The

AMERICAN HERITAGE®

ENGLISH *as a*

SECOND

LANGUAGE

DICTIONARY

HOUGHTON MIFFLIN COMPANY
BOSTON • NEW YORK

Words are included in this Dictionary on the basis of their usage. Words that are known to have current trademark registrations are shown with an initial capital and are also identified as trademarks. No investigation has been made of common-law trademark rights in any word, because such investigation is impracticable. The inclusion of any word in this Dictionary is not, however, an expression of the Publisher's opinion as to whether or not it is subject to proprietary rights. Indeed, no definition in this Dictionary is to be regarded as affecting the validity of any trademark.

American Heritage® and the eagle logo are registered trademarks of Forbes Inc. Their use is pursuant to a license agreement with Forbes Inc.

Charts and tables created by Graphic Chart & Map Co., Inc.

Printed in the U.S.A.

Library of Congress Cataloging-in-Publication Data

The American Heritage English as a second language dictionary.
    p.   cm.
    ISBN 0-395-88069-6 (hard). —ISBN 0-395-81873-7
    1. English language—Dictionaries.   2. English language—
Conversation and phrase books.   I. Houghton Mifflin Company.
PE1628.A6235   1998
423—dc21   97-41967
                                   CIP

Hardcover ISBN: 0-395-88069-6
Paperback ISBN: 0-395-81873-7

89-DOC-05 04 03

Table of Contents

Acknowledgments

COLLEGE DIVISION

Director of ESL Programs
Susan Maguire

Editorial Assistant
Lauren Wilson

**Senior Production/
Design Coordinator**
Sarah Ambrose

Senior Designer
Henry Rachlin

**Packaging Services
Supervisor**
Charline Lake

**Director of
Manufacturing**
Michael O'Dea

Marketing Manager
Elaine Uzan Leary

EDITORIAL DEVELOPMENT

Project Manager
Angela M. Castro

Editor
Kathleen Sands Boehmer

Lexical Reviewers
Julia Penelope
Jacqueline Russom

Pronunciation
Rima McKinzey

Contributors

Noreen Baker
Linda Butler
John Chapman

Katherine Isaacs
Robin Longshaw
Julia Penelope

Jacqueline Russom
Margaret Sokolik
Kristine Zaballos

Art/Photo Research
Patricia McTiernan

TRADE AND REFERENCE DIVISION

Vice President, Director of Lexical Publishing
Margery S. Berube

Editorial Staff Consultant
David Pritchard

Lexical Consultants
Joseph P. Pickett
Marion Severynse

Managing Editor
Christopher Leonesio

**Senior Art and
Production Coordinator**
Margaret Anne Miles

REVIEWERS

Victoria Badalamenti, *LaGuardia Community College, New York;*
David Bohlke, *Sejong University, Korea;* Young-Hee Chung, *Sejong University, Korea;*
Donald Bissonnette, *South Seattle Community College;* Marcia Cassidy, *Miami-Dade
Community College;* Pamela Caywood, *San Jose City College;* Leslie Crucil, *Santa Ana Unified
School District;* Daniele Dibie, *California State University at Northridge;*
Kathleen Flynn, *Glendale College, California;* Rachel Gader, *Georgetown University;*
Janet Goldstein, *Bramson ORT Technical Institute, New York;* Ann-Marie Hadzima,
National Taiwan University, Taiwan; Sheri Handel, *Columbia University;*
Barbara Hockman, *City College of San Francisco;* Grazyna Kenda, *The College of
Technology, New York;* Thomas Shu-hui Liao, *National Taiwan University, Taiwan;*
Anne Mari Hidalgo McCabe, *Saint Louis University in Madrid;* Kevin McClure, *ELS Language
Centers, San Francisco;* Donna McInnis, *Soka University, Japan;*
Mayra Nieuwlandt, *Chula Vista High School, California;* Susan Rodriguez, *Texas Intensive
English Program, Austin;* Terry Rapoport, *ELS Language Centers, Riverdale, New York;*
Jacqueline Russom, *Dorcas Place Parent Literacy Center, Inc., Providence;*
Barbara Smith-Palinkas, *University of South Florida;* Pearl Yang, *Cheng Senior High, Taiwan*

Special Thanks

This dictionary has been adapted from *The American Heritage® Student Dictionary* by the Houghton Mifflin Company College Division in collaboration with the Trade and Reference Division.

I would like to thank the Trade and Reference Division for agreeing to pursue this project. We are sincerely grateful and truly indebted to Margery Berube, Director of Lexical Publishing, for her undying spirit of cooperation, and to David Pritchard, Senior Editor, for his careful training, guidance, and assistance from the inception of the project to the final editing.

A special thanks goes to Angela Castro and her fine team of writers and proofreaders whose commitment, care, and attention to detail worked to create this fine new addition to the family of American Heritage® Dictionaries. I wish to express my sincere appreciation to Charline Lake, Sharon Ambrose, Henry Rachlin and Mike O'Dea for their expertise, cooperation, and tireless efforts, on the production and manufacturing stages of this Dictionary. They really made this project happen. A debt of gratitude also goes to Lauren Wilson for keeping the process flowing. Finally, I would like to thank Kristine Clerkin, Editorial Director of the College Division, for her continued support and encouragement throughout this project.

The American Heritage® ESL Dictionary is the product of a wonderful interdivisional team effort at Houghton Mifflin Company. I wish to express my heartfelt gratitude to all who worked to make this project a successful one.

Susan Maguire

Susan Maguire

Introduction

Over a quarter of a century ago, Houghton Mifflin published the first in a long line of innovative and successful American Heritage Dictionaries. For the new century, we are pleased to offer an outstanding addition to this family of reference books: *The American Heritage English as a Second Language Dictionary*. Continuing the rich American Heritage tradition, this Dictionary has been specially designed for you, students from all backgrounds and languages who are learning to master written and spoken English.

The American Heritage English as a Second Language Dictionary is the first of its kind to be based on such a respected and authoritative dictionary of American English. The words entered here are those found in the books, magazines, encyclopedias, and other materials used by students such as you. We carefully examined and revised every entry to be easy to understand and to show you how words are actually used in American English today.

Here are some reasons we think this Dictionary will help you understand and use English in the most effective way possible:

UP-TO-DATE WORDS. Your Dictionary contains the very latest vocabulary list. It has over 40,000 words and phrases, with special attention to new business, medical, science, and technology words. It has thousands of new meanings added, such as *Internet, ATM,* and *on-line.*

CLEAR DEFINITIONS. The definitions in your Dictionary have been written to get the meaning across quickly and clearly. Like other American Heritage books, your Dictionary always lists the most common meanings of a word first, where they can be found most easily.

ACCURATE SAMPLE SENTENCES. The simplest way to quickly understand the meaning of a word is to see it used in a typical sentence. For this reason, we have included thousands of carefully written sample sentences and phrases throughout your Dictionary. In addition to learning that a word like *fly* can be both a transitive and intransitive verb, you can actually see the difference by reading the sample sentences in the entry.

EASY PRONUNCIATION SYSTEM. The alphabetic pronunciation system in your Dictionary is standard for all American Heritage Dictionaries. It is easy to learn and will prepare you for using other American English dictionaries in the future. Look up the word *jellyfish* or *childbirth* and see how quickly you can learn how to pronounce these words. Don't forget to look at the pronunciation key at the bottom of the left-hand page.

SPECIAL ENTRIES. Your Dictionary is the only ESL dictionary to include prefixes, suffixes, and abbreviations as separate entries. This helps you find what you are looking for immediately.

SYNONYM AND HOMONYM BOXES. Your Dictionary has 100 Synonym Boxes that identify words with similar meanings and help you understand the differences of meaning among groups of related words. The Homonym Boxes show words that have the same sound but different meanings, and show you how to spell and pronounce these words correctly. What do *key* and *quay* have in common? Look them up in your dictionary; you may be surprised!

WORLD BUILDING NOTES. Over 80 Word Building Notes help you to understand difficult words. Some Notes show how prefixes and suffixes affect the meanings of various words. Other Notes show how words have a central meaning that goes back to a common root in an ancient language.

USAGE NOTES. Nearly 100 Usage Notes point out common problems that every writer must deal with and give advice on how to solve them. What is the difference between *few* and *less*? Is the word *each* used with a singular or a plural verb? The Usage Notes answer these and many other questions.

HUNDREDS OF ILLUSTRATIONS. The definitions in this Dictionary are illustrated by over 250 photos and drawings that make it easier to understand what the words mean and also make it fun to keep turning the pages.

These and other useful features make *The American Heritage ESL Dictionary* a book that will increase your knowledge about words and excite you to learn more. So read and enjoy!

Elements of the Dictionary

B The symbol for the element **boron**.

Ba The symbol for the element **barium**.

B.A. *abbr.* An abbreviation of Bachelor of Arts.

back•ward (băk′wərd) *adj.* **1.** In the direction of the rear: *a backward glance; a backward tumble.* **2.** Less advanced than others, as in economic or social progress: *backward technology.* —*adv.* or **back•wards** (băk′wərdz).

1. To or toward the back or rear: *He kept glancing backward to see who was coming.* **2.** With the back or rear first: *With its hind legs a toad can dig its way into the ground backward.* **3.** In reverse order or direction: *count backward from 100.* **4.** Toward a worse condition: *As prices rise, poor people slip backward.* ◆ **bend over backward.** To make an effort greater than is required: *They bent over backward to be fair.* **know backward and forward** or **backwards and forwards.** To know sthg. very well or perfectly: *We know the play backward and forward.*

bad (băd) *adj.* **worse** (wûrs), **worst** (wûrst). **1.** Being below an acceptable standard; poor: *a bad book; a bad painter.* **2.** Evil or wicked: *a bad man.* **3.** Disobedient; naughty: *bad behavior.* **4.** Unfavorable: *bad luck; bad weather.* **5.** Disagreeable or unpleasant: *a bad odor; bad news.* **6.** Incorrect; improper: *a bad choice of words.* **7.** Not working properly; defective: *a bad telephone connection.* **8.** Rotten; spoiled: *bad fish; bad milk.* **9.** Harmful in effect: *Candy is bad for your teeth.* **10.** Being in poor health or condition: *I feel bad today. The jogger has a bad knee.* **11.** Severe; intense: *a bad cold; a bad snowstorm; a bad temper.* **12.** Sorry; regretful: *I feel very bad about what happened.* —*n.* [U] Something bad: *You must learn to accept the bad with the good.* ◆ **not half bad** or **not so bad.** *Informal.* Reasonably good: *That meal was not half bad.* **too bad.** Regrettable; unfortunate: *It's too bad you can't come along.* —**bad′ness** *n.* [U]

USAGE: bad You should avoid using **bad** as an adverb. Instead of *We need water bad*, use *We need water badly.* Instead of *My tooth hurt bad*, use *My tooth hurt badly.*

HOMONYMS: bad, bade (past of bid).

bal•lis•tics (bə lĭs′tĭks) *n.* [U] *(used with a singular verb).* The scientific study of the characteristics of projectiles, such as bullets or missiles, and the way they move in flight.

bal·loon (bə lōōn′)
n. **1.** A large flexible bag filled with helium, hot air, or some other gas that is lighter than the surrounding air and designed to rise and float in the atmosphere, often with a gondola or scientific instruments. **2.** A small brightly colored rubber or plastic bag that is inflated and used as a toy. **3.** A rounded or irregularly shaped outline containing the words that a character in a cartoon is represented to be saying. —*intr.v.* **1.** To swell out like a balloon: *The tire ballooned as it was inflated with air.* **2.** To ride in a gondola suspended from a balloon: *scenic ballooning over the town.*

balloon
Hot-air balloons

bar·i·um (bâr′ē əm *or* băr′ē əm) *n.* [U] *Symbol* **Ba** A soft, silvery-white, metallic element that occurs only in combination with other elements. Barium compounds are used in making pigments and safety matches. Atomic number 56. See table at **element.**

beau·ty (byōō′tē) *n., pl.* **beau·ties. 1.** [U] A pleasing quality, especially with regard to form, that delights the senses and appeals to the mind: *the beauty of the snowcapped mountains.* **2.** [C] A person or thing that is beautiful: *Modern supermodels are generally thought of as great beauties.* **3.** [U] A feature that is good or effective: *The beauty of this scheme is that we come out ahead either way.*

be·gin (bǐ gǐn′) *v.* **be·gan** (bǐ găn′), **be·gun** (bǐ gŭn′), **be·gin·ning, be·gins.** —*intr.* **1.** To take the first step in doing sthg.; start; commence: *We began with the kitchen and cleaned the whole house.* **2.** To come into being; originate: *Education begins at home.* **3.** To accomplish in the least way; come near: *The little bit of paint won't begin to cover the ceiling.* —*tr.* **1.** To start doing (sthg.): *If we begin our work now, we'll have time to enjoy ourselves later.* **2.** To bring (sthg.) into being; originate: *The owner's grandfather began the newspaper many years ago.* **3.** To come first in (sthg.): *The letter A begins the alphabet.*

SYNONYMS: begin, commence, start, embark. These verbs mean to take the first step or to get working or moving. **Begin** is the most general word: *The play begins at eight o'clock.* **Commence** is a more formal word than **begin:** *Our meetings always commence with a call to order.* **Start** often means to begin from a standstill: *The train started as soon as we sat down.* **Embark** means to set out on a venture

art

caption

symbol

table cross-reference

inflected forms

example

or journey: *After getting her teaching certificate, my sister will embark on a new career.* **ANTONYM: end.**

---

be•sides (bĭ **sīdz′**) *adv*. In addition; also: *We had dinner and a late-night snack besides.* —*prep*. In addition to: *Dentists do other things besides drilling cavities.* —SEE NOTE at **together.**

Note cross-reference

SYNONYMS: besides, too, also, likewise, furthermore. These adverbs mean in addition to sthg. else. **Besides** often introduces sthg. that reinforces what has gone before it: *We don't feel like cooking; besides, there is no food in the house.* **Too** is the most casual, used in everyday speech: *If you're going to the library today, I'd like to go too.* **Also** is more formal than **too**: *My brother is usually very friendly, but he is also capable of holding a grudge.* **Likewise** is even more formal: *Their parents were likewise attending the ceremony.* **Furthermore** often stresses the clause following it as more important than the clause before it: *I don't want you to go to that place; furthermore, I forbid it.*

Synonym Note

---

prefix entry

bio– or **bi–** *pref*. A prefix that means: **1.** Life or living organism: *biography.* **2.** Biology or biological: *biophysics.*

WORD BUILDING: bio– The prefix **bio–** means "life." When used to form words in English, **bio–** generally refers to living organisms or to biology, the science of living organisms. Many of the words that begin with **bio–,** such as **bioethics** and **biotechnology,** have only come into being in the 20th century. Sometimes before an *o* **bio–** becomes **bi–: biopsy.**

Word Building Note

---

status label

breath•er (**brē′***th*ər) *n*. *Informal*. A short period of rest: *After this chore, let's take a breather.*

GUIDE TO USING
THE DICTIONARY

This Guide is designed to help you find and understand the information in this Dictionary.

The Alphabet

The English alphabet has 26 letters. Each letter has two forms. These are shown below. The first letter in each column is called a capital letter or an uppercase letter. The second letter in each column is called a small letter or a lowercase letter.

Aa	Nn
Bb	Oo
Cc	Pp
Dd	Qq
Ee	Rr
Ff	Ss
Gg	Tt
Hh	Uu
Ii	Vv
Jj	Ww
Kk	Xx
Ll	Yy
Mm	Zz

Capital letters are used as the first letter of proper nouns and at the beginning of sentences. Proper nouns are the names of people, places, or things. Some examples of each are shown below:

Mary, Uncle Sam
England, Barton Street
Jeep, Rollerblade

You can find more information about using capital letters on page xxiv of this guide.

Alphabetical Order

The order of the letters in the alphabet is called alphabetical order. In a list of words in alphabetical order, the letter *a* always comes before *b*, the letter *b* always comes before *c*, and so on. This is true for words that begin with capital letters as well as words that begin with small letters.

apple
bring
cat
do
English
fill

Of course, the letter *a* also comes before all the letters after *b*, and so on. Again, this is true for both capital letters and small letters.

aunt
French
live
new
show
yesterday

Many words begin with the same two or even three letters. When two or more words have the same first two letters, the words are alphabetized by the third letter. When two or more words have the same first three letters, they are alphabetized by the fourth letter.

angry	slide	strand
animal	slip	strange
answer	slit	stranger
ant	slither	strap

Some words share even more letters, but the words are still alphabetized by the next letter that is different.

underage
undergo
understand
underweight

All the entries in the Dictionary are in alphabetical order.

Guidewords

This Dictionary has just one alphabetical list. All the entries, including single words, phrases, compound words with hyphens, abbreviations, proper names, prefixes, and suffixes, are in alphabetical order. To help you find the word you want to look up, we have put two boldface guidewords at the top of each page in this book:

bother / bound

The guideword on the left is the first boldface entry on that page. The guideword on the right is the last boldface entry on that page. The entry words *bother* and *bound* and all the alphabetical entries between them are listed on the page that has these two guidewords.

The Entry Word

The word or phrase you look up in the dictionary is called an *entry word* or an *entry*, or sometimes a *main entry*. The entry words are printed in boldface a little to the left of the rest of the column. They are listed in alphabetical order. Words that begin with the same letter are put into alphabetical order using their second letter. If the first two letters are the same, the words are put in alphabetical order using the third letter, and so on. This is shown in the list below:

> beagle
> beak
> beaker
> beam

Some entries have more than one word. These may be written as phrases, such as *water fountain* and *water polo*, or as compound words with hyphens, such as *baby-sit* and *heavy-duty*. Phrases and compounds are listed in alphabetical order as if they were written as one word.

Superscript Numbers

Some words have one spelling but different meanings and histories. These words, called *homographs*, are entered separately. Each has a superscript, or raised, number printed after the entry word:

sole[1] (sōl) *n.* **1.** The bottom surface of the foot. **2.** The bottom surface of a shoe or boot, often excluding the heel.
sole[2] (sōl) *adj.* **1.** Being the only one; single; only: *Her sole purpose in coming is to see you.* **2.** Relating exclusively to one person or group: *She took sole command of the ship.*
sole[3] (sōl) *n.* A fish related to the flounder and used as food.

Syllables

Entry words that have more than one syllable are divided into syllables by centered dots:

clas•si•cal (klăs′ĭ kəl) *adj.*

Related word forms are also divided into syllables:

clas•si•fy (klăs′ə fī′) *tr.v.* **clas•si•fied, clas•si•fy•ing, clas•si•fies.**
1. To arrange (sthg.) in categories or classes; categorize: *A librarian classifies books according to subject matter.* **2.** To designate (information) as available only to authorized persons: *classify military documents.*
—**clas′si•fi′a•ble** *adj.* —**clas′si• fi′er** *n.*

At entries that have two or more words, the centered dots are omitted for words that are divided into syllables at their own alphabetical place as main entries in the dictionary:

an•swer•ing machine (ăn′sər ĭng) *n.*

For example, the word *machine*, which is a separate entry, has no centered dots at the entry for *answering machine*.

The syllabication of an entry word shows the traditional way that writers break words at the end of a line. The pronunciations are divided into syllables according to the way a word is pronounced. Therefore, the syllable divisions of an entry word are not always the same as those of its pronunciation:

serv•ice (sûr′vĭs) *n.*

Spelling Variations

Some words have two or more different spellings. The spelling variation or variations are shown in boldface after the entry word. The word *or* tells you that both spellings are equally common:

ad•vis•er or **ad•vi•sor** (ăd vī′zər) *n.*

The word *also* tells you that the variant form is less common than the main entry word:

a•lign also **a•line** (ə līn′) *tr.v.*

Variants that do not fall immediately before or after their main entry word in alphabetical order are entered at their own alphabetical places:

a•line (ə līn′) *v.* Variant of **align**.

British spellings. A number of spelling variations show the spellings preferred in England and other parts of the United Kingdom. These spelling variations, such as *defence* and *colour*, have the label *Chiefly British*. They are entered at their own alphabetical places but are not given as spelling variations at the entries to which they refer:

de•fence (dĭ fĕns′) *n. Chiefly British.* Variant of **defense**.

Parts of Speech

The following italicized labels indicate parts of speech:

adj.	adjective
adv.	adverb
conj.	conjunction
def. art.	definite article
indef. art.	indefinite article
interj.	interjection

n.	noun
prep.	preposition
pron.	pronoun
v.	verb

Plurals are indicated by the label *pl.* The label *pl.n.* appears at entries for words, such as *clothes* and *cattle*, that are only used in the plural.

These italicized labels are used for the traditional classification of verbs:

tr.	transitive
intr.	intransitive
aux.	auxiliary

A transitive verb is a verb that requires a direct object to complete its meaning. *Affect* and *elect* are examples of transitive verbs. An intransitive verb never takes an object; verbs such as *die* and *fall* are intransitive. Many verbs, of course, can be transitive or intransitive depending on how they are used. An auxiliary verb, such as *have* or *may*, is used with another verb to make a tense, mood, or voice.

The labels for word elements are:

pref.	prefix
suff.	suffix

Entries that are abbreviations, such as *A.M.* and *blvd.*, are labeled *abbr.*

Certain entries do not carry part-of-speech labels. They include contractions (*I'll*), symbols (*I^2*, the symbol for iodine), and trademarks (*Band-Aid*).

Parts of Speech in Combined Entries

Many words can be used as more than one part of speech. For example, *paint* can be both a verb (as in *to paint a wall*) and a noun (as in *a gallon of paint*). In such cases, the different parts of speech are defined in one entry called a *combined entry*. In an entry of this kind, each part of speech receives its own part-of-speech label. Each part of speech that follows the first part of speech is preceded by a dash (–).

If a piece of information, such as a pronunciation or a status label, appears before the first part of speech in an entry, that piece of information applies to all parts of speech in that entry. Examples of these status labels are *Slang* and *Formal*. Labels and pronunciations that appear after a part of speech apply to that part of speech only. Some entries, such as *contract*, have a different pronunciation for each part of speech.

con•tract (kŏn′trăkt′) *n*. [C; U] An agreement between two or more persons or groups, especially one that is written and enforceable by law: *a contract to sell the house; a new labor contract.* —*v*. (kən **trăkt′** or kŏn′trăkt′). —*tr*. **1.** To make (sthg.) smaller by drawing together: *Hot water contracted the wool fibers in my sweater, and it shrank.* **2.** To arrange or settle (sthg.) by a formal agreement: *contract a business deal.* **3.** To get (sthg.); acquire: *contract the mumps; contract a debt.* **4.** To shorten (a word or words) by omitting or combining some of the letters or sounds. *Most people contract "I am" to "I'm" when they speak.* —*intr*. **1.** To draw together; become smaller: *The pupils of the cat's eyes contracted.* **2.** To arrange by a formal agreement: *The developers contracted for construction of several new houses.*

Inflected Forms of Verbs, Nouns, Adjectives, and Adverbs

An inflected form of a word differs from the main entry form by the addition of a suffix or by a change in the normal spelling of the main entry. For example, the verb *walk* forms its past tense, *walked*, by the addition of the suffix -*ed*, and *swim* forms its past tense *swam* by changing its spelling.

In this Dictionary, inflected forms that are irregular or that have spelling changes are shown. They appear in boldface, have syllable divisions, and have pronunciations when necessary.

An inflected form immediately follows the part-of-speech label or the number of the definition to which it applies.

Forms of verbs. The forms of verbs that are irregular or that have spelling changes are shown. The forms are entered in this order: *past tense, past participle, present participle,* and *third person singular present tense.*

fly[1] (flī) *v*. **flew** (floo), **flown** (flōn), **fly•ing, flies** (flīz).

When the past tense and past participle are identical, one form represents both. For example, *thought* is the past tense and past participle of the verb *think*:

think (thĭngk) *v*. **thought** (thôt), **think•ing, thinks.**

Comparison of adjectives and adverbs. Adjectives and adverbs that form the comparative and superlative degrees by adding -*er* and -*est* and have spelling changes, such as a double consonant or a change from *y* to *i*, show these forms in full immediately after the part-of-speech label:

fine[1] (fīn) *adj*. **fin•er, fin•est. 1.** Of very good quality, skill, or appearance: *a fine day; a fine performance.* **2.** Being in a state of good health; quite well; *I'm fine, thank you.* **3.** Very small in size, weight, or thickness: *fine hair.* **4.** Very sharp: *a fine point on a pencil.* **5.** Showing delicate and careful artistry: *a fine painting; fine china.* **6.** Consisting of small particles; not coarse: *fine dust; the fine spray of a water hose.* **7.** So small as to be difficult to see or understand: *the fine differences between a rabbit and a hare.* —*adv*. **finer, finest.** *Informal.* **1.** In small pieces or parts: *Chop the onions fine.* **2.** Very well: *The two dogs are getting along fine.* —**fine′ness** *n*. [U]

Irregular comparative and superlative forms are also given in full:

good (gŏŏd) *adj*. **bet•ter** (bĕt′ər), **best** (bĕst).

Plural forms of nouns. Regular plurals formed by adding the suffixes -s or -es to a noun are not normally shown in this Dictionary, but irregular plurals are always shown following the label *pl.*:

mouse (mous) *n., pl.* **mice** (mīs).

When a noun has a regular and an irregular plural form, both forms appear, with the most common form shown first:

cer•e•brum (sĕr′ə brəm *or* sə-rē′brəm) *n., pl.* **cer•e•brums** or **cer•e•bra** (sĕr′ə brə *or* sə rē′brə).

Regular plurals are also shown when spelling might be a problem:

po•ta•to (pə tā′tō) *n., pl.* **po•ta•toes.**

Sometimes inflected forms apply only to certain meanings of a word. In such cases, the inflected form appears in boldface after the number or letter of the meaning to which it applies:

> **hang** (hăng) *v.* **hung** (hŭng), **hang•ing, hangs.** *— tr.* **1.** To fasten (sthg.) from above with no support from below; suspend: *hang clothes to dry on a clothesline.* **2.** To fasten (sthg.) to allow free movement at the point of contact: *hang a door.* **3.** *Past tense and past participle* **hanged** (hăngd). To kill (sbdy.) by suspending by a rope around the neck. **4.** To hold or bend (sthg.) downward: *hang one's head in sorrow.* **5.** To attach (sthg.) to a wall: *hang wallpaper. — intr.* **1.** To be attached from above with no support from below: *A sign hung over the door.*

From this example you can see that the verb *hang* usually has the past tense and the past participle *hung*, but when used in the sense of an execution of a criminal, it has *hanged* as its past tense and past participle.

Separate Entries for Inflected Forms

Irregular inflected forms that have a change in spelling of the main form of a word are entered separately when they are more than one entry away from the main entry form. For example, *flew*, the past tense of *fly*, and *men*, the plural of *man*, both have their own entries:

flew (flōō) *v.* Past tense of **fly**[1].

men (mĕn) *n.* Plural of **man**.

The Dictionary does not normally give separate entries for inflected forms of words ending in -y, such as *berry, happy,* and *carry,* because forms such as *berries, happiest,* and *carried* have a regular spelling change that is easy to recognize.

Labels

This Dictionary uses labels to identify words and meanings whose use is limited in some way—to a particular style of expression, for example. When a label applies to all parts of an entry, it appears before the first part of speech:

> **snitch** (snĭch) *Slang. v. —tr.* To steal (sthg. of little value): *snitch candy.* *—intr.* To tell on sbdy.; turn informer: *He snitched on his brother. —n.* **1.** A thief. **2.** An informer.

The positioning of the label *Slang* in the above example means that both the noun and verb senses of the word are slang.

A label may apply only to a single part of speech, in which case it follows the part-of-speech label. Sometimes a label applies only to a single definition, in which case it follows the number or letter of the meaning for which it applies:

> **hot** (hŏt) *adj.* **hot•ter, hot•test. 1.** Having great heat; being at a high temperature; very warm: *a hot stove; a horse that was hot after working in the sun; a forehead hot with fever.* **2.** Charged with electricity: *a hot wire.* **3.** Causing a burning sensation in the mouth: *hot chili; hot mustard.* **4.** Marked by intense feeling: *a hot temper; a hot argument.* **5.** *Informal.* Most recent; new or fresh: *a hot piece of news.* **6.** *Slang.* Stolen: *a hot television set. —adv.* In a hot manner; with much heat: *The engine runs hot.*

In this entry, the label *Informal* applies only to meaning 5 and the label *Slang* only to meaning 6.

Status Labels

Status labels indicate that an entry word or a definition is limited to a particular level or style of usage. All words and definitions not marked with such a label should be appropriate for use in all contexts.

Slang. This label indicates a style of language that uses unusual, often humorous expressions as a way of making an effect. Most people use some forms of slang but not in formal speech or writing. An example of a word labeled *Slang* follows:

> **rip-off** (rĭp′ôf′ *or* rĭp′ŏf′) *n. Slang.* **1.** A theft. **2.** Something that makes one feel cheated: *That movie was a rip-off.*

Informal. Words that people use commonly in conversation and in informal writing but not in formal writing are identified by the label *Informal*. Informal words are ones you might use in a letter to a friend but should not use in a paper written for school or in a letter to a teacher, business, or newspaper, for example:

> **fish•y** (fĭsh′ē) *adj.* **fish•i•er, fish• i•est. 1.** Tasting, resembling, or smelling of fish: *a fishy smell.* **2.** *Informal.* Causing doubt or suspicion: *There was something fishy about that excuse.* —**fish′i•ness** *n.* [U]

Formal. Words that people tend to use in more formal speech or writing have the label *Formal.* An example of a word labeled *Formal* is shown below:

> **lev•i•ty** (lĕv′ĭ tē) *n.* [U] *Formal.* A light humorous manner or attitude; frivolity: *Levity is often improper in a court of law.*

Offensive. This label is used for words and expressions that are extremely insulting and are not used in polite speech and writing.

English-Language Labels

These labels identify an entry as a form that is used in specific areas of the English-speaking world:

> **flat²** (flăt) *n. Chiefly British.* An apartment, usually on one floor of a building.

Cross-References

A cross-reference is a word that refers you to another word. It signals that more information can be found at another entry. A cross-reference is helpful in avoiding the repetition of information at two entries. It also may indicate where you can find additional information.

The word referred to in a cross-reference appears in bold type and is preceded by a short phrase:

> **bade** (băd *or* bād) *v.* A past tense of **bid.**

This cross-reference tells you that *bade* is a past tense of the word *bid.* This indicates that more information about the entry can be found at *bid.*

A cross-reference that refers to only one meaning of a word that has more than one meaning includes that meaning number:

> **tzar** (zär *or* tsär) *n.* Variant of **czar** (sense 1).

This cross-reference tells you that *tzar* is a variant spelling of *czar,* but it refers only to meaning 1.

Some cross-references refer to tables. The word or words in bold type tell you where the table can be found:

> **hy•dro•gen** (hī′drə jən) *n.* [U] *Symbol* **H** A colorless, highly flammable gaseous element present in most organic compounds. Hydrogen is the lightest, most abundant element and combines with oxygen to form water. Atomic number 1. See table at **element.**

Other cross-references refer you to a note that appears at another entry:

huge (hyo͞oj) *adj.* **hug·er, hug·est.** Of great size, extent, or quantity; tremendous: *a huge iceberg; a huge difference.* See Synonyms at **large.** —**huge′ly** *adv.* —**huge′ness** *n.* [U]

lit·tle (lĭt′l) *adj.* **lit·tler, lit·tlest** or **less** (lĕs), **least** (lēst). **1.** Small in size, amount, or degree: *a little boy; little money.* **2.** Short in duration: *We have little time left.* **3.** Young or younger: *my little brother.* **4.** Unimportant; trivial: *a little problem.* —*adv.* **less, least. 1.** Not much: *He slept very little that night.* **2.** Not at all: *Little did the class realize the teacher planned a surprise test.* —*n.* **1.** A small amount: *I received only a little of what they owe.* **2.** A short distance or time: *We waited a little.* ♦ **a little.** Somewhat; a bit: *She feels a little better now.* **little by little.** By small degrees; gradually: *We paid the loan little by little.* —SEE NOTE at **few.**

These cross-references tell you that there is more information about the word in a note at another entry.

Order of Meanings

Entries that have more than one meaning are arranged with the most common or central meanings first. In addition, meanings that are related are grouped together. For example, in the entry for *nice* shown below, the common meaning "Kind; friendly" appears first and the less common meaning "Done with skill" comes as meaning 4:

nice (nīs) *adj.* **nic·er, nic·est. 1.** Kind; friendly: *She's really nice.* **2.** Good; pleasant; agreeable: *a nice place to stay.* **3.** Having a pleasant appearance; attractive: *a nice dress.* **4.** Done with skill: *a nice bit of work.* **5.** Used as an intensive with *and*: *nice and warm; nice and easy.* —**nice′ly** *adv.* —**nice′-ness** *n.* [U]

Division of meanings. Letters that appear in bold type before meanings show that two or more submeanings are closely related:

par·a·lyze (păr′ə līz′) *tr.v.* **par·a·lyzed, par·a·lyz·ing, par·a·lyz·es. 1.** To affect (sbdy.) with paralysis; make unable to move or feel: *The accident paralyzed her.* **2.a.** To make (sbdy.) helpless or motionless: *The victim was paralyzed by fear.* **b.** To block the normal functioning of (sthg.); bring to a standstill: *The heavy snows paralyzed the city.*

When an entry has more than one part of speech, the definitions are numbered in separate sequence beginning with each new part of speech:

dream (drēm) *n.* **1.** A series of mental images, ideas, and emotions during sleep: *She awoke from a bad dream.* **2.** A daydream. **3.** A hope: *dreams of world peace.* **4.** Something especially pleasing, excellent, or useful: *The new car runs like a dream.* —*v.* **dreamed** or **dreamt** (drĕmt), **dream·ing, dreams.** —*intr.* **1.** To have a dream while sleeping. **2.** To daydream: *Stop dreaming and get to work.* **3.** To consider as reasonable or practical: *I wouldn't even dream of going.* —*tr.* **1.** To have a dream of (sthg.) during sleep: *Did it storm last night, or did I dream it?* **2.** To imagine (sthg.): *We never dreamed it might snow so hard.* ♦ **dream up.** *tr.v.* [sep.] To think of or invent (sthg. unusual or impractical): *He dreamed up a plan to get rich quick.* —**dream′er** *n.*

Grammar Usage

Many entries have added information that tells you more about how the word is used in a sentence. For example, many noun entries tell you whether the word takes a singular or plural verb or whether it is usually singular or usually plural. This information appears as a usage phrase in italics before the meaning or part of speech that it applies to:

ge·net·ics (jə nĕt′ĭks) *n.* [U] **1.** *(used with a singular verb).* The branch of biology that deals with the principles of heredity and the variation of inherited characteristics among similar or related living things. **2.** *(used with a plural verb).* The genetic makeup of an individual or a group.

In the entry *genetics* above, the usage phrase tells you that meaning 1 takes a singular verb only and meaning 2 takes a plural verb only.

Countable and uncountable nouns. Countable nouns are nouns that can be counted and that can be used with words such as *a/an* or specific numbers. Nouns that are always countable are not marked in this Dictionary. Uncountable nouns are those that cannot be counted and are used with words such as *some* or *much*. Nouns that are uncountable are marked with [U] in this Dictionary. Nouns that have some meanings that are countable and some that are uncountable are marked [C] or [U], depending on the meaning.

> **lan·guage** (lăng′gwĭj) *n.* **1.** [U] Human communication, using voice sounds and often written symbols representing these sounds in organized combinations. **2.** [C] A system of sounds and symbols used by a group of people: *Many languages are spoken in Africa.* **3.** [C] A system of signs, symbols, rules, or gestures used to convey information: *a computer language.* **4.** [U] The special words and expressions used by members of a group or profession: *medical language.*

If a noun is marked [C; U], this means that in some contexts the word is countable, in others it is not.

> **rank**[1] (răngk) *n.* **1.** [C; U] A position or degree of value in a group with different levels: *in the top rank of his class.* **2.** [C] (*usually plural*). A body of people classed together; numbers: *He has joined the ranks of factory workers.* —*v.* —*tr.* To give a particular order or position to (sbdy./sthg.); classify: *The teacher ranked the children according to age.* —*intr.* To hold a certain rank: *She ranked eighth in the class.* ♦ **pull rank.** To use one's superior rank to gain an advantage: *I wanted to watch a comedy, but my father pulled rank and we watched the news.*

Forms That Apply to Specific Meanings

Some nouns have meanings in which they are usually used in the plural. In these cases, the boldface plural form of the noun appears just before the definition to show you that it is used in the plural:

> **due** (do̅o̅) *adj.* **1.** Owed or owing as a debt: *We must pay the amount still due.* **2.** Fitting or appropriate; suitable: *Every citizen is required to show due respect for the law.* **3.** As much as needed; sufficient; adequate: *We left early, taking due care to be on time.* **4.** Expected or scheduled: *When is the train due to arrive?* **5.** Expecting or ready for sthg. as part of a normal course or sequence: *We're due for some rain.* —*n.* **1.** [U] Something that is owed or deserved: *a dedicated scholar who finally got his due.* **2. dues.** A charge or fee for membership, as in a club: *golfing dues of $30 per month.* —*adv.* Straight; directly: *The settlers traveled due west.*

In this entry, the meaning of *due* that refers to a charge or fee for membership occurs only in the plural form *dues*.

The same style is used for any change in the form of a word as it shifts from one meaning to another:

> **north** (nôrth) *n.* [U] **1.** The compass direction to the left of sunrise, directly opposite south. **2.** A region in this direction: *Better farmlands lie in the north of the state.* **3. North.** The northern part of the United States, especially the Union states during the Civil War. —*adj.* **1.** To, toward, or in the north: *the north shore of the island.* **2.** From the north: *a north wind.* —*adv.* In, from, or toward the north: *The house faces north.*

Here the capitalized boldface form of the word appears just before the definition it applies to, telling you that in this meaning the word only occurs in the capitalized form *North*.

Examples to Illustrate Definitions

In addition to giving clear definitions of words, this Dictionary also gives you thousands of examples showing how a word is used in context. These examples are especially useful for illustrating special meanings of a word, idioms, transitive and intransitive verbs, separable and inseparable phrasal verbs, and multiple meanings of very common words:

a·round (ə round′) *adv.* **1.** On all sides or in all directions: *We drove around looking for a parking place.* **2.** In a circle or circular motion: *The ice skater spun around twice.* **3.** In circumference: *The lake is two miles around.* **4.** In or toward the opposite direction: *The horse turned around and ran toward the barn.* **5.** From one place to another; here and there: *I wandered around.* **6.** In or near one's present location: *He waited around all day.* **7.** To a specific place or area: *when you come around again.* **8.** Approximately; about: *Around 20 people went to the party.* —*prep.* **1.** On all sides of: *There are trees around the field.* **2.** Encircling or enclosing: *He wore a belt around his waist.* **3.** All about; throughout: *The teacher looked around the room.* **4.** On or to the farther side of: *the house around the corner.* **5.** Close by; near: *She lives right around here.* **6.** So as to pass or avoid: *How can we get around the problem?* **7.** Approximately at: *I woke up around seven.* ♦ **around the clock.** Ongoing; without stopping: *They worked around the clock.*

do (do͞o) *v.* **did** (dĭd), **done** (dŭn), **do·ing, does** (dŭz). —*tr.* **1.** To perform, complete, or accomplish (sthg.): *do a good job; do a favor for a friend.* **2.** To create, produce, or make (sthg.): *do a painting; do a report.* **3.** To make (sthg.) happen: *Crying won't do any good.* **4.** To put (sthg.) into action: *I'll do everything in my power to help you.* **5.** To put (sthg.) into order: *do one's hair.* **6.** To work at (sthg.) to earn a living: *"What do you do?" "I'm a nurse."* **7.** To solve or work out the details of (a problem): *I did this equation.* **8.a.** To travel (a specified distance): *do a mile in seven minutes.* **b.** To travel at (a speed): *He was only doing 50 miles an hour on the high-*

way. **9.** To be enough or convenient for (sbdy.): *This room will do us very nicely.* **10.** *Informal.* To serve (a prison term): *Both men did time for theft.* —*intr.* **1.** To behave or conduct oneself: *You did well in the interview.* **2.** To get along; manage: *The new student is doing well.* **3.** To serve a purpose: *That old coat will do for now.* **4.** Used instead of repeating a verb or phrase: *She reads as much as I do. I like novels and she does, too.* —*aux.* **1.** Used to ask questions: *Do you want to go? Did you hear me?* **2.** Used to make negative statements: *I did not sleep at all. We do not understand.* **3.** Used to form inverted phrases: *Little did I know that he was planning to leave.* **4.** Used to emphasize or make stronger: *But we do want to go. You really do play well.* —*n., pl.* **do's** or **dos.** A statement of what should and should not be done: *a long list of do's and don'ts from my mother.* ♦ **do away with. 1.** To get rid of or put an end to sthg.: *doing away with unnecessary laws.* **2.** To kill or destroy sbdy./sthg.: *The landlord promises to do away with rats in the building.* **do (one) in.** *tr.v.* [sep.] **1.** *Slang.* To make (sbdy.) very tired: *That long walk really did me in.* **2.** To kill (sbdy./sthg.): *Nobody knows who did him in.* **do (one) out of.** *Informal.* To cheat sbdy. and take away sthg.: *His partners did him out of his fair share of the money.* **do (one's) own thing.** *Slang.* To do what one does best or likes most: *The art teacher gave the girls some paints and let each one do her own thing.* **do or die.** Requiring a very great effort: *The test is tomorrow, so it's do or die time.* **do over.** *tr.v.* [sep.] *Informal.* **1.** To redecorate (sthg.): *Professionals are doing over the room.* **2.** To do (sthg.) again: *His homework was messy, so he did it over.* **do well by.** To behave well when dealing with sbdy.: *The children have done well by their aged parents.* **do with.** *tr.v.* [insep.] **1.** To use (sthg.): *You can do with the money as you wish.* **2.** (*usually with* could). To need or want (sthg.): *I could do with a hot shower.* **3.** To be related or connected to (sbdy./sthg.): *The story had to do with a lost dog. Our troubles are nothing to do with you.* **do without.** *tr.v.* [insep.] To manage without (sbdy./sthg.): *We can do without his help.*

♦ Idioms and Phrasal Verbs

An idiom is a group of words whose meaning as a group cannot be understood from the meanings of the individual words in the group. In this Dictionary, idioms are defined at the entry for the first important word in the phrase. For example, *walk on air* is defined at *walk*.

In this Dictionary, idioms and phrasal verbs appear at the end of the definitions of an entry in alphabetical order. The symbol ◆ marks the beginning of this section. Each idiom or phrasal verb is shown in boldface.

Phrasal verbs are formed by adding adverbs or prepositions to the verb, as this example shows:

cheer (chîr) *v.* —*intr.* To shout in happiness, approval, encouragement, or enthusiasm: *The audience cheered and clapped.* —*tr.* To praise, encourage, or urge (sbdy./sthg.) by shouting: *The fans cheered the team's victory.* —*n.* **1.** [C] A shout of happiness, approval, encouragement, or enthusiasm: *The crowd gave a loud cheer for the winning team.* **2.** [C] A slogan or chant shouted in encouragement or approval, as for a school's team at a game. **3.** [U] Happiness, good spirits: *My grandparents are always full of cheer.* ◆ **cheer on.** *tr.v.* [sep.] To encourage or urge (sbdy.): *People watching the race cheered the tiring runner on.* **cheer up.** *intr.v.* To become cheerful: *In spite of my disappointment, I soon cheered up.* —*tr.v.* [sep.] To make (sbdy.) happier or more cheerful: *The good news cheered her up.*

Two-word phrasal verbs are marked as transitive or intransitive. The abbreviations used are *tr.* and *intr.* Transitive phrasal verbs in this Dictionary are also marked as separable or inseparable. This information appears in brackets as [sep.] or [insep.]. In a separable phrasal verb, a direct object may appear between the two parts of the verb. An inseparable phrasal verb cannot be separated by an object.

This Dictionary lists nonliteral or unusual senses of phrasal verbs. Thus,

in the example below, *back out,* meaning "to refuse or fail to complete sthg. planned or promised," is defined in that sense, but not in the sense "to leave a parking lot in reverse." You should be able to figure out this latter meaning of the phrase by the meanings of the two words themselves, and therefore we do not usually define it:

back (băk) *n.* . . . ◆ **back down.** *intr.v.* To retreat from a demand made or a position taken: *There was an argument because neither side was willing to back down.* **back off.** *intr.v.* To retreat or move away, as from a dangerous position: *The senator backed off from his support of the bill.* **back out.** *intr.v.* To refuse or fail to complete sthg. planned or promised: *They accepted the invitation but backed out at the last minute.* **back up.** *tr.v.* [sep.] **1.** To make a copy of (a computer program or file): *Did you remember to back up your files?* **2.** To give one's support to (sbdy./sthg.): *The police didn't believe the man's story until two witnesses backed him up.* —*intr.v.* To increase in size or amount behind sthg. that blocks the way: *Traffic backed up near the accident.* **behind (one's) back.** When one is not present: *Don't talk about me behind my back.*

Run-On Entries

This Dictionary includes many additional words formed from an entry word by the addition of a suffix. These are located at the end of the entry. These run-on entries are clearly related to the main entry word and have the essential meaning, but they have different endings and different parts of speech. Run-on entries appear in boldface followed by a part-of-speech label. Syllables and stress are indicated on all run-on words of more than one syllable, and pronunciations are given where needed. Uncountable nouns are identified as well.

sor·row·ful (sŏr′ō fəl) *adj.* Causing, feeling, or expressing sorrow: *a sor-*

rowful event; a sorrowful voice. See Synonyms at **sad**. —**sor′row•ful•ly** adv. —**sor′row•ful•ness** n. [U]

Two or more run-on forms are in alphabetical order:

rap•id (răp′ĭd) adj. Fast; swift: *rapid progress; walking with rapid strides.* See Synonyms at **fast¹**. —n. *(usually plural).* An extremely fast-moving part of a river, caused by a steep descent in the riverbed: *We took our boat down the rapids.* —**ra•pid′i•ty** (rə pĭd′ĭ tē) n. [U] —**rap′id•ly** adv. —**rap′id•ness** n. [U]

Homonyms

Some words such as *cent, scent,* and *sent,* sound the same, but have different spellings and meanings. These words are called *homonyms.* To help you, the Dictionary provides a list of words that sound alike in a box for each entry for a homonym. The homonyms are listed in alphabetical order with the main entry word first. Each homonym that follows the main entry in the list has a word or phrase in parentheses that shows its meaning. Proper nouns and foreign words are not entered as homonyms:

row¹ (rō) n. **1.** A series of persons or things placed next to each other, usually in a straight line: *a row of trees.* **2.** A line of connected seats, as in a theater: *Which row are we in?* **3.** A series without a break or gap in time: *She won the tennis title three years in a row.*

HOMONYMS: row (continuous line, use oars), **roe** (fish eggs).

In the entry *row¹,* you can see that the words *row¹* meaning "continuous line," *row²* meaning "to use oars," and *roe* meaning "fish eggs" all sound alike.

Synonym Paragraphs

This Dictionary has 100 Synonym Paragraphs that list and describe words that have similar meanings. Each

Paragraph follows the entry for the central word of each synonym group. The Paragraphs are introduced by the heading *Synonyms* and the synonyms themselves appear in boldface. A list of antonyms, or words with meanings opposite those of the synonyms, often appears in boldface at the end of the Paragraph.

There are two kinds of Paragraphs. The first gives a central meaning shared by the synonyms in the list, and examples for each word:

SYNONYMS: help, aid, assist. These verbs mean to contribute to fulfilling a need, furthering an effort, or achieving a purpose. **Help** and **aid** are the most general: *A new medicine has been developed to help* (or *aid*) *digestion.* **Help** often means to aid in an active way: *I'll help you move the sofa.* **Assist** often means to play a secondary role in aiding: *A few of the students assisted the professor in researching the data.*

The second kind explains the differences in meaning among synonyms and shows how these words are used in context:

SYNONYMS: obstinate, stubborn, mulish, headstrong. These adjectives mean unwilling to change or cooperate. **Obstinate** means extremely difficult to persuade: *My aunt is obstinate about doing things her own way.* **Stubborn** and **mulish** can mean that a person's personality makes him or her unwilling to cooperate: *He is too stubborn to admit he was wrong. It's mulish of you to refuse to look at the map until after we're lost.* **Headstrong** means impatient and stubborn: *That headstrong child will never follow advice.* **ANTONYMS: cooperative, flexible.**

Every word that is discussed in a Synonym Paragraph has at its own entry a cross-reference to the entry that has the Synonym Paragraph. For example, the entry for *headstrong* has a cross-reference to the Synonym list presented at *obstinate*:

head·strong (hĕd′strông′ or hĕd′-strŏng′) *adj.* **1.** Wanting to have one's own way; stubborn and willful: *a proud and headstrong person.* See Synonyms at **obstinate. 2.** Resulting from being willful or stubborn: *a headstrong decision.*

Notes

In this Dictionary you will find a variety of notes providing more information about individual words. These notes describe how words are and should be used and how their meanings can be understood from their parts. Some notes give additional information about certain entries—information that is too detailed to be included in a definition. The words *See Note* at the end of an entry direct you to a note discussing that entry.

Usage Notes. Some words are easily confused with others or present difficulties in how they should be used. These entries have Usage Notes that provide explanations and offer advice on how to avoid or solve usage problems. Here is an example of a Usage Note:

> USAGE: **some, somebody,** or **someone.**
> When you think the answer to a question will be "yes," use **some, somebody,** or **someone:** *Can I borrow some money? Was somebody at the door? Did someone call me?* If you are not sure what the answer to a question will be, use **any, anybody,** or **anyone:** *Do you have any money I can borrow? Is anybody we know going to be at the party? Can anyone give me a ride home?*

When a word is discussed in a Usage Note next to an entry in another place in the book, it has a cross-reference to that entry. For example, at the entry for *any* you are directed to the note at *some,* where *any* is also discussed.

an·y (ĕn′ē) *adj.* **1.** One or some; no matter which; of whatever kind: *Take any book you want. Do you have any information on Chinese cooking?* **2.** No matter how many or how few; some: *Are there any oranges left?* **3.** Every: *Any dog likes meat.* —*pron. (used with a singular or plural verb).* Any person or thing or any persons or things; anybody or anything: *We haven't any left. Any of the teachers can help you.* —*adv.* At all: *The patient doesn't feel any better.* —SEE NOTE at **some.**

Word Building Notes. Word Building Notes help you understand how word parts are joined together to make longer, more complex words. There are two kinds of Word Building Notes: Affix Notes and Word Root Notes. Word Root Notes describe how roots form the heart of many words that have different but related meanings. Affix Notes show how prefixes and suffixes are attached to words to make new words:

> WORD BUILDING: sub— The prefix **sub—** means "under." When **sub—** is used to form words, it can mean "under" (**submarine, subsoil, subway**), "subordinate" (**subcommittee, subplot, subset**), or "less than completely" (**subhuman, substandard**). The prefix **sub—** can combine with verbs as well as with adjectives and nouns, as in **subdivide, sublease,** and **sublet.**

Pronunciation

The pronunciation, which is enclosed in parentheses, appears immediately after the boldface entry word. If an entry word and a variant of that entry word have the same pronunciation, the pronunciation follows the variant.

If the variant or variants do not have the same pronunciation as the entry word, pronunciations follow the forms to which they apply.

If a word has more than one pronunciation, the pronunciations are separated within the parentheses by *or*. All pronunciations given are acceptable in all circumstances. When more than one pronunciation is given, the first is assumed to be the most common, but often they are equally common. Differing pronunciations are given within an entry wherever necessary, as when there is a change in part of speech and in other special cases. A Full Pronunciation Key appears on page xxiii. A shorter form of this Key appears in a block at the bottom of every other page. Another Key, which compares the system used in the Dictionary with the International Phonetic Alphabet (IPA), is on the inside front cover. The set of symbols used is designed to help you produce a satisfactory pronunciation with just a quick reference to the key.

Stress

In this Dictionary, stress, or the relative degree of emphasis with which the syllables of a word (or phrase) are spoken, is indicated in three different ways. A syllable with no marking has the weakest stress in the word. The strongest, or *primary*, stress is marked with a bold mark (′). The syllable that receives the primary stress is also set in boldface type. An intermediate level of stress, here called *secondary*, is marked with a lighter mark (′). One-syllable words show no stress mark because there is no other stress level to which the syllable is compared.

Pronunciation Key

A list of the pronunciation symbols used in this Dictionary is given below in the column headed **Symbol.** The column headed **Example** contains words that show how the symbols are pronounced. The letters that correspond in sound to the symbols are shown in boldface.

The symbol (ə) is called *schwa*. It is used to represent a reduced vowel, a vowel that receives the weakest level of stress within a word. The schwa sound varies, sometimes according to the vowel it is representing and often according to the sounds around it.

a·bun·dant (ə bŭn′dənt)

mo·ment (mō′mənt)

civ·il (sĭv′əl)

pro·pose (prə pōz′)

grate·ful (grāt′fəl)

Note that the consonants *l* and *n* in English can be complete syllables by themselves. Some examples of words in which syllabic *l* and *n* occur are **needle** (nēd′l), **rattle** (răt′l), **sudden** (sŭd′n), and **rotten** (rŏt′n).

Symbol	Example	Symbol	Example	Symbol	Example	Symbol	Example
ă	cat	îr	dear,	ŏŏ	took	y	yes
ā	pay		deer,	ōō	boot	z	zebra,
âr	care		pier,	ou	out		xylophone
ä	father		here	p	pop	zh	vision,
b	bib	j	judge	r	roar		pleasure,
ch	church	k	kick,	s	sauce		garage
d	dead,		cat,	sh	ship,	ə	about,
	filled		unique		dish		item,
ĕ	get	l	lid,	t	tight,		legible,
ē	be,		needle		stopped		gallop,
	see	m	mum	th	thin		circus
f	fife,	n	no,	th	this	ər	butter
	phase,		sudden	ŭ	cut		
	cough	ng	thing	ûr	urge,	**Foreign Symbols**	
g	gag	ŏ	got		term,	œ	*French* feu
h	hat	ō	go		firm,	ü	*French* tu
hw	when	ô	caught,		word,	KH	*French* loch
ĭ	sit		saw		heard	N	*French* bon
ī	nice,	oi	noise,	v	valve		
	by		boy	w	with		

Capitalization, Punctuation, and Style Guide

This section of the Dictionary presents some of the basic points of style used in written American English. The rules for the correct use of capital letters, punctuation marks, numbers, and italics or underlining are grouped together under headings and subheadings for easy reference. Each rule includes an example phrase or sentence.

At the end of this Guide, you will find a brief section on the styling of bibliographical information. If you want to know more about any of the points discussed in the Guide, you should consult your grammar or composition textbook or one of the many style manuals available.

Capitalization

Rules for Capitalization

Capitalize the names of geographical entities, such as cities, states, and countries, and geographical features, such as rivers, mountains, and lakes:

Boston	Western Hemisphere	the Midwest
Minnesota	South Pole	Mississippi River
Brazil	Middle East	Lake Geneva
Mountain States	Gulf Coast	Andes Mountains
Arctic Circle	the South	Pacific Ocean

But do not capitalize directions:

We live ten miles west of Philadelphia.

Capitalize titles or their abbreviations when used with a person's name:

Governor Richards   Senator Garcia
Dr. Lin   President Kennedy

Capitalize words showing a family relationship when used with a person's name:

Uncle Bob
Grandmother Jones
but
her uncle, Robert Smith
my grandmother, Dora Jones

Capitalize words derived from proper names:

We ate at a Chinese restaurant.
She is French.

Capitalize the names of nationalities, languages, religions, and tribes:

Japanese
Spanish
Old English

Maori
Bantu
Roman Catholic Church

Capitalize the names of months, holidays, and holy days:

Monday
January
Labor Day

Passover
Ramadan
Easter

Capitalize the names of specific school subjects when followed by a number:

History I   Geography 101

Capitalize the names of councils, congresses, organizations and their members, and historical periods and events:

the Free and Accepted Masons
a Mason
the Republican Party
the House of Representatives

the Potsdam Conference
the Battle of Bull Run
the Italian Renaissance
the Middle Ages

Capitalize the names of streets, highways, buildings, bridges, and monuments:

Fifth Avenue
Route 9
World Trade Center

Vietnam Veterans Memorial
Golden Gate Bridge
Eiffel Tower

Capitalize the first word and all words except conjunctions and prepositions of four letters or fewer and articles in the titles of documents and literary, dramatic, artistic, and musical works:

the novel *To Kill a Mockingbird*
the play *A Raisin in the Sun*
the short story "The Necklace"
Bartok's *Concerto for Orchestra*
Bill of Rights
an article entitled "The Exports of Italy"
Robert Frost's poem "The Road Not Taken"
Picasso's *Guernica*

Capitalize the first word of each main topic and subtopic in an outline:

   I. Types of libraries
      A. Large public library
      B. Bookmobile
      C. School library
  II. Library services

Capitalize the first word in the greeting and closing of a letter:

Dear Marcia,	Your friend,
Dear Ms. Olson:	Sincerely yours,

Capitalize the first word of a direct quotation:

The candidate said, "Actions speak louder than words."
Who said, "Give me liberty, or give me death"?

Punctuation

End Marks

A *period* (.) ends a declarative or imperative sentence. A *question mark* (?) follows an interrogative sentence. An *exclamation point* (!) is used after an exclamatory sentence and after an interjection that expresses strong feeling.

The book is on my desk. (declarative)
Look up the spelling of that word. (imperative)
How is the word spelled? (interrogative)
This is your best poem so far! (exclamatory)
Wow! We've just won the essay prize. (interjection)

Apostrophe

To form the possessive of a singular noun, add an apostrophe and *s*:

sister-in-law's	family's	Agnes's

To form the possessive of a plural noun that does not end in *s*, add an apostrophe and *s:*

women's	mice's	sisters-in-law's

To form the possessive of a plural noun that ends in *s*, add an apostrophe only:

sisters'	families'	Joneses'

Use an apostrophe and *s* to form the plural of letters, numerals, symbols, and words that are used as words:

s's   *i*'s   2's   *'s

Fill in the questionnaire with *yes*'s and *no*'s.

Use an apostrophe in contractions in place of dropped letters:

isn't (is not)	they've (they have)	it's (it is)

Colon	**Use a colon to separate the hour from the minute:**

        7:30 P.M.   8:15 A.M.

Use a colon after the greeting in a business letter:

Dear Ms. Trimby: Dear Sir or Madam:

Use a colon before a list introduced by words such as *the following* or *these:*

Call the following: Lucia, Wanda, John, and Carl.

But do not use a colon after a verb or a preposition:

Next year I am taking English, history, and math.

He arrived with a suitcase, a coat, and an umbrella.

Comma

Use commas to separate words in a series:

My cousin asked if we had any apples, peaches, or grapes.

Use commas between two or more adjectives that come before a noun unless the adjectives are used together to express a single idea:

He had a rusty, old car.

but

The bird had dark blue feathers on its head.

Use a comma to separate the independent clauses in a compound sentence:

Some student were at lunch, but others were studying.

Use commas after words, phrases, and clauses that come at the beginning of sentences:

No, you cannot avoid the deadline.

Following the applause, the speaker continued.

When you are in doubt, ask for advice.

Use commas to separate interrupters such as *of course,* *however,* and *by the way* from the rest of the sentence:

His friend, of course, was late for the bus again.

The driver, however, had forgotten the directions.

Use commas to set off an appositive from the rest of the sentence when the appositive is not necessary to the meaning of the sentence:

Texas, the Lone Star State, borders Mexico.
(The appositive is extra, not needed for meaning.)
but
The writer Charles Dickens created complex plots.
(The appositive is necessary to the meaning.)

Use commas to set off a nonrestrictive clause—one that adds optional information not necessary to the meaning of the sentence. If a phrase or clause is essential, do not use commas:

Emily Dickinson, who was born in 1830, was a poet.
(The clause is not necessary to the meaning)
The man who read the poem is my father.
(The clause is necessary to the meaning.)

Use a comma to set off a word in direct address:

Thank you, Joe, for your help.
How was your trip, Mom?

Use a comma to separate the month and day from the year. Use a comma to separate the year from the rest of the sentence. Do not use commas if a specific day is not included:

January 12, 1998, was the date of the banquet.
but
The comet Hale Bopp appeared last in March 1997.

Use a comma after an interjection that expresses emotion:

Oh, I didn't see you there!

Use a comma to set off short quotations and sayings:

Jo told him, "Come tomorrow for dinner."
"I don't know if I can," he said, "but maybe I will."

Use a comma between the names of a city and a state in an address. If the address is within a sentence, also use a comma after the name of the state. Do not use a comma before the ZIP code:

Does Chicago, Illinois, have the world's tallest building?
Denise lives at 10 Palm Court, Lima OH 45807-3212.

Use a comma after the greeting in a personal letter and after the closing in all letters:

Dear Deena,   Sincerely yours,

Semicolon	**Use a semicolon to connect independent clauses that are closely related in thought or that have commas within them:**

There were five movie tickets left; she needed six.
He bought nuts, dates, and apples; we ate them all.

Use a semicolon to join two independent clauses when the second clause begins with an adverb such as *however, therefore,* or *consequently:*

It was growing dark; however, there were no clouds.

Hyphen, Dashes, and Parentheses	**Use a hyphen to join the parts of compound numbers, to join two or more words that work together as one adjective before a noun, or to divide a word at the end of a line:**

thirty-two   long-range plans
Raphael is known as one of Italy's many magnificent painters.

Use a dash to show a sudden change of thought:

The sky grew dark—it might mean snow.

Use parentheses to enclose unnecessary information:

Geraldine was reelected (once more) as treasurer.

Quotation Marks	**Use quotation marks to set off titles of short stories, articles, songs, poems, and book chapters:**

"The Party" (short story)   "If" (poem)
"The Summer Garden" (article)   "Mayan Art" (chapter)
"America" (song)

Use quotation marks to enclose direct quotations:

"What was Berlin like during the war?" she asked.
Eleanor Roosevelt said, "We must do the things we think we cannot do."

Numbers

Spell out numbers *zero* through *ten* and *first* through *tenth* and numbers at the beginning of a sentence. Use numerals for numbers over *ten* or *tenth:*

My team has 25 players.
Two hundred people were in the audience.
There are 147 apartments in my building.
It happened in the tenth century B.C.
He came in 14th out of 200 in the race.

Italics

Titles of books, magazines, newspapers, long musical works and poems, plays, works of art, movies, and television series are italicized:

In a Pickle (book)   *As You Like It* (play)
Miami Herald (newspaper)   *Mona Lisa* (painting)
Requiem (musical work)   *Nature* (TV series)

Use italics to indicate a word, number, or letter used as such:

The word *straight* has two *t*'s.
A *6* looks like an inverted *9*.

Use italics to distinguish the New Latin names of genera and species in botany and zoology:

Homo sapiens (human being)
Lycopersicon esculentum (tomato)

Use italics to set off the names of ships, planes, and often spacecraft:

U.S.S. *Kitty Hawk*
Spirit of St. Louis
Voyager II

In word processed, typewritten, or handwritten copy, as in an essay or a book report, italics are often indicated by underlining:

Melville's <u>Moby Dick</u>

the movie <u>The Wizard of Oz</u>

Bibliography

The basic organization of a bibliography is alphabetical. If the author's name is not given, list the title first, and alphabetize it by the first important word of the title:

Books

List the author's name (last name first), the book title, the city where the publisher is located, the publisher's name, and the year of publication. Note the punctuation:

McQuaig, Donald J., and Patricia A. Bille. *College Accounting.* Boston: Houghton Mifflin Company, 1997.

Encyclopedia Articles

List the author's name (last name first), then the title of the article (in quotation marks). Next, give the title of the encyclopedia (in italics or underlined) and the year of publication of the edition you are using. Note the punctuation.

Shields, Dianne. "Learning Disabilities." *The World Book Encyclopedia.* 1992 ed.

If the author of the article is not given, begin your listing with the title of the article.

"Global Warming." *The Concise Columbia Encyclopedia.* 1994 ed.

Magazine and Newspaper Articles

When listing an article from a magazine or newspaper, give the information in the following order: Author, article title, magazine or newspaper title, volume number, date, section number, and pages. A colon always precedes the page numbers. Note the punctuation in the examples below.

Magazine: Gorman, Christine. "None but the Brave." *Time* 6 Oct. 1997: 76.

Newspaper: Tye, Larry. "To Prevent Injuries, Protect and Prepare." *Boston Globe* 30 Sept. 1997: A19.

If the author of the article is not given, begin your listing with the title of the article.

"Ultrasound Computer Gives Look Inside Heart." *Boston Globe* 16 March 1993: 12.

Aa

a¹ or **A** (ā) *n., pl.* **a's** or **A's. 1.** The first letter of the English alphabet. **2. A.** The best or highest grade: *get an A on a report; grade A eggs.* **3.** In music, the sixth tone in the scale of C major.

a² (ə; ā *when stressed*) *indef. art.* **1.** One: *I didn't say a single word.* **2.** The same: *two of a kind.* **3.** Any: *A cat will always eat fish.* **4.** An example of a kind of: *Water is a liquid.*

a³ (ə) *prep.* In each; for each; per: *once a month; ten dollars a trip.*

a—¹ *pref.* A prefix that means without or not: *apolitical; atypical.*

WORD BUILDING: a—¹ The basic meaning of the prefix **a—** is "without." For example, **achromatic** means "without color." Before vowels and sometimes *h*, **a—** becomes **an—: anaerobic.** Many of the words beginning with this prefix are used in science, such as **aseptic** and **asexual.** It is important not to confuse **a—** with other prefixes, such as **ad—**, that begin with the letter *a*.

---

a—² *pref.* A prefix that means: **1.** On or in: *aboard.* **2.** In a particular condition: *abuzz; afire.*

a•back (ə băk′) *adv.* ◆ **take aback.** To surprise (sbdy.): *I was taken aback by his angry words.*

ab•a•cus (ăb′ə kəs) *n.* A device for doing arithmetic made of a frame holding parallel rods with sliding beads: *The abacus is used in China, Japan, and Korea.*

a•ban•don (ə băn′dən) *tr.v.* **1.** To leave (sbdy./sthg.) and not intend to return; desert: *abandon a sinking ship.* **2.** To give (sthg.) up completely; stop trying to succeed at: *They abandoned the attempt to climb the mountain.* See Synonyms at **yield.** *—n.* [U] Uncontrolled enjoyment: *We skied down the hill with abandon.* **—a•ban′don•ment** *n.* [U]

a•ban•doned (ə băn′dənd) *adj.* Deserted or given up: *After the snowstorm, the highway was covered with abandoned cars.*

a•bate (ə bāt′) *v.* **a•bat•ed, a•bat•ing, a•bates.** *—tr.* To make (sthg.) less in amount, degree, or intensity: *The driver raced around the curve without abating speed.* *—intr.* To become less in degree or intensity: *The storm abated.* **—a•bate′ment** *n.* [C; U]

ab•bey (ăb′ē) *n.* A place where monks or nuns live; a monastery or convent.

ab•bot (ăb′ət) *n.* A monk who is the head of a monastery.

abbr. *abbr.* An abbreviation of abbreviation.

ab•bre•vi•ate (ə brē′vē āt′) *v.* **ab•bre•vi•at•ed, ab•bre•vi•at•ing, ab•bre•vi•ates.** *—tr.* **1.** To reduce (a word or group of words) to a shorter form: *You can abbreviate the word* hour *to* hr. **2.** To shorten (sthg.): *abbreviate a long explanation.* *—intr.* To use abbreviations or shorten sthg. by abbreviation: *No one will understand your writing if you abbreviate so much.*

ab•bre•vi•a•tion (ə brē′vē ā′shən) *n.* **1.** [U] The act or process of shortening sthg.: *His abbreviation of the story left out many details.* **2.** [C] A shortened form of a word or group of words, for example, *Mr.* for *Mister* and *U.S.A.* for *United States of America.*

ABC (ā′bē sē′) *n., pl.* **ABC's.** (*usually plural*). **1.** The alphabet: *That child knows her ABC's.* **2.** The basic facts of a subject: *After learning the ABC's of arithmetic, most students are ready for algebra.*

ab•di•cate (ăb′dĭ kāt′) *v.* **ab•di•cat•ed, ab•di•cates, ab•di•cat•ing.** *—tr.* To give up (power or responsibility) formally: *abdicate the throne.* *—intr.* To give up power or responsibility: *The king abdicated to allow his son to take his place.* **—ab′di•ca′tion** *n.* [C; U]

ab•do•men (ăb′də mən *or* ăb dō′mən) *n.* **1.** The middle part of the body below the chest or ribs. **2.** The last part of the body of an insect or similar creature: *A bee's stinger is in its abdomen.*

ab•dom•i•nal (ăb dŏm′ə nəl) *adj.* Relating to the abdomen: *abdominal muscles.*

ab•duct (ăb dŭkt′) *tr.v.* To carry (sbdy.) away by force; kidnap: *No one knew who abducted the child.* **—ab•duc′tor** *n.*

ab•er•rant (ă bĕr′ənt) *adj.* Differing from what is normal, right, or typical: *aberrant behavior.*

ab•er•ra•tion (ăb′ə rā′shən) *n.* An action or event that differs from what is normal, right, or typical: *Wearing a suit and tie to work is an aberration for him because he usually dresses in jeans.*

a•bet (ə bĕt′) *tr.v.* **a•bet•ted, a•bet•ting, a•bets.** *Formal.* To encourage or help (sbdy./sthg.): *They have abetted our efforts to build a new gym.*

ab•hor (ăb hôr′) *tr.v.* **ab•horred, ab•hor•ring, ab•hors.** *Formal.* To feel disgust, hatred, or loathing for (sbdy./sthg.): *I abhor arguments.*

ab·hor·rence (ăb hôr′əns or ăb hŏr′əns) n.
1. [U] A feeling of disgust or hatred: *The crime filled me with abhorrence.* **2.** [C] Something regarded with disgust or loathing: *Cheating in any form is an abhorrence.* —**ab·hor′rent** adj.

a·bide (ə bīd′) tr.v. **a·bid·ed, a·bid·ing, a·bides.** To put up with, bear, or tolerate (sbdy./sthg.): *Most gardeners can't abide weeds.* ♦ **abide by.** tr.v. [insep.] To accept and obey (sthg.): *We abided by the terms of the agreement.*

a·bid·ing (ə bī′dĭng) adj. Continuing; permanent: *The doctor had an abiding faith in good nutrition.*

a·bil·i·ty (ə bĭl′ĭ tē) n., pl. **a·bil·i·ties. 1.** [C] The power to do sthg.: *Monkeys don't have the ability to speak.* **2.** [U] A skill or talent: *a famous violinist of great musical ability.* —**ability** or —**ibility** suff. A suffix that means ability or appropriateness for some action or condition: *readability;accessibility.*

ab·ject (ăb′jĕkt′ or ăb jĕkt′) adj. **1.** Deserving no respect; contemptible: *an abject coward.* **2.** In a low condition; miserable: *in abject poverty.*

a·blaze (ə blāz′) adj. On fire; in flames; blazing: *The barn was ablaze.* —**a·blaze′** adv.

a·ble (ā′bəl) adj. **a·bler, a·blest. 1.** Having the power, ability, or means to do sthg.: *He is able to work part-time after school.* **2.** Capable; talented: *Most cats are extremely able hunters.* —**a′bly** adv. —**able** or —**ible** suff. A suffix that means: **1.** Likely to be affected by a certain action: *breakable; washable.* **2.** Deserving a certain action: *honorable; credible.* **3.** Tending to a certain action: *variable.*

WORD BUILDING: —able The suffix —**able**, which forms adjectives, means "capable or worthy of." Thus a **likable** person is one who is capable of or worthy of being liked. The suffix —**ible** is closely related to —**able** and has the same meaning, as in **flexible**. Because they sound exactly alike, it is important to consult your dictionary when spelling words that end in this suffix.

---

a·ble-bod·ied (ā′bəl bŏd′ēd) adj. Physically strong and healthy: *able-bodied workers.*

ab·nor·mal (ăb nôr′məl) adj. Differing from what is considered normal, usual, or expected; not standard or ordinary: *flooding caused by an abnormal amount of rain.* —**ab·nor′mal·ly** adv.

ab·nor·mal·i·ty (ăb′nôr măl′ĭ tē) n., pl. **ab·nor·mal·i·ties.** Something that is not normal: *I wear glasses because of abnormalities in my eyes.*

a·board (ə bôrd′) adv. On, onto, or in a ship, train, or other passenger vehicle: *It's time for passengers to go aboard.* —prep. On, onto, or in: *life aboard ship.*

a·bode (ə bōd′) n. Formal. The place where one lives; a home: *a humble abode.*

a·bol·ish (ə bŏl′ĭsh) tr.v. To end (sthg.) completely; do away with: *Let's abolish the rule that forbids eating in the study hall.*

ab·o·li·tion (ăb′ə lĭsh′ən) n. [U] **1.** The act or state of ending or stopping sthg: *Many people favor the abolition of smoking.* **2.** The ending of slavery in the United States: *a Northerner who favored abolition.* —**ab′o·li′tion·ist** n.

a·bom·i·na·ble (ə bŏm′ə nə bəl) adj. **1.** Causing disgust; horrible: *an abominable crime.* **2.** Very unpleasant: *The cold, windy day was abominable weather for a hike.* —**a·bom′i·na·bly** adv.

a·bom·i·na·tion (ə bŏm′ə nā′shən) n. **1.** A feeling of hatred or disgust: *an abomination of cruelty to animals.* **2.** Something that causes hatred or disgust: *Many of these ugly concrete buildings are abominations.*

ab·o·rig·i·nal (ăb′ə rĭj′ə nəl) adj. **1.** Of or relating to aborigines: *aboriginal customs.* **2.** Having existed in a region from the earliest times; native; indigenous: *aboriginal plants.* —n. An aboriginal person, plant, or animal.

ab·o·rig·i·ne (ăb′ə rĭj′ə nē) n. A member of a group of people who are the first known to have lived in a region: *the aborigines of Australia.*

a·bort (ə bôrt′) v. —tr. **1.** To cause (an embryo or a fetus) to be born at a stage of development too early to allow survival. **2.** To end (sthg.) before completion: *Heavy fog forced the pilot to abort the landing.* —intr. **1.** To give birth to an embryo or fetus before it has developed enough to survive. **2.** To end sthg.: *We decided to abort when it became clear the mission would fail.*

a·bor·tion (ə bôr′shən) n. [C; U] **1.** The birth of an embryo or fetus before it is developed enough to survive; a miscarriage. **2.** The deliberate ending of a pregnancy and expulsion of an embryo or fetus that cannot survive.

a·bor·tive (ə bôr′tĭv) adj. Not successful; fruitless: *an abortive attempt.* —**a·bor′tive·ly** adv.

a·bound (ə bound′) intr.v **1.** To be full: *The forest abounds in animals.* **2.** To be present in large numbers: *Books abound on the library shelves.*

a·bout (ə bout′) adv. **1.** Close to, more or less (a number or amount); approximately: *The river is about 600 yards wide.* **2.** Almost; nearly: *The new highway is just about completed.* **3.** From side to side: *Great waves tossed the ship about.* **4.** To or in a reverse direction: *Instantly the shark turned about.*

ă–cat; ā–pay; âr–care; ä–father; ĕ–get; ē–be; ĭ–sit; ī–nice; îr–here; ŏ–got; ō–go; ô–saw; oi–boy; ou–out;
ŏŏ–took; ōō–boot; ŭ–cut; ûr–word; th–thin; *th*–this; hw–when; zh–vision; ə–about; ɴ–French bon

5. In no particular direction: *We walked about all afternoon.* **6.** Everywhere; all around: *looking about for a hiding place.* —*prep.* **1.** Concerning; having to do with; relating to: *stories about animals; the need to be careful about handling broken glass.* **2.** Near; close to: *She is about my size.* **3.** On all sides of; all around: *Thick fog is all about our boat.* **4.** Over different parts of; around: *children ran about the playground.* —*adj.* **1.** Moving here and there: *School's closed, and there's no one about.* **2.** *(followed by the infinitive with* to*).* **a.** Close to starting: *We are just about to go.* **b.** *Informal.* Close to being ready or willing: *I'm not about to let you do that.*

a·bout-face (ə bout′fās′) *n.* **1.** The act of turning the body to face in the opposite direction, especially in a military drill. **2.** A change to an opposite attitude or opinion: *The candidate's sudden about-face on that issue surprised everyone.*

a·bove (ə bŭv′) *adv.* **1.** In or to a higher place; overhead: *Clouds floated above.* **2.** In an earlier part of a book, article, or other written piece: *in the paragraph noted above.* —*prep.* **1.** Over or higher than: *sea gulls flying just above the waves; a tree that rises above the others.* **2.a.** Higher in rank, degree, or number: *The President is above all military officers.* **b.** Too honorable to do such a thing as: *He is above telling a lie.* **3.** Farther on; beyond: *The road is closed above the bridge.* **4.** Beyond the level or reach of: *We could hear the noise above the music.* —*adj.* Appearing or stated earlier: *the above figures.* —*n.* *(used with a singular or plural verb).* Something that appeared or was stated earlier: *You may choose any one or all of the above.* ♦ **above all.** More importantly than everything else: *Above all, she is honest.*

a·bove·board (ə bŭv′bôrd′) *adv. & adj.* Without dishonesty or trickery; open: *In a democracy all dealings of government should be aboveboard.*

ab·ra·sion (ə brā′zhən) *n.* **1.** [U] The act or process of scraping off or rubbing away. **2.** [C] An injury in which part of the skin has been scraped or rubbed away: *abrasions on the knees from falling off a bicycle.*

ab·ra·sive (ə brā′sĭv *or* ə brā′zĭv) *adj.* **1.** Causing a rubbing away or wearing off: *Sand is an abrasive substance.* **2.** Harsh and rough in manner: *an abrasive personality.* —*n.* A substance used in rubbing, grinding, or polishing. —**a·bra′sive·ly** *adv.* —**a·bra′sive·ness** *n.* [U]

a·breast (ə brĕst′) *adv.* Side by side in a line: *The soldiers marched four abreast.* ♦ **abreast of** or **abreast with.** Having recent information about; up-to-date with: *keeping abreast of the latest news.*

a·bridge (ə brĭj′) *tr.v.* **a·bridged, a·bridg·ing, a·bridg·es.** To shorten or condense (sthg.): *abridge a long novel by leaving out some chapters.* —**a·bridg′ment** *n.* [C; U]

a·broad (ə brôd′) *adv. & adj.* **1.** Out of one's country; in or to foreign places: *traveling abroad.* **2.** Broadly or over a wide area: *The wind scattered seeds abroad.*

a·brupt (ə brŭpt′) *adj.* **1.** Unexpected; sudden: *an abrupt change in temperature.* **2.** Very steep: *The path ends in an abrupt drop to the river.* **3.** Short, brief, and suggesting rudeness or displeasure; brusque: *an abrupt answer made in anger.* —**a·brupt′ly** *adv.* —**a·brupt′ness** *n.* [U]

ab·scess (ăb′sĕs′) *n.* A mass of infected liquid that forms at one place in the body and is surrounded by inflamed tissue: *He had a painful abscess on his leg.*

ab·scessed (ăb′sĕst′) *adj.* Having an abscess: *an abscessed tooth.*

ab·scis·sa (ăb sĭs′ə) *n., pl.* **ab·scis·sas** or **ab·scis·sae** (ăb-sĭs′ē). The distance of a point from the y-axis on a graph. It is measured parallel to the x-axis.

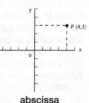

abscissa

ab·scond (ăb skŏnd′) *intr.v.* [with] *Formal.* To leave quickly and secretly and hide oneself; especially to avoid arrest: *The cashier absconded with the money.*

ab·sence (ăb′səns) *n.* **1.** [U] The state of being away: *Soccer practice was canceled because of the coach's absence.* **2.** [C] The period during which one is away: *an absence of four days.* **3.** [U] A lack: *The absence of reliable information caused rumors to spread.*

ab·sent (ăb′sənt) *adj.* **1.** Not present; away: *Two students are absent today.* **2.** [from] Lacking; missing: *Many important details were absent from the news report.* **3.** Not paying attention; absorbed in thought: *The boy had an absent look on his face and seemed not to hear his teacher.* —*tr.v.* (ăb sĕnt′). [from] *Formal.* To keep (oneself) away: *I absented myself from work because of illness.*

ab·sen·tee (ăb′sən tē′) *n.* A person who is absent: *Our class had four absentees.* —*adj.* **1.** Absent: *absentee students.* **2.** Not in residence: *an absentee landlord.*

ab·sen·tee·ism (ăb′sən tē′ĭz′ əm) *n.* [U] Repeated failure to appear, especially for work or other regular duty: *Absenteeism slowed production at the factory.*

ab·sent·ly (ăb′sənt lē) *adv.* As if lost in thought: *She stared absently out the window.*

ab·sent-mind·ed (ăb′sənt mīn′dĭd) *adj.* Tending to be lost in thought and to forget what one is doing; forgetful: *She is so absent-minded that she always forgets her keys.* —**ab′sent-mind′ed·ly** *adv.* —**ab′sent-mind′ed·ness** *n.* [U]

ab·so·lute (ăb′sə lōōt′) *adj.* **1.** Complete; total: *absolute silence.* **2.** Not limited in any way; unconditional: *absolute monarchy; absolute authority.* **3.** Not to be doubted; positive: *absolute proof.* —**ab·so·lute′ly** *adv.*

absolute value *n.* The value of a number without regard to its sign. For example, +3 and −3 each have the absolute value of 3.

absolute zero *n.* The temperature at which all molecules cease to move and at which no heat energy is present, equal to −459.67°F or −273.15°C.

ab·solve (əb zŏlv′ *or* əb sŏlv′) *tr.v.* **ab·solved, ab·solv·ing, ab·solves. 1.** To clear (sbdy.) of blame or guilt: *Evidence absolved the man of any connection to the crime.* **2.** To formally forgive (sbdy.) for sins committed. **3.** To release (sbdy.), as from a promise or responsibility: *Paying off the loan absolved her of her debt to the bank.*

ab·sorb (əb sôrb′ *or* əb zôrb′) *tr.v.* **1.** To take in or soak up (a liquid): *A paper towel absorbed the water.* **2.** To take (sthg.) in and make it a part of another thing: *New York absorbed a new wave of immigrants.* **3.** To take in or receive (sthg.) without transmitting or reflecting: *The color black absorbs heat.* **4.** To receive or withstand (sthg.) with little effect or reaction: *The car bumper absorbed the force of the collision.* **5.** To fill up or occupy (sthg.) completely: *My job after school absorbs all of my time.* —**ab·sorb′er** *n.*

ab·sorbed (əb sôrbd′ *or* əb zôrbd′) *adj.* Completely interested: *The absorbed look on their faces showed that they liked hearing the story.*

ab·sorb·ent (əb sôr′bənt *or* əb zôr′bənt) *adj.* Capable of taking in a liquid: *absorbent cotton.*

ab·sorb·ing (əb sôr′bĭng *or* əb zôr′bĭng) *adj.* Holding one's interest or attention: *an absorbing novel.* —**ab·sorb′ing·ly** *adv.*

ab·sorp·tion (əb sôrp′shən *or* əb zôrp′shən) *n.* [U] The act or process of absorbing sthg.: *Absorption of food is necessary in all living things.*

ab·stain (ăb stān′) *intr.v.* [*from*] To stay away from doing sthg. by one's own choice: *He abstains from eating meat.*

ab·sten·tion (ăb stĕn′shən) *n.* **1.** [U] The practice of abstaining: *Abstention from candy helps prevent tooth decay.* **2.** [C] An act of abstaining, especially the holding back of one's vote at an election: *one vote for, two against, and four abstentions.*

ab·sti·nence (ăb′stə nəns) *n.* [U] The act or practice of abstaining, especially by giving up certain drinks or foods or sexual contact. —**ab′sti·nent** *adj.*

ab·stract (ăb străkt′ *or* ăb′străkt′) *adj.* **1.**

Thought of apart from any particular object or thing. For example, *goodness* is an abstract word and *softness* is an abstract quality. **2.** Difficult to understand: *Your complicated explanation is too abstract for me.* **3.** In art, concerned with designs or shapes that do not realistically represent any person or thing: *an abstract painting full of strange shapes.* —*n.* (ăb′străkt′). A brief summary of the main points of a written or spoken text: *an abstract of the President's speech.* —*tr.v.* (ăb străkt′). **1.** To take away or remove (sthg.). **2.** [*from*] To think of (a quality, for example) apart from any particular instance or thing: *abstract a law of nature from a laboratory experiment.* **3.** To make a summary of (sthg.): *It was not easy to abstract his article.* ◆ **in the abstract.** In theory but not necessarily in reality: *In the abstract, fishing is relaxing, but we found it to be hard work.* —**ab·stract′ly** *adv.* —**ab·stract′ness** *n.* [U]

ab·strac·tion (ăb străk′shən) *n.* **1.** [C] An idea or quality thought of apart from any particular instance or thing: *Abstractions are hard to understand.* **2.** [U] Absent-mindedness: *In his abstraction, he didn't say hello.*

ab·surd (əb sûrd′ *or* əb zûrd′) *adj.* Clearly not true or sensible; ridiculous: *It would be absurd to walk backward all the time.* —**ab·surd′ly** *adv.*

ab·surd·i·ty (əb sûr′dĭ tē *or* əb zûr′dĭ tē) *n.* **1.** [U] The state of being absurd; foolishness. **2.** [C] An absurd action, thing, or idea: *The audience laughed at the absurdities in the film.*

a·bun·dance (ə bŭn′dəns) *n.* [C; U] A great amount or quantity; a plentiful supply: *The heavy spring rains gave us an abundance of water for the summer.*

a·bun·dant (ə bŭn′dənt) *adj.* Existing in great supply; very plentiful: *Abundant rainfall helped the farmers.* —**a·bun′dant·ly** *adv.*

a·buse (ə byōōz′) *tr.v.* **a·bused, a·bus·ing, a·bus·es. 1.** To use (sthg.) in a way it should not be used; misuse: *abuse a special privilege.* **2.** To hurt or injure (sbdy./sthg.) by physical violence; mistreat: *He abused his wife and was sent to jail.* **3.** To attack or injure (sbdy.) with words: *The candidates abused each other in sharp debate.* —*n.* (ə byōōs′). **1.** [U] Improper use; misuse: *drug abuse.* **2.** [U] Harsh or severe treatment: *child abuse; wife abuse.* **3.** [C] A practice or custom that is morally wrong: *Overworking an assistant is an abuse of power.* **4.** [U] Insulting language: *Baseball umpires have to take a lot of abuse from the crowd.* —**a·bus′er** (ə byōō′ zər) *n.*

a·bu·sive (ə byōō′sĭv) *adj.* **1.** Using rude

---

and insulting language: *abusive remarks.* **2.** Wrongly treated or incorrectly used: *the abusive powers of a dictator.* —**a•bu′sive•ly** *adv.* —**a•bu′sive•ness** *n.* [U]

a•but (ə bŭt′) *v.* **a•but•ted, a•but•ting, a•buts.** —*tr.* To border on or be next to (sthg.): *The garage abuts the house.* —*intr.* To touch at one end or side: *Our fence abuts on our neighbor's property.* —**a•but′ment** *n.*

a•buzz (ə bŭz′) *adj.* [*with*] **1.** Filled with a buzzing sound. **2.** Filled with activity or talk: *The classroom was abuzz with conversation.*

a•bys•mal (ə bĭz′məl) *adj.* **1.** Too deep to be measured; bottomless: *abysmal despair; abysmal ignorance.* **2.** Very bad, terrible: *an abysmal performance.* —**a•bys′mal•ly** *adv.*

a•byss (ə bĭs′) *n. (usually singular).* A very deep and large hole; a space that seems bottomless: *The scientists sent a probe into the abyss of the volcano.*

ac or **AC** *abbr.* An abbreviation of: **1.** Alternating current. **2.** Air conditioning.

ac•a•dem•ic (ăk′ə dĕm′ĭk) *adj.* **1.** Relating to a school or college: *an academic degree.* **2.** Relating to studies that are liberal or general rather than technical or vocational: *History and philosophy are academic studies.* **3.** Related only to theory and having no practical purpose: *The architects shifted from an academic discussion to a practical one.* —*n.* A professor or other member of a college or university. —**ac′a•dem′i•cal•ly** *adv.*

ac•a•de•mi•cian (ăk′ə də mĭsh′ən *or* ə kăd′ə mĭsh′ən) *n.* A member of an academy or a society for promoting literature, art, science, and other studies.

ac•a•dem•ics (ăk′ə dĕm′ĭks) *n.* [U] **1.** *(used with a plural verb).* College and university courses or studies: *Her parents wished she put more effort into academics.* **2.** *(used with a singular verb).* The academic environment, community, or profession: *The hard-working professor admits that acadmics is her life.*

a•cad•e•my (ə kăd′ə mē) *n., pl.* **a•cad•e•mies.** **1.** A school for a special field of study: *a naval academy.* **2.** A private high school. **3.** An association of educated persons or scholars for the purpose of advancing knowledge: *an academy of science.*

a cap•pel•la (ä′ kə pĕl′ə) *adv.* Using voices without musical instruments playing along: *The trio sang a cappella.*

ac•cede (ăk sēd′) *intr.v.* **ac•ced•ed, ac•ced•ing, ac•cedes.** [*to*] *Formal.* **1.** To consent; agree: *I acceded to her request that I attend although I had a cold.* **2.** To reach or come to a position of power or a public office: *The winning candidate acceded to the presidency.*

ac•cel•er•ate (ăk sĕl′ə rāt′) *v.* **ac•cel•er•at•ed, ac•cel•er•at•ing, ac•cel•er•ates.** —*tr.* To cause (sthg.) to go faster; speed up: *He accelerated his pace from a walk to*

a run. —*intr.* To increase in speed; quicken: *The car accelerated on the downhill slope.*

ac•cel•er•a•tion (ăk sĕl′ə rā′shən) *n.* [U] **1.** The act or process of accelerating. **2.** An increase in speed. **3.** The rate of change in the speed of a moving body with respect to time: *the acceleration of a falling object.*

ac•cel•er•a•tor (ăk sĕl′ə rā′tər) *n.* **1.** A device that controls the speed of a machine, especially the pedal that increases the flow of fuel to the motor of a car or truck: *The accelerator got stuck.* **2.** A substance or device that speeds up a chemical or atomic reaction.

ac•cent (ăk′sĕnt′) *n.* **1.** The stress or force with which a person says one or more syllables of a word compared with the other syllables of the word. For example, in the word *mother* the accent is on the first syllable. **2.** A mark showing accent or stress in pronouncing one or more syllables of a word. For example, in the word *résumé* there are accents over the *e*'s. **3.** A style of speech or pronunciation that is typical of a certain region or country: *She speaks with a French accent.* —*tr.v.* (ăk′sĕnt′ *or* ăk sĕnt′). **1.** To stress (sthg.) in speech or in music: *Accent the first syllable of the word.* **2.** To place an accent mark over (sthg.). **3.** To give emphasis or special notice to (sthg.); stress: *Her report accented the accomplishments made.*

ac•cen•tu•ate (ăk sĕn′chōō āt′) *tr.v.* **ac•cen•tu•at•ed, ac•cen•tu•at•ing, ac•cen•tu•ates.** To give stress to or emphasize (sthg.): *A red background accentuates the white letters of a stop sign.* —**ac•cen′tu•a′tion** *n.* [U]

ac•cept (ăk sĕpt′) *tr.v.* **1.** To receive (sthg.) offered: *accept a birthday gift.* **2.** To admit (sbdy.) to a group: *They accepted me as a new member of the club.* **3.** To think of (sthg.) as correct or true; believe in: *We accepted your explanation of what happened.* **4.** To have patience with or put up with (sbdy./sthg.): *You can accept the situation or do something to change it.* **5.** To say "yes" to (sthg.): *I accept your invitation.* **6.** To agree to take (responsibility): *You must accept the blame for your own actions.*

ac•cept•a•ble (ăk sĕp′tə bəl) *adj.* **1.** Welcome; agreeable: *an acceptable job offer.* **2.** Good enough; satisfactory: *Her schoolwork in chemistry is acceptable, but she could do better.* —**ac•cept′a•bly** *adv.*

ac•cep•tance (ăk sĕp′təns) *n.* [U] **1.** The act of taking sthg. offered: *the acceptance of a new job.* **2.** Agreement that sthg. is right; approval: *Acceptance of seat belts has greatly reduced injuries in car accidents.* **3.** Belief in sthg. as true: *Acceptance of the theory has been slow.*

ac•cess (ăk′sĕs) *n.* [U] **1.** The act of entering; entrance: *gain access to the building through the basement.* **2.** The right to enter, reach, or

A

use: *We have access to secret information.* **3.** A way of approaching or reaching: *The only access to the pond is by a dirt road.* —*tr.v.* To find and make available (data) from a computer: *The programmer accessed the file.*

access code *n.* A code that allows a person to use data stored in a computer.

ac·ces·si·ble (ăk sĕs′ə bəl) *adj.* **1.** Capable of being entered or reached: *easily accessible from the highway.* **2.** Easy to get: *The information is accessible on our computer.* —**ac·ces′si·bil′i·ty** *n.* [U] —**ac·ces′si·bly** *adv.*

ac·ces·so·ry (ăk sĕs′ə rē) *n.*, *pl.* **ac·ces·so·ries. 1.** Something that is not really needed but adds to the usefulness or appearance of sthg. else: *a car full of accessories including a CD player; a red scarf worn as an accessory with a black coat.* **2.** A person who is not present at the time a crime is committed but who helps a criminal either before or after the crime.

ac·ci·dent (ăk′sĭ dənt) *n.* **1.** [C] Something that happens without being planned or known in advance: *Our meeting each other was a lucky accident.* **2.** [C] An unexpected and undesirable event: *an automobile accident.* **3.** [U] Chance or coincidence: *She ran into an old friend by accident.*

ac·ci·den·tal (ăk′sĭ dĕn′tl) *adj.* Happening without being expected or intended: *the accidental discovery of gold in a river.* —**ac′ci·den′tal·ly** *adv.*

ac·ci·dent-prone (ăk′sĭ dənt prōn′) *adj.* Tending to have accidents: *She worries when her son uses tools because he is accident-prone.*

ac·claim (ə klām′) *tr.v.* To praise or greet (sbdy./sthg.) with loud approval: *All the film critics have acclaimed the new movie as the best of the year.* —*n.* [U] Loud or enthusiastic praise, applause, or approval: *public acclaim for her new book.*

ac·cli·mate (ə klī′mĭt *or* ăk′lə māt′) *tr. & intr.v.* **ac·cli·mat·ed, ac·cli·mat·ing, ac·cli·mates.** To accustom or become accustomed to new climate conditions or surroundings: *As time passed, they acclimated themselves to the tropical heat. Let's get acclimated before we unpack.*

ac·cli·ma·tion (ăk′lə mā′shən) *n.* [U] The process of acclimating or condition of being acclimated.

ac·cli·ma·tize (ə klī′mə tīz′) *tr. & intr.v.* **ac·cli·ma·tized, ac·cli·ma·tiz·ing, ac·cli·ma·tiz·es.** To acclimate: *He hasn't yet been acclimatized to life in the city. It takes time to acclimatize to living somewhere new.* —**ac·cli′ma·ti·za′tion** (ə klī′mə tĭ zā′shən) *n.* [U]

ac·co·lade (ăk′ə lād′ *or* ăk′ə läd′) *n.* An expression of approval; praise: *That movie received the Academy Award and other accolades.*

ac·com·mo·date (ə kŏm′ə dāt′) *v.* **ac·com·mo·dat·ed, ac·com·mo·dat·ing, ac·com·mo·dates.** —*tr.* **1.** To help or do a favor for (sbdy.): *I asked for an afternoon appointment, and she was able to accommodate me.* **2.** To provide (sbdy.) with lodging or living space: *accommodate guests at a hotel.* **3.** To have enough space for (sthg.); hold: *an airport built to accommodate the largest planes.* **4.** To adjust or adapt (oneself): *We must accommodate ourselves to changing conditions.* See Synonyms at **adapt.** —*intr.* To become adjusted, as the eyes do in focusing on objects at a distance.

ac·com·mo·dat·ing (ə kŏm′ə dā′tĭng) *adj.* Ready to help; obliging: *an agreeable and accommodating manner.* —**ac·com′-mo·dat′ing·ly** *adv.*

ac·com·mo·da·tion (ə kŏm′ə dā′shən) *n.* **1.** [U] The act of accommodating or the state of being accommodated; adjustment: *His accommodation to life in a new country was a painful experience.* **2. accommodations.** Room and board; lodging: *We requested accommodations at the hotel for two nights.*

ac·com·pa·ni·ment (ə kŭm′pə nē mənt *or* ə kŭmp′nē mənt) *n.* **1.** [C] Something added for use with another thing: *Crackers are a good accompaniment to soup.* **2.** [U] A musical part played as support, especially for a soloist: *a solo sung with piano accompaniment.*

ac·com·pa·nist (ə kŭm′pə nĭst *or* ə kŭmp′-nĭst) *n.* A musician who plays an accompaniment.

ac·com·pa·ny (ə kŭm′pə nē *or* ə kŭmp′nē) *tr.v.* **ac·com·pa·nied, ac·com·pa·ny·ing, ac·com·pa·nies. 1.** To go with (sbdy./sthg.): *The dog accompanied him through the woods.* **2.** To occur or happen in connection with (sthg.): *Heat accompanies fire.* **3.** To add to or supplement (sthg.): *The teacher accompanied the lesson with a slide presentation.* **4.** To play a musical accompaniment for (sbdy./sthg.): *Can you accompany this song on the guitar?*

ac·com·plice (ə kŏm′plĭs) *n.* A person who helps another person do sthg. wrong or illegal: *Police searched for the robber's accomplice.*

ac·com·plish (ə kŏm′plĭsh) *tr.v.* To complete, achieve, or carry out (sthg.): *We accomplished our goal of building a boat.*

ac·com·plished (ə kŏm′plĭsht) *adj.* **1.** Skilled because of practice or study; expert: *an accomplished musician.* **2.** Unquestionable: *It is an accomplished fact that smoking causes health problems.*

ă–cat; ā–pay; âr–care; ä–father; ĕ–get; ē–be; ĭ–sit; ī–nice; îr–here; ŏ–got; ō–go; ô–saw; oi–boy; ou–out; ŏŏ–took; ōō–boot; ŭ–cut; ûr–word; th–thin; *th*–this; hw–when; zh–vision; ə–about; N–French bon

ac·com·plish·ment (ə kŏm′plĭsh mənt) *n.*
1. [U] The act of completing or carrying out
sthg.: *the accomplishment of a task.* **2.** [C] An
achievement: *The first walk on the moon was
a great accomplishment in technology.* **3.** [C]
A skill acquired through training and practice: *Singing and painting are among the
actor's many accomplishments.*

ac·cord (ə kôrd′) *v. Formal.* —*tr.* To give or
grant (sthg.): *The U.S. Constitution accords
certain rights to citizens.* —*intr.* [with] To be
in agreement or harmony: *Your ideas accord
with mine.* —*n.* **1.** [U] Agreement; harmony:
His ideas are in accord with mine. **2.** [C] A
formal act of agreement; settlement between
conflicting parties: *The striking workers and
the employers reached an accord.* ◆ **of** or **on
(one's) own accord.** By one's own choice or
wish; voluntarily: *The children went to bed of
their own accord.*

ac·cor·dance (ə kôr′dns) *n.* [U] *Formal.*
Agreement; conformity: *in accordance with
your instructions.*

ac·cord·ing·ly (ə kôr′dĭng lē) *adv.* **1.** In
agreement with what is known, stated, or
expected: *Learn the rules and act accordingly.* **2.** As a result; therefore: *The student
was sick; accordingly, the teacher called the
parents.*

ac·cord·ing to (ə kôr′dĭng) *prep.* **1.** As said
or shown by; on the authority of: *According
to the weather report, it will rain tomorrow.* **2.**
In a way that agrees with: *Continue according to instructions.* **3.** As decided or regulated
by: *a list arranged according to the first letter
of each word.*

ac·cor·di·on (ə kôr′-
dē ən) *n.* A musical
instrument held at the
chest and played by
pressing keys while
pulling and pushing to
force air through.

ac·cost (ə kôst′ *or* ə-
kŏst′) *tr.v.* To come up
to and speak to (sbdy.),
often in a bold way: *A
stranger accosted me
for a quarter to make a phone call.*

accordion

ac·count (ə kount′) *n.* **1.** [C] A written or
spoken description of events; a narrative: *The
explorers gave an exciting account of their
adventures.* **2.** [C] A set of reasons; an explanation: *Give an account for your strange behavior.* **3.** [C] *(usually plural).* A record or
written statement of business dealings or
money received or spent: *A bookkeeper kept
the accounts of the company.* **4.** [C] A business arrangement, as with a bank or store, in
which money is kept, exchanged, or owed: *a
savings account in the local bank; a charge
account at a store.* **5.** [C] A customer or
client of a company or store: *an advertising
agency with several accounts that are big
manufacturing companies.* **6.** [U] Importance; worth: *Most gossip is of little account.*
◆ **account for.** *tr.v.* [insep.] **1.** To explain or
give the reason for (sthg.): *How do you
account for your absence from practice?* **2.**
To be the reason for (sthg.): *Bad weather
accounted for the delay in their arrival.* **on
account of.** Because of: *We were late on
account of the traffic jam.* **on no account.** At
no time; in no situation: *On no account
should you touch live wires.*

ac·count·a·ble (ə koun′tə bəl) *adj.* Expected or required to take responsibility for
one's actions: *Senators are accountable for
their actions to the people who elect them.*
—**ac·count′a·bil′i·ty** *n.* [U]

ac·count·ant (ə koun′tənt) *n.* A person
who keeps or inspects financial records, as of
a business, government agency, or person.

ac·count·ing (ə koun′tĭng) *n.* [U] The
occupation or methods of keeping financial
records, as of a business or government
agency.

ac·cred·it (ə krĕd′ĭt) *tr.v.* **1.** To consider
(sthg.) as the work of sbdy.: *We accredit the
discovery of radium to Marie Curie.* **2.** To
approve or record (sthg.) as good enough by
certain standards: *This college has been
accredited.*

ac·cred·i·ta·tion (ə krĕd′ĭ tā′shən) *n.*
[U] Approval of a school, a hospital, or an
agency as good enough by certain standards:
*The school lost its accreditation because of
overcrowding.*

ac·cru·al (ə krōō′əl) *n.* **1.** The process
of accruing; increase: *Education leads to an
accrual of knowledge.* **2.** Something that has
accrued.

ac·crue (ə krōō′) *intr.v.* **ac·crued, ac·cru·
ing, ac·crues.** **1.** To come to sbdy. as a gain
or an addition: *Interest accrues in my savings
account.* **2.** To increase or happen as a result
of growth: *Our knowledge of disease has
accrued from scientific research.*

ac·cu·mu·late (ə kyōōm′yə lāt′) *v.* **ac·
cu·mu·lat·ed, ac·cu·mu·lat·ing, ac·cu·
mu·lates.** —*tr.* To collect or gather (sthg.)
together: *By working hard and spending little,
she accumulated a great deal of money.* See
Synonyms at **gather.** —*intr.* To increase:
*During the storm, deep piles of snow accumu-
lated on the sidewalk.* —**ac·cu′mu·la′tion**
n. [C; U]

ac·cu·ra·cy (ăk′yər ə sē) *n.* [U] **1.** Freedom
from error or mistake; correctness: *Check
your math for accuracy.* **2.** Exactness; precision: *the accuracy of the clock.*

ac·cu·rate (ăk′yər ĭt) *adj.* **1.** Free from
errors or mistakes; correct: *accurate answers.*
2. Exact; precise: *an accurate description; an
accurate method of measurement.* —**ac′·
cu·rate·ly** *adv.* —**ac′cu·rate·ness** *n.* [U]

ac•cu•sa•tion (ăk′yo͞o zā′shən) *n.* **1.** [C] A statement or formal declaration that a person is guilty of wrongdoing: *The lawyer presented a written accusation against the suspected criminal.* **2.** [U] The act of accusing or the state of being accused of wrongdoing: *False accusation is a serious offense.*

ac•cuse (ə kyo͞oz′) *tr.v.* **ac•cused, ac•cus•ing, ac•cus•es.** [*of*] **1.** To charge (sbdy.) with doing sthg. wrong or illegal: *The city accused the company of polluting the river.* **2.** To find (sbdy.) to be at fault; blame: *She accused her little brother of messing up her room.* —**ac•cus′er** *n.*

ac•cused (ə kyo͞ozd′) *n., pl.* **ac•cused.** The defendant or defendants in a criminal case: *The accused were taken to trial for robbing the bank.*

ac•cus•tom (ə kŭs′təm) *tr.v.* [*to*] To get (sbdy.) used to; make familiar with: *Growing up in Florida had accustomed her to hot weather.*

ac•cus•tomed (ə kŭs′təmd) *adj.* Usual; familiar: *They all sat down to dinner in their accustomed places at the table.* ♦ **accustomed to.** Used to; in the habit of: *Farmers are accustomed to working long days.*

ace (ās) *n.* **1.** The highest or lowest value playing card with one figure of its suit in the center. **2.** A person who can do sthg. very well or is an expert in some field: *That man is the baseball team's pitching ace.* —*tr.v.* **aced, ac•ing, ac•es.** *Informal.* To achieve a grade of A on (a test): *She aced her quiz in English.* ♦ **ace in the hole.** A hidden advantage or resource kept in reserve until needed: *The secret file was her ace in the hole.*

ac•e•tate (ăs′ĭ tāt′) *n.* [U] A cellulose product used as a fabric or the fiber derived from it.

ache (āk) *intr.v.* **ached, ach•ing, aches. 1.** To hurt with a dull steady pain: *My tooth aches.* **2.** To want very much: *I am aching to get home. He ached for a cigarette.* —*n.* **1.** A dull, steady pain: *Growing pains often appear as aches in the legs.* **2.** A feeling of sadness or strong desire: *an ache in his heart.*

a•chieve (ə chēv′) *v.* **a•chieved, a•chiev•ing, a•chieves.** —*tr.* To succeed in completing, producing, or gaining (sthg.): *We achieved our goal.* See Synonyms at **reach.** —*intr.* To be successful: *They are eager for their children to achieve.* —**a•chiev′er** *n.*

a•chieve•ment (ə chēv′mənt) *n.* **1.** [U] The act or process of achieving sthg.: *The achievement of voting rights for women was the main focus of her life.* **2.** [C] Something that has been achieved, especially sthg. very difficult to do: *The development of the computer is a great achievement in technology.*

achievement test *n.* A test to measure how much a person has learned, especially at a particular grade level in school.

A•chil•les′ heel (ə kĭl′ēz) *n.* (*usually singular*). A weak point or vulnerable place: *Poor defense is the Achilles' heel of their team.*

Achilles tendon *n.* A strong tendon at the back of the leg connecting the calf muscles with the bone of the heel.

ach•ro•mat•ic (ăk′rə măt′ĭk) *adj.* **1.** Refracting white light without breaking it up into the colors of the spectrum: *an achromatic telescope.* **2.** Lacking color; colorless.

ach•y (ā′kē) *adj.* **ach•i•er, ach•i•est.** Filled with aches; having an ache: *Flu usually brings with it an achy feeling.*

ac•id (ăs′ĭd) *n.* **1.** [C; U] Any of a class of chemical substances that when dissolved in water are capable of reacting with a base to form salts and release hydrogen ions. Acids turn blue litmus paper red and have a sour taste. **2.** [U] *Slang.* LSD. —*adj.* **1.** Relating to or containing an acid: *an acid solution.* **2.** Having a sour taste: *Lemons have an acid taste.* **3.** Sharp and biting; sarcastic: *an acid tone of voice.* —**a•cid′ic** (ə sĭd′ĭk) *adj.* —**a•cid′i•ty** (ə sĭd′ĭ tē) *n.* [U] —**ac′id•ly** *adv.*

a•cid•i•fy (ə sĭd′ə fī′) *tr. & intr.v.* **a•cid•i•fied, a•cid•i•fy•ing, a•cid•i•fies.** To make or become acid: *Vinegar acidifies water. Milk becomes sour when it acidifies.*

acid rain *n.* [U] Rain, snow, or other precipitation containing a high amount of acidity resulting from air pollution and causing damage to forests, soils, lakes, and rivers. Acid rain is usually composed of a solution of sulfuric or nitric acid.

ac•knowl•edge (ăk nŏl′ĭj) *tr.v.* **ac•knowl•edged, ac•knowl•edg•ing, ac•knowl•edg•es. 1.** To admit or accept (sthg.) as real or true: *acknowledge one's mistakes.* **2.** To recognize the authority of (sbdy.): *The teacher was acknowledged as an expert on butterflies.* **3.a.** To express thanks for (sthg.): *acknowledge a favor.* **b.** To see or hear and reply to (sthg.): *acknowledge the cheers of the crowd.* **4.** To state that one has received (sthg.): *The college acknowledged my application with a post card.*

ac•knowl•edg•ment or **ac•knowl•edge•ment** (ăk nŏl′ĭj mənt) *n.* **1.** [C] Something done or given in answer to a gift, favor, or message from another person: *send an acknowledgment of an invitation.* **2.** [U] The act of admitting that sthg. is true: *His smile was acknowledgment that I had passed the test.*

ac•me (ăk′mē) *n.* (*usually singular*). The highest point; the greatest degree: *the acme of perfection.*

ă–cat; ā–pay; âr–care; ä–father; ĕ–get; ē–be; ĭ–sit; ī–nice; îr–here; ŏ–got; ō–go; ô–saw; oi–boy; ou–out; o͞o–took; o͞o–boot; ŭ–cut; ûr–word; th–thin; *th*–this; hw–when; zh–vision; ə–about; N–French bon

ac•ne (ăk′nē) *n.* [U] A condition in which the oil glands of the skin become blocked and infected, often causing pimples to form.

a•corn (ā′kôrn′) *n.* The nut of an oak tree, having a hard shell set in a woody base.

a•cous•tic (ə kōō′stĭk) also **a•cous•ti•cal** (ə kōō′stĭ kəl) *adj.* **1.** Relating to sound, the sense of hearing, or the science of sound: *the acoustic quality of a concert hall.* **2.** Designed to absorb or direct sound: *an acoustic ceiling.* **3.** Relating to a musical instrument that does not use electronic amplification of its sound: *an acoustic guitar.* —**a•cous′ti•cal•ly** *adv.*

a•cous•tics (ə kōō′stĭks) *n.* [U] **1.** *(used with a singular verb).* The scientific study of sound and its transmission. **2.** *(used with a plural verb).* The total effect of sound, especially as produced in a room or building: *The acoustics of the concert hall were improved when the new ceiling was added.*

ac•quaint (ə kwānt′) *tr.v.* [*with*] **1.** To tell or inform (sbdy.): *Acquaint us with your plans as soon as possible.* **2.** To make (sbdy.) familiar: *Let me acquaint myself with the facts of the case.*

ac•quain•tance (ə kwān′təns) *n.* **1.** [C] A person whom one knows but who is not a close friend: *We have many acquaintances in the neighborhood.* **2.** [U] Knowledge or information: *only a slight acquaintance with modern art.* ♦ **make (one's) acquaintance. 1.** *Formal.* To meet sbdy. for the first time: *I'm pleased to make your acquaintance.* **2.** To begin to know sbdy.: *We're making the acquaintance of our new neighbors.*

ac•quaint•ed (ə kwān′tĭd) *adj.* **1.** Known to each other: *We've been acquainted for years.* **2.** [*with*] Informed; familiar: *I am not acquainted with her novels.*

ac•qui•esce (ăk′wē ĕs′) *intr.v.* **ac•qui•esced, ac•qui•esc•ing, ac•qui•esc•es.** [*in; to*] To agree without protest: *acquiesce to a demand; acquiesce in a decision.*

ac•qui•es•cence (ăk′wē ĕs′əns) *n.* [U] Acceptance or obedience without protest; quiet agreement: *She promised acquiescence to her parents' wishes.* —**ac′qui•es′cent** *adj.*

ac•quire (ə kwīr′) *tr.v.* **ac•quired, ac•quir•ing, ac•quires. 1.** To gain possession of (sthg.): *acquire a valuable painting.* **2.** To get (sthg.) by one's own efforts: *acquire a second language.*

ac•qui•si•tion (ăk′wĭ zĭsh′ən) *n.* **1.** [U] The act or process of acquiring sthg.: *The museum's acquisition of a large art collection took many years.* **2.** [C] Something acquired, especially as an addition to a collection or one's possessions: *the newest acquisition to the library.*

ac•quit (ə kwĭt′) *tr.v.* **ac•quit•ted, ac•quit•ting, ac•quits. 1.** [*of*] To free or clear (sbdy.) from a formal accusation of wrongdo-

ing: *A jury acquitted the suspect of the crime.* **2.** To conduct (oneself); behave: *The firefighters acquitted themselves bravely during the crisis.*

ac•quit•tal (ə kwĭt′l) *n.* [C; U] The freeing of a person from an accusation of wrongdoing by the judgment of a court: *The vote of not guilty resulted in the defendant's acquittal.*

a•cre (ā′kər) *n.* **1.** A unit of area used in measuring land, equal to 43,560 square feet or 4,047 square meters. See table at **measurement. 2. acres.** Property in the form of land: *Their acres extend all the way to the river.*

a•cre•age (ā′kər ĭj *or* ā′krĭj) *n.* [U] Land area measured in acres: *a national park of vast acreage.*

ac•rid (ăk′rĭd) *adj.* **1.** Harsh or bitter to the sense of taste or smell: *Acrid smoke from the burning chemical plant filled the air.* **2.** Sharp or biting in tone or manner; nasty: *acrid criticism.*

ac•ri•mo•ni•ous (ăk′rə mō′nē əs) *adj.* Bitter and sharp in language or tone: *acrimonious exchanges among the candidates.* —**ac′ri•mo′ni•ous•ly** *adv.* —**ac′ri•mo′ni•ous•ness** *n.* [U]

ac•ri•mo•ny (ăk′rə mō′nē) *n.* [U] Bitterness or bad-tempered sharpness in manner or language: *signs of acrimony between jealous partners.*

ac•ro•bat (ăk′rə băt′) *n.* A person who can perform athletic feats requiring great agility and balance, such as swinging on a trapeze or walking a tightrope: *The acrobats and clowns performed in the circus.*

ac•ro•bat•ic (ăk′rə băt′ĭk) *adj.* Relating to acrobatics or seeming like an acrobat: *an acrobatic dive into the pool.*

ac•ro•bat•ics (ăk′rə băt′ĭks) *n.* [U] **1.** *(used with a singular or plural verb).* The art or performance of an acrobat. **2.** *(used with a plural verb).* A show of great skill and agility: *the singer's vocal acrobatics.*

ac•ro•nym (ăk′rə nĭm′) *n.* A word or name formed from the first letters or syllables of other words. For example, *radar* is an acronym for *radio detection and ranging* and *OPEC* is an acronym for *Organization of Petroleum Exporting Countries.*

a•cross (ə krôs′ *or* ə krŏs′) *prep.* **1.** On, at, or from the other side of sthg.: *a house across the road from ours.* **2.** From one side of sthg. to the other: *a bridge across a river.* **3.** Over; through: *Draw lines across the paper.* —*adv.* **1.** From one side to the other: *They drove across the bridge.* **2.** On or to the opposite side: *We came across by ferry.* **3.** In a way that is understood or accepted: *get one's point across.*

a•cross-the-board (ə krôs′ thə bôrd′ *or* ə krŏs′ thə bôrd′) *adj.* Including or affecting all members, levels, or departments, especially in an industry or a company: *an across-the-board pay increase.*

a•cryl•ic (ə krĭl′ĭk) n. **1.** [U] A type of plastic. **2.** [C] (usually plural). A paint made from acrylic. **3.** [U] A type of fiber: The sweater is made of acrylic.

act (ăkt) n. **1.** Something done; a completed action: an act of bravery. **2.** The process of doing sthg.: Police caught the robber in the act of stealing. **3.a.** A performance for an audience, often forming part of a longer show: a comedian's act. **b.** One of the main divisions of a play or other dramatic work: a play in three acts. **4.** Behavior that shows feelings one doesn't really have: His buying you flowers was just an act. **5.** A law, especially one created by a legislative body: an act of Congress. —v. —intr. **1.** To do sthg.; perform an action: By acting quickly, we stopped the fire from spreading. **2.** To serve or function: The heart acts like a pump. **3.** To behave; conduct oneself: She acts like a born leader. **4.** To perform in a dramatic presentation: act in a play. **5.** To behave in a way to fool sbdy.; pretend: He tried to look brave, but he was only acting. **6.** To have an effect: The medicine acts soon after it is taken. —tr. **1.** To play the part of (a character in a play or film): She acted Juliet in the play. **2.** To behave like (sbdy./sthg.): act the fool. **3.** To behave in a way that is right or suitable for (sthg.): Act your age. ♦ **act on** or **upon.** tr.v. [insep.] To do sthg. as a result of (sthg.): I finally acted on my doctor's advice and stopped smoking. **act out.** tr.v. [sep.] To perform (sthg.) in or as if in a play; dramatize: act out a story. **act up.** intr.v. **1.** To behave badly: The children were acting up all day, and their mother was upset. **2.** To fail to work or function as usual: The computer has been acting up.

act•ing (ăk′tĭng) adj. Serving for a limited time or in place of another person: the acting principal of the school. —n. [U] The occupation or performance of an actor: She studied acting in New York.

ac•tion (ăk′shən) n. **1.** [C] A thing done; a completed act: take responsibility for one's actions. **2.** [U] A tendency toward forceful activity: a man of action. **3.** [U] The process or fact of doing sthg.: an emergency requiring immediate action. **4.** [U] The series of events in a play or story: The action of the play takes place in Denmark. **5.** [C] A physical change, as in position, mass, or energy, that an object or system experiences: the action of a sail in the wind. **6.** [U] Fighting in a war; combat: send the soldiers into action. **7.** [C] A lawsuit.

action verb n. A verb that expresses action. Action verbs are either transitive, as activate (Electricity activates the fan's motor) or intransitive, as run (The fan's motor runs on electricity).

ac•ti•vate (ăk′tə vāt′) tr.v. **ac•ti•vat•ed, ac•ti•vat•ing, ac•ti•vates. 1.** To make (sthg.) active; start in motion: Press this button to activate the motor. **2.** To start or accelerate a chemical reaction in (sthg.), as by heating. —ac′ti•va′tion n. [U]

ac•tive (ăk′tĭv) adj. **1.** Moving or tending to move about: Nurses are more active than office workers. **2.** Performing or capable of performing an action or process; functioning: an active volcano. **3.** Involved in activities; participating: an active member of the club. **4.** Full of energy; busy: an active and useful life; an active mind. **5.** In grammar, relating to the active voice. —n. **1.** The active voice in grammar. **2.** A verb form in the active voice. —ac′tive•ly adv. —ac′tive•ness n. [U]

active voice n. In grammar, a form of a verb that shows that the subject is performing or causing the action expressed by the verb. For example, in the sentence John bought the book, the verb bought is in the active voice.

ac•tiv•ist (ăk′tə vĭst) n. A person who believes in or participates in direct action to make changes in government, social conditions, or a cause: environmental activists.

ac•tiv•i•ty (ăk tĭv′ĭ tē) n., pl. **ac•tiv•i•ties. 1.** [U] The condition or process of being active; action: mental or physical activity. **2.** [C] A particular kind of action or behavior: the nesting activities of birds. **3.** [C] A planned or organized thing to do, as in a school subject or social group: The children's after-school activities include sports and music lessons. **4.** [U] Energetic movement or action: The department store was a scene of great activity.

ac•tor (ăk′tər) n. A person who acts a part in a play, movie, or television program.

ac•tress (ăk′trĭs) n. A woman who is an actor.

ac•tu•al (ăk′chōō əl) adj. Existing or happening in fact; real: Actual sales were much greater than estimated sales.

ac•tu•al•i•ty (ăk′chōō ăl′ĭ tē) n., pl. **ac•tu•al•i•ties.** [C; U] Real existence; reality; fact: The human dream of walking on the moon became an actuality.

ac•tu•al•ly (ăk′chōō ə lē) adv. In fact; really: He said he was 21, but he was actually 19.

ac•tu•ar•y (ăk′chōō ĕr′ē) n., pl. **ac•tu•ar•ies.** A person who estimates risks and calculates how much an insurance company should charge for insurance.

ac•tu•ate (ăk′chōō āt′) tr.v. **ac•tu•at•ed, ac•tu•at•ing, ac•tu•ates.** Formal. **1.** To put (sthg.) into action or motion: Stepping on a pedal actuates the brake. **2.** To cause, inspire, or motivate (sbdy./sthg.): His remarks actuated a heated discussion. —ac′tu•a′tion n. [U] —ac′tu•a tor n.

ă–cat; ā–pay; âr–care; ä–father; ĕ–get; ē–be; ĭ–sit; ī–nice; îr–here; ŏ–got; ō–go; ô–saw; oi–boy; ou–out; ōō–took; ōō–boot; ŭ–cut; ûr–word; th–thin; th–this; hw–when; zh–vision; ə–about; N–French bon

a·cu·i·ty (ə kyōō′ĭ tē) *n.* [U] Sharpness of mind or perception: *With great acuity, the doctor diagnosed the patient's problem.*

a·cu·men (ə kyōō′mən *or* ăk′yə mən) *n.* [U] Quickness and wisdom in making judgments: *The owner's business acumen permitted the store to grow rapidly.*

ac·u·punc·ture (ăk′yōō pŭngk′chər) *n.* [U] The practice originating in traditional Chinese medicine in which thin needles are put into the body at specific points to relieve pain, treat a disease, or numb parts of the body during surgery.

a·cute (ə kyōōt′) *adj.* **1.** Able to see, hear, feel, or understand small differences; perceptive: *an acute sense of hearing; an acute awareness of one's surroundings.* **2.** Sharp and intense: *A toothache can cause acute pain.* **3.** Developing suddenly and having a short but intense course: *acute appendicitis.* **4.** Very serious; critical: *an acute lack of money.* —**a·cute′ly** *adv.* —**a·cute′ness** *n.* [U]

acute angle *n.* An angle whose measure in degrees is between 0° and 90°.

ad (ăd) *n.* An advertisement: *Let's look in the want ads for a used car.*

Homonyms: ad, add (combine to form a sum).

A.D. *abbr.* An abbreviation of anno Domini (in the year of the Lord; that is, after the birth of Jesus).

ad— *pref.* A prefix that means toward or to: *adapt; adhere.*

ad·age (ăd′ĭj) *n.* A short proverb or saying generally considered to be wise and true; for example, "Haste makes waste" is an adage.

a·da·gio (ə dä′jō *or* ə dä′jē ō′) *adv.* In music, slowly. —*adj.* In music, slow.

ad·a·mant (ăd′ə mənt) *adj.* [*about*] Firm and unwilling to change; not giving in easily: *Their parents were adamant about not letting them go.* —**ad′a·mant·ly** *adv.*

a·dapt (ə dăpt′) *v.* —*tr.* **1.** To change or adjust (sthg.) for a certain purpose: *They adapted the old truck for use as a camper.* **2.** [*to*] To make (oneself or sthg.) fit or suitable for a particular use or situation: *Her parents could not adapt themselves to living on an island.* —*intr.* [*to*] To change oneself so as to be right or fit; become adjusted: *The polar bear has adapted well to the Arctic climate.*

Synonyms: adapt, accommodate, adjust, conform. These verbs all mean to change sthg. to make it suitable. *Human beings can adapt themselves to a great variety of climates. I cannot accommodate myself to the new rules. If you adjust your seat belt you will be more comfortable. He wore shorts to school the first day but later conformed to the dress code.*

---

a·dapt·a·ble (ə dăp′tə bəl) *adj.* Able to change or be adjusted to fit in with new or different uses or situations: *an adaptable person; an adaptable schedule that is easy to rearrange.* —**a·dapt′a·bil′i·ty** *n.* [U]

ad·ap·ta·tion (ăd′ăp tā′shən) *n.* **1.** [U] The act or process of adapting; change or adjustment to meet new conditions: *The student's adaptation to a new country was easy and quick. The water wheel permitted adaptation of waterpower for the driving of early machinery.* **2.** [C] Something that is produced with changes from the original form: *The movie was an adaptation of a story written by Charles Dickens.* **3.** [C] The alteration of a body part or behavior that fits an animal or plant for a particular way of living: *Wings are an adaptation of the forelimbs of a bird for flight.*

a·dapt·ed (ə dăp′tĭd) *adj.* Fitted or suitable, especially for a certain purpose: *Some animals have claws well adapted for digging.*

a·dapt·er also **a·dap·tor** (ə dăp′tər) *n.* **1.** A device for putting together different parts of an apparatus that otherwise would not fit or work together: *He takes an adapter for his electric razor when he travels abroad.* **2.** A device for putting a machine or a piece of equipment to a different use.

a·dap·tive (ə dăp′tĭv) *adj.* **1.** Capable of or resulting from adaptation: *Adaptive changes in the penguin allow it to swim fast underwater.* **2.** Tending to change easily when necessary: *an adaptive good nature.*

add (ăd) *v.* —*tr.* **1.** To combine (two or more numbers) to form a sum: *Add 6 and 8 for a total of 14.* **2.** [*to*] To join or unite (sthg.) to increase, change, or improve sthg.: *add a suffix to a word; add an annex to a building.* **3.** To say or write (a word or words) as sthg. extra; say further: *Give them directions and add a note of caution.* —*intr.* **1.** To find a sum in arithmetic: *Most store clerks can add in their heads.* **2.** [*to*] To cause an increase or addition: *He adds to his savings each week.* ◆ **add up.** *intr.v.* To be reasonable, sensible, or logical: *What she said did not add up.* **add up to.** To result in: *A group of friends and some music add up to a good time.*

Homonyms: add, ad (advertisement).

---

ad·dend (ăd′ĕnd′ *or* ə dĕnd′) *n.* A number or quantity to be added to another number. For example, in $9 + 2 = 11$, the numbers 9 and 2 are addends.

ad·den·dum (ə dĕn′dəm) *n., pl.* **ad·den·da** (ə dĕn′də) A section added to a book or document, such as an appendix: *The client read the addendum to the contract.*

ad·dict (ə dĭkt′) *tr.v.* To cause (sbdy.) to become dependent on the use of a habit-forming substance, especially a narcotic drug. —*n.* (ăd′ĭkt). **1.** A person who has an uncontrollable desire for a harmful, habit-forming substance, especially a narcotic drug. **2.** A person who is very enthusiastic or cares greatly about sthg.: *a baseball addict.*

ad•dict•ed (ə dĭk′tĭd) *adj.* [*to*] **1.** Dependent on a harmful, habit-forming substance, especially a narcotic drug. **2.** Having a very strong liking and habit: *addicted to gossiping on the phone; addicted to a radio program.*

ad•dic•tion (ə dĭk′shən) *n.* [C; U] The condition of being addicted, especially dependence on harmful, habit-forming drugs.

ad•dic•tive (ə dĭk′tĭv) *adj.* Causing addiction; habit-forming: *Watching television can become addictive.*

ad•di•tion (ə dĭsh′ən) *n.* **1.** [U] The act, process, or operation of adding two or more numbers. **2.** [U] The act or process of adding sthg. extra to a thing: *the addition of seasoning to food.* **3.** [C] An added thing, part, or person: *The new baby is an addition to the family.* ◆ **in addition.** Also; too; as well: *We ate at a restaurant and saw a movie in addition.* **in addition to.** Besides; as well as: *In addition to riding her horse, she played her guitar this morning.*

ad•di•tion•al (ə dĭsh′ə nəl) *adj.* Added; extra; more: *The instructions are incomplete, and we need additional information to finish the project.* —**ad•di′tion•al•ly** *adv.*

ad•di•tive (ăd′ĭ tĭv) *n.* A substance added in small amounts to sthg. in order to improve its performance or quality, preserve its usefulness, or make it more effective: *a food additive to prevent spoiling.*

ad•dress (ə drĕs′) *tr.v.* **1.** To speak to (sbdy.): *The police officer addressed the speeder.* **2.** To give a speech to (sbdy./sthg.): *The President will address the nation on TV.* **3.** [*to*] To direct (sthg.) to a particular person, group, or place: *The teacher addressed her remarks to the new students.* **4.** To call or refer to (sbdy.) directly: *Address the judge as "Your Honor."* **5.** To write an address on (a piece of mail) to show where it should go: *address an envelope.* **6.** To take action about or deal with (sthg.): *We must address this problem.* —*n.* **1.** (*also* ăd′rĕs′). **a.** The place where a person lives or where a business is located: *your home address.* **b.** The information on a piece of mail, showing where it should go. **2.** A formal speech: *the President's inaugural address.* **3.** A number, label, or other symbol identifying a particular location where information is stored in the memory of a computer. ◆ **address (oneself) to.** To direct (one's efforts or attention): *The committee addressed itself to plans for a new town hall.*

ad•dress•ee (ăd′rĕ sē′ *or* ə drĕs′ ē′) *n.* The person to whom a letter or package is addressed.

a•dept (ə dĕpt′) *adj.* [*at*] Very skillful and effective: *Barbers are adept at cutting hair. The inventor was an adept mechanic.* See Synonyms at **proficient.** —**a•dept′ly** *adv.* —**a•dept′ness** *n.* [U]

ad•e•qua•cy (ăd′ĭ kwə sē) *n.* [U] The condition of being adequate; sufficiency or suitability: *The doctor doubted the adequacy of the sick child's diet.*

ad•e•quate (ăd′ĭ kwĭt) *adj.* **1.** As much as is needed for a particular purpose; enough: *We have an adequate supply of paper for our needs.* **2.** Not very good but just good enough: *That student's skills are just adequate to pass the test.* —**ad′e•quate•ly** *adv.* —**ad′e•quate•ness** *n.* [U]

ad•here (ăd hîr′) *intr.v.* **ad•hered, ad•her•ing, ad•heres.** [*to*] **1.** To stick or hold tightly: *The wallpaper adheres to the wall.* **2.** To remain faithful; support: *adhere to one's religious beliefs.* **3.** To act on or complete a plan without changes; hold firmly: *They adhered to their original plan.*

ad•her•ence (ăd hîr′əns *or* ăd hĕr′əns) *n.* [U] [*to*] **1.** The process or condition of adhering or sticking: *the glue's adherence to the paper.* **2.** Faithful attachment; devotion: *adherence to one's principles.*

ad•her•ent (ăd hîr′ənt *or* ăd hĕr′ənt) *n.* A loyal supporter or faithful follower: *Adherents of conservatism voted against more government spending.*

ad•he•sive (ăd hē′sĭv *or* ăd hē′zĭv) *adj.* **1.** Tending to hold tightly to another material; sticky. **2.** Coated with glue or other sticky substance: *adhesive tape.* —*n.* [U] An adhesive substance, such as paste or glue. —**ad•he′sion** (ăd hē′zhən) *n.* [C; U] —**ad•he′sive•ness** *n.* [U]

ad in•fi•ni•tum (ăd ĭn′fə nī′təm) *adv.* Without limit; forever; endlessly: *talk ad infinitum.*

a•di•os (ä′dē ōs′) *interj.* An expression used to say good-bye in Spanish.

adj. *abbr.* An abbreviation of adjective.

ad•ja•cent (ə jā′sənt) *adj.* **1.** [*to*] Next to; beside: *I can hear all the noise from the apartment adjacent to mine.* **2.** Lying near or close; nearby; neighboring: *the city and adjacent farmlands.*

adjacent angle *n.* Either of a pair of angles that have a vertex and a side in common so that they are located next to each other.

ad•jec•tive (ăj′ĭk tĭv) *n.* In grammar, a word used to modify a noun by describing it, limiting it, or adding to its meaning. For example, in the sentence *The young boy is very tall,* *young* and *tall* are adjectives. In English, adjectives usually appear before the noun they modify, but with verbs such as *act, seem,* and *be,* they often appear after the verb, as

ă-cat; ā-pay; âr-care; ä-father; ĕ-get; ē-be; ĭ-sit; ī-nice; îr-here; ŏ-got; ō-go; ô-saw; oi-boy; ou-out; ōo-took; ōō-boot; ŭ-cut; ûr-word; th-thin; *th*-this; hw-when; zh-vision; ə-about; N-French bon

in *The mouse acts nervous. The cat seems happy. The horse is thirsty.* —**ad′jec·ti′val** (ăj′ĭk tī′vəl) *adj.*

USAGE: adjective Words that modify nouns are called **adjectives.** If an adjective precedes a noun, it is called an **attributive adjective.** In the phrase *a blue coat, blue* is an attributive adjective. If an adjective follows a noun and a linking verb such as *be, grow,* or *seem,* the adjective is called a **predicate adjective,** as in the sentence *The sky grew dark.*

ad·join (ə join′) *v.* —*tr.* To be next to or connected with (sthg.): *The bath adjoins the bedroom.* —*intr.* To be side by side or connected: *These rooms adjoin.* —**ad·join′ing** *adj.*

ad·journ (ə jûrn′) *v.* —*tr.* To end (a meeting or session), leaving further business until later: *The judge adjourned the trial until after the holidays.* —*intr.* **1.** To stop official actions (of an organization or government body) until a later time: *The court adjourned for the weekend.* **2.** To move from one place to another: *The dinner guests adjourned to the living room.* —**ad·journ′ment** *n.* [U]

ad·junct (ăj′ŭngkt′) *n.* A separate, less important thing added to sthg.: *The gift shop is an adjunct of the museum.* —*adj.* Connected to or associated with a university: *She is an adjunct faculty member.*

ad·just (ə jŭst′) *v.* —*tr.* **1.** To change, set, or regulate (sthg.) in order to improve it: *I adjusted the seat belts in the car to fit the child.* See Synonyms at **adapt. 2.** To bring the parts of (a mechanism, for example) into a more effective arrangement: *The mechanic adjusted the carburetor on my car.* **3.** To change or adapt (oneself or sthg.) to be right or fit for present conditions: *Some wild animals do not adjust themselves to living in a cage.* **4.** To decide how much is to be paid on (an insurance claim). —*intr.* [*to*] To become accustomed or adapt to sthg.: *We can adjust to living in a smaller apartment.* —**ad·just′-a·ble** *adj.* —**ad·just′er** *n.*

ad·just·ment (ə jŭst′mənt) *n.* **1.** [C; U] The act of adjusting or the state of being adjusted: *Winter weather here requires adjustment to colder temperatures.* **2.** [C] A means by which a device can be adjusted: *Our TV set has several adjustments to regulate the color of the picture.* **3.** [C] A payment of or agreement about a claim or debt.

ad-lib (ăd lĭb′) *v.* **ad-libbed, ad-lib·bing, ad-libs.** —*tr.* To make up (words, music, or actions) while performing: *ad-lib a joke.* —*intr.* To make up words, music, or actions while performing; improvise: *The actor forgot his lines and ad-libbed.* —*n.* (ăd′lĭb′). A line, speech, action, or passage of music not prepared in advance but made up during a performance.

ad·min·is·ter (ăd mĭn′ĭ stər) *tr.v.* **1.** To manage or direct the affairs of (sthg.): *The mayor administers the city government.* **2.a.** To give out or dispense (sthg.): *A doctor administers medicine.* **b.** To give and supervise (sthg.): *administer a test.* **3.** To give (sthg.) formally or officially: *administer an oath of office.*

ad·min·is·tra·tion (ăd mĭn′ĭ strā′shən) *n.* **1.** [U] The act or process of directing the affairs of a business, school, or other institution; management. **2.** [U] The people who manage an institution or direct an organization: *The school administration is made up of the principal and a staff of teachers.* **3.** [C; U] Often **Administration.** The executive branch of a government, especially the President of the United States and the cabinet. **4.** [C] The time that a chief executive is in office or that a government is in power: *Many civil rights laws were enacted during President Johnson's administration.* **5.** [U] The act of administering: *administration of justice; administration of an oath.* —**ad·min′is·trate** (ăd mĭn′ĭ strāt′) *v.*

ad·min·is·tra·tive (ăd mĭn′ĭ strā′tĭv or ăd mĭn′ĭ strə tĭv) *adj.* Relating to government or management: *a manager with administrative ability; the President and other administrative officers of the government.* —**ad·min′is·tra′tive·ly** *adv.*

ad·mi·ra·ble (ăd′mər ə bəl) *adj.* Deserving admiration; excellent: *Honesty is an admirable quality.* —**ad′mi·ra·bly** *adv.*

ad·mi·ral (ăd′mər əl) *n.* The commanding officer of a navy or fleet of ships.

ad·mi·ra·tion (ăd′mə rā′shən) *n.* [U] A feeling of pleasure or approval: *The tourists looked at the Grand Canyon in admiration.*

ad·mire (ăd mīr′) *tr.v.* **ad·mired, ad·mir·ing, ad·mires. 1.** To look at (sbdy./sthg.) with pleasure and delight: *admire a beautiful picture.* **2.** To have a high opinion of or feel great respect for (sbdy./sthg.): *People admire her for her ability as a musician.* —**ad·mir′ing·ly** *adv.*

ad·mis·si·ble (ăd mĭs′ə bəl) *adj.* Accepted or permitted; allowable: *Admissible evidence in court must be based on fact.* —**ad·mis′-si·bil′i·ty** *n.* [U] —**ad·mis′si·bly** *adv.*

ad·mis·sion (ăd mĭsh′ən) *n.* **1.** [U] The act of allowing sbdy./sthg. to enter or join: *Congress must approve the admission of new states to the Union.* **2.** [U] **a.** The power or right to enter: *Admission to public school is open to all children.* **b.** Acceptance and entry of a person who applied to enter a school, profession, or club: *He received a letter of admission from the college.* **3.** [C] A price charged or paid to enter a place: *Visitors to the zoo paid an admission of five dollars each.* **4.** [C] A statement expressing one's guilt; a confession: *an admission of guilt.*

ad·mit (ăd mĭt′) *tr.v.* **ad·mit·ted, ad·mit·ting, ad·mits. 1.** To confess or express agreement to (sthg.) as being true or real: *I must admit that you are right. Never admit defeat.* **2.a.** To allow or permit (sbdy./sthg.) to enter: *This pass will admit one person free.* **b.** To accept and take in (sbdy.) as a new member, student, or patient: *The hospital admitted the accident victim.* **3.** To have enough space for (sthg.): *The harbor is large enough to admit many ships at once.*

ad·mit·tance (ăd mĭt′ns) *n.* [U] **1.** Permission or right to enter: *The sign said "no admittance."* **2.** The act of admitting: *The inspector gained admittance with a key.*

ad·mit·ted·ly (ăd mĭt′ĭd lē) *adv.* As generally admitted to be true; without denial: *They won, though admittedly they played badly.*

ad·mon·ish (ăd mŏn′ĭsh) *tr.v. Formal.* **1.** To criticize (sbdy.) for a fault in a kind but serious way: *Their uncle admonished the twins for their lateness.* **2.** To advise, warn, or caution (sbdy.): *She admonished us to be careful on the ice.* **—ad·mon′ish·ment** *n.* [C; U]

ad·mo·ni·tion (ăd′mə nĭsh′ən) *n.* A gentle criticism or friendly warning: *Remember the doctor's admonition to keep the bandage dry.*

a·do (ə dōō′) *n.* [U] Fuss; bother: *They said their good-byes and left quickly without further ado.*

a·do·be (ə dō′bē) *n.* **1.** [U] A building material made of clay and straw that is dried in the sun. **2.** [C] A house made of such material.

ad·o·les·cence (ăd′l ĕs′əns) *n.* [U] **1.** The period of growth and physical development that leads from childhood to adulthood. **2.** A period of change and development to maturity: *the adolescence of the computer industry.*

ad·o·les·cent (ăd′l ĕs′ənt) *adj.* Relating to or going through adolescence: *adolescent behavior.* *—n.* A boy or girl, especially a teenager, in the stage of growth and development between childhood and adulthood: *Adolescents face a great deal of peer pressure.*

a·dopt (ə dŏpt′) *tr.v.* **1.** To take (a new member) into one's family through legal means and treat as one's own: *Our neighbors adopted a baby girl.* **2.** To take (sthg.) for one's own: *Writer Samuel Clemens adopted the name Mark Twain.* **3.a.** To accept and use or follow (sthg.): *adopt a suggestion; adopt new methods.* **b.** To pass by vote or approve (sthg.) officially: *adopt a new constitution for our state government.* **4.** To put on or assume (an attitude or style): *Some people adopt a confident manner to hide their nervousness.* **—a·dopt′a·ble** *adj.*

a·dop·tion (ə dŏp′shən) *n.* [C; U] **1.** The act of adopting or the condition of being

adopted: *the adoption of a child; the adoption of new methods.* **2.** The state of being adopted; official approval: *The new math textbooks gained statewide adoption.*

a·dop·tive (ə dŏp′tĭv) *adj.* Related by adoption: *Some children have adoptive parents.*

a·dor·a·ble (ə dôr′ə bəl) *adj.* Delightful; lovable; charming: *an adorable puppy.* **—a·dor′a·bly** *adv.*

ad·o·ra·tion (ăd′ə rā′shən) *n.* [U] **1.** Great and devoted love: *Many famous actors have enjoyed the adoration of millions of fans.* **2.** Worship of God or of a divine being.

a·dore (ə dôr′) *tr.v.* **a·dored, a·dor·ing, a·dores. 1.** To love (sbdy.) deeply and devotedly: *The girl adored her mother.* See Synonyms at **revere. 2.** To like (sthg.) very much: *Audiences everywhere adore the circus.* **3.** To worship (sbdy./sthg.) as God or a god. **—a·dor′ing·ly** *adv.*

a·dorn (ə dôrn′) *tr.v. Formal.* [with] To decorate (oneself or sthg.): *The table was adorned with flowers.*

a·dorn·ment (ə dôrn′mənt) *n.* **1.** [U] The act of adorning; decoration: *jewelry worn for personal adornment.* **2.** [C] Something that adorns or beautifies; an ornament or a decoration: *They wore no jewels or other adornments.*

ad·re·nal gland (ə drē′nəl) *n.* Either of two endocrine glands, located one above each kidney, that produce adrenaline and certain other hormones.

a·dren·a·line (ə drĕn′ə lĭn) *n.* [U] A hormone released by the adrenal glands that quickens the heartbeat, raises blood pressure, and thereby prepares the body for forceful action, as in response to danger or other stress.

a·drift (ə drĭft′) *adv. & adj.* **1.** Drifting or floating without direction: *a boat set adrift for weeks in the lake.* **2.** Without direction or purpose: *The editorial department was adrift without a supervisor to guide it.*

a·droit (ə droit′) *adj.* Skillful or clever at doing or handling sthg. difficult: *an adroit answer to a complicated question.* **—a·droit′ly** *adv.* **—a·droit′ness** *n.* [U]

ad·u·la·tion (ăj′ə lā′shən) *n.* [U] Too much praise or admiration: *The leader wanted respect, not adulation, from his people.*

a·dult (ə dŭlt′ *or* ăd′ŭlt) *n.* **1.** An animal or a plant that is fully grown and developed. **2.** A person of legal age, usually 18 or 21 years old, having the right to vote, hold property, and take certain responsibilities: *All adults should vote in an election.* *—adj.* **1.** Fully developed; mature: *an adult cat and her kittens.* **2.** Intended or suitable for mature persons: *adult education; an adult movie.*

a·dul·ter·ant (ə dŭl′tər ənt) *n.* A substance used to adulterate sthg.

a·dul·ter·ate (ə dŭl′tə rāt′) *tr.v.* **a·dul·ter·at·ed, a·dul·ter·at·ing, a·dul·ter·ates.** To reduce the quality of (sthg.) by adding impure, inferior, or improper substances: *adulterate the town water supply.*

a·dul·ter·a·tion (ə dŭl′tə rā′shən) *n.* [C; U] **1.** The act or process of adulterating sthg.: *a regulation forbidding the adulteration of milk with water.* **2.** A product or substance that has been adulterated.

a·dul·ter·er (ə dŭl′tər ər) *n.* A person who commits adultery.

a·dul·ter·ess (ə dŭl′trĭs *or* ə dŭl′tər ĭs) *n.* An old term for a woman who commits adultery.

a·dul·ter·ous (ə dŭl′tər əs) *adj.* Relating to or guilty of adultery. —**a·dul′ter·ous·ly** *adv.*

a·dul·ter·y (ə dŭl′tə rē *or* ə dŭl′trē) *n.* [U] Voluntary sexual intercourse between a married person and another person who is not the person's husband or wife.

a·dult·hood (ə dŭlt′hŏŏd′) *n.* [U] The time or condition of being fully grown and developed; maturity.

adv. *abbr.* An abbreviation of adverb.

ad·vance (ăd văns′) *v.* **ad·vanced, ad·vanc·ing, ad·vanc·es.** —*tr.* **1.** To move (sthg.) forward, onward, or ahead: *In checkers, players advance their pieces one square at a time.* **2.** To help the growth or progress of (sthg.): *Scientific research advances knowledge.* **3.** To put forward, propose, or offer (sthg.): *advance a theory.* **4.a.** To move (sthg.) ahead to a later time: *Advance your watch one hour in the spring.* **b.** To move (sthg.) from a later to an earlier time: *advance a deadline from June to May.* **5.** To lend or pay (money) before the usual due date: *The company advanced him a week's pay.* —*intr.* **1.** To move forward or ahead: *A cat advanced toward the bird.* **2.** To make progress; improve or grow: *We are advancing in our studies.* **3.** To increase in amount or value: *As costs advance, prices go up.* —*n.* **1.** A movement forward: *the rapid advance of fire through the forest.* **2.** A step forward; an improvement or a development: *recent advances in science.* **3.** A loan or payment made before a due date or deadline: *Can you get an advance on your allowance?* **4.** An increase in price, amount, or value: *an advance of five cents per gallon in gasoline.* **5. advances. 1.** Efforts made to get friendship or favor: *advances to make up after an argument.* **2.** Generally unwelcome efforts to form a close, especially sexual, relationship: *She said her boss had made advances on many occasions.* —*adj.* **1.** Made or given ahead of time: *advance warning.* **2.** Going before sbdy./sthg.: *the advance guard.* ♦ **in advance.** Before in

time: *Make your travel plans in advance.* **in advance of.** In front of; ahead of: *She walked in advance of us, showing us the way.*

ad·vanced (ăd vănst′) *adj.* **1.** Very developed or complex: *advanced technology.* **2.** At a higher level than others: *an advanced student; advanced courses.* **3.** Far along in a process or time: *illness in its advanced stages; advanced age.*

ad·vance·ment (ăd văns′mənt) *n.* [C; U] **1.** The act of advancing or the condition of being advanced. **2.** A step forward; an improvement or a development: *new advancements in science.* **3.** A promotion at work or in a career: *opportunity for advancement to a higher position.*

ad·van·tage (ăd văn′tĭj) *n.* **1.** [C] A thing or condition that is helpful, useful, or can bring success: *Museums and libraries are some of the advantages of city life.* **2.** [U] Benefit or profit: *She learned from his mistake, turning it to her advantage.* **3.** [C] A favorable or preferred position: *The company's advertising gave them the advantage.* ♦ **to advantage.** To good effect; favorably: *The summer job let him use his talents to advantage.* —**ad′van·ta′geous** (ăd′vən tā′jəs) *adj.* —**ad′van·ta′geous·ly** *adv.*

ad·vent (ăd′vĕnt′) *n.* The coming or arrival of a new person or thing: *before the advent of the airplane.*

ad·ven·ture (ăd vĕn′chər) *n.* **1.** [C] An event that is unusual, exciting, or dangerous: *They went on a daring adventure in the wilderness.* **2.** [U] Excitement, danger, or discovery that comes from travel or new experience: *in search of adventure.*

ad·ven·tur·er (ăd vĕn′chər ər) *n.* **1.** A person who looks for or has adventures. **2.** A person who makes money in dangerous or dishonest ways: *The company founder was an old adventurer.*

ad·ven·tur·ous (ăd vĕn′chər əs) *adj.* Fond or full of adventure: *adventurous youths hiking in the wilderness.*

ad·verb (ăd′vûrb) *n.* In grammar, a word used to describe or add meaning to a verb, an adjective, or another adverb. In the sentences *They left early, The peacock is very pretty,* and *The dog ran very fast,* the words *early, very,* and *fast* are adverbs. —**ad·ver′bi·al** (ăd vûr′bē əl) *adj.*

ad·ver·sar·y (ăd′vər sĕr′ē) *n., pl.* **ad·ver·sar·ies.** An opponent or enemy: *The lawyers for the two sides were adversaries.*

ad·verse (ăd vûrs′ *or* ăd′vûrs′) *adj.* Not favorable; going against or in an opposite direction; hostile: *adverse criticism; an adverse reaction to medicine.* —**ad·verse′ly** *adv.*

ad·ver·si·ty (ăd vûr′sĭ tē) *n., pl.* **ad·ver·si·ties.** [C; U] Serious misfortune; trouble: *Faith helped them through times of adversity.*

ad·ver·tise (ăd′vər tīz′) *tr. & intr.v.* **ad·ver·tised, ad·ver·tis·ing, ad·ver·tis·es.** To call public attention to (a product or business) or to make a request for a worker as by a notice in a newspaper: *Manufacturers advertise their products. We advertised for a baby sitter.* —**ad′ver·tis′er** *n.*

ad·ver·tise·ment (ăd′vər tīz′mənt *or* ăd-vûr′tĭs mənt) *n.* A public notice, as in a newspaper or on television, to call attention to a product, a meeting, or an event.

ad·ver·tis·ing (ăd′vər tī′zĭng) *n.* [U] **1.** The act of calling public attention to a product, a meeting, or an event. **2.** The business of preparing and distributing advertisements: *Many people are employed in advertising.* **3.** Advertisements considered as a group: *How much advertising does the magazine have?*

ad·vice (ăd vīs′) *n.* [U] Opinion about how to solve a problem; guidance: *The pupil asked for advice from the teacher.*

ad·vis·a·ble (ăd vī′zə bəl) *adj.* Worth recommending or suggesting; wise; sensible: *It's not advisable to drive fast in the rain.* —**ad·vis′a·bil′i·ty** *n.* [U] —**ad·vis′a·bly** *adv.*

ad·vise (ăd vīz′) *tr.v.* **ad·vised, ad·vis·ing, ad·vis·es. 1.** To give advice to (sbdy.); recommend: *The doctor advised the patient to get some rest.* **2.** To inform (sbdy.); notify: *The radio advised us of the coming storm.* —**ad·vised′** *adj.*

ad·vis·er *or* **ad·vi·sor** (ăd vī′zər) *n.* **1.** A person who offers advice, especially officially or professionally: *The local doctor served as the school's health adviser.* **2.** A teacher who advises students in selecting courses and planning careers.

ad·vi·so·ry (ăd vī′zə rē) *adj.* Containing advice; having the power to advise: *an advisory committee.* —*n., pl.* **ad·vi·so·ries.** A report giving information, especially a warning: *a weather advisory.*

ad·vo·ca·cy (ăd′və kə sē) *n.* [U] Active support, as of an idea, a cause, or a policy: *His advocacy of the poor led him to start a free health clinic.*

ad·vo·cate (ăd′və kāt′) *tr.v.* **ad·vo·cat·ed, ad·vo·cat·ing, ad·vo·cates.** To be or speak in favor of (sthg.); support: *advocate changes in the law controlling air pollution.* —*n.* (ăd′və kĭt *or* ăd′və kāt′). A person who supports or speaks in favor of a cause: *an advocate of animal rights.*

aer·ate (âr′āt) *tr.v.* **aer·at·ed, aer·at·ing, aer·ates.** To let air into (sthg.); mix with air: *The lungs aerate the blood.* —**aer·a′tion** *n.* [U] —**aer′a′tor** *n.*

aer·i·al (âr′ē əl *or* ā îr′ē əl) *adj.* **1.** Relating to or caused by air: *aerial currents.* **2.** Relating to or carried out by aircraft: *aerial*

reconnaissance. —*n.* (âr′ē əl). An antenna, as for a radio or television.

aero— *or* **aer—** *pref.* A prefix that means: **1.** Air or atmosphere: *aerodynamics; aeroplane.* **2.** Gas: *aerosol.* **3.** Aviation: *aeronautics.*

aer·o·bic (â rō′bĭk) *adj.* **1.** Needing or using oxygen: *aerobic organisms.* **2.** Relating to exercise that improves the body's ability to use oxygen: *aerobic dancing.*

aer·o·bics (â rō′bĭks) *n.* [U] *(used with a singular or plural verb).* A system of exercises that involves dance routines and conditioning to promote the use of oxygen by the body.

aer·o·dy·nam·ics (âr′ō dī năm′ĭks) *n.* [U] *(used with a singular verb).* The scientific study of movement through the air: *the aerodynamics of a new car design.* —**aer′o·dy·nam′ic** *adj.* —**aer′o·dy·nam′i·cal·ly** *adv.*

aer·o·nau·tics (âr′ə nô′tĭks) *n.* [U] *(used with a singular verb).* The design, construction, or navigation of aircraft: *Improved aeronautics means that planes can fly faster.* —**aer′o·nau′ti·cal·ly** *adv.*

aer·o·plane (âr′ə plān′) *n. Chiefly British.* Variant of **airplane.**

aer·o·sol (âr′ə sôl′ *or* âr′ə sŏl′) *n.* A substance packaged under pressure in a can for use in a mist or spray form.

aer·o·space (âr′ō spās′) *adj.* **1.** Relating to Earth's atmosphere and the space beyond: *She does aerospace research for the government.* **2.** Relating to the science and technology of flight: *an aerospace engineer.*

aes·thet·ic *or* **es·thet·ic** (ĕs thĕt′ĭk) *adj.* Showing or relating to an appreciation or sense of beauty: *the aesthetic quality of a painting.*

aes·thet·ics *or* **es·thet·ics** (ĕs thĕt′ĭks) *n.* *(usually used with a singular verb).* The branch of philosophy that deals with the nature and expression of beauty, as in art: *My understanding of aesthetics changed after I studied modern art.*

AF *abbr.* An abbreviation of audio frequency.

a·far (ə fär′) *adv.* ♦ **from afar.** From a long distance: *We saw the boat from afar, so it was difficult to read its name.*

af·fa·ble (ăf′ə bəl) *adj.* Easy to speak to; pleasant; friendly: *I'm lucky; my boss is an affable sort.* —**af′fa·bil′i·ty** *n.* [U] —**af′fa·bly** *adv.*

af·fair (ə fâr′) *n.* **1.** A matter of concern: *Their argument was a private affair.* **2.** An occurrence, an action, an event, or a procedure: *Building a skyscraper is a long and costly affair.* **3. affairs.** Matters of business interest or public concern: *affairs of state.* **4.** A social gathering: *The wedding was a large affair.* **5.** A brief romantic relationship between two people: *His wife learned of his affair.*

ă–cat; ā–pay; âr–care; ä–father; ĕ–get; ē–be; ĭ–sit; ī–nice; îr–here; ŏ–got; ō–go; ô–saw; oi–boy; ou–out; ōō–took; ōō–boot; ŭ–cut; ûr–word; th–thin; *th*–this; hw–when; zh–vision; ə–about; ɴ–French bon

af·fect (ə fĕkt′) *tr.v.* **1.** To have an influence on (sbdy./sthg.); bring about a change in: *The drought has affected the fruit crop.* **2.** To touch the emotions of (sbdy.): *The movie affected us deeply.* **3.** To attack or infect (sbdy./sthg.): *Arthritis affects many older people.* **4.** To put on a false show of (sthg.); pretend to feel: *He affected indifference, though he was hurt by the remark.*

USAGE: affect The words **affect** and **effect** look and sound similar. Their meanings, however, are very different. The verb **affect** means "to influence": *That decision will affect my whole life.* The verb **effect** means "to make happen": *We effected some helpful changes.* The noun **effect** can mean "a result" or "an influence," but only the verb **affect** means "to influence."

---

af·fec·ta·tion (ăf′ĕk tā′shən) *n.* [C; U] Artificial behavior adopted to impress others; pretense: *He has many affectations, such as only drinking imported wine.*

af·fect·ed (ə fĕk′tĭd) *adj.* **1.** Acted upon, influenced, or changed: *Affected businesses lost clients in this recession.* **2.** Acted upon in an injurious way, as by disease or malfunction: *The affected toes were numbed by frostbite.* **3.** Speaking or behaving in an artificial way to make an impression: *an affected accent.*

af·fec·tion (ə fĕk′shən) *n.* [C; U] A fond or tender feeling toward sbdy./sthg.; fondness: *My affection for my aunt grew over the years.* —**af·fec′tion·ate** *adj.* —**af·fec′·tion·ate·ly** *adv.*

af·fi·da·vit (ăf′ĭ dā′vĭt) *n.* A written legal declaration made under oath before an authorized officer to be used as evidence or proof.

af·fil·i·ate (ə fĭl′ē āt′) *tr.v.* **af·fil·i·at·ed, af·fil·i·at·ing, af·fil·i·ates.** To associate or join (a larger or more important body): *The local unit of the Red Cross is affiliated with the national organization.* —**af·fil′i·ate** (ə fĭl′ē ĭt) *n.* —**af·fil′i·a′tion** *n.* [C; U]

af·fin·i·ty (ə fĭn′ĭ tē) *n., pl.* **af·fin·i·ties.** [C; U] **1.** [*for*] A natural attraction; a liking: *Our dog has an affinity for young children.* **2.** A close connection, relationship, or similarity: *The twins have a closer affinity than most members of their family.*

af·firm (ə fûrm′) *tr.v.* To declare (sthg.) positively; say firmly: *She affirmed her intention to run for the Senate.*

af·fir·ma·tion (ăf′ər mā′shən) *n.* **1.** [C; U] The act of declaring sthg. positively; assertion: *an affirmation of his love for her.* **2.** [C] Something declared to be true.

af·fir·ma·tive (ə fûr′mə tĭv) *adj.* Stating or declaring that sthg. is true, as with the answer "yes": *an affirmative response.* —*n.* A word or statement of agreement or assent. ♦ **in the affirmative.** Expressing agreement; saying "yes": *He answered in the affirmative.* —**af·fir′ma·tive·ly** *adv.*

affirmative action *n.* [U] The choosing of people for jobs or education based on race or gender to compensate for past discrimination.

af·fix (ə fĭks′) *tr.v.* To fasten (sthg.) to another thing; attach: *affix a label to a package.*

af·flict (ə flĭkt′) *tr.v.* [*with*] To cause physical or mental suffering to (sbdy.): *Human beings are afflicted with many diseases.*

af·flic·tion (ə flĭk′shən) *n. Formal.* **1.** [U] A condition of pain or distress: *offering help in times of affliction.* **2.** [C] A cause of pain or suffering: *Tuberculosis used to be a common affliction.*

af·flu·ence (ăf′lōō əns *or* ə flōō′əns) *n.* [U] A plentiful supply of goods or money; wealth. —**af·flu·ent** (ăf′lōō ənt *or* ə flōō′·ənt) *adj.* —**af′flu·ent·ly** *adv.*

af·ford (ə fôrd′) *tr.v.* **1.** To have enough time or money for (sthg.): *If we save our money, we can afford a new TV set.* **2.** *Formal.* To give or furnish (sthg.); provide: *This window affords a view of the mountains.*

af·front (ə frŭnt′) *tr.v.* To insult (sbdy.) on purpose or openly: *She affronted her hosts by asking how much dinner cost.* —*n.* An intentional insult or offense: *a personal affront.*

a·field (ə fēld′) *adv.* Away from one's usual environment or home; to or at a distance: *The children wandered far afield in search of butterflies.*

a·flame (ə flām′) *adv. & adj.* In flames or red as if in flames: *The spark set the tree aflame. Her mind was aflame with love for learning.*

AFL-CIO *abbr.* An abbreviation of American Federation of Labor and Congress of Industrial Organizations, a labor union.

a·float (ə flōt′) *adv. & adj.* **1.** Floating on air or water: *The raft was afloat on the lake.* **2.** Going from person to person, as rumors: *Talk of a change in managers is afloat.* **3.** Surviving financially; solvent: *That restaurant is barely staying afloat.*

a·foot (ə fŏŏt′) *adv. & adj.* **1.** An old term that meant on foot; walking: *We were afoot and arrived much later.* **2.** In the process of happening: *Something strange is afoot.*

a·fore·men·tioned (ə fôr′mĕn′shənd) *adj. Formal.* Spoken of earlier: *The aforementioned book is one that you should read.*

a·fraid (ə frād′) *adj.* **1.** Filled with fear; frightened: *afraid of the dark.* **2.** Doubtful about the future; reluctant; hesitant: *not afraid of work.* **3.** Full of concern; regretful: *I'm afraid that you don't understand.*

a·fresh (ə frĕsh′) *adv.* In a new way; again: *We must start our experiment afresh.*

Af·ri·can (ăf′rĭ kən) *adj.* Relating to Africa, its peoples, languages, or cultures. —*n.* **1.** A person born or living in Africa. **2.** A person whose ancestors are from Africa.

Af•ri•can A•mer•i•can or **African-Amer-ican** (ăf′rĭ kən ə měr′ĭ kən) *n.* An American whose ancestors are from Africa. —**Af′ri•can-A•mer′i•can** *adj.*

Af•ro-A•mer•i•can (ăf′rō ə měr′ĭ kən) *n.* An African American. —**Af′ro-A•mer′i•can** *adj.*

aft (ăft) *adv. & adj.* Toward or near the back of a ship or an aircraft: *going aft; the aft cabin.*

af•ter (ăf′tər) *prep.* **1.** Behind in place or order: *all in a row, one after another.* **2.** In pursuit of: *running after the fire engine.* **3.** About; concerning: *I asked after you.* **4.** At a later time than: *They arrived after dinner.* **5.** Past the hour of: *five minutes after three.* **6.** With the same name as; in honor of: *The baby was named after his grandfather.* **7.** Continuing without end: *week after week.* —*adv.* **1.** At a later time: *We left shortly after.* **2.** Behind; in the rear: *First came the tractor and then the wagon came rumbling after.* —*conj.* Following the time that: *We can eat after we get home.*

after all also **af•ter•all** (ăf′tər ôl′) *adv.* In spite of everything; nevertheless: *They struggled at the beginning of their marriage but made it a success after all.*

af•ter•ef•fect (ăf′tər ĭ fĕkt′) *n.* An effect (usually negative) that follows its cause after some delay: *The driver's nervousness was an aftereffect of the accident.*

af•ter•life (ăf′tər līf′) *n., pl.* **af•ter•lives** (ăf′tər līvz′). *(usually singular).* Life or existence after death: *belief in the afterlife.*

af•ter•math (ăf′tər măth′) *n. (usually singular).* A consequence or result, especially of a disaster or misfortune: *the aftermath of a hurricane.*

af•ter•noon (ăf′tər nōōn′) *n.* The part of the day from noon until sunset.

af•ter•shock (ăf′tər shŏk′) *n.* A less powerful quake coming after an earthquake.

af•ter•thought (ăf′tər thôt′) *n.* An idea thought of or added later: *Almost as an afterthought, he told us when we could expect him.*

af•ter•ward (ăf′tər wərd) also **af•ter•wards** (ăf′tər wərdz) *adv.* At a later time; after that: *We can go to the movie and have dinner afterward.*

Ag The symbol for the element silver.

a•gain (ə gĕn′) *adv.* **1.** Once more; another time: *If you don't win, try again.* **2.** To a previous place or position: *They left home but went back again.* **3.** On the other hand: *They might go, and again they might not.* ◆ **again and again.** Often; repeatedly: *I've read it again and again, but I can't understand it.*

a•gainst (ə gĕnst′) *prep.* **1.** In an opposite direction or course: *sailing against the wind.* **2.** In contact with; supporting: *waves wash-ing against the shore.* **3.** In opposition or resistance to: *struggling against prejudice.* **4.** In contrast to: *dark colors against a light background.* **5.** As a defense or safeguard from: *wearing gloves against the cold.*

ag•ate (ăg′ĭt) *n.* [C; U] A type of quartz found in various colors that are arranged in bands or in cloudy patterns.

age (āj) *n.* **1.** [C; U] The length of time during which a person or thing has existed; a lifetime or lifespan: *Elephants are famous for their great age.* **2.** [C] One of the stages of life: *the age of adolescence.* **3.** [U] The time in life when a person is allowed to assume adult rights and responsibilities, usually at 18 or 21 years: *People who are under age may not vote.* **4.** [U] The condition of being old; old age. **5.** Often **Age.** *(usually singular).* A period of history: *the Space Age.* **6. ages.** A long time: *It took ages to clean up after dinner.* —*v.* **aged, ag•ing, ag•es.** —*tr.* **1.** To cause (sbdy./sthg.) to grow old: *The crisis seemed to age the President.* **2.** To allow (sthg.) to mature or become flavorful: *They aged the wine in oak casks.* —*intr.* **1.** To become old: *She has aged well.* **2.** To take time to mature. Used of cheese, meat, or alcohol: *The cheese aged for three months.*

—**age** *suff.* A suffix that means: **1.** Collection; mass: *mileage.* **2.** Condition; state: *patronage.* **3.** Charge or fee: *postage.* **4.** Residence or place: *orphanage.* **5.** Act or result: *breakage; spoilage.*

ag•ed (ā′jĭd) *adj.* **1.** Old; elderly: *my aged aunts.* **2.** (ājd). Having the age of: *a child aged five.* **3.** (ājd). Ripe; mature: *aged cheese.* —*n.* [U] *(used with a plural verb).* Elderly people considered as a group: *Many of the aged continue to exercise.*

age•less (āj′lĭs) *adj.* Seeming never to grow old; existing forever; eternal: *ageless stories of daring and adventure.* —**age′less•ly** *adv.* —**age′less•ness** *n.* [U]

a•gen•cy (ā′jən sē) *n., pl.* **a•gen•cies.** A private business or governmental service authorized to act for others: *a real-estate agency.*

a•gen•da (ə jĕn′də) *n.* A list of things to be considered or done, as a program of business at a meeting: *Let's add that to our agenda for the next meeting.*

a•gent (ā′jənt) *n.* **1.** A person with the power or authority to act for another: *a ticket agent; a publicity agent.* **2.** A representative of a government or a governmental department: *an FBI agent.* **3.** A means by which sthg. is done or caused: *Wind and rain are agents of erosion.*

age-old (āj′ōld′) *adj.* Very old; ancient: *an age-old story.*

ag•gra•vate (ăg′rə vāt′) *tr.v.* **ag•gra•**

vat•ed, ag•gra•vat•ing, ag•gra•vates. 1. To make (sthg.) worse: *aggravate an injury.* **2.** To irritate (sbdy.); provoke: *Our constant noise aggravated the neighbors.* —**ag′‑ gra•vat′ing•ly** *adv.* —**ag′gra•va′tion** *n.* [C; U] —**ag′gra•va′tor** *n.*

ag•gre•gate (ăg′rĭ gĭt) *adj.* Gathered into or considered together as a whole; total: *an aggregate score.* —*n.* A collection or total: *A person's life is an aggregate of experiences.* ♦ **in the aggregate.** Taken as a whole; considered collectively: *We should look at the issues in the aggregate.* —**ag′gre•gate•ly** *adv.*

ag•gres•sion (ə grĕsh′ən) *n.* [U] The action of making an unprovoked attack on another person or country: *The war was started because of an act of aggression.*

ag•gres•sive (ə grĕs′ĭv) *adj.* **1.** Showing hostile behavior: *an aggressive person.* **2.** Vigorous; energetic: *an aggressive campaign to promote physical fitness.* —**ag•gres′‑ sive•ly** *adv.* —**ag•gres′sive•ness** *n.* [U] —**ag•gres′sor** *n.*

a•ghast (ə găst′) *adj.* [at] Filled with shock, fear, or surprise: *aghast at the accident.*

ag•ile (ăj′əl *or* ăj′īl′) *adj.* Physically or mentally able to move quickly: *an agile mountain climber.* —**ag′ile•ly** *adv.* —**a•gil′i•ty** (ə jĭl′‑ ĭ tē) *n.* [U]

ag•i•tate (ăj′ĭ tāt′) *v.* **ag•i•tat•ed, ag•i• tat•ing, ag•i•tates.** —*tr.* **1.** To shake or stir (sthg.) up violently: *The storm agitated the sea.* **2.** To disturb (sbdy.); upset: *Our quarrel agitated everyone present.* —*intr.* [for] To create public interest in a social or political issue: *agitate for civil rights.*

ag•i•tat•ed (ăj′ĭ tāt′əd) *adj.* Very nervous or excited: *You shouldn't be so agitated about her arrival.* —**ag′i•tat′ed•ly** *adv.*

ag•i•ta•tion (ăj′ĭ tā′shən) *n.* **1.** [U] The act of moving or shaking. **2.** [C; U] Great emotional excitement; anxiety. **3.** [U] Energetic action or discussion to create public interest in a social or political issue.

ag•i•ta•tor (ăj′ĭ tā′tər) *n.* **1.** A person who is active in creating interest in a social or political issue. **2.** A mechanism that stirs or shakes, as in a washing machine.

a•glow (ə glō′) *adv. & adj.* Brightly lit; shining: *a room aglow with lights; She's aglow with victory.*

ag•nos•tic (ăg nŏs′tĭk) *n.* A person who believes that there can be no proof that God exists. —*adj.* Relating to or being an agnostic. —**ag•nos′ti•cal•ly** *adv.* —**ag•nos′ti•cis′m** *n.* [U]

a•go (ə gō′) *adv. & adj.* In the past; back in time: *They lived there long ago.*

ag•o•nize (ăg′ə nīz′) *intr.v.* **ag•o•nized, ag•o•niz•ing, ag•o•niz•es.** [about; over] To be in serious physical or emotional pain or suffer great distress: *agonize over a decision.*

ag•o•niz•ing (ăg′ə nī′zĭng) *adj.* Causing great pain or worry: *an agonizing decision.* —**ag′o•niz′ing•ly** *adv.*

ag•o•ny (ăg′ə nē) *n., pl.* **ag•o•nies.** [C; U] Intense physical or emotional pain or suffering that lasts a long time.

a•grar•i•an (ə grâr′ē ən) *adj.* Relating to farmland or its ownership: *agrarian countries.*

a•gree (ə grē′) *intr.v.* **a•greed, a•gree•ing, a•grees. 1.** To have or share the same opinion: *I agree with you.* **2.** To consent: *He should never have agreed to such a crazy scheme.* **3.** To be the same; match: *The two versions of the story do not agree.* **4.** To come to an understanding or a settlement: *The jury could not agree on a verdict.* **5.** To be suitable, pleasing, or healthful: *The climate here agrees with most people.* **6.** In grammar, to have the same number, gender, case, or person: *In this sentence, the verb agrees with the subject.*

a•gree•a•ble (ə grē′ə bəl) *adj.* **1.** Pleasing; pleasant: *an agreeable smell.* **2.** [to] Willing to agree or consent: *The teacher was agreeable to the suggestion.* —**a•gree′a•bly** *adv.*

a•gree•ment (ə grē′mənt) *n.* **1.** [U] Similarity of opinion: *The neighboring countries were in agreement and signed a treaty.* **2.** [C] An arrangement or understanding between two people or groups: *an agreement between states over water rights.* **3.** [U] In grammar, correspondence between words in gender, number, case, or person.

ag•ri•busi•ness (ăg′rə bĭz′nĭs) *n.* [U] The business of producing, processing, and distributing agricultural products.

ag•ri•cul•tur•al (ăg′rĭ kŭl′chər əl) *adj.* Relating to farming; concerned with agriculture. —**ag′ri•cul′tur•al•ly** *adv.*

ag•ri•cul•ture (ăg′rĭ kŭl′chər) *n.* [U] The science, art, and business of growing useful crops and raising livestock; farming. —**ag′ri•cul′tur•ist** *n.*

a•gron•o•my (ə grŏn′ə mē) *n.* [U] The study of soil and the improvement of crop production; scientific farming. —**a•gron′o•mist** *n.*

a•ground (ə ground′) *adv. & adj.* Relating to a ship trapped in shallow water or on a reef or shoal: *During the storm, the ship ran aground near shore. The boat was aground.*

agt. *abbr.* An abbreviation of agent.

ah (ä) *interj.* An expression used to show surprise, delight, pity, or other emotions.

a•ha (ä hä′) *interj.* An expression used to show satisfaction, pleasure, or triumph: *Aha! Here are your keys!*

a•head (ə hĕd′) *adv.* **1.** At or to the front: *Let's move ahead to the front of the bus.* **2.** In advance: *To get tickets, you have to phone ahead.* **3.** For the future: *plan ahead.* **4.** Forward or onward: *The train moved ahead.* ♦ **ahead of.** In front of: *We were ahead of our friends in line.* **be ahead.** To be winning or in a superior position: *Our team is ahead by two goals.*

a·hem (ə hĕm′) *interj.* **1.** An expression used to attract attention or to express doubt or warning. **2.** The sound made when clearing the throat.

a·hoy (ə hoi′) *interj.* An expression used to hail a ship or person or to attract attention.

AI *abbr.* An abbreviation of artificial intelligence.

aid (ād) *tr.v.* To provide help or assistance to (sbdy.): *aid a friend in distress.* See Synonyms at **help.** —*n.* **1.** [U] Help; assistance: *foreign aid.* **2.** [C] A person or device that assists or helps: *She works as a teacher's aid. Because he is deaf, he uses a hearing aid.*

HOMONYMS: **aid, aide** (helper).

aide (ād) *n.* An assistant or helper: *a Presidential aide.*

AIDS (ādz) *n.* [U] *(from a*cquired *i*mmune *de*ficiency *syndrome).* A severe disease caused by HIV, a virus that attacks the body's immune system. The virus can be transmitted through bodily fluids such as semen and blood.

ail (āl) *v.* —*tr.* To make (sbdy.) ill; cause pain: *A high temperature is a sure sign that something is ailing you.* —*intr.* To be ill: *Their grandmother has been ailing for months.*

HOMONYMS: **ail, ale** (strong beer).

ai·le·ron (ā′lə rŏn′) *n.* A small section of the back edge of an airplane wing that can be moved up or down to control the plane's rolling and banking movements.

ail·ment (āl′mənt) *n.* A chronic illness or disease: *a heart ailment.*

aim (ām) *v.* —*tr.* To direct (a weapon or remark, for example) at sbdy./sthg.: *She aimed her rifle carefully at the target.* —*intr.* To propose; plan; intend: *aim to solve a problem.* —*n.* **1.** [U] The pointing of a weapon at a target: *take careful aim.* **2.** [C] Purpose; goal: *My aim is to be an actor.*

aim·less (ām′lĭs) *adj.* Without direction or purpose: *We spent an aimless afternoon strolling in the park.* —**aim′less·ly** *adv.* —**aim′less·ness** *n.* [U]

ain't (ānt). A nonstandard contraction of *am not, is not, are not, has not,* or *have not.*

air (âr) *n.* **1.** [U] The colorless, odorless, tasteless mixture of gases that surrounds the earth and which we breathe: *The air seems cleaner in the country than in the city.* **2.** [U] The open space above the earth; the sky: *a photograph taken from the air.* **3.** [U] Transportation by aircraft: *travel by air; ship goods by air.* **4.** [C] The appearance or manner of a person or thing: *The judge has*

a very dignified air. **5. airs.** An affected, unnatural way of acting, intended to impress people: *She is putting on airs by speaking with an accent.* —*v.* —*tr.* **1.** To put (sthg.) in the air to dry, cool, or freshen it; ventilate: *air a blanket.* **2.** To say (sthg.) publicly: *air your grievances.* **3.** To broadcast (a program): *The station aired the new show last night.* —*intr.* **1.** To become fresh or cool by exposure to the air: *give the room a chance to air out.* **2.** To be broadcast: *The news airs at 6:00 P.M.* ◆ **clear the air.** To settle an argument or end suspicion by giving facts: *The candidate cleared the air about her finances by publishing her tax records.* **in the air.** Being circulated; prevalent: *rumors in the air.* **off the air.** Not being broadcast: *Channel 11 goes off the air at 1 a.m.* **on the air.** Being broadcast: *The local news is on the air from 6:00 to 6:30 at night.* **up in the air.** Not yet decided; uncertain: *Our plans are still up in the air.*

HOMONYMS: **air, e'er** (ever), **ere** (before), **heir** (inheritor).

air bag *n.* A safety device in an automobile, consisting of a bag that inflates in a collision to keep a passenger or the driver from being injured.

air base *n.* A base for a military aircraft.

air·borne (âr′bôrn′) *adj.* **1.** Carried by air: *airborne viruses.* **2.** In flight; flying: *Drinks are served shortly after the plane is airborne.*

air brake *n.* A type of brake that is operated by compressed air.

air-con·di·tion (âr′kən dĭsh′ən) *tr.v.* **1.** To cool (a place) and regulate humidity using a mechanical device. **2.** To provide (a room or car, for example) with these devices: *We plan to air-condition our new house.* —**air′-con·di′tioned** *adj.*

air conditioning *n.* [U] A system of air conditioners.

air·craft (âr′krăft′) *n., pl.* **air·craft.** A machine, such as an airplane or helicopter, that is capable of flying.

aircraft carrier *n.* A naval ship with a long flat deck on which aircraft can take off and land.

air·field (âr′fēld′) *n.* A place, usually with paved runways, where aircraft can take off and land.

air·foil (âr′foil′) *n.* A part, such as an aircraft wing or propeller blade, designed to control direction or provide lift by changing how air flows around its surface.

air force or **Air Force** *n.* The branch of a country's military in charge of fighting war by using aircraft.

air·i·ly (âr′ə lē) *adv.* In a light or airy manner; gaily; jauntily: *She waved airily as she came in.*

air·less (âr′lĭs) *adj.* Lacking fresh air; stuffy: *a tiny and airless room.*

air·lift (âr′lĭft′) *n.* A system of transporting people or supplies by aircraft, especially to or from a place that is difficult to reach. —*tr.v.* To transport (sbdy./sthg.) by aircraft when ground routes are blocked: *The Army airlifted troops to the city.*

air·line (âr′līn′) *n.* A company that transports passengers and freight by air.

air·lin·er (âr′lī′nər) *n.* A large commercial passenger plane.

air·mail or **air mail** (âr′māl′) *n.* [U] **1.** The system of transporting mail by aircraft. **2.** Mail transported by aircraft. —*adj.* Relating to or for use with airmail: *an airmail letter.* —*tr.v.* To send (a letter, for example) by airmail: *You should airmail important papers overseas.*

air·plane (âr′plān′) *n.* Any of various vehicles that are heavier than air, have wings, and are powered by engines.

air pocket *n.* A downward current of air that makes an aircraft lose altitude suddenly.

air·port (âr′pôrt′) *n.* A level area for aircraft to take off and land, equipped with a control tower, buildings to store aircraft or cargo, and a passenger terminal.

air pressure *n.* [U] The force that air exerts.

air raid *n.* An attack by military aircraft usually armed with bombs: *The city was destroyed by air raids.*

air·ship (âr′shĭp′) *n.* A self-propelled aircraft, with an engine but without wings, that is filled with a gas so as to be lighter than air.

air·sick (âr′sĭk′) *adj.* Suffering from nausea because of the movement of an aircraft: *an airsick passenger.* —**air′sick′ness** *n.* [U]

air·space or **air space** (âr′spās′) *n.* [U] The space in the atmosphere above a country or region.

air speed *n.* The speed of an aircraft relative to the speed of the air it is traveling through.

air·strip (âr′strĭp′) *n.* A flat, clear area where aircraft can take off and land, usually only temporarily or in emergencies.

air·tight (âr′tīt′) *adj.* **1.** Allowing no air or other gas to pass in or out: *an airtight seal.* **2.** Having no weak points; without any possibility of being disproved: *an airtight excuse.*

air·way (âr′wā′) *n.* **1.** A passage through which air circulates, as in the throat: *The doctor checked the patient's airway.* **2.** A route for aircraft; an air lane.

air·y (âr′ē) *adj.* **air·i·er, air·i·est.** **1.** Open to the air: *The house was airy and full of light.* **2.** Similar to air: *airy silk; airy schemes.* —**air′i·ness** *n.* [U]

aisle (īl) *n.* **1.** A passageway between rows of seats, as in a church or theater. **2.** A similar passageway, as between counters in a department store.

a·jar (ə jär′) *adv. & adj.* Partially open: *Leave the door ajar. The door is ajar.*

AK *abbr.* An abbreviation of Alaska.

a·kin (ə kĭn′) *adj.* [*to*] Related; similar: *The word* maternal *is akin to the word* mother.

Al The symbol for the element **aluminum.**

AL *abbr.* An abbreviation of Alabama.

—**al** *suff.* A suffix that means of, relating to, or characterized by: *adjectival; postal.*

Ala. *abbr.* An abbreviation of Alabama.

al·a·bas·ter (ăl′ə băs′tər) *n.* [U] A smooth, hard, translucent marblelike stone that is white, tinted, or banded and used for decorative carvings.

à la carte also **a la carte** (ä′lə kärt′ *or* ăl′ə kärt′) *adv. & adj.* With a separate price for each item on the menu: *Breakfast is served à la carte. Meals in many high-priced restaurants are à la carte.*

à la mode (ä′lə mōd′ *or* ăl′ə mōd′) *adj.* **1.** According to or in the latest style or fashion; fashionable: *She can afford to dress à la mode.* **2.** Served with ice cream: *apple pie à la mode.*

a·larm (ə lärm′) *n.* **1.** [U] Sudden fear caused by a sense of danger: *There is no cause for alarm.* **2.** [C] A warning of approaching danger: *Rumors of fire were only a false alarm.* **3.** [C] A device that makes a noise to warn people of danger: *a fire alarm; a burglar alarm.* **4.** [C] An alarm clock. —*tr.v.* To fill (sbdy.) with alarm; frighten: *The loud noise alarmed the children.* See Synonyms at **frighten.**

alarm clock *n.* A clock that can be set to sound a bell or buzzer at a certain time in order to wake a person up.

a·larm·ing (ə lär′mĭng) *adj.* Causing great fear or anxiety: *The wind is increasing at an alarming rate.* —**a·larm′ing·ly** *adv.*

a·larm·ist (ə lär′mĭst) *n.* A person who frightens others needlessly or for little reason: *Don't be such an alarmist.*

a·las (ə lăs′) *interj. Formal.* An old expression used to show sorrow, regret, or grief.

al·be·it (ôl bē′ĭt *or* ăl bē′ĭt) *conj. Formal.* Even though; although: *They proposed an imaginative, albeit impractical, idea.*

al·bi·no (ăl bī′nō) *n.* A person or animal born without normal coloring, so that the skin and hair are white and the eyes are pink or blue: *an albino rabbit.* —**al′bi·nis′m** (ăl′bə nĭz′əm) *n.* [U]

al·bum (ăl′bəm) *n.* **1.** A book with blank pages on which to glue such things as photographs or stamps or to collect autographs. **2.** A phonograph record sold in a jacket.

al·che·my (ăl′kə mē) *n.* [U] A medieval system of chemistry that tried to change common metals into gold. —**al′che·mist** *n.*

al·co·hol (ăl′kə hôl′ *or* äl′kə hŏl′) *n.* [U]
1. Any of a large number of colorless, flammable liquids, especially those that occur in wines and liquors. **2.** Alcoholic beverages in general: *Some religions forbid the use of alcohol.*

al·co·hol·ic (ăl′kə hô′lĭk *or* äl′kə hŏl′ĭk) *adj.* Containing or resulting from alcohol: *the alcoholic odor of an antiseptic.* —*n.* A person who suffers from alcoholism.

al·co·hol·ism (ăl′kə hô lĭz′əm *or* ăl′kə-hŏ lĭz′əm) *n.* [U] Excessive drinking of or addiction to alcoholic beverages.

al·cove (ăl′kōv′) *n.* A small room that is part of a larger one without being separated from it by a wall or door: *There is a small alcove off the kitchen.*

ale (āl) *n.* [C; U] An alcoholic beverage similar to beer.

HOMONYMS: ale, ail (be ill).

---

a·lert (ə lûrt′) *adj.* Ready to speak or act; vigilant: *A good driver must remain alert.* —*n.* A warning signal against danger or attack: *They sounded the alert.* —*tr.v.* **1.** To warn (sbdy.) of approaching danger. **2.** To make (sbdy.) aware: *alert the public to the need for pollution control.* ◆ **on the alert.** [*for*] Watchful and prepared: *The police are on the alert for vandalism.*

al·fal·fa (ăl făl′fə) *n.* [U] A plant grown as feed for cattle and other livestock.

alg. *abbr.* An abbreviation of algebra.

al·ga (ăl′gə) *n., pl.* **al·gae** (ăl′jē). A water plant with a simple structure: *Algae can be as small as a single cell or as large as giant seaweed.*

al·ge·bra (ăl′jə brə) *n.* [U] A branch of mathematics that uses letters and other symbols to represent unknown numbers, especially in equations. —**al′ge·bra′ic** (ăl′-jə brā′ĭk) *adj.*

al·go·rithm (ăl′gə rĭth′əm) *n.* A mathematical rule or process for computing a desired result: *an algorithm used in a computer program.*

a·li·as (ā′lē əs) *n.* A false name used to hide a person's real identity: *She used several aliases while she was in hiding with her child.*

al·i·bi (ăl′ə bī′) *n.* **1.** A claim made by an accused person of being somewhere else when a crime was committed: *He had a good alibi on the night of the crime.* **2.** *Informal.* An excuse: *No more of your alibis!*

a·li·en (ā′lē ən *or* āl′yən) *n.* **1.** A person living in one country while remaining a citizen of another; a foreigner: *The new student registered as an alien.* **2.** A being from outer space: *In the movie, earth is invaded by aliens.* —*adj.* **1.** Belonging to or coming from another country; foreign. **2.** Not natural; unfamiliar; strange: *The new buildings make this town seem like an alien place.*

al·ien·ate (āl′yə nāt′ *or* ā′lē ə nāt′) *tr.v.* **al·ien·at·ed, al·ien·at·ing, al·ien·ates.** **1.** To lose the friendship or support of (sbdy.): *A barking dog tends to alienate the neighbors.* **2.** To cause (sbdy.) to become emotionally isolated: *Treating people as if they were just numbers in a computer will only alienate them.* —**al′ien·a′tion** *n.* [U]

a·lign also **a·line** (ə līn′) *tr.v.* **1.** To arrange (sthg.) in a straight line: *The chairs were aligned in two rows.* **2.** To commit (oneself) to one side of an argument or cause: *The allies usually align themselves behind the same position in foreign policy.* **3.** To adjust (a device or some of its parts) in order to produce a proper relationship or condition: *The mechanic aligned the wheels of my car.* —**a·lign′ment** also **a·line′ment** *n.* [U]

a·like (ə līk′) *adj.* Nearly the same; similar: *She and her mother are very much alike.* —*adv.* In the same way or to the same degree: *We must try to treat everyone alike.*

al·i·men·ta·ry (ăl′ə měn′tə rē *or* ăl′-ə měn′trē) *adj.* Relating to food, nutrition, or digestion: *the alimentary canal.*

al·i·mo·ny (ăl′ə mō′nē) *n.* [U] An amount of money that a court orders a divorced person to pay as support to a former husband or wife.

a·line (ə līn′) *v.* Variant of **align.**

a·live (ə līv′) *adj.* **1.** Having life; living: *The frog was alive, and it swam off as we came near.* **2.** In existence or operation; not extinct or inactive: *Keep your hopes alive.*

al·ka·li (ăl′kə lī′) *n.* A substance, such as ammonia or lye, that is soluble in water, neutralizes acids, and forms salts when combined with them. —**al′ka·line** (ăl′kə lĭn′) *adj.* —**al′ka·lin′i·ty** (ăl′kə lĭn′i tē) *n.* [U] —**al′ka·lize** *v.*

all (ôl) *adj.* **1.** The total number of: *All the windows are open.* **2.** The whole amount of: *We spent all day in the museum.* **3.** Any: *proven beyond all doubt.* **4.** Nothing but; only: *all skin and bones.* —*n.* [U] Everything one has: *The winning team gave their all.* —*pron.* **1.** The whole amount: *All of the flowers grew.* **2.** Each and every one: *All aboard the ship were saved.* —*adv.* **1.** Wholly; entirely: *The instructions are all wrong.* **2.** Each; apiece: *a score of five all.* ◆ **all along.** From the beginning; throughout: *I suspected all along that they were secretly in love.* **all for.** Completely in favor of: *The committee is all for changing the contest rules.* **all get-out.** *Informal.* The greatest degree possible: *She*

ă-**cat**; ā-**pay**; âr-**care**; ä-**father**; ĕ-**get**; ē-**be**; ĭ-**sit**; ī-**nice**; îr-**here**; ŏ-**got**; ō-**go**; ô-**saw**; oi-**boy**; ou-**out**;
ōō-**took**; ōō-**boot**; ŭ-**cut**; ûr-**word**; th-**thin**; *th*-**this**; hw-**when**; zh-**vision**; ə-**about**; ɴ-French **bon**

A

worked as hard as all get-out for her promotion. **all in.** Exhausted: *After a day working in the garden, I'm all in.* **all in all.** Everything being taken into account: *All in all, she's a good athlete.* **all of.** *Informal.* Not more than: *I was gone for all of an hour.* **all out.** With every possible effort; vigorously: *I studied all out and got an A in the course.* **all over. 1.** Over the whole area or extent: *a cloth embroidered all over with roses.* **2.** Everywhere: *He searched all over for the keys.* **3.** Finished in every respect: *Their marriage was all over.* **all that.** *Informal.* To the degree expected: *It's not all that hard.* **all there.** *Slang.* Alert; sane: *After the accident, she didn't seem to be all there.* **all the same.** Nevertheless; anyway: *It was hard, but I managed all the same.* **all told.** In total: *There were twenty people all told at the party.* **all wet.** *Informal.* Wrong; mistaken: *They were all wet when they told us they could help.* **at all. 1.** In any way: *I couldn't sleep at all.* **2.** To any extent; whatever: *not at all sorry.* **in all.** Altogether: *The two buses held 100 passengers in all.*

HOMONYMS: all, awl (pointed tool).

---

all— (ôl) *pref.* A prefix that means completely; totally: *all-American; all-knowing.*

Al·lah (ăl′ə *or* ä′lə) *n.* God, especially in Islam.

all-A·mer·i·can (ôl′ə mĕr′ĭ kən) *adj.* **1.** Typical of the United States: *an all-American hero.* **2.** In sports, chosen as the best amateur in the United States at a particular position or event: *an all-American fullback.* —*n.* An all-American athlete.

all-a·round (ôl′ə round′) *also* **all-round** (ôl′round′) *adj.* **1.** Able to do many or all things well: *an all-around athlete.* **2.** Comprehensive: *an all-around education.*

al·lay (ə lā′) *tr.v.* **1.** To lessen (sthg.); relieve: *allay pain.* **2.** To calm (fears or doubts): *allay one's fears.*

all clear *n.* [U] A signal, usually by siren, that an air raid, the threat of a tornado, or other danger is over: *We heard the all clear and came outside.*

al·le·ga·tion (ăl′ĭ gā′shən) *n.* A statement made without proof: *allegations of misconduct.*

al·lege (ə lĕj′) *tr.v.* **al·leged, al·leg·ing, al·leg·es.** To say that (sthg.) is true, usually without offering proof: *The newspaper alleges that the mayor took bribes.* —**al·leged′** *adj.* —**al·leg′ed·ly** *adv.*

al·le·giance (ə lē′jəns) *n.* [U] Loyalty or devotion, as to one's country; support: *The class pledged allegiance to the United States.*

al·le·go·ry (ăl′ĭ gôr′ē) *n., pl.* **al·le·go·ries.** A story, play, or picture in which characters or events stand for ideas or principles. —**al′le·gor′i·cal** (ăl′ĭ gôr′ĭ kəl *or*

ăl′ĭ gŏr′ĭ kəl) *adj.* —**al′le·gor′i·cal·ly** *adv.*

al·le·lu·ia (ăl′ə lōō′yə) *interj.* Hallelujah.

al·ler·gic (ə lûr′jĭk) *adj.* [*to*] **1.** Of or caused by an allergy: *an allergic reaction to dust.* **2.** Having an allergy: *a person who is allergic to tomatoes.* **3.** *Informal.* Having a dislike; averse: *allergic to hard work.* —**al·ler′gi·cal·ly** *adv.*

al·ler·gist (ăl′ər jĭst) *n.* A medical doctor who specializes in the diagnosis and treatment of allergies.

al·ler·gy (ăl′ər jē) *n., pl.* **al·ler·gies.** An unusual physical reaction to certain foods or substances, such as plant pollen or cat hair.

al·le·vi·ate (ə lē′vē āt′) *tr.v.* **al·le·vi·at·ed, al·le·vi·at·ing, al·le·vi·ates.** To make (sthg.) easier to bear; relieve; lessen: *Medicine will alleviate the pain.* —**al·le′vi·a′tion** *n.* [U]

al·ley (ăl′ē) *n., pl.* **al·leys. 1.** A narrow street or passageway between or behind buildings: *The truck blocked the alley.* **2.** A narrow area for playing games, such as a bowling alley.
♦ **up (one's) alley.** *Informal.* Suitable to one's interests or abilities: *This sort of project is right up their alley.*

al·li·ance (ə lī′əns) *n.* **1.** A formal agreement or union between nations, organizations, or individuals: *Britain and France formalized their alliance with a treaty.* **2.** A connection based on marriage, friendship, or common interest.

al·lied (ə līd′ *or* ăl′īd′) *adj.* **1.** Joined together in an alliance: *the allied countries of Europe.* **2.** Similar; related: *Biology and medicine are allied sciences.*

al·li·ga·tor (ăl′ĭ gā′tər) *n.* A large reptile that has tough skin, sharp teeth, and powerful jaws. An alligator's snout is shorter and rounder than that of the crocodile.

alligator

all-im·por·tant (ôl′ĭm pôr′tnt) *adj.* Very important; vital; crucial: *all-important efforts to keep the peace.*

al·lit·er·a·tion (ə lĭt′ə rā′shən) *n.* [U] The repetition of the same consonant sounds for poetic or rhetorical effect. The phrase *satiny smooth skin* is an example of alliteration. —**al·lit′er·a·tive** (ə lĭt′ər ə tĭv′) *adj.*

all-night (ôl′nīt′) *adj.* **1.** Continuing all night: *an all-night radio program.* **2.** Open all night: *an all-night diner.*

all-night·er (ôl′nī′tər) *n. Informal.* A project or event lasting all through the night.
♦ **pull an all-nighter.** To stay up all night working or studying: *He had to pull an all-nighter before the final.*

al·lo·cate (ăl′ə kāt′) *tr.v.* **al·lo·cat·ed,**

al·lo·cat·ing, al·lo·cates. To set (sthg.) aside for a particular purpose; allot: *allocate part of one's salary for entertainment.* —**al′lo·ca′tion** *n.* [U]

al·lot (ə lŏt′) *tr.v.* **al·lot·ted, al·lot·ting, al·lots. 1.** To distribute (sthg.): *The profits of the business were allotted equally to each partner.* **2.** To assign a portion of (sthg.) for a particular purpose; allocate: *We allotted 20 minutes for each speaker in the discussion.* —**al·lot′ment** *n.*

all-out (ôl out′) *adj.* Using all available resources; vigorous: *an all-out effort.*

al·low (ə lou′) *tr.v.* **1.a.** To let (sthg.) happen; permit: *We do not allow eating in the library.* **b.** To let (sbdy.) do sthg.; permit: *Please allow me to finish.* **2.** To let (sbdy.) have sthg.; permit to have: *We allowed ourselves a treat.* **3.** To let (sbdy./sthg.) in; permit the presence of: *We do not allow the dog upstairs.* ◆ **allow for.** To take (sthg.) into consideration and make a provision for it: *Our plans allow for changes in the weather.* —**al·low′a·ble** *adj.*

al·low·ance (ə lou′əns) *n.* **1.** The act of permitting. **2.** An amount of money or food, given at regular intervals or for a specific purpose: *a weekly allowance of five dollars; a travel allowance.* ◆ **make allowances for.** To consider or take (sbdy./sthg.) into account: *make allowances for inexperience.*

al·loy (ăl′oi′ *or* ə loi′) *n.* A metal made by mixing and fusing two or more metals. For example, bronze is an alloy.

all-pur·pose (ôl′pûr′pəs) *adj.* Useful in many ways: *Cotton is an all-purpose fabric.*

all right *adj.* **1.** Satisfactory; safe; uninjured; in good condition: *The tires are old but all right.* **2.** Average; mediocre: *This work is all right, but it could be better.* **3.** Correct: *These figures are perfectly all right.* —*adv.* **1.** In a satisfactory way: *The motor was running all right.* **2.** Yes: *All right, I'll go.* **3.** Without a doubt: *That's him, all right!*

all·spice (ôl′spīs′) *n.* [U] The fragrant strong-flavored berries of a tropical American tree, dried and used as a spice.

al·lude (ə lood′) *intr.v.* **al·lud·ed, al·lud·ing, al·ludes.** [*to*] To refer to sthg. indirectly; mention casually or in passing: *It is considered impolite to allude to how much money a person has.*

al·lure (ə loor′) *tr.v.* **al·lured, al·lur·ing, al·lures.** To attract (sbdy.); tempt: *I was allured by the ads.* —*n.* [U] Strong attraction; fascination: *the allure of sailing.*

al·lur·ing (ə loor′ĭng) *adj.* Attractive; inviting: *A vacation in the Caribbean is an alluring idea.* —**al·lur′ing·ly** *adv.*

al·lu·sion (ə loo′zhən) *n.* [C; U] An indirect reference: *allusions to Greek mythology in the poems.*

al·ly (ə lī′ *or* ăl′ī) *tr.v.* **al·lied, al·ly·ing, al·lies.** To join or unite (oneself) with sbdy. for a specific purpose: *The United States allied itself with the Soviet Union during World War II.* —*n., pl.* **al·lies.** People or countries that are allied to each other.

al·ma ma·ter (ăl′mə mä′tər *or* äl′mə mä′tər) *n.* (*usually singular*). **1.** The school, college, or university that a person has attended. **2.** The song or anthem of a school, college, or university.

al·ma·nac (ôl′mə năk′ *or* ăl′mə năk′) *n.* A book published once a year that includes calendars with weather forecasts, astronomical information, tide tables, and other related information.

al·might·y (ôl mī′tē) *adj.* All-powerful; omnipotent: *almighty God; the almighty dollar.* —*n.* **the Almighty.** God.

al·mond (ä′mənd *or* ăm′ənd) *n.* An oval edible nut with a soft light brown shell.

al·most (ôl′mōst′ *or* ôl mōst′) *adv.* Slightly short of; nearly: *almost done but not quite.*

alms (ämz) *pl.n. Formal.* An old expression for money or goods (such as food or clothes) given to the poor as charity.

a·loft (ə lôft′ *or* ə lŏft′) *adv.* In or into a high place; high or higher up: *Jet planes fly thousands of feet aloft.*

a·lo·ha (ə lō′ə *or* ä lō′hä) *interj.* A Hawaiian expression used to say hello or good-bye.

a·lone (ə lōn′) *adj.* **1.** Without the company of anyone else: *She returned to the room and found she was alone.* **2.** Without anyone or anything else; only: *The teacher alone knows when the quiz will be given.* —*adv.* **1.** Without others: *She likes to travel alone.* **2.** Without aid or help: *I can lift the rock alone.* ◆ **let alone.** Without taking into consideration: *We're too tired to walk, let alone run.* **leave** or **let well enough alone.** To be satisfied with things as they are and not try to change them: *It's best that we leave well enough alone.*

SYNONYMS: alone, solitary, lonesome, lonely. These adjectives describe being apart from others. **Alone** means lacking a companion but not necessarily feeling unhappy about it: *I walked alone on the beach while my brother went surfing.* **Solitary** often means being physically apart from others: *She thoroughly enjoyed her solitary dinner.* **Lonesome** means wishing for a companion: *I thought the goldfish looked lonesome in its glass bowl.* **Lonely** often means sad at being by oneself: *She felt lonely while all her friends were away on vacation.*

---

a·long (ə lông′ *or* ə lŏng′) *prep.* **1.** Over the length or course of: *walked along the path.* **2.** In accordance with: *Congress was split along party lines.* —*adv.* **1.** Forward; onward: *The train moved along, crossing the plains.* **2.** As a companion; together: *Bring your friend along.* ◆ **get along.** *intr.v.* [*with*] To be friendly with sbdy.: *We get along well with our neighbors.* **go along.** *intr.v.* [*with*] To agree to do sthg.: *He went along with the plan even though he was worried.*

a·long·side (ə lông′sīd′ *or* ə lŏng′sīd′) *adv.* At or near the side; to the side; side by side: *When I go for a run, my dog runs alongside.* —*prep.* By the side of; side by side with: *The car pulled up alongside the house.*

a·loof (ə lōōf′) *adj.* Distant, reserved, or indifferent in manner: *Her aloof manner offends some people.* —*adv.* At a distance but within view; apart: *The new student stood aloof from the others.* —**a·loof′ly** *adv.* —**a·loof′ness** *n.* [U]

a·loud (ə loud′) *adv.* **1.** With the voice; loud enough to be heard: *Read the story aloud.* **2.** In a loud tone; loudly: *If we talk aloud, it will awaken the baby.*

al·pac·a (ăl păk′ə) *n.* **1.** [C] A South American mammal related to the llama, with long silky wool. **2.** [U] Cloth made from the wool of this mammal.

al·pha·bet (ăl′fə bĕt′) *n.* The letters used to represent the different sounds of a language, arranged in a set order.

al·pha·bet·i·cal (ăl′fə bĕt′ĭ kəl) also **al·pha·bet·ic** (ăl′fə bĕt′ĭk) *adj.* Arranged in the order of the alphabet: *In a dictionary the words are listed in alphabetical order.* —**al′pha·bet′i·cal·ly** *adv.*

al·pha·bet·ize (ăl′fə bĭ tīz′) *tr.v.* **al·pha·bet·ized, al·pha·bet·iz·ing, al·pha·bet·iz·es.** To arrange (sthg.) in alphabetical order: *Alphabetize the names, please.* —**al′pha·bet′i·za′tion** (ăl′fə bĕt′ĭ zā′shən) *n.* [U]

al·pha·nu·mer·ic (ăl′fə nōō měr′ĭk *or* ăl′fə nyōō měr′ĭk) *adj.* Consisting of or using letters and numbers: *an alphanumeric computer code.*

al·read·y (ôl rĕd′ē) *adv.* **1.** By this time: *They are late and should be here already.* **2.** At an earlier time: *She's already paid her dues.* **3.** Earlier than expected: *Is it already time to leave?* **4.** Used to show impatience, frustration, or annoyance: *All right already! I'm moving as fast as I can!*

al·right (ôl rīt′) *adv. Informal.* All right.

al·so (ôl′sō) *adv.* **1.** In addition; besides: *The label not only lists the ingredients but also gives nutritional information.* See Synonyms at **besides.** **2.** Likewise: *If you will stay, I will also.* —*conj.* And in addition: *Many students studied French and math, also music and drawing.*

alt. *abbr.* An abbreviation of: **1.** Alternate. **2.** Altitude.

al·tar (ôl′tər) *n.* A table or similar structure in a church or temple, used in religious ceremonies.

HOMONYMS: altar, alter (change).

al·ter (ôl′tər) *v.* —*tr.* To make (sthg.) different; change: *We altered our plans for the weekend.* —*intr.* To become different; change: *Since the accident, his outlook on life has altered.*

al·ter·a·tion (ôl′tə rā′shən) *n.* **1.** [U] The act or process of changing or altering: *Alteration of the school took several months.* **2.** [C] A change: *The tailor made many alterations to the suit.*

al·ter·ca·tion (ôl′tər kā′shən) *n.* A noisy, angry quarrel: *The police stopped the altercation.*

al·ter·nate (ôl′tər nāt′) *v.* **al·ter·nat·ed, al·ter·nat·ing, al·ter·nates.** —*intr.v.* [*between; with*] **1.** To do sthg. or occur in turns: *Rain showers alternated with sunshine.* **2.** To pass back and forth from one state, action, or place to another: *alternate between hope and despair.* —*tr.* To do, perform, or use in turns: *We alternated running and walking.* —*adj.* (ôl′tər-nĭt). **1.** Occurring in turns (such as every other, every second); succeeding each other: *alternate periods of rain and sun.* **2.** In place of another: *an alternate route.* —*n.* (ôl′tər nĭt). A person acting in place of another: *She was chosen as an alternate on the team.* —**al′ter·nate·ly** *adv.*

al·ter·nat·ing current (ôl′tər nā′tĭng) *n.* [U] An electric current that reverses its direction of flow at regular intervals.

al·ter·na·tion (ôl′tər nā′shən) *n.* [C; U] Regular and repeated change between two or more things: *the alternation of the seasons.*

al·ter·na·tive (ôl tûr′nə tĭv) *n.* **1.** One of two or more possibilities from which to choose: *We had two alternatives: to continue driving or wait for the storm to pass.* **2.** A choice between two or more possibilities: *Your alternatives in this situation are limited.* See Synonyms at **choice.** —*adj.* Allowing a choice between two or more possibilities: *I can suggest two alternative plans.* —**al·ter′na·tive·ly** *adv.*

al·ter·na·tor (ôl′tər nā′tər) *n.* An electric generator that makes alternating current.

al·though (ôl thō′) *conj.* Regardless of the fact that; even though: *Although it was snowing, they went out without coats.*

al·tim·e·ter (ăl tĭm′ĭ tər) *n.* An instrument that measures and indicates the height at which an object, such as an aircraft, is located.

al·ti·tude (ăl′tĭ tōōd′) *n.* The height of a thing above a reference level, usually above sea level or the earth's surface.

al·to (ăl′tō) *n.* **1.** A low female singing voice; a contralto: *The choir has seven altos* and four sopranos. **2.** The range between soprano and tenor.

al·to·geth·er (ôl′tə gĕth′ər) adv. **1.** Completely; totally: *Soon the noise faded away altogether.* **2.** On the whole; with everything considered: *Altogether it was a successful field trip.*

USAGE: altogether The word **altogether** and the phrase **all together** sound alike, but their meanings differ. **Altogether** means "completely": *I was altogether amazed by her actions.* **All together** means "with everybody or everything together or acting at the same time": *My friends and I went all together.* **All together** can be used only if you can rephrase the sentence and separate **all** and **together** by other words: *The books lay all together in a heap. All the books lay together in a heap.*

al·tru·ism (ăl′trōō ĭz′əm) n. [U] Concern for the welfare of others. —**al′tru·ist** n. —**al′tru·is′tic** adj. —**al′tru·is′ti·cal·ly** adv.

al·u·min·i·um (ăl′yə mĭn′ē əm) n. *Chiefly British.* Variant of **aluminum.**

a·lu·mi·num (ə lōō′mə nəm) n. [U] *Symbol* **Al** A lightweight silvery white metallic element that is easily shaped and conducts electricity well. Atomic number 13. See table at **element.**

a·lum·na (ə lŭm′nə) n., pl. **a·lum·nae** (ə lŭm′nē′). A woman who has graduated from a certain school, college, or university: *She is an alumna of Smith College.*

a·lum·nus (ə lŭm′nəs) n., pl. **a·lum·ni** (ə lŭm′nī′). A man or a woman who has graduated from a certain school, college, or university: *We attended a meeting of alumni.*

al·ways (ôl′wāz *or* ôl′wĭz) adv. **1.** On every occasion; without exception: *I always leave at 6 o'clock.* **2.** For all time; forever: *They will always be friends.* **3.** At any time; in any event: *If the bus is late, we can always walk.*

Alz·heim·er's disease (älts′hī mərz *or* älts′hī mərz) n. A disease of the nervous system marked by memory loss and early senility.

am[1] (ăm) v. First person singular present tense of **be.**

am[2] *or* **AM** abbr. An abbreviation of amplitude modulation.

Am. abbr. An abbreviation of: **1.** America. **2.** American.

a.m. or **A.M.** abbr. An abbreviation of ante meridiem (before noon): *breakfast at 8:00 a.m.*

AMA abbr. An abbreviation of American Medical Association.

a·mal·gam (ə măl′gəm) n. **1.** [U] An alloy of mercury with other metals. **2.** [C] A combination or mixture.

a·mal·ga·mate (ə măl′gə māt′) tr.v. **a·mal·ga·mat·ed, a·mal·ga·mat·ing, a·mal·ga·mates.** To unite (sthg.) to make a unified whole; combine; merge: *The company amalgamated several of its divisions into one.* —**a·mal′ga·ma′tion** n. [C; U]

a·mass (ə măs′) tr.v. To gather (sbdy./sthg.); accumulate: *amass wealth; amass knowledge.*

am·a·teur (ăm′ə tûr′ *or* ăm′ə chŏŏr′ *or* ăm′ə tyŏŏr′) n. **1.** A person who engages in art, science, or sport for enjoyment rather than as a profession or for money. **2.** A person who does sthg. without professional skill: *The fact that the line was not straight showed that it was the work of an amateur.* —adj. **1.** Of or relating to an amateur: *an amateur gymnast.* **2.** Made up of amateurs: *an amateur orchestra.* **3.** Not skillful; amateurish: *an amateur performance.*

am·a·teur·ish (ăm′ə tûr′ĭsh *or* ăm′ə chŏŏr′ĭsh) adj. Without skill; imperfect; inexpert: *an amateurish attempt.* —**am′a·teur′is′m** n. [U]

a·maze (ə māz′) tr.v. **a·mazed, a·maz·ing, a·maz·es.** To fill (sbdy.) with surprise or wonder; astonish: *The size of the skyscrapers amazed the tourists.* See Synonyms at **surprise.** —**a·maze′ment** n. [U]

a·mazed (ə māzd′) adj. Surprised: *I'm amazed at how much a new car costs now.* —**a·maz′ed·ly** (ə mā′zĭd lē) adv.

a·maz·ing (ə māz′ĭng) adj. Very surprising: *She told us the most amazing story.* —**a·maz′ing·ly** adv.

am·bas·sa·dor (ăm băs′ə dər *or* ăm băs′ə dôr′) n. **1.** A diplomatic official of the highest rank who represents a government in another country. **2.** A messenger or representative: *a goodwill ambassador.*

am·ber (ăm′bər) n. [U] **1.** A hard, translucent, light or brownish yellow fossilized tree resin used for making jewelry and ornaments. **2.** A brownish yellow color. —adj. **1.** Made of amber: *an amber necklace.* **2.** Brownish yellow: *amber light.*

am·bi·ance also **am·bi·ence** (ăm′bē əns *or* äN byäNs′) n. [U] The atmosphere or mood surrounding a person, place, or thing: *the ambiance of Paris streets.*

am·bi·dex·trous (ăm′bĭ dĕk′strəs) adj. Able to use both the left and right hands equally well.

am·bi·gu·i·ty (ăm′bĭ gyōō′ĭ tē) n., pl. **am·bi·gu·i·ties.** **1.** [U] The condition of having two or more possible meanings. **2.** [C] Something that is ambiguous: *There were several ambiguities in their conflicting statements.*

am·big·u·ous (ăm bĭg′yōō əs) adj. Having two or more possible meanings; unclear; vague: *A number of ambiguous sentences made the*

ă–cat; ā–pay; âr–care; ä–father; ĕ–get; ē–be; ĭ–sit; ī–nice; îr–here; ŏ–got; ō–go; ô–saw; oi–boy; ou–out; ōō–took; ōō–boot; ŭ–cut; ûr–word; th–thin; th–this; hw–when; zh–vision; ə–about; N–French bon

report hard to understand. See Synonyms at **vague.** —**am•big′u•ous•ly** *adv.*

am•bi•tion (ăm bĭsh′ən) *n.* [C; U] A strong desire to achieve sthg.: *The student's ambition was to become a great scientist. Champion athletes must be people of great energy and ambition.*

am•bi•tious (ăm bĭsh′əs) *adj.* **1.** Full of ambition; eager to succeed: *The ambitious new worker learned very quickly.* **2.** Requiring great effort; challenging: *ambitious goals; an ambitious schedule.* —**am•bi′tious•ly** *adv.* —**am•bi′tious•ness** *n.* [U]

am•biv•a•lence (ăm bĭv′ə ləns) *n.* [U] The existence of two conflicting feelings at the same time; difficulty in deciding: *His hesitation to join the band was evidence of his ambivalence.*

am•biv•a•lent (ăm bĭv′ə lənt) *adj.* Showing or having conflicting feelings about sbdy./ sthg.: *She was ambivalent about taking the job on the night shift.* —**am•biv′a•lent•ly** *adv.*

am•ble (ăm′bəl) *intr.v.* **am•bled, am•bling, am•bles.** To walk or move along at a slow leisurely pace: *We ambled aimlessly down the street.*

am•bu•lance (ăm′byə ləns) *n.* A specially equipped vehicle used to transport sick and injured people.

am•bu•la•to•ry (ăm′byə lə tôr′ē) *adj.* Able to walk; not confined to one's bed: *an ambulatory patient.*

am•bush (ăm′boŏsh) *n.* [C; U] A surprise attack made from a hidden position: *The soldiers at the rear were victims of an ambush.* —*tr.v.* To attack (sbdy./sthg.) from a hidden position: *The soldiers hid among the rocks to ambush the pursuing forces.*

a•me•ba (ə mē′bə) *n.* Variant of **amoeba.**

a•men (ā mĕn′ *or* ä mĕn′) *interj.* An expression used at the end of a prayer or after a statement to express approval.

a•me•na•ble (ə mē′nə bəl *or* ə mĕn′ə bəl) *adj.* *Formal.* Willing to yield or cooperate; agreeable: *I am amenable to your suggestion.*

a•mend (ə mĕnd′) *tr.v.* **1.** To change (sthg.) for the better; improve: *I amended my earlier proposal to make it clearer.* **2.** To change or add to (a legislative motion, law, or constitution): *The U.S. Constitution has been amended many times.*

a•mend•ment (ə mĕnd′mənt) *n.* **1.** [C] A legally adopted change or addition to a law or body of laws: *Giving voting rights to women was accomplished in an amendment to the Constitution.* **2.** [U] The act of changing sthg. for the better; improvement: *Some treaties have provisions for amendment.*

a•mends (ə mĕndz′) *pl.n.* (*used with a singular or plural verb*). Something given or done to make up for an injury or insult: *By offering to pay for the repairs, they hoped to make amends for the damage.*

a•men•i•ty (ə mĕn′ĭ tē *or* ə mē′nĭ tē) *n., pl.* **a•men•i•ties.** **1. amenities.** Polite social behavior; courtesies: *When visiting a friend, it is wise to observe the social amenities.* **2.** [C] Something that provides or increases physical comfort; a convenience: *an apartment with all the amenities of modern living.* **3.** [U] The quality of being pleasant and agreeable: *the amenity of vacationing in the countryside.*

Amer. *abbr.* An abbreviation of: **1.** America. **2.** American.

Am•er•a•sian (ăm′ə rā′zhən *or* ăm′ə rā′-shən) *n.* A person whose ancestors are from America and Asia. —**Am′er•a′sian** *adj.*

A•mer•i•can (ə mĕr′ĭ kən) *adj.* **1.** Relating to the United States of America or its people, language, or culture: *American literature.* **2.** Relating to North or South America, the West Indies, or the Western Hemisphere: *American geology.* **3.** Relating to any of the Native American peoples: *American herbal medicine.* —*n.* A person born or living in the United States or the Americas.

A•mer•i•ca•na (ə mĕr′ə kä′nə *or* ə mĕr′-ə kăn′ə) *n.* [U] A collection of things relating to American history, folklore, or geography: *The local museum maintains a valuable collection of Americana.*

American cheese *n.* A smooth, mild, white or yellow processed cheddar cheese.

American Indian *n.* A Native American.

A•mer•i•can•ism (ə mĕr′ĭ kə nĭz′əm) *n.* **1.** A word or phrase that originates in American English or is unique to it. For example, the word *hotdog* is an Americanism for a frankfurter. **2.** A custom, trait, or tradition that originates in the United States.

A•mer•i•can•ize (ə mĕr′ĭ kə nīz′) *tr. & intr.v.* **A•mer•i•can•ized, A•mer•i•can• iz•ing, A•mer•i•can•iz•es.** To make or become typical of the United States in manner, customs, or speech: *The children of immigrants often Americanize more quickly than their parents.* —**A•mer′i•can•i•za′tion** (ə mĕr′ĭ kə nĭ zā′shən) *n.* [U]

American Revolution *n.* [U] The war fought from 1775 to 1783 between Great Britain and the American colonies in which the colonies won independence.

American Sign Language *n.* [U] An American system of communication for the hearing-impaired that uses the hands instead of the voice to communicate ideas.

am•e•thyst (ăm′ə thĭst) *n.* **1.** [C] A purple or violet form of transparent quartz used as a gemstone. **2.** [U] A purple or violet color. —*adj.* Purple or violet.

a•mi•a•ble (ā′mē ə bəl) *adj.* Friendly; good-natured: *an amiable laugh.* —**a′mi• a•bil′i•ty** *n.* [U] —**a′mi•a•bly** *adv.*

am•i•ca•ble (ăm′ĭ kə bəl) *adj.* Characterized by friendliness and goodwill; friendly: *an ami-*

cable discussion. —**am′i•ca•bil′i•ty** *n.* [U] —**am′i•ca•bly** *adv.*

a•mid (ə mĭd′) also **a•midst** (ə mĭdst′) *prep.* Surrounded by; in the middle of: *The swimmer's head appeared amid the waves.*

a•mi•no acid (ə mē′nō *or* ăm′ə nō′) *n.* Any of a large number of organic compounds that contain carbon, oxygen, hydrogen, and nitrogen and that form proteins. Certain essential amino acids cannot be produced by the body and must be obtained from food.

A•mish (ä′mĭsh *or* ăm′ĭsh) *n.* **1.** [U] An orthodox Christian religion, many of whose followers live in southeast Pennsylvania. **2. the Amish.** The followers of this religion considered as a group. —*adj.* Relating to this religion or its followers.

a•miss (ə mĭs′) *adv. & adj.* In an improper or defective way: *Your work is going amiss. Something is amiss when the train is this late.*

am•me•ter (ăm′mē′tər) *n.* An instrument that measures an electric current and indicates its strength in amperes.

am•mo•nia (ə mōn′yə) *n.* [U] **1.** A colorless gas, with a strongly irritating odor, that is composed of nitrogen and hydrogen and has the formula NH_3. It is used to manufacture fertilizers, explosives, and plastics. **2.** A solution of ammonia in water used for cleaning.

am•mu•ni•tion (ăm′yə nĭsh′ən) *n.* [U] **1.** Projectiles, such as bullets, that can be fired from guns. **2.** Explosive objects, such as bombs or rockets, that are used as weapons. **3.** Something that is used to attack or defend an argument or point of view: *The senator's poor voting record gave opponents ammunition during the election campaign.*

am•ne•sia (ăm nē′zhə) *n.* [U] A partial or total loss of memory, especially when caused by shock, brain injury, or some form of mental or physical illness: *She suffered from temporary amnesia for six months after the accident.*

am•nes•ty (ăm′nĭ stē) *n., pl.* **am•nes•ties.** [C; U] A pardon for past offenses: *The governor refused to grant amnesty to the convicted murderer.*

a•moe•ba also **a•me•ba** (ə mē′bə) *n.* A very small one-celled organism that has an indefinite changing shape. —**a•moe′bic** (ə mē′bĭk) *adj.*

a•mong (ə mŭng′) also **a•mongst** (ə-mŭngst′) *prep.* **1.** In the midst of; surrounded by: *an oak tree among the pines.* **2.** In the company of: *among friends.* **3.** In the number or class of: *I count myself among the lucky ones.* **4.** By many or all of: *a custom popular among the Greeks.* **5.** With portions to each of: *The soda was shared among them.* **6.** Each with the other: *The children were fighting among themselves.*

a•mor•al (ā môr′əl *or* ā mŏr′əl) *adj.* Without moral distinctions or judgments; neither moral nor immoral: *Nature is amoral.* —**a′mo•ral′i•ty** (ā′mô răl′ĭ tē) *n.* [U] —**a•mor′al•ly** *adv.*

am•o•rous (ăm′ər əs) *adj.* **1.** Strongly attracted to love, especially sexual love: *an amorous young man.* **2.** Feeling or expressing love: *an amorous look.* —**am′or•ous•ly** *adv.* —**am′or•ous•ness** *n.* [U]

a•mor•phous (ə môr′fəs) *adj.* Without definite form or shape: *an amorphous mass of mud and rock.* —**a•mor′phous•ly** *adv.* —**a•mor′phous•ness** *n.* [U]

a•mount (ə mount′) *n.* **1.** The total of two or more quantities: *The amount of your bill is $8.72.* **2.** A number; a sum: *Your total credit card charges add up to an enormous amount.* **3.** Quantity: *a small amount of rainfall.* —*intr.v.* [*to*] **1.** To add up in number or quantity: *Total sales for the day amounted to $655.* **2.** To be of importance: *Our effort to convince them didn't amount to much.* **3.** To be equal: *In some cases, disobeying orders amounts to treason.*

amp (ămp) *n. Informal.* **1.** An ampere. **2.** An amplifier, especially one used to amplify music.

am•per•age (ăm′pər ĭj *or* ăm′pîr′ĭj) *n.* [U] The strength of an electric current expressed in amperes.

am•pere (ăm′pîr′) *n.* A unit of electric current.

am•per•sand (ăm′pər sănd′) *n.* The character or sign (&) representing *and*.

am•phet•a•mine (ăm fĕt′ə mēn′ *or* ăm-fĕt′ə mĭn) *n.* A type of drug that is used to stimulate the central nervous system. Amphetamines are often manufactured and sold illegally.

am•phib•i•an (ăm-fĭb′ē ən) *n.* **1.** A cold-blooded animal that has a backbone and moist skin without scales, such as a frog, toad, or salamander. Most amphibians lay eggs in water, and their young breathe with gills in early life but develop lungs and breathe air as adults. **2.** A vehicle that is capable of traveling both on land and in water. —**am•phib′i•ous** *adj.*

amphibian

am•phi•the•a•ter (ăm′fə thē′ə tər) *n.* An oval or round structure with seats rising gradually outward from an open space, or arena, at the center.

am•ple (ăm′pəl) *adj.* **am•pler, am•plest.**

1. Of large or great size, amount, or capacity: *a rich nation with ample food for all.* **2.** Large in degree, kind, or quantity: *an enormous stadium with ample space for large crowds.* **3.** More than enough: *ample evidence to get a conviction.* —**am′ply** *adv.*

am·pli·fi·ca·tion (ăm′plə fĭ kā′shən) *n.* **1.a.** [U] The act or result of amplifying, enlarging, or extending sthg. **b.** [C] An increase in the magnitude or strength of an electric current, a force, or another physical quantity. **2.** [C] An expansion of a statement or idea: *The report is an amplification of the committee's views.*

am·pli·fi·er (ăm′plə fī′ər) *n.* A device, especially an electronic device, that produces amplification of an electric signal.

am·pli·fy (ăm′plə fī′) *tr.v.* **am·pli·fied, am·pli·fy·ing, am·pli·fies. 1.** To make (sthg.) louder: *A public-address system amplifies a speaker's voice.* **2.** To add to (sthg. spoken or written); expand; make complete: *amplify earlier remarks.*

am·pli·tude (ăm′plĭ tōōd′) *n.* **1.** [U] Greatness of size; extent. **2.** [U] Abundance; fullness. **3.** [C] The peak strength of an alternating electric current in a given cycle.

amplitude modulation *n.* [U] A system of radio transmission in which the amplitude of the carrier wave is adjusted so that it is proportional to the sound or other information that is to be transmitted.

am·pu·tate (ăm′pyōo tāt′) *tr.v.* **am·pu·tat·ed, am·pu·tat·ing, am·pu·tates.** To cut off (a part of the body), especially by surgery: *amputate a foot to save the leg.* —**am′pu·ta′tion** *n.* [C; U]

am·pu·tee (ăm′pyōo tē′) *n.* A person who has had a limb or limbs removed by amputation.

amt. *abbr.* An abbreviation of amount.

a·muck (ə mŭk′) also **a·mok** (ə mŭk′ or ə mŏk′) *adv.* In a wild manner, with intent to harm or kill: *The frightened dog ran amuck, biting its owners.*

am·u·let (ăm′yə lĭt) *n.* A charm worn to keep off evil or injury, especially one worn around the neck.

a·muse (ə myōoz′) *tr.v.* **a·mused, a·mus·ing, a·mus·es. 1.** To entertain (sbdy.) agreeably: *The explorer amused us with adventure stories.* **2.** To cause (sbdy.) to laugh or smile by giving pleasure: *The kitten's antics amused everyone.*

a·muse·ment (ə myōoz′mənt) *n.* **1.** [U] The state of being pleasantly entertained. **2.** [C] Something that amuses or entertains: *The carnival provides amusements for everyone.*

amusement park *n.* A commercially operated park that offers rides, games, and other forms of entertainment.

a·mus·ing (ə myōo′zĭng) *adj.* Pleasantly entertaining or comical: *an amusing trick.* —**a·mus′ing·ly** *adv.*

an (ən; ăn *when stressed*) *indef. art.* The form of *a* used before words beginning with a vowel sound or with an unpronounced *h*: *an elephant; an hour.*

—**an** *suff.* A suffix that means: **1.** Born in or being a citizen of: *Namibian; Mexican.* **2.** Belonging to, associated with, or expert in: *Unitarian; librarian; electrician.* **3.** Relating to or resembling: *Herculean; Shakespearean.*

a·nach·ro·nism (ə năk′rə nĭz′əm) *n.* Something that is out of its proper time: *Authors of historical novels must be careful to avoid anachronisms.* —**a·nach′ro·nis′tic** *adj.* —**a·nach′ro·nis′ti·cal·ly** *adv.*

an·aer·o·bic (ăn′ə rō′bĭk *or* ăn′âr ō′bĭk) *adj.* Living or growing where there is no atmospheric oxygen: *anaerobic bacteria.* —**an′aer·o′bi·cal·ly** *adv.*

an·a·gram (ăn′ə grăm′) *n.* A word or phrase formed by changing the order of the letters of another word or phrase. The words *trap, part,* and *rapt* are all anagrams.

a·nal (ā′nəl) *adj.* Relating to or near the anus. —**a′nal·ly** *adv.*

an·al·ge·sic (ăn′əl jē′zĭk *or* ăn′əl jē′sĭk) *n.* A painkiller: *Aspirin is a common analgesic.*

a·nal·o·gous (ə năl′ə gəs) *adj.* [*to*] Similar or parallel in certain ways: *The relation between addition and subtraction is analogous to the relation between multiplication and division.* —**a·nal′o·gous·ly** *adv.* —**a·nal′o·gous·ness** *n.* [U]

a·nal·o·gy (ə năl′ə jē) *n., pl.* **a·nal·o·gies. 1.** Similarity in some ways between things that are otherwise unalike. **2.** An explanation that is made by comparing one thing with sthg. similar: *The author uses the analogy of bees when describing the workers at the bakery.*

a·nal·y·sis (ə năl′ĭ sĭs) *n., pl.* **a·nal·y·ses** (ə năl′ĭ sēz′). **1.** The separation of sthg. into its parts in order to determine its nature: *An analysis of the theory shows it is based on faulty evidence.* **2.** A written report of the information obtained in this way.

an·a·lyst (ăn′ə lĭst) *n.* **1.** A person who performs an analysis: *a foreign policy analyst.* **2.** A psychoanalyst: *He is seeing an analyst.*

an·a·lyt·ic (ăn′ə lĭt′ĭk) *or* **an·a·lyt·i·cal** (ăn′ə lĭt′ĭ kəl) *adj.* Relating to analysis: *analytical chemistry.* —**an′a·lyt′i·cal·ly** *adv.*

an·a·lyze (ăn′ə līz′) *tr.v.* **an·a·lyzed, an·a·lyz·ing, an·a·lyz·es. 1.** To separate (sthg.) into parts in order to determine what it is or how it works: *They analyzed the metal and found it was gold.* **2.** To examine (sthg.) in detail: *The accountant analyzed past expenses to make a budget for next year.* **3.** To psychoanalyze (sbdy.). —**an′a·lyz′a·ble** *adj.* —**an′a·ly·za′tion** (ăn′ə lĭ zā′shən). [U] —**an′a·lyz′er** *n.*

an·ar·chism (ăn′ər kĭz′əm) *n.* [U] **1.** The theory that all forms of government lessen individual freedom and should be replaced by small cooperative groups of people. **2.** Rejection of all forms of coercive organization or authority. —**an′ar•chist** *n.*

an•ar•chy (ăn′ər kē) *n.* [U] **1.** Absence of any governmental authority: *Emma Goldman sometimes advocated anarchy in her writings.* **2.** Disorder and confusion resulting from lack of authority: *For several days after the hurricane, the region was in a state of anarchy.*

an•a•tom•i•cal (ăn′ə tŏm′ĭ kəl) also **an•a•tom•ic** (ăn′ə tŏm′ĭk) *adj.* **1.** Relating to anatomy or dissection: *anatomical comparison of similar fish.* **2.** Relating to the structure of a living thing as opposed to its functioning: *an anatomical abnormality.* —**an′a•tom′i•cal•ly** *adv.*

a•nat•o•my (ə năt′ə mē) *n., pl.* **a•nat•o•mies.** **1.** [U] The structure of an animal or a plant or any of its parts: *Bones and muscles are part of the human anatomy.* **2.** [U] The scientific study of the shape and structure of living things: *Anatomy has revealed many of the body's secrets to modern medicine.* **3.** [C] The human body: *the rugged anatomy of an athlete.*

—**ance** *suff.* A suffix that means: **1.** State or condition: *resemblance.* **2.** Action: *compliance.*

an•ces•tor (ăn′sĕs′tər) *n.* **1.** A person from whom one is descended, especially of a generation earlier than a grandparent: *His ancestors came to Canada from France.* **2.** An organism or a type of organism, either known or supposed to exist, from which later organisms evolved: *The mammoth is an ancestor of the modern elephant.* —**an•ces′tral** (ăn sĕs′trəl) *adj.* —**an•ces′tral•ly** *adv.*

an•ces•try (ăn′sĕs′trē) [U] **1.** A line of descent; lineage. **2.** Ancestors that are considered as a group: *My friend is of Russian ancestry.*

an•chor (ăng′kər) *n.* **1.** A heavy object attached to a boat by a cable and dropped overboard to keep the boat in place. **2.** A rigid point of support for securing a rope or cable. **3.** Something that helps one feel secure: *Religion has been his anchor in tough times.* **4.** An anchorman or anchorwoman. —*v.* —*tr.* **1.** To hold (sthg.) secure by an anchor: *We anchored our boat before we started to fish.* **2.** To act as an anchorman or anchorwoman on (a news broadcast) or in (a relay race): *More women now anchor the news.* —*intr.* To drop anchor or be held by an anchor.

anchor

an•chor•age (ăng′kər ĭj) *n.* A place where ships can anchor: *a safe anchorage in the harbor.*

an•chor•man (ăng′kər măn′) *n., pl.* **an•chor•men. 1.** In radio and television, a man who narrates or coordinates a news broadcast in which several correspondents give reports. **2.** A man who is the last member of a relay team in a race. —**an′chor•per′son** (ăng′kər pûr′sən) *n.* —**an′chor•wom′an** (ăng′kər wŏŏm′ən) *n.*

an•cho•vy (ăn′chō′vē *or* ăn chō′vē) *n., pl.* **anchovy** or **an•cho•vies.** A small sea fish related to the herring, often salted and canned.

an•cient (ān′shənt) *adj.* **1.** Very old; aged: *the ancient monuments at Stonehenge.* **2.** Relating to times long past: *ancient history.*

an•cil•lar•y (ăn′sə lĕr′ē) *adj.* Giving help or support but not of first importance: *an ancillary pump.*

—**ancy** *suff.* A suffix that means condition or quality: *buoyancy.*

and (ənd *or* ən; ănd *when stressed*) *conj.* **1.** Together with or along with; as well as: *The weather is clear and cold.* **2.** Added to; plus: *Two and two makes four.* **3.** As a result: *Go, and you will enjoy yourself.* **4.** *Informal.* To: *Try and find it.*

and/or (ănd′dôr′) *conj.* Used to indicate that either *and* or *or* may be used to connect words, phrases, or clauses depending upon what meaning is intended, as in the sentence *Make the rice with milk and/or water.*

an•dro•gen (ăn′drə jən) *n.* [U] A hormone, such as testosterone, that acts in the development and maintenance of masculine physical characteristics.

an•droid (ăn′droid′) *n.* A fictional robot that is created from biological materials and resembles a human being.

an•ec•dote (ăn′ĭk dōt′) *n.* A short story about an interesting or humorous event. —**an′ec•dot′al** *adj.* —**an′ec•dot′al•ly** *adv.*

a•ne•mi•a (ə nē′mē ə) *n.* [U] A diseased condition in which the blood cannot carry enough oxygen to the body tissues.

a•ne•mic (ə nē′mĭk) *adj.* **1.** Relating to or suffering from anemia. **2.** Lacking vitality; weak: *an anemic economic recovery.*

an•e•mom•e•ter (ăn′ə mŏm′ĭ tər) *n.* An instrument that measures the speed of the wind.

an•es•the•sia (ăn′ĭs thē′zhə) *n.* [U] A condition in which some or all of the senses, especially the sense of touch, stop functioning or are greatly diminished. This condition can be produced by the administration of drugs or acupuncture. —**an′es•the′si•ol′o•gist** *n.* —**an′es•the′si•ol′o•gy** *n.* [U]

ă–cat; ā–pay; âr–care; ä–father; ĕ–get; ē–be; ĭ–sit; ī–nice; îr–here; ŏ–got; ō–go; ô–saw; oi–boy; ou–out; ŏŏ–took; ōō–boot; ŭ–cut; ûr–word; th–thin; *th*–this; hw–when; zh–vision; ə–about; N–French bon

an·es·thet·ic (ăn′ĭs thĕt′ĭk) *adj.* Relating to or causing anesthesia. —*n.* A drug that causes anesthesia: *The dentist used a local anesthetic on my mouth.* —**an′es·thet′i·cal·ly** *adv.*

a·nes·the·tize (ə nĕs′thĭ tīz′) *tr.v.* **a·nes·the·tized, a·nes·the·tiz·ing, a·nes·the·tiz·es.** To put (sbdy./sthg.) into a condition of anesthesia, especially by means of a drug: *They anesthetized the injured dog in preparation for surgery.* —**a·nes′the·ti·za′tion** (ə nĕs′thĭ tĭ zā′shən) *n.* [U]

an·eu·rysm also **an·eu·rism** (ăn′yə rĭz′əm) *n.* A swelling in a weakened part of an artery or vein, caused by disease or injury.

a·new (ə nōō′) *adv.* Over again: *ready to start anew.*

an·gel (ān′jəl) *n.* **1.** One of the immortal beings serving as attendants or messengers of God. **2.** A guardian spirit. **3.** A kind and lovable person: *My aunt is such an angel.* —**an·gel′ic** (ăn jĕl′ĭk), **an·gel′i·cal** (ăn jĕl′ĭ kəl) *adj.*

an·ger (ăng′gər) *n.* [U] A feeling of great displeasure or hostility toward sbdy. or sthg.; rage: *surprise and then anger at being cheated.* —*tr. & intr.v.* To make or become angry: *I was angered by his rudeness. She angers slowly.*

SYNONYMS: anger, rage, fury, indignation. These nouns refer to different degrees of strong displeasure. **Anger** is the most general: *He wasn't shouting, but we could sense his anger.* **Rage** and **fury** mean strong and often destructive anger: *They'll go into a rage when they find out who wrecked their car. In her fury at being teased, she threw her sister's books down the stairs.* **Indignation** is anger at sthg. wrongful, unjust, or evil: *The ugly incident aroused the whole town's indignation.*

---

an·gle¹ (ăng′gəl) *n.* **1.** A geometric figure formed by two lines that begin at a common point or by two planes that begin at a common line. **2.** The space between such lines or planes, measured in degrees: *The walls meet at a 90° angle.* **3.** A projecting corner, as of a building: *The angle of the building blocked our view.* **4.** The place, position, or direction from which an object is seen; point of view: *a funny-looking hat from any angle.* **5.** A particular part of a problem; an aspect: *studying every angle of the question.* —*v.* **an·gled, an·gling, an·gles.** —*tr.* To move or hit (sthg.) at an angle: *angling the camera for a clearer view.* —*intr.* To turn or proceed at an angle: *The road angles sharply at the river.*

an·gle² (ăng′gəl) *intr.v.* **an·gled, an·gling, an·gles.** **1.** To fish with a hook and line. **2.** To try to get sthg. by using schemes or tricks: *By posing as a reporter, the tourist angled for a chance to meet the President.* —**an′gler, an′gling** *n.* [U]

An·gli·cize (ăng′glĭ sīz′) *tr.v.* **An·gli·cized, An·gli·ciz·ing, An·gli·ciz·es.** **1.** To adapt (a foreign word) to use in English, especially by changing its spelling or pronunciation: *My great-grandmother Anglicized her name.* **2.** To make (sthg.) English or similar to English in some form, style, or character of custom or habit.

An·glo (ăng′glō) *n. Informal.* An Anglo-American, especially a white resident of the United States who is not of Hispanic descent.

Anglo— *pref.* A prefix that means related to or descended from the English: *Anglo-American.*

an·gry (ăng′grē) *adj.* **an·gri·er, an·gri·est.** **1.** Feeling or showing anger: *an angry customer; an angry expression.* **2.** Seeming to threaten: *angry, dark storm clouds.* **3.** Inflamed; red and swollen: *an angry wound.* —**an′gri·ly** *adv.*

ang·strom (ăng′strəm) *n.* A unit of length equal to one hundred-millionth (10^{-8}) of a centimeter. It is used mainly in measuring wavelengths of light and shorter electromagnetic radiation.

an·guish (ăng′gwĭsh) *n.* [U] Strong pain or suffering of mind or body; torment; torture: *They were in anguish until their lost child was found.* —**an′guished** *adj.*

an·gu·lar (ăng′gyə lər) *adj.* **1.** Having, forming, or consisting of an angle or angles: *angular measurement.* **2.** Measured by an angle: *angular distance.* **3.** Bony and lean: *an angular face.* —**an′gu·lar′i·ty** (ăng′gyə lăr′ĭ tē) *n.* [U]

an·i·mal (ăn′ə məl) *n.* **1.** A living thing that is able to move from place to place, uses specialized sensory organs, and eats plants and other animals because it cannot make its own food. **2.** An animal organism other than a human: *In the past, humans had to protect themselves from animals.* **3.** *Informal.* A person whose behavior resembles an animal as distinguished from a human: *Only an animal would live in such a mess.* —*adj.* Relating to, characteristic of, or derived from animals: *animal behavior; animal fat.*

an·i·mate (ăn′ə māt′) *tr.v.* **an·i·mat·ed, an·i·mat·ing, an·i·mates.** **1.** To give interest or excitement to (sthg.): *The party was animated by the band's music.* **2.** To produce (sthg.) as an animated cartoon: *Many children's stories have been animated by motion picture companies.* —*adj.* (ăn′ə mĭt). **1.** Living: *The seabed is full of animate objects that grow out of the sand.* **2.** Belonging to the class of nouns that stand for living things. For example, the word *dog* is animate; the word *car* is inanimate.

an·i·mat·ed (ăn′ə mā′tĭd) *adj.* **1.** Lively: *The teacher's personality was energetic and animated.* **2.** Designed to appear alive and move in a lifelike manner: *animated cartoons.* —**an′i·mat′ed·ly** *adv.*

an·i·ma·tion (ăn′ə mā′shən) *n*. [U] **1.** The condition or quality of being alive; liveliness: *She can't sing well, but she sings with animation and great joy.* **2.** The process by which an animated cartoon is prepared. —**an′i·ma·tor** (ăn′ə mā′tər) *n*.

an·i·mos·i·ty (ăn′ə mŏs′ĭ tē) *n., pl.* **an·i·mos·i·ties.** [C; U] Hatred, anger, or hostility that is shown openly: *There was much animosity between the two nations even before war broke out.*

an·ise (ăn′ĭs) *n*. [U] An herb related to parsley, with small licorice-flavored seeds.

an·kle (ăng′kəl) *n*. **1.** The joint formed by the lower leg with the foot. **2.** The slender part of the leg just above this joint.

an·klet (ăng′klĭt) *n*. **1.** A bracelet or chain worn around the ankle as jewelry. **2.** A short sock reaching to just above the ankle.

an·nals (ăn′əlz) *pl.n*. **1.** A record of events written in the order of their occurrence, year by year. **2.** A descriptive account or record; a history: *the annals of the American Revolution.*

an·nex (ə nĕks′ *or* ăn′ĕks′) *tr.v.* **1.** To add or join (sthg.), especially to a larger or more significant thing: *The new gym will be annexed to the school.* **2.** To add (territory) to an existing country or other area: *The city is trying to annex two of the suburbs.* —*n*. (ăn′ĕks′). An extra building that is added to another bigger building and used for some related purpose: *The library has a special annex for historical documents.* —**an′nex·a′tion** (ăn′ek sā′shən) *n*. [C; U]

an·ni·hi·late (ə nī′ə lāt′) *tr.v.* **an·ni·hi·lat·ed, an·ni·hi·lat·ing, an·ni·hi·lates. 1.** To destroy (sthg.) completely; wipe out: *The use of nuclear weapons would annihilate all life on our planet.* **2.** To defeat (sbdy.) severely: *The Chicago Bulls annihilated all their opponents in the playoffs.* —**an·ni′hi·la′tion** *n*. [U]

an·ni·ver·sa·ry (ăn′ə vûr′sə rē) *n., pl.* **an·ni·ver·sa·ries. 1.** The yearly return of the date of an event that happened in an earlier year: *a wedding anniversary.* **2.** A celebration on this date.

an·no Dom·i·ni (ăn′ō dŏm′ə nī′ *or* ăn′ō- dŏm′ə nē) *adv. (used chiefly in abbreviated form).* In a specified year since the birth of Jesus: *500 A.D.*

an·no·tate (ăn′ō tāt′) *tr.v.* **an·no·tat·ed, an·no·tat·ing, an·no·tates.** To furnish (a written work) with explanatory notes: *Many textbooks are annotated with notes in the margin.* —**an′no·ta′tion** *n*. [C; U]

an·nounce (ə nouns′) *v*. **an·nounced, an·nounc·ing, an·nounc·es.** —*tr*. **1.** To bring (sthg.) to public notice; give formal notice of: *The teacher announced a change in our schedule.* **2.** To make known the presence or arrival of (sbdy./sthg.): *The doorman announced us by telephone.* **3.** To serve as an announcer of (sthg.): *announce soccer games on television.* —*intr*. To serve as an announcer on radio or television.

an·nounce·ment (ə nouns′mənt) *n*. **1.** A public declaration to make known sthg. that has happened or that will happen; an official statement: *An announcement concerning the policy changes will be made soon.* **2.** A printed or published notice: *a birth announcement.*

an·nounc·er (ə noun′sər) *n*. A person who announces, especially a person who introduces a show, makes comments, or reads the news on radio or television.

an·noy (ə noi′) *tr.v.* To bother or irritate (sbdy.): *The children's screaming annoyed the neighbors.*

an·noy·ance (ə noi′əns) *n*. **1.** [U] Irritation or displeasure: *Much to my annoyance, the bus was late.* **2.** [C] Something causing trouble or irritation; a nuisance: *Sunburn is a relatively minor annoyance.*

an·noy·ing (ə noi′ĭng) *adj*. Troublesome or irritating: *an annoying habit.* —**an·noy′ing·ly** *adv*.

an·nu·al (ăn′yōō əl) *adj*. **1.** Happening or done every year; yearly: *an annual medical examination.* **2.** Relating to or determined by a year's time: *I was offered an annual salary of $30,000.* **3.** Living and growing for just one year or season: *annual plants.* —*n*. **1.** A periodical published yearly; a yearbook: *She still has all of her high school annuals.* **2.** A plant that grows, flowers, produces seeds, and dies in a single year or season: *Pansies and petunias are popular annuals among home gardeners.* —**an′nu·al·ly** *adv*.

an·nu·i·ty (ə nōō′ĭ tē) *n., pl.* **an·nu·i·ties. 1.** An amount of money paid at regular intervals: *Some people retire and live off an annuity.* **2.** An investment on which one receives fixed payments during one's lifetime or for a certain number of years.

an·nul (ə nŭl′) *tr.v.* **an·nulled, an·nul·ling, an·nuls.** To make or declare (usually a marriage) void; cancel: *The court annulled their marriage.* —**an·nul′ment** *n*. [C; U]

an·ode (ăn′ōd′) *n*. **1.** The positively charged electrode of an electrolytic cell or electron tube. **2.** In a battery or other device that is supplying current, the negatively charged terminal.

a·noint (ə noint′) *tr.v.* **1.** To apply oil, ointment, or a similar substance to (sbdy./sthg.): *The nurse anointed the burn with salve.* **2.** To put oil on (sbdy.) in a religious ceremony as a means of making pure or holy: *anoint a king.* —**a·noint′ment** *n*. [U]

a·nom·a·ly (ə nŏm′ə lē) *n., pl.* **a·nom·a·lies.** Something that is unusual, irregular, or abnormal: *Flooding is an anomaly in desert regions of Africa.* —**a·nom′a·lous** (ə nŏm′ə ləs) *adj.*

a·non (ə nŏn′) *abbr.* An abbreviation of anonymous.

a·non·y·mous (ə nŏn′ə məs) *adj.* **1.** Nameless or unnamed: *The prize was awarded by a panel of anonymous judges.* **2.** Coming from an unknown source: *The anonymous letter was sent without a return address.* —**an′o·nym′i·ty** (ăn′ə nĭm′ĭ tē) *n.* [U] —**a·non′y·mous·ly** *adv.*

an·o·rex·i·a ner·vo·sa (ăn′ə rĕk′sē ə-nûr vō′sə) *n.* [U] A disorder, usually occurring in young women, that is characterized by an abnormal fear of gaining weight, a persistent aversion to food, and severe weight loss.

an·oth·er (ə nŭth′ər) *adj.* **1.** Additional; one more: *another cup of coffee.* **2.** Different: *He has been another man since his surgery.* **3.** Some other: *We'll discuss this another day.* **4.** New or similar but not exactly the same: *The coach thinks this player is another Pelé.* —*pron.* **1.** An additional one: *I had a drink of water and then another.* **2.** A different person or thing: *A baby is one thing to take care of; a six-year-old is another.* **3.** One of a group of things: *for one reason or another.*

an·swer (ăn′sər) *n.* **1.** A spoken or written reply to a question, request, or letter: *I wrote weeks ago but never got an answer.* **2.** An act that serves as a reply or response: *Their answer was to ignore me.* **3.** A solution to a problem: *We all got the right answer to that problem.* —*v.* —*intr.* **1.** To respond in words or action: *Answer to your name when it is called.* **2.** To be responsible for sthg.: *You will have to answer for this mess.* **3.** To match or correspond to sthg.: *The police saw a car answering to this description.* —*tr.* **1.** To reply to (sthg./sbdy.): *answer a letter.* **2.** To respond correctly to (sthg.): *I can't answer the question.* **3.** To fulfill the demands of (sthg.): *A good rest answered the weary traveler's needs.* **4.** To match or correspond to (sthg.): *That dog answers the description of the one you're looking for.*

SYNONYMS: answer, respond, reply, retort. These verbs refer to different kinds of reactions. **Answer, respond,** and **reply** mean to speak, write, or act in response to sthg.: *Please answer my question. I didn't expect the President to respond personally to my letter. The visiting team scored three goals, and the home team replied with two of its own.* **Retort** means to answer verbally in a quick, sharp, or angry way: *"My shoes may not be new, but at least they're clean!" she retorted.*

an·swer·a·ble (ăn′sər ə bəl) *adj.* **1.** Responsible; liable: *You are answerable for the money missing from the account.* **2.** Capable of being answered or proved wrong: *Some scientific questions are not wholly answerable.*

an·swer·ing machine (ăn′sər ĭng) *n.* A device attached to a telephone to record messages from callers.

answering service *n.* A business that answers a person's telephone calls and reports on the calls received.

ant (ănt) *n.* Any of various insects that live in highly organized colonies, often digging and tunneling in the ground or wood. Most ants are wingless and are known for being hardworking.

HOMONYMS: ant, aunt (sister of one's parent).

ant. *abbr.* An abbreviation of antonym.

ant— *pref.* Variant of **anti—.**

—ant *suff.* A suffix that means: **1.** Performing a certain action or being in a certain state: *defiant; compliant.* **2.** A person or thing that performs or causes a certain action: *coolant; deodorant.*

ant·ac·id (ănt ăs′ĭd) *adj.* Capable of neutralizing an acid; basic. —*n.* A substance that neutralizes acids or counteracts acidity, especially excess stomach acid: *He uses antacids because of his stomach problems.*

an·tag·o·nism (ăn tăg′ə nĭz′ əm) *n.* [C; U] **1.** Unfriendly feeling; hostility: *antagonism among rival factions.* **2.** Opposition, as between conflicting principles or forces: *Antagonism often arises between countries because of border disputes.*

an·tag·o·nist (ăn tăg′ə nĭst) *n.* A person who opposes and actively competes with another; an adversary: *Telling the truth can make an antagonist of a good friend.*

an·tag·o·nis·tic (ăn tăg′ə nĭs′tĭk) *adj.* **1.** Opposed; contending: *antagonistic points of view.* **2.** Unfriendly; hostile: *an antagonistic attitude.* —**an·tag′o·nis′ti·cal·ly** *adv.*

an·tag·o·nize (ăn tăg′ə nīz′) *tr.v.* **an·tag·o·nized, an·tag·o·niz·ing, an·tag·o·niz·es.** To earn the dislike of (sbdy.); provoke a feeling of irritation in: *Don't antagonize him by calling him names.*

ante— *pref.* A prefix that means prior to; earlier: *antedate.*

ant·eat·er (ănt′ē′tər) *n.* Any of several long-nosed tropical mammals that feed on ants and other insects, which they catch with a long, sticky tongue.

an·te·ce·dent (ăn′tĭ sēd′nt) *adj.* Formal. Going before; preceding: *She put in years of hard work antecedent to her promotion.* —*n.* **1.** A person or thing that comes before another: *The tremors were only the antecedents to the big quake.* **2.** The word, phrase, or clause to which a pronoun refers. In the sentence *My* cousin arrived yesterday, and I took her to the park, the word cousin is the antecedent of her.

an•te•date (ăn'tĭ dāt') tr.v. **an•te•dat•ed, an•te•dat•ing, an•te•dates.** Formal. To be of an earlier date than (sthg.): This novel antedates the writer's poetry.

an•te•lope (ăn'tl ōp') n. Any of various swift-running, often slender, horned mammals.

an•te me•rid•i•em (ăn'tē mə rĭd'ē əm) adv. & adj. (used chiefly in abbreviated form). Before noon: 9:00 a.m.

an•ten•na (ăn tĕn'ə) n. **1.** pl. **an•ten•nas.** A metallic device for sending and receiving radio or television signals: Most television antennas have been replaced by cable. **2.** pl. **an•ten•nae** (ăn ten'ē). One of a pair of long, slender structures growing on the head of an insect or a crustacean such as a lobster or shrimp. Most antennae are organs of touch, but some are sensitive to odors.

an•te•ri•or (ăn tîr'ē ər) adj. **1.** Placed in front; located forward: a small anterior room leading to the main hall. **2.** Prior in time; earlier.

an•them (ăn'thəm) n. A song of praise or loyalty: a national anthem.

ant•hill (ănt'hĭl') n. A mound of earth or sand formed by ants when they are digging or building a nest.

an•thol•o•gy (ăn thŏl'ə jē) n., pl. **an•thol•o•gies.** A collection of writings, such as poems or stories, by various authors: an anthology of short stories.

an•thro•poid (ăn'thrə poid') adj. Resembling a human being: Gorillas and chimpanzees are anthropoid apes. —n. An anthropoid ape.

an•thro•pol•o•gy (ăn'thrə pŏl'ə jē) n. [U] The scientific study of the origin, the behavior, and the physical, social, and cultural development of human beings. —**an'thro•po•log'i•cal** (ăn'thrə pə lŏj'ĭ kəl) adj. —**an'thro•po•log'i•cal•ly** adv. —**an'-thro•pol'o•gist** n.

anti— or **ant—** pref. A prefix that means: **1.** Opposite: antacid. **2.** Opposing: anti-Semitism. **3.** Counteracting: antibiotic.

WORD BUILDING: anti— The prefix **anti—** means "against." **Anti—** is so recognizable and its meaning is so clear that it is frequently used to make up new words. For example, the meanings of words such as **anticrime** and **antipollution** are easy to guess, even without a definition. Sometimes, when followed by a vowel, **anti—** becomes **ant—**: antacid.

---

an•ti•a•bor•tion (ăn'tē ə bôr'shən) adj. Opposed to the practice of ending a pregnancy by abortion.

an•ti•air•craft (ăn'tē âr'krăft') adj. De-signed for defense, especially from a position on the ground, against attack by aircraft: anti-aircraft missiles.

an•ti•bi•ot•ic (ăn'tĭ bī ŏt'ĭk) n. A substance, such as penicillin, that is capable of destroying or weakening harmful microorganisms. Antibiotics are widely used in the treatment and prevention of diseases. —adj. Relating to antibiotics: an antibiotic drug.

an•tic (ăn'tĭk) n. (usually plural). An odd or entertaining act or gesture: Kittens are known for their amusing antics.

an•tic•i•pate (ăn tĭs'ə pāt') tr.v. **an•tic•i•pat•ed, an•tic•i•pat•ing, an•tic•i•pates. 1.** To foresee or consider (sthg.) in advance: We hadn't anticipated such a crowd at the zoo. **2.** To deal with (sthg.) in advance: Store owners anticipated the storm by boarding up their windows. **3.** To look forward to (sthg.), especially with pleasure: I anticipated the opportunity to meet her for the first time. See Synonyms at **expect.**

an•tic•i•pa•tion (ăn tĭs'ə pā'shən) n. [U] **1.** Expectation, especially happy or eager expectation: She looked forward to vacation with great anticipation. **2.** Knowledge or concern about sthg. that has not yet happened: Anticipation of a rise in prices was mistaken.

an•ti•cli•max (ăn'tē klī'măks') n. (usually singular). **1.** A decline or end considered a disappointing contrast to what has gone before: The rest of the story was an anticlimax to the scene in the courtroom. **2.** A less important or trivial event that follows a series of significant ones: Rain showers were an anticlimax to the full force of the hurricane. —**an'ti•cli•mac'tic** (ăn'tē klī măk'tĭk) adj. —**an'ti•cli•mac'ti•cal•ly** adv.

an•ti•dote (ăn'tĭ dōt') n. **1.** A substance that counteracts the effects of poison. **2.** Something that relieves or counteracts: Baking soda is often used as an antidote to indigestion.

an•ti•freeze (ăn'tĭ frēz') n. [U] A substance added to a liquid, such as water, to lower its freezing point: Don't forget to change the antifreeze in your car before winter arrives.

an•ti•his•ta•mine (ăn'tē hĭs'tə mēn' or ăn'tē hĭs'tə mĭn) n. A type of drug that relieves symptoms of allergies or colds by interfering with the production or action of histamine in the body.

an•ti•nu•cle•ar (ăn'tē nōō'klē ər) adj. Opposed to the use of nuclear energy for military purposes or for generating electricity: He votes for candidates who are committed to antinuclear policies.

an•ti•pas•to (ăn'tē päs'tō) n., pl. **an•ti•pas•tos** or **an•ti•pas•ti** (ăn'tē päs'tē). A dish of assorted Italian appetizers.

an·ti·per·spi·rant (ăn′tē pûr′spər ənt) *n.* A preparation applied to the skin under the arm to reduce or prevent perspiration and odor.

an·ti·pov·er·ty (ăn′tē pŏv′ər tē) *adj.* Created or intended to reduce poverty: *antipoverty programs.*

an·ti·quat·ed (ăn′tĭ kwā′tĭd) *adj.* Too old to be useful, suitable, or fashionable: *I used to think my parents' ideas were antiquated.*

an·tique (ăn tēk′) *adj.* Belonging to, made in, or typical of an earlier period: *antique furniture.* —*n.* Something that has special value because of its age, especially a work of art or handicraft that is over 100 years old: *The writing table was a treasured antique.*

an·tiq·ui·ty (ăn tĭk′wĭ tē) *n., pl.* **an·tiq·ui·ties. 1.** [U] Ancient times, especially the times before the Middle Ages: *The pyramids of ancient Egypt belong to antiquity.* **2.** [U] The quality of being old: *a carving of great antiquity.* **3.** [C] *(usually plural).* Something, such as a relic, that dates from ancient times: *That museum has a collection of many antiquities from ancient Greece.*

an·ti-Sem·i·tism (ăn′tē sĕm′ĭ tĭz′əm) *n.* [U] Prejudice against or hostility toward Jews. —**an′ti-Se·mit′ic** (ăn′tē sə mĭt′ĭk) *adj.*

an·ti·sep·tic (ăn′tĭ sĕp′tĭk) *adj.* **1.** Preventing infection by stopping the growth and activity of microorganisms: *Alcohol and iodine have many antiseptic uses.* **2.** Without microorganisms: *Surgery is done under antiseptic conditions.* —*n.* An antiseptic substance or agent, such as alcohol. —**an′ti·sep′ti·cal·ly** *adv.*

an·ti·slav·er·y (ăn′tē slā′və rē *or* ăn′tē-slāv′rē) *adj.* Opposed to or against slavery: *Early feminists were vocal about their antislavery views.*

an·ti·so·cial (ăn′tē sō′shəl) *adj.* **1.** Avoiding the society or company of others; not sociable: *He has to try hard not to be antisocial.* **2.** Opposed to or interfering with society: *Criminal acts are aggressive antisocial behavior.* —**an′ti·so′cial·ly** *adv.*

an·tith·e·sis (ăn tĭth′ĭ sĭs) *n., pl.* **an·tith·e·ses** (ăn tĭth′ĭ sēz′). *(usually singular).* *Formal.* **1.** Direct contrast; opposition: *Your behavior stands in antithesis to your beliefs.* **2.** The direct or exact opposite: *Hope is the antithesis of despair.*

an·ti·tox·in (ăn′tē tŏk′sĭn) *n.* **1.** An antibody formed in response to and capable of acting against a biological toxin, such as one produced by bacteria. **2.** A serum containing such antibodies.

an·ti·trust (ăn′tē trŭst′) *adj.* Opposing or regulating trusts or similar business monopolies considered not in the best interests of the public: *Antitrust laws prevent unfair business practices.*

an·ti·ven·in (ăn′tē vĕn′ĭn) *n.* **1.** An antitoxin that counteracts the venom of a snake or other poisonous animal. **2.** A human or animal serum containing such an antitoxin.

an·ti·vi·ral (ăn′tē vī′rəl) *adj.* Destroying or slowing the growth and reproduction of viruses.

an·ti·war (ăn′tē wôr′) *adj.* Opposing war: *an antiwar demonstration.*

ant·ler (ănt′lər) *n.* *(usually plural).* A horny growth on the head of a deer, moose, elk, or other related animal, usually having one or more branches. Antlers usually grow only on males, and are shed and grown again from year to year.

antler
Moose

an·to·nym (ăn′tə nĭm′) *n.* A word having a sense opposite to a sense of another word. For example, *thick* is an antonym of *thin.*

ant·sy (ănt′sē) *adj.* **ant·si·er, ant·si·est.** *Slang.* Uneasy; anxious; restless: *My daughter can't sit through a movie without getting antsy.*

a·nus (ā′nəs) *n.* The opening at the lower end of the digestive tract through which solid waste is passed out of the body.

an·vil (ăn′vĭl) *n.* A heavy block of iron or steel, with a smooth flat top on which metals are shaped by hammering.

anx·i·e·ty (ăng zī′ĭ tē) *n., pl.* **anx·i·e·ties.** [C; U] A feeling of uneasiness and concern about sth. in the future; worry: *The settlers were filled with anxiety about food supplies in the coming winter.*

anx·ious (ăngk′shəs *or* ăng′shəs) *adj.* **1.** Having a feeling of uneasiness; worried: *They were anxious about the upcoming exam.* **2.** Marked by uneasiness or worry: *anxious moments.* **3.** Eagerly wanting sth.: *We were anxious to begin our vacation.* —**anx′ious·ly** *adv.* —**anx′ious·ness** *n.* [U]

an·y (ĕn′ē) *adj.* **1.** One or some; no matter which; of whatever kind: *Take any book you want. Do you have any information on Chinese cooking?* **2.** No matter how many or how few; some: *Are there any oranges left?* **3.** Every: *Any dog likes meat.* —*pron.* *(used with a singular or plural verb).* Any person or thing or any persons or things; anybody or anything: *We haven't any left. Any of the teachers can help you.* —*adv.* At all: *The patient doesn't feel any better.* —See Note at **some.**

an·y·bod·y (ĕn′ē bŏd′ē *or* ĕn′ē bŭd′ē) *pron.* Any person; anyone: *Invite anybody you like to the party.* —*n.* [U] A person of importance: *Everybody who is anybody came to the party.* —See Note at **some.**

an·y·how (ĕn′ē hou′) *adv.* **1.** In any case; at any rate; anyway: *The twins were sick, but*

A

they didn't want to go anyhow. **2.** Just the same; nevertheless; anyway: *You may know these words, but study them anyhow.*

an•y•more (ĕn′ē môr′) *adv.* **1.** Any longer; at the present: *Do they make this style of coat anymore?* **2.** From now on: *We promised not to shout in the library anymore.*

an•y•one (ĕn′ē wŭn′) *pron.* Any person; anybody: *I knocked on the door, but there wasn't anyone at home.* —SEE NOTE at **some.**

an•y•place (ĕn′ē plās′) *adv.* Anywhere: *I can go anyplace I like.*

an•y•thing (ĕn′ē thĭng′) *pron.* Any object, occurrence, or matter whatever: *Anything you order in this restaurant will be good.* —*adv.* To any degree or extent; at all: *Is your bike anything like mine?* ◆ **anything but.** By no means; not at all: *This room is anything but warm.*

an•y•time (ĕn′ē tīm′) *adv.* At any time: *Anytime we come inside we should wipe our feet.*

an•y•way (ĕn′ē wā′) *adv.* **1.** In any case; at least: *I don't know if the book is lost or stolen; anyway, it's gone.* **2.** In any manner whatever: *Get the job done anyway you can.* **3.** Just the same; nevertheless; anyhow: *The ball was slippery, but the goalie caught it anyway.*

an•y•where (ĕn′ē wâr′) *adv.* **1.** To, in, or at any place: *They travel anywhere they want to go.* **2.** At all: *We aren't anywhere near finished.*

A-OK (ā′ō kā′) *adj. Informal.* Perfectly OK: *Whatever you want to do is A-OK with me.*

A-one (ā′wŭn′) *adj. Informal.* First-class; excellent: *That painter always does an A-one job.*

a•or•ta (ā ôr′tə) *n.* The main artery of the body, starting at the left ventricle of the heart and branching to carry blood to all the organs of the body except the lungs.

a•pace (ə pās′) *adv.* At a rapid pace; swiftly: *The building of the new hospital is proceeding apace.*

a•part (ə pärt′) *adv.* **1.** Away from another in time or position: *two trees about ten feet apart.* **2.** In or into separate pieces; to pieces: *The box fell apart when it hit the floor.* **3.** One from another: *Can you tell the twins apart?* **4.** Aside or in reserve: *We've set money apart for a vacation.* ◆ **apart from.** Other than; aside from: *Apart from a little rain, we had fine weather on our vacation.*

a•part•heid (ə pärt′hīt′ *or* ə pärt′hāt′) *n.* [U] A former official policy of the Republic of South Africa involving legal and economic discrimination against nonwhites.

a•part•ment (ə pärt′mənt) *n.* A room or group of rooms to live in within a building: *Her new apartment is on the third floor.*

ap•a•thet•ic (ăp′ə thĕt′ĭk) *adj.* Feeling or showing little or no interest; indifferent: *Adults who are apathetic about politics should not complain about poor government.*

ap•a•thy (ăp′ə thē) *n.* [U] Lack of feeling or interest; indifference: *Apathy among our friends made it difficult to organize the ski trip.*

ape (āp) *n.* Any of various large primates such as the gorilla, chimpanzee, or orangutan. —*tr.v.* **aped, ap•ing, apes.** To imitate the actions of (sbdy.); mimic: *Many comedians ape the speech of famous people.*

a•pé•ri•tif (ä pĕr′ĭ tēf′) *n.* An alcoholic drink taken before a meal to stimulate the appetite.

ap•er•ture (ăp′ər chər) *n.* **1.** A hole or an opening: *an aperture in the wall.* **2.** The diameter of the opening through which light can pass into a camera, telescope, or other optical instrument: *Don't forget to check the aperture on the camera.*

a•pex (ā′pĕks) *n.* **1.** The peak or highest point of sthg.: *The runner won many victories at the apex of her great career.* **2.** The highest point of a geometric figure; a vertex.

a•phid (ā′fĭd *or* ăf′ĭd) *n.* Any of various small, soft-bodied insects that feed by sucking sap from plants: *The aphids damaged the roses.*

aph•ro•dis•i•ac (ăf′rə dĭz′ē ăk′ *or* ăf′rə-dē′zē ăk′) *n.* A drug or food that stimulates sexual desire. —*adj.* Sexually stimulating.

a•piece (ə pēs′) *adv.* To or for each one; each: *Give them an apple apiece.*

ap•ish (ā′pĭsh) *adj.* **1.** Resembling an ape. **2.** Silly; ridiculous: *an apish grin.* —**ap′ish•ly** *adv.* —**ap′ish•ness** *n.* [U]

a•plen•ty (ə plĕn′tē) *adj.* In abundance: *We'll have water aplenty when the rains come.*

a•plomb (ə plŏm′ *or* ə plŭm′) *n.* [U] Self-confidence; poise; assurance: *Our teacher handled the situation with aplomb.*

a•poc•a•lypse (ə pŏk′ə lĭps′) *n. (usually singular).* A prophecy or revelation, especially about the end of the world. —**a•poc′-a•lyp′tic** (ə pok′ə lĭp′tĭk) *adj.*

ap•o•gee (ăp′ə jē) *n.* **1.** The point farthest from the earth in the orbit of the moon or an artificial satellite. **2.** The highest point; apex: *the apogee of his career.*

a•pol•o•get•ic (ə pŏl′ə jĕt′ĭk) *adj.* Expressing or making an apology: *The student's excuse was offered with an apologetic smile.* —**a•pol′o•get′i•cal•ly** *adv.*

a•pol•o•gize (ə pŏl′ə jīz′) *intr.v.* **a•pol•o•gized, a•pol•o•giz•ing, a•pol•o•giz•es.** To make an apology; say one is sorry: *Did he apologize to you for being late?*

a•pol•o•gy (ə pŏl′ə jē) *n., pl.* **a•pol•o•gies. 1.** A statement expressing regret for an offense or fault: *make an apology for being late.* **2.** An inferior substitute: *That short note was a poor apology for a letter.*

a•pos•tle (ə pŏs′əl) *n.* **1.** Often **Apostle.** One of the twelve original followers of Jesus.

2. A person who leads or strongly supports a cause or movement: *an apostle of government reform.*

a·pos·tro·phe (ə pŏs'trə fē) *n.* A mark (') used to indicate that a letter or letters have been left out from a word or phrase, as in *aren't*, or to show possession, as in *Tom's hat*, or to show special plurals, especially those of numbers and letters, as in *A's.*

a·poth·e·car·y (ə pŏth'ĭ kĕr'ē) *n., pl.* **a·poth·e·car·ies.** An old word for a person trained in the preparation of drugs and medicines; a pharmacist.

ap·pall (ə pôl') *tr.v.* To fill (sbdy.) with horror and amazement; shock: *My mother was appalled when she saw the mess the workers made in the back yard.*

ap·pall·ing (ə pô'lĭng) *adj.* Causing fear or dismay: *the appalling working conditions of miners in the last century.* —**ap·pall'ing·ly** *adv.*

ap·pa·ra·tus (ăp'ə rā'təs *or* ăp'ə răt'əs) *n., pl.* **apparatus** or **ap·pa·ra·tus·es. 1.** *(usually singular).* The means by which some function or task is performed: *Congress has a complicated apparatus for making laws.* **2.** A device or mechanism for a particular purpose: *a laboratory full of scales and other scientific apparatus.*

ap·par·el (ə păr'əl) *n.* [U] Clothing: *The clothing store has a separate department of children's apparel.*

ap·par·ent (ə păr'ənt *or* ə pâr'ənt) *adj.* **1.** Readily understood or seen; obvious: *for no apparent reason.* **2.** Appearing to be sthg. but not necessarily so; seeming: *an apparent advantage.* —**ap·par'ent·ly** *adv.*

ap·pa·ri·tion (ăp'ə rĭsh'ən) *n.* A ghost; a specter: *People have reported seeing apparitions in the old cemetery.*

ap·peal (ə pēl') *n.* **1.** [C] An urgent or sincere request: *an appeal for help.* **2.** [U] The power to attract or create interest: *The waterfront has great appeal for tourists.* **3.** [C] The transfer of a legal case from a lower court to a higher court for a new hearing. —*v.* —*intr.* **1.** To make an urgent or sincere request: *I appeal to you to help us.* **2.** To be attractive or interesting: *The fine automobile appealed to the buyer.* **3.** To make or apply for a legal appeal: *We finally decided to appeal.* —*tr.* To make or apply for a legal appeal of (a case): *appeal a judge's decision.*

ap·peal·ing (ə pē'lĭng) *adj.* Attractive or interesting: *appealing clothes.*

ap·pear (ə pîr') *intr.v.* **1.** To come into view: *A ship appeared on the horizon.* **2.** To come before the public: *The violinist has appeared in two concerts.* **3.** To seem or look: *The senator appears to be in good health.* **4.** To present oneself formally before a court of law: *The criminal appeared before the judge.*

ap·pear·ance (ə pîr'əns) *n.* **1.** [C] The act

of appearing; a coming into sight: *the sudden appearance of storm clouds on the horizon.* **2.** [C] The act of coming into public view, especially for a performance: *nine years since the pianist's last personal appearance.* **3.** [C; U] The way a person or thing looks: *A neat appearance helps to make a good impression.* **4.** [C] A semblance, especially a false show: *an appearance of bravery.* **5. appearances.** Outward indications; circumstances: *By all appearances you would never know that she was sick.*

ap·pease (ə pēz') *tr.v.* **ap·peased, ap·peas·ing, ap·peas·es. 1.** To calm or pacify (sbdy.), especially by giving what is demanded: *The baby sitter appeased the crying baby with a bottle.* **2.** To satisfy (sbdy.); relieve: *Several glasses of water appeased his thirst.* —**ap·pease'ment** *n.* [C; U] —**ap·peas'er** *n.*

ap·pel·late (ə pĕl'ĭt) *adj.* Having the legal power to hear appeals and to reverse previous court decisions: *an appellate court.*

ap·pend (ə pĕnd') *tr.v.* To attach or add (sthg.): *The editor appended an index to the history book.*

ap·pend·age (ə pĕn'dĭj) *n.* **1.** Something that is appended or attached: *The handle on a coffee cup is a useful appendage.* **2.** A part or organ of the body that hangs or projects from another part: *A finger is an appendage of the hand.*

ap·pen·dec·to·my (ăp'ən dĕk'tə mē) *n., pl.* **ap·pen·dec·to·mies.** The removal of the appendix by surgery.

ap·pen·di·ci·tis (ə pĕn'dĭ sī'tĭs) *n.* [U] Inflammation of the appendix.

ap·pen·dix (ə pĕn'dĭks) *n., pl.* **ap·pen·dix·es** or **ap·pen·di·ces** (ə pĕn'dĭ sēz'). **1.** A section at the end of a book that contains additional material, tables, or other information relating to the subject of the book. **2.** The tubular projection attached to the large intestine near where it joins the small intestine.

ap·pe·tite (ăp'ĭ tīt') *n.* **1.** The desire for food or drink: *Hiking five miles really gave me an appetite!* **2.** A strong desire for sthg.: *an appetite for learning.*

ap·pe·tiz·er (ăp'ĭ tī'zər) *n.* A food or drink that is taken before a meal to stimulate the appetite: *I served appetizers to my guests before dinner.*

ap·pe·tiz·ing (ăp'ĭ tī'zĭng) *adj.* Stimulating or appealing to the appetite; tasty: *an appetizing meal.* —**ap'pe·tiz'ing·ly** *adv.*

ap·plaud (ə plôd') *v.* —*tr.* **1.** To express praise or approval of (sbdy./sthg.), as by clapping the hands: *applaud the actors.* **2.** To praise or approve of (sbdy./sthg.): *My parents applauded my decision to study physics.* —*intr.* To express approval, especially by clapping the hands: *The audience applauded for ten minutes.*

ap·plause (ə plôz′) *n.* [U] **1.** Praise or approval expressed by the clapping of hands: *The guitarist's performance was cheered with loud applause.* **2.** Public approval: *The vaccine for polio received applause from doctors everywhere.*

ap·ple (ăp′əl) *n.* A firm rounded edible fruit with a thin red, yellow, or green skin. ◆ **apple of (one's) eye.** A person or thing that is especially liked or loved by sbdy.: *Her grandson is the apple of her eye.*

ap·ple·sauce (ăp′əl sôs′) *n.* [U] Apples that have been cooked until they are soft and then mashed.

ap·pli·ance (ə plī′əns) *n.* A machine, such as a toaster or dishwasher, used to perform a household task.

ap·pli·ca·ble (ăp′lĭ kə bəl *or* ə plĭk′ə bəl) *adj.* Capable of being applied; appropriate: *The new rule is not applicable in your case.* —**ap′pli·ca·bil′i·ty** *n.* [U] —**ap′pli·ca·bly** *adv.*

ap·pli·cant (ăp′lĭ kənt) *n.* A person who applies for sthg.: *an applicant for a job.*

ap·pli·ca·tion (ăp′lĭ kā′shən) *n.* **1.** [C; U] The act of applying: *an application of paint on the wall.* **2.** [C; U] A method of applying or using; a specific use: *the application of science to industry.* **3.** [U] The capacity of being usable; relevance: *Geometry has practical application to flying an airplane.* **4.** [C] **a.** A request, as for a job, loan, or admittance to a school: *His application for a loan was approved.* **b.** The form or document upon which such a request is made: *fill out a job application.*

ap·pli·ca·tor (ăp′lĭ kā′tər) *n.* An instrument for applying sthg., such as medicine or glue.

ap·plied (ə plīd′) *adj.* Put into practice; used in a particular way: *The new car was designed using applied physics.*

ap·ply (ə plī′) *v.* **ap·plied, ap·ply·ing, ap·plies.** —*tr.* **1.** To put (sthg.) on or upon another thing: *Apply a little bit of glue to the paper.* **2.** To adapt or put (sthg.) to a special use: *The Red Cross applied all its money to medical supplies.* **3.** To put (sthg.) into action: *apply the brakes.* **4.** To use (a special word or phrase) in referring to sbdy./sthg.: *Underground Railroad was the name applied to the system that helped slaves escape.* **5.** To devote (oneself or one's efforts) to sthg.: *The students applied themselves to their homework.* —*intr.* **1.** To be pertinent or relevant: *This rule for quiet in the library does not apply during a fire drill.* **2.** To request employment, acceptance, or admission: *Several people applied for the same job.*

ap·point (ə point′) *tr.v.* To select or designate (sbdy.) for an office, position, or duty: *The Mayor will appoint a new police chief.*

ap·point·ee (ə poin′ tē′ *or* ăp′oin tē′) *n.* A person who is selected for an office, position, or duty: *I am the next appointee for club secretary.*

ap·point·ment (ə point′mənt) *n.* [C; U] **1.** An arrangement for a meeting at a particular time or place: *I called the dentist to change the time of my appointment.* **2.a.** The act of selecting sbdy. for an office or position: *The appointment of a school principal is an important decision.* **b.** The office or position to which a person has been appointed: *Our teacher accepted the appointment as director.*

ap·prais·al (ə prā′zəl) *n.* **1.** [C; U] The act of setting a value or price: *The carpenter's appraisal for fixing the door took only a few minutes.* **2.** [C] An official or expert estimate of sthg., as for quality or worth: *The jeweler gave me an appraisal of my diamonds.*

ap·praise (ə prāz′) *tr.v.* **ap·praised, ap·prais·ing, ap·prais·es.** **1.** To set a value on (sthg.); fix a price for: *The jeweler appraised the customer's ring.* **2.** To estimate the quality, amount, or size of (sthg.); judge: *The engineer appraised the condition of the bridge and found it was excellent.* —**ap·prais′er** *n.* —**ap·prais′ing·ly** *adv.*

ap·pre·cia·ble (ə prē′shə bəl) *adj.* Capable of being noticed or measured; noticeable: *an appreciable difference in the newly painted house.* —**ap·pre′cia·bly** *adv.*

ap·pre·ci·ate (ə prē′shē āt′) *v.* **ap·pre·ci·at·ed, ap·pre·ci·at·ing, ap·pre·ci·ates.** —*tr.* **1.** To recognize the worth, quality, or importance of (sbdy./sthg.); value highly: *The citizens of the new democracy appreciate their freedom.* **2.** To be aware of or sensitive to (sthg.); realize: *I appreciate the difficulty of your situation.* **3.** To be thankful for (sthg.): *The neighbors appreciated our help in moving the furniture.* —*intr.* To increase in price or value: *The value of the painting has appreciated over the last ten years.*

SYNONYMS: appreciate, value, prize, treasure, cherish. These verbs mean to have a favorable opinion of sbdy. or sthg. **Appreciate** means to judge highly in comparison with sthg. else: *That awful restaurant certainly taught me to appreciate home cooking.* **Value** means to have a high opinion of a thing's importance or worth: *A true democracy values the free exchange of ideas.* **Prize** often suggests feeling pride in owning sthg.: *He prizes the movie star's autograph so highly that he is making a frame for it.* **Treasure** and **cherish** both mean to care for attentively and affectionately: *She treasures that painting—it has been in her family for generations. A solid friendship is something to cherish.*

ă-**cat**; ā-**pay**; âr-**care**; ä-**father**; ĕ-**get**; ē-**be**; ĭ-**sit**; ī-**nice**; îr-**here**; ŏ-**got**; ō-**go**; ô-**saw**; oi-**boy**; ou-**out**; o͞o-**took**; o͞o-**boot**; ŭ-**cut**; ûr-**word**; th-**thin**; th-**this**; hw-**when**; zh-**vision**; ə-**about**; N-French **bon**

ap•pre•ci•a•tion (ə prē′shē ā′shən) n. **1.** [U] Recognition of the worth, quality, or importance of sthg.: *Your appreciation of her hard work has meant a lot to her.* **2.** [U] Gratitude; gratefulness: *They expressed their appreciation with a gift.* **3.** [C; U] Awareness of artistic value; understanding and enjoyment: *showing a great appreciation of music and sculpture.* **4.** [U] An increase in value or price: *Appreciation of land value has made some farmers wealthy.*

ap•pre•cia•tive (ə prē′shə tĭv *or* ə prē′-shē ā′tĭv) adj. Showing or feeling appreciation: *the applause of an appreciative audience.* —**ap•pre′cia•tive•ly** adv.

ap•pre•hend (ăp′rĭ hĕnd′) tr.v. **1.** To take (sbdy.) into custody; arrest: *Police officers apprehended the suspect.* **2.** To grasp (sthg.) mentally; understand: *We tried to apprehend the details of her theory.*

ap•pre•hen•sion (ăp′rĭ hĕn′shən) n. **1.** [U] Fear or dread of what may happen; anxiety about the future: *The fall in prices caused apprehension among the investors.* **2.** [U] The ability to understand; understanding. **3.** [C] The act of capturing; an arrest: *the apprehension of a criminal.*

ap•pre•hen•sive (ăp′rĭ hĕn′sĭv) adj. Anxious or fearful; worried; uneasy: *apprehensive about the future.* —**ap′pre•hen′sive•ly** adv. —**ap′-pre•hen′sive•ness** n. [U]

ap•pren•tice (ə prĕn′tĭs) n. **1.** A person, usually a member of a labor union, who is learning a trade. **2.** A beginner. —tr.v. **ap•pren•ticed, ap•pren•tic•ing, ap•pren•tic•es.** To place (sbdy.) as an apprentice: *In earlier times many children were apprenticed to craftspeople for no pay.*

ap•pren•tice•ship (ə prĕn′tĭs shĭp′) n. [C; U] **1.** The condition of learning a trade. **2.** The period during which a person is in training: *She acquired many skills in her long apprenticeship as an electrician.*

ap•prise (ə prīz′) tr.v. **ap•prised, ap•pris•ing, ap•pris•es.** Formal. [of] To inform (sbdy.) of sthg.: *Please apprise your teacher of the reason for your absence.*

ap•proach (ə prōch′) v. —intr. To come near or nearer in place or time: *As spring approached, we grew happier.* —tr. **1.** To come near or nearer to (sbdy./sthg.) in place or time: *The speaker approached the microphone. Our doctor is approaching retirement.* **2.** To come close to (sthg./sbdy.) in quality, appearance, or other characteristics; approximate: *What could approach the beauty of this lake?* **3.** To begin to deal with or work on (sthg.): *We approach the task with eagerness.* **4.** To make a proposal to (sbdy.): *I approached the owner for a job.* —n. **1.** The act of approaching sbdy./sthg.: *The pilot had to be cautious in his approach to the airport. Birds fly south at the approach of winter.* **2.** A way or method of dealing or working with

sbdy./sthg.: *a new approach to the problem.* **3.** A way of reaching a place; an access: *the approach to the bridge.*

ap•proach•a•ble (ə prō′chə bəl) adj. **1.** Capable of being reached; accessible: *a small town approachable only by a mountain road.* **2.** Easy to talk to; friendly: *an approachable person.* —**ap•proach′a•bil′i•ty** n. [U]

ap•pro•pri•ate (ə prō′prē ĭt) adj. Suitable for a particular person, occasion, or place; proper: *What are the appropriate clothes for the party?* —tr.v. (ə prō′prē āt′). **ap•pro•pri•at•ed, ap•pro•pri•at•ing, ap•pro•pri•ates.** **1.** To set (sthg.) apart for a particular use: *Congress appropriated money for education.* **2.** Formal. To take possession of (sthg.) exclusively for oneself, often without permission: *Another student appropriated my chair when I got up for a drink of water.* —**ap•pro′pri•ate•ly** adv. —**ap•pro′pri•ate•ness** n. [U]

ap•pro•pri•a•tion (ə prō′prē ā′shən) n. [C; U] **1.** The act of appropriating sthg.: *I didn't like the appropriation of my work for those purposes.* **2.** Public funds set aside for a specific purpose: *Congress increased appropriations for disaster relief.*

ap•prov•al (ə prōō′vəl) n. [U] **1.** A favorable response or attitude: *The voters expressed their approval by voting for our mayor again.* **2.** Official consent or agreement: *The article was published with the approval of the editors.* ◆ **on approval.** For examination or trial by a customer without the obligation to buy: *We bought our new furniture on approval.*

ap•prove (ə prōōv′) v. **ap•proved, ap•prov•ing, ap•proves.** —tr. **1.** To confirm or consent to (sthg.) officially: *The Senate approved the treaty.* **2.** To regard (sthg.) favorably; consider right or good: *The country approved the President's decision to fund more medical research.* —intr. [of] To feel, voice, or demonstrate approval: *His mother does not approve of their watching too much television.* —**ap•prov′ing•ly** adv.

approx. abbr. An abbreviation of: **1.** Approximate. **2.** Approximately.

ap•prox•i•mate (ə prŏk′sə mĭt) adj. Almost exact or accurate: *the approximate number of students.* —tr.v. (ə prŏk′sə māt′). **ap•prox•i•mat•ed, ap•prox•i•mat•ing, ap•prox•i•mates.** To come close to (sthg.); be nearly the same as: *The temperatures of the Mediterranean Sea approximate those of Caribbean waters.* —**ap•prox′i•mate•ly** adv. —**ap•prox′i•ma′tion** (ə prŏk′sə-mā′shən) n. [C; U]

Apr. or **Apr** abbr. An abbreviation of April.

a•pri•cot (ăp′rĭ kŏt′ *or* ā′prĭ kŏt′) n. **1.** [C] A small juicy yellow-orange fruit similar to a peach. **2.** [U] A yellowish orange color. —adj. Yellowish orange.

A•pril (ā′prəl) *n.* The fourth month of the year, with 30 days.

April Fools' Day (foolz) *n.* April 1, traditionally celebrated as a day for playing practical jokes.

a•pron (ā′prən) *n.* An article of clothing worn over the front of the body and usually tied in the back to protect the clothes while cooking or cleaning.

ap•ro•pos (ăp′rə pō′) *adj.* Relevant or fitting: *The teacher's explanation was apropos to the story we read.* —*adv.* At an appropriate time. —*prep.* Concerning; regarding: *Apropos our appointment, I'm afraid I can't make it.* ♦ **apropos of.** With regard to: *The candidate told a funny story apropos of politics.*

apt (ăpt) *adj.* **1.** Exactly suitable; appropriate: *The alert student gave an apt reply.* **2.** Having a tendency; inclined: *Most people are apt to accept the advice of an expert.* **3.** Quick to learn: *an apt student with high grades.* —**apt′ly** *adv.* —**apt′ness** *n.* [U]

apt. *abbr.* An abbreviation of apartment.

ap•ti•tude (ăp′tĭ tood′) *n.* **1.** [C; U] A natural ability or talent: *She has a remarkable aptitude for mathematics.* **2.** [U] Quickness in learning and understanding: *a student with high grades who shows unusual aptitude.*

aq•ua (ăk′wə *or* ä′kwə) *n.* [U] A light bluish green color. —*adj.* Light bluish green.

aq•ua•ma•rine (ăk′wə mə rēn′ *or* ä′kwə-mə rēn′) *n.* **1.** [C] A transparent blue-green stone. **2.** [U] A pale blue to light greenish blue color. —*adj.* Pale blue to light greenish blue.

a•quar•i•um (ə kwâr′ē əm) *n., pl.* **a•quar•i•ums** or **a•quar•i•a** (ə kwâr′ē ə). **1.** A glass tank or container such as a bowl filled with water for keeping and displaying fish or other animals and plants. **2.** A building where such animals and plants are displayed to the public.

A•quar•i•us (ə kwâr′ē əs) *n.* **1.** [U] The eleventh sign of the zodiac in astrology. **2.** [C] A person born under this sign, between January 20 and February 18.

a•quat•ic (ə kwăt′ĭk *or* ə kwŏt′ĭk) *adj.* **1.** Consisting of, relating to, or being in water: *Seaweed grows in an aquatic environment.* **2.** Living or growing in or on the water: *The whale is an aquatic mammal, and seaweeds are aquatic plants.* **3.** Taking place in or on the water: *swimming and other aquatic sports.*

aq•ue•duct (ăk′wĭ dŭkt′) *n.* **1.** A large pipe, canal, or channel that carries water from a distant source. **2.** A structure that supports, such a pipe or channel across low ground or a river.

a•que•ous (ā′kwē əs *or* ăk′wē əs) *adj.* Resembling, containing, or dissolved in water: *an aqueous solution of salt and water.*

aq•ui•fer (ăk′wə fər) *n.* An underground layer of sand, gravel, or spongy rock that collects water.

Ar The symbol for the element **argon.**

AR *abbr.* An abbreviation of Arkansas.

—ar *suff.* A suffix that means of, relating to, or resembling: *angular; linear.*

Ar•ab (ăr′əb) *n.* **1.** A member of a Semitic people inhabiting Arabia. **2.** A member of an Arabic-speaking people. —**Ar′ab** *adj.*

Ar•a•bic numeral (ăr′ə bĭk) *n.* One of the numerical symbols 1, 2, 3, 4, 5, 6, 7, 8, 9, or 0. They are called Arabic numerals because they were introduced into Western Europe from sources of Arabic scholarship.

ar•a•ble (ăr′ə bəl) *adj.* Suitable for cultivation: *Farmers need arable land for growing.*

a•rach•nid (ə răk′nĭd) *n.* An animal that resembles an insect but has eight legs, no wings or antennae, and a body divided into two parts. Spiders and scorpions are arachnids.

ar•bi•ter (ăr′bĭ tər) *n.* **1.** A person chosen to judge a dispute; an arbitrator. **2.** [*of*] A person or thing having the power to judge: *The buyer is the final arbiter of fashion.*

ar•bi•trar•y (ăr′bĭ trĕr′ē) *adj.* **1.** Based on impulse or chance, not on reason or law: *Drawing numbers out of a hat was an arbitrary way to select the captain of the team.* **2.** Not limited by law: *The dictator's arbitrary government jailed many of his political opponents.* —**ar′bi•trar′i•ly** *adv.* —**ar′bi•trar′i•ness** *n.* [U]

ar•bi•trate (ăr′bĭ trāt′) *v.* **ar•bi•trat•ed, ar•bi•trat•ing, ar•bi•trates.** —*tr.* **1.** To decide (sthg.) as a judge: *arbitrate the boundary dispute between the two neighbors.* **2.** To submit (sthg.) to judgment: *Management and labor agreed to arbitrate their differences.* —*intr.* **1.** To serve as a judge: *Even strong nations must allow others to arbitrate.* **2.** To submit a dispute to the judgment of outsiders. —**ar′bi•tra′tion** *n.* [U] —**ar′bi•tra′tor** *n.*

ar•bor (ăr′bər) *n.* A structure upon which climbing plants grow, providing shade: *a grape arbor; a rose arbor.*

ar•bo•re•al (är bôr′ē əl) *adj.* **1.** Relating to or resembling a tree. **2.** Living in trees: *monkeys, squirrels, and other arboreal animals.* —**ar•bo′re•al•ly** *adv.*

ar•bo•re•tum (är′bə rē′təm) *n.* A place for the study and exhibition of growing trees, especially rare trees.

arc (ärk) *n.* **1.** Something shaped like a curve or arch: *the arc of a rainbow.* **2.** A continuous part of a circle or other curve. **3.** A stream of brilliant light or sparks produced when electricity jumps across the gap between two electrodes. —*intr.v.* **arced** or **arcked** (ärkt), **arc•ing** or **arck•ing** (är′kĭng), **arcs.** To take or follow a curved path: *The shooting star arced across the sky.*

ă–**cat**; ā–**pay**; âr–**care**; ä–**father**; ĕ–**get**; ē–**be**; ĭ–**sit**; ī–**nice**; îr–**here**; ŏ–**got**; ō–**go**; ô–**saw**; oi–**boy**; ou–**out**; oo–**took**; oo–**boot**; ŭ–**cut**; ûr–**word**; th–**thin**; th–**this**; hw–**when**; zh–**vision**; ə–**about**; N–French **bon**

ar•cade (är kād′) n. **1.** A series of arches supported by columns or pillars. **2.** A roofed passageway, especially one with shops on either side. **3.** A business or room that has coin-operated games.

arch[1] (ärch) n. **1.a.** A curved structure that supports a roadway, ceiling, or similar load, so that the weight of the load is carried by the sides. **b.** A monument built in this form. **2.** Something curved like an arch: *the arch of leaves overhanging the path.* **3.** The middle of the bottom of the foot. —v. —tr. **1.** To cause (sthg.) to form an arch or a similar curve: *The cat arched its back.* **2.** To span (sthg.): *The bridge arched the river.* —intr. [*across; over*] To extend in an arch: *The bridge arched across the river.* —arched adj.

arch[2] (ärch) adj. Chief; principal; main: *our arch rivals.*

arch— pref. A prefix that means principal, main, or chief: *archdiocese; archenemy.*

ar•chae•ol•o•gy or **ar•che•ol•o•gy** (är′kē ŏl′ə jē) n. [U] The scientific recovery and study of the remains of past human activities, such as burials, buildings, and tools. —ar′chae•o•log′i•cal adj. —ar′chae•ol′o•gist n.

ar•cha•ic (är kā′ĭk) adj. **1.** Characteristic of a very early, often primitive, period: *archaic fish.* **2.** Out-of-date; antiquated. For example, The word *hath* is an archaic form of *have.* —ar′cha•ism n. —ar•cha′i•cal•ly adv.

arch•bish•op (ärch bĭsh′əp) n. A bishop of the highest rank, leading an archdiocese or church province.

arch•di•o•cese (ärch dī′ə sĭs or ärch dī′-ə sēs′) n. The area under a Christian archbishop's control.

arch•en•e•my (ärch ĕn′ə mē) n. A chief or most important enemy: *France was the archenemy of Britain in Colonial America.*

ar•che•ol•o•gy (är′kē ŏl′ə jē) n. Variant of **archaeology.**

arch•er (är′chər) n. A person who shoots with a bow and arrow.

arch•er•y (är′chə rē) n. [U] The sport or skill of shooting with a bow and arrow.

ar•che•type (är′kĭ tīp′) n. An original model after which similar things are patterned: *The first airplane served as the archetype for later airplanes.*

ar•chi•pel•a•go (är′kə pĕl′ə gō′) n. A string of islands, such as Indonesia.

ar•chi•tec•ture (är′kĭ tĕk′chər) n. [U] **1.** The art and occupation of designing and directing the construction of buildings and other large structures. **2.** A style of building: *government buildings patterned on classical architecture.* **3.** Buildings and other large structures: *the impressive architecture of New York City.* —ar′chi•tec′tur•al adj. —ar′chi•tec′tur•al•ly adv.

ar•chive (är′kīv′) n. (*usually plural*). **1.** A place where records and historical documents are kept: *We went to the film archives to research silent movies.* **2.** A collection of records and documents. —ar•chiv′al adj. —ar′chive′ v.

arch•way (ärch′wā′) n. **1.** A passageway covered by an arch. **2.** An arch that covers or encloses an entrance or passageway.

—archy suff. A suffix that means a kind of rule or government: *monarchy.*

arc•tic (ärk′tĭk or är′tĭk) adj. **1.** Extremely cold; frigid: *arctic weather.* **2. Arctic.** Referring to the region surrounding the North Pole: *the Arctic Circle.* —Arc′tic n.

ar•dent (är′dnt) adj. **1.** Expressing or full of passion, desire, or other strong emotion; passionate: *an ardent plea to save the whales.* **2.** Strongly enthusiastic; eager: *an ardent defender of freedom.* —ar′dent•ly adv.

ar•dor (är′dər) n. [U] Great warmth or intensity of passion, enthusiasm, or other emotion: *the ardor of a political candidate.*

ar•du•ous (är′jōō əs) adj. Demanding great effort; difficult: *Becoming a police officer requires arduous training.* —ar′du•ous•ly adv. —ar′du•ous•ness n. [U]

are (är) v. **1.** Second person singular present tense of **be. 2.** First, second, and third person plural present tense of **be.**

ar•e•a (âr′ē ə) n. **1.** A section or region, as of land or a building: *an industrial area full of factories; an eating area for employees.* **2.** A surface, especially a part of the earth's surface: *a mountainous area.* **3.** A surface or plane figure as measured in square units: *The area of a rectangle is measured by multiplying its length by its width.* **4.** A range of activity or study: *the area of medical research.*

area code n. In the United States and Canada, a three-digit number assigned to a telephone area and used to place a call to that area: *The area code for San Francisco is 415.*

a•re•na (ə rē′nə) n. **1.** A building for sports events: *The arena was filled for the championship game.* **2.** An area of conflict or activity: *into the political arena.*

aren't (ärnt or är′ənt). **1.** Contraction of *are not: They aren't there anymore.* **2.** *Informal.* Contraction of *am not.* Used in tag questions: *I'm dressed OK for school, aren't I?*

ar•gon (är′gŏn′) n. [U] *Symbol* **Ar** A colorless, odorless element that is an inert gas, used in electric light bulbs. Atomic number 18. See table at **element.**

ar•gue (är′gyōō) v. **ar•gued, ar•gu•ing, ar•gues.** —tr. **1.** To give reasons for or against (sthg.), such as an opinion or proposal); debate: *The lawyer argued the case in court.* **2.** To prove or attempt to prove (sthg.) by reasoning: *I argued that the vacant lot should be* turned into a park. —*intr.* **1.** To engage in a quarrel; fight with words: *The twins seldom argue.* **2.** To put forth reasons for or against sthg.: *argue against building a new airport.* —**ar′gu•a•ble** *adj.* —**ar′gu•a•bly** *adv.* —**ar′gu•er** *n.*

ar•gu•ment (är′gyə mənt) *n.* **1.** A quarrel or dispute: *an argument over who goes first.* **2.** A discussion of differing points of view; a debate: *a scientific argument.* **3.** A statement in support of a position; a reason: *an argument for going.*

ar•gu•men•ta•tive (är′gyə měn′tə tǐv) *adj.* **1.** Liking to argue: *an argumentative person.* **2.** Containing or full of arguments: *an argumentative paper.* **ar′gu•men′ta•tive•ly** *adv.* —**ar′gu•men′ta•tive•ness** *n.* [U]

a•ri•a (ä′rē ə) *n.* A musical piece written for a solo singer accompanied by instruments, as in an opera.

ar•id (ăr′ĭd) *adj.* **1.** Having little or no rainfall; dry: *an arid desert; an arid wasteland.* **2.** Lifeless; dull: *a long arid book.* —**a•rid′i•ty** (ə rĭd′ĭ tē) *n.* [U] —**ar′id•ly** *adv.* —**ar′id•ness** *n.* [U]

Ar•ies (âr′ēz) *n.* **1.** [U] The first sign of the zodiac in astrology. **2.** [C] A person born under this sign, between March 21 and April 19.

a•rise (ə rīz′) *intr.v.* **a•rose** (ə rōz′), **a•ris•en** (ə rĭz′ən), **a•ris•ing, a•ris•es. 1.** To get up: *He arose from his chair.* **2.** To come into being; appear: *Take advantage of opportunities as they arise.* **3.** To move upward: *Mist arose from the lake.* **4.** To result: *The accident arose from careless driving.*

ar•is•toc•ra•cy (ăr′ĭ stŏk′rə sē) *n., pl.* **ar•is•toc•ra•cies.** [C; U] **1.** A social class based on inherited wealth, status, and sometimes titles: *The queen belongs to the aristocracy.* **2.** A group considered superior to others: *the aristocracy of local landowners.*

a•ris•to•crat (ə rĭs′tə krăt′ *or* ăr′ĭs tə krăt′) *n.* **1.** A member of the nobility. **2.** A person with the tastes, preferences, or other characteristics of the aristocracy. —**a•ris′to•crat′ic** *adj.* —**a•ris′to•crat′i•cal•ly** *adv.*

a•rith•me•tic (ə rĭth′mĭ tĭk) *n.* [U] **1.** The study of numbers and their properties under the operations of addition, subtraction, multiplication, and division. **2.** Calculation using these operations. —**ar′ith•met′ic** *or* **ar′ith•met′i•cal** *adj.* —**ar′ith•met′i•cal•ly** *adv.* —**a•rith′me•ti′cian** *n.*

Ariz. *abbr.* An abbreviation of Arizona.

ark (ärk) *n.* A ship, especially an ancient wooden ship.

HOMONYMS: ark, arc (part of a curve).

Ark. *abbr.* An abbreviation of Arkansas.

arm¹ (ärm) *n.* **1.** An upper limb of the human body, connecting the hand and wrist to the shoulder. **2.** A part that branches or seems to branch from the main body of sthg.: *an arm of the sea; the arm of a starfish.* **3.** Something designed to cover or support a human arm: *the arm of a shirt; the arm of a chair.* **4.** Authority that extends from a main source: *the long arm of the law.* ◆ **an arm and a leg.** An excessively high price: *He charged me an arm and a leg for the gifts.* **at arm's length. 1.** With the arm extended straight out from the body: *The art dealer held the picture at arm's length and looked at it.* **2.** At a distance; not on friendly or intimate terms: *A shy person often keeps acquaintances at arm's length.* **with open arms.** In a very friendly manner: *We welcomed our friends with open arms.* —**armed** *adj.*

arm² (ärm) *n.* **1.** (*usually plural*). A weapon, especially a gun: *The soldiers carried the arms.* **2. arms.** Warfare or military power: *The city could not be taken by force of arms.* —*v.* —*tr.* **1.** To equip (sbdy.) with weapons or other means of defense: *The governor armed civilians during the emergency.* **2.** To equip or provide (sbdy.) with sthg. necessary or useful: *Many people do not arm themselves with the facts before getting into an argument.* **3.** To make (sbdy./sthg.) ready; prepare: *arm the mechanism.* —*intr.* To prepare for war, as by gathering weapons and training soldiers: *As the countries armed, the leaders reached a settlement.* ◆ **up in arms.** Very upset; angry: *The whole neighborhood was up in arms over the closing of the fire station.* —**armed** *adj.*

ar•ma•dil•lo (är′- mə dĭl′ō) *n.* A burrowing mammal of southern North America and South America, covered with jointed bony plates.

armadillo

ar•ma•ment (är′- mə mənt) *n.* **1.** [C; U] The weapons, ammunition, and other equipment to fight a war or battle. **2.** [C] (*usually plural*). All the military forces and war equipment of a country. **3.** [U] Preparation for war: *Armament is a function of national security in time of war.*

arm•band (ärm′bănd′) *n.* A piece of cloth worn around the upper arm, often as a sign of mourning for the dead.

arm•chair (ärm′châr′) *n.* A chair with supports on the sides for one's arms.

armed forces (ärmd) *pl.n.* The military

forces of a country: *After graduation, she plans to join the armed forces.*

arm•ful (ärm′fŏŏl′) *n.* An amount as much as both arms can hold: *an armful of flowers.*

arm•hole (ärm′hōl′) *n.* An opening in a piece of clothing for an arm: *The armholes in my blouse are too small.*

ar•mi•stice (är′mĭ stĭs) *n.* A temporary stop in fighting by mutual agreement; a truce: *The warring countries declared an armistice.*

ar•mor (är′mər) *n.* [U] **1.** In early times, a covering worn to protect the body in battle. **2.** A protective covering, such as the bony plates covering an armadillo or the metal plates on tanks or warships. **3.** The armored vehicles of an army. —*tr.v.* To cover or protect (sthg.) with armor: *armor a warship.* —**ar′mored** *adj.*

ar•mor•y (är′mə rē) *n., pl.* **ar•mor•ies. 1.** A storehouse for weapons; an arsenal. **2.** A building that serves as the headquarters of a military reserve force.

ar•mour (är′mər) *n. & v.* Chiefly British. Variant of **armor.**

arm•pit (ärm′pĭt′) *n.* The hollow place under the arm at the shoulder.

arm•rest (ärm′rĕst′) *n.* A support for the arm, as on a chair or couch.

ar•my (är′mē) *n., pl.* **ar•mies. 1.** A body of people organized and trained for warfare on land. **2.** Often **Army.** The entire military land forces of a country. **3.** A large organized group: *an army of construction workers.*

a•ro•ma (ə rō′mə) *n.* A pleasant, characteristic smell; a fragrance: *The wonderful aroma of baking bread filled the house.* See Synonyms at **scent.**

ar•o•mat•ic (ăr′ə măt′ĭk) *adj.* Having an aroma; fragrant: *the aromatic scent of roses.* —**ar′o•mat′i•cal•ly** *adv.*

a•rose (ə rōz′) *v.* Past tense of **arise.**

a•round (ə round′) *adv.* **1.** On all sides or in all directions: *We drove around looking for a parking place.* **2.** In a circle or circular motion: *The ice skater spun around twice.* **3.** In circumference: *The lake is two miles around.* **4.** In or toward the opposite direction: *The horse turned around and ran toward the barn.* **5.** From one place to another; here and there: *I wandered around.* **6.** In or near one's present location: *He waited around all day.* **7.** To a specific place or area: *when you come around again.* **8.** Approximately; about: *Around 20 people went to the party.* —*prep.* **1.** On all sides of: *There are trees around the field.* **2.** Encircling or enclosing: *He wore a belt around his waist.* **3.** All about; throughout: *The teacher looked around the room.* **4.** On or to the farther side of: *the house around the corner.* **5.** Close by; near: *She lives right around here.* **6.** So as to pass or avoid: *How can we get around the problem?* **7.** Approximately at: *I woke up around seven.*

♦ **around the clock.** Ongoing; without stopping: *They worked around the clock.*

a•rous•al (ə rou′zəl) *n.* [U] **1.** The act of waking or the condition of being awakened. **2.** The act of exciting or the condition of being excited, often sexually.

a•rouse (ə rouz′) *tr.v.* **a•roused, a•rous•ing, a•rous•es. 1.** To awaken (sbdy.) from sleep or rest: *The baby's crying aroused me from my nap.* **2.** To stimulate or excite (sbdy./sthg.), sometimes sexually: *Their comments about the movie aroused my interest.*

ar•raign (ə rān′) *tr.v.* To call (sbdy.) into a court of law to answer a charge or indictment: *The suspect was arraigned on charges of burglary.* —**ar•raign′ment** *n.* [C; U]

ar•range (ə rānj′) *v.* **ar•ranged, ar•rang•ing, ar•rang•es.** —*tr.* **1.** To put (things) in a specific order: *Arrange these words alphabetically.* **2.** To plan or prepare for (sthg.): *A travel agent arranges transportation for tourists.* **3.** To come to an agreement about (sthg.): *The dealers arranged prices for the items.* **4.** To prepare an arrangement of (music): *He arranged the piano piece for orchestra.* —*intr.* **1.** To come to an agreement: *The company arranged with the union to allow more holidays.* **2.** To make preparations; plan: *We arranged for a taxi to pick us up at the train station.*

ar•range•ment (ə rānj′mənt) *n.* **1.** [U] The act of putting in order: *The arrangement of a time and place for the meeting was difficult.* **2.** [C; U] The manner or style in which things are put together: *The arrangement of ideas in the essay was clear.* **3.** [C] A collection or set of things that have been organized: *a flower arrangement.* **4.** [C] An agreement: *We have an arrangement about who cooks dinner and who washes the dishes.* **5.** [C] (usually plural). A plan or preparation: *Make arrangements for a vacation.* **6.** [C] A version of a musical composition that differs from the original in style or use of instruments: *a jazz arrangement of a popular song.*

ar•ray (ə rā′) *tr.v.* **1.** To put (things) in an orderly arrangement. **2.** To dress (sbdy.) up, especially in fine clothes; adorn: *The dancers were arrayed in red velvet.* —*n.* **1.** [C] An orderly arrangement: *an array of data.* **2.** [C] An impressively large number or group: *The cast for the play is a true array of talent.* **3.** [U] Clothing or finery: *The bride and groom were dressed in rich array.*

ar•rears (ə rîrz′) *pl.n.* An unpaid or overdue debt: *You have arrears of $23.00.* ♦ **be in arrears.** To be behind in fulfilling payments or an obligation: *After this bill is paid, they will not be in arrears.*

ar•rest (ə rĕst′) *tr.v.* **1.** To seize and hold (sbdy.) under authority of law: *The police arrested the thief.* **2.** To stop the progress of (sthg.): *The antibiotic arrested the spread of* the infection. **3.** To capture and hold (sthg.): *The exciting chapter arrested the reader's attention.* —*n.* [C; U] The act of arresting or the state of being arrested: *Her arrest surprised everyone in town.* —**ar•rest′ing** *adj.*

ar•rhyth•mi•a (ə rĭth′mē ə) *n.* [U] An irregular beating of the heart.

ar•ri•val (ə rī′vəl) *n.* **1.** [C; U] The act of reaching or coming somewhere: *the arrival of the passengers at the airport.* **2.** [C; U] The reaching of a goal or an objective: *The director's arrival at a decision came after much thought.* **3.** [C] A person or thing that has come somewhere: *the newest arrivals at the video store.*

ar•rive (ə rīv′) *intr.v.* **ar•rived, ar•riv•ing, ar•rives. 1.** To reach a destination; come to a place: *They arrived in the city on time.* **2.** To come; take place: *Spring weather arrived early this year.* **3.** To achieve success or fame: *She has finally arrived as an artist.* ♦ **arrive at.** *tr.v.* [insep.] To reach (sthg.) through effort or a process: *The jury arrived at a decision.*

ar•ro•gance (ăr′ə gəns) *n.* [U] The quality or condition of being too proud: *His arrogance had cost him many friends.*

ar•ro•gant (ăr′ə gənt) *adj.* **1.** Excessively and unpleasantly proud of oneself: *a conceited, arrogant person.* **2.** Characteristic of excessive pride: *an arrogant refusal to listen to others.* See Synonyms at **proud.** —**ar′ro•gant•ly** *adv.*

ar•row (ăr′ō) *n.* **1.** A straight thin shaft with a pointed head at one end and feathers at the other end. An arrow can be shot from a bow. **2.** Something similar in shape, as a sign or mark used to show direction: *Follow the arrows to my house.*

ar•row•head (ăr′ō hĕd′) *n.* The pointed removable tip of an arrow.

ar•roy•o (ə roi′ō) *n.* **1.** A small stream. **2.** A dry streambed in the southwest United States.

ar•se•nal (ăr′sə nəl) *n.* **1.** A building for the storage, manufacture, or repair of arms or ammunition. **2.** A stock of weapons: *Police discovered an arsenal of guns.*

ar•se•nic (ăr′sə nĭk) *n.* [U] **1.** *Symbol* **As** A chemical element used in making alloys, semiconductors, solders, and certain medicines. Atomic number 33. See table at **element. 2.** A deadly poison.

ar•son (ăr′sən) *n.* [U] The crime of intentionally setting fire to a building or property: *Arson was suspected.* —**ar′son•ist** *n.*

art (ärt) *n.* **1.** [U] **a.** The creation or production of painting, sculpture, poetry, or music. **b.** The study of these activities, especially the study of the visual arts: *I studied art in school.* **c.** A work or works resulting from

these activities, as a painting or a piece of sculpture: *an exhibit of modern art.* **2.** [C] A practical skill; a craft: *the art of sewing.* **3.** [C] The body of knowledge of a particular field: *the art of medicine; the industrial arts.* **4. arts.** The liberal arts; the humanities: *a college of arts and sciences.* **5. arts.** Artful devices; tricks.

ar•te•ri•al (är tîr′ē əl) *adj.* **1.** Relating to or resembling an artery or arteries. **2.** Serving as a main route of transportation: *This highway is the major arterial route through town.*

ar•te•ri•o•scle•ro•sis (är tîr′ē ō sklə rō′sĭs) *n.* [U] A disease in which the walls of the arteries become thickened and hard and interfere with the circulation of the blood.

ar•ter•y (är′tə rē) *n., pl.* **ar•ter•ies. 1.** Any branch of a system of blood vessels that carry blood away from the heart to various parts of the body. **2.** A major transportation route from which other routes branch.

art•ful (ärt′fəl) *adj.* **1.** Showing art or skill; skillful: *an artful player.* **2.** Crafty; cunning: *an artful salesclerk.* —**art′ful•ly** *adv.* —**art′ful•ness** *n.* [U]

ar•thri•tis (är thrī′tĭs) *n.* [U] A disease that causes inflammation and stiffness of a joint or joints in the body. —**ar•thrit′ic** (är thrĭt′ĭk) *adj.*

ar•thro•scope (är′thrə skōp′) *n.* An instrument used to examine the interior parts of a joint. —**ar′thro•scop′ic** (är′thrə skŏp′ĭk) *adj.*

ar•ti•choke (är′tĭ chōk′) *n.* A plant whose flower head is covered with thick, fleshy scales and is eaten cooked.

ar•ti•cle (är′tĭ kəl) *n.* **1.** A piece of writing that is a part of a publication; a report; an essay: *Read an article about sports in the newspaper.* **2.** A section or an item of a written document: *an article of the Constitution.* **3.** An individual thing; an item: *A shirt is an article of clothing.* **4.** In grammar, a word that is used to introduce a noun. In English the indefinite articles are *a* and *an,* and the definite article is *the.*

USAGE: article The words **a, an,** and **the** are known as **articles. A** and **an,** the **indefinite articles,** refer to any one. *I want an apple* means that I do not care which apple I get. The form **a** is used before a word beginning with a consonant sound, no matter how it may be spelled (*a frog, a university*). The form **an** is used before a word beginning with a vowel sound (*an orange, an hour*). **The,** the **definite article,** refers to some specific or definite person or thing: *I want the apple that is on the table.*

---

ar·tic·u·late (är tĭk′yə lĭt) *adj.* **1.** Spoken clearly and distinctly: *A radio announcer usually has articulate speech.* **2.** Capable of speaking clearly and effectively: *Teachers and lawyers must be articulate people.* —*v.* (är tĭk′yə lāt′). **ar·tic·u·lat·ed, ar·tic·u·lat·ing, ar·tic·u·lates.** —*tr.* **1.** To utter (a speech sound or sounds) distinctly; enunciate: *Children usually begin to articulate words by age two.* **2.** To express (sthg.) verbally: *Our leader articulated the feelings of the group.* —*intr.* **1.** To speak clearly and distinctly: *The speaker articulated well so all could understand.* **2.** To be jointed; form a joint: *the bones that articulate in the shoulder.* —**ar·tic′u·late·ly** *adv.* —**ar·tic′u·late·ness** *n.* [U] —**ar·tic′u·la′tion** *n.* [U]

ar·ti·fact (är′tə făkt′) *n.* An object produced by human handiwork, especially an item of ancient art: *The archaeologists found many artifacts as they explored the temple.*

ar·ti·fice (är′tə fĭs) *n.* [C; U] **1.** A clever device or trick: *Through artifice, the actor made us believe the story was true.* **2.** Deception; trickery: *The general used artifice in the surprise attack.*

ar·ti·fi·cial (är′tə fĭsh′əl) *adj.* **1.** Made by human beings to imitate sthg. found in nature: *an artificial sweetener; artificial flowers.* **2.** Not genuine or natural; affected: *an artificial display of tears and sadness.* —**ar′ti·fi′ci·al′i·ty** (är′tə fĭsh′ē ăl′ĭ tē) *n.* [U] —**ar′ti·fi′cial·ly** *adv.*

artificial intelligence *n.* [U] **1.** A branch of computer science that explores and develops the ability of computers to imitate human reasoning processes. **2.** The ability of a computer to reason as humans do.

ar·til·ler·y (är tĭl′ə rē) *n.* [U] **1.** Large mounted guns, such as cannons. **2.** The branch of an army that specializes in the use of such guns.

ar·ti·san (är′tĭ zən) *n.* A person skilled in making a certain product; a craftsperson: *These artisans make colorful pottery for use in cooking.*

art·ist (är′tĭst) *n.* **1.** A person who produces works of art, especially in the fine arts such as painting, sculpture, or music. **2.** A person who works in one of the performing arts, such as dancing or acting. **3.** A person who shows skill and creativity in an occupation or pastime: *That surgeon is a real artist.* —**ar·tis′tic** *adj.* —**ar·tis′ti·cal·ly** *adv.*

art·ist·ry (är′tĭ strē) *n.* [U] **1.** Artistic quality or workmanship: *the subtle artistry of a poem.* **2.** Artistic ability: *a painter of superb artistry.*

art·less (ärt′lĭs) *adj.* **1.** Free from deceit; sincere: *an artless child.* **2.** Not artificial; natural: *the artless beauty of a sunset.* —**art′·less·ly** *adv.* —**art′less·ness** *n.* [U]

art·work (ärt′wûrk′) *n.* [U] **1.a.** The production of decorative or artistic objects: *The* painter does artwork every day. **b.** Decorations or objects of art: *The archaeologists saved the artwork on the walls of the cave.* **2.** The illustrations and decorative parts of a book or other publication as distinct from the text: *The artwork in my chemistry book shows different illustrations of molecules.*

as (ăz; əz *when unstressed*) *adv.* **1.** Equally: *You won't find someone as willing to help.* **2.** For instance; for example: *large cats, as tigers and lions.* —*conj.* **1.** To the same degree or quantity that; equally with: *sweet as sugar.* **2.** In the same way that: *When in Rome, do as the Romans do.* **3.** At the same time that; while: *They smiled as their eyes met.* **4.** Because; since: *I wanted to stay home as I was ill.* **5.** Though: *Nice as that coat is, I don't want it.* **6.** In accordance with which; a fact that: *The sun is hot, as everyone knows.* —*pron.* That; who; which: *I got the same grade as you did.* —*prep.* **1.** The same as; like: *They treated the old car as a family member.* **2.** In the role or function of: *The teacher was acting as a friend.* ♦ **as for.** With regard to; concerning: *As for me, I'll stay.* **as if. 1.** In the same way that it would be if: *She ran as if she would never stop.* **2.** That: *It seemed as if the day lasted forever.* **as is.** *Informal.* Just the way it is; without changes: *The cracked cup is being sold as is, so it is very cheap.* **as it is. 1.** In fact; in reality: *I thought I had gotten a good grade. As it is, I barely passed.* **2.** Already: *You can't stop to do that now; we're late as it is.* **as long as. 1.** Because; since: *As long as you're offering, I accept.* **2.** On the condition that: *I'll go on the camping trip as long as you lend me a tent.* **as much.** All that; the same: *I might have guessed as much.* **as of.** On; at: *The assignment is due as of Friday.* **as to. 1.** With regard to: *There is great controversy as to the safety of nuclear energy.* **2.** According to: *The pencils were arranged as to color.* **as well.** In addition; also: *Yes, I've seen the movie, and I've read the book as well.* **as well as.** In addition to: *The weather was humid as well as hot.* **such as.** For instance; for example: *For a cold take something such as aspirin.*

As The symbol for the element **arsenic** (sense 1).

ASAP or **a.s.a.p.** *abbr.* A spoken or written abbreviation for "as soon as possible": *Please finish the report ASAP.*

as·bes·tos (ăs běs′təs *or* ăz běs′təs) *n.* [U] A mineral that is resistant to heat, flames, and chemical action.

as·cend (ə sĕnd′) *v.* —*intr.* **1.** To go or move upward; rise: *The airplane ascended rapidly.* **2.** To move to a higher rank or level: *The prince ascended to the throne and became king.* —*tr.* To climb to or toward to the top of (sthg.): *The climbers ascended the mountain.* —**as·cen′dant** also **as·cen′dent** *adj.*

as·cend·ing (ə sĕn'dĭng) *adj.* Moving or growing upward: *listed in ascending order of importance.*

as·cen·sion (ə sĕn'shən) *n.* [U] The act or process of moving upward or rising; an ascent.

as·cent (ə sĕnt') *n.* [C; U] **1.** The act of rising or moving up: *the first stages of the rocket's ascent through the atmosphere.* **2.** An upward slope: *The woman climbed the steep ascent to the mountaintop.* **3.** The act or process of rising from a lower level, degree, or status; development: *the laborer's ascent to a job in management.*

HOMONYMS: ascent, assent (agreement).

---

as·cer·tain (ăs'ər tān') *tr.v. Formal.* To find (sthg.) out: *ascertain the truth.* —**as'cer·tain'a·ble** *adj.* —**as'cer·tain'a·bly** *adv.* —**as'cer·tain'ment** *n.* [U]

as·cet·ic (ə sĕt'ĭk) *n.* A person who gives up comforts and pleasures in order to practice self-denial, often as a religious act. —*adj.* Self-denying; austere: *Most monks lead an ascetic life.* —**as·cet'i·cal·ly** *adv.* —**as·cet'i·cis'm** (ə sĕt'ĭ sĭz'əm) *n.* [U]

ASCII (ăs'kē) *n.* A computer code that allows different types of computers to share information.

as·cribe (ə skrīb') *tr.v.* **as·scribed, as·crib·ing, as·cribes.** *Formal.* [*to*] To think of (sthg.) as belonging to or coming from a specific cause, origin, or source; attribute: *The farmers ascribed their poor harvest to the bad weather.* —**as·crib'a·ble** *adj.*

a·sep·tic (ə sĕp'tĭk *or* ā sĕp'tĭk) *adj.* Free from microorganisms that cause infection: *aseptic surgical methods.* —**a·sep'ti·cal·ly** *adv.*

a·sex·u·al (ā sĕk'shōō əl) *adj.* **1.** Neither male nor female; sexless: *an asexual organism such as an amoeba.* **2.** Not involving sex organs or the union of sex cells: *asexual reproduction.* —**a·sex'u·al·ly** *adv.*

ash (ăsh) *n.* **1.** [C; U] The grayish white powder left when sthg. is burned. **2.** [U] The fine particles of solid matter thrown out of a volcano in an eruption. **3. ashes.** Human remains, especially after cremation.

a·shamed (ə shāmd') *adj.* **1.** Feeling shame or guilt: *You should be ashamed for losing your temper.* **2.** Reluctant to do sthg. because of fear of shame or embarrassment: *Don't be ashamed to ask for help.* —**a·sham'ed·ly** (ə shā'mĭd lē) *adv.*

ash·en (ăsh'ən) *adj.* Resembling ashes; pale: *ashen gray; a face ashen with fear.*

a·shore (ə shôr') *adv.* **1.** To move onto the shore from the sea: *go ashore.* **2.** On land: *The sailors spent the day ashore.*

ash·tray (ăsh'trā') *n.* A small container for tobacco ashes.

A·sian (ā'zhen) *adj.* Relating to Asia or its peoples, languages, or cultures. —*n.* **1.** A person born or living in Asia. **2.** A person whose ancestors are from Asia.

Asian American *or* **Asian-American** *n.* An American of Asian descent. —**Asian-American** *adj.*

a·side (ə sīd') *adv.* **1.** To or toward one side: *step aside; put a book aside.* **2.** Apart: *a day set aside for relaxation.* **3.** In reserve: *money put aside for a vacation.* **4.** Out of one's thoughts or mind: *put one's fears aside.*

♦ **aside from.** Apart from; except for: *Aside from a miracle, nothing can save her.*

as·i·nine (ăs'ə nīn') *adj.* Stupid or silly: *an asinine comment.* —**as'i·nine'ly** *adv.*

ask (ăsk) *v.* —*tr.* **1.** To put a question to (sbdy.): *My friend asked me if I had ever played the piano.* **2.** To seek an answer to (sthg.): *You learn to ask questions as you become a good student.* **3.** To make a request to (sbdy.) or for (sthg.): *She asked me for help. Can I ask a favor of you?* **4.** To invite (sbdy.): *Why don't we ask them to our house for lunch?* **5.** To charge (a fee): *They are asking $20 for this book.* **6.** To expect or demand (sthg.): *Riding in a car all day is asking a lot of a small child.* —*intr.* **1.** To make a request for sthg.: *I asked for help.* **2.** To make inquiries about sthg.: *We asked about the train schedule.*

SYNONYMS: ask, inquire, question, examine, quiz. These verbs all mean to seek information. **Ask** and **inquire** are the most general: *We stopped at the gas station and asked for directions to the stadium. I went into the store to inquire about the "Help Wanted" sign in the window.* **Question** often means to ask a series of questions: *The lawyer questioned the witness in great detail about the robbery.* **Examine** often means to question in order to test someone's knowledge: *All real-estate agents have been examined and licensed by the state.* **Quiz** means to question students in an informal test: *The teacher will quiz us tomorrow on the verbs.* **ANTONYM: answer.**

---

a·skance (ə skăns') *adv. Formal.* With distrust or disapproval: *The reporter looked askance at the rumors.*

a·skew (ə skyōō') *adv. & adj.* Not straight; out of line; crooked: *The wind knocked the sign askew. Your hat is askew.*

ASL *abbr.* An abbreviation of American Sign Language.

a·sleep (ə slēp') *adj.* **1.** Sleeping: *You must have been asleep when the phone rang.* **2.** Numb; without sensation: *My foot is asleep.*

ă-**cat**; ā-**pay**; âr-**care**; ä-**father**; ĕ-**get**; ē-**be**; ĭ-**sit**; ī-**nice**; îr-**here**; ŏ-**got**; ō-**go**; ô-**saw**; oi-**boy**; ou-**out**; ōō-**took**; ōō-**boot**; ŭ-**cut**; ûr-**word**; th-**thin**; th-**this**; hw-**when**; zh-**vision**; ə-**about**; N-French **bon**

◆ **fall asleep.** To begin to sleep: *The campers fell asleep quickly after their long hike.*

as•par•a•gus (ə **spăr'**ə gəs) *n.* [U] The green stalks of a grass-like plant that are cooked and eaten.

as•par•tame (ăs'pər tām' *or* ə spär'tām') *n.* [U] An artificial sweetener, about 200 times as sweet as sugar.

as•pect (ăs'pĕkt) *n.* **1.** A way in which sthg. can be considered; a feature: *In prescribing a treatment, the doctor considered all aspects of the patient's history.* **2.** Appearance; look: *the barren aspect of the desert.*

as•pen (ăs'pən) *n.* [C; U] A type of poplar tree with small rounded leaves that flutter in the lightest breeze.

as•per•sion (ə spûr'zhən *or* ə spûr'shən) *n. Formal.* A damaging or slanderous report or remark: *The critic cast aspersions on my opinions.*

as•phalt (ăs'fôlt') *n.* [U] A thick, sticky, dark brown or black mixture of petroleum tars used in paving roads, roofing, and waterproofing. —*tr.v.* To pave or coat (a surface) with asphalt.

as•phyx•i•a (ăs fĭk'sē ə) *n.* [U] Death or loss of consciousness caused by a lack of oxygen.

as•phyx•i•ate (ăs fĭk'sē āt') *intr. & tr.v.* **as•phyx•i•at•ed, as•phyx•i•at•ing, as•phyx•i•ates.** To undergo or cause to suffer asphyxia; suffocate: *Without air, the insects in the jar will asphyxiate. The thick smoke nearly asphyxiated the firefighters.* —**as•phyx'i•a'tion** *n.* [U]

as•pic (ăs'pĭk) *n.* A jelly made from gelatin and chilled meat juices or vegetable juices and served as a molded dish.

as•pi•rate (ăs'pə rāt') *tr.v.* **as•pi•rat•ed, as•pi•rat•ing, as•pi•rates.** **1.** To remove (a liquid or gas) from a body cavity by suction: *aspirate the lungs.* **2.** To pronounce (a vowel or word) with a puff of breath, as in the first sound of *help.*

as•pi•ra•tion (ăs'pə rā'shən) *n.* **1.** [C] A strong desire, as for a goal or ideal: *To become a dancer was my friend's aspiration.* **2.** [U] The process of removing a liquid or gas from a body cavity by suction. **3.** [U] The pronunciation of certain speech sounds with a puff of breath, especially at the beginning of a word, such as the *h* in *hurry.*

as•pire (ə spīr') *intr.v.* **as•pired, as•pir•ing, as•pires.** [*to*] To have a great ambition; desire strongly: *aspire to become a good player; aspire to great knowledge.*

as•pir•ant (ăs'pər ənt) *n.* A person who desires or strives for a particular position or honor: *a political aspirant.*

as•pi•rin (ăs'pər ĭn *or* ăs'prĭn) *n.* **1.** [U] A commonly used drug to reduce fever and pain. **2.** [C; U] A tablet of aspirin: *Please take two aspirin with your meal.*

ass (ăs) *n.* **1.** A hoofed mammal related to the horse, but smaller and with longer ears; a donkey. **2.** *Offensive.* A silly or stupid person. **3.** *Offensive.* The buttocks.

as•sail (ə sāl') *tr.v. Formal.* To attack (sbdy./sthg.) physically or with words: *The candidate assailed her opponents with strong criticism.* —**as•sail'a•ble** *adj.*

as•sail•ant (ə sā'lənt) *n.* A person who attacks sbdy. either physically or with words: *An unknown assailant attacked the woman.*

as•sas•sin (ə săs'ĭn) *n.* A person who kills sbdy. by surprise attack, especially one who kills a public official or other prominent figure for political reasons.

as•sas•si•nate (ə săs'ə nāt') *tr.v.* **as•sas•si•nat•ed, as•sas•si•nat•ing, as•sas•si•nates.** To murder (a public figure) by surprise attack, usually for political reasons: *President Kennedy was assassinated in 1963.* —**as•sas'si•na'tion** *n.* [C; U]

as•sault (ə sôlt') *n.* [C; U] A violent physical or verbal attack: *The army made an assault upon the town. The senator launched an assault upon his opponent.* —*tr.v.* To attack (sbdy./sthg.) vigorously: *The troops assaulted the coastline.*

assault and battery *n.* In law, a crime in which a physical attack on another person is carried out: *charged with assault and battery.*

as•sem•ble (ə sĕm'bəl) *v.* **as•sem•bled, as•sem•bling, as•sem•bles.** —*tr.* **1.** To bring (things or people) together as a group: *The teachers assembled their classes in the auditorium.* See Synonyms at **gather. 2.** To put (sthg.) together: *The mechanic assembled the engine.* —*intr.* **1.** To come together; gather: *A group of friends assembled at the corner.* **2.** To fit together: *The bicycle assembles quite easily.* —**as•sem'bler** *n.*

as•sem•bly (ə sĕm'blē) *n., pl.* **as•sem•blies. 1.** [C] A group of people gathered together for a common purpose. **2. Assembly.** A legislative body: *the State Assembly.* **3.a.** [U] The process of putting together a number of parts to make up a complete unit: *Assembly of a new car usually takes less than a day.* **b.** [C] A set of parts that work together as a unit; an apparatus: *the steering assembly of a truck.*

as•sent (ə sĕnt') *intr.v.* [*to*] To express agreement: *Everyone assented to the arrangement.* —*n.* [U] Agreement, as to a proposal, especially in a formal or impersonal manner: *The governor wanted the voters' assent to the new law.*

HOMONYMS: assent, ascent (rising).

---

as•sert (ə sûrt') *tr.v.* **1.** To state or declare (sthg.) positively; claim: *By passing the consumer protection law, the senators asserted their independence from business leaders.* **2.** To insist upon (sthg.); defend or maintain:

The lawyer asserted the defendant's right to a fair trial. ◆ **assert (oneself).** To express oneself boldly or forcefully: *We decided to assert ourselves and refused to go.*

as•ser•tion (ə sûr′shən) n. **1.** [C; U] The act of asserting. **2.** [C] A positive statement or claim, especially one for which no proof is offered: *His assertions of innocence were later found to be true.*

as•ser•tive (ə sûr′tĭv) adj. Bold and self-confident, especially in putting forward one's opinions: *She was assertive in her request for a raise.* —**as•ser′tive•ly** adv. —**as•ser′-tive•ness** n. [U]

as•sess (ə sĕs′) tr.v. **1.** To estimate the value of (property) for taxation: *The apartment building was assessed at several million dollars.* **2.** To charge (sbdy.) with a tax, fine, or other special payment: *Each student will be assessed five dollars for use of the gym.* **3.** To analyze and determine the significance or value of (sthg.); evaluate: *Our teacher assessed our homework for errors.* —**as•sess′ment** n. [C; U] —**as•ses′sor** n.

as•set (ăs′ĕt′) n. **1.** A valuable quality or possession: *A friendly personality is a great asset.* **2. assets.** All the property owned by a person or business that has monetary value: *Most of her assets are in real estate.*

as•sign (ə sīn′) tr.v. **1.** To set (sthg.) apart for a particular purpose; designate: *assign a day for the test.* **2.** To select (sbdy./sthg.) for a duty or office; appoint: *The fire chief assigned a group of firefighters to the industrial area of the city.* **3.** To give (sthg.) out as a task: *The teacher assigned homework to all of us.* **4.** To regard (sthg.) as belonging: *We sorted the rocks and assigned them to different categories.*

as•sign•ment (ə sīn′mənt) n. **1.** [C; U] The act of selection: *The work was divided among us by assignment.* **2.** [C] Something given out, especially a task or job: *What's the chemistry assignment for tomorrow?* See Synonyms at **task. 3.** [C] A post of duty to which one is appointed: *The journalist will take an assignment outside the United States.*

as•sim•i•late (ə sĭm′ə lāt′) v. **as•sim•i•lat•ed, as•sim•i•lat•ing, as•sim•i•lates.** —*tr.* **1.** To take (sthg.) in; incorporate; absorb: *students trying to assimilate new knowledge.* **2.** To take (sbdy.) into the cultural or social tradition of a group: *The United States has assimilated immigrants of many nationalities.* —*intr.* **1.** To be taken into the mind: *concepts that are difficult to assimilate.* **2.** To be taken into a group: *Many ethnic groups assimilated rapidly.* —**as•sim′i•la′tion** n. [U]

as•sist (ə sĭst′) tr. & intr.v. To help; aid: *Our friends assisted us in fixing the car. I'll be*

happy to assist. See Synonyms at **help.** —n. An act of giving aid; help: *give someone a quick assist.* —**as•sist′er** n.

as•sis•tance (ə sĭs′təns) n. [U] Help; aid: *The government provided financial assistance to farmers.*

as•sis•tant (ə sĭs′tənt) n. A person who assists; a helper: *the President's special assistant.* —adj. Acting under the authority of another person: *an assistant director.*

assn. abbr. An abbreviation of association.

assoc. abbr. An abbreviation of: **1.** Associate. **2.** Association.

as•so•ci•ate (ə sō′shē āt′ *or* ə sō′sē āt′) v. **as•so•ci•at•ed, as•so•ci•at•ing, as•so•ci•ates.** —*tr.* **1.** To bring (things) together in one's mind or imagination; connect: *We associate the desert with dry weather.* **2.** To connect (oneself) with a cause, group, or partnership: *Many people associate themselves with clubs.* —*intr.* [*with*] To spend time together: *How long have you been associating with those people?* —n. (ə sō′ shē ĭt *or* ə sō′sē ĭt). **1.** A partner or colleague: *my business associate.* **2.** A member who has only partial status: *an associate of the museum society.*

associate degree n. A degree awarded by some colleges after completion of a two-year course of study.

as•so•ci•a•tion (ə sō′sē ā′shən *or* ə sō′-shē ā′shən) n. **1.** [C; U] The act of associating: *working in association with others; a new association of ideas.* **2.** [C] A partnership or friendship: *a close association with old schoolmates.* **3.** [C] A group of people joined together for a common purpose or interest: *a trade association; a teachers' association.* **4.** [C] An idea or a train of ideas inspired by another idea or by a thought, feeling, or sensation: *What associations does the word* summer *bring to your mind?*

as•so•ci•a•tive (ə sō′shē ā′tĭv *or* ə sō′sē-ā′tĭv *or* ə sō′shə tĭv) adj. **1.** Characterized by, resulting from, or causing association. **2.** In mathematics, relating to the associative property, a law that the combinations by which numbers are added or multiplied will not change the sum or product. —**as•so′-ci•a′tive•ly** adv.

as•sort•ed (ə sôr′tĭd) adj. Consisting of various kinds: *shirts of assorted sizes; assorted screws.*

as•sort•ment (ə sôrt′mənt) n. A collection of various kinds; a variety: *people with an unusual assortment of skills; an assortment of vegetables.*

asst. abbr. An abbreviation of assistant.

as•sume (ə sōōm′) tr.v. **as•sumed, as•sum•ing, as•sumes. 1.** To take (sthg.) for granted; suppose: *Let's assume that our guests will come on time.* **2.** To take (responsibility) upon oneself: *We assume responsibility for keeping the playground clean.* **3.** To take on the duties of (sthg.): *The new governor assumes office in January.* **4.** To take (sthg.) over; seize: *She assumed control of the project during the crisis.* **5.** To take (sthg.) on; put on: *assume a disguise.* **6.** To pretend (sthg.): *He is always assuming an attitude of indifference.*

as•sumed (ə sōomd') *adj.* **1.** Fictitious; adopted: *an assumed name.* **2.** Taken as true: *an assumed fact.*

as•sum•ing (ə sōo'mĭng) *adj.* Taking too much for granted; presumptuous; arrogant: *Only an assuming guest would open my closet and borrow a shirt.*

as•sump•tion (ə sŭmp'shən) *n.* **1.** [C; U] The act of assuming: *his assumption of responsibility.* **2.** [C] An idea or a statement accepted as true without proof: *Let's start with the assumption that all people have equal rights under the law.*

as•sur•ance (ə shoŏr'əns) *n.* **1.** [C; U] The act of declaring positively. **2.** [C] A statement or indication that gives confidence; a guarantee: *The student gave the teacher his assurance that his homework would be done by Monday.* **3.** [U] Self-confidence: *The actor played the part with complete assurance.*

as•sure (ə shoŏr') *tr.v.* **as•sured, as•sur•ing, as•sures.** **1.** To declare (sthg.) positively: *I can assure you that the train will be on time.* **2.** To cause (sbdy.) to feel sure; convince: *She assured me of her good intentions.* **3.** To make certain of (sthg.): *The bank lent us the money to assure the success of the business.* **4.** To give confidence to (sbdy.): *The doctor assured me that I would feel better soon.* —**as•sured'** *adj.* —**as•sur'ed•ly** (ə shoŏr'ĭd lē) *adv.*

USAGE: assure The words **assure, ensure,** and **insure** all mean "to make secure or certain," but **assure** and **insure** have more specific meanings as well. Of the three, only **assure** can mean "to cause to feel sure": *He assured the queen of his loyalty.* **Insure** is the only one used in the commercial sense of "to guarantee persons or property against risk," as in *We insured the car.*

as•ter•isk (ăs'tə rĭsk') *n.* A symbol (*) used in printed and written matter to indicate sthg., such as a reference to extra information or a footnote.

as•ter•oid (ăs'tə roid') *n.* Any of many small, often irregularly shaped bodies that orbit the sun, mainly in the region between Mars and Jupiter.

asth•ma (ăz'mə *or* ăs'mə) *n.* [U] A lung disease that causes tightness of the chest, coughing, and difficulty breathing.

asth•mat•ic (ăz măt'ĭk *or* ăs măt'ĭk) *adj.* **1.** Relating to asthma. **2.** Having asthma: *an asthmatic child.* —*n.* A person with asthma.

as though *conj.* As if: *They looked as though they were enjoying themselves.*

a•stig•ma•tism (ə stĭg'mə tĭz'əm) *n.* (*usually singular*). A structural defect of the eye that produces indistinct or imperfect images.

a•stir (ə stûr') *adj.* **1.** In motion; moving about: *The class was astir after the news of a party.* **2.** Out of bed; awake: *She was astir at sunrise.*

a•ston•ish (ə stŏn'ĭsh) *tr.v.* To fill (sbdy.) with wonder; amaze; surprise: *The results of the experiment astonished the researchers.* See Synonyms at **surprise.** —**a•ston'ish•ing** *adj.* —**a•ston'ish•ing•ly** *adv.* —**a•ston'ish•ment** *n.* [U]

a•stound (ə stound') *tr.v.* To astonish and bewilder (sbdy.): *The rise in stock prices astounded investors.* See Synonyms at **surprise.** —**a•stound'ing** *adj.* —**a•stound'ing•ly** *adv.*

a•stray (ə strā') *adv.* Away from the proper goal or path: *He was led astray by bad advice.*

a•stride (ə strīd') *adv.* With the legs on each side: *riding astride on a horse.* —*prep.* With a leg on each side of: *The cowboy sat astride the horse's back.*

as•trin•gent (ə strĭn'jənt) *adj.* Having the property of shrinking body tissue. —*n.* A chemical substance that draws together or contracts body tissues and thus slows or stops the flow of blood or other body fluids: *She likes to use a mild astringent on her face.*

astro— *pref.* A prefix that refers to stars or space: *astronaut; astrology.*

as•trol•o•gy (ə strŏl'ə jē) *n.* [U] The study of the positions of the stars and planets in the belief that they influence human events and natural occurrences on earth. —**as'tro•log'i•cal** (ăs'trə lŏj'ĭ kəl) *adj.* —**as'tro•log'i•cal•ly** *adv.* —**as•trol'o•ger** *n.*

as•tro•naut (ăs'trə nôt') *n.* A person trained to serve as a member of the crew of a spacecraft.

as•tron•o•mer (ə strŏn'ə mər) *n.* A person who specializes in astronomy.

as•tro•nom•i•cal (ăs'trə nŏm'ĭ kəl) also **as•tro•nom•ic** (ăs'trə nŏm'ĭk) *adj.* **1.** Of or relating to astronomy. **2.** Too large to be easily imagined; immense: *The budget for the military is astronomical.* —**as'tro•nom'i•cal•ly** *adv.*

as•tron•o•my (ə strŏn'ə mē) *n.* [U] The science that deals with the study of the sun, moon, planets, stars, and all other celestial bodies.

as•tro•phys•ics (ăs'trō fĭz'ĭks) *n.* [U] (*used with a singular verb*). The branch of astronomy that deals with physical processes, such as energy, that occur in space.

as·tute (ə stōōt′) *adj.* Having excellent judgment; shrewd: *The reporter was an astute observer.* —**as·tute′ly** *adv.* —**as·tute′ness** *n.* [U]

a·sy·lum (ə sī′ləm) *n.* **1.** [U] A place of refuge or shelter: *I found asylum from the storm in an old house.* **2.** [U] Protection given to a political refugee from another country: *The refugees asked for political asylum.* **3.** [C] A hospital or shelter for people with physical or mental disorders.

a·sym·met·ri·cal (ā′sĭ mĕt′rĭ kəl) also **a·sym·met·ric** (ā′sĭ mĕt′rĭk) *adj.* Not symmetrical; not the same on both halves; lacking symmetry: *The building was asymmetrical.* —**a′sym·met′ri·cal·ly** *adv.*

a·sym·me·try (ā sĭm′ĭ trē) *n.* [C; U] Lack of symmetry or balance.

at (ăt; ət *when unstressed*) *prep.* **1.** In or near the position or location of: *at home.* **2.** To or toward the direction or goal of: *She refused to look at us.* **3.** On, near, or by the time or age of: *at noon.* **4.** In the state or condition of: *He's at peace with himself.* **5.** In the activity or field of: *good at math.* **6.a.** Dependent upon: *at your mercy.* **b.** According to: *at the judge's discretion.* **7.** In the rate, extent, or amount of: *gas at two dollars a gallon.* **8.** Through; by way of: *Come in at the side entrance.*

ate (āt) *v.* Past tense of **eat.**

Homonyms: ate, eight (number).

—ate[1] *suff.* A suffix that means: **1.** Characterized by: *fortunate.* **2.** Rank; office: *consulate.* **3.** To act upon in a specified manner: *insulate; stimulate.*

—ate[2] *suff.* A suffix that means a derivative of a chemical compound or a salt: *acetate.*

a·the·ism (ā′thē ĭz′əm) *n.* [U] Disbelief in or denial of the existence of God. —**a′the·ist** *n.* —**a′the·is′tic** *adj.*

ath·er·o·scle·ro·sis (ăth′ə rō sklə rō′sĭs) *n.* [U] A disease in which fatty material accumulates on the interior walls of the arteries, making them narrower.

ath·lete (ăth′lēt′) *n.* A person who is trained for or naturally good at sports that require physical strength, endurance, and coordination.

ath·let·ic (ăth lĕt′ĭk) *adj.* **1.** Relating to sports or players: *athletic ability; an athletic club.* **2.** Physically strong; muscular: *an athletic build.* See Synonyms at **muscular.** —**ath·let′i·cal·ly** *adv.*

ath·let·ics (ăth lĕt′ĭks) *n.* [U] *(used with a singular or plural verb).* Athletic activities; sports.

—ation *suff.* A suffix that means: **1.** Action or process: *demonstration.* **2.** The state, condition, or quality of: *starvation.* **3.** The result of an action or process: *discoloration.*

Word Building: —ation The very common noun suffix **—ation** is added to a verb and changes that verb to a noun. At first **—ation** was added to verbs that ended in **—ate.** So, for example, we have the noun **creation,** formed from the verb **create.** But **—ation** has become so popular in English that it is used to form nouns from verbs that do not end in **—ate,** such as **civilization** from the verb **civilize** and **starvation** from the verb **starve.**

—ative *suff.* A suffix that means of, relating to, or associated with: *talkative; authoritative.*

at·las (ăt′ləs) *n.* A book or bound collection of maps.

ATM *abbr.* An abbreviation of automated teller machine: *My bank has an ATM at the mall.*

ATM

at·mos·phere (ăt′mə sfîr′) *n.* **1.** [U] The gases that surround Earth or some other celestial body. **2.** [C] A unit of pressure equal to the pressure of the air at sea level, about 1.01325×10^5 newtons per square meter or 14.7 pounds per square inch. **3.** [U] The air or climate of a place: *the dry atmosphere of the desert.* **4.** [C; U] A general feeling or mood: *the library's quiet atmosphere.* —**at′mos·pher′ic** (ăt′mə sfĕr′ĭk *or* ăt′mə sfîr′ĭk) also **at′mos·pher′i·cal** *adj.* —**at′mos·pher′i·cal·ly** *adv.*

at·om (ăt′əm) *n.* **1.** The smallest part of an element, consisting of protons and neutrons in a dense central nucleus surrounded by moving electrons. **2.** A bit or small amount: *There is not an atom of truth in that statement.* —**a·tom′ic** (ə tŏm′ĭk) *adj.*

a·tom·ic number (ə tŏm′ĭk) *n.* The number of protons in the atomic nucleus of a chemical element.

atomic weight *n.* The average weight of an atom of an element.

a·tone (ə tōn′) *intr.v.* **a·toned, a·ton·ing, a·tones.** [*for*] To make up for a sin, fault, or other wrong: *atone for bad manners by apologizing.* —**a·tone′ment** *n.* [U]

a·top (ə tŏp′) *prep. Formal.* On top of: *The apple is atop the table.*

a·tri·um (ā′trē əm) *n.* **1.** An airy open place with high ceilings in a house or building. **2.** One of the chambers of the heart.

a·tro·cious (ə trō′shəs) *adj.* **1.** Extremely

evil or cruel; wicked: *atrocious acts of violence.* **2.** Very bad; terrible: *atrocious weather.* —**a•tro′cious•ly** *adv.*

a•troc•i•ty (ə trŏs′ĭ tē) *n., pl.* **a•troc•i•ties.** An act of extreme cruelty and violence: *atrocities of war.*

at•ro•phy (ăt′rə fē) *tr. & intr.v.* **at•ro•phied, at•ro•phy•ing, at•ro•phies.** To waste away or cause to waste away because of poor nourishment or lack of use: *A month of inactivity had atrophied the patient's body. The muscle atrophied.* —*n.* [U] The wasting away because of lack of use.

at•tach (ə tăch′) *v.* —*tr.* **1.** To fasten or join (things) together; connect: *attach the wires.* **2.** To bind (people) by ties of affection or loyalty: *The brother and sister are very attached to each other.* **3.** To think of (sthg.) as belonging: *I attach no importance to our different points of view.* **4.** To add (sthg.) at the end; append: *The lawyer had all parties attach their signatures to the document.* **5.** To assign (military personnel) to a unit on a temporary basis: *attach soldiers to a fighting unit.* **6.** To take or seize (property) by court order: *The bank attached the debtor's salary.* —*intr.* [*to*] To adhere or belong to: *The handle attaches to the door.* —**at•tach′a•ble** *adj.*

at•ta•ché (ăt′ə shā′) *n.* A person assigned to the staff of a diplomatic mission: *a cultural attaché to the American Embassy.*

attaché case *n.* A briefcase resembling a small suitcase, with hinges and flat sides.

at•tach•ment (ə tăch′mənt) *n.* **1.** [U] The act of attaching or condition of being attached: *attachment of a horse to a wagon.* **2.** [C] Something that attaches as a supplementary part; an accessory: *This vacuum cleaner has several attachments.* **3.** [C] A bond of affection or loyalty: *a strong attachment to a friend.*

at•tack (ə tăk′) *v.* —*tr.* **1.** To assault (sbdy./sthg.) with violent force: *Even large animals will not attack elephants.* **2.** To criticize (sbdy./sthg.) strongly or in a hostile manner: *The politicians attacked each other in their debate.* **3.** To affect (sbdy./sthg.) harmfully; afflict: *An epidemic of flu attacked thousands of people.* **4.** To start work on (sthg.) with purpose and vigor: *attack the problem of health care.* —*intr.* To launch an assault: *The troops attacked at dawn.* —*n.* **1.** [C; U] The act of attacking; an assault: *an attack at dawn.* **2.** [C] A strong or hostile expression of criticism: *The politician survived many attacks on the way to reelection.* **3.** [C] An occurrence of a disease, especially when sudden: *an attack of asthma.* —**at•tack′er** *n.*

at•tain (ə tān′) *tr.v.* **1.** To gain, accomplish, or achieve (sthg.) by effort: *attain a degree by hard work.* See Synonyms at **reach.** **2.** To arrive at or reach (sthg.) through time, growth, or movement: *Today many people attain the age of 80.* —**at•tain′a•ble** *adj.* —**at•tain′ment** *n.* [C; U]

at•tempt (ə tĕmpt′) *tr.v.* To make an effort at (sthg.); try: *Inventors attempt to develop new devices that help humans live more easily.* —*n.* **1.** An effort or a try: *an attempt to solve the mystery.* **2.** [*on*] An attack; an assault: *an attempt on the king's life.*

at•tend (ə tĕnd′) *v.* —*tr.* **1.** To be present at (sthg.); go to: *Most pupils attend school all day.* **2.** To take care of (sbdy.): *Two nurses attended the sick boy.* —*intr.* **1.** To be present: *I wanted to go, but I was ill and could not attend.* **2.** To apply oneself to sthg.; give care and thought: *Please attend to the matter at hand.*

at•ten•dance (ə tĕn′dəns) *n.* **1.** [U] The act of being present: *The child's attendance at school has been perfect. Several famous scholars were in attendance.* **2.** [C] (*usually singular*). The people or number of people present: *an attendance of 50,000 at the football game.* **3.** [U] The act of taking care of sbdy., as at a hospital: *a physician in attendance.*

at•ten•dant (ə tĕn′dənt) *n.* A person who attends or waits on another: *a parking lot attendant.*

at•ten•tion (ə tĕn′shən) *n.* **1.** [U] Concentration of the mental powers upon sbdy./sthg.: *Pay attention to the details. The speaker held the listeners' attention for more than an hour.* **2.** [U] Consideration; notice: *Your suggestion has come to our attention.* **3. attentions.** Acts of courtesy or consideration, especially in trying to win a person's affection: *Do you think his attentions are sincere?* **4.** [U] The posture taken by a soldier, with the body erect, eyes to the front, arms at the sides, and heels together: *Stand at attention.* —*interj.* An expression used as a command to assume an erect military posture.

at•ten•tive (ə tĕn′tĭv) *adj.* **1.** Giving attention to sthg.; alert: *Only the most attentive students understood the explanation.* **2.** Marked by careful attention to the comfort of others; considerate: *an attentive host.* —**at•ten′tive•ly** *adv.* —**at•ten′tive•ness** *n.* [U]

at•test (ə tĕst′) *v.* —*tr.* **1.** To declare or state (sthg.) to be true, correct, or genuine, especially by signing one's name as a witness: *attest a will.* **2.** To give evidence or proof of (sthg.); prove: *Their rounded shapes attest the great age of the mountains.* —*intr.* [*to*] To bear witness: *I can attest to his presence at the concert.*

at•tic (ăt′ĭk) *n.* A level of a house or room just below the roof, often used for storage: *We stored our old clothes in a trunk in the attic.*

at•tire (ə tīr′) *Formal.* *n.* [U] Clothing, costume, or apparel: *white tennis attire.* —*tr.v.* **at•tired, at•tir•ing, at•tires.** To dress (sbdy.), especially in fine or formal clothing: *The king was attired in his finest robes.*

at•ti•tude (ăt′ĭ tōōd′) *n.* **1.** [C; U] A state of mind with regard to sbdy./sthg.; a point of view: *What is the neighborhood's attitude toward building a new city park?* **2.** [C] A position of the body indicating a mood or condition: *The kids sprawled on the couch in a relaxed attitude.* **3.** [C; U] The position of a vehicle, such as an aircraft or spacecraft, in relation to its direction of motion or some other point of reference. **4.** [U] *Informal.* An obvious confidence in oneself; arrogance: *Don't come in here with all that attitude!*

at·tor·ney (ə tûr′nē) *n., pl.* **at·tor·neys.** A person, especially a lawyer, legally appointed to act as agent for another person.

at·tract (ə trăkt′) *v.* —*tr.* To cause (sbdy./ sthg.) to draw near; draw by some quality or action: *A magnet attracts nails by magnetism. The fine beaches attract many tourists.* —*intr.* To have the power to draw to oneself or itself: *attract by magnetic force.*

at·trac·tion (ə trăk′shən) *n.* **1.** [U] The act or power of attracting sbdy./sthg.: *the attraction of a magnet; sexual attraction.* **2.** [C] *(often plural).* A popular place; entertainment: *Boston has many attractions.*

at·trac·tive (ə trăk′tĭv) *adj.* **1.** Pleasing to the eye or mind; appealing: *an attractive young couple; an attractive offer that should be profitable.* **2.** Having the power to attract: *the attractive forces of magnetism and gravity.* —**at·trac′tive·ly** *adv.* —**at·trac′tive·ness** *n.* [U]

at·trib·ute (ə trĭb′yōōt) *tr.v.* **at·trib·ut·ed, at·trib·ut·ing, at·trib·utes.** To consider (sthg.) as belonging to or resulting from sbdy./sthg.: *We attribute a lot of air pollution to cars and trucks. This piece of music is attributed to Mozart.* —*n.* (ăt′rə byōōt′). A quality or characteristic belonging to sbdy. or sthg.; a distinctive feature: *One of her best attributes is her sense of humor.* See Synonyms at **quality.** —**at·trib′ut·a·ble** *adj.* —**at′tri·bu′tion** (ăt′rə byōō′shən) *n.* [U]

at·tri·tion (ə trĭsh′ən) *n.* [U] A gradual loss of number or strength in membership or personnel, as through retirement, resignation, or death: *The company lost several jobs through attrition.*

at·tune (ə tōōn′) *tr.v.* **at·tuned, at·tun·ing, at·tunes.** To bring (sbdy./sthg.) into a harmonious relationship; adjust: *a person attuned to the times.*

atty. *abbr.* An abbreviation of attorney.

a·typ·i·cal (ā tĭp′ĭ kəl) *adj.* Not typical; abnormal: *atypical behavior.* —**a·typ′i·cal·ly** *adv.*

Au The symbol for the element **gold.**

au·burn (ô′bərn) *n.* [U] A reddish brown color, especially of hair. —*adj.* Reddish brown: *auburn hair.*

auc·tion (ôk′shən) *n.* A public sale in which goods or property is sold to the highest bidder. —*tr.v.* To sell (sthg.) at an auction: *auction a diamond ring.*

auc·tion·eer (ôk′shə nîr′) *n.* A person who conducts an auction.

au·da·cious (ô dā′shəs) *adj.* **1.** Fearlessly daring; bold: *an audacious explorer.* **2.** Arrogant; impudent: *a showoff's audacious behavior.* —**au·da′cious·ly** *adv.* —**au·da′cious·ness** *n.* [U]

au·dac·i·ty (ô dăs′ĭ tē) *n.* [U] **1.** Courage and resolution; boldness: *The explorer found the audacity to go on in spite of the blizzard.* **2.** Insolence; impudence: *She had the audacity to come to my party after insulting me.*

au·di·ble (ô′də bəl) *adj.* Loud enough to be heard: *Speak in an audible voice so that others can hear you.* —**au′di·bly** *adv.*

au·di·ence (ô′dē əns) *n.* **1.** The people gathered to see and hear a play, movie, concert, or other performance: *The actor spoke directly to the audience.* **2.** The readers, hearers, or viewers reached by a book, radio broadcast, or television program: *Television news reaches a wide audience.* **3.** A formal meeting: *an audience with the ambassador.*

au·di·o (ô′dē ō′) *adj.* **1.** Relating to sound or hearing. **2.** Relating to the reproduction of sound: *a CD player and other audio equipment.* —*n.* [U] Audible sound or an electric sound signal: *The TV audio was too loud, so we turned it down.*

audio frequency *n.* A frequency corresponding to audible sound vibrations, usually between 15 hertz and 20,000 hertz for human beings.

au·di·o·tape (ô′dē ō tāp′) *n.* A recording of sound on tape.

au·di·o·vis·u·al also **au·di·o·vis·u·al** (ô′dē ō vĭzh′ōō əl) *adj.* **1.** Both audible and visible. **2.** Relating to materials, such as videotapes, films, and compact disks, that use electronic equipment to present information in both visible and audible form.

au·dit (ô′dĭt) *n.* An examination of financial records or accounts to check accuracy: *Most taxpayers fear an audit.* —*tr.v.* **1.** To examine and verify (financial records). **2.** To attend a college course without receiving credit: *She plans to audit an accounting course.*

au·di·tion (ô dĭsh′ən) *n.* A test or trial performance by a musician or actor who is applying for employment: *The violinist was well prepared for the music school audition.* —*v.* —*intr.* To perform in an audition: *Several musicians auditioned for a place in the orchestra.* —*tr.* To give (a performer) an audition: *The director of the movie auditioned many actors.*

au·di·tor (ô′dĭ tər) *n.* **1.** A person who examines financial records or accounts in order to check their accuracy. **2.** A person who audits courses in college.

au•di•to•ri•um (ô'dĭ tôr'ē əm) *n.* **1.** A room that can seat a large audience in a building. **2.** A large building used for public meetings, performances, or concerts: *The auditorium seats 2,000 people.*

au•di•to•ry (ô'dĭ tôr'ē) *adj.* Relating to hearing or the organs of hearing: *the auditory canal of the ear.*

Aug. *abbr.* An abbreviation of August.

aug•ment (ôg měnt') *v. Formal.* —*tr.* To make (sthg.) larger; increase: *The library's collection has been augmented by 5,000 new books.* —*intr.* To become greater; increase. —**aug•ment'a•ble** *adj.* —**aug'men•ta'-tion** *n.* [U]

au gra•tin (ō grät'n) *adj.* Topped with bread crumbs and often grated cheese and browned in an oven: *potatoes au gratin.*

au•gust (ô gŭst') *adj.* Inspiring awe or reverence; majestic: *the august bearing of the king.*

Au•gust (ô'gəst) *n.* The eighth month of the year, with 31 days.

au jus (ō zhōōs' *or* ō zhü') *adj.* Served in its own gravy or juice from cooking: *roast beef au jus.*

aunt (ănt *or* änt) *n.* **1.** The sister of one's father or mother. **2.** The wife of one's uncle.

HOMONYMS: aunt, ant (insect).

---

au•ra (ôr'ə) *n.* A distinctive air or quality that characterizes a person or thing: *an aura of mystery about the old house.*

au•ral (ôr'əl) *adj.* Relating to or perceived by the ear: *aural stimulation.* —**au'ral•ly** *adv.*

HOMONYMS: aural, oral (of the mouth).

---

au•ri•cle (ôr'ĭ kəl) *n.* An atrium of the heart.

HOMONYMS: auricle, oracle (prophet).

---

aus•pi•ces (ô'spĭ sĭz *or* ô'spĭ sēz') *pl.n. Formal.* Protection and support; patronage: *The marathon was organized under the auspices of local athletic clubs.*

aus•pi•cious (ô spĭsh'əs) *adj. Formal.* Showing signs of a successful outcome or result; favorable: *Their first large orders were an auspicious beginning for the new business.* —**aus•pi'cious•ly** *adv.* —**aus•pi'cious•ness** *n.* [U]

aus•tere (ô stîr') *adj.* **1.** Having a stern personality or appearance; somber: *an unsmiling, austere judge.* **2.** Living very simply, with few comforts: *a desert nomad's austere life.* **3.** Lacking decoration; plain or bare: *Their austere apartment had no pictures on the walls.* —**aus•tere'ly** *adv.*

aus•ter•i•ty (ô stěr'ĭ tē) *n.* [U] **1.** The condition of being austere: *The austerity of the hotel was disappointing.* **2.** Lack of luxury; extreme restraint in spending: *wartime austerity.*

aut— *pref.* Variant of **auto—**.

au•then•tic (ô thěn'tĭk) *adj.* **1.** Believable; true; credible: *The characters were authentic and the situations realistic in the detective story.* **2.** Not counterfeit or copied; real; genuine: *an authentic gold piece.* —**au•then'ti•cal•ly** *adv.*

SYNONYMS: authentic, genuine, real, true. These adjectives all mean not counterfeit or copied. *An expert assured us that the chair is an authentic antique. The recipe calls for genuine Italian olive oil, but I only have an American brand. The bouquets were made with silk flowers instead of real ones. A true friend would be more understanding.*

---

au•then•ti•cate (ô thěn'tĭ kāt') *tr.v.* **au•then•ti•cat•ed, au•then•ti• cat•ing, au•then•ti•cates. 1.** To establish (sthg.) as being true; prove: *Witnesses will authenticate our account of the accident.* **2.** To establish (a painting, an antique, or another object) as being genuine: *I am sure that an expert can authenticate the old violin.* —**au•then'-ti•ca'tion** *n.* [U]

au•then•tic•i•ty (ô'thěn tĭs'ĭ tē) *n.* [U] The condition or quality of being authentic: *The authenticity of our claim is established by these old records.*

au•thor (ô'thər) *n.* **1.** A person who writes a book, a story, an article, or another written work. **2.** The creator or originator of sthg.: *the author of an idea.* —*tr.v.* To be the author of (sthg.): *The professor has authored several books.*

au•thor•i•tar•i•an (ə thôr'ĭ târ'ē ən *or* ə thŏr'ĭ târ'ē ən) *adj.* Characterized by or demanding absolute obedience to authority: *the authoritarian government of a dictator.* —*n.* A person who believes in or practices authoritarian behavior. —**au•thor'i•tar'i•an•is'm** *n.* [U]

au•thor•i•ta•tive (ə thôr'ĭ tā'tĭv *or* ə-thŏr'ĭ tā'tĭv) *adj.* **1.** Showing authority; commanding: *the judge's authoritative manner.* **2.** Known to be accurate or excellent; reliable: *authoritative sources for the newspaper article.* —**au•thor'i•ta'tive•ly** *adv.* —**au•thor'i•ta'tive•ness** *n.* [U]

au•thor•i•ty (ə thôr'ĭ tē *or* ə thŏr'ĭ tē) *n.*, *pl.* **au•thor•i•ties. 1.a.** [U] The power to enforce laws, command obedience, or judge: *The director has the authority to close the school during a snowstorm.* **b.** [C] A person or an organization having this power: *government authorities.* **2.** [C] An accepted source of expert information, such as a book or person: *an authority on colonial history.*

au•thor•i•za•tion (ô'thər ĭ zā'shən) *n.* [C; U] **1.** The act of authorizing. **2.** Legal or official power or right: *The President and*

Congress have authorization to govern from the Constitution.

au·thor·ize (ô'thə rīz') *tr.v.* **au·thor·ized, au·thor·iz·ing, au·thor·iz·es.** **1.** To grant authority or power to (sbdy.): *The company president authorized the marketing study.* **2.** To approve or give permission for (sthg.): *The state legislature authorized a highway project.*

au·thor·ship (ô'thər shĭp') *n.* [U] The origin of a speech or piece of writing: *a book of unknown authorship.*

au·to (ô'tō) *n.* An automobile.

auto— or **aut—** *pref.* A prefix that means: **1.** Self; same: *autobiography; autoimmune.* **2.** Automatic: *autopilot.*

au·to·bi·og·ra·phy (ô'tō bī ŏg'rə fē) *n., pl.* **au·to·bi·og·ra·phies.** The story of a person's life written by that person. —**au'to·bi'o·graph'ic** (ô'tō bī'ə grăf'ĭk), **au'to·bi'o·graph'i·cal** *adj.* —**au'to·bi'o·graph'i·cal·ly** *adv.*

au·toc·ra·cy (ô tŏk'rə sē) *n., pl.* **au·toc·ra·cies.** **1.** [U] Government by a person having absolute power: *Dictatorship is a form of autocracy.* **2.** [C] A country having this form of government: *The country feared invasion by the neighboring autocracy.*

au·to·crat (ô'tə krăt') *n.* **1.** A ruler having unlimited power. **2.** An arrogant person with unlimited power: *The boss is an autocrat.* —**au'to·crat'ic** *adj.* —**au'to·crat'i·cal·ly** *adv.*

au·to·graph (ô'tə grăf') *n.* A signature, usually of a famous person, that is saved by an admirer or collector: *the baseball player's autograph.* —*tr.v.* To write one's name or signature on (sthg.): *The player autographed the ball.*

au·to·im·mune (ô'tō ĭ myo͞on') *adj.* Caused by the production of antibodies that attack the body's own cells and tissues: *an autoimmune disease.*

au·to·im·mu·ni·ty (ô'tō ĭ myo͞o'nĭ tē) *n.* [U] The condition in which antibodies produced by an organism attack the organism's own cells and tissues.

au·to·mak·er (ô'tō mā'kər) *n.* A manufacturer of automobiles: *The big automakers all plan a price increase.*

au·to·mate (ô'tə māt') *v.* **au·to·mat·ed, au·to·mat·ing, au·to·mates.** —*tr.* To operate (a process, factory, or machine) with automatic machinery or processes: *automate an assembly line with robots.* —*intr.* To use automatic machinery and processes: *Costs of manufacturing were reduced after the factory automated.*

automated teller machine *n.* An electronic machine that allows bank customers to make deposits, withdraw cash, and perform other transactions, all by using a plastic identification card.

au·to·mat·ic (ô'tə măt'ĭk) *adj.* **1.** Acting or operating without the control of a human being; self-operating or self-regulating: *an automatic elevator.* **2.** Done or produced by the body without conscious control or awareness; involuntary: *the automatic shrinking of the pupils of the eyes in bright light.* **3.** Capable of firing continuously until ammunition is gone or the trigger is released: *an automatic rifle.* —*n.* A device or machine, especially a firearm, that is wholly or partially automatic: *The guard fired several rounds with an automatic.* —**au'to·mat'i·cal·ly** *adv.*

automatic pilot *n.* A navigation device that automatically keeps to a preset course.

au·to·ma·tion (ô'tə mā'shən) *n.* [U] The automatic operation or control of a process, machine, or system, often by electronic devices, such as computers or robots: *Automation has replaced many workers.*

au·to·mo·bile (ô'tə mō bēl') *n.* A passenger vehicle generally moving on four wheels and propelled by a gasoline engine on land. —*adj.* Relating to automobiles; automotive: *the automobile industry.*

au·to·mo·tive (ô'tə mō'tĭv) *adj.* Relating to self-propelled vehicles, such as automobiles and trucks: *automotive parts.*

au·to·nom·ic (ô'tə nŏm'ĭk) *adj.* Relating to the autonomic nervous system, the system in the body that controls involuntary functions: *autonomic breathing.*

au·ton·o·mous (ô tŏn'ə məs) *adj.* Self-governing; independent: *an autonomous organization; autonomous regions.* —**au·ton'o·mous·ly** *adv.*

au·ton·o·my (ô tŏn'ə mē) *n.* [U] **1.** Self-government: *former colonies working toward autonomy.* **2.** Independence: *He wanted greater autonomy in his job.*

au·to·pi·lot (ô'tō pī'lət) *n.* An automatic pilot.

au·top·sy (ô'tŏp'sē) *n., pl.* **au·top·sies.** A medical examination of a dead human or animal body to determine the cause of death.

au·tumn (ô'təm) *n.* [C; U] The season of the year between summer and winter, lasting from the autumnal equinox in late September to the winter solstice in late December: *The football season starts in autumn.* —*adj.* Occurring in or appropriate to the season of autumn: *autumn colors.* —**au·tum'nal** (ô tŭm'nəl) *adj.*

aux·il·ia·ry (ôg zĭl'yə rē *or* ôg zĭl'ə rē) *adj.* **1.** Giving assistance or support: *a sailboat with an auxiliary engine.* **2.** Additional or supplementary: *The city has auxiliary* branches of the fire department in outlying areas. —n., pl. **aux•il•ia•ries. 1.** A person or thing that helps; an assistant. **2.** An auxiliary verb. **3.** An organization that is part of a larger one: *Members of the hospital auxiliary visit patients and run errands.*

auxiliary verb n. A verb that comes first in a verb phrase and helps form the tense, mood, or voice of the main verb. *Do, have, may, can, must,* and *will* are examples of auxiliary verbs.

av. *abbr.* An abbreviation of: **1.** Average. **2.** Avoirdupois.

a•vail (ə vāl′) *Formal. v. —tr.* To be of use or advantage to (sbdy./sthg.); help: *Nothing can avail us now. —intr.* To be of use or value; help: *A calculator avails little if you don't understand the problem. —n.* [U] Use, benefit, or advantage: *Since all the doors were locked, the burglar's efforts were to no avail.*
◆ **avail (oneself) of.** To make use of (sthg.); take advantage of: *While visiting Paris, you must avail yourself of the museums.*

a•vail•a•ble (ə vā′lə bəl) *adj.* **1.** Capable of being obtained: *Tickets are available at the box office.* **2.** At hand and ready for use: *Keep a calculator available during the test.* **3.** Willing or able to serve: *All available volunteers were asked to help.* **—a•vail′a•bil′i•ty** n. [U]

av•a•lanche (ăv′ə lănch′) n. **1.** The fall or slide of a large mass of snow or rock down the side of a mountain: *Two skiers were buried in the avalanche.* **2.** A massive or overwhelming amount: *an avalanche of mail.*

a•vant-garde (ä′vänt gärd′) n. [U] A group of people who are the leaders in promoting new or unconventional styles, ideas, or methods, especially in the arts: *a new play especially popular with the avant-garde. —adj.* Showing new or unusual styles, ideas, or methods: *an avant-garde magazine.*

av•a•rice (ăv′ə rĭs) n. [U] Extreme desire for money or wealth; greed. **—av′a•ri′cious** (ăv′ə rĭsh′əs) *adj.*

ave. or **Ave.** *abbr.* An abbreviation of avenue.

a•venge (ə vĕnj′) *tr.v.* **a•venged, a•veng•ing, a•veng•es.** To take revenge or get satisfaction for (sthg.): *The soccer team avenged the loss to their rivals by beating them the next time they played. —a•veng′er n.*

av•e•nue (ăv′ə noō′ or ăv′ə nyoō′) n. **1.** A wide street, often a main street: *a store on Fifth Avenue.* **2.** A means of reaching or achieving sthg.: *We must seek many avenues for peace.*

av•er•age (ăv′ər ĭj or ăv′rĭj) n. [C; U] **1.** A number, especially the arithmetic mean, that is derived from and considered typical or representative of a set of numbers: *What was your average on the three tests?* **2.** A typical kind or usual level or degree: *That musician's abilities are above average. —v.* **av•er•**

aged, av•er•ag•ing, av•er•ag•es. —*tr.* **1.** To compute the average of (a set of numbers): *After the trip, we averaged the number of miles we drove each day.* **2.** To have or attain (a number) as an average: *The temperature averages about 75 degrees in the summer. —intr.* To be or amount to an average: *Our expenses averaged out to $100 a day. —adj.* **1.** Computed or determined as an average: *On our trip across the country our average speed was 50 miles per hour.* **2.a.** Typical, usual, or ordinary: *an average American family.* **b.** Not special or exceptional; undistinguished: *just an average student.*
◆ **on the average.** Using the average as a basis for judgment: *She earned—on the average—seventy dollars a day. —av′er•age•ly adv. —av′er•age•ness* n. [U]

a•verse (ə vûrs′) *adj.* [to] Opposed; reluctant; unwilling: *Cats are extremely averse to getting wet.*

a•ver•sion (ə vûr′zhən or ə vûr′shən) n. (usually singular). [to] A strong dislike: *I have an aversion to crowds.*

a•vert (ə vûrt′) *tr.v.* **1.** To turn (sthg.) away or aside: *When people stared at us, we averted our eyes.* **2.** To keep (sthg.) from happening; prevent: *She averted an accident by swerving away from the truck.*

avg. *abbr.* An abbreviation of average.

a•vi•an (ā′vē ən) *adj.* Relating to birds: *avian research.*

a•vi•ar•y (ā′vē ĕr′ē) n., pl. **a•vi•ar•ies.** A large cage or enclosure for birds, as in a zoo.

a•vi•a•tion (ā′vē ā′shən or ăv′ē ā′shən) n. [U] **1.** The art of operating and navigating aircraft. **2.** The design, development, and production of aircraft: *The Wright brothers were pioneers of aviation.*

a•vi•a•tor (ā′vē ā′tər or ăv′ē ā′tər) n. A person who flies an aircraft; a pilot.

av•id (ăv′ĭd) *adj.* Eager; enthusiastic: *an avid reader of the editorial page; an avid baseball fan. —av′id•ly adv.*

a•vi•on•ics (ā′vē ŏn′ĭks or ăv′ē ŏn′ĭks) n. [U] The science and technology of electronics as applied to aircraft and spacecraft.

av•o•ca•do (ăv′ə kä′dō or ä′və kä′dō) n. An edible, tropical American fruit, with leathery green or blackish skin, mild-tasting yellow-green pulp, and a single large seed.

a•void (ə void′) *tr.v.* **1.** To keep away from (sbdy./sthg.); shun: *avoid too many sweets; avoid the crowds at the mall.* **2.** To keep (sthg.) from happening; prevent: *avoid an accident. —a•void′a•ble adj. —a•void′a•bly adv. —a•void′ance* n. [U]

av•oir•du•pois weight (ăv′ər də poiz′) n. [U] A system of weights based on a pound, equal to 16 ounces, traditionally used in English-speaking countries.

a•vow (ə vou′) *tr.v.* To acknowledge (sthg.) openly; admit freely: *We avowed our support for the controversial law.*

a·vow·al (ə vou′əl) *n.* [C; U] An open admission or acknowledgment: *avowal of an unpopular opinion.*

aw (ô) *interj.* An expression used to show sympathy, doubt, or disgust: *"Aw, you poor thing."*

a·wait (ə wāt′) *tr.v.* **1.** To wait for (sbdy./sthg.): *We sat up awaiting news of the election results.* See Synonyms at **expect. 2.** To be in the future for (sbdy.): *The meeting with the new manager awaits us at the end of the week.*

a·wake (ə wāk′) *v.* **a·woke** (ə wōk′) or **a·waked, a·waked** or **a·wok·en** (ə wō′-kən), **a·wak·ing, a·wakes.** —*tr.* **1.** To waken (sbdy.) from sleep: *The alarm clock awoke me at seven.* **2.** To create interest in (sbdy.); excite: *New evidence about heart disease awoke most of us to the benefits of exercise.* **3.** To produce (a feeling or memory, for example): *Seeing the old car awoke memories of my grandfather.* —*intr.* **1.** To wake up: *I awoke at dawn.* **2.** To become aware of: *Americans are awaking to the need for recycling.* —*adj.* **1.** Not asleep: *We were awake all night.* **2.** Alert, vigilant, or watchful: *awake to the dangers of an unhealthy diet.*

a·wak·en (ə wā′kən) *v.* —*intr.* To wake up: *I awakened early because of the noise.* —*tr.* **1.** To cause (sbdy.) to wake up: *A barking dog awakened me during the night.* **2.** To stir up or produce (a feeling or memory, for example): *Becoming an aunt awakened in her a sense of responsibility.*

a·ward (ə wôrd′) *tr.v.* **1.** To give (a prize, medal, or other honor) for outstanding performance or quality: *The committee awarded a blue ribbon to the best dog in the show.* **2.** To give or grant (sthg.) by legal or governmental decision: *award damages to the injured driver; award a contract to the lowest bidder.* —*n.* **1.** Something, such as a prize or medal, given for outstanding performance or quality: *an award for bravery; a scholarship award.* **2.** Something judged as due by legal decision: *The jury decided on an award for damages of one million dollars.*

a·ware (ə wâr′) *adj.* Being mindful or conscious of sthg.; knowing: *Be aware of the abilities of each staff member.* —**a·ware′-ness** *n.* [U]

a·way (ə wā′) *adv.* **1.** From a particular thing or place: *They got in the car and drove away.* **2.** At or to a distance: *We live two miles away from the beach.* **3.** In a different direction: *Don't look away now. She backed away from me.* **4.** Into storage or a safe place: *Please put* the toys away. **5.** From one's presence or possession: *They gave away that old bicycle.* **6.** Out of existence: *The music faded away.* **7.** Continuously: *working away; inviting the audience to ask away.* —*adj.* **1.** Absent: *My brother is away from home.* **2.** Distant, as in space or time: *Those mountains are miles away. The game is a week away.* **3.** Played on the opposing team's home grounds: *home games and away games.*

awe (ô) *n.* [U] A feeling of wonder, fear, and respect inspired by sthg. mighty or majestic: *gazing in awe at the mountains; in awe of the great scientist.* —*tr.v.* **awed, aw·ing, awes.** To fill (sbdy.) with awe: *The size of the huge plane awed everyone.*

a·weigh (ə wā′) *adj.* A sailor's term meaning that the anchor is hanging clear of the bottom: *With the anchor aweigh, the boat began to drift.*

awe·some (ô′səm) *adj.* Inspiring awe or amazement: *an awesome sight.*

awe·struck (ô′strŭk′) *adj.* Full of awe: *They were awestruck by the beauty of the mountains.*

aw·ful (ô′fəl) *adj.* **1.** Very bad or unpleasant; horrible: *awful weather; an awful book.* **2.** Inspiring awe or fear: *the awful stillness before the tornado.* **3.** Great; considerable: *an awful lot of homework.* —*adv. Informal.* Very; extremely: *awful sick; awful hungry.* —**aw′ful·ness** *n.* [U]

aw·ful·ly (ô′fə lē or ô′flē) *adv.* **1.a.** In a manner that inspires awe: *The wind blew awfully.* **b.** *Informal.* Very badly: *She behaved awfully.* **2.** *Informal.* Very: *The tourists seemed awfully confused.*

a·while (ə wīl′) *adv.* For a short time: *We waited awhile until they returned.*

awk·ward (ôk′wərd) *adj.* **1.** Not graceful; clumsy: *an awkward dancer.* **2.** Causing embarrassment; uncomfortable: *An awkward silence fell over the class.* **3.** Difficult to handle or manage; cumbersome: *a large and awkward bundle to carry.* —**awk′ward·ly** *adv.* —**awk′ward·ness** *n.* [U]

awl (ôl) *n.* A pointed tool for making holes, as in wood or leather.

ă-cat; ā-pay; âr-care; ä-father; ĕ-get; ē-be; ĭ-sit; ī-nice; îr-here; ŏ-got; ō-go; ô-saw; oi-boy; ou-out; ōō-took; ōō-boot; ŭ-cut; ûr-word; th-thin; th-this; hw-when; zh-vision; ə-about; N-French bon

awn·ing (ô′nĭng) *n.* A protective structure set up over a window or door like a roof: *an awning over the store entrance.*

a·woke (ə wōk′) *v.* A past tense of **awake.**

a·wok·en (ə wō′kən) *v.* A past participle of **awake.**

AWOL or **awol** (ā′wôl′) *adj.* Absent without leave, as a soldier from an army base. —*n.* A person who is absent without leave.

a·wry (ə rī′) *adv.* **1.** Turned or twisted to one side or out of shape: *The wind blew the curtains awry.* **2.** Wrong; amiss: *Our plans went awry.*

ax or **axe** (ăks) *n., pl.* **ax·es** (ăk′sĭz). A tool consisting of a head with a sharp blade on a long handle, used for cutting trees or chopping wood. —*tr.v.* **axed, ax·ing, ax·es.** To cut or chop (sthg.) with an ax. ◆ **ax to grind.** A selfish or personal aim: *The politician had an ax to grind during the debate.* **get the ax.** To be fired from a job: *Several workers got the ax last month.*

ax

ax·i·al (ăk′sē əl) *adj.* Of, on, around, or forming an axis: *A wheel turns by axial motion.*

ax·i·om (ăk′sē əm) *n.* **1.** A statement that is accepted as true or assumed to be true without proof. "The whole is greater than any of its parts" is an example of an axiom. **2.** An established rule, principle, or law: *One of the axioms of driving in the United States is to stay to the right.* —**ax′i·o·mat′ic** (ăk′sē ə-măt′ĭk) *adj.*

ax·is (ăk′sĭs) *n., pl.* **ax·es** (ăk′sēz′). **1.** A straight line around which an object rotates or can be imagined to rotate: *The axis of the earth passes through both of its poles.* **2.** In geometry, a line, ray, or line segment with respect to which a figure or object is symmetrical: *the axis of a cone.* **3.** A reference line from which or along which distances or angles are measured in a system of coordinates: *the x-axis.*

ax·le (ăk′səl) *n.* A shaft or bar, on which one or more wheels revolve: *The car's front axle was bent in the accident.*

a·ya·tol·lah (ī′ə tō′lə *or* ī′ə tō lä′) *n.* A male Shiite Muslim religious leader of the highest rank.

aye also **ay** (ī) *n.* **1.** A vote of yes. **2. ayes.** Those who vote yes: *The ayes have it; the motion is approved.* —*adv.* Yes.

HOMONYMS: aye, eye (organ of sight), **I** (personal pronoun).

AZ *abbr.* An abbreviation of Arizona.

a·zal·ea (ə zāl′yə) *n.* Any of several evergreen shrubs related to the rhododendron and often cultivated for their funnel-shaped, variously colored flowers.

az·i·muth (ăz′ə məth) *n.* An arc measured clockwise from a reference point, usually the northern point of the horizon, to the point where a vertical circle passing through a celestial body crosses the horizon.

AZT (ā′zē tē′) *n.* [U] A drug used in the treatment of AIDS.

az·ure (ăzh′ər) *n.* [U] A light purplish blue color. —*adj.* Light purplish blue: *azure sky.*

Bb

b or **B** (bē) *n.*, *pl.* **b's** or **B's**. **1.** The second letter of the English alphabet. **2. B.** The second-best or second-highest grade: *I got a B on a test!* **3.** In music, the seventh tone in the scale of C major. **4.** One of the four types of blood in the ABO system.

B The symbol for the element **boron**.

Ba The symbol for the element **barium**.

B.A. *abbr.* An abbreviation of Bachelor of Arts.

baa (bă *or* bä) *intr.v.* To make the sound a sheep makes. —*n.* The sound made by a sheep: *The startled sheep let out a loud baa.*

bab•ble (băb′əl) *v.* **bab•bled, bab•bling, bab•bles.** —*intr.* **1.** To say unclear or meaningless words or sounds: *Babies babble before they can talk.* **2.** To talk for a long time about sthg. that is foolish or not important; chatter: *She bored everyone as she babbled on and on about her family.* **3.** To make a continuous low murmuring sound, as a brook. —*tr.* To utter (sthg.) unclearly: *babble an answer to a teacher.* —*n.* [C; U] **1.** Unclear or meaningless words or sounds: *a babble of voices as we walked through the crowd.* **2.** Idle or foolish talk; chatter: *Pay no attention to the gossip; it's all just babble.* **3.** A continuous low murmuring sound, as of a brook. —**bab′bler** *n.*

babe (bāb) *n.* **1.** A baby; an infant. **2.** *Slang.* A sometimes offensive term for an attractive young woman.

ba•bel also **Ba•bel** (băb′əl *or* bā′bəl) *n.* [C; U] A confusion of sounds, voices, or lan-;uages: *a babel of voices in the street below.*

ba•boon (bă bōōn′) *n.* A large monkey from Africa and Asia with a face like a dog and a short tail.

ba•by (bā′bē) *n.*, *pl.* **ba•bies. 1.** A very young child; an infant: *Babies are not able to care for themselves.* **2.** The youngest member of a family: *My sister in second grade is the baby of the family.* **3.** A person who acts like a baby: *Don't be a baby and cry.* **4.** *Slang.* A sometimes offensive term for an attractive young woman. —*tr.v.* **ba•bied, ba•by•ing, ba•bies.** To treat (sbdy./sthg.) like a baby; coddle: *baby a spoiled child.* See Synonyms at **pamper**.

ba•by•hood (bā′bē hŏŏd′) *n.* [U] The time or condition of being a baby.

ba•by•ish (bā′bē ĭsh) *adj.* **1.** Resembling a baby; childlike: *a little babyish whimper.* **2.** Childish; immature: *a babyish attitude about sharing.*

ba•by-sit (bā′bē sĭt′) *v.* **ba•by-sat** (bā′bē-săt′), **ba•by-sit•ting, ba•by-sits.** —*intr.* To care for a child or children when the parents are not at home: *baby-sit for the children in the apartment downstairs.* —*tr.* To take care of (sbdy.): *He baby-sat his younger brother.*

baby sitter *n.* A person hired to baby-sit: *The baby sitter watches the kids after school.*

bac•ca•lau•re•ate (băk′ə lôr′ē ĭt) *n.* **1.** A bachelor's degree. **2.** A farewell address delivered to a graduating class at a college or university.

bach•e•lor (băch′ə lər *or* băch′lər) *n.* **1.** A man who has not married. **2.** A person who has a bachelor's degree.

Bachelor of Arts *n.* A bachelor's degree in liberal arts.

Bachelor of Science *n.* A bachelor's degree in science or mathematics.

bach•e•lor's degree (băch′ə lərz *or* băch′-lərz) *n.* A degree given by a college or university to a person who has completed a four-year undergraduate program or its equivalent.

ba•cil•lus (bə sĭl′əs) *n.*, *pl.* **ba•cil•li** (bə-sĭl′ī′). **1.** Any of various rod-shaped bacteria. **2.** A bacterium.

back (băk) *n.* **1.** The rear part of the human body between the neck and the pelvis. **2.** The part of another animal that is like this part in humans. **3.** The spine or backbone: *He fell and broke his back.* **4.** The part or area farthest from the front: *the back of the theater.* **5.** The part or side that is not usually seen or used: *the back of a photograph.* —*v.* —*tr.* **1.** To cause (sbdy./sthg.) to move backward or in a reverse direction: *The driver backed the car out of the garage.* **2.** To give (sthg.) a back or backing, often to make it stronger: *back a picture with cardboard.* **3.** To support (sbdy./sthg.): *A majority of voters backed the independent candidate.* —*intr.* To move backward: *We backed away from the barking dog.* —*adj.* **1.** Located at the back or rear: *the back door to the house.* **2.** Distant from a center of activity; remote: *a back road.* **3.** Late in being paid; overdue: *trying to pay the back*

ă–**cat**; ā–**pay**; âr–**care**; ä–**father**; ĕ–**get**; ē–**be**; ĭ–**sit**; ī–**nice**; îr–**here**; ŏ–**got**; ō–**go**; ô–**saw**; oi–**boy**; ou–**out**; ŏŏ–**took**; ōō–**boot**; ŭ–**cut**; ûr–**word**; th–**thin**; th–**this**; hw–**when**; zh–**vision**; ə–**about**; N–French bon

rent. **4.** Of a past date; not current: *a back issue of the magazine.* —*adv.* **1.** At, to, or toward the rear: *She pushed her hair back, away from her face.* **2.** In, to, or toward a former place, time, or condition: *They went back to the town where they used to live.* **3.** In reserve or in hiding: *It is dishonest to hold back the truth.* **4.** In reply or return: *If you send me a letter, I'll write back to you.* ♦ **back down.** *intr.v.* To retreat from a demand made or a position taken: *There was an argument because neither side was willing to back down.* **back off.** *intr.v.* To retreat or move away, as from a dangerous position: *The senator backed off from his support of the bill.* **back out.** *intr.v.* To refuse or fail to complete sthg. planned or promised: *They accepted the invitation but backed out at the last minute.* **back up.** *tr.v.* [sep.] **1.** To make a copy of (a computer program or file): *Did you remember to back up your files?* **2.** To give one's support to (sbdy./sthg.): *The police didn't believe the man's story until two witnesses backed him up.* —*intr.v.* To increase in size or amount behind sthg. that blocks the way: *Traffic backed up near the accident.* **behind (one's) back.** When one is not present: *Don't talk about me behind my back.*

back•ache (băk′āk′) *n.* Pain or discomfort in the region of the spine or back: *He could not play basketball because he had a backache.*

back and forth *adv.* Backward and forward; to and fro: *The engineers went back and forth about how to test the new product.*

back•bit•ing (băk′bī′tĭng) *n.* [U] The practice of saying unkind or mean things about sbdy. who is not present: *Backbiting among members of the research group made it a very unpleasant place to work.* —**back′bit′er** *n.*

back•board (băk′bôrd′) *n.* **1.** In basketball, an elevated vertical sheet of wood or other material to which the basket is attached: *The ball bounced off the backboard into the net.* **2.** A board placed under or behind sthg. for support: *They brought the accident victim into the hospital on a backboard.*

back•bone (băk′bōn′) *n.* **1.** [C] The system of bones that forms the main support of a vertebrate; the spinal column. **2.** [C] A principal support; mainstay: *Manufacturing is the backbone of the economy.* **3.** [U] Strength of character; courage: *It takes backbone to refuse to go along with the crowd.*

back•break•ing (băk′brā′kĭng) *adj.* Requiring great physical effort; exhausting: *backbreaking work.*

back•drop (băk′drŏp′) *n.* **1.** A curtain, often painted to show a scene in the background, hung at the back of a stage. **2.** A background: *A slow economy was the backdrop for a close election.*

back•er (băk′ər) *n.* A person who supports or gives aid to a person, a group, or an enter-

prise: *The new business needs a backer if it is to succeed.*

back•fire (băk′fīr′) *n.* **1.** In a gasoline engine, an explosion of fuel that ignites too soon or an explosion of unburned fuel in the exhaust system. **2.** A controlled fire started in the path of an oncoming uncontrolled fire in order to deprive it of fuel and thereby extinguish it. —*intr.v.* **back•fired, back•fir•ing, back•fires.** **1.** To explode in or make the sound of a backfire: *The car backfired as it drove down the street.* **2.** To lead to a result opposite to that intended: *Their scheme to raise money backfired, and everybody lost in the end.*

back•gam•mon (băk′găm′ən) *n.* [U] A game for two persons using dice to move pieces on a specially marked board.

back•ground (băk′ground′) *n.* **1.a.** The part of a picture, scene, or view that appears in the distance: *a river painted in the background.* **b.** The general scene or surface upon which designs, figures, or other forms are seen or represented: *a blue background covered with white stars.* **2.** A position that is difficult to see: *The police remained in the background during the demonstration.* **3.** Soft music that accompanies the dialogue or action in a play or motion picture. **4.** The circumstances or events surrounding or leading up to sthg.: *The client filled in the lawyer on the background of the case.* **5.** A person's experience, training, and education: *a perfect background for the job.*

back•hand (băk′hănd′) *n.* In sports, a stroke, as of a racket, made with the back of the hand facing forward: *a great tennis backhand.* —*adj.* Backhanded: *a backhand shot.* —*adv.* With a backhand stroke or motion: *She hit the ball backhand.*

back•hand•ed (băk′hăn′dĭd) *adj.* **1.** With the motion or direction of a backhand: *a backhanded stroke in tennis.* **2.** Indirect or insincere: *a backhanded compliment.* —**back′hand′ed•ly** *adv.*

back•hoe (băk′hō′) *n.* A machine used for digging, with a bucket attached to a hinged arm.

back•ing (băk′ĭng) *n.* **1.** [C] Material that forms the back of sthg.: *a table mat with a felt backing.* **2.** [U] **a.** Support or aid: *financial backing for a new business.* **b.** Approval or endorsement: *a request with official backing from the mayor.*

back•lash (băk′lăsh′) *n.* **1.** A sudden or violent backward whipping motion. **2.** Strong and hostile reaction to an earlier action or event: *Lack of courtesy brought a backlash of complaints from the store's customers.*

back•log (băk′lŏg′ or băk′lôg′) *n.* An accumulation, especially of unfinished work: *They had a backlog of orders to fill after the vacation.*

B

back•pack (băk′păk′) *n.* A knapsack, sometimes on a lightweight frame, that is worn on the back, as to carry books or camping supplies. —*intr.v.* To hike or travel while carrying a backpack: *The children and their guide backpacked to the lake.* —**back′pack′er** *n.* —**back′pack•ing** *n.* [U]

back-seat driver (băk′sēt′) *n. Informal.* **1.** A passenger in a car who frequently advises, corrects, or nags the driver. **2.** A person who continually gives unwanted advice.

back•side (băk′sīd′) *n. Informal.* The buttocks.

back•slide (băk′slīd′) *intr.v.* **back•slid** (băk′slĭd′), **back•slid•ing, back•slides.** To lapse into improper habits or wrongdoing, especially in religious matters: *Although she had tried to stop smoking, she kept backsliding.* —**back′slid′er** *n.*

back•stage (băk′stāj′) *adv.* **1.** In or toward the area of a theater that is behind the section where the performance takes place: *Wait backstage until it is time for your speech.* **2.** In or toward a place closed to public view: *backstage at a political convention.* —*adj.* (băk′stāj′). **1.** Relating to or situated behind the performing area of a theater: *a backstage orchestra; backstage passes.* **2.** Not open or known to the public: *backstage political dealings.*

back•stroke (băk′strōk′) *n.* [U] A swimming stroke made while lying on the back and moving the arms alternately upward and backward: *She will swim backstroke in tomorrow's competition.*

back•track (băk′trăk′) *intr.v.* **1.** To return over the route by which one came: *We backtracked to find the trail we had missed.* **2.** To reverse one's position: *The President backtracked on his plan not to raise taxes.*

back•up (băk′ŭp′) *n.* **1.** A reserve, as of provisions: *They kept several cans of tuna as a backup.* **2.** A person standing by and ready to serve as a substitute: *The assistant fire chief is the backup for the chief.* **3.** A copy of a program, file, or other data in a computer memory or on a disk or tape, made to protect against loss of the original: *Keep a backup of the information on your computer.* **4.** An accumulation or overflow caused by the blockage or clogging of sthg.: *a backup in the drain; a traffic backup on the highway.* —*adj.* Ready as a substitute or in a case of emergency; extra; standby: *a backup pilot.*

back•ward (băk′wərd) *adj.* **1.** In the direction of the rear: *a backward glance; a backward tumble.* **2.** Less advanced than others, as in economic or social progress: *backward technology.* —*adv.* or **back•wards** (băk′wərdz). **1.** To or toward the back or rear: *He kept glancing backward to see who was coming.*

2. With the back or rear first: *With its hind legs a toad can dig its way into the ground backward.* **3.** In reverse order or direction: *count backward from 100.* **4.** Toward a worse condition: *As prices rise, poor people slip backward.* ◆ **bend over backward.** To make an effort greater than is required: *They bent over backward to be fair.* **know backward and forward** or **backwards and forwards.** To know sthg. very well or perfectly: *We know the play backward and forward.*

back yard also **back•yard** (băk′yärd′) *n.* A yard at the back of a house: *Go play in the back yard.*

ba•con (bā′kən) *n.* [U] The salted and smoked meat from the back and sides of a pig: *Bacon and eggs used to be a typical breakfast.*

bac•te•ri•a (băk tîr′ē ə) *pl.n.* Plural of **bacterium.**

bac•te•ri•al (băk tîr′ē əl) *adj.* Relating to or caused by bacteria: *a bacterial enzyme; a bacterial disease.*

bac•te•ri•ol•o•gy (băk tîr′ē ŏl′ə jē) *n.* [U] The scientific study of bacteria. —**bac•te′ri•o•log′i•cal** *adj.* —**bac•te′ri•ol′o•gist** *n.*

bac•te•ri•um (băk tîr′ē əm) *n., pl.* **bac•te•ri•a** (băk tîr′ē ə). Any of a large group of very small one-celled organisms. Some kinds can cause disease.

bad (băd) *adj.* **worse** (wûrs), **worst** (wûrst). **1.** Being below an acceptable standard; poor: *a bad book; a bad painter.* **2.** Evil or wicked: *a bad man.* **3.** Disobedient; naughty: *bad behavior.* **4.** Unfavorable: *bad luck; bad weather.* **5.** Disagreeable or unpleasant: *a bad odor; bad news.* **6.** Incorrect; improper: *a bad choice of words.* **7.** Not working properly; defective: *a bad telephone connection.* **8.** Rotten; spoiled: *bad fish; bad milk.* **9.** Harmful in effect: *Candy is bad for your teeth.* **10.** Being in poor health or condition: *I feel bad today. The jogger has a bad knee.* **11.** Severe; intense: *a bad cold; a bad snowstorm; a bad temper.* **12.** Sorry; regretful: *I feel very bad about what happened.* —*n.* [U] Something bad: *You must learn to accept the bad with the good.* ◆ **not half bad** or **not so bad.** *Informal.* Reasonably good: *That meal was not half bad.* **too bad.** Regrettable; unfortunate: *It's too bad you can't come along.* —**bad′ness** *n.* [U]

USAGE: bad You should avoid using **bad** as an adverb. Instead of *We need water bad,* use *We need water badly.* Instead of *My tooth hurt bad,* use *My tooth hurt badly.*

HOMONYMS: bad, bade (past of bid).

---

bade (băd *or* bād) *v.* A past tense of **bid.**

badge (băj) *n.* **1.** An emblem worn to show rank or membership: *The police officers flashed their badges.* **2.** An emblem given as an award or honor: *He wore his medal as a badge of honor.*

badg•er (băj′ər) *n.* A mammal with short legs, long claws on the front feet, and thick grayish fur. —*tr.v.* To trouble (sbdy.) with many questions or protests; pester: *The speaker was badgered by the angry audience.*

bad•lands (băd′lăndz′) *pl.n.* An area of barren land with rough ridges and peaks: *Australia is known for its badlands.*

bad•ly (băd′lē) *adv.* **1.** In a bad manner; poorly: *a job badly done.* **2.** Very much; greatly: *He misses his brother badly.* —SEE NOTE at **bad.**

bad•min•ton (băd′mĭn′tən) *n.* [U] A game in which players use a light long-handled racket to hit a small object, called a shuttlecock, back and forth over a high net.

bad•mouth or **bad-mouth** (băd′mouth′ or băd′mou*th*′) *tr.v.* To criticize (sbdy.), often unfairly or spitefully: *Badmouthing your coworkers won't make you very popular.*

baf•fle (băf′əl) *tr.v.* **baf•fled, baf•fling, baf•fles.** To confuse (sbdy.); puzzle: *Use the dictionary for any word that baffles you.* —**baf′fle•ment** *n.* [U] —**baf′fler** *n.*

bag (băg) *n.* **1.** A container made of flexible material, such as paper, cloth, or plastic, used for carrying various articles: *I will fill the bag with books.* **2.a.** A bag with sthg. in it: *buy a bag of onions.* **b.** The amount that a bag can hold: *eat a bag of peanuts.* **3.** A purse, handbag, or suitcase: *Many passengers carry their bags right onto the airplane.* —*v.* **bagged, bag•ging, bags.** —*tr.* **1.** To put (sthg.) into a bag: *I bag groceries at the supermarket.* **2.** To capture and kill (sthg., such as game): *They bagged two quail that day.* —*intr.* To hang loosely like a bag: *This shirt bagged at the waist.* ◆ **be (one's) bag.** *Slang.* To be one's area of interest or skill: *Cooking is not her bag.* **in the bag.** Assured of a successful outcome; virtually accomplished or won: *The election is in the bag.* **let the cat out of the bag.** To make a secret known, often accidentally: *She was not supposed to tell anyone about the surprise party, but she let the cat out of the bag.*

ba•gel (bā′gəl) *n.* A ring-shaped bread with a tough chewy texture: *Bagels are my favorite for a quick breakfast.*

bag•gage (băg′ĭj) *n.* [U] **1.** The trunks, bags, suitcases, or boxes in which one carries one's belongings while traveling; luggage. **2.** *Informal.* Ideas, beliefs, or habits that influence the way a person acts: *She failed at new relationships because she carried too much baggage from her divorce.*

bag•gy (băg′ē) *adj.* **bag•gi•er, bag•gi•est.** Bulging or hanging loosely; loose-fitting: *baggy pants.*

bag•pipes (băg′pīps′) *pl.n.* A musical instrument from Scotland that consists of a reed pipe and several other pipes in which air from a large bag is forced out to produce sounds. —**bag′pip′er** *n.*

bagpipes

bail[1] (bāl) *n.* [U] **1.** Money supplied for the temporary release of an arrested person and guaranteeing that person's appearance for trial: *Friends posted bail of $500.* **2.** The release so obtained: *The man was out on bail until the trial.* —*v.* ◆ **bail out.** *tr.v.* [sep.] **1.** To obtain the release of (an arrested person) by providing bail: *Friends bailed her out.* **2.** To help (sbdy./sthg.) out of a difficult situation: *The bank loan bailed out her business when sales dropped.*

HOMONYMS: bail (money, remove water), **bale** (bundle).

---

bail[2] (bāl) *v.* —*tr.* **1.** To remove (water) from a boat by repeatedly filling a container and emptying it: *bail water with a coffee can.* **2.** [*out*] To empty (a boat) of water by this means: *bail out the canoe.* —*intr.* To empty a boat of water: *He bailed as he tried to save the boat.* ◆ **bail out.** *intr.v.* **1.** To parachute from an aircraft; eject: *The pilot bailed out before the plane crashed.* **2.** To abandon a project or an enterprise: *The project was dropped when its financial backers bailed out.*

bail•iff (bā′lĭf) *n.* An official who guards prisoners and maintains order in a courtroom.

bail•i•wick (bā′lə wĭk′) *n.* **1.** [U] A person's specific area of interest, skill, or authority: *Accounting is not her bailiwick.* **2.** [C] The office or district of a bailiff.

bails•man (bālz′mən) *n.* A person who provides bail or security for another.

bait (bāt) *n.* [U] **1.** Food placed on a hook or in a trap to attract fish, birds, or other animals: *I always use worms for bait.* **2.** Something used to attract or entice sbdy.: *A free book was the bait to get people to attend the book fair.* —*tr.v.* **1.** To put bait on or in (sthg.): *bait a fishhook; bait the trap.* **2.** To torment (sbdy.) with repeated verbal attacks, insults, or ridicule: *They baited the new student until he cried.*

bake (bāk) *v.* **baked, bak•ing, bakes.** —*tr.* **1.** To cook (sthg.) in an oven with dry heat: *We baked several loaves of bread.* **2.** To harden or dry (sthg.) by heating in or as if in an oven: *bake bricks in the sun.* —*intr.* **1.** To

B

cook by dry heat: *The bread bakes for one hour.* **2.** To become hardened or dry by or as if by baking: *The ground baked in the hot sun.*

bak•er (bā′kər) *n.* A person who bakes and sells bread, cakes, and pastries.

bak•er's dozen (bā′kərz) *n.* A group of 13; one dozen plus one.

bak•er•y (bā′kə rē) *n., pl.* **bak•er•ies.** A place where products such as bread and cake are baked or sold: *Please stop at the bakery for a loaf of bread.*

bak•ing powder (bā′kĭng) *n.* [U] A powdered mixture of baking soda, starch, and a slightly acid compound that causes biscuits and other baked goods to become light: *The cake recipe calls for two teaspoons of baking powder.*

baking soda *n.* [U] A white compound used in baked goods; sodium bicarbonate: *He put a teaspoon of baking soda in the cookie dough.*

bal•ance (băl′əns) *n.*
1. [C] A device for measuring the weight of an object by putting it at one end of a rod that swings on a support at its center and putting known weights on the other side until the rod is

balance

level: *Chemists use a balance to weigh ingredients of a formula.* **2.** [C; U] A condition in which all forces or influences are equaled by opposite forces or influences: *The student kept a balance between her interests in science and music.* **3.** [U] A state of keeping one's body steady, as when standing: *I was thrown off balance by the wind and I fell.* **4.** [U] In mathematics or chemistry, a condition in which an equation represents a correct statement: *The balance in the equation is maintained as equal quantities are added to each side.* **5.** [C] **a.** An equality between the amounts added to and taken from an account: *Our bookkeeper achieves a balance in our account at the end of the month.* **b.** The difference between these amounts: *There is a balance of $50 to be paid.* **6.** [C] Something left over; a remainder: *After dinner the balance of the evening was spent playing cards.* **7.** [C] An action or influence that results in even shares: *Part of the U.S. system of checks and balances is the division of power between the Congress and the President.* —*v.* **bal•anced, bal•anc•ing, bal•anc•es.** —*tr.* **1.** To put or keep (sthg.) in a condition of balance: *I balanced the book on my head.* **2.** To compare (two things) in the mind: *We tried to balance the reasons for*

and against the change before deciding. **3.** To act as a weight or an influence that is equal to (sthg.): *Your skill in languages balances your lack of experience in foreign countries.* **4.** To make equal the amounts added to and taken from (an account): *balance a checking account.* —*intr.* **1.** To be equal or very similar, as in weight, force, or parts: *rewards that don't balance with the risks.* **2.** To be or come into a state of balance or stability: *He balanced on the top of the wall.* **3.** To be equal in amounts added to and taken from an account. ♦ **in the balance.** In an unknown position that may be dangerous: *The future safety of our environment hangs in the balance.* **on balance.** After thinking about all the facts; all in all: *On balance, I prefer working nights.*

balance of power *n.* A distribution of power whereby one nation is not able to dominate or interfere with others: *During the Cold War, the United States and the USSR maintained a balance of power.*

bal•co•ny (băl′kə nē) *n., pl.* **bal•co•nies. 1.** A platform extending from the wall of a building and surrounded by a railing: *The apartment had a balcony overlooking the street.* **2.** An upper section of seats in a theater or an auditorium: *Cheaper tickets are often for seats in the balcony.*

bald (bôld) *adj.* **1.** Without hair on the head: *Many men go bald as they grow older.* **2.** Plain; blunt: *a bald statement of unpleasant facts.* —**bald′ness** *n.* [U]

bald•ing (bôl′dĭng) *adj.* Losing hair; going bald: *a balding head.*

bald eagle *n.* A North American eagle with a dark body and wings and a white head and tail: *The U.S. national bird is the bald eagle.*

bale (bāl) *n.* A large bound package or bundle of raw or finished material: *a bale of hay.* —*tr.v.* **baled, bal•ing, bales.** To wrap (sthg.) in bales: *bale cotton.* —**bal′er** *n.*

HOMONYMS: bale, bail (money, remove water).

bale•ful (bāl′fəl) *adj.* **1.** Threatening; menacing: *a baleful look.* **2.** Producing evil or harm; harmful: *a baleful influence.* —**bale′-ful•ly** *adv.* —**bale′ful•ness** *n.* [U]

balk (bôk) *intr.v.* **1.** To stop short and refuse to go on: *The horse balked and wouldn't jump the fence.* **2.** [at] To refuse: *The workers balked at the low terms of the wage settlement.*

ball[1] (bôl) *n.* **1.** [C] **a.** Something that is round or nearly round: *The earth is shaped like a great ball.* **b.** A round object used in sports and games: *a tennis ball.* **c.** The way a round object is thrown, hit, or kicked: *a fly ball; a curve ball.* **2.** [U] A game, especially baseball, played with such an object: *We all played ball in the park.* **3.** [C] A rounded part of the body: *the ball of the foot.* **4. balls.** *Offensive Slang.* **a.** Testicles. **b.** Courage, especially when reckless. —*tr. & intr.v.* To form into a ball: *ball yarn for knitting.* ◆ **ball of fire.** *Informal.* Full of energy: *He is a ball of fire; he really gets his work done.* **keep the ball rolling.** *Informal.* To continue a process that is already underway; keep sthg. going: *Let's keep the ball rolling so the meeting will end on time.* **on the ball.** *Informal.* Alert, competent, or efficient: *I missed the mistake, but luckily my assistant was on the ball.* **play ball.** *Informal.* To cooperate: *The teacher wouldn't play ball and go along with the students' prank.* **the ball is in (one's) court.** *Informal.* A situation in which another person needs to take action: *I made an offer to buy the house; now the ball is in the owner's court.* **whole ball of wax.** *Informal.* The entire situation, usually unpleasant or difficult: *He never liked her family, but when they got married, he had to take the whole ball of wax.*

HOMONYMS: ball (round object, dance), **bawl** (cry).

ball² (bôl) *n.* **1.** A formal social dance: *a debutante ball; a charity ball.* **2.** *Informal.* A wonderful time: *We had a ball at the beach.*

bal·lad (băl′əd) *n.* **1.** A poem that tells a story in simple stanzas, often intended to be sung: *Many ballads have been collected in Appalachia.* **2.** A popular love song: *a rock 'n' roll ballad.*

bal·last (băl′əst) *n.* [U] Heavy material in a ship or a balloon to provide weight and steadiness: *Submarines use water as ballast in order to submerge.* —*tr.v.* To provide or stabilize (sthg.) with ballast: *They used heavy stones to ballast the ship.*

ball bearing *n.* **1.** A bearing, as for a turning shaft, in which the moving and stationary parts are held apart by small steel balls that turn in a collar around the moving parts and reduce friction. **2.** A small steel ball used in such a bearing.

bal·le·ri·na (băl′-ə rē′nə) *n.* A female dancer in a ballet company: *the star ballerina in "Swan Lake."*

bal·let (bă lā′ or băl′ā′) *n.* **1.** [U] A form of artistic dancing based on a technique of jumps, turns, and poses requiring great

ballerina

exactness and grace of movement: *He's been studying ballet for 10 years.* **2.** [C] A theatri-

cal performance of dancing to music, usually in costume, to convey a story or theme.

bal·lis·tic (bə lĭs′tĭk) *adj.* Relating to ballistics or projectiles. ◆ **go ballistic.** *Slang.* To be very excited or angry: *The director went ballistic when none of the singers knew the music.*

ballistic missile *n.* A projectile that is guided during the time that it is propelled and then allowed to fall or coast toward its target.

bal·lis·tics (bə lĭs′tĭks) *n.* [U] *(used with a singular verb).* The scientific study of the characteristics of projectiles, such as bullets or missiles, and the way they move in flight.

bal·loon (bə loon′) *n.* **1.** A large flexible bag filled with helium, hot air, or some other gas that is lighter than the surrounding air and designed to rise and float in the atmosphere, often with a gondola or scientific instruments. **2.** A

balloon
Hot-air balloons

small brightly colored rubber or plastic bag that is inflated and used as a toy. **3.** A rounded or irregularly shaped outline containing the words that a character in a cartoon is represented to be saying. —*intr.v.* **1.** To swell out like a balloon: *The tire ballooned as it was inflated with air.* **2.** To ride in a gondola suspended from a balloon: *scenic ballooning over the town.*

bal·loon·ist (bə loo′nĭst) *n.* A person who flies by means of a balloon.

bal·lot (băl′ət) *n.* **1.** [C] A piece of paper used to cast a vote, especially a secret vote: *Mark your ballot carefully.* **2.** [U] The act or method of voting: *In a democracy, many decisions are made by the ballot.* **3.** [U] The total of all votes cast in an election: *The ballot is especially heavy in the year of a presidential election.* —*intr.v.* To cast a ballot or ballots; vote: *The entire class balloted secretly.*

ball·park (bôl′pärk′) *n.* A stadium for playing baseball: *We went to the ballpark to see a game.* —*adj. Slang.* Approximately right; close: *I need the exact cost, not a ballpark figure.* ◆ **in the ballpark.** *Informal.* Approximately right or within the right range: *His price was in the ballpark, so the customer signed the contract.*

ball·play·er (bôl′plā′ər) *n.* A baseball player.

ball·point pen (bôl′point′) *n.* A pen that has a small ball bearing that transfers ink from a cartridge onto a writing surface.

ball·room (bôl′room′ or bôl′room′) *n.* A large room for dancing.

ballroom danc·ing (dăn′sĭng) *n.* [U] The act of dancing social dances such as the waltz in which couples follow a set pattern of steps.

balm (bäm) *n.* [C; U] **1.** A fragrant ointment or oil from certain kinds of plants, trees, or shrubs. **2.** Something that soothes or comforts: *The teacher's tender words were balm to the child's hurt feelings.*

balm·y (bä′mē) *adj.* **balm·i·er, balm·i·est. 1.** Having the quality or fragrance of balm; soothing. **2.** Mild and pleasant: *balmy subtropical climates; balmy weather.*

ba·lo·ney[1] (bə lō′nē) *n.* [U] A variant of **bologna.**

ba·lo·ney[2] (bə lō′nē) *n. Slang.* [U] Nonsense: *His story sounded like baloney, so I did not believe him.*

bal·sa (bôl′sə) *n.* [C; U] A tropical American tree with wood that is unusually light in weight: *Model airplanes are often made of balsa wood.*

bam·boo (băm bōō′) *n., pl.* **bam·boos. 1.** [C] Any of various tall grasses with hollow jointed stems: *Bamboo shoots are often found in Chinese food.* **2.** [C; U] The strong woody stems of this plant, used for construction, fishing poles, walking sticks, and many other purposes: *bamboo furniture.*

bam·boo·zle (băm bōō′zəl) *tr.v.* **bam·boo·zled, bam·boo·zling, bam·boo·zles.** *Informal.* To trick (sbdy.); cheat: *bamboozle a newcomer.*

ban (băn) *tr.v.* **banned, ban·ning, bans.** To prohibit (sbdy./sthg.) by law, decree, or rule; forbid: *The city council banned billboards on most streets. The principal banned the misbehaving student from class.* —*n.* A prohibition made by law or official decree: *a ban on cigarette smoking on airplanes.*

ba·nal (bə năl′ *or* bā′nəl) *adj.* Dull; trite: *Always talking about the weather makes for banal conversation.* —**ba·nal′i·ty** *n.* [C; U] —**ba·nal′ly** *adv.*

ba·nan·a (bə năn′ə) *n.* A tropical plant that bears a crescent-shaped fruit with sweet soft flesh and yellow to reddish skin that peels off easily.

band[1] (bănd) *n.* **1.a.** A strip of metal, cloth, or other material used to bind, support, or hold things together: *A band of metal held the wooden barrel together.* **b.** A stripe, a mark, or an area suggestive of such a strip: *the band of colors forming the rainbow.* **2.** A simple ungrooved ring, especially a wedding ring: *a plain gold band.* **3.** A specific range of wavelengths or frequencies used in radio broadcasting: *the shortwave band.* —*tr.v.* **1.** To tie, bind, or encircle (sthg.) with or as if with a band: *band a skirt with a red ribbon.* **2.** To put a band on the leg of (a bird) for purposes of identification: *band a migratory bird.*

band[2] (bănd) *n.* **1.** A group of people or animals: *a band of friends.* **2.** A group of musi-

cians who play together: *a rock 'n' roll band.* —*v.* ◆ **band together.** *intr.v.* To form or gather in a group or an association: *The neighbors banded together for protection.*

band·age (băn′dĭj) *n.* A strip of cloth or other material used to protect a wound or other injury. —*tr.v.* **band·aged, band·ag·ing, band·ag·es.** To cover or bind (sthg.) with a bandage: *bandage a wound.*

Band-Aid (bănd′ād′). A trademark for an adhesive bandage with a gauze pad in the center. —*adj. Informal.* Temporary or ineffective: *The curfew was a Band-Aid solution to teenage violence.*

ban·dan·na *or* **ban·dan·a** (băn dăn′ə) *n.* A large brightly colored handkerchief, often having a printed pattern on a red or blue background: *a bandanna around the farmer's neck.*

ban·dit (băn′dĭt) *n.* A robber, often one who is a member of a gang of outlaws. ◆ **make out like a bandit.** *Slang.* To be highly successful in a given enterprise: *Anyone who bought stock in computers early on has probably made out like a bandit by now.*

band·stand (bănd′stănd′) *n.* An outdoor platform, usually with a roof, generally used for concerts and other performances.

band·wag·on (bănd′wăg′ən) *n.* **1.** A brightly decorated wagon for carrying musicians in a parade. **2.** An informal term for a popular cause or party: *on the education reform bandwagon.*

ban·dy (băn′dē) *tr.v.* **ban·died, ban·dy·ing, ban·dies. 1.** To toss, throw, or strike (sthg.) back and forth: *We bandied the ball back and forth over the net.* **2.** To give and take (sthg.); exchange: *The opposing groups bandied insults at each other.* **3.** [*about*] To say or discuss (sthg.) in a casual manner: *The movie star's name was bandied about in idle gossip.*

bane (bān) *n.* ◆ **bane of (one's) existence.** A cause of great trouble or ruin: *Fleas were the bane of the cat's existence. His son has been the bane of his existence.*

bang (băng) *n.* **1.** A loud, sharp, sudden noise: *The door slammed with a bang.* **2.** A sudden forceful blow; a thump: *a bang on the knee.* **3.** *Slang.* A feeling of excitement; a thrill: *What a bang!* —*v.* —*tr.* **1.** To strike or hit (sthg.) with a loud sharp noise: *The cook banged the pots and pans together.* **2.** To hit or move (sthg.) suddenly and with great force: *I banged my knee against the table.* **3.** To close (sthg.) suddenly and loudly; slam: *bang the door shut.* —*intr.* **1.** To make a loud, sharp, sudden noise: *Firecrackers banged in the distance.* **2.** To crash noisily against or into sthg.: *The little toy car banged into the* *wall.* —*adv.* Directly; exactly: *The arrow hit bang on the target.* ◆ **bang away at. 1.** To ask a lot of questions of (sbdy.): *The curious students banged away at the visiting astronaut.* **2.** To work diligently and often at length at (sthg.): *We banged away at the project until it was finished.* **bang up.** *tr.v.* [sep.] To damage (sbdy./sthg.) extensively: *He banged the car up in the accident.* **get a bang out of.** *Slang.* To get a thrill from (sthg.): *Most kids get a bang out of the circus.*

ban•gle (băng′gəl) *n.* **1.** A bracelet worn around the wrist or ankle, especially one without a clasp. **2.** An ornament that hangs from a bracelet or necklace.

bangs (băngz) *pl.n.* Hair cut straight across the forehead: *She wears her hair pulled back, but her bangs nearly cover her eyes.*

bang-up (băng′ŭp) *adj.* Very good: *She did a bang-up job fixing the table's broken leg.*

ban•ish (băn′ĭsh) *tr.v.* **1.** To force (sbdy.) to leave a country or place; exile: *The king banished the outlaw.* **2.** To drive (sbdy./sthg.) away; cast out: *Banish all doubts from your mind.* —**ban′ish•ment** *n.* [C; U]

ban•is•ter also **ban•nis•ter** (băn′ĭstər) *n.* **1.** A handrail along with its supporting posts: *Sliding down the banister is usually not allowed.* **2.** One of the posts supporting a handrail on a staircase.

ban•jo (băn′jō) *n.,* *pl.* **ban•jos** or **ban•joes.** A stringed musical instrument with a narrow neck and a hollow circular body.

bank¹ (băngk) *n.* **1.** The rising ground next to a body of water, especially a river. **2.** A hillside or slope: *the*

banjo

steep bank leading down to the valley. **3.** A pile, small hill, or ridge of earth or other material: *a snow bank.* **4.** A pile or mass, as of clouds or fog. **5.** The sideways tilt of an aircraft in making a turn. —*v.* —*tr.* **1.** To put (earth, snow, or other matter) into a pile, ridge, or slope: *The plows banked snow along the edge of the road.* **2.** To tilt (an aircraft) in making a turn. —*intr.* **1.** To rise in or take the form of a bank: *The snow banked along the fence.* **2.** To tilt an aircraft in making a turn: *The pilot banked to the left before starting down.*

bank² (băngk) *n.* **1.** A place or a business organization in which money is kept. **2.** A small container in which money is saved: *She used a coffee can for a bank.* **3.** A supply for future use: *the blood bank of a hospital.* **4.** A place of safekeeping or storage: *a computer's memory bank.* —*v.* —*tr.* To put (money) in a bank: *Many workers bank a part of their salary.* —*intr.* To have an account or do business at a particular bank: *We bank at the Bank*

of America. ◆ **bank on.** *tr.v.* [insep.] To rely on or depend on (sbdy./sthg.): *I'm banking on you to get the job done.*

bank³ (băngk) *n.* A set or group arranged in a row: *a bank of elevators.*

bank•book (băngk′bŏŏk′) *n.* A book in which the amounts deposited in or taken out of a savings or checking account are entered; a passbook.

bank•card (băngk′kärd′) *n.* A card given by a bank to identify the holder, who can then use the card at an automated teller machine.

bank•er (băng′kər) *n.* A person who is an executive of a bank.

bank•ing (băng′kĭng) *n.* [U] The business or occupation of running a bank: *His career is in banking.*

bank•roll (băngk′rōl′) *n.* [U] Available money; funds. —*tr.v.* To provide the funds for (a business venture, for example): *Her wealthy brother bankrolled her new office building.*

bank•rupt (băngk′rŭpt′) *adj.* **1.** Legally declared unable to pay one's debts because of lack of money and having one's remaining property divided among the creditors. **2.** Completely without money; financially ruined. **3.** [*of*] Without valuable qualities: *a book bankrupt of original ideas; morally bankrupt.* —*tr.v.* To cause (sbdy./sthg.) to become bankrupt: *The month-long consumer boycott bankrupted the store.* —**bank′rupt•cy** *n.* [C; U]

ban•ner (băn′ər) *n.* **1.** A flag or piece of cloth, often having words or a special design on it: *Paraders marched with a banner for women's rights.* **2.** A headline spanning the width of a newspaper page. —*adj.* Unusually good; outstanding: *a banner year for our team.*

ban•nis•ter (băn′ĭstər) *n.* Variant of **banister.**

ban•quet (băng′kwĭt) *n.* A large elaborate meal; a feast: *They put on a banquet for the visiting royalty.*

ban•ter (băn′tər) *n.* [U] Playful good-humored conversation: *light-hearted banter between friends.* —*intr.v.* To exchange joking or teasing remarks: *bantering with the jovial professor.* —**ban′ter•er** *n.*

bap•tism (băp′tĭz′əm) *n.* **1.** A religious ceremony in which a person is sprinkled with or dipped in water as a sign of being cleansed of sin and admitted to a Christian church. **2.** A first experience. ◆ **baptism by fire.** A very difficult situation that sbdy. experiences for the first time: *Her first job was a baptism by fire.* —**bap•tis′mal** (băp tĭz′məl) *adj.*

Bap•tist (băp′tĭst) *n.* A member of a Protestant church that believes in baptism only for people old enough to understand its meaning. —**Bap′tist** *adj.*

bap•tize (băp tīz′ *or* băp′tīz′) *tr.v.* **bap•tized, bap•tiz•ing, bap•tiz•es. 1.** To ad-

B

mit (sbdy.) into Christianity or a particular Christian church by baptism. **2.** To give a name to (a person who is being baptized).

bar (bär) *n.* **1.** A narrow, straight, hard piece of material: *Bars covered the prison windows.* **2.** A block of a hard substance: *a chocolate bar; a bar of soap.* **3.** Something that blocks entry or progress; a barrier: *The fallen tree was a bar to our continuing along the road.* **4.** A ridge of sand or gravel in the water, formed by the action of tides or currents: *waves crashing on a sand bar.* **5.a.** A high long table at which drinks, especially alcoholic drinks, and sometimes food are served: *sit at the bar.* **b.** A restaurant or store where alcoholic drinks are served: *He works in a bar.* **6.** A measure of music: *Let's practice the final bars of this march.* *—tr.v.* **barred, bar•ring, bars. 1.** To secure or fasten (sthg.) with a bar or bars: *closed and barred the gate.* **2.** To block or close (sthg.) off: *Fallen branches barred the way.* **3.** To keep (sbdy./sthg.) out: *Hunters are barred from wildlife sanctuaries.* ♦ **bar none.** With no exceptions: *This is the best pizza I've ever had, bar none.*

barb (bärb) *n.* **1.** A sharp point projecting backward, as on a fishhook or an arrow. **2.** A sharp or biting remark: *The author saved her best barbs for her critics.*

bar•bar•i•an (bär bâr'ē ən) *n.* **1.** A member of a people considered by those of another nation or group to be primitive or uncivilized: *The ancient Greeks considered everyone else to be barbarians.* **2.** A crude, uncivilized, or brutal person: *The pirates were barbarians.*

bar•bar•ic (bär bär'ĭk) *adj.* **1.** Relating to barbarians: *The native peoples considered the explorers barbaric.* **2.** Crude or uncivilized: *a barbaric custom.*

bar•ba•rism (bär'bə rĭz'əm) *n.* **1.** [U] A barbarous uncivilized state. **2.** [C] A barbarous act or custom: *Imprisoning debtors is now considered a barbarism.*

bar•bar•i•ty (bär bär'ĭ tē) *n., pl.* **bar•bar•i•ties. 1.** [C] A cruel or savage act: *the barbarities of war.* **2.** [U] Crudeness; coarseness: *The barbarity of the speaker's remarks disgusted the audience.*

bar•ba•rous (bär'bər əs) *adj.* **1.** Primitive in culture and customs; uncivilized: *The barbarous invaders burned the village.* **2.** Brutal; cruel: *barbarous acts of war.* **—bar'ba•rous•ly** *adv.* **—bar'ba•rous•ness** *n.* [U]

bar•be•cue (bär'bĭ kyōō') *n.* **1.** [C] A social gathering at which food is cooked over an open fire: *Everybody came to the neighborhood barbecue.* **2.** [U] A whole animal or a piece of it roasted over an open fire: *Join us for barbecue.* **3.** [C] A grill, pit, or fireplace for roasting meat, often outdoors. *—tr.v.* **bar•be•cued, bar•be•cu•ing, bar•be•cues.** To cook (food) over an open fire, often with a spicy sauce: *We barbecued ribs and chops.*

barbed (bärbd) *adj.* **1.** Having barbs: *the barbed head of a harpoon.* **2.** Cutting; stinging: *barbed criticism.*

barbed wire *n.* [U] Twisted strands of wire with barbs at regular intervals, used in making fences: *Barbed wire was strung between posts to keep the cattle in.*

bar•bell (bär'bĕl') *n.* A bar with adjustable weights at each end, lifted for exercise.

bar•ber (bär'bər) *n.* A person whose work is cutting hair and shaving or trimming beards. *—v. —tr.* To cut the hair of or shave or trim the beard of (sbdy.). *—intr.* To work as a barber.

bar•ber•shop (bär'bər shŏp') *n.* A barber's place of business. *—adj.* Relating to singing sentimental songs in four-part harmony: *a barbershop quartet.*

bar•bi•tu•rate (bär bĭch'ər ĭt *or* bär bĭch'-ə rāt') *n.* A substance that is mainly used as a sedative or sleep-producing drug: *The doctor prescribed barbiturates.*

bar code *n.* A group of lines of varied thicknesses printed on a label for a computer scanner to read, such as a Universal Product Code.

bard (bärd) *n.* **1.** A poet of ancient times who composed and recited verses about heroes and heroic deeds. **2.** A poet: *Shakespeare is sometimes called the Bard of Avon.*

bare (bâr) *adj.* **bar•er, bar•est. 1.** Without clothing or covering; naked: *bare feet; a bare hillside.* **2.** Without the usual or expected furnishings or equipment: *bare shelves; bare walls.* See Synonyms at **empty. 3.** Having no addition or restriction; simple: *the bare facts.* **4.** Just sufficient or adequate; mere: *the bare necessities of life.* *—tr.v.* **bared, bar•ing, bares.** To uncover (sthg.); expose to view: *The dog bared its teeth. He bared his soul to his friends.* **—bare'ness** *n.* [U]

HOMONYMS: bare, bear (support, animal).

bare•back (bâr'băk') *also* **bare•backed** (bâr'băkt') *adv. & adj.* On a horse without a saddle: *riding bareback; a bareback rider.*

bare•faced (bâr'fāst') *adj.* Shameless; bold: *a barefaced lie.*

bare•foot (bâr'fŏot') *also* **bare•foot•ed** (bâr'fŏot'ĭd) *adv. & adj.* Without shoes or other covering on the feet: *running barefoot through the grass; a barefoot child.*

bare•hand•ed (bâr'hăn'dĭd) *adv. & adj.* With the hand or hands alone; without a glove, tool, weapon, or protection: *catching fish barehanded; a barehanded catch of a baseball.*

ă–cat; ā–pay; âr–care; ä–father; ĕ–get; ē–be; ĭ–sit; ī–nice; îr–here; ŏ–got; ō–go; ô–saw; oi–boy; ou–out; ōō–took; ōō–boot; ŭ–cut; ûr–word; th–thin; th–this; hw–when; zh–vision; ə–about; N–French bon

bare·head·ed (bâr′hĕd′ĭd) *adv. & adj.* Without a hat or other head covering: *walking bareheaded in the rain; bareheaded hikers.*

bare·leg·ged (bâr′lĕg′ĭd *or* bâr′lĕgd′) *adv. & adj.* With the legs uncovered: *running barelegged through the surf; barelegged children at the beach.*

bare·ly (bâr′lē) *adv.* **1.** By very little; hardly; just: *We could barely see the shore in the dark.* **2.** In a bare or scanty manner; sparsely: *a barely furnished room.*

barf (bärf) *Slang. intr.v.* To throw up; vomit. —*n.* Vomit.

bar·gain (bär′gĭn) *n.* **1.** An arrangement, often involving payment or trade; a deal: *We made a bargain that I would cut the grass for $10.* **2.** Something offered or bought at a low price: *The elegant dress that's now on sale is a bargain.* —*intr.v.* To argue over or discuss the terms of an agreement, especially a price to be paid: *The hotel's cook bargained for vegetables in the market.* ◆ **bargain for** *or* **on.** *tr.v.* [insep.] To count on (sthg.); expect: *That old car gave us more trouble than we bargained for.* **drive a hard bargain.** To negotiate an agreement strongly in one's own favor: *That car dealer drives a hard bargain.* **into** *or* **in the bargain.** Over and above what is expected; in addition: *We attended an interesting conference and got a free meal in the bargain.*

bar·gain·ing chip (bär′gə nĭng) *n.* Something of value that a person or group can use in a business or political situation to gain an advantage in negotiations: *Limits on foreign trade was the President's bargaining chip in his talks with business leaders.*

barge (bärj) *n.* A large flat-bottomed boat used to carry loads on rivers, canals, and coastal waters. —*intr.v.* **barged, barg·ing, barg·es.** [*in; into*] To move, enter, or intrude clumsily: *The demonstrators barged into the room and interrupted the meeting. I hate to barge in, but it is time to go.*

bar graph *n.* A graph consisting of parallel bars or rectangles drawn at lengths that are in proportion to the quantities they represent.

bar graph

bar·i·tone (băr′ĭ tōn′) *n.* **1.** A moderately low singing voice of a man, higher than a bass and lower than a tenor. **2.** A man with such a voice. **3.** A part written in the range of this voice.

bar·i·um (bâr′ē əm *or* băr′ē əm) *n.* [U] *Symbol* **Ba** A soft, silvery-white, metallic element that occurs only in combination with other elements. Barium compounds are used in making pigments and safety matches. Atomic number 56. See table at **element.**

bark[1] (bärk) *n.* **1.** The short gruff sound made by a dog and certain other animals such as seals and coyotes. **2.** A sound similar to this, such as a cough. —*v.* —*intr.* **1.** To make the sound of a bark: *The neighbor's dog barked all night.* **2.** To speak gruffly or sharply: *The sergeant barked at the new recruits.* —*tr.* To say (sthg.) in a loud harsh voice: *The team captain barked commands.* ◆ **bark up the wrong tree.** To misdirect one's energies or attention: *Looking for him in the library is barking up the wrong tree.* **(one's) bark is worse than (one's) bite.** An expression used when a person is less rough or dangerous than he or she seems: *He shouts a lot, but his bark is worse than his bite.*

bark[2] (bärk) *n.* [U] The protective outer covering of the trunk, branches, and roots of trees and other woody plants.

bark·er (bär′kər) *n.* **1.** A person or an animal that barks: *That dog is a loud barker.* **2.** A person who makes a loud colorful sales talk at the entrance to a show, carnival, or other attraction: *A barker sold tickets outside the circus.*

bar·ley (bär′lē) *n.* [U] A grain-bearing grass with seeds used as food and for making beer and whiskey.

bar magnet *n.* A permanent magnet in the shape of a bar: *A bar magnet suspended from a string will serve as a simple compass by pointing north.*

bar·maid (bär′mād′) *n.* A woman who serves drinks in a bar. —**bar′man** (bär′mən) *n.*

bar mitz·vah (bär mĭts′və) *n.* A ceremony in which a 13-year-old Jewish boy is admitted as an adult into the religious community.

barn (bärn) *n.* A large farm building used for storing grain, hay, and other farm products and for sheltering livestock: *We keep the horses in the barn.*

bar·na·cle (bär′nə kəl) *n.* A small hard-shelled sea animal that attaches itself to underwater objects, such as rocks, piers, and the bottoms of ships.

barn·storm (bärn′stôrm′) *tr. & intr.v.* To travel about the countryside appearing in shows or making political speeches: *During the campaign both candidates barnstormed the countryside.* —**barn′storm′er** *n.*

barn·yard (bärn′yärd′) *n.* The yard or area of ground around a barn.

ba·rom·e·ter (bə rŏm′ĭ tər) *n.* **1.** An instrument for measuring atmospheric pressure, used to determine height above sea level and in weather forecasting. **2.** Something that shifts and changes like those of the weather; an indicator: *Opinion polls are used as a barometer of public mood.*

barometer

bar·o·met·ric (băr′ə mĕt′rĭk) *adj.* Relating to or measured by a barometer: *take a barometric reading.*

barometric pressure *n.* Atmospheric pressure.

bar·on (băr′ən) *n.* **1.** A British nobleman of the lowest rank. **2.** A businessman of great wealth and influence: *a baron of industry; railroad barons of the 19th century.*

HOMONYMS: baron, barren (not productive).

bar·on·ess (băr′ə nĭs) *n.* The wife or widow of a baron.

ba·roque also **Baroque** (bə rōk′) *adj.* Relating to a style of art, architecture, and music developed in Europe from about 1550 to 1750, characterized by elaborate and ornate forms. *—n.* The baroque style or period in art, architecture, and music.

bar·racks (băr′əks) *pl.n.* A building or group of buildings used to house soldiers.

bar·ra·cu·da (băr′ə koō′də) *n.* An ocean fish with a long narrow body, a projecting jaw, and very sharp teeth, found mostly in tropical waters.

bar·rage (bə räzh′) *n.* **1.** A concentrated firing of guns or missiles, often as a screen or protection for military troops: *The kidnapper died in a barrage of gunfire.* **2.** An overwhelming outpouring of words: *a barrage of last-minute questions. —tr.v.* **bar·raged, bar·rag·ing, bar·rag·es.** To direct a barrage at (sbdy./sthg.): *Reporters barraged the speaker with questions.*

barred (bärd) *adj.* **1.** Having bars: *barred windows.* **2.** Having stripes: *the barred owl.*

bar·rel (băr′əl) *n.* **1.** A large container of wood, metal, plastic, or cardboard with round flat ends of equal size often held together by hoops: *a rain barrel.* **2.** The amount that a barrel can hold: *a barrel of oil.* **3.** Any of various measures of volume or capacity ranging from 31 to 42 gallons (about 120 to about 159 liters). See table at **measurement. 4.a.** The long tube of a gun, through which a bullet or shell travels. **b.** A cylindrical machine part. **5.** *Informal.* A great amount: *a barrel of fun. —v. —tr.* To put or pack (sthg.) in a barrel or barrels: *barrel vinegar for shipping to market. —intr. Informal.* To move at great speed: *The express train barreled along the tracks.*

bar·ren (băr′ən) *adj.* **1.** Without any plants or crops: *a barren desert; barren soil.* **2.** Unable to bear offspring or fruit: *an orchard of barren trees.* **3.** Not useful or productive: *barren efforts.* **4.** [*of*] Empty; bare: *a life barren of pleasure. —n. (often used in the plural).* An area of barren or unproductive

land: *the Pine Barrens of New Jersey. —bar′·ren·ness n.* [U]

HOMONYMS: barren, baron (nobleman).

bar·rette (bə rĕt′) *n.* A clip used by women and girls to hold the hair in place.

bar·ri·cade (băr′ĭ kād′ *or* băr′ĭ kād′) *n.* A structure set up to obstruct the passage of sbdy./sthg.: *a barricade around the construction site. —tr.v.* **bar·ri·cad·ed, bar·ri·cad·ing, bar·ri·cades.** To close off, block, or protect (sthg.) with a barricade: *barricade streets to control the crowd at a parade.*

bar·ri·er (băr′ē ər) *n.* **1.** A structure, such as a fence or wall, built to prevent passage: *Police set up a barrier at each end of the street the night before the fair began.* **2.** Something that blocks; an obstacle: *Lack of education can be a barrier to success.*

barrier reef *n.* A long narrow ridge of coral deposits parallel to the mainland and separated from it by a deep lagoon: *Divers are often astonished by the sea life around a barrier reef.*

bar·ring (bär′ĭng) *prep.* Apart from the occurrence of; excluding: *Barring any problems, we'll be the first to arrive.*

bar·ri·o (bä′rē ō′ *or* băr′ē ō) *n., pl.* **bar·ri·os.** A chiefly Spanish-speaking community or neighborhood in a U.S. city.

bar·ris·ter (băr′ĭ stər) *n. Chiefly British.* A lawyer who argues cases in a court of law.

bar·room (bär′roōm′ *or* bär′roōm′) *n.* A room or building in which alcoholic beverages are sold at a counter or bar.

bar·tend·er (bär′tĕn′dər) *n.* A person who mixes and serves alcoholic drinks at a bar.

bar·ter (bär′tər) *v. —intr.* To trade goods or services without using money: *We had no money, so we had to barter to get food. —tr.* To trade (goods or services) without using money: *We bartered homegrown vegetables for firewood. —n.* [U] The act or practice of bartering: *A fair exchange is the basis for barter. —adj.* Relating to or based on bartering: *a barter economy.*

bas·al (bā′səl *or* bā′zəl) *adj.* **1.** Basic; fundamental; primary: *Many schools use basal readers in the early grades.* **2.** Located at or forming a base: *a plant having large basal leaves.*

basal metabolism *n.* The amount of energy used by an organism at complete rest.

base[1] (bās) *n.* **1.** The lowest or bottom part: *the base of a mountain.* **2.a.** A part or layer on which sthg. rests or is placed for support; a foundation: *a house built on a base of solid rock.* **b.** A basic and important part; a basis: *an industrial base to the economy.* **3.** An important substance in sthg.: *a paint with an oil*

base. **4.** A starting point or central place for supplies or operations; a headquarters: *The Army has many bases around the country.* **5.** A starting point, safety area, or goal in certain games: *The baseball player raced to first base.* **6.** In a number system, the factor by which each place value of a number is multiplied to generate the next place value to the left. **7.** A word or word part to which other word parts may be added. For example, in *filled, refill,* and *filling, fill* is the base. **8.** A substance that, when dissolved in water, reacts with an acid to form a salt, turns litmus dye blue, and has a slippery feel and bitter taste. —*tr.v.* **based, bas•ing, bas•es. 1.** [*on*] To use sthg. as a reason for (sthg.): *He based his theory on the results of his experiments.* **2.** [*on*] To use sthg. as a base or starting point for (sthg.): *The composer based this piece of music on an old folk song.* **3.** To locate or place (sbdy./sthg.) at a center of activity: *The general based the troops in Europe.* ♦ **get to first base. 1.** To reach an early goal: *He tried to make friends with his classmate, but he couldn't get to first base.* **2.** *Slang.* To kiss. **off base.** Badly mistaken: *Your criticism of me is off base.*

HOMONYMS: base (lowest part, mean), **bass²** (lowest tones in music).

---

base² (bās) *adj.* **bas•er, bas•est. 1.** Having or showing a lack of decency; mean: *a base act.* **2.** Common or inferior in value or quality: *base metals such as iron and lead.* —**base′ly** *adv.* —**base′ness** *n.* [U]
base•ball (bās′bôl′) *n.* **1.** [U] A game played with a bat and ball on a field with four bases laid out in a diamond pattern. Two teams of nine players take turns at bat and in the field, the members of the team at bat trying to score runs by touching all four bases. **2.** [C] The ball used in this game.
base•board (bās′bôrd′) *n.* A molding along the lower edge of a wall, next to the floor.
base line *n.* **1.** A line serving as a base, as for measurement: *Resting pulse is used as a base line for medical tests on the heart.* **2.** In baseball, an area within which a base runner must stay when running between bases. **3.** A line bounding the back end of each side in a tennis court.
base•ment (bās′mənt) *n.* The lowest story of a building, often below ground level: *a basement apartment.*
ba•ses (bā′sēz′) *n.* Plural of **basis.**
bash (băsh) *tr.v.* **1.** To strike (sbdy./sthg.) with a heavy crushing blow: *The car skidded off the road and bashed the fence.* **2.** *Informal.* To criticize (a person or thing) harshly: *They bashed the absent politician.* —*n.* **1.** *Informal.* A heavy crushing blow: *a bash on the head.* **2.** *Slang.* A party: *a birthday bash.*

bash•ful (băsh′fəl) *adj.* Timid and embarrassed with other people; shy: *Some children are bashful around strangers.* —**bash′ful•ly** *adv.* —**bash′ful•ness** *n.* [U]
bash•ing (băsh′ĭng) *n.* [U] (*usually combined with a noun*). The act or practice of attacking a person or group using physical or verbal violence: *Gay-bashing is still common in the military.*
ba•sic (bā′sĭk) *adj.* **1.** Relating to or forming a base or basis; fundamental: *Basic changes in education do not occur very frequently. We need some basic information before coming to a decision.* **2.a.** Relating to a chemical base. **b.** Alkaline: *a basic solution.* —*n.* (*usually plural*). Something basic or fundamental: *Try to learn the basics of arithmetic before studying algebra.* —**ba′si•cal•ly** *adv.*
BA•SIC or **Ba•sic** (bā′sĭk) *n.* [U] A computer language using simple English and algebraic terms.
bas•il (băz′əl *or* bā′zəl) *n.* [U] A fragrant plant related to mint, with leaves used as a seasoning.
ba•sin (bā′sĭn) *n.* **1.** An open, usually round, shallow container used especially for holding liquids: *Fill the basin with warm water.* **2.** The amount that a basin can hold: *drenched by a basin of water.* **3.** A sink, as in a bathroom: *Take the plug out of the basin.* **4.** An enclosed area filled with water: *a basin at the foot of the falls.* **5.** A region drained by a river and the streams that flow into it: *the Amazon basin.*
ba•sis (bā′sĭs) *n., pl.* **ba•ses** (bā′sēz′). A foundation on which sthg. rests: *On what basis did you make this decision? Addition is a basis for higher math.*
bask (băsk) *intr.v.* **1.** To expose oneself to or enjoy a pleasant warmth: *turtles basking in the sun.* **2.** To take pleasure; live happily: *Many teachers bask in the glory of their students' achievements.*
bas•ket (băs′kĭt) *n.* **1.** A container made of interwoven twigs, strips of wood, or rushes. **2.** Something resembling such a container in shape or function: *a wastepaper basket; a fruit basket.* **3.** The amount that a basket can hold: *a basket of peaches.* **4.a.** A metal hoop from which is hung a net that is open at the bottom, used as a goal in basketball. **b.** A score made by throwing the ball through this hoop: *A basket is usually worth two points.*
bas•ket•ball (băs′kĭt bôl′) *n.* **1.** [U] A game played by two teams of five players in which players try to throw a ball through an elevated basket on the opponent's end of a rectangular court. **2.** [C] The ball used in this game.
bas mitz•vah (bäs mĭts′və) *n. & v.* Variant of **bat mitzvah.**
bass¹ (băs) *n., pl.* **bass.** Any of several freshwater or saltwater fish of North America, caught for food or sport.

bass² (bās) *n.* **1.** [C] A male singing voice in the lowest range. **2.** [C] A singer who has such a voice. **3.** [U] The lowest part in four-part harmony: *He sings bass in the choir.*

B

HOMONYMS: bass², base (lowest part, mean).

bass drum (bās) *n.* A large cylindrical drum that makes a deep booming sound when struck: *You can hear the marching band's bass drum from a long way away.*

bas·soon (bə sōōn′) *n.* A low-pitched woodwind instrument having a long wooden body connected to a double reed by a U-shaped metal tube. —**bas·soon′ist** *n.*

bas·tard (băs′tərd) *n.* **1.** A child born of parents who are not married to each other. **2.** *Slang.* An offensive term for sbdy. who is considered to be mean or disagreeable. —*adj.* Born of parents who are not married to each other; illegitimate.

baste¹ (bāst) *tr.v.* **bast·ed, bast·ing, bastes.** To sew (a seam, for example) with long loose stitches meant to be taken out when the final sewing is done: *baste a hem.*

baste² (bāst) *tr.v.* **bast·ed, bast·ing, bastes.** To moisten (meat) with liquid such as melted fat while roasting: *baste a chicken.*

bas·tion (băs′chən *or* băs′tē ən) *n.* **1.** A part built out from the main body of a fort or rampart enabling defenders to aim at those attacking along a wall. **2.** A strongly protected or well-defended position; a stronghold: *That magazine is a bastion of freedom of speech.*

bat¹ (băt) *n.* A wooden stick or club, especially one used for hitting a ball, as in baseball or cricket. —*v.* **bat·ted, bat·ting, bats.** —*tr.* **1.** To hit (sbdy./sthg.) with or as if with a bat: *The cat batted the toy mouse around the room.* **2.** In baseball, to have (a certain percentage) as a batting average: *He is batting .276 this season.* —*intr.* In baseball, to use a bat: *The whole team is batting well this season.* ♦ **at bat.** Taking one's turn to bat, as in baseball: *The home team's at bat.* **bat around.** *tr.v.* [sep.] To discuss (sthg.); consider: *batted some ideas around.* **go to bat for.** To help or defend (sbdy. in need): *The student went to bat for his friend who was wrongly accused.* **right off the bat.** Without hesitation; immediately: *We liked the new student right off the bat.*

bat² (băt) *n.* Any of various flying mammals that look like mice but have thin leathery wings. Most bats are active at night and eat insects or fruit.

bat³ (băt) *tr.v.* **bat·ted, bat·ting, bats.** To move (sthg.) with a flapping motion; blink: *bat one's eyelashes.* ♦ **bat an eye.** *(often used in*

the negative). To show surprise: *They didn't bat an eye when the firecracker exploded.*

batch (băch) *n.* **1.** An amount prepared at one time: *several loaves in a batch of homemade bread; mix a batch of cement.* **2.** A group or number of similar things: *recycle a batch of old newspapers.*

bated (bā′tĭd) *adj.* ♦ **with bated breath.** In an excited or a frightened way, as if holding one's breath: *She waited for the answer with bated breath.*

bath (băth) *n., pl.* **baths** (băthz *or* băths). **1.a.** The act of washing or soaking the body, as in water or steam: *She gave the baby a bath. Some people take a bath before they go to bed.* **b.** The water used for a bath: *run a hot bath.* **2.** A bathtub or bathroom: *an apartment with three rooms and a bath.* ♦ **take a bath.** To lose a large amount of money: *The entrepreneur took a bath when the company failed.*

bathe (bāth) *v.* **bathed, bath·ing, bathes.** —*intr.* **1.** To take a bath: *bathe before breakfast.* **2.** To go into the water for swimming or recreation: *bathe in the surf.* —*tr.* **1.** To wash (sbdy./sthg.) in water; give a bath to: *bathe the baby.* **2.** To soak (sthg.) in a liquid: *bathe a swollen leg.* **3.** To make (sthg.) wet; moisten: *Tears bathed the baby's cheeks.* —**bath′er** *n.*

bath·ing suit (bā′thĭng) *n.* A swimsuit.

bath·robe (băth′rōb′) *n.* A loose robe worn before and after bathing and for relaxing at home.

bath·room (băth′rōōm′ *or* băth′rŏŏm′) *n.* A room equipped for taking a bath or shower and usually also containing a sink and toilet: *a bathroom connected to the bedroom.*

bath·tub (băth′tŭb′) *n.* A tub for bathing, especially one installed in a bathroom.

ba·tik (bə tēk′ *or* băt′ĭk) *n.* [U] **1.** A method of dyeing a design on cloth by putting removable wax over the parts of the cloth not meant to be dyed. **2.** [C] Cloth dyed by batik.

bat mitz·vah (bät mĭts′və) *or* **bas mitz·vah** (bäs mĭts′və) *n.* A ceremony for a Jewish girl of 12 to 14 years of age in which she is admitted as an adult into the religious community.

ba·ton (bə tŏn′ *or* băt′n) *n.* **1.** A thin stick often used by a conductor in leading a band or an orchestra. **2.** A stick or staff such as that twirled by a drum major, passed in a relay race, or carried as a symbol of office.

bat·tal·ion (bə tăl′yən) *n.* **1.** A large group of soldiers organized as a unit, usually consisting of two or more companies of infantry or artillery. **2.** A large number: *a battalion of ants.*

bat·ter¹ (băt′ər) *v.* —*tr.* **1.** To strike or pound (sbdy./sthg.) repeatedly with heavy blows: *Heavy wind and rain battered the windows. The boxers battered each other in the fight.* **2.**

ă–**cat**; ā–**pay**; âr–**care**; ä–**father**; ĕ–**get**; ē–**be**; ĭ–**sit**; ī–**nice**; îr–**here**; ŏ–**got**; ō–**go**; ô–**saw**; oi–**boy**; ou–**out**; ōō–**took**; ōō–**boot**; ŭ–**cut**; ûr–**word**; th–**thin**; th–**this**; hw–**when**; zh–**vision**; ə–**about**; N–French **bon**

To injure or damage (sbdy./sthg.) by rough treatment or hard wear: *The dented old car was badly battered.* —*intr.* To hit heavily and repeatedly; pound: *Waves battered against the pier.*

bat·ter² (bắt′ər) *n.* The player at bat in baseball or cricket: *The next batter needs to hit a home run.*

bat·ter³ (bắt′ər) *n.* [U] A beaten mixture, as of flour, milk, and eggs, used in cooking: *a bowl of cake batter; pancake batter.*

bat·tered (bắt′ərd) *adj.* **1.** Physically harmed or beaten by sbdy. familiar or known: *a battered woman; a battered child.* **2.** Slightly damaged: *a battered old truck.*

bat·ter·y (bắt′ə rē) *n., pl.* **bat·ter·ies. 1.a.** Two or more connected electric cells that supply a direct current by converting chemical energy to electrical energy. **b.** A small dry cell designed to power a flashlight or other electric device: *We change the batteries in our smoke detector frequently.* **2.a.** A group or set of large guns, as of artillery: *The fort had a battery of cannons.* **b.** A place where such guns are set up: *the old battery at the end of Manhattan Island.* **c.** A unit of soldiers in the artillery, corresponding to a company in the infantry. **3.** A group of things or people used or doing sthg. together: *The celebrities faced a battery of cameras and reporters.* **4.** The unlawful touching or beating of another person, with the intention of doing harm: *the felony of battery.*

bat·tle (bắt′l) *n.* **1.** A fight between two armed forces, usually on a large scale: *famous battles of World War II.* **2.** A struggle or sharp conflict: *a political battle; a battle of wits.* —*v.* **bat·tled, bat·tling, bat·tles.** —*intr.* To fight in or as if in battle; struggle: *The firefighters battled bravely against the flames.* —*tr.* To fight against (sbdy./sthg.): *The sailors battled the storm for hours. The English battled the French at Agincourt.* —**bat′tler** *n.*

bat·tle·field (bắt′l fēld′) *n.* A field or an area where a battle is or was fought: *the battlefield at Gettysburg.*

bat·tle·front (bắt′l frŭnt′) *n.* The line or area in which armed forces engage opponents in battle: *The army was fighting on several battlefronts.*

bat·tle·ground (bắt′l ground′) *n.* A battlefield: *The inner-city park is a battleground for local gangs.*

bat·tle·ship (bắt′l shĭp′) *n.* Any of a class of warships of the largest size, having the heaviest guns and armor.

bat·ty (bắt′ē) *adj.* **bat·ti·er, bat·ti·est.** *Slang.* Crazy; insane: *She thinks I'm batty because I have seven cats.*

bau·ble (bô′bəl) *n.* A showy ornament or trinket of little value: *selling baubles to tourists.*

baud (bôd) *n., pl.* **baud.** A unit of speed in data transmission, usually equal to one bit per second.

baux·ite (bôk′sīt′) *n.* [U] A mixture of min-erals, often resembling clay, that is the principal ore of aluminum.

bawd·y (bô′dē) *adj.* **bawd·i·er, bawd·i·est.** Humorously crude: *bawdy jokes.* —**bawd′·i·ly** *adv.* —**bawd′i·ness** *n.* [U]

bawl (bôl) *v.* —*intr.* To cry or sob loudly; wail: *The unhappy baby kicked and bawled.* —*tr.* To utter or call (sthg.) in a loud strong voice: *The sentry bawled an order to halt.* —*n.* A loud wailing or bellowing cry: *the bawl of a stray calf.* ◆ **bawl out.** *tr.v.* [sep.] *Informal.* To scold (sbdy.) loudly or harshly: *She bawled out her son for misbehaving.*

HOMONYMS: bawl, ball (round object, dance).

---

bay¹ (bā) *n.* A body of water partially enclosed by land but having a wide outlet to the sea. A bay is usually smaller than a gulf and larger than a cove: *Beautiful white sand beaches dotted the bay.*

bay² (bā) *n.* **1.** A part of a building divided by vertical supports such as columns or pillars: *an arcade with ten bays.* **2.** A section or compartment, as of a building or an aircraft, set off for a specific purpose: *The cargo was stored in a loading bay.* **3.** A sickbay.

bay³ (bā) *adj.* Reddish brown: *a bay horse.* —*n.* **1.** [U] A reddish brown color. **2.** [C] A reddish brown horse.

bay⁴ (bā) *n.* A long howling bark: *The hound's bay echoed across the valley.* —*intr.v.* To bark with loud howling cries: *dogs baying at the moon.* ◆ **hold** or **keep at bay. 1.** To keep (sbdy./sthg.) in a position like that of an animal cornered by and facing its pursuers: *The barking dogs kept the horse at bay. The police officer held the suspect at bay.* **2.** To keep (sbdy./sthg.) at a distance: *Lights around the factory kept intruders at bay.*

bay⁵ (bā) *n.* A laurel tree with glossy fragrant leaves often used as a spice.

bay leaf *n.* The dried leaf of a kind of laurel, used as a seasoning in cooking: *He added a bay leaf to the stew.*

bay·o·net (bā′ə nĭt *or* bā′ə nĕt′) *n.* A knife attached to the muzzle of a rifle for use in close combat.

bay·ou (bī′ōō *or* bī′ō) *n.* A sluggish marshy stream connected with a river, lake, or gulf, common in the southern United States: *living on a bayou in Louisiana.*

ba·zaar (bə zär′) *n.* **1.** A market, usually consisting of a street lined with shops and stalls, especially in the Middle East: *One can buy almost anything in a bazaar.* **2.** A fair or sale, often to raise money for a charity: *a hospital bazaar.*

ba·zoo·ka (bə zōō′kə) *n.* A portable military weapon consisting of a tube from which antitank rockets are launched.

BBC (bē′bē sē′) *abbr.* An abbreviation of British Broadcasting Corporation.

B.C. *abbr.* An abbreviation of before Christ (in a specified year before the birth of Jesus in the Christian calendar).

be (bē) *v.* *Present tense*: first person singular **am** (ăm), second person singular **are** (är), third person singular **is** (ĭz), plural **are**, present participle **be•ing** (bē'ĭng). *Past tense*: first and third person singular **was** (wŭz *or* wŏz), second person singular **were** (wûr), plural **were**, past participle **been** (bĭn). —*intr.* **1.** To exist; have life or reality: *There are no dinosaurs now.* **2.** To have a position: *The food is on the table.* **3.** To happen or take place: *Where is the show?* **4.** To come or go: *Have you ever been to Alaska?* **5.a.** To equal in identity or meaning: *That experiment was a complete success.* **b.** To belong to a specified class or group: *Snakes are reptiles.* **c.** To have or show a specified quality or characteristic: *Please be quiet.* —*aux.* **1.** Used to form the passive voice in combination with the past participle of transitive verbs: *He was bitten by a dog.* **2.** Used in combination with the present participle of a verb to express: **a.** An action in process: *We are waiting for a bus. He was sleeping when I telephoned.* **b.** A temporary situation: *He is staying at a hotel.* **c.** A future action. Used in the present tense only: *She is leaving tomorrow.* **3.** Used to show a responsibility, possibility, or future event with the infinitive of another verb: *He was to meet us here at 6:00. How am I to know the answer? They are to be married next month.* **4.** Used to express a planned action in combination with **going to** and the infinitive of another verb: *I am going to read the newspaper. They were going to have a party.*

HOMONYMS: **be, bee** (insect, gathering).

be— *pref.* A prefix that means: **1.** Completely; thoroughly: *bemoan.* **2.** On; around; over: *besmirch.* **3.** Make; cause to become: *befit.* **4.** Affect or provide with: *befriend.*

beach (bēch) *n.* [C; U] The area of sand, stone, or gravel deposited above the water line at a shore by the action of waves: *Many families vacation at the beach.* —*tr.v.* To pull or run (sthg.) on to the beach: *The whale beached itself in shallow water.*

HOMONYMS: **beach, beech** (tree).

bea•con (bē'kən) *n.* **1.** A guiding or warning signal, such as a lighthouse located on a coast: *Each airport has a beacon to help pilots find it in the dark.* **2.** A radio transmitter that sends a guidance signal for aircraft.

bead (bēd) *n.* **1.** A small, often round piece of glass, wood, plastic, or other material that has a hole through it so that it can be placed on a string or wire. **2. beads.** A necklace of beads on a string: *wearing her beads to the dance.* **3.** A small round object, such as a drop of moisture: *beads of sweat on one's forehead.* —*tr.* & *intr.v.* To furnish with or collect into beads: *bead the collar around a sweater; water beading on the soda can.*

bead•y (bē'dē) *adj.* **bead•i•er, bead•i•est.** Small, round, and shining: *beady eyes.*

bea•gle (bē'gəl) *n.* A breed of small hound with long ears and a smooth coat with white, black, and tan markings.

beak (bēk) *n.* The hard, horny mouth of a bird; a bill.

beak•er (bē'kər) *n.* A cylindrical glass container with a pouring lip, used especially in laboratories.

beam (bēm) *n.* **1.** A long rigid piece of wood or metal used especially as a horizontal support in building. **2.** A stream of particles or waves, as of light, sound, or other radiation: *the beam of a flashlight; a laser beam.* **3.** One of the main horizontal supports of a building or ship. **4.** In a balance, the bar from which the weights are hung. —*v.* —*intr.* **1.** To give off light; shine: *The sun is beaming in the sky.* **2.** To smile broadly: *His face beamed with delight.* —*tr.* To emit or transmit (sthg.): *beam a TV program to Europe by satellite.*

bean (bēn) *n.* **1.a.** Any of various plants related to the pea, having seeds in pods that are usually long and narrow. **b.** The edible seed or pod of such a plant. **2.** A seed or pod similar to a bean: *a coffee bean; a vanilla bean.* —*tr.v.* To hit (sbdy.) on the head with a thrown object: *beaned with a baseball.* ◆ **full of beans.** *Slang.* **1.** Energetic; frisky: *The children were too full of beans to sit still.* **2.** Badly mistaken: *Don't believe him; he's full of beans.* **spill the beans.** *Informal.* To disclose a secret: *Don't spill the beans about the surprise party.*

bean sprouts *pl.n.* The tender shoots of certain bean plants, such as the soybean, used as food: *Do you want bean sprouts on your salad?*

bean•stalk (bēn'stôk') *n.* The stem of a bean plant.

bear[1] (bâr) *v.* **bore** (bôr), **borne** or **born** (bôrn), **bear•ing, bears.** —*tr.* **1.** To hold up or support (sthg. heavy): *The floor is able to bear the weight of heavy machinery.* **2.** To carry

bear

or transport (sbdy./sthg.): *The ships bearing cotton sailed to England.* **3.** To carry and tell (information): *bear good news.* **4.** To have responsibility for (sthg.): *We all shared in bearing the blame for our actions.* **5.** To behave (oneself) in a specified way: *Members of both teams bore themselves with pride.* **6.** To have (sthg.) in the heart or mind: *bear a grudge.* **7.** To show signs of (sthg.): *twins bearing a strong resemblance to each other.* **8.** To produce (sthg.): *Some trees bear fruit early in the spring.* **9.** To give birth to (sbdy./sthg.): *My grandmother bore seven children. That old dog has borne many pups.* **10.** To accept or put up with (sbdy./sthg.): *I can't bear his selfish attitude.* —*intr.* **1.** To produce fruit: *fruit trees that bear well.* **2.a.** To put pressure: *She bore so hard on the pencil that it broke.* **b.** To have and use influence: *bringing pressure to bear on companies that pollute.* **3.** To continue or turn in a given direction: *At the corner, bear right.* ♦ **bear down.** *intr.v.* **1.** To use or have heavy pressure: *Concern about water bears down heavily in times of no rain.* **2.** To work hard, make a special effort: *By bearing down, the workers were able to complete the job on time.* **bear down on. 1.** To affect (sbdy.) in a harmful way: *The large amount of work was bearing down on the entire department.* **2.** To move quickly toward (sbdy./sthg.): *The runners bore down on the finish line.* **bear on** or **upon.** *tr.v.* [insep.] To apply or have a connection to (sthg.): *How will the court's decision bear on future cases?* **bear out.** *tr.v.* [sep.] To prove (sbdy./sthg.) right: *The test results bear out our theory.* **bear up.** *intr.v.* To continue under difficulty or stress: *The patient bore up well during a long illness.* **bear with.** *tr.v.* [insep.] To be patient with (sbdy./sthg.): *Please bear with me while I find out where we are.*

Homonyms: bear (support, animal), **bare** (uncovered).

---

bear² (bâr) *n.* **1.** A large mammal with heavy fur, a very short tail, and a flat-footed walk. Bears usually eat both plants and other animals, especially insects. **2.** *Slang.* Something that is difficult or unpleasant: *That exam was a bear!* **3.** A person who sells stocks or other securities expecting their price to fall. —*adj.* Characterized by falling prices: *a bear market in stocks.* —**bear'ish** *adj.*

bear•a•ble (bâr'ə bəl) *adj.* Capable of being borne; tolerable: *Resting from time to time made the long hike bearable.* —**bear'a•bly** *adv.*

beard (bîrd) *n.* **1.** The hair on a man's chin, cheeks, and throat: *He looks younger since he shaved his beard.* **2.** A hairy growth on the face of certain mammals, as the chin tuft of a

goat. —*tr.v.* To face or defy (sbdy.) boldly: *He was so sure of himself, he bearded his opponents at their own meeting.*

bear•er (bâr'ər) *n.* **1.** A person who carries or supports sthg.: *a stretcher bearer; a message bearer.* **2.** A person who presents a check or other note for payment: *Checks direct a bank to pay the bearer a certain sum of money.*

bear•ing (bâr'ĭng) *n.* **1.** [C; U] The manner or way in which one carries oneself: *The judge has a dignified bearing.* **2.** [U] Relevance or relationship: *That issue has no bearing on my situation.* **3.** [C] A supporting part of a structure. **4.** [C] A mechanical part that supports a moving part, especially a turning shaft, and allows it to move with little friction: *a wheel bearing.* **5.** [C] *(usually plural).* The knowledge of one's position in relation to one's surroundings: *The hikers lost their bearings in the dark.*

beast (bēst) *n.* **1.** An animal other than a human being, especially a large four-footed animal: *the birds and the beasts of the jungle.* **2.** A cruel or brutal person.

beast•ly (bēst'lē) *adj.* **beast•li•er, beast•li•est. 1.** Relating to a beast; bestial. **2.** Unpleasant; disagreeable: *a beastly drive through heavy rain.* —*adv.* Chiefly British. To an extreme degree; very: *a beastly hot day.* —**beast'li•ness** *n.* [U]

beast of burden *n., pl.* **beasts of burden.** An animal, such as a horse, an ox, or a camel, used to carry loads or pull vehicles.

beat (bēt) *v.* **beat, beat•en** (bēt'n) or **beat, beat•ing, beats.** —*tr.* **1.** To strike or hit (sbdy./sthg.) repeatedly: *The baby beat the table with a spoon.* **2.** To produce sound by striking, hitting, or tapping (sthg.) repeatedly: *beat a drum.* **3.** To flap (sthg.) repeatedly: *Hummingbirds beat their wings very fast.* **4.** To mix (sthg.) rapidly with a utensil: *beat egg whites.* **5.** To defeat (sbdy.) as in a contest or battle: *We beat them 2 to 1 in the game.* **6.** To act ahead of or arrive before (sbdy./sthg.): *We beat you to the restaurant.* **7.** *Slang.* To baffle or perplex (sbdy.): *How the magician did that trick beats me.* **8.** *Informal.* To avoid or counter the effects of (sthg.): *Let's leave early to beat the traffic.* —*intr.* **1.** To pound forcefully and repeatedly; dash: *Huge waves beat against the pier.* **2.** To fall in torrents: *The rain beat down on the field.* **3.** To shine or glare intensely: *The summer sun beat down on the thirsty bikers.* **4.** To make a sound when struck: *The drums beat loudly.* **5.** To throb; pulsate: *My heart beat faster with excitement.* —*n.* **1.** A stroke or blow, especially one that makes a sound: *the beat of the drums in the parade.* **2.** A pulsation or throb: *the beat of your heart.* **3.** One of the succession of units that make up meter in music: *There are four beats in this measure.* **4.** An area regularly covered by a police officer, guard, or reporter. —*adj. Informal.* Tired; worn-out: *I'm really beat after a full day's work.* ◆ **beat around the bush.** To avoid a subject; delay in coming to the point: *I was beating around the bush because I didn't know what to say.* **beat it.** *Slang.* To leave hurriedly: *I think we should beat it before he comes home.* **beat up.** *tr.v.* [sep.] To hurt (sbdy.) physically: *He was beaten up badly in the fight.*

HOMONYMS: beat, beet (vegetable).

beat·en (bēt′n) *adj.* **1.** Mixed with a fork or other utensil: *beaten eggs.* **2.** Defeated: *a beaten army.* ◆ **off the beaten path.** Away from where people usually go: *They moved to a house off the beaten path because they like being alone.*

beat·er (bē′tər) *n.* A person or thing that beats, especially an instrument for beating: *Use an electric beater to mix bread dough.*

be·at·i·fy (bē ăt′ə fī′) *tr.v.* **be·at·i·fied, be·at·i·fy·ing, be·at·i·fies. 1.** To make (sbdy.) extremely happy. **2.** In the Roman Catholic Church, to declare (a deceased person) to be blessed and worthy of public veneration.

beat·ing (bē′tĭng) *n.* **1.** Punishment by hitting repeatedly: *The man was given a beating for stealing.* **2.** A defeat: *The defending champions gave our team a beating.* **3.** A throbbing or pulsation, as of the heart. ◆ **take a beating. 1.** To be hit very badly: *The boxer took a beating in the fight. The car took a beating on the rough roads.* **2.** To lose badly: *Our team took a beating in the championship.*

beat-up (bēt′ŭp′) *adj. Slang.* In bad condition; rundown: *a beat-up old car.*

beau (bō) *n., pl.* **beaus** or **beaux** (bōz). An outdated word for the boyfriend of a woman or girl.

HOMONYMS: beau, bow (weapon to shoot arrows).

beaut (byōot) *n. Slang.* Something outstanding of its kind: *I saw his new car; it's a beaut!*

HOMONYMS: beaut, butte (hill).

beau·ti·cian (byōo tĭsh′ən) *n.* A person who is skilled in the cosmetic services offered by a beauty parlor.

beau·ti·ful (byōo′tə fəl) *adj.* Showing or having beauty; pleasing to the senses or the mind: *beautiful scenery; beautiful music.* —**beau′ti·ful·ly** *adv.*

beau·ti·fy (byōo′tə fī′) *tr.v.* **beau·ti·fied, beau·ti·fy·ing, beau·ti·fies.** To make

(sthg.) beautiful: *Green parks beautify the city.* —**beau′ti·fi·ca′tion** (byōo′tə fĭ-kā′shən) *n.* [U] —**beau′ti·fi′er** *n.*

beau·ty (byōo′tē) *n., pl.* **beau·ties. 1.** [U] A pleasing quality, especially with regard to form, that delights the senses and appeals to the mind: *the beauty of the snowcapped mountains.* **2.** [C] A person or thing that is beautiful: *Modern supermodels are generally thought of as great beauties.* **3.** [U] A feature that is good or effective: *The beauty of this scheme is that we come out ahead either way.*

beauty parlor *n.* A business offering hair styling, manicures, and other cosmetic services, especially for women.

beauty salon *n.* A beauty parlor.

beauty shop *n.* A beauty parlor.

beaux (bōz) *n.* A plural of **beau.**

bea·ver (bē′vər) *n.*
1. [C] A mammal with thick fur, a flat broad tail, and large strong front teeth. Beavers live in lakes and streams and cut down trees with their teeth to build dams and lodges in the water. **2.** [U]

beaver

The fur of a beaver. ◆ **eager beaver.** An enthusiastic and energetic person: *His boss likes him because he is an eager beaver.*

be·came (bĭ kām′) *v.* Past tense of **become.**

be·cause (bĭ kôz′ *or* bĭ kŭz′) *conj.* For the reason that; since: *The room is uncomfortable because it is too hot.*

because of *prep.* On account of; by reason of: *I stayed home because of illness.*

beck (bĕk) *n.* A gesture of beckoning. ◆ **at (one's) beck and call.** Willing and obedient; ready to perform a service: *The staff of the hotel are generally at the beck and call of the guests.*

beck·on (bĕk′ən) *v.* —*tr.* **1.** To signal (sbdy.) to come, as by nodding or waving: *The principal beckoned us to her office.* **2.** To attract (sbdy.) because of an inviting appearance: *The lake beckoned me to dive in and cool off.* —*intr.* **1.** To signal to come: *The guide beckoned at the mouth of the cave.* **2.** To attract or entice: *Adventure beckoned down every road.*

be·come (bĭ kŭm′) *v.* **be·came** (bĭ kām′), **be·come, be·com·ing, be·comes.** —*intr.* To grow or come to be: *As winter approaches the temperature becomes colder.* —*tr.* **1.** To be appropriate or suitable to (sbdy./sthg.): *It becomes a judge to act with dignity.* **2.** To look good on or cause (sbdy.) to look good: *The new coat becomes you.* ◆ **what** or **what**

ever became of. Used to ask what happened to a person or thing: *What ever became of your friend who moved away?*

be•com•ing (bĭ kŭm′ĭng) *adj.* **1.** Appropriate; suitable: *a helpful and cheerful manner becoming to a nurse.* **2.** Pleasing or attractive to look at: *the baby's becoming smile; a becoming new hairstyle.* —**be•com′ing•ly** *adv.*

bed (bĕd) *n.* **1.a.** A piece of furniture for resting and sleeping, consisting usually of a flat rectangular frame and a mattress resting on springs. **b.** A mattress: *a feather bed.* **c.** A mattress and bedclothes: *make up a bed on the floor.* **2.a.** A small plot for cultivating or growing things: *a bed of flowers.* **b.** A similar plot on the bottom of a body of water: *an oyster bed.* **3.** The bottom of a body of water: *a stream bed; the ocean bed.* **4.** A part that is under sthg. and supports it: *Underneath the brick path is a bed of sand.* **5.** A mass of rock that extends under a large area and is bounded by different material: *a bed of coal.* —*tr.v.* **bed•ded, bed•ding, beds. 1.** To provide (sbdy.) with a bed or a place to sleep: *We bedded the guests in the living room.* **2.** To set or plant (sthg.) in a bed of soil: *bed tulip bulbs before the ground freezes.* ♦ **a bed of roses.** An easy situation: *Life is not a bed of roses.* **get up on the wrong side of the bed.** To be in a bad mood for no specific reason: *He must have gotten up on the wrong side of the bed; he's been grumpy all day.* **make (one's) bed.** To arrange the sheets and blankets neatly on a bed: *His mother told him to make his bed every morning.* **put to bed.** To take or send a child to bed: *The child was sick, so his father put him to bed.*

bed-and-break•fast (bĕd′n brĕk′fəst) *n.* A private residence that offers overnight lodging and breakfast as part of the charge: *We decided to stay at a bed-and-breakfast for the night.*

bed•clothes (bĕd′klōz′ *or* bĕd′klōthz′) *pl.n.* Coverings, such as sheets and blankets, used on a bed.

bed•ding (bĕd′ĭng) *n.* [U] **1.** Sheets, blankets, and mattresses for beds. **2.** Material, such as straw or hay, for animals to sleep on: *arrange bedding for the horses.*

bed•lam (bĕd′ləm) *n.* [U] A place or situation of confusion, noise, or disorder: *the bedlam of a one-day sale in the department store.*

Bed•ou•in (bĕd′ōō ĭn *or* bĕd′wĭn) *n., pl.* **Bedouin** or **Bed•ou•ins.** A member of a nomadic people of North African, Arabian, and Syrian deserts.

bed•pan (bĕd′păn′) *n.* A container used as a toilet by a person who has to stay in bed.

be•drag•gled (bĭ drăg′əld) *adj.* Very wet or messy: *bedraggled clothes; a bedraggled puppy pulled from a stream.*

bed•rid•den (bĕd′rĭd′n) *adj.* Having to stay in bed because of sickness or weakness: *He was bedridden for the last two months of his life.*

bed•rock (bĕd′rŏk′) *n.* [U] **1.** The solid rock that lies beneath the soil and other loose material on the surface of the earth. **2.** The lowest or bottom level: *Sales hit bedrock in the slow summer months.* **3.** The basis or foundation: *Making products of high quality is the bedrock of manufacturing.*

bed•roll (bĕd′rōl′) *n.* Blankets or a sleeping bag rolled up to be carried by a camper or a person who sleeps outdoors.

bed•room (bĕd′rōōm *or* bĕd′rŏŏm′) *n.* A room in which to sleep.

bed•side (bĕd′sīd′) *n.* The place along the side of a bed: *The nurse stood at the patient's bedside.* —*adj.* Near a bed: *a bedside table; a bedside conversation.*

bed•spread (bĕd′sprĕd′) *n.* A covering for a bed.

bed•time (bĕd′tīm′) *n.* [C; U] The time when a person usually goes to bed: *I get very tired when I'm up past my bedtime.*

bee[1] (bē) *n.* A winged, often stinging insect that has a hairy body and gathers pollen and nectar from flowers: *Some bees, such as the honeybee, live in colonies.* ♦ **a bee in (one's) bonnet.** An idea that persistently occupies one's mind; a notion: *My sister has a bee in her bonnet about buying a new car.*

HOMONYMS: bee (insect, gathering), **be** (exist).

bee[2] (bē) *n.* A gathering where people work together or compete against one another: *a quilting bee; a spelling bee.*

beech (bēch) *n.* **1.** [C] A tree with smooth gray bark, small edible nuts, and strong heavy wood. **2.** [U] The wood of such a tree.

HOMONYMS: beech, beach (area of sand).

beef (bēf) *n.* **1.** [U] The flesh of a full-grown steer, bull, ox, or cow, used as meat. **2.** [C] *Slang.* A complaint: *What is your beef now?* —*intr.v. Slang.* To complain: *He beefs every time he has to pay his share of the rent.* ♦ **beef up.** *tr.v.* [sep.] *Informal.* To make (sthg.) greater or stronger: *Police are beefing up efforts to combat crime.*

beef•y (bē′fē) *adj.* **beef•i•er, beef•i•est.** Heavy, strong, and muscular; brawny: *a beefy wrestler.*

bee•hive (bē′hīv′) *n.* **1.** A hive for bees. **2.** A very busy place: *The bus terminal is always a beehive of activity.*

bee•keep•er (bē′kē′pər) *n.* A person who keeps bees.

bee•line (bē′līn′) *n.* The fastest and most direct way, as one that might be taken by a bee going to its hive: *At noontime everybody made a beeline for the lunchroom.*

been (bĭn) v. Past participle of **be**.

---

beep (bēp) n. A short sound, as from an automobile's horn or a radio transmitter. —v. —intr. To make a beep: *The transmitter beeped steadily.* —tr. To cause (sthg.) to make a beep: *The drivers beeped their horns in the traffic jam.*

beep•er (bē'pər) n. A small electronic device that emits a signal when the person carrying it is being paged: *Many doctors carry beepers.*

beer (bîr) n. [C; U] **1.** An alcoholic beverage brewed from malt and hops. **2.** A drink such as root beer or birch beer.

bees•wax (bēz'wăks') n. [U] The yellowish or brownish wax produced by honeybees for making their honeycombs. ♦ **none of (one's) beeswax.** Used to tell sbdy. that some information is private: *It's none of his beeswax how much I earn.*

beet (bēt) n. **1.** A leafy plant with a thick, rounded, dark red root eaten as a vegetable. **2.** A form of this plant with a large whitish root from which sugar is made; the sugar beet.

---

bee•tle (bēt'l) n. Any of numerous insects that have biting mouthparts and hind wings folded and hidden under hard glossy front wings when not flying: *Many beetles are harmful to plants.*

be•fall (bĭ fôl') tr.v. **be•fell** (bĭ fĕl'), **be•fall•en** (bĭ fô'lən), **be•fall•ing, be•falls.** *Formal.* To happen to (sbdy.): *Many serious accidents befell the explorers.*

be•fit (bĭ fĭt') tr.v. **be•fit•ted, be•fit•ting, be•fits.** *Formal.* To be suitable to or appropriate for (sbdy./sthg.): *He wore a tuxedo befitting the formal occasion.*

be•fore (bĭ fôr') adv. **1.** Earlier in time: *I told you about this before.* **2.** In front; ahead: *The people who went before were turned away.* —prep. **1.** Previous to; earlier than: *They got there before me.* **2.** In front of: *Eat what's put before you.* **3.** Waiting for; awaiting: *You've got a great future before you.* **4.a.** Under the consideration of: *The case is now before the court.* **b.** Into or in the presence of: *Each prisoner was brought before the judge.* **5.** Instead of or in higher esteem than: *I'd take a hamburger before a hot dog any day.* —conj. **1.** In advance of the time when: *See me before you leave.* **2.** Sooner than; rather than: *I'd die before I'd give in.*

be•fore•hand (bĭ fôr'hănd') adv. & adj. Ahead of time: *The class starts at 9 o'clock, but I always get there beforehand.*

be•foul (bĭ foul') tr.v. *Formal.* To make (sthg.) dirty; soil: *Smokestacks befouled the air.*

be•friend (bĭ frĕnd') tr.v. *Formal.* To act as a friend to (sbdy.); assist: *A perfect stranger befriended the lost tourists.*

be•fud•dle (bĭ fŭd'l) tr.v. **be•fud•dled, be•fud•dling, be•fud•dles.** *Formal.* To confuse (sbdy.); perplex: *The problem befuddled even the experts.*

beg (bĕg) v. **begged, beg•ging, begs.** —tr. **1.** To ask for (sthg.) as charity: *begged money while sitting in a doorway.* **2.** To ask for (sthg.) humbly: *I beg your pardon.* **3.** To ask of (sbdy.): *We begged her for help.* —intr. **1.** To ask as help or charity. **2.** To ask earnestly; plead: *beg for another chance.* ♦ **beg off.** tr.v. [insep.] To ask to be excused from (sthg.): *We had to beg off the invitation to the party.* **beg to differ.** To disagree in a polite way: *I beg to differ; he did not arrive late.* **go begging.** To be available; be unwanted: *The last few doughnuts are going begging—won't you take one?*

be•gan (bĭ găn') v. Past tense of **begin**.

beg•gar (bĕg'ər) n. A person who begs as a means of living.

be•gin (bĭ gĭn') v. **be•gan** (bĭ găn'), **be•gun** (bĭ gŭn'), **be•gin•ning, be•gins.** —intr. **1.** To take the first step in doing sthg.; start; commence: *We began with the kitchen and cleaned the whole house.* **2.** To come into being; originate: *Education begins at home.* **3.** To accomplish in the least way; come near: *The little bit of paint won't begin to cover the ceiling.* —tr. **1.** To start doing (sthg.): *If we begin our work now we'll have time to enjoy ourselves later.* **2.** To bring (sthg.) into being; originate: *The owner's grandfather began the newspaper many years ago.* **3.** To come first in (sthg.): *The letter A begins the alphabet.*

SYNONYMS: begin, commence, start, embark. These verbs mean to take the first step or to get working or moving. **Begin** is the most general word: *The play begins at eight o'clock.* **Commence** is a more formal word than **begin:** *Our meetings always commence with a call to order.* **Start** often means to begin from a standstill: *The train started as soon as we sat down.* **Embark** means to set out on a venture or journey: *After getting her teaching certificate, My sister will embark on a new career.* **ANTONYM: end.**

---

be•gin•ner (bĭ gĭn'ər) n. A person who is just starting to learn or do sthg.; a novice: *A beginner at the piano plays simple pieces.*

be•gin•ning (bĭ gĭn'ĭng) n. [C; U] **1.** The act

---

of bringing or being brought into existence; a start: *The Declaration of Independence was the beginning of the nation.* **2.** The time or point when sthg. begins or is begun: *the beginning of the world.* **3.** The place where sthg. begins or is begun; an initial section, division, or part: *at the beginning of the play.* **4.a.** A source or an origin: *An early fort served as the beginning of the city of Chicago.* **b.** (*usually plural*). An early phase or rudimentary period: *the beginnings of life on Earth.*

be•grudge (bǐ grŭj') *tr.v.* **be•grudged, be•grudg•ing, be•grudg•es. 1.** To envy (sbdy.) for the possession or enjoyment of sthg.: *A generous person does not begrudge others their good fortune.* **2.** To give (sthg.) with reluctance: *He begrudged every penny spent on the repairs.* **—be•grudg′ing•ly** *adv.*

be•guile (bǐ gīl') *tr.v.* **be•guiled, be•guil• ing, be•guiles.** *Formal.* **1.** To deceive (sbdy.); trick: *The salesman beguiled me into buying more than I wanted.* **2.** To amuse (sbdy.); delight: *She beguiled us with song.*

be•gun (bǐ gŭn') *v.* Past participle of **begin.**

be•half (bǐ hǎf') *n.* [U] Interest; benefit: *On whose behalf did they act?* ◆ **in behalf of.** For the benefit of; in the interest of: *We raised money in behalf of the Red Cross.* **on behalf of.** As the agent of; on the part of: *The principal thanked the parents for their help on behalf of the entire teaching staff.*

be•have (bǐ hāv') *v.* **be•haved, be•hav•ing, be•haves. —***intr.* **1.** To act or function in a certain way: *The car behaves well on rough roads.* **2.** To conduct oneself in a specified way: *I'm sorry I behaved badly.* **—***tr.* **1.** To conduct (oneself) properly: *We behaved ourselves during the long boring lecture.* **2.** To conduct (oneself) in a specified way: *She behaved herself with dignity at the wedding.*

be•hav•ior (bǐ hāv′yər) *n.* **1.** [U] The way in which a person behaves; conduct: *on one's best behavior.* **2.** [C; U] The actions or reactions of persons or things under specific conditions: *the behavior of matter at extremely low temperatures; strange animal behaviors.* **—be• hav′ior•al** *adj.***—be•hav′ior•al•ly** *adv.*

be•hav•iour (bǐ hāv′yər) *n. Chiefly British.* Variant of **behavior.**

be•head (bǐ hĕd') *tr.v.* To cut off the head of (sbdy.); decapitate.

be•held (bǐ hĕld') *v.* Past tense and past participle of **behold.**

be•he•moth (bǐ hē′məth *or* bē′ə məth) *n.* **1.** A huge animal. **2.** Something enormous in size: *This problem is a behemoth.*

be•hind (bǐ hīnd') *adv.* **1.** In a place or condition that has been passed or left: *I left my gloves behind.* **2.** In, to, or toward the rear: *They did not see me because I was walking behind.* **3.** Below the standard or acceptable level: *The sick student fell behind in the class.*

—*prep.* **1.** At the back or in the rear of: *the shed behind the barn.* **2.** On the other side of: *The broom is behind the door.* **3.** In a place or time that has been passed or left by: *Their worries are behind them.* **4.** In a state less advanced than: *Many nations are behind the United States in space technology.* **5.** In the background of; underlying: *Behind the theory there is much research and observation.* **6.** In support of: *Most of the people are behind the President.* **—***n. Informal.* The buttocks or backside: *The child fell on his behind.*

be•hold (bǐ hōld') *tr.v.* **be•held** (bǐ hĕld'), **be•hold•ing, be•holds.** *Formal.* To gaze upon (sbdy./sthg.); look at; see: *In a tomb the treasure hunters beheld a rich store of gold and jewels.* **—be•hold′er** *n.*

be•hold•en (bǐ hōl′dən) *adj.* Indebted: *We were beholden to our neighbors for shelter in the storm.*

be•hoove (bǐ hōōv') *tr.v.* **be•hooved, be• hoov•ing, be•hooves.** *Formal.* To be necessary or proper for (sbdy. to do sthg.): *It behooves you to study for the test.*

beige (bāzh) *n.* [U] A light grayish or yellowish brown color: *Beige is a popular color for trousers.* **—***adj.* Light grayish or yellowish brown.

be•ing (bē′ĭng) *n.* **1.** [U] The state or quality of existing; existence: *Rock 'n' roll music came into being in the 1950s.* **2.** [C] A living organism, especially a person: *a human being.*

be•jew•eled (bǐ jōō′əld) *adj.* Decorated with jewels: *a bejeweled gown.*

be•la•bor (bǐ lā′bər) *tr.v.* **1.** To go over (sthg.) repeatedly; harp on: *The audience got bored as the politician belabored the point.* **2.** To attack (sbdy./sthg.) verbally: *The lawyer belabored the witness's testimony.*

be•lat•ed (bǐ lā′tĭd) *adj.* Tardy; too late: *belated birthday wishes.* **—be•lat′ed•ly** *adv.*

belch (bĕlch) *v.* **—***intr.* **1.** To expel gas noisily from the stomach through the mouth; burp: *The child belched loudly after drinking too much soda.* **2.** To gush out; pour out: *smoke belching from the truck's exhaust.* **—***tr.* To send out or eject (smoke or flames) violently: *The burning house belched smoke from its windows.* **—***n.* The act of belching: *The old car stopped with a belch of smoke.*

be•lea•guer (bǐ lē′gər) *tr.v. Formal.* **1.** To surround (sbdy./sthg.) with troops; besiege: *The king's troops beleaguered the city until the rebels surrendered.* **2.** To persecute (sbdy./sthg.) constantly, as by threats or demands; harass: *During the power outage the electric company was beleaguered by its customers. The hounds beleaguered the fox.*

bel•fry (bĕl′frē) *n., pl.* **bel•fries.** A tower or steeple in which one or more bells are hung.

be•lie (bǐ lī') *tr.v.* **be•lied, be•ly•ing, be• lies.** *Formal.* **1.** To give a wrong or false idea

B

of (sthg.): *A cheerful greeting belied the clerk's grumpy mood.* **2.** To be inconsistent with (sthg.); contradict: *The store's deceitful practices belied its good reputation.*

be·lief (bĭ lēf′) *n.* **1.** [U] An idea or condition that one accepts as true; conviction: *His explanation of what happened defies belief.* **2.** [U] The mental act or condition of placing trust or confidence in sbdy.: *My belief in you is as strong as ever.* **3.** [C] Something believed or accepted as true, especially by a group of people: *We sometimes take our beliefs for granted until we meet someone who does not share them.*

be·lieve (bĭ lēv′) *v.* **be·lieved, be·liev·ing, be·lieves.** —*tr.* **1.** To accept (sthg.) as true or real: *Everyone believes the earth is round.* **2.** To credit (sbdy.) with trust; trust: *I believe you.* **3.** To expect or suppose (sthg.); think: *I believe it will snow tomorrow.* —*intr.* **1.** To have faith, trust, or confidence: *We believe in getting plenty of sleep.* **2.** To have an opinion; think: *They have already left, I believe.* —**be·liev′a·ble** *adj.* —**be·liev′er** *adj.*

be·lit·tle (bĭ lĭt′l) *tr.v.* **be·lit·tled, be·lit·tling, be·lit·tles.** To represent or speak of (sbdy./sthg.) as small or unimportant: *Don't belittle their efforts just because they are children.*

bell (bĕl) *n.* A hollow metal instrument, usually shaped like a cup, that makes a metallic tone when struck. —*v.* —*tr.* To put a bell on (sthg.): *bell a cat that lives outdoors.* —*intr.* To flare like a bell: *pants that bell below the knee.*

Homonyms: bell, belle (girl or woman).

bell-bot·tom (bĕl′bŏt′ əm) *adj.* Having legs that flare out at the bottom: *bell-bottom pants.*
bell-bot·toms (bĕl′bŏt′ əmz) *pl.n.* Pants that flare out at the bottom.
bell·boy (bĕl′boi′) *n.* A bellhop.
belle (bĕl) *n.* A very attractive and popular girl or woman, especially the most attractive one of a group: *the belle of the ball.*

Homonyms: belle, bell (musical instrument).

bell·hop (bĕl′hŏp′) *n.* A person employed by a hotel to carry luggage, run errands, and do other chores.
bel·lig·er·ence (bə lĭj′ ər əns) *n.* [U] A warlike or hostile attitude: *The dictator's troop movement showed his belligerence.*
bel·lig·er·en·cy (bə lĭj′ ər ən sē) *n.* [U] **1.** The state of being at war. **2.** Belligerence.
bel·lig·er·ent (bə lĭj′ ər ənt) *adj.* Inclined to fight; hostile: *a belligerent bully.* —*n.* A person, group, or nation engaged in war or a con-

flict: *The United States and Germany were belligerents during World War II.* —**bel·lig′- er·ent·ly** *adv.*

bel·low (bĕl′ō) *v.* —*intr.* To shout or roar in a deep loud voice as a bull does: *I bellowed when I slammed my thumb with a hammer.* —*tr.* To utter (sthg.) in a loud voice: *The crowd bellowed its disapproval of the umpire's call.* —*n.* A loud sound like that made by a bull or certain other large animals: *bellows of outrage.*
bel·lows (bĕl′ōz *or* bĕl′əz) *pl.n. (used with a singular or plural verb).* A device for pumping or blowing air into sthg.: *stoked the fire using bellows.*
bel·ly (bĕl′ē) *n., pl.* **bel·lies.** **1.** In human beings and other mammals, the front part of the body below the chest; the abdomen. **2.** The stomach. **3.** A part that bulges or protrudes: *the belly of a sail.* ♦ **go belly up.** *Informal.* To fail: *The store went belly up when sales stayed low for a long time.*
bel·ly·ache (bĕl′ē āk′) *n.* A pain in the stomach or abdomen. —*intr.v.* **bel·ly·ached, bel·ly·ach·ing, bel·ly·aches.** *Slang.* To grumble or complain, especially in a whining way: *Stop bellyaching about how much work you have to do.* —**bel′ly·ach′er** *n.*
bel·ly·but·ton (bĕl′ē bŭt′n) *n. Informal.* The navel.
be·long (bĭ lông′ *or* bĭ lŏng′) *intr.v.* **1.a.** To be proper or suitable: *A napkin belongs at every place setting.* **b.** To be in proper or suitable place: *The suit belongs in the closet.* **2.** To be owned as property: *This watch belonged to my mother.* **3.** To be a member of a group: *Many students belong to that club.*
be·long·ings (bĭ lông′ĭngz *or* bĭ lŏng′ĭngz) *pl.n.* The things that belong to sbdy.; possessions: *We took all of our belongings when we moved out of state.*
be·lov·ed (bĭ lŭv′ĭd *or* bĭ lŭvd′) *adj.* Dearly loved: *the parents' beloved children.* —*n.* A person who is dearly loved.
be·low (bĭ lō′) *adv.* **1.** In a lower place: *They paused on the bridge to admire the river below.* **2.** On or to a lower floor: *The boxes were put on a shelf below.* **3.** Further down, as along a slope or stream: *There is a cabin in the valley below.* **4.** Following or farther down on a page: *A chart is printed below with an explanation.* —*prep.* **1.** Underneath; beneath: *We stood at the window watching the street below us.* **2.** Lower than, as in degree or rank: *temperatures below zero.*
belt (bĕlt) *n.* **1.** A band of leather, cloth, or plastic worn around the waist. **2.** A broad strip or band: *a belt of trees along the highway.* **3.** A seat belt. **4.** A band that passes over two or more wheels or pulleys to transmit motion from one to another or to convey

objects: *A belt connects the car motor to the fan.* **5.** *Slang.* A powerful blow: *a belt to the head from a falling branch.* **6.** *Slang.* A drink of hard liquor: *a belt of whiskey.* —*tr.v.* **1.** To encircle (sthg.) with or as if with a belt: *The equator belts the earth.* **2.** To fasten (sthg.) with a belt: *The hikers belted canteens around their waists.* **3.** To strike (sthg.); hit: *He belted three home runs in one game.* ♦ **below the belt.** Not according to the rules; unfair: *The candidate's false accusations were below the belt.* **belt out.** *tr.v.* [sep.] *Slang.* To sing (sthg.) loudly: *The audience belted out a song.* **tighten (one's) belt.** To become thrifty and frugal: *We can save money if we tighten our belts.*

be•moan (bǐ mōn') *tr.v. Formal.* To mourn over (sbdy./sthg.); grieve for: *He bemoaned his fate.*

bench (běnch) *n.* **1.** A long seat for two or more persons: *a picnic bench in the park.* **2.** A sturdy table on which a carpenter or other skilled person works. **3.** The seat for judges in a courtroom. **4.** The office or position of a judge: *appointed to the bench.* **5.** The judge or judges on a court: *put before the bench.* **6.** The place where the members of an athletic team sit when they are not playing. —*tr.v.* To remove or keep (a player) from a game: *The coach benched a player because of injuries.*

bench•mark (běnch'märk') *n.* **1.** A standard by which sthg. can be measured or judged: *use this temperature as a benchmark.* **2.** A surveyor's mark made on some stationary object, such as a boulder, used as a reference point for measurement.

bend (běnd) *v.* **bent** (běnt), **bend•ing, bends.** —*tr.* **1.** To make (sthg.) curved or crooked: *Bend the wire around the post. Bend light through a prism.* **2.** To turn or direct (sthg.): *bend one's steps toward home.* **3.** To force (sbdy.) to yield; subdue: *He bent his employees to his will.* **4.** To change (sthg.) deceptively; distort: *You must not bend the facts to fit a conclusion.* —*intr.* **1.** To become curved or crooked: *The trees bent in the wind.* **2.** To incline the body; stoop: *I bent over to pick up the ball.* **3.** To curve away from a straight line: *The road bends to the right at the bridge.* **4.** To submit; yield: *bend to someone's wishes.* —*n.* A turn, curve, or bent part: *a bend in the river.* ♦ **bend over backward.** To try harder than is required to please sbdy.: *The teacher bent over backward to help the new student.*

be•neath (bǐ nēth') *adv.* In a lower place; below: *From the top of the hill we looked down at the valley beneath.* —*prep.* **1.** Lower than; below: *Beneath the tall elm trees they planted flowers.* **2.** Covered or concealed by: *Most oil lies beneath the ground.* **3.** Under the force, control, or influence of: *The supervisor has six workers beneath her.* **4.** Unworthy of: *Lying is beneath me.*

ben•e•dic•tion (běn'ǐ dǐk'shən) *n.* A blessing, especially one recited at the end of a religious service.

ben•e•fac•tor (běn'ə fǎk'tər) *n.* A person who gives financial or other aid for worthwhile purposes: *An unknown benefactor paid her tuition.*

ben•e•fi•cial (běn'ə fǐsh'əl) *adj.* Bringing benefit; helpful: *Many bacteria are beneficial to human life.* —**ben'e•fi'cial•ly** *adv.*

ben•e•fi•ci•ar•y (běn'ə fǐsh'ē ěr'ē *or* běn'-ə fǐsh'ə rē) *n., pl.* **ben•e•fi•ci•ar•ies. 1.** A person who receives benefit from sthg.: *We are all beneficiaries of the large new library.* **2.** A person who receives money or property from an insurance policy or a will: *She was named as her father's beneficiary.*

ben•e•fit (běn'ə fǐt) *n.* **1.** [C; U] Something that is of help; an advantage: *The lecture was of great benefit to the students.* **2.** [C] A payment provided by a salary agreement, an insurance policy, or a public assistance program: *Her new job's benefits include three weeks of paid vacation.* **3.** [C] A social event held to raise money for a cause. —*v.* —*tr.* To be helpful or beneficial to (sbdy./sthg.): *The clean-air program will benefit the environment.* —*intr.* To receive help; profit: *You can benefit from studying with your classmates.* ♦ **benefit of the doubt.** A favorable judgment made when complete information is not available: *We gave her the benefit of the doubt because she had never lied before.*

be•nev•o•lence (bə něv'ə ləns) *n.* [U] **1.** A desire to do sthg. good; goodwill: *We donated money out of benevolence.* **2.** A generous act: *We appreciate your benevolence.*

be•nev•o•lent (bə něv'ə lənt) *adj.* Characterized by doing good; kindly: *a benevolent king; a benevolent attitude.* —**be•nev'o•lent•ly** *adv.*

be•nign (bǐ nīn') *adj.* **1.** Kind; gentle: *a benign face with a warm smile.* **2.** Mild; favorable: *the benign climate of the tropics.* **3.** Not seriously harmful or malignant: *a benign tumor.*

bent (běnt) *v.* Past tense and past participle of **bend.** —*adj.* **1.** Curved or crooked: *a bent nail.* **2.** [on] Resolved; determined: *a runner bent on becoming a champion.* —*n.* A tendency or an inclination: *a strong bent for studying science.* ♦ **bent out of shape.** *Informal.* Angry: *He got bent out of shape when he found out he had to work on a holiday.*

be•queath (bǐ kwēth' *or* bǐ kwēth') *tr.v. Formal.* **1.** To leave or give (property) by will: *He bequeathed the house to his grandson.* **2.** To pass on or hand down (sthg.) to sbdy.: *One generation bequeaths its knowledge to the next.*

be•quest (bǐ kwěst') *n.* **1.** The act of bequeathing: *From her bequest, he inherited great wealth.* **2.** Something that is bequeathed in a will: *a bequest of $1,000.*

be•rate (bĭ rāt′) *tr.v.* **be•rat•ed, be•rat•ing, be•rates.** To scold (sbdy.) severely: *The child was berated for spilling his milk.*

be•reave (bĭ rēv′) *tr.v.* **be•reaved** or **be•reft** (bĭ rĕft′), **be•reav•ing, be•reaves.** To leave (sbdy.) alone and sad, especially by death: *The woman was bereaved by the death of her husband.* —**be•reave′ment** *n.* [U]

be•reft (bĭ rĕft′) *v.* A past tense and a past participle of **bereave.** —*adj. Formal.* Deprived of sthg.: *an act that left him bereft of dignity.*

be•ret (bə rā′) *n.* A round, soft cap of wool or felt without a brim.

berm (bûrm) *n.* A bank of earth, often placed against the wall of a building to provide protection or insulation.

Ber•mu•da shorts (bər myōō′də) *pl.n.* Shorts that end slightly above the knees.

ber•ry (bĕr′ē) *n., pl.* **ber•ries.** A usually small juicy fruit with many seeds in fleshy pulp: *We picked wild berries.*

HOMONYMS: berry, bury (cover with earth).

---

ber•serk (bər sûrk′ *or* bər zûrk′) *adj. & adv.* In or into a crazed or violent frenzy: *He went berserk and started smashing windows.*

berth (bûrth) *n.* **1.** A built-in bed or bunk in a ship or train. **2.** A space at a wharf for a ship to dock or anchor. **3.** A job or position: *He hopes to earn a berth on the U.S. Olympic Team.*

HOMONYMS: berth, birth (act of being born).

---

ber•yl (bĕr′əl) *n.* A transparent to translucent mineral of varied colors. Transparent beryls, such as emeralds and aquamarines, are valued as gems.

be•seech (bĭ sēch′) *tr.v. Formal.* To ask (sbdy.) earnestly; implore: *They beseeched the authorities for help after the flood.* —**be•seech′ing•ly** *adv.*

be•set (bĭ sĕt′) *tr.v.* **be•set, be•set•ting, be•sets.** *Formal.* **1.** To trouble (sbdy.) persistently; harass: *He was beset by doubts about the right course to follow.* **2.** To attack (sbdy./sthg.) from all sides: *Enemy troops beset the fort.* **3.** To hem (sbdy./sthg.) in; surround: *Rising floodwaters beset the town.*

be•side (bĭ sīd′) *prep.* **1.** At the side of; next to: *The cat sat down beside me.* **2.** In comparison with: *The movie version is quite short beside the book.* **3.** Not relevant to: *a remark that was beside the point.* ♦ **beside (oneself).** Extremely excited or emotional: *The winners were beside themselves with joy.*

be•sides (bĭ sīdz′) *adv.* In addition; also: *We had dinner and a late-night snack besides.* —*prep.* In addition to: *Dentists do other*

things besides drilling cavities. —SEE NOTE at **together.**

SYNONYMS: besides, too, also, likewise, furthermore. These adverbs mean in addition to sthg. else. **Besides** often introduces sthg. that reinforces what has gone before it: *We don't feel like cooking; besides, there is no food in the house.* **Too** is the most casual, used in everyday speech: *If you're going to the library today, I'd like to go too.* **Also** is more formal than **too**: *My brother is usually very friendly, but he is also capable of holding a grudge.* **Likewise** is even more formal: *Their parents were likewise attending the ceremony.* **Furthermore** often stresses the clause following it as more important than the clause before it: *I don't want you to go to that place; furthermore, I forbid it.*

---

be•siege (bĭ sēj′) *tr.v.* **be•sieged, be•sieg•ing, be•sieg•es. 1.** To surround and blockade (sthg.) in order to capture: *The king's troops besieged the city until it surrendered.* **2.** To crowd around (sbdy./sthg.) and hem in: *A crowd of fans besieged the movie star.* **3.** To harass (sbdy.), as with requests: *The reporters besieged the police for information.* —**be•sieg′er** *n.*

be•smirch (bĭ smûrch′) *tr.v. Formal.* To ruin (sthg.); stain: *besmirch someone's good name by repeating slanderous remarks.*

best (bĕst) *adj.* Superlative of **good, well².** **1.** Surpassing all others in excellence: *the best singer in the choir.* **2.** Most satisfactory, suitable, or useful: *the best place to dig a well.* **3.** Largest or greatest: *We talked for the best part of the journey.* —*adv.* Superlative of **well². 1.** In the most excellent way: *Which of the three jackets fits best?* **2.** To the greatest degree or extent; most: *What do you like to eat best?* —*n.* [U] **1.** A person or thing that surpasses all others: *That skier is surely the best in the race.* **2.** The superior part or value: *The best is yet to come.* **3.** One's greatest effort or appearance: *do your best; look your best.* **4.** One's nicest clothing: *She put on her best and went to the dance.* **5.** One's warmest wishes or regards: *Give them my best.* —*tr.v.* To do better than (sbdy.); defeat: *besting their rivals in every game.* ♦ **at best. 1.** Viewed most favorably; at the most: *There were 20 people in the theater at best.* **2.** Under the most favorable conditions: *This car has a top speed of 40 miles per hour at best.* **for the best.** Having a positive or preferable result in the end: *Although we were sorry to miss the movie, it turned out for the best because we talked to our friends instead.* **get** or **have the best of.** To outdo or outwit (sbdy.); defeat: *Nobody's ever gotten the best of me at checkers.*

---

bes·tial (bĕs′chəl *or* bēs′chəl) *adj.* **1.** Characteristic of an animal. **2.** Without reason or intelligence. **3.** Brutal; cruel. —**bes′ti·al′i·ty** *n.* [C; U] —**bes′tial·ly** *adv.*

best man *n.* The chief attendant of the bridegroom at a wedding.

be·stow (bĭ stō′) *tr.v.* [*on*] *Formal.* To give or present (sthg.), especially as a gift or an honor: *bestowed awards on the best actors and plays each season.*

best·sell·er (bĕst′sĕl′ər) *n.* A product, such as a book, that sells a large number of copies: *reading the latest bestseller.*

best-sell·ing (bĕst′sĕl′ ĭng) *adj.* Selling in the largest numbers at a specific time: *a best-selling novel.*

bet (bĕt) *n.* **1.** An agreement, usually between two people or groups, that the one who has made an incorrect prediction about an event will give sthg., such as money, to the other: *He made a bet with his friend that their school team would win.* **2.** An object or amount of money risked in a wager; a stake: *a bet of ten dollars.* —*v.* **bet** *or* **bet·ted, bet·ting, bets.** —*tr.* **1.** To risk (sthg.) in a bet: *He bet two dollars on the game.* **2.** To make a bet with (sbdy.): *I bet my brother I'd finish the race first.* **3.** To state (sthg.) with confidence, as in a bet: *I bet you did well on the exam.* —*intr.* To make or place a bet: *They bet on the horses.* ◆ **best bet.** Best chance of succeeding: *If you want to get there quickly, your best bet would be to take the freeway.*

bet (one's) bottom dollar. To be sure: *You can bet your bottom dollar that they will be at the party.* **you bet.** *Informal.* Of course; surely: *You bet I'm going to the beach tomorrow.*

betcha (bĕ′chə) *Informal.* A shortened way of saying *I bet you,* used in rapid speech: *Betcha can't run as fast as I can!* ◆ **You betcha.** Used as a response to "thank you": *"Thank you." "You betcha."*

be·tray (bĭ trā′) *tr.v.* **1.** To give aid or information to an enemy of (a country, for example): *spies betraying their own countries.* **2.** To be disloyal to (sbdy./sthg.): *betray a friend; a corrupt politician betraying the confidence of the voters.* **3.** To give evidence of (sthg.); indicate: *The redness of her face betrayed her embarrassment over the mistake.* —**be·tray′er** *n.*

be·tray·al (bĭ trā′əl) *n.* [C; U] The act of betraying, especially through disloyalty and deception: *Telling the secret was an act of betrayal.*

be·troth·al (bĭ trō′thəl *or* bĭ trô′thəl) *n.* *Formal.* A promise to marry; an engagement.

be·trothed (bĭ trōthd′ *or* bĭ trôtht′) *adj.* *Formal.* Engaged to be married. —*n.* A person to whom one is engaged to be married.

bet·ter (bĕt′ər) *adj.* Comparative of **good.** **1.** Greater in excellence or higher in quality than sbdy./sthg.: *Which of the twins is the bet-*

ter skater? **2.** More useful, suitable, or desirable: *I know a better way to go.* **3.** Larger; greater: *It took the better part of an hour to get there.* **4.** Healthier than before: *Many days passed before I began to feel better.* —*adv.* Comparative of **well²**. **1.** In a superior way: *He sings better than his father.* **2.** To a greater extent or larger degree: *I like fish better when it's broiled.* **3.** More: *The play was first performed better than 20 years ago.* —*n.* **1.** [U] The superior of two: *Both are good, but which is the better?* **2.** [C] A superior: *I leave the more difficult work to my betters.* —*v.* —*tr.* **1.** To surpass or exceed (sbdy./sthg.): *The old record stood until another athlete bettered it.* **2.** To make (sbdy./sthg.) better; improve: *The purpose of education is to better ourselves.* —*intr.* To become better: *Conditions bettered with time.* ◆ **better off.** In a better condition: *With vaccines, people are better off than they were years ago.* **for the better.** Resulting in or aiming at an improvement: *Her condition took a turn for the better.* **get the better of.** To defeat (sbdy.): *He got the better of his opponent.* **had better. 1.** Ought to; should: *We had better leave before dark.* **2.** Used to express a threat: *You had better pay me back.*

HOMONYMS: better, bettor (one who bets).

---

bet·ter·ment (bĕt′ər mənt) *n.* [U] An improvement: *We work for the betterment of our children.*

bet·tor also **bet·ter** (bĕt′ər) *n.* A person who bets.

HOMONYMS: bettor, better (greater).

---

be·tween (bĭ twēn′) *prep.* **1.** In the position or interval separating two things: *between the trees; between 11 and 12 o'clock; water flowing between the banks.* **2.** Connecting through a space that is separating two things: *a long path between the house and the lake.* **3.** By the combined effect or effort of: *Between them, the friends finished the job.* **4.** As measured against: *Choose between milk and water.* —*adv.* In an intermediate space, position, or time: *The plane went from New York to Los Angeles, and several cities between.* ◆ **between you and me.** In the strictest confidence: *Just between you and me, I don't like the way she sings.* **few and far between.** Very uncommon; rare: *Truly brilliant composers are few and far between.* **in between.** In an intermediate situation: *There are two cities near each other, with a river running in between.*

USAGE: between When two people or objects are discussed, **between** is correct and **among** is wrong: *the friendship between Jill and Jane.* When more than two people or objects are involved, however, or when the number is not specified, use **between** to suggest distinct individuals and **among** for a group or mass. *Friendships between peers* refers to separate friendships between individuals, but *friendship among peers* suggests a single group of friends.

bev•el (bĕv′əl) *n.* A surface formed when two planes meet at a sloping edge. —*tr.v.* To cut a bevel on (sthg.): *bevel the edges of the picture frame.*

bev•er•age (bĕv′ər ĭj *or* bĕv′rĭj) *n.* A liquid for drinking, such as milk, tea, or juice, usually excluding water: *A free beverage comes with your meal.*

be•ware (bĭ wâr′) *v. (used in the imperative or infinitive).* —*tr.* To watch out for (sbdy./sthg.); be on guard against: *Beware the smooth talk of the salesman.* —*intr.* To be cautious: *Beware of the dog.*

be•wil•der (bĭ wĭl′dər) *tr.v.* To confuse (sbdy.) greatly; puzzle: *The city's complicated layout bewilders tourists.* —**be•wil′-der•ment** *n.* [U]

be•wil•dered (bĭ wĭl′dərd) *adj.* Very confused: *The bewildered man had no idea what to do.* —**be•wil′dered•ly** *adv.*

be•wil•der•ing (bĭ wĭl′dər ĭng) *adj.* Causing confusion: *a bewildering number of choices.*

be•witch (bĭ wĭch′) *tr.v.* **1.** To cast a spell over (sbdy.): *The prince was bewitched by a fairy.* **2.** To captivate (sbdy.) completely; fascinate; charm: *Her piano solo bewitched the audience.*

be•witch•ing (bĭ wĭch′ ĭng) *adj.* Fascinating; enchanting: *a bewitching smile.* —**be•witch′ing•ly** *adv.*

be•yond (bē ŏnd′ *or* bĭ yŏnd′) *prep.* **1.** On the far side of; past: *I planted carrots just beyond the fence.* **2.** To a degree or an amount greater than: *rich beyond his wildest dreams.* **3.** Later than: *Don't stay up beyond midnight.* **4.** Past the reach, scope, or understanding of: *beyond hope; beyond recall.* **5.** In addition to: *The retired couple asked for nothing beyond peace and quiet.* —*adv.* **1.** Farther along: *We walked under the trees into the bright sunlight beyond.* **2.** In addition; more: *I wanted my share but nothing beyond.* —*n.* [U] The world beyond death; the hereafter: *the great beyond.*

bi—[1] *or* **bin—** *pref.* A prefix that means: **1.** Two: *bifocal.* **2.** Both sides, parts, or directions: *bilateral.* **3.** Happening at intervals of two: *bicentennial.* **4.** Happening twice during: *bimonthly.*

bi—[2] *pref.* Variant of **bio—.**

bi•an•nu•al (bī ăn′yōō əl) *adj.* Happening twice each year; semiannual: *a biannual picnic held in April and October.* —**bi•an′-nu•al•ly** *adv.*

bi•as (bī′əs) *n.* [C; U] A prejudice: *a bias against white cars.* —*tr.v.* To cause (sbdy.) to have a bias: *His stubbornness biased the employer against him.*

bi•ased (bī′əst) *adj.* Marked by or showing bias; prejudiced: *Try not to write a biased review of the book.*

bib (bĭb) *n.* **1.** A piece of cloth or plastic worn under the chin, especially by small children, to protect the clothes while eating. **2.** The part of an apron or a pair of overalls worn over the chest.

Bi•ble (bī′bəl) *n.* **1.** The sacred book of Christianity and Judaism. **2. bible.** A book considered authoritative in its field: *the bible of French cooking.*

bib•li•cal (bĭb′lĭ kəl) *adj.* Relating to the nature of the Bible. —**bib′li•cal•ly** *adv.*

bib•li•og•ra•phy (bĭb′lē ŏg′rə fē) *n., pl.* **bib•li•og•ra•phies. 1.** A list of the works of a specific author or publisher. **2.** A list of the writings on a specific subject: *a bibliography of Latin American history.* —**bib′li•o•graph′ic** (bĭb′lē ə grăf′ĭk), **bib′li•o•graph′i•cal** *adj.* —**bib′li•o•graph′i•cal•ly** *adv.*

bi•cen•ten•ni•al (bī′sĕn tĕn′ē əl) *adj.* **1.** Relating to a 200th anniversary: *a bicentennial celebration.* **2.** Happening once every 200 years. —*n.* A 200th anniversary or its celebration: *The bicentennial of the United States was celebrated in 1976.*

bi•ceps (bī′sĕps′) *n., pl.* **biceps.** The muscle at the front of the upper arm that bends the forearm.

bick•er (bĭk′ər) *intr.v.* To argue over an unimportant matter; squabble: *We bickered over whose turn it was to wash dishes.*

bi•cy•cle (bī′sĭ kəl *or* bī′sĭk′əl) *n.* A vehicle consisting of a light metal frame mounted on two wheels and having a seat for the rider, who steers the front wheel by handlebars and pushes pedals that drive the rear wheel. —*intr.v.* **bi•cy•cled, bi•cy•cling, bi•cy•cles.** To ride on a bicycle: *I just bicycled down to the store.* —**bi′cy•cler, bi′cy•clist** *n.*

bicycle

bid (bĭd) *v.* **bade** (băd *or* bād) *or* **bid, bid•den** (bĭd′n) *or* **bid, bid•ding, bids.** —*tr.* **1.** *Past tense and past participle* **bid. a.** To offer (an amount of money) as a price for sthg. at an auction: *The collector bid $5,000 for the painting.* **b.** To offer to do work at (a certain price): *The contractor bid $20,000 on the project.* **2.** *Formal.* To request (sbdy.) to come; invite: *The neighbors bade us to have coffee with them.* **3.** *Formal.* To say or express (a greeting, wish, or farewell): *I bid you farewell.* —*intr.* **1.** *Past tense and past participle* **bid. a.** To make an offer to pay a certain price: *We bid on the old lamp.* **b.** To make an offer to do a job: *We bid on the project.* **2.** *Past tense and past participle* **bid.** To try to win or achieve sthg.: *Both candidates bid for election to Congress.* —*n.* **1.a.** An offer to pay a certain amount of money for sthg.: *The auctioneer called for bids on the antique desk.* **b.** An offer to do a job for a certain price: *Bids came in from three different companies.* **2.** An effort to win or attain sthg.: *Several candidates made a bid for the Presidency.* —**bid′der** *n.*

bid•ding (bĭd′ĭng) *n.* [U] **1.** An order or a command: *Orchestras start to play at the conductor's bidding.* **2.** *Formal.* A request to appear; an invitation: *At my bidding, they accepted.*

bide (bīd) *tr.v.* **bid•ed** or **bode** (bōd), **bid•ed, bid•ing, bides.** To wait for (sthg.). ◆ **bide (one's) time.** To wait for further developments: *If you bide your time, you may have a chance.*

bi•en•ni•al (bī ĕn′ē əl) *adj.* **1.** Lasting, living, or happening every two years: *biennial plants.* **2.** Happening every second year: *biennial elections to Congress.* —*n.* A plant that grows and produces leaves in its first year and then flowers, produces seeds, and dies in its second year. —**bi•en′ni•al•ly** *adv.*

bi•fo•cals (bī fō′kəlz *or* bī′fō′kəlz). *pl.n.* A pair of eyeglasses having lenses to correct both near and distant vision. —**bi•fo•cal** (bī-fō′kəl *or* bī′fō′kəl) *adj.*

big (bĭg) *adj.* **big•ger, big•gest. 1.** Of great size, number, quantity, or extent; large: *a big house; a big city; a big appetite.* See Synonyms at **large. 2.** Older: *Big brothers and sisters must look out for the little children in a family.* **3.** Important; powerful: *a big banker; a big figure in the peace movement.* **4.** Of great importance: *a big day in my life; practice for the big game.* **5.** Loud; resounding: *a big noise.* **6.** Full of self-importance; boastful: *a big talker.* —*adv.* **1.** With an air of self-importance; boastfully: *He always talks big about what he is going to do.* **2.** *Informal.* **a.** With considerable success: *The two of them made it big with their recent best-selling book.* **b.** In a thorough or unmistakable way: *That movie failed big at the box office.* ◆ **big deal.** Used to show one's lack of interest or concern: *"An exam? Big deal." ***big of.*** *Informal.* Kind or generous of: *It's big of you to help me.* **big on.** *Informal.* Excited about; partial to: *She's big on volleyball.* **bigger fish to fry.** More important things to do: *He has bigger fish to fry and doesn't want to deal with small problems.* —**big′ness** *n.* [U]

big•a•my (bĭg′ə mē) *n.* [U] The crime of marrying one person while still being legally married to another. —**big′a•mist** *n.* —**big′-a•mous** *adj.*

big-heart•ed (bĭg′här′tĭd) *adj.* Generous; kind: *Our big-hearted neighbor brought us all a piece of cake.* —**big′-heart′ed•ly** *adv.* —**big′-heart′ed•ness** *n.* [U]

big•horn (bĭg′hôrn′) *n.* A wild mountain sheep of western North America, with large curving horns in the male; the Rocky Mountain sheep.

big league *n.* *Informal.* **1.** A major league in a professional sport, especially in baseball. **2.** *(usually plural).* The highest level of accomplishment in a field: *made it to the big leagues of academia.* —**big′-league′** *adj.*

big•ot (bĭg′ət) *n.* A person who is intolerant of people who are different, as in religion, race, or politics: *She claims to be open-minded but is really a bigot.* —**big′ot•ed** *adj.*

big•ot•ry (bĭg′ə trē) *n.* [U] The attitude or behavior of a bigot; intolerance.

big shot *n.* *Slang.* A very important person.

big ticket *adj.* Very expensive: *Big ticket items such as cars are selling well.*

big time *n.* *Informal.* The highest level of success in a field, such as the arts, business, or sports: *He acted in small productions for years until he made it to the big time.*

bike (bīk) *n.* **1.** A bicycle. **2.** A motorbike or motorcycle. —*intr.v.* **biked, bik•ing, bikes.** To ride a bike: *They biked around the West during the summer.*

bik•er (bī′kər) *n.* **1.** A person who rides a bicycle, motorbike, or motorcycle. **2.** Somebody who is a member of a motorcycle gang.

bi•ki•ni (bĭ kē′nē) *n.* **1.** A very small two-piece bathing suit worn by women. **2.** Small underpants worn by men and women.

bi•lat•er•al (bī lăt′ər əl) *adj.* **1.** Having two sides; two-sided. **2.** Affecting two sides: *a bilateral agreement.* —**bi•lat′er•al•ly** *adv.*

bile (bīl) *n.* [U] **1.** A bitter greenish liquid that is produced by the liver and aids in digestion. **2.** Bitterness of temper; ill humor: *sarcastic remarks full of bile.*

bi•lin•gual (bī lĭng′gwəl) *adj.* **1.** Able to use two languages equally well: *Many diplomats are bilingual.* **2.** Relating to or expressed in two languages: *a bilingual dictionary.* —*n.* Somebody who uses or is able to use two languages: *I'm learning Spanish because I hope to become a bilingual.* —**bi•lin′gual•ly** *adv.*

bilk (bĭlk) *tr.v.* To cheat or defraud (sbdy.): *The art dealer bilked unsuspecting clients out of millions.*

bill¹ (bĭl) *n.* **1.** A statement of charges for goods supplied or work performed: *a telephone bill.* **2.** A piece of paper money worth a certain amount: *a ten-dollar bill.* **3.** An advertising poster: *Do not put any bills on the wall.* **4.** A draft of a law presented for

approval to a legislature: *a conservation bill.*
— *tr.v.* **1.a.** To give or send a statement
of charges to (sbdy./sthg.): *Bill me for the
amount due. Bill the company for the business lunch.* **b.** To prepare a bill of (sthg.):
Please bill these purchases to our account. **2.**
To advertise or schedule (sthg.) by public
notice or as part of a program: *I see that the
play is billed as a comedy.* ◆ **fill the bill.** To
be what is needed: *If you are looking for
someone hardworking, she fills the bill.* **foot
the bill.** *Informal.* To pay for sthg.: *He
offered to foot the bill for dinner.*

bill² (bĭl) *n.* The horny projecting mouth parts
of a bird; a beak: *The bills of birds differ
according to how they feed and what they eat.*

bill·board (bĭl′bôrd′) *n.* A large upright
board used to display advertisements in public places or alongside highways.

bill·fold (bĭl′fōld′) *n.* A small, flat case used
for carrying paper money and personal documents; a wallet.

bil·liards (bĭl′yərdz) *pl.n. (used with a singular verb).* A game played on a rectangular
cloth-covered table with raised cushioned
edges, in which a cue is used to hit three balls
against one another or the side cushions of
the table.

bill·ing (bĭl′ĭng) *n.* **1.** [U] The order in which
performers' names are listed in programs,
advertisements, and on theater marquees:
*The two actors share top billing in the new
play.* **2.** [U] Advertising; promotion: *the
product was given heavy billing.* **3.** [C] *(usually plural).* The total amount of business
done in a specific period, especially by a law
firm or advertising agency: *billings of
$10,000 last month.*

bil·lion (bĭl′yən) *n.* The number, written
as 10^9 or 1 followed by nine zeros, that is
equal to one thousand times one million.
— **bil′lionth** *n., adj. & adv.*

bil·lion·aire (bĭl′yə nâr′) *n.* A person
whose wealth equals at least a billion dollars,
pounds, or similar units in another currency.

bill of rights *n., pl.* **bills of rights. 1.** A formal statement of those rights and liberties
considered essential to a people or group of
people: *a consumer bill of rights.* **2.** Also **Bill
of Rights.** The first ten amendments to the
Constitution of the United States, guaranteeing certain rights and privileges to citizens,
such as freedom of speech.

bill of sale *n., pl.* **bills of sale.** A document
that transfers ownership of sthg. to a new
owner.

bil·low (bĭl′ō) *n.* A great swell or mass of
sthg.: *Billows of smoke could be seen coming
from the burning building.* — *v.* — *intr.* **1.** To
rise or surge in billows: *Flames and smoke*

billowed through the whole building. **2.** To
swell out; bulge: *At the open window there
were curtains billowing in the wind.* — *tr.* To
cause (sthg.) to swell out: *The wind billowed
the ship's sails.* — **bil′low·y** *adj.*

billy goat *n. Informal.* A male goat.

bi·month·ly (bī mŭnth′lē) *adj.* **1.** Happening once every two months: *There are six
bimonthly meetings of the club each year.* **2.**
Happening twice a month: *We meet bimonthly on the second and fourth Tuesdays of each
month.* — *adv.* **1.** Once every two months. **2.**
Twice a month: *Many businesses pay bimonthly, on the first and the fifteenth.* — *n.,
pl.* **bi·month·lies.** A publication issued bimonthly. — SEE NOTE at **biweekly.**

bin (bĭn) *n.* An enclosed space for storing
food, grain, coal, or other dry substances.

HOMONYMS: bin, been (existed).

---

bin— *pref.* Variant of **bi—**.

bi·na·ry (bī′nə rē) *adj.* **1.** Relating to the
number 2 or the binary number system: *a
binary numeral.* **2.** Involving two different
parts, kinds, or things: *a binary chemical
compound.*

bind (bīnd) *v.* **bound** (bound), **bind·ing,
binds.** — *tr.* **1.** To fasten or secure (sbdy./
sthg.) by tying, as with a rope or cord: *bind a
package with string; bind a prisoner in chains.*
2. To bandage (sthg.): *bound their wounds.* **3.**
To cause (sthg.) to stick together: *Cement
binds gravel to make concrete for paving
roads.* **4.** To compel, obligate, or unite (sbdy.):
Duty binds me to remain at my post. **5.** To
place (sbdy.) under legal obligation: *The terms
of the contract bind the author and the publisher.* **6.** To cover (sthg.) with a border or edging for added protection or decoration: *bind a
seam with tape.* **7.** To enclose and fasten
(sthg.) between covers: *bind a book.* — *intr.* **1.**
To become compact or solid; stick together:
Cement will not bind without water. **2.** To be
compelling or unifying: *We have family ties
that bind.* ◆ **in a bind.** *Informal.* In a difficult
or confining situation: *He was in a bind when
his car broke down.*

bind·er (bīn′dər) *n.* **1.** A notebook cover with
rings for holding sheets of paper. **2.** A person
who binds books. **3.** A payment or written
statement making an agreement legally binding until the completion of a contract, especially an insurance contract: *She must sign a
binder before the contract goes through.*

bind·ing (bīn′dĭng) *n.* **1.** The cover that holds
together the pages of a book. **2.** A strip of tape
or fabric sewn over an edge or a seam to protect or decorate it. — *adj.* Imposing a firm commitment; obligatory: *a binding agreement.*

ă–cat; ā–pay; âr–care; ä–father; ĕ–get; ē–be; ĭ–sit; ī–nice; îr–here; ŏ–got; ō–go; ô–saw; oi–boy; ou–out;
ŏŏ–took; ōō–boot; ŭ–cut; ûr–word; th–thin; th–this; hw–when; zh–vision; ə–about; N–French bon

binge (bĭnj) *n.* A period of uncontrolled activity, such as drinking or spending; uncontrolled self-indulgence: *a shopping binge.* —*intr.v.* To engage in an activity, especially eating, drinking, or spending, in an uncontrolled way: *After two months without a drink, he binged. She binges on chocolate on Valentine's Day.*

bin•go (bĭng'gō) *n.* [U] A game of chance played by covering numbers on a printed card as they are called out.

bin•oc•u•lar (bə nŏk'yə lər *or* bī nŏk'yə lər) *adj.* Involving both eyes at once: *Humans have binocular vision.* —*n. (usually plural).* An optical device, such as a pair of field glasses, designed for use by both eyes at once and consisting of two small telescopes: *Birdwatchers are rarely without their binoculars.*

bio— or **bi—** *pref.* A prefix that means: **1.** Life or living organism: *biography.* **2.** Biology or biological: *biophysics.*

WORD BUILDING: bio— The prefix **bio—** means "life." When used to form words in English, **bio—** generally refers to living organisms or to biology, the science of living organisms. Many of the words that begin with **bio—**, such as **bioethics** and **biotechnology,** have only come into being in the 20th century. Sometimes before an *o* **bio—** becomes **bi—:** *biopsy.*

---

bi•o•chem•ist (bī'ō kĕm'ĭst) *n.* A scientist who specializes in biochemistry.

bi•o•chem•is•try (bī'ō kĕm'ĭ strē) *n.* [U] The study of the chemical composition of substances that form living matter and of chemical processes that occur in living matter. —**bi'o•chem'i•cal** *adj.* —**bi'o•chem'i•cal•ly** *adv.*

bi•o•de•grad•a•ble (bī'ō dĭ grā'də bəl) *adj.* Able to be decomposed by biological agents, especially bacteria: *a biodegradable detergent.*

bi•o•eth•ics (bī'ō ĕth'ĭks) *n.* [U] *(used with a singular verb).* The study of the problems of behavior and conduct in biological and medical research.

bi•o•feed•back (bī'ō fēd'băk') *n.* [U] The use of monitoring devices in an attempt to gain some voluntary control over involuntary bodily functions, such as the heartbeat or blood pressure: *She used biofeedback to control her headaches.*

bi•og•ra•phy (bī ŏg'rə fē) *n., pl.* **bi•og•ra•phies.** An account of a person's life written by sbdy. else: *Reviewers praised the new biography of Eleanor Roosevelt.* —**bi'og'ra•pher** *n.* —**bi'o•graph'ic** (bī'ə grăf'ĭk), **bi'o•graph'i•cal** *adj.*

bi•o•log•i•cal (bī'ə lŏj'ĭ kəl) also **bi•o•log•ic** (bī'ə lŏj'ĭk) *adj.* **1.** Relating to living organisms: *biological processes such as growth and digestion.* **2.** Relating to biology: *the biological sciences.* —**bi'o•log'i•cal•ly** *adv.*

bi•ol•o•gist (bī ŏl'ə jĭst) *n.* A scientist who specializes in biology: *A biologist studies the processes of living organisms.*

bi•ol•o•gy (bī ŏl'ə jē) *n.* [U] The scientific study of living organisms and life processes, including growth, structure, and reproduction. Among the branches of biology are botany, zoology, and ecology.

bi•o•phys•ics (bī'ō fĭz'ĭks) *n.* [U] *(used with a singular verb).* The branch of biology that applies the laws and methods of physics to biological problems and phenomena.

bi•op•sy (bī'ŏp'sē) *n., pl.* **bi•op•sies.** The surgical removal of a sample of tissue from a living body for examination and diagnosis: *The biopsy shows no disease.*

bi•o•rhythm (bī'ō rĭth'əm) *n.* An inborn, cyclical biological process or function.

bi•o•sphere (bī'ə sfîr') *n.* **1.** The part of the earth and its atmosphere in which living organisms exist. **2.** The living organisms and their environment in the biosphere.

bi•o•tech•nol•o•gy (bī'ō tĕk nŏl'ə jē) *n.* [U] **1.** The use of living organisms or biological substances to perform certain industrial or manufacturing processes. **2.** The engineering and biological study of relationships between humans and machines. —**bi'o•tech'no•log'i•cal** (bī'ō tĕk'nə lŏj'ĭ kəl) *adj.*

bi•par•ti•san (bī pär'tĭ zən *or* bī pär'tĭ sən) *adj.* Composed of or supported by two political parties: *a bipartisan bill to fight crime.*

bi•ped (bī'pĕd') *n.* An animal with two feet, such as a bird or human.

bi•plane (bī'plān') *n.* An airplane with two sets of wings, one above the other.

bi•ra•cial (bī rā'shəl) *adj.* For or consisting of members of two racial groups: *a biracial committee for cooperation between African American and white residents.*

birch (bûrch) *n.* **1.** [C] Any of various trees of the Northern Hemisphere with toothed leaves and white papery bark that peels easily. **2.** [U] The hard wood of such a tree.

bird (bûrd) *n.* **1.** Any of numerous warm-blooded animals that lay eggs and have two wings and a body covered with feathers: *Pigeons, ducks, and sparrows are birds.* **2.** *Slang.* An odd or unusual person: *My neighbor is a strange bird.* ♦ **birds of a feather.** People who are similar, as in character, personality, or tastes: *They get along so well because they're birds of a feather.* **for the birds.** Objectionable or worthless: *This dead-end job is for the birds!* **kill two birds with one stone.** To take an opportunity to do two things at once: *I went to New York on business and visited my friend there too, so I killed two birds with one stone.*

bird•bath (bûrd'băth') *n.* A shallow basin filled with water for birds to drink or bathe in.

bird-brained (bûrd′brānd′) *adj. Informal.* Silly or foolish.

bird•house (bûrd′hous′) *n.* A box with one or more small holes, made as a nesting place for birds: *They put up birdhouses to attract birds.*

bird of prey *n., pl.* **birds of prey.** Any of various birds, such as a hawk, an eagle, or an owl, that hunt and kill other animals for food.

bird•seed (bûrd′sēd′) *n.* [U] A mixture of different kinds of seeds for feeding birds.

bird's-eye view (bûrdz′ī′) *n.* A view seen from high above: *From the airplane, we had a bird's-eye view of the countryside.*

bird watcher *n.* A person who observes and identifies birds in their natural surroundings. —**bird watching** *n.* [U]

birth (bûrth) *n.* **1.** [C] The emergence of offspring from the mother's body: *He was sickly from birth.* **2.** [C; U] The act or process of bearing young: *A second birth is usually easier than the first.* **3.** [U] A beginning or an origin: *the birth of an idea.* **4.** [U] Family background; ancestry: *an heir of noble birth.*

HOMONYMS: birth, berth (bed).

birth control *n.* [U] Control of the number of children born, especially by the planned use of contraceptive techniques; contraception.

birth•day (bûrth′dā′) *n.* The anniversary of the day of a person's birth: *What do you plan to do to celebrate your birthday?*

birth•mark (bûrth′märk′) *n.* A mark on the body present from birth.

birth•place (bûrth′plās′) *n.* The place where sbdy. is born or where sthg. originates: *Dayton, Ohio, is sometimes considered the birthplace of aviation.*

birth•rate (bûrth′rāt′) *n.* The number of total live births to total population in a specified area over a particular period of time, usually one year.

birth•stone (bûrth′stōn′) *n.* A jewel associated with the specific month of a person's birth: *The birthstone for April is the diamond.*

bis•cuit (bĭs′kĭt) *n.* **1.** A small flaky cake of bread leavened with baking powder or baking soda. **2.** *Chiefly British.* **a.** A cracker. **b.** A cookie.

bi•sect (bī′sĕkt′ *or* bī sĕkt′) *tr.v.* To cut or divide (sthg.) into two equal parts: *bisect a triangle.* —**bi•sec′tion** *n.* [U]

bi•sec•tor (bī′sĕk′tər *or* bī sĕk′tər) *n.* A straight line that bisects an angle or a line segment.

bi•sex•u•al (bī sĕk′shōō əl) *adj.* **1.** Having sexual interest in or attraction to persons of both sexes. **2.** Having male and female reproductive organs in a single individual; hermaphroditic: *Earthworms are bisexual.* —*n.* A bisexual person. —**bi•sex•u•al′i•ty** (bī′sĕk-shōō ăl′ĭ tē) *n.* [U] —**bi•sex′u•al•ly** *adv.*

bish•op (bĭsh′əp) *n.* **1.** A high-ranking Christian cleric, in modern churches usually in charge of a diocese. **2.** A chess piece that can only move diagonally.

bi•son (bī′sən *or* bī′zən) *n.* A large mammal of western North America similar to an ox and with a very large head, a shaggy dark-brown mane, and short curved horns; a buffalo.

bison

bisque (bĭsk) *n.* [C; U] A thick cream soup: *lobster bisque.*

bis•tro (bē′strō *or* bĭs′trō) *n., pl.* **bis•tros.** A small bar or nightclub.

bit[1] (bĭt) *n.* **1.** [C] A small piece or amount: *a bit of lint; a bit of luck.* **2.** [U] A brief amount of time; a moment: *Wait a bit.* ◆ **a bit.** To a small degree; somewhat: *The soup is a bit hot.* **bit by bit.** Little by little; gradually: *His writing has improved bit by bit.*

bit[2] (bĭt) *n.* **1.** A pointed tool for drilling that fits into a brace or an electric drill. **2.** The metal mouthpiece of a bridle, used to control the horse.

bit[3] (bĭt) *n.* **1.** In computer science, either of the binary digits 0 or 1. **2.** The smallest unit of information a computer can recognize; a binary digit.

bit[4] (bĭt) *v.* Past tense and a past participle of **bite.**

bitch (bĭch) *n.* **1.** *Offensive Slang.* **a.** A woman. **b.** Something very unpleasant or difficult. **2.** A female dog or related animal, such as a coyote. —*intr.v.* [*about*] *Offensive Slang.* To complain. —**bitch′y** *adj.* —**bitch′i•ness** *n.* [U]

bite (bīt) *v.* **bit** (bĭt), **bit•ten** (bĭt′n) *or* **bit, bit•ing, bites.** —*tr.* **1.** To cut, grip, or tear (sthg.) with the teeth: *He bit the bread and tore off a piece.* **2.** To pierce the skin of (a person or an animal) with the teeth, fangs, or mouthparts: *A mosquito bit me on the leg.* **3.** To cause (sbdy./sthg.) to sting or smart: *The cold wind was biting my face.* —*intr.* **1.** To cut or tear sthg. with or as if with the teeth: *The ax bit into the tree.* **2.** To take or swallow bait: *Fish seem to bite more just before it starts to rain.* **3.** To be deceived by a trick or scheme: *She tried to pass off the old car as a bargain, but no one would bite.* —*n.* **1.** The act of biting: *The dog's bark is worse than his bite.* **2.** A wound or an injury resulting from biting: *a mosquito bite.* **3.** An amount of food taken into the mouth at one time; a mouthful:

Let me have a bite of your sandwich. **4.** *Informal.* A light meal or snack: *We stopped for a bite.* ✦ **bite off more than (one) can chew.** *Informal.* To decide or agree to do more than one can accomplish: *When he volunteered to manage the whole festival, he bit off more than he could chew.* **bite the bullet.** *Slang.* To face a painful or difficult situation with bravery and determination: *Although she had sprained her ankle, she bit the bullet and continued to run the race.* **bite the dust.** *Slang.* **1.** To die: *The bad guy in the movie bit the dust.* **2.** To come to an end: *The project bit the dust because no one would support it.* —**bit′er** *n.*

HOMONYMS: bite, byte (unit of computer measure).

---

bit•ing (bī′tĭng) *adj.* **1.** Sharp; stinging: *The snow was accompanied by a biting wind.* **2.** Causing an unpleasant feeling; sarcastic; cutting: *biting criticism.* —**bit′ing•ly** *adv.*
bit•ten (bĭt′n) *v.* A past participle of **bite.**
bit•ter (bĭt′ər) *adj.* **1.** Having or being a taste that is sharp and unpleasant: *a bitter drink.* **2.** Causing sharp pain to the body; harsh: *a bitter wind.* **3.** Hard to accept, admit, or bear: *the bitter truth.* **4.** Showing or resulting from strong dislike or animosity: *bitter foes; a bitter fight.* **5.** Resulting from severe grief, anguish, or disappointment: *cry bitter tears.* **6.** Having or showing a resentful feeling: *bitter about being cheated.* —*n.* **1.** [U] *Chiefly British.* A sharp-tasting beer made with hops. **2. bitters.** A bitter, usually alcoholic liquid used in cocktails and as a tonic. —**bit′ter•ly** *adv.* —**bit′ter•ness** *n.* [U]
bit•ter•sweet (bĭt′ər swēt′) *adj.* **1.** Bitter and sweet at the same time: *bittersweet chocolate.* **2.** Pleasant and unpleasant at the same time: *She was left with bittersweet memories of the event.*
bi•week•ly (bī wēk′lē) *adj.* **1.** Happening every two weeks. **2.** Happening twice a week: *biweekly meetings on Tuesday and Thursday.* —*n., pl.* **bi•week•lies.** A publication issued biweekly: *The newspaper is a biweekly.* —*adv.* **1.** Once every two weeks: *The company pays biweekly.* **2.** Twice a week.

USAGE: biweekly The word **biweekly** means "every two weeks" or "twice a week" and **bimonthly** means "every two months" or "twice a month." **Semiweekly** means "twice a week" and **semimonthly** means "twice a month." Because many people confuse these **bi—** and **semi—** words, it is safest to use phrases like *every two weeks* or *twice a month.* A publication that comes out every two weeks, however, is always called a **biweekly.** One appearing every two months is a **bimonthly.**

bi•zarre (bĭ zär′) *adj.* Very strange or odd: *a bizarre hat; a bizarre idea.*
blab (blăb) *v.* **blabbed, blab•bing, blabs.** —*tr.* To tell (a secret), especially through careless talk: *He blabbed his boss's salary by mistake.* —*intr.* **1.** To reveal secret matters: *The secret was out when I blabbed without thinking.* **2.** To chatter indiscreetly: *He blabs all day long on the phone.*
blab•ber (blăb′ər) *intr.v.* To chatter. —*n.* **1.** [U] Idle chatter. **2.** [C] A person who blabs.
blab•ber•mouth (blăb′ər mouth′) *n.* *Informal.* A person who talks carelessly and at length: *Don't tell him the secret; he's such a blabbermouth it'll be all over town in a week.*
black (blăk) *adj.* **1.** Of the color black: *a black sweater; black tulips.* **2.** Without light: *a black moonless night.* **3.** Often **Black. a.** Relating to or belonging to a racial group having dark skin, especially a group of African origin. **b.** Relating to or belonging to an American group of people descended from African peoples having dark skin; African American. **4.** Gloomy; depressing: *a black day; black thoughts.* **5.** Often **Black.** Marked by disaster: *The stock market crashed on Black Friday.* **6.** Deserving censure or dishonor: *the industry's blackest record as a polluter of the rivers.* **7.** Evil; wicked: *black deeds.* **8.** Angry; sullen: *He gave me a black look.* **9.** Served without cream or milk: *black coffee.* —*n.* **1.** [U] The darkest extreme of the series of colors that runs through all the shades of gray to white, being the opposite of white. **2.** [C] A black paint, dye, or pigment. **3.** Often **Black.** [C] **a.** A member of a racial group having dark skin, especially one of African origin. **b.** An American descended from peoples of African origin having dark skin; an African American. —*v.* ✦ **black out.** *intr.v.* To lose consciousness or memory temporarily: *He felt lightheaded and then blacked out.* —*tr.v.* [sep.] **1.** To forbid or prevent the transmission of (a television program): *The baseball game broadcast was blacked out in the city where the game was being played.* **2.** To turn off or conceal all lights of (a city) that might help enemy aircraft find a target during an air raid: *The city was blacked out every night during the war.* **3.** To cause a failure of electrical power in (sthg.): *The storm blacked out the street lights.* **in the black.** Making a profit; prosperous: *The new business was in the black within a year.* —**black′ly** *adv.* —**black′ness** *n.* [U]

USAGE: black or **Black** Although using **black** or **Black** when talking about an individual's or a group's race was acceptable in the United States not so long ago, the usage is sometimes considered offensive now. When you are referring to people whose heritage is African, many people now prefer *African American.*

black-and-blue (blăk´ən blōō´) *adj. Informal.* Discolored by broken blood vessels under the skin; bruised: *Her leg was black-and-blue from the fall.*

black and white *n.* [U] **1.** Writing or printing: *She did not believe it until she read it in black and white.* **2.** Photography or printmaking that uses only black and white: *a movie shot in black and white.*

black-and-white (blăk´ən wīt´) *adj.* **1.** Being done, drawn, or photographed in shades of black and white: *a black-and-white picture.* **2.** Partly black and partly white: *a black-and-white cow.* **3.** Making judgments based on two rigid categories, such as right and wrong: *Nothing is ever as black-and-white as we would like.*

black•ball (blăk´bôl´) *n.* A negative vote. —*tr.v.* To shut (sbdy.) out from participation: *The actor was blackballed for her political views.*

black belt *n.* **1.** [U] The rank of expert in a system of self-defense, such as judo or karate. **2.** [C] A person who holds this rank.

black•ber•ry (blăk´běr´ē) *n.* A thorny shrub with a blackish, glossy, edible berry related to the raspberry.

black•bird (blăk´bûrd´) *n.* A bird with black or mostly black feathers.

black•board (blăk´bôrd´) *n.* A hard, smooth, dark-colored panel for writing on with chalk; a chalkboard: *write the example on the blackboard.*

black•en (blăk´ən) *v.* —*tr.* **1.** To make (sthg.) black: *Smoke blackened the sky.* **2.** To speak evil of (sbdy.): *The scandal blackened the athlete's reputation.* —*intr.* To become dark or black: *The sky blackened before the storm.*

black eye *n.* **1.** A black-and-blue discoloration of the skin around the eye, resulting from being hit. **2.** A bad name; a dishonored reputation: *Involvement in the scandal gave the politician a black eye.*

black•head (blăk´hěd´) *n.* A small spot of material that collects in and blocks one of the pores of the skin.

black•ish (blăk´ĭsh) *adj.* Somewhat black in color.

black•jack (blăk´jăk´) *n.* [U] A card game in which the object is to hold cards with a higher count than that of the dealer but not exceeding 21.

black•list (blăk´lĭst´) *n.* A list of persons or organizations to be disapproved or penalized: *In the 1950s many actors were placed on a Hollywood blacklist.* —*tr.v.* To place (a name) on a blacklist: *Many companies used to blacklist strikers.*

black magic *n.* [U] Magic practiced for evil purposes.

black•mail (blăk´māl´) *n.* [U] **1.** The extortion of money or sthg. valuable from a person by threat: *letters that could be used for blackmail.* **2.** Money or sthg. of value paid or demanded as blackmail: *twenty thousand dollars in blackmail.* —*tr.v.* To subject (sbdy.) to blackmail. —**black´mail´er** *n.*

black market *n.* The illegal business of buying or selling goods in violation of governmental restrictions, such as price controls or rationing: *My roommate bought blue jeans on the black market.*

black•out (blăk´out´) *n.* **1.** Lack of lighting caused by an electrical power failure. **2.** A temporary loss of consciousness or memory: *The driver's blackout caused the crash.* **3.** A suppression by censorship: *a news blackout.* **4.** The act of prohibiting the transmission of a television program. **5.** The act of putting out or concealing all lights that might help enemy aircraft find a target during a night raid.

black sheep *n.* A member of a family or group considered undesirable: *The criminal was considered the black sheep of her family.*

black•smith (blăk´smĭth´) *n.* A person who makes iron into horseshoes and other objects of metal.

black tie *n.* **1.** [C] A black bow tie worn with a dinner jacket or tuxedo. **2.** [U] Formal evening clothes for men: *He was dressed in black tie.* —**black´-tie** *adj.*

black•top (blăk´tŏp´) *n.* [U] A material, such as asphalt, used to pave roads. —*tr.v.* **black•topped, black•top•ping, black•tops.** To pave (a road) with blacktop.

black widow *n.* A spider of Central and North America, the female of which has a black body with a red mark on the underside and is poisonous.

blad•der (blăd´ər) *n.* Any of various sacs found in most animals and made of elastic membrane, especially the sac that stores urine from the kidneys.

blade (blād) *n.* **1.** The flat sharp-edged part of a cutting tool or weapon: *Never handle a knife by its blade.* **2.** A sword. **3.** The thin flat part of sthg.: *the blade of an oar.* **4.** The broad flattened part of a leaf: *a blade of glass.* **5.** The metal part of an ice skate.

blah (blä) *adj. Informal.* **1.** Dull and uninteresting: *a blah day.* **2.** Low in spirits or health: *I'm feeling blah.*

blame (blām) *tr.v.* **blamed, blam•ing, blames.** **1.** To hold (sbdy./sthg.) responsible or at fault: *They blamed the girl for breaking the window.* **2.** To find fault with (sbdy.); censure: *You cannot blame them for wanting to live on a lake.* —*n.* [U] The state of being responsible for a fault or an error: *I had to accept the blame for my mistake.* ♦ **be to**

B

blame. To deserve censure; be at fault: *Heavy rainfall was to blame for the crop failure.* **take the blame.** To accept guilt: *He took the blame for the accident because he was driving the car.* —**blam′a•ble** *adj.*

blame•less (blām′lǐs) *adj.* Without blame or guilt; innocent: *a blameless case of mistaken identity.* —**blame′less•ly** *adv.*

blanch (blǎnch) *v.* —*tr.* **1.** To place (fruits or vegetables) briefly in boiling water to remove the skins or soften them: *He blanched the tomatoes before canning them.* **2.** To cause (sbdy./sthg.) to become pale: *Fear blanched the startled child's face.* —*intr.* To turn pale: *They blanched when they heard the news.*

bland (blǎnd) *adj.* **1.** Pleasant or soothing in manner; gentle: *a bland smile.* **2.** Having a moderate, soft, or soothing quality; not irritating or stimulating: *a bland diet; a bland climate.* **3.** Lacking distinctive character; dull; flat: *a bland speech.* —**bland′ly** *adj.* —**bland′ness** *n.* [U]

blank (blǎngk) *adj.* **1.** Free of marks or writing: *a blank wall; a blank piece of paper.* **2.** Containing no information: *a blank tape.* See Synonyms at **empty. 3.** Showing no expression or interest: *a blank stare.* —*n.* **1.** An empty space or place; a void: *My mind was a complete blank on the subject.* **2.a.** An empty space on a document to be filled in with an answer or a comment: *Write your name in the blank.* **b.** A document or form with empty spaces to be filled in: *We need entry blanks for the contest.* **3.** A gun cartridge having a charge of powder but no bullet. —*tr.v. Informal.* To prevent (an opponent) from scoring in a game: *Our team blanked theirs 4–0.* ♦ **draw a blank.** To be unable to remember sthg.: *I tried to remember his name, but I drew a blank.* —**blank′ly** *adv.* —**blank′-ness** *n.* [U]

blan•ket (blǎng′kǐt) *n.* **1.** A large piece of cloth used as a covering for warmth: *I put extra blankets on the bed because it was cold.* **2.** A layer that covers: *a blanket of snow.* —*adj.* Covering a wide range of topics, conditions, or requirements: *They gave the proposals blanket approval.* —*tr.v.* To cover (sbdy./sthg.) with or as if with a blanket: *Snow blanketed the countryside. She blanketed the children.*

blare (blâr) *v.* **blared, blar•ing, blares.** —*intr.* To sound loudly and stridently: *horns blaring in the traffic jam.* —*tr.* To cause (sthg.) to sound loudly and stridently: *A brass band blared the national anthem.* —*n.* A loud strident noise: *a trumpet blare.*

bla•sé (blä zā′) *adj.* Uninterested or unexcited; without emotion: *People who live on the coast tend to be blasé about the ocean.*

blas•pheme (blǎs fēm′ *or* blǎs′fēm′) *v.* **blas•phemed, blas•phem•ing, blas•phemes.** —*tr.* To speak of (God or sthg. sacred) in a disrespectful way. —*intr.* To speak disrespectfully of God or sthg. sacred. —**blas•phem′er** *n.* —**blas′phe•mous** (blǎs′fə məs) *adj.* —**blas′phe•mous•ly** *adv.* —**blas′phe•my** (blǎs′fə mē) *n.* [C; U]

blast (blǎst) *n.* **1.** A strong gust of wind or air. **2.** A strong stream of air, gas, or steam from an opening: *a cold blast from the open door.* **3.** A loud sudden sound, especially one produced by forced air: *the blast of the steam whistle.* **4.** An explosion: *a blast of dynamite.* **5.** *Informal.* A great time: *We had a blast at the party.* —*v.* —*tr.* **1.a.** To knock down or tear apart (sthg.) with an explosive: *blasting rocks in a quarry.* **b.** To make or open (sthg.) by or as if by an explosion: *blast a road through the mountain.* **2.** To cause (sthg.) to sound loudly; blare: *The radio blasted music out the window.* **3.** To criticize (sbdy./sthg.) severely: *The reviewer blasted the movie.* —*intr.* **1.** To emit a loud unpleasant sound: *Car horns blasted from the street below.* **2.** To criticize or attack: *The paper blasted away at the corrupt city government.* ♦ **blast off.** *intr.v.* To take off, as a rocket: *The shuttle blasted off for another trip into space.* **full blast.** At full speed, volume, or capacity: *He turned the radio up full blast.*

blast furnace *n.* A furnace in which combustion is made more intense by a forced stream of air.

blast•off *also* **blast-off** (blǎst′ôf′ *or* blǎst′ŏf′) *n.* [C; U] The launching of a rocket or spacecraft: *A crowd watched the blastoff from several miles away.*

bla•tant (blāt′nt) *adj.* **1.** Offensively obvious: *a blatant lie.* **2.** Unpleasantly loud: *blatant revelers.* —**bla′tant•ly** *adv.*

blaze[1] (blāz) *n.* **1.** A destructive fire: *A blaze destroyed the building.* **2.** A bright or steady glare: *the blaze of the sun.* **3.** A brilliant display: *The flowers were a blaze of color.* **4.** Sudden activity or emotion: *in a blaze of speed; a blaze of anger.* —*intr.v.* **blazed, blaz•ing, blaz•es. 1.** To burn or shine brightly: *a fire blazing in the fireplace.* **2.** To be filled with color: *The garden blazed with colorful flowers.*

blaze[2] (blāz) *n.* **1.** A white spot on the face of an animal, such as a horse. **2.** A mark cut on a tree to indicate a trail. —*tr.v.* **blazed, blaz•ing, blaz•es. 1.** To indicate (a trail) by marking trees with cuts. **2.** To prepare or lead (sthg.): *blaze the way in space exploration.*

blaz•er (blā′zər) *n.* A lightweight sports jacket: *A blazer and tie will be suitable to wear to dinner.*

bldg. *abbr.* An abbreviation of building.

bleach (blēch) *v.* —*tr.* **1.** To remove the color from (fabric) by means of sunlight or chemicals; whiten: *bleach a shirt or blouse.* **2.** To lighten the color of (hair): *She bleached her hair blond.* —*intr.* To turn white or lose color:

wood bleaching in the desert sun. —*n.* [U] A chemical agent used for bleaching.

bleach•ers (blē′chərz) *pl.n.* Wooden planks set in tiers for spectators to sit on at a public event.

bleak (blēk) *adj.* **1.** Gloomy; dreary; depressing: *The prospects for success are bleak.* **2.** Cold and harsh: *a damp bleak valley.* —**bleak′ly** *adv.* —**bleak′ness** *n.* [U]

blear•y (blîr′ē) *adj.* **blear•i•er, blear•i•est. 1.** Blurred by or as if by tears: *bleary eyes.* **2.** Vague or indistinct; blurred: *a bleary photograph.* —**blear′i•ness** *n.* [U]

bleat (blēt) *n.* The hoarse broken cry of a goat, sheep, or calf. —*intr.v.* **1.** To make the cry of a goat, sheep, or calf: *a lamb bleating for its mother.*

bleed (blēd) *v.* **bled** (blĕd), **bleed•ing, bleeds.** —*intr.* **1.** To lose blood: *My finger bled when I cut it on the glass.* **2.** To feel sympathetic grief: *My heart bleeds for you in your sorrow.* **3.** To become mixed and run, as dye in wet cloth: *When I washed my new jeans, the dye bled and ruined a white shirt.* —*tr.* **1.a.** To take or remove blood from (sbdy.): *Long ago doctors bled patients as a cure.* **b.** To remove sap or juice from (a plant). **2.** To drain (a liquid or gas) from a container or pipe: *bleed air from tires that are overly inflated.*

blem•ish (blĕm′ĭsh) *tr.v.* To damage or mar (sthg.) by putting a mark on it; disfigure: *Scratches blemished the table.* —*n.* Something that mars; a flaw: *skin blemishes; a blemish on one's reputation.*

blend (blĕnd) *v.* —*tr.* **1.** To mix (sthg.) thoroughly: *The cook blended milk and flour.* See Synonyms at **mix. 2.** To combine (different varieties or grades) to make a mixture with unique qualities: *We blended the two coffees.* —*intr.* **1.** To form a mixture; be combined: *Oil does not blend with water.* **2.** To become merged into one; unite: *The blue blends into the green in this painting.* **3.** To be in harmony; go together: *Your tie blends well with your jacket.* —*n.* A harmonious mixture or combination: *a blend of colors; a blend of teas.*

blend•er (blĕn′dər) *n.* An electrical appliance used to blend or purée foods.

bless (blĕs) *tr.v.* **1.** To make (sthg.) holy: *The minister blessed the water for baptism.* **2.** To praise (sbdy.) as holy; glorify: *Bless the Lord.* **3.** To endow, favor, or enrich (sbdy.): *The artist was blessed with unusual talent.*

bless•ed (blĕs′ĭd *or* blĕst) *adj.* **1.** Worthy of worship; holy. **2.** (blĕst). Enjoying happiness; very fortunate: *I feel blessed.* **3.** Bringing happiness; pleasurable: *A new baby in a family is a blessed event.*

bless•ing (blĕs′ĭng) *n.* **1.** A prayer calling for

divine favor. **2.** Approval: *The expedition to explore the Northwest had the government's blessing.* **3.** A wish for happiness or success: *We gave our blessings to the bride and groom.*

blew¹ (bloo) *v.* Past tense of **blow¹.**

HOMONYMS: blew, blue (color).

---

blight (blīt) *n.* [C; U] **1.** Any of numerous plant diseases that cause plant tissues to die. **2.** Something that is harmful: *Corruption is a blight on government.* —*tr.v.* **1.** To cause (sthg.) to die: *A dry summer blighted the wheat.* **2.** To ruin (sthg.); destroy: *Several losses blighted the team's hopes of becoming the league champions.*

blimp (blĭmp) *n.* An airship that does not have a rigid framework: *The blimp flew over the stadium during the game.*

blimp
The Goodyear blimp *Spirit of Akron*

blind (blīnd) *adj.* **1.** Not able to see; sightless: *blind at birth.* **2.** Unwilling or unable to understand: *Many people are blind to their own faults.* **3.** Not based on reason or evidence: *blind faith.* **4.** Hidden from sight: *a blind driveway.* **5.** Closed at one end: *a blind alley.* —*n.* **1.** (used with a plural verb). The group of people who are blind: *a school for the blind.* **2.** Something that shuts out light or blocks vision: *We pull the blinds over the windows at night.* —*adv.* Without being able to see: *The pilot had to fly blind in the fog.* —*tr.v.* **1.** To take sight from (sbdy.): *Lights from the oncoming cars blinded me.* **2.** To leave (sbdy.) without judgment or reason: *Prejudice blinds them to the advantages of the plan.* ◆ **blind as a bat.** An expression used, often in a humorous way, to describe a person who cannot see well or misses the obvious: *Grandpa is getting to be as blind as a bat.* **the blind leading the blind.** Used to describe a situation in which no one knows enough to lead well: *I'll try to help you with the new software, but it's going to be* *the blind leading the blind.* —**blind′ly** *adv.* —**blind′ness** *n.* [U]

USAGE: Some people consider references to disabilities such as blindness or deafness offensive when used in an idiomatic or figurative way.

---

blind date *n.* A date between two people who have not previously met.

blind·fold (blīnd′fōld′) *tr.v.* To cover the eyes of (sbdy.) with a cloth: *blindfold a prisoner.* —*n.* A piece of cloth put over the eyes and tied around the head to prevent sbdy. from seeing. —**blind′fold′ed** *adj.*

blind spot *n.* **1.** A part of an area that cannot be seen directly: *The car was in his blind spot.* **2.** A subject about which a person is noticeably ignorant or prejudiced: *Neatness is his blind spot; he just can't see its importance.* **3.** An area where radio or television reception is poor.

blink (blĭngk) *v.* —*intr.* **1.** To close and open the eyes rapidly: *She blinked at the bright light.* **2.** To flash off and on: *lights blinking on the horizon.* **3.** To waver or back down in a contest of wills: *the first to blink in a confrontation.* —*tr.* **1.** To close and open (the eye or eyes) rapidly; wink: *The cat blinked its eyes in the bright light.* **2.** To make (sthg.) flash off and on: *Blink the lights of your car.* —*n.* A very brief closing of the eye or eyes. ◆ **on the blink.** Out of working order: *This old television is always on the blink.*

blink·er (blĭng′kər) *n.* A light that blinks as a means of sending a message or warning.

blintz (blĭnts) *n.* A thin rolled pancake with a filling such as cream cheese or fruit.

blip (blĭp) *n.* **1.** A spot of light on a radar or sonar screen indicating the position of a detected object, such as an aircraft. **2.** *Informal.* An interruption in the usual: *The loss was a small blip in an otherwise great season.*

bliss (blĭs) *n.* [U] Extreme happiness; joy: *She was in a state of bliss during her first year of marriage.*

bliss·ful (blĭs′fəl) *adj.* Full of or causing bliss: *a blissful silence; blissful ignorance of the problem.* —**bliss′ful·ly** *adv.* —**bliss′ful·ness** *n.* [U]

blis·ter (blĭs′tər) *n.* **1.** A thin fluid-filled bubble that forms on the skin as a result of a burn or an irritation. **2.** A raised bubble on a painted surface: *We had to repaint the house because the old job was full of blisters.* —*intr.* & *tr.v.* To form or cause to form blisters: *Her skin blistered from poison ivy. Tight shoes blistered the hiker's feet.* —**blis′ter·y** *adj.*

blis·ter·ing (blĭs′tər ĭng) *adj.* **1.** Extremely hot: *a blistering summer sun.* **2.** Very strong; intense: *blistering criticism.* **3.** Extremely fast: *a blistering pace.*

blithe (blīth *or* blĭth) *adj.* **1.** Carefree and lighthearted: *the blithe atmosphere of the birthday party.* **2.** Showing a lack of concern: *a blithe disregard of danger.* —**blithe′ly** *adv.* —**blithe′ness** *n.* [U]

blitz (blĭts) *n.* **1.** An intense effort or campaign: *an advertising blitz.* **2.** A sudden surprise military attack, especially by air. —*tr.v.* To subject (sbdy./sthg.) to a blitz.

blitz·krieg (blĭts′krēg′) *n.* A swift, sudden military attack, usually by air and land forces.

bliz·zard (blĭz′ərd) *n.* **1.** A very heavy snowstorm with strong winds: *Many cattle died in the blizzard.* **2.** A great number or an unusually heavy flow: *a blizzard of phone calls congratulating the winning candidate.*

bloat (blōt) *intr.* & *tr.v.* To swell or cause to swell or puff up, as with liquid or gas: *a stomach bloated by overeating.*

blob (blŏb) *n.* A soft formless mass: *A blob of wax fell from the burning candle.*

bloc (blŏk) *n.* A group of nations, parties, or persons united by common interests or political aims: *representatives forming the farm bloc in Congress.*

HOMONYMS: bloc, block (flat-sided object).

---

block (blŏk) *n.* **1.** A solid piece of wood or another hard substance having one or more flat sides: *a block of wood; blocks of marble.* **2.** Such a piece on which chopping or cutting is done: *a butcher's block.* **3.** A small wooden or plastic cube used as a building toy: *a set of blocks.* **4.** A set of like items sold or handled as a unit: *a block of tickets in the balcony.* **5.a.** An obstacle or a hindrance: *The accident caused a block in traffic.* **b.** In medicine, an obstruction of a bodily function: *an intestinal block.* **6.a.** A section of a city or town enclosed by connecting streets: *Walk the dog around the block.* **b.** The part of a street that lies between two successive cross streets: *Our home is in the middle of the block.* **7.** In sports, an act of obstructing an opponent. —*tr.v.* **1.a.** To stop the movement of (sbdy./sthg.): *Road work was blocking traffic.* **b.** To stop movement through (sthg.): *The stalled car blocked the intersection.* **2.** To be in the way of (sbdy./sthg.); obstruct visually: *You're blocking my view.* **3.** In medicine, to obstruct the functioning of (a nerve, for example): *The dentist blocked the nerve.* **4.** In sports, to stop or hinder the movement of (an opponent or the ball): *She blocked the player from scoring.* ◆ **be a chip off the old block.** To be like one's parents: *He's a chip off the old block; he wants to be a doctor like his father.*

block out. *tr.v.* [sep.] **1.** To remove (sbdy./sthg.) from one's mind: *She blocked out thoughts of her accident.* **2.** To indicate (sthg.) in a general way: *block out a plan of action; block out some time for a meeting.* **block up.** *tr.v.* [sep.] To prevent movement through (a passage); plug: *The rice blocked up the sink.*

B

block•ade (blŏ kād′) *n.* **1.** The closing off of a city, harbor, or country by troops or warships in order to prevent people and supplies from going in and out: *smuggling weapons through the blockade.* **2.** Something that closes off or obstructs; an obstacle: *set up a blockade of chairs behind the door.* — *tr.v.* **block•ad•ed, block•ad•ing, block•ades.** To set up a blockade against (sbdy./sthg.). —**block•ad′er** *n.*

block•age (blŏk′ĭj) *n.* **1.** [U] The act of obstructing. **2.** [C] An obstruction: *an intestinal blockage.*

block•bust•er (blŏk′bŭs′tər) *n. Informal.* Something, such as a movie or book, that is very popular or sells in large numbers: *The movie was a blockbuster that made millions for its stars.*

block•head (blŏk′hĕd′) *n. Informal.* An insulting term for a person who is considered stupid, often used in a humorous way.

blond also **blonde** (blŏnd) *adj.* Having light hair: *a blond baby.* —*n.* A blond person: *Some claim that blonds have more fun.* —**blond′-ness** *n.* [U]

blood (blŭd) *n.* [U] **1.** The fluid that moves through the body by the action of the heart, distributing oxygen, nutrients, and hormones and carrying wastes away: *The doctor tested iron levels in the patient's blood.* **2.** Temperament or disposition: *a person of hot blood and a fiery temper.* **3.** Family relationship; kinship: *related by blood.* **4.** Descent from a common ancestor; lineage. ♦ **bad blood.** Very negative feelings; hatred: *bad blood between the brothers.* **in cold blood.** Deliberately, coldly, and dispassionately: *He killed the family in cold blood.* **make (one's) blood boil.** To make sbdy. very angry: *Her insults made my blood boil.* **new blood.** New people with fresh ideas: *The company would be more successful if they hired new blood.* **out for blood.** Wanting revenge: *The brother of the man who was killed is out for blood.*

blood bank *n.* A place where blood is classified and stored for use in transfusions.

blood•bath (blŭd′băth′) *n.* Savage and widespread killing; a massacre.

blood count *n.* A count of the number of red and white blood cells and platelets in a sample of a person's blood.

blood•cur•dling (blŭd′kûrd′lĭng) *adj.* Causing great horror; terrifying: *a bloodcurdling scream.*

blood group *n.* A blood type.

blood•hound (blŭd′hound′) *n.* A breed of hound with a smooth coat, drooping ears, loose folds of skin around the face, and a keen sense of smell.

blood•less (blŭd′lĭs) *adj.* **1.** Lacking blood.

2. Pale and anemic in color: *cold and bloodless hands.* **3.** Accomplished without killing: *a bloodless revolution.* —**blood′less•ly** *adv.*

blood•line (blŭd′līn′) *n.* A direct line of descent: *traced the royal bloodline.*

blood•mo•bile (blŭd′mə bēl′) *n.* A motor vehicle equipped for collecting blood from donors.

blood pressure *n.* [U] The pressure that the blood exerts on the walls of the arteries or other blood vessels.

blood•shed (blŭd′shĕd′) *n.* [U] The shedding of blood, especially the injuring or killing of humans; slaughter: *War rarely occurs without massive bloodshed.*

blood•shot (blŭd′shŏt′) *adj.* Red and overfilled with blood, often with the small blood vessels enlarged: *bloodshot eyes.*

blood•stained (blŭd′stānd′) *adj.* Stained or spotted with blood: *a bloodstained handkerchief.*

blood•stream (blŭd′strēm′) *n.* [U] The blood as it flows through the body: *Oxygen circulates in the bloodstream.*

blood test *n.* An examination of a sample of blood to determine its contents, as for finding out the blood group or diagnosing illness.

blood•thirst•y (blŭd′thûr′stē) *adj.* Eager to cause or see the shedding of blood; cruel: *a bloodthirsty pirate.*

blood type *n.* Any of the four main types, A, B, AB, and O, into which human blood is divided on the basis of the presence or absence of certain proteins and antibodies; blood group.

blood vessel *n.* A tube or passage in the body through which blood moves; an artery, a vein, or a capillary.

blood•y (blŭd′ē) *adj.* **blood•i•er, blood•i•est. 1.** Bleeding: *a bloody nose.* **2.** Stained with blood: *bloody bandages.* **3.** Causing or marked by bloodshed: *a bloody fight.* —*adv. Chiefly British. Informal.* Used as a slightly rude intensive: *You're a bloody fool!* —*tr.v.* **blood•ied, blood•y•ing, blood•ies.** To make (sbdy./sthg.) bloody: *My elbow was bloodied in the fall.*

bloom (blo͞om) *n.* **1.** [C] The flower or blossom of a plant: *This lily has a lovely bloom.* **2.** [U] The condition or time of flowering: *a rosebush in bloom.* **3.** [U] A condition or time of great development, vigor, or beauty: *a boy in the full bloom of youth.* —*intr.v.* **1.** To bear flowers; blossom: *Tulips bloom in the spring.* **2.** To grow or flourish: *Volunteer groups to teach reading are blooming.*

bloom•ing (blo͞o′mĭng) *adv. & adj. Chiefly British. Informal.* Used as an intensive: *a blooming hot day; a blooming idiot.*

bloop•er (blo͞o′pər) *n.* A clumsy mistake, especially one made in public.

blos•som (blŏs′əm) *n.* **1.** [C] A flower or cluster of flowers: *apple blossoms.* **2.** [U] The condition or time of flowering: *spring flowers in blossom.* —*intr.v.* **1.** To come into flower; bloom: *Cherry trees blossom in the spring.* **2.** To develop and do well; flourish: *The public's interest in science blossomed with space flight.*

blot (blŏt) *n.* **1.** A stain or spot: *an ink blot.* **2.** A stain on one's character or reputation; a disgrace: *The failing grade was a blot on his record.* —*v.* **blot•ted, blot•ting, blots.** —*tr.* **1.** To spot or stain (sthg.): *Greasy fingerprints blotted the page.* **2.** To dry or soak up (sthg.) with absorbent material: *blot a spill with paper towels.* —*intr.* **1.** To spill or spread in a spot or stain. **2.** To become blotted or absorbed: *Watercolors blot easily.* ♦ **blot out.** *tr.v.* [sep.] **1.** To hide (sthg.) from view; obscure: *Storm clouds blotted out the sun.* **2.** To destroy (sthg.) completely; annihilate: *The frost blotted out the tomatoes.*

blotch (blŏch) *n.* **1.** A spot or blot; a splotch: *a blotch on the apple.* **2.** A discoloration on the skin; a blemish: *a blotch on his nose.* —**blotched, blotch′y** *adj.*

blot•ter (blŏt′ər) *n.* A piece or pad of thick absorbent paper used to dry a surface by soaking up excess ink.

blouse (blous *or* blouz) *n.* A loosely fitting shirt that extends to the waist.

blow¹ (blō) *v.* **blew** (blōo), **blown** (blōn), **blow•ing, blows.** —*intr.* **1.** *(used of the air or wind).* To be in motion: *The wind blew hard all night.* **2.** To be moved by a current of air: *My hat blew off.* **3.** To send out a current of air: *Blow on your soup to cool it.* **4.** To make a sound by air passing through sthg.: *The whistle blows at noon.* **5.** To break suddenly because of air pressure inside: *The tire blew when we hit a rock.* **6.** *(used of an electrical fuse).* To melt: *We were left in darkness when the fuse blew.* —*tr.* **1.** To cause (sbdy./sthg.) to move by a current of air: *The storm blew a tree across the power lines.* **2.** To push out (as air) from the mouth: *She blew a kiss from across the room.* **3.** To cause (a wind instrument) to sound by forcing breath through it: *blow a trumpet.* **4.** To cause (sthg.) to explode: *To build the tunnel they blew rock out of the way with dynamite.* **5.** To clear (sthg.) by forcing air through: *blowing his nose noisily.* **6.** To shape (a soft material, such as molten glass) by forcing air into it: *blow a bubble of chewing gum.* **7.** To cause (an electrical fuse) to melt and open a circuit. **8.** To lose or waste (sthg.) through mistakes or carelessness: *You blew your chance to go to Europe.* —*n.* The act or an instance of blowing: *He put the candle out with a blow.* ♦ **blow away.** *tr.v.* [sep.] *Informal.* **1.** To kill (sbdy.) by shooting, especially with a gun. **2.** To have a powerful effect on (sbdy.): *That concert blew me away.* **blow**

hot and cold. To like sthg. one minute and dislike it the next: *She blows hot and cold about going to college.* **blow in.** *intr.v. Slang.* To arrive, especially when unexpected: *He blew in late last night.* **blow off.** *tr.v.* [sep.] *Slang.* **1.** To treat (sbdy.) as unimportant: *They invited him to lunch, but he blew them off.* **2.** To choose not to do (sthg. one thinks of as unimportant): *She blew off her homework.* **blow off steam.** To express emotion that has been held inside: *The workers blew off steam by complaining to each other.* **blow (one's) cover.** *Informal.* To expose a person's true self or reasons for doing sthg.: *Don't blow my cover at the party tonight.* **blow (one's) mind.** *Slang.* To be difficult to believe: *It blows my mind that she would leave such a good job.* **blow (one's) own horn.** To speak well about oneself: *He blew his own horn about getting a promotion.* **blow (one's) top** or **stack.** To express anger suddenly and forcefully: *When I told him I'd wrecked the car, he blew his top.* **blow out.** *tr.v.* [sep.] To stop (sthg.) from burning by a current of air: *blow out the candles.* —*intr.v.* To fail, as an electrical device: *The TV blew out.* **blow over.** *intr.v.* To come to an end with little lasting effect: *The storm will blow over soon.* **blow the whistle on.** To report the improper behavior of (sbdy.): *He blew the whistle on his friend who had stolen the money.* **blow up.** *intr.v.* **1.** To come into being: *A storm blew up.* **2.** To express anger suddenly and forcefully: *He blows up when his children argue with him.* **3.** To explode: *The gas tank blew up.* —*tr.v.* [sep.] **1.** To fill (sthg.) with air: *blowing up balloons.* **2.** To enlarge (a photograph): *Can you blow this photo up for me?* **3.** To cause (sbdy./sthg.) to explode: *The enemy blew up the bridge.*

blow² (blō) *n.* **1.** A sudden hard stroke or hit, as with the fist or a weapon: *He suffered a blow to the head when he fell.* **2.** A sudden unexpected shock or piece of bad luck: *The closing of the museum was a blow to our weekend plans.* ♦ **blow-by-blow.** Having many details: *She gave us a blow-by-blow description of the accident.*

blow-dry (blō′drī′) *tr.v.* **blow-dried, blow-dry•ing, blow-dries.** To dry and often style (hair) with a blow dryer: *I always blow-dry my hair after I wash it.*

blow dryer *n.* A portable electric blower for drying and styling hair.

blow•er (blō′ər) *n.* A device that produces a flow of air or other gas through a duct or an enclosed space.

blown (blōn) *v.* Past participle of **blow¹**.

blow•out (blō′out′) *n.* **1.** A sudden and violent loss of air pressure, as from an automobile tire. **2.** *Informal.* A large party: *Their wedding reception was a blowout.* **3.** *Informal.* An easy, one-sided victory: *That loss yesterday was a blowout.*

B

blow•torch (blō′tôrch′) *n.* A torch using air to produce a flame hot enough to melt soft metals and remove paint.

blow•up (blō′ŭp′) *n.* **1.** An explosion: *Many people were killed in the blowup at the factory.* **2.** A photographic enlargement: *I made a blowup of my son's photograph and hung it on my wall.* **3.** An outburst of anger: *There was a blowup between the two friends when one of them wrecked the other one's car.*

blub•ber[1] (blŭb′ər) *v. —intr.* To cry or sob in a noisy manner: *a child blubbering for her mother.* See Synonyms at **cry.** *—tr.* To say (sthg.) while crying and sobbing: *The boy blubbered his name.*

blub•ber[2] (blŭb′ər) *n.* [U] **1.** The fat of whales and some other sea animals, lying under the skin and over the muscles, from which oil is obtained. **2.** Excessive body fat in a person.

bludg•eon (blŭj′ən) *tr.v.* To beat or strike (sbdy./sthg.) with a heavy object.

blue (blōō) *n.* [C; U] The color of the sky on a clear day; the color of the visible spectrum lying between green and violet. *—adj.* **blu•er, blu•est. 1.** Of the color blue. **2.** Having a gray or purplish color, as from cold or a bruise: *lips blue from the chill.* **3.** Gloomy; sad: *a sailor far from home, lonely and blue.* ◆ **blue in the face.** To the point or at the point of extreme exasperation: *I argued with them until I was blue in the face.* **into the blue.** At a far distance; into the unknown: *After college she disappeared into the blue.* **once in a blue moon.** Not very often: *I see my friend once in a blue moon.* **out of the blue. 1.** From an unexpected source: *a problem that came out of the blue.* **2.** At a completely unexpected time: *My friend showed up out of the blue last night.* *—***blue′ness** *n.* [U]

HOMONYMS: blue, blew (expelled air).

blue•ber•ry (blōō′bĕr′ē) *n.* A round, juicy, edible blue or purplish berry or the shrub that produces it.

blue•bird (blōō′bûrd′) *n.* A North American bird with blue feathers and a rust-colored breast in the male.

blue blood *n.* A member of the aristocracy or other high social group.

blue cheese *n.* [U] A strong-tasting cheese streaked with bluish mold: *a salad dressing with blue cheese.*

blue-col•lar (blōō′kŏl′ər) *adj.* Relating to wage earners whose jobs are performed in work clothes and often involve manual labor: *Plumbing is a blue-collar job.*

blue jay *n.* A North American bird with a crested head, blue feathers with white and black markings, and a harsh noisy cry.

blue jeans *pl.n.* Pants of blue denim or similar cloth: *students wearing old blue jeans.*

blue•print (blōō′prĭnt′) *n.* **1.** A photographic copy of architectural plans or technical drawings appearing as white lines on a blue background: *working from the blueprints.* **2.** A carefully worked-out plan: *a blueprint for success.*

blue ribbon *n.* The first prize or highest award: *Our dog won the blue ribbon at the dog show.*

blues (blōōz) *pl.n. (used with a singular or plural verb).* **1.** A type of popular music with a slow tempo that developed from southern African American songs: *Louisiana is famous for the blues.* **2.** Lowness of spirit: *The rainy weather is giving people the blues.*

bluff[1] (blŭf) *v. —tr.* To deceive or mislead (sbdy.): *He bluffed the guard into thinking he worked for the bank. —intr.* To give a false display of strength or confidence: *They were bluffing when the reporters said they knew the movie star. —n.* An example of deceiving or misleading by a false display of strength or confidence: *Their courage was all a bluff.* *—***bluff′er** *n.*

bluff[2] (blŭf) *n. (usually plural).* A steep headland, cliff, or riverbank: *climbed the bluffs along the river. —adj.* Gruff or blunt in manner but not unkind: *bluff speech.*

blu•ish (blōō′ĭsh) *adj.* Somewhat blue: *a bluish tint to the shirt.*

blun•der (blŭn′dər) *n.* A foolish or careless mistake: *Using the wrong medicine was a serious blunder. —intr.v.* **1.** To make a foolish mistake: *We blundered in estimating the cost of the repairs.* **2.** To move clumsily or blindly; stumble: *They blundered through the bushes into a stream.* *—***blun′der•er** *n.*

blunt (blŭnt) *adj.* **1.** Having a thick dull edge or end; not sharp: *a blunt knife.* **2.** Abrupt and frank in manner: *a blunt response. —tr.v.* To make (sthg.) less sharp or keen; dull: *The knife was blunted from so much use.* *—***blunt′ly** *adv. —***blunt′ness** *n.* [U]

blur (blûr) *v.* **blurred, blur•ring, blurs.** *—tr.* **1.** To make (sthg.) indistinct or hazy in outline; obscure: *Clouds blurred the mountain.* **2.** To smear or stain (sthg.); smudge: *My wet hands blurred the watercolors.* **3.** To reduce the ability to perceive (sthg.); dim: *Bright lights blurred the driver's vision. —intr.* To become indistinct, vague, or hazy: *The mountain blurred in the snowstorm. —n.* **1.** Something that is indistinct and hazy: *The crowd was a blur of colors in the distance.* **2.** A smear or blot; a smudge: *a blur on the camera lens.*

blurb (blûrb) *n.* A brief favorable publicity notice, as on the jacket of a book.

blur·ry (blûr′ē) *adj.* Indistinct and hazy: *blurry sounds; a blurry picture.*

blurt (blûrt) *tr.v.* [*out*] To say (sthg.) suddenly and without thought: *She blurted out the secret.*

blush (blŭsh) *intr.v.* [*at*] **1.** To become suddenly red in the face from modesty, embarrassment, or shame: *She blushed at the attention.* **2.** To feel ashamed: *I blushed at their rude remarks.* —*n.* **1.** [C] A sudden reddening of the face caused by modesty, embarrassment, or shame. **2.** [C] A reddish or rosy color: *The sun's last blushes tinted the hills.* **3.** [U] Makeup put on the cheeks: *That woman wears too much blush.*

blus·ter (blŭs′tər) *intr.v.* **1.** To blow in loud violent gusts: *Winds blustered on the mountain top.* **2.** To utter noisy boasts or threats: *The angry customer blustered at the sales clerk.* —*n.* [U] **1.** A violent gusty wind: *the bluster of a March storm.* **2.** Noisy confusion; commotion: *reporters amid the bluster of a political convention.* **3.** Loud, boastful, or threatening talk: *Don't pay attention to all that bluster about layoffs.* —**blus′ter·er** *n.* —**blus′ter·ous, blus′ter·y** *adj.*

blvd. or **Blvd.** *abbr.* An abbreviation of boulevard.

bo·a (bō′ə) *n.* **1.** A large nonpoisonous snake, such as the boa constrictor of tropical America, that coils around and crushes its prey. **2.** A long fluffy scarf of fur or feathers.

boar (bôr) *n.* **1.** A male pig. **2.** A wild pig that has dark hair and short tusks.

HOMONYMS: **boar, bore** (drill, make weary, supported).

board (bôrd) *n.* **1.** [C] A flat thin piece of sawed wood; a plank: *The side of the house was finished with oak boards.* **2.** [C] A flat piece of wood or other material for some special use: *a bulletin board; a chessboard.* **3.** [U] Food served daily to paying guests: *room and board.* **4.** [C] A group of persons organized to conduct business: *the board of education.* —*v.* —*tr.* **1.** To go aboard (a plane, train, or ship): *We boarded the plane at gate 4.* **2.** To provide (sbdy./sthg.) with food and lodging for a charge: *We boarded our dogs at a kennel.* —*intr.* **1.** To go aboard or allow to board a plane, ship, or train: *Your plane will be boarding in ten minutes.* **2.** To live as a paying guest: *board at the local hotel.* ◆ **board up.** *tr.v.* [sep.] To close (sthg.) with boards: *Everyone was boarding up the windows before the storm.*

HOMONYMS: **board, bored** (wearied).

board·er (bôr′dər) *n.* A person who pays for and receives both meals and lodging at another person's home.

HOMONYMS: **boarder, border** (edge).

board·ing house (bôr′dĭng) *n.* A private home that provides meals and lodging for paying guests.

boarding school *n.* A school where students live.

board·walk (bôrd′wôk′) *n.* A public walk along a beach, usually made of wooden planks.

boast (bōst) *v.* —*intr.* To speak with too much pride about oneself; brag: *The world-champion swimmer boasted about his medals.* —*tr.* To have (sthg.) as a desirable feature: *The area boasts great monuments and buildings.* —*n.* **1.** A bragging or boastful statement: *a boast not supported by fact.* **2.** A source of pride: *The city's main boast is its beautiful park.* —**boast′er** *n.* —**boast·ful** *adj.* —**boast′ful·ly** *adv.* —**boast′ful·ness** *n.* [U]

boat (bōt) *n.* **1.** A small open craft for traveling on water. **2.** A large vessel that travels on or under the water; a ship or submarine. —*intr.* To travel by boat; row or sail: *They boated across the lake.* ◆ **in the same boat.** In the same situation as sbdy. else: *We were all in the same boat because none of us had studied music before.*

boat people *pl.n.* People who leave their country by boat seeking refuge in some country that will allow them to enter.

bob¹ (bŏb) *v.* **bobbed, bob·bing, bobs.** —*tr.* To cause (sthg.) to move up and down: *bobbed their heads.* —*intr.* **1.** To move or jerk up and down: *a boat bobbing on the water.* **2.** [*for*] To grab at floating or hanging objects with the teeth: *bob for apples.* —*n.* A quick jerking movement of the head or body.

bob² (bŏb) *n.* **1.** A small hanging weight. **2.** A fishing float or cork. **3.** A short haircut for a girl or woman. —*v.* **bobbed, bob·bing, bobs.** —*intr.* To fish with a bob. —*tr.* To cut (a girl or woman's hair) short: *She bobbed her hair.*

bob·bin (bŏb′ĭn) *n.* A small spool or reel that holds thread or yarn.

bob·ble (bŏb′əl) *v.* **bob·bled, bob·bling, bob·bles.** —*intr.* To bob up and down: *The toy boat bobbled in the water.* —*tr.* To lose one's grip on (a ball) momentarily: *The catcher bobbled the ball.* —*n.* A mistake or blunder: *A serious bobble cost him the game.*

bob·by (bŏb′ē) *n., pl.* **bob·bies.** *Chiefly British.* A policeman.

bob·cat (bŏb′kăt′) *n.* A North American wildcat with spotted reddish brown fur and a short tail.

bob·sled (bŏb′slĕd′) *n.* A long racing sled with a steering device that controls the front runners. —*intr.v.* **bob·sled·ded, bob·sled·ding, bob·sleds.** To ride or race in a bobsled: *They like to bobsled in the winter.*

bode¹ (bōd) *tr.v.* **bod·ed, bod·ing, bodes.**
To be a sign or an omen of (sthg. to come): *A rough sea boded trouble for the passengers.* ♦ **bode ill.** To be a bad sign: *The coming hurricane bodes ill for many store owners along the beach.* **bode well.** To be a good sign: *A clear sky boded well for our trip.*

bode² (bōd) *v.* A past tense of **bide.**

bod·ice (bŏd'ĭs) *n.* The fitted upper part of a dress.

bod·i·ly (bŏd'l ē) *adj.* Relating to the body: *food and other bodily needs.* —*adv.* **1.** In person: *The sleepy student was present bodily but not mentally.* **2.** As a whole: *a rabbit lifted bodily by the eagle.*

bod·y (bŏd'ē) *n., pl.* **bod·ies. 1.a.** The entire physical structure and substance of a living thing, especially of a human or an animal: *His body weakened as his illness got worse.* **b.** A corpse or carcass: *a dead body.* **2.** The main part of a person or an animal not including the head, arms, and legs; the trunk or torso. **3.** A mass or collection of material that is distinct from other masses: *a body of water.* **4.** Persons or things considered as a group: *the student body; a body of information.* **5.** The main or central part of sthg.: *the body of the car.*

bod·y·build·ing (bŏd'ē bĭl'dĭng) *n.* [U] The process of building one's muscles through diet and exercise, such as weightlifting.

bod·y·guard (bŏd'ē gärd') *n.* A person who is responsible for protecting one or more specific persons against possible attack.

body language *n.* [U] Gestures and postures of the body and facial expressions by which an individual communicates with others.

bog (bôg *or* bŏg) *n.* [C; U] An area of soft wet ground, consisting mainly of decayed plant matter: *They decided not to continue their search because they could not cross the bog.* —*v.* **bogged, bog·ging, bogs.** —*tr.* To cause (sthg.) to sink in a bog: *Rain bogged our car in a sea of mud.* —*intr.* [*down*] To be hindered or slowed: *The plan to restore the building bogged down in government regulations.*

bog·ey·man also **bog·ie·man** (bŏog'ē măn' *or* bō'gē măn') *n.* A terrifying spirit: *The child thought he saw a bogeyman in his room and refused to be alone.*

bog·gle (bŏg'əl) *v.* **bog·gled, bog·gling, bog·gles.** —*intr.* To be fearful or astonished: *My mind boggles at the thought of inheriting a fortune.* —*tr.* To cause (sbdy./sthg.) to be overcome with fright or astonishment: *The number of bicycles stolen each year boggles the mind.*

bo·gus (bō'gəs) *adj.* Counterfeit; fake: *It is a crime to use bogus money.*

bo·he·mi·an (bō hē'mē ən) *n.* A person,

especially an artist, who does not follow the usual standards of behavior.

boil¹ (boil) *v.* —*intr.* **1.** To change from a liquid to a gas by being heated: *Water boils at 100°C or 212°F.* **2.** To be cooked by boiling or putting into boiling water: *The potatoes need to boil for about 15 minutes.* **3.** To have the contents at a boil: *The pot is boiling on the stove.* **4.** To be very angry or excited: *boil with anger at the insult.* —*tr.* **1.** To heat (a liquid) to a temperature at which it turns into a gas, with bubbles breaking though the liquid's surface: *Boil the water for tea.* **2.** To cook (sthg.) by boiling: *boil an egg.* —*n.* The condition or act of being boiled: *First you should bring the soup to a rapid boil.* ♦ **boil away.** *intr.v.* To boil until dried out and completely gone: *The water boiled away and the rice burned.* **boil down.** *tr.v.* [*sep.*] To reduce (sthg.) in volume or amount by boiling: *boil down the juice into syrup.* —*intr.v.* To be reduced to a simpler form: *The problem boils down to a lack of money.* **boil over.** *intr.v.* **1.** To overflow while boiling: *The soup boiled over.* **2.** To explode in rage; lose one's temper: *Tempers boiled over at the city council meeting.*

boil² (boil) *n.* A painful swelling of the skin and the tissue beneath it, filled with pus and caused by a bacterial infection.

boil·er (boi'lər) *n.* A container in which a liquid, usually water, is heated and often vaporized for use in an engine, a turbine, or a heating system.

boil·ing point (boi'lĭng) *n.* **1.** The temperature at which a liquid boils, especially as measured at sea level. **2.** *Informal.* The point at which one loses one's temper: *Her husband has a low boiling point.*

bois·ter·ous (boi'stər əs *or* boi'strəs) *adj.* **1.** Rough and stormy; violent: *boisterous winds.* **2.** Noisy and lacking restraint or discipline: *boisterous cheers of an excited crowd.* —**bois'ter·ous·ly** *adv.* —**bois'ter·ous·ness** *n.* [U]

bold (bōld) *adj.* **1.** Having no fear; brave; courageous: *bold explorers.* See Synonyms at **brave. 2.** Showing or requiring courage; daring: *a bold proposal.* **3.** Taking inappropriate liberties; forward: *a bold stare; a bold reply.* **4.** Vivid; clear: *bold colors; bold handwriting.* —**bold'ly** *adv.* —**bold'ness** *n.* [U]

bold·face (bōld'fās') *n.* [U] Letters made with thick heavy lines to make them immediately noticeable: *All entry words in this dictionary are in boldface.* —**bold'face'**, **bold'-faced'** *adj.*

bo·lo·gna (bə lō'nē *or* bə lō'nə) also **ba·lo·ney** *or* **bo·lo·ney** (bə lō'nē) *n.* [U] A seasoned cooked sausage, often made of mixed meats and usually eaten in sandwiches.

bol·ster (bōl′stər) *tr.v.* To support or rein-force (sthg.): *Visitors bolstered the patient's spirits.*

bolt (bōlt) *n.* **1.** A small metal rod with a head at one end and threads onto which a nut is screwed at the other end, used to hold two parts to-gether. **2.** A sliding wooden or metal bar used to close a door or gate: *Lock the bolt on the door.* **3.** A large roll of cloth: *We bought the last two yards of cloth on the bolt.* **4.** A flash of lightning; a thunder-bolt: *The bolt struck the tree.* —*v.* —*tr.* **1.** To attach or fasten (sthg.) with a bolt or bolts: *They bolted the shelf to the wall.* **2.** To lock (sthg.) with a bolt: *Bolt the door.* **3.** To eat (sthg.) quickly: *He was late, so he bolted his dinner.* —*intr.* **1.** To move or spring suddenly: *He bolted from the room and ran outside.* **2.** To break from a rider's control and run away: *Her horse became frightened and bolted.* ◆ **bolt upright.** Stiff and straight: *Realizing he was late, he sat bolt upright in bed.*

bolt
(fastener)

bolt
(lock)

bomb (bŏm) *n.* **1.** An explosive weapon: *The bomb exploded, destroying the entire building.* **2.** A container that holds a substance under pressure, as a preparation for killing insects, that can be released as a spray or gas: *The exterminator used a flea bomb to get rid of the pests in the carpet.* **3.** *Slang.* A failure: *That movie was a bomb.* —*tr.v.* To attack, damage, or destroy (sthg.) with a bomb or bombs: *bomb a bridge.*

bom·bard (bŏm bärd′) *tr.v.* **1.** To attack (a location) with bombs, shells, or other explosives: *bombard an enemy position.* **2.** To shower (sbdy.) with questions or insults: *Reporters bombarded the police with ques-tions.* —**bom·bard′ment** *n.*

bombed (bŏmd) *adj. Slang.* Drunk.

bomb·er (bŏm′ər) *n.* **1.** A military airplane that carries and drops bombs. **2.** A person who makes and sets off bombs: *the subway bomber.*

bomb·shell (bŏm′shĕl′) *n.* **1.** A bomb. **2.** A great surprise or shock: *The news of the assassination was a real bombshell.*

bo·na fide (bō′nə fīd′ *or* bŏn′ə fīd′) *adj.* **1.** Done or made in good faith; sincere: *a bona fide offer to buy.* **2.** Genuine; authentic: *a bona fide painting by Rembrandt.*

bo·nan·za (bə năn′zə) *n.* A source of great wealth: *The rise in stock prices was a bonanza to shareholders.*

bon·bon (bŏn′bŏn′) *n.* A piece of candy, often with a creamy center and a chocolate coating.

bond (bŏnd) *n.* **1.** (*usually plural*). Something that binds, ties, or fastens together, as a cord or rope: *bonds around the prisoner's wrists.* **2.** A force that unites; a tie; a link: *strong bonds between the parent and child.* **3.** A force of attraction that holds atoms or groups of atoms together in a molecule. **4.** Money paid as bail to release sbdy. from prison: *He had to pay a bond of $5,000 to avoid staying in jail until the trial.* **5.** A certificate of debt issued by a government or corporation that guarantees repayment of the original invest-ment with interest: *stocks and bonds.* —*v.* —*tr.* **1.** To join (pieces) together, as with glue. **2.** To connect (persons) by strong emo-tional or social ties: *Love for our grandpar-ents bonded us all.* —*intr.* To be joined together with a bond: *Oxygen bonds to hydro-gen to form water.*

bond·age (bŏn′dĭj) *n.* [U] The condition of being kept as a slave.

bone (bōn) *n.* **1.** [U] The hard, dense, calcified tissue that forms the skeleton of most verte-brates. **2. bones. a.** The skeleton. **b.** The body of sbdy. who has died: *May their bones rest in peace.* —*tr.v.* **boned, bon·ing, bones.** *Informal.* In cooking, to remove the bones from (sthg.): *bone fish.* ◆ **bone of con-tention.** The subject of a dispute: *Who goes first is often a bone of contention.* **bone up on.** *Informal.* To study (a subject) intensively; review: *I need to bone up on my math skills before I take the test.* **have a bone to pick.** To have a reason for a complaint or dispute: *I have a bone to pick with you about your study habits.* **make no bones about.** To show no reserve or embarrassment about (sthg.); com-plain: *She made no bones about telling them how she felt about the new rules.*

bone-dry (bōn′drī′) *adj.* Without any mois-ture; very dry: *She needed to water her plants because the soil was bone-dry.*

bone·head (bōn′hĕd′) *n. Slang.* An insult-ing term for a person thought to be stupid, often used in a friendly, humorous way. —**bone′head′ed** *adj.*

bon·er (bō′nər) *n. Slang.* A foolish mistake; a blunder.

bon·fire (bŏn′fīr′) *n.* A large outdoor fire.

bon·go drums (bŏng′gō *or* bông′gō) *pl.n.* A pair of small drums that are held between the knees and beaten with the hands.

bon·gos (bŏng′gōz *or* bông′gōz) *pl.n.* Bongo drums.

bon·net (bŏn′ĭt) *n.* **1.** A hat tied with rib-bons under the chin: *an Easter bonnet.* **2.** *Chiefly British.* The hood of an automobile.

bon·sai (bŏn sī′ *or* bŏn′sī′) *n.* **1.** [U] The art of growing miniature trees in small pots or dishes. **2.** [C] A tree grown in this way.

bo·nus (bō′nəs) *n.* Something given or paid in addition to what is usual: *Each worker got a bonus of three extra days off for the holidays.*

bon•y or **bon•ey** (bō′nē) *adj.* **bon•i•er, bon• i•est** or **bon•ey•er, bon•ey•est. 1.** Relating to or resembling bone. **2.** Full of bones: *a bony piece of fish.* **3.** Having bones that stick out or show through; thin: *bony cheeks.* —**bon′i•ness** *n.* [U]

boo (bōō) *n., pl.* **boos.** A sound uttered to show dislike or disapproval: *The singer received boos from the fans because they did not like her song.* —*interj.* An expression used to show dislike or disapproval or to frighten or surprise. —*v.* —*intr.* To utter a boo: *The disappointed audience booed angrily.* —*tr.* To say "boo" to (sbdy./sthg.); jeer: *The baseball spectators booed the umpire's decision.*

boob (bōōb) *n. Offensive Slang.* **1.** A stupid or foolish person. **2.** A woman's breast.

boo-boo also **boo•boo** (bōō′bōō) *n., pl.* **boo-boos** or **boo•boos.** *Informal.* **1.** A foolish or careless mistake; a blunder: *I made a boo-boo by forgetting to give him the message.* **2.** A slight physical injury, such as a scratch: *The child fell and got a boo-boo.*

boob tube *n. Slang.* Television: *He spends all day watching the boob tube.*

boo•by prize (bōō′bē) *n.* An award given to the person who has the worst score in a game or contest.

booby trap *n.* **1.** A hidden bomb or mine set to go off when a harmless-looking object attached to it is moved or touched: *The soldiers were killed when the booby trap exploded.* **2.** A situation for catching a person off guard; a trap: *Be careful; this could be a booby trap.*

boog•ie-woog•ie (bōōg′ē wōōg′ē or bōō′gē wōō′gē) *n.* [U] A style of jazz piano playing in which a distinctive rhythmic and melodic pattern is repeated over and over in the bass.

book (bōōk) *n.* **1.** A set of printed or blank pages fastened together along one edge and enclosed between covers. **2.a.** A printed or written literary work: *She's writing a new book about Mexico.* **b.** A main division of a larger written or printed work: *a book of the Old Testament.* **3.** A volume for recording financial transactions: *an account book; An accountant keeps books.* **4.** A small packet of similar things bound together: *a book of matches.* —*tr.v.* **1.** To arrange for (sthg.) in advance; reserve: *We booked tickets to the show.* **2.** To write down charges against (sbdy.) in a police record: *book a suspect.* ◆ **by the book.** Strictly according to the rules: *She runs the company by the book.* **in (one's) book.** In one's opinion: *In my book she was one of the all-time greats.* **like a book.** Thoroughly; completely: *I know the town like a book.* **throw the book at. 1.** To give (sbdy.) the worst punishment possible: *Because it was the*

thief's third conviction, the judge threw the book at her. **2.** *Informal.* To scold or punish (sbdy.) severely: *I was late for supper again, and my mother threw the book at me.*

book•case (bōōk′kās′) *n.* A piece of furniture with shelves for holding books.

booked (bōōkt) *adj.* **1.** Fully reserved: *The flight was completely booked.* **2.** Having one's time completely taken up; very busy: *I'd love to do lunch, but I'm booked until next year.*

book•end (bōōk′ĕnd′) *n.* An object placed at the end of a row of books to keep them upright.

book•ie (bōōk′ē) *n.* A person who accepts and pays off bets; a bookmaker.

book•ish (bōōk′ĭsh) *adj.* Fond of books and study; studious: *a bookish student.*

book•keep•ing (bōōk′kē′pĭng) *n.* [U] The work or skill of keeping records of money received, owed, or paid by a business. —**book′keep′er** *n.*

book•let (bōōk′lĭt) *n.* A small book or pamphlet, usually with a paper cover.

book•mak•er (bōōk′mā′kər) *n.* **1.** A person or business that edits, prints, or publishes books. **2.** A person who accepts and pays off bets, especially on sporting events such as horse races. —**book′mak′ing** *n.* [U]

book•mark (bōōk′märk′) *n.* An object, such as a ribbon or a strip of paper, placed between the pages of a book to mark the reader's place.

book•shelf (bōōk′shĕlf′) *n.* A shelf or set of shelves for holding books.

book•shop (bōōk′shŏp′) *n.* A bookstore.

book•store (bōōk′stôr′) *n.* A store where books are sold.

book•worm (bōōk′wûrm′) *n. Informal.* A person who spends a lot of time reading or studying.

boom (bōōm) *v.* —*intr.* **1.** To make a deep resonant sound: *The cannon boomed across the valley.* **2.** To grow or develop rapidly; thrive: *Business is booming.* —*tr.* To say (sthg.) with a loud sound: *Rescuers boomed a message over their loudspeaker.* —*n.* **1.** A deep hollow sound, as from an explosion: *We could hear the boom of the rocket from miles away.* **2.** A sudden increase, as in growth or production: *A boom in farm production filled the markets.* **3.** A time of economic prosperity: *California had a boom after gold was discovered.*

boo•mer•ang (bōō′mə răng′) *n.* A flat curved piece of wood that can be thrown so that it returns to the thrower. Boomerangs were originally used by the native people of Australia. —*intr.v.* To have the opposite effect of what was intended; backfire: *Our plan to increase profits boomeranged; we lost money instead.*

boon (boon) *n.* A help or blessing: *Delay would harm us and be a boon to our competitors.*

boon·docks (boon'dŏks') *pl.n. Informal.* Rural country; the backwoods.

boor (boor) *n.* A crude person with rude or clumsy manners: *He is such a boor; he insulted my friends at the party.* —**boor'ish** *adj.* —**boor'ish·ly** *adv.* —**boor'ish·ness** *n.* [U]

boost (boost) *tr.v.* **1.** To lift (sbdy./sthg.) by pushing up from below: *My friend boosted me into the tree.* **2.** To increase (sthg.); raise: *Advertising often boosts sales.* —*n.* **1.** Something that helps sbdy. be more successful, healthy, or confident: *The compliment on her writing was a boost to her morale.* **2.** A push upward or ahead: *Give me a boost up the wall.* **3.** An increase: *A boost in salary.*

boost·er (boo'stər) *n.* **1.** Something that increases the power or effectiveness of a system or device: *a power booster; a booster shot.* **2.** A rocket used to launch a missile or space vehicle. **3.** A person or thing that boosts: *Her good test score was a confidence booster.*

boot (boot) *n.* **1.** A kind of shoe that covers the foot and ankle and usually part of the leg. **2.** A kick: *Give the ball a good boot.* **3.** *Chiefly British.* The trunk of an automobile. —*tr.v.* To kick (sthg.): *The soccer player booted the ball down the field.* ♦ **boot up.** *intr.v. (used of computers),* To start up: *My computer's just booting up.* —*tr.v.* [sep.] To start (a computer): *I can't boot up my computer.* **to boot.** In addition; besides: *He got a T-shirt and a baseball cap to boot.*

boot camp *n.* A training camp for soldiers or sailors who have just joined the armed services.

boo·tee also **boo·tie** (boo'tē) *n.* A soft, usually knitted baby shoe.

HOMONYMS: bootee, booty (loot).

booth (booth) *n., pl.* **booths** (boothz or booths). **1.** A small enclosed compartment: *a telephone booth.* **2.** A small room or stand where things are sold or entertainment is provided: *a ticket booth.* **3.** A seating compartment consisting of a table enclosed by benches: *We ate in a booth at the restaurant.*

boot·leg (boot'lĕg') *v.* **boot·legged, boot·leg·ging, boot·legs.** —*tr.* To make, sell, or transport (products) illegally. —*intr.* To engage in bootlegging. —*n.* [U] A product that is illegally made, sold, or transported. —*adj.* Made, sold, or transported illegally: *bootleg music tapes.* —**boot'leg'ger** *n.*

boo·ty (boo'tē) *n.* [U] **1.** Possessions taken from an enemy: *The pirates took booty from the ship that they captured.* **2.** A valuable prize; a treasure: *Divers brought up booty from the ship that sank.*

HOMONYMS: booty, bootee (baby shoe).

booze (booz) *Slang. n.* [U] Alcoholic drink. —*intr.v.* **boozed, booz·ing, booz·es.** To drink alcoholic beverages excessively. —**booz'er** *n.*

bop (bŏp) *Informal. tr.v.* **bopped, bop·ping, bops.** To hit or strike (sbdy./sthg.): *That jerk bopped me on the head for no reason!* —*n.* A blow or punch: *a bop on the head.*

bor·der (bôr'dər) *n.* **1.** The line where one country, state, or region ends and another begins; a boundary: *the border between United States and Canada.* **2.** A margin or an edge: *They picnicked on the border of the lake.* See Synonyms at **margin. 3.** A strip put on or around an edge, as for ornament: *a border of lace around the tablecloth.* —*tr.v.* **1.** To lie along or next to (sthg.): *Canada and Mexico border the United States.* **2.** To put a border or an edging on (sthg.): *border a collar with lace.* ♦ **border on** or **upon.** *tr.v.* [insep.] **1.** To be next to (sthg.); touch: *France borders on Germany.* **2.** To come close to (sthg.); approach: *This weather borders on perfect!*

HOMONYMS: border, boarder (lodger).

bor·der·line (bôr'dər līn') *n.* **1.** A dividing line; a border or boundary. **2.** An indefinite line between two different conditions: *Your grade is on the borderline between A and B.* —*adj.* Not clearly within a certain class or limit; uncertain: *a borderline condition, perhaps ready for surgery.*

bore¹ (bôr) *v.* **bored, bor·ing, bores.** —*tr.* **1.** To make (a hole, tunnel, or well) by drilling or digging: *bore a tunnel through a mountain.* **2.** To make a hole in or through (sthg.), as with a drill or similar tool: *bore the mountain.* —*intr.* To make a hole by drilling or digging: *The miners bored through the rock to get at the coal.* —*n.* The inside diameter of a hole, tube, cylinder, or other hollow object: *a pipe with a bore of three inches.* —**bor'er** *n.*

HOMONYMS: bore (drill, make weary, supported), boar (male pig).

bore² (bôr) *v.* **bored, bor·ing, bores.** —*tr.* To make (sbdy.) weary by failing to interest or by being dull: *The speaker bored the audience by talking too long.* —*intr.* To become weary: *Teenagers bore easily.* —*n.* An uninteresting or tiresome person or thing: *He is such a bore.*

bore³ (bôr) *v.* Past tense of **bear¹.**

bored (bôrd) *adj.* Not interested: *We were bored by his long speech.* ♦ **bored stiff.** Very bored: *I was bored stiff by his story.*

bore•dom (bôr′dəm) *n.* [U] The condition of being bored; weariness of mind: *kids causing trouble out of boredom.*

bo•ric acid (bôr′ĭk) *n.* [U] A white or colorless compound, often used as an antiseptic.

bor•ing (bôr′ĭng) *adj.* Not interesting; dull: *The book was so long and boring that I could not finish it.*

SYNONYMS: **boring, dull, tedious, tiresome.** These adjectives mean without interest, liveliness, or imagination. **Boring** describes sthg. that makes one feel tired and unhappy: *The movie was so boring that half the audience fell asleep or walked out before the end.* **Dull** means uninteresting and unsurprising: *The lecturer somehow was able to give an enthusiastic presentation on a dull topic.* **Tedious** describes sthg. that is boring because of its slowness: *Our parents think train travel is romantic but we find it tedious.* **Tiresome** means tedious and repetitious: *I don't mind the tiresome job of returning bottles and cans because I want to help the environment.* ANTONYMS: **interesting, lively.**

---

born (bôrn) *v.* A past participle of **bear**[1]. —*adj.* **1.** Brought into life or existence: *She was born in 1980.* **2.** Having a natural talent from birth: *a born artist.* **3.** Destined from birth: *She was born to sing.* **4.** Coming or resulting from sthg.: *wisdom born of experience.* ♦ **born and bred.** A native, usually still living in the place where he or she was born and showing its traditions: *I'm a Californian, born and bred.* **born yesterday.** Inexperienced; naive: *I understand his tricks; I wasn't born yesterday.*

born-a•gain (bôrn′ə gĕn′) *adj.* **1.** Relating to or being a person who has made a conversion or renewed commitment to Jesus as his or her personal savior: *a born-again Christian.* **2.** Marked by renewed activity or revived interest or enthusiasm: *a born-again supporter of free speech.*

borne (bôrn) *v.* A past participle of **bear**[1].

bo•ron (bôr′ŏn′) *n.* [U] *Symbol* **B** A soft, brown element used in alloys, nuclear reactors, and abrasives. Atomic number 5. See table at **element.**

bor•ough (bûr′ō *or* bŭr′ō) *n.* A governmental division of an area or city: *the Borough of Queens.*

HOMONYMS: **borough, burro** (donkey), **burrow** (hole).

---

bor•row (bŏr′ō *or* bôr′ō) *v.* —*tr.* **1.** To take (sthg.) with the promise of returning or replacing it later: *He borrowed a book from the library. I borrowed money from my friend*

to go the movies. **2.** To take (a word, idea, or method) from another source and use it as one's own: *We borrowed the word kindergarten from German in the 19th century.* —*intr.* To obtain or receive sthg., especially money on loan: *I borrowed from the bank to buy a new car.* —**bor′row•er** *n.*

USAGE: **borrow** The word **borrow** means "to take (sthg.) temporarily with the promise of returning it"; **lend** means "to give (sthg.) temporarily on condition of having it returned." A library *lends* books; readers *borrow* them. Another verb very similar to **lend** is **loan,** meaning "to lend money or an object." **Lend** also has a figurative use, but **loan** does not: *The music lent spirit to the party; lend us your enthusiasm.*

---

bor•row•ing (bŏr′ō ĭng) *n.* Something that is borrowed, especially a word or phrase borrowed from another language: *The English word plateau is a borrowing from French.*

bos•om (boŏz′əm *or* boō′zəm) *n.* [U] The upper front part of a woman's body; the breast. ♦ **bosom buddy** *or* **friend.** A close friend: *We've been bosom buddies since first grade.*

boss (bôs *or* bŏs) *n.* **1.** A person who employs or directs workers. **2.** A person who is in charge or makes decisions: *His boss told him he needed to work harder.* —*tr.v.* **1.** To give orders to (sbdy.): *Their older cousin tried to boss the younger children.* **2.** To be in charge of (sbdy.); supervise: *A manager of a store usually bosses a group of salespeople.* ♦ **boss around.** *tr.v.* [sep.] To give orders to (sbdy.): *Stop bossing me around!*

boss•y (bô′sē *or* bŏs′ē) *adj.* **boss•i•er, boss•i•est.** Inclined to order others around; domineering: *I do not like my older sister because she is too bossy.* —**boss′i•ness** *n.* [U]

bo•tan•i•cal (bə tăn′ĭ kəl) *adj.* Relating to plants or botany: *a collection of botanical herbs.* —**bo•tan′i•cal•ly** *adv.*

bot•a•ny (bŏt′n ē) *n.* [U] The scientific study of plants. —**bot′a•nist** *n.*

botch (bŏch) *tr.v.* To spoil (sthg.) by careless or clumsy work; bungle: *botch a repair job.*

both (bōth) *adj.* One as well as the other; relating to or being two: *Both sides of the board are painted.* —*pron.* The one as well as the other: *Both of my friends skate well.* —*conj.* As well; equally: *The actor both sings and dances.*

USAGE: **both** The word **both** means "each of two, taken individually." *Both books weigh more than five pounds* means that each book weighs more than five pounds by itself, not that the two books weighed together come to more than five pounds. When **both** is used with **and** to

---

ă–cat; ā–pay; âr–care; ä–father; ĕ–get; ē–be; ĭ–sit; ī–nice; îr–here; ŏ–got; ō–go; ô–saw; oi–boy; ou–out; oō–took; ōō–boot; ŭ–cut; ûr–word; th–thin; *th*–this; hw–when; zh–vision; ə–about; N–French bon

connect two words or phrases in a sentence, these words or phrases should be grammatically parallel. *In both India and China* or *both in India and in China* are correct. *Both in India and China* is not correct.

both•er (bŏ*th*′ər) *v.* —*tr.* **1.** To disturb or anger (sbdy./sthg.); annoy: *Noise in the hall bothered the teacher while she was teaching.* **2.a.** To make (sbdy.) nervous or upset: *Being in high places bothers some people.* **b.** To puzzle (sbdy.): *A problem had been bothering them.* —*intr.* To take the trouble; concern oneself: *Don't bother to get up.* —*n. (usually singular).* An annoying thing; a nuisance: *Having to wait so long was a bother.*

both•er•some (bŏ*th*′ər səm) *adj.* Causing trouble; troublesome: *He raised several bothersome questions about the details of the plan.*

bot•tle (bŏt′l) *n.* **1.** A container, usually made of glass or plastic, having a narrow neck and an opening. **2.** A bottle with sthg. in it: *buy a bottle of wine.* **3.** A bottle for feeding a baby. —*tr.v.* **bot•tled, bot•tling, bot•tles.** To put (sthg.) in a bottle or bottles: *a machine that bottles water.* ◆ **bottle up.** *tr.v.* [sep.] To hold (sthg.) in or back; restrain: *bottle up one's anger; bottle traffic up for hours.* —**bot′tler** *n.*

bot•tle•neck (bŏt′l nĕk′) *n.* A narrow route or passage where movement is slowed down: *Highway construction caused a bottleneck on the highway this morning.*

bot•tom (bŏt′əm) *n.* **1.** The lowest or deepest part of sthg.: *the bottom of a page; the bottom of the hill.* **2.** The underside of sthg.: *the bottom of a shoe.* **3.** The solid surface under a body of water: *The diver went to the bottom of the lake.* **4.** The underlying truth or cause; the basis or heart: *get to the bottom of the mystery.* **5.** *Informal.* The buttocks: *She fell and hurt her bottom.* ◆ **at the bottom.** Having the lowest rank or level: *He started working for the company at the bottom and finally became the manager.* **bottom out.** *intr.v.* To reach the lowest point: *My grades bottomed out when I failed both chemistry and math.* **Bottoms up!** A toast before drinking: *The host said, "Bottoms up!" before we drank our toast.* **from the bottom of (one's) heart.** Sincerely: *I love you from the bottom of my heart.* **get to the bottom of.** To find the truth about (sthg.): *The police won't rest until they get to the bottom of the crime.*

bot•tom•less (bŏt′əm lĭs) *adj.* **1.** Having no bottom: *a bottomless barrel.* **2.** Too deep to be measured: *a bottomless lake.*

bottom line *n.* **1.** The last line in a financial statement that shows the amount of profit or loss for a business. **2.** The final result or main point: *After a long discussion with my mother, the bottom line is that I have to be home by ten.*

bot•u•lism (bŏch′ə lĭz′əm) *n.* [U] An often fatal form of food poisoning usually caused by bacteria that grow in improperly preserved foods.

bough (bou) *n.* A large or main branch of a tree.

HOMONYMS: bough, bow (front of a ship, bend).

bought (bôt) *v.* Past tense and past participle of **buy.**

bouil•la•baisse (boo′yə bäs′ or bool′yə-bäs′) *n.* [U] A thick soup made with several kinds of fish and shellfish.

bouil•lon (bool′yŏn′ or bool′yən) *n.* [U] A clear thin broth usually made by simmering meat in water with seasonings: *beef bouillon.*

HOMONYMS: bouillon, bullion (gold).

boul•der (bōl′dər) *n.* A large rock.

boul•e•vard (bool′ə värd′) *n.* A broad city street, often lined with trees.

bounce (bouns) *v.* **bounced, bounc•ing, bounc•es.** —*intr.* **1.** To hit a surface and spring back from it; rebound: *The ball bounced off the wall.* **2.** To move with a bobbing, jolting, or vibrating motion: *Cars bounced down the dirt road.* **3.** *Informal.* To be sent back by a bank as worthless: *The check bounced because there was not enough money in the account.* —*tr.* **1.** To cause (sthg.) to bounce: *Bounce the ball to me.* **2.** *Slang.* To throw (sbdy.) out forcefully: *The noisy group was bounced from the movie theater.* —*n.* **1.** [C] An act of bouncing or a bouncing movement: *Catch the ball on the first bounce.* **2.** [U] Capacity to bounce; springiness: *a rubber ball with plenty of bounce.* **3.** [U] Liveliness: *There is a certain bounce to march music.* ◆ **bounce back.** *intr.v.* To return to a normal condition; recover or begin anew: *bounce back after a serious illness.* —**bounc′y** *adj.* —**bounc′i•ly** *adv.*

bounc•er (boun′sər) *n.* A person employed to remove disorderly persons from a nightclub, bar, or similar place of entertainment.

bounc•ing (boun′sĭng) *adj.* Big and strong; healthy; thriving: *a happy bouncing baby.*

bound[1] (bound) *intr.v.* **1.** To leap, jump, or spring: *The dog bounded over the gate.* **2.** To move forward by leaps or springs: *The deer bounded into the woods.* —*n.* A leap or jump: *The deer ran away in a single bound.*

bound[2] (bound) *n. (usually plural).* A limit: *Their enthusiasm knew no bounds.* —*tr.v.* To be the limit of (sthg.): *Water bounds the city on three sides.*

bound[3] (bound) *v.* Past tense and past participle of **bind.** —*adj.* **1.** Being under obligation; obliged: *She felt bound by her promise.* **2.** Certain: *If we leave after dark, we are bound*

B

to be late for dinner. **3.** Held together by bonds; tied: *the bound hands of the prisoner.* **4.** Enclosed in a cover or binding: *a bound book.* ◆ **bound up with.** Closely associated or connected with: *The migration of birds is bound up with change in the seasons.* **bound and determined.** Strongly hoping or planning to do sthg.: *We are bound and determined to see a movie this week.*

bound⁴ (bound) *adj.* Headed or intending to go in a certain direction: *We are bound for Quebec.*

bound•a•ry (boun′də rē *or* boun′drē) *n., pl.* **bound•a•ries.** A border or limit: *the southern boundary of Montana; the boundary between right and wrong.*

bound•less (bound′lĭs) *adj.* **1.** Very great; limitless: *her boundless energy.* **2.** Without limits; infinite: *the boundless reaches of outer space.* —**bound′less•ness** *n.* [U]

boun•ti•ful (boun′tə fəl) *adj.* Plentiful; abundant: *bountiful crops.*

boun•ty (boun′tē) *n., pl.* **boun•ties. 1.** [U] A large or generous amount: *the bounty of the earth in a rich harvest.* **2.** [C] A reward for performing a service for the government, as for capturing an outlaw or killing a destructive animal.

bou•quet (bō kā′ *or* boo kā′) *n.* **1.** A bunch of flowers: *a bouquet of yellow roses.* **2.** A pleasant odor, especially of a wine.

bour•bon (bûr′bən) *n.* [U] A type of whiskey.

bour•geois (boor zhwä′ *or* boor′zhwä′) *n., pl.* **bourgeois.** A member of the middle class or bourgeoisie. —*adj.* **1.** Relating to or typical of the middle class: *bourgeois merchants and shopkeepers.* **2.** Caring too much about respectability and possessions: *bourgeois attitudes about social standing.*

bour•geoi•sie (boor′zhwä zē′) *n.* [U] The middle class in a society.

bout (bout) *n.* **1.** A contest, such as a boxing match. **2.** A period or spell: *a severe bout of the flu.*

bou•tique (boo tēk′) *n.* A small retail shop that sells fashionable clothes and other specialized merchandise.

bou•ton•niere (boo′tə nîr′ *or* boo′tən-yâr′) *n.* A flower worn by a man in a buttonhole, usually on a lapel of a jacket.

bo•vine (bō′vīn′ *or* bō′vēn′) *adj.* Related to a cow or cattle: *The veterinarian specializes in bovine diseases.*

bow¹ (bou) *n.* The front section of a ship or boat.

HOMONYMS: bow (front of a ship, bend), **bough** (branch).

---

bow² (bou) *v.* —*intr.* **1.** To bend the body, head, or knee, as in greeting, respect, or

agreement: *bow politely from the waist.* **2.** To bend downward; stoop: *The mover bowed beneath the heavy load.* **3.** To give in; yield: *They refused to bow to pressure.* —*tr.* To bend (the body, head, or knee), as in greeting, agreement, or respect: *He bowed his head in prayer.* —*n.* A bending of the body or head, as when showing respect or accepting applause. ◆ **bow out.** *intr.v.* To remove oneself; withdraw: *After the scandal, the candidate bowed out of the race for mayor.* **take a bow.** To acknowledge or accept applause, as by standing up or coming out on stage: *The actors took a bow at the end of the play.*

bow³ (bō) *n.* **1.** A weapon used to shoot arrows, made of a flexible curved strip of wood or plastic, with a string stretched tightly from end to end. **2.** A slender rod that has horsehair stretched between two ends, used in playing the violin and other stringed instruments. **3.** A knot usually having two loops and two ends: *Tie your shoes with a bow.* —*v.* —*tr.* **1.** To play (sthg.) with a bow: *bow a fiddle.* **2.** To bend (sthg.) into a curved shape: *The heavy snow bowed the branches until they broke.* —*intr.* **1.** To play a stringed instrument with a bow. **2.** To bend into a curved shape: *The branches bowed and then snapped in the high wind.*

bow (weapon)

bow (cello)

bow•el (bou′əl) *n.* **1.** *(usually plural).* The intestine, especially of a human being. **2.** **bowels.** The interior part of sthg.: *the bowels of a ship; the bowels of the earth.*

bow (knot)

bowl¹ (bōl) *n.* **1.** A rounded hollow container or dish that can hold liquid or food: *a soup bowl; a mixing bowl.* **2.** The amount that a bowl holds: *Eat a bowl of cereal.* **3.** One of several special football games played after the usual season ends: *The U.S. professional football championship is called the Super Bowl.*

ă-cat; ā-pay; âr-care; ä-father; ĕ-get; ē-be; ĭ-sit; ī-nice; îr-here; ŏ-got; ō-go; ô-saw; oi-boy; ou-out; oo-took; oo-boot; ŭ-cut; ûr-word; th-thin; *th*-this; hw-when; zh-vision; ə-about; N-French bon

bowl² (bōl) *v.* —*intr.* To play the game of bowling: *Do you like to bowl?* —*tr.* **1.** To play (a game) of bowling. **2.** To make (a score) in bowling: *The champion bowled a high score.* ◆ **bowl over.** *tr.v.* [sep.] **1.** To take (sbdy.) by surprise or overwhelm: *The unexpected announcement bowled them over.* **2.** To knock (sbdy.) down as if with a rolling ball: *The dog bowled the little girl over.* —**bowl′er** *n.*

bow•leg•ged (bō′lĕg′ĭd *or* bō′lĕgd′) *adj.* Having legs that curve outward at the knee: *a bowlegged horseman.*

bowl•ing (bō′lĭng) *n.* [U] A game played by rolling a large ball down a bowling alley to knock down wooden pins.

bowling alley *n.* **1.** A smooth level wooden lane used in bowling. **2.** A building or room with lanes for bowling.

bow tie (bō) *n.* A small necktie tied in a bow close to the neck.

box¹ (bŏks) *n.* **1.a.** A stiff container with four sides, a bottom, and often a top or lid. **b.** The amount that a box can hold: *eat a box of crackers.* **2.** A rectangle or square: *Draw a box around the right answer.* **3.** A separate compartment holding seats in a theater or stadium: *The tickets for the box seats were more expensive than the others.* **4.** A signaling device enclosed in a casing: *a fire-alarm box.* **5.** A compartment for mail: *a box in a post office.* —*tr.v.* To put or pack (sthg.) in a box: *box fruit before shipping.* ◆ **box in.** *tr.v.* [sep.] To slow or stop (sthg.): *The bus was boxed in by the traffic jam.* **box off.** *tr.v.* [sep.] To enclose (sthg.): *They boxed off the area where the construction was being done.*

box² (bŏks) *n.* A blow or slap with the hand: *a box on the ear.* —*v.* —*tr.* **1.** To take part in a boxing match with (an opponent). **2.** To hit or slap (sbdy.) with the hand: *He was so angry he boxed him.* —*intr.* To fight with the fists in a boxing match: *The champion boxed yesterday.*

box•car (bŏks′kär′) *n.* An enclosed railroad car used to carry freight.

box•er (bŏk′sər) *n.* **1.** A person who fights with the fists, especially to earn money. **2. boxers.** Boxer shorts: *She wears boxers to bed.* **3.** A medium-sized dog with a short, smooth, brownish coat and a square face.

boxer shorts *pl.n.* Loose-fitting shorts worn especially as underwear by men or for sport by both men and women.

box•ing (bŏk′sĭng) *n.* [U] The sport of fighting with the fists, especially when boxing gloves are worn and special rules are followed.

boxing glove *n.* One of two heavily padded leather gloves worn by a boxer to protect the fists while fighting.

box office *n.* A booth where tickets are sold in a theater, an auditorium, or a stadium.

box seat *n.* A seat in a box at a theater or stadium: *We had box seats for the circus.*

box spring *n.* A bedspring consisting of a frame enclosed with cloth, which supports a mattress.

box•y (bŏk′sē) *adj.* **box•i•er, box•i•est.** Resembling a box, as in shape: *a boxy car.*

boy (boi) *n.* **1.a.** A male child. **b.** A young man: *a college boy.* **2.a.** A son: *her youngest boy.* **b.** A brother or male cousin: *the Jones boys.* **c.** *Informal.* A fellow; a guy: *a night out with the boys.* —*interj.* An expression used to show astonishment, elation, or disgust: *Boy! What a great car!*

boy•cott (boi′kŏt′) *tr.v.* **1.** To act together in refusing to use, buy, or deal with (sbdy./ sthg.), especially as an expression of protest: *We boycotted that store because it was unfair to its workers.* **2.** To refuse to use, buy, or deal with (sbdy./sthg.): *boycott foreign-made goods.* —*n.* **1.** A refusal to buy from or deal with a person, business, or nation, especially as a form of protest. **2.** A refusal to buy or use a product or service.

boy•friend (boi′frĕnd′) *n.* *Informal.* A male sweetheart or favored companion.

boy•hood (boi′hŏŏd′) *n.* [C; U] The time of being a boy: *He spent his boyhood on a farm.*

boy•ish (boi′ĭsh) *adj.* Resembling or appropriate for a boy: *a boyish haircut.* —**boy′-ish•ly** *adv.* —**boy′ish•ness** *n.* [U]

Boy Scout *n.* A member of the Boy Scouts.

Boy Scouts *n.* *(used with a singular verb).* An organization for boys that attempts to develop self-reliance, good citizenship, and outdoor skills.

Br The symbol for the element **bromine.**

bra (brä) *n.* A women's undergarment worn to support the breasts; a brassiere.

brace (brās) *n.* **1.** A device that holds parts together or in place; a clamp. **2.** A medical device used to support a bodily part: *After the accident he needed a neck brace.* **3. braces.** Wires and bands attached to the teeth to straighten them: *The dentist put braces on her teeth.* —*tr.v.* **braced, brac•ing, brac•es.** **1.** To give support to (sthg.); strengthen: *brace a tent with poles.* **2.** To prepare (oneself) for a shock or difficulty: *The candidates braced themselves for the coming election.*

brace•let (brās′lĭt) *n.* A band or chain worn around the wrist or arm as an ornament.

brac•ing (brā′sĭng) *adj.* Giving strength and energy; refreshing: *a bracing wind.*

brack•et (brăk′ĭt) *n.* **1.** A support or fixture fastened to a wall and sticking out to hold sthg., such as a shelf. **2.** Either of the pair of symbols, [or], used to enclose printed or written material. **3.** A group, class, or range within a series: *the 9-to-12 age bracket; a high salary bracket.* —*tr.v.* **1.** To support (sthg.) with a bracket or brackets: *bracket* shelves to strengthen them. **2.** To place (sthg.) within brackets: *bracket words inserted in a quotation.* **3.** To classify or group (things) together: *bracket taxpayers according to the money they earn.*

brack·ish (brăk′ĭsh) *adj.* Slightly salty; briny: *brackish marsh waters near the ocean.*

brag (brăg) *v.* **bragged, brag·ging, brags.** —*intr.* To talk boastfully; boast: *He bragged about winning the race.* —**brag′ger** *n.*

brag·gart (brăg′ərt) *n.* A person who brags a lot.

Brah·ma (brä′mə) *n.* **1.** [U] In Hinduism, the god who created the world. **2.** [C] Variant of **Brahman.**

Brah·man (brä′mən) also **Brah·ma** (brä′mə) *n.* **1.** Variant of **Brahmin. 2.** Also **Brahmin.** One of a breed of cattle native to India with a hump between the shoulders and a fold of loose skin below the neck.

Brah·man·ism (brä′mə nĭz′əm) *n.* [U] **1.** The religion of ancient India. **2.** The religious and social system of the Brahmins of India.

Brah·min (brä′mĭn) *n.* **1.** Also **Brah·man** (brä′mən). A member of the highest Hindu class, responsible for officiating at religious rites. **2.** Variant of **Brahman** (sense 2).

braid (brād) *tr.v.* **1.** To weave or twist together three or more strands of (hair, fiber, or fabric); plait: *She braided her long hair.* **2.** To make (sthg.) by weaving strands together: *braid a straw rug.* —*n.* **1.** [C] A segment of braided hair, fabric, or other material. **2.** [U] Ornamental cord or ribbon, used especially for trimming clothes.

braid

Braille or **braille** (brāl) *n.* [U] A system of writing and printing for visually impaired or sightless people in which raised dots representing letters, numbers, and punctuation are read by touching them.

brain (brān) *n.* **1.** The large mass of nerve tissue enclosed in the skull of humans and other vertebrates: *The brain controls all the activities of the body.* **2.** The mind: *The plan took shape in his brain.* **3.** *(usually plural).* Intellectual power; intelligence: *It takes brains to be an economist.* **4.** *Informal.* A highly intelligent person: *That new student is a brain.* —*tr.v. Slang.* To hit (sbdy./sthg.) hard on the head: *She brained him with the tennis racket.*

brain·child (brān′chīld′) *n. Informal.* The product of a person's mind; an original plan,

idea, or invention: *The telephone was Bell's brainchild.*

brain-dead (brān′dĕd′) *adj.* Showing no electrical activity in the brain, indicating death of the cerebral cortex.

brain death *n.* Complete absence of electrical activity in the brain.

brain·less (brān′lĭs) *adj.* Without thought; stupid; foolish: *a brainless act of vandalism.* —**brain′less·ly** *adv.* —**brain′less·ness** *n.* [U]

brain·storm (brān′stôrm′) *Informal. n.* A sudden inspiration or clever idea: *After thinking about the problem for a long time, he suddenly had a brainstorm.* —*intr.v.* To hold an idea session: *Let's brainstorm for a while.*

brain·wash (brān′wŏsh′ or brān′wôsh′) *tr.v.* **1.** To indoctrinate (sbdy.) forcibly so that his or her beliefs are replaced with different ones: *Several prisoners of war were brainwashed to confess to spying.* **2.** To persuade (sbdy.) by intense means, such as repeated suggestions, to adopt a belief or behave in a certain way: *TV commercials brainwashed them into buying junk food.*

brain·wash·ing (brān′wŏsh′ĭng or brān′wô′shĭng) *n.* [U] The act or process by which a person is brainwashed.

brain·y (brā′nē) *adj.* **brain·i·er, brain·i·est.** *Informal.* Intelligent; smart: *a brainy child.*

braise (brāz) *tr.v.* **braised, brais·ing, brais·es.** To brown (meat or vegetables) in fat and then simmer in a liquid in a covered container.

brake (brāk) *n.* A device for slowing or stopping motion, as of a vehicle or machine: *The brakes failed, and the car ran off the road.* —*intr.v.* **braked, brak·ing, brakes.** To operate or apply a brake or brakes: *Slow down and brake before turning.*

HOMONYMS: brake, break (split).

bran (brăn) *n.* [U] The outer covering of wheat and other grains, removed from the flour after processing. Bran is used in some cereals and bread as a source of dietary fiber.

branch (brănch) *n.* **1.a.** One of the woody parts growing out from the trunk, limb, or main stem of a tree or shrub: *The branches of the tree were so long they were touching the house.* **b.** A part going out from a main part like a tree branch: *a stream that is a branch of this river.* **2.** A part or division of a larger whole: *Botany and zoology are branches of biology.* **3.** A local unit or office: *a bank branch.* —*intr.v.* **1.** To put forth branches. **2.** To develop as a branch or division; diverge: *The road branches into two forks.* ◆ **branch out.** *intr.v.* To expand one's interests or activities: *The store sells only men's clothing, but* *it is going to branch out and sell women's dresses.*

brand (brănd) *n.* **1.** A particular kind or make of product, especially as shown by a trademark: *a popular brand of soap.* **2.** A distinctive category or kind: *That comedian is known for a strange brand of humor.* **3.** A mark indicating ownership burned into the hide of cattle or other valuable animals with a hot iron. —*tr.v.* **1.** To mark (sthg.) with a hot iron: *Cowboys branded the calves.* **2.** To mark (sbdy./sthg.) with a label of disgrace: *The court branded the spies as traitors.*

bran•dish (brăn′dĭsh) *tr.v.* To wave or show (sthg.) in a dramatic or threatening way: *He brandished his fist in defiance.*

brand-new (brănd′nōo′) *adj.* Completely new; not used: *I decided to buy a brand-new car rather than a used one.*

bran•dy (brăn′dē) *n.* [U] An alcoholic liquor distilled from wine or fermented fruit juice.

brash (brăsh) *adj.* **1.** Bold; impudent: *a brash young newcomer.* **2.** Acting too quickly and without thinking; rash: *a brash move.* —**brash′ly** *adv.* —**brash′ness** *n.* [U]

brass (brăs) *n.* [U] **1.** A yellow alloy of copper and zinc: *brass doorknobs.* **2.** Ornaments, objects, or utensils made of such metal: *Polish all the brass including the doorknobs.* **3.** Wind instruments made of brass or some other metal, including the French horn, trumpet, trombone, and tuba: *She plays in the brass section of the band.* **4.** *Informal.* Shameless boldness; nerve: *She had the brass to ask for another raise three months after her first one.* **5.** *Slang.* Military officers or civilian officials of high rank: *The soldier had to get approval from the top brass.* ♦ **get down to brass tacks.** *Informal.* To look at only the essential facts: *Let's get down to brass tacks so we can make a decision.*

bras•siere (brə zîr′) *n.* A woman's undergarment worn to support the breasts.

brass•y (brăs′ē) *adj.* **brass•i•er, brass•i•est.** **1.** Made of, decorated with, or having the color of brass. **2.** Resembling or featuring the sound of brass instruments: *a brassy voice.* **3.** *Informal.* Shamelessly bold; impudent: *the brassy behavior of a showoff.* —**brass′i•ly** *adv.* —**brass′i•ness** *n.* [U]

brat (brăt) *n.* A child who behaves badly or is spoiled.

bra•va•do (brə vä′dō) *n.* [U] A show of pretended or defiant courage; false bravery: *the bravado of the coward before a fight.*

brave (brāv) *adj.* **brav•er, brav•est.** Having courage: *The brave soldier was not afraid to fight.* —*n.* A sometimes offensive term for a Native American warrior. —*tr.v.* **braved, brav•ing, braves.** To undergo or face (sthg.) with courage: *Firefighters brave many dangers in their work.* —**brave′ly** *adv.* —**brave′ness, bra′very** *n.* [U]

SYNONYMS: brave, courageous, fearless, bold, valiant. These adjectives mean having or showing courage in a difficult or dangerous situation. **Brave,** the most general, often refers to an inner quality: *I'm not brave enough to speak in front of such a large crowd.* **Courageous** means consciously depending on one's inner strength to face danger: *The courageous captain guided the ship through the terrible storm.* **Fearless** emphasizes the absence of fear: *The fearless tightrope walker does not use a net.* **Bold** often means being brave and showing a tendency to look for danger: *The bolder members of the search party went into the cave first.* **Valiant** means brave in a heroic way; it is usually used when describing a person: *The valiant firefighters had rescued everyone from the burning building.* **ANTONYM: cowardly.**

bra•vo (brä′vō *or* brä vō′) *interj.* An expression used to show approval, as for a musical performance. —*n., pl.* **bra•vos.** A shout or cry of "bravo."

brawl (brôl) *n.* A noisy quarrel or fight. —*intr.v.* To quarrel or fight noisily: *The two men violently disagreed and brawled in the alley.*

brawn (brôn) *n.* [U] Muscular strength and power.

brawn•y (brô′nē) *adj.* **brawn•i•er, brawn•i•est.** Strong and muscular: *My brother works out often and is quite brawny now.* See Synonyms at **muscular.** —**brawn′i•ness** *n.* [U]

bray (brā) *v.* —*intr.* To make the loud harsh cry of a donkey. —*tr.* To utter (sthg.) loudly or harshly: *The car's horn brayed its warning.* —*n.* **1.** The loud harsh cry of a donkey. **2.** A sound resembling this cry: *the bray of trumpets.*

bra•zen (brā′zən) *adj.* Rudely bold; impudent: *a brazen remark.* —**bra′zen•ly** *adv.* —**bra′zen•ness** *n.* [U]

bra•zier (brā′zhər) *n.* A metal pan for holding burning coals or charcoal.

Bra•zil nut (brə zĭl′) *n.* The edible oily nut of a tropical South American tree, having a hard, three-sided, dark brown shell.

breach (brēch) *n.* **1.** An open section or hole, especially in a solid structure: *The crowd poured through a breach in the fence.* **2.** A violation of a law or legal obligation: *a breach of contract.* **3.** A disruption of friendly relations: *An argument caused a breach between the friends.* —*tr.v.* To make a hole or gap in (sthg.); break through: *Floodwaters breached the dike.*

bread (brĕd) *n.* [U] **1.** A food made from flour mixed with liquid and other ingredients, usually combined with yeast and baked in a loaf: *He likes to eat bread with dinner.* **2.** Food in general, regarded as necessary to sustain life:

A farm family works long hours for its daily bread. **3.** The necessities of life; livelihood: *earn one's bread as a writer.* **4.** *Slang.* Money. —*tr.v.* To coat (food) with bread crumbs before cooking.

HOMONYMS: bread, bred (produced offspring).

bread•ing (brĕd′ĭng) *n.* [U] A mixture of bread crumbs used to coat meat or vegetables before frying.
breadth (brĕdth) *n.* [C; U] **1.** The distance from side to side of sthg.; width: *The breadth of the river is several meters, while its depth is only one meter.* **2.** Wide extent or scope: *Her breadth of knowledge is impressive.*
bread•win•ner (brĕd′wĭn′ər) *n.* A person who earns money to support a household.
break (brāk) *v.* **broke** (brōk), **bro•ken** (brō′kən), **break•ing, breaks.** —*tr.* **1.a.** To cause (sthg.) to separate into two or more pieces as the result of force: *break a mirror.* **b.** To take off (a part) with a sharp movement: *break a twig from a branch.* **2.** To fracture a bone of (a part of the body): *break an arm.* **3.** To make (sthg.) unusable: *I broke my watch when I sat on it.* **4.** To force a way through the surface of (sthg.): *break ground for a new building.* **5.** To cause (sthg.) to explode from pressure inside: *I broke the balloon with a pin.* **6.** To escape from (jail). **7.a.** To destroy the regularity, order, or completeness of (sthg.): *break a set of books by selling some of them.* **b.** To put an end to (sthg.), as by force, opposition, or change: *break a habit.* **c.** To end or interrupt (sthg.) suddenly: *A cry broke the silence.* **d.** To create a space in (sthg.) across which electricity cannot pass: *break a circuit.* **8.** To fail to keep, follow, or conform to (sthg.): *break a law; break a promise.* **9.** To make (sthg.) less in force or effect: *A big bush broke my fall.* **10.** *Informal.* To cause (sbdy./sthg.) to be without money: *Big bills and few customers broke the new business.* **11.** To exchange (a bill) for coins or smaller bills: *Break a dollar for change to pay the bus fare.* **12.** To train (an animal) to obey: *break a wild horse.* **13.** To find the solution or key to (a puzzle of some kind): *break a code.* **14.** To make (information) known: *break sad news gently.* —*intr.* **1.** To become separated into pieces or fragments: *Glass breaks easily.* **2.** To become unusable: *The radio broke.* **3.** To lose strength suddenly: *He broke after three hours of intense questioning.* **4.** To explode from pressure inside: *The bubble broke.* **5.** To move, change direction, or escape suddenly: *The racehorses broke from the starting gate.* **6.** To become known or noticed: *The story broke in the afternoon*

news. **7.** To interrupt or stop an activity: *Let's break for five minutes.* **8.** To come to an end: *The cold spell finally broke.* **9.** (used of voices). To change suddenly in sound: *Her voice broke with emotion.* —*n.* **1.** A result of breaking; a fracture or crack: *a break in a bone.* **2.** A separation or an opening: *a break in the clouds.* **3.** An interruption in sthg. regular or continuous: *a break in the conversation; a break in an electrical circuit.* **4.** A short stopping of an activity, such as work: *Take a break for a few minutes.* **5.** A sudden run: *The rabbit made a break for the safety of the bushes.* **6.** An attempt to escape: *a jail break.* **7.** A sudden change: *a break in the weather.* **8.** An ending of a relationship: *a break between families.* **9.** A surprising event or piece of luck: *a lucky break.* **10.** Generous or kind treatment: *I bought the car after the dealer gave me a break on the price.* ◆ **break a record.** To do sthg. faster or better than the best performance before that one: *She broke the school's high-jump record.* **break down.** *tr.v.* [sep.] **1.** To cause (sthg.) to fail or be destroyed: *break down one's resistence; break down a wall.* **2.** To analyze or consider (sthg.) in parts: *Break the exercise down into several steps.* —*intr.v.* **1.** To fail to function: *The truck broke down on the highway.* **2.** To separate chemically: *Plastic takes years to break down.* **3.** To become distressed or upset: *They broke down and cried when they got lost.* **break even.** To gain an amount of money equal to the amount spent, as in a business: *We broke even on the deal.* **break in.** *intr.v.* **1.** To enter a building or property illegally: *The burglars broke in but could not find the jewels.* **2.** To interrupt a conversation: *The waiter broke in to offer us more coffee.* —*tr.v.* [sep.] **1.** To train or instruct (sbdy.) for some purpose: *break in a new worker.* **2.** To soften (sthg.) with use: *break in new shoes.* **break into.** *tr.v.* [insep.] **1.** To enter (a place) by use of force: *The bear broke into the cabin.* **2.** To begin (sthg.) suddenly: *He broke into song.* **3.** To interrupt (sthg.): *He broke into our discussion to tell us it was time to go.* **break off.** *intr.v.* **1.** To stop suddenly, as in speaking: *break off in the middle of a sentence.* **2.** To stop being friendly: *When the soldiers returned home, they broke off with their old army friends.* —*tr.v.* [sep.] To take off (a part): *Break a piece of bread off for me.* **break out.** *intr.v.* **1.** To be affected with a skin irritation, such as a rash: *An allergy to wool makes me break out.* **2.** To begin suddenly: *Fire broke out during the night.* —*tr.v.* [sep.] To make (sthg.) ready for action or use: *Firefighters broke out the hoses.* **break (one's) heart.** To disappoint sbdy.

severely: *It broke her heart to have to sell the house.* **break up.** *intr.v.* **1.** To separate or move apart: *The clouds are breaking up.* **2.** To come to an end: *Their partnership broke up.* —*tr.v.* [sep.] **1.** To separate (sthg.) into smaller parts: *break up a word into syllables.* **2.** To bring (sthg.) to an end: *A fight started, but the police broke it up.* **3.** To interrupt (sthg.): *We broke up the long day by going swimming.* **give (one) a break.** *Informal.* **1.** To stop bothering (sbdy.): *Give me a break; I'm trying to do my work.* **2.** To give (sbdy.) a reduction in price: *He gave me a break on the car. He wanted $10,000, but he took $9,500.* **3.** To not punish (sbdy.): *They decided to give the man a break because it was his first offense.* **the breaks.** *Slang.* Bad luck: *He lost his job. That's the breaks.*

HOMONYMS: break, brake (device for stopping).

SYNONYMS: break, crack, split, splinter, shatter. These verbs mean to separate into parts or pieces. **Break** is the most general: *Take care not to break anything while you're dusting.* **Crack** means to break, often with a sharp snapping sound, without dividing into parts: *We heard the ice cracking as we walked on it.* **Split** means to divide along the length of sthg.: *These pants have split along the seam.* **Splinter** means to split into long, thin, sharp pieces: *Lightning struck the tree and splintered it.* **Shatter** means to break into many loose scattered pieces: *The perfume bottle fell and shattered on the floor.*

break•a•ble (brā′kə bəl) *adj.* Able to be broken; fragile.
break•age (brā′kĭj) *n.* [U] **1.** The act of breaking. **2.** A quantity broken: *Breakage during shipping was extensive.* **3.** Loss or damage as a result of breaking: *The fire resulted in breakage of most of the store's windows.*
break•down (brāk′doun′) *n.* **1.** The process or condition of failing to function properly: *The breakdown of train service caused many travelers to be delayed.* **2.** An analysis or a summary consisting of itemized data: *The sticker on the car window shows a breakdown of costs.*
break•fast (brĕk′fəst) *n.* The morning meal. —*intr.v.* To eat breakfast: *They breakfasted at the new restaurant.*
break•neck (brāk′nĕk′) *adj.* Dangerously fast: *The ambulance drove at breakneck speed.*
break•through (brāk′thrōō′) *n.* A major achievement or success that permits further progress, as in technology or medicine: *Development of the transistor was a breakthrough in electronics.*

break•up (brāk′ŭp′) *n.* **1.** The act of breaking up; a separation: *the breakup of an iceberg; the breakup of a large corporation.* **2.** The ending of a relationship: *the sudden breakup of their marriage.*
breast (brĕst) *n.* In mammals, especially humans, one of the glands in which a female produces milk to feed her young offspring.
breast-feed (brĕst′fēd′) *tr.v.* **breast-fed** (brĕst′ fĕd′), **breast-feed•ing, breast-feeds.** To feed (a baby) mother's milk from the breast; nurse: *She breast-fed her baby for six months.*
breast•stroke (brĕst′strōk′) *n.* [U] A swimming stroke in which one lies face down and extends the arms in front of the head, sweeping them back to the sides while kicking.
breath (brĕth) *n.* **1.** [C] The air inhaled into and exhaled from the lungs. **2.** [U] The ability to breathe, especially with ease: *I got short of breath as I ran.* **3.** [C] A single act of breathing, especially an inhalation: *The singer took a deep breath.* **4.** [C] Exhaled air, as shown by vapor, odor, or heat: *You can see your breath in the cold winter air.* **5.** [C] A slight breeze: *Not a breath of air stirred the leaves.* ♦ **a breath of fresh air.** A new person or attitude that adds energy to a situation: *The new employee was like a breath of fresh air in the company.* **catch (one's) breath.** To rest so as to breathe normally: *After running a mile, I had to stop and catch my breath.* **out of breath.** Breathing with difficulty, as from exertion; gasping: *I was out of breath when I got to the top of the hill.* **take (one's) breath away.** To cause sbdy. not to be able to speak because of beauty, love, or another strong reaction: *The view was so beautiful it took my breath away.* **under (one's) breath.** In a muted voice or whisper: *She was complaining under her breath.*
breathe (brēth) *v.* **breathed, breath•ing, breathes.** —*intr.* **1.** To take air in and out of the body: *As we climbed higher, it got harder to breathe.* **2.** To be alive; live: *As long as the dog breathed he was loyal to his master.* **3.** To stop to rest or to regain breath, as after action: *I was so busy, I barely had time to breathe.* —*tr.* **1.** To take (air, for example) in and out of the body: *You can breathe clean air in the country.* **2.** To say (sthg.), especially quietly; whisper: *Don't breathe a word of this.* ♦ **breathe a sigh of relief.** To stop worrying: *When they pulled the child from the swimming pool, everyone breathed a sigh of relief.* **breathe down (one's) neck.** To watch or monitor sbdy. closely, often annoyingly: *Stop breathing down my neck!* **breathe easy.** To stop worrying: *Now that the project has been completed, I can breathe easy.* **breathe (one's) last.** To die.
breath•er (brē′thər) *n. Informal.* A short period of rest: *After this chore, let's take a breather.*

breath•less (brĕth′lĭs) *adj.* **1.** Breathing with difficulty; gasping: *The runners were breathless after the race.* **2.** Holding the breath from excitement or suspense: *The audience was breathless as the firefighters tried to stop the fire.* **3.** Causing excitement that makes one hold the breath: *the breathless beauty of the mountains.* —**breath′less•ly** *adv.* —**breath′less•ness** *n.* [U]

breath•tak•ing (brĕth′tā′kĭng) *adj.* Inspiring awe; very exciting: *The fireworks are always a breathtaking spectacle.*

bred (brĕd) *v.* Past tense and past participle of **breed.**

HOMONYMS: bred, bread (food).

---

breech•es or **britch•es** (brĭch′ĭz *or* brē′chĭz). *pl.n.* **1.** Pants extending to or just below the knees. **2.** *Informal.* Pants of any kind.

breed (brēd) *v.* **bred** (brĕd), **breed•ing, breeds.** —*tr.* **1.** To produce (offspring): *Mice breed large litters.* **2.a.** To raise (animals or plants), often to produce new or improved types: *The researchers are trying to breed cattle with lean meat.* **b.** To arrange the mating of (animals) so as to produce offspring: *We hope to breed the dogs and sell the puppies.* **3.** To bring about (sthg.); give rise to: *Poverty breeds crime.* —*intr.* **1.** To produce or reproduce by giving birth or hatching: *Mosquitoes breed rapidly.* **2.** To originate and grow: *Discontent breeds in hunger and injustice.* —*n.* **1.** A group of organisms with common ancestors and certain characteristics: *a strong breed of cattle; a breed of hybrid corn.* **2.** A type or kind: *a new breed of politician.* —**breed′er** *n.*

breed•ing (brē′dĭng) *n.* [U] **1.** Training in the proper forms of conduct: *Good manners are a sign of good breeding.* **2.** The producing of offspring or young: *She is doing research in the breeding of corn plants.*

breeze (brēz) *n.* **1.** A light current of air; a gentle wind: *The breeze near the ocean was very pleasant.* **2.** *Informal.* Something that is easy to do: *That math test was a breeze; I got a perfect score.* —*v.* **breezed, breez•ing, breez•es.** —*intr.v.* To move quickly and confidently: *She breezed into my office. He breezed by on his way to dinner.* ♦ **breeze through.** *tr.v.* [insep.] *Informal.* To make rapid progress through (sthg.) without effort: *We breezed through the homework.*

breez•y (brē′zē) *adj.* **breez•i•er, breez•i•est.** **1.** Exposed to breezes; windy: *a breezy point along the shore.* **2.** Lively; sprightly: *a writer's breezy style.* —**breez′i•ly** *adv.* —**breez′i•ness** *n.* [U]

breth•ren (brĕth′rən) *n.* [U] A plural of **brother** (sense 2).

brev•i•ty (brĕv′ĭ tē) *n.* [U] Briefness, as of expression; shortness: *The brevity of the speaker's comments prevented boredom.*

brew (broō) *v.* —*tr.* **1.** To make (beer or ale). **2.** To make (a beverage) by boiling or mixing ingredients: *brew tea.* **3.** To devise or plan (sthg.): *Members of the opposing party brewed a plot to take control of the government.* —*intr.* **1.** To be brewed: *The tea brewed quickly.* **2.** To be imminent; threaten to occur: *A storm brewed on the horizon.* —*n.* **1.** [C; U] A beverage made by brewing: *a strong brew.* **2.** [C] A serving of such a beverage: *He ordered a brew.* —**brew′er** *n.*

brew•er•y (broō′ə rē *or* broōr′ē) *n., pl.* **brew•er•ies.** A place where malt liquors, such as beer and ale, are made.

brew•ing (broō′ĭng) *n.* [U] The act, process, or business of making malt liquors, such as beer and ale.

bribe (brīb) *n.* Something, such as money, property, or position, given to sbdy. in order to influence that person: *Corrupt police officers were dismissed for accepting bribes.* —*tr.v.* **bribed, brib•ing, bribes.** To give or offer a bribe to (sbdy.): *It is a criminal act to bribe a judge.* —**brib′er•y** *n.* [U]

brick (brĭk) *n., pl.* **bricks** or **brick. 1.** [C] An oblong block of clay, baked until hard and used as a building and paving material. **2.** [U] The material from which bricks are made: *My new fireplace is made of brick.* **3.** [C] An object shaped like such a block: *a brick of cheese.* —*v.* ♦ **like a ton of bricks.** *Informal.* With a lot of force: *The box was so heavy that it felt like a ton of bricks. Her words hit me like a ton of bricks.* **brick up.** *tr.v.* [sep.] To close or fill in (sthg.) with bricks: *The builder bricked up the window opening.*

brick•lay•er (brĭk′lā′ər) *n.* A person who builds buildings or structures with bricks. —**brick′lay′ing** *n.* [U]

bri•dal (brīd′l) *adj.* Relating to a bride or a marriage ceremony: *a bridal veil; the bridal party.*

HOMONYMS: bridal, bridle (straps for a horse's head).

---

bride (brīd) *n.* A woman who is about to be married or has recently been married.

bride•groom (brīd′groōm′ *or* brīd′groōm′) *n.* A man who is about to be married or has recently been married.

brides•maid (brīdz′mād′) *n.* A woman who assists the bride at a wedding.

bridge¹ (brĭj) *n.* **1.** A structure that goes across a river, railroad, or other obstacle: *Engineers are building a bridge over the river so that cars can go across it.* **2.a.** The upper bony ridge of the human nose. **b.** The part of a pair of eyeglasses that rests against this ridge. **3.** A structure that replaces one or more missing teeth. **4.** The area above the main deck

bridge
San Francisco–
Oakland Bay Bridge

of a ship from which the ship is controlled. —*tr.v.* **bridged, bridg·ing, bridg·es. 1.** To build a bridge over (sthg.): *bridge a river.* **2.** To cross (sthg.) by or as if by a bridge: *His career bridged two generations of technology.* ◆ **bridge the gap.** To reduce the differences: *They are trying to bridge the gap between the different cultures in the city.* **burn (one's) bridges.** To destroy old relationships or contacts. *You should not burn your bridges when you leave this job.*

bridge² (brĭj) *n.* [U] A card game for four players.

bridge·work (brĭj'wûrk') *n.* [U] One or more dental bridges used to replace missing teeth.

bri·dle (brīd'l) *n.* A harness, consisting of straps, a bit, and reins, that fits a horse's head and is used to control the animal. —*v.* **bri·dled, bri·dling, bri·dles.** —*tr.* **1.** To put a bridle on (a horse): *bridle a horse.* **2.** To control (sthg.) with or as if with a bridle: *Bridle your temper!* —*intr.* [*at*] To show anger; take offense: *The author bridled at the criticism.*

HOMONYMS: bridle, bridal (of a bride).

---

brief (brēf) *adj.* Short in time or duration: *I could only take a brief nap because I had a lot of work to do.* —*n.* **1.** A short statement or summary, especially a lawyer's summary of the facts. **2. briefs.** Short, tight-fitting underwear: *Do you prefer briefs or boxers?* —*tr.v.* To give instructions, information, or advice to (sbdy.): *The pilot was briefed on weather conditions before takeoff.* —**brief'ly** *adv.* —**brief'ness** *n.* [U]

brief·case (brēf'kās') *n.* A flat rectangular case for carrying books or papers.

brief·ing (brē'fĭng) *n.* The act of giving or receiving instructions, information, or advice: *The President's assistant gave him a briefing before the news conference.*

brig (brĭg) *n.* A military jail or prison: *The sailor was thrown into the brig.*

bri·gade (brĭ gād') *n.* **1.** A large army unit. **2.** A group organized for a specific purpose: *a fire brigade.*

brig·a·dier general (brĭg'ə dîr') *n.* A high-ranking general in the U.S. Army, Air Force, or Marine Corps.

bright (brīt) *adj.* **1.** Giving off or reflecting a lot of light; shining: *the bright sun shining in a cloudless sky.* **2.** Vivid or intense: *bright green.* **3.** Intelligent; smart: *a bright child; a bright idea.* See Synonyms at **smart. 4.** Happy; cheerful: *a bright smiling face; a bright tune.* **5.** Full of promise and hope: *a bright future.* ◆ **bright and early.** Near dawn or very early in the morning: *We have to catch our plane bright and early tomorrow.* —**bright'ly** *adv.* —**bright'ness** *n.* [U]

bright·en (brīt'n) *tr. & intr.v.* **1.** To make or become bright or brighter: *Sunlight brightened the room. Stars brighten as the sun goes down.* **2.** To make or become happy or more cheerful: *The gifts brightened the children's faces. Their faces brightened at the clown's approach.*

bril·liance (brĭl'yəns) *n.* [U] **1.** Extreme brightness: *the brilliance of the noonday sun.* **2.** Exceptional intelligence or inventiveness: *a scientist of great brilliance.*

bril·liant (brĭl'yənt) *adj.* **1.** Full of light; shining brightly: *A brilliant sun shone in the sky.* **2.** Very vivid in color: *The sky was a brilliant blue.* **3.** Extremely intelligent or inventive: *A brilliant scientist made the discovery.* See Synonyms at **smart. 4.** Excellent; wonderful: *The musicians gave a brilliant performance.* —**bril'liant·ly** *adv.*

brim (brĭm) *n.* **1.** The rim or uppermost edge of a hollow container, such as a cup or glass: *The cup was filled to the brim.* **2.** A projecting rim on a hat. —*intr.v.* **brimmed, brim·ming, brims.** To be full to the brim: *My cup is brimming with coffee.*

brim·stone (brĭm'stōn') *n.* [U] **1.** Sulfur. **2.** The torments of hell; hellfire: *fire and brimstone.*

brine (brīn) *n.* [U] Water that contains a large amount of dissolved salt. —**brin·y** *adj.*

bring (brĭng) *tr.v.* **brought** (brôt), **bring·ing, brings. 1.** To take or carry (sthg.) with oneself to a place: *I brought my books home from school.* **2.** To cause (sthg.) to result: *The flood brought much property damage.* **3.** To persuade or influence (sbdy.): *People were having such a good time they could not bring themselves to leave.* **4.** To attract or cause (sbdy./sthg.) to come: *Smoke from the barn brought the neighbors.* **5.** To make (sthg.) come to mind: *This song brings back memories.* **6.** To lead or force (sbdy./sthg.) into a particular situation, location, or condition: *The movie brought the audience to tears. Bring the potatoes to a boil.* ◆ **bring about.** *tr.v.* [sep.] To cause (sthg.) to happen: *Hard*

work brought about the success of the play.
bring around. *tr.v.* [sep.] **1.** To cause (sbdy.) to accept an idea or take a certain action: *We tried to bring him around, but he did what he wanted anyway.* **2.** To cause (sbdy.) to come back to consciousness; bring to: *When she fainted, the doctor brought her around.* **bring back memories.** To cause sbdy. to remember sthg.: *The photograph brought back memories of her childhood.* **bring down.** *tr.v.* [sep.] **1.** To cause (sbdy./ sthg.) to fall or lose power: *The revolution brought down the king.* **2.** To kill (sbdy./ sthg.): *The hunter brought down a deer with one shot.* **bring forth.** *Formal. tr.v.* [sep.] **1.** To produce (sthg.): *The bulbs brought forth flowers in the spring.* **2.** To give birth to (young). **bring forward.** *tr.v.* [sep.] To present or produce (sbdy./sthg.): *bring forward proof.* **bring in.** *tr.v.* [sep.] **1.** To give (a verdict) to a court. **2.** To produce, yield, or earn (profits or income): *He brings in a good salary.* **bring off.** *tr.v.* [sep.] To accomplish (sthg.): *We brought off a successful play.* **bring on.** *tr.v.* [sep.] To cause (sthg.) to appear: *Working in the rain brought on a cold.* **bring out.** *tr.v.* [sep.] **1.** To reveal or show (sthg.) openly: *The article in the newspaper brought out the seriousness of the problem.* **2.** To produce or publish (sthg.): *The company is bringing out a new book.* **3.** To make (a quality, for example) easier to see or experience: *She brings out the best in us.* **bring to.** *tr.v.* [sep.] To cause (sbdy.) to come back to consciousness: *The patient was brought to after surgery.* **bring up.** *tr.v.* [sep.] **1.** To take care of and educate (a child): *He is bringing up three children.* **2.** To introduce (a topic) into discussion: *I was surprised when they brought up such personal matters.*

brink (brĭngk) *n. (usually singular).* **1.** The upper edge of a steep or vertical slope: *He stood at the brink of the canyon.* **2.** The point at which sthg. is likely to begin; the verge: *on the brink of extinction; at the brink of success.* See Synonyms at **margin.**

bri•quette also **bri•quet** (brĭ kĕt′) *n.* A block of compressed charcoal used for fuel, especially in barbecues.

brisk (brĭsk) *adj.* **1.** Moving or acting quickly; lively; energetic: *a brisk walk to get to school on time.* **2.** Very active: *Business is brisk when the store has a sale.* **3.** Cool and invigorating: *a brisk fall morning.* **4.** Sharp in speech or manner: *He gave us a friendly but rather brisk reply.* —**brisk′ly** *adv.* —**brisk′ness** *n.* [U]

bris•ket (brĭs′kĭt) *n.* [C; U] Meat from the chest of an animal: *a brisket of beef.*

bris•tle (brĭs′əl) *n.* **1.** A short stiff hair. **2.** A short, often synthetic piece resembling a hair: *the plastic bristles of a hairbrush.* —*v.* **bris•tled, bris•tling, bris•tles.** —*intr.* **1.** To raise the hairs, as in anger or fright: *The dog bristled and showed his teeth.* **2.** To show sudden anger or annoyance: *The artist bristled at the criticism of his work.* —**bris′tly** (brĭs′lē) *adj.*

Brit. *abbr.* An abbreviation of: **1.** Britain. **2.** British.

britch•es (brĭch′ĭz) *pl.n. Informal.* Breeches; pants. ♦ **too big for (one's) britches.** Overconfident; cocky: *He has gotten too big for his britches since he got that new job.*

Brit•ish (brĭt′ĭsh) *adj.* Relating to Great Britain or its people, language, or culture: *My ancestors were British; they lived in London, England.* —*n.* [U] **1.** *(used with a plural verb).* The people of Great Britain: *The British are tea drinkers.* **2.** British English.

brit•tle (brĭt′l) *adj.* **brit•tler, brit•tlest.** Easy to break or snap: *a brittle plastic plate; a brittle fingernail.* —**brit′tle•ness** *n.* [U]

bro. *abbr.* An abbreviation of brother.

broach (brōch) *tr.v.* To talk or write about (sthg.) for the first time; begin to discuss: *She tried to broach the subject of his drinking.*

HOMONYMS: broach, brooch (pin).

---

broad (brôd) *adj.* **1.** Wide from side to side: *a broad river.* **2.** Clear; bright: *broad daylight.* **3.** Covering a wide scope; general: *a broad topic.* —**broad′ly** *adv.*

broad•cast (brôd′kăst′) *v.* **broad•cast** or **broad•cast•ed, broad•cast•ing, broad•casts.** —*tr.* **1.** To transmit (sthg.) by radio or television: *All the networks will broadcast the President's speech.* **2.** To make (sthg.) known over a wide area: *Rumors were broadcast all over town.* —*intr.* To transmit a radio or television program: *Many stations broadcast from tall buildings.* —*n.* A radio or television program or transmission. —*adj.* Relating to transmission by radio or television: *Broadcast time for commercials is expensive.* —**broad′cast′er** *n.*

broad•cloth (brôd′klôth′ or brôd′klŏth′) *n.* [U] **1.** A fine woolen cloth with a smooth glossy texture, used especially in making suits. **2.** A closely woven silk, cotton, or synthetic cloth with a narrow rib, used especially in making shirts.

broad•en (brôd′n) *tr. & intr.v.* To make or become wide or wider: *broaden a narrow street; His view of the world broadened after a trip to Asia.*

broad jump *n.* The long jump.

broad-mind•ed (brôd′mīn′dĭd) *adj.* Having liberal and tolerant views and opinions: *It's wise to keep a broad-minded attitude toward the politics of other people.* —**broad'•mind'ed•ly** *adv.* —**broad'mind'ed•ness** *n.* [U]

broad•side (brôd'sīd') *n.* A forceful written or verbal attack, as in an editorial or a speech. —*adv.* With the side turned toward a specified object: *The wave caught them broadside and filled the boat.* —*tr.v.* **broad•sid•ed, broad•sid•ing, broad•sides. 1.** To hit (a vehicle) along the side: *The drunk driver broadsided the car at the intersection.* **2.** To catch (sbdy.) unawares, especially in a hostile or unpleasant way: *I felt broadsided by her decision.*

bro•cade (brō kād') *n.* [U] A heavy cloth with a rich raised design.

broc•co•li (brŏk'ə lē) *n.* [U] A vegetable with dense clusters of green flower buds.

bro•chure (brō shŏŏr') *n.* A small pamphlet or booklet: *a travel brochure.*

broil (broil) *v.* —*tr.* **1.** To cook (sthg.) close to flame or direct heat: *broil the fish.* **2.** To expose (sthg.) to great heat: *The desert sun broiled everyone.* —*intr.* **1.** To be cooked by direct heat: *The fish broiled for ten minutes.* **2.** To be exposed to great heat: *The tourists broiled under the tropical sun.*

broil•er (broi'lər) *n.* **1.** A pan, grill, or part of a stove used for broiling. **2.** A young chicken suitable for broiling.

broke (brōk) *v.* Past tense of **break.** —*adj.* *Informal.* Without money: *I was broke after I bought a new car.*

bro•ken (brō'kən) *v.* Past participle of **break.** —*adj.* **1.** Separated into pieces by force; fractured: *broken pieces of glass; a broken leg.* **2.** Out of order; not functioning: *a broken watch.* **3.** Not kept; violated: *a broken promise.* **4.** Overwhelmed, as by sadness: *a broken heart.*

bro•ken-down (brō'kən doun') *adj.* **1.** In poor condition, as from old age: *a broken-down cart horse.* **2.** Out of working order: *a broken-down car.*

bro•ken•heart•ed (brō'kən här'tĭd) *adj.* Overwhelmed with sadness; very sad.

bro•ker (brō'kər) *n.* A person who acts as an agent for other people by negotiating contracts, purchases, or sales in return for a fee or commission: *a stockbroker.*

bro•ker•age (brō'kər ĭj) *n.* **1.** [C; U] The business of a broker: *a brokerage firm.* **2.** [C] A fee or commission paid to a broker.

bro•mine (brō'mēn) *n.* [U] *Symbol* **Br** A dark brownish red element that is a nonmetallic liquid. Atomic number 35. See table at **element.**

bron•chi (brŏng'kī' *or* brŏng'kē') *n.* Plural of **bronchus.**

bron•chi•al (brŏng'kē əl) *adj.* Relating to the bronchi.

bronchial tube *n.* A bronchus or any of the tubes branching from a bronchus.

bron•chi•tis (brŏn kī'tĭs *or* brŏng kī'tĭs) *n.* [U] Inflammation of the mucous membrane of the bronchial tubes.

bron•chus (brŏng'kəs) *n.*, *pl.* **bron•chi** (brŏng'kī' *or* brŏng'kē).* Either of the two large main branches of the windpipe, leading directly to the lungs.

bron•co (brŏng'kō) *n.*, *pl.* **bron•cos.** A small wild or half-wild horse of western North America.

bronze (brŏnz) *n.* **1.** [U] An alloy of copper and tin or aluminum. **2.** [C] A work of art made of bronze. **3.** [U] A yellowish or olive brown color. —*adj.* **1.** Yellowish or olive brown. **2.** Made of or containing bronze: *bronze tools; a bronze statue.* —*tr.v.* **bronzed, bronz•ing, bronz•es. 1.** To give the appearance of bronze to (sthg.): *The sun had bronzed the faces of the lifeguards.* **2.** To coat (sthg.) with bronze: *They bronzed the baby's first pair of shoes to keep them as a momento.*

brooch (brōch *or* brŏŏch) *n.* A large pin worn as an ornament, fastened to the clothing with a clasp.

HOMONYMS: brooch, broach (begin to discuss).

---

brood (brŏŏd) *n.* **1.** The young of certain animals, especially a group of young birds with the same mother. **2.** The children in one family: *The little house was too small for the neighbor's brood.* —*v.* —*intr.* **1.** To sit on and hatch eggs. **2.** To think at length and unhappily; worry: *It seems pointless to brood about the past.* —*tr.* To sit on and hatch (eggs).

brook (brŏŏk) *n.* A small natural stream of fresh water.

broom (brŏŏm *or* brŏŏm) *n.* A tool for sweeping, made of straw or plastic bound together and attached to a long stick: *He swept the floor with a broom.*

broom•stick (brŏŏm'stĭk' *or* brŏŏm'stĭk') *n.* The long handle of a broom.

bros. *abbr.* An abbreviation of brothers.

broth (brôth *or* brŏth) *n.*, *pl.* **broths** (brôths *or* brŏths *or* brôthz *or* brŏthz). [C; U] A clear soup made from the water in which meat, fish, or vegetables have been boiled.

broth•er (brŭth'ər) *n.* **1.** A boy or man having the same mother and father as another person: *I have one brother and one sister.* **2.** A fellow member of a group, such as a profession, fraternity, or labor union: *The brothers in our local chapter meet monthly.*

broth•er•hood (brŭth'ər hŏŏd') *n.* **1.** [U] The relationship of being a brother or brothers. **2.** [U] Brotherly feelings or friendship toward other human beings: *The United Nations promotes peace and brotherhood among countries.* **3.** [C] A group of people

B

united for a common purpose: *The carpenters formed a brotherhood.*

broth·er-in-law (brŭth′ər ĭn lô′) *n.*, *pl.* **broth·ers-in-law** (brŭth′ərz ĭn lô′). **1.** The brother of one's husband or wife: *My sister-in-law and brother-in-law moved into a new house.* **2.** The husband of one's sister. **3.** The husband of the sister of one's husband or wife.

broth·er·ly (brŭth′ər lē) *adj.* Characteristic of or appropriate to brothers; affectionate: *a warm brotherly greeting; brotherly love.* —**broth′er·li·ness** *n.* [U]

brought (brôt) *v.* Past tense and past participle of **bring.**

brou·ha·ha (brōō′hä hä′) *n.* [C; U] A lot of unnecessary noise and activity; a commotion: *Don't make such a brouhaha over nothing.*

brow (brou) *n.* **1.** The forehead. **2.** An eyebrow: *His colorful language didn't raise a brow.*

brow·beat (brou′bēt′) *tr.v.* **brow·beat, brow·beat·en** (brou′bēt′n), **brow·beat·ing, brow·beats.** To bully or intimidate (sbdy.), as with frightening looks or harsh words: *We were browbeaten into accepting the new proposal.*

brown (broun) *n.* [C; U] The color of chocolate or coffee. —*adj.* Of the color brown. —*tr. & intr.v.* To cook until brown on the outside: *The chef browned the meat. These cookies browned quickly.* —**brown′ness** *n.* [U]

brown·ie (brou′nē) *n.* **1.** A bar of moist chocolate cake, often with nuts: *She made brownies for dessert.* **2. Brownie.** A member of the Girl Scouts between six and eight years old.

brown·ish (brou′nĭsh) *adj.* Somewhat brown.

brown rice *n.* [U] Rice that still has the outer layer of bran on the grain.

brown·stone (broun′stōn′) *n.* **1.** [U] A brownish red sandstone used as a building material. **2.** [C] A house built or faced with such stone: *a row of brownstones.*

brown sugar *n.* [U] Unrefined or partially refined sugar with a flavor similar to that of molasses.

browse (brouz) *v.* **browsed, brows·ing, brows·es.** —*intr.* [through] To look at things in a slow and casual way: *browse through a book; browse through a department store.* —*tr.* To look through (sthg.) casually: *browse the Internet.*

brows·er (brou′zər) *n.* **1.** Someone who looks at sthg. casually: *She's a constant browser, always wandering through the stores.* **2.** A computer program that makes it possible to find and use information on the Internet: *a Web browser.*

bruise (brōōz) *v.* **bruised, bruis·ing, bruis·es.** —*tr.* **1.** To injure (a part of the

body) without breaking the skin, as by a blow: *When I fell off my bike, I bruised my knees.* **2.** To hurt (one's feelings); offend: *Criticism bruised the actor's pride.* —*intr.* To become bruised: *Fruit bruises easily.* —*n.* **1.** An injury in which the skin is injured by pressure or a blow, producing discoloration: *She got a bruise from a fall.* **2.** A similar injury to a fruit, vegetable, or plant: *There's a bruise on this peach, so don't buy it.*

brunch (brŭnch) *n.* A meal eaten late in the morning that combines breakfast and lunch: *We have a pancake brunch every Sunday.*

bru·nette (brōō nĕt′) *adj.* (*used of a girl or woman*). Having dark or brown hair. —*n.* A girl or woman with dark or brown hair.

brunt (brŭnt) *n.* [U] The main impact, force, or burden: *Towns along the shore bore the brunt of the storm.*

brush¹ (brŭsh) *n.* **1.** A tool made of bristles, hairs, or wire attached to a handle, used especially for scrubbing, applying paint, or grooming the hair. **2.** An application of a brush: *She gave her hair a good brush.* **3.** A light touch in passing; a graze: *the brush of a branch against my coat.* —*v.* —*tr.* **1.** To clean, polish, or groom (sthg.) with a brush: *brush shoes until they shine; brush one's teeth.* **2.** To apply (sthg.) with a brush: *brush paint on evenly.* **3.** To remove (sthg.) with or as if with a brush: *brush dirt off one's jacket.* **4.** To touch (sthg.) lightly in passing: *His arm brushed hers in the crowded hall.* —*intr.* To move past sthg. so as to touch it lightly: *The wet paint got on my clothes when I brushed against it.* ♦ **brush aside.** *tr.v.* [sep.] To pay no attention to (sbdy./sthg.); dismiss: *He brushed aside her objections and continued on.* **brush off.** *tr.v.* [sep.] To dismiss (sbdy./sthg.): *His boss brushed off his idea.* **brush up on. 1.** To refresh one's memory of (sthg.). **2.** To renew (a skill): *I'll have to brush up on my Spanish before going to Mexico.*

brush² (brŭsh) *n.* [U] **1.a.** A dense growth of shrubs or bushes: *He got scratched running through the brush.* **b.** Land covered with such growth. **2.** Broken or cut branches: *Pile the brush at the curb.* —**brush′y** *adj.*

brush³ (brŭsh) *n.* A brief, often hostile or frightening encounter: *a brush with the law.*

brush·off also **brush-off** (brŭsh′ôf′ or brŭsh′ŏf′) *n.* An abrupt dismissal; a snub: *She gave her old boyfriend the brushoff.*

brusque (brŭsk) *adj.* Rudely abrupt in manner or speech; curt; blunt: *The busy shopkeeper gave a brusque reply to the curious children.* —**brusque′ly** *adv.* —**brusque′-ness** *n.* [U]

ă–cat; ā–pay; âr–care; ä–father; ĕ–get; ē–be; ĭ–sit; ī–nice; îr–here; ŏ–got; ō–go; ô–saw; oi–boy; ou–out; ōō–took; ōō–boot; ŭ–cut; ûr–word; th–thin; *th*–this; hw–when; zh–vision; ə–about; N–French bon

Brus•sels sprouts (brŭs′əlz) *pl.n.* *(used with a singular or plural verb).* Small buds that look like cabbages, eaten as a vegetable.

bru•tal (brōōt′l) *adj.* Cruel; ruthless: *a brutal attack.* —**bru•tal•i•ty** (brōō tal′ĭ tē) *n.* [C; U] —**bru′tal•ly** *adv.*

bru•tal•ize (brōōt′l īz′) *tr.v.* **bru•tal•ized, bru•tal•iz•ing, bru•tal•iz•es.** To treat (sbdy.) cruelly or harshly: *The trucker refused to brutalize the animals by keeping them in narrow cages.*

brute (brōōt) *n.* **1.** An animal, especially a large one; a beast: *That dog is a big brute, isn't he?* **2.** A brutal person. —*adj.* Entirely physical: *the brute force of the athlete.* —**brut′ish** (brōō′tĭsh) *adj.* —**brut′ish•ly** *adv.* —**brut′ish•ness** *n.* [U]

B.S. *abbr.* An abbreviation of Bachelor of Science.

B.Sc. *abbr.* An abbreviation of Bachelor of Science.

Btu *abbr.* An abbreviation of British thermal unit, a unit of heat.

bu. *abbr.* An abbreviation of bushel.

bub•ble (bŭb′əl) *n.* **1.** A rounded thin film of liquid enclosing a pocket of air or other gas: *soap bubbles.* **2.** A small rounded pocket of gas that rises to the surface of a liquid or remains trapped in a solid or plastic material: *bubbles of air in ice cubes.* —*intr.v.* **bub•bled, bub•bling, bub•bles. 1.** To form or give off bubbles: *Steam rose as water bubbled in the pot.* **2.** To show lively activity or emotion: *As they entered the theater, the children bubbled with excitement.* —**bub′bly** *adj.*

bubble gum *n.* [U] Chewing gum that can be blown into bubbles.

buc•ca•neer (bŭk′ə nîr′) *n.* A pirate.

buck¹ (bŭk) *n.* **1.** A sudden leap forward and upward, as by a horse or mule. **2.** The adult male of certain animals, such as the deer, antelope, and rabbit. —*v.* —*intr.* **1.** To leap upward arching the back: *The horse bucked and kicked.* **2.** To resist; balk: *bucking against the trend in fashion.* —*tr.* **1.** To throw off (a rider) by bucking: *The young horse bucked the cowboy when he tried to ride it.* **2.** To struggle against (sthg.); oppose: *The rebel only seems happy when he is bucking the rules.* ◆ **buck up.** *intr.v.* To call on one's courage or spirits: *When we lost the game, the coach advised us to buck up and try harder.*

buck² (bŭk) *n. Informal.* A dollar.

buck•et (bŭk′ĭt) *n.* **1.** A round open container with a curved handle, used for carrying; a pail: *He filled the bucket with water.* **2.a.** The amount that a bucket holds: *Pour a bucket of sand on an icy sidewalk.* **b.** An unexpectedly great amount or quantity: *The rain came down in buckets.* ◆ **a drop in the bucket.** A small amount in comparison with what is needed: *The small donation was only a drop in the bucket.* **kick the bucket.** *Informal.* To die.

buck•et•ful (bŭk′ĭt fool′) *n.* The amount that a bucket can hold: *a bucketful of water.*

bucket seat *n.* A seat with a rounded padded back, as in sports cars.

buck•le (bŭk′əl) *n.* **1.** A clasp used to attach one end of a strap or belt to the other: *the buckle on the strap of a watch.* **2.** An ornament that looks like such a clasp, as one on top of a shoe. **3.** A bend, bulge, warp, or other distortion: *The buckle in the sidewalk needed to be fixed.* —*v.* **buck•led, buck•ling, buck•les.** —*tr.* **1.** To fasten (sthg.) with a buckle: *Buckle your seat belt before the car starts.* **2.** To cause (sthg.) to bend, warp, or crumple, as by pressure or heat: *Too much pressure buckled the sides of the box.* —*intr.* To sag, bend, or collapse: *Walls buckled in the heat of the fire.* ◆ **buckle down.** *intr.v.* To apply oneself with determination: *We need to buckle down and study before a big test.*

buck•skin (bŭk′skĭn′) *n.* **1.** [U] A soft, grayish yellow leather, made from the skins of deer or sheep. **2. buckskins.** Pants or shoes made of this leather.

buck•wheat (bŭk′wēt′) *n.* [U] A cereal plant of Asia with small triangular fruits that are often ground into flour.

bu•col•ic (byōō kŏl′ĭk) *adj.* Characteristic of country life; rustic: *a bucolic scene.*

bud (bŭd) *n.* **1.a.** A small swelling on a branch or stem, containing an undeveloped flower, shoot, or leaf. **b.** A partly opened flower or leaf. **2.** A stage of early or incomplete development: *the bud of a new idea.* —*intr.v.* **bud•ded, bud•ding, buds. 1.** To form or produce a bud: *Tulips bud in the very early spring.* **2.** To be in an early stage; begin to develop: *Businesses using new research are budding near the university.*

Bud•dhism (bōō′dĭz′əm *or* bōōd′ĭz′əm) *n.* [U] The religion, based on the teachings of Buddha, that holds that suffering is unavoidable in life and that extinguishing one's worldly desires leads to a state of understanding and compassion called nirvana. —**Bud′-dhist** *n. & adj.*

bud•dy (bŭd′ē) *n., pl.* **bud•dies.** *Informal.* A close friend; a comrade: *old army buddies.*

budge (bŭj) *intr. & tr.v.* **budged, budg•ing, budg•es. 1.** To move or cause to move slightly: *The sleeping dog did not budge. We cannot budge the rock.* **2.** To alter or cause to alter a position or an attitude: *They won't budge once they have reached a decision. After the prime minister had made up her mind no one could budge her.*

budg•et (bŭj′ĭt) *n.* A plan or an estimate of the amount of money that will be spent and received in a given time period: *They cannot spend more than the amount in their budget each month.* —*tr.v.* To plan in advance for the use of (resources, such as money or time): *We* budget *how much money we spend on food every month.* —*adj.* **1.** Relating to a budget: *Were these budget items approved by Congress?* **2.** Appropriate to a budget; inexpensive: *a budget car; budget meals.* —**bud′get•ar′y** (bŭj′ĭ tĕr′ē) *adj.*

buff¹ (bŭf) *n.* **1.** [U] A yellowish tan color. **2.** [C] A piece of soft material or an implement covered with such material used for polishing. —*tr.v.* To polish or shine (sthg.) with a piece of soft material: *Please buff my car and make it shine.* ◆ **in the buff.** Naked or nude: *We went swimming in the buff.*

buff² (bŭf) *n. Informal.* A person who has great interest in and some knowledge of a subject: *a car buff; science buffs.*

buf•fa•lo (bŭf′ə lō′) *n., pl.* **buffalo** or **buf•fa•loes** or **buf•fa•los. 1.** The North American bison. **2.** Any of several African or Asian mammals similar to the ox, with large outward-curving horns, as the domesticated water buffalo.

buff•er¹ (bŭf′ər) *n.* A soft pad or tool having a pad used to polish or shine objects: *He used a buffer to polish the table.*

buff•er² (bŭf′ər) *n.* **1.** Something that reduces the shock of a blow or collision: *a block of wood serving as a buffer when hammering.* **2.** A substance that minimizes change in the acidity of a solution when an acid or a base is added. **3.** Something that reduces the danger of conflict between two rivals or competitors: *She was a buffer for her brothers.* **4.** A device or an area of a computer used temporarily to store data being transferred between two machines that process data at different rates, such as a computer and a printer.

buf•fet¹ (bə fā′ *or* boo fā′) *n.* **1.** A large piece of furniture with drawers and cupboards for storing china, silverware, and table linens: *The buffet in her dining room was more than 100 years old.* **2.** A meal at which guests serve themselves from dishes arranged on a table: *They invited their friends to their house for a buffet.* —*adj.* Describing a meal at which people serve themselves: *a buffet lunch.*

buf•fet² (bŭf′ĭt) *tr.v.* To hit or strike against (sthg.) forcefully; batter: *The rough sea buffeted the small boat.*

buf•foon (bə foon′) *n.* **1.** A clown or jester. **2.** An insulting term for a person who seems ridiculous; a fool. —**buf•foon′er•y** *n.* [U]

bug (bŭg) *n.* **1.** An insect, a spider, or a similar organism: *Moths and other bugs flew around the light.* **2.a.** A microorganism that causes disease; a germ: *He caught a flu bug and got sick.* **b.** A disease caused by such a microorganism: *suffering from a bug.* **3.** A fault or defect in a system or device: *work the bugs out of a plan; a bug in the computer program.* **4.** A hidden electronic device that allows private conversations to be overheard: *The spy put a bug under the table to hear the conversation.* —*v.* **bugged, bug•ging, bugs.** —*intr.* [out] To grow large; bulge: *Their eyes bugged out with surprise.* —*tr. Slang.* **1.** To annoy, trouble, or pester (sbdy.): *TV commercials bug me.* **2.** To equip (a room or telephone circuit, for example) with a concealed electronic listening device: *The FBI bugged her office.* ◆ **put a bug in (one's) ear.** To give sbdy. an idea: *She put a bug in his ear about vacation.* **bug off.** *intr.v. Slang.* To leave sbdy. alone; go away: *I told my little brother to bug off because I needed to study.* **bug out.** *intr.v. Slang.* To leave quickly: *He bugged out when he saw how late it was.*

bug•gy (bŭg′ē) *n., pl.* **bug•gies. 1.** A small carriage with a single seat and four wheels, drawn by a horse. **2.** A baby carriage.

bu•gle (byoo′gəl) *n.* A brass wind instrument similar to a trumpet but without valves. —*intr.v.* **bu•gled, bu•gling, bu•gles.** To play a bugle. —**bu′gler** *n.*

build (bĭld) *v.* **built** (bĭlt), **build•ing, builds.** —*tr.* **1.** To make or form (sthg.) by fitting together materials or parts; construct: *It takes a long time to build a skyscraper.* **2.** To make (sthg.) steadily and gradually; create and add to: *Reading helps build a rich vocabulary.* —*intr.* To progress toward a peak; develop: *A good mystery builds from the first chapters to its climax.* —*n.* The physical makeup of a person or thing: *a muscular athletic build.* ◆ **build in** or **into.** *tr.v.* [sep.] To construct (sthg.) as a permanent part of: *build in kitchen cabinets.* **build on** or **onto.** *tr.v.* [insep.] To use (sthg.) as a basis or foundation: *We must build on our success.* **build up.** *tr.v.* [sep.] **1.** To develop (sthg.) in stages or by degrees: *build up a business; build up a strong vocabulary.* **2.** To cover (an area) with buildings: *The downtown area is getting built up.* —*intr.v.* To increase steadily: *His anger has been building up for days. The ashes are building up in the ashtray.*

build•er (bĭl′dər) *n.* **1.** A person or an animal that builds: *Beavers are great dam builders.* **2.** A person who constructs new buildings or develops land: *the architects and builders of a great city.*

build•ing (bĭl′dĭng) *n.* **1.** [C] Something that is built, such as a house or similar structure. **2.** [U] The act, process, or occupation of constructing.

build•up also **build-up** (bĭld′ŭp′) *n.* **1.** [U] The act or process of building up: *the buildup of ashes in a fireplace.* **2.** [C] Widely favorable publicity; high praise: *The newspaper gave the fundraising dance a nice buildup.*

built (bĭlt) *v.* Past tense and past participle of **build.** —*adj. Offensive Slang.* Having large breasts and a good figure.

built-in (bĭlt′ĭn′) *adj.* Constructed as a permanent part of a larger unit: *a built-in cupboard.*

built-up (bĭlt′ŭp′) *adj.* **1.** Made by fastening layers or sections one on top of the other: *a built-up roof.* **2.** Filled with buildings; developed: *a built-up neighborhood.*

bulb (bŭlb) *n.* **1.** A rounded plant bud that develops underground and contains the undeveloped shoots of a new plant that will grow from it: *an onion bulb; a tulip bulb.* **2.** A rounded part of sthg.: *the bulb of a thermometer.* **3.** A lamp or its glass container; a light bulb. —**bul′bous** *adj.*

bulge (bŭlj) *n.* A protruding part; a swelling: *A blister causes a bulge in the skin.* —*intr. & tr.v.* **bulged, bulg•ing, bulg•es.** To swell or cause to swell beyond the usual size: *eyes bulging with surprise; groceries bulging in a bag.* —**bulg′i•ness** *n.* [U] —**bulg′y** *adj.*

bu•lim•i•a (bōo lē′mē ə) *n.* [U] A disorder, usually occurring in young women, caused by fear of being fat, in which the person eats a lot of food and then vomits to get rid of the food. —**bu•lim′ic** *adj.*

bulk (bŭlk) *n.* [U] **1.** Great size, mass, or volume: *the whale's enormous bulk.* **2.** The major portion of sthg.; greater part: *The bulk of the dairy farm is pasture.* ◆ **in bulk. 1.** Unpackaged; loose: *That store sells rice in bulk.* **2.** In large numbers, amounts, or volume: *Offices buy paper in bulk.*

bulk•head (bŭlk′hĕd′) *n.* One of the vertical walls that divide the inside of a ship or aircraft into compartments: *His legs are long, so he asks for a bulkhead seat when he flies.*

bulk•y (bŭl′kē) *adj.* **bulk•i•er, bulk•i•est. 1.** Extremely large; massive: *Elephants and whales are bulky animals.* **2.** Taking up much space; clumsy: *The lamp came in a bulky package.* —**bulk′i•ly** *adv.* —**bulk′i•ness** *n.* [U]

bull (bōol) *n.* **1.** [C] **a.** The full-grown male of cattle. **b.** The male of certain other large mammals, such as the elephant, moose, or seal. **2.** [U] *Offensive Slang.* Bullshit. —*adj.* **1.** Male: *a bull seal.* **2.** Characterized by rising prices, especially in the stock market: *a bull market.* ◆ **take the bull by the horns.** To face a difficult situation directly: *She took the bull by the horns and asked her boss for a raise.*

bull•dog (bōol′dôg′ *or* bōol′dŏg′) *n.* A breed of stocky short-haired dog with a large head and strong square jaws.

bull•doze (bōol′dōz′) *tr.v.* **bull•dozed, bull•doz•ing, bull•doz•es. 1.** To clear, dig up, or move (sthg.) with a bulldozer: *bulldoze land for a new development.* **2.** To bully,

intimidate, or coerce (sbdy.): *He tried to bulldoze the committee into accepting his plan.*

bull•doz•er (bōol′dō′zər) *n.* A large powerful tractor with treads and a metal blade in front for moving earth and leveling land.

bul•let (bōol′ĭt) *n.* A small, rounded, usually pointed piece of metal to be fired from a gun: *The bullet went through the man's arm.*

bul•le•tin (bōol′ĭ tn) *n.* **1.** A statement on a matter of public interest, as in a newspaper, on television, or on radio: *a weather bulletin.* **2.** A newspaper, magazine, or pamphlet published regularly by an organization, such as a society or club: *Did you read the school bulletin this week?*

bulletin board *n.* **1.** A board, usually hung on a wall, on which notices are placed: *The help wanted ad is posted on the bulletin board.* **2.** A service for computer users that displays messages and other information and permits subscribers to communicate with each other through their computers.

bul•let•proof (bōol′ĭt prōof′) *adj.* Designed to stop or repel bullets: *bulletproof glass.*

bull•fight (bōol′fīt′) *n.* A spectacle, especially in Spain and Latin America, in which a bull is fought by a human and usually killed with a sword. —**bull′fight′er** *n.* —**bull′-fight′ing** *n.* [U]

bull•frog (bōol′frôg′ *or* bōol′frog′) *n.* A large frog of North America with a deep croak.

bull•head•ed (bōol′hĕd′ĭd) *adj.* Very stubborn; headstrong: *She's too bullheaded to go to the doctor for a checkup.* —**bull′-head′ed•ness** *n.* [U]

bull•horn (bōol′hôrn′) *n.* A portable device used to make the voice louder: *Police used a bullhorn to talk with the man holding the hostage.*

bul•lion (bōol′yən) *n.* [U] Gold or silver in the form of bars.

HOMONYMS: bullion, bouillon (soup).

---

bull•ish (bōol′ĭsh) *adj.* **1.a.** Causing, expecting, or characterized by rising stock market prices: *a bullish market.* **b.** Optimistic or confident: *Management is bullish on the prospects for a negotiated settlement.* —**bull′ish•ly** *adv.* —**bull′ish•ness** *n.* [U]

bull•pen (bōol′pĕn′) *n.* An area in a baseball stadium for pitchers to warm up during a game.

bull•ring (bōol′rĭng′) *n.* A circular arena for bullfighting.

bull's-eye *or* **bull's eye** (bōolz′ī′) *n.* **1.** The small central circle on a target: *Try to hit the bull's-eye.* **2.** A shot that hits its target: *Bull's-eye! You won the game!*

bull•shit (bōol′shĭt′) *Offensive Slang. n.* [U] Lies, deception, or nonsense. —**bull′shit′** *interj.*

bul·ly (bŏŏl'ē) *n., pl.* **bul·lies.** A person who enjoys frightening or hurting smaller or weaker people: *The bully was always picking on smaller boys.* —*tr.v.* **bul·lied, bul·ly·ing, bul·lies.** To hurt or frighten (sbdy.) as a bully does: *Stop bullying me!*

bum (bŭm) *n. Informal.* **1.** A tramp; a hobo: *He is a bum; he goes around town begging instead of working.* **2.** A person who avoids work; a loafer. **3.** Somebody who spends a large amount of time on an activity: *a beach bum; a ski bum.* —*v.* **bummed, bum·ming, bums.** —*tr.* **1.** *Informal.* To obtain (sthg.) by begging; mooch: *bum a quarter for a phone call.* **2.** *Informal.* To get (sthg.) by asking for a favor: *Can I bum a ride from you?* **3.** *Slang.* To make (sbdy.) sad; disappoint: *That bums me.* —*adj.* **1.** Worthless: *bum directions.* **2.** Disabled: *a bum knee.* **3.** Unfavorable or unfair: *a bum rap.* ◆ **bum around.** *intr.v. Informal.* To wander about: *He bummed around the country for several months after college.* **bum out.** *tr.v.* [sep.] *Slang.* To make (sbdy.) sad; disappoint: *I was bummed out when my favorite team lost.*

bum·ble·bee (bŭm'bəl bē') *n.* Any of various large hairy bees related to the honeybee that fly with a humming sound.

bum·bling (bŭm'blĭng) *adj.* Unable to do anything right: *a bumbling fool.*

bum·mer (bŭm'ər) *n. Slang.* [U] An unpleasant experience or situation: *Missing the bus home late at night was a real bummer.*

bump (bŭmp) *v.* —*tr.* **1.** To come up or knock against (sbdy./sthg.) forcefully: *They bumped heads as they both tried to pick up the dime.* **2.** To cause (sthg.) to knock against an obstacle: *I bumped the vacuum cleaner against the table.* **3.** To move (sbdy.) from a flight because more tickets have been sold than there are seats: *I was bumped from my flight because of overbooking.* —*intr.* **1.** To hit or knock against sthg. forcefully: *My knee bumped against the wall.* **2.** To proceed with jerks and jolts: *an old car bumping down the road.* —*n.* **1.** A light blow, collision, or jolt: *We felt a bump as the other car backed into us.* **2.** A small swelling, as from a blow or an insect sting: *a bump on the head.* **3.** A small place that rises above the level of the surface surrounding it: *a bump in the road.* ◆ **bump into.** *tr.v.* [insep.] To meet (sbdy.) by chance: *We bumped into each other at the store.*

bump·er (bŭm'pər) *n.* A horizontal metal or rubber bar attached to the front or rear of a vehicle to absorb the impact of a collision: *The front bumper of the car was damaged when he hit the pole.*

bumper crop *n.* An abundant crop: *The farmers had a bumper crop after the rains.*

bumper sticker *n.* A sticker with a printed message to display on a car or truck.

bumper-to-bumper *adj. & adv.* With a lot of traffic very close together: *Traffic is bumper-to-bumper during rush hour. They parked the cars bumper-to-bumper.*

bump·y (bŭm'pē) *adj.* **bump·i·er, bump·i·est.** **1.** Full of bumps: *a bumpy road.* **2.** Marked by or causing jerks and jolts: *a bumpy ride.* —**bump'i·ly** *adv.* —**bump'i·ness** *n.* [U]

bun (bŭn) *n.* **1.** A small bread roll: *a hamburger bun; a cinnamon bun.* **2.** A roll or coil of hair worn by a woman at the back of the head: *The ballerina had her hair in a bun.*

bunch (bŭnch) *n.* **1.** A group of things that are alike and growing, fastened, or placed together: *bunches of fresh grapes; a bunch of keys.* **2.** *Informal.* A group of people having a common interest: *My brother and his bunch like video games.* **3.** *Informal.* A considerable number or amount: *I have a whole bunch of work.* —*v.* —*tr.* To gather (things) into a bunch: *bunch flowers into a bouquet.* —*intr.* To form a cluster or group: *Cold hikers bunched around a campfire.* ◆ **bunch up.** *intr.v.* To gather in folds or knots: *Those pants bunch up at the waist.*

bun·dle (bŭn'dl) *n.* **1.** A number of objects bound, tied, or wrapped together: *a bundle of sticks.* **2.** Something tied up for carrying; a package. —*v.* **bun·dled, bun·dling, bun·dles.** —*tr.* **1.** To tie, wrap, or bind (sthg.) securely together: *bundle newspapers for recycling.* **2.** To send (sbdy./sthg.) quickly; hustle: *bundle the children off to school.* **3.** To dress (sbdy.) warmly: *She bundled up the baby and went outside.*

bun·ga·low (bŭng'gə lō') *n.* A small one-story house or cottage.

bun·gle (bŭng'gəl) *v.* **bun·gled, bun·gling, bun·gles.** —*intr.* To work or act in an incompetent manner. —*tr.* To manage or handle (sthg.) poorly; botch: *He bungled the mixing of the ingredients, and his cookies were terrible.* —**bun'gler** *n.* —**bun'gling** *adj.*

bun·ion (bŭn'yən) *n.* A painful inflamed swelling in the joint at the base of the big toe.

bunk¹ (bŭngk) *n.* A narrow bed. —*intr.v.* **1.** To sleep in a bunk. **2.** To occupy makeshift sleeping quarters: *bunk on the sofa tonight.*

bunk² (bŭngk) *n.* [U] *Informal.* Empty talk; nonsense: *That's nothing but bunk.*

bunk bed *n.* One of two single beds that are attached one above the other.

bun·ker (bŭng'kər) *n.* A fortification, as a deep trench or tunnel: *a concrete bunker.*

bunk·house (bŭngk'hous') *n.* A building with sleeping quarters on a ranch or in a camp.

ă–cat; ā–pay; âr–care; ä–father; ĕ–get; ē–be; ĭ–sit; ī–nice; îr–here; ŏ–got; ō–go; ô–saw; oi–boy; ou–out; ŏŏ–took; ōō–boot; ŭ–cut; ûr–word; th–thin; *th*–this; hw–when; zh–vision; ə–about; N–French bon

bun·ny (bŭn′ē) *n., pl.* **bun·nies.** *(used especially by or with children).* A rabbit, especially a young one: *the Easter bunny.*

buns (bŭnz) *pl.n. Slang.* Buttocks.

Bun·sen burner (bŭn′sən) *n.* A gas burner used in laboratories.

buoy (boo͞′ē *or* boi) *n.* **1.** A float used to warn ships of danger, such as a reef or sandbar, or to mark a channel or safe passage. **2.** A life buoy. —*tr.v.* **1.** To keep (sbdy./sthg.) afloat. **2.** To cheer (sbdy./sthg.); hearten: *The good news buoyed our spirits.*

buoy·an·cy (boi′ən sē *or* boo͞′yən sē) *n.* [U] **1.** The tendency or capacity to float in a liquid or to rise in air: *the buoyancy of wood in water.* **2.** The upward force that a fluid exerts on an object less dense than itself: *the buoyancy of salt water.* **3.** Lightness of spirit; cheerfulness: *The nurse's buoyancy cheered up the patient.*

buoy·ant (boi′ənt *or* boo͞′yənt) *adj.* **1.** Having buoyancy; tending to float or floating: *a buoyant cork.* **2.** Lighthearted; cheerful: *a buoyant mood.* —**buoy′ant·ly** *adv.*

bur *also* **burr** (bûr) *n.* A rough prickly covering that encloses the seeds or fruit of a plant: *Your pants are covered with burs.*

bur·den (bûr′dn) *n.* **1.** Something that is carried; a load: *horses carrying their heavy burden up the hill.* **2.** Something endured as a duty or responsibility: *Citizens carry the burden of taxation.* **3.** Something endured with difficulty: *Taking care of his elderly parents has been a financial burden.* —*tr.v.* To load (sbdy./sthg.) with or as if with sthg. difficult to bear: *heavy snow burdening the branches of the tree; a man burdened with sad memories.*

bur·den·some (bûr′dn səm) *adj.* Creating a burden; hard to bear: *the burdensome task of cleaning out the garage.*

bu·reau (byoor′ō) *n.* **1.** A chest of drawers, especially for holding clothes: *In his room, there is a bed and a bureau.* **2.** An office for a specific kind of business: *a travel bureau.* **3.** A department of a government: *the Federal Bureau of Investigation.*

bureau

bu·reauc·ra·cy (byoo͞ rŏk′rə sē) *n., pl.* **bu·reauc·ra·cies. 1.** [C] The administration of a government or an organization composed of bureaus and departments with appointed officials. **2.** [U] An administration, as of a business or government, in which the need to follow rules and regulations complicates and slows effective action: *Application for a refund was delayed in the bureaucracy of the accounting department.*

bu·reau·crat (byoor′ə krăt′) *n.* **1.** An official of a bureaucracy. **2.** A person who insists on rigid adherence to rules and routines. —**bu′reau·crat′ic** *adj.* —**bu′reau·crat′i·cal·ly** *adv.*

burg (bûrg) *n. Informal.* A small city or town: *I can hardly wait to leave this burg.*

bur·geon (bûr′jən) *intr.v.* To grow quickly and vigorously; flourish: *New ideas burgeon when people are allowed to talk freely.*

burg·er (bûr′gər) *n. Informal.* A hamburger.

bur·glar (bûr′glər) *n.* A person who commits burglary: *The police caught the burglar as he was leaving the house.*

bur·glar·ize (bûr′glə rīz′) *tr.v.* **bur·glar·ized, bur·glar·iz·ing, bur·glar·iz·es.** To enter and steal from (a building or home, for example): *My home was burglarized and some valuable antiques were taken.*

bur·gla·ry (bûr′glə rē) *n., pl.* **bur·gla·ries.** [C; U] The crime of breaking into a building, home, or some other place with the intention of stealing: *He committed three burglaries before he was caught. Burglary is a serious crime.*

bur·i·al (bĕr′ē əl) *n.* The act of placing a dead body in a grave, a tomb, or the sea.

bur·lap (bûr′lăp′) *n.* [U] A coarse cloth used to make bags, sacks, and coverings.

bur·lesque (bər lĕsk′) *n.* An old-fashioned variety show with singing, dancing, and comedy. —*adj.* Relating to burlesque entertainment: *a burlesque theater.*

bur·ly (bûr′lē) *adj.* **bur·li·er, bur·li·est.** Heavy and strong; muscular: *burly football players.* See Synonyms at **muscular.** —**bur′li·ness** *n.* [U]

burn (bûrn) *v.* **burned** *or* **burnt** (bûrnt), **burn·ing, burns.** —*tr.* **1.** To cause (sthg.) to undergo combustion: *The body burns food for energy.* **2.** To set (sthg.) on fire: *We burned logs for heat.* **3.** To destroy (sthg.) with fire: *Our town burns garbage to generate electricity.* **4.** To damage or injure (sbdy./sthg.) by fire, heat, a corrosive chemical such as acid, or some other means: *I burned my fingers with a match.* **5.** To use (sthg.) as fuel: *This furnace burns oil.* **6.** To give (sbdy./sthg.) a feeling of heat: *Some highly seasoned food burns my mouth.* —*intr.* **1.** To undergo combustion or be consumed as fuel: *Wood and paper burn easily.* **2.** To be damaged, injured, or destroyed by or as if by fire: *The house burned to the ground.* **3.** To produce light and heat by or as if by fire: *The sun burned bright in the sky.* **4.** To feel or look hot: *burning with fever.* **5.** To be irritated or painful: *My eyes are burning from the smoke.* **6.** To be overtaken with strong emotion: *burn with anger; burning with a desire to win.* —*n.* **1.** An injury produced by fire, heat, a chemical, radiation, or electricity: *I got a blister from the burn.* **2.** A burned place or area: *a burn in the tablecloth.* ◆ **burn out.**

B

intr.v. **1.** To stop burning from lack of fuel: *A campfire burns out if you don't keep putting wood on it.* **2.** To wear out or fail, especially because of heat: *The fan motor burned out from overuse.* **3.** To become exhausted, especially as a result of long-term stress: *She burned out from years of overwork.* **burn up.** *intr.v.* To be consumed by fire: *The books burned up in the fire.* —*tr.v.* [sep.] *Informal.* To make (sbdy.) furious; anger: *That child's lying burns me up!* **get burned.** To get hurt, often emotionally; suffer a loss: *I tried to help her, but I got burned.* —**burn′a·ble** *adj.*

burn·er (bûr′nər) *n.* **1.** A furnace or other device in which sthg. is burned: *An oil burner heats the house.* **2.** The part of a stove, furnace, or lamp in which a flame is produced.

burn·ing (bûr′nĭng) *adj.* **1.** On fire; flaming; hot: *a burning candle.* **2.** Inflamed with strong emotion; heated: *a burning desire; a burning issue.*

bur·nish (bûr′nĭsh) *tr.v.* To make (sthg.) smooth and shiny by rubbing; polish: *burnish a brass plate.*

burn·out (bûrn′out′) *n.* **1.** [C] A failure of a device because of burning, heat, or friction. **2.** [U] Exhaustion of physical or emotional strength: *He was suffering from burnout.*

burnt (bûrnt) *v.* A past tense and a past participle of **burn.**

burp (bûrp) *n.* A belch. —*intr. & tr.v.* To belch or cause to belch: *He burped after eating the spicy meal. He burped the baby.*

burr (bûr) *n.* **1.** A rough edge or spot left on metal or other material after it has been cast, cut, or drilled. **2.** Variant of **burr.**

bur·ri·to (boo rē′tō) *n., pl.* **bur·ri·tos.** A flour tortilla wrapped around a filling of meat, beans, or cheese.

bur·ro (bûr′ō *or* boor′ō *or* bŭr′ō) *n., pl.* **bur·ros.** A small donkey, usually used for carrying loads.

HOMONYMS: burro, borough (town), burrow (animal hole).

bur·row (bûr′ō *or* bŭr′ō) *n.* A hole or tunnel dug in the ground by a small animal, such as a rabbit or mole. —*intr.v.* **1.** To make a tunnel, hole, or shelter by digging or tunneling: *rabbits burrowing in the fields.* **2.** To live or hide in a burrow: *Some animals burrow under the ground during the winter.* **3.** To search: *If you burrow in your desk, you will surely find a pencil.* —**bur′row·er** *n.*

bur·si·tis (bər sī′tĭs) *n.* [U] Inflammation of a joint, especially the shoulder, elbow, or knee.

burst (bûrst) *v.* —*intr.* **1.** To break open suddenly and violently: *The balloon burst.* **2.** To

arrive suddenly and in full force: *The police burst into the room.* **3.** To seem to be full to the point of breaking open; swell: *He's bursting with pride.* **4.** To express an emotion or say sthg. suddenly: *burst out laughing; burst into tears.* —*tr.* To cause (sthg.) to break open suddenly and violently: *The heat of the lamp burst the balloon.* —*n.* **1.** A sudden outbreak or outburst; an explosion: *a burst of laughter.* **2.** A sudden and intense increase; a rush: *a burst of speed.* ◆ **burst at the seams.** To be full to the point of almost breaking: *Her bag was so full it was bursting at the seams.* **burst in on.** To interrupt (sbdy./sthg.): *They insisted on bursting in on the meeting.* **burst into.** *tr.v.* [insep.] To enter (sthg.) forcefully: *She was so excited she burst into the room.* **burst out.** *intr.v.* **1.** To do sthg. suddenly: *burst out laughing.* **2.** To leave suddenly: *The dog burst out of the bushes.*

bur·y (bĕr′ē) *tr.v.* **bur·ied, bur·y·ing, bur·ies.** **1.** To place (sthg.) in the ground: *The dog buried a bone.* **2.** To place (a dead body) in a grave: *He was buried in the town cemetery.* **3.** To conceal (sthg.); hide: *She buried her face in the pillow.* See Synonyms at **hide¹.** **4.** To occupy (oneself) with deep concentration; absorb: *I buried myself in my homework.* ◆ **bury the hatchet.** To agree to stop fighting; forgive: *Our argument had continued too long, so we decided to bury the hatchet and forget it.*

HOMONYMS: bury, berry (fruit).

bus (bŭs) *n., pl.* **bus·es** or **bus·ses.** **1.** A long motor vehicle with rows of seats for carrying passengers. **2.** A circuit that connects the major components of a computer, allowing the transfer of electric signals from one component to another. —*v.* **bused, bus·ing, bus·es** or **bussed, bus·sing, bus·ses.** —*tr.* To carry or transport (sbdy./sthg.) in a bus: *The club bused us to the beach.* —*intr.* To travel in a bus: *Many people bus to work and school.*

bus·boy also **bus boy** (bŭs′boi′) *n.* A waiter's helper who sets and clears the table in a restaurant: *Ask the busboy for more water.*

bush (boosh) *n.* **1.** [C] A shrub, especially one having many separate branches. **2.** [U] A thick growth of shrubs. **3.** [U] Land covered with dense shrubby growth. **4.** [U] Land that is remote from human settlement: *a journey through the Australian bush.*

bushed (boosht) *adj. Informal.* Extremely tired: *I was bushed after the race.*

bush·el (boosh′əl) *n.* **1.** A unit of volume or capacity, used in dry measure in the United States and equal to 4 pecks (about 35.24

liters) or 2,150.42 cubic inches: *Many fruits and vegetables are measured by the bushel for market.* See table at **measurement. 2.** A container that holds this amount.

bush·y (bŏŏsh′ē) *adj.* **bush·i·er, bush·i· est. 1.** Overgrown with bushes: *bushy undergrowth.* **2.** Thick and shaggy: *a squirrel's bushy tail.* ◆ **bright-eyed and bushy-tailed.** Alert and ready: *The workers arrived bright-eyed and bushy-tailed after having a week off.* —**bush′i·ness** *n.* [U]

bus·i·ly (bĭz′ə lē) *adv.* In a busy manner: *We worked busily in the kitchen.*

busi·ness (bĭz′nĭs) *n.* **1.** [U] The occupation, trade, or work that provides a person with a means of living: *a group of salespersons in the automobile business.* **2.** [U] Commercial, industrial, and professional dealings considered as a group: *Computers are now being used throughout business and industry.* **3.** [C] A commercial establishment, such as a store or factory: *Will you go into the family business?* **4.** [U] The volume or amount of trade: *Business falls off when summer begins.* **5.** [U] One's rightful or proper concern: *What he does with his money is none of our business.* **6.** [U] An affair; a matter: *The manager dealt with the business at hand.* ◆ **get down to business.** To start talking about the most important topic: *Let's get down to business and discuss the parking problem in the city.* **have no business.** To have no right or authority: *You have no business telling me what to do.* **mean business.** To be serious: *I could see on his face that he meant business.* **mind (one's) own business.** To not interfere in the life of another person or in a private matter: *When she asked me about my salary, I told her to mind her own business.*

SYNONYMS: business, industry, commerce, trade, traffic. These nouns mean activity that produces merchandise. **Business** means general commercial, financial, and industrial activity: *This article discusses why American business should invest more in research.* **Industry** means the manufacture of goods, especially on a large scale: *The automobile industry has experimented with robots on assembly lines.* **Commerce** and **trade** mean the exchange and distribution of goods: *The new economic treaties among European countries will have a profound effect on international commerce. Those rules don't apply to trade between those countries.* **Traffic** often means the business of transporting goods or people, but it can also suggest an illegal way of making money: *harbor improvements made to attract shipping traffic; the drug traffic.*

---

busi·ness·like (bĭz′nĭs līk′) *adj.* Efficient; orderly: *a friendly but businesslike manner.*

busi·ness·man (bĭz′nĭs măn′) *n.* A man

engaged in business: *That hotel caters to the businessman.* —**busi′ness·wom′an** (bĭz′nĭs wŏŏm′ən) *n.*

busi·ness·per·son (bĭz′nĭs pûr′sən) *n.* A businessman or businesswoman.

bus·ing or **bus·sing** (bŭs′ĭng) *n.* [U] The transportation of children by bus to schools outside their neighborhoods, especially as a means of achieving racial integration: *Most voters supported the busing referendum.*

bus·ses (bŭs′ĭz) *n.* A plural of **bus.**

bust[1] (bŭst) *n.* **1.** A sculpture of a person's head, shoulders, and upper chest: *a marble bust of Lincoln.* **2.** A woman's breasts. **3.** The measurement around a woman's breasts and back.

bust[2] (bŭst) *v.* —*tr.* **1.** *Slang.* To smash or break (sthg.): *I busted the ice with a hammer.* **2.** To cause (sbdy.) to become bankrupt or short of money: *The long drought busted many farmers.* **3.** To hit (sbdy.); punch: *One boxer busted another in the mouth.* **4.** *Slang.* To place (sbdy.) under arrest: *The cops busted the thief.* —*intr. Slang.* To become broken or unusable; break: *The bicycle chain busted as I went up the hill.* —*n.* **1.** A failure; a flop: *That movie is a real bust.* **2.** A financial depression: *times of boom and bust.* **3.** *Informal.* An arrest: *a drug bust.* ◆ **go bust.** *Informal.* To fail financially: *The company went bust.*

bus·tle (bŭs′əl) *intr.v.* **bus·tled, bus·tling, bus·tles.** To move busily and energetically: *The mechanics bustled about the airplane.* —*n.* [U] Excited activity; commotion: *the hustle and bustle of city streets.*

bus·y (bĭz′ē) *adj.* **bus·i·er, bus·i·est. 1.** Occupied with work; active: *The doctor was busy with a patient.* **2.** In use, as a telephone line: *Her phone is busy.* —*tr.v.* **bus·ied, bus·y·ing, bus·ies.** To make (oneself) busy; occupy: *I busied myself with my work.* —**bus′y·ness** *n.* [U]

bus·y·bod·y (bĭz′ē bŏd′ē) *n., pl.* **bus·y· bod·ies.** A nosy or meddling person interested in the affairs of others: *After he retired, my neighbor turned into a busybody.*

bus·y·work (bĭz′ē wûrk′) *n.* [U] An activity that takes up time but does not necessarily produce anything meaningful: *the busywork of sorting old newspapers.*

but (bŭt *or* bət *when unstressed*) *conj.* **1.a.** On the contrary; yet: *We organized our work but we completed very little.* **b.** Nevertheless: *The plan may not work, but we must try.* **2.** Without the result that: *It never rains but it pours.* **3.** That: *There is no doubt but that we will win.* **4.** With the exception that; except that: *The captives would have resisted but they lacked courage.* —*prep.* Other than; except: *No one went but me.* —*adv.* **1.** Only; merely: *This is but one class in many.* **2.** No more than: *They had run but a few meters when the teacher called.* —SEE NOTE at **not.**

bu•tane (byōō'tān') *n.* [U] A gaseous hydrocarbon produced from petroleum and used as a fuel: *a butane lighter.*

butch•er (bŏoch'ər) *n.* **1.** A person who kills animals and prepares their meat for food. **2.** A person who sells meat: *We buy steak from the local butcher.* **3.** A person who kills sbdy./sthg. cruelly or without reason. —*tr.v.* **1.** To slaughter or prepare (animals) for market. **2.** To kill (sbdy./sthg.) brutally and without reason: *The murderer butchered 12 victims.* **3.** To make mistakes with (sthg.); bungle: *The actor butchered the part by forgetting many lines.*

butch•er•y (bŏoch'ə rē) *n.* [U] Cruel or savage killing; slaughter.

but•ler (bŭt'lər) *n.* The chief male servant of a household.

butt[1] (bŭt) *tr.v.* To hit or push (sbdy./sthg.) with the head or horns: *The goat butted the farmer.* —*n.* A push or blow with the head or horns. ◆ **butt in** or **into.** *tr.v.* [insep.] *Informal.* To interfere in (sthg.); intrude: *Don't butt into other people's business.* —*intr.v.* To interrupt or intrude: *Stop butting in on our conversation!*

butt[2] (bŭt) *n.* A person or thing that is an object of ridicule or scorn: *The clown was the butt of his own jokes.*

butt[3] (bŭt) *n.* **1.** The thicker end of sthg.: *the butt of a rifle.* **2.** An unused or unburned end of a cigarette. **3.** *Slang.* The buttocks or backside.

butte (byōot) *n.* A steep-sided hill with a flat top, often standing alone.

but•ter (bŭt'ər) *n.* **1.** [U] A soft, yellowish, fatty food made from milk or cream. **2.** [C; U] A similar substance, such as a fruit spread: *apple butter.* —*tr.v.* To put butter on (sthg.): *Shall I butter your toast?* ◆ **butter up.** *tr.v.* [sep.] To flatter (sbdy.): *He's always buttering up the boss.*

but•ter•fat (bŭt'ər făt') *n.* [U] The fat that is contained in milk and from which butter is made.

but•ter•fin•gers (bŭt'ər fĭng'gərz) *pl.n.* (*used with a singular verb*). A clumsy or awkward person who often drops things: *The catcher is a butterfingers.*

but•ter•fly (bŭt'ər-flī') *n.* **1.** [C] An insect with four broad, colorful wings, a narrow body, and slender antennae. **2.** [U] A swimming stroke in which both arms are drawn upward out of the water and forward while the legs kick up and down.

butterfly

but•ter•milk (bŭt'ər mĭlk') *n.* [U] The thick sour liquid that remains after butter has been made from cream.

but•ter•scotch (bŭt'ər skŏch') *n.* [U] A candy or a flavoring made from brown sugar and butter. —*adj.* Made or flavored with butterscotch: *butterscotch pudding.*

but•ter•y (bŭt'ə rē) *adj.* **1.** Resembling butter: *buttery soft leather.* **2.** Having or covered with butter: *hot buttery muffins.*

but•tock (bŭt'ək) *n.* **1.** Either of the rounded fleshy parts of the rump. **2. buttocks.** The rump of the human body.

but•ton (bŭt'n) *n.* **1.** A disk sewn to cloth, usually fitting through an opening to fasten edges together or to serve as decoration: *I have wooden buttons on my coat.* **2.** A part that is pushed to work a switch: *Push the button to call the elevator.* **3.** Something resembling a button, as a round flat pin with words or a design on it: *a candidate's campaign button.* —*v.* —*tr.* To fasten (sthg.) with a button or buttons: *button up a coat.* —*intr.* To be or be capable of being fastened with buttons: *a coat that buttons down the front.* ◆ **on the button.** Exactly; precisely: *We arrived at three o'clock on the button.*

but•ton•hole (bŭt'n hōl') *n.* An opening in a piece of clothing used to fasten a button. —*tr.v.* **but•ton•holed, but•ton•hol•ing, but•ton•holes.** To make (sbdy.) stop and listen, as if grabbing the buttonhole in a garment: *The campaign worker buttonholed me and asked for a contribution.*

but•tress (bŭt'rĭs) *n.* A structure, often of brick or stone, built against a wall for support. —*tr.v.* **1.** To brace or reinforce (sthg.) with a buttress: *buttress the roof of a tunnel with poles.* **2.** To help sustain (sthg.): *The lawyer buttressed her argument with evidence.*

bux•om (bŭk'səm) *adj.* (*used of women*). With large breasts: *a buxom young woman.* —**bux'om•ness** *n.* [U]

buy (bī) *v.* **bought** (bôt), **buy•ing, buys.** —*tr.* **1.** To get (sthg.) in exchange for money or sthg. of equal value: *go to the store to buy food.* **2.** To be capable of purchasing (sthg.): *Money can buy comfort but not happiness.* **3.** *Informal.* To bribe (sbdy.): *Money will not* *buy an honest judge.* —*intr.* To purchase goods: *buy on sale.* —*n. Informal.* Something cheaper than usual; a bargain: *The coats on sale are a good buy.* ◆ **buy into.** *tr.v.* [insep.] To accept (sthg.) as true or good: *I bought into his plan to expand the building.* **buy off.** *tr.v.* [sep.] To bribe (sbdy.): *It is illegal to try to buy off a government official.* **buy out.** *tr.v.* [sep.] To purchase the stock, rights, or interests of (sbdy./sthg.): *He will buy out the company. My partner wants me to buy him out.* **buy up.** *tr.v.* [sep.] To purchase all that is available of (sthg.): *The day after the elections, people bought up all the newspapers early in the morning.*

HOMONYMS: buy, by (near).

buy·er (bī′ər) *n.* **1.** A person who buys goods; a customer. **2.** A person who buys merchandise for a retail store.
buzz (bŭz) *v.* —*intr.* **1.** To make a low droning sound like that of a bee: *Flies buzzed near the cherries.* **2.** To talk in excited low tones: *The audience buzzed in anticipation of the show.* —*tr.* To signal (sbdy.), as with a buzzer: *The patient buzzed the nurse.* —*n.* A low droning sound, such as the one made by a bee: *the buzz of a fly.* ◆ **buzz off.** *intr.v. Informal.* To leave quickly; go away: *I told my younger brother to buzz off because I needed to do my homework.*
buz·zard (bŭz′ərd) *n.* A vulture.
buzz·er (bŭz′ər) *n.* An electrical device that makes a buzzing noise to give a signal or warning.
buzz·word (bŭz′wûrd′) *n.* A word or phrase used in a specific subject that is popular for a brief time: *political buzzwords.*
by (bī) *prep.* **1.** Close to; near: *the chair by the window.* **2.** Up to and beyond; past: *A car drove by us.* **3.** Through the agency or action of: *a building destroyed by fire; a novel by a young author.* **4.** With the help or use of; through: *Come to our house by the back road.* **5.** According to: *playing by the rules.* **6.** In the course of; during: *sleeping by night and working by day.* **7.** In the amount of: *The President receives letters by the thousands.* **8.** Not later than: *finish by noon.* **9.** In the matter of; concerning: *They are storekeepers by trade.* **10.** After; following: *One by one they left.* **11.** Combined in multiplication, division, or measurement with: *Multiply 4 by 6.* —*adv.* **1.** Close at hand; nearby: *We just stood by watching.* **2.** Aside; away: *putting some money by for retirement.* **3.** Up to and beyond; past: *The car raced by.* ◆ **by and by.** Before long; later: *The weather always changes by and by.* **by and large.** On the whole; mostly: *By and large people are hon-*

est. **by oneself. 1.** Alone: *I walked by myself in the woods.* **2.** Without help: *I repaired the car by myself.* **by the way.** Incidentally: *By the way, we really should be leaving soon.*

HOMONYMS: by, buy (purchase).

by— or **bye—** *pref.* A prefix that means: **1.** Near; at hand: *bystander.* **2.** Out of the way; aside: *bypass.* **3.** Secondary: *byproduct.* **4.** Past: *bygone.*
bye-bye (bī′bī′ *or* bī bī′) *interj.* An expression used to say good-bye.
by·gone (bī′gôn′ *or* bī′gŏn′) *adj.* Gone by; past: *bygone days.* —*n. (usually plural).* A past occurrence. ◆ **let bygones be bygones.** To forgive what happened in the past: *It's time to let bygones be bygones.*
by·law (bī′lô′) *n.* A law or rule made by a local government, corporation, club, or other organization governing its own affairs.
by·line (bī′līn′) *n.* A printed line at the head of a newspaper or magazine article giving the writer's name.
BYOB *abbr.* An abbreviation of Bring Your Own Bottle; used to indicate that a party is one that will not provide alcoholic drinks for guests.
by·pass also **by-pass** (bī′păs′) *n.* **1.** A road that passes around a city or other congested area: *They built a bypass around the city to reduce traffic going through the downtown area.* **2.** A path that leads around some component of a system, as in an electric circuit or a system of pipes. **3.** A surgical operation to make a new passage for blood around old vessels that are blocked: *a coronary bypass around a blood vessel of the heart.* —*tr.v.* To go around (sbdy./sthg.) by or as if by means of a bypass: *We can bypass all the salespeople if we see the manager directly.*
by·prod·uct or **by-prod·uct** (bī′prŏd′əkt) *n.* **1.** Something produced in the making of sthg. else: *Asphalt and paraffin are byproducts of refining crude oil into gasoline.* **2.** A secondary result; a side effect: *Widespread illness and disease are byproducts of unsanitary conditions.*
by·stand·er (bī′stăn′dər) *n.* A person who is present at an event but does not take part: *Bystanders crowded around the scene of the accident.*
byte (bīt) *n.* **1.** A sequence of adjacent bits used by a computer. **2.** The amount of computer memory needed to store one character of a specified size.

HOMONYMS: byte, bite (grip with the teeth).

by·way (bī′wā′) *n.* A road not often used; a side road.

Cc

c or **C** (sē) *n.*, *pl.* **c's** or **C's. 1.** The third letter of the English alphabet: *There are two c's in the word* clock. **2. C.** The third best or third highest grade: *I got a C on a test.* **3.** In music, the first tone in the scale of C major.

C¹ (sē) *n.* [U] A computer programming language widely used on microcomputers.

C² 1. The symbol for the element **carbon** (sense 1). **2.** Also **c.** The Roman numeral for 100.

C³ *abbr.* An abbreviation of: **1.** Celsius. **2.** Centigrade.

c. or **C.** *abbr.* An abbreviation of: **1.** Cent. **2.** Century. **3.** Chapter. **4.** Circa.

ca *abbr.* An abbreviation of circa.

Ca The symbol for the element **calcium.**

CA *abbr.* An abbreviation of California.

cab (kăb) *n.* **1.** A taxicab. **2.** A covered compartment for the operator or driver of a heavy vehicle or machine, such as a truck or crane.

cab•a•ret (kăb′ə rā′) *n.* A restaurant or nightclub providing live entertainment.

cab•bage (kăb′ĭj) *n.* [C; U] A plant that has a large round head of tightly overlapping green or reddish leaves eaten raw or cooked.

cab•by or **cab•bie** (kăb′ē) *n.*, *pl.* **cab•bies.** A driver of a taxicab.

cab•driv•er (kăb′drī′vər) *n.* A driver of a taxicab.

cab•in (kăb′ĭn) *n.* **1.** A small, simply built house; a cottage or hut. **2.** A room in a ship used as living quarters. **3.** An enclosed compartment in a boat that serves as a shelter or as living quarters. **4.** The enclosed compartment in an airplane or a spacecraft for passengers, crew, or cargo.

cabin cruiser *n.* A motorboat with a cabin.

cab•i•net (kăb′ə nĭt) *n.* **1.** A case or cupboard with shelves or drawers for storing or displaying objects: *a kitchen cabinet; a filing cabinet.* **2.** Often **Cabinet.** A group of people appointed by a head of state or prime minister to act as official advisers and to head the various ous departments of state.

ca•ble (kā′bəl) *n.* **1.** [C] A strong thick rope made of steel wires or fiber. **2.** [C] A group of insulated electrical wires that are bound together. **3.** [U] Cable television: *Do you have cable?* **4.** [C] A cablegram. —*v.* **ca•bled, ca•bling, ca•bles.** —*tr.* To transmit (a message) by telegraph: *The reporter*

cabled the story to his newspaper. —*intr.* To send a cablegram.

cable car *n.* A vehicle pulled by a cable that runs either overhead or beneath rails.

ca•ble•gram (kā′bəl grăm′) *n.* A telegraph message sent by underwater cable.

cable television *n.* [U] A television system that is delivered by cable to subscribers who pay for the service: *CNN is found on cable television.*

ca•boose (kə bōōs′) *n.* The last car of a freight train.

ca•ca•o (kə kä′ō *or* kə kā′ō) *n.* A tropical American evergreen tree that produces seeds used to make chocolate, cocoa, and cocoa butter.

cache (kăsh) *n.* **1.** A hiding place, as for a supply of food or weapons. **2.** A supply of sthg. hidden in such a place: *a cache of food.* —*tr.v.* **cached, cach•ing, cach•es.** To hide or store (sthg.) away in a cache: *squirrels caching nuts for winter.*

HOMONYMS: cache, cash (money).

---

ca•chet (kă shā′) *n.* A quality, as of distinction or individuality: *Doctors have a certain cachet in the United States.*

cack•le (kăk′əl) *intr.v.* **cack•led, cack•les. 1.** To make a sound like a hen: *The chicken cackled after laying an egg.* **2.** To laugh or speak in a shrill manner. —*n.* **1.** The act or sound of cackling. **2.** Shrill laughter or foolish chatter.

cac•tus (kăk′təs) *n.*, *pl.* **cac•ti** (kăk′tī) *or* **cac•tus•es.** Any of various plants that have thick, leafless, often spiny stems and that grow in hot dry places, chiefly in North and South America.

cad (kăd) *n.* An old-fashioned expression for a dishonorable man.

CAD (kăd) *abbr.* An abbreviation of computer-aided design or computer-assisted design.

cactus

ca•dav•er (kə dăv′ər) *n.* A dead body, especially one that is to be dissected and studied.

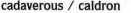

ca·dav·er·ous (kə dăv′ər əs) *adj.* Resembling a dead body; pale and very thin: *He had been sick so long that he looked cadaverous.*

cad·die also **cad·dy** (kăd′ē) *n., pl.* **cad·dies.** A person hired by a golfer to carry golf clubs. —*intr.v.* **cad·died, cad·dy·ing, cad·dies.** To serve as a caddie: *As a boy, he caddied at the local golf course.*

ca·dence (kād′ns) *n.* **1.** Measured rhythmic flow, as of poetry or music: *poetry written in short quick cadences.* **2.** The general rise and fall of the voice in speaking, as at the end of a question.

ca·det (kə dĕt′) *n.* A student at a military or naval academy who is training to be an officer.

cad·mi·um (kăd′mē əm) *n.* [U] *Symbol* **Cd** A soft bluish white element resembling tin that occurs only in combination with other elements and is used in plating metals to prevent corrosion, in making alloys, and in batteries. Atomic number 48. See table at **element.**

cae·sar·e·an (sĭ zâr′ē ən) *adj. & n.* Variant of **cesarean.**

ca·fé also **ca·fe** (kă fā′) *n.* A coffeehouse, restaurant, or bar.

caf·e·te·ri·a (kăf′ĭ tîr′ē ə) *n.* A restaurant in which the customers are served at a counter and carry their meals on trays to tables.

caf·feine (kă fēn′ *or* kăf′ēn′) *n.* [U] A bitter white substance that acts as a stimulant and is found in coffee, tea, and cola beverages.

cage (kāj) *n.* A structure made of wire or metal bars for holding birds or other animals. —*tr.v.* **caged, cag·ing, cag·es.** To put (sbdy./sthg.) in a cage: *cage a wild animal.*

ca·gey (kā′jē) *adj.* **ca·gi·er, ca·gi·est.** *Informal.* Shrewd; crafty: *a cagey lawyer with much experience.* —**cag′i·ly** *adv.* —**cag′i·ness** *n.* [U]

ca·hoots (kə hoōts′) *pl.n. Informal.* ♦ **in cahoots.** In a secret partnership: *a surprise party that she planned for him in cahoots with friends.*

CAI *abbr.* An abbreviation of computer-aided instruction.

ca·jole (kə jōl′) *tr.v.* **ca·joled, ca·jol·ing, ca·joles.** To persuade (sbdy.) by flattery or insincere talk; coax: *Immigrants were cajoled into going west by promises of great wealth.*

Ca·jun (kā′jən) *n.* A member of a group of people living in Louisiana and descended from French colonists. —*adj.* Relating to the Cajuns: *Cajun food is usually spicy.*

cake (kāk) *n.* **1.** [C; U] A sweet baked food made of flour, liquid, eggs, and other ingredients, often round or rectangular in shape and often with icing on the top and sides: *chocolate cake; a birthday cake.* **2.** [C] A flat rounded mass of dough or batter that is baked or fried: *a wheat cake.* **3.** [C] A flat rounded mass of chopped food that is baked or fried: *a fish* cake. **4.** [C] A shaped or molded piece, as of soap. —*v.* **caked, cak·ing, cakes.** —*tr.* To cover or fill (sthg.) with a thick layer; encrust: *My shoes are caked with mud.* —*intr.* To form into a compact mass: *The melted cheese caked on the plate as it cooled.* ♦ **be a piece of cake.** *Informal.* To be very easy: *The test was a piece of cake.* **have (one's) cake and eat it too.** *Informal.* To have all of the advantages of sthg. without any of the disadvantages: *He wants the security of the job without the responsibility, but he can't have his cake and eat it too.*

cal or **Cal** *abbr.* An abbreviation of calorie.

Cal. *abbr.* An abbreviation of California.

ca·lam·i·ty (kə lăm′ĭ tē) *n., pl.* **ca·lam·i·ties. 1.** An event that causes great distress and suffering; a disaster: *The long summer drought was a calamity for farmers.* **2.** Distress or misfortune: *the calamity of unemployment.* —**ca·lam′i·tous** *adj.* —**ca·lam′i·tous·ly** *adv.*

cal·ci·um (kăl′sē əm) *n.* [U] *Symbol* **Ca** A soft, silvery white element found in limestone, chalk, milk, and bone. It is essential for the normal growth and development of plants and animals. Calcium is used in alloys, plaster, and cement. Atomic number 20. See table at **element.**

cal·cu·late (kăl′kyə lāt′) *v.* **cal·cu·lat·ed, cal·cu·lat·ing, cal·cu·lates.** —*tr.* **1.** To find or determine (an answer or a result) by using mathematics: *calculate the total cost of the trip.* **2.** To make an estimate of (sthg.); figure out: *calculate the possibilities of succeeding.* **3.** To make (sthg.) for a specific purpose; design: *His remarks were calculated to please the stockholders.* —*intr.* To perform a mathematical process, such as addition.

cal·cu·lat·ed (kăl′kyə lā′tĭd) *adj.* **1.** Carefully estimated in advance: *Making money in the stock market involves taking a calculated risk.* **2.** Made or planned to accomplish a specific purpose: *insincere, calculated modesty.*

cal·cu·lat·ing (kăl′kyə lā′tĭng) *adj.* **1.** Used in performing calculation: *a calculating machine.* **2.** Selfish; scheming: *a cold and calculating criminal.* **3.** Cleverly planned; shrewd: *the calculating defense of an experienced attorney.*

cal·cu·la·tion (kăl′kyə lā′shən) *n.* **1.** [C; U] The act or result of calculating: *All the calculations in my math homework turned out to be correct.* **2.** [U] Careful thinking or planning: *They won the game by clever calculation.*

cal·cu·la·tor (kăl′kyə lā′tər) *n.* **1.** A machine that automatically performs mathematical computations. **2.** A person who calculates.

cal·cu·lus (kăl′kyə ləs) *n.* [U] The branch of advanced mathematics that extends the use of algebra.

cal·dron also **caul·dron** (kôl′drən) *n.* A large kettle for boiling.

cal•en•dar (kăl'ən dər) *n.* **1.** A chart showing the months, weeks, and days of the year. **2.** A list of dates, as of events or things to be done, arranged in order: *Doctors keep appointment calendars.*

calf¹ (kăf) *n., pl.* **calves** (kăvz). **1.** A young cow or bull. **2.** The young of certain other mammals, such as the elephant or whale.

calf² (kăf) *n., pl.* **calves** (kăvz). The muscular back part of the human leg between the knee and ankle.

cal•i•ber (kăl'ə bər) *n.* **1.** [C] **a.** The diameter of the inside of a tube. **b.** The inside diameter of a gun. **2.** [U] The diameter of a bullet: *a .45-caliber bullet.* **3.** [U] Degree of worth; quality: *A judge should be a citizen of high caliber.*

cal•i•brate (kăl'ə brāt') *tr.v.* **cal•i•brat•ed, cal•i•brat•ing, cal•i•brates.** To check, adjust, or standardize (a measuring instrument), usually by comparing with an accepted model: *calibrate an oven thermometer.* —**cal'i•bra'tion** *n.* [U]

cal•i•co (kăl'ĭ kō') *n., pl.* **cal•i•cos. 1.** [C; U] A cotton cloth with a brightly colored or closely printed pattern. **2.** [C] A cat with a coat that has tan, white, and black patches.

cal•i•per also **cal•li•per** (kăl'ə pər') *n. (usually plural).* An instrument with two hinged legs that can be adjusted to measure diameter, thickness, or the distance between two points, as on a map or scale.

cal•is•then•ics (kăl'ĭs thĕn'ĭks) *pl.n.* Exercises done to develop muscular strength and general health. —**cal'is•then'ic** *adj.*

calk (kôk) *v.* Variant of **caulk.**

call (kôl) *v.* —*tr.* **1.** To say (sthg.) in a loud voice: *call the name of someone across the room.* **2.** To ask or send for (sbdy.) to come: *call the fire department.* **3.** To bring (sthg.) into being, (effect, or action, as by giving an order: *call a meeting; call an end to a project.* **4.a.** To give a name to (sbdy./sthg.): *What did they call the baby?* **b.** To describe (sbdy./sthg.) as: *Horse racing is called "the sport of kings."* **5.** To telephone (sbdy.): *call a friend to talk.* **6.** To stop or interrupt (a sports event): *call a game on account of rain.* **7.** To correctly tell the future of (sthg.): *The reporter called the outcome of the election.* **8.** To demand payment of (money owed): *The bank called the loan.* —*intr.* **1.** To attract attention by shouting: *call until help comes.* **2.** To make a characteristic sound: *birds calling to each other.* **3.** To telephone sbdy.: *You've already called several times.* **4.** To make a short visit: *We called to see her in the hospital.* —*n.* **1.** A shout or loud cry: *A frightened call came from the woods.* **2.a.** The typical cry of an animal. **b.** An instrument or sound made to imitate

such a cry, used to attract the animal: *a duck call used by hunters.* **3.** A word or sound used as a signal: *a bugle call to meals.* **4.** The act or an instance of communicating or trying to communicate by telephone: *an afternoon spent making calls to friends.* **5.** A short visit: *a friendly call on new neighbors.* **6.a.** A strong urge or feeling: *She felt she had a call to become a teacher.* **b.** Attraction or appeal: *the call of camping in the wild.* **7.** Need, reason, or cause: *There was no call to be rude.* **8.** In sports, a decision made by an official. ◆ **call back.** *tr.v.* [sep.] **1.** To telephone (sbdy.) in return: *May I call you back?* **2.** To ask or order (sbdy.) to return: *The company called us back to work.* **call for.** *tr.v.* [insep.] **1.** To go and get (sbdy./sthg.): *The taxi will call for you at eight.* **2.** To require or demand (sbdy./sthg.): *The recipe calls for flour.* **call in.** *tr.v.* [sep.] To ask (sbdy.) to come and give help or advice: *call in a specialist.* —*intr.v.* **1.** To report by phone: *I called in to say I'd be late.* **2.** To make a telephone call to a radio or television station to give an opinion or ask a question: *Viewers often call in while her show is on the air.* **call into question.** To raise doubt about (sthg.): *The whole story is called into question by the lack of evidence.* **call it a day.** *Informal.* To stop what one has been doing for the rest of the day: *Let's call it a day and finish the job tomorrow.* **call off.** *tr.v.* [sep.] **1.** To cancel (sthg.): *call off a game.* **2.** To make (sbdy./sthg.) come back from an attack: *Call off your dogs!* **call on.** *tr.v.* [insep.] **1.** To ask or order (sbdy.) to speak: *The teacher called on the new student first.* **2.** To ask (sbdy.) to do sthg.: *The President called on each of us to do something for our country.* **call out.** *intr.v.* To say sthg. or yell in a loud voice: *Did you hear someone call out?* —*tr.v.* [sep.] **1.** To ask or summon (sbdy.) for a purpose: *He was suddenly called out on business.* **2.** To cause (a group) to come together: *The governor called out the National Guard after the earthquake struck.* **call out for. 1.** To say or yell sthg. in a loud voice: *The firefighters called out for more people to help them.* **2.** To need (sthg. in addition) to be better: *This sauce calls out for more garlic.* **call to account.** To demand an explanation from (sbdy.): *The student was called to account for being late.* **call to mind.** To cause sbdy. to remember: *The movie calls to mind other adventure stories.* **call up.** *intr.v.* To telephone: *She called up at noon.* —*tr.v.* [sep.] To order (sbdy.) into military service. **on call.** Available when called to come, as to work: *I'm on call this weekend.*

call•er (kô'lər) *n.* **1.** A person who makes a short visit or a telephone call: *Several callers came by to see the new baby.* **2.** A person who calls out numbers or directions, as in bingo or square dancing.

cal·lig·ra·phy (kə lĭg′rə fē) *n.* [U] The art of fine handwriting. —**cal·lig′ra·pher** *n.*

call·ing (kô′lĭng) *n.* **1.** An inner urge or strong impulse; a call: *Some people feel a calling to travel.* **2.** An occupation, profession, or career: *Writing poetry is her calling.*

cal·li·per (kăl′ə pər) *n.* Variant of **caliper.**

cal·lous (kăl′əs) *adj.* Unfeeling; unkind: *The callous man walked right by the crying puppy.* —**cal′lous·ly** *adv.* —**cal′lous·ness** *n.* [U]

HOMONYMS: callous, callus (hard skin).

---

cal·lus (kăl′əs) *n.* An area of the skin that has become hardened and thick, usually because of prolonged pressure or rubbing.

cal·lused (kăl′əst) *adj.* Having calluses from physical labor: *the callused hands of a farmer or logger.*

calm (käm) *adj.* **1.** Peacefully quiet; not excited: *The children remained calm throughout the storm.* **2.** Nearly motionless; still: *I took a walk along the calm lake.* —*n.* **1.** [U] A condition of being peaceful; tranquility: *Her calm was broken by the shouts in the street.* **2.** [C] Lack of motion; stillness: *We felt a calm in the air just before the storm hit.* —*tr. & intr.v.* To make or become calm or quiet: *calm a crying baby; calm down after an argument.* —**calm′ly** *adv.* —**calm′ness** *n.* [U]

SYNONYMS: calm, peaceful, tranquil, placid, serene. These adjectives all describe the absence of any disturbance. **Calm** and **peaceful** mean emotionally untroubled: *The other children tried to annoy her but the girl remained calm. Which decade was the most peaceful in American history?* **Tranquil** describes a more lasting calm: *The writer wanted a tranquil life in the country.* **Placid** means calm in a pleasant, lazy way: *We spent an idle, placid weekend at the shore.* **Serene** means spiritually calm: *It took talent to capture her serene expression in her portrait.* **ANTONYMS: turbulent, upset.**

---

cal·o·rie (kăl′ə rē) *n.* **1.** A unit of heat equal to the amount of heat needed to raise the temperature of one gram of water one degree Celsius. **2.** A unit for measuring the amount of heat energy supplied by food: *Chocolate cake has a lot of calories.* —**ca·lor′ic** (kə-lôr′ĭk *or* kə lŏr′ĭk) *adj.*

calve (kăv) *intr.v.* **calved, calv·ing, calves.** To give birth to a calf: *Cows usually calve in springtime.*

calves¹ (kăvz) *n.* Plural of **calf¹.**

calves² (kăvz) *n.* Plural of **calf².**

cam (kăm) *n.* An oddly shaped wheel or a projection on a wheel that is part of an engine.

CAM (kăm) *abbr.* An abbreviation of computer-aided manufacturing.

ca·ma·ra·der·ie (kä′mə rä′də rē *or* kăm′-ə răd′ə rē) *n.* [U] Goodwill and warm feeling between or among friends.

cam·cord·er (kăm′-kôr′dər) *n.* A videotape recorder combined with a TV camera: *The portable camcorder allows on-the-scene news coverage.*

camcorder

came (kām) *v.* Past tense of **come.**

cam·el (kăm′əl) *n.* A long-necked humped mammal of northern Africa and western Asia that can go without water for long periods of time.

ca·mel·lia (kə mēl′yə) *n.* A shrub or tree with glossy leaves and flowers that resemble roses.

Cam·em·bert (kăm′əm bâr′) *n.* [U] A creamy rich cheese that softens on the inside as it matures.

cam·e·o (kăm′ē ō′) *n., pl.* **cam·e·os. 1.** A gem, shell, or medallion that usually has a carved design on a background of a different color. **2.** A brief movie role played by a popular star.

cam·er·a (kăm′ər ə *or* kăm′rə) *n.* A device for taking photographs, film, or videotape consisting of a lightproof box with a lens through which light is focused to record an image on light-sensitive film.

cam·er·a·man (kăm′ər ə măn′ *or* kăm′-rə măn′) *n.* A man who operates a movie or television camera. —**cam′er·a·wom′an** *n.*

cam·i·sole (kăm′ĭ sōl′) *n.* A short sleeveless undergarment worn by a woman or girl.

cam·o·mile (kăm′ə mīl′ *or* kăm′ə mēl′) *n.* Variant of **chamomile.**

cam·ou·flage (kăm′ə fläzh′ *or* kăm′ə-fläj′) *n.* [U] **1.** A method of hiding military troops or equipment by making them appear to be part of the natural surroundings. **2.** Protective coloring or a disguise that hides: *An alligator's camouflage makes it look like a log floating in the water.* **3.** Cloth or other material used for camouflage. —*tr.v.* **cam·ou·flaged, cam·ou·flag·ing, cam·ou·flag·es.** To conceal or hide (sbdy./sthg.) by camouflage.

camp (kămp) *n.* **1.** A place where a group of people, such as vacationers or soldiers, live temporarily in tents, cabins, or outside. **2.** A cabin or shelter or group of such buildings: *Their family has a camp on a lake.* **3.** A place in the country that offers activities for fun or instruction, as for children on vacation: *When I was a child, I went to summer camp every year.* —*intr.v.* **1.** To make or set up a camp: *We camped next to the river.* **2.** To live in or as if in a camp: *The protesters camped on the Capitol steps until police forced them to leave.*

cam•paign (kăm pān′) *n.* **1.** Organized activity to reach a political, social, or commercial goal: *an advertising campaign; the presidential campaign.* **2.** A series of military operations: *The army's campaign secured the area.* —*intr.v.* To engage in a campaign: *The candidates campaigned on television.*

camp•er (kăm′pər) *n.* **1.** A person who camps outdoors. **2.** A boy or girl who attends a summer camp. **3.** A motor vehicle with a space equipped as a living area for camping on long trips.

camp•fire (kămp′fīr′) *n.* An outdoor fire in a camp, used for warmth or cooking.

camp•ground (kămp′ground′) *n.* An area used for setting up a camp or holding a camp meeting.

camp•site (kămp′sīt′) *n.* An area used for camping.

cam•pus (kăm′pəs) *n.* The grounds of a school, college, or university.

cam•shaft (kăm′shăft′) *n.* A shaft fitted with one or more cams, as in a gasoline engine.

can¹ (kăn; kən *when unstressed*) *aux.v.* Past tense **could** (kŏŏd). **1.** To know how to: *My cousin can speak Arabic.* **2.** To be able to: *I can skate backward.* **3.** To possess the right or power to: *The President can veto bills passed by Congress.* **4.** To have permission to; be allowed to: *You can borrow my pen if you like.*

can² (kăn) *n.* **1.a.** An airtight metal container in which food and beverages are preserved: *Recycle the empty cola cans.* **b.** The contents of such a container: *The baby ate a whole can of peaches.* **2.** A metal container: *a garbage can.* —*tr.v.* **canned, can•ning, cans. 1.** To preserve (food) in a sealed container: *They spent the morning canning beans.* **2.** *Slang.* To fire (sbdy.) from a job: *He was canned last week.*

Can. *abbr.* An abbreviation of: **1.** Canada. **2.** Canadian.

Can•a•da Day (kăn′ə də) *n.* July 1, observed in Canada in commemoration of the formation of the Dominion in 1867.

Canada goose or **Ca•na•di•an goose** (kə-nā′dē ən) *n.* A North American wild goose with gray, black, and white feathers and a white patch on its face.

ca•nal (kə năl′) *n.* **1.** A waterway that is created for irrigation, drainage, or navigation: *the Panama Canal.* **2.** A tube or duct in the body of an animal or plant, as for the passage of liquid, air, food, or other matter: *the ear canal.*

ca•nar•y (kə nâr′ē) *n., pl.* **ca•nar•ies. 1.** [C] A small yellow bird that is popular as a pet. **2.** [U] A yellow color. —*adj.* Yellow.

can•cel (kăn′səl) *v.* —*tr.* **1.** To call off (a planned event): *I canceled an appointment.* **2.** To cross (sthg.) out with lines or other

markings: *cancel items on a shopping list.* **3.** To mark or perforate (a postage stamp, for example) to show that it may not be used again. ◆ **cancel out.** *tr.v.* [sep.] To equal (sthg.) with an opposite effect so that a balance is kept; offset: *Two opposing votes cancel each other out.* —*intr.v.* To counterbalance each other: *Spending and saving often cancel out.*

can•cel•la•tion (kăn′sə lā′shən) *n.* [C; U] **1.** The act or process of canceling: *The flight is full, but maybe there will be a cancellation and I will get a seat.* **2.** A mark made, as on a stamp or check, to show that it has been canceled.

can•cer (kăn′sər) *n.* **1.** [C; U] Any of various diseases in which cells of the body grow in an abnormal way. **2.** [C] A mass of cells that grows and spreads in this manner; a malignant tumor. **3.** [C] A destructive, spreading evil: *Poverty is a social cancer.* —**can′cer•ous** (kăn′sər əs) *adj.*

Can•cer (kăn′sər) *n.* **1.** [U] The fourth sign of the zodiac in astrology. **2.** [C] A person born under this sign, between June 21 and July 22.

can•de•la•bra (kăn′dl ä′brə *or* kăn′dl-äb′rə) *n.* A large decorative candlestick that can hold many candles.

can•did (kăn′dĭd) *adj.* **1.** Direct and open; straightforward: *a candid opinion.* **2.** Not posed or rehearsed: *a candid photograph.* —**can′did•ly** *adv.* —**can′did•ness** *n.* [U]

can•di•da•cy (kăn′dĭ də sē) *n., pl.* **can•di•da•cies.** The fact or condition of being a candidate: *a presidential candidacy.*

can•di•date (kăn′dĭ dāt *or* kăn′dĭ dĭt) *n.* A person who seeks or is nominated for an office, a prize, or an honor.

can•died (kăn′dēd) *adj.* Cooked in or coated with sugar: *candied sweet potatoes; candied fruit.*

can•dle (kăn′dl) *n.* A solid stick of wax or other fatty substance with a wick inside that is lit and burned to provide light.

can•dle•light (kăn′dl līt′) *n.* [U] The light given off by a candle: *dine by candlelight.*

can•dle•stick (kăn′dl stĭk′) *n.* A holder with a cup or shallow base where a candle is placed.

can•dor (kăn′dər) *n.* [U] The quality of saying freely what one thinks; openness: *She criticized the plan with candor.*

can•dy (kăn′dē) *n., pl.* **can•dies. 1.** [C; U] A sweet food made with sugar and often combined with fruit or nuts. **2.** [C] A single piece of this food: *a box of chocolate candies.* —*tr.v.* **can•died, can•dy•ing, can•dies.** To cook, preserve, or coat (sthg.) with sugar or syrup: *candy apples.*

cane (kān) *n.* **1.** [C] A stick used as an aid in walking. **2.a.** [C] A thin hollow plant stem that is easily bent, such as bamboo or sugar cane. **b.** [U] Strips of such stems woven together to make chair seats or other objects. —*tr.v.* **caned, can·ing, canes. 1.** To make or repair (furniture, for example) with cane. **2.** To beat (sbdy.) with a cane as punishment.

ca·nine (kā′nīn) *adj.* Relating to dogs or related mammals. —*n.* **1.** An animal belonging to the canine family, such as a dog or wolf. **2.** One of the four pointed teeth in mammals.

can·is·ter (kăn′ĭ stər) *n.* A container for holding coffee, tea, flour, spices, and other dry foods or a gas.

can·ker (kăng′kər) *n.* A sore similar to an ulcer on the lips or in the mouth. —**can′ker·ous** *adj.*

canker sore *n.* A canker.

can·na·bis (kăn′ə bĭs) *n.* [U] The hemp plant; marijuana.

canned (kănd) *adj.* **1.** Preserved and sealed in an airtight can or jar: *canned vegetables.* **2.** *Informal.* Recorded or taped: *canned laughter on a TV comedy.*

can·ner·y (kăn′ə rē) *n., pl.* **can·ner·ies.** A factory where fish, fruit, vegetables, or other foods are canned.

can·ni·bal (kăn′ə bəl) *n.* **1.** A person who eats the flesh of other humans. **2.** An animal that feeds on others of its own kind. —**can′·ni·bal·ism** *n.* [U] —**can′ni·bal·is′tic** *adj.*

can·ni·bal·ize (kăn′ə bə līz′) *tr.v.* **can·ni·bal·ized, can·ni·bal·iz·ing, can·ni·bal·iz·es.** To remove useful parts from (a machine or equipment) to use in the repair of other equipment: *cannibalize an old truck for its motor.*

can·non (kăn′ən) *n., pl.* **cannon** or **can·nons.** A large gun that is mounted on wheels or on a fixed base and fires heavy ammunition.

can·non·ball (kăn′ən bôl′) *n.* An iron or steel ball fired from a cannon.

can·not (kăn′ŏt *or* kə nŏt′ *or* kă nŏt′) *aux. v.* A negative form of **can¹.**

can·ny (kăn′ē) *adj.* **can·ni·er, can·ni·est.** Careful and shrewd in one's actions and dealings; cautious: *a wise and canny judge of character.* —**can′ni·ly** *adv.* —**can′ni·ness** *n.* [U]

ca·noe (kə nōō′) *n.* A light narrow boat that has pointed ends and is propelled by paddles. —*intr.v.* **ca·noed, ca·noe·ing, ca·noes.** To paddle or travel in a canoe.

can·on (kăn′ən) *n.* **1.** A law or code of laws enacted by a church. **2.** A principle or standard: *He seems totally unaware of the canons of good behavior.*

canoe

can opener *n.* A device used for opening cans of food.

can·o·py (kăn′ə pē) *n., pl.* **can·o·pies. 1.** A covering, usually of cloth, hung above a bed or throne or supported by poles: *The king sat under a canopy.* **2.** A similar covering: *a canopy of leafy branches.* **3.** The transparent movable enclosure over a military aircraft's cockpit. —*tr.v.* **can·o·pied, can·o·py·ing, can·o·pies.** To cover (sthg.) with a canopy.

can't (kănt) *v.* Contraction of *can not.*

can·ta·loupe (kăn′tl ōp′) *n.* [C; U] A type of melon with a ribbed rough skin and sweet orange flesh.

can·tan·ker·ous (kăn tăng′kər əs) *adj.* Quarrelsome and ill-tempered; disagreeable: *a cantankerous professor who is difficult to study with.* —**can·tan′ker·ous·ly** *adv.* —**can·tan′ker·ous·ness** *n.* [U]

can·ta·ta (kən tä′tə) *n.* A musical composition centered around a story or poem that is sung.

can·teen (kăn tēn′) *n.* **1.** A container for carrying water or other liquid to drink. **2.** A place to get food or drinks in a school, factory, military base, or camp.

can·ter (kăn′tər) *n.* A slow easy gallop. —*intr. & tr.v.* To move or cause to move at a canter: *The horse and rider cantered down the road. She cantered her horse across the field.*

can·tor (kăn′tər) *n.* The official who leads the musical part of a Jewish religious service.

can·vas (kăn′vəs) *n.* **1.** [U] A heavy coarse cloth used for making tents and sails. **2.** [C] **a.** A piece of canvas used for painting. **b.** A painting on canvas: *That artist has several canvases hanging in this museum.*

can·vass (kăn′vəs) *v.* —*tr.* To visit (a person or region) asking for votes, opinions, sales, or contributions: *canvass voters before the election.* —*intr.* To go about a region asking for votes, sales, opinions, or contributions: *The candidate canvassed up and down the county for votes.* —*n.* The act of canvassing. —**can′vass·er** *n.*

can·yon (kăn′yən) *n.* A deep narrow valley with steep cliff walls, cut into the earth by running water.

cap (kăp) *n.* **1.** A usually soft, close-fitting head covering, either with no brim or with a visor: *a baseball cap.* **2.** A protective cover or seal: *a bottle cap; a cap on a tooth.* **3.a.** The top or highest part: *the polar cap.* **b.** A limit or restraint: *a cap on government spending.* **4.** A small explosive charge enclosed in paper for use in a toy gun. —*tr.v.* **capped, cap•ping, caps. 1.** To cover, protect, or seal (sthg.) with a cap: *cap a bottle.* **2.** To outdo (sthg.); excel: *Each joke capped the one before.*

cap. *abbr.* An abbreviation of: **1.** Capacity. **2.** Capital. **3.** Capital letter.

ca•pa•bil•i•ty (kā′pə bĭl′ĭ tē) *n., pl.* **ca•pa•bil•i•ties. 1.** [U] The quality of being able; ability: *prove one's capability for the job.* **2.** [C] *(usually plural).* Potential ability: *live up to one's capabilities.* **3.** [C; U] The capacity to be used or developed for a specific purpose: *To become more energy-efficient we must make full use of our technological capability.*

ca•pa•ble (kā′pə bəl) *adj.* **1.** Having ability; able; competent: *a capable teacher.* **2.** [*of*] Having the tendency or disposition: *She's just not capable of saying such a thing.* —**ca′•pa•bly** *adv.*

ca•pac•i•tor (kə păs′ĭ tər) *n.* A device used in an electric circuit to store a charge temporarily.

ca•pac•i•ty (kə păs′ĭ tē) *n., pl.* **ca•pac•i•ties. 1.** [C] The ability to hold, receive, or contain: *a bottle with a capacity of three quarts; a theater with a small seating capacity.* **2.** [U] The maximum amount that can be contained: *a trunk filled to capacity.* **3.** [U] The maximum amount that can be produced: *a machine operating at full capacity.* **4.** [C; U] Mental ability: *a person's capacity for learning.* **5.** [C] The position in which a person functions; a role: *in your capacity as sales manager.*

cape[1] (kāp) *n.* A long sleeveless outer garment fastened at the throat and worn hanging loose over the shoulders.

cape[2] (kāp) *n.* A point of land projecting into a body of water: *Cape Cod.*

ca•per[1] (kā′pər) *n.* **1.** A playful leap or hop: *the capers of a monkey.* **2.** A prank or trick: *childish capers.* **3.** *Slang.* A criminal plot or act, especially one involving theft: *a bank caper.* —*intr.v.* To jump about playfully: *The lambs capered about the meadow.*

ca•per[2] (kā′pər) *n.* A small green pickled flower bud of a Mediterranean shrub, used to season food.

cap•il•lar•y (kăp′ə lĕr′ē) *n., pl.* **cap•il•lar•ies.** One of the tiny blood vessels that connect the smallest arteries to the smallest veins. —*adj.* **1.** Relating to the capillaries in the body. **2.** Having a very small inside diameter.

cap•i•tal (kăp′ĭ tl) *n.* **1.** [C] A city that is the seat of a state or national government: *Every state has a capital.* **2.** [U] Wealth in the form of money or property that has accumulated in a business and is often used to create more wealth. **3.** [C] A capital letter. —*adj.* **1.**

Relating to a seat of government: *a capital city.* **2.** Involving wealth and its use in investment: *capital improvements in the factory.* **3.** Punishable by or involving death: *Murder is often a capital offense.* **4.** First and foremost; principal: *a decision of capital importance.* **5.** Excellent; first-rate: *a capital idea.*

HOMONYMS: capital, capitol (building).

capital gain *n.* *(usually plural).* The profit made by selling an investment, such as a stock or a piece of property.

cap•i•tal•ism (kăp′ĭ tl ĭz′əm) *n.* [U] An economic system in which the means of production and distribution are privately owned by individuals or groups and competition for business establishes the price of goods and services.

cap•i•tal•ist (kăp′ĭ tl ĭst) *n.* **1.** A person who invests capital in business, especially a large investor in an important business. **2.** A person who supports capitalism. —*adj.* Relating to capitalism or capitalists: *a capitalist country.* —**cap′i•tal•is′tic** *adj.*

cap•i•tal•ize (kăp′ĭ tl īz′) *v.* **cap•i•tal•ized, cap•i•tal•iz•ing, cap•i•tal•iz•es.** —*tr.* **1.** To write (sthg.) with a capital letter or letters: *capitalize the title of a report.* **2.** To supply (sbdy./sthg.) with capital or funds. ◆ **capitalize on.** *tr.v.* [insep.] To turn (sthg.) to advantage; profit by: *capitalize on an opponent's errors and win.* —**cap′i•tal•i•za′tion** (kăp′ĭ tl ĭ zā′shən) *n.* [U]

capital letter *n.* A letter, such as A or B, written or printed in a size larger than and often in a form differing from its corresponding lowercase letter. A person's name usually begins with a capital letter.

capital punishment *n.* [U] The death penalty for certain crimes, such as murder.

cap•i•tol (kăp′ĭ tl) *n.* **1. Capitol.** The building in Washington, D.C., where the Congress of the United States meets. **2.** A building in which a state legislature assembles.

HOMONYMS: capitol, capital (city).

ca•pit•u•late (kə pĭch′ə lāt′) *intr.v.* **ca•pit•u•lat•ed, ca•pit•u•lat•ing, ca•pit•u•lates.** To surrender under stated conditions: *The soldiers capitulated to the enemy after a long battle.*

ca•pit•u•la•tion (kə pĭch′ə lā′shən) *n.* **1.** [U] The act of capitulating: *capitulation in the face of defeat.* **2.** [C] A statement of the main points of a topic; an outline.

cap•let (kăp′lĭt) *n.* A tablet of medicine usually coated to make it easy to swallow.

cap•puc•ci•no (kăp′ə chē′nō) *n., pl.*

ă–cat; ā–pay; âr–care; ä–father; ĕ–get; ē–be; ĭ–sit; ī–nice; îr–here; ŏ–got; ō–go; ô–saw; oi–boy; ou–out; ŏŏ–took; ōō–boot; ŭ–cut; ûr–word; th–thin; th–this; hw–when; zh–vision; ə–about; N–French bon

cap·puc·ci·nos. [C; U] A drink made with espresso coffee and steamed milk.

ca·price (kə prēs′) *n.* An impulsive change of mind; a whim: *the caprices of an immature person.*

ca·pri·cious (kə prĭsh′əs *or* kə prē′shəs) *adj.* Subject to sudden unpredictable changes: *a capricious child; capricious weather.* —**ca·pri′cious·ly** *adv.* —**ca·pri′cious·ness** *n.* [U]

Cap·ri·corn (kăp′rĭ kôrn′) *n.* **1.** [U] The tenth sign of the zodiac in astrology. **2.** [C] A person born under this sign, between December 22 and January 19.

cap·size (kăp′sīz′ *or* kăp sīz′) *intr. & tr.v.* **cap·sized, cap·siz·ing, cap·siz·es.** To overturn or cause to overturn: *Our boat did not capsize in the storm. A huge wave capsized the ship.*

cap·sule (kăp′səl *or* kăp′sool) *n.* **1.** A small container, usually of gelatin or another material that dissolves, containing a dose of a medicine to be taken by mouth. **2.** A compartment that can be separated from the rest of a spacecraft, especially one designed for a crew.

Capt. *abbr.* An abbreviation of captain.

cap·tain (kăp′tən) *n.* **1.** The leader of a group; chief: *the captain of the football team.* **2.** The person in command of a ship or an aircraft: *the captain of a tugboat.* **3.** An officer in the military. **4.** An officer in a police or fire department. **5.** A leader in an enterprise: *a captain of industry.* —*tr.v.* To command or direct (sbdy./sthg.); lead: *captain a soccer team; captain a ship.*

cap·tion (kăp′shən) *n.* **1.** A short explanation written above or below an illustration or photograph: *a cartoon caption.* **2.** A subtitle in a motion picture: *Film captions can be hard to read.* —*tr.v.* To supply a caption or captions for (sthg.): *caption a television program for the hearing-impaired.*

cap·ti·vate (kăp′tə vāt′) *tr.v.* **cap·ti·vat·ed, cap·ti·vat·ing, cap·ti·vates.** To fascinate or charm (sbdy.), as with wit, beauty, or intelligence: *The movie captivated audiences everywhere.* —**cap′ti·va′tion** *n.* [U]

cap·tive (kăp′tĭv) *n.* A person or animal held under a restraint; a prisoner: *Her illness made her a captive in her own home.* —*adj.* **1.** Held as a prisoner: *The soldier was held captive for many years.* **2.** Kept under restraint or control; confined: *a captive audience.* —**cap·tiv′i·ty** *n.* [U]

cap·tor (kăp′tər *or* kăp′tôr′) *n.* A person who takes or holds another person as a captive: *The prisoners were forced to work by their captors.*

cap·ture (kăp′chər) *tr.v.* **cap·tured, cap·tur·ing, cap·tures.** **1.** To get hold of (sbdy./sthg.), as by force; seize: *Troops captured the rebels.* **2.** To gain possession or control of (sthg.): *The winner captured first prize.* **3.** To get or hold the interest of (sbdy./sthg.): *a mystery story that captures the imagination.* **4.** To hold or preserve (sthg.) in permanent form: *capture the sound of a howling wolf on tape.* —*n.* [C; U] The act of capturing or the process of being captured: *the capture of the lion.*

car (kär) *n.* **1.** An automobile: *a sports car.* **2.** A vehicle, such as a railroad car, that moves on rails: *the dining car.* **3.** The part of an elevator that holds passengers or cargo.

ca·rafe (kə răf′) *n.* A glass bottle for serving water or wine.

car·a·mel (kăr′ə məl *or* kär′məl) *n.* **1.** [C] A smooth chewy candy made with sugar, butter, and cream or milk. **2.** [U] Sugar heated to a brown syrup and used for coloring and sweetening foods.

car·at (kăr′ət) *n.* A unit of weight for precious stones, equal to 200 milligrams or about ¹⁄₁₄₀ of an ounce: *a one-carat diamond.*

HOMONYMS: carat, carrot (plant).

car·a·van (kăr′ə văn′) *n.* **1.** A group of travelers journeying together for safety in regions such as the desert. **2.** A group of vehicles or pack animals traveling together in single file: *The caravan of trucks crossed over the mountains.* —*intr.v.* To travel in or as if in a caravan: *We caravaned to the company's annual picnic.*

car·a·way (kăr′ə wā′) *n.* [U] A plant of Europe and Asia or its strong-tasting crescent-shaped seeds, used as flavoring in baking and cooking.

car·bide (kär′bīd′) *n.* A chemical compound, especially calcium carbide, consisting of carbon and a metal.

car·bo·hy·drate (kär′bō hī′drāt′) *n.* Any of a large class of compounds consisting of only carbon, hydrogen, and oxygen, produced in green plants by photosynthesis and composing a major type of food for animals: *Sugars, starches, and cellulose are carbohydrates.*

car·bon (kär′bən) *n.* **1.** [U] *Symbol* **C** A nonmetallic element that occurs in all plants and animals and in all organic compounds. Diamonds and graphite are pure carbon in the form of crystals; coal and charcoal are mostly carbon. Atomic number 6. See table at **element.** **2.** [C] **a.** A sheet of carbon paper. **b.** A copy made by using carbon paper.

car·bon·ate (kär′bə nāt′) *tr.v.* **car·bon·at·ed, car·bon·at·ing, car·bon·ates.** To charge (sthg.) with carbon dioxide gas, as a beverage: *Soda water is carbonated.* —**car′bon·a′tion** *n.* [U]

car·bon·at·ed (kär′bə nā′tĭd) *adj.* Containing carbon dioxide gas: *People in the United States drink a lot of carbonated beverages.*

carbon copy *n.* **1.** A duplicate of sthg. written or typed, made by using carbon paper. **2.** A person or thing that closely resembles another: *He grew up to be a carbon copy of his father, quiet and shy.*

carbon dioxide *n.* [U] A colorless odorless gas that does not burn. It is composed of carbon and oxygen in the proportion CO_2 and is present in the atmosphere or formed when any fuel containing carbon is burned.

carbon monoxide *n.* [U] A colorless odorless gas that is extremely poisonous and has the formula CO. Carbon monoxide is formed when carbon or a compound that contains carbon burns incompletely.

carbon paper *n.* [U] A lightweight paper coated on one side with a dark coloring matter, placed between two sheets of blank paper so that the bottom sheet will receive a copy of what is typed or written on the top sheet.

car•bu•re•tor (kär′bə rā′tər *or* kär′byə rā′tər) *n.* A device in a gasoline engine that mixes the gasoline with air to form an explosive mixture: *My car's carburetor was clogged with dirt.*

car•cass (kär′kəs) *n.* **1.** The dead body of an animal, especially one ready to be cut up for meat. **2.** The remains of sthg.: *the carcasses of old cars in a junkyard.*

car•cin•o•gen (kär sĭn′ə jən *or* kär′sə nə-jĕn′) *n.* A substance or agent that produces or tends to produce cancer: *Tobacco is a known carcinogen.* —**car′cin•o•gen′ic** (kär′sə nə-jĕn′ĭk) *adj.*

car•ci•no•ma (kär′sə nō′mə) *n.* A cancerous tumor of the skin or similar tissue of the body: *After his years of tanning, no one was surprised when he developed a carcinoma.*

card (kärd) *n.* **1.** A small, usually rectangular piece of stiff paper, cardboard, or plastic: *The address file is filled with business cards.* **2.** One of a set of 52 pieces of stiff heavy paper with numbers or figures and divided into four suits, used for various games; a playing card. **3. cards.** *(used with a singular or plural verb).* A game played with one or more sets of 52 cards: *Shall we play a game of cards?* **4.a.** A piece of stiff folded paper, often printed with a picture or message, used to send a note or greeting: *We sent her a birthday card.* **b.** A post card. **5.** A stiff piece of paper with a person's name, a book's title, or other information, used for indentification or classification: *a file card.* **6.** An outdated word for an amusing or eccentric person. —*v.* —*tr.* To check the identification of (sbdy.), especially for age: *The bartender carded all of us.* —*intr.* To check identification: *That bar cards every night.* ♦ **in the cards. 1.** Likely; probable: *A change in management seems to be in the*

cards. **2.** Destined to happen: *I really wanted the job, but I guess it wasn't in the cards.* **put** or **lay (one's) cards on the table.** To be frank and clear, as in one's intentions: *Let me put my cards on the table; I'm ready to meet your price.*

card•board (kärd′bôrd′) *n.* [U] Thick, stiff, heavy paper made of pressed paper pulp or pasted sheets of paper. —*adj.* Made of cardboard: *cardboard boxes.*

card catalog *n.* An alphabetical listing, especially of books in a library, made with a separate card for each item.

car•di•ac (kär′dē ăk′) *adj.* Relating to the heart: *a cardiac disorder.*

car•di•gan (kär′dĭ gən) *n.* A sweater or knitted jacket that opens down the front.

car•di•nal (kär′dn əl *or* kärd′nəl) *adj.* **1.** Of primary importance; chief: *A good design is the cardinal element of a successful building.* **2.** Deep or vivid red. —*n.* **1.** [C] A high official of the Roman Catholic Church. **2.** [U] A deep or vivid red color. **3.** [C] A North American bird with a crested head and bright red feathers in the male. **4.** [C] A cardinal number.

cardinal number *n.* A number, such as 3 or 11 or 412, used in counting to indicate quantity but not order.

cardinal point *n.* One of the four principal directions on a compass; north, south, east, or west.

car•di•o•gram (kär′dē ə grăm′) *n.* An electrocardiogram.

car•di•o•graph (kär′dē ə grăf′) *n.* An electrocardiograph.

car•di•ol•o•gy (kär′dē ŏl′ə jē) *n.* [U] The branch of medicine that deals with the heart, its diseases, and their treatment. —**car′di•ol′o•gist** *n.*

car•di•o•pul•mo•nar•y (kär′dē ō pool′-mə nĕr′ē *or* kär′dē ō pŭl′mə nĕr′ē) *adj.* Relating to the heart and lungs: *cardiopulmonary diseases.*

cardiopulmonary resuscitation *n.* [U] A procedure used to restore normal breathing and circulation after a person's heart has stopped beating. It uses mouth-to-mouth breathing and pushing on the chest to force blood from the heart.

car•di•o•vas•cu•lar (kär′dē ō văs′kyə lər) *adj.* Relating to or involving the heart and blood vessels: *cardiovascular disease.*

care (kâr) *n.* **1.** [U] A feeling of fear, doubt, or anxiety; worry: *on vacation and free from care.* **2.** [C] An object or source of worry, attention, or concern: *the cares of running a business.* **3.** [U] **a.** Serious attention or effort: *You should put more care into your work.* **b.** Caution to avoid harm or damage: *Glass* should be handled with care. **4.** [U] Protection or supervision; keeping: *The patient was left in the care of a nurse.* —*v.* **cared, car·ing, cares.** —*intr.* **1.** To be concerned or interested: *I don't care about going.* **2.** To object or mind: *Would you care if I turned on the radio?* **3.** To have a liking; like: *Some people don't care for fish.* **4.** *Formal.* To want; be inclined: *Would you care for another helping of peas?* **5.** To provide protection or help: *Who will care for the dog while we are away?* —*tr.* **1.** To be concerned about or interested in (sbdy./sthg.): *I don't care what they think.* **2.** *Formal.* To wish for (sthg.): *Would you care to go for a walk?* ◆ **in care of.** At the address of or in the name of: *Address all letters in care of my roommate.*

SYNONYMS: care, charge, keeping, trust. These nouns all refer to the function of watching, guarding, or overseeing sthg. *The neighbors left their dog in my care when they went on vacation. Who has charge of collecting today's homework? I left the key in our neighbors' keeping. The author committed her important papers to the bank's trust.*

---

ca·reen (kə rēn') *intr.v.* **1.** To swerve out of control while in fast motion: *The car careened on the icy road.* **2.** To lean to one side, as a ship: *The ship careened wildly in the heavy winds.*

ca·reer (kə rîr') *n.* **1.** A profession or an occupation: *She's considering a career in medicine.* **2.** The general progress or course of one's life, especially in one's profession: *a police officer with a distinguished career.*

care·free (kâr'frē') *adj.* Free of worries or responsibilities: *a carefree vacation.*

care·ful (kâr'fəl) *adj.* **1.** Attentive to possible danger; cautious; prudent: *Be careful not to eat too much.* **2.** Done with care; thorough; conscientious: *a careful job on one's homework.* **3.** Showing concern; mindful: *being careful of other people's feelings.* —**care'·ful·ly** *adv.* —**care'ful·ness** *n.* [U]

care·giv·er (kâr'gĭv'ər) *n.* A person who cares for older people, children, or the ill: *She is the primary caregiver for her elderly parents.*

care·less (kâr'lĭs) *adj.* **1.** Not taking enough care; negligent: *a careless worker; careless about one's appearance.* **2.** Done or made without care or attention: *a careless mistake.* **3.** Said or done without thought; inconsiderate: *a careless remark.* —**care'less·ly** *adv.* —**care'less·ness** *n.* [U]

ca·ress (kə rĕs') *n.* A gentle touch or gesture of fondness, tenderness, or love: *The child's caresses calmed the frightened cat.* —*tr.v.* To touch or stroke (sbdy./sthg.) affectionately: *He gently caressed the leather upholstery of his car.*

care·tak·er (kâr'tā'kər) *n.* Someone employed to look after and take care of a thing, place, or person: *the caretaker of a large estate.*

care·worn (kâr'wôrn') *adj.* Showing signs of worry or anxiety: *the parent's careworn face.*

car·fare (kär'fâr') *n.* [U] The amount charged for a ride, as on a subway or bus: *Do you have carfare to get to work?*

car·go (kär'gō) *n., pl.* **car·goes** or **car·gos.** The freight carried by a ship, an airplane, or another vehicle: *The freighter delivered its cargo at the wharf.*

car·hop (kär'hŏp') *n.* Someone who waits on customers in their cars at a drive-in restaurant.

car·i·bou (kär'ə bōō') *n.* Any of several deer of arctic regions of North America, having large spreading antlers in both the males and females.

car·i·ca·ture (kär'ĭ kə chŏor' *or* kär'ĭ kəchər) *n.* **1.** [C] A picture or description of a person or thing in which certain physical features are greatly exaggerated or distorted to produce a comic effect. **2.** [U] The art of creating such pictures or descriptions: *The cartoonist is a master of caricature.* **3.** [U] A bad example of sthg./sbdy.: *a caricature of justice; a caricature of his former self.* —*tr.v.* **car·i·ca·tured, car·i·ca·tur·ing, car·i·ca·tures.** To represent (sbdy./sthg.) in caricature: *He caricatures political figures.* —**car'i·ca·tur'ist** *n.*

car·mine (kär'mĭn *or* kär'mīn') *n.* [U] A deep or purplish red color. —*adj.* Deep or purplish red.

car·nage (kär'nĭj) *n.* [U] Great slaughter, especially in war; a massacre: *the carnage of battle.*

car·nal (kär'nəl) *adj. Formal.* **1.** Relating to the body or sex; sensual: *carnal desire.* **2.** Worldly or earthly: *the pursuit of carnal things.* —**car'nal·ly** *adv.*

car·na·tion (kär nā'shən) *n.* **1.** [C] A garden plant cultivated for its fragrant many-petaled white, pink, or red flowers. **2.** [U] A pinkish red color.

car·ni·val (kär'nə vəl) *n.* **1.** A traveling amusement show that offers rides, games, and sideshows. **2.** A time of merrymaking; a festival.

car·ni·vore (kär'nə vôr') *n.* **1.** An animal that feeds chiefly on the flesh of other animals and generally has large sharp canine teeth. Carnivores include predators, such as dogs and cats, and scavengers, such as hyenas and raccoons. **2.** A plant that eats insects.

car·niv·o·rous (kär nĭv'ər əs) *adj.* **1.** Feeding on the flesh of other animals: *Lions are carnivorous.* **2.** Having leaves or other parts that trap insects, allowing the plant to feed on them: *Carnivorous plants are rare.*

car•ob (kăr′əb) *n*. [U] An evergreen tree of the Mediterranean region that has long pods used as food. Carob is used as a replacement for chocolate.

car•ol (kăr′əl) *n*. A song of joy, especially for Christmas. —*intr.v*. **1**. To sing joyously. **2**. To go from house to house singing Christmas carols. —**car′ol•er** *n*.

HOMONYMS: carol, carrel (library nook).

ca•rouse (kə rouz′) *intr.v*. **ca•roused, ca•rous•ing, ca•rous•es**. To have a noisy and merry time, usually while drinking alcohol: *After the team's victory, the students caroused all night*. —**ca•rous′er** *n*.

car•ou•sel or **car•rou•sel** (kăr′ə sĕl′) *n*. **1**. A merry-go-round at an amusement park. **2**. A circular conveyor, on which objects are displayed or presented: *a baggage carousel at the airport*.

carp[1] (kärp) *intr.v*. To find fault or complain in a petty or disagreeable way: *He was carping about his boss again*.

carp[2] (kärp) *n*. A large freshwater fish often bred in ponds and lakes and used as food.

car•pen•ter (kär′pən tər) *n*. Someone who builds or repairs wooden objects and structures such as cabinets, houses, and ships. —**car′pen•try** *n*. [U]

car•pet (kär′pĭt) *n*. **1**. [C] A thick heavy covering for a floor, usually made of woven wool or synthetic fibers; a rug. **2**. [U] The fabric used for floor covering: *a roll of carpet*. **3**. [C] Something that covers a surface like a carpet: *a carpet of pine needles on the forest floor*. —*tr.v*. To cover (sthg.) with or as with a carpet: *carpet the stairs*.

car•pet•ing (kär′pĭ tĭng) *n*. [U] **1**. Material or fabric used for carpets: *pretty red carpeting*. **2**. A carpet or carpets: *a room with wall-to-wall carpeting*.

car pool *n*. **1**. An arrangement among a number of car owners who agree to take turns driving each other or their children to a regular destination, such as work or school: *Mothers are often responsible for children's car pools*. **2**. A group of people forming a car pool: *My car pool often stops for breakfast*.

car-pool (kär′pōōl′) *v*. —*intr*. To travel in a car pool: *Four of us car-pool to work every day*. —*tr*. To transport (sbdy.) by means of a car pool: *Several families car-pool their children to school*. —**car′-pool′er** *n*.

car•port (kär′pôrt′) *n*. A shelter for a car under a roof projecting from the side of a building, especially a house.

car•rel (kăr′əl) *n*. A small enclosed area with a desk for study in a library.

HOMONYMS: carrel, carol (song).

car•riage (kăr′ĭj) *n*. **1**. [C] A passenger vehicle with wheels, usually drawn by horses. **2**. [C] A small wheeled vehicle for a baby or a doll that is pushed by sbdy. walking behind it. **3**. [C] A wheeled structure on which a heavy object, such as a cannon, is moved. **4**. [U] The manner in which one's head or body is held; posture: *She has the poise and carriage of a model*.

car•ri•er (kăr′ē ər) *n*. **1**. A person or thing that transports or conveys: *a baggage carrier*. **2**. A person or business that deals in transporting passengers or goods: *Airlines, railroads, bus lines, and other carriers see an increase in business during holidays*. **3**. An aircraft carrier. **4**. A device or mechanism for moving or carrying sthg.: *We attached our bikes to the carrier on top of the car*. **5**. A person or an animal that is infected with a disease, but shows none of its symptoms and is capable of transmitting it to others: *Mosquitoes are carriers of malaria*.

carrier wave *n*. An electromagnetic wave whose amplitude or frequency is modulated to transmit a signal, as in radio broadcasting.

car•ri•on (kăr′ē ən) *n*. [U] The decaying flesh of dead animals: *Vultures feed on carrion*.

car•rot (kăr′ət) *n*. A plant with feathery leaves and a long, tapering, orange root eaten raw or cooked.

carrot

HOMONYMS: carrot, carat (weight of gems).

car•rou•sel (kăr′ə sĕl′) *n*. Variant of **carousel**.

car•ry (kăr′ē) *v*. **car•ried, car•ry•ing, car•ries**. —*tr*. **1**. To hold or support (sbdy./sthg.) while moving; bear: *carry the groceries into the house*. **2**. To take (sbdy./sthg.) from one place to another: *Airplanes carry passengers and freight*. **3**. To serve as a means of moving (sthg.): *The pipes carry water from the reservoir*. **4**. To cause (sthg.) to move; propel: *The wind carried the ball over the fence*. **5**. To support the weight or responsibility of (sthg.): *She is carrying a heavy load of courses this semester*. **6**. To be pregnant with (a child). **7**. To hold and move (oneself, one's body, or a part of it) in a certain way: *Dancers carry themselves very gracefully*. **8**. To keep a supply of (sthg.) for sale: *Drugstores carry many different health products*. **9**. To sing (a tune or melody) producing the right notes: *carry a tune.* **10.** To put (a number) into the next column to the left when performing addition: *carry the 5.* **11.** To have (sthg.) as a condition, a result, or an effect: *a washing machine carrying a guarantee for one year; a crime carrying a prison sentence.* **12.** To express or contain (sthg.): *a report carrying a warning; a package carrying a label.* **13.** To win a majority of the votes in (an area): *The President carried almost all the states.* **14.** To make (sthg.) last or continue: *carry a joke too far.* **15.** To print or broadcast (information): *All the papers carried the story.* — *intr.* **1.** To be transmitted; cover a distance: *a voice that carries well.* **2.** To be approved or accepted: *The proposal carried by a wide margin.* —*n., pl.* **car•ries.** The act of carrying in sports such as football: *The halfback averages four yards per carry.* ◆ **carry away.** *tr.v.* [sep.] To excite great emotion in (sbdy.): *I was carried away by the music.* **carry off.** *tr.v.* [sep.] **1.** To win (sthg.): *He carried off first prize.* **2.** To handle (sthg.) successfully: *The debate was carried off without any difficulty.* **carry on.** *tr.v.* [sep.] To be involved in or continue (sthg.): *carry on a conversation; carry on correspondence* — *intr.v.* **1.** To continue despite difficulties: *carry on even with a bad cold.* **2.** To behave in an excited or improper manner: *What are they carrying on about?* **carry out.** *tr.v.* [sep.] To do (sthg.) as planned or ordered: *carry out a mission; carry out instructions.*

car•ry•all (kăr′ē ôl′) *n.* A large bag, basket, or pocketbook.

car•ry•on (kăr′ē ŏn′) *adj.* Small or compact enough to be carried aboard an airplane, a train, or a bus by a passenger: *carryon luggage.* —*n.* A bag or other container small or compact enough to be carried aboard an airplane, a train, or a bus: *Carryons must be placed in the overhead compartment on an airplane.*

car•ry•out (kăr′ē out′) *adj.* Intended to be eaten away from a restaurant: *carryout pizza.*

car•sick (kär′sĭk′) *adj.* Nauseated by the motion of a car, bus, or other vehicle: *My sister gets carsick when she sits in the back seat of the car.* —**car′sick′ness** *n.* [U]

cart (kärt) *n.* **1.** A small wheeled vehicle pushed by hand: *a grocery cart.* **2.** A two-wheeled wooden vehicle pulled by a horse or other animal and used to transport goods or people. **3.** A light motorized vehicle: *a golf cart.* —*tr.v.* To carry (sbdy./sthg.) somewhere: *She carts her daughter everywhere she goes.*

carte blanche (kärt blänsh′ *or* kärt blänch′) *n.* [U] Complete freedom of action: *The teacher gave us carte blanche to organize the party.*

car•tel (kär tĕl′) *n.* An association of independent business firms or other groups, often from different countries, organized to control prices, production, and sales by its members: *the oil cartel; a drug cartel.*

Cartesian coordinate system *n.* A system for locating any point in a plane by giving its distances from two perpendicular lines that intersect at an origin, the distance from each line being measured along a straight line parallel to the other.

car•ti•lage (kär′tl ĭj) *n.* [U] A tough white connective tissue that forms a large part of the skeleton of humans and other vertebrates. It is more flexible than bone and not as hard: *cartilage in the nose.* —**car′ti•lag′i•nous** (kär′tl ăj′ə nəs) *adj.*

car•tog•ra•phy (kär tŏg′rə fē) *n.* [U] The art of making maps or charts. —**car•tog′-ra•pher** *n.*

car•ton (kär′tn) *n.* **1.** A cardboard or plastic box made in various sizes: *an egg carton; a juice carton.* **2.** The contents of a carton: *drink a carton of milk.*

car•toon (kär tōōn′) *n.* **1.** A drawing showing a humorous situation or illustrating an opinion on a public issue: *political cartoons.* **2.** An animated cartoon: *watching a Disney cartoon.* **3.** A comic strip.

car•toon•ist (kär tōōn′ĭst) *n.* A person who draws cartoons, as for a newspaper.

car•tridge (kär′trĭj) *n.* **1.** A cylindrical casing of metal or cardboard that holds the powder to propel a bullet or shot. **2.** A smaller unit designed to be inserted into a larger piece of equipment: *an ink cartridge for a pen; a toner cartridge for the copier.* **3.** A cassette containing magnetic tape.

cart•wheel (kärt′wēl′) *n.* A handspring in which the body turns over sideways with the arms and legs spread like the spokes of a wheel. —*intr.v.* To do cartwheels: *She cartwheeled across the stage.*

carve (kärv) *v.* **carved, carv•ing, carves.** —*tr.* **1.** To shape or decorate (sthg.) by cutting: *carve a block of marble into a statue.* **2.** To cut (meat or poultry) in pieces to be eaten: *carve a turkey.* **3.** To make (sthg.) by or as if by cutting: *The boys carved their names in the bark of the tree.* —*intr.* To slice meat or poultry to eat: *On Thanksgiving, my mother carves.* ◆ **carve out.** *tr.v.* [sep.] To create or establish (sthg.) by great effort: *It took time for the new player to carve out a place for himself on the team.* **carve up.** To divide (sthg.) into parts or shares: *The land is being carved up into plots for ten houses.* —**carv′er** *n.*

carv•ing (kär′vĭng) *n.* **1.** [U] The act or process of cutting wood or stone to form an object or design: *Wood carving is my uncle's hobby.* **2.** [C] An object or a design formed by cutting: *a wood carving.*

car wash *n.* An area or a building equipped for washing cars.

ca•sa•ba also **cas•sa•ba** (kə sä′bə) *n.* [C; U] A melon with a yellow skin and sweet whitish flesh.

cas•cade (kă skād') *n.* **1.** A waterfall or a series of small waterfalls that flows over steep rocks. **2.** Something resembling a cascade: *a cascade of sparks from the machine.* — *intr.v.* **cas•cad•ed, cas•cad•ing, cas•cades.** To fall in or as if in a cascade: *The cards cascaded to the floor.*

case¹ (kās) *n.* **1.** An instance or example of sth.: *It was a case of mistaken identity.* **2.** A situation or set of conditions: *In that case there is nothing more we can do.* **3.** A situation that requires investigation, especially by police: *the case of the missing diamonds.* **4.** An occurrence of a disease or disorder: *She had a bad case of chickenpox.* **5.** A person being assisted, treated, or studied, as by a doctor or a social worker: *The social worker took on several cases.* **6.** A legal action; a lawsuit: *The Supreme Court is the last court to consider a case.* **7.** A set of reasons or arguments offered in support of sth.: *There is a good case for changing the rules.* **8.** In grammar, a set of forms of a noun, pronoun, or adjective that show relationships among words in a sentence. English has three cases: nominative, objective, and possessive. ♦ **in any case.** No matter what happens: *In any case, we will have to leave soon.* **in case of.** If sth. happens: *In case of emergency, call the police.*

case² (kās) *n.* **1.** A container or receptacle: *a packing case.* **2.** A container and all its contents: *We bought a case of soda.* **3.** A container or protective cover for holding or carrying jewelry, eyeglasses, or other delicate items: *a camera case.*

case history *n.* In fields such as medicine and psychology, a detailed list of the facts affecting the condition of a person or group under treatment or study.

case•work (kās'wûrk') *n.* [U] Social work devoted to individual people or cases. — **case'work'er** *n.*

cash (kăsh) *n.* [U] **1.** Money in the form of bills and coins: *I have five dollars in cash in my pocket.* **2.** Payment in the form of currency or a check: *We decided not to charge our purchases and paid cash.* — *tr.v.* To exchange (sth.) for money: *cash a check.* ♦ **cash in on.** *Informal.* To take advantage of (sth.): *I think I'll cash in on the sunshine and go to the beach.*

HOMONYMS: cash, cache (hiding place).

---

cash•ew (kăsh'oo or kə shoo') *n.* The kidney-shaped edible nut of a tropical American tree.

cash•ier (kă shîr') *n.* A person employed to receive and pay out money, as in a store, restaurant, hotel, or bank.

ca•shier's check (kă shîrz') *n.* A check drawn by a bank on its own funds and signed by the bank's cashier: *Anyone can cash a cashier's check.*

cash machine *n.* An automated teller machine.

cash•mere (kăzh'mîr' *or* kăsh'mîr') *n.* [U] Yarn or cloth made from the fine soft wool of a goat native to India and Tibet: *The sweater was made of cashmere.*

cash register *n.* A machine that records the amount of each cash sale and contains a drawer for holding money.

ca•si•no (kə sē'nō) *n., pl.* **ca•si•nos.** An establishment for gambling and other entertainment.

cas•ket (kăs'kĭt) *n.* A coffin or box used to bury a dead person.

cas•sa•ba (kə să'bə) *n.* Variant of **casaba.**

cas•sa•va (kə să'və) *n.* [U] A tropical American plant having a large starchy root that is used as food.

cas•se•role (kăs'ə rōl') *n.* **1.** [C] A dish, usually of pottery or glass, in which food is both baked and served. **2.** [C; U] Food baked in such a dish: *The tuna casserole was delicious.*

cas•sette (kə sĕt') *n.* A small case containing magnetic tape for use in a tape recorder, VCR, or videocamera.

cast (kăst) *v.* **cast, cast•ing, casts.** — *tr.* **1.** To throw (sth.): *Tourists cast coins into the fountain.* **2.** To throw off or remove (sth.): *The snake casts its skin as it grows.* **3.** To cause (sth.) to fall in a certain direction: *cast a shadow; cast doubt upon the report.* **4.** To turn or direct (sth.): *cast a look in the mirror.* **5.** To give (one's ballot or vote) in an election. **6.** To give a role to (an actor): *The director cast the actor as a judge.* **7.** To form (an object) by pouring hot liquid or soft material into a mold and allowing it to harden: *The artist cast the sculpture in bronze.* — *intr.* **1.** To throw sth., especially a fishing net or line: *The fisherman cast in the river all morning.* **2.** To be shaped in a mold: *Some metals, such as lead, cast easily.* — *n.* **1.** The act or an instance of throwing or casting: *a cast of the dice.* **2.** The actors in a play or movie: *There were only four people in the cast.* **3.** A hard stiff covering used to keep a broken bone from moving while it heals. **4.** An object cast in or as if in a mold: *a cast of a statue.* **5.** A color: *The cloth has a slightly reddish cast.* ♦ **cast about for.** To look around for (sbdy./sth.): *cast about for a way to escape.* **cast aside.** *tr.v.* [sep.] To discard or throw away (sth. of no value): *cast aside a suggestion.* **cast lots.** To choose objects from a set of things used to determine sth. by chance: *We cast lots to decide*

ă-**cat**; ā-**pay**; âr-**care**; ä-**father**; ĕ-**get**; ē-**be**; ĭ-**sit**; ī-**nice**; îr-**here**; ŏ-**got**; ō-**go**; ô-**saw**; oi-**boy**; ou-**out**; oo-**took**; oo-**boot**; ŭ-**cut**; ûr-**word**; th-**thin**; th-**this**; hw-**when**; zh-**vision**; ə-**about**; N-French bon

who would go first. **cast off.** *intr.v.* [*from*] To release a ship from a dock: *They cast off from the dock at noon for the cruise.*

HOMONYMS: cast, caste (social class).

cast•a•way (kăst′ə wā′) *adj.* **1.** Lost at sea or shipwrecked: *castaway sailors.* **2.** Discarded; thrown away: *castaway clothes.* —*n.* **1.** A shipwrecked person: *The castaways were on that island for two years.* **2.** A person or thing that has been discarded: *He collected and sold castaways to make a living.*

caste (kăst) *n.* **1.** In India, one of the hereditary social classes in Hindu society. **2.** A social class as distinguished by rank, profession, or wealth: *the priestly caste of Aztec civilization.*

HOMONYMS: caste, cast (throw).

cast•ing (kăs′tĭng) *n.* **1.** [U] The act or process of making casts or molds. **2.** [C] An object that has been formed in a mold: *Bullets are lead castings.* **3.** [U] The selection of actors or performers, as for a play: *Who is in charge of casting for the play?*

cast iron *n.* [U] A hard brittle alloy of iron that contains carbon and small amounts of silicon, sulfur, manganese, and phosphorus.

cast-i•ron (kăst′ī′ərn) *adj.* **1.** Made of cast iron: *a cast-iron skillet.* **2.** Rigid or inflexible: *a cast-iron rule.* **3.** Hardy; strong: *With your cast-iron stomach you could eat anything!*

cas•tle (kăs′əl) *n.* **1.** A large building or group of buildings with high, thick walls, towers, and other defenses against attack. **2.** A building that resembles a castle in size or appearance, sometimes figuratively: *His home is his castle.*

cast•off (kăst′ôf′ *or* kăst′ŏf′) *n.* A person or thing that has been discarded or thrown away: *picking through other people's castoffs for valuables.* —**cast′-off** *adj.*

cas•trate (kăs′trāt′) *tr.v.* **cas•trat•ed, cas•trat•ing, cas•trates.** To remove the testicles of (a male); geld or emasculate. —**cas•tra′tion** *n.* [C; U]

ca•su•al (kăzh′ōō əl) *adj.* **1.** Not thought about beforehand: *a casual remark about the weather.* **2.** Suited for everyday wear or use; informal: *casual clothes.* **3.** Not serious or thorough: *a casual inspection.* **4.** Not close or intimate: *a casual friendship.* **5.** Happening by chance; not planned; accidental: *a casual meeting of friends on a street corner.* —**cas′-u•al•ly** *adv.* —**cas′u•al•ness** *n.* [U]

ca•su•al•ty (kăzh′ōō əl tē) *n.*, *pl.* **ca•su•al•ties.** **1.** A person who is killed or injured in an accident or a military action: *She was a casualty of drunk driving.* **2.** A serious accident, especially one in which sbdy. is serious-

ly injured or killed: *The latest airline casualty caused 90 deaths.*

cat (kăt) *n.* **1.** A small carnivorous mammal with soft fur and sharp claws, kept as a pet or for catching mice and rats. **2.** Any of various related mammals, such as a lion, tiger, leopard, or cougar. ♦ **let the cat out of the bag.** To give away a secret; let a secret be known: *It's a surprise birthday party, so don't let the cat out of the bag.*

cat•a•clysm (kăt′ə klĭz′ əm) *n.* **1.** A sudden and violent change in the earth's crust, as an earthquake or a volcanic eruption. **2.** A great upheaval or disaster, such as a revolution or war: *the cataclysm of a nuclear war.* —**cat′a•clys′mic** (kăt′ə klĭz′mĭk) *adj.*

cat•a•combs (kăt′ə kōmz′) *pl.n.* An underground cemetery consisting of chambers or tunnels with recesses used as graves.

cat•a•log *or* **cat•a•logue** (kăt′l ôg′ *or* kăt′l ŏg′) *n.* **1.** A book or pamphlet that contains descriptions and pictures of items for sale: *a mail-order catalog.* **2.** A list of items, usually in alphabetical order, with a description of each item: *The library catalog is now online.* —*tr.v.* **cat•a•loged, cat•a•log•ing, cat•a•logs** *or* **cat•a•logued, cat•a•logu•ing, cat•a•logues.** To list (things) in a catalog; make a catalog of: *catalog the books in a library.* —**cat′a•log′er** *or* **cat′a•logu′er** *n.*

cat•a•lyst (kăt′l ĭst) *n.* [C; U] **1.** A substance that increases the rate of a chemical reaction while undergoing no permanent change in composition itself. **2.** A person or thing that causes or speeds up a process or event: *Greed is often a catalyst of war.* —**cat′a•lyt′ic** (kăt′l ĭt′ĭk) *adj.*

catalytic converter *n.* A device that changes harmful exhaust gases from an automotive engine from hydrocarbons and carbon monoxide into carbon dioxide and water vapor.

cat•a•pult (kăt′ə pŭlt′ *or* kăt′ə pŏolt′) *n.* **1.** An ancient military machine for throwing stones, spears, arrows, or other missiles at an enemy. **2.** A mechanism for launching aircraft from the deck of a ship. —*v.* —*tr.* To throw or launch (sthg.) from or as if from a catapult: *The volcano catapulted large boulders high into the air.* —*intr.* To move suddenly as if thrown from a catapult: *When the firefighters heard the alarm, they catapulted out of bed.*

cat•a•ract (kăt′ə răkt′) *n.* **1.** (*usually plural*). A condition in which the lens of an eye turns cloudy, causing total or partial blindness. **2.** A large steep waterfall.

ca•tas•tro•phe (kə tăs′trə fē) *n.* **1.** A great and sudden disaster, such as an earthquake or a flood. **2.** A complete failure: *The party was a catastrophe.* —**cat′a•stroph′ic** (kăt′ə strŏf′ĭk) *adj.* —**cat′a•stroph′i•cal•ly** *adv.*

cat•call (kăt′kôl′) *n.* (*usually plural*). A loud shrill call or whistle expressing disapproval or

C

derision, usually directed from an audience toward a speaker or performer: *Catcalls and boos greeted the appearance of the new pitcher.*

catch (kăch *or* kĕch) *v.* **caught** (kôt), **catch‧ing, catch‧es.** —*tr.* **1.** To get hold of or grasp (sbdy./sthg.): *catch a ball.* **2.** To capture (sbdy./sthg.), especially after a chase: *The cat caught a mouse.* **3.** To find or come upon (sbdy./sthg.) suddenly: *We caught the puppy stealing the cat's food.* **4.** To reach (a bus, train, or plane) in time to board: *Can we still catch the 3 o'clock train?* **5.** To become infected with (a sickness): *catch a cold.* **6.** To cause (sthg.) to be hooked or entangled: *I caught my shirt on a nail.* **7.** To hit (sthg.); strike: *The falling tree caught a corner of the roof.* **8.** To attract (notice or interest): *They tried to catch our attention by yelling and waving their arms.* **9.** To take in or get (sthg.) momentarily: *catch sight of the robber; catch what was said over the noise.* **10.** To go to see (a play, movie, or other entertainment): *We caught the 7:30 show.* **11.** To stop (oneself) during an action: *I caught myself before laughing.* —*intr.* **1.** To become hooked or entangled: *My coat caught in the car door.* **2.** To burn; ignite: *The fire caught quickly.* —*n.* **1.** The act or an instance of catching in the hands: *The center fielder made a diving catch.* **2.** The amount of sthg. caught, especially fish: *a huge catch of tuna.* **3.** A device, such as a hook or latch, for fastening or closing sthg.: *a door catch.* **4.** A game in which two or more people throw a ball back and forth to each other: *They played catch until supper.* **5.** A choking or stoppage of the breath or voice: *She could hear the catch in his voice as he gave the sad news.* **6.** *Informal.* A hidden or tricky condition: *The offer is generous, but there must be a catch.* ◆ **catch fire. 1.** To begin to burn. **2.** To become popular: *a hobby that has caught fire around the country.* **catch on.** *intr.v.* **1.** [*to*] *Informal.* To understand; get the idea: *The dancers caught on to the new steps quickly.* **2.** To become fashionable or popular: *The new style hasn't caught on yet.* **catch (one's) breath.** To rest so as to be able to continue: *We caught our breath for a minute before climbing to the top of the mountain.* **catch up.** *intr.v.* **1.** To come up from behind; overtake: *We've almost caught up with the leaders.* **2.** To become up-to-date: *We have to catch up on the latest news.*

catch‧all (kăch′ôl′ *or* kĕch′ôl′) *n.* **1.** A place for keeping assorted objects, as a box, shelf, handbag, or closet. **2.** Something that covers many different situations, as a phrase, word, or law.

catch‧er (kăch′ər *or* kĕch′ər) *n.* A person or thing that catches, especially the baseball player stationed behind home plate who catches pitches.

catch‧ing (kăch′ĭng *or* kĕch′ĭng) *adj.* Easily passed from one person to another; contagious: *The flu is catching.*

catch‧word (kăch′wûrd′ *or* kĕch′wûrd′) *n.* A well-known word or phrase, especially one that sums up an idea or group: *Political speeches are little more than collections of catchwords.*

catch‧y (kăch′ē *or* kĕch′ē) *adj.* **catch‧i‧er, catch‧i‧est. 1.** Attractive or appealing: *a catchy idea for a new book.* **2.** Easily remembered: *a catchy tune.* **3.** Tricky; deceptive: *a catchy question.*

cat‧e‧chism (kăt′ĭ kĭz′əm) *n.* A book giving a brief summary of the basic principles of Christianity in the form of questions and answers.

cat‧e‧gor‧i‧cal (kăt′ĭ gôr′ĭ kəl *or* kăt′ĭ-gŏr′ĭ kəl) *adj.* Being without exception or qualification; absolute: *a categorical rejection of an offer.* —**cat′e‧gor′i‧cal‧ly** *adv.*

cat‧e‧go‧rize (kăt′ĭ gə rīz′) *tr.v.* **cat‧e‧go‧rized, cat‧e‧go‧riz‧ing, cat‧e‧go‧riz‧es.** To put (sbdy./sthg.) into a category; classify: *categorize news reports into those about domestic matters and those about international affairs.* —**cat′e‧go‧ri‧za′tion** (kăt′ĭ gər ĭ zā′shən) *n.* [C; U]

cat‧e‧go‧ry (kăt′ĭ gôr′ē) *n.,* *pl.* **cat‧e‧go‧ries.** A class or division in a system of classification: *several categories to describe kinds of human intelligence.*

ca‧ter (kā′tər) *v.* —*intr.* To provide and serve food and drinks: *His business caters for functions at the statehouse.* —*tr.* To supply and serve food and drinks for (sthg.): *cater a wedding.* ◆ **cater to.** *tr.v.* [insep.] To treat (sbdy./sthg.) with special consideration: *The governor was accused of catering to big business.* —**ca′ter‧er** *n.*

cat‧er‧pil‧lar (kăt′ər pĭl′ər *or* kăt′ə-pĭl′ər) *n.* The larva of a butterfly or moth, often resembling a hairy worm.

cat‧fish (kăt′fĭsh′) *n.* Any of numerous scaleless, mostly freshwater fish with feelers like cat whiskers near the mouth.

ca‧the‧dral (kə thē′drəl) *n.* **1.** The principal church of a bishop's diocese. **2.** A large or important church.

cath‧e‧ter (kăth′ĭ tər) *n.* A thin flexible tube inserted into a duct of the body to drain fluid.

cath‧ode (kăth′ōd′) *n.* **1.** A negative electrode. **2.** The positive terminal in a battery or other device that is supplying current.

cathode ray *n.* A stream of electrons from the cathode in a vacuum tube.

cath•ode-ray tube (kăth′ōd rā′) *n.* A vacuum tube in which a stream of electrons is directed against a screen where, under the influence of electric or magnetic fields, it traces a picture or display.

cath•o•lic (kăth′ə lĭk *or* kăth′lĭk) *adj.* **1.** Broad in sympathies, interests, and understanding: *a person with catholic tastes.* **2. Catholic.** Relating to the Roman Catholic Church. —*n.* **Catholic.** A Roman Catholic.

Ca•thol•i•cism (kə thŏl′ĭ sĭz′ əm) *n.* [U] The faith, teachings, practice, and organization of the Roman Catholic Church.

cat•nap (kăt′năp′) *n.* A short nap: *A catnap before supper will refresh you.* —*intr.v.* **cat•napped, cat•nap•ping, cat•naps.** To take a short nap: *The children catnapped during the long trip.*

cat•nip (kăt′nĭp′) *n.* [U] A plant related to mint, with a strong spicy smell that is very attractive to cats.

CAT scan (kăt) *n.* An x-ray picture of a cross section of the body or some organ of the body, made by a computer that assembles views of a body taken at a series of different angles. —**CAT scan′ner** *n.*

cat•sup (kăt′səp *or* kăch′əp *or* kĕch′əp) *n.* [U] Variant of **ketchup.**

cat•tail (kăt′tāl′) *n.* A tall marsh plant with long leaves and a dense tube-shaped cluster of tiny flowers that turn brown in the fall.

cat•tle (kăt′l) *pl.n.* Any of various horned, hoofed mammals bred and raised for beef and dairy products: *Cows, bulls, and oxen are cattle.*

cat•ty-cor•nered (kăt′ē kôr′nərd) *or* **kit•ty-cor•nered** (kĭt′ē kôr′nərd) *adj. & adv.* In a diagonal position: *He sits catty-cornered from me in class.*

cat•walk (kăt′wôk′) *n.* A narrow elevated platform or pathway.

Cau•ca•sian (kô kā′zhən) *adj.* Relating to a major division of people whose members characteristically have light or brown skin color and straight or wavy hair. —*n.* A Caucasian person.

cau•cus (kô′kəs) *n.* A meeting of members of a political party to decide on a question of policy or to choose a candidate for office: *The women held a caucus before the election.* —*intr.v.* To gather in or hold a caucus: *The representatives caucused to identify common concerns.*

caught (kôt) *v.* Past tense and past participle of **catch.** ◆ **caught up in.** Involved or absorbed in (sthg.): *He is caught up in his latest project.*

caul•dron (kôl′drən) *n.* Variant of **caldron.**

cau•li•flow•er (kô′lĭ flou′ər *or* kŏl′ĭ-flou′ər) *n.* [U] The compact whitish flower head of a plant closely related to the cabbage and broccoli, eaten raw or cooked.

caulk (kôk) *v.* —*tr.* To make (sthg.) watertight or airtight by filling or sealing with caulking: *caulk the cracks around the window.* —*intr.* To apply caulking. —*n.* [U] Caulking. —**caulk′er** *n.*

caulk•ing (kô′kĭng) *n.* [U] A material, such as tar or a plastic compound, used to fill or seal spaces, such as the seams around a window or the joints of pipes.

caus•al (kô′zəl) *adj.* Being a cause: *the causal connection between a scarcity of food and higher prices.* —**caus′al•ly** *adv.*

cause (kôz) *n.* **1.** [C] A person or thing that makes sthg. happen: *Scientists are investigating the cause of the extinction of the dinosaurs.* **2.** [U] A basis for a certain feeling, action, or decision: *There is no cause for alarm.* **3.** [C] An idea or a goal to which many people are dedicated: *the noble cause of peace.* —*tr.v.* **caused, caus•ing, caus•es.** To be the cause of (sthg.); make happen: *Many bacteria cause disease.* —**cause′less** *adj.*

cause•way (kôz′wā′) *n.* A raised roadway or bridge across marshland or water: *A series of causeways connects the Florida Keys.*

caus•tic (kô′stĭk) *adj.* **1.** Capable of burning or destroying living tissue: *Some acids are caustic substances.* **2.** Sarcastic; biting; cutting: *caustic remarks.* —*n.* A caustic material or substance. —**caus′ti•cal•ly** *adv.*

cau•tion (kô′shən) *n.* **1.** [U] Care to avoid danger or trouble: *climb icy steps with caution.* **2.** [C] A warning: *My doctor ended his advice with a caution about getting enough sleep.* —*tr.v.* To warn (sbdy.) against possible trouble or danger: *The sign cautioned drivers to go slowly.*

cau•tious (kô′shəs) *adj.* Showing or having caution; careful: *a slow and cautious driver.* —**cau′tious•ly** *adv.* —**cau′tious•ness** *n.* [U]

cav•al•ry (kăv′əl rē) *n., pl.* **cav•al•ries. 1.** In the past, troops trained to fight on horseback. **2.** A modern military unit using armored vehicles, such as tanks and helicopters.

cave (kāv) *n.* A natural passage under the earth or in the side of a hill or mountain with an opening to the surface. —*intr.v.* **caved, cav•ing, caves.** To give in; surrender: *After three days without talking to each other, he finally caved and phoned her.* ◆ **cave in.** *intr.v.* To fall in; collapse: *The ground above the old mine caved in.* —*tr.v.* [sep.] To cause (sthg.) to fall in: *A surge of water caved in the banks of the river.*

ca•ve•at (kăv′ē ăt′ *or* kä′vē ät′) *n. Formal.* A warning: *I will accept the job with one caveat: Don't tell me what to do.*

cave-in (kāv′ĭn′) *n.* **1.** A collapse, as of a tunnel: *The recent cave-in killed several miners.* **2.** A place where the ground has caved in.

cave•man *also* **cave man** (kāv′măn′) *n.* A prehistoric cave dweller.

cav•ern (kăv′ərn) *n.* A very large cave.

cav•ern•ous (kăv′ər nəs) *adj.* Resembling a cavern; huge, deep, and hollow: *the cavernous interior of a great cathedral.*

cav·i·ar (kăv′ē är′ *or* kä′vē är′) *n.* [U] The eggs of a sturgeon or other large fish, prepared with salt and eaten as a delicacy.

cav·i·ty (kăv′ĭ tē) *n., pl.* **cav·i·ties. 1.** A hollow or hole: *Some birds nest in tree cavities.* **2.** A hollow area within the body: *the abdominal cavity.* **3.** A pocket of decay in a tooth: *The dentist filled the cavity.*

ca·vort (kə vôrt′) *intr.v.* To leap about playfully; romp; frolic: *The children cavorted in the pool.*

caw (kô) *n.* The harsh sound made by a crow or similar bird. —*intr.v.* To make this sound.

cay (kē *or* kā) *n.* A small low island composed largely of coral or sand.

HOMONYMS: **cay, key** (lock opener, island), **quay** (wharf).

---

cay·enne pepper (kī ĕn′ *or* kā ĕn′) *n.* [U] A very strong sharp-tasting seasoning made from the ground pods of red peppers.

cc *abbr.* An abbreviation of cubic centimeter.

Cd The symbol for the element **cadmium.**

CD *abbr.* An abbreviation of compact disk.

CD-ROM (sē′dē′ rŏm′) *n.* A compact disk used for storing large amounts of computer data.

cease (sēs) *intr. & tr.v.* **ceased, ceas·ing, ceas·es.** To come or bring to an end; stop: *The noise ceased. The factory ceased production.* See Synonyms at **stop.**

cease-fire or **cease·fire** (sēs′fīr′) *n.* A suspension of fighting in a war; a truce: *She declared a cease-fire in the war with her coworker.*

cease·less (sēs′lĭs) *adj.* Having no pause; constant or continual: *Make that cat stop its ceaseless meowing.* —**cease′less·ly** *adv.*

ce·dar (sē′dər) *n.* **1.** [C] Any of several evergreen trees related to pines and firs, with reddish pleasant-smelling wood. **2.** [U] The wood of such a tree, used to make chests, pencils, and lining for closets.

cede (sēd) *tr.v.* **ced·ed, ced·ing, cedes.** *Formal.* To surrender possession of (sthg.), especially by treaty; give up: *France ceded Canada to Great Britain at the end of the French and Indian War.* See Synonyms at **yield.**

HOMONYMS: **cede, seed** (part that plants grow from).

---

ceil·ing (sē′lĭng) *n.* **1.** The inside upper surface of a room: *lights hung from the ceiling.* **2.** The maximum altitude at which an airplane can fly. **3.** The distance between the earth and the lowest clouds: *A ceiling of less than 500 feet gives poor visibility for an aircraft.* **4.** A maximum limit: *a ceiling on gasoline prices; a ceiling on crop production.*

cel·e·brant (sĕl′ə brənt) *n.* **1.** A person who officiates at a religious ceremony or rite. **2.** A participant in a celebration: *The celebrants gathered early for the party.*

cel·e·brate (sĕl′ə brāt′) *v.* **cel·e·brat·ed, cel·e·brat·ing, cel·e·brates.** —*tr.* **1.** To observe (a special occasion) with festive activity: *celebrate one's birthday.* **2.** To perform (a religious ceremony): *The priest celebrated Mass.* **3.** To praise (sbdy./sthg.) publicly; honor: *a poem that celebrates friendship.* —*intr.* **1.** To mark an occasion with proper ceremony or festivity: *After winning the lottery, she celebrated by quitting her job.* **2.** To engage in a party or other festive activity: *celebrate after hearing the good news.* —**cel′e·bra′tion** *n.* [C; U]

cel·e·brat·ed (sĕl′ə brā′tĭd) *adj.* Known and praised by many people: *a celebrated musician.* See Synonyms at **noted.**

ce·leb·ri·ty (sə lĕb′rĭ tē) *n., pl.* **ce·leb·ri·ties. 1.** [C] A famous person: *The singer is a celebrity wherever he goes.* **2.** [U] Fame; renown: *She achieved celebrity as an architect.*

cel·er·y (sĕl′ə rē) *n.* [U] The crisp, juicy, green or white stems of a plant related to parsley, eaten raw or cooked.

ce·les·tial (sə lĕs′chəl) *adj.* **1.** Relating to the sky: *Stars and planets are celestial bodies.* **2.** Of heaven; divine: *Angels are celestial beings.* —**ce·les′tial·ly** *adv.*

cel·i·ba·cy (sĕl′ə bə sē) *n.* [U] The condition of abstaining from sex, especially for religious reasons. —**cel′i·bate** (sĕl′ə bĭt) *n. & adj.*

cell (sĕl) *n.* **1.** A small confining room, as in a prison or convent: *a prison cell.* **2.** The basic unit of living matter in all organisms: *Some organisms consist of single cells.* **3.** A single unit that is capable of changing some form of energy, such as chemical energy, into electricity: *A flashlight battery is a single cell.*

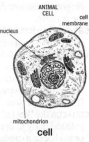

ANIMAL CELL

cell membrane

nucleus

mitochondrion

cell

HOMONYMS: **cell, sell** (give for money).

---

cel·lar (sĕl′ər) *n.* A storage room beneath a house: *a wine cellar; a root cellar.*

HOMONYMS: **cellar, seller** (one who gives sthg. for money).

---

cel·list (chĕl′ĭst) *n.* A person who plays the cello.

ă-cat; ā-pay; âr-care; ä-father; ĕ-get; ē-be; ĭ-sit; ī-nice; îr-here; ŏ-got; ō-go; ô-saw; oi-boy; ou-out; ŏŏ-took; ōō-boot; ŭ-cut; ûr-word; th-thin; th-this; hw-when; zh-vision; ə-about; ɴ-French bon

cel•lo (chĕl'ō) *n., pl.*
cel•los. A large musical instrument of the
violin family, having
four strings and a pitch
below that of the viola
but higher than that of
the double bass.

cello

cel•lo•phane (sĕl'ə-
fān') *n.* [U] A thin, flexible, transparent mate-
rial made from cellulose
that is used as a mois-
tureproof wrapping.
cell phone *n.* A cellular
telephone.
cel•lu•lar (sĕl'yə lər) *adj.* **1.** Relating to or
involving cells: *cellular division.* **2.** Made of
or containing cells: *the cellular structure of
the brain.*
cellular telephone *n.* A mobile telephone
unit that can be used over a large area covered
by a system of low-power radio transmitters.
cel•lu•lite (sĕl'yə līt') *n.* [U] A fatty deposit, as under the skin around the thighs.
cel•lu•loid (sĕl'yə loid') *n.* [U] A colorless
flammable material made from cellulose
and formerly used in making photographic
film.
cel•lu•lose (sĕl'yə lōs') *n.* [U] A carbohydrate that does not dissolve in water, is the
main component of plant tissues, and is used
in making products such as paper, cello-
phane, and textiles.
Cel•si•us (sĕl'sē əs *or* sĕl'shəs) *n.* A temperature scale on which the freezing point of
water is 0° and the boiling point of water is
100° under normal atmospheric pressure.
—*adj.* **1.** Relating to this scale: *at 0° Celsius.*
2. Centigrade.
ce•ment (sĭ mĕnt') *n.* [U] **1.** A building material made by grinding limestone with clay
to form a powder that can be mixed with
water and poured to harden. **2.** Concrete. **3.**
Something that unites or joins: *Mutual respect was the cement of their friendship.*
—*tr.v.* **1.** To join or cover (sthg.) with cement:
cement bricks in a wall. **2.** To make (sthg.)
binding; strengthen: *Signing the contract ce-
mented the partners' agreement.*
cem•e•ter•y (sĕm'ĭ tĕr'ē) *n., pl.* **cem•e•
ter•ies.** A place for burying the dead; a
graveyard.
cen•sor (sĕn'sər) *n.* A person who examines
books, movies, or other materials to remove
or prevent from becoming available anything
that is considered improper or harmful. —*tr.v.*
To remove material from or prevent the publication of (sthg.): *Military officials censor
classified information in letters.*
cen•sor•ship (sĕn'sər shĭp') *n.* [U] The act
or practice of censoring: *Censorship flourishes when people are afraid of ideas.*

cen•sure (sĕn'shər) *n.* [U] An expression of
strong disapproval or harsh criticism: *I was
shocked by my friends' censure.* —*tr.v.* **cen•
sured, cen•sur•ing, cen•sures.** To express
strong disapproval of (sbdy./sthg.); criticize:
*The press censured the city government for
corruption.* —**cen'sur•er** *n.*
cen•sus (sĕn'səs) *n.* An official counting of
population, usually made at regular intervals
and often including statistics on age, sex,
occupation, and other information: *Some
people are missed when the census is taken.*
cent (sĕnt) *n.* **1.** A coin of the United States,
Canada, Australia, New Zealand, and other
countries, that is ¹⁄₁₀₀ of a dollar. **2.** A coin
of other countries equal to ¹⁄₁₀₀ of the basic
monetary unit. **3.** A small sum of money: *I
haven't a cent to my name.* ♦ **put (one's) two
cents in.** *Informal.* To give an opinion even
when not asked for: *She always has to put her
two cents in.*

HOMONYMS: cent, scent (smell), **sent** (transmitted).

---

cent. *abbr.* An abbreviation of: **1.** Centigrade.
2. Central. **3.** Century.
cen•te•nar•i•an (sĕn'tə nâr'ē ən) *n.* A person who is one hundred years old or older.
cen•ten•ni•al (sĕn tĕn'ē əl) *n.* A 100th
anniversary or a celebration of it. —*adj.* **1.**
Relating to a period of 100 years. **2.** Happening once every 100 years: *The United
States has had two centennial celebrations of
its founding.*
cen•ter (sĕn'tər) *n.* **1.** [C] A point within a
circle or sphere that is equally distant from all
points of the circumference or surface. **2.** [C]
The middle position, part, or place of sthg.:
*the center of a table; chocolates with soft cen-
ters.* **3.** [C] A place of concentrated activity: *a
shopping center; a big city that is a trade center.* **4.** [C] A person or thing that is the chief
object of attention, interest, activity, or emotion: *Our guest was the center of the party.* **5.**
Often **Center.** [U] In politics, representing a
moderate view between those of the right and
left. **6.** [C] A player on a team positioned in or
near the middle of a playing area or forward
line, as in basketball and hockey. —*v.* —*tr.* **1.**
To place (sthg.) in or at the center: *center a
picture on a page.* **2.** To concentrate on
(sthg.): *The moderator centered the discussion on the most urgent problems.* —*intr.* **1.**
To be concentrated: *Support for the political
opposition centered in the cities.* **2.** To have as
a main theme, interest, or concern; focus: *The
conversation centered on air pollution.*
cen•ter•piece (sĕn'tər pēs') *n.* An ornamental object or bowl, as of flowers, placed
at the center of a dining table.
centi— *pref.* A prefix that means a hundredth:
centigram.

cen·ti·grade (sĕn′tĭ grād′) *n.* Celsius. —*adj.*

cen·ti·gram (sĕn′tĭ grăm′) *n.* A unit of weight equal to one hundredth (10^{-2}) of a gram.

cen·ti·me·ter (sĕn′tə mē′tər) *n.* A unit of length equal to one hundredth (10^{-2}) of a meter. See table at **measurement.**

cen·ti·pede (sĕn′tə pēd′) *n.* Any of various small animals with a body divided into many segments, each with a pair of legs.

cen·tral (sĕn′trəl) *adj.* **1.** Situated at, near, or in the center: *a central position from which to view the show.* **2.** Forming the center: *the central part of the state.* **3.a.** Having the dominant or controlling power: *the central office of the corporation.* **b.** Controlling all parts of a system from a particular place: *central air conditioning; central heating.* **4.** Essential or principal: *the central topic of a story.* —**cen′tral·ly** *adv.*

Central Intelligence Agency *n.* [U] An agency of the U.S. government that gathers information on matters affecting national security.

cen·tral·ize (sĕn′trə līz′) *v.* **cen·tral·ized, cen·tral·iz·ing, cen·tral·iz·es.** —*tr.* **1.** To bring (sthg.) into or toward a center: *centralize records in one office.* **2.** To bring (sthg.) under a central controlling authority: *The Constitution centralizes political power in the federal government.* —*intr.* To come together at a center; concentrate: *Their attention centralized on the essential problem.* —**cen′tral·i·za′tion** (sĕn′trə lĭ zā′shən) *n.* [U]

central nervous system *n.* In a vertebrate animal, the part of the nervous system that consists of the brain and spinal cord.

central processing unit *n.* The part of a computer that interprets and carries out instructions.

cen·tre (sĕn′tər) *n. & v. Chiefly British.* Variant of **center.**

cen·trif·u·gal (sĕn trĭf′yə gəl *or* sĕn trĭf′ə-gəl) *adj.* Moving or directed away from a center: *the centrifugal action of a spinning ball.* —**cen·trif′u·gal·ly** *adv.*

centrifugal force *n.* [U] The force that appears to cause a body turning around a center to move away from the center. Centrifugal force is not a true force, but is actually an example of inertia.

cen·tri·fuge (sĕn′trə fyōōj′) *n.* A machine for separating substances of different densities, as cream from milk or bacteria from a fluid, by rotating them at high speeds.

cen·trip·e·tal (sĕn trĭp′ĭ tl) *adj.* Directed or moving toward a center or axis. —**cen·trip′e·tal·ly** *adv.*

centripetal force *n.* The force that tends to move things toward the center around which they are turning. Gravitation acts as a centripetal force.

cen·trist (sĕn′trĭst) *n.* A person whose political views fall midway between liberal and conservative. —*adj.* Marked by or holding moderate political views: *a centrist policy; a centrist representative.*

cen·tu·ry (sĕn′chə rē) *n., pl.* **cen·tu·ries. 1.** A period of 100 years. **2.** Each of the 100-year periods counted forward or backward since the time of Jesus's birth: *the 20th century.*

CEO *abbr.* An abbreviation of Chief Executive Officer.

ce·ram·ic (sə răm′ĭk) *n.* **1.** [U] A hard breakable material that is made by baking clay or some other nonmetallic mineral at an extremely high temperature. **2.** [C] An object made of this material: *ceramics on display at the museum.* **3. ceramics.** [U] *(used with a singular verb).* The art or technique of making things from this material: *Ceramics is his hobby.* —**ce·ram′ic** *adj.*

ce·re·al (sîr′ē əl) *n.* [C; U] **1.** The seeds of certain grasses, such as wheat, rice, or corn, used as food. **2.** A food, such as oatmeal or other breakfast food, prepared from such seeds: *cereal and milk for breakfast.*

HOMONYMS: cereal, serial (a series).

---

cer·e·bel·lum (sĕr′ ə bĕl′əm) *n., pl.* **cer·e·bel·lums** *or* **cer·e·bel·la** (sĕr′ ə bĕl′ə). A part of the brain, located at the rear of the skull, that regulates and coordinates complex muscular movements.

cer·e·bral (sĕr′ə brəl *or* sə rē′brəl) *adj.* **1.** Relating to the brain or cerebrum: *a cerebral blood vessel.* **2.** Concerned with the intellect rather than the emotions: *Her approach to life is highly cerebral.*

cer·e·brum (sĕr′ə brəm *or* sə rē′brəm) *n., pl.* **cer·e·brums** *or* **cer·e·bra** (sĕr′ə brə *or* sə rē′brə). The large rounded structure of the brain that fills most of the skull. It is divided into two parts that are joined at the bottom, and it controls thought and voluntary muscular movements.

cer·e·mo·ni·al (sĕr′ə mō′nē əl) *adj.* Relating to a ceremony: *ceremonial dances.* —*n.* A set of ceremonies established for a specific occasion; a ritual: *We attended the ceremonial.*

cer·e·mo·ni·ous (sĕr′ə mō′nē əs) *adj.* **1.** Careful about ceremony and formality; formally polite: *Diplomats are usually ceremonious people.* **2.** In accordance with a set of customary forms or rites; formal: *Inauguration of the President is a ceremoni-*

---

ous occasion. —**cer′e•mo′ni•ous•ly** *adv.*
—**cer′e•mo′ni•ous•ness** *n.* [U]

cer•e•mo•ny (sĕr′ə mō′nē) *n., pl.* **cer•e•mo•nies. 1.** [C] A formal act or set of acts performed in honor or celebration of an occasion, such as a wedding, funeral, or national event: *The wedding ceremony will be held in the cathedral.* **2.** [U] Proper or polite behavior; formality: *Mexico's president was welcomed with great ceremony.*

cer•tain (sûr′tn) *adj.* **1.** Established or agreed upon; definite: *We save a certain amount each month.* **2.** Sure to come or happen; inevitable: *If the temperature falls, it is certain that the rain will turn to snow.* **3.** Proven beyond doubt; indisputable: *It is certain that the planets revolve around the sun.* **4.** Confident; assured: *Are you certain that you left the book here?* **5.** Not named but assumed to be known: *There are certain laws for automobile safety.* **6.** Named but not familiar or known: *a certain Mr. Smith.* **7.** Some but not much; limited: *The report is accurate to a certain degree.* —*pron.* A certain number; some: *Certain of the watches are waterproof.* ◆ **for certain.** Without doubt; definitely: *Winter will come for certain.*

cer•tain•ly (sûr′tn lē) *adv.* Surely; definitely: *I am certainly going to the movies.*

cer•tain•ty (sûr′tn tē) *n., pl.* **cer•tain•ties. 1.** [U] The condition or quality of being certain; sureness: *There is no certainty that the package will arrive today.* **2.** [C] A proven fact: *It is a certainty that the moon affects the tides.*

cer•tif•i•cate (sər tĭf′ĭ kĭt) *n.* **1.** An official document that is proof of some fact, such as a date of birth: *a marriage certificate.* **2.** A document stating that a person has completed the requirements to practice a certain profession: *a teaching certificate.* **3.** A document that certifies ownership: *an automobile registration certificate; a stock certificate.*

cer•ti•fi•ca•tion (sûr′tə fĭ kā′shən) *n.* **1.** [U] The act of certifying or the condition of being certified: *All states require the certification of doctors.* **2.** [C] A certified document or statement; a certificate: *Our doctor's certification hung in a frame on the wall.*

cer•ti•fy (sûr′tə fī′) *v.* **cer•ti•fied, cer•ti•fy•ing, cer•ti•fies.** —*tr.* **1.** To guarantee (sthg.) to be true or valid with an official document: *Your license certifies that you know how to drive a car.* **2.** To guarantee the quality, value, or standard of (sthg.): *The inspector certified the elevator as safe.* **3.** To issue a license or certificate to (sbdy.): *A state board of examiners certifies public accountants.* —*intr.* To testify or declare sthg.: *Their fine work certifies to their ability.*

cer•ti•tude (sûr′tĭ tōōd′ *or* sûr′tĭ tyōōd′) *n.* [U] *Formal.* The condition of being certain;

confidence: *She spoke with great certitude about her research.*

cer•vix (sûr′vĭks) *n.* **1.** The neck. **2.** The neck-shaped outer end of the uterus in the female: *The cervix opens during childbirth.* —**cer′vi•cal** (sûr′vĭ kəl) *adj.*

ce•sar•e•an also **cae•sar•e•an** (sĭ zâr′ē ən) *n.* A cesarean section. —*adj.* Of or relating to a cesarean section.

cesarean section *n.* A surgical operation in which a cut is made through the abdominal wall and uterus to remove a baby: *The baby was delivered by cesarean section.*

ces•sa•tion (sĕ sā′shən) *n. Formal.* The act of ceasing or stopping; a halt: *A computer failure caused a cessation of stock trading.*

cf. *abbr.* An abbreviation of compare.

CFO *abbr.* An abbreviation of Chief Financial Officer.

cg or **cgm** *abbr.* An abbreviation of centigram.

ch. *abbr.* An abbreviation of chapter.

chafe (chāf) *v.* **chafed, chaf•ing, chafes.** —*tr.* To irritate (sbdy./sthg.) by rubbing: *The diaper chafed the baby.* —*intr.* **1.** To become irritated or sore from rubbing: *My hands chafed from washing them with harsh soap.* **2.** To feel irritation; be impatient: *chafe at the delay.*

chaff (chăf) *n.* [U] **1.** The husks of grain separated from the seeds by threshing. **2.** Unimportant or worthless people or ideas: *Their picky criticisms were just a lot of chaff.* ◆ **separate the wheat from the chaff.** To find out what is valuable and what is worthless in order to save what is valuable and get rid of what is worthless: *Before we can start the project, we need to separate the wheat from the chaff so we don't waste time on ideas that won't work.*

cha•grin (shə grĭn′) *n.* [U] A strong feeling of unease or annoyance caused by disappointment, embarrassment, or humiliation, especially at a mistake or failure: *To her chagrin, she lost the election by a few votes.* —*tr.v.* To cause (sbdy.) to feel chagrin; annoy greatly: *I was chagrined at being corrected in front of my friends.*

chain (chān) *n.* **1.** A series of connected links, usually of metal: *a bicycle chain; a gold chain.* **2.** A series of connected or related things: *a chain of events.* **3.** A number of stores, restaurants, theaters, or other businesses under common ownership or management: *a chain of supermarkets around the state.* **4. chains.** Something that restrains or confines: *They threw off the chains of slavery.* —*tr.v.* To bind or confine (sbdy./sthg.) with or as if with a chain or chains: *chain an elephant to a stake; be chained to one's job.*

chain reaction *n.* **1.** A series of events, each of which causes or influences the next: *The car crash caused a chain reaction on the highway.* **2.** A continuous series of chemical or physical actions.

chain saw *n.* A power saw with teeth set on a circular chain.

chain store *n.* One store in a number of retail stores under the same ownership or management.

chair (châr) *n.* **1.** A piece of furniture on which one may sit, consisting of a seat, back, legs, and sometimes arms at the sides. **2.** A position of authority, as that of a professor: *The head of the department has the chair of ancient history.* **3.** A chairperson: *address questions to the chair.* —*tr.v.* To preside over (sth.): *chair a meeting; chair a committee.*

chain saw

chair lift *n.* A series of chairs suspended from an endless cable and used to carry skiers up a slope.

chair•man (châr′mən) *n.* A man who presides over a meeting or is the head of a committee, board, or similar group. —**chair′wom′an** (châr′wŏŏm′ən) *n.*

chair•man•ship (châr′mən shĭp′) *n.* [U] The job of a chairperson or the period during which a chairperson has the job.

chair•per•son (châr′pûr′sən) *n.* A person who presides over a meeting or is the head of a committee, board, or similar group.

chaise longue or **chaise lounge** (shāz lounj′ or shāz lông′) *n.* A long chair on which one can sit and stretch out one's legs.

cha•let (shă lā′ or shăl′ā) *n.* **1.** A wooden house with a gently sloping roof that extends beyond the walls. **2.** A mountain cabin in the Swiss Alps.

chal•ice (chăl′ĭs) *n.* A cup or goblet.

chalk (chôk) *n.* [U] **1.** A soft white limestone formed from fossil seashells. **2.** A piece of this material or a similar substance, used especially for writing on a chalkboard or other surface: *colored chalk.* —*v.* ◆ **chalk up.** *tr.v.* [sep.] To earn or score (sth.): *The team chalked up a victory.* **chalk up to.** To credit sth.: *Chalk that up to pure luck.* —**chalk′i•ness** *n.* [U] —**chalk′y** *adj.*

chalk•board (chôk′bôrd′) *n.* A panel, usually green or black, for writing on with chalk.

chal•lenge (chăl′ənj) *n.* **1.** A call to take part in a contest: *a challenge to a race.* **2.** A calling into question; a demand for an explanation: *The new evidence presents a challenge to their theory.* **3.** Something that tests a person's skills, efforts, or resources: *the challenge of studying advanced mathematics.* —*tr.v.* **chal•lenged, chal•leng•ing, chal•**

leng•es. 1. To call (sbdy.) to engage in a contest: *We challenged the other team to a game of basketball.* **2.** To question or dispute the truth or rightness of (sth.): *challenge a statement.* **3.** To call (sth.) into action or use: *a problem that challenges the imagination.* —**chal′leng•er** *n.*

chal•leng•ing (chăl′ən jĭng) *adj.* **1.** Requiring the full use of one's abilities or skills: *a challenging job.* **2.** Arousing one's interest or curiosity; intriguing: *a challenging idea.*

cham•ber (chām′bər) *n.* **1.** An old word for a bedroom. **2.** A room in which a person of high rank receives visitors: *the pope's audience chamber.* **3. chambers.** A judge's office in a courthouse: *Before the trial the lawyers met in the judge's chambers.* **4.** A legislative or judicial body: *The Senate is the upper chamber of the legislature.* **5.** An enclosed space or compartment in a machine or body: *a bullet in the chamber of a rifle; the four chambers of the heart.*

chamber of commerce *n., pl.* **chambers of commerce.** An association of businesspersons and merchants for the promotion of business interests in the community.

cha•me•leon (kə mēl′yən) *n.* **1.** Any of various small lizards that can change color rapidly to blend in with their surroundings. **2.** A changeable or inconstant person, especially one who changes mood or opinion quickly: *He is a political chameleon; he agrees with whoever wins the election.*

cham•o•mile or **cam•o•mile** (kăm′ə mīl′ or kăm′ə mēl′) *n.* [U] A strong-smelling plant with flowers similar to daisies and feathery leaves. The dried flowers are used to make chamomile tea.

champ[1] (chămp) *tr. & intr.v.* To chew or bite upon noisily: *a horse champing its oats; a horse chewing and champing with great vigor.* ◆ **champ at the bit.** To be impatient at being delayed: *The children were champing at the bit to start the party.*

champ[2] (chămp) *n. Informal.* A champion.

cham•pagne (shăm pān′) *n.* [C; U] A bubbly white wine produced in Champagne, a region of France, or in other areas.

cham•pi•on (chăm′pē ən) *n.* **1.** A person or thing that holds first place or wins first prize in a contest, especially in sports. **2.** A person who fights for or defends sth., such as a cause or movement: *a champion of human rights.* —*tr.v.* To fight for or defend (sbdy./sth.); support actively: *champion the rights of poor people.* —*adj.* Holding first place or prize: *the champion team.*

cham•pi•on•ship (chăm′pē ən shĭp′) *n.* **1.** [C] **a.** The position or title of a champion: *Who holds the championship?* **b.** A contest held to determine a champion: *tickets for the championship.* **2.** [U] Defense or support: *the championship of civil rights.*

chance (chăns) *n.* **1.** [U] The unknown or uncertain course of events that has no apparent cause: *Most card games are games of chance. By chance did you find your glasses?* **2.** [C] The possibility that sthg. will happen; probability: *We still have a good chance of catching the train.* **3.** [C] An opportunity: *We never miss a chance to go to the movies.* **4.** [C] A risk or gamble: *You're taking a chance that the store will still be open.* **5.** [C] A raffle or lottery ticket: *She bought five chances to win the trip to Alaska.* —*adj.* Caused by chance; not planned: *a chance meeting.* —*v.* **chanced, chanc•ing, chanc•es.** —*intr.* To happen by accident: *I chanced to find a quarter on the sidewalk.* —*tr.* To take a chance with (sthg.); risk: *They chanced crossing the river in a canoe.* ◆ **chance on** or **upon.** *tr.v.* [insep.] To find or meet (sbdy./sthg.) accidentally: *I chanced on an old friend yesterday.*

chan•cel•lor (chăn′sə lər *or* chăn′slər) *n.* **1.** A high government official in some European countries: *The German Chancellor attended the conference.* **2.** The president of certain U.S. universities.

chanc•y (chăn′sē) *adj.* **chanc•i•er, chanc•i•est.** Uncertain; risky: *Sailing in such weather is a chancy undertaking.*

chan•de•lier (shăn′də lîr′) *n.* A light that holds a number of bulbs or candles on branches, sometimes with glass or crystal prisms, and hangs from a ceiling.

change (chānj) *v.* **changed, chang•ing, chang•es.** —*tr.* **1.** To cause (sthg.) to be different; alter: *change the rules; change the color of a room.* **2.a.** To give and receive (one thing for another): *The twins changed places to fool everybody.* **b.** To exchange (a unit of money) for smaller units: *The machine changes a dollar bill into coins.* **3.** To put fresh clothes or coverings on (sbdy./sthg.): *It's your turn to change the baby. I'll show you how to change the bed.* —*intr.* **1.** To become different: *The town grew and changed over the years.* **2.** To make an exchange: *If you would rather sit in this seat, I'll change with you.* **3.** To put on other clothing: *They changed into work clothes.* **4.** To transfer from one vehicle to another: *We changed in Chicago when we flew to the coast.* **5.** To become deeper in tone: *The boy's voice has begun to change.* —*n.* **1.** [C; U] The act or result of changing: *a change in the schedule; little changes in the patient's condition.* **2.** [U] **a.** The money in smaller units given for an equal amount in larger bills or coins: *Can you give me change for a dollar?* **b.** The money returned when the amount given in paying for sthg. is more than enough: *The salesperson gave me back two dollars' change.* **c.** A num-

ber of coins: *a purse full of change.* **3.** [C] Something different from one's routine: *We finished dinner early for a change.* **4.** [C] A fresh set of clothing. ◆ **change hands.** To pass from one owner to another: *The store changed hands this year.* **change (one's) mind.** To make a new decision or form a different opinion. —**chang′er** *n.*

change•a•ble (chān′jə bəl) *adj.* **1.** Likely to change; unpredictable: *changeable moods.* **2.** Capable of being changed: *changeable habits.* —**change′a•bil′i•ty, change′a•ble•ness** *n.* [U] —**change′a•bly** *adv.*

change•less (chānj′lĭs) *adj.* Never changing; constant: *He was changeless in his opposition to our proposal.* —**change′less•ly** *adv.* —**change′less•ness** *n.* [U]

change•o•ver (chānj′ō′vər) *n.* A change from one way of doing sthg. to another: *a changeover from typewriters to computers.*

chan•nel (chăn′əl) *n.* **1.** A band of frequencies reserved for broadcasting or communication: *a television channel.* **2.** A course or way through which sthg., such as news, messages, or ideas, may travel: *opening new channels of information.* **3.** The bed or deepest part of a stream or river. **4.** A broad strait of water: *a channel between islands.* **5. channels.** Official routes of communication: *go through channels to get permission to enter the country.* —*tr.v.* **1.** To form a channel in or through (sthg.): *The stream channeled the limestone.* **2.** To direct or guide (sbdy./sthg.) along a desired route: *channel her thoughts toward passing the test.*

chant (chănt) *n.* **1.** A simple melody in which many words or syllables are sung on the same note. **2.** A religious text sung to such a melody. **3.** A sustained rhythmic call or shout: *the chant of the crowd at a soccer game.* —*v.* —*tr.* **1.** To sing (sthg.) to a chant: *The monks chanted a prayer.* **2.** To call out (sthg.) in a sustained rhythmic way: *fans chanting the team's name.* —*intr.* **1.** [*for*] To call in a chant: *The crowd chanted for the President.* **2.** To sing a chant: *The monks chanted during the service.* —**chant′er** *n.*

Cha•nu•kah (κHä′nə kə *or* hä′nə kə) *n.* Variant of **Hanukkah.**

cha•os (kā′ŏs′) *n.* [U] Great disorder or confusion: *The street was in chaos after the car accident.* —**cha•ot′ic** (kā′ŏt′ĭk) *adj.* —**cha•ot′i•cal•ly** *adv.*

chap[1] (chăp) *tr. & intr.v.* **chapped, chap•ping, chaps.** To make or become dry, scaly, and cracked: *Strong soaps can chap your hands. My lips chap easily in cold weather.*

chap[2] (chăp) *n. Chiefly British. Informal.* A man or boy; a fellow.

chap. *abbr.* An abbreviation of chapter.

chap•el (chăp′əl) *n.* **1.** [C] A small church: *a little chapel in the hills.* **2.** [C] A small place reserved for prayer or religious services: *The airport had a small chapel for travelers.* **3.**

[U] Religious services held at a chapel: *Students attended chapel before the holidays.*

chap·er·on or **chap·er·one** (shăp′ə rōn′) *n.* **1.** An older person who attends and supervises a dance, party, or trip for young people: *Two of the teachers were chaperons for the class trip.* **2.** A person, especially an older or married woman, who accompanies a young unmarried woman in public. —*tr.v.* **chaper·oned, chaper·on·ing, chaper·ones.** To act as a chaperon for (sbdy./sthg.): *chaperon a party.*

chap·lain (chăp′lĭn) *n.* A member of the clergy who conducts religious services and performs other duties for an institution, a military unit, or a school.

chaps (chăps *or* shăps) *pl.n.* Heavy leather coverings worn over trousers by cowhands to protect their legs.

chap·ter (chăp′tər) *n.* **1.** A main division of a book. **2.** A series of related events or a part of a person's life: *That was an exciting chapter in my life.* **3.** A local branch of a large club, fraternity, or other organization: *My mother joined our town's chapter of the League of Women Voters.*

char (chär) *tr.v.* **charred, char·ring, chars.** To blacken (sthg.) by burning: *Most of the house was charred by the fire.*

char·ac·ter (kăr′ək tər) *n.* **1.** [U] The combination of qualities or features that makes one person, group, or thing different from another: *The character of the town is calm and peaceful.* **2.** [U] One's moral nature: *an honest and upstanding student of fine character.* **3.** [U] Moral strength; integrity: *a respected citizen of character.* **4.** [C] A person portrayed in a work of art, such as a novel, play, or movie: *The hero is the chief character in the play.* **5.** [C] *Informal.* An odd or eccentric person: *He's known to be quite a character.* **6.** [C] A symbol, such as a letter or number, used to represent information, as in printing, writing, or a computer program: *Check each character on that line of the program.* ♦ **in character.** Consistent with one's general character or usual behavior: *Being late is in character for my brother.* **out of character.** Not consistent with one's general character or usual behavior: *Not returning phone calls is quite out of character for him.*

char·ac·ter·is·tic (kăr′ək tə rĭs′tĭk) *adj.* Being a feature or quality that distinguishes a person or thing: *the zebra's characteristic stripes; my friend's characteristic laugh.* —*n.* A feature or quality that distinguishes a person or thing: *A curved bill is a characteristic of parrots.* See Synonyms at **quality.** —**char′ac·ter·is′ti·cal·ly** *adv.*

char·ac·ter·ize (kăr′ək tə rīz′) *tr.v.* **char·**

acter·ized, character·iz·ing, character·iz·es. 1. To describe the character or qualities of (sbdy./sthg.): *The supervisor's report characterized the nurse as very efficient.* **2.** To be a characteristic or quality of (sbdy./sthg.): *Dense pine forests characterize that region.* —**char′ac·ter·i·za′tion** (kăr′ək tər ĭ zā′shən) *n.* [C; U]

cha·rade (shə rād′) *n.* **1. charades.** (*used with a singular or plural verb*). A game in which words or phrases are acted out in pantomime, often syllable by syllable, until guessed by the other players: *We played charades at the party.* **2.** Something done as a deception; a pretense: *Laughter is often a charade to hide nervousness.*

char·coal (chär′kōl′) *n.* **1.** [U] A black porous material composed chiefly of carbon, produced by heating wood or sometimes bone until the lighter materials in it are burned away. **2.** [C; U] A stick of this material, used for drawing: *The artist does drawings in charcoal.* **3.** [U] A dark gray color. —*adj.* Dark gray: *He wore a charcoal gray suit.*

charge (chärj) *v.* **charged, charg·ing, charg·es.** —*tr.* **1.a.** To ask (an amount) as a price: *The shop charges ten dollars for a new watch battery.* **b.** To demand payment from (sbdy.): *The store will charge you for wrapping the gift.* **2.** To buy (sthg.) on credit and pay later: *We can charge school supplies to our account at the bookstore.* **3.** To attack (sbdy./sthg.) violently: *The lion charged the herd of zebras.* **4.** To accuse or blame (sbdy.): *The police charged the driver with speeding.* **5.** To fill or load (sthg.): *The last scene of the movie was charged with excitement.* **6.** To fill (sthg.) with an amount of electrical energy: *We can charge the car battery at the gas station.* —*intr.* **1.** [*for*] To demand or ask payment: *They didn't charge for the repair.* **2.** To rush forward, in or as if in an attack: *The children charged out of the room.* —*n.* **1.** [C; U] An amount asked as payment: *There is no charge for this delivery.* **2.** [U] Care; supervision; control: *The scientist had charge of the laboratory.* See Synonyms at **care. 3.** [C] A person or thing for which one is responsible: *The baby sitter took her charges to the park.* **4.** [C] An accusation, especially one made formally, as in a legal case: *The defendant was found not guilty of the charges.* **5.** [C] A rushing, forceful attack: *the charge of a bull elephant.* **6.** [C] The amount of electrical energy contained in an object, a particle, or a region of space. A charge is positive if the object or space contains fewer electrons than protons. A charge is negative if the object or space contains more electrons than protons. **7.** [C] *Informal.* A feeling of excitement; a thrill: *They got a real*

ă-**cat**; ā-**pay**; âr-**care**; ä-**father**; ĕ-**get**; ē-**be**; ĭ-**sit**; ī-**nice**; îr-**here**; ŏ-**got**; ō-**go**; ô-**saw**; oi-**boy**; ou-**out**; o͝o-**took**; o͞o-**boot**; ŭ-**cut**; ûr-**word**; th-**thin**; *th*-**this**; hw-**when**; zh-**vision**; ə-**about**; N-French **bon**

charge from seeing the Grand Canyon. ◆ **in charge.** [*of*] In a position of authority or control: *The manager of the store is in charge. The recreation department is in charge of the annual fireworks display.*

charge account *n.* An arrangement of credit, as with a store, in which a customer receives goods or services before paying for them.

charge card *n.* A credit card.

char•i•ot (chăr′ē ət) *n.* A horse-drawn two-wheeled vehicle used in ancient times in battle, races, and processions.

cha•ris•ma (kə rĭz′mə) *n.* [U] A special quality of individuals who show an exceptional ability to lead and win the devotion of large numbers of people: *Some leaders have great charisma.* — **char′is•mat′ic** (kăr′ĭz-măt′ ĭk) *adj.*

char•i•ta•ble (chăr′ĭ tə bəl) *adj.* **1.** Showing love or good will; full of kindness: *a kind and charitable friend.* **2.** Generous in giving money or help to the needy: *a charitable impulse.* **3.** Tolerant or merciful in judging others: *Most parents are charitable about their children's mistakes.* **4.** Of or for helping the needy: *We made a donation to a charitable organization.* — **char′i•ta•ble•ness** *n.* [U] — **char′i•ta•bly** *adv.*

char•i•ty (chăr′ĭ tē) *n., pl.* **chari•ties. 1.** [U] Goodwill or kind feelings toward others: *She is well known for her charity and kindness.* **2.** [U] Tolerance and mercy in judging others: *President Lincoln urged charity for all after the Civil War.* **3.** [U] Help or relief to the needy: *raising money for charity.* **4.** [C] An institution or a fund established to help the needy: *a ten-dollar donation to a charity.*

char•la•tan (shär′lə tən) *n.* A person who deceives others by falsely claiming to have expert knowledge or skill; a quack: *Charlatans make their living off unsuspecting and ignorant people.*

charm (chärm) *n.* **1.** [U] The power or ability to please or delight; appeal: *Some people just don't have charm.* **2.** [C] A quality or manner that pleases or attracts: *Her wit is one of her many charms.* **3.** [C] A saying, action, or thing supposed to have magical power, as in warding off evil: *He carries a four-leaf clover as a good-luck charm.* **4.** [C] A small ornament worn hanging on a bracelet or chain. — *tr.v.* **1.** To please (sbdy.) greatly; delight: *The young piano player charmed the audience.* **2.** To affect (sbdy.) by or as if by magic; bewitch: *The children's laughter charmed us into playing the game again.* ◆ **work like a charm.** To bring very successful results: *Asking for a raise worked like a charm.* — **charm′er** *n.*

charm•ing (chär′mĭng) *adj.* Delightful; very pleasing: *a charming person; charming manners.* — **charm′ing•ly** *adv.*

chart (chärt) *n.* **1.** Something written or drawn, as a table or graph, that presents information in an organized, easily viewed form: *a chart showing rainfall for the last ten years.* **2.** A map showing coastlines, water depths, or other information of use to ships. — *tr.v.* **1.** To show or record (sthg.) on a chart; make a chart of: *chart the daily changes in temperature.* **2.** To plan (sthg.) in detail: *I hope to chart a course for success.*

char•ter (chär′tər) *n.* **1.** A written document from a ruler, government, or other group, giving certain rights to a person, a corporation, or an entire people: *The Magna Carta is a famous charter granted by King John of England in 1215 to his noblemen.* **2.** A document, such as a constitution, stating the principles, function, and form of a governing body or organization: *The United Nations is governed by a charter.* **3.** The hiring or renting of a bus, an aircraft, a boat, or another vehicle for a special use: *We arranged the charter of a fishing boat for our vacation.* — *tr.v.* **1.** To grant a charter to (sbdy.); establish by charter: *Congress chartered the bank for 20 years.* **2.** To hire or rent (sthg.) by charter: *The travel club chartered a plane.* — **char′ter•er** *n.*

char•treuse (shär trōōz′ *or* shär trōōs′) *n.* [U] A light yellowish green color. — *adj.* Light yellowish green.

chase (chās) *v.* **chased, chas•ing, chas•es.** — *tr.* **1.** To follow quickly and try to catch (sbdy./sthg.); pursue: *Our dog chased the cat.* **2.** [*from*] To force (sbdy./sthg.) to leave: *chased the rabbits from the garden.* — *intr.* **1.** [*after*] To follow and try to catch: *chase after a loose dog.* **2.** *Informal.* To hurry; rush: *chasing about doing last-minute errands.* — *n.* **1.** [C] The act of chasing; rapid pursuit: *The police arrested the driver after a short chase.* **2. the chase.** [U] The hunting of animals as a sport: *Some people enjoy the chase.*

chas•er (chā′sər) *n.* **1.** A person or thing that chases or pursues. **2.** *Informal.* A drink of water, beer, or other liquid taken after a drink of hard liquor.

chasm (kăz′əm) *n.* **1.** A deep crack or opening in the surface of the earth; a gorge. **2.** A large gap, such as that caused by a difference of opinion or attitude: *After their argument, a chasm developed between the two friends.*

chas•sis (shăs′ē *or* chăs′ē) *n., pl.* **chas•sis** (shăs′ēz *or* chăs′ēz). The frame of an automotive vehicle that supports the body and includes the motor, gears, axles, and wheels.

chaste (chāst) *adj.* **chast•er, chast•est. 1.** Morally pure in thought and conduct; modest: *a chaste life.* **2.** Abstaining from sex. — **chaste′ly** *adv.* — **chaste′ness** *n.* [U]

chas•ten (chā′sən) *tr.v. Formal.* To discipline or correct (sbdy./sthg.) by punishment: *She chastened her dog for not coming when she called.*

chas·tened (chā′sənd) *adj.* Feeling meek or subdued, especially after being criticized or disciplined: *The chastened child calmed down and behaved well.*

chas·tise (chăs tīz′ *or* chăs′tīz′) *tr.v.* **chas·tised, chas·tis·ing, chas·tis·es.** *Formal.* To punish or criticize (sbdy.) severely for misbehavior or wrongdoing: *We were chastised for being late to work.* —**chas·tise′-ment** *n.* [U] —**chas·tis′er** *n.*

chas·ti·ty (chăs′tǐ tē) *n.* [U] *Formal.* The condition or quality of being chaste or pure: *Nuns and monks agree to a life of chastity.*

chat (chăt) *intr.v.* **chat·ted, chat·ting, chats.** To talk in a relaxed, friendly, informal manner: *chat with friends.* —*n.* A relaxed, friendly, informal talk: *I've had several nice chats with my neighbor.*

chat·ter (chăt′ər) *intr.v.* **1.** To make short rapid sounds that resemble speech, as some animals and birds do: *Monkeys chattered in the trees.* **2.** To talk rapidly and at length about sthg. unimportant; jabber: *He chattered endlessly about this and that until we finally had to leave.* **3.** To make a rapid series of rattling or clicking noises: *My teeth chattered with cold.* —*n.* [U] **1.** Idle talk about unimportant matters: *All of that gossip is just neighborhood chatter.* **2.** The sharp rapid sounds made by some birds and animals: *the chatter of an angry squirrel.* **3.** A series of quick rattling or clicking sounds: *the chatter of typewriters.*

chat·ter·box (chăt′ər bŏks′) *n. Informal.* A person who seems to talk all the time: *Her little brother is an annoying chatterbox.*

chat·ty (chăt′ē) *adj.* **chat·ti·er, chat·ti·est. 1.** Often involved in informal conversation: *a chatty person full of gossip.* **2.** Having the tone or style of informal conversation: *a chatty newspaper column about movie celebrities.* —**chat′ti·ly** *adv.* —**chat′ti·ness** *n.* [U]

chauf·feur (shō′fər *or* shō fûr′) *n.* A person who is hired to drive an automobile. —*tr.v.* To serve as a driver for (sbdy.): *I spent the week chauffeuring visiting relatives to see the local sights.*

chau·vin·ism (shō′və nĭz′əm) *n.* [U] **1.** Extreme devotion to one's country or a cause: *Chauvinism is often an excuse to make war.* **2.** Unwarranted belief in the superiority of one's own group; prejudice: *male chauvinism.* —**chau′vin·ist** *n. & adj.* —**chau′vin·ist′ic** *adj.*

cheap (chēp) *adj.* **1.** Low in price; inexpensive or comparatively inexpensive: *Tomatoes are cheap and plentiful in the summer months.* **2.** Charging low prices: *a cheap restaurant.* **3.** Requiring little effort; easily

gotten: *a cheap victory.* **4.** Of little value or poor quality; inferior: *Cheap shoes wear out quickly.* **5.** Not spending or giving money generously; stingy: *a cheap boss who pays employees very little.* —*adv.* At a low price: *an old car that we bought cheap.* —**cheap′ly** *adv.* —**cheap′ness** *n.* [U]

HOMONYMS: cheap, cheep (sound of a bird).

---

cheap·en (chē′pən) *tr. & intr.v.* To make or become cheap or cheaper: *Rude behavior tends to cheapen one's reputation. Imports are expected to cheapen with the new trade agreement.*

cheap shot *n.* An unfair statement directed especially at a defenseless person or group: *The candidate took a cheap shot when he referred to his opponent's children.*

cheap·skate (chēp′skāt′) *n. Slang.* An insulting word for sbdy. thought to be stingy; a miser: *She's such a cheapskate; she always waits for someone else to pay for dinner.*

cheat (chēt) *v.* —*tr.* **1.** To deceive (sbdy.) by trickery: *The grocer cheated customers by selling old bread at full price.* **2.** To escape or get away from (sthg.) as if by a trick: *The daring mountain climbers cheated death.* —*intr.* To act dishonestly: *cheat to pass a test; cheat at cards.* —*n.* A person who cheats: *Laziness and greed will turn some people into cheats.* —**cheat′er** *n.*

check (chĕk) *v.* —*tr.* **1.** To test, examine, or make sure of (sthg.): *Check your answers after finishing the math problems.* **2.** To mark (sthg.) with a check: *Check each item on the list that is missing from the shelf.* **3.** To cause (sthg.) to stop suddenly: *A roadblock checked the flow of traffic.* **4.** To hold back or control (sthg.): *The angry driver checked a sudden urge to shout.* **5.** To place (sthg.) for temporary safekeeping or shipping: *They checked their baggage at the airport.* —*intr.* **1.** To make an examination; be sure sthg. is true or correct: *check in your pocket for your plane ticket; check with the teacher before leaving.* **2.** To agree in every point: *Our two lists checked exactly.* —*n.* **1.** [C] A careful look or study to see that sthg. is being done or working properly: *A check of the math homework showed several errors.* **2.** [U] The condition of being stopped or held back: *The dry weather kept the mosquitoes in check.* **3.** [C] A mark (√) made to show that sthg. has been noted, chosen, or is correct. **4.** [C] A written order to a bank to pay a certain amount from money held an account: *write a check to pay a bill.* **5.** [C] A ticket or slip of paper for identifying and claiming sthg.: *a baggage check.* **6.** [C] A bill at a restaurant. **7.** [C] A pattern of squares resembling a checkerboard: *a fabric of black and*

ă–cat; ā–pay; âr–care; ä–father; ĕ–get; ē–be; ĭ–sit; ī–nice; îr–here; ŏ–got; ō–go; ô–saw; oi–boy; ou–out; ōō–took; ōō–boot; ŭ–cut; ûr–word; th–thin; th–this; hw–when; zh–vision; ə–about; N–French bon

white checks. **8.** [U] In chess, the situation of the king when under direct attack by an opponent's piece. ♦ **check in.** *intr.v.* **1.** To register or sign in, as at a hotel: *check in at the airport before the flight.* **2.** To see or talk to sbdy. briefly: *The boss wants you to check in with her before you leave.* **check on.** *tr.v.* [insep.] To examine or look at (sbdy./sthg.) briefly: *The nurse checked on the patient.* **check out.** *intr.v.* **1.** To leave, as after paying a hotel bill: *Did you check out?* **2.** To be confirmed as true: *The suspect's story checks out.* —*tr.v.* [sep.] **1.a.** To take (sthg.) and pay the amount owed: *check out groceries at a supermarket.* **b.** To take (sthg.) and record what is being taken: *check books out from the library.* **2.** *Informal.* To look at (sbdy./sthg.): *checking out a new car.*

check•book (chĕk′bŏŏk′) *n.* A book containing blank checks, given by a bank to sbdy. who has a checking account.

checked (chĕkt) *adj.* Having a pattern of squares; checkered: *a checked shirt.*

check•er (chĕk′ər) *n.* **1.** A person or thing that checks, as for accuracy: *Our word processor has a checker for spelling.* **2.** A person who receives items for safekeeping or shipping: *a baggage checker.* **3.** A cashier in a supermarket. **4.a. checkers.** *(used with a singular verb).* A game played on a checkerboard by two players, each using 12 round, flat pieces of a different color. **b.** One of the pieces used in this game.

check•er•board (chĕk′ər bôrd′) *n.* A game board divided into 64 squares of alternating colors, on which the game of checkers is played.

check•ered (chĕk′ərd) *adj.* **1.** Marked with or divided into squares: *a checkered floor.* **2.** Full of many changes; varied: *a checkered career.*

check•ing account (chĕk′ĭng) *n.* A bank account from which payments may be made by writing checks against the amount on deposit.

check•list (chĕk′lĭst′) *n.* A list of items to be checked or remembered: *a checklist of phone calls to make.*

check•out (chĕk′out′) *n.* **1.** [C; U] The place in a supermarket where one pays: *I'll meet you at the checkout.* **2.** [U] The act of checking out, as at a supermarket, library, or hotel: *While you take care of checkout at the hotel's front desk, I'll get the car.* **3.** [C] A test or inspection, as of a machine, for working condition or accuracy: *We decided to give the used car a quick checkout before we bought it.*

check•point (chĕk′point′) *n.* A place where people on foot or in vehicles are stopped for inspection: *The police will set up several checkpoints.*

check•room (chĕk′rŏŏm′ *or* chĕk′rŏŏm′) *n.* A room where coats, packages, or baggage may be left temporarily.

check•up (chĕk′ŭp′) *n.* A thorough examination or inspection, as for health or general working condition: *regular medical checkups; an engine checkup.*

Ched•dar also **ched•dar** (chĕd′ər) *n.* [C; U] A firm, smooth, usually yellowish or orange-colored cheese: *I like mild cheddar, but my friend prefers sharp cheddar.*

cheek (chēk) *n.* **1.** The part of either side of the face below the eye and between the nose and ear. **2.** *Chiefly British.* Bold behavior; impudence: *have the cheek to tell one's boss what to do.*

cheek•bone (chēk′bōn′) *n.* A small bone on the side of the face just below the eye, forming the outermost point of the cheek.

cheek•y (chē′kē) *adj. Chiefly British.* **cheek•i•er, cheek•i•est.** Bold; impolite: *a cheeky response.* —**cheek′i•ness** *n.* [U]

cheep (chēp) *n.* A high-pitched chirp, like that of a young bird. —*intr.v.* To make such a sound.

HOMONYMS: cheep, cheap (inexpensive).

---

cheer (chîr) *v.* —*intr.* To shout in happiness, approval, encouragement, or enthusiasm: *The audience cheered and clapped.* —*tr.* To praise, encourage, or urge (sbdy./sthg.) by shouting: *The fans cheered the team's victory.* —*n.* **1.** [C] A shout of happiness, approval, encouragement, or enthusiasm: *The crowd gave a loud cheer for the winning team.* **2.** [C] A slogan or chant shouted in encouragement or approval, as for a school's team at a game. **3.** [U] Happiness; good spirits: *My grandparents are always full of cheer.* ♦ **cheer on.** *tr.v.* [sep.] To encourage or urge (sbdy.): *People watching the race cheered the tiring runner on.* **cheer up.** *intr.v.* To become cheerful: *In spite of my disappointment, I soon cheered up.* —*tr.v.* [sep.] To make (sbdy.) happier or more cheerful: *The good news cheered her up.*

cheer•ful (chîr′fəl) *adj.* **1.** In good spirits; happy: *Everyone was cheerful at breakfast.* See Synonyms at **glad. 2.** Producing a feeling of cheer; pleasant and bright: *a cozy, cheerful room.* **3.** Willing; good-humored: *cheerful acceptance of one's duty.* —**cheer′ful•ly** *adv.* —**cheer′ful•ness** *n.* [U]

cheer•lead•er (chîr′lē′dər) *n.* A person who leads the cheering of spectators, as at a football game.

cheer•less (chîr′lĭs) *adj.* Lacking cheer; gloomy and depressing: *a cheerless rainy day.* —**cheer′less•ly** *adv.* —**cheer′less•ness** *n.* [U]

cheer•y (chîr′ē) *adj.* **cheer•i•er, cheer•i•est.** Bright and cheerful: *a cheery smile; a cheery fire.* —**cheer′i•ly** *adv.* —**cheer′i•ness** *n.* [U]

cheese (chēz) *n.* [C; U] A food made from pressed curds of milk, often seasoned and aged.

cheese·burg·er (chēz'bûr'gər) *n.* A hamburger topped with melted cheese.

cheese·cake (chēz'kāk') *n.* [C; U] A dessert made with sweetened cream cheese or cottage cheese and often with various flavorings.

cheese·cloth (chēz'klôth' *or* chēz'klŏth') *n.* [C; U] A thin loosely woven cotton cloth, originally used for wrapping cheese.

chees·y (chē'zē) *adj.* **chees·i·er, chees·i·est. 1.** Containing or resembling cheese. **2.** *Informal.* Of poor quality; shoddy: *a cheap room with cheesy furniture.* —**chees'i·ness** *n.* [U]

chee·tah (chē'tə) *n.* A long-legged swift-running wild cat of Africa and southwest Asia that has tan fur with black spots.

chef (shĕf) *n.* A cook, especially the chief cook of a large kitchen staff, as in a restaurant.

chem. *abbr.* An abbreviation of: **1.** Chemical. **2.** Chemist. **3.** Chemistry.

chem·i·cal (kĕm'ĭ kəl) *adj.* **1.** Relating to chemistry: *a chemical discovery.* **2.** Used in or produced by means of chemistry: *a chemical symbol; a chemical change.* —*n.* A substance obtained by or used in a chemical process: *toxic chemicals.* —**chem'i·cal·ly** *adv.*

chem·ist (kĕm'ĭst) *n.* **1.** A scientist who specializes in chemistry. **2.** *Chiefly British.* A pharmacist.

chem·is·try (kĕm'ĭ strē) *n.* [U] **1.** The science that deals with the structure, properties, and reactions of the elements and the compounds they form. **2.** The chemical properties of a substance or a system of substances: *blood chemistry.*

che·mo·ther·a·py (kē'mō thĕr'ə pē) *n.* [U] The treatment, usually of cancer, by chemicals that have a specific poisonous effect on disease-producing organisms or malignant cells.

cheque (chĕk) *n. Chiefly British.* Variant of **check.**

cher·ish (chĕr'ĭsh) *tr.v.* **1.** To care for (sbdy./sthg.) gently and lovingly: *The children cherished the little kittens.* **2.** To regard (sbdy./sthg.) with appreciation; value highly: *Citizens of democratic countries cherish freedom.* See Synonyms at **appreciate.**

cher·ry (chĕr'ē) *n., pl.* **cher·ries. 1.** [C] Any of various small, rounded, fleshy fruits having a hard pit or stone and a smooth skin. Cherries range in color from yellow and bright red to a dark purple: *cherry pie.* **2.** [U] The wood of such a tree: *furniture made of cherry and maple.*

cher·ub (chĕr'əb) *n.* **1.** An angel, usually shown in pictures as a beautiful winged child with a chubby face. **2.** A sweet, pretty, or innocent-looking child. —**che·ru'bic** (chə-roo'bĭk) *adj.*

chess (chĕs) *n.* [U] A game played on a chessboard by two players, each starting with 16 pieces that are moved in various ways.

chess·board (chĕs'bôrd') *n.* A board with 64 squares in alternating colors, used in playing chess.

chest (chĕst) *n.* **1.** The front part of the body between the neck and the abdomen, enclosed by the ribs. **2.** A sturdy box with a lid, used especially for holding or storing things: *a tool chest.*

chest·nut (chĕs'nŭt') *n.* **1.** [C] A smooth, reddish brown, edible nut of a tree of northern regions: *We bought some roasted chestnuts.* **2.** [U] A reddish brown color. **3.** [C] A reddish brown horse. —*adj.* Reddish brown.

chest of drawers *n., pl.* **chests of drawers.** A piece of furniture with several drawers, used chiefly for keeping clothes; a bureau or dresser.

chew (choo) *v.* —*tr.* To bite and grind (sthg.) with the teeth: *chew food thoroughly.* —*intr.* To crush or grind sthg. with the teeth: *Don't chew so loudly.* —*n.* **1.** The act of chewing: *Puppies enjoy having a good chew on a bone.* **2.** Something held in the mouth and chewed: *a chew of tobacco.* —**chew'er** *n.*

chew·ing gum (choo'ĭng) *n.* [U] A sweet flavored gum for chewing.

chew·y (choo'ē) *adj.* **chew·i·er, chew·i·est.** Needing much chewing in order to swallow: *tough chewy meat.* —**chew'i·ness** *n.* [U]

chic (shēk) *adj.* **chic·er, chic·est.** Attractive and stylish; fashionable: *a chic dress.* —*n.* [U] Style and elegance in dress or manner: *She has a sense of chic.*

HOMONYMS: chic, sheik (Arab leader).

Chi·ca·na (chĭ kä'nə) *n.* A woman or girl in the United States who was born in Mexico or has Mexican ancestors. —**Chi·ca'na** *adj.*

chi·can·er·y (shĭ kā'nə rē *or* chĭ kā'nə rē) *n.* [U] *Formal.* Deception by trickery: *accusations of political chicanery.*

Chi·ca·no (chĭ kä'nō) *n., pl.* **Chi·ca·nos.** A person in the United States, especially a man or boy, who was born in Mexico or has Mexican ancestors. —**Chi·ca'no** *adj.*

chick (chĭk) *n.* **1.** A young chicken. **2.** The young of any bird. **3.** *Slang.* A term, considered offensive by some, for a woman.

chick·en (chĭk'ən) *n.* **1.** [C] The common farm bird raised for eggs or meat; a hen or rooster. **2.** [U] The meat of this bird. **3.** [C]

Slang. A person who is afraid or acts in a cowardly manner: *Only a chicken would not speak out against prejudice.* —*adj. Slang.* Afraid; cowardly. —*v.* ♦ **chicken out.** —*intr.v. Slang.* To lose one's nerve; act in a cowardly manner: *They chickened out at the last moment.*

chick·en·heart·ed (chĭk′ən här′tĭd) *adj.* Cowardly; timid: *a chicken-hearted lie.*

chick·en·pox or **chicken pox** (chĭk′ənpŏks′) *n.* [U] A contagious viral disease, mainly of young children, in which the skin breaks out in a rash and mild fever occurs.

chicken wire *n.* [U] A wire mesh used as light fencing, especially where chickens are kept.

chick·pea (chĭk′pē′) *n.* The round edible seed of a bushy plant related to the pea.

chide (chīd) *tr. & intr.v.* **chid·ed** or **chid** (chĭd), **chid·ing, chid·es.** To scold or reproach: *The director chided me for being late. Birds chided loudly from the trees.*

chief (chēf) *n.* A person with the highest rank or authority; a leader: *the chief of a Scottish clan; the chief of the fire department.* —*adj.* **1.** Highest in rank or authority: *The chief engineer is in charge of the power station.* **2.** Most important; main; principal: *What is the country's chief crop?*

Chief Executive *n.* The President of the United States.

Chief Executive Officer *n.* The highest-ranking person in a corporation.

Chief Financial Officer *n.* The top financial person in a corporation.

chief justice also **Chief Justice** *n.* A judge who presides over a court of several judges, as the United States Supreme Court.

chief·ly (chēf′lē) *adv.* **1.** Mainly; especially: *They went home early, chiefly to avoid the storm.* **2.** For the most part; mostly: *land used chiefly for farming.*

chief·tain (chēf′tən) *n.* The leader or head of a group, especially of a tribe or clan.

chif·fon (shĭ fŏn′ *or* shĭf′ŏn′) *n.* [U] A soft, sheer, light fabric of silk, nylon, or rayon, used for scarfs, veils, dresses, and blouses. —*adj.* **1.** Relating to or resembling chiffon. **2.** Made light and fluffy by the addition of beaten egg whites or gelatin: *lemon chiffon pie.*

chif·fo·nier (shĭf′ə nîr′) *n.* A narrow high chest of drawers, often with a mirror attached.

chig·ger (chĭg′ər) *n.* The tiny larva of any of various mites that clings to the skin of humans and animals, causing intense itching.

Chi·hua·hua (chĭ wä′wä) *n.* A tan dog with short hair and pointed ears, belonging to an ancient breed from Mexico. It is the smallest known dog.

child (chīld) *n., pl.* **chil·dren** (chĭl′drən). **1.** A young person between birth and physical maturity. **2.a.** A son or daughter; an offspring: *There are several children in that big family.* **b.** An infant; a baby: *a newborn child.*

c. An unborn baby; a fetus: *carrying a child.* **3.** An older person who behaves like a child; an immature person: *Don't be such a child!* **4.** A descendant: *children of Abraham.* **5.** A person or thing considered as the offspring of some condition, influence, or force: *a child of the 20th century.* ♦ **with child.** *Formal.* Pregnant.

child·bear·ing (chīld′bâr′ĭng) *n.* [U] Pregnancy and childbirth. —*adj.* Relating to childbirth: *a woman of childbearing age.*

child·birth (chīld′bûrth′) *n.* [U] The act or process of giving birth to a child.

child·hood (chīld′hŏŏd′) *n.* [C; U] The time or condition of being a child: *It's easy to make friends during childhood.*

child·ish (chīl′dĭsh) *adj.* **1.** Relating to or suitable for a child: *a high childish voice; childish games.* **2.** Immature; foolish or silly: *childish behavior.* —**child′ish·ly** *adv.* —**child′ish·ness** *n.* [U]

child·like (chīld′līk′) *adj.* Similar to or suitable for a child; innocent and simple: *childlike faith in others.*

child·proof (chīld′prŏŏf′) *adj.* **1.** Designed to resist opening or use by young children: *a childproof medicine bottle.* **2.** Made safe for young children: *Is the kitchen childproof?* —*tr.v.* To make (sthg.) childproof. *We childproofed the house when our daughter was small.*

chil·dren (chĭl′drən) *n.* Plural of **child.**

child's play (chīldz) *n.* [U] Something very easy to do: *These addition problems are mere child's play.*

chil·i (chĭl′ē) *n., pl.* **chil·ies. 1.** Also **chile. a.** [C] The very spicy sharp-tasting pod of any of several red peppers. **b.** [U] A seasoning made from the dried or ground pods of such a pepper. **2.** [U] A spicy dish made with chili, tomatoes, meat, and often beans: *He had a big bowl of chili for lunch.*

HOMONYMS: chili, chilly (cold).

chill (chĭl) *n.* **1.** A moderate coldness: *a chill in the fall air.* **2.** (*usually plural*). A feeling of coldness: *Chills and sneezing are signs of a cold.* **3.** Something that discourages enthusiasm: *The bad news put a chill on the celebration.* **4.** A feeling of fear: *We all felt a chill when the lights went out.* —*adj.* **1.** Moderately cold; chilly: *a chill north wind.* **2.** Not warm and friendly: *a chill greeting.* **3.** Discouraging: *My suggestions met with a chill response.* —*v.* —*tr.* **1.** To make (sbdy./sthg.) cold: *The icy wind chilled our faces.* **2.** To produce a feeling of cold or fear in (sbdy.): *The story chilled all who heard it.* **3.** To discourage (hope or desire): *Bad luck has chilled their enthusiasm.* —*intr.* To become cold: *Put the dessert in the refrigerator to chill.* —**chill′er** *n.*

chill•y (chĭl′ē) *adj.* **chill•i•er, chill•i•est. 1.** Cold enough to cause discomfort: *Damp chilly weather is common along the seacoast.* See Synonyms at **cold. 2.** Feeling cold; shivering. **3.** Not enthusiastic: *a chilly reaction to the new plan.* **4.** Unfriendly: *a chilly greeting.* —**chill′i•ness** *n.* [U]

HOMONYMS: chilly, chili (pepper).

chime (chīm) *n.* **1.** *(usually plural).* A set of bells tuned to different pitches and rung to make musical sounds. **2.** A single bell: *The chime in that clock strikes on the hour.* **3.** A musical sound produced by or as if by bells or chimes: *the chime of the doorbell.* —*v.* **chimed, chim•ing, chimes.** —*intr.* To ring, as a bell or set of chimes. —*tr.* **1.** To strike (a bell) to produce music: *chime the church bells in celebration of peace.* **2.** To announce (the time of day) by ringing bells: *The clock chimed three o'clock.* ◆ **chime in.** *intr.v.* To join in, as in song or conversation: *The audience chimed in on the chorus.*

chim•ney (chĭm′nē) *n., pl.* **chim•neys. 1.** A hollow, usually vertical structure for the passage of smoke and gases rising from a fireplace, stove, or furnace. **2.** The part of such a structure that rises above a roof.

chimp (chĭmp) *n. Informal.* A chimpanzee.

chim•pan•zee (chĭm′păn zē′ *or* chĭm păn′zē) *n.* A dark-haired African ape somewhat smaller than a gorilla, with a high degree of intelligence.

chin (chĭn) *n.* The front part of the face below the lips formed by the lower jaw and extending to the neck. ◆ **keep (one's) chin up.** To keep one's courage: *Keep your chin up; you'll get a job soon.*

chi•na (chī′nə) *n.* [U] **1.** A fine hard porcelain, made from a white clay, baked at high temperatures and often decorated with colored designs. **2.** Articles, such as dishes, vases, or figurines, made from this porcelain.

Chinese checkers (chī nēz′ *or* chī nēs′) *pl.n. (used with a singular or plural verb).* A game for two to six players in which marbles are moved from holes on one point of a star-shaped design on a board to the set of holes on the opposite point.

chink (chĭngk) *n.* **1.** A narrow crack or hole: *a chink in the brick wall.* **2.** A short clinking sound, as of metal striking together: *the chink of coins.* —*intr. & tr.v.* To make or cause to make such a sound: *Coins chinked in my purse. I chinked the coins in my pocket.*

chi•no (chē′nō) *n., pl.* **chi•nos. 1.** [U] A strong cotton cloth used chiefly for uniforms and sport clothes. **2. chinos.** Pants made of this material.

chintz (chĭnts) *n.* [C; U] A printed cotton fabric, usually of bright colors: *kitchen curtains made of chintz.*

chintz•y (chĭnt′sē) *adj.* **chintz•i•er, chintz•i•est.** Gaudy; cheap: *Don't buy that chintzy blouse.*

chin-up (chĭn′ŭp′) *n.* The act or exercise of pulling oneself up to the chin on an overhead bar: *She can do 50 chin-ups.*

chip (chĭp) *n.* **1.** A small piece cut or broken off; a fragment: *a chip of wood.* **2.** A dent or mark left when a small piece is broken off: *a chip in the cup.* **3.a.** A thin slice of food: *a potato chip.* **b. chips.** *Chiefly British.* French-fried potatoes: *fish and chips.* **4.** An electronic component used in building computers. **5.** A small disk used in gambling to represent money. —*v.* **chipped, chip•ping, chips.** —*tr.* **1.** To break off a small piece from (sthg.), as by hitting: *chip the edge of the glass.* **2.** To shape or carve (sthg.) by cutting or chopping: *I chipped my name in stone.* —*intr.* To become broken off: *These dishes chip if you are not careful.* ◆ **a chip off the old block.** A child that closely resembles one parent or the other. **chip in.** *intr.v.* To contribute money or labor: *How many people chipped in for the present?* **chip on (one's) shoulder.** A hostile attitude: *My cousin has had a chip on his shoulder since our argument.*

chip•munk (chĭp′mŭngk′) *n.* Any of several rodents of North America resembling a squirrel but smaller and with stripes on the back.

chipper (chĭp′ər) *adj.* Active; cheerful: *She's always chipper in the morning.*

chi•ro•prac•tic (kī′rə prăk′tĭk *or* kī′rə prăk′tĭk) *n.* [U] A method of treating diseases by manipulating the spinal column and other structures of the body, usually without the use of drugs or surgery. —**chi′ro•prac′tor** *n.*

chirp (chûrp) *n.* A short high-pitched sound, as that made by a small bird. —*intr.v.* To make such a sound: *The baby birds chirped noisily.*

chis•el (chĭz′əl) *n.* A metal tool with a sharp edge across the end of a thick blade, used to cut and shape stone, wood, or metal. —*v.* —*tr.* To shape (sthg.) with a chisel: *The sculptor chiseled the statue out of stone.* —*intr.* To use a chisel. ◆ **chisel (one) out of.** *Informal.* To cheat (sbdy.) of (sthg.): *He chiseled me out of 50 dollars.* —**chis′el•er** *n.*

chit•chat (chĭt′chăt′) *n.* [U] Casual conversation: *She doesn't have time for idle chitchat.* —*intr.v.* **chit•chat•ted, chit•chat•ting, chit•chats.** To engage in chitchat: *We chitchatted into the wee hours.*

chiv•al•rous (shĭv′əl rəs) *adj.* **1.** Brave, honorable, and courteous, especially toward women: *a chivalrous act.* **2.** Relating to the age of chivalry: *the chivalrous days of King Arthur.*

chiv·al·ry (shĭv′əl rē) *n.* [U] **1.** The qualities of the ideal knight, such as bravery, courtesy, and honor. **2.** The medieval institution of knighthood and its customs.

chive (chīv) *n.* **1.** A plant related to the onion, having long narrow leaves. **2. chives.** The onion-flavored leaves of this plant, used as seasoning.

chlo·ri·nate (klôr′ə nāt′) *tr.v.* **chlo·ri·nat·ed, chlo·ri·nat·ing, chlo·ri·nates.** To treat or combine (a substance) with chlorine, especially in order to kill bacteria in water: *The water in the school swimming pool is chlorinated.* —**chlo′ri·na′tion** *n.* [U]

chlo·rine (klôr′ēn′ *or* klôr′ĭn) *n.* [U] *Symbol* **Cl** A greenish yellow gaseous halogen element found chiefly in combination with sodium as common salt. Atomic number 17. See table at **element.**

chlo·ro·phyll also **chlo·ro·phyl** (klôr′ə-fĭl) *n.* [U] A green pigment composed of carbon, hydrogen, magnesium, nitrogen, and oxygen, found in green plants. Chlorophyll absorbs light that provides the energy used in photosynthesis to change carbon dioxide and water into carbohydrates.

chm. or **chmn** *abbr.* An abbreviation of chairman.

choc·o·late (chô′kə lĭt *or* chôk′lĭt *or* chŏk′-lĭt) *n.* **1.** [C; U] A food, especially candy, made from cacao seeds: *a bar of unsweetened chocolate; a box of chocolates.* **2.** [U] A sweetened drink made from this substance; cocoa: *hot chocolate.* **3.** [U] A brown to deep reddish brown color. —*adj.* **1.** Made of or flavored with chocolate: *a chocolate cake.* **2.** Deep brown or reddish brown.

choice (chois) *n.* **1.** [C] The act of choosing; selection: *Did price influence your choice?* **2.** [U] The power, right, or possibility to choose; option: *You leave me no choice in this matter.* **3.** [C] A person or thing chosen: *The customer's choices were roast beef, mashed potatoes, and peas.* **4.** [C] A variety from which to choose: *The cafeteria has a wide choice of sandwiches.* **5.** [C] An alternative: *What are my choices in this situation?* —*adj.* **choic·er, choic·est. 1.** Of fine quality; very good: *choice vegetables.* **2.** Selected with care: *reply in a few choice words.*

You pick the movie; I have no preference. **Selection** suggests a variety of things or persons to choose from: *Make your selection from the items on the menu.*

choir (kwīr) *n.* An organized group of singers, especially one that performs regularly in a church: *a children's choir; a cathedral choir.*

choke (chōk) *v.* **choked, chok·ing, chokes.** —*tr.* **1.** To stop the breathing of (a person or an animal) by squeezing or blocking the air passage in the throat. **2.** To slow down the movement or growth of (sthg.): *Weeds are choking the garden.* **3.** To stop (sthg.) as if by strangling: *Sobs choked her words.* —*intr.* To be unable to breathe, swallow, or speak normally, as when the throat is blocked: *choke on a piece of bread.* —*n.* **1.** The act or sound of choking. **2.** A device that controls the amount of air taken in by a gasoline engine. ♦ **choke back.** *tr.v.* [sep.] To hold back (sthg.); control: *choke back tears.* **choke off.** *tr.v.* [sep.] To put an end to (sthg.); stop: *Closing the train station would choke off business in the area.* **choke up.** *intr.v.* **1.** To be unable to speak because of strong emotion: *I choke up when I hear that old song.* **2.** To be unable to perform: *The actor choked up and had to leave the stage.* —*tr.v.* [sep.] **1.** To block or fill (sthg.); clog: *Scraps of food have choked the drain out again.* **2.** To overwhelm (sbdy.) with emotion: *That story always chokes me up.*

chok·er (chō′kər) *n.* **1.** A person or thing that chokes: *Some dogs are trained with collars that are chokers.* **2.** A short necklace that fits closely around the throat: *She bought a new pearl choker.*

chol·er·a (kŏl′ər ə) *n.* [U] A serious, often fatal disease of the intestines that is infectious and often epidemic.

cho·les·ter·ol (kə lĕs′tə rôl′) *n.* [U] A white fatty substance that is important in metabolism and hormone production and is found in many animal and plant tissues.

chomp (chŏmp) *v.* —*tr.* To chew or bite on (sthg.) noisily: *a horse chomping oats.* —*intr.* [on] To chew or bite noisily on sthg.: *chomping on a carrot.*

choose (chōōz) *v.* **chose** (chōz), **cho·sen** (chō′zən), **choos·ing, choos·es.** —*tr.* **1.** To select (sbdy./sthg.) from a greater number; pick out: *choose a book in the library.* **2.** To decide (sthg.); prefer: *choose to walk to work; choose to work at night.* —*intr.* To make a choice; select: *They had to choose for themselves.* —**choos′er** *n.*

choos·y also **choos·ey** (chōō′zē) *adj.* **choos·i·er, choos·i·est.** Very careful in choosing: *She's choosy about the film she uses in her camera.*

chop (chŏp) *v.* **chopped, chop·ping, chops.** —*tr.* **1.** To cut (sthg.) by striking with a heavy sharp tool, such as an ax: *chop wood.* **2.** To cut up (sthg.) into small pieces: *chop onions.* **3.** To cut (sthg.) short: reduce: *chop a report that is too long.* —*intr.* To make heavy cutting strokes: *chop away at a block of ice.* —*n.* **1.** A quick short cutting stroke: *A chop of the ax split the wood.* **2.** A small cut of meat that usually contains a bone: *My family likes pork chops.*

chop•per (chŏp′ər) *n.* **1.** *Informal.* A helicopter. **2.** A person or thing that chops: *a food chopper.*

chop•py (chŏp′ē) *adj.* **chop•pi•er, chop•pi•est. 1.** Full of short irregular waves: *choppy seas.* **2.** Not smooth; jerky: *choppy writing.* —**chop′pi•ness** *n.* [U]

chops (chŏps) *pl.n. Slang.* The jaws or cheeks: *The dog licked its chops.*

chop•sticks (chŏp′stĭks′) *pl.n.* A pair of slender sticks usually made of wood or plastic and used as eating utensils in eastern Asia and in restaurants serving Asian food.

cho•ral (kôr′əl) *adj.* For or sung by a chorus or choir: *a choral group.*

cho•rale also **cho•ral** (kə răl′) *n.* A hymn melody sung in unison or harmonized for the organ.

HOMONYMS: chorale, corral (fenced-in area).

chord¹ (kôrd) *n.* A combination of three or more musical tones sounded at the same time. —**chord′al** *adj.*

HOMONYMS: chord (musical tones, line segment), **cord** (string).

chord² (kôrd) *n.* A line segment whose end points lie on a curve or on the circumference of a circle.

chore (chôr) *n.* **1.** A routine or minor task: *Feeding the cat is a daily chore.* See Synonyms at **task. 2.** An unpleasant task: *Taking out the garbage is a chore that I hate doing.*

cho•re•o•graph (kôr′ē ə grăf′) *v.* —*tr.* To create the dance for (a ballet or other stage work.) —*intr.* To engage in the art of creating ballets or other dances. —**cho′re•o′graph•er** (kôr′ē ŏg′rə fər) *n.* —**cho′re•og′ra•phy** (kôr′ē ŏg′rə fē) *n.* [U]

chor•tle (chôr′tl) *n.* A happy, low laugh. —*intr.v.* **chor•tled, chor•tling, chor•tles.** To laugh in a happy manner: *The baby chortled in her crib.*

cho•rus (kôr′əs) *n.* **1.** A group of singers who perform together. **2.** A musical composition or a part of one that is written for such a group. **3.** A group of people who speak or sing a part in a play all at the same time. **4.** Singers and dancers who play a supporting role in a stage production. **5.** A section of music that is repeated after each verse of a song: *Join in on the chorus.* ◆ **in chorus.** All together: *The group responded to the suggestion in chorus.*

chose (chōz) *v.* Past tense of **choose.**

cho•sen (chō′zən) *v.* Past participle of **choose.** —*adj.* Selected from or preferred above others: *the chosen few.*

chow (chou) *n. Slang.* Food: *Let's grab some chow before the restaurants close.* ◆ **chow down.** *tr.v.* [sep.] *Slang.* To eat (sthg.) very quickly: *He chowed down his lunch.*

chow•der (chou′dər) *n.* [C; U] A thick soup or stew containing vegetables and often seafood, usually in a milk or tomato base: *clam chowder.*

chris•ten (krĭs′ən) *tr.v.* **1.** To baptize and give a name to (sbdy.) in a Christian church. **2.** To name (sthg.), especially at a ceremony: *christen a ship.* **3.** *Informal.* To use (sthg.) for the first time: *christen a new car with a ride around the block.*

chris•ten•ing (krĭs′ə nĭng) *n.* [C; U] The Christian ceremony of baptizing and naming a child.

Chris•tian (krĭs′chən) *adj.* **1.** Related to Jesus Christ or the religion based on his teachings: *a Christian religion.* **2.** Showing qualities characteristic of Jesus, such as gentleness or humility: *a Christian act of forgiveness.* —*n.* A person who follows a Christian religion.

Chris•ti•an•i•ty (krĭs′chē ăn′ĭ tē *or* krĭs′-tē ăn′ĭ tē) *n.* [U] The Christian religion, based on the life and teachings of Jesus.

Christ•mas (krĭs′məs) *n.* **1.** [C] December 25, celebrated by Christians in memory of the birth of Jesus. **2.** [U] Christmastime.

Christmas Eve *n.* The day and evening before Christmas.

Christ•mas•time (krĭs′məs tīm′) *n.* [U] The season of Christmas.

Christmas tree *n.* A natural or artificial evergreen tree decorated with ornaments and lights at Christmastime.

chrome (krōm) *n.* [U] **1.** A shiny, hard metal; chromium. **2.** A material plated with chromium or one of its alloys: *The chrome on the car shines in the sun.*

chro•mi•um (krō′mē əm) *n.* [U] *Symbol* **Cr** A grayish, hard, brittle metallic element that does not rust or become dull easily. Chromium is used in electroplating other metals, in making stainless steel, in making dyes and paints, and in photography. Atomic number 24. See table at **element.**

chro•mo•some (krō′mə sōm′) *n.* A small body in all living cells, contained in the nucleus and composed mainly of DNA. It carries the genes that determine heredity. —**chro′mo•so′mal** (krō′mə sō′məl) *adj.*

chron·ic (krŏn'ĭk) *adj.* **1.** Lasting for a long time or often repeated: *chronic bronchitis.* **2.** Having a habit a long time: *He is a chronic gossip.* —**chron'i·cal·ly** *adv.*

chron·i·cle (krŏn'ĭ kəl) *n.* A record of historical events arranged in the order in which they happened. —*tr.v.* **chron·i·cled, chron·i·cling, chron·i·cles.** To record (sthg.), as in a chronicle: *Explorers carefully chronicle the events of their trips.* —**chron'i·cler** *n.*

chron·o·log·i·cal (krŏn'ə lŏj'ĭ kəl) *adj.* Arranged in order of the time in which the events took place: *Keep all historical facts in chronological order.* —**chron'o·log'i·cal·ly** *adv.*

chro·nol·o·gy (krə nŏl'ə jē) *n., pl.* **chro·nol·o·gies. 1.** [U] The science that deals with determining the dates and order of events. **2.** [C] A chronological list or table: *a detailed chronology of modern history.* **3.** [U] The arrangement of events in time: *the chronology of her recovery from cancer.*

chro·nom·e·ter (krə nŏm'ĭ tər) *n.* A very accurate clock or other timepiece, especially as used in scientific experiments, navigation, or astronomical observations.

chry·san·the·mum (krĭ săn'thə məm) *n.* A plant that has many cultivated forms with showy, round, colored flowers.

chub·by (chŭb'ē) *adj.* **chub·bi·er, chub·bi·est.** Round and plump: *The baby has a chubby face.* —**chub'bi·ness** *n.* [U]

chuck[1] (chŭk) *tr.v.* **1.** To pat (a person or animal) affectionately under the chin. **2.** *Informal.* **a.** To throw or toss (sthg.): *chuck a stone in the pond.* **b.** To throw (sthg.) out: *chuck an old shoe; chuck a poor plan.* —*n.* **1.** An affectionate pat, especially under the chin. **2.** *Informal.* A toss or throw.

chuck[2] (chŭk) *n.* **1.** [U] A cut of beef extending from the neck to the ribs. **2.** [C] In a machine such as a drill or lathe, a rotating clamp that holds either a tool or the work.

chuck·le (chŭk'əl) *intr.v.* **chuck·led, chuck·ling, chuck·les.** To laugh quietly: *He chuckled to himself.* —*n.* A quiet laugh of amusement or satisfaction: *The crowd reacted to the joke with polite chuckles.*

chug (chŭg) *n.* A dull explosive sound made by or as if by an engine working hard. —*v.* **chugged, chug·ging, chugs.** —*tr. Informal.* To drink (sthg.) rapidly and with chugging sounds: *He chugged his beer.* —*intr.* **1.** To make chugging sounds: *The old truck's motor chugged under the hood.* **2.** To move making such sounds: *The little train chugged up the mountain.*

chum (chŭm) *n.* A close friend or companion; a pal. —*v.* **chummed, chum·ming, chums.** ◆ **chum around.** *intr.v.* To be on terms of close friendship: *That group of kids chums around a lot after school.*

chum·my (chŭm'ē) *adj.* **chum·mi·er,**

chum·mi·est. Friendly: *They have been chummy with each other for years.*

chump (chŭmp) *n. Slang.* A foolish or stupid person: *She felt like a chump for believing him.*

chunk (chŭngk) *n.* **1.** A thick piece of sthg.: *a chunk of ice.* **2.** A large portion or amount of sthg.: *They spent a chunk of their free time at the museum.*

chunk·y (chŭng'kē) *adj.* **chunk·i·er, chunk·i·est. 1.** Short, strong, and somewhat fat; stocky: *a chunky dog.* **2.** Containing small thick pieces: *chunky soup.* —**chunk'i·ness** *n.* [U]

church (chûrch) *n.* **1.** [C] A building for religious services, especially Christian worship. **2.** [U] The members who attend a particular Christian church: *Her church holds a children's fair each spring.*

church·go·er (chûrch'gō'ər) *n.* A person who attends church services.

churl·ish (chûr'lĭsh) *adj.* Rude; surly: *The criminal's churlish answer offended the judge.* —**churl'ish·ly** *adv.* —**churl'ish·ness** *n.* [U]

churn (chûrn) *n.* A container in which cream is stirred or beaten to make butter. —*v.* —*tr.* **1.** To move or swirl (sthg.) about violently: *Wind churned the leaves into piles.* **2.** To stir or beat (cream) to make butter. —*intr.* **1.** To stir or move violently: *Waves churned in the storm. My stomach was churning with nerves.* **2.** To make butter in a churn.

chute (shoot) *n.* **1.** A vertical or inclined passage down which things can be dropped or slid: *a laundry chute.* **2.** *Informal.* A parachute.

HOMONYMS: chute, shoot (fire a weapon).

---

chut·ney (chŭt'nē) *n.* [C; U] A spicy relish made of fruit and herbs: *mango chutney.*

chutz·pah (кно̄ot'spə *or* ho̅ot'spə) *n.* [U] *Informal.* Shameless boldness; nerve: *It took chutzpah to ask the teacher for a better grade.*

CIA *also* **C.I.A.** *abbr.* An abbreviation of Central Intelligence Agency.

—cide *suff.* A suffix that means: **1.** A killer of: *insecticide.* **2.** An act of killing: *suicide.*

ci·der (sī'dər) *n.* [U] The juice pressed from apples, used as a beverage or to produce vinegar.

ci·gar (sĭ gär') *n.* A large, tight roll of tobacco leaves prepared for smoking: *Cuba is famous for its fine cigars.*

cig·a·rette (sĭg'ə rĕt' *or* sĭg'ə rĕt') *n.* A small roll of finely cut tobacco enclosed in a wrapper of thin paper for smoking.

cinch (sĭnch) *n.* **1.** A type of belt that encircles a horse's body and is used for holding a saddle or pack. **2.** *Informal.* Something easy: *Riding a bike is a cinch when you know how.* —*tr.v.* **1.** To tighten the cinch on (a horse). **2.** *Informal.* To make (sthg.) certain: *That cinches it; I'm not going with you.*

cin·der (sĭn'dər) *n.* **1.** A burned or partly burned material, such as coal or wood. **2. cinders.** Ashes: *The house was reduced to cinders by the fire.*

cinder block or **cin·der·block** (sĭn'dər-blŏk') *n.* A large, gray hollow concrete block made with coal cinders and used in building.

cin·e·ma (sĭn'ə mə) *n.* **1.** [C] A movie theater. **2.** [U] The movie industry. —**cin'e·mat'ic** (sĭn'ə măt'ĭk) *adj.*

cin·e·ma·tog·ra·phy (sĭn'ə mə tŏg'rə-fē) *n.* [U] The art or technique of movie photography. —**cin'e·ma·tog'ra·pher** *n.*

cin·na·mon (sĭn'ə mən) *n.* [U] A reddish brown spice made from the dried and often ground bark of certain tropical Asian trees. —*adj.* Having a cinnamon color.

ci·pher (sī'fər) *n.* **1.** [C] The numerical symbol 0 representing zero. **2.** [U] A system of writing in code: *The secret information was sent in cipher.* —*tr.v.* To put (a message) into a code.

cir·ca (sûr'kə) *prep. Formal. (used with dates).* About: *a house built circa 1790.*

cir·ca·di·an (sər kā'dē ən) *adj.* Functioning or recurring in cycles of 24 hours: *sleep and wakeful periods in the human circadian rhythm.*

cir·cle (sûr'kəl) *n.*
1. A closed curve that has all of its points at the same distance from the center. **2.** A group of people sharing common interests or activities: *a doctor well known in scientific circles.* —*v.* **cir·cled, cir·cling, cir·cles.** —*tr.* **1.** To draw or form a circle around (sthg.): *Circle the right answer.* **2.** To move or travel in a circle around (sthg.): *A helicopter circled the city.* —*intr.* To move in a circle: *The eagle circled overhead.*

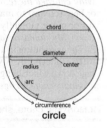

circle

circle graph *n.* A pie chart.

cir·cuit (sûr'kĭt) *n.* **1.** A path that forms a circle around sthg.: *the moon's circuit around the earth.* **2.** A closed path through which an electric current flows: *There are several appliances on the circuit in the kitchen.* **3.** A system of electrically connected parts or devices: *Microchips contain all the circuits for this computer.* **4.** A regular route followed from place to place: *a salesperson on the West Coast circuit.* **5.** An association of teams, clubs, or arenas of competition: *the professional tennis circuit.*

circuit board *n.* An insulated board on which circuits and electronic components are mounted.

circuit breaker *n.* A switch that automatic-

ally interrupts the flow of an electric current if the current becomes too strong.

cir·cu·i·tous (sər kyōō'ĭ təs) *adj.* Not direct; roundabout: *take a circuitous route to the store; a confusing and circuitous argument.* —**cir·cu'i·tous·ly** *adv.* —**cir·cu'i·tous·ness** *n.* [U]

cir·cuit·ry (sûr'kĭ trē) *n.* [U] **1.** The plan for an electric circuit. **2.** Electric circuits considered as a group: *The circuitry of television sets is complicated.*

cir·cu·lar (sûr'kyə lər) *adj.* **1.** Relating to or shaped like a circle: *Most coins are circular pieces of metal.* **2.** Forming or moving in a circle: *circular motion.* —*n.* A printed advertisement or notice for public distribution: *The newspaper contained many advertising circulars.* —**cir'cu·lar·ly** *adv.*

cir·cu·late (sûr'kyə lāt') *v.* **cir·cu·lat·ed, cir·cu·lat·ing, cir·cu·lates.** —*intr.* **1.** To move or flow in a closed path: *Blood circulates through the body.* **2.** To move or flow freely: *The fan helps the air circulate.* **3.** To spread widely among persons or places: *Rumors tend to circulate quickly.* —*tr.* **1.** To cause (sthg.) to move or flow: *The heart circulates blood throughout the body.* **2.** To spread or distribute (sthg.): *That opinion has been circulated widely in public discussion.*

cir·cu·la·tion (sûr'kyə lā'shən) *n.* **1.** [U] **a.** The act or process of circulating: *Opening the window will help the circulation of air.* **b.** The passage of sthg., such as money or news, from person to person or from place to place: *There aren't many two-dollar bills in circulation in the United States.* **2.** [U] The flow of the blood from the heart through the arteries and veins back to the heart: *a person with poor circulation.* **3.** [C; U] The distribution of printed matter, such as newspapers and magazines: *This popular magazine has a wide circulation.*

cir·cu·la·to·ry (sûr'kyə lə tôr'ē) *adj.* **1.** Of or involving circulation. **2.** Relating to the circulatory system: *The veins are sometimes damaged by circulatory disease.*

circulatory system *n.* The heart, blood vessels, and lymphatic system of the body.

circum— *pref.* A prefix that means around or about: *circumnavigate.*

cir·cum·cise (sûr'kəm sīz') *tr.v.* **cir·cum·cised, cir·cum·cis·ing, cir·cum·cis·es.** To remove the foreskin of the penis of (a male). —**cir'cum·ci'sion** (sûr'kəm sĭzh'ən) *n.* [C; U]

cir·cum·fer·ence (sər kŭm'fər əns) *n.* [C; U] **1.** The boundary of a circle. **2.** The boundary line of an area or object: *The circumference of the moon is about 6,800 miles.*

cir·cum·nav·i·gate (sûr'kəm năv'ĭ gāt') *tr.v.* **cir·cum·nav·i·gat·ed, cir·cum·nav·**

i·gat·ing, cir·cum·nav·i·gates. To sail completely around (the earth): *Sir Francis Drake was the first Englishman to circumnavigate the earth.* —**cir′cum·nav′i·ga′tion** *n.* [C; U]

cir·cum·scribe (sûr′kəm skrīb′) *tr.v.* **cir· cum·scribed, cir·cum·scrib·ing, cir·cum· scribes. 1.** To enclose (sthg.) within a line or surface: *circumscribe the number on each page.* **2.** To limit (sthg.): *Their plans for the future were circumscribed by their lack of money.*

cir·cum·spect (sûr′kəm spĕkt′) *adj.* Careful of consequences; cautious: *The President must be circumspect about statements made to reporters.* —**cir′cum·spec′tion** *n.* [U] —**cir′cum·spect′ly** *adv.*

cir·cum·stance (sûr′kəm stăns′) *n.* **1.** *(usually plural).* A condition or an event connected with and usually affecting another event: *Snow and cold created circumstances that made the trip difficult.* **2.** A fact or an event: *We'll never know the circumstances of his death.* **3. circumstances.** Financial condition: *a wealthy family in comfortable circumstances.* ◆ **under no circumstances.** In no case; never: *Under no circumstances should you touch this wire.* **under the circumstances.** Given these conditions: *A storm was expected, so under the circumstances we left for home.* —**cir′cum·stan′- tial** (sûr′kəm **stăn′**shəl) *adj.*

circumstantial evidence *n.* [U] Evidence not directly related to the facts in a case, but describing facts or events from which one might draw a conclusion about the case.

cir·cum·vent (sûr′kəm vĕnt′) *tr.v. Formal.* To find a way to avoid or get around (sbdy./sthg.): *They tried to circumvent the law.* —**cir′cum·ven′tion** *n.* [U]

cir·cus (sûr′kəs) *n.* **1.** A traveling show with acrobats, clowns, and trained animals: *We went to the circus last night.* **2.** *Informal.* Something suggestive of a circus, as in activity or disorder: *Holidays are a circus in our house.*

cis·tern (sĭs′tərn) *n.* A large tank or reservoir for the collection and storage of rainwater.

ci·ta·tion (sī tā′shən) *n.* **1.** A reference or quotation: *a report full of citations from books and scholarly articles.* **2.** A summons to appear in court for some offense: *The police officer issued a citation to the speeding driver.* **3.** An official certificate for bravery.

cite (sīt) *tr.v.* **cit·ed, cit·ing, cites. 1.** To quote (sbdy./sthg.) as an authority or example: *The professor cited several experts in astronomy.* **2.** To summon (sbdy.) before a court of law: *a driver cited for speeding.* **3.** To mention and commend (sbdy.) for doing sthg. important: *The firefighter was cited for bravery.*

HOMONYMS: cite, sight (vision), **site** (place).

cit·i·zen (sĭt′ĭ zən) *n.* **1.** A legal member of a given country: *citizens of African nations.* **2.** A resident of a city or town, especially one entitled to vote and enjoy other privileges there: *Citizens demanded an investigation of the mayor's finances.*

cit·i·zen·ship (sĭt′ĭ zən shĭp′) *n.* [U] The status of a citizen with its duties, rights, and privileges: *Citizenship has responsibilities as well as privileges.*

cit·ric acid (sĭt′rĭk) *n.* [U] A white odorless acid with a sour taste that has the formula $C_6H_8O_7$. It is found in oranges, grapefruit, lemons, and other fruit.

cit·rus (sĭt′rəs) *n.* **1.** [U] Any of various fruit with juicy flesh and a thick skin, as the orange, lemon, lime, or grapefruit. **2.** [C] An evergreen tree or shrub that bears such fruit. —*adj.* Relating to such trees or their fruit: *citrus groves.*

cit·y (sĭt′ē) *n., pl.* **cit·ies. 1.** A center of population, commerce, and culture: *Many people go into the city to work each day.* **2.** The people living in a city considered as a group: *The city voted for a new mayor.*

city hall *n.* **1.** [C] The building in which the offices of a city government are located. **2.** [U] City government officials as a group: *City hall released the budget for next year.*

civ·ic (sĭv′ĭk) *adj.* **1.** Relating to or belonging to a city: *Our town's Fourth of July parade is a major civic event.* **2.** Relating to citizenship: *It is a civic duty to vote in elections.*

civ·ics (sĭv′ĭks) *n.* [U] *(used with a singular verb).* The study of the purpose and function of local and national government and of the rights and duties of citizens.

civ·il (sĭv′əl) *adj.* **1.** Relating to a citizen or citizens: *voting and other civil responsibilities.* **2.** Relating to the general public rather than to military or religious matters: *a couple married in a civil ceremony at city hall.* **3.** Polite; courteous: *a civil reply.* See Synonyms at **polite.** —**civ′il·ly** *adv.*

civil engineer *n.* An engineer trained in the design and construction of bridges, roads, and dams. —**civil engineering** *n.* [U]

ci·vil·ian (sĭ vĭl′yən) *n.* A person not serving in the military. —*adj.* Relating to civilians: *civilian clothes; a civilian career.*

ci·vil·i·ty (sĭ vĭl′ĭ tē) *n., pl.* **ci·vil·i·ties. 1.** [U] Courteous behavior; politeness: *civility in daily life.* **2.** [C] An act or expression of politeness: *Saying "good morning" is a pleasant civility.*

civ·i·li·za·tion (sĭv′ə lĭ zā′shən) *n.* **1.** [U] A condition of human society in which there is a high level of development in the arts and sciences and political and social organization: *Warfare is not consistent with the idea of civilization.* **2.** [C] The kind of culture and society developed by a particular people or nation in some period of history: *ancient civilizations.* **3.** [U] *Informal.* Modern society with its conveniences: *We were glad to return to civilization after two weeks of camping.*

civ·i·lize (sĭv'ə līz') *tr.v.* **civ·i·lized, civ·i·liz·ing, civ·i·liz·es.** To bring (sbdy.) to a higher level of development in the arts, sciences, culture, and political organization.

civ·i·lized (sĭv'ə līzd') *adj.* **1.** Having or marked by a highly developed society and culture: *civilized life.* **2.** Polite or cultured: *a civilized person.*

civil rights *pl.n.* The rights belonging to an individual as a citizen, especially freedom from discrimination.

civil servant *n.* A person employed in the civil service.

civil service *n.* **1.** [C] All branches of government service that are not legislative, judicial, or military. **2.** [U] Those persons employed by the civil branches of the government: *Most people in the civil service in the United States government are hired after competitive examinations.*

civil war *n.* **1.** [C] A war between opposing groups of the same country. **2. Civil War.** [U] The war in the United States between the North and the South from 1861 to 1865.

Cl The symbol for the element **chlorine.**

clack (klăk) *intr. & tr.v.* To make or cause to make a sudden sharp sound, as that of objects struck together. —*n.* A sudden sharp sound: *the clack of a typewriter.*

clad (klăd) *v.* Formal. A past tense and a past participle of **clothe.**

claim (klām) *tr.v.* **1.** To demand or ask for (sthg.) as one's own: *claim luggage; claim a reward.* **2.** To declare (sthg.) to be true: *The witnesses claim that they saw the accident.* —*n.* **1.** A demand for sthg. as a right: *file an insurance claim for losses from the fire.* **2.** A statement of sthg. as fact: *an advertisement that makes false claims about certain products.* **3.** Something claimed, especially a piece of land claimed by a miner: *stake a claim.* ✦ **lay claim to.** To declare ownership of (sthg.): *The pioneers laid claim to the land along the river.*

clair·voy·ance (klâr voi'əns) *n.* [U] The supposed power to see objects or events that exist in other places or existed at other times. —**clair·voy'ant** *n. & adj.*

clam (klăm) *n.* A sea creature with a soft body covered by a double hinged shell. Clams burrow into sand or mud under fresh or salt water. The soft body of many kinds of clam is used as food. —*intr.v.* **clammed, clam·ming, clams.** To dig for clams: *clamming along the seashore at low tide.* ✦ **clam up.** *intr.v. Informal.* To refuse to talk; stop talking: *The suspect clammed up when the police started asking questions.*

clam·ber (klăm'bər) *intr.v.* To climb with difficulty, especially on all fours: *clamber up a rocky slope.*

clam·my (klăm'ē) *adj.* **clam·mi·er, clam·mi·est.** Unpleasantly damp, sticky, and usually cold: *clammy rain-soaked clothes; clammy feet in wet boots.* —**clam'mi·ness** *n.* [U]

clam·or (klăm'ər) *n.* [C; U] **1.** A loud, continuous, and usually confused noise: *the clamor of fans at a football game.* **2.** A strong or loud demand: *a public clamor for a new park.* —*intr.v.* To make a clamor: *The children clamored for more candy.* —**clam'or·ous** *adj.*

clamp (klămp) *n.* A tool for holding things together. —*tr.v.* To grip or fasten (sthg.) with or as if with a clamp: *glue and clamp two boards together.* ✦ **clamp down.** *intr.v.* [*on*] To become more strict; impose controls: *clamping down on polluters.*

clan (klăn) *n.* A group of families claiming a common ancestor: *the clans of Scotland.*

clan·des·tine (klăn děs'tĭn) *adj.* Done secretly or kept secret, often for some unlawful purpose: *a clandestine meeting.* —**clan·des'tine·ly** *adv.*

clang (klăng) *intr. & tr.v.* To make or cause to make a loud, metallic ringing sound: *Bells clanged to announce the new year.* —*n.* A clanging sound: *the clang of an alarm.*

clank (klăngk) *n.* A loud, metallic sound: *The gate closed with a clank.* —*intr.v.* To make a clank: *The old car clanked down the road.*

clap (klăp) *v.* **clapped, clap·ping, claps.** —*intr.* **1.** To strike the hands together with a sudden loud sound: *The audience clapped at the end of the song.* **2.** To make a sudden sharp sound: *The door clapped shut.* —*tr.* **1.** To strike (the hands) together with a sudden loud sound: *The crowd clapped their hands after she scored a goal.* **2.** To tap (sbdy.) with the open hand, as in hearty greeting: *clap a friend on the shoulder.* —*n.* **1.** The act or sound of clapping the hands. **2.** A loud, sharp, or explosive noise: *a clap of thunder.* **3.** A tap with an open hand: *a friendly clap on the back.*

clap·per (klăp'ər) *n.* **1.** The piece of metal inside a bell. **2.** A person or thing that claps.

clar·i·fy (klăr'ə fī') *v.* **clar·i·fied, clar·i·fy·ing, clar·i·fies.** —*tr.* **1.** To make (sthg.) clear or easier to understand: *a detailed explanation to clarify the instructions.* **2.** To make (a liquid, butter, or other substance) clear or pure by removing unwanted solid matter: *clarify butter by heating it; clarify vinegar by straining it.* —*intr.* To become clear: *We delayed our decision until the situation had clarified.* —**clar'i·fi·ca'tion** (klăr'ə fĭ kā'shən) *n.* [C; U]

clar·i·net (klăr'ə nĕt') *n.* A woodwind

instrument with a long cylindrical body, a flaring end, and a mouthpiece with a single reed. It is played by covering holes and pressing keys with the fingers. — **clar'i•net'ist** n.

clar•i•ty (klăr'ĭ tē) n. [U] The condition or quality of being clear: *clarity of speech.*

clash (klăsh) v. — intr. **1.** To strike or collide or come together violently: *The two armies clashed.* **2.** To be strongly out of harmony: *That pink shirt clashes with your green trousers.* — tr. To strike (two things) together with a loud harsh noise: *At the end of the march I clashed the cymbals together.* — n. **1.** A conflict or a disagreement: *a clash of different personalities; a clash between political parties.* **2.** A loud, harsh, metallic sound: *a clash of cymbals.*

clasp (klăsp) n. **1.** A fastener, such as a hook or buckle, used to hold two objects or parts together. **2.** A firm grasp or embrace: *He took my hand with a firm clasp.* — tr.v. **1.** To fasten (sthg.) with a clasp: *clasp a necklace.* **2.** To take hold of or embrace (sbdy./sthg.) tightly: *The child clasped his mother's hand.*

class (klăs) n. **1.** [C] A group of persons or things that are generally alike in some way: *a class of ships.* **2.** [C] A group of persons with approximately the same economic and social standing: *the working class.* **3.** [C] A group of plants or animals with similar characteristics: *All mammals belong to the same class of animals.* **4.** [C] **a.** A group of people graduated in the same year: *a reunion of the class of 1995.* **b.** A group of students who meet regularly to study the same subject: *Our biology class has 20 students.* **c.** The period during which such a group meets: *eat lunch before class; miss a class.* **5.** [C; U] **a.** A grade of mail: *A letter is sent first class and a magazine third class.* **b.** The quality of accommodations on a plane, train, or ship: *Going by business class on an airline costs more than tourist class.* **6.** [U] *Informal.* Great style or quality: *This restaurant has a lot of class.* — tr.v. To assign (sthg.) to a class; classify: *I would class this novel as a murder mystery.*

clas•sic (klăs'ĭk) adj. **1.** Considered an outstanding example of its kind: *a classic example of modern architecture.* **2.** Well-known and typical: *A runny nose is a classic sign of a cold.* **3.** Of ancient Greece and Rome or their literature or art; classical: *classic architecture.* — n. **1.** A work of literature, music, or art considered to be of the highest rank: *Many early rock 'n' roll recordings are now classics.* **2. classics.** The languages and literature of ancient Greece and Rome.

clas•si•cal (klăs'ĭ kəl) adj. **1.** Relating to the art, architecture, literature, and way of life of ancient cultures: *classical architecture; a classical scholar.* **2.** Relating to music that has developed over a long period of time in Europe: *a classical composer such*

as Mozart. **3.** Standard or traditional rather than new or experimental: *The calculator has replaced classical methods of doing arithmetic.* — **clas'si•cal•ly** adv.

clas•si•fi•ca•tion (klăs'ə fĭ kā'shən) n. **1.** [U] A grouping by categories: *The classification of books by subject is the work of a librarian.* **2.a.** [C] The result of classifying, as by category, name, or rating; a systematic arrangement: *chemical elements arranged in a classification by atomic weight.* **b.** [U] In botany and zoology, the systematic grouping of plants and animals by evolutionary or structural relationships.

clas•si•fied (klăs'ə fīd') adj. **1.** Arranged in classes; sorted; categorized: *You can find ads for jobs, cars, and pets in the classified section of a newspaper.* **2.** Available only to authorized persons; secret: *classified information.*

classified advertisement n. An advertisement, usually brief and in small type, printed in a newspaper along with others of the same category.

clas•si•fy (klăs'ə fī') tr.v. **clas•si•fied, clas•si•fy•ing, clas•si•fies. 1.** To arrange (sthg.) in categories or classes; categorize: *A librarian classifies books according to subject matter.* **2.** To designate (information) as available only to authorized persons: *classify military documents.* — **clas'si•fi'a•ble** adj. — **clas'si•fi'er** n.

class•mate (klăs'māt') n. A member of the same class in a school or college.

class•room (klăs'rōōm' or klăs'rŏŏm') n. A room in which classes are held in a school or college.

class•y (klăs'ē) adj. **class•i•er, class•i•est.** *Informal.* Stylish; elegant: *a classy hat.*

clat•ter (klăt'ər) v. — intr. **1.** To make a rattling sound: *The window shutters clattered as the storm approached.* **2.** To move with a rattling sound: *A rickety old wagon clattered down the road.* — tr. To cause (sthg.) to make a rattling sound: *The cook clattered pots and pans in the kitchen.* — n. **1.** [C] *(usually singular).* A rattling sound: *the clatter of dishes falling to the floor.* **2.** [U] Noisy talk: *the clatter of voices in the crowd.*

clause (klôz) n. **1.** In grammar, a group of words containing a subject and a verb phrase and forming part of a sentence. **2.** A separate part of a document containing some specific information: *The contract had several clauses, each outlining the duties of the partners.*

claus•tro•pho•bi•a (klô'strə fō'bē ə) n. [U] An abnormal fear of being in small or closed-in spaces: *Because of his claustrophobia, he always avoids elevators.*

claw (klô) n. **1.** A sharp curved nail on the toe of a mammal, reptile, or bird. **2.** A foot of an animal that has sharp hooked nails. **3.** A pincer, as of a lobster or crab, used for grasping. **4.** Something resembling a claw: *I pulled out* the nail with the *claw of the hammer.* —*tr. & intr.v.* To scratch, dig, tear, or hold with or as if with claws: *The cat clawed my hand. The dog clawed at the door to get in.*

clay (klā) *n.* [C; U] A stiff sticky earthy material that is soft and easy to shape when wet. It is used in making bricks, pottery, and tiles.

 clean (klēn) *adj.* **1.** Free from dirt or impurities: *clean clothing; clean air.* **2.** Producing little pollution: *The new law calls for clean fuels in all cars.* **3.** Free from wrongdoing; honorable: *a clean win; a clean record.* **4.** Having a smooth edge or surface: *A clean break in the bone heals quickly.* **5.** Entire; complete: *They made a clean escape, leaving no clues as to where they went.* **6.** Not yet used: *a clean page.* —*adv.* **1.a.** So as to be unsoiled: *We washed the wall clean.* **b.** In a fair manner: *They played the game clean.* **2.** *Slang.* Entirely; completely: *I clean forgot about the test.* —*v.* —*tr.* **1.** To take away dirt, stain, or disorder from (sthg.): *clean a room.* **2.** To prepare (food) for cooking, as by removing parts that are not eaten: *clean a fish.* **3.** To empty or remove the contents from (sthg.): *I cleaned my plate.* —*intr.* To become clean or perform cleaning: *A wool rug cleans easily. A damp rag cleans well.* ♦ **clean house.** *Slang.* To get rid of what is unwanted: *The new boss cleaned house and fired the unproductive workers.* **clean out.** *tr.v.* [scp.] **1.** To remove dirt, trash, or disorder from (sthg.): *clean out the garage.* **2.** *Slang.* To remove everything of value from (sbdy./sthg.): *Paying for college cleaned out my savings. Thieves broke into our apartment and cleaned us out.* **3.** To empty (sthg.) of its contents: *He cleaned out the refrigerator to make sandwiches.* **clean up.** *tr.v.* [sep.] To take away dirt or disorder from (sthg.): *clean up one's room; clean up the city government.* —*intr.v. Slang.* To make a large sum of money in a short period of time: *We cleaned up on the stock market.* —**clean′ness** *n.* [U]

clean-cut (klēn′kŭt′) *adj.* Neat and trim in appearance. Used of men and boys: *a clean-cut soldier.*

clean•er (klē′nər) *n.* **1.** Often **cleaners.** A person or business whose job it is to clean: *Take these clothes to the cleaners.* **2.** A machine or substance used in cleaning: *Ammonia is a good household cleaner.*

clean•li•ness (klĕn′lē nĭs) *n.* [U] The state

of being clean: *Personal cleanliness is important for good health.*

clean•ly (klĕn′lē) *adj.* **clean•li•er, clean•li•est.** Habitually and carefully neat and clean: *Her habits suggest that she's a cleanly person.* See Synonyms at **clean.** —*adv.* (klēn′lē). In a sharp, smooth-edged manner: *The fruit had been cut cleanly by the knife.*

cleanse (klĕnz) *tr.v.* **cleansed, cleans•ing, cleans•es.** To make (sthg.) clean or pure: *cleanse a wound.* —**cleans′er** *n.*

clean•up (klēn′ŭp′) *n.* The act or process of cleaning up: *a trash cleanup.*

clear (klîr) *adj.* **1.** Free from clouds, mist, or haze: *a clear sky.* **2.** Easy to see through; transparent: *clear water.* **3.** Free from anything that blocks the way: *We had a clear view of the valley from the mountains. The road was clear of snow.* **4.** Easily heard, seen, or understood: *a clear picture on the TV; the clear sound of church bells; clear directions.* **5.** Free from doubt or confusion; certain: *Are you clear about what you have to do?* **6.** Free from guilt; untroubled: *a clear conscience.* **7.** Free from errors, flaws, or imperfections: *clear skin.* —*adv.* **1.** Out of the way: *The cat jumped clear of the oncoming car.* **2.** Distinctly; clearly: *The announcer spoke loud and clear before the audience.* **3.** *Slang.* All the way; entirely: *The baby cried clear through the night.* —*v.* —*tr.* **1.** To make (sthg.) clear, light, or bright: *A fan will clear the room of smoke.* **2.a.** To make (sthg.) free of objects or things that block the way: *clear the table after dinner; clear the road of snow.* **b.** To take (such things) away: *clear the dishes from the table.* **3.** To pass by, under, or over (sthg.) without contact: *The horse cleared the fence.* **4.** To free (a defendant) from a legal charge. **5.a.** To win the approval of (an authority): *The bill cleared the Senate. We cleared customs.* **b.** To win approval for (sthg.): *clear a plan with the boss.* **6.** To earn (an amount of money) as net profit or earnings: *She cleared only $200 a week.* —*intr.* **1.** To become clear, light, or bright: *The sky cleared in the afternoon.* **2.** To go away; disappear: *The fog cleared.* **3.** To pass through a clearing-house. Used of bank checks or bills of exchange: *After you deposit a check in your bank account, you must wait for it to clear before you can take the money out.* ♦ **clear out.** *intr.v. Informal.* To leave a place, often quickly: *The crowd cleared out when the police arrived.* **clear the air.** To make a situation free of emotional tensions or differences: *A joke cleared the air.* **clear up.** *tr.v.* [sep.] To explain or remove doubts about (sthg.): *clear up a misunderstanding.* —*intr.v.* To clear completely: *The skies cleared up. My cold has cleared up.* **in the clear.** Free from dangers, guilt, or responsibility: *After the facts were known, the suspect was in the clear.* —**clear′ly** *adv.* —**clear′ness** *n.* [U]

clear•ance (klîr′əns) *n.* **1.** [U] The act of clearing: *The city has begun clearance of the abandoned buildings.* **2.** [C] A sale of old merchandise at reduced prices: *Department stores often have a clearance after the holidays.* **3.** [C; U] The distance or amount of space by which a moving object passes or clears sthg.: *a small clearance for trucks passing under the bridge.* **4.** [U] Permission for an airplane, ship, or other vehicle to proceed: *The control tower gave the pilot clearance to take off.* **5.** [U] Official certification of trustworthiness or fitness: *You need clearance to handle top-secret material.*

clear-cut (klîr′kŭt′) *adj.* **1.** Outlined in sharp distinct form: *a face with clear-cut features.* **2.** Not vague or confused; obvious: *a clear-cut statement of fact.*

clear•ing (klîr′ĭng) *n.* An area of land from which trees and other obstructions have been removed: *a clearing in the forest.*

cleat (klēt) *n.* A projecting piece of metal or rubber, attached to the sole of a shoe to keep it from slipping: *Shoes worn for soccer or baseball have cleats.*

cleav•age (klē′vĭj) *n.* **1.** [C; U] *Formal.* The act of splitting or state of being split: *Earthquakes are often accompanied by cleavage of the ground.* **2.** [U] *Informal.* The space between a woman's breasts: *The neckline of her gown revealed little cleavage.*

cleave[1] (klēv) *tr.v.* **cleft** (klĕft) or **cleaved** or **clove** (klōv), **cleft** or **cleaved** or **clo•ven** (klō′vən), **cleav•ing, cleaves.** *Formal.* **1.** To split (sthg.), as by a sudden blow: *The ax cleft the piece of wood.* **2.** To make or accomplish (sthg.) by or as if by cutting: *a ship cleaving its way through the ice.*

cleave[2] (klēv) *intr.v.* **cleaved, cleav•ing, cleaves.** *Formal.* **1.** To cling; adhere; stick fast: *The two pieces of paper cleaved together.* **2.** To remain faithful: *cleave to old beliefs.*

cleav•er (klē′vər) *n.* A tool with a broad heavy blade and a short handle, used especially by butchers for cutting meat.

clef (klĕf) *n.* A symbol on a set of musical lines that tells which pitch each of the various lines and spaces represents.

cleft (klĕft) *v.* A past tense and a past participle of **cleave**[1]. —*adj.* Divided; split: *a cleft chin.* —*n.* A crack or split: *My glasses fell into a cleft in the rock.*

clem•en•cy (klĕm′ən sē) *n.* [U] **1.** Mercy, as toward an offender or enemy; leniency: *The judge showed clemency in sentencing the defendant.* **2.** Mildness, especially of weather.

clench (klĕnch) *tr.v.* **1.** To close (a hand or the teeth) tightly: *I clenched my fists in anger.* **2.** To grasp or grip (sthg.) tightly: *The driver clenched the steering wheel.* —*n.* A tight grip:

The wrestler failed to get out of his opponent's clench.

cler•gy (klûr′jē) *n., pl.* **cler•gies.** The group of people trained for religious service, as ministers, mullahs, or rabbis: *Many religions ban women from the clergy.*

cler•gy•man (klûr′jē mən) *n.* A man who is a member of the clergy. —**cler′gy•wom′an** (klûr′jē wŏom′ən) *n.*

cler•ic (klĕr′ĭk) *n.* A member of the clergy: *Some clerics wear robes during services.*

cler•i•cal (klĕr′ĭ kəl) *adj.* **1.** Relating to clerks or office workers: *typing and other clerical work.* **2.** Relating to the clergy: *a priest dressed in clerical robes.* —**cler′i•cal•ly** *adv.*

clerk (klûrk) *n.* **1.** A person who works in an office doing such jobs as keeping records, filing, and typing. **2.** A person who keeps the records and performs the regular business of a court or legislative group. **3.** A person who sells merchandise in a store or works at a service desk, as in a hotel. —*intr.v.* To work or serve as a clerk: *clerk in a drugstore as a summer job.*

clev•er (klĕv′ər) *adj.* **1.** Having the capacity to learn and think quickly; bright; quickwitted: *A clever dog is easy to train.* **2.** Showing intelligence or ingenuity: *a clever plan; a clever trick.* **3.** Skilled at doing sthg., especially with the hands: *a clever magician.* —**clev′er•ly** *adv.* **clev′er•ness** *n.* [U]

clew (klŏo) *Chiefly British. n. & v.* Variant of **clue.**

cli•ché (klē shā′) *n.* An overused expression or idea that has lost its original quality or effect: *The politician's speech was full of old clichés.*

click (klĭk) *n.* A short sharp sound: *the click of train wheels over the tracks.* —*v.* —*intr.* **1.** To produce a click or a series of clicks: *The wheels of the train clicked over the rails.* **2.** *Slang.* To be a success: *The new comedian clicked with the audience.* **3.** *Slang.* To work well together or be in harmony: *We clicked as soon as we met.* **4.** *Slang.* To become understandable; make sense: *The name clicked when I saw the actor's picture.* —*tr.* To cause (sthg.) to make a clicking sound: *He clicked his ballpoint pen and started to write.*

cli•ent (klī′ənt) *n.* **1.** A person who uses the services of a professional person: *Lawyers have clients, but doctors are usually said to have patients.* **2.** A customer of a business: *That jewelry store has several wealthy clients.*

cli•en•tele (klī′ən tĕl′) *n.* (*usually singular*). The group of regular clients or customers: *a restaurant with a select clientele.*

cliff (klĭf) *n.* A high, steep, or overhanging face of rock or earth: *We stood on the cliffs overlooking the sea far below.*

cliff•hang•er (klĭf′hăng′ər) *n.* **1.** A suspenseful situation at the end of a chapter, a scene, or an episode of a story. **2.** A contest whose outcome is uncertain until the end: *The game was a cliffhanger; the two teams were tied until the last minute.*

cli·mac·tic (klī măk′tĭk) *adj.* Relating to or forming a climax: *climactic events leading to the end of the mystery story.*

cli·mate (klī′mĭt) *n.* **1.** The general or average weather conditions of a certain region, including temperature, rainfall, and wind: *The coast of the Mediterranean has a summer climate of warm breezes and sunshine.* **2.** A region having certain weather conditions: *They live in a tropical climate.* **3.** A general condition or attitude: *The new teacher created a climate of relaxation in the classroom.*

cli·mat·ic (klī măt′ĭk) *adj.* Relating to climate: *climatic changes; climatic regions.*

cli·ma·tol·o·gy (klī′mə tŏl′ə jē) *n.* [U] The scientific study of climates.

cli·max (klī′măks′) *n.* **1.** The point in a series of events that is of greatest importance, usually occurring near the end: *Winning the Presidency was the climax of a long political career.* **2.** An orgasm. —*tr. & intr.v.* To bring or come to a climax: *The appearance of a surprise guest climaxed the party.*

climb (klīm) *v.* —*intr.* **1.** To move upward, especially by using the hands and feet; ascend: *The hikers climbed all day to reach the top of the mountain.* **2.** To go higher; rise: *The morning sun climbed in the sky. The patient's fever began to climb.* **3.** To slant or slope upward: *The trail climbs to the top of the cliff.* **4.** To grow upward by clinging to or twining around sthg.: *The vine climbs around the tree.* —*tr.* **1.** To go up, over, or through (sthg.), especially by using the hands and feet; ascend: *Leopards can climb trees.* **2.** To grow up on (sthg.): *Roses climbed the trellis.* —*n.* **1.** The act of climbing: *a hard climb up the mountain; an executive's climb to power.* **2.** A place to be climbed: *That hill was a steep climb.* —**climb′a·ble** *adj.* —**climb′er** *n.*

HOMONYMS: climb, clime (climate).

clime (klīm) *n.* Climate: *Many older people move to warmer climes.*

clinch (klĭnch) *v.* —*tr.* To settle (sthg.) definitely: *clinch a deal; clinch a championship.* —*intr.* In boxing, to hold the opponent's body with one or both arms. —*n.* In boxing, the act or an instance of clinching: *The boxers went into a clinch at the end of the second round.*

clinch·er (klĭn′chər) *n. Informal.* A final and decisive point, fact, or remark, as in an argument: *The accusation of corruption was the clincher; he lost the election.*

cling (klĭng) *intr.v.* **clung** (klŭng), **cling·ing,**

clings. **1.** To hold tight or adhere to sthg.: *clinging to the rope.* **2.** To stay near; remain close: *We clung together during the storm.* **3.** To remain attached emotionally; hold on: *cling to old beliefs; cling to a hope.*

clin·ic (klĭn′ĭk) *n.* **1.** A medical facility. **2.** A place where medical specialists work together in research and treatment of particular illnesses: *an eye and ear clinic.* **3.** A special training session: *an acting clinic; a tennis clinic.*

clin·i·cal (klĭn′ĭ kəl) *adj.* **1.** Relating to or connected with a clinic: *a doctor on the clinical staff.* **2.** Involving or based on direct examination and treatment of patients: *a clinical diagnosis of disease.* **3.** Very objective; not emotional; analytical: *He was able to give a clinical account of the accident.* —**clin′i·cal·ly** *adv.*

clink¹ (klĭngk) *tr. & intr.v.* To make or cause to make a light, sharp, ringing sound: *clink glasses after a toast; ice clinking in a glass.* —*n.* A light, sharp, ringing sound: *the clink of glasses on a tray.*

clink² (klĭngk) *n. Slang.* A prison or prison cell: *He did three years in the clink.*

clink·er (klĭng′kər) *n. Slang.* A mistake; a blunder: *Not asking for more money was a clinker.*

clip¹ (klĭp) *v.* **clipped, clip·ping, clips.** —*tr.* **1.** To cut, cut off, or cut out (sthg.) with scissors or shears: *clip a picture out of the newspaper; clip rosebushes.* **2.** To stop or shorten (sthg.): *Our discussion was clipped by our need to go home.* **3.** *Informal.* To hit or strike (sthg.) with a quick sharp blow: *Their car clipped our front fender.* —*intr.* To move rapidly: *The sailboat clipped along in the strong wind.* —*n.* **1.** The act of clipping: *Just a few clips of the scissors will even your hair.* **2.** Something clipped off, as a scene from a movie film: *show several clips of the latest movie.* **3.** *Informal.* A quick sharp blow: *a clip on the chin.* **4.** A quick speed: *The train sped along at a good clip.*

clip² (klĭp) *n.* **1.** A device for gripping or holding things together: *A paper clip holds several pages together.* **2.** A holder for cartridges to be loaded into an automatic rifle or pistol. **3.** A piece of jewelry, such as a pin, that fastens with a clasp or clip. —*tr.v.* **clipped, clip·ping, clips.** To fasten (sthg.) with a clip: *clip the papers together.*

clip·board (klĭp′bôrd′) *n.* A small writing board with a spring clip at the top for holding papers or a writing pad.

clip·per (klĭp′ər) *n.* **1.** A person who clips, cuts, or shears. **2.** **clippers.** A tool for clipping, cutting, or shearing: *nail clippers; a barber's clippers.* **3.** A wooden sailing ship, formerly built for great speed.

clip·ping (klĭp′ĭng) *n.* Something cut or trimmed off, especially an article or a photograph clipped from a newspaper or magazine.

clique (klĭk) *n.* A small group of people who socialize together and remain apart from others: *a clique at school.*

cliqu·ish (klĭk′ĭsh) *adj.* Relating to or characteristic of a clique: *Some high-school groups become too cliquish.* —**cliqu′ish·ness** *n.* [U]

clit·o·ris (klĭt′ər ĭs) *n.* A small organ that forms part of the external genitals in female mammals.

cloak (klōk) *n.* **1.** A loose outer garment, usually without sleeves. **2.** Something that covers or hides: *A cloak of mystery surrounds their disappearance.* —*tr.v.* To cover (sthg.) with or as if with a cloak: *The airport was cloaked in fog.*

clob·ber (klŏb′ər) *tr.v. Slang.* **1.** To hit or pound (sbdy./sthg.) with great force: *The thief clobbered the store owner over the head.* **2.** To defeat (sbdy.) completely: *Our team was clobbered by theirs.*

clock (klŏk) *n.* An instrument other than a watch for measuring and showing time: *an alarm clock; a wall clock.* —*tr.v.* To record the time or speed of (sbdy./sthg.): *The bicyclist was clocked at 30 miles per hour.*

clock radio *n.* A radio with a built-in clock that can be set to turn the radio on automatically.

clock·wise (klŏk′wīz′) *adv. & adj.* In the same direction as the rotating hands of a clock: *turn clockwise; a clockwise movement.*

clock·work (klŏk′wûrk′) *n.* [U] A mechanism of gears driven by a spring, as in a mechanical clock. ◆ **like clockwork.** With perfect regularity and precision: *She eats lunch at 12:15 every day like clockwork.*

clod (klŏd) *n.* **1.** A lump of earth: *Break up the clods in the garden before you plant the seeds.* **2.** An insulting term for a person lacking manners: *Ignore the clods standing on the corner.*

clog (klôg *or* klŏg) *n.* **1.** Something that obstructs or hinders flow: *a clog in the drain; a clog in the flow of traffic.* **2.** A heavy shoe, usually with a wooden sole. —*v.* **clogged, clog·ging, clogs.** —*tr.* To cause (sthg.) to become obstructed or blocked: *Heavy traffic clogged the highway.* —*intr.* To become obstructed or blocked: *The drain clogs easily.*

clois·ter (kloi′stər) *n.* **1.** A covered walk along the side of a building, such as a church, with open arches facing into a courtyard. **2.** A place of religious seclusion, as a monastery or convent. —*tr.v.* To shut away or confine (sbdy.) in or as if in a cloister; seclude: *The author cloistered herself in the library all morning.*

clomp (klŏmp) *intr.v.* To walk heavily and noisily: *Don't clomp around the house when other people are sleeping.*

clone (klōn) *n.* **1.** An organism produced asexually from a single parent. **2.** A person or thing that copies or closely resembles another: *These computers are clones of a more expensive model.* —*v.* **cloned, clon·ing, clones.** —*tr.* To produce a copy of (sbdy./sthg.): *Many computers are cloned from an earlier model.* —*intr.* To reproduce or breed asexually.

clop (klŏp) *n.* The sound of horse's hoofs as they strike pavement. —*intr.v.* **clopped, clop·ping, clops.** To make or move with such a sound: *The children clopped noisily down the stairs.*

close (klōs) *adj.* **clos·er, clos·est. 1.** Near in space or time: *The airport is close to town. It was close to midnight when I got home.* **2.** Near in relationship: *They are close relatives.* **3.** Strongly connected by loyalties or affection: *close friends.* **4.** Having little space in between: *chairs arranged in close rows.* **5.** Very much like another or the original: *a close copy of an ancient statue.* **6.** Carefully done; thorough: *a close watch for forest fires.* **7.** Offering little space to move: *The room was close quarters for the three of us.* **8.** Very short or near to the surface: *a close haircut; a close shave.* **9.** Lacking fresh air: *It's very close in this room with the window shut.* **10.** Almost even, as in a contest: *a close race; a close election.* **11.** Secretive: *The accountant was very close about clients' affairs.* —*v.* (klōz). **closed, clos·ing, clos·es.** —*tr.* **1.** To move (a door, for example) so that an opening or a passage is blocked; shut. **2.** To stop the operations of (a business, for example): *Most shopkeepers close their stores around six o'clock.* **3.** To bring (sthg.) to an end: *close a letter; close a meeting.* See Synonyms at **complete. 4.** To bring together the edges of (an opening): *It took eight stitches to close the wound.* **5.** To succeed in completing (a business agreement): *close a deal; close a sale.* —*intr.* **1.** To become shut: *The window closed with a bang.* **2.** To come to an end: *The book closes with a love scene.* **3.** To stop business or operation: *The museum closes on Wednesdays.* **4.** To move near: *Our boat was closing fast on the one in front.* **5.** To come together: *The child's arms closed around the stuffed animal.* —*n.* (klōz). A conclusion; an end: *The meeting came to a quick close.* —*adv.* (klōs). **closer, closest.** In a close position or manner: *Let's stay close together.* ◆ **close call.** *Informal.* A situation in which sthg. dangerous or unwanted almost happens: *The car missed hitting my bicycle, but it was a close call.* **close down.** *intr.v.* To stop operating: *The old factory finally closed down.* —*tr.v.* [sep.] To stop (sbdy./sthg.) from operating: *A storm closed down the amusement park.* **close in.** *intr.v.* [on] To surround and move towards sbdy./sthg.: *The fog was quickly closing in on us.* **close out.** *tr.v.* [sep.]

To sell (sthg.) at a reduced price in order to clear it out of a business quickly: *The store closed out all its winter clothes in March.* **close to.** At a point when sthg. is likely to happen soon: *close to tears; close to signing a peace plan.* —**close′ly** *adv.* —**close′ness** *n.* [U]

HOMONYMS: close, clothes (things to wear).

closed (klōzd) *adj.* **1.** Blocked to passage or entry: *a closed port.* **2.** Producing only elements of the same set in a given mathematical operation. The set of whole numbers is closed under addition, but not under division because fractions may occur.

closed-cap•tioned (klōzd′ kăp′shənd) *adj.* With titles or captions that give the dialogue on a television program for people who cannot hear it: *a closed-captioned news program.*

closed circuit *n.* **1.** An electric circuit through which current can flow in an uninterrupted path. **2.** A television system that uses cable to send signals to a limited number of receivers: *We couldn't get into the auditorium, so we watched the conference on closed circuit in the lobby.*

closed shop *n.* A company or business that only hires union members or people who agree to join the union within a certain time.

close-knit (klōs′nĭt′) *adj.* Tightly joined by common interests, beliefs, or relationships: *a close-knit family.*

close-mouthed (klōs′mouthd′) *adj.* [*about*] Not talking much; giving away very little information: *She was close-mouthed about her new job.*

close•out (klōz′out′) *n.* [C; U] A sale in which goods are offered at greatly reduced prices in order to dispose of them: *find good prices at a closeout; buy furniture on closeout.*

clos•et (klŏz′ĭt *or* klô′zĭt) *n.* A small room or cabinet for storing things, such as clothes, supplies, or food: *a clothes closet; a broom closet.* —*adj.* Describing information that sbdy. wants to keep secret: *He's been a closet liberal for years.* ✦ **come out of the closet.** To make a secret about oneself known, especially about one's homosexuality: *She came out of the closet last year.*

close-up (klōs′ŭp′) *n.* **1.** A photograph taken from very near: *The portrait was a close-up of the President.* **2.** A close or intimate study, look, or view: *The interview presented a close-up of the actor.*

clo•sure (klō′zhər) *n.* [U] The act of closing; an ending: *Closure of the incision ended the operation.*

clot (klŏt) *n.* A thickened or solid mass or lump formed from a liquid: *a blood clot in*

her lung. —*intr. & tr.v.* **clot•ted, clot•ting, clots.** To form or cause to form into clots: *Blood clots when exposed to air. Lemon can be used to clot cream.*

cloth (klôth *or* klŏth) *n., pl.* **cloths** (klôths *or* klôthz *or* klŏths *or* klŏthz). **1.** [U] Fabric or material made by weaving, knitting, or matting fibers such as wool or cotton together. **2.** [C] A piece of cloth used for a special purpose, such as a tablecloth. ✦ **of the cloth.** *Formal.* Belonging to the clergy: *a man of the cloth.*

clothe (klōth) *tr.v.* **clothed, cloth•ing, clothes.** **1.** To put clothes on or provide clothes for (sbdy.); dress: *feed and clothe a family.* **2.** To cover (sthg.), as if with clothing: *trees clothed in their fall colors.*

clothes (klōz) *pl.n.* Coverings worn on the body, such as shirts, trousers, dresses, and coats.

HOMONYMS: clothes, close (shut).

clothes•line (klōz′līn′) *n.* A rope or wire on which clothes are hung to dry.

clothes•pin (klōz′pĭn′ *or* klōthz′pĭn′) *n.* A clip of wood or plastic used to hold clothes on a clothesline.

cloth•ing (klō′thĭng) *n.* [U] Clothes or garments such as shirts, pants, and skirts considered as a group: *fashionable clothing.*

cloud (kloud) *n.* **1.a.** A visible mass of water vapor or ice particles floating in the air. **b.** A similar mass of dust, steam, or smoke. **2.** A moving mass of things on the ground or in the air that is so large and dense that it resembles a cloud: *A cloud of insects swarmed the field.* **3.** Something that causes depression: *The bad news cast a cloud over the celebration.* **4.** A charge or other cause of suspicion: *The stockbroker was under a cloud of mistrust until he resigned.* —*v.* —*tr.* **1.** To cover (sthg.) with clouds: *Heavy mist clouded the hills.* **2.** To make (sthg.) gloomy or confused: *Superstition clouded their thinking.* **3.** To damage (a reputation): *A charge of corruption clouded the mayor's reputation.* —*intr.* [*over; up*] To become covered with clouds: *The sky clouded over. It's clouding up.*

cloud•burst (kloud′bûrst′) *n.* A sudden heavy rainstorm; a downpour: *A violent cloudburst ended the picnic.*

cloud•y (klou′dē) *adj.* **cloud•i•er, cloud•i•est.** **1.** Full of or covered with clouds; overcast: *a cloudy sky; a cloudy day.* **2.** Not clear; murky: *cloudy water.* —**cloud′i•ness** *n.* [U]

clout (klout) *n.* [U] *Informal.* Power, prestige, or influence: *The President has great political clout.*

clove[1] (klōv) *n.* The dried aromatic flower bud of a tropical Asian tree, used as a spice.

clove² (klōv) *n.* One of the sections of a garlic bulb or a similar plant bulb.

clo•ven (klō′vən) *adj.* Split or divided into two parts: *the cloven hoofs of deer or cattle.*

clo•ver (klō′vər) *n.* [U] Any of various plants with leaves divided into three leaflets and small, often fragrant white or purple flowers: *Many kinds of clover are grown to feed cattle and horses.*

clo•ver•leaf (klō′vər lēf′) *n.* A highway interchange whose exit and entrance ramps resemble a four-leaf clover.

clown (kloun) *n.* **1.** A performer in a circus or carnival who jokes and does tricks or humorous stunts. **2.** A person who is always making jokes or acting foolishly: *the office clown.* —*intr.v.* [*around*] To behave like a clown; act foolishly: *Practical jokers are always clowning around.* —**clown′ish** *adj.* —**clown′ish•ness** *n.* [U]

club (klŭb) *n.* **1.** A heavy stick, usually thicker at one end than at the other, used as a weapon. **2.** A stick used to hit a ball in certain games, especially golf. **3.a.** A black figure, shaped like the leaf of a clover, on a playing card. **b. clubs.** The suit in a deck of cards having this figure as its symbol. **4.a.** A group of people organized for a common purpose: *a chess club.* **b.** The room, building, or other facility used by such a group. —*tr.v.* **clubbed, clubbing, clubs.** To strike or beat (sbdy./sthg.) with a club: *The robbers clubbed their victim on the head.*

club•house (klŭb′hous′) *n.* A building used by a club or an athletic team.

club sandwich *n.* A sandwich made of two or three slices of bread with a filling of meat, tomato, lettuce, and mayonnaise.

club soda *n.* [C; U] Soda water.

cluck (klŭk) *n.* The deep short sound made by a chicken. —*intr.v.* **1.** To make such a sound. **2.** To make a sound similar to that of a chicken, as when urging a horse to move, or to show disapproval.

clue (klōō) *n.* A fact or an object that helps to solve a problem or mystery: *Identifying the virus was a clue to the prevention of polio.* —*v.* **clued, clue•ing** or **clu•ing, clues.** ♦ **clue (one) in on.** To give (sbdy.) information: *Clue me in on what's happening.* —**clue′less** *adj.*

clump (klŭmp) *n.* **1.** A thick mass, group, or cluster: *a clump of trees; a clump of mud.* **2.** A heavy dull sound, as of footsteps: *We heard the clump on the stairs.* —*v.* —*intr.* **1.** To walk with a heavy dull sound. **2.** To form clumps: *The flour clumped as the cook stirred it into the liquid.* —*tr.* To gather into or form clumps of (sthg.): *The trees were clumped together near the house.* —**clump′y** *adj.*

clum•sy (klŭm′zē) *adj.* **clum•si•er, clum•si•est. 1.** Lacking grace or skill; awkward: *a clumsy walk; clumsy animals.* **2.** Difficult to

handle or maneuver: *clumsy wooden shoes.* —**clum′si•ly** *adv.* —**clum′si•ness** *n.* [U]

clung (klŭng) *v.* Past tense and past participle of **cling.**

clunk (klŭngk) *n.* A dull heavy sound: *The can fell to the floor with a clunk.*

clun•ky (klŭng′kē) *adj.* Large and heavy: *She likes to wear big clunky bracelets.*

clus•ter (klŭs′tər) *n.* A group of similar things growing or grouped close together: *a cluster of grapes; a cluster of stars.* —*intr.v.* To gather or grow in clusters: *Everyone clustered around the fire.*

clutch¹ (klŭch) *v.* —*tr.* To hold or grasp (sbdy./sthg.) tightly: *I clutched the railing as I started down the stairs.* —*intr.* To try to grasp or seize sthg.: *I clutched at the chair as I started to fall.* —*n.* **1.** A tight hold or grip. **2.** (*usually plural*). Control or power; possession: *fall into the clutches of the enemy.* **3.** A device, usually a pedal, used to change gears in an automobile or a truck: *Put your foot on the clutch.* **4.** A critical situation: *our best hitter in a clutch.*

clutch² (klŭch) *n.* The eggs produced at a single laying.

clut•ter (klŭt′ər) *n.* [U] A collection of things scattered about in a disorderly way; a mess; a jumble: *She stumbled over the clutter on the floor.* —*tr.v.* To fill (sthg.) in such a way as to block movement or action: *On Sundays our living room floor is cluttered with newspapers.*

cm *abbr.* An abbreviation of centimeter.

Co The symbol for the element cobalt.

CO *abbr.* An abbreviation of Colorado.

co. or **Co.** *abbr.* An abbreviation of: **1.** Company. **2.** County.

c/o *abbr.* An abbreviation of in care of, used in addresses.

co– *pref.* A prefix that means: **1.** Together; jointly: *coexist.* **2.** Partner or associate: *co-author.*

WORD BUILDING: co– The prefix **co–** means "together, joint, jointly." In words such as *coproduce* and *coworker,* **co–** has simply been affixed to words that already existed to create new words whose meanings are easy to guess.

---

coach (kōch) *n.* **1.** [C] A large closed carriage on four wheels, pulled by horses. **2.** [C] A railroad passenger car or a bus. **3.** [U] A low-priced class for train or airplane travel. **4.** [C] A person who trains or teaches athletes or athletic teams: *a soccer coach.* **5.** [C] A person who gives private lessons, as in singing or acting: *a voice coach.* —*v.* —*tr.* To train or teach (sbdy.): *coach a swimming team.* —*intr.* To act as a coach: *He coaches for a living.*

co•ag•u•lant (kō ăg′yə lənt) *n.* A substance that causes coagulation.

co•ag•u•late (kō ăg′yə lāt′) *v.* **co•ag•u•lat•ed, co•ag•u•lat•ing, co•ag•u•lates.**

—*tr.* To change (a liquid) into a solid or nearly solid mass; clot: *Exposure to air coagulates the blood.* —*intr.* To become solid or nearly solid: *Egg whites coagulate when heated.* —**co•a′g•u•la′tion** *n.* [U]

coal (kōl) *n.* **1.** [U] A dark brown to black natural solid substance which consists mainly of carbon and is widely used as a fuel and raw material. **2.** [C] A glowing burnt piece of wood, coal, or other solid fuel; an ember: *Coals continue to give off heat long after the flame is out.*

co•a•lesce (kō′ə lĕs′) *intr.v.* **co•a•lesced, co•a•lesc•ing, co•a•lesc•es.** To grow or come together so as to form one mass or whole; unite: *Two local groups coalesced into a powerful national organization.* —**co′a•les′cense** *n.* [U]

co•a•li•tion (kō′ə lĭsh′ən) *n.* A united group of political parties or factions created for some special purpose: *A coalition of small business owners formed to defeat the sales tax.*

coarse (kôrs) *adj.* **coars•er, coars•est. 1.** Not smooth; rough; lumpy: *coarse skin; coarse material.* **2.** Not polite; crude; rude: *coarse and vulgar language.* **3.** Of low, common, or inferior quality: *coarse lumber good only for use in a barn.* —**coarse′ly** *adv.* —**coarse′ness** *n.* [U]

HOMONYMS: **coarse, course** (unit of study).

coars•en (kôr′sən) *tr. & intr.v.* To make or become coarse: *His beard coarsened as he got older. Working in the garden can coarsen one's hands.*

coast (kōst) *n.* **1.** The edge of the land next to the sea; the seashore. **2.** A region next to or near the sea: *The western coast of South America includes large parts of Chile, Peru, Ecuador, and Colombia.* —*intr.v.* **1.** To slide or continue to move without the use of power: *The car coasted to a stop.* See Synonyms at **slide. 2.** To move ahead or through with little effort: *Some students coast through math class.* —**coast′al** *adj.*

coast•er (kō′stər) *n.* A small disk or plate placed under a glass or cup to protect the surface of a table.

Coast Guard *n.* A U.S. military organization whose job is to patrol the coast, carry out rescue operations of ships in trouble, and enforce immigration, navigation, and customs laws.

coast•line (kōst′līn′) *n.* The shape or outline of a coast.

coat (kōt) *n.* **1.** An outer garment with sleeves, usually worn for warmth or protection. **2.** The hair or fur of an animal: *The cat's coat was thick and soft.* **3.** A layer of sthg. spread over a surface: *a coat of paint.* —*tr.v.* [with] To cover

(sbdy./sthg.) with a layer of sthg.: *Dust coated the table. He was coated with dirt.*

coat•ing (kō′tĭng) *n. (usually singular).* A layer of a substance spread over a surface, as for protection or decoration: *a sticky coating of varnish; a thin coating of ice on the streets.*

co•au•thor (kō ô′thər) *n.* One of two or more people who work together in writing a book, story, play, or other piece of writing. —*tr.v.* To be the coauthor of (sthg.): *I coauthored a book with him last year.*

coax (kōks) *tr.v.* **1.** To persuade or try to persuade (sbdy.) by gently urging: *The trainer coaxed the lion into the cage.* **2.** To obtain (sthg.) by this type of persuasion: *My jokes coaxed a smile from the unhappy child.*

co•ax•i•al cable (kō ăk′sē əl) *n.* A cable used to carry telephone, telegraph, and television signals.

cob (kŏb) *n.* The long hard central part of an ear of corn; a corncob.

co•balt (kō′bôlt′) *n.* [U] *Symbol* **Co** A hard silver-white metallic element used in alloys and pigments. Atomic number 27. See table at **element.**

cob•bled (kŏb′əld) Paved with cobblestones: *a cobbled street.*

cob•bler[1] (kŏb′lər) *n.* A shoemaker.

cob•bler[2] (kŏb′lər) *n.* [C; U] A large fruit pie baked in a deep dish: *apple cobbler.*

cob•ble•stone (kŏb′əl stōn′) *n.* A naturally rounded stone formerly used for paving streets.

CO•BOL (kō′bôl′) *n.* [U] A language based on English words and phrases, used in programming computers for various business applications.

co•bra (kō′brə) *n.* Any of several poisonous Asian or African snakes capable of spreading out the skin of the neck to form a flattened hood.

cob•web (kŏb′wĕb′) *n.* A web or single thread spun by a spider.

co•caine (kō kān′ *or* kō′kān′) *n.* [U] An addictive drug that is sometimes used as a local anesthetic, especially for the eyes, nose, and throat, or, illegally, for pleasure.

cock (kŏk) *n.* **1.** A full-grown male chicken; a rooster. **2.** An adult male of various other birds. **3.** A tilting or jaunty upward turn: *the cock of a sailor's cap.* —*tr.v.* **1.** To set (a device, such as a gun) in a position ready for use: *cock the shutter on a camera; cock a pistol.* **2.** To tilt or turn (sthg.) up to one side: *Birds often cock their heads to hear or see better.*

cock•er spaniel (kŏk′ər) *n.* A type of small dog with long drooping ears and a silky coat.

cock•eyed (kŏk′īd′) *adj. Informal.* **1.** Tilted or turned to one side; crooked: *The picture hung cockeyed on the wall.* **2.** Ridiculous; absurd: *cockeyed plans that are sure to fail.*

ă–cat; ā–pay; âr–care; ä–father; ĕ–get; ē–be; ĭ–sit; ī–nice; îr–here; ŏ–got; ō–go; ô–saw; oi–boy; ou–out; o͞o–took; o͞o–boot; ŭ–cut; ûr–word; th–thin; *th*–this; hw–when; zh–vision; ə–about; N–French bon

cock·pit (kŏk′pĭt′) *n.* **1.** The space in an airplane that has seats for the pilot and co-pilot and sometimes passengers. **2.** The space in a small boat from which the boat is steered.

cock·roach (kŏk′rōch′) *n.* A brownish or black insect with a flat body and usually long antennae. Cockroaches are common household pests.

cock·tail (kŏk′tāl′) *n.* **1.** An alcoholic drink made by mixing liquor with fruit juice, soda, or another liquor. **2.** An appetizer such as seafood, juice, or fruit: *a shrimp cocktail.*

cock·y (kŏk′ē) *adj.* **cock·i·er, cock·i·est.** Too sure of oneself; arrrogant: *a cocky young man.* —**cock′i·ly** *adv.* —**cock′i·ness** *n.* [U]

co·coa (kō′kō) *n.* [U] **1.** A powder made of cacao seeds, used as a chocolate flavoring. **2.** A drink made with this powder, sugar, and milk or water; hot chocolate. **3.** A reddish brown color. —**co′coa** *adj.*

co·co·nut (kō′kə nŭt′) *n.* **1.** [C] The large, hard-shelled nut of a palm, with sweet white meat and a hollow center filled with a milky liquid. **2.** [U] The meat of this nut, often used in baking and as a seasoning.

co·coon (kə kōōn′) *n.* **1.** A covering of silky strands spun by the larva of a moth or other insect as protection during its pupal stage. **2.** A similar protective covering or structure: *The baby was wrapped in a cocoon of blankets.*

cod (kŏd) *n.* [C; U] A large food fish of the northern Atlantic and Pacific oceans.

COD or **C.O.D.** *abbr.* An abbreviation of cash on delivery.

code (kōd) *n.* **1.** [C; U] A system of words, symbols, or letters used in place of ordinary writing to keep messages secret or to communicate with a computer, for example. **2.** [C] A system of numbers used to represent a geographic area: *a ZIP code.* **3.** [C] A system or collection of laws or rules and regulations: *a building code; an honor code.* —*tr.v.* **cod·ed, cod·ing, codes.** To put (a text, numbers, or information) into a code: *code information to store in a computer.*

co·deine (kō′dēn′) *n.* [U] A drug made from opium that is used to promote sleep and relieve coughing and pain.

co·ed or **co-ed** (kō′ĕd′) *n. Informal.* A woman who attends a college or university that is open to men and women. —*adj.* Relating to coeducation: *a coed school.*

co·ed·u·ca·tion (kō ĕj′ə kā′shən) *n.* [U] The system of educating male and female students together. —**co′ed·u·ca′tion·al** *adj.*

co·ef·fi·cient (kō′ə fĭsh′ənt) *n.* A number or symbol multiplying a variable or an unknown quantity in an algebraic term. In the term $4x$, 4 is the coefficient. In $x(a + b)$, x is the coefficient.

co·erce (kō ûrs′) *tr.v.* **co·erced, co·erc·ing, co·erc·es.** To force (sbdy.) to do sthg.

by pressure, threats, or intimidation: *The committee coerced the president to resign.* —**co·erc′er** *n.* —**co·er′cion** (kō ûr′zhən) *n.* [U] —**co·er′cive** *adj.*

co·ex·ist (kō′ĭg zĭst′) *intr.v.* To live or exist together, at the same time, or in the same place: *Bears and wolves coexist in the Alaskan wilderness. Many nations coexist on the European continent.* —**co′ex·is′tence** *n.* [U] —**co′ex·is′tent** *adj.*

cof·fee (kô′fē *or* kŏf′ē) *n.* **1.** [C; U] A drink made with hot water and the ground seeds of a tropical plant native to Africa. **2.** [C; U] The dried whole or ground seeds of this tree. **3.** [U] A dark or yellowish brown color. —*adj.* Dark or yellowish brown.

coffee break *n.* A short period of rest from work when coffee or other refreshments may be enjoyed.

cof·fee·house (kô′fē hous′ *or* kŏf′ē hous′) *n.* An informal restaurant where coffee and other refreshments are served.

cof·fee·pot (kô′fē pŏt′ *or* kŏf′ē pŏt′) *n.* A covered pot with a handle and spout, for making and pouring coffee.

coffee shop *n.* A small restaurant where inexpensive, light meals are served.

coffee table *n.* A low table, often placed in front of a sofa.

cof·fer (kô′fər *or* kŏf′ər) *n. Formal.* **1.** A strong box or chest for holding money or other valuables. **2. coffers.** A treasury, as of a nation; financial resources: *The state coffers were opened to aid the poor.*

cof·fin (kô′fĭn *or* kŏf′ĭn) *n.* A box in which a dead person is buried.

cog (kŏg *or* kôg) *n.* One of a series of teeth on a wheel that fit between the teeth on another wheel so that one wheel can move the other.

co·gent (kō′jənt) *adj.* Forceful and convincing in argument: *a cogent presentation based on facts.* —**co′gen·cy** (kō′jən′ sē) *n.* [U] —**co′gent·ly** *adv.*

co·gnac (kōn′yăk′) *n.* [C; U] A brandy, especially of a type from France.

cog·nate (kŏg′nāt′) *adj.* Related in origin: *French and Spanish are cognate languages.* —*n.* A cognate thing, especially a word related to one in another language: *The English word* cup, *the Dutch word* kopje, *and the Italian word* coppa *are cognates from the Late Latin word* cuppa.

cog·ni·tion (kŏg nĭsh′ən) *n.* [U] The mental process or faculty by which knowledge is acquired, including perception, awareness, and reasoning. —**cog′ni·tive** (kŏg′nĭ tĭv) *adj.*

cog·ni·zance (kŏg′nĭ zəns) *n.* [U] *Formal.* **1.** Knowledge or awareness: *We had no cognizance that a problem existed.* **2.** Ability to understand: *The origins of life are still beyond the cognizance of modern science.* —**cog′ni·zant** *adj.*

co·hab·it (kō hăb′ĭt) *intr.v. Formal.* To live together as if married. —**co·hab′i·ta′tion** *n.* [U]

co·here (kō hîr′) *intr.v.* **co·hered, co·her·ing, co·heres. 1.** To stick or hold together in a mass, such as mud or wet sand. **2.** To be logically connected: *He presented a careful argument in which one point cohered neatly with another.*

co·her·ence (kō hîr′əns *or* kō hĕr′əns) *n.* [U] The quality or state of being coherent: *After three glasses of wine, his speech lost its coherence.* —**co·her′en·cy** (kō hîr′ən sē) *n.* [U]

co·her·ent (kō hîr′ənt *or* kō hĕr′ənt) *adj.* **1.** Sticking together: *coherent particles of wet sand.* **2.** Logically connected; easy to understand: *The editorial provides a coherent argument for a tax increase.* —**co·her′ent·ly** *adv.*

co·he·sion (kō hē′zhən) *n.* [U] **1.** The attraction between molecules of the same kind: *The cohesion of molecules of H_2O produces drops of water.* **2.** The condition of holding together; unity: *The cohesion of so many different groups is the result of a common belief in the equality of all citizens.* —**co·he′sive** (kō hē′sĭv) *adj.* —**co·he′sive·ly** *adv.* —**co·he′sive·ness** *n.* [U]

co·hort (kō′hôrt′) *n.* **1.** A companion or an associate: *My cohorts on the newspaper staff agreed to publish the article.* **2.** A group or band: *A cohort of protesters assembled in front of city hall.*

coil (koil) *n.* A series of connected spirals or gathered loops: *a coil of rope.* —*v.* —*tr.* To wind (sthg.) into a series of spirals or loops: *The snake coiled itself around a branch.* —*intr.* **1.** To form spirals or loops: *The hose that I was using coiled and knotted.* **2.** To move in a spiral course: *The smoke coiled up into the sky.*

coin (koin) *n.* A piece of metal, usually flat and round, made by a government for use as money. —*tr.v.* **1.** To make (coins) from metal; mint: *The U.S. government coins dimes and quarters.* **2.** To invent (a word or phrase): *The computer industry has coined many new terms.* —**coin′age** *n.* [C; U]

co·in·cide (kō′ĭn sīd′) *intr.v.* **co·in·cid·ed, co·in·cid·ing, co·in·cides.** [*with*] **1.** To agree; be identical: *Our opinions of the movie coincided.* **2.** To happen at the same time or during the same period of time: *The date of your party coincides with my birthday.* **3.** To be in the same position or occupy the same space: *The park coincides with the location of an old town.*

co·in·ci·dence (kō ĭn′sĭ dəns) *n.* [C; U] A combination of events that is accidental but seems planned or arranged: *By a strange coinci-*

dence, all three brothers married women named *Ann.* —**co·in′ci·den′tal** (kō ĭn′sĭ dĕn′tl) *adj.* —**co·in′ci·den′tal·ly** *adv.*

coke (kōk) *n.* [U] *Slang.* Cocaine.

Coke (kōk) A trademark used for Coca-Cola.

col. *abbr.* An abbreviation of column.

Col. *abbr.* An abbreviation of **1.** Colonel. **2.** Colorado.

co·la (kō′lə) *n.* [C; U] A carbonated drink; a soda.

col·an·der (kŭl′ən dər *or* kŏl′ən dər) *n.* A bowl-shaped kitchen utensil with holes in the bottom, used for rinsing and draining liquids from foods such as pasta or fruit and vegetables.

cold (kōld) *adj.* **1.** Having a low temperature: *cold water; a cold day.* **2.** Feeling no warmth; chilled: *I am cold without a jacket.* **3.** Not friendly; aloof: *a cold and businesslike manner.* **4.** Showing no enthusiasm or interest: *a cold audience.* **5.** Faint; weak: *The thief's trail was cold.* —*adv.* **1.** Completely; absolutely: *Our suggestion was turned down cold.* **2.** Without preparation or prior notice: *We took the test cold.* —*n.* **1.** [U] Lack of warmth: *Cold slows down chemical reactions.* **2.** [U] Cold weather: *We were out in the cold all day.* **3.** [C] A viral infection that causes a runny or stuffy nose, coughing, sneezing, and sometimes a fever: *Everyone at the office has a bad cold.* ♦ **catch (a) cold.** To become sick with a cold: *She caught cold and had to stay home from work.* **get** *or* **have cold feet.** *Informal.* To lack courage; be or become timid or fearful: *Their friends got cold feet and wouldn't go skydiving with them.* **give the cold shoulder.** *Informal.* To behave with deliberate unfriendliness or disregard towards (sbdy.); snub: *After I forgot his birthday, he gave me the cold shoulder.* **out cold.** Unconscious: *He was out cold after being hit on the head.* **out in the cold.** Lacking benefits given to others; neglected: *Because she had just been hired, she was left out in the cold when raises were given.* —**cold′ly** *adv.* —**cold′ness** *n.* [U]

SYNONYMS: cold, chilly, frigid, frosty, icy. These adjectives all describe sthg. at a very low temperature. *The cold wind made me wish I had worn a coat. They walked to the store even though the autumn day felt chilly. We brought the heater into the frigid room. This frosty weather is perfect for sledding. The travelers warmed their icy hands by the fire.* **ANTONYM: hot.**

cold-blood·ed (kōld′blŭd′ĭd) *adj.* **1.** Having a body temperature that changes according to the temperature of the surroundings: *Fish, frogs, and reptiles are cold-blooded.* **2.** Having no feeling or emotion; cruel: *a cold-*

blooded dismissal of a long-time employee.
—**cold′-blood′ed•ly** *adv.* —**cold′-blood′-
ed•ness** *n.* [U]

cold cream *n.* [C; U] A creamy cosmetic for
cleansing and softening the skin.

cold cuts *pl.n.* Slices of cold cooked meat,
used to make sandwiches and appetizers.

cold-heart•ed (kōld′här′tĭd) *adj.* Without
sympathy or feeling; callous: *a cold-hearted
decision to sell the farm.* —**cold′-heart′-
ed•ly** *adv.* —**cold′-heart′ed•ness** *n.* [U]

cold sore *n.* A small sore on or near the lips
that often accompanies a fever or cold; a
fever blister.

cole•slaw (kōl′slô′) *n.* [U] A salad of shredded raw cabbage with a dressing.

col•ic (kŏl′ĭk) *n.* [U] Severe pain or cramping
in the abdomen. —**col′ick•y** *adj.*

col•i•se•um also **col•os•se•um** (kŏl′ĭ-
sē′əm) *n.* A large round stadium or hall for
sports events, exhibitions, or other public
entertainment.

col•lab•o•rate (kə lăb′ə rāt′) *intr.v.* **col•
lab•o•rat•ed, col•lab•o•rat•ing, col•
lab•o•rates. 1.** To work together on a
project: *The scientists collaborated by sharing their discoveries and planning a new
experiment.* **2.** [*with*] To cooperate with an
enemy that has invaded one's country: *Afraid
of being killed, they collaborated with the
enemy.* —**col•lab′o•ra′tion** *n.* [U] —**col•
lab′o•ra′tor** *n.*

col•lage (kə läzh′) *n.* [C; U] A work of art
made by pasting materials or objects, such as
pieces of cloth, metal, colored paper, string,
and pictures, onto a surface.

col•lapse (kə lăps′) *v.* **col•lapsed, col•
laps•ing, col•laps•es.** —*intr.* **1.** To fall
down or inward suddenly; cave in: *Part of the
roof collapsed after the fire.* **2.** To break
down or fail suddenly and completely: *She
collapsed from overwork and fatigue.
Negotiations collapsed as a result of disagreement.* **3.** To fold together compactly:
This folding chair collapses very easily. —*tr.*
To cause (sthg.) to collapse: *The weight of the
books collapsed the shelf.* —*n.* [C; U] **1.** The
act of collapsing: *the collapse of the building;
the collapse of a business deal.* **2.** A sudden
and complete loss of strength or stamina; a
breakdown: *He suffered a complete collapse.*

col•laps•i•ble (kə lăp′sə bəl) *adj.* Capable
of being collapsed or folded compactly: *a
collapsible chair.*

col•lar (kŏl′ər) *n.* **1.** The part of a shirt, coat,
or dress that goes around the neck. **2.** A
leather or plastic band put around the neck of
an animal: *a dog collar.* **3.** A band or marking
around the neck of an animal, resembling a
collar: *The condor has a collar of white feathers.* **4.** A device shaped like a ring and used to
guide or secure a machine part. —*tr.v.* **1.** To
put a collar on (sthg.): *collar a sheep to*

attach a bell. **2.** *Slang.* To seize, capture, or
arrest (sbdy.): *The police collared the thief a
few blocks away.*

col•lar•bone (kŏl′ər bōn′) *n.* A bone that
connects the breastbone and the shoulder
blade.

col•late (kə lāt′ *or* kŏl′āt′ *or* kō′lāt′) *tr.v.*
col•lat•ed, col•lat•ing, col•lates. To
arrange (papers) in proper order: *collate sections of the Sunday newspaper for delivery.*
—**col•la′tion** *n.* [U]

col•lat•er•al (kə lăt′ər əl) *adj.* **1.** Additional; supporting: *Further experiments provided collateral information to the scientists.*
2. Guaranteed by sthg. of value: *a collateral
loan.* —*n.* [U] Property, such as jewelry or
bonds, promised as security for a loan: *She
used her house as collateral for the loan.*
—**col•lat′er•al•ly** *adv.*

col•league (kŏl′ēg′) *n.* A fellow member of a
profession, staff, or organization; an associate.

col•lect (kə lĕkt′) *v.* —*tr.* **1.** To bring (sthg.)
together in a group; gather: *We collected firewood.* See Synonyms at **gather. 2.** To pick
up and take (sthg.) away: *collect garbage;
collect the laundry.* **3.** To get and keep (sthg.)
as a hobby or for study: *collect stamps; collect samples for a report about flowers.* **4.** To
take in or obtain payment of (money): *We collected a dollar from each student for the gift.*
5. To recover control of (oneself): *They finally collected themselves after the accident.*
—*intr.* **1.** To come together; congregate: *A
group of people collected on the sidewalk.*
2. To build up; accumulate: *A pile of snow
collected by the door.* **3.** To take in payments
or donations: *The band collected for new
uniforms.* —*adv. & adj.* With payment to
be made by the receiver: *call home collect; a
collect call.* —**col•lect′a•ble, col•lect′i•
ble** *adj.*

col•lect•ed (kə lĕk′tĭd) *adj.* **1.** In full control of oneself; calm: *He did his best to
remain cool and collected when speaking to a
crowd.* **2.** Gathered together: *the collected
works of Shakespeare.* —**col•lect′ed•ly** *adv.*
—**col•lect′ed•ness** *n.* [U]

col•lec•tion (kə lĕk′shən) *n.* **1.** [C; U] The
act or process of collecting: *Trash collection
is on Tuesday.* **2.** [C] A group of things
brought or kept together for study or use or as
a hobby: *a collection of folk songs; a coin
collection.* **3.** [C] A pile of sthg.; a deposit:
the collection of dust on the piano. **4.** [C; U]
Money collected, as at a church service.

col•lec•tive (kə lĕk′tĭv) *adj.* Relating to a
number of persons or nations acting as a
group: *the collective opinion of the committee; our collective security.* —*n.* A business
owned and controlled by its workers: *You can
buy vegetables more cheaply from the farm
collective than the supermarket.* —**col•lec′-
tive•ly** *adv.*

collective bar·gain·ing (bär′gə nĭng) *n*. [U] Negotiation between the representatives of workers in a labor union and their employer or employers to determine wages and working conditions: *When collective bargaining failed, the factory workers went on strike.*

collective noun *n*. A noun, such as *committee, family,* or *team,* that refers to a collection of persons or things regarded as a unit. Collective nouns usually take a singular verb.

USAGE: collective noun When referring to a collection considered as a whole, a collective noun takes a singular verb: *The family was united on this question.* A collective noun takes a plural verb when it refers to the members of the group as individuals, as in *My family are always fighting among themselves.* Among the common collective nouns are **committee, clergy, company, enemy, group, family, flock, public,** and **team.**

---

col·lec·tor (kə lĕk′tər) *n*. **1.** A person, thing, or business that collects sthg.: *a garbage collector; a solar collector.* **2.** A person who collects sthg., such as stamps or coins, as a hobby: *a collector of autographs.*

col·lege (kŏl′ĭj) *n*. **1.** A school of higher learning, entered after high school, that grants a bachelor's degree: *Where does your brother plan to go to college?* **2.** An undergraduate division within a university: *the College of Liberal Arts.* **3.** A school for special study, often connected with a university: *a teachers' college.* **4.** An official group of persons with a common purpose or shared duties: *a college of surgeons.*

col·le·gian (kə lē′jən *or* kə lē′jē ən) *n*. An old-fashioned term for a college student.

col·le·giate (kə lē′jĭt *or* kə lē′jē ĭt) *adj*. Relating to a college or college students: *collegiate activities.*

col·lide (kə līd′) *intr.v.* **col·lid·ed, col·lid·ing, col·lides.** **1.** To strike or bump together with violent direct impact: *The car was badly damaged when it collided with the tree.* **2.** To disagree strongly; clash: *The governments of the two nations collided over fishing rights in coastal waters.*

col·lie (kŏl′ē) *n*. A large dog with long white and tan hair and a narrow nose, originally used in Scotland to herd sheep.

col·li·sion (kə lĭzh′ən) *n*. [C; U] The act or process of colliding; a crash or conflict: *a fatal collision on the highway.*

col·lo·ca·tion (kŏl′ō kā′shən) *n*. An arrangement or a proper ordering, as of words: *Sample sentences in the dictionary illustrate common collocations.*

col·lo·qui·al (kə lō′kwē əl) *adj*. Characteristic of or suitable for informal spoken or written language: *It's a bad idea to use colloquial language in a research paper.* **—col·lo′qui·al·ly** *adv*.

col·lo·qui·al·ism (kə lō′kwē ə lĭz′əm) *n*. A colloquial expression. For example, *up a tree* is a colloquialism meaning "in a difficult situation."

col·lu·sion (kə lōō′zhən) *n*. [U] A secret agreement between persons seeking to deceive or cheat sbdy. else: *The company discovered she was in collusion with a competitor.* **—col·lu′sive** (kə lōō′sĭv) *adj*.

Colo. *abbr*. An abbreviation of Colorado.

co·logne (kə lōn′) *n*. [C; U] A scented liquid made of alcohol and fragrant oils, used as light perfume.

co·lon¹ (kō′lən) *n*. **1.** A punctuation mark (:) used after a word introducing a quotation, an explanation, an example, or a series. **2.** The sign (:) used between numbers or groups of numbers in expressions of time (2:30, read as "two thirty") and ratios (1:2, read as "one to two").

co·lon² (kō′lən) *n*. The lower part of the large intestine.

colo·nel (kûr′nəl) *n*. An officer in the U.S. Army, Air Force, or Marine Corps.

HOMONYMS: colonel, kernel (seed).

---

co·lo·ni·al (kə lō′nē əl) *adj*. **1.** Relating to a colony or colonies: *France and England were colonial powers in Africa and Asia.* **2.** Often **Colonial.** Relating to the 13 British colonies that became the United States of America: *the Colonial period.* **3.** Often **Colonial.** Relating to the style of architecture and furniture often found in the British colonies in North America. *—n.* A person who lives in a colony. **—co·lo′ni·al·ism** *n*. [U]

col·o·nist (kŏl′ə nĭst) *n*. An original settler or founder of a colony.

col·o·nize (kŏl′ə nīz′) *tr.v.* **col·o·nized, col·o·niz·ing, col·o·niz·es.** To establish or settle a colony in (a country or territory): *Norwegians originally colonized Iceland.* **—col′o·ni·za′tion** (kŏl′ə nĭ zā′shən) *n*. [U] **—col′o·niz′er** *n*.

col·o·ny (kŏl′ə nē) *n., pl.* **col·o·nies.** **1.** A group of people who settle in a distant land but are controlled by their native country: *The English Pilgrims founded a colony at Plymouth.* **2.** A territory ruled by a distant power: *The government built railroads in each of its colonies.* **3. Colonies.** The 13 British colonies that became the original United States of America. **4.** A group of people of the same nationality, religion, or interests, living together in one area: *the American*

ă-**cat**; ā-**pay**; âr-**care**; ä-**father**; ĕ-**get**; ē-**be**; ĭ-**sit**; ī-**nice**; îr-**here**; ŏ-**got**; ō-**go**; ô-**saw**; oi-**boy**; ou-**out**; ōō-**took**; ōō-**boot**; ŭ-**cut**; ûr-**word**; th-**thin**; *th*-**this**; hw-**when**; zh-**vision**; ə-**about**; N-French **bon**

colony in Paris. **5.** A group of the same kind of animals, plants, or one-celled organisms living or growing together: *a colony of ants; a colony of bacteria.*

col·or (kŭl′ər) *n.* **1.** [U] The sensation produced by light waves striking the retina of the eye. **2.** [C; U] A color other than black, white, or gray: *The drawings were not in color.* **3.** [C] A dye, pigment, paint, or other coloring substance: *I buy oil colors at an art supply store.* **4.** [C; U] The general appearance of the skin; a complexion: *She has the color of good health.* **5.** [U] The skin coloring of a person who is not classified as Caucasian: *There are laws against discrimination based on color.* **6. colors. a.** A flag or banner, as of a country or military unit: *At the beginning of the ceremony, they raised the colors.* **b.** A distinguishing symbol badge, ribbon, color, or mark of sthg.: *a tie with the college's colors on it.* **7.** [U] Vivid and interesting detail, as of a scene or an event: *The author's description of the political campaign had a great deal of color.* —*v.* —*tr.* **1.** To give color to or change the color of (sthg.): *color a picture with crayons; color hair.* **2.** To influence, distort, or misrepresent (sthg.): *Anger colored the witness's account of the accident.* —*intr.* **1.** To put on or change color: *The children sat on the floor coloring with crayons.* **2.** To blush: *Her face colored in embarrassment.* ◆ **people of color.** A unifying term for all people who are not Caucasian: *People of color are working together for common goals.* **show (one's) true colors.** To show the truth about oneself: *We thought she was shy, but she showed her true colors by talking to everyone at the party.* **with flying colors.** Extremely well: *He passed the examination with flying colors; he got an A+.*

col·or·a·tion (kŭl′ə rā′shən) *n.* [U] Arrangement of colors: *Protective coloration helps some animals to hide from their enemies.*

col·or·blind or **col·or-blind** (kŭl′ər blīnd′) *adj.* **1.** Partly or totally unable to see the difference between certain colors, such as red and green. **2.** Treating all people as equals; fair: *Judges should be colorblind in their courtrooms.* —**col′or·blind′ness** *n.* [U]

col·or-code (kŭl′ər kōd′) *tr.v.* **col·or-cod·ed, col·or-cod·ing, col·or-codes.** To color (sthg.) according to a code for easy identification: *color-code the sections of a telephone directory.*

col·ored (kŭl′ərd) *adj.* **1.** Having color: *colored paper; colored pencils.* **2.** Often **Colored.** *Offensive.* An out-of-date term that means belonging to an ethnic group that is not Caucasian. **3.** Distorted by prejudice or biased by self-interest: *The drivers each gave a very colored version of the accident.*

col·or·fast (kŭl′ər făst′) *adj.* Having color that will not run or fade after washing or wear: *a colorfast fabric.*

col·or·ful (kŭl′ər fəl) *adj.* **1.** Full of color or colors: *Many butterflies have colorful wings.* **2.** Rich in variety; vivid: *a colorful description of a castle.* —**col′or·ful·ly** *adv.* —**col′or·ful·ness** *n.* [U]

col·or·ing (kŭl′ər ĭng) *n.* **1.** [C; U] The process of applying color: *laws regulating the coloring of foods.* **2.** [C; U] A substance used to color sthg.: *hair coloring; food coloring.* **3.** [U] The color of skin, hair, or fur: *animals protected by their coloring.*

col·or·less (kŭl′ər lĭs) *adj.* **1.** Without color: *Air is colorless.* **2.** Without variety, interest, or distinction; dull: *a colorless account of his vacation trip.*

co·los·sal (kə lŏs′əl) *adj.* Very great in size, extent, or degree; enormous: *a city full of colossal buildings; a daring venture requiring colossal self-confidence.* —**co·los′sal·ly** *adv.*

col·os·se·um (kŏl′ĭ sē′əm) *n.* Variant of **coliseum.**

co·los·sus (kə lŏs′əs) *n.* **1.** A huge statue. **2.** Something of enormous size or importance: *a colossus among clothing manufacturers.*

col·our (kŭl′ər) *n. & v. Chiefly British.* Variant of **color.**

colt (kōlt) *n.* A young male horse.

col·umn (kŏl′əm) *n.* **1.** A pillar, usually shaped like a cylinder, used in a building as a support or as a decoration: *Greek columns.* **2.** Something that resembles a pillar in shape or use: *a column of mercury in a thermometer.* **3.** One of two or more vertical sections of a page: *Newspapers are often printed in six columns across the page.* **4.** A feature article that appears regularly in a newspaper or magazine: *a sports column.* **5.** A long row or line of sthg., such as numbers or trucks: *A column of soldiers marched down the road.*

col·um·nist (kŏl′əm nĭst) *n.* A person who writes a special section for a newspaper or magazine: *My uncle is an award-winning columnist.*

com. *abbr.* An abbreviation of: **1.** Commerce. **2.** Common. **3.** Commonly. **4.** Commissioner. **5.** Committee.

Com. *abbr.* An abbreviation of: **1.** Commissioner. **2.** Committee.

com— *pref.* A prefix that means together or with: *combine; compete.*

WORD BUILDING: com— The basic meaning of the prefix **com—** is "together, with." Before the consonants *l* and *r*, **com—** has changed to **col—** and **cor—**, as we see in the words **collaborate** and **correspond.** Before all other consonants except *p*, *b*, or *m*, **com—** became **con—**, as in **confide, conspire,** and **contribute.**

---

co·ma (kō′mə) *n.* A state of unnatural deep unconsciousness caused by disease, injury, or poisoning.

co•ma•tose (kō′mə tōs′ *or* kŏm′ə tōs′) *adj.* **1.** Being in a coma; deeply unconscious: *a comatose patient.* **2.** Relating to or resembling a coma: *a comatose trance.*

comb (kōm) *n.* **1.** A thin strip of plastic, metal, or hard rubber with teeth, used to arrange the hair or to keep it in place. **2.** Something resembling a comb in shape or use, as a device for arranging and cleaning wool. **3.** The brightly colored ridge on the top of the head of a rooster, hen, or certain other birds. **4.** A honeycomb. —*tr.v.* **1.** To style, arrange, or untangle (the hair) with a comb: *He combed his hair before leaving.* **2.** To search (sthg.) thoroughly: *We combed many books for information.*

com•bat (kəm băt′ *or* kŏm′băt′) *tr.v.* To fight or struggle against (sthg.): *new drugs that combat infection.* See Synonyms at **oppose.** —*n.* (kŏm′băt′). [C; U] A fight or struggle between two people, groups, or beliefs; a contest: *the combat between teenagers and parents.*

com•bat•ant (kəm băt′nt *or* kŏm′bə tnt) *n.* A person engaged in fighting or combat.

com•bat•ive (kəm băt′ĭv) *adj.* Ready or eager to fight: *the lawyer's combative personality.* —**com•bat′ive•ness** *n.* [U]

com•bi•na•tion (kŏm′bə nā′shən) *n.* **1.** [U] The act of combining: *The combination of fresh air and sunshine produced a beautiful day.* **2.** [C] Something that results from combining two or more things: *An alloy is a combination of metals.* **3.** [C] The series of numbers or letters used to open a lock or safe: *I memorized the combination for my bike lock.*

com•bine (kəm bīn′) *v.* **com•bined, com•bin•ing, com•bines.** —*tr.* To bring (two or more things) together; join: *a movie that combines an interesting story and a moral.* See Synonyms at **join.** —*intr.* **1.** To become united; come together: *Friends combined to help the family after the fire.* **2.** To form a compound: *Two atoms of hydrogen combine with one of oxygen to form water.*

com•bo (kŏm′bō) *n., pl.* **com•bos. 1.** A small group of musicians: *a jazz combo.* **2.** *Informal.* A combination: *We think pizza and beer is a great combo.*

com•bus•ti•ble (kəm bŭs′tə bəl) *adj.* Capable of catching fire and burning. —*n.* A substance that burns easily and quickly. —**com•bus′ti•bil′i•ty** *n.* [U]

com•bus•tion (kəm bŭs′chən) *n.* [U] The process of burning.

Comdr. *abbr.* An abbreviation of commander.

come (kŭm) *intr.v.* **came** (kām), **come, com•ing, comes. 1.** To move toward the speaker or toward a specified place: *Come here and sit by me.* **2.** [*to*] To arrive at a particular result or end: *The two countries came to an agreement.* **3.** [*to*] To move or be brought to a particular position: *The bus came to a stop.* **4.** To reach: *The snow came up to the window ledge.* **5.a.** To be located at a particular point or place: *The date of birth comes after the name in this listing.* **b.** To have importance; rank: *Work comes first. A comes before B.* **6.** To happen as a result: *Success often comes from hard work.* **7.** To occur in the mind: *I can't remember his name right now, but it will come to me.* **8.** To become: *The knot in my shoelace came loose.* **9.** To be available: *Shoes come in many styles.* **10.** *Slang.* To experience an orgasm. ◆ **come about.** *intr.v.* **1.** To occur or happen: *How did the change come about?* **2.** In sailing, to change tack or direction. **come across.** *tr.v.* [insep.] To meet or find (sbdy./sthg.) by chance: *We came across some letters in the attic.* —*intr.v.* To appear or make an impression: *She came across as being very nervous.* **come along.** *intr.v.* To progress: *The new garden is coming along well.* **come around.** *intr.v.* **1.** To recover; become conscious again. **2.** To change one's opinion or position: *The coach came around after hearing the whole story.* **come back.** *intr.v.* **1.** To return to memory: *The author's name came back to me.* **2.** To return to past success after a period of trouble: *The town came back after the flood.* **come between.** *tr.v.* [insep.] To cause trouble or a separation between (two people): *Don't let politics come between the two of you.* **come by.** *tr.v.* [insep.] To acquire or get (sthg.): *How did you come by that chair?* —*intr.v.* To make a visit: *Why don't you come by in the morning?* **come down.** *intr.v.* To be continued over time by tradition: *a custom that comes down from colonial times.* **come down with.** To become sick with (an illness): *I came down with a cold.* **come in.** *intr.v.* **1.** To become available for use: *New weather information just came in.* **2.** To arrive among those who finish a contest or race: *come in fifth.* **3.** To take on a role or responsibility: *When we need to develop a marketing plan, that's where you come in.* **come from.** *tr.v.* [insep.] **1.** To be a native or resident of (a place): *Her family comes from Georgia.* **2.** To be produced by (sthg.): *Wool comes from sheep.* **3.** To begin (in a place): *Where is that buzzing sound coming from?* **come in for.** *Informal.* To receive (blame, for example): *The reporter's work came in for criticism.* **come off.** *intr.v.* To happen; occur: *The celebration came off on schedule.* **come off it.** *Slang.* To stop being foolish. **come out.** *intr.v.* **1.** To become known: *The whole story came out in the trial.* **2.** To be issued or made available to the public: *The author's new book just came out.* **3.** To speak about sthg. publicly: *The president has come out for the tax*

ă-**cat**; ā-**pay**; âr-**care**; ä-**father**; ĕ-**get**; ē-**be**; ĭ-**sit**; ī-**nice**; îr-**here**; ŏ-**got**; ō-**go**; ô-**saw**; oi-**boy**; ou-**out**; ōō-**took**; ōō-**boot**; ŭ-**cut**; ûr-**word**; th-**thin**; *th*-**this**; hw-**when**; zh-**vision**; ə-**about**; N-French bon

proposal. **4.** To result: *Everything came out fine, as we expected.* **5.** To make a formal social debut. **6.** To reveal to people that one is gay or homosexual. **come through.** *intr.v.* To do what is required or expected: *I asked for their help, and they came through.* **come to.** *intr.v.* To return to consciousness: *He fainted but came to quickly.* —*tr.v.* [insep.] To total (an amount of money): *The bill came to $15.* **come up.** *intr.v.* To be spoken of: *The question didn't come up at the meeting.* **come up with.** *Informal.* To propose or produce (an idea or invention, for example): *The committee came up with some interesting new ideas.* **come upon.** *tr.v.* [insep.] To discover or meet (sbdy./sthg.) by accident: *We came upon an injured rabbit on our walk.* **how come.** *Informal.* Why: *How come they left early?*

come·back (kŭm′băk′) *n.* **1.** A return to success or high rank: *The tennis star made a comeback.* **2.** A reply, especially a quick, witty one; a retort: *I can never think of good comebacks in time.*

co·me·di·an (kə mē′dē ən) *n.* **1.** A professional entertainer who tells jokes or does other things in order to make audiences laugh. **2.** A person who tries to be funny; a clown: *the office comedian.*

come·down (kŭm′doun′) *n.* A drop in status or position: *Losing so badly was quite a comedown for the former champion.*

com·e·dy (kŏm′ĭ dē) *n., pl.* **com·e·dies.** **1.** [C] A play, a movie, or another work that has a funny story with humorous characters and a happy ending: *There are several new comedies out this summer.* **2.** [U] The branch of drama made up of such plays or other dramatic works: *The actor found comedy more difficult than tragedy.* —**co·me′dic** (kə mē′dĭk) *adj.*

come·ly (kŭm′lē) *adj.* **come·li·er, come·li·est.** *Formal.* Having a pleasing appearance; attractive: *a comely face* —**come′li·ness** *n.* [U]

come-on (kŭm′ŏn′ *or* kŭm′ôn′) *n. Slang.* Something offered to attract sbdy. to do sthg.; an inducement: *The come-on for renting cars was a free tank of gas.*

com·et (kŏm′ĭt) *n.* An object in the solar system with a bright halo and tail that travels around the sun: *Halley's comet appears about every 76 years.*

com·fort (kŭm′fərt) *tr.v.* **1.** To soothe (sbdy.) in time of grief or fear; console: *comfort a lost child.* **2.** To help relieve the pain and suffering of (sbdy.): *A nurse comforted the patient by putting a pillow behind her back.* —*n.* **1.** [U] A condition of ease or well-being:

comet

Pillows are available for the comfort of the passengers. **2.** [U] Relief in time of pain, grief, or fear: *The frightened child ran to her mother for comfort.* **3.** [C] A person or thing that provides relief, ease, or well-being: *Pets are a comfort to their owners.* **4.** [U] The capacity or ability to give ease or a sense of well-being: *Curtains and soft chairs added to the comfort of the room.*

com·fort·a·ble (kŭm′fər tə bəl *or* kŭmf′-tə bəl) *adj.* **1.** Providing physical comfort: *a comfortable chair.* **2.** Without worry or anxiety; relaxed: *I felt very comfortable on stage.* **3.** Enough to meet a need; sufficient: *a comfortable income for a small family.* —**com′fort·a·bly** *adv.*

com·fort·er (kŭm′fər tər) *n.* A thick warm quilt used as a bed cover: *During the storm, we snuggled under a comforter.*

com·fy (kŭm′fē) *adj.* **com·fi·er, com·fi·est.** *Informal.* Comfortable: *comfy shoes; a comfy chair.*

com·ic (kŏm′ĭk) *adj.* **1.** Relating to comedy: *comic writing.* **2.** Humorous; amusing: *a comic situation.* —*n.* **1.** A person who is funny or amusing, especially a comedian. **2. comics.** *Informal.* Comic strips: *Have you read the comics?*

com·i·cal (kŏm′ĭ kəl) *adj.* Causing amusement or laughter; funny: *She looked comical in the large hat.* —**com′i·cal·ly** *adv.*

comic book *n.* A booklet of comic strips, usually telling only one or two stories.

comic strip *n.* A series of cartoons that tells a joke or a story, usually printed in a newspaper: *Do you have a favorite comic strip?*

com·ing (kŭm′ĭng) *adj.* **1.** Approaching; next: *The coastal towns prepared for the coming storm.* **2.** Showing promise of fame or success: *a young and coming political leader.* —*n. (usually singular).* Arrival: *With the coming of spring, the days become longer.* ♦ **comings and goings.** *Informal.* The movements of people in preparation for some event: *With all the comings and goings as we got ready for the party, the carpet got very dirty.*

com·ma (kŏm′ə) *n.* A punctuation mark (,) used to indicate a separation of elements within a sentence, such as a series of items or an independent clause.

com·mand (kə mănd′) *v.* —*tr.* **1.** To direct (a person or group) with authority; give orders to: *The control tower commanded the pilot to land elsewhere.* **2.** To have control or authority over (a person or group); rule: *The general commands thousands of troops.* **3.** To deserve and receive (sthg.): *His bravery commands respect.* **4.** To have control over (sthg.) by position; overlook: *That mountain commands the valley below.* —*intr.* **1.** To give orders: *The coach commanded in a loud voice.* **2.** To exercise authority as a commander; be in control: *The general commanded through a staff of junior* *officers.* —*n.* **1.** [C] An order or a direction: *Dogs can be trained to follow commands.* **2.** [U] The possession or use of authority to command: *The admiral was in command of the navy.* **3.** [C; U] Ability to control or use; mastery: *She has a command of French and Russian.* —*adj.* **1.** Relating to or being a command: *a command decision.* **2.** Done in response to a command: *a command performance.*

com•man•deer (kŏm′ən dîr′) *tr.v.* To seize (property) for public use, especially for military use: *The police commandeered a taxi to chase the car thief.*

com•mand•er (kə măn′dər) *n.* **1.** A person who commands, especially a commanding military officer. **2.** An officer in the U.S. Navy or Coast Guard ranking below a captain.

commander in chief *n., pl.* **commanders in chief. 1.** The commander of all the armed forces of a nation: *The President is commander in chief of the armed forces of the United States.* **2.** The officer commanding a major armed force: *the commander in chief of Pacific forces.*

com•mand•ing (kə măn′dĭng) *adj.* **1.** Having command; in charge: *The captain is the commanding officer of an ocean liner.* **2.** Dominating, because of position or size: *a commanding lead over an opponent.*

com•mand•ment (kə mănd′mənt) *n.* **1. Commandment.** One of the Ten Commandments in the Bible. **2.** A command; an order.

com•man•do (kə măn′dō) *n., pl.* **com•man•dos** or **com•man•does.** A member of a small fighting force trained for making quick raids into enemy territory.

com•mem•o•rate (kə mĕm′ə rāt′) *tr.v.* **com•mem•o•rat•ed, com•mem•o•rat•ing, com•mem•o•rates. 1.** To honor the memory of (a person, group, or event): *A large crowd gathered in the park to commemorate the sacrifice of all American soldiers.* **2.** To be a memorial to (sthg.), as a holiday, ceremony, or statue: *The statue commemorates a military victory.* —**com•mem′-o•ra′tion** *n.* [U] —**com•mem′o•ra•tive** (kə mĕm′ər ə tĭv *or* kə mĕm′ə rā tĭv) *adj.*

com•mence (kə mĕns′) *intr. & tr.v.* **com•menced, com•menc•ing, com•menc•es.** *Formal.* To begin; start: *The festivities commenced with the national anthem. A lawsuit commences legal action.* See Synonyms at **begin.**

com•mence•ment (kə-mĕns′mənt) *n.* **1.** [C] A graduation ceremony in which students receive their diplomas: *Com-*

commencement
College graduation ceremony

mencement will be held at 1:00 in the auditorium. **2.** [C; U] A beginning; a start: *The commencement of the Olympic games is marked by a parade.*

com•mend (kə mĕnd′) *tr.v.* **1.** To speak highly of (sbdy.); praise: *The principal commended the students for their skill in algebra.* **2.** To put (sbdy./sthg.) in the care of sbdy.: *The sick patient was commended to the care of the doctor.*

com•mend•a•ble (kə mĕn′də bəl) *adj.* Praiseworthy: *a commendable performance of a difficult play.* —**com•mend′a•bly** *adv.*

com•men•da•tion (kŏm′ən dā′shən) *n.* *Formal.* An official award or citation, often for bravery: *The firefighter received a commendation.*

com•men•su•rate (kə mĕn′sər ĭt *or* kə-mĕn′shər ĭt) *adj.* [*with*] Equal; in proportion: *I want a salary commensurate with my performance.* —**com•men′su•rate•ly** *adv.*

com•ment (kŏm′ĕnt) *n.* **1.** [C] A written note or a remark that explains, interprets, or gives an opinion on sthg.: *a critic's comment on a play; the newspaper's comments on the governor's speech.* **2.** [U] Talk; gossip: *Their fighting caused much comment among friends.* —*intr.v.* To make a comment; remark: *He commented on my new red coat.*

com•men•tar•y (kŏm′ən tĕr′ē) *n., pl.* **com•men•tar•ies.** [C; U] An instance or a series of explanations, opinions, or interpretations: *He gave his commentary as we watched the movie. The scandal is a sad commentary on our city government.*

com•men•ta•tor (kŏm′ən tā′tər) *n.* A writer or broadcaster who explains or gives opinions of events: *The commentators gave opposing views at the end of the newscast.*

com•merce (kŏm′ərs) *n.* [U] The buying and selling of goods, especially on a large scale; trade. See Synonyms at **business.**

com•mer•cial (kə mûr′shəl) *adj.* **1.** Relating to commerce: *a commercial loan from the bank.* **2.** Done or created to make a profit: *The professor writes scholarly books, not commercial ones.* **3.** Sponsored by an advertiser or supported by advertising: *a commercial television station.* —*n.* An advertisement on radio or television. —**com•mer′cial•ly** *adv.* —**com•mer′cial•ism** *n.* [U]

com•mer•cial•ize (kə mûr′shə līz′) *tr.v.* **com•mer•cial•ized, com•mer•cial•iz•ing, com•mer•cial•iz•es. 1.** To apply business methods to (sthg.) in order to make a profit: *commercialize agriculture.* **2.** To do, make, or use (sthg.) mainly for profit: *Many of the island's beaches have been heavily commercialized and spoiled.* —**com•mer′cial•i•za′tion** (kə mûr′shə lĭ zā′shən) *n.* [U]

ă–cat; ā–pay; âr–care; ä–father; ĕ–get; ē–be; ĭ–sit; ī–nice; îr–here; ŏ–got; ō–go; ô–saw; oi–boy; ou–out; ōō–took; ōō–boot; ŭ–cut; ûr–word; th–thin; *th*–this; hw–when; zh–vision; ə–about; N–French bon

com·min·gle (kə mĭng′gəl) *tr. & intr.v.* **com·min·gled, com·min·gling, com·min·gles.** To blend or mix together; combine: *cities where people of many nationalities commingle.*

com·mis·er·ate (kə mĭz′ə rāt′) *tr. & intr.v.* **com·mis·er·at·ed, com·mis·er·at·ing, com·mis·er·ates.** To feel or express sorrow or pity for; sympathize: *defeated candidates commiserating with one another; commiserate a loss.* —**com·mis′er·a′tion** (kə mĭz′ə rā′shən) *n.* [U]

com·mis·sion (kə mĭsh′ən) *n.* **1.a.** [U] The act of granting authority to sbdy. to carry out a certain job or duty: *The commission of ambassadors is one of the duties of the President.* **b.** [C] The authority given by such a grant: *The artist was given a commission to paint the actor's picture.* **2.** [C] A group of people who have been given authority by law to perform certain duties: *The President set up a commission to investigate ways of improving education.* **3.** [U] The act of committing or doing sthg.: *the commission of a crime.* **4.** [C; U] Money in the form of a fee or a percentage of a price paid to a salesperson or agent for services: *The dealer's commission on the $500 sale was $50.* **5.** [C] Appointment to the rank of a commissioned officer in the armed forces: *The pilot received a commission in the air force.* —*tr.v.* **1.** To give a commission for (sthg.) or to (sbdy.): *The king commissioned the expedition. The Coast Guard commissioned new officers at graduation.* **2.** To place an order for (sthg.): *The duke commissioned a new symphony from the composer.* **3.** To put (a ship) into active service: *The ship was commissioned in 1940.* ♦ **in commission.** In use or in usable condition; available: *Only two computers are in commission.* **out of commission.** Not in working condition; not available: *Three machines are out of commission and need repairs.*

com·mis·sion·er (kə mĭsh′ə nər) *n.* **1.** A member of a commission: *one of the planning commissioners.* **2.** An official in charge of a governmental department or an organized professional sport: *a police commissioner; the baseball commissioner.*

com·mit (kə mĭt′) *tr.v.* **com·mit·ted, com·mit·ting, com·mits.** **1.** To do, perform, or be guilty of (a mistake or crime): *commit a crime; commit a serious blunder.* **2.** [*to*] To place (sbdy./sthg.) in the keeping of another; entrust: *commit oneself to the care of a doctor; commit responsibilities to an assistant.* **3.** To place (sbdy.) in confinement or custody by an official act: *The judge committed the criminal to prison for two years.* **4.** [*to*] To place (sthg.) for future use or preservation: *The spy committed the secret code to memory.* **5.** To promise or obligate (oneself): *He committed himself to finish the project by Friday.*

com·mit·ment (kə mĭt′mənt) *n.* **1.** [U] The act of committing: *the commitment of poems to memory.* **2.** [C; U] A promise or an obligation to keep certain beliefs or to follow a certain course of action: *The President takes an oath that is a binding commitment to uphold the laws of the United States.* **3.** [C] The state of being emotionally or mentally bound to another person or to a course of action: *a strong commitment to each other; a deep commitment to help clean up the environment.*

com·mit·tee (kə mĭt′ē) *n.* A group of people chosen to do a particular job or to fulfill specified duties: *A committee of five members is investigating the best ways of using computers to teach mathematics.* —SEE NOTE at **collective noun.**

com·mod·i·ty (kə mŏd′ĭ tē) *n., pl.* **com·mod·i·ties.** An article of trade or commerce, such as grains or minerals: *Wheat, oil, and aluminum are commodities of international trade.*

com·mon (kŏm′ən) *adj.* **1.** Belonging to, done by, shared by, or relating to all or most members of a community: *common interests in the neighborhood; health regulations enforced for the common good.* **2.** Found often and in many places; usual: *Gas stations became common as the use of cars grew.* **3.** Most widely known of its kind; ordinary: *the common field mouse.* **4.** Of no special quality; average: *Common sneakers cost less than running shoes.* **5.** Unrefined or coarse in manner; vulgar: *He thought her behavior was common.* —*n.* An area of land belonging to or used by a community as a whole: *The early New England town had a common for citizens to graze their sheep.* ♦ **common ground.** An area of agreement, shared values, or shared opinions: *Before we can work together, we need to find some common ground.* **in common.** Equally with another or others; jointly: *The partners have interests in common.* —**com′mon·ly** *adv.* —**com′mon·ness** *n.* [U]

common denominator *n.* A number that is a multiple of the denominators of a group of fractions: *When you find a common denominator, it is possible to add and subtract fractions.*

com·mon·er (kŏm′ə nər) *n.* A person without royal rank or title: *It isn't unusual for modern royalty to marry commoners.*

common noun *n.* A noun that is the name of a class or group of things or people. *Teacher, car,* and *crowd* are common nouns. —SEE NOTE at **noun.**

com·mon·place (kŏm′ən plās′) *adj.* Ordinary; common; uninteresting: *a commonplace story about good guys against bad guys.*

common sense *n.* [U] Good judgment gained from everyday experience: *She's very intelligent, but she doesn't have much common sense.*

com·mon·wealth (kŏm′ən wĕlth′) *n.* **1.** The people of a nation or state: *It is the duty of the commonwealth to defend the nation.* **2.** A nation or state governed by the people; a union of states; a republic: *Canada is one of the commonwealths of North America.* **3. Commonwealth.** The official title of some U.S. states, specifically Kentucky, Maryland, Massachusetts, Pennsylvania, and Virginia. **4. Commonwealth.** An organization of countries that were formerly British colonies; the Commonwealth of Nations.

com·mo·tion (kə mō′shən) *n.* [C; U] A disturbance or confusion; tumult: *The argument created a commotion in the hall.*

com·mu·nal (kə myōō′nəl *or* kŏm′yə nəl) *adj.* Belonging to, used by, or serving the people of a community: *the communal dining room of a dormitory.* —**com·mu′nal·ly** *adv.*

com·mune[1] (kə myōōn′) *intr.v.* **com·muned, com·mun·ing, com·munes.** [*with*] To feel a sense of closeness or intimacy; share: *a hiker communing with nature.*

com·mune[2] (kŏm′yōōn′ *or* kə myōōn′) *n.* A small community whose members have common interests and in which property is often shared or owned jointly: *an agricultural commune.*

com·mu·ni·ca·ble (kə myōō′nĭ kə bəl) *adj.* Capable of being passed from person to person: *Chicken pox and measles are communicable diseases.* —**com·mu′ni·ca·bly** *adv.*

com·mu·ni·cate (kə myōō′nĭ kāt′) *v.* **com·mu·ni·cat·ed, com·mu·ni·cat·ing, com·mu·ni·cates.** —*tr.* **1.** To make (sthg.) known; share: *A good speaker communicates ideas clearly.* **2.** To pass on (a disease); transmit. —*intr.* **1.** To have an exchange, as of ideas or information: *The telephone makes it possible to communicate over long distances.* **2.** To be connected: *a hallway that communicates with each bedroom.* —**com·mu′ni·ca′tor** *n.*

com·mu·ni·ca·tion (kə myōō′nĭ kā′shən) *n.* **1.** [U] The act of communicating; transmission: *Unsanitary conditions contribute to the communication of disease.* **2.** [U] The exchange of thoughts, information, or messages: *Communication between people of different cultures is often difficult.* **3.** [C] Something communicated; a message: *We have received no communication from him since last week.* **4. communications.** A system for sending and receiving messages, such as by mail, telephone, or radio: *During the earthquake communications were down.*

com·mu·ni·ca·tive (kə myōō′nĭ kā′tĭv *or* kə myōō′nĭ kə tĭv) *adj.* Willing to communicate thoughts or information; not secretive: *The frightened child was not very communicative.*

com·mun·ion (kə myōōn′yən) *n.* [U] **1.** *Formal.* The act or an instance of sharing, as of thoughts, feelings, or interests: *a communion of purpose among the employees.* **2. Communion.** The Christian sacrament in which people receive bread and wine.

com·mu·ni·qué (kə myōō′nĭ kā′ *or* kə-myōō′nĭ kā′) *n.* An official announcement, usually made to the press: *The government issued a communiqué stating that the economy was improving.*

com·mu·nism (kŏm′yə nĭz′əm) *n.* [U] **1.** An economic system characterized by common ownership of property for the benefit of all of society. **2. Communism.** A system of government in which the state owns all businesses and property, for the benefit of all citizens: *Communism fell in the Soviet Union in 1990.*

Com·mu·nist (kŏm′yə nĭst) *n.* **1.** A member of a Communist Party. **2.** Often **communist.** A person who believes in or supports communism. —*adj.* **1.** Relating to a Communist Party or its membership. **2.** Often **communist.** Relating to, characteristic of, or resembling communism or Communists.

com·mu·ni·ty (kə myōō′nĭ tē) *n.*, *pl.* **com·mu·ni·ties. 1.** [C] A group of people living in the same city or district and under the same government: *The community decided to build a public swimming pool.* **2.** [C] A group of people who have close ties, as through common nationality or interests: *the American community in Rome.* **3.** [C; U] Similarity or identity; closeness: *a community of interests; a spirit of community among neighbors.*

community college *n.* A two-year college established to serve a certain community and often funded in part by the government.

com·mu·ta·tive (kŏm′yə tā′tĭv *or* kə-myōō′tə tĭv) *adj.* Relating to the property of addition and multiplication, which states that the order in which numbers are added or multiplied will not change the result of the operation. For example, $2 + 3$ gives the same sum as $3 + 2$, and 2×3 gives the same product as 3×2.

com·mute (kə myōōt′) *v.* **com·mut·ed, com·mut·ing, com·mutes.** —*intr.* To travel between home and work or school on a regular basis: *She commutes 100 miles each day to work.* —*tr.* To reduce (a legal sentence) to a less severe one: *The governor commuted the sentence.* —*n.* A trip made by a commuter: *a commute of 15 miles to work.* —**com′mu·ta′tion** (kŏm′yə tā′shən) *n.* [C; U]

com·mut·er (kə myōō′tər) *n.* A person who travels regularly between a home in one community and work or school in another.

com·pact[1] (kəm păkt′ *or* kŏm′păkt′) *adj.*

1. Closely and firmly packed together; dense: *flowers growing in compact clusters.* **2.** Occupying little space or time in comparison with others of the same kind: *a compact camera; a compact weekly news summary.* —*tr.v.* (kəm **păkt′**). To press or join (sthg.) firmly together; pack together: *The dirt was compacted by the heavy trucks driving over it.* —*n.* (**kŏm′**păkt′). **1.** An automobile that is smaller than a standard model. **2.** A small case containing face powder. —**com•pact′ly** *adv.* —**com•pact′ness** *n.* [U]

com•pact² (**kŏm′**păkt′) *n.* A formal agreement or a covenant between two or more groups or countries: *a compact between nations to avoid war.*

com•pact disk (**kŏm′**păkt′) or **compact disc** *n.* A small optical disk containing data or music in digital form; a CD.

compact disk

com•pan•ion (kəm **păn′**yən) *n.* **1.** A person who goes or associates with another; a comrade: *He had three companions on his ski trip.* **2.** One of a pair or set of things; a mate: *I lost the companion to this sneaker.*

com•pan•ion•a•ble (kəm **păn′**yə nə bəl) *adj.* Suited to be a good companion; friendly: *Most dogs are companionable pets.* —**com•pan′ion•a•bly** *adv.*

com•pan•ion•ship (kəm **păn′**yən ship′) *n.* [U] The relationship of companions; fellowship: *Our companionship began in college.*

com•pa•ny (**kŭm′**pə nē) *n.*, *pl.* **com•pa•nies.** **1.** [C] A business enterprise; a firm: *That company makes many useful products.* **2.** [U] A guest or guests: *We're going to have company for dinner.* **3.** [U] **a.** A companion or companions: *I find them very interesting company.* **b.** Companionship; togetherness: *She went shopping with him, and he was grateful for the company.* **4.** [C] A group of people; a gathering: *A great company of admirers crowded around the baseball player.* **5.** [C] A group of performers organized to present plays, operas, and ballets, or to produce movies. **6.** [C] A military unit commanded by a captain or major. ♦ **part company.** To end a relationship or association: *They couldn't stop fighting, so they decided to part company.* —SEE NOTE at **collective noun.**

com•pa•ra•ble (**kŏm′**pər ə bəl) *adj.* [to] **1.** Capable of being compared: *Buying a house is comparable to investing in a business.* **2.** Worthy of being compared; similar: *Some photographs are comparable to fine paintings.* —**com′pa•ra•bly** *adv.*

com•par•a•tive (kəm **păr′**ə tĭv) *adj.* **1.** Relating to a comparison: *the comparative study of related languages.* **2.** Measured in relation to sthg. else; relative: *He is a com-*

parative beginner in computer skills. **3.** In grammar, showing greater quality or quantity expressed by an adjective or adverb: *Bigger is the comparative form of* big. —*n.* In grammar, the comparative form of an adjective or adverb: *Worse is the comparative of* bad *or* badly. —**com•par′a•tive•ly** *adv.*

com•pare (kəm **pâr′**) *v.* **com•pared, com•par•ing, com•pares.** —*tr.* **1.** [to] To describe (sbdy./sthg.) as similar to another; liken: *Shakespeare compared the world to a stage.* **2.a.** [with] To examine (sbdy./sthg.) for similarities and differences with another: *Let's compare cooking over heat with cooking in a microwave oven.* **b.** To examine (two or more people or things) for similarities and differences: *The magazine article compared brands of cameras.* —*intr.* [with] To be worthy of comparison: *His photographs do not compare with yours.* ♦ **compare apples and oranges.** To try to find similarity in two things so different that they cannot be compared: *Comparing the two cities is like comparing apples and oranges.*

com•par•i•son (kəm **păr′**ĭ sən) *n.* [C; U] **1.** The act or result of comparing: *My comparison of prices shows that you will save money if you shop downtown.* **2.** The quality of being similar; likeness: *There is no comparison between homemade bread and bread bought in a store.*

com•part•ment (kəm **pärt′**mənt) *n.* One of the parts or spaces into which sthg. is divided: *My wallet is divided into compartments for dollar bills and coins.*

com•pass (**kŭm′**pəs or **kŏm′**pəs) *n.* **1.a.** A device used to determine direction, with a magnetic needle that points to magnetic north. **b.** Any of several other devices, such as a radio compass, used to determine direction. **2.** A device used for drawing circles and arcs and for measuring distances, consisting of two legs hinged together at one end.

compass

com•pas•sion (kəm **păsh′**ən) *n.* [U] The deep awareness of the suffering of another, together with a desire to relieve it; pity: *compassion for the homeless.*

com•pas•sion•ate (kəm **păsh′**ə nĭt) *adj.* Feeling or showing compassion; sympathetic: *a compassionate doctor.* —**com•pas′sion•ate•ly** *adv.*

com•pat•i•ble (kəm **păt′**ə bəl) *adj.* [with] Capable of working or existing together; suitable: *They are very compatible with their cousins and enjoyed the trip together.* —**com•pat′i•bil′i•ty** *n.* [U] —**com•pat′i•bly** *adv.*

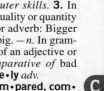

com·pa·tri·ot (kəm pā′trē ət) *n.* A person from one's own country: *We were both born in Canada; we're compatriots.*

com·pel (kəm pĕl′) *tr.v.* **com·pelled, com·pel·ling, com·pels.** To make (sbdy.) do sthg. by force, necessity, or powerful influence; make necessary: *The sudden storm compelled us to go indoors.*

com·pel·ling (kəm pĕl′ĭng) *adj.* Having a very strong influence or effect; powerful; forceful: *a compelling argument.* **—com·pel′ling·ly** *adv.*

com·pen·sate (kŏm′pən sāt′) *v.* **com·pen·sat·ed, com·pen·sat·ing, com·pen·sates.** **—** *tr.* To make satisfactory payment to (sbdy.); reimburse: *The store compensates its clerks for extra time worked during the holiday season.* **—** *intr.* To provide a balancing effect: *We worked extra hard to compensate for the hour lost.* **—com·pen′sa·to·ry** (kəm pĕn′sə tôr′ē) *adj.*

com·pen·sa·tion (kŏm′pən sā′shən) *n.* [U] **1.** Something given or received as payment or as a balance for a loss: *The firefighter's family received compensation when he was killed fighting a fire.* **2.** The act of compensating: *Worker compensation is handled by the payroll department.*

com·pete (kəm pēt′) *intr.v.* **com·pet·ed, com·pet·ing, com·petes.** To participate in a race or contest against another or others to attain sthg., such as a prize: *compete in a race; compete for someone's business.*

com·pe·tence (kŏm′pĭ təns) *n.* [U] The ability to do what is required; adequate skill or knowledge: *She demonstrated her competence by finishing the report early.*

com·pe·ten·cy (kŏm′pĭ tən sē) *n., pl.* **com·pe·ten·cies.** [C; U] Competence.

com·pe·tent (kŏm′pĭ tənt) *adj.* **1.** Able to do sthg. with adequate skill; capable: *a competent worker.* **2.** Legally qualified: *a competent physician registered to give medical treatment.* **—com′pe·tent·ly** *adv.*

com·pe·ti·tion (kŏm′pĭ tĭsh′ən) *n.* **1.** [U] The act of competing, as for a prize; rivalry: *a race in competition with ten contestants; competition in the jungle for food.* **2.** [C] A test of skill or ability; a contest: *a skating competition.* **3.** [U] A competitor: *Is the competition as good as our team?*

com·pet·i·tive (kəm pĕt′ĭ tĭv) *adj.* **1.** Involving or decided by competition: *competitive games.* **2.** Liking competition or inclined to compete: *Most athletes are competitive people.* **—com·pet′i·tive·ly** *adv.* **—com·pet′i·tive·ness** *n.* [U]

com·pet·i·tor (kəm pĕt′ĭ tər) *n.* A person, team, business organization, or other group that competes with another or others; an opponent or a rival: *We are better trained than our competitors, so we are sure to win the race.*

com·pi·la·tion (kŏm′pə lā′shən) *n.* **1.** [U] The act of compiling: *Computers are useful in the compilation of facts and figures.* **2.** [C] Something that has been compiled, such as a collection of written works or a record.

com·pile (kəm pīl′) *tr.v.* **com·piled, com·pil·ing, com·piles.** To put together (facts, information, or other matter from several sources) into a single collection, set, or record: *She is compiling family records for a book about her great-grandmother.* **—com·pil′er** *n.*

com·pla·cen·cy (kəm plā′sən sē) *n.* [U] A feeling of satisfaction with oneself or with what one has done; smugness: *The sudden drop in sales shook the business leaders out of their complacency.*

com·pla·cent (kəm plā′sənt) *adj.* Pleased or contented with oneself; self-satisfied; smug: *She wore the complacent look of someone who has won too often.* **—com·pla′cent·ly** *adv.*

com·plain (kəm plān′) *intr.v.* [*about*] To say that one is in pain or dissatisfied or that sthg. is wrong: *They worked hard all day and never complained. Complain to the telephone company about the mistake in your bill.*

com·plaint (kəm plānt′) *n.* **1.** [C; U] An expression of pain, dissatisfaction, or unhappiness: *a complaint about carelessness; no cause for complaint.* **2.** [C] A cause or reason for complaining; a grievance: *The tenants sent a list of their complaints to the landlord.* **3.** [C] A formal charge of the commission of a crime: *The storekeeper signed a complaint accusing the suspect of robbery.* **4.** [C] Something, such as an illness, that causes pain or discomfort: *Colds are a common winter complaint.*

com·ple·ment (kŏm′plə mənt) *n.* **1.** Something that completes, makes up a whole, or brings to perfection: *Attractive trees are a complement to a fine building.* **2.** The number or amount needed to make sthg. complete: *library shelves with a full complement of books.* **3.** In grammar, a word or group of words, such as adjectives or nouns, that follows a transitive or linking verb. For example, *worm* in *The robin ate the worm* and *cold* in *The water feels cold* are complements. **4.** An angle related to another so that their sum is 90°. If an angle measures 30°, its complement is 60°. **5.** Either of two complementary colors: *Blue is the complement of orange.* **—** *tr.v.* (kŏm′plə mĕnt′). To make (sthg.) complete; be a complement to: *That easy chair complements the furnishings of the room.*

USAGE: complement The word **complement** means "sthg. that completes or brings to perfection": *The flowers were a perfect complement to the beautifully set table.* **Compliment** means "an expression of courtesy or praise": *They gave us a compliment on our beautiful dinner table.*

HOMONYMS: complement, compliment (praise).

com·ple·men·ta·ry (kŏm′plə měn′tə rē *or* kŏm′plə měn′trē) *adj.* Serving as a complement; supplying what is lacking or needed: *a sofa and some complementary chairs.*

HOMONYMS: complementary, complimentary (praising).

complementary angles *pl.n.* Two angles whose sum is 90 degrees.

complementary color *n.* One of two colors, such as red and green, that form gray when mixed in the proper proportions.

com·plete (kəm plēt′) *adj.* **1.** Having all necessary or normal parts; entire: *We found a complete set of an encyclopedia at the yard sale.* **2.** Ended; finished: *A job is complete when all the tools are put away.* **3.** Absolute; total: *It was a complete shock to open the door and see you—I thought you were on a trip.* —*tr.v.* **com·plet·ed, com·plet·ing, com·pletes. 1.** To add what is missing from (sthg.); make whole *A year abroad will complete your education.* **2.** To bring (sthg.) to an end; finish: *The farmers completed the spring planting.* —**com·plete′ly** *adv.* —**com·plete′ness** *n.* [U]

SYNONYMS: complete, close, end, conclude. These verbs mean to bring to a stopping point. **Complete** means to bring sthg. to fulfillment: *The students will complete their science projects next week.* **Close** means to complete sthg. that has been going on for some time: *The orchestra closed the concert with an encore.* **End** emphasizes a definite conclusion: *The book was good, but it ended too quickly.* **Conclude** can mean to complete or close in a formal way: *The United Nations concluded the conference yesterday.*

com·ple·tion (kəm plē′shən) *n.* [U] The act of completing sthg.: *Completion of the building took only three weeks.*

com·plex (kəm plĕks′ *or* kŏm′plĕks) *adj.* **1.** Consisting of many connected parts or factors; intricate: *the complex wiring of a computer.* **2.** Difficult to understand or explain: *a complex theory.* —*n.* (kŏm′plĕks′). **1.** A system or unit consisting of a large number of parts: *a complex of businesses.* **2.** A group of related ideas, wishes, or emotions that influence a person's behavior and personality: *an inferiority complex.* —**com·plex′ly** *adv.*

complex fraction *n.* A fraction having a fraction in the numerator, denominator, or both.

com·plex·ion (kəm plĕk′shən) *n.* **1.** The color, texture, and appearance of the skin, especially of the face: *The skier had a tanned complexion from being outside.* **2.** The general character, aspect, or nature of sthg.: *The whole complexion of the situation improved with the good news.*

com·plex·i·ty (kəm plĕk′sĭ tē) *n., pl.* **com·plex·i·ties. 1.** [U] The condition of being complex: *the complexity of modern civilization.* **2.** [C] Something complex: *the complexities of the subway system.*

complex number *n.* A number that can be expressed as $a + bi$, where a and b are real numbers and i is an imaginary number whose square equals -1.

complex sentence *n.* A sentence containing an independent clause and one or more dependent clauses. For example, *When the rain ends, we will go home* is a complex sentence.

com·pli·ance (kəm plī′əns) *n.* [U] **1.** The act of complying: *Compliance with a country's laws is expected of all citizens.* **2.** A tendency to yield to others: *His colleagues take advantage of his compliance by giving him all the unpleasant jobs.*

com·pli·ant (kəm plī′ənt) *adj.* Inclined or willing to yield to the wishes or requests of others: *You need to stop being so compliant and learn to say "no."* —**com·pli′ant·ly** *adv.*

com·pli·cate (kŏm′plĭ kāt′) *tr.v.* **com·pli·cat·ed, com·pli·cat·ing, com·pli·cates.** To make (sthg.) more complex, confusing, or difficult to do: *The new information only complicates an already serious problem.*

com·pli·cat·ed (kŏm′plĭ kā′tĭd) *adj.* **1.** Made up of many intricately combined or involved parts: *a complicated computer program.* **2.** Not easy to understand or solve: *a long complicated explanation.*

com·pli·ca·tion (kŏm′plĭ kā′shən) *n.* **1.** [C] Something that increases difficulty, confusion, or complexity: *Your suggestions just add complications to an already difficult situation.* **2.** [C] A difficult or confused state or condition: *The executive tried to simplify the complications of the employees' vacation schedule.* **3.** [U] The act of complicating.

com·plic·i·ty (kəm plĭs′ĭ tē) *n.* [U] Participation in a crime or wrongdoing: *Complicity in the theft cost the accountants their reputation.*

com·pli·ment (kŏm′plə mənt) *n.* **1.** An expression of praise, admiration, or congratulation: *The author received many compliments on the new book.* **2.** An act showing honor or courtesy: *The neighbors paid us the compliment of an invitation to dinner.* **3.**

compliments. Good wishes; greetings: *Please extend my compliments to your parents.* —*tr.v.* To pay a compliment to (sbdy.): *The critic complimented both artists on their work.* —SEE NOTE at **complement.**

HOMONYMS: compliment, complement (sthg. that completes).

com·pli·men·ta·ry (kŏm′plə mĕn′tə rē *or* kŏm′plə mĕn′trē) *adj.* **1.** Expressing praise or admiration: *The reviewer was not very complimentary about the movie.* **2.** Given free: *a complimentary copy of a new book.*

HOMONYMS: complimentary, complementary (completing).

com·ply (kəm plī′) *intr.v.* **com·plied, com·ply·ing, com·plies.** [*with*] To act in accordance with a request, rule, or order: *Sick people should comply with their doctor's orders.*

com·po·nent (kəm pō′nənt) *n.* One of the parts that make up a whole: *Components such as batteries make up an electric circuit.* —*adj.* Being or functioning as a part or an ingredient: *The loudspeakers and amplifiers are component parts of our stereo system.*

com·pose (kəm pōz′) *v.* **com·posed, com·pos·ing, com·pos·es.** —*tr.* **1.** To make up the parts of (sthg.); form: *The heart, veins, arteries, and capillaries compose the circulatory system.* **2.** To make or create (sthg.) by putting parts or elements together: *She composed the speech from entries in her journal.* **3.** To create (a musical or literary work): *compose a symphony.* **4.** To make (oneself) calm, controlled, or orderly: *compose oneself before making a speech.* —*intr.* To create literary or musical pieces: *Chopin composed mostly for the piano.*

WORD BUILDING: compose The word root —pose— means "to put." Compose therefore literally means "to put together" (using the prefix com—, which means "with"). The word propose, as in *propose an idea*, contains a prefix, pro—, which means "forward," and the root —pose—, which means "put." *To propose an idea* is "to put an idea forward."

com·posed (kəm pōzd′) *adj.* Being in control of one's emotions; calm; serene.

com·pos·er (kəm pō′zər) *n.* A person who composes, especially a creator of musical works.

com·pos·ite (kəm pŏz′ĭt) *adj.* Made up of different parts: *The photograph was a composite picture of several snapshots of family members.* —*n.* Something made by combining different parts: *The report was a composite of many facts and tables from different sources.*

composite number *n.* A whole number divisible without a remainder by at least one whole number other than itself and 1.

com·po·si·tion (kŏm′pə zĭsh′ən) *n.* **1.** [U] The act or process of putting together parts or elements to form a whole: *The composition of a symphony can take months.* **2.** [C] A work created by such a process, as a musical work or a short essay: *My composition was six pages long.* **3.** [U] The parts or constituents forming a whole: *the chemical composition of a mineral.* **4.** [C] A mixture of substances: *Concrete is a composition of gravel and cement.*

com·post (kŏm′pōst′) *n.* [U] A mixture of decaying organic matter, such as leaves or manure, used as fertilizer.

com·po·sure (kəm pō′zhər) *n.* [U] Control over one's emotions; calmness: *Don't lose your composure over a mistake.*

com·pote (kŏm′pōt) *n.* Sweetened stewed fruit, served as a dessert.

com·pound¹ (kəm pound′ *or* kŏm′pound′) *tr.v.* **1.** To put (things) together to form a whole; combine: *compound ingredients to make paint.* **2.** To add to (sthg.); increase: *We compounded our difficulties by refusing to admit we had made a mistake.* —*adj.* (kŏm′-pound′ *or* kəm pound′). Consisting of two or more parts, ingredients, elements, or substances: *a compound word.* —*n.* (kŏm′-pound′). **1.** Something consisting of a combination of two or more parts or ingredients: *Cough syrup is usually a compound of alcohol, sweet flavoring, and some medicine.* **2.** A word consisting of a combination of two or more other words and forming a single unit with its own meaning. The words *loudspeaker, baby-sit,* and *high school* are compounds. **3.** A substance formed by chemical combination of two or more elements in definite proportions by weight: *Water is a compound of hydrogen and oxygen.*

com·pound² (kŏm′pound′) *n.* A group of houses or other buildings, enclosed by a wall, fence, or other barrier.

compound fracture *n.* A bone fracture in which a sharp piece of bone cuts through nearby soft tissue and makes an open wound.

compound interest *n.* [U] Interest computed on an amount of money constituting the principal plus all the unpaid interest already earned.

compound sentence *n.* A sentence of two or more independent clauses, usually joined by a conjunction such as *and, but,* or *or.* For example, *The problem was difficult, but I found the answer* is a compound sentence.

com·pre·hend (kŏm′prĭ hĕnd′) *tr.v.* To

understand (sthg.): *Many people do not comprehend how computers work.*

com·pre·hen·si·ble (kŏm′ prĭ hĕn′sə bəl) *adj.* Easily understood; understandable: *I was able to make the menu comprehensible to our visitor from Japan.* —**com′pre·hen′si·bil′i·ty** *n.* [U] —**com′pre·hen′si·bly** *adv.*

com·pre·hen·sion (kŏm′ prĭ hĕn′shən) *n.* [U] **1.** The act or fact of understanding sthg.: *Comprehension of basic chemistry is not as difficult as you think.* **2.** The capacity to understand sthg.: *Algebra is well within your comprehension.*

com·pre·hen·sive (kŏm′ prĭ hĕn′sĭv) *adj.* Including much; thorough: *The last chapter is a comprehensive review of the book's contents.* —**com′pre·hen′sive·ly** *adv.* —**com′pre·hen′sive·ness** *n.* [U]

com·press (kəm prĕs′) *tr.v.* **1.** To squeeze or press (things) together: *He compressed his lips into a thin line.* **2.** To make (sthg.) smaller or shorter by squeezing or pressing: *compress one's thoughts into a short statement.* —*n.* (kŏm′prĕs′). A soft pad of cotton or other material applied to a wound or injury: *The doctor put a cold compress on the bee sting.* —**com·pressed′** *adj.* —**com·pres′sion** *n.* [U]

com·pres·sor (kəm prĕs′ər) *n.* A device or machine that compresses, especially one used to compress a gas, as in a refrigerator.

com·prise (kəm prīz′) *tr.v.* **com·prised, com·pris·ing, com·pris·es. 1.** To consist of (one or more elements); include: *The United Nations comprises more than 130 countries.* **2.** To make up (sthg.); form; constitute: *Milk, butter, and cheese comprise the bulk of dairy products.*

com·pro·mise (kŏm′prə mīz′) *n.* [C; U] **1.** A settlement of an argument in which each side gives up some of what it wants: *By agreeing to share the cost, our neighbors reached a compromise over rebuilding the fence.* **2.** Something that combines qualities or elements of different things: *The design of the car is a compromise between style and safety.* —*v.* **com·pro·mised, com·pro·mis·ing, com·pro·mis·es.** —*tr.* **1.** To settle an argument by giving up some of (sthg. valued): *Those who often compromise their principles usually end up with none.* **2.** To expose (sbdy./sthg.) to dishonor or suspicion: *The scandal will surely compromise his reputation.* —*intr.* To make a compromise: *We compromised and bought both kinds of tea.*

comp·trol·ler (kən trō′lər) *n.* Variant of **controller** (sense 2).

com·pul·sion (kəm pŭl′shən) *n.* **1.** [U] The act of compelling or the state of being compelled: *In wartime, the government can use compulsion to obtain supplies and troops from the nation.* **2.** [C] An irresistible urge or impulse: *a compulsion to stay up late.*

com·pul·sive (kəm pŭl′sĭv) *adj.* Having or resulting from a strong irresistible impulse: *Some people have a compulsive desire to talk.* —**com·pul′sive·ly** *adv.* —**com·pul′sive·ness** *n.* [U]

com·pul·so·ry (kəm pŭl′sə rē) *adj.* Required by law, regulations, or duty: *Education is compulsory for children in most countries.*

com·punc·tion (kəm pŭngk′shən) *n.* [U] An uneasy feeling that one has done sthg. wrong; regret: *The children showed no compunction about eating all the cookies.*

com·pu·ta·tion (kŏm′ pyoo tā′shən) *n.* [C; U] The act of computing; mathematical calculation: *I can't do these computations in my head.*

com·pute (kəm pyoot′) *v.* **com·put·ed, com·put·ing, com·putes.** —*tr.* **1.** To find (a result, an answer, or a solution) by mathematics; calculate: *The bank computes the interest on savings accounts.* **2.** To determine (sthg.) by use of a computer: *compute the most efficient design of a sailboat.* —*intr.* To determine an amount or a number.

com·put·er (kəm pyoo′tər) *n.* An electronic device that stores and processes information according to a set of instructions stored within the device.

computer graphics *n.* *(used with a singular or plural verb).* Graphic artwork, such as maps, diagrams, or pictures, produced with a computer.

computer
Personal computer
with monitor, disk
drive, and keyboard

com·put·er·ize (kəm pyoo′tə rīz′) *tr.v.* **com·put·er·ized, com·put·er·iz·ing, com·put·er·iz·es. 1.** To process or store (information) in a computer: *We are trying to computerize the office files.* **2.** To furnish (a person or business) with a computer or a system of computers: *computerize an office.*

computer language *n.* A system of symbols, letters, and punctuation, along with a set of rules, that is used to tell a computer what to do and how to do it. BASIC and COBOL are computer languages.

computer literacy *n.* [U] The ability to operate a computer and to understand how a computer works.

computer science *n.* [U] The study of the design and operation of computers and their uses in science, business, and the arts.

com·rade (kŏm′răd′) *n.* **1.** A trusted companion, especially a person who shares school and other activities. **2.** Often **Comrade.** A fellow member of a group, especially a fellow member of the Communist Party. —**com′rade·ship′** *n.* [U]

con[1] (kŏn) *adv.* In disagreement; against: *arguing a question pro and con.* —*n. (usually plural).* An argument or a consideration against sthg.: *discussing the pros and cons of the subject.*

con[2] (kŏn) *tr.v.* **conned, con•ning, cons.** *Slang.* To trick or coax (sbdy.) into doing sthg. by first winning the person's confidence: *She'll con someone into buying her junky old car.* —*n.* An instance of cheating sbdy. out of money or property; a swindle: *He was involved in some type of con.*

con[3] (kŏn) *n. Slang.* A convict: *an ex-con.*

con•cave (kŏn kāv′ or kŏn′kāv′) *adj.* Curved inward like the inside of a circle or sphere. —**con• cave′ly** *adv.* —**con• cave′ness** *n.* [U]

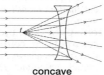

concave

Light passing through a double-concave lens, with f indicating the focus

con•cav•i•ty (kŏn-kăv′ĭ tē) *n.* [U] The condition of being concave: *The concavity of the mirror allows it to focus the rays of the sun into a beam.*

con•ceal (kən sēl′) *tr.v.* **1.** To keep (sbdy./sthg.) from being seen; put out of sight: *A bank of clouds concealed the setting sun.* See Synonyms at **hide**[1]. **2.** To keep (sthg.) secret: *conceal hurt feelings.* —**con•ceal′a•ble** *adj.* —**con•ceal′er** *n.* —**con•ceal′ment** *n.* [U]

con•cede (kən sēd′) *v.* **con•ced•ed, con• ced•ing, con•cedes.** —*tr.* **1.** To admit (sthg.) as true or real, often unwillingly or hesitantly; acknowledge: *The losing candidate finally conceded defeat the morning after election day.* **2.** To give, yield, or grant (sthg.) to sbdy.: *After the uprising, the government conceded the right to vote to its citizens.* —*intr.* To make a concession; yield: *The candidate refused to concede.*

con•ceit (kən sēt′) *n.* [U] An overly high opinion of one's abilities or worth; vanity: *The famous author's conceit was unpleasant.*

con•ceit•ed (kən sē′tĭd) *adj.* Holding or showing an overly high opinion of oneself: *a conceited actor who thinks he is better than anyone else.* —**con•ceit′ed•ly** *adv.* —**con• ceit′ed•ness** *n.* [U]

con•ceiv•a•ble (kən sē′və bəl) *adj.* Capable of being thought of; imaginable: *It is conceivable that life exists on other planets.*

con•ceive (kən sēv′) *v.* **con•ceived, con• ceiv•ing, con•ceives.** —*tr.* **1.** To form or develop (an idea) in the mind: *James Watt conceived the idea of using steam to drive an engine.* **2.** To imagine or think of (sthg.); consider: *We could not conceive such a strange*

place existed. **3.** *Formal.* To become pregnant with (offspring): *conceive a child.* —*intr.* **1.** [*of*] To have an idea or concept; think: *People in ancient times conceived of the earth as flat.* **2.** *Formal.* To become pregnant: *She conceived last month.*

con•cen•trate (kŏn′sən trāt′) *v.* **con• cen•trat•ed, con•cen•trat•ing, con•cen• trates.** —*intr.* **1.** To keep or direct one's thoughts, attention, or efforts: *It's hard to concentrate on writing a letter with the TV on.* **2.** To come toward or meet in a common center: *The migrating geese concentrate at ponds and streams.* —*tr.* **1.** To draw or gather (sthg.) toward one place or point; focus: *For centuries the population of Europe has been concentrated in large cities.* **2.** To make (a solution or mixture) stronger. —*n.* [C; U] Something that has been concentrated: *orange juice concentrate.*

con•cen•tra•tion (kŏn′sən trā′shən) *n.* **1.** [U] The act of concentrating; giving close undivided attention: *The secret of doing your work in less time is complete concentration.* **2.** [C] A close gathering or dense grouping: *Lights shone brightly from the concentration of houses in the new development.* **3.** [C] The amount of a particular substance in a given amount of a mixture: *the concentration of salt in seawater.*

con•cen•tric (kən sĕn′-trĭk) *adj.* Having the same center: *a set of concentric circles.* —**con•cen′tri• cal•ly** *adv.*

con•cept (kŏn′sĕpt′) *n.* A general idea or understanding, especially one based on known facts or observation: *the concept*

concentric

that all matter is made up of atoms. See Synonyms at **idea.**

con•cep•tion (kən sĕp′shən) *n.* **1.** [C; U] A general idea or understanding: *The study of astronomy has given us some conception of the age of the universe.* **2.** [U] A beginning or formation of an idea: *a history of the computer from its earliest conception to the most advanced models.* **3.** [C; U] The formation of a cell capable of developing into a new organism; fertilization: *Conception took place in March, and the baby was born in December.*

con•cep•tu•al (kən sĕp′chōō əl) *adj.* Consisting of or based on a concept or concepts: *The engineers came up with a conceptual proposal for a new electric car.* —**con•cep′tu•al•ly** *adv.*

con•cep•tu•al•ize (kən sĕp′chōō ə līz′) *tr. & intr.v.* **con•cep•tu•al•ized, con•cep•**

tu·al·iz·ing, con·cep·tu·al·iz·es. To form a general idea or a concept: *The architect conceptualizes plans for houses in her head first. He conceptualizes on paper.*

con·cern (kən sûrn′) *tr.v.* **1.** To relate to or be about (sbdy./sthg.): *The story concerns the struggles of a group of rabbits who establish a new community.* **2.** To be of importance or interest to (sbdy.); involve: *Cleaning up the environment concerns all of us.* **3.** To fill (sbdy.) with care or anxiety; worry: *The lack of rain deeply concerned the farmers.* —*n.* **1.** [C] Something of interest or importance: *The author's chief concern is to write the history of the plastics industry.* **2.** [U] Worry; anxiety: *the parents' concern for their sick child.* **3.** [C] A business establishment; a firm: *Repair shops and banks are concerns that provide more services than products.*

con·cerned (kən sûrnd′) *adj.* **1.** Interested or affected; involved: *Most concerned citizens recycle trash.* **2.** Worried; troubled: *a concerned expression on his face.*

con·cern·ing (kən sûr′nĭng) *prep.* In reference to; about: *science fiction stories concerning visitors from outer space.*

con·cert (kŏn′sərt) *n.* A musical performance usually given by one or more singers or instrumentalists or both. ♦ **work** or **act in concert.** To function as a single unit or group; work together: *Several nearby towns are working in concert to ease rush-hour traffic.*

con·cert·ed (kən sûr′tĭd) *adj.* Planned or accomplished together with others; combined: *The committee made a concerted effort to reelect the president.*

con·cer·to (kən chĕr′tō) *n.*, *pl.* **con·cer·tos.** A musical composition written for one or more solo instruments and an orchestra: *a violin concerto.*

con·ces·sion (kən sĕsh′ən) *n.* **1.** [U] An act of yielding, giving in, or conceding: *settle a dispute by concession on both sides.* **2.** [C] Something yielded or conceded: *The company offered more time off and other concessions to solve the dispute with its workers.* **3.** [C] A business that has the right to operate in a certain place: *We got hot dogs at the food concession in the ballpark.*

conch (kŏngk *or* kŏnch) *n.* A tropical sea animal related to the snail with a large, often brightly colored spiral shell.

HOMONYMS: conch, conk (hit).

---

con·cil·i·ate (kən sĭl′ē āt′) *v.* **con·cil·i·at·ed, con·cil·i·at·ing, con·cil·i·ates.** —*tr.* To overcome the anger or distrust of (sbdy.): *The baby sitter tried to conciliate the angry child by reading a story.* —*intr.* To gain friendship, goodwill, or favor by friendly behavior. —**con·cil′i·a′tion** *n.* [U] —**con·cil′i·a′tor** *n.*

con·cil·i·a·to·ry (kən sĭl′ē ə tôr′ē) *adj.* Done to conciliate or having the effect of conciliating: *a conciliatory attitude that helped restore peace.*

con·cise (kən sīs′) *adj.* Expressing much in a few words; brief and clear: *a concise summary of the main points of the meeting.* —**con·cise′ly** *adv.* —**con·cise′ness** *n.* [U]

con·clude (kən klōōd′) *v.* **con·clud·ed, con·clud·ing, con·cludes.** —*tr.* **1.** To form an opinion or judgment about (sthg.); decide: *The scientist concluded that the bones were those of a dinosaur.* **2.** To arrange or settle (sthg.) finally: *conclude an agreement on trade between two countries.* **3.** To bring (sthg.) to an end; close; finish: *conclude a religious service with a prayer.* See Synonyms at **complete.** —*intr.* To come to an end; close: *The conference concluded with a call for action.*

con·clu·sion (kən klōō′zhən) *n.* **1.** The close or last part of sthg.; the end: *the exciting conclusion of a story.* **2.** A judgment or decision reached by reasoning: *Scientists check their observations thoroughly to arrive at accurate conclusions.* **3.** A final arrangement or settlement: *the conclusion of a peace treaty.* ♦ **in conclusion.** As a last statement; finally: *In conclusion, we must work together for peace.*

con·clu·sive (kən klōō′sĭv) *adj.* Putting an end to doubt, question, or uncertainty: *The new piece of evidence was conclusive and proved that he was guilty.* —**con·clu′sive·ly** *adv.* —**con·clu′sive·ness** *n.* [U]

con·coct (kən kŏkt′) *tr.v.* **1.** To make (sthg.) by mixing or combining ingredients or parts: *She was able to concoct a stew from leftover meat and vegetables.* **2.** To invent (sthg.): *concoct an excuse to avoid going to the movie.* —**con·coc′tion** *n.* [C; U]

con·cord (kŏn′kôrd *or* kŏng′kôrd′) *n.* **1.** [U] A friendly or harmonious relationship: *The neighboring nations lived in peace and concord.* **2.** [C] An agreement establishing such a relationship.

con·course (kŏn′kôrs′) *n.* A large open space in which crowds gather or pass through, as in an airport or a railroad station.

con·crete (kŏn krēt′ *or* kŏn′krēt′) *adj.* **1.** Made of concrete: *a concrete sidewalk.* **2.** Existing in reality as sthg. that can be seen or touched: *concrete objects such as trees or rocks.* **3.** Relating to real, specific ideas, not vague, general ones: *We made concrete suggestions for how to save money.* —*n.* (kŏn′krēt′ *or* kŏn krēt′). [U] A building or paving material made of sand and pebbles or crushed stone, held together by cement. —**con·crete′ly** *adv.* —**con·crete′ness** *n.* [U]

con·cur (kən kûr′) *intr.v.* **con·curred, con·cur·ring, con·curs.** *Formal.* **1.** To have the same opinion; agree: *Most people concur on the need to stop pollution.* **2.** To happen at the

C

same time: *When rain concurs with a cold snap, icy conditions usually follow.*

con·cur·rence (kən **kûr'**əns *or* kən-**kûr'**əns) *n*. **1.** [U] Agreement of opinion: *Concurrence among all of the partners led to a satisfactory business arrangement.* **2.** [C; U] An occurrence, as of several events or actions, at the same time: *an unusual concurrence of events.*

con·cur·rent (kən **kûr'**ənt *or* kən **kûr'**ənt) *adj*. **1.** Happening at the same time: *concurrent events.* **2.** Similar; harmonious: *concurrent opinions.* **3.** Meeting or tending to meet at the same point: *the intersection of concurrent lines.* —**con·cur'rent·ly** *adv.*

con·cus·sion (kən **kŭsh'**ən) *n*. [C; U] **1.** A violent shock: *The strong concussion from the blast broke many windows.* **2.** An injury to the brain, resulting from a hard blow: *He suffered a concussion in the fall.*

con·demn (kən **dĕm'**) *tr.v.* **1.** To express strong disapproval of (sbdy./sthg.); denounce: *The governor condemned the waste of taxpayers' money.* **2.a.** To judge (sbdy.) to be guilty: *The suspect was condemned by the jury.* **b.** To sentence (sbdy.) to a particular punishment: *He was condemned to 15 years in prison.* **3.** To declare (sthg.) unfit for use: *The city condemned the old building after the fire.* **4.** To take over (private property) for public use: *The state condemned farms in the path of the new highway.*

con·dem·na·tion (kŏn'dĕm **nā'**shən) *n*. [C; U] The act of condemning: *The building was torn down after condemnation.*

con·den·sate (kŏn'dən sāt' *or* kən **dĕn'**sāt') *n*. A product of condensation.

con·den·sa·tion (kŏn'dən **sā'**shən) *n*. **1.** [U] A changing from a gas or vapor to a liquid: *Cooling causes the condensation of steam to water.* **2.** [U] A liquid or solid, especially water or ice, formed by this process: *condensation on the bathroom mirror.* **3.** [C; U] The act of shortening sthg.: *The author struggled in his condensation of the long story.*

con·dense (kən **dĕns'**) *v*. **con·densed, con·dens·ing, con·dens·es.** —*tr.* **1.** To cause (a gas or vapor) to change to a liquid or solid form: *A sudden drop in temperature may condense dew or even fog into ice crystals.* **2.** To make (sthg.) more concentrated or dense: *We boiled the soup to condense it.* **3.** To make (sthg. written) shorter or more concise: *The author condensed the book for publication in a magazine.* —*intr.* **1.** To become denser or more compact: *Stars may condense from matter scattered in space.* **2.** To change from a gas to a liquid: *Water vapor will often condense on windowpanes in the winter.*

con·densed milk (kən **dĕnst'**) *n*. Sweet-

ened cow's milk that has been made very thick by evaporation before canning.

con·dens·er (kən **dĕn'**sər) *n*. **1.** A person or thing that condenses. **2.** An apparatus used to condense a gas or vapor. **3.** A capacitor.

con·de·scend (kŏn'dĭ **sĕnd'**) *intr.v.* [*to*] **1.** To agree to do sthg. that is thought to be beneath one's social rank or dignity: *The famous author condescended to autograph books.* **2.** To act in a manner that shows one considers oneself superior to others: *The family in the big house condescends to all the neighbors.* —**con'de·scend'ing** *adj.* —**con'de·scend'ing·ly** *adv.* —**con'de·scen'sion** *n*. [U]

con·di·ment (kŏn'də mənt) *n*. A sauce, relish, or spice used as a seasoning for food: *Mustard is a popular condiment.*

con·di·tion (kən **dĭsh'**ən) *n*. **1.** [C] A state of being or existence: *They worked hard to restore the old house to its original condition.* **2.** [U] **a.** A state of health or fitness: *Exercise keeps you in good condition.* **b.** Readiness for use; working order: *A few repairs will put the car in condition.* **3.** [C] A disease or physical ailment: *a heart condition.* **4. conditions.** The existing circumstances: *The committee investigated complaints about working conditions.* —*tr.v.* **1.** To put (sbdy./sthg.) into good or proper condition: *Running five miles a day will condition the track team.* **2.** To adapt (sbdy./sthg.); accustom: *The visitors from Sweden were not conditioned to the hot weather here.* **3.** To train (an organism): *The researchers conditioned the chicken to go outside when a light was turned on.* ♦ **on (the) condition that.** Provided that: *She gave us permission to use the computer on condition that we report any problems with it.*

con·di·tion·al (kən **dĭsh'**ə nəl) *adj.* **1.** Depending on a condition or conditions: *While awaiting the response of parents, the committee gave conditional approval to the plan.* **2.** In grammar, expressing a condition that is necessary in order for sthg. to happen. In the sentence *We'll go swimming if it's sunny tomorrow,* the clause *if it's sunny tomorrow* is a conditional clause.

con·di·tioned (kən **dĭsh'**ənd) *adj.* **1.** Physically fit: *a well-conditioned athlete.* **2.** Trained or established by means of conditioning: *a conditioned reflex.*

con·di·tion·er (kən **dĭsh'**ə nər) *n*. [C; U] A device or substance used to improve sthg. in some way: *a bottle of hair conditioner; an air conditioner.*

con·di·tion·ing (kən **dĭsh'**ə nĭng) *n*. [U] A process of behavior modification by which a person or animal learns to behave in a certain way in response to a stimulus.

con•do (kŏn′dō′) *n.*, *pl.* **con•dos.** *Informal.* A condominium: *They bought a new condo.*

con•do•lence (kən dō′ləns) *n.* [C; U] Sympathy or an expression of sympathy for a person who has experienced sadness or loss: *When my cousin died, I sent my aunt and uncle a letter of condolence.*

con•dom (kŏn′dəm) *n.* A flexible cover for the penis to be worn during sexual intercourse to prevent pregnancy and sexually transmitted diseases. Condoms are usually made of thin rubber or latex.

con•do•min•i•um (kŏn′də mĭn′ē əm) *n.* **1.** An apartment building in which the individual apartments are owned by the tenants. **2.** An apartment in such a building.

con•done (kən dōn′) *tr.v.* **con•doned, con•don•ing, con•dones.** To forgive, overlook, or ignore (sthg.): *a police chief who condones corruption.* See Synonyms at **forgive.**

con•dor (kŏn′dôr′) *n.* A large vulture living in the mountains of California or the Andes, with a ruff of feathers on the neck and a bare head.

con•du•cive (kən dōō′sĭv) *adj.* Tending to cause or promote a specific result: *Noisy corridors in the school are not conducive to studying.* —**con•du′cive•ness** *n.* [U]

con•duct (kən dŭkt′) *tr.v.* **1.** To lead (sbdy./ sthg.); guide: *The guide conducted us through the art museum.* **2.** To direct the course of (sthg.); manage: *conduct an experiment; conduct negotiations.* **3.** To lead or direct (musicians or a musical work): *conduct an orchestra; conduct one of Mozart's symphonies.* **4.** To be a medium for (sthg., such as electricity); transmit: *Most metals conduct electricity well.* **5.** To behave (oneself) in a certain way: *In school most people conduct themselves in an orderly way.* —*n.* (kŏn′dŭkt′). [U] **1.** The way a person acts; behavior: *rude and disorderly conduct.* **2.** The act of directing or controlling; management: *The President is responsible for the conduct of foreign affairs.* —**con•duct′i•bil′i•ty** *n.* [U] —**con•duct′i•ble** *adj.*

con•duc•tion (kən dŭk′shən) *n.* [U] The transmission or passage of sthg., such as heat or electric charge, through a medium or along a path.

con•duc•tive (kən dŭk′tĭv) *adj.* Showing conductivity: *conductive metals.*

con•duc•tiv•i•ty (kŏn′dŭk tĭv′ĭ tē) *n.* [U] The ability or power to conduct heat, electricity, or sound: *The engineers measure the conductivity of insulating materials.*

con•duc•tor (kən dŭk′tər) *n.* **1.** A person who conducts, especially the leader or director of an orchestra or other group of musical performers. **2.** The person in charge of passengers on a train, bus, or streetcar. **3.** A material or an object that conducts heat, electricity, light, or sound: *Copper is a good conductor of heat and electricity.*

con•duit (kŏn′dōō ĭt *or* kŏn′dĭt) *n.* **1.** A channel or pipe for carrying fluids, such as water or natural gas. **2.** A tube or pipe through which electric wires or cables pass.

cone (kōn) *n.* **1.** A solid object in which the base is a circle and the sides narrow to form a point. **2.** Something having the shape of such a figure: *an ice-cream cone.* **3.** A rounded or long cluster containing the seeds of a pine, fir, hemlock, or related tree: *a pine cone.* **4.** One of a group of cone-shaped cells of the retina of the eye that is sensitive to bright light and color.

con•fec•tion (kən fĕk′shən) *n.* A sweet food or preparation, such as candy. —**con• fec′tion•er** *n.* —**con•fec′tion•er′y** (kən-fĕk′shə nĕr′ē) *n.*, *pl.* **con•fec′tion•er′ies.** [C; U]

con•fec•tion•ers′ sugar (kən fĕk′shə-nərz) *n.* [U] A fine powdery sugar with cornstarch added.

con•fed•er•a•cy (kən fĕd′ər ə sē) *n.*, *pl.* **con•fed•er•a•cies. 1.** A political union of peoples or states: *the powerful confederacy of Native American peoples called the Iroquois Nation.* **2. Confederacy.** The 11 Southern states that separated from the United States in 1860 and 1861.

con•fed•er•ate (kən fĕd′ər ĭt) *n.* **1.** An associate in a plot or crime; an accomplice: *The police arrested him and all his confederates.* **2.** A member of a confederacy. **3. Confederate.** A supporter of the American Confederacy. —*adj.* **1.** Belonging to a confederacy. **2. Confederate.** Relating to the American Confederacy: *Confederate soldiers.* —*tr. & intr.v.* (kən fĕd′ə rāt′). **con• fed•er•at•ed, con•fed•er•at•ing, con• fed•er•ates.** To form into or become part of a confederacy.

con•fed•er•a•tion (kən fĕd′ə rā′shən) *n.* **1.** [C] A group of confederates: *The teachers formed a national confederation to advance their interests.* **2.** [U] The act of confederating or the state of being confederated.

con•fer (kən fûr′) *v.* **con•ferred, con•fer• ring, con•fers.** —*intr.* To meet in order to discuss sthg. or compare opinions: *The President conferred with cabinet advisers.* —*tr.* [on] To bestow or award (sthg., especially a prize): *The mayor conferred a medal on the two heroic firefighters.*

con•fer•ence (kŏn′fər əns *or* kŏn′frəns) *n.* **1.** [C] A meeting to discuss a subject or a number of subjects: *a peace conference.* **2.** [C] A regional association of churches, athletic teams, or other groups. **3.** [U] The act of conferring: *The principal and teachers were in conference for hours.*

conference call *n.* A conference by telephone in which three or more persons participate: *He couldn't fly in for the meeting, so we had a conference call instead.*

confess / conform 184

con·fess (kən fĕs′) v. —tr. **1.** To state openly or admit (sthg. wrong or bad that one has done): *The children confessed that they broke the window.* **2.** To make known (one's sins) to a priest or to God. —intr. **1.** To admit or acknowledge sthg. wrong or bad that one has done: *The driver confessed to driving too fast.* **2.** To tell one's sins to a priest.

con·fes·sion (kən fĕsh′ən) n. **1.** [C; U] The act of confessing or admitting; acknowledgment: *The suspect's full confession of guilt cleared up the case.* **2.** [U] The act of telling one's sins to a priest or to God. **3.** [C] Something confessed: *Did the prisoner sign her confession?*

con·fet·ti (kən fĕt′ē) pl.n. (used with a singular verb). Small pieces of colored paper that are thrown on festive occasions.

con·fi·dant (kŏn′fĭ dänt′ or kŏn′fĭ dänt′) n. A person with whom a person discusses personal matters or secrets: *They have been close confidants for years.*

con·fide (kən fīd′) v. **con·fid·ed, con·fid·ing, con·fides.** —tr. **1.** To tell (sthg.) confidentially: *confide a secret to a friend.* **2.** To put (sthg.) into another's keeping; entrust: *Before going on vacation, he confided the task of watering his plants to a friend.* —intr. To tell or share one's secrets: *I know I can confide in you.*

con·fi·dence (kŏn′fĭ dəns) n. **1.** [U] A feeling of assurance, especially of self-assurance: *The lawyer argued the case with confidence.* **2.** [U] Trust or faith: *I am placing my confidence in your reliability.* **3.** [U] A trusting relationship: *I have decided to take you into my confidence.* **4.** [U] A feeling of assurance that sbdy. will keep a secret: *I am telling you this in strict confidence.* **5.** [C] Something confided; a secret: *the many confidences of close friends.*

con·fi·dent (kŏn′fĭ dənt) adj. Feeling or showing confidence, especially in being sure of oneself; certain: *The lawyer is confident of winning the case.* —**con′fi·dent·ly** adv.

con·fi·den·tial (kŏn′fĭ dĕn′shəl) adj. **1.** Told in confidence; secret: *A person's medical history is confidential information shared only with a doctor.* **2.** Entrusted with another person's secrets: *a confidential secretary.* **3.** Showing secrecy or intimacy: *a confidential tone of voice.* —**con′fi·den′tial·ly** adv. —**con′fi·den′ti·al′i·ty** n. [U]

con·fid·ing (kən fī′dĭng) adj. Having a tendency to confide; trusting: *a confiding nature.*

con·fig·u·ra·tion (kən fĭg′yə rā′shən) n. [C; U] The form or arrangement of the parts of sthg.: *The general configuration of the earth and other planets is that of a ball.*

con·fine (kən fīn′) tr.v. **con·fined, con·fin·ing, con·fines.** [to] **1.** To keep (sbdy./sthg.) within bounds; restrict; limit: *Firefighters confined the fire to the roof.* **2.** To shut or keep (sbdy./sthg.) inside, as in prison: *The dogs were confined to a backyard pen.*

con·fine·ment (kən fīn′mənt) n. [U] The act of confining or the condition of being confined: *a prisoner in solitary confinement.*

con·fines (kŏn′fīnz′) pl.n. The limits of a space or area; the borders: *The dog left the confines of the yard.*

con·firm (kən fûrm′) tr.v. **1.** To support or establish the truth or validity of (sthg.): *The results of the experiment confirmed the theory.* **2.** To make (sthg.) firmer; strengthen: *Reading about famous scientists confirmed her plan to study chemistry.* **3.** To make (sthg.) valid or binding by a formal or legal act: *The judge's appointment to the Supreme Court was confirmed by the Senate.* **4.** To admit (sbdy.) to full membership in a church by confirmation: *Their 13-year-old was confirmed last weekend.*

con·fir·ma·tion (kŏn′fər mā′shən) n. [C; U] **1.** The act of confirming: *The President needs the Senate's confirmation to appoint an ambassador.* **2.** Something that confirms; proof: *The driver's license was confirmation of the man's age.* **3.** A religious ceremony that allows sbdy. to be a full member of a church: *We held a reception to celebrate our son's confirmation.*

con·firmed (kən fûrmd′) adj. **1.** Firmly established; proved: *a confirmed theory.* **2.** Settled in a habit or condition: *a confirmed gossip.*

con·fis·cate (kŏn′fĭ skāt′) tr.v. **con·fis·cat·ed, con·fis·cat·ing, con·fis·cates. 1.** To seize (private property) from sbdy. by government authority: *The police confiscated the illegal goods.* **2.** To seize (sthg.) by authority; take away: *The teacher confiscated the knife.* —**con′fis·ca′tion** n. [U]

con·fla·gra·tion (kŏn′flə grā′shən) n. A large fire: *The conflagration destroyed the warehouse.*

con·flict (kŏn′flĭkt) n. [C; U] **1.** A state of fighting; a battle or war: *There have been few racial conflicts in this city.* **2.** A state of disagreement, as between persons, ideas, or interests: *a conflict between right and wrong.* —intr.v. (kən flĭkt′). [with] To be in opposition; clash: *The meeting conflicts with my dental appointment.*

con·flu·ence (kŏn′flōō əns) n. [C; U] A flowing or gathering together: *A confluence of little streams forms the river.* —**con′flu·ent** adj.

con·form (kən fôrm′) v. —intr. [to] **1.** To act in agreement with established customs,

ă-cat; ā-pay; âr-care; ä-father; ĕ-get; ē-be; ĭ-sit; ī-nice; îr-here; ŏ-got; ō-go; ô-saw; oi-boy; ou-out; ōō-took; ōō-boot; ŭ-cut; ûr-word; th-thin; th-this; hw-when; zh-vision; ə-about; N-French bon

rules, or styles: *Many young people do not like to conform to the way other people dress.* **2.** To correspond in form or character; be similar: *The computer conforms to the manufacturer's advertising claims.* —*tr.* To bring (sthg.) into agreement; make similar: *She doesn't often conform her thinking to the rest of the group.* See Synonyms at **adapt.**

con•for•ma•tion (kŏn′fər mā′shən) *n.* **1.** [C] The way sthg. is formed; shape or structure: *The conformation of a snake's skeleton is elongated.* **2.** [U] The act of conforming or the state of being conformed.

con•form•ist (kən fôr′mĭst) *n.* A person who conforms to current customs, rules, or styles: *He is a conformist, not an independent thinker.*

con•form•i•ty (kən fôr′mĭ tē) *n.* [U] **1.** Agreement; harmony: *act in conformity with established custom.* **2.** Action or behavior that is in agreement with current customs, rules, or styles.

con•found (kən found′ *or* kŏn found′) *tr.v.* **1.** To confuse or surprise (sbdy.): *The dog's strange behavior confounded her master.* **2.** To mistake (one thing) for another; mix up: *The confused witness confounded fiction and fact.*

con•front (kən frŭnt′) *tr.v.* To come face to face with (sbdy./sthg.), especially in conflict or opposition: *She finally confronted her rival on the tennis court.* —**con′fron•ta′tion** (kŏn′frŭn tā′shən) *n.* [C; U]

con•fuse (kən fyōōz′) *tr.v.* **con•fused, con•fus•ing, con•fus•es. 1.** To cause (a person or an animal) to be unable to think clearly; mislead: *The poorly organized presentation only confused the audience.* **2.** To fail to distinguish between (one person or thing and another); mistake: *The coach confused me with my brother.* —**con•fus′ing•ly** *adv.*

con•fused (kən fyōōzd′) *adj.* **1.** Bewildered; perplexed: *a confused look.* **2.** Mixed up; disordered: *a confused situation; a confused story.* —**con•fus′ed•ly** (kən fyōō′zĭd lē) *adv.*

con•fus•ing (kən fyōō′zĭng) *adj.* Hard to understand or figure out: *a confusing textbook; a confusing maze of streets.*

con•fu•sion (kən fyōō′zhən) *n.* [U] **1.** The act of confusing: *The confusion of the addresses meant the package was not delivered to the right place.* **2.** The state of being confused: *The unexpected news threw us all into confusion.*

con•geal (kən jēl′) *v.* —*intr.* **1.** To change from a liquid to a solid, as by freezing: *The diesel fuel congealed in the intense cold.* **2.** To thicken or coagulate: *Blood congeals on exposure to air.* **3.** To take shape: *The plans had begun to congeal.* —*tr.* To cause (sthg.) to change from a liquid to a solid.

con•gen•ial (kən jēn′yəl) *adj.* **1.** Having similar tastes, habits, or dispositions: *two con-*

genial persons. **2.** Of a pleasant nature; friendly: *a congenial host.* **3.** Pleasant; agreeable: *The bright airy room provided congenial surroundings.* —**con•ge′ni•al′i•ty** (kən jē′nē ăl′ĭ tē) *n.* [U] —**con•gen′ial•ly** *adv.*

con•gen•i•tal (kən jĕn′ĭ tl) *adj.* Existing before or from the time of birth: *Many congenital defects can now be corrected by surgery.* —**con•gen′i•tal•ly** *adv.*

con•gest (kən jĕst′) *v.* —*tr.* To overfill (sthg.); overcrowd: *Heavy traffic congested the highway.* —*intr.* [with] To become congested: *Pneumonia causes the lungs to congest with fluid.* —**con•ges′tive** *adj.*

con•gest•ed (kən jĕs′tĭd) *adj.* **1.** Too full or crowded because of too many people or vehicles: *congested city streets.* **2.** Filled with body fluids, especially mucus or blood: *I can't breathe well because of a congested nose.*

con•ges•tion (kən jĕs′chən) *n.* [U] **1.** A condition of overcrowding: *traffic congestion during rush hour.* **2.** A condition in which fluid collects in an organ or tissue of the body: *Cold medicines can relieve nasal congestion.*

con•glom•er•ate (kən glŏm′ər ĭt) *n.* **1.** [C] A business corporation made up of a number of separate companies that do different types of work: *My brother works in Europe for a huge conglomerate.* **2.** [U] A mass of material, such as small stones or wood particles, that clings together. —*adj.* **1.** Formed together into a mass: *This conglomerate rock is formed of sand and pebbles.* **2.** Made up of many parts: *The reformers were a conglomerate group from several political parties.*

con•glom•er•a•tion (kən glŏm′ə rā′shən) *n.* [C; U] A collection or an accumulation of many different things or people.

con•grat•u•late (kən grăch′ə lāt′ *or* kən grăj′ə lāt′) *tr.v.* **con•grat•u•lat•ed, con•grat•u•lat•ing, con•grat•u•lates.** To express joy or good wishes to (sbdy.) for an achievement or good fortune: *Everyone crowded around to congratulate the newly elected mayor.* —**con•grat′u•la•to′ry** (kən grăch′-ə lə tôr′ē *or* kən grăj′ə lə tôr′ē) *adj.*

con•grat•u•la•tions (kən grăch′ə lā′shənz *or* kən grăj′ə lā′shənz) *pl.n.* **1.** The act of congratulating: *a card of congratulations to the new parents.* **2.** An expression of joy or acknowledgement: *Congratulations on your promotion!*

con•gre•gate (kŏng′grĭ gāt′) *intr.v.* **con•gre•gat•ed, con•gre•gat•ing, con•gre•gates.** To come together in a crowd or mass; assemble: *Students congregate in the hall before class starts.*

con•gre•ga•tion (kŏng′grĭ gā′shən) *n.* [C; U] A gathering of people or things, especially a group of people gathered for religious worship: *The congregation bowed their heads in prayer.* —**con′gre•ga′tion•al** *adj.*

con·gress (kŏng′grĭs) *n.* **1.** A formal meeting of persons representing various nations, organizations, or professions to discuss problems: *a medical congress of heart specialists.* **2.** The lawmaking body of a republic. **3. Congress.** The national legislative body of the United States, consisting of the Senate and the House of Representatives: *She was elected to Congress two years ago.* —**con·gres′sion·al** (kən grĕsh′ə nəl *or* kəng-grĕsh′ə nəl) *adj.*

con·gress·man (kŏng′grĭs mən) *n.* A man who is a member of the United States Congress, especially of the House of Representatives. —**con′gress·wom′an** (kŏng′grĭs wŏŏm′ən) *n.*

con·gru·ent (kŏng′grŏŏ ənt *or* kən grŏŏ′-ənt) *adj.* **1.** In geometry, matching exactly; having the same size and shape: *congruent triangles.* **2.** Corresponding or agreeing; harmonious: *congruent objectives.* —**con·gru·ence** *n.* [U] —**con′gru·ent·ly** *adv.*

con·gru·i·ty (kən grŏŏ′ĭ tē) *n.* [U] **1.** Agreement; harmony: *The two leaders worked in congruity.* **2.** The state or fact of being congruent: *congruity of triangles.*

con·i·cal (kŏn′ĭ kəl) *adj.* Relating to or shaped like a cone. —**con′i·cal·ly** *adv.*

con·i·fer (kŏn′ə fər *or* kō′nə fər) *n.* Any of various trees or shrubs that bear cones. Conifers are usually evergreen and include the pine, fir, spruce, and yew. —**co·nif′er·ous** (kō nĭf′ər əs *or* kə nĭf′ər əs) *adj.*

conj. *abbr.* An abbreviation of conjunction.

con·jec·ture (kən jĕk′chər) *n.* [C; U] The formation of an opinion, an idea, or a conclusion from too little evidence; a guess: *The origin of language is a matter of conjecture. Can you make a conjecture about who will win?* —*intr.v.* **con·jec·tured, con·jec·tur·ing, con·jec·tures.** To make a conjecture; guess: *Several radio commentators were conjecturing on who would be the new mayor.* —**con·jec′tur·al** *adj.*

con·ju·gal (kŏn′jə gəl) *adj.* Relating to marriage or the relationship between husband and wife: *conjugal happiness.* —**con′ju·gal·ly** *adv.*

con·ju·gate (kŏn′jə gāt′) *tr.v.* **con·ju·gat·ed, con·ju·gat·ing, con·ju·gates.** To give the forms of (a verb), usually in a set order. For example, the verb "to be" is conjugated *I am, you are, he/she/it is, we are, you are, they are.*

con·ju·ga·tion (kŏn′jə gā′shən) *n.* [C; U] **1.** The inflection of a particular verb. **2.** A presentation of the complete set of inflected forms of a verb. **3.** A class of verbs having similar inflected forms.

con·junc·tion (kən jŭngk′shən) *n.* **1.** [U]

The act of joining or state of being joined; combination: *A happy conjunction of circumstances strengthened the economy.* **2.** [C] A word, such as *and, but, or,* or *yet,* that connects other words in a sentence.

con·junc·tive (kən jŭngk′tĭv) *adj.* **1.** Joined or serving to join together. **2.** In grammar, connecting or serving as a conjunction. Conjunctive adverbs, such as *however* and *therefore,* are used to connect sentences. —**con·junc′tive·ly** *adv.*

con·junc·ti·vi·tis (kən jŭngk′tə vī′tĭs) *n.* [U] Inflammation of the eye, often in the form of pinkeye.

con·jure (kŏn′jər *or* kən jŏŏr′) *v.* **con·jured, con·jur·ing, con·jures.** —*tr.* To make (sbdy./sthg.) appear or disappear using magic: *The magician conjured a dove out of a handkerchief.* —*intr.* To practice magic; perform magic tricks. ♦ **conjure up.** *tr.v.* [sep.] To call or bring (sthg.) to mind: *The mention of winter conjures up images of snowy hills.*

con·jur·er *also* **con·jur·or** (kŏn′jər ər *or* kŭn′ jər ər) *n.* A magician or sorcerer.

conk (kŏngk) *Slang. n.* A blow, especially on the head: *A hard conk knocked him out.* —*tr.v.* To hit (sbdy.), especially on the head: *The cartoon character conked himself on the head with a frying pan.* ♦ **conk out.** *intr.v.* **1.** To fail suddenly: *The engine conked out.* **2.** To fall asleep, especially suddenly: *He conked out while watching television.*

HOMONYMS: conk, conch (mollusk).

Conn. *abbr.* An abbreviation of Connecticut.

con·nect (kə nĕkt′) *v.* —*tr.* **1.** To join or fasten (two or more things or persons) together; link: *A new road connects the two towns.* See Synonyms at **join.** **2.** To consider (sthg.) as related to sthg. else; associate in the mind: *We connect summer with picnics and swimming.* **3.** To plug in (an electrical cord or device) to an outlet: *connect a television set.* **4.** To link (sbdy.) by telephone: *The operator connected me with the order department.* —*intr.* **1.** To be or become joined: *The two streams connected to form a river.* **2.** To be scheduled so that passengers can transfer from one bus, train, or airplane to another: *The two flights connected in Chicago.* —**con·nect′er** *n.* —**con·nect′i·ble** *adj.* —**con·nec′tor** *n.*

con·nec·tion (kə nĕk′shən) *n.* **1.** [U] The act of connecting: *Connection of the telephone cables took several hours.* **2.** [C] Something that connects or joins; a link: *a telephone connection; rail connections between the two cities.* **3.** [C; U] An association or a relationship: *There is a connection between good* *health and eating well.* **4.** [C] *(usually plural).* A person with whom one is associated by family or profession: *I heard about the job through family connections.* **5.** [C] A train, boat, bus, or airplane scheduled to leave soon after another arrives, so that passengers can keep traveling without delays: *I missed my connection in Chicago.*

con·nec·tive (kə nĕk′tĭv) *adj.* Connecting or serving to connect. —*n.* Something that connects, especially a word such as a conjunction that connects words, phrases, clauses, or sentences.

con·nois·seur (kŏn′ə sûr′ *or* kŏn′ə sŏŏr′) *n.* A person who has expert knowledge or excellent judgment of sthg., such as art or fine food: *an opera connoisseur; a connoisseur of fine wines.*

con·no·ta·tion (kŏn′ə tā′shən) *n.* A meaning suggested by a certain word in addition to its literal or most exact meaning: *The word* lamb *has connotations of simplicity and innocence.*

con·note (kə nōt′) *tr.v.* **con·not·ed, con·not·ing, con·notes.** To suggest or imply (sthg.) in addition to literal or exact meaning: *In a political leader, hesitation connotes weakness.*

con·quer (kŏng′kər) *v.* —*tr.* **1.** To defeat or take control of (an enemy or a territory) by force: *In 1066 the Norman French conquered England.* **2.** To gain control over (sthg.): *Scientists have conquered many diseases by developing vaccines.* —*intr.* To be victorious; win. —**con′quer·er, con′quer·or** *n.*

con·quest (kŏn′kwĕst′ *or* kŏng′kwĕst′) *n.* **1.** [U] An act of conquering: *the Spanish conquest of Mexico.* **2.** [C] Something conquered: *one of the empire's conquests.*

con·science (kŏn′shəns) *n.* [C; U] A sense of right and wrong: *Listen to your conscience and you'll do the right thing.*

con·sci·en·tious (kŏn′shē ĕn′shəs) *adj.* **1.** Guided by or done with a sense of what is right or proper: *a conscientious decision.* **2.** Careful and thorough: *a conscientious worker.* —**con′sci·en′tious·ly** *adv.* —**con′sci·en′tious·ness** *n.* [U]

con·scious (kŏn′shəs) *adj.* **1.** Able to perceive what is happening around oneself; awake: *The patient was fully conscious throughout the operation.* **2.** Aware of one's own existence, feelings, thoughts, and surroundings: *People are not always conscious of their talents.* **3.** Intentionally done; deliberate: *make a conscious effort to speak more clearly.* —**con′scious·ly** *adv.*

con·scious·ness (kŏn′shəs nĭs) *n.* [U] **1.** The condition of being conscious: *The doctor asked if the patient had lost consciousness.* **2.** All the ideas, opinions, feelings, and thoughts held by a person or group: *Love of freedom runs deep in the national consciousness.*

con·script (kŏn′skrĭpt′) *Formal. n.* A person who is drafted, especially into the armed forces. —*adj.* Conscripted; drafted. —*tr.v.* (kən skrĭpt′). To enroll (sbdy.) by force into service in the armed forces; draft: *conscript civilians into the army.* —**con·scrip′tion** *n.* [U]

con·se·crate (kŏn′sĭ krāt′) *tr.v.* **con·se·crat·ed, con·se·crat·ing, con·se·crates.** **1.** To declare or set apart (sbdy./sthg.) as sacred or holy: *consecrate a new church; consecrate a bishop.* **2.** To dedicate (sthg.) to a worthy purpose: *The nurse's life was consecrated to caring for the ill.* —**con′se·cra′tion** *n.* [U]

con·sec·u·tive (kən sĕk′yə tĭv) *adj.* Following one after another in order, without a break or interruption; successive: *It rained this week for five consecutive days.* —**con·sec′u·tive·ly** *adv.*

con·sen·sus (kən sĕn′səs) *n.* [C; U] Collective opinion; general agreement: *The consensus among voters is for building the school.*

con·sent (kən sĕnt′) *intr.v.* To give permission; agree: *My parents finally consented to let me go skiing.* —*n.* [U] Agreement and acceptance; permission: *Our teacher got the principal's consent to let us go home early.*

con·se·quence (kŏn′sĭ kwĕns′) *n.* **1.** [C] Something that follows from an action or a condition; an effect; a result: *Having a large vocabulary was a consequence of so much reading.* **2.** [U] Importance; significance: *a small matter of no consequence.*

con·se·quent (kŏn′sĭ kwĕnt′) *adj.* Following as an effect or result: *heavy rains and consequent flooding.*

con·se·quen·tial (kŏn′sĭ kwĕn′shəl) *adj.* Important; significant: *a consequential decision that affected us all.* —**con′se·quen′tial·ly** *adv.*

con·se·quent·ly (kŏn′sĭ kwĕnt′lē) *adv.* As a result; therefore: *I forgot my wallet and consequently had to go back home for it.*

con·ser·va·tion (kŏn′sûr vā′shən) *n.* [U] **1.** The act of saving or preserving sthg. **2.** Preservation from loss or damage, especially the controlled use and systematic protection of natural resources, such as forests, soil, and water: *the conservation of our rivers.*

con·ser·va·tion·ist (kŏn′sûr vā′shə nĭst) *n.* A person who supports or practices conservation, especially of natural resources.

con·ser·va·tism (kən sûr′və tĭz′əm) *n.* [U] The tendency, especially in politics, to maintain customs, traditions, and existing arrangements as they are: *U.S. voters almost never elect candidates who show extreme conservatism.*

con·ser·va·tive (kən sûr′və tĭv) *adj.* **1.** Favoring things as they are; opposing change: *a conservative attitude toward manners.* **2.** Traditional in style; not showy: *a conservative dark suit.* **3.** Moderate; cautious; restrained: *a conservative budget.* **4.**

C

Belonging to a political party or group that emphasizes respect for traditional institutions, distrusts governmental solutions to problems, and opposes sudden change in the established arrangement of power. —*n.* **1.** A person who is conservative. **2.** Often **Conservative.** A member of a conservative party. —**con·serv'a·tive·ly** *adv.*

con·ser·va·to·ry (kən sûr'və tôr'ē) *n., pl.* **con·ser·va·to·ries. 1.** A greenhouse in which plants are arranged for display. **2.** A school of music or dramatic art.

con·serve (kən sûrv') *tr.v.* **con·served, con·serv·ing, con·serves. 1.** To protect (sthg.) from loss or harm; preserve: *conserve one's energy; conserve forests and other natural resources.* **2.** To use (sthg.) carefully; avoid wasting: *We turned down the thermostat to conserve energy.* —*n.* (kŏn'sûrv'). [C; U] A jam made of fruits cooked in sugar.

con·sid·er (kən sĭd'ər) *v.* —*tr.* **1.** To think carefully about (sthg.); contemplate: *I will consider what you said and respond later.* **2.** To regard (sbdy./sthg.) as; believe to be: *I consider this the most beautiful park in town.* **3.** To take (sthg.) into account; keep in mind: *She sings well if you consider the fact that she never had lessons.* **4.** To be thoughtful of (sthg.); show consideration for: *Consider the feelings of other people.* —*intr.* To think carefully; reflect: *Give me time to consider.*

con·sid·er·a·ble (kən sĭd'ər ə bəl) *adj.* A lot of; much: *They gave considerable thought to the problem.* —**con·sid'er·a·bly** *adv.*

con·sid·er·ate (kən sĭd'ər ĭt) *adj.* Thinking of other people's feelings; thoughtful: *quiet and considerate neighbors.* —**con·sid'er·ate·ly** *adv.*

con·sid·er·a·tion (kən sĭd'ə rā'shən) *n.* **1.** [U] Careful thought: *The matter is complicated and needs consideration.* **2.** [C] Something to think about carefully in making a judgment or decision: *The health of the community should be an important consideration in voting for a new sewer system.* **3.** [U] Thoughtful concern: *consideration for people's feelings.* ◆ **in consideration of.** In return for: *payment in consideration of extra work.* **take into consideration.** To remember and make allowances for sthg. when making a judgment: *She's under a lot of stress, and you have to take that into consideration.*

con·sid·ered (kən sĭd'ərd) *adj.* Reached after careful thought: *my considered opinion.*

con·sid·er·ing (kən sĭd'ər ĭng) *prep.* In view of; taking into consideration: *Considering the mistakes that were made, it is amazing that the job was completed.*

con·sign (kən sīn') *tr.v.* [*to*] **1.** To give (sbdy./sthg.) to the care of another person;

entrust: *The criminals have been consigned to prison.* **2.** To deliver (sthg.) for sale: *The manufacturer consigned the cars to the dealer.*

con·sign·ment (kən sīn'mənt) *n.* [C; U] The delivery of sthg. for sale: *The store received a consignment of umbrellas.* ◆ **on consignment.** With the agreement that payment is expected only after sales have been made and that unsold items may be returned: *The store owner accepted the shipment on consignment.*

con·sist (kən sĭst') *intr.v.* [*of*] To be made up or composed of: *The United States consists of 50 states.*

con·sis·ten·cy (kən sĭs'tən sē) *n., pl.* **con·sis·ten·cies. 1.** [U] Agreement with the same principles or course of action: *There's no consistency between what he says and what he does.* **2.** [C; U] The degree of firmness or thickness: *mix water and clay to the consistency of thick cream.*

con·sis·tent (kən sĭs'tənt) *adj.* Continually following the same principles or course of action: *a consistent supporter of women's rights.* —**con·sis'tent·ly** *adv.*

con·so·la·tion (kŏn'sə lā'shən) *n.* **1.** [U] The act of comforting. **2.** [C] Something that comforts: *The one consolation in their leaving on a trip is that they will not be gone for long.*

con·sole¹ (kən sōl') *tr.v.* **con·soled, con·sol·ing, con·soles.** To comfort (sbdy.) in time of disappointment or sadness: *Friends consoled the widow at the funeral.*

con·sole² (kŏn'sōl') *n.* **1.** A cabinet for a radio, television set, or stereo system, designed to stand on the floor. **2.** The part of an organ facing the player, containing the keyboard, stops, and pedals. **3.** A panel housing the controls for a system of electronic or mechanical equipment.

con·sol·i·date (kən sŏl'ĭ dāt') *v.* **con·sol·i·dat·ed, con·sol·i·dat·ing, con·sol·i·dates.** —*tr.* **1.** To combine (two or more items) into one; unite: *The company was formed when four small firms were consolidated.* **2.** To make (sthg.) secure and strong: *She consolidated her power during her first year as president.* —*intr.* To be united or combined: *The two businesses consolidated into one large firm.* —**con·sol'i·da'tion** *n.* [C; U]

con·som·mé (kŏn'sə mā' *or* kŏn'sə mā') *n.* [C; U] A clear soup made of meat or vegetable broth.

con·so·nant (kŏn'sə nənt) *n.* **1.** A speech sound made by partially or completely blocking the flow of air through one's mouth. **2.** A letter of the alphabet representing such a sound, such as *b, c, d,* or *f.*

ă–cat; ā–pay; âr–care; ä–father; ĕ–get; ē–be; ĭ–sit; ī–nice; îr–here; ŏ–got; ō–go; ô–saw; oi–boy; ou–out; oo–took; oo–boot; ŭ–cut; ûr–word; th–thin; th–this; hw–when; zh–vision; ə–about; N–French bon

con•sort (kən sôrt′) v. Formal. ♦ **consort with.** tr.v. [insep.] To keep company with (sbdy.); associate: *a musician who consorts with movie stars.*

con•spic•u•ous (kən spĭk′yōō əs) adj. **1.** Easily seen; obvious: *a conspicuous spot on the front of my shirt.* **2.** Attracting attention; remarkable: *a conspicuous achievement.* —**con•spic′u•ous•ly** adv. —**con•spic′u•ous•ness** n. [U]

con•spir•a•cy (kən spĭr′ə sē) n., pl. **con•spir•a•cies.** [C; U] The act of making a secret plan to commit an unlawful act; a plot: *a conspiracy to overthrow the government.*

con•spir•a•tor (kən spĭr′ə tər) n. A person who takes part in a conspiracy.

con•spire (kən spīr′) intr.v. **con•spired, con•spir•ing, con•spires. 1.** To plan together secretly to commit an illegal act: *Traitors conspired to kill the king.* **2.** To work together to produce a certain result; combine: *Good weather and a new car conspired to make the trip a happy one.*

con•stant (kŏn′stənt) adj. **1.** Not changing; remaining the same: *An electric motor maintains a constant speed.* **2.** Happening continually; persistent: *constant interruptions; constant reminders.* **3.** Unchanging in loyalty or love; faithful: *a constant friend.* —n. **1.** Something that never changes: *Your friendship has been a constant in my life.* **2.** In mathematics: **a.** A number that has a fixed value in a specific situation: *In averaging final grades, the number of tests is a constant for each student.* **b.** A number that never varies: *The ratio of the circumference to the diameter of a circle is π, a constant.* —**con′stan•cy** n. [U] —**con′stant•ly** adv.

con•stel•la•tion (kŏn′stə lā′shən) n. **1.** A group of stars, especially one that has the name of an object or a mythological figure: *The Little Dipper and Orion are two well-known constellations.* **2.** A group or gathering of important persons or things: *The Nobel Prize ceremony is usually attended by a constellaton of scientists and scholars.*

con•ster•na•tion (kŏn′stər nā′shən) n. [U] Great fear, surprise, or dismay: *To our consternation, the dog ran out into the road.*

con•sti•pate (kŏn′stə pāt′) tr.v. **con•sti•pat•ed, con•sti•pat•ing, con•sti•pates.** To cause constipation in (sbdy.).

con•sti•pa•tion (kŏn′stə pā′shən) n. [U] Difficulty in passing waste from the bowels: *medicine to relieve constipation.*

con•stit•u•en•cy (kən stĭch′ōō ən sē) n., pl. **con•stit•u•en•cies. 1.** A group of voters: *His constituency repeatedly returned the Senator to office.* **2.** A district represented by an elected official: *a constituency of six counties.*

con•stit•u•ent (kən stĭch′ōō ənt) adj. Making up part of a whole: *An atom is a constituent element of a molecule.* —n. **1.** A con-

stituent part; a component: *Flour is the main constituent of bread.* **2.** A person represented by an elected official: *Senators are often contacted by their constituents.*

con•sti•tute (kŏn′stĭ tōōt′) tr.v. **con•sti•tut•ed, con•sti•tut•ing, con•sti•tutes. 1.** To be the elements or parts of (sthg.); compose: *Four quarters constitute a dollar.* **2.** To set (sthg.) up; establish: *Police departments are constituted to maintain law and order.*

con•sti•tu•tion (kŏn′stĭ tōō′shən) n. **1.** [U] The system of fundamental laws or principles by which a nation, government, or group is organized. **2.** [C] A document in which such a system is described. **3.** [U] The way in which sbdy./sthg. is made up, especially the physical makeup of a person or organization: *a healthy person with a strong constitution.*

con•sti•tu•tion•al (kŏn′stĭ tōō′shə nəl) adj. **1.** Relating to a constitution: *a constitutional amendment.* **2.** Permitted by a constitution: *The proposed law restricting the press is not constitutional.* **3.** Basic to one's makeup: *a constitutional weakness in his health.* —n. A walk taken regularly for one's health: *a daily constitutional.* —**con′sti•tu′tion•al•ly** adv.

con•sti•tu•tion•al•i•ty (kŏn′stĭ tōō′shə năl′ĭ tē) n. [U] Accordance with a constitution: *The Supreme Court upheld the constitutionality of the law guaranteeing equal rights to all citizens.*

con•strain (kən strān′) tr.v. **1.** To force (sbdy.) by physical or moral force; oblige: *I feel constrained to explain my opposition to the plan.* **2.** To hold (sbdy./sthg.) back; restrain: *The dog was constrained by a leash.*

con•straint (kən strānt′) n. [C; U] Something that restricts or prevents, as by the threat or use of force; a limitation: *Without moral constraints we would live in total confusion.*

con•strict (kən strĭkt′) tr. & intr.v. To make or become smaller or tighter, as by contracting; compress: *This drug constricts blood vessels. I could feel my muscles constrict with fright.* —**con•stric′tive** adj.

con•stric•tion (kən strĭk′shən) n. **1.** [U] The act of constricting. **2.** [C] A feeling of pressure or tightness: *a constriction in one's throat.* **3.** [C] Something that constricts: *The narrow section of the road was a constriction on traffic.*

con•stric•tor (kən strĭk′tər) n. Any of various snakes, such as the boa and python, that kill their prey by coiling around it and squeezing.

con•struct (kən strŭkt′) tr.v. To build or put (sthg.) together; erect or compose: *construct new houses; construct a plan.* —**con•struc′tor** n.

con•struc•tion (kən strŭk′shən) n. **1.** [U] The act of constructing: *Two new hotels are under construction.* **2.** [U] The way in which sthg. is put together; a design: *modern construction.* **3.** [C] The arrangement of words to form a meaningful phrase, clause, or sentence: *constructions using comparative forms.*

con·struc·tive (kən strŭk′tĭv) *adj.* Serving a useful purpose or helping to improve sthg.: *The boss gave me constructive suggestions on my work.* —**con·struc′tive·ly** *adv.* —**con·struc′tive·ness** *n.* [U]

con·strue (kən strōō′) *tr.v.* **con·strued, con·stru·ing, con·strues.** *Formal.* To determine or explain the meaning of (sthg.); interpret: *We construed her smile as approval.*

con·sul (kŏn′səl) *n.* An official appointed by a government to live in a foreign city, look after the government's interest, and help its citizens who live or travel there: *When we lost our passports, we called the consul's office.* —**con′su·lar** (kŏn′sə lər) *adj.*

con·su·late (kŏn′sə lĭt) *n.* The building or offices occupied by a consul.

con·sult (kən sŭlt′) *v.* —*tr.* **1.** To seek information or advice from (sbdy.): *Consult your doctor.* **2.** To look in (a book or other reference) for information: *We consulted the encyclopedia to settle the question.* —*intr.* To exchange views; confer: *The United States consulted with the Canadian government.*

con·sult·ant (kən sŭl′tənt) *n.* A person who gives expert or professional advice: *A lawyer is a consultant in legal matters.*

con·sul·ta·tion (kŏn′səl tā′shən) *n.* **1.** [U] An act of consulting: *Close consultation between the nurses and the doctor saved the patient.* **2.** [C] A meeting at which advice is given or views are exchanged: *Lawyers for the opposing sides in the case held a consultation.*

con·sume (kən sōōm′) *tr.v.* **con·sumed, con·sum·ing, con·sumes.** **1.** To eat or drink (sthg.) up: *The guests consumed all the spaghetti, so we made more.* **2.** To use (sthg.) up; expend: *The experiment consumed her entire summer.* **3.** To destroy (sthg.) totally, as by fire: *Flames consumed the factory.* **4.** To occupy the attention of (sbdy.): *The book consumed me for hours.* —**con·sum′a·ble** (kən sōō′mə bəl) *adj.*

con·sum·er (kən sōō′mər) *n.* A person or thing that consumes, especially a person who buys and uses goods and services: *The manufacturers increased the price consumers would have to pay.*

con·sum·mate (kŏn′sə māt′) *tr.v.* **con·sum·mat·ed, con·sum·mat·ing, con·sum·mates.** To bring (sthg.) to completion; conclude: *consummate a business deal.* —*adj.* (kən sŭm′ĭt *or* kŏn′sə mət). **1.** Complete or perfect in every respect: *consummate happiness.* **2.** Highly skilled: *a consummate musician.*

con·sump·tion (kən sŭmp′shən) *n.* [U] **1.** The act of consuming: *Much manufacturing is based on the consumption of oil.* **2.** A quantity consumed: *The consumption of wood used for paper can be reduced by recycling.*

cont. *abbr.* An abbreviation of continued.

con·tact (kŏn′tăkt′) *n.* **1.** [U] The touching or coming together of persons or things: *Don't let the chemicals come in contact with your skin.* **2.** [U] The condition of being in communication: *We lost contact with our former neighbors after they moved.* **3.** [C] A person who is in a position to be of help; a connection: *His uncle has numerous contacts in the government.* **4.** [C] **a.** A connection between two conductors that allows an electric current to flow. **b.** A part or device that makes or breaks a connection in an electrical circuit: *the contacts of a switch.* **5.** [C] A contact lens: *Have you seen my contacts?* —*v.* (kŏn′tăkt′ *or* kən tăkt′). —*tr.* **1.** To bring (sthg.) into contact with sthg. else; touch: *If water contacts the paper, it will leave a mark.* **2.** To get in touch with (sbdy.); communicate with: *The salesman contacted several customers by telephone.* —*intr.* To be or come into contact: *Bare wires that contact might cause a fire.*

contact lens *n.* A thin plastic or glass lens designed to correct a vision problem, worn directly on the eye.

con·ta·gion (kən tā′jən) *n.* **1.** [U] The spreading of disease by direct or indirect contact between individuals: *Lack of sanitary conditions may lead to widespread contagion.* **2.** [C] A disease that is or can be transmitted in this way: *Flu is a common contagion in winter.* **3.** [U] The tendency to spread, especially of an influence or emotional state: *the contagion of panic.*

con·ta·gious (kən tā′jəs) *adj.* **1.** Capable of being spread by direct or indirect contact: *Chicken pox is a highly contagious disease.* **2.** Capable of carrying or spreading disease: *He stayed home until he was no longer contagious.* **3.** Tending to spread from person to person: *contagious laughter.*

con·tain (kən tān′) *tr.v.* **1.** To have (sthg.) within; hold: *The document contains important information.* **2.** To consist of (sthg.); include: *A gallon contains four quarts.* **3.** To hold (sthg., such as feelings) back: *I could scarcely contain my laughter.*

con·tain·er (kən tā′nər) *n.* Something, such as a box, can, jar, or barrel, used to hold sthg.: *a container of juice.*

con·tain·ment (kən tān′mənt) *n.* [U] The act or fact of containing sthg.: *underground facilities for the containment of radioactive waste.*

con·tam·i·nant (kən tăm′ə nənt) *n.*

ă–**cat**; ā–**pay**; âr–**care**; ä–**father**; ĕ–**get**; ē–**be**; ĭ–**sit**; ī–**nice**; îr–**here**; ŏ–**got**; ō–**go**; ô–**saw**; oi–**boy**; ou–**out**; ōō–**took**; ōō–**boot**; ŭ–**cut**; ûr–**word**; th–**thin**; th–**this**; hw–**when**; zh–**vision**; ə–**about**; N–French **bon**

Something that contaminates: *Contaminants polluted the nearby stream.*

con•tam•i•nate (kən tăm′ə nāt′) *tr.v.* **con•tam•i•nated, con•tam•i•nat•ing, con•tam•i•nates.** To make (sthg.) impure or unclean by mixture or contact; pollute: *The waters were contaminated with oil from a leaking tanker.* —**con•tam′i•na′tion** *n.* [U]

contd. *abbr.* An abbreviation of continued.

con•tem•plate (kŏn′təm plāt′) *v.* **con•tem•plat•ed, con•tem•plat•ing, con•tem•plates.** —*tr.* **1.** To look at (sbdy./sthg.) carefully and thoughtfully: *contemplate the stars in wonder.* **2.** To think about (sthg.) carefully: *I contemplated the offer of a job.* **3.** To think about doing (sthg.): *We contemplated a trip to Africa.* —*intr.* To ponder; med tate: *He sat in the garden contemplating.* —**con•tem′pla•tive** (kən tĕm′plə tĭv *or* kŏn′təm plā′tĭv) *adj.*

con•tem•pla•tion (kŏn′təm plā′shən) *n.* [U] **1.** The act of looking at or thinking about sthg. thoughtfully: *We spent several days in contemplation before deciding.* **2.** Meditation on spiritual or religious matters: *monks that spend hours in contemplation.*

con•tem•po•rar•y (kən tĕm′pə rĕr′ē) *adj.* Current; modern: *contemporary style furniture.* —*n., pl.* **con•tem•po•rar•ies.** A person living at the same time as another: *George Washington and Thomas Jefferson were contemporaries.*

con•tempt (kən tĕmpt′) *n.* [U] **1.** A feeling that a person or thing is low or worthless; scorn: *She has contempt for all criminals.* **2.** *Formal.* Open disobedience to a court of law: *Failure to appear before the judge put the witness in contempt of court.*

con•tempt•i•ble (kən tĕmp′tə bəl) *adj.* Deserving contempt; despicable: *contemptible behavior.*

con•temp•tu•ous (kən tĕmp′chōō əs) *adj.* Feeling or showing contempt: *a contemptuous refusal to listen.*

con•tend (kən tĕnd′) *v.* —*intr.* **1.** To struggle against difficulties: *Doctors contend with disease.* **2.** To compete: *The two teams contended for the championship.* —*tr.* To claim or maintain (sthg.): *The witness contended that his statement was true.* —**con•tend′er** *n.*

con•tent[1] (kŏn′tĕnt′) *n.* **1.** [C] *(usually plural).* Something that is held in a container: *the contents of a jar.* **2.** [C] *(usually plural).* The subject matter of a written work, such as a document or book: *The contents of the report were not revealed.* **3.** [U] The meaningful part of sthg.: *The content of the paper is fine, but the style needs work.* **4.** [C] *(usually singular).* The amount of a substance contained in sthg.: *the fat content of milk.*

con•tent[2] (kən tĕnt′) *adj.* Wanting no more than one has; satisfied: *He was content to live in the small apartment.* —*tr.v.* [with] To make (oneself) content or satisfied: *I contented myself with a cup of tea and a book.* —**con•tent′ment** *n.* [U]

con•tent•ed (kən tĕn′tĭd) *adj.* Satisfied with things as they are; content: *Few things are more peaceful than a contented look on a child's face.* —**con•tent′ed•ly** *adv.*

con•ten•tion (kən tĕn′shən) *n.* **1.** [U] The act of striving or contending: *The rival teams played in fierce but friendly contention.* **2.** [C] A statement put forward in an argument: *The lawyer's contention was that the evidence was confusing.*

con•ten•tious (kən tĕn′shəs) *adj.* Inclined to argue; quarrelsome: *One of the newspaper editors was a contentious troublemaker.* —**con•ten′tious•ly** *adv.* —**con•ten′tious•ness** *n.* [U]

con•test (kŏn′tĕst′) *n.* **1.** A struggle for victory or superiority between rivals: *The struggle for American independence was a long contest.* **2.** A competition between entrants who perform separately and are rated by judges: *an essay contest; a skating contest.* —*v.* (kən tĕst′ *or* kŏn′tĕst′). —*tr.* **1.** To struggle, compete, or strive for (sthg.): *The two birds contested a nesting place.* **2.** To dispute (sthg.); challenge: *contest a parking ticket; contest a will.* See Synonyms at **oppose.** —*intr.* To struggle or compete: *rival teams contesting for first place.*

con•tes•tant (kən tĕs′tənt) *n.* A person who takes part in a contest.

con•text (kŏn′tĕkst′) *n.* [C; U] **1.** The part of a statement or text that surrounds a particular word or passage and makes its meaning clear: *In some contexts mad means "insane"; in other contexts it means "angry."* **2.** A general setting or set of circumstances in which a particular event occurs; a situation: *Horses are out of place in the context of modern city life.*

con•tex•tu•al (kən tĕks′chōō əl) *adj.* Of or depending on context: *contextual meaning.* —**con•tex′tu•al•ly** *adv.*

con•tig•u•ous (kən tĭg′yōō əs) *adj.* **1.** With a common boundary; adjoining: *New Hampshire is contiguous with Maine.* **2.** Connected in time or space without a break: *the 48 contiguous states.*

con•ti•nent (kŏn′tə nənt) *n.* **1.** One of the seven great land masses of the earth, including Africa, Antarctica, Asia, Australia, Europe, North America, and South America. **2. Continent.** The mainland of Europe.

con•ti•nen•tal (kŏn′tə nĕn′tl) *adj.* **1.** Relating to or characteristic of a continent: *the continental United States.* **2.** Often **Continental.** Relating to the mainland of Europe: *continental breakfast.*

con•tin•gen•cy (kən tĭn′jən sē) *n., pl.* **con•tin•gen•cies.** An event that may happen but is not likely or intended; a possibility: *People who work in emergency medical service must be prepared for any contingency.*

C

con·tin·gent (kən tĭn′jənt) *adj.* **1.** Possible but not certain to happen; uncertain: *a contingent move of company offices.* **2.** [*on; upon*] Dependent on circumstances not yet known; conditional: *The success of our picnic is contingent on the weather.* —*n.* **1.** A representative group; a delegation: *the Maine contingent at the Democratic national convention.* **2.** A group, as of troops, that is part of a general effort: *The international medical team at the earthquake site included a contingent of American doctors.*

con·tin·u·al (kən tĭn′yoo əl) *adj.* **1.** Repeated regularly and frequently: *the continual banging of the door in the wind.* **2.** Not stopping; steady: *continual noise.* —**con·tin′u·al·ly** *adv.*

con·tin·u·a·tion (kən tĭn′yoo ā′shən) *n.* **1.** [U] The act of going on or persisting: *Continuation of the heavy rain will cause flooding.* **2.** [C] The act or an instance of beginning again after stopping; a resumption: *After a delay of several weeks there was a continuation of work on the highway.*

con·tin·ue (kən tĭn′yoo) *v.* **con·tin·ued, con·tin·u·ing, con·tin·ues.** —*intr.* **1.** To keep on or persist: *We continue in our efforts to improve our products.* **2.** To go on after stopping; resume: *Our program continues after these commercials.* **3.** To remain in the same condition or place: *The rainy weather continued for weeks.* —*tr.* **1.** To carry on or persist in (sthg.): *The police continued their investigation.* **2.** To begin with (sthg.) again after stopping; resume: *We will continue our discussion tomorrow.* **3.** To cause (sthg.) to remain or last; maintain: *continue a family business.* **4.** *Formal.* In law, to postpone or adjourn (sthg.): *The judge continued the beginning of the trial for another week.*

con·ti·nu·i·ty (kŏn′tə noo′ĭ tē) *n.* [U] An uninterrupted series: *A telephone call broke the continuity of my thoughts.*

con·tin·u·ous (kən tĭn′yoo əs) *adj.* Continuing without interruption; unbroken: *Living cells must have a continuous supply of oxygen.* —**con·tin′u·ous·ly** *adv.*

con·tin·u·um (kən tĭn′yoo əm) *n.* [U] Something that continues or extends without interruption: *the continuum of colors in the rainbow; the space–time continuum.*

con·tort (kən tôrt′) *tr.v.* To twist or bend (sthg.) severely out of shape: *The pain of a toothache contorted his face.* —**con·tor′tion** *n.* [C; U]

con·tor·tion·ist (kən tôr′shə nĭst) *n.* An acrobat who twists into contorted positions.

con·tour (kŏn′toor′) *n.* The outline of a figure, body, or mass: *the irregular contour of the coastline.*

contra— *pref.* A prefix that means against or opposite: *contradiction.*

con·tra·band (kŏn′trə bănd′) *n.* [U] **1.** Goods prohibited by law from being imported or exported: *Customs officers seized contraband from the travelers.* **2.** Smuggling: *They were engaged in contraband.* —*adj.* Prohibited from being imported or exported: *a contraband shipment.*

con·tra·cep·tion (kŏn′trə sĕp′shən) *n.* [U] The intentional prevention of conception and pregnancy, as by the use of drugs or a device such as a condom.

con·tra·cep·tive (kŏn′trə sĕp′tĭv) *adj.* Capable of preventing conception: *contraceptive creams.* —*n.* A contraceptive substance or device: *Most modern contraceptives are safe and effective.*

con·tract (kŏn′trăkt′) *n.* [C; U] An agreement between two or more persons or groups, especially one that is written and enforceable by law: *a contract to sell the house; a new labor contract.* —*v.* (kən trăkt′ or kŏn′trăkt′). —*tr.* **1.** To make (sthg.) smaller by drawing together: *Hot water contracted the wool fibers in my sweater, and it shrank.* **2.** To arrange or settle (sthg.) by a formal agreement: *contract a business deal.* **3.** To get (sthg.); acquire: *contract the mumps; contract a debt.* **4.** To shorten (a word or words) by omitting or combining some of the letters or sounds: *Most people contract "I am" to "I'm" when they speak.* —*intr.* **1.** To draw together; become smaller: *The pupils of the cat's eyes contracted.* **2.** To arrange by a formal agreement: *The developers contracted for construction of several new houses.*

con·trac·tion (kən trăk′shən) *n.* **1.** [U] The act of contracting: *Cold air causes the contraction of most substances.* **2.** [C] A condensed word or phrase, formed by omitting or combining some of the letters or sounds. For example, *isn't* is a contraction of *is not.* **3.** [C] The shortening and thickening of a muscle in action, especially of the uterus during labor: *The pregnant woman's contractions were ten minutes apart.*

con·trac·tor (kŏn′trăk tər or kən trăk′tər) *n.* A person who contracts to do sthg., especially to provide materials and labor for a construction job: *We hired a contractor to remodel the kitchen.*

con·trac·tu·al (kən trăk′choo əl) *adj.* Relating to a contract: *a contractual arrangement between a carpenter and a house builder.* —**con·trac′tu·al·ly** *adv.*

con·tra·dict (kŏn′trə dĭkt′) *tr.v.* **1.** To say or assert the opposite of (a statement): *The witness gave information that contradicted previous* *testimony.* **2.** To deny the statement of (sbdy.): *The two scientists contradicted each other in a heated debate.* **3.** To be contrary to or inconsistent with (sthg.): *The results of the experiments contradicted his predictions.*

con•tra•dic•tion (kŏn′trə dĭk″shən) *n.* **1.** [U] The act of contradicting: *His contradiction of the teacher embarrassed us.* **2.** [C] An inconsistency; a discrepancy: *There's a contradiction between what you say and what your report states.*

con•tra•dic•to•ry (kŏn′trə dĭk′tə rē) *adj.* **1.** Involving a contradiction; opposing: *Contradictory reports about the vaccine's effectiveness confused the doctors.* **2.** Given to contradicting: *a quarrelsome and contradictory nature.*

con•trap•tion (kən trăp′shən) *n. Informal.* A complex mechanical device; a gadget.

con•trar•y (kŏn′trĕr′ē) *adj.* **1** Completely different; opposed: *The debaters held contrary opinions.* **2.** Adverse; unfavorable: *A contrary wind made sailing difficult.* **3.** Also (kən trâr′ē). Stubbornly willful: *Little children often become contrary when they need a nap.* —*n.* [U] Something that is opposite: *Their theory made sense at first, but experimentation proved the contrary to be true.* ◆ **on the contrary.** In opposition to the previous statement; conversely: *I'm not sick; on the contrary, I'm quite healthy.* —**con′trar′i•ly** *adv.* —**con′trar′i•ness** *n.* [U]

con•trast (kən trăst′ *or* kŏn′trăst′) *v.* —*tr.* To compare differences between (two things): *The essay contrasts city and country life.* —*intr.* To show differences when compared: *light colors that contrast with a dark background.* —*n.* (kŏn′trăst′). **1.** [U] Comparison, especially in order to reveal differences: *Our new car seems roomy in contrast with our old one.* **2.** [C] A striking difference between things compared: *the startling contrast between modern life and that of pioneer times.* **3.** [C] Something that is strikingly different from sthg. else: *Driving a truck is quite a contrast to driving a compact car.*

con•trib•ute (kən trĭb′yo͞ot) *v.* **con•trib•ut•ed, con•trib•ut•ing, con•trib•utes.** [to] —*tr.* To give or supply (sthg.) in common with others: *We contributed a lot of time to the project.* —*intr.* **1.** To give or supply sthg. along with others: *contribute to the Red Cross.* **2.** To help in bringing about a result: *Exercise contributes to better health.* —**con•trib′u•tor** *n.*

con•tri•bu•tion (kŏn′trĭ byo͞o′shən) *n.* **1.** [U] The act of contributing: *Contribution by several people is necessary to hold a good discussion.* **2.** [C] Something that is contributed: *The clothes were a small contribution to the homeless.*

con•trib•u•to•ry (kən trĭb′yə tôr′ē) *adj.* Contributing toward a result; helping to bring about a result: *Carelessness was a contributory factor in the accident.*

con•trite (kən trīt′ *or* kŏn′trīt′) *adj.* Feeling deep regret and sadness for one's wrongdoing: *a contrite expression on her face; contrite tears.* —**con•trite′ly** *adv.* —**con•trite′ness** *n.* [U]

con•tri•tion (kən trĭsh′ən) *n.* [U] *Formal.* A deep feeling of sadness about having done sthg. wrong; deep regret.

con•tri•vance (kən trī′vəns) *n.* **1.** [U] *Formal.* The act of contriving: *the contrivance of friends to give a surprise party.* **2.** [C] Something that is contrived, such as a mechanical device or a clever plan: *A mechanical pencil is a useful contrivance.*

con•trive (kən trīv′) *tr.v.* **con•trived, con•triv•ing, con•trives.** **1.** To plan or devise (sthg.) cleverly: *contrive an excuse for being late.* **2.** To bring (sthg.) about, especially by scheming: *contrive a victory by surprise attack.* **3.** To make (sthg.), especially by improvisation: *contrive a tent out of a blanket and rope.*

con•trived (kən trīvd′) *adj.* Seeming false or unnatural: *His excuse for not marrying her seemed contrived.*

con•trol (kən trōl′) *tr.v.* **con•trolled, con•trol•ling, con•trols.** **1.** To exercise authority or influence over (sbdy./sthg.); direct: *The mayor controls the city government.* **2.** To adjust or regulate (sthg.): *This valve controls the flow of water.* —*n.* **1.** [U] Authority or power to regulate, direct, or dominate: *the coach's control over the team.* **2.** [C] A means of restraint; a check: *A leash is a control over a dog.* **3.** [C] A standard of comparison for testing the results of a scientific experiment: *The patients who received no medication were used as controls in the testing.* **4.** [C] *(usually plural).* A device or set of devices used to operate, regulate, or guide a machine or vehicle: *The pilot was sitting at the controls of the airplane.* ◆ **be in control.** [of] To be in charge of (sbdy./sthg.); have command: *She's in control of two departments at work.* **be** or **get out of control.** To behave badly because of a lack of control: *After the teacher left the room, the children got totally out of control.* —**con•trol′la•ble** *adj.*

con•trol•ler (kən trō′lər) *n.* **1.** A person who controls or regulates sthg.: *an air-traffic controller.* **2.** Also **comp•trol•ler** (kən trō′lər). An officer who supervises the financial affairs of a business or a governmental body.

control tower *n.* A tower at an airport from which the landing and takeoff of aircraft are controlled by radio and radar.

con•tro•ver•sial (kŏn′trə vûr′shəl *or* kŏn′trə vûr′sē əl) *adj.* Causing argument or debate: *controversial writing; a controversial issue.* —**con′tro•ver′sial•ly** *adv.*

con·tro·ver·sy (kŏn'trə vûr'sē) n., pl.
con·tro·ver·sies. [C; U] A dispute, especially a public one between sides holding
opposite views: *a controversy over the school
budget; a matter of great controversy.*

con·va·les·cence (kŏn'və lĕs'əns) n. **1.**
[U] Gradual return to health and strength
after illness or injury: *a period of convalescence.* **2.** [C] *(usually singular).* The time
needed for this: *a short convalescence in
bed.* —**con'va·lesce'** v.

con·va·les·cent (kŏn'və lĕs'ənt) adj. **1.**
Relating to convalescence: *a convalescent
home.* **2.** Recovering from illness or injury: *a
convalescent patient.* —n. A patient who is
recovering.

con·vec·tion (kən vĕk'shən) n. [U] The
transfer of heat from one place to another by
the circulation of heated currents within a gas
or liquid.

con·vene (kən vēn') intr. & tr.v. **con·vened,
con·ven·ing, con·venes.** To assemble or
cause to assemble: *Members of the committee
convene monthly. The governor convened the
legislature.*

con·ven·ience (kən vēn'yəns) n. **1.** [U] The
quality of being convenient; suitability: *the
convenience of doing all of one's food shopping at a supermarket.* **2.** [U] Personal comfort or advantage: *Each hotel room has a
telephone for the convenience of the guests.*
3. [C] Something that provides comfort or
saves effort, such as a device or service: *A
microwave oven is a modern convenience.*

con·ven·ient (kən vēn'yənt) adj. **1.** Suited
or favorable to one's comfort, needs, or purpose: *An electric mixer is a convenient
kitchen appliance.* **2.** Easy to reach or close
by: *a bank with many convenient locations.*
—**con·ven'ient·ly** adv.

con·vent (kŏn'vənt) n. **1.** A community of
nuns. **2.** The building or buildings occupied
by nuns.

con·ven·tion (kən vĕn'shən) n. **1.** [C] A formal meeting of a group for a particular purpose: *a political convention for nominating
candidates.* **2.** [C; U] General agreement on or
acceptance of certain practices or attitudes:
*Convention allows for much more casual dress
today.* **3.** [C] A formal agreement or compact,
as between nations: *Prisoners of war are protected by the Geneva Convention.*

con·ven·tion·al (kən vĕn'shə nəl) adj. **1.**
Based on or approved by general usage; customary: *Saying "Hello" is a conventional way
of answering the telephone.* **2.** Following
accepted practice so closely as to be dull
or unimaginative: *a conventional plan for a
house.* —**con·ven'tion·al·i·ty** (kən vĕn'-
shə năl'ĭ tē) n. [U] —**con·ven'tion·al·ly** adv.

con·verge (kən vûrj') v. **con·verged, con·
verg·ing, con·verg·es.** —intr. **1.** To come
together in one place; meet: *The three roads
converge in the center of town.* **2.** To tend or
move toward each other or toward the same
conclusion or result: *Their minds converged
on the same point.* —tr. To cause (things) to
converge: *A magnifying glass converges rays
of light.* —**con·ver'gence** n. [U] —**con·
ver'gent** adj.

con·ver·sant (kən vûr'sənt or kŏn'vər sənt)
adj. [with] Familiar, especially because of
study: *She is conversant with ancient history.*

con·ver·sa·tion (kŏn'vər sā'shən) n.
[C; U] An informal spoken exchange of
thoughts and feelings; a talk: *When we
entered the party, all conversation stopped.*

con·ver·sa·tion·al (kŏn'vər sā'shə nəl)
adj. **1.** Relating to conversation: *in a normal
conversational tone.* **2.** Skilled at or liking
conversation: *Friendly people are generally
more conversational than others.*

con·ver·sa·tion·al·ist (kŏn'vər sā'shə-
nə lĭst) n. A person who is fond of or skilled
at conversation: *He's not much of a conversa-
tionalist.*

con·verse¹ (kən vûrs') intr.v. **con·versed,
con·vers·ing, con·vers·es.** To talk informally with others: *converse about family
matters.* See Synonyms at **speak.**

con·verse² (kən vûrs' or kŏn'vûrs') adj.
Reversed in order; contrary: *The converse
order of the alphabet is hard to repeat.* —n.
(kŏn'vûrs'). *(usually singular).* Something
that has been reversed; an opposite: *Dark is
the converse of light.* —**con·verse'ly** adv.

con·ver·sion (kən vûr'zhən or kən vûr'-
shən) n. **1.** [U] The process of changing one
thing, use, or purpose into another: *A generator is used for the conversion of water power
into electricity.* **2.** [C] A change in which
a person adopts a new belief, opinion, or
religion: *His conversion was caused by his
sister's illness.*

con·vert (kən vûrt') v. —tr. **1.** To change
(sthg.) into another form, substance, or condition: *convert water into ice.* **2.** To change
(sthg.) from one use to another; adapt to a
new purpose: *convert a bedroom into a study.*
3. To persuade (sbdy.) to adopt a particular
religion or belief: *Spanish and French priests
tried to convert the native peoples of the
Americas to Christianity.* **4.a.** To exchange
(sthg.) for sthg. else of equal value: *Since we
are going to France, we need to convert our
dollars into francs.* **b.** To express (a quantity)
in alternative units: *convert 100 yards into
meters.* —intr. **1.** To undergo a change; be
converted: *This sofa converts easily into a
bed.* **2.** To adopt a particular religion or

ă–**cat**; ā–**pay**; âr–**care**; ä–**father**; ĕ–**get**; ē–**be**; ĭ–**sit**; ī–**nice**; îr–**here**; ŏ–**got**; ō–**go**; ô–**saw**; oi–**boy**; ou–**out**;
ōō–**took**; ōō–**boot**; ŭ–**cut**; ûr–**word**; th–**thin**; th–**this**; hw–**when**; zh–**vision**; ə–**about**; N–French **bon**

belief: *Many people in Europe converted to Christianity in the Middle Ages.* —*n.* (**kŏn′**vûrt′). A person who has adopted a new religion or belief.

con•vert•er (kən vûr′tər) *n.* **1.** A machine that changes alternating current to direct current or direct current to alternating current. **2.** An electronic device that changes the frequency of a radio or other electromagnetic signal.

con•vert•i•ble (kən vûr′tə bəl) *adj.* **1.** Capable of being converted: *The convertible couch is also a bed.* **2.** Having a top that can be folded back or removed: *a convertible sports car.* —*n.* A car with a convertible top: *She bought a new red convertible.*

con•vex (kŏn′vĕks′ or kən vĕks′) *adj.* Curving outward like the outer boundary of a circle or sphere: *Rain rolled off the convex surface of the dome.*

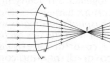

convex
Light passing through a double-convex lens, with f indicating the focus

con•vey (kən vā′) *tr.v.* **1.** To take or carry (sbdy./sthg.) from one place to another; transport: *A helicopter conveyed the skiers to the top of the mountain.* **2.** To make (sthg.) known; communicate: *His smile conveyed his pleasure.* **3.** To transfer ownership of (sthg.): *The deed conveyed the land to a close relative.*

con•vey•ance (kən vā′əns) *n. Formal.* **1.** [U] The act of conveying: *Airlines now serve as the chief means of conveyance for transatlantic passengers.* **2.** [C] Something used to convey, especially a vehicle such as an automobile or a bus.

con•vey•er also **con•vey•or** (kən vā′ər) *n.* **1.** A person or thing that conveys: *a conveyer of good news.* **2.** A mechanical device, such as a moving belt, that carries things from one place to another: *put the suitcases on the conveyer.*

con•vict (kən vĭkt′) *tr.v.* To find or prove (sbdy.) guilty of an offense, especially in a court of law: *The judge convicted the polluter of endangering public health* —*n.* (**kŏn′**vĭkt′). A person who has been found guilty of a crime and sentenced to prison: *an escaped convict.*

con•vic•tion (kən vĭk′shən) *n.* **1.** [C] The judgment of a judge or jury that a person is guilty of a crime. **2.** [U] The state of being found or proven guilty: *a trial ending in the terrorist's conviction.* **3.** [C; U] A strong opinion or belief: *act according to one's convictions; a speech that lacked conviction.*

con•vince (kən vĭns′) *tr.v.* **con•vinced, con•vinc•ing, con•vinc•es.** To cause (sbdy.) to believe sthg.; persuade: *More clues convinced us we were on the right track.*

con•vinc•ing (kən vĭn′sĭng) *adj.* Serving to convince; persuasive: *a convincing argument.* —**con•vinc′ing•ly** *adv.*

con•vo•lut•ed (kŏn′və loo′tĭd) *adj.* **1.** Complicated; intricate: *a convoluted argument that is hard to understand.* **2.** Having many turns or twists: *a convoluted path winding around streams and rocks.*

con•vo•lu•tion (kŏn′və loo′shən) *n.* A winding or folding: *the convolutions of a coiled snake.*

con•voy (kŏn′voi) *n.* **1.** A group of ships or motor vehicles, traveling together: *a convoy of trucks on the highway at night.* **2.** An accompanying and protecting force: *a convoy of warships protecting the supply ships.*

con•vulse (kən vŭls′) *tr.v.* **con•vulsed, con•vuls•ing, con•vuls•es.** **1.** To shake (sthg.) violently; rock: *An explosion convulsed the area.* **2.** To cause (sbdy.) to laugh uproariously: *Her comic impersonations convulsed the audience.* **3.** To cause (a person or animal) to have violent involuntary muscle contractions: *The patient was convulsed by high fever.* —**con•vul′sive** *adj.* —**con•vul′sive•ly** *adv.*

con•vul•sion (kən vŭl′shən) *n. (usually plural).* **1.** A violent involuntary muscular contraction: *convulsions resulting from high fever.* **2.** An uncontrolled fit of laughter: *The audience went into convulsions watching the clown.* **3.** A violent upheaval: *convulsions of the earth's crust.*

coo (koo) *intr.v.* **1.** To make the murmuring sound of a pigeon or dove: *The doves cooed in the cage.* **2.** To make a similar sound: *The baby cooed at her mother.*

HOMONYMS: coo, coup (action).

---

cook (kook) *v.* —*tr.* To prepare (food) for eating by using heat: *He cooked bacon and eggs for breakfast.* —*intr.* **1.** To undergo cooking: *Fish cooks quickly.* **2.** To prepare food for eating by using heat: *He often cooks for the family.* —*n.* A person who prepares food for eating: *Dinner was delicious! You're a great cook!* ♦ **cook up.** *tr.v.* [sep.] **1.** *Informal.* To invent (sthg.); concoct: *He needed to cook up an excuse.* **2.** To prepare (food) for eating, especially quickly and without planning: *I'm hungry. Let's see what we can find to cook up.*

cook•book (kook′book′) *n.* A book containing recipes and other information about cooking.

cook•er (kook′ər) *n.* A utensil or an appliance for cooking: *a pressure cooker.*

cook•ie (kook′ē) *n., pl.* **cook•ies.** A small, usually flat and crisp cake made from sweetened dough: *chocolate-chip cookies.*

cook•out (kook′out′) *n.* A meal cooked and eaten outdoors: *Our neighbors invited us to a cookout.*

cool (kōol) *adj.* **1.** Moderately cold; neither warm nor very cold: *cool fall weather.* **2.** Giving or allowing relief from heat: *a cool summer breeze; a cool light blouse.* **3.** Calm; unexcited: *a cool head in a crisis.* **4.** Indifferent; unfriendly; unenthusiastic: *They were cool to the idea of hosting the party.* **5.** *Slang.* Excellent; first-rate: *It's a really cool movie.* **6.** *Informal.* Entire; full: *The deal brought the company a cool million in profit.* —*tr. & intr.v.* **1.** To make or become less warm: *cool a room by opening a window; let the pie cool.* **2.** To make or become less intense: *Having to wait cooled their enthusiasm. My anger cooled as time went by.* —*n.* [U] A cool place, part, or time: *the cool of the evening.* ◆ **cool it.** *Slang.* To calm down; relax: *You need to cool it. You're too upset.* **cool (one's) heels.** *Informal.* To wait or be kept waiting: *His boss left him cooling his heels for an hour.* **keep** or **lose (one's) cool.** *Slang.* To stay calm or become upset or angry: *Keep your cool no matter what he says. Be careful not to lose your cool when you call him.* —**cool′ly** *adv.* —**cool′ness** *n.* [U]

cool·ant (kōo′lənt) *n.* [C; U] Something that cools, especially a fluid that circulates through a machine or over some of its parts in order to draw off heat.

cool·er (kōo′lər) *n.* A device or container for cooling sthg.: *a water cooler.*

cool-head·ed (kōol′hĕd′ĭd) *adj.* Not easily excited or flustered; calm: *be cool-headed in an emergency.* —**cool′-head′ed·ly** *adv.* —**cool′-head′ed·ness** *n.* [U]

coon (kōon) *n. Informal.* A raccoon.

coop (kōop) *n.* A structure or cage for poultry: *a chicken coop.* —*v.* ◆ **coop up.** *tr.v.* [sep.] To confine (sbdy./sthg.); shut in: *The author has been cooped up in that little room all day.*

co-op (kō′ŏp′) *n.* A cooperative: *I shop at a food co-op.*

co·op·er·ate (kō ŏp′ə rāt′) *intr.v.* **co·op·er·at·ed, co·op·er·at·ing, co·op·er·ates.** To work or act with another or others for a common purpose: *Everyone cooperated in decorating for the party.*

co·op·er·a·tion (kō ŏp′ə rā′shən) *n.* [U] The act of working together toward a common end or purpose: *international cooperation to reduce air pollution.*

co·op·er·a·tive (kō ŏp′ər ə tĭv *or* kō ŏp′ə-rā′tĭv *or* kō ŏp′rə tĭv) *adj.* **1.** Done with others: *a cooperative effort.* **2.** Willing to help or cooperate: *a cooperative and helpful assistant.* **3.** Relating to a cooperative: *a cooperative apartment.* —*n.* **1.** A business, farm, store, or residence owned jointly by those who use it: *That apartment house is a cooperative in which the residents share the costs of operat-*

ing the building. **2.** An apartment in a building jointly owned by the residents: *a three-room cooperative on the first floor.* —**co·op′er·a·tive·ly** *adv.* —**co·op′er·a·tive·ness** *n.* [U]

co·or·di·nate (kō ôr′dn āt′ *or* kō ôr′dn ĭt) *n.* **1.** A person or thing that is equal in importance, rank, or degree. **2.** In mathematics, one of a set of numbers that determines the position of a point on a line, in a plane, or in space. —*adj.* (kō ôr′dn ĭt *or* kō ôr′dn āt′). **1.** Of equal importance, rank, or degree: *A compound sentence has two or more coordinate clauses.* **2.** Of or involving coordinates: *a coordinate system.* —*intr. & tr.v.* (kō ôr′dn-āt′). **co·or·di·nat·ed, co·or·di·nat·ing, co·or·di·nates.** To work or cause to work together efficiently in a common cause or effort; harmonize: *The nursing staff of the hospital coordinates well. The nervous system coordinates activities of the body.* —**co·or′di·nate·ly** *adv.*

co·or·di·nat·ing conjunction (kō ôr′dn-ā′tĭng) *n.* A conjunction that connects two identical grammatical elements. For example, in the phrase *books and pencils,* the word *and* is a coordinating conjunction.

co·or·di·na·tion (kō ôr′dn ā′shən) *n.* [U] **1.** An act of coordinating or a condition or being coordinated: *Coordination among the rescue workers saved many of the earthquake victims.* **2.** The organized action of groups of muscles in the performance of complicated movements: *Gymnastics requires a great deal of coordination.*

co·or·di·na·tor (kō ôr′dn ā′tər) *n.* A person who organizes the activities of others.

cop (kŏp) *n. Informal.* A police officer: *kids playing cops and robbers.*

cope (kōp) *intr.v.* **coped, cop·ing, copes.** To face difficulty and function, especially successfully: *I just can't cope today.* ◆ **cope with.** *tr.v.* [insep.] To deal well with (sbdy./sthg.): *Computers help us cope with vast amounts of information.*

cop·i·er (kŏp′ē ər) *n.* A machine that makes photocopies; a photocopier.

co·pi·lot (kō′pī′lət) *n.* The second pilot of an aircraft: *When the pilot became ill, the copilot took control of the airplane.*

co·pi·ous (kō′pē əs) *adj.* Large in quantity; abundant: *Rainfall is copious in the tropics.* —**co′pi·ous·ly** *adv.*

cop·per (kŏp′ər) *n.* **1.** [U] *Symbol* **Cu** A tough reddish brown metallic element that is an excellent conductor of heat and electricity and is widely used for electrical wiring and water piping. Atomic number 29. See table at **element.** **2.** [U] A reddish brown color: *curls of shining copper.* —*adj.* Reddish brown. —**cop′per·y** *adj.*

cop·per·head (kŏp'ər hĕd') *n*. A poisonous snake of the eastern United States, with reddish brown markings.

cop·ter (kŏp'tər) *n. Informal.* A helicopter.

cop·u·late (kŏp'yə lāt') *intr.v.* **cop·u·lat·ed, cop·u·lat·ing, cop·u·lates.** To engage in sexual intercourse. — **cop'u·la'-tion** *n.* [U]

cop·y (kŏp'ē) *n., pl.* **cop·ies. 1.** [C] An imitation or a reproduction of stng. original; a duplicate. **2.** [C] One specimen or example of a printed text or picture: *a copy of the June issue of the magazine.* **3.** [U] Written material to be set in type and printed: *Reporters hand in copy for newspaper articles* — *v.* **cop·ied, cop·y·ing, cop·ies.** — *tr.* **1.** To make sthg. that is exactly like (an original); reproduce: *I copied my paper over again.* **2.** To follow (sthg.) as a model or pattern; imitate: *The builder copied the house next door.* See Synonyms at **imitate.** — *intr.* To make a copy or copies: *Good authors don't copy from others.*

cop·y·cat (kŏp'ē kăt') *n. Slang.* A person who mimics or imitates others, as in speech, dress, or action: *He's such a copycat— I don't think he's ever had an original thought.*

cop·y·right (kŏp'ē rīt') *n.* [C; U] The legal right to be the only one to publish, produce, sell, or distribute a literary, musical, dramatic, or artistic work. — *tr.v.* To get a copyright for (sthg.): *She copyrighted her new novel.*

cor·al (kôr'əl *or* kŏr'əl) *n.* [U] **1.** A hard stony substance formed by the skeletons of tiny, usually tropical sea animals massed together in great numbers. Coral is often white, pink, or reddish, and some kinds are used for making jewelry. **2.** A yellowish pink or reddish orange color. — *adj.* **1.** Made of coral: *a coral bracelet.* **2.** Yellowish pink or reddish orange.

coral

cord (kôrd) *n.* **1.** [C; U] A string or small rope of twisted strands. **2.** [C] An insulated flexible electric wire fitted with a plug or plugs: *a power cord.* **3.** [C] A structure of the body, such as a nerve or tendon, that resembles a cord: *the spinal cord.*

cor·dial (kôr'jəl) *adj.* Warm and sincere; friendly: *cordial relations with the neighbors.* — *n.* [C; U] A liqueur: *We had a glass of cherry cordial after dinner.* — **cor'cial·ly** *adv.*

cord·less (kôrd'lĭs) *adj.* Having no cord; using batteries: *a cordless telephone.*

cor·don (kôr'dn) *n.* A line of police officers, military posts, or soldiers stationed around an area to enclose or guard it. — *v.* ◆ **cordon off.** *tr.v.* [sep.] To enclose and protect (sthg.) by surrounding: *The firefighters had cordoned off the burned-out building.*

cor·du·roy (kôr'də roi') *n.* **1.** [U] A heavy cotton fabric with raised ribs or ridges. **2.** **corduroys.** Pants made of this fabric: *I bought some navy corduroys.*

core (kôr) *n.* **1.** The hard or stringy central part of certain fruits, such as an apple or a pear, containing the seeds: *He ate the apple and threw the core in the trash.* **2.** The innermost part of sthg.; the heart: *the core of the nuclear reactor.* **3.** The basic or most important part of sthg.; the essence: *The core of the problem was a lack of funds.* **4.** The central or innermost portion of Earth. **5.** A piece of magnetic material, such as a rod of soft iron, placed inside an electrical coil or transformer to intensify and provide a path for the magnetic field produced by the windings. — *tr.v.* **cored, cor·ing, cores.** To remove the core of (sthg.): *core apples.* — **cor'er** *n.*

co·ri·an·der (kôr'ē ăn'dər) *n.* [U] **1.** A plant related to and resembling parsley, or its spicy fruits similar to seeds, dried and used as a seasoning. **2.** The young shoots of this plant, used in salads and as a garnish.

cork (kôrk) *n.* **1.** [U] The light spongy outer bark of the cork oak, used for bottle stoppers. **2.** [C] **a.** Something made of cork, especially a bottle stopper: *He pulled the cork out of the wine bottle.* **b.** A bottle stopper made of other material, such as rubber or plastic. — *tr.v.* To close up or stop (sthg.) with a cork: *cork a bottle.*

cork·screw (kôrk'skroō') *n.* A device for removing corks from bottles, consisting of a pointed metal spiral attached to a handle. — *adj.* Spiral in shape; twisted: *the corkscrew motion of a slowly spinning top.*

corn[1] (kôrn) *n.* [U] A tall cereal grass with edible grains or kernels on large ears; maize: *corn on the cob.*

corn[2] (kôrn) *n.* A hard thickening of the skin, usually on or near a toe, resulting from pressure or rubbing.

corn·bread (kôrn'brĕd') *n.* [U] Bread made from cornmeal.

corn·cob (kôrn'kŏb') *n.* The long hard central part of an ear of corn, bearing the kernels.

cor·ne·a (kôr'nē ə) *n.* The tough transparent outer coat of the eyeball that covers the iris and the pupil.

corned beef (kôrnd) *n.* Beef that has been preserved in brine, often used in sandwiches.

cor·ner (kôr'nər) *n.* **1.a.** The point at which two lines, edges, or surfaces meet: *the upper left-hand corner of the page; the corner of a* *table.* **b.** The area enclosed by the intersection of two lines, edges, or surfaces: *I sat in the corner.* **2.** The place where two roads or streets meet: *Meet me at the corner of Oak Street and Pine.* **3.** A remote or secluded place: *Americans have come from all corners of the world.* **4.** A monopoly, as of a stock or commodity, that enables the supplier to control the price: *a corner on the wheat market.* —*tr.v.* **1.** To force (sbdy./sthg.) into a threatening or difficult position: *The dog cornered the cat in a closet.* **2.** To gain a monopoly over (sthg.): *He attempted to corner the market in silver.* —*adj.* **1.** Located at a street corner: *the corner bookstore.* **2.** Designed for or used in a corner: *a corner cupboard for dishes.* ♦ **cut corners.** To do sthg. easily and quickly, usually by ignoring common practice or using cheaper materials: *They tried to save money on building their new house by cutting corners.* **in a corner.** In a difficult situation: *We were in a corner when we ran out of money on our vacation.* **just around the corner.** Very close in time or space: *I'm sure better days are just around the corner.* **turn the corner.** To overcome a critical point in a process or an illness: *The President says that the economy is going to turn the corner very soon.*

corn•field (**kôrn′**fēld′) *n.* A field where corn is grown.

corn flakes *pl.n.* A crisp, flaky, cold cereal prepared from coarse cornmeal.

corn•husk (**kôrn′**hŭsk′) *n.* The leafy covering surrounding an ear of corn.

corn•meal also **corn meal** (**kôrn′**mēl′) *n.* [U] Coarse meal made from ground corn kernels.

corn•stalk (**kôrn′**stôk′) *n.* The stem of the corn plant.

corn•starch (**kôrn′**stärch′) *n.* [U] A starchy flour made from corn, used as a thickener in cooking.

corn syrup *n.* [U] A thick sweet syrup that is made from corn starch.

cor•nu•co•pi•a (kôr′nə kō′pē ə) *n.* A cone-shaped container overflowing with fruit, vegetables, and flowers, symbolizing prosperity and abundance.

corn•y (**kôr′**nē) *adj.* **corn•i•er, corn•i•est.** *Slang.* Silly, outdated, or sentimental: *He likes to listen to corny songs from the 1940s.*

cor•ol•lar•y (**kôr′**ə lĕr′ē *or* **kŏr′**ə lĕr′ē) *n., pl.* **cor•ol•lar•ies.** **1.** A statement that follows with little or no proof required from an already proven statement: *If we know A equals B, then the corollary is that B equals A.* **2.** A natural consequence or effect; a result: *Disease and suffering are the corollaries of unclean living conditions.*

co•ro•na (kə rō′nə) *n.* A faintly colored shining ring seen around a celestial body, especially the moon or sun, when seen through a thin cloud or haze.

cor•o•nar•y (**kôr′**ə nĕr′ē *or* **kŏr′**ə nĕr′ē) *adj.* Relating to the heart: *Many hospitals have coronary care units.* —*n., pl.* **cor•o•nar•ies.** A heart attack.

coronary artery *n.* Either of the two arteries that supply blood directly to the heart.

cor•o•na•tion (kôr′ə nā′shən *or* kŏr′ə nā′shən) *n.* [C; U] The ceremony of crowning a king or queen.

cor•o•ner (**kôr′**ə nər *or* **kŏr′**ə nər) *n.* A public official who investigates any death not clearly due to natural causes: *The police called the coroner after they discovered the body.*

corp. *abbr.* An abbreviation of corporation.

cor•po•ral[1] (**kôr′**pər əl *or* **kôr′**prəl) *adj.* Relating to the body: *corporal punishment.*

cor•po•ral[2] (**kôr′**pər əl *or* **kôr′**prəl) *n.* A noncommissioned officer in the U.S. Army or Marine Corps ranking below a sergeant.

cor•po•rate (**kôr′**pər ĭt *or* **kôr′**prĭt) *adj.* **1.** Relating to a corporation: *The government taxes corporate profits.* **2.** United or combined; collective: *a corporate effort of the citizens to clean up the parks.* —**cor′po•rate•ly** *adv.*

cor•po•ra•tion (kôr′pə rā′shən) *n.* A large business organization; a company.

corps (kôr) *n., pl.* **corps** (kôrz). **1.** A section or branch of the armed forces with a special function: *The medical corps is trained to take care of the wounded.* **2.** A group of people working together: *the press corps.*

HOMONYMS: corps, core (central part).

---

corpse (kôrps) *n.* A dead body, especially of a human.

cor•pu•lent (**kôr′**pyə lənt) *adj. Formal.* Overweight; fat. —**cor′pu•lence** *n.* [U]

cor•pus (**kôr′**pəs) *n., pl.* **cor•po•ra** (**kôr′**pər ə). A large collection of writings on a specific subject.

cor•ral (kə răl′) *n.* An enclosed area for keeping cattle, horses, or sheep. —*tr.v.* **cor•ralled, cor•ral•ling, cor•rals.** **1.** To drive (sthg.) into a corral and hold there: *corral cattle for shipment to market.* **2.** *Informal.* To surround or seize (sbdy./sthg.): *We corralled the children into the bus.*

HOMONYMS: corral, chorale (music).

---

cor•rect (kə rĕkt′) *tr.v.* **1.a.** To remove the mistakes from (sthg.); make right: *Correct your paper before you hand it in.* **b.** To indicate or mark the errors in (sthg.): *The teacher corrected our tests.* **2.** To fix (sthg.): *Glasses will correct*

ă–**cat**; ā–**pay**; âr–**care**; ä–**father**; ĕ–**get**; ē–**be**; ĭ–**sit**; ī–**nice**; îr–**here**; ŏ–**got**; ō–**go**; ô–**saw**; oi–**boy**; ou–**out**; ŏŏ–**took**; ōō–**boot**; ŭ–**cut**; ûr–**word**; th–**thin**; th–**this**; hw–**when**; zh–**vision**; ə–**about**; N–French **bon**

your vision. **3.** To punish (sbdy.) for the purpose of improving behavior or performance: *The teacher corrected the children for running in the halls.* —*adj.* **1.** Free from error; accurate: *Your answers are absolutely correct.* **2.** Conforming to approved standards; proper: *the correct way to give artificial respiration.* —**cor·rect'ly** *adv.* —**cor·rect'ness** *n.* [U]

cor·rec·tion (kə rĕk'shən) *n.* **1.** [U] The act or process of correcting: *Correction of all my spelling mistakes did not take long.* **2.** [C] Something that is offered or substituted for a mistake or fault; an improvement: *Several corrections are written in the margin.* **3.** [U] Punishment intended to correct or improve. **4. corrections.** The care of criminals in a prison system.

cor·rec·tion·al facility (kə rĕk'shə nəl) *n.* A jail or prison.

correctional officer *n.* A prison guard.

cor·rec·tive (kə rĕk'tĭv) *adj.* Intended or tending to correct: *corrective lenses.*

cor·re·late (kôr'ə lāt' *or* kŏr'ə lāt') *v.* **cor·re·lat·ed, cor·re·lat·ing, cor·re·lates.** —*tr.* To put or bring (sthg.) into a meaningful relationship (with sthg. else): *We correlated the new data from our experiment with the old data and changed our theory.* —*intr.* To be related; to fit together: *The new data correlates perfectly with earlier studies.*

cor·re·la·tion (kôr'ə lā'shən *or* kŏr'ə-lā'shən) *n.* **1.** [C] A relation or connection: *a correlation between smoking and lung disease.* **2.** [U] An act of correlating: *The navigator's correlation of speed and position helped guide the ship.*

cor·rel·a·tive (kə rĕl'ə tĭv) *adj.* **1.** Related; corresponding: *Reading and writing are correlative language skills.* **2.** In grammar, indicating a relation and usually used in pairs. In the sentence, *Neither Jim nor Joe went along, neither* and *nor* are correlative conjunctions.

cor·re·spond (kôr'ĭ spŏnd' *or* kŏr'ĭ spŏnd') *intr.v.* **1.** [with] To be in agreement; match or compare closely: *This rainy weather hardly corresponds with yesterday's sunny forecast.* **2.** [to] To be very similar or equivalent: *The eyelids correspond to the shutter of a camera.* **3.** To communicate by letter over a period of time: *We can correspond over the summer.*

cor·re·spon·dence (kôr'ĭ spŏn'dəns *or* kŏr'ĭ spŏn'dəns) *n.* **1.** [U] Agreement: *Correspondence in the wording of the documents shows one is a copy of the other.* **2.** [C; U] Resemblance, as in function or structure; similarity: *Scientists classify animals and plants partly by the correspondences of their forms.* **3.** [U] **a.** Communication by the exchange of letters. **b.** The letters exchanged: *a drawer full of old correspondence.*

cor·re·spon·dent (kôr'ĭ spŏn'dənt *or* kŏr'-ĭ spŏn'dənt) *n.* **1.** A person who communicates by letter, often on a regular basis. **2.** A

person hired by a newspaper or radio or television station to report on news from a particular place: *the London correspondent for a U.S. newspaper.*

cor·re·spond·ing (kôr'ĭ spŏn'dĭng *or* kôr'ĭ spŏn'dĭng) *adj.* Matching closely; similar: *the corresponding function of feathers and fur.* —**cor·re·spond'ing·ly** *adv.*

cor·ri·dor (kôr'ĭ dər *or* kŏr'ĭ dər) *n.* **1.** A hall with rooms opening onto it. **2.** An open area of land forming a passageway: *a corridor for trains through the city.*

cor·rob·o·rate (kə rŏb'ə rāt') *tr.v.* **cor·rob·o·rat·ed, cor·rob·o·rat·ing, cor·rob·o·rates.** *Formal.* To support or confirm (sthg.) by new evidence: *Similar results of several experiments corroborated the new scientific theory.* —**cor·rob'o·ra'tion** *n.* [U] —**cor·rob'o·ra'tive** *adj.*

cor·rode (kə rōd') *v.* **cor·rod·ed, cor·rod·ing, cor·rodes.** —*tr.* To dissolve or wear away (a metal or alloy), especially by chemical action: *Salt corrodes metal.* —*intr.* To be dissolved or worn away: *Most metals corrode in a solution of salt.*

cor·ro·sion (kə rō'zhən) *n.* [U] **1.** The process of corroding: *Corrosion caused the pipe to leak.* **2.** A substance, such as rust, produced by corroding: *Clean the corrosion from the metal door.*

cor·ro·sive (kə rō'sĭv) *adj.* Capable of producing corrosion: *The salt used to melt snow and ice on highways is corrosive to cars.* —*n.* A corrosive substance. —**cor·ro'sive·ly** *adv.* —**cor·ro'sive·ness** *n.* [U]

cor·ru·gat·ed (kôr'ə gā'tĭd *or* kŏr'ə-gā'tĭd) *adj.* Having parallel ridges and grooves: *corrugated cardboard.*

cor·rupt (kə rŭpt') *adj.* **1.** Immoral: *the corrupt life of a criminal.* **2.** Willing to take money in exchange for special treatment; dishonest: *a corrupt government.* **3.** Containing errors or changes: *a corrupt translation of a poem.* —*tr.v.* **1.** To ruin (sbdy.) morally; cause to behave badly: *Greed corrupts some people.* **2.** To destroy the honesty of (sbdy.): *They corrupted the senator with offers of money.* **3.** To infect or spoil (sthg.): *Several chemical spills corrupted the water supply.* **4.** To change the original form of (a text, word, or language): *Careless copying corrupted later versions of the poem.* —**cor·rupt'ly** *adv.* —**cor·rupt'ness** *n.* [U]

cor·rupt·i·ble (kə rŭp'tə bəl) *adj.* Capable of being corrupted. —**cor·rupt'i·bil'i·ty** *n.* [U] —**cor·rupt'i·bly** *adv.*

cor·rup·tion (kə rŭp'shən) *n.* [U] **1.** The act of corrupting: *corruption of a powerful official.* **2.** Dishonesty or improper behavior, as by a person in a position of authority: *a police officer accused of corruption.* **3.** A corrupted form, as of a word: *The word* lite *to describe some diet foods is a corruption of* light.

cor·sage (kôr säzh′ *or* kôr säj′) *n.* A flower or small bouquet worn by a woman, especially on the shoulder or wrist.

cor·ti·sone (kôr′tĭ sōn′ *or* kôr′tĭ zōn′) *n.* [U] A hormone produced by the adrenal cortex or produced synthetically, used in treating arthritis, allergies, and other illnesses.

cos *abbr.* An abbreviation of cosine.

co·sign (kō sīn′) *tr.v.* To sign (a legal document, such as a contract) with one or more partners: *cosign a loan.* —**co·sign′er** *n.*

co·sine (kō′sīn′) *n.* The ratio of the length of the side adjacent to an acute angle of a right triangle to the length of the hypotenuse.

cos·met·ic (kŏz mĕt′ĭk) *n. (usually plural).* A preparation, such as face powder or skin cream, designed to beautify the body. —*adj.* Done or used to improve the appearance, as of a person or building: *cosmetic surgery to remove a scar; a little paint and some other cosmetic repairs on the house.*

cos·mic (kŏz′mĭk) *adj.* **1.** Relating to the universe or outer space: *cosmic dust.* **2.** Extremely large: *Overpopulation of the planet is an issue of cosmic importance.* —**cos′mi·cal·ly** *adv.*

cos·mo·naut (kŏz′mə nôt′) *n.* An astronaut from Russia or the former Soviet Union.

cos·mo·pol·i·tan (kŏz′mə pŏl′ĭ tn) *adj.* **1.** Made up of persons or elements from many different parts of the world: *Montreal is a cosmopolitan city.* **2.** Having broad interests or wide experience; sophisticated: *A cosmopolitan guest made the party interesting.*

cos·mos (kŏz′məs *or* kŏz′mōs′) *n.* [U] The universe regarded as an orderly and harmonious whole.

cost (kôst) *n.* **1.** [C; U] An amount paid or charged for a purchase; a price: *The cost of a fishing license is going up.* **2.** [C; U] The loss or sacrifice necessary to achieve a goal: *He worked day and night at the cost of his health.* **3. costs.** The expenses of a business: *We need to cut costs.* —*tr.v.* **1.** To have or require (sthg.) as a price: *A subscription to the magazine costs $15.* **2.** To cause (sbdy.) to lose or sacrifice (sthg.): *Years without rain cost them their farm.* ◆ **at any cost.** No matter what happens or what the price: *The team wanted to win at any cost.* **cost an arm and a leg.** *Informal.* To be very expensive: *The new car cost us an arm and a leg.*

cost·ly (kôst′lē) *adj.* **cost·li·er, cost·li·est.** **1.** High-priced; expensive: *costly jewelry.* **2.** Involving great loss or sacrifice: *Leaving their native country is a costly decision for many immigrant families.* —**cost′li·ness** *n.* [U]

cos·tume (kŏs′tōōm′ *or* kŏs′tyōōm′) *n.* **1.** [C; U] An outfit or a disguise worn on special occasions such as Halloween: *a costume party.* **2.** [C; U] The style of clothing and hair typical of a certain time, place, or people: *the costume of the ancient Romans.* **3.** [C] A set of clothes suitable for a certain occasion or season: *a skating costume.* —*tr.v.* **cos·tumed, cos·tuming, cos·tumes.** To dress (sbdy.) in a costume: *Everyone was costumed for our Halloween party.*

costume jewelry *n.* [U] Jewelry made of inexpensive materials, such as colored glass, plated metals, and imitation stones.

co·sy (kō′zē) *adj. & n.* Variant of **cozy.**

cot (kŏt) *n.* A narrow bed usually made of canvas stretched over a folding frame.

co·tan·gent (kō tăn′jənt) *n.* The ratio of the length of the adjacent side of an acute angle in a right triangle to the length of the opposite side.

cot·tage (kŏt′ĭj) *n.* **1.** A small house, usually in the country. **2.** A small house for summer use.

cottage cheese *n.* [U] A soft white cheese made of curds of sour skim milk.

cot·ton (kŏt′n) *n.* [U] **1.** A woody plant grown in warm regions for the downy white fibers that surround the seeds. **2.** Thread or cloth made of cotton fibers. —*v.* ◆ **cotton to.** *tr.v.* [insep.] *Informal.* To take a liking to (sbdy.); become friendly: *Our dog doesn't cotton to strangers.*

cotton candy *n.* [U] A candy made of sugar spun into thin fibers that form a fluffy mass.

cot·ton·tail (kŏt′n tāl′) *n.* A rabbit.

cot·ton·wood (kŏt′n wŏŏd′) *n.* Any of several American poplar trees with triangular leaves and seeds with cottony tufts.

cot·ton·y (kŏt′n ē) *adj.* **1.** Of or resembling cotton; fluffy or downy: *cottony filling.* **2.** Covered with fibers resembling cotton.

couch (kouch) *n.* A sofa. —*tr.v.* [in] To word (sthg.) in a certain manner: *The bank robbers couched their demands in polite language.*

cou·gar (kōō′gər) *n.* The mountain lion.

cough (kôf *or* kŏf) *v.* —*intr.* To force air from the lungs suddenly and noisily, usually to clear mucus or other matter from the throat or lungs: *cough from breathing smoke.* —*tr.* [up] To clear (sthg.) from the respiratory tract by coughing: *cough up mucus.* —*n.* **1.** The act of coughing: *The student's cough disturbed the class.* **2.** An illness marked by coughing: *A deep cough kept me out of school.* ◆ **cough up.** *tr.v.* [sep.] *Informal.* To pay or give (sthg.): *Where's that $10 I loaned you? Cough it up!*

could (kŏŏd) *aux.v.* Past tense of **can**[1]. **1.** Used to show possibility: *It could rain tomorrow.* **2.** Used to show ability in the past: *I could run faster back then.* **3.** Used to show permission in the past: *Only friends of the* musicians could go backstage after the concert. **4.** Used to show politeness: *Could I have some more juice?*

could•n't (kŏŏd′nt). Contraction of *could not.*

coun•cil (koun′səl) *n.* **1.** A gathering of people called together to discuss a problem or give advice: *the UN Security Council.* **2.** A group of people elected or appointed to make laws, policies, or decisions: *The President has a council of economic advisers.*

HOMONYMS: council, counsel (advice).

USAGE: council The word **council** refers to a decision-making assembly, as in *city council* or *student council*; its members are known as **councilors.** The word **counsel,** on the other hand, means "advice and guidance"; a person who provides such counsel, as at a summer camp or in a legal dispute, is a **counselor.**

---

coun•cil•man (koun′səl mən) *n.* A man who is part of a council, especially of the group that makes the laws of a city. —**coun′cil•wom′an** (koun′səl wŏŏm′ən) *n.*

coun•cil•or also **coun•cil•lor** (koun′sə lər *or* koun′slər) *n.* A member of a council. —SEE NOTE at **council.**

HOMONYMS: councilor, counselor (adviser).

---

coun•sel (koun′səl) *n.* [U] **1.** Advice; guidance: *I will not make a decision without your counsel.* **2.** A lawyer or group of lawyers giving legal advice. —*tr.v.* **1.** To give (sbdy.) advice; advise: *The school counseled parents to keep children at home during the storm.* **2.** To recommend (sthg.): *They counsel swift action.* —SEE NOTE at **council.**

HOMONYMS: counsel, council (group).

---

coun•sel•or also **coun•sel•lor** (koun′sə lər *or* koun′slər) *n.* **1.** A person who advises or guides; an adviser: *a school counselor.* **2.** A lawyer. **3.** A person who supervises children at a summer camp. —SEE NOTE at **council.**

HOMONYMS: counselor, councilor (member of a council).

---

count¹ (kount) *v.* —*tr.* **1.** To find the total of (sthg.); add up: *Count your change before leaving the store. Count the books before you return them to the library.* **2.** To name the numbers in order up to and including (a particular number): *Count three and jump.* **3.** To take account of (sbdy./sthg.); include: *There are seven in my family, counting me.* —*intr.* **1.** To name numbers in order or list items: *count*

from 1 to 10. **2.** To have importance or value: *It is not how much you write but how well you write that counts.* —*n.* **1.** The act of counting or calculating: *A count showed that most of the class came.* **2.** (usually singular). A number reached by counting: *The count of students on the bus was low.* **3.** In law, any of the separate charges listed in an indictment: *The thief was tried on five counts of robbery.*
♦ **count down.** *intr.v.* To count the seconds backwards, especially before beginning a race, or launching a rocket: *I'll count down from three and say "Go!"* **count in.** *tr.v.* [sep.] To include (sbdy./sthg.): *If you are going camping, count me in.* **count off.** *intr.v.* To separate people or things into groups by counting: *count off by twos.* **count on.** *tr.v.* [insep.] **1.** To rely on (sbdy./sthg.): *You can count on me to help.* **2.** To be confident of (sbdy./sthg.); anticipate: *I am counting on an A in history.* **count out.** *tr.v.* [sep.] To exclude (sbdy./sthg.): *If there's going to be any roughness, you can count me out.*

count² (kount) *n.* A nobleman in some European countries.

count•a•ble (koun′tə bəl) *adj.* That can be counted: *countable items.*

countable noun *n.* A noun such as *pen* or *child* that has a singular and plural form and can be counted.

count•down (kount′doun′) *n.* **1.** The counting backward from a starting number to mark the time remaining before a scheduled event, such as the launching of a rocket. **2.** The preparations carried out during this process.

coun•te•nance (koun′tə nəns) *Formal. n.* Appearance, especially the expression of the face: *a grim countenance.* —*tr.v.* **coun•te•nanced, coun•te•nanc•ing, coun•te•nanc•es.** To give approval to (sthg.); condone: *She won't countenance bad manners.*

coun•ter¹ (koun′tər) *adj.* Contrary; opposing: *views counter to public opinion.* —*tr.* **1.** To move or act in opposition to (sbdy./sthg.); oppose: *They countered our plan with one of their own.* **2.** To return (a blow) with another blow. **3.** To offer or say (sthg.) in response: *She countered that she was too busy to write a long paper.* —*intr.* [with] **1.** To move, act, or respond in opposition: *They countered with a weak argument.* **2.** To give a blow in return, as in boxing. —*adv.* [to] In a contrary manner or direction: *a new method that runs counter to the regular way.*

count•er² (koun′tər) *n.* **1.** A flat surface on which goods are sold or money is counted: *The clerk rang up the items on the counter.* **2.** A flat surface where food is prepared, usually on top of a low kitchen cabinet.

count•er³ (koun′tər) *n.* A person or thing that counts, especially a mechanical or electronic device that automatically counts.

counter– *pref.* A prefix that means: **1.** Contrary or opposite: *counteract; counterclockwise.* **2.** In return or opposing: *counterattack.* **3.** Corresponding or matching: *counterpart.*

coun·ter·act (koun′tər ăkt′) *tr.v.* To oppose and lessen the effects of (sthg.) by contrary action: *Aspirin often counteracts a fever.*

coun·ter·at·tack (koun′tər ə tăk′) *n.* An attack made in return for another attack. —*intr. & tr.v.* (koun′tər ə tăk′). To attack in return.

coun·ter·bal·ance (koun′tər băl′əns) *n.* **1.** A force or an influence that counteracts another. **2.** A weight that balances another. —*tr.v.* (koun′tər băl′əns). **coun·ter·bal·anced, coun·ter·bal·anc·ing, coun·ter·bal·anc·es.** To act as a counterbalance to (sthg.): *His caution counterbalances his partner's daring.*

coun·ter·clock·wise (koun′tər klŏk′wīz′) *adv. & adj.* In a direction opposite to that of the movement of the hands of a clock: *move counterclockwise; counterclockwise motion.*

coun·ter·feit (koun′tər fĭt′) *v.* —*tr.* **1.** To make a copy of (sthg.) in order to deceive: *The defendant was found guilty of counterfeiting money.* **2.** To pretend (sthg.); fake: *We counterfeited surprise to please the host.* —*intr.* **1.** To carry on a deception; pretend. **2.** To make fake copies, especially of money. —*adj.* **1.** Made in imitation of what is genuine in order to deceive: *a counterfeit dollar bill.* **2.** Pretended; simulated: *counterfeit friendliness.* —*n.* Something counterfeited: *That $20 bill is a counterfeit.* —**coun′ter·feit′er** *n.*

coun·ter·in·tel·li·gence (koun′tər ĭn·těl′ə jəns) *n.* [U] The work of preventing enemy spies from gathering secret political and military information.

coun·ter·of·fer (koun′tər ô′fər *or* koun′tər ŏf′ər) *n.* An offer made in return by sbdy. who rejects an unsatisfactory offer.

coun·ter·part (koun′tər pärt′) *n.* **1.** A person or thing that corresponds to another in function, relation, or position: *The ancient counterpart to the car was the chariot.* **2.** A person or thing that is a natural complement to another: *He has one sock but lost its counterpart.*

coun·ter·pro·duc·tive (koun′tər prə·dŭk′tĭv) *adj.* Not useful; troublesome: *His comments were counterproductive.*

coun·ter·sign (koun′tər sīn′) *tr.v.* To sign (a document previously signed by another) to guarantee authenticity: *The property deed was signed by the new owner and countersigned by a notary public.*

coun·ter·spy (koun′tər spī′) *n., pl.* **coun·ter·spies.** A spy working to uncover or oppose enemy spies.

coun·ter·weight (koun′tər wāt′) *n.* A weight used as a counterbalance.

count·ess (koun′tĭs) *n.* **1.** A woman holding the title of count or earl. **2.** The wife or widow of a count or earl.

count·less (kount′lĭs) *adj.* Too many to be counted: *the countless stars.*

count noun *n.* A noun, such as *chair* or *dog,* that refers to a single person or thing and can be used in the plural or with the article *a* or *an.*

coun·try (kŭn′trē) *n., pl.* **coun·tries. 1.** [C] **a.** A nation or state: *Mexico and Canada are two countries in the Western Hemisphere.* **b.** The land of a nation or state: *Switzerland is a mountainous country.* **2.** [C] The land of one's birth or citizenship: *The sailors returned to their country at the end of the voyage.* **3.** [C] The people of a nation or state: *The country will benefit from his invention.* **4.** [U] A large area of land distinguished by certain physical, geographic, or cultural features: *hill country.* **5.** [U] The region outside of cities or heavily populated districts; a rural area: *go to the country for a vacation.* —*adj.* Relating to or typical of the country: *country life.*

country and western *n.* [U] A type of popular music based on folk music of the southern rural United States or on the music of cowboys in the American West.

country club *n.* A suburban club with facilities for social and sports activities, usually with a golf course.

coun·try·man (kŭn′trē mən) *n.* A man from one's own country. —**coun′try·wom′an** (kŭn′trē wŏŏm′ən) *n.*

country music *n.* [U] **1.** Country and western. **2.** A type of music originating in the Southern United States.

coun·try·side (kŭn′trē sīd′) *n.* [U] **1.** A rural region. **2.** The people who live in the countryside: *The whole countryside resisted building the highway.*

coun·ty (koun′tē) *n., pl.* **coun·ties. 1.** [C] In the United States, a subdivision of a state. **2.** [C] A major territorial division in Great Britain and Ireland. **3.** [U] The people living in a county.

county seat *n.* A town or city that is the center of government in its county.

coup (kōō) *n., pl.* **coups** (kōōz). **1.** A brilliantly executed move or action that achieves the desired results: *Quickly restoring peace between the enemy nations was a real coup for the ambassador.* **2.** A coup d'état.

HOMONYMS: coup, coo (murmuring sound).

---

coup d'é·tat (dā tä′) *n., pl.* **coups d'état** or **coup d'é·tats** (dā tä′). The sudden overthrow of a government, bringing a new group into power: *Military control of the government started as a coup d'état.*

cou•ple (kŭp′əl) *n.* **1.** Two things of the same kind; a pair: *a couple of shoes.* **2.** Two people united, as in marriage or interests: *a young couple just starting a family; a dance couple.* **3.** *Informal.* A few; several: *vacation for a couple of days.* —*v.* **cou•pled, cou•pling, cou•ples.** —*tr.* To attach or link (two things) together: *couple the cars of a train.* —*intr.* [*with*] To form pairs; join: *Hard work coupled with good luck to make a successful business.*

cou•pling (kŭp′lĭng) *n.* A device that links or connects.

cou•pon (kōō′pŏn′ *or* kyōō′pŏn′) *n.* A part of a ticket, card, or advertisement that permits the person holding it certain benefits, such as a cash refund or a gift: *Supermarket coupons can save shoppers money.*

cour•age (kûr′ĭj *or* kŭr′ĭj) *n.* [U] The quality of mind or spirit that helps one to face danger or difficulty; bravery: *It takes courage to do something that frightens you.*

cou•ra•geous (kə rā′jəs) *adj.* Having or showing courage; brave. See Synonyms at **brave. —cou•ra′geous•ly** *adv.* **—cou•ra′geous•ness** *n.* [U]

cou•ri•er (kōōr′ē ər *or* kûr′ē ər) *n.* A messenger, especially one on official diplomatic business: *Government requests for peace talks were sent by courier.*

course (kôrs) *n.* **1.** Onward movement in a particular direction or in time: *the course of events; in the course of a week.* **2.** The route or direction taken by sbdy. or sthg.: *the course of a stream; a southern course.* **3.** An area of land or water on which a race is held or a sport is played: *a golf course.* **4.** A way of behaving or acting: *Your best course is to do what was asked.* **5.** The usual way that sthg. develops or is done: *The disease ran its course.* **6.** A planned series of actions: *a course of medical treatments.* **7.** A complete series of lessons on a subject in a school, college, or university: *an algebra course; a four-year course in engineering.* **8.** A part of a meal served as a unit at one time: *Soup was our first course.* —*intr.v.* **coursed, cours•ing, cours•es.** To flow or move swiftly: *Blood courses through the veins.* ♦ **in due course.** At the proper or right time: *We will learn the results in due course.* **of course. 1.** In the natural or expected order of things; naturally: *That student is smart and works hard, so of course she gets good grades.* **2.** Without any doubt; certainly: *Of course we'll come to your party.*

---

court (kôrt) *n.* **1.** An area of open ground with walls or buildings on some or all sides; a courtyard. **2.** A short street, especially with buildings on three sides. **3.a.** A person or group of officials who make decisions on legal cases: *the Supreme Court.* **b.** The room or building in which such cases are heard; a courthouse or courtroom. **4.** A king or queen's group of ministers and state advisers. **5.** The people who attend a king or queen, including family, servants, advisers, and friends. **6.** An open level area marked with lines for games such as tennis, handball, or basketball. —*v.* —*tr.* **1.** An old-fashioned word meaning to try to get the love of (sbdy.), especially with hopes of marrying: *He courted her for a year before the wedding.* **2.** To seek the support or favor of (sbdy.): *Columbus courted the Queen and King of Spain to help pay for his expeditions.* **3.** To look for or try to get (sthg.), often foolishly or without thinking: *court danger.* —*intr.* To pay loving attention: *The young couple courted in secret.*

cour•te•ous (kûr′tē əs) *adj.* Considerate toward other people; polite: *a kind and courteous manner.* See Synonyms at **polite. —cour′te•ous•ly** *adv.* **—cour′te•ous•ness** *n.* [U]

cour•te•sy (kûr′tĭ sē) *n., pl.* **cour•te•sies. 1.** [U] Polite behavior: *We try to treat all of our customers with courtesy.* **2.** [C] An act or a gesture showing politeness: *Our host's many courtesies made our visit with him very enjoyable.*

court•house (kôrt′hous′) *n.* **1.** A building in which courts of law are held. **2.** A building that houses a county government.

court-mar•tial (kôrt′mär′shəl) *n., pl.* **courts-mar•tial** (kôrts′mär′shəl). [C; U] **1.** A military court of officers who examine and judge persons accused of offenses under military law. **2.** A trial by such a court. —*tr.v.* To try (sbdy.) by court-martial: *The officer was court-martialed.*

court•room (kôrt′rōōm′ *or* kôrt′rōōm′) *n.* A room in which a court of law functions.

court•ship (kôrt′shĭp′) *n.* [C; U] The act or period of courting.

court•yard (kôrt′yärd′) *n.* An open space with walls or buildings on all sides.

courtyard

cous•in (kŭz′ĭn) *n.* **1.** A child of one's aunt or uncle. **2.** A family member connected by a shared grandparent or an earlier ancestor.

cove (kōv) *n.* **1.** A small protected bay in the shoreline of a sea, river, or lake. **2.** A small valley in the side of a mountain.

cov•en (kŭv′ən *or* kō′vən) *n.* A gathering or meeting of witches.

C

cov•e•nant (kŭv′ə nənt) *n.* A formal agreement made by two or more persons or groups: *a covenant between nations to preserve peace.*

cov•er (kŭv′ər) *tr.v.* **1.** To place sthg. on or over (sthg.), so as to protect or hide: *cover a table; cover one's ears.* **2.** To spread over the surface of (sthg.): *Dust covered the table.* **3.** To hide (sthg.) from other people: *He tried to cover up his mistakes.* **4.** To include (an area or subject): *a farm covering 100 acres; a book covering the American Revolution.* **5.** To travel or pass over (a distance): *We covered 200 miles a day.* **6.** To be responsible for reporting the details of (an event or a situation), as for a newspaper: *The reporter covered the crisis in the Middle East.* **7.** To be enough money for (sthg.): *Will five dollars cover the cost of it?* **8.** To include (sthg.) under the protection of insurance: *We have fire insurance to cover our house.* **9.a.** To aim a gun at (sbdy.): *The police officer covered the suspect.* **b.** To protect (sbdy./sthg.) with guns: *The entrance to the harbor is covered by the guns of the fort.* **10.** In sports: **a.** To guard the play of (an opposing player). **b.** To defend (an area or a position): *In baseball, the pitcher covers first base when the first baseman cannot.* —*n.* **1.** [C] Something placed on or attached to sthg. else, as to close in or protect it: *the cover of a teapot; the covers of a book.* **2.** [U] A place or thing that gives protection: *The rabbit ran for the cover of the tall grass.* **3.** [U] Something that hides or disguises: *The enemy retreated under the cover of darkness.* **4.** [U] A cover charge. ◆ **cover for.** *tr.v.* [insep.] *Informal.* To act as a substitute for (sbdy. who is absent): *A coworker covered for me while I was at lunch.* **cover up for.** To hide sthg. in order to save sbdy. from punishment, embarrassment, or loss: *cover up for a friend who made a mistake.* **take cover.** To get into a hiding place, as in escaping from enemy attack: *The soldiers took cover from the planes.* **under cover.** Secretly: *Spies work under cover.*

cov•er•age (kŭv′ər ĭj) *n.* [U] **1.** The amount to which or the way in which sthg. is reported: *television news coverage of local events.* **2.** The amount or area of protection given by an insurance policy: *We carry accident and theft coverage on our car.*

cover charge *n.* A fixed amount charged for entrance to a nightclub or restaurant with entertainment: *There's a cover charge of $10.*

cov•er•ing (kŭv′ər ĭng) *n.* Something that covers, protects, or hides: *a covering for a bed.*

cov•er•let (kŭv′ər lĭt) *n.* A bedspread.

cover letter *n.* A letter sent with another letter, document, or package to explain it: *To apply for the job, send a résumé and cover letter.*

cov•ert (kŭv′ərt *or* kō′vərt) *adj.* Hidden; secret: *a covert mission behind enemy lines.* —*n.* **1.** A covered or protected place; a hiding place. **2.** Thick low plants that provide protection from hunters for animals or birds. —**cov′ert•ly** *adv.* —**cov′ert•ness** *n.* [U]

cov•er-up *or* **cov•er•up** (kŭv′ər ŭp′) *n.* An effort or plan to hide sthg., such as a crime or scandal, that could be harmful or embarrassing if made public.

cov•et (kŭv′ĭt) *tr.v.* **1.** To desire (sthg. belonging to another person): *She covets her friend's money.* **2.** To wish for (sthg.) strongly: *an ambitious person who coveted success.*

cov•et•ous (kŭv′ĭ təs) *adj. Formal.* Having a strong desire for sthg. belonging to another person. —**cov′et•ous•ly** *adv.* —**cov′et•ous•ness** *n.* [U]

cow[1] (kou) *n.* **1.** The mature female of domestic cattle. **2.** The mature female of certain other large mammals, such as elephants or moose.

cow[2] (kou) *tr.v.* To frighten or control (sbdy.) with threats or a show of force: *The approach of the army cowed the rioting crowd.*

cow•ard (kou′ərd) *n.* A person who doesn't have the courage to face danger or pain, or shows fear in a shameful way.

cow•ard•ice (kou′ər dĭs) *n.* [U] Lack of courage or a shameful show of fear when facing danger or pain.

cow•ard•ly (kou′ərd lē) *adj.* **1.** Failing to show courage: *a cowardly liar.* **2.** Usual for a coward: *cowardly behavior.* —**cow′ard•li•ness** *n.* [U] —**cow′ard•ly** *adv.*

cow•boy (kou′boi′) *n.* A man or boy who tends cattle, especially in the western United States, often working on horseback. —**cow′girl′** (kou′gûrl′) *n.*

cow•er (kou′ər) *intr.v.* To crouch or draw back, as from fear or pain; cringe: *The dog cowered under the table in the thunderstorm.*

cow•hand (kou′hănd′) *n.* A cowboy or cowgirl.

cow•hide (kou′hīd′) *n.* [U] **1.** The skin or hide of a cow. **2.** Leather made from this hide.

cow•lick (kou′lĭk′) *n.* A group of hairs that stands up from the head and will not lie flat.

co•work•er (kō′wûr′kər) *n.* A person with whom one works; a fellow worker.

cow•poke (kou′pōk′) *n. Informal.* A cowhand.

coy (koi) *adj.* **1.** Not direct and confident; shy. **2.** Pretending to be shy or modest, especially to attract attention: *She gave him a coy smile.* —**coy′ly** *adv.* —**coy′ness** *n.* [U]

coy•o•te (kī ō′tē *or* kī′ōt′) *n.* A mammal similar to the wolf, common in western North America.

co•zy (kō′zē) *adj.* **co•zi•er, co•zi•est. 1.** Comfortable and warm: *a cozy chair by the fire.* **2.** Friendly; intimate: *a cozy circle of friends.* **3.** *Informal.* Marked by close association for dishonest purposes: *a cozy deal between management and union leaders.* —*n., pl.* **co•zies.** A thick covering placed over a teapot to keep the tea hot. ◆ **cozy up.** *intr.v.* [*to*] *Informal.* To try to become friendly and close: *He's been cozying up to the boss.* —**co′zi•ly** *adv.* —**co′zi•ness** *n.* [U]

CPA *also* **C.P.A.** *abbr.* An abbreviation of certified public accountant.

Cpl. *abbr.* An abbreviation of corporal.

CPR *abbr.* An abbreviation of cardiopulmonary resuscitation.

cps *abbr.* An abbreviation of cycles per second.

CPU *abbr.* An abbreviation of central processing unit.

Cr The symbol for the element chromium.

crab[1] (krăb) *n.* **1.** Any of various primarily marine animals related to the lobster and shrimp, with a broad flat body and five pairs of legs, of which the front pair are claws. **2.** Any of various similar related animals, such as the horseshoe crab or the hermit crab. —*intr.v.* **crabbed, crab•bing, crabs.** To hunt or catch crabs. —**crab′ber** *n.*

crab[2] (krăb) *n.* **1.** A crab apple tree or its small, sour fruit. **2.** *Informal.* A bad-tempered complaining person; a grouch. —*intr.v.* **crabbed, crab•bing, crabs.** *Informal.* To complain irritably.

crab•by (krăb′ē) *adj.* **crab•bi•er, crab•bi•est.** *Informal.* Irritable and difficult to please: *She's crabby until she's had her coffee.* —**crab′bi•ly** *adv.* —**crab′bi•ness** *n.* [U]

crack[1] (krăk) *v.* —*intr.v.* **1.** To break with a sharp sound: *The tree limb cracked in the storm.* See Synonyms at **break. 2.** To make a sharp snapping sound: *My knees cracked when I got down on the floor.* **3.** To break without dividing into parts: *The mirror cracked.* **4.** (*used of voices*). To change sharply in sound: *The reporter's voice cracked with emotion.* **5.** To lose mental or emotional self-control: *The young doctor cracked under the strain of long hours.* —*tr.* **1.** To break (sthg.) with a sharp sound: *We cracked walnuts.* **2.** To cause (sthg.) to make a sharp snapping sound: *The coach driver cracked a whip.* **3.** To cause (sthg.) to break without dividing into parts: *The hot tea cracked the cup.* **4.** To hit (sthg.) with a sudden sharp sound: *I cracked my head on the low ceiling.* **5.** To open (a safe) illegally. **6.** To solve or find the answer to (sthg.): *crack a spy's code; crack a police case.* **7.** *Informal.* To tell or say (a joke or sthg. witty). —*n.* **1.** A sharp snapping sound: *a loud crack of thunder.* **2.** An incomplete split or break: *a crack in a plate.* **3.** A narrow space: *The door was opened just a crack.* **4.** A sharp blow: *a crack on the head.* **5.** A sudden change in sound: *a crack in the singer's voice.* **6.** *Informal.* A try or an attempt: *Take a crack at the job.* **7.** A witty or sarcastic remark: *What kind of crack is that?* —*adj.* Having excellent skill: *The hunter was a crack shot.* ◆ **crack down.** *intr.v. Informal.* To become more severe or strict: *The principal cracked down on students' arriving late.* **crack up.** *Informal. tr.v.* [sep.] **1.** To damage or wreck (sthg.): *I cracked up the car.* **2.** To make (sbdy.) laugh: *That comedian always cracks me up.* —*intr.v.* **1.** To have a mental or physical breakdown: *crack up from overwork.* **2.** To start laughing: *I cracked up when I heard the story.*

crack[2] (krăk) *n.* [U] A strong form of cocaine.

crack•down (krăk′doun′) *n.* An action taken to stop an illegal or disapproved activity: *a crackdown on gambling.*

cracked (krăkt) *adj.* **1.** Having a crack or cracks: *a cracked dish.* **2.** Broken into pieces: *cracked ice.* **3.** Changing or uneven in sound: *a cracked voice.* **4.** *Informal.* An insulting term for sbdy. thought to be very strange or irrational.

crack•er (krăk′ər) *n.* **1.** A thin crisp wafer or biscuit: *Have some cheese and crackers.* **2.** An offensive term for a poor white person of the rural southeastern United States.

crack•er•jack (krăk′ər jăk′) *Slang. n.* A person or thing of excellent quality or ability. —*adj.* Of the highest quality or ability: *a crackerjack pilot.*

crack•le (krăk′əl) *intr.v.* **crack•led, crack•ling, crack•les.** To make slight sharp snapping sounds, as a small fire does: *The oil crackled as I heated it in the pan.* —*n.* The act or sound of crackling: *the crackle of dry leaves underfoot.* —**crack′ly** *adj.*

crack•ling (krăk′lĭng) *n.* **1.** Sharp snapping sounds like those produced by a fire or by the crushing of paper. **2. cracklings.** Crisp bits remaining after fat from meat has been melted down, as in making lard.

crack•pot (krăk′pŏt′) *n.* An insulting term for a person with very strange ideas.

crack•up *or* **crack-up** (krăk′ŭp′) *n.* **1.** *Informal.* A collision, as of an aircraft or an automobile. **2.** A sudden loss of emotional, mental, or physical strength.

cra•dle (krād′l) *n.* **1.** A small bed for a baby, usually on rockers for side-to-side movement. **2.** A place of origin; a birthplace: *Boston was the cradle of the American Revolution.* —*tr.v.* **cra•dled, cra•dling, cra•dles.** To place or hold (sbdy./sthg.) in or as if in a cradle: *cradle a baby in one's arms.*

craft (krăft) *n.* **1.** [C; U] Special skill or ability: *a table made with craft; the craft of fine* *needlework.* **2.** [U] Skill in tricking or avoiding others, such as an enemy: *With great craft the spy escaped capture.* **3.** [C] An occupation or a trade requiring special skill: *learning his craft as a printer.* **4.** *pl.* **craft.** A boat, ship, aircraft, or spacecraft. —*tr.v.* **1.** To make (sthg.) by hand: *craft fine watches.* **2.** To make or arrange (sthg.) with great care and skill: *craft an agreement between two nations at war.*

crafts•man (krăfts′mən) *n.* A man who practices a craft with great skill. —**crafts′-man•ship′** *n.* [U]

crafts•wom•an (krăfts′wŏom′ən) *n.* A woman who practices a craft with great skill.

craft•y (krăf′tē) *adj.* **craft•i•er, craft•i•est.** Having or showing skill at tricking people: *a crafty thief.* —**craft′i•ly** *adv.* —**craft′i•ness** *n.* [U]

crag (krăg) *n.* A steep projection of rock forming part of a cliff or mountain.

crag•gy (krăg′ē) *adj.* **crag•gi•er, crag•gi•est.** **1.** Having crags; steep and rugged: *a craggy mountain.* **2.** Having strong and uneven features: *an old sailor's craggy face.* —**crag′gi•ness** *n.* [U]

cram (krăm) *v.* **crammed, cram•ming, crams.** —*tr.* **1.** To force, press, or squeeze (persons or things) into too small a space: *I crammed my clothes into the suitcase.* **2.** To fill or crowd (sthg.) too tightly: *Cars crammed the street so that no traffic moved.* —*intr. Informal.* [*for*] To study in a hurry before an examination: *cramming for a test.*

cramp[1] (krămp) *n.* **1.** A sudden painful contraction of a muscle, often resulting from strain or chill: *A leg cramp forced the runner to quit the race.* **2.** A temporary condition of muscles that are used too much and so can't move: *My fingers had writer's cramp after the test.* **3. cramps.** Sharp continuing pains in the abdomen: *An upset stomach and cramps made me feel sick.* —*intr. & tr.v.* To have or cause to have a cramp or cramps: *The runner's leg cramped in the cold. Swimming so many laps eventually cramped her legs.*

cramp[2] (krămp) *n.* A force or an influence that restrains: *The rain put a cramp in our picnic plans.* —*tr.v.* To confine or hold (sthg.) back: *We were cramped on the crowded bus.*
♦ **cramp (one's) style.** To stop (sbdy.) from acting or speaking freely: *His parents' presence cramped the boy's style.*

cramped (krămpt) *adj.* **1.** Confined and limited in space: *a cramped little apartment.* **2.** Hard to read: *cramped handwriting.*

cran•ber•ry (krăn′bĕr′ē) *n.* The tart, shiny, red berry of an evergreen shrub that grows in damp places, used in making jelly and baked goods.

crane (krān) *n.* **1.** Any of various large wading birds having a long neck, long legs, and a long bill. **2.** A machine for lifting heavy objects by means of ropes or wires attached to a long movable arm. **3.** Any of various devices in which a swinging arm or rod is used to support a load. —*v.* **craned, cran•ing, cranes.** —*tr.* To strain and stretch (the neck) in order to see better: *She had to crane her neck to see.* —*intr.* To stretch one's neck toward sthg. for a better view: *He craned to see the movie screen.*

crane
Black-crowned crane

crane
Mechanical crane

cra•ni•a (krā′nē ə) *n.* A plural of **cranium.**

cra•ni•al (krā′nē əl) *adj.* Relating to the skull: *cranial nerves.*

cra•ni•um (krā′nē əm) *n.*, *pl.* **cra•ni•ums** or **cra•ni•a** (krā′nē ə). **1.** The bones that form the head of a vertebrate animal; skull. **2.** The part of the skull that encloses the brain.

crank (krăngk) *n.* **1.** A rod and handle that can be attached to a shaft and turned to start or operate a machine. **2.** *Informal.* **a.** An irritable person; a grouch. **b.** A person with odd ideas. —*tr.v.* **1.** To start or operate (an engine or a device) by means of a crank: *Electric starters replaced the need to crank early car motors.* **2.** To move or operate (a window, for example) by or as if by turning a handle: *Crank the window open a little.* —*adj.* Produced by an odd person: *a crank phone call.*
♦ **crank out.** *tr.v.* [sep.] To produce (sthg.), especially mechanically and rapidly: *The printing press is cranking out copies of the pamphlet.* **crank up.** *tr.v.* [sep.] **1.** To start (an engine): *Crank up the engine and let's get out of here.* **2.** To make (sthg.) louder: *Crank up the music! Let's party!*

crank•case (krăngk′kās′) *n.* The bottom part of a gasoline engine that covers the crankshaft and holds the oil to lubricate it.

crank•shaft (krăngk′shăft′) *n.* A shaft that turns or is turned by a crank. In a gasoline engine it is connected to and rotated by the pistons.

crank•y (krăng′kē) *adj.* **crank•i•er, crank•i•**

est. Easily annoyed; irritable: *Some children are cranky when they are tired.* —**crank′i•ly** *adv.* —**crank′i•ness** *n.* [U]

cran•ny (krăn′ē) *n., pl.* **cran•nies.** A small opening; a crevice: *We searched for the missing money in every nook and cranny.*

crap (krăp) *Slang. n.* [U] **1.** Excrement. **2.** A mildly offensive word for sthg. that is of poor quality or worthless: *Why did you leave all your crap in my car?* **3.** A mildly offensive word for sthg. that one feels is untrue: *That's just a bunch of crap; he can't possibly have a million dollars.* —**crap′py** *adj.*

crash (krăsh) *v.* —*intr.* **1.** To break violently and noisily: *The dishes crashed to pieces on the floor.* **2.** To be damaged or destroyed by hitting sthg. violently: *The car crashed into the tree.* **3.** To move noisily or violently: *The elephants crashed through the trees.* **4.** To fail suddenly: *The stock market crashed in 1929. My computer just crashed again.* **5.** To make a sudden loud noise: *waves crashing on the rocky shore.* —*tr.* **1.** To cause (sthg.) to fall or hit sthg. else suddenly, violently, and noisily: *The boy crashed his bike into the garage door.* **2.** *Informal.* To join or enter (a social event) without being invited: *crash a party.* —*n.* **1.** A violent meeting of two moving objects: *Their car was destroyed in a crash.* **2.** A loud noise from such a crash: *a crash of thunder.* **3.** A sudden severe drop in business: *the crash of 1929.* **4.** The sudden failure of a computer or computer program. —*adj. Informal.* Marked by a strong effort to produce or accomplish sthg. quickly: *a crash diet to lose weight.*

crass (krăs) *adj.* Offensive and unfeeling: *a crass remark about his looks.* —**crass′ly** *adv.* —**crass′ness** *n.* [U]

—**crat** *suff.* A suffix that means one who is involved in or supports a certain form of government: *bureaucrat; democrat.*

crate (krāt) *n.* A large packing case made of narrow pieces of wood. —*tr.v.* **crat•ed, crat•ing, crates.** To pack (sthg.) into a crate: *crate a painting to be sent to a museum; crate oranges for shipping.*

cra•ter (krā′tər) *n.* **1.** A bowl-shaped area at the mouth of a volcano or geyser. **2.** A pit that looks like this, as one made by an explosion or found on the surface of the moon.

crave (krāv) *tr.v.* **craved, crav•ing, craves. 1.** To have a very strong desire for (sthg.): *The thirsty runners craved water.* See Synonyms at **desire. 2.** To ask or beg for (sthg.) with strong feeling: *crave a favor of someone.*

crav•ing (krā′vĭng) *n.* [*for*] A very strong desire: *a craving for something sweet.*

crawl (krôl) *intr.v.* **1.** To move slowly on the hands and knees or by dragging the body along the ground: *The baby crawled across the room.* **2.** To move or advance slowly or with many stops: *The bus crawled along in* the heavy traffic. **3.a.** [*with*] To be covered with or as if with crawling things: *The scene of the crime was crawling with police.* **b.** To feel as if covered with crawling things: *The story made my skin crawl.* —*n.* **1.** A very slow pace: *Traffic moved at a crawl.* **2.** A rapid swimming stroke performed face down with alternating overarm strokes and a flutter kick. —**crawl′er** *n.*

cray•fish (krā′fĭsh′) also **craw•fish** (krô′fĭsh′) *n.* [C; U] Any of various freshwater shellfishes that resemble a small lobster, often used as food.

cray•on (krā′ŏn′ or krā′ən) *n.* A stick of colored wax used for drawing, especially by children: *The children sat quietly coloring with their crayons.*

craze (krāz) *tr.v.* **crazed, craz•ing, craz•es.** To make (sbdy.) become insane or seem mentally ill: *The prisoner was crazed by a lack of contact with other people.* —*n.* Something very popular for a brief time; a fad.

cra•zy (krā′zē) *adj.* **cra•zi•er, cra•zi•est. 1.a.** An insulting term describing sbdy. who is mentally ill. **b.** Very distressed or upset: *They were crazy with worry when their son didn't return.* **2.** *Informal.* Not sensible; impractical or unwise: *a crazy idea for making money fast.* **3.** *Informal.* [*about*] Full of enthusiasm or excitement: *The whole family is crazy about their new car.* ♦ **like crazy.** *Informal.* In an extremely active way: *The singer's newest recording is selling like crazy.* —**cra′zi•ly** *adv.* —**cra′zi•ness** *n.* [U]

creak (krēk) *intr.v.* To make or move with a grating or squeaking sound: *The rusty gate creaked as it swung open.* —*n.* A grating or squeaking sound: *We heard creaks in the old wooden stairs.* —**creak′i•ly** *adv.* —**creak′i•ness** *n.* [U]

HOMONYMS: creak, creek (stream).

---

creak•y (krē′kē) *adj.* **creak•i•er, creak•i•est.** Likely to creak or making creaking sounds: *I oiled the creaky hinges of the door.*

cream (krēm) *n.* **1.** [U] The yellowish fatty part of milk that rises to the top, used in cooking and making butter. **2.** [U] A yellowish white color. **3.** [C; U] Any of various substances that contain or look like cream: *cream of spinach soup; skin cream.* —*adj.* Yellowish white. —*tr.v.* **1.** To mix (foods) together until they resemble cream: *Cream the butter and sugar before adding the eggs.* **2.** To remove the cream from (milk). **3.** *Slang.* To defeat (sbdy.) in an overpowering way: *We creamed them at the last basketball game.* ♦ **cream of the crop.** The best part: *These juicy tomatoes are the cream of the crop.*

cream cheese *n.* [U] A soft white cheese made of cream and milk: *cream cheese spread on a bagel.*

cream•er (krē′mər) *n.* **1.** [C] A small pitcher for cream. **2.** [U] A powdered or liquid substitute for cream, used in coffee or tea: *non-dairy creamer.*

cream•er•y (krē′mə rē) *n.*, *pl.* **cream•er•ies.** A place where dairy products are prepared or sold.

cream•y (krē′mē) *adj.* **cream•i•er, cream•i•est.** **1.** Rich in cream: *a creamy filling for a cake.* **2.** Like cream in richness, texture, or color: *a creamy white.* —**cream′i•ly** *adv.* —**cream′i•ness** *n.* [U]

crease (krēs) *n.* **1.** A line or mark made by pressing or folding: *a crease in his trousers.* **2.** A wrinkle: *creases on the old man's face.* —*tr. & intr.v.* **creased, creas•ing, creas•es.** To make or become creased, folded, or wrinkled: *a face creased with age; fabric that creases easily.*

cre•ate (krē āt′) *tr.v.* **cre•at•ed, cre•at•ing, cre•ates.** **1.** To bring (sth.) into being; cause to exist: *She created the school to teach cooking.* See Synonyms at **establish. 2.** To produce (sth.) through artistic effort: *create a poem.* —**cre•a′tor** *n.*

cre•a•tion (krē ā′shən) *n.* **1.** [U] The act of creating: *the creation of islands by volcanoes.* **2.** [C] Something produced by invention and imagination: *The x-ray machine and the computer are creations of modern science.* **3.** [U] The universe, the world, and all created beings and things: *He says he is the happiest man in all creation.* **4. Creation.** [U] In various religions, the act of God by which the world began.

cre•a•tion•ism (krē ā′shə nĭz′əm) *n.* [U] The belief that all living things were created by God in the form they now have and did not develop by evolution.

cre•a•tive (krē ā′tĭv) *adj.* **1.** Having the ability or power to create things: *a creative writer.* **2.** Showing imagination or originality: *creative work.* —**cre•a′tive•ly** *adv.* —**cre•a′tive•ness** *n.* [U]

cre•a•tiv•i•ty (krē′ā tĭv′ĭ tē) *n.* [U] The quality of being creative; originality and inventiveness.

crea•ture (krē′chər) *n.* **1.** A living being, especially an animal: *birds, rabbits, and other creatures of the woods.* **2.** A human being who is totally dependent on or influenced by sth.: *a creature of habit.*

cre•dence (krēd′ns) *n.* [U] Acceptance as true; belief: *Don't put any credence in that rumor.*

cre•den•tial (krĭ dĕn′shəl) *n.* **1.** Something that serves as proof of a person's good char-

acter, experience, or abilities: *An honest face was the borrower's only credential.* **2. credentials.** Letters or other papers that show a person's official position: *The guard asked for credentials before letting the professor into the library of rare books.*

cred•i•bil•i•ty (krĕd′ə bĭl′ĭ tē) *n.* [U] The condition, quality, or power of being credible: *The leader lost his credibility by failing to follow his threats with action.*

cred•i•ble (krĕd′ə bəl) *adj.* Deserving confidence or belief: *a credible news report; a credible witness.* —**cred′i•bly** *adv.*

cred•it (krĕd′ĭt) *n.* **1.** [U] Belief or confidence; trust: *We place full credit in our employees.* **2.** [U] Approval or praise for some act or quality: *The authors shared the credit for the book's success.* **3.a.** [U] Formal acceptance that a student has done the required work for a course of study: *credit towards a college degree.* **b.** A unit of study: *a four-credit course.* **4.** [C] *(usually plural).* A statement noting work done, as in the production of a film or play: *a long list of credits at the end of the movie.* **5.** [U] A system of buying goods or services with payment made at a later time: *buy a car on credit.* **6.** [U] The amount of money in the account of a person or group, as at a bank. —*tr.v.* **1.** To trust or believe in (sth.): *They credited my explanation of what happened.* **2.a.** [*with*] To regard (sbdy.) as having done sth. good: *Two Canadian scientists are credited with the discovery of insulin.* **b.** [*to*] To regard (sth.) as the work of a person: *Some historians credit the song to Haydn.* **3.** To give educational credits to (a student). **4.a.** To give credit for (a payment) in an account: *The store credited $100 to my account.* **b.** To give credit to (a person's account): *When I paid my bill, the company credited my account.* ♦ **be a credit to.** To be a source of honor or distinction to (sbdy./sth.): *This fine athlete is a credit to his team.* **have good** or **bad credit.** To have a reputation for repaying or not repaying debts: *I have good credit at all the local stores.* **to (one's) credit. 1.** As a sign of one's good character: *It is to their credit that they worked so hard without complaining.* **2.** As sth. for one to be proud of: *That poet has several awards to her credit.*

cred•it•a•ble (krĕd′ĭ tə bəl) *adj.* Deserving praise or credit: *They made a creditable attempt to solve the problem.* —**cred′it•a•bly** *adv.*

credit card *n.* A card given to a person by a bank or business permitting him or her to buy goods or services on credit.

credit line or **line of credit** *n.* The greatest amount of money available to a customer as credit: *The company asked the r bank to increase their credit line.*

cred·i·tor (krĕd′ĭ tər) *n.* A person or firm to whom money is owed.

cre·do (krē′dō *or* krä′dō) *n., pl.* **cre·dos.** A statement of belief; a creed: *The store owner's credo is "The customer always comes first."*

cre·du·li·ty (krĭ dōō′lĭ tē *or* krĭ dyōō′lĭ tē) *n.* [U] The tendency to believe anything people say: *The young boy's credulity led him to believe many stories that weren't true.*

cred·u·lous (krĕj′ə ləs) *adj.* Tending to believe too easily; gullible: *A credulous person is easily fooled.* **—cred′u·lous·ly** *adv.* **—cred′u·lous·ness** *n.* [U]

creed (krēd) *n.* **1.** A formal statement of religious belief. **2.** A system of belief or principles that guides a person's actions: *The creed of modern science says that a theory must be tested by experimentation.*

creek (krēk *or* krĭk) *n.* A small stream, often leading to a river.

HOMONYMS: creek, creak (squeak).

---

creep (krēp) *intr.v.* **crept** (krĕpt), **creep·ing, creeps. 1.** To move slowly or carefully with the body close to the ground: *The cat crept toward the mouse.* **2.** To move in a shy, careful, or secretive way: *The father crept out of the sleeping baby's room.* **3.** To advance or spread slowly: *Traffic was creeping along during rush hour.* **4.** To have a feeling on the skin, as if covered with crawling things: *Thinking of ghosts makes my flesh creep.* *—n.* **1.** The act of creeping: *the silent creep of a tiger.* **2.** *Slang.* An unpleasant or annoying person. **3. creeps.** *Informal.* A sensation of fear and strong discomfort, as if things were crawling on one's skin: *This old house gives me the creeps.*

creep·er (krē′pər) *n.* **1.** A person or thing that creeps. **2.** A plant having stems that grow along the ground or cling to a surface for support.

creep·y (krē′pē) *adj.* **creep·i·er, creep·i·est.** *Informal.* Producing a feeling of worry or fear, as if things were creeping on one's skin: *a dark and creepy old house.* **—creep′i·ly** *adv.* **—creep′i·ness** *n.* [U]

cre·mate (krē′māt *or* krĭ māt′) *tr.v.* **cre·mat·ed, cre·mat·ing, cre·mates.** To burn (a dead person's body) to ashes. **—cre·ma′tion** *n.* [C; U]

cre·ma·to·ri·um (krē′mə tôr′ē əm) *n.* A furnace or building with a furnace for burning bodies of dead people.

cre·ma·to·ry (krē′mə tôr′ē *or* krĕm′ə tôr′ē) *n., pl.* **cre·ma·to·ries.** A crematorium.

Cre·ole (krē′ōl′) *n.* **1.** [C] A person of European family origin born in the West Indies. **2.a.** [C] A person whose relatives were the original French settlers of the south-

ern United States, especially Louisiana. **b.** [U] The French dialect spoken by these people. **3. creole.** [C] A language formed when two or more groups of people speaking different languages have contact with one another for a long time: *Several different creoles are found in the Caribbean Islands.* *—adj.* **1.** Relating to the Creoles or their languages and cultures. **2. creole.** Cooked with a spicy sauce containing tomatoes, green peppers, and onions: *shrimp creole.*

crepe also **crêpe** (krāp) *n.* **1.** [C; U] A light, soft, thin cloth with a wrinkled surface, made of silk, cotton, or another fiber. **2.** [U] A band of black crepe, worn or hung in honor of sbdy. who has died. **3.** [C] A very thin pancake, usually served folded with a filling: *crepes filled with strawberries.*

crepe paper *n.* [U] Colored paper like crepe with wrinkles in it, used for decorations.

crept (krĕpt) *v.* Past tense and past participle of **creep.**

cres·cen·do (krə shĕn′dō) *n., pl.* **cres·cen·dos.** In music, a gradual increase in loudness. *—adj. & adv.* Gradually increasing in loudness: *a crescendo passage.*

cres·cent (krĕs′ənt) *n.* **1.** The thin figure of the moon as it appears in its first quarter. **2.** Something shaped like such a figure: *The ancient Middle East is known as the Fertile Crescent.* *—adj.* **1.** Shaped like a crescent: *crescent rolls.* **2.** Increasing: *the crescent phase of the moon.*

crescent
Of the moon

crest (krĕst) *n.* **1.** A group of feathers or hairs that stick up on the head of a bird or other animal. **2.a.** The top of sthg., such as a mountain or wave. **b.** The highest point, as of a process or action: *The novelist was at the crest of a long career.* *—v. —tr.* To reach the top of (sthg.): *The climbers crested the mountain.* *—intr.* **1.** To form into a crest: *Waves crested over the sea wall.* **2.** To reach a high point before decreasing: *The river crested after the heavy rain.*

cre·vasse (krĭ văs′) *n.* A deep, wide crack, as in a glacier.

crev·ice (krĕv′ĭs) *n.* A narrow crack or opening: *Snow blew through the crevice under the door.*

crew (krōō) *n.* **1.** A group of people who work together: *a crew of volunteers.* **2.a.** The people working together to operate a ship, plane, spacecraft, or train. **b.** All the people working together to operate a ship, plane, or spacecraft under the direction of the officers: *the captain and crew.* **3.** A team of rowers. *—intr.v.* To serve as a member of a crew.

crew cut or **crew·cut** (kroō′kŭt′) *n.* A very short haircut.

crib (krĭb) *n.* **1.** A small bed with high sides for a baby or young child. **2.** *Informal.* A list of answers or information used dishonestly by a student during an examination. —*v.* **cribbed, crib·bing, cribs.** *Informal.* —*intr.* To use a secret list of answers or information in examinations. —*tr.* To copy (sthg.) dishonestly: *crib answers from a friend.*

crick·et¹ (krĭk′ĭt) *n.* A small black insect related to the grasshopper. The male produces a chirping sound by rubbing the front wings together.

crick·et² (krĭk′ĭt) *n.* [U] **1.** An outdoor game played with bats and a ball by two teams of 11 players each: *Cricket is popular in Great Britain, India, and Australia.* **2.** *Informal.* Fair play: *That's not cricket.* —**crick′et·er** *n.*

crime (krīm) *n.* **1.** [C] **a.** An act that is against the law: *the crime of murder.* **b.** A failure to do what the law requires: *It's a crime not to pay taxes.* **2.** [U] Unlawful activity: *There is too much crime in our society.* **3.** [C] A shameful or senseless act: *It's a crime to waste good food.*

crim·i·nal (krĭm′ə nəl) *adj.* **1.** Of or involving crime: *criminal behavior.* **2.** Relating to criminal law and the punishment of crime: *criminal court.* **3.** *Informal.* Shameful; shocking: *a criminal waste of energy.* —*n.* A person who has committed or been found guilty of a crime: *The judge sentenced the criminal to jail for stealing a car.* —**crim′i·nal·ly** *adv.*

crim·i·nol·o·gy (krĭm′ə nŏl′ə jē) *n.* [U] The scientific study of crime, criminals, criminal behavior, and corrections. —**crim′i·nol′o·gist** *n.*

crimp (krĭmp) *tr.v.* To press or bend (sthg.) into small regular folds or waves: *crimp the edges of a pie crust.* —*n.* Something produced by crimping, as a fold or crease.

crim·son (krĭm′zən) *n.* [U] A bright purplish red color. —*adj.* Bright purplish red.

cringe (krĭnj) *intr.v.* **cringed, cring·ing, cring·es.** To pull oneself back, as in fear or embarrassment: *The puppy cringed when I tried to pet it.*

crin·kle (krĭng′kəl) *v.* **crin·kled, crin·kling, crin·kles.** —*intr.* **1.** To form wrinkles or ripples: *Her face crinkles when she smiles.* **2.** To make a crackling sound: *The foil crinkled as I wrapped the leftover food.* —*tr.* **1.** To cause (sthg.) to form wrinkles or ripples: *I crinkled the wrapping paper when my hand slipped.* **2.** To cause (sthg.) to crackle. —*n.* A wrinkle or crease: *Crinkles form around the eyes from laughter.* —**crin′kly** *adj.*

crip·ple (krĭp′əl) *n.* **1.** A term used in the past, and now considered offensive, for a per-son who was partially disabled or unable to use one or more arms or legs. **2.** A crippled animal. —*tr.v.* **crip·pled, crip·pling, crip·ples.** **1.** To cause (sbdy.) to lose the use of one or both arms and/or legs. **2.** To damage or disable (sthg.): *The storm crippled the ship.* —**crip′pler** *n.*

cri·sis (krī′sĭs) *n., pl.* **cri·ses** (krī′sēz). **1.** A situation of great difficulty or danger, especially involving political or economic conditions: *a political crisis.* **2.** A sudden change in the course of a serious illness: *The patient suffered a crisis.* **3.** A difficult or stressful event or change in a person's life: *the crisis of a divorce.*

crisp (krĭsp) *adj.* **1.** Firm but easily broken or crumbled: *crisp toast; crisp fried chicken.* **2.** Fresh and firm: *crisp lettuce.* **3.** Clean and new: *a crisp dollar bill.* **4.** Refreshing: *crisp mountain air.* **5.** Sharp, clear, and short: *a crisp reply.* —*tr. & intr.v.* To make or become crisp, as by heating or cooking. —**crisp′ly** *adv.* —**crisp′ness** *n.* [U]

crisp·y (krĭs′pē) *adj.* **crisp·i·er, crisp·i·est.** Firm but easily broken or crumbled: *a bowl of crispy breakfast cereal.* —**crisp′i·ness** *n.* [U]

criss·cross (krĭs′krôs′ or krĭs′krŏs′) *v.* —*tr.* **1.** To mark (sthg.) with a pattern of crossing lines: *Animal trails crisscross the woods.* **2.** To move back and forth over or through (sthg.): *Ships crisscrossed the sea.* —*intr.* To move back and forth and often meet: *Our paths crisscrossed throughout the day.* —*n.* A mark or pattern made of crossing lines. —*adj.* Crossing one another: *crisscross lines.* —*adv.* In crossing directions: *umbrellas leaning crisscross in the stand.*

cri·te·ri·on (krī tîr′ē ən) *n., pl.* **cri·te·ri·a** (krī tîr′ē ə). A rule or standard on which a judgment can be based: *Clarity of expression and organization of ideas are two important criteria for judging an essay.*

crit·ic (krĭt′ĭk) *n.* **1.** A person who expresses judgments about the qualities of sthg., especially an artistic work such as a painting, play, or musical performance: *a movie critic.* **2.** A person who often criticizes people or things.

crit·i·cal (krĭt′ĭ kəl) *adj.* **1.** Tending to criticize and find fault: *A critical person is rarely pleased with anything.* **2.** Showing or using careful judgment: *critical analysis of a poem.* **3.** Extremely important or decisive: *a critical point in the political campaign.* **4.** Related to a medical crisis: *High fever is the critical point of pneumonia.* **5.** Extremely serious or dangerous: *a critical shortage of food.* —**crit′i·cal·ly** *adv.*

crit·i·cism (krĭt′ĭ sĭz′əm) *n.* **1.** [U] The art

ă–**cat**; ā–**pay**; âr–**care**; ä–**father**; ĕ–**get**; ē–**be**; ĭ–**sit**; ī–**nice**; îr–**here**; ŏ–**got**; ō–**go**; ô–**saw**; oi–**boy**; ou–**out**; ŏŏ–**took**; ŏŏ–**boot**; ŭ–**cut**; ûr–**word**; th–**thin**; *th*–**th**is; hw–**when**; zh–**vision**; ə–**about**; N–French bon

or profession of forming and expressing judgments, especially about literary or artistic works. **2.** [C; U] Expression of disapproval: *constant criticism with no encouragement.* **3.** [C] A comment, article, or review that expresses judgments: *Several reporters wrote criticisms of the new movie.*

crit·i·cize (krĭt′ĭ sīz′) *v.* **crit·i·cized, crit·i·ciz·ing, crit·i·ciz·es.** —*tr.* **1.** To judge the good and bad points of (sbdy/sthg.): *The painter stepped back to criticize her last hour's work.* **2.** To express disapproval of or find fault with (sbdy./sthg.): *Newspapers criticized the library closing.* —*intr.* To express negative criticism: *He didn't help us, so he has no right to criticize.* —**crit′i·ciz′er** *n.*

cri·tique (krĭ tēk′) *n.* A critical review or report, such as an evaluation of an artistic work.

crit·ter (krĭt′ər) *n. Informal.* A creature, especially an animal.

croak (krōk) *n.* A low hoarse sound, such as that made by a frog. —*v.* —*intr.* **1.** To make such a sound: *Bullfrogs croaked in the pond.* **2.** To speak with a low hoarse voice: *The patient weakly croaked.* **3.** *Slang.* To die. —*tr.* To say (sthg.) in a low hoarse voice: *croak an answer.*

cro·chet (krō shā′) *v.* **cro·cheted** (krō shād′), **cro·chet·ing** (krō shā′ĭng), **cro·chets** (krō-shāz′). —*tr.* To make (sthg.) by looping thread or yarn into connected links with a hooked needle: *crochet a sweater.* —*intr.* To crochet a piece of needlework: *She crochets as a hobby.* —*n.* [U] Needlework made by crocheting.

crock (krŏk) *n.* **1.** A pot or jar made of clay. **2.** *Slang.* Nonsense: *That story is nothing but a crock!*

croc·o·dile (krŏk′ə dīl′) *n.* **1.** [C] Any of various large water reptiles with rough thick skin, sharp teeth, and long narrow jaws, living in the tropical regions of the Americas, Africa, Asia, and Australia. **2.** [U] Leather made from crocodile skin.

crocodile tears *pl.n.* A show of grief or tears that is not sincere.

cro·cus (krō′kəs) *n.* A small garden plant with purple, yellow, or white flowers that bloom early in spring.

crois·sant (krə sänt′) *n.* A buttery crescent-shaped roll.

Cro-Mag·non (krō măg′nən *or* krō măn′-yən) *n.* An early form of modern human being. The Cro-Magnons made tools of stone and bone and are noted for cave paintings.

cro·ny (krō′nē) *n., pl.* **cro·nies.** *Informal.* A close friend or companion: *old cronies.*

crook (krŏok) *n.* **1.** A tool with a hook or hooked part: *a shepherd's crook.* **2.** Something bent or curved: *a bag of groceries held in the crook of one's arm.* **3.** A curve or bend: *a crook in the road.* **4.** *Informal.* A person who gets money dishonestly. —*tr. & intr.v.*

To curve or become curved: *crook one's arm around a package; a road that crooks sharply to the right.*

crook·ed (krŏok′ĭd) *adj.* **1.** Not straight; bent or curved: *a crooked street.* **2.** *Informal.* Dishonest: *a crooked politician.* —**crook′ed·ly** *adv.* —**crook′ed·ness** *n.* [U]

croon (krōon) *v.* —*tr.* To sing or hum (sthg.) softly: *croon a lullaby to the baby.* —*intr.* **1.** To sing or hum a melody softly. **2.** To sing popular songs in a sentimental manner. —**croon′er** *n.*

crop (krŏp) *n.* **1.a.** Farm plants or plant products such as grain, fruit, and vegetables: *Wheat is a common crop.* **b.** The amount of such a product grown or gathered in a single season or place: *Our orchard produced a huge crop of cherries last year.* **2.** A group or quantity appearing at one time: *a promising crop of new students.* **3.** A short whip used in horseback riding. —*tr.v.* **cropped, crop·ping, crops.** **1.** To cut or bite off the tops or ends of (sthg.): *Sheep cropped the grass very short.* **2.** To cut (hair, for example) short. **3.** To cut off edges of (a photograph, for example). ◆ **crop up.** *intr.v.* To appear unexpectedly: *Even when I'm careful, spelling errors crop up in my work.*

cro·quet (krō kā′) *n.* [U] A lawn game in which each player uses a mallet to hit a wooden ball through a set of wire arches stuck into the ground.

cross (krôs *or* krŏs) *n.* **1.** A wooden post with a piece across it near the top, used in ancient times in putting people to death. **2.** Any of various statues, medals or other objects in the shape of a cross. **3.a.** A mark or pattern formed by the intersection of two lines. **b.** Such a mark (X) used as a signature by a person who cannot read or write. **4.** An animal or a plant produced by crossbreeding: *A mule is a cross between a horse and a donkey.* **5.** A combination of two different things: *The novel is a cross between a romance and a mystery.* —*v.* —*tr.* **1.** To go or extend across (sthg.): *The chicken crossed the road. The bridge crosses the river.* **2.** To place (two things) so one passes over or intersects the other: *cross one's legs.* **3.** To oppose or block (sbdy.): *Some people feel angry when they have been crossed.* **4.** To crossbreed (animals or plants): *cross a horse with a donkey.* **5.** To draw a line across (sthg.): *Cross your T's.* —*intr.* **1.** To extend across; intersect: *The stream crosses through our yard.* **2.** To move across sthg.; make a crossing: *We crossed into Mexico.* **3.** To meet or pass while going in different directions: *Our letters crossed in the mail.* —*adj.* **1.** Lying crosswise; intersecting: *a cross street.* **2.** Showing anger or irritation; annoyed: *Slow traffic makes some people very cross.* **3.** Opposing or opposite: *opponents with cross interests.* ◆ **cross off.** *tr.v.*

[sep.] To delete or remove (sthg.) by drawing a line through it: *cross the names off the list.*
cross out. *tr.v.* [sep.] To mark (sthg.) with a line through it to show that it was in error: *She crossed out the misspelled word.* —**cross′ly** *adv.* —**cross′ness** *n.* [U]

cross– *pref.* **1.** Going across or between: *cross-cultural; cross-country.* **2.** Placed so as to cross or intersect: *cross-legged; crossroad.* **3.** In opposition: *cross-purposes; cross-examine.*

cross•bar (krôs′bär′ *or* krŏs′bär′) *n.* A horizontal bar: *the crossbar of a men's bicycle.*

cross•bones (krôs′bōnz′ *or* krŏs′bōnz′) *pl.n.* A picture of two bones placed crosswise, usually under a skull, used as a symbol of death or a warning of danger.

cross•bow (krôs′bō′ *or* krŏs′bō′) *n.* A weapon consisting of a bow fixed across a short strong length of wood, used to shoot arrows.

cross•breed (krôs′brēd′ *or* krŏs′brēd′) *v.* **cross•bred** (krôs′brĕd′ *or* krŏs′brĕd′), **cross•breed•ing, cross•breeds.** —*tr.* To produce (a hybrid animal or plant) by mating two individuals of different breeds. —*intr.* To mate so as to produce a hybrid. —*n.* An animal or a plant produced by crossbreeding; a hybrid or cross: *A mule is a crossbreed.*

cross-coun•try (krôs′kŭn′trē *or* krŏs′-kŭn′trē) *adj.* **1.** Moving or directed across open countryside rather than following roads or tracks: *a cross-country race.* **2.** Going from one side of a country to the other: *a cross-country trip.* —**cross′-coun′try** *adv.*

cross-cul•tur•al (krôs′kŭl′chər əl *or* krŏs′kŭl′chər əl) *adj.* Comparing or dealing with two or more different cultures: *a cross-cultural study.*

cross-dress (krôs′drĕs′ *or* krŏs′drĕs′) *intr.v.* To wear the clothes of the other sex. —**cross′-dress′er** *n.* —**cross′-dress′ing** *n.* [U]

cross-ex•am•ine (krôs′ĭg zăm′ĭn *or* krŏs′ĭg zăm′ĭn) *tr.v.* **cross-ex•am•ined, cross-ex•am•in•ing, cross-ex•am•ines.** **1.** To question (a witness already examined by the opposing side) in court. **2.** To question (sbdy.) very closely, especially in order to check the answers against answers given before. —**cross′-ex•am′i•na′tion** *n.* [C; U] —**cross′-ex•am′in•er** *n.*

cross-eyed (krôs′īd′ *or* krŏs′īd′) *adj.* Having one or both of the eyes turned inward toward the nose: *a cross-eyed kitten.*

cross•fire (krôs′fīr′ *or* krŏs′fīr′) *n.* **1.** [U] Lines of gunfire crossing each other at a single point: *soldiers caught in the crossfire.* **2.** [C] A rapid, often angry discussion: *a crossfire of loud accusations.*

cross•ing (krô′sĭng *or* krŏs′ĭng) *n.* **1.** A place at which sthg., such as a street, railroad,

or river, may be crossed: *a pedestrian crossing.* **2.** A place where two or more things cross; an intersection: *a traffic light at the street crossing.* **3.** The act of crossing, especially a voyage or flight across an ocean.

cross-leg•ged (krôs′lĕg′ĭd *or* krŏs′lĕg′ĭd) *adv. & adj.* **1.** With legs or ankles crossed and knees spread wide, as when sitting on the ground: *sitting cross-legged around the fire.* **2.** With one leg lying across the other: *She sat cross-legged.*

cross•o•ver (krôs′ō′vər *or* krŏs′ō′vər) *n.* Something, such as a bridge over a highway or a short stretch of connecting railroad track, that makes a crossing. —*adj.* Moving from one group, style, or period to another: *crossover voters; a crossover band.*

cross-pur•pose (krôs′pûr′pəs *or* krŏs′-pûr′pəs) *n.* A conflicting purpose. ♦ **at cross-purposes.** Misinterpreting or failing to understand each other's purposes: *The two committees were at cross-purposes.*

cross-ref•er•ence (krôs′rĕf′ər əns *or* krŏs′rĕf′ər əns) *n.* A note directing the reader from one part of a book, catalogue, index, or file, to another part that has related information.

cross•road (krôs′rōd′ *or* krŏs′rōd′) *n.* **1.** A road that crosses another road. **2.** **crossroads.** *(used with a singular verb).* **a.** A place, often in the countryside, where two or more roads meet: *The bus for the city stops at the crossroads near our farm.* **b.** A very important point or place, especially one where different courses of action may be taken: *I'm at a crossroads in my career.*

cross section *n.* **1.a.** A slice or section of an object made by cutting straight through it, usually at right angles to its length: *the rings of growth in the cross section of a tree trunk.* **b.** A piece cut in this way or a picture or drawing of such a piece: *The picture is a cross section of the eye.* **2.** A small group of people or things that is representative of the whole group: *They surveyed a cross section of voters.*

cross-stitch (krôs′stĭch′ *or* krŏs′stĭch′) *n.* **1.** [C] A stitch shaped like an X, used in sewing and embroidery. **2.** [U] Needlework made with the cross-stitch. —*tr. & intr.v.* To make or embroider with cross-stitches.

cross-town *or* **cross•town** (krôs′toun′ *or* krŏs′toun′) *adj.* Running, extending, or going across a city or town: *a cross-town bus.* —*adv.* Across a city or town: *We got snarled in traffic going cross-town.*

cross•walk (krôs′wôk′ *or* krŏs′wôk′) *n.* A path marked with painted lines for people walking across a street.

cross•wise (krôs′wīz′ *or* krŏs′wīz′) also

cross·ways (krôs′wāz′ *or* krŏs′wāz′) *adv.* So as to be or lie in a cross direction; across: *logs laid crosswise on the fire.*

cross·word puzzle (krôs′wûrd′ *or* krŏs′wûrd′) *n.* A puzzle in which numbered squares, running down and across, must be filled with letters of words than numbered clues.

crotch (krŏch) *n.* **1.a.** The place where the human body branches into two legs. **b.** The place in a piece of clothing, such as pants, where the leg seams meet. **2.** The place where a branch separates from a tree; a fork: *The bird nested in the crotch of the tree.*

crotch·et·y (krŏch′ĭ tē) *adj.* **1.** Opposed to others in desires and ideas. **2.** Irritable and tending to complain: *I'm getting crotchety in my old age!* —**crotch′et·i·ness** *n.* [U]

crouch (krouch) *intr.v.* **1.** To lower the body by bending the legs: *The tiger crouched in the grass waiting for its prey.* **2.** To lower the body in fear: *The kittens crouched in the corner while the dog growled at them.* —*n.* The act or posture of crouching: *skiing in a crouch.*

croup (krōōp) *n.* [U] A sickness that affects the throat and windpipe, especially in children, producing difficult and noisy breathing and a hoarse cough. —**croup′y** *adj.*

crou·ton (krōō′tŏn′ *or* krōō tŏn′) *n.* A small piece of toasted bread, used on soups and salads.

crow[1] (krō) *n.* A large bird with shiny black feathers and a harsh hoarse call. ♦ **as the crow flies.** In a straight line: *It would be ten miles to town as the crow flies, but winding roads make it a 20-mile drive.*

crow[2] (krō) *intr.v.* **1.** To make the loud cry of a rooster: *A rooster crowed at sunrise.* **2.** To make a loud sound of pleasure or delight: *The happy baby kicked and crowed in his crib.* **3.** To boast, especially about sbdy. else's defeat: *The winners crowed over their victory to all their friends.* —*n.* **1.** The loud high-pitched cry of a rooster. **2.** A loud sound expressing pleasure or delight.

crow·bar (krō′bär′) *n.* A straight iron or steel bar, usually having one end bent or curved with a narrow edge, used as a lever for lifting or forcing things apart.

crowd (kroud) *n.* **1.** A large number of people gathered together: *A crowd had gathered in front of the building.* **2.** The common people; people in general: *Do what you want to do and don't follow the crowd.* **3.** A group of people of one type: *the college crowd.* —*v.* —*tr.* **1.** To fill (a place) to overflowing: *Shoppers crowded the store.* **2.** To press or push (things) tightly together: *He crowded his old magazines in a cabinet.* **3.** To press or push against (sbdy.): *Subway riders crowd each other.* —*intr.* **1.** To gather together in a limited space: *Fans crowded around the rock star.* **2.** To move forward by shoving: *Everybody crowded into the cafeteria.*

crown (kroun) *n.* **1.** A head covering, often made of gold set with jewels, worn by a king or queen as a symbol of power. **2.** Often **Crown.** The authority, power, or position of a king or queen: *the power of the Crown.* **3.** A wreath worn on the head: *a crown of laurel.* **4.** The top part of sthg., especially of the head. **5.** The top part of a hat. **6.** An artificial substitute for the top part of a tooth. **7.** A former British coin worth five shillings. **8.** A title, honor, or reward: *win the heavyweight boxing crown.* —*tr.v.* **1.** To place a crown or wreath on the head of (sbdy.): *crown the victor of the marathon.* **2.** To give the power of a king or queen to (sbdy.): *The king was crowned at the age of 15.* **3.** To give honor or recognition to (sbdy.): *The critics crowned her as the best pianist of all.* **4.** To cover or form the top of (sthg.): *Snow crowned the mountain peaks.* **5.** To be the highest achievement of (sthg.): *The Nobel Prize crowned the scientist's career.* **6.** To put a crown on (a tooth).

cru·cial (krōō′shəl) *adj.* Of the greatest importance; decisive: *the crucial moment in the trial; a crucial win.* —**cru′cial·ly** *adv.*

cru·ci·fix (krōō′sə fĭks′) *n.* An image or a figure of Jesus on the cross.

cru·ci·fix·ion (krōō′sə fĭk′shən) *n.* [C; U] The act of putting a person to death on a cross.

cru·ci·fy (krōō′sə fī′) *tr.v.* **cru·ci·fied, cru·ci·fy·ing, cru·ci·fies.** **1.** To kill (sbdy.) by nailing or tying to a cross: *Roman soldiers crucified two thieves.* **2.** To punish or torment (sbdy.), as by very strong criticism: *The newspapers crucified the senator for his mistakes.*

crud (krŭd) *n.* Slang. [U] **1.** Something that is very unpleasant to see, touch, taste, or smell: *You call this crud food?* **2.** Silliness; nonsense: *Cut the crud and get back to work.* —**crud′dy** *adj.*

crude (krōōd) *adj.* **crud·er, crud·est.** **1.** Being in an unrefined or natural state: *crude oil.* **2.** Showing a lack of knowledge or skill; rough: *a quick crude sketch.* **3.** Rough and insensitive: *a crude person with no manners; a crude remark made with little feeling.* —**crude′ly** *adv.* —**crude′ness, cru′di·ty** *n.* [U]

cru·el (krōō′əl) *adj.* Causing pain or suffering: *a cruel dictator; a cruel joke.* —**cru′el·ly** *adv.* —**cru′el·ness** *n.* [U]

cru·el·ty (krōō′əl tē) *n.* [U] The condition or quality of being cruel: *cruelty to animals.*

cruise (krōōz) *v.* **cruised, cruis·ing, cruis·es.** —*intr.* **1.** To sail or travel about in an unhurried way: *A tourist boat cruised along the coast.* **2.** To move or travel about in no fixed direction: *Taxis cruised through the business district looking for customers.* **3.** To travel at maximum efficient speed: *After takeoff the plane cruised at a high altitude.* —*tr.* To travel about or journey over (sthg.): *A police car cruised the streets of the town.* —*n.* A sea voyage for pleasure: *We enjoyed our cruise to Bermuda.*

C

cruis·er (krōō′zər) *n.* **1.** A medium-sized warship of high speed and a large cruising range. **2.** A large motorboat. **3.** A police car.

crumb (krŭm) *n.* **1.** *(usually plural).* A tiny piece of food: *We tossed crumbs of bread to the squirrels.* **2.** A little bit; a fragment: *She has not a crumb of sympathy for him.*

crum·ble (krŭm′bəl) *v.* **crum·bled, crum·bling, crum·bles.** —*tr.* To break (sthg.) into small pieces or crumbs: *He always crumbles crackers into his soup.* —*intr.* **1.** To break up into small pieces: *The lump of dry dirt crumbled easily.* **2.** To fall apart: *The old barn finally crumbled to the ground.*

crum·bly (krŭm′blē) *adj.* **crum·bli·er, crum·bli·est.** Easily crumbled: *crumbly old cake.* —**crum′bli·ness** *n.* [U]

crum·my (krŭm′ē) *adj.* **crum·mi·er, crum·mi·est.** *Slang.* **1.** Of poor quality: *a crummy movie.* **2.** Miserable; very uncomfortable: *feeling crummy all afternoon.*

crum·ple (krŭm′pəl) *v.* **crum·pled, crum·pling, crum·ples.** —*tr.* To crush (sthg.) so as to form creases or wrinkles: *Don't crumple that freshly ironed shirt.* —*intr.* **1.** To become wrinkled or crushed: *Tissue paper crumples easily.* **2.** To lose strength suddenly and fall: *Stomach cramps caused the runner to crumple.*

crunch (krŭnch) *v.* —*tr.* To chew (sthg.) with a noisy sound: *crunch peanuts.* —*intr.* **1.** To chew noisily: *crunch on celery.* **2.** To move with a crushing or grinding sound: *We crunched through the snow.* **3.** To make a crushing sound: *The snow crunched under my boots.* —*n.* **1.** The act of crunching. **2.** A crushing sound: *the crunch of gravel as the car drove up the driveway.* **3.** A critical situation, especially one resulting from a lack of time, money, or resources: *an oil crunch; a time crunch.*

crunch·y (krŭn′chē) *adj.* **crunch·i·er, crunch·i·est.** Crisp and noisy when chewed or crushed: *crunchy potato chips.*

cru·sade (krōō sād′) *n.* **1.** A campaign or movement for a belief or ideal: *a crusade for women's rights.* **2.** Often **Crusade.** Any of a series of military expeditions against the Muslims by European Christians in the 11th, 12th, and 13th centuries. —*intr.v.* **cru·sad·ed, cru·sad·ing, cru·sades.** To join in a campaign or movement for social change: *The parents crusaded for better schools.* —**cru·sad′er** *n.*

crush (krŭsh) *v.* —*tr.* **1.** To press or squeeze (sthg.) with enough force to break or injure: *The falling tree crushed the front of the car.* **2.** To break, grind, or pound (sthg.) into small pieces or powder: *crush rocks into gravel.* **3.** To wrinkle (sthg.): *Packing the suitcase too tight will crush your clothes.* **4.** To crowd or press (sbdy./sthg.): *I was crushed against the wall of the crowded elevator.* **5.** To end or oppress (sthg.) by force or pressure: *crush a rebellion; crush someone's spirit.* —*intr.* **1.** To be or become crushed: *The ice crushed under my feet.* **2.** To move by crowding or pressing: *The commuters crushed into the train.* —*n.* **1.** [C] The act of crushing; extreme pressure: *The crush of the collision destroyed the car's engine.* **2.** [C] A great crowd: *I was caught in the crush and couldn't get through the market.* **3.** [C; U] A substance prepared by or as if by crushing: *orange crush.* **4.** [C] *Informal.* A strong, often foolish and brief liking for sbdy: *a teenage crush.* —**crush′er** *n.*

crust (krŭst) *n.* **1.a.** [C; U] The hard outside part of bread. **b.** [C] A hard dry piece of bread: *a few crusts to feed the birds.* **2.** [C; U] A pastry shell, as of a pie: *pizza crust.* **3.** [C] A hard outer layer or covering: *Snow with a firm crust.* **4.** [U] The solid outer layer of the earth. —*v.* —*tr.* **1.** To cover (sthg.) with a crust: *Snow and ice crusted the mountain trail.* **2.** To form (sthg.) into a crust: *Rust was crusted on the pipes.* —*intr.* To become covered with a crust: *The snow crusted over.*

crus·ta·cean (krŭ stā′shən) *n.* Any of a group of animals, such as a lobster, crab, or shrimp, that live mostly in water and have a hard shell and jointed bodies and legs. —*adj.* Belonging to this group of animals.

crust·y (krŭs′tē) *adj.* **crust·i·er, crust·i·est.** **1.** Having a crust: *crusty bread.* **2.** Speaking or acting with few words in an unfriendly way: *The crusty old soldier was easily angered.* —**crust′i·ly** *adv.* —**crust′i·ness** *n.* [U]

crutch (krŭch) *n.* A staff or support used by injured or disabled persons when walking, often having a padded top that fits under the arm.

crux (krŭks *or* krōōks) *n.* *(usually singular).* A basic or essential point: *Let's try to locate the crux of the problem.*

cry (krī) *v.* **cried** (krīd), **cry·ing, cries** (krīz). —*intr.* **1.** To have tears flow and make sounds of sadness or pain. **2.** To call loudly; shout: *We cried to our friends across the street.* **3.** To make a characteristic sound or call: *The monkeys cried in the treetops.* —*tr.* **1.** To call (sthg.) out loudly: *The crowd cried, "Long live the king!"* **2.** To bring (oneself) into a particular condition by crying: *She cried herself to sleep.* —*n.*, *pl.* **cries** (krīz). **1.** A loud call; a shout: *a cry of warning.* **2.** A loud sound expressing fear, grief, or pain. **3.** A period of crying: *After a short cry the baby was fast asleep.* **4.** The characteristic sound or call of an animal: *the cry of an eagle.* **5.** A public or general demand or complaint: *a cry*

for reform in city politics. ♦ **cry over spilled milk.** To regret what cannot be changed or repaired: *It's no use crying over spilled milk.*
cry out. *intr.v.* To produce a loud cry as in pain or anger: *She cried out in pain when she fell.* **cry wolf.** To call for help when there is no real danger: *She has cried wolf too often, so now nobody listens to her.*

SYNONYMS: cry, weep, blubber, sob, whimper. These verbs mean to make sounds that show grief, unhappiness, or pain. **Cry** and **weep** both involve tears: *Loud, sudden noises make the baby cry. No one wept at the dictator's funeral.* **Blubber** refers to noisy crying mixed with speech that cannot be understood: *The child blubbered over the broken toy.* **Sob** refers to weeping and speech marked by gasps for air: *Stop sobbing for a minute and take a deep breath.* **Whimper** means to make low, sorrowful cries: *The poor dog came home limping and whimpering.* **ANTONYM: laugh.**

---

crypt (krĭpt) *n.* An underground vault or room, especially one that is used as a tomb beneath a church.
cryp•tic (krĭp′tĭk) *adj.* Having a hidden meaning or secret nature; mysterious; puzzling: *a cryptic message.* See Synonyms at **vague.** —**cryp′ti•cal•ly** *adv.*
cryp•tog•ra•phy (krĭp tŏg′rə fē n. [U] The study and use of secret codes and ciphers. —**cryp•tog′ra•pher** *n.*
crys•tal (krĭs′təl) *n.* **1.a.** [C] A regular geometric shape formed by some substances: *sugar crystals; salt crystals.* **b.** [U] A transparent colorless mineral, especially a form of pure quartz. **2.** [U] **a.** A clear colorless glass of high quality. **b.** An object or objects made of this glass: *a table set with fine china and crystal.* **3.** [C] A transparent cover that protects the face of a watch or clock: *I scratched the crystal on my watch.* —*adj.* Clear; transparent: *I could see to the bottom in the crystal water of the lake.*
crystal ball *n.* A globe of crystal or glass in which images supposedly appear and give information about the future.
crys•tal•line (krĭs′tə lĭn *or* krĭs′ ə līn′) *adj.* **1.** Made of or looking like crystal. **2.** Made of crystals: *Snowflakes are crystalline.*
crys•tal•lize (krĭs′tə līz′) *v.* **crys•tal•lized, crys•tal•liz•ing, crys•tal•liz•es.** —*tr.* **1.** To cause (sthg.) to form crystals or change into crystalline structure: *The researchers had to crystallize the protein before they could determine its structure.* **2.** To give a definite, clear, and permanent form to (sthg.): *The architect helped us crystallize our ideas about the design for the house.* —*intr.* **1.** To change into crystalline form. **2.** To take on a definite and usually permanent form: *New political parties crystallized in eastern Europe after*

the Communist governments fell. —**crys′tal•li•za′tion** (krĭs′tə lĭ zā′shən) *n.* [U]
CT *abbr.* An abbreviation of Connecticut.
ct. *abbr.* An abbreviation of cent.
Ct. *abbr.* An abbreviation of Connecticut.
Cu The symbol for the element **copper** (sense 1).
cu. *abbr.* An abbreviation of cubic.
cub (kŭb) *n.* The young of certain animals, such as the bear, wolf, or lion: *a lion cub.* ♦ **cub reporter.** A beginner in newspaper reporting.
cub•by•hole (kŭb′ē hōl′) *n.* A small storage space or a room that is like one: *She hated trying to work in a cubbyhole of an office.*
cube (kyoōb) *n.* **1.** A solid having six equal square faces or sides. **2.** Something having this shape or almost this shape: *a sugar cube.* **3.** A cubicle. **4.** The product that results when the same number is used three times as a factor. For example, the cube of 4, written 4^3, is equal to $4 \times 4 \times 4$. —*tr.v.* **cubed, cub•ing, cubes.** **1.** To form the cube of (a number). **2.** To express or measure the volume of (a container or space) in cubic units. **3.** To cut or form (sthg.) into a cube or cubes: *cube potatoes.*

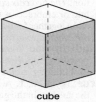
cube

cube root *n.* The number that produces a given number when cubed: *The cube root of 125 is 5.*
cu•bic (kyoō′bĭk) *adj.* **1.** Shaped like or nearly like a cube: *Dice have a cubic form.* **2.** Having length, width, and depth or height; three-dimensional: *If you measure the volume of a room, you will express it in cubic feet or meters.*
cu•bi•cal (kyoō′bĭ kəl) *adj.* Cubic: *a room of cubical shape.*

HOMONYMS: cubical, cubicle (small room).

---

cu•bi•cle (kyoō′bĭ kəl) *n.* A very small room or compartment, especially in a large office.
cubic measure *n.* A unit for measuring volume, such as a cubic foot.
cub•ism (kyoō′bĭz′əm) *n.* [U] A style of 20th-century painting, drawing, and sculpture that shows natural forms as abstract, often geometric forms. —**cub′ist** *adj. & n.*
Cub Scout *n.* A member of a younger group in the Boy Scouts, for boys of ages eight through ten.
cuck•oo (koō′koō *or* koŏk′oō) *n., pl.* **cuck•oos.** A European bird with grayish feathers and a call of two notes that sounds like its name. It lays its eggs in the nests of birds of other species. —*adj. Slang.* Ridiculous; foolish.
cuckoo clock *n.* A wall clock that marks the time with a mechanical whistle that sounds

like a cuckoo's call as a toy bird comes out of a small door.

cu•cum•ber (kyōō′kŭm′bər) *n.* [C; U] The long rounded fruit of a climbing plant, having a green skin and white watery insides, eaten in salads and used for making pickles.

cud (kŭd) *n.* [U] Food that has been brought back up from the first stomach to the mouth for more chewing by mammals such as cattle and sheep.

cud•dle (kŭd′l) *v.* **cud•dled, cud•dling, cud•dles.** —*tr.* To hold (sbdy./sthg.) gently and lovingly: *cuddle a baby in one's arms.* —*intr.* To be or get close together for warmth or affection: *The two cats cuddled near the fire.* —*n.* A hug or embrace. ◆ **cuddle up.** *intr.v.* To get close together for warmth or affection: *The couple cuddled up in front of the fire.*

cud•dly (kŭd′lē) *adj.* **1.** Fond of cuddling: *a couple of cuddly old cats.* **2.** Lovable; inviting cuddling: *a cuddly teddy bear.*

cue¹ (kyōō) *n.* **1.** A long thin stick used to hit the cue ball in the games of billiards and pool. **2.** A line of waiting people or vehicles.

HOMONYMS: cue (stick, signal), **queue** (line of people).

---

cue² (kyōō) *n.* **1.** A word or signal marking the moment for an actor or singer to speak, sing, or do sthg. during a performance: *The actor missed his cue.* **2.** A signal for action: *We all sat down at the teacher's cue.* **3.** A hint or suggestion as to how to behave or what should be done: *Our host's yawn was a cue that it was time for us to go home.* —*tr.v.* **cued, cu•ing, cues.** To give (sbdy.) a cue: *Cue me when it's my turn.* ◆ **(right) on cue.** At exactly the right moment: *She returned with snacks for everyone right on cue. We were hungry!* **take (one's) cue from.** To do what sbdy. else does in order to behave in an appropriate way: *Take your cue from her; she knows what she's doing.*

cue ball *n.* The white ball used to strike other balls in billiards and pool.

cuff¹ (kŭf) *n.* **1.** A band or fold of cloth at the bottom of a sleeve. **2.** The turned-up fold at the bottom of a leg of a pair of pants. **3.** A handcuff. ◆ **off the cuff.** With little or no preparation; not rehearsed: *remarks made off the cuff.*

cuff² (kŭf) *tr.v.* To hit (sbdy./sthg.) with or as if with the open hand: *The bear cuffed her cubs.* —*n.* A blow or slap made with or as if with the open hand.

cuff link or **cuff•link** (kŭf′lĭngk′) *n.* One of a pair of fasteners for shirt cuffs, with a chain or straight metal piece that passes through the buttonholes and connects two buttonlike parts.

cui•sine (kwĭ zēn′) *n.* **1.** [C; U] A style of cooking or preparing food: *French cuisine.* **2.** [U] Food cooked in a restaurant or hotel: *a restaurant with excellent cuisine.*

cul-de-sac (kŭl′dĭ săk′ *or* kōōl′dĭ săk′) *n.* A narrow street closed at one end.

cu•li•nar•y (kyōō′lə nĕr′ē *or* kŭl′ə nĕr′ē) *adj.* Relating to a kitchen or cooking: *a chef of great culinary skill.*

cull (kŭl) *tr.v.* **1.** To pick out or choose (sthg.) from others: *cull the prettiest flowers.* **2.** To remove unwanted members or parts from (sthg.): *cull a herd of sheep.* —*n.* Something picked out from others as inferior: *Set the culls aside and freeze the rest of the strawberries.*

cul•mi•nate (kŭl′mə nāt′) *intr.* **cul•mi•nat•ed, cul•mi•nat•ing, cul•mi•nates.** To reach the highest point or degree, often just before ending: *The celebration culminated in a huge fireworks show.* —*tr.* To bring (sthg.) to the highest point or degree, often just before completion: *An appearance by the President culminated the political convention.* —**cul′mi•na′tion** *n.* [U]

cul•prit (kŭl′prĭt) *n.* A person or thing guilty of a fault or crime: *The culprit who took the basketball net should put it back.*

cult (kŭlt) *n.* **1.a.** A system of religious beliefs and customary acts: *the ancient cults of Egypt.* **b.** A religion or religious group whose followers live in an unusual way under a leader who demands complete obedience. **2.** A great or too strong attachment to a person, principle, or thing: *A cult of physical fitness has created large numbers of joggers and bikers nationwide.*

cul•ti•vate (kŭl′tə vāt′) *tr.v.* **cul•ti•vat•ed, cul•ti•vat•ing, cul•ti•vates.** **1.a.** To prepare and improve (land), as by plowing or fertilizing, for raising farm crops. **b.** To loosen or dig soil around (growing plants). **2.** To grow or take care of (plants or crops): *cultivate flowers.* **3.** To develop (sthg.) by study or teaching: *cultivate a love of music.* **4.** To try to get the approval or friendship of (sbdy.): *cultivate the new neighbors.*

cul•ti•vat•ed (kŭl′tə vā′tĭd) *adj.* **1.** Prepared and used to grow plants: *cultivated land ready for planting.* **2.** Grown by cultivation; not wild: *Many roses are cultivated flowers.* **3.** Improved by study or developed by training: *a cultivated appreciation of music.* **4.** Well educated about the arts: *cultivated people with a love of opera.*

cul•ti•va•tion (kŭl′tə vā′shən) *n.* [U] **1.** The process of growing: *the cultivation of fruits and vegetables.* **2.** Development or improvement by training: *cultivation of one's mind.* **3.** Education about and love of the arts; culture: *a person of great cultivation.*

---

cul•ti•va•tor (kŭl′tə vā′tər) *n.* **1.** A person who cultivates. **2.** A machine for loosening the earth and destroying weeds around growing plants: *A cultivator works faster than a hoe.*

cul•tur•al (kŭl′chər əl) *adj.* Relating to culture: *Paris is the cultural center of France. Cultural influences affect individual behavior.* —**cul′tur•al•ly** *adv.*

cul•ture (kŭl′chər) *n.* **1.** [C] The arts, beliefs, customs, institutions, and all other products of human work and thought at a particular time: *the various cultures of Africa.* **2.** [U] The qualities of mind and the tastes that result from appreciation of the arts and sciences: *a writer of great culture.* **3.** [U] The breeding of animals or growing of plants, especially to improve their development: *bee culture.* **4.a.** [U] The growing of microorganisms or tissues under special conditions for scientific study or use in medicines. **b.** [C] Such a growth, as of bacteria or tissue: *a culture of penicillin-producing mold.* —*tr.v.* **cul•tured, cul•tur•ing, cul•tures.** To grow (microorganisms, tissues, or other living matter) for scientific study.

cul•tured (kŭl′chərd) *adj.* **1.** Well educated; having appreciation for the arts: *a cultured supporter of the ballet.* **2.** Grown or produced under artificial and controlled conditions: *cultured pearls.*

culture shock *n.* [U] A condition of confusion and anxiety that can affect a person who enters an unfamiliar culture or environment.

cul•vert (kŭl′vərt) *n.* A pipe that carries water under a road or railroad tracks, for example.

cum•ber•some (kŭm′bər səm) *adj.* Hard to carry or manage: *cumbersome baggage.* —**cum′ber•some•ness** *n.* [U]

cum•in (kŭm′ĭn *or* kōō′mĭn *or* kyōō′mĭn) *n.* [U] A plant of the Mediterranean region that is related to parsley or its spicy seeds, used for seasoning food.

cum lau•de (kŏŏm lou′də) *adv. & adj.* With academic honor: *She graduated cum laude. He is a cum laude graduate.*

cu•mu•la•tive (kyōōm′yə lā′tĭv *or* kyōōm′-yə lə tĭv) *adj.* Increasing or growing by steady addition or in stages: *The cumulative efforts of many people helped clean up the river.* —**cu′mu•la•tive•ly** *adv.*

cun•ning (kŭn′ĭng) *adj.* **1.** Smart and designed to trick people: *a cunning plan.* **2.** *Informal.* Charming; cute: *a cunning little child.* —*n.* [U] **1.** Skill in tricking people: *It takes great cunning to be a spy.* **2.** Skill in performance; cleverness: *a mystery writer of wonderful cunning.* —**cun′ning•ly** *adv.*

cup (kŭp) *n.* **1.** A small open container, usually having a handle, from which to drink liquids: *The baby can now drink from a cup.* **2.** The contents of such a container: *drink a cup of cocoa.* **3.** In cooking, a measure equal to ½ pint, 8 ounces, or 16 tablespoons (237 milliliters). See table at **measurement. 4.**

Something similar in shape to a cup: *the cup of a flower.* **5.** A cup-shaped prize or trophy: *She won the cup at the tennis tournament.* —*tr.v.* **cupped, cup•ping, cups. 1.** To form (sth.) in such a way as to look like a cup: *cup one's hands to get a drink.* **2.** To place (sth.) in or as if in a cup: *I cupped my ear with my hand to show I couldn't hear her.* ♦ **(one's) cup of tea.** Something that one enjoys or does well: *Opera is not my cup of tea.*

cup•board (kŭb′ərd) *n.* A closet or cabinet, usually having shelves for storing food, dishes, or other small items: *a kitchen cupboard.*

cup•cake (kŭp′kāk′) *n.* A small cake baked in a cup-shaped container.

cup•ful (kŭp′fŏŏl′) *n.* The amount that a cup can hold.

cur•a•ble (kyŏŏr′ə bəl) *adj.* Capable of being healed or cured: *a curable illness.*

cu•ra•tor (kyŏŏ rā′tər *or* kyŏŏr′ə tər) *n.* A person who manages a museum, library, or zoo.

curb (kûrb) *n.* **1.** A concrete or stone border along the edge of a street: *Don't trip over the curb!* **2.** Something that stops or holds back: *a curb on spending.* —*tr.v.* To hold back or control (sth.): *curb one's temper.*

curd (kûrd) *n.* [C; U] The thick part of milk that separates from the whey and is used to make cheese.

cur•dle (kûr′dl) *v.* **cur•dled, cur•dling, cur•dles.** —*intr.* **1.** To form into curds: *The milk curdled overnight.* **2.** To seem to thicken and stop flowing, as because of fear or shock: *My blood curdled at the scream in the night.* —*tr.* To cause (sth.) to form into curds: *Don't curdle the milk by leaving it out too long.*

cure (kyŏŏr) *n.* **1.** A return to health; a recovery from illness. **2.** A medical treatment or a series of such treatments used to bring sbdy. back to health: *Penicillin is used as a cure for infections.* **3.** Something that brings back health or improves a condition: *A trip was the perfect cure for overwork.* —*v.* **cured, cur•ing, cures.** —*tr.* **1.** To bring (sbdy.) back to health: *Strong medicine cured the patient quickly.* **2.** To cause a recovery from (an illness): *cure a cold.* **3.** To remove (a harmful condition or influence): *cure a social problem.* **4.** To prepare, preserve, or finish (a substance or material) by a special process: *cure wood; cure fish in a smokehouse.* —*intr.* **1.** To cause a return to good health: *a medicine that cures.* **2.** To be prepared, preserved, or finished by a chemical or physical process: *The fish cured in the sun.*

cur•few (kûr′fyōō) *n.* **1.** A regulation requiring certain people to be off the streets and indoors at a certain hour: *a midnight curfew for teenagers.* **2.** The time at which such a regulation is in effect. **3.** The signal, such as the ringing of a bell, announcing the beginning of this regulation.

C

cu•rie (**kyŏŏr′ē** or **kyŏŏ rē′**) n. A unit for measuring the intensity of radioactivity.

cu•ri•os•i•ty (**kyŏŏr′ē ŏs′ĭ tē**) n., pl. **cu•ri•os•i•ties. 1.** [U] A desire to know or learn: *She was full of curiosity over who had sent the letter.* **2.** [C] Something unusual or extraordinary: *curiosities in the museum's collection.*

cu•ri•ous (**kyŏŏr′ē əs**) adj. **1.** Eager to learn more: *curious detectives.* **2.** Interesting and strange: *We found a curious shell at the beach.* **—cu′ri•ous•ly** adv. **—cu′ri•ous•ness** n. [U]

SYNONYMS: curious, inquisitive, snoopy, nosy. These adjectives describe persons who show a strong desire for information or knowledge. **Curious** refers to a strong desire to know or learn: *If you are curious about a particular subject, the librarian can help you find a book about it.* **Inquisitive** often means too curious: *The inquisitive student asked a question every time the teacher paused for breath.* **Snoopy** means curious in a sneaky way: *The snoopy reporter searched through the movie star's garbage for evidence.* **Nosy** means rudely curious: *She is so nosy she will even read other people's mail.* **ANTONYM: indifferent.**

---

curl (**kûrl**) v. —tr. **1.** To twist or form (sthg.) into coils or a curved shape: *curl one's hair; curl a ribbon.* **2.** To make (sthg.) curved or coiled: *I curled my hand around my coffee cup.* —intr. **1.** To form ringlets or curls: *Her hair curls when it dries.* **2.** To move in a curve or spiral: *Smoke curled from the chimney.* —n. **1.** A coil or ringlet of hair. **2.** Something with a spiral or coiled shape: *a curl of smoke.* ◆ **curl up.** intr.v. **1.** To sit or lie down with the legs bent and pulled towards the upper body: *He curled up on the sofa to read.* **2.** To form curls: *Her hair curls up in the rain.*

curl•er (**kûr′lər**) n. A roller that strands of hair are wrapped around for curling.

curl•y (**kûr′lē**) adj. **curl•i•er, curl•i•est.** Having curls or tending to curl: *curly hair.* **—curl′i•ness** n. [U]

cur•rant (**kûr′ənt** or **kŭr′ənt**) n. **1.a.** The small, sour, usually red or blackish fruit of any of various prickly shrubs, used especially for making jelly. **b.** A shrub that produces such fruit. **2.** A small seedless raisin, used mostly in baking.

HOMONYMS: currant, current (belonging to the present time).

---

cur•ren•cy (**kûr′ən sē** or **kŭr′ən sē**) n., pl. **cur•ren•cies. 1.** [C; U] Money in any form when in actual use in a country: *U.S. currency is in dollars, and French currency is in francs.* **2.** [U] General acceptance or use: *Many slang words and expressions have currency for only a short time.* **3.** [U] A passing from one person to another; circulation: *coins now in currency.*

cur•rent (**kûr′ənt** or **kŭr′ənt**) adj. **1.** Belonging to the present time: *a person's current address.* **2.** Passing from one to another; circulating, as money or a rumor. **3.** Commonly accepted or used: *Use of hand calculators is current in schools today.* —n. **1.** A mass of liquid or gas that is in motion: *the current of a river; a current of cool air flowing through the room.* **2.a.** A flow of electric charge. **b.** The amount of electric charge that passes a point in a unit of time, usually expressed in amperes. **3.** A general tendency or movement in one direction, as of events or opinions: *The current of voter opinion supports the President.* **—cur′rent•ly** adv.

HOMONYMS: current, currant (fruit).

---

cur•ric•u•la (**kə rĭk′yə lə**) n. A plural of **curriculum.**

cur•ric•u•lum (**kə rĭk′yə ləm**) n., pl. **cur•ric•u•la** (**kə rĭk′yə lə**) or **cur•ric•u•lums.** A set of courses of study offered at a particular educational institution or department: *The curriculum in engineering at that college is strong.* **—cur•ric′u•lar** adj.

curriculum vi•tae (**vī′tē** or **vē′tī**) n., pl. **cur•ric•u•la vi•tae** A summary of one's education, professional history, and job qualifications, as for a possible employer.

cur•ry¹ (**kûr′ē** or **kŭr′ē**) tr.v. **cur•ried, cur•ry•ing, cur•ries.** To comb the hair of (a horse). ◆ **curry favor.** To look for or gain favor by flattery: *The new worker tried to curry favor with the boss.*

cur•ry² (**kûr′ē** or **kŭr′ē**) n., pl. **cur•ries. 1.** [U] A mixture of sharp-flavored powdered spices; curry powder. **2.** [C; U] A strongly-flavored sauce or dish seasoned with curry powder: *We ate lamb curry for dinner.* —tr.v. **cur•ried, cur•ry•ing, cur•ries.** To give flavor to (food) with curry.

curse (**kûrs**) n. **1.a.** An appeal or a prayer for evil or harm to happen to a person or thing. **b.** The evil or harm that follows or seems to follow such an appeal. **2.** A word or group of words expressing great anger; an oath. **3.** Something that causes great evil or harm: *Greed is a great curse of the human race.* —v. **cursed** or **curst** (**kûrst**), **curs•ing, curs•es.** —tr. **1.** To wish evil or harm on (sbdy.) with a curse. **2.** To bring great harm to (sbdy.): *The farmers were cursed with bad weather at*

ă–cat; ā–pay; âr–care; ä–father; ĕ–get; ē–be; ĭ–sit; ī–nice; îr–here; ŏ–got; ō–go; ô–saw; oi–boy; ou–out; ŏŏ–took; ōō–boot; ŭ–cut; ûr–word; th–thin; th–this; hw–when; zh–vision; ə–about; N–French bon

harvest time. **3.** To swear at (sbdy. sthg.): *He often curses other drivers.* —*intr.* To speak curses; swear.

curs·ed (kûr′sĭd *or* kûrst) *also* **curst** (kûrst) *adj.* Deserving to be cursed: *Will this cursed rain never end?* —**curs′ed·ly** *adv.*

cur·sive (kûr′sĭv) *adj.* Written or printed with connected letters: *cursive handwriting.* —*n.* A cursive character or letter.

cur·sor (kûr′sər) *n.* A small square, dot, or bar of light on a computer screen that can be moved to the point where the next operation takes place, such as taking out or typing in a letter.

cur·so·ry (kûr′sə rē) *adj.* Hurried and incomplete; not thorough: *He made a cursory search for a familiar face in the crowd.* —**cur′so·ri·ly** *adv.*

curt (kûrt) *adj.* Rudely brief in speech or manner; brusque: *They gave me only a curt greeting in their rush to catch the train.* —**curt′ly** *adv.* —**curt′ness** *n.* [U]

cur·tail (kər tāl′) *tr.v.* To reduce or limit (sthg.): *We had to curtail our spending on the rest of the trip.* —**cur·tail′ment** *n.* [U]

cur·tain (kûr′tn) *n.* **1.** Cloth or other material hanging in a window or door as a decoration, shade, or screen: *The wind was blowing the curtains at the open window.* **2.** Something that acts as a screen or cover: *mountains hidden by a thick curtain of fog.* **3.** The movable cloth or screen in a theater that separates the stage from the audience. **4. curtains.** *Slang.* The end: *It'll be curtains for him if he's late again.* —*tr.v.* [off] To provide or shut off (sthg.) with or as if with a curtain: *The first-class cabin was curtained off from the rest of the passengers.*

curt·sy *or* **curt·sey** (kûrt′sē) *n., pl.* **curt·sies** *or* **curt·seys.** A gesture of respect made in the past by women by bending the knees with one foot forward and lowering the body. —*intr.v.* **curt·sied, curt·sy·ing, curt·sies** *or* **curt·seyed, curt·sey·ing, curt·seys.** To make a curtsy: *The dancer curtsied to her partner.*

cur·va·ture (kûr′və chŏŏr′ *or* kûr′və chər) *n.* **1.a.** [U] The act of curving or the condition of being curved: *the curvature of the moon's orbit.* **b.** [C] The degree to which sthg. is curved: *a small curvature in the wooden table top.* **2.** [C; U] A curving or bending of a body part, especially when abnormal: *curvature of the spine.*

curve (kûrv) *n.* **1.** A line or surface that bends in a smooth continuous way without sharp angles. **2.** Something that has the shape of a curve: *a curve in the road.* **3.** In mathematics, a line of a set of points defined by a function drawn on a surface or plane. —*v.* **curved, curv·ing, curves.** —*intr.* To move in or take the shape of a curve: *The ball curved to the right. The road curves sharply just ahead.*

—*tr.* To cause (sthg.) to curve: *curve a metal band.*

cush·ion (kŏŏsh′ən) *n.* **1.** A pad or pillow with a soft filling, used to sit, lie, or rest on: *Something spilled on the cushion of the sofa.* **2.** Something used as a rest, support, or shock absorber. **3.** Something shaped like or used as a cushion: *He slept on a cushion of dried leaves.* **4.** Something used to lessen a bad effect: *We have a savings account as a cushion against a drop in business.* —*tr.v.* **1.** To place or seat (sthg.) on a cushion: *The cat cushioned itself on our pillows.* **2.** To supply (sthg.) with a cushion or cushions: *Soft pillows cushioned the chair.* **3.** To lessen or soften the impact of (sthg.): *My thick coat cushioned the fall.*

cuss (kŭs) *Informal. intr. & tr.v.* To curse. —*n.* **1.** A strange and easily angered person: *an unpleasant cuss.* **2.** A curse.

cus·tard (kŭs′tərd) *n.* [C; U] A pudding of milk, sugar, eggs, and flavoring that is baked or boiled: *vanilla custard.*

cus·to·di·an (kŭ stō′dē ən) *n.* **1.** A person who has responsibility for sthg.; a caretaker or guardian: *custodian of a museum collection.* **2.** A person who takes care of a building; a janitor.

cus·to·dy (kŭs′tə dē) *n.* [U] **1.** [of] Supervision; care: *The children were in the custody of their aunt and uncle while their parents were away.* **2.** The condition of being held under guard, especially by the police: *The suspect was held in custody for questioning.* **3.** [of] The legal right to care for a child or children: *The divorce court granted the mother full custody of the children.*

cus·tom (kŭs′təm) *n.* **1.** An accepted practice or usual way followed by people of a particular group or region: *Shaking hands when meeting someone is a common custom.* **2.** A usual practice of an individual; a habit: *Their custom is to go to bed early.* See Synonyms at **habit. 3. customs.** *(used with a singular verb).* **a.** A duty or tax imposed on goods imported from another country. **b.** The government agency that collects these duties and inspects imported goods. —*adj.* **1.** Made for a particular customer: *custom suits made to the instructions of the buyer.* **2.** Making or selling things as they are ordered by customers: *a custom tailor.*

cus·tom·ar·y (kŭs′tə měr′ē) *adj.* Set by custom; usual: *The customary place for a judge to sit is at the head of a courtroom.* —**cus′tom·ar′i·ly** (kŭs′tə mâr′ə lē) *adv.*

cus·tom-built (kŭs′təm bĭlt′) *adj.* Built according to the orders of the buyer: *custom-built cabinets.*

cus·tom·er (kŭs′tə mər) *n.* **1.** A person who buys goods or services, especially on a regular basis. **2.** *Informal.* A difficult person with whom one must interact or deal: *a tough customer.*

cus·tom·ize (kŭs′tə mīz′) *tr.v.* **cus·tom·ized, cus·tom·iz·ing, cus·tom·iz·es.** To make or change (sthg.) to meet the wishes of an individual: *customize a van.*

cus·tom-made (kŭs′təm mād′) *adj.* Made according to the orders of the buyer: *custom-made furniture.*

cut (kŭt) *v.* **cut, cut·ting, cuts.** —*tr.* **1.** To make an opening in (sthg.) with a sharp edge or instrument: *I cut my finger on a piece of broken glass.* **2.** To separate or divide (sthg.) by using a sharp instrument: *cut the paper in half with scissors.* **3.** To separate (sthg.) from what it was attached to: *cut a branch from a tree.* **4.** To pass through or across (sthg.): *The path cuts the neighbor's yard.* **5.** To shorten or trim (sthg.): *cut hair; cut the lawn.* **6.** To interrupt or stop (sthg.): *A bad storm cut our electric power for two hours.* **7.** To reduce the size or amount of (sthg.): *cut taxes; cut one's losses.* **8.** To remove or take away (sthg.): *The director cut several scenes from the play.* **9.** To hurt the feelings of (sbdy.): *Their unfriendly remarks cut me deeply.* **10.** *Informal.* To fail to attend (sthg.) purposely: *I cut my classes today.* —*intr.* **1.** To make an opening or a separation: *The knife cut right through the apple.* **2.** To allow an opening or severing: *Butter cuts easily.* **3.** To be like a sharp instrument: *The cold wind cut through my thin jacket.* **4.a.** To go by a short or direct route: *cut across the park to get home quickly.* **b.** To go across; cross: *This road cuts through the mountains.* **5.** To change direction abruptly: *The driver suddenly cut to the right.* —*n.* **1.** The result of cutting; an opening or a wound. **2.** A blow or stroke, as with a sharp instrument: *a few cuts of the ax.* **3.** A part that has been cut from the main body of sthg.: *an expensive cut of beef.* **4.** A removal of a part: *He made several cuts in the speech.* **5.** A decrease in the amount of sthg.: *I had to take a cut in pay.* **6.** *Informal.* A share of profits or earnings: *The salesman gets a five percent cut.* **7.** A wounding remark; an insult: *That was an unkind cut you directed at me.* ◆ **be cut out.** To be right or have the necessary qualities: *He's not cut out to be a leader.* **cut back.** *tr.v.* [sep.] **1.** To shorten (sthg.) by cutting parts off: *cut back a rosebush.* **2.** To reduce or decrease (sthg.): *cut back prices in a sale.* **cut corners.** To do sthg. in a way that saves time, work, or money, often with poor results. **cut down.** *tr.v.* [sep.] **1.** To cut through (the main stem of a tree) and cause it to fall. **2.** To kill or strike (sbdy.) down: *The cannon fire cut down the charging troops.* **3.** To make (sthg.) less; reduce: *cut down one's spending.* **cut down to size.** To show a self-important person that she or he is not as special as she or he thinks: *If he starts bragging*

again, I'll cut him down to size. **cut in.** *intr.v.* **1.** To move into a line of people or things out of turn: *cut in at the head of the line for tickets.* **2.** To interrupt: *That rude man cut in on our conversation.* **3.** To interrupt a dancing couple in order to dance with one of them: *May I cut in?* **cut off.** *tr.v.* [sep.] **1.** To stop or shut off (sthg.) suddenly: *cut off the electricity.* **2.** To block (sbdy.) from inheriting one's money after one dies: *He cut off his children without a cent.* **3.** To separate or isolate (sbdy./sthg.): *People on the island were cut off from the mainland during the storm.* **cut out.** *tr.v.* [sep.] **1.** To form or shape (sthg.) by cutting: *cut out pieces of cloth for a coat.* **2.** To stop doing (sthg.): *Cut it out!* **3.** To keep (sbdy.) out of a will to prevent him or her from inheriting money. —*intr.* **1.** *(used of motors).* To stop working: *The engine cut out when I slowed down.* **2.** *Slang.* To leave: *I need to cut out soon.* **cut up.** *tr.v.* [sep.] To cut (sthg.) into smaller pieces: *Cut up the potatoes so I can put them in the soup.* —*intr.v. Informal.* To behave playfully: *Those two boys are always cutting up in class.*

cut-and-dried (kŭt′n drīd′) *adj.* **1.** Prepared and arranged in advance: *There are no cut-and-dried rules for good writing.* **2.** Lacking freshness or imagination; ordinary: *His advice was full of cut-and-dried old phrases.*

cut·back (kŭt′băk′) *n.* A decrease; a reduction: *a cutback in government spending.*

cute (kyo͞ot) *adj.* **cut·er, cut·est.** **1.** Delightfully small and pretty: *a cute puppy.* **2.** Obviously designed to charm: *a cute remark.* **3.** Clever; shrewd: *a cute trick.* —**cute′ly** *adv.* —**cute′ness** *n.* [U]

cu·ti·cle (kyo͞o′tĭ kəl) *n.* The hard skin around the sides and base of a fingernail.

cut·ler·y (kŭt′lə rē) *n.* [U] **1.** Cutting instruments and tools, such as knives and scissors. **2.** Knives, forks, and spoons used as tableware.

cut·let (kŭt′lĭt) *n.* A thin slice of meat, as of veal, cut from the leg or ribs.

cut·off (kŭt′ôf′ *or* kŭt′ŏf′) *n.* **1.** A set limit or stopping point: *Saturday is the cutoff for new job applications.* **2.** The act or an instance of cutting sthg. off: *a cutoff of electricity.* **3.** A device used to stop a flow, as of a liquid or gas: *That valve is the cutoff for our water.* **4.** A shortcut or bypass: *use the cutoff through the park.* **5. cutoffs.** Pants made into shorts by cutting off part of the legs. —*adj.* Marking a limit or deadline: *a cutoff date.*

cut-rate (kŭt′rāt′) *adj.* **1.** Sold or on sale at a reduced price. **2.** Cheap and of poor quality: *cut-rate furniture.*

cut·ter (kŭt′ər) *n.* **1.** A worker whose job involves cutting some material, such as cloth, glass, or stone. **2.** A cutting device or machine: *a cookie cutter.* **3.** A small, lightly armed boat used by the Coast Guard.

cut•throat (kŭt′thrōt′) *n.* A person with no principles or mercy. —*adj.* **1.** Cruel; murderous: *a cutthroat band of thieves.* **2.** Without concern for fairness or kindness in competition: *a cutthroat business.*

cut•ting (kŭt′ĭng) *adj.* **1.** Capable of or designed for cutting: *a cutting blade.* **2.** Injuring the feelings of others: *a cutting remark.* —*n.* **1.** A part cut off from a main body: *a collection of newspaper cuttings.* **2.** A stem, twig, or leaf removed from a plant and placed in soil, sand, or water to form roots and develop into a new plant.

cut•up (kŭt′ŭp′) *n. Informal.* A person who behaves in a playful way to amuse others.

C.V. *abbr.* An abbreviation of curriculum vitae.

—cy *suff.* A suffix that means: **1.** State; condition; quality: *bankruptcy; urgency.* **2.** Rank; office: *presidency.*

cy•a•nide (sī′ə nīd′) *n.* **1.** [C] Any of a large group of salts and esters. Cyanides are used in making plastics and extracting and treating metals. **2.** [U] A very strong poison of this group.

cy•ber•net•ics (sī′bər nĕt′ĭks) *n.* [U] (*used with a singular verb*). The study of communication and control processes in biological, mechanical, and electronic systems.

cy•ber•space (sī′bər spās) *n.* [U] The worldwide collection of computer networks and bulletin board systems that carry online messages: *My home computer lets me travel in cyberspace.*

cy•cle (sī′kəl) *n.* **1.a.** A series of events that is periodically repeated: *the moon's cycle from new moon to full moon.* **b.** The time during which such a series of events occurs: *a four-year cycle.* **2.** A long period of time; an age. **3.** The set of traditional poems or stories about a central theme or hero: *the Arthurian cycle.* **4.** A bicycle, motorcycle, or similar vehicle. —*intr.v.* **cy•cled, cy•cling, cy•cles. 1.** To occur in or pass through a cycle. **2.** To ride a bicycle, motorcycle, or similar vehicle.

cy•clic (sī′klĭk *or* sĭk′lĭk) or **cy•cli•cal** (sī′klĭ kəl *or* sĭk′lĭ kəl) *adj.* **1.** Relating to or happening in cycles: *the cyclic motion of the tides.* **2.** Relating to or containing an arrangement of atoms in a ring or closed chain.

cy•clist (sī′klĭst) *n.* A person who rides a motorcycle, bicycle, or similar vehicle.

cy•clone (sī′klōn′) *n.* **1.** A storm or winds moving around and toward a calm center of

low pressure, which also moves. **2.** A violent rotating windstorm, such as a hurricane or tornado.

cyl•in•der (sĭl′ən dər) *n.* **1.** A solid figure bounded by a curved surface and two parallel circles of equal size at the ends. **2.** An object or container having such a shape, as a can or a roller on a typewriter. **3.** The enclosed space in which a piston moves up and down, as in an engine or pump: *a four-cylinder engine.*

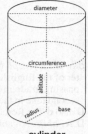
cylinder

cy•lin•dri•cal (sə lĭn′drĭ kəl) also **cy•lin•dric** (sə lĭn′drĭk) *adj.* Relating to or having the shape of a cylinder. —**cy•lin•dri•cal•ly** *adv.*

cym•bal (sĭm′bəl) *n.* One of a pair of brass musical instruments made into the shape of a plate. Cymbals are sounded either by striking them together or by hitting them with a drumstick or brush.

HOMONYMS: cymbal, symbol (sign).

---

cyn•ic (sĭn′ĭk) *n.* A person who believes that people act mostly because of selfish interests.

cyn•i•cal (sĭn′ĭ kəl) *adj.* Refusing to believe in goodness or honesty in people's actions: *distrusting and cynical remarks about politics.* —**cyn′i•cal•ly** *adv.*

cyn•i•cism (sĭn′ĭ sĭz′əm) *n.* [U] An attitude of refusing to believe in goodness in people and laughing at those who believe: *Recent scandals have increased cynicism about politics.*

cy•press (sī′prĭs) *n.* **1.a.** [C] Any of various evergreen trees of warm regions of Asia, Europe, and North America, with hard wood and small leaves. **b.** [U] The wood of any of these trees. **2.** [C] Any of several similar or related trees that grow in swamps and lose their needles each year.

cyst (sĭst) *n.* An abnormal sac in the body, composed of thin tissue surrounding a gas, liquid, or soft solid material. —**cys′tic** *adj.*

czar (zär *or* tsär) *n.* **1.** Also **tsar** or **tzar.** Any of the emperors who ruled Russia until the revolution of 1917. **2.** A person who has great authority or power: *He is the President's drug policy czar.*

cza•ri•na (zä rē′nə *or* tsä rē′nə) *n.* The wife of a Russian czar.

czar•ist (zär′ĭst) *adj.* Relating to or in the time of the Russian czars: *czarist Russia.*

Dd

d or **D** (dē) *n., pl.* **d's** or **D's. 1.** The fourth letter of the English alphabet. **2. D.** The lowest passing grade in school. **3. D.** In music, the second tone in the scale of C major.

D also **d** The Roman numeral for 500.

D.A. *abbr.* An abbreviation of district attorney.

dab (dăb) *v.* **dabbed, dab·bing, dabs.** —*tr.* **1.** To apply (sth.) with short light strokes: *dab paint on a wall.* **2.** To pat (sth.) quickly and lightly: *He dabbed the stain on his shirt with a cloth.* —*intr.* To tap gently; pat: *She dabbed lightly at the spot on her dress.* —*n.* A small amount or lump: *a dab of butter.*

dab·ble (dăb′əl) *v.* **dab·bled, dab·bling, dab·bles.** —*tr.* To splash (sth.) in and out of water: *The children dabbled their feet in the lake.* —*intr.* **1.** To splash or play in water: *The ducks dabbled in the shallow water.* **2.** [*in*] To do or work on sth. without serious intent: *I dabbled in photography for a time.* —**dab′bler** *n.*

dachs·hund (däks′hŏŏnt′ *or* dăk′sənt) *n.* A small dog with a long body, long ears, and very short legs.

dad (dăd) *n. Informal.* Father.

dad·dy (dăd′ē) *n., pl.* **dad·dies.** *Informal.* Father.

daf·fo·dil (dăf′ə dĭl) *n.* A yellow spring flower with a trumpet-shaped center.

daffodil

daf·fy (dăf′ē) *adj.* **daf·fi·er, daf·fi·est.** *Informal.* Silly; ridiculous.

dag·ger (dăg′ər) *n.* A short pointed knife, used as a weapon. ♦ **with daggers in (one's) eyes.** With anger or hatred: *He looked at me with daggers in his eyes.*

dai·ly (dā′lē) *adj.* Done, happening, or appearing every day or weekday: *a daily walk.* —*adv.* Every day: *She tries to exercise daily.* —*n., pl.* **dai·lies.** A newspaper published every day or every weekday.

dain·ty (dān′tē) *adj.* **dain·ti·er, dain·ti·est. 1.** Delicately beautiful: *dainty lace.* **2.** Very careful in choosing; fussy: *The cat is a dainty eater.* —**dain′ti·ly** *adv.* —**dain′ti·ness** *n.* [U]

dair·y (dâr′ē) *n., pl.* **dair·ies. 1.** A room or building where milk and cream are stored, prepared for use, or made into butter and cheese. **2.** A business, farm, or store that prepares or sells milk and milk products. —*adj.* Relating to milk or milk products: *You can find butter in the dairy case at the supermarket.*

da·is (dā′ĭs *or* dī′ĭs) *n.* A raised platform for a throne, a speaker, or a group of special guests.

dai·sy (dā′zē) *n., pl.* **dai·sies.** A flower that has many narrow petals, usually white, surrounding a flat round yellow center.

dal·ly (dăl′ē) *intr.v.* **dal·lied, dal·ly·ing, dal·lies. 1.** To waste time: *After class, we dallied in the hall.* **2.** To flirt playfully; toy: *Don't dally with your food.*

Dal·ma·tian (dăl mā′shən) *n.* A medium-sized dog with a short, smooth white coat with many small black spots.

dam¹ (dăm) *n.* A barrier across a waterway to control the flow or raise the level of the water. —*tr.v.* **dammed, dam·ming, dams. 1.** To hold (sth.) back by means of a dam: *Engineers dammed the river.* **2.** To hold back or restrain (sth.): *dam up emotions.*

HOMONYMS: dam (barrier, female animal), **damn** (condemn).

---

dam² (dăm) *n.* The female parent of a four-legged animal.

dam·age (dăm′ĭj) *n.* **1.** [U] Harm or injury: *The storm did great damage to the houses.* **2. damages.** In law, money to be paid to make up for an injury or loss: *After the car hit me, I decided to sue the driver for damages.* —*tr.v.* **dam·aged, dam·ag·ing, dam·ag·es.** To hurt or injure (sbdy./sth.): *Some insects damage plants.* See Synonyms at **hurt.**

dam·ag·ing (dăm′ĭ jĭng) *adj.* Having a very bad effect on sbdy. or sth.: *The news about her campaign finances was damaging to her political career.*

dame (dām) *n.* **1.** *Chiefly British.* **a.** A woman given a title by the queen or king as an honor. **b.** The wife or widow of a knight. **2.** *Slang.* A mildly offensive outdated word for a woman.

damn (dăm) *v.* —*tr.* **1.** To condemn (sth.) as being very bad: *Reviewers damned the new movie.* **2.a.** To condemn (sbdy./sth.) to failure or ruin: *Without money the project was damned.* **b.** To condemn (sbdy.) to everlasting punish-

---

ment in hell: *The priest damned the sinner.*
—*interj. Offensive.* An expression used to show
anger, irritation, or disappointment: *Damn! I
forgot my keys.* —*adj. & adv. Offensive.* Very;
damned: *a damn fool; a damn good joke.* —*n.
Offensive.* The least bit: *not worth a damn.*
◆ **damned if.** *Offensive.* Used to show strong
opposition to sthg. happening or to emphasize a
lack of information: *Damned if you'll get away
with lying to me again! Damned if I know
what's going on around here!* **damned if (one)
does, damned if (one) doesn't.** Used to say
that whatever one does in a situation, it will be
wrong: *I don't know whether to tell her; I'm
damned if I do, and damned if I don't.* **damn
well.** *Offensive.* Absolutely: *You know damn
well what time it is!* **give a damn.** *Offensive.* To
care at all about sthg.: *He doesn't give a damn
what people say about him. Do you give a damn
about your health?* **I'll be damned.** *Offensive.*
Used to show shock or surprise: *I'll be damned!
You're on time for once!*

HOMONYMS: damn, dam (barrier, female animal).

---

damned (dămd) *adj.* **1.** Condemned or
doomed. **2.** *Offensive.* Dreadful; awful: *this
damned weather.* **3.** *Offensive.* Used as an
intensive: *a damned fool.* —*adv. Offensive.*
Very; damn: *a damned good idea.*
damned•est (dăm′dĭst) *adj.* A mildly offensive word meaning surprising or very strange:
It was the damnedest thing. ◆ **do (one's)
damnedest.** To do everything possible: *He
did his damnedest to keep her from hearing
the news.*
damn•ing (dăm′ĭng) *adj.* **1.** Showing clearly: *damning evidence of the accused's guilt.*
2. Revealing that sthg. is very bad or wrong:
a damning speech.
damp (dămp) *adj.* Slightly wet; humid: *a
damp towel; damp air.* See Synonyms at **wet.**
—*n.* [U] Moisture in the air; humidity: *Don't
go out in the damp.* —*tr.v.* **1.** To extinguish
(a fire, for example) by cutting off air: *We
damped the flame by putting sand on it.* **2.**
To discourage (sbdy./sthg.): *a cold mist that
damped the hiker's spirits.* —**damp′ly** *adv.*
—**damp′ness** *n.* [U]
damp•en (dăm′pən) *tr.v.* **1.** To moisten
(sthg.): *dampen a sponge.* **2.** To reduce (positive feelings such as excitement or happiness): *The delay dampened their excitement.*
—**damp′en•er** *n.*
damp•er (dăm′pər) *n.* A movable plate in
the flue of a furnace, stove, or fireplace for
controlling the flow of air. ◆ **put a damper
on.** To ruin plans: *The rain put a damper on
their vacation plans.*
dance (dăns) *v.* **danced, danc•ing,
danc•es.** —*intr.* **1.** To move with rhythmic
steps and motions, especially in time to
music. **2.** To leap, skip, or prance about: *The*

excited children danced about the room. —*tr.*
To engage in or perform (a dance): *They
danced a waltz.* —*n.* **1.** [C] A set of rhythmic
steps and motions, usually performed to
music. **2.** [C] A party at which people dance:
Are you going to the dance? **3.** [C] One
round or turn of dancing: *May I have this
dance?* **4.** [U] The art of dancing: *They study
dance at a ballet school.* **5.** [C] A piece of
music composed as an accompaniment for
dancing. —**danc′er** *n.*
dan•de•li•on (dăn′dl ī′ən) *n.* A common
weed with bright yellow flowers and long
leaves that are sometimes eaten in salads.
After the flowers have bloomed, the ripe
seeds form a fluffy rounded mass.
dan•druff (dăn′drəf) *n.* [U] Small white pieces
of dead skin that are shed from the scalp.
dan•dy (dăn′dē) *n., pl.* **dan•dies. 1.** *Informal.*
Something very good: *This car is a dandy.* **2.**
An old-fashioned word for a man who wears
fine elegant clothes. —*adj.* **dan•di•er, dan•
di•est.** *Informal.* Very good; fine: *That's a
dandy idea!*
dan•ger (dān′jər) *n.* **1.** [U] The chance or
risk of harm: *The house was in danger of
being swept into the sea.* **2.** [C] A possible
cause or chance of harm; a threat or hazard:
Fog is a danger to pilots.
dan•ger•ous (dān′jər əs) *adj.* **1.** Involving
danger; hazardous: *a dangerous job.* **2.** Able
or likely to cause harm: *The crocodile is a
dangerous animal.* —**dan′ger•ous•ly** *adv.*
—**dan′ger•ous•ness** *n.* [U]
dan•gle (dăng′gəl) *v.* **dan•gled, dan•
gling, dan•gles.** —*intr.* To hang loosely and
swing or sway: *A key dangled from the chain.*
—*tr.* To cause (sbdy./sthg.) to swing loosely:
The children dangled their feet in the water.
Dan•ish pastry (dā′nĭsh) *n.* A sweet buttery
pastry made with raised dough, often with a
fruit or cheese filling.
dank (dăngk) *adj.* Uncomfortably damp;
chilly and wet: *a dank old cellar.* —**dank′ly**
adv. —**dank′ness** *n.* [U]
dap•per (dăp′ər) *adj.* Neatly dressed; trim:
dapper soldiers on parade.
dap•ple (dăp′əl) *tr.v.* **dap•pled, dap•pling,
dap•ples.** To mark (sthg.) with spots or
patches of a different color: *Sunlight filtering
through the leaves dappled the ground.*
dap•pled (dăp′əld) *adj.* Marked with spots or
patches of a different color: *a dappled horse.*
dare (dâr) *tr.v.* **dared, dar•ing, dares. 1.** To
have the courage necessary for (sthg.); be bold
enough to try: *She dared her most difficult
dive. I didn't dare go into the house.* **2.** To
challenge (sbdy.) to do sthg. requiring courage: *They dared me to dive off the high board.*
3. To confront or oppose (sbdy./sthg.) boldly;
defy: *The swimmers dared the freezing waters.*
—*n.* A challenge: *I took their dare and swam
across the pond.* ◆ **how dare (one).** Used

dare·dev·il (dâr′dĕv′əl) *n.* A person who takes unnecessary risks. —*adj.* Willing to take unnecessary risks; fearless: *The man performed daredevil stunts on his motorcycle.*

dar·ing (dâr′ĭng) *adj.* Willing to take risks; bold: *a daring test pilot.* —*n.* [U] Fearless bravery; boldness: *Climbing the mountain requires great daring.* —**dar′ing·ly** *adv.*

dark (därk) *adj.* **1.** With little or no light: *a dark tunnel.* **2.** A shade of color that is closer to black than it is to white: *dark gray.* **3.** Gloomy; dismal: *a dark view of the future.* **4.** Evil; threatening: *a story full of dark deeds.* —*n.* **1.** [U] Absence of light; darkness: *Many children are afraid of the dark.* **2.** [U] Night or nightfall: *Come home before dark.* **3.** [C] A dark shade or color: *the darks and lights in a photograph.* ◆ **get dark.** To lose light: *It's getting dark now. I hope he gets home soon.* **in the dark.** Not told; uninformed: *We were totally in the dark about the surprise party.* —**dark′ly** *adv.* —**dark′ness** *n.* [U]

SYNONYMS: dark, dim, murky, dusky, shady, shadowy. These adjectives describe the absence of light. **Dark** means not lighted enough to see well: *The room was so dark I thought there had been a blackout.* **Dim** means so dark that the outlines of things cannot be seen clearly: *I stumbled down the dim hallway.* **Murky** means dark in a smoky or foggy way: *It was difficult to see through the murky water.* **Dusky** describes decreasing light, as at twilight: *The children hurried down the dusky streets, trying to get home by dinnertime.* **Shady** describes sthg. sheltered from light, especially sunlight: *We found a shady spot in the park for our picnic.* **Shadowy** often describes blocked light or shifting, mysterious shadows: *My sister shone her flashlight into the shadowy well.* **ANTONYMS:** light, bright.

dark·en (där′kən) *tr. & intr.v.* **1.** To make or become dark or darker: *Clouds darkened the sky. Twilight darkens into night.* **2.** To make or grow gloomy or sad: *News of the defeat darkened their faces. His mood darkened.*

dark horse *n.* **1.** A little-known entrant, as in a horse race. **2.** A person who receives unexpected support and success as a political candidate, especially during a convention.

dark·room (därk′rōōm′ *or* därk′rŏŏm′) *n.* A room in which photographs are developed.

dar·ling (där′lĭng) *n.* **1.** A dearly loved person. **2.** A favorite: *That star was a darling of the theater for years.* —*adj.* **1.** Dearest; beloved: *my darling child.* **2.** *Informal.* Charming; adorable: *The little kittens are darling.*

darn¹ (därn) *tr.v.* To mend (cloth) by sewing a hole closed: *darn socks.* —**darn′er** *n.*

darn² (därn) *interj. Informal.* An expression used to show displeasure or annoyance: *Darn! I forgot my pencil.* —*adj. & adv.* A milder word for damn: *That darn dog ran away again. That soup tastes darn good.*

dart (därt) *v.* —*intr.* To move suddenly and swiftly: *A dog darted across the road.* —*tr.* To shoot out or send (sthg.) forth with a swift sudden movement: *The bear darted a paw at the fish.* —*n.* **1.** A thin object with a sharp point that is thrown at a target by hand or shot from a blowgun, crossbow, or other device. **2. darts.** (*used with a singular or plural verb*). A game in which darts are thrown at a board or other target. **3.** A quick rapid movement: *The cat made a sudden dart at the mouse.*

dash (dăsh) *v.* —*intr.* **1.** To race or rush with sudden speed: *The children dashed down the stairs.* **2.** To strike, knock, or hurl with violent force: *Heavy rain dashed against the windows.* —*tr.* **1.** To throw (sthg.) with sudden force: *The storm dashed the ship against the rocks.* **2.** To break or smash (sthg.) by striking violently: *The angry man dashed the bottle on the floor.* **3.** To destroy (sthg.): *Illness dashed their hopes for a vacation.* —*n.* **1.** A sudden movement; a rush: *We made a dash for shelter from the rainstorm.* **2.** A short footrace: *the 100-meter dash.* **3.** A small amount; a bit: *a dash of salt.* **4.** A punctuation mark (—) used to show a pause, break, or omission or to set off part of a sentence from the rest. **5.** A long sound or signal used in Morse code in combination with the dot and silent intervals to represent letters, numbers, or punctuation. **6.** A dashboard. ◆ **dash off.** *intr.v.* To leave a place very quickly: *I have to dash off; I'm late for work.* —*tr.v.* [sep.] To do or complete (sthg.) quickly: *I dashed off a reply to his letter before lunch.*

dash·board (dăsh′bôrd′) *n.* The panel beneath the windshield in an automobile, containing instruments and controls.

dash·ing (dăsh′ĭng) *adj.* **1.** Brave, bold, and daring: *a dashing hero.* **2.** Showy or stylish: *The band wore dashing uniforms.*

da·ta (dā′tə *or* dăt′ə) *pl.n.* (*used with a singular or plural verb*). **1.** Information, especially when it is to be analyzed or used as the basis for a decision. **2.** Information, usually in numerical form, suitable for processing by computer. **3.** Plural of **datum.**

da·ta·base also **data base** (dā′tə bās′ *or* dăt′ə bās′) *n.* A collection of data arranged for easy and speedy retrieval.

data processing *n.* [U] Sorting, analysis, and other operations performed on data by computers.

date¹ (dāt) *n.* **1.a.** Time stated in terms of

the day, month, and year: *The date of his birthday is April 13, 1987.* **b.** A statement of calendar time: *The date on the coin is 1950.* **2.** A specified day of the month: *What is today's date?* **3.** A point or period of time in history: *At that date radio hadn't been invented.* **4.** An agreement to meet sbdy. at a particular time and place, especially as a social engagement: *We made a date to have lunch on Thursday.* **5.** A person with whom one has a romantic engagement: *I met my date at the restaurant.* —*v.* **dat·ed, dat·ing, dates.** —*tr.* **1.** To mark (sthg.) with a date: *He dated the letter May 1.* **2.** To determine the age, time, or origin of (sthg.): *They dated the rock by studying the fossils in it.* **3.** *Informal.* To go on dates with (sbdy.): *She's been dating him for two months* —*intr.* **1.** To come from a particular time in the past: *This statue dates from about 500 B.C.* **2.** To go on dates: *They dated a lot during vacation.* ◆ **to date.** Up to the present time: *To date, we have received no new information.*

date² (dāt) *n.* **1.** The dark, sweet, one-seeded fruit of the date palm. **2.** The date palm.

dat·ed (dā'tĭd) *adj.* **1.** Marked with a date: *a dated receipt.* **2.** Old and therefore not valid: *The information in the book was dated.* **3.** Old-fashioned: *a dated style.*

date·line (dāt'līn') *n.* A phrase at the beginning of a news story or report that gives its date and place of origin.

da·tum (dā'təm *or* dăt'əm) *n.*, *pl.* **da·ta.** A fact used to draw a conclusion or make a decision.

daub (dôb) *tr.v.* **1.** To cover (sbdy./sthg.) with a soft sticky substance such as clay, plaster, or mud: *He daubed the cracks in the wall with mortar.* **2.** To paint (sthg.) with crude or careless strokes: *He daubed the walls quickly to hide the dirt.* —*n.* **1.** Something daubed on: *A daub of glue will mend the cup.* **2.** A spot of sthg., such as paint: *You have a daub of mustard on your tie.*

daugh·ter (dô'tər) *n.* **1.** A person's female child. **2.** A female descendant. **3.** A woman considered as if in a relationship of child to parent: *She is a daughter of the rebellion.*

daugh·ter-in-law (dô'tər ĭn lô') *n.*, *pl.* **daugh·ters-in-law** (dô'tərz ĭn lô'). The wife of one's son.

daunt (dônt *or* dŏnt) *tr.v. Formal.* To frighten or discourage (sbdy.): *The chance of failure did not daunt the scientist.*

daunt·ing (dônt'tĭng *or* dŏn'tĭng) *adj.* Dangerous or scary; intimidating: *a daunting responsibility.*

daunt·less (dônt'lĭs *or* dŏrt'lĭs) *adj.* Not easily frightened or discouraged; fearless: *a dauntless explorer.* —**daunt'less·ly** *adv.* —**daunt'less·ness** *n.* [U]

dav·en·port (dăv'ən pôrt') *n.* A large sofa.

daw·dle (dôd'l) *intr.v.* **daw·dled, daw·dling, daw·dles.** To take more time than

necessary: *If you dawdle at the restaurant, you'll miss the movie.* ◆ **dawdle away.** *tr.v.* [sep.] To waste (time): *He dawdled away the morning.* —**daw'dler** *n.*

dawn (dôn) *n.* **1.** The time of the first appearance of daylight in the morning: *She gets up at dawn.* **2.** A first appearance of sthg.; a beginning: *the dawn of recorded history.* —*intr.v.* **1.** To begin to grow light in the morning: *We awoke when the day dawned.* **2.** To come into existence; start: *a new age dawned with the first flights to the moon.* ◆ **dawn on.** *tr.v.* [insep.] To begin to be seen by (sbdy.); become clear to: *It suddenly dawned on me that I had left my keys on the desk.*

day (dā) *n.* **1.** The period of light between sunrise and sunset: *a clear sunny day.* **2.** The 24-hour period during which the earth makes one complete rotation on its axis: *It rained for three days without stopping.* **3.** The part of the day devoted to work or study: *They work a seven-hour day; the school day.* **4.** A particular period of time: *before the days of automobiles.* ◆ **call it a day.** *Informal.* **1.** To finish working for the day: *It's 5:30; let's call it a day.* **2.** To give up on sthg.: *You've worked hard in your marriage but you still aren't happy; it's time to call it a day.* **day after day.** For many days in succession: *Day after day they marched across the desert.* **day by day.** Gradually; little by little: *Day by day she regained her self-confidence.* **day in, day out.** Every day without a break: *Feeding a pet must be done day in, day out.* **from day to day.** From one day to the next; constantly: *I never know what you'll do from day to day.* **make (one's) day.** *Informal.* To make one very happy: *The flowers made her day.*

day·break (dā'brāk') *n.* [U] The time each morning when light first appears; dawn: *Farmers often get up before daybreak.*

day·care *or* **day care** (dā'kâr') *n.* [U] Daytime care for children of preschool age, the elderly, or the disabled.

day·dream (dā'drēm') *n.* A pleasant, waking collection of thoughts, often about things one wishes would become reality. —*intr.v.* **day·dreamed** *or* **day·dreamt** (dā'drĕmt'), **day·dream·ing, day·dreams.** To have daydreams: *daydreaming of an expensive vacation on an island.* —**day'dream'er** *n.*

day·light (dā'līt') *n.* [U] **1.** The light of day; sunlight: *We don't have much daylight left, so let's hurry.* **2.** Dawn: *The bus driver is often at work before daylight.* **3.** Daytime: *He stole the car in broad daylight.* ◆ **beat the daylights out of.** *Slang.* To beat sbdy. up severely: *He beat the daylights out of the boy who had teased his sister.* **scare the daylights out of.** *Slang.* To frighten sbdy. severely: *She scared the daylights out of her father when she jumped out of the box.*

day·light-sav·ing time (dā'līt sā'vĭng) *n.* [U] Time during which clocks are set one hour ahead of standard time, providing extra daylight at the end of the working day during spring, summer, and fall.

day·time (dā′tīm′) *n.* [U] The time between sunrise and sunset. —*adj.* Occurring during the day or appropriate to the daytime: *daytime activities; daytime TV.*

day-to-day (dā′tə dā′) *adj.* **1.** Happening every day; daily: *a day-to-day routine.* **2.** Surviving one day at a time with little thought of the future: *The lost mountain climbers were existing on a day-to-day basis.* —*adv.* From one day to the next; daily: *The homeless must live day-to-day.*

daze (dāz) *tr.v.* **dazed, daz·ing, daz·es.** To stun or confuse (sbdy.), as with a blow, shock, or surprise: *The explosion dazed and deafened them.* —*n.* [U] A stunned or confused condition: *The news left us all in a daze.*

dazed (dāzd) *adj.* Unable to think clearly; confused: *The dazed victims were simply glad to be alive.* —**daz′ed·ly** (dā′zĭd lē) *adv.*

daz·zle (dăz′əl) *tr.v.* **daz·zled, daz·zling, daz·zles.** **1.** To make (sbdy.) almost or momentarily blind with too much bright light: *The ranger's searchlight dazzled the eyes of the campers.* **2.** To amaze or impress (sbdy.) with a spectacular display: *The pianist dazzled us with his superb technique.* —*n.* [U] Blinding brightness; glare: *the dazzle of sunlight on the water.*

daz·zling (dăz′lĭng) *adj.* Impressive; exciting: *a dazzling ballet performance.* —**daz′-zling·ly** *adv.*

dB *abbr.* An abbreviation of decibel.

dc or **DC** *abbr.* An abbreviation of direct current.

DC or **D.C.** *abbr.* An abbreviation of District of Columbia.

D.D.S. *abbr.* An abbreviation of Doctor of Dental Surgery.

DDT (dē′dē tē′) *n.* [U] A powerful insecticide that is also poisonous to humans and animals.

DE *abbr.* An abbreviation of Delaware.

de— *pref.* A prefix that means: **1.** Reverse: *decode.* **2.** Remove: *defrost.* **3.** Reduce: *demote.* **4.** Out of: *deplane.*

WORD BUILDING: de— The prefix **de—** means "from, off, apart, away, down, out." It usually indicates reversal, removal, or reduction. Thus **deactivate** means "to make inactive," **decontaminate** means "to remove the contamination in," and **decompress** means "to remove or reduce pressure."

dea·con (dē′kən) *n.* A Protestant layperson who assists the minister. —**dea′con·ess** (dē′kə nĭs) *n.*

de·ac·ti·vate (dē ăk′tə vāt′) *tr.v.* **1.** To

make (sthg.) inactive or ineffective: *deactivate a bomb.* **2.** To remove (sbdy.) from active military duty: *deactivate soldiers in time of peace.*

dead (dĕd) *adj.* **1.** No longer alive or living: *A dead tree cannot grow new leaves.* **2.** Having no life or living things; lifeless: *the dead moon.* **3.** Without feeling; numb: *My cold toes felt dead.* **4.** Not moving or circulating; motionless: *the dead air in a closed room.* **5.a.** No longer in existence, operation, or use: *a dead language.* **b.** No longer active: *a dead volcano.* **c.** Unexciting: *a dead party.* **6.** Out of operation; broken down: *The car is dead.* **7.** Lacking electric power or charge: *a dead battery.* **8.** Weary and worn-out; exhausted: *After finishing work I was dead.* **9.** Complete; absolute: *dead silence; a dead stop.* **10.** Sure; certain: *She's a dead shot who always hits the mark.* **11.** In sports, out of play: *When it crosses the sideline, the ball is dead.* —*n.* [U] **1.** Those who have died; dead people: *The soldiers buried the dead.* **2.** The darkest, quietest, or coldest part: *the dead of night; the dead of winter.* —*adv.* **1.** Completely; absolutely: *You can be dead sure of that.* **2.** Straight; directly: *A huge boulder lay dead ahead.* **3.** Suddenly: *We stopped dead in our tracks.* ♦ **dead meat.** *Slang.* In very serious trouble: *He's dead meat if I catch him taking my car again.* **dead on (one's) feet.** Very tired: *After cleaning the house and doing the laundry I was dead on my feet.* **dead to the world.** Asleep or unconscious: *I went to bed very late and was dead to the world until ten this morning.* **go dead.** To stop working: *The phone suddenly went dead.*

dead·beat (dĕd′bēt′) *n. Slang.* **1.** A person who does not pay debts. **2.** A lazy person; a loafer.

dead·en (dĕd′n) *tr.v.* **1.** To make (sthg.) less sensitive, intense, or strong: *Anesthetics deaden pain.* **2.** To make (sthg.) soundproof: *Rugs helped deaden the sound in the room.*

dead end *n.* **1.** A street, alley, or other passage that is closed or blocked off at one end: *She lives on a dead end.* **2.** A point after which no movement or progress can be made: *We reached a dead end in our argument.*

dead·line (dĕd′līn′) *n.* A set time by which sthg. must be finished; a time limit: *No one could enter the contest after the deadline.*

dead·lock (dĕd′lŏk′) *n.* A standstill that occurs when opposing forces are equally strong and no agreement can be reached: *The negotiations ended in a deadlock.* —*tr. & intr.v.* To bring or come to a deadlock: *The negotiations were deadlocked over a disagreement on salaries. The peace talks deadlocked over treaty terms.*

dead·ly (dĕd′lē) *adj.* **dead·li·er, dead·li·est.** **1.** Dangerous enough to cause death: *a* *deadly weapon.* **2.** Intending to kill or destroy; mortal: *deadly enemies.* **3.** With the appearance of death: *a face with an ashen, deadly look.* **4.** Absolute; complete: *deadly earnestness.* **5.** *Slang.* Very dull and boring: *a deadly play.* —*adv.* **1.** Extremely; utterly: *I'm deadly serious.* **2.** Suggesting death: *deadly pale.* —**dead′li•ness** *n.* [U]

dead•pan (dĕd′păn′) *adj.* Showing no emotion or amusement: *a deadpan expression.*

deaf (dĕf) *adj.* **1.** Not able to hear: *Many deaf people learn to use sign language.* **2. Deaf.** Relating to the Deaf or their culture. **3.** Unwilling to listen: *The principal was deaf to our complaints.* —*n.* [U] *(used with a plural verb).* **1.** Deaf people considered as a group: *a school for the deaf.* **2. Deaf.** The community of deaf people who use American Sign Language as their main means of communication.
♦ **fall on deaf ears.** To not be listened to: *His mother's advice fell on deaf ears.* **turn a deaf ear.** To refuse to listen: *I tried to apologize, but she turned a deaf ear.* —**deaf′ly** *adv.* —**deaf′ness** *n.* [U] —SEE NOTE at **blind.**

deaf•en (dĕf′ən) *tr.v.* To make (sbdy.) deaf: *The loud siren deafened us temporarily.*

deaf-mute also **deaf mute** (dĕf′myoōt′) *n.* *Offensive.* A person who can neither hear nor speak.

deal (dēl) *v.* **dealt** (dĕlt), **deal•ing, deals.** —*intr.* **1.** To buy and sell illegal drugs: *He'd been dealing for years before he was caught.* **2.** To distribute playing cards: *It's your turn to deal.* —*tr.* **1.** To buy and sell (illegal drugs): *They were dealing cocaine and went to jail.* See Synonyms at **distribute. 2.** To give or deliver (sthg.): *The champion dealt the opponent a mighty blow.* **3.** To hand out (cards) to players in a card game: *Deal the cards.* —*n.* **1.** [C] *Informal.* **a.** An agreement, as in business or politics: *We made a deal with our neighbors to buy their car.* **b.** A favorable sale; a bargain: *I got a real deal on a TV.* **2.** [C] A corrupt or secret arrangement: *The inspector made a deal to ignore the building's unsafe condition.* **3.** [U] *Informal.* Treatment received: *a fair deal from the judge.* **4.** [U] **a.** The distribution of playing cards. **b.** A player's turn to deal: *It's your deal.* **c.** A hand of cards dealt: *lose because of a bad deal.* ♦ **a good deal** or **a great deal. 1.** A large amount; a lot: *We learned a great deal from our older sister.* **2.** Much; considerably: *She was a good deal thinner after her illness.* **deal in.** *tr.v.* [insep.] **1.** To do business with (an item); trade: *a salesman who deals in watches.* **2.** [sep.] To include (sbdy.), as in a card game: *Deal me in!* **deal out.** *tr.v.* [sep.] **1.** To give (sthg.) as a share: *We dealt out pencils to the students.* **2.** To exclude (sbdy.), as in a card game: *Deal me out. I don't have time to play another hand.* **deal with.** *tr.v.* [insep.] **1.** To be concerned with or

to involve (sthg.): *This book deals with architecture.* **2.** To behave toward (sbdy.): *The counselor dealt fairly with the students about their absences.* **3.** To take action regarding (sthg.): *deal with an emergency.* **4.** To do business with (sbdy.): *We will never deal with that company again.* **5.** To bear or endure (sthg.): *I can't deal with all this guilt.*

deal•er (dē′lər) *n.* **1.** A person engaged in buying and selling: *a furniture dealer; a drug dealer.* **2.** A person who distributes the playing cards in a game of cards.

deal•ing (dē′lĭng) *n.* **1.** [U] The buying and selling of drugs: *Drug dealing has spread to small towns.* **2.** [U] A way of acting or doing business; conduct toward others: *That store is known for its fair dealing.* **3. dealings.** Agreements or relations with others, especially when involving money or trade: *business dealings.*

dealt (dĕlt) *v.* Past tense and past participle of **deal.**

dean (dēn) *n.* **1.** An official of a college or university in charge of a certain school or faculty: *dean of the medical school.* **2.** An official of a college or high school who counsels students and enforces rules.

dear (dîr) *adj.* **1.** Loved and cherished: *my dear friend.* **2.** Greatly valued; precious: *Her dearest possessions are in the cabinet.* —*adv.* Fondly or affectionately: *memories of old friends held dear to one's heart.* —*n.* A dearly loved person or animal: *the poor dear.* —*interj.* An expression used to show distress or surprise: *Oh dear!*

HOMONYMS: dear, deer (animal).

---

dearly (dîr′lē) *adv.* **1.** With deep feelings: *I love my son dearly.* **2.** Very much: *You will pay dearly for that mistake.*

dearth (dûrth) *n.* *(usually singular).* A lack or scarcity of sthg.: *a dearth of knowledge about distant planets.*

death (dĕth) *n.* **1.** [C; U] The act of dying; the end of life: *She remained busy and active until death.* **2.** [U] The condition of being dead: *Death is nothing to fear.* **3.** [U] A cause of dying: *A fall from that height is certain death.* **4.** [C; U] The ending, destruction, or extinction of sthg.: *the death of ancient customs.* ♦ **put to death.** To kill (sbdy.); execute. **to death.** *Informal.* To an unbearable degree; extremely: *We were bored to death by the long slide show.*

death•bed (dĕth′bĕd′) *n.* A person's last hours of life: *He confessed on his deathbed.*

death•ly (dĕth′lē) *adj.* Characteristic of death: *a deathly appearance.* —*adv.* **1.** In a way that resembles death: *She was deathly pale.* **2.** Very; extremely: *deathly ill; deathly afraid.*

death penalty *n.* [U] The legal taking of a person's life as punishment for a serious crime: *supporters of the death penalty.*

D

death rate *n.* The ratio of total deaths to total population in a certain community over a specified period of time.

death row *n.* [U] The part of a prison where prisoners are kept while waiting to be put to death: *The prisoner has been on death row for four years.*

de•bark (dĭ bärk′) *v.* —*tr.* To unload (sbdy./sthg.), as from a ship; disembark: *debark passengers.* —*intr.* To get off a ship; land: *Tourists debarked at the port.* —**de′-bar•ka′tion** (dē′bär kā′shən) *n.* [U]

de•base (dĭ bās′) *tr.v.* **de•based, de•bas•ing, de•bas•es.** To lower (sbdy./sthg.) in character, quality, or importance: *Don't debase yourself by cheating on a test.* —**de•base′-ment** *n.* [U]

de•bat•a•ble (dĭ bā′tə bəl) *adj.* Open to question, argument, or dispute; doubtful: *an unproven and debatable theory.*

de•bate (dĭ bāt′) *v.* **de•bat•ed, de•bat•ing, de•bates.** —*intr.* **1.** To consider sthg.; try to decide about sthg.: *We debated about which trail to take.* **2.** To present or discuss arguments for and against sthg.: *We debated about the fairness of the school's rules.* —*tr.* **1.** To consider (sthg.); try to decide: *I debated what to do next.* **2.** To discuss or argue about (sthg.): *We debated the issue of states' rights.* —*n.* **1.** A discussion of the arguments for and against sthg.: *the debate about changing the health care system.* **2.** A formal contest in which opponents argue for opposite sides of an issue: *The political candidates held a debate.* —**de•bat′er** *n.*

de•bauch•er•y (dĭ bô′chə rē) *n., pl.* **de•bauch•er•ies.** Too much eating, drinking, and other sensual pleasures: *a night of debauchery.*

de•bil•i•tate (dĭ bĭl′ĭ tāt′) *tr.v.* **de•bil•i•tat•ed, de•bil•i•tat•ing, de•bil•i•tates.** To weaken (sbdy./sthg.): *A long illness usually debilitates a person.* —**de•bil′i•tat′ing** *adj.* —**de•bil′i•ta′tion** *n.* [U]

de•bil•i•ty (dĭ bĭl′ĭ tē) *n., pl.* **de•bil•i•ties.** [C; U] The condition of extreme bodily weakness.

deb•it (dĕb′ĭt) *n.* **1.** A debt charged to and recorded in an account. **2.** The side of an account book showing such debt. —*tr.v.* To charge (an account) with a debt: *The bank debited my account for the checks I wrote.*

deb•o•nair also **deb•o•naire** (dĕb′ə nâr′) *adj.* Gracious and charming in a cheerful, carefree way: *The tall debonair professor was very popular.* —**deb′o•nair′ly** *adv.* —**deb′o•nair′ness** *n.* [U]

de•brief (dē brēf′) *tr.v.* To question (sbdy.) in order to obtain knowledge, especially knowledge gathered on a mission: *The astro-*nauts were debriefed after returning from their flight.*

de•bris (də brē′ *or* dā′brē′) *n.* [U] The remains of sthg. broken, destroyed, or discarded: *Debris from the storm was spread all over the beach.*

debt (dĕt) *n.* [C; U] Something, such as money, that is owed by a person: *I will pay my debts as soon as I get paid. The people owe a great debt of thanks to soldiers of their country.* ◆ **in debt.** Owing sthg.; under obligation: *They are in debt to the bank for their loan.* **out of debt.** Owing nothing: *After I pay this money to the bank, I will be out of debt.*

debt•or (dĕt′ər) *n.* A person who owes sthg.

de•bug (dē bŭg′) *tr.v.* **de•bugged, de•bug•ging, de•bugs.** To search for and fix errors in (a computer program).

de•bunk (dē bŭngk′) *tr.v.* To show that (sthg.) is false or exaggerated: *It took centuries to debunk the theory that the sun revolves around the earth.*

de•but also **dé•but** (dā byōō′ *or* dā′byōō′) *n.* **1.** The first public appearance: *a new actor's stage debut; the debut of a new line of computers.* **2.** The formal presentation of a young woman into society. —*intr.v.* To make a first public appearance: *The movie debuted on Friday.*

deb•u•tante (dĕb′yōō tänt′) *n.* A young woman making a debut into society.

Dec. or **Dec** *abbr.* An abbreviation of December.

deca— *pref.* A prefix that means ten: *decaliter.*

dec•ade (dĕk′ād′) *n.* A period of ten years.

dec•a•dence (dĕk′ə dəns) *n.* [U] A condition or period of decay or decline, as in morals or art.

dec•a•dent (dĕk′ə dənt) *adj.* Having low moral standards; decaying: *a decadent society with a high crime rate.* —**dec′a•dent•ly** *adv.*

de•caf (dē′kăf′) *n.* [C; U] Decaffeinated coffee or tea: *I'll take a decaf, please.*

de•caf•fein•at•ed (dē kăf′ə nā′tĭd) *adj.* With most of the caffeine removed: *decaffeinated coffee.*

dec•a•gon (dĕk′ə gŏn′) *n.* A flat geometric shape with ten sides.

de•cal (dē′kăl′ *or* dĭ kăl′) *n.* A picture or design printed on adhesive material that can be transferred to another surface such as glass, metal, or plastic.

dec•a•li•ter (dĕk′ə lē′tər) *n.* A unit of volume equal to ten liters.

de•cant•er (dĭ kăn′tər) *n.* A decorative glass bottle with a stopper, used for holding liquids such as wine.

de•cap•i•tate (dĭ kăp′ĭ tāt′) *tr.v.* **de•**

cap·i·tat·ed, de·cap·i·tat·ing, de·cap·i·tates. To cut off the head of (a person or an animal); behead. —**de·cap′i·ta′tion** n. [C; U]

de·cath·lon (dǐ kǎth′lən or dǐ kǎth′lǒn′) n. An athletic contest in which each contestant participates in ten different track-and-field events. The contestant scoring the most total points for all events is the winner.

de·cay (dǐ kā′) v. —intr. **1.** To rot or become rotten; decompose: Dead trees gradually decay. **2.** To fall into ruin: Why did this ancient civilization decay? —tr. To cause (sthg.) to decay: Fungus will decay wood. —n. [U] **1.** The act of rotting: tooth decay; decay of old buildings through neglect. **2.** A deterioration or decline, as in health or strength: the decay of physical fitness after an injury.

de·ceased (dǐ sēst′) adj. No longer living; dead: my deceased grandparents. —n., pl. **deceased.** A dead person or persons: We spoke with members of the deceased's family. The deceased are remembered in our prayers.

de·ceit (dǐ sēt′) n. **1.** [U] The act of deceiving; deception: A successful spy is an expert in deceit. **2.** [C] A trick used to deceive sbdy. else: an unfaithful friend's many deceits. **3.** [U] The quality of being deceitful: a swindler full of deceit. —**de·ceit′ful** adj —**de·ceit′ful·ly** adv. —**de·ceit′ful·ness** n. [U]

de·ceive (dǐ sēv′) tr.v. **de·ceived, de·ceiv·ing, de·ceives.** To make (sbdy.) believe sthg. that is not true; trick: The fox ran back on its own trail to deceive the pursuing dogs. Why would he deceive us instead of being honest? —**de·ceiv′er** n.

de·cel·er·ate (dē sěl′ə rāt′) v. **de·cel·er·at·ed, de·cel·er·at·ing, de·cel·er·ates.** —tr. To decrease the speed or rate of (sthg.): The driver decelerated the car by putting on the brakes. —intr. To decrease in speed; slow down: The train decelerated slowly. —**de·cel′er·a′tion** n [C; U] —**de·cel′er·a′tor** n.

De·cem·ber (dǐ sěm′bər) n. The 12th month of the year, with 31 days.

de·cen·cy (dē′sən sē) n., pl. **de·cen·cies. 1.** [U] The condition of being decent: the decency to act in an honest and proper manner. **2. decencies. a.** Decent or proper acts; correct observances: the social decencies such as courtesy and good manners. **b.** The things needed for a respectable and proper way of living: A refrigerator is one of the decencies of life in a developed nation.

de·cent (dē′sənt) adj. **1.** Following the rules and conventions of society: Decent people obey the law. **2.** Kind; considerate: It was very decent of you to help in time of trouble. **3.** Adequate; passable: a decent salary. **4.** Informal. Properly or modestly dressed: Parents want their children to look decent when they go to school. —**de′cent·ly** adv.

de·cen·tral·ize (dē sěn′trə līz′) tr.v. **de·cen·tral·ized, de·cen·tral·iz·ing, de·cen·tral·iz·es. 1.** To distribute the functions or powers of (a government or central authority) among several local authorities. **2.** To reorganize (sthg.) into smaller units of operation: decentralize a school system. —**de·cen′tral·i·za′tion** (dē sěn′trə lǐ zā′shən) n. [U]

de·cep·tion (dǐ sěp′shən) n. **1.** [U] The use of deceit: False advertising is a form of deception. **2.** [C] Something that deceives, as a trick or lie: Her deception shocked her classmates because they had always trusted her.

de·cep·tive (dǐ sěp′tǐv) adj. Dishonest; designed to hide the truth: the deceptive calm before the storm. —**de·cep′tive·ly** adv. —**de·cep′tive·ness** n. [U]

deci– pref. A prefix that means one tenth: deciliter.

de·ci·bel (děs′ə bəl or děs′ə běl′) n. A unit used in measuring the loudness of sounds: The speaking voice of most people ranges from 45 to 75 decibels.

de·cide (dǐ sīd′) v. **de·cid·ed, de·cid·ing, de·cides.** —tr. **1.** To bring (sthg.) to a conclusion by resolving a conflict: The court decided the case. **2.** To influence or determine the outcome of (sthg.): A single goal decided the game. —intr. **1.** To make up one's mind: We decided to go to the movies. **2.** To give a judgment: The judge decided against the defendant.

de·cid·ed (dǐ sī′dǐd) adj. Definite; undoubted: a decided advantage. —**de·cid′ed·ly** adv.

de·cid·u·ous (dǐ sǐj′ōō əs) adj. Losing leaves at the end of the growing season: Maples and oaks are deciduous trees.

dec·i·li·ter (děs′ə lē′tər) n. A unit of volume equal to one tenth (10^{-1}) of a liter.

dec·i·mal (děs′ə məl) n. A number containing a decimal fraction, such as 66.03 or .099. —adj. Based on 10; proceeding by tens: The system of decimal notation is an invention of mathematicians in India.

decimal fraction n. A fraction in which the denominator is 10 or a power of 10. Expressed as decimal fractions, $^{29}/_{100}$ is .29, and $^{29}/_{1000}$ is .029.

decimal place n. The position of a digit in a decimal fraction. In .079, for example, 0 is in the first decimal place, 7 is in the second decimal place, and 9 is in the third decimal place.

decimal point n. A period placed to the left of a decimal fraction and used in decimals to separate whole numbers from fractions. For example, 1.3 represents $1 + ^3/_{10}$.

decimal system n. [U] A number system based on units of 10.

dec·i·mate (děs′ə māt′) tr.v. **dec·i·mat·ed, dec·i·mat·ing, dec·i·mates.** To destroy or kill a large part of (a population): The hurricane decimated the bird population of the small island. —**dec′i·ma′tion** n. [U]

dec·i·me·ter (dĕs′ə mē′tər) *n.* A unit of length equal to one tenth (10⁻¹) of a meter.

de·ci·pher (dĭ sī′fər) *tr.v.* **1.** To change (a message) from a code to ordinary language; decode: *Telegraph operators must be able to decipher dots and dashes.* **2.** To read or interpret (sthg. hard to understand or illegible): *I can't decipher your handwriting.* —**de·ci′·pher·a·ble** *adj.*

de·ci·sion (dĭ sĭzh′ən) *n.* **1.** The act of deciding: *Our friends have not come to a decision about going on the trip with us.* **2.** A conclusion or judgment: *The judge handed down a decision of not guilty.*

decision-mak·ing (dĭ sĭzh′ən mā′kĭng) *n.* [U] The action of deciding or the ability to make decisions: *He leaves most of the decision-making to his wife.*

de·ci·sive (dĭ sī′sĭv) *adj.* **1.** Able to make decisions quickly and confidently: *A police officer should be a decisive person.* **2.a.** Having the power to settle sthg.; conclusive: *a decisive argument.* **b.** Without doubt; unmistakable: *a decisive victory.* —**de·ci′·sive·ly** *adv.* —**de·ci′sive·ness** *n.* [U]

deck¹ (dĕk) *n.* **1.** A platform extending from one side of a ship to the other. **2.** A platform like the deck of a ship: *a deck on the side of the house.* **3.** A pack of playing cards: *shuffle the deck and deal.* **4.** A tape deck. —*tr.v.* *Informal.* To knock (sbdy.) down with force: *The fighter decked his opponent.* ♦ **on deck.** **1.** On hand; present: *Be on deck an hour before we leave.* **2.** Waiting to take one's turn, especially as a batter in baseball.

deck² (dĕk) *tr.v.* To decorate (sthg.): *decking the halls for the holidays.* ♦ **deck out.** *tr.v.* [sep.] To put fine clothes on (sbdy.) or decorate (sthg.): *She decked herself out for the party. The house is decked out for the party.*

dec·la·ra·tion (dĕk′lə rā′shən) *n.* **1.** The act of stating sthg.: *a declaration of love.* **2.** A formal statement or announcement: *the declaration of one's candidacy for political office.* **3.** A document listing goods that are taxable or subject to duty: *Travelers made out declarations before going through customs.*

de·clar·a·tive (dĭ klâr′ə tĭv *or* dĭ klăr′ə tĭv) *adj.* Making a statement, as opposed to a question or an order: *a declarative sentence such as "I'm going home."*

de·clare (dĭ klâr′) *tr.v.* **de·clared, de·clar·ing, de·clares.** **1.** To state (sthg.) with emphasis; affirm: *The teacher declared the exam would be postponed.* **2.** To state (sthg.) officially or formally: *Congress has the power to declare new national holidays.* **3.** To list (goods) when entering a country at customs: *You need to declare expensive gifts before entering the country.*

de·cline (dĭ klīn′) *v.* **de·clined, de·clin·ing, de·clines.** —*tr.* To refuse (sthg.) politely: *They declined my offer to help.* See Synonyms at **refuse¹.** —*intr.* **1.** To refuse politely to do or accept sthg.: *I asked them home for a snack, but they declined.* **2.** To decrease in strength, value, or importance: *Her health declined until she saw the doctor. Prices tend to decline when business is poor.* —*n.* [C; U] **1.** A decrease in strength or importance; decay: *The country was in a period of decline.* **2.** A change to a lower level or state, as in value: *a decline in prices.*

de·code (dē kōd′) *tr.v.* **de·cod·ed, de·cod·ing, de·codes.** To change (information) from a code into ordinary language; decipher: *decode the military communication.* —**de·cod′er** *n.*

de·com·pose (dē′kəm pōz′) *v.* **de·com·posed, de·com·pos·ing, de·com·pos·es.** —*tr.* To cause (sthg.) to rot: *Water decomposed the dead plants.* —*intr.* To decay; rot: *Flowers decompose easily.* —**de·com′po·si′tion** (dē kŏm′pə zĭsh′ən) *n.*

de·com·press (dē′kəm prĕs′) *intr.v.* To return gradually to normal atmospheric pressure: *Scuba divers decompress by swimming to the ocean surface.* —**de′com·pres′sion** *n.* [U]

de·con·ges·tant (dē′kən jĕs′tənt) *n.* A medication that eliminates or reduces congestion in the nose or bronchial passages.

de·con·tam·i·nate (dē′kən tăm′ə nāt′) *tr.v.* **de·con·tam·i·nat·ed, de·con·tam·i·nat·ing, de·con·tam·i·nates.** To remove harmful substances, such as bacteria, poisonous chemicals, or radioactive materials, from (sthg.): *After the oil spill, the entire coast had to be decontaminated.* —**de′con·tam′i·na′tion** *n.* [U]

de·con·trol (dē′kən trōl′) *tr.v.* **de·con·trolled, de·con·trol·ling, de·con·trols.** To free (sthg.) from control, especially from government control: *The government decontrolled the telephone company, opening the market to competition.*

de·cor (dā kôr′ *or* dā′kôr′) *n.* [C; U] The style of a room, home, restaurant, or other area: *Her new house has very modern decor.*

dec·o·rate (dĕk′ə rāt′) *tr.v.* **dec·o·rat·ed, dec·o·rat·ing, dec·o·rates.** **1.** To furnish (an area) with sthg. attractive or beautiful; adorn: *The students decorated the auditorium with flowers for graduation.* **2.** To paint, paper, or select and organize the furnishings of (a room, house, or other area): *They decorated the hall in a soft green color.* **3.** To give a medal or other honor to (sbdy.): *The chief decorated the firefighter for bravery.* —**dec′o·ra·tive** (dĕk′ər ə tĭv *or* dĕk′ə-rā′tĭv) *adj.* —**dec′o·ra·tive·ly** *adv.* —**dec′-o·ra′tor** *n.*

dec·o·ra·tion (dĕk′ə rā′shən) *n.* **1.** [U] The act of decorating sthg.: *Decoration of the auditorium for graduation took most of the morning.* **2.** [C] Something that adorns or beautifies; an ornament: *We put up wreaths, streamers, and other decorations.* **3.** [C] A medal, badge, or ribbon awarded as an honor: *The police officer received a decoration for bravery.*

dec·o·rous (dĕk′ər əs *or* dĭ kôr′əs) *adj.* Characterized by proper behavior: *decorous manners.* —**dec′o·rous·ness** *n.* [U]

de·co·rum (dĭ kôr′əm) *n.* [U] Proper behavior: *Conduct yourself with decorum.*

de·coy (dē′koi′ *or* dĭ koi′) *n.* **1.** A person or thing used to lead another into danger or a trap: *The police officer was dressed like a tourist to act as a decoy to catch pickpockets.* **2.** A model of a duck or other bird, used by hunters to attract wild birds

de·crease (dĭ krēs′) *tr. & intr.v.* **de·creased, de·creas·ing, de·creas·es.** To make or become gradually less or smaller; diminish: *We must decrease spending to conserve our money. Oil supplies decreased during the winter.* —*n.* (dē′krēs′). **1.** [C] The act of decreasing; a decline: *A decrease in sales forced the owners to close the store.* **2.** [U] The amount by which sthg. becomes less or smaller: *a decrease in the price of gasoline of five cents a gallon.*

SYNONYMS: decrease, lessen, reduce, diminish, dwindle. These verbs mean to become or cause to become smaller or less. **Decrease** and **lessen** both mean to become smaller or less at a steady, gradual rate: *City traffic decreases on holidays. My appetite lessens as the weather gets warmer.* **Reduce** means to bring down, as in size, degree, or strength: *Maybe you should reduce the amount of sugar in the cake recipe.* **Diminish** means to decrease by taking away sthg.: *Each new scandal diminishes our respect for the senator.* **Dwindle** means to decrease gradually until no more or almost no more is left: *Their savings dwindled over the years.* **ANTONYM: increase.**

---

de·cree (dĭ krē′) *n.* An official order: *The falsely accused prisoner was released by court decree.* —*tr.v.* **de·creed, de·cree·ing, de·crees.** To order or decide (sthg.) by decree: *The governor decreed a state holiday.*

de·crep·it (dĭ krĕp′ĭt) *adj.* Weakened, worn-out, or broken down because of old age or long use: *a decrepit old car.* —**de·crep′it·ly** *adv.*

de·crim·i·nal·ize (dē krĭm′ə nə līz′) *tr.v.* **de·crim·i·nal·ized, de·crim·i·nal·iz·ing, de·crim·i·nal·iz·es.** To remove the legal penalties for doing or possessing (sthg.): *Gambling was decriminalized in many states.*

de·cry (dĭ krī′) *tr.v.* **de·cried, de·cry·ing,**

de·cries. To disapprove of (sbdy./sthg.) strongly: *The judge decried the criminal's behavior.*

ded·i·cate (dĕd′ĭ kāt′) *tr.v.* **ded·i·cat·ed, ded·i·cat·ing, ded·i·cates.** **1.** To set (sthg.) apart for a special purpose: *This park is dedicated to the soldiers of World War I.* **2.** To give or commit (oneself) fully to sthg.; devote: *Nurses dedicate their lives to the care of the sick.* **3.** To address or inscribe (a book, performance, or other creative work) to sbdy. as a mark of respect or affection: *The writer dedicated her book to an old friend.*

ded·i·cat·ed (dĕd′ĭ kā′tĭd) *adj.* Strongly committed to sthg.: *We need dedicated teachers in our schools.*

ded·i·ca·tion (dĕd′ĭ kā′shən) *n.* **1.** [U] The act of dedicating or the state of being dedicated: *her dedication to helping others.* **2.** [C] A ceremony dedicating sthg.: *We went to the dedication of the new library.* **3.** [C] A note in a book or other creative work dedicating it to sbdy.: *He included a dedication to his father in his book.*

de·duce (dĭ dōōs′) *tr.v.* **de·duced, de·duc·ing, de·duc·es.** To reach (a conclusion) by reasoning, especially from a general principle: *The engineers deduced from the laws of physics that the new airplane would fly.*

de·duct (dĭ dŭkt′) *tr.v.* To take away (a quantity from another); subtract: *The dealer deducted the amount of our earlier deposit from the final payment for the car.*

de·duct·i·ble (dĭ dŭk′tə bəl) *n.* [C; U] An amount that an owner of an insurance policy must pay on a claim before the insurance company begins to pay: *I have a $200 deductible on my health insurance.* —*adj.* Capable of being deducted, especially from one's taxable income.

de·duc·tion (dĭ dŭk′shən) *n.* **1.** [C] An amount that is deducted: *a deduction from one's taxable income for medical expenses.* **2.a.** [U] The process of reaching a conclusion by reasoning, especially from general principles: *the judge's deduction that the law violated the Constitution.* **b.** [C] A conclusion reached by this process: *a brilliant deduction.*

de·duc·tive (dĭ dŭk′tĭv) *adj.* Involving logical deduction: *deductive reasoning.* —**de·duc′-tive·ly** *adv.*

deed (dēd) *n.* **1.** An act or action: *Returning the lost money was a good deed.* **2.** A legal document showing ownership of property: *the deed for the land.* —*tr.v.* To transfer or give (property) by means of a deed: *The government deeded land to the miners.*

dee·jay (dē′jā′) *n. Informal.* A disc jockey.

deem (dēm) *tr.v. Formal.* To judge, consider, or believe (sthg.): *The doctor deemed it important for me to get more exercise.*

deep (dēp) *adj.* **1.** Extending far down below a surface: *a deep hole in the earth.* **2.**

Extending from front to rear, or from the outside to the inside: *a deep closet.* **3.** Extending a specified distance in a given direction: *snow three feet deep.* **4.** Far down or in: *The campers were deep in the woods.* **5.** Extreme; intense: *a deep silence; a deep sleep.* **6.** Very much absorbed or involved: *She was deep in thought.* **7.** Showing much thought or feeling; strongly felt: *a deep understanding; a deep love of books.* **8.** Rich and vivid in shade of color: *a deep red.* **9.** Low in pitch: *a deep voice.* —*adv.* **1.** To a great depth: *dig deep into the earth.* **2.** Well along in time; late: *The students worked deep into the night.* —*n.* [U] **1.** A deep place, such as the ocean or a place in the ocean: *We know little of life in the deep.* **2.** The most intense or extreme part: *the deep of night.* ◆ **go off the deep end.** To do sthg. extreme: *He went off the deep end when he gave away all his furniture.* **in deep water.** In serious trouble: *She's in deep water because of her grades.* —**deep′ly** *adv.* —**deep′ness** *n.* [U]

deep•en (dē′pən) *tr. & intr.v.* To make or become deep or deeper: *More digging slowly deepened the hole. Floodwaters deepened as the rain continued.*

deep-fried *adj.* Cooked in very hot oil: *deep-fried shrimp.* —**deep′-fry′** *v.*

deep-root•ed (dēp′roo̅′tĭd *or* dēp′root′ĭd) *adj.* **1.** Firmly implanted below the surface: *a deep-rooted oak tree.* **2.** Firmly fixed; deep-seated: *deep-rooted beliefs.*

deep-seat•ed (dēp′sē′tĭd) *adj.* **1.** Deeply implanted below the surface: *a deep-seated infection.* **2.** Firmly fixed; deeply rooted: *We've struggled with a deep-seated problem for many years.*

deer (dîr) *n., pl.* **deer.** A hoofed mammal, such as the elk or the white-tailed deer; the males usually have antlers.

deer

Homonyms: deer, dear (loved one).

---

de•face (dĭ fās′) *tr.v.* **de•faced, de•fac•ing, de•fac•es.** To damage the surface or appearance of (sthg.); disfigure: *deface a wall with graffiti.* —**de•face′ment** *n.* [U]

def•a•ma•tion (dĕf′ə mā′shən) *n.* [U] The act of damaging a person's reputation by saying sthg. that is not true; slander or libel: *defamation of a person's character.* —**de•fam′a•to′ry** (dĭ făm′ə tôr′ē) *adj.*

de•fame (dĭ fām′) *tr.v.* **de•famed, de•fam•ing, de•fames.** To attack or damage the reputation of (sbdy.) with lies: *He defamed her by spreading false rumors about her behavior.*

de•fault (dĭ fôlt′) *n.* [U] **1.** A failure to do what is required, especially a failure to pay a debt: *The company is guilty of default on its loans.* **2.** A setting used by a computer unless the user chooses a different setting. —*intr.v.* **1.** To fail to do what is required: *default on a business contract.* **2.** To fail to pay money when it is due: *default on a loan.* **3.** To lose a contest by failing to participate in or complete it: *Illness caused the tennis star to default in the match.* ◆ **by default.** Because sbdy. else failed to do what is required: *The other team didn't show up, so we won by default.*

de•feat (dĭ fēt′) *tr.v.* **1.** To win victory over (sbdy./sthg.); beat: *The mayor defeated all opponents in the last election.* **2.** To prevent the success of (sbdy./sthg.): *A misunderstanding defeated our efforts at a compromise.* —*n.* **1.** [C] The act of defeating or the state of being defeated: *The veto was a defeat of the new environmental measures.* **2.** [U] Failure to win: *We had to admit defeat.*

de•feat•ism (dĭ fē′tĭz′əm) *n.* [U] Acceptance of the idea of defeat: *Defeatism can prevent success.* —**de•feat′ist** *n.*

def•e•cate (dĕf′ĭ kāt′) *intr.v.* **def•e•cat•ed, def•e•cat•ing, def•e•cates.** To empty the bowels of waste matter. —**def′-e•ca′tion** *n.* [U]

de•fect (dē′fĕkt′ *or* dĭ fĕkt′) *n.* An imperfection; a flaw: *A defect in the engine caused an explosion.* —*intr.v.* (dĭ fĕkt′). **1.** To leave one's country and take up residence in another, especially for political reasons: *a pilot who defected.* **2.** To abandon a position or an association, often to join an opposing group: *The American general Benedict Arnold defected to the British side.* —**de•fec′tion, de•fec′tor** *n.*

de•fec•tive (dĭ fĕk′tĭv) *adj.* Having a defect or flaw; faulty: *The defective clock never kept time well.* —**de•fec′tive•ly** *adv.*

de•fence (dĭ fĕns′) *n.* Chiefly British. Variant of **defense.**

de•fend (dĭ fĕnd′) *tr.v.* **1.** To make or keep (sbdy./sthg.) safe from attack or harm; guard: *The ants defended their colony against the invading predators.* **2.** To support or maintain (sbdy./sthg.), as by argument; justify: *The scientist defended the theory that germs cause disease.* **3.** To represent (a defendant) in a court of law: *the right to be defended by a lawyer.* —**de•fend′er** *n.*

Synonyms: defend, protect, guard, preserve, shield. These verbs mean to make or keep safe from danger, attack, or harm. **Defend** suggests taking measures to drive back an attack: *A small army was formed to defend the island against invasion.* **Protect** suggests providing

---

some kind of cover for safety or comfort: *Wear a seat belt to protect yourself in case of an accident.* **Guard** means to keep watch over sthg.: *The family bought three big dogs to guard the house.* **Preserve** means to act to keep sthg. safe: *Ecologists work to preserve the rain forests.* **Shield** means to protect the way armor would by standing in between the threat and the threatened: *The suspect's lawyers tried to shield him from the angry reporters.*

---

de•fen•dant (dǐ fĕn′dənt) *n.* A person who is accused of doing sthg. illegal and is taken to court.

de•fense (dǐ fĕns′) *n.* **1.** [U] The act of defending (sbdy./sthg.) against attack, harm, or danger: *The patriots fought in defense of their freedom.* **2.** [C; U] **a.** A method of defending or protecting sthg.: *A heavy coat is a good defense against the cold.* **b.** An argument in support or justification of sthg.: *The newspaper article is a strong defense for freedom of the press.* **3.** [U] **a.** The response of a defendant in opposition to a complaint. **b.** The defendant and his or her legal counsel. **4.** [C; U] In sports, the team or those players on the team attempting to keep the opposition from scoring.

de•fense•less (dǐ fĕns′lĭs) *adj.* Having no defense; unprotected: *a defenseless infant.*

de•fen•si•ble (dǐ fĕn′sə bəl) *adj.* Capable of being defended, protected, or justified: *Blaming others for one's mistakes is not a defensible position.*

de•fen•sive (dǐ fĕn′sǐv) *adj.* **1.** Intended for defense: *a defensive moat surrounding the castle.* **2.** Intended to protect against aggression or attack: *a defensive attitude.* **3.** Relating to defense in sports: *That was a great defensive play!* —*n.* [U] A means of defense. ♦ **on the defensive.** Prepared to protect sbdy./sthg. against aggression or attack. —**de•fen′sive•ly** *adv.* —**de•fen′sive•ness** *n.* [U]

de•fer (dǐ fûr′) *tr.v.* **de•ferred, de•fer•ring, de•fers. 1.** To put off (sthg.); postpone: *Let's defer going until we know what the weather will be.* **2.** To submit to the wishes, opinion, or decision of (sbdy.), as through recognition of authority or knowledge: *Let's defer to an expert on that matter.* —**de•fer′ra•ble** *adj.* —**de•fer′ral** *n.*

def•er•ence (dĕf′ər əns *or* dĕf′rəns) *n.* [U] **1.** Yielding to the opinion, wishes, or judgment of another. **2.** Courteous respect: *The guests showed deference to their host by standing until he was seated.* —**def′er•en′tial** (dĕf′ə rĕn′shəl) *adj.* —**def′er•en′tial•ly** *adv.*

de•fer•ment (dǐ fûr′mənt) *n.* [C; U] The act of delaying or putting off sthg.: *the deferment of payments on a loan.*

de•fi•ance (dǐ fī′əns) *n.* [U] The act of defy-

ing; resistance to an opposing force or authority: *shook their fists in a gesture of defiance.* ♦ **in defiance of.** In spite of; contrary to: *We went on the picnic in defiance of bad weather forecasts.*

de•fi•ant (dǐ fī′ənt) *adj.* Showing defiance; boldly resisting: *The rebels took a defiant stance.* —**de•fi′ant•ly** *adv.*

de•fi•cien•cy (dǐ fĭsh′ən sē) *n., pl.* **de•fi•cien•cies.** [C; U] **1.** The quality of being deficient. **2.** A lack or shortage, especially of sthg. essential to health: *A vitamin deficiency made the patient weak.*

de•fi•cient (dǐ fĭsh′ənt) *adj.* **1.** Without an essential quality or element: *a deficient diet.* **2.** Not enough; insufficient: *a deficient education.*

def•i•cit (dĕf′ĭ sĭt) *n.* The amount by which a sum of money is less than the required or expected amount; a shortage: *The deficit in the club's funds was caused by spending too much money on parties.*

de•file (dǐ fīl′) *tr.v.* **de•filed, de•fil•ing, de•files. 1.** To make (sthg.) dirty; pollute: *Sewage seeping into the lake defiled the water.* **2.** To spoil the sacredness or purity of (sthg.): *The invaders defiled the temple.* —**de•file′ment** *n.* [U]

de•fine (dǐ fīn′) *tr.v.* **de•fined, de•fin•ing, de•fines. 1.** To state the exact meaning of (a word or phrase, for example): *Dictionaries define words.* **2.** To make a clear outline of (sthg.): *The hills were defined against the bright morning sky.* **3.** To describe (sthg.); specify clearly: *The Constitution defines the powers of the President.*

def•i•nite (dĕf′ə nĭt) *adj.* **1.** Certain: *It's still not definite whether they are going.* **2.** Having specific limits: *definite restrictions on using the credit cards.* **3.** Clearly defined; precise and exact: *a definite plan; a definite time.* —**def′i•nite•ly** *adv.* —**def′i•nite•ness** *n.* [U]

definite article *n.* A word used to introduce and refer to a particular noun or noun phrase. In English *the* is the definite article. —SEE NOTE at **article.**

def•i•ni•tion (dĕf′ə nĭsh′ən) *n.* **1.** [C] A statement that explains the meaning of sthg., such as a word or phrase, as in a dictionary entry. **2.** [U] The act of making (sthg.) clear and distinct: *a definition of one's purposes.*

de•fin•i•tive (dǐ fĭn′ĭ tĭv) *adj.* **1.** Clear and conclusive: *a definitive answer; a definitive victory.* **2.** Authoritative and complete: *a definitive biography based on diaries and personal papers.* —**de•fin′i•tive•ly** *adv.* —**de•fin′i•tive•ness** *n.* [U]

de•flate (dǐ flāt′) *v.* **de•flat•ed, de•flat•ing, de•flates.** —*tr.* **1.** To release air or gas from (sthg.): *A pin deflated the balloon.* **2.** To reduce the size or importance of (sthg.): *The crowd's jeers soon deflated the speaker's con-*

fidence. **3.** To reduce the amount or availability of (currency or credit), causing a decline in prices. —*intr.* To lose air: *As the tire deflated, we pulled off to the side of the road.* —**de·fla′tion** *n.* [U]

de·flect (dǐ flěkt′) *intr. & tr.v.* **1.** To turn aside or cause to turn aside: *A sunbeam deflected as it struck the window. Constant interruptions deflected the speaker's thoughts from his main purpose.* **2.** To change direction or cause to change direction: *The ball deflected off the wall. The vest she wore deflected the bullet.* —**de·flec′tion, de·flec′tor** *n.*

de·fo·li·ant (dē fō′lē ənt) *n.* A chemical applied to plants to make their leaves fall off, such as a chemical that is used to control weeds in farming.

de·fo·li·ate (dē fō′lē āt′) *tr.v.* **de·fo·li·at·ed, de·fo·li·at·ing, de·fo·li·ates.** To cause the leaves of (a plant or tree, for example) to fall off, especially by the use of a chemical. —**de·fo′li·a′tion** *n.* [U]

de·for·est (dē fôr′ĭst *or* dē fŏr′ĭst) *tr.v.* To cut down and clear away the trees or forests from (the land). —**de·for′es·ta′tion** *n.* [U]

de·form (dǐ fôrm′) *tr.v.* **1.** To spoil the natural form of (sthg.); misshape: *The heat of the fire deformed the candles.* **2.** To spoil the beauty or appearance of (sthg.); disfigure.

de·for·ma·tion (dē′fôr mā′shən *or* dĕf′ər mā′shən) *n.* **1.** [C] The act or process of deforming: *the deformation of plastic by heat.* **2.** [U] The condition of being deformed. **3.** [C] A change in form for the worse: *deformations in plants caused by harsh weather.*

de·formed (dǐ fôrmd′) *adj.* Misshapen or distorted in form.

de·for·mi·ty (dǐ fôr′mǐ tē) *n., pl.* **de·for·mi·ties.** **1.** [C; U] A condition of being improperly formed. **2.** [C] A deformed person or thing.

de·fraud (dǐ frôd′) *tr.v.* To take sthg. from (sbdy.) by dishonest methods; swindle: *The developer defrauded people by selling them worthless land.*

de·fray (dǐ frā′) *tr.v.* To make the payment of (a cost or an expense): *Contributions will defray the cost of a new library.*

de·frost (dē frôst′ *or* dē frŏst′) *v.* —*tr.* **1.** To remove ice or frost from (sthg.): *defrost the refrigerator by turning it off.* **2.** To cause (sthg.) to thaw: *defrost the pork chops.* —*intr.* **1.** To become free of ice or frost: *a refrigerator that defrosts quickly.* **2.** To become thawed: *The chicken defrosted in less than an hour.*

de·frost·er (dē frô′stər *or* dē frŏs′tər) *n.* A heating device that removes frost from sthg., as a car windshield.

deft (dĕft) *adj.* Quick and skillful: *the deft hands of a good surgeon.* —**deft′ly** *adv.* —**deft′ness** *n.* [U]

de·funct (dǐ fŭngkt′) *adj.* No longer in existence or use; dead: *a defunct business that failed years ago.*

de·fy (dǐ fī′) *tr.v.* **de·fied, de·fy·ing, de·fies.** **1.** To oppose or resist (sbdy./sthg.) openly: *defy the law; defy tradition.* **2.** To be beyond the power of (sbdy./sthg.): *That story defies belief.* **3.** To challenge or dare (sbdy.) to do sthg.: *I defy you to find an error in this report.*

deg or **deg.** *abbr.* An abbreviation of degree.

de·gen·er·ate (dǐ jĕn′ər ĭt) *adj.* Having fallen into an inferior or low state, especially in mental or moral qualities: *a degenerate society.* —*n.* A corrupt or immoral person. —*intr.v.* (dǐ jĕn′ə rāt′). **de·gen·er·at·ed, de·gen·er·at·ing, de·gen·er·ates.** To sink into a much worse or lower condition; decline in quality: *The quality of her work degenerated during her illness.* —**de·gen′er·ate·ly** *adv.* —**de·gen′er·a′tion** *n.* [U]

de·grad·a·ble (dǐ grā′də bəl) *adj.* Capable of being broken down or decayed by stages.

de·grade (dǐ grād′) *tr.v.* **de·grad·ed, de·grad·ing, de·grades.** **1.** To lower the quality of (sthg.): *He degraded the value of his car when he dented it.* **2.** To lower (sbdy./sthg.) in dignity; dishonor or disgrace: *I refuse to degrade myself by arguing over trivia.* —**deg′ra·da′tion** (dĕg′rə dā′shən) *n.* [C; U]

de·grad·ing (dǐ grā′dǐng) *adj.* Causing sbdy. to lose dignity; humiliating: *Losing by so many points was a degrading experience for our team.*

de·gree (dǐ grē′) *n.* **1.** [C] A unit of measurement on a temperature scale: *The temperature of water at freezing is 32 degrees Fahrenheit.* **2.** [C] **a.** A unit for measuring an angle or an arc of a circle. One degree is ¹⁄₃₆₀ of the circumference of a circle. **b.** This unit used to measure latitude or longitude on the earth's surface. **3.** [C] One of a series of steps in a process, course, or progression: *a second-degree black belt.* **4.** [U] Relative amount: *a high degree of accuracy; various degrees of skill in acting.* **5.** [C] An academic title awarded by a college or university for completing a required course of study: *a degree in chemistry.* **6.** [U] In law, classification of a crime according to its seriousness: *Accidental murder is murder in the second degree.* ♦ **by degrees.** Little by little; gradually: *improved on the guitar by degrees.* **the third degree.** An intense, severe process of questioning: *When I got home an hour late, my mother gave me the third degree.*

de·hu·man·ize (dē hyōō′mə nīz′) *tr.v.* **de·hu·man·ized, de·hu·man·iz·ing,**

ă–**cat**; ā–**pay**; âr–**care**; ä–**father**; ĕ–**get**; ē–**be**; ĭ–**sit**; ī–**nice**; îr–**here**; ŏ–**got**; ō–**go**; ô–**saw**; oi–**boy**; ou–**out**; ōō–**took**; ōō–**boot**; ŭ–**cut**; ûr–**word**; th–**thin**; *th*–**this**; hw–**when**; zh–**vision**; ə–**about**; N–French **bon**

de·hu·man·iz·es. To take away human qualities such as individuality or compassion from (sbdy./sthg.): *Some people think that computers dehumanize our lives.* —**de·hu'man·i·za'tion** (dē hyŏō'mə nĭ zā'shən) *n.* [U]

de·hu·mid·i·fy (dē'hyŏō mĭd'ə fī') *tr.v.* **de·hu·mid·i·fied, de·hu·mid·i·fy·ing, de·hu·mid·i·fies.** To decrease the humidity of (the air): *An air conditioner dehumidifies the air.* —**de'hu·mid'i·fi·er** *n.*

de·hy·drate (dē hī'drāt') *v.* **de·hy·drat·ed, de·hy·drat·ing, de·hy·drates.** —*tr.* To cause (sbdy./sthg.) to lose water or moisture; make dry: *dehydrate vegetables.* —*intr.* To lose water or moisture; become dry: *Some illnesses cause people to dehydrate.* —**de'hy·dra'tion** *n.* [U]

de·ice (dē īs') *tr.v.* **de·iced, de·ic·ing, de·ic·es.** To remove the ice from (sthg.): *deice the wings of an airplane.* —**de·ic'er** *n.*

de·i·fy (dē'ə fī') *tr.v.* **dei·fied, dei·fy·ing, dei·fies.** To make (sbdy./sthg.) into a god: *Some religions deify volcanoes and stars.*

deign (dān) *intr.v. Formal.* To do sthg. that is below one's dignity: *The speaker deigned to answer the rude man's questions.*

de·i·ty (dē'ĭ tē) *n., pl.* **de·i·ties.** A god or goddess.

de·ject·ed (dĭ jĕk'tĭd) *adj.* In low spirits; sad: *The students felt dejected when they did poorly on the exam.* —**de·ject'ed·ly** *adv.*

de·jec·tion (dĭ jĕk'shən) *n.* [U] Sadness; low spirits: *Dejection set in after we got the bad news.*

Del. *abbr.* An abbreviation of Delaware.

de·lay (dĭ lā') *v.* —*tr.* **1.** To put off (sthg.) until a later time; postpone: *We will have to delay dinner an hour.* **2.** To cause (sbdy./sthg.) to be late: *A traffic jam delayed my arrival.* —*intr.* To move slowly; put off an action or a decision: *Buy your books today; don't delay.* —*n.* **1.** [U] The act of delaying or the condition of being delayed: *loss of time: Your order will be filled without delay.* **2.** [C] A period of time during which one is delayed: *We had a delay of 15 minutes waiting for the bus to arrive.*

de·lec·ta·ble (dĭ lĕk'tə bəl) *adj.* Delicious; enjoyable: *a delectable chocolate cake.*

del·e·gate (dĕl'ĭ gāt' or dĕl'ĭ gĭt) *n.* **1.** A person chosen to speak and act for another person; a representative or an agent: *Delegates to the convention were elected at the meeting.* **2.** A representative of a U.S. territory in the House of Representatives who is entitled to speak but not vote. —*tr.v.* (dĕl'ĭ gāt'). **del·e·gat·ed, del·e·gat·ing, del·e·gates. 1.** To give (sbdy.) authority to be one's representative: *The class delegated six students to serve on the committee.* **2.** To give or entrust (sthg.) to another person: *We delegated responsibility for feeding the animals to our sister.*

del·e·ga·tion (dĕl'ĭ gā'shən) *n.* **1.** [C] A person or persons chosen to represent another or others: *Each state sends a delegation to the convention.* **2.** [U] The act of giving authority: *delegation of power to a representative.* **3.** [U] The condition of being delegated; appointment.

de·lete (dĭ lēt') *tr.v.* **de·let·ed, de·let·ing, de·letes.** To remove (sthg.) by erasing or canceling: *You should delete the last sentence of the paragraph.*

de·le·tion (dĭ lē'shən) *n.* **1.** [U] The act of deleting. **2.** [C] A part that has been removed, such as a word, sentence, or paragraph.

del·i (dĕl'ē) *n., pl.* **del·is.** *Informal.* A delicatessen.

de·lib·er·ate (dĭ lĭb'ər ĭt) *adj.* **1.** Done or said on purpose; intentional: *a deliberate lie.* **2.** Decided by careful consideration: *a deliberate choice.* **3.** Not hasty or hurried; slow: *He crossed the bridge with deliberate steps.* —*v.* (dĭ lĭb'ə rāt'). **de·lib·er·at·ed, de·lib·er·at·ing, de·lib·er·ates.** —*intr.* **1.** To think carefully and often slowly; reflect: *He deliberated over buying a new car.* **2.** To discuss sthg. in order to reach a decision: *The Senate deliberated throughout the night.* —*tr.* To consider (sthg.) carefully and often slowly: *We deliberated the purchase of a new house for months.* —**de·lib'er·ate·ly** *adv.* —**de·lib'er·ate·ness** *n.* [U]

de·lib·er·a·tion (dĭ lĭb'ə rā'shən) *n.* **1.** [U] The act of deliberating. **2. deliberations.** Formal discussion and consideration of all sides of an issue: *The deliberations of Congress are printed in the* Congressional Record. **3.** [U] Thoughtfulness in decision or action: *The mountain climber took each step with deliberation.*

del·i·ca·cy (dĕl'ĭ kə sē) *n., pl.* **del·i·ca·cies. 1.** [C] Food that is considered delicious and is difficult to find: *Caviar is considered a delicacy.* **2.** [U] Fineness of quality, appearance, construction, or performance: *embroidery of great delicacy.* **3.** [U] Weakness of body or health: *The delicacy of small children makes them subject to many diseases.* **4.** [U] Sensitivity to the feelings of others; tact: *She phrased the apology with delicacy.*

del·i·cate (dĕl'ĭ kĭt) *adj.* **1.** Pleasing to the senses, especially in a subtle way: *a delicate pink; a delicate flavor.* **2.** Very fine in quality or appearance; dainty: *delicate lace.* **3.** Weak in health: *The patient is delicate and must get plenty of rest.* **4.** Easily broken or damaged; fragile: *a delicate glass figurine.* **5.** Requiring consideration or tactful treatment: *a delicate matter that could embarrass one's friends.* **6.** Fine or soft in touch or skill: *a delicate surgeon.* **7.** Very responsive or sensitive: *a delicate control on the heater.* —**del'i·cate·ly** *adv.* —**del'i·cate·ness** *n.* [U]

del·i·ca·tes·sen (dĕl′ĭ kə tĕs′ən) n. A store that sells cooked or prepared foods ready for serving, such as cheeses, salads, and smoked meats.

de·li·cious (dĭ lĭsh′əs) adj. Very pleasing or agreeable, especially to the senses of taste or smell: *delicious fresh fruit; a delicious supper.* —**de·li′cious·ly** adv. —**de·li′cious·ness** n. [U]

de·light (dĭ līt′) n. **1.** [U] Great pleasure; joy: *The child's face beamed with delight.* **2.** [C; U] Something that gives great pleasure or enjoyment: *The birthday party was a delight to the whole family.* —v. —intr. [in] To take great pleasure or joy: *Most people delight in going to the circus.* —tr. To please (sbdy.) greatly: *Paris delights the visitor.*

de·light·ed (dĭ lī′tĭd) adj. Greatly pleased; happy: *The delighted winner waved to the crowd.* —**de·light′ed·ly** adv.

de·light·ful (dĭ līt′fəl) adj. Greatly pleasing: *We had a delightful time at the party.* —**de·light′ful·ly** adv. —**de·light′ful·ness** n. [U]

de·lin·e·ate (dĭ lĭn′ē āt′) tr.v. **de·lin·e·at·ed, de·lin·e·at·ing, de·lin·e·ates.** **1.** To draw or trace the outline of (sthg.): *delineate the state of California on a map.* **2.** To represent (sbdy./sthg.) in a picture; depict. **3.** To state or describe (sbdy./sthg.) in words or gestures: *The instructions delineate my duties carefully.*

de·lin·quen·cy (dĭ lĭng′kwən sē) n. [U] Behavior that is contrary to the requirements of the law, especially by young people.

de·lin·quent (dĭ lĭng′kwənt) adj. **1.** Failing to do what law or duty requires: *The delinquent owners let their dog run free.* **2.** Overdue in payment: *a delinquent account.* —n. A person who fails to do what law or duty requires, especially a young person. —**de·lin′quent·ly** adv.

de·lir·i·ous (dĭ lîr′ē əs) adj. **1.** Affected by delirium; confused: *a delirious patient.* **2.** In a state of uncontrolled excitement; overjoyed: *delirious happiness.* —**de·lir′i·ous·ly** adv. —**de·lir′i·ous·ness** n. [U]

de·lir·i·um (dĭ lîr′ē əm) n. [U] **1.** A temporary state of confusion resulting from high fever, poisoning, or shock: *the delirium of patients suffering from malaria.* **2.** A state of uncontrolled excitement or emotion: *the delirium of winning the gold medal.*

de·liv·er (dĭ lĭv′ər) v. —tr. **1.** To take or carry (sthg.) to the proper place or person: *deliver the mail; deliver a package.* **2.** To surrender (sbdy./sthg.); hand over: *deliver a criminal to the authorities.* **3.** To strike (a blow): *The logger delivered a blow of the ax that split the log completely.* **4.** To express

(sthg.) in words; say: *deliver a speech to an audience.* **5.a.** To give birth to (sbdy.): *She delivered a baby girl.* **b.** To help with the birth of (sbdy.): *The doctor delivered the baby.* —intr. **1.** To take goods to the proper place; make deliveries: *Only a few stores deliver nowadays.* **2.** To give birth: *The woman delivered a week early, but the baby was healthy.* —**de·liv′er·ance** n. [U] —**de·liv′er·er** n.

de·liv·er·y (dĭ lĭv′ə rē or dĭ lĭv′rē) n., pl. **de·liv·er·ies.** [C; U] **1.a.** The act of delivering: *The post office makes deliveries every day but Sunday.* **b.** Something that is delivered: *There is a delivery for you downstairs.* **2.** The act of giving birth: *The woman had a natural delivery of a healthy baby.* **3.** The manner of speaking or singing: *The content of his speech was excellent, but his delivery was poor.*

de·lude (dĭ lood′) tr.v. **de·lud·ed, de·lud·ing, de·ludes.** To deceive (sbdy.): *Clever ads delude people into buying worthless products.*

del·uge (dĕl′yooj) n. **1.** A great flood or heavy downpour: *The deluge from spring rains flooded fields and roads for miles around.* **2.** An excessive amount of sthg.: *a deluge of mail in response to the editorial.* —tr.v. **del·uged, del·ug·ing, del·ug·es.** **1.** To flood (sthg.) with water. **2.** To inundate (sbdy./sthg.) with an excessive number or amount of sthg.: *deluged the graduate with words of congratulation.*

de·lu·sion (dĭ loo′zhən) n. **1.** [U] The act of deluding or the state of being deluded: *the delusion of a swindler's victim.* **2.** [C] A false belief or opinion: *under the delusion that the moon is made of cheese.*

de·luxe (dĭ lŭks′ or dĭ looks′) adj. Of especially fine quality; luxurious: *They stayed in a deluxe hotel as part of the grand prize.*

delve (dĕlv) intr.v. **delved, delv·ing, delves.** To search deeply and thoroughly: *She delved into the court records.* —**delv′er** n.

Dem. abbr. An abbreviation of: **1.** Democrat. **2.** Democratic.

dem·a·gogue (dĕm′ə gôg′ or dĕm′ə gŏg′) n. A leader who wins people's favor by appealing to their emotions and prejudices: *The demagogue's speech worked the crowd into a frenzy.* —**dem′a·gog′ic** (dĕm′ə gŏj′ĭk or dĕm′ə gŏg′ĭk) adj.

de·mand (dĭ mănd′) tr.v. **1.** To ask for (sthg.) strongly: *She demanded that they leave immediately.* **2.** To claim (sthg.) as due: *demand repayment of a loan.* **3.** To require (sthg.): *A lawyer's work demands skill and concentration.* —n. **1.** [U] The act of demanding sthg. **2.** [C] Something that is asked for strongly:

striking workers making new wage demands.
3. [C] A requirement, need, or claim: *This project has made many demands on my time.*
4. [U] The state of being needed: *Firewood is in great demand during winter months.*

de·mand·ing (dĭ măn′dĭng) *adj.* Requiring much effort or attention: *a very demanding child; a demanding job.*

de·mean (dĭ mēn′) *tr.v.* To lower (oneself or sbdy.), as in dignity or social standing: *I wish he wouldn't demean himself by continually asking for favors.*

de·mean·ing (dĭ mē′nĭng) *adj.* Making sbdy. feel lower in dignity or worth: *a demeaning job.*

de·mean·or (dĭ mē′nər) *n.* [U] The way in which sbdy. behaves; conduct: *As head librarian, she has a demeanor of quiet authority.*

de·ment·ed (dĭ měn′tĭd) *adj.* Having a serious mental disorder: *The man talked to himself so much that he seemed demented.* **—de·ment′ed·ly** *adv.*

de·mer·it (dĭ měr′ĭt) *n.* A mark against one's record for a fault or misconduct: *The students received demerits for being late to class.*

demi— *pref.* A prefix that means partly: *demigod.*

dem·i·god (děm′ē gŏd′) *n.* A mythological male being, such as a minor god or the offspring of a god and a human being. **—dem′i·god′dess** (děm′ē gŏd′ĭs) *n.*

de·mil·i·ta·rize (dē mĭl′ĭ tə rīz′) *tr.v.* **de·mil·i·ta·rized, de·mil·i·ta·riz·ing, de·mil·i·ta·riz·es.** To ban military forces in (an area): *demilitarize a country.* **—de·mil′i·ta·ri·za′tion** (dē mĭl′ĭ tər ĭ zā′shən) *n.* [U]

de·mise (dĭ mīz′) *n.* [U] **1.** Death. **2.** The end of existence; termination: *The loss of customers caused the demise of the department store.*

dem·o (děm′ō) *n., pl.* **dem·os.** *Informal.* **1.** A demonstration, as of a product or service. **2.** Something used for demonstration, such as an automobile or a recording that shows a musician's qualities: *We bought the demo at a great price.*

de·moc·ra·cy (dĭ mŏk′rə sē) *n., pl.* **de·moc·ra·cies.** [C; U] Government by the people, exercised either directly or through representatives: *the principles of democracy; the former monarchy became a democracy.*

dem·o·crat (děm′ə krăt′) *n.* **1.** A person who advocates democracy. **2. Democrat.** A member of the Democratic Party.

dem·o·crat·ic (děm′ə krăt′ĭk) *adj.* **1.** Characteristic of or advocating democracy. **2.** Of or for the people in general; popular: *a democratic movement.* **3. Democratic.** Relating to or characteristic of the Democratic Party. **—dem′o·crat′i·cal·ly** *adv.*

Democratic Party *n.* One of the two major political parties of the United States.

de·moc·ra·tize (dĭ mŏk′rə tīz′) *tr.v.* **de·moc·ra·tized, de·moc·ra·tiz·ing, de·moc·ra·tiz·es.** To make (a country or organization) democratic. **—de·moc′ra·ti·za′tion** (dĭ mŏk′rə tĭ zā′shən) *n.* [U]

dem·o·graph·ics (děm′ə grăf′ĭks) *n.* [U] *(used with a plural verb).* The characteristics of human populations, especially when used to identify consumer markets: *The demographics of that region are changing.*

de·mog·ra·phy (dĭ mŏg′rə fē) *n.* [U] The study of the characteristics of human populations, such as growth, density, distribution, and birth and death rates. **—dem′o·graph′ic** (děm′ə grăf′ĭk) *adj.*

de·mol·ish (dĭ mŏl′ĭsh) *tr.v.* **1.** To tear (sthg.) down completely; level: *demolish an old building.* **2.** To destroy (sthg.) completely; put an end to: *demolish an argument.* See Synonyms at **ruin.** **—dem′o·li′tion** (děm′ə lĭsh′ən) *n.* [U]

de·mon (dē′mən) *n.* **1.** An evil supernatural being; a devil. **2.** A tormenting force or passion: *She has faced her personal demons and will perform well.* **3.** A person who is very energetic, skillful, or diligent: *He has been working like a demon.* **—de·mon′ic** (dĭ mŏn′ĭk) *adj.*

de·mon·stra·ble (dĭ mŏn′strə bəl) *adj.* Able to be demonstrated or proved: *a demonstrable theory.*

dem·on·strate (děm′ən strāt′) *v.* **dem·on·strat·ed, dem·on·strat·ing, dem·on·strates.** **—tr. 1.** To show (sthg.) clearly and deliberately: *She demonstrated her skill as an artist.* **2.** To show (sthg.) to be true; prove: *demonstrate one's ability to do the job.* **3.a.** To describe or explain (sthg.) by experiment, practical application, or example: *We performed an experiment to demonstrate the effect of light on plants.* **b.** To show the use of (a product) to a prospective buyer: *The salesperson demonstrated the washing machine.* **—intr.** [*for; against*] To take part in a public display of opinion: *The residents demonstrated against the new law by carrying signs and shouting.*

dem·on·stra·tion (děm′ən strā′shən) *n.* **1.** [C; U] The act of showing or making evident. **2.** [C] Clear and conclusive proof; evidence. **3.** [C] An explanation or a description, as of a theory or product: *the demonstration of the use of the new dishwasher.* **4.** [C; U] A display or an outward show, as of one's feelings: *a demonstration of love for one's sisters.* **5.** [C] A public display of group opinion, such as a rally or march.

de·mon·stra·tive (dĭ mŏn′strə tĭv) *adj.* **1.** Serving to prove: *Her good grades are demonstrative of her excellent talents.* **2.** Openly expressing one's feelings, especially affection: *The demonstrative performer wept when she received the award.* **3.** In grammar, specifying the person or thing referred to; for example, the word *these* is a demonstrative pronoun in *These are my books* and a demonstrative adjective in *These books are mine.* —*n.* A demonstrative pronoun or adjective. —**de·mon'stra·tive·ly** *adv.* —**de·mon'stra·tive·ness** *n.* [U]

dem·on·stra·tor (dĕm'ən strā'tər) *n.* A person who demonstrates, such as a participant in a public display of opinion.

de·mor·al·ize (dĭ môr'ə līz' *or* dĭ mŏr'ə-līz') *tr.v.* **de·mor·al·ized, de·mor·al·iz·ing, de·mor·al·iz·es.** 1. To weaken the confidence or morale of (sbdy.); discourage: *Reading the negative reviews of the movie demoralized its director.* 2. To weaken the morals of (sbdy.); corrupt: *Offers of favors have demoralized many politicians.* —**de·mor'al·i·za'tion** (dĭ môr'ə lĭ zā'shən *or* dĭ mŏr'ə lĭ zā'shən) *n.* [U]

de·mote (dĭ mōt') *tr.v.* **de·mot·ed, de·mot·ing, de·motes.** To reduce (sbdy.) in rank, grade, or status: *demoted from captain to lieutenant.* —**de·mo'tion** *n.* [C; U]

de·mur (dĭ mûr') *intr.v.* **de·murred, de·mur·ring, de·murs.** *Formal.* To raise objections; object: *When the boss asked us to work late, we demurred.*

de·mure (dĭ myo͝or') *adj.* Reserved and modest in behavior: *She is a pleasant and demure person.* —**de·mure'ly** *adv.* —**de·mure'ness** *n.* [U]

den (dĕn) *n.* 1. The place where a wild animal lives; a lair: *The fox was safe in its den.* 2. A room for study, recreation, or relaxation.

de·ni·al (dĭ nī'əl) *n.* [C; U] 1. A refusal to satisfy a request. 2. A refusal to accept the truth of an accusation: *The charges of corruption resulted in an immediate denial from the mayor.*

den·i·grate (dĕn'ĭ grāt') *tr.v.* **den·i·grat·ed, den·i·grat·ing, den·i·grates.** To attack the reputation or character of (sbdy./sthg.): *To make himself look better, he denigrates opponents.* —**den'i·gra'tion** *n.* [U]

den·im (dĕn'ĭm) *n.* [U] A heavy cotton cloth, usually used to make jeans, overalls, and work uniforms.

den·i·zen (dĕn'ĭ zən) *n.* A person or an animal that lives in a particular place; an inhabitant: *Lions and giraffes are denizens of the African plains.*

de·nom·i·na·tion (dĭ nŏm'ə nā'shən) *n.* 1. An organized religious group with a common faith and name: *People of several denominations met to worship together.* 2. One of a series of values or sizes, as in a system of currency: *bills of different denominations.* —**de·nom'i·na'tion·al** *adj.*

de·nom·i·na·tor (dĭ nŏm'ə nā'tər) *n.* The

number below the line in a fraction that indicates the number of equal parts into which one whole is divided: *In the fraction* $^2/_7$, *7 is the denominator.*

de·note (dĭ nōt') *tr.v.* **de·not·ed, de·not·ing, de·notes.** 1. To be a sign of (sthg.); mark: *The blue areas on the map denote water.* 2. To refer to (sthg.) specifically: *The teacher denoted the chapters we should study.* —**de'no·ta'tion** (dē'nō tā'shən) *n.*

de·nounce (dĭ nouns') *tr.v.* **de·nounced, de·nounc·ing, de·nounc·es.** 1. To condemn (sbdy./sthg.) openly: *The Senator denounced the policy as wasteful and foolish.* 2. To accuse (sbdy.) formally: *denounced the thief to the police.*

dense (dĕns) *adj.* **dens·er, dens·est.** 1. Having relatively high density. 2. Crowded closely together; compact: *a dense population in the city.* 3. Difficult to penetrate; thick: *a dense forest; a dense fog.* 4. Difficult to understand: *a dense novel.* 5. *Informal.* Slow to comprehend: *My little brother seems very dense; he doesn't understand anything!* —**dense'ly** *adv.* —**dense'ness** *n.* [U]

den·si·ty (dĕn'sĭ tē) *n., pl.* **den·si·ties.** 1. [C] In physics, the mass per unit of volume of a substance: *Lead has a greater density than water.* 2. [C] The amount of sthg. in a unit or measure of length, volume, or area: *The population density in New York City is greater than in many other U.S. cities.* 3. [U] Thickness: *The density of the grass made the tiger invisible.*

dent (dĕnt) *n.* A hollow place in a surface, usually caused by pressure or a blow: *a dent in a car from an accident.* —*v.* —*tr.* To make a dent in (sthg.): *When I hit the tree, I dented the car's fender.* —*intr.* To become dented: *Aluminum cans dent easily.* ◆ **make a dent in.** *Informal.* 1. To make meaningful progress doing sthg.: *If we work all day, we will make a significant dent in this assignment.* 2. To reduce in amount: *That new car didn't make a dent in his lottery winnings.*

den·tal (dĕn'tl) *adj.* 1. Relating to or for the teeth: *a dental tool.* 2. Relating to or intended for dentistry: *a dental school.*

dental floss *n.* [U] A type of thread used to clean between the teeth.

dental hygienist *n.* A person who is trained to clean and examine the teeth.

den·tist (dĕn'tĭst) *n.* A doctor who is trained and licensed to practice dentistry.

den·tist·ry (dĕn'tĭ strē) *n.* [U] 1. The scientific study and treatment of diseases and disorders of the mouth and teeth. 2. The practice of this science as a profession.

den·tures (dĕn'chərz) *pl.n.* A set of artificial teeth.

de·nun·ci·a·tion (dĭ nŭn′sē ā′shən) *n.* [C; U] **1.** The act of denouncing or speaking against sbdy./sthg., especially publicly: *a denunciation of corruption in government.* **2.** The act of accusing another of a crime before a public prosecutor: *the denunciation of the spy.*

de·ny (dĭ nī′) *tr.v.* **de·nied, de·ny·ing, de·nies. 1.** To declare (sthg.) to be untrue: *deny an accusation.* **2.** To refuse to acknowledge (sthg.): *deny a friendship.* **3.** To refuse to grant or allow (sthg.): *The prisoners were denied food and water.* **4.** To restrain (oneself), especially from pleasures: *I denied myself a rest and bicycled all the way home.*

de·o·dor·ant (dē ō′dər ənt) *n.* A preparation used to hide or cover up odors: *a room deodorant; a body deodorant.*

de·o·dor·ize (dē ō′də rīz′) *tr.v.* **de·o·dor·ized, de·o·dor·iz·ing, de·o·dor·iz·es.** To remove the odor of (sthg.). —**de·o′dor·i·za′tion** (dē ō′dər ĭ zā′shən) *n.* [U] —**de·o′dor·iz′er** *n.*

de·ox·y·ri·bo·nu·cle·ic acid (dē ŏk′sē-rī′bō nōō klē′ĭk *or* dē ŏk′sē rī′bō nōō-klā′ĭk) *n.* DNA.

de·part (dĭ pärt′) *intr.v.* To go away; leave: *I depart for work early each morning. The plane will depart at 6:35.* ◆ **depart from.** *tr.v.* [insep.] **1.** To vary from (a regular habit or course); deviate: *We departed from our custom of eating pizza on Saturdays.* **2.** To leave from (a place): *Our plane departs from gate 3.*

de·part·ed (dĭ pär′tĭd) *n.* [U] **1.** A dead person: *a service for the dearly departed.* **2.** Dead people considered as a group; the dead. —*adj.* Dead.

de·part·ment (dĭ pärt′mənt) *n.* **1.** A separate division of an organization, such as a government, company, or college: *the fire department; the personnel department; the English department.* **2.** A section of a department store selling a particular line of merchandise: *the shoe department.* —**de′part·men′tal** *adj.*

department store *n.* A large store selling many kinds of goods and services and organized in separate departments.

de·par·ture (dĭ pär′chər) *n.* [C; U] **1.** The act of going away: *Our departure was delayed by a flat tire.* **2.** A difference in an established rule, plan, or procedure: *Going to bed early was a departure from our usual habit.*

de·pend (dĭ pĕnd′) *v.* ◆ **depend on** or **upon.** *tr.v.* [insep.] **1.** To rely on (sbdy./sthg.), especially for support or maintenance: *Many students depend on their parents for money.* **2.** To place trust or confidence in (sbdy.): *You can depend on me to be on time.* **3.** To be determined by (sthg.): *Our plans depend on the weather.* **that** or **it depends.** Used as an answer when a speaker has not yet decided what to do: *Do you plan to go with us? That depends. I don't know what time I'll be home.*

de·pend·a·ble (dĭ pĕn′də bəl) *adj.* Trustworthy: *He is the best employee because he is the most dependable; he always finishes on time.* —**de·pend′a·bil′i·ty** *n.* [U] —**de·pend′a·bly** *adv.*

de·pend·ence (dĭ pĕn′dəns) *n.* [U] **1.** The state of being dependent, as for support. **2.** Reliance; trust: *I place little dependence in the accuracy of this watch.* **3.** The state of being determined, influenced, or controlled by sthg. else: *the dependence of a storekeeper on suppliers.* **4.** An addiction: *She has a dependence on alcohol.* —**de·pend′en·cy** *n.* [C; U]

de·pend·ent (dĭ pĕn′dənt) *adj.* **1.** Determined by some other event or fact: *The outcome is dependent on the voters.* **2.** Subordinate: *a dependent clause in a sentence.* —*n.* A person who relies on another, especially for financial support: *My parents have three dependents including me.* ◆ **be dependent on** or **upon.** To need the help of another for support: *Plants are dependent on sunlight. Children are dependent upon their parents.* —**de·pend′ent·ly** *adv.*

dependent clause *n.* A clause that cannot stand alone as a full sentence; a subordinate clause. For example, in the sentence *When I saw him he was feeling fine, when I saw him* is a dependent clause.

de·pict (dĭ pĭkt′) *tr.v.* To represent (sthg.) in words or pictures; describe or show: *a book depicting life in ancient Rome; a painting that depicts a historical event.* —**de·pic′tion** *n.*

de·plane (dē plān′) *intr.v.* **de·planed, de·plan·ing, de·planes.** To exit from an airplane: *After the jet landed, we deplaned quickly.*

de·plete (dĭ plēt′) *tr.v.* **de·plet·ed, de·plet·ing, de·pletes.** To empty (sthg.) out; use up: *This cold weather has depleted oil supplies.* —**de·ple′tion** *n.* [U]

de·plor·a·ble (dĭ plôr′ə bəl) *adj.* **1.** Worthy of strong disapproval or condemnation: *rude and deplorable behavior.* **2.** Bad; unfortunate: *The kitchen was in a deplorable condition after we finished cooking. The city has deplorable rundown housing.* —**de·plor′a·bly** *adv.*

de·plore (dĭ plôr′) *tr.v.* **de·plored, de·plor·ing, de·plores. 1.** To feel or express strong disapproval of (sthg.); condemn: *We deplore cruelty to animals.* **2.** To express sorrow or grief over (sthg.): *The world deplored the loss of the great actor.*

de·ploy (dĭ ploi′) *tr.v.* To put (sbdy./sthg.) in a position ready for combat: *deploy troops for a battle.* —**de·ploy′ment** *n.* [U]

de·pop·u·late (dē pŏp′yə lāt′) *tr.v.* **de·pop·u·lat·ed, de·pop·u·lat·ing, de·pop·u·lates.** To sharply reduce the population of (an area): *Severe flooding depopulated much of the region.* —**de·pop′u·la′tion** *n.* [U]

D

de·port (dĭ pôrt′) *tr.v.* **1.** To expel (sbdy.) from a country; banish: *Government authorities deported the spy.* **2.** *Formal.* To behave (oneself) in a certain manner: *Visitors usually deport themselves with quiet respect while in the cathedral.*

de·por·ta·tion (dē′pôr tā′shən) *n.* [C; U] The act or an instance of deporting: *He faces deportation for being in the country illegally.*

de·port·ment (dĭ pôrt′mənt) *n. Formal.* A manner of personal conduct; behavior: *She has a very dignified deportment.*

de·pos·it (dĭ pŏz′ĭt) *tr.v.* **1.** To put or set (sthg.) down; place: *Please deposit books returned to the library at the front desk.* **2.** To lay (sthg.) down or leave behind by a natural process: *The flooding river deposited mud and debris in the roads.* **3.** To put (money) in a bank or financial account: *She deposited her paycheck.* —*n.* **1.** Something, such as money, put in a place for safekeeping: *a bank deposit.* **2.a.** A partial or initial payment of a cost or debt: *She left a deposit on the coat.* **b.** An amount of money given as security for sthg. rented: *a deposit on a rented lawn mower; a security deposit on an apartment.* **3.a.** Solid material left by a natural process: *Deposits of mud and sticks blocked the stream.* **b.** A mass of a naturally occurring mineral: *gold deposits in the mountains.* ◆ **on deposit.** Placed somewhere for safekeeping: *money on deposit in a bank account.* **put down a deposit.** To give sbdy. an initial payment on an item that one wishes to buy or rent so that the item will not be sold or rented to sbdy. else: *We had to put down a deposit of $100 on the car to hold it for 24 hours.* —**de·pos′i·tor** *n.*

de·pot (dē′pō *or* dĕp′ō) *n.* **1.** A railroad or bus station: *a train depot.* **2.** A warehouse or storehouse: *a trucking depot for freight.*

de·praved (dĭ prāvd′) *adj.* Morally corrupt; perverted.

de·prav·i·ty (dĭ prăv′ĭ tē) *n., pl.* **de·prav·i·ties. 1.** [U] Wickedness; evil: *The depravity of the criminals was clear.* **2.** [C; U] A depraved act or condition.

de·pre·ci·ate (dĭ prē′shē āt′) *intr.v.* **de·pre·ci·at·ed, de·pre·ci·at·ing, de·pre·ci·ates.** To go down in price or value: *The house had depreciated in value because of its poor condition.* —**de·pre′ci·a′tion** *n.* [U]

de·press (dĭ prĕs′) *tr.v.* **1.** To make (sbdy.) sad: *The news of his friend's death depressed him.* **2.** To press (sthg.) down: *Depress the brake pedal to stop the car.* **3.a.** To weaken (sthg.): *Widespread layoffs have depressed the economy.* **b.** To lower prices in (a stock market): *The economic news depressed the stock market and stock prices fell.*

de·pres·sant (dĭ prĕs′ənt) *n.* A drug that tends to slow body processes: *Sleeping pills are depressants.*

de·pressed (dĭ prĕst′) *adj.* **1.** Very sad; low in spirits: *The news of the accident left me feeling very depressed.* **2.** Suffering from social and economic problems, as from poverty and unemployment: *a program of aid for depressed areas of the country.*

de·press·ing (dĭ prĕs′ĭng) *adj.* Causing emotional depression: *depressing news.*

de·pres·sion (dĭ prĕsh′ən) *n.* **1.** [C; U] The act of depressing or the state of being depressed. **2.** [C; U] The condition of feeling sad and sorrowful: *a mood of depression and despair.* **3.** [C] A period of severe decline in an economy: *A depression brings unemployment and hardship to many people.* **4.** [C; U] A lowering in amount, degree, or position: *a depression in the temperature.* **5.** [C] An area that is sunk below its surroundings; a hollow: *Depressions in the sidewalk made it hard to walk on.*

dep·ri·va·tion (dĕp′rə vā′shən) *n.* [C; U] **1.** The act or an instance of depriving; a loss. **2.** The condition of being deprived.

de·prive (dĭ prīv′) *tr.v.* **de·prived, de·priv·ing, de·prives. 1.** To take sthg. away from (sbdy./sthg.): *Revolution deprived the government of its power.* **2.** To prevent (sbdy./sthg.) from having; deny: *Heavy snow deprived the birds of food.*

de·prived (dĭ prīvd′) *adj.* Lacking things needed to be healthy or happy: *deprived children.*

dept. *abbr.* An abbreviation of department.

depth (dĕpth) *n.* **1.** [U] The quality or condition of being deep. **2.** [C] The measure or distance downward, backward, or inward: *The closet has a depth of two meters.* **3.** [C] *(usually plural).* A deep part or place: *the ocean depths.* **4.** [C] The severest or worst part: *in the depth of despair.* **5.** [U] Intellectual complexity: *He wrote poetry and plays of unusual depth.* **6.** [U] Complete detail; thoroughness: *an interview conducted in great depth.*

dep·u·ty (dĕp′yə tē) *n., pl.* **dep·u·ties. 1.** A person appointed to act in place of another: *The health officer has several deputies to help enforce environmental laws.* **2.** A police officer who works for a sheriff.

de·rail (dē rāl′) *intr. & tr.v.* To go off or cause to go off the tracks: *The train derailed near Buffalo. A fallen tree on the tracks derailed the express.* —**de·rail′ment** *n.* [C; U]

de·range (dĭ rānj′) *tr.v.* **de·ranged, de·rang·ing, de·rang·es. 1.** To upset the arrangement, functioning, or order of (sthg.): *The flood completely deranged the furniture.* **2.** To unbalance (sbdy.) mentally; make insane: *The loss of her daughter deranged her.*

de·ranged (dĭ rānjd′) *adj.* Mentally unstable

ă–cat; ā–pay; âr–care; ä–father; ĕ–get; ē–be; ĭ–sit; ī–nice; îr–here; ŏ–got; ō–go; ô–saw; oi–boy; ou–out; ŏŏ–took; ōō–boot; ŭ–cut; ûr–word; th–thin; th–this; hw–when; zh–vision; ə–about; N–French bon

or insane: *His odd behavior made me believe he was deranged.*

der·by (dûr′bē) *n., pl.* **der·bies. 1.** An annual horse race. **2.** A stiff felt hat with a round crown and a narrow curved brim.

der·e·lict (dĕr′ə lĭkt′) *adj.* **1.** Deserted by an owner; abandoned: *a derelict building crumbling with the years.* **2.** Neglectful; careless: *derelict in one's duty.* —*n.* A homeless or jobless person.

der·e·lic·tion (dĕr′ə lĭk′shən) *n.* [U] *Formal.* Willful neglect, as of duty.

de·ride (dĭ rīd′) *tr.v.* **de·rid·ed, de·rid·ing, de·rides.** To laugh at (sbdy./stng.) with contempt or scorn; mock: *Many people deride customs they don't understand.*

de·ri·sion (dĭ rĭzh′ən) *n.* [U] Contemptuous or jeering laughter; ridicule.

de·ri·sive (dĭ rī′sĭv *or* dĭ rī′zĭv) *adj.* Expressing ridicule; mocking: *Talk of the plan was silenced by derisive laughter.* —**de·ri′sive·ly** *adv.* —**de·ri′sive·ness** *n.* [U]

der·i·va·tion (dĕr′ə vā′shən) *n.* **1.** [U] The act of deriving. **2.** [C] The source from which sthg. is derived; origin: *The polka is a dance of eastern European derivation.* **3.** [C] The historical origin and development of a word; an etymology: *Derivations are given for many of the words in some dictionaries.*

de·riv·a·tive (dĭ rĭv′ə tĭv) *adj.* Resulting from or using derivation: *English has many derivative words.* —*n.* **1.** Something derived: *Gasoline is a derivative of oil.* **2.** A word formed from another, such as *electricity* from *electric.*

de·rive (dĭ rīv′) *v.* **de·rived, de·riv·ing, de·rives.** —*tr.* **1.** To obtain or receive (sthg.) from a source: *derive pleasure from music.* **2.** To trace the origin of (a word): *The linguists derived that word from ancient Greek.* —*intr.* [*from*] To issue from a source; originate: *French derives from Latin.*

der·ma·tol·o·gy (dûr′mə tŏl′ə jē) *n.* [U] The medical study of the skin, its diseases, and their treatment. —**der′ma·tol′o·gist** *n.*

der·mis (dûr′mĭs) *n.* [U] The layer of skin, beneath the epidermis, that contains nerve endings, sweat glands, and blood and lymph vessels.

de·rog·a·to·ry (dĭ rŏg′ə tôr′ē) *adj.* Making sthg. seem inferior; belittling: *He made a derogatory remark.* —**de·rog′a·to′ri·ly** *adv.*

der·rick (dĕr′ĭk) *n.* **1.** A machine for lifting and moving heavy objects. **2.** A tall framework that supports the equip-

derrick

ment used in drilling an oil well or a similar hole.

de·sal·i·nize (dē săl′ə nīz′) *tr.v.* **de·sal·i·nized, de·sal·i·niz·ing, de·sal·i·niz·es.** To remove salt from (seawater or soil, for example).

de·scend (dĭ sĕnd′) *v.* —*intr.* **1.** To move from a higher to a lower place; go or come down: *The airplane descended for a landing.* **2.** To slope or incline downward: *The path descended along the side of the cliff.* **3.** To come from an ancestor or ancestry: *Our neighbor descends from African royalty.* **4.** To lower oneself; stoop: *Both candidates chose not to descend to the level of personal accusations.* **5.** To arrive or attack suddenly or with overwhelming effect: *Our relatives descended on us this weekend.* —*tr.* To move from a higher to a lower part of (sthg.); go down: *We descended a fire escape.*

de·scen·dant (dĭ sĕn′dənt) *n.* A person or an animal descended from specified ancestors: *Her descendants settled in Oregon.*

de·scent (dĭ sĕnt′) *n.* **1.** [C; U] The act or an instance of descending: *the descent from the mountain.* **2.** [C] A downward incline or slope: *Rocks and mud slid down the steep descent.* **3.** [U] Ancestry: *Many Americans are of mixed descent.* **4.** [U] A sudden visit or attack: *The descent of the children on the candy store sent the cashier running.*

HOMONYMS: descent, dissent (disagreement).

de·scribe (dĭ skrīb′) *tr.v.* **de·scribed, de·scrib·ing, de·scribes. 1.** To give an account of (sbdy./sthg.) in words; tell or write about: *a newspaper report describing the fire; an oral report describing one's experiences.* **2.** To convey an impression of (sbdy./sthg.); characterize: *described him as gentle and kind.* —**de·scrib′a·ble** *adj.*

de·scrip·tion (dĭ skrĭp′shən) *n.* [C; U] **1.** An account or a statement describing sthg.: *The newspaper carried a description of the plane crash.* **2.** A kind or variety; a sort: *The zoo has animals of every description.*

de·scrip·tive (dĭ skrĭp′tĭv) *adj.* Involving or characterized by description; serving to describe: *descriptive words; a descriptive passage in a guidebook.* —**de·scrip′tive·ly** *adv.* —**de·scrip′tive·ness** *n.* [U]

des·e·crate (dĕs′ĭ krāt′) *tr.v.* **des·e·crat·ed, des·e·crat·ing, des·e·crates.** To damage (sthg. sacred): *The vandals desecrated the cemetery.* —**des′e·crat′er** *n.* —**des′e·cra′tion** *n.* [U]

de·seg·re·gate (dē sĕg′rĭ gāt′) *tr.v.* **de·seg·re·gat·ed, de·seg·re·gat·ing, de·seg·re·gates.** To abolish racial separation in (a school or workplace, for example): *Schools were desegregated by the government.* —**de·seg′re·ga′tion** *n.* [U]

des·ert[1] (dĕz′ərt) n. [C; U] **1.** A dry region, often covered with sand and with little or no vegetation. **2.** An empty or isolated place; a wasteland: *a cultural desert.* —adj. **1.** Relating to, characteristic of, or inhabiting a desert: *the desert life of a nomad; a desert animal.* **2.** Empty and uninhabited: *a desert island.*

de·sert[2] (dĭ zûrt′) v. —tr. **1.** To leave (sbdy./sthg.) empty or alone; abandon: *Miners deserted the valley after the gold ran out.* **2.** To abandon (a military post, for example) in violation of orders or an oath: *The soldiers deserted their posts just before the attack.* —intr. To abandon one's duty or post, especially without intending to return: *The frightened sailors deserted after the battle.* —de·sert′er n. —de·ser′tion n. [U]

HOMONYMS: desert (abandon), **dessert** (last course of a meal).

---

de·serve (dĭ zûrv′) tr.v. **de·served, de·serv·ing, de·serves.** To be worthy of (sthg.); merit: *The rescuers deserved a reward for their courageous act.*

de·served (dĭ zûrvd′) adj. Merited or earned: *a richly deserved reward.* —de·serv′ed·ly (dĭ zûr′vĭd lē) adv.

de·serv·ing (dĭ zûr′vĭng) adj. Worthy, as of aid, reward, or praise: *Scholarships are available for deserving students.*

des·ic·cate (dĕs′ĭ kāt′) tr.v. **des·ic·cat·ed, des·ic·cat·ing, des·ic·cates.** *Formal.* To dry (sthg.) out thoroughly: *A long period without rain desiccated most of the farmland.*

de·sign (dĭ zīn′) v. —tr. **1.** To draw up plans, sketches, or drawings for (sthg.): *design a building; design dresses.* **2.** To intend or set (sthg.) apart for a specific purpose: *This room was designed as a workshop.* **3.** To have (sthg.) as a goal or purpose; intend: *That chair was never designed to be used as a ladder.* —intr. To make or execute plans: *Engineers design for automobile manufacturers.* —n. **1.** [C] A plan, drawing, or sketch, especially a detailed plan showing how sthg. is to be made: *She drew up designs for the new gym.* **2.** [U] The art of creating designs by making patterns, drawings, or sketches: *Engineers and architects are specialists in design.* **3.** [C] An ornamental pattern: *a design on wallpaper.* ♦ **by design.** Purposely: *We left early by design to meet the train.* **have designs on.** To have a secretive plan or scheme to get sbdy./sthg.: *My sister has designs on my new leather jacket.* —de·sign′er n.

des·ig·nate (dĕz′ĭg nāt′) tr.v. **des·ig·nat·ed, des·ig·nat·ing, des·ig·nates. 1.** To indicate or specify (sthg.); point out: *The fence designates the boundary of our prop-*erty. **2.** To give a name or title to (sthg.); characterize: *a period of history designated as the Space Age.* **3.** To select (sbdy./sthg.) for a duty, an office, or a purpose; appoint: *We designated two delegates to represent us at the meeting.* —des′ig·na′tion n. [C; U]

de·sign·ing (dĭ zī′nĭng) adj. Scheming; crafty: *He was fooled by a designing partner.*

de·sir·a·ble (dĭ zīr′ə bəl) adj. Worthwhile; good: *a desirable neighborhood; desirable changes in the law.* —de·sir′a·bil′i·ty, de·sir′a·ble·ness n. [U] —de·sir′a·bly adv.

de·sire (dĭ zīr′) tr.v. **de·sired, de·sir·ing, de·sires. 1.** To wish or long for (sbdy./sthg.); want: *The puppy seemed to desire only attention.* **2.** To express a wish for (sbdy./sthg.); request: *The customer desired information on the new product.* —n. [C; U] **1.** A wish or longing: *She had a lifelong desire to fly airplanes.* **2.** A request or petition: *The citizens made their desires known to the mayor.* —de·sir′ous adj.

SYNONYMS: desire, crave, want, wish. These verbs all mean to feel a strong longing for sthg. *After years of fighting, both nations desire peace. His brother went to Hollywood craving fame and fortune. Do you want to come along? I wish summer vacation were here.*

---

de·sist (dĭ sĭst′ *or* dĭ zĭst′) intr.v. *Formal.* To stop doing (sthg.): *Please desist from interrupting others.*

desk (dĕsk) n. **1.** A piece of furniture usually with a flat top for writing and often drawers or compartments. **2.** A table, counter, or booth at which a service is offered: *an information desk; a reservation desk.*

desk·top (dĕsk′tŏp′) n. The top of a desk. —adj. Designed for use on a desk or table: *a desktop lamp; a desktop computer.*

desktop publishing n. [U] The design and production of publications, such as newsletters and brochures, using a microcomputer with graphics capability.

des·o·late (dĕs′ə lĭt) adj. **1.** Having few or no inhabitants; deserted: *an abandoned shack on a desolate road.* **2.** Having little or no vegetation; not fertile: *a desolate stretch of desert land.* **3.** Dreary; depressing: *a desolate climate of rain and fog.* **4.** Without friends or hope; sad and lost: *He was desolate when all of his friends went away.* See Synonyms at **sad.** —tr.v. (dĕs′ə lāt′). **des·o·lat·ed, des·o·lat·ing, des·o·lates. 1.** To rid or deprive (an area) of inhabitants. **2.** To lay waste to (an area): *A fire desolated the forest.* **3.** To make (sbdy.) lonely or sad: *The loss of our old dog desolated us.* —des′o·late·ly adv. —des′o·la′tion (dĕs′ə lā′shən) n. [U]

ă–cat; ā–pay; âr–care; ä–father; ĕ–get; ē–be; ĭ–sit; ī–nice; îr–here; ŏ–got; ō–go; ô–saw; oi–boy; ou–out; ōō–took; ōō–boot; ŭ–cut; ûr–word; th–thin; th–this; hw–when; zh–vision; ə–about; N–French bon

de·spair (dĭ spâr′) *intr.v.* [*of*] To lose all hope: *He despaired of returning on the early train.* —*n.* [U] **1.** Complete lack of hope: *The hikers gave up in despair as their supplies began to run out.* **2.** A person or thing that causes loss of hope: *The leaky boat was the despair of the crew.*

de·spair·ing (dĭ spâr′ĭng) *adj.* Marked by or resulting from despair: *despairing glances.* —**de·spair′ing·ly** *adv.*

des·per·ate (dĕs′pər ĭt) *adj.* **1.** Having lost all hope; despairing: *a desperate look.* **2.** Willing to do or try anything as the result of a lack of hope: *desperate owners looking for their lost dog.* **3.** Nearly hopeless; critical: *a desperate illness.* **4.** Suffering or driven by a great need for sthg.: *desperate for medical attention.* **5.** Extremely intense: *in desperate need.* —**des′per·ate·ly** *adv.* —**des′per·a′tion** (dĕs′pə rā′shən) *n.* [U]

des·pi·ca·ble (dĕs′pĭ kə bəl *or* dĭ spĭk′-ə bəl) *adj.* Deserving contempt or scorn; hateful: *Stealing is despicable behavior.* —**des′pi·ca·bly** *adv.*

de·spise (dĭ spīz′) *tr.v.* **de·spised, de·spis·ing, de·spis·es. 1.** To regard (sbdy./sthg.) with contempt or scorn: *Everyone despises a thief.* **2.** To dislike (sbdy./sthg.) intensely: *She despises her ex-husband.*

de·spite (dĭ spīt′) *prep.* In spite of; notwithstanding: *We took a hike despite the rainy skies.*

de·spon·dent (dĭ spŏn′dənt) *adj.* Feeling or expressing a lack of hope; depressed: *became despondent during his long absence from home.* —**de·spon′dence, de·spon′den·cy** *n.* [U] —**de·spon′dent·ly** *adv.*

des·pot (dĕs′pət) *n.* **1.** A ruler with absolute power. **2.** A person who wields power oppressively; a tyrant. —**des·pot·ic** (dĭ spŏt′ĭk) *adj.* —**des·pot′i·cal·ly** *adv.* —**des′pot·is′m** (dĕs′pə tĭz′əm) *n.* [U]

des·sert (dĭ zûrt′) *n.* [C; U] The last course of a meal, usually consisting of a sweet dish such as fruit, ice cream, or pastry.

Homonyms: dessert, desert (abandon).

---

des·ti·na·tion (dĕs′tə nā′shən) *n.* The place to which sbdy./sthg. is going or is sent: *The destination of that package is written on the label. His destination was Rome.*

des·tine (dĕs′tĭn) *tr.v.* **des·tined, des·tin·ing, des·tines. 1.** To determine (sthg.) beforehand: *The movie is destined to become a classic.* **2.** To set (sthg.) aside for a specific use or purpose: *This land was destined to be a park.*

des·ti·ny (dĕs′tə nē) *n.*, *pl.* **des·ti·nies. 1.** [C] The fortune or fate of a person or thing considered inevitable or necessary: *Her destiny was to become a doctor.* **2.** [U] The power believed to determine events in

advance: *events shaped by destiny.*

des·ti·tute (dĕs′tĭ tōōt′) *adj.* **1.** [*of*] Having none; empty: *a barren land destitute of trees.* **2.** Being without food, shelter, or other means of subsistence; completely impoverished: *The fire left the inhabitants destitute.* —**des′ti·tu′tion** *n.* [U]

de·stroy (dĭ stroi′) *tr.v.* **1.** To ruin (sbdy./sthg.) completely; spoil: *The explosion destroyed several homes.* **2.** To put an end to (sthg.); eliminate: *Hostile action destroyed all hope of a peaceful settlement.* **3.** To put (sthg.) to death; kill: *The severely injured cat had to be destroyed.* See Synonyms at **ruin.**

de·stroy·er (dĭ stroi′ər) *n.* **1.** A person or thing that destroys. **2.** A small, fast, highly maneuverable warship.

de·struc·ti·ble (dĭ strŭk′tə bəl) *adj.* Breakable or easily destroyed: *The children's toys are easily destructible.*

de·struc·tion (dĭ strŭk′shən) *n.* [U] **1.** The act of destroying sthg.: *Destruction of the old house was completed in two days.* **2.** The condition of having been destroyed; ruin: *The tornado caused great destruction.* **3.** The cause or means of destroying sthg.: *An unwillingness to discuss problems is the destruction of many good friendships.*

de·struc·tive (dĭ strŭk′tĭv) *adj.* **1.** Causing destruction: *a destructive storm.* **2.** Designed or intending to discredit: *Destructive criticism did not help the child.* —**de·struc′tive·ly** *adv.* —**de·struc′tive·ness** *n.* [U]

de·tach (dĭ tăch′) *tr.v.* To separate (sthg.); disconnect: *detach the trailer from the car.* —**de·tach′a·bil·i·ty** *n.* [U] —**de·tach′a·ble** *adj.* —**de·tach′a·bly** *adv.*

de·tached (dĭ tăcht′) *adj.* **1.** Standing apart; disconnected; separate: *a house with a detached garage.* **2.** Without emotional involvement: *a detached view of this problem.*

de·tach·ment (dĭ tăch′mənt) *n.* **1.** [U] The act of separating or disconnecting. **2.** [U] Emotionally removed from others: *He sat through the lecture with bored detachment.* **3.** [U] Without prejudice or bias: *A judge must consider legal matters with detachment.* **4.** [C] A group sent out for a special purpose: *A detachment set up camp.*

de·tail (dĭ tāl′ *or* dē′tāl′) *n.* [C; U] **1.** An individual part or item; a particular: *The story has many details about life on an island.* **2.** A minor or unimportant item or aspect: *We need to focus on the main idea of the story, not just the details.* **3.** An assigned duty: *We have cleanup detail all week.* —*tr.v.* (dĭ tāl′). **1.** To report or describe (sthg.) fully: *The chief detailed the fire to the reporters.* **2.** To assign (sbdy./sthg.) to a special duty: *The highway department detailed extra plows to clear the snow.* ◆ **in detail.** With attention to particulars; minutely: *The planning board examined the design of the new park in detail.*

D

de•tailed (dĭ tāld′ *or* dē′tāld′) *adj.* Marked by abundant use of detail or thoroughness of treatment: *a detailed drawing; a detailed study of the evidence in the case.*

de•tain (dĭ tān′) *tr.v.* **1.** To keep (sbdy./sthg.) from going on; delay: *Friends detained me awhile at lunch.* **2.** To keep (sbdy.) in custody; confine temporarily: *Police detained several suspects overnight.* —**de•tain′ment** *n.* [U]

de•tect (dĭ tĕkt′) *tr.v.* To discover or determine the existence of (sbdy./sthg.): *detect the smell of smoke; detect errors in a report.* —**de•tect′a•ble, de•tect′i•ble** *adj.* —**de•tec′tion** *n.* [U]

de•tec•tive (dĭ tĕk′tĭv) *n.* A police officer or private investigator who investigates crimes and obtains evidence or information. —*adj.* Relating to detectives or their work: *a detective story.*

de•tec•tor (dĭ tĕk′tər) *n.* A thing that detects, especially a mechanical, chemical, or electrical device that indicates the presence of a particular substance or agent: *a metal detector in an airport; a smoke detector on the ceiling.*

dé•tente (dā tänt′) *n.* [U] A relaxation or lessening of tensions between nations: *A policy of détente has increased trade between the two countries.*

de•ten•tion (dĭ tĕn′shən) *n.* [C; U] **1.** The act of detaining or holding back. **2.** The state of being detained, especially a period of custody: *The prisoners were held in detention.*

de•ter (dĭ tûr′) *tr.v.* **de•terred, de•ter•ring, de•ters.** To prevent or discourage (sbdy.) from doing sthg.: *The threat of rain deterred us from picnicking.*

de•ter•gent (dĭ tûr′jənt) *n.* [C; U] A liquid or powdered soap used for washing clothing, dishes, or other items: *dishwasher detergent; laundry detergent.* —*adj.* Having cleansing power: *a detergent soap.*

de•te•ri•o•rate (dĭ tîr′ē ə rāt′) *tr. & intr.v.* **de•te•ri•o•rat•ed, de•te•ri•o•rat•ing, de•te•ri•o•rates.** To make or become inferior in quality, character, or value; worsen: *Moisture deteriorated the cover of the old book. The railroads deteriorated as air travel grew.* —**de•te′ri•o•ra′tion** *n.* [U]

de•ter•mi•na•tion (dĭ tûr′mə nā′shən) *n.* **1.** [C; U] The act of making a decision: *The determination of the judges is final.* **2.** [U] Firmness of purpose; resolve: *The determination of the team helped them to win.* **3.** [C] The act of finding out the quality, quantity, position, or character of sthg.: *the determination of the ship's position.*

de•ter•mine (dĭ tûr′mĭn) *tr.v.* **de•ter•mined, de•ter•min•ing, de•ter•mines.**

1. To settle or decide (sthg.) firmly and conclusively: *determine whether a statement is true or false.* **2.** To establish (sthg.) definitely after consideration, calculation, or investigation: *determine the answer to a math problem.* **3.** To be the cause of (sthg.); regulate: *Climate determines how people in different parts of the world live.* **4.** To limit (sthg.) in scope or extent: *Time will determine how much we can do.*

de•ter•mined (dĭ tûr′mĭnd) *adj.* Having determination: *a determined leader; a determined effort.* —**de•ter′mined•ly** *adv.*

de•ter•min•er (dĭ tûr′mə nər) *n.* A word belonging to a class of noun modifiers that includes articles, demonstrative pronouns, possessive adjectives, and other words such as *any, both,* and *whose.*

de•ter•rence (dĭ tûr′əns *or* dĭ tŭr′əns) *n.* [U] The act or a means of deterring: *The fence around the yard served as a deterrence to dogs.*

de•ter•rent (dĭ tûr′ənt *or* dĭ tŭr′ənt) *n.* A person or thing that deters: *The supervisor's lack of interest was a deterrent to the rest of us to work hard.*

de•test (dĭ tĕst′) *tr.v.* To dislike (sbdy./sthg.) strongly; abhor: *Many people detest snakes.*

de•throne (dē thrōn′) *tr.v.* **de•throned, de•thron•ing, de•thrones.** **1.** To remove (royalty) from the throne: *The new democratic leaders dethroned the king.* **2.** To remove (sbdy.) from a position of power: *The committee members dethroned their leader because of his frequent absences.* —**de•throne′ment** *n.* [U]

det•o•nate (dĕt′n āt′) *intr. & tr.v.* **det•o•nat•ed, det•o•nat•ing, det•o•nates.** To explode or cause to explode: *The explosives detonated in sequence. The miners detonated a charge of explosives.* —**det′o•na′tion** *n.*

det•o•na•tor (dĕt′n ā′tər) *n.* A device used to set off an explosive charge.

de•tour (dē′tŏŏr′ *or* dĭ tŏŏr′) *n.* **1.** A road used temporarily instead of a main route: *We took the detour around the construction site.* **2.** An indirect way or course: *a detour through the country on a nice day.* —*intr. & tr.v.* To go or cause to go by an indirect way: *We detoured around the traffic accident. Police detoured traffic because of heavy flooding.*

de•tox•i•fy (dē tŏk′sə fī′) *tr.v.* **de•tox•i•fied, de•tox•i•fy•ing, de•tox•i•fies.** **1.** To counteract or destroy the toxic properties of (sthg.): *Nuclear waste cannot be detoxified.* **2.** To remove poison or other harmful substances from (sthg.): *Fasting is a good way to detoxify the body.* —**de•tox′i•fi•ca′tion** *n.* [U]

ă–cat; ā–pay; âr–care; ä–father; ĕ–get; ē–be; ĭ–sit; ī–nice; îr–here; ŏ–got; ō–go; ô–saw; oi–boy; ou–out; ŏŏ–took; ōō–boot; ŭ–cut; ûr–word; th–thin; *th*–this; hw–when; zh–vision; ə–about; ɴ–French bon

de·tract (dǐ trăkt′) *intr.v.* To reduce the importance or quality of sthg.: *The old curtains detract from the beauty of the room.* —**de·trac′tion, de·trac′tor** *n.*

det·ri·ment (dĕt′rə mənt) *n.* **1.** [U] Damage, harm, or loss: *My brother was out sick a week without detriment to his grades.* **2.** [C] Something that causes damage, harm, or loss: *Oil spills are a serious detriment to coastal wildlife.* —**det′ri·men′tal** (dĕt′rə mĕn′tl) *adj.* —**det′ri·men′tal·ly** *adv.*

deuce (dōōs) *n.* A playing card with two marks; a two.

deut·sche mark (doich *or* doi′chə) *n.* The basic monetary unit of Germany.

de·val·ue (dē văl′yōō) *tr.v.* **de·val·ued, de·val·u·ing, de·val·ues. 1.** To lower the exchange value of (a currency). **2.** To lessen or cancel the value of (sthg.): *The scientist never devalued the contributions of his assistants.* —**de·val′u·a′tion** *n.* [C; U]

dev·as·tate (dĕv′ə stāt′) *tr.v.* **dev·as·tat·ed, dev·as·tat·ing, dev·as·tates. 1.** To destroy (sthg.): *The storms devastated much of the countryside.* **2.** To overwhelm (sbdy.); harm: *The loss of her sister devastated my mother.* —**dev′as·ta′tion** (dĕv′ə-stā′shən) *n.* [U]

dev·as·tat·ing (dĕv′ə stā′tĭng) *adj.* **1.** Very damaging or harmful: *A devastating storm erased hope for a good harvest.* **2.** Causing great sadness or grief: *He cried after the devastating news of his child's death.* —**dev′as·tat′ing·ly** *adv.*

de·vel·op (dǐ vĕl′əp) *v.* —*tr.* **1.** To help (sthg.) grow or become stronger: *develop muscle by exercising.* **2.** To increase the complexity or quality of (sthg.): *develop one's vocabulary from reading.* **3.a.** To bring (sthg.) into existence gradually: *develop a new industry.* **b.** To design or clarify (sthg.) by degrees: *develop a plan; develop a story.* **4.a.** To come to have (sthg.) gradually: *develop a taste for citrus fruits.* **b.** To become affected with (sthg.); contract: *She developed a rash.* **5.** To cause (a tract of land) to serve a particular purpose: *They developed the land as a mall.* **6.** To treat (photographic film) with chemicals to make images recorded on it appear: *My friend can develop the pictures for us.* —*intr.* **1.** To grow by degrees into a more advanced or mature state: *A student's mind develops with education and time.* **2.** To increase or expand: *The town developed into a city over the years.* **3.** To come gradually into existence or activity: *A friendship soon developed between the two.* **4.** To become clear; be disclosed: *I'll give you the details as they develop.*

de·vel·oped (dǐ vĕl′əpt) *adj.* **1.** Made larger or stronger or otherwise improved: *well-developed biceps; a developed sense of what is right.* **2.** Having many industries and better living conditions: *the developed nations of the world.*

de·vel·op·er (dǐ vĕl′ə pər) *n.* **1.** A person or thing that develops, especially a person who develops real estate by preparing a site for residential or commercial use. **2.** A chemical used in developing a photographic film or similar material.

de·vel·op·ing (dǐ vĕl′ə pǐng) *adj.* **1.** Growing or changing: *a developing embryo; developing news.* **2.** Having a relatively low level of economic and industrial development: *a developing nation.*

de·vel·op·ment (dǐ vĕl′əp mənt) *n.* **1.** [U] The act of developing: *The development of a vaccine requires much research.* **2.** [U] The state of being developed: *The plans for the project are in development.* **3.** [C] A significant event, happening, or change: *The newspaper related the latest developments in the peace talks.* **4.** [C] A group of buildings made by the same contractor: *The development includes homes and a shopping center.* —**de·vel′op·men′tal** *adj.*

de·vi·ant (dē′vē ənt) *adj.* Differing from conventional social standards: *deviant behavior.* —*n.* An insulting word for a person whose attitude, character, or behavior differs from conventional social standards, especially in a sexual way.

de·vi·ate (dē′vē āt′) *intr.v.* **de·vi·at·ed, de·vi·at·ing, de·vi·ates.** [*from*] To move away, as from a norm or purpose; stray: *Their plans deviated from what we originally agreed to do.* —*n.* (dē′vē ĭt). A deviant.

de·vi·a·tion (dē′vē ā′shən) *n.* [C; U] **1.** The act of deviating or turning aside. **2.** An abnormality; a departure: *Staying up late is a deviation from our routine.*

de·vice (dǐ vīs′) *n.* **1.** An object designed or used for a particular purpose; a mechanism: *A telephone is a handy device.* **2.** A plan, scheme, or trick: *The child used crying and other devices to get his way.* ◆ **leave to (one's) own devices.** To allow sbdy. to do as he or she pleases: *We left the child to her own devices for an hour.*

dev·il (dĕv′əl) *n.* **1.** In many religions, the personified spirit of evil who is often also the ruler of Hell and the enemy of God. **2.** An evil spirit; a demon. **3.** A wicked or bad-tempered person. **4.** *Informal.* A person: *The young man is a handsome devil.* **5.** A person who is daring, clever, or full of mischief. —**dev′il·ish** *adj.* —**dev′il·ish·ly** *adv.* —**dev′il·ish·ness** *n.* [U]

dev·il-may-care (dĕv′əl mā kâr′) *adj.* Very careless; reckless: *We didn't approve of his devil-may-care attitude.*

dev·il's advocate (dĕv′əlz) *n.* A person who argues against a position simply for the sake of argument or to test the validity of the position.

dev·il's food cake *n.* A rich chocolate cake.

D

de·vi·ous (dē′vē əs) *adj.* **1.** Not direct; shifty: *a devious character.* **2.** Not following the correct or accepted way: *They achieved success by devious means.* —**de′vi·ous·ly** *adv.* —**de′vi·ous·ness** *n.* [U]

de·vise (dĭ vīz′) *tr.v.* **de·vised, de·vis·ing, de·vis·es.** To figure out or arrange (sthg.); plan: *She devised a way to keep the window open with a stick.*

de·void (dĭ void′) *adj.* [*of*] Completely lacking; empty: *a person devoid of humor.*

de·vote (dĭ vōt′) *tr.v.* **de·vot·ed, de·vot·ing, de·votes.** **1.** To give or apply (one's time, attention, or self) entirely to a certain activity, cause, or person: *a musician who devotes time to helping students.* **2.** To set (sthg.) apart for a specific purpose; dedicate: *He devotes a few hours each week to working on the vegetable garden.*

de·vot·ed (dĭ vō′tĭd) *adj.* **1.** Showing strong affection or attachment; loving: *a devoted friend.* **2.** Dedicated: *a devoted scientist.* —**de·vot′ed·ly** *adv.* —**de·vot′ed·ness** *n.* [U]

dev·o·tee (dĕv′ə tē′) *n.* A person who is strongly devoted to sthg.; a fan: *A devotee of fishing will be out in all kinds of weather.*

de·vo·tion (dĭ vō′shən) *n.* **1.** [U] Strong affection and dedication, as to a person: *the devotion of a parent to a child.* **2.** [C] *(usually plural).* An act of religious observance or prayer, especially when private. **3.** [U] The act of devoting or the state of being devoted: *devotion of time to teaching English to immigrants.* —**de·vo′tion·al** *adj.* —**de·vo′tion·al·ly** *adv.*

de·vour (dĭ vour′) *tr.v.* **1.** To eat (sthg.) greedily: *The hungry campers devoured their dinner.* **2.** To destroy or consume (sthg.): *Flames devoured the building.* **3.** To take (sthg.) in greedily: *devour an exciting mystery story.*

de·vout (dĭ vout′) *adj.* **1.** Devoted to religion or to religious obligations: *a devout monk.* **2.** Sincere; earnest: *a devout wish for peace.* —**de·vout′ly** *adv.* —**de·vout′ness** *n.* [U]

dew (dōō) *n.* [U] **1.** Water droplets condensed from the air, mostly at night, onto cool surfaces. **2.** Moisture appearing in small drops, as tears or perspiration. —**dew′i·ness** *n.* [U] —**dew′y** *adj.*

HOMONYMS: dew, do (perform), **due** (owing).

---

dew point *n.* [U] The temperature at which air becomes saturated with water vapor and dew forms.

dex·ter·i·ty (dĕk stĕr′ĭ tē) *n.* [U] Skill or grace in using the hands, body, or mind: *Her dexterity has made her a great basketball player.*

dex·ter·ous (dĕk′stər əs *or* dĕk′strəs) also **dex·trous** (dĕk′strəs) *adj.* Skillful in the use of the hands or mind: *a dexterous carpenter.* —**dex′ter·ous·ly** *adv.* —**dex′ter·ous·ness** *n.* [U]

di— *pref.* A prefix that means two, twice, or double: *dioxide; dioxin.*

dia— or **di—** *pref.* A prefix that means through or across: *diagonal.*

di·a·be·tes (dī′ə bē′tĭs *or* dī′ə bē′tēz) *n.* [U] A metabolic disorder in which the body cannot control the level of sugar in the blood. —**di′a·bet′ic** (dī′ə bĕt′ĭk) *adj. & n.*

di·a·bol·i·cal (dī′ə bŏl′ĭ kəl) also **di·a·bol·ic** (dī′ə bŏl′ĭ k) *adj.* Extremely clever, evil, or cruel: *The terrorists used a diabolical plan to shut down the power plant.* —**di′a·bol′i·cal·ly** *adv.*

di·a·crit·i·cal mark (dī′ə krĭt′ĭ kəl) *n.* A mark added to a letter to indicate a certain pronunciation or stress.

di·ag·nose (dī′əg nōs′ *or* dī′əg nōz′) *tr.v.* **di·ag·nosed, di·ag·nos·ing, di·ag·nos·es.** To make a careful examination of (sbdy./sthg.); identify and study: *Doctors diagnose disease, and mechanics diagnose car trouble.*

di·ag·no·sis (dī′əg nō′sĭs) *n., pl.* **di·ag·no·ses** (dī′əg nō′sēz) [C; U] **1.** The act of identifying or determining the nature and cause of a disease or injury by examining a patient, analyzing a patient's medical history, and reviewing the results of laboratory tests: *the doctor's diagnosis.* **2.** A close analysis of the nature of sthg. or the conclusions reached by such an analysis: *When the computer broke down, the diagnosis was a bad memory chip.* —**di′ag·nos′tic** (dī′əg nŏs′tĭk) *adj.* —**di′ag·nos′ti·cal·ly** *adv.* —**di′ag·nos·ti′cian** (dī′əg nŏ stĭsh′ən) *n.*

di·ag·o·nal (dī- ăg′ə nəl) *adj.* **1.** Connecting two nonadjacent corners in a geometric figure: *a diagonal line drawn in a square.* **2.** Slanting: *the diagonal stripes on a tie.* —*n.* **1.** A diagonal line segment: *She drew a diagonal.* **2.** Something having a sloping or slanting direction, as a row, course, or part: *The path across the field was a diagonal. Cut the carrots on the diagonal.* —**di·ag′o·nal·ly** *adv.*

diagonal

di·a·gram (dī′ə grăm′) *n.* A plan, drawing, or sketch that shows how sthg. works or indicates how parts are put together: *A diagram of the machine shows what each part is called.* —*tr.v.* **di·a·grammed, di·a·gram·ming, di·a·grams** or **di·a·gramed, di·**

---

a·gram·ing, di·a·grams. To show or represent (sthg.) by a diagram: *diagram a floor plan.*

di·al (dī′əl) *n.* **1.** A usually round surface on which a measurement, such as speed, is indicated by a moving needle or pointer. **2.** The control that selects the station to which a radio or television is tuned. **3.** A movable disk on a rotary telephone with numbers and letters, used to signal the number to which a call is made. —*v.* —*tr.* **1.** To operate (sthg.) by using a dial, as in a combination lock: *We dialed the combination, and the lock opened.* **2.** To call (sbdy.) on a telephone: *Dial '0' to reach an operator.* —*intr.* To use a dial, as on a telephone: *Dial until you get an answer.*

di·a·lect (dī′ə lĕkt′) *n.* A variety of a language spoken in a particular region or by a particular group of people: *There are many dialects of English.* —**di′a·lec′tal** (dī′ə-lĕk′təl) *adj.*

USAGE: dialect One language may have several dialects that differ from each other in such things as pronunciation or choice of words. The dialect of English that is taught in your school and used by newspapers, magazines, radio, and television is called Standard English. In different parts of the country, people pronounce words in a certain way and even use certain words because of the dialect they speak. For example, people who live in the Northeast or the South of the United States usually call carbonated soft drink **soda.** People who live in the Midwest or West usually call it **pop.** People in Boston call it **tonic.**

---

di·a·logue or **di·a·log** (dī′ə lôg′ or dī′ə-lŏg′) *n.* **1.** [C] A conversation between two or more people: *a friendly dialogue.* **2.** [U] The words spoken by the characters of a play or story: *The dialogue of the comedy was witty.*

dial tone *n.* A low steady tone in a telephone receiver, telling the user that a number may be dialed.

di·al·y·sis (dī ăl′ĭ sĭs) *n.* [U] The removal of wastes from the bloodstream by a machine when the kidneys do not function properly.

diam. *abbr.* An abbreviation of diameter.

di·am·e·ter (dī ăm′ĭ tər) *n.* **1.** A straight line segment that passes through the center of a circle or sphere from one side to the other. **2.** The length of such a line segment.

di·a·met·ri·cal (dī′ə mĕt′rĭ kəl) also **di·a·met·ric** (dī′ə mĕt′rĭk) *adj.* **1.** Of or along a diameter: *a diametrical measurement.* **2.** Exactly opposite; contrary: *debaters with diametrical points of view.* —**di′a·met′ri·cal·ly** *adv.*

di·a·mond (dī′ə mənd or dī′mənd) *n.* **1.a.** [U] A form of pure carbon that occurs as a clear crystal and is the hardest of all known

minerals. **b.** [C] A gemstone made from diamond crystal. **2.** [C] **a.** A figure with four equal sides forming two inner obtuse angles and two inner acute angles. **b.** *(often used in the plural).* Playing cards bearing a red figure shaped like this ♦: *the four of diamonds.* **3.** [C] **a.** A baseball infield. **b.** The whole playing field in baseball.

di·a·per (dī′ə pər or dī′pər) *n.* A folded piece of absorbent material, such as paper or cloth, used as underpants for a baby. —*tr.v.* To put a diaper on (a baby): *He diapered the baby and gave her a bottle.*

di·a·phragm (dī′ə frăm′) *n.* **1.** A muscle that separates the chest cavity from the abdominal cavity and forces air into and out of the lungs. **2.** A birth control device used by women.

di·ar·rhe·a (dī′ə rē′ə) *n.* [U] A condition in which bowel movements are frequent and watery.

di·a·ry (dī′ə rē) *n., pl.* **di·a·ries.** **1.** A daily record, especially a personal record of experiences, observations, and events. **2.** A book of blank pages for keeping such a record.

di·a·tribe (dī′ə trīb′) *n.* A severe criticism; a verbal attack: *a diatribe against smoking.*

dibs (dĭbz) *pl.n. Slang.* A claim; rights: *I have dibs on the last cookie.*

dice (dīs) *n., pl.* **dice.** A small cube with a different number of spots on each side, used in games: *It's your turn to roll the dice.* —*v.* **diced, dic·ing, dic·es.** To cut (food) into small cubes: *dice vegetables for soup.*

dic·ey (dī′sē) *adj. Informal.* Risky: *a dicey situation.*

dick (dĭk) *n. Offensive Slang.* **1.** The penis. **2.** An insulting term for a man who is ill-mannered or rude.

dict. *abbr.* An abbreviation of dictionary.

dic·tate (dĭk′tāt′ or dĭk tāt′) *v.* **dic·tat·ed, dic·tat·ing, dic·tates.** —*tr.* **1.** To say or read (words) aloud to be recorded or written by another person: *dictate an order over the phone; dictate a letter.* **2.** To establish (sthg.) with authority; impose: *Hospital rules dictate visiting hours.* —*intr.* **1.** To say or read aloud material to be recorded or written by another person: *The reporter dictated into the tape recorder.* **2.** To issue orders or commands.

dic·ta·tion (dĭk tā′shən) *n.* **1.** [U] The act of dictating material to be written down or recorded by sbdy. else: *dictation of a letter over the telephone.* **2.** [C] The material that is dictated.

dic·ta·tor (dĭk′tā′tər or dĭk tā′tər) *n.* **1.** An absolute ruler. **2.** A tyrant; a despot. —**dic′-ta·to′ri·al** (dĭk′tə tôr′ē əl) *adj.* —**dic′ta·to′ri·al·ly** *adv.*

dic·ta·tor·ship (dĭk tā′tər shĭp′ or dĭk′-tā′tər shĭp′) *n.* **1.** [C] The office of a dictator. **2.** [C] A state or government under the rule of a dictator. **3.** [U] Absolute control or power.

D

dic·tion (dĭk'shən) *n.* [U] Degree of clearness and distinctness in pronouncing words: *The singer had good diction, so we could enjoy both the words and the music.*

dic·tion·ar·y (dĭk'shə nĕr'ē) *n., pl.* **dic·tion·ar·ies. 1.** A reference book containing an alphabetical list of words with information given for each word. Such information usually includes meaning, pronunciation, and sample sentences. **2.** A book containing a list of words in one language translated into another language: *a Russian–English dictionary.* **3.** A book listing words in a particular subject or category with information about each word: *a medical dictionary.*

did (dĭd) *v.* Past tense of **do**[1].

di·dac·tic (dī dăk'tĭk) *adj.* **1.** Intended to teach: *Many children's stories have a didactic purpose.* **2.** Teaching or moralizing too much: *didactic poetry.* —**di·dac'ti·cal·ly** *adv.*

did·n't (dĭd'nt). Contraction of *did not.*

die[1] (dī) *intr.v.* **died, dy·ing** (dī'ĭng), **dies. 1.** To stop living; become dead: *The flowers died after the first frost.* **2.** To cease existing; become extinct: *We don't know why the dinosaurs died.* **3.** To experience an agony; suffer: *He nearly died of embarrassment.* **4.** To stop working or operating: *The motor died when we ran out of gas.* ◆ **be dying to.** To want to do sthg. very much: *I'm dying to see that movie.* **die away** or **down.** *intr.v.* To become weaker and disappear gradually: *The comedian continued to speak after the laughter died down.* **die for.** *tr.v.* [insep.] **1.** To give one's life for (sbdy./sthg.): *He was willing to die for his country.* **2.** To want (sthg.) very much: *The cake looks so good; I am dying for a piece.* **die laughing.** To laugh hard: *The joke was so funny that I thought I would die laughing.* **die off.** *intr.v.* To undergo a sudden sharp decline in population: *When temperature decreases, many plants die off.* **die out.** *intr.v.* To cease living completely; become extinct: *Some customs survive and others just die out.* **to die for.** *Slang.* Very wonderful or desirable: *They live in a house that's to die for.* **until (one's) dying day.** For the rest of one's life; with strong lasting commitment: *I will remember my parents' advice until my dying day.*

HOMONYMS: die (stop living, tool for shaping material), **dye** (color).

die[2] (dī) *n., pl.* **dies.** A tool or device that shapes materials by stamping, cutting, or punching: *Dies are used to make coins.*

die-hard also **die·hard** (dī'härd') *adj.* Stubbornly resisting change or holding on to a belief: *a die-hard supporter.* —*n.* A person who stubbornly refuses to give up a cause or resists change: *Those die-hards don't know when to quit.*

die·sel (dē'zəl or dē'səl) *n.* **1.** [C] A type of engine. **2.** [U] The fuel to power a diesel engine.

diesel engine *n.* An internal-combustion engine in which the fuel oil is ignited by the heat of air that has been highly compressed in the cylinder.

di·et (dī'ĭt) *n.* **1.** [C; U] The usual food and drink eaten by a person or an animal: *a healthy diet.* **2.** [C] A specific selection of foods: *The diet of a diabetic excludes most fatty foods.* —*intr.v.* To eat and drink according to a regulated system: *I need to wear my old suit, so I'm dieting to lose weight.* —**di·e·tar'y** (dī'ĭ tĕr'ē) *adj.* —**di·et·er** *n.*

di·e·tet·ic (dī'ĭ tĕt'ĭk) *adj.* **1.** Relating to diet or its regulation. **2.** Made for restricted diets: *dietetic foods prepared with less salt and sugar.*

dif·fer (dĭf'ər) *intr.v.* **1.** To be unlike in nature or amount: *The weather often differs from one part of a state to another.* **2.** [*over; about*] To be of a different opinion; disagree: *Members of the committee differed over what plan to accept.*

dif·fer·ence (dĭf'ər əns or dĭf'rəns) *n.* **1.** [U] The quality or condition of being unlike: *the difference between summer and winter.* **2.** [C] An instance of being unlike or different: *the differences were obvious.* **3.** [U] A noticeable change or effect: *Exercise has made a big difference in her health.* **4.** [C] (*usually plural*). A disagreement or controversy: *We settled our differences amicably.* **5.** [U] The amount by which one quantity is greater or less than another; what is left when one number is subtracted from another: *The difference between 10 and 4 is 6.*

dif·fer·ent (dĭf'ər ənt or dĭf'rənt) *adj.* **1.** Unlike in form, quality, amount, or nature: *The two breeds of dog are very different.* **2.** Distinct or separate: *We ran into each other on three different occasions today.* **3.** Differing from all others; unusual: *The penguin is a very different bird.* —**dif'fer·ent·ly** *adv.*

USAGE: different When you are making a comparison between two persons or things, **different** should be followed by **from** instead of **than**: *My book is different from* (not *than*) *yours.*

dif·fer·en·ti·ate (dĭf'ə rĕn'shē āt') *v.* **dif·fer·en·ti·at·ed, dif·fer·en·ti·at·ing, dif·fer·en·ti·ates.** —*tr.* **1.** To be the difference between (things): *Red shirts and* *blue shirts differentiate the teams.* **2.** To understand or show the differences between (things): *We learned to differentiate the various wildflowers.* —*intr.* **1.** To become distinct or specialized: *Cells differentiated into new forms.* **2.** [*between*] To make distinctions; discriminate: *A doctor can differentiate between a rash and chickenpox.* —**dif•fer•en'ti•a'tion** *n.* [C; U]

dif•fi•cult (dĭf'ĭ kŭlt') *adj.* **1.** Hard to do or perform: *a difficult task.* **2.** Hard to understand or solve: *a difficult math problem.* **3.** Hard to please, satisfy, or manage: *a difficult person to live with.*

dif•fi•cul•ty (dĭf'ĭ kŭl'tē *or* dĭf'ĭ kəl tē) *n.*, *pl.* **dif•fi•cul•ties. 1.** [U] The quality or condition of being difficult: *The difficulty of the subject made the chemistry book hard to understand.* **2.** [C] (*usually plural*) A troublesome or embarrassing state of affairs: *The store was having financial difficulties and had to close.* **3.** [U] A laborious effort; a struggle: *I finished the exam with difficulty.* **4.** [C] A disagreement or dispute: *There was a small difficulty over the boundary line.*

dif•fuse (dĭ fyōōz') *v.* **dif•fused, dif•fus•ing, dif•fus•es.** —*tr.* **1.** To cause (sthg.) to spread out freely: *The lamp diffuses light over the table.* **2.** To scatter (sthg.): *diffuse ideas; diffuse knowledge.* —*intr.* **1.** To become spread out or scattered: *A lighthouse beam diffuses far out over the ocean.* **2.** To become mixed together: *Water and air diffuse to create fog.* —*adj.* (dĭ fyōōs'). Widely spread or scattered: *Diffuse light is often hard to read by.* —**dif•fu'sion** *n.* [U]

dig (dĭg) *v.* **dug** (dŭg), **dig•ging, digs.** —*tr.* **1.** To break, turn over, or remove (earth, for example), as with a shovel or the hands: *The dog was digging the dirt to crawl under the fence.* **2.** To make or form (sthg.) by removing earth or other material: *A rabbit dug a hole in the garden.* **3.** To get (sthg.) by digging: *dig clams.* **4.** To poke or thrust (nails or claws, for example): *The cat dug its claws into a tree. She dug her fingers into my arm in fear.* **5.** *Slang.* **a.** To understand (sthg.) fully: *Do you dig what I mean?* **b.** To appreciate (sthg.): *Dig that fantastic car!* —*intr.* **1.** To loosen, turn over, or remove earth or other material: *I'm going out to the garden to dig.* **2.** To make one's way by pushing aside or removing material: *dig through the trash to find a lost earring.* **3.** *Slang.* To have an understanding: *Do you dig?* —*n.* **1.** A poke or thrust: *a dig in the ribs.* **2.** A sarcastic taunting remark: *a nasty dig about my accent.* **3.** An archaeological excavation. **4.** *Slang.* **digs.** The place where one lives: *You have to see my new digs!* ◆ **dig in.** *intr.v.* **1.** To dig trenches for protection: *The army dug in for battle.* **2.** To begin to eat heartily: *We were hungry and quickly dug in.* **dig up.** *tr.v.* [sep.]

1. To learn or discover (sthg.) by investigation or research: *dig up information in a library.* **2.** To turn over soil in (sthg.): *dig up the garden.* —**dig'ger** *n.*

di•gest (dĭ jĕst' *or* dī jĕst') *v.* —*tr.* **1.** To break down (food) chemically into materials that the body can use as nourishment: *As carbohydrates are digested, the body turns them into sugar and starch.* **2.** To absorb (ideas) mentally; comprehend: *Reporters must digest facts quickly in order to write their stories.* —*intr.* To be taken in as food or as if food: *Some foods do not digest easily.* —*n.* (dī'jĕst'). A collection of previously published materials, such as essays or reports, usually in condensed form: *Many scientific groups publish digests of their members' work.* —**di•gest'i•bil'i•ty** *n.* [U] —**di•gest'i•ble** *adj.* —**di•ges'tion** *n.* [C; U] —**di•ges'tive** *adj.* —**di•ges'tive•ly** *adv.*

dig•it (dĭj'ĭt) *n.* **1.** A finger or toe. **2.** One of the ten Arabic numerals, 0 through 9: *a ten-digit number.*

dig•i•tal (dĭj'ĭ tl) *adj.* **1.** Relating to or resembling a digit, especially a finger. **2.** Expressed in digits, especially for use by a computer: *digital information.* **3.** Using or giving a reading in digits: *a digital clock; a digital speedometer.* —**dig'i•tal•ly** *adv.*

dig•ni•fied (dĭg'nə fīd') *adj.* Having dignity: *the careful and dignified manner of an ambassador.*

dig•ni•fy (dĭg'nə fī') *tr.v.* **dig•ni•fied, dig•ni•fy•ing, dig•ni•fies. 1.** To give dignity or honor to (sbdy./sthg.): *The mayor's presence dignified our school ceremony.* **2.** To raise the status of (sthg. unworthy and lowly): *My parents would not dignify the gossip by responding to it.*

dig•ni•tar•y (dĭg'nĭ tĕr'ē) *n.*, *pl.* **dig•ni•tar•ies.** A person of high rank or position.

dig•ni•ty (dĭg'nĭ tē) *n.* [U] **1.** The state of being worthy of esteem or respect. **2.** A stately or poised manner: *The judge maintained his dignity in the court at all times.*

di•gress (dī grĕs' *or* dĭ grĕs') *intr.v.* To turn aside, especially from the main subject in writing or speaking: *The professor digressed from the lecture to tell a personal story.* —**di•gres'sion** (dī grĕsh'ən *or* dĭ grĕsh'ən) *n.* [C; U]

dike (dīk) *n.* A structure built to hold back water and prevent flooding from a river or the sea.

di•lap•i•dat•ed (dĭ lăp'ĭ dā'tĭd) *adj.* In a condition of decay or disrepair, as through neglect: *The dilapidated building was beyond repair.* —**di•lap'i•da'tion** *n.* [U]

di•late (dī lāt' *or* dī'lāt') *tr. & intr.v.* **di•lat•ed, di•lat•ing, di•lates.** To make or become larger or wider; expand: *The doctor dilated the pupils of my eyes to do an* *examination. His pupils dilated in the darkness.* —**di•la′tion** *n.* [U]

di•lem•ma (dĭ lĕm′ə) *n.* A situation that requires a person to choose between options that seem equally difficult or unfavorable: *After the company was sold, the manager faced the dilemma of taking a cut in pay or losing her job.*

dil•i•gence (dĭl′ə jəns) *n.* [U] Earnest and persistent application or effort: *It took a lot of diligence to stick with such a difficult project.*

dil•i•gent (dĭl′ə jənt) *adj.* Marked by dedicated and persistent effort: *A diligent search of the records revealed new evidence.* —**dil′i•gent•ly** *adv.*

dill (dĭl) *n.* [U] The very fine leaves or spicy seeds of a plant related to parsley, dried and used as seasoning.

dill pickle *n.* A pickled cucumber flavored with dill.

dil•ly-dal•ly (dĭl′ē dăl′ē) *intr.v.* **dil•ly-dal•lied, dil•ly-dal•lying, dil•ly-dal•lies.** *Informal.* To waste time, especially in indecision; dawdle: *Hurry to class and don't dilly-dally.*

di•lute (dī lōōt′ *or* dĭ lōōt′) *tr.v.* **di•lut•ed, di•lut•ing, di•lutes. 1.** To make (a substance) thinner or less concentrated by adding a liquid such as water: *dilute thick soup.* **2.** To weaken the force, intensity, purity, or condition of (sthg.): *A lack of facts diluted the argument.* —**di•lu′tion** *n.* [U]

dim (dĭm) *adj.* **dim•mer, dim•mest. 1.** Lacking in brightness: *a dim corner of the big room.* See Synonyms at **dark. 2.** Giving off only a small amount of light: *a dim star.* **3.** Lacking luster; dull and faded: *dim colors faded by the sun.* **4.** Faintly outlined; not distinct: *I could just make out the dim shape of a ship in the mist.* **5.** Not sharp or clear; lacking keenness of understanding or perception: *dim eyesight; a dim idea for a story.* **6.** Not favorable: *The coach took a dim view of my excuses.* —*tr. & intr.v.* **dimmed, dim•ming, dims.** To make or become dim: *Drivers must dim their headlights in traffic. The lights dimmed as the play began.* —**dim′ly** *adv.* —**dim′ness** *n.* [U]

dime (dīm) *n.* A coin of the United States or Canada worth ten cents. ◆ **a dime a dozen.** Overly abundant; commonplace: *Personal computers are a dime a dozen these days.* **stop** or **turn on a dime.** To stop or turn at a precise point or within a narrowly defined area: *This car stops on a dime. The skater seems to turn on a dime.*

di•men•sion (dĭ mĕn′shən *or* dī mĕn′shən) *n.* **1.** The measurement of a length, width, or thickness: *The dimensions of the window are 2 feet by 4 feet.* **2.** (*usually plural*). Extent or

magnitude; scope: *a problem of huge dimensions.* **3.** A physical quantity, such as mass, length, or time, on which other measurements are based. —**di•men′sion•al** *adj.*

di•min•ish (dĭ mĭn′ĭsh) *tr. & intr.v.* To make or become smaller or less; reduce or decrease: *A drought diminished their water supply. Light diminished steadily as the sun went down.* See Synonyms at **decrease. —di•min′ish•ing** *adj.*

dim•i•nu•tion (dĭm′ə nōō′shən *or* dĭm′ə nyōō′shən) *n.* [U] The act or process of diminishing; a reduction: *Lack of exercise leads to the diminution of physical strength.*

di•min•u•tive (dĭ mĭn′yə tĭv) *adj.* **1.** Extremely small in size; tiny: *diminutive plates and cups in a dollhouse.* **2.** Relating to a suffix that expresses smallness, youth, or affection, as *-let* in *booklet* and *-ie* in *dearie.* —*n.* A diminutive suffix, word, or name. For example, *Bobby* is a diminutive of *Robert.* —**di•min′u•tive•ly** *adv.*

dim•mer (dĭm′ər) *n.* A device used to control the brightness of an electric light.

dim•ple (dĭm′pəl) *n.* A small hollow or dent in the flesh of the human body, especially in the cheek: *She has dimples when she smiles.* —*intr.v.* **dim•pled, dim•pling, dim•ples.** To form dimples by smiling.

din (dĭn) *n.* A combination of loud, unpleasant sounds: *We couldn't hear them speaking over the din of the traffic.* See Synonyms at **uproar.**

dine (dīn) *v.* **dined, din•ing, dines.** —*intr.* To have dinner: *We dined early. They dined on lobster and salad.* —*tr.* To give dinner to (sbdy.); entertain at dinner: *They wined and dined the visiting senators.* ◆ **dine in** or **out.** *intr.v.* To eat in one's home or out at a restaurant: *Do you want to dine in or dine out tonight?*

din•er (dī′nər) *n.* **1.** A person who dines. **2.** An inexpensive restaurant that has a long counter and booths, usually in a building designed to look like a railroad car.

ding (dĭng) *intr. & tr.v.* To ring or cause to ring with a metallic sound: *The timer on the stove dinged when the cake was done. Ding the bell on the front desk to call the bellhop.* —*n.* A ringing sound: *the ding of a timer.*

ding-dong (dĭng′dông′ *or* dĭng′dŏng′) *n.* The sound of a bell.

din•ghy (dĭng′ē) *n., pl.* **din•ghies.** A small open boat, especially a rowboat carried by a larger boat.

din•gy (dĭn′jē) *adj.* **din•gi•er, din•gi•est.** Darkened or discolored with dirt: *a dark and dingy room in need of paint.* —**din′gi•ly** *adv.* —**din′gi•ness** *n.* [U]

din•ing room (dī′nĭng) *n.* A room, as in a house or hotel, in which meals are eaten.

ă–**cat**; ā–**pay**; âr–**care**; ä–**father**; ĕ–**get**; ē–**be**; ĭ–**sit**; ī–**nice**; îr–**here**; ŏ–**got**; ō–**go**; ô–**saw**; oi–**boy**; ou–**out**; ōō–**took**; ōō–**boot**; ŭ–**cut**; ûr–**word**; th–**thin**; *th*–**this**; hw–**when**; zh–**vision**; ə–**about**; N–French **bon**

din•ky (dĭng′kē) *adj.* **din•ki•er, din•ki• est.** *Informal.* Of small size or little importance: *a dinky little car.*

din•ner (dĭn′ər) *n.* **1.** The main meal of the day, eaten at midday or in the evening. **2.** A formal meal in honor of a person or an event: *We held a dinner in a restaurant to celebrate his birthday.*

di•no•saur (dī′nə sôr′) *n.* One of a large group of meat- or plant-eating reptiles that lived many millions of years ago. The fossil remains of their bones show that the dinosaurs included the largest land animals ever known to live.

di•o•cese (dī′ə sĭs *or* dī′ə sēs′) *n.* The district or group of churches under the control of a bishop.

di•ox•ide (dī ŏk′sīd) *n.* A compound with two atoms of oxygen per molecule.

di•ox•in (dī ok′sĭn) *n.* A cancer-causing substance that can be found in chemicals for killing unwanted plants.

dip (dĭp) *v.* **dipped, dip•ping, dips.** —*tr.* **1.** To put (sthg.) briefly in or into a liquid: *dip a cracker into soup.* **2.** To pick (sthg.) up by pushing the hand or a cup below the surface, as of a liquid: *dip water from a stream to get a drink.* **3.** To lower and raise (sthg.) briefly: *dip one's head under the doorway.* —*intr.* **1.** To go briefly into water or other liquid: *The oars dipped in and out of the water.* **2.** To put the hand or a cup into liquid or a container, especially so as to take sthg. out: *dip into one's pocket for 25 cents.* **3.** To drop down suddenly: *The temperature dipped below freezing.* **4.** To slope downward: *The path dips to the river.* —*n.* **1.** A quick swim: *a dip in the pool.* **2.** A liquid into which sthg. is dipped, as for dyeing or disinfecting: *a flea dip for dogs.* **3.** A creamy food mixture into which crackers or other foods may be dipped: *a spicy vegetable dip; chips and dip.* **4.** An amount taken up by dipping; a scoop: *a double dip of ice cream.* **5.** A downward slope: *a dip in the road.*

diph•the•ri•a (dĭf thîr′ē ə *or* dĭp thîr′ē ə) *n.* [U] A serious contagious disease with symptoms that include high fever and difficulty in breathing.

diph•thong (dĭf′thông′ *or* dĭf′thŏng *or* dĭp′thông′ *or* dĭp′thŏng) *n.* A speech sound blending two vowels in the same syllable. For example, the speech sounds represented by *oy* in *boy* and *i* in *nice* are diphthongs.

di•plo•ma (dĭ plō′mə) *n.* A paper or certificate given by a school showing that a person has earned a degree or completed a course of study: *a high-school diploma.*

di•plo•ma•cy (dĭ plō′mə sē) *n.* [U] **1.** The art or practice of managing relations between countries: *Diplomacy includes making alliances, treaties, and trade agreements.* **2.** Skill in dealing with other people in a sensitive way: *The lawyer was known for her diplomacy.*

dip•lo•mat (dĭp′lə măt′) *n.* **1.** A person, such as an ambassador, who represents a government in its dealings with other governments. **2.** A person who uses sensitivity and skill in dealing with other people. —**dip′lo•mat′ic** *adj.* —**dip′lo•mat′i• cal•ly** *adv.*

dip•per (dĭp′ər) *n.* **1.** A person or thing that dips. **2.** A cup with a handle for taking up liquids.

dire (dīr) *adj.* **dir•er, dir•est. 1.** Warning of or having terrible results: *a dire accident.* **2.** Extremely serious and urgent: *in dire need of food and medicine.*

di•rect (dĭ rĕkt′ *or* dī rĕkt′) *v.* —*tr.* **1.** To manage or guide (sthg.): *direct a business.* **2.** To instruct, order, or command (sbdy.): *The general directed the soldiers to free all prisoners.* **3.** To cause (sbdy.) to move toward a goal: *Please direct your eyes to the blackboard.* **4.** To show (sbdy.) the way: *I directed them to the post office.* **5.** To make (remarks, for example) to a particular person or audience: *The principal directed a few words of welcome to the new students.* —*intr.* **1.** To give commands or directions: *police officers directing at an intersection.* **2.** To lead a performance or rehearsal: *The conductor is directing in front of the orchestra.* —*adj.* **1.** Moving in a straight course or line: *The dancers moved in a direct line across the stage.* **2.** Open and honest; frank: *They gave direct answers to my questions.* **3.** Having no persons or conditions to interrupt or influence: *direct sunlight; a direct line to the President.* **4.** Decided by action of the voters rather than through representatives: *direct election.* **5.** Consisting of the exact words of a writer or speaker: *a direct quote from the article.* **6.** Complete and absolute: *direct opposites.* —*adv.* Straight; directly: *He arrived direct from the airport.* —**di•rect′ness** *n.* [U]

direct current *n.* An electric current flowing in one direction only, as that of a battery.

di•rec•tion (dĭ rĕk′shən *or* dī rĕk′shən) *n.* **1.** [U] Management, control, or guidance of an action or operation: *The fire department is under the direction of the chief.* **2.** [C] (*usually plural*). An instruction or a series of instructions for doing or finding sthg.: *directions for fixing the car; directions to the train station.* **3.** [C] An order or a command: *My whistle was a direction for my dog to come.* **4.** [C] The line or course along which a person or thing moves or is located: *traveling in a northerly direction; in the direction of the city.* **5.** [C] A course of development: *We can see the artist taking a different direction in her new paintings.*

di•rec•tion•al (dĭ rĕk′shə nəl *or* dī rĕk′- shə nəl) *adj.* **1.** Showing direction: *a car's directional signals.* **2.** Able to receive or send

D

signals in one direction only: *a directional radar antenna.* —**di·rec′tion·al·ly** *adv.*

di·rec·tive (dĭ rĕk′tĭv *or* dī rĕk′tĭv) *n.* An order or instruction, especially one given by a central authority: *a directive from the coach to all team members about attendance.*

di·rect·ly (dĭ rĕkt′lē *or* dī rĕkt′lē) *adv.* **1.** In a direct line or manner; straight: *The cat headed directly for its food.* **2.** Without anything or anyone coming between: *The students spoke directly to the superintendent about the issue.* **3.** Exactly or totally: *His ideas on this issue are directly opposite to mine.* **4.** Without delay: *I'll meet you there directly after work.*

direct object *n.* The word or words in a sentence that show the person or thing receiving the action of a transitive verb. For example, in the sentence *I wrote a poem,* the direct object is *poem.*

di·rec·tor (dĭ rĕk′tər *or* dī rĕk′tər) *n.* **1.** A person who controls or manages: *The magazine has a new art director.* **2.** A member of a group of persons chosen to control or govern a company or an institution: *a meeting of the board of directors of the hospital.* **3.** A person who guides and controls the actors and others involved in a play, film, or other performance. —**di·rec′tor′i·al** (dĭ rĕk′tôr′ē əl *or* dī rĕk′tôr′ē əl) *adj.*

di·rec·tor·ate (dĭ rĕk′tər ĭt *or* dī rĕk′tər ĭt) *n.* **1.** The office or position of a director. **2.** A board of directors, as of a corporation.

di·rec·to·ry (dĭ rĕk′tə rē *or* dī rĕk′tə rē) *n.,* *pl.* **di·rec·to·ries. 1.** A book containing a list of names, addresses, or other facts, such as telephone numbers, in alphabetical or other order: *A building directory lists the offices of different companies.* **2.** A listing of the data files stored in a computer memory.

dirge (dûrj) *n.* A sad, serious piece of music, such as a funeral hymn.

dirt (dûrt) *n.* [U] **1.** Earth or soil: *The gardener was digging in the dirt.* **2.** A substance such as mud, dust, or grease that soils a clean surface: *A detergent removes dirt from clothes.* **3.** *Informal.* Information about a person's private life, especially embarrassing information; gossip: *This magazine publishes all the dirt about movie stars.*

dirt-cheap (dûrt′chēp′) *adv. & adj. Informal.* Very inexpensive: *buy a truck dirt-cheap; a dirt-cheap hotel.*

dirt·y (dûr′tē) *adj.* **dirt·i·er, dirt·i·est. 1.** Soiled, as with dirt; unclean: *dirty water; dirty clothes.* **2.** Mean, dishonorable, or obscene: *a dirty trick; a dirty movie.* **3.** Not playing fair: *a dirty card player.* **4.** Expressing disapproval or hostility: *a dirty look.* —*tr. & intr.v.* **dirt·ied, dirt·y·ing, dirt·ies.**

To make or become soiled: *The baby dirtied the tablecloth. White clothes dirty easily.*
♦ **dirty linen** or **laundry.** *Informal.* Personal affairs that could cause embarrassment if made public: *Don't air your dirty linen in public.* **dirty work. 1.** A job that causes sbdy. to become soiled or unclean: *Fixing a car can be dirty work.* **2.** A job that is unpleasant, dishonest, or dishonorable: *The boss always gets someone to do his dirty work for him.* **give a dirty look.** To look at sbdy. with disapproval: *When I came in late, he gave me a dirty look.*

dis– *pref.* A prefix that means: **1.** Not: *dissimilar.* **2.** Not any: *discomfort.* **3.** Opposite of: *distrust.* **4.** Do the opposite of: *disapprove.* **5.** Remove or deprive sbdy. of: *disarm.*

WORD BUILDING: dis– The prefix **dis–** has several senses, but its basic meaning is "not, not any." Thus **disbelieve** means "to refuse to believe" and **discomfort** means "a lack of comfort." **Dis–** occurs very frequently in English in words such as **discredit, disrepair,** and **disrespect.**

---

dis·a·bil·i·ty (dĭs′ə bĭl′ĭ tē) *n.,* *pl.* **dis·a·bil·i·ties. 1.** [U] The condition of being disabled: *She is learning to live with her disability.* **2.** [C] Something that disables: *Loss of one's eyesight is a serious disability.*

dis·a·ble (dĭs ā′bəl) *tr.v.* **dis·a·bled, dis·a·bling, dis·a·bles.** To weaken or reduce the capacity or abilities of (sbdy./sthg.): *The storm disabled the steamer's engine.*

dis·a·bled (dĭs ā′bəld) *adj.* **1.** Having one's physical abilities reduced or lessened, as from injury: *a disabled veteran.* **2.** Unable to function: *a disabled car.* —*n.* [U] Physically disabled people considered as a group: *We have laws to protect the rights of the disabled.*

dis·ad·van·tage (dĭs′əd văn′tĭj) *n.* **1.** [C] An unfavorable condition, situation, or position: *I arrived late, so I felt at a disadvantage in the discussion.* **2.** [U] Damage or harm: *The shorter library hours worked to the disadvantage of the public.*

dis·ad·van·taged (dĭs′əd văn′tĭjd) *adj.* Without some of the basic necessities of life, such as good housing, health care, or education: *disadvantaged children.*

dis·ad·van·ta·geous (dĭs ăd′vən tā′jəs *or* dĭs′ăd vən tā′jəs) *adj.* Causing harm; unfavorable: *disadvantageous living conditions.* —**dis·ad′van·ta′geous·ly** *adv.*

dis·af·fect·ed (dĭs′ə fĕk′tĭd) *adj.* Angry about conditions that seem unfair: *The disaffected workers voted to go on strike.*

dis·a·gree (dĭs′ə grē′) *intr.v.* **dis·a·greed,**

ă–cat; ā–pay; âr–care; ä–father; ĕ–get; ē–be; ĭ–sit; ī–nice; îr–here; ŏ–got; ō–go; ô–saw; oi–boy; ou–out; ōō–took; ōō–boot; ŭ–cut; ûr–word; th–thin; *th*–this; hw–when; zh–vision; ə–about; N–French bon

dis•a•gree•ing, dis•a•grees. 1. To fail to match; differ: *Your answer to the math problem disagrees with mine.* **2.** To have a differing opinion: *Scientists disagree on why dinosaurs died out.* **3.** To argue or quarrel: *Rival countries often disagree about international trade.* **4.** To cause bad effects: *Fried food disagrees with me.*

dis•a•gree•a•ble (dĭs′ə grē′ə bəl) *adj.* **1.** Not pleasing; unpleasant or offensive: *a strong and disagreeable smell.* **2.** Having an unfriendly or bad-tempered manner: *Many people are disagreeable when they first wake up.* —**dis′a•gree′a•ble•ness** *n.* [U] —**dis′-a•gree′a•bly** *adv.*

dis•a•gree•ment (dĭs′ə grē′mənt) *n.* **1.** [U] A failure or refusal to agree: *The peace talks ended in disagreement.* **2.** [C] A conflict or argument: *Their disagreement ended in loud words.*

dis•al•low (dĭs′ə lou′) *tr.v. Formal.* **1.** To refuse to allow (sthg.): *disallow eating in one's room.* **2.** To refuse to accept (sthg.) as true or proper: *The judge will disallow an unsigned will as evidence in court.*

dis•ap•pear (dĭs′ə pîr′) *intr.v.* **1.** To pass out of sight: *The ship disappeared into the distance.* **2.** To stop existing: *The dinosaurs disappeared millions of years ago.*

SYNONYMS: disappear, evaporate, fade, vanish. These verbs mean to pass out of sight or existence. *The small plane disappeared in the fog. His courage evaporated when the time came to go to the dentist. As I watched the runners ahead of me, my hopes of winning the race faded away. No one could understand how the magician made the coin vanish.* **ANTONYM: appear.**

---

dis•ap•pear•ance (dĭs′ə pîr′əns) *n.* [C; U] The act or an example of disappearing: *the sudden disappearance of a ship during a storm.*

dis•ap•point (dĭs′ə point′) *tr.v.* **1.** To fail to satisfy the hope, desire, or expectation of (sbdy.): *The ads for the movie were exciting, but the movie itself disappointed me.* **2.** To block (sthg.) from happening: *So far our efforts to get payment have been disappointed.*

dis•ap•point•ed (dĭs′ə poin′tĭd) *adj.* Sad because of failed hopes: *a disappointed lover; disappointed in their son for failing to graduate.*

dis•ap•point•ing (dĭs′ə poin′tĭng) *adj.* Not as good as hoped or expected: *a disappointing 12th-place finish in the race.*

dis•ap•point•ment (dĭs′ə point′mənt) *n.* **1.** [U] The act of disappointing. **2.** [U] The condition or feeling of being disappointed: *The children couldn't hide their disappointment.* **3.** [C] A person or thing that disappoints: *The picnic was a disappointment.*

dis•ap•prov•al (dĭs′ə prōō′vəl) *n.* [U] The act of disapproving: *She made clear her disapproval of smoking.*

dis•ap•prove (dĭs′ə prōōv′) *v.* **dis•ap•proved, dis•ap•prov•ing, dis•ap•proves.** —*tr.* **1.** [*of*] To have an unfavorable opinion of (sbdy./sthg.): *Her parents disapprove of her new boyfriend.* **2.** To refuse to accept (sthg.): *The state disapproved the city's building proposal.* —*intr.* To have an unfavorable opinion: *I prefer to dress casually, but my boss disapproves.*

dis•arm (dĭs ärm′) *v.* —*tr.* **1.** To take a weapon from (sbdy.): *The police officer disarmed the robber.* **2.** To make (sthg.) harmless: *disarm a bomb.* **3.** To end the distrust and win the confidence of (sbdy.): *Her kind words disarmed us right away.* —*intr.* **1.** To lay down weapons. **2.** To reduce or get rid of armed forces: *The countries voted to disarm.*

dis•ar•ma•ment (dĭs är′mə mənt) *n.* [U] The reduction of a country's armed forces or weapons of destruction.

dis•arm•ing (dĭs är′mĭng) *adj.* Serving to end distrust or unfriendliness; winning favor or confidence: *a disarming smile.* —**dis•arm′ing•ly** *adv.*

dis•ar•ray (dĭs′ə rā′) *n.* [U] A state of disorder; confusion: *The mail lay in disarray on the desk.*

dis•as•sem•ble (dĭs′ə sĕm′bəl) *v.* **dis•as•sem•bled, dis•as•sem•bling, dis•as•sem•bles.** —*tr.* To take (sthg.) apart: *We have to disassemble the engine to repair it.* —*intr.* To come apart: *This telephone disassembles easily.*

dis•as•ter (dĭ zăs′tər) *n.* **1.** Something that causes great destruction and terrible trouble: *Tornadoes, earthquakes, and floods are natural disasters.* **2.** *Informal.* A total failure: *The party was a disaster.*

dis•as•trous (dĭ zăs′trəs) *adj.* **1.** Related to a disaster: *a disastrous forest fire.* **2.** *Informal.* Related to a total failure: *a disastrous performance.* —**dis•as′trous•ly** *adv.*

dis•a•vow (dĭs′ə vou′) *tr.v. Formal.* To deny knowledge of, responsibility for, or association with (sthg.): *He disavowed any connection to the crime.* —**dis′a•vow′al** *n.*

dis•band (dĭs bănd′) *v.* —*tr.* To break apart and end the organization of (a corporation, for example): *disband an orchestra.* —*intr.* To stop functioning as an organization: *The club disbanded last year.*

dis•be•lief (dĭs′bĭ lēf′) *n.* [U] Refusal or inability to believe: *I can't help but express disbelief at such a strange story.*

dis•be•lieve (dĭs′bĭ lēv′) *v.* **dis•be•lieved, dis•be•liev•ing, dis•be•lieves.** —*tr.* To refuse to believe in (sthg.): *I generally disbelieve stories about visitors from other planets.* —*intr.* To hold back or refuse belief. —**dis′be•liev′ing** *adj.*

dis·burse (dĭs bûrs′) *tr.v.* **dis·bursed, dis·burs·ing, dis·burs·es.** *Formal.* To pay out (money), as from a fund: *disburse large sums to advertise a product.* —**dis·burse′ment** *n.* [C; U]

disc (dĭsk) *n.* Variant of **disk.**

dis·card (dĭ skärd′) *v.* —*tr.* **1.** To throw (sthg.) away: *discard old shoes; discard a childish habit.* **2.** In card games, to throw out (a playing card) from one's hand: *She discarded an ace.* —*intr.* To throw out a playing card: *It's your turn to discard.* —*n.* (dĭs′kärd′). Something that is thrown away as unwanted: *Charities will usually accept discards such as old clothes and furniture.*

dis·cern (dĭ sûrn′ *or* dĭ zûrn′) *v. Formal.* —*tr.* **1.** To see (sbdy./sthg.) in spite of difficulty: *discern a figure in the shadows.* **2.** To recognize or understand (an idea, for example): *to discern that he was correct.* —*intr.* To see or understand differences; distinguish: *discern between right and wrong.*

dis·cern·i·ble (dĭ sûr′nə bəl *or* dĭ zûr′nə bəl) *adj.* Able to be seen or understood: *There are few discernible differences between the two theories.* —**dis·cern′i·bly** *adv.*

dis·cern·ing (dĭ sûr′nĭng *or* dĭ zûr′nĭng) *adj.* Showing the ability to observe and make good judgments; perceptive: *a discerning mind.* —**dis·cern′ing·ly** *adv.*

dis·charge (dĭs chärj′) *v.* **dis·charged, dis·charg·ing, dis·charg·es.** —*tr.* **1.** To dismiss (sbdy.): *The steel plant closed and discharged its workers from their jobs.* **2.** To send or pour (sthg.) forth: *Pipes discharge water into the lake.* **3.** To unload or empty (contents): *The ship discharged its cargo.* **4.** To shoot (sthg.): *discharge a gun.* **5.** To do what is required by (an office, a duty, or a job): *discharge the duties of mayor.* **6.** To pay (money owed): *discharged the loan by making regular payments.* **7.** To take an electric charge from (sthg.): *We discharged the battery while trying to start the car.* —*intr.* **1.** To get rid of a burden, load, or weight. **2.** *(used of a gun).* To go off; fire. **3.** To pour forth contents: *Several streams discharge into the river.* **4.** To give off or lose an electric charge: *Flashlight batteries discharge when the light is on.* —*n.* (dĭs′chärj′ *or* dĭs chärj′). **1.** [U] The act of removing a load or burden: *a discharge of freight from the ship.* **2.** [C] The act of firing or shooting: *We could hear the discharges of a distant cannon.* **3.** [U] **a.** Something pouring out: *a discharge of water from a pipe.* **b.** Something that oozes: *a watery discharge from the eyes.* **4.** [C] Completion of sthg. promised, such as payment of a loan. **5.** [U] Dismissal or release: *a discharge from the hospital.* **6.** [C; U] **a.** A release of electric charge. **b.** The conversion

of chemical energy to electric energy in a battery.

dis·ci·ple (dĭ sī′pəl) *n.* A person who accepts and helps to spread the teachings of a leader.

dis·ci·pli·nar·i·an (dĭs′ə plə när′ē ən) *n.* A person who uses or believes in strict discipline.

dis·ci·pline (dĭs′ə plĭn) *n.* **1.** [U] **a.** Training expected to produce a specific skill, behavior, or character. **b.** Controlled behavior resulting from such training: *the discipline of an Olympic athlete.* **c.** A system for controlling behavior: *military discipline.* **2.** [U] Punishment intended to correct or train: *The high-school vice principal is responsible for discipline.* **3.** [C] A branch of knowledge or of teaching: *Mathematics and computer science are related disciplines.* —*tr.v.* **dis·ci·plined, dis·ci·plin·ing, dis·ci·plines.** **1.** To train (a person or an animal) by instruction and practice. **2.** To punish (a person or an animal) in order to gain control or enforce obedience: *discipline a child who behaves badly in class.* —**dis′ci·pli·nar′y** *adj.*

dis·ci·plined (dĭs′ə plĭnd) *adj.* Having or showing the effects of strong training: *a disciplined set of work habits.*

disc jockey *n.* An announcer who presents and talks about popular recorded music, especially on the radio.

dis·claim (dĭs klām′) *v.* —*tr.* **1.** To deny or give up any claim to or connection with (sthg.): *He modestly disclaimed credit for our success.* **2.** To deny the truth of (sthg.): *disclaimed the story.* **3.** To give up one's legal right or claim to (sthg.): *His first wife disclaimed any part of the inheritance.*

dis·claim·er (dĭs klā′mər) *n.* A statement denying any responsibility or connection: *The manufacturer had a disclaimer printed on the side of the package.*

dis·close (dĭ sklōz′) *tr.v.* **dis·closed, dis·clos·ing, dis·clos·es.** **1.** To make visible or uncover (sthg.): *The digging disclosed remains of an ancient city.* **2.** To make known (sthg. that had been kept secret): *His report disclosed that the sale had been illegal.*

dis·clo·sure (dĭ sklō′zhər) *n.* **1.** [U] The act or process of revealing or uncovering: *The company delayed disclosure of information about its new car.* **2.** [C] Something uncovered, shown, or told for the first time: *A series of disclosures about the candidate's past hurt his chances of being elected.*

dis·co (dĭs′kō) *n., pl.* **dis·cos. 1.** [C] A discotheque. **2.** [U] Popular dance music having strong repetitive bass rhythms. —*intr.v.* To dance to disco music: *They discoed until 2:00 A.M.*

---

dis·col·or (dĭs kŭl′ər) tr. & intr.v. To change or become changed in color; stain: *Flood waters discolored the walls. Metal discolors with rust.*

dis·col·or·a·tion (dĭs kŭl′ə rā′shən) n. **1.** [U] The act of discoloring or the condition of being discolored: *the discoloration of teeth from smoking.* **2.** [C] A stain: *Water damage left several large discolorations on the carpet.*

dis·com·fort (dĭs kŭm′fərt) n. **1.** [U] A lack of comfort; uneasiness: *a patient in discomfort.* **2.** [C] Something that disturbs comfort: *the discomforts of life in the tropics.*

dis·con·cert (dĭs′kən sûrt′) tr.v. Formal. To upset the self-confidence or calm of (sbdy.): *All of the horns honking disconcerted the student driver.* —**dis′con·cert′ed, dis′con·cert′ing** adj. —**dis′con·cert′ing·ly** adv.

dis·con·nect (dĭs′kə někt′) tr.v. [from] To break or interrupt a connection of (sthg.): *Disconnect the TV from the outlet before you repair it.* —**dis′con·nec′tion** n. [C; U]

dis·con·nect·ed (dĭs′kə něk′tĭd) adj. **1.** Not connected; separate: *disconnected buildings.* **2.** Not clear or logical: *He seemed confused and gave a disconnected account of the accident.* —**dis′con·nect′ed·ly** adv. —**dis′con·nect′ed·ness** n. [U]

dis·con·so·late (dĭs kŏn′sə lĭt) adj. Formal. Very sad; hopeless: *We were disconsolate when our cat disappeared.* —**dis·con′so·late·ly** adv.

dis·con·tent (dĭs′kən tĕnt′) n. [U] Lack of contentment; dissatisfaction: *Not getting a raise caused discontent among the workers.* —**dis′con·tent′ment** n. [U]

dis·con·tent·ed (dĭs′kən tĕn′tĭd) adj. Not contented; unhappy: *Discontented tenants refused to pay rent until they got heat.* —**dis′con·tent′ed·ly** adv.

dis·con·tin·u·a·tion (dĭs′kən tĭn′yōō ā′shən) n. [C; U] A stopping or an ending: *discontinuation of bus service during the storm.*

dis·con·tin·ue (dĭs′kən tĭn′yōō) v. **dis·con·tin·ued, dis·con·tin·u·ing, dis·con·tin·ues.** —tr. To stop or put an end to (sthg.): *discontinue publication of a magazine.* —intr. To come to an end: *Bus service discontinued after midnight.*

dis·con·tin·u·ous (dĭs′kən tĭn′yōō əs) adj. Not continuous; interrupted: *The stove worked badly because of a discontinuous supply of natural gas.* —**dis′con·tin′u·ous·ly** adv.

dis·cord (dĭs′kôrd′) n. **1.** [U] Lack of agreement or harmony: *an angry meeting filled with discord.* **2.** [C; U] A combination of musical tones that sounds unpleasant. **3.** [U] A confused or unpleasant mixing of sounds: *the early morning discord of rush-hour traffic.*

dis·cor·dant (dĭ skôr′dnt) adj. **1.** Not in agreement; conflicting: *a discordant meeting.*

2. Unpleasant in sound: *discordant sounds of the city streets.* —**dis·cor′dance** n. [U] —**dis·cor′dant·ly** adv.

dis·co·theque (dĭs′kə těk′ or dĭs′kə těk′) n. A nightclub where people dance to recorded music.

dis·count (dĭs′kount′ or dĭs kount′) tr.v. **1.** To subtract (a percentage) from a cost or price of an item: *The dealer discounted 25 percent off the original price of the rug.* **2.** To sell or offer (sthg.) for sale at a reduced price: *The store discounts its coats each spring.* **3.** To consider (sthg.) with doubt or disbelief: *The scientist discounted the rumors of a new energy source.* —n. (dĭs′kount′). A reduction from the full amount of a price or debt: *That store gives customers a discount.*

dis·cour·age (dĭ skûr′ĭj or dĭ skŭr′ĭj) tr.v. **dis·cour·aged, dis·cour·ag·ing, dis·cour·ag·es. 1.** To make (sbdy.) less hopeful or confident: *The difficulty of the job discouraged me.* **2.** [from] To try to prevent (sthg. from happening or sbdy. from doing sthg.) by disapproval, warnings, or advice: *Friends discouraged them from going.* —**dis·cour′aged, dis·cour′ag·ing** adj.

dis·cour·age·ment (dĭ skûr′ĭj mənt or dĭ skŭr′ĭj mənt) n. **1.** [U] A condition of being or feeling discouraged: *Discouragement and hardship destroyed the hopes of many pioneers.* **2.** [C] Something that discourages: *Harsh winters are a discouragement to living in the far north.* **3.** [U] The act of discouraging: *The discouragement of my family made me more determined to be an actor.*

dis·course (dĭs′kôrs′) n. **1.** [U] Talking; conversation: *cheerful discourse among friends.* **2.** [C] A formal discussion, either spoken or written: *The minister gave a long discourse on morality.* —intr.v. (dĭ skôrs′). **dis·coursed, dis·cours·ing, dis·cours·es.** To speak or write formally and often at length: *The mayor discoursed on the role of the government in improving city life.*

dis·cour·te·ous (dĭs kûr′tē əs) adj. Lacking courtesy; not polite: *discourteous drivers who don't signal turns.* —**dis·cour′te·ous·ly** adv.

dis·cour·te·sy (dĭs kûr′tĭ sē) n., pl. **dis·cour·te·sies. 1.** [U] Lack of courtesy; rudeness. **2.** [C] A rude or impolite act: *the discourtesy of interrupting people who are talking.*

dis·cov·er (dĭ skŭv′ər) tr.v. **1.** To find or see (sthg.) for the first time: *The explorers discovered the source of the river.* **2.** To learn of (sthg.); gain knowledge of: *discover errors by checking one's math.* —**dis·cov′er·er** n.

dis·cov·er·y (dĭ skŭv′ə rē) n., pl. **dis·cov·er·ies. 1.** [U] The act of discovering: *Discovery of a polio vaccine ended fear of the disease.* **2.** [C] Something discovered: *Atomic energy is one of the most important scientific discoveries of the 1900s.*

dis·cred·it (dĭs krĕd'ĭt) *tr.v.* **1.** To hurt the reputation of (sbdy.): *The report of dishonesty discredits our politicians.* **2.** To cause (sthg.) to be distrusted: *The new scientific evidence discredits earlier theories.* **3.** To refuse to believe in (sthg.): *discredit a story as mere gossip.* —*n.* [U] **1.** Loss or damage to one's reputation: *Dishonest officials brought discredit to the city government.* **2.** Lack or loss of trust or belief: *An account from a new witness brought the earlier accounts into discredit.* **3.** Something that brings disgrace or distrust: *He is a discredit to his family.* —**dis·cred'it·a·ble** *adj.* —**dis·cred'it·a·bly** *adv.*

dis·creet (dĭ skrēt') *adj.* With caution or self-control in one's speech or behavior; prudent: *The teacher was discreet in discussing the student's mistake.* —**dis·creet'ly** *adv.* —**dis·creet'ness** *n.* [U]

HOMONYMS: discreet, discrete (distinct).

---

dis·crep·an·cy (dĭ skrĕp'ən sē) *n., pl.* **dis·crep·an·cies.** Lack of agreement; inconsistency: *There was a large discrepancy between their statement about the accident and the facts.*

dis·crete (dĭ skrēt') *adj.* Separate from others; distinct: *The police commissioner is responsible for several discrete departments.* —**dis·crete'ly** *adv.*

HOMONYMS: discrete, discreet (prudent).

---

dis·cre·tion (dĭ skrĕsh'ən) *n.* [U] **1.** The quality of being discreet; prudence: *Diplomats must use great discretion in negotiating treaties.* **2.** Freedom of action or judgment: *Choosing a captain for the team was left to the players' discretion.*

dis·cre·tion·ar·y (dĭ skrĕsh'ə nĕr'ē) *adj.* Left to or determined by one's own discretion or judgment: *The governor has a discretionary fund for emergencies.*

dis·crim·i·nate (dĭ skrĭm'ə nāt') *v.* **dis·crim·i·nat·ed, dis·crim·i·nat·ing, dis·crim·i·nates.** —*intr.* **1.** To see clear differences: *discriminate among the possible choices.* **2.** [*against*] To show preference or prejudice based on a person's race, age, or sex, for example, instead of individual merit: *Some employers discriminate against older workers.* —*tr.* To make or see a clear difference between (things): *A critic discriminates good books from poor ones.* —**dis·crim'i·na'tor** *n.*

dis·crim·i·nat·ing (dĭ skrĭm'ə nā'tĭng) *adj.* **1.** Showing careful judgment or fine taste: *a discriminating critic of modern music.* **2.** Serving to mark sbdy./sthg. as different from others; distinctive: *a discriminating characteristic.* **3.** Marked by or showing bias; discriminatory. —**dis·crim'i·nat'ing·ly** *adv.*

dis·crim·i·na·tion (dĭ skrĭm'ə nā'shən) *n.* [U] **1.** The ability to see or understand small differences, as in quality: *clothes bought without care or discrimination; an artist's discrimination of color.* **2.** Unfair treatment of people based on their belonging to a class or category, such as race, age, or sex, rather than on individual merit: *The U.S. Constitution protects citizens from racial and religious discrimination.*

dis·crim·i·na·to·ry (dĭ skrĭm'ə nə tôr'ē) *adj.* Showing prejudice; biased: *discriminatory treatment of minorities.* —**dis·crim'i·na·to'ri·ly** *adv.*

dis·cus (dĭs'kəs) *n., pl.* **dis·cus·es.** A heavy disk of wood and metal that is thrown for distance in athletic contests.

dis·cuss (dĭ skŭs') *tr.v.* To talk or write about (sbdy./sthg.): *We met to discuss plans for a new park.*

dis·cus·sion (dĭ skŭsh'ən) *n.* [C; U] A conversation or an exchange of views on a subject by different people.

dis·dain (dĭs dān') *tr.v.* To consider or treat (sthg.) as deserving no respect: *The composer disdained the judgments of critics in the press.* —*n.* [U] The feeling that sbdy. or sthg. deserves no attention or respect: *She responded with disdain to all offers of money for telling her life story.*

dis·dain·ful (dĭs dān'fəl) *adj.* Feeling or showing disdain; scornful. —**dis·dain'ful·ly** *adv.*

dis·ease (dĭ zēz') *n.* [C; U] A condition of a person or other living thing that prevents functioning in the normal or proper way; sickness: *Malaria is one of the most common diseases in the world.*

dis·eased (dĭ zēzd') *adj.* Affected with or suffering from disease: *a diseased tree.*

dis·em·bark (dĭs'ĕm bärk') *v.* —*intr.* To get off a ship or an airplane: *We disembark at Montreal's airport.* —*tr.* [*from*] To put or let (sbdy.) off a ship or an airplane: *The captain disembarked passengers from the ship.* —**dis·em'bar·ka'tion** *n.* [U]

dis·en·chant (dĭs'ĕn chănt') *tr.v.* To free (sbdy.) from illusion or false belief: *A close look at the old house was enough to disenchant any serious buyer.* —**dis'en·chant'ment** *n.* [U]

dis·en·chant·ed (dĭs'ĕn chăn'tĭd) *adj.* [*with*] No longer believing in (sbdy./sthg. admired or valued): *He became disenchanted with the project and quit.*

ă–cat; ā–pay; âr–care; ä–father; ĕ–get; ē–be; ĭ–sit; ī–nice; îr–here; ŏ–got; ō–go; ô–saw; oi–boy; ou–out; ōō–took; ōō–boot; ŭ–cut; ûr–word; th–thin; *th*–this; hw–when; zh–vision; ə–about; N–French bon

dis·en·fran·chise (dĭs′ĕn frăn′chīz′) tr.v. **dis·en·fran·chised, dis·en·fran·chis·ing, dis·en·fran·chis·es.** To take or keep away a privilege or a right from (sbdy.), especially the right to vote. —**dis′en·fran′chise′ment** n. [U]

dis·en·gage (dĭs′ĕn gāj′) v. **dis·en·gaged, dis·en·gag·ing, dis·en·gag·es.** —tr. To make (sthg.) free from sthg. that holds it in place: disengage the car's clutch. —intr. To become free or separate: As the brakes disengaged, the car rolled backwards. —**dis′en·gage′ment** n. [U]

dis·en·tan·gle (dĭs′ĕn tăng′gəl) tr.v. **dis·en·tan·gled, dis·en·tan·gling, dis·en·tan·gles.** To free (sthg.) from tangles or confusion: disentangle a knotted fishing line; disentangle fact from fiction in his stories. —**dis′en·tan′gle·ment** n. [U]

dis·fa·vor (dĭs fā′vər) n. [U] **1.** Disapproval: a look of disfavor on her face. **2.** The condition of being regarded with dislike or disapproval: The governor was in disfavor with voters. —tr.v. To view or treat (sthg.) with dislike or disapproval: The company disfavored spending any of its profits to clean up the environment.

dis·fig·ure (dĭs fĭg′yər) tr.v. **dis·fig·ured, dis·fig·ur·ing, dis·fig·ures.** To spoil the appearance of (sbdy./sthg.): Vandals disfigured the statue with paint.

dis·grace (dĭs grās′) n. **1.** [U] Loss of honor, respect, or reputation: The boy's arrest brought disgrace on his family. **2.** [U] The condition of being strongly disapproved: in disgrace for telling a secret. **3.** [C; to] A person or thing that brings dishonor or disfavor: The dirty streets are a disgrace to the city. —tr.v. **dis·graced, dis·grac·ing, dis·grac·es.** To bring shame or dishonor upon (sbdy./sthg.): She disgraced herself by cheating on an exam.

dis·grace·ful (dĭs grās′fəl) adj. Causing or deserving disgrace; shameful: disgraceful behavior. —**dis·grace′ful·ly** adv. —**dis·grace′ful·ness** n. [U]

dis·grun·tle (dĭs grŭn′tl) tr.v. **dis·grun·tled, dis·grun·tling, dis·grun·tles.** To make (sbdy.) discontented or displeased: Loss of two vacation days disgruntled all the employees. —**dis·grun′tled** adj. —**dis·grun′tle·ment** n. [U]

dis·guise (dĭs gīz′) tr.v. **dis·guised, dis·guis·ing, dis·guis·es. 1.** To hide the identity of (sbdy.) by changing the appearance: The princess disguised herself as a boy. **2.** To hide (sthg.) or cause it to appear different: She disguised her embarrassment with a smile. —n. [C; U] **1.** Clothes or other effects used to hide one's true identity: The two spies wore the disguise of repairmen. **2.** An act or a manner of behaving that is designed to hide sthg.: Their laughter was a disguise for nervousness.

dis·gust (dĭs gŭst′) tr.v. To cause (sbdy.) to have feelings of sickening dislike or annoyance: Your refusal to cooperate has disgusted everyone on the project. —n. [U] A feeling of extreme dislike, distaste, or annoyance: The baseball fans showed their disgust with the umpire's decision by booing loudly.

dis·gust·ed (dĭs gŭs′tĭd) adj. Filled with disgust: She had a disgusted look on her face. —**dis·gust′ed·ly** adv.

dis·gust·ing (dĭs gŭs′tĭng) adj. Causing disgust: disgusting food; a disgusting joke. —**dis·gust′ing·ly** adv.

dish (dĭsh) n. **1.a.** A shallow container for holding or serving food. **b.** The amount that a dish can hold: I ate two dishes of ice cream. **2.** A particular kind or preparation of food: Texas chili is our favorite dish. **3.** A radio, television, or radar antenna having the shape of a dish: a satellite dish on the roof. —tr.v. To serve (food) in a dish or dishes: dish the vegetables. ◆ **dish out.** tr.v. [sep.] Informal. To give (sthg.) out freely: She likes to dish out advice. **dish up.** tr.v. [sep.] To put (food) out to be eaten: I'm going to dish it up before it gets cold. **do the dishes.** To wash all the plates, pots, and utensils used for a meal: You cooked, so I'll do the dishes.

dish
(plate for food)

dish
(radar dish antenna)

dis·heart·en (dĭs här′tn) tr.v. To cause (sbdy.) to lose courage and hope: Lack of public interest in their new battery disheartened the inventors. —**dis·heart′ened, dis·heart′en·ing** adj. —**dis·heart′en·ing·ly** adv.

di·shev·eled or **di·shev·elled** (dĭ shĕv′əld) adj. (used of one's appearance). Messy or disorderly: disheveled clothes; a disheveled look.

dis·hon·est (dĭs ŏn′ĭst) adj. **1.** Inclined to lie, cheat, or deceive: a dishonest art dealer. **2.** Showing or resulting from a lack of truth or an attempt to deceive: a dishonest answer; dishonest dealings. —**dis·hon′est·ly** adv.

dis·hon·es·ty (dĭs ŏn′ĭ stē) n. [U] Lack of honesty or truthfulness: guilty of dishonesty.

dis·hon·or (dĭs ŏn′ər) n. **1.** Loss of honor, respect, or reputation; shame: He brought dishonor on his family. **2.** A person or thing that causes loss of honor: His poor

D

sportsmanship was a dishonor to the whole team. —tr.v. To bring shame or disgrace on (sbdy./sthg.): *His rude behavior dishonors the reputation of his company.*

dis·hon·or·a·ble (dĭs ŏn′ər ə bəl) *adj.* Characterized by or causing dishonor: *a dishonorable discharge from the army.* —**dis·hon′or·a·bly** *adv.*

dish·wash·er (dĭsh′wŏsh′ər *or* dĭsh′wô′shər) *n.* **1.** A machine that washes dishes. **2.** A person who washes dishes, especially in a restaurant.

dis·il·lu·sion (dĭs′ĭ lōō′zhən) *tr.v.* To free (sbdy.) from a false idea or belief: *Many newcomers to the country were disillusioned when they discovered the high cost of living.* —**dis′·il·lu′sion·ment** *n.* [U]

dis·il·lu·sioned (dĭs′ĭ lōō′zhənd) *adj.* Lacking hope or belief: *The disillusioned child never trusted her father again.*

dis·in·fect (dĭs′ĭn fĕkt′) *tr.v.* To clean (sthg.) so as to destroy microorganisms that cause disease: *disinfect a cut.* —**dis′in·fec′tion** *n.* [U]

dis·in·fec·tant (dĭs′ĭn fĕk′tənt) *n.* [C; U] A substance that kills microorganisms that cause disease: *wash a wound with disinfectant.* —*adj.* Destroying or slowing the growth of microorganisms that cause disease: *disinfectant soap.*

dis·in·for·ma·tion (dĭs ĭn′fər mā′shən) *n.* [U] False information from a government or especially an intelligence agency intended to mislead or influence the public or another government.

dis·in·her·it (dĭs′ĭn hĕr′ĭt) *tr.v.* To take away an inheritance or the right to inherit money or property from (sbdy.): *The millionaire disinherited his daughter for disobeying him.*

dis·in·te·grate (dĭs ĭn′tĭ grāt′) *v.* **dis·in·te·grat·ed, dis·in·te·grat·ing, dis·in·te·grates.** —*intr.* To break or separate into very small pieces: *rock disintegrating into sand.* —*tr.* To cause (sthg.) to break into small separate pieces: *Water disintegrated the cement to pebble-sized pieces.*

dis·in·te·gra·tion (dĭs ĭn′tĭ grā′shən) *n.* [U] **1.** The act or process of disintegrating: *Freezing and thawing caused disintegration of the concrete.* **2.** The condition of being disintegrated: *Disintegration will continue until repairs are made.*

dis·in·ter·est·ed (dĭs ĭn′trĭ stĭd *or* dĭs·ĭn′tə rĕs′tĭd) *adj.* **1.** Free of selfish bias and self-interest; impartial: *the disinterested decision of an umpire.* **2.** Uninterested or unconcerned: *My friends are totally disinterested in the movie.* —**dis·in′ter·est** *n.* [U] —**dis·in′ter·est′ed·ly** *adv.*

dis·joint·ed (dĭs join′tĭd) *adj.* Lacking

order or good connections between parts: *a disjointed paragraph.* —**dis·joint′ed·ly** *adv.*

disk *also* **disc** (dĭsk) *n.* **1.** A thin, flat, circular object, such as a plate or coin. **2.** A round, flattened structure in an animal, as between the bones of the human spine. **3.** Often **disc. a.** A round flat plate coated with a magnetic substance on which computer data is stored. **b.** An optical disk, such as a compact disk (CD).

disk drive *n.* A device in a computer that stores or gets data from a rotating disk.

disk·ette (dĭ skĕt′) *n.* A floppy disk.

disk jockey *n.* Variant of **disc jockey.**

disk operating system *n.* Software that controls the transfer of information between a computer and a program.

dis·like (dĭs līk′) *tr.v.* **dis·liked, dis·lik·ing, dis·likes.** To not like (sbdy./sthg.): *I dislike his idea.* —*n.* [C; U] A feeling of not liking sbdy./sthg.: *I have a strong dislike of green peas.*

dis·lo·cate (dĭs′lō kāt′ *or* dĭs lō′kāt) *tr.v.* **dis·lo·cat·ed, dis·lo·cat·ing, dis·lo·cates.** **1.** To put (a part of the body) out of joint: *I dislocated my thumb catching the ball.* **2.** To throw (sthg.) into confusion or disorder: *The snowstorm dislocated rail and air traffic.* —**dis′lo·ca′tion** *n.* [C; U]

dis·lodge (dĭs lŏj′) *tr.v.* **dis·lodged, dis·lodg·ing, dis·lodg·es.** To move or force (sthg.) out of position: *Heavy rains dislodged big rocks from the hillside.*

dis·loy·al (dĭs loi′əl) *adj.* Lacking loyalty; unfaithful: *disloyal fans of the losing team.* —**dis·loy′al·ly** *adv.*

dis·loy·al·ty (dĭs loi′əl tē) *n., pl.* **dis·loy·al·ties.** **1.** [U] Lack of loyalty; unfaithfulness: *a soldier accused of disloyalty.* **2.** [C] A disloyal act: *Taking all the credit for the discovery was a disloyalty to fellow researchers.*

dis·mal (dĭz′məl) *adj.* **1.** Causing low spirits or depression: *a dismal fog.* **2.** Depressed or miserable: *A bad cold makes me feel dismal.* —**dis′mal·ly** *adv.*

dis·man·tle (dĭs măn′tl) *tr.v.* **dis·man·tled, dis·man·tling, dis·man·tles.** To take (sthg.) apart: *We dismantled the table to get it through the door.*

dis·may (dĭs mā′) *tr.v.* **1.** To make (sbdy.) anxious or afraid: *Fear of the river flooding dismayed the whole city.* **2.** To discourage or upset (sbdy.): *The low grade dismayed the student.* —*n.* [U] A sudden loss of courage or confidence in the face of danger or trouble: *Being lost filled the hikers with dismay.*

dis·mem·ber (dĭs mĕm′bər) *tr.v.* **1.** To cut, tear, or pull off the parts of (a body): *The fox dismembered the chicken.* **2.** To divide into

---

ă–cat; ā–pay; âr–care; ä–father; ĕ–get; ē–be; ĭ–sit; ī–nice; îr–here; ŏ–got; ō–go; ô–saw; oi–boy; ou–out; ōō–took; ōō–boot; ŭ–cut; ûr–word; th–thin; *th*–this; hw–when; zh–vision; ə–about; N–French bon

pieces: *The Roman Empire was dismembered into numerous states.* —**dis•mem′ber•ment** *n.* [U]

dis•miss (dĭs mĭs′) *tr.v.* **1.** To direct or allow (sbdy.) to leave: *The students were dismissed for the holidays.* **2.** To end the employment or service of (sbdy.): *Several workers were dismissed from the shop for sleeping on the job.* **3.** To put (sthg.) out of one's thoughts or consider as unimportant: *We dismissed the story as gossip.*

dis•miss•al (dĭs mĭs′əl) *n.* **1.** [C; U] The act of dismissing: *the principal's dismissal of students because of the coming snowstorm.* **2.** [U] The condition of being dismissed. **3.** [C] An order or a notice of an end to employment: *Two workers received their dismissals by mail.*

dis•mount (dĭs mount′) *intr.v.* To get off or down, as from a horse or bicycle: *The riders dismounted.*

dis•o•be•di•ence (dĭs′ə bē′dē əns) *n.* [U] Refusal or failure to obey: *a soldier punished for disobedience.* —**dis′o•be′di•ent** *adj.* —**dis′o•be′di•ent•ly** *adv.*

dis•o•bey (dĭs′ə bā′) *tr. & intr.v.* To refuse or fail to obey: *Drivers must not disobey traffic signals. A trained horse seldom disobeys.*

dis•or•der (dĭs ôr′dər) *n.* **1.** [U] Lack of order or regular arrangement: *Your desk is always in a state of disorder.* **2.** [C; U] A public argument or fight: *Police responded to a disorder in our neighborhood.* **3.** [C] A sickness of the body or mind: *a nervous disorder; a digestive disorder.*

dis•or•der•ly (dĭs ôr′dər lē) *adj.* **1.** Lacking orderly arrangement; messy: *a disorderly room.* **2.** Lacking order or control: *a disorderly crowd.* —**dis•or′der•li•ness** *n.* [U]

dis•or•gan•ize (dĭs ôr′gə nīz′) *tr.v.* **dis•or•gan•ized, dis•or•gan•iz•ing, dis•or•gan•iz•es.** To destroy the organization or orderly arrangement of (sthg.): *The sudden airline strike disorganized air schedules.* —**dis•or′gan•i•za′tion** (dĭs ôr′gə nĭ zā′shən) *n.* [U]

dis•or•ga•nized (dĭs ôr′gə nīzd) *adj.* Lacking order; confused; messy: *Can you find anything in this disorganized clutter?*

dis•o•ri•ent (dĭs ôr′ē ĕnt′) *tr.v.* To confuse (sbdy.) so as to take away all sense of direction: *Walking around in a strange part of the city disoriented us.* —**dis•o′ri•en•ta′tion** *n.* [U]

dis•o•ri•ent•ed (dĭs ôr′ē ĕn′tĭd) *adj.* Unable to orient oneself; confused: *The disoriented people stumbled off the Ferris wheel.*

dis•own (dĭs ōn′) *tr.v.* To refuse to claim or accept (sbdy./sthg.) as one's own: *The father disowned his son for refusing to join the family business.*

dis•par•age (dĭ spăr′ĭj) *tr.v.* **dis•par•aged, dis•par•ag•ing, dis•par•ag•es.** To speak

of (sbdy./sthg.) as unimportant or of poor quality: *He disparages the work done by other people.* —**dis•par′age•ment** *n.* [U]

dis•par•a•ging (dĭ spăr′ĭ jĭng) *adj.* Intended to show lack of respect or disdain; unkind: *He stopped writing after the disparaging reviews of his first novel.* —**dis•par′ag•ing•ly** *adv.*

dis•pa•rate (dĭs′pər ĭt *or* dĭ spăr′ĭt) *adj.* Completely distinct or different in kind: *voters with disparate interests.* —**dis′pa•rate•ly** *adv.*

dis•par•i•ty (dĭ spăr′ĭ tē) *n., pl.* **dis•par•i•ties.** [C; U] **1.** Inequality; difference: *the disparity in population between one city and another.* **2.** Lack of similarity; unlikeness: *a great disparity between his story of what happened and hers.*

dis•pas•sion•ate (dĭs păsh′ə nĭt) *adj.* Not influenced by strong feelings or emotions: *the dispassionate decision of a judge.* —**dis•pas′sion•ate•ly** *adv.*

dis•patch (dĭ spăch′) *tr.v.* **1.** To send (sbdy./sthg.) off to a specific place or on specific business: *dispatch a letter; dispatch a police car to the scene of a crime.* **2.** To complete or settle (sthg.) promptly: *The police dispatched their duty and left.* **3.** To put (sbdy./sthg.) to death quickly and coolly: *The hunter dispatched the injured deer.* —*n.* **1.** [C] The act of sending off: *the dispatch of a representative to the conference.* **2.** [U] Quickness and efficiency in performance: *The owl killed the mouse with dispatch.* **3.** [C] A written message, especially an official communication, sent with speed: *The messenger carried a dispatch from headquarters.* **4.** [C] A news report sent to a newspaper or broadcasting station.

dis•patch•er (dĭ spăch′ər) *n.* A person who controls the departure and movements of trains, taxicabs, or delivery trucks.

dis•pel (dĭ spĕl′) *tr.v.* **dis•pelled, dis•pel•ling, dis•pels.** To cause (sthg.) to disappear by or as if by scattering: *His confident words dispelled my fears.*

dis•pen•sa•ble (dĭ spĕn′sə bəl) *adj.* Not essential; unimportant: *To shorten the report, I removed all of the dispensable comments.* —**dis•pen′sa•bil′i•ty** *n.* [U]

dis•pen•sa•ry (dĭ spĕn′sə rē) *n., pl.* **dis•pen•sa•ries.** **1.** An office in a hospital, school, or other institution where medicines and medical supplies are given out. **2.** A place where medicines and medical treatment are provided, usually at little or no cost.

dis•pen•sa•tion (dĭs′pən sā′shən) *n.* [C; U] **1.** The act or process of giving out; distribution: *dispensation of medicine by the local clinic.* **2.** Freedom or a release from an obligation or a rule, permitted in a particular case: *a dispensation from taxes to help new businesses grow.*

dis•pense (dĭ spĕns´) *tr.v.* **dis•pensed, dis• pens•ing, dis•pens•es. 1.** To deal out or distribute (sthg.) in or as if in parts or shares: *food dispensed to refugees; a judge dispensing justice.* **2.** To prepare and give out (medicines). ◆ **dispense with.** *tr.v.* [insep.] To manage without (sthg.): *Let's dispense with the formalities and get started on the job.*

dis•pens•er (dĭ spĕn´sər) *n.* A person or thing that dispenses: *a paper cup dispenser.*

dis•per•sal (dĭ spûr´səl) *n.* [U] The act of dispersing or the condition of being dispersed: *the dispersal of a crowd by police; dispersal of aid among the needy.*

dis•perse (dĭ spûrs´) *v.* **dis•persed, dis• pers•ing, dis•pers•es.** —*tr.* **1.** To drive off or scatter (people or things) in different directions: *The rain dispersed the crowd.* **2.** To cause (sthg.) to vanish or disappear: *Winds dispersed the clouds.* —*intr.* **1.** To move or scatter in different directions: *The protesters dispersed when the police arrived.* **2.** To vanish or disappear: *The mist dispersed with the morning sun.*

dis•per•sion (dĭ spûr´zhən *or* dĭ spûr´shən) *n.* [U] The act of dispersing or the state of being dispersed: *Bright sunlight caused dispersion of the fog.*

dis•pir•it (dĭ spĭr´ĭt) *tr.v.* To discourage or lower the spirits of (sbdy.): *Heavy rains dispirited the vacationers.*

dis•pir•it•ed (dĭ spĭr´ĭ tĭd) *adj.* Depressed; discouraged: *feeling tired and dispirited.*

dis•place (dĭs plās´) *tr.v.* **dis•placed, dis• plac•ing, dis•plac•es. 1.** To change the place or position of (sbdy./sthg.): *The refugees were displaced by the war.* **2.** To replace or take the place of (sbdy.): *Many workers have been displaced in their jobs by robots.* **3.** To take the space of (a quantity of liquid or gas): *An equal amount of oxygen displaced the carbon dioxide.*

dis•place•ment (dĭs plās´mənt) *n.* [U] **1.** The weight or volume of fluid displaced by an object floating in it. **2.** The act of displacing or the condition of being displaced: *Flooding caused the displacement of many people.*

dis•play (dĭ splā´) *tr.v.* **1.** To put (sthg.) to be seen in public: *The library displays its new books in a case.* **2.** To show or let (sthg.) be noticed: *display good humor.* —*n.* **1.** [C] The act of displaying: *a display of kindness.* **2.** [C] A public exhibition: *a display of Native American art.* **3.** [C; U] A show designed to impress or to attract attention: *The big party was just a display of wealth.* **4.** [C] A device, such as a computer screen, that gives information for people to see.

dis•please (dĭs plēz´) *tr.v.* **dis•pleased,**

dis•pleas•ing, dis•pleas•es. To cause annoyance or irritation to (sbdy.): *Bad manners displease me.* —**dis•pleased´, dis•pleas´ing** *adj.* —**dis•pleas´ure** (dĭs plĕzh´ər) *n.* [U]

dis•pos•a•ble (dĭ spō´zə bəl) *adj.* Designed to be thrown away after use: *disposable razors.*

dis•pos•al (dĭ spō´zəl) *n.* **1.** [U] The act of getting rid of sthg.: *The disposal of garbage is a serious problem for cities.* **2.** [U] The act of attending to or settling a matter: *The mayor's decision led to a quick disposal of the problem.* **3.** [C] An electric device placed below a sink that grinds food waste so it can be washed away: *a garbage disposal.* ◆ **at (one's) disposal.** Available for one's use: *The university library books are at the disposal of students and faculty.*

dis•pose (dĭ spōz´) *tr.v.* **dis•posed, dis• pos•ing, dis•pos•es. 1.** To place or arrange (sthg.) in a particular order: *The gardeners disposed the rosebushes throughout the park.* **2.** [*to*] **a.** To make (sbdy.) willing or ready: *a friend disposed to forgive a mistake.* **b.** To make (sbdy.) easily affected by: *My brother is disposed to ear infections.* ◆ **dispose of.** *tr.v.* [insep.] **1.** To get rid of (sthg. unwanted): *We disposed of the leftovers in the garbage.* **2.** To sell or give away (sthg.): *The dealer disposed of the cars.* **3.** To settle or decide (sthg.): *We disposed of the problem quickly.*

dis•posed (dĭ spōzd´) *adj. Formal.* Tending or inclined; willing: *I'm not disposed to party all night these days.* ◆ **well** or **favorably disposed.** Liking: *The boss seems favorably disposed to your idea.*

dis•po•si•tion (dĭs´pə zĭsh´ən) *n.* [C; U] **1.** The usual mood or attitude of a person or an animal: *a young child's affectionate disposition.* **2.** Arrangement or distribution: *the disposition of books by subject on library shelves.* **3.** *Formal.* An act of settling; settlement: *disposition of legal matters at the lawyer's office.*

dis•pos•sess (dĭs´pə zĕs´) *tr.v. Formal.* To take away from (sbdy.) the possession of sthg., such as land or a house: *The bank may dispossess a person of land for failure to make payment on a loan.* —**dis´pos• ses´sion** (dĭs´pə zĕsh´ən) *n.* [U]

dis•pro•por•tion (dĭs´prə pôr´shən) *n.* A lack of proportion; imbalance: *the disproportion between the size of a piece of balsa wood and its very light weight.*

dis•pro•por•tion•ate (dĭs´prə pôr´shə nĭt) *adj.* Out of proportion to sthg. else, as in size or shape: *The child demanded a disproportionate share of the teacher's attention.* —**dis´pro•por´tion•ate•ly** *adv.*

---

dis·prove (dĭs prōov') *tr.v.* **dis·proved,
dis·prov·ing, dis·proves.** To prove (sthg.)
to be false or in error: *Shadows of buildings in
the photograph disprove the witness's claim
that it was a cloudy day.*

dis·put·a·ble (dĭ spyōo'tə bəl) *adj.* Open
to argument; questionable: *The facts are well
known, but your interpretation of them is dis-
putable.* —**dis·put'a·bil'i·ty** *n.* [U]

dis·pute (dĭ spyōot') *v.* **dis·put·ed, dis·
put·ing, dis·putes.** —*tr.* **1.** To debate or
argue about (sthg.): *The editors disputed the
importance of the news story.* **2.** To doubt or
question the truth or validity of (sthg.): *We
disputed her story of what happened.* —*intr.*
To engage in discussion; argue: *The candidates disputed over where city expenses
should be cut.* —*n.* **1.** A debate; an argument:
*Each scientist in the dispute had a different
theory.* **2.** A quarrel: *Police quieted the dispute.* —**dis·pu'tant** *n.*

dis·qual·i·fy (dĭs kwŏl'ə fī') *tr.v.* **dis·
qual·i·fied, dis·qual·i·fy·ing, dis·qual·
i·fies. 1.** To make (sbdy.) unqualified or
unfit: *Poor eyesight disqualifies many people
who would like to become pilots.* **2.** To
declare or call (sbdy.) unqualified or unable
to participate: *The judges disqualified the
swimmer from the race.* —**dis·qual'i·fi·
ca'tion** (dĭs kwŏl'ə fĭ kā'shən) *n.*

dis·qui·et (dĭs kwī'ĭt) *tr.v.* To make uneasy;
trouble; worry: *Strange noises disquieted the
guard.* —*n.* Worry, uneasiness, or anxiety:
*Rumors of engine trouble caused disquiet
among the airplane passengers.*

dis·re·gard (dĭs'rĭ gärd') *tr.v.* To pay little
or no attention to (sbdy./sthg.): *They disre-
garded the warnings not to go out in the boat.*
—*n.* [U] Lack of attention or regard: *a disregard for safety.*

dis·re·pair (dĭs'rĭ pâr') *n.* [U] The condition of being in need of repair: *an old house
in disrepair.*

dis·rep·u·ta·ble (dĭs rĕp'yə tə bəl) *adj.*
Having a bad reputation; not respectable: *He
made the mistake of trusting a disreputable
building contractor.* —**dis·rep'u·ta·bly** *adv.*

dis·re·pute (dĭs'rĭ pyōot') *n.* [U] *Formal.*
Damage to or loss of reputation; disgrace:
*That company is in disrepute because it has
polluted the town's water.*

dis·re·spect (dĭs'rĭ spĕkt') *n.* [U] Lack of
respect or courtesy; rudeness: *The child's
behavior in class showed disrespect for
school rules.*

dis·re·spect·ful (dĭs'rĭ spĕkt'fəl) *adj.*
Having or showing a lack of respect; rude:
disrespectful words. —**dis·re·spect'ful·ly**
adv.

dis·rupt (dĭs rŭpt') *tr.v.* To force (sthg.) into
confusion or disorder: *The noise from the
construction disrupted the class.* —**dis·
rupt'er** *n.* —**dis·rup'tion** *n.* [C; U]

dis·rup·tive (dĭs rŭp'tĭv) *adj.* Causing confusion or disorder: *The street repairs were
disruptive to city traffic.* —**dis·rup'tive·ly**
adv. —**dis·rup'tive·ness** *n.* [U]

dis·sat·is·fac·tion (dĭs săt'ĭs făk'shən) *n.*
[U] The feeling of being displeased or dissatisfied: *There is a great deal of dissatisfaction
among teachers and parents over the closing
of the library.*

dis·sat·is·fied (dĭs săt'ĭs fīd') *adj.* Feeling
or showing a lack of contentment or satisfaction: *The dissatisfied customer returned the
clock he had bought.*

dis·sat·is·fy (dĭs săt'ĭs fī') *tr.v.* **dis·
sat·is·fied, dis·sat·is·fy·ing, dis·sat·
is·fies.** To fail to satisfy (sbdy.); displease:
Your careless work dissatisfies me.

dis·sect (dĭ sĕkt' *or* dī sĕkt' *or* dī'sĕkt')
tr.v. **1.** To cut apart (tissue) for study or
examination: *dissect an animal in a lab.* **2.** To
examine, analyze, or criticize (sthg.) in detail:
*We dissected the plan to see where it might go
wrong.* —**dis·sec'tion** *n.* [C; U]

dis·sem·i·nate (dĭ sĕm'ə nāt') *tr.v.* **dis·
sem·i·nat·ed, dis·sem·i·nat·ing, dis·
sem·i·nates.** To make (information) known
widely: *The TV newscast disseminated the
report instantly.* —**dis·sem'i·na'tion** *n.* [U]

dis·sen·sion (dĭ sĕn'shən) *n.* [U] Difference of opinion; disagreement: *There was
dissension among the union members over
the contract.*

dis·sent (dĭ sĕnt') *intr.v.* [*from*] To think or
feel differently; disagree: *Many angry citizens dissented from the government action of
raising taxes.* —*n.* [U] Difference of opinion
or feeling; disagreement): *dissent over the
British right to tax the American colonists.*
—**dis·sent'er** *n.*

HOMONYMS: dissent, descent (ancestry).

---

dis·ser·ta·tion (dĭs'ər tā'shən) *n.* A long
and formal discussion of a subject, especially
one written at a university: *a doctoral disser-
tation.*

dis·serv·ice (dĭs sûr'vĭs) *n.* [U] A harmful
action; an injury: *He did us a disservice by
telling everyone that our play is boring.*

dis·si·dent (dĭs'ĭ dənt) *adj.* Disagreeing, as
in opinion or belief: *Dissident opinions were
heard before the final vote was taken.* —*n.* A
person who disagrees; a dissenter: *The dictator had political dissidents put in jail.*
—**dis'si·dence** *n.* [U]

dis·sim·i·lar (dĭ sĭm'ə lər) *adj.* Unlike;
different: *We have dissimilar views.* —**dis·
sim'i·lar·ly** *adv.*

dis·sim·i·lar·i·ty (dĭ sĭm'ə lăr'ĭ tē) *n., pl.*
dis·sim·i·lar·i·ties. 1. [U] The quality or
condition of being unlike; difference: *There
is great dissimilarity of climate between the
wet coastal regions and the dry inland plains.*

D

2. [C] A point where two things differ: *Even identical twins have some dissimilarities.*

dis·si·pate (dĭs′ə pāt′) *v.* **dis·si·pat·ed, dis·si·pat·ing, dis·si·pates.** *Formal.* —*tr.* **1.** To drive (sth.) away by or as if by sending in different directions: *A strong wind dissipated the clouds.* **2.** To waste or use (sth.) up unwisely: *They dissipated their wealth on fast cars and big parties.* —*intr.* To separate and disappear: *The fog dissipated soon after sunrise.* —**dis′si·pa′tion** *n.* [U]

dis·so·ci·ate (dĭ sō′shē āt′ *or* dĭ sō′sē āt′) *v.* **dis·so·ci·at·ed, dis·so·ci·at·ing, dis·so·ci·ates.** —*tr.* To break association with (sbdy./sth.); part: *We dissociated ourselves from the committee because we disagree with its report.* —*intr.* In chemistry, to undergo dissociation. —**dis·so′ci·a′tion** *n.* [U]

dis·so·lu·tion (dĭs′ə lōō′shən) *n.* [U] *Formal.* **1.** The act or process of breaking up into parts: *Failure to take in new members caused the slow dissolution of the club.* **2.** The ending of a formal or legal connection: *dissolution of a business partnership.*

dis·solve (dĭ zŏlv′) *v.* **dis·solved, dis·solv·ing, dis·solves.** —*tr.* **1.** To change a (solid matter) to a liquid: *Warm weather dissolved the ice on the lake.* **2.** To bring (sth.) to an end: *dissolve a partnership.* **3.** To cause (sth.) to disappear: *Growing older dissolves fear of the dark for most children.* —*intr.* **1.** To become part of a solution: *Alcohol dissolves in water, but oil does not.* **2.** To change from a solid into a liquid: *The ice cubes dissolved in the warm tea.* **3.** To break up and disappear: *After a bad loss, the team's confidence dissolved quickly.* **4.** To lose self-control emotionally: *The lost child dissolved into tears.* —**dis·solv′a·ble** *adj.*

dis·so·nant (dĭs′ə nənt) *adj.* **1.** Having a harsh combination of sounds: *a dissonant passage in the symphony.* **2.** Lacking agreement: *a dissonant meeting.* —**dis′so·nance** *n.* [U] —**dis′so·nant·ly** *adv.*

dis·suade (dĭ swād′) *tr.v.* **dis·suad·ed, dis·suad·ing, dis·suades.** [*from*] To discourage (sbdy.) from doing something by persuasion or advice: *Friends dissuaded me from leaving early.* —**dis·sua′sion** (dĭ-swā′zhən) *n.* [U]

dist. *abbr.* An abbreviation of: **1.** Distance. **2.** District.

dis·tance (dĭs′təns) *n.* **1.** [C; U] The length of the space between two points or things: *The distance between my house and the post office is half a mile.* **2.** [U] A stretch of space without definite limits: *We could see a whale swimming in the distance.* —*v.* **dis·tanced, dis·tanc·ing, dis·tanc·es.** ♦ **distance (oneself) from.** To place or keep oneself at

or as if at a distance: *He distanced himself from old friends when he became famous.*

dis·tant (dĭs′tənt) *adj.* **1.** Far away; remote: *a distant planet.* **2.** Separate or apart in space: *Our house is two miles distant from the station.* **3.** Far away or apart in time: *the distant past.* **4.** Far apart in relationship: *a distant cousin.* **5.** Unfriendly in manner; aloof: *The new neighbors appeared cold and distant until we got to know them.* —**dis′tant·ly** *adv.*

dis·taste (dĭs tāst′) *n.* [U; *for*]A dislike or strong objection: *a distaste for modern music.*

dis·taste·ful (dĭs tāst′fəl) *adj.* Unpleasant; disagreeable: *Cleaning the basement is a distasteful job.* —**dis·taste′ful·ly** *adv.* —**dis·taste′ful·ness** *n.* [U]

dis·tend (dĭ stĕnd′) *v.* —*intr.* To swell or expand from or as if from internal pressure: *The puppies ate until their stomachs distended.* —*tr.* To cause (sth.) to expand by or as if by internal pressure: *Fluid distends a blister.*

dis·till (dĭ stĭl′) *v.* —*tr.* **1.** To treat (a substance) by the process of distillation: *distill water to purify it.* **2.** To separate or bring out the central or most important part of (sth.): *distill the important points of a book in a report.* —*intr.* To go through or be produced by distillation.

dis·til·la·tion (dĭs′tə lā′shən) *n.* **1.** [U] The process of boiling a liquid and condensing and collecting the vapor: *Distillation is used to purify liquids, such as seawater.* **2.** [C; U] Something distilled from another substance or from a more complex form: *a distillation of the philosopher's ideas.*

dis·till·er (dĭ stĭl′ər) *n.* A person or company that produces alcoholic liquors.

dis·till·er·y (dĭ stĭl′ə rē) *n.,* *pl.* **dis·till·er·ies.** A company or factory for distilling, especially for producing alcoholic liquors.

dis·tinct (dĭ stĭngkt′) *adj.* **1.** Different and separate from all others; separate: *We discussed the problem on two distinct occasions.* **2.** Easily noticed and recognized by the senses or mind: *Onions have a distinct odor.* **3.** Clear; unquestionable: *Doctors have distinct limitations on their time.* —**dis·tinct′ly** *adv.* —**dis·tinct′ness** *n.* [U]

dis·tinc·tion (dĭ stĭngk′shən) *n.* **1.** [U] The act of distinguishing: *Employers must hire without distinction of age or race.* **2.** [C] The condition or fact of being different and separate: *a distinction between studying and casual reading.* **3.** [C] (*usually singular*). A mark or quality that sets one apart: *the distinction of being the best singer in the group.* **4.** [U] Excellence, as of performance, character, or reputation: *a composer of distinction.*

dis·tinc·tive (dĭ stĭngk′tĭv) *adj.* Serving to

ă-cat; ā-pay; âr-care; ä-father; ĕ-get; ē-be; ĭ-sit; ī-nice; îr-here; ŏ-got; ō-go; ô-saw; oi-boy; ou-out; ōō-took; ōō-boot; ŭ-cut; ûr-word; th-thin; *th*-this; hw-when; zh-vision; ə-about; N-French bon

identify, characterize, or set apart from others: *Your team wears a distinctive uniform.* —**dis•tinc′tive•ly** *adv.* —**dis•tinc′tive•ness** *n.* [U]

dis•tin•guish (dĭ stĭng′gwĭsh) *v.* —*tr.* **1.** To recognize (sthg.) as being different or distinct: *learning how to distinguish crocodiles from alligators.* **2.** To see or hear (sthg.) clearly: *the ear's ability to distinguish musical notes.* **3.** To make (sbdy./sthg.) noticeable or different: *The beaver is distinguished by its broad flat tail.* **4.** To cause (oneself) to gain fame, respect, or honor: *Some artists distinguished themselves as great portrait painters.* —*intr.* To recognize differences: *distinguish between right and wrong.* —**dis•tin′guish•a•ble** *adj.*

dis•tin•guished (dĭ stĭng′gwĭsht) *adj.* **1.** Recognized as excellent: *a distinguished composer.* **2.** Dignified in manner or appearance: *the distinguished air of a great dancer.*

dis•tort (dĭ stôrt′) *tr.v.* **1.** To twist (sthg.) out of the usual shape: *a grin that distorted the clown's face.* **2.** To give a false report of (sthg.); misrepresent: *distort the facts.* **3.** To change (an electronic signal) so as to result in poor quality sound, as of radio or recorded music.

dis•tor•tion (dĭ stôr′shən) *n.* **1.** [U] **a.** The act of distorting: *His distortion of the facts gave us a false idea of what actually happened.* **b.** The condition of being distorted: *distortion of an object in a poor photograph.* **2.** [C] Something distorted: *Their report was full of lies and distortions.*

dis•tract (dĭ străkt′) *tr.v.* **1.** To draw (the attention, for example) away from sthg.: *The noise distracted the students in the library.* **2.** To pull (sbdy.) in opposite emotional directions; unsettle: *Worries about moving to a new city distracted the whole family.* —**dis•tract′ed** *adj.*

dis•trac•tion (dĭ străk′shən) *n.* **1.** [C] Something that distracts or draws attention away: *The new kittens were a continuous distraction from homework.* **2.** [U] Great mental confusion and disturbance: *Worry over paying the bills nearly drove the shopkeeper to distraction.* **3.** [C] *(usually singular).* The act of drawing away the attention: *the distraction of watching TV.* **4.** [U] Relief from worry or work: *A good book brings distraction to the reader.*

dis•traught (dĭ strôt′) *adj.* Very upset or worried: *She was distraught over the divorce.*

dis•tress (dĭ strĕs′) *tr.v.* To cause (sbdy.) to suffer in mind or body: *It distresses me to see you cry.* —*n.* [U] **1.** Pain or suffering of mind or body: *Injuries from the accident caused the victim severe distress.* **2.** Something that causes emotional discomfort: *Seeing an animal suffering is a great distress to me.* —**dis•tress′ful** *adj.* —**dis•tress′ful•ly** *adv.*

dis•trib•ute (dĭ strĭb′yŏot) *tr.v.* **dis•trib•ut•ed, dis•trib•ut•ing, dis•trib•**utes. **1.** To divide and give (sthg.) out in regular amounts or shares: *distribute newspapers to the door of each apartment.* **2.** To supply or send out (sthg.): *distribute fresh vegetables to other parts of the country.* **3.** To spread (sthg.) over an area: *The storm distributed heavy snow throughout the region.*

SYNONYMS: distribute, divide, dispense, deal, ration. These verbs mean to give out in parts or shares. **Distribute** is the most general: *In the 19th century the United States government distributed land to settlers.* **Divide** means to give out amounts on the basis of a plan or a purpose: *The old man's money will be divided among the heirs.* **Dispense** often means to give carefully measured or weighed amounts: *The pharmacist dispensed the medicine.* **Deal** means to distribute sthg. in a orderly way: *Each player was dealt five cards.* **Ration** means to deal out items in short supply: *The government had to ration food during the war.* ANTONYM: **gather.**

dis•tri•bu•tion (dĭs′trə byŏo′shən) *n.* [U] **1.** The act of distributing: *the distribution of mail to each house.* **2.** The way in which sthg. is distributed: *a map showing the distribution of population in Asia.* **3.** The process of marketing and supplying goods, especially to retailers, for sale to the public.

dis•trib•u•tive (dĭ strĭb′yə tĭv) *adj.* Relating to distribution: *We studied the distributive function of the bloodstream.* —**dis•trib′u•tive•ly** *adv.*

dis•trib•u•tor (dĭ strĭb′yə tər) *n.* **1.** A person or company that markets or sells goods, especially a wholesaler. **2.** A device that applies electric current at the proper time to each spark plug in an engine.

dis•trict (dĭs′trĭkt) *n.* **1.** A part of an area marked out by law for a particular purpose: *our school district.* **2.** An area, especially one having a special characteristic or function: *a shopping district.*

district attorney *n.* The attorney who represents the government in a judicial district, especially the attorney who prosecutes people accused of a crime.

dis•trust (dĭs trŭst′) *n.* [U] Lack of confidence or trust; suspicion: *a distrust of strangers.* —*tr.v.* To lack confidence or trust in (sbdy./sthg.): *I distrust TV commercials that make products seem too good.* —**dis•trust′ful** *adj.* —**dis•trust′ful•ly** *adv.*

dis•turb (dĭ stûrb′) *tr.v.* **1.** To break up or destroy the order or settled state of (sthg.): *a breeze that disturbed the papers on my desk.* **2.** To make (sbdy.) anxious or upset: *I was disturbed when I didn't know where you were.* **3.** To interrupt or bother (sbdy.): *The visitors disturbed the musician's practice.* —**dis•turbed′** *adj.*

dis·tur·bance (dĭ stûr′bəns) n. **1.** [U] The act of disturbing or the condition of being disturbed: *a disturbance in the TV signal.* **2.** [C; U] Something that interrupts, bothers, or upsets: *The coughing of a few was a disturbance to the rest of the audience.* **3.** [C] A noisy argument or fight: *Angry fans created a disturbance at the game.*

dis·u·ni·ty (dĭs yōō′nĭ tē) n. [U] Lack of unity or agreement: *a troubling disunity among team members.*

dis·use (dĭs yōōs′) n. [U] The condition of not being used or of being no longer in use: *a road fallen into disuse.*

ditch (dĭch) n. A long narrow trench dug in the ground: *Water ran through the ditch by the road.* —*v.* —*tr.* **1.** *Slang.* To get rid of (sthg.): *The thief kept the money and ditched the wallet.* **2.** To bring (an aircraft) to a forced landing on water. —*intr.* To be forced to land an aircraft on water: *The helicopter pilot ditched in the harbor.*

dith·er (dĭth′ər) n. [U] A condition of nervous excitement or indecision: *in a dither about getting ready for the party.* —*intr.v.* To be nervously unable to make a decision or act on sthg.: *She dithered about what to wear to her interview.*

dit·to (dĭt′ō) n., pl. **dit·tos. 1.** *Informal.* The same as stated above or before: *"I'm tired. What about you?" "Ditto."* **2.** A ditto mark.

ditto mark n. (*usually plural*). A pair of marks (″) used directly below a word to be repeated instead of writing it again, as on long lists.

dive (dīv) *intr.v.* **dived** or **dove** (dōv), **dived, div·ing, dives. 1.** To throw oneself into water, especially headfirst. **2.** To go toward the bottom of a body of water: *The submarine dived.* **3.** To go downwards rapidly at a steep angle: *The airplane turned and dived.* **4.** To begin an activity with energy: *She dove into the project with great enthusiasm.* —*n.* **1.** A plunge into water, especially headfirst. **2.** A sharp downward movement, as of an airplane or a submarine. **3.** *Informal.* A run-down bar or nightclub. —SEE NOTE at **wake**[1].

div·er (dī′vər) n. **1.** A person who dives into water: *a champion diver.* **2.** A person who works underwater, as in gathering pearl oysters or recovering lost objects.

di·verge (dĭ vûrj′ or dī vûrj′) *intr.v.* **di·verged, di·verg·ing, di·verg·es. 1.** To go in different directions from a shared point: *a small dirt road that diverged into two tracks.* **2.** [*from*] To move away from a fixed order, standard, or norm: *Today's class diverged from the usual because we had a debate.* **3.** To differ, as in opinion or manner: *The twins diverged in their interests as they grew older.* —**di·ver′gence** n. [U] —**di·ver′gent** adj. —**di·ver′gent·ly** adv.

di·verse (dĭ vûrs′ or dī vûrs′ or dī′vûrs′) adj. Distinct in kind; different: *Members of the same family can have diverse personalities.* —**di·verse′ly** adv.

di·ver·si·fy (dĭ vûr′sə fī′ or dī vûr′sə fī′) v. **di·ver·si·fied, di·ver·si·fy·ing, di·ver·si·fies.** —*tr.* To give diversity or variety to (sthg.): *After becoming successful as a writer, she diversified the kinds of books she wrote.* —*intr.* To become diversified, especially by making or dealing in different products: *The soap company diversified into producing a line of perfumes.* —**di·ver′si·fi·ca′tion** (dĭ vûr′sə fĭ kā′shən) n. [U]

di·ver·sion (dĭ vûr′zhən or dī vûr′zhən) n. **1.** [U] The act of diverting: *the diversion of traffic from a road under repair.* **2.** [C] Something that relaxes or entertains; recreation: *Playing music has been a wonderful diversion for me.* **3.** [C] Something that draws the attention to a different direction or action: *The movie star was able to leave the hotel unseen because his manager created a diversion by arguing with reporters.*

di·ver·si·ty (dĭ vûr′sĭ tē or dī vûr′sĭ tē) n., pl. **di·ver·si·ties. 1.** [U] The quality of being diverse; difference. **2.** [C] Variety: *a diversity of foods on a menu.* **3.** [U] Variety among people in race, culture, and religion, for example: *The college president spoke of the value of diversity.*

di·vert (dĭ vûrt′ or dī vûrt′) v. —*tr.* **1.** To turn (sthg.) away from a course or direction: *divert traffic around a fallen tree on the road.* **2.** [*from*] To draw (the mind or attention) to another direction: *A passing fire truck diverted our attention from the game.* **3.** *Formal.* To amuse or entertain (sbdy.): *divert children by singing songs on a rainy afternoon.* —*intr.* To turn aside: *The pilot had to divert from the airport closed in by fog.*

di·vest (dĭ vĕst′ or dī vĕst′) *tr.v.* [*of*] **1.** To free (oneself) of sthg.: *They divested themselves of their heavy winter coats. He divested himself of several properties.* **2.** To take (rights or property) away from sbdy.: *A person convicted of a serious crime is divested of the right to vote.* —**di·vest′i·ture** (dĭ vĕs′tĭ chər), **di·vest′ment** n. [U]

di·vide (dĭ vīd′) v. **di·vid·ed, di·vid·ing, di·vides.** —*tr.* **1.** [*into*] To separate (sthg.) into parts, groups, or kinds: *The teacher divided the class into four groups.* **2.** To separate or keep (sthg.) apart: *A mountain chain divides France and Spain.* **3.** [*among; between*] To share or distribute (sthg.) among members of a group: *Volunteers divided the* *different jobs among themselves.* **4.** [*by; into*] To find how many times (one number) contains another: *I divided 24 by 4 and got 6.* —*intr.* **1.** To become separated into parts, groups, or factions: *The country divided on the issue of how to improve the economy.* **2.** To perform the mathematical operation of division. —*n.* A long high area of land separating two areas each drained by a different river system: *Hills form a divide between the rivers flowing eastward and westward.*

div·i·dend (dĭv′ĭ dĕnd′) *n.* **1.** A number or quantity that is to be divided: *In the fraction ¼, 1 is the dividend.* **2.a.** Profits earned by a company during a certain period of time and divided among the stockholders or owners. **b.** A share of profits paid to a stockholder of a company: *a dividend paid by check.* **3.** *Informal.* A benefit or an advantage; a bonus: *Cleaning up our environment will provide dividends for us all.*

di·vid·er (dĭ vī′dər) *n.* A person or thing that divides, especially a screen or other partition: *a room divider.*

div·i·na·tion (dĭv′ə nā′shən) *n.* **1.** [U] The art of telling the future by using magic powers. **2.** [C] Something that has been predicted by this art: *There have been many divinations about the end of the world.* **3.** [C] *Formal.* A clever guess.

di·vine (dĭ vīn′) *adj.* **1.** Related to God or a god: *divine wisdom; divine guidance.* **2.** *Informal.* Exceptionally good: *This dessert is divine.* —*n. Formal.* A Christian minister, priest, or scholar. —*tr.v.* **di·vined, di·vin·ing, di·vines. 1.** To predict (sthg. about the future) by divination: *prophets that divined disasters from the flights of birds.* **2.** *Formal.* To guess (sthg.): *The mechanic divined my car's problem after looking at the tires.* —**di·vine′ly** *adv.* —**di·vine′ness** *n.* [U] —**di·vin′er** *n.*

div·ing board (dī′vĭng) *n.* A flexible board from which a person can dive, secured at one end with the other sticking out over the water.

di·vin·i·ty (dĭ vĭn′ĭ tē) *n., pl.* **di·vin·i·ties. 1.** [U] The quality or condition of being divine. **2.** [C] A god or goddess. **3.** [U] The study of God and religion; theology: *a school of divinity for Christian ministers.*

di·vis·i·ble (dĭ vĭz′ə bəl) *adj.* Capable of being divided, especially with no remainder: *Even numbers are divisible by two.* —**di·vis′i·bil′i·ty** *n.* [U] —**di·vis′i·bly** *adv.*

di·vi·sion (dĭ vĭzh′ən) *n.* **1.** [U] The act of dividing or the condition of being divided; separation into parts: *the division of a book into chapters.* **2.** [C] One of the parts or groups into which sthg. is divided: *a division in a company.* **3.** [C] Something, such as a partition or line, that divides: *The wall marked the division between east and west Berlin.* **4.** [U] Disagreement; disunity: *The*

meeting was marked by deep division among representatives from different parts of the country. **5.** [U] The operation of dividing one number or quantity by another.

divi·sion sign *n.* A symbol (÷) placed between two numbers to show that the first is to be divided by the second.

di·vi·sive (dĭ vī′sĭv) *adj.* Creating or tending to create disagreement or a lack of unity: *a divisive political issue.* —**di·vi′sive·ly** *adv.* —**di·vi′sive·ness** *n.* [U]

di·vi·sor (dĭ vī′zər) *n.* The number or quantity by which another is to be divided: *In the fraction ¼, 4 is the divisor.*

di·vorce (dĭ vôrs′) *n.* [C; U] The legal ending of a marriage. —*v.* **di·vorced, di·vorc·ing, di·vorc·es.** —*tr.* **1.** To end the marriage of (persons): *The judge divorced the husband and wife.* **2.** To end a marriage legally with (one's husband or wife): *She divorced her husband.* **3.** To separate or remove (sthg.): *We cannot divorce a good diet from fitness.* —*intr.* To end one's marriage legally: *They divorced in 1990.*

di·vor·cé (dĭ vôr sā′) *n.* A man who is divorced.

di·vor·cée (dĭ vôr sā′) *n.* A woman who is divorced.

di·vulge (dĭ vŭlj′) *tr.v.* **di·vulged, di·vulg·ing, di·vulg·es.** To tell or make (sthg.) known, especially a secret: *The reporter wouldn't divulge the source of her information.* —**di·vulg′er** *n.*

div·vy (dĭv′ē) *v.* **div·vied, div·vy·ing, div·vies.** ◆ **divvy up.** *tr.v.* [sep.] *Informal.* To divide or share (sthg.): *We divvied up the pizza so that each of us got a piece.*

diz·zy (dĭz′ē) *adj.* **diz·zi·er, diz·zi·est. 1.** Having a feeling of turning quickly or feeling about to fall: *A ride on the roller coaster made me feel dizzy.* **2.** Very confused: *dizzy with excitement.* —*tr.v.* **diz·zied, diz·zy·ing, diz·zies.** To make (sbdy./sthg.) dizzy: *Listening to so many facts and figures dizzied my brain.* —**diz′zi·ly** *adv.* —**diz′zi·ness** *n.* [U]

DJ *abbr.* An abbreviation of disc jockey: *We hired a DJ for the party.*

DNA (dē′ĕn ā′) *n.* [U] An acid found in all living cells that looks like a twisted ladder and forms the main component of chromosomes; deoxyribonucleic acid: *DNA is the genetic material controlling all cells and many viruses.*

do (do͞o) *v.* **did** (dĭd), **done** (dŭn), **do·ing, does** (dŭz). —*tr.* **1.** To perform, complete, or accomplish (sthg.): *do a good job; do a favor for a friend.* **2.** To create, produce, or make (sthg.): *do a painting; do a report.* **3.** To make (sthg.) happen: *Crying won't do any good.* **4.** To put (sthg.) into action: *I'll do everything in my power to help you.* **5.** To put (sthg.) into order: *do one's hair.* **6.** To work at (sthg.) to earn a living: *"What do you do?" "I'm a nurse."* **7.** To solve or work out the

details of (a problem): *I did this equation.*
8.a. To travel (a specified distance): *do a mile in seven minutes.* **b.** To travel at (a speed): *He was only doing 50 miles an hour on the highway.* **9.** To be enough or convenient for (sbdy.): *This room will do us very nicely.* **10.** *Informal.* To serve (a prison term): *Both men did time for theft.* —*intr.* **1.** To behave or conduct oneself: *You did well in the interview.* **2.** To get along; manage: *The new student is doing well.* **3.** To serve a purpose: *That old coat will do for now.* **4.** Used instead of repeating a verb or phrase: *She reads as much as I do. I like novels and she does, too.* —*aux.* **1.** Used to ask questions: *Do you want to go? Did you hear me?* **2.** Used to make negative statements: *I did not sleep at all. We do not understand.* **3.** Used to form inverted phrases: *Little did I know that he was planning to leave.* **4.** Used to emphasize or make stronger: *But we do want to go. You really do play well.* —*n.*, *pl.* **do's** or **dos.** A statement of what should and should not be done: *a long list of do's and don'ts from my mother.* ◆ **do away with. 1.** To get rid of or put an end to sthg.: *doing away with unnecessary laws.* **2.** To kill or destroy sbdy./sthg.: *The landlord promises to do away with rats in the building.* **do (one) in.** *tr.v.* [sep.] **1.** *Slang.* To make (sbdy.) very tired: *That long walk really did me in.* **2.** To kill (sbdy./sthg.): *Nobody knows who did him in.* **do (one) out of.** *Informal.* To cheat sbdy. and take away sthg.: *His partners did him out of his fair share of the money.* **do (one's) own thing.** *Slang.* To do what one does best or likes most: *The art teacher gave the girls some paints and let each one do her own thing.* **do or die.** Requiring a very great effort: *The test is tomorrow, so it's do or die time.* **do over.** *tr.v.* [sep.] *Informal.* **1.** To redecorate (sthg.): *Professionals are doing over the room.* **2.** To do (sthg.) again: *His homework was messy, so he did it over.* **do well by.** To behave well when dealing with sbdy.: *The children have done well by their aged parents.* **do with.** *tr.v.* [insep.] **1.** To use (sthg.): *You can do with the money as you wish.* **2.** (*usually with* could). To need or want (sthg.): *I could do with a hot shower.* **3.** To be related or connected to (sbdy./sthg.): *The story had to do with a lost dog. Our troubles are nothing to do with you.* **do without.** *tr.v.* [insep.] To manage without (sbdy./sthg.): *We can do without his help.*

doc (dŏk) *n. Informal.* A doctor: *I need to see the doc.*

doc•ile (dŏs′əl *or* dŏs′īl′) *adj.* Easy to train or handle; submissive: *She chose a docile horse with a good disposition.* —**doc′ile•ly** *adv.* —**do•cil′i•ty** (dŏ sĭl′ĭ tē *or* dō sĭl′ĭ tē) *n.* [U]

dock¹ (dŏk) *n.* **1.a.** A structure built out from a shore over water and used for loading and unloading ships: *We all went fishing off the dock.* **b.** A platform attached to a building, used for loading and unloading trucks or trains. **2.** (*often plural*). A group of piers that serve as the landing area of a harbor: *He works on the docks of New York.* —*v.* —*tr.* To move (a ship, for example) into position at a dock: *It is very tricky to dock a big ocean liner.* —*intr.* **1.** To come into dock: *The ferry docked late in the evening.* **2.** To join together two or more spacecraft while in space: *The two ships docked.*

dock² (dŏk) *tr.v.* **1.a.** To hold back a part of (a salary): *The restaurant docked the waiter's pay to make up for dishes he broke.* **b.** To punish (a worker) by such deduction: *That company docks workers who are late.* **2.** To cut off (an animal's tail, for example): *Some people dock the tail of their dog.*

dock³ (dŏk) *n.* (*usually singular*). An enclosed place where the defendant stands or sits in a criminal court.

doc•tor (dŏk′tər) *n.* **1.** A person who is trained and licensed to practice any of the healing arts, such as medicine or dentistry. **2.** A person who holds the highest degree given by a university. —*tr.v.* **1.** *Informal.* To give medical treatment to (sbdy.): *She doctored my wounds and told me to rest.* **2.** *Slang.* To change or falsify (official documents, for example): *The researcher doctored the results of the experiment.*

doc•tor•ate (dŏk′tər ĭt) *n.* The degree or status of a doctor as awarded by a university: *a doctorate in English literature.* —**doc′tor•al** *adj.*

doc•trine (dŏk′trĭn) *n.* **1.** A principle or set of principles held and taught by a religious or philosophical group: *He follows the doctrines of his church.* **2.** A statement of government policy, especially in foreign affairs: *a new trade doctrine.* —**doc′tri•nal** *adj.*

doc•u•ment (dŏk′yə mənt) *n.* A written or printed paper that can be used to give evidence or information: *A birth certificate is an important personal document.* —*tr.v.* (dŏk′yə mĕnt′). To prove or support (sthg.) with evidence: *document a report with photographs and letters.*

doc•u•men•ta•ry (dŏk′yə mĕn′tə rē) *adj.*

Relating to or based on documents: *documentary evidence. —n., pl.* **doc·u·men·ta·ries.** A motion picture or television program giving a factual account of some subject and often showing actual events: *We watched a documentary on African elephants.*

doc·u·men·ta·tion (dŏk′yə mĕn tā′shən) *n.* [U] **1.** The act of supplying documents or records of decisive information: *documentation of the experiments.* **2.** The documents or records provided: *documentation for the trial.* **3.** The information and instructions that serve as the basis for a computer program and explain its design: *documentation on the software.*

dodge (dŏj) *v.* **dodged, dodg·ing, dodg·es.** *—tr.* **1.** To avoid (sbdy./sthg.) by moving quickly aside or out of the way: *The dog dodged the cars as it ran across the street.* **2.** To escape (a duty or sthg. unpleasant) by trickery or other means: *The candidate dodged the reporter's questions. —intr.* To move by jumping suddenly to the side: *The boy dodged through the crowd. —n.* **1.** The act of dodging. **2.** A trick to cheat or avoid: *a tax dodge.*

doe (dō) *n., pl.* **doe** or **does. 1.** A female deer. **2.** The female of certain other animals, such as the hare or kangaroo.

HOMONYMS: doe, dough (flour mixture).

---

do·er (dōo′ər) *n.* A person who does sthg., especially an active and energetic person: *She is a doer and does not hesitate to act when people need her help.*

does (dŭz) *v.* Third person singular present tense of **do.**

does·n't (dŭz′ənt). Contraction of *does not.*

dog (dôg *or* dŏg) *n.* A four-legged mammal that eats meat and can be any of many varieties, some of which look like the wolf: *For thousands of years dogs have been kept as pets and trained to hunt or guard. —tr.v.* **dogged, dog·ging, dogs.** To follow (sbdy./sthg.) persistently: *The detective dogged the suspect's every move.* ◆ **dog-eat-dog.** Very competitive and completely without kindness: *a dog-eat-dog business environment.*

dog

dog-eared (dôg′îrd′ *or* dŏg′îrd′) *adj.* Describing book pages that are turned down at the corners or torn.

dog·ged (dô′gĭd *or* dŏg′ĭd) *adj.* Not giving up easily; stubborn: *The doctor's dogged efforts succeeded in discovering a cure for the disease.* **—dog′ged·ly** *adv.* **—dog′ged·ness** *n.* [U]

dog·gone (dôg′gôn′ *or* dôg′gŏn′ *or* dŏg′-

gôn′ *or* **dŏg′**gŏn′) *Informal. interj.* An expression used when one is mildly annoyed: *Doggone it! I forgot my wallet. —adj. & adv.* Very: *This cake is doggone good.*

dog·gy bag or **dog·gie bag** (dô′gē *or* **dŏg′**ē) *n.* A bag for leftover food taken home from a restaurant.

dog·house (dôg′hous′ *or* **dŏg′**hous′) *n.* A small house or shelter for a dog. ◆ **in the doghouse.** *Slang.* In disfavor; in trouble: *He's in the doghouse for forgetting to call.*

dog·ma (dôg′mə *or* **dŏg′**mə) *n.* [C; U] **1.** An idea or a system of beliefs taught by a religion. **2.** A belief, an opinion, or an idea considered to be true: *Political dogmas of the past often seem unreasonable today.*

dog·mat·ic (dôg măt′ĭk *or* dŏg măt′ĭk) *adj.* **1.** Relating to dogma: *a dogmatic idea.* **2.** Having or showing a proud insistence on the truth of one's beliefs or opinions: *a dogmatic person.* **—dog·mat′i·cal·ly** *adv.* **—dog′ma·tis′m** (dôg′mə tĭz′əm *or* **dŏg′**mə tĭz′əm) *n.* [U]

dog·wood (dôg′wŏod′ *or* **dŏg′**wŏod′) *n.* A tree that has showy white or pink flowers in the spring.

doi·ly (doi′lē) *n., pl.* **doi·lies.** A small fancy mat, as of lace, linen, or paper, often used to protect or decorate a tabletop.

do·ings (dōo′ĭngz) *pl.n.* Activities, especially social activities: *doings at the club.*

do-it-your·self (dōo′ĭt yər sĕlf′) *adj.* Relating to or designed to be done by an average untrained person: *do-it-yourself home repairs.* **—do′it-your·self′er** *n.*

dol·drums (dōl′drəmz′ *or* dŏl′drəmz′) *pl.n. (used with a singular or plural verb).* **1.** A period or condition of depression or inactivity: *in the doldrums over some bad luck.* **2.** A region of the ocean near the equator where there is little or no wind: *Several sailing ships were delayed by being caught in the doldrums.*

dole (dōl) *n.* [U] The free distribution of goods to poor people, especially of money, food, or clothing. *—v.* **doled, dol·ing, doles.** ◆ **dole out.** *tr.v.* [sep.] **1.** To distribute (sthg.) free to people in need: *The organization doles out food and medicine.* **2.** To give out (sthg.) in small amounts: *The boss rarely doles out praise.*

dole·ful (dōl′fəl) *adj.* Filled with or expressing sadness or grief: *the cat's doleful cry in the rain.* **—dole′ful·ly** *adv.*

doll (dŏl) *n.* **1.** A child's usually small toy representing a person. **2.** *Slang.* A sweetheart or darling: *You're a doll to help me with dinner.*

dol·lar (dŏl′ər) *n.* The basic monetary unit in the United States and many other countries, including Australia, Canada, Fiji, New Zealand, Taiwan, and Zimbabwe.

dollar sign *n.* The symbol ($) for a dollar or dollars, placed before a number.

D

dol·lop (dŏl′əp) *n.* A large lump or portion of soft food: *a dollop of whipped cream.*

dol·ly (dŏl′ē) *n., pl.* **dol·lies.** **1.** *Informal.* A child's doll. **2.** A hand truck or low movable platform on small wheels, used for moving heavy loads.

dol·phin (dŏl′fĭn *or* dôl′fĭn) *n.* Any of various marine mammals related to the whales but smaller: *Dolphins are noted for their intelligence.*

dolphin
Calf (*top*) and adult female (*bottom*)

—dom *suff.* A suffix that means: **1.** Condition; state: *stardom.* **2.** Domain; position: *kingdom.*

do·main (dō mān′) *n.* **1.** A territory or area of rule or control: *the duke's domain; public domain.* **2.** An area of interest or activity: *The new teacher's domain is math.*

dome (dōm) *n.* **1.** A rounded roof or vault built in the shape of a hemisphere: *the dome of the Capitol in Washington.* **2.** A structure or other object resembling such a roof: *the dome of the sky.* **—domed** *adj.*

do·mes·tic (də mĕs′tĭk) *adj.* **1.** Relating to the family or household: *domestic chores.* **2.** Tame or domesticated. Used of animals: *cats and other domestic animals.* **3.** Produced in or native to a particular country; not foreign or imported: *domestic cars.* **—do·mes′-ti·cal·ly** *adv.*

do·mes·ti·cate (də mĕs′tĭ kāt′) *tr.v.* **do·mes·ti·cat·ed, do·mes·ti·cat·ing, do·mes·ti·cates.** To train (an animal) to live with or be of use to humans; tame: *Human beings domesticated cattle long ago.* **—do·mes′ti·cat′ed** *adj.* **—do·mes′ti·ca′tion** *n.* [U]

do·mes·tic·i·ty (dō′mĕ stĭs′ĭ tē) *n.* [U] **1.** The quality or condition of being domestic. **2.** Home life or pleasure in it: *the comforts of domesticity.*

dom·i·cile (dŏm′ĭ sīl′ *or* dō′mĭ sīl′) *n.* *Formal.* **1.** A place where sbdy. lives; a home. **2.** A person's legal home.

dom·i·nant (dŏm′ə nənt) *adj.* **1.** Having the most influence or control: *the dominant dog in a pack.* **2.** Most easily seen, as because

of position: *The tallest buildings are dominant in a city's skyline.* **3.** Relating to the gene in any pair of differing genes that masks or dominates the other. **—dom′in·ance** *n.* [U] **—dom′i·nant·ly** *adv.*

dom·i·nate (dŏm′ə nāt′) *v.* **dom·i·nat·ed, dom·i·nat·ing, dom·i·nates.** *—tr.* **1.** To rule over (sbdy./sthg.) by superior power or authority: *Great Britain dominated about one-fourth of the world in the 19th century.* **2.** To have a commanding position in or over (sthg.): *The mountain dominates the countryside for miles around.* *—intr.* **1.** To have or exert strong authority or influence. **2.** To have the most prominent or superior position: *Tall people dominate in a crowd.* **—dom′i·na′tion** *n.* [U]

dom·i·neer (dŏm′ə nîr′) *intr. & tr.v.* To rule over or control with force and self-interest: *Some rulers domineer. That country domineers its smaller neighbors.*

dom·i·neer·ing (dŏm′ə nîr′ĭng) *adj.* Tending to domineer: *His domineering manner offended many people.* **—dom′i·neer′ing·ly** *adv.*

do·min·ion (də mĭn′yən) *n.* **1.** [U; *over*] Power to control or use of control. **2.** [C] A territory or area of influence or control: *Parts of the Americas were once the dominions of Spain.*

dom·i·no (dŏm′ə- nō′) *n., pl.* **dom·i·noes** *or* **dom·i·nos.** **1.** A small rectangular block, each half of which is blank or marked by one to six dots. **2.** **dominoes.** (*used with a singular or plural verb*). A game played with a set of these small blocks.

domino

domino effect *n.* (*usually singular*). An effect produced when one event starts a chain of similar events: *Increasing the speed limit in one state will probably have a domino effect on neighboring states.*

do·nate (dō′nāt′ *or* dō nāt′) *tr.v.* **do·nat·ed, do·nat·ing, do·nates.** To present (sthg.) as a gift to a fund or cause: *We often donate clothing to the Red Cross.*

do·na·tion (dō nā′shən) *n.* **1.** [U] The act of giving to a fund or cause. **2.** [C] A gift or contribution: *make a small donation to UNICEF.*

done (dŭn) *v.* Past participle of **do.** *—adj.* **1.** Completely accomplished or finished: *a done deal.* **2.** Cooked enough: *Is the fish done?* ◆ **done for.** Sure to meet death or destruction: *When the brakes failed, I thought we were done for.* **done in.** Very tired: *She felt done in by the end of the day.*

HOMONYMS: done, dun (ask for payment).

don·key (dŏng′kē- or dông′kē) n., pl. don·keys. A mammal related to the horse but smaller and having longer ears, used as a pack animal.

donkey

do·nor (dō′nər) n. 1. A person who gives sthg., such as money, to a cause or fund. 2. A person from whom blood, tissue, or an organ is taken to help sbdy. in need of a transfusion or transplant.

do-no·thing (dōō′nŭth′ĭng) Informal. adj. Making no effort for change: a do-nothing mayor. —n. An inactive or lazy person.

don't (dōnt). Contraction of do not.

do·nut (dō′nŭt′ or do′nət) n. Variant of doughnut.

doo·dle (dōōd′l) v. doo·dled, doo·dling, doo·dles. —intr. To draw pictures without thinking: He doodles during phone calls. —tr. To draw (a design or figure) while thinking of other things: She doodles fish constantly. —n. A design or figure drawn in such a way while preoccupied. —doo′dler n.

doom (dōōm) n. [C; U] 1. Fate or ending, especially a sad or destructive one: The revolution was poorly planned and soon met its doom. 2. A decision or judgment, especially one that carries severe punishment: the prisoner's doom. —tr.v. [to] 1. To make a severe judgment against (sbdy.): doomed the prisoner to life behind bars. 2. To force (sbdy.) to an unhappy end: The injury doomed the patient to several weeks in bed.

door (dôr) n. 1. A movable structure used to close off an entrance, typically made of a panel that swings on hinges or slides to one side. 2. The entrance to a room or building: They stood in the door and talked. 3. The room or building to which a door belongs: The deli is several doors down the street. 4. A way to approach or reach sthg.: An education can be a door to success. ◆ show (one) the door. To force sbdy. to leave: After I complained, she showed me the door.

door·bell (dôr′bĕl′) n. A buzzer or bell outside a door that a visitor rings upon arrival.

door·knob (dôr′nŏb′) n. A knob-shaped handle for opening and closing a door.

door·nail (dôr′nāl′) n. A large-headed nail. ◆ dead as a doornail. Clearly dead: The mouse was dead as a doornail.

door·step (dôr′stĕp′) n. A step leading up to or down from a door.

door·way (dôr′wā′) n. The entrance to a room or building.

dope (dōp) n. 1. [U] Slang. A narcotic or other drug, especially one sold and used ille-

gally. 2. [C] Informal. A stupid person. 3. [U] Informal. Information, especially a person: He gave me the dope on the new teacher. —tr.v. doped, dop·ing, dopes. Informal. To give a narcotic drug to (sbdy.): She was doped for the operation. ◆ doped up. Slang. High on drugs: He spends most of his time doped up.

dop·ey (dō′pē) adj. dop·i·er, dop·i·est. Slang. Stupid or silly: a dopey idea.

dorm (dôrm) n. Informal. A dormitory.

dor·man·cy (dôr′mən sē) n. [U] The condition of being dormant: Winter is a time of dormancy for many plants.

dor·mant (dôr′mənt) adj. 1. In an inactive state in which growth and development stop, only to start again when conditions are favorable: Seeds are dormant during winter. 2. Not active but capable of becoming active again: a dormant volcano.

dor·mi·to·ry (dôr′mĭ tôr′ē) n., pl. dor·mi·to·ries. 1. A building for housing a number of persons, as at a school. 2. A large room designed to sleep a number of people.

dor·sal (dôr′səl) adj. On or near the back or upper surface of a part or the body of an animal: the dorsal fin of a shark.

DOS (dôs or dŏs) abbr. An abbreviation of disk operating system.

dos·age (dō′sĭj) n. 1. [C] (usually singular). The giving or applying of medicine in measured amounts: the dosage of a drug three times a day. 2. [U] The amount given or applied at one time: The doctor reduced my dosage of painkiller.

dose (dōs) n. 1. The amount of medicine or other substance given or taken at one time: a dose of medicine every four hours. 2. Informal. An amount, especially of sthg. unpleasant, that one receives: a dose of hard luck. —tr.v. dosed, dos·ing, dos·es. To give or prescribe (medicine) in specified amounts.

dos·si·er (dŏs′ē ā′ or dô′sē ā′) n. A collection of papers giving detailed information about a person or subject: Army records included a dossier on each soldier.

dot (dŏt) n. 1. A small round mark; a spot: a dot over the letter i. 2. The short sound or signal used in Morse code in combination with the dash and silent intervals to represent letters, numbers, or punctuation. —tr.v. dot·ted, dot·ting, dots. To cover or mark (sthg.) with or as if with dots: Dandelions dotted the green field. ◆ on the dot. Exactly at the appointed time: I arrived at 9 o'clock on the dot.

dote (dōt) v. dot·ed, dot·ing, dotes. ◆ dote on. tr.v. [insep.] To show a great or foolish amount of love or attention: They doted on their only grandchild.

dou·ble (dŭb′əl) adj. 1. Twice as much in size, strength, number, or amount: a double dose. 2. Composed of two similar parts: double doors. 3. Composed of two unlike parts: a double meaning. **4.** Designed for two people: *a double hotel room.* —*n.* **1.** Something increased to twice as much: *His cone had a single scoop of ice cream, but I got a double.* **2.** A person or thing that looks very much like another: *She's her sister's double.* **3. doubles.** A form of a game, such as tennis or handball, having two players on each side. —*v.* **dou·bled, dou·bling, dou·bles.** —*tr.* **1.** To make (sthg.) twice as great: *Double the amount of food if both of you go hiking.* **2.** To do sthg. that is twice as much as (sthg.): *I'll double whatever they offered to pay you.* **3.** To fold (sthg.) in two: *double the blanket to get more warmth.* **4.** To close (one's fist) tightly. **5.** To duplicate or repeat (sthg.): *Double the t in* hit *when you spell* hitting. —*intr.* **1.** To be increased to twice as much: *Our rent has doubled in ten years' time.* **2.** To go back over or retrace a path in the direction from which one has come: *The bear doubled back on its trail.* **3.** To serve in a second role: *My bed doubles as a couch.* **4.** To be a substitute: *The stunt man doubled for the film star in dangerous scenes.* —*adv.* **1.** To twice the amount or extent: *My uncle paid double for the customized car.* **2.** Two together: *ride double on a horse.* ◆ **double up.** *intr.v.* **1.** To bend suddenly, as in pain or laughter: *The joke made us double up.* **2.** To share sthg., such as a room meant for one person: *We're short of space, so you'll have to double up.* **on the double.** Immediately or quickly: *We need help on the double!*

dou·ble-breast·ed (dŭb'əl brĕs'tĭd) *adj.* Describing a piece of clothing, especially a jacket, that has two rows of buttons and is fastened by lapping one edge of the front of a garment well over the other.

dou·ble-check (dŭb'əl chĕk') *tr.v.* To inspect or examine (sthg.) again; verify: *Don't forget to double-check your subtraction.*

dou·ble-cross (dŭb'əl krôs' *or* dŭb'əl-krŏs') *tr.v.* To betray (sbdy./sthg.) by acting against a promise or an agreement: *The thief double-crossed his partners and took all the money for himself.* —*n.* An act of betrayal. —**dou'ble-cross'er** *n.*

dou·ble-dig·it (dŭb'əl dĭj'ĭt) *adj.* Being between 10 and 99 percent: *double-digit inflation.*

dou·ble-park (dŭb'əl pärk') *tr. & intr.v.* To park beside another vehicle already parked parallel to the curb: *We double-parked the car for just a few minutes. The police officer gave a ticket to the driver who double-parked.*

double standard *n.* A set of standards that allows greater freedom or opportunity to one group than another, especially one giving more sexual freedom to men than to women.

double take *n.* A delayed reaction to sthg.

unexpected or unusual: *He did a double take when he saw her in the bank.*

double talk *n.* [U] Talk that is intentionally confusing or meaningless: *campaign double talk.*

dou·bly (dŭb'lē) *adv.* To a double degree; twice: *Make doubly sure the totals are right.*

doubt (dout) *v.* —*tr.* **1.** To be undecided or unsure about (sbdy./sthg.): *doubt a report; doubt someone as a true friend.* **2.** To think of (sthg.) as unlikely: *I doubt that we'll arrive on time.* —*intr.* To be undecided or disbelieving. —*n.* **1.** [C] *(often plural).* A lack of certainty: *doubts about our future.* **2.** [U] A lack of trust. **3.** [U] The condition of being undecided or unresolved: *The winner of the horse race is still in doubt.* ◆ **beyond** or **without a doubt.** Without question; certainly: *This is beyond a doubt the best party I've ever been to.* **no doubt.** Certainly or probably: *No doubt you'll see him there.*

doubt·ful (dout'fəl) *adj.* **1.** Causing doubt: *a doubtful claim.* **2.** Having or showing doubt: *We were doubtful about the proposed plan.* —**doubt'ful·ly** *adv.*

doubt·less (dout'lĭs) *adv.* **1.** Certainly: *The bad weather was doubtless a reason for the delay.* **2.** Probably: *They will doubtless reject our proposal.* —**doubt'less·ly** *adv.*

dough (dō) *n.* [U] **1.** A soft thick mixture of ingredients such as flour and water that is used in baking bread or pastry. **2.** *Slang.* Money. —**dough'y** *adj.*

HOMONYMS: dough, doe (deer).

---

dough·nut also **do·nut** (dō'nŭt' *or* dō'nət) *n.* A small ring-shaped cake made of rich dough that is fried in deep fat.

dour (dŏor *or* dour) *adj.* Silent and unsmiling: *He had a dour personality that won him few friends.* —**dour'ly** *adv.*

douse (dous) *tr.v.* **doused, dous·ing, dous·es.** **1.** To wet (sbdy./sthg.) thoroughly: *The runner doused his head with cool water.* **2.** To put out (a light or fire): *douse the flames.*

dove[1] (dŭv) *n.* **1.** Any of various birds, including pigeons, with a small head and a cooing call. **2.** A person who is in favor of peaceful ways to solve international problems.

dove[2] (dōv) *v.* A past tense of **dive.**

dow·dy (dou'dē) *adj.* **dow·di·er, dow·di·est.** Lacking stylishness or neatness; shabby: *dowdy old clothes.* —**dow'di·ly** *adv.* —**dow'di·ness** *n.* [U]

Dow Jones average (dou'jōnz') A trademark used for numbers that represent the prices of selected stocks and show stock market conditions.

down[1] (doun) *adv.* **1.a.** From a higher to a lower place: *hiked down from the mountain top.* **b.** To,

---

ă–**cat**; ā–**pay**; âr–**care**; ä–**father**; ĕ–**get**; ē–**be**; ĭ–**sit**; ī–**nice**; îr–**here**; ŏ–**got**; ō–**go**; ô–**saw**; oi–**boy**; ou–**out**; ōō–**took**; ōō–**boot**; ŭ–**cut**; ûr–**word**; th–**thin**; th–**this**; hw–**when**; zh–**vision**; ə–**about**; N–French bon

toward the ground, floor, or bottom: *fell ˌn.* **2.** In or to a lower position: *sat down; lay own on the grass.* **3.** Toward or in the south: *going down to Florida.* **4.** Away from a center of activity: *down on the farm.* **5.** Toward or at a lower point on a scale: *turn down the volume.* **6.** To or into an inferior condition: *Our team went down in defeat.* **7.** From an earlier to a later time: *traditions handed down through the years.* **8.** As payment in part at the time of purchase: *put $50 down on the TV set.* **9.** In writing: *The reporter took the statement down.* **10.** Seriously or intensely: *Let's get down to work.* —*adj.* **1.a.** Moving or directed downward: *a down elevator.* **b.** Low or lower: *The room is dark because the blinds are down.* **2.** Sick; not feeling well: *He is down with a bad cold.* **3.** In low spirits; depressed: *feeling down today.* **4.** Not functioning or operating, especially temporarily: *They can't issue report cards because the school's computers are down.* —*prep.* **1.** In a descending direction upon, along, through, or into; *ran down the stairs; went down to the cellar.* **2.** Along the course of: *walking down the road.* —*tr.v.* **1.** To bring, strike, or throw (sbdy./sthg.) down: *down an enemy plane.* **2.** To swallow (sthg.) fast: *I downed a lot of water before the race.* ◆ **down in the mouth** or **down at the mouth.** Discouraged; sad: *You're looking sort of down in the mouth. Are you okay?* **down on.** Informal. Angry or negative toward: *She was down on jogging after her injury.* **down to.** Left with only a small amount of sthg.: *He was down to his last dollar.*

down² (doun) *n.* [U] **1.** The soft feathers of a bird: *a down-filled ski jacket.* **2.** Fine soft hair, as on some plants and fruits: *the down on a peach.* —**down'y** *adj.*

down-and-out (doun'ănd out' *or* doun'ən-out') *adj.* Having no luck and no money: *She was down-and-out after the loss of her job.*

down·er (dou'nər) *n. Slang.* **1.** A depressing experience or situation: *Failing the test was a real downer.* **2.** A depressant.

down·fall (doun'fôl') *n.* **1.** [C; U] A sudden big loss of money, power, or happiness: *An investigation resulted in the downfall of the dishonest banker.* **2.** [U] A cause of sudden ruin: *Careless spending was the treasurer's downfall.* **3.** [C] A fall of rain or snow, especially one that is heavy or unexpected.

down·grade (doun'grād') *n.* A descending slope, as in a road: *The truck gained speed on the downgrade.* —*tr.v.* **down·grad·ed, down·grad·ing, down·grades.** **1.** To lower the status or salary of (sbdy.): *downgrade an employee.* **2.** To make (sthg.) seem less valuable or important than it is: *She downgraded their contribution.*

down·heart·ed (doun'här'tĭd) *adj.* Low in spirits; sad. —**down'heart'ed·ly** *adv.* —**down'heart'ed·ness** *n.* [U]

down·hill (doun'hĭl') *adv.* **1.** Down the slope of a hill: *We raced downhill.* **2.** Toward a lower or worse position: *His health has gone downhill since the accident.* —*adj.* (doun'hĭl'). Sloping downward; descending: *a downhill direction.*

down·load (doun'lōd') *tr.v.* To transfer (data) from a central computer to another computer or to a terminal: *I downloaded information from the Internet to my diskette.*

down payment *n.* A payment in part made at the time of purchase, with the rest of the money to be paid later: *a down payment on a car.*

down·play (doun'plā') *tr.v.* To make (sthg.) seem less important: *The media downplayed the severity of the earthquake.*

down·pour (doun'pôr') *n.* A heavy fall of rain.

down·right (doun'rīt') *adj.* Thoroughgoing; complete: *a downright scoundrel.* —*adv.* Thoroughly; absolutely: *They acted downright unpleasant.*

down·size (doun'sīz') *v.* **down·sized, down·siz·ing, down·siz·es.** —*intr.* (used of a company or an organization). To become smaller: *The company downsized by laying off 100 employees.* —*tr.* To make (sthg.) smaller, especially to lower costs in a company or organization: *a plan to downsize the work force.*

down·stairs (doun'stârz') *adv.* **1.** Down the stairs: *I slipped going downstairs.* **2.** To or on a lower floor: *I ran downstairs to answer the phone.* —*adj.* (doun'stârz'). Located on a lower floor: *a downstairs bedroom.* —*n.* (doun'stârz'). (used with a singular verb). The lower or main floor of a building: *The whole downstairs was a mess after the party.*

down·stream (doun'strēm') *adj.* In the direction of a river or stream's current: *a downstream boat race.* —*adv.* (doun'strēm'). Along with a stream's current: *The raft floated downstream.*

down·time (doun'tīm') *n.* The period of time when sthg., such as a factory or a piece of machinery, is not in operation.

down-to-earth (doun'tə ûrth') *adj.* Realistic; sensible: *a calm and down-to-earth manner.*

down·town (doun'toun') *n.* The lower part or the business center of a city or town. —*adv.* (doun'toun'). Toward or in the lower part or business center of a city or town: *Let's walk downtown.* —*adj.* (doun'toun'). Being in or going toward the business center of a city or town: *a downtown restaurant; a downtown bus.*

down·turn (doun'tûrn') *n.* A move or tendency downward, especially in business or economic activity: *In a recession there is a marked downturn in business.*

down·ward (doun'wərd) *adv. & adj.* From a higher to a lower place, level, or condition: *floating downward; a downward trend.*

down·wind (doun'wĭnd') *adv.* In the direction toward which the wind blows.

dow·ry (dou'rē) *n., pl.* **dow·ries.** Money or property brought by a bride to her husband at marriage.

doz. *abbr.* An abbreviation of dozen.

doze (dōz) *v.* **dozed, doz·ing, doz·es.** —*intr.* To sleep lightly; nap: *doze on the porch in the sun.* —*tr.* To spend (time) dozing or as if dozing: *doze the afternoon away.* —*n.* A short light sleep; a nap. ◆ **doze off.** *intr.v.* To fall into a light sleep: *I dozed off during the play's first act.*

doz·en (dŭz'ən) *n., pl.* **dozen. 1.** A set of 12: *Two dozen eggs are 24 eggs.* **2.** *pl.* **dozens.** A large undetermined number: *Dozens of fish swam below.* —*adj.* Twelve: *a dozen eggs.*

dpt. *abbr.* An abbreviation of department.

Dr. *abbr.* An abbreviation of: **1.** Doctor. **2.** Drive (street).

drab (drăb) *adj.* **drab·ber, drab·best.** Faded and dull in appearance: *These drab walls need a coat of paint.* —**drab'ly** *adv.* —**drab'ness** *n.* [U]

draft (drăft) *n.* **1.** [C] A current of air indoors: *feel a cold draft on one's feet.* **2.** [C] A rough outline or a version of a plan, document, or picture: *a draft of a report; an architect's first draft of a building.* **3.** [C; U] **a.** The process of choosing one or more individuals from a group, as for a service or duty. **b.** A system of requiring people to serve in the armed forces. **4.** [C] The taking out of a liquid, as from a cask or keg, or an amount of such a liquid: *a draft of ale.* **5.** [C] A document, such as a check, for directing the payment of money from an account or fund. **6.** [C; U] The depth of a boat's lowest point below the surface of the water. —*tr.v.* **1.** To choose (sbdy.) from a group for some usually required service: *draft volunteers to clean up the neighborhood.* **2.** To draw up a plan, sketch, or version of (sthg.): *drafted several versions of a speech.* —*adj.* Suited for or used for pulling heavy loads: *a team of draft horses.*

draft·ee (drăf tē') *n.* A person who is drafted, especially into the armed forces.

drafts·per·son (drăfts'pûr'sən) *n.* A person who drafts plans or designs, as of structures to be built. —**drafts'man** (drăfts'mən) *n.* —**drafts'man·ship'** *n.* [U] —**drafts'-wom'an** (drăfts'wŏom'ən) *n.*

draft·y (drăf'tē) *adj.* **draft·i·er, draft·i·est.** With unwanted drafts of air: *a drafty old house.* —**draft'i·ly** *adv.* —**draft'i·ness** *n.* [U]

drag (drăg) *v.* **dragged, drag·ging, drags.**
—*tr.* **1.** To pull (sthg.) along the ground or floor with difficulty: *dragged the heavy box out of the way.* **2.** To cause (sthg.) to follow, touching the ground: *Don't drag your coat in the mud.* **3.** To search the bottom of (a body of water), as with a hook or net: *Police dragged the river for the sunken boat.* —*intr.* **1.** To follow, touching the ground: *The chain dragged along behind the tractor.* **2.** To move slowly or with difficulty: *The exhausted hikers dragged back to camp.* —*n.* **1.** [C] Something that is pulled along the ground, especially sthg. for carrying loads: *The horse was harnessed to the drag.* **2.** [C] A person or thing that slows or stops motion or progress: *High interest rates can act as a drag on the economy.* **3.** [U] The force produced by friction that slows motion through air or a liquid. **4.** [C] *Slang.* A person or thing that is very boring or annoying: *This party is such a drag!* ◆ **drag on.** *intr.v.* To pass or proceed too slowly: *The long speech dragged on and on.* **drag (one's) feet.** To act or work with intentional slowness: *drag one's feet about completing a chore.* **drag out.** *tr.v.* [sep.] To make (sthg.) last too long: *They dragged the discussion out.* **drag up.** *tr.v.* [sep.] To discuss (sthg.) unnecessarily: *Whenever we disagree, you drag up things I did ten years ago!* **in drag.** *Informal.* Describing the wearing of women's clothing by a man.

drag·on (drăg'ən) *n.* An imaginary giant reptile often described in stories as a winged fire-breathing monster.

drag·on·fly (drăg'ən flī') *n.* A large insect with a long body and four narrow clear wings.

drag race *n.* A short race between cars to see which can speed up faster from a standing start.

drain (drān) *v.* —*tr.* **1.** To take away (a liquid) gradually: *drain water from a sink.* **2.** To make (sthg.) dry or empty by taking away liquid: *drain the pond.* **3.** To completely use up the energy of (sbdy.): *The performance drained the singers.* —*intr.* **1.** To flow off or out: *Melted snow drained off the roof.* **2.** To become empty by the removal of liquid: *The bathtub drained slowly.* **3.** To send out surface or excess water: *Most large rivers drain into the sea.* —*n.* **1.** A pipe or channel by which liquid is drained off: *the drain from the kitchen sink.* **2.** Something that causes a gradual loss: *Building a new school is a drain on the city's resources.* ◆ **down the drain.** To or into the condition of being wasted or lost: *When our first plan went down the drain, we quickly thought of another.*

drain·age (drā'nĭj) *n.* [U] **1.** The action or a method of draining: *farmland with good*

...**age. 2.** Material that is drained off: *...m sewers carried the drainage away.*

...**ke** (drāk) *n.* A male duck.

...**ram** (drăm) *n.* **1.** A unit of weight in the U.S. Customary System equal to ¹⁄₁₆ of an ounce or 27.34 grains (about 1.77 grams). See table at **measurement. 2.** A small drink.

dra·ma (drä′mə *or* drăm′ə) *n.* **1.** [C] A literary work that tells a story and is meant to be performed by actors on stage. **2.** [U] **a.** Theatrical plays of a particular kind or period: *modern drama.* **b.** The art and practice of writing and producing plays. **3.** [U] An exciting or emotional situation in real life: *the daily drama within Congress.*

dra·mat·ic (drə măt′ĭk) *adj.* **1.** Relating to drama or the theater: *dramatic performances.* **2.** Resembling a drama in action, emotion, or effect: *the dramatic events that led to Lincoln's election.* —**dra·mat′i·cal·ly** *adv.*

dra·mat·ics (drə măt′ĭks) *n.* **1.** [U] *(used with a singular or plural verb).* The art or practice of acting in or staging plays: *Dramatics is the actor's great interest.* **2.** [C] *(used with a plural verb).* Dramatic or exaggerated behavior: *I have no patience for his dramatics.*

dram·a·tist (drăm′ə tĭst *or* drä′mə tĭst) *n.* A person who writes plays; a playwright.

dram·a·tize (drăm′ə tīz′ *or* drä′mə tīz′) *tr.v.* **dram·a·tized, dram·a·tiz·ing, dram·a·tiz·es. 1.** To adapt (a literary work) into a play or screenplay: *dramatize a novel.* **2.** To present or view (sthg.) in a way that affects one's emotions: *The report dramatizes the situation of the flood victims.* —**dram′a·ti·za′tion** (drăm′ə tĭ zā′shən *or* drä′mə tĭ zā′shən) *n.* [C; U]

drank (drăngk) *v.* Past tense of **drink.**

drape (drāp) *v.* **draped, drap·ing, drapes.** —*tr.* **1.** To cover (sthg.) with or as if with cloth hanging in loose folds: *The artist draped the painting with a cloth.* **2.** To hang or let (sthg.) rest loosely: *I draped my legs over the back of the chair.* —*intr.* To fall or hang in loose folds: *Silk drapes easily.* —*n.* **1.** [C] A curtain: *pull the drapes over the window.* **2.** [U] The way in which cloth falls or hangs: *the drape of fine suit material.*

drap·er·y (drā′pə rē) *n., pl.* **drap·er·ies.** A piece or pieces of fabric hanging straight in loose folds, as for a curtain.

dras·tic (drăs′tĭk) *adj.* Severe or extreme in nature: *Calling out the military was a drastic measure to quiet protesters.* —**dras′ti·cal·ly** *adv.*

drat (drăt) *interj. Informal.* An expression used to show mild annoyance: *Oh, drat. I forgot my keys.*

draw (drô) *v.* **drew** (drōō), **drawn** (drôn), **drawing, draws.** —*tr.* **1.a.** To pull or move (sthg.) after or toward oneself by applying force: *a team of horses drawing a load.* **b.** To cause (sbdy.) to move, as by leading: *She* drew us into the room to show us her presents. **2.** To cause (sthg.) to flow forth: *a deep scratch that drew blood.* **3.** To suck or take in (air, for example): *The singer drew a deep breath.* **4.** To pull or take (sthg.) out: *He drew his wallet from his pocket.* **5.** To attract (sbdy./sthg.): *Our beaches draw many tourists.* **6.** To get (sthg.) as a response: *The comic drew laughter from the audience.* **7.** To earn or gain (money): *draw interest on a saving account.* **8.** To take out (money) from an account. **9.** To take or receive (sthg.) by chance: *I drew the lucky number.* **10.** To make a picture of (sbdy./sthg.), using mostly lines: *drawing illustrations for a new book.* **11.** To create or decide on (sthg.) based on evidence: *draw a comparison; draw a conclusion from the facts.* —*intr.* **1.** To continue or move steadily: *The boat drew near shore.* **2.** To contract or tighten: *The smile drew into a frown.* **3.** To end a contest with the score tied: *The chess players drew after 32 moves.* **4.** To make a picture with lines: *Several students draw especially well.* —*n.* **1.** Something that attracts interest or customers: *That movie was a good draw at the box office.* **2.** A contest ending in a tie: *The game ended in a draw.* **3.** A naturally low area of land that water drains into. ◆ **draw on.** *intr.v.* To come nearer: *The days get shorter as winter draws on.* —*tr.v.* [insep.] To make use of (sbdy./sthg.) as a resource: *It was a great help to draw on her experience.* **draw out.** *tr.v.* [sep.] **1.** To make (sthg.) last: *The committee chair drew out the meeting until we were quite bored.* **2.** To get (sbdy.) to talk freely: *The child was shy, but she managed to draw him out.* **draw the line.** To set a limit, as on behavior: *You can borrow $10 more, but that's where I draw the line.* **draw up.** *tr.v.* [sep.] **1.** To write up (sthg.) in a set form: *draw up a will.* **2.** To bring (oneself) into a straight up position: *He drew himself up as the guests entered the room.* —*intr.v.* To bring or come to a stop: *The truck drew up at the gate.*

draw·back (drô′băk′) *n.* A disadvantage or inconvenience: *The pay was good, but the long hours were a drawback.*

draw·bridge (drô′brĭj′) *n.* A bridge that can be raised up or pulled aside either to close it off or to permit boats to pass under it.

drawbridge

draw·er (drô′ər) n. **1.** A storage compartment that can be pulled in and out of a piece of furniture by a handle. **2. drawers** (drôrz). *Informal.* An old-fashioned term for underpants.

draw·ing (drô′ĭng) n. **1.** [U] The art of making pictures on a surface by means of lines: *students of drawing, painting, and sculpture.* **2.** [C] A work produced by this art: *There are several fine drawings of horses on the wall.*

drawl (drôl) intr. & tr.v. To say sthg. or speak with lengthened or drawn-out vowels. —n. The speech or manner of speaking of one who drawls: *The actor spoke with a drawl.*

drawn (drôn) v. Past participle of **draw.** —adj. Having a very tired or ill look: *The survivors looked drawn after their rescue.*

dread (drĕd) tr.v. **1.** To be in terror of (sbdy./sthg.): *Many people dread snakes.* **2.** To think of (sthg. in the future) with dislike or fear: *We were dreading the long drive home.* —n. [U] **1.** Strong fear; terror: *a dread of high places.* **2.** Fear or displeasure about sthg. coming in the future: *They lived in dread of an earthquake.* —adj. Causing people to feel fear or awe: *a dread disease.*

dread·ful (drĕd′fəl) adj. **1.** Horrible; terrible: *a dreadful accident.* **2.** Extremely unpleasant: *dreadful furniture; dreadful behavior.* —**dread′ful·ly** adv. —**dread′ful·ness** n. [U]

dread·locks (drĕd′lŏks′) pl.n. Hair worn in thin dense long braids or natural locks.

dream (drēm) n. **1.** A series of mental images, ideas, and emotions during sleep: *She awoke from a bad dream.* **2.** A daydream. **3.** A hope: *dreams of world peace.* **4.** Something especially pleasing, excellent, or useful: *The new car runs like a dream.* —v. **dreamed** or **dreamt** (drĕmt), **dream·ing, dreams.** —intr. **1.** To have a dream while sleeping. **2.** To daydream: *Stop dreaming and get to work.* **3.** To consider as reasonable or practical: *I wouldn't even dream of going.* —tr. **1.** To have a dream of (sthg.) during sleep: *Did it storm last night, or did I dream it?* **2.** To imagine (sthg.): *We never dreamed it might snow so hard.* ♦ **dream up.** tr.v. [sep.] To think of or invent (sthg. unusual or impractical): *He dreamed up a plan to get rich quick.* —**dream′er** n.

dreamt (drĕmt) v. A past tense and a past participle of **dream.**

dream·y (drē′mē) adj. **dream·i·er, dream·i·est. 1.** Vague or unclear, like a dream: *a dreamy memory of early childhood.* **2.** Tending to daydream: *a dreamy person who seldom pays attention.* **3.** Pleasant and calming: *soft dreamy music.* —**dream′i·ly** adv. —**dream′i·ness** n. [U]

drea·ry (drîr′ē) adj. **drea·ri·er, drea·ri·**

est. 1. Cheerless and depressing: *a drea[ry] January rain.* **2.** Boring; dull: *the drear[y] tasks of housekeeping.* —**drear′i·ly** adv[.] —**drear′i·ness** n. [U]

dredge¹ (drĕj) n. A machine or ship equipped with an underwater digging or suction device, used especially to deepen a harbor or waterway. —v. **dredged, dredg·ing, dredg·es.** —tr. **1.** To clean, deepen, or widen (a harbor, for example) with a dredge. **2.** To bring (sthg.) up with a dredge: *dredge dirt and rock out of the river to make a channel.* —intr. To use a dredge. ♦ **dredge up.** tr.v. [sep.] To find out or speak of (information about the past): *Let's not dredge up stories about her childhood while she's here.*

dredge² (drĕj) tr.v. **dredged, dredg·ing, dredg·es.** [in] To coat (food) by covering it with a powder, such as flour or bread crumbs: *Dredge the chicken in flour.*

dregs (drĕgz) pl.n. **1.** The unwanted sediment at the bottom of a liquid: *rinse the dregs out of the coffeepot.* **2.** The part of sthg. that is least wanted or lowest in quality: *They did the easy part of the job and left us the dregs.*

drench (drĕnch) tr.v. To wet (sthg.) completely: *A thunderstorm drenched everyone outside.* —**drenched** (drĕncht) adj.

dress (drĕs) v. —tr. **1.** To put clothes on (sbdy.): *Dress the baby warmly.* **2.** To apply medicine or bandages to (a wound): *After the operation the nurse dressed the incision.* **3.** To arrange or style (the hair). **4.** To decorate (sthg.): *dress a Christmas tree.* **5.** To prepare (sthg.) for cooking or eating: *dress a turkey; dress a salad.* —intr. **1.** To put on clothes: *I got up late and dressed in a hurry.* **2.** To wear clothes of a certain kind or style: *She dresses casually.* **3.** To wear formal clothes: *dress for dinner.* —n. **1.** A style of clothing: *in military dress.* **2.** A one-piece article of clothing usually worn by women and girls: *She had a new dress for the party.* —adj. Suitable as or requiring formal clothes: *a dress shirt; a dress reception.* ♦ **dress down.** tr.v. [sep.] To scold or criticize (sbdy.), often harshly: *The boss called him into the office to dress him down for his mistake.* —intr.v. To wear casual clothes: *We always dress down when we are on vacation.* **dress up.** intr.v. **1.** To wear formal or fancy clothes: *They dressed up for the party.* **2.** To wear another person's clothes for fun: *The children dressed up as clowns.* —tr.v. [sep.] To make (sbdy./sthg.) more attractive: *She dressed herself up. I'll dress the room up with new curtains.*

dress code n. A set of rules, as in a school, telling how people should dress: *Most U.S. public schools have very informal dress codes.*

dress·er (drĕs′ər) n. A chest of drawers,

often with a mirror above it and typically used for holding clothing and personal items.

dress•ing (drĕs′ĭng) *n.* **1.** [C] Medicine or bandages applied to a wound. **2.** [C; U] A sauce for certain dishes, such as salads: *blue cheese dressing.* **3.** [U] A stuffing, as for cooking inside poultry or fish.

dressing room *n.* A room, as in a theater, for changing costumes or clothes and applying makeup.

dress•mak•ing (drĕs′mā′kĭng) *n.* [U] The act or occupation of making women's clothing, especially dresses: *She studied dressmaking in Paris.* —**dress′mak′er** *n.*

dress rehearsal *n.* A complete rehearsal of a play as a final practice.

dress•y (drĕs′ē) *adj.* **dress•i•er, dress•i•est.** Showy or stylish in clothes or appearance: *a dressy shirt.* —**dress′i•ly** *adv.* —**dress′i•ness** *n.* [U]

drew (drōō) *v.* Past tense of **draw.**

drib•ble (drĭb′əl) *intr. & tr.v.* **drib•bled, drib•bling, drib•bles.** **1.** To fall or cause to fall in drops or an unsteady stream: *Water dribbled out of the leaky faucet. I dribbled gravy on the potatoes.* **2.** To move a ball or puck with repeated light bounces or kicks, as in basketball or soccer: *The player dribbled around an opponent. The forward dribbled the ball right past the defender.* —*n.* **1.** A small quantity; a drop: *a dribble of milk.* **2.** The act of dribbling a ball: *a fast dribble down the court.* —**drib′bler** *n.*

dri•er also **dry•er** (drī′ər) *n.* A person or thing that dries: *a new clothes drier; She washed the dishes, and I was the drier.*

drift (drĭft) *v.* —*intr.* **1.** To be carried along by a current of water or air: *The boat drifted slowly toward shore.* **2.** To proceed or move unhurriedly and without a fixed purpose: *drift through the summer.* **3.** To move away from a direct course or a point of attention: *My attention drifted from my homework.* **4.** To be piled up by the force of a current: *snow drifting against a stone wall.* —*tr.* **1.** To cause (sbdy./sthg.) to be carried in a current: *Waves drifted debris all along the shore.* **2.** To pile (sthg.) up in heaps or banks: *The winds drifted the snow.* —*n.* **1.** [U] The act or condition of drifting: *a continuous drift of sand.* **2.** [C] The mass of material, such as sand or snow, piled up by a current of air or water: *snow drifts that were six feet high.* **3.** [U] A general meaning or direction of thought: *The drift of their conversation was hard to follow.* ◆ **catch** or **get (one's) drift.** To understand the general meaning of sthg.: *Do you catch my drift?*

drift•er (drĭf′tər) *n.* A person who moves from place to place or from job to job with no fixed purpose.

drift•wood (drĭft′wŏŏd′) *n.* [U] Wood washed up onto land or floating in the water.

drill (drĭl) *n.* **1.** A tool used to force holes in materials, usually by a rotating action or by repeated blows: *a dentist's drill.* **2.** A task or an exercise for teaching a skill or procedure by repetition: *a fire drill.* —*v.* —*tr.* **1.** To make a hole with a drill in (a hard material): *drilling wood.* **2.** To make (a hole) with or as if with a drill. **3.** To teach or train (sbdy.) by continuous repetition: *drill a company of soldiers.* —*intr.* **1.** To make a hole with or as if with a drill: *drill into a board.* **2.** To perform a training exercise: *The astronauts drill before trying to make repairs in space.*

drill

drink (drĭngk) *v.* **drank** (drăngk), **drunk** (drŭngk), **drink•ing, drinks.** —*tr.* **1.** To take into the mouth and swallow (a liquid): *I drink water every day.* **2.** To swallow the liquid contents of (a container): *I drank a cup of hot cocoa.* **3.** To take in or soak up (a liquid): *The dry earth drank up the rain.* —*intr.* **1.** To swallow liquid: *The thirsty hikers drank from a clear stream.* **2.** To drink alcoholic beverages: *Don't drink and drive.* —*n.* **1.** A liquid for drinking; a beverage: *Orange juice is a popular breakfast drink.* **2.** An amount of liquid swallowed: *He took a small drink of water.* **3.** An alcoholic beverage: *One drink is enough for me.* ◆ **drink in.** *tr.v.* [sep.] To take (sthg.) in eagerly through the senses or the mind: *The tourists drank in the beauty of the mountains.* **drink to.** *tr.v.* [insep.] To honor (a person or an occasion) with a toast: *We drank to their future happiness.* —**drink′a•ble** *adj.* —**drink′er** *n.*

drip (drĭp) *intr. & tr.v.* **dripped, drip•ping, drips.** To fall or let fall in drops: *Water dripped from the faucet. I dripped paint on the floor.* —*n.* **1.** The process of forming and falling in drops: *the drip of water from a leaky roof.* **2.** Liquid or moisture that falls in drops: *Drips of paint spattered the floor.* **3.** The sound made by liquid falling in drops: *The constant drip of the faucet was annoying.*

drive (drīv) *v.* **drove** (drōv), **driv•en** (drĭv′ən), **driv•ing, drives.** —*tr.* **1.a.** To push or press (sbdy./sthg.) onward with force: *drove the sheep into the barn.* **b.** To force (sbdy./sthg.) to go away: *The loud music drove us out of the room.* **2.a.** To guide, control, or direct (a vehicle): *They drive their car to work every day.* **b.** To carry or transport (sbdy.) in a vehicle: *The neighbors drove me to the store.* **3.a.** To supply the force or power to make (sthg.) work: *Electricity drives many motors.* **b.** To force (sbdy.) to work, often too much: *The desire for power drives him.* **c.** To provide the underlying cause for (sthg.): *Satisfying our customers drives this business.* **d.** To force (sbdy.) into a particular state or act: *Constant interruptions drove me crazy.* **4.** To force (sthg.) to go into sthg. solid: *drive a nail into wood.* **5.** To hit (a ball) hard: *The batter drove the ball right over the fence.* —*intr.* **1.** To move along or advance quickly as if pushed by a force: *The car drove into a tree.* **2.** To guide or control a vehicle or an animal: *Many people drive too fast on this road.* **3.** To go or be carried in a vehicle: *We drove to the supermarket.* **4.** To make an effort to reach or achieve a goal: *The author drove hard to complete the book on time.* —*n.* **1.** [C] A trip or journey in a vehicle: *go for a quiet drive in the country.* **2.** [C] **a.** A narrow road: *Cars may use the drive in the park.* **b.** A drive-way. **3.** [U] The means for transmitting power from an engine to operate a movable part of a machine: *a vehicle with four-wheel drive.* **4.** [C] **a.** An organized effort to accomplish sthg.: *a drive to raise money for a museum.* **b.** A military offensive. **5.a.** [U] Energy, mental force, or aggressiveness: *People who have drive and ambition often achieve their goals.* **b.** [C] A strong basic instinct: *the basic drive to satisfy one's hunger and thirst.* **6.** [C] A computer device that transfers data to and from storage, as on a floppy disk. ◆ **drive at.** *tr.v.* [insep.] To mean (sthg.): *I'm not sure what you are driving at.* **drive home.** *tr.v.* [sep.] To make (sthg.) well understood in a forceful way: *drive home one's point in an argument.* **drive off** or **away.** *tr.v.* [sep.] To force (sbdy./sthg.) to go away: *Nothing we used was strong enough to drive the mosquitoes off.* —*intr.v.* To leave in a car: *She waved once and drove off.*

drive-by (drīv′bī′) *adj.* Driving past a place, especially to shoot sbdy./sthg.: *Her daughter was killed in a drive-by shooting.* —*n.* An instance of driving past a place and shooting at sbdy./sthg.: *He's been involved in several drive-bys.*

drive-in (drīv′ĭn′) *n.* An establishment, such as an outdoor movie theater or a restaurant, designed to allow customers to stay in their cars while seeing a movie or getting food.

driv•en (drĭv′ən) *v.* Past participle of **drive.** —*adj.* Seeming to be forced to do sthg. by an inner need; compelled: *The driven athlete practiced every day of the week.*

driv•er (drī′vər) *n.* **1.** A person who drives a motor vehicle, such as a car. **2.** A tool, such as a screwdriver or a hammer, that is used to give forceful pressure to another object.

drive-through (drīv′thrōō′) *adj.* Constructed so that customers can conduct business without getting out of a vehicle: *a drive-through window at a bank; a drive-through insurance office.* —*n.* A place where customers can conduct business without getting out of a vehicle: *The drive-through at that restaurant is open all night.*

drive•way (drīv′wā′) *n.* A private road connecting a house, a garage, or another building with the street.

driz•zle (drĭz′əl) *intr.v.* **driz•zled, driz•zling, driz•zles.** To rain gently in a fine mist. —*n.* [U] A fine gentle misty rain. —**driz′zly** *adj.*

droll (drōl) *adj. Formal.* Quietly amusing in an unusual way: *a droll sense of humor.* —**droll′ness** *n.* [U]

drone[1] (drōn) *n.* **1.** A male bee, especially a honeybee that mates with the queen: *Drones have no stings and do not produce honey.* **2.** *Informal.* A lazy person who lives off the work of other people.

drone[2] (drōn) *intr.v.* **droned, dron•ing, drones.** To make a continuous low dull humming sound: *An airplane droned far overhead.* —*n.* *(usually singular).* A continuous low humming or buzzing sound: *the drone of the bumblebee.* ◆ **drone on.** *intr.v.* To speak in a dull tone: *The professor droned on for an hour.*

drool (drōōl) *intr.v.* **1.** To let saliva drip from the mouth: *The hungry dog was drooling.* **2.** [over] To show great appreciation or desire: *They drooled over the expensive bicycles in the window.* —*n.* [U] Saliva: *Wipe the drool from the baby's chin.*

droop (drōōp) *intr.v.* **1.** To bend or hang downward: *The flowers are beginning to droop.* **2.** To become tired or disappointed: *The tourists began to droop toward the end of the day.* —*n.* The act or condition of drooping.

droop•y (drōō′pē) *adj.* Bending or hanging downward: *droopy heads of tired children.* —**droop′i•ly** *adv.* —**droop′i•ness** *n.* [U]

drop (drŏp) *n.* **1.** A small mass of liquid in a rounded shape: *drops of paint.* **2.** A small quantity of a substance: *There isn't a drop of juice left.* **3. drops.** Liquid medicine given in drops: *eye drops.* **4.** A very small amount: *not a drop of pity.* **5.** Something like a drop in shape or size, especially a small piece of candy: *a lemon drop.* **6.** A sudden fall or decrease, as in quality, quantity, or intensity: *a drop in temperature; a drop in prices.* **7.** The vertical distance from a higher to a lower level: *a drop of 200 feet.* —*v.* **dropped, drop•ping, drops.** —*intr.* **1.** To fall in drops: *rain dropping on the roof.* **2.** To fall from a higher to a lower place or position: *I heard the plate drop on the floor.* **3.** To become less, as in intensity or number: *The temperature dropped as the sun went down.* **4.** To go down from one level to another: *The sun dropped toward the western hills.* **5.** To fall due to a complete loss of strength: *I was so tired I was ready to drop.* —*tr.* **1.** To let

---

ă–**cat**; ā–**pay**; âr–**care**; ä–**father**; ĕ–**get**; ē–**be**; ĭ–**sit**; ī–**nice**; îr–**here**; ŏ–**got**; ō–**go**; ô–**saw**; oi–**boy**; ou–**out**; ōō–**took**; ōō–**boot**; ŭ–**cut**; ûr–**word**; th–**thin**; *th*–**this**; hw–**when**; zh–**vision**; ə–**about**; N–French **bon**

(sthg.) fall: *I dropped the hot frying pan.* **2.** To say or write (sthg.) in an informal way: *drop a suggestion; drop a note.* **3.** To stop thinking of or planning on (sthg.): *Let's drop the matter.* **4.** To end a relationship with (sbdy.): *drop one's friends.* **5.** To leave out (a letter, for example) in speaking or writing. **6.** To set (sbdy./sthg.) down at a particular place: *drop passengers at the station.* ◆ **a drop in the bucket.** An amount too small to be useful: *Your help is appreciated but it is really just a drop in the bucket.* **drop** or **fall behind.** *intr.v.* To fail to move ahead as fast as expected: *I have to work hard to keep from dropping behind.* **drop by.** *intr.v.* To make a short informal visit: *She dropped by after work.* **drop in on.** To make an informal, usually unexpected, visit to sbdy.: *I dropped in on her on my way home.* **drop off.** *intr.v.* **1.** To fall asleep: *She drops off on the couch every night.* **2.** To decrease: *Temperatures usually drop off in the evening.* —*tr.v.* [sep.] To deliver (sbdy./sthg.): *Can I drop that off at the cleaners for you? She drops her children off at her mother's every day.* **drop out.** *intr.v.* To stop participating, as in a game, competition, or school: *His family convinced him not to drop out.*

drop•let (drŏp′lĭt) *n.* A tiny drop.

drop•out (drŏp′out′) *n.* A person who quits school or college: *a high-school dropout.*

drop•per (drŏp′ər) *n.* A small glass or plastic tube with a suction bulb at one end for drawing in a liquid and releasing it in drops.

drop•pings (drŏp′ĭngz) *pl.n.* Feces produced by small animals or birds.

drought (drout) *n.* A long period of little or no rainfall: *The drought lasted for two years.*

drove[1] (drōv) *v.* Past tense of **drive.**

drove[2] (drōv) *n.* A large group of people or animals moving or acting as one: *droves of visitors on their way to the White House.*

drown (droun) *v.* —*tr.* **1.** To kill (sbdy.) by keeping in water or another liquid so as to prevent breathing. **2.** To cover (sthg.) completely with or as if with a liquid: *They drowned their meat in gravy.* **3.** To ease (one's pain), especially by drinking: *He drowns his disappointment in the company of friends.* —*intr.* To die from being unable to breathe in water or other liquid: *Many animals drowned in the flood.* ◆ **drown out.** *tr.v.* [sep.] To cover or mask (a sound) with a louder sound: *Their laughter drowned out the speaker's voice.*

drowse (drouz) *intr.v.* **drowsed, drows•ing, drows•es.** To be half-asleep: *The cat drowsed in the sun.*

drows•y (drou′zē) *adj.* **drows•i•er, drows•i•est.** Dull with sleepiness: *feeling drowsy after dinner.* —**drows′i•ly** *adv.* —**drows′i•ness** *n.* [U]

drudge (drŭj) *n.* A person who does bor-

ing, unpleasant, or low-level work. —*intr.v.* **drudged, drudg•ing, drudg•es.** To do tedious, unpleasant, or menial work. —**drudg′er•y** *n.* [U]

drug (drŭg) *n.* **1.** A substance used in medicine, as for curing disease. **2.** A narcotic or other substance whose main effect is on the nervous system, especially one causing changes in behavior and often addiction. —*tr.v.* **drugged, drug•ging, drugs. 1.** To give a drug to (sbdy.): *drug a patient with an anesthetic before an operation.* **2.** To mix a drug into (food or drink): *drug her drink.*

drug•gist (drŭg′ĭst) *n.* A pharmacist.

drug•store (drŭg′stôr′) *n.* A store where prescriptions are filled and medical supplies and other items are sold.

drum (drŭm) *n.* **1.** A musical instrument made of a hollow container shaped like a cylinder or bowl with an animal skin or similar material stretched across it. **2.** Something having a shape or structure like a drum: *an oil drum.* —*v.* **drummed, drum•ming, drums.** —*intr.* **1.** To play a drum or drums. **2.** To hit a surface rhythmically or continually: *I drummed on the table with my pencil.* —*tr.* To perform (a musical part or piece) on or as if on a drum. ◆ **drum into.** *tr.v.* [sep.] To force sbdy. to learn (sthg.) by constant repetition: *I drummed the facts into my head to pass the test.* **drum out.** *tr.v.* [sep.] To send (sbdy.) away in disgrace: *They drummed the soldier out of the army.* **drum up.** *tr.v.* [sep.] To gain (sthg.) by continuous effort: *Students drummed up support for their trip.*

drum•beat (drŭm′bēt′) *n.* The sound produced by beating a drum.

drum•mer (drŭm′ər) *n.* A person who plays a drum, as in a band.

drum•stick (drŭm′stĭk′) *n.* **1.** A stick for beating a drum. **2.** The lower part of the leg of a cooked chicken or turkey.

drunk (drŭngk) *v.* Past participle of **drink.** —*adj.* **1.** Under the effects of alcoholic liquor. **2.** Overpowered by strong feeling or emotion: *The dictator is drunk with power.* —*n.* A drunken person; drunkard.

drunk•ard (drŭng′kərd) *n.* A person who is habitually drunk.

drunk•en (drŭng′kən) *adj.* Involving or happening under the effects of alcoholic liquor: *a drunken argument.* —**drunk′en•ly** *adv.* —**drunk′en•ness** *n.* [U]

dry (drī) *adj.* **dri•er** (drī′ər), **dri•est** (drī′ĭst) or **dry•er, dry•est. 1.** Free from liquid or moisture: *dry clothes; dry air.* **2.** With little or no rainfall: *the dry season.* **3.** With all or almost all of the liquid or water drained away or used up: *a dry stream; a dry well.* **4.** Needing or desiring drink: *My throat is dry.* **5.** Not sweet: *a dry white wine.* **6.** Plain; without decoration: *a dry speaker; dry facts.* **7.** Quietly amusing: *a dry sense of humor.* **8.**

Not permitting the sale or drinking of alcoholic beverages: *a dry town.* —*v.* **dried** (drīd), **dry•ing, dries** (drīz). —*tr.* To remove the wetness or moisture from (sthg.): *We dried the dishes after supper.* —*intr.* To become dry: *The laundry dried quickly in the sun.* ♦ **dry out.** *intr.v.* **1.** To become dry: *We resumed our hike after our clothes dried out.* **2.** To give up drinking: *He went to a clinic to dry out.* **dry up.** *intr.v.* **1.** To lose water or other moisture gradually: *Many lakes and rivers are drying up.* **2.** To become unproductive, especially to do so gradually: *Support for the plan dried up as costs rose.* **3.** *Informal.* Used to tell sbdy. to stop talking: *Would you just dry up!* —**dry′ly** *adv.* —**dry′ness** *n.* [U]

dry-clean (drī′klēn′) *tr.v.* To clean (clothing or fabrics) with chemical solvents that have little or no water: *This suit must be dry-cleaned.*

dry cleaners *pl.n. (used with a singular verb).* A business that dry-cleans clothes.

dry cleaning *n.* [U] **1.** The cleaning of fabrics with chemical solvents. **2.** Clothes that have been dry-cleaned: *He picks up his dry cleaning on Mondays.*

dry•er (drī′ər) *n.* **1.** An appliance that removes moisture by heating or another process: *a clothes dryer; a hair dryer.* **2.** Variant of **drier.**

dry goods *pl.n.* Cloth, clothing, and related items.

dry ice *n.* [U] Carbon dioxide compressed and chilled into a solid and used as a cooling agent.

dry•ly (drī′lē) *adv.* In a dry way; unemotionally: *They speak dryly of political affairs.*

du•al (dōō′əl) *adj.* Composed of two parts; double: *This plane provides dual controls for pilot and copilot.* —**du•al′it•y** *n.* [C; U] —**du′al•ly** *adv.*

HOMONYMS: dual, duel (combat).

---

dub (dŭb) *tr.v.* **dubbed, dub•bing, dubs. 1.** To give a name or nickname to (sbdy./sthg.): *The children dubbed their new kitten Mittens.* **2.** To insert (new sounds) into an existing recording, as on magnetic tape or the sound track of a film: *The editor dubbed the music for the movie.* **3.** To provide (a film) with a new soundtrack, often with the dialogue in a different language: *They dubbed the Russian film into English for U.S. audiences.*

du•bi•ous (dōō′bē əs) *adj.* **1.** Feeling or showing doubt or uncertainty; uncertain: *I am still dubious of the answer.* **2.** Questionable in character; suspicious: *His schemes to get rich quickly sounded dubious.* —**du′bi•ous•ly** *adv.* —**du′bi•ous•ness** *n.* [U]

duch•ess (dŭch′ĭs) *n.* The wife or widow of a duke.

duck[1] (dŭk) *n.* **1.** [C] A domesticated water bird with a broad flat bill, short neck and legs, and webbed feet. **2.** [C] A female duck, as distinguished from a drake. **3.** [U] The meat of a duck, eaten as food.

duck[2] (dŭk) *v.* —*tr.* **1.** To lower (the head and body) quickly: *She ducked her head getting into the car.* **2.** To evade (sbdy./sthg.); avoid: *duck a responsibility.* **3.** To push (sbdy./sthg.) suddenly under water: *duck someone in the pool.* —*intr.* **1.** To lower the head or body quickly: *The boy ducked under the table.* **2.** To push or dip suddenly under water: *He ducked under.* ♦ **duck in** or **out.** *intr.v. Informal.* To enter or leave quickly or temporarily: *duck out of a meeting.*

duck•ling (dŭk′lĭng) *n.* A young duck.

duct (dŭkt) *n.* **1.** A tube through which sthg. flows: *Ducts carry heat from the furnace to the rest of the house.* **2.** A tube in the body that carries a bodily fluid: *tear ducts.*

duc•tile (dŭk′təl *or* dŭk′tīl′) *adj.* **1.** Easily molded or shaped: *Plastic pipe is ductile if heated.* **2.** Easily persuaded or influenced.

dud (dŭd) *n.* **1.** A bomb or firework that fails to explode. **2.** A person or thing that turns out to be ineffective or unsuccessful: *Our hasty plan was a real dud.* **3.** **duds.** *Informal.* Someone's clothing or personal belongings: *all dressed up in new duds.*

dude (dōōd) *n.* **1.** A city person who vacations on a ranch in the American West. **2.** *Slang.* A fellow; a man.

due (dōō) *adj.* **1.** Owed or owing as a debt: *We must pay the amount still due.* **2.** Fitting or appropriate; suitable: *Every citizen is required to show due respect for the law.* **3.** As much as needed; sufficient; adequate: *We left early, taking due care to be on time.* **4.** Expected or scheduled: *When is the train due to arrive?* **5.** Expecting or ready for sthg. as part of a normal course or sequence: *We're due for some rain.* —*n.* **1.** [U] Something that is owed or deserved: *a dedicated scholar who finally got his due.* **2.** **dues.** A charge or fee for membership, as in a club: *golfing dues of $30 per month.* —*adv.* Straight; directly: *The settlers traveled due west.*

HOMONYMS: due, dew (water droplets), **do** (perform).

---

du•el (dōō′əl) *n.* **1.** A type of combat in the past, arranged between two people, usually fought to settle an argument or a point of honor: *The rivals fought a duel.* **2.** A struggle between two opponents: *a duel of wits between lawyers in the courtroom.* —*tr. &*

ă–cat; ā–pay; âr–care; ä–father; ĕ–get; ē–be; ĭ–sit; ī–nice; îr–here; ŏ–got; ō–go; ô–saw; oi–boy; ou–out; ōō–took; ōō–boot; ŭ–cut; ûr–word; th–thin; *th*–this; hw–when; zh–vision; ə–about; N–French bon

intr.v. To fight in a duel: *They dueled to the death.* —**du′el•er, du′el•ist** *n.*

du•et (dōō ĕt′) *n.* A musical composition for two voices or two instruments.

due to *prep.* Because of: *The concert was canceled due to bad weather.*

duf•fel bag (dŭf′əl) *n.* A large cylindrical cloth bag for carrying personal belongings.

dug (dŭg) *v.* Past tense and past participle of **dig.**

dug•out (dŭg′out′) *n.* **1.** A boat or canoe made by hollowing out a log. **2.** A rough shelter dug into the ground or on a hillside and used especially in battle for protection.

duh (dŭ) *interj.* Used sarcastically to show that the speaker thinks sthg. just said is so obvious that it is not worth commenting on: *"I think we should pay our bills." "Duh."*

DUI *abbr.* An abbreviation of driving under the influence: *She was charged with DUI.*

duke (dōōk) *n.* A nobleman of the highest rank.

dull (dŭl) *adj.* **1.** Not sharp or pointed; blunt: *a dull knife; a dull pencil.* **2.** Not interesting; boring: *a dull book; dull work.* See Synonyms at **boring. 3.** Mentally weak: *a dull student.* **4.** Not intensely felt: *a dull ache in my throat.* **5.** Not bright or vivid; dim: *a dull red.* **6.** Not loud or clear; muffled: *the dull sound of distant thunder.* —*tr. & intr.v.* To make or become dull: *Cutting paper dulled the scissors. The saw blade dulled from use.* —**dull′ness** *n.* [U] —**dull′y** *adv.*

du•ly (dōō′lē) *adv.* **1.** In a proper manner; rightfully: *a duly elected candidate.* **2.** At the expected time; punctually: *The loan was duly repaid.*

dumb (dŭm) *adj.* **1.** *Offensive.* Incapable of using speech; mute. **2.** Unwilling to speak; silent: *The witness remained dumb under questioning.* **3.** Unintelligent; stupid. —**dumb′ly** *adv.* —**dumb′ness** *n.* [U]

dumb•bell (dŭm′bĕl′) *n.* **1.** A weight lifted for exercise, consisting of a short bar with a metal ball or plate at each end. **2.** *Slang.* A person regarded as stupid or ignorant.

dumb•found (dŭm′found′) *tr.v.* To make (sbdy.) speechless with astonishment; amaze: *The man's answers dumbfounded the experts.*

dum•my (dŭm′ē) *n., pl.* **dum•mies. 1.** A model of the human body, used as a substitute for a person: *A dummy was used to test the seat belt.* **2.** A person or organization secretly working for another: *That organization is a dummy; they really work for our competitors.* **3.** A stupid or foolish person. —*adj.* **1.** Made to work like or resemble a real object; imitation; fake: *dummy appliances in the kitchen display at the store.* **2.** Secretly in the service of another: *a dummy corporation covering up their criminal activities.*

dump (dŭmp) *tr.v.* **1.** To release or throw down (sthg.) in a mass: *The factory illegally dumped waste into the river. Don't dump your books on the table.* **2.** To empty out (a container or vehicle): *dump a wastebasket.* **3.** *Informal.* To get rid of or reject (sbdy./sthg.): *dumped the plan for a new highway; dumped her boyfriend.* **4.** To sell (goods) in large quantities and at a low price: *The company dumped computers in several countries.* **5.** To print out or transfer (information stored in computer memory) without processing it: *He dumped the data to the disk before turning off the computer.* —*n.* **1.** [C] A place where garbage or trash is discarded: *The town dump is nearly full.* **2.** [U] An untidy accumulation of things; a pile: *That messy storage closet is a dump.* **3.** [C] A military storage place: *an ammunition dump.* **4.** [C] A shabby rundown place: *The old house is a dump.* ◆ **down in the dumps.** Depressed; sad: *After he failed the test, he felt down in the dumps.*

dump•ing (dŭm′pĭng) *n.* [U] The selling of goods at a low price or below cost, often in another country: *The company was accused of dumping by its competitors.*

dump•ling (dŭmp′lĭng) *n.* **1.** A small ball of dough cooked in soup or steamed. **2.** Sweetened baked dough wrapped around fruit: *an apple dumpling.*

Dump•ster (dŭmp′stər). A trademark used for large containers designed to hold garbage.

dump truck *n.* A heavy-duty truck with a bed that tilts upward to dump loose material, such as sand or gravel.

dump•y (dŭm′pē) *adj.* **dump•i•er, dump•i•est.** An insulting word used to describe sbdy. who is short and fat: *That dress makes her look dumpy.* —**dump′i•ly** *adv.* —**dump′i•ness** *n.* [U]

dun (dŭn) *tr.v.* **dunned, dun•ning, duns.** To ask (sbdy. who owes unpaid debts) again and again for payment.

dunce (dŭns) *n.* A person regarded as stupid.

dune (dōōn) *n.* A hill or ridge of windblown sand: *From the top of the dunes, you can see the ocean.*

dung (dŭng) *n.* [U] **1.** The excrement of animals. **2.** Manure.

dun•ga•rees (dŭng′gə rēz′) *pl.n.* Jeans made of sturdy blue denim fabric: *She wore holes in her dungarees sliding down the hill.*

dun•geon (dŭn′jən) *n.* A dark, usually underground room used in the past to confine prisoners.

dunk (dŭngk) *tr.v.* **1.** To dip (sthg.) in a liquid: *dunk a doughnut in coffee.* **2.** To submerge (sbdy.) playfully, as in a swimming pool: *dunk the child in the swimming pool.* —*n.* A brief swim: *a dunk in the pool.*

dun•no (də nō′) *Informal.* **I dunno.** A spoken form of *I do not know.*

du•o (dōō′ō) *n., pl.* **du•os.** Two people who do sthg. together, usually musical performers.

dupe (dōōp) *n.* A person who is tricked or deceived. —*tr.v.* **duped, dup•ing, dupes.** [*into*] To deceive (sbdy.); trick: *The false advertisement duped us into believing the bicycles were on sale.*

du•plex (dōō′plĕks′) *n.* A house or apartment divided into two living units, usually with separate entrances.

du•pli•cate (dōō′plĭ kĭt) *adj.* Copied from an original: *a duplicate key.* —*n.* An exact copy; a double: *That letter is a duplicate of the original.* —*tr.v.* (dōō′plĭ kāt′). **du•pli•cat•ed, du•pli•cat•ing, du•pli•cates. 1.** To make an exact copy of (sthg.): *duplicate a key.* **2.** To do or perform (sthg.) again; repeat: *duplicate an experiment.*

du•pli•ca•tion (dōō′plĭ kā′shən) *n.* **1.** [U] The act or condition of being duplicated: *Duplication of the experiment confirmed the original results.* **2.** [C] A duplicate; a replica: *This statue is a duplication of a Roman statue of Caesar.*

du•pli•ca•tor (dōō′plĭ kā′tər) *n.* A machine that makes exact copies of printed matter.

du•plic•i•ty (dōō plĭs′ĭ tē) *n.* [U] Deliberate deceptiveness in behavior or speech; deceit: *The spy used duplicity to get information.*

du•ra•ble (dōōr′ə bəl) *adj.* **1.** Capable of staying in good condition for a long time; sturdy: *Denim is a durable fabric used for work clothes.* **2.** Lasting or enduring; stable: *a durable peace.* —**du′ra•bil′i•ty** *n.* [U] —**du′ra•bly** *adv.*

du•ra•tion (dōō rā′shən) *n.* [U] The period of time during which sthg. lasts: *the duration of a storm.*

du•ress (dōō rĕs′) *n.* [U] ◆ **under duress.** The use of force or threat to make sbdy. do sthg.: *The prisoner confessed under duress.*

dur•ing (dōōr′ĭng) *prep.* **1.** Throughout the course or duration of sthg.: *We talked during the entire evening.* **2.** Within the time of sthg.; at some time in: *He composed his music during the last half of the 19th century.*

dusk (dŭsk) *n.* [U] The time of evening just before darkness: *Only a few stars shine at dusk.*

dusk•y (dŭs′kē) *adj.* **dusk•i•er, dusk•i•est. 1.** Dark in color: *dusky fur.* **2.** With little light; dim: *a dusky room.* See Synonyms at **dark.** —**dusk′i•ness** *n.* [U]

dust (dŭst) *n.* [U] Fine dry particles of matter: *clouds of dust raised by cattle; the dust gathering on old books.* —*v.* —*tr.* **1.** To remove dust from (sthg.) by wiping or brushing: *We dusted the shelves.* **2.** To sprinkle (sthg.) with a powdery substance: *She dusted the rose-bushes with insecticide. The police dusted the weapon for fingerprints.* —*intr.* To clean by removing dust: *The cleaning staff must dust every day.* ◆ **dust off.** *tr.v.* [sep.] **1.** To restore or revise (sthg.) for current use: *dust off an old essay for publication.* **2.** To remove the dust from (sthg.): *He dusted off the table.*

dust•y (dŭs′tē) *adj.* **dust•i•er, dust•i•est.** Covered or filled with dust: *a dusty road; a dusty room.* —**dust′i•ness** *n.* [U]

Dutch (dŭch) *n.* **1. the Dutch.** *(used with a plural verb).* The people of the Netherlands. **2.** [U] The language of the Netherlands. —*adj.* Relating to the Netherlands or its people, language, or culture. ◆ **go dutch.** To pay one's own expenses, as on a date: *Let's go dutch; you paid for lunch last time.* **in dutch.** In trouble or disfavor: *in dutch for being late.*

du•ti•ful (dōō′tĭ fəl) *adj.* Careful to perform one's duty; obedient: *a dutiful child.* —**du′ti•ful•ly** *adv.*

du•ty (dōō′tē) *n., pl.* **du•ties.** [C; U] **1.** Something that a person must or should do; an obligation: *In a democracy, one duty of a citizen is to vote.* **2.** Moral obligation: *We went to the ceremony out of duty.* **3.** A task or assignment that is part of one's work: *Dish-washing is a household duty. We posted a notice listing the job duties.* **4.** A tax charged by a government on imported or exported goods: *the duty on alcohol and cigarettes.* ◆ **on** or **off duty.** Required or not required to work: *Get it yourself; I'm off duty now. She'll be on duty at noon.*

du•ty-free (dōō′tē frē′) *adj.* Describing goods that can be brought into another country without being charged duty.

dwarf (dwôrf) *n., pl.* **dwarfs** or **dwarves** (dwôrvz). **1.a.** An insulting term for a person who is very small as an adult. **b.** An unusually small plant or animal: *a dwarf pine tree.* **2.** In fairy tales and legends, a tiny, often ugly creature who has magical powers. —*tr.v.* **1.** To make (sbdy./sthg.) seem small by comparison with sbdy./sthg. else: *The skyscraper dwarfed the old church.* **2.** To slow the natural growth of (sthg.); stunt: *Lack of water dwarfed the trees.*

dwell (dwĕl) *v.* **dwelt** (dwĕlt) or **dwelled, dwell•ing, dwells.** —*intr.* To live as a resident; reside: *dwell in a city.* ◆ **dwell on** or **upon.** *tr.v.* [insep.] To speak, think, or write about (sthg.) at length: *Don't dwell on one subject for too long in your report.* —**dwell′er** *n.*

dwell•ing (dwĕl′ĭng) *n.* A place to live in; a residence: *Our house is a two-story dwelling.*

dwelt (dwĕlt) *v.* A past tense and a past participle of **dwell.**

DWI *abbr.* An abbreviation of driving while intoxicated: *The driver was put in jail on DWI charges.*

dwin·dle (dwĭn′dl) *intr.v.* **dwin·dled, dwin·dling, dwin·dles.** To become gradually less until little is left: *Without steady work, their savings dwindled.* See Synonyms at **decrease.**

dye (dī) *n.* A substance used to color food, hair, cloth, or other materials. —*v.* **dyed, dye·ing, dyes.** —*tr.* To color (sthg.) with a dye: *I need to dye the fabric red. She dyed her hair blond.* —*intr.* To become colored by a dye: *Some fabrics dye more easily than others.* ◆ **dyed-in-the-wool.** Not likely to change; completely committed: *a dyed-in-the-wool liberal.*

HOMONYMS: dye, die (stop living, device for shaping material).

---

dy·ing (dī′ĭng) *v.* Present participle of **die**[1]. —*adj.* **1.** About to die: *the shriveled leaves of the dying plant.* **2.** Drawing to an end: *a dying day.* **3.** Done or said just before death: *dying words.*

dyke (dīk) *n. Offensive Slang.* A lesbian.

dy·nam·ic (dī năm′ĭk) *adj.* **1.** Marked by intensity; forceful: *the dynamic personality of a political leader.* **2.** Changing; active: *a dynamic stock market.* **3.** Relating to energy or to objects in motion. —**dy·nam′i·cal·ly** *adv.*

dy·nam·ics (dī năm′ĭks) *n.* **1.** [U] *(used with a singular verb).* The branch of physics that deals with the effects of forces on the motions of bodies. **2.** [C] *(used with a plural verb).* The forces that produce activity and change in a particular area: *the dynamics that have increased international trade.*

dy·na·mism (dī′nə mĭz′əm) *n.* [U] Continuous change or activity; energy: *the dynamism of a new government administration.*

dy·na·mite (dī′nə mīt′) *n.* [U] **1.** A powerful explosive used in blasting. **2.** *Slang.* Something that is especially exciting or wonderful: *These new video games are dynamite!* —*tr.v.* **dy·na·mit·ed, dy·na·mit·ing, dy·na·mites.** To blow up or destroy (sthg.) with dynamite: *The old office building was dynamited to make space for a new building.* —**dy′na·mit′er** *n.*

dy·na·mo (dī′nə mō′) *n., pl.* **dy·na·mos. 1.** An electric generator. **2.** *Informal.* An extremely energetic and forceful person: *He's a dynamo in the office.*

dy·nas·tic (dī năs′tĭk) *adj.* Relating to a dynasty: *a long tradition of dynastic rule.*

dy·nas·ty (dī′nə stē) *n., pl.* **dy·nas·ties.** A succession of rulers from the same family: *the Ming dynasty of China.*

dys·en·ter·y (dĭs′ən tĕr′ē) *n.* [U] An infection of the lower intestines that produces pain, fever, and severe diarrhea.

dys·func·tion (dĭs fŭngk′shən) *n.* [C; U] Abnormal functioning of a system, a social unit, or an organ of the body: *a kidney dysfunction; dysfunction in the family.* —**dys·func′tion·al** *adj.*

dys·lex·i·a (dĭs lĕk′sē ə) *n.* [U] A learning disorder that interferes with the ability to recognize and comprehend written words. —**dys·lex′ic** *adj. & n.*

dz. *abbr.* An abbreviation of dozen.

Ee

e or **E** (ē) *n.*, *pl.* **e's** or **E's. 1.** The fifth letter of the English alphabet. **2.** In music, the third tone in the scale of C major.

E *abbr.* An abbreviation of: **1.** East. **2.** Eastern. **3.** Energy. **4.** English.

ea. *abbr.* An abbreviation of each.

each (ēch) *adj.* Referring to one of two or more persons or things considered individually; every: *The teacher talked to each student for ten minutes.* —*pron.* Every one of a group of persons or things: *Each of us took a turn looking in the telescope.* —*adv.* For or to each one; apiece: *The apples cost 25¢ each.*

USAGE: each When the subject of a sentence begins with **each**, the verb and following pronouns must be singular: *Each of the rooms has its own bath.* When **each** follows a plural subject, however, the verb and pronouns are in the plural: *The rooms each have their own baths.*

---

each other *pron.* Used to show that each person or thing does the same as the other: *The girls greeted each other. The brothers haven't spoken to each other since their father died.*

ea•ger (ē'gər) *adj.* Having or showing great interest or desire: *Thousands of eager sports fans cheered the players.* —**ea'ger•ly** *adv.* —**ea'ger•ness** *n.* [U]

ea•gle (ē'gəl) *n.* A large bird of prey with a strong bill, sharp vision, and broad wings: *The bald eagle is the symbol of the United States.*

eagle

ea•gle-eyed (ē'gəl īd') *adj.* Having very good eyesight: *an eagle-eyed guard.*

ear¹ (îr) *n.* **1.** [C] The organ of hearing in humans and other animals. **2.** [U] The sense of hearing: *The singing sounded pleasant to my ear.* **3.** [C; U] The ability to distinguish tones or sounds very accurately: *the sensitive ear of a musician.* **4.** [C; U] Attention: *Give me your ear until I finish the explanation.* ◆ **all ears.** Listening eagerly; paying

ear
(outer ear)

careful attention: *The children were all ears when they heard about the circus.* **be up to (one's) ears.** *Informal.* To be very busy with sthg.: *They were up to their ears in work.* **go in one ear and out the other.** To have no influence or effect: *I could tell that my instructions went in one ear and out the other.* **play it by ear.** To act according to the circumstances; improvise: *I'm not sure what the schedule is, so we'll have to play it by ear.*

ear² (îr) *n.* The part of a cereal plant, such as corn, that bears flowers from which grains develop: *She bought six ears of corn for dinner.*

ear
(corn)

ear•ache (îr'āk') *n.* A pain in the ear: *The baby cried all night because of an earache.*

ear•drum (îr'drŭm') *n.* The membrane in the ear that vibrates when sound waves strike it.

ear•ful (îr'fŏŏl') *n. (usually singular).* **1.** A large amount of gossip or information: *I got an earful about the scandal from a neighbor.* **2.** A scolding or strong criticism: *The gardener gave me an earful for walking across the lawn.*

earl (ûrl) *n.* A British nobleman.

ear•lobe (îr'lōb') *n.* The soft fleshy part at the bottom of the external ear of humans.

ear•ly (ûr'lē) *adj.* **ear•li•er, ear•li•est. 1.** Happening near the beginning of sthg.: *the early morning; people in their early twenties; the early stages of an animal's growth.* **2.** Belonging to a previous time: *Early humans made simple tools.* **3.** Before the usual or expected time: *We had an early spring this year.* **4.** Happening in the near future: *Lawyers predict an early end to the trial.* —*adv.* **ear•li•er, ear•li•est. 1.** Near the beginning of a period of time: *The hikers left early in the morning.* **2.** Before the usual or expected time: *They arrived early.* **3.** Far back in time; long ago: *The Greek islands were settled as early as 5000 B.C.* —**ear'li•ness** *n.* [U]

early bird *n. Informal.* A person who wakes up, arrives, or starts being active before most

---

ă–c**at**; ā–p**ay**; âr–c**are**; ä–f**ather**; ĕ–g**et**; ē–b**e**; ĭ–s**it**; ī–n**ice**; îr–h**ere**; ŏ–g**ot**; ō–g**o**; ô–s**aw**; oi–b**oy**; ou–**out**; ŏŏ–t**ook**; ōō–b**oot**; ŭ–c**ut**; ûr–w**ord**; th–**thin**; *th*–**this**; hw–**when**; zh–vi**si**on; ə–**about**; N–French b**on**

others: *The office early birds are usually in at 7:00.*

ear•mark (îr′märk′) *n.* A special quality or mark that sets sbdy./sthg. apart: *Careful observation is one of the earmarks of a good scientist.* —*tr.v.* To set (sthg., especially money) aside for some purpose: *We earmarked part of the bonus money for a new car.*

ear•muff (îr′mŭf′) *n.* One of a pair of coverings for the ears, used in cold weather: *She wore earmuffs to protect her ears from the cold wind.*

earn (ûrn) *tr.v.* **1.** To get (sthg.) by working or by supplying a product or service: *earn money by selling cars.* **2.** To deserve or win (sthg.) by one's efforts or actions: *earn a reputation for being very thoughtful; earn a scholarship.* **3.** To produce (sthg.) as income or profit: *A savings account earns interest on your money.* —**earn′er** *n.*

HOMONYMS: earn, urn (container).

---

ear•nest (ûr′nĭst) *adj.* Sincere or serious: *an earnest offer to help.* ◆ **in earnest.** With serious purpose or intent: *After a slow start, we began working on the project in earnest.* —**ear′nest•ly** *adv.* —**ear′nest•ness** *n.* [U]

earn•ings (ûr′nĭngz) *pl.n.* **1.** Money earned for work; wages: *They saved 5% of their earnings.* **2.** Profits, as from a business or an investment: *Earnings were up for small businesses last year.*

ear•phones (îr′fōnz′) *pl.n.* A piece of electronic equipment that is worn over the ear and is used to listen to sthg., such as a radio or tape.

ear•plug (îr′plŭg′) *n. (usually plural).* A small piece of material, such as rubber, foam, or wax, placed inside the ear to protect against noise or water.

earphones

ear•ring (îr′rĭng) *n.* A piece of jewelry worn on or hanging from a hole or holes in the earlobe.

ear•shot (îr′shŏt′) *n.* [U] The range or distance within which sound can be heard: *Their shouts were out of earshot and went unnoticed.*

ear•split•ting (îr′splĭt′ĭng) *adj.* Loud enough to hurt the ears; deafening: *the earsplitting sound of the jet engines.*

earth (ûrth) *n.* [U] **1.** Often **Earth.** The planet on which human beings live, the third planet from the sun. **2.** Dry land; the ground: *snowflakes falling to the earth.* **3.** Dirt; soil: *seeds sprouting in the moist earth.* **4.** All of the human inhabitants of the world: *The earth rejoiced at the news of peace.*

earth•en (ûr′thən) *adj.* Made of soil or clay: *the earthen floor of a cabin; an earthen pot.*

earth•ling (ûrth′lĭng) *n.* A person who lives on the earth, especially as compared to beings from other planets.

earth•ly (ûrth′lē) *adj.* **1.** Relating to the earth rather than heaven: *the everyday earthly business of earning a living.* **2.** Possible; imaginable: *a remark with no earthly meaning.* —**earth′li•ness** *n.* [U]

earth•quake (ûrth′kwāk′) *n.* A sudden violent movement of the earth's surface, caused by volcanic action or by the release of built-up stress within the rocks along geologic faults.

earth•worm (ûrth′wûrm′) *n.* A common worm that has a segmented body and burrows in soil.

earth•y (ûr′thē) *adj.* **earth•i•er, earth•i•est.** **1.** Relating to earth or soil: *the earthy smell of the woods after rain.* **2.** Hearty; natural: *an earthy enjoyment of life.* **3.** Crude; indecent: *earthy humor.* —**earth′i•ness** *n.* [U]

ease (ēz) *n.* [U] **1.** Freedom from difficulty, strain, or great effort: *I solved the problem with ease. She lifted the heavy book with ease.* **2.** Freedom from pain or worry: *Her mind was at ease, knowing the children had returned safely.* **3.** Freedom from awkwardness or embarrassment; naturalness: *She spoke before the crowd with ease.* —*v.* **eased, eas•ing, eas•es.** —*tr.* **1.** To free sbdy. from the pain or worry of (sthg.): *The medication eased his earache.* **2.** To make (sthg.) less difficult: *The school eased its entrance requirements.* **3.** To cause (sthg.) to move slowly and carefully: *The student driver eased the car into the garage.* **4.** To reduce the pressure or strain of (sthg.); loosen: *ease the dog's collar.* —*intr.* To relax; let up: *The tension eased when the angry customer left the store.*

ea•sel (ē′zəl) *n.* An upright stand used to display or support an artist's canvas.

eas•i•ly (ē′zə lē) *adv.* **1.** In an easy manner; with ease: *Libraries are arranged so that you can find books easily.* **2.** Without doubt; surely: *That is easily the best book I have ever read.* **3.** Very likely: *If we beat their team, we could easily win the championship.*

east (ēst) *n.* [U] **1.** The direction in which the sun is seen to rise, directly opposite west. **2.** Often **East.** A region or part of a country lying in the east: *He moved to Texas from somewhere in the East.* **3.** Often **East.** Eastern Asia: *trade with the East.* —*adj.* **1.** Of, in, or toward the east: *the east bank of the river; the east road to town.* **2.** From the east: *An east wind is blowing.* —*adv.* In, from, or toward the east: *a river flowing east.*

east•bound (ēst′bound′) *adj.* Going toward the east: *an eastbound train.*

east•er•ly (ē′stər lē) *adj.* **1.** Situated toward the east: *the most easterly point of land;*

E

flying in an easterly direction. **2.** Coming from the east: *easterly wind.* —*n., pl.* **east‧er‧lies.** A storm or wind from the east. —**east′er‧ly** *adv.*

east‧ern (ē′stərn) *adj.* **1.** Of, in, or toward the east: *eastern Europe; the eastern slope of a mountain.* **2.** From the east: *an eastern wind.* **3.** Often **Eastern.** Relating to or characteristic of eastern regions or the East: *the Eastern attitude toward business.*

east‧ern‧er also **East‧ern‧er** (ē′stər nər) *n.* A person who lives in or comes from the east, especially the eastern United States.

east‧ward (ēst′wərd) *adv. & adj.* To or toward the east: *a river flowing eastward; the eastward flow of the current.* —*n.* A direction or region to the east: *The fields are located to the eastward.* —**east′wards** *adv.*

eas‧y (ē′zē) *adj.* **eas‧i‧er, eas‧i‧est. 1.** Requiring little or no effort or trouble: *an easy task; handwriting that is easy to read.* **2.** Free from worry, strain, or pain: *an easy life; an easy mind.* **3.** Not forced, hurried, or strenuous: *within easy walking distance; an easy drive.* **4.** Relaxed; comfortable: *a natural easy manner; an easy smile.* **5.** Not strict or demanding; lenient: *Some teachers are easy on new students.* —*adv.* **1.** Without haste or worry: *Take it easy and you'll do a better job.* **2.** With little effort; easily: *Playing the banjo came easy to her.* **3.** Without much hardship: *He got off easy with only a small fine.* ◆ **easier said than done.** Easy to talk about but hard to do: *Winning this election will be easier said than done.* **easy as pie.** *Informal.* Very easy to do: *With everyone helping, finishing that project was easy as pie!* **easy does it.** Used to tell sbdy. to move slowly or carefully, especially when moving sthg.: *Easy does it. We're almost up the stairs.* —**eas′i‧ness** *n.* [U]

SYNONYMS: easy, simple, effortless, smooth. These adjectives mean requiring little effort. **Easy** describes tasks that are not difficult: *It's easy to take care of a pet hamster.* **Simple** describes sthg. that is easy because it is not complex: *She gave us simple directions to her house.* **Effortless** means seeming to be easy because of the strength or skill applied: *The skater performed an effortless jump.* **Smooth** means free from difficulties or obstacles: *The road to success is hardly ever smooth.*

---

easy chair *n.* A large comfortable upholstered chair.

eas‧y‧go‧ing (ē′zē gō′ĭng) *adj.* Relaxed; carefree: *an easygoing life; an easygoing manner of speech.*

eat (ēt) *v.* **ate** (āt), **eat‧en** (ēt′n), **eat‧ing,**

eats. —*tr.* **1.** To take (solid food) into the body through the mouth: *Cats eat mice.* **2.** To wear away, corrode, or destroy (sthg.) by or as if by eating: *Rust has eaten away the iron pipes.* **3.** To make (sthg.) by eating: *Moths ate holes in the blanket.* —*intr.* **1.** To take food; have a meal: *They usually eat at 7 o'clock.* **2.** To wear away; corrode: *Home improvements ate into their savings.* ◆ **eat up.** *tr.v.* [sep.] To enjoy (sthg.) greatly; be greedy for: *The actor eats up compliments.* **eat (one's) words.** To withdraw sthg. that one has said: *After promising to work Saturday, I had to eat my words and help my mother instead.* **eating out of (one's) hand.** Controlled or dominated by sbdy.: *That pretty girl has the boys eating out of her hand.* —**eat′er** *n.*

eat‧en (ēt′n) *v.* Past participle of **eat.**

eat‧er‧y (ē′tə rē) *n., pl.* **eat‧er‧ies.** *Informal.* A lunchroom; a diner.

eaves‧drop (ēvz′drŏp′) *intr.v.* **eaves‧dropped, eaves‧drop‧ping, eaves‧drops.** [*on*] To listen secretly to the private conversation of others: *He hid behind the door to eavesdrop on his sister.* —**eaves′drop′per** *n.*

ebb (ĕb) *n.* [U] **1.** The period when the tide is flowing away from the shore. **2.** A period of decline: *The family's fortunes were at their lowest ebb.* —*intr.v.* **1.** To flow back; recede: *The flood waters began to ebb after the storm passed.* **2.** To fade or fall away; decline: *The hooked fish struggled less as its strength ebbed.*

eb‧on‧y (ĕb′ə nē) *n., pl.* **eb‧on‧ies. 1.a.** [C] A tropical tree with hard black or blackish wood. **b.** [U] The wood of this tree. **2.** [U] A black color. —*adj.* **1.** Made of ebony: *an ebony cabinet.* **2.** Black: *ebony hair.*

ec‧cen‧tric (ĭk sĕn′trĭk) *adj.* **1.** Odd or unusual in appearance, behavior, or manner; strange: *The eccentric man wore old-fashioned clothes and ate only soup.* **2.** Not perfectly circular; elliptical: *an eccentric orbit.* —*n.* A person who is odd or unusual in behavior: *She is considered an eccentric for her odd habits.* —**ec‧cen′tri‧cal‧ly** *adv.* —**ec′cen‧tric′i‧ty** (ĕk′sĕn trĭs′ĭ tē) *n.* [C; U]

ech‧e‧lon (ĕsh′ə lŏn′) *n.* A level of command or authority: *a job in the lowest echelon of the corporation.*

ech‧o (ĕk′ō) *n., pl.* **ech‧oes. 1.** A repeated sound that is caused by the reflection of sound waves from a surface: *an echo bouncing back from the far cliff.* **2.** A repetition or imitation of sthg.: *New fashions in dress usually have echoes of earlier styles.* —*v.* —*tr.* **1.** To repeat (a sound) by an echo: *The mountain echoed their shouts.* **2.** To repeat or imitate (sthg.): *She echoed our feelings in her state-*

ă–cat; ā–pay; âr–care; ä–father; ĕ–get; ē–be; ĭ–sit; ī–nice; îr–here; ŏ–got; ō–go; ô–saw; oi–boy; ou–out; ŏŏ–took; ōō–boot; ŭ–cut; ûr–word; th–thin; *th*–this; hw–when; zh–vision; ə–about; N–French bon

ment to the teacher. —*intr.* **1.** To be repeated by an echo: *The shouts echoed from the mountainside.* **2.** To resound with an echo; reverberate: *The long hallway echoed with many footsteps.*

é·clair (ā klâr′ *or* ā′klâr′) *n.* A long pastry filled with custard or whipped cream and usually topped with chocolate.

e·clec·tic (ĭ klĕk′tĭk) *adj.* Choosing the best from various sources: *eclectic music combining jazz and classical styles.* —*n.* A person whose opinions and beliefs are drawn from several sources. —**e·clec′ti·cal·ly** *adv.*

e·clipse (ĭ klĭps′) *n.* **1.** The partial or total blocking of light from one celestial body as it passes behind or through the shadow of another celestial body. In a solar eclipse, the moon comes between the sun and the earth. In a lunar eclipse, the moon enters the earth's shadow. **2.**

eclipse
Solar eclipse

A decline in importance, use, or fame: *The singer's popularity has suffered an eclipse since her retirement.* —*tr.v.* **e·clipsed, e·clips·ing, e·clips·es. 1.** To cause an eclipse of (sthg.): *When the moon eclipsed the sun it caused partial darkness.* **2.** To obscure or overshadow (sbdy./sthg.) in importance, fame, or reputation; surpass: *The war eclipsed all other news for a while.*

e·col·o·gist (ĭ kŏl′ə jĭst) *n.* A scientist who specializes in ecology.

e·col·o·gy (ĭ kŏl′ə jē) *n.* [U] **1.** The branch of biology that studies the relationships between living things and their environments. **2.** The relationship between living things and their environments. —**ec′o·log′i·cal** (ĕk′ə lŏj′ĭ kəl *or* ē′kə lŏj′ĭ kəl) *adj.* —**ec′o·log′i·cal·ly** *adv.*

ec·o·nom·ic (ĕk′ə nŏm′ĭk *or* ē′kə nŏm′ĭk) *adj.* **1.** Relating to the production, development, and management of wealth, as of a country, household, or business: *A government's economic policy is supposed to support new businesses.* **2.** Relating to the science of economics: *economic theories of how money works in society.*

ec·o·nom·i·cal (ĕk′ə nŏm′ĭ kəl *or* ē′kə-nŏm′ĭ kəl) *adj.* Not wasteful; thrifty: *an economical use of time; an economical way to produce better crops.* —**ec′o·nom′i·cal·ly** *adv.*

ec·o·nom·ics (ĕk′ə nŏm′ĭks *or* ē′kə-nŏm′ĭks) *n.* [U] **1.** (*used with a singular verb*). The study of the ways in which goods and services are produced, transported, sold,

and used. **2.** (*used with a singular or plural verb*). Economic matters, especially those relating to cost and profit: *the economics of running a store.*

e·con·o·mist (ĭ kŏn′ə mĭst) *n.* A person who specializes in economics.

e·con·o·mize (ĭ kŏn′ə mīz′) *v.* **e·con·o·mized, e·con·o·miz·ing, e·con·o·miz·es.** —*intr.* To be thrifty; reduce expenses or avoid waste: *You could economize by bringing your own lunch to work.* —*tr.* To use or manage (sthg.) with thrift: *Economize your time to get more done.*

e·con·o·my (ĭ kŏn′ə mē) *n., pl.* **e·con·o·mies. 1.** [U] The careful use or management of resources, such as money, materials, or labor: *She practices economy in running the household.* **2.** [C] The economic system of a country, region, or state: *The rise in housing prices boosted the city's economy.* **3.** [C] A specific kind of economic system: *an industrial economy.*

ec·o·sys·tem (ĕk′ō sĭs′təm *or* ē′kō sĭs′-təm) *n.* An ecological community, including plants, animals, and microorganisms, considered together with their environment: *A pond is an example of a complex ecosystem.*

ec·sta·sy (ĕk′stə sē) *n., pl.* **ec·sta·sies.** [C; U] Intense joy or delight: *The runner was in ecstasy over winning an Olympic gold medal.*

ec·stat·ic (ĕk stăt′ĭk) *adj.* In a state of ecstasy: *I was ecstatic over the chance to go to Europe.* —**ec·stat′i·cal·ly** *adv.*

ecto— *pref.* A prefix that means outer or external: *ectoderm.*

ec·to·derm (ĕk′tə dûrm′) *n.* The outer cell layer of an early embryo that develops into the outer skin, hair, nails, and parts of the nervous system.

ec·u·men·i·cal (ĕk′yə mĕn′ĭ kəl) *adj.* **1.** Relating to the worldwide Christian church: *an ecumenical council.* **2.** Worldwide in range or relevance; universal: *an ecumenical view of environmental planning.* —**ec′u·men′i·cal·ly** *adv.*

ec·ze·ma (ĕk′sə mə *or* ĕg′zə mə) *n.* [U] An inflammation of the skin, marked by redness, itching, and sores.

ed. *abbr.* An abbreviation of: **1.** Edition. **2.** Editor. **3.** Edited. **4.** Education.

—ed¹ *suff.* A suffix that forms the past tense of regular verbs: *cared; carried.*

—ed² *suff.* A suffix that forms the past participle of regular verbs: *ended; expected.*

—ed³ *suff.* A suffix that means having, characterized by, or resembling: *hardhearted; wretched.*

edge (ĕj) *n.* **1.** The thin sharpened side of a blade: *the edge of a knife.* **2.** The line or point where two surfaces meet: *the edge of a table.* **3.a.** A dividing line; a border: *a house on the edge of town.* See Synonyms at **margin. b.**

The area or part farthest from the middle: *the edge of the carpet.* **4.** An advantage: *We had a slight edge over the other team.* —*v.* **edged, edg·ing, edg·es.** —*tr.* **1.** To give an edge to (sthg.); sharpen: *edge a dull knife.* **2.** To be the edge of (sthg.): *Flowers edged the lawn.* **3.** To put a border or an edge on (sthg.): *edge a sleeve with lace.* **4.** To advance or move (sbdy./sthg.) gradually; push: *The photographers edged their way through the crowd.* —*intr.* To move gradually: *The child edged slowly toward the door.* ✦ **be on edge. 1.** To be nervous about sthg. that may happen or is about to happen: *She has been on edge about her parents' visit.* **2.** To be tense or irritable: *He was on edge from listening to the baby cry.* **edge out.** *tr.v.* [sep.] To beat (sbdy.) by a small margin: *She edged out her rival for the position.*

edge·wise (ĕj′wīz′) *adv.* With the edge forward: *Turn the table edgewise to get it through the door.* ✦ **get a word in edgewise.** To manage to say sthg. in a conversation dominated by another person: *The others talked so much I couldn't get a word in edgewise.*

edg·ing (ĕj′ĭng) *n.* [C; U] Something that forms an edge or a border: *an edging of bricks along the path.*

edg·y (ĕj′ē) *adj.* **edg·i·er, edg·i·est.** Nervous or irritable: *We got edgy waiting for the concert to begin.* —**edg′i·ness** *n.* [U]

ed·i·ble (ĕd′ə bəl) *adj.* Fit to be eaten: *The spoiled cheese was no longer edible.* —*n.* (usually plural). Something to be eaten; food: *Look in the refrigerator for some edibles.*

e·dict (ē′dĭkt′) *n.* An official order or decree issued by a person in authority: *an edict on acceptable behavior.*

ed·i·fice (ĕd′ə fĭs) *n. Formal.* A building, especially one that is large and impressive.

ed·it (ĕd′ĭt) *tr.v.* **1.** To make (written material) ready for publication by clarifying and marking corrections for a printer: *The staff edited reporters' stories for publication in the newspaper.* **2.** To supervise the publication of (a newspaper or magazine): *My professor edits a literary magazine.* **3.** To put together or cut out parts of (a film, videotape, or musical recording): *We edited our videotape of the wedding down to a 30-minute show.*

edit. *abbr.* An abbreviation of: **1.** Edition. **2.** Editor.

e·di·tion (ĭ dĭsh′ən) *n.* **1.** A single printing of a book or newspaper: *today's edition of the newspaper.* **2.** Any of the forms in which a publication is issued: *a paperback edition of a novel.*

ed·i·tor (ĕd′ĭ tər) *n.* **1.** A person who edits written material for publication: *a textbook editor.* **2.** A person who prepares a film, videotape, or musical recording by assem-

bling its parts. **3.** A person who directs the writing and preparation of a newspaper or magazine or supervises one of its departments: *the entertainment editor.*

ed·i·to·ri·al (ĕd′ĭ tôr′ē əl) *n.* An article in a newspaper or magazine or a commentary on television or radio expressing the opinions of the editors or owners: *an editorial promoting public education.* —*adj.* **1.** Relating to an editor or editing: *an editorial position in a publishing company.* **2.** Expressing opinion rather than reporting news: *the editorial page of the newspaper.* —**ed′i·to′ri·al·ly** *adv.*

ed·i·to·ri·al·ize (ĕd′ĭ tôr′ē ə līz′) *intr.v.* **ed·i·to·ri·al·ized, ed·i·to·ri·al·iz·ing, ed·i·to·ri·al·iz·es.** To express an opinion in or as if in an editorial: *Most newspapers editorialize in each issue.*

ed·u·cate (ĕj′ə kāt′) *v.* **ed·u·cat·ed, ed·u·cat·ing, ed·u·cates.** —*tr.* To provide (sbdy.) with knowledge or training, especially through formal schooling; teach: *a campaign to educate people about the dangers of smoking.* See Synonyms at **teach.** —*intr.* To provide instructions and training: *Their purpose is to educate through the use of visual aids.* —**ed′u·ca·ble** (ĕj′ə kə bəl) *adj.*

ed·u·cat·ed (ĕj′ə kā′tĭd) *adj.* **1.** Having an education, especially one above the average: *Librarians are educated people.* **2.** Based on experience or factual knowledge: *an educated guess.*

ed·u·ca·tion (ĕj′ə kā′shən) *n.* [U] **1.a.** The process of obtaining knowledge or skill: *Many people want to continue their education after high school.* **b.** The knowledge or skill obtained by such a process; learning: *It takes a lot of education to be an engineer.* **2.** A program of instruction of a specified kind or level: *a college education.* **3.** The field of study that is concerned with teaching and learning: *Many teachers are graduates of schools of education.* —**ed′u·ca′tion·al** *adj.* —**ed′u·ca′tion·al·ly** *adv.*

ed·u·ca·tor (ĕj′ə kā′tər) *n.* A person who is trained in teaching; a teacher.

—ee *suff.* A suffix that means: **1.** A person who receives or benefits from an action: *appointee; trainee.* **2.** A person or an animal that performs an action: *absentee; escapee.*

eel (ēl) *n.* A long fish that lacks scales and resembles a snake.

—eer *suff.* A suffix that means a person who is associated with or involved in: *auctioneer; racketeer.*

e'er (âr) *adv.* A literary form of ever.

HOMONYMS: e'er, air (gas), **ere** (before), **heir** (inheritor).

---

ee•rie or **ee•ry** (îr′ē) *adj.* **ee•ri•er, ee•ri•est.** Strange and frightening: *The eerie old house made us feel uneasy.* —**ee′ri•ly** *adv.* —**ee′ri•ness** *n.* [U]

ef•fect (ĭ fĕkt′) *n.* [C; U] **1.** Something brought about by a cause; a result: *The effect of advertising should be an increase in sales.* **2.** The power to bring about a result; influence: *The new regulation had no effect on improving air quality.* **3.** An artistic technique that produces a specific impression: *Thunder and lightning and other special effects can be used in making a movie.* **4. effects.** *Formal.* Movable belongings; goods: *She searched for the book among her effects.* —*tr.v.* *Formal.* To produce (sthg.) as a result; cause to occur: *New technologies have effected many changes in the way people live.* ◆ **in effect. 1.** In essence; actually: *By turning off the lights they were in effect telling us to go home.* **2.** In active force: *The new law is now in effect.* **take effect.** To come into active force: *The law will take effect at midnight tomorrow.*

ef•fec•tive (ĭ fĕk′tĭv) *adj.* **1.** Having an intended effect: *a vaccine effective against polio.* **2.** Operative; in effect: *The law will be effective as soon as the governor signs it.* **3.** Producing a strong impression or response: *The President made an effective speech that united the country behind him.* —**ef•fec′tive•ly** *adv.* —**ef•fec′tive•ness** *n.* [U]

ef•fec•tu•al (ĭ fĕk′chŏŏ əl) *adj.* Producing a desired effect; fully adequate: *Practice is the only effectual method of learning to play a musical instrument.* —**ef•fec′tu•al•ly** *adv.*

ef•fem•i•nate (ĭ fĕm′ə nĭt) *adj.* An offensive term used to describe a man or boy who has qualities associated with women rather than men. —**ef•fem′i•nate•ly** *adv.*

ef•fer•vesce (ĕf′ər vĕs′) *intr.v.* **ef•fer•vesced, ef•fer•vesc•ing, ef•fer•vesc•es. 1.** To give off bubbles of gas, as a carbonated liquid. **2.** To show high spirits; be lively. —**ef′fer•ves′cent** *adj.*

ef•fer•ves•cence (ĕf′ər vĕs′əns) *n.* [U] **1.** The process of giving off small bubbles of gas: *the effervescence of soda water.* **2.** Sparkling high spirits; vivacity.

ef•fi•ca•cious (ĕf′ĭ kā′shəs) *adj.* *Formal.* Effective: *an efficacious treatment of a disease.* —**ef′fi•ca′cious•ly** *adv.* —**ef′fi•ca′cious•ness** *n.* [U]

ef•fi•ca•cy (ĕf′ĭ kə sē) *n.* [U] Effectiveness: *The efficacy of most medicines declines over time.*

ef•fi•cien•cy (ĭ fĭsh′ən sē) *n.* [U] **1.** The condition or quality of being efficient: *Tired people can't work with efficiency.* **2.** The ratio of useful work a machine does to the energy required to operate it: *A car with greater fuel efficiency travels farther per gallon of fuel.*

ef•fi•cient (ĭ fĭsh′ənt) *adj.* Acting or producing effectively with a minimum of waste, expense, or effort: *an efficient worker; an efficient motor.* —**ef•fi′cient•ly** *adv.*

ef•fi•gy (ĕf′ə jē) *n., pl.* **ef•fi•gies. 1.** [C; U] A crude figure or dummy of a hated person, often burned: *Protesters burned the former leader in effigy.* **2.** [C] A likeness or sculpture of a person: *a stone effigy on a tomb.*

ef•flu•ent (ĕf′lōō ənt) *n.* *Formal.* [U] The liquid waste or sewage that flows from a factory or other system: *Effluent from the mill flowed directly into the stream, polluting it.*

ef•fort (ĕf′ərt) *n.* **1.** [C; U] The use of physical or mental energy to do sthg.; exertion: *It took a lot of effort to edit this book.* **2.** [C] An attempt, especially an earnest attempt: *We made an effort to arrive on time.* **3.** [C] Something done or produced through exertion; an achievement: *This painting is the artist's best and latest effort.*

ef•fort•less (ĕf′ərt lĭs) *adj.* Requiring or showing little or no effort: *Watching TV is an effortless activity. The skater glided in effortless turns around the ice.* See Synonyms at **easy.** —**ef′fort•less•ly** *adv.* —**ef′fort•less•ness** *n.* [U]

ef•fu•sive (ĭ fyōō′sĭv) *adj.* Unrestrained or excessive in emotional expression: *His effusive display of gratitude embarrassed his friend.* —**ef•fu′sive•ly** *adv.* —**ef•fu′sive•ness** *n.* [U]

EFL *abbr.* An abbreviation of English as a foreign language.

e.g. *abbr.* An abbreviation of exempli gratia (for example): *Some holidays are celebrated only in the United States, e.g., the Fourth of July.*

egg[1] (ĕg) *n.* **1.** A female sex cell of humans and many kinds of animals from which an embryo develops. **2.** A hard-shelled egg, the contents of which are used for food, especially a chicken egg: *Scrambled eggs are a favorite of mine.* ◆ **egg on (one's) face.** Embarrassment; humiliation: *If you promise that and can't deliver it, you'll end up with egg on your face.* **good egg.** *Informal.* A nice person: *What a good egg she is!* **put** or **have all (one's) eggs in one basket.** To risk everything on a single venture: *Investing all your savings in the new company is putting all your eggs in one basket.*

egg[2] (ĕg) *v.* ◆ **egg on.** *tr.v.* [sep.] To encourage or urge (sbdy.): *If my best friend hadn't egged me on, I never would have tried to ski down that hill.*

egg•beat•er (ĕg′bē′tər) *n.* A kitchen utensil with rotating blades for beating eggs, whipping cream, or mixing ingredients together.

egg•head (ĕg′hĕd′) *n.* *Informal.* An insulting term for sbdy. who is an intellectual.

egg•nog (ĕg′nŏg′) *n.* [C; U] A drink made of milk and beaten eggs, served especially during the Christmas season and often mixed with an alcoholic liquor such as rum or brandy: *They served eggnog at the Christmas party.*

egg·plant (ĕg′plănt′)
n. [C; U] The large egg-
shaped fruit of a bushy
plant, usually having a
purple skin and eaten
cooked.

egg·shell (ĕg′shĕl′) *n.*
1. [C] The thin hard
outer covering of the
egg of a bird or reptile.
2. [U] A light yellowish white color. —*adj.*
Light yellowish white.

eggplant

egg white *n.* [C; U] The transparent part of
an egg.

e·go (ē′gō) *n.*, *pl.* **e·gos. 1.** [C] The awareness of oneself as separate and different from
other things; the self: *a healthy ego.* **2.** [U]
Egotism; conceit: *Self-important people are
often full of ego.*

e·go·cen·tric (ē′gō sĕn′trĭk) *adj.* Concerned
only with oneself; self-centered: *An egocentric
person usually does not work well in a group.*

e·go·ism (ē′gō ĭz′ əm) *n.* [U] The tendency
to think or act with only one's own interests
in mind; selfishness. —**e′go·ist** *n.*

e·go·tism (ē′gə tĭz′əm) *n.* [U] An exaggerated sense of one's own importance; conceit:
*Her idea that she alone runs the company is
sheer egotism.* —**e′go·tist′** *n.* —**e′go·tis′-
ti·cal** *adj.* —**e′go·tis′ti·cal·ly** *adv.*

e·gre·gious (ĭ grē′jəs) *adj.* Extremely bad
or offensive; outrageous: *an egregious error.*
—**e·gre′gious·ly** *adv.* —**e·gre′gious·ness**
n. [U]

e·gress (ē′grĕs′) *n.* [U] *Formal.* **1.** An exit:
*When fire blocked the doorway there was no
egress from the building.* **2.** The right to go
out: *The guard denied them egress.*

eight (āt) *n.* **1.** The number, written 8, that is
equal to 7 + 1. **2.** The eighth in a set or
sequence. —**eight** *adj. & pron.*

eight·een (ā tēn′) *n.* **1.** The number, written
18, that is equal to 17 + 1. **2.** The 18th in a
set or sequence. —**eight·een′** *adj. & pron.*

eight·eenth (ā tēnth′) *n.* **1.** The ordinal
number matching the number 18 in a series.
2. One of 18 equal parts: *One eighteenth of
180 is 10.* —**eight·eenth′** *adj. & adv.*

eighth (ātth *or* āth) *n.* **1.** The ordinal number
matching the number eight in a series. **2.** One
of eight equal parts: *One eighth of 800 is 100.*
—**eighth** *adj. & adv.*

eight·y (ā′tē) *n., pl.* **eight·ies. 1.** The number, written 80, that is equal to 8 × 10. **2.**
eighties. a. Often **Eighties.** The ten years
from 80 to 89 in a century. **b.** A decade or the

numbers from 80 to 89: *My grandfather is in
his eighties.* —**eight′y** *adj. & pron.*

ei·ther (ē′thər *or* ī′thər) *pron.* One or the
other of two: *It was a while before either of
them spoke.* —*conj.* Used before the first of
two or more words or groups of words linked
by *or: Either we go now or we forget about
going.* —*adj.* **1.** One or the other; any one of
two: *Wear either coat.* **2.** One and the other;
each of the two: *Candles stood on either end
of the shelf.* —*adv.* Any more than the other;
also: *I didn't go to the movies, and my friends
didn't either.*

e·jac·u·late (ĭ jăk′yə lāt′) *tr. & intr.v.*
**e·jac·u·lat·ed, e·jac·u·lat·ing, e·jac·
u·lates.** To discharge semen from the penis.
—**e·jac′u·la′tion** *n.* [C; U]

e·ject (ĭ jĕkt′) *tr.v.* **1.** To throw (sbdy./sthg.)
out; expel: *Active volcanoes eject hot ash and
lava.* **2.** To drive (sbdy./sthg.) out; force out:
*The noisy people were ejected from the the-
ater.* —**e·jec′tion** *n.* —**e·jec′tor** *n.*

eke (ēk) *v.* ◆ **eke out.** *tr.v.* [sep.] To get
(sthg.) with great effort or strain: *The farmers
managed to eke out an existence during the
drought.*

EKG *abbr.* An abbreviation of: **1.** Electrocardiogram. **2.** Electrocardiograph.

el. *abbr.* An abbreviation of elevation.

e·lab·o·rate (ĭ lăb′ər ĭt) *adj.* Planned or
made with great attention to many parts or
details; intricate: *We made elaborate preparations for the party.* —*v.* (ĭ lăb′ə rāt′).
**e·lab·o·rat·ed, e·lab·o·rat·ing, e·lab·
o·rates.** *Formal.* —*tr.* To work (sthg.) out
with care and detail; develop thoroughly: *It
may take scientists many years to elaborate a
theory.* —*intr.* To express oneself at greater
length or in greater detail; provide more
information: *The author elaborated on the
difficulty of writing the book.* —**e·lab′o·
rate·ly** *adv.* —**e·lab′o·rate·ness** *n.* [U]
—**e·lab′o·ra′tion** *n.* [U]

e·lapse (ĭ lăps′) *intr.v.* **e·lapsed, e·laps·ing,**

e·laps·es. To pass; go by: *Months elapsed before I heard from my friend again.*

e·las·tic (ĭ lăs′tĭk) *adj.* **1.** Able to return to its original shape after being stretched: *an elastic band.* **2.** Capable of adapting or being adapted to change or a variety of circumstances; flexible: *An elastic interpretation of the rules allows some children to come to school early.* —*n.* **1.** [U] A fabric woven with strands of rubber or a similar synthetic fiber to make it stretch: *Elastic held the sleeves of my jacket around my wrists.* **2.** [C] A rubber band. —**e·las′ti·cal·ly** *adv.*

e·las·tic·i·ty (ĭ lă stĭs′ĭ tē *or* ē′lă stĭs′ĭ tē) *n.* [U] The condition or property of being elastic: *The rubber band broke when it lost its elasticity.*

e·late (ĭ lāt′) *tr.v.* **e·lat·ed, e·lat·ing, e·lates.** To raise the spirits of (sbdy.); make very happy or joyful: *The news of victory elated the candidate's supporters.* —**e·la′tion** (ĭ lā′shən) *n.* [U]

e·lat·ed (ĭ lā′tĭd) *adj.* Joyful; happy; in high spirits: *the elated feeling of winning a race.* —**e·lat′ed·ly** *adv.*

el·bow (ĕl′bō′) *n.* **1.** The joint or bend between the forearm and the upper arm. **2.** Something having a bend or sharp angle, especially a length of pipe that has a sharp bend in it: *The plumber used an elbow to run the pipe around the corner.* —*tr.v.* **1.** To push, jostle, or shove (sbdy.) with the elbows: *She elbowed me in the ribs to get me to stop laughing.* **2.** To make (one's way) by pushing as with the elbows: *The police elbowed their way through the crowd.*

elbow grease *n.* [U] *Informal.* Strenuous physical effort: *Polishing a car requires elbow grease.*

el·bow·room (ĕl′bō rōōm′ *or* ĕl′bō rŏŏm′) *n.* [U] Room to move around; ample space: *Their cramped cubicles didn't give the artists enough elbowroom to work.*

eld·er (ĕl′dər) *adj.* Born before another; older; senior: *my elder sister; an elder statesman.* —*n.* (*usually plural*). **1.** An older person *Children rely on their elders for guidance and support.* **2.** An older influential person of a family, tribe, or community: *a council of elders governing community affairs.*

eld·er·ly (ĕl′dər lē) *adj.* Approaching old age; rather old: *an elderly person.* —*n.* (*used with a plural verb*). Older people considered as a group: *The elderly are a strong political force.*

eld·est (ĕl′dĭst) *adj.* Oldest: *My eldest sister still treats us all as children.*

e·lect (ĭ lĕkt′) *tr.v.* **1.** To choose (sbdy.) by vote for an office or for membership: *The citizens of each state vote to elect two senators.* **2.** To choose or decide (sthg.): *I elected an art course. I elected to take geology, too.* —*adj.* Elected but not yet installed in office:

The governor-elect will take office in January. —*n.* (*used with a plural verb*). A chosen or privileged group: *one of the elect who have influence in the organization.*

e·lec·tion (ĭ lĕk′shən) *n.* **1.** The act of voting for candidates to fill an office or a position: *The election of representatives takes place every two years.* **2.** The fact of being chosen for such an office: *She celebrated her election to the city council.*

e·lec·tive (ĭ lĕk′tĭv) *adj.* **1.** Filled or obtained by election: *The Presidency is an elective office.* **2.** Not required; optional: *Italian is an elective course in my major.* —*n.* An optional course in school: *My electives are music and French.*

e·lec·tor (ĭ lĕk′tôr) *n.* **1.** A person who has the right to vote in an election. **2.** A member of the Electoral College of the United States.

e·lec·tor·al (ĭ lĕk′tər əl) *adj.* Relating to election: *Electoral reforms will make it easier to vote.*

Electoral College *n.* A group of electors chosen by the voters to elect the President and Vice President of the United States. The number of electors each state can have is based on population.

e·lec·tor·ate (ĭ lĕk′tər ĭt) *n.* (*used with a singular or plural verb*). All those persons qualified to vote in an election: *The United States has a huge electorate, but not all voters vote.*

e·lec·tric (ĭ lĕk′trĭk) *adj.* **1.** Also **e·lec·tri·cal** (ĭ lĕk′trĭ kəl). Relating to or operated by electricity: *electric power; an electrical appliance.* **2.** Filled with emotion; exciting; thrilling: *the electric feeling of watching a very close race.* —**e·lec′tri·cal·ly** *adv.*

electrical engineering *n.* [U] The branch of engineering that deals with the practical uses of electricity and their effects. —**electrical engineer** *n.*

e·lec·tri·cian (ĭ lĕk trĭsh′ən *or* ē′lĕk-trĭsh′ən) *n.* A person who installs, maintains, repairs, or operates electric equipment and electrical circuits: *Call an electrician to check the wiring.*

e·lec·tric·i·ty (ĭ lĕk trĭs′ĭ tē *or* ē′lĕk trĭs′-ĭ tē) *n.* [U] **1.** The physical effects resulting from charged particles and their interactions. **2.** Electric current used as a source of power: *Electricity lights our homes.* **3.** Emotional excitement: *Electricity filled the air during the soccer game.*

e·lec·tri·fy (ĭ lĕk′trə fī′) *tr.v.* **e·lec·tri·fied, e·lec·tri·fy·ing, e·lec·tri·fies. 1.** To charge (sthg.) with electricity: *throw the switch to electrify a circuit.* **2.** To wire or equip (sthg.) for the use of electric power: *electrify a building.* **3.** To thrill, startle, or shock (sbdy.): *The actor's performance electrified the audience.* —**e·lec′tri·fi·ca′tion** (ĭ lĕk′trə fĭ kā′shən) *n.* [U]

electro– or **electr–** *pref.* A prefix that means: **1.** Electric: *electromagnet.* **2.** Electric or electrically: *electrocute.*

e·lec·tro·car·di·o·gram (ĭ lĕk'trō kär'dē ə grăm') *n.* The result of an electrocardiograph, used to determine how well a heart is working or what is wrong with it.

e·lec·tro·car·di·o·graph (ĭ lĕk'trō kär'dē ə grăf') *n.* An instrument that records the electrical activity of the heart.

e·lec·tro·cute (ĭ lĕk'trə kyoōt') *tr.v.* **e·lec·tro·cut·ed, e·lec·tro·cut·ing, e·lec·tro·cutes.** To kill or execute (sbdy.) with electricity: *The workers shut off the power to avoid any danger of being electrocuted.* —**e·lec'tro·cu'tion** *n.*

e·lec·trode (ĭ lĕk'trōd') *n.* A conductor through which an electric current enters or leaves a liquid or gas.

e·lec·trol·y·sis (ĭ lĕk trŏl'ĭ sĭs *or* ē'lĕk·trŏl'ĭ sĭs) *n.* [U] **1.** Chemical change, especially decomposition, produced when an electric current is passed through a chemical compound. **2.** Destruction of living tissue, such as the roots of hairs, by an electric current: *permanent hair removal by electrolysis.*

e·lec·tro·lyte (ĭ lĕk'trə līt') *n.* **1.** A substance that when dissolved or melted conducts electricity. **2.** An ion, such as sodium, potassium, magnesium, or chloride, required by cells to regulate the electric charge and flow of water molecules.

e·lec·tro·mag·net (ĭ lĕk'trō măg'nĭt) *n.* A magnet that consists of a coil of insulated wire wrapped around an iron core that becomes magnetized only when an electric current flows through the wire. —**e·lec'tro·mag·net'ic** *adj.*

e·lec·tro·mag·net·ism (ĭ lĕk'trō măg'nĭ tĭz'əm) *n.* [U] **1.** Magnetism produced by an electric charge in motion. **2.** The scientific study of electricity and magnetism and the relationships between them.

e·lec·tro·mo·tive (ĭ lĕk'trō mō'tĭv) *adj.* **1.** Producing an electric current. **2.** Relating to electromotive force.

electromotive force *n.* [U] **1.** A force that produces electric current. **2.** The energy, usually measured in volts, that is converted into electrical form by a battery, generator, or similar device.

e·lec·tron (ĭ lĕk'trŏn') *n.* A subatomic particle with the smallest unit of negative charge, which is equal in strength but opposite in sign to that of a proton. All atoms have electrons grouped around the nucleus.

e·lec·tron·ic (ĭ lĕk trŏn'ĭk *or* ē'lĕk trŏn'ĭk) *adj.* Relating to electrons or electronics: *an electronic calculator; electronic equipment.* —**e·lec·tron'i·cal·ly** *adv.*

electronic mail *n.* [U] **1.** A system for sending messages by computer. **2.** Messages sent or received by this system.

e·lec·tron·ics (ĭ lĕk' trŏn'ĭks *or* ē'lĕk trŏn'ĭks) *n.* [U] *(used with a singular verb).* The study of electrons in motion and the development of devices operated by a controlled flow of electrons: *Electronics has made the computer possible.*

el·e·gance (ĕl'ĭ gəns) *n.* [U] Refinement, grace, and beauty in appearance or behavior: *The old castle still had signs of past elegance in its great staircase.*

el·e·gant (ĕl'ĭ gənt) *adj.* Showing elegance: *elegant clothes; an elegant restaurant.* —**el'e·gant·ly** *adv.*

el·e·ment (ĕl'ə mənt) *n.* **1.** A part of a whole, especially a fundamental or essential part: *The story contains elements of a detective novel and a romance.* **2. elements.** The basic principles: *Composers must learn the elements of music.* **3.** In chemistry, a substance that cannot be broken down into simpler substances by chemical means: *Oxygen, carbon, and sulfur are chemical elements.* See table on pages 292–293. **4. elements.** The forces of the weather, especially the cold, wind, and rain: *The rescuers braved the elements to hunt for the lost children.* **5.** An environment to which a person or thing is suited or adapted: *The sea was as much the sailors' element as the land.*

el·e·men·tal (ĕl'ə mĕn'tl) *adj.* **1.** Of or resembling a force of nature in power or effect: *the elemental fury of the hurricane.* **2.** Fundamental; basic: *Most students are familiar with the elemental concepts of physics.*

el·e·men·ta·ry (ĕl'ə mĕn'tə rē *or* ĕl'ə·mĕn'trē) *adj.* Relating to or involving the basic or simplest aspects of a subject: *an elementary textbook in math.*

elementary school *n.* A school attended for the first five to seven years of a child's formal classroom instruction.

el·e·phant (ĕl'ə fənt) *n.* Either of two mammals of Asia and Africa with thick skin, a long flexible trunk, and long tusks: *Elephants are the largest living land animals.*

el·e·vate (ĕl'ə vāt') *tr.v.* **ele·vat·ed, ele·vat·ing, ele·vates.** **1.** To raise (sbdy./sthg.) to a higher place or position; lift up: *A nurse elevated the head of the bed so the patient could sit up to read.* **2.** To promote (sbdy.) to a higher rank: *The publisher elevated him to editor in chief.*

el·e·vat·ed (ĕl'ə vā'tĭd) *adj.* **1.** Raised or placed above a given level: *The speaker stood on an elevated platform.* **2.** Exalted; dignified: *elevated thought; the elevated position of vice president.*

el•e•va•tion (ĕl′ə vā′shən) *n.* **1.** [C] An elevated place or position: *That hill is the highest elevation for miles around.* **2.** [C] The height to which sthg. is elevated, especially the height above sea level: *The ridge rises to an elevation of 100 meters.* **3.** [U] The act of elevating: *Elevation to a high position in government is a great honor.*

el•e•va•tor (ĕl′ə vā′tər) *n.* An enclosed car, platform, or cage raised or lowered in a vertical shaft to carry people or heavy things from floor to floor in a building: *We took the elevator to the 11th floor.*

e•lev•en (ĭ lĕv′ən) *n.* **1.** A number, written 11, that is equal to 10 + 1. **2.** The eleventh in a set or sequence. —**e•lev′en** *adj. & pron.*

e•lev•enth (ĭ lĕv′ənth) *n.* **1.** The ordinal number matching the number 11 in a series. **2.** One of 11 equal parts: *One eleventh of 33 is 3.* —**e•lev′enth** *adj. & adv.*

eleventh hour *n.* [U] The latest possible time: *They waited until the eleventh hour to buy tickets for the concert.*

elf (ĕlf) *n., pl.* **elves** (ĕlvz). A tiny, mythical creature with magical powers. —**elf′in,** —**elf′ish** *adj.* —**elf′ish•ly** *adv.*

e•lic•it (ĭ lĭs′ĭt) *tr.v.* To bring (sthg.) out; evoke: *The lawyer elicited the truth from the witness through careful questioning.*

HOMONYMS: elicit, illicit (illegal).

---

el•i•gi•ble (ĕl′ĭ jə bəl) *adj.* Qualified or suited: *Eligible voters may go to the polls to vote on election day.* —**el′i•gi•bil′i•ty** *n.* [U]

e•lim•i•nate (ĭ lĭm′ə nāt′) *tr.v.* **e•lim•i•nat•ed, e•lim•i•nat•ing, e•lim•i•nates.** **1.** To get rid of (sbdy./sthg.); remove: *We must make greater efforts to eliminate disease and poverty.* **2.** To leave out or omit (sbdy./sthg.) from consideration; reject: *The police eliminated two of the four suspects in the case.* **3.** *Formal.* To rid the body of (waste products); excrete.

e•lim•i•na•tion (ĭ lĭm′ə nā′shən) *n.* [U] The act of eliminating: *elimination of language barriers; elimination from the contest.*

e•lite (ĭ lēt′ *or* ā lēt′) *n.* [U] *(used with a plural verb).* Those considered as the best, superior, or wealthiest members of a society or group: *the elite of the sports world.* —**e•lite′** *adj.*

e•lit•ism (ĭ lē′tĭz′əm *or* ā lē′tĭz′əm) *n.* [U] The belief that certain persons of a group deserve special treatment because they are superior to others. —**e•lit′ist** *adj. & n.*

e•lix•ir (ĭ lĭk′sər) *n.* **1.** A sweetened and flavored solution of alcohol and water taken as medicine. **2.** A substance believed to have the power to cure all ills: *selling phony elixirs to gullible patients.*

elk (ĕlk) *n.* A type of very large deer.

ell (ĕl) *n.* A wing of a building at right angles to the main structure.

e•lipse (ĭ lĭps′) *n.* A geometric shape that forms a closed curve shaped like an oval with both ends alike. —**el•lip′ti•cal** (ĭ lĭp′-tĭ kəl) *adj.*

ellipse

el•lip•sis (ĭ lĭp′sĭs) *n., pl.* **el•lip•ses** (ĭ lĭp′-sēz). A mark or series of marks (...) used in writing or printing to show the omission of a word or phrase.

elm (ĕlm) *n.* **1.** [C] A tall shade tree with curving branches. **2.** [U] The hard wood of such a tree.

e•lon•gate (ĭ lông′gāt′ *or* ĭ lŏng′gāt′) *tr.v.* **e•lon•gat•ed, e•lon•gat•ing, e•lon•gates.** To make (sthg.) longer; lengthen: *The artist often elongates faces and figures in cartoons.* —*adj.* Or **elongated.** Long and thin; lengthened: *an elongated shape.* —**e•lon′-ga′tion** *n.* [U]

e•lope (ĭ lōp′) *intr.v.* **e•loped, e•lop•ing, e•lopes.** To run away with a lover to get married: *They eloped to avoid the expense of a big wedding.* —**e•lope′ment** *n.*

el•o•quence (ĕl′ə kwəns) *n.* [U] **1.** Persuasive powerful speaking: *The lawyer's eloquence influenced the jury.* **2.** The skill or power of using such speaking: *a poet known for her eloquence.* —**el′o•quent** *adj.* —**el′o•quent•ly** *adv.*

else (ĕls) *adj.* **1.** Other; different: *Somebody else can have my share.* **2.** Additional; more: *Would you like something else to eat?* —*adv.* **1.** Differently: *How else could it have been done?* **2.** If not; otherwise: *Run, else you will be caught in the rain.* ♦ **or else.** An expression used to indicate the need to do sthg. or suffer negative consequences: *Do your homework for tomorrow, or else!*

else•where (ĕls′wâr′) *adv.* In or to a different or another place: *We decided to go elsewhere.*

e•lude (ĭ lood′) *tr.v.* **e•lud•ed, e•lud•ing, e•ludes.** **1.** To avoid or escape from (sbdy./sthg.) by skill or daring: *The fox eluded the hunters.* **2.** To escape the understanding or notice of (sbdy.): *Very small details often elude us.*

e•lu•sive (ĭ loo′sĭv) *adj.* **1.** Tending to escape: *an elusive butterfly.* **2.** Hard to define or describe: *an elusive phrase.* —**e•lu′sive•ly** *adv.* —**e•lu′sive•ness** *n.*

HOMONYMS: elusive, illusive (unreal).

---

elves (ĕlvz) *n.* Plural of **elf.**

em— *pref.* Variant of **en—.**

'em (əm) *pron. Informal.* Them, especially in spoken language.

e•ma•ci•at•ed (ĭ mā′shē ā təd) *adj.* Extremely thin, especially from starvation. —**e•ma′ci•a′tion** *n.* [U]

PERIODIC TABLE OF THE ELEMENTS

The periodic table arranges the chemical elements in two ways. The first is by atomic number, the number of protons in each element's nucleus. The elements are arranged so that their atomic numbers increase as you read across each row, or period, from left to right. The second is by chemical families. Each column, or group, contains elements with similar chemical properties.

The first periodic table was devised by Dmitri Mendeleev in 1869. At that time, only 63 elements were known. Mendeleev left empty spaces in his table to make the known elements fit in the correct columns. He correctly predicted that the spaces would later be filled in as more elements were discovered. The modern periodic table is basically the same as Mendeleev's chart, with some improvements.

In the table as shown here, elements that are nonmetals have light shading. Darker shading indicates the metalloids. Elements with no shading are metals. The lanthanide series (elements 57–71) and the actinide series (elements 89–103) do not match the way the other elements fit into the table. They are placed below the main body of the table to make it easier to read.

Period										
1	1 **H** Hydrogen									
2	3 **Li** Lithium	4 **Be** Beryllium								
3	11 **Na** Sodium	12 **Mg** Magnesium								
4	19 **K** Potassium	20 **Ca** Calcium	21 **Sc** Scandium	22 **Ti** Titanium	23 **V** Vanadium	24 **Cr** Chromium	25 **Mn** Manganese	26 **Fe** Iron	27 **Co** Cobalt
5	37 **Rb** Rubidium	38 **Sr** Strontium	39 **Y** Yttrium	40 **Zr** Zirconium	41 **Nb** Niobium	42 **Mo** Molybdenum	43 **Tc** Technetium	44 **Ru** Ruthenium	45 **Rh** Rhodium
6	55 **Cs** Cesium	56 **Ba** Barium	57–71* **Lanthanides**	72 **Hf** Hafnium	73 **Ta** Tantalum	74 **W** Tungsten	75 **Re** Rhenium	76 **Os** Osmium	77 **Ir** Iridium
7	87 **Fr** Francium	88 **Ra** Radium	89–103** **Actinides**	104	105				

* LANTHANIDES	57 **La** Lanthanum	58 **Ce** Cerium	59 **Pr** Praseodymium	60 **Nd** Neodymium	61 **Pm** Promethium	62 **Sm** Samarium	63 **Eu** Europium

** ACTINIDES	89 **Ac** Actinium	90 **Th** Thorium	91 **Pa** Protactinium	92 **U** Uranium	93 **Np** Neptunium	94 **Pu** Plutonium	95 **Am** Americium

TABLE OF THE ELEMENTS

ELEMENT	SYMBOL	ATOMIC NUMBER	ELEMENT	SYMBOL	ATOMIC NUMBER	ELEMENT	SYMBOL	ATOMIC NUMBER	ELEMENT	SYMBOL	ATOMIC NUMBER
Actinium	Ac	89	Cadmium	Cd	48	Element 104	–	104	Holmium	Ho	67
Aluminum	Al	13	Calcium	Ca	20	Element 105	–	105	Hydrogen	H	1
Americium	Am	95	Californium	Cf	98	Erbium	Er	68	Indium	In	49
Antimony	Sb	51	Carbon	C	6	Europium	Eu	63	Iodine	I	53
Argon	Ar	18	Cerium	Ce	58	Fermium	Fm	100	Iridium	Ir	77
Arsenic	As	33	Cesium	Cs	55	Fluorine	F	9	Iron	Fe	26
Astatine	At	85	Chlorine	Cl	17	Francium	Fr	87	Krypton	Kr	36
Barium	Ba	56	Chromium	Cr	24	Gadolinium	Gd	64	Lanthanum	La	57
Berkelium	Bk	97	Cobalt	Co	27	Gallium	Ga	31	Lawrencium	Lr	103
Beryllium	Be	4	Copper	Cu	29	Germanium	Ge	32	Lead	Pb	82
Bismuth	Bi	83	Curium	Cm	96	Gold	Au	79	Lithium	Li	3
Boron	B	5	Dysprosium	Dy	66	Hafnium	Hf	72	Lutetium	Lu	71
Bromine	Br	35	Einsteinium	Es	99	Helium	He	2	Magnesium	Mg	12

E

INERT GASES

BORON GROUP	CARBON GROUP	NITROGEN GROUP	OXYGEN GROUP	HALOGENS	2 **He** Helium
5 **B** Boron	6 **C** Carbon	7 **N** Nitrogen	8 **O** Oxygen	9 **F** Fluorine	10 **Ne** Neon
13 **Al** Aluminum	14 **Si** Silicon	15 **P** Phosphorus	16 **S** Sulfur	17 **Cl** Chlorine	18 **Ar** Argon

28 **Ni** Nickel	29 **Cu** Copper	30 **Zn** Zinc	31 **Ga** Gallium	32 **Ge** Germanium	33 **As** Arsenic	34 **Se** Selenium	35 **Br** Bromine	36 **Kr** Krypton
46 **Pd** Palladium	47 **Ag** Silver	48 **Cd** Cadmium	49 **In** Indium	50 **Sn** Tin	51 **Sb** Antimony	52 **Te** Tellurium	53 **I** Iodine	54 **Xe** Xenon
78 **Pt** Platinum	79 **Au** Gold	80 **Hg** Mercury	81 **Tl** Thallium	82 **Pb** Lead	83 **Bi** Bismuth	84 **Po** Polonium	85 **At** Astatine	86 **Rn** Radon

64 **Gd** Gadolinium	65 **Tb** Terbium	66 **Dy** Dysprosium	67 **Ho** Holmium	68 **Er** Erbium	69 **Tm** Thulium	70 **Yb** Ytterbium	71 **Lu** Lutetium
96 **Cm** Curium	97 **Bk** Berkelium	98 **Cf** Californium	99 **Es** Einsteinium	100 **Fm** Fermium	101 **Md** Mendelevium	102 **No** Nobelium	103 **Lr** Lawrencium

ELEMENT	SYMBOL	ATOMIC NUMBER	ELEMENT	SYMBOL	ATOMIC NUMBER	ELEMENT	SYMBOL	ATOMIC NUMBER	ELEMENT	SYMBOL	ATOMIC NUMBER
Manganese	Mn	25	Palladium	Pd	46	Rubidium	Rb	37	Terbium	Tb	65
Mendelevium	Md	101	Phosphorus	P	15	Ruthenium	Ru	44	Thallium	Tl	81
Mercury	Hg	80	Platinum	Pt	78	Samarium	Sm	62	Thorium	Th	90
Molybdenum	Mo	42	Plutonium	Pu	94	Scandium	Sc	21	Thulium	Tm	69
Neodymium	Nd	60	Polonium	Po	84	Selenium	Se	34	Tin	Sn	50
Neon	Ne	10	Potassium	K	19	Silicon	Si	14	Titanium	Ti	22
Neptunium	Np	93	Praseodymium	Pr	59	Silver	Ag	47	Tungsten	W	74
Nickel	Ni	28	Promethium	Pm	61	Sodium	Na	11	Uranium	U	92
Niobium	Nb	41	Protactinium	Pa	91	Strontium	Sr	38	Vanadium	V	23
Nitrogen	N	7	Radium	Ra	88	Sulfur	S	16	Xenon	Xe	54
Nobelium	No	102	Radon	Rn	86	Tantalum	Ta	73	Ytterbium	Yb	70
Osmium	Os	76	Rhenium	Re	75	Technetium	Tc	43	Yttrium	Y	39
Oxygen	O	8	Rhodium	Rh	45	Tellurium	Te	52	Zinc	Zn	30
									Zirconium	Zr	40

e-mail or **email** (ē′māl′) *n.* [U] **1.** A system for sending messages by computer; electronic mail. **2.** Messages sent or received through a computer system: *I have to read my e-mail.* —*tr.v.* **1.** To send electronic messages to (sbdy.): *She e-mailed her boss.* **2.** To send (sthg.) as e-mail: *I'll e-mail the information to everyone on the committee.*

em·a·nate (ĕm′ə nāt′) *intr.* & *tr.v.* **em·a·nat·ed, em·a·nat·ing, em·a·nates.** *Formal.* To come or send forth, as from a source: *The sound of a piano emanated from the house.*

e·man·ci·pate (ĭ măn′sə pāt′) *tr.v.* **e·man·ci·pat·ed, e·man·ci·pat·ing, e·man·ci·pates.** To free (sbdy.) from slavery or oppression; liberate: *U.S. President Abraham Lincoln emancipated the slaves in 1863.* —**e·man′ci·pa′tor** *n.* —**e·man′ci·pa′tion** *n.* [U]

em·balm (ĕm bäm′) *tr.v.* To treat (a dead body) with preservatives in order to prevent or slow decay: *Ancient Egyptians embalmed their kings.* —**em·balm′er** *n.*

em·bank·ment (ĕm băngk′mənt) *n.* A mound of earth or stone built to hold back water or to support a roadway: *We climbed down the embankment and waded into the river.*

em·bar·go (ĕm bär′gō) *n., pl.* **em·bar·goes.** A prohibition by a government on some or all trade with a foreign nation: *an embargo on trade with Cuba.* —*tr.v.* To place an embargo on (sthg.): *The Senate will embargo imports if that country doesn't sign the agreement.*

em·bark (ĕm bärk′) *intr.v.* **1.** To go aboard an aircraft or a ship: *The captain ordered the passengers to embark, as the ship was leaving port soon.* **2.** [on] To set out on a venture; begin: *embark on a campaign to clean up the environment.* See Synonyms at **begin.** —**em′bar·ka′tion** (ĕm′bär kā′shən) *n.* [C; U]

em·bar·rass (ĕm băr′əs) *tr.v.* To cause (sbdy.) to feel self-conscious or uncomfortable; disconcert: *Not knowing the answer to the question embarrassed me.*

em·bar·rassed (ĕm băr′əst) *adj.* Made to feel ashamed or uncomfortable: *The embarrassed child fled the playground.*

em·bar·rass·ing (ĕm băr′ə sĭng) *adj.* Causing shame or discomfort: *an embarrassing remark.* —**em·bar′rass·ing·ly** *adv.*

em·bar·rass·ment (ĕm băr′əs mənt) *n.* **1.** [U] The condition of being embarrassed: *My face turned red with embarrassment.* **2.** [C] Something that embarrasses: *Their argument in public was an embarrassment.*

em·bas·sy (ĕm′bə sē) *n., pl.* **em·bas·sies. 1.** A building containing the offices of an ambas-

sador and staff: *We went to the embassy to get our visas.* **2.** A staff of diplomatic representatives headed by an ambassador.

em·bat·tled (ĕm băt′ld) *adj.* **1.** Prepared for battle or engaged in battle: *the embattled countries of Europe during World War II.* **2.** Suffering from criticism or controversy: *an embattled candidate fighting to win election.*

em·bed (ĕm bĕd′) *tr.v.* **em·bed·ded, em·bed·ding, em·beds.** To fix (sthg.) firmly in a surrounding mass or object: *The splinter was deeply embedded in my finger.*

em·bel·lish (ĕm bĕl′ĭsh) *tr.v.* **1.** To make (sthg.) beautiful by ornamentation; decorate: *embellish a tablecloth with fine designs.* **2.** To add imaginative details to (sthg.): *embellish a true story with some invented characters.* —**em·bel′lish·ment** *n.* [C; U]

em·ber (ĕm′bər) *n.* A piece of glowing coal or wood, as in a dying fire: *The forest fire started from an ember.*

em·bez·zle (ĕm bĕz′əl) *tr.v.* **em·bez·zled, em·bez·zling, em·bez·zles.** To take (money) for one's own use in violation of a trust: *The bank president was caught embezzling money from the account.* —**em·bez′·zle·ment** *n.* [U] —**em·bez′zler** *n.*

em·bit·tered (ĕm bĭt′ərd) *adj.* Having bitter feelings: *The long feud with his brothers left him embittered and alone.*

em·bla·zon (ĕm blā′zən) *tr.v.* **1.** To decorate (a surface) richly with bold markings: *The players wore jackets emblazoned across the back with the team's name.* **2.** To make (sthg.) brilliant with colors: *Fireworks emblazoned the sky.*

em·blem (ĕm′bləm) *n.* An object or a representation that functions as a symbol: *The bald eagle is an emblem of the United States.*

em·blem·at·ic (ĕm′blə măt′ĭk) *adj.* Relating to or serving as an emblem; symbolic: *The dove is emblematic of peace.*

em·bod·i·ment (ĕm bŏd′ē mənt) *n.* [U] *Formal.* **1.** The act of embodying or the state of being embodied. **2.** A person or thing that embodies: *That dancer is the embodiment of grace.*

em·bod·y (ĕm bŏd′ē) *tr.v.* **em·bod·ied, em·bod·y·ing, em·bod·ies. 1.** To give a bodily form to (sthg.); personify: *A hero embodies our ideal of bravery.* **2.** To make (sthg.) part of a system or whole; incorporate: *Our constitution embodies a plan for democratic government.*

em·boss (ĕm bôs′ *or* ĕm bŏs′) *tr.v.* To decorate (sthg.) with a raised design: *emboss a leather belt with a name.*

em·brace (ĕm brās′) *v.* **em·braced, em·brac·ing, em·brac·es.** —*tr.* **1.** To hold (sbdy./sthg.) close with the arms, usually as a

---

ă–cat; ā–pay; âr–care; ä–father; ĕ–get; ē–be; ĭ–sit; ī–nice; îr–here; ŏ–got; ō–go; ô–saw; oi–boy; ou–out; ŏŏ–took; ōō–boot; ŭ–cut; ûr–word; th–thin; *th*–this; hw–when; zh–vision; ə–about; N–French bon

sign of affection; hug: *embrace a child.* **2.** To surround (sbdy./sthg.): *The warm water of the pool embraced us.* **3.** To accept or take (sthg.) up willingly: *The newcomers embraced the hectic life of the big city.* —*intr.* To join in an embrace: *The twins embraced at their reunion.* —*n.* The act of holding close with the arms; a hug: *the loving embrace of old friends.*

em·broi·der (ĕm broi′dər) *v.* —*tr.* **1.** To decorate (sthg.) with needlework: *embroider a shirt with initials.* **2.** To make (sthg.) by means of needlework: *embroider a design on a handkerchief.* **3.** To add imaginative details to (sthg.): *The author embroidered the general's biography with exciting dialogue.* —*intr.* To make needlework: *My grandmother likes to embroider in her spare time.*

em·broi·der·y (ĕm broi′də rē) *n.* [U] **1.** The act or art of embroidering. **2.** A piece of embroidered fabric: *He has embroidery on most of his shirts.*

em·broil (ĕm broil′) *tr.v.* [in] To involve (sbdy.) in an argument: *The reporter embroiled the candidate in a debate.*

em·bry·o (ĕm′brē ō′) *n., pl.* **em·bry·os.** An organism in its earliest stages of development, especially before it has reached a distinctively recognizable form.

em·bry·on·ic (ĕm′brē ŏn′ĭk) *adj.* **1.** Relating to an embryo: *the stages of embryonic development.* **2.** In an early undeveloped state: *an embryonic outline.*

em·cee (ĕm′sē′) *n.* A master of ceremonies. —*tr. & intr.v.* **em·ceed, em·cee·ing, em·cees.** To serve as master of ceremonies of: *My sister emceed our variety show. The director asked me to emcee because of my clear speaking voice.*

em·er·ald (ĕm′ər əld *or* ĕm′rəld) *n.* **1.** [C] A brilliant green transparent mineral that is used as a gem. **2.** [U] A strong yellowish green color. —*adj.* Of a strong yellowish green color: *We sailed on the emerald sea.*

e·merge (ĭ mûrj′) *intr.v.* **e·merged, e·merg·ing, e·merg·es.** **1.** To rise out of sthg., such as water: *Sea mammals must emerge from the water to breathe.* **2.** To come out or forward: *The new nation soon emerged as an important power.* **3.** To become known or visible: *The truth emerged at the hearing.*

e·mer·gence (ĭ mûr′jəns) *n.* [U] The act of emerging: *the emergence of a butterfly from a cocoon; emergence of the truth under questioning.*

e·mer·gen·cy (ĭ mûr′jən sē) *n., pl.* **e·mer·gen·cies.** A serious situation that happens suddenly and calls for immediate action: *A fire extinguisher is kept in the hall for use in case of an emergency.*

e·mer·gent (ĭ mûr′jənt) *adj.* Coming into existence, view, or attention: *an emergent political leadership.*

e·mer·i·tus (ĭ mĕr′ĭ təs) *adj.* Retired but keeping an honorary title: *a professor emeritus.*

em·i·grant (ĕm′ĭ grənt) *n.* A person who emigrates: *The United States accepts emigrants from other countries.*

em·i·grate (ĕm′ĭ grāt′) *intr.v.* **em·i·grat·ed, em·i·grat·ing, em·i·grates.** To leave one country or region to settle in another: *My parents emigrated from Japan.*

em·i·gra·tion (ĕm′ĭ grā′shən) *n.* [C; U] The act of emigrating: *Emigration has brought many people to the United States.*

em·i·nence (ĕm′ə nəns) *n.* [U] A position of great distinction or superiority: *She rose to eminence as a scientist.*

em·i·nent (ĕm′ə nənt) *adj.* Standing out above others in performance, character, or rank: *an eminent surgeon.* —**em′i·nent·ly** *adv.*

e·mir (ĕ mîr′ *or* ĭ mîr′ *or* ā mîr′) *n.* A prince or governor, especially in the Middle East.

e·mir·ate (ĕ′mər ĭt *or* ĭ mîr′ĭt *or* ĭ mîr′āt′) *n.* **1.** [U] The office of an emir. **2.** [C] The nation or territory ruled by an emir.

em·is·sar·y (ĕm′ĭ sĕr′ē) *n., pl.* **em·is·sar·ies.** A person sent on a mission as the representative of another: *The President sent an emissary to discuss the terms of a new trade agreement.*

e·mis·sion (ĭ mĭsh′ən) *n.* **1.** [U] The act of emitting: *For environmental safety we must try to reduce the factory's emission of fumes and smoke.* **2.** [C] *(usually plural).* Something that is emitted: *Harmful emissions from automobiles kill plants.*

e·mit (ĭ mĭt′) *tr.v.* **e·mit·ted, e·mit·ting, e·mits.** **1.** To release or send out (matter or energy): *Volcanoes emit lava and hot gases.* **2.** To give or let out (a sound); express: *The baby emitted a cry.*

e·mol·lient (ĭ mŏl′yənt) *adj.* Softening and soothing, especially to the skin: *an emollient cream.* —*n.* Something that softens and soothes the skin: *Various oils act as emollients.*

e·mo·tion (ĭ mō′shən) *n.* [C; U] A feeling that arises without conscious effort, such as love, sorrow, happiness, or anger: *He read the lines of the poem with great emotion. The child had trouble controlling her emotions.* See Synonyms at **feeling.**

e·mo·tion·al (ĭ mō′shə nəl) *adj.* **1.** Relating to emotion: *an emotional conflict.* **2.** Easily affected by emotion: *an emotional person who is easily upset.* —**e·mo′tion·al·ly** *adv.*

em·pa·thy (ĕm′pə thē) *n.* [U] Understanding of another's situation, feelings, and motives: *empathy between parent and child; empathy for the novel's main character.*

em·per·or (ĕm′pər ər) *n.* A man who is the ruler of an empire.

em·pha·sis (ĕm′fə sĭs) *n., pl.* **em·pha·ses** (ĕm′fə sēz′). [C; U] **1.** Special forcefulness

E

of expression that gives importance or focus: *a lecture on computers with emphasis on new software.* **2.** Stress given to a syllable, word, or phrase: *Put the emphasis on the first syllable of* father.

em•pha•size (ĕm′fə sīz′) *tr.v.* **em•pha•sized, em•pha•siz•ing, em•pha•siz•es.** To give emphasis to (sthg.); stress: *You can emphasize an idea by repeating it in several different ways.*

em•phat•ic (ĕm făt′ĭk) *adj.* **1.** Expressed or performed with emphasis: *an emphatic nod of the head.* **2.** Forceful and definite in expression or action: *an emphatic person.* —**em•phat′i•cal•ly** *adv.*

em•phy•se•ma (ĕm′fĭ sē′mə *or* ĕm′fĭ zē′mə) *n.* [U] A disease that affects the lungs, resulting in severe difficulty breathing.

em•pire (ĕm′pīr′) *n.* **1.** A group of territories or nations headed by a single authority: *the empire of Alexander the Great.* **2.** A group of businesses united under one authority: *a publishing empire of newspapers and magazines.*

em•pir•i•cal (ĕm pîr′ĭ kəl) *adj.* Coming from observation or experiment rather than theory: *empirical results that support the hypothesis.* —**em•pir′i•cal•ly** *adv.*

em•ploy (ĕm ploi′) *tr.v.* **1.** To put (sbdy.) to work: *The store employs many salespeople.* **2.** To put (sbdy./sthg.) to use: *They employed all their skills to build the bridge.* —*n.* [U] The condition of being employed: *in the employ of the government; hundreds of people in their employ.* —**em•ploy′a•ble** *adj.*

em•ploy•ee (ĕm ploi′ē *or* ĕm′ploi ē′) *n.* A person who works for another in return for money or other compensation: *The store owner treats her employees well.*

em•ploy•er (ĕm ploi′ər) *n.* A person or business that employs people for money or other compensation: *The workers took their complaints to their employer.*

em•ploy•ment (ĕm ploi′mənt) *n.* [U] **1.** The act of employing: *the employment of new technology in industry.* **2.** The work in which a person is engaged; an occupation: *He found employment as a carpenter.*

em•po•ri•um (ĕm pôr′ē əm) *n.* **1.** A place where various goods are bought and sold; a marketplace. **2.** A large retail store or place of business.

em•pow•er (ĕm pou′ər) *tr.v.* To invest (sbdy.) with power, especially legal power or official authority: *The state legislature empowered the governor to raise taxes.*

em•press (ĕm′prĭs) *n.* **1.** A woman who is the ruler of an empire. **2.** The wife or widow of an emperor.

emp•ty (ĕmp′tē) *adj.* **emp•ti•er, emp•ti•est.** **1.** Holding or containing nothing: *an*

empty box; an empty gas tank. **2.** Not occupied or used by anyone; vacant: *an empty house; an empty parking lot.* **3.** Lacking force or power: *an empty threat.* **4.** Lacking purpose or substance; meaningless: *Everything you said was empty talk.* —*v.* **emp•tied, emp•ty•ing, emp•ties.** —*tr.* To remove the contents of (sthg.): *I emptied the dishwasher.* —*intr.* **1.** To become empty: *The sink emptied when the plumber opened the drain.* **2.** To discharge or flow out: *The river empties into a bay.* —*n., pl.* **emp•ties.** *Informal.* An empty beverage container: *We recycled the empties.* —**emp′ti•ly** *adv.* —**emp′ti•ness** *n.* [U]

SYNONYMS: empty, vacant, blank, void, bare. These adjectives describe what contains nothing and therefore lacks what it could have or should have. **Empty** means having no contents or substance: *I thought there were some cherries left, but the bowl was empty.* **Vacant** can mean not occupied: *There are many vacant seats left in the auditorium.* **Blank** means missing sthg. meaningful or important, especially on a surface: *Every poem starts out as a blank piece of paper.* **Void** means absolutely empty: *The guard's face was void of all expression.* **Bare** means lacking surface covering or detail: *We found bare walls without paint or wallpaper.* It also means stripped of contents: *I need to go to the supermarket; the kitchen shelves are all bare.*

---

emp•ty-hand•ed (ĕmp′tē hăn′dĭd) *adj.* **1.** Holding or bringing nothing: *They arrived at the birthday party empty-handed.* **2.** Having received or gained nothing: *We came out of the meeting empty-handed.*

em•u•late (ĕm′yə lāt′) *tr.v.* **em•u•lat•ed, em•u•lat•ing, em•u•lates.** To try to equal or do better than (sbdy./sthg.), especially through imitation: *I tried to emulate the expert's style.* —**em′u•la′tion** *n.* [U]

e•mul•si•fy (ĭ mŭl′sə fī′) *tr.v.* **e•mul•si•fied, e•mul•si•fy•ing, e•mul•si•fies.** To make (sthg.) into an emulsion: *Soap emulsifies oils in warm water.* —**e•mul′si•fi•ca′tion** (ĭ mŭl′sə fĭ kā′shən) [U]

e•mul•sion (ĭ mŭl′shən) *n.* [C; U] **1.** A suspension of small droplets of one liquid in another with which the first does not mix, as the suspension of cream in homogenized milk. **2.** The coating of a photographic film or paper that is sensitive to light.

en— *or* **em—** *or* **in—** *pref.* A prefix that means: **1.** To put into or onto: *endanger.* **2.** To cover or provide with: *encase.* **3.** To cause to be: *endear.* **4.** Thoroughly: *entangle.*

—**en**[1] *suff.* A suffix that means: **1.** To cause to

ă–cat; ā–pay; âr–care; ä–father; ĕ–get; ē–be; ĭ–sit; ī–nice; îr–here; ŏ–got; ō–go; ô–saw; oi–boy; ou–out; o͞o–took; o͞o–boot; ŭ–cut; ûr–word; th–thin; *th*–this; hw–when; zh–vision; ə–about; N–French bon

be: *cheapen.* **2.** To become: *redden.* **3.** To cause to have: *hearten.* **4.** To come to have: *lengthen.*

WORD BUILDING: —en[1] and —en[2] The basic meaning of the suffix —en[1] is "to cause to be" or "to become." When added to nouns and adjectives, —en[1] forms verbs: **threaten, widen, soften.** The suffix —en[2], meaning "made of; resembling," is an adjective suffix. That is, —en[2] changes nouns into adjectives: **wooden, golden.**

—en² *suff.* A suffix that means made of or resembling: *earthen; wooden.*

en•a•ble (ĕ nā′bəl) *tr.v.* **en•a•bled, en•a•bling, en•a•bles.** To give (sbdy./sthg.) the ability or opportunity to do sthg.: *The new computer system enables the store owners to keep better records of their merchandise.*

en•act (ĕn ăkt′) *tr.v.* To make (sthg.) into law: *The Senate enacted a recycling bill.* —**en•act′ment** *n.* [C; U]

e•nam•el (ĭ năm′əl) *n.* **1.** [U] A glassy coating baked onto the surface of metal, porcelain, or pottery for decoration or protection. **2.** [C; U] A paint that dries to a hard glossy surface. **3.** [U] The hard substance that covers the outer part of a tooth. —*tr.v.* To coat or decorate (sthg.) with enamel: *a bracelet of enameled beads.*

en•am•ored (ĭ năm′ərd) *adj.* [with; of] *Formal.* Inspired with love; captivated: *We were enamored with the beautiful landscape.*

en•camp (ĕn kămp′) *v.* —*intr.* To set up camp or live in a camp: *encamp in the woods.* —*tr.* To provide living space for (sbdy.) in a camp: *encamp soldiers.*

en•camp•ment (ĕn kămp′mənt) *n.* **1.** [U] The act of encamping. **2.** [C] A camp or campsite: *The encampment is just down the road.*

en•cap•su•late (ĕn kăp′sə lāt′) *tr.v.* **en•cap•su•lat•ed, en•cap•su•lat•ing, en•cap•su•lates.** **1.** To enclose (sthg.) in or as if in a capsule: *Manufacturers encapsulate drugs to make them easier to swallow.* **2.** To express (sthg.) in a brief summary: *The statement encapsulated the long committee report.* —**en•cap′su•la′tion** *n.* [C; U]

en•case (ĕn kās′) *tr.v.* **en•cased, en•cas•ing, en•cas•es.** To enclose (sthg.) in or as if in a case: *The skull encases the brain.*

—ence *suff.* A suffix that means: **1.** State or condition: *dependence.* **2.** Action: *emergence.*

en•ceph•a•li•tis (ĕn sĕf′ə lī′tĭs) *n.* [U] Inflammation of the brain.

en•chant (ĕn chănt′) *tr.v.* **1.** To attract and delight (sbdy.); charm: *The play enchanted everyone who saw it.* **2.** To cast a spell on (sbdy./sthg.); bewitch: *In fairy tales, witches often enchant princes.* —**en•chant′er** *n.* —**en•chant′ment** *n.* [C; U]

en•chant•ed (ĕn chănt′əd) *adj.* Under a magic spell: *an enchanted castle.*

en•chant•ing (ĕn chăn′tĭng) *adj.* Having the power to enchant; charming: *an enchanting melody.*

en•chi•la•da (ĕn′chə lä′də) *n.* A rolled tortilla with a cheese or meat filling and served with a spicy sauce.

en•cir•cle (ĕn sûr′kəl) *tr.v.* **en•cir•cled, en•cir•cling, en•cir•cles.** To form a circle around (sbdy./sthg.); surround: *Trees encircled the house.*

en•clave (ĕn′klāv′ *or* ŏn′klāv′) *n.* **1.** A country or part of a country that lies completely within the boundaries of another. **2.** A distinctly separated area enclosed within a larger unit: *ethnic enclaves in a large city.*

en•close (ĕn klōz′) *tr.v.* **en•closed, en•clos•ing, en•clos•es** **1.** To surround (sthg.) on all sides; close in: *A high fence encloses the yard.* **2.** To contain (sthg.), especially to shelter: *We enclosed the porch so that we could use it in the winter.* **3.** To insert (sthg.) in the same envelope or package: *I enclosed a check for twenty-five dollars with the order.*

en•clo•sure (ĕn klō′zhər) *n.* **1.** [U] The act of enclosing: *enclosure of a payment in an envelope.* **2.** [C] Something enclosed: *a garden in the middle of the enclosure; a business letter with enclosures.* **3.** [C] Something that encloses, as a wall or fence: *The zoo had a high enclosure to keep the animals in.*

en•code (ĕn kōd′) *tr.v.* **en•cod•ed, en•cod•ing, en•codes.** To put (a message, for example) into code: *The spy encoded the note.* —**en•cod′er** *n.*

en•com•pass (ĕn kŭm′pəs) *tr.v.* **1.** To form a circle or ring about (sthg.); surround: *Tall fences encompass the garden.* **2.** To include (sthg.): *The report encompassed a number of different subjects.*

en•core (ŏn′kôr′) *n.* An additional performance in response to a demand by an audience, usually expressed by applause: *The singer came back on stage for an encore.* —*interj.* An expression used to demand an additional performance: *The audience shouted "Encore!"*

en•coun•ter (ĕn koun′tər) *n.* **1.** An unexpected meeting: *a frightening encounter with a bear.* **2.** A hostile meeting or confrontation: *an encounter between rival gangs.* —*tr.v.* **1.** To meet (sbdy./sthg.), especially unexpectedly: *She encountered a snake on the path.* **2.** To meet with or come up against (sthg.): *encounter many problems.*

en•cour•age (ĕn kûr′ĭj *or* ĕn kŭr′ĭj) *tr.v.* **en•cour•aged, en•cour•ag•ing, en•cour•ag•es.** **1.** To give hope, courage, or confidence to (sbdy.): *The good grade encouraged me to study more.* **2.** To stimulate (sthg.): *Fertilizer encourages the growth of plants.* —**en•cour′age•ment** *n.* [U]

en•cour•ag•ing (ĕn kûr′ə jĭng *or* ĕn-kŭr′ə jĭng) *adj.* Giving courage, hope, or confidence: *Our spirits rose when we heard the encouraging news.*

en·croach (ĕn krōch′) *intr.v.* [*on*] **1.** To take another's possessions or rights gradually: *encroach on a neighbor's land.* **2.** To advance beyond former limits: *the ocean encroaching on the shore.* —**en·croach′ment** *n.* [U]

en·crust (ĕn krŭst′) *tr.v.* To cover (sthg.) with or as if with a crust or hard layer: *Ice encrusted the windowpanes.*

en·cum·ber (ĕn kŭm′bər) *tr.v. Formal.* **1.** To put a heavy load on (sbdy.); burden: *The heavy pack encumbered the hiker.* **2.** To hinder or make difficult the action or performance of (sbdy./sthg.): *restrictions that encumber police work.* **3.** To burden (sbdy.) with legal or financial obligations: *They were encumbered by debt from credit cards.*

en·cum·brance (ĕn kŭm′brəns) *n. Formal.* A person or thing that encumbers; a burden or an obstacle.

—**ency** *suff.* A suffix that means quality or condition: *dependency; emergency.*

en·cy·clo·pe·di·a (ĕn sī′klə pē′dē ə) *n.* A book or set of books containing articles, usually arranged in alphabetical order and covering one particular field or a wide variety of subjects. —**en·cy′clo·pe′dic** *adj.*

end (ĕnd) *n.* **1.a.** Either point where sthg. that has length begins or stops: *They sat at opposite ends of the table.* **b.** The extreme edge or limit of a space or area; a boundary: *The highway starts at the end of town.* **2.** The finish or conclusion of sthg.: *I get paid at the end of the month.* **3.** Something one tries to achieve; a goal: *Financial stability is her ultimate end.* **4.** Death or ruin: *He came to his end in an auto accident.* **5.** The final limit of sthg.: *at the end of one's savings; at the end of one's patience.* **6.** A share of a responsibility: *your end of the bargain.* —*v.* —*tr.* **1.** To bring (sthg.) to a conclusion; finish: *a nice way to end a trip.* See Synonyms at **complete. 2.** To form the last part of (sthg.): *A chase ends the movie.* —*intr.* To come to a finish; conclude: *The game ended in a tie.* ◆ **end up.** *intr.v.* To come to a finish or a final position: *After all their traveling, they ended up living back in their hometown.* **in the end.** Eventually; ultimately: *There were many problems, but everything worked out in the end.* **make ends meet.** To have enough money for one's living expenses: *Since he lost his job, he's been having trouble making ends meet.* **no end.** A great deal: *We have no end of stories to tell after all our adventures.*

en·dan·ger (ĕn dān′jər) *tr.v.* To put (sbdy./sthg.) in danger: *Forest fires endanger wildlife.*

en·dan·gered (ĕn dān′jərd) *adj.* In danger of extinction: *The rhinoceros is an endangered species.*

en·dear (ĕn dîr′) *tr.v.* To make (sbdy./sthg.) become loved by others: *The kitten quickly endeared itself to the whole family.* —**en·dear′ing·ly** *adv.*

en·dear·ment (ĕn dîr′mənt) *n.* An expression of affection, especially a word or gesture: *Words like* honey *and* darling *are endearments.*

en·deav·or (ĕn dĕv′ər) *n.* A serious attempt: *They were successful in their business endeavors.* —*tr.v. Formal.* To make an effort (to do or accomplish sthg.); try: *Their parents endeavored to improve their quality of life.*

en·dem·ic (ĕn dĕm′ĭk) *adj.* Common in a particular region, area, country, or group of people: *a disease endemic in that country.* —*n.* An endemic disease.

end·ing (ĕn′dĭng) *n.* **1.** The concluding part, especially of a book, play, or film: *The comedy has a happy ending.* **2.** A letter or letters added to the end of a word to change the meaning or show some relationship of grammar, as in adding *-ed* to *walk* to make the past tense *walked.*

en·dive (ĕn′dīv′ *or* ŏn′dēv′) *n.* [C; U] A plant with crisp or curly leaves used in salads.

end·less (ĕnd′lĭs) *adj.* **1.** Being or seeming to be without an end; infinite: *endless stretches of sandy beaches.* **2.** Formed with the ends joined; continuous: *an endless chain.* —**end′·less·ly** *adv.* —**end′less·ness** *n.* [U]

endo— or **end—** *pref.* A prefix that means inside or within: *endocrine; endoscope.*

en·do·crine (ĕn′də krĭn *or* ĕn′də krēn′) *adj.* Relating to endocrine glands or the hormones they secrete. —*n.* An endocrine gland or the secretion of an endocrine gland.

endocrine gland *n.* Any of various glands, such as the thyroid gland or adrenal gland, that produce hormones that pass directly into the bloodstream or lymphatic system.

en·dor·phin (ĕn dôr′fĭn) *n.* Any of a group of chemicals present in the brain that affect various bodily responses, such as pain or emotion.

en·dorse (ĕn dôrs′) *tr.v.* **en·dorsed, en·dors·ing, en·dors·es. 1.** To write one's signature on the back of (a check): *She endorsed the check before she deposited it.* **2.** To give approval of (sbdy./sthg.); support: *Many people have endorsed the idea of national health care. Environmental groups endorsed the candidate.* —**en·dorse′ment** *n.* [C; U] —**en·dors′er** *n.*

en·do·scope (ĕn′də skōp′) *n.* An optical instrument for examining the inside of a hollow organ or tube, such as the urethra or rectum.

en·dow (ĕn dou′) *tr.v.* **1.** To provide (sbdy./sthg.) with property, income, or a source of income: *endow a school.* **2.** To provide (sbdy.) with a talent or quality: *Nature endowed him with a good singing voice.* —**en·dow′ment** *n.* [C; U]

en·dur·ance (ĕn dŏŏr′əns) *n.* [U] **1.** The ability to withstand stress or hardship: *Running a marathon requires endurance.* **2.** Continuing existence: *the endurance of democracy.*

en·dure (ĕn dŏŏr′ *or* ĕn dyŏŏr′) *v.* **en·dured, en·dur·ing, en·dures.** —*tr.* **1.** To carry on or continue through (sthg.), despite hardships: *The pioneers endured long cold winters.* **2.** To put up with (sbdy./sthg.); tolerate: *I could no longer endure such rudeness.* —*intr.* **1.** To continue to exist; last: *a name that will endure forever.* **2.** To suffer patiently: *The prisoners endured in spite of terrible conditions.* —**en·dur′a·ble** *adj.*

en·dur·ing (ĕn dŏŏr′ĭng *or* ĕn dyŏŏr′ĭng) *adj.* Lasting; durable: *the enduring friendship of the old schoolmates.*

end·wise (ĕnd′wīz′) *also* **end·ways** (ĕnd′wāz′) *adv.* **1.** On end; upright: *Stand the books endwise on the shelf.* **2.** Lengthwise: *a couch placed endwise along a wall.* **3.** End to end: *Lay the bricks endwise to make the wall.*

en·e·ma (ĕn′ə mə) *n.* The injection of a liquid into the rectum through the anus for cleansing, as a laxative, or for other therapeutic purposes.

en·e·my (ĕn′ə mē) *n., pl.* **en·e·mies. 1.** A person who feels hatred toward, intends injury to, or opposes the interests of another; a foe. **2.** A hostile power or force, such as a nation: *During a war, neighboring nations may be enemies.* **3.** Something harmful or destructive: *Disease is an enemy of plant and animal life.* —*adj.* Relating to a hostile power or force: *enemy soldiers.* —SEE NOTE at **collective noun.**

en·er·get·ic (ĕn′ər jĕt′ĭk) *adj.* Possessing or showing energy: *The energetic efforts of the volunteers got the cleanup done.* —**en′er·get′i·cal·ly** *adv.*

en·er·gize (ĕn′ər jīz′) *tr.v.* **en·er·gized, en·er·giz·ing, en·er·giz·es.** To give energy to (sbdy./sthg.); activate: *This switch energizes the electric circuit. The excitement of the game energized both teams.* —**en′er·giz′er** *n.*

en·er·gy (ĕn′ər jē) *n., pl.* **en·er·gies. 1.** [U] The capacity for work or vigorous activity; power: *They lacked the energy to finish the job.* **2.** [C; U] Use of power or vigor; effort: *She's devoting all her energies to caring for her family.* **3.** [U] Usable heat or power: *Do we have enough energy to run the computer?* **4.** [U] The capacity for doing work, as turning, pushing, or raising sthg.: *chemical energy; solar energy.*

en·force (ĕn fôrs′) *tr.v.* **en·forced, en·forc·ing, en·forc·es.** To force observance of or obedience to (sthg.): *The police enforce parking regulations.* —**en·force′a·ble** *adj.* —**en·force′ment** *n.* [U]

eng. *abbr.* An abbreviation of: **1.** Engine. **2.** Engineer. **3.** Engineering.

Eng. *abbr.* An abbreviation of: **1.** England. **2.** English.

en·gage (ĕn gāj′) *v.* **en·gaged, en·gag·ing, en·gag·es.** —*tr.* **1.** *Formal.* To contract for the services of (sbdy.); employ: *engage a carpenter to build a house.* **2.** *Formal.* To arrange for the use of (sthg.); reserve: *engage a room for a meeting.* **3.** To attract and hold the attention of (sbdy.): *The parade engaged us for an hour.* **4.** *Formal.* To require the use of (sthg.); occupy: *Studying engages much of my time.* **5.** To enter into conflict with (sbdy./sthg.): *Our planes engaged the enemy over the bay.* **6.** To cause (sthg.) to interlock; mesh: *A lever engages the gears.* —*intr.* To involve oneself or become occupied; participate: *They engaged in a lively conversation.* **2.** To become meshed or interlock: *The gears engaged.*

en·gaged (ĕn gājd′) *adj.* **1.** Promised to marry: *an engaged couple.* **2.** *Formal.* Employed, occupied, or busy: *I can't come to the phone right now; I'm otherwise engaged.* **3.** Being in gear; meshed: *Third gear is engaged.*

en·gage·ment (ĕn gāj′mənt) *n.* **1.** An act of engaging or the state of being engaged. **2.** An agreement to marry; betrothal: *The couple announced their engagement.* **3.** A promise to be at a particular place at a certain time: *a dinner engagement.* **4.** Employment, especially for a set length of time: *an actor's two-week engagement in a play.* **5.** A battle; a military encounter.

en·gag·ing (ĕn gā′jĭng) *adj.* Charming; attractive: *an engaging smile.* See Synonyms at **interesting.** —**en·gag′ing·ly** *adv.*

en·gine (ĕn′jĭn) *n.* **1.** A machine that turns energy into mechanical force or motion, especially one that gets its energy from the burning of a fuel: *a car engine; a jet engine.* **2.** A railroad locomotive: *The freight train was drawn by a diesel engine.*

en·gi·neer (ĕn′jə nîr′) *n.* **1.** A person who is specially trained or works in a branch of engineering: *a mechanical engineer.* **2.** A person who operates an engine: *a locomotive engineer.* **3.** A person who skillfully manages a project: *The head of our advertising department was the engineer of this sales campaign.* —*tr.v.* **1.** To plan, construct, or manage (sthg.) as an engineer: *engineer a new bridge.* **2.** To plan, manage, and accomplish (sthg.) by skill: *Her secretary engineered the entire surprise party.*

en·gi·neer·ing (ĕn′jə nîr′ĭng) *n.* [U] The use of scientific and mathematical principles to design and build structures, machines, and systems.

Eng·lish (ĭng'glĭsh) *adj.* Relating to or characteristic of England or its people or culture. —*n.* **1. the English.** The people of England. **2.** [C; U] The language of England, the United States, Canada, and other countries: *American English; world Englishes.*

Eng·lish·man (ĭng'glĭsh mən) *n.* **1.** A man born or living in England. **2.** A man of English descent. —**Eng'lish·wom'an** (ĭng'glĭsh woŏm'ən) *n.*

English muffin *n.* A flat round muffin made of yeast dough, usually cut in half and served toasted for breakfast.

en·gorge (ĕn gôrj') *tr.v.* **en·gorged, en·gorg·ing, en·gorg·es. 1.** To eat up (sthg.) greedily: *The dogs engorged a meal in just minutes.* **2.** To congest or overfill (sthg.) with blood or other fluid: *The tick was engorged with blood.* —**en·gorge'ment** *n.* [U]

en·grave (ĕn grāv') *tr.v.* **en·graved, en·grav·ing, en·graves. 1.** To carve, cut, or etch (sthg.) into a material: *engrave a name on a wristwatch.* **2.** To print (an image) from a block or plate that has been carved, cut, or etched into: *engrave invitations on heavy paper.* **3.** To impress (sthg.) deeply as if by carving: *engrave rules of safety in a child's mind.* —**en·grav'er** *n.*

en·grav·ing (ĕn grā'vĭng) *n.* **1.** [U] The art or technique of one who engraves. **2.** [C] A design or text engraved on a surface. **3.** [C] A print made from an engraved plate or block: *a show of the artist's engravings.*

en·gross (ĕn grōs') *tr.v.* To occupy the complete attention of (sbdy.); absorb: *The interesting new book engrossed him.*

en·gross·ing (ĕn grō'sĭng) *adj.* Occupying one's complete attention: *an engrossing movie.*

en·gulf (ĕn gŭlf') *tr.v.* To swallow up or overwhelm (sbdy./sthg.) by overflowing and enclosing: *Flood waters engulfed the land near the river.*

en·hance (ĕn hăns') *tr.v.* **en·hanced, en·hanc·ing, en·hanc·es.** To make (sthg.) greater, as in value, beauty, or reputation: *The gardens enhanced the grounds around the museum.* —**en·hance'ment** *n.* [C; U]

e·nig·ma (ĭ nĭg'mə) *n.* A person or thing that is puzzling or hard to explain: *The extinction of the dinosaurs remains an enigma.*

en·ig·mat·ic (ĕn'ĭg măt'ĭk) *adj.* Resembling an enigma; puzzling: *the enigmatic behavior of an eccentric person.* —**en'ig·mat'i·cal·ly** *adv.*

en·join (ĕn join') *tr.v. Formal.* **1.** [*to*] To direct (sbdy.) with authority and emphasis: *The doctor enjoined the patient to walk one mile each day.* **2.** [*from*] To prohibit or forbid (sbdy.): *The court enjoined the company from merging with its competitor.*

en·joy (ĕn joi') *tr.v.* **1.** To receive pleasure or satisfaction from (sbdy./sthg.): *I enjoy living in the country.* See Synonyms at **love. 2.** To have the use or benefit of (sthg.): *You seem to enjoy good health.* ◆ **enjoy (oneself).** To have a good time: *I enjoyed myself at the ball game.* —**en·joy'ment** *n.* [U]

en·large (ĕn lärj') *v.* **en·larged, en·larg·ing, en·larg·es.** —*tr.* To make (sthg.) larger; add to: *enlarge a house.* —*intr.* To become larger; grow: *The town enlarged as new businesses moved in.* See Synonyms at **increase.** ◆ **enlarge on** or **upon.** *tr.v.* [insep.] To speak or write about (sthg.) more thoroughly: *The second article enlarged on the subject of the first.*

en·large·ment (ĕn lärj'mənt) *n.* **1.** [U] An act of enlarging or the state of being enlarged: *Enlargement of the library will permit the school to buy more books.* **2.** [C] Something that has been enlarged, especially a photograph: *He ordered several enlargements of the family photographs.*

en·light·en (ĕn līt'n) *tr.v.* To give spiritual or intellectual understanding to (sbdy.): *The movie enlightened us about the difficulties of improving health care.* —**en·light'en·ment** *n.* [U]

en·list (ĕn lĭst') *v.* —*tr.* **1.** To bring (sbdy.) into service in the armed forces: *The army enlisted three people from the same neighborhood.* **2.** To engage the support or cooperation of (sbdy./sthg.): *The committee leader enlisted our help in giving food to the homeless.* —*intr.* **1.** To enter the armed forces: *enlist in the army after high school.* **2.** To participate actively in a cause or an enterprise: *Many volunteers enlisted as drivers.* —**en·list'ment** *n.* [C; U]

en·liv·en (ĕn lī'vən) *tr.v.* To make (sthg.) lively or spirited; animate: *Music enlivened the party.*

en masse (ŏn măs') *adv.* In a group or as a body; all together: *Our guests arrived en masse by taxi.*

en·mesh (ĕn mĕsh') *tr.v.* To entangle or catch (sbdy./sthg.) in or as if in a net: *He has been enmeshed in local politics.*

en·mi·ty (ĕn'mĭ tē) *n., pl.* **en·mi·ties.** [C; U] Deep-seated, often mutual hatred: *centuries of enmity between the two countries.*

e·nor·mi·ty (ĭ nôr'mĭ tē) *n.* [U] Very great size or seriousness: *People were horrified at the enormity of the crime.*

e·nor·mous (ĭ nôr'məs) *adj.* Very great in size, extent, number, or degree: *an enormous elephant; the enormous cost of building a sports arena.* See Synonyms at **large.** —**e·nor'mous·ly** *adv.*

e·nough (ĭ nŭf') *adj.* Able to meet a need or

satisfy a desire: *There is enough food for every-body.* —*pron.* An adequate amount or quantity *The hungry hiker ate enough for two people* —*adv.* **1.** To a satisfactory amount or degree sufficiently: *Are you warm enough?* **2.** Tolerably; rather: *The songs were good enough, but the show didn't draw a big audience.*

en•rage (ĕn rāj′) *tr.v.* **en•raged, en•rag•ing, en•rag•es.** To put (sbdy.) into a rage; infuriate: *The plan to put a highway right through town enraged the residents.*

en•rich (ĕn rĭch′) *tr.v.* **1.** To make (sbdy. sthg.) rich or richer: *Foreign words have enriched the English language.* **2.** To add fertilizer to (soil): *Nitrogen enriches garden soil.* **3.** To add nutrients, such as vitamins and minerals, to (food): *The baker enriched the bread with iron.* —**en•rich′ment** *n.* [U]

en•roll (ĕn rōl′) *v.* —*tr.* To enter or register (sbdy.) in a list, record, or roll: *enroll a child in kindergarten; enroll new students for an art class.* —*intr.* To place one's name on a roll or register: *enroll as a voter before the elections; enroll in the advanced Spanish class.*

en•roll•ment (ĕn rōl′mənt) *n.* **1.** [U] The act or process of enrolling: *enrollment in the university.* **2.** [C] The number enrolled: *The school has an enrollment of 600.*

en route (ŏn rōōt′ *or* ĕn rōōt′) *adv. & adj.* On or along the way: *We'll pick you up en route to the theater. We were en route when the accident happened.*

en•sem•ble (ŏn sŏm′bəl) *n.* **1.** A coordinated outfit or costume: *a colorful ensemble of dress, shoes, and hat.* **2.** A group of musicians, singers, dancers, or actors who perform together: *a string ensemble.*

en•slave (ĕn slāv′) *tr.v.* **en•slaved, en•slav•ing, en•slaves.** To make (sbdy.) into or as if into a slave: *The farmers' work seems to enslave them to the land.* —**en•slave′ment** *n.* [U]

en•snare (ĕn snâr′) *tr.v.* **en•snared, en•snar•ing, en•snares.** To catch (sbdy./sthg.) in or as if in a trap or snare: *False claims ensnare customers into buying things they don't need.*

en•sue (ĕn sōō′) *intr.v.* **en•sued, en•su•ing, en•sues.** *Formal.* To follow as a consequence or result: *After their angry words, a fight ensued.* See Synonyms at **follow.**

en•sure (ĕn shōōr′) *tr.v.* **en•sured, en•sur•ing, en•sures.** To make (sthg.) sure or certain; guarantee: *I need to ensure that you will arrive on time.* —SEE NOTE at **assure.**

—ent *suff.* A suffix that means: **1.** Performing, promoting, or causing a specified action: *absorbent.* **2.** Being in a specified state or condition: *independent.* **3.** A person or thing that performs, promotes, or causes a specified action: *superintendent; correspondent.*

en•tail (ĕn tāl′) *tr.v.* To require (sthg.) as a necessary accompaniment or result: *Building a new university will entail great expense.*

en•tan•gle (ĕn tăng′gəl) *tr.v.* **en•tan•gled, en•tan•gling, en•tan•gles. 1.** To make (sthg.) tangled; snarl: *The cat entangled the string.* **2.** To involve (sbdy./sthg.) as if in a tangle: *She became entangled in a neighborhood quarrel.* —**en•tan′gle•ment** *n.* [C; U]

en•ter (ĕn′tər) *v.* —*tr.* **1.** To come or go into (sthg.): *The train entered the tunnel.* **2.** To become a part of or participant in (sthg.): *enter a discussion; enter a contest.* **3.** To cause (sbdy./sthg.) to become a participant, member, or part of; enroll: *enter a child in kindergarten; enter a poodle in a dog show.* **4.** To make a beginning in (sthg.); start: *enter a profession.* **5.a.** To write or put (sthg.) in: *enter names in a guest book; enter data into a computer.* **b.** To place (sthg.) formally upon the records: *The defendant entered a plea of not guilty.* —*intr.* To come or go in: *We entered at the side of the building.* ♦ **enter into.** *tr.v.* [insep.] **1.** To participate in (sthg.): *enter into conversation; enter into an agreement.* **2.** To be a factor in (sthg.): *Many considerations entered into the decision to buy a new house.*

en•ter•prise (ĕn′tər prīz′) *n.* **1.** [C] A task or venture, especially of some importance, complication, and risk: *a new business enterprise.* **2.** [C] A business or organization. **3.** [U] Readiness to start new things; initiative: *The student showed real enterprise in this assignment.*

en•ter•pris•ing (ĕn′tər prī′zĭng) *adj.* Showing initiative and willingness to begin new projects: *An inventor must be an enterprising person.* —**en′ter•pris′ing•ly** *adv.*

en•ter•tain (ĕn′tər tān′) *v.* —*tr.* **1.** To hold the attention of (sbdy.) with sthg. amusing: *A country music band entertained us.* **2.** To extend hospitality toward (sbdy.): *entertain friends at dinner.* **3.** To consider or keep (sthg.) in mind: *We entertained the idea of visiting Texas.* —*intr.* To show hospitality to guests: *We entertained last night.*

en•ter•tain•er (ĕn′tər tā′nər) *n.* A person, such as a singer or comic, who performs for an audience.

en•ter•tain•ing (ĕn′tər tā′nĭng) *adj.* Amusing and interesting: *Her uncle told many entertaining stories.* —**en′ter•tain′ing•ly** *adv.*

en•ter•tain•ment (ĕn′tər tān′mənt) *n.* [U] **1.** The act of entertaining: *The expenses of entertainment add up.* **2.** Something intended to amuse, especially a performance or show: *A magician provided the entertainment at the party.* **3.** The pleasure that comes from being entertained; amusement: *She offered to play the piano for our entertainment.*

en•thrall (ĕn thrôl′) *tr.v.* To hold the attention of (sbdy.) completely; captivate: *The magic show enthralled everyone.* —**en•thrall′ment** *n.* [U]

en·thu·si·asm (ĕn thōō′zē ăz′əm) *n.* [U] Great interest in or excitement for a subject or cause: *The audience applauded with enthusiasm.*

en·thu·si·ast (ĕn thōō′zē ăst′) *n.* A person who follows an interest or a pursuit seriously: *a tennis enthusiast.*

en·thu·si·as·tic (ĕn thōō′zē ăs′tĭk) *adj.* Having or showing enthusiasm: *an enthusiastic welcome; enthusiastic support of a team.* —**en·thu′si·as′ti·cal·ly** *adv.*

en·tice (ĕn tīs′) *tr.v.* **en·ticed, en·tic·ing, en·tic·es.** To attract (sbdy.) by creating hope or desire; lure: *Advertising entices people to buy things.* —**en·tice′ment** *n.* [C; U] —**en·tic′ing** *adj.*—**en·tic′ing·ly** *adv.*

en·tire (ĕn tīr′) *adj.* **1.** Having no part missing; whole: *the entire country; his entire savings.* **2.** Without reservation or limitation; complete: *The plan has my entire approval.*

en·tire·ly (ĕn tīr′lē) *adv.* **1.** Wholly; completely: *an argument entirely forgotten.* **2.** Solely or exclusively: *He was entirely to blame.*

en·tire·ty (ĕn tī′rĭ tē *or* ĕn tīr′tē) *n.* [U] **1.** The condition of being entire; completeness: *I'd like to see the plan in its entirety.* **2.** The entire amount or extent; the whole: *They wasted the entirety of their evening watching television.*

en·ti·tle (ĕn tīt′l) *tr.v.* **en·ti·tled, en·ti·tling, en·ti·tles. 1.** To give a name or title to (sthg.): *The book was entitled* The History of the World. **2.** To give (sbdy.) a right or privilege to sthg.: *This coupon entitles you to a discount.*

en·ti·ty (ĕn′tĭ tē) *n., pl.* **en·ti·ties.** Something that exists and may be distinguished from other things: *American English and British English are distinct entities.*

en·tomb (ĕn tōōm′) *tr.v.* To place (sbdy./sthg.) in or as if in a tomb or grave; bury: *The eruption of the volcano entombed whole buildings.* —**en·tomb′ment** *n.* [C; U]

en·to·mol·o·gy (ĕn′tə mŏl′ə jē) *n.* [U] The scientific study of insects. —**en′to·mol′o·gist** *n.*

en·tou·rage (ŏn′tōō räzh′) *n.* A group of associates or attendants who accompany an important person: *The President arrived with an entourage of bodyguards.*

en·trance¹ (ĕn′trəns) *n.* **1.** [C] The act or an instance of entering: *an actor's dramatic entrance onstage.* **2.** [C] A means or point by which to enter: *Use the back entrance of the building for deliveries.* **3.** [U] The permission or power to enter; admission: *Entrance to the meeting was free.*

en·trance² (ĕn trăns′) *tr.v.* **en·tranced, en·tranc·ing, en·tranc·es.** To fill (sbdy.) with delight, enchantment, or wonder; fascinate: *The exciting movie entranced us all.* —**en·tranc′ing** *adj.*

en·trant (ĕn′trənt) *n.* A person or an animal that enters a competition, such as a race or contest: *There were 75 entrants in the race.*

en·trap (ĕn trăp′) *tr.v.* **en·trapped, en·trap·ping, en·traps. 1.** To catch (sbdy./ sthg.) in a trap: *A net entrapped the fish.* **2.** To attract (sbdy.) into danger or difficulty: *The criminal claimed she had been entrapped by the undercover police officer.* —**en·trap′-ment** *n.* [U]

en·treat (ĕn trēt′) *tr.v. Formal.* To ask (sbdy.) earnestly; beg: *She entreated her son not to go.*

en·treat·y (ĕn trē′tē) *n., pl.* **en·treat·ies.** *(usually plural).* An earnest request; a plea: *He paid no attention to her entreaties.*

en·trée *or* **en·tree** (ŏn′trā) *n.* **1.** [C] The main course of a meal: *I chose the steak for my entrée.* **2.** [U] The power, permission, or liberty to enter; admittance: *The new club members gained entrée to the meeting.*

en·trench (ĕn trĕnch′) *tr.v.* **1.** To provide (sbdy.) with a trench, especially to fortify or defend: *The general entrenched the forces and waited for an attack.* **2.** To fix (sthg.) firmly or securely: *Their opinions are so entrenched they cannot change.* —**en·trench′ment** *n.* [C; U]

en·tre·pre·neur (ŏn′trə prə nûr′ *or* ŏn′trə-prə nōōr′) *n.* A person who organizes and operates a business enterprise and takes the risks involved.

en·trust (ĕn trŭst′) *tr.v.* To give (sthg.) to another for safekeeping, care, or action: *Our neighbors entrusted the care of their dog to me.*

en·try (ĕn′trē) *n., pl.* **en·tries. 1.** [C; U] The act or right of entering; entrance: *A visa is needed for entry into the country.* **2.** [C] A means or place by which to enter: *The entry is a narrow hall.* **3.** [C] An item written in a diary, register, list, or other record: *Each sale is an entry in this account book.* **4.** [C] A word, phrase, or term entered and defined, as in a dictionary or an encyclopedia. **5.** [C] A person or thing entered in a contest: *That horse was a late entry in the race.*

en·try·way (ĕn′trē wā′) *n.* A passage or an opening by which to enter: *You can leave your boots in the entryway.*

en·twine (ĕn twīn′) *tr.v.* **en·twined, en·twin·ing, en·twines.** To twine around (sthg.): *Ivy entwined the pillars of the porch.* ◆ **be entwined.** To be closely connected in many ways: *The friends' lives have been entwined since they were small children.*

e·nu·mer·ate (ĭ nōō′mə rāt′) *tr.v.* **e·nu·mer·at·ed, e·nu·mer·at·ing, e·nu·mer·**

ates. *Formal.* **1.** To count off or name (things) one by one; list: *My list of objectives is too long to enumerate.* **2.** To determine the number of (sthg.); count: *enumerate your concerns.* —**e·nu′mer·a′tion** *n.* —**e·nu′mer·a′tor** *n.*

e·nun·ci·ate (ĭ nŭn′sē āt′) *v.* **e·nun·ci·at·ed, e·nun·ci·at·ing, e·nun·ci·ates.** *Formal.* —*tr.* **1.** To pronounce (sthg.); articulate: *The speaker enunciated every word clearly.* **2.** To state (sthg.) precisely or systematically: *The governor's speech enunciated a new program of education reforms.* —*intr.* To make clear and distinct sounds: *The actors enunciated so poorly that we could hardly understand the play.* —**e·nun′ci·a′tion** *n.* [C; U]

en·vel·op (ĕn vĕl′əp) *tr.v.* To enclose or encase (sbdy./sthg.) completely as if with a covering: *Fog enveloped the buildings.* —**en·vel′op·ment** *n.* [U]

en·ve·lope (ĕn′və lōp′ *or* ŏn′və lōp′) *n.* A flat folded paper container, especially one used for mailing a letter.

en·vi·a·ble (ĕn′vē ə bəl) *adj.* Admirable or desirable enough to be envied: *an enviable achievement.* —**en′vi·a·bly** *adv.*

en·vi·ous (ĕn′vē əs) *adj.* Feeling, expressing, or characterized by envy: *Other contestants were envious of the winner.* —**en′vi·ous·ly** *adv.* —**en′vi·ous·ness** *n.* [U]

en·vi·ron·ment (ĕn vī′rən mənt *or* ĕn·vī′ərn mənt) *n.* **1.a.** All of the surroundings and conditions that affect the growth and development of living things: *Fish and birds, like all living things, must adapt to their environments.* **b.** The condition of the surroundings, such as water, soil, and air in which living things exist: *a clean environment without industrial pollution.* **2.** The social and cultural conditions affecting the nature of a person or community: *a friendly environment.* —**en·vi′ron·men′tal** *adj.* —**en·vi′ron·men′tal·ly** *adv.*

en·vi·rons (ĕn vī′rənz *or* ĕn vī′ərnz) *pl.n.* A surrounding area, especially a city: *The historical environs of Boston include Lexington and Concord.*

en·vi·sion (ĕn vĭzh′ən) *tr.v.* To picture (sbdy./sthg.) in the mind; imagine: *He envisioned how pleasant his vacation was going to be.*

en·voy (ĕn′voi′ *or* ŏn′voi′) *n.* **1.** A representative of a government who is sent on a special diplomatic mission. **2.** A messenger; an agent: *The rebels sent an envoy with a list of demands.*

en·vy (ĕn′vē) *n.* [U] **1.** A feeling of discontent and resentment caused by wanting sthg. that sbdy. else owns or has achieved: *The girl felt envy for her friend's new baseball glove.* **2.** The object of such a feeling: *The racing bike was the envy of everyone who saw it.* —*tr.v.* **en·vied, en·vy·ing, en·vies. 1.** To

feel envy toward (sbdy.): *I envy you for the chance to travel to Mexico.* **2.** To regard (sthg.) with envy: *envy the talent of a great musician.*

en·zyme (ĕn′zīm) *n.* A protein produced in living cells that acts as a catalyst in the chemical processes of living organisms. Some enzymes help break down food so that it can be digested.

e·on (ē′ŏn′ *or* ē′ən) *n.* **1.** *(usually plural).* An extremely long period of time; an eternity: *It seems like eons since I last saw you.* **2.** A division of geologic time.

ep·au·let also **ep·au·lette** (ĕp′ə lĕt′ *or* ĕp′ə lĕt′) *n.* An ornamental strap worn on the shoulder of an officer's uniform.

e·phem·er·al (ĭ fĕm′ər əl) *adj.* Lasting only a brief time; short-lived: *Fame is often ephemeral, lasting only so long as the public remembers.* —**e·phem′er·al·ly** *adv.*

epi— or **ep—** *pref.* A prefix that means: **1.** On; upon: *epitaph.* **2.** Over; above: *epicenter.*

ep·ic (ĕp′ĭk) *n.* A long poem about the lives and actions of heroic characters: *Beowulf is an Old English epic.* —*adj.* **1.** Relating to an epic: *an epic film.* **2.** Grand; tremendous: *an epic achievement.* —**ep′i·cal·ly** *adv.*

ep·i·cen·ter (ĕp′ĭ sĕn′tər) *n.* The part of the earth's surface that is directly above the point where an earthquake begins.

ep·i·dem·ic (ĕp′ĭ dĕm′ĭk) *adj.* Spreading rapidly and widely among the people who live in an area: *Measles is a dangerous epidemic disease.* —*n.* **1.** An outbreak of a contagious disease that spreads rapidly: *news of a cholera epidemic.* **2.** A rapid spread or development: *There were so many strikes that the country had an epidemic of labor troubles.*

ep·i·der·mis (ĕp′ĭ dûr′mĭs) *n.* [C; U] The outer protective layer of the skin of vertebrates.

ep·i·lep·sy (ĕp′ə lĕp′sē) *n.* [U] A brain disorder that causes seizures, and sometimes involves convulsions or loss of consciousness.

ep·i·lep·tic (ĕp′ə lĕp′tĭk) *adj.* Of or suffering from epilepsy: *an epileptic attack.* —*n.* A person who has epilepsy.

ep·i·logue also **ep·i·log** (ĕp′ə lôg′ *or* ĕp′ə lŏg′) *n.* A short section at the end of a literary work, often discussing what happens to the characters after the main story.

E·pis·co·pal Church (ĭ pĭs′kə pəl) *n.* [U] The church in the United States that agrees with the Church of England in beliefs and most practices.

E·pis·co·pa·lian (ĭ pĭs′kə pāl′ē ən *or* ĭ pĭs′kə pāl′yən) *adj.* Relating to the Episcopal Church. —*n.* A member of the Episcopal Church. —**E·pis′co·pal** *adj.*

ep·i·sode (ĕp′ĭ sōd′) *n.* **1.** An event or incident in the course of a larger series: *Living in India was an exciting episode in her life.* **2.** A part of a novel or radio or television program presented as a series: *The story was divided*

E

into six episodes for TV. —**ep′i•sod′ic** (ĕp′ĭ sŏd′ĭk) *adj.*

ep•i•taph (ĕp′ĭ tăf′) *n.* Writing carved on a tombstone or monument in memory of the person buried there: *An epitaph often includes a person's birth and death dates.*

ep•i•thet (ĕp′ə thĕt′) *n.* A term used to describe the nature of a person or thing; for example, *The Big Apple* is an epithet for New York City.

e•pit•o•me (ĭ pĭt′ə mē) *n.* ◆ **the epitome of.** A person or thing that is a typical example of an entire class or type: *Her remark was the epitome of good judgment.*

e•pit•o•mize (ĭ pĭt′ə mīz′) *tr.v.* **e•pit•o•mized, e•pit•o•miz•ing, e•pit•o•miz•es.** To be a typical example of (a class of persons or things): *Abraham Lincoln epitomizes the strong leader.*

ep•och (ĕp′ək *or* ē′pŏk′) *n.* **1.** A period, especially one in history marked by certain important events or developments; an era: *the epoch of space exploration.* **2.** A unit of time that is a division of a geologic period.

ep•ox•y (ĭ pŏk′sē) *n., pl.* **ep•ox•ies.** [C; U] A synthetic resin that is tough and strongly adhesive, used in making protective coatings and glues.

eq•ua•ble (ĕk′wə bəl *or* ē′kwə bəl) *adj.* **1.** Not varying; steady: *the equable climate of the Caribbean.* **2.** Even-tempered; calm: *Our teacher has an equable disposition.* —**eq′ua•bil′i•ty** *n.* [U] —**eq′ua•bly** *adv.*

e•qual (ē′kwəl) *adj.* **1.** Having the same amount, number, size, rank, or value as another: *equal strength; equal size.* **2.** Being the same for all members of a group; even: *Every player had an equal chance to win.* —*n.* A person or thing that is equal to another: *Most people want to be treated as equals.* —*tr.v.* **1.** To be equal to (sthg.): *Two pints equal a quart. My ability equals theirs.* **2.** To do, make, or produce sthg. equal to (sthg. else): *The athlete equaled the world's record in the mile run.* —**e′qual•ly** *adv.*

e•qual•i•ty (ĭ kwŏl′ĭ tē) *n.* [U] The condition of being equal, especially the condition of having equal rights: *equality under the law.*

e•qual•ize (ē′kwə līz′) *tr.v.* **e•qual•ized, e•qual•iz•ing, e•qual•iz•es.** **1.** To make (sthg.) equal: *Opening the bottle equalizes the pressure with the outside air.* **2.** To make (sthg.) even or uniform: *Move this box to equalize the weight on both sides of the car.* —**e′qual•i•za′tion** (ē′kwə lĭ zā′shən) *n.* [U] —**e′qual•iz′er** *n.*

equal sign *n.* The symbol (=) used in mathematics to show that sthg. is equal to sthg. else, as in $a = b$ and $2 + 2 = 4$.

e•qua•nim•i•ty (ē′kwə nĭm′ĭ tē *or* ĕk′wə-nĭm′ĭ tē) *n.* [U] The condition or quality of being calm and even-tempered; composure: *Judges are expected to show equanimity in court.*

e•quate (ĭ kwāt′) *tr.v.* **e•quat•ed, e•quat•ing, e•quates.** To make or consider (sthg.) the same or equivalent: *Many people equate fame with success.*

e•qua•tion (ĭ kwā′zhən *or* ĭ kwā′shən) *n.* **1.** A mathematical statement of the equality of two expressions. For example, $3 \times 2 = 6$, $y = 2 + 8$, and $x + y = 18$ are all equations. **2.** An expression using chemical formulas and symbols to show the quantities and substances in a chemical reaction. For example, two hydrogen molecules reacting with an oxygen molecule to form two molecules of water is expressed by the equation $2H_2 + O = 2H_2O$.

e•qua•tor (ĭ kwā′tər) *n.* [U] The imaginary line around the earth halfway between the North and South poles: *The equator divides the earth into the Northern Hemisphere and the Southern Hemisphere.*

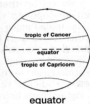

equator

e•qua•to•ri•al (ē′kwə-tôr′ē əl *or* ĕk′wə tôr′ē əl) *adj.* **1.** Of or near the equator: *an equatorial region of Brazil.* **2.** Characteristic of conditions at the earth's equator: *equatorial heat.*

e•ques•tri•an (ĭ kwĕs′trē ən) *adj.* Relating to horseback riders or horseback riding: *equestrian ability; an equestrian statue of the king.* —*n.* A person who rides a horse or performs on horseback.

equi— *pref.* A prefix that means equal or equally: *equidistant.*

WORD BUILDING: equi— The prefix **equi—** means "equal" or "equally." Thus **equidistant** means "equally distant." **Equinox** means "having the night equal (to the day)." **Equivalent** means literally "being equal."

---

e•qui•dis•tant (ē′kwĭ dĭs′tənt) *adj.* Equally distant from or between two places: *Switzerland is about equidistant from Paris and Rome.* —**e′qui•dis′tant•ly** *adv.*

e•qui•lat•er•al (ē′kwə lăt′ər əl) *adj.* With all sides equal: *an equilateral triangle.* —**e′qui•lat′er•al•ly** *adv.*

e•qui•lib•ri•um (ē′kwə lĭb′rē əm) *n.* [U] A condition of balance or stability: *Ideally, the supply of a product should be in equilibrium with the demand for it.*

e•quine (ē′kwīn′ *or* ĕk′wīn′) *adj.* Relating to horses: *equine medicine.*

e·qui·nox (ē′kwə nŏks′ *or* ĕk′wə nŏks′) *n.* Either of the times of year when the sun crosses the celestial equator and day and night are about equal in length. In the Northern Hemisphere, equinoxes occur about March 21 and September 23.

e·quip (ĭ kwĭp′) *tr.v.* **e·quipped, e·quip·ping, e·quips.** To supply (sbdy./sthg.) with what is needed; provide: *The expedition was equipped with warm clothes for the bitterly cold weather.*

e·quip·ment (ĭ kwĭp′mənt) *n.* [U] **1.** The things needed or used for a particular purpose: *a tent, sleeping bag, and other camping equipment.* **2.** The act of equipping: *The equipment of the expedition took a month to complete.*

eq·ui·ta·ble (ĕk′wĭ tə bəl) *adj.* Fair and just: *Judges are expected to make equitable decisions.* —**eq′ui·ta·bly** *adv.*

eq·ui·ty (ĕk′wĭ tē) *n.* [U] **1.** Justice; fairness: *The law relies on the equity of a jury.* **2.** The value of a business or property after debts and mortgages on it are subtracted: *Rising home values have helped increase my home equity.*

e·quiv·a·lent (ĭ kwĭv′ə lənt) *adj.* **1.** Equal in value, meaning, or force: *The wish of the king is equivalent to a command.* **2.** Having a one-to-one correspondence, as between parts; identical: *equivalent geometric figures.* —*n.* Something that is equivalent: *A dime is the equivalent of two nickels.* —**e·quiv′a·lence** *n.* [U]

e·quiv·o·cal (ĭ kwĭv′ə kəl) *adj.* **1.** Having more than one interpretation; ambiguous or misleading: *The politician gave an equivocal answer to the reporter's question.* **2.** Not certain; undecided: *He was equivocal about how to solve the problem.* **3.** Of uncertain meaning: *The experiment gave equivocal results that we could not interpret with certainty.* —**e·quiv′o·cal·ly** *adv.*

e·quiv·o·cate (ĭ kwĭv′ə kāt′) *intr.v.* **e·quiv·o·cat·ed, e·quiv·o·cat·ing, e·quiv·o·cates.** *Formal.* To use language that can be interpreted in more than one way, especially in order to mislead: *Stop equivocating and tell us what you really think.* —**e·quiv′o·ca′tion** *n.* [C; U]

—**er**[1] *suff.* A suffix that means: **1.** A person or thing that does a specified action: *swimmer; blender.* **2.** A person who is born in or lives in a place: *islander; New Yorker.* **3.** A person or thing that is: *foreigner; six-footer.* **4.** A person or thing that is associated or involved with: *banker; gardener.*

—**er**[2] *suff.* A suffix used to form the comparative degree of adjectives and adverbs: *neater; slower.*

e·ra (îr′ə *or* ĕr′ə) *n.* **1.** A period of time beginning at a specific date or event: *The atomic era and the postwar era began with* the conclusion of World War II in 1945. **2.** A period of time characterized by particular circumstances, events, or persons: *These events took place during the Colonial era of U.S. history.* **3.** The longest division of geologic time, containing one or more periods.

e·rad·i·cate (ĭ răd′ĭ kāt′) *tr.v.* **e·rad·i·cat·ed, e·rad·i·cat·ing, e·rad·i·cates.** **1.** To get rid of (sthg.); destroy: *Vaccination has eradicated smallpox.* **2.** To tear (sthg.) up by the roots: *The gardener eradicated that patch of weeds.* —**e·rad′i·ca′tion** *n.* [U]

e·rase (ĭ rās′) *tr.v.* **e·rased, e·ras·ing, e·ras·es.** **1.** To remove (sthg. written or drawn) by rubbing, scraping, or wiping: *erase a mistake.* **2.** To remove writing or a recording from (sthg.): *erase a tape; erase a blackboard.* **3.** To remove or destroy (sthg.) as if by wiping out: *Time will erase hurt feelings.*

e·ras·er (ĭ rā′sər) *n.* An implement that erases marks made with pencil, ink, or chalk.

e·ra·sure (ĭ rā′shər) *n.* **1.** The act of erasing. **2.** Something erased, as a word or number: *The paper had many erasures.*

ere (âr) *prep.* In poetic or older usage, previous to; before. —*conj.* Sooner than; rather than.

HOMONYMS: ere, air (gas), e'er (ever), heir (inheritor).

---

e·rect (ĭ rĕkt′) *adj.* In a vertical or upright position: *a soldier's erect posture.* —*tr.v.* **1.** To build (sthg.); construct: *erect a skyscraper.* **2.** To raise (sthg.) upright; set on end: *erect a new telephone pole.* —**e·rect′ly** *adv.* —**e·rect′ness** *n.* [U]

e·rec·tion (ĭ rĕk′shən) *n.* **1.** [C] The stiffening of tissues in the penis during sexual stimulation. **2.** [U] The act of erecting, building, or raising upright: *The erection of the new building took nearly two years.*

e·rode (ĭ rōd′) *v.* **e·rod·ed, e·rod·ing, e·rodes.** —*tr.* **1.** To wear (sthg.) away by or as if by rubbing or scraping: *Wind eroded the hillside.* **2.** To eat into (sthg.); corrode: *The acidity of the water eroded the pipes.* **3.** To cause (sthg.) to lessen or disappear: *The bookkeeper's mistakes eroded their trust in his work.* —*intr.* To become worn away gradually: *Dust storms are caused by soil that erodes in a strong wind.*

e·ro·sion (ĭ rō′zhən) *n.* [U] The gradual wearing away by the action of water or wind: *farmland lost by soil erosion.*

e·rot·ic (ĭ rŏt′ĭk) *adj.* Arousing sexual desire. —**e·rot′i·cal·ly** *adv.* —**e·rot′i·cis′m** (ĭ rŏt′ĭ sĭz′əm) *n.* [U]

err (ûr *or* ĕr) *intr.v.* *Formal.* [in] To make a mistake or an error; be incorrect: *We erred in thinking the bus would be on time.*

er·rand (ĕr′ənd) *n.* A short trip taken to do sthg.: *Our neighbor asked me to run an errand to the store downtown.*

E

er·rant (ĕr′ənt) *adj.* **1.** Roving or wandering: *errant knights seeking adventure.* **2.** Moving away from the proper course or standards: *a golfer's errant shot; an errant youth.*

er·rat·ic (ĭ răt′ĭk) *adj.* **1.** Irregular or uneven, as in quality or progress: *erratic work.* **2.** Not in keeping with the general course of behavior or opinion; eccentric: *His erratic behavior worried his parents.* —**er·rat′i·cal·ly** *adv.*

er·ro·ne·ous (ĭ rō′nē əs) *adj.* Containing or resulting from error; mistaken: *an erroneous belief.* —**er·ro′ne·ous·ly** *adv.*

er·ror (ĕr′ər) *n.* Something that is incorrect, wrong, or false; a mistake: *The waiter made an error in adding up our bill.* ♦ **in error.** Incorrect or wrong: *The statement is in error.*

er·u·dite (ĕr′yə dīt′ *or* ĕr′ə dīt′) *adj.* Having great knowledge or learning; scholarly: *an erudite book; an erudite person.* —**er′u·dite′ly** *adv.* —**er′u·dite′ness** *n.* [U]

er·u·di·tion (ĕr′yə dĭsh′ən *or* ĕr′ə dĭsh′ən) *n.* [U] Extensive learning.

e·rupt (ĭ rŭpt′) *intr.v.* **1.** To become violently active: *The volcano erupted with little warning.* **2.** To appear or develop suddenly and violently; explode: *War erupted between the two nations.* **3.** To force out or release sthg. violently or suddenly: *The water heater erupted in a burst of steam.* **4.** To appear on the skin: *A rash erupted on the child's back.*

e·rup·tion (ĭ rŭp′shən) *n.* **1.** An instance of erupting: *the eruption of a volcano.* **2.** A sudden, almost violent outburst: *an eruption of anger.* **3.** A rash or blemish on the skin: *an eruption caused by a virus.*

—**ery** *or* —**ry** *suff.* A suffix that means: **1.** A place for: *bakery.* **2.** A collection or type: *greenery.* **3.** A state or condition: *slavery.* **4.** Act or practice: *bribery.*

—**es**[1] *suff.* Variant of —**s**[1].

—**es**[2] *suff.* Variant of —**s**[2].

es·ca·late (ĕs′kə lāt′) *tr. & intr.v.* **es·ca·lat·ed, es·ca·lat·ing, es·ca·lates.** To increase or cause to increase by stages, as in value, scope, or intensity: *Congress has escalated the fight against pollution over the last ten years. Rents escalated during the 1990s.* —**es′ca·la′tion** *n.* [C; U]

es·ca·la·tor (ĕs′kə lā′tər) *n.* A moving stairway consisting of steps attached to a continuously circulating belt.

es·ca·pade (ĕs′kə pād′) *n.* A carefree or dangerous action: *youthful escapades.*

es·cape (ĭ skāp′) *v.* **es·caped, es·cap·ing, es·capes.** —*intr.* **1.** To get away from sbdy./sthg. that holds or confines; get free: *The prisoners escaped by climbing the wall.* **2.** [*from*] To leak or come out: *All the air escaped from the balloon.* —*tr.* **1.** To get free

of (sbdy./sthg.): *A vacation will allow me to escape the noise of the city.* **2.** To succeed in avoiding (capture, danger, or harm): *I barely escaped injury when the ladder fell.* **3.** To be unnoticed or forgotten by (sbdy.): *The name of the new worker escapes me.* **4.** To be let out from (sbdy./sthg.) involuntarily: *A cry of delight escaped the child's lips.* —*n.* [C; U] **1.** The act or means of escaping: *prisoners with little chance of escape.* **2.** A means of escaping: *An open gate provided the dog's escape.* **3.** An activity that provides temporary freedom from worry, care, or unpleasantness: *For her, running provides an escape from everyday problems.*

es·cap·ee (ĭ skā′ pē′) *n.* A person who has escaped, especially an escaped prisoner.

—**escence** *suff.* A suffix that means the state or process: *convalescence; obsolescence.*

—**escent** *suff.* A suffix that means beginning to be or becoming: *adolescent; luminescent.*

es·cap·ism (ĭ skăp′ĭz′ əm) *n.* [U] The desire to ignore or forget unpleasant facts or events in the world: *Escapism may not be the best way to deal with serious problems.* —**es·cap′ist** *n. & adj.*

es·cort (ĕs′kôrt′) *n.* **1.** A person or group that goes with another in order to give protection or to pay honor: *The visiting foreign leader was given a police escort.* **2.** One or more airplanes, warships, or other vehicles accompanying another or others to provide protection. **3.** A man who is the companion of a woman, especially on a social occasion: *Her friend was her escort for her cousin's wedding.* —*tr.v.* (ĭ skôrt′ *or* ĕs′kôrt′). To accompany (sbdy./sthg.) as an escort: *An honor guard escorted the President during the parade.*

es·crow (ĕs′krō′ *or* ĕ skrō′) *n.* [U] Money, property, or a deed put into the keeping of a bank, for example, until certain conditions of a deal or agreement are fulfilled. ♦ **in escrow.** In the care of another until various conditions are met: *The bank is holding the deposit in escrow until the purchase of the house is approved.*

—**ese** *suff.* A suffix that means: **1.** Of or relating to a certain place: *Japanese.* **2.** Native or inhabitant of: *Chinese.* **3.** A language or dialect of: *Portuguese.*

Es·ki·mo (ĕs′kə mō′) *n., pl.* **Eskimo** or **Es·ki·mos.** **1.** [C] A member of a group of peoples living in the Arctic coastal regions of North America and parts of Greenland and northeast Siberia. **2.** [U] Any of the languages of the Eskimo peoples. —**Es′ki·mo′** *adj.*

ESL *abbr.* An abbreviation of English as a second language.

e·soph·a·gus (ĭ sŏf′ə gəs) *n., pl.* **e·soph·a·gi** (ĭ sŏf′ə jī′). The tube that connects the throat and the stomach for the passage of food.

es·o·ter·ic (ĕs′ə tĕr′ĭk) *adj.* Intended for, known to, or understood by only a small group of people: *an esoteric book on astrophysics.* —**es′o·ter′i·cal·ly** *adv.*

ESP¹ *abbr.* An abbreviation of English for specific purposes.

ESP² *abbr.* An abbreviation of extrasensory perception.

esp. *abbr.* An abbreviation of especially.

es·pe·cial·ly (ĭ spĕsh′ə lē) *adv.* To a notable extent or degree; particularly: *He seemed especially tired after school today.*

es·pi·o·nage (ĕs′pē ə näzh′ *or* ĕs′pē ə-nĭj) *n.* [U] The act of spying; use of spies: *Many countries engage in espionage in time of war.*

es·pres·so (ĕ sprĕs′ō) *n., pl.* **es·pres·sos.** [C; U] A strong coffee made by forcing steam through long-roasted, powdered coffee beans: *Espresso is a popular after-dinner drink.*

—esque *suff.* A suffix that means in the manner of or resembling: *statuesque.*

—ess *suff.* A suffix that means female: *heiress; lioness.*

es·say (ĕs′ā′) *n.* **1.** A short written work on a single subject, usually presenting the personal views of the author. **2.** (*or* ĕ sā′). *Formal.* An attempt; a try: *He made a brief essay at politics before settling on a teaching career.*

es·sence (ĕs′əns) *n.* **1.** [U] The quality or qualities of a thing that give it its identity or character: *The essence of democracy is freedom to choose.* **2.** [C; U] A concentrated form or extract of a substance: *Turpentine is an essence of pine tar.* **3.** [C] A perfume or scent.

es·sen·tial (ĭ sĕn′shəl) *adj.* **1.** Very important; necessary: *Good food is essential for good health.* **2.** Being the essence of sthg.; fundamental: *The essential work of the police is to protect the citizens from harm.* —*n.* (*usually plural*). Something fundamental or necessary: *Take along only the essentials when traveling.* —**es·sen′tial·ly** *adv.*

—est *suff.* A suffix used to form the superlative degree of adjectives and adverbs: *greatest; earliest.*

es·tab·lish (ĭ stăb′lĭsh) *tr.v.* **1.** To settle (sbdy./sthg.) securely in a position or condition; install: *It took several years for the new business to establish itself in this town.* **2.** To begin or set up (sthg.); found: *Their ancestors established the company in 1789.* **3.** To show (sthg.) to be true; prove: *Several witnesses established the suspect's innocence.* **4.** To cause (sbdy./sthg.) to be recognized and accepted without question: *His transatlantic flight established Charles Lindbergh as a national hero.*

es·tab·lish·ment (ĭ stăb′lĭsh mənt) *n.* **1.** [U] The act of establishing: *The new government's first priority was the establishment of peace.* **2.** [C] An organization or institution, such as a business, hospital, or school: *Most of the town's commercial establishments contributed to the fund for the new playground.* **3.** Often **Establishment.** [C] (*usually singular*). A group of people holding most of the power and influence in a government, society, or field of endeavor: *young people protesting against the Establishment.*

es·tate (ĭ stāt′) *n.* **1.** A large piece of land, usually with a large house: *Their family owns several estates in Europe.* **2.** Everything one owns, especially all of the property and debts left by sbdy. who has died: *When the shopkeeper died, the family inherited a small estate.*

es·teem (ĭ stēm′) *tr.v.* **1.** To regard (sbdy./sthg.) with respect; value: *Judges are esteemed for their fairness and honesty.* **2.** To judge to be (sthg.); consider: *Improving public transportation was esteemed the best way to deal with the parking problem.* —*n.* [U] Favorable regard; respect: *The doctor is held in high esteem.*

es·thet·ic (ĕs thĕt′ĭk) *adj.* Variant of **aesthetic.**

es·thet·ics (ĕs thĕt′ĭks) *n.* Variant of **aesthetics.**

es·ti·ma·ble (ĕs′tə mə bəl) *adj.* Deserving great respect; admirable: *Patience, honesty, and fairness are estimable characteristics.* —**es′ti·ma·bly** *adv.*

es·ti·mate (ĕs′tə māt′) *tr.v.* **es·ti·mat·ed, es·ti·mat·ing, es·ti·mates.** **1.** To make a judgment about the approximate cost, quantity, or size of (sthg.); calculate roughly: *I estimate that 25 people will come to the party.* **2.** To form an opinion about (sbdy./sthg.); evaluate: *We estimated her singing ability and decided to give her the lead role in the show.* —*n.* (ĕs′tə mĭt). **1.** An approximate calculation: *Our estimate is that we will arrive in about an hour.* **2.** A calculation of the cost of work to be done: *The plumber's estimate to fix the pipe was reasonable.* **3.** An opinion; an evaluation: *The critic's estimate of the play was that it needed work.*

es·ti·ma·tion (ĕs′tə mā′shən) *n.* [U] **1.** The act of estimating: *Estimation of the storm damage took several weeks.* **2.** An opinion; a judgment: *In my estimation that is a good painting.*

es·trange (ĭ strānj′) *tr.v.* **es·tranged, es· trang·ing, es·trang·es.** To cause (sbdy.) to change from friendly to unfriendly or indifferent: *The neighbors were estranged over differences about who was responsible for repairing the fence.* —**es·trange′ment** *n.* [C; U]

es·tro·gen (ĕs′trə jən) *n.* [U] A hormone that causes the development of female characteristics and regulates the female reproductive cycle.

—**et** *suff.* A suffix that means small: *eaglet.*

et al. *abbr.* An abbreviation of et alii (and others): *a book by Falbel, Perkins, et al.*

etc. *abbr.* An abbreviation of et cetera: *cars, buses, trucks, etc.*

et cet·er·a (ĕt sĕt′ər ə *or* ĕt sĕt′rə). And other things of the same type; and so forth: *grapes, raspberries, plums, peaches, et cetera.*

etch (ĕch) *v.* —*tr.* **1.** To cut into (metal, glass, or other material) by using acid. **2.** To imprint (sthg.) clearly: *The sight of that waterfall is etched in my memory.* —*intr.* To practice the art of etching.

etch·ing (ĕch′ĭng) *n.* **1.** [U] The art or technique of making etched metal plates and printing pictures and designs from them. **2.** [C] A design or picture etched on or printed from such a plate: *The artist finished the etching.*

e·ter·nal (ĭ tûr′nəl) *adj.* **1.** Having no beginning or end; existing outside of time: *eternal love.* **2.** Continuing without interruption or change: *the eternal tides.* **3.** Seemingly endless: *eternal complaining.* —**e·ter′nal·ly** *adv.*

e·ter·ni·ty (ĭ tûr′nĭ tē) *n., pl.* **e·ter·ni· ties. 1.** [U] All of time without beginning or end; infinite time: *We cannot measure eternity.* **2.** [U] The timeless state following death: *She wanted to be with him for all eternity.* **3.** [C; U] A very long or seemingly very long time: *It was an eternity before they opened the doors of the theater.*

—**eth** *suff.* Variant of —**th.**

e·ther (ē′thər) *n.* [U] A colorless flammable liquid that is used as a solvent and an anesthetic: *Hold a cloth soaked in ether to the patient's mouth.*

e·the·re·al (ĭ thîr′ē əl) *adj.* **1.** Delicate; light and airy: *ethereal music.* **2.** Of heaven; heavenly: *Angels are ethereal beings.* —**e·the′re·al·ly** *adv.*

eth·ic (ĕth′ĭk) *n.* **1.** [C; U] A set of principles of correct behavior; a system of moral values: *Our company is ruled by the work ethic.* **2. ethics.** [U] *(used with a singular verb).* The branch of philosophy that deals with the general nature of morals and moral choices. **3. ethics.** [C; U] *(used with a singular or plural verb).* Standards of right

behavior or conduct; moral principles: *The code of ethics in the medical profession prohibits doctors from discussing individual patients by name.*

eth·i·cal (ĕth′ĭ kəl) *adj.* **1.** Following accepted standards of behavior or conduct; morally right: *It is not considered ethical for a lawyer to represent both sides in a dispute.* **2.** Relating to ethics: *ethical standards of right and wrong.* —**eth′i·cal·ly** *adv.*

eth·nic (ĕth′nĭk) *adj.* Relating to a group of people that have the same racial, national, religious, linguistic, or cultural background: *a survey on ethnic background.* —*n.* A member of a particular ethnic group. —**eth′ni· cal·ly** *adv.*

eth·nic·i·ty (ĕth nĭs′ĭ tē) *n.* [U] The condition of belonging to a particular ethnic group: *Many Americans are of mixed ethnicity.*

eth·nol·o·gy (ĕth nŏl′ə jē) *n.* [U] The study and comparison of the characteristics, history, and development of human cultures and of the origins of ethnic groups and the relations among them. —**eth′no·log′i·cal** (ĕth′nə lŏj′ĭ kəl) *adj.* —**eth·no′lo·gist** *n.*

et·i·quette (ĕt′ĭ kĕt′ *or* ĕt′ĭ kĭt) *n.* [U] The forms and rules of proper behavior required by custom among people: *Good etiquette requires a person to thank another for a gift or favor.*

—**ette** *suff.* A suffix that means: **1.** Small: *kitchenette.* **2.** Female: *majorette.* **3.** Imitation or substitute: *leatherette.*

et·y·mol·o·gy (ĕt′ə mŏl′ə jē) *n., pl.* **et·y· mol·o·gies. 1.** [C] The origin and development of a word as shown by its earliest use and changes in form and meaning: *Many medical terms have etymologies that go back to ancient Greek.* **2.** [U] The study of the origin and history of words: *Etymology requires a knowledge of many languages.* —**et′y· mo·log′i·cal** (ĕt′ə mə lŏj′ĭ kəl) *adj.* —**et′y·mo·log′i·cal·ly** *adv.*

eu·lo·gize (yōō′lə jīz′) *tr.v.* **eu·lo·gized, eu·lo·giz·ing, eu·lo·giz·es.** To praise (sbdy.) highly in speech or writing: *She eulogized her dear friend at the funeral.*

eu·lo·gy (yōō′lə jē) *n., pl.* **eu·lo·gies.** A speech or piece of writing praising a person or thing, especially a person who has just died: *A lifelong friend delivered the eulogy at the memorial service.*

eu·nuch (yōō′nək) *n.* A castrated man.

eu·phe·mism (yōō′fə mĭz′ əm) *n.* **1.** [C] An inoffensive or indirect word or expression used instead of another expression that is considered offensive or too direct. For example, *pass away* is a euphemism for *die.* **2.** [U] The use of such words or expressions. —**eu′phe·mis′tic** (yōō′fə mĭs′tĭk) *adj.*

ă–cat; ā–pay; âr–care; ä–father; ĕ–get; ē–be; ĭ–sit; ī–nice; îr–here; ŏ–got; ō–go; ô–saw; oi–boy; ou–out; ōō–took; ōō–boot; ŭ–cut; ûr–word; th–thin; th–this; hw–when; zh–vision; ə–about; N–French bon

Eu·ro·pe·an (yoor'ə pē'ən) *n.* **1.** A person born or living in Europe. **2.** A person of European descent. —*adj.* Relating to Europe or its peoples, languages, or cultures.

eu·sta·chian tube (yoo stā'shən *or* yoo-stā'shē ən) *n.* The narrow passage that connects the middle ear and the pharynx and allows the pressure on both sides of the eardrum to equalize.

eu·tha·na·sia (yoo'thə nā'zhə *or* yoo'thə-nā'zhē ə) *n.* [U] The act of ending the life of a person who is suffering from an incurable illness or injury; mercy killing.

e·vac·u·ate (ĭ văk'yoo āt') *tr.v.* **e·vac·u·at·ed, e·vac·u·at·ing, e·vac·u·ates.** **1.** To send away or withdraw (people) from an area: *evacuate families threatened by the flood.* **2.** To withdraw or depart from (sthg.); vacate: *The firefighters quickly evacuated the burning building.* —**e·vac'u·a'tion** *n.* [C; U]

e·vac·u·ee (ĭ văk'yoo ē') *n.* A person evacuated from a dangerous area.

e·vade (ĭ vād') *tr.v.* **e·vad·ed, e·vad·ing, e·vades.** **1.** To escape or avoid (sbdy./sthg.) by cleverness or dishonesty: *evade arrest.* **2.** To avoid giving a direct answer to (sthg.): *The mayor evaded the question by talking about something else.*

e·val·u·ate (ĭ văl'yoo āt') *tr.v.* **e·val·u·at·ed, e·val·u·at·ing, e·val·u·ates.** To find out or estimate the value of (sbdy./sthg.); examine and appraise: *evaluate paintings for sale; evaluate a job candidate.* —**e·val'u·a'tion** *n.* [C; U]

e·van·gel·i·cal (ē'văn jĕl'ĭ kəl) *also* **e·van·gel·ic** (ē'văn jĕl'ĭk) *adj.* **1.** Of or in accordance with the Christian gospel, especially the four Gospels of the New Testament. **2. Evangelical.** Of or being a Protestant group that stresses belief solely in the authority of the Bible and salvation through faith in Jesus. —*n.* **Evangelical.** A member of an evangelical church. —**e'van·gel'i·cal·ly** *adv.*

e·vap·o·rate (ĭ văp'ə rāt') *v.* **e·vap·o·rat·ed, e·vap·o·rat·ing, e·vap·o·rates.** —*tr.* **1.** To cause (sthg.) to change from a liquid into a vapor, especially without boiling: *The sun evaporates water from the ocean.* **2.** To extract water or other liquid from (sthg.): *evaporate milk.* —*intr.* **1.** To change from a liquid into a vapor: *The dew evaporated as the sun came up.* **2.** To disappear; vanish: *My fear evaporated as the airplane took off.* See Synonyms at **disappear.** —**e·vap'o·ra'tion** *n.* [U]

e·va·sion (ĭ vā'zhən) *n.* **1.** [U] The act of evading: *His tax evasion led to his imprisonment.* **2.** [C] A means of evading; an excuse: *His father saw through his evasions and insisted that he go to church.*

e·va·sive (ĭ vā'sĭv) *adj.* **1.** Tending or intended to escape: *The submarine took eva-*

sive action to get away from the enemy. **2.** Intentionally misleading or ambiguous: *The journalist grew more and more impatient with the candidate's evasive answers to her questions.* —**e·va'sive·ly** *adv.* —**e·va'sive·ness** *n.* [U]

eve (ēv) *n.* [U] **1.** The evening or day before a special day, such as a holiday: *New Year's Eve.* **2.** The period immediately before a certain event: *the eve of war.*

e·ven (ē'vən) *adj.* **1.a.** Having a horizontal surface; flat: *An even field is best for playing sports.* **b.** Having no roughness, dents, or bumps; smooth: *an even board.* **c.** Being in the same plane or line; parallel: *Is your writing even with the top of the page?* **2.** Having no variation; uniform: *keeping an even speed.* **3.** Calm; peaceful: *an even temper.* **4.a.** Equally matched: *an even fight.* **b.** Equal in degree, value, or amount: *even portions of a meal.* **5.** Containing 2 as a factor; exactly divisible by 2. For example, 8 is an even number. **6.** Having equal probability: *Our team has an even chance of winning.* **7.** Having an equal score or ranking: *The teams are even.* **8.** With nothing owed or due: *Pay me one dollar, and we are even.* **9.** Having an exact amount, extent, or number: *an even pound.* —*adv.* **1.** To a higher or greater degree; still: *an even better idea.* **2.** At the same time as; just: *Even as we watched, the tree fell.* **3.** Indeed; moreover: *She was relieved, even happy, to see us.* **4.** Used to emphasize sthg. that is unexpected: *He wouldn't even consider our idea.* —*tr.v.* To make (sthg.) even: *even the soil with a rake.* ◆ **break even.** To come out of a situation without winning or losing money: *We broke even when we sold the house, getting just what we had paid for it.* **even if.** Whether or not: *Even if it rains, we'll go to the beach.* **even out.** *tr.v.* [sep.] To make (sthg.) equal or level: *We evened out the pieces of candy among the children.* —*intr.v.* To become equal or stable: *Business has been up and down, but we hope things will even out after a while.* **even so.** Nevertheless: *The team lost their best player, but even so, they won the game.* **even up.** *tr.v.* [sep.] To make (sthg.) equal: *I had to even up his haircut because one side had been cut shorter than the other.* **get even with.** To have revenge on (sbdy.): *He tried to get even with the manager who fired him.* **on an even keel.** In a stable state: *The new contract put the relationship between the company and its workers on an even keel.* —**e'ven·ly** *adv.* —**e'ven·ness** *n.* [U]

e·ven·hand·ed (ē'vən hăn'dĭd) *adj.* Dealing fairly with everyone; impartial: *Parents should be evenhanded with children.*

eve·ning (ēv'nĭng) *n.* [C; U] **1.** The period of decreasing daylight between afternoon and

night: *At evening the moon rose over the lake.*
2. The period between sunset and bedtime:
We spent a quiet evening at home.
evening dress *n.* **1.** [U] Formal clothing, for
men or women, worn for evening social
events. **2.** [C] An evening gown.
evening gown *n.* A woman's formal dress,
usually reaching to the floor or close to it.
e·vent (ĭ vĕnt′) *n.* **1.** An occurrence, incident, or experience, especially an important
one: *A trip to Brazil was the great event of her
life.* **2.** An item in a program of sports: *I like
to watch the jumping events at a horse show.*
◆ **in any event.** In any case; anyhow: *You
should come in any event.* **in the event.** If it
should happen; in case: *In the event of the
President's death, the Vice President takes
over.*
e·vent·ful (ĭ vĕnt′fəl) *adj.* **1.** Full of events:
an eventful afternoon. **2.** Important; momentous: *She made an eventful decision to change
jobs.* —**e·vent′ful·ly** *adv.* —**e·vent′ful·
ness** *n.* [U]
e·ven·tu·al (ĭ vĕn′cho͞o əl) *adj.* Happening
at an unspecified future time; ultimate: *We
never lost hope of eventual victory.* —**e·ven′-
tu·al·ly** *adv.*
e·ven·tu·al·i·ty (ĭ vĕn′cho͞o ăl′ĭ tē) *n.*,
pl. **e·ven·tu·al·i·ties.** Something that
may happen; a possibility: *One prepares for
the worst eventuality and hopes for the best
outcome.*
ev·er (ĕv′ər) *adv.* **1.** At all times; always:
They lived happily ever after. **2.** At any time:
Have you ever visited Pittsburgh? **3.** By any
chance; in any possible case or way: *How
could they ever have thought they would succeed at that?* **4.** *(used for emphasis, often
with* so*).* To a great extent or degree: *She's
ever so sorry.*
ev·er·green (ĕv′ər grēn′) *adj.* Having green
leaves or needles all year: *evergreen trees.*
—*n.* An evergreen tree, shrub, or plant: *Pine,
holly, and rhododendron are evergreens.*
ev·er·last·ing (ĕv′ər lăs′tĭng) *adj.* **1.**
Lasting forever; eternal: *everlasting life.* **2.**
Continuing for a long time: *everlasting happiness.* **3.** Lasting too long; wearisome: *everlasting work.* —**ev′er·last′ing·ly** *adv.*
ev·er·more (ĕv′ər môr′) *adv.* Forever; always: *They promised to be friends evermore.*
eve·ry (ĕv′rē) *adj.* **1.** Each: *every student in
the class.* **2.** Each in a specified series or at
specific intervals: *Take the medicine every
four hours.* **3.** The highest degree of; the
utmost: *I have every confidence they will succeed.* ◆ **every bit.** *Informal.* In all ways;
equally: *every bit as clever as we thought.*
every last or **single.** Without exception: *She
finally paid every last bill. She ate every sin-*

gle cookie. **every now and then** or **again.**
From time to time; occasionally: *The whole
family goes camping every now and then.*
every other. Each alternate: *The group meets
every other Tuesday.* **every so often.** At
intervals; occasionally: *We exchange letters
every so often.* —SEE NOTE at **she.**
eve·ry·bod·y (ĕv′rē bŏd′ē *or* ĕv′rē bŭd′ē)
pron. (used with a singular verb). Every person; everyone: *Everybody we knew was at the
party.*
eve·ry·day (ĕv′rē dā′) *adj.* **1.** Suitable for
ordinary days or occasions: *everyday clothes.*
2. Ordinary; usual: *an everyday event.*
eve·ry·one (ĕv′rē wŭn′) *pron. (used with a
singular verb).* Every person; everybody:
Everyone has bought a ticket.
eve·ry·thing (ĕv′rē thĭng′) *pron. (used with
a singular verb).* **1.** All things or all of a
group of things: *Everything in this room must
be packed.* **2.** The most important fact; the
thing that matters most: *When telling a joke,
timing is everything.*
eve·ry·where (ĕv′rē wâr′) *adv.* In any or
every place; in all places: *People were celebrating the news everywhere in town.*
e·vict (ĭ vĭkt′) *tr.v.* To force out (a tenant)
from an apartment, a house, or a building by
legal process: *The landlord evicted the man
who was living in that apartment because he
didn't pay his rent.* —**e·vic′tion** *n.* [C; U]
ev·i·dence (ĕv′ĭ dəns) *n.* [U] **1.** A thing or
things helpful in making a judgment or coming to a conclusion: *The fossils of seashells
were evidence that the region had once been
covered by water.* **2.** The statements, objects,
and facts accepted for consideration in a court
of law: *The evidence was not clear enough to
convince the jury that the defendant was
guilty.* **3.** Something that indicates; a sign:
*Constant laughter was evidence that the
show was very funny.* —*tr.v.* **ev·i·denced,
ev·i·denc·ing, ev·i·denc·es.** *Formal.* To
show (sthg.) clearly; prove: *Cheers and
applause evidenced the audience's approval.*
◆ **in evidence.** Plainly visible; to be seen:
*The welcome signs were in evidence among
the crowd at the airport.*
ev·i·dent (ĕv′ĭ dənt) *adj.* Easily seen or
understood; clear: *From the warm temperature and abundant flowers, it is evident
that spring is here.* —**ev′i·dent·ly** or
ev′i·dent′ly *adv.*
e·vil (ē′vəl) *adj.* **1.** Morally bad or wrong;
wicked: *evil deeds.* **2.** Causing pain or injury;
harmful: *an evil temper; an evil tongue.* —*n.*
1. [U] Wickedness: *a story about good and
evil.* **2.** [C] Something that causes harm: *the
social evils of poverty.* —**e′vil·ly** *adv.*
—**e′vil·ness** *n.* [U]

ă-cat; ā-pay; âr-care; ä-father; ĕ-get; ē-be; ĭ-sit; ī-nice; îr-here; ŏ-got; ō-go; ô-saw; oi-boy; ou-out;
o͞o-took; o͞o-boot; ŭ-cut; ûr-word; th-thin; *th*-this; hw-when; zh-vision; ə-about; N-French bon

e·vil·do·er (ē′vəl dōō′ər) *n.* A person who does evil things.

e·voke (ĭ vōk′) *tr.v.* **e·voked, e·vok·ing, e·vokes. 1.** To bring or call forth (sthg.); inspire: *The question evoked a long and complicated reply.* **2.** To call (sthg.) to mind by naming or suggesting: *a song that evokes memories.* —**e·voc′a·tive** (ĭ vōk′ə tĭv) *adj.*

ev·o·lu·tion (ĕv′ə lōō′shən) *n.* [U] **1.** A gradual process by which sthg. develops or changes into a different form: *the evolution of jazz.* **2.** The process by which groups of living things, such as species, change over a long period of time through natural selection, so that descendants are different from their ancestors. —**ev′o·lu′tion·ar′y** *adj.*

e·volve (ĭ vŏlv′) *v.* **e·volved, e·volv·ing, e·volves.** —*tr.* **1.** To develop (sthg.) gradually: *Several bankers evolved a plan to save the city from bankruptcy.* **2.** To develop (a characteristic) by biological evolution: *Cats have evolved an extraordinary sense of balance.* —*intr.* To undergo biological evolution: *Birds may have evolved from reptiles.*

ewe (yōō) *n.* A full-grown female sheep.

HOMONYMS: ewe, yew (shrub), **you** (pronoun).

ex. *abbr.* An abbreviation of example.

ex— *pref.* A prefix that means: **1.** *(often used with a hyphen).* Former: *ex-President; ex-wife.* **2.** Outside; out of; away from: *exit; exhale.*

WORD BUILDING: ex— The prefix **ex—** means "out of, from." Thus combining *ex—* with the root *—tend—*, "to stretch," gives us **extend**, "to stretch out." Similarly, in **express**, *ex—* combines with the root *—press—*, which means "to squeeze." So when we express ourselves, we "to squeeze out" our thoughts. Sometimes **ex—** takes the form of **e—**, as in **emit** (*e—* plus the root *—mit—*, "to send") meaning "to send out."

ex·ac·er·bate (ĭg zăs′ər bāt′) *tr.v.* **ex·ac·er·bat·ed, ex·ac·er·bat·ing, ex·ac·er·bates.** *Formal.* To make (sthg.) worse or more severe; aggravate: *The rumor exacerbated tensions between the two friends.* —**ex·ac′er·ba′tion** *n.* [C; U]

ex·act (ĭg zăkt′) *adj.* **1.** In complete agreement with fact or an original: *a person's exact words; an exact duplicate.* **2.** Accurate; precise: *An exact reading of these instruments is necessary in this experiment.* —*tr.v.* **1.** [*from*] To force the payment of (sthg.): *The king exacted new taxes from the people.* **2.** To require or demand (sthg.), especially by force or authority: *The teacher exacts strict discipline in class.* —**ex·act′ness** *n.* [U]

ex·act·ing (ĭg zăk′tĭng) *adj.* **1.** Making great demands; demanding: *I learn the most from an exacting teacher.* **2.** Requiring great effort, attention, or care: *A medical operation is an exacting procedure.* —**ex·act′ing·ly** *adv.*

ex·ac·ti·tude (ĭg zăk′tĭ tōōd) *n.* [U] *Formal.* The quality of being exact; exactness.

ex·act·ly (ĭg zăkt′lē) *adv.* **1.** In an exact manner; precisely: *The cake did not rise because I did not follow the recipe exactly.* **2.** In all respects; just: *Do exactly as you wish.* **3.** I agree; as you say: *"Exactly," he replied, "I feel the same way."*

ex·ag·ger·ate (ĭg zăj′ə rāt′) *v.* **ex·ag·ger·at·ed, ex·ag·ger·at·ing, ex·ag·ger·ates.** —*tr.* **1.** To speak or write about (sthg.) as if greater or more important than is really the case: *He exaggerated his accomplishments in order to get the job.* **2.** To enlarge or increase (sthg.) to an abnormal degree: *The unusually high tides exaggerated the destructive force of the hurricane.* —*intr.* To make overstatements: *It's important not to exaggerate when writing stories for a newspaper.* —**ex·ag′ger·at′ed** *adj.* —**ex·ag′ger·a′tion** *n.* [C; U]

ex·alt (ĭg zôlt′) *tr.v. Formal.* **1.** To raise (sbdy.) in position, status, rank, or regard; elevate: *The emperor exalted the faithful servant to a place among his most trusted advisors.* **2.** To praise (sbdy.); glorify. —**ex′al·ta′tion** (ĕg′zôl tā′shən) *n.* [U]

ex·alt·ed (ĭg zôl′tĭd) *adj.* **1.** Having high rank or status; dignified: *The emperor is an exalted person.* **2.** Elevated in style or condition; noble: *the exalted style of epic poetry.*

ex·am (ĭg zăm′) *n.* An examination.

ex·am·i·na·tion (ĭg zăm′ə nā′shən) *n.* **1.** [C; U] The act of examining; inspection: *Close examination of the diamond showed it was a fake.* **2.** [C] A set of questions or exercises testing knowledge or skill; a test: *Final examinations are next week.* **3.** [C] A formal questioning: *the lawyer's examination of the witness in a trial.*

ex·am·ine (ĭg zăm′ĭn) *tr.v.* **ex·am·ined, ex·am·in·ing, ex·am·ines. 1.** To observe (sbdy./sthg.) carefully; inspect or study: *Examine the plant cells under a microscope.* **2.** To inspect or test (sbdy./sthg.) for evidence of disease, abnormality, or defects: *The inspector examined the bridge for cracks.* **3.** To question (sbdy.) formally to obtain information or facts: *The prosecutor examined the witness in court.* **4.** To ask (sbdy.) questions to test knowledge: *State boards examine teachers before giving them teaching licenses.* See Synonyms at **ask.** —**ex·am′in·er** *n.*

ex·am·ple (ĭg zăm′pəl) *n.* **1.** A person or thing that is typical of a whole class or group; a sample or specimen: *The Empire State Building is an example of a graceful skyscraper.* **2.** A person or thing that is worthy of imitation; a model: *This article is an example of good writing.* **3.** A person or thing that is intended to serve as a warning to others: *They lost their scholarships because of cheating—let that be an example to you!* **4.** A completed problem or exercise given to illustrate a principle or method: *an example of multiplication; an example of the form of a composition.* ◆ **for example.** As an illustration; for instance: *We have several team sports, for example, baseball and soccer.* **make an example of.** To punish (sbdy.) in order to warn others: *The court made an example of the dishonest dealer by imposing heavy fines on him.* **set an example.** To give or be a model of good behavior: *We set an example for the school children by cleaning up their playground.*

ex·as·per·ate (ĭg zăs′pə rāt′) *tr.v.* **ex·as·per·at·ed, ex·as·per·at·ing, ex·as·per·ates.** To make (sbdy.) angry or impatient; irritate greatly: *The dog's constant barking exasperated the neighbors.* —**ex·as′per·a′tion** *n.* [U]

ex·ca·vate (ĕk′skə vāt′) *tr.v.* **ex·ca·vat·ed, ex·ca·vat·ing, ex·ca·vates.** **1.** To make a hole in (sthg.); hollow out: *excavate a hillside to build a tunnel.* **2.** To create or uncover (sthg.) by digging: *excavate the foundation for a house.* **3.** To expose or uncover (sthg.) by digging: *The researchers excavated the remains of an ancient settlement.*

ex·ca·va·tion (ĕk′skə vā′shən) *n.* **1.** [U] The act of excavating: *Excavation of the basement will begin soon.* **2.** [C] A hole formed by excavation: *a deep excavation for the new skyscraper.*

ex·ca·va·tor (ĕk′skə vā′tər) *n.* A person or thing that excavates, especially a backhoe.

ex·ceed (ĭk sēd′) *tr.v.* **1.** To be greater than (sthg.); surpass: *The play's tremendous success exceeded everyone's hopes.* **2.** To go beyond the limits of (sthg.): *Do not exceed the speed limit.*

ex·ceed·ing (ĭk sē′dĭng) *adj.* Extreme; extraordinary: *a night of exceeding darkness.*

ex·ceed·ing·ly (ĭk sē′dĭng lē) *adv.* To an advanced or unusual degree; extremely: *exceedingly hot weather; exceedingly delicate work.*

ex·cel (ĭk sĕl′) *v.* **ex·celled, ex·cel·ling, ex·cels.** —*tr.* To be better than (sthg.); surpass: *Their performance excelled all the others.* —*intr.* To be better than others: *Few people excel at every sport.* ◆ **excel (one-self).** To do even better than one usually does: *The director has excelled himself with his latest film.*

ex·cel·lence (ĕk′sə ləns) *n.* [U] The condition or quality of excelling; superiority: *artistic excellence; a prize given for excellence in writing.*

ex·cel·lent (ĕk′sə lənt) *adj.* Of the highest quality; superb: *an excellent report; an excellent musician.* —**ex′cel·lent·ly** *adv.*

ex·cept (ĭk sĕpt′) *prep.* Not including; excluding; but: *All the rooms except one are clean.* —*conj.* **1.** If it were not for the fact that; only: *I could go with you except that I have to study.* **2.** Otherwise than: *He would not open his mouth except to argue.* —*tr.v. Formal.* [*from*] To leave (sbdy./sthg.) out; exclude: *I had helped earlier and was excepted from staying to clean up.*

ex·cept·ing (ĭk sĕp′tĭng) *prep. Formal.* With the exception of: *No one excepting our father wanted to go fishing in the rain.*

ex·cep·tion (ĭk sĕp′shən) *n.* **1.** [U] The act of excepting or the condition of being excepted: *All our guests have arrived with the exception of two.* **2.** [C] A person or thing that is excepted: *I like all my classes with one exception.* **3.** [U] An objection or a criticism: *opinions that are open to exception.* ◆ **make an exception.** To allow the breaking of a rule: *Animals are not allowed in the restaurant, but for a guide dog they'll make an exception.* **take exception to.** To be angered or upset by (sthg.): *take exception to a tasteless joke.*

ex·cep·tion·al (ĭk sĕp′shə nəl) *adj.* **1.** Being an exception; uncommon: *The speaker discussed the topic with exceptional frankness.* **2.** Very much above average; extraordinary: *an exceptional memory.* —**ex·cep′tion·al·ly** *adv.*

ex·cerpt (ĕk′sûrpt′) *n.* A passage or scene selected from a longer work, such as a book, film, or piece of music: *The author read an excerpt from her book.* —*tr.v.* (ĭk sûrpt′). To select or use (a passage or segment from a longer work): *The author excerpted parts of several famous speeches.*

ex·cess (ĭk sĕs′ *or* ĕk′sĕs′) *n.* **1.** [U] The state of going beyond what is normal or sufficient: *The waiter filled my glass to excess and it spilled over.* **2.** [U] An amount or a quantity that is more than what is needed; a surplus: *I used too much glue and had to wipe away the excess.* **3.** [C] The amount or degree by which one amount is greater than another: *an excess of four pounds.* —*adj.* Being more than what is usual, permitted, or required: *Remove the excess fat.* ◆ **in excess of.** Greater than; more than: *a package weighing in excess of 40 pounds.*

ex·ces·sive (ĭk sĕs′ĭv) *adj.* Going beyond a normal, usual, or proper limit: *Excessive rains caused flooding.* —**ex·ces′sive·ly** *adv.*

ex·change (ĭks chānj′) *tr.v.* **ex·changed, ex·chang·ing, ex·chang·es.** **1.** To give (sthg.) in return for sthg. received: *I exchanged my pesos for dollars.* **2.** To give and receive (sthg.) mutually: *exchange glances; exchange letters.* **3.** To turn (sthg.) in for replacement: *I exchanged the tie for a belt at the store.* —*n.* **1.** [C; U] An act of exchanging: *an exchange of ideas; gifts given in exchange.* **2.** [C] A thing that is exchanged: *The watch seemed a fair exchange for the compass.* **3.** [C] A place where things, especially stocks or commodities, are exchanged or traded: *a stock exchange.* —**ex•change′-a•ble** *adj.*

ex•cise (ĭk sīz′) *tr.v.* **ex•cised, ex•cis•ing, ex•cis•es.** *Formal.* [*from*] To remove (sthg.) by cutting: *excise two scenes from a movie.* —**ex•ci′sion** (ĭk sĭzh′ən) *n.* [C; U]

ex•cise tax (ĕk′sīz′) *n.* A tax on production, sale, or use of certain items or services within a country: *The government raised excise taxes on liquor and tobacco.*

ex•cit•a•ble (ĭk sī′tə bəl) *adj.* Easily excited: *a jumpy and excitable cat.* —**ex•cit′a•bil′-i•ty** *n.* [U] —**ex•cit′a•bly** *adv.*

ex•cite (ĭk sīt′) *tr.v.* **ex•cit•ed, ex•cit•ing, ex•cites.** **1.** To cause strong feeling in (sbdy.): *The speaker excited the audience.* **2.** To cause (a reaction or an emotion, for example): *The news report excited our curiosity.* **3.** To move or stir (sbdy./sthg.) to activity: *The vaccine excites the immune system to produce antibodies against the disease.*

ex•cit•ed (ĭk sī′tĭd) *adj.* Full of happy interest and eagerness: *The astronomers were very excited about their discovery of a new star.* —**ex•cit′ed•ly** *adv.*

ex•cite•ment (ĭk sīt′mənt) *n.* [U] **1.** The act of exciting or the state of being excited. **2.** Nervous activity and expectation: *There was excitement in the air before the performance.*

ex•cit•ing (ĭk sī′tĭng) *adj.* Creating or producing excitement: *an exciting trip across country.* —**ex•cit′ing•ly** *adv.*

ex•claim (ĭk sklām′) *tr. & intr.v.* To say or cry out suddenly, from surprise, pleasure, impatience, or other emotion: *"How nice of you to stop by!" he exclaimed. She exclaimed with pleasure when she saw the new bike.*

ex•cla•ma•tion (ĕk′sklə mā′shən) *n.* [C; U] Something that is said suddenly or forcefully: *exclamations of surprise; sounds of exclamation.*

exclamation mark *n.* An exclamation point.

exclamation point *n.* A punctuation mark (!) used after an exclamation.

ex•clude (ĭk sklōōd′) *tr.v.* **ex•clud•ed, ex•clud•ing, ex•cludes.** [*from*] **1.** To prevent (sbdy./sthg.) from entering; keep out: *a rule that excludes young children from the big swimming pool.* **2.** To prevent (sthg.) from being included, considered, or accepted: *Let's not exclude the possibility of rain in making our plans.* —**ex•clu′sion** *n.* [U]

ex•clu•sive (ĭk sklōō′sĭv) *adj.* **1.** Not shared with others: *exclusive ownership of*

the estate. **2.** Undivided; complete: *The audience gave the diver their exclusive attention.* **3.** Excluding some or most people, as from membership or participation; restricted: *an exclusive school.* —**ex•clu′sive•ly** *adv.* —**ex•clu′sive•ness** *n.* [U]

exclusive of *prep.* Not including; besides: *Exclusive of last-minute changes, this book is finished.*

ex•com•mu•ni•cate (ĕks′kə myōō′nĭ kāt′) *tr.v.* **ex•com•mu•ni•cat•ed, ex•com•mu•ni•cat•ing, ex•com•mu•ni•cates.** To take away the right of church membership from (sbdy.) by official authority: *In 1533 the Pope excommunicated Henry VIII.* —**ex′com•mu′-ni•ca′tion** *n.* [C; U]

ex•cre•ment (ĕk′skrə mənt) *n.* [U] Solid waste matter that passes out of a person's or an animal's body after digestion.

ex•crete (ĭk skrēt′) *tr.v.* **ex•cret•ed, ex•cret•ing, ex•cretes.** *Formal.* To pass (waste matter) out of the body: *Sweat and urine are excreted from the body.*

ex•cru•ci•at•ing (ĭk skrōō′shē ā′tĭng) *adj.* Intensely painful; excruciating pain of a toothache. —**ex•cru′ci•at′ing•ly** *adv.*

ex•cur•sion (ĭk skûr′zhən) *n.* **1.** A short journey made for pleasure; an outing: *an excursion to the park.* **2.** A round trip on a passenger vehicle at a special reduced fare: *Excursions are a cheap way to travel abroad.*

ex•cuse (ĭk skyōōz′) *tr.v.* **ex•cused, ex•cus•ing, ex•cus•es.** **1.** To try to remove the blame from (sbdy./sthg.): *She excused herself for being late.* **2.** To forgive (sbdy.); pardon: *Excuse me for taking your chair.* See Synonyms at **forgive. 3.** To serve as an apology for (sthg.); justify: *Nothing excuses such rudeness.* **4.** To free or release (sbdy.) from a duty, an activity, or an obligation: *All seniors will be excused from school early today.* —*n.* (ĭk skyōōs′). **1.** [C] An explanation that is given to justify or obtain forgiveness: *I offered my excuses.* **2.** [C; U] Something that serves to excuse; a justification: *There is no excuse for such thoughtless behavior.* **3.** [C] A note explaining an absence: *You'll need an excuse from your doctor.* ♦ **a poor excuse for.** An inferior example of (sthg.): *Their old station wagon is a poor excuse for a car.* —**ex•cus′a•ble** *adj.* —**ex•cus′a•bly** *adv.*

exec. *abbr.* An abbreviation of executive.

ex•e•cute (ĕk′sĭ kyōōt′) *tr.v.* **ex•e•cut•ed, ex•e•cut•ing, ex•e•cutes.** **1.** To put (sthg.) into effect; carry out: *execute a program on computer; execute the law fairly.* **2.** To perform (sthg.); do: *execute a U-turn.* **3.** To make (sthg.) valid, as by signing: *execute a deed.* **4.** To kill (sbdy.), especially by carrying out a legal sentence: *execute a convicted criminal.*

ex•e•cu•tion (ĕk′sĭ kyōō′shən) *n.* **1.** [U] The act of executing sthg.: *administrators* responsible for the execution of a new school policy. **2.** [U] The manner, style, or result of completing or carrying sthg. out: *the design and execution of a plan.* **3.** [C; U] The act of putting a person to death as a lawful penalty. **4.** [U] The validation of a legal document by finishing all necessary formalities: *the execution of a deed.*

ex·e·cu·tion·er (ĕk′sĭ kyōō′shə nər) *n.* A person who legally puts a person to death as punishment for a crime.

ex·ec·u·tive (ĭg zĕk′yə tĭv) *n.* A person or group that manages an organization, especially a corporation or government division: *an executive responsible for the running of a company.* —*adj.* **1.** Relating to or capable of carrying out plans, duties, or other tasks: *a committee having executive powers.* **2.** Relating to the branch of government concerned with putting laws into effect or managing the country: *The President leads the executive branch of the U.S. government.*

ex·ec·u·tor (ĭg zĕk′yə tər) *n.* A person who is responsible for carrying out the terms of a will.

ex·em·pla·ry (ĭg zĕm′plə rē) *adj.* **1.** Worthy of imitation; commendable: *exemplary behavior.* **2.** Serving as an illustration; typical: *an exemplary Supreme Court case.* **3.** Serving as a warning: *an exemplary glance.* —**ex·em′pla′ri·ly** *adv.*

ex·em·pli·fy (ĭg zĕm′plə fī′) *tr.v.* **ex·em·pli·fied, ex·em·pli·fy·ing, ex·em·pli·fies.** *Formal.* To be an example of (sthg.); illustrate: *a movie that exemplifies a director's style.*

ex·empt (ĭg zĕmpt′) *tr.v.* [*from*] To free (sbdy.) from a duty or an obligation; excuse: *Regulations exempt certain people from serving on juries.* —*adj.* Freed from a duty or an obligation that is required of others; excused: *Church property is exempt from taxes.*

ex·emp·tion (ĭg zĕmp′shən) *n.* [C; U] The act of exempting or the condition of being exempt: *the exemption of food from the sales tax.*

ex·er·cise (ĕk′sər sīz′) *n.* **1.** [C; U] An activity that requires strenuous physical effort, especially to maintain or develop fitness: *stretching exercises for the back; a healthy form of exercise.* **2.** [C] A lesson, problem, or task performed to develop, maintain, or increase skill: *a book with vocabulary exercises at the end of each chapter.* **3.** [U] The active use or performance of sthg.: *the exercise of good judgment; the exercise of official duties.* **4. exercises.** A ceremony or program for an audience: *college graduation exercises.* —*v.* **ex·er·cised, ex·er·cis·ing, ex·er·cis·es.** —*tr.* To make active use of (sthg.); employ: *By voting we exercise our*

rights as citizens. **2.** To cause (sbdy./sthg.) to practice or work in order to train, strengthen, or develop: *exercise a horse; exercise your stiff muscles.* —*intr.* To take exercise: *We exercise at our health club for an hour daily.*

ex·ert (ĭg zûrt′) *tr.v.* **1.** To use (force or energy); put forth: *I exerted all my strength to move the box.* **2.** To put (oneself) to serious mental or physical effort: *The hikers exerted themselves to climb the mountain by noon.* —**ex·er′tion** *n.* [C; U]

ex·hale (ĕks hāl′ *or* ĕk sāl′) *v.* **ex·haled, ex·hal·ing, ex·hales.** —*intr.* To breathe out: *The doctor told the patient to exhale slowly.* —*tr.* To breathe out or blow forth (sthg.): *The dragon exhaled fire and smoke.*

ex·haust (ĭg zôst′) *tr.v.* **1.** To tire (sbdy.) greatly: *Moving the heavy furniture exhausted us all.* **2.** To use (sthg.) completely: *Tickets and snacks exhausted our money.* **3.** To let out or draw off (sthg.): *exhaust harmful gases through a pipe.* **4.** To cover (sthg.) completely: *exhaust a topic of conversation.* —*n.* **1.** [U] The escape or release of waste gases or vapors, as from an engine: *The fan is too small to ensure quick exhaust of the fumes.* **2.** [U] The vapors or gases so released: *A cloud of exhaust came from the bus.* **3.** [C] An exhaust pipe or tailpipe: *It sounds like your car needs a new exhaust.* —**ex·haust′ed·ly** *adv.*

ex·haust·ed (ĭg zô′stĭd) *adj.* Very tired: *I was exhausted after the long trip.*

ex·haust·ing (ĭg zô′stĭng) *adj.* Causing sbdy. to be very tired: *The long trip was exhausting.*

ex·haus·tion (ĭg zôs′chən) *n.* [U] **1.** An act of exhausting: *exhaustion of the water supply.* **2.** The state of being very tired; extreme fatigue: *The runner collapsed from exhaustion.*

ex·haus·tive (ĭg zô′stĭv) *adj.* Complete; thorough: *an exhaustive search for a solution.* —**ex·haus′tive·ly** *adv.* —**ex·haus′tive·ness** *n.* [U]

ex·hib·it (ĭg zĭb′ĭt) *tr.v.* **1.** To present (sthg.) for the public to view; display: *exhibit new artworks at a gallery.* **2.** To give evidence of (sthg.); demonstrate: *The doctors exhibited great skill in repairing the patient's knee.* —*n.* **1.** Something exhibited; a display: *She studied the museum's fossil exhibits for her new book.* **2.** A public showing; an exhibition: *The art exhibit will open next month.* **3.** Something formally introduced as evidence in a court of law: *The knife was presented as exhibit A.* —**ex·hib′i·tor** *n.*

ex·hi·bi·tion (ĕk′sə bĭsh′ən) *n.* **1.** [C; U] The act of exhibiting: *an exhibition of poor taste.* **2.** [C] A large-scale public showing: *In Miami he attended an exhibition of boating equipment.*

ex·hi·bi·tion·ism (ĕk′sə bĭsh′ə nĭz′əm) *n.* [U] The act or practice of deliberately behaving in a way that attracts attention, often sexual in nature. —**ex′hi·bi′tion·ist′** *n.*

ex·hil·a·rate (ĭg zĭl′ə rāt′) *tr.v.* **ex·hil·a·rat·ed, ex·hil·a·rat·ing, ex·hil·a·rates. 1.** To cause (sbdy.) to feel happy: *The victory exhilarated the whole school.* **2.** To make (sbdy.) feel more lively; stimulate: *A walk in the cold will exhilarate us.* —**ex·hil′a·ra′tion** *n.* [U]

ex·hil·a·rat·ed (ĭg zĭl′ə rā′tĭd) *adj.* **1.** Feeling very happy and excited: *We were exhilarated when our school won the championship.* **2.** Feeling stimulated: *They were exhilarated by a swim in the ocean.*

ex·hil·a·rat·ing (ĭg zĭl′ə rā′tĭng) *adj.* **1.** Causing sbdy. to feel happy and excited: *The race was exhilarating.* **2.** Causing sbdy. to feel stimulated: *Our early morning walk was exhilarating.*

ex·hort (ĭg zôrt′) *tr.v. Formal.* [*to*] To urge (sbdy.) to do sthg.: *The candidate exhorted the crowd to vote.* —**ex′hor·ta′tion** *n.* [C; U]

ex·hume (ĭg zōōm′) *tr.v.* **ex·humed, ex·hum·ing, ex·humes.** *Formal.* To dig up or remove (a body) from a grave: *a court order to exhume the body.*

ex·ile (ĕg′zīl′ *or* ĕk′sīl′) *n.* **1.** [U] Enforced or voluntary absence from one's native country: *Exile was the punishment for any opposing political activities.* **2.** [U] The condition or a period of living away from one's native country: *The author's exile lasted ten years.* **3.** [C] A person who lives away from his or her native country: *The exiles published a magazine in their native language.* —*tr.v.* **ex·iled, ex·il·ing, ex·iles.** To send (sbdy.) into exile; banish: *The dictator exiled members of the opposition party.*

ex·ist (ĭg zĭst′) *intr.v.* **1.** To be real: *How many chemical elements have been shown to exist?* **2.** To have life; live: *Dinosaurs existed millions of years ago.* **3.** To continue; persist: *old traditions that still exist in parts of the country.* **4.** To be present; occur: *A new spirit of cooperation existed on both sides.* —**ex·is′tent** *adj.*

ex·is·tence (ĭg zĭs′təns) *n.* **1.** [U] The fact or condition of existing; being: *a group no longer in existence.* **2.** [U] The fact or condition of continued being; life: *our existence on Earth.* **3.** [C] A manner of existing: *The former star lived an ordinary existence.* **4.** [U] Occurrence; presence: *The existence of oil deposits in the rocks brought many drilling companies to the region.*

ex·ist·ing (ĭg zĭs′tĭng) *adj.* Present, alive, or now visible: *Are you aware of existing conditions in that country? How many existing species are there?*

ex·it (ĕg′zĭt *or* ĕk′sĭt) *n.* **1.** The act of going away or out: *I made a quick exit from the snake house at the zoo.* **2.** A passage or way out: *Exits must be clearly marked.* —*v.* —*intr.* To make one's exit; depart: *Please exit to the left.* —*tr.* To go out of (sthg.); leave: *We exited the plane through a rear door.*

exo— *pref.* A prefix that means outside or external: *exoskeleton.*

ex·o·dus (ĕk′sə dəs) *n. (usually singular).* A departure of a large number of people: *an exodus from the cities to the suburbs.*

ex·on·er·ate (ĭg zŏn′ə rāt′) *tr.v.* **ex·on·er·at·ed, ex·on·er·at·ing, ex·on·er·ates.** *Formal.* To free (sbdy.) from blame: *The jury's decision exonerated the defendant.* —**ex·on′er·a′tion** *n.* [U]

ex·or·bi·tant (ĭg zôr′bĭ tənt) *adj.* Going beyond normal limits, as of custom or fairness; too much: *an exorbitant price on an imported car.* —**ex·or′bi·tance** *n.* [U] —**ex·or′bi·tant·ly** *adv.*

ex·or·cise (ĕk′sôr sīz′) *tr.v.* **ex·or·cised, ex·or·cis·ing, ex·or·cis·es. 1.** To drive away (an evil spirit), usually by incantation, prayer, or command. **2.** To free (sbdy./sthg.) from evil spirits: *the exorcising of an old house.* —**ex′or·cis′m** *n.* [U] —**ex′or·cist′** *n.*

ex·o·skel·e·ton (ĕk′sō skĕl′ĭ tn) *n.* A hard protective outer body covering, as the shell of a crab; an external skeleton.

ex·ot·ic (ĭg zŏt′ĭk) *adj.* **1.** From another part of the world; foreign: *exotic imported birds.* **2.** Strikingly unfamiliar or unusual: *the exotic beauty of the Galápagos Islands.* —*n.* A thing that is exotic: *Many exotics were exhibited at the flower show.* —**ex·ot′i·cal·ly** *adv.* —**ex·ot′ic·ness** *n.* [U]

ex·pand (ĭk spănd′) *v.* —*tr.* **1.** To increase the size, number, volume, or scope of (sthg.); enlarge: *expand a balloon with air; expand the business into new areas.* **2.** To express (sthg.) at greater length or in more detail; enlarge upon: *She promised to expand her ideas in her next presentation.* **3.** To open (sthg.) up or out; unfold: *The owl expanded its wings and flew away.* —*intr.* **1.** To become greater in size, volume, quantity, or scope: *Gases expand when heated.* See Synonyms at **increase. 2.** To open up or out; unfold: *The sofa expands into a bed.* **3.** To speak or write at length or in detail: *Committee members expanded on the issues at the meeting.* —**ex·pand′a·ble** *adj.*

ex·panse (ĭk spăns′) *n.* A wide and open area, as of surface, land, or sky: *a vast expanse of desert.*

ex·pan·sion (ĭk spăn′shən) *n.* **1.** [U] The act of expanding: *the growth and expansion of industry.* **2.** [C] Something formed or produced by expansion: *These suburbs are an expansion of the city.* **3.** [C] The extent or amount by which sthg. has increased: *a 40 percent expansion in sales.*

E

ex·pan·sive (ĭk spăn′sĭv) *adj.* **1.** Able or tending to expand: *Balloons are made of expansive material.* **2.** Broad in size or extent; comprehensive: *an expansive view of world affairs.* **3.** Open, communicative, and generous: *Expansive hosts make their guests feel at home.* **4.** Grand in scale: *the calm expansive lake.* **—ex·pan′sive·ly** *adv.* **—ex·pan′-sive·ness** *n.* [U]

ex·pa·tri·ate (ĕk spā′trē āt′) *tr.v.* **ex·pa·tri·at·ed, ex·pa·tri·at·ing, ex·pa·tri·ates.** *Formal.* **1.** To send (sbdy.) into exile. **2.** To voluntarily remove (oneself) from one's native land: *Many American writers expatriated themselves to France in the 1920s.* **—n.** (ĕk spā′trē ĭt). A person who has gone to live in a foreign country: *The community of expatriates grew after the war.* **—ex·pa′tri·a′tion** *n.* [U]

ex·pect (ĭk spĕkt′) *tr.v.* **1.** To believe or hope that (sthg.) will happen: *expecting a telephone call.* **2.** To consider (sthg.) reasonable or due: *The host will expect an apology for your breaking the dish.* **3.** *Informal.* To assume (sthg.) to be true; suppose: *I expect you're right.*

Synonyms: expect, anticipate, hope, await. These verbs have to do with looking ahead to sthg. in the future. **Expect** means to look forward to sthg. that is likely to happen: *My brother expects to get his braces removed next week.* **Anticipate** often means to take advance action, such as to prevent sthg. expected from happening: *The cook anticipated trouble and put the pot roast out of the dog's reach.* **Hope** means to look forward to sthg. with desire and usually to trust that it will actually happen: *We hope to see you at the annual meeting.* **Await** means to wait expectantly for sthg.: *I am eagerly awaiting your letter.*

---

ex·pec·tant (ĭk spĕk′tənt) *adj.* **1.** Having or showing a feeling of expectation: *an expectant audience; an expectant look.* **2.** Awaiting the birth of a child: *expectant parents.* **—ex·pec′tant·ly** *adv.*

ex·pec·ta·tion (ĕk′spĕk tā′shən) *n.* **1.** [U] The act of expecting: *waiting by the phone in expectation of a call.* **2.** [U] Anticipation: *eyes shining with expectation.* **3. expectations.** Belief in future success or gain: *He graduated with a degree in engineering and high expectations.*

ex·pe·di·ence (ĭk spē′dē əns) *n.* [U] Expediency.

ex·pe·di·en·cy (ĭk spē′dē ən sē) *n., pl.* **ex·pe·di·en·cies. 1.** [C; U] Appropriateness to the purpose at hand; fitness: *We agreed on the expediency of selling the land.*

2. [U] Self-interest: *Their political views seem to be nothing but expediency.*

ex·pe·di·ent (ĭk spē′dē ənt) *adj.* **1.** Suited to a particular purpose; appropriate: *It was expedient to replace the old building with a park.* **2.** Promoting one's own interests; self-serving: *We try to do what is right, not what is merely expedient.* **—n.** Something that is a means to an end: *Shopping by mail is a useful expedient for people in remote areas.* **—ex·pe′di·ent·ly** *adv.*

ex·pe·dite (ĕk′spĭ dīt′) *tr.v.* **ex·pe·dit·ed, ex·pe·dit·ing, ex·pe·dites.** *Formal.* **1.** To speed up the progress of (sthg.); make easier: *My telephone call expedited delivery of the package.* **2.** To perform (sthg.) quickly and efficiently: *expedite a job.* **—ex′pe·dit′er, ex′pe·di′tor** *n.*

ex·pe·di·tion (ĕk′spĭ dĭsh′ən) *n.* **1.** A trip made by a group of people with a definite purpose: *a geological expedition through the canyon.* **2.** The group making such a trip: *The expedition set off at dawn.*

ex·pe·di·tious (ĕk′spĭ dĭsh′əs) *adj.* Done with speed and efficiency: *The most expeditious transportation over long distances is by airplane.* **—ex′pe·di′tious·ly** *adv.* **—ex′pe·di′tious·ness** *n.* [U]

ex·pel (ĭk spĕl′) *tr.v.* **ex·pelled, ex·pel·ling, ex·pels. 1.** To force or drive (sbdy./ sthg.) out; eject forcefully: *expel air from the lungs.* **2.** To force (sbdy.) to leave; deprive of membership: *The dean expelled several students for cheating.*

ex·pend (ĭk spĕnd′) *tr.v.* **1.** To spend (sthg.): *expend tax money on health care.* **2.** To use (sthg.); consume: *expend energy.*

ex·pend·a·ble (ĭk spĕn′də bəl) *adj.* **1.** Likely to be used or consumed: *an expendable source of energy.* **2.** Not worth saving or reusing: *After 20 years of service the boat was considered expendable and wasn't repaired.* **3.** Likely to be given up or sacrificed, usually to gain an objective: *In peacetime, some army bases are expendable.*

ex·pen·di·ture (ĭk spĕn′də chər) *n.* **1.** [U] The act or process of spending or using; outlay: *the expenditure of city funds for a recycling plant.* **2.** [C] An amount expended: *The council must account for all expenditures.*

ex·pense (ĭk spĕns′) *n.* **1.** [C; U] Something spent to achieve a purpose: *an expense of time and effort on the project.* **2.** [U] A loss for the sake of sthg. gained; a sacrifice: *He devoted himself to work at the expense of time with his family.* **3.** [C] An expenditure of money; a cost: *With so many visitors, food is our biggest expense.* **4. expenses.** Charges paid for an employee in doing a job, especially while away from the office: *My travel expenses*

---

include food and lodging. **5.** [C] Something requiring one to spend money: *Owning a car can be a big expense.* ◆ **at (one's) expense.** Causing pain or financial loss to sbdy.: *He told a joke at my expense.*

ex·pen·sive (ĭk spĕn′sĭv) *adj.* **1.** High-priced; costly: *an expensive perfume.* **2.** Marked by high prices: *an expensive store.* —**ex·pen′sive·ly** *adv.* —**ex·pen′sive·ness** *n.* [U]

ex·pe·ri·ence (ĭk spîr′ē əns) *n.* **1.** [U] **a.** Active participation in events or activities: *I learned more from experience than from reading books.* **b.** The knowledge or skill gained from such participation: *a carpenter with a lot of experience.* **2.** [C] An event or series of events participated in or lived through: *That trip was an unforgettable experience.* —*tr.v.* **ex·per·i·enced, ex·per·i·enc·ing, ex·per·i·enc·es.** To participate in (sthg.) personally; undergo: *experience a great adventure; experience the excitement of winning a race.*

ex·pe·ri·enced (ĭk spîr′ē ənst) *adj.* Having knowledge as a result of active participation or practice: *an experienced teacher.*

ex·per·i·ment (ĭk spĕr′ə mənt) *n.* A test to find out about or show sthg.: *experiments in the use of color for road signs; medical experiments with new drugs to fight infection.* —*intr.v.* (ĭk spĕr′ə mĕnt′). **1.** To conduct an experiment; make tests or trials: *experiment on different breeds of mice.* **2.** To try sthg. new, especially in order to gain experience: *We experimented with different kinds of paint.* —**ex·per′i·ment′er** *n.*

ex·per·i·men·tal (ĭk spĕr′ə mĕn′tl) *adj.* **1.** Relating to experiments: *Physics and chemistry are experimental sciences.* **2.** Of the nature of an experiment; being or undergoing a test: *an experimental cancer treatment.* —**ex·per′i·men′tal·ly** *adv.*

ex·per·i·men·ta·tion (ĭk spĕr′ə mĕn·tā′shən) *n.* [U] The act, process, or practice of experimenting: *I discovered how to make good biscuits after much experimentation.*

ex·pert (ĕk′spûrt) *n.* A person with great knowledge or skill in a particular field: *Doctors are experts in medicine.* —*adj.* (ĕk′spûrt *or* ĭk spûrt′). Having great knowledge or skill as a result of experience or training: *The forest ranger was an expert guide.* See Synonyms at **proficient.** —**ex′pert·ly** *adv.*

ex·per·tise (ĕk′spûr tēz′) *n.* [U] Expert advice, opinion, skill, or knowledge: *the expertise of a fine jeweler.*

ex·pire (ĭk spîr′) *intr.v.* **ex·pired, ex·pir·ing, ex·pires.** **1.** To come to an end; terminate: *When our dog's license expires, we have to renew it.* **2.** *Formal.* To die: *The injured bird expired before we could get help for it.* —**ex′pi·ra′tion** (ĕk′spə rā′shən) *n.* [U]

ex·plain (ĭk splān′) *v.* —*tr.* **1.** To make (sthg.) clear or easy to understand: *explain the rules of a game; explain a job to a substitute.* **2.** To give reasons for (sthg.); justify: *We were asked to explain our noisy behavior during class.* —*intr.* To make sthg. clear or easy to understand: *Listen. I'll explain.* ◆ **explain away.** *tr.v.* [sep.] To get rid of (sthg.) by explaining: *There is no way to explain away my carelessness.* —**ex·plain′a·ble** *adj.*

ex·pla·na·tion (ĕk′splə nā′shən) *n.* **1.** [U] The act of explaining: *So much time was spent on explanation that the class was boring.* **2.** [C] Something that explains: *The police looked for an explanation for the crime.*

ex·plan·a·to·ry (ĭk splăn′ə tôr′ē) *adj.* Serving or intended to explain: *The math book has explanatory notes to go along with some problems.*

ex·ple·tive (ĕk′splĭ tĭv) *n.* A word or phrase used in exclamation, especially one that is vulgar or obscene: *By law, some expletives cannot be broadcast on radio or TV.*

ex·pli·ca·ble (ĕk′splĭ kə bəl *or* ĭk splĭk′ə bəl) *adj.* Possible to explain: *He disappeared for no explicable reason.*

ex·plic·it (ĭk splĭs′ĭt) *adj.* **1.** Fully and clearly expressed; complete: *an explicit statement of their plans for a new school.* **2.** Showing nudity, sex, or violence: *sexually explicit photographs.* —**ex·plic′it·ly** *adv.* —**ex·plic′it·ness** *n.* [U]

ex·plode (ĭk splōd′) *v.* **ex·plod·ed, ex·plod·ing, ex·plodes.** —*intr.* **1.** To release energy in an explosion; blow up: *Fireworks exploded all around.* **2.** To burst violently as a result of internal pressure: *Suddenly the bottle of soda water exploded.* **3.** To burst forth or break out suddenly: *The farmer exploded with anger at the hunters.* **4.** To increase suddenly and sharply: *The population has exploded in the past decade.* —*tr.* **1.** To cause (sthg.) to undergo an explosion; set off: *The engineers exploded the dynamite to open a passage through the rock.* **2.** To show (sthg.) to be false or unreliable: *explode a hypothesis.*

ex·ploit (ĕk′sploit′) *n.* An act, especially a brilliant or heroic one: *the exploits of legendary figures such as Robin Hood.* —*tr.v.* (ĭk sploit′). **1.** To make use of (sbdy./sthg.) selfishly or unethically: *They exploit unskilled workers when they pay them so little.* **2.** To use (sthg.) to the greatest possible advantage: *exploit an idea to make a profit.* —**ex·ploit′a·ble** *adj.* —**ex·ploit′er** *n.*

ex·ploi·ta·tion (ĕk′sploi tā′shən) *n.* [U] **1.** The use of a person or group for selfish purposes: *the exploitation of immigrant labor.* **2.** The act of using sthg. to the greatest possible advantage: *the exploitation of oil fields.*

ex·plo·ra·tion (ĕk′splə rā′shən) *n.* [C; U] The act of exploring: *Arctic exploration; an*

E

exploration of new medical treatments.
—**ex•plor′a•to′ry** (ĭk **splôr′**ə tôr′ē) *adj.*

ex•plore (ĭk splôr′) *v.* **ex•plored, ex•plor•ing, ex•plores.** —*tr.* **1.** To investigate (sthg.) systematically; examine: *Our representatives explored the possibilities of a new trade agreement.* **2.** To travel in or search (an area) for the purpose of discovery: *explore a vast region of rain forest.* —*intr.* To make a careful examination or search: *Geologists were hired to explore for oil.* —**ex•plor′er** *n.*

ex•plo•sion (ĭk splō′zhən) *n.* **1.** The act of bursting apart or blowing up with a sudden violent release of energy: *an explosion of fireworks.* **2.** The loud sharp sound made by such a release: *an explosion heard for miles.* **3.** A sudden, often emotional outbreak: *an explosion of laughter.* **4.** A sudden great increase: *a population explosion.*

ex•plo•sive (ĭk splō′sĭv) *adj.* **1.** Having the nature of an explosion: *an explosive laugh; an explosive fit of temper.* **2.** Capable of exploding: *an explosive powder.* —*n.* A substance that tends to explode or is capable of exploding: *Explosives were used to make the tunnel through the mountain.* —**ex•plo′sive•ly** *adv.* —**ex•plo′sive•ness** *n.* [U]

ex•po (ĕk′spō) *n. Informal.* A public exposition: *a computer expo.*

ex•po•nent (ĭk spō′nənt *or* ĕk′spō′nənt) *n.* **1.** A person who represents or believes in sthg.; an advocate: *exponents of this new method of surgery.* **2.** A number or symbol that shows the number of times a mathematical expression is used as a factor. For example, the exponent 3 in 5^3 means $5 \times 5 \times 5$.

ex•po•nen•tial (ĕk′spə nĕn′shəl) *adj.* **1.** Containing or involving one or more exponents in a mathematical expression. **2.** Large and growing: *an exponential increase in population in the past ten years.*

ex•port (ĭk spôrt′ *or* ĕk′spôrt′) *tr.v.* To send or transport (goods or products) to another country, especially for trade or sale: *export fruit to England.* —*n.* (ĕk′spôrt′). **1.** [U] Exportation. **2.** [C] Something that is exported: *Exports have fallen in the last ten years.* —**ex•port′a•ble** *adj.* —**ex•port′er** *n.*

ex•por•ta•tion (ĕk′spôr tā′shən) *n.* [U] The act of exporting: *The exportation of automobiles is an important element of the Japanese economy.*

ex•pose (ĭk spōz′) *tr.v.* **ex•posed, ex•pos•ing, ex•pos•es.** **1.** To open or subject (sbdy./sthg.) to an influence: *expose young children to literature; expose a visitor to a cold.* **2.** To allow (a photographic film, for example) to be acted on by light: *The film on this roll has already been exposed, so I'm sending it to the lab for developing.* **3.** To

make (sthg.) visible; reveal: *Paint remover exposed the old wood underneath.* **4.** To make known (sthg. negative) or reveal the guilt of (sbdy.): *expose the nature of the crime; expose a dishonest official.*

ex•po•sé (ĕk′spō zā′) *n.* A story, as in a newspaper or on TV, that makes public sthg. negative: *a magazine exposé of corruption in government.*

ex•po•si•tion (ĕk′spə zĭsh′ən) *n.* **1.** [C; U] An exact and detailed explanation of difficult material: *The astronomer gave a long exposition on the nature of the eclipse.* **2.** [C] A large public show or fair: *an international computer exposition.* —**ex•pos′i•to′ry** (ĭk-spŏz′ĭ tôr′ē) *adj.*

ex•po•sure (ĭk spō′zhər) *n.* **1.** The act of exposing, put as: **a.** [C; U] An act of putting or being put in contact with an action or influence: *a child's exposure to measles; her exposure to danger.* **b.** [U] Appearance in public or in the mass media: *The candidate enjoyed high levels of TV exposure.* **c.** [C; U] An act of making known sthg. that was secret, especially a crime or sthg. wrong: *Her exposure as a tax cheat lost her many friends.* **2.** [C] A position in relation to weather conditions or points of the compass: *Our house has a southern exposure.* **3.a.** [U] The act of exposing a photographic film or plate. **b.** [C] An exposed section of a roll of film: *We took several exposures.*

ex•pound (ĭk spound′) *v. Formal.* —*tr.* To explain (sthg.) in detail: *Debaters must always expound their views clearly.* —*intr.* To make a detailed statement: *The candidate expounded on the need for good government.*

ex•press (ĭk sprĕs′) *tr.v.* **1.** To make (sthg.) known, by words or gestures; communicate: *A good speaker expresses ideas clearly. The winner's face expressed great joy.* **2.** To represent (sthg.) by a sign or symbol: *In arithmetic, the minus sign expresses subtraction.* **3.** To squeeze or press (sthg.) out, as juice from an orange: *a machine that expresses juice from berries and fruits.* **4.** To send (sthg.) by special messenger or rapid transport: *express a letter to the office in Atlanta.* —*adj.* **1.** Clearly stated; explicit: *She ignored my express wish to go home.* **2.** Particular; specific: *The express object of the exercise was to teach cooperation.* **3.a.** Direct or rapid: *an express train.* **b.** Relating to or sent by rapid travel: *an express package; an express lane on the highway.* —*adv.* By express transport or delivery: *Send that package express.* —*n.* **1.** A system or company that provides rapid and direct delivery of goods and mail: *Call the local express to handle that box of fruit.* **2.** A method of transportation, such as a train, that travels rapidly, usually with no stops: *Take an express to the airport.* —**ex•press'i•ble** *adj.*

ex•pres•sion (ĭk sprĕsh′ən) *n.* **1.** [U] The act of expressing, as in words, art, action, or movement: *the expression of one's opinion by means of voting.* **2.** [C] Something, as a facial aspect or look, that expresses or communicates: *We could see the expression of joy in the child's eyes.* **3.** [C] A symbol or arrangement of symbols that indicates a mathematical operation or quantity. For example, $x + y$ is an algebraic expression. **4.** [U] A manner of speaking or performing that expresses particular feeling or meaning: *The poet read several poems with great expression.* **5.** [C] A particular word or phrase: *Raining cats and dogs is a familiar expression.*

ex•pres•sion•less (ĭk sprĕsh′ən lĭs) *adj.* Without expression: *a dull expressionless voice.*

ex•pres•sive (ĭk sprĕs′ĭv) *adj.* **1.** Expressing or showing: *The kitten's crying was expressive of its hunger.* **2.** Full of meaning; significant: *an expressive smile.* —**ex•pres′sive•ly** *adv.* —**ex•pres′sive•ness** *n.* [U]

ex•press•ly (ĭk sprĕs′lē) *adv.* **1.** In a clear or definite manner; explicitly: *The rules expressly say that only four can play at a time.* **2.** Especially; particularly: *He needs scissors made expressly for left-handed people.*

ex•press•way (ĭk sprĕs′wā′) *n.* A major divided highway for high-speed travel.

ex•pro•pri•ate (ĕk sprō′prē āt′) *tr.v.* **ex•pro•pri•at•ed, ex•pro•pri•at•ing, ex•pro•pri•ates.** *Formal.* To take (land or other property) away from sbdy., especially for public use: *The government expropriated the home of the tax evaders.* —**ex•pro′pri•a′tion** *n.* [C; U]

ex•pul•sion (ĭk spŭl′shən) *n.* [C; U] The act of expelling: *expulsion of gases from a jet engine; a student facing expulsion from school.*

ex•qui•site (ĕk′skwĭ zĭt *or* ĭk skwĭz′ĭt) *adj.* **1.** Intricate and beautiful: *an exquisite vase.* **2.** Very sensitive or perceptive: *exquisite taste in art.* **3.** Intense; keen: *They took exquisite pleasure in the success of their children.* —**ex′qui•site•ly** *adv.*

ex•tem•po•ra•ne•ous (ĭk stĕm′pə rā′nē-əs) *adj.* Done or made with little or no preparation; unplanned: *The scientist stood up at the meeting and gave an extemporaneous speech.* —**ex•tem′po•ra′ne•ous•ly** *adv.* —**ex•tem′po•ra′ne•ous•ness.** [U]

ex•tend (ĭk stĕnd′) *v.* —*tr.* **1.** To open or straighten (sthg.) out: *Extend your left arm.* **2.** To make (sthg.) longer: *Better living conditions have extended the average life span.* **3.** To enlarge the area, scope, or range of (sthg.): *extend the boundaries of the park.* See Synonyms at **increase**. **4.** To offer or provide (sthg.): *extend congratulations to the gradu-*

ates; extend aid to an underdeveloped country. —*intr.* To be long, large, or comprehensive: *The beach extends for miles. The influence of our democracy extends around the world.*

ex•tend•ed (ĭk stĕn′dĭd) *adj.* **1.** Stretched or pulled out: *extended arms.* **2.** Continued for a long period of time; prolonged: *an extended vacation in the Caribbean.* **3.** Enlarged or broad in meaning, scope, or influence: *extended television coverage of the trial.*

extended family *n.* A family that includes parents, children, and other close relatives, often living near each other.

ex•ten•sion (ĭk stĕn′shən) *n.* **1.** [U] The act of extending: *Extension of the highway has snarled traffic.* **2.** [U] The act of straightening or extending a part of the body by a muscle: *extension of the leg to relieve muscle cramps.* **3.** [C] Something that extends from a main part; an addition: *An extension was added to the back of the building.* **4.** [C] An additional telephone connected to a main line: *We have two extensions to our telephone.*

extension cord *n.* A long electric cord with a socket and plug, used to connect an electric device to a wall socket.

ex•ten•sive (ĭk stĕn′sĭv) *adj.* Large in extent, range, or amount: *An extensive park runs along the ocean. We made extensive renovations to the old building.* —**ex•ten′-sive•ly** *adv.* —**ex•ten′sive•ness** *n.* [U]

ex•tent (ĭk stĕnt′) *n.* [*of*] **1.** [U] The area or distance over which sthg. extends; size: *increase the extent of their lands; underestimate the extent of the damage.* **2.** [C] *(usually singular).* Degree: *The state prosecuted the criminal to the fullest extent of the law.* **3.** [C] An extensive space or area: *an extent of pine forest.*

ex•ten•u•ate (ĭk stĕn′yōō āt′) *tr.v.* **ex•ten•u•at•ed, ex•ten•u•at•ing, ex•ten•u•ates.** *Formal.* To lessen the size or seriousness of (sthg. negative), especially by providing a partial excuse: *Lack of experience extenuated the fault of the goalie in the team's loss.*

♦ **extenuating circumstances.** Conditions that partly excuse bad behavior: *The principal considered the extenuating circumstances and gave the boy a mild punishment.*

ex•te•ri•or (ĭk stîr′ē ər) *adj.* **1.** Outer; external: *the exterior walls of a building.* **2.** Coming from the outside: *exterior pressures.* **3.** Suitable for outside use: *an exterior paint able to withstand sun and rain.* —*n.* **1.** A part or surface that is outside: *the exterior of the house.* **2.** An outward appearance: *The town had a cheerful exterior.*

ex•ter•mi•nate (ĭk stûr′mə nāt′) *tr.v.* **ex•ter•mi•nat•ed, ex•ter•mi•nat•ing, ex•ter•mi•nates.** To destroy (sthg.) completely; wipe out: *exterminate rats.* —**ex•ter′mi•na′tion** *n.* [U]

ex·ter·mi·na·tor (ĭk stûr′mə nā′tər) *n.* A person whose job is exterminating insects, rodents, or other pests.

ex·ter·nal (ĭk stûr′nəl) *adj.* **1.** Relating to the outside or an outer part; exterior: *external repairs on a house.* **2.** Relating to an outer surface: *a cream for external use only.* **3.** Acting or coming from the outside: *an external force.* **4.** Relating primarily to outward appearance; superficial: *an external display of pleasure.* **5.** Relating to foreign affairs or foreign countries: *external affairs.* —**ex·ter′nal·ly** *adv.*

ex·tinct (ĭk stĭngkt′) *adj.* **1.** No longer existing or living: *an extinct species.* **2.** No longer burning or active: *an extinct volcano.*

ex·tinc·tion (ĭk stĭngk′shən) *n.* [U] **1.** The act of extinguishing. **2.** The fact of being extinct: *Early trappers hunted the beaver almost to extinction.*

ex·tin·guish (ĭk stĭng′gwĭsh) *tr.v.* **1.** To put out (a fire, for example): *extinguish a candle; extinguish the lights.* **2.** To put an end to (hopes, for example); destroy: *Low grades extinguished her hopes of going to medical school.* —**ex·tin′guish·a·ble** *adj.*

ex·tin·guish·er (ĭk stĭng′gwĭ shər) *n.* A portable device for spraying and extinguishing a fire with chemicals.

ex·tol also **ex·toll** (ĭk stōl′) *tr.v.* **ex·tolled, ex·tol·ling, ex·tols** or **ex·tolls.** *Formal.* To praise (sbdy./sthg.) highly; laud: *extol the achievements of a great humanitarian.*

ex·tort (ĭk stôrt′) *tr.v.* [*from*] To obtain (sthg.) from another person by threats or force: *The blackmailer extorted money from a man who had lied about his past.*

ex·tor·tion (ĭk stôr′shən) *n.* [U] **1.** The act of extorting. **2.** Illegal use of one's official position to obtain property or funds: *The governor was charged with extortion after she gave her friends jobs in exchange for payment.* —**ex·tor′tion·ist** *n.*

ex·tra (ĕk′strə) *adj.* More than what is usual or expected; additional: *earn extra money by working a second job.* —*n.* **1.** *(usually plural).* Something additional, for which one pays an added charge: *We bought a new car with all the extras.* **2.** A special edition of a newspaper: *The extra gave the latest news of the crisis.* **3.** A performer hired to play a minor part in a film, as in a crowd scene. —*adv.* To an exceptional degree; unusually: *The audience was extra quiet during the vocalist's solo.*

extra— or **extro**— *pref.* A prefix that means outside or beyond: *extracurricular; extraterrestrial.*

ex·tract (ĭk străkt′) *tr.v.* **1.** To obtain or draw (sthg.) out with force; pull out: *extract a tooth.* **2.** To obtain (sthg.) by clever or persuasive methods; coerce: *The detectives finally extracted a confession from the suspect.* **3.** To obtain (sthg.) from a substance by a chemical or physical process: *extract iron ore; extract the juice of berries.* **4.** To select (sthg.) such as from a book or musical work for separate consideration or publication; excerpt. —*n.* (ĕk′străkt′). **1.** [C] A passage from a literary or musical work; an excerpt: *The book is made up of extracts from other works.* **2.** [C; U] A concentrated substance from a food used for flavoring: *vanilla extract; an extract of coffee.* —**ex·trac′tor** *n.*

ex·trac·tion (ĭk străk′shən) *n.* **1.** [C; U] The act or result of extracting: *The extraction of impacted wisdom teeth is quite common.* **2.** [U] Descent; origin: *of French-Canadian extraction.*

ex·tra·cur·ric·u·lar (ĕk′strə kə rĭk′yə-lər) *adj.* Outside the regular course of study of a school or college: *Debating is an extracurricular activity.*

ex·tra·dite (ĕk′strə dīt′) *tr.v.* **ex·tra·dit·ed, ex·tra·dit·ing, ex·tra·dites. 1.** To send (a prisoner or fugitive, for example) to another state or country for trial. **2.** To obtain (a prisoner) in this way. —**ex·tra·di′tion** (ĕk′strə dĭsh′ən) *n.* [C; U]

ex·tra·ne·ous (ĭk strā′nē əs) *adj.* **1.** Not basic, directly connected, or essential; irrelevant: *These minor points are extraneous to my report.* **2.** Coming from the outside: *Extraneous material in the blood sample made the test invalid.* —**ex·tra′ne·ous·ly** *adv.* —**ex·tra′ne·ous·ness** *n.* [U]

ex·traor·di·nar·y (ĭk strôr′dn ĕr′ē or ĕk′strə ôr′dn ĕr′ē) *adj.* Very unusual; remarkable: *Landing on the moon was an extraordinary accomplishment.* —**ex·traor′di·nar′i·ly** (ĭk strôr′dn âr′ə lē or ĕk′strə ôr′dn âr′ə lē) *adv.*

ex·trap·o·late (ĭk străp′ə lāt′) *v.* **ex·trap·o·lat·ed, ex·trap·o·lat·ing, ex·trap·o·lates.** *Formal.* —*tr.* To guess or estimate (sthg. unknown) using known information: *We extrapolated next year's expenses from a review of this year's bills.* —*intr.* To make an estimate or prediction on the basis of known information: *Try to extrapolate from what you've read.* —**ex·trap′o·la′tion** *n.* [U]

ex·tra·sen·so·ry (ĕk′strə sĕn′sə rē) *adj.* Outside the normal range of the senses: *He claims he has extrasensory powers and can predict the future.*

extrasensory perception *n.* [U] Perception by means other than the usual senses: *People who seem to know what others are thinking sometimes claim they have extrasensory perception.*

ex·tra·ter·res·tri·al (ĕk′strə tə rĕs′trē əl) *adj.* Beyond the earth or outside its atmosphere: *extraterrestrial bodies such as stars and comets.* —*n.* A creature from outer space.

ex·trav·a·gance (ĭk străv′ə gəns) *n.* **1.** [U] The quality or practice of being extravagant. **2.** [C] Something that is too costly: *Their latest extravagance is an expensive race car.*

ex·trav·a·gant (ĭk străv′ə gənt) *adj.* **1.** Tending to spend money lavishly or inappropriately: *an extravagant executive.* **2.** Unreasonably high; too much: *extravagant fees for the service.* —**ex·trav′a·gant·ly** *adv.*

ex·trav·a·gan·za (ĭk străv′ə găn′zə) *n.* A large and impressive display or entertainment: *The circus is one huge extravaganza.*

ex·treme (ĭk strēm′) *adj.* **1.** The farthest possible; outermost: *the extreme end of the room.* **2.** Very great or intense: *use extreme caution; suffer from the extreme cold.* **3.** Extending far beyond the norm: *She holds extreme opinions in politics.* —*n.* **1.** [U] The greatest degree or point: *eager to the extreme.* **2.** [C] Either end of a range or scale: *His opinions go from one extreme to the other.* **3.** [C] An action that goes beyond normal limits, taken to achieve sthg.: *resort to extremes in an emergency.* ◆ **go to extremes.** To do sthg. that is beyond what is considered right or necessary: *If you don't go to extremes when you renovate your house, you'll save money.* —**ex·treme′ly** *adv.*

ex·trem·ist (ĭk strē′mĭst) *n.* A person with opinions extending far beyond the norm, especially in politics: *That fundamentalist organization is full of extremists.* —**ex·trem′ism** *n.* [U]

ex·trem·i·ty (ĭk strĕm′ĭ tē) *n., pl.* **ex·trem·i·ties.** **1.** The outermost or farthest point; a limit: *Patagonia is at the southern extremity of South America.* **2.** (*usually singular*). The greatest degree: *an extremity of sorrow.* **3.** An extreme or severe action to achieve sthg.: *resort to extremities in a crisis.* **4.** A hand or foot: *Frostbite often affects the extremities first.*

ex·tri·cate (ĕk′strĭ kāt′) *tr.v.* **ex·tri·cat·ed, ex·tri·cat·ing, ex·tri·cates.** [*from*] To set (sbdy./sthg.) free from a difficult situation: *extricate oneself from embarrassing circumstances.* —**ex′tri·ca′tion** *n.* [U]

ex·trin·sic (ĭk strĭn′sĭk *or* ĭk strĭn′zĭk) *adj.* **1.** Not essential or basic; extraneous: *Your arguments are extrinsic to the discussion.* **2.** Originating from the outside; external: *extrinsic forces on the elephants' environment.* —**ex·trin′si·cal·ly** *adv.*

ex·tro·vert (ĕk′strə vûrt′) *n.* A person interested mainly in other people or outside circumstances rather than his or her own thoughts and feelings: *To succeed in sales, it helps to be an extrovert instead of an introvert.* —**ex′tro·vert′ed** *adj.*

ex·u·ber·ance (ĭg zōō′bər əns) *n.* [U] The condition or quality of being exuberant: *The crowd cheered in wild exuberance.*

ex·u·ber·ant (ĭg zōō′bər ənt) *adj.* Full of or showing enthusiasm or joy: *Spectators of the parade were in an exuberant mood.* —**ex·u′ber·ant·ly** *adv.*

ex·ude (ĭg zōōd′ *or* ĭk sōōd′) *tr. & intr.v.* **ex·ud·ed, ex·ud·ing, ex·udes.** To give or come out by or as if by oozing: *The body exudes sweat through the pores. Confidence exuded in their cocky manner.*

ex·ult (ĭg zŭlt′) *intr.v.* To be joyful or triumphant; rejoice: *The entire town exulted in the team's victory.*

ex·ul·tant (ĭg zŭl′tənt) *adj.* Showing great joy or jubilation: *an exultant victor.* —**ex·ult′ant·ly** *adv.* —**ex′ul·ta′tion** (ĕk′səl tā′shən *or* ĕg′zəl tā′shən) *n.* [U]

—**ey** *suff.* Variant of —**y**[1].

eye (ī) *n.* **1.a.** An organ of the body by means of which an animal is able to see or sense light. **b.** The outer visible part of this organ, especially the colored iris: *People may have blue, green, or brown eyes.*

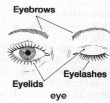

Eyebrows

Eyelashes

Eyelids

eye

2. Sight; vision: *A lifeguard must have a sharp eye.* **3.** The ability to estimate, judge, or note: *The coach has an eye for new talent.* **4.** A way of regarding sthg.; a point of view or an opinion: *She saw the world with a critical eye.* **5.** Something that resembles an eye, such as a bud on a potato or a spot on a peacock's tail feather. **6.** The hole in a needle through which the thread goes. **7.** The relatively calm area at the center of a hurricane or similar storm: *When the eye of the hurricane was directly overhead, the wind stopped.* —*tr.v.* **eyed, eye·ing** *or* **ey·ing** (ī′ĭng), **eyes.** To look at (sbdy./sthg.); watch: *The child eyed the big dog suspiciously.* ◆ **an eye for an eye.** Punishment in which an offender suffers what the victim has suffered: *Execution of the murderer was defended as no more than an eye for an eye.* **be up to (one's) eyes in.** To be very busy or occupied with (sthg.): *I'm up to my eyes in paperwork!* **close (one's) eyes to.** To ignore or refuse to see (sthg.): *The government has closed its eyes to corruption.* **in the public eye.** Frequently seen in public or in the media: *It is impossible to relax when one is always in the public eye.* **keep an eye on.** To watch (sbdy./sthg.): *Can you keep an eye on the baby while I go to the store?* **keep an eye out.** [*for*] To be alert: *Keep an eye out for your brother—he should be home at 5:00.* **lay** or **set eyes on.** To see (sbdy./sthg.): *Have you laid eyes on my lost glasses?* **see eye to eye.** [*on*] To be in agreement: *We see eye to eye on most issues.* **under** or **before (one's) very eyes.** In front of or in plain sight of: *They took the money from under our very eyes!* **with an eye to.** Planning on: *We left early with an*

E

eye to getting home before dark. **with (one's) eyes (wide) open.** Fully aware of circumstances or consequences: *If you decide to invest, do it with your eyes wide open.*

HOMONYMS: eye, aye (yes), **I** (pronoun).

eye•ball (ī′bôl′) *n.* The part of the eye shaped like a ball and enclosed by the socket behind the eyelids. —*tr.v. Informal.* **1.** To look (sbdy./sthg.) over carefully; examine: *People eyeballed the newcomers to the party.* **2.** To measure or estimate (sthg.) roughly by sight: *The painter eyeballed the area of the walls to be painted.*

eye•brow (ī′brou′) *n.* The line of short hairs above the eye: *He raised his eyebrows in disbelief.*

eye-catch•ing (ī′kăch′ĭng) *adj.* Unusual or attractive: *an eye-catching car; an eye-catching outfit.*

eye•drop•per (ī′drŏp′ər) *n.* A dropper for applying liquid medicine to the eye.

eye•drops (ī′drŏps) *pl.n.* A liquid medicine used to treat the eyes.

eye•ful (ī′fŏŏl′) *n.* **1.** An amount of sthg. that gets into the eye: *The wind was blowing and I got an eyeful of dust.* **2.** A complete view; a good look: *We got a real eyeful during the tour of the auto plant.*

eye•glass•es (ī′glăs′ĭz) *pl.n.* A pair of lenses worn in front of the eyes to correct vision; glasses.

eye•lash (ī′lăsh′) *n.* **1. eyelashes.** A row of hairs on the edge of the eyelid. **2.** One of the hairs in this row.

eye•lid (ī′lĭd′) *n.* Either the upper or lower piece of skin that can cover the eye: *Her eyelids grew heavy with sleep.*

eye•lin•er (ī′lī′nər) *n.* [C; U] Makeup used to outline the eyes.

eye opener *n. Informal.* A surprising or shocking piece or source of information: *The article about the water shortage was an eye opener.*

eye•piece (ī′pēs′) *n.* The lens or group of lenses closest to the eye in a telescope, microscope, or similar optical instrument.

eye shadow *n.* [C; U] A cosmetic applied to the eyelids to color them.

eye•sight (ī′sīt′) *n.* [U] **1.** The ability to see; vision; sight: *People wear glasses to correct poor eyesight.* **2.** Range of vision; view: *a stream within eyesight of the house.*

eye•sore (ī′sôr′) *n.* An ugly or unpleasant sight: *That junkyard is an eyesore.*

eye•wit•ness (ī′wĭt′nĭs) *n.* A person who has seen sbdy./sthg. and can swear to the fact, as in a trial or other legal proceeding: *The eyewitness described the accident for the police.*

Ff

f or **F** (ĕf) *n.*, *pl.* **f's** or **F's. 1.** The sixth letter of the English alphabet. **2. F.** A failing grade in school. **3.** In music, the fourth tone in the scale of C major.

F¹ The symbol for the element **fluorine.**

F² *abbr.* An abbreviation of Fahrenheit.

f. *abbr.* An abbreviation of: **1.** Female. **2** Feminine.

F. *abbr.* An abbreviation of: **1.** French. **2** Friday.

fa·ble (fā′bəl) *n.* **1.** [C] A story that teaches a lesson about human nature, often with animal characters that speak and act like humans. **2** [C; U] A legend or myth: *A moral at the end of a story is a common device in fables.*

fa·bled (fā′bəld) *adj.* Made famous by fables legendary: *the fabled city of El Dorado.*

fab·ric (făb′rĭk) *n.* **1.** [C; U] A cloth: *Lace silk, and cotton are different types of fabric* **2.** [U] A basic structure: *Crime is threatening the fabric of society.*

fab·ri·cate (făb′rĭ kāt′) *tr.v.* **fab·ri·cat·ed fab·ri·cat·ing, fab·ri·cates. 1.** To make or manufacture (sthg.), especially by assembling parts: *fabricate refrigerators in a factory.* **2.** To make (sthg.) up; invent, especially in order to deceive: *The student fabricated an excuse for being late.* —**fab′ri·ca′tion** *n.* [U]

fab·u·lous (făb′yə ləs) *adj.* **1.** *Informal* Extremely pleasing or successful; wonderful *a fabulous vacation.* **2.** Difficult to believe astonishing: *a fabulous rise to fame.* **3** Famous in old stories; legendary: *the fabulous lands of Asia.* —**fab′u·lous·ly** *adv* —**fab′u·lous·ness** *n.* [U]

fa·çade also **fa·cade** (fə säd′) *n.* **1.** The front of a building: *the decorated façade of a great cathedral.* **2.** An artificial or false manner: *The salesman's friendly manner was only a façade to gain our confidence.*

face (fās) *n.* **1.** The front of the head: *She had a mask over her face.* **2.** The expression of the face: *a friendly face.* **3.** The surface presented to view; the front: *the face of a building.* **4.** An outer surface: *the face of the earth.* **5.** The outward appearance; look *With so many new buildings, the face of the city has changed.* —*v.* **faced, fac·ing fac·es.** —*tr.* **1.** To have or turn the face or front toward (sbdy./sthg.): *The actor faced the audience. The cathedral faces the square* **2.** To meet or deal with (sbdy./sthg.) boldly or bravely: *Police officers face danger every*

day. **3.** To recognize and be ready to deal with (sthg.): *You've got to face the facts.* **4.** To cover (a surface) with a different material: *face the front of the fireplace with marble.* —*intr.* **1.** To be turned or placed with the front in a certain direction: *The house faces toward the west. Put the test paper face down on your desk.* **2.** To turn the face in a certain direction: *I faced into the wind.* ◆ **face down.** *tr.v.* [sep.] To meet (an enemy) without fear: *He faced the robber down.* **face off.** *intr.v.* **1.** To start play in hockey, lacrosse, and other games by releasing the puck or ball between two opposing players. **2.** To compete against another team or opponent: *The two rivals will face off in the finals.* **face the music.** To accept unpleasant results of one's actions: *The child had to face the music for breaking the window.* **face to face.** In the presence of sbdy.: *I was pleased to finally meet him face to face.* **face up to.** To confront (an unpleasant situation) boldly: *His parents finally faced up to his drug problem.* **in the face of.** In spite of; despite: *The team won in the face of strong competition.* **keep a straight face.** To keep oneself from smiling or laughing in a situation that is not supposed to be funny: *When I saw what they were wearing, I couldn't keep a straight face.* **on the face of it.** Based on appearances: *On the face of it, this is an easy game, but it's really quite difficult.* **save** or **lose face.** To maintain or lose one's dignity after sthg. embarrassing has happened: *They saved face by saying they had been lied to.*

face card *n.* A king, queen, or jack in a deck of playing cards.

face·less (fās′lĭs) *adj.* Unidentified or unidentifiable: *the faceless crowds.*

face-lift (fās′lĭft′) *n.* **1.** An operation to tighten wrinkles or loose skin of the face. **2.** A change to improve the appearance of a building.

fac·et (făs′ĭt) *n.* **1.** One of the flat polished surfaces cut on a gem or occurring naturally in a crystal: *the facets of a diamond.* **2.** One of the ways of considering sthg.; an aspect: *a complex problem with many facets to consider.*

fa·ce·tious (fə sē′shəs) *adj.* Meant to be funny but annoying instead: *a facetious remark.* —**fa·ce′tious·ly** *adv.* —**fa·ce′tious·ness** *n.* [U]

face value *n.* **1.** [C; U] The value shown on postage stamps, money, checks, bonds, or other paper securities: *an old coin worth ten times its face value*. **2.** [U] The apparent value or meaning: *Take their compliments at face value.*

fa·cial (fā′shəl) *adj.* Relating to the face: *facial expressions.* —*n.* A cosmetic treatment for the face, usually including a massage.

fac·ile (făs′əl) *adj. Formal.* **1.** Done with little effort or difficulty; easy: *a facile task.* **2.** Working, acting, or speaking effortlessly: *a facile speaker; a facile writer.* **3.** Arrived at without proper care or effort; superficial: *We don't need another facile solution to the problem.*

fa·cil·i·tate (fə sĭl′ĭ tāt′) *tr.v.* **fa·cil·i·tat·ed, fa·cil·i·tat·ing, fa·cil·i·tates.** To make (sthg.) easier; assist: *The bank loans will facilitate the building of a new sports arena.* —**fa·cil′i·ta′tion** *n.* [U]

fa·cil·i·ty (fə sĭl′ĭ tē) *n., pl.* **fa·cil·i·ties. 1.** [C] *(usually plural).* Something built or designed to provide a service or convenience: *The building has good storage facilities.* **2.** [C; U] Ease in moving, acting, or doing; aptitude: *She has a facility for learning foreign languages.*

fac·sim·i·le (făk sĭm′ə lē) *n.* An exact copy or reproduction of sthg.: *The exhibit contained facsimiles of historic documents.*

facsimile machine *n.* A fax machine.

fact (făkt) *n.* **1.** [C] Something known to be true or to have actually happened: *The fact is that the bridge collapsed.* **2.** [U] The quality of being true or real: *This movie mixes fact and fiction.* **3.** [C] A piece of information about sthg. actual or real: *a book full of facts.* **4.** [C] A thing that has been done, especially a crime: *an accessory after the fact.* ◆ **in fact** or **as a matter of fact.** In reality; in truth: *In fact, I did try to call you.*

fac·tion (făk′shən) *n.* A group of people who have certain interests that are not shared with others in a larger group: *Factions form in organizations when members feel unhappy with things as they are.* —**fac′tion·al** *adj.* —**fac′tion·al·ism** *n.* [U]

fac·tor (făk′tər) *n.* **1.** Something that helps cause a certain result; an element or ingredient: *Many factors contributed to the success of the celebration.* **2.** In mathematics, one of two or more numbers or expressions that are multiplied to obtain a given product. For example, both 2 and 3 are factors of 6, and $a + b$ and $a - b$ are factors of $a^2 - b^2$. —*tr.v.* To find the factors of (a number or an expression). ◆ **factor in.** *tr.v.* [sep.] To consider (sthg.): *We factored in the possibility of getting stuck in traffic when we scheduled the meeting.* —**fac′tor·a·ble** *adj.*

fac·to·ry (făk′tə rē) *n., pl.* **fac·to·ries.** A building or group of buildings in which goods are manufactured, especially in large numbers; a plant: *The new automobile factory is filled with automated machines.*

fac·tu·al (făk′chōō əl) *adj.* Based on facts: *a factual account of what happened.* —**fac′tu·al·ly** *adv.*

fac·ul·ty (făk′əl tē) *n., pl.* **fac·ul·ties. 1.a.** The teaching staff of a school, college, or university: *The faculty voted to change the curriculum.* **b.** One of the divisions or departments of learning at a college or university: *the science faculty.* **2.** One of the powers of the mind or body: *the faculty of speech.* **3.** A special ability or skill: *He has a faculty for doing impersonations.*

fad (făd) *n.* Something that is done or adopted with great enthusiasm by many people for a brief period of time: *Wearing baggy pants far down on the hips was a fad.*

fade (fād) *v.* **fad·ed, fad·ing, fades.** —*intr.* **1.** To lose brightness; dim: *The colors faded in the wash.* **2.** To lose freshness; wither: *The flowers are beginning to fade.* **3.** To disappear slowly; vanish: *The sound of footsteps gradually faded.* See Synonyms at **disappear.** —*tr.* To cause (sthg.) to lose brightness: *The sun faded the colors in the quilt.* ◆ **fade away.** *intr.v.* To disappear slowly: *All hope has now faded away.* **fade in.** *intr.v.* To become visible or audible gradually: *The movie fades in to the next scene, 20 years later.* **fade out.** *intr.v.* To become invisible or inaudible gradually: *The music faded out in the distance.*

fag (făg) *n.* **1.** *Slang.* An old word for a cigarette. **2.** *Offensive Slang.* A homosexual man; a faggot.

fag·got (făg′ət) *n. Offensive Slang.* A homosexual man.

Fahr·en·heit (făr′ən hīt′) *n.* [U] A temperature scale that indicates the freezing point of water as 32° and the boiling point of water as 212° under standard atmospheric pressure. —*adj.* Relating to such a scale.

fail (fāl) *v.* —*intr.* **1.** To be unsuccessful at sthg., especially sthg. wanted or expected: *Their first attempt at climbing the mountain failed.* **2.** To be lacking or not enough: *After months of drought the water supply failed.* **3.** To receive a grade that is less than acceptable in school: *If he doesn't study, he's going to fail.* **4.** To stop functioning correctly; break down: *The brakes on the car failed.* **5.** To weaken or decline: *Her health failed after her heart attack.* **6.** To become bankrupt: *A number of downtown stores failed in the recession.* —*tr.* **1.** To leave (sthg.) undone; neglect: *The defendant failed to appear in court.* **2.** To disappoint or prove undependable to (sbdy.): *I won't fail you this time.* **3.**

To abandon (sbdy./sthg.): *His strength failed him in the last mile of the race.* **4.a.** To receive an academic grade that is below the acceptable minimum in (a course or test, for example): *Did any students fail geometry?* **b.** To give an academic grade indicating an unacceptable performance by (sbdy.): *The professor failed several students in the class.* ◆ **without fail.** Definitely; certainly: *The job will be finished tomorrow without fail.*

fail·ing (fā′lĭng) *n.* **1.** A fault or weakness; a shortcoming: *One of my failings is being late with library books.* **2.** The act of sbdy./sthg. that fails; a failure: *a failing of the water supply.* —*prep. Formal.* In the absence of; without: *Failing directions, we will have to find the office on our own.*

fail-safe (fāl′sāf′) *adj.* **1.** Capable of stopping operation in case of a failure, as in a mechanism: *Fail-safe switches on machinery have saved many workers from injury.* **2.** Guaranteed not to fail: *a fail-safe plan.*

fail·ure (fāl′yər) *n.* **1.** [U] The condition of not achieving sthg. desired; lack of success: *Early airplane experiments ended in failure.* **2.** [C; U] The neglect or inability to do sthg.: *My failure to return library books meant a large fine.* **3.** [C] The condition of not being enough: *a crop failure during a drought.* **4.** [C] A stopping of function: *an electric power failure.* **5.** [C] Bankruptcy: *The failure of the shop put several people out of work.* **6.** [C] A person or thing that has failed: *I'm a failure as an actor.*

faint (fānt) *adj.* **1.** Lacking brightness; dim: *a faint light.* **2.** Lacking strength; weak: *a faint odor; a faint resemblance.* **3.** Likely to become unconscious; dizzy and weak: *Extreme hunger made the hiker feel faint.* **4.** Lacking courage; cowardly: *faint attempts to succeed.* —*n.* A sudden, usually short loss of consciousness: *a faint caused by fear.* —*intr.v.* To lose consciousness for a short time: *The dancer fainted in the heat.* —**faint′ly** *adv.* —**faint′ness** *n.* [U]

HOMONYMS: **faint, feint** (movement).

fair¹ (fâr) *adj.* **1.** Without favoritism; just: *a fair price; a fair trial.* **2.** Light in color: *fair hair.* **3.** Clear and sunny; free of clouds or storms: *fair weather.* **4.** Somewhat good; acceptable: *The movie was only fair.* **5.** Pleasing to look at; beautiful: *a fair face.* —*adv.* In a fair manner; properly: *I believe in playing fair.* ◆ **fair and square.** In a just and honest manner: *Our team won the championship fair and square.* **no fair.** Something contrary to the rules: *No fair! I saw you take the last cookie!* —**fair′ness** *n.* [U]

HOMONYMS: **fair** (just, market), **fare** (travel cost).

fair² (fâr) *n.* **1.** A gathering for the buying and selling of goods, often held at a particular time and place; a market: *We went to the annual book fair.* **2.** An exhibit, as of agricultural and home products, often together with entertainment: *a county fair.*

fair²

fair game *n.* [U] A person or thing that seems suitable for pursuit or attack: *Politicians are fair game for reporters, especially during a campaign.*

fair·ground (fâr′ground′) *n.* (*usually plural*). An outdoor space where fairs, exhibitions, or other public events are held: *The fairgrounds were filled with people attending the state fair.*

fair-haired (fâr′hârd′) *adj.* **1.** Having blond hair. **2.** Favorite: *the fair-haired member of the family.*

fair·ly (fâr′lē) *adv.* **1.** In a fair or just manner: *treating everyone fairly.* **2.** Moderately; rather: *I am feeling fairly well today.* **3.** Actually; positively: *The walls fairly shook from the wind.*

fair-mind·ed (fâr′mīn′dĭd) *adj.* Just and impartial; not prejudiced: *a fair-minded judge.* —**fair′-mind′ed·ness** *n.* [U]

fair·y (fâr′ē) *n., pl.* **fair·ies. 1.** A tiny imaginary being in human form, supposed to have magical powers: *Children expect the tooth fairy to leave them money when they lose their baby teeth.* **2.** *Offensive Slang.* A homosexual man.

fair·y·land (fâr′ē lănd′) *n.* **1.** An imaginary place where fairies are supposed to live. **2.** An enchanting place; a wonderland: *Snow turned the woods into a fairyland.*

fairy tale *n.* **1.** A story about fairies, magical creatures, or legendary deeds, usually intended for children. **2.** An explanation that is not true.

fait ac·com·pli (fā′tä kôn plē′) *n.* [U] *Formal.* Something done that cannot be undone: *The decision to close the factory is already a fait accompli.*

faith (fāth) *n.* **1.** [U] Confidence or trust: *You must have faith in yourself.* **2.** [U] Belief in

God: *a person of great faith.* **3.** [C; U] The set of teachings of a religion: *the Muslim faith.* **4.** [U] Loyalty to a person or thing: *keeping faith with one's supporters.* **5.** [C; U] A set of principles or beliefs: *A democratic faith guides this country.* ◆ **bad faith.** Deceit; insincerity: *The striking union said that management had negotiated in bad faith.* **good faith.** Sincerity; honesty: *A signature is a token of one's good faith.* **on faith.** With trust; confidently: *You'll have to accept my promise on faith.*

faith•ful (fāth′fəl) *adj.* **1.** Loyal: *a faithful friend; faithful performance of duty.* **2.** Accurate; exact: *a faithful copy of the original letter.* —*pl.n.* **1.** The members of a religion: *Several hundred of the faithful attended the service.* **2.** Loyal followers or supporters: *The faithful journeyed to the huge rock concert in the park.* —**faith′ful•ly** *adv.* —**faith′ful•ness** *n.* [U]

faith•less (fāth′lĭs) *adj.* **1.** Disloyal: *The candidate was betrayed by a faithless friend.* **2.** Having no religious faith. —**faith′less•ly** *adv.* —**faith′less•ness** *n.* [U]

fake (fāk) *adj.* False; counterfeit: *a fake document; a fake diamond.* —*n.* **1.** A person who makes false claims; a faker: *The doctor turned out to be a fake.* **2.** Something that looks authentic but is not; a forgery: *Experts discovered a fake in the museum's art collection.* —*tr.v.* **faked, fak•ing, fakes.** **1.** To pretend (sthg.): *fake illness.* **2.** To make (sthg.) in order to deceive; counterfeit: *fake an identification card.* —**fak′er** *n.*

fal•con (făl′kən *or* fôl′kən) *n.* Any of various swift, small to medium-sized hawks with long pointed wings and long tails: *People have been training falcons to hunt for thousands of years.*

fal•con•er (făl′kə nər *or* fôl′kə nər) *n.* A person who raises, trains, or hunts with falcons.

fal•con•ry (făl′kən rē *or* fôl′kən rē) *n.* [U] Training or using falcons for hunting: *Falconry is an ancient sport.*

fall (fôl) *intr.v.* **fell** (fĕl), **fall•en** (fô′lən), **fall•ing, falls.** **1.** To drop or come down: *The snow fell silently to the ground.* **2.** To come down from an upright position suddenly: *Several people slipped on the ice and fell.* **3.** To be wounded or killed, especially in battle: *Thousands could fall in the first battles of a major war.* **4.** To come as if by descending suddenly: *Darkness fell and all was quiet. Silence fell over the crowd.* **5.** To slope downward: *The fields fall steeply toward the river.* **6.** To hang down: *The girl's hair fell to her waist.* **7.** To assume a sad look: *The child's face fell when she saw the injured puppy.* **8.** To become lower in value, intensity, or amount: *The temperature fell below freezing.* **9.** To suffer defeat, destruction, capture, or overthrow: *The monarchy fell in the revolution.* **10.** To occur at a specific place: *The stress of* control *falls on the last syllable.* **11.** To happen; occur: *Thanksgiving always falls on a Thursday in November.* **12.** To pass from one state or condition into another: *fall asleep; fall ill.* **13.** To be given, as a task, a right, an assignment, or a duty: *The task of cleaning the room fell to us.* **14.** To come by chance: *The papers fell into the enemy's hands.* **15.** To be divided or put into categories: *The books fall into three categories: novels, biographies, and scholarly works.* **16.** To be said; come out: *Angry words fell from my lips.* —*n.* **1.** [C; U] A dropping or coming down from a higher place: *the fall of leaves from trees; a heavy fall of snow.* **2.** [C] A sudden drop from an upright position: *a bad fall on the ice.* **3.** [C] The distance that sth. falls: *a fall of ten feet.* **4.** [C] An amount of sth. that has fallen: *We expect a fall of two inches of snow.* **5.** [C; U] A downward movement or slope: *the gentle fall of fields toward the river.* **6.** [C; U] The season of the year occurring between summer and winter. In the Northern Hemisphere, it lasts from September until December: *Last fall we traveled to the mountains to see the leaves on the trees change color.* **7. falls.** *(used with a singular or plural verb).* A waterfall: *The falls are just ahead.* **8.** [C] A reduction in amount, intensity, or value: *a fall in water pressure.* **9.** [C] A capture, an overthrow, or a collapse: *the fall of a corrupt government.* **10.** [C] A decline in standing, rank, or importance: *a story of one family's fall from wealth to poverty.* —*adj.* Happening in or appropriate to the season of fall: *fall fashions.* ◆ **fall back.** *intr.v.* To give ground; retreat: *fall back before an attack.* **fall back on.** To rely on (sbdy./sthg.): *They had to fall back on their savings.* **fall behind.** *tr.v.* [insep.] To fail to keep up with (sbdy./sthg.): *We fell behind the group we were traveling with.* —*intr.v.* To not do sthg. on time: *They fell behind in their bills.* **fall flat.** To produce no result; fail: *Their hasty plans fell flat.* **fall for.** *tr.v.* [insep.] **1.** To become infatuated with (sbdy./sthg.); fall in love with: *He fell for her in college.* **2.** To be tricked by (sthg.): *They fell for the swindler's scheme.* **fall in.** *intr.v.* To take one's place in a military formation: *The soldiers were ordered to fall in.* **fall in with.** **1.** To associate or begin to associate with (sbdy.): *She fell in with a new crowd at school.* **2.** To agree to (sthg.): *They immediately fell in with my suggestions.* **fall off.** *intr.v.* To become smaller or fewer; decline: *Attendance fell off in the* *spring.* **fall on** or **upon.** *tr.v.* [insep.] **1.** To attack (sbdy./sthg.) suddenly: *The cat fell on the mice.* **2.** To find (sthg.); come upon: *They fell upon the ruins of an ancient city in the desert.* **3.** To meet with (sthg.): *They fell on hard times.* **fall out.** *intr.v.* **1.** To quarrel: *The cousins fell out over an inheritance.* **2.** To leave one's place in a military formation: *The troops fell out of line.* **fall prey to.** To be a victim of (sbdy./sthg.): *Elderly people often fall prey to dishonest businessmen.* **fall short. 1.** To fail to reach a specified amount or degree: *Sales fell short of expectations.* **2.** To be inadequate: *Food supplies fell short.* **fall through.** *intr.v.* To fail; collapse: *Their plans for a vacation fell through.* **fall through the cracks.** To go unnoticed, neglected, or unchecked: *Several details fell through the cracks as we rushed to finish the project.*

fal·la·cious (fə lā′shəs) *adj. Formal.* Based on sthg. that is not true: *fallacious arguments based on a misunderstanding of the facts.* —**fal·la′cious·ly** *adv.*

fal·la·cy (făl′ə sē) *n., pl.* **fal·la·cies. 1.** [C] A false idea or mistaken belief: *It is a fallacy that money can buy happiness.* **2.** [C; U] False reasoning, belief, or argument.

fall·en (fô′lən) *v.* Past participle of **fall.**

fal·li·ble (făl′ə bəl) *adj.* Capable of making mistakes: *Each of us is a fallible human being.* —**fal′li·bil′i·ty** *n.* [U] —**fal′li·bly** *adv.*

fall·ing-out (fô′lĭng out′) *n., pl.* **fall·ings-out** or **fall·ing-outs.** A disagreement; a quarrel: *He had a falling-out with his parents and hasn't spoken to them for a month.*

fall·out (fôl′out′) *n.* [U] **1.** The tiny particles discharged into the atmosphere from an explosion, especially radioactive debris from a nuclear explosion: *The fallout after the accident ruined crops in a 50-mile radius.* **2.** The fall of such particles back to earth. **3.** Unexpected results or consequences: *People stopped buying that company's products as fallout from their negative ad compaign.*

false (fôls) *adj.* **fals·er, fals·est. 1.** Not true; incorrect: *The information she gave you is false.* **2.** Deliberately untrue or meant to deceive: *false testimony; a false promise.* **3.** Based on mistaken ideas or information: *The early news report raised false hopes.* **4.** Unfaithful; disloyal: *a false friend.* **5.** Not natural or genuine; not real: *a false signature.* —**false′ly** *adv.* —**false′ness** *n.* [U]

false·hood (fôls′hŏŏd′) *n.* **1.** [C] *Formal.* An untrue statement; a lie: *a report filled with falsehoods.* **2.** [U] The quality of being false; untruthfulness: *the falsehood of the accusation.* **3.** [U] The practice of making false statements; lying.

fal·set·to (fôl sĕt′ō) *n., pl.* **fal·set·tos.** The high-pitched upper register of a man's singing voice.

fal·si·fy (fôl′sə fī′) *tr.v.* **fal·si·fied, fal·**si·fy·ing, fal·si·fies. 1.** To lie about (sthg.); misrepresent: *It is a crime to falsify the facts when testifying under oath.* **2.** To change (a document, for example) in order to deceive; counterfeit: *falsify a driver's license.* —**fal′si·fi·ca′tion** (fôl′sə fĭ kā′shən) *n.* [U] —**fal′si·fi′er** *n.*

fal·ter (fôl′tər) *intr.v.* **1.** To lose confidence, strength, or purpose; hesitate: *My determination faltered as the work became more difficult.* **2.** To speak or move with hesitation: *Several times the speaker faltered from embarrassment. The child faltered, then fell off the bicycle.* —**fal′ter·ing·ly** *adv.*

fame (fām) *n.* [U] Great reputation; public esteem or renown: *Early fame brought many problems to the young author.* —**famed** *adj.*

fa·mil·ial (fə mĭl′yəl) *adj.* Relating to a family: *familial responsibilities.*

fa·mil·iar (fə mĭl′yər) *adj.* **1.** Well-known; often encountered; common: *a familiar sight.* **2.** [with] Having some knowledge; acquainted: *I am familiar with those streets in your neighborhood.* **3.** [with] Of established friendship; close: *We are on familiar terms with the neighbors.* **4.** [with] Overly friendly; presumptuous: *It is a mistake to be too familiar with one's boss.* —**fa·mil′iar·ly** *adv.*

fa·mil·iar·i·ty (fə mĭl′ yăr′ĭ tē or fə mĭl′-ē ăr′ĭ tē) *n., pl.* **fa·mil·iar·i·ties. 1.** [U] Knowledge of sthg.: *Familiarity with the city's streets is important for a cab driver.* **2.** [U] Friendship or informality: *the familiarity of close associates.* **3.** [C] Improper friendliness; forwardness: *I was offended by the salesperson's familiarities on the telephone.*

fa·mil·iar·ize (fə mĭl′yə rīz′) *tr.v.* **fa·mil·iar·ized, fa·mil·iar·iz·ing, fa·mil·iar·iz·es. 1.** [with] To make (sbdy.) acquainted with (sthg.): *They familiarized themselves with the new library.* **2.** To make (sthg.) known: *TV familiarized the special vocabulary of the space program.*

fam·i·ly (făm′ə lē or făm′lē) *n., pl.* **fam·i·lies. 1.** A social group usually consisting of parents and their offspring: *Most of my family lives in Arizona.* **2.** All the members of a household living under one roof: *His family includes his grandmother and his uncle, who live on the first floor.* **3.** The children of the same father and mother: *They raised a large family.* **4.** A group of persons sharing common ancestors; relatives: *Each year our whole family gets together for a cookout.* **5.** Line of descent; ancestry: *I come from an old Virginia family.* **6.** A group of things, such as animals, plants, or languages, that are alike or have a shared origin; a class: *The family of brass instruments includes the trumpet and trombone. French and Spanish are of the same language family.* **7.** A group of related plants or animals ranking above a genus and below an order: *Dogs, wolves, coyotes, and*

F

foxes belong to the same family. —SEE NOTE at **collective noun.**

family name *n.* A surname; last name: *Write your first name and your family name.*

family planning *n.* [U] The planning of the number and timing of children in a family through birth control.

family tree *n.* A diagram showing the relationships among the ancestors of a family.

fam·ine (făm′ĭn) *n.* [C; U] A serious, widespread shortage of food: *Famine may strike after a prolonged drought.*

fam·ished (făm′ĭsht) *adj.* Extremely hungry; starving: *I didn't stop working to have lunch, and now I'm famished.*

fa·mous (fā′məs) *adj.* Widely known; famed: *a country famous for its beautiful mountains.* See Synonyms at **noted.**

fan[1] (făn) *n.* **1.** An electrical device that moves air, especially for cooling, by means of rotating metal or plastic blades: *She sat in front of the fan.* **2.** A collapsible flat device, usually shaped like a half-circle, waved in the hand to create a cooling breeze: *paper fans.* **3.** Something that resembles an open fan: *The turkey's tail feathers spread into a fan.* —*v.* **fanned, fan·ning, fans.** —*tr.* **1.** To direct a current of air to blow upon (sbdy./sthg.), especially in order to cool: *We sat fanning ourselves under a tree.* **2.** To move or create a current of (air) with a fan. **3.** To stir up (sthg.) by or as if by fanning: *Rumors fanned smoldering anger in the crowd.* **4.** To open or spread (sthg.) out into the shape of a fan: *The peacock fanned its tail.* ◆ **fan out.** *intr.v.* To spread like a fan: *The search parties fanned out in different directions.*

fan[2] (făn) *n. Informal.* Someone who is an enthusiastic follower or admirer; an enthusiast: *a baseball fan; an opera fan.*

fa·nat·ic (fə năt′ĭk) *n.* A person with extreme beliefs or devotion to a cause: *soccer fanatics; religious fanatics.* —*adj.* Extremely enthusiastic. —**fa·nat′i·cal** *adj.* —**fa·nat′i·cal·ly** *adv.* —**fa·nat′i·cism** (fə năt′ĭ-sĭz′əm) *n.* [U]

fan·ci·er (făn′sē ər) *n.* A person with a special interest in sthg.: *a cat fancier.*

fan·ci·ful (făn′sĭ fəl) *adj.* **1.** Created in the mind; imaginary; unreal: *fanciful tales.* **2.** Using or tending to use the imagination: *a fanciful mind.* **3.** Original in design; imaginative: *fanciful figures made with pieces of cloth.* —**fan′ci·ful·ly** *adv.* —**fan′ci·ful·ness** *n.* [U]

fan·cy (făn′sē) *n., pl.* **fan·cies. 1.** [U] Imagination, especially of a playful type: *The characters are all creations of the author's fancy.* **2.** [C] An impulsive idea or thought; a whim: *We had a sudden fancy to go to the*

diner. **3.** [C] A liking, a fondness, or an inclination: *The stray dog took a fancy to our family.* —*adj.* **fan·ci·er, fan·ci·est. 1.** Very decorated; elaborate: *fancy carvings around the door.* **2.** Done with great skill; complex; intricate: *a dancer's fancy footwork.* **3.** Of superior quality; fine: *fancy fruits and vegetables.* **4.** Exorbitant; excessive: *That store charges very fancy prices.* —*tr.v.* **fan·cied, fan·cy·ing, fan·cies.** *Formal.* **1.** To picture (sbdy./sthg.) in the mind; imagine: *I tried to fancy myself as an actor.* **2.** To have a liking for (sbdy./sthg.); enjoy: *Would you fancy a movie tonight?* See Synonyms at **love. 3.** To suppose (sthg.); guess: *I fancy the meeting will end soon.* —**fan′ci·ly** *adv.* —**fan′ci·ness** *n.* [U]

fan·fare (făn′fâr′) *n.* **1.** [C] A short song played by one or more brass instruments; a flourish. **2.** [U] A spectacular public display or ceremony: *The astronauts were welcomed home with great fanfare.*

fang (făng) *n.* A long pointed tooth, such as that of a dog or poisonous snake: *The angry dog showed its fangs.*

fan·ny (făn′ē) *n., pl.* **fan·nies.** *Informal.* A person's buttocks: *Get off your fannies and get to work!*

fanny pack *n. Informal.* A small pack for carrying personal items, worn strapped around the waist.

fan·tas·tic (făn tăs′tĭk) *adj.* **1.** Based on fantasy; unreal: *a fantastic story of life in another galaxy.* **2.** Strange; weird: *dancers dressed in fantastic costumes.* **3.** Remarkable; outstanding: *The carpenter did a fantastic job of restoring the old house.* —**fan·tas′ti·cal·ly** *adv.*

fan·ta·sy (făn′tə sē *or* făn′tə zē) *n., pl.* **fan·ta·sies. 1.** [U] The creative imagination: *Her fantasy is at work in her latest science fiction novel.* **2.** [C] Something that is a creation of the imagination, as a fanciful work of fiction: *He likes to read fantasies.* **3.** [C] An imagined event or situation, especially one that fulfills a wish: *He has this fantasy about becoming a movie star.* —**fan′ta·size** *v.*

far (fär) *adv.* **far·ther** (fär′thər), **far·thest** (fär′thĭst) or **fur·ther** (fûr′thər), **fur·thest** (fûr′thĭst). **1.** To, from, or at a distance: *My home is located far from town.* **2.** To or at a specific distance, degree, or position: *How far do you intend to take this argument?* **3.** To a large degree; much: *I feel far better today than I did yesterday.* —*adj.* **farther, farthest** or **further, furthest. 1.** At great distance in space or time: *a far country halfway around the world; the far past.* **2.** More distant than another; opposite: *the far side of the mountain.* **3.** Politically extreme: *the far right.* ◆ **a**

far cry from. Very different from: *His second movie was a far cry from his first.* **as far as.** To the distance, extent, or degree that: *As far as I know they left an hour ago.* **by far.** To a great degree: *Their grades are better than mine by far.* **far and away.** By a wide margin: *This is far and away the best movie we've seen.* **far and wide.** Everywhere: *They traveled far and wide looking for a place to call home.* **far from.** Not at all: *His reply was far from honest.* **far off. 1.** At a great distance in time or space: *They traveled from far off to make their pilgrimage.* **2.** Inaccurate; incorrect: *Early predictions about the process were far off.* **go far.** To be successful: *They're so clever that their business is sure to go far.* **so far. 1.** Up to the present moment: *We haven't heard from anyone so far.* **2.** To a limited extent: *You can only go so far on $10.*

far·a·way (fär′ə wā′) *adj.* **1.** Very distant; remote: *The explorer spent years traveling in faraway places.* **2.** Dreamy; preoccupied: *a faraway look in his eyes.*

farce (färs) *n.* **1.** [C; U] A type of comic play with an unlikely story and characters exaggerated for humorous effect: *a political farce.* **2.** [C] Something ridiculous or laughable; a mockery: *Baseball practice turned into a farce after the coach left.*

far·ci·cal (fär′sĭ kəl) *adj.* Resembling a farce; foolish: *farcical errors.*

fare (fâr) *n.* **1.** [C] The money charged for transportation from one place to another: *The subway fare has gone up.* **2.** [C] A passenger who pays a fare: *The taxi stopped to pick up a fare.* **3.** [U] *Formal.* Food and drink: *The fare at this inn is excellent.* —*intr.v.* **fared, far·ing, fares.** To get along; progress: *How are you faring with your project?*

---

fare·well (fâr wĕl′) *interj. Formal.* An old-fashioned expression used to say good-bye. —*n.* **1.** [U] The act of saying good-bye, usually with good wishes: *a nod of farewell.* **2.** [C] An expression at parting; good-bye: *It was hard to say our farewells.*

far-fetched (fär′fĕcht′) *adj.* Hard to believe; improbable: *a far-fetched story.*

far-flung (fär′flŭng′) *adj.* Covering a large area: *the far-flung operations of an international airline.*

farm (färm) *n.* **1.** An area of land on which crops or animals are raised. **2.** An area of water used for raising aquatic animals: *a trout farm.* —*v.* —*tr.* To cultivate or produce a crop on (an area of land): *We farm 1,000 acres.* —*intr.* To engage in farming; grow crops or raise livestock: *They farm for a living.* ♦ **farm out.** To send (work) out to be done by another business: *All the sewing done by hand is farmed out by the manufacturer.*

farm

farm·er (fär′mər) *n.* A person who owns or operates a farm.

farm·ers' market (fär′mərz) *n.* A market at which farmers sell their produce directly to customers.

farm hand *n.* A person who works on a farm.

farm·yard (färm′yärd′) *n.* An area surrounded by or next to farm buildings: *Chickens and geese wandered freely in the farmyard.*

far-off (fär′ôf′ *or* fär′ŏf′) *adj.* Faraway; distant: *Home seemed very far-off.*

far-out (fär′out′) *adj. Slang.* Extremely unconventional; very unusual: *a far-out movie.*

far-reach·ing (fär′rē′chĭng) *adj.* Having a wide influence or effect: *A tax on energy will have far-reaching effects in the economy.*

far·sight·ed or **far-sight·ed** (fär′sī′tĭd) *adj.* **1.** Able to see distant objects better than close objects: *I am farsighted and wear glasses to read.* **2.** Planning wisely for the future; having foresight: *a farsighted plan to stop pollution.* —**far′sight′ed·ness** *n.* [U]

fart (färt) *Offensive Slang. intr.v.* To expel gas through the anus; break wind. —*n.* **1.** A release of gas from the anus. **2.** An insulting term for sbdy. who is annoying, usually an older man.

far·ther (fär′thər) *adv.* A comparative of **far**. **1.** To or at a greater distance: *We walked farther than we had expected.* **2.** To a greater extent or degree: *I've read farther in the book and I like it now.* —*adj.* A comparative of **far**. More distant; remoter: *at the farther end of the street.*

---

far·thest (fär′thĭst) *adj.* A superlative of **far**. Most remote or distant: *the farthest regions of the Arctic.* —*adv.* A superlative of **far**. **1.** To or at the greatest distance in space or time: *The Chinese had come farthest to this meeting.* **2.** By the greatest extent or degree; most: *Their team of climbers had progressed farthest of all.*

F

F

fas•ci•nate (făs′ə nāt′) *tr.v.* To capture and hold the interest and attention of (sbdy.); captivate: *This book fascinates me so much I cannot put it down. I've always been fascinated by history.* —**fas′ci•na′tion** *n.* [U]

fas•ci•nat•ing (făs′ə nā′tĭng) *adj.* Attracting great interest; captivating: *a fascinating story.* See Synonyms at **interesting.** —**fas′ci•nat′ing•ly** *adv.*

fas•cism or **Fascism** (făsh′ĭz′ əm) *n.* [U] A political movement that advocates a system of government with a dictatorship, government control of the economy, strong nationalism, and often violent suppression of all opposition. —**fas′cist** or **Fascist** *n.*

fash•ion (făsh′ən) *n.* **1.** [C; U] A style or custom, as in dress or behavior, that is popular at a certain time: *an idea now in fashion.* **2.** [C] Something, such as a garment, that is popular at a certain time: *a store carrying the latest fashions.* **3.** [C] A manner of doing sthg.; a way: *She works in an organized fashion.* —*tr.v.* To shape or form into (sthg.): *fashion figures from clay.* ◆ **after a fashion.** In some way or other; to some extent: *We sing after a fashion but have little training.* **in fashion.** Popular: *Simple black dresses are always in fashion.*

fash•ion•a•ble (făsh′ə nə bəl) *adj.* **1.** According to the latest style; stylish: *a fashionable wardrobe.* **2.** Used by stylish people: *a fashionable hotel.* —**fash′ion•a•bly** *adv.*

fast[1] (făst) *adj.* **1.** Quick; swift: *a fast train; a fast computer.* **2.** Done or finished in very little time: *We ate a fast lunch.* **3.** Suitable for rapid movement: *a fast racetrack.* **4.** Ahead of the correct time: *My watch is fast.* **5.** Firmly fixed or fastened: *Keep a fast grip on the rope.* **6.** Permanent; not likely to fade: *Fast colors will not run in the wash.* **7.** Loyal; firm: *fast friends.* **8.** Disregarding moral standards; wild: *He hangs out with a fast crowd.* —*adv.* **1.** Quickly; rapidly: *You are driving too fast.* **2.** Firmly; securely: *Hold fast to the railing.* **3.** So as to run ahead of the correct time: *My watch runs fast.* **4.** Deeply; soundly: *The child is fast asleep.* ◆ **hard and fast.** Without exception; strict: *It is a hard and fast rule that only adults can become members of the club.* **live in the fast lane.** To live intensely: *People who work hard and play hard live in the fast lane.* **on the fast track.** Progressing quickly in a career: *He is on the fast track in that company; after two months he's already in management.*

SYNONYMS: fast, rapid, swift, quick, hasty. These adjectives describe sthg. marked by great speed. **Fast** often describes the person or thing in motion: *You would become a fast runner if you stayed in shape.* **Rapid** often describes the activity or movement involved: *Rapid advances in technology have changed daily life in a short period of time.* **Swift** describes smoothness and sureness of movement: *Be careful of the swift current while you're swimming.* **Quick** usually describes what takes little time: *Her quick reaction prevented the accident.* **Hasty** describes hurried action and often a lack of care or thought: *The contest judges came to regret their hasty decision.*

---

fast[2] (făst) *intr.v.* To eat little or no food or only certain foods, especially for religious reasons or as a form of protest: *They fasted all day long.* —*n.* The act or a period of fasting: *She ended her fast at sundown.*

fas•ten (făs′ən) *v.* —*tr.* **1.** To attach (sthg.) firmly; connect: *fasten a button to a shirt; unable to fasten blame on anyone.* **2.** To make (sthg.) fast or secure: *Fasten your seat belts.* **3.** To fix or direct (sthg.) steadily: *She fastened her gaze on the stranger.* —*intr.* **1.** To become attached, fixed, or joined: *The helmet fastens under your chin.* **2.** To fix or focus steadily: *My eyes fastened on the approaching plane.* —**fas′ten•er** *n.*

fas•ten•ing (făs′ə nĭng) *n.* Something, such as a hook, used to fasten things together.

fast food *n.* [C; U] Restaurant food prepared and served quickly.

fast-food (făst′fo͞od′) *adj.* Specializing in foods that are prepared and served quickly: *a fast-food restaurant.*

fast-forward (făst′fôr′wərd) *n.* [U] **1.** The button on a magnetic tape player that causes the tape to wind more quickly than it does at normal speed. **2.** The condition or process of moving forward very quickly: *She's certainly put her career in fast-forward.* —*v.* —*tr.* To cause (a magnetic tape) to wind very quickly. —*intr.* **1.** To advance a magnetic tape: *I always fast-forward through the commercials.* **2.** To move quickly, especially in time: *Let's fast-forward and eat now!*

fas•tid•i•ous (fă stĭd′ē əs *or* fə stĭd′ē əs) *adj.* **1.** Careful in all details: *Reporters must pay fastidious attention to the facts.* **2.** Difficult to please; choosy or finicky: *a fastidious eater.* —**fas•tid′i•ous•ly** *adv.* —**fas•tid′i•ous•ness** *n.* [U]

fat (făt) *n.* **1.** [C; U] Any of a large number of oily white or yellow compounds that are found in plant and animal tissues and that store energy. **2.** [U] Animal tissue containing such compounds: *Cut the fat off the steak.* **3.** [C; U] A solid animal or vegetable oil: *French fries are cooked in fat.* **4.** [U] Plumpness or obesity: *Exercise will take off the fat.*

—*adj.* **fat·ter, fat·test. 1.** Having much or too much body fat; obese: *At five feet six inches and 250 pounds, he was clearly too fat.* **2.** Full of fat or oil; greasy: *Fat foods are not good for you.* **3.** *Informal.* Big; generous: *a fat paycheck.* ◆ **fat chance.** *Slang.* Very little or no chance: *Fat chance I'll get an A!* **live off the fat of the land.** To live well, especially with plenty to eat: *Few of the early settlers were able to live off the fat of the land.* —**fat′ness** *n.* [U]

fa·tal (fāt′l) *adj.* **1.** Causing or capable of causing death: *a fatal disease.* **2.** Causing ruin or destruction; disastrous: *The investment was a mistake that proved fatal to the business.* **3.** Most decisive; fateful: *the fatal moment of going onstage to perform.* —**fa′tal·ly** *adv.*

fa·tal·ism (fāt′l ĭz′ əm) *n.* [U] **1.** The belief that all events are determined in advance by fate and cannot be altered. **2.** Acceptance of this belief; submission to fate: *His fatalism prevented him from acting to improve the situation.* —**fa′tal·ist** *n.* —**fa′tal·is′tic** *adj.*

fa·tal·i·ty (fā tăl′ĭ tē *or* fə tăl′ĭ tē) *n., pl.* **fa·tal·i·ties. 1.** [C] A death resulting from an accident or a disaster: *Three fatalities occurred in the fire.* **2.** [U] The ability to cause death: *a disease known for its fatality.*

fate (fāt) *n.* **1.** [U] A force or power that is believed to control events: *She believes in fate.* **2.** [C] Something believed to be caused by fate, especially sthg. bad; a destiny: *It was his fate never to defeat his rival.* **3.** [C] A final result; an outcome: *The fate of the plane is still not known.*

Homonyms: fate, fete (festival).

fate·ful (fāt′fəl) *adj.* **1.** Decisive and important; momentous: *the fateful decision to go to war.* **2.** Indicating trouble or disaster; prophetic: *The fever was a fateful sign that the patient was getting worse.* **3.** Bringing death or disaster; fatal: *a fateful battle in which thousands died.* **4.** Controlled by fate: *a fateful journey.* —**fate′ful·ly** *adv.*

fa·ther (fä′thər) *n.* **1.** A male parent or guardian of a child. **2.** A man who acts as a father, especially an older responsible person: *My older brother became a father to me when Dad got sick.* **3.** A male ancestor; a forefather: *the land of our fathers.* **4.** A male leader or official: *the city fathers.* **5.** A man who creates, starts, or founds sthg.: *Chaucer is considered the father of English poetry.* **6. Father.** God. **7. Father.** Used as a title and form of address for a priest or other clergyman. —*tr.v.* **1.** To be the male parent of (sbdy.): *father two children.* **2.** To act or serve as a father to (sbdy.): *He gladly undertook the duties of fathering his new stepchildren.* **3.** To create, start, or found (sthg.): *an*

organization fathered by a group of scientists.

fat-free (făt′frē′) *adj.* Having no fat: *Fat-free foods are becoming more popular.*

fa·ther·hood (fä′thər hŏŏd′) *n.* [U] The condition of being a father.

fa·ther-in-law (fä′thər ĭn lô′) *n., pl.* **fa·thers-in-law** (fä′thərz ĭn lô′). The father of one's husband or wife.

fa·ther·land (fä′thər lănd′) *n.* **1.** A person's native land; the country of one's birth. **2.** The land of one's ancestors.

fa·ther·less (fä′thər lĭs) *adj.* Without a living or known father: *a fatherless child.*

fa·ther·ly (fä′thər lē) *adj.* Resembling or appropriate to a father: *a fatherly interest in my progress in school.*

Fa·ther's Day (fä′thərz) *n.* The third Sunday in June, observed in the United States and Canada in honor of fathers.

fath·om (făth′əm) *n.* A distance equal to six feet (1.8 meters), used to measure water depth. —*tr.v.* To understand (sbdy./sthg.); comprehend: *We can't fathom his motives.*

fa·tigue (fə tēg′) *n.* **1.** [U] Weariness or exhaustion resulting from hard work or great effort: *She was suffering from fatigue.* **2.** [U] The weakening or failure of a material, such as metal, resulting from continual stress: *metal fatigue.* **3. fatigues.** Clothing worn by soldiers for heavy work or field duty. —*tr.v.* **fa·tigued, fa·tigu·ing, fa·tigues.** To tire (sbdy.) out physically or mentally; exhaust: *The long hike fatigued us.*

fat·ten (făt′n) *tr. & intr.v.* To make or become fat: *The farmer fattened the cattle. People fatten on a rich diet.*

fat·ten·ing (făt′nĭng *or* făt′ən ĭng) *adj.* Causing fat: *All my favorite foods are fattening!*

fat·ty (făt′ē) *adj.* **fat·ti·er, fat·ti·est. 1.** Composed of or containing fat: *fatty food.* **2.** Characteristic of fat; greasy. —**fat′ti·ness** *n.* [U]

fau·cet (fô′sĭt) *n.* A device that controls the flow of liquid from a pipe; a tap: *a leaky faucet at the kitchen sink.*

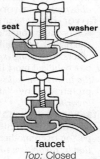

faucet
Top: Closed
Bottom: Open

fault (fôlt) *n.* **1.** A defect: *A fault in the book is its length.* **2.** A mistake; an error: *a fault in addition.* **3.** Responsibility for a mistake or an error: *The mix-up was all my fault.* **4.** A break in a rock mass caused by a movement of the earth's surface: *The houses built along the fault were destroyed in the earthquake.* —*tr.v.* To criticize (sbdy./sthg.): *No one can fault such a fine performance.* ◆ **at fault.** Deserving of blame;

guilty: *He admitted to being at fault.* **find fault with.** To criticize (sbdy./sthg.): *You're always finding fault with my ideas!* **to a fault.** To an excessive degree: *She is generous to a fault.*

fault·y (fôl′tē) *adj.* **fault·i·er, fault·i·est.** Having a fault or faults; imperfect or defective: *faulty electric wiring; a faulty argument.* —**fault′i·ly** *adv.* —**fault′i·ness** *n.* [U]

fau·na (fô′nə) *n.* [U] All the animals of a particular region or time period: *tropical fauna; prehistoric fauna.*

fa·vor (fā′vər) *n.* **1.** [C] A kind or helpful act: *My friend agreed to go with me as a favor.* **2.** [U] Approval or support; liking: *The plan is fast gaining favor.* **3.** [C] A small gift given to each guest, as at a party or wedding: *We all got small ivy plants as favors at the wedding.* **4.** [U] Friendly regard; partiality: *A judge cannot show favor in the court.* **5.** [U] Behalf; interest: *The cashier made an error in our favor.* —*tr.v.* **1.** [*with*] To perform a kindness or service for (sbdy.); oblige: *The singer favored us with two more songs.* **2.** To approve or support (sthg.): *I favor longer vacations.* **3.** To be partial to (sbdy./sthg.): *favor the youngest child.* **4.** To make (sthg.) easier or more likely; promote: *The climate there favors fruit farming.* **5.** To be gentle with (sthg.); treat with care: *The goalie favored his left leg while walking off the field.* **6.** To resemble (sbdy.); look like: *She favors her father.* ◆ **in favor of. 1.** In support of (sthg.): *All those in favor of the motion say "aye."* **2.** To the advantage of (sbdy.): *The judge decided in favor of the defendant.* **in (one's) favor.** To one's advantage: *The decision was in my favor.*

fa·vor·a·ble (fā′vər ə bəl *or* fāv′rə bəl) *adj.* **1.** Helpful; advantageous: *a favorable climate for growing crops.* **2.** Pleasing; promising: *The new student made a favorable impression on us.* **3.** Approving or praising: *favorable reviews of a movie.* **4.** Granting what has been desired or requested: *a favorable reply.* —**fa′vor·a·bly** *adv.*

fa·vor·ite (fā′vər ĭt *or* fāv′rĭt) *n.* **1.** A person or thing considered or treated with special regard, especially one preferred above all others: *That song is my favorite.* **2.** A contestant believed most likely to win: *Our team is the favorite in today's game.* —*adj.* Liked or preferred above all others: *Green is my favorite color.*

fa·vor·it·ism (fā′vər ĭ tĭz′əm *or* fāv′rĭ-tĭz′əm) *n.* [U] Better treatment given to one person over another; partiality: *gain promotion by favoritism rather than by skill.*

fa·vour (fā′vər) *n. & v.* Chiefly British. Variant of **favor**.

fawn[1] (fôn) *intr.v.* [*on; over*] **1.** To show affection or attempt to please: *She fawns over*

her husband. **2.** To seek favor by flattery or servile behavior: *The clerk fawned on the customer, hoping to make a sale.*

fawn[2] (fôn) *n.* **1.** [C] A young deer, especially one less than a year old. **2.** [U] A yellowish or reddish brown color. —*adj.* Yellowish or reddish brown.

fax (făks) *n.* **1.** A fax machine. **2.** A copy of material sent or received by a fax machine: *a fax of a business contract.* —*tr.v.* To send (sthg.) by a fax: *Businesses fax new information in minutes to their sales staff.*

fax

fax machine *n.* An electronic device that sends and receives exact copies of documents over telephone lines.

faze (fāz) *tr.v.* **fazed, faz·ing, faz·es.** To upset (sbdy.); bother: *Some people do not let anything faze them.*

HOMONYMS: faze, phase (aspect).

FBI also **F.B.I.** *abbr.* An abbreviation of Federal Bureau of Investigation.

FCC *abbr.* An abbreviation of Federal Communications Commission.

FDA *abbr.* An abbreviation of Food and Drug Administration.

Fe The symbol for the element **iron** (sense 1).

fear (fîr) *n.* **1.** [U] A feeling of fright: *She felt her fear increase as the sound grew louder.* **2.** [U] A state or condition marked by this feeling: *The citizens of the town lived in fear.* **3.** [C; U] An anxious feeling; concern: *a fear of looking foolish.* **4.** [C] A cause for fear; dread: *My greatest fears are poverty and loneliness.* —*v.* —*tr.* **1.** To be afraid of (sbdy./sthg.); be frightened of: *The boy does not fear spiders.* **2.** To feel anxious or concerned about (sthg.); worry: *We fear mistakes will show up.*

fear·ful (fîr′fəl) *adj.* **1.** Feeling or showing fear; afraid: *I was fearful of losing my way in the forest.* **2.** Causing fear; terrible: *We heard a fearful explosion.* **3.** *Informal.* Very bad; dreadful: *a fearful mistake.* —**fear′ful·ly** *adv.* —**fear′ful·ness** *n.* [U]

fear·less (fîr′lĭs) *adj.* Having no fear; brave: *a fearless explorer.* See Synonyms at **brave**. —**fear′less·ly** *adv.* —**fear′less·ness** *n.* [U]

fear·some (fîr′səm) *adj.* Causing fear; frightening: *A tornado is a fearsome sight.*

fea·si·ble (fē′zə bəl) *adj.* **1.** Capable of being done; possible: *Development of rockets*

---

made space exploration feasible. **2.** Likely; logical: *That answer seems feasible enough.* —**fea·si·bil·i·ty** *n.* [U] —**fea·si·bly** *adv.*

feast (fēst) *n.* **1.** A large elaborate meal, especially one prepared for a special occasion; a banquet: *a wedding feast.* **2.** A religious festival. —*v.* —*intr.* [on] To eat heartily: *feast on the first corn of summer.* —*tr.* To give a feast for (sbdy.); entertain lavishly: *The couple feasted all their friends with an elaborate dinner party.* ◆ **feast (one's) eyes on.** *Informal.* To look at (sbdy./sthg.) with pleasure: *Feast your eyes on the beautiful landscape.*

feat (fēt) *n.* An outstanding deed or accomplishment, especially one that requires much skill or daring: *The dam is a remarkable feat of engineering.*

HOMONYMS: feat, feet (plural of foot).

---

feath·er (fĕth'ər) *n.* One of the light flat growths that cover the skin of birds. —*tr.v.* To cover or fit (sthg.) with a feather or feathers: *feather an arrow.* ◆ **a feather in (one's) cap.** Something to be proud of; a great achievement: *The sales award was a feather in her cap.* **as light as a feather.** Very light: *The package looked heavy, but it was as light as a feather.* **feather (one's) nest.** To get rich by taking advantage of circumstances: *He feathered his nest after the war.* **ruffle (one's) feathers.** To make (sbdy.) angry: *The critic's negative remarks ruffled the author's feathers.*

feath·ered (fĕth'ərd) *adj.* Covered or trimmed with feathers: *a feathered hat.*

feath·er·y (fĕth'ə rē) *adj.* **1.** Made of or covered with feathers. **2.** Resembling a feather as in form or lightness: *feathery leaves.*

fea·ture (fē'chər) *n.* **1.** A prominent part or characteristic: *Dust and craters are features of the moon's surface. Several features of the plan caught our attention.* **2.a.** Any of the distinct parts of the face: *I couldn't make out his features from a distance.* **b.** The appearance of the face or its parts: *our friend's cheerful features.* **3.** The main film of a motion-picture program: *Today's feature is a Western.* **4.** A special article or column in a newspaper or magazine. —*tr.v.* **fea·tured, fea·tur·ing, fea·tures.** To give special attention to (sbdy./sthg.): *an exhibit that features Native American pottery.*

Feb. also **Feb** *abbr.* An abbreviation of February.

Feb·ru·ar·y (fĕb'rōō ĕr'ē *or* fĕb'yōō ĕr'ē) *n., pl.* **Feb·ru·ar·ies.** The second month of the year, with 28 days or, in leap years, 29 days.

fe·ces (fē'sēz) *pl.n.* Waste matter excreted from the bowels; excrement. —**fe'cal** (fē'kəl) *adj.*

fed (fĕd) *v.* Past tense and past participle of **feed.**

Fed (fĕd) *n.* *Informal.* **1.** *(usually singular).*

The Federal Reserve System. **2.** A federal agent or official.

fed·er·al (fĕd'ər əl *or* fĕd'rəl) *adj.* **1.** Relating to a form of government in which separate states retain control over local affairs but are united under a central government that manages affairs of common concern to all the states: *federal courts; federal laws applying to all the states.* **2.** Often **Federal.** Relating to the central government of the United States: *a Federal Court of Appeals; Federal income tax.* —**fed'er·al·ly** *adv.*

Federal Bureau of Investigation *n.* The U.S. government agency responsible for enforcing Federal laws.

fed·er·al·ism (fĕd'ər ə lĭz'əm *or* fĕd'-rə lĭz'əm) *n.* [U] A system of government in which power is divided between a central government and member states. —**fed'er·al·ist** *n.*

fed·er·a·tion (fĕd'ə rā'shən) *n.* **1.** [U] The act of joining together in a league, federal union, or other association. **2.** [C] A league or an association formed by combining several groups: *a federation of independent small business owners.*

fee (fē) *n.* A charge or payment for a service or privilege: *an admission fee to the movies; a fee for advice from our lawyer; a tuition fee for school.*

fee·ble (fē'bəl) *adj.* **fee·bler, fee·blest.** **1.** Lacking strength; weak: *a very old and feeble person recovering from surgery.* **2.** Without adequate force or intensity; inadequate: *a feeble attempt; a feeble voice.* —**fee'ble·ness** *n.* [U] —**fee'bly** *adv.*

feed (fēd) *v.* **fed** (fĕd), **feed·ing, feeds.** —*tr.* **1.** To give food to (sbdy./sthg.): *People feed the birds in the park.* **2.** To provide (sthg.) as food or nourishment: *We fed the leftover turkey to the cat.* **3.** To produce or serve as food for (sbdy./sthg.): *a turkey large enough to feed a dozen people.* **4.** To supply (material needed for growth, maintenance, or operation): *We fed more wood to the fire. Scientists fed data into a computer.* —*intr.* [on] To use as food; eat: *Young turtles feed on insects.* —*n.* [C; U] **1.** Food for animals or birds: *feed for the horses.* **2.** *Informal.* A meal, especially a large one: *The family sits down to a great feed every Thanksgiving.* ◆ **be fed up.** To be unable or unwilling to put up with sthg. any longer; annoyed: *The manager was fed up with his excuses for being late.*

feed·back (fēd'băk') *n.* [U] A response or reaction: *We asked the employees for feedback on the new cafeteria.*

feed·er (fē'dər) *n.* **1.** A person or thing that supplies feed: *a bird feeder on a window ledge.* **2.** Something that feeds materials into a machine to be processed.

feel (fēl) *v.* **felt** (fĕlt), **feel·ing, feels.** —*tr.* **1.** To be aware of or experience (sthg.) as a physical sensation: *feel a sharp pain; feel the cold.* **2.** To be aware of (sthg.) through the sense of touch: *feel the softness of velvet.* **3.** To touch or examine (sbdy./sthg.) by touching in order to find sthg. out: *The nurse felt the patient's forehead for fever.* **4.** To sense or experience (sthg.): *They felt my annoyance over their loud music.* **5.** To be affected by (sthg.): *She still feels the loss of her cat.* **6.** To believe (sthg.); consider: *We feel the idea is worth trying.* —*intr.* **1.** To experience sensations of touch: *The doctor poked my foot to see if I could feel.* **2.** To produce a particular sensation or feeling: *The sheets felt cool and smooth. It feels good to be home.* **3.** To be aware of a quality or an emotional state: *We all felt satisfied with the results of our work.* **4.** To try to find sthg. by touching: *We felt around for the light switch.* —*n.* [U] **1.** Awareness or sensation caused by physical touch: *the feel of raindrops.* **2.** A quality that can be sensed by touching: *the smooth and slippery feel of satin.* ◆ **feel as if** or **as though.** To give or have the impression that sthg. will happen: *He felt as if he was going to faint. It feels as though it's going to rain.* **feel for.** *tr.v.* [insep.] **1.** To sympathize with (sbdy.): *I know you're disappointed and I really feel for you.* **2.** To try to find (sthg.) by touching: *I'm feeling for the light switch.* **feel free.** To be encouraged: *Feel free to ask any questions you might have.* **feel in (one's) bones.** To have an intuition: *I feel in my bones that this project will succeed.* **feel like.** *Informal.* **1.** To be in the mood for (sthg.): *I did not feel like going for a walk.* **2.** To have the appearance of (sthg.): *Does it feel like rain to you? This feels like silk.* **feel like a million dollars.** To feel very good: *I felt like a million dollars after getting some rest.* **feel (oneself)** or **feel like (oneself).** To be in the usual state of health or spirits: *I don't feel quite myself this morning.* **feel (one's) way.** To move ahead cautiously: *When he first came to the United States, he had to feel his way around in social situations.* **feel out.** *tr.v.* [sep.] To try cautiously to find out the viewpoint of (sbdy.): *We felt them out about playing a football game.* **feel up to. 1.** To be well enough for (sthg.): *With his cold, he doesn't feel up to going to the party.* **2.** To be prepared to do (sthg. unpleasant or hard): *I never feel up to cleaning the garage.* **get the feel of.** To become comfortable with (sthg.): *He walked around to get the feel of the new shoes.*

feel•er (fē′lər) *n.* **1.** A remark, question, or suggestion used to find out the attitude or intention of others: *The letter was a feeler sent to see if there was any interest in our project.* **2.** A slender body part, such as the antenna of an insect, used for touching or feeling.

feel•ing (fē′lĭng) *n.* **1.** [U] The sense of touch: *I had no feeling in my cut finger.* **2.** [C; U] A physical sensation, especially one produced by touch: *the feeling of ice.* **3.** [C; U] An emotion, such as joy or sorrow: *a feeling of excitement.* **4.** [C] An awareness; an impression: *a feeling of danger nearby.* **5.** [C] An opinion: *The engineer's feeling is that the bridge is still strong.* ◆ **hurt (one's) feelings.** To injure (sbdy.) emotionally: *His lack of concern hurt my feelings.*

SYNONYMS: feeling, emotion, passion, sentiment. These nouns refer to an intense, complicated mental state such as love or hate. **Feeling** is the most general and neutral: *A feeling of relief came over the audience when the performer regained her balance.* **Emotion** is a stronger term; it often means an excited or agitated feeling: *The thought of returning home after so many years filled them with emotions.* **Passion** means an intense, compelling emotion: *Getting carried away by passions can lead to serious harm.* **Sentiment** often refers to delicate, sensitive, refined feelings: *Don't let your sentiments get the better of you.*

feet (fēt) *n.* Plural of **foot.**

HOMONYMS: feet, feat (accomplishment).

feign (fān) *tr. & intr.v.* To make or give a false appearance; pretend: *The child feigned illness so he could stay home from school. The bird isn't really dead; it's only feigning to fool the dog.*

feint (fānt) *n.* A movement that is meant to deceive by diverting attention from the real target: *With a feint to the left, she fooled the goalie and scored.* —*intr.v.* To make a feint: *My opponent feinted as if to take a shot at the basket.*

HOMONYMS: feint, faint (dim).

feist•y (fī′stē) *adj.* **feist•i•er, feist•i•est.** Having a lot of energy; frisky: *a feisty little puppy.*

fe•line (fē′līn′) *adj.* **1.** Belonging to the family of carnivorous mammals that includes the cats, lions, tigers, and leopards. **2.** Like a cat: *walking with feline grace.* —*n.* An animal in the feline family: *The cat is a feline.*

fell[1] (fĕl) *tr.v.* To cause (sthg.) to fall; cut or knock down: *They felled trees to build a cabin.* ◆ **in one fell swoop.** All at once: *They bought a car and a boat in one fell swoop.*

fell[2] (fĕl) *v.* Past tense of **fall.**

fel·low (fĕl′ō) *n.* **1.** A man or boy: *The little fellow was afraid of the thunder.* **2.** A comrade or an associate: *Robin Hood and his fellows hid in the forest.* **3.** A graduate student who receives a grant of money for further study. **4.** A member of a scholarly society: *She was elected a fellow of the art institute.* —*adj.* Being of the same kind, group or class; sharing certain characteristics or interests: *our fellow workers.*

fel·low·ship (fĕl′ō shĭp′) *n.* **1.** [U] Friendly association of people; companionship: *We enjoyed the fellowship of the other workers.* **2.** [C] A group of people sharing common interests. **3.** [C] A grant of money awarded a graduate student in a college or university.

fel·on (fĕl′ən) *n.* A person who has committed a felony.

fe·lo·ni·ous (fə lō′nē əs) *adj.* Relating to a felony: *carrying a gun with felonious intent.*

fel·o·ny (fĕl′ə nē) *n.*, *pl.* **fel·o·nies.** [C; U] A serious crime, such as murder, rape, or burglary: *He was found guilty of a felony and was sent to prison.*

felt¹ (fĕlt) *n.* [U] A smooth firm cloth made by pressing wool, fur, or other fibers together instead of weaving them. —*adj.* Made of felt: *a felt hat.*

felt² (fĕlt) *v.* Past tense and past participle of **feel.**

fem. *abbr.* An abbreviation of: **1.** Female. **2.** Feminine.

fe·male (fē′māl′) *adj.* **1.** Relating to the sex that produces eggs or gives birth to offspring: *a female duck with her ducklings.* **2.** Composed of women or girls: *a female choir.* —*n.* **1.** A female animal or plant: *The female of the horse is called a mare.* **2.** A woman or girl: *Females and males sat on opposite sides of the room.*

fem·i·nine (fĕm′ə nĭn) *adj.* **1.** Relating to women or girls: *Requirements for feminine nutrition are different from those for men.* **2.** Having qualities traditionally attributed to a woman: *The lace curtains gave the house a feminine feeling.* **3.** In grammar, relating to the gender of nouns that refers to females or to things classified as female. For example, in German, the word for *world* is feminine. —**fem′i·nine·ly** *adv.*

fem·i·nin·i·ty (fĕm′ə nĭn′ĭ tē) *n.* [U] The quality or condition of being feminine.

fem·i·nism (fĕm′ə nĭz′əm) *n.* [U] **1.** Belief in the same rights for women and men in all aspects of public and private life. **2.** The movement organized around this belief. —**fem′i·nist** *n. & adj.*

fe·mur (fē′mər) *n.* The long bone in the upper part of the leg; the thighbone.

fence (fĕns) *n.* **1.** A structure that serves as an enclosure, a boundary, or a barrier. **2.** A person who receives and sells stolen goods. —*v.* **fenced, fenc·ing, fenc·es.** —*tr.* To sur-

round or separate (sthg.) with a fence: *fence a pasture to keep cows in.* —*intr.* To practice the sport of fencing: *Both actors fenced with skill.* ◆ **fence in.** *tr.v.* [sep.] **1.** To restrict the freedom of (sbdy.): *She feels fenced in by all the demands of her family.* **2.** To surround (sthg.) with a fence: *fence in the yard; fenced in the dogs for the night.* **on the fence.** *Informal.* Undecided as to which of two sides to support; uncommitted: *We're still on the fence about going on vacation.* —**fenc′er** *n.*

fenc·ing (fĕn′sĭng) *n.* [U] **1.** The art or sport of using a sword: *an Olympic fencing champion.* **2.** Material used to construct fences: *That lumber yard sells fencing.* **3.** A barrier or an enclosure of fences: *Low stone fencing surrounds the park.*

fend (fĕnd) *v.* ◆ **fend for (oneself).** To attempt to manage without help: *He'll have to fend for himself until his parents get home from work.* **fend off.** *tr.v.* [insep.] To protect oneself from (sbdy./sthg.): *fend off an attack.*

fend·er (fĕn′dər) *n.* A guard over each wheel of an automobile or other vehicle that keeps mud or water from splashing up.

fend·er-bend·er or **fender bender** (fĕn′dər bĕn′dər) *n. Informal.* A minor collision between two or more automobiles.

fer·ment (fûr′mĕnt′) *n.* **1.** [C] A substance that causes fermentation, such as a yeast, a mold, or an enzyme. **2.** [U] A state of agitation; unrest. —*tr. & intr.v.* (fər mĕnt′). To undergo or cause to undergo fermentation: *Yeast ferments starch and sugar. Our apple cider had fermented overnight.*

fer·men·ta·tion (fûr′mĕn tā′shən) *n.* [U] A chemical reaction in which enzymes break down complex organic compounds into simpler compounds: *Sugar is made into alcohol through the process of fermentation.*

fern (fûrn) *n.* Any of numerous plants with feathery fronds divided into many leaflets: *We saw many types of ferns on our hike in the woods.*

fe·ro·cious (fə rō′shəs) *adj.* **1.** Extremely savage; fierce: *the tiger's ferocious attack.* **2.** Extreme; intense: *ferocious heat.* —**fe·ro′-cious·ly** *adv.* —**fe·ro′cious·ness** *n.* [U]

fe·roc·i·ty (fə rŏs′ĭ tē) *n.* The state or quality of being ferocious; fierceness: *the lion's ferocity.*

fer·ret (fĕr′ĭt) *n.* A North American mammal similar to the weasel and with brown fur and dark feet, now sometimes kept as a pet. —*v.* ◆ **ferret out.** *tr.v.* [sep.] To bring (sbdy./sthg.) to light by searching; uncover: *ferreted out the solution to the mystery; ferret out the enemy.*

fer·ric (fĕr′ĭk) *adj.* Relating to or containing iron.

Fer·ris wheel (fĕr′ĭs) *n.* An amusement ride consisting of an upright wheel with seats that remain horizontal as the wheel revolves.

F

F

fer·rous (fĕr′əs) *adj.* Relating to or containing iron.

fer·ry (fĕr′ē) *tr.v.* **fer·ried, fer·ry·ing, fer·ries. 1.** To transport (people, vehicles, or goods) by boat across a body of water: *ferry cars and trucks across the bay.* **2.** To cross (a body of water) by a ferry: *We ferried the river before a bridge was built.* **3.** To transport (people or things), especially by aircraft: *Volunteers ferried everyone from the disaster area to the hospital.* —*n., pl.* **fer·ries. 1.** A boat used to transport passengers, vehicles, or goods across a body of water; a ferryboat. **2.** A place where passengers or goods are transported across a body of water by a ferry: *There was a crowd waiting at the ferry.*

fer·ry·boat (fĕr′ē bōt′) *n.* A boat used to transport passengers, vehicles, or goods across a body of water.

fer·tile (fûr′tl) *adj.* **1.** Able to produce offspring, seeds, or fruit: *a fertile cow; a fertile plant.* **2.** Able to develop into a complete organism; fertilized: *A fertile egg from a hen will produce a chick.* **3.** Favorable to the growth of crops and plants: *fertile soil; a fertile valley.* **4.** Very productive or active; inventive: *the writer's fertile imagination.* —**fer·til′i·ty** (fər tĭl′ĭ tē) *n.* [U]

fer·til·ize (fûr′tl īz′) *tr.v.* **fer·til·ized, fer·til·iz·ing, fer·til·iz·es. 1.** To cause (an egg cell) to become fertile, especially by a union with sperm. **2.** To make (soil, for example) fertile: *Last fall's leaves will fertilize the ground.* **3.** To spread fertilizer on (soil, for example): *fertilize the garden.* —**fer′til·i·za′tion** (fûr′tl ĭ zā′shən) *n.* [U]

fer·til·iz·er (fûr′tl ī′zər) *n.* [C; U] A material, such as manure, compost, or a chemical compound, added to soil to increase its productivity or fertility.

fer·vent (fûr′vənt) *adj.* Having great emotion or zeal; passionate: *the fervent leaders of the reform movement; a fervent plea for help.* —**fer′vent·ly** *adv.*

fer·vor (fûr′vər) *n.* [U] Strong emotion or belief: *religious fervor.*

fes·ter (fĕs′tər) *intr.v.* **1.** To form pus, as an infected wound does: *An unclean cut will fester and become painful.* **2.** To be or become a source of irritation: *His anger festered.*

fes·ti·val (fĕs′tə vəl) *n.* **1.** An occasion for feasting or celebration, especially a day or time of religious significance. **2.** A series of cultural performances, exhibitions, or competitions that occur regularly: *an international film festival.*

fes·tive (fĕs′tĭv) *adj.* Merry; joyous: *a festive party; festive decorations.* —**fes′tive·ly** *adv.* —**fes′tive·ness** *n.* [U]

fes·tiv·i·ty (fĕ stĭv′ĭ tē) *n., pl.* **fes·tiv·i·ties. 1.** [U] The joy and gaiety of a celebration or festival: *a holiday full of festivity.* **2.** [C] *(usually plural).* The activities of a festival: *Mardi gras festivities included parades, banquets, and balls.*

fes·toon (fĕ stoon′) *n.* A string or garland, as of leaves or flowers, suspended in a curve between two points. —*tr.v.* To decorate (sthg.) with or as if with festoons: *festooned the room with balloons.*

fet·a (fĕt′ə *or* fē′tə) *n.* [U] A white Greek cheese made usually of goat's or sheep's milk and preserved in brine.

fe·tal (fēt′l) *adj.* Relating to a fetus: *a fetal heartbeat.*

fetch (fĕch) *v.* —*tr.* **1.** To go after and bring back (sbdy./sthg.); get: *Shall I fetch your bags for you?* **2.** To bring in (an amount of money) as a price: *The painting fetched $200 at the auction.* —*intr.* To go after sthg. and return with it: *If you throw the ball, the dog will fetch.*

fetch·ing (fĕch′ĭng) *adj.* Very attractive; charming: *a fetching smile.* —**fetch′ing·ly** *adv.*

fete (fāt *or* fĕt) *n.* **1.** A festival or feast. **2.** An elaborate party. —*tr.v.* **fet·ed, fet·ing, fetes.** To honor (sbdy.) with a festival, a feast, or an elaborate entertainment: *They feted the veterans on Memorial Day.*

HOMONYMS: fete, fate (destiny).

---

fet·id (fĕt′ĭd *or* fē′tĭd) *adj.* Having an offensive odor; stinking: *a fetid pond.* —**fet′id·ly** *adv.*

fet·ish (fĕt′ĭsh) *n.* **1.** An object that is believed to have magical or spiritual powers. **2.** An object of too much attention or reverence, often sexual in nature: *a foot fetish.*

fet·ter (fĕt′ər) *n. Formal. (usually plural).* **1.** A chain or shackle for the ankles or feet. **2.** Something that restricts or restrains: *the fetters of city life.* —*tr.v.* **1.** To put fetters on (sbdy./sthg.); shackle. **2.** To restrict the freedom of (sbdy./sthg.): *Bad weather fettered our travel plans.*

fe·tus (fē′təs) *n.* The unborn young of a mammal at the later stages of its development.

feud (fyood) *n.* A bitter quarrel or state of hostility between two people or groups: *An ancient feud came between the families.* —*intr.v.* [over; about] To carry on a feud: *The neighbors feuded about the fence.*

feu·dal (fyood′l) *adj.* Relating to feudalism.

feu·dal·ism (fyood′l ĭz′əm) *n.* [U] A political and economic system in Europe during the Middle Ages, in which a landowner permitted people of a lower class to use land in exchange for various duties. —**feu′dal·is′tic** *adj.*

ă-**cat**; ā-**pay**; âr-**care**; ä-**father**; ĕ-**get**; ē-**be**; ĭ-**sit**; ī-**nice**; îr-**here**; ŏ-**got**; ō-**go**; ô-**saw**; oi-**boy**; ou-**out**; oo-**took**; oo-**boot**; ŭ-**cut**; ûr-**word**; th-**thin**; *th*-**this**; hw-**when**; zh-**vision**; ə-**about**; ɴ-French **bon**

fe•ver (fē′vər) *n*. **1.** [C] A body temperature that is higher than normal: *a high fever*. **2.** [U] A disease in which a high body temperature is one of the main symptoms: *yellow fever*. **3.** [C] A condition of great activity or excitement: *a fever of enthusiasm during the game*.

fe•ver•ish (fē′vər ĭsh) *adj*. **1.a.** Relating to, causing, or resembling a fever. **b.** Having a fever or symptoms characteristic of a fever: *The sick child was feverish*. **2.** Intensely excited or active: *The team was struck with a feverish desire to win*. —**fe′ver•ish•ly** *adv*.

few (fyoo) *adj*. Amounting to a small number; not many: *Few people like to swim in cold water*. —*n*. (used with a plural verb). **1.** A small number of persons or things: *I invited only a few to my party*. **2.** A limited group; a minority: *the happy few*. —*pron*. (used with a plural verb). A small number of persons or things: *Many felt it was an interesting idea, but few seemed willing to do anything about it*. ◆ **few and far between**. Rare: *True friends are few and far between*. **quite a few**. A fairly large number; several: *Quite a few people were interested in taking the class*.

USAGE: few The word **fewer** is used with expressions that refer to things that can be counted: *fewer than four players*; **less** is used with uncountable nouns: *less paper; less water*. **Less**, however, is the correct word in the expression *less than* when it is used before a plural noun referring to a measure of time, amount, or distance, as in *less than 50 miles*.

fez (fĕz) *n*., *pl*. **fez•zes**. A red felt cap in the shape of a flat-topped cone with a black tassel, worn chiefly in the eastern Mediterranean region.

fi•an•cé (fē′än sā′ *or* fē än′sā′) *n*. A man engaged to be married.

fi•an•cée (fē′än sā′ *or* fē än′sā′) *n*. A woman engaged to be married.

fi•as•co (fē ăs′kō) *n*., *pl*. **fi•as•coes** or **fi•as•cos**. A complete failure: *Without enough rehearsal, the play was a fiasco*.

fib (fĭb) *n*. A lie about sthg. unimportant or small: *Their excuse is just a fib*. —*intr.v*. **fibbed, fib•bing, fibs**. To tell a small lie. —**fib′ber** *n*.

fi•ber (fī′bər) *n*. **1.** [C] A thin strand; a thread: *Cotton, wool, and nylon fibers may be spun into yarn*. **2.** [C] Any of various elongated cells in the body, especially one of muscle or nerve tissue. **3.** [U] Basic strength: *a person of moral fiber*. **4.** [U] The part of grains, fruits, and vegetables not easily absorbed or digested, containing cellulose and stimulating the muscles of the intestinal walls. —**fi′brous** (fī′brəs) *adj*.

fi•ber•board (fī′bər bôrd′) *n*. [U] A building material made from wood chips glued together.

fi•ber•glass (fī′bər glăs′) *n*. [U] A material made up of very fine glass fibers, used in making various products, such as building insulation and boats.

fiber optics *n*. [U] (used with a singular or plural verb). The technology based on the use of fine glass or plastic fibers that are capable of transmitting light around curves: *Fiber optics are used in communications equipment*.

fi•bre (fī′bər) *n*. *Chiefly British*. Variant of **fiber**.

fib•u•la (fĭb′yə lə) *n*. The smaller of the two bones between the knee and the ankle in humans and other vertebrate animals.

—fic *suff*. A suffix that means making or causing: *horrific*.

fick•le (fĭk′əl) *adj*. Frequently changing; not stable or constant, especially with affections: *fickle teenagers*.

fic•tion (fĭk′shən) *n*. **1.** [U] A literary work based on the imagination and not on fact. **2.** [U] Something that is invented by the imagination: *The story seems real but is complete fiction*. **3.** [C] A lie: *The story he told the police is a complete fiction*. —**fic′tion•al** *adj*. —**fic′tion•al•ize′** (fĭk′shə nə līz′) *v*.

fic•ti•tious (fĭk tĭsh′əs) *adj*. Relating to fiction; imaginary: *a fictitious character*. —**fic•ti′tious•ly** *adv*. —**fic•ti′tious•ness** *n*. [U]

fid•dle (fĭd′l) *n*. A violin, especially one that is used to play folk music. —*v*. **fid•dled, fid•dling, fid•dles**. —*intr*. **1.** To play the fiddle: *We sang while they fiddled*. **2.** [*with*] To move one's fingers or hands nervously: *I was fiddling with my hat*. **3.** [*with*] To attempt to adjust sthg.: *Don't fiddle with the television!* —*tr*. To play (a tune) on a violin: *The musicians fiddled a reel*. ◆ **fiddle away**. *tr.v*. [sep.] To waste or squander (sthg.): *We fiddled away the last week of summer vacation*. **play second fiddle**. To accept being treated as less important than sbdy. else: *She doesn't play second fiddle to anyone*. —**fid′dler** *n*.

fi•del•i•ty (fĭ dĕl′ĭ tē *or* fī dĕl′ĭ tē) *n*. [U] **1.** Loyalty to obligations or duties: *a soldier's fidelity to duty*. **2.** Exact correspondence with the facts; accuracy: *the fidelity of the witness's account of the accident*.

fidg•et (fĭj′ĭt) *intr.v*. To behave or move nervously: *I fidgeted while waiting for the play to start*. —**fidg′et•y** *adj*.

field (fēld) *n*. **1.** A broad, level, open expanse of land: *We walked across the field*. **2.** A meadow: *a field of wildflowers*. **3.** A cultivated area of land, especially one for a particular crop: *cotton fields; a field ready for spring planting*. **4.** An area of land or a geologic formation containing a natural resource: *oil fields; a goldfield*. **5.** A battleground: *Thousands died on Flanders field during World War I*. **6.** A background area, as on a flag or painting: *a flag with white stars on a field of blue*. **7.** All the contestants or participants in a sports event: *a large field of* *athletes in the Olympics.* **8.** An area in which an athletic event takes place: *a ball field; a soccer field.* **9.** An area of human activity, study or interest; profession: *the field of American history.* **10.** Profession, employment, or business: *What field are you in?* **11.** A scene of practical work or observation outside an office, a school, a factory, or a laboratory: *The engineer is out in the field.* **12.** The area of space in which a physical force operates: *The moon is within the earth's gravitational field.* **13.** The area in which an image is visible to the eye or an optical instrument: *the field of a microscope; the field of vision.* —*adj.* **1.** Growing, living, or cultivated in fields or open land: *a field mouse.* **2.** Made, used, or done in the field: *field operations; field research.* —*tr.v.* **1.** In sports, especially baseball, to stop or catch (a ball): *fielded several fly balls.* **2.** *Informal.* To handle (sthg.) successfully: *field a difficult question well.*

field day *n.* A day set aside for sports or athletic competition. ◆ **have a field day.** To take advantage of sbdy./sthg.: *The press had a field day with the poorly prepared speaker.*

field glasses *pl.n.* Portable binoculars used especially outdoors for viewing distant objects.

field goal *n.* In football, a score worth three points made by a place kick that goes through the goal posts.

field hockey *n.* [U] A game played on a field in which two opposing teams of players using wooden sticks try to drive a ball into the opponents' goal.

field house *n.* A large building at an athletic field for indoor events and training.

field test *n.* A test of a new product under actual operating conditions.

field-test (fēld′tĕst′) *tr.v.* To test (a technique or product, for example) under conditions of actual operation: *field-test a new kind of lawn mower.*

field trip *n.* A group excursion for the purpose of firsthand observation, as to a museum, the woods, or a historic place.

fiend (fēnd) *n.* **1.** An evil spirit; a demon. **2.** An evil or wicked person. **3.** *Informal.* A person absorbed in or obsessed with a certain thing: *a baseball fiend; a fresh-air fiend.*

fiend·ish (fēn′dĭsh) *adj.* **1.** Relating to a fiend; evil, wicked, or cruel: *a fiendish weapon.* **2.** Extremely bad, disagreeable, or difficult: *a fiendish problem.* —**fiend′ish·ly** *adv.*

fierce (fîrs) *adj.* **fierc·er, fierc·est. 1.** Having a violent and savage nature; ferocious: *a fierce beast.* **2.** Extremely severe or intense; terrible: *a fierce snowstorm.* **3.** Extremely intense or ardent: *fierce loyalty.* —**fierce′ly** *adv.* —**fierce′ness** *n.* [U]

fier·y (fīr′ē *or* fī′ə rē) *adj.* **fier·i·er, fier·i·est. 1.** Flaming or on fire: *the fiery crater of the volcano.* **2.** Having the color of fire: *a fiery sunset.* **3.** Very hot: *the fiery hot peppers.* **4.** Easily excited or provoked; passionate: *a fiery temper.* **5.** Charged with emotion; high-spirited: *a fiery speech.* —**fier′i·ly** *adv.* —**fier′i·ness** *n.* [U]

fi·es·ta (fē ĕs′tə) *n.* A festival or religious holiday, especially a saint's day celebrated in Spanish-speaking countries.

fif·teen (fĭf tēn′) *n.* **1.** The number, written 15, that is equal to 14 + 1. **2.** The 15th in a series or sequence. —**fif′teen′** *adj. & pron.*

fif·teenth (fĭf tēnth′) *n.* **1.** The ordinal number matching the number 15 in a series. **2.** One of 15 equal parts. —**fif·teenth′** *adj. & adv.*

fifth (fĭfth) *n.* **1.** The ordinal number matching the number five in a series. **2.** One of five equal parts. **3.** One fifth of a gallon of liquor. —**fifth** *adj. & adv.*

fif·ty (fĭf′tē) *n., pl.* **fif·ties. 1.** The number, written 50, that is equal to 5 × 10. **2.** **fifties. a.** Often **Fifties.** The ten years from 50 to 59 in a century. **b.** A decade or the numbers from 50 to 59: *a man in his fifties.* —**fif′ty** *adj. & pron.*

fif·ty-fif·ty (fĭf′tē fĭf′tē) *adj.* **1.** Divided or shared equally: *The partners agreed on a fifty-fifty split of the money.* **2.** Equally balanced between favorable and unfavorable: *had a fifty-fifty chance to win the game.* —**fif′ty-fif′ty** *adv.*

fig (fĭg) *n.* A sweet pear-shaped fruit with many seeds that grows on trees or shrubs in warm regions: *Figs can be eaten fresh, dried, or canned.*

fig. *abbr.* An abbreviation of figure.

fight (fīt) *v.* **fought** (fôt), **fight·ing, fights.** —*intr.* **1.** To participate in combat or battle: *fought bravely against the invaders.* **2.** To box or wrestle: *They fought for the gold medal.* **3.** To engage in a quarrel; argue: *The neighbors fought for years over the boundary.* **4.** To try very hard to get sthg.: *fought for freedom.* —*tr.* **1.** To contend with (sbdy./ sthg.) physically or in battle: *The United States fought Germany in both world wars.* **2.** To carry on or engage in (a battle): *fought the war on two fronts.* **3.** To box or wrestle against (sbdy.) in a ring: *fight a contender in the Olympics.* **4.** To struggle against (sthg.): *fight illiteracy; fight rising floodwaters.* See Synonyms at **oppose.** —*n.* **1.** [C] A conflict between two or more individuals; a struggle: *a fight over who would empty the trash.* **2.** [C] A battle waged between opposing forces. **3.** [C] A boxing or wrestling match. **4.** [C] A struggle to achieve a goal: *the fight for free-*

ă–**cat**; ā–**pay**; âr–**care**; ä–**father**; ĕ–**get**; ē–**be**; ĭ–**sit**; ī–**nice**; îr–**here**; ŏ–**got**; ō–**go**; ô–**saw**; oi–**boy**; ou–**out**;
ōō–**took**; ōō–**boot**; ŭ–**cut**; ûr–**word**; th–**thin**; *th*–**this**; hw–**when**; zh–**vision**; ə–**about**; N–French bon

dom. **5.** [U] The power or will to battle or struggle: *We had no fight left in us.* ◆ **fight back against.** To defend oneself from (sthg.): *The city fought back against crime.* **fight fire with fire.** To combat one difficult or evil thing or person with another: *The company fought fire with fire and lowered its prices again.* **fight off.** *tr.v.* [sep.] To defend against (a hostile force, for example): *A fever is one way in which the body fights off germs. She fought her attacker off and fled.* **fight out.** *tr.v.* [sep.] To settle (sthg.), such as a dispute, by fighting: *I'm not going to fight everything out with you.*

fight·er (fī′tər) *n.* **1.** A soldier; a warrior *The colonists were brave fighters.* **2.** A boxer or wrestler. **3.** A fast airplane used in combat

fig·ment (fĭg′mənt) *n.* Something invented or imagined: *It was nothing but a figment of the imagination.*

fig·u·ra·tive (fĭg′yər ə tĭv) *adj.* **1.** Based on or using figures of speech; metaphorical: *figurative language.* **2.** Represented by a symbol or figure; emblematic: *An oil lamp is a figurative representation of knowledge.* **—fig′ur·a·tive·ly** *adv.*

fig·ure (fĭg′yər) *n.* **1.** A written symbol, especially a numeral, representing sthg. that is not a letter. **2. figures.** Mathematical calculations: *An accountant needs to have a good head for figures.* **3.** An amount represented in numbers: *priced at a high figure.* **4.** In geometry, any combination of points, lines, or surfaces: *Circles and triangles are plane figures.* **5.** The shape or form of a human body: *People buy clothes to suit their figures.* **6.** A person, especially a well-known one: *The President is an important public figure.* **7.** A drawing or diagram: *On that page the figure shows a bird in flight.* —*v.* **fig·ured, fig·ur·ing, fig·ures.** —*tr.* **1.** To calculate (sthg.) with numbers; compute: *figured the cost of a new car.* **2.** *Informal.* To conclude, believe, or predict (sthg.); consider to be reasonable or expected: *I figured that you'd want to go swimming.* —*intr.* **1.** To calculate; compute: *Most store clerks can figure quickly and accurately.* **2.** To be or seem important: *The opening of the store figured in the local news.* **3.** *Informal.* To seem reasonable or expected: *It figures that they decided to work as a team because they work well together.* ◆ **figure in.** *tr.v.* [sep.] To include (sbdy./sthg.): *He figured in 15% of the bill for a tip.* **figure on.** *Informal. tr.v.* [insep.] To plan on (sthg.): *You can always figure on some guests to be late.* **figure out.** *tr.v.* [sep.] To solve, decipher, or discover (sthg.): *figure out a puzzle.* **That figures.** *Informal.* That is logical: *That figures! I knew you would forget his birthday.*

fig·ure·head (fĭg′yər hĕd′) *n.* **1.** A person in a position of leadership who has no real authority: *The Queen of England is really a figurehead and can make no governmental decisions.* **2.** A carved figure on the prow of a ship.

figure of speech *n., pl.* **figures of speech.** An expression in which words are used in unusual or nonliteral ways to create vivid or dramatic effects: *"To talk until you're blue in the face" is a figure of speech that means to talk a great deal.*

figure skat·ing (skā′tĭng) *n.* [U] Ice skating in which the skater makes movements or elaborate figures. **—fig′ure skat′er** *n.*

fil·a·ment (fĭl′ə mənt) *n.* A thin thread, wire, or fiber: *The filament in the light bulb burned out.*

filch (fĭlch) *tr.v.* To steal (sthg. of little value) in a sly manner; pilfer: *She filched a pencil from my desk.* **—filch′er** *n.*

file¹ (fīl) *n.* **1.** A container, such as a cabinet or folder, for keeping papers in order: *drawings stored in large files.* **2.a.** A collection of papers or published materials kept or arranged in convenient order: *Please get me the file on this case.* **b.** A collection of related data for a computer: *How many files are there now on your diskette?* **3.** A row or single line of people or things arranged one behind the other: *The ducks waddled across the road in a file.* —*v.* **filed, fil·ing, files.** —*tr.* **1.** To put or keep (papers, for example) in useful order for storage or reference: *I filed the report.* **2.** To submit or send (sthg.) in an official manner: *Reporters file newspaper stories daily. I'd like to file a complaint.* —*intr.* **1.** To march or walk in a line: *The nine justices solemnly filed in.* **2.** To make application; apply: *Candidates for election must file with the county clerk.* ◆ **on file.** Kept in a file: *Her application is on file.* **—fil′er** *n.*

file² (fīl) *n.* Any of several steel tools having a series of sharp ridges, used to smooth, shape, or grind down sthg. —*tr.v.* **filed, fil·ing, files.** To smooth, reduce, or remove (sthg.) with a file: *If you file the edge of the knife it will cut better.*

fi·let (fĭ lā′ *or* fĭl′ā′) *n. & v.* Variant of **fillet.**

fi·let mi·gnon (fĭ lā′ mēn yôɴ′) *n., pl.* **fi·lets mi·gnons** (fĭ lā′ mēn yôɴ′). [C; U] A round, very choice cut of beef.

fil·i·bus·ter (fĭl′ə bŭs′tər) *n.* The use of delaying tactics, such as making a long speech in an attempt to prevent the passage of a piece of legislation. —*intr. & tr.v.* To delay or obstruct by filibuster. **—fil′i·bus′ter·er** *n.*

fil·i·gree (fĭl′ĭ grē′) *n.* Delicate and intricate ornamental work of twisted gold or silver wire: *filigree earrings.* —*tr.v.* To decorate (sthg.) with or as if with filigree: *Frost filigreed the windowpanes.*

fil·ing (fī′lĭng) *n.* A particle or shaving removed by a file: *metal filings.*

F

fill (fĭl) *v.* —*tr.* **1.** To put as much into (sthg.) as it can hold: *fill a glass; fill an album with pictures.* **2.a.** To stop or plug up (an opening, for example): *fill a hole in the road.* **b.** To repair a cavity in (a tooth). **3.** To satisfy or meet (sthg.); fulfill: *fill the requirements for a job.* **4.** To supply (sthg.) as required: *fill a prescription; fill an order for 20 books.* **5.** To place a person in (a job, for example): *We filled the job with an experienced worker.* **6.** To take up the whole of (sbdy./sthg.); occupy: *Music filled the room. He was filled with happiness.* **7.** To engage or occupy (sbdy./sthg.) completely: *Memories of the summer filled my mind.* —*intr.* To become full: *The boat quickly filled with water.* —*n.* [U] **1.** An amount that is needed to make complete or satisfied: *We ate our fill of the blueberries.* **2.** Earth, gravel, or other material used to build up or fill in land. ◆ **fill in.** *tr.v.* [sep.] **1.** To provide (sbdy.) with information that is essential or newly acquired: *We filled in the police chief on the details of the theft. Can you fill me in?* **2.** To complete (sthg.): *I'll stitch the pattern first and fill in the background later. Fill in the blanks on the test.* —*intr.v.* To act as a substitute for sbdy.; stand in: *an understudy who filled in at the last minute.* **fill (one's) shoes.** To take sbdy.'s position or duties: *It will be hard to fill the manager's shoes.* **fill out.** *tr.v.* [sep.] To complete (a form, for example) by providing required information: *Did you fill out the job application?* —*intr.v.* To become more fleshy: *The pup filled out to become a full-grown dog.* **fill the bill.** To be or do exactly what is needed: *Your suggestions fill the bill.* **fill up.** *tr.v.* [sep.] To make (sthg.) completely occupied: *She filled up the mug with tea.* **fill up on.** To eat so much (of sthg.) that one is no longer hungry: *The children filled up on snacks.*

fill•er (fĭl'ər) *n.* [U] **1.** Something added to increase weight or size or to fill space: *They use cartoons and advertisements as filler in the newspaper.* **2.** A stack of loose papers used to fill a notebook or binder.

fil•let also **fi•let** (fĭ lā' *or* fĭl'ā') *n.* A piece of meat or fish without bones, especially the beef tenderloin. —*tr.v.* Also **filet** (fĭ lā' *or* fĭ'lā'). To slice, bone, or make (sthg.) into fillets: *I watched the fisherman fillet a trout.*

fill-in (fĭl'ĭn') *n. Informal.* A person or thing that serves as a substitute: *The understudy was a fill-in for the star.*

fill•ing (fĭl'ĭng) *n.* **1.** [C] Something used to fill a space, cavity, or container: *a gold filling in a tooth.* **2.** [U] An edible mixture used to fill pastries, sandwiches, or cakes: *a pie with an apple filling.*

filling station *n.* A service station.

fil•ly (fĭl'ē) *n.*, *pl.* **fil•lies.** A young female horse.

film (fĭlm) *n.* **1.** [C] A thin coating: *a film of oil over the puddle; a film of dust on a tabletop.* **2.** [U] A thin, flexible, transparent sheet, as of plastic, used in wrapping or packaging. **3.** [U] A thin flexible roll or sheet of material coated with a substance that is sensitive to light, used to make photographs. **4.** [C] A motion picture; a movie. —*v.* —*tr.* **1.** To cover (sthg.) with a film: *filmed the surface of the water.* **2.** To make a movie of (sthg.): *We filmed porpoises swimming alongside our boat.* —*intr.* **1.** [*over; up*] To become coated or obscured with or as if with a film: *My glasses filmed over when I came in from the cold.* **2.** To make or shoot scenes for a movie: *They're filming downtown today.*

film•y (fĭl'mē) *adj.* **film•i•er, film•i•est.** **1.** Resembling or made of film; gauzy: *filmy curtains.* **2.** Covered as if by a film; hazy: *a filmy sky.* —**film'i•ly** *adv.* —**film'i•ness** *n.* [U]

fil•ter (fĭl'tər) *n.* **1.** A device that separates solid particles from a liquid or gas passing through it: *A filter on the faucet collects particles of dirt from the water.* **2.** Porous material used in such a device for this purpose. **3.** A device that allows certain frequencies of waves to pass and stops the passage of others: *Filters on photographic lenses allow only certain colors of light to enter the camera.* —*v.* —*tr.* **1.** To pass (a liquid or gas) through a filter: *filter water for drinking.* **2.** To remove (sthg.) by passing through a filter: *The screen filters leaves from the water.* —*intr.* To flow through or as if through a filter: *Light filtered through the blinds.*

filth (fĭlth) *n.* [U] **1.** Dirty matter or refuse: *The kitchen, which had not been used for years, was covered with filth.* **2.** Something, such as language, considered obscene or immoral: *There is too much filth on television.*

filth•y (fĭl'thē) *adj.* **filth•i•er, filth•i•est.** **1.** Covered with filth; extremely dirty: *filthy streets with litter everywhere.* **2.** Obscene: *filthy language.*

fil•tra•tion (fĭl trā'shən) *n.* [U] The process of filtering.

fin (fĭn) *n.* **1.** One of the movable parts of the body of a fish or other aquatic animal that is used for swimming. **2.** Something shaped or used like a fin, as the tail of an aircraft.

fi•nal (fī'nəl) *adj.* **1.** Occurring at the end; last: *final preparations before leaving on a trip; the exciting final moments of a game.* **2.** Not to be changed; conclusive: *The judge's decision is final.* —*n.* **1.** The last or one of the last in a series of contests: *the finals for the championship.* **2.** The last examination of an academic course: *Our final covered a whole year's work.*

fi•nal•e (fə năl′ē or fə nä′lē) n. The concluding part, especially of a musical composition.

fi•nal•ist (fī′nə lĭst) n. A contestant in the final session of a competition.

fi•nal•i•ty (fī năl′ĭ tē or fə năl′ĭ tē) n. [U] The fact or condition of being final: a decision given with finality; the finality of leaving.

fi•nal•ize (fī′nə līz′) tr.v. **fi•nal•ized, fi•nal•iz•ing, fi•nal•iz•es.** To put (sthg.) into final form; complete: finalize travel plans; finalize an agreement.

fi•nal•ly (fī′nə lē) adv. At last; at the end: After much delay, the taxi finally arrived.

fi•nance (fə năns′ or fī′năns′) n. **1.** [U] The fact or of the management of money and other financial assets: An economist is a specialist in finance. **2. finances.** Monetary resources; funds: My finances were getting low. —tr.v. **fi•nanced, fi•nanc•ing, fi•nanc•es.** To provide or obtain funds or capital for (sthg.): We financed our new car with a bank loan.

finance company n. A company that makes loans to clients.

fi•nan•cial (fə năn′shəl or fī năn′shəl) adj. Relating to finance: The treasurer is responsible for the financial affairs of our club. —**fi•nan′cial•ly** adv.

fin•an•cier (fĭn′ən sîr′ or fə năn′ sîr′) n. A person who works in or is an expert in large-scale financial affairs.

fi•nanc•ing (fə năn′sĭng or fī′năn sĭng) n. [U] Money provided by an individual, a bank, or a group to support a purchase, project, or business: financing for a new car.

finch (fĭnch) n. Any of various songbirds with a short thick bill used for cracking seeds: I often see finches at my bird feeder.

find (fīnd) tr.v. **found** (found), **find•ing, finds.** **1.** To come upon (sbdy./sthg.), often by accident: I found a quarter on the sidewalk. **2.** To discover or come upon (sbdy./sthg.) after a search: At last I found my glasses. **3.** To perceive (sbdy./sthg.) to be, after observation or experience: found the book entertaining; found her interesting. **4.** To recover the use of (sthg.); regain: I found my voice and shouted for help. **5.** To succeed in reaching (sthg.); arrive at: The arrow found its mark. **6.** To obtain or acquire (sthg.) by effort: find the money to make the trip. **7.** To decide on and make a declaration about (sbdy./sthg.): The jury found the accused innocent of all charges. **8.** To furnish (sthg.); supply: We can find a bed for you in the house tonight. **9.** To understand (oneself) to be in a specific location or condition: The lost hikers found themselves in difficulty. —n. Something that is found, especially an unexpectedly valuable discovery: news of oil finds in Alaska. ◆ **find out.** tr.v. [sep.] **1.** To get (information): I found out when she's arriving. **2.** To learn the true nature or character of (sbdy./sthg.): The employee who was stealing was soon found out.

find•ing (fīn′dĭng) n. Something that has

been found especially after an examination or investigation: a finding in the investigation of an airplane crash.

fine¹ (fīn) adj. **fin•er, fin•est. 1.** Of very good quality, skill, or appearance: a fine day; a fine performance. **2.** Being in a state of good health; quite well: I'm fine, thank you. **3.** Very small in size, weight, or thickness: fine hair. **4.** Very sharp: a fine point on a pencil. **5.** Showing delicate and careful artistry: a fine painting; fine china. **6.** Consisting of small particles; not coarse: fine dust; the fine spray of a water hose. **7.** So small as to be difficult to see or understand: the fine differences between a rabbit and a hare. —adv. **finer, finest.** Informal. **1.** In small pieces or parts: Chop the onions fine. **2.** Very well: The two dogs are getting along fine. —**fine′ness** n. [U]

fine² (fīn) n. A sum of money that has to be paid as a penalty for an offense: a $15 fine for overtime parking. —tr.v. **fined, fin•ing, fines.** To order (sbdy.) to pay a fine: fine a borrower who doesn't return library books.

fine art n. (usually plural). Any of the art forms, such as painting, sculpture, and music, that are used to create works intended for beauty rather than utility.

fine•ly (fīn′lē) adv. **1.** In a fine manner; splendidly: a finely decorated room. **2.** In small pieces or parts: The recipe calls for finely chopped onions.

fi•nesse (fə nĕs′) n. [U] **1.** Exact performance, creation, or craft: the finesse of an experienced glass blower. **2.** Clever handling of a situation; tact and skill: the lawyer's finesse in getting the partners to agree. —tr.v. **fi•nessed, fi•ness•ing, fi•ness•es.** To accomplish or handle (sthg.) with finesse: The gymnast finessed her dance routine.

fin•ger (fĭng′gər) n. **1.** One of the five parts of the hand that extend outward, especially one that is not the thumb. **2.** Something that looks like a finger: a finger of land extending into the ocean; the fingers of a glove. **3.** The length or width of a finger: Add about two fingers of juice. —tr.v. **1.** To handle or feel (sthg.) with the fingers; touch: The farmer fingered the dry soil. **2.** To play (a musical instrument) by using the fingers in a particular way. **3.** Slang. To point out (sbdy.) as responsible: finger a thief for the police. ◆ **give (one) the finger.** To make an obscene gesture at (sbdy.) with the middle finger. **have** or **keep (one's) fingers crossed.** To hope for a successful or advantageous result: I'm keeping my fingers crossed that our team will win the game. **not put (one's) finger on. 1.** To not be able to remember sthg.: I can't put my finger on his name right now. **2.** To not be able to see exactly what is wrong or different: He couldn't put his finger on what was new about her looks. —**fing′er•ing** n.

F

fin·ger·nail (fĭng′gər nāl′) *n.* The thin hard covering on the back of the tip of each finger.

fin·ger·print (fĭng′gər prĭnt′) *n.* An impression of the patterns in the skin on the tips of the fingers, especially such an impression made in ink and used to identify sbdy. —*tr.v.* To take the fingerprints of (sbdy.): *The police fingerprinted the new prisoners.*

fin·ger·tip (fĭng′gər tĭp′) *n.* The extreme tip or end of a finger.

fin·ick·y (fĭn′ĭ kē) *adj.* Very fussy; hard to please: *finicky about certain foods.*

fin·ish (fĭn′ĭsh) *v.* —*tr.* **1.** To arrive at or reach the end of (sthg.): *finish a race.* **2.** To bring (sthg.) to an end; complete: *Finish your homework before going outside.* **3.** To consume all of (sthg.) completely; use up: *finish a bottle of ketchup.* **4.** To give (a surface) a desired texture: *finish a floor with clear varnish.* —*intr.* **1.** To come to an end; stop: *Call me when the washing machine finishes.* **2.** To reach the end of a task, course, or relationship: *The runner finished well ahead of the pack.* —*n.* **1.** [C] *(usually singular).* The conclusion of sthg.; the end: *The finish of the play was exciting.* **2.** [C] **a.** The surface or texture produced by preparing or coating sthg.: *a shiny finish to the waxed floor.* **b.** The material used in surfacing or coating sthg.: *Paint is a good finish for wood.* **3.** [U] Accuracy, skill, or smoothness of performance; polish: *The musicians lacked finish.* ◆ **finish off.** *tr.v.* [sep.] **1.** To use (sthg.) up completely: *There's no more milk, because we finished it off at breakfast.* **2.** To kill (a living thing) that is already weak or hurt: *The lion finished off the zebra.* **finish up.** *tr.v.* [sep.] **1.** To bring (sthg.) to an end: *finished up his work for the day.* **2.** To eat, drink, or use all of (sthg.): *Finish up your vegetables.* —**fin′ish·er** *n.*

fin·ished (fĭn′ĭsht) *adj.* **1.** Highly skilled or accomplished: *a finished actor.* **2.** Showing a high degree of skill or polish: *a finished essay.*

fi·nite (fī′nīt′) *adj.* Limited in number or amount: *a finite list of choices.* —**fi′nite·ly** *adv.* —**fi′nite·ness** *n.* [U]

fir (fûr) *n.* **1.** [C] Any of various evergreen trees with flat needles and producing cones. **2.** [U] The wood of such a tree.

fir
Douglas fir

fire (fīr) *n.* **1.** [C] The flame, light, and heat produced when sthg. is burning: *The fire was bright enough to read by.* **2.** [C] Something that is burning, especially a pile of burning fuel, such as wood: *We started a fire in the fireplace.* **3.** [U] Intense feeling; enthusiasm: *The veterans played with the fire of young players.* **4.** [U] The discharge of weapons, such as guns: *heard the fire of cannon.* —*v.* **fired, fir·ing, fires.** —*tr.* **1.** To maintain or fuel a fire in (sthg.): *fire a furnace with oil.* **2.** To bake (sthg.) in a kiln: *fire clay pots to harden them.* **3.** To excite (sthg.); stimulate: *The book fired my interest in science.* **4.** To discharge (a firearm) or launch (a missile): *fire a cannon at the enemy; fire a rocket.* **5.** *Informal.* To throw (sthg.) with force and speed: *fire a baseball at a teammate.* **6.** *Informal.* To discharge (sbdy.) from a job; dismiss: *The company fired several workers today.* —*intr.* **1.** To shoot a weapon: *The soldiers fired into the air as a warning.* **2.** To ignite fuel, as in an engine: *The car motor will not fire properly when it's wet.* ◆ **on fire. 1.** Burning: *Thousands of acres of forest were on fire.* **2.** Filled with enthusiasm or excitement: *The team was on fire after scoring a goal.* **under fire.** Under attack or criticism: *The new regulation came under fire. The soldiers were under fire.*

fire·arm (fīr′ärm′) *n.* A weapon, especially a gun, that uses an explosive charge to fire an object.

fire·crack·er (fīr′krăk′ər) *n.* A small explosive charge and a fuse in a heavy paper casing, exploded to make noise, as at celebrations: *lighting firecrackers in the street.*

fire drill *n.* An exercise to practice using firefighting equipment or getting people out of a building in case of a fire.

fire engine *n.* Any of various large motor vehicles that carry firefighters and equipment to a fire.

fire escape *n.* A metal stairway or ladder attached to the outside of a building and used as an emergency exit in case of a fire.

fire extinguisher *n.* A portable container filled with chemicals to spray on a small fire to put it out.

fire escape

fire·fight·er also **fire fighter** (fīr′fī′tər) *n.* A person whose job is fighting fires. —**fire′-fight′ing** *n.* [U]

fire·fly (fīr′flī′) *n.* Any of various insects that fly at night and give off a flashing light from the rear part of the body.

fire hydrant *n.* A large upright pipe usually placed near a street for drawing water to fight fires.

fire·man (fīr′mən) *n.* A firefighter.

fire·place (fīr′plās′) *n.* An area in a room, usually set into a wall at floor level, for holding a fire.

fire·pow·er (fīr′pou′ər) *n.* [U] The capacity, as of a weapon, military unit, or position, for shooting projectiles.

fire·proof (fīr′prōōf′) *adj.* Made of material that is not affected by or is resistant to fire: *Many fireproof buildings are made of concrete.* —*tr.v.* To make (sthg.) fireproof: *The builder fireproofed the wall behind the stove.*

fire station *n.* A building for firefighters and firefighting equipment.

fire·trap (fīr′trăp′) *n.* A building that can catch fire easily or is hard to escape from if there is a fire: *Many old buildings become firetraps.*

fire truck *n.* A fire engine.

fire·wood (fīr′wŏŏd′) *n.* [U] Wood used as fuel: *The campers collected firewood.*

fire·works (fīr′wûrks′) *pl.n.* An explosive device, often attached to a small rocket, set off to create bright lights and loud noises for amusement.

fir·ing line (fīr′ĭng) *n.* The line of positions from which gunfire is directed against a target. ◆ **on the firing line.** In a position where one is likely to be attacked, criticized, or blamed: *As company president, he was on the firing line during the strike.*

firm¹ (fûrm) *adj.* **1.** Resistant to pressure from outside: *a firm mattress; an athlete's firm muscles.* **2.** Securely fixed in place; not easily moved: *a firm foundation for a building.* **3.** Showing or having determination or a fixed idea: *a firm voice; a firm belief.* **4.** Constant and dependable: *a firm friendship; a firm partnership.* **5.** Not able to be changed; fixed and definite: *a firm price on the car.* —*tr. & intr.v.* To make or become firm: *One must firm the dirt around newly potted plants. His muscles firmed with exercise.* —*adv.* With determination; steadily: *She stood firm in her refusal to go.* ◆ **firm up.** *tr.v.* [sep.] To make (sthg.) more definite: *We've talked about the plans, but we still need to firm things up.* —**firm′ly** *adv.* —**firm′ness** *n.* [U]

firm² (fûrm) *n.* A business partnership of two or more persons: *She is a partner in a law firm.*

first (fûrst) *n.* [U] **1.** The ordinal number matching the number one in a series. **2.** [C] A person or thing coming or ranking before or above all others: *the first of its kind.* **3.** [U] The beginning: *At first he was afraid of the water, but now he enjoys swimming.* **4.** [U] The transmission gear used to produce the lowest range of speeds in a motor vehicle: *Start the car and shift into first.* —*adj.* **1.** Corresponding in order to the number one. **2.** Coming before all others in order or location: *January is the first month of the year.* **3.** Having the greatest importance or the highest quality: *first in her class.* **4.** Relating to the transmission gear used to produce the lowest range of speeds in a motor vehicle: *in first gear.* —*adv.* **1.** Before or above all others: *Who will speak first?* **2.** For the first time: *When did you first meet the new neighbors?* **3.** More willingly; preferably: *The musicians said they would quit first before they would accept lower pay.* **4.** In the first place; to begin with: *First, let me introduce you.*

first aid *n.* [U] Emergency care given to an injured or sick person before professional medical care is available. —**first′-aid′** *adj.*

first base *n.* [U] **1.** In baseball, the base that must be touched first by a batter running around the bases after hitting the ball. **2.** *Slang.* The first step or stage toward completion or success: *The reform bill never got to first base.*

first-born (fûrst′bôrn′) *adj.* First in order of birth: *a first-born child.* —*n.* The child in a family who is born first: *her first-born.*

first class *n.* [U] **1.** The first, highest, or best group in a system of classification: *a restaurant of the first class.* **2.** The best and most expensive type of service or accommodations on a train, a ship, or an airplane: *She always flies in first class.* **3.** A class of mail including letters and packages sent quickly, often by air. —**first class** *adv.*

first-class (fûrst′klăs′) *adj.* **1.** Of the first, highest, or best group in a system of classification: *first-class mail; a first-class hotel.* **2.** Of the highest quality; first-rate: *a first-class author.*

first-de·gree burn (fûrst′dĭ grē′) *n.* A mild burn that produces redness of the skin.

first floor *n.* The ground-level floor of a building.

first·hand (fûrst′hănd′) *adj.* Received from the original source: *He saw the accident, so he could give firsthand information.* —**first′-hand′** *adv.*

first lady *n.* **1.** Often **First Lady.** The wife of the chief executive of a country, state, or city. **2.** The most important woman of a profession or an art: *the first lady of modern dance.*

first name *n.* The name or names given to a person, coming before his or her last name or family name: *Her first name is Mary and her last name is Smith.*

first·ly (fûrst′lē) *adv.* In the first place; to begin with: *Firstly, we have to decide what we want to accomplish.*

first person *n.* [U] **1.** A group of words or word forms, such as verbs and pronouns, referring to the speaker or writer of the sentence in which they appear. *I* and *we* are pronouns in the first person. **2.** The style of writing in which forms in the first person are used: *The novel* Moby Dick *is written in the first person; Chapter I begins, "Call me Ishmael."*

first-rate (fûrst′rāt′) *adj.* Very high in quality, rank, skill, or importance: *a first-rate hotel; a first-rate mechanic.*

first-string (fûrst′strĭng′) *adj.* In sports, being a regular player for a team rather than a substitute: *the first-string quarterback.*

fis•cal (fĭs′kəl) *adj.* **1.** Relating to the treasury or finances of a government: *Carefully controlled spending is the fiscal policy during an economic slowdown.* **2.** Relating to finance or finances: *The accountant is the company's fiscal agent.* —**fis′cal•ly** *adv.*

fiscal year *n.* A period of 12 months for which an organization plans the use of its funds: *The college's fiscal year ends June 30.*

fish (fĭsh) *n., pl.* **fish** or **fish•es. 1.** [C] Any of numerous cold-blooded animals that live in water and have a backbone, gills for breathing, and a vertical tail. **2.** [U] The flesh of a fish used as food. —*v.* —*intr.* **1.** To catch or try to catch fish: *He enjoys fishing.* **2.** [*for*] To look for sthg. by feeling one's way: *I fished in my pocket for a quarter.* **3.** [*for*] To try to get sthg. in a sly or indirect way: *She was always fishing for compliments.* —*tr.* **1.** To catch or try to catch fish in (sthg.): *We fished the lake for several hours.* **2.** To catch or pull (sthg.) as if fishing: *fish the keys out of the drawer.* ◆ **like a fish out of water.** Completely unfamiliar with one's surroundings or activity: *She was like a fish out of water in her new profession.*

fish and chips *pl.n.* Fried fillets of fish and French-fried potatoes.

fish•bowl (fĭsh′bōl′) *n.* **1.** A glass container where pet fish are kept. **2.** A situation in which everything one does can be seen: *The President lives in a fishbowl.*

fish•er•man (fĭsh′ər mən) *n.* A person who fishes for work or fun.

fish•er•y (fĭsh′ə rē) *n., pl.* **fish•er•ies.** A place where fish or other underwater animals are caught or bred: *the cod and haddock fisheries of the northwest Atlantic.*

fish•hook (fĭsh′hŏŏk′) *n.* A barbed hook for catching fish.

fish•ing (fĭsh′ĭng) *n.* [U] The act, occupation, or sport of catching fish.

fishing rod *n.* A rod of wood, steel, or fiberglass used with a line for catching fish.

fish•net (fĭsh′nĕt′) *n.* **1.** [C; U] Netting used to catch fish. **2.** [U] A fabric that looks like such netting: *fishnet stockings.*

fish•pond (fĭsh′pŏnd′) *n.* A pond with fish for catching and eating.

fish stick *n.* A strip of fish fillet covered with bread crumbs.

fish story *n. Informal.* A boastful story that is probably not true: *I've heard all his fish stories a hundred times.*

fish•y (fĭsh′ē) *adj.* **fish•i•er, fish•i•est. 1.** Tasting, resembling, or smelling of fish: *a fishy smell.* **2.** *Informal.* Causing doubt or suspicion: *There was something fishy about that excuse.* —**fish′i•ness** *n.* [U]

fis•sion (fĭsh′ən) *n.* [U] **1.** The act of splitting into parts. **2.** A nuclear reaction in which an atomic nucleus splits into two parts, releasing tremendous energy. **3.** A reproductive process in which a single cell divides to form two independent cells that later grow to full size.

fis•sure (fĭsh′ər) *n.* A long narrow crack or opening, as in the face of a rock.

fist (fĭst) *n.* The hand closed tightly with the fingers bent against the palm: *The winner raised his fist.*

fist•fight (fĭst′fīt′) *n.* A fight with the bare fists.

fist•ful (fĭst′fŏŏl′) *n., pl.* **fist•fuls.** The amount a fist can hold: *a fistful of coins.*

fit¹ (fĭt) *v.* **fit•ted** or **fit, fit•ted, fit•ting, fits.** —*tr.* **1.** To be the proper size and shape for (sbdy./sthg.): *Do the shoes fit you?* **2.** To be appropriate for or suitable to (sbdy./sthg.): *A dignified appearance fitted the judge's high office.* **3.** To equip or provide (sthg.): *We fitted the car with new tires.* **4.** To provide a time or place for (sbdy./sthg.): *The doctor can fit you in at 2:00. Can you fit all of your books in one bag?* —*intr.* **1.** To be the proper size and shape: *If the key fits, open the door.* **2.** To be suited; belong: *Their happy mood fit with the joyous occasion.* —*adj.* **fit•ter, fit•test. 1.** Suited, adapted, or acceptable for a given purpose or situation: *Late at night is not a fit time for a meeting. The dinner was not fit to eat.* **2.** Physically sound; healthy: *Fresh air and exercise help keep people fit.* —*n.* (*usually singular*). **1.** The state, quality, or way of being fitted: *a perfect fit.* **2.** The way sthg. fits: *The fit of the sweater was too tight.* ◆ **see** or **think fit.** To determine; decide: *Each person must vote as he or she sees fit.*

fit² (fĭt) *n.* **1.** A sudden appearance of a symptom of an illness: *a fit of coughing.* **2.** A sudden burst of strong emotion: *a fit of jealousy.* **3.** A sudden period of vigorous activity: *a fit of housekeeping.* ◆ **by fits and starts.** With irregular periods of action and inaction; not continuously: *practice the piano by fits and starts.* **have** or **throw a fit.** *Informal.* To become very angry about sthg.: *She's going to have a fit when she sees the car.*

fit•ful (fĭt′fəl) *adj.* Marked by activity that starts and stops; irregular: *fitful coughing; fitful sleep.* —**fit′ful•ly** *adv.* —**fit′ful•ness** *n.* [U]

fit•ness (fĭt′nĭs) *n.* [U] **1.** The state or condition of being physically fit, especially as the result of exercise and proper nutrition. **2.** The quality of being capable; competence: *There is no doubt about his fitness for the mission.*

fit•ting (fĭt′ĭng) *adj.* Right for a situation; appropriate: *a fitting remark.* —*n.* **1.** The act of trying on clothes whose fit is being adjusted: *It took several fittings to get the sleeves right.* **2.** A small part for a machine or mechanical device: *a box of nuts, washers, joints, and other fittings.*

five (fīv) *n.* **1.** The number, written 5, that is equal to 4 + 1. **2.** The fifth in a set or sequence. —**five** *adj. & pron.*

fix (fĭks) *v.* —*tr.* **1.** To set (sthg.) right; repair: *fix a car; fix a misspelling.* **2.** To make (sthg.) ready; prepare: *We are fixing dinner.* **3.** To place (sthg.) securely; make stable or firm: *fix a post in the ground.* **4.** To establish (sthg.) definitely; specify: *fix a time for the meeting.* **5.** To direct (sthg.) steadily: *We fixed our eyes on the screen.* **6.** To treat (a photographic image) with a chemical that prevents it from fading or changing color. **7.** *Informal.* To take revenge upon (sbdy.): *After he wrecked my bike, I fixed my brother.* **8.** *Informal.* To influence the result of (sthg.) by unlawful means: *fix a horse race.* **9.** To neuter (an animal); castrate or spay: *Both of my cats have been fixed.* —*intr.* **1.** To direct one's attention or concentration: *Let's fix on finding a solution to the problem.* **2.** To become rigid or firm: *The plaster will fix in a few hours.* —*n.* **1.** The act of adjusting, correcting, or repairing: *a quick fix.* **2.** The position, as of a ship or an aircraft, determined by sight or by radio signals: *get a fix on a disabled ship.* **3.** A difficult or embarrassing situation: *We lost our oars and were in a fix out in the middle of the lake.* **4.** *Slang.* An amount of sthg., especially a narcotic drug: *The cocaine addict was desperate for a fix. I need a caffeine fix.* ◆ **a fixer-upper.** *Slang.* A house that is in need of major repairs: *They bought a fixer-upper and spent the next two years renovating the house.* **a quick fix.** A temporary repair or solution: *This problem requires more than a quick fix.* **be in a fix.** To have a problem that is difficult to solve: *They were in a fix when the car broke down on the way to the wedding.* **fix up.** *tr.v.* [sep.] **1.** To improve the appearance or condition of (sthg.): *They fixed up the old house with a fresh coat of paint.* **2.** To supply (sthg.); provide: *We fixed up a bed for our guests.* **3.** To find a date for (sbdy.): *She fixed him up with her cousin.* —**fix′a•ble** *adj.* —**fix′er** *n.*

fix•a•tion (fĭk sā′shən) *n.* An unnaturally strong interest in or attachment to sbdy./sthg.: *The child had a fixation on a particular blanket.* —**fix′ate** *v.*

fixed (fĭkst) *adj.* **1.** Firmly in position; stationary: *a row of fixed desks.* **2.** Not changing; constant: *Most retired people live on a fixed income.* **3.** Firmly held; steady: *a fixed stare; old and fixed ideas.* **4.** With the result illegally controlled: *a fixed election.*

fix•ed•ly (fĭk′sĭd lē) *adv.* Without looking at or thinking about anything else: *She stared fixedly at my face.*

fix•ings (fĭk′sĭngz) *pl.n. Informal.* Things that contribute to an effect; trimmings: *a Thanksgiving dinner with all the fixings.*

fix•ture (fĭks′chər) *n.* **1.** Something that is fixed in a permanent location: *a plumbing fixture; a lighting fixture.* **2.** A person or thing that stays in one place: *After 30 years of teaching, he is a fixture at the school.*

fizz (fĭz) *intr.v.* To make a hissing or bubbling sound: *Baking soda will fizz if you pour water on it.* —*n.* [U] **1.** A hissing or bubbling sound: *the fizz of soda.* **2.** *Informal.* High spirits; excitement: *Put some fizz into your life.* —**fizz′y** *adj.*

fiz•zle (fĭz′əl) *intr.v.* **fiz•zled, fiz•zling, fiz•zles.** **1.** To make a hissing or sputtering sound: *The hot coals of our campfire fizzled in the rain.* **2.** *Informal.* To fail or end weakly, especially after a hopeful beginning: *Their relationship fizzled after only two months.* —*n. Informal.* A failure: *That whole evening was a fizzle.* ◆ **fizzle out.** *intr.v.* To fail: *I think plans for the party are going to fizzle out.*

fjord (fyôrd) *n.* A long narrow area from the sea between steep slopes.

fl or **fl.** *abbr.* An abbreviation of fluid.

FL *abbr.* An abbreviation of Florida.

Fla. *abbr.* An abbreviation of Florida.

flab (flăb) *n.* [U] Soft fatty body tissue: *Exercises will reduce flab.* —**flab′bi•ness** *n.* [U] —**flab′by** *adj.*

flab•ber•gast (flăb′ər găst′) *tr.v.* To cause (sbdy.) to be extremely surprised or shocked: *The news flabbergasted us.*

flac•cid (flăk′sĭd *or* flăs′ĭd) *adj.* Lacking firmness, resilience, or muscle tone: *a flaccid handshake.* —**flac•cid′i•ty, flac′cid•ness** *n.* [U] —**flac′cid•ly** *adv.*

flag[1] (flăg) *n.* A piece of cloth of a particular color or design, used as a signal or as a symbol: *flags of member nations flying at the United Nations.* —*tr.v.* **flagged, flag•ging, flags.** To signal (sbdy.) with a flag: *flagged a motorist to get help.* ◆ **flag down.** *tr.v.* [sep.] To signal (sbdy./sthg.) to stop: *flag down a passing car.*

flag[2] (flăg) *intr.v.* **flagged, flag•ging, flags.** To lose energy or strength; weaken: *Our spirits flagged when we saw how much we had to do.*

F

flag·man (flăg′mən) *n.* A person who signals with or carries a flag: *a flagman on road construction.*

fla·grant (flā′grənt) *adj.* Openly offensive; blatant: *a flagrant misuse of public funds.* —**fla′grant·ly** *adv.*

flag·ship (flăg′shĭp′) *n.* A ship that carries a fleet or squadron commander and flies the commander's flag.

flail (flāl) *v.* —*tr.* **1.** To beat or strike (sbdy./ sthg.) with an object: *He flailed the horse with the reins.* **2.** To wave or swing (sthg.) vigorously: *I flailed my arms to get their attention.* —*intr.* To move in a vigorous or erratic way: *arms flailing helplessly in the water.*

flair (flâr) *n.* **1.** [C] A natural talent: *a flair for imitating voices.* **2.** [U] Special style or elegance: *They served our dinner with flair.*

HOMONYMS: flair, flare (blaze).

---

flak (flăk) *n.* [U] **1.** Antiaircraft guns or the bursting shells fired from such guns: *Many of the planes were hit by flak.* **2.** *Informal.* Criticism; opposition: *Our suggestion got a lot of flak.*

flake (flāk) *n.* **1.** A thin piece of sthg.: *Large flakes of paint had fallen on the floor.* **2.** A snowflake. **3.** *Slang.* A person who is odd or strange: *My sister is a total flake.* —*intr.v.* **flaked, flak·ing, flakes.** To come off in flakes; chip off: *The paint is flaking off the fence.*

flak·y (flā′kē) *adj.* **flak·i·er, flak·i·est. 1.** Forming or tending to form flakes or thin crisp fragments: *flaky crackers.* **2.** *Slang.* Strange; odd: *All her friends are just as flaky as she is.* —**flak′i·ly** *adv.* —**flak′i·ness** *n.* [U]

flam·boy·ant (flăm boi′ənt) *adj.* **1.** Having an exaggerated or showy style: *With many large gestures, the actor gave a flamboyant performance.* **2.** Brilliant; vivid: *flamboyant colors.* —**flam·boy·ance** *n.* [U] —**flam·boy′ant·ly** *adv.*

flame (flām) *n.* **1.** [C] A hot glowing mass of burning gas or vapor: *cooked over a low flame.* **2.** [C; U] The condition of active burning: *burst into flame.* **3.** [C] An intense feeling; a passion: *a flame of enthusiasm.* **4.** [C] *Informal.* A sweetheart: *She unexpectedly met an old flame.* *v.* **flamed, flam·ing, flames.** —*intr.* **1.** To burn brightly; blaze: *The logs flamed as I fanned them.* **2.** To flush; acquire color: *My cheeks flamed with embarrassment.* —*tr. Informal.* To attack (sbdy.) on the Internet: *As soon as people read his crazy ideas, he'll get flamed.*

flam·ing (flā′mĭng) *adj.* **1.** On fire; blazing: *flaming logs.* **2.** Similar to a flame in brilliance, color, or form: *flaming red and yellow autumn leaves.*

fla·min·go (flə mĭng′gō) *n., pl.* **fla·min·gos** or **fla·min·goes.** A long-legged, long-necked tropical water bird with reddish or pinkish feathers.

flamingo

flam·ma·ble (flăm′ə-bəl) *adj.* Easily set on fire and able to burn rapidly: *Alcohol is flammable.*

flank (flăngk) *n.* **1.a.** [C] The side of the body between the ribs and the hip. **b.** [U] Meat from this part of an animal. **2.** [C] A side part: *The flank of the mountain rose steeply from the valley.* —*tr.v.* **1.** To attack or move around the side of (sbdy./ sthg.): *flank an opposing force.* **2.** To be at the side of (sbdy./sthg.): *Two chairs flanked the fireplace.*

flan·nel (flăn′əl) *n.* [C; U] **1.** A soft cotton cloth used for sheets, light blankets, and baby clothes. **2.** A soft woolen cloth used especially in making coats, jackets, and trousers.

flap (flăp) *n.* **1.** A flat piece attached along one side only: *the flap over a pocket.* **2.** A section of the rear edge of an aircraft wing that moves up and down. **3.** The sound or action of waving or fluttering: *the flap of a bird's wings.* **4.** *(usually singular). Slang.* A state of emotional upset or nervous excitement: *We all got into a flap when no one could find the car keys.* —*v.* **flapped, flap·ping, flaps.** —*tr.* **1.** To move (the wings or arms) up and down: *The baby bird flapped its wings as it tried to fly.* **2.** To cause (sthg.) to move with a waving or fluttering motion: *A brisk wind flapped the clothes on the line.* —*intr.* **1.** To wave about while attached to sthg. that is not moving: *A flag flapped softly in the breeze.* **2.** To wave the arms or wings up and down.

flap·jack (flăp′jăk′) *n.* A pancake.

flare (flâr) *intr.v.* **flared, flar·ing, flares. 1.** To burn with a sudden or unsteady flame: *The candle flared briefly and went out.* **2.** To come out suddenly and forcefully; erupt: *Tempers flared during the tense meeting.* **3.** To spread outward in shape: *A horn flares at the end.* —*n.* **1.** A brief wavering blaze of light. **2.** A device that produces a bright light for signaling or lighting: *Police placed flares on the road around the scene of the crash.* **3.** An outbreak, as of emotion or activity: *a flare of anger.* **4.** A shape or form that spreads out: *the flare of a trumpet.*

HOMONYMS: flare, flair (talent).

---

flare-up (flâr′ŭp′) *n.* **1.** A sudden outbreak of flame or light. **2.** A sudden show of strong emotion: *a flare-up of anger.* **3.** Another sudden or brief occurrence of a problem, especially of a health problem: *a flare-up of arthritis.*

flash (flăsh) *v. —intr.* **1.** To give off a sudden bright light: *Bursts of fireworks flashed in the sky.* **2.** To be lighted on and off: *A lighthouse flashed in the distance.* **3.** To appear or occur suddenly: *an idea for a story flashed through my mind.* **4.** To move rapidly: *A shooting star flashed across the sky. —tr.* **1.** To send (sthg.) forth suddenly or for an instant: *flash a smile.* **2.** To make (sthg.) known or signal by flashing lights: *The yellow light flashed a warning.* **3.** To send (a message) at great speed: *flash a news bulletin to the world capitals. —n.* **1.** A short sudden show of light: *a flash of lightning.* **2.** A sudden brief burst: *a flash of understanding.* **3.** A second; an instant: *I ran to the phone in a flash.* **4.** A brief important news item broadcast over radio or television: *Stations broadcast flashes about the election all day.* **5.** A flashbulb or flashbulb attachment on a camera: *The flash didn't go off.* ◆ **flash in the pan.** A person or thing that promises great success but fails: *Their latest idea was just another flash in the pan.* **in a flash.** Quickly: *I'll be back in a flash.*

flash·back (flăsh′băk′) *n.* **1.** A scene or an episode showing an earlier event that is placed in a story, play, or movie: *The movie included a flashback to the main character's childhood.* **2.** A vivid mental image of a past experience: *having flashbacks of an accident.*

flash·bulb or **flash bulb** (flăsh′bŭlb′) *n.* An electric bulb that produces a flash of light for taking photographs.

flash card *n.* One of a set of cards marked with words, numbers, or other symbols to be learned through memorization.

flash·er (flăsh′ər) *n.* **1.** (*usually plural*). A light on a vehicle that flashes when turned on and warns other drivers that it is disabled: *The truck had its flashers on.* **2.** *Informal.* A man who gets sexual pleasure from exposing his genitals to women in public places.

flash flood *n.* A sudden violent flood after a heavy rain.

flash·light (flăsh′līt′) *n.* A portable electric light that uses batteries.

flash point *n.* **1.** The lowest temperature at which the vapor of a flammable liquid can be made to catch fire in air. **2.** The point at which sthg., such as a disagreement, becomes an open conflict: *Border disputes became the flash point for war between the two countries.*

flash·y (flăsh′ē) *adj.* **flash·i·er, flash·i·est.** **1.** Brilliant: *the acrobat's flashy performance.* **2.** Cheap and showy: *a flashy tie.* **flash′i·ly** *adv.* **—flash′i·ness** *n.* [U]

flask (flăsk) *n.* **1.** A small bottle with a flat-

tened shape, made to fit in one's pocket. **2.** A rounded container, made of glass, with a long neck, used in laboratories.

flat¹ (flăt) *adj.* **flat·ter, flat·test.** **1.** With a smooth even surface; level: *flat land.* **2.** With a broad surface and little thickness or depth: *a flat dish.* **3.** Extending or lying full length; horizontal: *flat on my back in bed.* **4.** Having lost air; deflated: *a flat tire.* **5.** Without interest or excitement; dull: *a flat performance.* **6.** Having lost fizz or sparkle: *flat soda.* **7.** Complete; absolute: *a flat refusal to help.* **8.** Not changing; fixed: *The taxi charges a flat rate.* **9.** Not glossy; dull: *finished with a flat paint.* **10.** Lower in musical pitch than the natural tone or key: *D flat.* **11.** Lacking or slow in business activity: *flat sales for the month. —adv.* **flatter, flattest.** **1.** On or against a flat surface: *Press the pizza dough flat.* **2.** Exactly: *He ran the race in 50 seconds flat.* **3.** Completely: *I'm flat broke.* **4.** Below the correct pitch: *Don't sing flat. —n.* **1.** A flat surface or part: *the flat of my hand.* **2.** (*usually plural*). An area of level low-lying tidal ground: *dig clams in the mud flats.* **3.** A tire that has lost air: *The car has a flat.* **4.** A woman's shoe with a flat heel: *She always wears flats.* **5.a.** A musical note or tone that is a half step lower than a corresponding natural tone or key. **b.** The symbol (♭) attached to a note or tone to indicate that it is flat. **—flat′ness** *n.* [U]

flat² (flăt) *n. Chiefly British.* An apartment, usually on one floor of a building.

flat-foot·ed (flăt′fŏŏt′ĭd) *adj.* **1.** Having feet with low arches so that most or all of the sole touches the ground. **2.** Unable to react quickly; unprepared: *The question caught me flat-footed.* **—flat′-foot′ed·ly** *adv.* **—flat′-foot′ed·ness** *n.* [U]

flat·land (flăt′lănd′) *n.* **1.** Land that has almost no hills or valleys. **2. flatlands.** A geographic area made up chiefly of flatland.

flat·ly (flăt′lē) *adv.* **1.** Directly and absolutely: *He flatly refused to lend the money.* **2.** Without any show of emotion: *She told me flatly what had happened.*

flat·ten (flăt′n) *v. —tr.* **1.** To make (sthg.) flat or flatter: *A rolling pin flattens dough.* **2.** To knock (sbdy./sthg.) down: *The wind flattened the old shed. —intr.* To become flat: *All the wrinkles flattened out when the shirt was ironed.*

flat·ter (flăt′ər) *v. —tr.* **1.** To praise (sbdy.) insincerely, especially in order to win favor. **2.** To please or gratify (sbdy.): *The award flattered me.* **3.** To show (sbdy.) favorably: *This photograph flatters her.* **—flat′ter·er** *n.*

flat·ter·y (flăt′ə rē) *n.* [U] Excessive or insincere praise: *Flattery will open many doors.*

flat·u·lent (flăch′ə lənt) *adj.* Suffering from too much gas in the digestive tract. **—flat′u·lence** *n.* [U]

F

flat·ware (flăt'wâr') *n.* [U] Tableware or utensils such as plates, knives, forks, and spoons.

flaunt (flônt) *tr.v.* To show (sthg.) with too much pride: *flaunt one's knowledge.* —**flaunt'ing·ly** *adv.*

fla·vor (flā'vər) *n.* **1.** Distinctive taste of sthg.: *the spicy flavor of cinnamon.* **2.** A seasoning or flavoring: *Vanilla is a common flavor.* **3.** A quality that is characteristic of a place or thing: *a story full of the flavor of India.* —*tr.v.* To give flavor to (sthg.): *Vinegar flavored the salad.* —**fla'vor·ful** *adj.*

fla·vor·ing (flā'vər ĭng) *n.* [C; U] A substance used to flavor food: *raspberry flavoring.*

flaw (flô) *n.* A defect or an imperfection: *The dish broke where there was a flaw in it. Their argument had many flaws and did not convince anyone.*

flawed (flôd) *adj.* With errors or imperfections: *a flawed performance.*

flaw·less (flô'lĭs) *adj.* Without any defect; perfect: *a flawless diamond.* See Synonyms at **perfect.** —**flaw'less·ly** *adv.* —**flaw'less·ness** *n.* [U]

flea (flē) *n.* A small, wingless, jumping insect that lives on the bodies of animals and sucks their blood.

HOMONYMS: **flea, flee** (run away).

---

flea collar *n.* A collar, for a cat or dog, that contains a substance for killing fleas.

flea market *n.* A market, usually held outdoors, where old or used goods are sold.

fleck (flĕk) *n.* A small mark or spot: *flecks of grey paint on the floor.* —*tr.v.* To mark (sthg.) with flecks; spot: *Spots of paint flecked the floor.*

fled (flĕd) *v.* Past tense and past participle of **flee.**

fledg·ling (flĕj'lĭng) *n.* **1.** A young bird that has just grown the feathers needed to fly. **2.** A young or inexperienced person. —*adj.* New and inexperienced: *a fledgling skier.*

flee (flē) *v.* **fled** (flĕd), **flee·ing, flees.** —*intr.* To run away from trouble or danger: *The thieves fled when they heard the police car.* —*tr.* To run away from (sbdy./sthg.); escape from: *flee the burning house.*

HOMONYMS: **flee, flea** (insect).

---

fleece (flēs) *n.* [U] **1.** The coat of wool of a sheep or similar animal. **2.** Soft fabric used in coats, boots, and other cold-weather clothing. —*tr.v.* **fleeced, fleec·ing, fleec·es. 1.** To cut away the fleece from (a sheep). **2.** To swindle or cheat (sbdy.) of money or belongings: *A dishonest salesman fleeced the car buyer.*

fleec·y (flē'sē) *adj.* **fleec·i·er, fleec·i·est.** Resembling fleece: *fleecy blankets; fleecy clouds.*

fleet[1] (flēt) *n.* **1.** A group of warships under one commander. **2.** A number of boats or vehicles owned or operated as a group: *a fishing fleet; a fleet of taxis.*

fleet[2] (flēt) *adj.* Moving very quickly and lightly: *fleet as a deer.* —*intr.v.* To move very quickly: *clouds fleeting across the sky.* —**fleet'ly** *adv.* —**fleet'ness** *n.* [U]

fleet·ing (flē'tĭng) *adj.* Passing quickly; very brief: *a fleeting look from a passing stranger.* —**fleet'ing·ly** *adv.*

flesh (flĕsh) *n.* [U] **1.** The skin of a human or animal body and the tissue under it. **2.** The pulpy part of a fruit or vegetable used as food: *the sweet flesh of a ripe melon.* **3.** The human body as distinguished from the mind or soul: *desires of the flesh.* ◆ **flesh and blood.** A close relative or relatives: *Of course I trust him; he's my own flesh and blood.* **flesh out.** *tr.v.* [sep.] To add missing details to (sthg.): *You need to flesh out the report.* **in the flesh.** In person; actually present: *I have never seen the President in the flesh, only on TV.*

flesh·y (flĕsh'ē) *adj.* **flesh·i·er, flesh·i·est. 1.** Relating to flesh. **2.** Having much flesh; plump: *fleshy cheeks.*

flew (flōō) *v.* Past tense of **fly**[1].

HOMONYMS: **flew, flu** (influenza), **flue** (pipe).

---

flex (flĕks) *tr.v.* **1.** To bend (sthg.): *Flex your elbow.* **2.** To cause (a muscle) to contract: *The weight lifter flexed his muscles.*

flex·i·ble (flĕk'sə bəl) *adj.* **1.** Capable of being bent; pliable: *a flexible hose.* **2.** Capable of or willing to change; adaptable: *Our plans are flexible. I'm flexible.* —**flex'i·bil'i·ty** *n.* [U] —**flex'i·bly** *adv.*

flex·time (flĕks'tīm') *n.* [U] An arrangement by which employees may set their own work schedules, especially their starting and finishing hours: *Many companies now offer their workers flextime.*

flick (flĭk) *n.* **1.** A light quick blow, jerk, or touch: *turn on a light with a flick of the finger.* **2.** The sound made by such a light blow or stroke: *We heard the flick of the switch.* —*tr.v.* **1.** To touch or hit (sbdy./sthg.) with a light quick blow: *The horse flicked flies with its tail.* **2.** To cause (sthg.) to move with a light blow: *flick a mosquito off your arm.*

flick·er (flĭk'ər) *intr.v.* **1.** To burn or shine unsteadily: *The candles flickered in the breeze.* **2.** To move unevenly; flutter: *Shadows flick-*

ă–cat; ā–pay; âr–care; ä–father; ĕ–get; ē–be; ĭ–sit; ī–nice; îr–here; ŏ–got; ō–go; ô–saw; oi–boy; ou–out; ŏŏ–took; ōō–boot; ŭ–cut; ûr–word; th–thin; *th*–this; hw–when; zh–vision; ə–about; N–French bon

ered on the wall. —*n.* **1.** An uneven or unsteady light: *Only the flicker of a candle lit our way.* **2.** A brief or slight feeling: *a flicker of disappointment.* **3.** A short quick movement: *the flicker of a butterfly's wings.*

fli·er also **fly·er** (flī′ər) *n.* **1.** A person or thing that flies, especially a pilot or an aviator. **2.** A printed sheet or sheets of paper with information or advertising: *We distributed fliers for the candidate.*

flight[1] (flīt) *n.* **1.** [U] The act of flying: *a bird in flight.* **2.** [C] A scheduled airline trip: *My flight to Milwaukee is set for Friday.* **3.** [C] The distance covered in such a trip: *The flight was 3,000 miles.* **4.** [C] A group, especially of birds or aircraft, flying together: *a flight of geese.* **5.** [C] Something that goes beyond the ordinary: *a brilliant flight of the imagination.* **6.** [C] A series of stairs, as between floors: *We climbed three flights to get to the top floor.*

flight[2] (flīt) *n.* [U] An act of running away; an escape: *a criminal's flight from the police.*

flight attendant *n.* A person who takes care of passengers in an airplane.

flight·less (flīt′lĭs) *adj.* Not able to fly: *Ostriches and penguins are flightless birds.*

flight recorder *n.* An electronic device that records information about the operation of each flight of an aircraft and is kept in a sealed box so that it can be recovered after a crash.

flight·y (flī′tē) *adj.* **flight·i·er, flight·i·est.** Tending to behave unsteadily and impulsively: *Flighty people cannot be relied on.* —**flight′i·ness** *n.* [U]

flim·sy (flĭm′zē) *adj.* **flim·si·er, flim·si·est. 1.** Thin or light: *flimsy cloth.* **2.** Not solid or strong; likely to fall apart: *a flimsy table.* **3.** Not believable; unconvincing: *a flimsy excuse.* —**flim′si·ly** *adv.* —**flim′si·ness** *n.* [U]

flinch (flĭnch) *intr.v.* To make a small movement back, as from pain or fear: *The patient flinched when the doctor put medicine on the cut.*

fling (flĭng) *v.* **flung** (flŭng), **fling·ing, flings.** —*tr.* To throw (sbdy./sthg.) forcefully: *We were flinging small stones into the river.* See Synonyms at **throw.** —*intr.* To go quickly or angrily; rush: *The insulted guest flung out of the room without saying good-bye.* —*n.* **1.** The act of flinging; a throw. **2.** A brief period of doing whatever one wants: *a final fling before school starts.* **3.** *Informal.* A brief attempt or try: *take a fling at skiing.* **4.** A short, casual sexual relationship: *He didn't know their affair was only a fling for her.*

flint (flĭnt) *n.* [C; U] A very hard, gray to black quartz that makes sparks when it is struck with steel.

flint·y (flĭn′tē) *adj.* **flint·i·er, flint·i·est. 1.** Composed of or containing flint: *gray flinty hills.* **2.** Unyielding; stony: *a cold flinty look.* —**flint′i·ness** *n.* [U]

flip (flĭp) *v.* **flipped, flip·ping, flips.** —*tr.* **1.** To toss (sbdy./sthg.) with a light quick motion, especially with a spin or turn: *flip a coin.* **2.** To turn (sthg.) over with a light quick motion: *flip the pages of a magazine.* —*intr.* **1.** To turn over: *The canoe flipped in the river.* **2.** To move in twists and turns: *The fish flipped in the net.* **3.** To turn a somersault in the air: *This dog flips for treats.* —*n.* **1.** An act of flipping, especially a quick turning movement: *give the pancake a flip.* **2.** A somersault: *The gymnast did a back flip.* —*adj.* **flip·per, flip·pest.** *Informal.* Disrespectful; flippant: *a flip attitude.*

flip-flop (flĭp′flŏp′) *n.* **1.** The movement or sound of sthg. waving back and forth repeatedly: *the flip-flop of a shade against a window.* **2.** *Informal.* A reversal of opinion or direction: *The mayor's flip-flop on the important issue left everyone wondering what he was thinking.* **3.** A rubber sandal or thong: *She wears flip-flops at home and on the beach.*

flip·pant (flĭp′ənt) *adj.* Marked by disrespect in a careless or lightly humorous way: *flippant remarks.* —**flip′pan·cy** *n.* [U] —**flip′pant·ly** *adv.*

flip·per (flĭp′ər) *n.* **1.** A wide flat limb, as of a sea mammal such as a seal or dolphin, adapted for swimming. **2.** A rubber covering for the foot with a wide flat part extending from the toes, used for swimming.

flirt (flûrt) *intr.v.* **1.** To act romantically, especially in a playful or teasing way: *He's always flirting with women at parties.* **2.** To deal in a playful way, as if sthg. were of little importance: *Bullfighters flirt with danger.* —*n.* A person who likes romantic flirting: *Just tell the flirt to leave you alone.*

flir·ta·tion (flûr tā′shən) *n.* **1.** [U] The act or practice of flirting. **2.** [C] A casual or brief romance. —**flir·ta′tious** (flûr tā′shəs) *adj.* —**flir·ta′tious·ly** *adv.* —**flir·ta′tious·ness** *n.* [U]

flit (flĭt) *intr.v.* **flit·ted, flit·ting, flits. 1.** To move quickly and lightly: *Birds flitted around in the thicket.* **2.** To pass quickly: *A smile flitted across the child's face.*

float (flōt) *v.* —*intr.* **1.** To rest on the surface of a liquid: *The air mattress floated until we all got on.* **2.** To move or drift supported by or as if by a fluid: *The spacecraft floated toward the distant planet. The balloon floated through the air.* —*tr.* **1.** To cause (sthg.) to float or move on the surface of a fluid: *float logs down the river.* **2.** To offer (sthg.) for sale: *float a new company.* **3.** To arrange for (a loan): *Could you float me a loan of $50?* —*n.* **1.** An object designed to float, especially a buoy or a raft fixed in place. **2.** A hollow ball attached to a lever to regulate the water level in a tank, as in a toilet tank. **3.** A decorated exhibit displayed on a large flat vehicle in a parade: *floats covered with flowers for the parade.* **4.** A soft drink with ice cream in it: *a root-beer float.* **—float′er** *n.*

flock (flŏk) *n.* **1.** A group of birds, sheep, or goats that live, travel, or feed together: *The shepherd watched his flock.* **2.** A large crowd or number: *A flock of weekend visitors crowded into the museum.* **3.** The members of a church. *—intr.v.* To gather or travel in a flock or crowd: *People flocked to the cities for jobs.* **—SEE NOTE at collective noun.**

floe (flō) *n.* A mass or sheet of floating ice.

HOMONYMS: floe, flow (run freely).

flog (flŏg *or* flôg) *tr.v.* **flogged, flog·ging, flogs.** To beat (sbdy./sthg.) harshly with a whip or rod. **—flog′ger** *n.*

flood (flŭd) *n.* **1.** An overflowing of water onto land that is normally dry. **2.** A large number: *a flood of job applications.* *—v. —tr.* **1.** To cover (sthg.) with or as if with a flood: *The heavy rain flooded the cellar.* **2.** To fill or overwhelm (sbdy./sthg.) with too much of sthg.: *Telephone calls flooded the electric company during the power outage.* *—intr.* To overflow; pour forth: *The stream floods every spring. Her eyes flooded with tears.* ◆ **flood the market.** To sell a large amount or too much of sthg., causing the price to go down: *flooding the market with cheaply made products.*

flood·light (flŭd′līt′) *n.* **1.** An electric lamp that produces a broad, intensely bright beam of light: *We had floodlights installed for security.* **2.** The beam of light produced by such a lamp: *The fountain sparkled in the floodlight.*

flood·lit (flŭd′līt′) *adj.* Lit with a floodlight: *a floodlit parking lot.*

flood·plain (flŭd′plān′) *n.* Flatlands bordering a river and made up of soil deposited during floods.

flood·wa·ter (flŭd′wô′tər *or* flŭd′wŏ′tər) *n.* (usually plural). The water of a flood: *Floodwaters threatened the town.*

floor (flôr) *n.* **1.** The surface of a room on which one stands: *an oak floor.* **2.** The ground or bottom surface of a forest or an ocean: *explore the ocean floor.* **3.** A story or level of a building: *Our apartment is on the fifth floor.* **4. the floor.** The right to speak to a group in a formal setting: *The representative from Hawaii has the floor.* *—tr.v.* **1.** To provide (sthg.) with a floor: *floor a deck.* **2.** To knock (sbdy.) down: *The boxer was floored twice.* **3.** To shock (sbdy.) who then cannot speak or move: *The thrilling news floored me.*

floor·board (flôr′bôrd′) *n.* **1.** A board in a floor: *a broken floorboard.* **2.** The floor of a motor vehicle: *a rusted floorboard.*

floor·ing (flôr′ĭng) *n.* [U] **1.** Material, such as lumber, used to make floors. **2.** A floor or floors: *The house had flooring of fine wood.*

floor·show (flôr′shō′) *n.* A series of acts, such as singing or comedy acts, presented in a nightclub.

flop (flŏp) *v.* **flopped, flop·ping, flops.** *—intr.* **1.** To fall heavily and noisily: *I flopped on my bed.* **2.** To move about loosely or limply: *The dog's ears flopped as it ran.* **3.** *Informal.* To fail: *The musical comedy flopped in New York.* *—tr.* To cause (sthg.) to fall down heavily or drop noisily: *I flopped the heavy package on the table.* *—n.* **1.** The action or sound of flopping: *The whale's tail gave a flop as it dove.* **2.** *Informal.* A failure: *The play was a complete flop.*

flop·py (flŏp′ē) *adj.* **flop·pi·er, flop·pi·est.** Tending to flop: *floppy ears; big floppy sleeves.* *—n., pl.* **flop·pies.** A floppy disk: *What size floppy do you need?* **—flop′pi·ness** *n.* [U]

floppy disk *n.* A flexible plastic disk coated with magnetic material and covered by a protective jacket, used to store computer data: *Insert the floppy disk into the disk drive.*

floppy disk
Top: 3.5-inch floppy disk
Bottom: 5.25-inch floppy disk

flo·ra (flôr′ə) *n.* [U] All the plants of a particular region or time period considered as a group: *desert flora.*

flo·ral (flôr′əl) *adj.* Relating to flowers: *a floral arrangement; floral perfume.*

flor·id (flôr′ĭd *or* flŏr′ĭd) *adj.* **1.** Having a rosy color; ruddy: *a florid complexion.* **2.** Elaborate; flowery: *a florid style of writing.*

flo·rist (flôr′ĭst *or* flŏr′ĭst) *n.* A person who raises or sells ornamental plants and flowers.

floss (flôs *or* flŏs) *n.* [U] **1.** Thread, often waxed, used to clean between the teeth; dental floss. **2.** Soft, loosely twisted silk or cotton thread used in embroidery. *—tr. & intr.v.* To clean with dental floss: *Floss your teeth carefully. I brushed and flossed.*

flo·ta·tion (flō tā′shən) *n.* [U] The act of floating.

flounce (flouns) *intr.v.* **flounced, flounc·ing, flounc·es.** **1.** To move in a lively or bouncy manner: *The children flounced about the room.* **2.** To walk with a show of anger or impatience: *She felt insulted, so she flounced out of the room.*

floun·der¹ (floun′dər) *intr.v.* **1.** To move clumsily or with difficulty: *floundering through* *deep snow.* **2.** To struggle clumsily in confusion or embarrassment: *flounder through a speech.*

floun·der² (floun′dər) *n.* [C; U] A type of flat-bodied ocean fish used as food.

flour (flour) *n.* [U] A fine powdery food product made by grinding and sifting grain, especially wheat: *whole-wheat flour; white flour.* —*tr.v.* To coat (sthg.) with flour: *flour chicken before frying it.*

flour·ish (flûr′ĭsh *or* flŭr′ĭsh) *v.* —*intr.* **1.** To grow or develop well or in great amounts; thrive: *Most flowers flourish in full sunlight.* **2.** To do well; prosper: *The lawyer's practice flourished.* —*tr.* To wave (sthg.) vigorously or dramatically: *The bank robber flourished a gun.* —*n.* **1.** A dramatic action or gesture: *the flourish of a sword.* **2.** An added decorative touch; an unnecessary ornament: *handwriting with many flourishes.*

flout (flout) *tr.v.* To show contempt or a lack of respect for (sthg.): *flout the law.*

flow (flō) *intr.v.* **1.** To move or run smoothly in a stream: *Oil flowed from the well.* **2.** To proceed steadily and easily: *The preparations for the party flowed smoothly.* **3.** To be full or overflow: *Their hearts flowed with warm feelings.* **4.** To hang loosely and gracefully: *The judges' robes flowed behind them.* —*n.* **1.** [C] A stream or current: *a lava flow.* **2.** [U] A continuous movement: *the flow of traffic.* **3.** [U] The act of flowing: *Doctors could not stop the flow of blood.* **4.** [U] The rising of the tide toward shore.

HOMONYMS: flow, floe (ice mass).

flow chart *also* **flow·chart** (flō′chärt′) *n.* A diagram that shows the order of parts in a system or sequence of tasks for solving a problem or managing a complex project. —**flow′chart′** *v.*

flow·er (flou′ər) *n.* **1.** [C] The part of a plant that produces seeds, usually surrounded by brightly colored petals; a blossom. **2.** [C] A plant that is grown mainly for its flowers: *The flowers made a colorful garden.* **3.** [U] Time or period of coming into bloom: *an apple tree in full flower.* **4.** [C] *(usually singular).* The best example or representative of sthg.: *We're studying Shakespeare, who was the flower of Elizabethan England.* —*intr.v.* **1.** To produce flowers; bloom: *These fruit trees all flower in spring.* **2.** To develop fully; reach a high point: *His artistic talents flowered early in life.*

flow·er·y (flou′ə rē) *adj.* **flow·er·i·er, flow·er·i·est.** **1.** Full of or suggestive of flowers: *flowery meadows; a flowery fragrance.* **2.** Full of fancy words or expressions: *a flowery speech.* —**flow′er·i·ness** *n.* [U]

flown (flōn) *v.* Past participle of **fly¹.**

fl oz *or* **fl. oz.** *abbr.* An abbreviation of fluid ounce.

flu (flōō) *n.* [C; U] *Informal.* Influenza.

HOMONYMS: flu, flew (moved through the air), **flue** (pipe).

flub (flŭb) *tr.v.* **flubbed, flub·bing, flubs.** To fail to handle (sthg.) successfully: *He flubbed the pass and dropped the ball.* —*n.* A clumsy mistake; an error: *After several flubs, she solved the problem.*

fluc·tu·ate (flŭk′chōō āt′) *intr.v.* **fluc·tu·at·ed, fluc·tu·at·ing, fluc·tu·ates.** To change or vary irregularly; waver: *In summer the temperature fluctuates a great deal.* —**fluc′tu·a′tion** *n.* [C; U]

flue (flōō) *n.* A pipe, tube, or other channel for carrying smoke, steam, or waste gases, as from a fireplace to a chimney.

HOMONYMS: flue, flew (moved through the air), **flu** (influenza).

flu·en·cy (flōō′ən sē) *n.* [U] Smoothness and ease, especially in speaking or writing: *Fluency in more than one language is useful in many careers.*

flu·ent (flōō′ənt) *adj.* **1.** Able to express oneself smoothly and effortlessly: *a fluent speaker; fluent in German and French.* **2.** Flowing or moving smoothly; graceful: *an expensive boat with fluent lines.* —**flu′ent·ly** *adv.*

fluff (flŭf) *n.* **1.** [U] Soft, light material such as down or fuzz: *the fluff from a woolen sweater.* **2.** [U] Something having a very light or downy appearance: *The ducklings were little balls of fluff.* **3.** [C] *Informal.* An error: *My fluff in the ninth inning lost us the baseball game.* **4.** [U] Something having little substance or importance: *Her speech was nothing but fluff.* —*tr.v.* **1.** To make (sthg.) light and puffy by patting or shaking: *fluff a pillow.* **2.** *Informal.* To make an error in (sthg.); spoil: *fluff an exam; fluff a speech.*

fluff·y (flŭf′ē) *adj.* **fluff·i·er, fluff·i·est.** **1.** Resembling or covered with fluff or down: *a fluffy blanket; a fluffy baby bird.* **2.** Light and airy; soft: *fluffy whipped potatoes; fluffy curls.* —**fluff′i·ness** *n.* [U]

flu·id (flōō′ĭd) *n.* [C; U] A substance, such as air or water, that flows easily and takes the shape of its container: *All liquids and gases are fluids.* —*adj.* **1.** Capable of flowing; liquid or gaseous: *The waters of this lake remain fluid all winter.* **2.** Able to be changed easily: *Our vacation plans remained fluid until we knew how much time we had.* —**flu·id′i·ty** (flōō ĭd′ĭ tē) *n.* [U]

fluid ounce *n.* A liquid measure equal to ¹⁄₁₆ of a pint (29.57 milliliters). See table at **measurement.**

fluke (flōōk) *n.* Something happening by chance, especially sthg. good: *It was a fluke that we all arrived at the same time.*

flung (flŭng) *v*. Past tense and past participle of **fling**.

flunk (flŭngk) *Informal. v. —intr.* **1.** To fail, especially in an examination or a course. **2.** [*out*] To be forced to leave a college or university, for example, because of low grades: *The courses were so hard that many students flunked out. —tr.* **1.** To fail (a test or subject in school): *She flunked English twice.* **2.** To give (sbdy.) a failing grade: *Our teacher flunks students who cheat.*

flun·ky (flŭng′kē) *n., pl.* **flun·kies. 1.** A person who eagerly obeys another to win favor: *Rock stars are surrounded by willing flunkies.* **2.** A person who does a servant's work: *He's nothing but a flunky for the lawyers where he works.*

fluo·res·cence (floo rĕs′əns *or* flô rĕs′əns) *n.* [U] **1.** The giving off of light by a substance when it receives electromagnetic radiation, such as ultraviolet rays or x-rays. **2.** The light produced in this way.

fluo·res·cent (floo rĕs′ənt *or* flô rĕs′ənt) *adj.* Relating to, showing, or produced by fluorescence: *fluorescent light.*

fluorescent lamp *n.* A lamp that produces visible light by fluorescence, especially a glass tube coated on the inside with a fluorescent material and filled with an ionized gas that emits ultraviolet rays.

fluor·i·date (floor′ĭ dāt′ *or* flôr′ĭ dāt′) *tr.v.* **fluor·i·dat·ed, fluor·i·dat·ing, fluor·i·dates.** To add a compound of fluorine to (drinking water) to prevent tooth decay. **—fluor′i·da′tion** *n.* [U]

fluor·ide (floor′īd′ *or* flôr′īd′) *n.* [U] A chemical compound of fluorine and another element or radical.

fluor·ine (floor′ēn′ *or* flôr′ēn′) *n.* [U] *Symbol* **F** A pale yellow, poisonous gas that is highly corrosive. Atomic number 9. See table at **element.**

fluor·o·car·bon (floor′ō kär′bən *or* flôr′ō kär′bən) *n.* A liquid or gas containing fluorine and carbon, used in aerosol sprays, refrigerants, solvents, and lubricants: *Fluorocarbons have been linked to damage to the ozone layer.*

flur·ry (flûr′ē *or* flŭr′ē) *n., pl.* **flur·ries. 1.** A brief light fall of snow: *We're expecting snow flurries tonight.* **2.** A sudden burst of confusion, excitement, or activity: *a flurry of interest in the new product. —tr.v.* **flur·ried, flur·ry·ing, flur·ries.** To confuse, excite, or agitate (sbdy.): *Unexpected questions flurried the speaker.*

flush¹ (flŭsh) *v. —intr.* **1.** To turn red in the face; blush: *Her face flushed with excitement.* **2.** To be emptied or cleaned by a rapid gush of water: *The toilet's not working; it won't flush. —tr.* **1.** To cause (sbdy./sthg.) to red-

den or glow: *The disappointed customer was flushed with annoyance.* **2.** To excite (sbdy.), as with a feeling of pride or accomplishment: *The winning team was flushed with victory.* **3.** To wash, empty, or purify (sthg.) with a sudden rapid flow of water: *The nurse flushed the patient's wound. —n.* **1.** A flow or rush of water. **2.** A blush or rosy glow: *She had a healthy flush to her checks.* **3.** A rush of strong feeling or excitement: *a flush of enthusiasm.* **4.** A state of freshness or vigor: *the first flush of youth. —adj.* **1.** *Informal.* Having a large supply of money: *The company was flush with cash from sales of its latest product.* **2.** Marked by a great supply; plentiful: *rivers flush with spring rains.* **3.** Having surfaces that are even, level, or close together: *sections of the sidewalk that are flush. —adv.* Evenly placed in a line: *Set the margins of the document and align it flush right.*

flush² (flŭsh) *v. —tr.* To cause (a bird or an animal) to dart or fly from a hiding place: *Our noise flushed several ducks from the tall grass. —intr.* To rush out or fly from a hiding place: *The dog barked and a rabbit flushed from the thicket.*

flus·ter (flŭs′tər) *tr.v.* To make (sbdy.) nervous, excited, or confused: *Shouts from the protesters flustered the speaker. —n.* A state of excitement, confusion, or nervous upset: *The heavy city traffic put the driver in a fluster.*

flute (floot) *n.* A woodwind instrument consisting of a tube with finger holes and keys on the side, played by blowing across a hole near one end. **—flut′ist** *n.*

flute

flut·ter (flŭt′ər) *v. —intr.* **1.** To wave or flap rapidly and lightly: *Curtains fluttered in the breeze.* **2.a.** To fly with a quick light flapping of the wings: *Moths fluttered around the light.* **b.** To flap the wings while making short hops: *The chicken fluttered across the yard.* **3.** To beat rapidly or in an irregular way: *When I was scared, my heart fluttered wildly.* **4.** To move quickly in a nervous or excited way: *Clerks fluttered about the store trying to look busy.* **5.** To fall or move lightly with an irregular motion: *Hundreds of feathers fluttered to the floor after the pillow fight. —tr.* To cause (sthg.) to flutter: *A light breeze fluttered the curtain. —n.* **1.** [U] An act of fluttering: *the flutter of a butterfly.* **2.** [C] A condition of nervous excitement or expectation: *We were in a flutter getting ready for the party.*

flux (flŭks) *n.* **1.** [U] Continual change: *The price of gold is in flux.* **2.** [C] A substance applied to a metal surface that is to be soldered or welded. **3.** [U] The rate of flow of fluids, particles, or energy across a given surface or area.

fly[1] (flī) *v.* **flew** (flo͞o), **flown** (flōn), **fly•ing, flies** (flīz). —*intr.* **1.** To move through the air by means of wings: *Birds fly south in winter.* **2.a.** To move or travel by air: *We flew to Seattle for vacation.* **b.** To pilot an aircraft or a spacecraft: *The crew flew from New York to Mexico City.* **3.a.** To be carried by the wind: *Dust flew through the air.* **b.** To float or flutter in the air: *pennants flying from buildings.* **4.** To be sent through the air with great speed or force: *The plate flew from my hands when I fell.* **5.** To rush or run away: *flew down the hall; fly from danger.* **6.** To pass by fast: *a vacation flying by.* —*tr.* **1.** To cause (sthg.) to float in the air: *fly a kite.* **2.a.** To pilot (an aircraft or a spacecraft): *learning to fly a plane.* **b.** To carry or transport (sbdy./sthg.) in an aircraft or a spacecraft: *fly supplies to a remote area.* **3.** To rush away or escape from (sbdy./sthg.): *Many people flew the country.* —*n.* A zipper or set of buttons on the front of trousers: *Excuse me. I think your fly is open.* ◆ **fly at.** *tr.v.* [insep.] To attack (sbdy.) fiercely: *The angry shopper just flew at the salesclerk.* **fly-by-night.** Dishonest and unlikely to be around long: *a fly-by-night business.* **fly into a rage.** To get very angry suddenly: *He flew into a rage when he found out that his car had been stolen.* **fly off the handle.** *Informal.* To get angry: *She flies off the handle easily.* **fly the coop.** To leave quickly: *He took the money and flew the coop.* **let fly. 1.** To shoot, throw, or release (a weapon): *The archer let fly an arrow.* **2.** To express sudden strong criticism: *The mayor let fly with an attack on her critics.* **on the fly. 1.** While moving; in a hurry: *I ate a sandwich on the fly.* **2.** While in the air; in flight: *The hawk caught the pigeon on the fly.*

fly[2] (flī) *n.* **1.** Any of numerous two-winged insects, especially one of a group that includes the housefly. **2.** A fishhook made to look like such an insect, as by attaching bits of feathers. ◆ **fly on the wall.** A secret observer: *I would like to be a fly on the wall at their meeting.*

fly•er (flī′ər) *n.* Variant of **flier.**

fly-fish•ing (flī′fĭsh′ĭng) *n.* The sport of fishing using artificial flies for bait.

fly•ing (flī′ĭng) *adj.* **1.** Capable of or engaged in flight: *a flying insect.* **2.** Swiftly moving: *the pianist's flying fingers.* **3.** Relating to aviation: *flying lessons.* —*n.* [U] **1.** Flight, as in an aircraft: *Flying is an exciting way to travel.* **2.** The operation of an aircraft: *A pilot is an expert in flying.* ◆ **off to a flying start.** Making a good beginning: *The team was off to a flying start, scoring a goal in the first minute of the game.* **with flying colors.** Very successfully: *She passed her test with flying colors, getting a perfect score.*

flying fish *n.* Any of various fishes having large side fins that spread out like wings as they leap out of the ocean.

flying saucer *n.* An unidentified flying object from another planet, usually said to be shaped like a disk: *He claimed he had seen flying saucers from outer space.*

fly•pa•per (flī′pā′pər) *n.* [U] Paper coated with a sticky, sometimes poisonous substance, used to catch flies.

fly swat•ter (swŏt′ər) *n.* A tool used to hit and kill flies or other insects, usually consisting of plastic or wire mesh attached to a long handle.

FM or **fm** *abbr.* An abbreviation of frequency modulation: *My favorite FM radio station plays jazz all night.*

foal (fōl) *n.* The young offspring of a horse, zebra, or similar animal, especially one less than a year old. —*intr.v.* To give birth to a foal: *a mare ready to foal.*

foam (fōm) *n.* [U] **1.** A mass of very small bubbles on the surface of a liquid, as in the ocean, liquid soap, and certain drinks: *foam on the hot chocolate; foam on the waves.* **2.** A spongy plastic or rubber formed with many tiny airholes in it: *a pillow made of foam.* —*intr.v.* **1.** To form foam or come forth in foam: *The soap foamed as I sprayed water on it. The animal was foaming at the mouth.* **2.** To be extremely angry: *He was foaming over the delays.*

foam•y (fō′mē) *adj.* **foam•i•er, foam•i•est.** Full of, covered with, or resembling foam: *foamy shaving cream.* —**foam′i•ness** *n.* [U]

fo•cal (fō′kəl) *adj.* Relating to a focus: *The focal point of the discussion was the subject of rights for minority groups.*

fo•cus (fō′kəs) *n.* **1.** [C] A center of interest, attention, or activity: *The senator was the focus of attention at the assembly.* **2.** [C] Concentration or emphasis: *The narrator's focus is on the characters in the story rather than the action.* **3.** [C] A point at which rays of light come together or from which they spread apart, as after passing through a lens. **4.** [U] The condition or adjustment in which an eye or optical instrument gives its best image: *The camera is out of focus.* —*v.* —*tr.* **1.** To adjust (the eyes or an optical instrument) to produce a clear image: *Focus the telescope on the moon.* **2.** To concentrate, center, or fix (sthg.): *Focus your attention on the lesson.* —*intr.* **1.** To adjust one's eyes or an optical instrument to produce a clear image: *This camera focuses automatically.* **2.** To concentrate attention or energy: *Let's focus on the problem at hand.*

fod•der (fŏd′ər) *n.* [U] Food, such as chopped cornstalks or hay, for livestock.

F

foe (fō) *n.* An enemy, opponent, or adversary: *Foes of the new city dump met to fight the plan.*

fog (fôg *or* fŏg) *n.* [C; U] **1.** Condensed water vapor in cloudy masses lying close to the surface of the ground or water: *It was difficult driving because of the fog.* **2.** A cloud of material, such as dust or smoke, that floats in the air: *a fog of insect spray.* **3.** A confused or unthinking condition: *A fog of anger prevented me from thinking clearly.* —*v.* **fogged, fog·ging, fogs.** —*tr.* **1.** To cover (sthg.) with fog: *Steam fogged the bathroom mirror.* **2.** To make (sthg.) uncertain or unclear; confuse: *The strong medicine fogged the patient's mind.* —*intr.* To become covered with fog: *The car windows fogged up in the rain.*

fo·gey (fō′gē) *n.* Variant of **fogy.**

fog·gy (fô′gē *or* fŏg′ē) *adj.* **fog·gi·er, fog·gi·est. 1.** Full of or surrounded by fog: *a foggy valley.* **2.** Confused or vague; clouded: *I have only a foggy memory of what happened.* —**fog′gi·ly** *adv.* —**fog′gi·ness** *n.* [U]

fog·horn (fôg′hôrn′ *or* fŏg′hôrn′) *n.* A horn, usually with a deep tone, blown to warn ships of danger in foggy weather.

fo·gy *also* **fo·gey** (fō′gē) *n., pl.* **fo·gies** *also* **fo·geys.** *Informal.* A person with old-fashioned or narrow-minded ideas.

foi·ble (foi′bəl) *n.* A minor personal fault or habit: *Laughing too loudly is an annoying foible.*

foil¹ (foil) *tr.v.* To prevent (sbdy./sthg.) from being successful; frustrate: *an alarm system to foil thieves.*

foil² (foil) *n.* **1.** [U] A thin flexible sheet of metal: *aluminum foil.* **2.** [C] A person or thing that makes another person look good by contrast: *The serious official was a perfect foil for the comedian.*

foist (foist) *v.* ◆ **foist on** *or* **upon.** *tr.v.* [sep.] To present (sthg.) as genuine, valuable, or worthy when the opposite is true: *The dishonest merchant tried to foist damaged goods on his customers.*

fold¹ (fōld) *v.* —*tr.* **1.** To bend over or double up (sthg.) so that one part lies over another: *Fold your paper in half.* **2.** To close or flatten (sthg.) by bending, pressing, or doubling jointed or connected parts: *The bird folded its wings. The sunbathers folded their chairs and left.* **3.a.** To take and hold (sbdy.) gently: *I folded the infant in my arms.* **b.** To enclose or wrap (sthg.): *fold the garbage in a newspaper.* **4.** To blend (an ingredient) into a mixture by gently turning one part over another: *Fold the beaten egg whites into the batter.* —*intr.* **1.** To be folded or be capable of being folded: *My wallet folds in the middle.* **2.** *Informal.* To

fail and close: *The business folded during the recession.* —*n.* **1.** A line or crease formed by folding: *Tear the paper along the fold.* **2.** A folded edge or part: *The little child hid in the folds of the curtain.* ◆ **fold out.** *tr.v.* [sep.] To bring (sthg.) to an extended position; unfold: *I folded out the map to see where we were.*

fold² (fōld) *n.* **1.** An established group, such as a church or political party, whose members share the same beliefs, aims, or interests: *Some party members rebelled but later returned to the fold.* **2.** A pen for sheep.

—**fold** *suff.* A suffix that means: **1.** Multiplied by a specified number: *a fivefold increase in sales.* **2.** Divided into a specified number of parts: *a threefold problem.*

fold·er (fōl′dər) *n.* **1.** A folded sheet of cardboard or heavy paper used to hold loose papers: *a file folder.* **2.** A booklet of information made of one or more folded sheets of paper: *travel folders.* **3.** A collection of related documents stored on computer: *I store copies of my personal letters in a folder named "Friends."*

fo·li·age (fō′lē ĭj *or* fō′lĭj) *n.* [U] Plant leaves, especially tree leaves, considered as a group: *colorful autumn foliage.*

folk (fōk) *n., pl.* **folk** *or* **folks.** *(used with a plural verb).* **1.** People: *city folk; honest folk.* **2. folks.** *Informal.* **a.** People considered as a group: *The warning sign scared folks away.* **b.** One's parents or relatives: *My folks are coming to visit.* —*adj.* Of or coming from the common people or their culture: *a folk hero; a folk tune.*

folk dance *n.* A traditional dance originating among the common people of a country or region: *The mazurka is a Polish folk dance.* —**folk danc′ing** *n.* [U]

folk·lore (fōk′lôr′) *n.* [U] The traditional beliefs, legends, and customs of a group or nation, passed from generation to generation.

folk·sing·er (fōk′sĭng′ər) *n.* A person who specializes in singing folksongs. —**folk sing′ing** *n.* [U]

folk·song (fōk′sông′ *or* fōk′sŏng′) *n.* **1.** A song that is part of the folk music of a people. **2.** A song composed in the style of such a song.

folk·sy (fōk′sē) *adj.* **folk·si·er, folk·si·est.** *Informal.* Simple and informal: *folksy people.*

folk·tale (fōk′tāl′) *n.* A traditional story or legend passed down by the people of a country or region from one generation to the next.

fol·li·cle (fŏl′ĭ kəl) *n.* A small cavity, sac, or gland in the body from which hairs grow.

fol·low (fŏl′ō) *v.* —*tr.* **1.** To go or come after (sbdy./sthg.): *Follow the usher to your seats. Night follows day.* **2.** To chase or trail (sbdy./

sthg.): *The detectives followed the suspect at a distance.* **3.** To move along the same course as (sthg.): *We followed a path to the beach.* **4.** To occur as a result of (sthg.): *General agreement followed the discussion.* **5.** To act in agreement with (an order, a guide, or a model); obey: *Follow the rules of the game. Follow my example.* **6.** To accept, believe in, or support (sbdy./sthg.): *follow a religion.* **7.** To listen to or watch (sthg.) closely: *Weather forecasters followed the progress of the storm on their radar screens.* **8.** To stay informed about (sthg.): *Scientists follow new developments in genetics.* **9.** To grasp the meaning of (sbdy./sthg.); understand: *Do you follow what I'm saying? Are you following me?* —*intr.* **1.** To come, move, or take place after another person or thing in order or time: *A picnic followed after the baseball game.* **2.** To occur as a result: *Success will follow if you keep practicing.* ♦ **as follows.** An expression used to introduce a list: *The directions to my house are as follows: Go two miles; turn left at the light; turn into the second house on the right.* **follow through.** *intr.v.* To carry sthg. to completion: *She followed through on her promise.* **follow up.** *tr.v.* [sep.] **1.** To make (a previous action) more effective by doing sthg. else: *He followed up his interview with a thank-you letter.* **2.** To carry (sthg.) to completion: *After they made their recommendation, we followed it up with a plan.*

SYNONYMS: follow, succeed, ensue, result. These verbs mean to come after sbdy. or sthg. in time or order. **Follow** is the most general: *I followed my friends to the restaurant because I didn't know the way.* **Succeed** means to follow, especially in a planned order determined by rank, inheritance, or election: *His daughter succeeded him as publisher of the local newspaper.* **Ensue** means to follow as an effect or logical development: *If you do not cleanse the wound, an infection may ensue.* **Result** means to follow as a direct effect: *Failure to return a library book on time will result in a fine.*

---

fol•low•er (fŏl′ō ər) *n.* **1.** A person who follows the beliefs or ideas of another: *a follower of Ghandi.* **2.** A close observer, a fan, or an enthusiast: *a follower of new developments in computers.*

fol•low•ing (fŏl′ō ĭng) *adj.* Coming next in order or time: *the following afternoon.* —*n.* **1.** [C] *(usually singular).* A group of admirers, supporters, or disciples: *a popular politician with a large following.* **2.** **the following.** *(used with a plural verb).* The items or people to be mentioned next: *The following are what you'll need to buy: milk, cheese, fruit, bread, and eggs.* —*prep.* After: *Following dinner, we watched a movie.*

fol•low-up or **fol•low•up** (fŏl′ō ŭp′) *n.*

(usually singular). Something that strengthens or improves a previous action or event: *The software was a successful follow-up to the original product.* —**fol′low-up′** *adj.*

fol•ly (fŏl′ē) *n., pl.* **fol•lies.** **1.** [U] Lack of good sense or judgment; foolishness: *accused of folly for quitting school.* **2.** [C] A foolish act or idea: *Sometimes important inventions are treated as follies at first.*

fo•ment (fō mĕnt′) *tr.v. Formal.* To stir up (sthg.); arouse; provoke: *The protesters were charged with fomenting a riot.*

fond (fŏnd) *adj.* **1.** [*of*] Having a strong liking: *Are you fond of gardening?* **2.** Loving or affectionate: *a fond smile from his mother.* **3.** Foolishly affectionate: *fond and doting pet owners.* **4.** Cherished; dear: *my fondest hopes.* —**fond′ly** *adv.*

fon•dle (fŏn′dl) *tr.v.* **fon•dled, fon•dling, fon•dles.** To touch or stroke (sbdy./sthg.) lovingly; caress: *fondle a puppy.*

fond•ness (fŏnd′nĭs) *n.* [U] **1.** Liking or inclination: *a fondness for the outdoors.* **2.** Warm affection: *a smile full of fondness.*

font[1] (fŏnt) *n.* **1.** A basin that holds holy water or water used in baptism. **2.** A source or an origin: *The professor is a font of knowledge.*

font[2] (fŏnt) *n.* A complete set of printing characters of one size and style: *Computers provide users with a variety of fonts for creating documents.*

food (fōōd) *n.* **1.** [C; U] Material that a plant or an animal can take in and use for energy and to maintain life and growth. **2.** [C; U] A particular kind of nourishment: *some plant food; my favorite foods.* **3.** [U] Something that stimulates or encourages some activity or growth: *The movie gave them food for thought.*

Food and Drug Administration *n.* The U.S. government agency responsible for checking the safety of foods and medicines.

food chain *n.* A series of living things in an environment, in which each one in the series is eaten by another kind higher up in the chain.

food poisoning *n.* [U] A painful stomach and intestinal disorder that results from eating food that has become contaminated with bacteria.

food proc•es•sor (prŏs′ĕs′ər *or* prō′sĕs′ər) *n.* An appliance with blades that processes food, as by slicing or shredding, at high speeds.

food stamp *n.* A stamp, issued by the U.S. government to people with low incomes, that can be used to buy food at stores.

food•stuff (fōōd′stŭf′) *n. Formal. (usually plural).* A substance that can be used or prepared for use as food: *These utensils should be used only with foodstuffs.*

fool (fōōl) *n.* **1.** A person who lacks judgment or good sense: *She was a fool to lend him the* *money.* **2.** In the past, a member of a royal or noble household who provided entertainment by telling jokes and clowning; a jester. —*v.* —*tr.* **1.** To deceive or trick (sbdy.); mislead: *They fooled me into thinking they had left.* **2.** To surprise (sbdy.): *We were sure their plan would fail, but they fooled us.* —*intr.* **1.** *Informal.* To behave with a lack of seriousness or purpose: *If you continue fooling, you'll never finish your homework.* **2.** To act or speak in a joking way: *My friend thought I was serious, but I was only fooling.* **3.** To play or handle sthg. foolishly: *Don't fool with the knobs on the oven.* ◆ **fool around.** *intr.v. Informal.* **1.** To waste time: *Stop fooling around and get to work.* **2.** To pass time in carefree fun: *fooling around with friends on a summer afternoon.* **3.** To be unfaithful in a romantic relationship: *Whenever he is away from home, he fools around.*

fool·har·dy (fo͞ol′här′dē) *adj.* Foolishly bold; reckless: *a foolhardy beginner trying to ski down the steepest slopes.* —**fool′har′di·ness** *n.* [U]

fool·ish (fo͞o′lĭsh) *adj.* **1.** Lacking in good sense or judgment; unwise: *a foolish choice.* **2.** Deserving of laughter; ridiculous: *I looked foolish dressed as a clown.* —**fool′ish·ly** *adv.* —**fool′ish·ness** *n.* [U]

fool·proof (fo͞ol′pro͞of′) *adj.* So safe, simple, and reliable that error or misuse is impossible: *a foolproof plan.*

foot (fo͝ot) *n., pl.* **feet** (fēt). **1.** The part of the leg that rests on or touches the ground or floor in standing or walking. **2.** A part or base resembling a foot, as the end of a table leg. **3.** The lowest part of sthg. high or long; the bottom: *the foot of the stairs; the foot of the page.* **4.** The end opposite the head in position: *the foot of the bed.* **5.** The part of a boot or stocking that covers the foot: *The foot is too long.* **6.** A unit of length equal to ⅓ of a yard or 12 inches (about 30.5 centimeters). See table at **measurement.** —*tr.v. Informal.* To pay (an expense): *I'll foot the bill.* ◆ **on foot.** Walking or running: *We're going to the restaurant on foot.*

foot·age (fo͝ot′ĭj) *n.* [U] A length or an amount of sthg. as measured in feet: *film footage.*

foot·ball (fo͝ot′bôl′) *n.* **1.a.** [U] A game played by two teams of 11 players each on a rectangular field with goals at either end. The object is to carry the ball across the opponent's goal line or to kick it between the opponent's goal posts. **b.** [C] The inflated oval ball used in this game. **2.** *Chiefly British.* **a.** [U] Soccer or Rugby. **b.** [C] The ball used in soccer or Rugby.

foot·ed (fo͝ot′ĭd) *adj.* Having a foot or feet: *a footed sofa; a four-footed animal.*

foot·hill (fo͝ot′hĭl′) *n.* (*usually plural*). A low hill located near the base of a mountain or mountain range: *the foothills of the Rocky Mountains.*

foot·hold (fo͝ot′hōld′) *n.* **1.** A place to put the foot so that it won't slip, especially when climbing a mountain. **2.** A firm secure position from which it is possible to advance: *He got a foothold in business by first working as an assistant.*

foot·ing (fo͝ot′ĭng) *n.* **1.** [U] A firm placing of the feet allowing one to stand or move without falling: *Be careful not to lose your footing.* **2.** [U] The condition of a surface for walking or running: *The sidewalk was icy and the footing dangerous.* **3.** [C] A basis or standing: *You'll be on an equal footing with the other job applicants.*

foot·lights (fo͝ot′līts′) *pl.n.* Lights placed in a row along the front of a stage floor.

foot·lock·er (fo͝ot′lŏk′ər) *n.* A trunk, usually of metal, for storing clothes and other personal belongings: *a soldier's footlocker.*

foot·loose (fo͝ot′lo͞os′) *adj.* Having no responsibilities to others; free to do as one pleases. ◆ **footloose and fancy free.** Free to do as one pleases: *You won't be footloose and fancy free for long; once you get married things will change.*

foot·note (fo͝ot′nōt′) *n.* A note at the bottom of a page explaining sthg. in the text or giving the source of a quotation, a fact, or an idea. —*tr.v.* **foot·not·ed, foot·not·ing, foot·notes.** To provide (sthg.) with footnotes: *Students were required to footnote their research papers.*

foot·path (fo͝ot′păth′) *n.* A narrow path for people to walk on.

foot·print (fo͝ot′prĭnt′) *n.* A mark left by a foot or shoe, as in sand or snow: *We looked for footprints of animals in the fresh snow.*

foot·race or **foot race** (fo͝ot′rās′) *n.* A race run by people on foot.

foot·rest (fo͝ot′rĕst′) *n.* A low stool, metal bar, or other support on which to rest the feet.

foot·step (fo͝ot′stĕp′) *n.* **1.** A step taken by a foot. **2.** The sound of a foot stepping: *I heard their footsteps on the stairs.* ◆ **follow in (one's) footsteps.** To continue the behavior, work, or tradition of (sbdy.): *She is following in her father's footsteps by going into medicine.*

foot·stool (fo͝ot′sto͞ol′) *n.* A low stool on which to rest the feet while sitting.

foot·wear (fo͝ot′wâr′) *n.* [U] Coverings for the feet, such as shoes or boots.

foot·work (fo͝ot′wûrk′) *n.* [U] **1.** The movement of the feet, as in boxing or dancing: *The dancer was known for his fancy footwork.* **2.** Clever scheming to achieve some

---

ă–cat; ā–pay; âr–care; ä–father; ĕ–get; ē–be; ĭ–sit; ī–nice; îr–here; ŏ–got; ō–go; ô–saw; oi–boy; ou–out; o͝o–took; o͞o–boot; ŭ–cut; ûr–word; th–thin; th–this; hw–when; zh–vision; ə–about; N–French bon

purpose: *His footwork has enabled him to remain untainted by scandal.*

for (fôr; fər *when unstressed*) *prep.* **1.a.** With the purpose or goal of: *swimming for exercise; studying for the exam.* **b.** Directed or addressed to: *a letter for you.* **2.** In the direction of; having as a destination: *Let's head for home.* **3.** As a result of: *They were rewarded for their hard work.* **4.** As the agent or representative of: *She spoke for all of us.* **5.** In favor or support of: *Are you for or against the idea?* **6.** In place of: *She used her coat for a blanket.* **7.** In the amount of; at the price of: *a bill for five dollars; a radio bought for ten dollars.* **8.** To the extent of or through a distance or time of: *We drove for miles. We talked for an hour.* **9.** At the stated time of: *I have an appointment for 2 o'clock.* **10.a.** As regards; concerning: *He has a talent for making money.* **b.** Considering the usual nature or character of: *The child is tall for her age.* **c.** In honor of: *She was named for her aunt.* **11.** Right or suitable to: *It's really for her to decide.* **12.** In spite of: *For all his complaining, he seems to like his job.* —*conj. Formal.* Because; since: *We must be careful measuring the windows, for it's easy to make mistakes.*

HOMONYMS: for, fore (at the front), **four** (number).

for·age (fôr′ĭj *or* fŏr′ĭj) *n.* **1.** [U] Food for horses, cattle, or other animals: *The rancher supplied forage for his cattle during the long winter.* **2.** [C] A search to find available food or supplies: *a forage for wood to build a fire.* —*v.* **for·aged, for·ag·ing, for·ag·es.** —*intr.* **1.** To search for food: *Bears forage for food.* **2.** To search or hunt about, as for sthg. needed or desired: *foraging in a drawer for a sock.* —*tr.* **1.** To get (sthg.) by searching about: *We foraged cookies from the kitchen cabinet.* **2.** To get food, supplies, or other goods from (sbdy./sthg.), often by force: *Pirates foraged the coastal towns.* —**for′ag·er** *n.*

for·ay (fôr′ā′ *or* fŏr′ā′) *n.* **1.** A venture into a new place or a first try at sthg. outside one's usual area: *an actor's foray into politics.* **2.** A sudden raid or military expedition. —*intr.v.* To make a raid: *foray into enemy territory.*

for·bear (fôr bâr′) *tr. & intr.v.* **for·bore** (fôr-bôr′), **for·borne** (fôr bôrn′), **for·bear·ing, for·bears.** *Formal.* To keep from or resist doing sthg.; hold back: *forbear telling him the truth; forbear from replying in anger.*

for·bear·ance (fôr bâr′əns) *n.* [U] *Formal* Patience, tolerance, or restraint: *He showed forbearance in speaking gently to the rude children.*

for·bid (fôr bĭd′) *tr.v.* **for·bade** (fôr băd′ *or* fôr bād′) *or* **for·bad** (fôr băd′), **for·bid·den** (fôr bĭd′n) *or* **for·bid, for·bid·-**

ding, **for·bids. 1.** To refuse to allow (sthg.); prohibit: *The law forbids robbery.* **2.** To order (sbdy.) not to do sthg.: *I forbid you to go.*

for·bid·ding (fôr bĭd′ĭng) *adj.* Looking threatening, dangerous, or unfriendly: *a forbidding desert; a forbidding expression.*

force (fôrs) *n.* **1.** [U] Strength; power; energy: *the force of an explosion.* See Synonyms at **strength.** **2.** [U] Power, pressure, or violence used on a person or thing that resists: *use force in driving a nail; a promise obtained by force.* **3.** [C] In science, sthg. that causes a change in the speed or direction of an object's motion, or a quantity that measures this change in motion: *the attractive force between two opposite electric charges.* **4.** [C] **a.** A group of people organized or available for a certain purpose: *a large labor force; a police force.* **b. forces.** Military units, as of an army: *Napoleon's forces.* **5.** [C] A strong influence acting as an urge or a restraint: *forces affecting modern life.* **6.** [U] The power to influence or persuade; effectiveness: *the force of the lawyer's arguments.* —*tr.v.* **forced, forc·ing, forc·es. 1.** To make (sbdy.) do sthg., as through pressure or necessity: *The storm forced us to cancel our meeting.* **2.** To get (sthg.) by the use of force: *I forced the ball from his hand.* **3.** [*on*] To make (sthg. be suffered by sbdy.); impose: *The invaders forced their laws on the peoples they conquered.* **4.** To move, push, or drive (sthg.) by pressure: *The pump forces water through the pipe.* **5.** To make (sthg.) happen through effort or pressure: *I forced a smile on my face.* **6.** To break (sthg.) open by using violence: *force the door; force a lock.* ♦ **by** or **from force of habit.** Automatically without thinking: *He drinks a cup of coffee every morning from force of habit.* **in force. 1.** In effect; valid: *The rule is no longer in force.* **2.** In a large group: *The protesters arrived at city hall in force.* **join forces.** To come together with another person or group to achieve a goal: *If we join forces, we will be able to finish the job sooner.*

forced (fôrst) *adj.* **1.** Done under force, not by free choice; compulsory: *forced labor* **2.** Not natural; strained: *the forced laughter of a nervous man.*

force·ful (fôrs′fəl) *adj.* Full of force; effective: *The winning candidate is a forceful speaker.* —**force′ful·ly** *adv.* —**force′ful·ness** *n.* [U]

for·ceps (fôr′səps) *n., pl.* **forceps.** A pair of special pincers or tongs used especially by surgeons or dentists for picking up, holding, or pulling: *The doctor used forceps to deliver the baby.*

forc·i·ble (fôr′sə bəl) *adj.* **1.** Accomplished through the use of force: *The firefighters broke into the building by forcible entry.* **2.** Having force; forceful: *a forcible personality.* —**for′ci·bly** *adv.*

ford (fôrd) *n.* A shallow place in a stream or river where one can walk, ride, or drive across. —*tr.v.* To cross (a stream or river) by wading, riding, or driving through a ford: *The settlers forded the river.* —**ford′a·ble** *adj.*

fore (fôr) *adj.* In, at, or toward the front; forward: *The fore part of the new building faces the avenue.* —*n.* [U] **1.** Something that is located at or toward the front. **2.** The front part: *The sailors checked the ropes at the fore.* —*adv.* At, toward, or near the front; forward: *ran fore to check the damage.* —*interj.* An expression used by golfers to warn others on the course that the ball is about to be hit in their direction. ◆ **to the fore.** In, into, or toward a position of importance or influence: *New issues bring new leaders to the fore.*

HOMONYMS: fore, for (with the purpose of), **four** (number).

---

fore— *pref.* A prefix that means: **1.** Before; earlier: *foresight; forefather.* **2.** Front; in front of: *forehead.*

WORD BUILDING: fore— The prefix **fore—** means "before, in front." A **forerunner** is "one that goes before," and a **foreleg** is "a front leg of an animal." It is important not to confuse **fore—** with the prefix *for—* (sometimes spelled *fore—*), which appears in many English words but is no longer used to form words in English. This prefix has the meaning of exclusion or rejection and survives in words like **forbid** and **forswear.**

---

fore·arm (fôr′ärm′) *n.* The part of the arm between the wrist and elbow.

fore·bod·ing (fôr bō′dĭng) *n.* [U] A sense that sthg. bad will soon happen: *The empty house seemed full of foreboding.*

fore·cast (fôr′kăst′) *tr.v.* **fore·cast** or **fore·cast·ed, fore·cast·ing, fore·casts.** To tell in advance (sthg. that might or will happen, especially weather conditions): *forecast snow for the weekend.* —*n.* A prediction, as of coming events or conditions: *the weather forecast.* —**fore′cast′er** *n.*

fore·close (fôr klōz′) *v.* **fore·closed, fore·clos·ing, fore·clos·es.** —*tr.* **1.** To take away (a mortgage), as when payments have not been made: *The bank foreclosed the mortgage on his house and took away the property.* **2.** To exclude (sthg.): *foreclose an option.* —*intr.* To take away the right to pay off a mortgage and take ownership of the property: *The bank will foreclose tomorrow if we can't make the payment.*

fore·clo·sure (fôr klō′zhər) *n.* The act of foreclosing, especially a legal proceeding by which a mortgage is foreclosed: *Numerous foreclosures are a sign of a weak economy.*

fore·fa·ther (fôr′fä′thər) *n.* An ancestor.

fore·fin·ger (fôr′fĭng′gər) *n.* The finger next to the thumb; the index finger.

fore·front (fôr′frŭnt′) *n.* [U] The most important or most advanced position: *at the forefront in the fight against crime.*

fore·go·ing (fôr gō′ĭng *or* fôr′gō′ĭng) *adj. Formal.* Said, written, or seen just before; previous: *Refer to the foregoing figures.*

fore·gone (fôr′gôn′ *or* fôr′gŏn′) *adj.* Having gone before; previous. ◆ **a foregone conclusion.** An end or a result seen as certain or inevitable: *The victory was a foregone conclusion.*

fore·ground (fôr′ground′) *n.* [U] The part of a scene or picture that is nearest to and in front of the viewer.

fore·head (fôr′hĕd′ *or* fŏr′hĕd′) *n.* The part of the face above the eyebrows.

for·eign (fôr′ĭn *or* fŏr′ĭn) *adj.* **1.** Relating to or from another country or place: *a foreign language; foreign customs.* **2.** Conducted or involved with other governments: *foreign service; foreign trade.* **3.** [*to*] Not naturally belonging; alien: *Jealousy is foreign to her nature.*

for·eign·er (fôr′ə nər *or* fŏr′ə nər) *n.* **1.** A person from a foreign country or place: *Millions of foreigners have immigrated to the United States.* **2.** An outsider: *a foreigner to the lives of factory workers.*

fore·knowl·edge (fôr nŏl′ĭj *or* fôr′nŏl′ĭj) *n.* [U] Knowledge of sthg. before it happens or comes into existence: *The witness swore that he'd had no foreknowledge of the crime.*

fore·leg (fôr′lĕg′) *n.* One of the front legs of a four-legged animal.

fore·lock (fôr′lŏk′) *n.* A lock of hair that grows from or falls on the forehead.

fore·man (fôr′mən) *n.* **1.** A person who has charge of a group of workers, as in a factory. **2.** A person who is chosen to lead and speak for a jury.

fore·most (fôr′mōst′) *adj.* First in time, place, rank, or position; most important or leading: *the world's foremost authority on the subject.* —*adv.* In the first or front position: *First and foremost, we must consider safety concerns.*

fo·ren·sic (fə rĕn′sĭk *or* fə rĕn′zĭk) *adj.* Relating to or used in courts of law or public discussion: *forensic evidence; forensic skills.*

fore·play (fôr′plā′) *n.* [U] Sexual activities such as kissing and touching that are done before sexual intercourse.

fore·run·ner (fôr′rŭn′ər) *n.* **1.** A person or thing that comes or goes before, as in time: *Roller skates were the forerunners of skate-*

---

boards. **2.** A warning sign or symptom: *A sore throat is often the forerunner of a cold.*

fore·see (fôr sē′) *tr.v.* **fore·saw** (fôr sô′), **fore·seen** (fôr sēn′), **fore·see·ing, fore·sees.** To see or know (sthg.) in advance: *As the mountain got steeper, the hikers foresaw a difficult climb.* —**fore·see′a·ble** *adj.*

fore·shad·ow (fôr shăd′ō) *tr.v.* To present a sign or suggestion of (sthg.) in advance: *Everyone hoped that the border dispute did not foreshadow a wider war.*

fore·sight (fôr′sīt′) *n.* [U] **1.** Understanding of the importance and nature of events before they happen: *The city planners were later credited with great foresight.* **2.** Care in providing for the future: *Spending all of your money at once shows little foresight.* —**fore′sight′ed** *adj.*

fore·skin (fôr′skĭn′) *n.* The loose fold of skin that covers the end of the penis.

for·est (fôr′ĭst *or* fŏr′ĭst) *n.* A dense growth of trees and plants covering a large area: *a vast pine forest.* —**for′es·ta′tion** *n.* [U]

fore·stall (fôr stôl′) *tr.v.* To prevent, delay, or hinder (sbdy./sthg.) by acting in advance: *The Senator ended the news conference to forestall any more questions.*

for·est·ry (fôr′ĭ strē *or* fŏr′ĭ strē) *n.* [U] The science or work of cultivating, developing, and maintaining forests.

fore·taste (fôr′tāst′) *n.* A small taste or sample of sthg. coming in the future: *Her first published story was a foretaste of later successful novels.*

fore·tell (fôr tĕl′) *tr.v.* **fore·told** (fôr tōld′), **fore·tell·ing, fore·tells.** To tell or indicate (sthg.) in advance; predict: *Can you foretell what will happen?*

fore·thought (fôr′thôt′) *n.* [U] Thought, planning, or consideration for the future; foresight: *With a little forethought, you can avoid many accidents.*

fore·told (fôr tōld′) *v.* Past tense and past participle of **foretell.**

for·ev·er (fər ĕv′ər) *adv.* **1.** For always; eternally: *No one can live forever.* **2.** At all times; without stopping or pausing: *The baby is forever fussing.* ◆ **take forever.** To require what seems to be a very long time: *The bus is taking forever to come.*

for·ev·er·more (fər ĕv′ər môr′) *adv.* Forever.

fore·warn (fôr wôrn′) *tr.v.* To warn (sbdy.) in advance: *Dark clouds forewarned them of an approaching storm.*

fore·word (fôr′wərd) *n.* A preface or an introductory note, as for a book.

for·feit (fôr′fĭt) *n.* [C; U] Something lost or taken away as a punishment or a penalty: *Our last two games were forfeits because we had too few players.* —*tr.v.* To lose or give up the right to (sthg.) as a penalty or punishment for a crime, an error, or an offense: *By failing to*

come to the ballpark on time, the opposing team forfeited the game.

for·fei·ture (fôr′fĭ chŏŏr′ *or* fôr′fĭ chər) *n.* [U] *Formal.* The act of giving up sthg. as a forfeit: *To avoid forfeiture of the car, make your payments on time.*

for·gave (fər gāv′ *or* fôr gāv′) *v.* Past tense of **forgive.**

forge[1] (fôrj) *n.* A furnace or hearth where metal is heated so that it can be hammered into shape. —*tr.v.* **forged, forg·ing, forg·es. 1.** To form (metal, for example) by heating in a forge and hammering into shape: *A blacksmith forges iron.* **2.** To form or build (sthg.), especially with careful effort: *The coach forged a close relationship with his players.* **3.** To reproduce or copy (sthg.) for dishonest purposes; counterfeit: *forge a signature on a document.* —**forg′er** *n.*

forge[2] (fôrj) *intr.v.* **forged, forg·ing, forg·es. 1.** To move forward gradually but steadily: *The explorers forged through the swamp.* **2.** To advance with increase in speed: *The runner forged into first place at the finish line.* ◆ **forge ahead.** *intr.v.* To make progress in spite of difficulties: *We decided to forge ahead with the plans even though our advisers disagreed.*

for·ger·y (fôr′jə rē) *n., pl.* **for·ger·ies. 1.** [U] The act of forging, especially the illegal production of sthg. fake that is presented as real: *the forgery of a painting.* **2.** [C] Something counterfeit, forged, or fraudulent: *All of those stock certificates are forgeries.*

for·get (fər gĕt′ *or* fôr gĕt′) *tr.v.* **for·got** (fər gŏt′ *or* fôr gŏt′), **for·got·ten** (fər gŏt′n *or* fôr gŏt′n) *or* **for·got, for·get·ting, for·gets. 1.** To be unable to remember (sthg.): *I forget the telephone number. He completely forgot his lines in the play.* **2.** To pay no attention to or neglect (sthg.); fail to do or mention: *I forgot to give you the message.* **3.** To fail to bring (sthg.) by mistake: *I forgot my toothbrush.* ◆ **forget about.** *tr.v.* [insep.] To decide not to do (sthg.): *He decided to forget about the party.* **forget it.** *Informal.* **1.** To stop worrying about sthg.: *She apologized for her mistake, and I told her to forget it.* **2.** To put sthg. impossible out of one's mind: *If you think I'm going to pay your way, you can forget it.* **forget oneself.** To lose one's reserve, temper, or self-restraint: *The students touring the White House forgot themselves and ran to shake the President's hand.* **I forget.** *Informal.* I have forgotten: *I bought this shirt last week, but I forget how much it cost.* —**for·get′ta·ble** *adj.*

for·get·ful (fər gĕt′fəl *or* fôr gĕt′fəl) *adj.* **1.** Often forgetting things: *When I am sleepy, I can be forgetful.* **2.** Neglectful; thoughtless: *forgetful of one's responsibilities.* —**for·get′ful·ly** *adv.* —**for·get′ful·ness** *n.* [U]

F

for·giv·a·ble (fər gĭv′ə bəl *or* fôr gĭv′ə bəl) *adj.* Referring to sthg. that can be forgiven: *a forgivable loan; What he did was not forgivable.*

for·give (fər gĭv′ *or* fôr gĭv′) *v.* **for·gave** (fər gāv′ *or* fôr gāv′), **for·giv·en** (fər-gĭv′ən *or* fôr gĭv′ən), **for·giv·ing, for·gives.** —*tr.* **1.** To excuse (sbdy.) for a fault or an offense; pardon: *Our friends forgave us for making them late.* **2.** To free (sbdy.) from the requirement to repay (a debt, for example). —*intr.* To grant forgiveness: *A parent usually forgives easily.*

SYNONYMS: forgive, pardon, excuse, condone. These verbs mean to decide not to punish an offender. **Forgive** means to grant pardon without resentment: *He forgave you because he knew you didn't mean what you said.* **Excuse** and **pardon** both mean to forgive by agreeing to forget a mistake or bad manners: *Please excuse the child for her bad manners. Pardon me for interrupting.* **Pardon** also means to free from a penalty: *After the revolution all political prisoners were pardoned.* **Condone** means to excuse an offense, usually a serious one: *I cannot condone such horrible behavior by ignoring it.*

---

for·give·ness (fər gĭv′nĭs *or* fôr gĭv′nĭs) *n.* [U] The act of forgiving; pardon: *She asked for her mother's forgiveness.*

for·giv·ing (fər gĭv′ĭng *or* fôr gĭv′ĭng) *adj.* Inclined or able to forgive: *a kind, forgiving person.*

for·go (fôr gō′) *tr.v.* **for·went** (fôr-wĕnt′), **for·gone** (fôr gôn′ *or* fôr gŏn′), **for·go·ing, for·goes.** To give up (sthg.); do without: *I will forgo the trip to the beach and finish my work instead.*

for·got (fər gŏt′ *or* fôr gŏt′) *v.* Past tense and a past participle of **forget.**

for·got·ten (fər gŏt′n *or* fôr gŏt′n) *v.* A past participle of **forget.**

fork (fôrk) *n.* **1.** A utensil with two or more prongs, used to serve or eat food. **2.** A large farm tool of similar shape, used to pick up hay or dig up ground. **3.a.** A separation into two or more branches, as of a stream or road: *a sign at the fork in the road.* **b.** One of the branches of such a separation: *the right fork of the road.* —*intr.v.* To divide into two or more branches: *The road forks beyond the hill.* ♦ **fork out** or **over.** *tr.v.* [sep.] *Informal.* To pay (money demanded): *His boss forked over the money to cover the dinner expenses.*

forked (fôrkt *or* fôr′kĭd) *adj.* Having a fork or forks; divided: *a forked river; a snake's forked tongue.*

fork·lift (fôrk′lĭft′) *n.* A small vehicle with a pair of prongs in front that can be slid under a load to lift and move it: *a forklift for moving boxes from trucks into the warehouse.*

forklift

for·lorn (fər lôrn′ *or* fôr lôrn′) *adj.* Appearing sad or lonely because of being abandoned: *a forlorn puppy.* —**for·lorn′ly** *adv.*

form (fôrm) *n.* **1.** [C] The shape and structure of an object: *the form of a snowflake.* **2.** [U] The body or outward appearance of a person or an animal; the figure: *a statue of the human form.* **3.** [U] The manner in which a thing exists, acts, or shows itself: *Our negotiations took the form of private talks. I arranged my ideas in outline form.* **4.** [C] A document with blanks that are to be filled in: *The patient's condition is recorded on a medical form. Did you fill out the form?* **5.** [U] Fitness or condition of mind or body: *The athlete is in top form this season.* **6.** [C] One of the ways a word may be spelled or pronounced: *Feet is the plural form of foot.* **7.** [U] Behavior according to an accepted standard: *It is not good form to talk during a movie.* —*v.* —*tr.* **1.** To give form to (sthg.); shape: *form clay into figures.* **2.** To develop (sthg.) in the mind: *form an opinion.* **3.** To organize or arrange (sthg.): *form a students' committee.* **4.** To develop or acquire (sthg.): *form a bad habit.* **5.** To produce (a tense, for example) by adding certain elements: *form a plural by adding an s to the singular.* —*intr.* To come into being by taking form: *Ice forms on the lake in winter.*

for·mal (fôr′məl) *adj.* **1.** Structured according to rules or conventions: *He had little formal education. They held a formal meeting.* **2.** Executed, carried out, or done in proper or regular form: *a formal document.* **3.** Marked by stiff attention to ceremony: *His formal manner makes him seem unfriendly.* —*n.* Something, such as a long dress or a social affair, that is formal in nature: *She bought a formal for her junior prom.* —**for′mal·ly** *adv.*

for·mal·de·hyde (fôr măl′də hīd′) *n.* [U] A colorless gas with the formula CH_2O. It is used in making plastics and in solution as a preservative for biological specimens and as a disinfectant.

for·mal·i·ty (fôr măl′ĭ tē) *n., pl.* **for·mal·i·ties. 1.** [U] Strict observance of accepted rules, or customs: *There was no formality at our dinner table.* **2.** [C; U] An established

---

rule or custom, especially one followed even though it has no practical importance: *the legal formalities of a trial.*

for·mal·ize (fôr′mə līz′) *tr.v.* **for·mal·ized, for·mal·iz·ing, for·mal·iz·es. 1.** To give a definite form or shape to (sthg.): *formalize the style of a book report.* **2.** To make (sthg.) formal or official: *They formalized the treaty by signing it.*

for·mat (fôr′măt′) *n.* **1.** A plan for the organization or arrangement of sthg.: *The format of the new television program was a series of interviews.* **2.** The form or layout of a publication or computer document: *the format of a newspaper.* —*tr.v.* **for·mat·ted, for·mat·ting, for·mats. 1.** To plan or arrange (sthg.) in a specified form: *format a conference.* **2.** To divide (a computer disk) into sectors so that it will store data: *You need to format the disk before you can use it.*

for·ma·tion (fôr mā′shən) *n.* **1.** [U] The act of forming sthg. or of taking form: *the formation of political parties.* **2.** [C] Something formed: *a cloud formation.* **3.** [C] A specified arrangement: *The geese flew overhead in a V formation.*

form·a·tive (fôr′mə tǐv) *adj.* **1.** Forming or capable of forming: *Childhood experiences often have a formative influence on writers.* **2.** Relating to growth or development: *The growth of industry marked a formative period in U.S. history.*

for·mer (fôr′mər) *adj.* **1.** Relating to or taking place in the past: *the tools of former civilizations; our former president.* **2.** Coming before in place or order: *the former part of the book.* **3.** Being the first of two people or things mentioned: *Of the two plans, I prefer the former rather than the latter.*

for·mer·ly (fôr′mər lē) *adv.* At an earlier time; once: *Machines do work formerly done by people.*

for·mi·da·ble (fôr′mǐ də bəl) *adj.* **1.** Causing fear or alarm: *the formidable prospect of major surgery.* **2.** Inspiring respect or admiration: *a formidable musical talent.* **3.** Difficult to do, accomplish, or defeat: *a formidable challenge.* —**for′mi·da·bly** *adv.*

form·less (fôrm′lǐs) *adj.* Having no definite form; shapeless: *a formless mist.* —**form′less·ly** *adv.* —**form′less·ness** *n.* [U]

for·mu·la (fôr′myə lə) *n., pl.* **for·mu·as** or **for·mu·lae** (fôr′myə lē′). **1.** [C] A method of doing or treating sthg. that uses a set, accepted model or approach: *A balanced diet is part of the formula for healthy living.* **2.** [C] A set of symbols showing the composition of a chemical compound: H_2O *is the formula for water.* **3.** [C] A set of symbols in mathematics that expresses a rule or principle. For example, the formula for the area of a rectangle is $a = lw$, where a *is the area,* l *the length, and* w *the width.* **4.** [C] A list of the

ingredients and processes used in making sthg.; a recipe: *the formula for making toothpaste.* **5.** [C; U] A liquid food for infants, containing many of the nutrients in human milk: *She gave the baby his formula in a bottle.* —**for′mu·la′ic** (fôr′myə lā′ǐk) *adj.*

for·mu·late (fôr′myə lāt′) *tr.v.* **for·mu·lat·ed, for·mu·lat·ing, for·mu·lates.** To express (sthg.) in or as if in a formula; plan in an orderly way: *formulate a process; formulate an idea.* —**for′mu·la′tion** *n.* [C; U]

for·sake (fôr sāk′) *tr.v.* **for·sook** (fôr sŏŏk′), **for·sak·en** (fôr sā′kən), **for·sak·ing, for·sakes.** *Formal.* **1.** To give up (sthg. formerly loved or valued): *forsaking cigarettes.* **2.** To leave (sbdy./sthg.) completely; abandon: *Do not forsake us when we need help.*

for·swear (fôr swâr′) *tr.v.* **for·swore** (fôr-swôr′), **for·sworn** (fôr swôrn′), **for·swear·ing, for·swears.** *Formal.* **1.** To renounce (sthg.) seriously: *We forswore all junk food.* **2.** To disavow (sthg.) under oath; deny.

fort (fôrt) *n.* A fortified place or position used for military purposes.

HOMONYMS: fort, forte (strong point).

forte (fôrt *or* fôr′tā′) *n.* Something in which a person excels; a strong point: *Jazz was the trumpet player's forte.*

forth (fôrth) *adv. Formal.* **1.** Forward in time, place, or order: *from this time forth.* **2.** Out into view: *After the movie the audience poured forth from the theater.*

HOMONYMS: forth, fourth (number).

forth·com·ing (fôrth kŭm′ǐng) *adj. Formal.* **1.** Soon to appear or take place; approaching: *The authors gave an interview about their forthcoming book.* **2.** Available when required or as promised: *More funds were not forthcoming.* **3.** Willing to speak openly and cooperate: *The Senator was not forthcoming about his future plans.*

forth·right (fôrth′rīt′) *adj.* Direct and honest; straightforward: *She gave a forthright answer to my question.*

for·ti·fi·ca·tion (fôr′tə fǐ kā′shən) *n.* **1.** [U] The act of fortifying: *the fortification of the city against enemy invaders.* **2.** [C] Something that fortifies or defends, especially military works constructed to protect a position or place.

for·ti·fy (fôr′tə fī′) *v.* **for·ti·fied, for·ti·fy·ing, for·ti·fies.** —*tr.* **1.** To strengthen and secure (a position) with fortifications: *The soldiers fortified the position.* **2.** To make (oneself) feel stronger physically: *The hikers fortified themselves with a hearty breakfast.* **3.** To strengthen or improve (food, for example), as by adding vitamins; enrich:

Bread and milk are often fortified. —*intr.* To build fortifications: *fortify against intrusion.*

for·ti·tude (fôr′tĭ tōōd′) *n.* [U] Strength of mind that allows one to deal with pain or difficulties with courage: *He endured the long recovery from illness with fortitude and determination.*

for·tress (fôr′trĭs) *n.* A fortified place, especially a large military stronghold.

for·tu·i·tous (fôr tōō′ĭ təs) *adj.* **1.** Happening by chance; unplanned: *a fortuitous meeting with an old friend.* **2.** Lucky; fortunate: *A fortuitous change in the weather made the picnic possible.* —**for·tu′i·tous·ly** *adv.* —**for·tu′i·tous·ness** *n.* [U]

for·tu·nate (fôr′chə nĭt) *adj.* **1.** Bringing sthg. good and unexpected: *Coming home from the party early turned out to be a fortunate decision.* **2.** Having good fortune; lucky: *I am fortunate in having good friends.* —**for′tu·nate·ly** *adv.*

for·tune (fôr′chən) *n.* **1.** [U] The chance happening of favorable or unfavorable events; chance: *I had the good fortune to meet interesting people during my visit.* **2.** [C] Very large amounts of material possessions or wealth; riches: *make a fortune playing the stock market.* **3.** [C] The course of one's future; fate: *told fortunes at the fair.*

for·tune·tell·er (fôr′chən tĕl′ ər) *n.* A person who predicts future events. —**for′tune·tell′ing** *n.* [U]

for·ty (fôr′tē) *n., pl.* **for·ties. 1.** The number, written 40, that is equal to 4 × 10. **2. forties. a.** Often **Forties.** The ten years from 40 to 49 in a century: *the U.S. effort in World War II in the Forties.* **b.** A decade or the numbers from 40 to 49: *They stopped smoking in their forties.* —**for′ty** *adj. & pron.*

fo·rum (fôr′əm) *n.* **1.a.** [*on*] A public meeting or presentation involving a discussion: *a forum on the environment.* **b.** [*for*] A medium of open discussion or voicing of ideas, such as a newspaper or a radio or television program: *the best forum for such a debate.* **2.** The public square of an ancient Roman city.

for·ward (fôr′wərd) *adj.* **1.** At, near, or belonging to the front of sthg.: *the forward section of an airplane.* **2.** Going or moving toward the front: *a bad forward fall.* **3.a.** Prompt; eager: *a forward student wanting to answer every question.* **b.** Too aggressive; bold: *I resented the clerk's forward manner in suggesting what I needed.* **4.** Being ahead of current economic, political, or technological trends; progressive: *forward ideas about recycling.* —*adv.* **1.** In the direction of the front: *All volunteers please step forward.* **2.** In or toward the future: *set the clock forward.* —*n.* A player in certain sports, such as bas-

ketball or soccer, who is part of the front line of offense. —*tr.v.* **1.** To send (mail) on to a further destination or address: *The post office will forward letters to a new address.* **2.** To promote or advance (sthg.): *She always forwards her own interests.* —**for′ward·ly** *adv.* —**for′ward·ness** *n.* [U]

for·wards (fôr′wərdz) *adv.* In the direction of the front; forward: *passengers facing forwards.*

for·went (fôr wĕnt′) *v.* Past tense of **forgo.**

fos·sil (fŏs′əl) *n.* **1.** Something left of or by a plant or an animal that lived long ago: *dinosaur fossils found in layers of rock.* **2.** *Informal.* A person or thing that is seen as old-fashioned or outdated: *In the computer age, typewriters are fossils.*

fossil

fossil fuel *n.* [C; U] A fossil material that burns, such as coal, petroleum, or natural gas.

fos·sil·ize (fŏs′ə līz′) *tr. & intr.v.* **fos·sil·ized, fos·sil·iz·ing, fos·sil·iz·es.** To change into or become a fossil: *The shells of many prehistoric sea animals have fossilized in layers of rock.* —**fos′sil·i·za′tion** (fŏs′ə lĭ zā′shən) *n.* [U]

fos·ter (fô′stər *or* fŏs′tər) *tr.v.* To help (sthg.) to grow or develop: *The teacher fostered the students' interest in writing.* —*adj.* Giving parental care to or receiving it from sbdy. not legally related: *a foster child; a foster parent.*

fought (fôt) *v.* Past tense and past participle of **fight.**

foul (foul) *adj.* **1.** Offensive or unpleasant to the taste or smell: *the foul flavor of spoiled food; a foul smell of automobile exhaust.* **2.** Morally offensive; wicked: *foul rumors.* **3.** Bad or unfavorable: *foul weather.* **4.** Of a vulgar or obscene nature: *foul language.* **5.** In sports, against the rules of a game: *A foul blow in boxing is one below the waist.* —*n.* In sports, a violation of the rules of play: *a foul in a game of basketball.* —*adv.* In a foul manner: *Don't play foul with me.* —*v.* —*tr.* **1.** To make (sthg.) dirty or foul: *Factory smoke fouls the air.* **2.** To block (sthg.) by filling: *Leaves fouled the drainpipe.* **3.** To entangle or catch (a rope, for example): *The dog fouled its leash in trying to get at the cat.* **4.** In sports, to commit a foul against (another player).* —*intr.* **1.** To become foul: *All the meat in our freezer fouled when the electrici-*

ty went off. **2.** In sports, to commit a foul. **3.** To become entangled or twisted: *The anchor line fouled on a rock.* ◆ **foul out.** *intr.v.* In sports, to be put out of a game for making too many fouls: *He fouled out in the first half of the game.* **foul up.** *intr.v. Informal.* To make a mistake: *I'm sorry I fouled up.* —*tr.v.* [sep.] To cause a seriouus problem in (sthg.) because of mistakes or poor judgment: *I fouled up the recipe by adding too much milk.*

HOMONYMS: foul, fowl (bird).

foul play *n.* [U] Unfair or treacherous action, especially when involving violence: *a victim of foul play.*

foul-up (**foul′**ŭp′) *n. Informal.* **1.** A mistake caused by poor judgment: *Her life is one foul-up after another.* **2.** A mechanical failure: *a computer foul-up.*

found[1] (found) *tr.v.* **1.** To create or establish (sthg.); set up: *founded the college in 1871.* See Synonyms at **establish. 2.** To establish the foundation or basis of (sthg.): *The report was founded on concrete facts.*

found[2] (found) *v.* Past tense and past participle of **find.**

foun•da•tion (foun dā′shən) *n.* **1.** [U] The act of founding or establishing: *the foundation of a research program.* **2.** [C] The basis on which sthg. stands, is founded, or is supported: *the foundations of modern science; the foundation of a building.* **3.** [C] An institution that is founded and supported by an endowment.

foun•der[1] (foun′dər) *intr.v.* **1.** To sink below the water: *Several ships foundered in the storm.* **2.** To collapse or fall apart: *The building foundered in the earthquake.* **3.** To fail: *Their business foundered.*

found•er[2] (foun′dər) *n.* A person who founds or helps to establish sthg.: *the founders of the school.*

Found•ing Father (foun′dĭng) *n.* A member of the convention that drafted the U.S. Constitution in 1787.

found•ling (found′lĭng) *n.* A deserted or abandoned child whose parents are not known.

foun•dry (foun′drē) *n., pl.* **foun•dries.** A place in which metals are melted and shaped.

foun•tain (foun′tən) *n.* **1.** A structure, often decorative, from which a jet or stream of water rises and flows: *the beautiful fountains of Rome; a drinking fountain.* **2.** A point of origin; a source, as of information: *The zookeeper was a fountain of knowledge about animals.*

fountain pen *n.* A pen with a container of ink inside that feeds the writing point.

four (fôr) *n.* **1.** The number, written 4, that is equal to 3 + 1. **2.** The fourth in a set or sequence. ◆ **all fours.** All four limbs of an animal or a person: *Babies crawl around on all fours.*

HOMONYMS: four, for (with the purpose of), **fore** (front part).

four-let•ter word (fôr′lĕt′ər) *n.* Any of several short English words with four letters, generally considered offensive or obscene: *an R-rated movie full of four-letter words.*

401(K) plan (fôr′ō wŭn′kā′) *n.* A retirement plan offered by some businesses, allowing an employee to have part of his or her pretax pay withheld and invested.

four•score (fôr′skôr′) *adj. Formal.* Four times twenty; eighty.

four•some (fôr′səm) *n.* **1.** A group of four persons or things: *We organized a foursome to play cards every week.* **2.** A game, especially a golf match, played by four persons, two on each side.

four•teen (fôr tēn′) *n.* **1.** The number, written 14, that is equal to 13 + 1. **2.** The 14th in a set or sequence. —**four•teen′** *adj. & pron.*

fourth (fôrth) *n.* **1.** [C] The ordinal number matching the number four in a series. **2.** [C] One of four equal parts: *a fourth of a pie.* **3.** [U] The transmission gear used to produce speeds next higher to those of third in a motor vehicle. **4. the Fourth.** The Fourth of July; Independence Day: *We spent the Fourth at the beach.* —**fourth** *adv. & adj.*

HOMONYMS: fourth, forth (forward).

Fourth of July *n.* Independence Day.

four-wheel drive (fôr′wēl′) *n.* [U] An automotive drive system in which mechanical power is transmitted from the drive shaft to all four wheels.

fowl (foul) *n., pl.* **fowl. 1.** A bird, such as a chicken, duck, or turkey, that is raised or hunted for food. **2.** The meat of any of these birds used as food.

HOMONYMS: fowl, foul (rotten).

fox (fŏks) *n.* **1.** [C] A meat-eating mammal related to the dog and the wolf with a long bushy tail. **2.** [U] The fur of this mammal. **3.** [C] A crafty, clever, or sly person, usually referring to a man: *The old fox fooled everyone.* **4.** [C] *Informal.* An attractive person, usually referring to a woman.

fox•y (fŏk′sē) *adj.* **fox•i•er, fox•i•est. 1.** Slyly clever; smart and tricky: *Bureaucracy often forces people to become quite foxy in their efforts to deal with it.* **2.** *Slang.* Sexually attractive: *a foxy woman.* —**fox′i•ly** *adv.* —**fox′i•ness** *n.* [U]

foy•er (foi′ər *or* foi′ā′) *n.* **1.** A lobby or an anteroom, as of a theater or hotel. **2.** An entrance hall, as of a private house or an apartment.

fr. *abbr.* An abbreviation of: **1.** Franc. **2.** From.

Fr. *abbr.* An abbreviation of: **1.** France. **2.** French. **3.** Friday.

fra·cas (frā′kəs *or* frăk′əs) *n. Informal.* A noisy disturbance: *What a fracas our neighbors caused last night!*

frac·tion (frăk′shən) *n.* **1.** A number that compares part of sthg. with the whole, especially the result of dividing two whole numbers, and written in the form %: *The fraction ½ can represent 10 pencils out of a box of 20, or 50 cents out of a dollar.* **2.** A part or bit of sthg.: *A fraction of the people voted.*

frac·tion·al (frăk′shə nəl) *adj.* **1.** Of, relating to, or composed of a fraction or fractions. **2.** Very small; of no importance: *a fractional share of the vote.* —**frac′tion·al·ly** *adv.*

frac·tious (frăk′shəs) *adj.* **1.** Causing trouble: *a fractious worker.* **2.** Cross; easily upset; cranky: *a fractious child.* —**frac′tious·ly** *adv.* —**frac′tious·ness** *n.* [U]

frac·ture (frăk′chər) *n.* **1.** [U] The act of breaking: *enough pressure to cause the fracture of solid rock.* **2.** [C] A break or crack, as in bone: *The fracture in her jaw healed slowly.* —*tr. & intr.v.* **frac·tured, frac·tur·ing, frac·tures.** To break or cause to break: *I fractured my arm in the fall. The foundation of the building fractured in the earthquake.*

frag·ile (frăj′əl *or* frăj′īl′) *adj.* **1.** Easily damaged or broken; frail: *a fragile glass vase.* **2.** Without physical or emotional strength; delicate: *The illness has left him in a fragile condition.* —**frag′ile·ly** *adv.* —**fra·gil′i·ty** (frə jĭl′ĭ tē) *n.* [U]

frag·ment (frăg′mənt) *n.* **1.** A small part broken off from a whole: *a fragment of a shattered china plate.* **2.** An incomplete or isolated part; a bit: *We could overhear fragments of their conversation.* —*tr. & intr.v.* (frăg′mĕnt′). To break or become broken into fragments: *An explosion had fragmented the sinking ship. After the election, the committee fragmented.*

frag·men·tar·y (frăg′mən tĕr′ē) *adj.* Consisting of small disconnected parts: *We could read only fragmentary sentences of the damaged document.*

frag·men·ta·tion (frăg′mən tā′shən) *n.* [U] The act of fragmenting or breaking into pieces: *A tremendous volcanic explosion caused the fragmentation of enormous rocks.*

fra·grance (frā′grəns) *n.* [C; U] A sweet or pleasant odor; a scent: *the fresh fragrance of pine.* —**fra′grant** *adj.* —**fra′grant·ly** *adv.*

frail (frāl) *adj.* Physically weak; not strong: *frail health.* —**frail′ness** *n.* [U]

frail·ty (frāl′tē) *n., pl.* **frail·ties.** **1.** [U] The quality or condition of being frail; weakness: *physical frailty.* **2.** [C] A fault coming from human weakness; a failing: *Envy and greed are common human frailties.*

frame (frām) *tr.v.* **framed, fram·ing, frames.** **1.** To build (sthg.) by putting together structural parts: *frame an agreement; frame a house.* **2.** To enclose (sthg.) in a frame: *frame a picture.* **3.** *Informal.* To invent evidence to make (sbdy.) appear to be guilty: *The witness was paid to frame an innocent person for the crime.* —*n.* **1.a.** A structure that shapes or supports sthg.: *the frame of a car.* **b.** An open structure or rim used to hold or border sthg.: *a door frame; a picture frame.* **c.** The structure of a human or animal body: *his tall frame.* **2.** A single picture on a roll of film. ♦ **frame of mind.** An attitude or mood at a certain point in time: *He's in no frame of mind to listen to anyone's suggestions.* **frame of reference.** A set of ideas that serve as the basis for understanding new information: *We study history because it gives us a frame of reference for interpreting current events.* —**fram′er** *n.*

frame-up (frām′ŭp′) *n. Informal.* A plot to make an innocent person seem guilty of a crime: *The accountant didn't steal the money; it was a frame-up to protect the owner of the company.*

frame·work (frām′wûrk′) *n.* **1.** A structure that shapes or supports sthg.; a frame: *The building was constructed on a framework of steel girders.* **2.** A fundamental structure, as for a written work or a system of ideas: *Education is the framework on which to build a productive life.*

franc (frăngk) *n.* The basic monetary unit of Belgium, France, Mali, Niger, Switzerland, and many other countries.

HOMONYMS: franc, frank (sincere, frankfurter).

fran·chise (frăn′chīz′) *n.* Permission given to a person or group to sell a product within a district or to serve a territory: *They have the local franchise for that restaurant.* —**fran·chis′ee′, fran′chis′er** *n.*

frank¹ (frăngk) *adj.* Open and sincere in expression; straightforward: *The boss made several frank remarks about the quality of their work.* —**frank′ness** *n.* [U]

HOMONYMS: frank (sincere, frankfurter), **franc** (money).

frank² (frăngk) *n. Informal.* A frankfurter: *franks and beans.*

frank·furt·er (frăngk′fər tər) *n.* A smoked sausage of beef or beef combined with other meats.

frank·in·cense (frăng′kĭn sĕns′) *n.* [U] A tree gum with a pleasant spicy odor, burned as incense.

ă–cat; ā–pay; âr–care; ä–father; ĕ–get; ē–be; ĭ–sit; ī–nice; îr–here; ŏ–got; ō–go; ô–saw; oi–boy; ou–out; ŏŏ–took; ōō–boot; ŭ–cut; ûr–word; th–thin; *th*–this; hw–when; zh–vision; ə–about; N–French bon

frank•ly (frăngk′lē) *adv.* **1.** In a frank manner; candidly: *Speaking frankly, the manager warned the employees about the decrease in sales.* **2.** Honestly; in truth: *Frankly, I don't know.*

fran•tic (frăn′tĭk) *adj.* Very excited with fear or anxiety; desperate: *frantic with worry.* —**fran′ti•cal•ly** *adv.*

frat (frăt) *n. Informal.* A college fraternity.

fra•ter•nal (frə tûr′nəl) *adj.* **1.** Relating to brothers: *a close fraternal tie.* **2.** Consisting of a fraternity: *The Masons are a fraternal society.* **3.** Relating to twins that develop from separately fertilized egg cells, have distinct hereditary characteristics, and can be of different sexes: *fraternal twins.* —**fra•ter′nal•ly** *adv.*

fra•ter•ni•ty (frə tûr′nĭ tē) *n., pl.* **fra•ter•ni•ties.** **1.** [C] A social organization of male college or university students. **2.** [C] A group of people with similar interests, backgrounds, or occupations: *the local business fraternity; the medical fraternity.* **3.** [U] The quality or condition of being brothers: *A sense of fraternity often develops among members of a team.*

frat•er•nize (frăt′ər nīz′) *intr.v.* **frat•er•nized, frat•er•niz•ing, frat•er•niz•es.** **1.** To associate with others in a friendly way: *Teachers and students fraternize in the cafeteria.* **2.** To associate on friendly terms with the people of an enemy or opposing group: *People who fraternized with the enemy were severely punished after the war.* —**frat′er•ni•za′tion** (frăt′ ər nĭ zā′shən) *n.* [U]

frat•ri•cide (frăt′rĭ sīd′) *n.* [U] The killing of one's brother or sister.

fraud (frôd) *n.* **1.** [U] Dishonesty practiced in order to make unfair or unlawful gains: *A government agency protects consumers against fraud.* **2.** [C] An incidence of trickery; a trick: *He claims that the vote was a fraud.* **3.** [C] A person who practices deception and trickery; an impostor or a swindler: *The professor turned out to be a fraud who had put his name on someone else's work.*

fraud•u•lent (frô′jə lənt) *adj.* Gained by or engaging in fraud; dishonest: *a fraudulent scheme; a fraudulent merchant.* —**fraud′u•lence** *n.* [U] —**fraud′u•lent•ly** *adv.*

fraught (frôt) *adj.* [*with*] *Formal.* Filled with a specified element; charged: *fraught with danger; Every moment is fraught with significance.*

fray[1] (frā) *n.* ◆ **the fray.** A quarrel or fight: *Several people who had been watching joined the fray.*

fray[2] (frā) *v.* —*tr.* **1.** To wear away (the edges of fabric, for example) by rubbing: *Wearing and washing the shirt every day soon frayed the collar.* **2.** To strain (sthg.); irritate: *The constant noise of traffic frayed the driver's nerves.* —*intr.* To become worn away along the edges: *The rope frayed and then broke.*

fraz•zle (frăz′əl) *Informal. tr.v.* **fraz•zled, fraz•zling, fraz•zles.** **1.** To wear (sthg.) away along the edges; fray: *Repeated rubbing frazzled the rope.* **2.** To exhaust (sbdy.) physically or emotionally: *frazzled by hard work and pressure.* —*n. (usually singular).* A condition of physical or emotional exhaustion: *The long day wore us to a frazzle.*

freak (frēk) *n.* **1.** A thing or an event that is unusual or irregular: *The summer snowstorm was a freak of nature.* **2.** A sometimes offensive term for an organism, especially a person or an animal, that develops in an abnormal way: *Two-headed calves are freaks.* **3.** *Slang.* A person who is very enthusiastic about sthg.: *a movie freak; a running freak.* —*v.* ◆ **freak out.** *Slang. intr.v.* To behave uncontrollably suddenly: *She'll freak out when she hears he's in the hospital.* —*tr.v.* [*sep.*] To cause (sbdy.) to become greatly upset or frightened: *The special effects in the horror movie really freaked me out.*

freak•ish (frē′kĭsh) *adj.* Markedly abnormal or unusual; strange: *freakish warm weather in winter.* —**freak′ish•ly** *adv.* —**freak′ish•ness** *n.* [U]

freck•le (frĕk′əl) *n.* A small spot of dark pigment in the skin, often caused by exposure to the sun. —*tr. & intr.v.* **freck•led, freck•ling, freck•les.** To mark or become marked with freckles or spots of color: *She has red hair and she freckles easily in the sun.* —**freck′led** *adj.*

free (frē) *adj.* **fre•er, fre•est.** **1.** At liberty; not imprisoned or enslaved: *The political prisoner will soon be free.* **2.a.** Having political independence: *a free country.* **b.** Not under limits forced by a government: *a free press.* **3.** Not affected, troubled, or burdened: *free from worry; Medicine is free of sales tax.* **4.** Costing nothing; given without charge: *a free meal.* **5.** Not busy or used: *free space; a free hour at lunchtime.* **6.** Unguarded in expression or manner; frank: *too free with her opinions.* **7.** Liberal or generous: *very free with the inherited money.* **8.** In chemistry, not combined with sthg. else: *Oxygen exists free in air.* **9.** Not literal or exact: *a free translation.* —*adv.* **1.** In a free manner; without restraint: *The rope swung free.* **2.** Without charge: *We were admitted free to the museum.* —*tr.v.* **freed, free•ing, frees.** **1.** To set (sbdy./sthg.) at liberty: *The convict was freed from prison.* **2.** To relieve (sbdy./sthg.) of a burden, an obligation, or a restraint: *Vacation frees us from daily jobs for a short time.* **3.** To unfasten or untangle (sbdy./sthg.); detach: *We freed the rope caught on a nail.* ◆ **for free.** *Informal.* Without charge: *I used a special coupon to get tickets for free.* **free up.** *tr.v.* [*sep.*] *Informal.* To make (sbdy./sthg.) available: *She freed up some time in her busy schedule to help us.* —**free′ly** *adv.*

F

free•dom (frē′dəm) *n.* **1.** [U] The condition of being free from restraints: *freedom of speech.* **2.** [U] Liberty of a person from slavery, confinement, or oppression. **3.** [C; U] The capacity to make choices; free will: *the freedom to do what we want.* **4.** [C; U] Frankness or boldness; lack of reserve: *a casual freedom in their manner.* **5.** [U] The use of or access to sthg.: *Investigators were given the freedom of the files.*

free enterprise *n.* [U] The freedom of private businesses to compete for profit with little government regulation.

free fall *n.* [U] The fall of sthg. toward the earth without any force keeping it back other than the drag produced by the atmosphere.

free-for-all (frē′fər ôl′) *n.* A disorderly quarrel, fight, or competition that anyone can join: *What began as a friendly argument turned into a violent free-for-all.*

free•hand (frē′hănd′) *adj.* Drawn by hand without the aid of tracing or drafting tools: *She showed us a freehand plan of the house.* —**free′hand′** *adv.*

free•lance (frē′lăns′) *intr.v.* **free•lanced, free•lanc•ing, free•lanc•es.** To work as an artist, a writer, an editor, or another trained person who sells his or her services to different employers as the work is needed. —*adj.* Relating to or working as a professional who freelances: *a freelance editor.* —**free′lanc′er** *n.*

free•load (frē′lōd′) *intr.v.* Slang. To make repeated use of other people's generosity with money, food, or housing: *Why does she continue to let them freeload off her?* —**free′load′er** *n.*

free•stand•ing (frē′stăn′dĭng) *adj.* Standing without support or attachment; able to stand alone: *a freestanding garage.*

free•style (frē′stīl′) *n.* [U] **1.** A competitive sports event, especially in swimming or skiing, in which any style or movement may be used by the competitor. **2.** A swimming stroke that combines overarm strokes and a rapid kick without bending the knees. —**free′style′** *adv. & adj.*

free•think•er (frē′thĭng′kər) *n.* A person who forms opinions independently and does not follow a set of traditional beliefs, especially in matters of politics and religion. —**free′think′ing** *adj. & n.* [U]

free•way (frē′wā′) *n.* A highway for high-speed travel, with several lanes: *The state is building a new freeway outside of town.*

free•wheel•ing (frē′wē′lĭng) *adj.* Free of restraints or limits; acting freely: *freewheeling television advertising campaigns.*

free will *n.* [U] The power to make one's own choices; free choice: *I decided of my own free will to join the navy.*

freeze (frēz) *v.* **froze** (frōz), **fro•zen** (frō′zən), **freez•ing, freez•es.** —*intr.* **1.** To change from a liquid to a solid by loss of heat: *Pure water freezes at a higher temperature than salt water.* **2.** To have ice form in or on sthg.: *The pond freezes early in winter. The pipes froze.* **3.** To be harmed or killed by cold or frost: *Many fruits freeze in very cold weather.* **4.** To be very cold: *We froze without sweaters.* **5.** To become motionless or unable to move: *The climber froze with fear on the slippery rocks.* **6.** To become icily silent in manner: *We froze after the harsh words.* —*tr.* **1.** To change (a liquid) into ice. **2.** To cause ice to form upon (sthg.): *The cold snap froze the river.* **3.** To preserve (food, for example) at a freezing temperature: *freeze vegetables.* **4.** To harm or kill (sthg.) by cold: *The deep cold froze the oranges.* **5.** To make (sbdy./sthg.) very cold: *The winter wind froze my fingers.* **6.** To make (sbdy./sthg.) motionless or unable to move: *Fear froze the deer in the beam of our lights.* **7.** To set (prices or wages) at a certain amount: *The company froze wages at last year's levels.* —*n.* **1.a.** The act of freezing: *a freeze on hiring.* **b.** The state of being frozen: *a price freeze.* **2.** A period of cold weather; a frost: *crops ruined by the early freeze.* ♦ **freeze out.** *tr.v.* [sep.] To shut out or exclude (sbdy./sthg.), as by cold or unfriendly treatment: *Chain stores sometimes freeze out small shops.* **freeze up.** *intr.v.* To become unable to move because of nervousness: *The actor froze up in front of the large audience.*

freeze-dry (frēz′drī′) *tr.v.* **freeze-dried, freeze-dry•ing, freeze-dries.** To preserve (food, for example) by rapid freezing and drying in a vacuum. —**freeze′-dried** *adj.*

freez•er (frē′zər) *n.* A refrigerated compartment that is kept at a very low temperature for freezing and storing food: *Put the ice cream back into the freezer.*

freez•ing (frē′zĭng) *adj.* Very cold: *It was freezing last night.*

freezing point *n.* The temperature at which liquid freezes.

freight (frāt) *n.* [U] **1.a.** Goods carried as cargo by truck, train, ship, or aircraft: *load freight on a ship.* **b.** The charge for transporting such goods: *The freight for shipping by air is very expensive.* **2.** Commercial transportation of goods: *laws regulating freight.* —*tr.v.* **1.** To transport (sthg.) commercially as cargo: *Trucks freight fruit across the country.* **2.** To load or fill (sthg.) with cargo: *ships waiting to be freighted.*

freight car *n.* A railroad car designed to carry freight.

freight•er (frā′tər) *n.* A ship or an airplane for carrying freight.

freight train *n.* A railroad train made up of freight cars.

ă–cat; ā–pay; âr–care; ä–father; ĕ–get; ē–be; ĭ–sit; ī–nice; îr–here; ŏ–got; ō–go; ô–saw; oi–boy; ou–out; ōō–took; ōō–boot; ŭ–cut; ûr–word; th–thin; *th*–this; hw–when; zh–vision; ə–about; N–French bon

French fry (frĕnch) *n. pl.* **French fries.** A thin strip of potato fried in hot oil: *a hamburger and French fries.*

French-fry (frĕnch′frī′) *tr.v.* **French-fried, French-fry·ing, French-fries.** To fry (potato strips, for example) in hot oil.

French horn *n.* A brass musical instrument with a long coiled tube ending in a wide bell.

French toast *n.* [U] Sliced bread soaked in a batter of milk and egg and lightly fried, often served for breakfast.

fre·net·ic (frə nĕt′ĭk) *adj.* Wildly active or excited; frenzied: *She worked at a frenetic pace to get the project done.* —**fre·net′i·cal·ly** *adv.*

fren·zied (frĕn′zēd) *adj.* Marked by frenzy; frantic: *a frenzied rush for the exit.* —**fren·zied·ly** *adv.*

fren·zy (frĕn′zē) *n., pl.* **fren·zies.** A state of violent agitation or wild excitement: *The frightened horses dashed about in a frenzy.*

fre·quen·cy (frē′kwən sē) *n., pl.* **fre·quen·cies. 1.** [U] Repetition at short intervals: *The frequency of the buyers' calls is proof of their interest in the property.* **2.** [U] The number of times some event occurs within a specified period: *accidents happening with increasing frequency.* **3.** [C] The number of complete cycles of a wave, such as a radio wave, that occur per second.

frequency modulation *n.* [U] A method of broadcasting in which the frequency of radio waves is varied and static is reduced.

fre·quent (frē′kwənt) *adj.* Happening or appearing quite often: *While my teeth were being fixed, I made frequent visits to the dentist.* —*tr.v.* (*also* frē **kwĕnt′**). To make frequent visits to (a place): *They frequented the museum on weekends.* —**fre′quent·ly** *adv.*

fres·co (frĕs′kō) *n., pl.* **fres·coes** *or* **fres·cos. 1.** [U] The art of painting on fresh moist plaster. **2.** [C] A painting done in this manner.

fresh (frĕsh) *adj.* **1.** Recently made, produced, or gathered; not stale or spoiled: *fresh bread; fresh fruit.* **2.** Not preserved, as by canning, smoking, or freezing: *fresh vegetables.* **3.** Not salty: *fresh water.* **4.** New to one's experience; not known before: *fresh reports from the scene of the earthquake.* **5.** Unusual or different; novel: *a fresh approach to old problems.* **6.** Not yet used or soiled; clean: *fresh paper towels.* **7.** Bright and clear; not dull or faded: *recent experiences that are fresh in one's memory.* **8.** Not tired; refreshed; rested: *I felt fresh after a short nap.* **9.** *Informal.* Bold; impudent: *a fresh child.* —**fresh′ly** *adv.* —**fresh′ness** *n.* [U]

fresh·en (frĕsh′ən) *tr.v.* To make (sthg.) fresh: *Rain freshened the air.* ◆ **freshen (oneself) up.** *tr. & intr.v.* To make (oneself) look better by washing or by changing one's clothes, makeup, or hair: *I'm going upstairs to freshen up before dinner.*

fresh·man (frĕsh′mən) *n.* A student in the first-year class of a high school, university, or college.

fresh·wa·ter (frĕsh′wô′tər *or* frĕsh′wŏt′ər) *adj.* Relating to or living in water that is not salty: *freshwater fish; a freshwater pond.*

fret[1] (frĕt) *intr.v.* **fret·ted, fret·ting, frets.** To be uneasy, troubled, or worried: *The director fretted over each detail.* —*n.* The act or an instance of fretting: *in a fret about money.*

fret[2] (frĕt) *n.* One of several ridges on the neck of a stringed instrument, such as a guitar. —**fret′ted** *adj.*

fret·ful (frĕt′fəl) *adj.* Feeling or showing worry and distress; troubled: *The fever made the baby fretful.* —**fret′ful·ly** *adv.* —**fret′ful·ness** *n.* [U]

Fri. *abbr.* An abbreviation of Friday.

fri·ar (frī′ər) *n.* A man who is a member of certain Roman Catholic orders.

HOMONYMS: friar, fryer (young chicken).

---

fric·tion (frĭk′shən) *n.* [U] **1.** The rubbing of one object or surface against another: *Friction of flint and steel can produce sparks.* **2.** The force that resists motion between two objects in contact: *By oiling the wheels, we reduced the friction.* **3.** Conflict between people who have different opinions or beliefs: *The debate caused friction between the two senators.*

Fri·day (frī′dē *or* frī′dā′) *n.* The sixth day of the week.

fridge (frĭj) *n. Informal.* A refrigerator.

fried (frīd) *adj.* Cooked by frying: *Fried foods are high in fat.*

friend (frĕnd) *n.* **1.** A person who is known and liked by another: *My friends came to my birthday party.* **2.** A person who supports a group, cause, or movement: *Their support of conservation made them friends of the environmental agency.* ◆ **make friends.** To establish a relationship with a person that one likes: *It was difficult to make friends when he moved to a new city.*

friend·ly (frĕnd′lē) *adj.* **friend·li·er, friend·li·est. 1.** Relating to or suitable for a friend or friends: *friendly cooperation.* **2.** Giving support; comforting: *friendly words.* —**friend′li·ness** *n.* [U]

—**friend·ly** (frĕnd′lē) *suff.* (*used with a hyphen*). A suffix that means easy or comfortable for: *user-friendly software; a child-friendly environment.*

friend·ship (frĕnd′shĭp′) *n.* **1.** [C] The condition or fact of being friends: *a friendship from childhood.* **2.** [U] A feeling of warmth toward another; friendliness: *friendship between people who like the same things.*

fri·er (frī′ər) *n.* Variant of **fryer.**

fries (frīz) *pl.n.* Potatoes cut in strips and fried; French fries.

fright (frīt) *n.* **1.** [U] Sudden intense fear, as of sthg. immediately threatening: *Fright caused the flock of birds to fly away.* **2.** [C] *Informal.* Something with a very messy or strange appearance: *She looked a fright with her dirty wind-blown hair.*

fright•en (frīt′n) *v.* —*tr.* **1.** To fill (sbdy./ sthg.) with fear: *A loud noise frightened me.* **2.** To drive or force (sbdy./sthg.) by arousing fear: *The police frightened him into making a confession.* —*intr.* To become afraid: *The child frightens easily.*

SYNONYMS: frighten, scare, alarm, terrify, panic. These verbs mean to cause fear in a person or thing. **Frighten** is the most general: *It's hard to believe that elephants are frightened of mice.* **Scare** is also general, but less formal: *Don't let the amount of homework scare you.* **Alarm** means to frighten suddenly: *Her loss of ten pounds in a month alarmed her doctor.* **Terrify** means to overwhelm with fear: *We were terrified that the footbridge would collapse as we walked on it.* **Panic** means to alarm to the point of losing self-control: *False reports of an invasion panicked the whole city.*

fright•ened (frīt′nd) *adj.* [*of*] Filled with fear; afraid: *She was frightened of getting lost.*

fright•en•ing (frīt′n ĭng) *adj.* Causing fright or sudden alarm: *a frightening thunderstorm.* —**fright′en•ing•ly** *adv.*

fright•ful (frīt′fəl) *adj.* **1.** Causing disgust or shock; horrifying: *The number of hungry refugees is frightful.* **2.** Causing fright; terrifying: *frightful Halloween masks.* —**fright′ful•ly** *adv.* —**fright′ful•ness** *n.* [U]

frig•id (frĭj′ĭd) *adj.* **1.** Extremely cold: *frigid temperatures in Antarctica.* See Synonyms at **cold. 2.** Stiff and formal in manner: *the frigid manner of a judge.* —**fri•gid′i•ty** (frĭ jĭd′-ĭ tē), **frig′id•ness** *n.* [U] —**frig′id•ly** *adv.*

frill (frĭl) *n. (usually plural).* **1.** A ruffled or gathered piece of fancy trimming, as on a fabric edge: *frills on a doll's dress.* **2.** *Informal.* Something desirable but unnecessary added on as an extra: *a simple speech without any frills; a cheap ticket on an airplane flight that offered no frills.* —**frill′y** *adj.*

fringe (frĭnj) *n.* **1.** A decorative border or edging of hanging threads or cords, often attached to a separate band: *a fringe at each end of a rug.* **2.** Something that looks like such a border or edging: *a fringe of eyelashes.* **3.** An outer part; an edge: *stand on the fringe of the crowd.* —*tr.v.* **fringed, fring•ing, fring•es.** To decorate (sthg.) with or as if with a fringe: *fringe curtains.*

fringe benefit *n. (usually plural).* An em-ployment benefit, such as medical insurance, given in addition to wages or salary: *The company offers terrific fringe benefits.*

Fris•bee (frĭz′bē). A trademark used for a disk-shaped object that players throw and catch.

frisk (frĭsk) *v.* —*intr.* To move about quickly and playfully: *Squirrels frisked in the trees.* —*tr.* To search (sbdy.) for sthg. concealed, especially a weapon: *frisk a prisoner.*

frisk•y (frĭs′kē) *adj.* **frisk•i•er, frisk•i•est.** Energetic, lively, and playful: *a frisky kitten.* —**frisk′i•ly** *adv.* —**frisk′i•ness** *n.* [U]

frit•ter¹ (frĭt′ər) *v.* ◆ **fritter away.** *tr.v.* [sep.] To reduce or waste (sthg.) little by little: *We frittered the day away watching TV and playing solitaire.*

frit•ter² (frĭt′ər) *n.* A small fried cake of batter that often contains fruit, vegetables, or seafood.

fri•vol•i•ty (frĭ vŏl′ĭ tē) *n., pl.* **fri•vol•i•ties. 1.** [U] The quality or condition of being frivolous: *Holidays are times for play and frivolity.* **2.** [C] A frivolous act or thing: *no time for frivolities.*

friv•o•lous (frĭv′ə ləs) *adj.* **1.** Not deserving of serious attention: *wasting time on frivolous ideas.* **2.** Inappropriately silly: *a frivolous purchase.* —**friv′o•lous•ly** *adv.* —**friv′o•lous•ness** *n.* [U]

frizz (frĭz) *tr. & intr.v.* To form or be formed into small tight tufts or curls: *The humidity frizzed my hair. Her hair frizzed.*

friz•zy (frĭz′ē) *adj.* **friz•zi•er, friz•zi•est.** Tightly curled: *Her hair gets frizzy on rainy days.*

fro (frō) *adv.* ◆ **to and fro.** Away and back: *A pendulum swings to and fro.*

frock (frŏk) *n.* **1.** An outdated term for a woman's dress. **2.** A long loose outer garment, such as a priest's robe or an artist's smock.

frog (frôg *or* frŏg) *n.* Any of numerous amphibious animals with smooth moist skin, webbed feet, long hind legs used for leaping, and no tail when fully grown: *Frogs are amphibians, and many kinds live chiefly in water.*

frog

◆ **have a frog in (one's) throat.** *Informal.* To have hoarseness in the throat: *I can't sing tonight because I have a frog in my throat.*

frol•ic (frŏl′ĭk) *n.* **1.** [U] Happiness; merriment: *The children's party was all fun and frolic.* **2.** [C] A happy, carefree time: *summertime frolics.* —*intr.v.* **frol•icked, frol•ick•ing, frol•ics.** To behave playfully: *The rabbits frolicked in the grass.*

from (frŭm or frŏm; frəm *when unstressed*) *prep.* **1.** Used to indicate a specified place or time as a starting point: *walked home from the station; from midnight until dawn.* **2.** Used to indicate a source, a cause, or an instrument: *a gift from a friend; milk from cows.* **3.** Because of: *faint from hunger.* **4.** Out of or off of: *taking a book from the shelf.* **5.** Out of the control or possession of: *They took the ball from us.* **6.** So as not to be doing: *kept from playing.* **7.** As opposed to: *knowing right from wrong.*

frond (frŏnd) *n.* **1.** The leaf of a fern or palm tree, usually divided into smaller leaflets. **2.** A part that looks like a leaf, as of seaweed.

front (frŭnt) *n.* **1.** The forward part or surface: *a shirt with buttons down the front; a desk at the front of the room.* **2.** The area, location, or position directly before or ahead: *We had hoped to be at the front of the long line. The Jamaican runner was in front.* **3.** A person's outward manner, behavior, or appearance: *keeping up a brave front despite his bad luck.* **4.** Land bordering a lake, river, or street: *a house on the lakefront.* **5.** In warfare, an area where a battle is taking place. **6.** The boundary between two air masses having different temperatures: *a cold front.* **7.** A field of activity: *Conditions on the economic front are poor.* **8.** A group or movement uniting persons or organizations that seek a common goal: *Several unions formed a labor front.* **9.** A person or business that seems respectable but serves as a cover for secret or illegal activity: *That business is a front for selling drugs.* —*adj.* Relating to, directed at, or located in the front: *the front door; the front pages; the front view.* —*v.* —*tr.* To face or look out upon (sthg.): *The building fronts the main street.* —*intr.* **1.** To have a front; face onto sthg. else: *The motel fronts on the highway.* **2.** *Informal.* To serve as a cover or substitute for: *He fronts for the drug dealers in town.*

front•age (frŭn′tĭj) *n.* **1.** [C] The front part of a piece of property. **2.** [U] The land next to sthg., such as a building, street, or body of water: *100 feet of lake frontage.*

fron•tal (frŭn′tl) *adj.* **1.** At or concerning the front: *a frontal assault.* **2.** Relating to the forehead: *the frontal lobe of the brain.* —**fron′tal•ly** *adv.*

fron•tier (frŭn tîr′ or frŭn′tîr′) *n.* **1.** A boundary between countries or the land along such a boundary; a border: *guards at the frontier.* **2.** A region just beyond or at the edge of a settled area: *pioneers settling on the frontier.* **3.** An undeveloped area or field of research or interest: *exploring new frontiers in space.*

front•line (frŭnt′līn′) *n.* A front or boundary, especially one between political or military positions: *troops on the frontline.* —*adj.* **1.** Located or used at a military front: *front-*line troops. **2.** Relating to the most advanced position in a field or an effort: *frontline research.*

front office *n.* The officers of an organization who make management and policy decisions: *That question will have to be decided by the front office.*

front-run•ner also **front-run•ner** (frŭnt′-rŭn′ər) *n.* A person who leads in a race or other competition: *Neither candidate is a front-runner at this time.*

frost (frôst or frŏst) *n.* **1.** [U] A deposit of small ice crystals, formed from frozen water vapor, covering a surface: *the frost on the car windshield in early morning.* **2.** [C] A temperature low enough to cause frost: *We had a frost last night.* —*v.* —*tr.* **1.** To cover (sthg.) with frost. **2.** To cover or decorate (a cake, cupcake, or other baked goods) with icing. —*intr.* To become covered with frost: *The windows frosted up.*

f°**ost•bite** (frôst′bīt′ or frŏst′bīt′) *n.* [U] Injury to a part of the body as a result of freezing temperatures: *The climber lost two toes to frostbite.* —**frost′bit′ten** *adj.*

frost•ing (frô′stĭng or frŏs′tĭng) *n.* [C; U] A sweet mixture of sugar and other ingredients, used to cover and decorate cakes or cookies; icing: *chocolate frosting.*

frost•y (frô′stē or frŏs′tē) *adj.* **frost•i•er,** **frost•i•est.** **1.** Producing or characterized by frost: *A sudden chill made the night frosty and cold.* See Synonyms at **cold. 2.** Covered with frost or having a surface resembling frost: *the frosty bedroom window; a frosty texture.* **3.** Cold in manner; unfriendly: *The hostility between the neighbors was clear from their frosty greeting.* —**frost′i•ly** *adv.* —**frost′i•ness** *n.* [U]

froth (frôth or frŏth) *n.* [U] **1.** A mass of bubbles in or on a liquid; foam. **2.** Something lacking in substance or depth: *Most gossip is mere froth.* —*intr.v.* (*also* frôth *or* frŏth). To give off or form foam: *The sick dog frothed at the mouth.* —**froth′i•ness** *n.* [U] —**froth′y** *adj.*

frown (froun) *v.* —*intr.* **1.** To pull down and wrinkle the eyebrows, as in thought or displeasure. **2.** [on] To disapprove of sthg.: *Most people frown on rudeness.* —*tr.* To show (sthg.) by a frown: *He frowned his displeasure at being interrupted.* —*n.* The act of frowning: *The teacher silenced the children with a frown.*

froze (frōz) *v.* Past tense of **freeze.**

fro•zen (frō′zən) *v.* Past participle of **freeze.** —*adj.* **1.a.** Made into ice: *frozen orange juice.* **b.** Covered with or surrounded by ice: *a frozen pool.* **2.** Very cold: *the frozen North.* **3.** Preserved by freezing: *frozen strawberries.* **4.** Not able to move, as from fright: *frozen with fear.* **5.** Damaged or killed by frost: *frozen crops.* **6.** Unfriendly; cold: *a frozen stare.*

fruc·tose (frŭk′tōs′ *or* froŏok′tōs′) *n.* [U] A very sweet sugar found in honey and in many fruits, having the chemical formula $C_6H_{12}O_6$.

fru·gal (froō′gəl) *adj.* **1.** Careful in spending or in using resources; thrifty: *Frugal use of energy saves natural resources.* **2.** Costing little; inexpensive: *a frugal lunch.* —**fru· gal′i·ty** (froō găl′ĭ tē) *n.* [U] —**fru′gal·ly** *adv.*

fruit (froōt) *n.* [C; U] **1.a.** The ripened part of a flowering plant that contains the seeds: *Berries and pods are fruit.* **b.** A fleshy, often sweet plant part of this kind, eaten as food: *Apples and oranges are fruits. Would you like a piece of fruit?* **2.** A plant crop or product: *the fruit of this year's planting.* **3.** A result or outcome: *at last enjoying the fruits of our labor.* **4.** An insulting term for a person who is different. —*intr.v.* To produce fruit: *Apple trees fruit in the fall.* ◆ **bear fruit.** To have a successful result: *The investigation finally bore fruit when they discovered who the murderer was.*

fruit·cake (froōt′kāk′) *n.* **1.** A rich spiced cake containing various dried and preserved fruits and nuts. **2.** *Informal.* A strange person: *Those fruitcakes are never on time.*

fruit·ful (froōt′fəl) *adj.* **1.** Producing or bearing fruit: *a fruitful orchard.* **2.** Producing sthg. in large amounts; productive: *Thomas Edison was a fruitful inventor.* **3.** Producing good results; beneficial or profitable: *Going into business for themselves proved to be a fruitful idea.* —**fruit′ful·ly** *adv.* —**fruit′ful· ness** *n.* [U]

fru·i·tion (froō ĭsh′ən) *n.* [U] **1.** The achievement of sthg. desired or worked for; accomplishment: *Our idea for a student newspaper finally reached fruition.* **2.** The condition of bearing fruit: *These plants require two months to come to fruition.*

fruit·less (froōt′lĭs) *adj.* **1.** Having little or no result; unproductive: *Only after many fruitless attempts did explorers reach the South Pole.* **2.** Producing no fruit: *a fruitless orchard.* —**fruit′less·ly** *adv.* —**fruit′less· ness** *n.* [U]

fruit·y (froō′tē) *adj.* **fruit·i·er, fruit·i·est.** **1.** Tasting or smelling of fruit: *the fruity smell of ripe peaches.* **2.** *Slang.* Strange or foolish: *Arguing with the teacher was a fruity thing to do.* —**fruit′i·ness** *n.* [U]

frus·trate (frŭs′trāt′) *tr.v.* **frus·trat·ed, frus·trat·ing, frus·trates.** **1.** To prevent (sbdy./sthg.) from accomplishing sthg.: *Lack of money frustrated my efforts to continue studying the piano.* **2.** To cause feelings of discouragement or confusion in (sbdy.): *The scientists were frustrated by the negative results of the experiment.* **3.** To bring (sthg.) to nothing; defeat: *Bad weather frustrated our plans to go fishing.* —**frus·tra′tion** *n.* [C; U]

frus·trat·ed (frŭs′trā′tĭd) *adj.* **1.** [*with*] Upset and impatient: *I was frustrated with the slow-moving traffic.* **2.** Prevented from developing or using a particular skill: *a frustrated novelist who writes for a newspaper instead.*

frus·trat·ing (frŭs′trā′tĭng) *adj.* Causing annoyance and impatience by blocking one's efforts: *a frustrating wait.*

fry (frī) *v.* **fried** (frīd), **fry·ing, fries** (frīz). —*tr.v.* To cook (food) over direct heat in hot oil or fat: *We fried potatoes in a pan.* —*intr.v.* To be cooked over direct heat in hot oil or fat: *Eggs fry quickly.* —*n., pl.* **fries** (frīz). **1.** A French fry. **2.** An informal gathering where food is fried and eaten: *a fish fry.*

fry·er *also* **fri·er** (frī′ər) *n.* **1.** A small young chicken suitable for frying. **2.** A pot or pan with a basket for frying foods.

HOMONYMS: fryer, friar (member of a religious order).

---

fry·ing pan (frī′ĭng) *n.* A shallow pan with a long handle, used for frying food.

ft. *abbr.* An abbreviation of foot.

fudge (fŭj) *n.* [U] A soft rich candy, often flavored with chocolate. —*v.* *Informal.* **fudged, fudg·ing, fudg·es.** —*tr.* **1.** To avoid being clear about (sthg.): *The politician fudged his responses about toxic waste dumps.* **2.** To change (sthg.) dishonestly: *The scientist fudged the results of the experiment.* —*intr.* To act in an indecisive manner: *The mayor always fudged on the important issues.*

fu·el (fyoō′əl) *n.* [C; U] **1.** A substance, such as coal, wood, oil, or gas, that is burned to produce useful heat or energy. **2.** A substance that can be made to undergo a nuclear reaction and produce energy. **3.** Something that feeds or encourages a feeling: *Being insulted added fuel to his anger.* —*v.* —*tr.* **1.** To provide (sthg.) with fuel: *A tank truck fueled the plane.* **2.** To make (sthg.) more intense: *The other team's confidence fueled our desire to beat them.* —*intr.* To take in fuel: *The freighter fueled at the nearest port.*

fu·gi·tive (fyoō′jĭ tĭv) *n.* A person who flees: *The escaped criminal was a fugitive from the law.* —*adj.* **1.** Running or having run away, as from the law or justice: *fugitive criminals.* **2.** Passing quickly: *relaxing for a few fugitive hours.*

—**ful** *suff.* A suffix that means: **1.** Full of: *eventful; playful.* **2.** Characterized by: *boastful.* **3.** Tending or able to: *helpful; useful.* **4.** A quantity that fills: *armful; cupful.*

ă–cat; ā–pay; âr–care; ä–father; ĕ–get; ē–be; ĭ–sit; ī–nice; îr–here; ŏ–got; ō–go; ô–saw; oi–boy; ou–out; ōo–took; ōō–boot; ŭ–cut; ûr–word; th–thin; th–this; hw–when; zh–vision; ə–about; N–French bon

ful·crum (fŏŏl′krəm *or* fŭl′krəm) *n.*, *pl.* **ful·crums** or **ful·cra** (fŏŏl′krə *or* fŭl′-krə). The point or support on which a lever turns.

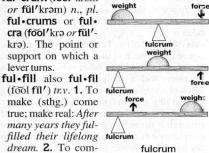

weight
force
fulcrum
weight
force
fulcrum
force
weight
fulcrum
fulcrum

ful·fill also **ful·fil** (fŏŏl fĭl′) *tr.v.* **1.** To make (sthg.) come true; make real: *After many years they fulfilled their lifelong dream.* **2.** To complete (a duty or order): *Citizens should fulfill their duty as voters.* **3.** To perform in a way that satisfies (wishes or demands): *fulfilling all requirements.* —**ful·fill′ment** *n.* [U]

full (fŏŏl) *adj.* **1.** Containing all that is normal or possible; filled: *a full bucket.* **2.** Not lacking; complete: *I need your full attention.* **3.** Of highest degree or development: *at full speed; in full bloom.* **4.** Having a large number or amount of sthg.: *shelves full of books.* **5.** Rounded in shape: *a full face and figure.* **6.** Having or made with a generous amount of fabric: *a full skirt.* **7.** Filled with food; completely fed: *The guests were full after the huge banquet.* —*adv.* **1.** Completely; entirely: *Fill the pitcher full.* **2.** Exactly; directly: *The tree fell full across the middle of the road.* ◆ **be full of (oneself).** To have an excessively high opinion of oneself: *Since he got his new car, he has been full of himself.* **full blast.** As much as possible: *He was so excited that he ran home full blast to tell his parents the news. She had the sound on full blast.* **full well.** Certainly: *He knows full well that he should not be doing that.* **in full.** Completely: *She paid the bill in full.* —**full′ness** *n.* [U]

full-blown (fŏŏl′blōn′) *adj.* Fully matured or developed: *A full-blown cold kept him home.*

full-fledged (fŏŏl′flĕjd′) *adj.* **1.** Fully developed; mature. **2.** With full status or rank: *She must pass the bar exam to become a full-fledged lawyer.*

full-length (fŏŏl′lĕngkth′ *or* fŏŏl′lĕngth′) *adj.* **1.** Covering the entire length of a person or thing: *a full-length mirror; a full-length coat.* **2.** Of normal or standard length: *a full-length motion picture.*

full moon *n.* **1.** [C] The moon when it is fully visible: *in the light of the full moon.* **2.** [U] The time of the month when this occurs: *planting after the full moon.*

full-scale (fŏŏl′skāl′) *adj.* **1.** Of the full size; not reduced: *The design for the new car was produced in a full-scale model.* **2.** Not limited; complete: *Everyone came to city hall for a full-scale demonstration against local water pollution.*

full-size (fŏŏl′sīz′) *adj.* Of the standard or normal size: *a full-size refrigerator.*

full-time (fŏŏl′tīm′) *adj. & adv.* Employed for or involving a standard number of hours of working time: *a full-time editor; a full-time job; works full-time.*

ful·ly (fŏŏl′ē) *adv.* **1.** Totally or completely: *The deer was fully aware of our presence.* **2.** At least; no less than: *Fully half the students had to take the test again.*

fum·ble (fŭm′bəl) *v.* **fum·bled, fum·bling, fum·bles.** —*intr.* **1.** To touch or handle sthg. nervously or idly: *The driver fumbled with the car keys.* **2.** To feel around awkwardly while searching: *The child fumbled for the light switch in the dark.* **3.** In sports, to mishandle or drop a ball: *He fumbled at the end of the game.* —*tr.* **1.** To handle (sthg.) clumsily: *She fumbled the glass and it broke.* **2.** To ruin (sthg.) through clumsy mistakes: *The bank robber fumbled the job.* **3.** In sports, to mishandle or drop (a ball): *The player fumbled the ball.* —*n.* **1.** An act of fumbling. **2.** A ball that has been fumbled.

fume (fyŏŏm) *n.* Smoke, vapor, or gas, especially if irritating, harmful, or smelly: *the choking fumes from a smokestack.* —*intr.v.* **fumed, fum·ing, fumes. 1.** To produce or give off fumes: *A volcano fumed in the distance.* **2.** To feel or show anger or agitation: *After his appointment was postponed for the third time, he was fuming.*

fu·mi·gate (fyŏŏ′mĭ gāt′) *tr.v.* **fu·mi·gat·ed, fu·mi·gat·ing, fu·mi·gates.** To expose (a room or an object) to fumes in order to kill insects, rats, or other pests. —**fu′mi·ga′tion** *n.* [U] —**fu′mi·ga′tor** *n.*

fun (fŭn) *n.* [U] **1.** Enjoyment; amusement: *We had fun at the picnic.* **2.** A source of enjoyment or amusement: *The birthday party was fun.* —*adj. Informal.* Enjoyable; amusing: *She's a fun person.* ◆ **for** or **in fun.** As a joke; playfully: *I tease my friend, but it is all in fun.*

func·tion (fŭngk′shən) *n.* **1.** The normal or proper activity of sbdy. or sthg.; a purpose: *The function of the heart is to pump blood.* **2.** An assigned duty or activity: *Creating a menu is part of her function as head chef.* **3.** A quantity whose value depends on the value given to one or more related quantities: *The area of a square is a function of the length of its sides.* **4.** A formal social gathering or official ceremony: *attend university functions.*

F

F

—*intr.v.* **1.** To have or perform a function; serve: *She functioned as ambassador to Greece.* **2.** To work; operate: *The elevator isn't functioning properly.*

func•tion•al (fŭngk′shə nəl) *adj.* **1.** Relating to a function: *the functional responsibilities of a manager.* **2.** Having or able to complete a function; working: *Is this clock functional?* **3.** Intended for a particular purpose or use: *The log cabin is an example of functional architecture.* —**func′tion•al•ly** *adv.*

func•tion•ar•y (fŭngk′shə něr′ē) *n., pl.* **func•tion•ar•ies.** A person who holds a position of authority or trust; an official: *The tax collector is a functionary in the local government.*

fund (fŭnd) *n.* **1.** A sum of money for a certain purpose: *Our library has a new book fund each year.* **2. funds.** Available money; ready cash: *We have no funds to pay our bills.* **3.** A source of supply; a stock: *An encyclopedia is a fund of knowledge.* —*tr.v.* To provide money for (sthg.): *Several citizens of the town funded our sports program.*

fun•da•men•tal (fŭn′də měn′tl) *adj.* Relating to or forming a foundation; basic: *A fundamental knowledge of mathematics should be part of everyone's education.* —*n. (usually plural).* Something that is a basic part; an essential: *the fundamentals of good cooking.* —**fun′da•men′tal•ly** *adv.*

fun•da•men•tal•ism (fŭn′də měn′tl ĭz′-əm) *n.* [U] **1.** Belief in the Bible as a complete and accurate historical record and statement of prophecy. **2.** Strict observance of the basic principles of a religion. —**fun′da•men′tal•ist** *n. & adj.*

fund•rais•er or **fund-rais•er** (fŭnd′rā′zər) *n.* A person, organization, or event that collects money for a purpose: *a fundraiser held to benefit the museum.*

fu•ner•al (fyōō′nər əl) *n.* The ceremonies that accompany burial or cremation of the dead.

funeral director *n.* A person whose business is to prepare the dead for burial or cremation and to assist at funerals.

funeral home *n.* A building in which the dead are prepared for burial or cremation, and in which wakes and funerals are held.

fu•ne•re•al (fyōō nîr′ē əl) *adj.* Relating to or suitable for a funeral: *dressed in funereal black.*

fun•gal (fŭng′gəl) also **fun•gous** (fŭng′gəs) *adj.* **1.** Of, relating to, or typical of a fungus or fungi: *the fungal life cycle.* **2.** Caused by a fungus: *a fungal infection.*

fun•gi•cide (fŭn′jĭ sīd′ *or* fŭng′gĭ sīd′) *n.* [C; U] A chemical substance that destroys or prevents the growth of fungi.

fun•gus (fŭng′gəs) *n., pl.* **fun•gi** (fŭn′jī *or* fŭng′gī) or **fun•gus•es.** Any of a class of living things, including mushrooms, molds, yeasts, and mildews, that have no green coloring and get food from living or dead plant or animal matter.

funk (fŭngk) *n.* **1.** [U] A type of popular music that combines elements of jazz and blues. **2.** [C] *Informal.* A state of depression: *They were in a funk because their trip was canceled.*

funk•y (fŭng′kē) *adj.* **1.** *Slang.* Having qualities of music similar to the blues: *funky jazz.* **2.** *Slang.* Original and unusual: *a funky shirt.* **3.** *Informal.* Having a moldy or musty smell: *Those old tennis shoes smell funky.* —**funk′i•ness** *n.* [U]

fun•nel (fŭn′əl) *n.* **1.** A utensil with a wide opening at one end and a tube at the other, used to pour liquids or other substances into a container with a small mouth. **2.** The smokestack of a ship or steam engine. **3.** Something shaped like a funnel: *the funnel of a tornado.* —*tr. & intr.v.* To move through or as if through a funnel: *You'll need to funnel the juice into a bottle. Tourists funneled through the museum exhibit.*

fun•nies (fŭn′ēz) *pl.n.* A newspaper section containing comic strips.

fun•ny (fŭn′ē) *adj.* **fun•ni•er, fun•ni•est. 1.** Causing laughter or amusement: *a funny cartoon.* **2.** Strange; odd; curious: *It's funny that I can't remember where I left my shoes.* —**fun′ni•ly** *adv.* —**fun′ni•ness** *n.* [U]

funny bone *n. Informal.* **1.** [C] A point near the elbow where a nerve can be pressed against the bone, producing a numb or tingling feeling in the arm. **2.** [U] A sense of humor: *That joke really hit my funny bone.*

fur (fûr) *n.* **1.** [U] The thick soft hair covering the body of a mammal, such as a rabbit, cat, or fox. **2.** [C] The skin and hair of such a mammal, treated and used for clothing. **3.** [C] A coat, cape, or hat made of fur. **4.** [U] A coating similar to the fur of an animal.

Homonyms: fur, fir (evergreen).

---

fu•ri•ous (fyoor′ē əs) *adj.* **1.** Very angry: *Her brother was furious because she borrowed his jacket.* **2.** Done with extreme energy or anger; violent: *They worked at a furious pace.* —**fu′ri•ous•ly** *adv.* —**fu′ri•ous•ness** *n.* [U]

furl (fûrl) *v.* —*tr.* To roll up and fasten (a flag or sail) to a pole, yard, or mast. —*intr.* To become rolled up: *The flag furled around the pole in the wind.*

fur•lough (fûr′lō) *n.* [C; U] A vacation or leave of absence, especially one granted to a member of the armed forces: *The sailor was on furlough.* —*tr.v.* To grant a leave to (sbdy.): *The worker was furloughed.*

ă–cat; ā–pay; âr–care; ä–father; ĕ–get; ē–be; ĭ–sit; ī–nice; îr–here; ŏ–got; ō–go; ô–saw; oi–boy; ou–out; ōō–took; ōō–boot; ŭ–cut; ûr–word; th–thin; th–this; hw–when; zh–vision; ə–about; N–French bon

fur•nace (fûr′nĭs) *n.* An enclosed chamber in which fuel is burned to produce heat. Furnaces are used to heat buildings and to manufacture metal and glass.

fur•nish (fûr′nĭsh) *tr.v.* **1.** To provide (a room or building) with furniture and other necessities: *furnish each room of an apartment.* **2.** To supply (sthg.); give: *The lamp furnished enough light to read.* —**fur′nish•er** *n.*

fur•nish•ings (fûr′nĭ shĭngz) *pl.n.* The furniture, appliances, and other movable articles in a house or other building.

fur•ni•ture (fûr′nĭ chər) *n.* [U] The movable articles, such as chairs, tables, or appliances, that make a room fit for living or an office suitable for working.

fu•ror (fyŏor′ôr′ *or* fyŏor′ər) *n.* **1.** [C] (*usually singular*). A noisy outburst; a commotion or an uproar: *Rumors of the President's arrival caused a furor of excitement.* **2.** [U] Violent anger; frenzy: *the furor of the mob.*

fur•row (fûr′ō *or* fŭr′ō) *n.* **1.** A long narrow groove made in the ground by a plow or other tool: *furrows cut in the field for planting.* **2.** A rut, groove, or depression: *The car's tires made deep furrows in the dirt road.* —*tr.v* **1.** To make furrows in (sthg.); plow: *furrowed the cornfield into neat rows.* **2.** To form deep wrinkles in (the face, especially the forehead): *Months of worry had furrowed the banker's brow.*

fur•ry (fûr′ē *or* fŭr′ē) *adj.* **fur•ri•er, fur•ri•est. 1.** Consisting of or resembling fur: *a furry coat.* **2.** Covered with fur: *a furry kitten.* —**fur′ri•ness** *n.* [U]

fur•ther (fûr′thər) *adj.* A comparative of **far. 1.** More distant in space, time, or degree: *You couldn't be further from the truth.* **2.** Additional; more: *Call for further information.* —*adv.* A comparative of **far. 1.** To a greater extent; more: *We will explore the matter further at a later time.* **2.** In addition; also: *He stated further that he thought the mayor's remarks were unfair.* **3.** Past a certain point: *I read five pages further.* —*tr.v.* To help the progress of (sthg.); advance: *The dedicated teacher furthered the careers of many students with sound advice.* —SEE NOTE at **farther.**

fur•ther•more (fûr′thər môr′) *adv.* Moreover; in addition; besides: *Furthermore, the storm knocked down several large trees.*

fur•ther•most (fûr′thər mōst′) *adj.* Most distant or remote: *the furthermost stars from our galaxy.*

fur•thest (fûr′thĭst) *adj.* A superlative of **far.** Most distant in space, time, or degree: *Quitting is the furthest thing from my mind.* —*adv.* A superlative of **far. 1.** To the greatest extent or degree: *The scientist's explanation went furthest toward providing a solution.* **2.** At or to the most distant or advanced point: *He advanced the furthest in his research.*

fur•tive (fûr′tĭv) *adj.* Done or acting in a secretive manner: *He cast a furtive glance at the clock.* —**fur′tive•ly** *adv.* —**fur′tive•ness** *n.* [U]

fu•ry (fyŏor′ē) *n., pl.* **fu•ries. 1.** [C; U] Violent anger; rage. See Synonyms at **anger. 2.** [U] Violent and uncontrolled action: *the storm's fury.*

fuse[1] also **fuze** (fyŏoz) *n.* **1.** A cord of easily burned material that is used to carry a flame to make a charge explode: *He put the dynamite in place and lit the fuse.* **2.** Often **fuze.** A device used to set off an explosive device, such as a bomb or grenade. ♦ **blow a fuse. 1.** To cause a fuse to break: *We blew a fuse when we plugged in the stereo and the television at the same time.* **2.** To become angry suddenly: *He blew a fuse when he heard how much money his son had spent.* **have a short fuse.** To get angry easily: *I don't like talking to him; he has a short fuse.*

fuse[2] (fyŏoz) *v.* —*tr.* **1.** To melt (sthg.) by heating. **2.** To blend (things) by or as if by melting: *The music fuses African and Caribbean rhythms.* See Synonyms at **mix.** —*intr.* **1.** To become liquid from heat; melt. **2.** To become mixed or united by or as if by melting together: *The two cultures fused over the years to produce a new civilization.* —*n.* A safety device that protects an electric circuit, containing a wire that melts and breaks the circuit when the current reaches an unsafe level: *We were using too many appliances at the same time, so the fuse blew.* —**fu′si•ble** *adj.*

fu•se•lage (fyŏo′sə läzh′ *or* fyŏo′zə läzh′) *n.* The main body of an airplane that holds cargo, passengers, and crew.

fu•sion (fyŏo′zhən) *n.* **1.** [U] The process of melting or mixing different things into one by heat: *the fusion of copper and zinc to produce brass.* **2.** [C] A mixture or blend formed by fusing two or more things: *An alloy is a fusion of two or more metals.* **3.** [U] A nuclear reaction in which light nuclei combine to form heavier nuclei, releasing large amounts of energy.

fuss (fŭs) *n.* **1.** [U] Unnecessary nervous activity: *There was a lot of fuss in the confusion of moving to a new office.* **2.** [C] An expression of concern or worry, especially over an unimportant matter: *Why make a fuss about a harmless remark?* —*intr.v.* **1.** To be excessively careful or concerned: *My grandmother fussed over dinner.* **2.** To protest, complain, or act in an upset manner: *The baby was fussing all night.*

fuss•y (fŭs′ē) *adj.* **fuss•i•er, fuss•i•est. 1.** Easily upset; tending to cry or complain: *a fussy baby.* **2.** Paying great or too much attention to small details: *She is fussy about her clothes.* —**fuss′i•ly** *adv.* —**fuss′i•ness** *n.* [U]

fu•tile (fyōōt′l *or* fyōō′tīl′) *adj.* Useless; hopeless: *It is futile to argue that the earth is flat.* —**fu′tile•ly** *adv.* —**fu•til′i•ty** (fyōō-tĭl′ĭ tē) *n.* [U]

fu•ton (fōō′tŏn) *n.* A pad of cotton batting or similar material used on a floor or on a raised platform as a mattress or comforter.

fu•ture (fyōō′chər) *n.* **1.** [U] The period of time still to come: *Let's try to do better in the future.* **2.** [C] Something that will happen in time to come: *The business's future is in the hands of new management.* **3.** [C; U] Chance of success or advancement: *The young doctor faced a bright future.* **4.** [U] The future tense. —*adj.* That will be or happen in time to come: *Let's review our progress at some future date.*

future perfect tense *n.* A verb tense expressing action or a state completed by a specified time in the future. It is formed by combining *will have* or *shall have* with a past participle, as in the sentence *By noon tomorrow, the train will have arrived there.*

future tense *n.* A verb tense used to express action or a state in the future. In English, it is formed by combining the auxiliary verbs *shall* and *will* with the simple form of a verb, as in the sentences *I shall be back tonight* and *They will leave in half an hour.*

fu•tur•is•tic (fyōō′chə rĭs′tĭk) *adj.* Relating to the future: *futuristic architecture.* —**fu′tur•is′ti•cal•ly** *adv.*

fuze (fyōōz) *n.* Variant of **fuse**[1].

fuzz (fŭz) *n.* [U] Soft short fibers or hairs: *the fuzz on a peach; You have some fuzz on your jacket.*

fuzz•y (fŭz′ē) *adj.* **fuzz•i•er, fuzz•i•est. 1.** Covered with fuzz: *a fuzzy peach.* **2.** Of or resembling fuzz: *the fuzzy hair of a kitten.* **3.** Not clear; blurred: *I have only a fuzzy memory of the crash.* —**fuzz′i•ly** *adv.* —**fuzz′i•ness** *n.* [U]

—fy *or* **—ify** *suff.* A suffix that means to make or cause to become: *beautify; solidify.*

WORD BUILDING: —fy The verb suffix **—fy** means "to make or cause sthg. to become." Thus **purify** means "to make pure, cleanse." In English the suffix **—fy** normally takes the form **—ify: acidify, humidify.** Verbs ending in **—fy** often have related nouns ending in *—fication* or *—faction:* **magnify, magnification; satisfy, satisfaction.**

FYI *abbr.* An abbreviation of for your information: *I'll send you a copy of my letter to the boss, FYI.*

Gg

g¹ or **G** (jē) *n.*, *pl.* **g's** or **G's.** **1.** The seventh letter of the English alphabet. **2.** In music, the fifth tone in the scale of C major.

g² *abbr.* An abbreviation of: **1.** Gravity. **2.** Gram.

G (jē) *n.* A movie rating that recommends admission to persons of all ages: *a family cartoon rated G.*

GA also **Ga.** *abbr.* An abbreviation of Georgia.

gab (găb) *intr.v.* **gabbed, gab·bing, gabs.** *Informal.* To talk without purpose and often too much: *The neighbors gabbed over the fence.*

gab·by (găb′ē) *adj.* **gab·bi·er, gab·bi·est.** *Informal.* Tending to talk too much. —**gab′·bi·ness** *n.* [U]

ga·ble (gā′bəl) *n.* The triangular section of wall between the two slopes of a roof. —**ga′bled** *adj.*

gadg·et (găj′ĭt) *n.* A small mechanical device: *can openers, corkscrews, and other kitchen gadgets.*

gag (găg) *n.* **1.** Something put into or over a person's mouth to prevent speaking or crying out. **2.** *(usually singular).* Something, such as a law or ruling, that limits or censors free speech: *The judge put a gag on press reporting while the trial was in progress.* **3.** A humorous remark or practical joke intended to make people laugh. —*v.* **gagged, gag·ging, gags.** —*tr.* **1.** To prevent (sbdy.) from speaking or crying out by using a gag: *gagging a hostage.* **2.** To prevent (sbdy.) from exercising free speech: *The judge gagged the reporters.* —*intr.* To choke or feel unable to swallow: *The gasoline smell made us gag. The baby gagged on the peas.*

gage (gāj) *n. & v.* Variant of **gauge.**

gai·e·ty (gā′ĭ tē) *n.* [U] **1.** The condition of being gay or merry; cheerfulness: *the gaiety of the laughing children.* **2.** Showiness or brightness in dress or appearance: *The gaiety of the colorful flowers brightened the room.*

gai·ly (gā′lē) *adv.* **1.** In a joyful, cheerful, or happy manner; merrily: *singing gaily around the piano.* **2.** Brightly; colorfully; showily: *The parade moved down the gaily decorated streets.*

gain (gān) *v.* —*tr.* **1.** To get or acquire (sbdy./sthg.): *I've gained a new friend. We gained experience by working during the summer.* **2.** To win (sthg.) in competition: *Our team gained a decisive victory in the soccer game.* **3.** To get an increase of (sthg.): *Students gain knowledge by reading.* See Synonyms at **reach.** —*intr.* **1.** To increase; grow: *Has your house gained in value?* **2.** To become better; improve: *The recovering patient is gaining in strength.* **3.** [*on*] To come nearer; get closer: *The hounds gained on the fleeing fox.* —*n.* [C; U] **1.** Progress; advancement: *We have made great social gains since the early 1900s.* **2.** An increase, as in wealth: *the financial gains made from careful investment.* **3.** The act of acquiring sthg.: *a slow gain in weight.* ◆ **gain ground.** To move forward; advance: *The company was once the clear leader in computer software, but now its competitors are gaining ground.*

gain·ful (gān′fəl) *adj.* Providing an income or advantage; profitable: *gainful employment.* —**gain′ful·ly** *adv.*

gait (gāt) *n.* **1.** A way of walking or running: *a shuffling gait.* **2.** The way in which a horse moves, as a walk, trot, or gallop: *The trainer showed off the horse's gaits.*

HOMONYMS: gait, gate (entrance).

gal (găl) *n. Informal.* A girl.

gal. *abbr.* An abbreviation of gallon.

ga·la (gā′lə *or* găl′ə *or* gä′lə) *n.* A festive occasion or celebration: *We attended a gala to raise funds for the museum.* —*adj.* Festive: *The city greeted the home team's victory with a gala celebration.*

ga·lac·tic (gə lăk′tĭk) *adj.* Relating to a galaxy, especially the Milky Way.

gal·ax·y (găl′ək sē) *n.*, *pl.* **gal·ax·ies.** **1.** A vast grouping of stars, gas, and dust held together by the force of gravity: *A galaxy has billions of stars.* **2.** An assembly of well-known or distinguished persons or things: *a galaxy of television stars.*

gale (gāl) *n.* **1.** A very strong wind, especially one having a speed between 32 and 63 miles (50–102 kilometers) per hour: *A gale warning was issued as the storm came closer to land.* **2.** A noisy outburst: *gales of laughter.*

gall (gôl) *n.* **1.** Bitter feeling; spite: *The feuding neighbors were full of gall.* **2.** Insulting boldness; nerve: *They had the gall to come to the party uninvited.* —*tr.v.* To annoy (sbdy.): *It really galls me when people use the express checkout at the supermarket even though they have too many items.*

gal·lant (găl′ənt) *adj.* **1.** Brave and noble; courageous: *a gallant knight on horseback.* **2.**

Stately or majestic; grand: *a gallant ship.* **3.** (gə **lănt'** *or* gə **lănt'**). Used of a man who is polite and attentive to women: *our host's gallant manner.* —**gal'lant•ly** *adv.*

gal•lant•ry (găl'ən trē) *n.* [U] *Formal.* **1.** Heroic courage or brave and honorable behavior. **2.** Considerate attention to women: *His gallantry made him the hit of the party.*

gall•blad•der also **gall bladder** (gôl'blăd'ər) *n.* A small muscular sac, located near the liver, in which bile is stored.

gal•le•on (găl'ē ən *or* găl'yən) *n.* A large sailing ship of the 15th to 17th centuries, used especially by the Spanish.

gal•ler•y (găl'ə rē) *n., pl.* **gal•ler•ies. 1.** A building or hall for displaying works of art: *a new art show at a downtown gallery.* **2.** A long narrow walk or passage, often with a roof and windows along one side: *galleries surrounding a courtyard.* **3.** An enclosed passageway, such as a hall or corridor: *a shooting gallery.*

gal•ley (găl'ē) *n., pl.* **gal•leys. 1.** The kitchen on a ship or an airliner. **2.** A long narrow ship driven by sails and oars.

gall•ing (gô'lĭng) *adj.* Very irritating or annoying: *A mechanical problem caused another galling delay in our flight.*

gal•li•vant (găl'ə vănt') *intr.v. Informal.* [*about; around*] To travel about in search of pleasure or amusement: *spending the summer gallivanting around Europe.*

gal•lon (găl'ən) *n.* **1.** A unit of volume or capacity used for measuring liquids, equal to 4 quarts (3.785 liters). See table at **measurement. 2.** A container with a capacity of one gallon or the amount of liquid that can be held in such a container: *a gallon of milk.*

gal•lop (găl'əp) *n.* [U] The fastest gait of a horse or other four-footed animal. —*v.* —*tr.* To cause (a horse) to gallop: *The rider galloped the horse around the track.* —*intr.* **1.** To ride at a gallop: *gallop around the field.* **2.** To move or progress very quickly: *Summer is galloping by.*

gal•lop•ing (găl'ə pĭng) *adj.* Increasing very quickly; out of control: *galloping inflation.*

gal•lows (găl'ōz) *pl.n.* An upright framework from which a rope with a noose is suspended, used for execution by hanging: *a criminal sentenced to the gallows.*

ga•lore (gə lôr') *adj.* In great numbers; in large supply: *The streets were filled with shoppers galore.*

ga•losh (gə lŏsh') *n.* (*usually plural*). A waterproof overshoe: *It's going to rain, so don't forget your galoshes.*

gal•va•nize (găl'və nīz') *tr.v.* **gal•va•nized, gal•va•niz•ing, gal•va•niz•es. 1.** To cause (sbdy.) to act quickly: *Knowing that the other boat was gaining on them galva-*

nized the crew. **2.** To treat (a metal) so that it does not rust.

gam•bit (găm'bĭt) *n.* An action or a remark designed to bring about a desired result: *a political gambit.*

gam•ble (găm'bəl) *v.* **gam•bled, gam•bling, gam•bles.** —*intr.* [*on*] **1.** To bet money on the result of a game, contest, or other event: *gamble on a horse race.* **2.** To take a risk in the hope of gaining an advantage: *The builder is gambling on the need for more houses soon.* —*tr.* **1.** To risk (sthg.) in gambling: *gambled the house in a risky investment.* **2.** To expose (sthg.) to danger; risk: *The soldier gambled a promising career in refusing to obey an order.* —*n. (usually singular).* **1.** A bet or wager: *took a gamble on a motorcycle race.* **2.** An act of doing sthg. uncertain; a risk: *Quitting her job was a gamble, but she felt sure she could find a new one.* —**gam'bler** *n.*

gam•bling (găm'blĭng) *n.* [U] The activities of making or accepting bets on contests or games of chance.

game¹ (gām) *n.* **1.** [C] An activity or sport that provides entertainment or amusement: *The children made a game of counting cars that passed.* **2.** [C] A single contest between two opponents or teams: *a football game on Saturday.* **3.** [C] The equipment, such as a board and pieces, needed for playing certain games: *The game came with its own box.* **4.** [U] Wild animals, birds, or fish hunted for food or sport: *hiked through the woods in search of game.* **5.** [C] *Informal.* A plan or scheme: *He can't fool anyone with that old game.* —*adj.* **gam•er, gam•est. 1.** Courageous; spirited: *The smaller boy put up a game fight.* **2.** Ready and willing: *I'm game for climbing the mountain.* ♦ **play games.** To convince people to do sthg. by changing decisions and being tricky: *She played games on him all the time and got him to go on vacation.* —**game'ly** *adv.* —**game'ness** *n.* [U]

game² (gām) *adj.* **gam•er, gam•est.** Lame or injured: *a game leg.*

game plan *n.* A plan of action for winning a game or sporting event or for achieving success in business: *The coach outlined the game plan for the players.*

game show *n.* A television show in which contestants compete for prizes by playing a game, such as a quiz: *She won a trip to Hawaii on a game show.*

gam•ete (găm'ēt' *or* gə mēt') *n.* A cell that unites with another to form a fertilized cell that develops into a new organism.

gam•ing (gā'mĭng) *n.* [U] The playing of games of chance; gambling.

gam•ut (găm'ət) *n.* [U] The complete range

---

of sthg.: *the gamut of feelings from high hope to utter despair.*

gan·der (gănʹdər) *n.* **1.** A male goose. **2.** *(usually singular). Informal.* A look or glance: *Take a gander at this report and tell us what you think.*

gang (găng) *n.* **1.** A group of young people who band together, especially a group of delinquents: *Members of the gang served time in jail.* **2.** *Informal.* A group of friends: *The whole gang went to see a movie.* *v.* —*intr.* To band together in a group or gang: *Reporters ganged around the governor.* ◆ **gang up.** *intr.v.* To act together as a group: *Workers ganged up to stop the flood.* **gang up on** or **against.** To fight or pressure (sbdy.) as a group: *The older children ganged up on the younger child.*

gang·bust·ers (găngʹbŭsʹtərz) *pl.n.* ◆ **like gangbusters.** *Informal.* Very quickly and forcefully: *That business is growing like gangbusters.*

gan·gling (găngʹglĭng) *adj.* Tall and awkward; lanky: *a gangling 15-year-old boy.*

gang·plank (găngʹplăngkʹ) *n.* A board or ramp used as a bridge between a ship and a pier.

gan·grene (găngʹgrēnʹ *or* găng grēnʹ) *n.* [U] Decay of tissue in a living body: *The soldier's wound went untreated, and gangrene set in.* —**gan·gre·nous** (găngʹgrə nəs) *adj.*

gang·ster (găngʹstər) *n.* A member of an organized group of criminals.

gang·way (găngʹwāʹ) *n.* **1.** A gangplank. **2.** A passage along either side of a ship's upper deck.

gaol (jāl) *n. Chiefly British.* Variant of **jail.**

gap (găp) *n.* **1.** An opening or a break, as in a wall or fence: *She climbed through the gap in the fence.* **2.** A break in sthg. continuous: *There are many gaps in our knowledge of the universe.* **3.** A pass through mountains: *the Cumberland Gap.* **4.** A wide difference or imbalance: *There is a gap between what he says and what he does.* —*intr.v.* **gapped, gap·ping, gaps.** To have a gap: *These pants gap at the waist.* ◆ **bridge the gap.** To fill a space between two things: *Her salary was not enough to live on, so she got a second job to bridge the gap.*

gape (gāp *or* găp) *intr.v.* **gaped, gap·ing, gapes.** **1.** To open the mouth wide, as if to bite: *The fish gaped at the bait.* **2.** To stare in amazement, often with the mouth open: *The fans gaped as the ball went soaring towards the stands in right field.* **3.** To open wide; form a gap: *Cracks gaped in the ground after the earthquake.* —*n.* The act or an instance of gaping: *The gape of the lion's yawn made us cringe.*

ga·rage (gə răzhʹ *or* gə räjʹ) *n.* **1.** A building or an indoor space in which to park a motor vehicle: *The house has a two-car garage.* **2.** A business where cars are repaired or serviced: *I need to take the car to the garage.*

—*tr.v.* **ga·raged, ga·rag·ing, ga·rag·es.** To put or keep (a vehicle) in a garage: *garage the car during the snowstorm.*

garage sale *n.* A sale of used household items or clothing held outside the home of the seller.

garb (gärb) *n.* [U] A style or form of clothing: *the informal garb of most tourists.* —*tr.v.* To clothe or dress (sbdy.): *The judge was garbed in robes of court.*

gar·bage (gärʹbĭj) *n.* [U] **1.** Waste material, such as old food and used paper: *Don't forget to take out the garbage.* **2.** *Informal.* Worthless or inferior material; trash: *That novel is nothing but garbage.*

gar·ban·zo (gär bänʹzō) *n., pl.* **gar·ban·zos.** The chickpea.

gar·ble (gärʹbəl) *tr.v.* **gar·bled, gar·bling, gar·bles.** To distort, confuse, or mix up (sthg.): *The report sounded great, but it garbled the facts.* —*n.* The act or an instance of garbling: *a confused garble of voices.*

gar·den (gärʹdn) *n.* **1.** A piece of land used for growing flowers, vegetables, herbs, or fruit. **2.** A park or other public place ornamented with flowers and other plants: *a botanical garden.* —*intr.v.* To plant or tend a garden: *She gardens as a hobby.*

gar·den·er (gärdʹnər *or* gärʹdn ər) *n.* A person who works in or takes care of a garden.

gar·de·nia (gär dēnʹyə) *n.* A shrub with glossy evergreen leaves and large, fragrant, usually white flowers.

gar·den-va·ri·e·ty (gärʹdn və rīʹĭ tē) *adj.* Common; ordinary: *It's nothing special, just another garden-variety TV comedy show.*

gar·gan·tu·an (gär gănʹchoo ən) *adj.* Of very great size; enormous: *a stadium of gargantuan proportions.*

gar·gle (gärʹgəl) *v.* **gar·gled, gar·gling, gar·gles.** —*intr.* To wash or rinse the mouth or throat by exhaling air through a liquid held there: *gargled to soothe a sore throat.* —*tr.* To circulate (a liquid) in the mouth or throat by gargling: *She gargled the mouthwash.* —*n.* A liquid used for gargling: *The nurse suggested a saltwater gargle.*

gar·goyle (gärʹgoilʹ) *n.* A stone figure, just below the roof of a building, usually in the form of a strange animal.

gar·ish (gârʹĭsh *or* gărʹĭsh) *adj.* Too bright or ornamented; gaudy: *His garish tie looked foolish with his dark suit.* —**garʹish·ly** *adv.* —**garʹish·ness** *n.* [U]

gar·land (gärʹlənd) *n.* A wreath or chain of flowers or leaves worn as a crown or used for ornament: *The little girl wore a garland of daisies in her hair.* —*tr.v.* To decorate (sbdy./sthg.) with a garland: *The official garlanded the winner with a laurel wreath.*

gar·lic (gärʹlĭk) *n.* [U] The bulb of a plant related to the onion with a strong taste and odor and used as seasoning.

gar·ment (gär′mənt) *n.* An article of clothing: *He washed several garments.*

gar·ner (gär′nər) *tr.v. Formal.* To gather or acquire (sthg.); amass: *She has garnered many awards.*

gar·net (gär′nĭt) *n.* [C; U] A common crystalline silicate mineral that is usually red and used as a gem.

gar·nish (gär′nĭsh) *tr.v.* **1.** To decorate (sthg.): *garnish mashed potatoes with parsley.* **2.** To take (pay or property) legally for payment of a debt: *garnished his wages for unpaid child support.* —*n.* Ornamentation; decoration: *a garnish of lemon wedges on the plate.*

gar·ri·son (găr′ĭ sən) *n.* The troops stationed at a military post: *The garrison was put on full alert.* —*tr.v.* To assign (troops) to a military post: *Soldiers were garrisoned at the border.*

gar·ru·lous (găr′ə ləs) *adj.* Too talkative, especially about unimportant matters: *a garrulous person.* —**gar′ru·lous·ness** *n.* [U]

gar·ter (gär′tər) *n.* An elastic band or strap worn on the leg to hold up a stocking or sock.

garter snake *n.* A small, striped, harmless North American snake that is brownish or greenish in color.

gas (găs) *n.* **1.** [C; U] One of the three basic forms of matter, composed of molecules in constant random motion, and with no fixed shape or volume. **2.** [U] A gas or mixture of gases burned as fuel for cooking or heating: *propane gas for the grill.* **3.** [U] Gasoline. **4.** [U] A chemical gas that chokes, irritates, or poisons, used as a weapon: *tear gas; nerve gas.* **5.** [U] An anesthetic that is in the form of gas: *The nurse gave the patient gas before the operation.* **6.** [U] Flatulence: *Some foods give me gas.* —*v.* **gassed, gas·sing, gas·es** or **gas·ses.** —*tr.* To injure or poison (sbdy./sthg.) with gas: *The enemy gassed the opposing forces.* ◆ **gas up.** *tr.v.* [sep.] To supply (a vehicle) with gasoline: *We gassed the car up before going on our trip.* —*intr.v.* To supply a vehicle with gasoline: *We gassed up before getting on the highway.*

gas·e·ous (găs′ē əs *or* găsh′əs) *adj.* Relating to or existing as a gas: *The sun is in a gaseous state.*

gas-guz·zler (găs′gŭz′lər) *n. Informal.* An automobile that uses a lot of gas: *My old car was a gas-guzzler.*

gash (găsh) *tr.v.* To make a long deep cut or wound in (sthg.): *She gashed her leg on the rocks.* —*n.* A long deep cut or wound.

gas·ket (găs′kĭt) *n.* A seal or packing placed between machine parts or around pipe joints to prevent the escape of gas or fluid.

gas mask *n.* A mask that covers the face and has an air filter as protection against poisonous gases.

gas·o·line (găs′ə lēn′ *or* găs′ə lēn′) *n.* [C; U] A very flammable liquid that evaporates easily and is used chiefly as a fuel for engines in automobiles, motorcycles, and small trucks.

gasp (găsp) *v.* —*intr.* To breathe in air in a sudden, sharp way, as from shock, surprise, or exercise: *She gasped when she heard the bad news.* —*tr.* To say (sthg.) in a breathless manner: *The runner gasped out his message.* —*n.* A sudden or violent intake of the breath: *a gasp of horror.*

gas station *n.* A service station.

gas·sy (găs′ē) *adj.* **gas·si·er, gas·si·est.** Resembling, containing, or filled with gas: *bubbles in a gassy liquid.*

gas·tric (găs′trĭk) *adj.* Relating to or concerning the stomach: *a gastric disorder.*

gas·tro·in·tes·ti·nal (găs′trō ĭn tĕs′tə-nəl) *adj.* Relating to the stomach and intestines.

gas·tron·o·my (gă strŏn′ə mē) *n.* [U] The art or science of good eating. —**gas′tro·nom′ic** (găs′trə nŏm′ĭk), **gas′tro·nom′i·cal** *adj.*

gate (gāt) *n.* **1.** A hinged or sliding barrier that serves as a door in a wall or fence: *a swinging gate at the end of the walk.* **2.** The number of people attending an event or a performance: *a gate of 500 people.* **3.** The total amount of money paid for people attending an event or a performance: *The gate for the game was $750.*

HOMONYMS: gate, gait (way of walking).

gate·crash·er (gāt′krăsh′ər) *n. Slang.* A person who attends a gathering, performance, private party, or sports event without being invited or without paying.

gate·way (gāt′wā′) *n.* **1.** An opening, as in a wall or fence, that may be closed with a gate. **2.** Something that serves as an entrance: *Denver is thought of as the gateway to the Rockies.*

gath·er (găth′ər) *v.* —*tr.* **1.** To bring (people or things) together in a group: *The teacher gathered the students around the exhibit.* **2.** To pick or collect (things): *Squirrels gather nuts.* **3.** To bring (mental or physical powers) together or into use: *gathering my thoughts.* **4.** To gain or increase (sthg.) gradually: *The truck gathered speed as it moved down the mountain.* **5.** To conclude (that sthg. is true): *I gather that you didn't like the movie.* **6.** To run a thread through (cloth) so as to draw it up into small folds or pleats: *gather material at the waist of a full skirt.* —*intr.* **1.** To come together in a group; assemble: *The children gathered to wait for the school bus.* **2.** To grow or increase bit by bit; accumulate: *Dust gathered under* *the couch.* —*n. (usually plural).* One of the small folds or pleats made in cloth by gathering it. —**gath′er•er** *n.*

SYNONYMS: gather, collect, assemble, accumulate. These verbs mean to bring together in a group or mass. **Gather** is the most general: *I gathered sticks to build a fire.* **Collect** often means to select like or related things that then become part of an organized whole: *Many people like to collect stamps and coins from around the world.* **Assemble** means to gather persons or things that have a definite and usually close relationship: *We assembled all the parts before beginning to build our model.* **Accumulate** describes the increase of like or related things over an extended period of time: *We accumulated piles of old newspapers in the basement.*

gath•er•ing (găth′ər ĭng) *n.* **1.** [C] An assembly of persons; a meeting: *a family gathering.* **2.** [U] The act of a person or thing that gathers: *the gathering of dust over time.*

gauche (gōsh) *adj.* Lacking social grace; tactless: *Talking about people when they can hear you is gauche.*

gaud•y (gô′dē) *adj.* **gaud•i•er, gaud•i•est.** Too brightly colored and showy to be in good taste: *That tie is too gaudy to wear to a job interview.* —**gaud′i•ly** *adv.* —**gaud′i•ness** *n.* [U]

gauge *also* **gage** (gāj) *n.* **1.** An instrument for measuring or testing: *The motorist measured the air pressure with a tire gauge.* **2.** A standard or scale of measurement. **3.** A means of estimating or evaluating; a test: *How a person handles a difficult situation is a good gauge of character.* **4.** The diameter of a shotgun barrel: *a 12-gauge shotgun.* **5.** Thickness or diameter, as of sheet metal or wire: *What gauge wire do you need for the speaker?* —*tr.v.* **gauged, gaug•ing, gaug•es** *also* **gaged, gag•ing, gag•es.** **1.** To measure (sth.) precisely: *gauge the depth of the ocean.* **2.** To evaluate or judge (sbdy./sth.): *gauge a person's ability; gauge a job candidate.*

gaunt (gônt) *adj.* Unhealthily thin and bony: *The fashion model looked gaunt and malnourished.* —**gaunt′ness** *n.* [U]

gaunt•let (gônt′lĭt *or* gänt′lĭt) *n.* **1.** A heavy leather glove worn with medieval armor. ◆ **run the gauntlet.** To withstand an attack or severe trial: *Presidential candidates run the gauntlet of public scrutiny.* **throw down the gauntlet.** To challenge or invite to a fight or debate: *He threw down the gauntlet when he said no woman could ever make the climb.*

gauze (gôz) *n.* [U] A loosely woven, somewhat transparent cloth used especially for bandaging. —**gauz′i•ness** *n.* [U] —**gauz′y** *adj.*

gave (gāv) *v.* Past tense of **give.**

gav•el (găv′əl) *n.* A small wooden mallet used by a presiding officer or an auctioneer to

signal for attention or to mark the close of a transaction.

gawk (gôk) *intr.v.* To stare stupidly: *The performer gawked at the sea of people.*

gawk•y (gô′kē) *adj.* **gawk•i•er, gawk•i•est.** Awkward; clumsy: *a gawky colt.* —**gawk′i•ly** *adv.* —**gawk′i•ness** *n.* [U]

gay (gā) *adj.* **1.** Relating to homosexuals: *a gay newspaper.* **2.** Merry; lighthearted: *a gay mood; gay music.* **3.** Bright or lively, especially in color: *The package was tied with gay ribbons.* —*n.* A homosexual person, especially a man.

gaze (gāz) *intr.v.* **gazed, gaz•ing, gaz•es.** To look intently, as with wonder or curiosity; stare: *The visitors gazed in awe at the beauty of the scenery.* —*n.* An intent steady look: *The crowd fixed their gaze on the speaker.*

ga•ze•bo (gə zā′bō *or* gə zē′bō) *n.*, *pl.* **ga•ze•bos.** An outdoor structure that provides a shady resting place.

ga•zelle (gə zĕl′) *n.* A slender swift-running antelope.

ga•zette (gə zĕt′) *n.* A newspaper or periodical.

G.B. *abbr.* An abbreviation of Great Britain.

gear (gîr) *n.* **1.a.** [C] A wheel with teeth around its rim that mesh with the teeth of another wheel to transmit motion: *the gears of a bicycle.* **b.** [U] An arrangement of such interlocking wheels, as in a watch, a machine, or an auto-

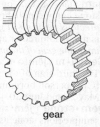

gear

mobile, used to transmit power or change the direction of motion in a mechanism: *Start the car, and then put it in gear.* **c.** [U] An assembly of gears or moving parts that serves a particular function in a larger machine: *the landing gear of an aircraft.* **2.** [U] Equipment, such as tools or clothing, needed for a particular activity: *fishing gear; camping gear.* —*v.* —*tr.* **1.** To connect (sth.) by gears: *gear a motor to a propeller.* **2.** [to] To adjust or adapt (sth.): *The scientists geared their remarks to a youthful audience.* —*intr.* To be or become in gear; mesh: *The cogs of an automobile transmission gear into each other.* ◆ **gear up for.** To get ready for a coming action or event: *We are gearing up for our family's camping trip.*

gear•shift (gîr′shĭft′) *n.* A device for changing from one gear to another in a transmission, as in an automobile.

GED *abbr.* An abbreviation of general equivalency diploma, which one receives for having passed a test that covers what is generally learned in high school: *She quit high school before graduating, but she later passed the exam to earn a GED.*

gee (jē) *interj.* An expression used as an exclamation of surprise: *Gee, I wish I'd known about the sale.*

geese (gēs) *n.* Plural of **goose.**

gel (jĕl) *n.* [C; U] **1.** A semisolid mixture such as that formed when boiled fruit juices thicken and cool. **2.** A thick wet substance like jelly used in beauty and cleaning products: *hair gel.—intr.v.* **gelled, gel·ling, gels. 1.** To form a gel. **2.** To become defined: *Their vacation plans have begun to gel.*

Homonyms: gel, jell (congeal).

---

gel·a·tin (jĕl′ə tn) *n.* [C; U] **1.** An odorless colorless substance that forms a gel when mixed with hot water and allowed to cool: *Gelatin is used in foods, drugs, glue, and photographic film.* **2.** A flavored jelly made with gelatin, often used as a dessert or salad.

ge·lat·i·nous (jə lăt′n əs) *adj.* Similar in texture to gelatin; thick and sticky: *The vegetables were overcooked and became gelatinous.*

geld (gĕld) *tr.v.* To remove the testicles of (a male horse).

geld·ing (gĕl′dĭng) *n.* A gelded male horse.

gem (jĕm) *n.* **1.** A precious or semiprecious stone cut and polished as a jewel: *a ring of precious gems set in gold.* **2.** Something that is much admired or appreciated: *This painting is the gem of the museum's collection.*

Gem·i·ni (jĕm′ə nī′ *or* jĕm′ə nē′) *n.* **1.** [U] The third sign of the zodiac in astrology. **2.** [C] A person born under this sign, between May 21 and June 20.

gem·stone (jĕm′stōn′) *n.* A precious or semiprecious stone used as a jewel when cut and polished: *mining gemstones.*

gen. *abbr.* An abbreviation of general.

Gen. *abbr.* An abbreviation of General.

gen·der (jĕn′dər) *n.* [C; U] **1.** In grammar, one of the categories used to classify nouns, pronouns, adjectives, and in some languages verbs. Gender includes the categories feminine, masculine, and neuter, and the gender of many words corresponds to their sexual classification. **2.** Sexual identity: *the male gender; social roles determined by gender.*

gene (jēn) *n.* A segment of DNA, located at a particular point on a chromosome, that determines hereditary characteristics. *Genes control eye color in human beings.*

ge·ne·al·o·gy (jē′nē ŏl′ə jē *or* jē′nē ăl′ə jē) *n.,* *pl.* **ge·ne·al·o·gies. 1.** [C] A record of the descent of a family or person from an ancestor or ancestors: *traced the family's genealogy.* **2.** [U] The study of ancestry and family histories. **—ge′ne·a·log′i·cal** (jē′nē ə lŏj′ĭ kəl) *adj.* **—ge′ne·al′o·gist** *n.*

gen·er·a (jĕn′ər ə) *n.* Plural of **genus.**

gen·er·al (jĕn′ər əl) *adj.* **1.** Concerned with, applying to, or affecting all members of a category: *An election is supposed to express the general will.* **2.** Affecting a majority of those involved; widespread: *general satisfaction.* **3.** Not limited in area or application: *as a general rule; general studies.* **4.** Involving only the main features of sthg. rather than details or particulars: *The witness could only give a general account of what happened.* **5.** Highest or superior in rank: *the general manager. —n.* An officer in the military. ◆ **in general.** Generally; in most situations: *In general, it is best to eat dinner before dessert.*

gen·er·al·ist (jĕn′ər ə lĭst) *n.* A person with general knowledge and skills in several fields: *The best teachers are usually generalists.*

gen·er·al·i·ty (jĕn′ə răl′ĭ tē) *n.,* *pl.* **gen·er·al·i·ties. 1.** [U] The state or quality of being general. **2.** [C] A statement or an idea that is vague or imprecise: *a speech full of generalities and empty phrases.*

gen·er·al·i·za·tion (jĕn′ər ə lĭ zā′shən) *n.* **1.** [U] The act of generalizing: *A reporter must be careful of generalization and should stick to the facts.* **2.** [C] A general statement or principle: *generalizations about French cooking based on one French restaurant.*

gen·er·al·ize (jĕn′ər ə līz′) *v.* **gen·er·al·ized, gen·er·al·iz·ing, gen·er·al·iz·es. —tr. 1.** To consider or state (sthg.) in terms of a general form or principle. **2.** To draw (a general conclusion) from particular facts: *generalize a rule from a series of experiments. —intr.* To draw a general conclusion from particular facts: *Scientists generalize about dinosaurs from their fossilized bones and other evidence.*

gen·er·al·ly (jĕn′ər ə lē) *adv.* **1.** Usually: *I generally go for a walk before breakfast.* **2.** Widely; commonly: *The fact is not generally known.* **3.** In general terms: *Generally speaking, there are two ways to handle the problem.*

general practitioner *n.* A doctor who does not specialize in one field but treats a variety of medical problems.

gen·er·ate (jĕn′ə rāt′) *tr.v.* **gen·er·at·ed, gen·er·at·ing, gen·er·ates.** To bring (sthg.) into being; produce: *generate heat; generate interest among voters.*

gen·er·a·tion (jĕn′ə rā′shən) *n.* **1.** [C] A group of people who grow up at about the same time, often thought to have similar social and cultural attitudes: *the younger generation.* **2.** [C] The average length of time between the birth of parents and the birth of their offspring: *Many generations have passed since this town was founded.* **3.** [C] A class of things produced based on an earlier class, usually by making improvements: *the*

---

new generation of computers. **4.** [U] The act or process of generating: *the generation of electric power; the generation of new ideas.*

generation gap *n.* The difference in values and attitudes between one generation and the next, especially between young people and their parents: *Popular music is often a visible symbol of a generation gap.*

gen•er•a•tor (jĕn′ə rā′tər) *n.* A person or thing that generates, especially a machine that converts mechanical energy into electrical energy: *The hospital keeps an emergency generator in case the power goes out.*

ge•ner•ic (jə nĕr′ĭk) *adj.* **1.** Relating to an entire group or class; general: *Stress is a generic term that covers a variety of pressures in modern life.* **2.** Relating to a genus: *Cats and dogs show generic differences.* **3.** Relating to or descriptive of an entire class of products: *Aspirin is the generic name for a certain kind of drug.* —**ge•ner′i•cal•ly** *adv.*

gen•er•os•i•ty (jĕn′ə rŏs′ĭ tē) *n.*, *pl.* **gen•er•os•i•ties. 1.** [U] The quality or condition of being generous: *Teachers are known for their generosity in giving help to students.* **2.** [U] Thought or behavior that shows high moral character: *The coach speaks of our rivals with generosity.* **3.** [C] A generous act: *a kind leader known for many generosities.*

gen•er•ous (jĕn′ər əs) *adj.* **1.** Willing to give or share; unselfish: *a generous contributor.* **2.** Large; abundant: *They serve generous portions.* —**gen′er•ous•ly** *adv.*

gen•e•sis (jĕn′ĭ sĭs) *n.*, *pl.* **gen•e•ses** (jĕn′ĭ sēz′). **1.** Often **Genesis.** The first book of the Bible. **2.** The coming into being of sthg.; the origin: *the genesis of an idea.*

ge•net•ic (jə nĕt′ĭk) *adj.* Relating to genes or genetics: *genetic research.* —**ge•net′i•cal•ly** *adv.*

genetic engineering *n.* [U] The science of changing of genes or genetic material to produce desirable new traits in plants, animals, or human beings or to eliminate undesirable traits: *trying to stop hereditary diseases through genetic engineering.*

ge•net•i•cist (jə nĕt′ĭ sĭst) *n.* A scientist who specializes in genetics.

ge•net•ics (jə nĕt′ĭks) *n.* [U] **1.** *(used with a singular verb).* The branch of biology that deals with the principles of heredity and the variation of inherited characteristics among similar or related living things. **2.** *(used with a plural verb).* The genetic makeup of an individual or a group.

gen•ial (jēn′yəl) *adj.* Cheerful, friendly, and good-humored: *an enthusiatic and genial personality.* —**gen′ial•ly** *adv.*

ge•nie (jē′nē) *n.* A spirit that appears in human form and fulfills wishes with magic powers.

gen•i•tal (jĕn′ĭ tl) *adj.* **1.** Relating to biological reproduction: *the genital organs.* **2.** Relating to the genitals.

gen•i•ta•li•a (jĕn′ĭ tā′lē ə *or* jĕn′ĭ tāl′yə) *pl.n. Formal.* The genitals.

gen•i•tals (jĕn′ĭ tlz) *pl.n.* The external sex organs.

gen•ius (jēn′yəs) *n.* **1.** [U] Extraordinary mental ability or creative power: *Artists of genius are remembered centuries after their deaths.* **2.** [C] A person of extraordinary mental ability or creative power: *The great inventor was a genius.* **3.** [U] A strong natural talent or ability: *a genius for leadership.*

gen•o•cide (jĕn′ə sīd′) *n.* [U] The deliberate destruction or killing off of a racial, religious, political, or cultural group. —**gen′o•cid′al** *adj.*

gen•re (zhän′rə) *n.* A particular type or class of literary, musical, or artistic composition: *Novels and plays are of different literary genres.*

gent (jĕnt) *n. Informal.* A man or gentleman.

gen•teel (jĕn tēl′) *adj.* Refined in manner; very polite: *a genteel young man.* —**gen•teel′ly** *adv.* —**gen•til′i•ty** (jĕn tĭl′ĭ tē) *n.* [U]

gen•tile (jĕn′tīl′) *n.* Often **Gentile.** A person who is not a Jew, especially a Christian.

gen•tle (jĕn′tl) *adj.* **gen•tler, gen•tlest. 1.** Considerate or kindly in manner; thoughtful: *The police officer was gentle with the frightened child.* **2.** Not harsh or severe; mild and soft: *a gentle tap on the shoulder.* **3.** Not steep or sudden; gradual: *a gentle slope.* **4.** Easily managed or handled; docile: *a gentle horse.* —**gen′tle•ness** *n.* [U] —**gen′tly** *adv.*

gen•tle•man (jĕn′tl mən) *n.*, *pl.* **gen•tle•men. 1.** A man with very good manners and behavior. **2.** A man: *The gentleman sitting at their table would like spaghetti.* **3. gentle-men.** Used as a form of address for men in a group: *Good evening, ladies and gentlemen.*

gen•tle•man's agreement or **gen•tle•men's agreement** (jĕn′tl mənz) *n.* An informal agreement guaranteed only by the promise of the people involved to honor it.

gen•tri•fi•ca•tion (jĕn′trə fĭ kā′shən) *n.* [U] The repair and improvement of older or run-down city housing by the middle classes, often with the result that people with low incomes have to move away: *Gentrification has made housing in many old neighborhoods too expensive.* —**gen′tri•fy′** (jĕn′trə fī′) *v.*

gen•try (jĕn′trē) *n.* [U] People of high social standing.

gen•u•ine (jĕn′yōō ĭn) *adj.* **1.** Not false; real or pure: *a necklace of genuine gold.* See Synonyms at **authentic. 2.** Sincere; honest: *genuine affection.* —**gen′u•ine•ly** *adv.* —**gen′u•ine•ness** *n.* [U]

ge•nus (jē′nəs) *n.*, *pl.* **gen•er•a** (jĕn′ər ə). **1.** A group of related plants or animals ranking below a family and above a species: *Dogs, wolves, and coyotes belong to the same genus.* **2.** A class, group, or kind with common characteristics: *the genus of boats known as pleasure crafts.*

geo— or **ge—** *pref.* A prefix that means: **1.** Earth: *geology; geothermal.* **2.** Geography: *geopolitical.*

WORD BUILDING: geo— The basic meaning of the prefix **geo—** is "earth." Thus **geography** is "the study of the earth and its surface features." When used to form words in English, **geo—** can mean either "earth" or "geography." For example, **geomagnetism** refers to the magnetism of the earth, and **geopolitics** refers to the relationship between politics and geography.

---

geog. *abbr.* An abbreviation of geography.
ge·og·ra·pher (jē ŏg′rə fər) *n.* A person who specializes in geography.
ge·og·ra·phy (jē ŏg′rə fē) *n.* [U] **1.** The study of the earth's surface and its various climates, continents, countries, peoples, resources, industries, and products. **2.** The physical features of a region or place: *We studied the geography of Hawaii.* —**ge′o·graph′ic** (jē′ə grăf′ĭk), **ge′o·graph′i·cal** *adj.* —**ge′o·graph′i·cal·ly** *adv.*
ge·ol·o·gist (jē ŏl′ə jĭst) *n.* A scientist who specializes in geology.
ge·ol·o·gy (jē ŏl′ə jē) *n.* [U] **1.** The science that studies the origin, history, and structure of the earth. **2.** The structure of a specific region, including its rocks, soils, mountains, and other features: *The geology of New England was affected by the glaciers of the Ice Age.* —**ge′o·log′ic** (jē′ə lŏj′ĭk), **ge′o·log′i·cal** *adj.* —**ge′o·log′i·cal·ly** *adv.*
geom. *abbr.* An abbreviation of geometry.
ge·o·met·ric (jē′ə mĕt′rĭk) also **ge·o·met·ri·cal** (jē′ə mĕt′rĭ kəl) *adj.* **1.** Relating to geometry and its methods and principles: *a geometric problem.* **2.** Consisting of or using simple shapes formed from straight lines or curves: *a geometric design with many circles and squares.* —**ge′o·met′ri·cal·ly** *adv.*
ge·om·e·try (jē ŏm′ĭ trē) *n.* [U] The mathematical study of the properties, measurement, and relationships of points, lines, planes, surfaces, angles, and solids.
ge·o·phys·ics (jē′ō fĭz′ĭks) *n.* [U] *(used with a singular verb).* The application of physics to the study of the earth and its environment. —**ge′o·phys′i·cal** *adj.*
ge·o·pol·i·tics (jē′ō pŏl′ĭ tĭks) *n.* [U] *(used with a singular verb).* The study of the relationship among politics and geography, demographics, and economics. —**ge′o·po·lit′i·cal** (jē′ō pə lĭt′ĭ kəl) *adj.*
ge·o·ther·mal (jē′ō thûr′məl) *adj.* Relating to the internal heat of the earth: *geothermal energy.*
Ger. *abbr.* An abbreviation of: **1.** German. **2.** Germany.

ge·ra·ni·um (jə rā′nē əm) *n.* A plant with rounded leaves and showy clusters of red, pink, purplish, or white flowers, often grown as potted plants.
ger·bil (jûr′bəl) *n.* A small rodent somewhat like a mouse, with long hind legs and a long tail, and often kept as a pet.
ger·i·at·rics (jĕr′ē ăt′rĭks) *n.* [U] *(used with a singular verb).* The medical study of the biological process of aging and the treatment of diseases of old age.
ger·i·at·ric (jĕr′ē ăt′rĭk) *adj.* Relating to old age: *a geriatric patient.*
germ (jûrm) *n.* **1.** A microscopic organism, especially one that causes disease, such as bacteria and viruses: *killing germs with soap and hot water.* **2.** The earliest form of sthg.; the basis: *The discovery that the earth orbits the sun was the germ of a revolution in astronomy.*
ger·mane (jər mān′) *adj. Formal.* Closely or naturally related; pertinent: *Their comments were not germane to the discussion.*
Ger·man measles (jûr′mən) *n. (used with a singular or plural verb).* A contagious disease that causes fever and red spots on the body; rubella.
German shepherd *n.* A large dog with a thick black or brownish coat and often trained to help police officers or guide the blind.
ger·mi·cide (jûr′mĭ sīd′) *n.* [C; U] A substance that kills germs, especially disease germs. —**ger′mi·cid′al** (gûr′mĭ sīd′l) *adj.*
ger·mi·nate (jûr′mə nāt′) *intr. & tr.v.* **ger·mi·nat·ed, ger·mi·nat·ing, ger·mi·nates.** To begin or cause to begin to grow; sprout: *Seeds need water and warmth to germinate. We germinated several types of seeds for our experiment.* —**ger′mi·na′tion** *n.* [U]
ger·und (jĕr′ənd) *n.* A noun formed from a verb. In English the gerund ends in *-ing.* In the sentence *Hitting a ball hard requires strength,* the word *hitting* is a gerund.
ges·ta·tion (jĕ stā′shən) *n.* **1.** [U] The carrying and development of young in the uterus from conception to birth; pregnancy: *a nine-month gestation.* **2.** [U] The period of gestation. **3.** [C] The conception or development of a plan or an idea: *The writer's idea for the novel had its gestation in a casual conversation.*
ges·tic·u·late (jĕ stĭk′yə lāt′) *intr.v.* **ges·tic·u·lat·ed, ges·tic·u·lat·ing, ges·tic·u·lates.** To make gestures in order to emphasize meaning or express one's feelings: *The angry speaker gesticulated wildly with his hands.* —**ges·tic′u·la′tion** *n.* [U]
ges·ture (jĕs′chər) *n.* **1.** Movement of the arms, hands, head, or body to help express meaning: *A mime must rely on gestures to tell a story.* **2.** Something done or said for its

effect on the feelings or opinions of others: *Sending someone a birthday card is a thoughtful gesture.* —*v.* **ges•tured, ges•tur•ing, ges•tures.** —*intr.* To make a gesture or gestures: *The police officer gestured for the car to proceed.* —*tr.* To express or signal (sthg.) by gesture: *With a nod, the judge gestured a willingness to listen.*

get (gĕt) *v.* **got** (gŏt), **got•ten** (gŏt′n) or **got, get•ting, gets.** —*tr.* **1.** To receive (sthg.): *She got skates for her birthday.* **2.** To go after and obtain (sthg.): *I got some food at the supermarket.* **3.** To gain or earn (sthg.): *The student got a prize for high achievement.* **4.** To experience or become affected with (sthg.): *He got a broken ankle.* **5.** To cause (sbdy.) to be or become: *Sad movies get me down.* **6.** To make (sthg.) ready; prepare: *get lunch for a crowd.* **7.a.** To cause (sbdy.) to do (sthg.): *We got the guide to give us the complete tour.* **b.** To cause (sthg.) to be done: *We got the house painted.* **8.** To hit or strike (sbdy./sthg.): *The snowball got me on the arm.* **9.** To understand (sbdy./sthg.): *I don't get my homework assignment.* **10.** To make contact with (sbdy.): *We got the manager on the telephone.* **11.** *Informal.* To annoy or irritate (sbdy.): *His rudeness really gets me.* **12.** (used with the present participle). To start: *We should get going or we'll be late.* —*intr.* **1.** To reach or arrive: *get to the airport; get to school on time.* **2.** To be or become: *get well; get adjusted.* **3.** To come or go: *get up the icy steps.* **4.** To be able or permitted: *I never got to see the movie.* —*aux.* Used as the auxiliary verb, instead of *be*, in a passive sentence, and indicating that the object of the passive verb is responsible for what happened: *A woman got raped last night. The students got caught cheating.* ◆ **get ahead.** *intr.v.* To make progress or succeed: *He'll never get ahead if he doesn't save his money.* **get along.** *intr.v.* **1.** To have a friendly relationship: *The two little children got along well.* **2.** To manage with reasonable success: *We're not rich, but we're getting along.* **3.** To advance; progress: *How's your project getting along?* **4.** To leave: *I think I'll be getting along now.* **get around.** *tr.v.* [insep.] **1.** To deal with (sbdy./sthg.) in a dishonest, evasive way: *Many lazy people try to get around rules.* **2.** To travel from place to place: *He gets around on his bicycle.* —*intr.v.* To become widely known; spread: *Rumors get around quickly.* **get around to.** To do sthg. after a delay: *When do you think you can get around to fixing the sink?* **get at.** *tr.v.* [insep.] **1.** To reach (sthg.): *The book fell behind the bookcase where I can't get at it.* **2.** To express or mean (sthg.): *Do you understand what I am getting at?* **get away.** *intr.v.* **1.** To go away: *We want to get away on a trip to the mountains.* **2.** To escape: *The lion got away from the zoo.* **get away with.** To do

sthg. without being punished or found out: *get away with a crime.* **get back at.** To take revenge on sbdy.: *The players wanted to get back at the team that beat them.* **get behind.** *tr.v.* [insep.] To help support (sbdy.): *My friends got behind that candidate too.* **get behind on** or **with.** To fail to do sthg. on time: *He got behind on his car payments. I try not to get behind with my homework.* **get by.** *intr.v.* **1.** To manage; survive: *They were unprepared for rain but got by somehow.* **2.** To pass without being noticed: *The prisoners got by the guards.* **3.** To succeed but at the lowest acceptable level: *just getting by in school.* **get down.** *tr.v.* [sep.] *Informal.* To make (sbdy.) sad: *He really got me down when he told us about his misfortunes.* **get down to.** To give one's attention to sthg.: *Let's get down to work.* **get in.** *intr.v.* **1.** To enter or be allowed to enter: *Can we get in without a ticket?* **2.** To arrive: *The plane gets in at midnight.* **get it. 1.** To understand sthg.: *I just don't get it; it's too difficult.* **2.** *Informal.* To be punished or scolded: *You're really going to get it when your mother comes home.* **get off.** *intr.v.* **1.** To have permission to leave: *Tomorrow all employees get off early.* **2.** To escape punishment or obligation: *The student who cheated got off with just a warning.* **get on.** *intr.v.* **1.** To be on friendly terms: *The neighbors got on for years and then suddenly had a fight.* **2.** To grow old: *The old dog is getting on in years.* **3.** To continue, proceed, or progress: *I got on with the work.* **get out.** *intr.v.* **1.** To leave or escape: *Our dog got out of the yard.* **2.** To become known: *The secret finally got out.* —*tr.v.* [sep.] To produce (sthg.): *That band gets out a new CD every year.* **get over.** *tr.v.* [insep.] To recover from (sthg.): *get over a cold.* **get over with.** To do sthg. unpleasant so that it will be finished: *Go to the dentist today and get it over with.* **get through.** *tr.v.* [insep.] To finish (sthg.): *trying to get through a big job.* —*intr.* To succeed in making contact: *I telephoned twice, but couldn't get through.* **get together.** To meet; assemble: *getting together for supper tonight.* **get up.** *intr.v.* **1.** To arise from bed: *They got up early to see the sunrise.* **2.** To sit or stand up: *He got up from the chair.*

get•a•way (gĕt′ə wā′) *n.* The act of getting away; an escape: *a vacation getaway at the beach; make a fast getaway.*

get-to•geth•er (gĕt′tə gĕth′ər) *n. Informal.* A small party or gathering: *a quiet get-together with friends.*

get•up (gĕt′ŭp′) *n. Informal.* A set of clothes or a costume, especially one that is odd or different: *Have you seen the getup our teacher is wearing today?*

get-up-and-go (gĕt′ŭp′ən gō′) *n.* [U] *Informal.* Ambition and energy: *That young executive shows plenty of get-up-and-go.*

gey·ser (gī′zər) *n.* A natural hot spring that regularly sends a spray of steam and boiling water up into the air.

ghast·ly (găst′lē) *adj.* **ghast·li·er, ghast·li·est. 1.** Terrifying; horrible: *a ghastly crime.* **2.** Resembling a ghost; extremely pale: *The patient had a ghastly complexion.* **3.** Extremely unpleasant or bad: *His cooking is ghastly.* —**ghast′li·ness** *n.* [U]

ghet·to (gĕt′ō) *n., pl.* **ghet·tos** or **ghet·toes.** A section of a city where a minority group lives because it is poor or under social pressure: *This neighborhood was the Irish ghetto in the early days of the city.*

ghost (gōst) *n.* **1.** The spirit of a dead person, supposed to haunt or appear to living persons: *She thought she saw the ghost of her Aunt Martha, who'd been dead for 20 years.* **2.** A slight trace; a bit: *a ghost of a smile; a ghost of a chance.* —**ghost′li·ness** *n.* [U] —**ghost′ly** *adj.*

ghost town *n.* A town, especially one of the western frontier in the United States, that has been abandoned.

ghost·write (gōst′rīt′) *tr.v.* **ghost·wrote** (gōst′rōt′), **ghost·writ·ten** (gōst′rĭt′n), **ghost·writ·ing, ghost·writes.** To write (sthg., such as an article or a speech) for another person who is credited as the author: *The movie star's autobiography was ghostwritten by a professional writer.* —**ghost′·writ′er** *n.*

ghoul (gool) *n.* **1.** An evil spirit. **2.** A person who delights in brutal or horrible things: *Only a ghoul could watch the murder scene in that movie!* —**ghoul′ish** *adj.* —**ghoul′ish·ly** *adv.* —**ghoul′ish·ness** *n.* [U]

GI (jē′ī′) *n., pl.* **GIs** or **GI's.** An enlisted person in or a veteran of any of the U.S. armed forces. —*adj.* Relating to or characteristic of a GI: *a GI uniform; the GI bill.*

gi·ant (jī′ənt) *n.* **1.** A person or thing of great size, ability, or importance: *a musical giant.* **2.** A being of great size and strength with human form and found in myth or folklore: *Giants are common characters in fairy tales.* —*adj.* Gigantic; huge: *a giant airport.*

gib·ber·ish (jĭb′ər ĭsh) *n.* [U] Meaningless or nonsensical talk or writing: *The auctioneer was speaking so fast it all sounded like gibberish.*

gid·dy (gĭd′ē) *adj.* **gid·di·er, gid·di·est. 1.** Having a whirling sensation in the head; dizzy: *The climber became giddy at the top of the mountain.* **2.** Lighthearted; not serious: *The good news put everyone in a giddy mood.* —**gid′di·ly** *adv.* —**gid′di·ness** *n.* [U]

gift (gĭft) *n.* **1.** Something given; a present: *a birthday gift.* **2.** A special talent, aptitude, or ability: *a gift for mathematics; the gift of gab.*

gift certificate *n.* A certificate from a certain store or business, usually bought as a gift, that allows sbdy. to choose goods or services valued at the amount shown: *a $50 gift certificate to a local restaurant.*

gift·ed (gĭf′tĭd) *adj.* With great natural ability, intelligence, or talent: *a gifted athlete.*

gift-wrap (gĭft′răp′) *tr.v.* **gift-wrapped, gift-wrap·ping, gift-wraps.** To wrap (sthg. intended as a gift) with fancy paper, ribbon, or other trimmings.

gig (gĭg) *n. Slang.* A job for a musician, especially at a club: *The band has a gig playing at a wedding next week.*

gig·a·byte (gĭg′ə bīt′ *or* jĭg′ə bīt′) *n.* A unit of computerized information equal to one billion bytes.

gig·a·hertz (gĭg′ə hûrtz′ *or* jĭg′ə hûrtz′) *n., pl.* **gig·a·hertz.** A unit of frequency equal to one billion hertz.

gi·gan·tic (jī găn′tĭk) *adj.* Suggestive of a giant; huge: *a gigantic basketball player; a gigantic factory.* —**gi·gan′ti·cal·ly** *adv.*

gig·gle (gĭg′əl) *intr.v.* **gig·gled, gig·gling, gig·gles.** To laugh in a silly or nervous way: *The children giggled at the clown's funny expression.* —*n.* A short silly laugh. —**gig′gler** *n.* —**gig′gly** *adj.*

gild (gĭld) *tr.v.* **gild·ed** or **gilt** (gĭlt), **gild·ing, gilds. 1.** To cover (sthg.) with a thin layer of gold: *gild the frame of a mirror.* **2.** To give a falsely attractive or improved appearance to (sthg.): *In gilding the facts, the author made the commander seem less cruel.*

HOMONYMS: gild, guild (association).

---

gill (gĭl) *n.* The organ that enables fish and certain other water animals to take oxygen from the water, consisting of a series of membranes through which oxygen and carbon dioxide pass into and out of the bloodstream. ♦ **to the gills.** *Informal.* As full as possible; completely: *I ate so much I'm stuffed to the gills.*

gilt (gĭlt) *v.* A past tense and a past participle of **gild.** —*n.* [U] A thin layer of gold or sthg. similar to gold, like gold-colored paint, applied to a surface. —*adj.* Covered with gold or sthg. resembling gold; gilded: *a picture in a gilt frame.*

HOMONYMS: gilt, guilt (remorse).

---

gim·mick (gĭm′ĭk) *n. Informal.* A clever idea, scheme, or device, often used to promote sthg.: *an advertising gimmick.*

gin (jĭn) *n.* [C; U] A strong alcoholic liquor distilled from grain and flavored with juniper berries.

ă–cat; ā–pay; âr–care; ä–father; ĕ–get; ē–be; ĭ–sit; ī–nice; îr–here; ŏ–got; ō–go; ô–saw; oi–boy; ou–out; oo–took; oo–boot; ŭ–cut; ûr–word; th–thin; *th*–this; hw–when; zh–vision; ə–about; N–French bon

gin·ger (jĭn′jər) n. [U] **1.** A tropical plant having a root with a sharp spicy flavor often preserved and used for flavoring or candied. **2.** Informal. Liveliness; vigor: a kitten full of ginger.

ginger ale n. [U] A soft drink flavored with ginger.

gin·ger·bread (jĭn′jər brĕd′) n. [U] **1.** A cake or cookie flavored with ginger and molasses. **2.** Elaborate and detailed ornamentation, especially in architecture or furniture: a beach cottage covered in gingerbread.

gin·ger·ly (jĭn′jər lē) adv. Cautiously; carefully: The cat rubbed herself gingerly against the horse's legs. —adj. Cautious; careful: It is best to offer advice in a gingerly fashion.

ging·ham (gĭng′əm) n. [U] A light cotton cloth woven with colored thread in small squares.

gi·raffe (jə răf′) n. A tall African mammal with a very long neck and legs, a tan coat with brown patches, and short horns. The giraffe is the tallest living mammal.

gird·er (gûr′dər) n. A horizontal beam, as of steel, that acts as one of the main supports of a building, bridge, or other structure.

gir·dle (gûr′dl) n. **1.** A woman's elastic undergarment, worn over the waist and hips. **2.** Something that surrounds like a belt: a girdle of mountains around the valley. —tr.v. **gir·dled, gir·dling, gir·dles.** To encircle (sbdy./sthg.) as if with a belt: Embroidery girdled the waist of the dress.

girl (gûrl) n. **1.** A female child. **2.** A daughter: our youngest girl. **3.** Informal. A term that can be used offensively by a man or playfully by another woman when referring to a woman: an evening out with the girls; the girls in the typing pool. —**girl′hood′** n. [C; U]

girl·friend also **girl friend** (gûrl′frĕnd′) n. **1.** A favored female companion or sweetheart: a teenage boy and his girlfriend. **2.** A female friend: She invited her closest girlfriends to lunch. **3.** Used as a friendly term of address by one woman to another: Girlfriend, you need to pull yourself together.

girl·ish (gûr′lĭsh) adj. Characteristic of or suitable for a girl: a woman with a girlish laugh. —**girl′ish·ly** adv. —**girl′ish·ness** n. [U]

Girl Scout n. A member of the Girl Scouts.

Girl Scouts pl.n. An organization for girls whose goals include helping girls develop self-reliance, good citizenship, and outdoor skills.

girth (gûrth) n. **1.** [C; U] The distance around sthg.; the circumference: a large tree 15 feet in girth. **2.** [C] A strap encircling the body of a horse or pack animal in order to hold a load or saddle on its back.

gist (jĭst) n. [U] The central idea; the main point: the gist of a message.

give (gĭv) v. **gave** (gāv), **giv·en** (gĭv′ən),

giv·ing, gives. —tr. **1.** To make a present of (sthg.): My sister gave me a new watch. **2.** To place (sthg.) in the hands of (sbdy.): Please give me the magazine. **3.** To deliver (sthg.) in exchange or in payment; sell or pay: We gave them the bike for $25. They gave us $25 for the bike. **4.** To present (sthg.) as an award: They gave first prize to the best artist. **5.** To administer or deliver (sthg.) by physical action: The doctor gave me a shot. My mother gave me a hug. **6.** To provide or supply (sthg.): Green vegetables give us vitamins and minerals. **7.** To offer or present (sthg.): Could you give us your ideas on the economy? **8.** To tell (sthg.): give an order; give him a message. **9.** To infect (sbdy.) with an illness or disease, or cause discomfort: Who gave you that cold? This work always gives me a headache. **10.** To produce or yield (sthg.): Their cows give milk and cream. —intr. **1.** To make a gift or donation: They give generously to local charities. **2.** To yield to force or pressure: The roof gave under the weight of the snow. —n. [U] Elasticity; flexibility: The diving board has a lot of give. ◆ **give away.** tr.v. [sep.] **1.** To make a gift of (sthg.): We gave away many of the vegetables from our garden. **2.** To present (a bride) to the bridegroom at a wedding ceremony: The bride's father gave her away. **3.** To tell or make (sthg.) known, often by accident: I gave away the surprise party when I mentioned buying balloons and other decorations. **give back.** tr.v. [sep.] To return (sthg.): Give me back my book. **give birth to.** To bear a child: She gave birth to twins. **give in.** intr.v. To surrender; yield: The baby sitter gave in and let the children watch TV. **give it to.** Informal. To punish or scold sbdy. severely: My dad's going to give it to me when he sees the window I broke. **give off.** tr.v. [sep.] To send (sthg.) forth: The moon gave off an eerie light. **give or take.** Plus or minus a small amount: He's six feet tall, give or take an inch. **give out.** tr.v. [sep.] **1.** To let (sthg.) be known: gave out the bad news. **2.** To distribute (sthg.): give out paychecks to employees. —intr.v. **1.** To stop working; fail: The water pump gave out. **2.** To become used up: The runner's energy gave out after five miles. **give over.** tr.v. [sep.] **1.** To release or entrust (sthg.) to sbdy.: He has given over his responsibilities to the new president. **2.** Make (sthg.) available for a purpose: The last part of the program is given over to questions from the audience. **give rise to.** To be the cause or origin of sthg.: give rise to doubts. **give up.** tr.v. [sep.] **1.** To surrender (oneself): The thieves gave themselves up to the police. **2.** To stop doing (sthg.): My uncle has given up smoking. **3.** To let go any hope for (sbdy./sthg.): We gave the cat up as lost. —intr.v. To admit defeat and stop trying: They finally gave up and stopped looking for the ring. **give way.**

G

1. To move back or away; retreat: *The animals gave way before the advancing fire.* **2.** To lose one's self-control: *Don't give way to panic.* **3.** To collapse; break: *The old flooring might give way under so much weight.* —**giv′er** *n.*

give-and-take also **give and take** (gĭv′ən-tāk′) *n.* [U] Willingness on both sides to agree to each other's wishes; compromise: *the give-and-take necessary to reach an agreement.*

give•a•way (gĭv′ə wā′) *n. Informal.* **1.** Something given away or sold at a very low price: *At ten cents a pound these potatoes are a real giveaway.* **2.** Something that reveals hidden information, often by accident: *His refusal to answer the question was a giveaway that he knew more about what happened.*

giv•en (gĭv′ən) *v.* Past participle of **give.** —*adj.* **1.** Specified; stated: *obtain all the facts on one given country.* **2.** Considering: *Given the condition of the car, it's a wonder it runs at all.* **3.** [*to*] Having a tendency; inclined: *given to talking too much.* —*n.* Something that is assumed or taken to be true: *Her ability to lead is a given, but I question her desire to do so.*

given name *n.* The name given to a person at birth; a first name: *Elizabeth is her given name; Morrison is her family name.*

giz•mo (gĭz′mō) *n., pl.* **giz•mos.** *Informal.* A small device whose name is forgotten or not yet known: *We need a few more of these gizmos to finish putting the model together.*

gla•cial (glā′shəl) *adj.* **1.** Relating to or produced by a glacier: *Glacial lakes are scattered around the area.* **2.** Suggesting the extreme slowness of a glacier: *Political reform often moves at a glacial pace.* **3.** Lacking warmth or friendliness: *a glacial stare.* —**gla′cial•ly** *adv.*

gla•cier (glā′shər) *n.* A large mass of ice slowly moving over a mountain or through a valley, formed over many years from packed snow in areas where snow accumulates faster than it melts: *glaciers in Alaska.*

glad (glăd) *adj.* **glad•der, glad•dest. 1.** Experiencing, showing, or providing joy and pleasure: *We were so glad to get your letter.* **2.** Pleased; willing: *I would be glad to help.* —**glad′ly** *adv.* —**glad′ness** *n.* [U]

SYNONYMS: glad, happy, cheerful, lighthearted, joyful. These adjectives mean being in or showing good spirits. **Glad** often means satisfied with immediate circumstances: *I am so glad we finally met.* **Happy** can mean feeling pleasurable contentment, as from a sense of fulfillment: *The veterinarian is happy with her new job.* **Cheerful** means having good spirits, as from being pleased: *The child tried to remain cheerful while he was in the hospital.* **Lighthearted**

means free of cares and worries: *Summertime always puts me in a lighthearted mood.* **Joyful** means having great happiness and liveliness: *Their wedding was a joyful occasion.*

---

glad•den (glăd′n) *tr.v. Formal.* To make (sbdy./sthg.) glad: *The good news gladdened our hearts.*

glade (glād) *n.* An open space in a forest.

glad•i•a•tor (glăd′ē ā′tər) *n.* In ancient Rome, a person, especially a slave, captive, or criminal, who had to fight to the death in an arena to entertain the public.

glad•i•o•la (glăd′ē ō′lə) *n.* A plant with leaves shaped like swords and a long cluster of showy, variously colored flowers.

glam•or also **glam•our** (glăm′ər) *n.* [U] A feeling of romance or excitement surrounding a person or thing: *the glamor of being a movie star.*

glam•or•ize (glăm′ə rīz′) *tr.v.* **glam•or•ized, glam•or•iz•ing, glam•or•iz•es.** To make (sthg.) glamorous: *Hollywood movies have glamorized the life of gangsters.*

glam•or•ous (glăm′ər əs) *adj.* Having or showing glamor; fascinating: *a glamorous life of wealth and adventure.* —**glam′or•ous•ly** *adv.* —**glam′or•ous•ness** *n.* [U]

glance (glăns) *intr.v.* **glanced, glanc•ing, glanc•es. 1.** To look briefly or hastily: *I glanced over the contract, but I didn't study it carefully.* **2.** [*off*] To strike a surface at such an angle as to fly off to one side: *The ax glanced off the log and struck the ground.* —*n.* **1.** A brief or hasty look: *a quick glance over the shoulder.* **2.** A glancing off; a deflection. ◆ **at first glance.** On first thinking about sthg.: *At first glance it seemed impossible, but then I saw how we could make it work.*

gland (glănd) *n.* **1.** An organ in the body, such as the liver, kidneys, or thyroid, that produces some special substance, such as a hormone or an enzyme. **2.** A lymph node or other organ of the body that resembles a gland. —**glan′du•lar** (glăn′jə lər) *adj.*

glare (glâr) *v.* **glared, glar•ing, glares.** —*intr.* **1.** To stare fiercely or angrily: *The angry customer glared at the sales clerk.* **2.** To shine intensely: *The sun glared off the windshield.* —*tr.* To express (sthg.) with a fierce or angry stare: *The prisoners glared defiance at their guards.* —*n.* **1.** [C] A fixed angry stare: *The angry child greeted her teacher with a glare.* **2.** [U] A very strong and blinding light: *the sun's glare.*

glar•ing (glâr′ĭng) *adj.* **1.** Staring fiercely or angrily: *glaring eyes.* **2.** Shining intensely: *a glaring summer sun.* **3.** Very easily seen or noticed; obvious: *a glaring error.* —**glar′ing•ly** *adv.*

ă–cat; ā–pay; âr–care; ä–father; ĕ–get; ē–be; ĭ–sit; ī–nice; îr–here; ŏ–got; ō–go; ô–saw; oi–boy; ou–out; ŏŏ–took; ōō–boot; ŭ–cut; ûr–word; th–thin; *th*–this; hw–when; zh–vision; ə–about; N–French bon

glass (glăs) *n.* **1.** [U] A hard, transparent or translucent material made by melting sand with soda and lime: *windows made of glass.* **2.** [C] Something made of glass, as a mirror or a windowpane: *When I threw the ball it broke the glass.* **3.** [C] A container used for drinking, especially one made of glass: *Here's a glass for your drink.* **4.** [C] The amount contained in a drinking container; a glassful: *spill a whole glass of milk.* **5. glasses.** Eyeglasses: *I wear glasses only when I read.*

glass•ful (glăs′fŏŏl′) *n.* The quantity that a glass can hold.

glass•ware (glăs′wâr′) *n.* [U] Objects, especially containers, made of glass.

glass•y (glăs′ē) *adj.* **glass•i•er, glass•i•est. 1.** Resembling glass; smooth: *the glassy surface of a highly polished table.* **2.** Having no expression; blank: *a glassy stare.* —**glass′i•ly** *adv.* —**glass′i•ness** *n.* [U]

glau•co•ma (glou kō′mə *or* glô kō′mə) *r.* [U] An eye disease that often damages the optic nerve and leads eventually to blindness.

glaze (glāz) *n.* [C; U] **1.** A thin, smooth, shiny coating: *A glaze of ice covered the roads. I covered the cake with chocolate glaze.* **2.** A coating of colored material applied to ceramics before firing in a kiln. —*v.* **glazed, glaz•ing, glaz•es.** —*tr.* **1.** To apply a glaze to (sthg.): *The baker glazed the buns with egg white. The potter glazed the mugs and bowls.* **2.** To fit or supply (sthg.) with glass: *glaze a window.* —*intr.* [*over*] To become glazed or glassy: *His eyes glazed over from boredom.*

gleam (glēm) *n.* **1.** A flash of light: *occasional gleams of sunshine through the clouds.* **2.** A steady glow: *the soft pale gleam of moonlight.* **3.** A brief indication; a trace: *a gleam of hope.* —*intr.v.* To give off a gleam; shine: *The snow gleamed like diamonds.*

glean (glēn) *tr.v.* To gather (sthg.) bit by bit: *After weeks of investigation, the reporter gleaned enough information for the article.*

glee (glē) *n.* A feeling of delight; joy: *She accepted her prize with glee.* —**glee′ful** *adj.* —**glee′ful•ly** *adv.* —**glee′ful•ness** *n.* [U]

glee club *n.* A group of singers who perform usually short pieces of choral music.

glen (glĕn) *n.* A valley: *a farm nestled in the glen.*

glib (glĭb) *adj.* **glib•ber, glib•best.** Speaking or writing smoothly but suggesting lack of thought or sincerity: *a glib reply to a serious question.* —**glib′ly** *adv.* —**glib′ness** *n.* [U]

glide (glīd) *v.* **glid•ed, glid•ing, glides.** —*intr.* **1.** To move smoothly and with little effort: *The skaters glided over the ice.* See Synonyms at **slide. 2.** To pass or happen without notice: *The weekend had glided by.* **3.** To fly without using propelling power: *The hot-air balloon glided overhead.* —*tr.* To cause (sthg.) to move smoothly and with little effort: *glide a canoe through the water.* —*n.* **1.** [U] The act or process of gliding. **2.** [C] A smooth effortless movement: *a glide across the dance floor.*

glid•er (glī′dər) *n.* **1.** An aircraft that has no engine and is designed to glide after being towed up into the air by an airplane. **2.** A long swinging seat that hangs in a vertical frame.

glim•mer (glĭm′ər) *n.* **1.** A dim or unsteady light; a flicker: *the glimmer of candles in the breeze.* **2.** A very small sign or indication; a trace: *a glimmer of understanding; a glimmer of hope.* —*intr.v.* To give off a dim or flickering light: *A single lamp glimmered in the window.*

glimpse (glĭmps) *n.* A brief incomplete view or look: *We caught just a glimpse of the sun on the cloudy day.* —*tr.v.* **glimpsed, glimps•ing, glimps•es.** To obtain a brief incomplete view of (sbdy./sthg.): *glimpsed a speeding car.*

glint (glĭnt) *n.* A brief flash of light; a sparkle: *a glint in her eyes.* —*intr.v.* To gleam or flash; sparkle: *The lake glinted in the moonlight.*

glis•ten (glĭs′ən) *intr.v.* To shine with a sparkling reflected light: *The snow glistened in the sunlight.* —*n.* A shine or sparkle.

glitch (glĭch) *n.* A malfunction or problem, often technical: *a glitch in the computer program; a glitch in our plans.*

glit•ter (glĭt′ər) *n.* [U] **1.** A sparkling light or brightness: *the glitter of polished silver.* **2.** Brilliance or showiness: *the glitter of a movie star's party.* **3.** Small pieces of light-reflecting decorative material: *eye shadow sparkling with glitter.* —*intr.v.* **1.** To sparkle brilliantly: *The stars glittered in the night sky.* **2.** To be brilliantly, often falsely attractive: *The chance of making a fortune glittered in front of them.* —**glit′ter•y** *adj.*

gloat (glōt) *intr.v.* [*over*] To feel or express great pleasure, often because of somebody's misfortune: *The team gloated over the victory.*

glob (glŏb) *n.* A thick drop or rounded mass or lump: *a glob of mashed potatoes.*

glob•al (glō′bəl) *adj.* **1.** Of the entire earth; worldwide: *a global population figure.* **2.** Considering all parts: *a global study.* —**glob′al•ly** *adv.*

global warm•ing (wôr′mĭng) *n.* [U] A rise in the earth's temperature, caused by increasing amounts of carbon dioxide in the atmosphere.

globe (glōb) *n.* **1.** An object with the general shape of a ball or sphere, especially a representation of the earth: *We learned geography from maps and globes.* **2.** The earth: *The space station is designed to circle the globe constantly.* **3.** A spherical container, especially a glass sphere covering a light bulb: *You have to remove the globe before you can replace the burned-out light bulb.*

glob•ule (glŏb′yŏŏl) *n.* A very small rounded mass, especially a small drop of liquid. —**glob′u•lar** (glŏb′yə lər) *adj.*

G

gloom (glōōm) *n.* [U] **1.** Partial or total darkness; dimness: *He peered into the gloom of the night.* **2.** Lowness of spirit; sadness: *She sank into gloom after losing her job.*

gloom·y (glōō′mē) *adj.* **gloom·i·er, gloom·i·est. 1.** Partially or totally dark; dismal: *a gloomy deserted castle.* **2.** Showing or filled with gloom; sad: *His gloomy face showed that the news was not good.* **3.** Causing low spirits; depressing: *a gloomy atmosphere.* —**gloom′·i·ly** *adv.* —**gloom′i·ness** *n.* [U]

glo·ri·fy (glôr′ə fī′) *tr.v.* **glo·ri·fied, glo·ri·fy·ing, glo·ri·fies. 1.** To give honor or high praise to (sbdy./sthg.): *The Egyptians glorified their king by building a pyramid.* **2.** To make (sthg.) seem more glorious or excellent than it really is: *Their description glorified the old house as a mansion.* —**glo′ri·fi·ca′tion** (glôr′ə fĭ kā′shən) *n.* [U]

glo·ri·ous (glôr′ē əs) *adj.* **1.** Having or deserving glory; famous: *the glorious achievements of the Renaissance.* **2.** Having great beauty or splendor; magnificent: *a glorious sunset.* —**glo′ri·ous·ly** *adv.*

glo·ry (glôr′ē) *n., pl.* **glo·ries. 1.** [U] Great honor or praise given by others; fame: *The swimmer won glory by breaking the world record.* **2.** [C] Something that brings honor, praise, or fame: *a symphony that is one of the glories of 18th-century music.* **3.** [U] Great beauty: *The sun was setting in a blaze of glory.* **4.** [U] A period of highest achievement or prosperity: *Rome in its greatest glory.* —*intr.v.* **glo·ried, glo·ry·ing, glo·ries.** [*in*] To rejoice: *The team gloried in its victory.*

gloss[1] (glôs *or* glŏs) *n.* [C; U] **1.** A shine on a surface; a sheen: *the gloss of a polished table.* **2.** An attractive appearance intended to hide the real nature of sthg.: *The new coat of paint was merely a gloss concealing the house's many structural problems.* —*tr.v.* **1.** To give a bright shine or luster to (sthg.). **2.** [*over*] To make sbdy./sthg. attractive or acceptable by hiding or falsely presenting (sthg.): *The committee glossed over serious problems in its report.*

gloss[2] (glôs *or* glŏs) *n.* A brief note that explains or translates a difficult word or phrase: *The Spanish book includes glosses in the reading.* —*tr.v.* To provide (a text) with glosses: *This science textbook glosses all technical terms.*

glos·sa·ry (glô′sə rē *or* glŏs′ə rē) *n., pl.* **glos·sa·ries.** A list of specialized words with their definitions: *a glossary of computer terms.*

gloss·y (glô′sē *or* glŏs′ē) *adj.* **gloss·i·er, gloss·i·est.** Smooth and shiny: *Satin is a glossy fabric.* —**gloss′i·ly** *adv.* —**gloss′i·ness** *n.* [U]

glove (glŭv) *n.* **1.** A covering for the hand, with a separate section for each finger and the thumb. **2.** A special covering for the hand, often of padded leather, used in baseball, handball, boxing, or some other sport. —*tr.v.* **gloved, glov·ing, gloves.** To cover (a hand or hands) with a glove: *He gloved his hands to keep them warm.* ◆ **fit like a glove.** To fit perfectly: *My new dress fits like a glove.*

glow (glō) *intr.v.* **1.** To shine brightly and steadily, especially with heat: *The embers glowed in the fireplace.* **2.** To have a bright warm color: *The skier's cheeks glowed in the cold.* **3.** To be radiant with emotion: *glow with happiness.* —*n.* [U] **1.** A light given off by sthg. that is hot or brilliant: *the glow of coals in the furnace.* **2.** A feeling of warmth, especially when caused by emotion: *the glow on a child's happy face.*

glow·er (glou′ər) *intr.v.* [*at*] To look or stare angrily: *The unfriendly neighbors glowered at us.* —*n.* An angry or threatening stare: *the glower of a driver stuck in traffic.*

glow·ing (glō′ĭng) *adj.* **1.** Giving or reflecting brilliant light: *glowing coals.* **2.** Having a rich warm color, as from health or strong emotion: *a glowing complexion.* **3.** Enthusiastic; highly favorable: *We received glowing reports of their success.* —**glow′ing·ly** *adv.*

glu·cose (glōō′kōs′) *n.* [U] **1.** A common kind of sugar found in plant and animal tissue. **2.** A thick mixture of different sugars and water, used in commercial baking.

glue (glōō) *n.* [C; U] A thick sticky substance used to join things together: *His mother used glue to fix the broken toy.* —*tr.v.* **glued, glu·ing, glues. 1.** To stick or fasten (sthg.) together with glue: *glue the broken leg of a chair.* **2.** To fix or hold (sbdy./sthg.) firmly as if with glue: *The dog glued its eyes on the stranger. The child was glued to the television all evening.*

glum (glŭm) *adj.* **glum·mer, glum·mest.** Feeling or appearing sad or gloomy: *a glum look on his face.* —**glum′ly** *adv.*

glut (glŭt) *tr.v.* **glut·ted, glut·ting, gluts. 1.** To fill (sbdy./sthg.) beyond capacity, especially with food: *The lions slept after glutting themselves on their kill.* **2.** To provide (a market) with too many goods so that the supply is much greater than the demand: *glutted the oil market by expanding production.* —*n.* A too great amount; an oversupply: *A glut of gasoline caused lower prices.*

glu·ten (glōōt′n) *n.* [U] A tough sticky plant protein found in grains such as oats and wheat, used as an adhesive and as a flour substitute.

glu·ti·nous (glōōt′n əs) *adj.* Resembling glue; thick and sticky: *a glutinous mixture of flour and water.*

glut•ton (glŭt′n) *n.* **1.** A person who eats to excess: *That glutton had six eggs for break-fast—and a steak!* **2.** A person with an unusually great capacity to receive or tolerate sthg.: *a glutton for work.* ◆ **glutton for punishment.** Somebody who appears to enjoy sthg. unpleasant: *a glutton for punishment who kept working long hours for low pay.* —**glut′ton•ous** *adj.* —**glut′ton•ous•ly** *adv.*

glut•ton•y (glŭt′n ē) *n.* [U] Excess in eating or drinking: *His gluttony resulted in health problems.*

gm. *abbr.* An abbreviation of gram.

gnarled (närld) *adj.* Knotty and misshapen; deformed: *the old man's gnarled hands.*

gnash (năsh) *tr.v.* To grind (the teeth) together: *She gnashed her teeth in frustration.*

gnat (năt) *n.* A very small winged insect that gives itching bites.

gnaw (nô) *v.* —*tr.* **1.** To bite or chew (sthg.) continuously with the teeth: *animals gnawing the bark of trees; a dog gnawing a bone.* **2.** To reduce (sthg.) gradually as if by gnawing: *The waves gnawed the base of the cliff during high tide.* **3.** To cause distress or pain to (sbdy./ sthg.): *Frustration gnawed his stomach.* —*intr.* **1.** [*on*] To bite or chew: *The dog gnawed on a bone.* **2.** [*at*] To trouble or distress: *The lack of success gnawed at the scientist for weeks.*

gnome (nōm) *n.* In folklore, a dwarf that lives underground and guards treasure.

GNP *abbr.* An abbreviation for gross national product: *The President announced a large increase in the GNP.*

gnu (nōō) *n.* A large African antelope with a beard and mane, a long tufted tail, and curved horns.

HOMONYMS: gnu, knew (had knowledge), **new** (not used).

---

go (gō) *v.* **went** (wĕnt), **gone** (gôn *or* gŏn), **go•ing, goes** (gōz). —*intr.* **1.** To move along or forward; travel: *The bus went along steadily in the rain.* **2.** To move or advance to a specified place: *I am going to New York.* **3.** To move from a place; leave: *We must go now.* **4.** To function, operate, move, or work: *A battery makes the watch go.* **5.** To travel somewhere for an activity: *go study; go skating.* **6.** To follow a course of action: *go to a lot of trouble; go too far.* **7.a.** To belong in a definite place or position: *This book goes on that shelf.* **b.** To be suitable: *Do this shirt and tie go together?* **8.** To extend between two points or in a certain direction: *The windows go from the ceiling to the floor. The road goes north.* **9.** To pass: *Time goes quickly when you are busy.* **10.** To be given or marked for a purpose: *First prize went to my friend. This money goes for the homeless in our town.* **11.** To pass or end in a particular way: *How did your day go? How does the rest of the story go?* **12.** To become weak; fail: *My eyes are going.* **13.** To enter into a certain state or condition: *go mad; go to sleep; a tire going flat.* **14.** Used to indicate intention or expectation in combination with the infinitive of another verb: *I am going to become a doctor. We were going to play tennis but it rained.* —*n., pl.* **goes.** *Informal.* **1.** An attempt; an effort: *Let's have a go at the puzzle.* **2.** A success: *They tried to make a go of their store.* —*adj. Informal.* Ready for action or working correctly: *Everything is go for the parade.* ◆ **go about.** *tr.v.* [insep.] **1.** To begin to do (sthg.) complex: *How does one go about building a house?* **2.** To continue (sthg.) as usual: *go about one's business.* **go along.** *intr.v.* To cooperate: *She decided to go along with their plans for the surprise party.* **go around.** *intr.v.* **1.** To satisfy a demand or requirement: *We have enough food to go around.* **2.** To move from place to place: *She goes around complaining about her job.* **3.** To circulate: *rumors going around.* **go at.** *tr.v.* [insep.] **1.** To attack (sbdy./ sthg.), especially with energy: *He went at the meat with a sharp knife.* **2.** To begin to do (sthg.): *He went at the assignment right away.* **go back on.** To fail to honor or keep sthg., such as a promise: *Don't go back on your word!* **go by.** *intr.v.* To pass: *Time goes by fast sometimes.* —*tr.v.* [insep.] To follow or be guided by (sthg.): *go by appearances.* **go down.** *intr.v.* **1.a.** To drop below the horizon; set: *The sun went down.* **b.** To sink: *The ship went down in a storm.* **2.** To be easy to swallow: *This ice cream goes right down.* **3.** To come to be remembered much later: *He went down in history as a famous inventor.* **go for.** *tr.v.* [insep.] **1.** *Informal.* To have a special liking for (sbdy./ sthg.): *I really go for jazz.* **2.** To attack (sbdy./ sthg.): *When the whistle blew, the teams went for each other.* **go in for.** To have an interest or take part in sthg.: *She goes in for water skiing.* **go into.** *tr.v.* [insep.] **1.** To discuss or explain (sthg.): *I asked what had happened, but she refused to go into it.* **2.** To enter (a profession); start (a career): *She's going into law.* **go off.** *intr.v.* **1.** To explode: *fireworks going off.* **2.** To make a noise; sound: *The fire alarm went off, but it was just a test.* **3.** To leave: *They went off for a walk.* **go off on.** To lose one's temper: *Don't go off on me because you lost your car keys!* **go on.** *intr.v.* **1.** To take place; happen: *What's going on?* **2.** To continue: *How long has this discussion been going on? They went on talking.* **3.** *Informal.* To talk too much: *He does go on about his car.* **go out.** *intr.v.* **1.** To stop working, burning, or glowing: *The lights all went out in the storm.* **2.** To take part in social life outside the home: *Let's go out to the movies.* **3.** To date: *They've been going out now for months.* **4.** To become unfashionable: *That dance went out years ago.* **go out of (one's) way.** To inconvenience oneself in doing more than what is required: *He went out of his way to help us.* **go over.** *intr.v.* To gain acceptance or approval: *My idea went over well.* —*tr.v.* [insep.] To examine (sthg.): *Did you go over my paper yet?* **go steady.** To date one person and nobody else: *We went steady for three months.* **go through.** *tr.v.* [insep.] **1.** To examine (sthg.) carefully: *I've gone through your paper and it's great!* **2.** To experience (sthg.): *We all go through some sad times.* **go through with.** To do sthg. as promised or planned: *He says he'll quit, but do you think he'll go through with it?* **go under.** *intr.v.* To fail: *The business went under.* **go without saying.** To be clear without any discussion needed: *Some rules go without saying.* **on the go.** Constantly busy or active: *My mother is always on the go.* **to go. 1.** To be taken out, as restaurant food or drink: *He ordered a pizza to go.* **2.** Remaining: *We've painted one room and we have two rooms to go.* —SEE NOTE at **gonna.**

goad (gōd) *tr.v.* To push or urge (sbdy./sthg.): *The bad grade goaded us to study harder.*

go•a•head (gō′ə hĕd′) *n. Informal.* Permission to begin or proceed: *waiting for the go-ahead from the boss.*

goal (gōl) *n.* **1.** The purpose toward which one is working; an objective: *The student's goal was to become a doctor.* **2.a.** In certain sports, a structure or an area into which players must send the ball or puck in order to score: *a soccer goal; a hockey goal.* **b.** The score awarded for doing this: *scored three goals in the game.*

goal•ie (gō′lē) *n.* A goalkeeper.

goal•keep•er (gōl′kē′pər) *n.* The player who defends the goal in sports such as hockey and soccer.

goat (gōt) *n.* A hoofed mammal with hollow horns and a beard, related to the sheep and raised in many parts of the world for wool, milk, and meat.

goat•ee (gō tē′) *n.* A small beard ending in a point just below a man's chin.

gob (gŏb) *n.* **1.** A small piece or lump: *a gob of wax.* **2.** *(usually plural). Informal.* A large quantity, as of money: *gobs of cash.*

gob•ble¹ (gŏb′əl) *tr.v.* **gob•bled, gob•bling, gob•bles.** To eat or consume (sthg.) in big greedy bites: *He is rude to gobble his food.* ◆ **gobble up.** *tr.v.* [sep.] To take or grab (sthg.) greedily: *Fans gobbled up the few remaining tickets.*

gob•ble² (gŏb′əl) *n.* The throaty sound made by a male turkey. —*intr.v.* **gob•bled, gob•bling, gob•bles.** To make this sound. —**gob′bler** *n.*

gob•ble•dy•gook also **gob•ble•de•gook** (gŏb′əl dē gook′) *n.* [U] *Informal.* Unclear, complicated speech or writing: *The contract was nothing but meaningless gobbledygook.*

go-be•tween (gō′bĭ twēn′) *n.* A person who acts as an intermediary or a messenger between two sides: *When my friends were fighting, I acted as a go-between.*

gob•let (gŏb′lĭt) *n.* A drinking glass with a stem and base: *a wine goblet.*

gob•lin (gŏb′lĭn) *n.* A small ugly creature of folklore, thought to cause mischief or evil.

god (gŏd) *n.* **1. God.** A being regarded as the creator and ruler of the universe, the object of worship in many religions. **2.** A being of supernatural powers, worshiped by a people, especially a male being thought to control some part of nature. **3.** Something considered to be of great value or high importance: *Absolute power was his god.*

god•child (gŏd′chīld′) *n., pl.* **god•child•ren.** A child for whom a person serves as sponsor at baptism. —**god′daugh′ter** (gŏd′dô′tər), **god′son′** (gŏd′sŭn′) *n.*

god•dess (gŏd′ĭs) *n.* A female being of supernatural powers, worshiped by a people.

god•fa•ther (gŏd′fä′thər) *n.* A man who serves as sponsor at one's baptism.

god•for•sak•en (gŏd′fər sā′kən) *adj.* Describing a remote place where not much is happening: *She lives in a godforsaken little town in the middle of the desert.*

god•like (gŏd′līk′) *adj.* Resembling or of the nature of God or a god; divine: *godlike wisdom.*

god•ly (gŏd′lē) *adj.* **god•li•er, god•li•est.** Having great reverence for God; pious: *known as a godly man.* —**god′li•ness** *n.* [U]

god•moth•er (gŏd′mŭth′ər) *n.* A woman who serves as sponsor at one's baptism.

god•par•ent (gŏd′pâr′ənt *or* gŏd′păr′ənt) *n.* A godfather or godmother.

god•send (gŏd′sĕnd′) *n.* Something wanted or needed that comes or happens unexpectedly: *Her brother's volunteering to watch the baby was a godsend when she needed to study.*

go-get•ter (gō′gĕt′ər *or* gō′gĕt′ər) *n. Informal.* An energetic person with much determination and ambition: *Her brother is a real go-getter who will go far in life.*

gog•gles (gŏg′əlz) *pl.n.* A pair of eyeglasses worn tight against the head to protect the eyes: *Always wear safety goggles when using power tools.*

goggles
Ski goggles

go•ing (gō′ĭng) *n.* **1.** [C] The act of leaving or moving away; departure: *comings and goings of passengers in the terminal.* **2.** [U] The condition of the ground or road as it affects how one walks or rides: *It was rough going over the icy roads, but we made it.* **3.** [U] *Informal.*

Progress toward a goal: *Learning this new computer program has been easy going.* —*adj.* **1.** Working; running: *The clock is in going order.* **2.** In full operation; flourishing: *Our business is at last a going operation.* **3.** Available or now in existence: *We make the best bikes going.* **4.** Most common at present; current: *The going rates for bank loans will soon increase.* ◆ **while the going's good.** While sthg. is still possible: *It will be dark soon. Let's leave while the going's good.*

gold (gōld) *n.* **1.** [U] *Symbol* **Au** A soft, shiny, yellow element that resists chemical change, much used in making fine jewelry and coins. Atomic number 79. See table at **element. 2.** [C; U] A deep, strong, or metallic yellow color: *when fall leaves turn to red and gold.* **3.** [U] Gold coins. **4.** [U] Money; riches: *With that much gold they'll never starve.* —*adj.* **1.** Relating to or containing gold: *a gold ring; a gold coin.* **2.** Having a deep, strong, or metallic yellow color. ◆ **have a heart of gold.** To be thought of as kind and good: *She helped everyone in our neighborhood with their problems; she has a heart of gold.*

gold•en (gōl′dən) *adj.* **1.** Relating to or containing gold: *golden earrings.* **2.** Having the color of gold: *a golden wheat field.* **3.a.** Of great value or importance; precious: *golden memories of a happy childhood.* **b.** Very favorable; excellent: *a golden opportunity.* **4.** Marked by peace, prosperity, and often creativeness: *a golden era in our past.*

gold•en•rod (gōl′dən rŏd′) *n.* [U] A wild plant with clusters of small yellow flowers that bloom on the ends of tall stalks in late summer or fall.

golden rule *n.* The rule of conduct that one should behave toward other people as one would like others to behave toward oneself.

gold-filled (gōld′fĭld′) *adj.* Made of hard metal with an outer layer of gold: *a gold-filled watch.*

gold•finch (gōld′fĭnch′) *n.* A small North American bird; the male has yellow feathers with a black forehead, wings, and tail.

gold•fish (gōld′fĭsh′) *n.* A small freshwater fish, usually orange or reddish, often kept in outdoor ponds and home aquariums.

gold•mine (gōld′mīn′) *n.* **1.** A business or activity that produces a lot of money: *The restaurant has turned out to be a goldmine.* **2.** A mine from which gold is taken.

gold•smith (gōld′smĭth′) *n.* A person who makes or deals in objects of gold.

golf (gŏlf *or* gôlf) *n.* [U] A game played over a large outdoor course with a series of 9 or 18 holes spaced far apart. A player, using various clubs, tries to take as few strokes as possible in hitting a ball into one hole after another. —*intr.v.* To play golf: *The two friends golf every Wednesday.* —**golf′er** *n.*

golf club *n.* **1.** One of a set of clubs, made

with a long stick and a head of wood or iron, used in golf. **2.** An association of golfers.

golf course *n.* A large piece of land designed for golf.

—gon *suff.* A suffix that means a specified number of angles: *octagon.*

go•nad (gō′năd′) *n.* An organ in which egg cells or sperm cells are produced; an ovary or a testis.

gon•do•la (gŏn′dl ə *or* gŏn dō′lə) *n.* **1.** A long narrow boat pushed by sbdy. in the stern with a single oar and used on the canals of Venice. **2.** A basket attached to the underside of a hot-air balloon. **3.** An enclosed car suspended from a cable used for transporting passengers, as up a mountain for skiing.

gon•do•lier (gŏn′dl îr′) *n.* The person who pushes a gondola.

gone (gôn *or* gŏn) *v.* Past participle of **go.** —*adj.* **1.** Away from a place; absent: *I'll be gone for a few days.* **2.** Dead: *I'm afraid all of the goldfish are gone.* **3.** Used up or consumed: *When natural resources are gone, they cannot be replaced.*

gon•er (gô′nər *or* gŏn′ər) *n. Slang.* A person or thing that is ruined or certain to be doomed or ruined: *We were afraid he was a goner.*

gong (gông *or* gŏng) *n.* A saucer-shaped metal disk that produces a loud ringing tone when struck: *a dinner gong to call everyone in.*

gon•na (gô′nə *or* gə′nə) *aux.v. Informal.* One of the pronunciations of *going to* used in rapid speech (see **go,** sense 14) to show strong possibility or expectation with the infinitive of another verb: *I'm gonna leave when you do. When are you gonna wash the dishes?*

USAGE: gonna In speech, two pronunciations of **going to** are used to show a difference in meaning that is not obvious in written English. Although both ways of pronouncing **going to** indicate strong intention and high probability, the pronunciation **gonna** is the auxiliary use, and **gonta** (gŭn′tə *or* gôn′tə), in which the *t* is clearly pronounced, shows that the form retains its meaning as a progressive verb. For example, compare the difference in meaning between the spoken sentences *I'm gonta the store now,* in which *going to* is a verb with its object (store), and *She's gonna rest for a while,* in which *going to* functions as an auxiliary of the verb *rest.*

gon•or•rhe•a (gŏn′ə rē′ə) *n.* [U] A sexually transmitted bacterial disease that causes inflammation of the genitals and urinary tract.

goo (gōō) *n.* [U] *Informal.* A sticky wet substance: *What have you been doing? These shoes are covered in goo!*

good (gŏŏd) *adj.* **bet•ter** (bĕt′ər), **best** (bĕst). **1.** Having positive or desirable qualities; not bad or poor: *a good book; good food.* **2.** Providing a benefit; helpful: *Rain is* *good for the crops.* **3.** Superior to average; skilled: *She's good at math. He's good with children.* **4.** In usable condition: *The milk is still good.* **5.** Valid; true: *a good reason.* **6.** In effect; valid: *The warranty on that car is good for 10,000 miles.* **7.** Attractive; handsome: *good looks.* **8.a.** Of moral excellence: *a good honest person.* **b.** Deserving respect; honorable: *a good name.* **c.** Kind: *It was good of you to call.* **9.** Well-behaved: *Be good, children!* **10.** Proper; correct: *good manners.* **11.** Not less than; full: *It is a good mile to the station.* **12.** Thorough; complete: *a good housecleaning.* —*n.* **1.** [U] Something good: *You must learn to accept the bad with the good.* **2.** [U] Benefit; welfare: *for the good of the country.* **3.** [U] Value; use: *What good is a bicycle without a chain?* **4.** **goods. a.** Things that can be bought and sold; merchandise. **b.** Personal belongings: *They lost all their household goods in the fire.* ◆ **a good deal.** A lot: *a good deal of money.* **as good as.** Nearly; almost: *This car is as good as new.* **for good.** Permanently; forever: *They left town for good.* **good and.** *Informal.* Very; entirely: *I'll do the job when I'm good and ready.* **no good.** Useless; worthless: *It's no good arguing with them.* **to the good.** In one's favor, especially a better financial position: *We have $20 to the good from the bake sale.*

good afternoon *interj. Formal.* An expression of greeting used in the afternoon when meeting sbdy. or speaking on the telephone: *"Good afternoon. This is Customer Service. How may I help you?"*

good-bye or **good•bye** also **good-by** (gŏŏd-bī′) *interj.* An expression used when leaving or to sbdy. who is leaving. —*n., pl.* **good-byes** also **good-bys.** An expression of farewell: *They said their good-byes early to avoid being late to the airport.*

good evening *interj. Formal.* An expression of greeting used in the evening: *"Good evening, ladies and gentlemen."*

good-for-noth•ing (gŏŏd′fər nŭth′ĭng) *Informal. n.* A person considered worthless or useless. —*adj.* Having little worth; useless.

good•heart•ed (gŏŏd′här′tĭd) *adj.* Kind and generous: *a goodhearted person.* —**good′heart′ed•ly** *adv.* —**good′heart′ed•ness** *n.* [U]

good-hu•mored (gŏŏd′hyŏŏ′mərd) *adj.* Cheerful; amiable: *a good-humored remark.* —**good′-hu′mored•ly** *adv.*

good-look•ing (gŏŏd′lŏŏk′ĭng) *adj.* Having a pleasing appearance; attractive: *a good-looking young man.*

good morning *interj.* An expression of greeting used in the morning when meet-

ing sbdy. or speaking on the telephone: *The teacher welcomed her students with a cheerful "Good morning!"*

good-na•tured (gŏŏd′nā′chərd) *adj.* Having a pleasant disposition; cheerful: *He accepted our jokes about his tie with goodnatured patience.* —**good′-na′tured•ly** *adv.* —**good′-na′tured•ness** *n.* [U]

good•ness (gŏŏd′nĭs) *n.* [U] **1.** The quality or condition of being good; excellence: *He came out of the goodness of his heart.* **2.** The best or nutritious part: *Overcooking takes the goodness out of vegetables.* —*interj.* An expression used to show surprise: *Goodness! You surprised me.*

good night *interj.* An expression used when going to bed or to sbdy. who is going to bed.

Good Samaritan *n.* A person who unselfishly helps others: *A Good Samaritan helped us change the flat tire.*

good-sized (gŏŏd′sīzd′) *adj.* Of a fairly large size: *a good-sized rabbit.*

good•will also **good will** (gŏŏd′wĭl′) *n.* [U] **1.** An attitude of kindliness or friendliness: *Her goodwill made us feel welcome in the neighborhood.* **2.** A good relationship of a nation with other nations or a business with its customers: *You can't put a price on a business's goodwill.*

good•y (gŏŏd′ē) *Informal. interj.* An expression used to show delight: *The child said "Oh goody" when invited to the zoo.* —*n.* also **good•ie,** *pl.* **good•ies.** Something attractive, especially sthg. good to eat: *Let's have some goodies.*

goo•ey (gŏŏ′ē) *adj.* **goo•i•er, goo•i•est.** Thick and sticky: *gooey icing on the cake; gooey mud.*

goof (gŏŏf) *Informal. n.* **1.** A careless mistake: *I'm afraid I made a big goof.* **2.** A silly person: *She can be such a goof sometimes!* —*intr.v.* To make a careless or silly mistake: *I must have goofed when I dialed the number.* ◆ **goof off** or **around** *intr.v.* To waste time: *We goofed off all afternoon.* **goof up.** *tr.v.* [sep.] To spoil (sthg.), as through silly mistakes or clumsiness: *He goofed up his lines in the play.* —**goof′i•ness** *n.* [U] —**goof′y** *adj.*

goon (gŏŏn) *n. Slang.* **1.** A stupid or awkward person. **2.** A rough man hired to frighten or harm people, especially workers on strike: *Management goons terrorized the picket line.*

goose (gŏŏs) *n., pl.* **geese** (gēs). **1.a.** [C] A large water bird related to the duck with a long neck and a short pointed bill. **b.** [C] The female of such a bird: *The goose and her gander made a nest by the lake.* **c.** [U] The meat of such a bird, used as food: *a holiday goose.* **2.** [C] *Informal.* A silly person.

goose bumps *pl.n.* Tiny bumps that form on the skin as a temporary reaction to cold or fear: *I got goose bumps listening to the scary story.*

GOP or **G.O.P.** *abbr.* An abbreviation of Grand Old Party (the Republican Party).

go•pher (gō′fər) *n.* **1.** A burrowing North American rodent with large cheek pouches. **2.** A ground squirrel. **3.** Often **Gopher.** An information searching tool used on the Internet.

gore¹ (gôr) *tr.v.* **gored, gor•ing, gores.** To pierce or stab (sbdy./sthg.) with a horn or tusk: *gored by a bull.*

gore² (gôr) *n.* [U] Blood, especially blood from a wound: *a horror movie full of gore.*

gorge (gôrj) *n.* A deep narrow valley with steep rocky sides, often with a stream flowing through it: *The gorge was the only way through the mountains.* —*v.* **gorged, gorg•ing, gorg•es.** —*tr.* To stuff (oneself) with food: *gorged themselves with spaghetti.* —*intr.* To eat greedily: *The bear gorged on the fish.*

gor•geous (gôr′jəs) *adj.* Incredibly beautiful or magnificent: *The snowcapped mountains were gorgeous in the sunset.* —**gor′geous•ly** *adv.* —**gor′geous•ness** *n.* [U]

go•ril•la (gə rĭl′ə) *n.* A large, powerful ape of the central African forests and mountains with a heavy stocky body and dark hair: *The gorilla is the largest and most powerful of the apes.*

HOMONYMS: **gorilla, guerrilla** (fighter).

---

gor•y (gôr′ē) *adj.* **gor•i•er, gor•i•est. 1.** Covered with gore; bloody: *a gory crime scene.* **2.** Full of or marked by bloodshed and violence: *a gory movie.* —**gor′i•ly** *adv.* —**gor′i•ness** *n.* [U]

gosh (gŏsh) *interj. Informal.* An expression used to show mild surprise or delight: *Gosh, that's a nice bike!*

gos•ling (gŏz′lĭng) *n.* A young goose.

gos•pel (gŏs′pəl) *n.* **1.** [C] Often **Gospel.** One of the first four books of the New Testament, describing the life and teachings of Jesus. **2.** [U] Something, such as an idea or a principle, believed to be unquestionably true: *They took her explanation as gospel.*

gospel music *n.* [U] A kind of religious music developed by southern African Americans that combines elements of folk music, jazz, and spirituals.

gos•sa•mer (gŏs′ə mər) *n.* [U] **1.** A soft, sheer, gauzy cloth. **2.** Something delicate and light: *wings like gossamer.* —*adj.* Light, sheer, or delicate: *a gossamer dress.*

gos•sip (gŏs′əp) *n.* **1.** [U] Trivial talk, often involving rumors of people and their personal affairs: *He heard some gossip about the neighbors.* **2.** [C] A person who often enters into in such talk: *She's been a gossip for*

years. —*intr.v.* [*about*] To engage in or spread gossip: *gossip about one's neighbors.* —**gos′sip•er** *n.*

got (gŏt) *v.* Past tense and a past participle of **get.**

got•cha (gŏ′chə) *interj.* **1.** An expression used in rapid speech that means "I've got you": *She yelled "gotcha" when she caught her little sister. "Gotcha! You believed that story I told you!"* **2.** Used to mean "I understand you" or "all right": *"You want me to take the garbage out now? Gotcha!"*

got•ta (gŏt′ə) *aux.v.* A rapid pronunciation of *got to,* used in speech as an auxiliary verb to show obligation: *I gotta do my homework now. She's gotta study, or she'll fail the course.*

got•ten (gŏt′n) *v.* A past participle of **get.**

gouge (gouj) *n.* **1.** A chisel with a rounded grooved blade. **2.** A groove or hole made with or as if with a chisel: *a deep gouge in the wood.* —*tr.v.* **gouged, goug•ing, goug•es. 1.** To cut or scoop out (sthg.) as if with a gouge: *gouge out watermelon seeds; gouge prices.* **2.** *Slang.* To cheat (sbdy.), especially out of money: *That business is known for gouging its customers with high prices.* —**goug′er** *n.*

gou•lash (gōō′läsh′ or gōō′läsh′) *n.* [C; U] A meat and vegetable stew seasoned with paprika.

gourd (gôrd or gōōrd) *n.* **1.** The fruit of a vine related to the pumpkin, squash, and cucumber, with a hard skin and often an irregular shape. **2.** The dried hollowed-out shell of such a fruit, used as a ladle, bowl, or cup.

gourd

gour•met (gōōr mā′ or gōōr′mā′) *n.* A person who enjoys and is knowledgeable about fine food and drink.

gout (gout) *n.* [U] A painful disease in which hard deposits of salts from urine form in the joints, especially of the legs, feet, and hands.

gov. or **Gov.** *abbr.* An abbreviation of governor.

gov•ern (gŭv′ərn) *v.* —*tr.* **1.** To control the public policy and affairs of (a state or nation): *In elections the voters decide who will govern the country.* **2.** To have or use a determining influence on (sthg.): *The weather governs the success or failure of crops.* —*intr.* To exercise political authority: *She governs with a firm hand.* —**gov′ern•a•ble** *adj.*

gov•er•ness (gŭv′ər nĭs) *n. Formal.* A woman employed to teach and train the children of a household.

gov•ern•ment (gŭv′ərn mənt) *n.* **1.** [U] The act or process of governing, especially the control and administration of a political unit. **2.** [C; U] A system by which a political unit is governed: *democratic government.* **3.** [U] The people who make up a governing body: *There will be a change of government with the next elections.* —**gov′ern·men′tal** (gŭv′ərn měn′tl) *adj.*

gov·er·nor (gŭv′ər nər) *n.* The chief executive of a state in the United States: *The governors of the 50 states held a conference.*

gov·er·nor·ship (gŭv′ər nər shĭp′) *n.* [U] The office or duties of a governor or the period during which a governor is in office.

govt. or **Govt.** *abbr.* An abbreviation of government.

gown (goun) *n.* **1.** A long, loose, flowing garment, such as a nightgown. **2.** A woman's dress, especially a long formal one: *a velvet gown for the opera.* **3.** An outer robe for official ceremonies: *academic gowns.*

G.P. or **GP** *abbr.* An abbreviation of general practitioner.

GPA *abbr.* An abbreviation of grade point average.

gr. *abbr.* An abbreviation of: **1.** Gram. **2.** Gross.

Gr. *abbr.* An abbreviation of Greek.

grab (grăb) *v.* **grabbed, grab·bing, grabs.** —*tr.* **1.** To take (sthg.) suddenly: *The monkey grabbed the peanut out of my hand.* **2.** To take (sthg.) by means of force: *The dictator grabbed power.* **3.** *Informal.* To take a quick opportunity to get or do (sthg.): *Just give me a minute to grab my coat.* —*intr.* To make a quick, rough attempt to take sthg.: *She grabbed for the dog's leash.* —*n.* The act of grabbing: *I made a grab at the frog.* ◆ **up for grabs.** *Informal.* Available for anyone to take or win: *He sold his car, so his parking space is up for grabs.*

grace (grās) *n.* **1.** [U] Beauty of movement, form, or manner: *the grace of a swan swimming across a lake.* **2.** [C; U] A charming or pleasing quality or characteristic: *a boorish person, lacking in social graces.* **3.** [U] In Christianity, the state of being protected by the favor and love of God. **4.** [C; U] A short prayer said before or after a meal. **5.** [U] A temporary immunity or exemption from penalty: *You have seven days' grace after the payment due date before you'll be charged a fine.* —*tr.v.* **graced, grac·ing, grac·es.** *Formal.* **1.** To honor or favor (sbdy./sthg.): *The governor's presence graced the meeting.* **2.** To give beauty, elegance, or charm to (sthg.): *A bouquet of fresh flowers graced the table.* ◆ **in (one's) good graces.** In favor with sbdy.: *The child is trying to get back in his parents' good graces after breaking a lamp.*

grace·ful (grās′fəl) *adj.* Showing grace of movement, form, or proportion: *a graceful dance; a graceful gymnast.* —**grace′ful·ly** *adv.* —**grace′ful·ness** *n.* [U]

grace·less (grās′lĭs) *adj.* **1.** Lacking grace; clumsy: *a graceless fall.* **2.** Without a sense of what is proper or polite: *a rude and graceless remark.* —**grace′less·ly** *adv.* —**grace′less·ness** *n.* [U]

gra·cious (grā′shəs) *adj.* **1.** Characterized by kindness and courtesy: *a gracious and thoughtful host.* **2.** Characterized by tact and politeness: *She responded to the insult with gracious good humor.* —*interj.* An expression used to show surprise or mild emotion: *Goodness gracious! My gracious!* —**gra′cious·ly** *adv.* —**gra′cious·ness** *n.* [U]

grad (grăd) *Informal.* *n.* A graduate of a school or college: *the job market for recent grads.* —*adj.* Graduate: *grad school; a grad student.*

gra·da·tion (grā dā′shən) *n.* A series of gradual stages or steps in a series: *the gradation in shading from light to dark.*

grade (grād) *n.* **1.** A mark showing the quality of a student's work: *I always get good grades in science.* **2.** A division of the course of study in elementary and high school, usually a year's work: *the ninth grade.* **3.** A level of quality, size, rank, or intensity: *a poor grade of olive oil; grade A eggs.* **4.a.** A slope or an incline, as of a road on a hill: *The truck couldn't stop on the grade.* **b.** The degree to which sthg., such as a road or railroad track, slopes: *the steep grade of a mountain road.* —*v.* **grad·ed, grad·ing, grades.** —*tr.* **1.** To give a grade to (a student or an assignment, for example): *grade book reports.* **2.** To level or smooth (an area of land) to a desired gradient: *bulldozers grading a road.* **3.** To arrange (sthg.) in a series or according to a scale: *graded the lumber according to quality.* —*intr.* To change or progress gradually: *The various types of sandpaper grade from coarse to fine.* ◆ **make the grade.** To succeed: *After a lot of work, he made the grade as a professional football player.*

grad·er (grā′dər) *n.* **1.** A student in a specific grade at school: *a fifth grader; a seventh grader.* **2.** A piece of heavy equipment used to level or smooth road or other surfaces.

grade point average *n.* The average grade earned by a student, figured by dividing the points given for grades earned by the number of credits for courses attempted: *He got an A in every course, so his grade point average is 4.0.*

grade school *n.* Elementary school.

gra·di·ent (grā′dē ənt) *n.* **1.** The degree to which sthg. inclines; a slope: *the steep gradient of the hillside.* **2.** The rate of change of a variable, such as temperature or pressure, with distance: *The pilot measured the temperature gradient as the airplane ascended.*

grad·u·al (grăj′o͞o əl) *adj.* Happening in small stages or degrees or by even continuous change: *the gradual increase in prices; a gradual recuperation from illness.* —**grad′u·al·ly** *adv.*

grad·u·ate (grăj′o͞o āt′) *v.* **grad·u·at·ed, grad·u·at·ing, grad·u·ates.** —*intr.* To receive an academic degree or diploma: *graduate from high school.* —*tr.* **1.** To grant an academic degree or diploma to (sbdy.): *Our high school graduated 100 students.* **2.** To divide or mark (sthg.) into steps showing measures, as of length or volume: *A thermometer is graduated into degrees.* —*n.* (grăj′o͞o ĭt). A person who has received an academic degree or diploma: *She's a recent Harvard graduate.* —*adj.* (grăj′o͞o ĭt). **1.** Having an academic degree or diploma: *a graduate student.* **2.** Relating to studying beyond the bachelor's degree: *graduate courses leading to a Ph.D.*

grad·u·a·tion (grăj′o͞o ā′shən) *n.* **1.** [U] The giving or receiving of an academic degree or a diploma. **2.** [C] Any of the marks made on a container or an instrument to show amounts or measures: *This thermometer is marked with fine graduations.*

graf·fi·ti (grə fē′tē) *n.* [U] A drawing or writing on a wall or other surface, usually so as to be seen by the public: *graffiti on the subway cars.*

graft[1] (grăft) *tr.v.* **1.** To join (a part of a plant) to another living plant so that the two grow together as a single plant: *grafted roses in the garden.* **2.** To transplant (tissue or an organ) by means of surgery from one part of the body to another or from one person to another: *Doctors grafted skin from her leg to the burns on her arms.* —*n.* **1.** A part of a plant that has been grafted onto another plant: *The graft on the apple tree produced excellent fruit.* **2.** An organ or a piece of tissue transplanted by surgery: *a skin graft.*

graft[2] (grăft) *n.* [U] **1.** The dishonest use of one's position of power to gain profit or advantage: *city officials accused of graft.* **2.** Money or an advantage gained by such use.

grain (grān) *n.* **1.** [C] A small hard seed, especially of wheat, rice, or other cereal plants: *a single grain of rice.* **2.** [U] Cereal plants, such as wheat or rye, considered as a group: *a field of grain.* **3.** [C] **a.** A small particle similar to a seed: *a grain of salt.* **b.** A small amount or the smallest possible amount: *not a grain of sense in what they say.* **4.** [C] A unit of weight equal to 0.002285 ounce (0.065 gram). See table at **measurement. 5.** [U] **a.** The markings, pattern, or texture in wood: *the fine grain of hard woods.* **b.** The direction of such markings: *It's harder to cut a board across the grain.* ♦ **against the grain.**

Against one's nature or liking: *It went against the grain for him to do a poor job.* **with a grain of salt.** Without complete belief or trust; skeptically: *Take everything he says with a grain of salt.*

grain·y (grā′nē) *adj.* **grain·i·er, grain·i·est. 1.** Consisting of or resembling grains: *grainy flour; a grainy photo.* **2.** Resembling the grain of wood: *a grainy surface.*

gram (grăm) *n.* A unit of mass or weight in the metric system, equal to about ¹/₂₈ ounce. See table at **measurement.**

—**gram** *suff.* A suffix that means something written or drawn: *cardiogram; telegram.*

gram·mar (grăm′ər) *n.* **1.** [U] The study of the structure of words, the relationships among words, and the arrangement of words to make sentences. **2.** [C; U] The system of rules for making sentences in a given language: *Latin grammar.* **3.** [U] The use of words according to educated speakers of a language: *The teacher criticized my paper for bad grammar.*

gram·mar·ian (grə mâr′ē ən) *n.* A specialist in grammar.

grammar school *n.* **1.** An elementary school. **2.** *Chiefly British.* A secondary or preparatory school.

gram·mat·i·cal (grə măt′ĭ kəl) *adj.* **1.** Relating to grammar: *grammatical principles.* **2.** Following the rules of grammar: *a grammatical sentence.* —**gram·mat′i·cal·ly** *adv.*

grand (grănd) *adj.* **1.** Large and impressive; magnificent: *The bridge that crosses the bay is a grand structure.* See Synonyms at **magnificent. 2.** *Formal.* Very pleasing or wonderful: *We had a grand time.* **3.** Being the most important of a category: *the grand prize.* **4.** Showing high moral character; noble: *The United Nations has a grand purpose.* **5.** Including or covering all units or aspects: *the grand total.* —*n.* **1.** [C] A grand piano: *a baby grand.* **2.** [U] *Slang.* A thousand dollars: *The car cost about 18 grand.* —**grand′ly** *adv.*

grand·aunt (grănd′ănt′ *or* grănd′änt′) *n.* A great-aunt.

grand·child (grănd′chīld′ *or* grăn′chīld′) *n., pl.* **grand·child·ren.** A child of one's daughter or son.

grand·dad (grăn′dăd′) *n. Informal.* A grandfather.

grand·dad·dy (grăn′dăd′ē) *n. Informal.* A grandfather.

grand·daugh·ter (grăn′dô′tər) *n.* A daughter of one's daughter or son.

gran·deur (grăn′jər *or* grăn′jo͞or′) *n.* [U] The quality or condition of being grand; magnificence: *the grandeur of the pyramids in Egypt.*

grand·fa·ther (grănd′fä′thər *or* grăn′fä′thər) *n.* The father of one's mother or father.

grandfather clock *n.* A pendulum clock enclosed in a tall narrow cabinet.

G

grand·fa·ther·ly (grănd′fä′thər lē *or* grăn′fä′thər lē) *adj.* Typical of or suitable to a grandfather: *treated us in a grandfatherly manner.*

gran·di·ose (grăn′dē ōs′ *or* grăn′dē ōs′) *adj.* **1.** Characterized by greatness of size or intent; grand: *grandiose architecture.* See Synonyms at **magnificent. 2.** Pretending to be better than sthg. really is; pompous: *a grandiose style of writing.* —**gran′di·ose′ly** *adv.* —**gran′di·os′i·ty** (grăn′dē ŏs′ĭ tē) *n.* [U]

grand jury *n.* A jury of 12 to 23 people that meets in private to evaluate accusations against a person charged with a crime and determines whether an indictment should be made: *Without a grand jury indictment, the case would not go to trial.*

grand·ma (grănd′mä′ *or* grăn′mä′ *or* grăm′mä′) *n. Informal.* A grandmother.

grand·moth·er (grănd′mŭth′ər *or* grăn′-mŭth′ər) *n.* The mother of one's father or mother.

grand·moth·er·ly (grănd′mŭth′ər lē *or* grăn′mŭth′ər lē) *adj.* Typical of or suitable to a grandmother: *She hugged us with grandmotherly joy.*

grand·neph·ew (grănd′něf′yoō *or* grăn′-něf′yoō) *n.* A son of one's nephew or niece.

grand·niece (grănd′nēs′ *or* grăn′nēs′) *n.* A daughter of one's nephew or niece.

grand·pa (grănd′pä′ *or* grăn′pä′ *or* grăm′-pä′) *n. Informal.* A grandfather.

grand·par·ent (grănd′pâr′ənt *or* grănd′-pär′ənt) *n.* A parent of one's mother or father.

grand piano *n.* A large piano in a frame supported on three legs, usually used for concerts.

grand·son (grănd′sŭn′ *or* grăn′sŭn′) *n.* A son of one's daughter or son.

grand·stand (grănd′stănd′ *or* grăn′stănd′) *n.* A roofed stand for people watching an event at a stadium or racetrack: *The empty grandstand seems to be waiting for the race day.* —*intr.v.* To perform for effect, especially to impress an audience: *The lawyer was grandstanding for the jury.*

grand·un·cle (grănd′ŭng′kəl) *n.* A great-uncle.

gran·ite (grăn′ĭt) *n.* [U] A common, coarse-grained, hard rock used in buildings and monuments.

gran·ny or **gran·nie** (grăn′ē) *n., pl.* **gran·nies.** *Informal.* A grandmother.

gra·no·la (grə nō′lə) *n.* [U] Oats mixed with various ingredients, such as dried fruit, brown sugar, and nuts, and used especially as a breakfast cereal.

grant (grănt) *tr.v.* **1.** To give or allow (sthg. asked for): *grant a request.* **2.** To give (sthg.) as a favor or privilege: *The Constitution* grants certain powers to the Supreme Court. **3.** To concede or admit (sthg. to be true): *I'll grant that it's not the best car, but it's reliable.* —*n.* Something granted, especially money: *a grant of $3,000 for college tuition.*

gran·u·lar (grăn′yə lər) *adj.* Made of or appearing to be made of grains or granules: *the granular surface of a rock; the granular consistency of rice.*

gran·u·late (grăn′yə lāt′) *tr.v.* **gran·u·lat·ed, gran·u·lat·ing, gran·u·lates.** To form (sthg.) into grains or granules: *granulated sugar.* —**gran′u·la′tion** *n.* [U]

gran·ule (grăn′yoōl) *n.* A small hard grain or pellet: *granules of sand.*

grape (grāp) *n.* A small, rounded, juicy fruit with smooth, usually purple or green skin that grows in clusters on a vine.

grape·fruit (grāp′froōt′) *n.* A large round citrus fruit of an evergreen tree related to the orange, with a yellow skin and a sour taste.

grape·vine (grāp′vīn′) *n.* **1.** A vine on which grapes grow. **2.** The informal system of passing gossip, rumor, or information from person to person: *I heard through the grapevine that we may soon have a new boss.*

graph (grăf) *n.* A diagram or chart in which lines, bars, or proportional areas represent how one quantity depends on or changes with another quantity: *a line graph showing population increases.* —*tr.v.* To make a graph of (sthg.): *graph the sales figures for the past six months.*

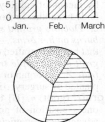

graph

—**graph** *suff.* A suffix that means: **1.** Something that writes or records: *seismograph; telegraph.* **2.** Something written or drawn: *autograph.*

—**grapher** *suff.* A suffix that means someone who writes or records: *stenographer; lexicographer.*

graph·ic (grăf′ĭk) *adj.* **1.a.** Relating to written or drawn representations, such as letters, signs, or pictures: *A pronunciation key in a dictionary has graphic symbols of speech.* **b.** Relating to graphics: *a graphic display of data.* **c.** Relating to the graphic arts: *a graphic designer for a magazine.* **2.** Described in clear and vivid detail: *The witness*

gave a graphic description of the incident.
—**graph'i•cal•ly** *adv.*

graphic arts *pl.n.* The visual arts that involve making images: *Among the graphic arts are drawing, engraving, and woodcutting.*

graph•ics (grăf'ĭks) *n.* [U] *(used with a singular verb).* **1.** The making of drawings that follow the rules of mathematics, as in engineering and architecture. **2.** The process by which a computer produces and displays information as pictures, diagrams, and charts, rather than as letters and numerals.

graph•ite (grăf'īt') *n.* [U] A rather soft form of carbon that is steel gray to black in color and is used in making lubricants, paints, and pencils.

—**graphy** *suff.* A suffix that means: **1.** A writing or representation produced in a certain way: *photography.* **2.** A writing about a specific subject: *oceanography.*

grap•ple (grăp'əl) —*intr.v.* **grap•pled, grap•pling, grap•ples.** To fight or struggle with sbdy. as if in wrestling: *The wrestlers grappled on the mat.* ♦ **grapple with.** *tr.v.* [insep.] To try to solve (a difficult problem): *The committee grappled with the problem of finding a new leader.*

grasp (grăsp) *v.* —*tr.* **1.** To take and hold (sbdy./sthg.) firmly with the hands: *Grasp the rope and pull.* **2.** To understand (sthg.): *You fail to grasp the problem.* —*intr.* [at; for] **1.** To make a motion of seizing, snatching, or clutching: *The sailor in the water grasped for the line thrown to him.* **2.** To show eager acceptance: *grasped at the opportunity to go to college.* —*n.* *(usually singular).* **1.** A firm hold or grip: *The puppy wriggled out of my grasp.* **2.** The ability to get sthg.; reach: *Victory was within the team's grasp.* **3.** Understanding; comprehension: *The teacher has a thorough grasp of the subject.*

grasp•ing (grăs'pĭng) *adj.* Eager for money and unwilling to share; greedy: *a grasping miser.* —**grasp'ing•ly** *adv.*

grass (grăs) *n.* **1.** [C; U] Any of various plants with narrow green leaves: *horses grazing on tall grass.* **2.** [U] Such plants covering a lawn or pasture: *using a lawnmower to cut the grass.* **3.** *Slang.* Marijuana.

grass•hop•per (grăs'hŏp'ər) *n.* An insect with two pairs of wings and long hind legs used for jumping.

grass•land (grăs'lănd') *n.* An area, such as a prairie or meadow, covered with grass.

grass•roots (grăs'rōots' *or* grăs'rŏots') *pl.n.* *(used with a singular or plural verb).* People or society at a local level rather than at the national level: *True political change must come from the grassroots.*

grass•y (grăs'ē) *adj.* **grass•i•er, grass•i•est.** **1.** Covered with or rich in grass: *a grassy plain.* **2.** Resembling or suggestive of grass, as in color or odor: *a grassy green color.*

grate¹ (grāt) *v.* **grat•ed, grat•ing, grates.**

—*tr.* **1.** To reduce (sthg.) to small pieces, shreds, or powder by rubbing against a rough surface: *Grate the cheese for pizza.* **2.** To cause (sthg.) to make a harsh grinding or rasping sound by rubbing: *She grated her teeth in anger.* —*intr.* [on] **1.** To make a harsh grinding or rasping sound by rubbing: *The wagon grated on its rusty wheels.* **2.** To cause irritation or annoyance: *Your sarcasm grates on my nerves.*

HOMONYMS: grate (shred, framework), **great** (large).

grate² (grāt) *n.* **1.** A framework of parallel or interwoven bars for blocking an opening: *an iron grate over the window.* **2.** A similar framework used to hold fuel or food in a stove, furnace, or fireplace: *wood piled on the grate in the fireplace.*

grate•ful (grāt'fəl) *adj.* **1.** [for] Appreciative or thankful for some good received: *grateful for needed help.* **2.** Expressing thanks or gratitude: *a grateful look.* —**grate'ful•ly** *adv.* —**grate'ful•ness** *n.* [U]

grat•er (grā'tər) *n.* A kitchen utensil with slits and perforations on which to grate food: *a cheese grater.*

grat•i•fi•ca•tion (grăt'ə fĭ kā'shən) *n.* [U] The act of gratifying or the condition of being gratified: *immediate gratification of the king's wishes.*

grat•i•fy (grăt'ə fī') *tr.v.* **grat•i•fied, grat•i•fy•ing, grat•i•fies.** **1.** To please or satisfy (sbdy.): *The excellent test results gratified the patient.* **2.** To give what is desired to (sbdy.); indulge: *gratify one's curiosity.*

grat•ing (grā'tĭng) *n.* A grill or network of bars set across an opening, such as a window or a street drain; a grate: *Window gratings help keep children from falling out.*

grat•is (grăt'ĭs *or* grā'tĭs) *adv. & adj.* Without charge: *We went to the show gratis. The tickets are gratis.*

grat•i•tude (grăt'ĭ tōod') *n.* [U] The state of being grateful; thankfulness: *The family was full of gratitude for the neighbor's help during the fire.*

gra•tu•i•tous (grə tōo'ĭ təs) *adj.* Unnecessary and undeserved; unjustified: *gratuitous criticism.* —**gra•tu'i•tous•ly** *adv.* —**gra•tu'i•tous•ness** *n.* [U]

gra•tu•i•ty (grə tōo'ĭ tē) *n., pl.* **gra•tu•i•ties.** *Formal.* A favor or gift, usually of money, given in return for service; a tip: *a gratuity for the waiter.*

grave¹ (grāv) *n.* **1.** A hole dug in the ground for the burial of a dead body. **2.** A place of burial: *The sea is the grave of many sailors.* **3.** Death or extinction: *Dinosaurs went to their graves many thousands of years ago.*

grave² (grāv) *adj.* **grav•er, grav•est.** **1.** Requiring serious thought: *a grave decision.*

2. Filled with danger or harm: *a grave illness.* **3.** Dignified and serious in behavior or character: *The judge looked grave.* —**grave′ly** *adv.*

grav·el (grăv′əl) *n.* [U] A loose mixture of pebbles or small pieces of rock, often used for roads and walks: *Gravel can make bicycle riding more difficult.* —*tr.v.* To cover (sthg.) with gravel: *gravel a driveway.*

grav·el·ly (grăv′ə lē) *adj.* **1.** Covered with or containing gravel: *gravelly soil.* **2.** Having a harsh rasping sound: *a low gravelly voice.*

grave·stone (grāv′stōn′) *n.* A stone placed over a grave as a marker; a tombstone.

grave·yard (grāv′yärd′) *n.* A cemetery.

graveyard shift *n.* **1.** A work shift that runs during the early morning hours, as from midnight to 8 A.M. **2.** The workers on such a shift.

grav·i·tate (grăv′ĭ tāt′) *intr.v.* **grav·i·tat·ed, grav·i·tat·ing, grav·i·tates.**
♦ **gravitate toward.** *tr.v.* [insep.] **1.** To move under or as if under the influence of gravity toward (sthg.): *a meteoroid gravitating toward the earth.* **2.** To be attracted to (sbdy./sthg.) by an irresistible force: *The baby gravitated toward the cookies.*

grav·i·ta·tion (grăv′ĭ tā′shən) *n.* [U] **1.** The force of attraction that tends to draw together any two objects in the universe: *Gravitation is the force responsible for the earth's orbit around the sun.* **2.** A movement toward a source of attraction: *the gravitation of the middle class to the suburbs.* —**grav′i·ta′tion·al** *adj.*

grav·i·ty (grăv′ĭ tē) *n.* [U] **1.** The natural force that causes objects to move or tend to move toward the center of the earth as a result of gravitation. **2.** Seriousness; importance: *The students realized the gravity of the test and its effect on their grades.*

gra·vy (grā′vē) *n.* [U] A sauce made from the juices from cooking meat and thickened, as with flour: *turkey gravy on mashed potatoes.*

gray also **grey** (grā) *n.* [C; U] A color made by mixing black and white. —*adj.* **1.** Having the color gray. **2.** Having gray hair: *a middle-aged man going gray.* **3.** Lacking in cheer; gloomy: *a gray mood; a gray day.* —*tr. & intr.v.* To make or become gray: *Age grays the hair. The driftwood grayed in the sun.* —**gray′ly** *adv.* —**gray′ness** *n.* [U]

gray·ish (grā′ĭsh) *adj.* Somewhat gray: *grayish hair.*

gray matter *n.* [U] *Informal.* Brains; intellect: *Try to use your gray matter to solve the problem.*

graze¹ (grāz) *v.* **grazed, graz·ing, graz·es.** —*intr.* To feed on growing grasses: *Cattle grazed in the field.* —*tr.* **1.** To feed on the grass of (a piece of land): *The goats grazed the mountain pasture.* **2.** To put (farm or ranch animals) out to feed on growing grasses: *grazed their cattle on the plains.*

graze² (grāz) *v.* **grazed, graz·ing, graz·es.** —*tr.* **1.** To touch (sbdy./sthg.) lightly in passing: *His suitcase just grazed my leg as he moved by me. The report only grazes the surface of the problem.* **2.** To scrape or scratch (sthg.) slightly: *I fell off my bike and grazed my knees and elbows.* —*intr.* To scrape or touch sthg. lightly in passing. —*n.* **1.** The act of brushing or scraping along a surface. **2.** A minor scratch or scrape.

grease (grēs) *n.* [U] **1.** Animal fat when melted or soft, often used in cooking: *eggs fried in bacon grease.* **2.** A thick sticky oil or similar material, used to lubricate moving parts, as of a machine: *black bicycle grease.* —*tr.v.* (grēs or grēz). **greased, greas·ing, greas·es.** To apply grease to (sthg.): *grease the pan before cooking; grease the track of a sliding door.*

greas·y (grē′sē or grē′zē) *adj.* **greas·i·er, greas·i·est.** **1.** Coated or soiled with grease: *greasy pots and pans.* **2.** Containing grease; oily: *a greasy hamburger.* **3.** Slippery: *I dropped the greasy dish.* —**greas′i·ly** *adv.* —**greas′i·ness** *n.* [U]

great (grāt) *adj.* **1.** Very large in size, number, amount, or extent: *a great crowd of fans.* See Synonyms at **large.** **2.** Remarkable or special because of large size or extreme degree: *a great crisis.* **3.** Important; significant: *The signing of the treaty was a great moment in history.* **4.** *Informal.* Very good; wonderful: *a great party; a great time.* —**great′ness** *n.* [U]

HOMONYMS: great, grate (shred, framework).

great-aunt or **great aunt** (grāt′ănt′ or grăt′ănt′) *n.* A sister of one's grandparent.

great-grand·child (grāt′ grănd′chĭld′ or grāt′ grăn′chĭld′) *n., pl.* **great-grand·child·ren.** A child of one's grandchild.

great-grand·daughter (grāt′ grăn′dô′tər) *n.* A daughter of one's grandchild.

great-grand·father (grāt′ grănd′fä′thər or grāt′ grăn′fä′thər) *n.* The father of one's grandparent.

great-grand·mother (grāt′ grănd′mŭth′ər or grāt′ grăn′mŭth′ər) *n.* The mother of one's grandparent.

great-grand·parent (grāt′ grănd′pâr′ənt or grāt′ grănd′păr′ənt) *n.* The parent of one's grandparent.

great-grand·son (grāt′ grănd′sŭn′ or grāt′ grăn′sŭn′) *n.* A son of one's grandchild.

great·ly (grāt′lē) *adv.* To a great degree; very much: *Families vary greatly in size.*

great-uncle or **great uncle** (grāt′ŭng′kəl) *n.* A brother of one's grandparent.

ă–cat; ā–pay; âr–care; ä–father; ĕ–get; ē–be; ĭ–sit; ī–nice; îr–here; ŏ–got; ō–go; ô–saw; oi–boy; ou–out; ŏŏ–took; ōō–boot; ŭ–cut; ûr–word; th–thin; *th*–this; hw–when; zh–vision; ə–about; N–French bon

greed (grēd) *n.* [U] A selfish desire for more than one needs or deserves: *Greed often makes people take foolish risks with their money.*

greed·y (grē′dē) *adj.* **greed·i·er, greed·i·est.** Filled with greed; wanting more than one needs or deserves: *The greedy child refused to share with his friends.* —**greed′i·ly** *adv.* —**greed′i·ness** *n.* [U]

Greek (grēk) *n.* **1.** [U] The ancient or modern language of Greece. **2.** [C] A person born or living in Greece. **3.** [U] *Informal.* Something that is hard to understand: *Computer programming language is Greek to me.* —*adj.* Relating to Greece or its people, language, or culture.

green (grēn) *n.* [C; U] **1.** The color of most plant leaves and growing grass. In the color spectrum it is between yellow and blue. **2. greens. a.** The branches and leaves of green plants used for decoration: *holiday greens.* **b.** Leafy plants or plant parts eaten as vegetables: *salad greens.* **3.** A grassy area located usually at the center of a town or city; a common: *the village green.* —*adj.* **1.** Of the color green: *green leaves.* **2.** Covered with growing plants, grass, or foliage: *green meadows.* **3.** Not mature or ripe: *a green banana.* **4.** Lacking training or experience: *green musicians.* **5.** Not aged, cured, dried, seasoned, or otherwise prepared for use: *green wood.*

green·back (grēn′băk′) *n. Informal.* A piece of paper money of U.S. currency.

green bean *n.* A long, thin green vegetable that is eaten before the bean inside is mature; a string bean.

green card *n.* An official document issued by the U.S. government to a person who is not a U.S. citizen, giving the legal right to live and work in the United States.

green·er·y (grē′nə rē) *n.* [U] Green plants or leaves: *We decorated the house with greenery.*

green·horn (grēn′hôrn′) *n. Informal.* An inexperienced or immature person, especially one who is easily fooled: *playing tricks on the greenhorns.*

green·house (grēn′hous′) *n.* A room or building with a glass roof and sides, used for growing plants that need an even, usually warm temperature; a hothouse.

greenhouse effect *n.* [U] The trapping of the sun's radiation in the earth's atmosphere. It is caused by the buildup of carbon dioxide and water vapor in the atmosphere, which traps heat on the earth's surface.

green·ish (grē′nĭsh) *adj.* Somewhat green: *a greenish tint to the water.*

green pepper *n.* The unripened green fruit of any of various varieties of the pepper plant.

green thumb *n.* An ability to make plants grow well: *All her houseplants are healthy because she has a green thumb.*

Green·wich time (grĕn′ĭch *or* grĭn′ĭj) *n.* [U] Universal time.

greet (grēt) *tr.v.* **1.** To address (sbdy.) in a friendly way, as upon meeting or in opening a letter: *The hosts greeted their guests.* **2.** To receive (sbdy./sthg.) with a specified reaction: *Our parents greeted the news with great joy.* **3.** To be perceived by (sbdy./sthg.): *A cry of "Surprise!" greeted our ears.*

greet·ing (grē′tĭng) *n. (often plural).* A gesture or word of welcome or a hello: *a friendly greeting for the new arrivals; calling out greetings.*

greeting card *n.* A folded card printed with a message of greeting, for example, of congratulations, and usually sent or given to mark a special event or holiday.

gre·gar·i·ous (grĭ gâr′ē əs) *adj.* **1.** Looking for and enjoying the company of others; sociable: *a gregarious person.* **2.** Referring to animals that live in flocks, herds, colonies, or similar groups with others of their own kind: *Zebras are gregarious.* —**gre·gar′i·ous·ly** *adv.* —**gre·gar′i·ous·ness** *n.* [U]

grem·lin (grĕm′lĭn) *n.* An imaginary creature whose mischief is said to cause mechanical failures: *He joked that gremlins had stalled the car again.*

gre·nade (grə nād′) *n.* A small bomb thrown by hand or fired from a launcher.

grew (grōō) *v.* Past tense of **grow.**

grey (grā) *n., adj., & v.* Variant of **gray.**

grey·hound (grā′hound′) *n.* A tall thin dog with long legs, a smooth coat, and a narrow head and used for hunting and racing.

grid (grĭd) *n.* **1.** A framework of parallel or crisscrossed bars; a grating. **2.** A pattern of regularly spaced horizontal and vertical lines forming squares of equal size, such as those on a map or graph: *city streets arranged as a grid.* **3.** A system for distribution of electricity over a wide area.

grid·dle (grĭd′l) *n.* A heavy flat metal surface, such as a pan, that is used for cooking by dry heat: *pancakes cooked on the griddle.*

grid·dle·cake (grĭd′l kāk′) *n.* A pancake.

grid·i·ron (grĭd′ī′ərn) *n.* A football field.

grid·lock (grĭd′lŏk′) *n.* [U] **1.** A complete halt in the movement of traffic, especially at an intersection of major streets: *gridlock in the streets of Manhattan.* **2.** A complete halt in an activity resulting in a backup: *legislative gridlock.*

grief (grēf) *n.* [U] **1.** Deep mental suffering and pain such as that caused by a death: *grief over the loss of their child in an accident.* **2.** A cause of deep mental pain: *Failure in business was her greatest grief.* **3.** *Informal.* **a.** Trouble or criticism: *Her boss gave her grief for coming to work late.* **b.** Teasing or playful criticism: *His new hairstyle earned him a lot of grief from his friends.*

griev·ance (grē′vəns) *n.* **1.** A real or imagined wrong seen as a good reason for protest: *Lack of affordable housing is a legitimate* *grievance.* **2.** A complaint based on such a situation: *delivered a list of grievances to the mayor.*

grieve (grēv) *v.* **grieved, griev·ing, grieves.** —*tr.* To cause (sbdy.) to be very sad: *The news grieved us deeply.* —*intr.* To experience or express grief: *They grieved silently.*

griev·ous (grē′vəs) *adj.* **1.** Causing grief, pain, or sorrow: *a grievous loss.* **2.** Serious or grave: *a grievous crime.* —**griev′ous·ly** *adv.* —**griev′ous·ness** *n.* [U]

grif·fin (grĭf′ən) *n.* An imaginary animal in stories from the past, with the head and wings of an eagle and the body of a lion.

grill (grĭl) *tr.v.* **1.** To cook (sthg.) on a grill: *grill fish in the back yard.* **2.** *Informal.* To question (sbdy.) closely and repeatedly; cross-examine: *The lawyer grilled a witness in court.* —*n.* **1.** A cooking device with parallel metal bars. **2.** An informal restaurant where grilled foods are served: *a bar and grill.*

grille also **grill** (grĭl) *n.* **1.** A metal or wood grating, often decorative, that covers a door, window, or other opening. **2.** The metal covering on the front end of a motor vehicle: *a dent in the grille of the car.*

grim (grĭm) *adj.* **grim·mer, grim·mest. 1.** Marked by hard and continuous effort: *They worked with grim determination.* **2.** Uninviting, disagreeable, or frightening in appearance: *The judge was grim when passing the severe sentence.* **3.** Dark and cheerless: *We started out on a cold, dark, and grim morning.* **4.** Suggesting trouble or evil: *grim reminders of war.* —**grim′ly** *adv.*

grim·ace (grĭm′ĭs *or* grĭ mās′) *n.* A movement of the face, expressing pain, disgust, or contempt: *His face contracted in a grimace.* —*intr.v.* **grim·aced, grim·ac·ing, grim·ac·es.** To make a sharp movement of the face into an expression as of pain: *Most people grimace when tasting a lemon.*

grime (grīm) *n.* [U] Black dirt covering a surface. —**grim′i·ly** *adv.* —**grim′i·ness** *n.* [U] —**grim′y** *adj.*

grin (grĭn) *intr.v.* **grinned, grin·ning, grins.** To smile broadly, showing the teeth: *grin with delight.* —*n.* A broad smile: *a happy grin.* ◆ **grin and bear it.** To tolerate or suffer sthg. unpleasant: *I hate going to the dentist, but I try to grin and bear it.*

grind (grīnd) *v.* **ground** (ground), **grind·ing, grinds.** —*tr.* **1.** To crush (sthg.) into small bits or a fine powder: *grind wheat into flour; grind coffee.* **2.** To shape, smooth, or sharpen (sthg.) by rubbing on a rough surface: *grind scissors to a fine edge; grind lenses for eyeglasses.* **3.** To rub (two surfaces) together: *grind the teeth.* —*intr.* **1.** To become crushed or powdered by rubbing: *The rocks ground away over the years.* **2.** To move with noisy friction; grate: *The train ground to a halt.* —*n.* **1.** The act of grinding: *a grind of the brakes.* **2.** A specific grade or degree of crushing: *a fine grind of coffee.* **3.** (*usually singular*). *Informal.* A laborious task, routine, or study: *the daily grind of homework.* **4.** *Informal.* A student who works or studies all the time: *Her brother is a total grind; he has no social life.* ◆ **grind away at.** *Informal.* To work tirelessly at sthg.: *grind away at the long report.* **grind down.** *tr.v.* [sep.] To wear (sbdy./sthg.) out; crush: *The team's spirit was ground down by ten straight losses.* **grind out.** *tr.v.* [sep.] To produce (sthg., such as music or poetry) without inspiration: *I've been grinding out short stories all year.*

grind·er (grīn′dər) *n.* **1.** A thing or person that grinds: *a meat grinder; a lens grinder.* **2.** A submarine sandwich.

grind·stone (grīnd′stōn′) *n.* A revolving stone disk, used for polishing or sharpening tools. ◆ **put** or **have (one's) nose to the grindstone.** *Informal.* To work hard and steadily: *She put her nose to the grindstone and finished the report in three days.*

grip (grĭp) *n.* **1.** [C] A tight hold; a firm grasp: *a good grip on the rope.* **2.** [C] A part of a device designed to be held; a handle: *the grips on the handlebars of a bicycle.* **3.** [U] Understanding; great skill: *He now has a good grip on Spanish.* —*tr.v.* **gripped, grip·ping, grips. 1.** To grasp and hold (sthg.) tightly; seize firmly: *He gripped my hand in a warm handshake when I arrived.* **2.** To hold the interest and attention of (sbdy.): *a real-life drama that gripped the nation.* ◆ **come to grips with.** To deal with a difficult situation: *She'll have to come to grips with the loss of her job.* **get a grip on (oneself).** To regain control of one's emotions: *Get a grip on yourself! We'll find your wallet.*

gripe (grīp) *intr.v.* **griped, grip·ing, gripes.** *Informal.* To complain; grumble: *Everyone griped about the new regulations.* —*n.* *Informal.* A complaint: *Everyone has some gripe about winter weather.*

gris·ly (grĭz′lē) *adj.* **gris·li·er, gris·li·est.** Causing horror, terror, or disgust: *That movie had too many grisly scenes for my taste.* —**gris′li·ness** *n.* [U]

Homonyms: grisly, grizzly (grayish).

gris·tle (grĭs′əl) *n.* [U] Tough tissue or cartilage, especially when found in meat: *She cut the gristle off the steak.* —**gris′tly** (grĭs′lē) *adj.*

grit (grĭt) *n.* [U] **1.** Tiny rough particles, as of sand or stone: *Grit had collected on the hood* *of the car.* **2.** *Informal.* A brave spirit; great courage and will: *She has the grit she needs to be a good athlete.* —*tr.v.* **grit•ted, grit•ting, grits.** To clamp or grind (the teeth) together, especially when faced with a difficult situation: *My leg hurt, but I gritted my teeth and kept walking.* —**grit′ti•ness** *n.* [U] —**grit′ty** *adj.*

grits (grĭts) *pl.n.* Coarsely ground corn kernels cooked and served for breakfast or as a side dish: *Grits are popular in the South.*

griz•zled (grĭz′əld) *adj.* Streaked with or partly gray: *a grizzled beard.*

griz•zly (grĭz′lē) *adj.* **griz•zli•er, griz•zli•est.** Grayish or flecked with gray. —*n., pl.* **griz•zlies.** A grizzly bear.

<hr>

Homonyms: grizzly, grisly (horrifying).

<hr>

grizzly bear *n.* A large brown bear of the mountainous regions of western North America.

groan (grōn) *v.* —*intr.* **1.** To make a deep and drawn out sound, as of pain, grief, or displeasure: *groan over a toothache.* **2.** To make a low creaking sound that resembles this: *The floorboards groaned.* —*tr.* To communicate (sthg.) by groaning: *The audience groaned their dissatisfaction at the play's ending.* —*n.* The sound made in groaning.

<hr>

Homonyms: groan, grown (past tense of grow).

<hr>

gro•cer (grō′sər) *n.* A storekeeper who sells food and household supplies.

gro•cer•y (grō′sə rē) *n.* **1.** A store selling food and household supplies: *Do you need anything at the grocery?* **2. groceries.** The goods sold by a grocer.

grog•gy (grŏg′ē) *adj.* **grog•gi•er, grog•gi•est.** Unsteady and dazed; shaky: *still groggy with sleep.* —**grog′gi•ly** *adv.* —**grog′gi•ness** *n.* [U]

groin (groin) *n. (usually singular).* The fold where the thigh joins the body, including the area nearby.

groom (grōōm *or* grŏŏm) *n.* **1.** A person employed to take care of horses. **2.** A bridegroom. —*tr.v.* **1.** To make (oneself) neat, especially in personal appearance: *They groomed themselves in front of the mirror before going to the party.* **2.** To clean and brush (an animal): *She groomed the horse before riding.* **3.** To teach (sbdy.) the skills needed for a certain job or position: *She was groomed by her father to take over the company.*

groove (grōōv) *n.* **1.** [C] A long narrow channel: *The drawer moves in and out on grooves.* **2.** [U] *Slang.* A normal routine: *We got out of the groove over vacation.* —*tr.v.* **grooved, groov•ing, grooves.** To cut a groove or grooves in: *groove the surface of a highway.*

groov•y (grōō′vē) *adj.* **groov•i•er, groov•**

i•est. *Slang.* An expression from the 1960s meaning very pleasing; wonderful: *a groovy song.* —**groov′i•ly** *adv.* —**groov′i•ness** *n.* [U]

grope (grōp) *v.* **groped, grop•ing, gropes.** —*intr.* [*for*] To reach about or search for uncertainly or questioningly: *grope for the light switch; grope for an answer.* —*tr.* To make (one's way) by reaching about uncertainly: *She groped her way down the long dark hall.*

gross (grōs) *adj.* **1.** With nothing subtracted; total: *gross pay of $6.00 an hour.* **2.** Very easy to see; obvious: *a gross error.* **3.** Offensive; disgusting: *gross table manners.* —*n., pl.* **gross. 1.** The entire amount of income before any deductions have been made: *The company's gross was impressive, but after expenses were figured in, it didn't seem so great.* **2.** A group of 144 items; 12 dozen: *This box holds a gross of pencils.* —*tr.v.* To earn (money) as a total income or profit before deductions: *She grossed $30,000 last year.* ◆ **gross out.** *tr.v.* [sep.] To fill (sbdy.) with disgust; nauseate: *The violent scene in the movie grossed me out.* —**gross′ly** *adv.* —**gross′ness** *n.* [U]

gross national product *n. (usually singular).* The total market value of all goods and services produced by a nation during a specified period.

gro•tesque (grō tĕsk′) *adj.* **1.** Very strange or odd in character or appearance: *The grotesque clown made us laugh.* **2.** Characterized by extreme ugliness or unpleasantness in appearance or manner: *He made a grotesque effort to get her attention.* —**gro•tesque′ly** *adv.* —**gro•tesque′ness** *n.* [U]

grot•to (grŏt′ō) *n., pl.* **grot•toes** *or* **grot•tos.** A small cave or cavern.

grouch (grouch) *n.* A person who habitually complains or grumbles: *Our neighbor is a grouch who never smiles.* —*intr.v.* To complain; grumble: *Why grouch about the weather?* —**grouch′i•ly** *adv.* —**grouch′i•ness** *n.* [U] —**grouch′y** *adj.*

ground[1] (ground) *n.* **1.** [U] The solid surface of the earth; land; soil: *The ground is still frozen.* **2.** [C] *(often plural).* An area of land set aside for a special purpose: *camp grounds; a burial ground.* **3.** [C] *(usually plural).* The land surrounding a house or other building: *the school grounds.* **4.** [C] *(usually plural).* The basis or reason for a belief or an action: *grounds for making an accusation.* **5.** [U] An area of reference or discussion; a subject: *covered new ground in today's talk.* **6. grounds.** The sediment that settles at the bottom of a liquid: *coffee grounds.* **7.** [U] A connection between an electrical conductor and the earth. —*v.* —*tr.* **1.** To run (a boat) onto land: *We grounded our boat by accident.* **2.** To instruct (sbdy.) in fundamentals or basics: *This class grounds students in basic science.* **3.** To provide a basis for (a theory, for example); justify: *grounded his argument on facts.* **4.** To connect (an electric circuit or conductor) with the earth: *To avoid an electrical shock, you should ground your tools.* **5.** To prevent (an aircraft or a pilot) from flying: *Bad weather grounded all flights.* **6.** *Informal.* To punish (sbdy.) by limiting freedom or privileges: *His parents grounded him because of his bad grades in school.* ♦ **gain** or **lose ground.** To progress or fall behind: *The candidate gained ground on his opponent.* **get off the ground.** To begin: *The new school hasn't yet gotten off the ground.*

ground² (ground) *v.* Past tense and past participle of **grind.**

ground•break•ing (ground′brā′kĭng) *n.* [U] The act or ceremony of turning up ground to start construction: *Groundbreaking for the new hospital is to begin today.* —*adj.* Showing originality and innovation: *groundbreaking technology.*

ground crew *n.* A team of mechanics and technicians responsible for the maintenance and service of aircraft on the ground.

ground floor *n.* **1.** [C] The floor of a building at or nearest ground level. **2.** [U] *Informal.* The lowest level of sthg., as a job: *I started on the ground floor of publishing, working in the mail room.* **3.** [U] *Informal.* The start of sthg., as a project or business: *getting in on the ground floor of land development in this country.*

ground•hog (ground′hôg′ *or* ground′hŏg′) *n.* The woodchuck.

Groundhog Day *n.* February 2, which predicts that there will be an early spring if the groundhog does not see its shadow when it comes out of its burrow or that there will be six weeks more of winter weather if the groundhog does see its shadow.

ground•less (ground′lĭs) *adj.* Having no basis in fact; unsupported by the facts: *Her worries about being fired turned out to be groundless.* —**ground′less•ly** *adv.* —**ground′less•ness** *n.* [U]

ground rule *n.* (*usually plural*). A basic rule: *ground rules for tennis; set ground rules for a club.*

ground•swell (ground′swĕl′) *n.* A sudden gathering of force, as of public opinion: *a groundswell of support for the proposed law.*

ground•work (ground′wûrk′) *n.* [U] Early or beginning work that becomes the basis for sthg.: *His research on violence laid the groundwork for the new gun control law.*

group (grōōp) *n.* **1.** A number of people or things gathered or located together: *a group of students in a museum; a group of islands*

off the coast of Alaska. **2.** A number of people or things classed together because of common or shared features: *a small group of supporters across the country.* —*v.* —*tr.* To place or arrange (sbdy./sthg.) in a group: *group books on the same topic together.* —*intr.* To belong to or form a group: *The class grouped on the steps for their picture.*

group•ie (grōō′pē) *n. Informal.* A person who follows rock musicians from concert to concert.

group•ing (grōō′pĭng) *n.* (*usually singular*). **1.** The act or process of bringing together in groups: *The grouping of the children into teams took several minutes.* **2.** A collection of things or persons brought together in a group: *There is a large grouping of reference books in the library.*

grouse¹ (grous) *n.* A small fat bird with spotted brown or grayish feathers on the body and legs, often hunted as game.

grouse² (grous) *intr.v.* **groused, grous•ing, grous•es.** *Informal.* [at; about] To complain; grumble: *My parents groused about the poor hotel service.*

grove (grōv) *n.* A group of trees, as in an orchard: *an orange grove.*

grov•el (grŏv′əl *or* grŭv′əl) *intr.v.* **1.** To behave in an extremely humble manner; cower: *Be proud of yourself and do not grovel.* **2.** To lie flat or crawl on one's belly, as in giving in or submitting to another's power: *The dog began to grovel at its owner's feet.* —**grov′el•er** *n.*

grow (grō) *v.* **grew** (grōō), **grown** (grōn), **grow•ing, grows.** —*intr.* **1.** To develop by a natural process: *The seedlings grew into plants. The sky grew dark.* **2.** To be capable of growth: *Banana trees grow well in tropical climates.* —*tr.* **1.** To cause (sthg.) to grow; cultivate: *grow vegetables in a garden.* **2.** To allow (sthg.) to develop or increase by a natural process: *grow a beard.* ♦ **grow on.** *tr.v.* [insep.] To become more and more pleasing to (sbdy.): *Your new haircut is growing on me.* **grow out of. 1.** To develop or come into existence from (sthg.): *The book grew out of our scribbled notes.* **2.** To become too old or too big for (sthg.): *She grew out of her shoes. We grew out of our childish games.* **grow up.**

intr.v. To become an adult: *Most children can't wait to grow up.*

grow•er (grō′ər) *n.* **1.** A person who grows sthg., especially a person who grows a particular crop for sale: *a fruit grower.* **2.** A plant that grows in a particular way: *Most weeds are fast growers.*

growl (groul) *n.* **1.** A low warning sound made by an animal: *the growl of a dog.* **2.** Something said in a rude, unfriendly way: *He answered my question with a growl.* —*v.* —*intr.* **1.** To make a low throaty sound: *The dog growled menacingly.* **2.** To speak in a rude or angry manner: *The officer growled at the soldiers.* —*tr.* To express (sthg.) by growling: *The dog growled a warning.*

grown (grōn) *v.* Past participle of **grow.** —*adj.* **1.** At full growth; mature: *act like a grown person.* **2.** Produced or cultivated: *locally grown produce.*

Homonyms: grown, groan (moan).

---

grown•up *also* **grown-up** (grōn′ŭp′) *n.* An adult: *She finally felt like a grownup.* —**grown′-up′** *adj.*

growth (grōth) *n.* **1.** [U] The process of growing; progress: *the growth of a child.* **2.** [C] Something that grows or has grown: *A thick growth of weeds covered the yard.* **3.** [U] An amount of sthg. grown; an increase: *measure the growth of a country's population.* **4.** [C] An abnormal mass of tissue growing in or on a living organism: *a growth on the lung.*

grub (grŭb) *intr.v.* **grubbed, grub•bing, grubs.** **1.** To dig in the ground: *grub for potatoes.* **2.** To work hard: *grub for a living.* —*n.* **1.** [C] The thick worm-like larva of certain beetles and other insects. **2.** *Slang.* [U] Food: *buy the grub for a camping trip.*

grub•by (grŭb′ē) *adj.* **grub•bi•er, grub•bi•est.** Dirty; grimy: *grubby work clothes.* —**grub′bi•ly** *adv.* —**grub′bi•ness** *n.* [U]

grudge (grŭj) *tr.v.* **grudged, grudg•ing, grudg•es.** To be unwilling to give or admit (sthg.): *grudged me a small discount for paying in cash.* —*n.* A deep-seated feeling of anger about sthg.: *She still holds a grudge about the accident.*

grudg•ing•ly (grŭj′ĭng lē) *adv.* In an unwilling manner: *The children grudgingly went to bed.*

gru•el (grōō′əl) *n.* [U] A thin watery porridge eaten by poor or sick people in the past.

gru•el•ing (grōō′ə lĭng *or* grōō′lĭng) *adj.* Physically or mentally tiring: *Working in a coal mine is a grueling job.*

grue•some (grōō′səm) *adj.* Causing horror and shock; frightful: *a gruesome accident.* —**grue′some•ly** *adv.*

gruff (grŭf) *adj.* **1.** Abrupt or stern in manner or appearance: *a gruff answer.* **2.** Harsh-sounding; hoarse: *a gruff voice.* —**gruff′ly** *adv.* —**gruff′ness** *n.* [U]

grum•ble (grŭm′bəl) *v.* **grum•bled, grum•bling, grum•bles.** —*intr.* **1.** To complain in a rude or unfriendly manner; mutter unhappily: *They grumbled about the store's prices.* **2.** To rumble or growl: *I was so hungry that my stomach grumbled.* —*tr.* To express (sthg.) in a rude or unhappy manner: *grumbled a response.* —*n.* **1.** A muttered complaint: *A grumble rose from the unfriendly crowd.* **2.** A rumble; a growl: *the grumble of distant thunder.* —**grum′bler** *n.*

grump•y (grŭm′pē) *adj.* **grump•i•er, grump•i•est.** Unfriendly and impatient; cranky: *a grumpy mood.* —**grump′i•ly** *adv.* —**grump′i•ness** *n.* [U]

grunt (grŭnt) *v.* —*intr.* **1.** To make a deep throaty sound, as a pig does. **2.** To make a sound similar to a grunt: *The workers grunted under their heavy loads.* —*tr.* To say or express (sthg.) with a deep throaty sound: *The unfriendly clerk grunted a reply.* —*n.* A deep throaty sound, as that made by a pig.

gua•no (gwä′nō) *n.* [U] The dung of certain sea birds or bats, used as fertilizer.

guar•an•tee (găr′ən tē′) *n.* **1.** Something that assures a particular condition or outcome: *Money is not a guarantee of happiness.* **2.** A promise or an assurance of a product's quality or durability: *Our new car has a five-year guarantee.* —*tr.v.* **1.** To make (sthg.) certain or sure: *The rains guarantee a good crop.* **2.** To try to accomplish (sthg.) for another: *Jefferson wanted to guarantee freedom of speech for future generations.* **3.** To take responsibility for the quality or performance of (sthg.): *The manufacturer guarantees these microwave ovens for five years.* **4.** To provide security for (sbdy./sthg.): *Insurance guarantees a car owner against costs of injury or of repairs.* —**guar′an•tor′** (găr′ən tôr′) *n.*

guard (gärd) *v.* —*tr.* **1.** To protect (sbdy./sthg.) from harm or danger: *guard a building after dark.* See Synonyms at **defend.** **2.** To watch over (sbdy.) so as to prevent escape or violence: *guard a prisoner.* —*intr.* To try to avoid sthg.: *guard against illness by getting plenty of rest and taking vitamins.* —*n.* [C] **1.** Something that protects against or prevents sthg.: *a guard against tooth decay.* **2.** [C] A person who keeps watch or protects: *a security guard.* **3.** [U] Protection or watch: *The sheepdog kept guard over the herd.* ♦ **be on guard** *or* **be on (one's) guard.** To be alert and watchful; cautious: *be on guard for patches of ice on the sidewalk.* **catch off guard** *or* **catch off (one's) guard.** To be unprepared; not alert: *The thunder caught me off guard, and I jumped.*

guard•ed (gär′dĭd) *adj.* **1.** Defended; protected: *a heavily guarded border.* **2.** Cautious; controlled: *The witness gave a guarded answer.* —**guard′ed•ly** *adv.*

guard•i•an (gär′dē ən) *n.* **1.** A person or thing that guards, protects, or watches over sbdy./sthg.: *The courts act as a guardian of the law.* **2.** A person who is legally responsible for the care of sbdy. who cannot manage his or her own affairs: *He's the guardian of two children.*

guard•rail (gärd′rāl′) *n.* A protective railing, as on a highway or stairway: *The car hit the guardrail.*

gua•va (gwä′və) *n.* The sweet fruit of a tropical American tree, used to make jelly and preserves.

gu•ber•na•to•ri•al (gōō′bər nə tôr′ē əl) *adj.* Relating to a governor: *She's one of three gubernatorial candidates.*

guer•ril•la or **gue•ril•la** (gə rĭl′ə) *n.* A member of a military force operating in small bands in occupied territory to attack the enemy, as by surprise raids.

HOMONYMS: guerrilla, gorilla (ape).

guess (gĕs) *v.* —*tr.* **1.** To assume (sthg.) without sufficient information: *The reporter guessed that 6,000 people were at the concert.* **2.** To form a correct estimate or judgment of (sthg.): *I guessed the answer to the math problem.* **3.** To suppose (sthg.); think: *I guess you're right.* —*intr.* To make an estimate or offer an opinion: *We can only guess at their reason for staying home.* —*n.* A conclusion or decision arrived at by guessing: *If you're not sure of the answer, at least make a guess.* —**guess′er** *n.*

guess•ti•mate (gĕs′tə mĭt) *n. Informal.* An estimate based on reasoning from incomplete information: *At this stage, we can only give you a guesstimate of when we'll arrive.* —**guess′ti•mate′** (gĕs′tə māt′) *v.*

guess•work (gĕs′wûrk′) *n.* [U] **1.** The process of making guesses: *There is a lot of guesswork involved in predicting sales of a new product.* **2.** An estimate or a judgment made by guessing: *Judging a student's skill is no matter for guesswork.*

guest (gĕst) *n.* **1.a.** A person who receives courtesy and kindness at the home or table of another: *We invited several guests for dinner.* **b.** A person who is treated well or entertained by a host or hostess, as at a party. **2.** A person who pays for meals or lodging at a restaurant, hotel, or other businesses.

guf•faw (gə fô′) *n.* A hearty loud burst of laughter: *a loud guffaw from the back of the room.* —*intr.v.* To laugh heartily and loudly: *The audience guffawed at the jokes.*

guid•ance (gīd′ns) *n.* [U] **1.** The act of guiding: *Success of the expedition depended on the guidance of their scouts.* **2.** Counseling, as on vocational, educational, or personal problems: *We look to her for guidance.* **3.** A process by which the course of a missile can be controlled in flight.

guide (gīd) *n.* **1.** A person or thing that shows the way, directs, leads, or advises sbdy./sthg.: *a tour guide; a guide to good manners.* **2.** A guidebook. —*tr.v.* **guid•ed, guid•ing, guides.** **1.** To serve as a guide for (sbdy.); conduct: *The ranger guided the tourists through the park.* **2.** To direct the course of (sthg.); steer: *guide a car down a narrow street.* **3.** To exert control or influence over (sbdy./sthg.): *Lincoln guided our nation through the Civil War.*

SYNONYMS: guide, lead, shepherd, steer, usher. These verbs all mean to conduct on the way or direct to the way. *We were guided to our seats. The teacher led the students in a discussion of the novel's themes. The tourists were shepherded to the chartered bus. The secretary steered the applicant to the proper department. The host now usher the guests to the table.*

guide•book (gīd′bŏŏk′) *n.* A handbook of directions and information, especially for travelers and tourists.

guide dog *n.* A dog trained to lead a person who needs help seeing or hearing.

guide•line (gīd′līn′) *n. (usually plural).* A statement or other indication of policy or way of doing sthg., intended to give practical guidance: *The President presented guidelines for economic development and aid to other countries.*

guide•word (gīd′wûrd′) *n.* A word or term at the top of a column or page in a reference book to indicate the first or last entry on the page.

guild (gĭld) *n.* A group of people who share a trade, formed to protect mutual interests and maintain standards.

HOMONYMS: guild, gild (cover with gold).

guile (gīl) *n.* [U] Dangerous cunning; skillful deceit: *Their plans showed a great deal of guile.*

guile•less (gīl′lĭs) *adj.* Free of guile; innocent: *a guileless victim.*

guil•lo•tine (gĭl′ə tēn′ *or* gē′ə tēn′) *n.* A device made of a heavy blade held up between two upright guides and dropped to cut off the head of the person below. —*tr.v.* **guil•lo•tined, guil•lo•tin•ing, guil•lo•tines.** To behead (sbdy.) with a guillotine.

guilt (gĭlt) *n.* [U] **1.** Responsibility for an offense: *Thorough investigation proved the suspect's guilt.* **2.** Regretful awareness of having done sthg. wrong: *the guilt he felt for his sister's death.* **3.** Guilty behavior: *the guilt on the child's face.*

HOMONYMS: guilt, gilt (layer of gold).

guilt·less (gĭlt′lĭs) *adj.* Free of guilt; innocent: *a guiltless associate.*

guilt·y (gĭl′tē) *adj.* **guilt·i·er, guilt·i·est. 1.** Having done wrong; deserving of blame: *The thief was found guilty.* **2.** Caused by a sense of guilt: *a guilty conscience.* —**guilt′i·ly** *adv.* —**guilt′i·ness** *n.* [U]

guin·ea pig (gĭn′ē) *n.* **1.** A small rodent with short ears, short legs, and little or no tail: *Guinea pigs are often kept as pets or used as laboratory animals.* **2.** A person who is used as a subject for research.

guise (gīz) *n. Formal.* **1.** Outward appearance; aspect: *Her guise revealed her sadness.* **2.** False appearance; pretense: *They spoke to me under the guise of friendship.* **3.** Manner or style of clothing: *The spy entered the enemy castle in the guise of a beggar.*

gui·tar (gĭ tär′) *n.* A stringed musical instrument with a long neck and a large, pear-shaped sound box with a flat back. —**gui·tar′ist** *n.*

guitar

gulch (gŭlch) *n.* A deep narrow gap in the earth's surface, especially one cut by the course of a stream.

gulf (gŭlf) *n.* **1.** A large body of ocean or sea water that is partly surrounded by land: *Gulf of Mexico.* **2.** A deep wide opening in the earth; a large hole: *Eruption of the volcano blew a gulf in the side of the mountain.* **3.** A wide gap, as in understanding: *the gulf between one generation and the next.*

gull (gŭl) *n.* A coastal water bird with a strong curved beak, webbed feet, long wings, and usually gray and white feathers.

gul·li·ble (gŭl′ə bəl) *adj.* Easily deceived or tricked: *Ignorance often makes people gullible.* —**gul′li·bil′i·ty** *n.* [U]

gul·ly (gŭl′ē) *n., pl.* **gul·lies.** A ditch or channel cut in the earth by running water, especially after heavy rain.

gulp (gŭlp) *v.* —*tr.* To swallow (food or liquid) greedily or rapidly in large amounts: *We were late and had to gulp our lunch.* —*intr.* **1.** To choke or gasp, as in swallowing large amounts of liquid. **2.** To swallow air, as in nervousness: *She gulped when she saw the snarling dog.* —*n.* **1.** The act of gulping: *His bag of peanuts disappeared in just a few gulps.* **2.** An amount swallowed at one time: *a large gulp of water.* ◆ **gulp back.** *tr.v.* [sep.] To control (strong emotions): *I gulped back my fears about the operation.* **gulp down.** *tr.v.* [sep.] To eat or swallow (sthg.) very quickly: *He gulped his sandwich down before returning to class.*

gum¹ (gŭm) *n.* **1.** [U] A sweet substance that is chewed for a long time but not swallowed; chewing gum: *a stick of gum.* **2.** [C; U] A thick, sticky substance produced by certain plants and trees used to stick things together: *Gum on the flap of an envelope gets sticky after you lick it.* **3.** [U] Rubber made from a plant substance. —*v.* **gummed, gum·ming, gums.** ◆ **gum up.** *tr.v.* [sep.] To cover, smear, seal, fill, or fasten (sthg.) in place with or as if with gum: *Grease has gummed up the drain.* —*intr.v.* To become sticky or clogged: *The machine's gears are gummed up.* —**gum′mi·ness** *n.* [U] —**gum′my** *adj.*

gum² (gŭm) *n. (usually plural).* The firm connective tissue that surrounds and supports the bases of the teeth.

gum·bo (gŭm′bō) *n., pl.* **gum·bos.** [C; U] A thick soup or stew made with meat or seafood, okra, and other vegetables.

gum·drop (gŭm′drŏp′) *n.* A small sugar-coated candy made of sweetened gum or gelatin.

gump·tion (gŭmp′shən) *n.* [U] *Informal.* Boldness, courage, or spirit: *It took gumption to admit her mistake.*

gun (gŭn) *n.* **1.** A weapon that shoots bullets or shells through a heavy metal tube, usually by the explosion of gunpowder. **2.** A device that resembles a gun, as in its ability to project sthg. under pressure: *Painting with a spray gun is quick.* —*tr.v.* **gunned, gun·ning, guns.** To open the throttle of (an engine) so as to accelerate: *He gunned the engine and sped away.* ◆ **be gunning for. 1.** To look for a way to harm sbdy.: *That bully is gunning for you now.* **2.** To try to obtain sthg., as an increase in wages or a better position: *She's gunning for her boss's job.* **gun down.** *tr.v.* [sep.] To shoot (sbdy.): *He gunned down three people before the police caught him.* **jump the gun.** To do sthg. before other people or before the proper time: *Don't jump the gun selling your car; wait until you can get a fair price.* **stick to (one's) guns.** To continue to believe sthg. or hold an opinion even though other people disagree: *In spite of a heated argument, she stuck to her guns and the committee approved her plan.*

gun·fire (gŭn′fīr′) *n.* [U] The firing of guns: *The sound of gunfire woke everyone in the neighborhood.*

gung ho (gŭng′ hō′) *adj. Slang.* Extremely devoted or eager: *a gung ho baseball fan; We were all gung ho about getting started.*

gun·man (gŭn′mən) *n.* A man armed with a gun, especially a killer or criminal.

gun·ny·sack (gŭn′ē săk′) *n.* A strong bag or sack made of a coarse burlap cloth.

gun·pow·der (gŭn′pou′dər) *n.* [U] An explosive powder used in guns, fireworks, and blasting.

gun·shot (gŭn′shŏt′) *n.* **1.** [C] A shot fired from a gun. **2.** [U] The range of a gun: *within gunshot.* **3.** [C] The shooting of a gun: *They ran when they heard gunshots.*

gun·smith (gŭn′smĭth′) *n.* A person who makes or repairs firearms.

G

gup·py (gŭp′ē) *n., pl.* **gup·pies.** A very small tropical freshwater fish that is often kept in home aquariums.

gur·gle (gûr′gəl) *v.* **gur·gled, gur·gling, gur·gles.** *—intr.* **1.** To flow in an irregular current, making a bubbling sound: *A stream gurgled over the rocks.* **2.** To make such a bubbling sound: *The baby gurgled with contentment.* *—tr.* To express (sthg.) with an irregular bubbling sound: *The baby gurgled its delight.*

gu·ru (gōŏr′ōō *or* gŏŏ rōō′) *n., pl.* **gu·rus. 1.** A Hindu spiritual teacher. **2.** A person who is followed as a leader or teacher: *a financial guru.*

gush (gŭsh) *v.* *—intr.* **1.** [*from*] To flow forth suddenly in great volume: *Water gushed from the broken pipe.* **2.** [*over*] To make a show of too much eagerness or emotion: *Be sincere when thanking people, but don't gush over them.* *—tr.* To release (sthg.) in great quantity; pour out: *The new well gushed oil.* *—n.* **1.** A sudden outpouring: *a gush of tears.* **2.** A show of too much eagerness or emotion: *He greeted us with a gush of affection.*

gush·er (gŭsh′ər) *n.* An oil or gas well that pours out a steady flow without pumping.

gush·y (gŭsh′ē) *adj.* **gush·i·er, gush·i·est.** Showing too much eagerness or emotion: *a gushy birthday card.* *—***gush′i·ly** *adv.* *—***gush′i·ness** *n.* [U]

gust (gŭst) *n.* **1.** A sudden strong rush of wind. **2.** A sudden burst, as of rain or smoke. **3.** An outburst of feeling: *a gust of anger.* *—***gust′i·ly** *adv.* *—***gust′i·ness** *n.* [U] *—***gust′y** *adj.*

gus·to (gŭs′tō) *n.* [U] Great pleasure; intense joy: *We were hungry and ate lunch with gusto.*

gut (gŭt) *n.* **1.** (*usually singular*). The digestive tract or any of its parts, especially the stomach or intestines. **2. guts.** The intestines; bowels. **3. guts.** *Slang.* Courage, strength, or nerve: *She had guts to stand up to her boss.* *—tr.v.* **gut·ted, gut·ting, guts. 1.** To remove the intestines of (sthg.): *gut a fish.* **2.** To destroy the contents or inside of (sthg.), usually by fire: *The fire gutted their apartment.* *—adj. Slang.* Arousing or involving basic emotions: *The student's gut reaction was to protest the test score.*

gut·less (gŭt′lĭs) *adj. Slang.* Lacking courage, drive, or inner strength: *a gutless approach to life.* *—***gut′less·ness** *n.* [U]

gut·ter (gŭt′ər) *n.* **1.a.** A channel next to a street curb for draining off water: *She dropped her glove in the gutter.* **b.** An open pipe along the edge of a roof for draining water: *He cleans the leaves from the gutters every fall.* **2.** (*usually singular*). The bad social conditions of certain areas: *the language of the gutter.* **3.** A groove on either side of a bowling alley.

gut·tur·al (gŭt′ər əl) *adj.* Relating to or produced in the throat: *a deep guttural voice.* *—***gut′tur·al·ly** *adv.*

guy (gī) *n. Informal.* **1.** A man or boy; a fellow: *I work with a guy from New Jersey.* **2. guys.** People of either sex: *What do you guys want now?*

guz·zle (gŭz′əl) *tr.v.* **guz·zled, guz·zling, guz·zles.** To drink (sthg.) greedily or often: *guzzle a can of soda.*

guz·zler (gŭz′lər) *n. Informal.* A person or thing, usually a car, that uses too much of sthg.: *a beer-guzzler; a gas-guzzler.*

gym (jĭm) *n.* **1.** [C] A gymnasium. **2.** [U] A class in physical education: *I have gym at 10:15.*

gym·na·si·um (jĭm nā′zē əm) *n.* A room or building equipped for indoor sports: *play basketball in the gymnasium.*

gym·nast (jĭm′năst′ *or* jĭm′nəst) *n.* A person skilled in gymnastics.

gym·nas·tics (jĭm năs′tĭks) *n.* [U] (*used with a singular verb*). Physical exercises designed to develop and display strength, balance, and agility, especially those performed on or with special equipment, such as parallel bars. *—***gym·nas′tic** *adj.*

gy·ne·col·o·gy (gī′nĭ kŏl′ə jē) *n.* [U] The branch of medicine that deals with the diagnosis and treatment of disorders of the female reproductive system. *—***gy′ne·col′o·gist** *n.* *—***gy′ne·co·log′i·cal** (gī′nĭ kə lŏj′ĭ kəl) *adj.*

gyp (jĭp) *Slang. tr.v.* **gypped, gyp·ping, gyps.** To deprive (sbdy.) of sthg. by fraud; cheat or swindle: *He gypped me out of twenty dollars.* *—n.* A fraud or swindle: *That movie was a gyp.*

gyp·sum (jĭp′səm) *n.* [U] A white mineral containing calcium.

gyp·sy (jĭp′sē) *n., pl.* **gyp·sies. 1.** A sometimes offensive term for a member of a nomadic people who originally migrated to Europe from India around the 14th century. **2.** *Informal.* A person who does not like to stay in the same place for long.

gy·rate (jī′rāt′) *intr.v.* **gy·rat·ed, gy·rat·ing, gy·rates. 1.** To turn around a fixed point or axis: *The earth gyrates about its axis.* **2.** To move in a spiral or circular path: *The dancers gyrated around the room.* *—***gy·ra′tion** *n.* [C; U]

gy·ro (jī′rō) *n., pl.* **gy·ros.** A gyroscope.

gy·ro·scope (jī′rə skōp′) *n.* An instrument consisting of a disk or wheel that spins rapidly about an axis like a top. The gyroscope is an accurate navigational instrument and an effective stabilizing device in ships and airplanes.

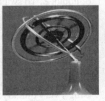

gyroscope

ă–cat; ā–pay; âr–care; ä–father; ĕ–get; ē–be; ĭ–sit; ī–nice; îr–here; ŏ–got; ō–go; ô–saw; oi–boy; ou–out; ŏŏ–took; ōō–boot; ŭ–cut; ûr–word; th–thin; *th*–this; hw–when; zh–vision; ə–about; ɴ–French bon

Hh

h¹ or **H** (āch) *n., pl.* **h's** or **H's**. The eighth let-ter of the English alphabet.

h² *abbr.* An abbreviation of hour.

H The symbol for the element **hydrogen**.

h. also **H.** *abbr.* An abbreviation of: **1.** Height. **2.** Hundred.

ha also **hah** (hä) *interj.* An expression used to show surprise, wonder, triumph, or puzzle-ment: *Ha! I knew you'd say that!*

hab·it (hăb'ĭt) *n.* **1.** [C] A pattern of behavior that occurs repeatedly and is often done with-out thinking: *Many people have a habit of fidgeting when they are nervous.* **2.** [U] A usual practice or manner: *in the habit of tak-ing an early-morning walk.* **3.** [C] An addic-tion to sthg.: *a smoking habit.*

SYNONYMS: habit, practice, custom. These nouns refer to a pattern of behavior that appears repeatedly. **Habit** means a way of acting that has been repeated so many times it no longer involves conscious thought: *My dog has the habit of turning in circles before she lies down.* **Practice** means a routine, often chosen, way of acting: *It is their practice to eat dinner early.* **Custom** means a usually long-standing practice in line with social conventions: *It is a Japanese custom not to wear shoes in the house.*

---

hab·it·a·ble (hăb'ĭ tə bəl) *adj.* Suitable to live in: *Is the old house still habitable?* —**hab'it·a·bil'i·ty** *n.* [U]

hab·i·tat (hăb'ĭ tăt') *n.* The area or natural environment in which an animal or a plant normally lives or grows: *Bears are usually found in cooler northern habitats.*

hab·i·ta·tion (hăb'ĭ tā'shən) *n.* **1.** [C] *Formal.* A place in which to live; a residence. **2.** [U] The act of inhabiting a place or the condition of being inhabited by sbdy.: *The Antarctic climate is not suitable for human habitation.*

hab·it-form·ing (hăb'ĭt fôr'mĭng) *adj.* Leading to or causing addiction: *a habit-forming drug.*

ha·bit·u·al (hə bĭch'ᴏᴏ əl) *adj.* **1.** Of the nature of habit; done constantly or repeated-ly: *Their habitual lateness annoyed everyone.* **2.** Established by long use; usual: *his habitu-al confusion.* —**ha·bit'u·al·ly** *adv.*

hack¹ (hăk) *v.* —*tr.* **1.** To cut or chop (sbdy./ sthg.) with repeated and irregular blows: *hacked weeds.* **2.** *Slang.* To cut (sthg.) as if by hacking: *hacked a large amount from the*

budget. —*intr.* **1.** To chop or cut by hacking: *hack at a tree stump.* **2.** To work on or use a computer with great skill, especially in new ways: *hacked into bank records.* **3.** To cough roughly or harshly: *hacking with a bad cold.* —*n.* **1.** A rough irregular cut or notch made by hacking. **2.** A rough dry cough.

hack² (hăk) *n.* **1.** A horse, especially one for hire, that is used for riding or driving. **2.** A person, especially a writer, who does routine work for hire.

hack·er (hăk'ər) *n.* A person skilled in the use of a computer, especially one who gains access to computer systems to steal informa-tion or money: *The FBI arrested a group of hackers for getting into university records.*

hack·neyed (hăk'nēd) *adj.* Overfamiliar through overuse: *writing full of hackneyed phrases.*

hack·saw (hăk'sô') *n.* A saw used espe-cially for cutting metal.

had (hăd) *v.* Past tense and past participle of **have.** ♦ **be had.** To be cheated or lied to: *You aren't a detective! I've been had!*

had·dock (hăd'ək) *n.* A food fish of the northern Atlantic Ocean.

had·n't (hăd'nt) *v.* Contraction of *had not.*

hag (hăg) *n.* **1.** An insulting term for an old woman who is perceived to be ugly or fright-ful. **2.** A witch; a sorceress.

hag·gard (hăg'ərd) *adj.* Appearing worn and exhausted; gaunt: *a haggard face.* —**hag'-gard·ly** *adv.* —**hag'gard·ness** *n.* [U]

hag·gle (hăg'əl) *intr.v.* **hag·gled, hag·gling, hag·gles.** To bargain, as over the price of sthg.: *a shopper haggling with a fruit seller.* —**hag'gler** *n.*

hah (hä) *interj.* Variant of **ha.**

hail¹ (hāl) *n.* [U] **1.** Water that falls to the earth in the form of rounded balls of ice and hard snow that usually occurs during thun-derstorms. **2.** Something that falls with the force of a shower of ice and hard snow: *a hail of pebbles; a hail of criticism.* —*v.* —*intr.* To fall as hail: *It hailed this afternoon.* —*tr.* To pour (sthg.) down or forth: *The two drivers hailed insults at each other.*

HOMONYMS: hail (ice, greeting), **hale** (healthy, force).

---

hail² (hāl) *tr.v.* **1.** To salute or greet (sbdy.): *hail a friend across the street.* **2.** To signal or call loudly in order to catch the attention of (sbdy./sthg.): *hail a cab.* ◆ **hail from.** *tr.* [insep.] To come or originate from (a place): *They hail from Ohio.*

hail•stone (hāl′stōn′) *n.* A piece of hail.

hail•storm (hāl′stôrm′) *n.* A storm in which hail falls.

hair (hâr) *n.* **1.** [C] One of the fine strands that grows from the skin of human beings and other mammals: *a piece of hair.* **2.** [U] A mass of such fine strands: *My cat has soft hair.* **3.** [C] *(usually singular).* A tiny distance or narrow margin: *We won by a hair.* ◆ **get in (one's) hair.** To bother sbdy.: *The children got in their baby sitter's hair.* **let (one's) hair down.** To relax; behave wildly: *After we finished our exams, we let our hair down.* **make (one's) hair stand on end.** To frighten or terrify sbdy.: *That film made my hair stand on end.* **split hairs.** To be too concerned with small details: *Let's just sign the contract—don't split hairs.* **—hair′like′** *adj.*

HOMONYMS: hair, hare (rabbit).

hair•brush (hâr′brŭsh′) *n.* A brush for the hair.

hair•cut (hâr′kŭt′) *n.* **1.** The act or instance of cutting the hair: *You need a haircut.* **2.** A style in which hair is cut: *a short haircut.*

hair•do (hâr′dōō′) *n., pl.* **hair•dos.** A hairstyle.

hair•dress•er (hâr′drĕs′ər) *n.* A person who cuts or arranges hair.

hair dryer *n.* A mechanical device used to dry hair.

hair•less (hâr′lĭs) *adj.* With little or no hair.

hair•line (hâr′līn′) *n.* The edge of hair growing above the forehead or around the head. —*adj.* A very thin line: *a hairline scratch.*

hair•piece (hâr′pēs′) *n.* Human or artificial hair worn to hide a bald spot or as part of a hairdo.

hair-rais•ing (hâr′rā′zĭng) *adj.* Causing excitement, terror, or thrills: *a hair-raising ride on a roller coaster.*

hair•split•ting (hâr′splĭt′ĭng) *n.* [U] The making of distinctions that are too fine to be important: *The hairsplitting between the lawyers annoyed the judge.*

hair spray *n.* [C; U] A substance sprayed on the hair to keep it in place.

hairstyle (hâr′stīl′) *n.* A style of cutting or arranging the hair.

hair•y (hâr′ē) *adj.* **hair•i•er, hair•i•est. 1.** Covered with hair or projections similar to hair: *a hairy caterpillar.* **2.** Made of or looking like hair: *a hairy blanket.* **3.** *Slang.* Full of problems or hardship; dangerous: *a hairy escape.* **—hair′i•ness** *n.* [U]

hale¹ (hāl) *adj.* ◆ **hale and hearty.** Free from weakness or illness; healthy: *Regular exercise has made her hale and hearty.*

HOMONYMS: hale (healthy, force), **hail** (greeting, ice).

hale² (hāl) *tr.v.* **haled, hal•ing, hales.** To force (sbdy.) to go: *hale an offender into court.*

half (hăf) *n., pl.* **halves** (hăvz). **1.** [C] One of two equal, or nearly equal, parts that together make up a whole: *Fifty cents is one half of a dollar.* **2.** [C] In sports, either of the two equal time periods that make up a game. **3.** [U] Half an hour: *at half past one.* —*adj.* **1.** Being one of two equal, or nearly equal, parts: *a half glass of milk.* **2.** Partial or incomplete: *a half truth.* —*adv.* **1.** To exactly or nearly 50 percent: *a half-empty tank.* **2.** Not completely; partly: *Your work is only half done.* ◆ **half and half.** Of nearly equal parts: *"Is your dog a terrier or a collie?" "Half and half."* **in half.** Into halves: *cut a slice of bread in half.* **not half bad.** Not bad at all: *This soup is not half bad.*

half-a•sleep (hăf′ə slēp′) *adj.* Not fully asleep: *I can't think when I'm half-asleep.*

half-assed (hăf′ast′) *adj. & adv. Slang.* A rude expression used when sbdy. thinks sthg. has been done poorly or without enough care: *She did a half-assed job on her paper.*

half-baked (hăf′bākt′) *adj.* **1.** Only partly baked: *half-baked pizza.* **2.** *Informal.* Not fully thought out; poorly conceived: *a half-baked idea.*

half brother *n.* A brother related through one parent only.

half-dol•lar (hăf′dŏl′ər) *n.* A U.S. silver coin worth 50 cents.

half-heart•ed (hăf′här′tĭd) *adj.* Showing or feeling little enthusiasm, interest, or desire: *With so much work left, I made only a halfhearted attempt to finish it.* **—half′heart′ed•ly** *adv.*

half-hour (hăf′our′) *n.* **1.** A period of 30 minutes. **2.** The middle point of an hour: *News bulletins are broadcast on the half-hour.*

half-mast (hăf′măst′) *n.* [U] The position halfway up a mast or pole at which a flag is flown as a symbol of mourning for sbdy. important who has died.

half sister *n.* A sister related through one parent only.

half•time (hăf′tīm′) *n.* [U] In sports, the pause between halves in certain games.

half•way (hăf′wā′) *adj.* **1.** Midway between two points or conditions: *the halfway point on the trail to the summit.* **2.** Reaching or including only half or a portion; partial: *halfway measures to control pollution.* —*adv.* **1.** To or at half the distance: *I'll meet you halfway* between your house and mine. **2.** Partially: *I halfway gave in to their demands.*

halfway house *n.* A place in which people just released from a prison or other institution can live for a short period of time while they adjust to life outside.

hall (hôl) *n.* **1.** A corridor or passageway in a building: *The hall had several classrooms off it.* **2.** An entrance room or inside passage in a building; a lobby: *We waited in the hall at the elevators.* **3.** A building where meetings, parties, concerts, or other gatherings are held: *a lecture hall.* **4.** A school, college, or university building: *Students live in three halls at the back of campus.*

hal·le·lu·jah (hăl′ə lōō′yə) *interj.* An expression used to show praise or joy. —*n.* An exclamation of "hallelujah."

hall·mark (hôl′märk′) *n.* **1.** A mark that indicates excellence or quality. **2.** A distinguishing characteristic, feature, or trait: *Good design and quality materials are hallmarks of fine automobiles.*

hal·lowed (hăl′ōd) *adj.* Sacred; holy: *hallowed ground.*

Hal·low·een (hăl′ə wēn′ *or* hŏl′ə wēn′) *n.* October 31, celebrated by children going door to door in costumes and asking for treats and playing pranks.

hal·lu·ci·na·tion (hə lōō′sə nā′shən) *n.* [C; U] An illusion of seeing, hearing, or otherwise being aware of sthg. that does not really exist: *People with high fevers may have hallucinations.* —**hal·lu′ci·nate′** *v.* —**hal·lu′ci·na·to′ry** (hə lōō′sə nə tôr′ē) *adj.*

hal·lu·cin·o·gen (hə lōō′sə nə jən) *n.* A drug that produces or tends to produce hallucinations. —**hal·lu′cin·o·gen′ic** (hə lōō′sə nə jĕn′ĭk) *adj.*

hall·way (hôl′wā′) *n.* **1.** A corridor in a building: *a hallway full of trash.* **2.** An entrance hall: *The mail is left in the hallway of our apartment building.*

ha·lo (hā′lō) *n., pl.* **ha·los** *or* **ha·loes**. **1.** A circular band of light that surrounds the sun, the moon, a star, or another light source. **2.** A ring or disk of light surrounding the heads or bodies of sacred figures in religious paintings: *an angel's halo.*

hal·o·gen (hăl′ə jən) *n.* A group of elements with similar properties, including fluorine, chlorine, bromine, iodine, and astatine.

halt (hôlt) *n.* A temporary stop of movement or progress: *The car rolled to a halt when it stalled.* —*intr. & tr.v.* To stop or cause to stop: *The hikers halted for lunch and some rest. The government hopes to halt air pollution.* See Synonyms at **stop**.

hal·ter (hôl′tər) *n.* **1.** A rope or leather strap that fits around the head or neck of an animal

---

and is used to lead or secure the animal. **2.** A piece of women's clothing that ties behind the neck and leaves the back, arms, and shoulders bare.

halt·ing (hôl′tĭng) *adj.* Hesitant or trembling: *a low and halting voice.*

halve (hăv) *tr.v.* **halved, halv·ing, halves. 1.** To divide (sthg.) into two equal portions or parts: *A friend and I halved the remaining apple.* **2.** To reduce or lessen (sthg.) by half: *The storekeeper halved the prices for the sale.*

halves (hăvz) *n.* Plural of **half**.

ham (hăm) *n.* **1.** [C; U] A cut of meat from the thigh of a hog. **2.** [C] An actor who overacts or a performer who exaggerates. **3.** [C] A licensed amateur radio operator. —*v.* **hammed, ham·ming, hams. ◆ ham it up.** *Informal.* To exaggerate or overdo a dramatic role, for example; overact: *The children were hamming it up in front of the mirror.*

ham·burg·er (hăm′bûr′gər) *n.* **1.** [U] Ground meat, usually beef. **2.** [C] A patty of such meat. **3.** [C] A sandwich made with a patty of ground meat usually in a roll or bun.

ham·mer (hăm′ər) *n.* A hand tool usually made of an iron head attached to a handle, used primarily for pounding in nails. —*v.* —*tr.* **1.** To hit (sthg.), especially repeatedly, as if with a hammer: *hammer a nail.* **2.** To beat (sthg.) into shape as if with a hammer: *hammer a dent out of a fender.* **3.** To force upon (sbdy.) by repeated use: *hammer grammar into their heads.* —*intr.* To deal repeated blows with or as if  **hammer** with a hammer; beat: *hammer on a door.* **◆ hammer away at.** *Informal.* To keep at sthg. continuously: *We hammered away at our homework.* **hammer out.** *tr.v.* [sep.] To arrive at (an agreement) after long negotiations: *hammer out a contract.*

ham·mock (hăm′ək) *n.* A hanging bed made of strong fabric hung by cords between two trees or other supports.

hammock

ham·per¹ (hăm′pər) *tr.v.* To prevent the progress, free movement, or action of (sbdy./sthg.): *The snowstorm hampered our plane's flight.*

ham·per² (hăm′pər) *n.* A large basket with a cover, used for holding dirty clothes before washing.

ham·ster (hăm′stər) *n.* A small rodent with soft fur, large cheek pouches, and a short tail, often kept as a pet.

ham·string (hăm′strĭng′) *n.* A large tendon at the back of the human knee. —*tr.v.*

ham·strung (hăm′strŭng′), **ham·string·ing, ham·strings.** To destroy or hinder the efficiency of (sbdy.sthg.); frustrate: *Poor education and lack of resources have hamstrung the development of many nations.*

hand (hănd) *n.* **1.a.** The part of the human arm that is below the wrist consisting of a palm, four fingers, and a thumb. **b.** A similar part in other animals, such as monkeys or raccoons, that can hold things. **2.** Something like a hand in shape or use, especially a pointer on a dial: *the hands of a clock.* **3.** Side or direction based on the way a person is facing: *At my right hand you see a door.* **4.** Physical assistance; help: *Give me a hand with this heavy box.* **5.** A person who does manual labor; a laborer: *Many hired hands worked in the field.* **6.** A member of a group or crew: *All hands on deck!* **7.** An aptitude or ability: *I decided to try my hand at painting.* **8.** An influence or effect: *She had a hand in the decision.* **9.** A round of applause: *The audience gave us a big hand.* **10.** A promise of marriage or permission to marry: *ask for someone's hand in marriage.* **11. a.** The cards dealt to and held by a player in a card game: *Don't look at my hand.* **b.** One round of a card game: *I'll play one more hand of poker.* **12.** *(often plural).* Possession, ownership, or keeping: *The books should be in your hands by noon.* —*tr.v.* To give or pass (sthg.) with the hands: *Hand the flashlight to me.* ♦ **at hand. 1.** Close by; near: *Remain close at hand.* **2.** Soon to happen: *Spring is at hand.* **at the hand** or **hands of.** By the action of: *He died at the hands of an assassin.* **by hand.** With the hands rather than by machine: *These dresses have been sewn by hand.* **change hands.** To transfer from one owner to another: *That restaurant changes hands nearly every year.* **hand down.** *tr.v.* [sep.] **1.** To give or pass (sthg.) on, as an inheritance to one's heirs: *The family handed the painting down from generation to generation.* **2.** To make and pronounce (an official decision, especially a court verdict): *The judge handed down her decision.* **hand in.** *tr.v.* [sep.] To submit or turn (sthg.) in: *Hand in your term papers by May 1.* **hand in hand.** In cooperation; jointly: *Proper diet and good health go hand in hand.* **hand it to.** *Informal.* To give credit or praise to (sbdy.): *You've got to hand it to her; she knows what she's doing.* **hand out.** *tr.v.* [sep.] To distribute or give out (sthg.): *He handed out invitations to the party.* **hand over.** *tr.v.* [sep.] To release or relinquish (sthg.) to another person: *Hand over the stolen property to the police.* **hand over fist.** *Informal.* At a very fast rate: *They were making money hand over fist.* **hands down.** With no trouble; easily: *win the award hands down.*

hand to mouth. Using all of one's salary to live, without any money left over: *The artist sold very few paintings and lived hand to mouth.* **have (one's) hands full.** To have a lot or too much to do: *He has his hands full right now with opening his new store.* **in hand. 1.** Under control: *We succeeded in keeping the situation in hand.* **2.** Ready; within reach: *I arrived at my exam room with pencil in hand.* **on hand.** Present; available: *Will you be on hand for the meeting Friday?* **on** or **off (one's) hands.** In or out of one's care and area of responsibility: *He has a difficult case on his hands. That project is finally off my hands.* **on the one hand.** From one point of view. **on the other hand.** From another point of view: *On the one hand, he works awfully slowly, but on the other hand, he does nice careful work.* **out of hand.** Out of control: *We can't let our expenses get out of hand.* **wait on hand and foot.** To serve sbdy. with never-ending effort; completely: *We waited on them hand and foot.* **wash (one's) hands of.** To refuse to be responsible for sbdy./sthg.: *She washed her hands of the trick her brother was playing on their neighbors.*

hand·bag (hănd′băg′) *n.* A woman's purse used to hold personal items.

hand·ball (hănd′bôl′) *n.* [U] A game in which two or more players hit a ball against a wall with the hand usually while wearing a special glove.

hand·book (hănd′bŏŏk′) *n.* A small reference book or manual providing specific information on a certain subject: *a handbook on golf.*

hand·craft (hănd′krăft′) *n.* Variant of **handicraft.** —*tr.v.* (hănd krăft′). To fashion or make (sthg.) by hand: *They handcraft wooden toys.* —**hand′craft·ed** *adj.*

hand·cuff (hănd′kŭf′) *n.* *(usually plural).* A restraining device made of a pair of metal hoops that are chained together and that can be locked around the wrists: *The policeman put handcuffs on the prisoner.* —*tr.v.* **1.** To restrain (sbdy.) with handcuffs: *The sheriff handcuffed the prisoner.* **2.** To make (sbdy./ sthg.) useless or powerless: *The change in rules handcuffed our plans to get the project.*

handcuffs

hand·ed (hăn′dĭd) *adj.* Relating to skill or preference with respect to a hand or hands: *left-handed.*

hand·ful (hănd′fŏŏl′) *n., pl.* **hand·fuls. 1.** The amount that a hand can hold: *a handful of coins.* **2.** A small but unspecified amount or number: *a handful of people.* **3.** A person or thing that is difficult to control or handle easily: *The spoiled baby is a real handful.*

hand•gun (hănd′gŭn′) *n.* A gun that can be used with one hand.

hand•i•cap (hăn′dē kăp′) *n.* **1.** A physical or mental disability. **2.** Something that gets in the way of sthg.: *Disorganization is my chief handicap.* **3.** A race or contest in which advantage is given to different contestants to equalize the chances of winning: *a golf handicap.* —*tr.v.* **hand•i•capped, hand•i•cap•ping, hand•i•caps. 1.** To cause (sbdy.) to be at a disadvantage: *A sore throat handicapped the singer.* **2.** To give a handicap to (sbdy.) in a game or sport: *handicap a contestant in a golf match.*

hand•i•capped (hăn′dē kăpt′) *adj.* Physically or mentally disabled.

hand•i•craft (hăn′dē krăft′) *also* **hand•craft** (hănd′krăft′) *n. (usually plural).* **1.** A craft or job requiring skilled use of the hands, as weaving or basketry. **2.** Work produced by skilled hands: *The shop sells handicrafts from many countries.*

hand•i•ly (hăn′dĭ lē *or* hăn′dl ē) *adv.* In an easy manner: *The student answered the test questions handily.*

hand•i•work (hăn′dē wûrk′) *n.* [U] **1.** Work performed by hand: *Knitting is handiwork that requires skilled hands.* **2.** The product of a person's efforts and actions: *Friends came to admire our handiwork, a new porch.*

hand•ker•chief (hăng′kər chĭf *or* hăng′-kər chēf′) *n., pl.* **hand•ker•chiefs** *also* **hand•ker•chieves** (hăng′kər chĭvz *or* hăng′kər chēvz′). A small square of cloth, used especially to wipe the nose and mouth.

han•dle (hăn′dl) *v.* **han•dled, han•dling, han•dles.** —*tr.* **1.** To touch, hold, operate, or lift (sthg.) with the hands: *Please do not handle the merchandise.* **2.** To manage, deal with, or treat (sbdy./sthg.) in a specified way, especially successfully: *handles problems well.* **3.** To deal in (sthg.); buy and sell: *Drugstores handle a wide variety of goods.* —*intr.* To act or function in a given way while in operation: *This new car handles well on the highway.* —*n.* A part that is designed to be held or operated with the hand: *carry a pail by its handle; a cup handle; a broom handle.* ◆ **fly off the handle.** To become very angry; lose one's temper: *While training the new employee, the supervisor flew off the handle many times.* **get** *or* **have a handle on.** To reach an understanding of sthg.; gain control of sthg.: *I finally got a handle on the problem.*

han•dle•bar (hăn′dl bär′) *n. (usually plural).* A metal steering bar, often curved, as on a bicycle: *Hold onto the handlebars!*

han•dler (hănd′lər) *n.* A person who handles a person or thing; especially an animal.

hand•made (hănd′mād′) *adj.* Made by hand rather than by machine: *a handmade quilt.*

hand-me-down (hănd′mē doun′) *n. (often plural).* Something, such as an article of clothing, passed on from one person to another: *The sweater is a hand-me-down from my sister.*

hand•out (hănd′out′) *n.* **1.** A folder or leaflet given out free of charge: *The student passed out the handouts.* **2.** Food, clothing, or money given to the needy: *asking for a handout.*

hand•pick (hănd′pĭk′) *tr.v.* **1.** To gather or pick (sthg.) by hand: *We handpicked the fruit.* **2.** To select (sbdy./sthg.) personally: *handpick members of a committee.*

hand•rail (hănd′rāl′) *n.* A narrow railing to be held with the hand for support, usually along a stairway.

hand•shake (hănd′shāk′) *n.* The taking of hands by two people, as in greeting or leave-taking: *a firm handshake.*

hand•some (hăn′səm) *adj.* **hand•som•er, hand•som•est. 1.** Pleasing and appealing in form and appearance: *a handsome couple.* **2.** Generous or liberal: *a handsome reward.* —**hand′some•ly** *adv.* —**hand′some•ness** *n.* [U]

hands-on (hăndz′ŏn′ *or* hăndz′ôn′) *adj.* Involving active participation; applied, as opposed to theoretical knowledge: *We use computers in the classroom in hands-on job training.*

hand•stand (hănd′stănd′) *n.* The act of balancing on the hands with one's feet in the air.

hand•writ•ing (hănd′rī′tĭng) *n.* [U] The writing style of a particular person: *Your handwriting is unreadable.*

hand•y (hăn′dē) *adj.* **hand•i•er, hand•i•est. 1.** Skillful in using one's hands: *A carpenter must be handy with tools.* **2.** Readily available: *a handy supply of wood for the fireplace; a handy place for the telephone directory.* **3.** Useful and easy to use: *a handy reference book.* ◆ **come in handy.** To be useful: *That flashlight came in handy on our camping trip.*

hang (hăng) *v.* **hung** (hŭng), **hang•ing, hangs.** —*tr.* **1.** To fasten (sthg.) from above with no support from below; suspend: *hang clothes to dry on a clothesline.* **2.** To fasten (sthg.) to allow free movement at the point of contact: *hang a door.* **3.** *Past tense and past participle* **hanged** (hăngd). To kill (sbdy.) by suspending by a rope around the neck. **4.** To hold or bend (sthg.) downward: *hang one's head in sorrow.* **5.** To attach (sthg.) to a wall: *hang wallpaper.* —*intr.* **1.** To be attached from above with no support from below: *A sign hung over the door.* **2.** To be fastened to allow free movement from a hinge or hook: *The gate hangs on its hinges.* **3.** To die as a result of hanging. **4.** To remain unresolved or uncertain: *His future hangs in the balance.* **5.** [on]

To be dependent; depend: *A great deal hangs on your decision.* **6.** To stay suspended in the air over a place or an object: *A rain cloud hangs over the field.* **7.** To be exhibited: *Many famous paintings hang in this museum.* **8.** [on] To pay strict attention: *The student hung on the teacher's every word.* —*n.* The way in which sthg. hangs: *the hang of a skirt.* ◆ **get the hang of.** *Informal.* The proper way of doing, handling, or using sthg.: *I can't get the hang of this new camera.* **hang around.** *tr. & intr.v.* [insep.] *Informal.* To spend time doing nothing: *I'd love to hang around the beach all day with you. We hung around waiting for her.* **hang around with.** To keep company: *hang around with old friends.* **hang back.** *intr.v.* To hold oneself back, as if nervous or unwilling: *When the teacher asked a question, several students hung back.* **hang on.** *intr.v.* **1.** To cling tightly to sthg.: *When the mountain climber slipped, he hung on by his fingers.* **2.** To remain on the telephone; hold the line: *Hang on. I'll see if he's here.* **3.** To continue persistently: *This fever keeps hanging on.* **hang on to.** To hold tightly to sthg.: *Hang on to your money.* **hang out.** *intr.v.* *Slang.* To spend one's free time: *She hangs out at the mall with her friends.* **hang out to dry.** To leave sbdy. without help or support, especially by trickery: *The spy was killed because his partner hung him out to dry.* **hang together.** To make sentences as a whole; be understandable: *The sentences hang together to form a good paragraph.* **hang up.** *intr.v.* To end a telephone conversation: *I have to hang up now.* —*tr.v.* [sep.] **1.** To suspend (clothing) on a hook or hanger: *Before class begins, the children hang their coats up.* **2.** To delay or block the progress of (sthg.): *Budget problems hung up the project for months.*

han•gar (hăng′ər *or* hăng′gər) *n.* A building used for housing or repairing aircraft.

___

HOMONYMS: hangar, hanger (hook).

hanged (hăngd) *v.* Past tense and past participle of **hang** (sense 3).

hang•er (hăng′ər) *n.* A frame or hook on which an article of clothing can be hung.

hang•er-on (hăng′ər ŏn′ *or* hăng′ər ôn′) *n., pl.* **hang•ers-on** (hăng′ərz ŏn′ *or* hăng′ərz ôn′). A person who seeks the friendship of a powerful person in the hope of achieving personal gain.

hang glider *n.* A device resembling a kite from which a rider hangs in a harness while gliding from a high place. —**hang gliding** *n.* [U]

hang•ing (hăng′ĭng) *n.* **1.** Execution on a gallows: *death by hanging.* **2.** Something, such as a tapestry, that is hung: *a wall hanging.* —*adj.* Extending downward; overhanging: *a hanging lamp; hanging moss.*

hang•nail (hăng′nāl′) *n.* A small flap of dead skin that hangs from the side or base of a fingernail.

hang•out (hăng′out′) *n.* *Slang.* A frequently visited place: *The mall is a favorite hangout of teenagers.*

hang•o•ver (hăng′ō′vər) *n.* A sick feeling, often characterized by nausea and a headache, that results the day after drinking too much alcohol.

hang-up (hăng′ŭp′) *n.* *Informal.* **1.** An inhibition or emotional difficulty with sthg.: *He has a hang-up about learning to swim.* **2.** An obstacle or inconvenience: *A few hang-ups delayed our arrival.*

han•ker (hăng′kər) *intr.v.* *Informal.* To have a longing or yearning; desire: *I hanker to travel abroad.*

Ha•nuk•kah or **Ha•nu•kah** also **Cha•nu•kah** (KHä′nə kə *or* hä′nə kə) *n.* A Jewish festival lasting eight days and celebrating an ancient victory.

hap•haz•ard (hăp hăz′ərd) *adj.* Dependent on chance; random: *He had left the papers in a haphazard arrangement on the desk.* —**hap•haz′ard•ly** *adv.* —**hap•haz′ard•ness** *n.* [U]

hap•less (hăp′lĭs) *adj.* Unfortunate; unlucky: *a hapless business scheme.* —**hap′less•ly** *adv.* —**hap′less•ness** *n.* [U]

hap•pen (hăp′ən) *intr.v.* **1.** To occur or take place by chance: *The accident happened last night.* **2.** To result from an action or situation: *What will happen if we leave now?* ◆ **happen on** or **upon.** *tr.v.* [insep.] To come upon (sthg.) by chance: *I happened upon an interesting article in the newspaper last week.*

hap•pen•ing (hăp′ə nĭng) *n.* Something that happens; an event or occurrence: *an interesting recent happening.*

hap•pi•ly (hăp′ə lē) *adv.* **1.** In a happy way; with pleasure, joy, and gladness: *The children happily played in the park.* **2.** By luck; with good fortune: *Happily, the parts I needed were all in stock at the hardware store.*

hap•py (hăp′ē) *adj.* **hap•pi•er, hap•pi•est.** **1.** Having, showing, or marked by a feeling of joy or pleasure: *a happy child; the happiest day of my life.* See Synonyms at **glad. 2.** Characterized by good luck; fortunate: *a happy series of events.* **3.** Cheerful; willing: *We'll be happy to help.* —**hap′pi•ness** *n.* [U]

hap•py-go-luck•y (hăp′ē gō lŭk′ē) *adj.* Taking things easily; carefree: *a happy-go-lucky attitude.*

ha•rangue (hə răng′) *n.* A long loud, often attacking, speech: *The dictator delivered a*

___

ă–cat; ā–pay; âr–care; ä–father; ĕ–get; ē–be; ĭ–sit; ī–nice; îr–here; ŏ–got; ō–go; ô–saw; oi–boy; ou–out; ōō–took; ōō–boot; ŭ–cut; ûr–word; th–thin; *th*–this; hw–when; zh–vision; ə–about; N–French bon

harangue against enemies of the government. —*tr. & intr.v.* **ha•rangued, ha•rangu•ing, ha•rangues.** To deliver a harangue to: *The boss harangues his employees for their short-comings. She can harangue for hours.*

har•ass (hăr′əs *or* hə răs′) *tr.v.* **1.** To annoy or torment (sbdy.) repeatedly: *harass a speaker with whistles and shouts.* **2.** To carry out repeated attacks and raids against (sbdy./sthg.): *The pirates harassed ships carrying gold and other treasures.* —**ha•rass′ment** *n.* [U]

har•bor (här′bər) *n.* **1.** A sheltered part of a body of water deep enough to serve as a port for ships. **2.** A place of shelter; a refuge: *Home is always a safe harbor.* —*tr.v.* **1.** To give shelter to (sbdy.): *harbor a fugitive.* **2.** To have (a specified thought or feeling): *harboring a grudge against an old enemy.*

hard (härd) *adj.* **1.** Resistant to pressure; not easily penetrated: *a hard surface; hard as a rock.* **2.** Difficult to understand or express: *a hard question; a hard concept to explain.* **3.a.** Requiring great effort or endurance: *A cross-country race is a hard run.* **b.** Showing effort, endurance, or force: *a hard worker.* **4.** Bad; harmful; unfavorable: *hard times.* **5.** Intense; forceful: *a hard blow; a hard kick.* **6.** Strict and demanding: *a hard teacher.* **7.** Showing careful concentration: *take a hard look at the facts.* **8.** Definite or real; true and unchangeable: *the hard facts of the evidence.* **9.** Causing damage to; tending to wear down quickly: *Road salt is hard on a car.* **10.** Bitter; resentful: *There are hard feelings between the brothers.* **11.** Easily exchanged for gold or other currency: *hard currency.* **12.** Designating the sound represented by the letters *c* and *g* as they are pronounced in *cat* and *go.* **13.** Having high alcoholic content: *hard liquor.* **14.** Containing dissolved salts that interfere with the action of soap: *hard water of high mineral content.* —*adv.* **1.** With much effort; intently; earnestly: *work hard.* **2.** With great force, vigor, or energy: *Press hard on the handle.* **3.** In such a way as to cause great damage or hardship: *A number of towns were hard hit by the storm.* **4.** With great distress, grief, pain, or resentment: *took the news hard.* **5.** Toward or into a solid condition: *The little lake is frozen hard all winter.* ♦ **hard and fast.** Defined, fixed, and invariable: *a hard and fast rule.* **hard of hearing.** Having a partial loss of hearing: *Grandma is getting more and more hard of hearing.* **hard put to.** Having great difficulty: *I'm hard put to explain what he meant.* **hard up.** *Informal.* Without money: *After she lost her job, she was hard up and couldn't pay the rent.* —**hard′ness** *n.* [U]

hard•back (härd′băk′) *adj.* Bound in cloth, cardboard, or leather rather than paper: *Hardback books last longer than paperback books do.* —*n.* A book bound in cloth, cardboard, or leather: *Hardbacks cost more than paperbacks.*

hard•ball (härd′bôl′) *n.* [U] *Informal.* The use of tough and aggressive means to obtain a goal: *The negotiator played hardball to get the opposition to give in.*

hard-boiled (härd′boild′) *adj.* **1.** Boiled in the shell to a solid texture: *a hard-boiled egg for breakfast.* **2.** *Informal.* Lacking emotion; practical; tough: *a hard-boiled newspaper reporter.*

hard-core (härd′kôr′) *adj.* **1.** Intensely dedicated or loyal: *a hard-core golfer.* **2.** Opposed to improvement or change: *a hard-core criminal.* **3.** Extreme: *hard-core pornography.*

hard•cov•er (härd′kŭv′ər) *adj. & n.* Hard-back: *Do you have this book in hardcover?*

hard disk *n.* A computer disk that cannot be removed from the processor.

hard•en (här′dn) *v.* —*tr.* **1.** To make (sthg.) hard or harder: *harden steel.* **2.** To toughen (sbdy.): *harden young athletes by long periods of exercise.* **3.** To make (sbdy.) unfeeling, unsympathetic, or unkind: *Seeing so much poverty and disease hardened the young doctor's heart.* —*intr.* To become hard or harder: *Allow the mixture to cool until it hardens.*

hard•hat *or* **hard-hat** (härd′hăt′) *n.* **1.** A lightweight protective helmet worn by workers in construction or industrial settings. **2.** *Informal.* A construction worker.

hard•head•ed (härd′hĕd′ĭd) *adj.* **1.** Stubborn: *a hardheaded mule.* **2.** Practical; realistic: *a hardheaded business manager.* —**hard′head′ed•ly** *adv.* —**hard′head′ed•ness** *n.* [U]

hard•heart•ed (härd′här′tĭd) *adj.* Lacking in feeling or sympathy; without pity: *a hard-hearted view of the world.* —**hard′heart′ed•ly** *adv.* —**hard′heart′ed•ness** *n.* [U]

hard•ly (härd′lē) *adv.* **1.** Barely; only just: *We hardly noticed it was getting late.* **2.** Probably or almost surely not: *I would hardly expect visitors on such a snowy day.*

USAGE: hardly The words **hardly, rarely,** and **scarcely** act like negatives, so they should not be used with other negatives. You should write or say *I could hardly believe it* rather than *I couldn't hardly believe it.*

---

hard•ship (härd′shĭp′) *n.* [C; U] A cause of suffering or difficulty: *The settlers suffered great hardships.*

hard•ware (härd′wâr′) *n.* [U] **1.** Equipment and tools used for home repair and gardening: *Hardware such as ladders, nails, and hammers are sold at a hardware store.* **2.** A computer and related equipment, such as the keyboard, monitor, disk drive, and printer: *computer hardware and software.*

hard•wood (härd′wŏŏd′) *n.* [C; U] Any of various trees with compact wood and leaves that usually fall each year: *Maple and oak are hardwoods.*

H

har·dy (här′dē) *adj.* **har·di·er, har·di·est.**
1. Strong and in good health: *a hardy puppy.*
2. Capable of surviving in harsh or difficult conditions: *A hardy rosebush can survive freezing temperatures.*

hare (hâr) *n.* A mammal similar to the rabbit but with longer ears and legs.

HOMONYMS: hare, hair (strands on the head).

---

hare·brained (hâr′brānd′) *adj.* Foolish; not fully thought out: *a hare-brained idea.*

har·em (hâr′əm *or* här′əm) *n.* **1.** The part of a Muslim house in which the women live. **2.** The women who live in a Muslim household.

hark (härk) *intr.v. Formal.* To listen carefully: *Hark to what she has to say.* ◆ **hark back.** To recall or return to an earlier time or event: *hark back to happier days.*

har·lot (här′lət) *n. Formal.* An old-fashioned word for a prostitute.

harm (härm) *n.* [U] **1.** Injury or damage: *Insects often cause great harm to crops.* **2.** Wrong; evil: *There was no harm meant in their careless mistake.* —*tr.v.* To do harm to (sbdy./sthg.): *Your remarks can't harm me.*

harm·ful (härm′fəl) *adj.* Causing or able to cause harm; damaging: *harmful insects.* —**harm′ful·ly** *adv.* —**harm′ful·ness** *n.* [U]

harm·less (härm′lĭs) *adj.* Unable to cause harm: *a harmless kitten.* —**harm′less·ly** *adv.* —**harm′less·ness** *n.* [U]

har·mon·i·ca (här-mŏn′ĭ kə) *n.* A small, rectangular musical instrument that has a series of tuned metal reeds set back in air holes, played by exhaling or inhaling.

har·mo·ni·ous (här-mō′nē əs) *adj.* **1.** Showing accord in feeling or action: *a harmonious gathering of friends.* **2.** Having elements pleasingly or appropriately combined: *a harmonious arrangement of colors.* **3.** Characterized by harmony of sound; melodious. —**har·mo′ni·ous·ly** *adv.*

harmonica

har·mo·nize (här′mə nīz′) *v.* **har·mo·nized, har·mo·niz·ing, har·mo·niz·es.** —*tr.* **1.** To be in or bring (sthg.) into agreement; make harmonious: *harmonize different ideas into a plan.* **2.** To provide written, played, or sung harmony for (a melody). —*intr.* **1.** To be in agreement; be harmonious. **2.** To sing or play in harmony: *The choir harmonized in song.* —**har′mo·ni·za′tion** (här′mə nĭ zā′shən) *n.* [U]

har·mo·ny (här′mə nē) *n., pl.* **har·mo·nies. 1.** [C; U] The combination of notes forming a chord: *The piano fills in the harmony for the voice part of the singer.* **2.** [C] A combination of musical sounds considered to be pleasing: *The quartet's close harmonies delighted the audience.* **3.** [C] A pleasing combination of elements that form a whole: *The developers destroyed the harmony of the beautiful mountain scenery.* **4.** [U] Agreement in feeling or opinion; accord: *a family that lives in harmony.*

har·ness (här′nĭs) *n.* **1.** A set of leather straps and metal pieces used to attach an animal to a vehicle or plow. **2.** Something that looks like a harness, as the arrangement of straps used to hold a parachute to the body. —*tr.v.* **1.** To put a harness on (a working animal): *harness a horse to a wagon.* **2.** To bring under control and direct the force of (sthg.): *harness the sun's energy.*

harp (härp) *n.* A musical instrument with an upright triangular frame on which a series of strings are played by plucking with the fingers. —*intr.v.* ◆ **harp on.** *intr.v.* To write or talk about a subject to an excessive or boring degree: *harping on how much it costs to go to the movies.* —**harp′ist** (här′pĭst) *n.*

har·poon (här pōōn′) *n.* A weapon like a spear that is used in hunting sea mammals and large fish. —*tr.v.* To strike, kill, or catch (sthg.) with or as if with a harpoon. —**har·poon′er** *n.*

harp·si·chord (härp′sĭ kôrd′) *n.* An old-fashioned keyboard instrument that resembles a piano, but with strings that are plucked.

har·row·ing (hăr′ō ĭng) *adj.* Extremely worrying: *a harrowing experience.*

har·ry (hăr′ē) *tr.v.* **har·ried, har·ry·ing, har·ries.** To disturb or distress (sbdy./sthg.) by or as if by repeated attacks; harass: *harried me with constant phone calls.*

harsh (härsh) *adj.* **1.** Unpleasantly coarse or rough: *harsh detergents.* **2.** Unpleasant to the senses: *a harsh angry voice.* **3.** Extremely mean or cruel; stern: *harsh words of criticism.* —**harsh′ly** *adv.* —**harsh′ness** *n.* [U]

har·vest (här′vĭst) *n.* **1.** The act, time, or process of gathering a crop: *The cotton harvest began late this year.* **2.** The crop that ripens or is gathered in a season: *a large corn harvest.* —*v.* —*tr.* **1.** To gather (a crop): *harvest wheat; harvest an apple orchard.* **2.** To receive (the benefits or consequences of an action): *harvest the rewards of hard work.* —*intr.* To gather a crop: *They finally harvested last week.* —**har′vest·er** *n.*

has (hăz) *v.* Third person singular present tense of **have.**

has-been (hăz′bĭn′) *n., pl.* **has-beens.** *Informal.* A person whose fame, popularity, or success has passed: *The actor is a has-been.*

---

hash (hăsh) n. [U] **1.** A dish of chopped meat and potatoes or other vegetables browned and cooked together. **2.** *Informal.* Hashish. —v. ♦ **hash out.** *tr.v.* [sep.] *Informal.* To discuss (sthg.) carefully; review: *hash out a solution to the problem.*

hash•ish also **hash•eesh** (hăsh′ēsh′ or hă shēsh′) n. [U] A dry resinous extract prepared from the hemp plant, smoked as an illegal drug.

has•n't (hăz′ənt). Contraction of *has not.*

has•sle (hăs′əl) *Informal.* n. **1.** An argument or a fight: *I don't want any hassles.* **2.** Trouble or bother: *Driving in the snow is a real hassle.* —v. **has•sled, has•sling, has•sles.** —*intr.v.* [*over; about*] To argue or fight: *We hassled over who would go first.* —*tr.* To bother or harass (sbdy.): *The bully hassled the boy on his way to school.*

haste (hāst) n. [U] Swiftness of motion or action; speediness: *Haste caused her to drop the plate.* ♦ **in haste.** To act without thinking: *She had acted in haste and now regretted her decision.*

has•ten (hā′sən) *intr. & tr.v.* To hurry or cause to hurry swiftly; hurry: *I hastened to tell them the good news. The medicine hastened my recovery.*

hast•y (hā′stē) *adj.* **hast•i•er, hast•i•est.** Done or made too quickly to be accurate or wise: *hasty judgments.* —**hast′i•ly** *adv.* —**hast′i•ness** n. [U]

hat (hăt) n. A covering for the head: *She wore a big straw hat to protect her head from the sun.* ♦ **at the drop of a hat.** At the slightest cause or reason: *She'll argue at the drop of a hat.* **old hat.** Old-fashioned; out of style: *His ideas are too old hat to take seriously.* **pass the hat.** To collect donations of money: *The musician passed the hat.* **take (one's) hat off to.** To respect, admire, or congratulate: *I take my hat off to anyone who can get a high mark on that test.*

hatch¹ (hăch) n. An opening, as in the deck of a ship or in an airplane.

hatch² (hăch) v. —*intr.* To come out of an egg: *Ten chicks hatched today.* —*tr.* **1.** To cause (young animals) to come out of an egg: *The hen hatched a brood of eight chicks.* **2.** To plan or plot (sthg.), especially in secret: *hatching a plan of escape.*

hatch•et (hăch′ĭt) n. A small ax with a short handle used with one hand.

hate (hāt) *tr.v.* **hat•ed, hat•ing, hates. 1.** To have a great dislike for (sbdy.); detest: *She hates her ex-husband.* **2.** To feel dislike or distaste for (sthg.): *We hate washing dishes. I hate onions.* —n. [U] Intense dislike; hatred: *Hate is a dangerous emotion.* —**hat′er** n.

hate•ful (hāt′fəl) *adj.* **1.** Arousing or deserving hatred: *Child abuse is a hateful crime.* **2.** Feeling or showing hatred; full of hate: *They*

stared at me in a hateful manner. —**hate′ful•ly** *adv.* —**hate′ful•ness** n. [U]

ha•tred (hā′trĭd) n. [U] Intense animosity or hostility: *They are fighting against racial hatred.*

hat•ter (hăt′ər) n. A person who makes, sells, or repairs hats. ♦ **as mad as a hatter.** Completely insane: *His war experience left him as mad as a hatter.*

haugh•ty (hô′tē) *adj.* **haugh•ti•er, haugh•ti•est.** Behaving as though one is better than others; insultingly proud: *The haughty waiter offended many customers.* See Synonyms at **proud.** —**haugh′ti•ly** *adv.* —**haugh′ti•ness** n. [U]

haul (hôl) v. —*tr.* **1.** To pull or drag (sthg.) with force; tug: *We hauled the wood into the shed.* **2.** To transport (sthg.), as with a truck or cart: *used trucks to haul away the dirt.* **3.** To bring (sbdy.) before a judge or other authority for punishment: *He was hauled into court for unpaid parking tickets.* —*intr.* To pull or tug: *They hauled on the rope for what seemed like hours.* —n. **1.** The act of pulling or dragging. **2.** A distance over which sthg. is transported or pulled: *a long haul across country.* **3.** Everything collected or acquired by a single effort; the take: *a big haul of fish.* ♦ **haul off** or **away.** *intr.v. Informal.* To draw back one's arm before hitting sbdy.: *She hauled off and slapped him.* —*tr.v.* [sep.] **1.** To take (sbdy.) away unwillingly: *He was hauled off to jail.* **2.** To carry (trash) away: *We hauled it off to the dump.* **long haul. 1.** An action or series of actions that requires great effort: *Becoming a doctor is a long haul.* **2.** A long period of time: *They're committed to this project for the long haul.* **short haul.** A brief period of time: *They're only in business for the short haul.* —**haul′er** n.

HOMONYMS: haul, hall (corridor).

---

haunch (hônch *or* hŏnch) n. *(usually plural).* The hip, buttock, and upper thigh of a person or an animal: *The dog settled back on its haunches.*

haunt (hônt *or* hŏnt) *tr.v.* **1.** To visit or appear to (sbdy./sthg.) in the form of a ghost or other supernatural being: *spirits haunting the woods.* **2.** To visit (a place) often: *haunts the local bookstores.* **3.** To come to (one's mind) continually: *That bad experience has haunted me ever since.* —n. A place that is visited often: *This café is a favorite haunt of artists.*

haunt•ing (hôn′tĭng *or* hŏn′tĭng) *adj.* Coming again and again to the mind; unforgettable: *a haunting melody.* —**haunt′ing•ly** *adv.*

have (hăv) v. **had** (hăd), **hav•ing, has** (hăz). —*tr.* **1.** To own or be in possession of (sthg.): *My family has an old car.* **2.** To possess (sthg.) as a characteristic, function, or quality: *That* singer has a good voice. **3.** To possess or contain (sthg.) as a part: *This typewriter has a correction key.* **4.** To be in a certain relationship to (sbdy.): *I have a brother and a sister.* **5.** To possess knowledge of or experience in (sthg.): *I have had no science or math this semester.* **6.** To hold (sthg.) in the mind: *I have many doubts about this trip.* **7.** To accept or take (sthg.): *Will you have some coffee?* **8.** To experience (sthg.): *I had a good summer.* **9.** To allow or permit (sthg.): *Our teacher won't have sloppy writing.* **10.a.** To cause (sbdy.) to do sthg.: *He had the taxi driver wait for him.* **b.** To cause (sthg. to be done): *We had the house cleaned for the party.* **11.** To participate or engage in (sthg.): *We have arguments but are still good friends.* **12.** To give birth to (young): *Our cat is having kittens soon.* **13.** *(used with the infinitive of another verb).* To be forced or obliged (to do sthg.); must: *We have to leave now.* **14.** To eat or drink (sthg.): *I'd like to have a snack.* —*aux.* Used with a past participle to form the perfect tenses: *They have already had their lunch. She has been trying to reach you. We had just finished dinner when they arrived. We will have finished the job by the end of next week.* ◆ **have at.** *tr.v.* [insep.] To attack (sbdy./sthg.): *We watched two birds have at each other.* **have done with.** To stop (sthg.): *Let's have done with this nonsense.* **have got.** *Informal. (used in the present tense).* To possess (sthg.): *He's got a new car. They've got a good reputation.* **have got to.** *Informal. (used in the present tense).* To need to (do sthg.); must: *You have got to see a doctor.* **have had it.** To have endured all that one can: *I've had it with this traffic.* **have it in for.** To intend to harm (sbdy.); especially because of a grudge: *He has it in for her because she tricked him.* **have it out.** To settle (sthg.) decisively, especially through discussion or argument: *We had it out and decided we would share all our chores.* **have on.** *tr.v.* [sep.] To wear (sthg.): *The girls have on their new outfits.* **have to do with.** To be concerned or associated with (sbdy./sthg.): *The book has to do with the U.S. Civil War.* **haves and have-nots.** People or countries that are rich and those that are not: *The gap between the haves and have-nots seems to be increasing.*

ha•ven (hā′vən) *n.* A place of refuge or safety; a sanctuary: *The library is a haven from noise.*

have-not (hăv′nŏt′) *n.* A person or country with little or no material wealth: *the have-nots of this society.*

have•n't (hăv′ənt). Contraction of *have not.*

hav•oc (hăv′ək) *n.* [U] Very great destruc-

tion; ruin: *The hurricane created havoc throughout the coastal area.*

hawk[1] (hôk) *n.* **1.** Any of various birds with a short hooked bill, keen eyesight, and strong claws with which they catch small birds and animals for food. **2.** *Informal.* A person who

hawk[1]

favors aggressive action or policy: *The Senator is a hawk on U.S. trade policy.* —*intr.v.* To hunt with a trained hawk.

hawk[2] (hôk) *tr.v.* To sell (goods) in the street by calling out; peddle: *She hawks hot dogs for a living.* —**hawk′er** *n.*

hawk[3] (hôk) *intr.v. Informal.* To clear or try to clear the throat by coughing: *He hawked loudly before he spoke.*

hawk-eyed (hôk′īd′) *adj.* Having very sharp eyesight: *That hawk-eyed teacher misses nothing.*

hay (hā) *n.* [U] Grasses that are cut and dried for use as food for horses and cattle. —*v.* —*intr.* To cut and dry grasses to make them into hay: *We have to hay before it rains.* —*tr.* To feed (grazing animals) with hay: *The rancher hayed the cattle during winter.* ◆ **hit the hay.** *Informal.* To go to sleep: *It's getting late, so we should hit the hay.*

hay fever *n.* [U] A severe irritation of the eyes, nose, and throat, caused by an allergy to pollens.

hay•ride (hā′rīd′) *n.* A ride taken for pleasure in a wagon partly filled with hay.

hay•wire (hā′wīr′) *n.* [U] Wire used for tying up bales of hay. —*adj. Informal.* **1.** Not functioning properly; broken: *The gauge went haywire.* **2.** Mentally confused; upset: *The writer went haywire when told he would have to revise the article again.*

haz•ard (hăz′ərd) *n.* A chance of being injured or harmed; danger: *the hazards of skiing; The stacks of old newspapers were a fire hazard.* —*tr.v.* To expose (sbdy./sthg.) to danger; risk: *Firefighters hazard their lives for the safety of others.* ◆ **hazard a guess.** To make a guess about sthg.: *I'm not sure why he's absent, but I'll hazard a guess.*

haz•ard•ous (hăz′ər dəs) *adj.* Full of danger; risky: *a hazardous voyage.*

haze[1] (hāz) *n.* **1.** [C; U] Fine dust, smoke, or water vapor suspended in the air: *The skyscrapers were hidden in the haze.* **2.** *(usually singular).* A vague or confused state of mind: *Many people are in a haze just after waking up.*

haze² (hāz) *tr.v.* **hazed, haz•ing, haz•es.** To play rough or humiliating jokes on (sbdy.); force to perform humiliating or unpleasant tasks: *haze new members of the club.*

ha•zel (hā′zəl) *n.* **1.** [C] A small tree, with edible nuts. **2.** [U] A greenish brown color. —*adj.* Greenish brown.

ha•zel•nut (hā′zəl nŭt′) *n.* The edible nut of a hazel, with a hard brown shell.

haz•y (hā′zē) *adj.* **haz•i•er, haz•i•est. 1.** Marked by the presence of haze; misty: *a hazy sun.* **2.** Not clear; vague: *a hazy memory of an event long past.* —**haz′i•ly** *adv.* —**haz′i•ness** *n.* [U]

H-bomb (āch′bŏm′) *n.* A hydrogen bomb.

he (hē) *pron.* **1.** The man or boy mentioned before: *Tom worked here last summer, but now he is back in school.* **2.** The male animal mentioned before: *Our cat usually sleeps outside, but he slept in my room last night.* **3.** A person whose gender is not specified or known: *He who laughs last laughs best.* —*n.* A male animal or person: *If the puppy is a he, we'll call him Shep.* —SEE NOTE at **she.**

He The symbol for the element **helium.**

head (hĕd) *n.* **1.** The top or front part of the body containing the brain, eyes, ears, nose, and mouth. **2.** The brain or mind: *I can do all the math in my head.* **3.** A weight, fixture, or part that sticks out at the end of an object: *the head of a pin.* **4.** The working part of a tool: *the head of a hammer.* **5.** A rounded mass of leaves, buds, or flowers growing from the main stem of a plant: *a head of cabbage.* **6.** A person who leads, rules, or is in charge of sthg.; a leader or director: *the head of the corporation.* **7.** The most important part or leading position: *The girl marched at the head of the parade.* **8.** The top part of sthg.: *Look at the head of each column.* **9.** A point when sthg. decisive happens: *Continual smog over the city brought the matter of air pollution to a head.* **10.** *pl.* **head.** A single animal or person: *seven head of cattle; tickets costing ten dollars a head.* **11.** (*often used in the plural with a singular verb*). The side of a coin with the principal design and the date: *We'll flip a coin; heads is yes and tails is no.* **12.** Water that forms the source of a river or stream: *the little stream that forms the head of a great river.* **13.** Part of a tape or CD player: *Maybe you need to clean the heads on your tape player.* —*adj.* **1.** Most important; ranking first; chief: *the head coach.* **2.** Placed on top or in the front: *the head name on a list.* —*v.* —*tr.* **1.** To aim, point, or turn (sbdy./sthg.) in a certain direction: *They headed the team of horses up the hill.* **2.** To lead or be in charge of (sthg.): *The mayor headed the committee.* **3.** To be in the first or foremost position of (sthg.): *She heads the list of candidates for the job.* —*intr.* [*for; towards*] To proceed or go in a certain direction: *head for home.* ◆ **a**

good head for. A mental ability or aptitude: *a good head for business.* **go to** (one's) **head. 1.** To become conceited: *His sudden fame went to his head.* **2.** To become intoxicated: *The woman at the bar had one drink, and it went to her head.* **head off.** *tr.v* [sep.] To block the progress of (sbdy./sthg.); intercept: *They tried to head him off before he went home.* **head over heels. 1.** Rolling, as in a somersault: *He tripped and fell head over heels.* **2.** Completely; hopelessly: *Those two are head over heels in love.* **keep** (one's) **head.** To stay calm: *During an emergency, it's important to keep your head.* **lose** (one's) **head.** To lose one's self-control: *He tends to lose his head in a crisis.* **out of** (one's) **head.** Insane; crazy: *If you believe his story you're out of your head!* **over** (one's) **head.** Beyond one's understanding or financial ability: *He is in over his head.*

head•ache (hĕd′āk′) *n.* **1.** A pain in the head. **2.** *Informal.* Something that causes trouble: *Those children are a real headache.*

head•band (hĕd′bănd′) *n.* A band worn around the head to absorb sweat or hold hair in place.

head•board (hĕd′bôrd′) *n.* A board, frame, or panel that stands at the head of a bed.

head•ed (hĕd′ĭd) *adj.* (*usually used with a number or an adjective and a hyphen*). **1.** Having hair of a certain kind or color: *the red-headed twins.* **2.** Having a specified kind or number of heads: *a three-headed monster.* **3.** Having a specified kind of disposition: *a cool-headed surgeon; a wrong-headed plan.*

head•first (hĕd′fûrst′) *adv.* **1.** With the head leading: *She dove headfirst into the water.* **2.** Hastily and with little thought; rashly: *We must avoid rushing headfirst into a complicated project.*

head•gear (hĕd′gîr′) *n.* [U] A covering for the head, as a hat or helmet: *The right headgear can protect you when you cycle.*

head•hunt (hĕd′hŭnt′) *v.* —*tr.* To look for (people) to place in high-level jobs for companies: *She headhunts programmers for multinational corporations.* —*intr.* To earn a living placing people in high-level jobs: *He used to headhunt for large manufacturers.* —**head′hunt′er** *n.*

head•ing (hĕd′ĭng) *n.* **1.** A title, subtitle, or topic put at the head of a page, chapter, or section of a printed or written work: *Each chapter has a heading on the first page.* **2.** The course or direction in which a ship or an aircraft is moving: *The ship's heading was due south.*

head•less (hĕd′lĭs) *adj.* **1.** Having no head. **2.** Lacking a leader or director: *Her decision to retire has left the committee headless.*

head•light (hĕd′līt′) *n.* A bright light on the front of an automobile, a train, or another vehicle.

H

head·line (hĕd′līn′) *n.* The title of a newspaper article, usually printed in large type. —*tr.v.* **head·lined, head·lin·ing, head·lines. 1.** To give a headline to (a page or an article). **2.** To announce (sbdy./sthg.) widely: *headline a new product.*

head·long (hĕd′lông′ *or* hĕd′lŏng′) *adv.* **1.** With the head leading; headfirst: *He slid headlong into third base.* **2.** At dangerous speed or with uncontrolled force: *The wolf ran headlong in pursuit.* **3.** Hastily and without thinking: *They jumped headlong into the new business.* —*adj.* (hĕd′lông′ *or* hĕd′lŏng′). **1.** Done with the head first: *a headlong fall down the steps.* **2.** Dangerously fast or uncontrollably forceful: *a headlong race to the finish.* **3.** Done in a rush; with little thought: *a headlong decision to go.*

head-on (hĕd′ŏn′ *or* hĕd′ôn′) *adj.* **1.** With the front end receiving the impact: *a head-on crash of two cars.* **2.** Facing forward; direct: *the head-on fury of the storm.* —*adv.* **1.** With the head or front first: *The truck ran head-on into the fence.* **2.** In open conflict; directly: *Their opponent attacked the idea head-on.*

head·phone (hĕd′fōn′) *n. (usually plural).* A receiver, as for a radio, held to the ears by a headband.

head·quar·ters (hĕd′kwôr′tərz) *pl.n. (used with a singular or plural verb).* The building or offices from which a commander, company president, or police force issues orders.

head·room (hĕd′rōōm′ *or* hĕd′rŏŏm′) *n.* [U] The amount of space above one's head, usually in a car: *That model car has very little headroom.*

head·rest (hĕd′rĕst′) *n.* The top part of a chair or seat that supports the head: *Most front seats in cars have adjustable headrests.*

head·set (hĕd′sĕt′) *n.* A pair of headphones.

head·stand (hĕd′stănd′) *n.* A position in which one balances oneself vertically on one's head, placing the hands on the floor for support.

head start *n. (usually singular).* An early start that provides some advantage: *We got a head start on planting our vegetable garden this year.*

head·stone (hĕd′stōn′) *n.* A memorial stone set at the head of a grave.

head·strong (hĕd′strông′ *or* hĕd′strŏng′) *adj.* **1.** Wanting to have one's own way; stubborn and willful: *a proud and headstrong person.* See Synonyms at **obstinate. 2.** Resulting from being willful or stubborn: *a headstrong decision.*

head·wait·er (hĕd′wā′tər) *n.* A waiter who is in charge of other waiters.

head·way (hĕd′wā′) *n.* [U] **1.** Movement forward: *The canoe barely made headway against the strong current.* **2.** Progress toward a goal: *We made a great deal of headway in planning our experiment.*

head·wind (hĕd′wĭnd′) *n.* A wind blowing in the direction opposite the course of a ship or an aircraft.

head·word (hĕd′wûrd′) *n.* A word used as the heading of an entry in a dictionary or an encyclopedia.

head·y (hĕd′ē) *adj.* **head·i·er, head·i·est. 1.** Tending to make one dizzy or foolish: *the heady effects of alcohol.* **2.** Marked by hasty action or willfully dangerous behavior; headstrong: *a heady outburst of resentment.* —**head′i·ly** *adv.* —**head′i·ness** *n.* [U]

heal (hēl) *tr. & intr.v.* To make or become healthy and sound: *Doctors heal the sick. Most cuts heal in a short time.* —**heal′er** *n.*

HOMONYMS: heal, heel (foot part), **he'll** (he will).

health (hĕlth) *n.* [U] **1.** The overall condition of an organism or a thing at a particular time: *the health of the economy.* **2.** Freedom from disease, injury, or defect; soundness of body and mind: *Rest is important to your health.*

health food *n.* [U] Food that is usually grown organically.

health·ful (hĕlth′fəl) *adj.* **1.** Tending to promote good health: *a healthful diet.* **2.** Healthy: *a healthful athlete.* —**health′ful·ly** *adv.* —**health′ful·ness** *n.* [U]

health maintenance organization *n.* An organization that provides health care to members who pay insurance premiums to cover costs and agree to certain limits in treatment, as in choosing of doctors.

health·y (hĕl′thē) *adj.* **health·i·er, health·i·est. 1.** In a state of good health: *a healthy student.* **2.** Promoting good health; healthful: *a healthy climate.* **3.** Showing good health: *a healthy appearance.* **4.** Large: *a healthy portion of meat.* —**health′i·ly** *adv.* —**health′i·ness** *n.* [U]

heap (hēp) *n.* **1.** A group of things thrown together; a pile: *a trash heap.* **2.** *Informal. (usually plural).* A great amount; a lot: *The game was heaps of fun.* —*tr.v.* **1.** To put or throw (sthg.) in a heap; pile up: *They heaped wood by the fireplace.* **2.** To fill (sthg.) to overflowing; pile high: *They heaped the cart with groceries.* **3.** To give (sthg.) in large amounts: *The critics heaped compliments on the popular author.*

hear (hîr) *v.* **heard** (hûrd), **hear·ing, hears.** —*tr.* **1.** To be aware of or receive (sound) by the ears: *Did you hear the phone ring?* **2.** To learn (sthg.) by hearing; be told by others: *We heard the news from a friend.* —*intr.* To be capable of receiving sound by the ear: *I don't hear well.* ♦ **have heard of.** To know that sbdy./sthg. exists but not having much information about the person or thing: *I've heard of him, but I've never met him.* **hear from.** *tr.v.* [insep.] To get a letter, telephone call, or message from (sbdy.): *I haven't heard from her in years.*

HOMONYMS: hear, here (at this place).

heard (hûrd) *v.* Past tense and past participle of **hear.**

HOMONYMS: heard, herd (cattle).

hear•ing (hîr′ĭng) *n.* **1.** [U] The sense by which sound is perceived; the capacity to hear: *Dogs have excellent hearing.* **2.** [U] The region within which sounds from a particular source can be heard; earshot: *They were talking within my hearing.* **3.** [C] *(usually singular).* A chance to be heard: *The students deserve a hearing on their concerns.* **4.** [C] A formal session for listening to testimony or arguments: *Congress holds hearings before passing new laws.*

hearing aid *n.* A small electronic device used to amplify sound for persons who have difficulty hearing.

hear•ing-im•paired (hîr′ĭng ĭm pārd′) *adj.* **1.** Having a weakened sense of hearing; hard of hearing. **2.** Completely unable to hear; deaf. —*n. (used with a plural verb).* People who don't hear well or are deaf considered as a group.

hear•say (hîr′sā′) *n.* [U] Information or news heard from another person: *The police couldn't arrest the man on hearsay alone.*

hearse (hûrs) *n.* A special vehicle for carrying a dead person to a cemetery.

heart (härt) *n.* **1.** [C] **a.** The muscular organ in the chest that pumps blood throughout the body of a human or other vertebrate. **b.** A similar organ in invertebrate animals. **2.** [C] The vital center and source of one's emotions: *I could feel joy in my heart.* **3.a.** [C] Emotional state or mood: *I walked to the park with a heavy heart.* **b.** [C] Love; affection: *The children won their teacher's heart.* **c.** [U] The capacity to feel sympathy, kindness, or concern: *Have you no heart for these people?* **4.** [U] Courage; determination: *The captain's talk before the battle gave the soldiers heart.* **5.** [U] The central or essential part: *the heart of the city; the heart of the matter.* **6.** [C] A figure that represents the heart, often colored red or pink. **7.** [C] A playing card bearing this figure. ◆ **by heart.** Memorized completely: *He knows that poem by heart.* **from the bottom**

heart
(symbol)

heart
(organ)

of (one's) heart. Most sincerely: *I apologize from the bottom of my heart.* **have a change of heart.** To change one's mind about an earlier decision: *The teacher gave the class two assignments and then had a change of heart and only gave one assignment.* **have (one's) heart in the right place.** To be well-intentioned: *She doesn't always act wisely, but her heart's in the right place.* **in (one's) heart of hearts.** According to one's truest feelings: *I hate to admit it, but in my heart of hearts I know he's right.* **near** or **close to (one's) heart.** Loved by or important to one: *My nephew is near to my heart.* **take to heart.** To take sthg. seriously and be affected or troubled by it: *Don't take my criticism too much to heart.* **to (one's) heart's content.** To one's entire satisfaction; without limitation: *On Halloween the children ate candy to their hearts' content.* **with all (one's) heart.** With the deepest feeling or devotion: *I thank you with all my heart.*

heart•ache (härt′āk′) *n.* [U] Deep sorrow or sadness: *Their child's illness caused them much heartache.*

heart attack *n.* A sudden dangerous interruption in the normal functioning of the heart.

heart•beat (härt′bēt′) *n.* [C; U] The rate of the heart's movement: *a weak and rapid heartbeat.* ◆ **in a heartbeat.** With great speed; quickly: *I'll be there in a heartbeat.*

heart•break (härt′brāk′) *n.* [U] Great sorrow, grief, or disappointment: *Drunken drivers cause great heartbreak to others.*

heart•break•ing (härt′brā′kĭng) *adj.* Causing great sorrow, grief, or disappointment: *heartbreaking news.*

heart•bro•ken (härt′brō′kən) *adj.* Suffering from great sorrow, grief, or disappointment: *Our team was heartbroken when we lost the championship.*

heart•burn (härt′bûrn′) *n.* [U] A burning feeling in the chest area, usually caused by excess acid in the stomach.

heart•en (här′tn) *tr.v.* To give strength or courage to (sbdy.); encourage: *The improvement in the patient heartened the family.*

heart failure *n.* [U] A condition in which the heart loses its ability to pump enough blood to the body.

heart•felt (härt′fĕlt′) *adj.* Deeply felt; sincere: *I offered my heartfelt sympathy at the death of his mother.*

hearth (härth) *n.* **1.** [C] The floor of a fireplace, often extending into a room. **2.** [U] *Formal.* Family life; the home: *The weary travelers longed for the comfort of the hearth.*

heart•i•ly (här′tl ē) *adv.* **1.** In a warm and friendly manner; sincerely: *They welcomed their old friends heartily.* **2.** With great energy, appetite, or eagerness: *Everyone ate heartily.*

heart•land (härt′lănd′) *n.* [U] A central geographical region that is thought of as vital to a nation's well-being.

heart·less (härt′lĭs) *adj.* Without sympathy or mercy; without pity: *To lengthen the suffering of the dying is heartless.* —**heart′less·ly** *adv.* —**heart′less·ness** *n.* [U]

heart-rend·ing or **heart·rend·ing** (härt′rĕn′dĭng) *adj.* Causing grief or suffering: *The U.S. Civil War was a heart-rending conflict for many families.* —**heart′-rend′ing·ly** *adv.*

heart·sick (härt′sĭk′) *adj.* Extremely disappointed; very unhappy: *The news about her loss made us heartsick.*

heart·strings (härt′strĭngz′) *pl.n.* A person's deepest feelings: *The actor's expression of grief tugged at the audience's heartstrings.*

heart-to-heart (härt′tə härt′) *adj.* Personal and sincere; frank: *We need to have a heart-to-heart talk.*

heart·y (här′tē) *adj.* **heart·i·er, heart·i·est. 1.** Showing warm feelings; cheerful and friendly: *a hearty greeting.* **2.** Strong; energetic: *We gave the team our hearty support.* **3.** Giving much nourishment; substantial: *a hearty soup.* —**heart′i·ness** *n.* [U]

heat (hēt) *n.* **1.** [U] A form of energy produced by the motion of molecules. **2.** [U] The condition of being hot; warmth: *feel the heat of the sun.* **3.** [U] A furnace or other source of warmth: *Is the heat on?* **4.** [U] The most intense or active stage: *In the heat of their debate both candidates were shouting.* **5.** [C] A single contest in a competition, such as a race: *The competition was reduced to six runners after the first heat.* **6.** [U] A time in which a female mammal, other than a human, is ready to mate: *The mare is in heat.* —*tr. & intr.v.* To make or become warm or hot: *The sun heats the earth. The soup is heating on the stove.* ◆ **heat up.** *tr.v.* [sep.] To warm (sthg.): *Do you want this stew cold, or do you want me to heat it up?* —*intr.v. Informal.* To become acute or intense: *Their quarrel heated up rapidly.*

heat·ed (hē′tĭd) *adj.* Excited or angry: *a heated debate.* —**heat′ed·ly** *adv.* —**heat′ed·ness** *n.* [U]

heat·er (hē′tər) *n.* A device, such as a furnace or stove, that supplies heat.

hea·then (hē′thən) *n., pl.* **hea·thens** or **heathen. 1.** [C; U] An outdated insulting expression for a person or group of people that does not believe in one's own religion: *The missionary had a strong desire to convert the heathen.* **2.** [C] A person considered to be uncivilized or uncultured.

heath·er (hĕth′ər) *n.* [U] A low shrub with tiny evergreen leaves and small purple or pink flowers.

heat wave *n.* A period of unusually hot weather.

heave (hēv) *v.* **heaved** or **hove, heav·ing, heaves.** —*tr.* **1.** To raise or lift (sbdy./sthg.) with effort or force; hoist: *heaved the pack onto the mule's back.* **2.** To throw (sthg.) with force or effort; hurl: *heave rocks down the hill.* —*intr.* **1.** To pull with force or effort; haul: *We heaved on the rope to raise the flag.* **2.** To rise and fall repeatedly: *Seaweed heaved on the gentle waves.* **3.** To be forced upward; bulge: *Parts of the sidewalk heaved after the ground froze.* **4.** *Informal.* To vomit. —*n.* **1.** An act or effort of heaving; a throw: *Each heave on the line loosened the anchor a bit more.* **2. the heaves.** *Informal.* A long period of vomiting: *He had the heaves all day.* ◆ **heave a sigh.** To produce a long sigh: *He heaved a great sigh of relief when his daughter got home safely.*

heav·en (hĕv′ən) *n.* **1.** [C] *(usually plural).* The sky or universe as seen from the earth: *a star shooting across the heavens.* **2.** [U] Often **Heaven.** In certain religions, the place where a deity lives with other holy beings and where the souls of the good reside after death. **3. heavens.** Used in exclamations to express surprise: *Good heavens! Look at that crowd!* **4.** [U] A place or condition of great happiness; bliss: *It'll be heaven to vacation in the quiet of the country.* ◆ **for heaven's sake.** An expression used when one is annoyed: *For heaven's sake, children! Please share.*

heav·en·ly (hĕv′ən lē) *adj.* **1.** Relating to heaven: *the planets and other heavenly bodies.* **2.** Very pleasing; delightful; lovely: *a heavenly summer's day.* —**heav′en·li·ness** *n.* [U]

heav·y (hĕv′ē) *adj.* **heav·i·er, heav·i·est. 1.** With great weight: *a heavy package; a heavy skillet.* **2.** Large in amount: *a heavy rain; heavy traffic.* **3.** Having great power or force; violent: *a heavy blow; heavy seas.* **4.** With considerable thickness, body, or strength: *a heavy winter coat; drew a heavy line.* **5.** Weighed down with sthg.: *branches heavy with apples; eyelids heavy with sleep.* **6.** Sad, as from grief or depression: *a heavy heart.* **7.** Deserving careful thought; serious: *a heavy issue; heavy reading.* **8.** Not easily digested; too rich: *a heavy dessert.* **9.** Moving with difficulty: *the heavy steps of the elephant.* **10.** Involving large-scale manufacturing of basic products, such as steel: *heavy industry.* —*adv.* **heavier, heaviest.** Heavily: *These thoughts weigh heavy on his mind.* —*n., pl.* **heav·ies.** A villain in a story or play: *She is often cast as the heavy, though in real life she's quite nice.* —**heav′i·ly** *adv.* —**heav′i·ness** *n.* [U]

heav·y-dut·y (hĕv′ē dōo′tē) *adj.* Made to withstand hard use or wear: *heavy-duty boots; a heavy-duty truck.*

heav·y-hand·ed (hĕv′ē hăn′dĭd) *adj.* **1.** Awkward or clumsy: *a heavy-handed per-*

formance on the piano. **2.** Unkind in treating others; oppressive: *heavy-handed discipline.* —**heav′y-hand′ed•ness** *n.* [U]

heav•y•set (hĕv′ē sĕt′) *adj.* Having a heavy build; stocky: *The wrestler was heavyset and muscular.*

heav•y•weight (hĕv′ē wāt′) *n.* **1.** [U] A thing of more than average weight: *heavyweight paper; heavyweight fabric.* **2.** [C] A boxer, wrestler, or weight lifter in the heaviest weight class, often weighing more than 175 pounds.

He•brew (hē′brōō) *n.* **1.** [C] A member of the Semitic people claiming descent from Sarah and Abraham; an Israelite; a Jew. **2.** [U] The Semitic language of ancient Israel. —**He′brew** *adj.*

heck•le (hĕk′əl) *tr.v.* **heck•led, heck•ling, heck•les.** To harass or bother (sbdy.) with questions or annoying remarks: *The crowd heckled the speaker at the rally.* —**heck′ler** *n.*

hec•tare (hĕk′târ′) *n.* A unit of area in the metric system, equal to 2.471 acres or 10,000 square meters. See table at **measurement.**

hec•tic (hĕk′tĭk) *adj.* Full of intense activity, confusion, or excitement: *Because they overslept, they had a hectic departure for their vacation.* —**hec′ti•cal•ly** *adv.*

he'd (hēd) Contraction of *he had* or *he would.*

HOMONYMS: he'd, heed (listen).

---

hedge (hĕj) *n.* **1.** A row of closely planted shrubs or small trees forming a fence or boundary. **2.** *(usually singular).* A means of protection or defense: *They put some of their savings in stocks as a hedge against inflation.* —*v.* **hedged, hedg•ing, hedg•es.** —*tr.* **1.** To enclose or separate (sthg.) with a hedge or hedges: *hedge a yard.* **2.** To restrict or confine (sbdy./sthg.); hem in: *The flooded river hedged us in on one side.* **3.** To protect (oneself) against possible losses on (a bet, an investment, or another risk) by balancing one risk against another: *She hedged her investment in stocks by investing in bonds.* —*intr.* To avoid giving a clear or direct answer or statement: *When asked if she would run for office again, the mayor hedged.*

hedge•hog (hĕj′hôg′ *or* hĕj′hŏg′) *n.* A small mammal that feeds on insects and is covered with short stiff spines.

heed (hēd) *tr.v.* To pay attention to (sbdy./ sthg.); listen to and consider: *I did not heed his warning.* —*n.* [U] *Formal.* Close attention or consideration; notice: *They gave no heed to my greeting. Take heed while crossing the highway.*

HOMONYMS: heed, he'd (he would).

---

heed•less (hēd′lĭs) *adj. Formal.* [*of*] Paying little or no attention to: *heedless of danger.*

—**heed′less•ly** *adv.* —**heed′less•ness** *n.* [U]

hee•haw (hē′hô′) *n.* **1.** The loud harsh sound made by a donkey. **2.** *Informal.* A rude noisy laugh. —*intr.v.* To make such a sound: *The audience heehawed at the clown's antics.*

heel (hēl) *n.* **1.** The rear part of the foot or leg below the ankle in humans and animals. **2.** The part of a sock, shoe, or stocking that covers or supports the heel of the foot. **3.** A lower or back part, such as the crusty end of a loaf of bread: *a heel of bread.* **4.** *Informal.* A dishonest person: *He behaved like a heel.* —*v.* —*tr.* To put a heel or heels on (shoes or boots): *The cobbler heeled the old shoes.* —*intr.* To follow at one's heels: *I taught the dog to heel.* ♦ **cool (one's) heels.** To wait for sthg./sbdy., usually unwillingly: *I had to cool my heels in the dentist's office for an hour.* **on** or **upon the heels of.** Directly behind or immediately following: *The first spring birds come on the heels of winter.* **take to (one's) heels.** To run away; flee: *The boy who broke the window took to his heels.*

HOMONYMS: heel, heal (make healthy), **he'll** (he will).

---

heft•y (hĕf′tē) *adj.* **heft•i•er, heft•i•est.** **1.** Weighty; heavy: *a truck carrying a hefty load.* **2.** Big and strong; muscular: *a hefty sailor.* **3.** *Informal.* Large in size or amount: *The boys ate a hefty meal.*

heif•er (hĕf′ər) *n.* A young female cow that has not given birth to a calf.

height (hīt) *n.* **1.** [U] The distance from the top to the bottom of sthg.; elevation: *The height of that tree is more than 60 feet.* **2.** [U] The condition of being relatively high or tall: *Height is an advantage in basketball.* **3.** [C] *(usually singular).* The highest point or most advanced degree: *Late summer is the height of the tourist season.*

height•en (hīt′n) *intr. & tr.v.* **1.** To rise or cause to rise in degree or amount; become more intense: *The excitement heightened during the last quarter of the game. His angry glare heightened the tension.* **2.** To become or cause to become high or higher; raise or be raised: *The kite heightened in the strong wind. The barber heightened the chair for the little boy.*

hei•nous (hā′nəs) *adj. Formal.* Very wicked or evil; horrible: *a heinous crime.* —**hei′nous•ly** *adv.* —**hei′nous•ness** *n.* [U]

heir (âr) *n.* A person who inherits or is legally entitled to inherit the property or title of another.

HOMONYMS: heir, air (gas), **e'er** (ever), **ere** (before).

---

heir•ess (âr′ĭs) *n.* A woman who inherits or is legally entitled to inherit the property or title of another.

heir•loom (âr′lo͞om′) *n.* A possession passed down through succeeding generations of a family: *My ring is a family heirloom.*

heist (hīst) *n. Informal.* An armed robbery; a burglary: *a bank heist; a jewel heist.*

held (hĕld) *v.* Past tense and past participle of **hold**[1].

hel•i•cop•ter (hĕl′ĭ kŏp′tər) *n.* A wingless aircraft that is lifted by blades that rotate horizontally above the aircraft.

helicopter

he•li•um (hē′lē əm) *n.* [U] *Symbol* **He** A very light, colorless, odorless, gaseous element. It has the lowest boiling point of any substance and is the second most abundant element in the universe. Atomic number 2. See table at **element.**

hell (hĕl) *n.* [U] **1.** A place where the spirits of the dead remain for eternity; the underworld. **2.** Often **Hell.** In certain religions, the place where devils and the souls of the wicked reside after death. **3.** Misery, torment, or anguish: *the hell of battle.*

he'll (hēl). Contraction of *he will* or *he shall.*

HOMONYMS: **he'll, heal** (make healthy), **heel** (part of a foot).

hell•ish (hĕl′ĭsh) *adj.* Resembling or worthy of hell; terrible: *hellish confusion and noise.* —**hell′ish•ly** *adv.* —**hell′ish•ness** *n.* [U]

hel•lo (hĕ lō′ *or* hə lō′) *interj.* An expression used to greet sbdy., answer the telephone, or express surprise. —*n., pl.* **hel•los.** A call or greeting of "hello."

helm (hĕlm) *n.* The steering apparatus of a ship, especially the wheel.

hel•met (hĕl′mĭt) *n.* A protective covering of metal, plastic, or other hard material for the head: *I always wear a bicycle helmet.*

help (hĕlp) *v.* —*tr.* **1.** To assist or support (sbdy.); aid: *The salesperson helped the customer buy a bicycle helmet.* **2.** To give aid

helmet

to (sthg.); further the progress of: *His cheerful attitude helped heal the bad feelings between them.* **3.** To relieve (sthg.); ease: *This medicine will help your cold.* **4.** To avoid, prevent, or change (sthg.): *I cannot help it if the train is late.* —*intr.* To be of service; assist: *Do what you can to help.* —*n.* [U] **1.** The act of helping; assistance; aid: *With the help of a dictionary, you can find out what words mean.* **2.** A person or a group of people hired to work as a helper or helpers: *The restaurant needs kitchen help.* **3.** Relief; cure: *There is no help for certain diseases.* ♦ **cannot help but.** To have to; be unable to avoid or resist: *I cannot help but admire their efforts to assist those in need.* **help (oneself) to.** To take what one wants, sometimes without permission: *The guests were told to help themselves to the punch.* **help out.** *tr.v.* [sep.] To aid or assist (sbdy.), especially in a crisis: *We helped the flood victims out for a week.* —**help′er** *n.*

SYNONYMS: **help, aid, assist.** These verbs mean to contribute to fulfilling a need, furthering an effort, or achieving a purpose. **Help** and **aid** are the most general: *A new medicine has been developed to help* (or *aid*) *digestion.* **Help** often means to aid in an active way: *I'll help you move the sofa.* **Assist** often means to play a secondary role in aiding: *A few of the students assisted the professor in researching the data.*

help•ful (hĕlp′fəl) *adj.* Providing assistance; useful: *The advisor gave me some helpful advice.* —**help′ful•ly** *adv.* —**help′ful•ness** *n.* [U]

help•ing (hĕl′pĭng) *n.* A portion of food for one person: *He took two helpings of meat.*

helping verb *n.* An auxiliary verb.

help•less (hĕlp′lĭs) *adj.* **1.** Unable to manage by oneself; powerless: *as helpless as a baby.* **2.** Lacking protection; defenseless: *The townspeople were helpless in the violent storm.* **3.** Puzzled; confused: *a helpless glance.* —**help′less•ly** *adv.* —**help′less•ness** *n.* [U]

hel•ter-skel•ter (hĕl′tər skĕl′tər) *adv.* In disorderly haste: *The toys were strewn helter-skelter in the living room.* —*adj.* Hurried and confused: *a helter-skelter retreat from the sudden storm.*

hem (hĕm) *n.* An edge or a border of a garment or piece of cloth, made by folding the edge under and sewing it down. —*tr.v.* **hemmed, hem•ming, hems.** To fold back and sew down the edge of (sthg.): *The tailor hems skirts and pants.* ♦ **hem in.** *tr.v.* [sep.] To surround and shut in (sbdy./sthg.); enclose: *a valley hemmed in by high mountains.*

hemi— *pref.* A prefix that means half: *hemisphere.*

hem•i•sphere (hĕm′ĭ sfîr′) *n*. **1.** One half of a sphere formed by a plane that passes through the center of the sphere. **2.** A half of the human brain. **3.** One half of the earth's surface. —**hem′i•spher′ic** (hĕm′ĭ sfîr′ĭk *or* hĕm′ĭ sfĕr′ĭk) or **hem′i•spher′i•cal** *adj.*

hem•lock (hĕm′lŏk′) *n*. **1.** An evergreen tree with short flat needles and small cones. **2.** A poisonous plant with feathery leaves and clusters of small white flowers or the poison from this plant.

hemo— or **hema—** or **hem—** *pref.* A prefix that means blood: *hemophilia.*

he•mo•glo•bin (hē′mə glō′bĭn) *n*. [U] The substance that gives the red blood cells their characteristic color and that carries oxygen to the body.

he•mo•phil•i•a (hē′mə fĭl′ē ə *or* hē′mə-fēl′yə) *n*. [U] An inherited blood disease, affecting males, in which the blood does not clot properly, making it very difficult to stop bleeding. —**he′mo•phil′i•ac** (hē′mə fĭl′-ē ăk′ *or* hē′mə fē′lē ăk′) *n*.

hem•or•rhage (hĕm′ər ĭj) *n*. [C; U] A large amount of bleeding. —*intr.v.* **hem•or•rhaged, hem•or•rhag•ing, hem•or•rhag•es.** To have a hemorrhage; bleed heavily.

hem•or•rhoids (hĕm′ə roidz′) *pl.n.* Itching or painful swollen tissue and enlarged veins near the anus.

hemp (hĕmp) *n*. [U] A plant that produces tough fiber used for making rope, cord, and coarse cloth.

hen (hĕn) *n*. **1.** An adult female chicken: *Our hens lay eggs daily.* **2.** The female of various other birds: *peahen.*

hence (hĕns) *adv. Formal.* **1.** For this reason; therefore: *These dolls are handmade and hence expensive.* **2.** From this time; from now: *thirty years hence.*

hence•forth (hĕns′fôrth′) *adv. Formal.* From this time on; from now on.

hence•for•ward (hĕns fôr′wərd) *adv. Formal.* Henceforth.

hench•man (hĕnch′mən) *n*. A loyal and trusted follower, as of a politician or a criminal gang.

hen•na (hĕn′ə) *n*. [U] **1.** A brownish red dye used to color the hair. **2.** A brownish red color.

hep•a•ti•tis (hĕp′ə tī′tĭs) *n*. [U] Inflammation of the liver caused by infection.

hepta— or **hept—** *pref.* A prefix that means seven: *heptagon.*

hep•ta•gon (hĕp′tə gŏn′) *n*. A flat geometric shape with seven sides.

her (hər *or* ər; hûr *when stressed*) *adj.* The possessive form of **she.** Belonging to her: *She picked up her package.* —*pron.* The objective form of **she.** **1.** Used as the direct object of a verb: *We brought her to the train station.* **2.** Used as the indirect object of a verb: *I wrote her a letter.* **3.** Used as the object of a preposition *I gave all the popcorn to her.* —SEE NOTE at **me.**

her•ald (hĕr′əld) *n*. **1.** A person who carries messages or makes announcements. **2.** A person or thing that indicates sthg. to come: *The crocus is a herald of spring.* —*tr.v.* To indicate the coming of (sbdy./sthg.); announce: *The evening star heralds the arrival of nightfall.*

herb (ûrb *or* hûrb) *n*. Any of various plants used in medicine or as a seasoning.

herb•al (ûr′bəl *or* hûr′bəl) *adj.* Relating to or containing herbs: *herbal medicine.*

her•bi•cide (hûr′bĭ sīd′ *or* ûr′bĭ sīd′) *n*. [C; U] A chemical substance used to destroy or reduce the growth of plants.

her•bi•vore (hûr′bə vôr′ *or* ûr′bə vôr′) *n*. An animal that feeds mainly on plants: *Cows, deer, and rabbits are herbivores.* —**her•biv′o•rous** (hûr bĭv′ ər əs *or* ûr bĭv′ ər əs) *adj.*

herd (hûrd) *n*. A group of domestic or wild animals of a single kind, feeding or traveling together: *a herd of elephants; a herd of goats.* —*v.* —*tr.* **1.** To gather, keep, or flock (sthg.) together: *Dogs herded the sheep into the pen. We were herded into the room.* **2.** To tend or watch over (sheep or cattle): *He herds sheep in the mountains.* —*intr.* To come together in a herd: *Buffalo herded together on the plains.* —**herd′er** *n*.

HOMONYMS: herd, heard (past tense of hear).

---

here (hîr) *adv.* **1.** At or in this place: *Put the box here.* **2.** At this time; now: *Let's stop practicing here and break for lunch.* **3.** To this place: *Come here and sit beside me.* —*interj.* An expression used to answer to one's name in a roll call, to call to an animal, or to get sbdy.'s attention: *Here, now! Stop talking and listen to me.* —*n*. [U] **1.** This place: *I went from here to the store.* **2.** This life or this state: *We should think more about the here and now than about what might happen.* ♦ **here goes.** Used to show one is going to do sthg. risky or unfamiliar: *I've never gone scuba diving before, but here goes!* **here you are** or **go.** Used as a polite expression when sbdy. gives sthg., often in connection with service in a restaurant or in a store. **neither here nor there.** Not to the point; off the subject; unimportant: *Their vague remarks were neither here nor there.*

HOMONYMS: here, hear (listen).

---

here•a•bouts (hîr′ə bouts′) *adv.* In this area; around here: *The ball rolled hereabouts.*

here•af•ter (hîr ăf′tər) *adv. Formal.* From now on; after this: *Hereafter, when you write use my full address.* —*n*. [U] Life after death: *gone to the hereafter.*

here•by (hîr bī′) *adv. Formal.* By virtue of this; by this means: *All drivers are hereby required to have an eye test.*

he•red•i•tar•y (hə rĕd′ĭ tĕr′ē) *adj.* **1.** Passed or capable of being passed from parent to offspring by means of genes: *a heredi-tary illness.* **2.** Passed down by inheritance to a legal heir: *a hereditary title.*

he·red·i·ty (hə rĕd′ĭ tē) *n.* [U] The passage of traits or characteristics from parents to offspring by biological inheritance through genes.

here·in (hîr ĭn′) *adv. Formal.* In this thing, matter, fact, or place: *She likes to read, and herein lies the source of her large vocabulary.*

her·e·sy (hĕr′ĭ sē) *n., pl.* **her·e·sies. 1.** [C] An opinion or belief that is different from the established beliefs of a religion: *In the past, sci-entists were often accused of heresy.* **2.** [C] An opinion that is contrary to prevailing views, as in politics or science: *What is considered heresy one day may be accepted the next.* **3.** [U] The holding of such a belief or opinion: *The idea that some people are better than others would be a heresy in a democracy.*

her·e·tic (hĕr′ĭ tĭk) *n.* A person who holds beliefs or opinions that are different from accepted beliefs or opinions, as of a church or a political party: *It is better to be a heretic than to accept socially approved evil.*

he·ret·i·cal (hə rĕt′ĭ kəl) *adj.* Relating to heresy or heretics.

here·with (hîr wĭth′ *or* hîr wĭth′) *adv. Formal.* Along with this: *I am sending here-with the requested documents.*

her·i·tage (hĕr′ĭ tĭj) *n. (usually singular).* **1.** Something other than property passed down from preceding generations; a tradition: *Our country has a great heritage of folk music.* **2.** Property that is or can be inherited.

her·mit (hûr′mĭt) *n.* A person who has with-drawn from society and lives a solitary exis-tence: *He has lived as a hermit for the last 20 years.*

her·ni·a (hûr′nē ə) *n.* A condition in which an organ pushes through an opening in the wall that normally holds it; a rupture.

he·ro (hîr′ō) *n., pl.* **he·roes. 1.** In mythol-ogy and legend, a man of great courage and strength who is famous for his bold deeds. **2.** A person who is famous for courageous acts or significant achievements: *a sports hero.* **3.** A submarine sandwich. —**he·ro·ic** (hĭ rō′ĭk) *adj.* —**he·ro′i·cal·ly** *adv.*

her·o·in (hĕr′ō ĭn) *n.* [U] A highly addictive drug derived from morphine.

HOMONYMS: heroin, heroine (courageous woman).

---

her·o·ine (hĕr′ō ĭn) *n.* A woman who is famous for courageous acts or significant achievements.

her·o·ism (hĕr′ō ĭz′ əm) *n.* [U] Brave con-duct or action; courage: *She was awarded a medal for heroism.*

her·on (hĕr′ən) *n.* A wading bird with a long neck, long legs, and a long pointed bill, which lives near water.

her·pes (hûr′pēz) *n.* [U] Any of several dis-eases caused by viruses in which blisters form on the skin or a mucous membrane.

her·ring (hĕr′ĭng) *n.* A fish found in Atlantic and Pacific waters, used as a fresh or pre-served food.

hers (hûrz) *pron. (used with a singular or plural verb).* The one or ones belonging to her: *If his desk is occupied, use hers. Hers must be over there.*

her·self (hûr sĕlf′) *pron.* **1.** The one that is the same as her: **a.** Used as the direct object or indirect object of a verb or as the object of a preposition to show that the action of the verb refers back to the subject: *She pulled herself up by the rope. She bought herself a new pen.* **b.** Used to give emphasis: *Mother herself is going.* **2.** Her normal or healthy self: *She has not been herself since her friend left town.*

hertz (hûrts) *n., pl.* **hertz.** A unit of frequency of vibrations and waves equal to one cycle per second.

he's (hēz). Contraction of *he is* or *he has.*

hes·i·tant (hĕz′ĭ tənt) *adj.* Inclined or tend-ing to hesitate; reluctant: *We were hesitant to fly in such bad weather.* —**hes′i·tan·cy** *n.* [U] —**hes′i·tant·ly** *adv.*

hes·i·tate (hĕz′ĭ tāt′) *intr.v.* **hes·i·tat·ed, hes·i·tat·ing, hes·i·tates. 1.** To be slow to act, speak, or decide: *We hesitated about whether to go skiing on the icy mountain.* **2.** To be reluctant or unwilling: *They hesitated to ask for help when they saw how busy I was.* —**hes′i·ta′tion** (hĕz′ĭ tā′shən) *n.* [C; U]

hetero— or **heter—** *pref.* A prefix that means other or different: *heterogeneous.*

het·er·o·ge·ne·ous (hĕt′ər ə jē′nē əs *or* hĕt′ər ə jēn′yəs) *adj.* Different in kind; not alike: *the heterogeneous collection of art in the museum.* —**het′er·o·ge·ne′i·ty** (hĕt′-ə rō jə nē′ĭ tē) *n.* [U]

het·er·o·sex·u·al (hĕt′ə rō sĕk′shoo əl) *adj.* Relating to or having sexual feelings for members of the opposite sex. —*n.* A hetero-sexual person. —**het′er·o·sex′u·al′i·ty** (hĕt′ə rō sĕk′shoo ăl′ĭ tē) *n.* [U]

hew (hyoo) *v.* **hewed, hewn** (hyoon) *or* **hewed, hew·ing, hews.** —*tr.* To make or shape (sthg.) with an ax: *We hewed our way through the bushes.* —*intr.* To adhere to sthg., such as rules or norms; keep: *Hew closely to the regulations.*

HOMONYMS: hew, hue (color).

---

hexa— or **hex—** *pref.* A prefix that means six: *hexagon.*

hex•a•gon (hĕk'sə gŏn') *n.* A flat geometric shape with six sides. **—hex•ag'o•nal** (hĕk săg'ə nəl) *adj.*

hey (hā) *interj.* An expression used to show surprise, appreciation, or wonder, or to call attention: *Hey, that's nice! Hey, you!*

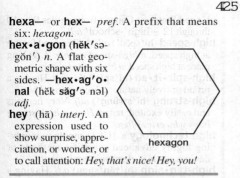
hexagon

HOMONYMS: hey, hay (dried grass).

---

hey•day (hā'dā') *n. (usually singular).* The period of greatest popularity, success, or power: *the heyday of very large cars.*

HF or **hf** *abbr.* An abbreviation of high frequency.

Hg The symbol for the element **mercury** (sense 1).

hi (hī) *interj. Informal.* An expression used as a greeting: *Hi, how are you today?*

HOMONYMS: hi, high (elevated).

HI *abbr.* An abbreviation of Hawaii.

hi•a•tus (hī ā'təs) *n. (usually singular). Formal.* A gap in time, space or a series; a break or an interruption: *Rain caused a hiatus in the game.*

hi•ber•nate (hī'bər nāt') *intr.v.* **hi•ber•nat•ed, hi•ber•nat•ing, hi•ber•nates.** To spend the winter in an inactive state like deep sleep: *Bears and some other wild animals hibernate.* **—hi'ber•na'tion** *n.* [U]

hic•cup (hĭk'əp) *n. (usually plural).* A sudden repeated stopping of the breath. *—intr.v.* **hic•cupped, hic•cup•ping, hic•cups.** To make a hiccup.

hick (hĭk) *n. Informal.* An insulting word for a person from the country who is believed to be unsophisticated, inexperienced, or ignorant: *He's just a hick from the country. —adj.* Considered ignorant and unsophisticated: *a hick town.*

hide¹ (hīd) *v.* **hid** (hĭd), **hid•den** (hĭd'n) or **hid, hid•ing, hides.** *—tr.* **1.** To put or keep (sbdy./sthg.) out of sight; conceal: *I hid his birthday present in my closet.* **2.** To prevent (sthg.) from being known; keep secret: *She wanted to hide her true identity.* **3.** To cover up (sthg.): *Clouds hid the stars. —intr.* To keep oneself out of sight: *The lion hid in the tall grass.* ◆ **hide out.** *tr.v.* [sep.] To be in hiding, especially from a pursuer: *The bank robbers hid out in a remote cabin until it was safe to return to the city.*

SYNONYMS: hide, conceal, screen, bury. These verbs mean to keep from the sight or

knowledge of others. **Hide** and **conceal** are the most general: *She smiled to hide her hurt feelings. A throw rug concealed the stain on the carpet.* **Screen** means to shield or block sbdy./sthg. from the view of others: *Tall shrubs screen the actor's home from inquisitive tourists.* **Bury** means to conceal sthg. by covering it: *He buried his hands in his pockets so the teacher couldn't see his dirty fingernails.*

---

hide² (hīd) *n.* The skin of an animal, especially the thick tough skin of a large animal.

hide-and-seek (hīd'n sēk') *n.* [U] A children's game in which one player tries to find and catch the other players who are hiding.

hide•a•way (hīd'ə wā') *n.* A secluded or isolated place: *spend a vacation at a hideaway in the mountains.*

hid•e•ous (hĭd'ē əs) *adj.* Horribly ugly; revolting; disgusting: *a hideous monster; a hideous murder.* **—hid'e•ous•ly** *adv.* **—hid'e•ous•ness** *n.* [U]

hide•out (hīd'out') *n.* A place of shelter or concealment: *The children built a hideout in the trees.*

hi•er•ar•chy (hī'ə rär'kē or hī'rär'kē) *n., pl.* **hi•er•ar•chies.** [C; U] A group of persons or things classified according to rank or grade: *We made a chart to show the hierarchy of positions in the corporation.* **—hi'er•ar'chic, hi'er•ar'chi•cal** *adj.* **—hi'er•ar'chi•cal•ly** *adv.*

hi•er•o•glyph (hī'ər ə glĭf' or hī'rə glĭf') *n. (usually plural).* A picture or symbol used in hieroglyphic writing.

hi•er•o•glyph•ic (hī'ər ə glĭf'ĭk or hī'rə glĭf'ĭk) *adj.* Related to a system of writing in which pictures or symbols are used to represent words or sounds: *The ancient Egyptians used hieroglyphic writing. —n.* **1.** A hieroglyph. **2. hieroglyphics.** Hieroglyphic writing.

high (hī) *adj.* **1.a.** Being a great distance above a certain level, as above sea level or the surface of the earth: *These high mountains are over 5,000 meters.* **b.** Extending a specified distance upward: *The table is three feet high.* **2.** Greater than usual in degree, amount, quality, force, or intensity: *high temperature; a high standard of living; high winds.* **3.** Above the middle range of musical pitch: *the high notes on the piano.* **4.** Being at or near the top: *Election to the Presidency was the high point of a long career in politics.* **5.** Advanced in development or complexity: *higher forms of animal life.* **6.** Greater than others in rank, status, or importance: *a high official; a high priority.* **7.** Showing joy or excitement: *high spirits.* **8.** Affected by or as if by a drug: *Having just one beer made him high. —adv.* At, in, or to a high position, level, or degree: *Planes fly high in the sky. —n.* **1.** A high degree or level: *Gold prices reached a new high.* **2.** A high-pressure mass of atmospheric

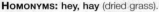

air: *This clear dry weather is the result of a high from the West.* **3.** *Informal.* A state of very good feeling or well-being: *The runner was on a high after winning the race.* ◆ **high and dry.** Helpless and alone: *When our car broke down on a deserted road, we were left high and dry.* **high and low.** Everywhere: *I looked high and low for the keys.*

HOMONYMS: high, hi (greeting).

---

high blood pressure *n.* [U] A condition in which the pressure of the blood circulating in the body is higher than it should be; hypertension.

high frequency *n.* [U] A radio wave frequency in the range between 3 and 30 megahertz.

high-grade (hī′grād′) *adj.* Of superior quality: *high-grade beef.*

high·hand·ed (hī′hăn′dĭd) *adj.* Using power without considering others; arrogant; overbearing: *The manager's highhanded rejection of my idea annoyed me.* —**high′hand′ed·ly** *adv.* —**high′hand′ed·ness** *n.* [U]

high·land (hī′lənd) *n.* *(usually plural).* A mountainous or hilly part of a country, or a region at a high elevation. —*adj.* Relating to a highland.

high·light (hī′līt′) *n.* The most outstanding event or part: *The highlight of the trip was visiting the botanical gardens.* —*tr.v.* **1.** To emphasize (sthg.): *She highlighted key parts of the plan for the audience.* **2.** To mark important passages of (text) with a usually fluorescent marker for later reference: *highlight the important passages.*

high·ly (hī′lē) *adv.* **1.** To a great degree; extremely; very: *highly developed; highly amusing.* **2.** In a good or favorable way: *I think highly of the candidate.* **3.** At a high price, cost, or rate: *a highly paid executive.*

high-mind·ed (hī′mīn′dĭd) *adj.* Having high ideals; noble: *high-minded citizens.* —**high′-mind′ed·ness** *n.* [U]

High·ness (hī′nĭs) *n.* Used as a title and form of address for a prince or princess: *Her Royal Highness the Princess Margaret.*

high noon *n.* [U] Exactly noon; the very middle of the day.

high-pitched (hī′pĭcht′) *adj.* Relating to sound that is high in pitch; shrill: *a high-pitched flute.*

high-pres·sure (hī′prĕsh′ər) *adj.* **1.** Having, using, or tolerating pressures higher than normal: *a high-pressure tire; a high-pressure job.* **2.** *Informal.* Using aggressive methods of persuasion: *a high-pressure sales pitch.*

high-rise (hī′rīz′) *adj.* Very tall and having many stories: *high-rise apartment building.* —*n.* or **high rise.** A high-rise building.

high school *n.* A secondary school in the United States or Canada from grades 9 or 10 through 12. —**high′-school′** *adj.*

high-speed (hī′spēd′) *adj.* **1.** Designed for use at high speed: *a high-speed washer.* **2.** Taking place at high speed: *a high-speed chase.*

high-spir·it·ed (hī′spĭr′ĭ tĭd) *adj.* Having a proud or lively nature: *a high-spirited horse.*

high-strung (hī′strŭng′) *adj.* Very nervous and easily excited; tense: *He is a high-strung baby who cries often.*

high technology *n.* [U] Technology involving highly advanced scientific methods or devices, such as electronic equipment.

high-ten·sion (hī′tĕn′shən) *adj.* Having a high voltage: *high-tension wires.*

high tide *n.* [C; U] The tide or the time of day when the water reaches its highest level.

high time *n.* [U] The time when sthg. must begin, before it is too late: *If you want to catch the train, it's high time we go.*

high-wa·ter mark (hī′wô′tər *or* hī′wŏt′ər) *n.* *(usually singular).* **1.** A mark showing the highest level reached by a flood or body of water. **2.** The highest point of sthg.; the peak: *The band reached a high-water mark with its third CD.*

high·way (hī′wā′) *n.* A main public road: *A highway connects the cities.*

hi·jack (hī′jăk′) *tr.v.* **1.** To force to stop and rob (sthg.), such as a vehicle. **2.** To steal (goods) from a vehicle in transit: *The rebels hijacked medical supplies.* **3.** To seize or take control of (a moving vehicle) by use of force, especially in order to reach a different destination: *hijack an airplane.* —**hi′jack′er** *n.*

hike (hīk) *v.* **hiked, hik·ing, hikes.** —*intr.* To go on an extended walk, especially for pleasure: *hike through the woods.* —*n.* **1.** A long walk or trip on foot. **2.** A pull or tug upward: *Give your socks a hike.* **3.** A rise; an increase: *a hike in gasoline prices.* ◆ **hike up.** *tr.v.* [sep.] To pull, increase, or raise (sthg.), especially with a sudden motion: *I hiked up my socks. The new sales tax will hike up prices.* **take a hike.** To go away: *He wouldn't leave me alone, so I told him to take a hike.* —**hik′er** *n.*

hi·lar·i·ous (hĭ lâr′ē əs *or* hī lâr′ē əs) *adj.* Very funny; causing much laughter: *a hilarious story.* —**hi·lar′i·ous·ly** *adv.* —**hi·lar′i·ous·ness** *n.* [U]

hi·lar·i·ty (hĭ lăr′ĭ tē *or* hī lâr′ĭ tē) *n.* [U] Great merriment or fun: *We greeted her costume with hilarity.*

hill (hĭl) *n.* **1.** A part of the earth's surface rising above the level of the land, but not as high as a mountain. **2.** A small heap, mound, or pile: *an ant hill.* ◆ **over the hill.** *Informal.* Too old to do sthg. well: *At age 24, he was already over the hill as a swimmer.*

ă–**cat**; ā–**pay**; âr–**care**; ä–**father**; ĕ–**get**; ē–**be**; ĭ–**sit**; ī–**nice**; îr–**here**; ŏ–**got**; ō–**go**; ô–**saw**; oi–**boy**; ou–**out**; ŏŏ–**took**; ōō–**boot**; ûr–**word**; th–**thin**; *th*–**this**; hw–**when**; zh–**vision**; ə–**about**; ɴ–French **bon**

hill•bil•ly (hĭl′bĭl′ē) *n.*, *pl.* **hill•bil•lies.**
Informal. An insulting term for a person who lives in a remote mountain area.

hill•y (hĭl′ē) *adj.* **hill•i•er, hill•i•est.** Having many hills: *Northern Missouri is hilly.*

hilt (hĭlt) *n.* The handle of a sword or dagger.
◆ **to the hilt.** To the limit; completely: *They played their roles to the hilt.*

him (hĭm) *pron.* The objective form of **he. 1.** Used as the direct object of a verb: *We helped him.* **2.** Used as the indirect object of a verb: *She gave him a ride.* **3.** Used as the object of a preposition: *This package is for him.* —SEE NOTE at **me.**

HOMONYMS: him, hymn (song).

---

him•self (hĭm sĕlf′) *pron.* **1.** That one that is the same as him: **a.** Used as the direct object or indirect object of a verb or as the object of a preposition to show that the action of the verb refers back to the subject: *He dressed himself. He gave himself plenty of time. He saved some popcorn for himself.* **b.** Used to give emphasis: *He took care of his problem himself.* **2.** His real, normal, or healthy self: *He looks more like himself after the vacation.*

hind (hīnd) *adj.* Located at or forming the rear or back, especially of an animal: *a horse's hind legs.*

hin•der (hĭn′dər) *tr.v.* To prevent the action or progress of (sbdy./sthg.); hamper: *Heavy rains hindered traffic on the highway.*

hind•quar•ter (hīnd′kwôr′tər) *n.* (*usually plural*). The back part of a four-footed animal.

hin•drance (hĭn′drəns) *n.* A person or thing that hinders; an obstacle: *The heavy backpack was a hindrance to the hiker.*

hind•sight (hīnd′sīt′) *n.* [U] The understanding of the significance of a past event: *In hindsight I know I should have ignored their rude remarks.*

Hin•du (hĭn′dōō) *n.* **1.** An inhabitant of India, especially of northern India. **2.** A believer in Hinduism. —*adj.* **1.** Relating to the Hindus or their culture. **2.** Relating to Hinduism.

Hin•du•ism (hĭn′dōō ĭz′əm) *n.* [U] A religion that is predominant in India and characterized by belief in reincarnation and in multiple gods.

hinge (hĭnj) *n.* A joint on which a door, gate, lid, or cover turns or swings. —*v.* **hinged, hing•ing, hing•es.** —*tr.* To attach (sthg.) by a hinge or hinges: *The carpenter hinged the door.* ◆ **hinge on** or **upon.** *intr.v.* To depend: *Their grades hinge on this exam.*

hint (hĭnt) *n.* **1.** A slight indication or an indirect suggestion; a clue: *Can't you give me a hint about when the test will be?* **2.** A small amount; a trace: *There is just a hint of vanilla in these cookies.* —*v.* —*tr.* To make (sthg.) known in an indirect manner: *Our host hinted*

that it was time to leave. —*intr.* To give a hint: *She refused to hint at what really happened.*

hin•ter•land (hĭn′tər lănd′) *n.* (*usually plural*). Land away from a seacoast; an inland area: *They live in the hinterlands.*

hip¹ (hĭp) *n.* The projecting part of the body where the leg joins the body.

hip² (hĭp) *adj.* **hip•per, hip•pest.** *Slang.* Knowledgeable; aware: *We're hip to your tricks.*

hip•bone (hĭp′bōn′) *n.* Either of the large, flat, irregularly shaped bones that with the lower backbone form the pelvis.

hip•pie (hĭp′ē) *n.*, *pl.* **hip•pies.** *Slang.* A person who opposes conventional standards and customs, such as those of behavior and dress.

hip•po (hĭp′ō) *n.*, *pl.* **hip•pos.** *Informal.* A hippopotamus.

hip•po•pot•a•mus (hĭp′ə pŏt′ə məs) *n.*, *pl.* **hip•po•pot•a•mus•es** or **hip•po•pot•a•mi** (hĭp′ə pŏt′ə mī′). A large, very heavy African river mammal with thick skin, short legs, and a wide mouth.

hire (hīr) *tr.v.* **hired, hir•ing, hires. 1.** To pay (sbdy.) for working or performing a service; employ: *hire teachers for the new school.* **2.** To pay for the use of (sthg.) for a limited time; rent: *hire a car.* —*n.* [U] Payment for doing work or for the use of sthg.: *The day's hire for the car is $100.*

his (hĭz) *adj.* The possessive form of **he.** Belonging to him: *His house was not far from ours. The boy was careful to see that his studies came first.* —*pron.* (*used with a singular or plural verb*). The one or ones belonging to him: *The book is his. I am a friend of his. If you can't find your book, borrow his.*

His•pan•ic (hĭ spăn′ĭk) *adj.* Relating to the culture or people of Spain or Spanish-speaking Latin America. —*n.* A person of Spanish or Latin-American descent, especially one living in the United States.

hiss (hĭs) *n.* A sound like that made by pronouncing the letter *s*: *the hiss of air escaping from a tire.* —*intr.v.* **1.** To make a sound like that of the letter *s*: *A cat will hiss when frightened.* **2.** To express dislike or disapproval with such a sound: *"You're making too much noise," someone hissed from behind.*

his•to•ri•an (hĭ stôr′ē ən or hĭ stōr′ē ən) *n.* A person who writes about or studies history.

his•tor•ic (hĭ stôr′ĭk or hĭ stōr′ĭk) *adj.* **1.** Important or famous in history: *the historic city of Williamsburg.* **2.** Historical.

his•tor•i•cal (hĭ stôr′ĭ kəl or hĭ stōr′ĭ kəl) *adj.* **1.** Relating to history: *historical events.* **2.** Based on or concerned with events in history: *a historical novel.* —**his•tor′i•cal•ly** *adv.*

his•to•ry (hĭs′tə rē) *n.*, *pl.* **his•to•ries. 1.** [C] A written account or record of past events. **2.** [U] The study of past events as a

special field of knowledge: *History is a favorite subject among students.* **3.** [U] The events that form the subject matter of a historical account: *printing and other important inventions in history.*
hit (hĭt) *v.* **hit, hit·ting, hits.** —*tr.* **1.** To give a blow to (sbdy./sthg.); strike with a blow or stroke: *I hit the tennis ball with the racket.* **2.** To strike against (sthg.) with force; crash into: *The car hit the fence.* **3.** To cause (sthg.) to come against a person or thing: *He hit his fist against the table.* **4.** To get to (sthg.); reach: *hit a high note; going smoothly until we hit a bumpy road.* **5.** To affect (sbdy./sthg.) painfully or severely, as if by a blow: *A period of bad business hit the store hard.* —*intr.* **1.** To come against a person or thing; collide: *The two boats hit in the fog.* **2.** To happen or occur: *The blizzard hit during the night.* **3.** To achieve or find sthg. desired or sought: *We hit on the right answer.* —*n.* **1.** A blow that strikes sthg.: *Two or three hits of the hammer will drive the nail in.* **2.** A person or thing that is a popular success: *The new musical is the hit of the season.* ♦ **hit it off.** To get along well together: *We hit it off as soon as we met.* **hit on.** *tr.v.* [insep.] *Informal.* To talk to (sbdy. one is sexually attracted to), often when the other person is not interested: *He was hitting on every woman at the party.* **hit (one) up.** *tr.v.* [sep.] *Informal.* To ask (sbdy.) for sthg., usually money: *My brother hit me up for a loan.* **hit the nail on the head.** To be absolutely right: *You hit the nail on the head when you predicted a tax increase.* **hit the road.** To leave: *It's getting late, so I guess I'll hit the road.* **hit the roof** or **ceiling.** To be very angry: *When she told me she'd borrowed my bike without asking and lost it, I hit the roof.* **hit upon** or **on.** *tr.v.* [insep.] To find (sthg.) unexpectedly; resolve (a problem) by chance: *He hit upon a solution to our problems while he was out walking.* —**hit′ter** *n.*
hit-and-run (hĭt′n rŭn′) *adj.* Involving a driver of a vehicle who hits sbdy. or damages sthg. and leaves the scene to avoid responsibility: *a hit-and-run accident.*
hitch (hĭch) *v.* —*tr.* **1.** To tie or fasten (sthg.) with a rope, strap, or loop: *The trapper hitched a dog team to the sled.* **2.** To raise or pull (sthg.) with a tug or jerk: *The driver hitched the heavy branch out of the way.* **3.** *Informal.* To get (a ride): *We hitched a lift to the gas station.* —*intr. Informal.* To hitchhike: *We hitched all the way to Seattle.* —*n.* **1.** A short pull or jerk; a tug. **2.** A delay or problem; a snag: *a hitch in our plans.* **3.** *Informal. (usually singular).* A ride obtained by hitchhiking: *They got a hitch to the game.* ♦ **get hitched.** *Informal.* To get married: *They got hitched in Las Vegas.*

hitch up. *tr.v.* [sep.] To adjust or pull (sthg.) up: *He hitched up his pants.*
hitch·hike (hĭch′hīk′) *intr.v.* **hitch·hiked, hitch·hik·ing, hitch·hikes.** To travel by getting a free ride from drivers of passing cars or trucks: *They hitchhiked across the country.* —**hitch′hik′er** *n.*
hith·er (hĭth′ər) *adv. Formal.* To or toward here: *Come hither.* ♦ **hither and thither** or **hither and yon.** In or to many places; here and there: *running hither and thither all day.*
hith·er·to (hĭth′ər tōo′) *adv. Formal.* Until this time; up to now: *hitherto unknown species of plants.*
hit-or-miss (hĭt′ər mĭs′) *adj.* Careless or unplanned; random: *a hit-or-miss approach to studying.*
HIV *abbr.* An abbreviation of human immunodeficiency virus, the virus that causes AIDS by destroying the body's immune system.
hive (hīv) *n.* **1.** A colony of bees living in a special structure. **2.** A crowded place full of activity: *The supermarket was a hive of frantic last-minute shopping.*
hives (hīvz) *pl.n. (used with a singular or plural verb).* An itching red skin rash, usually caused by allergies or nervousness.
HMO *abbr.* An abbreviation of health maintenance organization: *At our company employees can choose among several different HMOs for their health care.*
hoard (hôrd) *n.* A hidden supply that is stored for future use: *the squirrel's hoard of nuts for winter.* —*tr.v.* To save and store (sthg.) away; accumulate: *Our neighbor hoarded old newspapers.* —**hoard′er** *n.*

HOMONYMS: hoard, horde (crowd).

hoarse (hôrs) *adj.* **hoars·er, hoars·est.** Low and gruff in sound; husky: *The cold reduced my voice to a hoarse whisper.* —**hoarse′ly** *adv.* —**hoarse′ness** *n.* [U]

HOMONYMS: hoarse, horse (animal).

hoax (hōks) *n.* A trick or an act intended to deceive others, often in the form of a practical joke or false report: *The report that the store was going out of business proved to be a hoax.* —**hoax′er** *n.*
hob·ble (hŏb′əl) *v.* **hob·bled, hob·bling, hob·bles.** —*intr.* [along] To walk with difficulty; limp: *The patient hobbled along with one leg in a cast.* —*tr.* **1.** To put a rope or strap around the legs of (an animal) to make movement more difficult: *hobble a camel; hobble a horse.* **2.** To make (sthg.) difficult; hinder: *Quarreling hobbled the efforts of the committee to reach a decision.*

hob·by (hŏb′ē) *n.*, *pl.* **hob·bies.** An activity that is for pleasure, not to earn a living: *I collect stamps as a hobby.* —**hob′by·ist** *n.*

hob·by·horse (hŏb′ē hôrs′) *n.* A rocking horse.

hob·gob·lin (hŏb′gŏb′lĭn) *n.* **1.** A mischievous or troublesome elf; a goblin. **2.** A source of fear or dread: *The thought of losing his job is the hobgoblin that keeps him up at night.*

hob·nob (hŏb′nŏb′) *intr.v.* **hob·nobbed, hob·nob·bing, hob·nobs.** [*with*] To meet, talk, or spend time together in a friendly manner: *hobnobbing with friends in the park.*

ho·bo (hō′bō) *n.*, *pl.* **ho·boes** or **ho·bos.** A person who wanders from place to place and does odd jobs or begs for a living: *A hobo knocked on the kitchen door to ask for a drink of water.*

hock[1] (hŏk) *n.* The joint of the hind leg of a horse or other animal having hoofs, corresponding to the human ankle.

hock[2] (hŏk) *tr.v. Slang.* To pawn (sthg.): *I hocked my ring for some cash.* ◆ **in hock.** In debt: *No matter how much money I make, I'm always in hock.*

hock·ey (hŏk′ē) *n.* [U] **1.** Ice hockey. **2.** Field hockey.

ho·cus-po·cus (hō′kəs pō′kəs) *n.* [U] Meaningless speech or behavior used to deceive: *the hocus-pocus of a swindler.*

hodge·podge (hŏj′pŏj′) *n.* [U] A mixture of various things; a jumble: *a hodgepodge of items in a desk drawer.*

hoe (hō) *n.* A tool with a flat blade on a long handle, used to loosen the soil and weed around plants. —*tr. & intr.v.* **hoed, hoe·ing, hoes.** To use a hoe to weed or dig up: *We hoed the garden. We hoed for an hour.*

hog (hôg *or* hŏg) *n.* **1.** A pig, especially a full-grown pig raised for meat. **2.** *Informal.* A greedy, selfish, or filthy person: *He made a hog of himself at lunch.* —*tr.v.* **hogged, hog·ging, hogs.** *Informal.* To take more than one's fair share of (sthg.): *Some thoughtless drivers hog the road.* ◆ **go whole hog.** *Informal.* To do sthg. completely: *When they redecorated their house, they went whole hog.* **live high on the hog.** To live in an expensive way: *For someone with such a small salary, she lives high on the hog.*

hoist (hoist) *tr.v.* To raise or haul (sthg.) up, usually with the help of a pulley or machinery: *A tall crane hoisted bricks to the top of the new building.* —*n.* A device for hoisting, as a crane, winch, or rope and pulley.

hold[1] (hōld) *v.* **held** (hĕld), **hold·ing, holds.** —*tr.* **1.** To have and keep (sbdy./sthg.) in one's grasp: *The baby can hold her bottle now.* **2.** To keep (sbdy./sthg.) from moving or escaping: *He held the dog by a leash.* **3.** To restrain, stop, or control (sbdy./sthg.): *Please hold your questions until the end of the presentation.* **4.** To occupy (a place) by force:

The army held the town for a month. **5.** To have or take (a number or an amount of sthg.) as contents; contain: *This box holds a dozen eggs.* **6.** To support or bear (sbdy./sthg.): *Will that wagon hold such a heavy load?* **7.** To have (sthg.) as a position or privilege: *Thomas Jefferson held the office of President for two terms.* **8.** To have (sthg.) as an achievement: *She holds the school record for diving.* **9.** To cause (sthg.) to happen; engage in: *hold elections; hold a conversation.* **10.** To keep or capture the interest of (sbdy.): *The movie held our attention.* **11.** To consider or judge (sbdy./sthg.): *That painting was held to be the best.* **12.** To state or affirm (an idea): *The court holds that the law is not constitutional.* —*intr.* **1.** To continue in a state or condition; last: *The good weather held for two weeks.* **2.** To remain firm or secure: *The knot held against the strain.* **3.** To be true or correct: *The theory holds in all cases.* —*n.* **1.** [C; U] The act or a means of grasping: *keep a firm hold on the handle.* **2.** [C] Something that may be grasped or used for support: *The rocks had many holds for climbers.* **3.** [U] A very strong influence or power: *England's hold over the American colonies ended with the Revolution.* ◆ **get hold of. 1.** To get possession of sthg.; find: *Where can I get hold of a copy of that book?* **2.** To communicate with sbdy., especially by telephone: *I tried to get hold of you.* **3. (oneself).** To gain control of (oneself): *Get hold of yourself.* **hold against.** *tr.v.* [sep.] To allow (sthg.) to influence unfavorably one's judgment of sbdy.: *She held the accident against her brother for years.* **hold down.** *tr.v.* [sep.] **1.** To have and keep (a job): *He can't seem to hold down a job.* **2.** To limit (sthg.): *Please hold the noise down.* **hold forth.** *intr.v.* To talk at great length; make a long speech: *The candidate held forth for two hours.* **hold off.** *intr.v.* To delay or wait: *I hope the rain holds off until after the picnic.* **hold on.** *intr.v.* **1.** To keep a grip; cling: *Hold on or you'll fall out of the boat!* **2.** To continue to do sthg., especially sthg. difficult: *It was a long race, but everyone held on to the end.* **3.** To stop or wait for sbdy./sthg.: *Hold on a minute, I'm coming, too.* **hold (one's) own.** To do well despite difficulty: *He's the smallest boy in the group, but he holds his own.* **hold out.** *intr.v.* **1.** To last: *How long will our water supply hold out?* **2.** To continue to resist: *The strikers held out against the management.* **hold over.** *tr.v.* [sep.] **1.** To delay or postpone (sthg.): *They held over the launch of the space shuttle.* **2.** To keep (sthg.) for an additional period of time: *The play was held over for another week.* **hold up.** *intr.v.* To remain in good condition; function well: *This car should hold up for many years.* —*tr.v.* [sep.] **1.** To stop or delay (sthg.): *What's holding up traffic?* **2.**

To show (sthg.) as an example: *The essay was held up as an example of good writing.* **3.** To rob (sbdy./sthg.) by threatening with harm or force: *Robbers held up a bank.* **no holds barred.** Using any and all means to do sthg., without limits or restraints: *It'll be a tough election campaign, with no holds barred.*

hold² (hōld) *n.* The lower inside part of a ship or an aircraft, where cargo or luggage is stored.

hold•er (hōl′dər) *n.* **1.** A person who holds, owns, or possesses sthg.: *a ticket holder; a job holder.* **2.** A device for holding sthg.: *a napkin holder.*

hold•ing (hōl′dĭng) *n. (usually plural).* Legally owned property, such as land, stocks, or bonds: *His uncle has huge holdings in the oil industry.*

hold•up (hōld′ŭp′) *n.* **1.** [U] A stopping of progress or activity; a delay: *a holdup in production.* **2.** [C] A robbery committed by a person with a gun: *a bank holdup.*

hole (hōl) *n.* **1.** An opening or open place; a gap: *a hole in the elbow of a sweater; a hole in a fence.* **2.** A hollowed place in sthg. solid, such as the ground or a wall: *dig a hole to plant the tree; a mouse's hole in the wall.* **3.** *Slang.* An ugly, dirty, or depressing dwelling: *She lives in a real hole.* **4.** A bad or troublesome situation; a difficulty: *help a friend out of a hole.* **5.** A fault or defect: *Let's find the holes in that argument.* —*tr.v.* **holed, hol•ing, holes.** ◆ **be in the hole.** To owe money: *She bought too many gifts for her family, and she's really in the hole now.* **hole up.** *intr.v.* To sleep, hide, or take shelter in or as if in a burrow or other shelter: *We holed up until the storm passed.*

HOMONYMS: hole, whole (complete).

---

hol•i•day (hŏl′ĭ dā′) *n.* **1.** A day on which general business activity is stopped to celebrate a particular event: *May 1 is a holiday in many countries.* **2.** *Chiefly British.* A period of time for relaxing away from work; a vacation.

ho•li•ness (hō′lē nĭs) *n.* [U] The condition or quality of being holy.

ho•lis•tic (hō lĭs′tĭk) *adj.* Emphasizing the importance of the whole of sthg. over any one of its parts: *holistic medicine.*

hol•ler (hŏl′ər) *tr. & intr.v. Informal.* To yell or shout: *Don't holler at me. She hollered a greeting to friends across the street.* See Synonyms at **shout.** —*n.* A shout or yell: *Give a holler when you're ready.*

hol•low (hŏl′ō) *adj.* **1.** Having a space or opening inside: *a hollow log.* **2.** Sounding as if coming from an empty place: *the hollow sound of far-off thunder.* **3.** Not true or sincere; empty: *a hollow promise.* —*n.* An opening or a space; a hole: *The rabbits made a hollow at the*

foot of the tree. —*tr.v.* ◆ **hollow out.** *tr.v.* [sep.] **1.** To make (sthg.) hollow: *hollow out a log.* **2.** To scoop or form (sthg.) by making into the shape of a bowl or cup: *We hollowed out a pumpkin and put a candle in it for Halloween.* —**hol′low•ly** *adv.* —**hol′low•ness** *n.* [U]

hol•ly (hŏl′ē) *n., pl.* **hol•lies.** An evergreen shrub with leaves that have prickly edges and bright red berries.

hol•o•caust (hŏl′ə kôst′ *or* hō′lə kôst′) *n.* **1.** Great or total destruction, as by fire. **2. Holocaust.** The mass killing of European Jews and others by the Nazis during World War II.

hol•o•gram (hŏl′ə grăm′ *or* hō′lə grăm′) *n.* The photographic record of an image produced by holography.

ho•log•raph•y (hō lŏg′rə fē) *n.* [U] A method of producing a three-dimensional image of an object by using a laser. —**hol′o•graph′ic** (hŏl′ə grăf′ĭk *or* hō′lə grăf′ĭk) *adj.*

hol•ster (hōl′stər) *n.* A case to hold a handgun or tools, usually made of leather and worn on a belt.

ho•ly (hō′lē) *adj.* **ho•li•er, ho•li•est.** **1.** Associated with a divine power; sacred: *The Bible and the Koran are holy books.* **2.** Living according to highly moral or religious principles; saintly: *a holy person.*

HOMONYMS: holy, wholly (completely).

---

hom•age (hŏm′ĭj *or* ŏm′ĭj) *n.* [U] *Formal.* Special honor or respect; reverence: *The President paid homage to the poet by quoting her in his speech.*

home (hōm) *n.* **1.** A place in which a person lives: *Our home is in that apartment building.* **2.** A group of people, especially a family, that lives together in a dwelling place; a household: *Those children come from a loving home.* **3.** The place in which one was born, grew up, or has lived a long time: *No matter where I live, I will always think of New York as my home.* **4.** *(usually singular).* The region or place in which an animal, a plant, or a thing is commonly found; a native habitat: *The forest is the home of many plants and animals.* **5.** A place where people are cared for: *a home for the elderly.* **6.** In baseball, home plate. —*adj.* **1.** Relating to or taking place in a home: *home life; home cooking.* **2.** Played on the grounds where a team originates or plays most of its games: *a home game.* —*adv.* **1.** At, to, or toward one's home: *The children raced home from school.* **2.** To the center or heart of sthg.; deeply: *Their arguments struck home.* —*intr.v.* **homed, hom•ing, homes.** ◆ **at home. 1.** In one's home or country: *While abroad, we read about problems at*

---

home. 2. Comfortable and relaxed; at ease: *She felt at home with strangers.* **bring** or **come home to.** To make (sbdy.) aware of sthg.: *Her illness brought home to us how much we loved her.* **hit home.** To disturb sbdy. deeply: *Their problems hit home with us.* **home in on.** To be guided directly to a destination or target: *These birds home in on their nesting grounds each spring.*

home·com·ing (hōm′kŭm′ĭng) *n.* **1.** A return to one's home: *The soldier's homecoming was a joyous occasion.* **2.** In some high schools and colleges, a yearly celebration held for returning graduates.

home·grown (hōm′grōn′) *adj.* Made or grown at home: *homegrown tomatoes from our garden.*

home·land (hōm′lănd′) *n.* The country in which one was born or has lived for a long time.

home·less (hōm′lĭs) *adj.* Having no home. —*n.* [U] *(used with a plural verb).* People who have no home considered as a group: *a shelter for the homeless.*

home·ly (hōm′lē) *adj.* **home·li·er, home·li·est.** Not attractive or good-looking: *a homely dog.* —**home′li·ness** *n.* [U]

home·made (hōm′mād′) *adj.* Made at home: *delicious homemade bread.*

home·mak·er (hōm′mā′kər) *n.* A person who manages a household. —**home′mak′-ing** *n.* [U]

home·page (hōm′pāj′) *n.* A place on the Internet where one can find information about a specific person, group, or company.

home plate *n.* [U] In baseball, the base at which the batter stands, which must be touched by a runner in order to score a run.

home·room (hōm′rōōm′ *or* hōm′rŏŏm′) *n.* A classroom in which a group of students are required to gather each day.

home run *n.* In baseball, a hit that allows the batter to touch all the bases and score a run.

home·sick (hōm′sĭk′) *adj.* Longing for home: *I was homesick during the whole trip.* —**home′sick′ness** *n.* [U]

home·spun (hōm′spŭn′) *adj.* **1.** Spun or woven at home: *homespun cloth.* **2.** Plain and simple; folksy: *homespun humor.*

home·stead (hōm′stĕd′) *n.* **1.** A farm, especially one on land that was given by the government, together with the land and buildings belonging to it. **2.** *Informal.* One's childhood home: *It's always a pleasure to get back to the old homestead.* —*intr.v.* To settle on land claimed as a homestead: *My grandparents homesteaded.* —**home′-stead′er** *n.*

home·stretch (hōm′strĕch′) *n.* [U] **1.** The part of a racetrack from the last turn to the finish line. **2.** The last stage of sthg.: *I am finally in the homestretch of writing this report.*

home·ward (hōm′wərd) *adj.* Toward or at home: *the homeward journey.* —*adv.* also **home·wards.** Toward home: *They headed homeward.*

home·work (hōm′wûrk′) *n.* [U] School assignments that are done at home or outside the classroom.

hom·ey (hō′mē) *adj.* **hom·i·er, hom·i·est.** *Informal.* Suggesting a home; cheerful and comfortable: *a restaurant with a homey atmosphere.*

hom·i·cide (hŏm′ĭ sīd′ *or* hō′mĭ sīd′) *n.* [C; U] The killing of one person by another. —**hom′i·cid′al** *adj.*

homo— or **hom—** *pref.* A prefix that means same or similar: *homogeneous; homosexual.*

ho·mo·ge·ne·ous (hō′mə jē′nē əs *or* hō′mə jēn′yəs) *adj.* Of the same or similar kind; uniform throughout: *a homogeneous class of students having about the same ability.* —**ho′mo·ge·ne′i·ty** (hō′mə jə nē′ĭ tē *or* hō′mə jə nā′ĭ tē) *n.* [U] —**ho′mo·ge′ne·ous·ly** *adv.*

ho·mog·e·nize (hə mŏj′ə nīz′) *tr.v.* **ho·mog·e·nized, ho·mog·e·niz·ing, ho·mog·e·niz·es.** To make (sthg.) homogeneous or uniform throughout: *homogenized milk.* —**ho·mog′e·ni·za′tion** (hə mŏj′ə nĭ zā′shən) *n.* [U]

hom·o·graph (hŏm′ə grăf′) *n.* A word that has the same spelling as another word but differs in meaning, origin, and sometimes in pronunciation; for example, *ring* (circle) and *ring* (sound) and *bass* (fish) and *bass* (deep tone) are homographs.

hom·o·nym (hŏm′ə nĭm′) *n.* A word that has the same sound and sometimes the same spelling as another word but a different meaning and origin; for example, *die* (stop living), *die* (stamping), and *dye* (color) are all homonyms.

hom·o·phone (hŏm′ə fōn′) *n.* A word that has the same sound as another word but differs in spelling, meaning, and origin; for example, *for, fore,* and *four* are homophones.

ho·mo·sex·u·al (hō′mə sĕk′shōō əl) *adj.* Relating to or having sexual feelings for members of the same sex. —*n.* A homosexual person. —**ho·mo·sex·u·al·i·ty** (hō′mə-sĕk′shōō ăl′ĭ tē) *n.* [U]

hone (hōn) *tr.v.* **honed, hon·ing, hones. 1.** To sharpen (a knife or other sharp tool) on a fine-grained stone. **2.** To make (sthg.) more effective: *Authors must hone their skills by writing a great deal.*

hon·est (ŏn′ĭst) *adj.* **1.** Not lying, stealing, or cheating; trustworthy: *The bank teller is an honest worker.* **2.** Done or obtained without lying, cheating, or stealing: *an honest profit.* **3.** Not hiding anything; sincere: *an honest opinion.* —**hon′est·ly** *adv.*

hon·es·ty (ŏn′ĭ stē) *n.* [U] The quality of being honest; truthfulness: *No one questioned the honesty of the judge's statement.*

hon·ey (hŭn′ē) n. [U] **1.** A sweet, thick, syrupy substance made by bees and used as food. **2.** Informal. Sweetheart; dear.

hon·ey·bee (hŭn′ē bē′) n. A bee that produces honey and beeswax: Honeybees swarmed around the hive.

hon·ey·comb (hŭn′ē kōm′) n. [C; U] **1.** A wax structure with many small six-sided compartments, made by honeybees to hold honey, pollen, and eggs. **2.** Something full of openings or spaces like those in a honeycomb: The building was a honeycomb of small rooms and passages. —tr.v. To fill (sthg.) with openings or spaces like those in a honeycomb: Tiny shops and stalls honeycombed the village.

hon·ey·dew melon (hŭn′ē dōo′) n. A melon with a smooth whitish skin and sweet green flesh.

hon·ey·moon (hŭn′ē mōon′) n. **1.** A trip taken by a newly married couple. **2.** A period of harmony early in a relationship: the honeymoon between the new President and Congress. —intr.v. To have or spend a honeymoon: They honeymooned in the Caribbean. —**hon′ey·moon′er** n.

hon·ey·suck·le (hŭn′ē sŭk′əl) n. A vine with fragrant yellow, white, or pink flowers.

honk (hôngk or hŏngk) n. A loud harsh sound, such as that made by a goose or an automobile horn. —intr. & tr.v. To make or cause to make a honk: A flock of geese honked overhead. The impatient driver honked the car horn. —**honk′er** n.

hon·or (ŏn′ər) n. **1.** [U] Special respect or high regard: The award is given to show honor to great film directors. **2.** [C] An act that shows respect or high regard; recognition for outstanding work: a hero's funeral with full honors. **3.** [U] A sense of what is right; high principles; integrity: A person of honor does not lie, cheat, or steal. **4.** Often **Honor.** Used as a title and form of address for certain officials, such as judges and mayors: her Honor the mayor. —tr.v. **1.** To show special respect or recognition to (sbdy./sthg.); treat with honor: We honored the volunteers with a party. **2.** To think highly of (sbdy.); esteem: a doctor who was honored everywhere for achievements in medicine. **3.** To accept (sthg.) as payment: honor a check. ◆ **on (one's) honor.** Under a solemn pledge to be truthful and do what is right: I'll do what you ask, on my honor. **with honors.** With high academic standing: graduated from college with honors.

hon·or·a·ble (ŏn′ər ə bəl) adj. **1.** Deserving honor and respect: Teaching is an honorable profession. **2.** Having or showing a sense of what is right or just: an honorable person; an honorable solution to a difficult problem. **3.** Done with or accompanied by marks of honor: an honorable burial. —**hon′or·a·ble·ness** n. [U] —**hon′or·a·bly** adv.

hon·o·rar·i·um (ŏn′ə râr′ē əm) n., pl. **hon·o·rar·i·ums** or **hon·o·rar·i·a** (ŏn′ə râr′ē ə). A payment made to a professional person for services, such as a lecture.

hon·or·ar·y (ŏn′ə rĕr′ē) adj. Given or holding as an honor: an honorary degree from a university.

hood[1] (hōod) n. **1.** A soft covering for the head and neck, often attached to a coat or cape: a winter coat with a hood attached. **2.** The hinged metal lid over the engine of an automobile: I'll look under the hood. —tr.v. To supply or cover (sthg.) with a hood: The men hooded the kidnap victim. —**hood′like′** adj.

hood[2] (hōod) n. Slang. A hoodlum.

—**hood** suff. A suffix that means: **1.** Condition or quality: girlhood; falsehood. **2.** A group sharing a certain condition or quality: sisterhood; priesthood.

hood·ed (hōod′ĭd) adj. Covered with or having a hood: a hooded cape.

hood·lum (hōod′ləm or hŏod′ləm) n. A gangster or criminal.

hood·wink (hōod′wĭngk′) tr.v. Informal. To deceive or mislead (sbdy.); trick: They were hoodwinked into buying useless land.

hoof (hōof or hŏof) n., pl. **hoofs** or **hooves** (hōovz, hŏovz). The whole foot or tough horny covering on the lower part of the foot of certain mammals, such as horses, cattle, deer, and pigs. —intr.v. Slang. To dance, especially to tap-dance. ◆ **hoof it.** Slang. To walk quickly: We hoofed it into town.

hoofed (hōoft or hŏoft) adj. Having hoofs: hoofed animals.

hook (hōok) n. **1.** A curved or sharply bent piece of metal or other stiff material, used to catch, hold, fasten, or pull sthg.: Coats hung on hooks in the hall. **2.** A fishhook. **3.** Something shaped or used like a hook. —v. —tr. **1.** To catch, hang, or connect (sthg.) with a hook: hook a tuna while fishing; hook a picture on the wall. **2.** To make (a rug, for example) by looping yarn through a loosely woven material with a hook. —intr. **1.** To move, throw, or extend in a curve: The road hooks toward the river. **2.** To be fastened by means of a hook: The gate hooks on the post. ◆ **by hook or by crook.** By whatever means possible, fair or unfair: They plan to win the election by hook or by crook. **hook up.** tr.v. [sep.] To connect or make a connection between (two or more things): The electricity was hooked up to the house. **off the hook.** Informal. Free of blame or obligation: We are off the hook for now.

hooked (hōokt) adj. **1.** Curved or bent like a hook: the owl's hooked beak. **2.** Made with a hook: *a hooked rug.* **3.** *Slang.* Addicted or devoted to sthg.: *hooked on drugs; She's hooked on golf.*

hook•up (hŏŏk'ŭp') *n.* A connection or an arrangement, especially of parts in a system: *a nationwide radio and television hookup; a hookup between buyer and seller.*

hook•y (hŏŏk'ē) *n.* [U] *Informal.* Absence without permission: *play hooky from school.*

hoo•li•gan (hōō'lĭ gən) *n. Informal.* A person who causes public disturbances, vandalism, etc. —**hoo'li•gan•is'm** *n.* [U]

hoop (hŏŏp *or* hōōp) *n.* A circular band or ring of wood, metal, bone, or plastic: *an embroidery hoop; a basketball hoop.* ◆ **shoot some hoops.** *Slang.* To play basketball: *Let's shoot some hoops after class.*

HOMONYMS: hoop, whoop (shout).

hoop•la (hōōp'lä' *or* hŏŏp'lä') *n.* [U] *Slang* **1.** Noisy or confusing commotion. **2.** Extravagant publicity: *There was a lot of hoopla over that movie, but it wasn't really that good.*

hoo•ray (hŏŏ rā' *or* hə rā') *interj., n., & v* Variant of **hurrah.**

hoot (hōōt) *v.* —*intr.* **1.** To make the cry of an owl. **2.** [*at*] To make a shout or loud cry of contempt or disapproval: *Demonstrators hooted at the speaker.* —*tr.* **1.** To shout at or drive (sbdy.) away with scornful cries or jeers: *The hecklers hooted the candidate off the platform.* **2.** To express (sthg.) by hooting: *The fans hooted their disappointment.* —*n.* **1.** The sound of an owl. **2.** A shout: *She gave a hoot when our team scored.* ◆ **give a hoot.** To care; be concerned about: *I don't give a hoot if it rains. Do you give a hoot about your grades?*

hooves (hŏŏvz *or* hōōvz) *n.* A plural of **hoof.**

hop¹ (hŏp) *v.* **hopped, hop•ping, hops** —*intr.* **1.** To move with light springing jumps or skips: *The frightened rabbit hopped away.* **2.** To jump on one foot. —*tr.* **1.** To jump over (sthg.): *hopped the fence in a single bound.* **2.** *Informal.* To jump aboard (sthg.), especially a vehicle: *hop a train.* —*n.* **1.** A hopping motion; a springy jump: *The squirrel crossed the lawn in short hops.* **2.** A short trip, especially by air: *It is a short hop between Boston and New York.* **3.** A short bounce: *The ball took a bad hop.* ◆ **be hopping mad.** To be extremely angry: *She was hopping mad that I wore her new sweater.*

hop² (hŏp) *n. (usually plural).* A vine with green flower clusters that are dried and used in making beer.

hope (hōp) *v.* **hoped, hop•ing, hopes.** —*intr.* To trust or wish for a favorable outcome: *I think I can win the race; at least I hope so.* —*tr.* **1.** To look forward to (sthg.) with a feeling of expectation or confidence: *I hope to be there by five o'clock.* See

Synonyms at **expect.** **2.** To desire (sthg.) very much; wish earnestly: *I hope that I have not misspelled any of the words on the test.* —*n.* **1.** [C; U] A feeling of confident expectation: *The young doctor is full of hope for success.* **2.** [C] A reason for or cause of such a feeling: *A home run is the team's only hope for victory.* **3.** [C] *(usually plural).* Something that is hoped for or desired: *I have high hopes of becoming a singer.* ◆ **hold out hope.** To offer encouragement that sthg. will happen: *The coach held out little hope of our winning.* **raise (one's) hopes.** To encourage sbdy. to believe that sthg. is possible, especially when it seems unlikely: *raised our hopes of getting a new car.*

hope•ful (hōp'fəl) *adj.* **1.** Feeling hope: *The immigrants arrived hopeful of a better life.* **2.** Inspiring hope; encouraging: *hopeful signs of peace.* —*n.* A person who wishes to succeed in sthg.: *Several hopefuls tried out for the lead in the play.* —**hope'ful•ness** *n.* [U]

hope•ful•ly (hōp'fə lē) *adv.* **1.** In a hopeful manner: *The children watched hopefully out the window for their parents' car.* **2.** *Informal.* It is to be hoped: *Hopefully, you'll do better next time.*

hope•less (hōp'lĭs) *adj.* Having or offering no hope: *After many hours of wandering in the forest the lost hikers felt hopeless.* **2.** Having no hope of improvement: *My room is a hopeless mess.* —**hope'less•ly** *adv.* —**hope'less•ness** *n.* [U]

hop•scotch (hŏp'skŏch') *n.* [U] A children's game in which players toss a small object into the numbered squares drawn on the ground and then hop into the squares to pick up the object and return.

horde (hôrd) *n.* A large group, crowd, or swarm: *hordes of people at the fair.*

HOMONYMS: horde, hoard (store away).

ho•ri•zon (hə rī'zən) *n.* **1.** The line along which the earth and sky appear to meet. **2.** The limit of one's experience, knowledge, or interests: *Lack of education often narrows a person's horizons.*

hor•i•zon•tal (hôr'ĭ zŏn'tl *or* hŏr'ĭ zŏn'tl) *adj.* Parallel to or in the plane of the horizon; level: *Draw two horizontal lines on your paper.* —**hor'i•zon'tal•ly** *adv.*

hor•mone (hôr'mōn') *n.* A substance produced by an endocrine gland and carried in the bloodstream to tissues and other organs: *Hormones control basic bodily processes and functions such as growth and metabolism.* —**hor•mon'al** *adj.*

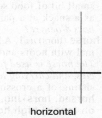

horizontal

horn (hôrn) *n.* **1.** A hard bony growth on the heads of cattle, sheep, and goats. **2.** A wind instrument such as a trombone or tuba: *the English horn.* **3.** A warning device that produces a loud sound: *an automobile horn.* —*intr.v.* ◆ **horn in on.** *Slang.* To join in sthg. without being invited; intrude: *The older children horned in on the game of tag.* —**horn′less** *adj.* —**horn′like′** *adj.*

horned (hôrnd) *adj.* Having a horn, horns, or a hornlike growth: *a horned snail.*

hor•net (hôr′nĭt) *n.* Any of various large stinging wasps that live in colonies and build large papery nests.

horn•y (hôr′nē) *adj.* **horn•i•er, horn•i•est. 1.** Having horns or hornlike projections. **2.** *Informal.* Sexually excited or interested.

hor•o•scope (hôr′ə skōp′ *or* hŏr′ə skōp′) *n.* **1.** The relative position of the planets and stars at a given moment, as the hour of a person's birth, for example. **2.** A prediction, especially of a person's future: *What does your horoscope for today say?*

hor•ren•dous (hô rĕn′dəs *or* hə rĕn′dəs) *adj.* Terrible; dreadful: *horrendous weather.* —**hor•ren′dous•ly** *adv.*

hor•ri•ble (hôr′ə bəl *or* hŏr′ə bəl) *adj.* **1.** Causing horror; dreadful: *a horrible crime.* **2.** Extremely unpleasant: *a horrible noise.* —**hor′ri•bly** *adv.*

hor•rid (hôr′ĭd *or* hŏr′ĭd) *adj.* **1.** Causing horror; horrible: *a horrid murder.* **2.** Extremely disagreeable; offensive: *What a horrid person!* —**hor′rid•ly** *adv.*

hor•ri•fy (hôr′ə fī′ *or* hŏr′ə fī′) *tr.v.* **hor•ri•fied, hor•ri•fy•ing, hor•ri•fies. 1.** To cause (sbdy.) to feel horror: *The possibility of a violent earthquake horrified people.* **2.** To surprise (sbdy.) unpleasantly; shock: *The class's poor performance on the test horrified the teacher.*

hor•ror (hôr′ər *or* hŏr′ər) *n.* **1.** [U] A feeling of fear and disgust; terror: *She felt horror at the thought of what might have happened.* **2.** [C] Something that causes horror: *the horrors of war.*

hors d'oeuvre (ôr dûrv′) *n., pl.* **hors d'oeuvres** (ôr dûrvz′) *or* **hors d'oeuvre.** A small bit of food served before a meal or as a snack at a party: *Would you like an hors d'oeuvre?*

horse (hôrs) *n.* **1.** A large four-legged mammal with hoofs and a long mane and tail: *The horse is used for riding, pulling vehicles, and carrying loads.* **2.** A support consisting of a crossbar and four legs. —*v.* **horsed, hors•ing, hors•es.** ◆ **be** or **get on (one's) high horse.** To be or become arrogant or conceited about sthg.: *He's on his high horse about winning a scholarship.*

beat a dead horse. To continue discussing a matter that has already been decided: *We've already decided not to go, so why beat a dead horse?* **hold (one's) horses.** To hold back from an unwise action: *Hold your horses! Don't spend money you haven't earned yet!* **horse around.** *intr.v. Informal.* To engage in rough play or other playful activity: *Stop horsing around!* **horse of a different color.** Something completely different and unexpected: *They invited us to an elegant dinner, but when they served hot dogs, that was a horse of a different color!* **look a gift horse in the mouth.** To examine a gift critically: *You might not like the book she gave you, but you shouldn't look a gift horse in the mouth.* **put the cart before the horse.** To do things in the wrong order: *If you frost the cake before it bakes, you'll be putting the cart before the horse.* **straight from the horse's mouth.** Information or advice directly from the source: *"How do you know we're all getting a raise?" "I got it straight from the horse's mouth—the boss told me."*

HOMONYMS: horse, hoarse (husky).

horse•back (hôrs′băk′) *n.* [U] The back of a horse: *police officers on horseback.* —*adv. & adj.* On the back of a horse: *ride horseback; horseback riding.*

horse•fly (hôrs′flī′) *n.* A large fly that bites horses, cattle, and other animals.

horse•play (hôrs′plā′) *n.* [U] Rough or rowdy play: *Horseplay around water is dangerous.*

horse•pow•er (hôrs′pou′ər) *n., pl.* **horsepower.** A unit for measuring the power of engines and motors.

horse•rad•ish (hôrs′răd′ĭsh) *n.* [U] A plant with a large whitish root that has a sharp taste, often used grated as a condiment.

horse sense *n.* [U] *Informal.* Common sense: *Use horse sense when you buy a car.*

horse•shoe (hôrs′shoo′ *or* hôrsh′shoo′) *n.* **1.** A flat U-shaped metal plate fitted and nailed to a horse's hoof for protection. **2.** **horseshoes.** *(used with a singular verb).* A game in which the players try to toss horseshoes around a stake in the ground.

hor•ti•cul•ture (hôr′tĭ kŭl′chər) *n.* [U] The science or art of raising and caring for plants, especially flowers, fruits, and vegetables. —**hor′ti•cul′tur•al** *adj.* —**hor′ti•cul′tur•ist** (hôr′tĭ kŭl′chər ĭst) *n.*

hose (hōz) *n.* **1.** *pl.* **hose.** *(used with a plural verb).* Women's stockings: *My new hose are ruined.* **2.** *pl.* **hos•es.** A flexible tube for carrying liquids or gases under pressure: *use an air hose to fill the car tires.* —*tr.v.* **hosed,**

hos·ing, hos·es. ◆ hose down. *tr.v.* [sep.] To wash or spray (sthg.) with water from a hose: *hose down a car while washing it.*

ho·sier·y (hō′zhə rē) *n.* [U] Stockings and socks; hose.

hos·pice (hŏs′pĭs) *n.* A program providing care and support for people who are suffering from terminal illness.

hos·pi·ta·ble (hŏs′pĭ tə bəl *or* hŏ spĭt′ə-bəl) *adj.* Treating guests with warmth and generosity: *The hotel staff is extremely hospitable.* —**hos′pi·ta·bly** *adv.*

hos·pi·tal (hŏs′pĭ tl *or* hŏs′pĭt′l) *n.* An institution that provides medical, surgical, or psychiatric care and treatment for those who are sick and injured.

hos·pi·tal·i·ty (hŏs′pĭ tăl′ĭ tē) *n.* [U] Welcoming or generous treatment of guests: *We thanked our friends for their hospitality.*

hos·pi·tal·i·za·tion (hŏs′pĭ tl ĭ zā′shən) *n.* **1.** [C; U] The act of placing a person in a hospital as a patient. **2.** [U] The condition of being hospitalized: *Her hospitalization after the accident lasted for seven months.* **3.** [U] Insurance that fully or partially covers a patient's hospital expenses: *He has no hospitalization, so he'll have to pay all his own costs.*

hos·pi·tal·ize (hŏs′pĭt l īz′) *tr.v.* **hos·pi·tal·ized, hos·pi·tal·iz·ing, hos·pi·tal·iz·es.** To place (sbdy.) in a hospital for treatment or care: *I was hospitalized for two days with appendicitis.*

host[1] (hōst) *n.* **1.** A person who receives or is in charge of an event in a social, business, or official capacity: *The new neighbors were our hosts for the evening.* **2.** A living plant or animal on or in which a parasite lives and feeds. —*tr.v.* To serve as host to (sbdy.) or at (sthg.): *host a party; host an interview on TV.*

host[2] (hōst) *n. Formal.* A great number; a multitude: *a host of angels.*

hos·tage (hŏs′tĭj) *n.* A person who is held by another or by a group in a conflict as security that a specified demand will be met: *The robbers took several bank employees as hostages.*

hos·tel (hŏs′təl) *n.* A supervised inexpensive lodging place for travelers, especially young travelers: *a youth hostel.*

host·ess (hō′stĭs) *n.* A woman who receives guests or is in charge of an event in a social or business capacity: *The café hostess took us to a table.*

hos·tile (hŏs′təl *or* hŏs′tīl′) *adj.* **1.** Relating to or characteristic of an enemy: *hostile forces.* **2.** Unfriendly: *a hostile crowd.* —**hos′tile·y** *adv.*

hos·til·i·ty (hŏ stĭl′ĭ tē) *n., pl.* **hos·til·i·ties. 1.** [U] The state of being hostile; antagonism: *The hostility of the former enemies was felt by everyone.* **2. hostilities.** Acts of war; open warfare: *Hostilities broke out between the two countries.*

hot (hŏt) *adj.* **hot·ter, hot·test. 1.** Having great heat; being at a high temperature; very warm: *a hot stove; a horse that was hot after working in the sun; a forehead hot with fever.* **2.** Charged with electricity: *a hot wire.* **3.** Causing a burning sensation in the mouth: *hot chili; hot mustard.* **4.** Marked by intense feeling: *a hot temper; a hot argument.* **5.** *Informal.* Most recent; new or fresh: *a hot piece of news.* **6.** *Slang.* Stolen: *a hot television set.* —*adv.* In a hot manner; with much heat: *The engine runs hot.* ◆ **hot on (one's) trail.** Close to catching (sbdy.): *hot on the robbers' trail.* **hot under the collar.** Very angry or irritated: *If the printer won't work, don't get hot under the collar. Just turn it off.* **in the hot seat.** In a position of responsibility that is extremely difficult: *When the workers went on strike the union leaders were in the hot seat.* —**hot′ly** *adv.* —**hot′ness** *n.* [U]

hot air *n.* [U] *Slang.* Empty exaggerated talk: *The promises made by politicians are nothing but hot air.*

hot·bed (hŏt′bĕd′) *n.* **1.** A place that leads to rapid and excessive growth or development, especially of sthg. bad: *a hotbed of intrigue.* **2.** A bed of soil covered with glass and used for growing seeds or protecting young plants.

hot-blood·ed (hŏt′blŭd′ĭd) *adj.* Easily excited; passionate: *hot-blooded teenagers.*

hot·cake (hŏt′kāk′) *n. (usually plural).* A pancake. ◆ **go** or **sell like hotcakes.** *Informal.* To go or sell quickly and in great amounts: *The raffle tickets are selling like hotcakes.*

hot dog or **hot·dog** (hŏt′dôg′ *or* hŏt′dŏg′) *n.* **1.** A long type of sausage served hot in a long roll. **2.** A showoff. —*interj.* Used to show approval, agreement, or pleasure: *Hot dog! She says we can go to the movies.*

hot·dog (hŏt′dôg′ *or* hŏt′dŏg′) *intr.v.* **hot·dogged, hot·dog·ging, hot·dogs.** To perform in a showy or reckless way; show off: *He's always hotdogging on his motorcycle.*

ho·tel (hō tĕl′) *n.* A building that provides rooms and often meals and other services for paying guests: *When we went on vacation, we stayed in the best hotels.*

hot·head (hŏt′hĕd′) *n.* A person who does things without thinking: *a dangerous hothead.*

hot·head·ed (hŏt′hĕd′ĭd) *adj.* **1.** Easily angered; quick-tempered: *a crowd of hot-*

headed protestors. **2.** Not carefully planned; rash: *a hotheaded plan.* —**hot′head′ed·ly** *adv.* —**hot′head′ed·ness** *n.* [U]

hot·house (hŏt′hous′) *n.* A warm building with a glass roof and sides, used for growing plants; a greenhouse. —*adj.* Grown in a hothouse: *hothouse tomatoes.*

hot line or **hot·line** (hŏt′līn′) *n.* A telephone line for crises, or that provides information or help: *a suicide-prevention hot line.*

hot·ly (hŏt′lē) *adv.* In an intense or fiery manner: *a hotly debated subject.*

hot plate *n.* A small electric stove for cooking or warming food.

hot rod *n. Slang.* An automobile rebuilt or modified for greater acceleration and speed.

hot·shot (hŏt′shŏt′) *n. Slang.* A person who is highly successful and self-assured: *a hotshot lawyer.*

hot spot *n.* **1.** A dangerous or hostile place: *Los Angeles has been a political hot spot lately.* **2.** *Slang.* A lively and popular place, such as a nightclub: *a downtown hot spot for food and dancing.*

hot water *n.* [U] *Informal.* A difficult or uncomfortable situation; trouble: *He's in hot water with his parents for coming home late.*

hound (hound) *n.* **1.** Any of various breeds of dog, originally used for hunting: *a foxhound.* **2.** A person who eagerly follows sthg.; enthusiast: *a mystery hound.* —*tr.v.* **1.** To pursue (sbdy.) without stopping: *Reporters hounded the actor all over town.* **2.** To urge (sbdy.) to do sthg. insistently; nag: *The children hounded their parents to let them go to the movies.*

hour (our) *n.* **1.** A unit of time equal to one of the 24 equal parts of a day; 60 minutes. **2.** The distance that can be traveled in an hour: *When we cross the bridge, we will only be two hours from our destination.* **3.** A particular time: *At what hour does the store open?* **4.** A customary or fixed time for a specific activity: *the dinner hour; open hours from eight to three; keeps office hours.* ♦ **after hours.** Later than regular business hours: *an after-hours bar; The boss annoys us by scheduling meetings after hours.* **at all hours.** At any time of day or night: *She calls us at all hours.* **at the eleventh hour.** At a time that is almost too late: *They reached a peace agreement at the eleventh hour.* **on the hour.** At an exact time, such as 12 o'clock: *Trains leave every hour on the hour.* **the wee hours.** The hours just after midnight (1 to 3 A.M.): *The party lasted into the wee hours.*

HOMONYMS: hour, our (of us).

hour·glass (our′glăs′) *n.* An instrument for measuring time, made with two glass chambers connected by a narrow neck and containing an amount of sand or another substance that passes from the top chamber to the bottom one in a fixed amount of time, often an hour.

hourglass

hour·ly (our′lē) *adj.* **1.** Happening every hour: *hourly temperature readings; hourly news reports during the hurricane.* **2.** By the hour as a unit: *an hourly wage.* **3.** Frequent; continual: *hourly changes to the report.* —*adv.* At or during every hour: *doses of medicine given hourly.*

house (hous) *n., pl.* **hous·es** (hou′zĭz or hou′sĭz). **1.** A structure in which one or more persons lives; a residence. **2.** A building used for some special purpose: *an opera house; a movie house.* **3.** The people in an audience: *The actors played to a full house.* **4.** Often **House.** An assembly having the power of making laws; a legislature: *The two houses of the U.S. Congress are the Senate and the House of Representatives.* —*tr.v.* (houz). **housed, hous·ing, hous·es. 1.** To provide living quarters for (sbdy.): *The apartment building houses ten families.* **2.** To keep or store (sthg.) in a house or other shelter: *house our car in the garage.* ♦ **bring the house down.** To cause everyone at a performance to clap or laugh: *Their singing brought the house down.* **like a house afire.** Very quickly: *We raced down the stairs like a house afire.* **on the house.** Paid for by the owner of a bar, restaurant, etc.: *If you buy dinner and a drink, dessert is on the house.*

house arrest *n.* [U] Being held in one's house, rather than prison, by court order: *a dissident under house arrest for ten years.*

house·boat (hous′bōt′) *n.* A special type of boat used as a residence.

house·break (hous′brāk′) *tr.v.* **house·broke** (hous′brōk′), **house·bro·ken** (hous′brō′kən), **house·break·ing, house·breaks.** To train (a dog) not to use the house as a bathroom: *We are trying to housebreak our new puppy.* —**house′bro′ken** *adj.*

house·break·ing (hous′brā′kĭng) *n.* [U] The act of unlawfully breaking into and entering another's house.

house call *n.* A professional visit made to a home, especially by a doctor.

house·clean·ing (hous′klē′nĭng) *n.* [U] The cleaning of a house and its contents.

house·hold (hous′hōld′) *n.* The members of a family and others living together in a house.

—*adj.* Relating to or used in a household: *household appliances; household expenses.*

house•hus•band (hous'hŭz'bənd) *n.* A married man who manages a household as his main occupation.

house•keep•er (hous'kē'pər) *n.* A person who takes care of a home or supervises cleaning a hospital, hotel, or similar institution.

house•keep•ing (hous'kē'pĭng) *n.* [U] Cleaning and other chores necessary to keep a house clean.

house•plant (hous'plănt') *n.* A plant grown indoors, often for decorative purposes.

house•top (hous'tŏp') *n.* The roof of a house.

house•wares (hous'wârz') *pl.n.* Articles used especially in the kitchen, such as cooking utensils and dishes: *We shopped for housewares after we moved into the apartment.*

house•warm•ing (hous'wôr'mĭng) *n.* A party to celebrate moving into a new home: *We were invited to a housewarming at our friends' new house.*

house•wife (hous'wīf') *n.* A married woman who manages the household as her main occupation.

house•work (hous'wûrk') *n.* [U] The tasks performed to maintain a house, such as cleaning and cooking.

hous•ing (hou'zĭng) *n.* [U] **1.** Buildings in which people live: *housing for the poor.* **2.** Payment of costs for a place to live, often by an employer: *The employment agreement included housing.*

housing development *n.* A number of houses built in the same area, often in the suburbs.

housing project *n.* A group of publicly funded houses or apartment buildings, usually for people with low incomes.

hov•el (hŭv'əl *or* hŏv'əl) *n.* A small miserable house: *hovels by the river.*

hov•er (hŭv'ər *or* hŏv'ər) *intr.v.* **1.** To stay floating, suspended, or fluttering in the air: *Hummingbirds hover in the air as they feed.* **2.** To remain close by: *She hovered over her son when he had a fever.*

how (hou) *adv.* **1.** In what manner or way; by what means: *The teacher showed us how to use a compass.* **2.** In what state or condition, especially of health: *How do you feel today?* **3.** To what extent, amount, or degree: *How strong is the rope? How much do these shoes cost?* **4.** For what reason; why: *How did you manage to miss the train?* **5.** With what meaning: *How should I take that remark?* —*conj.* The manner or way in which: *I forgot how the song goes.* —*n.* The way sthg. is done: *I am more interested in the how than the why of a thing.* ♦ **and how.** Very much indeed: *"Are you hungry?" "And how!"* **how about.** Used to ask about one's thoughts, feeling, or desire

regarding sthg.: *How about some ice cream?*

how come. *Informal.* How is it that; why: *How come you're late?*

how•dy (hou'dē) *interj. Informal.* An expression used in greeting sbdy.

how•ev•er (hou ev'ər) *adv.* **1.** To whatever extent or degree: *However long it takes, an education is absolutely necessary.* **2.** In whatever way or manner: *However you manage it, the job must be done.* **3.** Nevertheless; yet: *It was a difficult time; however, there were amusing moments.*

howl (houl) *intr.v.* **1.** To produce a long, mournful, sad sound: *The dogs howled at the loud siren.* **2.** To cry or wail loudly, as in pain, sorrow, or anger: *The patient howled when the dentist pulled the tooth.* See Synonyms at **shout. 3.** *Slang.* To laugh heartily: *The audience howled at the comedian's jokes.* —*n.* A long wailing cry.

howl•ing (hou'lĭng) *adj.* **1.** Marked by the sound of howling: *a howling wind.* **2.** *Slang.* Very great: *The party was a howling success.*

hp *abbr.* An abbreviation of horsepower.

HQ *or* **h.q.** *or* **H.Q.** *abbr.* An abbreviation of headquarters.

hr *abbr.* An abbreviation of hour.

ht *abbr.* An abbreviation of height.

hub (hŭb) *n.* **1.** The center part of a wheel, fan, or propeller. **2.** A center of activity or interest; a focal point: *The kitchen was the hub of the party.*

hub•bub (hŭb'ŭb') *n.* [U] *Informal.* Noisy confusion; uproar: *the hubbub of traffic; the hubbub in a crowded room.*

hub•cap (hŭb'kăp') *n.* A round covering over an automobile wheel.

hud•dle (hŭd'l) *n.* **1.** A densely packed group or crowd of people or animals: *a huddle of reporters on the hospital steps.* **2.** A small private conference or meeting: *The two lawyers went into a huddle.* —*intr.v.* **hud•dled, hud•dling, hud•dles. 1.** To crowd together, as from cold or fear: *The sheep huddled into a small pen.* **2.** To draw one's limbs close to one's body: *The rabbit huddled under some leaves.* **3.** *Informal.* To confer; meet: *The football players huddled and talked about the next play.*

hue (hyōō) *n.* The property of color that distinguishes it from another color; color: *all the hues of the rainbow; the basic hues of red, blue, and yellow.*

HOMONYMS: hue, hew (shape with an ax).

---

huff (hŭf) *n.* A fit of anger or annoyance: *She left the room in a huff.* —*intr.v.* To puff; blow: *They huffed all the way up the hill.*

huff•y (hŭf'ē) *adj.* **huff•i•er, huff•i•est.** Easily offended; touchy: *Why are you so huffy today?* —**huff'i•ly** *adv.* —**huff'i•ness** *n.* [U]

hug (hŭg) *tr.v.* **hugged, hug·ging, hugs. 1.** To hold (sbdy.) closely; embrace: *hug a child.* **2.** To keep or stay close to (sthg.): *This car hugs the road well on corners.* —*n.* An affectionate or tight embrace: *Give me a hug!*

huge (hyōoj) *adj.* **hug·er, hug·est.** Of great size, extent, or quantity; tremendous: *a huge iceberg; a huge difference.* See Synonyms at **large.** —**huge′ly** *adv.* —**huge′ness** *n.* [U]

huh (hŭ) *interj. Informal.* An expression used to ask a question or show surprise: *"Huh? I didn't hear what you said."*

hulk (hŭlk) *n.* **1.** The hull of an old, unseaworthy, or wrecked ship. **2.** A large clumsy person or thing: *a hulk of a football player; a big bus that is a hulk.*

hulk·ing (hŭl′kĭng) *adj.* Unwieldy or bulky; massive: *a great hulking dog.*

hull (hŭl) *n.* **1.** The framework or body of a ship or plane. **2.** The outer covering of certain seeds or fruits. **3.** The cluster of leaflets at the stem end of certain fruits, such as the strawberry. —*tr.v.* To remove the hulls of (fruit or seeds): *hull berries.*

hul·la·ba·loo (hŭl′ə bə lōo′) *n., pl.* **hul·la·ba·loos.** *Informal.* Great noise or excitement; uproar: *There was a hullabaloo when we heard the good news.*

hum (hŭm) *v.* **hummed, hum·ming, hums.** —*intr.* **1.** To make the continuous droning sound of a bee in flight; buzz: *Bees hummed around the flower.* **2.** To sing without words, with the lips kept closed: *hum while working.* **3.** To be full of or alive with activity: *The street hums with traffic.* —*tr.* To sing (a tune) without opening the lips: *hum a melody.* —*n.* The sound produced by humming: *The TV has a strange hum.*

hu·man (hyōo′mən) *adj.* **1.** Relating to or characteristic of people: *the human body.* **2.** Made up of people: *People linked their arms in a human chain.* —*n.* A person. —**hu′man·ness** *n.* [U]

human being *n.* A person; a woman, man, or child.

hu·mane (hyōo mān′) *adj.* Characterized by kindness or mercy: *a humane judge.* —**hu·mane′ly** *adv.* —**hu·mane′ness** *n.* [U]

hu·man·ism (hyōo′mə nĭz′əm) *n.* [U] **1.** A system of thought that is concerned with human welfare, interests, and values. **2.** The study of the humanities; learning in the liberal arts. —**hu′man·ist** *n. & adj.*

hu·man·i·tar·i·an (hyōo mǎn′ĭ târ′ē ən) *n.* A person who promotes human welfare and the advancement of social reforms; a philanthropist. —*adj.* Related to the belief that it is important to work for the improvement of human welfare: *humanitarian goals and ideals.* —**hu·man′i·tar′i·an′ism** *n.* [U]

hu·man·i·ty (hyōo mǎn′ĭ tē) *n., pl.* **hu·man·i·ties. 1.** [U] Human beings considered as a group; the human race: *The measles vaccine is of benefit to humanity.* **2.** [U] The quality of being humane; kindness: *Taking in the war refugees was an act of great humanity.* **3. humanities.** *(used with a singular or plural verb).* The areas of study, such as art, philosophy, and literature, that are concerned with human thought and culture.

hu·man·ize (hyōo′mə nīz′) *tr.v.* **hu·man·ized, hu·man·iz·ing, hu·man·iz·es.** To make (sth.) human: *The writer humanizes animal characters by showing how they feel.* —**hu′man·i·za′tion** *n.* [U]

hu·man·kind (hyōo′mən kīnd′) *n.* [U] All human beings as a group; humanity.

hu·man·ly (hyōo′mən lē) *adv.* **1.** In a human way. **2.** Within the scope of human means, abilities, or powers: *I'll do it as soon as is humanly possible.*

human resources *pl.n.* The department in a company that handles employment and training.

human rights *pl.n.* The basic rights of all human beings: *She devoted her life to human rights.*

hum·ble (hŭm′bəl) *adj.* **hum·bler, hum·blest. 1.** Modest or unassuming in behavior, attitude, or spirit: *a humble manner; humble thanks.* **2.** Low in rank, quality, or station: *My career began as a humble clerk.* —*tr.v.* **hum·bled, hum·bling, hum·bles.** To cause (sbdy.) to be meek or modest in spirit; humiliate: *Defeat humbled the proud tennis player.* —**hum′ble·ness** *n.* [U] —**hum′bly** *adv.*

hum·drum (hŭm′drŭm′) *adj.* Without variety or excitement; dull: *the humdrum work of filing papers.*

hu·mer·us (hyōo′mər əs) *n., pl.* **hu·mer·i** (hyōo′mə rī′). The bone of the upper arm or forelimb, extending from the shoulder to the elbow.

HOMONYMS: humerus, humorous (funny).

---

hu·mid (hyōo′mĭd) *adj.* Containing a large amount of water or water vapor; damp: *humid air before a shower of rain.* See Synonyms at **wet.**

hu·mid·i·fy (hyōo mĭd′ə fī′) *tr.v.* **hu·mid·i·fied, hu·mid·i·fy·ing, hu·mid·i·fies.** To make (sth.) moist or damp: *humidify the air in a greenhouse.* —**hu·mid′i·fi′er** *n.*

hu·mid·i·ty (hyōo mĭd′ĭ tē) *n.* [U] The condition of being humid; dampness: *The paintings were damaged by the humidity of the warehouse.*

hu·mil·i·ate (hyōo mĭl′ē āt′) *tr.v.* **hu·mil·i·at·ed, hu·mil·i·at·ing, hu·mil·**

ă–cat; ā–pay; âr–care; ä–father; ĕ–get; ē–be; ĭ–sit; ī–nice; îr–here; ŏ–got; ō–go; ô–saw; oi–boy; ou–out; ōo–took; ōo–boot; ŭ–cut; ûr–word; th–thin; th–this; hw–when; zh–vision; ə–about; N–French bon

i•ates. To lower the pride or self-respect of (sbdy.): *I was humiliated by the rude behavior of my children.*

hu•mil•i•a•tion (hyōō mǐl′ē ā′shən) *n.* **1.** [C] The act of humiliating; degradation: *the humiliation of an opponent.* **2.** [U] The condition of being humiliated; disgrace: *After that defeat, the team's humiliation was complete.*

hu•mil•i•ty (hyōō mǐl′ǐ tē) *n.* [U] The quality or condition of being humble: *The officer accepted the award with humility.*

hum•ming•bird (hŭm′ǐng bûrd′) *n.* A very small, brightly colored bird that drinks nectar from flowers.

hu•mor (hyōō′mər) *n.* [U] **1.** The quality of being funny or comical: *We laughed at the humor of the story.* **2.** An often temporary state of mind; a mood: *The beautiful day put me in good humor.* —*tr.v.* To go along with the wishes or ideas of (sbdy.); indulge: *The baby sitter humored the child.*

hu•mor•ist (hyōō′mər ǐst) *n.* A person with a sharp sense of humor, especially a writer or performer of humorous material.

hu•mor•less (hyōō′mər lǐs) *adj.* Without humor: *humorless remarks.* —**hu′mor•less•ness** *n.* [U]

hu•mor•ous (hyōō′mər əs) *adj.* Characterized by humor; funny: *a humorous writer; a humorous story.* —**hu′mor•ous•ly** *adv.* —**hu′mor•ous•ness** *n.* [U]

HOMONYMS: humorous, humerus (arm bone).

---

hu•mour (hyōō′mər) *n. & v. Chiefly British.* Variant of **humor.**

hump (hŭmp) *n.* A rounded lump, as on the back of a camel. —*tr.v.* To bend or make (sthg.) into a hump; arch: *The cat humped its back when it saw the dog.* ◆ **hump day.** Wednesday: *Well, we made it to hump day!* **over the hump.** Past the worst or hardest part or stage: *Once our exams are finished, we'll finally be over the hump.*

hu•mus (hyōō′məs) *n.* [U] A dark brown or black substance made up of decayed leaves and other organic material.

hunch (hŭnch) *n.* A suspicion or an intuition: *I had a hunch it would get chilly, so I brought a sweater.* —*v.* —*tr.* To draw up or bend (sthg.) into a hump: *I hunched my shoulders against the cold wind.* —*intr.* To go into a crouched or cramped posture: *The cat hunched in the corner.*

hunch•back (hŭnch′băk′) *n.* A person with a hump on the back caused by a curved spine. —**hunch′backed′** *adj.*

hun•dred (hŭn′drǐd) *n., pl.* **hundred** or **hun•dreds. 1.** The number, written as 100 or 10², that is equal to 10 x 10. **2. hundreds.** Many: *hundreds of faces in the crowd.*

hun•dredth (hŭn′drǐdth) *n.* **1.** (*singular only*). The ordinal number matching the num-

ber 100 in a series. **2.** One of one hundred equal parts. —**hun′dredth** *adj. & adv.*

hung (hŭng) *v.* Past tense and a past participle of **hang.**

hun•ger (hŭng′gər) *n.* [U] **1.** A strong desire or need for food: *Hunger drove the lions to hunt closer to the town.* **2.** A strong desire or craving: *The young child has a real hunger for knowledge.* —*intr.v.* **1.** To have a need or desire for food: *The hikers hungered for something hot and delicious.* **2.** To have a strong desire or craving: *Our team hungered for victory.*

hun•gry (hŭng′grē) *adj.* **hun•gri•er, hun•gri•est. 1.** Experiencing a need or desire for food. **2.** Having a strong desire or craving: *The students were hungry for knowledge.* **3.** Showing or feeling hunger or need: *a hungry look at my sandwich.* —**hun′gri•ly** *adv.* —**hun′gri•ness** *n.* [U]

hunk (hŭngk) *n.* **1.** A large piece; a chunk: *I broke a hunk of freshly baked bread off the loaf.* **2.** *Slang.* An attractive man: *My sister is dating a real hunk.*

hunt (hŭnt) *v.* —*tr.* **1.** To chase (animals) for food or sport: *hunt deer.* **2.** To search for (sthg.); seek out: *hunting bargains at the local stores.* —*intr.* [*for*] **1.** To pursue animals. **2.** To search thoroughly; seek: *I hunted for the book at the library.* —*n.* **1.** The act or sport of hunting animals: *a fox hunt.* **2.** A focused search or pursuit: *a hunt for my missing glasses.* ◆ **hunt down.** *tr.v.* [sep.] To find (a criminal or enemy) after much searching: *Police hunted down the escaped prisoners.* —**hunt′er** *n.*

hunt•ing (hŭn′tǐng) *n.* [U] The activity or sport of pursuing and killing animals.

hur•dle (hûr′dl) *n.* **1.** A light portable barrier over which runners must jump in certain races: *The runner cleared all the hurdles to win the race.* **2.** An obstacle or a problem to be overcome: *Getting the money was the chief hurdle I had in going to college.* —*v.* **hur•dled, hur•dling, hur•dles.** —*tr.* **1.** To jump over (a barrier) as if in a race: *The dog hurdled the fence after the rabbit.* **2.** To overcome or deal with (sthg.) successfully: *We hurdled his objections easily.* —*intr.* To jump over a hurdle or other barrier. —**hur′dler** *n.*

hurl (hûrl) *tr.v.* **1.** To throw (sthg.) with great force; fling: *The volcano hurled smoke and ash high into the air.* See Synonyms at **throw. 2.** To say (sthg.) forcefully: *The baseball players hurled insults at each other.* **3.** *Slang.* To vomit (sthg.): *I hurled my lunch.*

hur•rah (hŏŏ rä′ *or* hə rä′) *also* **hoo•ray** (hŏŏ rā′ *or* hə rā′) *interj.* An expression used to show approval, pleasure, or victory. —*n.* A shout of "hurrah." —*intr.v.* To applaud or cheer with shouts of "hurrah": *The crowd hurrahed when she broke the world record.*

hur•ri•cane (hûr′ǐ kān′ *or* hŭr′ǐ kān′) *n.* A severe tropical storm with heavy rains and winds exceeding 74 miles (119 kilometers) per hour. Hurricanes originate in the tropical parts of the Atlantic Ocean or the Caribbean Sea and move generally northward.

hur·ried (hûr′ēd *or* hŭr′ēd) *adj.* Done very quickly or in haste; rushed: *Because we got up late, we ate a hurried breakfast.* —**hur′ried·ly** *adv.*

hur·ry (hûr′ē *or* hŭr′ē) *v.* **hur·ried, hur·ry·ing, hur·ries.** —*intr.* To move or act very quickly: *The children hurried with their homework.* —*tr.* **1.** To cause (sbdy.) to move or act with speed: *Parents hurried their children to the bus stop.* **2.** To cause (sbdy.) to move or act too quickly; rush: *She hurried me into making a choice.* —*n.* [U] The act or an instance of hurrying: *In my hurry to get to the train, I forgot my wallet.* ◆ **hurry up.** An expression used to order a person to move more quickly: *Hurry up! We're late!* —*tr.v.* [sep.] To cause (sbdy.) to move more quickly: *We'll have to hurry them up.* —*intr.v.* To move more quickly: *I wish the bus would hurry up.*

hurt (hûrt) *v.* **hurt, hurt·ing, hurts.** —*tr.* **1.** To cause physical pain to (sbdy./sthg.); injure: *The fall hurt my leg.* **2.** To cause mental or emotional suffering to (sbdy.); distress: *The bitter argument hurt both of us.* **3.** To damage or impair (sthg.): *The dry summer hurt this year's corn crop.* —*intr.* **1.** To have a feeling of physical pain or discomfort: *When I have a cold, my head often hurts.* **2.** To cause distress or damage: *It hurt not to be picked for the team.* —*n.* [U] Something that hurts or harms: *The hurt of smaller paychecks discouraged many people from shopping.*

SYNONYMS: hurt, injure, damage, spoil. These verbs mean to affect sbdy./sthg. in a bad way. **Hurt** can mean to cause pain, distress, or loss: *Don't try to lift the heavier boxes because you might hurt your back.* **Injure** can mean to harm health, well-being, appearance, or expectations: *The runner didn't want a heavy lunch to injure her chances of winning the race.* **Damage** can mean to injure sthg. in a way that decreases value or usefulness: *The movers must have damaged the piano because I never noticed that scratch before now.* **Spoil** means to damage sthg. so that its value, excellence, or strength is completely destroyed: *The heavy rains spoiled our picnic.* **ANTONYMS: heal, help, improve.**

---

hurt·ful (hûrt′fəl) *adj.* Causing injury or suffering; painful: *That was a hurtful thing to say.* —**hurt′ful·ly** *adv.* —**hurt′ful·ness** *n.* [U]

hur·tle (hûr′tl) *intr. & tr.v.* **hur·tled, hur·**

tling, hur·tles. To move or cause to move with great speed and a rushing noise: *The speeding train hurtled through the tunnel. The player hurtled the ball.*

hus·band (hŭz′bənd) *n.* A man married to a woman.

hush (hŭsh) *v.* —*tr.* To make (sbdy.) silent or quiet: *The parents tried to hush the infant.* —*intr.* To be or become silent or still: *The audience hushed as the curtain went up.* —*n.* [U] A silence or stillness; quiet: *When the teacher returned, a hush fell over the classroom.* ◆ **hush money.** Money paid to keep sbdy. from revealing an evil or illegal action: *The criminal used hush money to conceal his illegal deals.* **hush up.** *tr.v.* [sep.] To keep (sthg.) from public knowledge; suppress: *The mayor tried to hush up news about the hotel to be built in the city.*

husk (hŭsk) *n.* The dry outer covering of certain seeds or fruits, such as an ear of corn: *corn husks.* —*tr.v.* To remove the husk from (sthg.): *I always helped to husk the ears of corn before cooking them.*

husk·y[1] (hŭs′kē) *adj.* **husk·i·er, husk·i·est.** **1.** Hoarse or deep in quality: *a husky voice.* **2.** Strongly built; burly: *a husky football player.* —**husk′i·ly** *adv.* —**husk′i·ness** *n.* [U]

hus·ky[2] (hŭs′kē) *n., pl.* **hus·kies.** A strong medium-sized work dog with a thick coat, used in Arctic regions for pulling sleds.

hus·tle (hŭs′əl) *v.* **hus·tled, hus·tling, hus·tles.** —*tr.* **1.** To push or shove (sbdy.) roughly: *The guards hustled the prisoner into a cell.* **2.** To move (sbdy./sthg.) hurriedly; rush: *We hustled the letter to the post office.* —*intr.* **1.** To move and push: *We hustled through the shopping mall.* **2.** To work or move energetically and rapidly: *You need to hustle to get the job done.* **3.** *Slang.* To sell or obtain sthg. by deceitful or illegal methods: *He was arrested for hustling drugs.* —*n.* [U] Energetic activity; drive: *The new player shows lots of hustle.* —**hus′tler** *n.*

hut (hŭt) *n.* A small crudely made house or shelter; a shack.

hutch (hŭch) *n.* **1.** A pen for small animals, especially rabbits. **2.** A cupboard used for storage.

hwy *abbr.* An abbreviation of highway.

hy·a·cinth (hī′ə sĭnth) *n.* A spring plant that grows from a bulb and has a long cluster of fragrant flowers.

hy·brid (hī′brĭd) *n.* A plant or an animal that has parents of different varieties, or species: *Hybrids are more disease resistant.* —*adj.* Relating to a hybrid: *hybrid varieties of wheat.* —**hy′brid·ize**[1] *v.* —**hy′brid·i·za′tion** (hī′brĭ dĭ zā′shən) *n.* [U]

ă-**cat**; ā-**pay**; âr-**care**; ä-**father**; ĕ-**get**; ē-**be**; ĭ-**sit**; ī-**nice**; îr-**here**; ŏ-**got**; ō-**go**; ô-**saw**; oi-**boy**; ou-**out**; ŏŏ-**took**; ōō-**boot**; ŭ-**cut**; ûr-**word**; th-**thin**; *th*-**this**; hw-**when**; zh-**vision**; ə-**about**; N-French bon

hy·dran·gea (hī drān′jə *or* hī drăn′jə) *n.*
[C; U] A shrub with large rounded clusters of
white, pink, or blue flowers.

hy·drant (hī′drənt) *n.* A large water pipe,
with a valve and usually placed near a street,
used for fighting fires.

hy·drau·lic (hī drô′lĭk) *adj.* Operated by the
pressure of water or other liquids in motion,
especially when forced through an opening:
a hydraulic brake; a hydraulic jack. **—hy·
drau′li·cal·ly** *adv.*

hy·drau·lics (hī drô′lĭks) *n. (used with a
singular verb).* The science that deals with
water and other liquids at rest or in motion,
their uses in engineering, and their behavior.

hydro— *or* **hydr—** *pref.* A prefix that means:
1. Water: *hydroelectric.* **2.** Hydrogen: *hydrocarbon.*

hy·dro·car·bon (hī′drə kär′bən) *n.* An
organic compound that contains only carbon
and hydrogen. Hydrocarbons form a large
class of chemical compounds and include
gasoline, benzene, and butane.

hy·dro·chlo·ric acid (hī′drə klôr′ĭk) *n.*
[U] A corrosive solution of hydrogen chloride in water, used in industrial processes.

hy·dro·e·lec·tric (hī′drō ĭ lĕk′trĭk) *adj.*
Generating electricity through the use of
water power: *a hydroelectric power station*

hy·dro·gen (hī′drə jən) *n.* [U] *Symbol* **H** A
colorless, highly flammable gaseous element
present in most organic compounds. Hydrogen
is the lightest, most abundant element and
combines with oxygen to form water. Atomic
number 1. See table at **element.**

hydrogen bomb *n.* An extremely destructive
type of bomb.

hydrogen peroxide *n.* [U] A colorless compound of hydrogen and oxygen having the
formula H_2O_2, often used in water solution as
an antiseptic and a bleaching agent.

hy·dro·pho·bi·a (hī′drə fō′bē ə) *n.* [U] **1.**
Rabies. **2.** An abnormal fear of water.

hy·dro·plane (hī′drə plān′) *n.* **1.** A motorboat
with a flattened bottom that moves quickly over
the surface of water. **2.** A seaplane.

hy·dro·pon·ics (hī′drə pŏn′ĭks) *n. (used
with a singular verb).* The growing of plants
in nutrient solution rather than in soil.

hy·dro·ther·a·py (hī′drə thĕr′ə pē) *n.* [U]
The use of water to treat an injury or disease.

hy·e·na (hī ē′nə) *n.* A dog-like, meat-eating
Asian or African mammal with coarse, sometimes spotted or striped hair and a piercing
cry that sounds like a laugh.

hy·giene (hī′jēn′) *n.* [U] Practices that promote
good health and the prevention of disease.

hy·gi·en·ic (hī′jē ĕn′ĭk *or* hī jĕn′ĭk *or*
hī jē′nĭk) *adj.* **1.** Relating to hygiene. **2.**
Tending to promote good health; clean; sanitary: *a hygienic kitchen; food preparation
following hygienic practices.* **—hy′gi·en′-
i·cal·ly** *adv.*

hy·gien·ist (hī jē′nĭst *or* hī jĕn′ĭst) *n.* A specialist in hygiene, especially a person who is
trained to clean and examine the teeth: *a dental hygienist.*

hy·grom·e·ter (hī grŏm′ĭ tər) *n.* An instrument that measures the humidity of the air.

hy·men (hī′mən) *n.* A membrane that partly
closes the opening of the vagina.

hymn (hĭm) *n.* A song of praise or joy to
a deity.

Homonyms: hymn, him (pronoun).

---

hym·nal (hĭm′nəl) *n.* A book or collection of
church hymns.

hyper— *pref.* A prefix that means excessively: *hypercritical; hypersensitive.*

hy·per·ac·tive (hī′pər ăk′tĭv) *adj.* Highly
or excessively active: *a hyperactive child; a
hyperactive gland.*

hy·per·bo·le (hī pûr′bə lē) *n.* A figure of
speech in which exaggeration is used for
effect. The sentence *It rained last night and
our yard is a lake* makes use of hyperbole.
—hy′per·bol′ic (hī′pər bŏl′ĭk) *adj.*

hy·per·crit·i·cal (hī′pər krĭt′ĭ kəl) *adj.*
Too ready to find fault; overly critical: *Our
instructor is hypercritical of our work.* **—hy′-
per·crit′i·cal·ly** *adv.*

hy·per·sen·si·tive (hī′pər sĕn′sĭ tĭv) *adj.*
Unusually or overly sensitive: *skin that is
hypersensitive to the sun.* **—hy′per·sen′-
si·tiv′i·ty** (hī′pər sĕn′sĭ tĭv′ĭ tē) *n.* [U]

hy·per·son·ic (hī′pər sŏn′ĭk) *adj.* Moving
or able to move at a speed at least five times
the speed of sound: *a new hypersonic fighter
plane.*

hy·per·ten·sion (hī′pər tĕn′shən) *n.* [U] An
illness characterized by high blood pressure.

hy·phen (hī′fən) *n.* A punctuation mark (-)
used between words or syllables of a word.

hy·phen·ate (hī′fə nāt′) *tr.v.* **hy·phen·
at·ed, hy·phen·at·ing, hy·phen·ates.**
To divide or connect (syllables, word elements, or names) with a hyphen. **—hy′phen·
a′tion** *n.* [U]

hyp·no·sis (hĭp nō′sĭs) *n.* [U] **1.** A condition resembling sleep in which a person
becomes very responsive to suggestions from
another: *Hypnosis is often used in psychotherapy.* **2.** Hypnotism. **—hyp·not′ic** (hĭp-
nŏt′ĭk) *adj.* **—hyp·not′i·cal·ly** *adv.*

hyp·no·tism (hĭp′nə tĭz′əm) *n.* [U] **1.** The
theory, method, or process of putting a person
into a state of hypnosis. **2.** The act of inducing hypnosis. **—hyp′no·tist** *n.*

hyp·no·tize (hĭp′nə tīz′) *tr.v.* **hyp·no·
tized, hyp·no·tiz·ing, hyp·no·tiz·es.**
1. To put (sbdy.) into a state of hypnosis: *The patient was hypnotized to relieve
pain.* **2.** To fascinate (sbdy.) by or as if by
hypnosis: *The exciting movie hypnotized the
audience.*

H

hypo— or **hyp—** *pref.* A prefix that means: **1.** Beneath or below: *hypodermic.* **2.** Less than normal: *hypoglycemia.*

hy·po·chon·dri·a (hī′pə kŏn′drē ə) *n.* [U] A condition in which a healthy person believes that he or she is ill or worries too much about becoming ill.

hy·po·chon·dri·ac (hī′pə kŏn′drē ăk′) *n.* A person who has hypochondria. —*adj.* Relating to hypochondria.

hy·poc·ri·sy (hĭ pŏk′rĭ sē) *n.* [U] The practice of showing or expressing feelings, beliefs, or virtues that one does not actually hold or possess: *If you criticize government, but you never vote, that's hypocrisy.*

hyp·o·crite (hĭp′ə krĭt′) *n.* A person who practices hypocrisy. —**hyp′o·crit′i·cal** *adj.* —**hyp′o·crit′i·cal·ly** *adv.*

hy·po·der·mic (hī′pə dûr′mĭk) *adj.* Injected or used to inject beneath the skin: *a hypodermic needle.* —*n.* A needle used to give such an injection.

hy·po·gly·ce·mi·a (hī′pō glī sē′mē ə) *n.* [U] An abnormally low level of sugar in the blood.

hy·pot·e·nuse (hī pŏt′n ōōs′) *n.* The side of a right triangle opposite the right angle.

hy·po·thal·a·mus (hī′pō thăl′ə məs) *n.* The region of the brain that controls temperature, hunger, and thirst and produces hormones.

hypotenuse

hy·poth·e·sis (hī pŏth′ĭ sĭs) *n., pl.* **hy·poth·e·ses** (hī pŏth′ĭ sēz′). A statement that appears to explain a set of facts; a theory: *If a hypothesis is proved true, it becomes an accepted fact.*

hy·poth·e·size (hī pŏth′ĭ sīz′) *intr.v.* **hy·poth·e·sized, hy·poth·e·siz·ing, hy·poth·e·siz·es.** To make a hypothesis: *Scientists hypothesize that there may be water on other planets.*

hy·po·thet·i·cal (hī′pə thĕt′ĭ kəl) also **hy·po·thet·ic** (hī′pə thĕt′ĭk) *adj.* Relating to or based on a hypothesis; theoretical: *The lawyer made up a hypothetical case to prove a point.* —**hy′po·thet′i·cal·ly** *adv.*

hys·ter·ec·to·my (hĭs′tə rĕk′tə mē) *n., pl.* **hys·ter·ec·to·mies.** Surgical removal of the uterus.

hys·ter·i·a (hĭ stĕr′ē ə *or* hĭ stîr′ē ə) *n.* [U] **1.** A mental disorder in which physical symptoms as extreme as blindness or partial paralysis can occur without physical cause. **2.** Uncontrollable excitement or emotion: *The crowd went into hysteria when the star arrived.*

hys·ter·ic (hĭ stĕr′ĭk) *n.* **1.** A person who suffers from hysteria. **2. hysterics.** *(used with a singular or plural verb).* Uncontrollable laughing or crying.

hys·ter·i·cal (hĭ stĕr′ĭ kəl) *adj.* **1.** Resulting from hysteria: *hysterical paralysis.* **2.** Having or subject to hysterics: *a screaming and hysterical child.* **3.** *Informal.* Extremely funny: *She told a hysterical story.* —**hys·ter′i·cal·ly** *adv.*

Hz *abbr.* An abbreviation of hertz.

ă–cat; ā–pay; âr–care; ä–father; ĕ–get; ē–be; ĭ–sit; ī–nice; îr–here; ŏ–got; ō–go; ô–saw; oi–boy; ou–out; ōō–took; ōō–boot; ŭ–cut; ûr–word; th–thin; *th*–this; hw–when; zh–vision; ə–about; ɴ–French bon

I i

i or **I** (ī) *n.*, *pl.* **i's** or **I's**. **1.** The ninth letter of the English alphabet.

I¹ (ī) *pron.* The person who is speaking or writing. — SEE NOTE at **me.**

HOMONYMS: **I**, **aye** (yes), **eye** (organ of sight).

I² **1.** The symbol for the element **iodine** (sense 1). **2.** Also **i.** The Roman numeral for 1.

IA *abbr.* An abbreviation of Iowa.

—ian *suff.* A suffix that means: **1.** Relating to or resembling: *Bostonian.* **2.** One relating to, belonging to, or resembling: *pediatrician.*

—ible *suff.* Variant of **—able.**

—ic *suff.* A suffix that means relating to or characterized by: *allergic; atomic.*

ice (īs) *n.* **1.** [U] Water frozen solid: *Put some ice in the lemonade.* **2.** [C] A dessert consisting of sweetened and flavored crushed ice: *We ate lemon and raspberry ices.* —*v.* **iced,** **ic•ing, ic•es.** —*tr.* **1.** To coat or cover (sthg.) with ice; freeze: *Sleet iced the road.* **2.** To chill (sthg.) with ice: *After catching the fish, we iced them.* **3.** To decorate (a cake or cookies) with icing. ♦ **ice over** or **up.** *intr.v.* To turn into or become covered or blocked with ice; freeze: *The river iced over during the cold spell. Drive carefully; it's really icing up out there.*

ice•berg (īs'bûrg') *n.* A massive body of floating ice that has broken away from a glacier.

ice•break•er (īs'brā'kər) *n.* **1.** A powerful ship built for breaking a path through ice. **2.** An activity used to overcome shyness or strangeness: *Dancing is often an icebreaker at a party.*

ice•cap (īs'kăp') *n.* A glacier covering a large area: *the polar icecaps.*

ice chest *n.* An insulated boxlike container into which ice is put to cool and preserve food.

ice cream *n.* [C; U] A smooth sweet frozen food made of a mixture of milk or cream and flavoring: *vanilla and strawberry ice cream.*

ice-cream cone (īs'krēm') *n.* **1.** An edible cone-shaped wafer used to hold ice cream. **2.** One of these wafers with ice cream in it.

ice hockey *n.* [U] A game played on ice in which two teams of skaters use curved sticks to try to drive a small, round disk into the goal of the opposing team.

ice pick *n.* A hand tool with a sharp point, used for chipping or breaking ice.

ice skate *n.* A boot with a metal blade attached to the sole, used for skating on ice.

ice-skate (īs'skāt') *intr.v.* **ice-skat•ed, ice-skat•ing, ice-skates.** To skate on ice with ice skates. —**ice skater** *n.*

i•ci•cle (ī'sĭ kəl) *n.* A thin, pointed hanging piece of ice that is formed by the freezing of dripping or falling water.

ic•ing (ī'sĭng) *n.* [U] A sweet covering used to decorate cakes or cookies; frosting.

i•con (ī'kŏn') *n.* **1.** A small image on a computer screen that the user selects for a function: *Click on the printer icon.* **2.** A well-known person or thing that represents an idea or a philosophy: *The Beatles are rock icons.* **3.** A religious image in the Eastern Orthodox Church.

—ics *suff.* A suffix that means: **1.** Art, science, or field of study: *graphics; mathematics.* **2.** Activities, actions, or practices of: *athletics; ceramics.*

ic•y (ī'sē) *adj.* **ic•i•er, ic•i•est. 1.** Containing or covered with ice; frozen: *an icy sidewalk.* **2.** Very cold: *icy waters.* See Synonyms at **cold. 3.** Unfriendly: *an icy stare.* —**i'ci•ly** *adv.* —**i'ci•ness** *n.* [U]

ID *abbr.* An abbreviation of: **1.** Idaho. **2.** Also **I.D.** Identification.

I'd (īd). Contraction of *I had, I would,* or *I should.*

i•de•a (ī dē'ə) *n.* **1.** A product of mental activity, such as a thought, opinion, belief, or fantasy: *She developed her idea for the project when she was in college.* **2.** A plan, scheme, or method: *My idea is to travel to Japan this summer.* **3.** The point or purpose of sthg.: *The idea of the essay is to get people concerned about pollution.*

SYNONYMS: **idea, thought, notion, concept.** These nouns mean sthg. formed or represented in the mind, a product of mental activity. **Idea** is the most general: *Writers sometimes have many ideas before they begin work.* **Thought** can mean an idea produced by contemplation and reason as opposed, for example, to emotion: *The thoughts of great philosophers are worth our attention.* **Notion** means a vague or general idea: *My grandparents have a notion to travel someday.* **Concept** means an idea on a large scale: *He seems to have an very different concept of time.*

i•de•al (ī dē'əl *or* ī dēl') *n.* **1.** A standard of perfection: *Equality and justice are two of our society's ideals.* **2.** A person or thing that is regarded as an example of excellence or perfection: *She remains the ideal among mathematics teachers.* —*adj.* **1.** Perfect or the best possible: *The hot summer sun made this an ideal day for swimming.* **2.** Existing only in the mind; imaginary: *ideal love.*

i•de•al•ism (ī dē′ə lĭz′ əm) *n.* [U] The practice of or belief in living according to personal standards: *His idealism lessened as he grew older.* —**i•de′al•ist** *n.* —**i•de′al•is′tic** (ī dē′-ə lĭs′tĭk) *adj.* —**i′de•al•is′ti•cal•ly** *adv.*

i•de•al•ize (ī dē′ə līz′) *tr.v.* **i•de•al•ized, i•de•al•iz•ing, i•de•al•iz•es.** To regard (sbdy./sthg.) as ideal or perfect: *Sometimes we idealize our friends so much that we do not see their faults.* —**i•de′al•i•za′tion** (ī dē′ə lĭ zā′shən) *n.* [U]

i•de•al•ized (ī dē′ə līzd′) *adj.* Made to seem or thought to be perfect or better: *an idealized portrayal of the family.*

i•de•al•ly (ī dē′ə lē) *adv.* **1.** In agreement with an ideal; perfectly: *The two friends were ideally suited to each other.* **2.** In theory or imagination: *Ideally, each room should have a VCR.*

i•den•ti•cal (ī děn′tĭ kəl) *adj.* **1.** Exactly equal and alike: *identical twins.* **2.** The very same: *The mayor used those identical words in his speech.* —**i•den′ti•cal•ly** *adv.*

i•den•ti•fi•ca•tion (ī děn′tə fĭ kā′shən) *n.* [U] **1.** The act of identifying (sbdy./sthg.) or the condition of being identified: *identification of a new species of insect.* **2.** Evidence of a person's identity: *A driver's license is the most common form of personal identification.*

i•den•ti•fy (ī děn′tə fī′) *v.* **i•den•ti•fied, i•den•ti•fy•ing, i•den•ti•fies.** —*tr.* **1.** To establish or recognize (sbdy./sthg.) as a certain person or thing: *We identified the bird as an eagle.* **2.** [*with*] To associate or connect (sbdy./sthg.) closely: *That economist is identified with conservative political groups.* —*intr.* [*with*] To be or feel closely associated with a person or thing: *He identifies strongly with his grandfather.* —**i•den′ti•fi′a•ble** *adj.*

i•den•ti•ty (ī děn′tĭ tē) *n., pl.* **i•den•ti•ties.** [C; U] Who or what a person or thing is: *The police tried to establish the suspect's identity.*

i•de•ol•o•gy (ī′dē ŏl′ə jē *or* ĭd′ē ŏl′ə jē) *n., pl.* **i•de•ol•o•gies.** [C; U] A set of ideas or beliefs that are shared by members of a group, such as a political party or social class: *communist ideology.* —**i′de•o•log′i•cal** (ī′dē ə lŏj′ĭ kəl *or* ĭd′ē ə lŏj′ĭ kəl) *adj.* —**i′de•o•log′i•cal•ly** *adv.*

id•i•o•cy (ĭd′ē ə sē) *n., pl.* **id•i•o•cies.** **1.** [U] Great foolishness or stupidity: *Playing soccer with an injured knee is idiocy.* **2.** [C] A foolish or stupid action or remark: *We're tired of your idiocies.*

id•i•om (ĭd′ē əm) *n.* A phrase or expression with a special meaning that cannot be understood from the individual meanings of its words. *Fly off the handle is an idiom that means lose one's temper.* —**id′i•o•mat′ic** (ĭd′ē ə măt′ĭk) *adj.*

id•i•o•syn•cra•sy (ĭd′ē ō sĭng′krə sē) *n., pl.* **id•i•o•syn•cra•sies.** A way of acting or thinking that is peculiar to an individual: *One of my cousin's idiosyncrasies is always taking an umbrella when going out.* —**id′i•o•syn•crat′ic** (ĭd′ē ō sĭn krăt′ĭk) *adj.* —**id′i•o•syn•crat′i•cal•ly** *adv.*

id•i•ot (ĭd′ē ət) *n.* A very foolish or stupid person: *They were idiots for not letting us help them.* —**id′i•ot′ic** (ĭd′ē ŏt′ĭk) *adj.* —**id′i•ot′i•cal•ly** *adv.*

i•dle (īd′l) *adj.* **i•dler, i•dlest.** **1.** Not employed or busy: *idle employees; idle machines; idle time on the holiday.* **2.** Worthless, useless, or untrue: *idle talk.* —*v.* **i•dled, i•dling, i•dles.** —*intr.* To run at a low speed or in neutral gear: *The car's engine idled smoothly.* —*tr.* To cause (sbdy./sthg.) to be unemployed or inactive: *The drivers' strike idled every bus in the city.* ◆ **idle away.** *tr.v.* [sep.] To pass (time) without working or in order to avoid work: *I idled the afternoon away without touching my homework.* —**i′dle•ness** *n.* [U] —**i′dly** *adv.*

HOMONYMS: idle, idol (image).

i•dol (īd′l) *n.* **1.** An image or object that is worshiped as a god. **2.** A person or thing adored or greatly admired, often to an excessive degree: *That actress is my idol—I want to be just like her!*

i•dol•ize (īd′l īz′) *tr.v.* **i•dol•ized, i•dol•iz•ing, i•dol•iz•es.** **1.** To regard (sbdy.) with unthinking admiration or devotion: *Many fans idolize their favorite performers.* **2.** To worship or treat (sbdy./sthg.) as an idol: *Early Egyptians idolized cats.* See Synonyms at **revere.**

i•dyl•lic (ī dĭl′ĭk) *adj.* Charming and peaceful: *idyllic countryside; an idyllic moment.* —**i•dyl′li•cal•ly** *adv.*

i.e. *abbr.* An abbreviation of id est (that is).

—**ie** *suff.* Variant of —**y³.**

if (ĭf) *conj.* **1.** In the event that; supposing that: *If it rains, we won't take a walk.* **2.** On condition that: *I'll go only if you do.* **3.** Whether: *I asked if they were coming.* **4.** Indicating a strong wish: *If only they had come sooner!*

if•fy (ĭf′ē) *adj.* **if•fi•er, if•fi•est.** *Informal.* Doubtful; uncertain: *Our experiment produced some iffy results.*

—**ify** *suff.* Variant of —**fy.**

ig•loo (ĭg′lōō) *n., pl.* **ig•loos.** An Eskimo dwelling, especially a dome-shaped house built of blocks of packed snow.

ig·nite (ĭg nīt′) v. **ig·nit·ed, ig·nit·ing, ig·nites.** —tr. To cause (sthg.) to start burning: A lightning bolt ignited the forest fire. —intr. To begin to burn; catch fire: Wet logs do not ignite easily.

ig·ni·tion (ĭg nĭsh′ən) n. **1.** [U] The act or process of igniting a substance. **2.** [C] (usually singular). A switch that activates an electrical system that starts an internal-combustion engine: Pump the gas pedal and turn the ignition.

ig·no·min·i·ous (ĭg′nə mĭn′ē əs) adj. **1.** Characterized by shame or embarrassment; humiliating: The candidate suffered an ignominious defeat at the polls. **2.** Deserving disgrace or shame; despicable: an ignominious crime.

ig·no·rance (ĭg′nər əns) n. [U] The condition of being ignorant; lack of knowledge: Ignorance of the law is no excuse for committing a crime.

ig·no·rant (ĭg′nər ənt) adj. **1.** Lacking education or knowledge: Many pioneers were ignorant of the hardships they were to face. **2.** Showing or arising from a lack of knowledge; rude: an ignorant mistake. —**ig′no·rant·ly** adv.

ig·nore (ĭg nôr′) tr.v. **ig·nored, ig·noring, ig·nores.** To pay no attention to (sbdy./sthg.); disregard: I ignored the sound of the television in the next room.

i·gua·na (ĭ gwä′nə) n. A large tropical American lizard with a ridge of spines along the back.

IL abbr. An abbreviation of Illinois.

il— pref. Variant of in—¹ or in—².

ilk (ĭlk) n. [U] Type or kind; sort; class: Flies, mosquitoes, and other insects of that ilk can be annoying.

ill (ĭl) adj. **worse** (wûrs), **worst** (wûrst). **1** Not healthy; sick: be ill with a cold. **2.** Not normal; unsound: ill health. **3.** Bad, harmful, or destructive: ill feeling between rivals. —adv. **worse, worst.** In a sickly or unsound manner; unwell: I feel ill. —n. Formal. **1.** [U] Evil; wrongdoing: the choice between doing good or doing ill. **2.** [C] A misfortune; an affliction: the ills of living in an overcrowded city. **3.** [U] Unfavorable or unkind words: Do not speak ill of him. ◆ **ill afford.** To be able to do sthg. only with difficulty: We can ill afford another mistake. **ill at ease.** Uncomfortable or embarrassed: He is ill at ease when he has to speak in public. **fall ill** or **be taken ill.** To become ill: We fell ill after eating undercooked meat.

Ill. abbr. An abbreviation of Illinois.

I'll (īl). Contraction of I will or I shall.

ill-ad·vised (ĭl′əd vīzd′) adj. Done with bad advice or with insufficient thinking: an ill-advised trip across country.

il·le·gal (ĭ lē′gəl) adj. **1.** Against the law; not legal: Selling heroin is illegal. **2.** Against the official rules, as of a game: Pushing is illegal in soccer. —**il′le·gal′i·ty** (ĭl′ē gǎl′ĭ tē) n. [C; U] —**il·le′gal·ly** adv.

il·leg·i·ble (ĭ lĕj′ə bəl) adj. Impossible or very difficult to read: an illegible note. —**il·leg′i·bil′i·ty** (ĭ lĕj′ə bĭl′ə tē) n. [U] —**il·leg′i·bly** adv.

il·le·git·i·mate (ĭl′ĭ jĭt′ə mĭt) adj. **1.** Born of parents who are not married to each other. **2.** Against the law; illegal: an illegitimate seizure of property. —**il′le·git′i·ma·cy** (ĭl′ĭ jĭt′ə mə sē) n. [U] —**il′le·git′i·mate·ly** adv.

ill-e·quipped (ĭl′ĭ kwĭpt′) adj. Lacking the skills or ability to do sthg.: He's ill-equipped for managing so many people.

ill-fat·ed (ĭl′fā′tĭd) adj. **1.** Destined for misfortune; doomed: The ill-fated ship never reached port. **2.** Marked by or causing misfortune; unlucky: an ill-fated decision to leave.

il·lic·it (ĭ lĭs′ĭt) adj. Not permitted by law; unlawful: an illicit affair. —**il·lic′it·ly** adv. —**il·lic′it·ness** n. [U]

il·lit·er·ate (ĭ lĭt′ər ĭt) adj. **1.** Unable to read and write: In earlier generations, education was rare, and most people were illiterate. **2.** Showing a lack of knowledge in a certain subject: illiterate about computers. —**il·lit·er·a·cy** (ĭ lĭt′ər ə sē) n. [U]

ill-man·nered (ĭl′mǎn′ərd) adj. Showing a lack of good manners; impolite; rude: The ill-mannered man cut into line without asking.

ill-na·tured (ĭl′nā′chərd) adj. Disagreeable or mean: My ill-natured neighbor often scolds the neighborhood children. —**ill′-na′tured·ly** adv.

ill·ness (ĭl′nĭs) n. [C; U] **1.** An unhealthy condition; poor health: Her son often misses school because of illness. **2.** A disease: AIDS is a fatal illness.

il·log·i·cal (ĭ lŏj′ĭ kəl) adj. Having or showing a lack of sound reasoning; not logical: Your argument is illogical. —**il·log′i·cal·ly** adv.

ill-tem·pered (ĭl′tĕm′pərd) adj. Having a bad temper; irritable: The man felt ill-tempered after a hard day at work. —**ill′-tem′pered·ly** adv.

ill-timed (ĭl′tīmd′) adj. Done or happening at the wrong time; untimely: The party was ill-timed; it was the night before the math test.

ill-treat (ĭl′trēt′) tr.v. To treat (sbdy./sthg.) badly or cruelly; mistreat: You should not ill-treat your books; they must last all year. —**ill′-treat′ment** n. [U]

il·lu·mi·nate (ĭ lōō′mə nāt′) tr.v. **il·lu·mi·nat·ed, il·lu·mi·nat·ing, il·lu·mi·nates. 1.** To provide (sbdy./sthg.) with light: A lamp illuminated the steps. **2.** To make (sthg.) clear; explain: *The film illuminated the events leading up to the war.* —il•lu′mi•na′tion *n.* [U]

il•lu•sion (ĭ lōō′zhən) *n.* **1.** An unreal or misleading appearance: *The painting gives the illusion that we are really looking out to sea.* **2.** An idea or a belief that is mistaken: *His illusion that he did not need to study for tests did not last long.* —il•lu′sive *adj.*

il•lus•trate (ĭl′ə strāt′ *or* ĭ lŭs′trāt′) *tr.v.* il•lus•trat•ed, il•lus•trat•ing, il•lus•trates. **1.** To make (sthg.) clear or explain, as by using examples or comparisons: *The teacher illustrated how the earth circles the sun by using a model.* **2.** To provide (sthg.) with pictures or diagrams that explain or decorate: *The artist illustrated the story.* —il′lus•tra′tor *n.*

il•lus•tra•tion (ĭl′ə strā′shən) *n.* **1.** Something, such as a picture, diagram, or chart, that explains or decorates sthg. else: *The illustrations improve the book.* **2.** Something serving as an example or a proof: *A ball falling is an illustration of gravity.* —il•lus′tra•tive (ĭ lŭs′trə tĭv *or* ĭl′ə strā′tĭv) *adj.*

il•lus•tri•ous (ĭ lŭs′trē əs) *adj.* Famous: *an illustrious author.* See Synonyms at **noted.**

ill will *n.* [U] Unfriendly feeling; hostility: *Ever since our fight I've felt nothing but ill will for him.*

im— *pref.* Variant of in—¹ or in—².

I'm (īm). Contraction of *I am.*

im•age (ĭm′ĭj) *n.* **1.** A representation of sbdy./sthg., especially a picture, photograph, or statue. **2.** A mental picture of sthg. not real or present: *We had an image of what our new teacher would look like.* **3.** *(usually plural).* A vivid description in words, especially a metaphor or simile: *The poem is full of images of country life.* **4.** The concept of a person or thing that is held by the public, especially as a result of advertising or publicity: *The toy company has a friendly image.*

im•age•ry (ĭm′ĭj rē) *n.* [U] Vivid descriptions in writing or speaking.

i•mag•i•na•ble (ĭ măj′ə nə bəl) *adj.* Capable of being imagined: *a book that has information on every imaginable topic.* —i•mag′i•na•bly *adv.*

i•mag•i•nar•y (ĭ măj′ə nĕr′ē) *adj.* Existing only in the imagination; not real: *an imaginary illness.*

i•mag•i•na•tion (ĭ măj′ə nā′shən) *n.* [C; U] **1.** The act of forming or ability to form mental images of sthg. that is not real or present: *Children have a lot of imagination.* **2.** The ability to use the mind effectively; creativity: *We solved the city's budget problems with imagination.*

i•mag•i•na•tive (ĭ măj′ə nə tĭv *or* ĭ măj′ə-nā′tĭv) *adj.* **1.** Having a strong imagination, especially creative imagination: *an imaginative person.* **2.** Marked by originality and creativity: *an imaginative solution to a problem.* —i•mag′i•na•tive•ly *adv.*

i•mag•ine (ĭ măj′ĭn) *v.* i•mag•ined, i•mag•in•ing, i•mag•ines. —*tr.* **1.** To form a mental picture of (sbdy./sthg.): *Can you imagine what it is like to live in a rain forest?* **2.** To make a guess at (sthg.); suppose: *I imagine this bad weather will make them late.* —*intr.* To use the imagination: *The mind is able to think, remember, and imagine.*

i•mam also I•mam (ĭ mäm′) *n.* **1.** A male prayer leader in a mosque. **2.** A male Muslim leader.

im•bal•ance (ĭm băl′əns) *n.* A lack of balance.

im•be•cile (ĭm′bə sĭl) *n.* An insulting term for a person thought to be stupid or foolish.

im•bibe (ĭm bīb′) *tr. & intr.v.* im•bibed, im•bib•ing, im•bibes. To drink, especially alcoholic beverages: *I imbibe more than my share of lemonade on these hot summer days. He has been imbibing again.*

im•i•tate (ĭm′ĭ tāt′) *tr.v.* im•i•tat•ed, im•i•tat•ing, im•i•tates. **1.** To follow (sbdy./sthg.) as a model or an example: *Your little brother imitates you because he likes you.* **2.** To copy the speech or actions of (sbdy.); mimic: *The actor imitated the President perfectly.* —im′i•ta′tor *n.*

SYNONYMS: imitate, copy, mimic, simulate. These verbs mean to follow sbdy./sthg. as a model. **Imitate** means to act like another: *Can you imitate a British accent?* **Copy** means to duplicate an original as closely as possible: *If you were absent, copy the notes from a classmate.* **Mimic** often means to imitate in order to make fun of a person or thing: *The class clown mimicked the teacher in our play about school.* **Simulate** means to falsely take on the appearance or character of sthg.: *They painted the wall to simulate marble.*

---

im•i•ta•tion (ĭm′ĭ tā′shən) *n.* [C; U] **1.** The act or an instance of imitating: *I learned the song through imitation.* **2.** Something made to look like sthg. else; a copy: *This is an imitation of the painting.* —*adj.* Made to look like another thing: *imitation leather.*

im•mac•u•late (ĭ măk′yə lĭt) *adj.* **1.** Perfectly clean: *the doctor's immaculate white coat.* See Synonyms at **clean. 2.** Free from fault or error; flawless: *an immaculate record as governor.* —im•mac′u•late•ly *adv.* —im•mac′u•late•ness *n.* [U]

im•ma•te•ri•al (ĭm′ə tîr′ē əl) *adj.* Of no importance: *After losing the tickets, it became immaterial what we decided to do.*

ă–cat; ā–pay; âr–care; ä–father; ĕ–get; ē–be; ĭ–sit; ī–nice; îr–here; ŏ–got; ō–go; ô–saw; oi–boy; ou–out; ōō–took; ōō–boot; ŭ–cut; ûr–word; th–thin; *th*–this; hw–when; zh–vision; ə–about; N–French bon

im·ma·ture (ĭm′ə tŏŏr′ *or* ĭm′ə chŏŏr′) *adj.* Not fully grown or developed; not mature: *immature corn; immature behavior.* —**im′ma·ture′ly** *adv.* —**im′ma·tur′i·ty** *n.* [U]

im·meas·ur·a·ble (ĭ mĕzh′ər ə bəl) *adj.* Impossible to measure: *the immeasurable number of stars in the sky.* —**im·meas′ur·a·bly** *adv.*

im·me·di·ate (ĭ mē′dē ĭt) *adj.* **1.** Taking place at once or very soon: *needing immediate medical care in an emergency room.* **2.** Close at hand; near: *our immediate surroundings.* ◆ **immediate family.** One's parents, spouse, children, and brothers and sisters: *The invitation was for the immediate family only.* —**im·me′di·ate·ly** *adv.* —**im·me′di·ate·ness** *n.* [U]

im·mense (ĭ mĕns′) *adj.* Of great size, extent, or degree; huge: *immense rocks; an immense length of time.* —**im·mense′ly** *adv.* —**im·men′si·ty** *n.* [U]

im·merse (ĭ mûrs′) *tr.v.* **im·mersed, im·mers·ing, im·mers·es. 1.** To cover (sbdy./sthg.) completely with a liquid; submerge: *immerse pots and pans in soapy water.* **2.** To involve (sbdy., especially oneself) deeply; absorb: *I immersed myself in the exciting story.* —**im·mer′sion** (ĭ mûr′zhən *or* ĭ mûr′shən) *n.* [U]

im·mi·grant (ĭm′ĭ grənt) *n.* A person who leaves one country and settles in another: *a nation of immigrants.*

im·mi·grate (ĭm′ĭ grāt′) *intr.v.* **im·mi·grat·ed, im·mi·grat·ing, im·mi·grates** To come into a foreign country to live: *People from many parts of the world immigrate to the United States each year.* —**im′mi·gra′tion** *n.* [U] —SEE NOTE at **emigrate.**

im·mi·nent (ĭm′ə nənt) *adj.* About to happen: *It is cold and windy, and snow seems imminent.* —**im′mi·nence** *n.* [U] —**im′m·nent·ly** *adv.*

im·mo·bile (ĭ mō′bəl) *adj.* Not moving or not able to be moved: *The deer stood immobile in the field.* —**im′mo·bil′i·ty** (ĭm′ō-bĭl′ĭ tē) *n.* [U]

im·mo·bi·lize (ĭ mō′bə līz′) *tr.v.* **im·mo·bi·lized, im·mo·bi·liz·ing, im·mo·bi·liz·es.** To make (sthg.) immobile or incapable of moving: *The doctor immobilized my broken finger with a splint.* —**im·mo′bi·li·za′tion** (ĭ mō′bə lĭ zā′shən) *n.* [U]

im·mor·al (ĭ môr′əl *or* ĭ mŏr′əl) *adj.* Contrary to what is considered moral: *immoral behavior.* —**im′mor·al′i·ty** (ĭm′-ô răl′ĭ tē *or* ĭm′ə ral′ĭ tē) *n.* [U] —**im·mor′al·ly** *adv.*

im·mor·tal (ĭ môr′tl) *adj.* **1.** Never dying; living forever: *The Greek gods were believed to be immortal.* **2.** Having eternal fame: *the immortal words of Shakespeare.* —*n.* **1.** An

immortal being: *The ancient Greeks believed their gods were immortals.* **2.** A person with enduring fame: *Mozart and Beethoven are immortals in the field of music.* —**im′mor·tal′i·ty** (ĭm′ôr tăl′ĭ tē) *n.* [U] —**im·mor′tal·ize** *v.* —**im·mor′tal·ly** *adv.*

im·mov·a·ble (ĭ mŏŏ′və bəl) *adj.* Not capable of moving or of being moved: *Mountains are immovable objects.*

im·mune (ĭ myoōn′) *adj.* **1.** Protected from disease naturally or by vaccination: *I'm immune to chickenpox because I had it when I was young.* **2.** Protected; guarded; safe: *The fort made the harbor immune from attack.*

im·mu·ni·ty (ĭ myoō′nĭ tē) *n.* [U] **1.** The ability of an animal or a plant to resist disease. **2.** Freedom from certain duties, penalties, or restrictions: *Diplomatic immunity protects ambassadors from being prosecuted for most crimes.*

im·mu·nize (ĭm′yə nīz′) *tr.v.* **im·mu·nized, im·mu·niz·ing, im·mu·niz·es.** To produce immunity in (sbdy.), as by vaccination. —**im′mu·ni·za′tion** (ĭm′yə nĭ zā′shən) *n.* [C; U]

im·mu·ta·ble (ĭ myoō′tə bəl) *adj.* Not subject to change; unchangeable: *nature's immutable laws.*

imp (ĭmp) *n.* A mischievous child: *That little imp took a handful of candy!*

im·pact (ĭm′păkt′) *n.* **1.** The action of one object striking another; collision: *the impact of the cars.* **2.** The effect of sthg.: *the impact of science on modern society.* —*tr.v. Informal.* To have an effect on (sthg.): *The rain impacted our plans for a picnic.*

im·pair (ĭm pâr′) *tr.v.* To diminish (sthg.) in strength, quantity, or quality: *An ear infection impaired my hearing for a week.* —**im·pair′ment** *n.* [C; U]

im·paired (ĭm pârd′) *adj.* Less good or strong; damaged: *Drinking too much causes impaired reflexes.*

im·pale (ĭm pāl′) *tr.v.* **im·paled, im·pal·ing, im·pales.** To pierce (sbdy./sthg.) with a sharp stake or point: *That poor victim had been impaled by the pole.*

im·part (ĭm pärt′) *tr.v. Formal.* **1.** To give a quality to (sthg.): *Bright sunlight imparted a cheerful feeling to the room.* **2.** To make (sthg.) known; reveal: *impart a secret.*

im·par·tial (ĭm pär′shəl) *adj.* Not favoring either side; unprejudiced: *Sports officials must be impartial in their judgments.* —**im′par·ti·al′i·ty** (ĭm′ pär shē ăl′ĭ tē) *n.* [U] —**im·par′tial·ly** *adv.*

im·pass·a·ble (ĭm păs′ə bəl) *adj.* Impossible to travel across or over; not passable: *The flood made the road impassable.*

im·passe (ĭm′păs′) *n.* A difficult situation that has no practical solution: *When members could not agree, the committee reached an impasse.*

im•pas•sioned (ĭm păsh′ənd) *adj.* Filled with intense feeling: *an impassioned plea for human rights.*

im•pas•sive (ĭm păs′ĭv) *adj.* Feeling or showing no emotion; calm: *The judge was impassive through all the lawyer's dramatic arguments.* —**im•pas′sive•ly** *adv.* —**im•pas′sive•ness** *n.* [U]

im•pa•tient (ĭm pā′shənt) *adj.* **1.** Unable to wait patiently: *When the line for tickets did not move, she grew impatient and left.* **2.** Expressing or produced by impatience: *an impatient answer.* —**im•pa′tience** *n.* [U] —**im•pa′tient•ly** *adv.*

im•peach (ĭm pēch′) *tr.v.* **1.** To charge (a public official) formally with misconduct in office: *The President of the United States can be impeached only by Congress.* **2.** To challenge or discredit (sbdy./sthg.); attack: *Scientists impeached the accuracy of the report.* —**im•peach′ment** *n.* [U]

im•pec•ca•ble (ĭm pĕk′ə bəl) *adj.* Having no flaws; faultless: *She has impeccable table manners.* See Synonyms at **perfect.** —**im•pec′ca•bly** *adv.*

im•pede (ĭm pēd′) *tr.v.* **im•ped•ed, im•ped•ing, im•pedes.** To obstruct or slow (sbdy./sthg.) down; hinder: *Road repairs impeded traffic all summer.*

im•ped•i•ment (ĭm pĕd′ə mənt) *n.* **1.** Something that impedes or slows progress: *Youth is no impediment to success in sports and music.* **2.** A physical defect that prevents clear speech: *A lisp is a speech impediment.*

im•pel (ĭm pĕl′) *tr.v.* **im•pelled, im•pel•ling, im•pels.** To urge (sbdy.) to action; drive: *Their curiosity impelled them to investigate the noise.*

im•pend•ing (ĭm pĕn′dĭng) *adj.* About to happen: *her impending retirement.*

im•pen•e•tra•ble (ĭm pĕn′ĭ trə bəl) *adj.* **1.** Impossible to penetrate or enter: *an impenetrable jungle.* **2.** Impossible to understand; incomprehensible: *an impenetrable mystery.*

im•per•a•tive (ĭm pĕr′ə tĭv) *adj.* **1.** In grammar, relating to the mood of a verb that expresses a command, an order, or a request. *Do* in *Please do it!* and *go* in *Go at once!* are in the imperative mood. **2.** Unavoidable; urgent: *It is imperative that we arrive on time.* —*n.* **1.** [C; U] In grammar, the imperative mood or a verb form in this mood. In the sentence *Please do it,* the word *do* is an imperative. **2.** [C] A command; an order: *The boss's suggestions are really imperatives.*

im•per•cep•ti•ble (ĭm′pər sĕp′tə bəl) *adj.* Impossible or difficult to perceive or feel: *the ant's imperceptible movement through the grass.* —**im′per•cep′ti•bly** *adv.*

im•per•fect (ĭm pûr′fĭkt) *adj.* **1.** Not perfect; having faults or defects. **2.** Relating to the imperfect tense. —*n.* **1.** [C; U] The imperfect tense. **2.** [C] A verb in the imperfect tense. —**im•per•fec′tion** (ĭm′pər fĕk′shən) *n.* [C; U] —**im•per′fect•ly** *adv.*

im•pe•ri•al (ĭm pîr′ē əl) *adj.* Relating to an empire, emperor, or empress: *the days of imperial China; the imperial court.* —**im•pe′ri•al•ly** *adv.*

im•pe•ri•al•ism (ĭm pîr′ē ə lĭz′əm) *n.* [U] The policy of increasing a nation's authority by acquiring territories or by establishing economic and political dominance over other nations. —**im•pe′ri•al•ist** *n.* —**im•pe′ri•al•is′tic** *adj.* —**im•pe′ri•al•is′ti•cal•ly** *adv.*

im•per•il (ĭm pĕr′əl) *tr.v. Formal.* To put (sbdy./sthg.) into peril; endanger: *Pollution imperils the fish in the sea.*

im•pe•ri•ous (ĭm pîr′ē əs) *adj.* Overly proud; arrogant; domineering: *The boss's imperious treatment of the workers caused many to quit.* —**im•pe′ri•ous•ly** *adv.* —**im•pe′ri•ous•ness** *n.* [U]

im•per•son•al (ĭm pûr′sə nəl) *adj.* **1.** Not referring to or intended for any particular person: *The speaker's remarks were general and impersonal.* **2.** Showing no emotion; impassive: *a cold and impersonal manner.* **3.** Having no subject or having the indefinite *it* as subject. For example, in the construction *It is snowing, snow* is an impersonal verb. —**im•per′son•al•ly** *adv.*

im•per•son•ate (ĭm pûr′sə nāt′) *tr.v.* **im•per•son•at•ed, im•per•son•at•ing, im•per•son•ates.** To assume the character or appearance of (sbdy.): *It is illegal to impersonate a police officer.* —**im•per′son•a′tion** *n.* [C; U] —**im•per′son•a′tor** *n.*

im•per•ti•nent (ĭm pûr′tn ənt) *adj.* Offensively bold; rude: *The clerk's impertinent manner offended me.* —**im•per′ti•nence** *n.* [U] —**im•per′ti•nent•ly** *adv.*

im•per•turb•a•ble (ĭm′pər tûr′bə bəl) *adj.* Unshakably calm and collected: *The senator remained imperturbable even in the heat of the debate.* —**im′per•turb′a•bil′i•ty** (ĭm′pər tûrb′ə bĭl′ə tē) *n.* [U] —**im′per•turb′a•bly** *adv.*

im•per•vi•ous (ĭm pûr′vē əs) *adj.* **1.** Impossible to penetrate: *A good raincoat should be impervious to water.* **2.** Impossible to affect: *The jet pilot seemed impervious to fear.* —**im•per′vi•ous•ly** *adv.* —**im•per′vi•ous•ness** *n.* [U]

im•pet•u•ous (ĭm pĕch′ōō əs) *adj.* Characterized by hasty actions; impulsive: *This impetuous decision has brought disaster.* —**im•pet•u•os′i•ty** (ĭm pĕch′ōō ŏs′i tē) *n.* [U] —**im•pet′u•ous•ly** *adv.*

ă–cat; ā–pay; âr–care; ä–father; ĕ–get; ē–be; ĭ–sit; ī–nice; îr–here; ŏ–got; ō–go; ô–saw; oi–boy; ou–out; ōō–took; ōō–boot; ŭ–cut; ûr–word; th–thin; th–this; hw–when; zh–vision; ə–about; N–French bon

im·pe·tus (ĭm′pĭ təs) *n.* **1.** [U] A driving force; a cause of action: *A sense of fairness is often the impetus for reform.* **2.** [C] The force or energy of a moving body; momentum: *The impetus of the speeding train made it difficult to stop quickly.*

im·pinge (ĭm pĭnj′) *v.* **im·pinged, im·ping·ing, im·ping·es.** ◆ **impinge on** or **upon.** *tr.v.* [insep.] *Formal.* To have an effect, often a negative one, on (sthg.): *Censorship impinges on our right of free speech.* —**im·pinge′ment** *n.* [U]

imp·ish (ĭm′pĭsh) *adj.* Playful: *the child's impish grin.* —**imp′ish·ly** *adv.* —**imp′ish·ness** *n.* [U]

im·plac·a·ble (ĭm plăk′ə bəl) *adj.* Impossible to calm or satisfy: *implacable workers.* —**im·plac′a·bly** *adv.*

im·plant (ĭm plănt′) *tr.v.* **1.** To place (a tissue or a device) within the body: *Surgeons implanted a new valve in the heart.* **2.** To establish (sthg.) securely: *The parents tried to implant a strong sense of values in their children.* —*n.* (ĭm′plănt′). A tissue or device that has been surgically grafted or inserted within the body: *breast implants.* —**im′plan·ta′-tion** (ĭm′plăn tā′shən) *n.* [U]

im·plau·si·ble (ĭm plô′zə bəl) *adj.* Hard to believe; not plausible: *an implausible excuse.* —**im·plau′si·bly** *adv.*

im·ple·ment (ĭm′plə mənt) *n.* A tool or an instrument used in doing a task: *Pencils and pens are writing implements.* —*tr.v.* (ĭm′plə-mĕnt′). To put (sthg.) into effect; carry out: *We need money in order to implement your idea.* —**im′ple·men·ta′tion** (ĭm′plə mən-tā′shən) *n.* [U]

im·pli·cate (ĭm′plĭ kāt′) *tr.v.* **im·pli·cat·ed, im·pli·cat·ing, im·pli·cates.** To show (sbdy.) to be involved or connected with an activity, especially a crime: *The witness implicated several people in the crime.*

im·pli·ca·tion (ĭm′plĭ kā′shən) *n.* [C; U] **1.** Something implied; an indirect indication: *Although he did not say so directly, his implication was that the operation was a success.* **2.** The act of implying or the condition of being implied: *The writer's thoughts were conveyed more by implication than by direct statement.*

im·plic·it (ĭm plĭs′ĭt) *adj.* **1.** *Formal.* Implied or understood without being directly expressed: *The threat of a lawsuit was implicit in the lawyer's letter.* **2.** Having no doubts; unquestioning: *We have implicit trust in your judgment.* —**im·plic′it·ly** *adv.*

im·plore (ĭm plôr′) *tr.v.* **im·plored, im·plor·ing, im·plores.** *Formal.* To appeal to (sbdy.) earnestly or anxiously; beg: *The students implored the teacher to postpone the test.*

im·ply (ĭm plī′) *tr.v.* **im·plied, im·ply·ing, im·plies.** **1.** To say or express (sthg.) indirectly: *The closed door implied that they*

wanted to be left alone. *Are you implying that you don't want to go?* **2.** To involve (sthg.) as a necessary part or consequence: *Life implies growth and eventual death.* —SEE NOTE at **infer.**

im·po·lite (ĭm′pə līt′) *adj.* Not polite; discourteous: *an impolite remark.* —**im′po·lite′ly** *adv.* —**im′po·lite′ness** *n.* [U]

im·port (ĭm pôrt′ or ĭm′pôrt′) *tr.v.* To bring in (goods) from a foreign country for sale or use: *That country imports grain and exports meat.* —*n.* (ĭm′pôrt′). **1.** [C] Something imported for sale or use: *clothing imports.* **2.** [U] The act of importing; importation: *The import of fruits and vegetables is strictly regulated.* **3.** [U] *Formal.* Importance; meaning: *an event of enormous import.*

im·por·tance (ĭm pôr′tns) *n.* [U] The quality or condition of being important; significance: *the importance of good nutrition.*

im·por·tant (ĭm pôr′tnt) *adj.* **1.** Marked by or having great value, significance, or influence: *Coffee is an important crop in South America.* **2.** Having high social rank or influence; powerful: *important business leaders.* —**im·por′tant·ly** *adv.*

im·por·ta·tion (ĭm′pôr tā′shən) *n.* [U] The act of importing, especially as a business: *importation of cars and TVs from Japan.*

im·port·er (ĭm pôr′tər) *n.* A person, company, or country that imports goods: *Japan is a large importer of North American timber.*

im·pose (ĭm pōz′) *v.* **im·posed, im·pos·ing, im·pos·es.** —*tr.* **1.** To place (a burden or an obligation) on sbdy.: *impose a tax; impose a punishment.* **2.** To bring (sthg.) about by exercising authority: *The United Nations imposed peace on the warring countries.* **3.** To force (oneself) on another or others: *Our visitors have imposed themselves on us for too long.* —*intr.* To force oneself on another or others; take unfair advantage: *We don't mean to impose, but could we stay for dinner?* ◆ **impose on** or **upon.** *tr.v.* [insep.] To take advantage of (sbdy./sthg.): *The guests imposed on their hosts by asking to borrow the car.* —**im·po·si′tion** (ĭm′pə zĭsh′ən) *n.* [C; U]

im·pos·ing (ĭm pō′zĭng) *adj.* Causing awe or admiration; impressive: *The Statue of Liberty is an imposing sight.* See Synonyms at **magnificent.** —**im·pos′ing·ly** *adv.*

im·pos·si·ble (ĭm pŏs′ə bəl) *adj.* **1.** Not capable of happening or existing: *A square circle is impossible.* **2.** Not capable of being done: *an impossible task.* **3.** Difficult to tolerate: *That dog is impossible.* —**im·pos′si·bil′i·ty** *n.* [U] —**im·pos′si·bly** *adv.*

im·pos·tor (ĭm pŏs′tər) *n.* A person who deceives others by pretending to be sbdy. else: *an impostor pretending to be a doctor.*

im·po·tent (ĭm′pə tənt) *adj.* **1.** Lacking strength, power, or effectiveness: *a govern-*

ment *impotent to deal with the crisis.* **2.** Referring to a male's inability to have an erection for sexual intercourse. —**im′po·tence** *n.* [U] —**im·po′tent·ly** *adv.*

im·pound (ĭm pound′) *tr.v.* To take and hold (sthg.) in legal custody: *The police impounded the illegally parked car.*

im·pov·er·ish (ĭm pŏv′ər ĭsh) *tr.v.* **1.** To make (sbdy./sthg.) very poor: *Bad harvests impoverished the family.* **2.** To use up the natural richness, strength, or resources of (sthg.): *Overplanting had impoverished the soil.* —**im·pov′er·ish·ment** *n.* [U]

im·pov·er·ished (ĭm pŏv′ə rĭsht) *adj.* **1.** Very poor: *impoverished people.* **2.** Lacking some vital element or ability: *an impoverished view of the world.*

im·prac·ti·cal (ĭm prăk′tĭ kəl) *adj.* **1.** Unwise or foolish to do: *an impractical plan.* **2.** Unable to deal well with practical matters: *an impractical dreamer.* —**im·prac′ti·cal′i·ty** (ĭm prăk′tĭ kăl′ĭ tē) *n.* [U]

im·pre·cise (ĭm′prĭ sīs′) *adj.* Not precise or clear: *an imprecise description.* —**im′pre·cise′ly** *adv.*

im·preg·na·ble (ĭm prĕg′nə bəl) *adj.* Impossible to capture or enter by force: *an impregnable city.*

im·preg·nate (ĭm prĕg′nāt) *tr.v.* **im·preg·nat·ed, im·preg·nat·ing, im·preg·nates.** **1.** To make (a female) pregnant. **2.** To fill (sthg.) completely: *The smell of roses impregnated the whole room.* —**im′preg·na′tion** *n.* [U]

im·press (ĭm prĕs′) *tr.v.* **1.** To have a strong, often favorable effect on the mind or feelings of (sbdy.): *The worker's performance impressed the manager.* **2.** To mark or stamp (sthg.) with pressure: *impress a design on soft clay.* ◆ **impress on** or **upon.** *tr.v.* [insep.] To fix (sthg.) firmly in the mind by force or influence: *The coach impressed upon the team the importance of teamwork.*

im·pres·sion (ĭm prĕsh′ən) *n.* **1.** An effect, image, or feeling that stays in the mind: *The new worker made a good impression on everyone.* **2.** A vague memory or feeling: *I have the impression that we've met before.* **3.** A mark or an imprint made on a surface by pressure: *There was an impression left on the cushion where the dog had slept.* **4.** A humorous imitation of a person's speech and manner: *He did impressions of movie stars as part of his act.*

im·pres·sion·a·ble (ĭm prĕsh′ə nə bəl) *adj.* Easily influenced or affected; suggestible: *Young children are impressionable and will usually believe anything you tell them.* —**im·pres′sion·a·bil′i·ty** *n.* [U]

im·pres·sive (ĭm prĕs′ĭv) *adj.* Making a strong impression; commanding attention: *an impressive monument.* —**im·pres′sive·ly** *adv.*

im·print (ĭm prĭnt′) *tr.v.* **1.** To make (a mark or pattern) on a surface by pressing: *imprint a name with a rubber stamp.* **2.** To establish (sthg.) firmly, as on the mind or memory: *Memories of childhood are often deeply imprinted on our minds.* —*n.* (ĭm′prĭnt′). **1.** A mark or pattern made by pressing sthg. on a surface: *the imprints of feet in the sand.* **2.** An influence or effect; an impression: *Spanish culture has left its imprint on the Southwestern states.*

im·pris·on (ĭm prĭz′ən) *tr.v.* To put (sbdy.) in prison; confine: *The thief was imprisoned for two years.* —**im·pris′on·ment** *n.* [U]

im·prob·a·ble (ĭm prŏb′ə bəl) *adj.* Not probable; unlikely: *an improbable story.* —**im·prob′a·bly** *adv.*

im·promp·tu (ĭm prŏmp′tōō) *adj.* Spoken or done with little or no preparation: *The student gave an impromptu presentation explaining his research.*

im·prop·er (ĭm prŏp′ər) *adj.* **1.** Not meeting accepted standards; incorrect: *an improper diet.* **2.** Unsuitable: *A swamp is an improper place to build a house.* **3.** Not behaving politely: *It is improper to interrupt a speaker.* —**im·prop′er·ly** *adv.*

im·pro·pri·e·ty (ĭm′prə prī′ĭ tē) *n., pl.* **im·pro·pri·e·ties.** *Formal.* **1.** [U] The condition of being improper: *the impropriety of playing a radio in the library.* **2.** [C] An improper act or expression: *a politician accused of campaign improprieties.*

im·prove (ĭm prōōv′) *v.* **im·proved, im·prov·ing, im·proves.** —*tr.* To make (sthg.) better: *The teacher's explanation improved my understanding of algebra.* —*intr.* To become or get better: *The patient improved after receiving treatment.*

im·prove·ment (ĭm prōōv′mənt) *n.* **1.** [C] A change or an addition that improves sthg.: *A new kitchen was one of our improvements to the house.* **2.** [U] The act or process of improving: *The student's homework shows great improvement.* **3.** [C] A person or thing that is better than another: *This governor is an improvement over the previous one.*

im·pro·vise (ĭm′prə vīz′) *v.* **im·pro·vised, im·pro·vis·ing, im·pro·vis·es.** —*tr.* **1.** To perform (sthg.) without preparation: *The comedian improvised several skits.* **2.** To make (sthg.) from materials found nearby: *improvise a bridge out of fallen trees.* —*intr.* To compose or perform sthg. without preparation: *The musicians finished a song by improvising.* —**im·prov′i·sa′tion** *n.* [C; U]

im·pu·dent (ĭm′pyə dənt) *adj.* Rude and

disrespectful; insolent: *The impudent student demanded to be assigned another instructor.* —**im′pu•dence** *n.* [U] —**im′pu•dent•ly** *adv.*

im•pulse (ĭm′pŭls′) *n.* **1.** A strong motivation; a drive or an instinct: *Most animals have a natural impulse to care for their young.* **2.** A sudden wish or urge: *We had a sudden impulse to go to the movies.* **3.** A surge of electrical power in one direction.

im•pul•sive (ĭm pŭl′sĭv) *adj.* **1.** Tending to act on impulse rather than careful thought: *Impulsive shoppers buy more items than they need.* **2.** Motivated or caused by impulse: *The wealthy industrialist was given to impulsive acts of generosity.* —**im•pul′sive•ly** *adv.* —**im•pul′sive•ness** *n.* [U]

im•pu•ni•ty (ĭm pyōo′nĭ tē) *n.* [U] Freedom from punishment, harm, or injury: *Did she really expect to break the law with impunity?*

im•pure (ĭm pyōor′) *adj.* **1.** Not pure or clean; contaminated: *Polluted water is impure.* **2.** Immoral or corrupt; bad: *Many people view gambling and games of chance as impure.* —**im•pure′ly** *adv.*

im•pu•ri•ty (ĭm pyōor′ĭ tē) *n., pl.* **im•pu•ri•ties. 1.** [U] The quality or condition of being impure. **2.** [C] A substance that makes another substance impure: *The treatment plant filters all the impurities out of our water.*

in¹ (ĭn) *prep.* **1.a.** Within the limits or area of; inside: *The students are all in the classroom.* **b.** From outside to a point within; into: *couldn't get in the house.* **2.** Within the time of; after: *I will finish in an hour.* **3.** To or at the condition of: *fall in love; be in good health.* **4.** Wearing: *in a bathing suit.* **5.** Having the activity or function of: *a career in politics.* **6.** With the purpose of; for: *in aid of a friend.* **7.** Made with or through the medium of: *a note written in Spanish.* **8.** With reference to; as to: *ten feet in length.* **9.** Among; out of: *One person in five can play a musical instrument.* —*adv.* **1.** To or toward the inside: *coming in out of the rain.* **2.** To or toward a goal: *The TV camera zoomed in on the singer's face.* **3.** Within a specified or understood place, situation, or activity: *Is the doctor in? The water is cold and the children won't be in long.* **4.** So as to include: *The cook forgot to put the salt in.* —*adj.* **1.** *Informal.* Fashionable; popular: *Short haircuts are in.* **2.** Having influence or power: *He's in with the leaders of the new government.* **3.** Incoming; inward: *the in bus; the in door.* —*n.* **1.** *Informal.* A means of access or influence: *The musician has an in with the conductor.* **2.** A person having power or influence: *The ins are always at an advantage over the outs.* ◆ **be in. 1.** To be at home or the office: *I'll be in all night long.* **2.** To arrive: *The plane will be in at noon.* **be in**

for. To get or have (sthg.) for sure: *We're in for a cold winter.* **be in on.** To be aware of (sthg. secret from others): *Who's in on the plans for his surprise party?* **in that.** *Formal.* For the reason that; because: *Their arguments are unconvincing in that their reasons are so weak.* **ins and outs.** *Informal.* The details of an activity or a process: *He had to learn the ins and outs of his new job.*

HOMONYMS: in, inn (hotel).

---

in² or **in.** *abbr.* An abbreviation of inch.

IN *abbr.* An abbreviation of Indiana.

in—¹ or **il—** or **im—** or **ir—** *pref.* A prefix that means not: *inaccurate; illegible; immoral; irresponsible.*

WORD BUILDING: in—¹ The basic meaning of the prefix **in—¹** is "not." Thus **inactive** means "not active." **In—¹** is related to and sometimes confused with the prefix **un—¹**, which also means "not." In fact, sometimes **in—¹** is used interchangeably with **un—¹**, as when *incommunicative* is used instead of **uncommunicative.** Before the consonants *l* and *r*, **in—¹** becomes **il—** and **ir—** respectively: **illogical, irregular.** Before the consonants *b*, *m*, and *p*, **in—¹** becomes **im—**: **imbalanced, immeasurable, impossible.**

in—² or **il—** or **im—** or **ir—** *pref.* **1.** A prefix that means "in": *inbound; infield.* **2.** Variant of **en—.**

WORD BUILDING: in—² The basic meaning of the prefix **in—²** is "in, within, or into." For example, **inlay** means "to set sthg. in sthg. else." **In—²** is also a form of the prefix **en—.** And in pairs such as **enclose/inclose** and **enquire/inquire,** the two prefixes can be used somewhat interchangeably. As with the prefix **in—¹**, before the consonants *l* and *r*, **in—²** becomes **il—** and **ir—** respectively: **illocutionary, irradiate.** And before the consonants *b*, *m*, and *p*, **in—²** becomes **im—**: **imbed, immerse, imprison.**

in•a•bil•i•ty (ĭn′ə bĭl′ĭ tē) *n.* [U] Lack of ability or means: *inability to sleep.*

in•ac•ces•si•ble (ĭn′ăk sĕs′ə bəl) *adj.* Not accessible; hard to reach: *an inaccessible road high in the mountains.*

in•ac•cu•ra•cy (ĭn ăk′yər ə sē) *n., pl.* **in•ac•cu•ra•cies. 1.** [U] The quality or condition of being inaccurate: *The report was criticized for its inaccuracy.* **2.** [C] An error; a mistake: *There are many inaccuracies in his research.*

in•ac•cu•rate (ĭn ăk′yər ĭt) *adj.* Wrong or incorrect; not accurate: *The student gave an inaccurate definition of the word.* —**in•ac′cu•rate•ly** *adv.*

in·ac·tion (ĭn ăk′shən) *n.* [U] Lack or absence of action: *The committee's inaction angered us.*

in·ac·tive (ĭn ăk′tĭv) *adj.* Not active; not functioning; idle: *an inactive volcano; an inactive life.* —**in·ac′tive·ly** *adv.*

in·ad·e·quate (ĭn ăd′ĭ kwĭt) *adj.* Not enough; insufficient: *We lost because of inadequate training.* —**in·ad′e·qua·cy** *n.* [C; U] —**in·ad′e·quate·ly** *adv.*

in·ad·mis·si·ble (ĭn′əd mĭs′ə bəl) *adj.* Not admissible or allowed: *Inadmissible evidence cannot be used in a trial.* —**in′ad·mis′si·bil′i·ty** *n.* [U]

in·ad·ver·tent (ĭn′əd vûr′tnt) *adj.* Not meant or intended: *an inadvertent error in the bill.* —**in′ad·ver′tent·ly** *adv.*

in·ad·vis·a·ble (ĭn′əd vī′zə bəl) *adj.* Not advised; unwise: *It is inadvisable to swim alone.*

in·al·ien·a·ble (ĭn āl′yə nə bəl *or* ĭn ā′lē-ə nə bəl) *adj.* Impossible to give up or take away: *the inalienable rights listed in the Declaration of Independence.*

in·ane (ĭn ān′) *adj.* Lacking sense or meaning; empty: *The critic made an inane comment about the movie.* —**in·ane′ly** *adv.*

in·an·i·mate (ĭn ăn′ə mĭt) *adj.* **1.** Not living: *A stone is an inanimate object.* **2.** Not lively; dull: *The crowd was inanimate during the long, dull concert.*

in·ap·pro·pri·ate (ĭn′ə prō′prē ĭt) *adj.* Not appropriate; unsuitable: *It's inappropriate to smoke around people who are sick.* —**in′ap·pro′pri·ate·ly** *adv.* —**in′ap·pro′pri·ate·ness** *n.* [U]

in·ar·tic·u·late (ĭn′är tĭk′yə lĭt) *adj.* Unable to speak clearly or effectively: *She always feels inarticulate speaking in front of a group.* —**in′ar·tic′u·late·ly** *adv.*

in·as·much as (ĭn′əz mŭch′) *conj. Formal.* Because of the fact that: *I decided to go swimming inasmuch as it was hot and sunny.*

in·at·ten·tive (ĭn′ə tĕn′tĭv) *adj.* Not paying attention; careless: *Students are sometimes sleepy and inattentive after lunch.* —**in′at·ten′tion** *n.* [U] —**in′at·ten′tive·ly** *adv.* —**in′at·ten′tive·ness** *n.* [U]

in·au·di·ble (ĭn ô′də bəl) *adj.* Impossible to hear: *an inaudible conversation.* —**in·au′di·bly** *adv.*

in·au·gu·ral (ĭn ô′gyər əl) *adj.* **1.** Relating to an inauguration: *the President's inaugural address.* **2.** First; initial: *an inaugural flight of a new plane.* —*n.* An inaugural ceremony or activity.

in·au·gu·rate (ĭn ô′gyə rāt′) *tr.v.* **in·au·gu·rat·ed, in·au·gu·rat·ing, in·au·gu·rates. 1.** To install (sbdy.) in office by a formal ceremony: *inaugurate a President.* **2.** To

open (sthg.) new with a ceremony; dedicate: *inaugurate a new office building.* —**in·au′gu·ra′tion** *n.* [C; U]

in·aus·pi·cious (ĭn′ô spĭsh′əs) *adj. Formal.* Not favorable or promising; not auspicious: *Despite an inauspicious beginning, the business grew.* —**in′aus·pi′cious·ly** *adv.*

in·born (ĭn′bôrn′) *adj.* Present in a person or an animal from birth: *an inborn talent for music.*

in·bound (ĭn′bound′) *adj.* Incoming; arriving: *an inbound train.*

in·bred (ĭn′brĕd′) *adj.* **1.** Produced by breeding generations of closely related individuals. **2.** Existing from birth; inborn: *The painter had an inbred sense of color.* —**in′breed′ing** *n.* [U]

inc. *abbr.* also **Inc.** An abbreviation of incorporated.

in·cal·cu·la·ble (ĭn kăl′kyə lə bəl) *adj.* Too great or too large in number to be counted or described; enormous: *incalculable damage from the earthquake; incalculable worth.* —**in·cal′cu·la·bly** *adv.*

in·can·des·cent (ĭn′kən dĕs′ənt) *adj.* Heated to such a high temperature that it gives off light; glowing with heat. —**in′can·des′cence** *n.* [U] —**in′can·des′cent·ly** *adv.*

in·can·ta·tion (ĭn′kăn tā′shən) *n.* Words or sounds recited or chanted to cast a spell or perform magic.

in·ca·pa·ble (ĭn kā′pə bəl) *adj.* Lacking the required power or ability; not capable: *Humans are incapable of breathing under water.*

in·ca·pac·i·tate (ĭn′kə păs′ĭ tāt′) *tr.v.* **in·ca·pac·i·tat·ed, in·ca·pac·i·tat·ing, in·ca·pac·i·tates.** To deprive (sbdy./sthg.) of power or ability; disable: *A knee injury incapacitated the wrestler.* —**in′ca·pac′i·ty** *n.* [U]

in·car·cer·ate (ĭn kär′sə rāt′) *tr.v.* **in·car·cer·at·ed, in·car·cer·at·ing, in·car·cer·ates.** To put (sbdy.) in jail; imprison: *The robber was incarcerated for two years.* —**in·car′cer·a′tion** *n.* [U]

in·car·nate (ĭn kär′nĭt) *adj.* Embodied in flesh, especially in human form; personified: *a villain who seemed evil incarnate.* —**in′car·na′tion** *n.* [U]

in·cen·di·ar·y (ĭn sĕn′dē ĕr′ē) *adj.* **1.** Able to cause fires: *an incendiary bomb.* **2.** Arousing anger or conflict; inflammatory: *After the incendiary speech, the mob rampaged through the streets.*

in·cense¹ (ĭn sĕns′) *tr.v.* **in·censed, in·cens·ing, in·cens·es.** To make (sbdy.) very angry; enrage: *The errors in the story incensed the editor.*

in•cense² (ĭn′sĕns′) *n.* [U] A substance that is burned to produce a pleasant odor.

in•cen•tive (ĭn sĕn′tĭv) *n.* Something that encourages action or effort: *The company gives bonuses as an incentive to good workers.*

in•cep•tion (ĭn sĕp′shən) *n.* [U] *Formal.* The beginning of sthg.; a start: *September usually marks the inception of a new school year.*

in•ces•sant (ĭn sĕs′ənt) *adj.* Continuing without stopping; constant: *The incessant sound of the traffic made it difficult to sleep.* —**in•ces′sant•ly** *adv.*

in•cest (ĭn′sĕst′) *n.* [U] Sexual relations between two people who are so closely related that they cannot be legally married. —**in•ces•tu•ous** (ĭn sĕs′chŏŏ əs) *adj.*

inch (ĭnch) *n.* **1.** A unit of length equal to ¹⁄₁₂ of a foot (2.54 centimeters). See table at **measurement. 2.** A very small degree or amount. —*intr.v.* To move or proceed very slowly: *We are inching closer to an understanding of the origin of the universe.* ♦ **every inch.** In every detail; entirely: *The actor looked every inch the role.* **inch by inch.** Little by little; very gradually: *Inch by inch, we finished the big project.* **(not) give an inch.** To refuse to yield or change an opinion: *Neither side would give an inch.* **within an inch of.** Almost to the point of; very near: *The team was within an inch of winning the state championship.*

in•ci•dence (ĭn′sĭ dəns) *n.* [U] The number of times sthg. occurs: *The incidence of polio has fallen since vaccines became available.*

in•ci•dent (ĭn′sĭ dənt) *n.* Something unusual or dangerous that happens: *Police were called to investigate the incident.* ♦ **without incident.** With no serious problems: *The damaged plane managed to land without incident.*

in•ci•den•tal (ĭn′sĭ dĕn′tl) *adj.* **1.** Occurring as a minor cost: *In addition to the costs of food and lodging, there were many incidental expenses.* **2.** Happening unexpectedly: *My weekend included several incidental encounters with old friends.* —*n. (usually plural).* A minor item or expense: *We must be careful not to spend our entire budget on mere incidentals.*

in•ci•den•tal•ly (ĭn′sĭ dĕn′tl ē) *adv.* **1.** Apart from the main subject; by the way: *Incidentally, what time is it?* **2.** As a minor matter: *She is a writer and only incidentally a runner.*

in•cin•er•ate (ĭn sĭn′ə rāt′) *tr.v.* **in•cin•er•at•ed, in•cin•er•at•ing, in•cin•er•ates.** To destroy (sthg.) by burning; burn to ashes: *We incinerate our trash.* —**in•cin′er•a′tion** *n.* [U]

in•cin•er•a•tor (ĭn sĭn′ə rā′tər) *n.* A furnace or other device for burning trash.

in•cip•i•ent (ĭn sĭp′ē ənt) *adj. Formal.* Beginning to exist or appear: *The darkening clouds were the signs of an incipient storm.*

in•ci•sion (ĭn sĭzh′ən) *n.* A cut made into sthg., especially a cut made by a doctor: *The surgeon made an incision in the patient's chest.*

in•ci•sive (ĭn sī′sĭv) *adj.* Sharp and clear; penetrating: *The incisive analysis was thorough and to the point.* —**in•ci′sive•ly** *adv.* —**in•ci′sive•ness** *n.* [U]

in•ci•sor (ĭn sī′zər) *n.* A tooth with a sharp edge adapted for cutting, located in mammals in the front of the mouth between the canine teeth.

in•cite (ĭn sīt′) *tr.v.* **in•cit•ed, in•cit•ing, in•cites.** To provoke (sbdy./sthg.); stir up: *The announcement of a cut in pay incited the workers to strike.* —**in•cite′ment** *n.* [U]

in•clem•ent (ĭn klĕm′ənt) *adj.* Stormy; rough: *inclement weather.*

in•cli•na•tion (ĭn′klə nā′shən) *n.* **1.** [C; U] A natural tendency to act in a certain way: *Many people have an inclination to sleep late on weekends.* **2.** [U] A slant or slope: *the steep inclination of the roof.*

in•cline (ĭn klīn′) *v.* **in•clined, in•clin•ing, in•clines.** —*intr.* **1.** To slant or slope: *a road that inclines steeply.* **2.** To lower the head or body, as in a nod or bow: *The baby's head inclined on his chest.* —*tr.* **1.** To cause (sthg.) to lean, slant, or slope: *We inclined the boards against the side of the building.* **2.** To cause (sthg.) to bend or bow: *The conductor inclined his head as a signal for us to get ready to play.* —*n.* (ĭn′klīn′). A surface that slants; a slope: *The car skidded down the icy incline of the street.* ♦ **be inclined to.** To be likely: *You might be inclined to change your mind after you read this.*

in•clined (ĭn klīnd′) *adj.* **1.** Sloping, slanting, or leaning: *a ramp inclined at 15 degrees.* **2.** Tending or likely: *a man inclined to act too quickly.*

in•clude (ĭn klŏŏd′) *tr.v.* **in•clud•ed, in•clud•ing, in•cludes. 1.** To have (sbdy./sthg.) as a part or member; contain: *The museum's collection includes many masterpieces.* **2.** To put (sbdy./sthg.) into a group, class, or total: *I included your whole family in the photograph I took at the party.*

in•clud•ing (ĭn klŏŏ′dĭng) *prep.* In or a part of a group or set: *There will be five of us, including my parents.*

in•clu•sion (ĭn klŏŏ′zhən) *n.* **1.** [U] The act of including or the condition of being included: *Inclusion on the list does not guarantee quality.* **2.** [C] Something that is included: *All inclusions are final.*

in•clu•sive (ĭn klŏŏ′sĭv) *adj.* **1.** Taking everything into account; comprehensive: *an all-inclusive list of doctors in the area.* **2.** Including the stated limits as well as what is between them: *Read Chapters 1 to 4 inclusive* means one should read from the beginning of Chapter 1 to the end of Chapter 4. —**in•clu′sive•ly** *adv.* —**in•clu′sive•ness** *n.* [U]

in·cog·ni·to (ĭn′kŏg nē′tō *or* ĭn kŏg′nĭ-tō′) *adv. & adj.* With one's identity hidden or disguised: *The movie star stayed at the hotel incognito. The incognito spy escaped across the border.*

in·co·her·ent (ĭn′kō hîr′ənt) *adj.* **1.** Lacking order or logical connection; not coherent: *an incoherent jumble of confused thoughts.* **2.** Unable to think or express one's thoughts in a clear or orderly manner: *The feverish patient was incoherent and confused.* —**in′co·her′ence** *n.* [U] —**in′co·her′ent·ly** *adv.*

in·come (ĭn′kŭm′) *n.* [C; U] The amount of money received for work, from the sale of property or goods, or from financial investments: *One's monthly income is all the money one receives in a month.*

income tax *n.* [C; U] A tax on the income of a person or business.

in·com·ing (ĭn′kŭm′ĭng) *adj.* **1.** Coming in; entering: *an incoming flight.* **2.** About to come in; next: *the incoming president.*

in·com·mu·ni·ca·do (ĭn′kə myōō′nĭ-kä′dō) *adv. & adj.* Without the possibility of communicating with others: *The jury was kept incommunicado until the trial was over.*

in·com·pa·ra·ble (ĭn kŏm′pər ə bəl) *adj.* Better than all others in comparison: *an incomparable performance.* —**in·com′pa·ra·bly** *adv.*

in·com·pat·i·ble (ĭn′kəm păt′ə bəl) *adj.* **1.** Not capable of existing with sthg. else: *Speeding is incompatible with safe driving.* **2.** Not capable of living or working together happily or smoothly: *The roommates were incompatible, so one moved to a new apartment.* —**in′com·pat′i·bil′i·ty** *n.* [C; U] —**in′com·pat′i·bly** *adv.*

in·com·pe·tent (ĭn kŏm′pĭ tənt) *adj.* Not having the abilities or qualifications to do sthg.; incapable: *an incompetent engineer.* —*n.* An incompetent person: *an office run by incompetents.* —**in·com′pe·tence** *n.* [U] —**in·com′pe·tent·ly** *adv.*

in·com·plete (ĭn′kəm plēt′) *adj.* Not complete; unfinished: *The writer's last novel is incomplete.* —**in′com·plete′ly** *adv.*

in·com·pre·hen·si·ble (ĭn′kŏm prĭ hĕn′-sə bəl) *adj.* Difficult or impossible to understand: *an incomprehensible sentence.* —**in′-com·pre·hen′si·bly** *adv.*

in·con·ceiv·a·ble (ĭn′kən sē′və bəl) *adj.* Hard or impossible to understand or imagine: *It would be inconceivable for them to complain about the hotel room.* —**in′con·ceiv′-a·bly** *adv.*

in·con·clu·sive (ĭn′kən klōō′sĭv) *adj.* Not conclusive: *The inconclusive election returns left both candidates unsure of victory.* —**in′-con·clu′sive·ly** *adv.*

in·con·gru·ous (ĭn kŏng′grōō əs) *adj.* **1.** Not fitting; incompatible or inconsistent: *Your proposal is incongruous with our plans.* **2.** Not in keeping with what is correct, proper, or logical; inappropriate: *incongruous behavior.* —**in·con·gru′i·ty** (ĭn′kŏn grōō′-ĭ tē) *n.* [C; U] —**in·con′gru·ous·ly** *adv.* —**in·con′gru·ous·ness** *n.* [U]

in·con·se·quen·tial (ĭn kŏn′sĭ kwĕn′-shəl) *adj.* Not important; trivial: *an inconsequential and boring newspaper story.*

in·con·sid·er·ate (ĭn′kən sĭd′ər ĭt) *adj.* Not considerate; thoughtless: *It is inconsiderate to make noise while we're trying to read.* —**in′con·sid′er·ate·ly** *adv.*

in·con·sis·tent (ĭn′kən sĭs′tənt) *adj.* **1.** Not in agreement with sthg.: *Her version of the story is inconsistent with the facts.* **2.** Not predictable, as in a course of action; not regular: *inconsistent behavior.* —**in′con·sis′-ten·cy** *n.* —**in′con·sis′tent·ly** *adv.*

in·con·sol·a·ble (ĭn′kən sō′lə bəl) *adj.* Hard or impossible to console or comfort: *The children were inconsolable at the loss of their dog.* —**in′con·sol′a·bly** *adv.*

in·con·spic·u·ous (ĭn′kən spĭk′yōō əs) *adj.* Not easily noticeable; not obvious: *The late student tried to be inconspicuous when she entered the class.* —**in′con·spic′u·ous·ly** *adv.* —**in′con·spic′u·ous·ness** *n.* [U]

in·con·tro·vert·i·ble (ĭn kŏn′trə vûr′tə-bəl *or* ĭn′kŏn trə vûr′tə bəl) *adj.* Impossible to argue about; unquestionable: *Incontrovertible evidence pointed to the suspect's guilt.* —**in·con′tro·vert′i·bly** *adv.*

in·con·ven·ience (ĭn′kən vēn′yəns) *n.* **1.** [C; U] The quality or condition of being inconvenient: *Forgetting my keys caused a great deal of inconvenience.* **2.** Something that causes difficulty or trouble: *Lack of an automobile is an inconvenience.* —*tr.v.* **in·con·ven·ienced, in·con·ven·ienc·ing, in·con·ven·ienc·es.** To cause inconvenience to (sbdy.); bother: *Road construction inconvenienced many drivers.*

in·con·ven·ient (ĭn′kən vēn′yənt) *adj.* Not convenient; causing difficulty: *It is inconvenient to have no cafeteria in this building.* —**in′con·ven′ient·ly** *adv.*

in·cor·po·rate (ĭn kôr′pə rāt′) *tr.v.* **in·cor·po·rat·ed, in·cor·po·rat·ing, in·cor·po·rates.** **1.** To include (sbdy./sthg.) as a part in a whole; combine with sthg. else: *a new car that incorporates features of earlier models.* **2.** To form (sbdy./sthg.) into a legal corporation: *incorporate a business.*

in·cor·po·rat·ed (ĭn kôr′pə rā′tĭd) *adj.* Organized and maintained as a legal corporation: *an incorporated business.*

in·cor·rect (ĭn′kə rĕkt′) *adj.* **1.** Not correct; wrong: *The test had many incorrect answers.* **2.** Inappropriate or improper: *Our dress was incorrect for the occasion.* **—in′·cor·rect′ly** *adv.* **—in′cor·rect′ness** *n.* [U]

in·cor·ri·gi·ble (ĭn kôr′ĭ jə bəl *or* ĭn kŏr′ĭ jə bəl) *adj.* Not capable of being corrected or changed: *an incorrigible child who breaks the rules.* **—n.** A person who cannot be changed.

in·cor·rupt·i·ble (ĭn′kə rŭp′tə bəl) *adj.* Not capable of being morally corrupted: *The honest judge is incorruptible.*

in·crease (ĭn krēs′) *tr. & intr.v.* **in·creased, in·creas·ing, in·creas·es.** To make or become greater or larger in size, number, or power: *Machines increase the rate at which goods are manufactured. The world's population increased rapidly over the last century.* **—n.** (ĭn′krēs′). [C; U] **1.** The act of increasing; growth: *a steady increase in sales.* **2.** The amount or rate by which sthg. is increased: *a ten percent increase in tax rates.* ◆ **on the increase.** Becoming greater or more frequent; increasing: *Crime is on the increase in that neighborhood.*

SYNONYMS: increase, expand, enlarge, extend, multiply. These verbs mean to become or make greater or larger. **Increase,** the most general, often means to grow steadily: *The number of students here has increased every year.* **Expand** means to increase in size, volume, or amount: *That pizza parlor expanded its delivery service to cover many more neighborhoods.* **Enlarge** means to make larger: *His mother likes that photograph so much that she wants to enlarge and frame it.* **Extend** means to increase in length: *The transit authority extended the subway line to the airport.* **Multiply** means to increase in number: *One of the zoo's roles is to help endangered species multiply.* **ANTONYM: decrease.**

---

in·creased (ĭn krēst′ *or* ĭn′krēst) *adj.* Greater or more than before: *increased applications to medical schools; an increased concern for saving endangered species.*

in·creas·ing·ly (ĭn krē′sĭng lē) *adv.* More and more: *Our wetlands are becoming increasingly fragile.*

in·cred·i·ble (ĭn krĕd′ə bəl) *adj.* Hard to believe; unbelievable: *The new plane flies at an incredible speed.* **—in·cred′i·bly** *adv.*

in·cred·u·lous (ĭn krĕj′ə ləs) *adj.* **1.** Not believing; skeptical: *We are incredulous of stories about flying saucers.* **2.** Expressing disbelief or surprise: *incredulous gasps at the gymnast's performance.* **—in′cre·du′li·ty** (ĭn′krĭ dōō′lĭ tē *or* ĭn′krĭ dyōō′lĭ tē) *n.* [U] **—in·cred′u·lous·ly** *adv.*

in·cre·ment (ĭn′krə mənt *or* ĭng′krə mənt) *n.* [C; U] An increase in number, size, amount, or extent: *The increment in sales made the company profitable.*

in·crim·i·nate (ĭn krĭm′ə nāt′) *tr.v.* **in·crim·i·nat·ed, in·crim·i·nat·ing, in·crim·i·nates.** To cause (sbdy.) to appear guilty of a crime or fault; implicate: *The suspect incriminated other people in the robbery.* **—in·crim′i·nat·ing** *adj.* **—in·crim′i·na′tion** *n.* [U]

in·cu·bate (ĭn′kyə bāt′ *or* ĭng′kyə bāt′) *v.* **in·cu·bat·ed, in·cu·bat·ing, in·cu·bates.** **—tr.** **1.** To keep (eggs, organisms, or other living tissue) in conditions favorable to growth and development: *The biologist incubated the microorganisms.* **2.** To form or consider (sthg.) slowly: *The writer incubated an idea for a new novel.* **—in·cu·ba′tion** *n.* [U]

in·cu·ba·tor (ĭn′kyə bā′tər *or* ĭng′kyə bā′tər) *n.* **1.** A machine in which desired conditions, such as temperature and humidity, can be maintained for hatching eggs and growing cultures of microorganisms. **2.** A similar machine supplied with oxygen for the special care of very small or premature babies.

in·cum·bent (ĭn kŭm′bənt) *adj.* Currently holding a specified office: *the incumbent mayor.* **—n.** A person currently holding an office: *Many incumbents lost in the last election.* ◆ **incumbent on** or **upon.** Imposed as an obligation or duty; required: *It is incumbent on all citizens to pay their taxes.* **—in·cum′ben·cy** *n.* [U]

in·cur (ĭn kûr′) *tr.v.* **in·curred, in·cur·ring, in·curs.** To acquire or become responsible for (sthg.): *The man incurred many debts when he bought a new house.*

in·cur·a·ble (ĭn kyŏŏr′ə bəl) *adj.* Not capable of being cured: *an incurable disease; an incurable romantic.* **—in·cur′a·bly** *adv.*

in·cur·sion (ĭn kûr′zhən *or* ĭn kûr′shən) *n.* A sudden attack on a foreign territory; a raid: *The pirates made many incursions along the coast.*

Ind. *abbr.* An abbreviation of Indiana.

in·debt·ed (ĭn dĕt′ĭd) *adj.* Owing another person money or gratitude for a loan, gift, or useful service: *We are indebted to you for your hospitality.* **—in·debt′ed·ness** *n.* [U]

in·de·cent (ĭn dē′sənt) *adj.* **1.** Not in good taste; not proper; unsuitable: *Our dinner guest told an indecent joke, which offended my mother.* **2.** Morally offensive; immodest: *indecent behavior.* **—in·de′cen·cy** *n.* [C; U] **—in·de′cent·ly** *adv.*

in·de·ci·sion (ĭn′dĭ sĭzh′ən) *n.* [U] The condition of being unable to make decisions: *His indecision cost him the job.*

in·de·ci·sive (ĭn′dĭ sī′sĭv) *adj.* **1.** Unable to make decisions: *The indecisive customer couldn't choose which camera to buy.* **2.** Having no clear result; inconclusive: *an indecisive election in which no candidate received a clear majority of the votes.* **—in′de·ci′sive·ly** *adv.* **—in′de·ci′sive·ness** *n.* [U]

in·deed (ĭn dēd′) *adv.* **1.** Without a doubt; certainly: *They were indeed happy.* **2.** In fact; in reality: *I said the car would break down and indeed it did.* —*interj.* An expression used to show surprise, emphasis, or disbelief: *You are expecting triplets? Indeed!*

in·de·fen·si·ble (ĭn′dĭ fĕn′sə bəl) *adj.* **1.** Easy to attack: *an indefensible town in the middle of a valley.* **2.** Not capable of being justified or excused; inexcusable: *rude and indefensible behavior.* —**in′de·fen′si·bly** *adv.*

in·de·fin·a·ble (ĭn′dĭ fī′nə bəl) *adj.* Impossible to define or describe: *a vague and indefinable feeling of suspicion.* —**in′de·fin′a·bly** *adv.*

in·def·i·nite (ĭn dĕf′ə nĭt) *adj.* **1.** Not fixed or limited: *an indefinite period of time.* **2.** Not clear or exact; vague: *indefinite outlines of people standing in the shadows.* **3.** Not decided; uncertain: *indefinite plans.* —**in·def′i·nite·ly** *adv.*

indefinite article *n.* An article, in English either *a* or *an,* that does not specify the identity of the noun modified. —SEE NOTE at *a².*

indefinite pronoun *n.* A pronoun, as English *any* or *some,* that does not specify the identity of its object.

in·del·i·ble (ĭn dĕl′ə bəl) *adj.* **1.** Impossible to remove, erase, or wash away; permanent: *an indelible stain.* **2.** Making a mark that cannot be removed: *an indelible pen.* —**in·del′i·bly** *adv.*

in·del·i·ca·cy (ĭn dĕl′ĭ kə sē) *n., pl.* **in·del·i·ca·cies. 1.** [U] The quality or condition of being indelicate. **2.** [C] Something that is indelicate.

in·del·i·cate (ĭn dĕl′ĭ kĭt) *adj.* Lacking good taste; crude or improper: *indelicate language.* —**in·del′i·cate·ly** *adv.*

in·dent (ĭn dĕnt′) *tr.v.* To set (the first line of a paragraph) in from the margin: *Please indent each paragraph five spaces.* —*n.* (ĭn′dĕnt′ *or* ĭn′dĕnt′). An indentation.

in·den·ta·tion (ĭn′dĕn tā′shən) *n.* **1.** [C; U] The act of indenting or the condition of being indented. **2.** [C] The blank space between a margin and the beginning of an indented line.

in·de·pend·ence (ĭn′dĭ pĕn′dəns) *n.* [U] **1.** The quality or condition of being independent: *Teenagers value their independence.* **2.** Political freedom from another country: *Many countries of colonial Africa won their independence from European nations during the last 50 years.*

Independence Day *n.* A U.S. national holiday celebrated on July 4 to commemorate the adoption of the Declaration of Independence in 1776.

in·de·pend·ent (ĭn′dĭ pĕn′dənt) *adj.* **1.** Not governed by a foreign country; ruling or governing itself: *The United States became an independent nation after the Revolution.* **2.** Not controlled, supported, or guided by others: *an independent mind; independent of one's parents.* **3.** Not dependent on or connected with a larger or controlling group; separate: *an independent drugstore; an independent plan.* **4.** Not committed to any one political party: *an independent voter.* —**in′de·pend′ent·ly** *adv.*

independent clause *n.* A clause in a sentence that can stand alone as a complete sentence; a main clause. In the sentence *When the sun came out, we went for a walk,* the clause *we went for a walk* is an independent clause.

in-depth (ĭn′dĕpth′) *adj.* Detailed; thorough: *an in-depth interview with the candidate.*

in·de·scrib·a·ble (ĭn′dĭ skrī′bə bəl) *adj.* Impossible to describe: *indescribable beauty.* —**in′de·scrib′a·bly** *adv.*

in·de·struc·ti·ble (ĭn′dĭ strŭk′tə bəl) *adj.* Impossible to destroy: *an indestructible stone house.* —**in′de·struc′ti·bly** *adv.*

in·de·ter·mi·nate (ĭn′dĭ tûr′mə nĭt) *adj.* Not precisely determined; vague: *a person of indeterminate age.* —**in′de·ter′mi·nate·ly** *adv.*

in·dex (ĭn′dĕks′) *n., pl.* **in·dex·es** or **in·di·ces** (ĭn′dĭ sēz′). A list of names or subjects in alphabetical order at the end of a book, along with the page numbers on which each item is mentioned: *We found references to our subject by looking in the index.* —*tr.v.* To furnish (sthg.) with an index: *index a history textbook.*

index finger *n.* The finger next to the thumb; the forefinger.

In·di·an (ĭn′dē ən) *adj.* **1.** Relating to India or the East Indies or to their peoples, languages, or cultures. **2.** Relating to any of the Native American peoples or their languages or cultures. —*n.* **1.** A person from India or the East Indies. **2.** A Native American.

Indian summer *n.* A period of warm weather occurring in late autumn.

in·di·cate (ĭn′dĭ kāt′) *tr.v.* **in·di·cat·ed, in·di·cat·ing, in·di·cates. 1.** To show or point (sthg.) out: *indicate a route on a map.* **2.** To serve as a sign or symptom of (sthg.): *Dark clouds indicate rain. Fever indicates illness.*

in·di·ca·tion (ĭn′dĭ kā′shən) *n.* **1.** [C; U] The act of indicating: *His indication of refusal came in a letter.* **2.** [C] Something that indicates; a sign: *flowers, birds, and other indications of spring.*

in·dic·a·tive (ĭn dĭk′ə tĭv) *adj.* **1.** [*of*] Serving to indicate: *A cough is often indicative of a cold.* **2.** Relating to the mood of a

---

ă–cat; ā–pay; âr–care; ä–father; ĕ–get; ē–be; ĭ–sit; ī–nice; îr–here; ŏ–got; ō–go; ô–saw; oi–boy; ou–out; ŏŏ–took; ōō–boot; ŭ–cut; ûr–word; th–thin; *th*–this; hw–when; zh–vision; ə–about; N–French bon

verb used in ordinary statements of fact or in factual questions. In *We went* and *Did they go?,* the words *went* and *go* are in the indicative mood. —*n.* **1.** [U] The indicative mood. **2.** [C] A verb form in this mood.

in·di·ca·tor (ĭn′dĭ kā′tər) *n.* A person or thing that indicates, especially: **1.** A meter or gauge that tells about the operation of an engine or other machine or system: *Look at the pressure on the indicator.* **2.** The needle or dial of such a meter or gauge: *Where is the indicator pointing? What does the indicator read?*

in·di·ces (ĭn′dĭ sēz′) *n.* A plural of **index.**

in·dict (ĭn dīt′) *tr.v.* To accuse (sbdy.) of wrongdoing: *a book that indicts advertisers on charges of corrupting our society.* —**in·dict′a·ble** *adj.*

in·dict·ment (ĭn dīt′mənt) *n.* **1.** [C; U] The act of indicting or the condition of being indicted: *a bank officer under indictment for embezzlement.* **2.** [C] A written statement issued by a grand jury that charges a person with a crime: *The grand jury handed down several indictments.*

in·dif·fer·ence (ĭn dĭf′ər əns *or* ĭn dĭf′rəns) *n.* [U] **1.** Lack of concern or interest: *the government's indifference to the poor.* **2.** Lack of importance; insignificance: *Their opinion is a matter of indifference to me.*

in·dif·fer·ent (ĭn dĭf′ər ənt *or* ĭn dĭf′rənt) *adj.* **1.** Having or showing no interest; not caring: *indifferent to the troubles of others; indifferent to weather conditions.* **2.** Showing no preference; fair: *A jury should be indifferent in viewing the facts of a trial.* **3.** Neither good nor bad; mediocre: *The orchestra gave an indifferent performance.* —**in·dif′fer·ent·ly** *adv.*

in·dig·e·nous (ĭn dĭj′ə nəs) *adj.* Originally living or growing in a region or environment; native: *The turkey and the tomato are indigenous to North America.*

in·di·gent (ĭn′dĭ jənt) *Formal. n.* [C; U] A poor or needy person or the group as a whole: *help for the indigent.* —*adj.* Poor; needy. —**in′di·gence** *n.* [U]

in·di·gest·i·ble (ĭn′dĭ jĕs′tə bəl *or* ĭn′dī jĕs′tə bəl) *adj.* Difficult or impossible to digest: *indigestible fatty foods.*

in·di·ges·tion (ĭn′dĭ jĕs′chən *or* ĭn′dī jĕs′chən) *n.* [U] Discomfort or illness resulting from the inability to digest or difficulty in digesting food: *Eating too much too fast will surely give you indigestion.*

in·dig·nant (ĭn dĭg′nənt) *adj.* Feeling or expressing indignation: *I was indignant over their thoughtlessness remarks.* —**in·dig′nant·ly** *adv.*

in·dig·na·tion (ĭn′dĭg nā′shən) *n.* [U] Anger aroused by sthg. unfair or mean: *The students expressed their indignation over the new rules at the school.* See Synonyms at **anger.**

in·dig·ni·ty (ĭn dĭg′nĭ tē) *n., pl.* **in·dig·ni·ties.** Something that offends a person's pride and sense of dignity; an insult: *She felt it was an indignity to be asked to wash windows for her boss.*

in·di·go (ĭn′dĭ gō′) *n.* [U] A dark violet-blue color. —*adj.* Dark violet blue.

in·di·rect (ĭn′dĭ rĕkt′ *or* ĭn′dī rĕkt′) *adj.* **1.** Not following a direct course: *The taxi took an indirect route to the airport.* **2.** Not straight to the point, as in talking: *an indirect answer.* **3.** Not directly connected; secondary: *The increase in bicycle sales was an indirect effect of the new gasoline tax.* —**in′di·rect′ly** *adv.* —**in′di·rect′ness** *n.* [U]

indirect object *n.* A word or words indirectly affected by the action of a verb. In the sentences *Sing me a song* and *We fed the dog meat,* the words *me* and *dog* are both indirect objects.

in·dis·creet (ĭn′dĭ skrēt′) *adj.* Lacking good judgment; unwise or tactless: *an indiscreet remark about his age.* —**in′dis·creet′ly** *adv.*

in·dis·cre·tion (ĭn′dĭ skrĕsh′ən) *n.* **1.** [U] Lack of discretion: *Her indiscretion has cost her friends.* **2.** [C] An indiscreet act or remark: *The governor had to resign because of public indiscretions.*

in·dis·crim·i·nate (ĭn′dĭ skrĭm′ə nĭt) *adj.* **1.** Showing lack of care in making choices: *an indiscriminate shopper who buys anything on sale.* **2.** Not sorted or put in order; random or confused: *an indiscriminate pile of papers on a desk.* —**in′dis·crim′i·nate·ly** *adv.*

in·dis·pen·sa·ble (ĭn′dĭ spĕn′sə bəl) *adj.* Essential; necessary: *A good education is indispensable to becoming a doctor.* —**in′dis·pen′sa·bly** *adv.*

in·dis·posed (ĭn′dĭ spōzd′) *adj.* **1.** Mildly ill: *indisposed with a slight cold.* **2.** Unwilling; reluctant: *indisposed to help anyone.*

in·dis·put·a·ble (ĭn′dĭ spyōō′tə bəl) *adj.* Beyond doubt; unquestionable: *an indisputable fact.* —**in′dis·put′a·bly** *adv.*

in·dis·tinct (ĭn′dĭ stĭngkt′) *adj.* Not clearly heard, seen, or understood: *an indistinct sound heard from far away; I saw an indistinct figure in the distance.* —**in′dis·tinct′ly** *adv.*

in·dis·tin·guish·a·ble (ĭn′dĭ stĭng′gwĭ shə bəl) *adj.* Lacking clear differences; impossible to tell apart: *a little store indistinguishable from any other on the street.*

in·di·vid·u·al (ĭn′də vĭj′ōō əl) *adj.* **1.** Relating to a single human, animal, or plant: *for each individual child.* **2.** By or for one person: *an individual portion of food.* **3.** Existing as a separate unit; distinct: *individual drops of rain.* **4.** Having a special quality; distinct: *Each variety of apple has its individual flavor.* —*n.* A single human: *a pleasant and friendly individual.* —**in′di·vid′u·al·ly** *adv.*

in·di·vid·u·al·ism (ĭn'də vĭj'ōō ə lĭz'əm) *n.* [U] **1.** Belief in following one's own interests without concern for the opinions of others or the usual way of doing things. **2.** A way of living based on this belief; personal independence. —**in'di·vid'u·al·ist** *n.* —**in'di·vid'u·al·is'tic** *adj.* —**in'di·vid·u·al·is'ti·cal·ly** *adv.*

in·di·vid·u·al·i·ty (ĭn'də vĭj'ōō ăl'ĭ tē) *n.* [U] **1.** The condition of being individual; distinctness: *While working on the assembly line, she felt at times she was losing her individuality.* **2.** The qualities that make sbdy./sthg. different from others; identity: *He expresses his individuality in the way he dresses.*

in·di·vid·u·al·ize (ĭn'də vĭj'ōō ə lĭz') *tr.v.* **in·di·vid·u·al·ized, in·di·vid·u·al·iz·ing, in·di·vid·u·al·iz·es.** **1.** To give individuality to (sbdy./sthg.): *She individualized her dorm room with plants.* **2.** To change (sthg.) to fit or satisfy an individual: *individualize exercises according to each person's ability.*

in·di·vis·i·ble (ĭn'də vĭz'ə bəl) *adj.* **1.** Not capable of being divided: *It was thought for many years that the atom was indivisible.* **2.** Not capable of being divided without leaving a remainder; for example, 7 is indivisible by 3. —**in'di·vis'i·bil'i·ty** *n.* [U] —**in'di·vis'i·bly** *adv.*

in·doc·tri·nate (ĭn dŏk'trə nāt') *tr.v.* **in·doc·tri·nat·ed, in·doc·tri·nat·ing, in·doc·tri·nates.** To instruct (sbdy.) in the doctrines or beliefs of a particular group: *The club indoctrinated the new members.* —**in·doc'tri·na'tion** *n.* [U]

in·dom·i·ta·ble (ĭn dŏm'ĭ tə bəl) *adj.* Not capable of being overcome or defeated; unconquerable: *an indomitable determination to finish the race.* —**in·dom'i·ta·bly** *adv.*

in·door (ĭn'dôr') *adj.* Situated in or done inside a house or other building: *an indoor pool; an indoor party.*

in·doors (ĭn dôrz') *adv.* In or into a house or building: *staying indoors because of a cold.*

in·duce (ĭn dōōs') *tr.v.* **in·duced, in·duc·ing, in·duc·es.** **1.** To persuade (sbdy.); influence: *Nothing could induce me to stay in that awful job.* **2.** To cause (sthg.) to happen; bring about: *induce vomiting in a patient who has swallowed poison; induce labor.* **3.** To arrive at (a conclusion or general principle) by a reasoned examination of particular facts. **4.** To produce (electricity or magnetism) by induction.

in·duce·ment (ĭn dōōs'mənt *or* ĭn dyōōs'mənt) *n.* **1.** [U] The act or process of inducing: *the inducement of labor in a pregnant*

woman. **2.** [C] Something that helps bring about an action; an incentive: *Free samples are an inducement to try new products.*

in·duct (ĭn dŭkt') *tr.v.* **1.** To admit (sbdy.) as a member; initiate: *The club inducts new students in the spring.* **2.** To enter (sbdy.) into military service: *He was inducted into the army.* **3.** To place (sbdy.) formally in office; install: *inducted the officer as treasurer.*

in·duct·ee (ĭn'dŭk tē') *n.* A person inducted or about to be inducted into the military.

in·duc·tion (ĭn dŭk'shən) *n.* [U] **1.** The act of installing sbdy. formally in office: *the induction of the new president.* **2.** The process of being enrolled in the military. **3.** A method of reasoning in which a conclusion is reached or a general principle is discovered on the basis of particular facts. **4.** The process by which an object having electrical or magnetic properties produces similar properties in a nearby object without direct contact.

in·duc·tive (ĭn dŭk'tĭv) *adj.* **1.** Relating to or using logical induction: *inductive reasoning.* **2.** Relating to or caused by electric or magnetic induction. —**in·duc'tive·ly** *adv.*

in·dulge (ĭn dŭlj') *v.* **in·dulged, in·dulg·ing, in·dulg·es.** —*tr.* **1.** To yield to the desires of (sbdy.); humor; pamper: *indulge a crying child.* See Synonyms at **pamper.** **2.** To give in to or satisfy (a desire): *indulge a desire for ice cream.* —*intr.* [in] To allow oneself some special pleasure; have or do what one wants: *indulge in a nap; indulge in an afternoon watching old movies.*

in·dul·gence (ĭn dŭl'jəns) *n.* **1.** [U] The act of indulging: *an occasional indulgence in junk food.* **2.** [C] Something indulged in: *A long vacation is a worthwhile indulgence.* **3.** [U] Liberal or mild treatment; favor: *The child expects to be treated with indulgence.*

in·dul·gent (ĭn dŭl'jənt) *adj.* Showing, marked by, or given to indulgence; lenient: *The indulgent owner spoiled the puppy.* —**in·dul'gent·ly** *adv.*

in·dus·tri·al (ĭn dŭs'trē əl) *adj.* **1.** Relating to industry: *industrial products.* **2.** Having highly developed industries: *an industrial nation.* **3.** Used in industry: *industrial tools and equipment.* —**in·dus'tri·al·ly** *adv.*

in·dus·tri·al·ist (ĭ dŭs'trē ə lĭst) *n.* A person who owns or runs an industrial company.

in·dus·tri·al·ize (ĭn dŭs'trē ə lĭz') *v.* **in·dus·tri·al·ized, in·dus·tri·al·iz·ing, in·dus·tri·al·iz·es.** —*tr.* To develop industries in (an area): *Many governments are working to industrialize their economies.* —*intr.* To become industrial: *That nation hopes to industrialize soon.* —**in·dus'tri·al·i·za'tion** (ĭn dŭs'trē ə lĭ zā'shən) *n.* [U]

in·dus·tri·ous (ĭn dŭs'trē əs) *adj.* Working

hard as a steady habit; diligent: *An indus-trious student can get good grades at this school.* —**in•dus′tri•ous•ly** *adv.* —**in•dus′tri•ous•ness** *n.* [U]

in•dus•try (ĭn′də strē) *n., pl.* **in•dus•tries. 1.a.** [U] The manufacture or production of goods on a large scale: *Industry has expand-ed in many Asian nations.* See Synonyms at **business. b.** [C] A specific branch of such activity: *the computer hardware industry.* **2.** [U] Hard work; steady effort: *Most people admire industry and thrift.*

in•e•bri•at•ed (ĭn ē′brē āt′ əd) *adj. Formal.* Intoxicated; drunk. —**in•e′bri•a′tion** *n.* [U]

in•ed•i•ble (ĭn ĕd′ə bəl) *adj.* Not fit to be eaten; not edible: *The peel of a banana is inedible.*

in•ef•fec•tive (ĭn′ĭ fĕk′tĭv) *adj.* **1.** Not ef-fective; not producing results: *Their attempt to push the disabled car proved ineffective.* **2.** Not performing satisfactorily; incompetent: *The medicine was an ineffective way to treat the disease.* —**in′ef•fec′tive•ly** *adv.* —**in′-ef•fec′tive•ness** *n.* [U]

in•ef•fec•tu•al (ĭn′ĭ fĕk′chōō əl) *adj.* Not having the desired effect; useless: *Our protests were ineffectual in changing the teacher's mind.* —**in′ef•fec′tu•al•ly** *adv.*

in•ef•fi•cient (ĭn′ĭ fĭsh′ənt) *adj.* **1.** Wast-ing time, energy, or materials: *an inefficient gasoline engine.* **2.** Lacking in skill or ability: *an inefficient manager.* —**in′ef•fi′cien•cy** *n.* [C; U] —**in′ef•fi′cient•ly** *adv.*

in•el•i•gi•ble (ĭn ĕl′ĭ jə bəl) *adj.* Not eli-gible; not qualified: *ineligible to vote; ineligi-ble for citizenship.* —**in•el′i•gi•bil′i•ty** *n.* [U] —**in•el′i•gi•bly** *adv.*

in•ept (ĭn ĕpt′) *adj.* **1.** Awkward or clumsy; lacking skill: *an inept actor; an inept per-formance.* **2.** Not suitable; inappropriate: *an inept suggestion.* —**in•ep′ti•tude′** (ĭn ĕp′-tĭ tōōd′) *n.* [U] —**in•ept′ly** *adv.* —**in•ept′-ness** *n.* [U]

in•e•qual•i•ty (ĭn′ĭ kwŏl′ĭ tē) *n., pl.* **in•e•qual•i•ties.** [C; U] The condition of being unequal, as in size, rank, or amount: *the great inequality between the rich and the poor.*

in•eq•ui•ty (ĭn ĕk′wĭ tē) *n., pl.* **in•eq•ui•ties.** [C; U] *Formal.* Lack of fairness injustice: *She complained about the inequity of having to cook while her brother sat.* —**in•eq′ui•ta•ble** *adj.* —**in•eq′ui•ta•bly** *adv.*

in•ert (ĭn ûrt′) *adj.* **1.** Incapable of reacting with other elements to form chemical com-pounds: *Helium is an inert gas.* **2.** Unable to move or act: *Rock is inert matter.* **3.** Slow to move, act, or respond; sluggish: *the inert dogs sleeping in the sun.* —**in•ert′ly** *adv.*

in•er•tia (ĭ nûr′shə) *n.* [U] **1.** In science, the tendency of a body at rest to remain at rest or of a body in motion to continue moving in a straight line unless a force is applied to it. **2.** Resistance to motion, action, or change: *There is enormous inertia in a big company.*

in•es•cap•a•ble (ĭn′ĭ skā′pə bəl) *adj.* Not capable of being escaped or avoided; in-evitable: *the inescapable duties of parents.* —**in′es•cap′a•bly** *adv.*

in•ev•i•ta•ble (ĭn ĕv′ĭ tə bəl) *adj.* Im-possible to avoid or prevent; certain to hap-pen: *the inevitable delays in driving across town during rush hour.* —**in•ev′i•ta•bly** *adv.*

in•ex•act (ĭn′ĭg zăkt′) *adj.* Not exact; not accurate or precise: *Because of inexact direc-tions, I got lost going to the party.* —**in′ex•act′ly** *adv.*

in•ex•cus•a•ble (ĭn′ĭk skyōō′zə bəl) *adj.* Impossible to excuse or justify: *an inexcus-able error.* —**in′ex•cus′a•bly** *adv.*

in•ex•haust•i•ble (ĭn′ĭg zô′stə bəl) *adj.* Not capable of being used up; unlimited: *an inexhaustible supply of food.* —**in′ex•haust′i•bly** *adv.*

in•ex•o•ra•ble (ĭn ĕk′sər ə bəl) *adj. For-mal.* Not capable of being stopped: *the inex-orable passage of time.* —**in•ex′o•ra•bly** *adv.*

in•ex•pen•sive (ĭn′ĭk spĕn′sĭv) *adj.* Not high in price; cheap. —**in′ex•pen′sive•ly** *adv.* —**in′ex•pen′sive•ness** *n.* [U]

in•ex•pe•ri•ence (ĭn′ĭk spîr′ē əns) *n.* [U] Lack of experience or knowledge gained from experience: *The inexperience of the young doctor caused him to hesitate in his decision.*

in•ex•pe•ri•enced (ĭn′ĭk spîr′ē ənst) *adj.* Lacking experience or the knowledge gained from experience: *an inexperienced driver.*

in•ex•pli•ca•ble (ĭn′ĭk splĭk′ə bəl) *adj.* Not capable of being explained or under-stood: *the inexplicable nature of certain vio-lent crimes.* —**in′ex•pli′ca•bly** *adv.*

in•fal•li•ble (ĭn făl′ə bəl) *adj.* **1.** Not capa-ble of making a mistake: *We had an infallible guide on our journey.* **2.** Not capable of fail-ing; sure: *an infallible cure for the infection.* —**in•fal′li•bil′i•ty** *n.* [U] —**in•fal′li•bly** *adv.*

in•fa•mous (ĭn′fə məs) *adj.* **1.** Having a very bad reputation; notorious: *an infamous murderer.* **2.** Deserving condemnation; shocking; outrageous: *infamous criminal deeds.* —**in′fa•mous•ly** *adv.*

in•fa•my (ĭn′fə mē) *n.* [U] **1.** The condition of being infamous: *a name that will live in infamy.* **2.** Evil reputation; disgrace: *The infamy of the dishonest politician was known far and wide.*

in•fan•cy (ĭn′fən sē) *n.* [U] **1.** The earliest period of childhood, especially before being able to walk: *Their first child died in infancy.* **2.** The earliest stage of sthg.: *Space explo-ration is still in its infancy.*

in·fant (ĭn′fənt) *n.* A child in the earliest period of life, especially before being able to walk; a baby. —*adj.* **1.** Relating to an infant: *infant years.* **2.** Intended for infants: *infant clothing.* **3.** Newly begun or formed: *The manufacturing of superconductors is an infant industry.*

in·fan·tile (ĭn′fən tīl′ *or* ĭn′fən tĭl) *adj.* **1.** Relating to infants or infancy: *infantile stages of development.* **2.** Lacking in maturity; childish: *The two leaders behaved in an infantile way.*

in·fan·try (ĭn′fən trē) *n.* [U] The branch of an army made up of units trained to fight on the ground.

in·fat·u·ate (ĭn făch′ōō āt′) *tr.v.* **in·fat·u·at·ed, in·fat·u·at·ing, in·fat·u·ates.** To fill (sbdy.) with foolish love or attachment: *He was infatuated with the famous actress.* —**in·fat′u·a′tion** *n.* [C; U]

in·fect (ĭn fĕkt′) *tr.v.* **1.** To cause disease or illness in (sbdy./sthg.) by introducing bacteria, viruses, or other organisms: *infected with HIV.* **2.** To transmit a disease to (sbdy./sthg.): *The sick child infected the rest of the class.*

in·fect·ed (ĭn fĕk′tĭd) *adj.* Having bacteria that prevent healing: *an infected wound.*

in·fec·tion (ĭn fĕk′shən) *n.* **1.** [C; U] The occurrence of disease or illness in people, animals, and plants from the introduction of bacteria, viruses, or other organisms: *Infection is spread in many ways.* **2.** [C] An infectious disease: *a viral infection.* **3.** [C; U] The state or condition of being infected: *ear infections.*

in·fec·tious (ĭn fĕk′shəs) *adj.* **1.** Caused or spread by infection: *an infectious disease.* **2.** Capable of causing infection: *infectious microorganisms.* **3.** Tending to spread easily or catch on: *infectious laughter.* —**in·fec′tious·ly** *adv.* —**in·fec′tious·ness** *n.* [U]

in·fer (ĭn fûr′) *tr.v.* **in·ferred, in·fer·ring, in·fers.** To arrive at (an opinion or idea) based on evidence; conclude: *I inferred from their laughter that they were having fun.*

───────────

USAGE: infer When we say that a speaker or sentence **implies** sthg., we mean that it is suggested without actually being said. *Even though you say you like sports, your lack of enthusiasm implies that you don't.* To **infer** sthg., on the other hand, is to draw conclusions that are not explicit in what is said: *Even though you say you like sports, I infer from your lack of enthusiasm that you really don't.*

───────────

in·fer·ence (ĭn′fər əns) *n.* **1.** [U] The act or process of inferring: *arrive at a conclusion by inference.* **2.** [C] Something inferred; a conclusion: *There is too little evidence to draw any inferences.*

in·fe·ri·or (ĭn fîr′ē ər) *adj.* [to] **1.** Low or lower in order, rank, or importance: *A captain is inferior to a general.* **2.** Low or lower in quality, value, or estimation: *A grade of C is inferior to a grade of B.* —*n.* A person lower in rank, status, or accomplishment than another. —**in·fe′ri·or′i·ty** (ĭn fîr′ē ôr′ĭ tē *or* ĭn fîr′ē ôr′i tē) *n.* [U]

in·fer·no (ĭn fûr′nō) *n., pl.* **in·fer·nos.** A place or condition suggestive of hell, as in being chaotic, noisy, or intensely hot: *The fire quickly grew to a raging inferno.*

in·fer·tile (ĭn fûr′tl) *adj.* **1.** Not fertile; unproductive: *infertile soil.* **2.** Describing a person or animal that is unable to have babies: *an infertile couple.* —**in′fer·til′i·ty** (ĭn′fər tĭl′ĭ tē) *n.* [U]

in·fest (ĭn fĕst′) *tr.v.* To be present in (sthg.) in large numbers so as to be harmful or unpleasant: *Insects infested the garden.* —**in′fes·ta′tion** (ĭn′fĕ stā′shən) *n.*

in·fi·del (ĭn′fĭ dəl *or* ĭn′fĭ dĕl′) *n.* An outdated expression for a person who does not believe in a particular religion: *Throughout history, people believed to be infidels were punished by religious groups.*

in·fi·del·i·ty (ĭn′fĭ dĕl′ĭ tē) *n., pl.* **in·fi·del·i·ties.** [C; U] Unfaithfulness to one's husband or wife, especially by having sexual relations with another person.

in·fight·ing (ĭn′fī′tĭng) *n.* Competition or argument among associates in a group or an organization: *political infighting.*

in·fil·trate (ĭn fĭl′trāt′ *or* ĭn′fĭl trāt′) *tr.v.* **in·fil·trat·ed, in·fil·trat·ing, in·fil·trates.** **1.** To move through (sthg.) with hostile intentions: *Enemy troops infiltrated our lines.* **2.** To enter (sthg.) without being noticed for purposes such as spying: *Government agents infiltrated the criminal operation.* —**in′fil·tra′tion** *n.* [C; U]

in·fi·nite (ĭn′fə nĭt) *adj.* **1.** Having no limit; endless: *The universe seems infinite.* **2.** Greater in value than any countable number, however large: *an infinite number.* **3.** Very great; immense: *His joy was infinite.* —**in′fi·nite·ness** *n.* [U]

in·fi·nite·ly (ĭn′fə nĭt lē) *adv.* Very much: *My brother is infinitely more patient than I am.*

in·fin·i·tes·i·mal (ĭn′fĭn ĭ tĕs′ə məl) *adj.* Extremely small; minute: *a high-grade steel with only infinitesimal amounts of impurities; infinitesimal differences.* —**in′fin·i·tes′i·mal·ly** *adv.*

in·fin·i·tive (ĭn fĭn′ĭ tĭv) *n.* A verb form that is not inflected to indicate person, number, or tense. In English, it is usually preceded by *to* or by an auxiliary verb. In the phrases *wanted*

───────────

to leave and *will play tomorrow,* the words *leave* and *play* are infinitives.

in·fin·i·ty (ĭn fĭn′ĭ tē) *n.* [U] A space, period of time, or quantity that is without a limit: *Space continues out into infinity.*

in·firm (ĭn fûrm′) *adj. Formal.* Weak in body, as from old age or sickness; feeble: *My grandmother is aged and infirm.*

in·fir·ma·ry (ĭn fûr′mə rē) *n., pl.* **in·fir·ma·ries.** A place for the care of sick or injured persons, especially a small hospital or clinic in a large institution.

in·fir·mi·ty (ĭn fûr′mĭ tē) *n., pl.* **in·fir·mi·ties.** *Formal.* **1.** [U] The condition of being infirm; weakness; frailty: *The doctor hesitated to perform surgery because of the patient's infirmity.* **2.** [C] A sickness; an illness.

in·flame (ĭn flām′) *tr.v.* **in·flamed, in·flam·ing, in·flames. 1.** To cause redness, swelling, and soreness in (sthg.): *The infection inflamed his skin.* **2.** To stir up (anger or other strong emotion); excite: *The speech inflamed the crowd.*

in·flamed (ĭn flāmd′) *adj.* **1.** Being very red and swollen: *an inflamed wound.* **2.** Too excited or angry: *the inflamed mob.*

in·flam·ma·ble (ĭn flăm′ə bəl) *adj.* Tending to catch fire easily and burn rapidly; flammable: *Gasoline is very inflammable.*

in·flam·ma·tion (ĭn′flə mā′shən) *n.* [C; U] Redness, swelling, heat, and soreness in a part of the body, resulting from injury, infection, or irritation.

in·flam·ma·to·ry (ĭn flăm′ə tôr′ē) *adj.* **1.** Arousing strong emotion: *a speaker's inflammatory language.* **2.** Characterized by or causing inflammation: *Arthritis is an inflammatory disease.*

in·flat·a·ble (ĭn flā′tə bəl) *adj.* Capable of being inflated: *an inflatable rubber boat.*

in·flate (ĭn flāt′) *v.* **in·flat·ed, in·flat·ing, in·flates.** —*tr.* **1.** To cause (sthg.) to expand with air or gas: *Did you inflate the tires on your bicycle?* **2.** To enlarge or raise (sthg.) abnormally or improperly: *All the attention from the reporters inflated the athlete's confidence in his abilities.* —*intr.* To become inflated: *The balloon inflated quickly.*

in·flat·ed (ĭn flā′tĭd) *adj.* **1.** Full of air or gas: *an inflated tire.* **2.** Too high or exaggerated: *her inflated idea of her own worth; inflated rhetoric.*

in·fla·tion (ĭn flā′shən) *n.* [U] **1.** The act of inflating; a swelling: *The inflation of the giant balloon took an hour.* **2.** A continuing rise in prices, caused by an increase in the amount of money or credit that is available: *annual inflation at four percent.*

in·fla·tion·ar·y (ĭn flā′shə nĕr′ē) *adj.* Relating to economic inflation: *inflationary prices.*

in·flect (ĭn flĕkt′) *tr.v.* **1.** To vary the tone or pitch of (the voice), especially in speaking. **2.** To change the form of (a word) to show

number, tense, person, comparison, or other grammatical function. For example, *book* is inflected to *books* in the plural.

in·flec·tion (ĭn flĕk′shən) *n.* **1.** [C; U] A change in the tone or pitch of the voice, especially in speech: *Simple yes–no questions end with a rising inflection.* **2.a.** [U] The process that changes the form of a word to indicate number, tense, person, comparison, or other grammatical function. For example, the comparative *quicker* is formed from *quick* by inflection. **b.** [C] A word formed by this process; an inflected form. For example, *drives, drove,* and *driven* are all inflections of the word *drive.* **c.** [C] A suffix used in this process. —**in·flec′tion·al** *adj.*

in·flex·i·ble (ĭn flĕk′sə bəl) *adj.* **1.** Not flexible; rigid: *An iron bar is inflexible.* **2.** Refusing to change; unyielding: *Workers were inflexible in their demands.* —**in·flex·i·bil′i·ty** *n.* [U] —**in·flex′i·bly** *adv.*

in·flict (ĭn flĭkt′) *tr.v.* **1.** To give (sthg.) as if by attack: *Bees inflict severe stings. A toothache inflicts pain.* **2.** To cause (sthg. unpleasant); impose: *The law inflicts penalties for criminal behavior.* —**in·flic′tion** *n.* [U]

in·flu·ence (ĭn′flōō əns) *n.* **1.** [U] The power to cause changes or have an effect without any apparent use of force: *Public opinion has a great influence on TV programs.* **2.** [U] Power that results from wealth or high position: *He got the job because of his uncle's influence.* **3.** [C] A person or thing that causes change without the use of force: *His wife has been a good influence on him.* —*tr.v.* **in·flu·enced, in·flu·enc·ing, in·flu·enc·es.** To have an effect on (sbdy./sthg.); change: *The automobile has greatly influenced the way people live.*

in·flu·en·tial (ĭn′flōō ĕn′shəl) *adj.* Having or exercising influence: *an influential newspaper.* —**in′flu·en′tial·ly** *adv.*

in·flu·en·za (ĭn′flōō ĕn′zə) *n.* A contagious viral disease that causes fever, inflammation of the respiratory system, irritation of the intestines, and muscle pain; flu.

in·flux (ĭn′flŭks′) *n.* An arrival of large numbers of people or things: *an influx of tourists to the park.*

in·fo (ĭn′fō) *n. Informal.* Information.

in·form (ĭn fôrm′) *tr.v.* To give information to (sbdy.); tell; notify: *The notice informed us of the time and place of the meeting.* ◆ **inform on** or **against.** *tr.v.* [insep.] To give secret or damaging information about (sbdy.): *The gang was captured after one of its members informed on the others.*

in·for·mal (ĭn fôr′məl) *adj.* **1.** Not following or requiring fixed ceremonies or rules; unofficial: *an informal agreement made with a handshake.* **2.** Suitable for everyday use or for casual occasions: *informal dress.* **3.** Not suitable for formal writing but frequently

I

used in conversation and ordinary writing. The use of *kid* to mean *a child* is informal.
—**in·for·mal·i·ty** (ĭn´fôr măl´ĭ tē) *n.* [C; U]
—**in·for·mal·ly** *adv.*

in·form·ant (ĭn fôr´mənt) *n.* A person who provides secret information to another: *a police informant.*

in·for·ma·tion (ĭn´fər mā´shən) *n.* [U] **1.** Knowledge or facts learned, especially about a certain event or subject: *The newspaper provides information on the day's events.* **2.** The act of informing or the condition of being informed: *This memo is for your information.*

in·form·a·tive (ĭn fôr´mə tĭv) *adj.* Providing information; instructive: *an informative TV series on dinosaurs.*

in·formed (ĭn fôrmd´) *adj.* Provided with information; knowledgeable: *That reporter is well informed on the facts of the issue.*

in·form·er (ĭn fôr´mər) *n.* A person who notifies authorities of secret and often illegal activities: *a paid informer.*

infra— *pref.* A prefix that means below or beneath: *infrastructure.*

in·frac·tion (ĭn frăk´shən) *n. Formal.* A breaking of a law or rule; a violation: *Speeding is a serious infraction of traffic laws.*

in·fra·red (ĭn´frə rĕd´) *adj.* Relating to the invisible part of the electromagnetic spectrum with wavelengths longer than those of visible red light but shorter than those of microwaves: *infrared light.*

in·fra·struc·ture (ĭn´frə strŭk´chər) *n.* A base or foundation for sthg., especially the basic systems necessary for a community to function, including roads and bridges, water pipes, and power lines.

in·fre·quent (ĭn frē´kwənt) *adj.* Not occurring often; occasional or rare: *an infrequent visitor.* —**in·fre´quent·ly** *adv.*

in·fringe (ĭn frĭnj´) *tr.v.* **in·fringed, in·fring·ing, in·fring·es.** To break or violate (a law, a right, or an obligation); fail to obey: *Censorship infringes the right to free speech.*
♦ **infringe on** or **upon.** *tr.v.* [insep.] To intrude upon; trespass on: *Reading someone else's mail infringes on that person's privacy.* —**in·fringe´ment** *n.* [C; U]

in·fu·ri·ate (ĭn fyoŏr´ē āt´) *tr.v.* **in·fu·ri·at·ed, in·fu·ri·at·ing, in·fu·ri·ates.** To make (sbdy.) furious; enrage: *I was infuriated by their rude remarks.*

in·fu·ri·at·ed (ĭn fyoŏr´ē āt ĭd) *adj.* Very angry: *The infuriated teacher could only sputter.*

in·fu·ri·at·ing (ĭn fyoŏr ē āt ĭng) *adj.* Causing great anger: *the child's infuriating behavior.* —**in·fu´ri·at´ing·ly** *adv.*

in·fuse (ĭn fyoōz´) *tr.v.* **in·fused, in·fus·ing, in·fus·es.** *Formal.* **1.** To fill (sbdy./

sthg.); inspire; instill: *Winning the game infused us with hope that we might win the championship.* **2.** To put (sthg.) into or introduce; instill: *The executive infused new life into the company.* **3.** To steep or soak (sthg.) in liquid without boiling in order to extract a substance: *Tea is made by infusing tea leaves in hot water.* —**in·fu´sion** *n.* [C; U]

—ing[1] *suff.* A suffix that forms: **1.** The present participle of verbs: *living.* **2.** Adjectives resembling present participles but not formed from verbs: *swashbuckling.*

—ing[2] *suff.* A suffix that means: **1.** An action or a process: *dancing; thinking.* **2.** An instance of an action or a process: *a meeting.* **3.** The result of an action or a process: *a painting.* **4.** Something used in an action or a process: *roofing.*

in·gen·ious (ĭn jēn´yəs) *adj.* **1.** Clever at making; creative: *an ingenious storyteller.* **2.** Planned, made, or done with originality and imagination: *The telephone is an ingenious device.* —**in·gen´ious·ly** *adv.* —**in·gen´ious·ness** *n.* [U]

in·ge·nu·i·ty (ĭn´jə noō´ĭ tē) *n.* [U] Inventive skill or imagination; cleverness: *Her ingenuity helped her solve the problem.*

in·gen·u·ous (ĭn jĕn´yoō əs) *adj.* Frank and open; candid: *They were being ingenuous in telling us the story.* —**in·gen´u·ous·ly** *adv.* —**in·gen´u·ous·ness** *n.* [U]

in·gest (ĭn jĕst´) *tr.v. Formal.* To take (food or drugs) into the body for digestion: *The baby had ingested some kind of harmful substance.* —**in·ges´tion** *n.* [U]

in·got (ĭng´gət) *n.* A mass of metal shaped in the form of a bar or block for convenient storage or transportation: *a gold ingot.*

in·grain (ĭn grān´) *tr.v.* To fix or impress (sthg.) deeply, as in the mind: *ingrain a sense of fairness.* —**in·grained´** *adj.*

in·grate (ĭn´grāt´) *n. Informal.* An ungrateful person: *She didn't even thank me; what an ingrate!*

in·gra·ti·ate (ĭn grā´shē āt´) *tr.v.* **in·gra·ti·at·ed, in·gra·ti·at·ing, in·gra·ti·ates.** To gain favor for (oneself) from another; make agreeable to another: *The class tried to ingratiate itself with the new teacher by being especially attentive.*

in·gra·ti·at·ing (ĭn grā´shē ā´tĭng) *adj.* **1.** Agreeable; pleasing: *an ingratiating smile.* **2.** Intended to win favor: *an ingratiating remark.* —**in·gra´ti·at´ing·ly** *adv.*

in·grat·i·tude (ĭn grăt´ĭ toōd´) *n.* [U] Lack of gratitude; ungratefulness.

in·gre·di·ent (ĭn grē´dē ənt) *n.* An element in a mixture: *The main ingredient of bread is flour.*

in·hab·it (ĭn hăb´ĭt) *tr.v.* To live in (a place);

ă–cat; ā–pay; âr–care; ä–father; ĕ–get; ē–be; ĭ–sit; ī–nice; îr–here; ŏ–got; ō–go; ô–saw; oi–boy; ou–out; oō–took; ōō–boot; ŭ–cut; ûr–word; th–thin; *th*–this; hw–when; zh–vision; ə–about; N–French bon

have as a dwelling place: *Dinosaurs inhabited the earth millions of years ago.* —**in•hab′it•a•ble** *adj.* —**in•hab′i•tant** *n.*

in•ha•lant (ĭn hā′lənt) *n.* Something, such as a medicine, that is inhaled.

in•hale (ĭn hāl′) *v.* **in•haled, in•hal•ing, in•hales.** —*tr.* To draw (air, for example) into the lungs by breathing: *inhaling fresh air.* —*intr.* To breathe in: *inhale deeply.* —**in′ha•la′tion** (ĭn′hə lā′shən) *n.*

in•hal•er (ĭn hā′lər) *n.* A device used to inhale a medicine.

in•her•ent (ĭn hîr′ənt *or* ĭn hĕr′ənt) *adj.* Being part of the basic nature of a person or thing; essential: *The student's inherent curiosity led to an interest in science.* —**in•her′ent•ly** *adv.*

in•her•it (ĭn hĕr′ĭt) *tr.v.* **1.** To receive (property) from a person who has died, usually through a will: *He inherited his wealth from his mother.* **2.** To receive or take over (sthg.) from sbdy. else: *Upon taking office, the mayor inherited many serious problems.* **3.** To acquire (characteristics) by genetic transmission from one's parents or ancestors: *I inherited my father's hair color.* —**in•her′i•tor** *n.*

in•her•i•tance (ĭn hĕr′ĭ təns) *n.* **1.** [U] The act of inheriting: *They gained their wealth by inheritance.* **2.** [C] Something that is inherited or is to be inherited at a person's death: *Her inheritance included money and property.*

in•hib•it (ĭn hĭb′ĭt) *tr.v.* To restrain or hold (sthg.) back; prevent: *Shyness inhibited the new student from talking freely in class.* —**in′hi•bi′tion** (ĭn′hə bĭsh′ən) *n.* [C; U]

in•hib•it•ed (ĭn hĭ′bĭt əd) *adj.* Lacking confidence; shy: *He was too inhibited to dance in public.*

in•hib•it•ing (ĭn hĭb′ĭt ĭng) *adj.* **1.** Making relaxed behavior or motion hard or impossible: *inhibiting clothes.* **2.** Tending to make sthg. hard or impossible: *The trip was slowed by inhibiting factors such as rain.*

in•hos•pi•ta•ble (ĭn hŏs′pĭ tə bəl *or* ĭn′-hŏ spĭt′ə bəl) *adj.* **1.** Showing no hospitality to others; unfriendly: *an inhospitable neighbor.* **2.** Not providing shelter or food; barren: *the inhospitable Arctic winter.* —**in′hos•pi′ta•bly** *adv.*

in•hu•man (ĭn hyōō′mən) *adj.* **1.** Lacking kindness or compassion; cruel: *The strict judge is often accused of being inhuman and without mercy.* **2.** Not suited for human needs: *The moon is an inhuman environment.* —**in′hu•man′i•ty** (ĭn′hyōō măn′ĭ tē) *n.* [C; U] —**in•hu′man•ly** *adv.*

in•hu•mane (ĭn′hyōō mān′) *adj.* Lacking pity or compassion: *The law punishes inhumane treatment of animals.* —**in′hu•mane′•ly** *adv.*

in•im•i•ta•ble (ĭ nĭm′ĭ tə bəl) *adj.* Impossible to imitate; unique: *a singer's inimitable style.* —**in•im′i•ta•bly** *adv.*

in•iq•ui•ty (ĭ nĭk′wĭ tē) *n., pl.* **in•iq•ui•ties. 1.** [U] Extreme injustice; wickedness: *The iniquity of the crime aroused great public anger.* **2.** [C] An immoral act; a sin. —**in•iq′ui•tous** *adj.* —**in•iq′ui•tous•ly** *adv.*

in•i•tial (ĭ nĭsh′əl) *adj.* Relating to or occurring at the beginning; first: *The initial attempts to correct the problem failed.* —*n.* The first letter of a word or name: *Please write your initials on your paper.* —*tr.v.* To mark or sign (sthg.) with initials: *Please initial each page of the contract to show you understand.* —**in•i′tial•ly** *adv.*

in•i•ti•ate (ĭ nĭsh′ē āt′) *tr.v.* **in•i•ti•at•ed, in•i•ti•at•ing, in•i•ti•ates. 1.** To begin or start (sthg.): *The company initiated a new line of clothes.* **2.** [*into*] To introduce (sbdy.) to a new subject, interest, skill, or activity: *My music teacher initiated me into the world of opera.* **3.** [*into*] To admit (sbdy.) into a group, often with a special ceremony: *Several new members were initiated into the club.* —*n.* (ĭ nĭsh′ē ĭt). A person who is being initiated. —**in•i′ti•a′tion** *n.* [C; U] —**in•i′ti•a′tor** *n.*

in•i•tia•tive (ĭ nĭsh′ə tĭv) *n.* **1.** [U] The ability to make decisions and put into effect a plan: *Starting one's own business requires a lot of initiative.* **2.** [C] The process by which citizens can propose a new law by petition and have it voted on: *The townspeople voted on the new anti-smoking initiative.* ♦ **on (one's) own initiative.** Without direction from others; by oneself: *The little boy bought his mother flowers on his own initiative.* **take the initiative.** To be in a position to make the first move: *She took the initiative and asked the new student for a date.*

in•ject (ĭn jĕkt′) *tr.v.* **1.a.** To force (a liquid or gas) into sthg.: *a mechanism that injects fuel into a cylinder of an engine.* **b.** To introduce (a fluid or medicine) into a body part, especially by a hypodermic needle: *The doctor injected the boy with the flu vaccine.* **2.** To introduce (sthg.); insert: *By mentioning cost, I tried to inject some realism into our planning.* —**in•jec′tor** *n.*

in•jec•tion (ĭn jĕk′shən) *n.* **1.** [C; U] The act of injecting: *medicine given by injection.* **2.** [C] Something that is injected, especially a dose of a liquid medicine injected into the body: *allergy injections.*

in•junc•tion (ĭn jŭngk′shən) *n.* An order, often from a court of law, or a command: *The judge issued an injunction stopping the strike and requiring further negotiations.*

in•jure (ĭn′jər) *tr.v.* **in•jured, in•jur•ing, in•jures.** To cause physical or emotional harm to (sbdy./sthg.); hurt: *She injured her arm in the accident.* See Synonyms at **hurt.**

in•ju•ry (ĭn′jə rē) *n., pl.* **in•ju•ries.** Damage or harm done to a person or thing: *I received only minor injuries in the accident.* —**in•ju′ri•ous** (ĭn jŏŏr′ē əs) *adj.*

in·jus·tice (ĭn jŭs′tĭs) n. 1. [U] Lack of justice; unfairness: *They fought against injustice.* 2. [C] A specific unjust act; a wrong: *Having the children taken away was an injustice.*

ink (ĭngk) n. [C; U] A black or colored liquid, used especially for writing or printing. —tr.v. To cover (sthg.) with ink; spread ink on: *The rubber stamp must be inked often.*

in·kling (ĭng′klĭng) n. A slight indication or hint; a vague idea: *He didn't have an inkling of how much it costs to build a house.*

ink·y (ĭng′kē) adj. 1. Stained or smeared with ink: *inky fingers.* 2. Like ink; dark; murky: *inky shadows.* —**ink′i·ness** n. [U]

in·laid (ĭn′lād′) v. Past tense and past participle of **inlay.** —adj. 1. Set into a surface to form a decoration: *inlaid decorative tile in a bathroom wall.* 2. Decorated with a pattern set into the surface: *a table with an inlaid top of wood.*

in·land (ĭn′lənd) adj. Relating to or located in the interior of a country or region: *The Great Lakes are inland waterways.* —adv. In, toward, or into the interior of a country or region: *You must travel inland to find the source of a river.*

in-law (ĭn′lô′) n. A relative by marriage: *My in-laws will visit my wife and me.*

in·lay (ĭn′lā′ *or* ĭn lā′) tr.v. **in·laid** (ĭn′lād′), **in·lay·ing, in·lays.** 1. To set (pieces of wood, for example) into a surface to form a design: *inlay strips of gold.* 2. To decorate (sthg.) by setting in such designs: *The floor was inlaid with different kinds of wood.* —n. Contrasting material set into a surface in pieces to form a design: *There is a rich inlay of silver and gold on the chair.*

in·let (ĭn′lĕt′ *or* ĭn′lĭt) n. 1. A narrow body of water between islands or leading inland. 2. An opening through which a liquid or gas can flow: *Don't forget to close the inlet on the tank.*

in-line skate (ĭn′līn′ skāt′) n. A type of skate with a single row of wheels.

in·mate (ĭn′māt′) n. A person confined to a prison or jail: *The inmates at the county jail all wear special clothing.*

inn (ĭn) n. A small hotel, especially one in a town or small city.

HOMONYMS: inn, in (inside).

in·nards (ĭn′ərdz) pl.n. Informal. 1. The internal organs of the body, especially of the abdomen. 2. The inner parts of a machine: *The computer's innards remain a mystery to me.*

in·nate (ĭ nāt′ *or* ĭn′āt′) adj. 1. Possessed at birth; inborn: *innate intelligence.* 2. Existing as a basic or essential characteristic; inherent: *Mountain climbing has certain innate dangers.* —**in·nate′ly** adv.

in·ner (ĭn′ər) adj. 1. Located farther inside: *The inner core of the earth lies very deep.* 2. Relating to the spirit or mind: *Sitting beside the brook, he felt an inner peace.* 3. More exclusive, private, or important: *the inner circles of government.*

inner city n. The older central part of a city, especially an area that is poor and in need of repair.

in·ner·most (ĭn′ər mōst′) adj. 1. Located farthest within: *the innermost room in the palace.* 2. Most private or intimate: *innermost feelings.*

inner tube n. A hollow rubber ring that can be inserted inside a tire and inflated.

in·ning (ĭn′ĭng) n. One of the nine divisions of a baseball game during which both teams have a turn at bat.

inn·keep·er (ĭn′kē′pər) n. A person who owns or manages an inn.

in·no·cence (ĭn′ə səns) n. [U] The condition, quality, or fact of being innocent, especially freedom from guilt.

in·no·cent (ĭn′ə sənt) adj. 1. Not guilty of a crime: *The jury found the defendant innocent.* 2. Not experienced in life; naive: *innocent children.* 3. Not intended to cause harm: *an innocent joke.* —n. A person, especially a child, who is free of evil or has done no wrong: *laws designed to protect the innocent.* —**in′no·cent·ly** adv.

in·noc·u·ous (ĭ nŏk′yōō əs) adj. Harmless; innocent: *an innocuous remark.* —**in·noc′u·ous·ly** adv.

in·no·vate (ĭn′ə vāt′) v. **in·no·vat·ed, in·no·vat·ing, in·no·vates.** —tr. To begin or introduce (sthg.) for the first time: *The scientist innovated new methods in research.* —intr. To begin or introduce sthg. new. —**in′no·va′tor** n.

in·no·va·tion (ĭn′ə vā′shən) n. 1. [C; U] The act of innovating: *The Industrial Revolution was a time of great innovation.* 2. [C] Something newly introduced: *Automatic transmission was a major innovation in automobiles.* —**in′no·va′tive** adj.

in·nu·en·do (ĭn′yōō ĕn′dō) n., pl. **in·nu·en·does.** [C; U] An indirect hint or suggestion, usually intended to hurt the reputation of sbdy.; an insinuation: *She had been hurt by lies and innuendoes.*

in·nu·mer·a·ble (ĭ nōō′mər ə bəl) adj. Too numerous to be counted: *innumerable difficulties.* —**in·nu′mer·a·bly** adv.

in·oc·u·late (ĭ nŏk′yə lāt′) tr.v. **in·oc·u·lat·ed, in·oc·u·lat·ing, in·oc·u·lates.** To inject (a person or an animal) with a vaccine in order to make the body resistant to a particular disease. —**in·oc′u·la′tion** n.

in·of·fen·sive (ĭn′ə fĕn′sĭv) adj. Giving no

offense; harmless: *an inoffensive joke.* **—in′·of·fen′sive·ly** *adv.* **—in′of·fen′sive·ness** *n.* [U]

in·op·er·a·ble (ĭn ŏp′ər ə bəl *or* ĭn ŏp′rə bəl) *adj.* **1.** Not suitable for surgery: *His cancer was inoperable.* **2.** Not functioning; inoperative: *The newest plan was inoperable.*

in·op·er·a·tive (ĭn ŏp′ər ə tĭv *or* ĭn ŏp′rə tĭv) *adj.* Not working or functioning: *The computer is inoperative at this time.*

in·op·por·tune (ĭn ŏp′ər tōōn′) *adj.* Coming at the wrong time; inappropriate: *a telephone call at a most inopportune moment.*

in·or·di·nate (ĭn ôr′dn ĭt) *adj.* Exceeding reasonable limits; excessive: *a talk of inordinate length.* **—in·or′di·nate·ly** *adv.*

in·or·gan·ic (ĭn′ôr găn′ĭk) *adj.* Not involving living organisms or the products of their life processes: *Inorganic matter contains no hydrocarbons.* **—in′or·gan′i·cal·ly** *adv.*

in·pa·tient (ĭn′pā′shənt) *n.* A patient who stays overnight in a hospital or clinic for treatment.

in·put (ĭn′pŏŏt′) *n.* [U] **1.** Ideas, money, or work put into a project or process: *The study requires input from many people.* **2.** The data or programs put into a computer. **3.** The power supplied to an electronic circuit or device. **—***tr.v.* **in·put·ted** *or* **in·put, in·put·ting, in·puts.** To enter (data or a program) into a computer: *We input the list of names.*

in·quest (ĭn′kwĕst′) *n.* A legal investigation into the cause of a death: *a coroner's inquest.*

in·quire (ĭn kwīr′) *intr.v.* **in·quired, in·quir·ing, in·quires.** *Formal.* **1.** To request information; try to find out by asking questions: *If you can't find your size, inquire at the sales desk.* See Synonyms at **ask. 2.** To make a search or study; investigate: *inquire into a case.* **—in·quir′er** *n.*

in·quir·ing (ĭn kwīr′ĭng) *adj.* Wanting to know more; curious: *the prying questions of inquiring people.* **—in·quir′ing·ly** *adv.*

in·quir·y (ĭn kwīr′ē *or* ĭn′kwə rē) *n., pl.* **in·quir·ies. 1.** The act of inquiring: *engaged in scientific inquiry.* **2.** A request for information; a question: *many inquiries about the new mail rates.* **3.** A detailed examination of a matter; an investigation: *an inquiry into why water bills are so high.*

in·qui·si·tion (ĭn′kwĭ zĭsh′ən) *n. (usually singular).* An investigation that violates the privacy or rights of individuals, often by thorough, harsh questioning: *She felt like she was being put through an inquisition.*

in·quis·i·tive (ĭn kwĭz′ĭ tĭv) *adj.* Eager to learn; curious: *an inquisitive mind.* See Synonyms at **curious. —in·quis′i·tive·ly** *adv.* **—in·quis′i·tive·ness** *n.* [U]

in·road (ĭn′rōd′) *n.* **1.** A hostile invasion; a raid. **2.** *(usually plural).* An advance at another's expense; an encroachment: *Our company has made inroads into the competing market.*

ins. *abbr.* An abbreviation of: **1.** Inches. **2.** Insurance.

in·sane (ĭn sān′) *adj.* **1.** Mentally ill: *The defendant was found not guilty because he was insane.* **2.** *Slang.* Very foolish; not sensible: *an insane stunt.* **—in·sane′ly** *adv.* **—in·san′i·ty** (ĭn săn′ĭ tē) *n.* [U]

in·sa·tia·ble (ĭn sā′shə bəl) *adj.* Impossible to satisfy; never satisfied: *an insatiable appetite.* **—in·sa′tia·bly** *adv.*

in·scribe (ĭn skrīb′) *tr.v.* **in·scribed, in·scrib·ing, in·scribes. 1.** To write, carve, or engrave (words, letters, or a design) on a surface: *Inscribe the winners' names on a trophy.* **2.** To impress (sthg.) deeply on the mind: *Our last day of school is inscribed on my memory.*

in·scrip·tion (ĭn skrĭp′shən) *n.* **1.** [U] The act or an example of inscribing: *the inscription of the names of war heroes on a monument.* **2.** [C] Something inscribed: *a wall covered with ancient Egyptian inscriptions.* **3.** [C] A short signed message in a book or on a picture given as a gift.

in·scru·ta·ble (ĭn skrōō′tə bəl) *adj.* Difficult to understand; mysterious: *an inscrutable smile; an inscrutable coded message.* **—in·scru′ta·bly** *adv.*

in·sect (ĭn′sĕkt′) *n.* Any of numerous, usually small animals that in the adult stage have six legs, a body with three main divisions, and usually two pairs of wings. Flies, bees, grasshoppers, butterflies, and moths are insects.

insect
Top to bottom:
Ant, bumblebee,
cockroach, and
grasshopper

in·sec·ti·cide (ĭn sĕk′tĭ sīd′) *n.* [C; U] A chemical used to kill insects.

in·se·cure (ĭn′sĭ kyŏŏr′) *adj.* **1.** Not sure or certain; doubtful: *an insecure future.* **2.** Not secure or safe; not fully protected: *an insecure apartment building with faulty locks.* **3.** Lacking self-confidence: *an insecure person.* **—in′se·cure′ly** *adv.* **—in′se·cu′ri·ty** (ĭn′sĭ kyŏŏr′ĭ tē) *n.* [C; U]

in·sem·i·nate (ĭn sĕm′ə nāt′) *tr.v.* **in·sem·i·nat·ed, in·sem·i·nat·ing, in·sem·i·nates.** To introduce semen into (a female); impregnate. **—in·sem′i·na′tion** *n.* [U]

in·sen·si·tive (ĭn sĕn′sĭ tĭv) *adj.* **1.** Lacking in sensitivity for others; unfeeling: *Her remark about older people was very insensitive.* **2.** Not physically sensitive (to pain); numb: *An injection made the tooth insensitive.* **—in·sen′si·tive·ly** *adv.* **—in·sen′si·tiv′i·ty** *n.* [U]

in·sep·a·ra·ble (ĭn sĕp′ər ə bəl *or* ĭn sĕp′rə bəl) *adj.* Impossible to separate:

inseparable friends. —**in•sep′a•ra•bil′i•ty**
n. [U] —**in•sep′a•ra•bly** *adv.*

in•sert (ĭn sûrt′) *tr.v.* To put (sthg.) into,
between, or among: *insert a key in a lock;
insert pictures between chapters in the book.*
—*n.* (ĭn′sûrt′). Something inserted or meant
to be inserted: *An advertising insert fell out of
the magazine.* —**in•ser′tion** *n.* [C; U]

in•side (ĭn sīd′ *or* ĭn′sīd′) *n.* **1.** An inner part,
side, or surface: *the inside of a house; articles
on the inside of a magazine.* **2. insides. a.**
Informal. The inner organs, especially those
of the abdomen: *Something is wrong with my
insides.* **b.** The inner workings: *the insides of
a TV set.* —*adj.* **1.** Inner; interior: *the inside
pocket of a jacket.* **2.** Coming from or known
by those within a group: *inside information; a
theft that was definitely an inside job.* —*adv.*
Into or in the interior; within: *go inside; staying inside.* —*prep.* Into or in the interior of:
inside the package; go inside the house.
♦ **inside of.** Within the limits of: *He should
be here inside of an hour.* **inside out. 1.** With
the inner surface turned out; reversed: *wearing his shirt inside out.* **2.** Thoroughly: *A taxi
driver must know the city inside out.*

in•sid•er (ĭn sī′dər) *n.* A person who has
special knowledge or access to private information: *The theft must have been the work of
an insider.*

in•sid•i•ous (ĭn sĭd′ē əs) *adj.* **1.** Intended to
trap; sneaky: *an insidious plot.* **2.** Working or
spreading harmfully in a subtle or hidden
manner: *insidious rumors; an insidious disease.* —**in•sid′i•ous•ly** *adv.* —**in•sid′i•
ous•ness** *n.* [U]

in•sight (ĭn′sīt′) *n.* **1.** [U] The ability to
understand the true nature of sthg.: *Einstein's
insight into the workings of the universe.* **2.**
[C] An understanding of the true nature of
sthg.: *The critic had a brilliant insight about
the meaning of the movie.* —**in•sight′ful** *adj.*

in•sig•ni•a (ĭn sĭg′nē ə) *n., pl.* **insignia** or
in•sig•ni•as. A badge of office, rank, membership, or nationality; an emblem: *She wore
the insignia of an officer.*

in•sig•nif•i•cant (ĭn′sĭg nĭf′ĭ kənt) *adj.* **1.** Of
no importance; trivial: *an insignificant detail.* **2.**
Small in size, power, or value: *an insignificant
amount of money.* —**in′sig•nif′i•cance** *n.* [U]
—**in′sig•nif′i•cant•ly** *adv.*

in•sin•cere (ĭn′sĭn sîr′) *adj.* Not sincere;
false: *an insincere apology.* —**in′sin•cere′ly**
adv. —**in′sin•cer′i•ty** (ĭn′sĭn sĕr′ĭ tē) *n.* [U]

in•sin•u•ate (ĭn sĭn′yōō āt′) *tr.v.* **in•sin•
u•at•ed, in•sin•u•at•ing, in•sin•u•ates.**
To introduce or suggest (sthg.) in a sly or
indirect way: *Are you insinuating that I'm not
good enough for the team?* —**in•sin′u•
a′tion** *n.* [C; U]

in•sip•id (ĭn sĭp′ĭd) *adj.* **1.** Lacking flavor;
bland: *an insipid watery soup.* **2.** Lacking
excitement or interest; dull: *an insipid movie.*
—**in•sip′id•ly** *adv.*

in•sist (ĭn sĭst′) *v.* —*intr.* [on] To be firm in a
plan or demand: *I insist on paying my share of
the expenses.* —*tr.* To demand (sthg.): *We insist
that you stay for dinner.* —**in•sis′tence** *n.* [U]
—**in•sis′tent** *adj.* —**in•sis′tent•ly** *adv.*

in•so•far as (ĭn′sō fär′) *conj.* To the extent
that: *Insofar as I am able, I will help you with
the move.*

in•so•lent (ĭn′sə lənt) *adj.* Disrespectfully
bold; rude: *an insolent reply.* —**in′so•lence**
n. [U] —**in′so•lent•ly** *adv.*

in•sol•u•ble (ĭn sŏl′yə bəl) *adj.* **1.** Difficult or
impossible to solve or explain: *an insoluble
problem.* **2.** Not capable of being dissolved in a
liquid: *Some salts are insoluble.* —**in•sol′u•
bil′i•ty** *n.* [U] —**in•sol′u•bly** *adv.*

in•sol•vent (ĭn sŏl′vənt) *adj. Formal.* Unable to pay one's debts; bankrupt: *an insol-
vent bank.* —**in•sol′ven•cy** *n.* [U]

in•som•ni•a (ĭn sŏm′nē ə) *n.* [U] Inability
to sleep; sleeplessness: *She has suffered from
insomnia for years.*

in•spect (ĭn spĕkt′) *tr.v.* **1.** To examine
(sthg.) carefully: *We inspect all of our products.* **2.** To examine or review (sbdy./sthg.)
formally; evaluate officially: *An officer inspects the troops every Saturday.* —**in•spec′-
tion** *n.* [C; U] —**in•spec′tor** *n.*

in•spi•ra•tion (ĭn′spə rā′shən) *n.* **1.** The
excitement of the mind, emotions, or imagination, as in creating sthg. or solving a problem: *Some writers get inspiration for a story
from reading the newspaper.* **2.** A person or
thing that excites the mind or the emotions of
others: *The brilliant scientist was an inspiration to younger colleagues.* —**in′spi•ra′-
tion•al** *adj.*

in•spire (ĭn spīr′) *v.* **in•spired, in•spir•
ing, in•spires.** —*tr.* **1.** To fill (sbdy.) with
great emotion: *The violinist's performance
inspired the entire audience.* **2.** To stimulate
(sbdy.) to creativity or action: *The discovery
inspired us to look for fossils.* **3.** To cause (a
feeling or an attitude) in another or others;
influence: *The candidate inspired confidence
in the voters.* **4.** To be the cause or source of
(sthg.): *The book inspired a movie.*

in•spired (ĭn spīrd′) *adj.* Excellent; brilliant:
an inspired performance.

in•spir•ing (ĭn spīr′ĭng) *adj.* Having an
influence; stimulating: *an inspiring story of
courage.*

in•sta•bil•i•ty (ĭn′stə bĭl′ĭ tē) *n.* [U] Lack
of stability; unsteadiness: *The roof collapsed
because of the instability of the walls.*

in•stall (ĭn stôl′) *tr.v.* **1.** To set (equipment) in position and connect for use: *The company installed the new phones yesterday.* **2.** To place (sbdy.) in an office, a rank, or a position, usually with ceremony: *The new officers of the club were installed.* —**in′stal‧la′tion** (ĭn′stə‑lā′shən) *n.* [C; U]

in‧stall‧ment (ĭn stôl′mənt) *n.* **1.** One of a series of payments on a debt: *We paid for our television set in four installments of $100 each.* **2.** A portion of sthg. issued or presented at intervals: *The book came out in installments in a magazine.*

in‧stance (ĭn′stəns) *n.* A case or an example: *This is another instance of her great leadership.* ◆ **for instance.** For example: *There are a lot of ways to invest money. For instance, you could buy shares in a mutual fund.*

in‧stant (ĭn′stənt) *n. (usually singular).* **1.** A brief period of time; a moment: *The accident happened in an instant.* **2.** A particular point in time: *Please call the instant they arrive.* —*adj.* **1.** Immediate: *an instant success.* **2.** Prepared by a manufacturer for quick preparation by the consumer: *instant soup.* —**in′stant‧ly** *adv.*

in‧stan‧ta‧ne‧ous (ĭn′stən tā′nē əs) *adj.* Happening without delay; immediate: *an instantaneous reaction.* —**in′stan‧ta′ne‧ous‧ly** *adv.*

in‧stead (ĭn stĕd′) *adv.* In place of sthg. previously mentioned; as a substitute or an alternative: *They didn't have tea, so I got coffee instead.*

instead of *prep.* In place of; rather than: *They walked home instead of taking the bus.*

in‧step (ĭn′stĕp′) *n.* **1.** The arched middle part of the foot between the toes and the ankle. **2.** The part of a shoe covering this part of the foot: *This shoe is too tight in the instep.*

in‧sti‧gate (ĭn′stĭ gāt′) *tr.v.* **in‧sti‧gat‧ed, in‧sti‧gat‧ing, in‧sti‧gates.** To make (sthg.) start to happen; provoke: *instigate a prison riot.* —**in′sti‧ga′tion** *n.* [U] —**in′‑sti‧ga′tor** *n.*

in‧still (ĭn stĭl′) *tr.v.* To introduce (sthg.) little by little; implant: *The parents instilled good values in their children.*

in‧stinct (ĭn′stĭngkt′) *n.* **1.** An inborn pattern of behavior that is characteristic of a given species: *the cat's instinct to chase mice.* **2.** A natural talent or ability: *an instinct for science.* —**in‧stinc′tive** *adj.* —**in‧stinc′tive‧ly** *adv.*

in‧sti‧tute (ĭn′stĭ tōōt′) *tr.v.* **in‧sti‧tut‧ed, in‧sti‧tut‧ing, in‧sti‧tutes.** *Formal.* To establish, organize, or set (sthg.) in operation; begin: *The government instituted a new trade policy.* See Synonyms at **establish.** —*n.* **1.** An organization established to promote a cause: *a research institute.* **2.** An educational institution: *an art institute.*

in‧sti‧tu‧tion (ĭn′stĭ tōō′shən) *n.* **1.** [U] The act of instituting: *the institution of new school rules for student conduct.* **2.** [C] A

custom, practice, or pattern of behavior that is important in the cultural life of a society: *the institution of marriage.* **3.** [C] An organization or foundation, especially one dedicated to public service: *an educational institution.* —**in′sti‧tu′tion‧al** *adj.*

in‧sti‧tu‧tion‧al‧ize (ĭn′stĭ tōō′shə nə‑līz′) *tr.v.* **in‧sti‧tu‧tion‧al‧ized, in‧sti‧tu‧tion‧al‧iz‧ing, in‧sti‧tu‧tion‧al‧iz‧es.** **1.** To make into, treat as, or give the character of an institution to (sbdy./sthg.). **2.** To place (a person) in the care of an institution: *He's been institutionalized most of his life.*

in‧sti‧tu‧tion‧al‧ized (ĭn′stĭ tōō′shə nə‑līzd′) *adj.* **1.** Accepted as normal or usual in a society: *institutionalized racism.* **2.** Placed in an institution, such as a hospital or prison, for a long time: *Institutionalized people often have problems adjusting to life outside when they're released.*

in‧struct (ĭn strŭkt′) *tr.v.* **1.** To give knowledge or skill to (sbdy.); teach: *The teacher will instruct the class in how to use these new computers.* See Synonyms at **teach.** **2.** To give orders to (sbdy.); direct: *The coach instructed us to run around the track.*

in‧struc‧tion (ĭn strŭk′shən) *n.* **1.** Something that is taught; a lesson: *instructions in music.* **2.** The act of teaching or instructing; education. **3. instructions.** Directions; orders: *The model airplane came with clear instructions.* —**in‧struc′tion‧al** *adj.*

in‧struc‧tive (ĭn strŭk′tĭv) *adj.* Providing knowledge or information: *an instructive example.* —**in‧struc′tive‧ly** *adv.*

in‧struc‧tor (ĭn strŭk′tər) *n.* **1.** A person who instructs; a teacher. **2.** A college or university teacher ranking below an assistant professor.

in‧stru‧ment (ĭn′strə mənt) *n.* **1.** An object used to do work, especially one used by a physician, dentist, or scientist. **2.** A device used for making music: *the instruments of an orchestra.* **3.** A device for recording or measuring: *A fuel gauge and a compass are important instruments in an aircraft.*

instrument
Clockwise from upper left: Tambourine, triangle, bass drum, and xylophone

I

in·stru·men·tal (ĭn′strə mĕn′tl) *adj.* **1.** Serving as the means; helpful: *Our teacher was instrumental in getting the club a place to meet.* **2.** Performed on or written for musical instruments: *instrumental music.* —**in′stru·men′tal·ist** *n.* —**in′stru·men′tal·ly** *adv.* —**in′stru·men·ta′tion** *n.* [U]

in·sub·or·di·nate (ĭn′sə bôr′dn ĭt) *adj.* Not obedient to authority: *fired for being insubordinate to his boss.* —**in′sub·or′di·nate·ly** *adv.* —**in′sub·or′di·na′tion** (ĭn′sə bôr′dn ā′shən) *n.* [U]

in·sub·stan·tial (ĭn′səb stăn′shəl) *adj.* **1.** Lacking substance or reality; imaginary: *not facts, but insubstantial visions.* **2.** Not firm; flimsy: *an insubstantial cardboard wall.* —**in′sub·stan′tial·ly** *adv.*

in·suf·fer·a·ble (ĭn sŭf′ər ə bəl *or* ĭn-sŭf′rə bəl) *adj.* Difficult or impossible to endure; intolerable: *insufferable rudeness.* —**in·suf′fer·a·bly** *adv.*

in·suf·fi·cient (ĭn′sə fĭsh′ənt) *adj.* Not enough; inadequate: *insufficient rainfall for a good harvest.* —**in′suf·fi′cien·cy** *n.* [U] —**in′suf·fi′cient·ly** *adv.*

in·su·lar (ĭn′sə lər *or* ĭns′yə lər) *adj.* Formal. Alone; isolated: *the insular life of a hermit.* —**in′su·lar′i·ty** (ĭn′sə lăr′ĭ tē *or* ĭns′yə lăr′ĭ tē) *n.*

in·su·late (ĭn′sə lāt′) *tr.v.* **in·su·lat·ed, in·su·lat·ing, in·su·lates. 1.** To cover or surround (sthg.) with a material that prevents the passage of heat, electricity, or sound into or out of: *We insulated our attic to keep out the cold.* **2.** To detach (sbdy./sthg.); isolate: *The mountain valley is insulated from outside influences.* —**in′su·la′tion** *n.* [U] —**in′su·la′tor** *n.*

in·su·lin (ĭn′sə lĭn) *n.* [U] A hormone that is produced in the pancreas and regulates the amount of sugar in the blood.

in·sult (ĭn sŭlt′) *tr.v.* To treat (sbdy./sthg.) with contempt; offend: *She insulted me by saying hello to everyone but me.* —*n.* (ĭn′sŭlt′). An offensive action or remark: *They shouted insults at each other.* —**in·sult′ing·ly** *adv.*

in·sur·ance (ĭn shoŏr′əns) *n.* [U] **1.** The business of guaranteeing to pay for specified losses in the future, as for accident, illness, theft, or death, in return for payment: *We need to buy auto insurance.* **2.a.** A contract making such guarantees in return for regular payments. **b.** The total amount to be paid to the person insured: *We bought $100,000 of life insurance.*

in·sure (ĭn shoŏr′) *tr.v.* **in·sured, in·sur·ing, in·sures. 1.** To provide (sbdy./sthg.) with insurance: *insure a car.* **2.** To make sure of (sthg.); guarantee; ensure: *Proper diet helps to insure good health.* —**in·sur′er** *n.*

in·sur·gent (ĭn sûr′jənt) *adj.* Rising in revolt: *The insurgent forces overthrew the government.* —*n.* A person who revolts against authority; a rebel. —**in·sur′gence** *n.* [U]

in·sur·mount·a·ble (ĭn′sər moun′tə bəl) *adj.* Impossible to overcome: *an insurmountable obstacle.*

in·sur·rec·tion (ĭn′sə rĕk′shən) *n.* [C; U] An uprising against an established authority or government; a rebellion. —**in′sur·rec′tion·ist** *n.*

in·tact (ĭn tăkt′) *adj.* Not weakened, injured, or damaged; whole: *The contents were intact in spite of the damage to the box.*

in·take (ĭn′tāk′) *n.* **1.** [C] An opening through which a liquid or gas enters a container or pipe: *an intake clogged with dirt.* **2.** [U] **a.** The act of taking in: *an efficient air intake.* **b.** Something, or the amount of sthg., taken in: *an adequate intake of food.*

in·tan·gi·ble (ĭn tăn′jə bəl) *adj.* Not capable of being touched; lacking physical substance: *Personal satisfaction is one of the intangible rewards of community service.* —*n.* Something intangible: *The intangibles of life, such as happiness, are hard to measure.* —**in·tan′gi·bly** *adv.*

in·te·ger (ĭn′tĭ jər) *n.* A positive or negative whole number or zero: *The number 5 is an integer; 5.5 is not.*

in·te·gral (ĭn′tĭ grəl *or* ĭn tĕg′rəl) *adj.* Necessary to form a whole or make sthg. complete: *Practice is an integral part of language learning.*

in·te·grate (ĭn′tĭ grāt′) *v.* **in·te·grat·ed, in·te·grat·ing, in·te·grates.** —*tr.* **1.** To make (sthg.) into a whole by bringing all parts together; unify: *The school integrated math and computer courses last fall.* **2.** To open (sthg.) to people of all races or ethnic groups without restriction; desegregate: *Schools were integrated to provide equal opportunity.* —*intr.* To become integrated. —**in′te·gra′tion** *n.* [U] —**in′te·gra′tion·ist** *n.*

in·teg·ri·ty (ĭn tĕg′rĭ tē) *n.* [U] **1.** Moral principles; honesty: *A judge must be a person of integrity.* **2.** Formal. Completeness; unity: *The country maintained its integrity by defending its borders.*

in·tel·lect (ĭn′tl ĕkt′) *n.* **1.** [U] The power of the mind to think, reason, and learn. **2.** [U] Great intelligence or mental ability: *We admire people of intellect.* **3.** [C] A person of great intellectual ability: *a gathering of scientific intellects.*

in·tel·lec·tu·al (ĭn′tl ĕk′choō əl) *adj.* **1.** Using the intellect: *an intellectual discussion.* **2.** Having or showing intelligence: *an intellectual person.* See Synonyms at **smart.** —*n.*

A person of intelligence, especially a person who is informed and interested in many things. —**in·tel·lec·tu·al·ly** adv.

in·tel·li·gence (ĭn tĕl′ə jəns) n. [U] **1.** The capacity to gain and use knowledge; mental ability: The ape is an animal of high intelligence. **2.** Information or news, especially secret information about an enemy or opponent.

in·tel·li·gent (ĭn tĕl′ə jənt) adj. **1.** Having intelligence, especially of a high degree: an intelligent history student. See Synonyms at **smart**. **2.** Showing intelligence; wise or thoughtful: an intelligent decision. —**in·tel′li·gent·ly** adv.

in·tel·li·gi·ble (ĭn tĕl′ĭ jə bəl) adj. Capable of being understood; comprehensible: We need someone to write intelligible instructions on using this computer program. —**in·tel′li·gi·bly** adv.

in·tend (ĭn tĕnd′) tr.v. **1.** To have (sthg.) as a purpose; plan: We intend to get an early start. **2.** To design (sthg.) for a specific purpose or use: That book is intended for beginners.

in·tend·ed (ĭn tĕn′dĭd) adj. Planned; intentional: an intended result. —n. Informal. A person who is engaged to be married: My sister and her intended came along.

in·tense (ĭn tĕns′) adj. **1.** Existing in an extreme degree; very strong: an intense blue; intense heat. **2.** Having deep feeling: an intense look; intense words. —**in·tense′ly** adv.

USAGE: intense The words **intense** and **intensive** mean two different things in the two phrases his intense study of English and his intensive study of English. **Intense** suggests that he himself is responsible for his concentrated activity, whereas **intensive** suggests that his concentration of activity is set by a program that covers a great deal of material in a brief period.

in·ten·si·fy (ĭn tĕn′sə fī′) tr. & intr.v. **in·ten·si·fied, in·ten·si·fy·ing, in·ten·si·fies.** To make or become intense or more intense: The police intensified their investigation. Our review sessions intensified as exams drew near. —**in·ten′si·fi·ca′tion** (ĭn tĕn′sə fĭ kā′shən) n. [U]

in·ten·si·ty (ĭn tĕn′sĭ tē) n. [U] Extreme force, strength, or concentration: Our team played with emotional intensity. **2.** The strength of a color: The two colors vary in intensity. **3.** The amount of strength of electricity, heat, light, or sound per unit of area, volume, or mass.

in·ten·sive (ĭn tĕn′sĭv) adj. Marked by intensity; deep: intensive study. —**in·ten′sive·ly** adv. —See NOTE at **intense**.

in·tent (ĭn tĕnt′) n. [U] **1.** A purpose; an intention: It was never my intent to start an argument. **2.** Meaning; significance: The

intent of your message is clear. —adj. **1.** Showing concentration; intense: He had an intent expression on his face while studying. **2.** Firmly fixed on some purpose; determined: We are intent on securing a new trade agreement. ◆ **for all intents and purposes.** In every practical sense; almost: With only two minutes left to play, for all intents and purposes the game is over. —**in·tent′ly** adv. —**in·tent′ness** n. [U]

in·ten·tion (ĭn tĕn′shən) n. **1.** A plan, purpose, or design: I have no intention of calling her. **2. intentions.** Purposes or motives in mind: She had the best of intentions. —**in·ten′tion·al** adj. —**in·ten′tion·al·ly** adv.

in·ter (ĭn tûr′) tr.v. **in·terred, in·ter·ring, in·ters.** Formal. To place (a body) in a grave; bury: ancient burials where the dead were interred in tombs. —**in·ter′ment** n. [U]

inter— pref. A prefix that means: **1.** Between; among: international. **2.** Together; interact.

in·ter·act (ĭn′tər ăkt′) intr.v. To act on or affect each other: The two groups interact smoothly. —**in′ter·ac′tion** n. [C; U]

in·ter·ac·tive (ĭn′tər ăk′tĭv) adj. Relating to a computer program or other entertainment in which the user and the program interact: Computer games are interactive.

in·ter·cede (ĭn′tər sēd′) intr.v. **in·ter·ced·ed, in·ter·ced·ing, in·ter·cedes.** To speak or act to help another: The teacher interceded with my parents to let me go on the trip.

in·ter·cept (ĭn′tər sĕpt′) tr.v. To stop (sbdy./sthg.) from going from one place to another: intercept a messenger; intercept a phone call. —**in′ter·cep′tion** n. [C; U] —**in′ter·cep′tor** n.

in·ter·change (ĭn′tər chānj′) tr.v. **in·ter·changed, in·ter·chang·ing, in·ter·chang·es. 1.** To give and receive (things) mutually; exchange: An open discussion is the best way to interchange ideas. **2.** To switch each of (two things) into the place of the other: If you interchange the first and last letters of the word pal, it becomes lap. —n. (ĭn′tər chānj′). **1.** [U] The act of interchanging: Trade is the interchange of goods or services. **2.** [C] A highway intersection that allows traffic to move from one road to another without crossing another line of traffic.

in·ter·change·a·ble (ĭn′tər chān′jə bəl) adj. Capable of being switched or interchanged: These two cars have interchangeable parts. —**in′ter·change′a·bly** adv.

in·ter·col·le·giate (ĭn′tər kə lē′jĭt) adj. Involving two or more colleges or universities: intercollegiate athletic events.

in·ter·com (ĭn′tər kŏm′) n. An electronic communication system, as between rooms of a building.

in·ter·con·nect (ĭn′tər kə nĕkt′) *intr.* & *tr.v.* To connect or be connected with each other. —**in′ter·con·nec′tion** [C; U] *n.*

in·ter·con·ti·nen·tal (ĭn′tər kŏn′tə nĕn′tl) *adj.* Involving two or more continents: *intercontinental weather patterns; an intercontinental airline.*

in·ter·course (ĭn′tər kôrs′) *n.* [U] *Formal.* The act of having sexual relations.

in·ter·de·pend·ent (ĭn′tər dĭ pĕn′dənt) *adj.* Dependent on one another; mutually dependent: *The two companies are interdependent; each produces something that the other needs.* —**in′ter·de·pend′ence** *n.* [U] —**in′ter·de·pend′ent·ly** *adv.*

in·ter·est (ĭn′trĭst *or* ĭn′tər ĭst) *n.* **1.a.** [U] A feeling of curiosity or concern about sthg.: *An exciting story will hold the reader's interest.* **b.** [C] A subject that creates such a feeling: *Music and computer games are among my interests.* **2.** [U] **a.** A charge for borrowing money, usually a percentage of the amount borrowed: *The interest on my credit card is 18 percent.* **b.** An amount paid by a bank to the owner of an account that earns money, usually a percentage of the amount on deposit: *My bank is paying four percent interest.* **3.** [U] Ownership in sthg.: *She has a 50 percent interest in that business.* **4.** [C] Something in which a right, claim, or share is held: *American interests overseas.* —*tr.v.* **1.** To create curiosity in or hold the attention of (sbdy.): *Modern art interests me a lot.* **2.** To cause (sbdy.) to become involved or concerned: *The salesperson tried to interest us in the car.* ◆ **in (one's) interest.** Advantage; benefit: *The company's decision to burn coal is not in the public interest.* **in the interest of.** To the advantage of; for the sake of: *I agreed to pick her up in the interest of saving time.*

in·ter·est·ed (ĭn′trĭ stĭd *or* ĭn′tə rĕs′tĭd) *adj.* **1.** Having or showing interest or concern: *Good teaching usually produces interested students.* **2.** Having a right, claim, or share: *The interested parties met to settle the dispute.*

in·ter·est·ing (ĭn′trĭ stĭng *or* ĭn′tə rĕs′tĭng) *adj.* Causing or holding interest or attention; absorbing: *an interesting movie.* —**in′ter·est·ing·ly** *adv.*

SYNONYMS: interesting, intriguing, fascinating, engaging. These adjectives all mean capable of capturing and holding one's attention. *You may write your report on any subject you find interesting. She thought my idea was intriguing and wanted to know more about it. How fascinating that lasers can be used to perform surgery! All the characters in the play are engaging.*

in·ter·face (ĭn′tər fās′) *n.* A point at which two systems or groups interact, especially the point at which a computer interacts with another computer or with a human operator. —*tr.* & *intr.v.* (ĭn′tər fās′). **in·ter·faced, in·ter·fac·ing, in·ter·fac·es.** To work together or communicate, especially with a computer or other electronic device.

in·ter·faith (ĭn′tər fāth′) *adj.* Involving people of different religions: *We attended an interfaith gathering.*

in·ter·fere (ĭn′tər fîr′) *intr.v.* **in·ter·fered, in·ter·fer·ing, in·ter·feres.** **1.** To get in the way of sthg.: *The rain interfered with our plans to go on a picnic.* **2.** To intrude in the affairs of others; meddle: *I wish you wouldn't interfere; it's none of your business.*

in·ter·fer·ence (ĭn′tər fîr′əns) *n.* [U] **1.** The act of interfering: *Human interference has upset the balance in the environment.* **2.** In electronics: **a.** The distortion of one broadcast signal by others. **b.** The distorted part of a broadcast signal; static: *I couldn't hear the game on the radio because of interference.*

in·ter·im (ĭn′tər ĭm) *n.* An interval of time between two events, periods, or processes: *During the interim, you can stay with me.* —*adj.* During an interval; temporary: *After an interim job as a cook, he returned to college.*

in·te·ri·or (ĭn tîr′ē ər) *adj.* **1.** Located in the inside; inner: *The interior walls of the building need paint.* **2.** Located away from a coast or border; inland: *Interior Australia is sparsely populated.* —*n.* **1.** The inner part of sthg.; the inside: *We plan to paint the interior of the house.* **2.** The inland part of a country or geographical area: *The interior of Alaska is very mountainous.*

interior decorator or **interior designer** *n.* A person who specializes in the decoration and furnishing of the interiors of homes, offices, or other buildings.

interj. *abbr.* An abbreviation of interjection.

in·ter·ject (ĭn′tər jĕkt′) *tr.v.* To put (sthg., such as a comment) between or among other things being said: *The speaker paused during her speech to interject a personal remark.*

in·ter·jec·tion (ĭn′tər jĕk′shən) *n.* **1.** A sudden phrase or remark that is interjected; an exclamation. **2.** In grammar, a word or phrase that expresses emotion and can stand alone. The words *Ouch!* and *Hurrah!* are interjections.

in·ter·lock (ĭn′tər lŏk′) *tr.* & *intr.v.* To unite two or more things firmly: *The dancers formed a circle and interlocked hands. These pieces don't interlock well.*

in·ter·lop·er (ĭn′tər lō′pər) *n.* *Formal.* A person who interferes in the lives of others; a meddler.

in·ter·lude (ĭn′tər lōōd′) *n.* **1.** An episode or period of time coming between other things: *There was a brief interlude of sunshine on this mostly cloudy day.* **2.** A short piece of music that occurs between parts of a longer composition.

in·ter·mar·ry (ĭn′tər măr′ē) *intr.v.* **in·ter·mar·ried, in·ter·mar·ry·ing, in·ter·mar·ries.** To marry (sbdy.) of another religion, nationality, or ethnic group: *The neighboring tribes have intermarried for many years.* —**in′ter·mar′riage** (ĭn′tər măr′ĭj) *n.*

in·ter·me·di·ar·y (ĭn′tər mē′dē ĕr′ē) *adj.* **1.** Acting to help settle disagreements: *A labor negotiator plays an intermediary role between management and workers.* **2.** Existing or occurring between; intermediate: *A tadpole is an intermediary stage in the development of a frog.* —*n., pl.* **in·ter·me·di·ar·ies.** A person or group acting as a mediator between opposing parties to bring about an agreement.

in·ter·me·di·ate (ĭn′tər mē′dē ĭt) *adj.* Being or occurring between; in the middle: *Middle school is intermediate between elementary school and high school.*

in·ter·mi·na·ble (ĭn tûr′mə nə bəl) *adj.* Seeming to have no end; endless: *I fell asleep during the second hour of the interminable movie.* —**in′ter′mi·na·bly** *adv.*

in·ter·min·gle (ĭn′tər mĭng′gəl) *tr. & intr.v.* **in·ter·min·gled, in·ter·min·gling, in·ter·min·gles.** To mix or become mixed together: *The pieces of the two puzzles were intermingled. A party presents a good chance to intermingle with others.*

in·ter·mis·sion (ĭn′tər mĭsh′ən) *n.* A short time between periods of activity; a pause: *The orchestra took a brief intermission during the concert.* See Synonyms at **pause.**

in·ter·mit·tent (ĭn′tər mĭt′nt) *adj.* Stopping and starting repeatedly; not continuous: *The alarm sounded intermittent blasts at intervals of 15 seconds.* —**in′ter·mit′·tent·ly** *adv.*

in·tern (ĭn′tûrn′) *n.* An advanced student or recent graduate in practical training, especially a medical school graduate who is in training in a hospital or clinic. —*v.* —*intr.* To train or serve as an intern: *He interned for a year at City Hospital.* —*tr.* (*also* ĭn **tûrn′**). To force (sbdy./ sthg.) to stay within a country or place, especially in wartime: *intern an enemy ship.* —**in·tern·ee** (ĭn′tûr nē′) *n.* —**in·tern′ment** *n.* [U]

in·ter·nal (ĭn tûr′nəl) *adj.* **1.** Located within the limits or inside of sthg.; inner; interior: *the internal workings of a clock.* **2.** Located or acting inside the body: *pills and other internal medicines.* **3.** Relating to domestic issues within a country or an organization: *Environmental issues are no longer internal political matters but require global attention.* —**in·ter′nal·ly** *adv.*

in·ter·nal-com·bus·tion engine (ĭn-tûr′nəl kəm bŭs′chən) *n.* An engine whose fuel is burned inside the engine itself rather than in an outside furnace or burner: *A gasoline or diesel engine is an internal-combustion engine; a steam engine is not.*

internal medicine *n.* [U] The branch of medicine that deals with the diagnosis and nonsurgical treatment of diseases affecting the internal organs of the body.

In·ter·nal Rev·e·nue Ser·vice *n.* [U] The division of the U.S. government responsible for collecting income taxes.

in·ter·na·tion·al (ĭn′tər năsh′ə nəl) *adj.* Relating to or between two or more nations: *The United Nations is an international organization.* —**in′ter·na′tion·al·ly** *adv.*

in·ter·na·tion·al·ism (ĭn′tər năsh′ə nə lĭz′əm) *n.* [U] A policy or principle of cooperation among nations for the benefit of all.

in·ter·na·tion·al·ize (ĭn′tər năsh′ə nə līz′) *tr.v.* **in·ter·na·tion·al·ized, in·ter·na·tion·al·iz·ing, in·ter·na·tion·al·iz·es.** To put (sthg.) under international control; make international: *a peace treaty that internationalized the Panama Canal.*

In·ter·net (ĭn′tər nĕt′) *n.* [U] A worldwide network of computers: *I have access to the Internet from my home computer, so I can send e-mail, do research, and browse the World Wide Web.*

in·ter·nist (ĭn tûr′nĭst) *n.* A doctor who specializes in internal medicine.

in·tern·ship (ĭn′tûrn shĭp′) *n.* A period of service as an intern: *She graduated from medical school and began serving her internship.*

in·ter·plan·e·tar·y (ĭn′tər plăn′ĭ tĕr′ē) *adj.* Located or occurring between planets; in the region of the planets: *interplanetary flight.*

in·ter·play (ĭn′tər plā′) *n.* [U] The action or influence of two people or things on each other; interaction: *The interplay between the two main characters provided most of the humor in the movie.*

in·ter·pose (ĭn′tər pōz′) *v.* **in·ter·posed, in·ter·pos·ing, in·ter·pos·es.** *Formal.* —*tr.* **1.** To put (sthg. or oneself) between two things: *Winter ice interposes a barrier between the harbor and the islands.* **2.** To add (sthg., such as a remark), during a conversation: *May I interpose a question?* —*intr.* To come between parties in a dispute: *The baby sitter interposed in the arguments between the children.*

in·ter·pret (ĭn tûr′prĭt) *v.* —*tr.* **1.** To translate (sthg.): *She interpreted the French film for her English-speaking friend.* **2.** To explain the meaning of (sthg.): *The critic interprets the poem in an essay.* **3.** To understand (sthg.) in one's own way: *We interpreted his smile to be an agreement.* **4.** To present the meaning of (sthg.), especially through artistic performance: *an actor interpreting a role.* —*intr.* To serve as an interpreter for speakers of a foreign language: *He interprets at the UN.* —**in•ter′pre•tive** (ĭn tûr′prĭ tĭv) also **in•ter′pre•ta′tive** (ĭn tûr′prĭ tā′tĭv) *adj.*

in•ter•pre•ta•tion (ĭn tûr′prĭ tā′shən) *n.* **1.** [U] The act of interpreting: *Interpretation of statistical data requires training.* **2.** [C] An explanation of the meaning of sthg., especially of a work of art: *Her interpretation of the movie gave us a lot to think about.* **3.** [C] A performer's own version of a work of art, such as a song or dance: *The dancer gave a unique interpretation of the ballet.*

in•ter•pret•er (ĭn tûr′prĭ tər) *n.* A person who translates orally from one language to another.

in•ter•ra•cial (ĭn′tər rā′shəl) *adj.* Relating to or involving different races: *an interracial committee.*

in•ter•re•late (ĭn′tər rĭ lāt′) *tr. & intr.v.* **in•ter•re•lat•ed, in•ter•re•lat•ing, in•ter•re•lates.** To place in or come into relationship: *Mental and physical health are interrelated. She studies how education and public health interrelate.* —**in′ter•re•la′-tion, in′ter•re•la′tion•ship** *n.* [C; U]

in•ter•re•lat•ed (ĭn′tĕr rĭ lā′tĭd) *adj.* Being connected or related and having mutual effects: *Global economies are now interrelated.*

in•ter•ro•gate (ĭn tĕr′ə gāt′) *tr.v.* **in•ter•ro•gat•ed, in•ter•ro•gat•ing, in•ter•ro•gates.** To question (sbdy.) formally and closely: *The police interrogated witnesses at the scene of the accident.* —**in•ter′-ro•ga′tion** *n.* [C; U] —**in•ter′ro•ga′tor** *n.*

in•ter•rog•a•tive (ĭn′tə rŏg′ə tĭv) *adj.* **1.** Asking a question: *an interrogative sentence.* **2.** Used in asking a question. *When, why,* and *where* can be used as interrogative pronouns. —*n.* A word or form used in asking a question. In the questions *Where did you go?* and *Whom did you see?* the words *where* and *whom* are interrogatives. —**in′ter•rog′-a•to•ry** (ĭn′tə rŏg′ə tôr′ ē) *adj.*

in•ter•rupt (ĭn′tə rŭpt′) *v.* —*tr.* **1.** To stop the action of (sbdy./sthg.): *I was about to fin-ish the joke when my brother interrupted me.* **2.** To cause (sthg.) to stop, usually tempo-rarily: *Rain interrupted our baseball game.* —*intr.* To stop sthg., especially a conversa-tion: *It is impolite to interrupt when others are talking.* —**in′ter•rup′tion** *n.* [C; U]

in•ter•scho•las•tic (ĭn′tər skə lăs′tĭk) *adj.* Existing or conducted between or among schools: *Eight high-school tennis teams com-peted at the interscholastic tournament.*

in•ter•sect (ĭn′tər sĕkt′) *v.* —*tr.* To cross (sthg.); divide: *A path intersects the park.*

—*intr.* To cross each other; overlap: *The road intersects with the highway north of town.*

in•ter•sec•tion (ĭn′tər sĕk′shən) *n.* **1.** [U] The act of intersecting. **2.** (*also* ĭn′tər sĕk′-shən). [C] A place where two or more things intersect, especially a place where two or more roads cross: *traffic lights at an intersec-tion.* **3.** [U] In geometry, the point where one line, surface, or solid crosses another: *The intersection of two planes determines a straight line.* **4.** [U] In mathematics, the set that contains only those elements shared by two or more sets.

in•ter•sperse (ĭn′tər spûrs′) *tr.v.* **in•ter•spersed, in•ter•spers•ing, in•ter•spers•es.** To vary (sthg.) by distributing things here and there: *The magazine is interspersed with advertisements.*

in•ter•state (ĭn′tər stāt′) *adj.* Involving or connecting two or more states: *An interstate highway runs between cities in different states.*

in•ter•stel•lar (ĭn′tər stĕl′ər) *adj.* Between or among the stars: *interstellar gases.*

in•ter•twine (ĭn′tər twīn′) *tr. & intr.v.* **in•ter•twined, in•ter•twin•ing, in•ter•twines.** To join or become joined by twisting together: *She intertwined the strands of hair into a braid. The dancers' arms intertwined.*

in•ter•twined (ĭn′tər twīnd′) *adj.* Woven or closely connected: *Their lives have gradually become intertwined.*

in•ter•val (ĭn′tər vəl) *n.* **1.** The amount of time between two events: *The alarm sounded at 60-second intervals.* **2.** The space between two objects, points, or units: *She planted tomatoes at intervals of one foot.* **3.** In mathe-matics and statistics, the set of all numbers between two given numbers.

in•ter•vene (ĭn′tər vēn′) *intr.v.* **in•ter•vened, in•ter•ven•ing, in•ter•venes.** **1.** [*between*] To come between two events: *A period of calm intervened between stormy sessions of the legislature.* **2.a.** To come between so as to change a course of events: *The teacher intervened to settle the argument.* **b.** To enter, usually with force, into the af-fairs of another nation: *Other countries refused to intervene in the civil war.*

in•ter•ven•tion (ĭn′tər vĕn′shən) *n.* [C; U] **1.** The act or an instance of intervening: *The governor's intervention saved the park from destruction.* **2.** Interference in the affairs of another nation, usually with force: *The UN felt that intervention in the war was not necessary.*

in•ter•view (ĭn′tər vyōō′) *n.* **1.** A face-to-face meeting for a specified purpose: *an interview for a job.* **2.** A conversation, such as one between a reporter and another person, for the purpose of getting information: *The* movie star grants no interviews. —*tr.v.* To ask questions in an interview with (sbdy.): *The committee interviewed candidates for the job.* —**in′ter·view′er** *n.*

in·ter·weave (ĭn′tər wēv′) *v.* **in·ter·wove** (ĭn′tər **wōv′**), **in·ter·wo·ven** (ĭn′tər-wō′vən), **inter·weav·ing, inter·weaves.** —*tr.* **1.** To weave (things) together: *Cloth is made by interweaving threads.* **2.** To blend or intermix (things that are different): *The author skillfully interweaves two plots in a single story.* —*intr.* To become joined by twisting together: *Our fingers interwove.*

in·tes·tine (ĭn tĕs′tĭn) *n.* The part of the digestive tract that extends from the stomach to the anus, consisting of the large intestine and small intestine. —**in·tes·ti·nal** (ĭn-tĕs′tə nəl) *adj.* —**in·tes′ti·nal·ly** *adv.*

in·ti·ma·cy (ĭn′tə mə sē) *n.* [C; U] The condition of being intimate, especially personal closeness: *intimacy between friends.*

in·ti·mate¹ (ĭn′tə mĭt) *adj.* **1.** Marked by close association or familiarity: *an intimate understanding of children.* **2.** Very personal; private: *an intimate letter.* —*n.* A close friend: *The two friends were long-time intimates.* —**in′ti·mate·ly** *adv.*

in·ti·mate² (ĭn′tə māt′) *tr.v.* **in·ti·mat·ed, in·ti·mat·ing, in·ti·mates.** To hint or imply (sthg.): *He intimated that the award would go to someone in our class.* —**in′ti·ma′tion** *n.* [C; U]

in·tim·i·date (ĭn tĭm′ĭ dāt′) *tr.v.* **in·tim·i·dat·ed, in·tim·i·dat·ing, in·tim·i·dates.** To fill (sbdy.) with fear; frighten or discourage: *The new coach intimidated the players.* —**in·tim′i·da′tion** *n.* [U]

in·tim·i·dat·ed (ĭn tĭm′ĭ dā′tĭd) *adj.* Easily frightened or threatened: *An intimidated teacher cannot be effective in the classroom.*

in·tim·i·dat·ing (ĭn tĭm′ĭ dā′tĭng) *adj.* Frightening; threatening: *an intimidating look.*

in·to (ĭn′tōō) *prep.* **1.** To the inside of: *going into the house.* **2.** So as to be in or within: *enter into an agreement.* **3.** To the occupation of: *go into banking as a career.* **4.** To the condition or form of: *break into pieces.* **5.** Toward; in the direction of: *looking into the distance.* **6.** Against: *crashed into a tree.* **7.** *Informal.* Interested in or involved with: *They are into health foods.* **8.** As a divisor of: *5 into 30 is 6.*

in·tol·er·a·ble (ĭn tŏl′ər ə bəl) *adj.* Impossible to tolerate; unbearable: *We found the noise in the factory intolerable.* —**in·tol′er·a·bly** *adv.* —**in·tol′er·ance** *n.* [U]

in·tol·er·ant (ĭn tŏl′ər ənt) *adj.* [*of*] Unwilling to accept different opinions or beliefs, or persons of other races, religions, or backgrounds; prejudiced: *My neighbor is intolerant of people with different political views.*

in·to·na·tion (ĭn′tə nā′shən) *n.* The way in which the speaking voice rises or falls in pitch in order to convey meaning. In English, rising intonation shows that *He's sick?* is a question.

in·tox·i·cant (ĭn tŏk′sĭ kənt) *n.* Something that intoxicates, especially an alcoholic drink.

in·tox·i·cate (ĭn tŏk′sĭ kāt′) *tr.v.* **in·tox·i·cat·ed, in·tox·i·cat·ing, in·tox·i·cates.** **1.** To cause (sbdy.) to lose control of physical or mental powers by means of a chemical substance, such as alcohol: *One glass of wine can intoxicate him.* **2.** *Formal.* To fill (sbdy.) with great excitement or enthusiasm; exhilarate: *The beauty of the mountain scenery intoxicated the tourists.* —**in·tox·i·ca·tion** (ĭn tŏk′sĭ kā′shən) *n.* [U]

in·tox·i·cat·ed (ĭn tŏk′sĭ kā′tĭd) *adj.* **1.** Drunk: *Intoxicated people are dangerous drivers.* **2.** Excited; happy: *Intoxicated with their victory, the team celebrated for hours.*

in·tox·i·cat·ing (ĭn tŏk′sĭ kā′tĭng) *adj.* **1.** Able to make sbdy. drunk: *intoxicating drinks.* **2.** Able to excite or make sbdy. feel happy: *an intoxicating victory.*

intra— *pref.* A prefix that means inside of or within: *intravenous.*

in·trac·ta·ble (ĭn trăk′tə bəl) *adj.* *Formal.* Difficult to manage or control: *an intractable problem.* —**in·trac′ta·bly** *adv.*

in·tra·mu·ral (ĭn′trə myōōr′əl) *adj.* Involving members of the same school or institution: *An intramural athletic program involves no competition between schools.*

in·tran·si·gent (ĭn trăn′sə jənt *or* ĭn-trăn′zə jənt) *adj.* *Formal.* Refusing to compromise; stubborn: *We hoped to reach an agreement, but they were completely intransigent.* —**in·tran′si·gence** *n.* [U] —**in·tran′s·i·gent·ly** *adv.*

in·tran·si·tive (ĭn trăn′sĭ tĭv *or* ĭn trăn′-zĭ tĭv) *adj.* Relating to a verb that does not require a direct object to complete its meaning. In the sentence *The bell rang loudly,* the verb *rang* is intransitive. —**in·tran′si·tive·ly** *adv.* —SEE NOTE at **verb.**

in·tra·ve·nous (ĭn′trə vē′nəs) *adj.* Within or into a vein: *The patient needed intravenous feeding.* —**in′tra·ve′nous·ly** *adv.*

in·trep·id (ĭn trĕp′ĭd) *adj.* Brave; fearless: *Early explorers of Antarctica were intrepid and resourceful.* —**in·trep′id·ly** *adv.*

in·tri·ca·cy (ĭn′trĭ kə sē) *n., pl.* **in·tri·ca·cies.** **1.** [U] The quality of being intricate or complex: *The intricacy of the puzzle makes it hard to solve.* **2.** [C] Something intricate; a complication: *The intricacies of human anatomy require years of study.*

in·tri·cate (ĭn′trĭ kĭt) *adj.* **1.** Having a complicated structure or pattern: *the intricate arrangement of gears in a clock.* **2.** Hard to understand: *The document is so intricate that it requires a great deal of study.* —**in′tri·cate·ly** *adv.*

in·trigue (ĭn'trēg' *or* ĭn trēg') *n.* **1.a.** [U] Planning or scheming done in secret: *political intrigue.* **b.** [C] A secret plot or scheme: *Their intrigues were discovered and the revolution failed.* **2.** [C] A secret love affair. —*v.* (ĭn trēg'). **in·trigued, in·trigu·ing, in·trigues.** —*intr.* [*against*] To plot or scheme secretly: *The political rivals intrigued against one another.* —*tr.* To excite the interest and curiosity of (sbdy.); fascinate: *The mystery of hibernation has long intrigued biologists.*

in·trigu·ing (ĭn trē'gĭng) *adj.* Exciting the interest or curiosity; fascinating: *an intriguing mystery.* See Synonyms at **interesting.**

in·trin·sic (ĭn trĭn'zĭk *or* ĭn trĭn'sĭk) *adj.* Relating to the basic nature of a thing; inherent: *He recommended the shoes on their intrinsic merits, not because they bear a famous athlete's name.* —**in·trin'si·cal·ly** *adv.*

in·tro (ĭn'trō') *n., pl.* **in·tros.** *Informal.* An introduction.

intro— *pref.* A prefix that means inward: *introvert.*

in·tro·duce (ĭn'trə dōōs') *tr.v.* **in·tro·duced, in·tro·duc·ing, in·tro·duc·es.** [*to*] **1.** To present (sbdy.) by name to another person at their first meeting: *Please introduce me to your old friend.* **2.** To bring (sth.) into use or practice: *That company has introduced several new products.* **3.** To provide (sbdy.) with a first experience of sth.: *My father introduced me to classical music.* **4.** To present (sth.) for consideration: *introduce legislation in Congress.* **5.** To talk or write about (sbdy./sth.) in advance: *The professor introduced the movie with a short lecture.* **6.** To bring or put (sth.) in a new place or environment; add: *Many European plants were introduced to North America.*

in·tro·duc·tion (ĭn'trə dŭk'shən) *n.* **1.** [C; U] The act of introducing: *the introduction of printing in the 15th century; making introductions at a party.* **2.** [C] Something introduced or brought into use: *The computer is a recent introduction in our office.* **3.** [C] The first part of a book, speech, or musical composition. **4.** [U] A first part of a course of study: *This book is an introduction to physics.*

in·tro·duc·to·ry (ĭn'trə dŭk'tə rē) *adj.* Serving to introduce a subject or person: *a few introductory remarks by the speaker; introductory French.*

in·tro·spec·tion (ĭn'trə spĕk'shən) *n.* [U] The examination of one's own thoughts and feelings: *He's an active, outgoing man who spends little time in introspection.*

in·tro·spec·tive (ĭn'trə spĕk'tĭv) *adj.* Tending to spend time examining one's own thoughts and feelings: *an introspective*

philosopher. —**in'tro·spec'tive·ly** *adv.*

in·tro·vert (ĭn'trə vûrt') *n.* A person who directs his or her thoughts and feelings inward rather than toward other people or the outside world: *He is an introvert who rarely shows his feelings.*

in·tro·vert·ed (ĭn'trə vûr'tĭd) *adj.* Very shy; withdrawn: *My introverted brother has no social life.*

in·trude (ĭn trōōd') *v.* **in·trud·ed, in·trud·ing, in·trudes.** —*tr.* To put or force (sth.) in without invitation: *They intruded their opinions into our conversation.* —*intr.* [*on*] To break or come in without being wanted or asked: *The new neighbors were always intruding on her quiet afternoons.* —**in·trud'er** *n.*

in·tru·sion (ĭn trōō'zhən) *n.* [C; U] The act of intruding: *Your entering my room uninvited is an intrusion on my privacy.*

in·tru·sive (ĭn trōō'sĭv) *adj.* Intruding or tending to intrude: *a rude intrusive question.* —**in·tru'sive·ly** *adv.*

in·tu·i·tion (ĭn'tōō ĭsh'ən) *n.* [U] The power of knowing or understanding sth. without reasoning or proof: *My intuition tells me that the experiment will work if we try it again.*

in·tu·i·tive (ĭn tōō'ĭ tĭv) *adj.* **1.** Based on intuition: *She hasn't studied musical harmony but shows an intuitive understanding of it.* **2.** Having or showing intuition: *an intuitive mind.* —**in·tu'i·tive·ly** *adv.*

in·un·date (ĭn'ŭn dāt') *tr.v.* **in·un·dat·ed, in·un·dat·ing, in·un·dates.** **1.** To cover (sth.) with water; flood: *The storm tide inundated the waterfront.* **2.** To overpower (sbdy./sth.) as if with a flood: *The store was inundated with shoppers during the holiday sale.* —**in'un·da'tion** *n.* [C; U]

in·vade (ĭn vād') *v.* **in·vad·ed, in·vad·ing, in·vades.** —*tr.* **1.** To enter (a place) by force in order to attack or conquer: *The Romans invaded Britain.* **2.** To enter and spread harm through (sth.): *Viruses invade cells of the body.* **3.** To enter (a place) as if to take control of: *On winter weekends, skiers invade the mountain town.* **4.** To violate or break in on (sth.): *Teenagers hate to have their privacy invaded.* —*intr.* To make an invasion: *When the war began, the large nation invaded.* —**in·vad'er** *n.*

in·va·lid¹ (ĭn'və lĭd) *n.* A person disabled by disease or injury: *My grandfather has been an invalid since his heart attack.* —*adj.* Disabled by disease or injury: *She cares for her invalid mother.*

in·val·id² (ĭn văl'ĭd) *adj.* **1.** Not valid or proper; without legal authority: *Unless a contract is signed, it is invalid.* **2.** Not based on fact or good reasoning: *He made only invalid arguments against our plan.* —**in·val′id·ly** *adv.*

in·val·i·date (ĭn văl′ĭ dāt′) *tr.v.* **in·val·i·dat·ed, in·val·i·dat·ing, in·val·i·dates.** To make (sthg.) invalid or worthless: *The lack of a signature invalidated the check.* —**in·val′i·da′tion** *n.* [U]

in·val·u·a·ble (ĭn văl′yōō ə bəl) *adj.* Of a value greater than can be measured; priceless: *invaluable art treasures.* —**in·val′u·a·bly** *adv.*

in·var·i·a·ble (ĭn vâr′ē ə bəl) *adj.* Not changing or varying; constant: *the invariable return of spring.* —**in·var′i·a·bil′i·ty** *n.* [U] —**in·var′i·a·bly** *adv.*

in·va·sion (ĭn vā′zhən) *n.* **1.** [C; U] The act of invading, especially the entry of an armed force in order to take control of another country. **2.** [C] An intrusion or a violation: *The loud music from next door is an invasion of our privacy.*

in·va·sive (ĭn vā′sĭv) *adj.* **1.** Tending to invade, especially tending to invade healthy cells or tissues: *an invasive form of cancer.* **2.** Involving entry into a part of the body, as by surgical incision: *invasive techniques for curing a heart defect.* **3.** Tending to intrude: *The reporter was asked to stop his invasive questioning of the victim's family.* —**in·va′sive·ness** *n.* [U]

in·vent (ĭn vĕnt′) *tr.v.* **1.** To produce or create (sthg. new) by using the imagination: *Thomas Edison invented the light bulb.* **2.** To imagine or make (sthg.) up: *They invented an excuse for having to leave earlier than usual.*

in·ven·tion (ĭn vĕn′shən) *n.* **1.** [C] Something invented, as a new device or process: *The computer is a modern invention.* **2.** [U] The act of inventing: *The invention of printing presses made books widely available.* **3.** [C] Something that is made up, especially a lie: *The excuse she gave was a complete invention.* —**in·ven′tor** *n.*

in·ven·tive (ĭn vĕn′tĭv) *adj.* **1.** Skillful at inventing; creative: *An inventive writer is able to keep the reader's attention.* **2.** Relating to or characterized by invention: *an inventive mind.* —**in·ven′tive·ly** *adv.*

in·ven·to·ry (ĭn′vən tôr′ē) *n., pl.* **in·ven·to·ries. 1.** [C] A detailed list of goods or possessions, especially of all goods and materials in stock. **2.** [U] The process of making such a survey or list: *The storekeeper took inventory of everything in the store.* **3.** [C] The supply of goods available; stock: *The store's inventory is getting low.* —*tr.v.* **in·ven·to·ried, in·ven·to·ry·ing, in·ven·to·ries.** To make a detailed list of the contents of (sthg.): *The store inventories its stock twice a year.*

in·verse (ĭn vûrs′ or ĭn′vûrs′) *adj.* Opposite or reversed, as in character or order: *CBA is ABC in inverse order.* —*n.* (ĭn′vûrs′ or ĭn vûrs′). [U] Something exactly opposite in order or character: *Her warm friendliness is the inverse of her husband's cool formality.* —**in·verse′ly** *adv.*

in·vert (ĭn vûrt′) *tr.v.* **1.** To turn (sthg.) upside down: *invert a glass.* **2.** To reverse the order, position, or condition of (sthg.): *A mirror inverts the placement of things in its reflection.* —**in·ver·sion** (ĭn vûr′zhən or ĭn vûr′shən) *n.* [C; U]

in·ver·te·brate (ĭn vûr′tə brĭt or ĭn vûr′tə brāt′) *adj.* Having no backbone or spinal column: *Invertebrate animals include shellfish and worms.* —*n.* An animal, such as an insect or a worm, that has no backbone or vertebrae: *An octopus is an invertebrate.*

in·vest (ĭn vĕst′) *v.* —*tr.* **1.** To put (money) into sthg., such as property, stocks, or a business, in order to earn interest or make a profit: *Many people invest their savings in mutual funds.* **2.** To spend (sthg.) for future advantage or benefit: *The candidates invested much time and energy in the election campaign.* **3.** *Formal.* To entrust (sbdy.) with a right or power: *The Constitution invests Congress with the power to make laws.* —*intr.* [*in*] To make an investment: *The bank invested heavily in real estate.* —**in·ves′tor** *n.*

in·ves·ti·gate (ĭn vĕs′tĭ gāt′) *v.* **in·ves·ti·gat·ed, in·ves·ti·gat·ing, in·ves·ti·gates.** —*tr.* To try to find the truth about (sthg.) by searching carefully for facts or information: *The police investigate crimes to learn who committed them.* —*intr.* To make an investigation: *When we heard the strange noise, we went downstairs to investigate.*

in·ves·ti·ga·tion (ĭn vĕs′tĭ gā′shən) *n.* A careful examination or search in order to discover facts or gain information.

in·ves·ti·ga·tor (ĭn vĕs′tĭ gā′tər) *n.* A person who investigates, especially a detective.

in·vest·ment (ĭn vĕst′mənt) *n.* **1.** [C; U] The act of investing money for profit or advantage: *The company made an investment in new equipment.* **2.** [C] A sum of money invested: *interest earned on an investment.* **3.** [C] Something in which money is invested: *Land is a good investment.* **4.** [C; U] A commitment, as of time or effort: *I've got a big investment in music lessons.*

in·vet·er·ate (ĭn vĕt′ər ĭt) *adj.* **1.** Fixed in a habit or practice: *An inveterate reader needs no persuasion to pick up a good book.* **2.** Firmly established for a long time; deep-rooted: *an inveterate liar.*

in·vig·or·ate (ĭn vĭg′ə rāt′) *tr.v.* **in·vig·or·at·ed, in·vig·or·at·ing, in·vig·or·ates.** To fill (sbdy.) with energy or vigor: *The cool autumn air invigorated us.* —**in·vig′or·a′tion** *n.* [U]

in·vig·or·at·ing (ĭn vĭg′ə rā′tĭng) *adj.* Able to make sbdy. feel healthy; energizing: *the invigorating mountain air.*

in·vin·ci·ble (ĭn vĭn′sə bəl) *adj.* Not capable of being defeated or overpowered: *an invincible army; invincible courage.* —**in·vin′ci·bil′i·ty** *n.* [U] —**in·vin′ci·bly** *adv.*

in·vis·i·ble (ĭn vĭz′ə bəl) *adj.* Impossible to see; not visible: *Air is colorless and invisible.* —**in·vis′i·bil′i·ty** *n.* [U] —**in·vis′i·bly** *adv.*

in·vi·ta·tion (ĭn′vĭ tā′shən) *n.* A spoken or written request for a person to do sthg.: *an invitation to a party.*

in·vite (ĭn vīt′) *tr.v.* **in·vit·ed, in·vit·ing, in·vites. 1.** To ask (sbdy.) politely to do sthg.: *invite guests to a party.* **2.** To welcome (sthg.): *The author invited questions from the audience.* **3.** To tend to cause (sthg.): *Exercising too much invites injury.*

in·vit·ing (ĭn vī′tĭng) *adj.* Attractive; tempting: *A swimming pool looks inviting on a hot day.* —**in·vit′ing·ly** *adv.*

in vi·tro (ĭn vē′trō) *adv. & adj.* In an artificial environment, such as a test tube, instead of inside a living organism: *grow tissue in vitro; in vitro fertilization.*

in·vo·ca·tion (ĭn′və kā′shən) *n.* **1.** [C; U] The act of invoking, especially an appeal for help from a higher power: *ancient peoples' invocation of their gods for a successful harvest.* **2.** [C] A prayer or an appeal used in asking for help or protection, as at the opening of a religious service.

in·voice (ĭn′vois′) *n.* A detailed list of goods shipped to a buyer, with an account of all costs and charges: *The publisher enclosed an invoice in the box of books I ordered.* —*tr.v.* **in·voiced, in·voic·ing, in·voic·es.** To send an invoice to (sbdy.); bill: *The company invoiced us for the shipment.*

in·voke (ĭn vōk′) *tr.v.* **in·voked, in·vok·ing, in·vokes.** *Formal.* **1.** To call on (a higher power) for help or protection: *Viking sailors invoked their gods before long voyages at sea.* **2.** To ask or call for (sthg.) earnestly: *The defendant invoked the mercy of the court.* **3.** To use or apply (sthg.) for support or protection: *In defending their right to protest, the lawyer invoked the Constitution.*

in·vol·un·tar·y (ĭn vŏl′ən tĕr′ē) *adj.* **1.** Not under one's conscious control; automatic: *Sneezing is involuntary.* **2.** Not done willingly or on purpose; unintentional or accidental: *an involuntary gesture; an involuntary participant in an argument.* —**in·vol′un·tar′i·ly** *adv.*

in·volve (ĭn vŏlv′) *tr.v.* **in·volved, in·volv·ing, in·volves. 1.** To contain (sthg.) as a part; include: *The play involved ten students.* **2.** To have (sthg.) as a necessary feature or result: *His new job involves a lot of travel.* **3.** To draw or bring (sbdy./sthg.) in: *By asking my opinion, he involved me in their argument. Her car was involved in an accident.* **4.** To hold the interest of (sbdy.): *The children were completely involved in their game.* —**in·volve′ment** *n.* [U]

in·volved (ĭn vŏlvd′) *adj.* [U] Complicated; complex: *a long involved sentence.* ♦ **involved in.** Being an active participant in sthg.: *She's very involved in sports.* **involved with.** Having an emotional commitment or romantic relationship: *She's involved with a man she met in college.*

in·vul·ner·a·ble (ĭn vŭl′nər ə bəl) *adj.* Impossible to attack, damage, or hurt: *an invulnerable position; an invulnerable argument.* —**in·vul′ner·a·bil′i·ty** *n.* [U] —**in·vul′ner·a·bly** *adv.*

in·ward (ĭn′wərd) *adj.* **1.** Directed toward or located on the inside: *an inward flow of air.* **2.** Relating to the thoughts or mind: *inward feelings.* —*adv.* **1.** Toward the inside or center: *The door opened inward.* **2.** Toward one's own mind or self: *His thoughts turned inward.* —**in′wards** *adv.*

in·ward·ly (ĭn′wərd lē) *adv.* **1.** On or in the inside; internally. **2.** To oneself; privately: *His face was serious but he was laughing inwardly.*

i·o·dide (ī′ə dīd′) *n.* [U] A chemical compound of iodine with another element or radical.

i·o·dine (ī′ə dīn′ *or* ī′ə dĭn) *n.* [U] **1.** *Symbol* **I** An element of the halogen group. In the body, iodine occurs as part of the thyroid hormones that control the rate of growth. Atomic number 53. See table at **element. 2.** An antiseptic solution containing iodine: *The nurse used iodine on my cut.*

i·o·dize (ī′ə dīz′) *tr.v.* **i·o·dized, i·o·diz·ing, i·o·diz·es.** To treat or combine (sthg.) with iodine or an iodide: *iodize table salt.*

i·on (ī′ən *or* ī′ŏn′) *n.* An atom or a group of atoms that has an electric charge: *Positive ions are formed by the loss of electrons; negative ions are formed by the gain of electrons.*

—ion *suff.* A suffix that means: **1.** Action or process: *completion.* **2.** Result of an action or a process: *decision.* **3.** State or condition: *elation.*

i·on·ize (ī′ə nīz′) *v.* **i·on·ized, i·on·iz·ing, i·on·iz·es.** —*tr.* To produce ions in (sthg.): *Lightning ionizes the air it moves through.* —*intr.* To break apart or change into ions: *Acids, bases, and salts ionize when they are dissolved in a solution.* —**i′on·i·za′tion** (ī′ə nĭ zā′shən) *n.* [U]

i·on·o·sphere (ī ŏn′ə sfîr′) *n.* [U] The region of the atmosphere extending about 30 miles (50 kilometers) to more than 250 miles (400 kilometers) above the earth and composed of layers of ionized gases.

ă–cat; ā–pay; âr–care; ä–father; ĕ–get; ē–bē; ĭ–sit; ī–nice; îr–here; ŏ–got; ō–go; ô–saw; oi–boy; ou–out; ōō–took; ōō–boot; ŭ–cut; ûr–word; th–thin; *th*–this; hw–when; zh–vision; ə–about; N–French bon

i·o·ta (ī ō'tə) *n. (always singular).* A very small amount; a bit: *There is not an iota of truth in that gossip.*

IOU (ī'ō yōō') *n., pl.* **IOU's** or **IOUs.** A written promise to pay a debt; IOU stands for "I owe you": *He borrowed five dollars and wrote me an IOU.*

ip·e·cac (ĭp'ĭ kăk') *n.* [U] A medicine used chiefly to make sbdy. vomit, as when a child has accidentally swallowed a poison.

IQ or **I.Q.** *abbr.* An abbreviation of intelligence quotient: *A genius has a very high IQ.*

ir— *pref.* Variant of **in—**[1] or **in—**[2].

i·ras·ci·ble (ĭ răs'ə bəl *or* ī răs'ə bəl) *adj.* Easily angered; highly irritable: *The irascible old man yelled at the noisy children.* **—i·ras'ci·bly** *adv.*

i·rate (ī rāt' *or* ī'rāt') *adj.* Angry; enraged: *A group of irate citizens protested the tax increase.* **—i·rate'ly** *adv.*

ire (īr) *n.* [U] *Formal.* Anger; wrath: *People feared the king's ire.*

ir·i·des·cent (ĭr'ĭ dĕs'ənt) *adj.* Showing a display of shining or glowing colors: *iridescent soap bubbles.* **—ir'i·des'cence** *n.* [U] **—ir'i·des'cent·ly** *adv.*

i·ris (ī'rĭs) *n.* **1.** The colored part of the eye, located around the pupil and between the cornea and lens: *The iris regulates the amount of light entering the eye.* **2.** A tall plant with long leaves and showy, often purple, flowers.

irk (ûrk) *tr.v.* To annoy, bother, or irritate (sbdy.): *Waiting for an hour irked me.*

i·ron (ī'ərn) *n.* **1.** [U] *Symbol* **Fe** A hard, gray metallic element from which steel is made. Iron occurs in red blood cells, helping to carry oxygen to all parts of the body. Atomic number 26. See table at **element.** **2.** [C] **a.** A metal appliance with a handle and flat bottom, used when heated to press wrinkles from cloth. **b.** An implement made of iron or a similar metal: *a curling iron.* **3.** [U] Great strength, firmness, or hardness: *a grip of iron; a will of iron.* **4. irons.** Heavy metal devices worn by a prisoner to limit movement: *a prisoner restrained by handcuffs and leg irons.* **—adj. 1.** Very hard, strong, or determined: *an iron fist; an iron determination.* **2.** Made of or containing iron: *an iron gate.* **—v. —tr.** To press or smooth (cloth items) with a heated iron: *iron a shirt.* **—intr.** To press clothes with a heated iron: *I ironed all morning.* ◆ **iron out.** *tr.v.* [sep.] To settle (sthg.) through discussion or compromise: *Labor and management ironed out their differences.*

iron

i·ron·clad (ī'ərn klăd') *adj.* **1.** Covered with iron plates for protection: *an ironclad ship.* **2.** Not easily broken or changed: *an ironclad rule.*

i·ron·ing (ī'ər nĭng *or* īr'nĭng) *n.* [U] The task of taking the wrinkles out of clothes with an iron: *I didn't get my ironing done this week.*

ironing board *n.* A padded board, usually on collapsible legs, for ironing clothing.

i·ro·ny (ī'rə nē *or* ī'ər nē) *n., pl.* **i·ro·nies.** **1.** [U] The use of words to express sthg. different and often opposite from what they mean literally. Referring to a mess as "a pretty sight" is an example of irony. **2.** [C; U] A conflict between what might be expected and what really happens: *We noted the irony that the boy who always complained about the cold weather became a famous skier.* **—i·ron·ic** (ĭ rŏn'ĭk) *adj.* **—i·ron'i·cal·ly** *adv.*

ir·ra·tion·al (ĭ răsh'ə nəl) *adj.* **1.** Not capable of reasoning or thinking clearly: *The announcement of his award so surprised him that he was irrational for several minutes.* **2.** Not based on or guided by reason; unreasonable; illogical: *an irrational fear of heights.* **—ir·ra·tion·al·i·ty** (ĭ răsh'ə năl'ĭ tē) *n.* [U] **—ir·ra'tion·al·ly** *adv.*

ir·rec·on·cil·a·ble (ĭ rĕk'ən sī'lə bəl *or* ĭ rĕk'ən sī'lə bəl) *adj.* Impossible to bring together in agreement: *irreconcilable enemies; irreconcilable differences of opinion.*

ir·ref·u·ta·ble (ĭ rĕf'yə tə bəl *or* ĭr'ĭ fyōō'tə bəl) *adj.* Impossible to refute or disprove: *irrefutable facts.* **—ir·ref'u·ta·bly** *adv.*

ir·reg·u·lar (ĭ rĕg'yə lər) *adj.* **1.** Not done according to rule, accepted order, or general practice: *The factory was accused of irregular hiring practices.* **2.** Uneven in how often or how fast sthg. happens: *an irregular heartbeat.* **3.** Not straight or balanced: *an irregular coastline.* **4.** In grammar, not following the usual pattern of inflected forms. *Do* is an irregular verb and has the irregular principal parts *did* and *done.* **5.** Not in standard condition because of imperfections: *The shirts on sale are marked "irregular" because of flaws in the fabric.* **—ir·reg'u·lar·ly** *adv.*

ir·reg·u·lar·i·ty (ĭ rĕg'yə lăr'ĭ tē) *n., pl.* **ir·reg·u·lar·i·ties.** **1.** [U] The quality or condition of being irregular. **2.** [C] Something irregular: *irregularities in the earth's surface.* **3.** [U] Constipation: *She suffers from irregularity.*

ir·rel·e·vant (ĭ rĕl'ə vənt) *adj.* Having no relation to the matter being discussed: *an irrelevant question.* **—ir·rel'e·vance** *n.* [U] **—ir·rel'e·vant·ly** *adv.*

ir·rep·a·ra·ble (ĭ rĕp'ər ə bəl) *adj.* Impossible to remedy or set right: *The statue has suffered irreparable damage.* **—ir·rep'a·ra·bly** *adv.*

ir·re·place·a·ble (ĭr'ĭ plā'sə bəl) *adj.* Impossible to replace: *irreplaceable antique photographs.*

ir·re·press·i·ble (ĭr′ĭ prĕs′ə bəl) *adj.* Impossible to hold back or control: *irrepressible laughter.* —**ir′re·press′i·bly** *adv.*

ir·re·proach·a·ble (ĭr′ĭ prō′chə bəl) *adj.* Perfect or blameless: *irreproachable behavior.* —**ir′re·proach′a·bly** *adv.*

ir·re·sis·ti·ble (ĭr′ĭ zĭs′tə bəl) *adj.* Too great or overpowering to be resisted: *an irresistible impulse.* —**ir′re·sist′i·bil′i·ty** *n.* [U] —**ir′re·sist′i·bly** *adv.*

ir·res·o·lute (ĭ rĕz′ə lōōt′) *adj.* Unsure of how to act; indecisive: *The irresolute manager was always asking for advice from his colleagues.* —**ir′res′o·lute′ly** *adv.* —**ir·res′o·lute′ness, ir·res′o·lu′tion** *n.* [U]

ir·re·spec·tive of (ĭr′ĭ spĕk′tĭv) *prep.* Formal. Regardless of: *Anyone can try out for a part in this play, irrespective of past acting experience.*

ir·re·spon·si·ble (ĭr′ĭ spŏn′sə bəl) *adj.* **1.** Showing a lack of responsibility: *Much of our pollution comes from irresponsible manufacturing processes.* **2.** Lacking a sense of responsibility; unreliable or untrustworthy: *It was irresponsible of him to drive after drinking alcohol.* —**ir′re·spon′si·bil′i·ty** *n.* [U] —**ir′re·spon′si·bly** *adv.*

ir·re·triev·a·ble (ĭr′ĭ trē′və bəl) *adj.* Hard or impossible to retrieve or get back: *Once the ring fell down the drain, it was irretrievable.* —**ir′re·triev′a·bly** *adv.*

ir·rev·er·ent (ĭ rĕv′ər ənt) *adj.* Having or showing a lack of reverence or respect; disrespectful: *People were shocked by his irreverent attitude during the ceremony.* —**ir·rev′er·ence** *n.* [U] —**ir·rev′er·ent·ly** *adv.*

ir·re·vers·i·ble (ĭr′ĭ vûr′sə bəl) *adj.* Impossible to reverse: *an irreversible decision.* —**ir′re·vers′i·bly** *adv.*

ir·rev·o·ca·ble (ĭ rĕv′ə kə bəl) *adj.* Not capable of being changed or undone: *an irrevocable decision.* —**ir·rev′o·ca·bly** *adv.*

ir·ri·gate (ĭr′ĭ gāt′) *tr.v.* **ir·ri·gat·ed, ir·ri·gat·ing, ir·ri·gates.** **1.** To supply (land) with water by means of streams, ditches, or pipes: *Ancient Egyptians used water from the Nile to irrigate land for farming.* **2.** To wash out (a wound or an opening) with water or a medicated solution: *The dentist irrigated the infected area around the tooth.* —**ir′ri·ga′tion** *n.* [U]

ir·ri·ta·bil·i·ty (ĭr′ĭ tə bĭl′ĭ tē) *n.* [U] The quality or condition of being easily angered or annoyed: *His irritability is due to hunger.*

ir·ri·ta·ble (ĭr′ĭ tə bəl) *adj.* **1.** Easily annoyed or angered: *Lack of sleep will make anyone irritable.* **2.** Very sensitive: *irritable skin around a scrape.* —**ir′ri·ta·ble·ness** *n.* [U] —**ir′ri·ta·bly** *adv.*

ir·ri·tant (ĭr′ĭ tənt) *n.* Something that irritates: *They found the city air full of irritants such as dust, soot, and smoke.*

ir·ri·tate (ĭr′ĭ tāt′) *tr.v.* **ir·ri·tat·ed, ir·ri·tat·ing, ir·ri·tates.** **1.** To make (sbdy.) angry or impatient; annoy: *The reporter's repeated questions irritated the speaker.* **2.** To make (sth.) sore or inflamed: *The smoke irritated the firefighter's eyes.* —**ir·ri·ta·tion** (ĭr′ĭ tā′shən) *n.* [C; U]

ir·ri·tat·ing (ĭr′ĭ tā′tĭng) *adj.* Annoying: *the irritating buzz of flies.* —**ir′ri·tat′ing·ly** *adv.*

IRS *abbr.* Internal Revenue Service.

is (ĭz) *v.* Third person singular present tense of **be.**

is. or **Is.** *abbr.* An abbreviation of island.

—ise *suff.* Variant of **—ize.**

—ish *suff.* A suffix that means: **1.** Relating to: *English.* **2.** Having the character of; like: *sheepish; childish.* **3.** Approximately; somewhat: *greenish.* **4.** Tending toward; interested in: *selfish.*

Is·lam (ĭs läm′ *or* ĭz läm′ *or* ĭs′läm′ *or* ĭz′läm′) *n.* A religion marked by belief in a single God and acceptance of Muhammad as the chief and last prophet of God. —**Is·lam′ic** *adj.*

is·land (ī′lənd) *n.* **1.** A body of land smaller than a continent, entirely surrounded by water: *Iceland is an island in the Atlantic Ocean.* **2.** Something like an island that is separated or different from what surrounds it: *The library is an island of quiet in the noisy city.*

is·land·er (ī′lən dər) *n.* A person who lives on an island.

isle (īl) *n.* An island, especially a small one.

HOMONYMS: isle, aisle (passageway), **I'll** (I will).

—ism *suff.* A suffix that means: **1.** Action, practice, or process: *criticism.* **2.** State or condition: *optimism.* **3.** Characteristic behavior or quality: *heroism.* **4.** A distinctive or characteristic trait, as of a language or people: *Americanism.* **5.** A doctrine, theory, or system: *pacifism.*

WORD BUILDING: —ism The suffix **—ism** is a noun suffix; that is, when added to words or word roots, **—ism** forms nouns. It means roughly "the act, state, or theory of." Nouns that end in **—ism** often have related verbs that end in **—ize** (criticism/criticize), related agent nouns that end in **—ist** (optimism/optimist), and related adjectives that end in **—istic** (optimistic).

---

isn't (ĭz′ənt). Contraction of *is not.*

i·so·late (ī′sə lāt′) *tr.v.* **i·so·lat·ed, i·so·lat·ing, i·so·lates.** **1.** To separate (sbdy./sth.) from others; set apart: *In the ancient*

ă–cat; ā–pay; âr–care; ä–father; ĕ–get; ē–be; ĭ–sit; ī–nice; îr–here; ŏ–got; ō–go; ô–saw; oi–boy; ou–out; ōō–took; ōō–boot; ŭ–cut; ûr–word; th–thin; *th*–this; hw–when; zh–vision; ə–about; N–French bon

world large distances isolated peoples from each other. **2.** To place (sbdy./sthg.) in quarantine: *isolate patients with contagious diseases.*

i•so•lat•ed (ī′sə lā′tĭd) *adj.* **1.** Not close to other things: *an isolated cabin in the mountains.* **2.** Feeling alone or cut off from other people: *It is not unusual to feel isolated in a large city.* **3.** Seldom happening: *an isolated example of political corruption.*

i•so•la•tion (ī′sə lā′shən) *n.* [U] **1.** The condition of being isolated: *a woodsman living in isolation from the modern world.* **2.** The act of isolating: *the isolation of patients with tuberculosis.*

i•so•la•tion•ism (ī′sə lā′shə nĭz′əm) *n.* [U] The policy or principle that a nation should avoid political and economic relationships with other countries. —**i′so•la′tion•ist** *n.*

i•so•met•ric (ī′sə mĕt′rĭk) *adj.* Involving contraction of a muscle with little movement: *He does isometric exercises at his desk.*

i•sos•ce•les triangle (ī sŏs′ə lēz′) *n.* A triangle with two sides of equal length.

isosceles triangle

i•so•tope (ī′sə tōp′) *n.* One of two or more forms of an element that have the same chemical properties and the same atomic number but different atomic weights. —**i′so•top′ic** (ī′sə-tŏp′ĭk) *adj.*

is•sue (ĭsh′ōō) *n.* **1.** [C] A subject being discussed; a question under debate: *the issue of reforming campaign laws.* **2.** [C] Something, especially printed, that is distributed or put into circulation: *a new issue of postage stamps; the June issue of the magazine.* **3.** [U] **a.** The act of flowing out, or a place of outflow: *the issue of water from the spring; a lake with no issue to the sea.* **b.** The act of distributing or putting out; release: *The date of issue is on the front of the newspaper.* —*v.* **is•sued, is•su•ing, is•sues.** —*intr.* To come out; flow out: *Water issued from the broken pipe.* —*tr.* **1.** To put (sthg.) in circulation; publish: *The Postal Service issues stamps.* **2.** To give (sthg.) out; distribute: *The school will issue uniforms to members of the team.* **3.** To cause (sthg.) to flow out: *The factory issues its waste water into tanks for treatment.* ✦ **at issue** Being discussed or questioned: *Your conduct is not at issue here.* **take issue with.** To disagree with (sbdy./sthg.): *He took issue with my view of the problem.* —**is′su•ance** *n.* [U] —**is′su•er** *n.*

—**ist** *suff.* A suffix that means: **1.** A person who performs an action: *bicyclist.* **2.** A person who produces, operates, plays, or is connected with a specified thing: *novelist.* **3.** A person who specializes in a specified art, sc-

ence, or skill: *biologist.* **4.** A person who believes in a certain philosophy or system: *socialist.* **5.** A person seen as having a certain characteristic: *romanticist.*

WORD BUILDING: —ist The suffix **—ist** forms agent nouns, that is, nouns that denote sbdy. who does sthg. Although **—ist** frequently forms agent nouns from verbs ending in **—ize** or nouns ending in **—ism**, it has also come to be combined with words that do not end in **—ize** or **—ism.** In some cases **—ist** can be used like the suffix **—er.** In pairs such as **conformer/conformist, copier/copyist,** and **cycler/cyclist, —ist** and **—er** may be used interchangeably.

isth•mus (ĭs′məs) *n.* A narrow strip of land with water on both sides, connecting two larger masses of land: *the isthmus of Panama.*

it (ĭt) *pron.* **1.** The thing, animal, or person last mentioned or thought to be understood: *I polished the table until it shone. They played with the puppy until it got tired. Whatever you choose, give it your best. I couldn't find out who it was on the telephone.* **2.** Used as the subject of an impersonal verb: *It is snowing.* **3.** Used as the subject of a clause that introduces a phrase or clause presenting the idea of the sentence: *It is important to get enough exercise.* —*n.* In some children's games, the player who must perform a certain act, such as chasing the other players: *You're it!*
✦ **that's it.** Used to indicate that nothing more can be said or tolerated: *I refuse to say anything more about the subject. That's it!*

It. *abbr.* An abbreviation of: **1.** Italian. **2.** Italy.

ital. *abbr.* An abbreviation of italic.

Ital. *abbr.* An abbreviation of: **1.** Italian. **2.** Italy.

i•tal•ic (ĭ tăl′ĭk *or* ī tăl′ĭk) *adj.* Referring to a style of printing type with the letters slanting to the right: *This sentence is written in italic print.* —*n. (usually plural).* Italic print or typeface: *This sentence is printed in italics.*

i•tal•i•cize (ĭ tăl′ĭ sīz′ *or* ī tăl′ĭ sīz′) *tr.v.* **i•tal•i•cized, i•tal•i•ciz•ing, i•tal•i•ciz•es.** To print (sthg.) in italic type: *italicize the title of a book.*

itch (ĭch) *n.* **1.** An irritated feeling in the skin that causes a desire to scratch. **2.** *Informal.* A restless desire: *Every spring I get an itch to go sailing.* —*v.* —*intr.* **1.** To feel, have, or cause an itch: *I itch all over from mosquito bites.* **2.** *Informal.* To have a restless desire: *They were just itching to show the teacher what they had done.* —*tr.* To cause (sbdy./sthg.) to have an itch: *This wool shirt itches my back.*

itch•y (ĭch′ē) *adj.* **itch•i•er, itch•i•est. 1.** Having or causing an itch: *an itchy bug bite.* **2.** Restless; jumpy: *I get itchy if I have to sit for a long period of time.* —**itch′i•ness** *n.* [U]

−ite *suff.* A suffix that means: **1.** A native or resident of: *urbanite.* **2.** Descendant of: *Israelite.* **3.** Rock; mineral: *graphite.*

i·tem (ī'təm) *n.* **1.** A single thing or unit: *I bought a shirt and several other items of clothing.* **2.** A piece of news or information: *an interesting item in the newspaper.*

i·tem·ize (ī'tə mīz') *tr.v.* **i·tem·ized, i·tem·iz·ing, i·tem·iz·es.** To set down (a series of things) item by item; list: *itemizing all charges on the bill.*

i·tin·er·ant (ī tĭn'ər ənt *or* ĭ tĭn'ər ənt) *adj.* Traveling from place to place and job to job: *At harvest time many farmers employ itinerant workers.* —*n.* A person who travels in this way: *They work as itinerants.*

i·tin·er·ar·y (ī tĭn'ə rĕr'ē *or* ĭ tĭn'ə rĕr'ē) *n., pl.* **i·tin·er·ar·ies.** A schedule of places to be visited during a journey: *The tourists' itinerary includes stops in Denver and Salt Lake City.*

−itis *suff.* A suffix that means an inflammation or inflammatory disease of: *bronchitis; tonsillitis.*

it'll (ĭt'l). Contraction of *it will* or *it shall.*

its (ĭts) *adj.* The possessive form of **it.** Belonging to the thing just mentioned: *How does the picture look? We just changed its frame.*

HOMONYMS: its, it's (it is, it has).

USAGE: its The word **its,** the possessive form of the pronoun **it,** is never written with an apostrophe: *I like my house because of its many windows.* The contraction **it's** (for *it is* or *it has*) is always written with an apostrophe: *It's because my house has many windows that I like it.*

---

it's (ĭts). Contraction of *it is* or *it has.*

it·self (ĭt sĕlf') *pron.* **1.** That one that is the same as it: **a.** Used as the direct object or indirect object of a verb or as the object of a preposition to show that the action of the verb refers back to the subject: *The cat scratched itself. Congress voted itself a pay raise. The robot moves by itself.* **b.** Used to give emphasis: *The trouble is in the motor itself.* **2.** Its normal or healthy condition or state: *The car has not been itself since its last tune-up.*

−ity *suff.* A suffix that means a quality or condition: *adversity; complexity.*

−ive *suff.* A suffix that means tending toward or performing a specified action: *administrative; constructive.*

I've (īv). Contraction of *I have.*

i·vo·ry (ī'və rē *or* īv'rē) *n., pl.* **i·vo·ries. 1.** [U] The hard, smooth, yellowish white substance forming the tusks of elephants and certain other animals: *Ivory was formerly used for making piano keys and decorative objects.* **2.** [U] A yellowish white color. **3. ivories.** *Slang.* The keys of a piano: *tickle the ivories.* —*adj.* **1.** Made of or resembling ivory: *ivory chess pieces.* **2.** Yellowish white.

i·vy (ī'vē) *n.* [U] A climbing or trailing plant with evergreen leaves.

−ize *suff.* A suffix that means: **1.** To cause to be or become: *dramatize.* **2.** To become; become like: *crystallize.* **3.** To treat like: *idolize.* **4.** To subject to or with: *anesthetize.*

WORD BUILDING: −ize The suffix **−ize** has become very important in English as a way of turning nouns and adjectives into verbs. **Formalize, jeopardize, legalize,** and **modernize** are examples of words that appeared in English hundreds of years ago. Other words that appeared in the 19th and 20th centuries, such as **emphasize, hospitalize, industrialize,** and **computerize,** are now also well established. Words ending in **−ize** often have related nouns ending in **−ization:** dramatize/dramatization.

Jj

j or **J** (jā) *n., pl.* **j's** or **J's.** The tenth letter of the English alphabet.

jab (jăb) *tr. & intr.v.* **jabbed, jab·bing, jabs.** **1.** To give a short hard push, especially with sthg. sharp: *He jabbed the fork into the meat.* **2.** To stab or pierce (sbdy./sthg.): *He jabbed the meat with his fork.* **3.** To punch with short quick blows: *The boxer jabbed at a punching bag.* —*n.* **1.** A sudden hard push, as with a finger or sthg. sharp: *The man sitting next to me gave me a jab in the side to get my attention.* **2.** A short quick blow.

jab·ber (jăb′ər) *intr.v.* To talk quickly without making any sense; chatter: *They jabbered on about their neighbors.* —*n.* [U] Fast or meaningless talk.

jack (jăk) *n.* **1.** A portable device used to raise heavy objects: *Raise the car with a jack to change a flat tire.* **2.** A socket that a plug can be pushed into to make an electrical connection: *a telephone jack.* **3.** A playing card showing a picture of a young man and ranking below a queen. **4.** A person who works in a specified manual trade: *a lumberjack.* —*v.* ◆ **jack-of-all-trades.** A person who is skilled at many things: *My uncle is a jack-of-all-trades who does carpentry, plumbing, and all sorts of repairs.* **jack up.** *tr.v.* [sep.] **1.** To raise (sthg. heavy) by means of a jack: *The mechanic jacked the rear of the car up to fix the tire.* **2.** To raise (sthg.) to a higher level, as in cost: *The landlord jacked up rents, causing much concern among tenants.*

jack·al (jăk′əl *or* jăk′ôl′) *n.* A type of wild dog of Africa and Asia that hunts and scavenges for food.

jack·ass (jăk′ăs′) *n.* **1.** A male donkey. **2.** *Informal.* A mildly offensive word for a foolish or stupid person: *He acted like a jackass when he was drunk.*

jack·et (jăk′ĭt) *n.* **1.** A short coat usually coming down only to the hips: *a winter jacket.* **2.** An outer covering: *a book jacket.*

jack·ham·mer (jăk′hăm′ər) *n.* A machine powered by compressed air, used especially to drill rock or break up concrete: *The worker broke up the street with a jackhammer.*

jack·knife (jăk′nīf′) *n.* A pocketknife with blades that can be folded back into the handle. —*intr.v.* **jack·knifed, jack·knif·ing, jack·knifes.** To fold or bend like a jackknife: *The trailer truck jackknifed on the icy road.*

jack-o'-lan·tern (jăk′ə-lăn′tərn) *n., pl.* **jack-o'-lanterns.** A hollowed out pumpkin with a carved face and a light inside, used at Halloween: *The children carved a jack-o'-lantern.*

jack-o'-lantern

jack·pot (jăk′pŏt′) *n.* The largest prize or award in a game or contest: *My grandmother hit the jackpot in Las Vegas.*

jack·rab·bit or **jack rabbit** (jăk′răb′ĭt) *n.* A hare of western North America with long ears and long very strong back legs.

jade (jād) *n.* [U] A hard mineral that is pale green or white: *Jade is often carved and used as a gemstone.*

jad·ed (jā′dĭd) *adj.* **1.** Tired or worn out: *a jaded look.* **2.** No longer interested after having too much of sthg.: *a jaded appetite.*

jag·ged (jăg′ĭd) *adj.* Uneven or irregular, often with sharp points: *jagged edges of broken glass; a jagged coastline.* —**jag′ged·ly** *adv.* —**jag′ged·ness** *n.* [U]

jag·uar (jăg′wär′) *n.* A large wild cat of tropical America with a black-spotted coat of light brown fur.

jail (jāl) *n.* A place in which persons await trial or serve a prison sentence: *The city built a new jail.* —*tr.v.* To put (sbdy.) into jail; imprison: *Police jailed the man for robbery.* —**jail′er** *n.*

jail·break (jāl′brāk′) *n.* An escape from jail or prison: *Two prisoners escaped in last week's jailbreak.*

ja·lop·y (jə·lŏp′ē) *n., pl.* **ja·lop·ies.** *Informal.* An outdated expression for an old automobile that is in bad condition.

jam¹ (jăm) *v.* **jammed, jam·ming, jams.** —*tr.* **1.** To force or drive (sthg.) into a tight space: *jam a cork into a wine bottle.* **2.** To fill (sthg.) too much: *Holiday shoppers jammed the store.* **3.** To cause (sthg.) to lock in an unworkable position: *Dirt jammed the bicycle's gears, and I couldn't ride it.* **4.** To apply or use (sthg.) with sudden force: *The child accidentally jammed his finger in his eye.* **6.** To make (electronic signals) difficult or impossible to receive by broadcasting an interfering signal: *jamming the enemy's radio messages.* —*intr.* **1.** To become fixed or stuck in a tight space: *The coin jammed in the slot.* **2.** To lock in an unworkable position: *The* *film jammed in the camera.* **3.** To force one's way into a limited space: *Everyone jammed into the elevator.* **4.** *Slang.* To get involved at a gathering by playing music or dancing: *The kids were jamming to the music.* —*n.* A large number of people or things in a limited space, making it difficult or impossible to move: *a traffic jam.* ◆ **in a jam.** *Informal.* In a difficult situation: *We're really in a jam because our car won't start.*

HOMONYMS: jam (wedge, preserve), **jamb** (door post).

---

jam² (jăm) *n.* [C; U] A preserve made from whole fruit boiled with sugar: *toast with strawberry jam.*

jamb (jăm) *n.* One of the vertical posts or pieces that form the sides of a door or window: *a door jamb.*

HOMONYMS: jamb, jam (wedge, preserve).

J

jam·bo·ree (jăm′bə rē′) *n.* A large party or celebration: *Several musical groups played at the jamboree.*

jammed (jămd) *adj.* Hard to move because sthg. is stuck in place: *I can't get the window open because it's jammed again!*

jam-packed (jăm păkt′) *adj.* Very full: *a movie jam-packed with action.*

Jan. *abbr.* An abbreviation of January.

jan·gle (jăng′gəl) *v.* **jan·gled, jan·gling, jan·gles.** —*intr.* To make a harsh metallic sound: *The coins jangled in my pocket.* —*tr.* **1.** To cause (sthg.) to make a harsh metallic sound: *I jangled my keys.* **2.** To have an irritating effect on (nerves): *The noise from the street jangled my nerves.* —*n.* A harsh metallic sound: *the jangle of keys.*

jan·i·tor (jăn′ĭ tər) *n.* A person whose job is to clean and take care of a building.

Jan·u·ar·y (jăn′yōō ĕr′ē) *n.*, *pl.* **Jan·u·ar·ies.** The first month of the year, with 31 days.

jar¹ (jär) *n.* **1.** A container made of glass or plastic with a wide mouth and usually no handles: *tomato sauce in a jar on the shelf.* **2.** The amount that a jar can hold: *We ate a jar of peanut butter in two weeks.*

jar² (jär) *v.* **jarred, jar·ring, jars.** —*intr.* **1.** [*on*] To have an irritating effect: *The loud music jars on my nerves.* **2.** To conflict; clash: *The statements of the opposing candidates frequently jarred.* —*tr.* **1.** To bump or cause (sbdy./sthg.) to shake: *An earthquake jarred the city.* **2.** To unsettle or shock (sbdy.): *The defeat jarred everyone on the team.* —*n.* A jolt or shock.

jar·gon (jär′gən) *n.* **1.** [U] Nonsensical or

meaningless talk: *The politician's talk was all jargon.* **2.** [C; U] The specialized language of a trade, profession, or group: *I can't understand the jargon those engineers use.*

jar·ring (jär′ĭng) *adj.* Very irritating or strange: *the jarring sounds of city traffic.*

jaun·dice (jôn′dĭs *or* jän′dĭs) *n.* [U] An abnormal yellow color of the body, resulting when the liver does not function properly.

jaun·diced (jôn′dĭst *or* jän′dĭst) *adj.* **1.** Affected with jaundice: *The baby looked jaundiced.* **2.** Showing or feeling envy, jealousy, prejudice, or hostility: *a jaundiced viewpoint.*

jaunt (jônt *or* jänt) *n.* A short pleasure trip; an outing: *a short weekend jaunt.* —*intr.v.* To make a short pleasure trip: *jaunting off to Europe on vacation.*

jaun·ty (jôn′tē *or* jän′tē) *adj.* **jaun·ti·er, jaun·ti·est.** Having a carefree self-confident air: *a jaunty young actor with a successful career.* **2.** Stylish in appearance: *a jaunty hat.* —**jaun′ti·ly** *adv.* —**jaun′ti·ness** *n.* [U]

ja·va (jăv′ə *or* jä′və) *n.* [U] *Informal.* Brewed coffee: *How about a cup of java?*

jave·lin (jăv′lĭn *or* jăv′ə lĭn) *n.* A light spear, especially one that is thrown for distance in an athletic contest.

jaw (jô) *n.* **1.** The parts of the body that serve to open and close the mouth. **2. jaws.** Something resembling a pair of jaws: *the jaws of a large wrench.*

jaw·bone (jô′bōn′) *n.* One of the bones in which the teeth are set, especially the lower jaw: *I found the jawbone of a cat in my yard.*

jay (jā) *n.* A bird often with a crest, brightly colored feathers, and a loud harsh call, such as the blue jay of North America.

jay·walk (jā′wôk′) *intr.v.* To cross a street in violation of the traffic rules, as in the middle of the block or when the light is red: *He was hit by a car when he jaywalked.* —**jay′walk′er** *n.* —**jay′walk′ing** *n.* [U]

jazz (jăz) *n.* [U] A style of music native to the United States that has strong, complex rhythms and melodies: *New Orleans jazz.* —*v.* ◆ **jazz up.** *tr.v.* [sep.] *Informal.* To make (sthg.) more interesting, lively, or bright: *Adding color to a room will jazz it up.*

jazz·y (jăz′ē) *adj.* **jazz·i·er, jazz·i·est. 1.** Resembling jazz. **2.** *Slang.* Showy; flashy: *a jazzy car.*

jeal·ous (jĕl′əs) *adj.* **1.** Fearful of losing affection or position to another: *He gets jealous when his girlfriend talks to other boys.* **2.** [*of*] Resenting another's success or advantages; envious: *Don't be jealous of his success.* —**jeal′ous·ly** *adv.*

jeal·ous·y (jĕl′ə sē) *n.*, *pl.* **jeal·ous·ies.** [C; U] A jealous attitude or feeling: *Her brother's good luck filled her with jealousy.*

ă–cat; ā–pay; âr–care; ä–father; ĕ–get; ē–be; ĭ–sit; ī–nice; îr–here; ŏ–got; ō–go; ô–saw; oi–boy; ou–out; ōō–took; ōō–boot; ŭ–cut; ûr–word; th–thin; *th*–this; hw–when; zh–vision; ə–about; N–French **bon**

jeans (jēnz) *pl.n.* Pants made of denim: *He bought a new pair of jeans.*

Jeep (jēp) A trademark for a rugged motor vehicle with four-wheel drive.

jeer (jîr) *v.* —*intr.* [*at*] To shout in a mocking way: *The crowd jeered at the losing team.* —*tr.* To shout at (sbdy.) in a mocking way: *The audience jeered the speaker off the stage.* —*n.* A mocking or insulting remark or shout: *A jeer rose from the stands.*

jell (jĕl) *intr.v.* **1.** To thicken or become solid: *The gravy jelled as it cooled.* **2.** To become clear and fixed; take shape: *Our plans for the weekend haven't jelled yet.*

HOMONYMS: jell, gel (jellylike mixture).

---

jel·lied (jĕl′ēd) *adj.* **1.** Turned into jelly, especially by cooling: *a jellied sauce.* **2.** Coated or spread with jelly: *a slice of jellied toast.*

Jell-O (jĕl′ō) [U] A trademark for a gelatin dessert.

jel·ly (jĕl′ē) *n., pl.* **jel·lies.** [C; U] **1.** A soft clear sweet food made by boiling fruit juice and sugar: *grape jelly on toast.* **2.** A substance resembling this: *petroleum jelly.* —**jel′ly·like′** *adj.*

jel·ly·bean (jĕl′ē bēn′) *n.* A small chewy candy, shaped like a bean, with a colored sugar coating.

jel·ly·fish (jĕl′ē fĭsh′) *n.* Any of numerous sea animals with a soft, often umbrella-shaped body: *Many jellyfish have tentacles that can cause a painful sting.*

jeop·ard·ize (jĕp′ər dīz′) *tr.v.* **jeop·ard·ized, jeop·ard·iz·ing, jeop·ard·iz·es.** To put (sbdy./sthg.) at risk of loss or injury; endanger: *Not getting enough sleep can jeopardize one's health.*

jeop·ard·y (jĕp′ər dē) *n.* [U] Risk of loss or injury; danger: *The volcano put the nearby city in jeopardy.*

jerk (jûrk) *v.* —*tr.* To move (sbdy./sthg.) with a quick pull or push: *I jerked my foot out of the cold water.* —*intr.* To move in sudden uneven motions: *The train jerked as we left the station.* —*n.* **1.** A sudden forceful motion, such as a pull or twist: *A jerk of the knob opened the door.* **2.** *Slang.* A stupid or foolish person: *Don't be such a jerk!*

jerk·y (jûr′kē) *adj.* **jerk·i·er, jerk·i·est. 1.** Making sudden starts and stops: *jerky movements.* **2.** *Slang.* Silly; foolish: *He's always playing childish jerky tricks on people.* —**jerk′-i·ly** *adv.* —**jerk′i·ness** *n.* [U]

jer·ry·built (jĕr′ē bĭlt′) *adj.* Built hastily, cheaply, and poorly: *We refused to live in a jerrybuilt house like that one.*

jer·sey (jûr′zē) *n., pl.* **jer·seys. 1.** [C; U] A soft knitted fabric of wool, cotton, or rayon, used for clothing. **2.** [C] A shirt made of this or a similar fabric: *a soccer jersey.*

jest (jĕst) *n.* **1.** [C] A mocking or humorous comment; a joke: *His jests are often made at his friends' expense.* **2.** [U] A playful mood or manner: *Their teasing was only done in jest.* —*intr.v.* To act or speak in a playful way: *The singer jested with the audience.*

jest·er (jĕs′tər) *n.* A person who jests, especially a person in the past who entertained a king or queen by joking: *the court jester.*

jet¹ (jĕt) *n.* **1.** An aircraft powered by a jet engine. **2.** A stream of liquid or gas forced through a small opening under pressure: *A jet of water shot out of the hose.* **3.** An opening or a nozzle through which a stream is forced: *a gas jet.* —*intr.v.* **jet·ted, jet·ting, jets. 1.** To travel by jet plane: *jetting from New York to Paris.* **2.** To move very quickly: *a boat that jets across the lake.*

jet² (jĕt) *n.* [U] **1.** A dense black stone that can be polished and used to make jewelry and other ornaments: *beads of jet.* **2.** A deep black color. —*adj.* Deep black.

jet engine *n.* An engine that develops its thrust from a jet of exhaust gases produced by burning fuel.

jet lag *n.* [U] A tired and confused feeling resulting from high-speed air travel through several time zones: *The tourists were suffering from jet lag.*

jet-pro·pelled (jĕt′prə pĕld′) *adj.* Powered by one or more jet engines: *a jet-propelled airplane.* —**jet pro·pul′sion** *n.* [U]

jet stream *n.* [U] A strong wind, often reaching very high speeds, that blows from a westerly direction: *The plane made good time because the jet stream was behind it.*

jet·ti·son (jĕt′ĭ sən *or* jĕt′ĭ zən) *tr.v.* **1.** To throw (sthg.) off a ship or aircraft, especially as a means of lightening it when it is in danger: *The ship jettisoned its cargo in the storm.* **2.** *Informal.* To discard (unwanted things): *The new manager quickly jettisoned many old practices and policies of the store.*

jet·ty (jĕt′ē) *n., pl.* **jet·ties. 1.** A structure of stone, earth, or timbers in the water and used to change a current or to protect a harbor or shoreline: *waves breaking against the jetty.* **2.** A wharf: *cargo on the jetty.*

Jew (jōō) *n.* **1.** A person whose religion is Judaism. **2.** A member of the people descended from the ancient Hebrews.

jew·el (jōō′əl) *n.* **1.** A precious stone, such as a diamond or sapphire; a gem. **2.** (*often plural*). An ornament, such as a ring or necklace, made of precious metal and gems: *The queen wore her finest jewels.* **3.** A person or thing that is greatly admired or valued: *The only grandchild is the jewel of the family.*

jew·eled (jōō′əld) *adj.* Covered or decorated with jewels: *the queen's jeweled crown.*

jew·el·er (jōō′ə lər) *n.* A person who makes, repairs, or sells jewelry: *We took the ring to the jeweler.*

J

jew·el·ry (jōō′əl rē) *n.* [U] Ornaments, such as bracelets or rings, made of precious metals and gems or of cheap or fake materials: *costume jewelry.*

Jew·ish (jōō′ĭsh) *adj.* Relating to the Jews or their culture or religion.

jibe (jīb) *intr.v.* **jibed, jib·ing, jibes.** [*with*] *Informal.* To be the same; agree: *The account of the other witness doesn't jibe with yours.*

jif·fy (jĭf′ē) *n.* [U] *Informal.* A moment; an instant: *I'll have this fixed in a jiffy.*

jig (jĭg) *n.* A lively dance or the music written for such a dance: *She danced a jig.* — *intr.v.* **jigged, jig·ging, jigs. 1.** To dance a jig: *The clown jigged around the ring.* **2.** To move up and down or back and forth in a quick, jerky way: *The fish jigged up and down on the line.*

jig·ger (jĭg′ər) *n.* A small cup that holds 1½ ounces (44 milliliters) of liquor: *a jigger of rum.*

jig·gle (jĭg′əl) *tr. & intr.v.* **jig·gled, jig·gling, jig·gles.** To shake or cause to shake up and down or back and forth with short quick jerks: *She jiggled the wire to get the light to work. My knees jiggled as I sat waiting nervously.* — *n.* A jiggling motion: *I gave the light a jiggle.*

jig·saw (jĭg′sô′) *n.* A saw with a narrow blade that moves up and down, used for cutting curves.

jigsaw puzzle *n.* A puzzle made of pieces of wood or cardboard of different shapes that form a picture when fitted together.

jilt (jĭlt) *tr.v.* To end a relationship with (a lover or sweetheart) suddenly: *She jilted him for another man.*

jin·gle (jĭng′gəl) *intr. & tr.v.* **jin·gled, jin·gling, jin·gles.** To make or cause to make a ringing metallic sound: *Coins jingled in her purse as she walked down the stairs. The jailor jingled the keys as he unlocked the gate.* — *n.* **1.** A ringing sound made by small metal objects striking together: *the jingle of small bells.* **2.** A rhyme or verse often used in radio and television commercials: *The boy whistled the catchy jingle from the candy bar ad on TV.*

jinx (jĭngks) *n.* A person or thing that is felt to bring bad luck: *The other sailors saw him as a jinx after he joined ship and bad weather began.* — *tr.v* To bring bad luck to (sbdy./ sthg.): *Don't jinx me!*

jit·ters (jĭt′ərz) *pl.n.* A feeling of nervousness: *The exam gave me a case of the jitters.*

jit·ter·y (jĭt′ə rē) *adj.* Very nervous: *The team was jittery before the big game.*

jive (jīv) *n.* [U] *Slang.* Meaningless or deceitful talk: *Don't listen to his jive.*

job (jŏb) *n.* **1.** A task that must be done: *My job is to fix lunch; your job is to wash the dishes.* See Synonyms at **task. 2.** A position at which sbdy. works for pay: *I enjoy my job in the bookstore.* **3.** Something resulting from or produced by work: *You did a fine job on the report.*

job·less (jŏb′lĭs) *adj.* **1.** Having no job; unemployed: *jobless workers.* **2.** Relating to people who are without jobs: *The state jobless rate continues to go up.* — *n.* (used with a plural verb). Unemployed people considered as a group: *The jobless are always looking for work.* — **job′less·ness** *n.* [U]

jock (jŏk) *n. Informal.* **1.** An athlete, especially in college: *The jocks live in a special dorm.* **2.** An athletic supporter; a jockstrap.

jock·ey (jŏk′ē) *n., pl.* **jock·eys.** A person who rides horses in races, especially as a profession. — *v.* — *tr.* **1.** To direct, move, or position (sthg.) by cleverness or skill: *The rowers jockeyed the boat into a good position at the start of the race.* **2.** To ride (a horse) in a race: *She jockeyed the horse to a win.* — *intr.* **1.** To ride a horse as a jockey. **2.** To move around in order to get a certain position or advantage: *The race cars jockeyed for position at the starting line.*

jock·strap (jŏk′străp′) *n.* A tight-fitting undergarment worn by males to protect the sexual organs; an athletic supporter.

joc·u·lar (jŏk′yə lər) *adj.* **1.** Tending to make jokes: *a jocular radio show host.* **2.** Meant as a joke; humorous: *a jocular remark.* — **joc′u·lar′i·ty** (jŏk′yə lăr′ĭ tē) *n.* [U] — **joc′u·lar·ly** *adv.*

jog (jŏg) *v.* **jogged, jog·ging, jogs.** — *intr.* To run at a steady slow pace, especially for exercise: *She jogs every day after work.* — *tr.* **1.** To move (sbdy./sthg.) by shoving or bumping; jar: *The old horse trotted along jogging me up and down.* **2.** To stir or shake up (sthg.): *Let's see if I can jog your memory.* — *n.* A slow steady pace: *The horse moved along at a jog.* — **jog′ger** *n.*

jog·ging (jŏg′ĭng) *n.* [U] The practice of running as a kind of exercise: *She enjoys jogging early in the morning.*

join (join) *v.* — *tr.* **1.** To put or bring (sbdy./sthg.) together; connect: *The bridge joins the island with the mainland. The children joined hands.* **2.** To meet and merge with (sthg.): *The Missouri River joins the Mississippi near St. Louis.* **3.** To become a member of (sthg.): *My brother joined the photography club.* **4.** To enter into the company of (sbdy.): *Can you join us for lunch?* **5.** To put or bring (sbdy./sthg.) into close association: *The two families were joined by marriage.* — *intr.* **1.** To come together: *The roads join just before the bridge.* **2.** To act together; join forces: *The two groups joined to oppose* *the new law.* **3.** [*in*] To take part; participate: *Everyone joined in the celebration.* **4.** To become a member of a group: *She joined last fall.* ◆ **join up.** *intr.v.* To enlist in the military or become a member of another organization: *After meeting the members of the neighborhood group, we decided to join up.*

SYNONYMS: join, combine, unite, link, connect. These verbs mean to fasten or attach two or more things together. **Join** can mean to bring separate things together physically: *We joined the pipes together and turned on the water.* **Combine** often means to mix or merge different things for a specific purpose: *The cook combined oil, vinegar, and herbs to make a salad dressing.* **Unite** suggests the joining of separate parts into a thoroughly blended whole with its own identity: *The prince united the villages to form a nation.* **Link** and **connect** can mean to attach firmly without taking away the special characteristics of each part: *The train's engine and wagons are linked together with strong bolts. The tunnel under the English Channel connects Great Britain and France.* **ANTONYMS: separate, divide.**

joint (joint) *n.* **1.** A place where two or more things are joined, such as the movable body parts in an animal: *a joint in a pipe; a knee joint.* **2.** The way in which two parts are joined: *A flexible joint allows the table leg to move.* **3.** *Slang.* A cheap gathering place: *They had drinks at the joint down by the river.* **4.** *Slang.* A marijuana cigarette. *—adj.* Shared by two or more people or groups: *a joint effort; a joint bank account.* ◆ **have (one's) nose out of joint.** *Informal.* To be in bad spirits or annoyed: *He has his nose out of joint because of his speeding ticket.*

joint·ly (joint′lē) *adv.* Together: *The business is owned jointly by three partners.*

joke (jōk) *n.* **1.** Something said or done to cause laughter, especially an amusing story with a surprise ending: *She tells great jokes.* **2.** A mischievous trick; a prank: *We played a joke on our teacher by pretending we all forgot our homework.* *—intr.v.* **joked, jok·ing, jokes.** To tell or play jokes: *They are always joking with each other.*

jok·er (jō′kər) *n.* **1.** A person who tells or plays jokes. **2.** A playing card with a picture of a jester, used as the highest card or as any card the holder desires: *I played the joker and won the game.*

jol·ly (jŏl′ē) *adj.* **jol·li·er, jol·li·est.** Full of fun and good spirits; cheerful: *a jolly fellow.* *—adv. Chiefly British.* Very: *That's a jolly good idea!*

joker

jolt (jōlt) *v.* *—tr.* To shake (sbdy./sthg.) violently: *The bicycle jolted me off the seat as it bumped over some rocks.* *—intr.* To move in a bumpy or jerky fashion: *The bus jolted to a stop as the driver jammed on the brakes.* *—n.* **1.** A sudden jerk or bump: *The car stopped with a jolt.* **2.** A sudden shock or surprise: *The news of their arrival came as quite a jolt.*

josh (jŏsh) *v.* *—tr.* To tease (sbdy.) in a lighthearted playful way: *We often josh our little brother about all his girlfriends.* *—intr.* To make or exchange jokes: *They josh around all the time.*

jos·tle (jŏs′əl) *v.* **jos·tled, jos·tling, jos·tles.** *—tr.* To push and come into rough contact with (sbdy.) while moving; bump: *They jostled each other on the crowded dance floor.* *—intr.* **1.** To come into rough contact while moving: *The people jostled on the platform as the train approached.* **2.** [*through*] To make one's way by pushing or elbowing: *I jostled through the crowd and left the lobby.*

jot (jŏt) *v.* **jot·ted, jot·ting, jots.** ◆ **jot down.** *tr.v.* [*sep.*] To write (sthg.) down briefly and hastily: *I jotted down a few notes.*

jour·nal (jûr′nəl) *n.* **1.** A daily record of events; a diary or log: *The teacher keeps a journal of the students' progress.* **2.** A newspaper or magazine containing articles on a particular subject: *a medical journal.*

jour·nal·ism (jûr′nə lĭz′əm) *n.* [U] The gathering, writing, and presentation of news in newspapers or magazines or in radio or television broadcasts. *—***jour′nal·ist** *n.* *—***jour′nal·is′tic** *adj.*

jour·ney (jûr′nē) *n., pl.* **jour·neys. 1.** A trip, especially one over a great distance: *a long journey across Europe and Asia.* **2.** The distance traveled on a journey or the time required for such a trip: *a thousand-mile journey; a three-day journey.* *—intr.v.* To travel; make a trip: *We journeyed throughout India.*

jo·vi·al (jō′vē əl) *adj.* Full of fun and good cheer; jolly: *a jovial host.* *—***jo′vi·al′i·ty** (jō′vē ăl′ĭ tē) *n.* [U] *—***jo′vi·al·ly** *adv.*

jowl (joul) *n.* *(usually plural).* The flesh under the lower jaw, especially when plump or hanging loosely: *a man with heavy jowls.*

joy (joi) *n.* **1.** [U] A feeling of great happiness: *She felt intense joy at the birth of her child.* **2.** [C] A source of joy: *Some books are a joy to read.*

joy·ful (joi′fəl) *adj.* Full of joy: *a joyful celebration.* See Synonyms at **glad.** *—***joy′ful·ly** *adv.* *—***joy′ful·ness** *n.* [U]

joy·less (joi′lĭs) *adj.* Cheerless; dismal: *a joyless existence.*

joy·ous (joi′əs) *adj.* Full of joy; joyful: *a joyous occasion.* *—***joy′ous·ly** *adv.* *—***joy′ous·ness** *n.* [U]

jr. or **Jr.** *abbr.* An abbreviation of junior.

ju·bi·lant (jōō′bə lənt) *adj.* Full of great joy: *A jubilant crowd celebrated their team's* *victory.* **—ju′bi·lant·ly** *adv.* **—ju′bi·la′tion** (jo͞o′bə lā′shən) *n.* [U]

ju·bi·lee (jo͞o′bə lē′ *or* jo͞o′bə lē′) *n.* A special anniversary, especially a 50th or 75th anniversary, or the celebration of it: *The city is celebrating its diamond jubilee.*

Ju·da·ic (jo͞o dā′ĭk) *adj.* Relating to or characteristic of Jews or Judaism: *Judaic traditions.*

Ju·da·ism (jo͞o′dē ĭz′əm) *n.* [U] The religion of the Jewish people, based on belief in one God and on the teachings set forth in the Bible and the Talmud.

judge (jŭj) *tr.v.* **judged, judg·ing, judg·es. 1.** To hear and decide (a case) in a court of law: *The jury judged the man.* **2.** To determine the winners of (a contest or an issue): *A panel of experts judged the political debate.* **3.** To form an opinion about or an evaluation of (sbdy./sthg.): *The critic judged the movie to be outstanding.* *—n.* **1.** A public official who hears and decides cases in a court of law: *a Supreme Court judge.* **2.** A person who gives an opinion about the value or quality of sthg.: *a good judge of character; a poor judge of painting.*

judg·ment *also* **judge·ment** (jŭj′mənt) *n.* **1.** [U] The ability to make good decisions: *Saving money shows good judgment.* **2.** [C] An opinion or estimate made after careful consideration: *We await the judgment of the referee.* **3.** [C] A decision reached in a court of law: *The high court handed down a judgment holding certain practices illegal.*

ju·di·cial (jo͞o dĭsh′əl) *adj.* Relating to courts of law: *the judicial branch of government.* **—ju·di′cial·ly** *adv.*

ju·di·ci·ar·y (jo͞o dĭsh′ē ĕr′ē *or* jo͞o dĭsh′-ə rē) *n.,* *pl.* **ju·di·ci·ar·ies.** A system of courts of law and judges: *a member of the judiciary.*

ju·di·cious (jo͞o dĭsh′əs) *adj.* Showing wise judgment; prudent: *Conservation involves the judicious use of resources.* **—ju·di′cious·ly** *adv.* **—ju·di′cious·ness** *n.* [U]

ju·do (jo͞o′dō) *n.* [U] A sport and method of self-defense developed in Japan and based on jujitsu.

jug (jŭg) *n.* **1.** A container with a narrow mouth, a handle, and usually a cap: *a milk jug.* **2.** The amount that a jug can hold: *We drank a jug of cider.*

jug·gle (jŭg′əl) *v.* **jug·gled, jug·gling, jug·gles.** *—tr.* **1.** To keep (two or more objects) in the air at one time by alternately tossing and catching them: *The clown juggled the balls.* **2.** To have difficulty holding or balancing (sthg.): *The tourist was juggling luggage and cameras.* **3.** To change or rearrange (amounts of money) so as to mislead or cheat: *The owner juggled the figures in the account*

books. *—intr.* To perform as a juggler: *He juggled for the children.* **—jug′gler** *n.*

jug·u·lar (jŭg′yə lər) *adj.* Relating to or located in the neck or throat: *the jugular vein.* *—n.* A jugular vein: *The lion bit the zebra's jugular.* ♦ **go for the jugular.** To try to destroy sthg.: *The lawyer went for the jugular with her last question to the witness.*

jugular vein *n.* Either of the two large veins on either side of the neck that drain blood from the head.

juice (jo͞os) *n.* **1.** [C; U] A liquid naturally contained in plant tissue: *orange juice.* **2.** [C] A fluid secreted within an organ of the body: *gastric juices.* **3.** [U] *Slang.* Electric current: *Don't forget to turn off the juice before you check the wires.*

juic·er (jo͞o′sər) *n.* An appliance used to extract juice from fruits and vegetables: *I bought a new juicer.*

juic·y (jo͞o′sē) *adj.* **juic·i·er, juic·i·est. 1.** Full of juice: *juicy berries.* **2.** Causing interest or excitement: *I heard a juicy piece of gossip.* **—juic′i·ly** *adv.* **—juic′i·ness** *n.* [U]

ju·jit·su *also* **jiu·jit·su** (jo͞o jĭt′so͞o) *n.* [U] An art of unarmed self-defense, developed in China and Japan, that exploits an opponent's weight and strength to one's own advantage.

juke·box (jo͞ok′bŏks′) *n.* An automatic phonograph or CD player operated by inserting money and pressing a button for the desired song: *Put a quarter in the jukebox and pick a song.*

Ju·ly (jo͞o lī′) *n.* The seventh month of the year, with 31 days.

jum·ble (jŭm′bəl) *tr.v.* **jum·bled, jum·bling, jum·bles.** To mix (things) in a confused way; throw together carelessly: *The shoes were all jumbled together in a heap on the floor.* *—n.* (*usually singular*). **1.** A confused or disordered mass: *a jumble of socks in a drawer.* **2.** A disordered state; a muddle: *The words came out in a jumble.*

jum·bo (jŭm′bō) *n.,* *pl.* **jum·bos.** A very large animal or thing: *Some boxes are called jumbos.* *—adj.* Very large: *a jumbo jet.*

jump (jŭmp) *v.* *—intr.* **1.** To rise off a surface by pushing with the legs and feet: *The frog jumped into the pond.* **2.** To move suddenly and in one motion: *He jumped out of bed.* **3.** To move quickly or involuntarily, as in fear or surprise: *I jumped at the sudden noise.* **4.a.** To enter eagerly into an activity: *She jumped into the race for mayor.* **b.** [*at*] To respond or accept quickly and eagerly: *I jumped at the chance to go skiing.* **5.** To increase suddenly: *Prices jumped during the past month.* **6.** [*on; at*] To make a sudden verbal attack: *She jumped on her employees for their carelessness.* *—tr.* **1.** To leap across (sthg.): *The deer jumped the stream.* **2.** *Slang.* To attack

J

(sbdy.): *The police jumped the thief in the parking lot.* **3.** To leave (a track): *Two subway cars jumped the tracks.* —*n.* **1.** A leap: *The cat made a graceful jump from the floor to the shelf.* **2.** The distance covered by a leap: *a jump of 16 feet.* **3.** Any of several track-and-field events in which competing athletes jump: *the long jump.* **4.** A sudden rise: *a jump in temperature.* **5.** A sudden involuntary movement: *He gave a jump in surprise.* ◆ **get** or **have the jump on.** To start sthg. ahead of (a competitor): *One daily newspaper got the jump on the others in reporting the story.* **jump ahead.** *intr.v.* To pass from one part to another further on; skip: *We jumped ahead to the middle chapters.* **jump out.** *intr.v* To be very easy to notice: *A misspelled word on the sign jumped out at me.* **jump the gun.** To start doing sthg. too soon: *Let's not jump the gun—we need to make a plan.* **jump to conclusions.** To form an opinion or a judgment too quickly: *Many people jump to conclusions about new ideas.*

jump•er¹ (jŭm′pər) *n.* **1.** A person or thing that jumps: *That horse is a good jumper.* **2.** *(usually plural).* Jumper cable.

jump•er² (jŭm′pər) *n.* A sleeveless dress worn over a blouse or sweater.

jumper cable *n.* A wire used to transfer electricity from a live car battery to a dead car battery: *I always carry jumper cables in my trunk.*

jump rope *n.* **1.** [C] A rope held at each end and twirled so that sbdy. can jump over it as it touches the ground: *The boxer trained with a jump rope.* **2.** [U] The game or activity played with a jump rope: *The children played jump rope during recess.*

jump-start (jŭmp′stärt′) *tr.v.* To start (the engine of a motor vehicle) by using a jumper cable or by pushing the vehicle downhill: *We had to jump-start the car.* —*n.* The act of jump-starting a motor vehicle: *My neighbor helped me with a jump-start.*

jump•suit (jŭmp′sōōt′) *n.* A single piece of clothing that consists of a shirt and attached pants: *a blue silk jumpsuit.*

jump•y (jŭm′pē) *adj.* **jump•i•er, jump•i•est.** Easily upset or excited; nervous: *The upcoming test made us all jumpy.* —**jump′i•ness** *n.* [U]

junc•tion (jŭngk′shən) *n.* The place at which two things join or meet: *There is a motel at the junction of the two highways.*

junc•ture (jŭngk′chər) *n.* **1.** The place where two things join: *Many small animals live along the juncture between fields and woods.* **2.** A point in time, especially a crisis or turning point: *At this juncture, a new government was formed.*

June (jōōn) *n.* The sixth month of the year, with 30 days.

jun•gle (jŭng′gəl) *n.* **1.** [C] An area of land with a dense growth of tropical trees and

plants: *Many undiscovered insect species live in the jungles of South America.* **2.** [C; U] A place of intense competition or violence: *He felt totally out of place in the corporate jungle.*

jun•ior (jōōn′yər) *adj.* **1.** Intended for young people: *the junior skating championship.* **2.** Used to distinguish a son from his father when both have the same name: *Do you want to speak to John junior or John senior?* **3.** Lower in rank or shorter in length of service: *a junior partner in a law firm; the junior senator from Texas.* **4.** Relating to the third year of a four-year high school or college: *the junior class.* —*n.* **1.** A person who is younger than another: *I am my aunt's junior by twenty-five years.* **2.** A student in the third year at a four-year high school or college: *a junior in high school.*

junior college *n.* An educational institution offering a two-year course of undergraduate training: *Many students transfer from a junior college to a four-year college.*

junior high school *n.* A school between elementary and high school in the United States and Canada that includes the seventh, eighth, and sometimes ninth grades.

ju•ni•per (jōō′nə pər) *n.* [C; U] An evergreen tree or shrub related to the pine with small cones used for flavoring alcohol.

junk¹ (jŭngk) *n.* [U] **1.** Material of any kind that is old, worn-out, and ready to be thrown away; trash: *Please get rid of this box of old newspapers—it's just junk!* **2.** *Informal.* Something cheap or poorly made: *That cheap toaster is nothing but junk.* —*tr.v.* To throw away (sthg.) as worn-out or useless: *We finally junked the old car.* —*adj.* Cheap, poorly made, or worthless: *junk jewelry.*

junk² (jŭngk) *n.* A Chinese flat-bottomed ship with a high stern and sails.

jun•ket (jŭng′kĭt) *n.* A trip made by a government official at public expense: *a congressional junket to Europe.*

junk food *n.* [C; U] Food that is high in calories but low in nutritional value: *Cookies and candy are considered junk food.*

junk•ie (jŭng′kē) *n. Slang.* **1.** A person addicted to narcotics: *The junkie stole to support his drug habit.* **2.** A person who has an extreme interest in sthg.: *a video game junkie.*

junk mail *n.* [U] Unrequested mail, such as advertisements and catalogs, sent to large numbers of people: *Junk mail fills my mailbox every day.*

junk•yard (jŭngk′yärd′) *n.* An open area used to store junk: *Old cars and rusted appliances fill the junkyard.*

jun•ta (hōōn′tə *or* jŭn′tə) *n.* A group of military leaders who jointly govern a nation after seizing power.

ju•ris•dic•tion (jōōr′ĭs dĭk′shən) *n.* **1.** [U] Authority or control; power: *Schools come under the jurisdiction of the state education*

J

department. **2.** [C] The range or extent of authority or control: *Cases of treason are beyond the jurisdiction of local courts.*

ju·rist (jŏŏr′ĭst) *n.* A person who is skilled in the law, especially a judge, lawyer, or legal scholar.

ju·ror (jŏŏr′ər *or* jŏŏr′ôr′) *n.* A member of a jury: *I was called to serve as a juror in a trial.*

ju·ry (jŏŏr′ē) *n.*, *pl.* **ju·ries.** A group of citizens sworn to hear evidence and to hand down a verdict in a case presented in a court of law: *the right to trial by jury.*

just (jŭst) *adj.* **1.** Honorable and fair: *a just ruler of the people.* **2.** Morally or legally right: *a just cause; a just verdict.* **3.** Deserved: *The criminal received just punishment.* **4.** Based on good reason; well-founded: *a just appraisal of his work.* —*adv.* (jəst *or* jĭst; jŭst *when stressed*). **1.** Exactly: *Everything went just as we had hoped.* **2.** A short time ago: *We just ran out of milk.* **3.** By a small amount; barely: *We ran and just made the bus. It's just after six o'clock.* **4.** Only; merely: *It was just a dream.* **5.** Perhaps; possibly: *I just may go.* ♦ **just about.** Almost; very nearly: *We are just about finished.* —**just′ly** *adv.* —**just′ness** *n.* [U]

jus·tice (jŭs′tĭs) *n.* **1.** [U] The quality of being just or fair: *A sense of justice forced the reporter to investigate both sides of the story.* **2.** [U] Fair treatment in accordance with honor or the law: *We only seek justice for the accused.* **3.** [U] The carrying out of the law: *the administration of justice through local and county courts.* **4.** [C] A judge: *a local justice; a justice of the Supreme Court.* ♦ **do justice to.** To treat (sbdy./sthg.) adequately or fairly: *I cannot do justice to her research in this brief report.*

justice of the peace *n.*, *pl.* **justices of the peace.** A local official with authority to try minor offenses, perform marriages, and administer oaths.

jus·ti·fi·a·ble (jŭs′tə fī′ə bəl *or* jŭs′tə-fī′ə bəl) *adj.* Capable of being justified; defensible: *The high price of this furniture is justifiable when one considers the fine workmanship.* —**jus′ti·fi′a·bil′i·ty** *n.* [U] —**jus′ti·fi′a·bly** *adv.*

jus·ti·fi·ca·tion (jŭs′tə fĭ kā′shən) *n.* **1.** [U] The act of justifying. **2.** [C] Something that justifies; a good reason: *Illness is a justification for not finishing your report on time.*

jus·ti·fied (jŭs′tə fīd) *adj.* Based on evidence or good reasoning: *a justified distrust of political promises.*

jus·ti·fy (jŭs′tə fī′) *tr.v.* **jus·ti·fied, jus·ti·fy·ing, jus·ti·fies.** To show or prove (sbdy./sthg.) to be right, just, or valid: *The increase in sales justified spending more on advertising.*

jut (jŭt) *intr.v.* **jut·ted, jut·ting, juts.** To extend sharply outward or upward; project: *The branches of that huge tree jut over the street.*

jute (jŏŏt) *n.* [U] A strong fiber used to make rope, twine, and coarse cloth such as burlap.

ju·ve·nile (jŏŏ′və nīl′ *or* jŏŏ′və nəl) *adj.* **1.** Not fully grown; young: *Tadpoles are juvenile frogs.* **2.** Relating to children or young people: *the juvenile section of the library; a juvenile court.* **3.** Immature; childish: *Stop that juvenile behavior.* —*n.* A young person or animal: *We saw three eagles yesterday— an adult and two juveniles.*

juvenile delinquency *n.* [U] Antisocial or criminal behavior by children or adolescents.

juvenile delinquent *n.* A child or an adolescent guilty of juvenile delinquency.

jux·ta·pose (jŭk′stə pōz′) *tr.v.* **jux·ta·posed, jux·ta·pos·ing, jux·ta·pos·es.** *Formal.* To place (two things) side by side or close together, especially for comparison: *We juxtaposed the two photographs of the house to see how it had changed.* —**jux′ta·po·si′tion** (jŭk′stə pə zĭsh′ən) *n.* [C; U]

Kk

k¹ or **K** (kā) *n.*, *pl.* **k's** or **K's.** The 11th letter of the English alphabet.

k² or **km** *abbr.* An abbreviation of kilometer: *He ran a 10k race.*

K¹ *n.*, *pl.* **K's.** *Slang.* One thousand dollars.

K² The symbol for the element **potassium.**

K³ *abbr.* An abbreviation of: **1.** Kelvin. **2.** Kilobyte.

ka•bob (kə bŏb′) *n.* Variant of **kebab.**

ka•lei•do•scope (kə lī′də skōp′) *n.* **1.** A mirrored tube with bits of loose colored glass contained at one end, which form symmetrical designs when the tube is rotated. **2.** A series of changing phases or events: *American politics is a kaleidoscope of ideas.* —**ka•lei′do•scop′ic** (kə lī′ də skŏp′ĭk) *adj.*

kan•ga•roo (kăng′gə rōō′) *n.* An Australian mammal with short front legs, long hind legs used for leaping, and a long strong tail. The female kangaroo carries her young in a pouch on the outside of her body.

Kans. *abbr.* An abbreviation of Kansas.

ka•ra•te (kə rä′tē) *n.* [U] A self-defense art developed in Japan, in which sharp blows and kicks are delivered to sensitive points on the body of an opponent.

kar•ma (kär′mə) *n.* [U] **1.** In Hinduism and Buddhism, the effect of a person's conduct, which is believed to determine a person's destiny. **2.** *Informal.* Fate; destiny: *Amazingly, a stray cat appeared at my door just days after my old cat had died—it was karma, I guess.*

kay•ak (kī′ăk′) *n.* A watertight, covered Eskimo canoe with a small opening for the paddler to sit in. —*intr.v.* To travel or race in a kayak.

ke•bab, ke•bob, or **ka•bob** (kə bŏb′) *n.* Shish kebab.

kayak

keel (kēl) *n.* A strong beam of wood or metal that runs along the center line of a boat from one end to the other. —*v.* ◆ **keel over.** *intr.v.* To collapse or fall down: *I almost keeled over with surprise.* **on an even keel.** Working well; stable: *Regular exercise will keep you on an even keel.*

keen (kēn) *adj.* **1.** Intense; piercing: *a keen wind; a keen glance.* **2.** Acute; sensitive: *the*

keen eyes of the owl. **3.** Having a sharp edge or point: *A keen knife cut the heavy canvas.* **4.** Intellectually sharp; bright: *a keen observer of politics.* **5.** Eager; enthusiastic: *He's really keen on golf.* —**keen′ly** *adv.* —**keen′-ness** *n.* [U]

keep (kēp) *v.* **kept** (kĕpt), **keep•ing, keeps.** —*tr.* **1.** To continue to have (sthg.): *I keep my old photographs.* **2.** To hold (sthg.) for future use; save: *I kept some food for you.* **3.** To put (sthg.) in a customary place: *Where do you keep your bike?* **4.** To cause (sbdy./sthg.) to continue in a certain position or condition: *Please keep me informed.* **5.** To continue or maintain (an activity): *keep watch.* **6.** To make regular entries in (a record book, for example): *I keep a diary.* **7.** To perform or fulfill (an agreement): *keep a promise.* **8.** To hold back from telling (sthg.): *Can you keep a secret?* —*intr.* **1.** To remain in a state or condition: *keep warm; keep in touch.* **2.** To stay fresh or unspoiled: *Fruit doesn't keep well.* —*n.* [U] **1.** The things needed to live: *There are many ways to earn one's keep.* **2.** Care; charge: *The child was in my keep for the day.* ◆ **for keeps.** Permanently: *The kitten was mine for keeps.* **keep at.** *tr.v.* [insep.] **1.** To continue working at (sthg. difficult): *If you keep at a task long enough, you can master it.* **2.** To ask (sbdy.) to do sthg. over and over; nag: *I had to keep at him to clean his room.* **keep back.** *tr.v.* [sep.] **1.** To withhold (information); refuse to tell: *She kept the full story back because she was so embarrassed.* **2.** To save (sthg.): *Keep back a little money for an emergency.* **keep company.** To go or stay with (sbdy.) to be friendly or prevent loneliness: *She drove me to the station and kept me company until my train came.* **keep down.** *tr.v.* [sep.] **1.** To stop (sthg.) from increasing or spreading: *Pulling weeds is one way to keep them down in a garden.* **2.** To treat (sbdy.) badly; oppress: *Some corporations keep workers down in order to make a profit.* **keep from.** *tr.v.* **1.** [sep.] To prevent or stop (sbdy./sthg.) from (doing sthg.): *We kept the kite from hitting the tree.* **2.** [insep.] To hold oneself back from (doing sthg.): *I could not keep from laughing.* **keep house.** To take care of household tasks, such as cleaning: *I keep house for several of my neighbors.* **keep on (doing).** To continue (doing sthg.): *Even after we asked him to shut up, he kept on talking.* **keep (one's) eyes**

K

open or **peeled.** To watch carefully: *Keep your eyes peeled for rabbits.* **keep (one's) head above water.** To survive or continue by constant effort: *He has so much work to do that it's all he can do to keep his head above water.* **keep (one's) sanity.** To be able to remain calm: *It's hard to keep my sanity with so many children yelling.* **keep the faith.** *Informal.* To continue to be loyal: *We kept the faith even while our leader was in jail.* **keep to (oneself).** *intr.v.* To avoid other people; remain alone: *a quiet man who keeps to himself.* —*tr.v.* [sep.] To hold (sthg.) back from others: *We could not keep such good news to ourselves.* **keep up.** *tr.v.* [sep.] To maintain (sthg.) in good condition: *keep the gardens up.* —*intr.v.* **1.** To continue at the same level or pace: *The storm kept up all night.* **2.** [*with*] To match others in success or lifestyle: *Our company must keep up with the competition.*

SYNONYMS: keep, retain, withhold, reserve. These verbs mean to maintain sthg. in one's possession or control. **Keep** is the most general: *Sometimes it's easier to earn money than to keep it.* **Retain** means to continue to hold sthg., especially when in danger of losing it: *No matter what goes wrong, she manages to retain her sense of humor.* **Withhold** means to refuse to give or allow sthg.: *The tenants withheld their rent until the landlord repaired the furnace.* **Reserve** means to hold sthg. for future use: *Please reserve your questions for the discussion period.*

---

keep·er (kē′pər) *n.* **1.** A person who watches over or guards sbdy./sthg.: *Am I my brother's keeper?* **2.** A person who takes care of or manages sthg.: *the keeper of a small shop.*

keep·ing (kē′pĭng) *n.* [U] **1.** Care; custody: *documents in the keeping of my lawyer.* See Synonyms at **care. 2.** Agreement; conformity: *They wore formal clothes in keeping with the important occasion.*

keep·sake (kēp′sāk′) *n.* Something kept in memory of the person who gave it or the place from which it came; a memento: *My teacher brought home a carved statue from Africa as a keepsake.*

keg (kĕg) *n.* A small barrel with a capacity of about 30 gallons (114 liters): *a keg of beer.*

kelp (kĕlp) *n.* [U] Brown, often very large seaweed.

Kel·vin scale (kĕl′vĭn) *n.* [U] The temperature scale that has its zero at absolute zero and uses degrees that are the same as those of the Celsius scale: *On the Kelvin scale, water freezes at 273.15 degrees and boils at 373.15 degrees.*

Ken. *abbr.* An abbreviation of Kentucky.

ken·nel (kĕn′əl) *n.* **1.** A shelter for dogs: *They built a kennel in the yard so the dog could stay dry when it rained.* **2.** A business establishment for the breeding, training, or boarding of dogs.

kept (kĕpt) *v.* Past tense and past participle of **keep.**

ker·chief (kûr′chĭf *or* kûr′chēf′) *n., pl.* **ker·chiefs** also **ker·chieves** (kûr′chĭvz *or* kûr′chēvz). **1.** A square piece of fabric worn over the head or around the neck. **2.** A handkerchief.

kerchief

ker·nel (kûr′nəl) *n.* **1.** A grain or seed, especially of corn, wheat, or a similar cereal plant. **2.** The softer, edible part inside the shell of a nut. **3.** The most important part; the core: *I recognized the kernel of truth in the proverb.*

HOMONYMS: kernel, colonel (officer).

---

ker·o·sene (kĕr′ə sēn′) *n.* [U] A thin light-colored oil that is used chiefly as a fuel.

ketch·up (kĕch′əp *or* kăch′əp) also **cat·sup** *n.* [U] A thick spicy sauce, usually made with tomatoes: *I need some ketchup for my French fries.*

ket·tle (kĕt′l) *n.* **1.** A metal pot, usually with a lid, for cooking: *a kettle of soup.* **2.** A teakettle.

key¹ (kē) *n., pl.* **keys. 1.** A small piece of metal, with notches or grooves, that is inserted into a lock to open or close it: *a house key.* **2.** Something that solves a problem or explains a mystery: *evidence that became the key to solving the crime; the answer key of a test.* **3.** An explanatory table, such as that explaining colors and symbols on a map. **4.** An important or essential person or thing: *Hard work is the key to her success.* **5.** Any of the buttons or levers moved by the fingers to run a machine or play a musical instrument: *a computer key; piano keys.* **6.** A scale or group of musical tones related to a primary tone: *a piece written in the key of D.* —*adj.* Very important; significant: *key decisions.* —*tr.v.* To adapt (sthg.) to special conditions; adjust: *farming methods keyed to local weather conditions.* ◆ **keyed up.** Nervous; excited: *I was too keyed up about my trip to eat.*

HOMONYMS: key (lock opener, island), cay (island), quay (wharf).

---

key² (kē) *n., pl.* **keys.** A low-lying island or reef along a coast, especially in the Gulf of Mexico.

ă–**cat**; ā–**pay**; âr–**care**; ä–**father**; ĕ–**get**; ē–**be**; ĭ–**sit**; ī–**nice**; îr–**here**; ŏ–**got**; ō–**go**; ô–**saw**; oi–**boy**; ou–**out**; o͞o–**took**; o͞o–**boot**; ŭ–**cut**; ûr–**word**; th–**thin**; *th*–**this**; hw–**when**; zh–**vision**; ə–**about**; ɴ–French **bon**

key·board (kē'bôrd') *n.* A set of keys, as on a piano or a computer. —*tr.v.* To enter (information) into a computer by using a keyboard. —**key'board'er** *n.*

key·hole (kē'hōl') *n.* The opening in a lock into which a key fits.

key·note (kē'nōt') *n.* The basic idea or theme, as of a speech, book, or political campaign.

key ring *n.* A metal ring on which keys are kept.

key·stone (kē'stōn') *n. (usually singular).* The essential element that supports a whole: *The keystone of their business was their downtown store.*

key·stroke (kē'strōk') *n.* A stroke of a key, as on a typewriter or word processor.

kg *abbr.* An abbreviation of kilogram.

khak·i (kăk'ē *or* kä'kē) *n.* **1.** [U] A heavy, yellowish brown cloth. **2. khakis. a.** Pants made of this cloth. **b.** A uniform made of this cloth. **3.** [U] A yellowish brown color. —*adj.* Yellowish brown.

kib·itz (kĭb'ĭts) *intr.v. Informal.* **1.** To look on and offer unwanted advice: *My grandfather always looks over my shoulder and kibitzes when I play cards.* **2.** To chat; converse. —**kib'itz·er** *n.*

kick (kĭk) *v.* —*intr.* **1.** To strike out with the foot. **2.** To move back sharply when fired: *The rifle kicked after he pulled the trigger.* —*tr.* **1.** To strike (sbdy./sthg.) with the foot: *The mule kicked the barn door.* **2.** To spring back against (sbdy./sthg.) suddenly: *The rifle kicked her shoulder when she fired it.* **3.** *Slang.* To free oneself of (a bad habit or an addiction): *She's trying to kick cigarettes.* —*n.* **1.** A blow with the foot: *The cow gave the bucket a kick.* **2.a.** The action of kicking a ball: *a hard kick on goal.* **b.** The distance covered by a kicked ball: *a thirty-yard kick.* **3.** The backward movement of a cannon or gun after firing. **4.** *Informal.* A feeling of pleasure: *They will get a kick out of this greeting card.* ♦ **for kicks.** For fun: *For kicks we decided to surprise him.* **kick around.** *Informal. tr.v.* [sep] **1.** To treat (sbdy.) badly; abuse: *Don't let anyone kick you around.* **2.** To think about or discuss (sthg.): *Several new ideas were kicked around at the meeting.* —*intr.v.* To move from place to place: *We could kick around at the mall for a while.* **kick back.** *intr.v.* To relax: *On weekends he likes to kick back and do nothing.* **kick in.** *tr.v.* [sep.] *Informal.* To contribute (one's share) to a common fund: *We will each kick in a few dollars for the office party.* —*intr.v.* To start: *The new prices kick in next week.* **kick off.** *tr.v.* [sep.] *Informal.* To start (sthg.): *We kicked off the day with a big breakfast.* **kick out.** *tr.v.* [sep.] *Informal.* To throw (sbdy.) out; dismiss: *The boy was kicked out of the library for talking.* **kick up.** *tr.v.* [sep.] To produce (sthg.) by striking with the foot: *a herd of cattle that kicked up dust.* —*intr.v.* To

start to hurt: *Her arthritis kicked up.* **kick up a fuss.** *Informal.* To create trouble: *Our cats kick up a fuss at night.* **kick up (one's) heels.** *Informal.* To have a good time; celebrate: *When they want to kick up their heels, they fly to Amsterdam.* **kick the bucket.** *Slang.* To die: *When I kick the bucket, I want to go quickly.* —**kick'er** *n.*

kick·back (kĭk'băk') *n. Slang.* A part of a payment returned by agreement to the payer, especially in the form of a bribe: *a mayor accused of taking kickbacks from developers.*

kick·off (kĭk'ôf' *or* kĭk'ŏf') *n. (usually singular).* **1.** A kick in football or soccer that begins play. **2.** *Informal.* A beginning: *The speech was the kickoff for the presidential campaign.*

kid (kĭd) *n.* **1.a.** [C] A young goat. **b.** [U] Leather made from the skin of a young goat. **2.** [C] *Informal.* A child or young person. —*adj.* **1.** Made of kid: *kid gloves.* **2.** Younger than oneself: *my kid brother.* —*v.* **kid·ded, kid·ding, kids.** *Informal.* —*tr.* To make fun of (sbdy.); tease: *My friends like to kid me.* —*intr.* [around] To engage in teasing or good-humored fooling: *Stop kidding around!*

kid·nap (kĭd'năp') *tr.v.* **kid·napped, kid·nap·ping, kid·naps.** To seize and keep (sbdy.) by force, usually for ransom. —**kid'nap'per** *n.*

kid·ney (kĭd'nē) *n.* Either of a pair of abdominal organs that maintain the proper amount of water in the body of a vertebrate and filter out wastes from the bloodstream in the form of urine.

kidney bean *n.* A large reddish bean, shaped somewhat like a kidney.

kill (kĭl) *v.* —*tr.* **1.** To cause the death of (sbdy./sthg.): *The man was killed by the car.* **2.** To put an end to (sthg.); destroy: *The rainy weekend killed our plans for a picnic.* **3.** To hurt (sbdy./sthg.) intensely: *These new shoes are killing my feet.* **4.** To pass (time) in idle activity: *kill an hour looking at magazines.* **5.** To cause (sthg.) to stop working: *kill a motor.* **6.** To take (sthg.) out; delete: *The editor decided to kill several paragraphs of the news story.* —*intr.* To cause death: *Speed kills.* —*n.* An animal that has just been killed: *the lion's kill.* ♦ **kill off.** *tr.v.* [sep.] To destroy (sthg.) totally or on a large scale: *Continued pollution could kill off several species of fish.*

kill·er (kĭl'ər) *n.* **1.** Somebody or sthg. that kills. **2.** *Slang.* Something that is extremely difficult to deal with or withstand: *That test was a killer!*

killer whale *n.* A black and white mammal found in the Pacific Ocean and related to the dolphin.

kill·ing (kĭl'ĭng) *n.* Murder; homicide. —*adj.* **1.** Apt to kill; fatal. **2.** *Informal.* Exhausting: *walk at a killing pace.* ♦ **make a killing.**

K

Informal. To earn a sudden large profit: *make a killing in the stock market.*

kiln (kĭln) *n.* An oven used to harden, burn, or dry things such as grain, lumber, or pottery.

ki·lo (kē′lō) *n., pl.* **ki·los.** A kilogram.

kilo— *pref.* A prefix that means one thousand: *kilowatt.*

kil·o·byte (kĭl′ə bīt′) *n.* A unit of measurement of the memory capacity of a computer, equal to 1,024 (2^{10}) bytes.

kil·o·cal·o·rie (kĭl′ə kăl′ ə rē) *n.* The quantity of heat needed to raise the temperature of one kilogram of water one degree Celsius.

kil·o·cy·cle (kĭl′ə sī′kəl) *n.* **1.** A unit equal to 1,000 cycles. **2.** A kilohertz.

kil·o·gram (kĭl′ə grăm′) *n.* The basic unit of mass in the metric system equal to 1,000 grams (about 2.2046 pounds). See table at **measurement.**

kil·o·hertz (kĭl′ə hûrts′) *n.* A unit of frequency equal to 1,000 cycles per second, used to express the frequency of radio waves.

kil·o·me·ter (kĭ lŏm′ ĭ tər or kĭl′ə mē′tər) *n.* A unit of length equal to 1,000 meters (0.62 mile). See table at **measurement.**

kil·o·watt (kĭl′ə wŏt′) *n.* A unit of power, especially electric power, equal to 1,000 watts.

kilt (kĭlt) *n.* A knee-length pleated skirt, of plaid wool, traditionally worn by men in the Highlands of Scotland.

kil·ter (kĭl′tər) *n.* [U] Good condition; proper form: *programs designed to bring the economy back into kilter.* ◆ **off kilter.** Not in proper position: *That painting is hanging slightly off kilter.*

ki·mo·no (kə mō′nə or kə mō′nō) *n., pl.* **ki·mo·nos.** A long loose robe with wide sleeves and a broad sash, traditionally worn by the Japanese as an outer garment.

kin (kĭn) *pl.n.* A person's relatives; family: *The kin of many immigrants remained in their native land.* —*adj.* [*to*] Related; kindred: *The panda is kin to the raccoon.*

kind¹ (kīnd) *adj.* **1.** Having a friendly, generous, or warm-hearted nature: *It was kind of you to offer to baby-sit.* **2.** Showing understanding for others: *kind words.*

kind² (kīnd) *n.* **1.** [C; *of*] A particular sort or type: *What kind of toothpaste do you use?* **2.** [U] A group sharing common traits or characteristics: *Seals gather with their own kind on this island.* ◆ **in kind. 1.** With goods or services as payment rather than money: *paying in kind.* **2.** In the same manner: *return a polite remark in kind.* **kind of.** *Informal.* Rather; somewhat: *I'm kind of hungry.*

USAGE: kind² When the plural **kinds** is used, the demonstrative pronoun and the verb must also be plural: *These* (or *those*) *kinds of films are*

popular. When both **kind** and the noun following it are singular, the verb must be singular: *This* (or *that*) *kind of film is popular.*

kin·der·gar·ten (kĭn′dər gär′tn) *n.* A class for children from four to six years of age that prepares them for elementary school: *Children sometimes learn to read in kindergarten.*

kind·heart·ed (kīnd′här′tĭd) *adj.* Gentle and generous by nature: *A kindhearted man lent me change for the bus even though he didn't know me.* —**kind′heart′ed·ly** *adv.* —**kind′heart′ed·ness** *n.* [U]

kin·dle (kĭn′dl) *v.* **kin·dled, kin·dling, kin·dles.** —*tr.* **1.** To build and start (a fire). **2.** To arouse (sthg.); excite: *The teacher used experiments to kindle our interest in science.* —*intr.* To catch fire: *The paper kindled on the third match.*

kin·dling (kĭnd′lĭng) *n.* [U] Sticks and other small pieces of material used to start a fire: *The trees burst into flame like dry kindling as the fire spread through the forest.*

kind·ly (kīnd′lē) *adj.* **kind·li·er, kind·li·est.** Considerate and helpful; kind: *a kindly and warm-hearted friend; kindly advice.* —*adv.* **1.** Out of kindness: *She kindly offered to help.* **2.** In a kind way; warmly: *The nurse greeted them kindly.* **3.** As a matter of courtesy; please: *Kindly read the notice aloud.* —**kind′li·ness** *n.* [U]

kind·ness (kīnd′nĭs) *n.* **1.** [U] The quality or state of being kind; generosity. **2.** [C] A kind act or kind treatment; a favor: *We are grateful for your many kindnesses.*

kin·dred (kĭn′drĭd) *n.* [U] A group of related persons, such as a clan. —*adj.* Having a similar origin or nature: *kindred feelings.*

ki·net·ic (kĭ nĕt′ĭk) *adj.* Relating to or produced by motion: *kinetic energy.*

kinetic energy *n.* [U] The energy possessed by a body because it is in motion.

ki·net·ics (kĭ nĕt′ĭks) *n.* [U] *(used with a singular verb).* The branch of physics that deals with forces and motion; dynamics.

kin·folk (kĭn′fōk′) *pl.n.* A person's relatives; kindred: *My kinfolk all live in Georgia.*

king (kĭng) *n.* **1.** A man who rules a nation. **2.** Somebody who is the most outstanding or important in a particular group: *That reporter is king of sportswriters.* **3.** Something that is regarded as the most powerful or important: *In the South, cotton was once king.*

king·dom (kĭng′dəm) *n.* **1.** A country that is ruled by a king or queen. **2.** The highest classification into which living organisms are grouped: *There are thousands of different species in the plant kingdom.*

king·ly (kĭng′lē) *adj.* **king·li·er, king·li·**

est. Of or fit for a king; regal; royal: *a kingly manner.* —*adv.* As a king; royally. —**king'li•ness** *n.* [U]

king•pin (kĭng'pĭn') *n.* The most important person or part in an organization or system: *Police arrested the drug kingpin.*

king•ship (kĭng'shĭp') *n.* **1.** [U] The position or power of a king. **2.** [C] The period during which a king rules; a reign.

king-size (kĭng'sīz') or **king-sized** (kĭng'sīzd') *adj.* Extra large: *a king-size bed.*

kink (kĭngk) *n.* **1.** A tight curl or twist, as in a hair, wire, or rope: *A kink in the wire may cause it to break.* **2.** A painful cramp or stiffness in a muscle, especially of the neck or back; a crick. **3.** A flaw or difficulty, as in a plan: *Technicians finally got the kinks out of the new computer program.* —*intr. & tr.v.* To form or cause to form a kink; curl or twist sharply: *When the hose kinks, water can't flow through it.*

kink•y (kĭng'kē) *adj.* **kink•i•er, kink•i•est. 1.** Full of kinks; tightly curled or twisted: *We could not pull the kinky wire through the hole.* **2.** *Informal.* Peculiar or eccentric, especially in a sexual sense; odd. —**kink'i•ness** *n.* [U]

kin•ship (kĭn'shĭp') *n.* [U] **1.** The condition of being related by blood, marriage, or adoption; family relationship: *Anthropologists study kinship.* **2.** A connection or similarity between persons or things: *kinship among students.*

kins•man (kĭnz'mən) *n.* A male relative. —**kins'wom'an** (kĭnz'wŏŏm'ən) *n.*

ki•osk (kē'ŏsk') *n.* **1.** A small structure often open on one side and used as a newsstand: *The newspaper kiosk on the corner sells papers and magazines in several languages.* **2.** A cylindrical structure on which advertisements are posted.

kiosk

kiss (kĭs) *v.* —*tr.* To touch (sbdy./sthg.) with the lips as a sign of affection, greeting, or reverence: *A medieval knight would often kiss the sword of his king as a sign of loyalty.* —*intr.* To engage in mutual touching or caressing with the lips: *The lovers kissed.* —*n.* **1.** A touch with the lips as a token of affection, greeting, or reverence: *a goodbye kiss.* **2.** A small piece of candy, especially of chocolate.

kiss•er (kĭs'ər) *n.* **1.** A person who kisses. **2.** *Slang.* The mouth or face, especially in boxing: *The boxer landed a punch on his opponent's kisser.*

kit (kĭt) *n.* **1.** A box or bag of articles or tools for a certain purpose: *a first-aid kit; a sewing kit.* **2.** A set of parts or materials to be assembled: *a model airplane kit.*

kitch•en (kĭch'ən) *n.* A room or an area where food is prepared or cooked.

kitch•en•ette (kĭch'ə nĕt') *n.* A small kitchen: *The studio apartment had just a kitchenette.*

kite (kīt) *n.* A light frame, usually of wood, covered with paper or cloth and designed to be flown in the wind at the end of a long string.

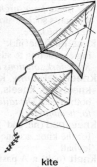

kite

kit•ten (kĭt'n) *n.* A young cat: *The cat carried her four kittens one by one from the barn to the house.*

kit•ty¹ (kĭt'ē) *n., pl.* **kit•ties.** A sum of money usually consisting of small contributions from a number of people, such as the players in a card game.

kit•ty² (kĭt'ē) *n., pl.* **kit•ties.** *Informal.* A kitten or cat: *Don't chase the kitties!*

kit•ty-cor•nered (kĭt'ē kôr'nərd) *adj. & adv.* Variant of **catty-cornered.**

ki•wi (kē'wē) *n.* **1.** An oval, brown, fuzzy fruit with sweet green pulp. **2.** A flightless bird of New Zealand with a long slender bill, a rounded body, and brownish feathers.

KKK or **K.K.K.** *abbr.* An abbreviation of Ku Klux Klan.

Kleen•ex (klē'nĕks') A trademark for a soft paper tissue.

klep•to•ma•ni•a (klĕp'tə mā'nē ə) *n.* [U] An uncontrollable urge to steal, especially when there is no personal need or desire for the things stolen. —**klep'to•ma'ni•ac'** (klĕp'tə mā'nē ăk') *n.*

klutz (klŭts) *n. Slang.* A clumsy person: *What a klutz! I just spilled coffee on myself.*

km *abbr.* An abbreviation of kilometer.

knack (năk) *n.* (*usually singular*). [*for*] A special talent or skill: *The mechanic has a knack for fixing cars.*

knap•sack (năp'săk') *n.* A bag made of sturdy material with shoulder straps for carrying small items on the back; a backpack.

knead (nēd) *tr.v.* **1.** To mix and work (a substance) into a pliable mass by folding, stretching, and pressing: *The cook kneaded the pizza dough. The potter kneaded the clay.* **2.** To squeeze, press, or roll (sthg.) with the hands, as in massaging: *The coach kneaded the runner's sore leg muscles.*

HOMONYMS: knead, need (necessity).

knee (nē) *n.* The joint at which the thigh and lower leg come together. —*tr.v.* **kneed, knee•ing, knees.** To push or strike (sbdy./sthg.) with the knee: *The waiter kneed the kitchen door open.*

knee·cap (nē′kăp′) *n.* The patella.

knee-deep (nē′dēp′) *adj.* **1.** Reaching as high as the knees: *The prairie grass was knee-deep.* **2.** Deeply occupied or engaged: *I'm knee-deep in work.*

knee-high (nē′hī′) *adj.* Reaching as high as the knee: *knee-high boots.* —*n.* (nē′hī′). A woman's sock or stocking that extends to just below the knee.

knee-jerk (nē′jûrk′) *adj. Informal.* Responding or reacting to sthg. without thinking first: *Knee-jerk solutions are sure to fail.*

kneel (nēl) *intr.v.* **knelt** (nĕlt) or **kneeled, kneel·ing, kneels.** To rest or fall on one or both knees: *The tailor knelt to mark the pants for hemming.*

knee·pad (nē′păd′) *n.* A protective covering for the knee, as one used by a player in volleyball.

knelt (nĕlt) *v.* A past tense and a past participle of **kneel.**

knew (nōō) *v.* Past tense of **know.**

HOMONYMS: knew, gnu (antelope), **new** (not old).

K

knick·ers (nĭk′ərz) *pl.n.* **1.** Loose pants formerly worn by boys or men that are gathered in with a band just below the knees. **2.** Long loose pants formerly worn as underwear by women and girls.

knick·knack also **nick·nack** (nĭk′năk′) *n.* A small ornamental article; a trinket: *My grandparents have many knickknacks in their living room.*

knife (nīf) *n., pl.* **knives** (nīvz). A tool made of a sharp blade with a handle, used for cutting, carving, or spreading. —*v.* **knifed, knif·ing, knifes.** —*tr.* To stab (sbdy./sthg.) with a knife. —*intr.* To cut or slash a way through sthg.: *The shark's fin knifed through the water.*

knight (nīt) *n.* **1.** In the Middle Ages, a gentleman soldier who served a king: *Lancelot was one of King Arthur's knights.* **2.** A man given a rank of honor by a king or queen for personal merit or service to the country. —*tr.v.* To make (a man) a knight: *The famous actor was knighted by the queen.* —**knight′ly** *adj. & adv.*

HOMONYMS: knight, night (darkness).

knight·hood (nīt′hŏŏd′) *n.* **1.** The rank of a knight. **2.** Knights considered as a group.

knit (nīt) *v.* **knit** or **knit·ted, knit·ting, knits.** —*tr.* **1.** To make (a fabric or garment) by looping yarn or thread: *I knit a sweater.* **2.** To join (sthg.) closely: *Shared interests knitted the group together.* **3.** To draw (the eyebrows) together in wrinkles: *knit one's brows in thought.* —*intr.* **1.** To make a fabric or garment by knitting: *I would like to learn to knit.* **2.** To grow or come together: *A broken bone knits fairly quickly.* —**knit′ter** *n.*

knit·ting (nĭt′ĭng) *n.* [U] **1.** The act of making knitted fabric or garments: *Knitting is a practical hobby.* **2.** Fabric or a garment in the process of being knitted: *I brought along my knitting.*

knitting needle *n.* One of two long thin needles, pointed at one or both ends, used in knitting by hand.

knives (nīvz) *n.* Plural of **knife.**

knob (nŏb) *n.* **1.** A rounded structure: *a brass knob on top of a bedpost.* **2.** A rounded handle on a door or piece of furniture or a dial on an appliance: *a control knob on a stove.* —**knob′by** *adj.*

knock (nŏk) *v.* —*tr.* **1.** To strike (sthg.) with a hard blow: *knock the baseball out of the park.* **2.** To produce (a hole) by striking: *knocked a hole in the wall.* **3.** *Slang.* To criticize (sbdy./sthg.); find fault with: *The critic knocked the actor's performance.* —*intr.* **1.** To strike a blow or series of blows causing a noise: *The neighbor knocked on our door.* **2.** To make a pounding noise: *The old car's engine knocks whenever we drive up a hill.* —*n.* **1.** A sharp blow: *The doctor gave me a knock on the knee.* **2.** The sound of a blow on a hard surface; a rap: *a loud knock at the door.* **3.** A pounding noise, as of an engine: *engine knocks.* ◆ **knock around** or **about.** *tr.v.* [sep.] To treat (sbdy.) roughly or brutally: *Her husband had knocked her around, so she called the police.* —*intr.v.* To wander from place to place: *knocking about Europe for the summer.* **knock dead.** *Slang.* To affect (sbdy.) strongly and positively: *You look great! You're going to knock everyone dead!* **knock down.** *tr.v.* [sep.] To break (sthg.) up or take (sthg.) apart: *We knocked down the tent and packed it in the car.* **knock for a loop.** To surprise (sbdy.) greatly: *Losing all that money really knocked me for a loop.* **knock it off.** *Slang.* To stop doing sthg. annoying: *I told the kids to knock it off.* **knock off.** *tr.v.* [sep.] *Informal.* **1.** To stop (sthg.): *Let's knock off work for today.* **2.** To complete or dispose of (sthg.) hastily or easily; finish: *I knocked off several letters this afternoon.* **3.** To eliminate (sthg.); deduct: *Using the coupon knocked five dollars off our bill.* **knock on wood.** *Informal.* An expression used in conversation that refers to the superstition that a knock on wood can prevent a bad thing from happening: *The weather should be sunny tomorrow, knock on wood.* **knock out.** *tr.v.* [sep.] **1.** To make (sbdy.) uncon-

---

ă–c**at**; ā–p**ay**; âr–c**are**; ä–f**ather**; ĕ–g**et**; ē–b**e**; ĭ–s**it**; ī–n**ice**; îr–h**ere**; ŏ–g**ot**; ō–g**o**; ô–s**aw**; oi–b**oy**; ou–**out**; ŏŏ–t**ook**; ōō–b**oot**; ŭ–c**ut**; ûr–w**ord**; th–**thin**; *th*–**this**; hw–**when**; zh–vi**si**on; ə–**about**; N–French b**on**

scious, as by a blow. **2.** To make (sthg.) useless or prevent from working: *The storm knocked out power in our neighborhood.* **3.** *Informal.* To exhaust (sbdy.) completely: *That long math exam really knocked me out.* **4.** To take (sbdy.) out of a competition, race, or game: *I was knocked out of the match.* **5.** *Informal.* To impress (sbdy.) greatly: *Your new outfit really knocks me out.* **knock over.** *tr.v.* [sep.] To hit and cause (sbdy./sthg.) to fall: *I accidentally knocked the glass of water over.* **knock together.** *tr.v.* [sep.] To put (sthg.) together quickly and without being careful: *They knocked together their proposal in a hurry, and it's not very good.* **knock up.** *tr.v.* [sep.] *Slang.* To make (a woman) pregnant.

knock•er (nŏk′ər) *n.* A metal device attached to a door so that visitors can use it to announce their presence.

knock•out (nŏk′out′) *n.* **1.** A hit or blow that leaves a person unconscious or results in a boxing victory. **2.** *Informal.* A strikingly attractive person or thing: *Your cousin is a real knockout with that haircut.*

knoll (nōl) *n.* A small rounded hill: *The cows stood grazing on the knoll.*

knot (nŏt) *n.* **1.** A tangle of thread, hair, or similar material: *She combed the knots out of her hair.* **2.** A fastening made by tying material such as ribbon, string, rope, or cord in a certain way: *a square knot.* **3.** A tight group of persons or things: *a knot of guests at the party.* **4.** The hard dark spot in wood where a branch grew from a tree trunk. **5.** A unit of speed equal to one nautical mile per hour, used especially by ships and aircraft. —*v.* **knot•ted, knot•ting, knots.** —*tr.* **1.** To tie or fasten (sthg.) in or with a knot: *We knotted the rope around the post.* **2.** To entangle (sthg.) in knots: *The strong current knotted our fishing lines together.* —*intr.* **1.** To become snarled or entangled. **2.** To form a knot or knots: *The chain had knotted in my pocket.*

knot

---

knot•hole (nŏt′hōl′) *n.* A hole in a board where a knot has come out.

knot•ty (nŏt′ē) *adj.* **knot•ti•er, knot•ti•est. 1.** Tied or tangled in knots: *knotty string.* **2.** With many knots: *knotty lumber.* **3.** Difficult to solve: *a knotty algebra problem.*

know (nō) *v.* **knew** (nōō), **known** (nōn), **know•ing, knows.** —*tr.* **1.** To be aware of (sthg.); realize: *I know what the answer is.* **2.** To regard (sthg.) as true; be sure of: *I know that the play will be a success.* **3.** To

have skill in (sthg.): *I know how to make ice cream.* **4.** To be acquainted or familiar with (sbdy./sthg.): *I know my neighbors well.* **5.** To recognize (sthg.): *I know the tune, but I can't remember the name of it.* **6.** To have (sthg.) memorized: *The actors must know their lines well.* —*intr.* [about] **1.** To possess knowledge or understanding: *My sister knows about the history of photography.* **2.** To be aware: *I knew about their plans for the weekend.* ♦ **in the know.** *Informal.* In possession of special or secret information: *My job with the city put me in the know about local politics.* **know better (than).** To have enough education or understanding not to do sthg.: *At your age, you should know better than to talk with your mouth full!* **know from.** *tr.v.* [sep.] To recognize or understand the difference between (one person or thing and another): *We know a good deal from a bad one.* **you know.** *Informal.* Used in conversation to fill pauses or to get the listener's agreement: *Please try to be, you know, a little quieter.* —**know′a•ble** *adj.*

---

know-how (nō′hou′) *n.* [U] Practical knowledge; skill: *Building a house requires a lot of know-how.*

know•ing (nō′ĭng) *adj.* **1.** With knowledge or awareness: *a knowing hiker, wise in the ways of the woods.* **2.** Suggestive of inside or secret information: *a knowing look.* —**know′ing•ly** *adv.*

know-it-all (nō′ĭt ôl′) *n. Informal.* A person who claims or pretends to know everything: *My assistant is a know-it-all with an opinion on everything.*

knowl•edge (nŏl′ĭj) *n.* [U] **1.** Awareness or understanding gained through experience or study: *He has an excellent knowledge of carpentry.* **2.** The fact or state of knowing: *Knowledge of the company's bad sales record made investors cautious.*

knowl•edge•a•ble (nŏl′ĭ jə bəl) *adj.* Well informed: *The secretary of state is knowledgeable about foreign policy.*

known (nōn) *v.* Past participle of **know.** —*adj.* Generally recognized: *a musician of known talent.*

knuck•le (nŭk′əl) *n.* A joint of a finger: *I scraped my knuckles when I fell.* —*v.* **knuck•led, knuck•ling, knuck•les.** ♦ **knuckle down.** *intr.v.* To apply oneself earnestly to a task: *We knuckled down and studied for the test.* **knuckle under.** *intr.v.* To yield to pressure; give in: *I knuckled under and agreed to go to the store.*

KO (kā′ō′) *Slang. tr.v.* **KO'd, KO'ing, KO's.** To knock (sbdy.) out. —*n.* (kā ō′ *or* kā′ō′). *pl.* **KO's.** A knockout, as in boxing.

ko•a•la (kō ä′lə) *n.* A
small Australian mam-
mal that resembles a
bear and has thick
grayish fur, large ears,
and sharp claws. The
female koala carries
her young in a pouch.

kook (kŏŏk) *n. Slang.*
An odd or crazy per-
son: *My history profes-
sor is brilliant but a
bit of a kook.* —**kook′i•ness** *n.* [U] —**kook′y**
adj.

koala
Adult female and
young koala

ko•sher (kō′shər) *adj.* **1.** Conforming to or
prepared in accordance with Jewish dietary
laws: *We eat only kosher beef.* **2.** *Slang.*
Proper; correct: *It's not kosher to copy someone else's homework.*

kow•tow (kou tou′ *or* kou′tou′) *intr.v.* **1.**
To kneel and touch the forehead to the
ground in expression of deep respect, worship, or submission: *Everyone kowtowed
before the emperor.* **2.** To show exaggerated
respect or obedience: *We all kowtowed to the
boss, hoping to please him.*

Kr The symbol for the element **krypton.**

kryp•ton (krĭp′tŏn′) *n.* [U] *Symbol* **Kr** A
colorless element that is an inert gas, used
chiefly in fluorescent lamps and lasers.
Atomic number 36. See table at **element.**

KS *abbr.* An abbreviation of Kansas.

ku•dos (kōō′dōz′ *or* kōō′dōs′) *n.* [U] *(used
with a singular or plural verb).* Praise, fame,
or renown for exceptional achievement: *The
diplomat received kudos for settling the dispute.*

Ku Klux Klan (kōō′ klŭks klăn′) *n.* A secret
society founded in the southern United States
to fight against civil rights for minorities
through the use of terrorism.

kung fu (kŭng′ fōō′) *n.* [U] A Chinese system of unarmed self-defense resembling
karate: *She's learning kung fu.*

kW *abbr.* An abbreviation of kilowatt.

KY or **Ky.** *abbr.* An abbreviation of Kentucky.

K

ă–cat; ā–pay; âr–care; ä–father; ĕ–get; ē–be; ĭ–sit; ī–nice; îr–here; ŏ–got; ō–go; ô–saw; oi–boy; ou–**out**;
ōō–took; ōō–boot; ŭ–cut; ûr–word; th–thin; *th*–**th**is; hw–**when**; zh–vision; ə–about; N–French bon

Ll

l¹ or **L** (ĕl) *n., pl.* **l's** or **L's.** The 12th letter of the English alphabet.

l² *abbr.* An abbreviation of: **1.** Liter. **2.** Or **L.** Large.

L also **l** The Roman numeral for 50.

l. *abbr.* An abbreviation of: **1.** Left. **2.** Length.

LA or **La.** *abbr.* An abbreviation of Louisiana.

L.A. also **LA** *abbr.* An abbreviation of Los Angeles.

lab (lăb) *n.* A laboratory.

la·bel (lā'bəl) *n.* **1.** A tag or piece of paper attached to sthg. to identify it: *the label on a can of peaches; the address label on a package.* **2.** A descriptive word or phrase: *the political labels* liberal *and* conservative. —*tr.v.* **1.** To attach a label to (sthg.): *Label the package for mailing.* **2.** To identify or describe (sbdy./sthg.) with a label: *The government labeled the writers traitors.*

la·bor (lā'bər) *n.* **1.** [U] Physical or mental effort; work: *the labor involved in climbing a hill.* **2.** [C] A specific task or piece of work: *Knitting him a sweater was a labor of love.* **3.** [U] People who work for wages: *negotiations between labor and management.* **4.** [C; U] (*usually singular*). The process of childbirth: *My sister had a difficult labor.* —*intr.v.* **1.** To work: *Many workers labored in the fields picking lettuce.* **2.** To move slowly and with difficulty; struggle: *The freight train labored over the mountain pass.* ◆ **labor under.** *tr.v.* [insep.] To suffer from (a burden or disadvantage): *They are laboring under the misconception that others will cooperate.* —**la'bor·er** *n.*

lab·o·ra·to·ry (lăb'rə tôr'ē) *n., pl.* **lab·o·ra·to·ries.** A room or building equipped for scientific research or experiments.

Labor Day *n.* The first Monday in September, celebrated as a holiday in honor of working people.

la·bored (lā'bərd) *adj.* Showing great effort; forced: *labored breathing.*

la·bor-in·ten·sive (lā'bər ĭn tĕn'sĭv) *adj.* Requiring more labor than machines or materials: *a labor-intensive project.*

la·bo·ri·ous (lə bôr'ē əs) *adj.* **1.** Needing great effort; difficult: *a laborious task.* **2.** Hardworking; industrious: *The members of the staff are skilled and laborious workers.* —**la·bo'ri·ous·ly** *adv.* —**la·bo'ri·ous·ness** *n.* [U]

la·bor-sav·ing (lā'bər sā'vĭng) *adj.* Designed to reduce human labor: *A dishwasher is a laborsaving device.*

labor union *n.* An organization of workers formed to protect their mutual interests by bargaining as a group with their employers over wages, working conditions, and benefits.

la·bour (lā'bər) *n. & v. Chiefly British.* Variant of **labor.**

lab·y·rinth (lăb'ə rĭnth') *n.* **1.** A complex structure of connected passages through which it is difficult to find one's way; a maze: *The cave was a dark labyrinth.* **2.** Something complicated or confusing in design or construction: *a labyrinth of streets.*

lace (lās) *n.* **1.** [C; U] A delicate fabric of fine threads woven in an open pattern with fancy designs: *Brussels is famous for its lace.* **2.** [C] A cord or string used to tie or fasten sthg., such as a shoe. —*v.* **laced, lac·ing, lac·es.** —*tr.* **1.** To pull a lace through the eyelets or around the hooks of (sthg.): *I laced the shoe before trying it on.* **2.** To weave, twist, or twine (sthg.) together: *She laced strands of hair into a braid.* —*intr.* To be fastened or tied with a lace or laces: *The children's sneakers lace easily.*

lac·er·ate (lăs'ə rāt') *tr.v.* **lac·er·at·ed, lac·er·at·ing, lac·er·ates.** *Formal.* To rip or tear (sthg.), especially in an injury: *He lacerated his arm falling through the window.* —**lac'er·a'tion** *n.* [C; U]

lack (lăk) *n.* (*usually singular*). A shortage or an absence: *The lack of electricity during the long power outage made life very hard.* —*v.* —*tr.* To have very little of or be without (sthg.): *Some streets lack trees.* —*intr.* [in] To be needing or deficient: *A diet of nothing but rice is lacking in protein.*

lack·a·dai·si·cal (lăk'ə dā'zĭ kəl) *adj.* Without spirit or interest: *a lackadaisical attitude.* —**lack'a·dai'si·cal·ly** *adv.*

lack·ey (lăk'ē) *n., pl.* **lack·eys.** An insulting expression for a follower who behaves like a servant; a flunky: *She brought her lackeys to the meeting.*

lack·lus·ter (lăk'lŭs'tər) *adj.* Lacking luster, brightness, or interest; dull: *lackluster conversation.*

lac·quer (lăk'ər) *n.* [C; U] A material similar to varnish that is applied to metal or wood and leaves a hard, shiny finish when dry. —*tr.v.* To coat (sthg.) with lacquer.

la·crosse (lə krôs' *or* lə krŏs') *n.* [U] A game played on a field in which players use sticks with nets to carry and pass a ball: *Lacrosse was played by Native Americans.*

lac·tate (lăk'tāt') *intr.v.* **lac·tat·ed, lac·tat·ing, lac·tates.** To produce milk.

lac·ta·tion (lăk tā′shən) *n.* [U] **1.** The secretion or formation of milk by the mammary glands. **2.** The period during which the mammary glands secrete milk.

lac·tic (lăk′tĭk) *adj.* Relating to milk: *lactic acid.*

lac·y (lā′sē) *adj.* **lac·i·er, lac·i·est.** Relating to or resembling lace: *a lacy covering of leaves overhead.*

lad (lăd) *n.* A word used in the past for a boy or young man: *I've known him since he was a lad.*

lad·der (lăd′ər) *n.* **1.** A device for climbing up or down, made of two long side pieces joined by steps: *We used a 6-foot ladder to pick apples.* **2.** A series of levels or stages: *She's high on the corporate ladder.*

lad·en (lād′n) *adj.* Weighed down with a load; heavy: *a ship laden with goods from China.*

la·dle (lād′l) *n.* A long-handled spoon with a deep bowl used for serving liquids. —*tr.v.* **la·dled, la·dling, la·dles.** To lift out and pour (sthg.) with a ladle: *I ladled the hot soup into the bowl.*

la·dy (lā′dē) *n., pl.* **la·dies. 1.** A woman of high social standing, good taste, or polite manners. **2.** A woman, especially when spoken about in a polite way: *the lady who lives next door.* **3. Lady.** *Chiefly British.* A feminine title of nobility.

la·dy·bug (lā′dē bŭg′) *n.* A small beetle, often red with black spots, that eats other insect pests.

la·dy·like (lā′dē līk′) *adj.* Characteristic of a lady: *Dancing on the table is not ladylike behavior.*

lag (lăg) *intr.v.* **lagged, lag·ging, lags. 1.** To move or develop more slowly than sbdy./sthg.: *Several runners began to lag behind the main group in the race.* **2.** To become weaker; diminish: *Our enthusiasm for the hike lagged as rain began to fall.* —*n.* **1.** The act or condition of lagging: *The cold weather caused a lag in interest in the field trip.* **2.** The extent or degree of lagging; a gap: *A huge lag separated the first and second place finishers in the race.*

la·ger (lä′gər) *n.* [C; U] A type of light beer.

lag·gard (lăg′ərd) *n.* A person who lags behind; a straggler: *The laggard fell farther behind on each lap of the race.*

la·goon (lə gōōn′) *n.* A shallow body of water separated from the sea by sandbars or reefs: *a tropical lagoon.*

laid (lād) *v.* Past tense and past participle of **lay**[1]: *He laid his hat on the chair.*

laid-back (lād′băk′) *adj. Informal.* Casual or relaxed: *It's going to be a laid-back party.*

lain (lān) *v.* Past participle of **lie**[1]: *The money has lain in the bank untouched for years.*

HOMONYMS: lain, lane (path).

lair (lâr) *n.* The place where a wild animal lives; a den: *a fox's lair.*

lais·sez faire (lĕs′ā fâr′) *n.* [U] An economic doctrine that opposes government regulation of commerce and industry beyond the minimum necessary for free enterprise to operate.

lake (lāk) *n.* A large inland body of fresh or salt water: *a cabin by the lake.*

la·ma (lä′mə) *n.* A Buddhist monk of Tibet or Mongolia.

HOMONYMS: lama, llama (pack animal).

lamb (lăm) *n.* **1.** [C] A young sheep. **2.** [U] The meat of a young sheep: *roast lamb.* **3.** [C] A sweet mild-mannered person: *She's such a lamb that she never quarrels with anyone.* —*intr.v.* To give birth to a lamb.

lamb

lame (lām) *adj.* **lam·er, lam·est. 1.** Unable to walk easily: *A leg injury made me lame.* **2.** *Informal.* Weak; unsatisfactory: *He gave a lame excuse for missing our meeting.* —*tr.v.* **lamed, lam·ing, lames.** To make (sbdy./sthg.) lame; disable: *The rock lamed the horse.* —**lame′ly** *adv.* —**lame′ness** *n.* [U]

lame duck *n.* A public officeholder who has not been reelected and is finishing a term of office: *The President is now a lame duck.*

la·ment (lə mĕnt′) *v.* —*tr.* **1.** To express grief for (sthg.); mourn: *lament the death of a loved one.* **2.** To regret (sthg.) deeply: *Architects lamented the state of the city.* —*intr.* To express grief; mourn: *The mourners began to lament.* —*n.* **1.** An expression of grief: *tears and laments.* **2.** A sorrowful song or poem: *a lament for his dead wife.* —**lam·en·ta·tion** (lăm′ən tā′shən) *n.* [C; U]

la·men·ta·ble (lə mĕn′tə bəl *or* lăm′ən-tə bəl) *adj.* Deserving of regret: *a lamentable mistake.* —**lam′en·ta·bly** *adv.*

lam·i·nate (lăm′ə nāt′) *tr.v.* **lam·i·nat·ed, lam·i·nat·ing, lam·i·nates. 1.** To beat or press (wood or metal, for example) into a thin plate or sheet. **2.** To make (plywood, glass, or plastics) by joining several layers. **3.** To cover (sthg.) with thin layers or sheets: *laminate a document with plastic.* —*n.* [C; U] Something, such as plywood, made by joining layers together. —**lam′i·na′tion** *n.* [C; U] —**lam′i·na′tor** *n.*

lamp (lămp) *n.* **1.** A device that gives off light by using oil, gas, or electricity: *When the lights went out, we lit a kerosene lamp.* **2.** A device that uses light for heating: *a sun lamp.*

lam•poon (lăm pōōn′) *n.* A piece of writing that makes fun of a person, group, idea, or institution. *—tr.v.* To make fun of (sbdy./ sthg.) with a lampoon: *The comedy lampooned the manners of the upper class.*

lance (lăns) *n.* **1.** A weapon with a sharp metal head, used by horsemen. **2.** A tool with a similar shape used for spearing fish or in surgery, for example. *—tr.v.* **lanced, lanc•ing, lanc•es. 1.** To pierce (sthg.) with a lance. **2.** To make a surgical incision in (sthg.): *The doctor lanced the swelling.*

land (lănd) *n.* **1.** [U] The part of the earth's surface not covered by water: *Only one third of the earth's surface is land.* **2.** [U] Ground or soil: *Farmers plow the land.* **3.** [C] A particular part of the earth, especially a region or country: *Venezuela is a land of great beauty.* **4.** [C] The people of a nation, district, or region: *Many lands participate in the Olympics.* **5.** [U] Property; real estate: *buy land in Hawaii.* *—v. —tr.* **1.** To set (a vehicle) down on the ground or another surface: *The pilot landed the plane in New York.* **2.** To get, catch, or win (sthg.): *She landed a good job. He landed a fish on the riverbank.* **3.** *Informal.* To deliver (a blow): *He landed a punch on the other boxer's chin.* *—intr.* **1.** To come to shore: *The boat landed in heavy surf.* **2.** To go ashore: *We landed on the dock.* **3.** To come down to the ground or another surface: *The plane landed on the lake.* ◆ **land in.** *intr.v.* To arrive in a place or condition: *I landed in trouble with the boss.* *—tr.v.* (sep.) To cause (sbdy.) to arrive in a place or condition: *Their protest landed them in jail.* **land on (one's) feet.** To come out of a bad or dangerous situation safely; be lucky: *I thought I was going to lose money on that investment, but I landed on my feet.*

land•ed (lăn′dĭd) *adj.* Owning land: *the landed gentry.*

land•fill (lănd′fĭl′) *n.* A place where garbage and trash are buried between layers of dirt: *Trucks haul garbage to the landfill.*

land•hold•er (lănd′hōl′dər) *n.* A person who owns land. *—***land′hold′ing** *n.* [U]

land•ing (lăn′dĭng) *n.* **1.** The act of coming to land after a voyage or flight: *the landing of a spacecraft on the moon.* **2.** A wharf or pier: *an old boat landing.* **3.** An area at the top or bottom of a set of stairs: *She stopped on the landing to catch her breath.*

landing gear *n.* [U] The equipment that supports an aircraft on land.

landing strip *n.* An aircraft runway without airport facilities.

land•la•dy (lănd′lā′dē) *n.* A woman who owns or runs buildings rented to tenants: *The landlady gave the new tenants the key to the apartment.*

land•locked (lănd′lŏkt′) *adj.* Entirely surrounded by land: *Switzerland is a landlocked country.*

land•lord (lănd′lôrd′) *n.* A person or a business that rents buildings to tenants: *My landlord raised my rent.*

land•mark (lănd′märk′) *n.* **1.** A familiar or easily recognized feature of a landscape: *The red barn is a well-known local landmark.* **2.** A building, place, or event that is important in history: *The discovery of penicillin was a landmark in the treatment of certain diseases. Philadelphia has many colonial landmarks.*

land•mass (lănd′măs′) *n.* A large area of land: *the landmass of Eurasia.*

land mine *n.* A small bomb buried in the ground and set to explode when stepped on or run over by a vehicle.

land•own•er (lănd′ō′nər) *n.* A person who owns land: *local landowners.* *—***land′own′ing** *adj.*

land•scape (lănd′skāp′) *n.* **1.** An area of scenery that can be seen from or in one place: *The Vermont landscape is lovely in autumn.* **2.** A painting or picture showing such a scene: *the landscapes of photographer Ansel Adams.* *—tr.v.* **land•scaped, land•scap•ing, land•scapes.** To change or improve the appearance of (a piece of land) by planting trees, shrubs, or flowers.

land•slide (lănd′slīd′) *n.* **1.** The loosening and fall of a large mass of soil and rock: *A landslide roared down the mountain.* **2.** A very large number of votes resulting in victory for a candidate or political party: *We expected him to win, but not by a landslide.*

lane (lān) *n.* **1.** A narrow path or road: *a country lane.* **2.** A set course used by ships or aircraft: *the shipping lanes of the Atlantic.* **3.** A strip marked off on a street or highway for one line of traffic: *a four-lane highway.* **4.** A similar strip marked off for contestants in a race: *the swimmer in lane three.* **5.** A bowling alley.

HOMONYMS: lane, lain (placed oneself flat).

lan•guage (lăng′gwĭj) *n.* **1.** [U] Human communication, using voice sounds and often written symbols representing these sounds in organized combinations. **2.** [C] A system of sounds and symbols used by a group of people: *Many languages are spoken in Africa.* **3.** [C] A system of signs, symbols, rules, or gestures used to convey information: *a computer language.* **4.** [U] The special words and expressions used by members of a group or profession: *medical language.*

lan•guid (lăng′gwĭd) *adj.* Without energy or spirit; weak or slow: *a languid wave of the hand.* *—***lan′guid•ly** *adv.*

lan·guish (lăng′gwĭsh) *intr.v.* **1.** To lose strength; grow weak: *Crops languished from lack of rain.* **2.** To suffer from miserable or depressing conditions: *The political prisoners languished in dark cells.*

lan·guor (lăng′gər) *n.* [U] A dreamy, lazy mood or quality: *the languor of a summer afternoon.* —**lan′guor·ous** *adj.*

lank (lăngk) *adj.* **1.** Long and lean; slender: *the athlete's lank body.* **2.** Long, straight, and limp: *lank hair.* —**lank′ly** *adv.*

lank·y (lăng′kē) *adj.* **lank·i·er, lank·i·est.** Tall, thin, and gawky: *a lanky young man.* —**lank′i·ness** *n.* [U]

lan·o·lin (lăn′ə lĭn) *n.* [U] A fatty substance from wool, used in soaps and cosmetics.

lan·tern (lăn′tərn) *n.* A portable case or container that protects a light from the weather: *We took a kerosene lantern on our camping trip.*

lantern

lap¹ (lăp) *n.* The flat place formed by the front part of the legs above the knees of a person who is sitting: *The puppy curled up in my lap.*

lap² (lăp) *tr.v.* **lapped, lap·ping, laps.** [*over*] To place or extend (sthg.) partly over sthg. else; overlap: *The worker laps the shingles over one another to keep the roof from leaking.* —*n.* **1.** A part folded or extending over sthg. else: *the front lap of a jacket.* **2.a.** One complete trip around a track, or up and down a pool: *a race of four laps.* **b.** A part or stage of a journey: *The first lap of our trip across the country was from New York to Ohio.*

lap³ (lăp) *v.* **lapped, lap·ping, laps.** —*tr.* **1.** To take up and swallow (a liquid) by using the tongue: *The dog lapped water from the bowl.* **2.** To wash or splash (sthg.) with a light slapping sound: *The sea lapped the shore gently.* —*intr.* [*against*] To wash or splash against sthg. with a light slapping sound: *Waves lapped against the dock.* —*n.* The act or sound of lapping: *each lap of the kitten's tongue; the lap of the waves.* ◆ **lap up.** *tr.v.* [*sep.*] **1.** To lap (a liquid) eagerly: *The kitten lapped up the milk.* **2.** To accept (praise) quickly and eagerly: *We lapped up their compliments.*

la·pel (lə pĕl′) *n.* One of the two folds that extend from the collar of a coat or jacket: *a narrow lapel.*

lapse (lăps) *intr.v.* **lapsed, laps·ing, laps·es.** **1.** [*into*] To fall to a lower or worse condition: *lapse into bad habits.* **2.** [*into*] To pass gradually or smoothly; slip: *He lapsed into unconsciousness.* **3.** To be no longer valid or active; end or expire: *I let my membership in the club lapse.* —*n.* **1.** A slip or failure, especially a

minor one: *a lapse of memory.* **2.** A fall into a lower or worse condition: *a lapse into bad habits.* **3.** A period of time: *a lapse of three months between trips.* **4.** The ending of an agreement, right, or custom because of lack of use or the passage of time: *the lapse of a lease.*

lap·top (lăp′tŏp′) *n.* A portable computer small enough to use on one's lap.

lar·ce·ny (lär′sə nē) *n., pl.* **lar·ce·nies.** [C; U] *Formal.* The crime of taking another's property; theft: *He was convicted of larceny.* —**lar′ce·nous** *adj.*

lard (lärd) *n.* [U] A white substance made from melted pig fat and used in cooking: *Few people cook with lard anymore.*

large (lärj) *adj.* **larg·er, larg·est.** Greater than average in size, amount, or number; big: *The blue whale is the largest mammal. The federal budget is a large sum of money.* ◆ **at large. 1.** Not in captivity; at liberty: *The bank robber was still at large.* **2.** In general: *The economy at large is doing well.* **3.** Representing a whole nation, state, or district: *a councilor-at-large.* —**large′ness** *n.* [U]

SYNONYMS: large, big, enormous, great, huge. These adjectives mean notably above the average in size or magnitude. *Los Angeles is a large city. Factory outlet stores usually offer big discounts. A computer can store an enormous amount of information. I'd like to take a cruise on a great ocean liner. Everyone had huge helpings of potato salad at the picnic.* **ANTONYM: small.**

large·ly (lärj′lē) *adv.* For the most part; mainly: *The hills are largely covered with trees.*

large-scale (lärj′skāl′) *adj.* **1.** Large in size or effect; extensive: *large-scale farming of crops for export.* **2.** Drawn or made larger in size than average, especially to show detail: *a large-scale map.*

lar·gess also **lar·gesse** (lär zhĕs′ *or* lär jĕs′) *n.* [U] Generosity in giving gifts: *She was known for her largess.*

lark¹ (lärk) *n.* A small brown songbird: *Larks often sing while flying.*

lark² (lärk) *n.* Something done just for fun or adventure: *We went to the zoo on a lark.*

lar·va (lär′və) *n., pl.* **lar·vae** (lär′vē) or **lar·vas.** The immature wormlike form of certain insects: *A caterpillar is the larva of a butterfly or moth.* —**lar′val** *adj.*

lar·yn·gi·tis (lăr′ən jī′tĭs) *n.* [U] A swelling of the larynx, causing difficulty in speaking.

lar·ynx (lăr′ĭngks) *n.* The upper part of the windpipe, containing the vocal cords; the voice box.

la·sa·gna (lə zän′yə) *n.* [U] **1.** Flat wide strips of pasta. **2.** A dish made by baking this pasta with layers of tomato sauce, cheese, and other fillings.

las·civ·i·ous (lə sĭv′ē əs) *adj.* Feeling or showing lust; lewd. —**las·civ′i·ous·ly** *adv.* —**las·civ′i·ous·ness** *n.* [U]

la·ser (lā′zər) *n.* A device that produces a very narrow and intense beam of light or other radiation.

lash¹ (lăsh) *n.* **1.** A blow given with a whip. **2.** An eyelash. —*v.* —*tr.* **1.** To strike (sbdy./sthg.) with or as if with a whip: *The man was lashed.* **2.** To strike (sthg.) with force or violence: *The storm lashed the shore with high winds.* —*intr.* **1.** To move rapidly or violently; dash: *The waves lashed against the shore.* **2.** To strike with or as if with a whip: *The mule's tail lashed at the flies.* ◆ **lash out against** or **at. 1.** To attack (sbdy.) violently with a hand, foot, or weapon: *He lashed out at the people who surrounded him.* **2.** To attack (sbdy./sthg.) verbally or in print: *The President lashed out against critics of the government.*

lash² (lăsh) *tr.v.* To fasten or secure (sthg.), with a rope or cord: *The crew lashed the cargo onto the ship's deck.*

lass (lăs) *n.* A word used in the past for a girl or young woman: *She moved to the city when she was a lass.*

las·si·tude (lăs′ĭ tōōd′) *n.* [U] A feeling of weakness or exhaustion; tiredness: *The disease brought on a long period of lassitude and inactivity.*

last¹ (lăst) *adj.* **1.** After all others; final: *the last day of the school year; my last dime.* **2.** Most recent; just passed: *last week.* **3.** Most unlikely; least expected: *The last thing you would expect is snow during the summer.* —*adv.* **1.** After all others; at the end: *The recipe says to add the flour last.* **2.** Most recently; latest: *I last saw them when I was a child.* —*n.* [U] **1.** A person or thing that is last: *I've read every chapter but the last.* **2.** The end: *They held out until the last.* ◆ **at last.** After a long time; finally: *At last we fell asleep.* **at long last.** After a lengthy or difficult wait or delay: *At long last the storm was over.* **last but not least.** Coming at the end but still important: *There are lots of reasons to stop working now; last but not least, I'm hungry.* **last straw.** The last in a series of annoyances or disappointments that finally leads to loss of patience, trust, or hope: *It was the last straw when he missed our date today.* **last word.** The newest or most up-to-date style or development; the latest thing: *This model is the last word in racing bikes.* —**last′ly** *adv.*

last² (lăst) *v.* —*intr.* **1.** To continue; go on: *The song lasted three minutes.* **2.** To remain in good condition; endure: *This table won't last; it's so flimsy.* **3.** To be enough: *The food supply should last for a long time.* —*tr.* To supply (sbdy./sthg.) adequately; be enough

for: *One loaf of bread can't last us a week.*

last·ing (lăs′tĭng) *adj.* Continuing for a long time; enduring: *a lasting peace between nations.*

lat. *abbr.* An abbreviation of latitude.

Lat. *abbr.* An abbreviation of Latin.

latch (lăch) *n.* A movable bar used to close a door, gate, or window: *Make sure the latch is secured.* —*tr. & intr.* To close or be closed with a latch: *Latch the door. Does the door latch securely?* ◆ **latch on to** or **onto.** *tr.v.* [insep.] To get hold of (sbdy./sthg.): *They latched onto us at a party, and it took us hours to get rid of them.*

late (lāt) *adj.* **lat·er, lat·est. 1.** Happening after the expected, usual, or proper time: *I am late for my appointment.* **2.** Happening toward the end of a time period: *It was late in the meeting when we discussed that plan.* **3.** Recent: *a late model car.* **4.** Dead, especially if only recently: *her late husband.* —*adv.* **later, latest. 1.** After the usual, expected, or proper time: *The train arrived late.* **2.** At the end or at an advanced stage: *Our team scored the winning run late in the game.* **3.** Recently: *as late as last week.* ◆ **of late.** Recently; lately: *The trains have been running on a new schedule of late.* —**late′ness** *n.* [U]

late·com·er (lāt′kŭm′ər) *n.* A person or thing that arrives later than others or has arrived recently: *Latecomers to the show may have difficulty finding seats.*

late·ly (lāt′lē) *adv.* Not long ago; recently: *The weather has been cold lately.*

la·tent (lāt′nt) *adj.* Present but not evident or active; hidden: *Many of a child's latent talents become visible only in adulthood.* —**la′ten·cy** *n.* [U]

lat·er·al (lăt′ər əl) *adj.* Located on or coming from the side: *lateral growth on a plant.* —**lat′er·al·ly** *adv.*

la·tex (lā′tĕks′) *n.* [U] **1.** The milky, sticky liquid produced by certain trees and plants, such as the rubber tree. **2.** A synthetic liquid similar to this, used in paints, adhesives, and other products.

lathe (lā*th*) *n.* A machine on which a piece of wood, metal, or plastic is turned and shaped by a cutting tool.

lath·er (lă*th*′ər) *n.* [C; U] Foam formed from soap or heavy sweating, especially on a horse: *He was in a lather.* —*tr.v.* To cover (sthg.) with lather: *The barber lathered the man's face.*

Lat·in American (lăt′n) *n.* **1.** A person born or living in Latin America. **2.** A person of Latin-American descent. —**Lat′in-A·mer′i·can** *adj.*

La·ti·no (lə tē′nō) *n., pl.* **La·ti·nos. 1.** A person born in or from Latin America. **2.** A person of Hispanic, especially Latin-American, descent. —**La·ti′na** *n., adj.* —**La·ti′no** *adj.*

L

lat•i•tude (lăt′ĭ tōōd′) *n.* **1.** [U] Distance north or south of the equator measured in degrees. **2.** [C] A region of the earth indicated by its approximate latitude: *Some of the coldest temperatures on earth occur in the polar latitudes.* **3.** [U] Freedom in thought, action, or opinion: *The police chief gave his staff latitude in investigating this case.* —**lat′-i•tu′di•nal** *adj.*

la•trine (lə trēn′) *n.* A hole in the ground used as a toilet in camps or military barracks.

lat•ter (lăt′ər) *adj.* **1.** Referring to the second of two people or things that are mentioned: *Apples and oranges both taste good, but I prefer the latter.* **2.** Closer to the end: *November comes in the latter part of the year.* —**lat′ter•ly** *adv.*

lat•tice (lăt′ĭs) *n.* An open framework made of strips of wood, metal, or a similar material: *The lattice covered the window.* —*tr.v.* **lat•ticed, lat•tic•ing, lat•tic•es.** To form (sthg.) into a lattice: *We latticed strips of cane to make the chair seat.* —**lat′ticed** *adj.*

laud (lôd) *tr.v. Formal.* To praise (sbdy./sthg.) highly: *The principal lauded the school's graduates during commencement.* —**laud′a•ble** *adj.* —**laud′a•bly** *adv.*

laugh (lăf) *v.* —*intr.* To make sounds and facial movements to express happiness, amusement, scorn, or nervousness: *He laughed about his problems.* —*tr.* To influence (sthg.) by laughter: *We laughed our worries away.* —*n.* The act or sound of laughing: *a good-natured laugh.* ◆ **have the last laugh.** To win after apparently losing: *We had the last laugh when we beat the undefeated team.* **laugh at.** *tr.v.* [insep.] To treat (sbdy./sthg.) lightly: *They laughed at my proposal.*

laugh•a•ble (lăf′ə bəl) *adj.* Causing or deserving of laughter: *a laughable suggestion.* —**laugh′a•bly** *adv.*

laugh•ing•stock (lăf′ĭng stŏk′) *n.* A person or thing that is made fun of; an object of ridicule: *the laughingstock of the office.*

laugh•ter (lăf′tər) *n.* [U] The act or sound of laughing: *Laughter filled the air.*

launch[1] (lônch) *v.* —*tr.* **1.** To throw or propel (sthg.) into the air or sky: *launch a rocket.* **2.** To put (a boat or ship) into the water. **3.** To start (sthg.): *The institute launched a new research program.* —*intr.* **1.** To set out; make a start: *He launched out on a new career.* **2.** To enter energetically into sthg.: *He launched into a review of the new movie.* —*n.* The act of launching sthg., such as a rocket or spacecraft: *The launch went smoothly.* —**launch′er** *n.*

launch[2] (lônch) *n.* A large open motorboat: *He crossed the river in the launch.*

launch pad *n.* The platform or base from which a rocket or space vehicle is launched.

laun•der (lôn′dər) *tr. & intr.v.* To wash or be washed in a specific way: *We launder our clothes on Mondays. This fabric launders easily in cold water.*

Laun•dro•mat (lôn′drə măt′). A trademark for a self-service laundry where clothes are washed and dried in coin-operated machines.

laun•dry (lôn′drē) *n., pl.* **laun•dries. 1.** [U] Clothes that have just been or will be washed: *Sort the laundry by color.* **2.** [C] A place where clothes and linens are washed and ironed.

lau•re•ate (lôr′ē ĭt *or* lŏr′ē ĭt) *n.* A person who has been honored for achievements, especially in literature or science.

lau•rel (lôr′əl *or* lŏr′əl) *n.* **1.** [C; U] A small shrub or tree native to the Mediterranean region, with glossy, spicy-smelling, evergreen leaves. **2.** [C] A wreath of laurel given as a symbol of honor. **3.** [C] *(usually plural).* Honors and glory won for great achievement: *She was given laurels for improving so much in math.* ◆ **rest on (one's) laurels.** To be content with one's achievements; show no sign of future ambition: *After he won the prize for sales, he decided to rest on his laurels.*

la•va (lä′və *or* lăv′ə) *n.* [U] **1.** Liquid rock that flows from a volcano or from a crack in the earth. **2.** The rock formed when this substance cools and hardens.

lav•a•to•ry (lăv′ə tôr′ē) *n., pl.* **lav•a•to•ries.** *Formal.* A room with a sink and a toilet; a bathroom: *The lavatory is down the hall.*

lav•en•der (lăv′ən dər) *n.* **1.** [C; U] A plant with small, fragrant purplish flowers. **2.** [U] A pale or light purple color. —*adj.* Pale or light purple.

lav•ish (lăv′ĭsh) *adj.* **1.** Given or provided very plentifully: *a party with lavish refreshments.* **2.** Very generous or free in giving: *Be lavish with praise.* —*tr.v.* To give (sthg.) in abundance: *The grandparents lavished affection on their grandchildren.* —**lav′ish•ly** *adv.* —**lav′ish•ness** *n.* [U]

law (lô) *n.* **1.** [C] A rule that controls conduct or activities, made by an authority: *Corporate laws govern business.* **2.** [U] Social order created by obedience to such rules: *a breakdown of law and order.* **3.** [U] The study of such rules: *a professor of law.* **4.** [U] The profession of a lawyer: *practice the law.* **5.** [U] A person or an agency, such as the police or a court, responsible for enforcing or administering the law: *a criminal pursued by the law.* **6.** [C] A generally accepted rule, principle, or practice: *the laws of good health.* **7.** [C] A statement or set of statements describing what will always happen when certain conditions exist: *the law of gravity; the laws of physics.*

ă–**cat**; ā–**pay**; âr–**care**; ä–**father**; ĕ–**get**; ē–**be**; ĭ–**sit**; ī–**nice**; îr–**here**; ŏ–**got**; ō–**go**; ô–**saw**; oi–**boy**; ou–**out**; ōō–**took**; ōō–**boot**; ŭ–**cut**; ûr–**word**; th–**thin**; *th*–**this**; hw–**when**; zh–**vision**; ə–**about**; N–French **bon**

law·a·bid·ing (lô′ə bī′dĭng) *adj.* Obeying the law: *law-abiding citizens.*

law·ful (lô′fəl) *adj.* **1.** Allowed by law: *lawful acts.* **2.** Established or recognized by the law: *a lawful heir.* **—law′ful·ly** *adv.* **—law′ful·ness** *n.* [U]

law·less (lô′lĭs) *adj.* **1.** Not governed by law: *the lawless frontier.* **2.** Disregarding or violating the law: *a lawless mob.* **—law′less·ly** *adv.* **—law′less·ness** *n.* [U]

law·mak·er (lô′mā′kər) *n.* A person who participates in creating laws; a legislator. **—law′mak′ing** *n.* [U]

lawn (lôn) *n.* A piece of ground around a house planted with grass that is usually cut regularly: *The lawn needs to be mowed.*

lawn mower also **lawn·mow·er** (lôn′mō′ər) *n.* A machine that has rotating blades for cutting grass.

law·suit (lô′soōt′) *n.* A suit or case brought to a court of law for settlement: *The woman won the lawsuit.*

law·yer (lô′yər) *n.* A person who gives legal advice to clients and represents them in a court of law; an attorney: *Our lawyer helped us write a will.*

lax (lăks) *adj.* **1.** Not careful or strict; negligent: *Some people are lax about paying bills.* **2.** Not firm; loose: *a lax cable.* **—lax′i·ty** *n.* [U] **—lax′ly** *adv.* **—lax′ness** *n.* [U]

lax·a·tive (lăk′sə tĭv) *n.* A medicine that causes the bowels to empty. *—adj.* Causing bowel movements.

lay¹ (lā) *v.* **laid** (lād), **lay·ing, lays.** *—tr.* **1.** To place or put (sbdy./sthg.) on a flat surface or in a horizontal position: *I laid the baby in the crib.* **2.** To put (sthg.) in place; set down: *We will lay tiles for flooring.* **3.** To produce (an egg): *The bird laid three eggs.* **4.** To place (a bet); wager: *She laid her bet.* *—intr.* To produce an egg or eggs: *The hens stopped laying suddenly.* *—n.* (*usually singular*). The organization or arrangement of sthg.: *the lay of the land.* ♦ **lay aside.** *tr.v.* [sep.] **1.** To give (sthg.) up; abandon: *Let's lay this disagreement aside.* **2.** To save (sthg.) for future use: *lay aside a portion of your salary for vacation.* **lay away.** *tr.v.* [sep.] To reserve (merchandise) until completely paid for: *I laid the computer away until Christmas.* **lay down.** *tr.v.* [sep.] **1.** To give up and surrender (sthg.): *The soldiers laid down their arms.* **2.** To specify (sthg.): *lay down rules by which to live.* **lay in.** *tr.v.* [sep.] To store (sthg.) for future use: *They laid in supplies for a blizzard.* **lay into.** *tr.v.* [insep.] *Slang.* **1.** To scold (sbdy.) harshly: *My parents laid into me for lying.* **2.** To attack (sbdy.) physically: *The boys laid into each other.* **lay off.** *tr.v.* **1.** [sep.] To dismiss or suspend (sbdy.) from a job: *Her boss laid her off a month ago.* **2.** [insep.] *Slang.* To stop (doing sthg.): *lay off working and go eat.* **lay out.** *tr.v.* [sep.] **1.** To

arrange (sthg.) according to plan: *laying out the streets of a new housing development.* **2.** *Informal.* To spend (money): *She laid out $10,000 for a car.* **lay over.** *intr.v.* To make a stopover in a journey: *The plane laid over for two hours in Chicago.* **lay up.** *tr.v.* [sep.] **1.** To store (sthg.) for future needs: *Grandma laid up tomatoes from the garden.* **2.** *Informal.* To keep (sbdy.) in bed or out of action with an illness or injury: *He was laid up with the flu.*

HOMONYMS: lay (put, not of the clergy, placed oneself flat), **lei** (garland).

USAGE: lay¹ The words **lay** ("to put or place") and **lie** ("to recline or be situated") are frequently confused. **Lay** is basically a transitive verb and takes an object: *I always lay my glasses down carefully. He laid* (not *lay*) *the newspaper on the table. She was laying carpet.* **Lie** is an intransitive verb and does not take an object: *She often lies down after lunch. When I lay down, I fell asleep. The rubbish had lain there a week. I was lying in bed when he called.*

---

lay² (lā) *adj.* **1.** Relating to people who are not members of the clergy: *a lay missionary.* **2.** Not belonging to a particular profession: *A lay observer accompanied the scientific expedition.*

lay³ (lā) *v.* Past tense of **lie¹**: *He lay in bed.*

lay·a·way (lā′ə wā′) *n.* A way of reserving merchandise by making payments until the item is paid in full: *I put a coat on layaway.*

lay·er (lā′ər) *n.* **1.** A single thickness of material lying between others or covering a surface: *a cake with three layers.* **2.** A person or thing that lays sthg.: *a carpet layer.* *—tr. & intr.v.* To form, arrange, or split into layers. **—lay′er·ing** *n.* [U]

lay·man (lā′mən) *n.* **1.** A man who does not have the specialized knowledge or training of a member of a profession: *in layman's terms.* **2.** A man who is not a member of the clergy. **—lay′wo·man** *n.*

lay·off (lā′ôf′ *or* lā′ŏf′) *n.* A firing or suspension of employees, especially because there is not enough work to be done: *Layoffs have cost thousands of workers their jobs.*

lay·out (lā′out′) *n.* A planned arrangement of parts or areas: *the layout of a factory.*

lay·o·ver (lā′ō′vər) *n.* A short stop or break in a journey: *a three-hour layover in Toronto.*

laze (lāz) *intr.* **lazed, laz·ing, laz·es.** To relax lazily; loaf: *laze away a summer's afternoon.*

la·zy (lā′zē) *adj.* **la·zi·er, la·zi·est. 1.** Not willing to work or be energetic: *a lazy person.* **2.** Causing idleness or a lack of energy: *lazy summer afternoons.* **3.** Slow-moving: *lazy clouds floating overhead.* **—la′zi·ly** *adv.* **—la′zi·ness** *n.* [U]

lb. *abbr.* An abbreviation of pound.

leach (lēch) *tr.v.* **1.** To dissolve (soluble materials) by passing a liquid through soil or other matter: *Heavy rains leached minerals from the soil.* **2.** To pass a liquid through (a substance), dissolving the soluble materials in it: *Heavy rains have leached the soil of minerals and other nutrients.*

HOMONYMS: leach, leech (worm).

lead¹ (lēd) *v.* **led** (lĕd), **lead·ing, leads.** —*tr.* **1.** To show the way to (sbdy.) by going ahead: *The guide will lead us to the top of the mountain.* See Synonyms at **guide. 2.** To guide (sbdy./sthg.) by the hand or an attached rope: *I led the horse out of the barn.* **3.** To serve as a channel or passage for (sthg.): *This pipe leads the water away from the house.* **4.** To be first in (a competition, for example): *She's still leading the race.* **5.** To direct (sbdy./sthg.): *He led the group in a song.* **6.** To cause (sbdy.) to think or act in a certain way: *His remarks led me to believe that he was a musician.* **7.** To live or experience (a life of a particular kind): *A pilot often leads an exciting life.* —*intr.* **1.** To go first as a guide: *The teacher led and the children followed.* **2.** To be first; be ahead: *Only one runner is now leading in the race.* **3.** To be or form a way, route, or passage: *The trail leads to a little stream.* —*n.* **1.** The front or winning position: *Our team took the lead in the game.* **2.** The amount by which one is ahead: *a five-point lead.* **3.** An example or a preceding event: *They followed the committee's lead and voted against the amendment.* **4.** A clue or piece of information that guides a search: *leads that helped solve the crime.* **5.** The main role, as in a play or movie: *She played the lead.* ♦ **lead off.** *intr.v.* To begin; start: *The speaker led off with a funny story.* **lead on.** *tr.v.* [sep.] To draw (sbdy.) into unwise action or mistaken opinion; deceive: *They led the investors on with false claims of oil discoveries.* **lead to.** *tr.v.* [insep.] To tend toward or result in (sthg.): *The discovery of oil led to the development of a city here.* **lead up to.** To result in (sthg.) by a series of steps: *These events led up to a change in management of the company.*

lead² (lĕd) *n.* **1.** [U] *Symbol* **Pb** A soft, heavy, dull gray metallic element that is easily worked and shaped. It is used in radiation shields, as a solder, in alloys, and in many other products. Atomic number 82. See table at **element. 2.** [C; U] A material, often made mostly of graphite, used as the writing substance in pencils. **3.** [U] Bullets from or for guns: *The sheriff filled the outlaw with lead.* —*tr.v.* To cover, join, or weight (sthg.) with lead: *church windows of leaded glass.*

HOMONYMS: lead², led (guided).

lead·en (lĕd'n) *adj.* **1.** Made of lead: *a leaden fishing weight.* **2.** Dull dark gray: *leaden skies.* **3.** Dull, heavy, or slow: *leaden feet worn out from a long hike; leaden spirits.*

lead·er (lē'dər) *n.* A person who leads, guides, or has power over others: *a natural leader.*

lead·er·ship (lē'dər shĭp') *n.* [U] **1.** The position or office of a leader: *He's part of the student leadership.* **2.** Ability to lead: *The mayor showed strong leadership during the crisis.*

lead·ing (lē'dĭng) *adj.* **1.** Having the first or front position: *the leading swimmer in the race.* **2.** Most important; main; principal: *the leading industrial countries.*

leaf (lēf) *n., pl.* **leaves** (lēvz). **1.** [C] A thin, usually flat green plant part that grows on the stem or up from the roots. **2.** [C] A sheet of paper in a book. **3.** [U] A very thin sheet of metal: *gold leaf.* **4.** [C] A movable or removable part of a table top. —*intr.v.* To produce leaves: *Most trees leafed early this spring.* ♦ **leaf through.** *tr.v.* [insep.] To turn pages in (a book or magazine): *I leafed through the new book.* **turn over a new leaf.** To make a new start: *It's time to give up junk food and turn over a new leaf.* —**leaf'less** *adj.*

leaf·let (lē'flĭt) *n.* **1.** A small leaf or leaflike part of a plant. **2.** A booklet or small pamphlet: *a fire-prevention leaflet.*

leaf·y (lē'fē) *adj.* **leaf·i·er, leaf·i·est. 1.** Covered with many leaves: *leafy branches.* **2.** Consisting of leaves: *You should eat three servings of green, leafy vegetables.*

league¹ (lēg) *n.* **1.** An association of nations, organizations, or people working to help one another. **2.** An association of sports teams or clubs that usually compete with each other: *My son plays in an after-school baseball league.* ♦ **in league.** Joined or working together: *They've been in league with drug dealers for years.*

league² (lēg) *n.* A unit of distance, approximately equal to three miles (4.8 kilometers).

leak (lēk) *v.* —*intr.* **1.** To allow sthg. to pass through an opening or openings: *The roof leaks in a heavy rain.* **2.** To pass through an opening or a break: *Water leaked from the rusty pail.* **3.** To become known through a break in secrecy: *The news leaked out.* —*tr.* **1.** To let (sthg.) pass through a hole or opening: *The roof leaks water.* **2.** To disclose (secret information) without permission: *Someone leaked the story to the newspapers.* —*n.* **1.** A hole or crack through which sthg. can pass: *I fixed the leak in the roof.* **2.** The passage of sthg. through such an opening or break: *The leak of oil is about a quart every week.* **3.** A release of secret information: *The leak came from the White House.*

leak•age (lē′kĭj) *n.* [C; U] **1.** The act or an instance of leaking. **2.** Something that escapes or enters by leaking.

leak•y (lē′kē) *adj.* **leak•i•er, leak•i•est.** Having or allowing a leak: *a leaky valve.*

lean[1] (lēn) *v.* —*intr.* **1.** To slant from an upright position: *The tree leaned in the high wind.* **2.** To rest one's weight on or against sthg. for support: *I leaned against the wall to rest.* —*tr.* To set or place (sthg.) in a slanting or supported position: *I leaned the ladder against the tree.* —*n.* A slant or an inclination: *The lean of the ladder makes it look as if it will fall.* ♦ **lean on** or **upon.** *tr.v.* [insep.] To depend on (sbdy.): *She leaned on her family during her illness.* **lean toward.** *tr.v.* [insep.] To prefer (sbdy./sthg.): *We're leaning toward going to the mountains next vacation.*

lean[2] (lēn) *adj.* **1.** Not fat; thin: *a lean cat.* **2.** Containing little or no fat: *lean meat.* **3.** Not productive or satisfying: *The long dry period brought a lean harvest.* —**lean′ness** *n.* [U]

SYNONYMS: lean, thin, slender, spare, skinny, scrawny. These adjectives mean having little or no excess flesh. **Lean** means lacking fat: *Leaner cuts of meat are better for your health.* **Thin** and **slender** mean having a lean body: *It's amazing that some people can eat ice cream every day and stay thin. A century ago, heavier bodies were considered more beautiful than slender ones.* **Spare** often means trim with good muscle tone: *She has the spare figure of a marathon runner.* **Skinny** and **scrawny** mean unattractively thin, as if undernourished: *The boy had skinny legs with prominent knees. If you exercise more instead of dieting, you won't look so scrawny.* **ANTONYM: fat.**

lean•ing (lē′nĭng) *n.* A tendency; a preference: *I don't have a strong leaning toward either candidate.*

leap (lēp) *v.* **leaped** or **leapt** (lĕpt *or* lēpt), **leap•ing, leaps.** —*intr.* **1.** To jump upward; spring: *The frog leaped from my hand.* **2.** To move suddenly from one state or subject to another: *You can't leap to conclusions without any evidence.* —*tr.* **1.** To jump or spring over (sthg.): *The deer leapt our garden fence.* **2.** To cause (sthg.) to jump: *You must leap the horse over a fence.* —*n.* **1.** The act of leaping; a spring or jump. **2.** The distance covered in a jump: *a leap of ten feet.*

leap•frog (lēp′frôg′ *or* lēp′frŏg′) *n.* [U] A game in which one player bends over while the next in line jumps over him or her. —*tr.v.* **leap•frogged, leap•frog•ging, leap•frogs.** **1.** To leap over (sbdy.) in a game of leapfrog. **2.** To advance past (sbdy.), especially to gain an advantage: *He leapfrogged the rest of us to get a promotion.*

leapt (lĕpt *or* lēpt) *v.* A past tense and a past participle of **leap.**

leap year *n.* A year in which there are 366 days, the extra day being February 29.

learn (lûrn) *v.* —*tr.* **1.** To gain knowledge or skill in (sthg.) through study or experience: *Is it hard to learn to speak French?* **2.** To find (sthg.) out: *We learned who won the election from the newspaper.* **3.** To memorize (sthg.): *Learn the tune and then add the words.* —*intr.* [*of; about*] To gain knowledge or skill: *I learned of their plans from my friend.*

learn•ed (lûr′nĭd) *adj.* Having deep knowledge; scholarly: *a learned history professor.*

learn•ing (lûr′nĭng) *n.* [U] **1.** Instruction; education: *Learning was a lot easier when the noise stopped.* **2.** Complete knowledge or skill gained by study: *Fortunately I have teachers of great learning.*

lease (lēs) *n.* A written agreement granting use of property for a certain time in exchange for rent: *We signed a two-year lease.* —*tr.v.* **leased, leas•ing, leas•es. 1.** To grant the use of (property) by lease: *The landlord leased the house to new tenants.* **2.** To acquire or hold (property) by lease: *We leased the house from the landlord.*

leash (lēsh) *n.* A cord or chain used to hold or lead a dog: *Put the dog on the leash.* —*tr.v.* To restrain (an animal) with a leash: *Keep your dog leashed.*

least (lēst) *adj.* A superlative of **little.** Smallest in degree, size, or importance: *We want to spend the least money possible.* —*adv.* Superlative of **little.** To the smallest degree: *I like vanilla ice cream least.* —*n.* [U] The smallest thing or amount: *The least you could do would be to apologize.* ♦ **at least. 1.** Not less than: *I go running at least three days a week.* **2.** In any event; anyway: *You might at least call before you come over.* **in the least.** At all: *I'm not in the least concerned.*

leath•er (lĕth′ər) *n.* [U] A material made by tanning the skin of an animal: *I always buy shoes made of leather.* —**leath′er•y** *adj.*

leave[1] (lēv) *v.* **left** (lĕft), **leav•ing, leaves.** —*tr.* **1.** To go out of or go away from (a place): *She just left the room. He left town on Thursday.* **2.** To end one's relationship with (sbdy./sthg.): *He left our band and started another.* **3.** To go without taking (sbdy./sthg.); forget: *I left my umbrella on the train.* **4.** To allow (sthg.) to remain unused: *I left some milk in the glass.* **5.** To allow (sthg.) to remain in a certain condition or place: *I left the light on all night.* **6.** To give (sthg.) to another person to do or use; entrust: *Leave the job to me.* **7.** To give (sthg.) by will; bequeath: *His uncle left him a piece of land.* **8.** To have (a sum) as a remainder after subtraction: *12 minus 5 leaves 7.* —*intr.* To go away: *We left after lunch.* ◆ **leave alone.** *tr.v.* [sep.] To keep from disturbing or interfering with (sbdy./sthg.): *Leave the puzzle alone.* **leave off.** *intr.v.* To stop; cease: *Let's start the story where we left off.* **leave out.** *tr.v.* [sep.] To omit (sbdy./sthg.): *Don't leave out the pepper from the recipe.*

leave² (lēv) *n.* **1.** [U] *Formal.* Permission; consent: *My parents gave me leave to stay up late.* **2.** [C; U] Official permission to be absent from work or duty: *My sister is on leave from the Navy.* **3.** [C] The length of such an absence: *a thirty-day leave.*

leav•en (lĕv′ən) *tr.v.* **1.** To add yeast or another fermenting agent to (dough or batter): *The baker used yeast to leaven the bread.* **2.** To spread through (sthg.) so as to change or make lively: *Her quick wit leavened an otherwise dull evening.*

leav•en•ing (lĕv′ə nĭng) *n.* [C; U] Something that leavens: *Yeast is used as a leavening.*

leaves (lēvz) *n.* Plural of **leaf.**

leave-tak•ing (lēv′tā′kĭng) *n. (usually singular).* An exchange of good-byes; a farewell: *a sad leave-taking.*

lech•er•y (lĕch′ə rē) *n.* [U] Too much indulgence in sexual activity; lewdness. —**lech′er•ous** *adj.* —**lech′er•ous•ly** *adv.*

lec•tern (lĕk′tərn) *n.* A desk with a slanted top for holding books or supporting the notes of a speaker: *The professor stood at the lectern.*

lec•ture (lĕk′chər) *n.* **1.** A prepared talk about a given subject, delivered to an audience or a class: *a boring lecture on plants.* **2.** A serious lengthy warning or scolding: *The judge gave the reckless driver a lecture in court.* —*v.* **lec•tured, lec•tur•ing, lec•tures.** —*intr.* To deliver a lecture: *My friend is lecturing at the university.* —*tr.* **1.** To give a lecture to (an audience or a class): *Our teacher lectured us for the whole hour.* **2.** To scold or warn (sbdy.) at length: *My mother lectured me about being late.* —**lec′tur•er** *n.*

led (lĕd) *v.* Past tense and past participle of **lead¹.**

HOMONYMS: led, lead² (element).

---

ledge (lĕj) *n.* A narrow shelf projecting from a wall or the side of a cliff: *a window ledge; ledges that broke the cliff's smooth surface.*

ledg•er (lĕj′ər) *n.* An account book in which money received and paid out by a business is recorded: *Enter the checks in the ledger.*

leech (lēch) *n.* **1.** A worm that lives in water and sucks blood from other animals, including humans. **2.** *Slang.* A person who constantly tries to gain from sbdy. else; a parasite: *He is a leech, living off the kindness of friends.*

HOMONYMS: leech, leach (dissolve out).

---

leek (lēk) *n.* A vegetable related to the onion, with a narrow white bulb and long, dark green leaves: *leek and potato soup.*

HOMONYMS: leek, leak (escape).

---

leer (lîr) *n.* A sly or lustful look. —*intr.v.* [at] To look at sbdy. with a leer: *Don't leer at waitresses.*

leer•y (lîr′ē) *adj.* **leer•i•er, leer•i•est.** Suspicious; cautious: *I am leery of schemes that promise instant money.* —**leer′i•ly** *adv.*

lee•way (lē′wā′) *n.* [U] Extra space, time, or resources for safety: *We left plenty of leeway to reach the airport during rush hour.*

left¹ (lĕft) *adj.* **1.** Relating or directed toward the side of the body that is located on the west when facing north: *She writes with her left hand.* **2.** Belonging to the political left; leftist. —*n.* **1.a.** [U] The direction or position on the left side: *The river was on my left as I drove north.* **b.** [U] The left side: *The judge sat to my left at lunch.* **c.** [C] A turn in the direction of the left hand or side: *Go two miles and make a left.* **2.** Often **Left.** [U] Liberal or radical groups in politics. —*adv.* On or to the left: *Turn left at the next stoplight.*

left² (lĕft) *v.* Past tense and past participle of **leave¹.**

left field *n.* [U] In baseball, the section of the field that is to the left. ◆ **out in left field.** Odd; not in touch with reality: *Don't listen to him; he's always out in left field.* **out of left field.** Not expected: *The question came out of left field.*

left-hand (lĕft′hănd′) *adj.* **1.** Located on the left: *the upper left-hand corner.* **2.** Intended for the left hand or for use by a left-handed person: *a left-hand can opener.*

left-hand•ed (lĕft′hăn′dĭd) *adj.* **1.** Using the left hand more skillfully or easily than the right hand. **2.** Made for use by the left hand: *left-handed scissors.* **3.** Done with the left hand: *a left-handed catch.* **4.** Insincere or mildly insulting: *a left-handed compliment.* —*adv.* With the left hand: *He made the catch left-handed.* —**left′-hand′er** *n.*

left•ist (lĕf′tĭst) *n.* A person who has liberal or radical political views: *Leftists aren't popular in some countries.* —*adj.* With liberal or radical political views: *leftist publications.*

left•o•ver (lĕft′ō′vər) *adj.* Remaining unused

ă–cat; ā–pay; âr–care; ä–father; ĕ–get; ē–be; ĭ–sit; ī–nice; îr–here; ŏ–got; ō–go; ô–saw; oi–boy; ou–out; ōō–took; ōō–boot; ŭ–cut; ûr–word; th–thin; th–this; hw–when; zh–vision; ə–about; ɴ–French bon

or uneaten: *leftover fabric; leftover rice.* —*n. (usually plural).* Something remaining unused or uneaten: *We had leftovers for dinner.*

left wing also **Left Wing** *n.* [U] The liberal or radical faction of a group, especially of a political group: *the left wing of the party.* —**left′-wing′** *adj.* —**left′-wing′er** *n.*

left·y (lĕf′tē) *n., pl.* **left·ies.** *Informal.* A person who is left-handed: *Her children are both lefties.*

leg (lĕg) *n.* **1.** A limb of an animal or a human used for support and for walking. **2.** The part of a garment, especially of a pair of trousers, that covers the leg: *Your pant legs are too long.* **3.** A supporting part resembling a leg in shape or function: *a table leg.* **4.** A stage, especially of a journey: *We were on the first leg of our trip to New York.* ♦ **have a leg to stand on.** To have a basis for a claim: *She doesn't have a leg to stand on; she'll never win the case.* **on (one's) last legs.** At the end of one's strength or resources; ready to collapse, fail, or die: *After working all day, she was on her last legs.* **stretch (one's) legs.** To take a walk or stand after sitting for a long time: *Let's stretch our legs during the break.* —**leg′less** *adj.*

leg·a·cy (lĕg′ə sē) *n., pl.* **leg·a·cies.** Something, such as money or values, passed on to those who come later in time; a heritage: *a legacy of religious freedom.*

le·gal (lē′gəl) *adj.* **1.** Relating to the law: *legal knowledge.* **2.** Permitted by law: *legal activities.* —**le′gal·ly** *adv.*

le·gal·i·ty (lē gǎl′ĭ tē) *n., pl.* **le·gal·i·ties. 1.** [U] The state of being legal; lawfulness: *We questioned the legality of his actions.* **2.** [C] Something required by law: *observe the legalities.*

le·gal·ize (lē′gə līz′) *tr.v.* **le·gal·ized, le·gal·iz·ing, le·gal·iz·es.** To make (sthg.) legal: *legalize gambling.* —**le′gal·i·za′tion** (lē′gə lĭ zā′shən) *n.* [U]

leg·end (lĕj′ənd) *n.* **1.** A story handed down from earlier times, often believed to be historically true: *the legend of King Arthur.* **2.** A person or thing that is famous enough to inspire legends: *He's a legend in his own time.* **3.** An explanatory caption under a map or a chart: *The legend shows major roads as solid yellow lines.*

leg·en·dar·y (lĕj′ən dĕr′ē) *adj.* **1.** Based on a legend: *legendary heroes.* **2.** Celebrated in legends: *The fox's cunning is legendary.* **3.** Very well-known; famous: *the legendary actor.*

leg·ged (lĕg′ĭd *or* lĕgd) *adj.* Having a certain kind or number of legs: *four-legged animals; a long-legged woman.*

leg·ging (lĕg′ĭng) *n. (usually plural).* A leg covering of cloth or leather, usually extending from the waist or knee to the ankle: *warm leggings.*

leg·gy (lĕg′ē) *adj.* **leg·gi·er, leg·gi·est.** Having long legs: *a leggy young horse.*

leg·i·ble (lĕj′ə bəl) *adj.* Capable of being read: *legible handwriting.* —**leg′i·bil′i·ty, leg′i·ble·ness** *n.* [U] —**leg′i·bly** *adv.*

le·gion (lē′jən) *n.* **1.** A large group or number of persons or things; a multitude: *Legions of insects settled on the fields.* **2.** Often **Legion.** A national organization of people who serve or once served in the armed forces.

leg·is·late (lĕj′ĭ slāt′) *v.* **leg·is·lat·ed, leg·is·lat·ing, leg·is·lates.** —*intr.* To make or pass laws: *Only Congress has the power to legislate.* —*tr.* To create or bring about (sthg.) by making laws: *They are working to legislate reforms in the housing code.*

leg·is·la·tion (lĕj′ĭ slā′shən) *n.* [U] **1.** The act of making laws: *Our Constitution gives Congress the authority of legislation.* **2.** Proposed or enacted laws: *legislation being discussed in Congress.*

leg·is·la·tive (lĕj′ĭ slā′tĭv) *adj.* **1.** Relating to making laws: *legislative powers.* **2.** Having power to make laws: *the legislative branch of government.*

leg·is·la·tor (lĕj′ĭ slā′tər) *n.* A member of a government body that makes laws: *Senators and representatives are legislators.*

leg·is·la·ture (lĕj′ĭ slā′chər) *n.* A body of persons with the power to make and change the laws of a nation or state: *She ran for election to the state legislature.*

e·git (lə jĭt′) *adj.* *Slang.* Legitimate: *That's not legit.*

e·git·i·mate (lə jĭt′ə mĭt) *adj.* **1.** In accordance with the law; lawful: *the legitimate owner of the property.* **2.** Supported by logic or common sense; reasonable: *Some problems have more than one legitimate solution.* **3.** Authentic; real: *We have a legitimate complaint.* **4.** Born of legally married parents: *a legitimate child.* —**le·git′i·ma·cy** (lə jĭt′ə mə sē) *n.* [U] —**le·git′i·mate·ly** *adv.*

le·git·i·mize (lə jĭt′ə mīz′) *tr.v.* **le·git·i·mized, le·git·i·miz·ing, le·git·i·miz·es.** To make (sthg.) legitimate: *That judge's decision legitimizes the new ownership.*

leg·room (lĕg′rōōm′ *or* lĕg′rŏŏm′) *n.* [U] Space for one's legs when sitting: *Most airplane seats have little legroom.*

leg·ume (lĕg′yōōm′ *or* lə gyōōm′) *n.* Any of a group of related plants with pods that contain a large number of seeds: *Beans and peas are legumes.*

leg·work (lĕg′wûrk′) *n.* [U] The work needed to collect information: *We did a lot of legwork before deciding to buy the car.*

lei (lā) *n., pl.* **leis.** A garland of flowers worn around the neck as an ornament.

HOMONYMS: lei, lay (put, not of the clergy, placed oneself flat).

lei·sure (lē′zhər *or* lĕzh′ər) *n.* [U] Freedom from work or time-consuming tasks: *Vacation is usually a time of leisure and relaxation.* ◆ **at (one's) leisure.** When one has free time; at one's convenience: *You can respond to this letter at your leisure.*

lei·sure·ly (lē′zhər lē *or* lĕzh′ər lē) *adj.* Characterized by leisure; unhurried: *a leisurely lunch.* —*adv.* In an unhurried manner; slowly: *We strolled leisurely toward town.*

lem·on (lĕm′ən) *n.* **1.** [C] An oval yellow citrus fruit with sour juicy pulp. **2.** [U] A bright clear yellow color. **3.** [C] *Informal.* A thing that does not function properly: *That car is a lemon and needs to be repaired every two months.* —*adj.* Bright clear yellow.

lem·on·ade (lĕm′ə nād′) *n.* [U] A cold drink made of lemon juice, water, and sugar: *Would you rather have lemonade or iced tea?*

lend (lĕnd) *tr.v.* **lent** (lĕnt), **lend·ing, lends.** **1.** To give or allow the use of (sthg.) with the understanding that it is to be returned: *My parents lent me the car to go to the movies.* **2.** To provide (money) temporarily on condition that the amount borrowed be returned, usually with an interest fee: *Banks lend money to students.* **3.** To contribute (sthg.): *The painting lent a feeling of warmth to the room.* **4.** To make (sthg.) available for another's use: *The neighbors lent their help after the storm.* ◆ **lend a hand.** To help: *Let me know if I can lend a hand with packing.* **lend itself to.** To be suitable for: *This novel lends itself to several interpretations.* —**lend′er** *n.* See Note at **borrow.**

length (lĕngkth *or* lĕngth) *n.* **1.** [U] The measured distance of a thing from end to end: *the length of the house.* **2.** [U] The extent of sthg.: *The explorers traveled the length of the Nile River.* **3.** [U] The amount of time sthg. takes; duration: *the length of the meeting.* **4.** [U] The quality of being long: *The length of the journey wore us out.* **5.** [C] The measure of sthg. used as a unit to estimate distances: *two car lengths.* **6.** [C] A piece of sthg., often of a standard size: *a length of wire.* ◆ **at length. 1.** After some time; eventually: *At length we arrived at the dock.* **2.** In detail; fully: *She spoke at length about her travels.*

length·en (lĕngk′thən *or* lĕng′thən) *tr. & intr.v.* To make or become longer: *lengthen pant legs; shadows that lengthen as sunset approaches.*

length·wise (lĕngkth′wīz′ *or* lĕngth′wīz′) *adv.* Along the direction of the length: *Fold a sheet of paper lengthwise.* —*adj.* In the direction of the length: *Make lengthwise folds in the paper.*

length·y (lĕngk′thē *or* lĕng′thē) *adj.* **length· i·er, length·i·est.** Long, especially too long:

a lengthy explanation. —**length′i·ly** *adv.* —**length′i·ness** *n.* [U]

le·ni·ent (lē′nē ənt *or* lēn′yənt) *adj.* Inclined to forgive; generous: *a lenient judge; lenient parents.* —**le′ni·ence, le′ni·en·cy** *n.* [U]

lens (lĕnz) *n.* **1.** A piece of glass or plastic shaped to focus light rays that pass through it to form an image: *a camera lens.* **2.** A transparent structure behind the iris of the eye that focuses light entering the eye on the retina.

lent (lĕnt) *v.* Past tense and past participle of **lend.**

len·til (lĕn′təl) *n.* The round flat edible seed of a plant related to beans and peas: *lentil soup.*

leop·ard (lĕp′ərd) *n.* A large, meat-eating, wild cat of Africa and Asia that has tan fur with black spots or black fur.

le·o·tard (lē′ə tärd′) *n.* A tight-fitting garment, sometimes with sleeves, originally worn by dancers and acrobats.

lep·er (lĕp′ər) *n.* A person who has the disease leprosy: *In the past, lepers had to live away from other people.*

lep·re·chaun (lĕp′rĭ kŏn′) *n.* In Irish folklore, an elf who can reveal hidden treasure if caught: *He loved stories about leprechauns.*

lep·ro·sy (lĕp′rə sē) *n.* [U] An infectious disease caused by bacteria that attack the skin and nerves and form sores on the body: *People have always feared leprosy.* —**lep′rous** *adj.*

les·bi·an (lĕz′bē ən) *n.* A woman whose sexual feelings are directed toward other women; a homosexual woman. —*adj.* Relating to a lesbian. —**les′bi·an·ism** *n.* [U]

le·sion (lē′zhən) *n.* A wound or an abnormal change in body tissue, caused by disease or injury: *The doctor examined the skin lesions.*

less (lĕs) *adj.* A comparative of **little. 1.** Smaller in amount, quantity, or degree; not so much: *less time to spare; less food to eat.* **2.** Lower in importance or rank: *No less a person than the President gave the order.* —*adv.* Comparative of **little.** To a smaller extent, degree, or amount: *The game was less enjoyable than I had hoped.* —*prep.* Minus; without: *Five less three is two.* —*n.* [U] A smaller amount or quantity: *The house sold for less than we thought.* ◆ **less than.** Not at all: *He gave a less than satisfactory answer.* **much less** or **still less.** Certainly not: *I'm not blaming anyone, much less you.* —See Note at **few.**

—less *suff.* A suffix that means: **1.** Without or lacking: *motherless; nameless.* **2.** Not able to act in a certain way: *relentless.*

Word Building: —less The suffix **—less** means "without." **—less** is often used to convey the negative or opposite of words ending in **—ful**, as in **careful/careless** and **fearful/fearless**. But **—less** is also used to form words that have no counterpart ending in **—ful**: **headless, loveless, motherless**. Although **—less** normally forms adjectives by attaching to nouns, sometimes it attaches to verbs, as in **tireless**.

les·see (lě sē′) n. Formal. A tenant holding a lease: *The new lessee picked up the key to the apartment.*

less·en (lěs′ən) tr. & intr.v. To make or become less: *a drug to lessen the pain; pair that lessened immediately.* See Synonyms at **decrease**.

HOMONYMS: lessen, lesson (instruction).

---

less·er (lěs′ər) adj. A comparative of **little** Smaller in amount, value, or importance: *a lesser evil; lesser gods.*

les·son (lěs′ən) n. **1.** Something to be learned, especially an assignment or exercise *an algebra textbook divided into 40 lessons* **2.** A period of time for teaching or learning a certain subject: *three piano lessons a week.* **3.** An experience or example from which one can learn: *The poor grades taught me a lesson in the value of studying.*

HOMONYMS: lesson, lessen (make less).

---

les·sor (lěs′ôr′ or lě sôr′) n. Formal. A person who rents property to another by lease: *The lessors reached an agreement with the lessees.*

lest (lěst) conj. Formal. For fear that: *Be careful with the hammer lest you hit your thumb.*

let (lět) tr.v. **let, let·ting, lets. 1.a.** To grant permission to (sbdy.); permit: *The crowd let the speaker continue without interruption.* **b.** To permit (sthg.) to happen; allow: *Let your hot cocoa cool a bit.* **2.** To cause (sthg.); make: *Let me know what happened.* **3.** Used as an auxiliary verb to express a request, command, or warning: *Let's finish the job!* **4.** Used as an auxiliary verb to express a proposal or an assumption: *Let x equal 3.* **5.** To permit (sthg.) to move in a specified way: *Let the cat out.* **6.** To rent or lease (a dwelling): *They let rooms to students.* ♦ **let down.** tr.v. [sep.] To fail to satisfy (sbdy.); disappoint: *Don't let me down.* **let off.** tr.v. [sep.] **1.** To excuse (sbdy.) from work or duty: *They let me off so I could go home early.* **2.** To release (sbdy.) with little or no punishment: *They were let off with a warning.* **let on.** tr.v. [insep.] To allow (sthg.) to be known; admit: *Don't let on that I'm going too.* **let out.** intr.v. To come to a close; end: *School lets out next week.* —tr.v. [sep.] **1.** To make (sthg.) known; reveal: *Who let that information out?* **2.** To increase

the size of (a garment, for example): *The tailor let the pants out.* **let up.** intr.v. To slow down or stop: *The rain finally let up.*

—let suff. A suffix that means: **1.** A small one: *booklet.* **2.** Something worn on: *armlet; anklet.*

let·down (lět′doun′) n. **1.** A decrease or slowing down, as in energy or effort: *I've had such a letdown since the semester ended.* **2.** A disappointment: *Losing that game was a real letdown.*

le·thal (lē′thəl) adj. Causing or capable of causing death: *a lethal weapon.* **—le′thal·ly** adv.

leth·ar·gy (lěth′ər jē) n. [U] Drowsy or sluggish indifference; apathy: *After working for hours, she quickly sank into a state of lethargy.* **—le·thar′gic** (lə thär′jĭk) adj. **—le·thar′gi·cal·ly** adv.

let's (lěts). Contraction of *let us: Let's watch the game.*

let·ter (lět′ər) n. **1.** [C] A written mark that represents a speech sound and is one of the characters of an alphabet: *How many letters are in your first name?* **2.** [C] A written message addressed to a person: *I wrote three letters to friends this week.* **3.** [U] The exact or literal meaning: *the letter of the law.* —tr.v. To mark or write (sthg.) with letters: *He carefully lettered our name on the mailbox.* ♦ **to the letter.** To the last detail; exactly: *We followed the instructions to the letter.*

let·ter·head (lět′ər hěd′) n. [U] Letter paper with a printed heading at the top of the sheet usually consisting of the name and address of the sender: *Send the recommendation on letterhead.*

let·ter·ing (lět′ər ĭng) n. [U] **1.** The act of forming letters. **2.** The letters formed, drawn, or painted, as on a sign: *The lettering was crooked.*

let·ter·per·fect (lět′ər pûr′fĭkt) adj. Perfect in every detail: *Her report was letter-perfect.*

let·tuce (lět′əs) n. [C; U] Any of various plants cultivated for their large edible green or red leaves used in salad: *leaf lettuce; Romaine lettuce.*

let·up (lět′ŭp′) n. [C; U] (usually singular). A reduction in pace, force, or intensity: *There was no letup in the storm.*

leu·ke·mi·a (loo kē′mē ə) n. [U] A cancer of the blood characterized by uncontrolled growth in the number of white blood cells.

lev·ee (lěv′ē) n. A bank of earth or other material built up along a river to keep it from flooding: *The floodwaters broke through the levee.*

HOMONYMS: levee, levy (collect).

---

lev·el (lěv′əl) n. **1.** Relative position or rank on a scale: *Science gets more complex at the* *college level.* **2.** *(usually singular).* **a.** A horizontal line or plane, often used to measure heights or depths: *The plane flew at tree level.* **b.** Height or depth: *The divers descended to a level of 60 feet.* **3.** A story or floor of a building: *The mall has three levels.* **4.** An instrument for determining whether a surface is horizontal or vertical, used especially by carpenters and masons. —*adj.* **1.** Having a flat even surface: *level farmland.* **2.** Horizontal: *Is the picture on this wall level?* **3.** Steady; uniform: *a level tone of voice.* **4.** At the same height, rank, or position; even: *The two tabletops are level with each other.* **5.** Reasonable and careful; sensible: *a level head.* —*tr.v.* **1.** To make (sth.) smooth, flat, or horizontal: *The contractor leveled the ground for a new building.* **2.** To cut or knock (sbdy./sthg.) down to the ground: *A tornado leveled several buildings.* **3.** To aim (a weapon) carefully: *level a rifle at the target.* ◆ **level with.** *Informal. tr.v.* [insep.] To be frank and open with (sbdy.): *Let's level with each other.* **on the level.** *Informal.* Without deception, honest: *On the level now, was I wrong?* **(one's) level best.** The best one can do: *We did our level best to save the child.* —**lev′el·ly** *adv.* —**lev′el·ness** *n.* [U]

lev·el·head·ed (lĕv′əl hĕd′ĭd) *adj.* With common sense and good judgment; sensible: *She's too levelheaded to do anything foolish.* —**lev′el·head′ed·ness** *n.* [U]

lev·er (lĕv′ər *or* lē′vər) *n.* **1.** A bar that moves on a fixed support or fulcrum and is used to transmit effort and motion. **2.** A handle or bar used in such a manner: *A crowbar is a simple tool used as a lever.* **3.** A projecting handle used to control, adjust, or operate a device or machine, as a gearshift lever: *Move the lever to the left.*

lev·er·age (lĕv′ər ĭj *or* lē′vər ĭj) *n.* [U] **1.** The action of a lever: *Use the pole for leverage.* **2.** An advantage in position or in power: *Great wealth gives a person leverage in many business situations.*

le·vi·a·than (lə vī′ə thən) *n.* Something of enormous size or bulk: *The leviathan rose from the deep.*

Le·vi's (lē′vīz′). A trademark for pants made of denim.

lev·i·tate (lĕv′ĭ tāt′) *intr.* & *tr.v.* **lev·i·tat·ed, lev·i·tat·ing, lev·i·tates.** To rise or cause to rise into the air and float: *The great balloon quickly levitated. The magician levitated the table.*

lev·i·ty (lĕv′ĭ tē) *n.* [U] *Formal.* A light humorous manner or attitude; frivolity: *Levity is often improper in a court of law.*

lev·y (lĕv′ē) *tr.v.* **lev·ied, lev·y·ing, lev·ies.** To impose or collect (a tax): *levy a sales tax;*

levy tariffs. —*n., pl.* **lev·ies. 1.** The act of levying a tax: *a new levy on imports.* **2.** Money collected as a tax, tariff, or other fee: *That levy will pay for new schools.*

HOMONYMS: levy, levee (bank of earth).

---

lewd (lo͞od) *adj.* Obscene; indecent: *His lewd comments shocked us.* —**lewd′ly** *adv.* —**lewd′ness** *n.* [U]

lex·i·cog·ra·phy (lĕk′sĭ kŏg′rə fē) *n.* [U] The process or work of writing or compiling a dictionary. —**lex′i·cog′ra·pher** *n.*

lex·i·con (lĕk′sĭ kŏn′) *n.* **1.** A dictionary, especially one giving translations of words from an ancient language. **2.** A set of terms used in a particular subject or profession; a vocabulary: *the lexicon of physics.*

Li The symbol for the element **lithium.**

li·a·bil·i·ty (lī′ə bĭl′ĭ tē) *n., pl.* **li·a·bil·i·ties. 1.** [C] Something that one owes; an obligation or a debt: *financial liabilities.* **2.** [C; U] Something that holds one back; a disadvantage: *Poor spelling is a liability for a secretary.*

li·a·ble (lī′ə bəl) *adj.* **1.** Legally obligated or responsible: *The drivers argued about who was liable for the accident.* **2.** Likely: *Without sleep you are liable to make mistakes.*

li·ai·son (lē′ā zŏn′ *or* lē ā′zŏn′) *n.* **1.** [U] A means of communication between different groups or units: *military liaison.* **2.** [C] A person who maintains communication: *I work as the company's liaison with the people who sell our line of products.* **3.** [C] A sexual or romantic relationship: *He had numerous liaisons in the past.*

li·ar (lī′ər) *n.* A person who tells lies: *You can never believe a liar.*

li·bel (lī′bəl) *n.* [U] The act or crime of making statements that unjustly damage a person's reputation: *charged with libel.* —*tr.v.* To write or publish a false or damaging statement about (sbdy.): *libel the new mayor.* —**li′bel·er** *n.* —**li′bel·ous** also **li′bel·lous** *adj.*

lib·er·al (lĭb′ər əl *or* lĭb′rəl) *adj.* **1.** Open to new ideas and tolerant of the ideas and behavior of others; broad-minded: *a person with liberal attitudes.* **2.** Tending to give generously: *a liberal contributor to the charity.* **3.** Not strict or literal; approximate: *The movie is a liberal adaptation of the novel.* **4.** Relating to the liberal arts. —*n.* A person with liberal political opinions. —**lib′er·al·ly** *adv.* —**lib′er·al·ness** *n.* [U]

liberal arts *pl.n.* College studies such as languages, history, philosophy, and science that provide general knowledge and the ability to think analytically, rather than practical or professional skills.

ă-**cat**; ā-**pay**; âr-**care**; ä-**father**; ĕ-**get**; ē-**be**; ĭ-**sit**; ī-**nice**; îr-**here**; ŏ-**got**; ō-**go**; ô-**saw**; oi-**boy**; ou-**out**; o͝o-**took**; o͞o-**boot**; ŭ-**cut**; ûr-**word**; th-**thin**; *th*-**this**; hw-**when**; zh-**vision**; ə-**about**; N-French **bon**

lib·er·al·ism (lĭb′ər ə lĭz′ əm *or* lĭb′rə lĭz′ əm) *n.* [U] Liberal political views and policies: *How can liberalism be a bad idea?*

lib·er·al·ize (lĭb′ər ə lĭz′ *or* lĭb′rə lĭz′) *tr.v.* **lib·er·al·ized, lib·er·al·iz·ing, lib·er·al·iz·es.** To make (sthg.) more liberal: *liberalize government regulations.* —**lib′er·al·i·za′tion** (lĭb′ər ə lĭ zā′shən *or* lĭb′rə lĭ zā′shən) *n.* [U]

lib·er·ate (lĭb′ə rāt′) *tr.v.* **lib·er·at·ed, lib·er·at·ing, lib·er·ates. 1.** To set (sbdy./sthg.) free from confinement or control: *The Emancipation Proclamation liberated the slaves.* **2.** To set (sthg.) free as a result of chemical combination: *liberate a gas.* —**lib′er·a′tion** *n.* [U] —**lib′er·a′tor** *n.*

lib·er·ty (lĭb′ər tē) *n., pl.* **lib·er·ties. 1.** [U] Freedom from imprisonment, slavery, or forced labor: *All people have the right to liberty.* **2.** [C; U] The right and power to act, believe, and express oneself as one chooses: *Too often, we take our liberties for granted.* **3.** [U] Political freedom from the control of another government; independence: *In 1776, the United States fought for liberty from Britain.* **4.** [C] A legal right to engage in a certain kind of action without control or interference: *liberties of citizens protected by the Bill of Rights.* **5.** *(usually plural).* An action that is improper or unreasonable: *He takes liberties with history to make his argument sound better.* ◆ **at liberty.** Not in confinement or under constraint; free: *You are at liberty to go where you wish.*

li·brar·y (lī′brĕr′ē) *n., pl.* **li·brar·ies. 1.** A building or room where books, magazines, records, and other materials are kept for reading or borrowing. **2.** A collection of such materials: *an extensive library.* —**li·brar′i·an** (lī brâr′ē ən) *n.*

lice (līs) *n.* Plural of **louse** (sense 1).

li·cense (lī′səns) *n.* **1.a.** [U] Legal permission to do or own a specified thing: *The group has license to run a daycare center.* **b.** [C] A document, card, or other proof that such permission has been granted: *The doctor's license is hung on the wall.* **2.** [U] Freedom of action: *I took the license to stop by without calling beforehand.* —*tr.v.* **li·censed, li·cens·ing, li·cens·es.** To grant a license to (sbdy.) or for (sthg.): *The state licenses drivers.*

lick (lĭk) *tr.v.* **1.a.** To pass the tongue over (sthg.): *The dog licks her pups.* **b.** To lap (sthg.) up: *The cat licked cream from a dish.* **2.** To touch or move over (sthg.) like a tongue: *Flames lick the burning logs.* **3.** *Slang.* To defeat (sbdy.); beat: *We licked the other team.* **4.** *Slang.* To punish (sbdy.) with a beating. —*n.* **1.** A movement of the tongue over sthg.: *a kitten's wet lick.* **2.** A small amount; a bit: *We couldn't find a lick of evidence.* ◆ **a lick and a promise.** A careless, quick attempt: *He gave his homework a lick and a promise and went out to play.*

lic·o·rice (lĭk′ər ĭs *or* lĭk′ər ĭsh) *n.* [U] **1.** A plant with a sweet strong-tasting root used as a flavoring. **2.** A chewy, often black candy flavored with an extract from this root.

lid (lĭd) *n.* **1.** A removable cover or top for a hollow container: *the lid for a jar; the lid of a box.* **2.** An eyelid: *Put the eye shadow on your lids.*

lie¹ (lī) *intr.v.* **lay** (lā), **lain** (lān), **ly·ing** (lī′ĭng), **lies. 1.** To place oneself in a flat or resting position: *The cow lay down in the pasture.* **2.** To be in a flat or resting position: *I was lying on the floor.* **3.** To be on a surface: *Forks and spoons lay on the table.* **4.** To be located: *Many tiny islands lie off the coast.* **5.** To be a basic quality or feature of sthg.: *The answer lay in further research.*

HOMONYMS: lie (be flat, untrue statement), **lye** (alkaline solution).

---

lie² (lī) *n.* An untrue statement made to deceive sbdy.: *The little boy was caught telling a lie.* —*intr.v.* **lied, ly·ing** (lī′ĭng), **lies. 1.** To tell a lie or lies: *The suspect lied to the police.* **2.** To create an illusion or a false impression: *Even photographs can lie.*

lien (lēn) *n.* A legal claim on the property of a person as payment for a debt: *The bank holds the lien on the property.*

HOMONYMS: lien, lean (bend, thin).

---

lieu (lōō) *n.* ◆ **in lieu of.** *Formal.* In place of; instead of: *She received a check in lieu of cash.*

lieu·ten·ant (lōō tĕn′ənt) *n.* **1.** An officer in a military group or in a police or fire department. **2.** A chief assistant; a deputy: *a staff member acting as the President's lieutenant.*

life (līf) *n., pl.* **lives** (līvz). **1.** [U] The property or quality that distinguishes living organisms from dead organisms and nonliving matter. **2.** [C] The fact of being alive: *risk one's life.* **3.** [C] The period of time between birth and death; a lifetime: *a long and interesting life.* **4.** [C] *(usually singular).* The time during which sthg. exists and works: *the life of a car.* **5.** [U] Living organisms considered as a group: *plant life; marine life.* **6.** [C] A living being; a person: *That doctor has saved hundreds of lives.* **7.** [U] A way of living: *the outdoor life; city life.* **8.** [U] Liveliness; spirit: *a puppy, curious and full of life.* ◆ **bring to life. 1.** To cause (sbdy.) to regain life or consciousness. **2.** To make (sthg.) lively or lifelike: *A good actor brings a character to life.* **come to life.** To become lively; grow excited: *She always came to life when talking about her favorite writer.* **for life.** Till the end of one's life: *He's in prison for life.* **life of the party.** An entertaining person: *Be sure to invite Ann; she's always the life of the party.*

take (one's) life. To commit murder or suicide. **true to life.** Accurately representing real life: *The movie is true to life.*

life·blood (līf′blŭd′) *n.* [U] An important or necessary part: *The conductor is the lifeblood of the orchestra.*

life·boat (līf′bōt′) *n.* A strong boat carried on a ship, used if the ship has to be abandoned: *We escaped the sinking ship in lifeboats.*

life·guard (līf′gärd′) *n.* A person hired to watch for the safety of swimmers at a beach or pool: *The lifeguard rescued the drowning child.*

life insurance *n.* [U] Insurance on a person's life, paid for by regular premiums and guaranteeing a certain amount of money to a specified person on the death of the holder: *$100,000 in life insurance.*

life jacket *n.* A life preserver in the form of a jacket or vest: *The children wore life jackets.*

life·less (līf′lĭs) *adj.* **1.** Having no life; dead or inanimate: *a lifeless body.* **2.** Not supporting life; having no living organisms: *a lifeless planet.* **3.** Lacking spirit or vitality; dull: *a lifeless party.* —**life′less·ly** *adv.* —**life′·less·ness** *n.* [U]

life·like (līf′līk′) *adj.* Accurately representing real life: *a lifelike statue.*

life·line (līf′līn′) *n.* **1.** An anchored line thrown as a support to sbdy. falling or drowning. **2.** A means or route for transporting needed supplies: *Railroads were once the lifeline of this country.*

life·long (līf′lông′ *or* līf′lŏng′) *adj.* Lasting a lifetime: *a lifelong friend; a lifelong ambition to become a doctor.*

life preserver *n.* A device, usually a belt, jacket, or tube filled with a buoyant material, designed to keep a person afloat in the water.

life·sav·er (līf′sā′vər) *n.* **1.** A lifeguard or other person who saves the lives of others. **2.** A person or thing that provides help in a crisis or emergency: *Their call to the fire department was a lifesaver.*

life·sav·ing (līf′sā′vĭng) *n.* [U] The skills and methods used in saving lives, especially in keeping people from drowning.

life-size (līf′sīz′) also **life-sized** (līf′sīzd′) *adj.* Being of the same size as the person or object represented: *a life-size statue of a person.*

life span *n.* **1.** The average or longest period of time that an organism can be expected to live: *the life span of the African elephant.* **2.** A lifetime: *a healthy life span.*

life·style (līf′stīl′) *n.* The way of life or style of living of a person or group, including diet, tastes, work, and interests: *the lifestyles of the famous.*

life·time (līf′tīm′) *n.* The period of time that a person lives or a thing exists or works properly: *the average lifetime of a person; the lifetime of our car.*

lift (lĭft) *v.* —*tr.* **1.** To raise (sbdy./sthg.) to a higher position; elevate: *I lifted the suitcase out of the car.* **2.** To raise or improve (sbdy./sthg.) in condition, status, or estimation: *The news lifted everybody's spirits.* **3.** To end or stop (sthg.): *The government lifted the curfew.* **4.** *Informal.* To steal (sthg.): *The robber lifted a priceless painting.* **5.** To copy (sthg.) from sthg. already published; plagiarize: *The reporter lifted the paragraph from a magazine article.* —*intr.* **1.** To rise or become raised: *The balloon slowly lifted into the air.* **2.** To rise and disappear: *The heavy fog finally lifted.* —*n.* **1.** The act of lifting or being lifted: *Give me a lift into the saddle.* **2.** A short ride in a vehicle: *Can I have a lift to the store?* **3.** A rising of the spirit: *Good grades give students a big lift.* **4.** *Chiefly British.* An elevator. ◆ **lift a finger.** To make an effort: *He just stood watching and didn't lift a finger to help.* **lift off.** *intr.v.* To begin flight: *The rocket lifted off at dawn.*

lift·off (lĭft′ôf′ *or* lĭft′ŏf′) *n.* [C; U] The takeoff of a rocket from its launch pad: *a smooth liftoff.*

lig·a·ment (lĭg′ə mənt) *n.* A sheet or band of tough fibers that connects two bones or holds an organ of the body in place: *a torn ligament in the knee.*

light¹ (līt) *n.* **1.** [U] A form of radiant energy made up of electromagnetic waves that can usually be seen: *Light travels at a speed of about 186,282 miles (299,728 kilometers) per second.* **2.** [U] Radiant energy that cannot be seen, such as infrared light and ultraviolet light. **3.** [U] Illumination; brightness: *The fireworks produced bursts of light.* **4.** [C] A source of light, such as the sun or a lamp: *a light in the window.* **5.** [U] Daylight: *Flowers need a lot of light to bloom.* **6.** [C] *Informal.* A source of fire, such as a match: *Excuse me, have you got a light?* **7.** [U] Understanding through knowledge and information: *Research shed new light on the solar system.* **8.** [U] Public attention; general knowledge: *Reports brought to light the need for improvements in the schools in our town.* —*v.* **light·ed** or **lit** (lĭt), **light·ing**, **lights.** —*tr.* **1.** To start (sthg.) burning: *light a fire.* **2.** To cause (sthg.) to give out light: *light a lamp.* **3.** To provide, cover, or fill (sthg.) with light: *Let's light the room with candles.* **4.** To make (sthg.) lively or bright: *A smile lighted the child's face.* **5.** To guide or direct (sbdy./sthg.) by means of a light: *A flashlight was enough to light our way along the path.* —*intr.* To start to burn: *The oven won't light for some reason.* —*adj.* **1.** Having light: *a nice light room to work in.* **2.** Bright; not dark: *light*

ă–**cat**; ā–**pay**; âr–**care**; ä–**father**; ĕ–**get**; ē–**be**; ĭ–**sit**; ī–**nice**; îr–**here**; ŏ–**got**; ō–**go**; ô–**saw**; oi–**boy**; ou–**out**; ŏŏ–**took**; ōō–**boot**; ŭ–**cut**; ûr–**word**; th–**thin**; *th*–**this**; hw–**when**; zh–**vision**; ə–**about**; N–French **bon**

gray; light hair. ◆ **in a different** or **new light.** With a changed way of looking at a certain matter: *We viewed him in a different light after we heard how he treated his family.* **in light of.** In consideration of; in relationship to: *In light of the report, let's try a different approach to the problem.* **light up.** *intr.v.* **1.** To become light or bright: *The neon sign lighted up after dark.* **2.** To become cheerful or lively: *Her face lit up when he gave her the flowers.* **3.** *Informal.* To start smoking a cigarette, cigar, or pipe: *He always lights up after dinner.* —**light′ness** *n.* [U]

light² (līt) *adj.* **1.** Having little weight; not heavy: *a light suitcase; a light jacket.* **2.** Having little force or impact: *a light breeze; a light blow.* **3.** Low in intensity or amount: *a light rain; a light lunch.* **4.** Not serious; with little meaning, importance, or feeling: *light comedy.* **5.** Free from care or worry: *a light heart.* **6.** Moving easily and quickly: *light on one's feet.* **7.** Requiring little effort: *light household chores.* **8.** A little unsteady or faint; dizzy: *I feel light in the head.* **9.** Having fewer calories; not fatty or rich: *light foods; light soft drinks.* **10.** Easily awakened: *a light sleeper.* —*adv.* Lightly, especially with little baggage: *We always travel light.* —*intr.v.* **light·ed** or **lit** (lĭt), **light·ing, lights. 1.** To come to rest; land: *The bird lit on the feeder.* **2.** To get down, as from a mount or vehicle: *Several passengers lighted from the rear of the plane.* ◆ **light into.** *tr.v.* [insep.] *Informal.* To attack (sbdy.) verbally or physically: *She lit into him when he criticized her decision.* **light out.** *intr.v. Informal.* To leave in a hurry: *The robbers lit out, with the police close behind.* —**light′ness** *n.* [U]

light bulb *n.* A glass-covered electric light source in which a wire is heated by an electric current so that it gives off light: *The light bulb burned out.*

light·en¹ (līt′n) *tr. & intr.v.* To make or become lighter in color or brighter: *He lightened the blue paint by mixing in some white. The clouds thinned and the sky lightened quickly.*

light·en² (līt′n) *v.* —*tr.* **1.** To make (sthg.) less heavy; reduce the weight of: *Leaving out those books will lighten the load.* **2.** To make (sthg.) less troublesome or oppressive: *You should hire an assistant to lighten the load of work.* **3.** To gladden or cheer (sthg.): *A song will lighten everyone's heart.* —*intr.* **1.** To become less in weight: *The hikers' backpacks lightened from day to day.* **2.** To become less troublesome or oppressive: *Our mood lightened when we heard the good news.* **3.** To become cheerful: *The party lightened as soon as she arrived.* ◆ **lighten up.** *intr.v.* To become less serious; be less gloomy: *Lighten up! It's summertime!*

light·er (līt′tər) *n.* A person or device that lights or ignites sthg.: *a cigarette lighter.* —*adj.* The comparative form of **light.**

light·head·ed (līt′hĕd′ĭd) *adj.* **1.** Dizzy or faint, as from fever: *The decrease in oxygen made the climbers lightheaded.* **2.** Silly or foolish in one's manner or behavior; flighty: *lightheaded with joy.* —**light′head′ed·ly** *adv.* —**light′head′ed·ness** *n.* [U]

light·heart·ed (līt′här′tĭd) *adj.* Carefree and cheerful: *a lighthearted attitude.* See Synonyms at **glad.** —**light′heart′ed·ly** *adv.* —**light′heart′ed·ness** *n.* [U]

light·house (līt′-hous′) *n.* A tower with a powerful light at the top, used to guide ships and warn ships of dangerous waters.

lighthouse

light·ing (līt′tĭng) *n.* [U] **1.** Light supplied, as for a room or an area: *good lighting for reading.* **2.** The arrangement or equipment that provides light: *outdoor lighting.*

light·ly (līt′lē) *adv.* **1.** With little pressure or force: *Walk lightly on the floor to avoid waking the baby.* **2.** To a small amount or degree: *The streets were lightly covered with snow.* **3.** In a carefree manner; cheerfully: *They took the news lightly.* **4.** With grace; seemingly without effort: *The deer leaped lightly over the fence.*

light·ning (līt′nĭng) *n.* [U] A flash of light in the sky caused by an electrical discharge between clouds or between a cloud and the earth's surface: *We watched the lightning in the distance.*

light·weight (līt′wāt′) *n.* **1.** A person or thing that weighs relatively little. **2.** A person of little ability, importance, or influence: *Ignore them; they're all lightweights.* —*adj.* Not heavy; weighing relatively little: *a lightweight jacket.*

light-year (līt′yîr′) *n.* The distance that light travels in a year, about 5.88 trillion miles (9.46 trillion kilometers).

lik·a·ble also **like·a·ble** (lī′kə bəl) *adj.* Easy to like; with a pleasing personality: *a pleasant likable classmate.*

like¹ (līk) *v.* **liked, lik·ing, likes.** —*tr.* **1.** To be fond of (sbdy.): *We are old friends and like each other.* See Synonyms at **love. 2.** To find (sthg.) pleasant; enjoy: *They liked the place and decided to stay.* **3.** To feel about (sbdy./ sthg.): *How do you like your new school?* **4.** To want to have (sbdy./sthg.): *Would you like some gravy? I'd like you to be my guest.* —*intr.* To have a desire or preference: *If you like, we can go home now.* —*n.* Something that is liked; a preference: *We share many of the same likes and dislikes.*

like² (līk) *prep.* **1.** Resembling; similar to: *You look a lot like your mother.* **2.** In the same way as: *Don't act like a clown.* **3.** In the typical manner of: *It's not like him to give up easily.* **4.** Such as: *I draw things like buildings and street scenes.* **5.** As if it is likely to be: *It looks like a good year for farmers.* —*adj.* **1.** Having the same or almost the same characteristics; similar: *We made this and like repairs to the car.* **2.** Equivalent: *The company will donate a like amount to charity.* —*adv.* As if: *We worked like crazy to get the job done on time.* —*n.* [U] Something equal or similar to sthg. else: *Owls eat mice, chipmunks, and the like.* —*conj. Informal.* **1.** In the same way that: *To dance like she does takes lots of practice.* **2.** As if: *It looks like we'll finish on time.* ◆ **feel like (doing).** To be in the mood for (doing sthg.): *I felt like going home.*

—**like** *suff.* A suffix that means similar to or characteristic of: *childlike; lifelike.*

like·li·hood (līk′lē hoŏd′) *n.* [U] The chance of a thing happening; probability: *The likelihood of snow in July is remote.*

like·ly (līk′lē) *adj.* **like·li·er, like·li·est. 1.** Showing a tendency or probability: *It is likely to rain at any moment.* **2.** Seeming to be true; believable: *a likely excuse for being late.* **3.** Appropriate or suitable: *She seems a likely choice for the job.* —*adv.* Probably: *Most likely the barn will need some repairs.*

lik·en (lī′kən) *tr.v.* [to] *Formal.* To describe (sthg.) as resembling sthg. else; compare: *He likened his youth to a summer day.*

like·ness (līk′nĭs) *n.* **1.** [C; U] Similarity or resemblance: *an amazing likeness between brothers; There is little likeness in our tastes or interests.* **2.** [C] A copy or picture of sbdy. or sthg.: *The portrait is a perfect likeness of you.* **3.** [C; *of*] *(usually singular).* Appearance; form: *At once the prince took on the likeness of a frog.*

like·wise (līk′wīz′) *adv.* **1.** In the same way; in like manner: *Once he saw her open her package, he did likewise.* **2.** Moreover; besides: *I enjoyed living in France and likewise learned to speak French.* See Synonyms at **besides.**

lik·ing (lī′kĭng) *n. (usually singular).* A feeling or fondness or affection; a preference: *a special liking for apples.*

li·lac (lī′lək *or* lī′lŏk *or* lī′lăk) *n.* **1.** [C] A shrub that has clusters of fragrant purple or white flowers. **2.** [U] A pale purple color. —*adj.* Pale purple.

lilt (lĭlt) *n.* A cheerful lively manner of speaking or walking: *She has a pleasing lilt in her voice.*

lil·y (lĭl′ē) *n., pl.* **lil·ies.** Any of various plants with showy flowers shaped like trumpets.

li·ma bean (lī′mə) *n.* The flat edible light green kidney-shaped seed of a tropical American plant.

limb (lĭm) *n.* **1.** *Formal.* A leg, an arm, or a wing of an animal: *The dog had lost a limb.* **2.** One of the larger branches of a tree: *The limb fell from the weight of the snow.*

lim·ber (lĭm′bər) *adj.* Bending or moving easily; flexible: *limber muscles; a limber athlete.* —*v.* ◆ **limber up.** *tr. & intr.v.* To exercise to make or become limber: *She stretched slowly to limber up her muscles.* —**lim′ber·ness** *n.* [U]

lim·bo¹ (lĭm′bō) *n.* [U] A place or condition of neglect or doubt: *Construction of the new pool was kept in limbo until new funds were found.*

lim·bo² (lĭm′bō) *n., pl.* **lim·bos.** A West Indian dance in which the dancers bend over backward and pass under a horizontal pole.

lime¹ (līm) *n.* **1.** [C] An oval citrus fruit related to the lemon, with a green skin and sour juice used as flavoring. **2.** [U] A yellowish green color. —*adj.* Yellowish green.

lime² (līm) *n.* [U] Calcium oxide: *I put some lime on the garden.*

lime·light (līm′līt′) *n.* [U] The center of public attention: *The President is always in the limelight.*

lim·er·ick (lĭm′ər ĭk) *n.* A humorous five-line poem that follows the rhyme scheme *aabba: Many limericks begin with the words There once was a.*

lime·stone (līm′stōn′) *n.* [U] A form of sedimentary rock that consists mainly of calcium carbonate, used as a building material and in making lime and cement.

lim·it (lĭm′ĭt) *n.* **1.** A point or line beyond which sthg. ends: *the 12-mile fishing limit; the limit of my patience.* **2. limits.** The boundary surrounding a certain area: *within the city limits.* **3.** The greatest amount of sthg. allowed: *a speed limit.* —*tr.v.* To place a limit on (sbdy./sthg.); confine: *Try to limit your talk to ten minutes.*

lim·i·ta·tion (lĭm′ĭ tā′shən) *n.* **1.** [C] Something that limits; a restriction: *Poor road conditions put limitations on how fast the car could go.* **2.** [U] The act of limiting sbdy./sthg. or the state of being limited.

lim·it·ed (lĭm′ĭ tĭd) *adj.* **1.** Small in area; restricted: *a small house with limited space.* **2.** Not able to perform at the highest level; not showing the best talent: *a popular but limited actor.*

lim·it·less (lĭm′ĭt lĭs) *adj.* Having no limit or boundary; unrestricted or infinite: *the limitless space of the high plains.*

lim·ou·sine (lĭm′ə zēn′ *or* lĭm′ə zēn′) *n.* A large luxurious automobile, often with a glass partition between the driver and the passengers: *The actor stepped out of the limousine.*

limp (lĭmp) *intr.v.* **1.** To walk lamely: *After my knee injury, I limped for several days.* **2.** To move with difficulty: *The damaged ship limped back to port.* —*n.* A lame or irregular way of walking: *My brother walks with a slight limp.* —*adj.* **1.** Not stiff: *a limp wet towel.* **2.** Not active or strong; weak: *He has a limp handshake.* —**limp′ly** *adv.* —**limp′ness** *n.* [U]

lim·pid (lĭm′pĭd) *adj.* Perfectly clear; transparent: *limpid water.*

linch·pin (lĭnch′pĭn′) *n.* **1.** An iron pin inserted in the end of an axle to prevent a wheel from slipping off. **2.** Something that keeps different parts together and functioning: *The linchpin of the candidate's campaign was his proposal for improving the economy.*

line¹ (līn) *n.* **1.a.** A thin continuous mark, as one made on paper by a pen or pencil. **b.** Something that looks like such a mark: *a face marked with deep lines.* **2.** A border or boundary: *the state line.* **3.** A group of people or things arranged in a row: *a line of customers at the counter.* **4.** Often **lines.** Outline, contour, or styling: *the lines of a new car.* **5.a.** A row of words printed or written across a page or column: *Read the fifth line.* **b.** A short letter: *I'll drop you a line.* **6. lines.** The words to be spoken by an actor in a film or a play. **7.** A cable, rope, or wire: *a fishing line.* **8.** A course or direction; a route: *the line of flight of migrating birds.* **9.** A series of persons or things following one another in time: *the line of French kings; our family line.* **10.** A system of transportation: *a bus line.* **11.** A telephone connection: *Their line is busy.* **12.** A pipe or wire used to carry water, gas, or electricity from one point to another. **13.** A collection of goods for sale in several styles and sizes: *a line of fashionable dresses.* **14.** A person's trade or occupation: *What is your line of work?* **15.** The area of a person's ability or interests: *That sort of work is out of my line.* **16.** *(usually plural).* The battle area or soldiers closest to the enemy: *The wounded were taken behind the lines.* **17.** *(usually singular). Informal.* False or exaggerated talk intended to deceive: *Her boyfriend fed her a line about who he was with at the party.* —*v.* **lined, lin·ing, lines.** —*tr.* **1.** To mark or cover (a surface) with lines: *Line the paper.* **2.** To form a line (along): *Thousands of people lined the sidewalks.* **3.** To place (people or things) in a line or row: *Line the children up by the door.* ◆ **all along the**

line graph

line. At every stage or moment: *Building the house has been difficult all along the line.* **in line for.** Next in order for: *She's in line for a promotion.* **line up.** *intr.v.* To form a line: *customers lining up to pay.* —*tr.v.* [sep.] To organize and make (sthg.) ready: *We lined up support for our candidate.* **on the line.** At risk: *If he doesn't increase his sales, then his job is on the line.* **out of line.** Not expected or acceptable; improper. Used of words and actions: *That remark was out of line.*

line² (līn) *tr.v.* **lined, lin·ing, lines. 1.** [with] To cover the inside surface of (a piece of clothing) with a layer of material: *The tailor lined the coat with satin.* **2.** To serve as a lining for or in (sthg.): *Tissue paper lined the box.* **3.** To fill (sthg.) completely: *Toys lined every shelf in the store.*

lin·e·age (lĭn′ē ĭj) *n.* **1.** [C] Direct descent from a particular ancestor; ancestry: *a lineage traced back to the Pilgrims.* **2.** [U] All of the descendants of a particular ancestor: *the lineage of kings.*

lin·e·al (lĭn′ē əl) *adj.* Being in the direct line of descent: *Without children, the couple had no lineal descendants.* —**lin′e·al·ly** *adv.*

lin·e·ar (lĭn′ē ər) *adj.* **1.** Relating to or resembling a line, especially a straight line: *linear distance.* **2.** Consisting of or using lines: *a linear design.* **3.** Relating to length: *The meter is a unit of linear measurement.* —**lin′e·ar·ly** *adv.*

lin·en (lĭn′ən) *n.* **1.** [U] Strong smooth cloth made of flax fibers. **2.** Also **linens.** Articles, such as bedsheets and tablecloths: *We change the bed linens once a week.*

lin·er¹ (lī′nər) *n.* A commercial ship or airplane carrying passengers on a regular route.

lin·er² (lī′nər) *n.* Something used as a lining: *My winter coat has a zip-out liner.*

line·up also **line-up** (līn′ŭp′) *n.* **1.** A group of persons lined up, as for purposes of identification: *a police lineup.* **2.** The members of a team chosen to play a game: *My sister is in the starting lineup for her softball team.*

—**ling** *suff.* A suffix that means: **1.** A person connected with: *earthling.* **2.** A person or thing having a specified quality: *foundling.* **3.** A person or thing that is small, young, or inferior: *duckling.*

lin·ger (lĭng′gər) *intr.v.* **1.** To be slow in acting or leaving: *The children lingered in the toy shop until closing.* See Synonyms at **stay¹. 2.** To continue or persist: *The taste of cherries lingered in my mouth.*

lin·ge·rie (län′zhə rā′) *n.* [U] Women's underclothes: *silk lingerie.*

lin·go (lĭng′gō) *n., pl.* **lin·goes.** Language of a special group that is difficult to understand: *Doctors have a lingo all their own.*

lin·guis·tics (lĭng gwĭs′tĭks) *n.* [U] *(used with a singular verb).* The study of the nature and structure of human language. —**lin′guist**

n. —**lin·guis′tic** *adj.* —**lin·guis′ti·cal·ly** *adv.*

lin·i·ment (lĭn′ə mənt) *n.* [U] A liquid medicine rubbed on the skin to soothe pain or relieve stiffness: *Some liniment will help your sore muscles.*

lin·ing (lī′nĭng) *n.* An inner covering or coating: *the stomach lining; the lining in a coat.*

link (lĭngk) *n.* **1.a.** One of the rings or loops forming a chain. **b.** One of a series of connected units: *a sausage link; text links.* **2.** Something that joins or connects: *a new rail link between the city and the airport.* —*v.* —*tr.* To connect or join (sbdy./sthg.) as if with a link: *The telephone links the far corners of the globe.* See Synonyms at **join.** —*intr.* **1.** To become connected: *The two expeditions plan to link up by radio.* **2.** *Informal.* To get together: *Did you two ever link up?*

link·age (lĭng′kĭj) *n.* **1.** [U] The act or process of linking: *linkage of tax reform to a balanced budget.* **2.** [C; U] The state or condition of being linked: *The agreement establishes economic linkages among several countries.*

link·ing verb (lĭng′kĭng) *n.* In grammar, a verb that connects the subject of a sentence with a predicate noun or adjective. In the sentences *The children are happy* and *You seem sleepy,* the verbs *are* and *seem* are linking verbs. —SEE NOTE at **adjective.**

links (lĭngks) *pl.n. Informal.* A golf course: *She spends all her free time on the links.*

HOMONYMS: links, lynx (wild cat).

---

li·no·le·um (lĭ nō′lē əm) *n.* [U] A sturdy washable material made in sheets, used for covering floors.

lint (lĭnt) *n.* [U] Small clinging pieces of fiber and fluff from fabrics: *My shirt was covered with lint from the wash.*

li·on (lī′ən) *n.* **1.** A very large, meat-eating, wild cat of Africa and India, with a tan coat and a heavy mane around the neck and shoulders in the male. **2.** A very brave person. **3.** A famous person; a celebrity: *a social lion.*
◆ **lion's share.** The greatest or best part: *The star player received the lion's share of the sportswriters' attention.*

li·on·ess (lī′ə nĭs) *n.* A female lion.

li·on·ize (lī′ə nīz′) *tr.v.* **li·on·ized, li·on·iz·ing, li·on·iz·es.** To treat (sbdy.) as very important: *The public lionized the popular author.*

lip (lĭp) *n.* **1.** [C] Either of the two fleshy muscular folds of tissue that together surround the mouth. **2.** [C] The edge or rim that surrounds an opening: *the lip of a cup.* **3.** [U] *Slang.* Disrespectful talk: *Don't give your teachers any lip.*

lip-read (lĭp′rēd′) *intr.v.* **lip-read** (lĭp′rĕd′), **lip-read·ing, lip-reads.** To interpret speech by lip reading: *He is able to lip-read and sign.*

lip reading *n.* [U] The skill of understanding unheard speech by interpreting movements of the lips and face of the speaker.

lip service *n.* [U] Agreement expressed in words but without sincerity or the intention of doing anything: *He paid lip service to the suggestion that we should volunteer to clean the park.*

lip·stick (lĭp′stĭk′) *n.* [C; U] A stick of waxy coloring matter used by women and applied to the lips: *She bought a new tube of lipstick.*

liq·ue·fac·tion (lĭk′wə făk′shən) *n.* [U] The act or process of liquefying: *Liquefaction of the metal allowed us to pour it.*

liq·ue·fy (lĭk′wə fī′) *tr. & intr.v.* **liq·ue·fied, liq·ue·fy·ing, liq·ue·fies.** To make or become liquid: *First, we liquefied the lead. Butter liquefies at low heat.*

li·queur (lĭ kûr′ *or* lĭ kyŏŏr′) *n.* A sweet alcoholic beverage: *an after-dinner liqueur.*

liq·uid (lĭk′wĭd) *n.* A substance that is neither a solid nor a gas, with molecules that move freely within the container in which it is put: *Water is a liquid.* —*adj.* **1.** In a liquid state: *a liquid rocket fuel.* **2.** Easily changed into cash: *liquid assets such as savings bonds.*

liq·ui·date (lĭk′wĭ dāt′) *tr.v.* **1.** To pay off or settle (sthg.): *liquidate one's debts.* **2.** To close down (a business) by settling its accounts and dividing up any remaining assets: *The furniture store must liquidate all its merchandise.* **3.** To put an end to (sthg.): *Development has liquidated vast forests.* —**liq′ui·da′tion** *n.* [C; U]

li·quid·i·ty (lĭ kwĭd′ĭ tē) *n.* [U] **1.** The quality or condition of being liquid. **2.** The quality of being easily changed into cash: *Stocks and bonds have high liquidity.*

liq·uor (lĭk′ər) *n.* [C; U] An alcoholic beverage, such as whiskey or gin, made by distillation: *He never drinks liquor.*

lisp (lĭsp) *n.* A speech defect in which the sounds *s* and *z* are pronounced *th* as in *thin* and *then.* —*intr. & tr.v.* To speak or say with a lisp.

list¹ (lĭst) *n.* A series of names, words, or other items written one after the other: *a guest list; a shopping list.* —*tr.v.* To make a list of (things); include in a list: *The hotel's guests are listed in the register.*

list² (lĭst) *n.* A tilt to one side, as of a ship: *a ship's sudden list to the starboard side.* —*intr. & tr.v.* To lean or cause to lean to one side, as a ship: *The ship listed heavily in the wind.*

lis·ten (lĭs′ən) *intr.v.* [*to*] **1.** To make an effort to hear: *I always listen to music in the evening.* **2.** To pay attention: *No one listened*

ă–**cat**; ā–**pay**; âr–**care**; ä–**father**; ĕ–**get**; ē–**be**; ĭ–**sit**; ī–**nice**; îr–**here**; ŏ–**got**; ō–**go**; ô–**saw**; oi–**boy**; ou–**out**; ŏŏ–**took**; ōō–**boot**; ŭ–**cut**; ûr–**word**; th–**thin**; *th*–**this**; hw–**when**; zh–**vision**; ə–**about**; N–French **bon**

to my advice. ◆ **listen in.** *intr.v.* **1.** To listen to a conversation between others; eavesdrop: *My mother listened in on my brother's phone call.* **2.** To tune in and listen to a radio or television broadcast: *We listened in to station KPIX this morning.* —**lis'ten•er** *n.*

list•ing (lĭs'tĭng) *n.* **1.** An entry in a list or directory: *a telephone listing.* **2.** A list: *a listing of dentists.*

list•less (lĭst'lĭs) *adj.* Without energy or enthusiasm: *The long days spent indoors made us feel bored and listless.* —**list'less•ly** *adv.* —**list'less•ness** *n.* [U]

list price *n.* A basic price published in a price list, often reduced by a seller: *We bought the TV at 20% below list price.*

lit (lĭt) *v.* A past tense and a past participle of **light**[1] and **light**[2].

lit. *abbr.* An abbreviation of: **1.** Liter. **2.** Literature.

lit•a•ny (lĭt'n ē) *n., pl.* **lit•a•nies. 1.** A prayer consisting of phrases recited by a leader alternating with responses by the congregation. **2.** A similar repetitive series: *Each employee recited a familiar litany of complaints.*

li•ter (lē'tər) *n.* A unit of volume equal to about 1.056 liquid quarts or 0.908 dry quart. See table at **measurement.**

lit•er•a•cy (lĭt'ər ə sē) *n.* [U] **1.** The ability to read or write: *Literacy is necessary for most jobs.* **2.** The understanding or knowledge a person has in a particular field: *computer literacy.*

lit•er•al (lĭt'ər əl) *adj.* **1.** Following the exact meaning of a word or group of words: *The literal interpretation of a poem is often too narrow.* **2.** Corresponding word for word with the original: *A literal translation of an idiom often doesn't make sense.* **3.** Factual: *She gave a literal account of events.* —**lit'er•al•ly** *adv.*

lit•er•ar•y (lĭt'ə rĕr'ē) *adj.* **1.** Relating to literature: *a literary critic.* **2.** Relating to writers or the profession of writing: *The writer John Steinbeck has been called a literary genius.*

lit•er•ate (lĭt'ər ĭt) *adj.* **1.** Able to read and write: *A job as a news reporter requires you to be literate.* **2.** Well educated: *literate in architecture.*

lit•er•a•ture (lĭt'ər ə chŏor' *or* lĭt'ər ə-chər) *n.* [U] **1.** A body of writing, especially writing with recognized artistic value: *She has read much American literature of the 20th century.* **2.** A body of writing on a given subject: *medical literature.* **3.** Printed material: *election campaign literature.*

lithe (līth) *adj.* **lith•er, lith•est.** Easily bent limber: *a lithe dancer.* —**lithe'ly** *adv.* —**lithe'ness** *n.* [U]

lith•i•um (lĭth'ē əm) *n.* [U] *Symbol* Li A soft, silvery metallic element. Lithium is the lightest of all metals. Atomic number 3. See table at **element.**

lith•o•graph (lĭth'ə grăf') *n.* A print produced by lithography. —**li•thog'ra•pher** (lĭ thŏg'rə fər) *n.* —**lith'o•graph'ic** *adj.*

li•thog•ra•phy (lĭ thŏg'rə fē) *n.* [U] A printing process in which an image is drawn on a flat surface such as a metal plate and treated to hold ink. The other areas of the surface are treated to repel ink.

lit•i•gant (lĭt'ĭ gənt) *n.* A person or group involved in a lawsuit: *The litigants could not agree on a settlement.*

lit•i•gate (lĭt'ĭ gāt') *intr. & tr.v.* To carry on a lawsuit: *Attorneys often litigate their cases in court.* —**lit'i•ga'tion** *n.* [U]

lit•mus (lĭt'məs) *n.* [U] A dye that changes to red in an acid solution and to blue in an alkaline solution.

litmus test *n.* **1.** A chemical test used to distinguish acid and alkaline solutions. **2.** A figurative test for truth or sincerity: *Her willingness to support the plan was a litmus test.*

li•tre (lē'tər) *n. Chiefly British.* Variant of **liter.**

lit•ter (lĭt'ər) *n.* **1.** [U] Carelessly scattered scraps of paper or other waste material: *Pick up that litter!* **2.** [C] Several young born to a mammal at a single time: *The dog had a litter of six puppies.* **3.** [U] Loose material spread for animals to sleep on or to absorb urine and feces: *kitty litter.* **4.** [C] A stretcher used to carry a sick or wounded person: *The soldier was carried on the litter.* —*tr. & intr.v.* To make untidy by scattering things about: *The people at the parade littered the street with trash. Don't litter!*

lit•ter•bug (lĭt'ər bŭg') *n. Informal.* A person who litters public areas with trash: *Litterbugs can be arrested and fined.*

lit•tle (lĭt'l) *adj.* **lit•tler, lit•tlest** *or* **less** (lĕs), **least** (lēst). **1.** Small in size, amount, or degree: *a little boy; little money.* **2.** Short in duration: *We have little time left.* **3.** Young or younger: *my little brother.* **4.** Unimportant; trivial: *a little problem.* —*adv.* **less, least. 1.** Not much: *He slept very little that night.* **2.** Not at all: *Little did the class realize the teacher planned a surprise test.* —*n.* **1.** A small amount: *I received only a little of what they owe.* **2.** A short distance or time: *We waited a little.* ◆ **a little.** Somewhat; a bit: *She feels a little better now.* **little by little.** By small degrees; gradually: *We paid the loan little by little.* —SEE NOTE at **few.**

Little League *n.* [C; U] An organization of baseball teams for children: *My youngest sister plays in Little League.*

lit·ur·gy (lĭt′ər jē) *n.*, *pl.* **lit·ur·gies.** The established form for public Christian ceremonies. —**li·tur′gi·cal** *adj.*

liv·a·ble also **live·a·ble** (lĭv′ə bəl) *adj.* **1.** Suitable for living in: *a livable house.* **2.** Acceptable; bearable: *a life of hardship that was barely livable.*

live¹ (lĭv) *v.* **lived, liv·ing, lives.** —*intr.* **1.** To be alive; exist: *Fish live in water.* **2.** To continue to remain alive: *My parents have lived for half a century.* **3.** To support oneself; subsist: *It takes hard work to live on a farm.* **4.** To reside or dwell: *They live in an apartment.* **5.** To conduct one's life in a certain manner: *They live happily.* —*tr.* To spend or pass (a life): *I have lived my whole life in this town.* ◆ **live and let live.** To accept others' actions: *You should learn to live and let live.* **live down.** *tr.v.* [sep.] To overcome or reduce the shame of (a misdeed, for example) over a period of time: *We thought we'd never live down losing the game.* **live it up.** To celebrate; enjoy oneself: *After winning the game, we decided to live it up and go out for an expensive dinner.* **live through.** *tr.v.* [insep.] To survive or endure (sthg.): *My grandfather lived through the war.* **live up to. 1.** To live or act in accordance with (sthg.): *I try to live up to my ideals.* **2.** To prove equal to (sthg.): *The new car did not live up to our expectations.* **3.** To fulfill (sthg.): *She lived up to her part of the bargain.* **live with.** *tr.v.* [insep.] To tolerate (sbdy./sthg.); resign oneself to: *We'll just have to live with the problem for now.*

live² (līv) *adj.* **1.** Alive; living: *live animals in the zoo.* **2.** Glowing; burning: *live coals.* **3.** Carrying electric current: *a live circuit.* **4.** Capable of exploding: *live ammunition.* **5.** Broadcast while actually being performed: *a live television program.* ◆ **live wire.** *Informal.* Somebody with a lot of energy: *My boss is a real live wire.*

live·li·hood (līv′lē hood′) *n.* *(usually singular).* The means of supporting life; a way of earning a living: *She earns her livelihood by selling cars.*

live·ly (līv′lē) *adj.* **live·li·er, live·li·est. 1.** Full of life or energy: *a lively puppy.* **2.** Full of spirit; exciting: *a lively discussion.* ◆ **step lively.** To move in a brisk and lively manner: *The marchers had to step lively to keep up.* —**live′li·ness** *n.* [U]

li·ven (lī′vən) *v.* ◆ **liven up.** *tr.v.* [sep.] To make (sthg.) lively: *Music livens me up.* —*intr.v.* To become lively: *The party livened up.*

liv·er (lĭv′ər) *n.* **1.** [C] A large, reddish brown organ that acts in the formation of blood and is located in the abdomen of vertebrates. **2.** [U] The liver of an animal used as food.

lives (līvz) *n.* Plural of **life.**

live·stock (līv′stŏk′) *n.* [U] Domestic animals, such as cattle, horses, sheep, or pigs, raised and kept on a farm or ranch: *My aunt and uncle raise livestock on their ranch.*

liv·id (lĭv′ĭd) *adj.* **1.** Extremely angry; furious: *He was livid when his friend forgot to call him.* **2.** Pale or ashen, as from shock: *livid from fear.* —**liv′id·ly** *adv.*

liv·ing (lĭv′ĭng) *adj.* **1.** Having life; alive: *oldest living person.* **2.** Relating to life: *the difficult living conditions of the desert.* **3.** Currently existing or in use: *a living language.* —*n.* **1.** [U] The condition of being alive: *the high cost of living.* **2.** [U] A manner or style of life: *We prefer simple living.* **3.** [C] A means of maintaining life; livelihood: *They make their living by fishing.*

living room *n.* A room in a home usually for entertaining guests and general use: *Is your TV in the living room?*

liz·ard (lĭz′ərd) *n.* Any of numerous reptiles with scaly skin, a long tail, and usually four legs: *Iguanas and chameleons are lizards.*

lla·ma (lä′mə) *n.* A South American mammal related to the camel, raised for its soft, woolly hair and used for carrying loads.

HOMONYMS: llama, lama (Buddhist monk).

---

load (lōd) *n.* **1.** The weight or force supported by a structure or some part of it: *the load on an arch.* **2.** A quantity or an amount that is carried, as by a vehicle, a person, or an animal: *a load of firewood on the horse's back.* **3.** The amount of work done by a person or machine: *a heavy load of homework; a load of laundry in the washing machine.* **4.** The mechanical resistance that a machine must overcome. **5.** The power output of a generator or power plant. **6.** *Informal. (usually plural).* A great number or amount: *She gets invited to loads of parties.* —*v.* —*tr.* **1.a.** To put (sthg.) into or onto a structure or vehicle: *The workers loaded grain onto a train.* **b.** To put sthg. into or onto (a structure or vehicle): *load a ship.* **2.** To cover or fill (sthg.) with a large amount: *Our hosts loaded the table with food.* **3.** To weigh (sbdy.) down, as with work to do: *The teachers loaded the students with homework.* **4.a.** To put (sthg. necessary) into a device: *load film into a camera.* **b.** To put sthg. necessary into (a device): *load a camera with film.* **c.** To put (a computer program or data) into a computer's memory. **d.** To put ammunition into (a gun). —*intr.* **1.** To receive a load: *The ship loaded in port.* **2.** To fill a gun with

---

ă–cat; ā–pay; âr–care; ä–father; ĕ–get; ē–be; ĭ–sit; ī–nice; îr–here; ŏ–got; ō–go; ô–saw; oi–boy; ou–out; oo–took; oo–boot; ŭ–cut; ûr–word; th–thin; *th*–this; hw–when; zh–vision; ə–about; N–French bon

ammunition. ◆ **a load off (one's) mind.** The removal of a responsibility or source of worry: *We've found an apartment, so that's a load off my mind.* **get a load of.** *Slang.* To notice or get a good look at (sbdy./sthg.): *Did you get a load of her new car?* **load up on.** To get a good supply of (sthg.): *People loaded up on emergency supplies before the hurricane.*

HOMONYMS: load, lode (ore deposit).

---

load•ed (lō′dĭd) *adj.* **1.** Carrying a load: *Our car was loaded with our belongings.* **2.** Intended to trick or trap by carrying hidden meaning: *a loaded question.* **3.** *Slang.* Very rich: *My uncle is loaded.* **4.** *Slang.* Very drunk: *The man at the bar was loaded.*

loaf[1] (lōf) *n., pl.* **loaves** (lōvz). A round or oblong mass of bread or food baked in one piece: *a loaf of bread; a meat loaf.*

loaf[2] (lōf) *intr.v.* To spend time lazily or aimlessly: *We loafed all morning.*

loaf•er (lō′fər) *n.* **1.** A person who spends time lazily or idly: *Don't be such a loafer!* **2.** A casual shoe that has no laces.

loam (lōm) *n.* [U] Rich soil used for planting: *The garden has rich, sandy loam that is ideal for growing vegetables.*

loan (lōn) *n.* **1.** The act of lending: *the loan of a raincoat to a friend.* **2.a.** Something lent for temporary use: *The lamp is a loan from my neighbor.* **b.** A sum of money lent at interest: *a loan from the bank.* —*tr.v.* To lend (sthg.): *Public libraries loan books.* —SEE NOTE at **borrow.**

HOMONYMS: loan, lone (solitary).

---

loath (lōth *or* lōth) *adj.* *Formal.* Not willing; reluctant: *They were loath to accept the offer of help from their rivals.*

HOMONYMS: loath, loathe (dislike).

---

loathe (lōth) *tr.v.* **loathed, loath•ing, loathes.** To dislike (sbdy./sthg.) greatly; detest: *I loathe cleaning the bathroom.* —**loath′ing** *n.* [U]

loath•some (lōth′səm *or* lōth′səm) *adj.* Detestable; extremely unpleasant: *a loathsome chore.* —**loath′some•ly** *adv.* —**loath′some•ness** *n.* [U]

loaves (lōvz) *n.* Plural of **loaf**[1].

lob (lŏb) *tr.v.* **lobbed, lob•bing, lobs.** To hit, throw, or propel (a ball) in a high arc: *In tennis, she often lobs the ball.* —*n.* A ball hit or thrown in a high arc.

lob•by (lŏb′ē) *n., pl.* **lob•bies. 1.** An entrance hall or a waiting room in a large building: *the hotel lobby; a theater lobby.* **2.** A group of persons who try to influence lawmakers in favor of a cause: *the agriculture lobby.* —*v.* **lob•bied, lob•by•ing, lob•**

bies. —*intr.* To try to influence lawmakers for or against a cause: *Environmental groups often lobby for antipollution laws.* —*tr.* To try to influence (lawmakers) in their voting: *Several groups lobbied Congress to approve the bill.* —**lob′by•ist** *n.*

lobe (lōb) *n.* A rounded projecting part, as of a leaf or an organ of the body: *ear lobe.* —**lobed** *adj.*

lob•ster (lŏb′stər) *n.* [C; U] A sea animal related to crabs and shrimps, with a long hard-shelled body and large claws, and used as food.

lobster

lo•cal (lō′kəl) *adj.* **1.** Relating to a particular area or place: *local governments; a local storm.* **2.** Making all stops on a route; not express: *a local train.* **3.** Limited to one part of the body: *a local infection.* —*n.* **1.** *(usually plural).* A person who lives in a certain region or neighborhood: *The locals are concerned about the town's growth.* **2.** A local branch of an organization, especially of a labor union: *Union locals voted on the contract.* **3.** A train or bus that makes all stops along its route: *The local is much slower than the express.* —**lo′cal•ly** *adv.*

lo•cale (lō kăl′) *n.* A place, especially with reference to a particular event or circumstance: *The locale in many of Dickens' stories is London.*

lo•cal•i•ty (lō kăl′ĭ tē) *n., pl.* **lo•cal•i•ties.** A certain neighborhood, place, or region: *She lives in a nice locality.*

lo•cal•ize (lō′kə līz′) *tr. & intr.v.* **lo•cal•ized, lo•cal•iz•ing, lo•cal•iz•es.** To confine or become restricted to a particular area: *The pain was localized in my stomach.*

lo•cate (lō′kāt′ *or* lō kāt′) *v.* **lo•cat•ed, lo•cat•ing, lo•cates.** —*tr.* **1.** To show the position of (sthg.): *Locate Austria on a map.* **2.** To find (sbdy./sthg.) by searching or examining: *You can locate information in the library.* **3.** To place or situate (sthg.): *We located the vegetables in a sunny corner of the garden.* —*intr.* To go and live somewhere; settle: *The family located in California.*

lo•ca•tion (lō kā′shən) *n.* **1.** [C] A place where sthg. is or could be located; a site: *The view makes this a good location for a house.* **2.** [U] The act of locating: *the location of water by drilling.* ◆ **on location.** At a site away from a movie studio where filming occurs: *The movie was filmed on location in Spain.*

lo•ci (lō′sī′) *n.* Plural of **locus.**

lock[1] (lŏk) *n.* **1.** A device used to fasten and secure sthg., operated by a key, combination, or card. **2.** A section of a waterway, closed off with gates, in which a ship can be raised or lowered by pumping water in or out. —*v.* —*tr.*

1. To fasten or secure (sthg.) with a lock: *Lock the door.* **2.** To confine (sbdy./sthg.) by means of a lock: *The keepers locked the animals in their cages.* **3.** To fix (sthg.) in place so that movement is impossible: *The ship was locked in the ice.* **4.** To join or link (things) firmly: *We locked arms and walked on.* — *intr.* **1.** To become fastened or secured: *The door locks automatically.* **2.** To become joined: *The railroad cars locked as they came together.*

lock² (lŏk) *n.* **1.** A strand or curl of hair. **2. locks.** The hair of the head: *the baby's red locks.*

lock•er (lŏk'ər) *n.* **1.** A compartment, as in a gymnasium, that can be locked to keep clothes or valuables safe. **2.** A refrigerated cabinet or room for storing frozen foods: *a meat locker.*

lock•et (lŏk'ĭt) *n.* A small case, usually for a picture, worn on a chain around the neck as jewelry: *The locket held a picture of her grandparents.*

lock•jaw (lŏk'jô') *n.* [U] Tetanus.

lock•smith (lŏk'smĭth') *n.* A person who makes or repairs locks: *The locksmith changed the lock on the front door.*

lo•co•mo•tion (lō'kə mō'shən) *n.* [U] The act or power of moving from place to place.

lo•co•mo•tive (lō'kə mō'tĭv) *n.* An engine that moves on its own power and is used to pull railroad cars. — *adj.* Relating to locomotion: *locomotive power.*

lo•cus (lō'kəs) *n.*, *pl.* **lo•ci** (lō'sī'). A place or locality: *the locus of activity.*

locust (lō'kəst) *n.* One of several types of grasshoppers that travel in large groups, often damaging crops.

lo•cu•tion (lō kyōō'shən) *n.* [U] *Formal.* A manner or style of speaking: *The actor practiced her locution.*

lode (lōd) *n.* A deposit of a metal, such as gold or silver, in another type of rock: *The miners dug into a rich lode of silver.*

HOMONYMS: lode, load (weight).

---

lodge (lŏj) *n.* **1.** A house or an inn used during a vacation or for recreational activity: *a fishing lodge.* **2.** The den of certain animals: *a beaver lodge.* **3.** A meeting place of an organization. — *v.* **lodged, lodg•ing, lodg•es.** — *tr.* **1.** To provide (sbdy.) with a place to stay temporarily: *We can lodge many guests in our home.* **2.** To fix or implant (sthg.): *The construction workers lodged stakes in the ground at the corners of the property.* **3.** To present (a complaint) to an appropriate official or office: *The angry tenant lodged a complaint with the housing agency.* — *intr.* **1.** To live in a place temporarily: *We lodged in an old*

hotel. **2.** To become stuck: *The saw blade lodged in the wood.* — **lodg'er** *n.*

lodg•ing (lŏj'ĭng) *n.* **1.** [U] A temporary place to live or stay: *The vacationers found lodging for the weekend.* **2. lodgings.** A rented room or rooms: *The students looked for affordable lodgings.*

loft (lôft *or* lŏft) *n.* **1.** A large, open area in a building or warehouse often used as an apartment or artist's studio. **2.** An open space under a roof: *a sleeping loft.* **3.** A gallery or balcony, as in a church: *a choir loft.* — *tr.v.* To send (a ball) in a high arc: *He lofted the tennis ball over the net.*

loft•y (lôf'tē *or* lŏf'tē) *adj.* **loft•i•er, loft•i•est.** **1.** Of great height; towering: *lofty mountains.* **2.** Elevated in character or spirit; noble: *lofty thoughts; lofty principles.* **3.** Arrogant: *Lofty treatment of others does not win friends.* — **loft'i•ly** *adv.* — **loft'i•ness** *n.* [U]

log¹ (lôg *or* lŏg) *n.* **1.** A long thick piece of a tree, used for building, firewood, or lumber. **2.** A journal or record of events: *The captain kept a log.* — *tr.v.* **logged, log•ging, logs.** — *tr.* **1.** To cut down trees on (a section of land): *The timber company logged the forestland.* **2.** To enter (sthg.) in a logbook: *I logged my mileage.* **3.** To travel (a certain distance or at a certain speed): *We logged several hundred miles in our two-day journey.* ◆ **log off.** *intr.v.* To enter into a computer the command to exit the system: *After working on the computer, I logged off and took a break.* **log on.** *intr.v.* To enter a computer system, usually with a password: *I logged on to the network and read my e-mail.* **sleep like a log.** To sleep deeply: *I was sleeping like a log and never heard the alarm.*

log² (lôg *or* lŏg) *n.* A logarithm.

log•a•rithm (lô'gə rĭth'əm *or* lŏg'ə-rĭth'əm) *n.* The power to which a base, usually 10, must be raised to produce a given number: *If the base is 10, then 2 is the logarithm of 100.* — **log'a•rith'mic** *adj.*

log•book (lôg'bŏŏk' *or* lŏg'bŏŏk') *n.* The official record book of a ship or an aircraft.

log•ger (lô'gər *or* lŏg'ər) *n.* A person who logs; a lumberjack: *My grandfather worked as a logger.*

log•ger•head (lô'gər hĕd' *or* lŏg'ər hĕd') *n.* ◆ **at loggerheads.** In disagreement; at odds: *The two brothers are at loggerheads about sharing their chores.*

log•ging (lô'gĭng *or* lŏg'ĭng) *n.* [U] The work of cutting down trees, sawing them into logs, and moving the logs to a mill.

log•ic (lŏj'ĭk) *n.* [U] **1.** The study of the principles of reasoning; the science of reasoning and of proof. **2.** Sound thinking; clear reasoning: *Their logic is undeniable when it comes to this issue.*

ă–**cat**; ā–**pay**; âr–**care**; ä–**father**; ĕ–**get**; ē–**be**; ĭ–**sit**; ī–**nice**; îr–**here**; ŏ–**got**; ō–**go**; ô–**saw**; oi–**boy**; ou–**out**; ŏŏ–**took**; ōō–**boot**; ŭ–**cut**; ûr–**word**; th–**thin**; *th*–**this**; hw–**when**; zh–**vision**; ə–**about**; N–French **bon**

log·i·cal (lŏj'ĭ kəl) adj. **1.** Using or agreeing with the principles of logic: a logical conclusion. **2.** Reasonably expected: A small apartment is a logical choice for a single person. —**log'i·cal·ly** adv.

lo·gi·cian (lō jĭsh'ən) n. A person who practices or is skilled in logic.

lo·gis·tics (lō jĭs'tĭks or lə jĭs'tĭks) n. [U] (used with a singular or plural verb). The planning and carrying out of a military operation or a business: We considered the logistics of getting everyone together for the meeting. —**lo·gis'tic, lo·gis'ti·cal** adj.

lo·go (lō'gō') n. A name, symbol, or trademark designed for easy recognition: He created the logo for the company.

—**logy** suff. A suffix that means: **1.** Oral or written expression: phraseology. **2.** Science, theory, or study: sociology.

loin (loin) n. **1.** [C] The sides and back of a person or animal between the ribs and hipbones. **2.** [C; U] A cut of meat taken from this part of an animal: pork loin. **3. loins.** The region of the hips, groin, and lower abdomen.

loin·cloth (loin'klôth' or loin'klŏth') n. A strip of cloth worn around the hips and groin.

loi·ter (loi'tər) intr.v. To stand about idly: I loitered at the station, waiting for the train to come. —**loi'ter·er** n. —**loi'ter·ing** n. [U]

loll (lŏl) v —intr. **1.** To move, stand, sit, or rest in a lazy way: The swimmers lolled about at the side of the pool. **2.** To hang loosely or droop: The limp flag lolled from the pole. —tr. To allow (sthg.) to hang or droop: The calf lolled its tongue on the hot day.

lol·li·pop also **lol·ly·pop** (lŏl'ē pŏp') n. A piece of hard candy on the end of a stick: The little girl offered a lick of her cherry lollipop.

lone (lōn) adj. Alone; solitary: a lone traveler on the deserted road.

Homonyms: lone, loan (something lent).

---

lone·ly (lōn'lē) adj. **lone·li·er, lone·li·est. 1.** Sad at being alone: feeling lonely with no friends. **2.** Without companions; alone: a lonely traveler. See Synonyms at **alone. 3.** Not used or visited by people; remote: a lonely road. —**lone'li·ness** n. [U]

lone·some (lōn'səm) adj. Sad at being alone: He felt lonesome when his best friend moved away. See Synonyms at **alone.**

long¹ (lông or lŏng) adj. **1.** Measuring a large amount from end to end; having great distance: The Nile is a long river. **2.** Of great duration: The presidential candidate gave a long speech. **3.** Of a certain extent or duration: The movie was two hours long. **4.** Relating to the vowel sounds in words such as mate, meet, mite, mote, moot, and mute. —adv. **1.** During or for a large amount of time: Stay as long as you like. **2.** At a very distant time: Long after the movie, I remembered that scene. —n. [U] A long time: It

won't be long before we leave. ◆ **as long as. 1.** Since: As long as you're going out, buy me a newspaper. **2.** On the condition that; if: You can go as long as you come home early. **be long on.** To have a lot of (sthg.): My grandmother is long on patience. **in the long run.** At the end: His health improved in the long run. **long ago.** At a time or during a period well before the present: I read that book long ago.

long² (lông or lŏng) intr.v. [for] To have a strong desire; wish very much: The students longed for summer vacation.

long. abbr. An abbreviation of longitude.

long-dis·tance (lông'dĭs'təns or lŏng'-dĭs'təns) adj. **1.** Covering a great distance: a long-distance race. **2.** Involving telephone connections to a distant telephone: a long-distance phone call. —adv. By telephone to a distant telephone: They talked long-distance.

lon·gev·i·ty (lŏn jĕv'ĭ tē or lôn jĕv'ĭ tē) n. [U] **1.** Long life: His family is known for longevity. **2.** Duration, as in an occupation: Few people can expect to achieve much longevity in their jobs today.

long·hand (lông'hănd' or lŏng'hănd') n. [U] Ordinary handwriting in which the words are fully written out: He wrote letters to his mother in longhand.

long·ing (lông'ĭng or lŏng'ĭng) n. [C; U] A deep yearning; a strong desire: a longing for success. —**long'ing·ly** adv.

lon·gi·tude (lŏn'jĭ tōōd' or lôn'jĭ tōōd') n. [C; U] Distance east or west on the earth's surface, measured in degrees from an imaginary line called the prime meridian. —**lon'gi·tu'di·nal** adj. —**lon'gi·tu'di·nal·ly** adv.

long-lived (lông'līvd' or lông'lĭvd' or lŏng'-līvd' or lŏng'lĭvd') adj. Having a long life; existing for a long time: a long-lived marriage.

long-lost (lông'lôst' or lŏng'lôst') adj. Not seen or heard from for a long time: a long-lost cousin.

long-range (lông'rānj' or lŏng'rānj') adj. **1.** Involving a lengthy period; not immediate: long-range goals and plans. **2.** Designed for covering great distances: long-range transport planes.

long·shore·man (lông'shôr'mən or lŏng'-shôr'mən) n. A dock worker who loads and unloads ships.

long shot n. **1.** An entry, as in a horse race, with only a slight chance of winning: I bet on the long shot and won. **2.** Something that is risky but rewarding if successful: It was a long shot, but he guessed at the answer on his test. ◆ **not by a long shot.** Not at all: He didn't win the tennis game, not by a long shot.

long-stand·ing (lông'stăn'dĭng or lŏng'-stăn'dĭng) adj. Of long duration: a long-standing business partnership.

long-term (lông'tûrm' or lŏng'tûrm') adj. Involving a long period of time: a long-term investment.

L

long-wind·ed (lông′wĭn′dĭd *or* lŏng′-wĭn′dĭd) *adj.* Writing or talking at great length; tiresome: *a long-winded candidate.* —**long′-wind′ed·ly** *adv.* —**long′-wind′-ed·ness** *n.* [U]

look (lŏŏk) *v.* —*intr.* **1.** To use the eyes to see: *I looked at the photograph.* **2.** To turn one's eyes or attention: *Everyone looked toward the camera. You must look carefully at all of the facts.* **3.** To appear; seem: *These bananas look ripe.* —*tr.* **1.** To turn one's eyes upon (sbdy./sthg.): *The teacher looked me in the eye.* **2.** To show (sthg.) by one's appearance: *He looks his age.* —*n.* **1.** The action of looking: *a quick look at the map.* **2.** An expression or appearance: *The dark clouds have a threatening look.* **3. looks.** Personal appearance: *The children have their parents' good looks.* ◆ **look after.** *tr.v.* [insep.] To take care of (sbdy./sthg.): *Someone must look after the baby.* **look alive** or **sharp.** *Informal.* To act or respond quickly: *We have to look alive if we want to finish on time.* **look down on.** To regard (sbdy./sthg.) with no respect: *looking down on players who cheat.* **look for.** *tr.v.* [insep.] To search for (sbdy./sthg.); seek: *a bird looking for food.* **look forward to.** To think of (a future event) with pleasure and excitement: *looked forward to vacation.* **look on** or **upon.** *tr.v.* [insep.] To regard or consider (sbdy./sthg.): *We look on you as a model student.* **look out.** *intr.v.* [*for*] To be watchful or careful: *Look out for cars as you cross the street.* **look the other way.** To permit illegal or improper behavior while pretending it is not happening: *The police looked the other way, and the drug traffic continued.* **look up.** *tr.v.* [sep.] **1.** To search for and find (sthg.), as in a reference book: *Look up the word in the dictionary.* **2.** To visit (sbdy.): *look up an old friend.* —*intr.v.* To become better; improve: *Things are looking up for the company.* **look up to.** To admire (sbdy.): *I look up to my grandfather.* —**look′er** *n.*

look·out (lŏŏk′out′) *n.* **1.** The act of looking or watching: *Keep a sharp lookout.* **2.** A high place with a wide view used to keep watch. **3.** A person assigned to watch for sthg.: *The captain sent a lookout to the edge of the camp.*

loom¹ (lŏŏm) *intr.v.* **1.** To come into view, often with a threatening appearance: *Storm clouds loomed over the mountains.* **2.** To seem close at hand; be about to happen: *The examination loomed before the students.*

loom² (lŏŏm) *n.* A machine or frame on which threads or yarns are woven to make cloth.

loon (lŏŏn) *n.* **1.** A large diving bird with a pointed bill, webbed feet, and a cry that resembles a laugh. **2.** *Informal.* A simple-minded or crazy person. ◆ **crazy as a loon.** *Informal.* Tending to act in a crazy manner; not sensible: *My uncle whistles himself to sleep every night; he's as crazy as a loon.*

loon·y (lŏŏ′nē) *Informal. adj.* **loon·i·er, loon·i·est. 1.** Very foolish or crazy: *Going hiking in the rain is a loony idea.* —*n., pl.* **loon·ies.** An extremely foolish person.

loop (lŏŏp) *n.* **1.** A piece of rope, thread, or wire that crosses over itself, making an opening. **2.** A circular or oval path: *The car followed a loop around the town.* —*v.* —*tr.* **1.** To make (sthg.) into a loop: *Loop the string and tie the ends.* **2.** To fasten or join (objects) with a loop: *We looped together the pieces of string.* —*intr.* To form a loop: *I prefer yarn that loops easily for knitting.* ◆ **in the loop.** Having all necessary information: *My cousin keeps me in the loop, and I hear all the family news.*

loop·hole (lŏŏp′hōl′) *n.* A means of escape, especially by unclear language in a law or contract: *A loophole in these laws allowed the defendant to escape prosecution.*

loose (lŏŏs) *adj.* **loos·er, loos·est. 1.** Not tightly fastened or secured: *a loose shoelace; loose bricks.* **2.** Free from confinement or bonds: *The horse was loose in the field.* **3.** Not tight-fitting: *a loose robe.* **4.** Not tightly packed; not compact: *loose gravel.* **5.** Not bound or gathered together: *loose notebook pages.* **6.** Not strict or exact: *a loose translation.* —*adv.* In a loose manner or condition: *We set the captured birds loose.* —*tr.v.* **loosed, loos·ing, loos·es.** To set (sbdy./sthg.) free; release: *We loosed our dog from her leash.* —**loose′ly** *adv.* —**loose′ness** *n.* [U]

loose-leaf (lŏŏs′lēf′) *adj.* Relating to pages that can be easily removed or replaced: *a loose-leaf notebook; loose-leaf paper.*

loos·en (lŏŏ′sən) *v.* —*tr.* **1.** To untie or make (sthg.) looser: *Loosen your tie and relax a while.* **2.** To free (sthg.) of restraint or strictness: *The school loosened its student dress code.* —*intr.* To become loose or looser: *The knot loosened easily.*

loot (lŏŏt) *n.* [U] **1.** Stolen goods: *The thieves escaped with the loot.* **2.** Valuable things taken in time of war. **3.** *Slang.* Money: *How much loot do you have?* —*v.* —*tr.* To rob (a place) of valuable things by violent means; plunder: *The burglar looted our house.* —*intr.* To take or steal goods; pillage. —**loot′er** *n.*

HOMONYMS: loot, lute (musical instrument).

---

lop (lŏp) *tr.v.* **lopped, lop·ping, lops.** To cut off (a part); remove: *The gardener lopped dead branches from the tree.*

lope (lōp) *intr.v.* **loped, lop·ing, lopes.** To

run in an easy way with long strides: *The horse loped along the trail.* —*n.* An easy way of running.

lop-eared (lŏp'îrd') *adj.* Having bent or drooping ears: *a lop-eared rabbit.*

lop·sid·ed (lŏp'sī'dĭd) *adj.* Heavier or larger on one side than on the other: *a lopsided cake; a lopsided win.*

lord (lôrd) *n.* **1.** In feudal times, a nobleman. **2. Lord.** *Chiefly British.* A general masculine title of nobility. **2. Lord.** A name for the Christian God. ◆ **lord it over.** To behave in a domineering manner toward (sbdy.): *The older students lorded it over the newcomers.*

lore (lôr) *n.* [U] The accumulated facts, traditions, or beliefs about sthg.: *sea lore; animal lore.*

lor·ry (lôr'ē *or* lŏr'ē) *n., pl.* **lor·ries.** *Chiefly British.* A truck.

lose (lo͞oz) *v.* **lost** (lôst *or* lŏst), **los·ing, los·es.** —*tr.* **1.** To be unable to find (sbdy./sthg.): *I lost my gloves yesterday.* **2.** To be deprived of (sbdy./sthg.) by accident, death, or other circumstance: *We lost our peach trees during the storm.* **3.** To be unable to maintain, sustain, or keep (sbdy./sthg.): *Our idea for the party lost the support of our friends when they saw how much it would cost.* **4.** To fail to win (sthg.): *They lost the game.* **5.** To fail to use (sthg.); waste: *lose a chance by hesitating.* **6.** To stray or wander from (sthg.): *lose one's way in the forest.* —*intr.* **1.** To suffer loss or destruction: *Many investors lost heavily in the recession.* **2.** To be defeated: *Their team lost because they were not in good shape.* ◆ **lose (one's) cool.** To become upset or emotional: *My boss lost his cool when I was late for work.* **lose (one's) shirt.** To lose everything, especially money: *He gambled all his money and lost his shirt.* **lose out.** *intr.v.* To be unsuccessful: *She had a chance at the job but she lost out to another candidate.* **lose out on.** To fail to win or get (sthg.); miss: *He lost out on the opportunity because he did not say he was interested.* —**los'er** *n.*

los·ing (lo͞o'zĭng) *adj.* Failing to win: *the losing team; a losing season.*

loss (lôs *or* lŏs) *n.* **1.** [C; U] The act or an instance of losing: *a loss of memory; the loss of a game.* **2.** [C] A person or thing that is lost: *Because of the accident, our car was a complete loss.* **3.** [C] The suffering or damage caused by losing a person or thing: *The doctor's retirement is a great loss to the community.* **4. losses.** Soldiers killed or wounded; casualties: *Both sides suffered great losses.* ◆ **at a loss. 1.** Below the actual cost: *They sold the old car at a loss.* **2.** Confused; puzzled: *I am at a loss to explain his behavior.*

lost (lôst *or* lŏst) *v.* Past tense and past participle of **lose.** —*adj.* **1.** Unable to find the way: *a lost tourist.* **2.a.** No longer possessed: *a lost*

fortune; a lost opportunity. **b.** No longer known or practiced: *a lost art.* **3.** Confused; bewildered: *At first we were lost in the advanced class.* **4.** Ruined or destroyed: *lost ships.* ◆ **lost in thought.** Completely involved or preoccupied: *She was lost in thought as she was reading a book.*

lot (lŏt) *n.* **1.** [C] A piece of land: *the empty lot behind the house.* **2.** [C] A number of people or things considered as a group: *We packed this lot of fruit for shipment.* **3.** [U] Fortune in life; luck: *It was his lot to struggle for a living.* ◆ **a lot of** *or* **lots of.** *Informal.* A large amount or number of: *I have a lot of work to do. We made lots of new friends.* **draw lots.** To use a set of objects to determine sthg. by chance: *They drew lots to see who would go first.*

lo·tion (lō'shən) *n.* [C; U] A liquid applied to the skin to heal, soften, cleanse, or soothe: *Put some lotion on your sunburn.*

lot·ter·y (lŏt'ə rē) *n., pl.* **lot·ter·ies.** A contest in which tickets are sold. The winning ticket or number is picked randomly.

lo·tus (lō'təs) *n.* A plant related to the water lily, with large white, pink, or yellow flowers and large, often floating, leaves.

loud (loud) *adj.* **1.** Characterized by high volume and intense sound: *That band plays loud music.* **2.** Too bright; flashy: *a loud suit.* —*adv.* In a loud manner: *Speak louder, please.* —**loud'ly** *adv.* —**loud'ness** *n.* [U]

loud·mouth (loud'mouth') *n. Informal.* A person who speaks loudly or rudely, or who tells secrets: *That loudmouth told the teacher that I didn't do my homework!*

loud·speak·er (loud'spē'kər) *n.* A device used to broadcast sound: *The director welcomed students over the loudspeaker.*

lounge (lounj) *intr.v.* **lounged, loung·ing, loung·es.** To act in a lazy or relaxed way: *She lounged in a comfortable chair.* —*n.* An informal room for relaxing or gathering: *the new student lounge.* ◆ **lounge around.** *intr.v.* To pass time idly: *I lounged around at home on my day off.* —*tr.v.* [insep.] To pass time idly in (a place): *The students lounged around the cafeteria after lunch.*

louse (lous) *n.* **1.** *pl.* **lice** (līs). A small, wingless insect that often lives on the bodies of other animals, including humans. **2.** *pl.* **lous·es.** *Slang.* A person who cannot be trusted: *Only a louse would break his promise.* —*v.* ◆ **louse up.** *tr.v.* [sep.] *Slang.* To damage (sthg.): *The call loused up our plans.*

lous·y (lou'zē) *adj.* **lous·i·er, lous·i·est. 1.** Of low quality: *a lousy car with a faulty engine.* **2.** Very bad: *I feel lousy today.* —**lous'i·ly** *adv.* —**lous'i·ness** *n.* [U]

lout (lout) *n.* An awkward, often angry and stupid person: *Her new boyfriend is an uncaring lout.*

lov·a·ble *also* **love·a·ble** (lŭv'ə bəl) *adj.* Having qualities that attract affection;

L

endearing: *a lovable kitten.* **—lov′a•ble• ness** *n.* [U] **—lov′a•bly** *adv.*

love (lŭv) *n.* **1.** [C; U] A feeling of affection, concern, or devotion toward a person: *a mother's love.* **2.** [C; U] A strong liking for sthg.: *a love of reading.* **3.** [C] A beloved person: *She is the love of my life.* **—** *tr.v.* **loved, lov•ing, loves. 1.** To feel love or strong affection for (sbdy./sthg.): *We love our parents.* **2.** To like (sbdy./sthg.) enthusiastically; delight in: *The audience loved the performance.* ◆ **a labor of love.** A job done for reasons other than money: *Her work in the theater is a labor of love.* **in love.** Feeling love and devotion toward sbdy.: *My parents are still in love with each other.*

SYNONYMS: love, like, enjoy, relish, fancy. These verbs mean to be attracted to or to find agreeable. **Love** means to feel a strong emotional attachment or intense affection for: *They love their cat as if it were their child.* **Like** is a less forceful word; it means to be interested in, to approve of, or to favor sthg.: *My sister likes her new school much better than the old one.* **Enjoy** means to feel personal satisfaction or pleasure from: *I would have enjoyed the movie more if the people behind me hadn't been talking so loudly.* **Relish** means to appreciate keenly: *We always relish hearing a good joke.* **Fancy** means to find sthg. appealing to one's taste or imagination: *The boys fancied big flashy cars.*

---

love•bird (lŭv′bûrd′) *n.* **1.** Any of various small parrots that are often kept as pets and seem to show great fondness between mates. **2. lovebirds.** An affectionate human couple: *The lovebirds held hands.*

love•less (lŭv′lĭs) *adj.* Showing or feeling no love: *a loveless tone in his voice.*

love•lorn (lŭv′lôrn′) *adj.* Deprived of love or one's lover: *a lovelorn person needing advice.*

love•ly (lŭv′lē) *adj.* **love•li•er, love•li•est. 1.** Having attractive qualities of character or appearance; beautiful: *a lovely person; a lovely house.* **2.** Enjoyable; delightful: *We spent a lovely evening with old friends.* **—love′li•ness** *n.* [U]

lov•er (lŭv′ər) *n.* **1.** A person who loves another person in a sexual relationship. **2.** A person who is fond of sthg.: *a lover of jazz.*

love seat or **love•seat** (lŭv′sēt′) *n.* A small sofa that seats two people.

love•sick (lŭv′sĭk′) *adj.* Unable to act normally as a result of being in love: *She was lovesick and couldn't eat or sleep.*

lov•ing (lŭv′ĭng) *adj.* Feeling or showing love; affectionate: *a loving parent.* **—lov′- ing•ly** *adv.*

low¹ (lō) *adj.* **1.** Of little height; not high or tall: *a low wall.* **2.** Near to the ground or horizon: *low branches; low clouds.* **3.** Of less than usual depth or degree: *The river is low. We had a record low temperature.* **4.** Inferior in rank, position, or status: *a low grade of oil.* **5.** Deep in pitch: *the low tones of a tuba.* **6.** Not loud; soft: *Speak in a low voice.* **7.** Inadequate in amount; almost gone: *Our supplies are low.* **8.** Immoral or contemptible: *a low trick.* **9.** Depressed: *in low spirits.* **10.** Not favorable; disapproving: *She has a low opinion of his work.* **—** *adv.* **1.** In or to a low position, level, or space: *The plane flew low over the runway.* **2.** In or to a low condition or rank: *The price of corn fell low after the good harvest.* **3.** Softly; quietly: *Speak low.* **4.** With a deep pitch: *The men in the choir sang low.* **—** *n.* **1.** [C] A low level, position, or degree: *The price of peanuts fell to a new low.* **2.** [U] The gear in a transmission that produces the slowest speed of the vehicle: *Put the car in low.* **—low′ness** *n.* [U]

low² (lō) *n.* The deep sound made by cattle; a moo. **—** *intr.v.* To make such a sound; moo: *The cows are lowing in the meadow.*

low•down (lō′doun′) *n.* [U] *Slang.* The whole truth: *Give me the lowdown on the scandal.*

low-down (lō′doun′) *adj.* *Informal.* Despicable; nasty: *a low-down, dirty trick.*

low•er (lō′ər) *adj.* Comparative of **low¹. 1.** Situated below a similar or comparable thing: *a lower shelf.* **2.** Less advanced in development by evolution: *lower life forms, such as worms.* **3.** Below another in rank, position, or authority: *the lower court.* **—** *v.* **—** *tr.* **1.** To let, bring, or move (sthg.) down: *lower the flag; lower one's head.* **2.** To reduce (sthg.), as in height, amount, degree, or quality: *The company lowered its prices.* **3.** To reduce (sthg.) in strength or intensity: *Lower your voice.* **—** *intr.* **1.** To move down: *The helicopter lowered over the building.* **2.** To become less: *The temperature lowered after dark.* ◆ **lower (oneself).** To act so as to reduce one's standing or self-respect: *I wouldn't lower myself to do that.*

low•er•case or **lower-case** (lō′ər kās′) *adj.* Relating to a letter that is smaller than its capital letter. For example, in the word *Mexico,* all the letters except *M* are lowercase. **—** *n.* [U] Lowercase letters: *written in lowercase.*

low-key (lō′kē′) *adj.* Quiet and calm; understated: *a low-key person who never boasts.*

low•land (lō′lənd) *n.* (*usually plural*). An area of land that is lower than the surrounding country. **—** *adj.* Relating to or characteristic of a lowland: *lowland people.* **—low′land•er** *n.*

low•ly (lō′lē) *adj.* **low•li•er, low•li•est.**

Humble or low in rank: *a person of lowly birth.* —**low′li·ness** *n.* [U]

low·pres·sure (lō′prĕsh′ər) *adj.* **1.** Having or using less than the usual pressure: *a low-pressure tire; a low-pressure system developing in the atmosphere.* **2.** Not anxiety-producing: *a low-pressure job at the library.*

low profile *n.* Behavior or activity carried out so as not to attract attention: *The thief kept a low profile so the police would not catch him.*

lox (lŏks) *n.* [U] Smoked salmon.

loy·al (loi′əl) *adj.* **1.** Faithful to a person, an idea, or a duty: *a loyal worker.* **2.** Faithful to a country or government: *a loyal citizen.* —**loy′al·ly** *adv.*

loy·al·ist (loi′ə lĭst) *n.* A person who remains loyal to the established government, political party, or ruler, especially during a civil war or revolution.

loy·al·ty (loi′əl tē) *n.*, *pl.* **loy·al·ties.** [C; U] The condition of being faithful: *Their loyalties lie with their families.*

loz·enge (lŏz′ĭnj) *n.* A small tablet that contains medicine or is used as a candy: *throat lozenges.*

LSD (ĕl′ĕs dē′) *n.* [U] A powerful drug that causes hallucinations and distorted perceptions.

Lt. *abbr.* An abbreviation of lieutenant.

ltd. or **Ltd.** *abbr.* An abbreviation of limited.

lu·bri·cant (lōo′brĭ kənt) *n.* [C; U] A slippery substance, such as oil, used to coat surfaces to reduce friction and wear: *Oil and grease are lubricants.*

lu·bri·cate (lōo′brĭ kāt′) *tr.v.* **lu·bri·cat·ed, lu·bri·cat·ing, lu·bri·cates. 1.** To apply oil or some other lubricant to (sthg.): *lubricate a car.* **2.** To make (sthg.) slippery or smooth: *lubricate skin with oil.* —**lu′bri·ca′tion** *n.* [U] —**lu′bri·ca′tor** *n.*

lu·cid (lōo′sĭd) *adj.* **1.** Easily understood; clear: *a lucid explanation.* **2.** Mentally sound; rational: *Though unable to speak, the patient was still lucid.* —**lu·cid′i·ty** (lōo sĭd′ĭ tē) *n.* [U] —**lu′cid·ly** *adv.* —**lu′cid·ness** *n.* [U]

luck (lŭk) *n.* [U] **1.** The chance happening of good or bad events; fortune: *Luck favored our team with a winning season.* **2.** Good fortune; success: *beginner's luck.* —*v.* ♦ **in luck.** Enjoying success; fortunate: *You're in luck; we still have that size.* **luck into.** *tr.v.* [insep.] To achieve (sthg.) through chance alone: *He really lucked into his new job.* **luck out.** *intr.v.* To have good fortune, especially when not deserved: *We didn't study for the exam, so we really lucked out when it was postponed.* **out of luck.** Lacking good fortune: *They must be out of luck; nothing is going right for them.*

luck·y (lŭk′ē) *adj.* **luck·i·er, luck·i·est. 1.** Marked by or having good luck; fortunate: *a lucky day; a lucky person.* **2.** Seeming to cause good luck: *a lucky penny.* —**luck′i·ly** (lŭk′ə lē) *adv.* —**luck′i·ness** *n.* [U]

lu·cra·tive (lōo′krə tĭv) *adj.* Producing wealth; profitable: *a lucrative business; a lucrative investment.* —**lu′cra·tive·ly** *adv.*

lu·di·crous (lōo′dĭ krəs) *adj.* Absurd; ridiculous: *a ludicrous idea with no merit.* —**lu′di·crous·ly** *adv.*

lug[1] (lŭg) *n.* **1.** A projecting part, as on a machine, used to support sthg.: *Take the nuts off the lugs to remove the tire.* **2.** *Slang.* A clumsy fool; a blockhead.

lug[2] (lŭg) *tr.v.* **lugged, lug·ging, lugs.** To drag or haul (sthg.) with great difficulty: *We lugged the boxes up the stairs.*

lug·gage (lŭg′ĭj) *n.* [U] The bags, suitcases, or trunks for carrying belongings on a trip; baggage: *I bought a new set of luggage.*

luke·warm (lōok′wôrm′) *adj.* **1.** Neither hot nor cold; mildly warm: *lukewarm water.* **2.** Lacking in enthusiasm; indifferent: *a lukewarm greeting.*

lull (lŭl) *tr.v.* To cause (sbdy.) to sleep or rest; calm; soothe: *a song to lull a baby to sleep.* —*n.* A temporary lessening of activity or noise; a calm interval: *a lull in the storm; a lull in sales.*

lull·a·by (lŭl′ə bī′) *n.*, *pl.* **lull·a·bies.** A soothing song meant to lull a child to sleep: *What lullaby did your mother sing to you as a child?*

lum·ber[1] (lŭm′bər) *n.* [U] Trees that have been cut down and sawed into boards: *My father bought lumber to make a deck.*

lum·ber[2] (lŭm′bər) *intr.v.* To walk or move in a clumsy or noisy manner: *The truck lumbered down the bumpy road.*

lum·ber·jack (lŭm′bər jăk′) *n.* A person whose work is to cut down trees and transport them to a sawmill.

lum·ber·yard (lŭm′bər yärd′) *n.* A business that sells lumber and other building materials: *The lumberyard sells boards in different sizes and types of wood.*

lu·mi·nar·y (lōo′mə nĕr′ē) *n.*, *pl.* **lu·mi·nar·ies.** A famous person, especially one noted for high achievement: *a film luminary.*

lu·mi·nes·cence (lōo′mə nĕs′əns) *n.* [U] The production of light accompanied by little heat. Fluorescence and phosphorescence are examples of luminescence that can be produced by biochemical or chemical processes. —**lu′mi·nes′cent** *adj.*

lu·mi·nous (lōo′mə nəs) *adj.* **1.** Giving off its own light; shining: *the luminous firefly.* **2.** Full of light; bright: *a full luminous moon.* **3.** Easily understood; clear: *simple luminous prose.* —**lu′mi·nos′i·ty** (lōo′mə nŏs′ĭ tē) *n.* [U] —**lu′mi·nous·ly** *adv.* —**lu′mi·nous·ness** *n.* [U]

lump (lŭmp) *n.* **1.** An irregularly shaped mass: *a lump of rock.* **2.** A small cube of sugar: *Do you take one or two lumps in your tea?* **3.** A swelling or bump: *A lump appeared on my finger where I was stung by the bee.*

L

—*adj.* **1.** Formed into a lump or lumps: *lump sugar.* **2.** Not divided into parts; whole: *We want the entire payment in one lump sum.* —*intr.v.* To form into a lump or lumps: *The sauce lumped because we didn't stir it.* ◆ **lump together.** *tr.v.* [sep.] To put (people or things that are different) in a group: *The coach lumped the boys and girls together in one gym class.*

lump•y (lŭm′pē) *adj.* **lump•i•er, lump•i•est.** Full of or covered with lumps: *lumpy gravy; a lumpy bed.* —**lump′i•ness** *n.* [U]

lu•na•cy (lōō′nə sē) *n.* [U] **1.** Foolish or reckless behavior: *Driving so fast was sheer lunacy.* **2.** Insanity.

lu•nar (lōō′nər) *adj.* Relating to the moon: *a lunar eclipse.*

lu•na•tic (lōō′nə tĭk) *n.* **1.** An extremely foolish or excited person: *Don't act like such a lunatic!* **2.** An insane person. —*adj.* **1.** Wildly or recklessly foolish: *a lunatic idea.* **2.** Insane.

lunch (lŭnch) *n.* [C; U] **1.** A meal eaten between breakfast and dinner, usually at midday: *I usually eat lunch at 12:30.* **2.** The food for this meal: *What do you want for lunch?* —*intr.v. Formal.* To eat lunch: *We lunched at our favorite restaurant.*

lunch•eon (lŭn′chən) *n.* Lunch, often a formal lunch: *Fifty people attended the luncheon.*

lunch•eon•ette (lŭn′chə nĕt′) *n.* A restaurant that serves light meals such as breakfast or lunch: *We had a sandwich at the luncheonette.*

lunch•room (lŭnch′rōōm′ *or* lŭnch′rōōm′) *n.* The cafeteria or room in a building where light meals are eaten: *The lunchroom at the office has several snack and drink machines.*

lung (lŭng) *n.* Either of two respiratory organs in the chest cavity of vertebrates: *His lungs were damaged by years of smoking.*

lunge (lŭnj) *n.* A sudden forward movement: *The goalie made a lunge for the ball.* —*intr.v.* **lunged, lung•ing, lung•es.** To make a sudden forward movement: *The cat lunged at the bird.*

lurch (lûrch) *intr.v.* **1.** To move suddenly and unsteadily; stagger: *He lurched forward under the heavy load of his backpack.* **2.** To roll or pitch suddenly: *The ship lurched as the wave hit it.* —*n.* A sudden rolling or pitching: *The train gave a lurch and started out of the station.* ◆ **leave (one) in the lurch.** To leave (sbdy.) in a difficult or embarrassing position: *We were left in the lurch when our tenants moved out without notice.*

lure (lōōr) *n.* **1.** A strong attraction or appeal: *the lure of fame.* **2.** A decoy used to catch animals, especially one used to attract and catch

fish: *My father attached the lure to his fishing line.* —*tr.v.* **lured, lur•ing, lures.** To attract or tempt (sbdy./sthg.), especially with a bait: *We lured the cat inside with a dish of food.*

lu•rid (lōōr′ĭd) *adj.* Causing shock or horror: *a lurid description of a train crash.* —**lu′rid•ly** *adv.*

lurk (lûrk) *intr.v.* **1.** To wait out of view; lie in wait: *The cat lurked in the grass, waiting for the mouse to approach.* **2.** To move about secretly; sneak: *The burglar lurked outside the house.*

lus•cious (lŭsh′əs) *adj.* Having a delicious taste or smell: *a luscious peach.* —**lus′cious•ly** *adv.* —**lus′cious•ness** *n.* [U]

lush (lŭsh) *adj.* **1.** Covered in thick plant growth: *a lush green lawn.* **2.** Luxurious; abundant and rich: *lush decorations.* —**lush′ly** *adv.* —**lush′ness** *n.* [U]

lust (lŭst) *n.* **1.** [U] Intense sexual desire. **2.** [C] An overwhelming desire or craving: *a lust for power.* —*intr.v.* [after] To have an intense or overwhelming desire: *The pirates lusted after riches.* —**lust′ful** *adj.* —**lust′ful•ly** *adv.*

lus•ter (lŭs′tər) *n.* [U] **1.** Soft reflected light; gloss: *the luster of pearls.* **2.** Glory; splendor: *The scientist's newest discoveries add luster to her name.* —**lus′trous** (lŭs′trəs) *adj.* —**lus′trous•ly** *adv.*

lus•tre (lŭs′tər) *n. Chiefly British.* Variant of **luster.**

lust•y (lŭs′tē) *adj.* **lust•i•er, lust•i•est.** Full of strength and vitality; robust: *a lusty laugh.* —**lust′i•ly** *adv.* —**lust′i•ness** *n.* [U]

lute (lōōt) *n.* A stringed instrument with a body shaped like a pear. The lute is played by plucking the strings.

HOMONYMS: lute, loot (stolen goods).

---

lux•u•ri•ant (lŭg zhŏŏr′ē ənt *or* lŭk shŏŏr′ē ənt) *adj.* **1.** Growing abundantly; lush: *luxuriant vegetation.* **2.** Highly ornamented: *a luxuriant dining room.* —**lux•u′ri•ance** *n.* [U] —**lux•u′ri•ant•ly** *adv.*

lux•u•ri•ate (lŭg zhŏŏr′ē āt′ *or* lŭk shŏŏr′ē āt′) *intr.v.* **lux•u•ri•at•ed, lux•u•ri•at•ing, lux•u•ri•ates.** *Formal.* **1.** To indulge oneself in fine or expensive things: *We luxuriated by taking a room in the expensive hotel.* **2.** To take great pleasure or delight: *My cats luxuriate in the warm sunshine.* **3.** To grow in abundance; thrive: *Plants luxuriate in a greenhouse.*

lux•u•ri•ous (lŭg zhŏŏr′ē əs *or* lŭk shŏŏr′ē əs) *adj.* **1.** Fond of luxury: *a luxurious taste for expensive clothes.* **2.** Marked by luxury; lavish: *a luxurious apartment.* —**lux•u′ri•ous•ly** *adv.* —**lux•u′ri•ous•ness** *n.* [U]

lux•u•ry (lŭg′zhə rē *or* lŭk′shə rē) *n., pl.*

ă–**cat**; ā–**pay**; âr–**care**; ä–**father**; ĕ–**get**; ē–**be**; ĭ–**sit**; ī–**nice**; îr–**here**; ŏ–**got**; ō–**go**; ô–**saw**; oi–**boy**; ou–**out**; ōō–**took**; ōō–**boot**; ŭ–**cut**; ûr–**word**; th–**thin**; th–**this**; hw–**when**; zh–**vision**; ə–**about**; N–French **bon**

lux•u•ries. 1. [C] Something that is not essential but gives pleasure or comfort: *Eating in a good restaurant is a luxury I can't afford these days.* **2.** [U] A way of living that brings comfort; use of the best or most costly things: *live in luxury.*

—ly¹ *suff.* A suffix that means: **1.** Having the characteristics of; like: *sisterly.* **2.** Recurring at a specified interval of time: *hourly.*

—ly² *suff.* A suffix that means: **1.** In a specified manner: *gradually.* **2.** At a specified interval: *weekly.*

lye (lī) *n.* [U] A strong alkaline solution used in making soap and in cleaning.

HOMONYMS: lye, lie (be flat, untrue statement).

---

ly•ing¹ (lī′ĭng) *v.* Present participle of **lie¹.**

ly•ing² (lī′ĭng) *v.* Present participle of **lie².** —*adj.* Given to telling lies or marked by falsehood: *a lying witness.*

lymph (lĭmf) *n.* [U] A nearly colorless liquid that flows through the lymphatic system and bathes and nourishes the tissues.

lym•phat•ic (lĭm făt′ĭk) *adj.* Carrying or relating to lymph: *the lymphatic system.*

lynch (lĭnch) *tr.v.* To execute (sbdy.), especially by hanging, without respect for the law: *In the movie, the bank robbers were lynched by the angry mob.*

lynx (lĭngks) *n.* A wild cat with thick soft fur and a short tail.

HOMONYMS: lynx, links (golf course).

---

lyre (līr) *n.* A stringed instrument related to the harp and used to accompany a singer or reciter of poetry.

lyr•ic (lĭr′ĭk) *adj.* Relating to poetry that expresses personal feelings and thoughts. —*n.* **1.** A lyric poem. **2.** Often **lyrics.** The words of a song: *Those are beautiful lyrics.*

lyr•i•cal (lĭr′ĭ kəl) *adj.* Expressing deep personal feelings or thoughts: *a lyrical description of her youth.*

lyr•i•cist (lĭr′ĭ sĭst) *n.* A writer of lyric poetry or songs: *The lyricist won an award for his songs.*

L

Mm

m¹ or **M** (ĕm) *n., pl.* **m's** or **M's.** The 13th letter of the English alphabet.

m² *abbr.* An abbreviation of: **1.** Mass. **2.** Meter (measurement). **3.** or **M.** Medium.

M also **m** The Roman numeral for 1,000.

m. *abbr.* An abbreviation of: **1.** Male. **2.** Masculine.

ma (mä *or* mô) *n. Informal.* Mother.

MA *abbr.* An abbreviation of Massachusetts.

M.A. or **MA** *abbr.* An abbreviation of Master of Arts: *She's studying for an M.A. in English literature.*

ma'am (măm) *n.* Madam: *Thank you, ma'am.*

ma•ca•bre (mə kä′brə *or* mə käb′) *adj.* Suggesting death and decay: *a macabre play about life in a city during a war.*

mac•a•ro•ni (măk′ə rō′nē) *n.* [U] A pasta made of wheat flour, usually in the shape of hollow tubes cut into short pieces.

ma•caw (mə kô′) *n.* A large, often brightly colored Central and South American parrot with a long tail and a strong beak.

mace (mās) *n.* [U] A spice made from the covering of the seed of the nutmeg.

Mace (mās). A trademark for a spray that causes irritation to the eyes and skin and makes breathing hard, used to protect oneself from an attacker: *The mail carrier sprayed the attacking dog with Mace.* —*tr.v.* **Maced, Mac•ing, Mac•es.** To spray (sbdy./sthg.) with Mace.

ma•chet•e (mə shĕt′ē *or* mə chĕt′ē) *n.* A large heavy knife with a broad blade, used as a weapon and as a cutting tool: *Machetes are used to clear paths and cut sugar cane.*

Mach•i•a•vel•li•an (măk′ē ə vĕl′ē ən) *adj.* **1.** Relating to the political theories of Niccolò Machiavelli. **2.** Using dishonest and clever ways to gain power: *a Machiavellian mind.*

mach•i•na•tion (măk′ə nā′shən) *n. (usually plural).* A secret plan to do sthg. harmful: *That group's machinations failed to affect the election results.*

ma•chine (mə shēn′) *n.* **1.** A device with fixed and moving parts used for specific tasks: *a washing machine.* **2.** A simple device that applies force or changes its direction: *The gear, lever, and screw are all simple machines.* **3.** An organized group that controls a political party in an area: *key members of the local political machine.* —*tr.v.* **ma•chined, ma•chin•ing, ma•chines.** To cut, shape, or finish (sthg.) by machine: *The workers machine metal at the factory.*

machine gun *n.* A gun that fires rapidly and repeatedly when the trigger is pressed.

ma•chine-gun (mə shēn′gŭn′) *tr.v.* **ma•chine-gunned, ma•chine-gun•ning, ma•chine-guns.** To fire at (sbdy./sthg.) with a machine gun: *machine-gunning the enemy.*

ma•chin•er•y (mə shē′nə rē *or* mə shēn′rē) *n.* [U] **1.** Machines considered as a group: *The factory is full of machinery.* **2.** The working parts of a particular machine: *The machinery of an automobile engine includes pistons and gears.* **3.** A system of persons or things that operate together to keep sthg. going: *the complex machinery of modern society.*

ma•chin•ist (mə shē′nĭst) *n.* A person who makes, operates, or repairs machines.

ma•chis•mo (mä chēz′mō) *n.* [U] Behavior or an attitude that stresses male strength, courage, and aggressiveness: *A display of machismo led to a fight.*

Mach number also **mach number** (mäk) *n.* The ratio of the speed of an aircraft to the speed of sound: *An aircraft flying at twice the speed of sound has a Mach number of 2.*

ma•cho (mä′chō) *adj.* Showing machismo: *The cowboy has a macho image.*

mack•er•el (măk′ər əl *or* măk′rəl) *n.* A silvery ocean fish with dark markings on the back, used as food.

macro— *pref.* A prefix that means large: *macrocosm.*

mac•ro•bi•ot•ics (măk′rō bī ŏt′ĭks) *n.* [U] *(used with a singular verb).* The philosophy of eating whole grains and natural foods to promote good health and a long life. —**mac′ro•bi•ot′ic** *adj.*

mac•ro•cosm (măk′rə kŏz′əm) *n.* A large system, especially the world or the universe: *Earth can be viewed as a macrocosm.*

mac•ro•ec•o•nom•ics (măk′rō ĕk′ə nŏm′ĭks *or* măk′rō ē′kə nŏm′ĭks) *n.* [U] *(used with a singular verb).* The study of the overall aspects and workings of a national economy: *Business majors need to study macroeconomics.*

mad (măd) *adj.* **mad•der, mad•dest.** **1.**

ă–cat; ā–pay; âr–care; ä–father; ĕ–get; ē–be; ĭ–sit; ī–nice; îr–here; ŏ–got; ō–go; ô–saw; oi–boy; ou–out; ōō–took; ōō–boot; ŭ–cut; ûr–word; th–thin; *th*–this; hw–when; zh–vision; ə–about; N–French bon

Informal. [*at; about*] Very angry: *His negative attitude made me mad at him.* **2.** Suffering from an illness of the mind; insane: *The war drove him mad.* **3.** Very foolish: *a mad idea.* **4.** [*about*] Filled with strong liking or enthusiasm: *mad about skiing.* **5.** Affected by rabies: *a mad dog.* ◆ **like mad.** *Informal.* With great energy or speed: *We ran like mad.* —**mad′ness** *n.* [U]

Mad•am (măd′əm) *n. Formal.* Used as a polite form of address for a woman: *Your table is this way, Madam.*

mad•cap (măd′kăp′) *adj.* Not sensible; impulsive: *A madcap idea got her into trouble.*

mad•den (măd′n) *tr.v.* To make (sbdy./sthg.) mad: *Heat and the flies maddened the horse.*

mad•den•ing (măd′n ĭng) *adj.* Causing great anger: *A maddening noise outside my window kept me awake.* —**mad′den•ing•ly** *adv.*

made (măd) *v.* Past tense and past participle of **make.** —*adj.* [*of*] Constructed, shaped, or formed: *carefully made plans; houses made of wood.* ◆ **have it made.** *Informal.* To have complete success and security: *If our company can win these contracts, we'll have it made.* **made for.** Perfectly suited for: *Those two are made for each other.*

Homonyms: made, maid (servant).

---

made-to-or•der (măd′tōō ôr′dər) *adj.* Made in agreement with particular instructions; custom-made: *a made-to-order suit.*

made-up (măd′ŭp′) *adj.* **1.** Not real; invented: *made-up stories.* **2.** Covered with cosmetics or makeup: *the clown's made-up face.*

mad•house (măd′hous′) *n.* **1.** A word used in the past for a hospital for mentally ill people. **2.** *Informal.* A place of great confusion or disorder: *The house was full of unpacked boxes and newspapers; it was a madhouse.*

mad•ly (măd′lē) *adv.* In a wild or foolish way: *They fell madly in love.*

mad•man (măd′măn′ *or* măd′mən) *n.* A man who is or seems mentally ill and dangerous: *The gunman was behaving like a madman, shooting everything that moved.* —**mad′wo′man** (măd′wŏŏm′ən) *n.*

mael•strom (māl′strəm) *n.* **1.** A large and violent whirlpool. **2.** A violent and dangerous situation: *the maelstrom of war.*

maes•tro (mīs′trō) *n., pl.* **maes•tros.** A famous conductor, composer, or music teacher.

Ma•fi•a (mä′fē ə) *n.* A secret organization involved in criminal activities, especially in Italy and the United States.

mag•a•zine (măg′ə zēn′ *or* măg′ə zēn′) *n.* **1.** A weekly or monthly publication that contains articles or stories and usually pictures and advertising. **2.** A storage area for guns and ammunition. **3.** In some guns, a container that holds cartridges.

ma•gen•ta (mə jĕn′tə) *n.* [U] A bright purplish red color. —*adj.* Bright purplish red.

mag•got (măg′ət) *n.* The larva of any of various flies, resembling a worm.

mag•ic (măj′ĭk) *n.* [U] **1.** The art that claims to use secret powers to control events. **2.** The art or skill of using tricks to produce entertaining and surprising effects: *He used magic to pull a rabbit out of a hat.* **3.** A mysterious or charming quality: *the magic of the woods in the fall.* —*adj.* Relating to magic and its practice: *a magic trick.* —**mag′i•cal** *adj.* —**mag′i•cal•ly** *adv.*

ma•gi•cian (mə jĭsh′ən) *n.* **1.** A person who uses magic; a wizard: *A magician told the king's future.* **2.** An entertainer who performs tricks of magic.

mag•is•te•ri•al (măj′ĭ stîr′ē əl) *adj.* Relating to a magistrate or a magistrate's official functions: *magisterial duties.*

mag•is•trate (măj′ĭ strāt′ *or* măj′ĭ strĭt′) *n.* An official, such as a judge or a justice of the peace, with the authority to administer the law: *The driver appeared before the magistrate to appeal the ticket.*

mag•ma (măg′mə) *n.* [U] The liquid rock material under the earth's surface. Magma is called lava when it comes to the surface.

mag•na cum lau•de (măg′nə kōōm lou′də) *adv.* With great honor: *She graduated magna cum laude.*

mag•na•nim•i•ty (măg′nə nĭm′ĭ tē) *n.* [U] *Formal.* The quality of being magnanimous: *The winner was admired for his magnanimity toward his opponent.*

mag•nan•i•mous (măg năn′ə məs) *adj. Formal.* Generous and unselfish: *a magnanimous person.* —**mag•nan′i•mous•ly** *adv.*

mag•nate (măg′nāt′ *or* măg′nĭt) *n.* A powerful and influential person, especially in business: *a real estate magnate.*

mag•ne•si•um (măg nē′zē əm *or* măg-nē′zhəm) *n.* [U] *Symbol* **Mg** A silvery metallic element that burns with an intense flame. Atomic number 12. See table at **element.**

mag•net (măg′nĭt) *n.* **1.** A stone, piece of metal, or other solid that attracts iron or steel through natural or electric power. **2.** An electromagnet. **3.** A person or place that has a powerful attraction: *Our garden is a magnet for rabbits.*

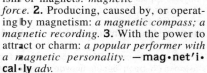

magnet

mag•net•ic (măg nĕt′ĭk) *adj.* **1.** Relating to magnetism or magnets: *magnetic force.* **2.** Producing, caused by, or operating by magnetism: *a magnetic compass; a magnetic recording.* **3.** With the power to attract or charm: *a popular performer with a magnetic personality.* —**mag•net′i•cal•ly** *adv.*

M

magnetic field *n.* A condition in the space around a magnet or an electric current in which a magnetic force exists.

magnetic pole *n.* Either of two points on the earth's surface toward which a compass needle points. The North Magnetic Pole is in the Arctic, and the South Magnetic Pole is in Antarctica.

mag•net•ism (măg′nĭ tĭz′ əm) *n.* [U] **1.** The properties or effects of magnets: *Magnetism causes a compass needle to point north.* **2.** The study of magnets and their effects. **3.** An unusual power to attract or influence: *The magnetism of the leader's personality drew many followers.*

mag•net•ize (măg′nĭ tīz′) *tr.v.* **mag•net•ized, mag•net•iz•ing, mag•net•iz•es.** To make (an object) magnetic: *Magnetize a nail by wrapping it in a wire that will carry an electric current.* —**mag′net•i•za′tion** (măg′nĭ tĭ zā′shən) *n.* [U]

mag•ni•fi•ca•tion (măg′nə fĭ kā′shən) *n.* [C; U] The act or degree of magnifying: *The biologist looked at the insect under magnification.*

mag•nif•i•cent (măg nĭf′ĭ sənt) *adj.* **1.** Grand; remarkable: *the king's magnificent palace.* **2.** Outstanding; excellent: *a magnificent athlete.* —**mag•nif′i•cence** *n.* [U] —**mag•nif′i•cent•ly** *adv.*

SYNONYMS: **magnificent, grand, majestic, imposing, grandiose.** These adjectives mean large and impressive. **Magnificent** means full of luxurious splendor on a large scale: *The Taj Mahal is a magnificent palace in India.* **Grand** and **majestic** suggest dignity or nobility: *The President welcomed the foreign officials with a grand ceremony. The mountain climbers struggled up the majestic Alps.* **Imposing** means impressive because of size, character, or power: *We stared up at the imposing statue of Abraham Lincoln.* **Grandiose** often means imposing in a negative way: *The politician's grandiose speech about world peace was nothing but empty words.*

mag•ni•fy (măg′nə fī′) *tr.v.* **mag•ni•fied, mag•ni•fy•ing, mag•ni•fies. 1.** To make (sthg.) appear larger than it really is: *A microscope magnifies cells so that scientists can study them.* **2.** To cause (sthg.) to appear greater or seem more important; exaggerate: *The wind magnifies the effect of the cold.* —**mag′ni•fi′er** *n.*

mag•ni•fy•ing glass (măg′nə fī′ĭng) *n.* A lens or combination of lenses that makes objects appear larger than they really are: *The investigator examined the fingerprints with a magnifying glass.*

mag•ni•tude (măg′nĭ tōōd′) *n.* [U] **1.**

Greatness of position, size, or importance: *Our boss finally understood the magnitude of the problem.* **2.** The relative brightness of a star or another celestial body. **3.** The force of an earthquake as measured on the Richter scale.

mag•no•lia (măg nōl′yə) *n.* Any of numerous evergreen trees or shrubs with large white, pink, or yellow flowers: *Magnolias are common in the South.*

ma•hog•a•ny (mə hŏg′ə nē) *n., pl.* **ma•hog•a•nies. 1.a.** [C] A tropical American tree with hard reddish brown wood. **b.** [U] The wood of such a tree, used for making furniture. **2.** [U] A reddish brown color. —*adj.* Reddish brown.

maid (mād) *n.* **1.** A female servant: *The maid does the laundry and cleans the house.* **2.** A term used in the past for an unmarried girl or young woman.

HOMONYMS: **maid, made** (created).

---

maid•en (mād′n) *n.* A term used in the past for an unmarried girl or young woman. —*adj.* **1.** A term used in the past to mean unmarried. Used of women: *a maiden aunt.* **2.** First or earliest: *a ship's maiden voyage.*

maid•en•hood (mād′n hŏŏd′) *n.* [U] The quality or condition of being a maiden.

maiden name *n.* A woman's family name before she changes it to her husband's name: *Mrs. Smith's maiden name was Jackson.*

maid of honor *n., pl.* **maids of honor.** An unmarried woman who is the bride's chief attendant at a wedding: *My sister was maid of honor at my wedding.*

mail¹ (māl) *n.* [U] **1.** Letters, postcards, packages, and printed material sent through the postal system of a country: *What came in the mail today?* **2.** A government system that handles the postal materials of a country: *the U.S. mail.* —*tr.v.* To send (sthg.) by mail: *I mailed him a letter.*

HOMONYMS: **mail** (postal material, armor), **male** (man).

---

mail² (māl) *n.* [U] Flexible armor made of connected metal rings or loops of chain: *In the Middle Ages, knights wore mail to protect themselves in battle.*

mail•box (māl′bŏks′) *n.* **1.** A public box for putting mail to be sent: *Please drop this letter in the mailbox.* **2.** A private box where incoming mail is delivered: *Did you check the mailbox?*

mail carrier *n.* A person who delivers mail or collects it from mailboxes: *Mail carriers work the same route each day.*

---

mail·er (mā′lər) *n.* An envelope or tube used to hold material to be mailed: *Put the disk in this mailer to send it.*

mail·ing (mā′lĭng) *n.* A batch of mail sent out at one time, usually for advertising or as notice to members of an organization: *The club sent out a new mailing to members.*

mail·man (māl′măn′ *or* māl′mən) *n.* A man who carries and delivers mail.

mail order *n.* [U] A request for goods to be shipped through the mail: *I saw this shirt in a catalog and bought it by mail order.*

maim (mām) *tr.v.* To disable (sbdy.), usually by causing the loss of the use of an arm or leg: *Accidents maim many people each year.*

main (mān) *adj.* Most important; principal: *Look for the main idea in each paragraph.* —*n.* A large pipe, duct, or conductor used to carry water, oil, gas, or electricity: *Workers repaired the broken water main.* ◆ **in the main.** For the most part: *Your ideas are, in the main, useful.*

<hr>

HOMONYMS: main, mane (neck hair).

<hr>

main clause *n.* In grammar, an independent clause that can stand alone.

main·frame (mān′frām′) *n.* A powerful computer that can quickly perform many operations and store large amounts of information: *Large companies often use mainframes that serve the entire company.*

main·land (mān′lănd′ *or* mān′lənd) *n.* (*usually singular*). The land mass of a country or continent without its islands: *A ferry runs between the island and the mainland.*

main·ly (mān′lē) *adv.* Most importantly; for the most part: *Homework for history class consists mainly of reading.*

main·spring (mān′sprĭng′) *n.* (*usually singular*). **1.** The spring that drives a mechanism, especially a clock or watch. **2.** The most important cause or force: *A desire for justice was the mainspring of the reform movement.*

main·stay (mān′stā′) *n.* A key person or element: *This player is the mainstay of the team. Meat and potatoes are the mainstays of his diet.*

main·stream (mān′strēm′) *n.* (*usually singular*). The current or most widely held ideas or beliefs in a group: *Her ideas are outside the mainstream.*

main·tain (mān tān′) *tr.v.* **1.** To continue (sthg.): *The train maintains its speed on hills.* **2.** To keep (sthg.) in good condition: *maintain public roads.* **3.** To pay the expenses of (sbdy./sthg.): *He maintains a large family.* **4.** To defend (sthg.): *She maintained her independence.* **5.** To say (sthg.) is true: *We maintain our innocence.*

main·te·nance (mān′tə nəns) *n.* [U] **1.** The act of maintaining: *maintenance of family*

traditions. **2.** The work involved in maintaining sthg.: *maintenance of an old building.*

maize (māz) *n.* [U] **1.** The corn plant or its edible kernels. **2.** A light to strong yellow color. —*adj.* Yellow.

<hr>

HOMONYMS: maize, maze (labyrinth).

<hr>

Maj. *abbr.* An abbreviation of major (military rank).

ma·jes·tic (mə jĕs′tĭk) *adj.* Having or showing majesty: *the majestic Rocky Mountain peaks.* See Synonyms at **magnificent.** —**ma·jes′tic·al·ly** *adv.*

maj·es·ty (măj′ĭ stē) *n., pl.* **maj·es·ties. 1.** [U] Magnificence, splendor, or grandeur: *the majesty of the Rocky Mountains.* **2.** [C] **Majesty.** Used as a title for a sovereign, such as a king or queen: *Your Majesty.*

ma·jor (mā′jər) *adj.* **1.** Greater or more important than others: *a major American novelist.* **2.** Relating to a major musical scale: *a major chord.* —*n.* **1.** In schools and colleges, a field of study chosen as a specialty: *My major is French.* **2.** An officer in the military ranking above a captain and below a colonel. —*intr.v.* [*in*] To study or specialize in a subject: *I am majoring in Spanish.*

ma·jor·i·ty (mə jôr′ĭ tē *or* mə jŏr′ĭ tē) *n., pl.* **ma·jor·i·ties. 1.** [U] The greater number or part of sthg.: *The majority of the class did well on the test.* **2.** [C] (*usually singular*). The number of votes by which a candidate wins: *The candidate won by a majority of 5,000 votes.* **3.** [U] The age of legal responsibility, usually 18 or 21.

<hr>

USAGE: majority When **majority** refers to a number of votes, it takes a singular verb: *Her majority was five votes.* When it refers to a group of persons or things, it may take either a singular or plural verb. It depends on whether the group is considered as a whole or as a set of people considered individually. So we say *The majority elects the candidate it wants,* because the group acts as a whole; but we say *The majority of the voters live in the city,* because living in the city is sthg. that each voter does individually.

<hr>

major league *n.* A league of principal importance in professional sports in the United States.

ma·jor-league (mā′jər lēg′) *adj.* **1.** Relating to a major league: *a major-league player.* **2.** Excellent or outstanding: *a major-league performance.*

make (māk) *v.* **made** (mād), **mak·ing, makes.** —*tr.* **1.** To cause (sthg.) to exist or happen; create: *make noise; make a wall of stones; make rules.* **2.** To cause (sbdy.) to be or become: *The invitation made us happy.* **3.** To cause (sbdy.) to act in a specified way: *The pepper made me*

M

sneeze. His mother made him stay home. **4.** To prepare (sthg.): *make breakfast.* **5.** To perform, complete, or engage in (sthg.): *make a telephone call; make war.* **6.** To reach (sthg.) in time: *We just made the bus.* **7.** To gain or acquire (sthg.): *make money; make friends.* **8.** To be suited for (sthg.): *This area would make a good soccer field.* **9.** To develop into (sthg.): *She will make a fine doctor.* **10.** To form or add up to (sthg.): *Two and two make four.* —*intr.* **1.** To cause sthg. to be in a specified manner: *The actors made ready for the play.* **2.** To go or move in a certain direction: *make for home; make after the thief.* —*n.* **1.** A style or manner in which sthg. is made: *She disliked the make of the coat.* **2.** A specific line of manufactured goods; a brand: *Three makes of small trucks are available.* ◆ **make away with.** To carry (sthg.) off; steal: *Thieves made away with the jewels.* **make believe.** To pretend: *The children made believe they were cowboys.* **make do.** [*with*] To manage; get along: *We'll have to make do with what little time we have.* **make ends meet.** To make enough money to pay one's expenses: *We can't seem to make ends meet.* **make for.** *tr.v.* [insep.] To be favorable to or promote (sthg.): *The steady breeze made for excellent sailing.* **make fun of.** To make jokes about or ridicule (sbdy./sthg.): *Please don't make fun of me.* **make good.** **1.** To perform sthg. successfully: *He made good his escape.* **2.** To make compensation for sthg.; make up for: *It was his fault, so he made good the loss.* **3.** To succeed: *She made good as an artist.* **make it.** *Informal.* To be successful: *You'll never make it as an actor.* **make light of.** To treat (sthg.) as unimportant: *He made light of his promotion.* **make love.** To have sexual intercourse: *The couple made love.* **make much of.** To treat (sbdy./sthg.) as very important: *They all made much of the baby's first tooth.* **make off with.** To quickly take or steal (sthg.): *The thief made off with the woman's purse.* **make out.** *tr.v.* [sep.] **1.** To see or identify (sbdy./sthg.), especially with difficulty: *Can you make out that sign?* **2.** To understand (sthg.): *I can't make out what she means in the letter.* **3.** To write out or fill out (sthg.): *make out a tax form.* —*intr.v.* **1.** To get along or progress in a given way: *How are you making out with the dance lessons?* **2.** *Slang.* To kiss and touch like lovers: *They made out after the dance.* **make over.** *tr.v.* [sep.] **1.** To redo or renovate (sthg): *make over the kitchen of an old house.* **2.** To change or transfer the ownership of (sthg.), usually by means of a legal document: *They made the house over to their children.* **make (sthg.) of.** To give a label of importance or

meaning to (an event or a situation): *Let's not make an issue of her mistake. I don't know what to make of this news.* **make the best of.** To treat (a bad situation) in a positive way: *We'll have to make the best of the fact that she can't afford the trip.* **make the most of.** To use (sthg.) to the greatest advantage: *She had only one chance to talk to the boss, so she made the most of it.* **make up.** *tr.v.* [sep.] **1.** To put (sthg.) together; construct or compose: *We made up a model of the new building.* **2.** To compose or form (sthg.): *A basketball team is made up of five players.* **3.** To apply cosmetics to (sbdy./sthg.): *make up an actor to look older.* **4.** To create (sthg.) as a fiction or falsehood; invent: *make up a story.* **5.** To compensate for (sthg.): *We made up the lost time by taking a shortcut.* **6.** To take (an examination or a course) again or at a later time. —*intr.v.* To put an end to a quarrel: *They talked over their differences and made up.* **make up (one's) mind.** To come to a definite decision or opinion: *I couldn't make up my mind about which car to buy.*

make-be•lieve (māk'bĭ lēv') *n.* [U] Playful imagining: *Fairies exist in the land of make-believe.* —*adj.* Imaginary; fictional: *The little girl poured some make-believe tea.*

mak•er (mā'kər) *n.* **1.** A person or thing that makes sthg.: *a shirt maker; the maker of fine furniture.* **2. Maker.** ◆ **go to meet (one's) Maker.** To die: *She went to meet her Maker at peace with herself.*

make•shift (māk'shĭft') *adj.* Serving as a temporary substitute until sthg. better is available: *We used the box as a makeshift table.*

make•up or **make-up** (māk'ŭp') *n.* **1.** [U] Cosmetics, especially for the face. **2.** [U] The way in which sthg. is put together: *What is the makeup of the police department?* **3.** [C] *(usually singular).* The qualities that make up a personality: *It's just not in her makeup to complain.*

mak•ing (mā'kĭng) *n.* [U] The act of creating or producing sthg.: *the making of a film; dressmaking.* ◆ **(all) the makings.** The materials needed to make or do sthg.: *We have all the makings for an apple pie.* **have the makings of.** To show the abilities or qualities needed to become (sthg.): *She has the makings of a fine teacher.* **in the making.** Developing; coming into existence: *He sensed trouble in the making.*

mal— *pref.* A prefix that means bad or wrongly: *malpractice; malformed.*

mal•ad•just•ed (măl'ə jŭs'tĭd) *adj.* Poorly adjusted to one's environment or to one's circumstances: *a maladjusted child who doesn't play well with others.* —**mal'ad•just'ment** *n.* [U]

mal•a•dy (măl′ə dē) *n.*, *pl.* **mal•a•dies.** *Formal.* A disease, a disorder, or an ailment: *a rare malady.*

mal•aise (mă lāz′) *n.* [U] *Formal.* **1.** A vague feeling of physical discomfort or illness: *The patient complained of malaise, but had no specific symptoms.* **2.** A general sense of depression or discomfort: *a malaise among employees after the slowdown of production.*

mal•a•prop•ism (măl′ə prŏp ĭz′əm) *n.* A funny misuse of a word, especially by confusion with a similar sound: *The comic was famous for using malapropisms.*

ma•lar•i•a (mə lâr′ē ə) *n.* [U] An infectious disease characterized by chills, fever, and sweating: *Malaria is passed from one person to another by mosquito bites.* —**ma•lar′i•al** *adj.*

mal•con•tent (măl′kən tĕnt′) *n.* A dissatisfied or rebellious person: *You shouldn't listen to anything he says about politics; he's a terrible malcontent.*

male (māl) *adj.* **1.** Relating to the sex that can fertilize egg cells and father offspring. **2.** Composed of men or boys: *a male singing group.* **3.** In machines and tools, designed to make a connection by fitting into an opening: *a male plug.* —*n.* **1.** A man or boy: *The dance company includes both males and females.* **2.** A male animal. —**male′ness** *n.* [U]

HOMONYMS: **male, mail** (postal material, armor).

ma•lev•o•lent (mə lĕv′ə lənt) *adj. Formal.* Wishing harm to others; malicious: *fear of a malevolent spirit.* —**ma•lev′o•lence** *n.* [U] —**ma•lev′o•lent•ly** *adv.*

mal•formed (măl fôrmd′) *adj.* With an imperfect or abnormal form: *Disease causes malformed ears of corn.* —**mal′for•ma′tion** (măl′fôr mā′shən) *n.* [C; U]

mal•func•tion (măl fŭngk′shən) *intr.v.* To fail to work properly: *The flight was delayed because the engine malfunctioned.* —*n.* [C; U] A failure to work well: *a computer malfunction.*

mal•ice (măl′ĭs) *n.* [U] The desire to harm others or to see others suffer: *She felt malice toward the people who hurt her.*

ma•li•cious (mə lĭsh′əs) *adj.* Showing, feeling, or motivated by malice: *She tried to hurt me with a malicious lie.* —**ma•li′cious•ly** *adv.* —**ma•li′cious•ness** *n.* [U]

ma•lign (mə līn′) *tr.v.* To speak evil of (sbdy./sthg.): *malign a person's reputation.*

ma•lig•nan•cy (mə lĭg′nən sē) *n.*, *pl.* **ma•lig•nan•cies.** **1.** [U] The quality or condition of being malignant. **2.** [C] A malignant tumor or condition.

ma•lig•nant (mə lĭg′nənt) *adj.* **1.** Tending to grow and spread throughout the body; cancerous: *a malignant tumor.* **2.** Feeling a desire to hurt others; malicious: *malignant thoughts.* —**ma•lig′nant•ly** *adv.*

ma•lin•ger (mə lĭng′gər) *intr.v.* To pretend to be ill or injured in order to avoid work or duty: *Her boss suspected her of malingering.* —**ma•lin′ger•er** *n.*

mall (môl) *n.* **1.** A large shopping center containing different kinds of stores and businesses: *Do you prefer shopping at the mall or downtown?* **2.** A street lined with stores, where cars are not allowed: *a pedestrian mall.*

HOMONYMS: **mall, maul** (injure).

mal•lard (măl′ərd) *n.* A type of wild duck.

mal•le•a•ble (măl′ē ə bəl) *adj.* **1.** Capable of being shaped by pressure or hammering: *Copper is a malleable metal.* **2.** Easily controlled or influenced: *The boss wanted a malleable assistant.* —**mal′le•a•bil′i•ty** *n.* [U]

mal•let (măl′ĭt) *n.* **1.** A hammer with a wooden head and a short handle. **2.** A long-handled hammer used to strike the ball in the games of croquet and polo.

mal•nour•ished (măl nûr′ĭsht *or* măl nŭr′-ĭsht) *adj.* Suffering from a lack of nutritious food: *Emergency food shipments were sent to the malnourished people in the refugee camps.*

mal•nu•tri•tion (măl′nōō trĭsh′ən) *n.* [U] A condition in which the body does not have the necessary foods: *The refugee children were suffering from malnutrition.*

mal•o•dor•ous (măl ō′dər əs) *adj. Formal.* Having a bad odor: *a malodorous swamp.*

mal•prac•tice (măl prăk′tĭs) *n.* [U] Improper, careless, or illegal behavior by a doctor or another professional: *The lawyer was accused of malpractice and lost many clients.*

malt (môlt) *n.* [U] Barley or other grain that has been allowed to sprout, used chiefly in brewing beer.

malt•ed (môl′tĭd) *adj.* Mixed, flavored, or prepared with malt: *malted milk chocolates.*

mal•treat (măl trēt′) *tr.v.* To treat (sbdy./ sthg.) cruelly: *They were fined for maltreating their animals.* —**mal•treat′ment** *n.* [U]

ma•ma (mä′mə *or* mə mä′) *n. Informal.* Mother.

mam•mal (măm′əl) *n.* Any of various warm-blooded animals that have a backbone, hair or fur, and that feed their young with milk: *Cats, dogs, cows, elephants, whales, and human beings are all mammals.* —**mam•ma′li•an** (mă mā′lē ən) *adj. & n.*

mam•mo•gram (măm′ə grăm′) *n.* An x-ray image of the human breast.

mam•moth (măm′əth) *n.* An extinct elephant that had long tusks and thick hair and that lived during the Ice Age. —*adj.* Huge; gigantic: *a mammoth project.*

man (măn) *n.*, *pl.* **men** (měn). **1.** An adult male human being: *Boys grow into men.* **2.** A human being without regard to sex or age:

M

The foreman put another man on the job. **3.** Human beings considered as a group; humanity: *Scientific research has benefited man.* **4.** A male person with qualities, such as bravery or strength, considered characteristic of manhood: *He is her idea of a real man.* **5.** A husband or lover: *She won't leave her man.* **6.** A piece used in a board game, such as chess or checkers: *I put my man on the wrong square.* —*tr.v.* **manned, man•ning, mans. 1.** To take one's place at (sthg.); work or operate: *Over the holiday, there weren't enough people to man the office.* **2.** To supply (sthg.) with men: *The captain manned the ship with a new crew of sailors.* ♦ **the man in the street.** A person who represents people in general; an average person: *How will the man in the street view the election results?* **to a man.** Without exception: *They supported the new labor contract to a man.*

USAGE: man The use of **man** to mean "a human being of either gender" has a long history, but many feel that the sense of "male" dominates the sense of "human being," making this use sexist. For that reason, many job titles in which **man** occurs are being replaced by neutral terms. For example, *firefighter* is often used instead of *fireman* and *Member of Congress* replaces *Congressman.* In addition, compounds formed with **woman,** as in *businesswoman, policewoman,* and *chairwoman,* are now used as parallel terms to the compounds formed with **man.**

---

man•a•cle (măn′ə kəl) *n. (usually plural).* Handcuffs. —*tr.v.* **man•a•cled, man•a•cling, man•a•cles.** To put manacles on (sbdy.): *The police officer manacled the thief.*

man•age (măn′ĭj) *v.* **man•aged, man•ag•ing, man•ag•es.** —*tr.* **1.** To have control over (sbdy./sthg.); be in charge of: *She manages a restaurant.* **2.** To succeed in doing or accomplishing (sthg.): *Despite the bitter cold, I managed to stay warm.* —*intr.* **1.** To direct business affairs: *The book offers advice to executives on how to manage effectively.* **2.** To carry on; get along: *I don't know how we managed without your help.*

man•age•a•ble (măn′ĭ jə bəl) *adj.* Capable of being handled or controlled: *a manageable problem.* —**man′age•a•bil′i•ty** *n.* [U]

man•age•ment (măn′ĭj mənt) *n.* [U] **1.** The act of managing: *hotel management.* **2.** The persons who manage a business or an organization: *I talked to the management.*

man•ag•er (măn′ĭ jər) *n.* **1.** A person who is in charge of a business. **2.** A person who is in charge of the business affairs of an entertainer or of the training of an athlete or a

team: *The musicians consulted their manager before signing the contract.* —**man′a•ge′-ri•al** (măn′ĭ jîr′ē əl) *adj.*

man•a•tee (măn′ə tē′) *n.* A large plant-eating water mammal found along the tropical Atlantic coast.

man•date (măn′dāt) *n.* **1.** The support of the voters given to their representatives through an election: *a broad mandate for change.* **2.** An official order or instruction, especially one issued by a court. —*tr.v.* **man•dat•ed, man•dat•ing, man•dates.** To make (sthg.) mandatory; require: *The law mandates desegregation in all schools.*

man•da•to•ry (măn′də tôr′ē) *adj.* Required; obligatory: *A college degree is mandatory for most teaching jobs.*

man•di•ble (măn′də bəl) *n.* **1.** A jaw of a vertebrate, especially the bone of the lower jaw. **2.** An organ in the mouth of many insects for seizing and biting food.

man•do•lin (măn′də lĭn′ *or* măn′dl ĭn) *n.* A musical instrument with a body shaped like a pear and four pairs of strings.

mane (mān) *n.* The long hair on the neck and head of certain animals, such as a horse or a male lion.

HOMONYMS: mane, main (chief).

---

ma•neu•ver (mə nōō′vər) *n.* **1.a.** A planned movement of troops or of an airplane or a ship: *By a series of brilliant maneuvers, the general defeated the enemy.* **b.** *(usually plural).* A large-scale military exercise to practice battle movements: *The soldiers are on maneuvers.* **2.** A movement or procedure that involves skill or cunning: *a political maneuver that gained him power.* —*v.* —*intr.* **1.** To use tactics to try to gain sthg.; plan skillfully: *Our lawyer maneuvered in order to get the trial postponed.* **2.** To make planned changes in movement or direction: *The ship had to maneuver very carefully to avoid the icebergs.* —*tr.* **1.** To direct (sthg.) skillfully by changes in course or in position: *They taught me how to maneuver a car on an icy road.* **2.** To manage or direct (sbdy./sthg.), especially by tricks: *She maneuvered her opponent into taking a position that lost him the election.* —**ma•neu′ver•a•bil′i•ty** *n.* [U] —**ma•neu′ver•a•ble** *adj.*

man•ga•nese (măng′gə nēz′) *n.* [U] *Symbol* **Mn** A gray brittle metallic element used in making steel alloys and other industrial products. Atomic number 25. See table at **element.**

mange (mānj) *n.* [U] A skin disease of dogs and other mammals, characterized by itching and loss of hair.

---

man·ger (mān′jər) n. An open box in which feed for horses or cattle is placed.

man·gle (măng′gəl) tr.v. **man·gled, man·gling, man·gles. 1.** To ruin the appearance of (sthg.) by crushing or tearing: *The accident mangled our car terribly.* **2.** To ruin or spoil (sthg.): *The orchestra completely mangled the music.*

man·go (măng′gō) n., pl. **man·goes** or **man·gos.** A tropical tree and its fruit with a smooth rind and sweet, juicy, yellow-orange flesh.

man·grove (măn′grōv′ or măng′grōv′) n. A tropical tree or shrub with many roots growing above the ground that look like extra trunks.

mang·y (mān′jē) adj. **mang·i·er, mang·i·est. 1.** Having or appearing to have mange: *a mangy dog.* **2.** With many bare spots; shabby: *a mangy old coat.* —**man′gi·ness** n. [U]

man·han·dle (măn′hăn′dl) tr.v. **man·han·dled, man·han·dling, man·han·dles.** To handle (sbdy./sthg.) in a rough way: *The porters manhandled the suitcases.*

man·hole (măn′hōl′) n. A hole in a street, with a removable cover, that allows a person to reach underground pipes or other structures for repair or inspection.

man·hood (măn′hŏŏd′) n. [U] **1.** The condition of being an adult male person: *He has reached manhood.* **2.** Male qualities: *Courage is often considered essential to one's manhood.*

man-hour (măn′our′) n. The work that can be done by one person in one hour, used to measure industrial production and costs.

ma·ni·a (mā′nē ə) n. **1.** [C] An intense enthusiasm: *He has a mania for horror movies.* **2.** [U] A form of mental illness in which a patient becomes excessively active and has rapidly changing ideas.

ma·ni·ac (mā′nē ăk′) n. **1.** An insane person. **2.** A person who acts in a wildly irresponsible way: *There are too many maniacs driving cars.* —**ma·ni·a·cal** (mə nī′ə kəl) adj.

man·ic (măn′ĭk) adj. Relating to mania: *a manic-depressive patient.*

man·i·cure (măn′ĭ kyŏŏr′) n. A cosmetic treatment for the fingernails, including shaping and polishing: *She got a manicure.* —tr.v. **man·i·cured, man·i·cur·ing, man·i·cures.** To trim, clean, and polish (the fingernails): *She manicures her nails once a week.* —**man′i·cur′ist** n.

man·i·fest (măn′ə fĕst′) adj. Formal. Clear and plain to see; obvious: *His pleasure in receiving the invitation was manifest.* —tr.v. Formal. To reveal (sthg.); show: *Her nervous gestures manifested her discomfort with the situation.* —n. A list of cargo or passengers: *Customs officials checked the ship's manifest.* —**man′i·fest·ly** adv.

man·i·fes·ta·tion (măn′ə fĕ stā′shən) n. [C; U] Formal. **1.** The showing or proving of sthg.: *a manifestation of bravery.* **2.** Something that shows a sign: *Rust on the pipes was a manifestation of leaks.*

man·i·fes·to (măn′ə fĕs′tō) n., pl. **man·i·fes·toes** or **man·i·fes·tos.** Formal. A public statement of principles and aims, especially of a political nature: *The leaders published the party's manifesto.*

man·i·fold (măn′ə fōld′) adj. Of many kinds; with many parts: *A knowledge of many subjects demonstrates manifold intelligence.* —n. A pipe or tube that has several openings for multiple connections: *The exhaust manifold of an engine connects to each cylinder.*

ma·nil·a or **ma·nil·la** (mə nĭl′ə) n. [U] Stiff paper or thin cardboard, of a yellow or brown color. —adj. Made of this kind of paper: *a manila envelope.*

ma·nip·u·late (mə nĭp′yə lāt′) tr.v. **ma·nip·u·lat·ed, ma·nip·u·lat·ing, ma·nip·u·lates. 1.** To operate or control (sthg.), especially with skill: *The pilot manipulated the controls of the airplane.* **2.** To influence or manage (sbdy./sthg.) in a clever or dishonest way: *He manipulated public opinion in his favor.* —**ma·nip′u·la′tion** n. [C; U] —**ma·nip′u·la′tive** (mə nĭp′yə lā′tĭv or mə nĭp′yə lə′tĭv) adj. —**ma·nip′u·la′tor** n.

man·kind (măn′kīnd′) n. [U] The human race; humankind.

USAGE: mankind The word **mankind** has long been used to mean "the human race," but many people feel it is a sexist term and prefer to use the term **humankind.**

man·ly (măn′lē) adj. **man·li·er, man·li·est.** With qualities traditionally seen as good and right for a man: *manly courage.* —**man′li·ness** n. [U]

man-made (măn′mād′) adj. Made by human beings rather than by nature; synthetic: *a man-made lake.*

manned (mănd) adj. Occupied or operated by a person: *manned spacecraft.*

man·ne·quin (măn′ĭ kĭn) n. A life-size model of the human body, used mainly for displaying clothes: *a mannequin in a shop window.*

man·ner (măn′ər) n. **1.** (usually singular). The way sthg. is done or happens: *We always work in a careful manner.* See Synonyms at **method. 2.** (usually singular). A way of acting; behavior: *The new boss has a friendly manner.* **3. manners.** Proper behavior with other people; etiquette: *Did no one ever teach him able manners?* ◆ **all manner of.** Many kinds of: *We had all manner of problems on our long trip.* **in a manner of speaking.** Not exactly but in a way: *His brother is his financial advisor, in a manner of speaking.*

HOMONYMS: manner, manor (estate).

man•nered (măn′ərd) *adj.* With manners of a specific kind: *ill-mannered people.*

man•ner•ism (măn′ə rĭz′əm) *n.* A distinctive personal gesture or habit, especially one that is exaggerated; a quirk: *People say I have a mannerism of scratching my chin.*

man•ner•ly (măn′ər lē) *adj.* With good manners; polite: *a mannerly boy.* See Synonyms at **polite.**

man•nish (măn′ĭsh) *adj.* Resembling or suitable for a man rather than a woman; masculine: *She has a rather mannish way of walking.* —**man′nish•ly** *adv.* —**man′nish•ness** *n.* [U]

man•or (măn′ər) *n.* **1.** A large fine house and its lands. **2.** The main house on an estate.

HOMONYMS: manor, manner (way of acting).

man•pow•er (măn′pou′ər) *n.* [U] **1.** The power supplied by human physical effort: *Lifting that piano requires a lot of manpower.* **2.** The people working or available for work: *Most of the company's manpower is now used to develop new products.*

man•sion (măn′shən) *n.* A large stately house: *He inherited a mansion from his rich aunt.*

man•slaugh•ter (măn′slô′tər) *n.* [U] The killing of a person without meaning to do so, as when a driver accidentally kills a person on the street.

man•tel also **man•tle** (măn′tl) *n.* A decorative shelf over a fireplace.

man•tis (măn′tĭs) *n.* A large insect that looks somewhat like a grasshopper. Mantises prey on other insects and hold their front legs up as if praying.

man•tle (măn′tl) *n.* **1.** Something that covers or conceals sthg. else: *a soft mantle of snow on the houses.* **2.** The layer of the earth between the crust and the core. **3.** Variant of **mantel.**

man•u•al (măn′yōō əl) *adj.* **1.** Relating to the hands: *a job requiring fine manual skills.* **2.** Operated with the hands: *manual controls.* —*n.* A small book of instructions: *Read the manual before setting up the computer.* —**man′u•al•ly** *adv.*

man•u•fac•ture (măn′yə făk′chər) *tr.v.* **man•u•fac•tured, man•u•fac•tur•ing, man•u•fac•tures.** To make or process (a product), especially with the use of machines: *a factory that manufactures cars.* —*n.* [U] The act of manufacturing products: *The manufacture of computer chips requires a clean, dust-free environment.*

man•u•fac•tur•er (măn′yə făk′chər ər) *n.* A person or company that manufactures sthg., especially the owner of a factory: *Manufacturers met to discuss changes in pollution laws.*

ma•nure (mə nŏŏr′) *n.* [U] Animal dung, especially the dung of cattle, often used as fertilizer.

man•u•script (măn′yə skrĭpt′) *n.* **1.** The form of a book or an article before it is published: *You should send your manuscript to a publisher.* **2.** A book or document written by hand, especially one made before the invention of printing: *a rare twelfth-century manuscript.*

man•y (mĕn′ē) *adj.* **more** (môr), **most** (mōst). *(used with count nouns).* **1.** Amounting to a large number; numerous: *Many friends were at the party.* **2.** Being one of a large number: *Many a person has failed that class.* —*n. (used with a plural verb).* A large number of persons or things: *Many of us were at the party.* —*pron. (used with a plural verb).* A large number of persons or things: *Many were invited but few came.* ◆ **a good** or **great many.** A lot: *A good many people drive carelessly.* **one too many.** One more than is correct or acceptable: *She has tricked us one too many times.*

map (măp) *n.* A drawing or chart of a place on the earth, often showing political divisions such as countries and physical features such as roads, mountains, and rivers. —*tr.v.* **mapped, map•ping, maps.** To make a map of (a place): *Early explorers mapped this region.* ◆ **map out.** *tr.v.* [sep.] To plan (sthg.) in detail: *Let's map out our schedule.* **put on the map.** To cause (a place) to be important: *The concert put our town on the map.* **wipe off the map.** To destroy (a place) completely: *The earthquake wiped many villages off the map.*

ma•ple (mā′pəl) *n.* **1.** [C] A tall tree with broad leaves that produces a sweet sap. **2.** [U] The hard wood of a maple, often used in making furniture.

maple syrup *n.* [U] A sweet syrup made from the sap of the sugar maple tree: *a breakfast of pancakes with maple syrup.*

mar (mär) *tr.v.* **marred, mar•ring, mars.** To spoil, ruin, or damage (sthg.): *I accidentally marred the top of the table with a knife.*

Mar. *abbr.* An abbreviation of March.

mar•a•thon (măr′ə thŏn′) *n.* **1.** A cross-country footrace of 26 miles, 385 yards (41.3 kilometers). **2.** A contest of endurance: *a dance marathon.*

ma•raud•ing (mə rô′dĭng) *adj.* Roaming in search of sthg. to steal or destroy: *Homes were burned and crops destroyed by marauding soldiers.* —**ma•raud′er** *n.*

mar•ble (mär′bəl) *n.* **1.** [U] A type of hard stone used for buildings, sculpture, and monuments. **2.a.** [C] A small ball made of a hard substance such as glass. **b. marbles.** *(used with a singular verb).* A children's game played with small glass balls. —*adj.* Made of or looking like marble: *a marble floor; marble cake.*

march (märch) *v.* —*intr.* **1.** To walk with regular forceful steps, as in a parade: *The band marched down the street.* **2.** To advance with a steady movement: *Time marches on.* —*tr.* To cause (sbdy./sthg.) to walk quickly: *The duck marched its ducklings to the edge of the lake.* —*n.* **1.** The act of marching: *the army's rapid march to the fort.* **2.** The distance covered by marching: *We were still a two-hour march from camp.* **3.** *(usually singular).* Forward movement; progress: *the dramatic march of modern science.* **4.** A piece of music written for marching.

March (märch) *n.* The third month of the year, with 31 days.

Mar•di gras or **Mar•di Gras** (mär′dē grä′) *n.* The day before Lent, celebrated as a holiday in many places with carnivals and parades: *New Orleans is famous for its Mardi gras parades.*

mare (mâr) *n.* An adult female horse or donkey: *The mare and her foal were in the pasture.*

mar•ga•rine (mär′jər ĭn) *n.* [U] A food used like butter, made from vegetable oils and other ingredients: *You can use either margarine or butter in the cake.*

mar•gin (mär′jĭn) *n.* **1.** The blank space around the written or printed area on a page: *Leave one-inch margins on the right and left of your paper.* **2.** An extra amount beyond what is needed: *You should allow a ten-minute margin for delays in getting to school.* **3.** A difference between two amounts: *We won the election by a large margin.* **4.** *(usually plural).* An edge or a border: *the margins of the forest.*

SYNONYMS: margin, border, edge, brink, rim. These nouns mean the line or narrow area that marks the outside limit of sthg. **Margin** means an outside area that is different somehow from the inside: *Flowers grow along the margin of the field.* **Border** can mean a boundary line: *The farmer built a fence along the border of the property.* **Edge** can mean the precise line where two different surfaces meet: *Move your cup away from the edge of the table.* **Brink** means the upper edge of sthg. steep: *We looked down from the brink of the canyon.* **Rim** often means the edge of sthg. that is circular or curved: *There is a small crack in the rim of the glass.*

---

mar•gin•al (mär′jə nəl) *adj.* **1.** Written or printed in the margin: *marginal notes through the whole book.* **2.** Barely acceptable: *marginal writing ability.* **3.** Making little profit: *a marginal business.* —**mar′gin•al•ly** *adv.*

mar•i•gold (mär′ĭ gōld′) *n.* A common garden plant with orange, yellow, or reddish flowers.

mar•i•jua•na (mär′ə wä′nə) *n.* [U] The hemp plant or its dried leaves or flowers, which contain an intoxicating drug: *Marijuana is an illegal substance.*

ma•ri•na (mə rē′nə) *n.* An area of a harbor that has docks, supplies, and repair facilities for small boats.

mar•i•nade (mär′ə nād′) *n.* [C; U] A mixture of oil, vinegar or wine, and spices, used to soak meat, fish, or vegetables before cooking.

mar•i•nate (mär′ə nāt′) *tr.v.* **mar•i•nat•ed, mar•i•nat•ing, mar•i•nates.** To soak (food) in a marinade: *Marinate the chicken for at least an hour.*

ma•rine (mə rēn′) *adj.* **1.** Relating to the sea: *marine biology.* **2.** Living in the sea: *marine life.* **3.** Relating to shipping or navigation: *a marine chart.* —*n.* **Marine.** A member of the U.S. Marine Corps.

Marine Corps *n.* A branch of the U.S. armed forces whose troops are specially trained for fighting on land and sea.

mar•i•ner (mär′ə nər) *n. Formal.* A sailor.

mar•i•o•nette (mär′ē ə nĕt′) *n.* A puppet moved by strings or wires attached to its arms, legs, and head.

mar•i•tal (mär′ĭ tl) *adj.* Relating to marriage: *What is your marital status?*

mar•i•time (mär′ĭ tīm′) *adj.* **1.** Located near the sea: *a maritime fishing village.* **2.** Relating to shipping or navigation by sea: *maritime law.*

mar•jo•ram (mär′jər əm) *n.* [U] A plant that is related to the mint, with leaves used in cooking.

mark¹ (märk) *n.* **1.** A visible line or spot, left on a surface: *The mug left a wet mark on the table.* **2.** A written symbol used in punctuation: *a question mark.* **3.** A letter or number used to show the quality of a person's work: *excellent marks in arithmetic.* **4.** A sign of some quality: *Taking responsibility for your own mistakes is a mark of maturity.* **5.** Something that is aimed at; a target: *The arrow found its mark.* **6.** A starting line or position, as in a track race: *The runners went to their marks at the starter's signal.* —*v.* —*tr.* **1.** To make a mark on (sthg.): *Someone had marked the important pages of the book.* **2.** To form, make, or write (sthg.) by a mark: *We marked a square in the garden.* **3.** To give evidence of (sthg.); signal: *The cool winds mark the beginning of fall.* **4.** To be a feature of (sthg.); characterize: *Her painting is marked by an unusual use of color.* **5.** To determine the quality of (sthg.) according to a grade: *The teacher is marking the tests now.* —*intr.* To give grades for school work: *I've never had a teacher who marks easily.*

♦ **make (one's) mark.** To have an influence or make an impression: *Her singing helped* *her make her mark on Broadway.* **mark down.** *tr.v.* [sep.] To mark (sthg.) for sale at a lower price: *All shoes are marked down 50%.* **mark off.** *tr.v.* [sep.] To define an area for (sthg.) by making marks: *We marked off a six-foot square for the garden.* **mark time. 1.** To move the feet in a marching step without advancing. **2.** To wait and do nothing: *The building crew marked time while the architects changed the plans.* **mark up.** *tr.v.* [sep.] **1.** To cover (sthg.) with marks: *An editor marked up the article with a red pen.* **2.** To mark (sthg.) for sale at a higher price: *Blankets are marked up in October.*

mark² (märk) *n.* The currency of Germany.

mark·down (märk′doun′) *n.* A reduction in price: *a 40% markdown on sofas.*

marked (märkt) *adj.* **1.** Having a mark or marks: *Pedestrians use the marked crosswalk.* **2.** Noticeable; easily seen: *a marked difference in price.* **3.** Selected for terrible punishment: *a marked man.*

mark·ed·ly (mär′kĭd lē) *adv.* In a manner that is easily seen: *When he worked hard, his grades improved markedly.*

mark·er (mär′kər) *n.* **1.** A thick, often colored pen used to write or draw marks on a surface: *We used markers to make posters for the science fair.* **2.** Something that marks a place: *a mile marker.*

mar·ket (mär′kĭt) *n.* **1.a.** A regular public meeting for buying and selling goods: *The farmer took vegetables to the Saturday market.* **b.** A place where goods are offered for sale: *We walked by the market before going home.* **2.** The stock market: *The market has been down lately.* **3.** The business of buying and selling a particular product: *the international coffee market.* **4.a.** A region or country where goods are sold: *We produce computers for foreign markets.* **b.** A particular group of buyers: *The college market includes people 16 to 22 years old.* **5.** A desire to buy; demand: *There is always a market for our bicycles.* —*tr.v.* To sell or offer (sthg.) for sale: *The company markets its products in Canada and Mexico.* ◆ **a buyer's** or **seller's market.** Conditions that are favorable to either buyers or sellers: *It's a good time to get a new car because it's a buyer's market.* **in the market.** [*for*] Interested in buying: *We are in the market for a new car.* **on the market. 1.** Available for buying: *There are several good brands of skis on the market.* **2.** For sale: *He put the family business on the market.* —**mar′ket·er** *n.*

mar·ket·a·ble (mär′kĭ tə bəl) *adj.* Ready for sale or of interest to purchasers or employers: *She has many marketable skills.* —**mar′ket·a·bil′i·ty** *n.* [U]

mar·ket·ing (mär′kĭ tĭng) *n.* [U] The business activity involved in selling, advertising, and packaging products: *The company president has a genius for marketing.*

mar·ket·place (mär′kĭt plās′) *n.* **1.** An open public area where products are sold: *We bought oranges when we visited the marketplace.* **2.** The general process of buying and selling; business activities: *New U.S. trade laws affect the international marketplace.*

mark·ing (mär′kĭng) *n.* The special colors on an animal or a plant: *a bird with beautiful markings.*

marks·man·ship (märks′mən shĭp′) *n.* [U] Skill at shooting a gun or another weapon. —**marks′man, marks′wom′an** (märks′wŏom′ən) *n.*

mark·up (märk′ŭp′) *n.* **1.** [C] The amount added to the cost of an item by a store to figure its selling price: *If you can buy from the manufacturer, you don't have to pay the store's markup.* **2.** [U] Annotation of a text's structural features for print or electronic publication.

mar·ma·lade (mär′mə lād′) *n.* [U] A jam made from citrus fruits: *orange marmalade.*

ma·roon¹ (mə rōōn′) *tr.v.* **1.** To put (sbdy.) off a boat and onto an island with no people: *The sailor was marooned on the island for three months.* **2.** To leave (sbdy.) alone and helpless: *I was marooned with a cold while everyone else went skating.*

ma·roon² (mə rōōn′) *n.* [U] A dark purplish red color. —*adj.* Dark purplish red.

mar·quee (mär kē′) *n.* A structure above the entrance to a building and often with a sign: *The names of the current films are listed on the theater marquee in large letters.*

mar·riage (mär′ĭj) *n.* [C; U] **1.** The state of being married: *My parents have a happy marriage.* **2.** A close union: *Poetry is a marriage of beautiful sound and intense meaning.* —**mar′riage·a·ble** *adj.*

mar·ried (mär′ēd) *adj.* **1.** With a husband or wife: *a married man.* **2.** Joined by marriage: *a married couple.* **3.** Relating to marriage: *married life.*

mar·row (mär′ō) *n.* [U] **1.** The soft material that fills most bones: *The dog ate the marrow from the bone.* **2.** The essential or most important part of sthg.: *We got to the marrow of the argument.*

mar·ry (mär′ē) *v.* **mar·ried, mar·ry·ing, mar·ries.** —*tr.* **1.** To take (sbdy.) as a husband or wife; wed: *She married him in Paris.* **2.** To unite (a couple) as husband and wife: *The judge married them.* —*intr.* To take a husband or wife: *They married in June.*

marsh (märsh) *n.* An area of low-lying wet land; a swamp: *The birds waded in the marsh.* —**marsh′land** *n.* —**marsh′y** *adj.*

ă–**cat**; ā–**pay**; âr–**care**; ä–**father**; ĕ–**get**; ē–**be**; ĭ–**sit**; ī–**nice**; îr–**here**; ŏ–**got**; ō–**go**; ô–**saw**; oi–**boy**; ou–**out**; ōō–**took**; ōō–**boot**; ŭ–**cut**; ûr–**word**; th–**thin**; *th*–**this**; hw–**when**; zh–**vision**; ə–**about**; N–French **bon**

mar·shal (mär′shəl) *n.* **1.** An officer with duties like those of a sheriff: *The Federal marshals took the prisoner from California to New York.* **2.** A person in charge of a ceremony or parade: *The marshall rode in the first car in the parade.* —*tr.v.* To place (sbdy./ sthg.) in proper order; organize: *The research team marshaled facts to defend its theory.*

HOMONYMS: marshal, martial (of war).

marsh·mal·low (märsh′mĕl′ō) *n.* **1.** A soft white candy with a spongy texture: *The campers toasted marshmallows over the campfire.* **2.** A mild-tempered, agreeable person.

mar·su·pi·al (mär sōō′pē əl) *n.* Any of various mammals, such as the kangaroo or opossum, whose young are carried in a pouch on the outside of the female's body. —*adj.* Relating to marsupials.

mart (märt) *n.* A market or trading center: *a fruit and vegetable mart.*

mar·tial (mär′shəl) *adj.* Relating to war or the military: *martial music.*

HOMONYMS: martial, marshal (law enforcement officer).

martial art *n.* Any of several arts of attack or self-defense that originated in eastern Asia: *Karate and judo are both martial arts.*

martial law *n.* [U] Military rule over a civilian population in an emergency or during a war.

Mar·tian (mär′shən) *adj.* Relating to the planet Mars. —*n.* A being that was thought to live on the planet Mars: *People used to think that Martians might be small and green.*

mar·tyr (mär′tər) *n.* **1.** A person who suffers and dies for religious beliefs: *saints and martyrs of the Christian church.* **2.** A person who suffers for a belief or cause: *She is a martyr to her children's needs.* **3.** A person who suffers or appears to suffer greatly: *She acts like such a martyr when she is sick.* —*tr.v.* To kill or cause (sbdy.) to suffer: *Joan of Arc was martyred by being burned at the stake.*

mar·tyr·dom (mär′tər dəm) *n.* [U] The condition of being a martyr: *Constant money troubles made her old age a martyrdom.*

mar·vel (mär′vəl) *n.* A person or thing that causes surprise or wonder: *The digital computer is a marvel of technology.* —*intr.v.* [at] To be filled with surprise or wonder: *We marveled at the gymnast's strength and grace.* See Synonyms at **wonder**.

mar·vel·ous (mär′və ləs) *adj.* **1.** Causing wonder or astonishment: *a marvelous cure for the disease.* **2.** Excellent; superior: *a marvelous performance of the play.* —**mar′vel·ous·ly** *adv.*

Marx·ism (märk′sĭz′əm) *n.* [U] The political, economic, and social theories of Karl Marx that predict the change of society from capitalism to communism. —**Marx′ist** *n.* & *adj.*

mar·zi·pan (mär′zə păn′) *n.* [U] A very sweet candy paste of sugar and ground almonds. It is often molded into shapes and colored to look like fruit.

masc. *abbr.* An abbreviation of masculine.

mas·car·a (mă skăr′ə) *n.* [U] A cosmetic used to darken the eyelashes.

mas·cot (măs′kŏt′) *n.* An animal, a person, or a thing believed to bring good luck, especially as a symbol of a sports team.

mas·cu·line (măs′kyə lĭn) *adj.* **1.** Relating to men or boys: *The group of volunteers was mostly masculine.* **2.** Suggestive of a man; mannish: *a masculine hairstyle.* **3.** In grammar, relating to the gender of nouns that refer to males or to things classified as male: *In French the word for boat is masculine.*

mas·cu·lin·i·ty (măs′kyə lĭn′ĭ tē) *n.* [U] The quality or condition of being masculine.

mash (măsh) *n.* [C; U] A soft wet mixture. —*tr.v.* To press (sthg.) into a soft, wet mixture: *Mash the potatoes for dinner.* —**mash′er** *n.*

mask (măsk) *n.* **1.** A covering worn over part or all of the face as a disguise: *a Halloween mask.* **2.** A protective covering for the face: *a welder's mask.* **3.** Something that disguises or hides: *The smile was a mask for the student's disappointment.* —*tr.v.* **1.** To cover (sthg.) with a mask: *The robbers masked their faces.* **2.** To cover (sthg.) in order to hide or protect: *The boy tried to mask his hurt feelings.*

mask

masked (măskt) *adj.* **1.** Wearing a mask: *a masked bandit.* **2.** Disguised; hidden: *masked disappointment.*

mask·ing tape (măs′kĭng) *n.* [U] An easily removed adhesive tape used for securing objects and covering areas not to be painted: *Where is the roll of masking tape?*

mas·och·ism (măs′ə kĭz′əm) *n.* [U] A psychological disorder in which a person gets pleasure from being hurt by another person. —**mas′o·chist′** *n.* —**mas′och·is′tic** *adj.*

ma·son (mā′sən) *n.* **1.** A person who builds or works with stone or brick: *The mason built a wall behind the house.* **2.** **Mason.** A member of the Freemasons, a secret men's organization.

ma·son·ry (mā′sən rē) *n.* [U] Work done by a mason; stonework or brickwork: *We need to hire someone to repair the masonry.*

mas·quer·ade (măs′kə rād′) *n.* **1.a.** A dance or party at which masks and fancy costumes are worn. **b.** A costume worn at such a dance or party. **2.** A disguise or false pretense: *The spy succeeded in his masquerade.* —*intr.v.* **mas·quer·ad·ed, mas·quer·ad·ing, mas·quer·ades.** [*as*] To disguise oneself: *The undercover police officer masqueraded as a taxi driver.*

mass (măs) *n.* **1.** [C] A quantity of matter with no specific shape: *a mass of clay.* **2.** [C] A large amount or number that is not specified: *A mass of people entered the stadium.* **3.** [U] The physical bulk or size of sthg. solid: *the huge mass of the ocean liner.* **4.** [U] A measure of the amount of matter contained in sthg.: *Mass is independent of gravity and therefore is different from weight.* **5. the masses.** The common people: *a political figure with great support among the masses.* —*tr. & intr.v.* To bring or come together in a mass: *The army massed its troops at the country's borders. The people massed downtown to watch the parade.* —*adj.* **1.** Involving large numbers of people: *a mass demonstration in the street outside the Capitol.* **2.** Done on a large scale: *mass production.*

Mass *also* **mass** (măs) *n.* In the Roman Catholic Church and some Protestant churches, the ceremony in celebration of Holy Communion.

Mass. *abbr.* An abbreviation of Massachusetts.

mas·sa·cre (măs′ə kər) *n.* The killing of a large number of people or animals who cannot defend themselves: *the scene of a massacre.* —*tr.v.* **mas·sa·cred, mas·sa·cring, mas·sa·cres.** To kill (sbdy./sthg.) cruelly; slaughter: *The troops massacred the villagers.*

mas·sage (mə săzh′ *or* mə säj′) *n.* [C; U] The rubbing or pressing of muscles and joints of the body to relieve pain and relax muscles: *I need to make an appointment with the masseuse to get a massage.* —*tr.v.* **mas·saged, mas·sag·ing, mas·sag·es.** To give a massage to (sbdy./sthg.): *I massaged my sore leg.*

mas·seur (mă sûr′ *or* mə sûr′) *n.* A man who gives massages professionally.

mas·seuse (mă soos′) *n.* A woman who gives massages professionally.

mas·sive (măs′ĭv) *adj.* **1.** Large, heavy, and solid: *a massive building.* **2.** Unusually large or impressive: *a massive dose of penicillin.* —**mas′sive·ly** *adv.* —**mas′sive·ness** *n.* [U]

mass media *pl.n.* The means of public communication, such as television, radio, films, and newspapers.

mass noun *n.* In grammar, a noun that refers to sthg. that cannot be counted. The words *furniture, honesty,* and *milk* are mass nouns.

mass-pro·duce (măs′prə doos′) *tr.v.* **mass-pro·duced, mass-pro·duc·ing, mass-pro·duc·es.** To produce (sthg.) in large quantities, especially on an assembly line: *mass-produce cars.* —**mass production** *n.* [U]

mass transit *n.* [U] The public transportation system of a city and the area around it: *Buses, subways, and trains are forms of mass transit.*

mast (măst) *n.* An upright pole, such as one that supports the sails of a ship.

mas·tec·to·my (mă stĕk′tə mē) *n., pl.* **mas·tec·to·mies.** A surgical operation to remove all or part of a breast, usually as a treatment for cancer: *My aunt had to undergo a mastectomy.*

mas·ter (măs′tər) *n.* **1.** A person who directs, rules, or controls others: *The dog followed its master.* **2.** A person of great learning, skill, or ability; an expert: *a master in metal work.* —*adj.* **1.** Highly skilled; expert: *a master carpenter.* **2.** Principal; chief: *a master bedroom.* **3.** Related to a part of a mechanism that controls all other parts: *a master switch.* **4.** Relating to the original from which copies are made: *a master recording.* —*tr.v.* **1.** To bring (sthg.) under control: *He can't seem to master his emotions.* **2.** To become skilled in the use of (sthg.): *She has mastered three foreign languages.*

mas·ter·ful (măs′tər fəl) *adj.* **1.** Acting to control; domineering: *a masterful approach to training dogs.* **2.** Expert; skillful: *a masterful performance of the concerto.* —**mas′ter·ful·ly** *adv.*

mas·ter·ly (măs′tər lē) *adj.* Showing the skill of a master: *a masterly player.*

mas·ter·mind (măs′tər mīnd′) *n.* A person who plans or directs sthg.: *She is the mastermind of their sales strategy.* —*tr.v.* To plan or direct (sthg.): *The coach masterminded the team's victory.*

Master of Arts *n.* A master's degree in liberal arts.

master of ceremonies *n., pl.* **masters of ceremonies.** A person who acts as the host at a formal gathering and introduces the speakers and entertainers: *The master of ceremonies introduced the speakers.*

Master of Science *n.* A master's degree in science or mathematics.

mas·ter·piece (măs′tər pēs′) *n.* **1.** An outstanding work; sthg. done with great skill: *The bridge was a masterpiece of engineering.* **2.** The greatest work of an artist: *Michelangelo's masterpiece.*

mas·ter's degree (măs′tərz) *n.* A degree above a bachelor's degree and below a doctorate, awarded by a college or university.

mas·ter·y (măs′tə rē) *n.* [U] Great skill, knowledge, or technique: *the musician's mastery of the piano.*

mas·ti·cate (măs′tĭ kāt′) *tr.v.* **mas·ti·cat·ed, mas·ti·cat·ing, mas·ti·cates.** *Formal.* To chew (food). —**mas′ti·ca′tion** *n.* [U]

mas·tur·bate (măs′tər bāt′) *intr.v.* **mas·tur·bat·ed, mas·tur·bat·ing, mas·tur·**

bates. To produce sexual pleasure by touch-ing the genitals, especially one's own genitals. —**mas′tur•ba′tion** *n.* [U]

mat¹ (măt) *n.* **1.** A flat piece of coarse material, used as a floor covering or for wiping one s shoes: *a bathmat; a welcome mat outside the front door.* **2.** A small piece of material used to protect the top of a table: *Put the plates on the place mats.* **3.** A thick pad used on the floor for wrestling or acrobatics. **4.** A dense or tangled mass: *a mat of hair.* —*v.* **mat•ted, mat•ting, mats.** —*tr.* **1.** To tangle (sthg.) into a thick mass: *The machine mats fibers together to make felt.* **2.** To cover (sthg.) with a mat or with matting: *They matted the floor of the gymnasium.* —*intr.* To become tangled into a thick compact mass: *The cat's fur matted because we didn't brush it.*

mat² (măt) *n.* A piece of cardboard or other material placed around a picture inside its frame. —*tr.v.* **mat•ted, mat•ting, mats.** To put a mat around (a picture): *We matted and framed the photos.* —*adj.* also **matte.** With a dull finish: *You have a choice of mat or glossy photos.*

mat•a•dor (măt′ə dôr′) *n.* The person who fights and kills the bull in a bullfight.

match¹ (măch) *n.* **1.a.** A person or thing exactly like another: *I can't find a match for this sock.* **b.** A person or thing that goes well with another: *This tie is a good match for your shirt.* **2.** A person or thing with similar ability: *The runners were a good match and ran a very close race.* **3.** A sports contest: *a wrestling match; a tennis match.* **4.a.** A marriage or an arrangement of marriage: *a love match.* **b.** A person viewed as a possible partner in marriage: *She's a great match for you.* —*v.* —*tr.* **1.** To be like (sthg.) or go well with (sthg.): *This sock doesn't match that one.* **2.** To fit (things) together: *Match the edges of the paper and glue them together.* **3.** To find or provide a match for (sthg.): *We could not match the color of the old paint.* **4.** To put (sbdy.) in competition with another: *The teacher matched one group against the other in a spelling contest.* —*intr.* To be alike or equal: *Your socks never match.*

match² (măch) *n.* A small strip of wood or cardboard coated at one end with a substance that catches fire easily when scratched against a rough surface: *Children playing with matches started the fire.*

match•book (măch′bŏŏk′) *n.* A small cardboard folder containing matches and a surface for striking them: *I like to collect matchbooks from places I visit.*

match•box (măch′bŏks′) *n.* A box for matches that usually has a surface for striking them.

match•less (măch′lĭs) *adj.* With no equal: *a matchless player.*

match•mak•er (măch′mā′kər) *n.* A person who arranges or tries to arrange marriages for others.

mate (māt) *n.* **1.** One of a matched pair: *I can't find the mate to this sock.* **2.** A husband or wife: *I'll ask my mate about your invitation.* **3.** The male or female of a pair of animals or birds that are breeding: *The mates both help care for the young.* **4.** *(usually used in a compound word).* A companion; a partner: *roommate; classmate.* **5.** An officer on a ship ranking below the captain. —*intr.v.* **mat•ed, mat•ing, mates.** To pair a male and a female animal for breeding; breed: *Many animals mate in the spring.*

ma•te•ri•al (mə tîr′ē əl) *n.* **1.** [C; U] The substance or substances from which sthg. is made: *Hemp is often used as material for ropes.* **2.** [C; U] Cloth or fabric: *She bought a yard of silk material.* **3.** [U] An idea or information that is used or developed to make sthg. else: *Historical material was used for the novel.* **4.** **materials.** Tools and supplies needed to perform a certain task: *building materials; educational materials.* —*adj.* **1.** Relating to the physical and not the spiritual or intellectual: *I did it not for material gain but for personal satisfaction.* **2.** Important; relevant: *Is your remark material to this discussion?* —**ma•te′ri•al•ly** *adv.*

ma•te•ri•al•ism (mə tîr′ē ə lĭz′əm) *n.* [U] **1.** The tendency to be interested in money and possessions rather than in spiritual or intellectual things. **2.** The set of beliefs that physical matter is the only reality. —**ma•te′ri•al•ist** *n.* —**ma•te′ri•al•is′tic** *adj.* —**ma•te′ri•al•is′ti•cal•ly** *adv.*

ma•te•ri•al•ize (mə tîr′ē ə līz′) *intr.v.* **ma•te•ri•al•ized, ma•te•ri•al•iz•ing, ma•te•ri•al•iz•es.** **1.** To become real or actual; become a fact: *Support for the project never materialized.* **2.** To appear in bodily form: *A mouse materialized in the corner of the room.*

ma•ter•nal (mə tûr′nəl) *adj.* **1.** Relating to or like a mother or motherhood: *the maternal instinct of a lioness.* **2.** Related through one's mother: *maternal aunts and uncles.* —**ma•ter′nal•ly** *adv.*

ma•ter•ni•ty (mə tûr′nĭ tē) *n.* [U] **1.** The state of being a mother. **2.** The feelings or characteristics that are part of being a mother; motherliness. —*adj.* Relating to pregnancy, childbirth, or the first months of motherhood: *a maternity dress; maternity leave.*

math (măth) *n.* [U] *Informal.* Mathematics.

math•e•ma•ti•cian (măth′ə mə tĭsh′ən) *n.* A person who is skilled in or who specializes in mathematics.

math•e•mat•ics (măth′ə măt′ĭks) *n.* [U] *(used with a singular verb).* The study of the relationships and properties of quantities, using numbers and symbols: *Arithmetic, algebra, and geometry are branches of mathematics.* —**math′e•mat′i•cal** *adj.* —**math′e•mat′i•cal•ly** *adv.*

M

mat·i·nee (măt′n ā′) *n.* A show or perform-ance given in the afternoon: *We got tickets for this afternoon's matinee.*

ma·tri·arch (mā′trē ärk′) *n.* A woman who rules a family, clan, or tribe.

ma·tri·ar·chy (mā′trē är′kē) *n.*, *pl.* **ma·tri·ar·chies.** [C; U] A society in which women have most of the power and authority. —**ma′tri·ar′chal** *adj.*

ma·tric·u·late (mə trĭk′yə lāt′) *tr. & intr.v.* **ma·tric·u·lat·ed, ma·tric·u·lat·ing, ma·tric·u·lates.** *Formal.* To enroll or allow (sbdy.) to enroll in a college or university: *The college will matriculate 500 students this year. When did he matriculate in the university?* —**ma·tric′u·la′tion** *n.* [U]

mat·ri·mo·ny (măt′rə mō′nē) *n.*, *pl.* **mat·ri·mo·nies.** [C; U] *Formal.* The act or con-dition of being married; marriage: *Are you ready to enter into matrimony?* —**mat′ri·mo′ni·al** *adj.*

ma·trix (mā′trĭks) *n.*, *pl.* **ma·tri·ces** (mā′trĭ sēz′ *or* măt′rĭ sēz′) *or* **ma·trix·es.** **1.** A situation or substance that contains, origi-nates, or develops sthg.: *The dinosaur fossils were embedded in a matrix of rock.* **2.** A dis-play of quantities arranged in columns and rows: *a computer matrix.*

ma·tron (mā′trən) *n.* **1.** A married woman or a widow, especially one of mature age or high social position. **2.** A woman who acts as a supervisor or guard in a school, hospital, or prison. —**ma′tron·ly** *adv. & adj.*

matron of honor *n.*, *pl.* **matrons of honor.** A married woman who serves as chief atten-dant of the bride at a wedding.

matte (măt) *adj.* Variant of **mat²**.

mat·ted (măt′ĭd) *adj.* Formed into a mass; tangled: *matted underbrush.*

mat·ter (măt′ər) *n.* **1.** [U] Something that occupies space, has mass, and can exist as a solid, liquid, or gas: *organic matter.* **2.** [C] A subject of concern or attention: *They debated matters of foreign policy. For me, this exam is a serious matter.* See Synonyms at **subject**. **3.** [U] Something written or printed: *reading matter.* —*intr.v.* To be of importance: *Your success matters to me.* ◆ **a matter of.** Ap-proximately: *I saw her for a matter of ten minutes.* **a matter of course.** Something that is expected; a natural or logical result: *It's a matter of course that you want a big lunch; you didn't have any breakfast.* **a mat-ter of opinion.** A subject on which people have different ideas. **as a matter of fact.** In fact; actually: *I thought the weather would be too hot there, but as a matter of fact, it was very nice.* **no laughing matter.** Something very serious: *Being arrested is no laughing matter.* **no matter.** Regardless of: *No matter*

where you go, I'll be thinking of you. **take matters into (one's) own hands.** To act to handle a problem because other people have not: *When the police failed to arrest the drug dealer, neighbors took matters into their own hands.* **the matter with.** The trouble or dif-ficulty that affects (sbdy./sthg.): *What's the matter with them?*

mat·ter-of-fact (măt′ər əv făkt′) *adj.* **1.** Keeping only to the facts: *They gave a mat-ter-of-fact description of the party.* **2.** Showing no emotion: *She had a matter-of-fact tone of voice.* —**mat′ter-of-fact′ly** *adv.*

mat·ting (măt′ĭng) *n.* **1.** [U] A coarse fabric used especially for making mats or covering floors. **2.** [C; U] Material formed into a mat: *a matting of leaves on the forest floor.*

mat·tress (măt′rĭs) *n.* A pad of heavy cloth filled with soft material or a group of springs, used on a bed: *This mattress isn't very com-fortable.*

ma·ture (mə tyoor′ *or* mə toor′ *or* mə-choor′) *adj.* **1.** Completely grown or devel-oped: *a mature tree.* **2.** With the mental and emotional qualities of an adult: *a mature young person.* **3.** Worked out completely in the mind: *a mature plan of action.* **4.** Having reached the limit of its time: *a mature savings bond.* —*v.* **ma·tured, ma·tur·ing, ma·tures.** —*tr.* To bring (sbdy./sthg.) to full development: *Working in the hospital has matured him.* —*intr.* **1.** To reach full growth or development: *She has matured into a fine actress.* **2.** To become due for payment: *This bond matures in seven years.* —**mat′u·ra′tion** (măch′ə rā′shən) *n.* [U] —**ma·ture′ly** *adv.*

ma·tur·i·ty (mə tyoor′ĭ tē *or* mə toor′ĭ tē *or* mə choor′ĭ tē) *n.* [U] **1.** The condition of being mature; full growth or development: *Tomatoes reach maturity in late summer here.* **2.** The time at which payment of a loan or bond becomes due: *The loan reaches maturi-ty in five years.*

mat·zo *or* **mat·zah** (măt′sə) *n.*, *pl.* **mat·zos** *or* **mat·zahs** (măt′səz). A flat piece of unleavened bread, eaten especially during Passover.

maud·lin (môd′lĭn) *adj.* Overly or foolishly sentimental: *Her friend enjoys crying over maudlin romantic novels.*

maul (môl) *tr.v.* **1.** To injure or damage (sbdy./sthg.) severely: *The bear cub mauled the sal-mon before eating it.* **2.** To handle (sbdy./sthg.) roughly: *The package was mauled in the mail.*

HOMONYMS: maul, mall (shopping center).

mau·so·le·um (mô′sə lē′əm *or* mô′zə-lē′əm) *n.* A building used as a tomb or monument for the dead: *In the United States, mausoleums were only used by the wealthy.*

mauve (mōv) *n.* [U] A light rosy or grayish purple color. —*adj.* Light rosy or grayish purple.

ma·ven (mā′vĭn) *n.* A person with special knowledge or experience; an expert: *Foreign policy mavens advise the President.*

mav·er·ick (măv′ər ĭk *or* măv′rĭk) *n.* A person who refuses to accept and follow the policies or views of a group: *a maverick in business.*

max (măks) *Slang. n.* [U] The maximum: *The car can seat five, but that's the max.* —*adv.* At the most: *We'll pay $250 max.* ◆ **max out.** *tr.v.* [sep.] To reach one's limit: *She maxed out her credit cards.*

max. *abbr.* An abbreviation of maximum.

max·im (măk′sĭm) *n.* A brief statement of a basic principle; a proverb: *"Haste makes waste" is a well-known maxim.*

max·i·mize (măk′sə mīz′) *tr.v.* **max·i·mized, max·i·miz·ing, max·i·miz·es.** To make (sthg.) as great or large as possible: *Hard work will maximize your opportunities.*

max·i·mum (măk′sə məm) *n., pl.* **max·i·mums** or **max·i·ma** (măk′sə mə). The greatest known or greatest possible number or measure: *You are allowed a maximum of three unexcused absences.* —*adj.* Relating to the greatest possible number or measure: *The train has a maximum speed of 120 miles per hour.*

may (mā) *aux.v.* Past tense **might** (mīt). **1.** To be allowed or permitted to (do sthg.): *May I go outside?* **2.** Used to show possibility: *It may rain today.* **3.** *Formal.* Used to express a desire or wish: *May your days be filled with laughter.* ◆ **may as well.** To have no reason not to (do sthg.): *If you're tired, you may as well go to bed.*

May (mā) *n.* The fifth month of the year, with 31 days.

may·be (mā′bē) *adv.* Possibly; perhaps: *Maybe we can go swimming tomorrow.* —*n.* An answer indicating possibility: *Is that a "no" or a "maybe"?*

may·day (mā′dā′) *n.* An international word used to call for help, especially for planes or ships in trouble: *The ship responded to the mayday.*

May Day *n.* May 1, celebrated in some countries as a spring holiday, and in others in honor of workers.

may·hem (mā′hĕm′ *or* mā′əm) *n.* [U] **1.** In law, causing serious injury to a person deliberately: *She was charged with mayhem.* **2.** A state of confusion or destructive disorder: *The riots caused mayhem in the city.*

may·o (mā′ō) *n. Informal.* Mayonnaise: *Give me lettuce and mayo on that sandwich, please.*

may·on·naise (mā′ə nāz′ *or* mā′ə nāz′) *n.* [U] A thick sauce made of eggs, oil, lemon juice or vinegar, and seasonings, used on cold foods and sandwiches.

may·or (mā′ər *or* mâr) *n.* The highest official of a city or town: *The mayor hired a new police chief.* —**may′or·al** *adj.*

maze (māz) *n.* **1.** A complicated and confusing network of paths: *The streets were like a maze.* **2.** A confused situation: *She had to work her way through the maze of paperwork.*

HOMONYMS: maze, maize (corn plant).

MC (em′se′) *n.* A master of ceremonies: *He's the MC of a TV game show.*

Md. *abbr.* An abbreviation of Maryland.

MD *abbr.* An abbreviation of: **1.** Maryland. **2.** Doctor of Medicine.

M.D. *abbr.* An abbreviation of Doctor of Medicine. —*n. Informal.* A doctor: *She plans to become an M.D.*

me (mē) *pron.* The object form of I. **1.** Used as the direct object of a verb: *He helped me.* **2.** Used as the indirect object of a verb: *She sent me a letter.* **3.** Used as the object of a preposition: *They brought the books to me.*

ME or **Me.** *abbr.* An abbreviation of Maine.

mead·ow (mĕd′ō) *n.* An open area of grassy ground, such as one used as a pasture or for growing hay: *The deer walked out of the forest into the meadow.*

mea·ger (mē′gər) *adj.* Small in quantity: *a meager dinner.* —**mea′ger·ly** *adv.* —**mea′ger·ness** *n.* [U]

meal¹ (mēl) *n.* **1.** The food served and eaten in one sitting: *a meal of chicken and biscuits.* **2.** The customary time for eating food: *Don't eat between meals.*

meal² (mēl) *n.* [U] **1.** Grain that has been coarsely ground: *cornmeal.* **2.** A substance that has been ground: *bone meal.*

meal·time (mēl′tīm′) *n.* The usual time for eating a meal: *What is your evening mealtime?*

meal·y (mē′lē) *adj.* **meal·i·er, meal·i·est. 1.** Resembling meal in texture and consistency; dry and granular: *a soft and mealy apple.* **2.** Lacking color; pale: *a mealy complexion.* —**meal′i·ness** *n.* [U]

meal·y-mouthed (mē′lē mouthd′ *or* mē′lē moutht′) *adj. Informal.* Unwilling to say directly or simply what one thinks is right or true: *He gave me a mealy-mouthed answer.*

mean¹ (mēn) *tr.v.* **meant** (mĕnt), **mean·ing, means. 1.** To have the sense of (sthg.); signify: *The Spanish word frijol means bean.* **2.** To intend to give or show (information or an idea, for example): *What did you mean by that statement?* **3.** To have (sthg.) as a purpose: *They mean no harm.* **4.** To design or intend (sthg.) for a certain purpose: *This building was meant for storage.* **5.** To be likely to result in (sthg.): *Dark clouds often mean a storm.* **6.** To be of importance by (a specified amount); matter: *Your friendship means a great deal to me.* ◆ **mean well.** To have good intentions despite the result: *She means well, despite her mistakes.*

HOMONYMS: mean (signify, unkind, middle point), **mien** (manner).

---

mean² (mēn) *adj.* **1.** Without kindness or goodwill: *The teacher was not being mean when he asked you to be quiet.* **2.** Cruel; hurtful: *a mean remark made in anger.* **3.** Not generous: *mean with money.* **4.** Low in rank or value; inferior: *She rose from mean origins to fame and success.* **5.** *Slang.* Excellent: *She plays a mean game of chess.*

mean³ (mēn) *n.* **1.** Something that is halfway between two extremes. **2.** An average, especially an arithmetic mean: *The mean of the grades on the exam was 75%.* **3. means. a.** A method or course of action used to gain an end or result: *We need a practical means of using the sun's energy to generate electricity.* **b.** Money, property, or other wealth: *a person of means.* —*adj.* Occupying a middle position between two extremes: *mean test scores.* ◆ **by all means.** Without fail; certainly: *You're the guest of honor, so by all means you must be there.* **by any means.** In any way possible: *We must fix this problem by any means.* **by means of.** With the use of: *They crossed the river by means of a raft.* **by no means.** In no way; certainly not: *By no means should you go sailing in bad weather.*

USAGE: mean³ When **means** has the sense of "a way to an end," it can be singular or plural. **Means** is singular when it refers to a particular method: *The best means of traveling there is by plane.* **Means** is plural when it refers to a group of methods: *What are the most effective means for doing this project?* When **means** has the meaning of "financial resources," it takes a plural verb: *Her means are more than adequate.*

---

me·an·der (mē ăn′dər) *intr.v.* **1.** To follow a winding and turning path: *The river meanders through the valley.* **2.** To wander without any clear purpose: *We meandered through the shops.* See Synonyms at **wander.**

mean·ing (mē′nĭng) *n.* Something that is meant or intended: *The word head has several meanings. What is the meaning of all this noise?*

mean·ing·ful (mē′nĭng fəl) *adj.* Full of meaning; significant: *a meaningful discussion.* —**mean′ing·ful·ly** *adv.* —**mean′ing·ful·ness** *n.* [U]

mean·ing·less (mē′nĭng lĭs) *adj.* Without meaning or significance: *a meaningless*

phrase. —**mean′ing·less·ly** *adv.* —**mean′ing·less·ness** *n.* [U]

mean·ness (mēn′nĭs) *n.* [U] **1.** The condition of being inferior in quality, character, or value: *She was depressed by the meanness of her surroundings.* **2.** Selfishness; lack of generosity: *She made him stay home out of meanness.*

meant (mĕnt) *v.* Past tense and past participle of **mean¹.**

mean·time (mēn′tīm′) *n.* *(usually singular).* The time between one event and another: *In the meantime, keep practicing your music.*

mean·while (mēn′wīl′) *adv.* **1.** During or in the time between two events: *Meanwhile, she continued to improve her swimming stroke.* **2.** At the same time: *I'll put the food on the plates, and meanwhile, you set the table.*

meas. *abbr.* An abbreviation of measure.

mea·sles (mē′zəlz) *n.* *(used with a singular or plural verb).* A contagious viral illness with symptoms that include coughing, fever, and a rash: *Children must be vaccinated against measles.*

mea·sly (mēz′lē) *adj.* **mea·sli·er, mea·sli·est.** *Slang.* Small in size, value, or quantity; meager: *A measly dollar is all they gave me.*

meas·ure (mĕzh′ər) *n.* **1.** [C] The size or amount of sthg. as compared with a standard: *What are the measures of that window?* **2.** [C] A unit of measure specified by a scale, as an inch or a pint: *A kilometer is a measure of distance.* **3.** [C; U] The extent or degree of sthg.: *There is a large measure of planning involved in having a wedding.* **4.** [C] A standard of evaluation or basis for comparison: *A book's sales shouldn't be the only measure of its success.* **5.** [U] Limit; bounds: *His generosity knows no measure.* **6.** [C] *(usually plural).* Action taken for a specified purpose or end: *It took drastic measures to clean up the harbor.* **7.** [C] A legislative bill or act; a law: *The Senate will vote on the measure.* —*v.* **meas·ured, meas·ur·ing, meas·ures.** —*tr.* **1.** To find the size, amount, capacity, or degree of (sthg.): *Measure this board for me.* **2.** To serve as a measure of (sthg.): *Inches and feet measure length.* **3.** [*off; out*] To mark off or distribute (sthg.) by measuring: *measure off a yard of fabric.* **4.** To form an opinion about (sthg.) by comparison or evaluation: *Try to measure the importance of a problem.* **5.** To choose (sthg.) with care; weigh: *I measured my words before answering the question.* —*intr.* **1.** To have a measurement: *The paper measures 8 by 12 inches.* **2.** To take measurements: *Measure carefully before cutting the wood.* ◆ **for good measure.** In addition to the required amount:

ă–cat; ā–pay; âr–care; ä–father; ĕ–get; ē–be; ĭ–sit; ī–nice; îr–here; ŏ–got; ō–go; ô–saw; oi–boy; ou–out; o͝o–took; o͞o–boot; ŭ–cut; ûr–word; th–thin; *th*–this; hw–when; zh–vision; ə–about; N–French bon

I packed my raincoat and hat and added an umbrella for good measure. **measure up.** *intr.v.* [*to*] To be good enough or meet a standard: *Did the concert measure up to your expectations?* —**meas´ur·a·ble** *adj.* —**meas´ur·a·bly** *adv.*

meas·ured (mĕzh´ərd) *adj.* **1.** Found out by measuring: *the measured distance of almost a mile.* **2.** Regular in rhythm and number: *a measured beat.* **3.** Careful; deliberate: *She used measured and precise words.*

meas·ure·less (mĕzh´ər lĭs) *adj.* With no limits; infinite: *Space is measureless.*

meas·ure·ment (mĕzh´ər mənt) *n.* **1.** [U] The act of measuring: *careful measurement of a dose of medicine.* **2.** [C] (*usually plural*). Numbers that express the size, amount, speed, or volume found by measuring: *The tailor took my measurements for a suit.* See table on pages 546–547.

meat (mēt) *n.* **1.** [U] The flesh of an animal eaten as food: *Do you want meat or fish?* **2.** [C] (*usually plural*). The edible part of a nut: *Chop the nutmeats.* **3.** [U] *Formal.* Food: *meat and drink.* **4.** [U] The essential part of sthg.: *the meat of the story.*

HOMONYMS: meat, meet (come upon), mete (distribute).

meat·ball (mēt´bôl´) *n.* A small ball of ground meat combined with seasonings and cooked: *I love spaghetti and meatballs.*

meat·y (mē´tē) *adj.* **meat·i·er, meat·i·est.** **1.** Full of meat; fleshy: *They cooked a large meaty turkey.* **2.** Full of meaning: *a meaty book.* —**meat´i·ness** *n.* [U]

me·chan·ic (mĭ kăn´ĭk) *n.* A worker skilled in making, using, or repairing machines: *The mechanic opened the hood of the car.*

me·chan·i·cal (mĭ kăn´ĭ kəl) *adj.* **1.** Relating to machines or tools: *mechanical difficulties with the power saw.* **2.** Operated, produced, or performed by machine. **3.** Performed as if by a machine; dull: *These routine mechanical tasks bore me.* —**me·chan´i·cal·ly** *adv.*

me·chan·ics (mĭ kăn´ĭks) *n.* [U] **1.** (*used with a singular verb*). The branch of physics that studies motion and force. **2.** (*used with a plural verb*). The technical aspects of sthg., such as an activity or a sport: *the mechanics of swimming.*

mech·a·nism (mĕk´ə nĭz´əm) *n.* **1.** The working parts of a machine: *an old clock's simple mechanism.* **2.** A system of parts that work together: *the mechanism of the solar system.* **3.** A process or means to do or create sthg.: *A constitution is a mechanism for establishing a democratic government.*

mech·a·nis·tic (mĕk´ə nĭs´tĭk) *adj.* **1.** Relating to mechanics as a branch of physics. **2.** Relating to the philosophy that all natural events can be explained by material causes and mechanical principles.

mech·a·nize (mĕk´ə nīz´) *tr.v.* **mech·a·nized, mech·a·niz·ing, mech·a·niz·es.** To equip (sthg.) with machinery: *The owners decided to mechanize the bakery.* —**mech´a·ni·za´tion** (mĕk´ ə nĭ zā´shən) *n.* [U]

med. *abbr.* An abbreviation of: **1.** Medical. **2.** Medicine. **3.** Medium.

med·al (mĕd´l) *n.* A flat piece of metal with a special design, given as an award: *a medal for bravery.*

HOMONYMS: medal, meddle (interfere).

med·al·ist (mĕd´l ĭst) *n.* A person who has received a medal: *an Olympic gold medalist.*

me·dal·lion (mĭ dăl´yən) *n.* **1.** A large medal. **2.** A round or oval ornament or design like a large medal: *a religious medallion.*

med·dle (mĕd´l) *intr.v.* **med·dled, med·dling, med·dles.** [*in; with*] **1.** To interfere in other people's business: *Stop meddling in my life!* **2.** To handle sthg. without care or understanding: *Don't meddle with my computer!* —**med´dler** *n*

HOMONYMS: meddle, medal (award).

med·dle·some (mĕd´l səm) *adj.* Tending to interfere in other people's business: *He is an annoying, meddlesome neighbor.*

me·di·a (mē´dē ə) *n.* **1.** A plural of **medium. 2.** (*used with a singular or plural verb*). Journalists as a group: *The police criticized the news media for their handling of the story.*

♦ **media event.** An event or occasion that attracts much attention from news organizations: *The actor's wedding became a media event.*

me·di·an (mē´dē ən) *adj.* Located in the middle: *the median strip down the center of the highway.* —*n.* Something that lies halfway between two extremes: *Your test result is exactly at the median.*

me·di·ate (mē´dē āt´) *v.* **me·di·at·ed, me·di·at·ing, me·di·ates.** —*tr.* To resolve (differences) by working with all sides: *The lawyer mediated the dispute.* —*intr.* To help the opposing sides in an argument come to an agreement: *The teacher mediated between the two students.* —**me´di·a´tion** *n.* [U]

me·di·a·tor (mē´dē ā´tər) *n.* A person or an agency that mediates in a dispute: *The company hired a mediator.*

med·ic (mĕd´ĭk) *n.* A person in a medical corps of the military.

Med·i·caid (mĕd´ĭ kād´) *n.* [U] A program in the United States, jointly funded by the federal government and the states, that pays hospitals and doctors for giving medical care to poor people.

M

TABLE OF MEASUREMENTS

UNIT	RELATION TO OTHER U.S. CUSTOMARY UNITS	METRIC EQUIVALENT
LENGTH		
inch	1/12 foot	2.54 centimeters
foot	12 inches or 1/3 yard	0.3048 meter
yard	36 inches or 3 feet	0.9144 meter
mile (statute)	5,280 feet or 1,760 yards	1.6093 kilometers
mile (nautical)	6,076 feet or 2,025 yards	1.852 kilometers
VOLUME OR CAPACITY (LIQUID MEASURE)		
ounce	pint	29.574 milliliters
cup	8 ounces	0.2366 liter
pint	16 ounces	0.4732 liter
quart	2 pints or 1/2 gallon	0.9463 liter
gallon	128 ounces or 8 pints	3.7853 liters
barrel (oil)	42 gallons	159.98 liters
VOLUME OR CAPACITY (DRY MEASURE)		
cup	1/2 pint	0.2753 liter
pint	2 cups or 1/2 quart	0.5506 liter
quart	4 cups or 2 pints	1.1012 liters
peck	8 quarts or 1/4 bushel	8.8098 liters
bushel	4 pecks	35.239 liters
WEIGHT		
grain	1/7000 pound	64.799 milligrams
dram	1/16 ounce	1.7718 grams
ounce	16 drams	28.350 grams
pound	16 ounces	453.6 grams
ton (short)	2,000 pounds	907.18 kilograms
ton (long)	2,240 pounds	1,016.0 kilograms
GEOGRAPHIC AREA		
acre	43,560 square feet or 4,840 square yards	4,047 square meters

COOKING MEASURES

UNIT	RELATION TO OTHER COOKING MEASURES	CONVERSION TO METRIC UNITS
teaspoon	76 drops or 1/3 tablespoon	4.9288 milliliters
tablespoon	3 teaspoons	14.786 milliliters
cup	16 tablespoons or 1/2 pint	0.2366 liter
pint	2 cups	0.4732 liter
quart	4 cups or 2 pints	0.9463 liter

MEASUREMENT CONVERSIONS

FROM METRIC TO U.S. CUSTOMARY

WHEN YOU KNOW	MULTIPLY BY	TO FIND
millimeters	0.04	inches
centimeters	0.39	inches
meters	3.28	feet
	1.09	yards
kilometers	0.62	miles
milliliters	0.03	fluid ounces
liters	1.06	quarts
	0.26	gallons
cubic meters	35.32	cubic feet
grams	0.035	ounces
kilograms	2.21	pounds
metric ton (1,000 kg)	1.10	short ton
square centimeters	0.16	square inches
square meters	1.20	square yards
square kilometers	0.39	square miles
hectares	2.47	acres

FROM U.S. CUSTOMARY TO METRIC

WHEN YOU KNOW	MULTIPLY BY	TO FIND
inches	25.4	millimeters
	2.54	centimeters
feet	30.48	centimeters
yards	0.91	meters
miles	1.61	kilometers
fluid ounces	29.57	milliliters
cups	0.24	liters
pints	0.47	liters
quarts	0.95	liters
gallons	3.79	liters
cubic feet	0.028	cubic meters
ounces	28.35	grams
pounds	0.45	kilograms
short ton (2,000 lbs)	0.91	metric tons
square inches	6.45	square centimeters
square feet	0.09	square meters
square yards	0.84	square meters
square miles	2.60	square kilometers
acres	0.40	hectares

TEMPERATURE CONVERSION BETWEEN CELSIUS AND FAHRENHEIT

$$°C = (°F - 32) \div 1.8 \qquad °F = (°C \times 1.8) + 32$$

METRIC PREFIXES

A multiple of a unit in the metric system is formed by adding a prefix to the name of that unit. The prefixes change the magnitude of the unit by orders of 10 from 10^9 to 10^{-9}.

PREFIX	SYMBOL	MULTIPLYING FACTOR
giga-	G	$10^9 = 1,000,000,000$
mega-	M	$10^6 = 1,000,000$
kilo-	K	$10^3 = 1,000$
hecto-	h	$10^2 = 100$
deca-	da	$10 = 10$
deci-	d	$10^{-1} = 0.1$
centi-	c	$10^{-2} = 0.01$
milli-	m	$10^{-3} = 0.001$
micro-	μ	$10^{-6} = 0.000,001$
nano-	n	$10^{-9} = 0.000,000,001$

M

med·i·cal (mĕd′ĭ kəl) *adj.* Relating to the study or practice of medicine: *a medical problem; medical school.* —**med′i·cal·ly** *adv.*

Med·i·care (mĕd′ĭ kâr′) *n.* [U] A program in the United States, funded by the federal government, that pays hospitals and doctors for medical care given to people over 65 years old.

med·i·cate (mĕd′ĭ kāt′) *tr.v.* **med·i·cat·ed, med·i·cat·ing, med·i·cates.** To treat (a person, an injury, or a part of the body) with medicine: *The doctor medicated the injured patient.*

med·i·cat·ed (mĕd′ĭ kāt′ĭd) *adj.* Containing medicine: *medicated skin cream.*

med·i·ca·tion (mĕd′ĭ kā′shən) *n.* **1.** [C; U] A substance that helps to cure a disease, heal an injury, or relieve pain; a medicine: *prescription medications.* **2.** [U] The act of medicating.

me·dic·i·nal (mĭ dĭs′ə nəl) *adj.* **1.** Relating to medicine: *medicinal plants.* **2.** Having a bitter taste like many medicines: *That drink left a medicinal taste.* —**me·dic′i·nal·ly** *adv.*

med·i·cine (mĕd′ĭ sĭn) *n.* **1.** [U] The science of studying, treating, and preventing diseases and disorders of the body. **2.** [C; U] A drug or other substance used to treat an illness or an injury: *cough medicine.* **3.** [U] A group of practices or beliefs believed to control nature, influence spiritual beings, or prevent or cure disease.

me·di·e·val (mē′dē ē′vəl *or* mĕd′ē ē′vəl) *adj.* Relating to the Middle Ages: *medieval history.*

me·di·o·cre (mē′dē ō′kər) *adj.* Neither good nor bad; ordinary: *He is nothing but a mediocre actor.* —**me′di·oc′ri·ty** (mē′dē ŏk′rĭ tē) *n.* [U]

med·i·tate (mĕd′ĭ tāt′) *v.* **med·i·tat·ed, med·i·tat·ing, med·i·tates.** —*intr.* **1.** [about; on] To think deeply and quietly; reflect: *The engineer meditated on the problem and changed the design of the car.* **2.** To think deeply on spiritual or religious matters. —*tr.* To consider (sthg.) completely: *She meditated a change of jobs.*

med·i·ta·tion (mĕd′ĭ tā′shən) *n.* [C; U] **1.** The process of meditating: *The poet stared out the window, lost in meditation.* **2.** Deep reflection on spiritual or religious matters.

me·di·um (mē′dē əm) *n., pl.* **me·di·a** (mē′dē ə) *or* **me·di·ums.** **1.** A means to do, transport, or transfer sthg.: *English is used as the medium of instruction.* **2.** The substance or environment in which sthg. lives: *Water is the medium of fish.* **3.** A technique or material used by artists: *a*

painter who works in a variety of media. **4.** *pl.* **mediums.** A person who claims to be able to communicate with the spirits of the dead: *The medium tried to communicate with the woman's dead husband.* **5.** *pl.* **media.** A way of sending information to large numbers of people: *Television is a good advertising medium.* **6. media.** *(used with a singular or plural verb).* Journalists as a group. —*adj.* Halfway between extremes; intermediate: *of medium height.* ◆ **happy medium.** A position, choice, or course of action that is balanced halfway between extremes: *We enjoyed a happy medium between hot and cold weather.* **medium of exchange.** Money or sthg. commonly used as money: *Gold is a medium of exchange.*

med·ley (mĕd′lē) *n.* **1.** A mixture or variety: *a medley of events in the program.* **2.** A musical piece that uses a series of melodies from different but related sources: *a medley of Beatles songs.*

meek (mēk) *adj.* **1.** Showing patience and humility; gentle: *as meek as a mouse.* **2.** Submissive: *Meek customers often don't dare to demand good service.* —**meek′ly** *adv.* —**meek′ness** *n.* [U]

meet¹ (mēt) *v.* **met** (mĕt), **meet·ing, meets.** —*tr.* **1.** To come together with (sbdy.) by chance or arrangement: *I will meet you at the restaurant.* **2.** To be introduced to (sbdy.): *Have you met my teacher?* **3.** To come into contact with (sthg.): *The stream meets the river at the rapids.* **4.** To handle or deal with (sthg.) effectively: *We have met every problem and continued our progress.* **5.** To satisfy (a requirement, for example): *You meet all the conditions for getting the loan.* **6.** To pay (an amount due): *Is there enough money to meet our expenses?* —*intr.* **1.** To come together; come face-to-face: *We'll meet tonight at 6 o'clock.* **2.** To become introduced: *My parents met at a dance.* **3.** To come into contact; be joined: *The edges meet at a right angle.* —*n.* A meeting or contest: *a gymnastics meet.* ◆ **meet with.** *tr.v.* [insep.] **1.** To experience or undergo (sthg.): *The explorers met with great difficulty when crossing the mountains.* **2.** To receive (sthg.): *Our plan met with their approval.*

HOMONYMS: meet, meat (animal flesh), **mete** (distribute).

meet·ing (mē′tĭng) *n.* **1.** A coming together: *a chance meeting of friends; a business meeting.* **2.** A point where two or more things come together: *the meeting of two railroad lines.* ◆ **meeting of the minds.** Agreement:

We started with different ideas, but then we reached a meeting of the minds.

mega– *pref.* A prefix that means: **1.** One million: *megahertz.* **2.** Large: *megaphone.*

meg•a•byte (mĕg′ə bīt′) *n.* A unit of computer memory equal to one million bytes.

meg•a•hertz (mĕg′ə hûrts′) *n., pl.* **megahertz.** A unit of frequency equal to one million cycles per second.

meg•a•lo•ma•ni•a (mĕg′ə lō mā′nē ə) *n.* [U] A mental disorder in which a person has mistaken ideas of being very rich or powerful. **—meg′a•lo•ma′ni•ac′** (mĕg′ə lō mā′-nē ăk′) *n.*

meg•a•phone (mĕg′ə fōn′) *n.* A large funnel-shaped horn, used to direct the voice and make it louder: *He spoke through a megaphone to the crowd.*

meg•a•ton (mĕg′ə tŭn′) *n.* A unit of power equal to the explosive force of one million metric tons of TNT: *Nuclear weapons are measured in megatons.*

meg•a•watt (mĕg′ə wŏt′) *n.* A unit of electrical power equal to one million watts: *The power plant produces a million megawatts a day.*

mel•an•chol•y (mĕl′ən kŏl′e) *n.* [U] Sadness or depression. —*adj.* **1.** Sad; gloomy: *a melancholy personality.* See Synonyms at **sad. 2.** Causing sadness; depressing: *the melancholy notes of the funeral march.* **—mel′an•chol′ic** *adj.*

me•lee (mā′lā′ *or* mā lā′) *n. (usually singular).* A confused fight among a number of people: *The soccer match ended in a melee.*

mel•low (mĕl′ō) *adj.* **1.** Rich and full in flavor: *mellow wine.* **2.** Rich and soft in quality: *the mellow colors of autumn.* **3.** With gentleness and tolerance: *a mellow personality.* —*tr. & intr.v.* To make or become mellow: *Time often mellows youthful intolerance. Wine mellows over a period of years.* **—mel′low•ly** *adv.* **—mel′low•ness** *n.* [U]

me•lod•ic (mə lŏd′ĭk) *adj.* Relating to melody: *a melodic poem.* **—me•lod′i•cal•ly** *adv.*

me•lo•di•ous (mə lō′dē əs) *adj.* With pleasant sounds; pleasant to listen to: *a melodious voice.* **—me•lo′di•ous•ly** *adv.* **—me•lo′di•ous•ness** *n.* [U]

mel•o•dra•ma (mĕl′ə drä′mə *or* mĕl′-ə drăm′ə) *n.* **1.** [C; U] A drama with exaggerated emotions, conflicts between characters, and often a happy ending: *She watches melodramas on daytime TV.* **2.** [U] Behavior or events full of exaggerated emotions: *I'm tired of the melodrama in our relationship.* **—mel′o•dra•mat′ic** (mĕl′ə drə măt′ĭk) *adj.* **—mel′o•dra•mat′i•cal•ly** *adv.*

mel•o•dy (mĕl′ə dē) *n., pl.* **mel•o•dies. 1.** A song or tune: *a folk melody.* **2.** The main part in a musical composition that has multiple parts: *The sopranos sing the melody.*

mel•on (mĕl′ən) *n.* [C; U] Any of several large fruits, such as a cantaloupe or watermelon, that grow on a vine and have a hard skin and juicy edible flesh.

melon

melt (mĕlt) *v.* —*intr.* **1.** To be changed from a solid to a liquid by heat: *The ice melted in the sun.* **2.** To dissolve: *Sugar melts in water.* **3.** To become gentle in feeling; soften: *Their hearts melted at the sight of the baby.* —*tr.* **1.** To change (a solid) to a liquid by heat: *The warm sun melted the snow.* **2.** To make (sthg.) gentler or milder; soften: *A look from the baby melted his hard heart.* ♦ **melt away.** *intr.v.* To disappear gradually: *The crowd melted away after the rally.* **—melt′er** *n.*

melt•ing pot (mĕl′tĭng) *n.* **1.** A container in which metals are melted. **2.** A place where people of different cultures or races form a single culture: *the American melting pot.*

mem•ber (mĕm′bər) *n.* **1.** A person or thing that belongs to a group: *a member of the cat family; a member of the United Nations.* **2.** A part of an animal or a human body, especially a leg or an arm: *The starfish had several missing members.*

mem•ber•ship (mĕm′bər shĭp′) *n.* **1.** [C; U] The state of being a member: *They're applying for membership in the organization.* **2.** [U] The total number of members in a group: *The membership elected a new club president.*

mem•brane (mĕm′brān′) *n.* A thin flexible layer of plant or animal tissue: *cell membrane.*

me•men•to (mə mĕn′tō) *n., pl.* **me•men•tos** *or* **me•men•toes.** A reminder of the past; a keepsake: *These seashells are mementos of our trip to the beach.*

mem•o (mĕm′ō) *n., pl.* **mem•os.** *Informal.* A memorandum: *a memo from the president to all employees.*

mem•oir (mĕm′wär′) *n. Formal.* **1.** An account of the personal experiences of an author: *a memoir of childhood on a farm.* **2.** *(usually plural).* An autobiography: *His memoirs were published just before his death last year.*

mem•o•ra•bil•i•a (mĕm′ər ə bĭl′ē ə) *pl.n.* Things from the past that are worth remembering or keeping: *a collection of memorabilia at the Baseball Hall of Fame.*

mem•o•ra•ble (mĕm′ər ə bəl) *adj.* Worth being remembered: *Memorable events are sometimes shown on stamps.* **—mem′o•ra•bly** *adv.*

mem•o•ran•dum (mĕm′ə răn′dəm) *n., pl.* **me•mo•ran•dums** *or* **me•mo•ran•da**

(měm′ə răn′də). An informal letter or note sent to members or offices of an organization: *The personnel department sent all employees a memorandum describing the new health insurance.*

me·mo·ri·al (mə môr′ē əl) *n.* Something, such as a monument or holiday, made or done in memory of a person or an event: *a memorial to war heroes.* —*adj.* Serving as a remembrance of a person or an event: *a memorial celebration.* —**me·mo′ri·al·ize** *v.*

Memorial Day *n.* May 30, celebrated in the United States in honor of those members of the armed forces killed in war.

mem·o·rize (měm′ə rīz′) *tr.v.* **mem·o·rized, mem·o·riz·ing, mem·o·riz·es.** To commit (sthg.) to memory; learn by heart: *You should memorize important phone numbers.* —**mem′o·ri·za′tion** (měm′ə rĭ zā′shən) *n.* [U]

mem·o·ry (měm′ə rē) *n., pl.* **mem·o·ries.** **1.** [C] The power or ability to remember: *Thanks to a good memory, I could tell the police what I saw.* **2.** [U] The part of the mind where knowledge is stored: *I committed the poem to memory.* **3.** [C] Something remembered: *a pleasant memory of summer vacation.* **4.** [U] The period of time that a group of people can remember: *the worst storm in living memory.* **5.** [U] A unit of a computer in which data is stored for later use: *How much memory does this computer have?*

men (měn) *n.* Plural of **man.**

men·ace (měn′ĭs) *n.* **1.** [C; U] A threat or danger: *rocks that are a menace to passing ships.* **2.** [C] A troublesome or annoying person: *The judge called the criminal a menace to society.* —*tr.v.* **men·aced, men·ac·ing, men·ac·es.** To threaten or put (sbdy./sthg.) in danger: *The erupting volcano menaced the nearby town.*

men·ac·ing (měn′əs ĭng′) *adj.* Frightening or threatening: *a menacing glance; menacing clouds.* —**men′ac·ing·ly** *adv.*

me·nag·er·ie (mə năj′ə rē *or* mə nǎzh′ə rē) *n.* **1.** A collection of animals kept in cages or pens to show people: *We visited the menagerie.* **2.** A strange group of people: *She lives in a menagerie.*

mend (měnd) *v.* —*tr.* **1.** To make repairs to (sthg.); fix: *I need to mend a torn jacket.* **2.** To improve or correct (bad behavior, for example): *The judge always warns criminals to mend their ways.* —*intr.* To heal: *Her broken ankle mended slowly.* ♦ **mend fences.** To improve poor relations, especially in politics: *The candidate needs to mend fences within his party before the election.* **on the mend.** Improving, especially in health: *She's home from the hospital and on the mend.*

me·ni·al (mē′nē əl) *adj.* Related to low-level, unskilled work; lowly: *They would only let me run errands and do other menial tasks for them.* —**me′ni·al·ly** *adv.*

men·in·gi·tis (měn′ĭn jī′tĭs) *n.* [U] An infection of the membranes that enclose the brain and spinal cord, often resulting in death.

men·o·pause (měn′ə pôz′) *n.* [U] The time at which a woman stops menstruating, usually between 45 and 55 years of age.

me·no·rah (mə nôr′ə) *n.* A candlestick used in Jewish religious ceremonies, especially one with nine branches used in the celebration of Hanukkah.

men's room (mǎnz) *n.* A public toilet for men.

men·stru·al (měn′strōō əl *or* měn′strəl) *adj.* Relating to menstruation: *menstrual cramps.*

men·stru·ate (měn′strōō āt′ *or* měn′strāt) *intr.v.* **men·stru·at·ed, men·stru·at·ing, men·stru·ates.** To experience menstruation: *She began to menstruate at age twelve.*

men·stru·a·tion (měn′strōō ā′shən *or* měn′strā′shən) *n.* [C; U] The passing of blood from the uterus that occurs in women who are not pregnant approximately every four weeks from puberty to menopause.

—ment *suff.* A suffix that means: **1.** Act or process: *statement; government.* **2.** State of being acted upon: *amazement; involvement.* **3.** Result of an action or a process: *advancement.*

WORD BUILDING: —ment The suffix —ment forms nouns, primarily by attaching to verbs. It can have several meanings, the most common being "an act of doing something" or "the state of being acted upon." Thus **entertainment** can be "an act of entertaining," and **amazement** is "the state of being amazed."

---

men·tal (měn′tl) *adj.* **1.** Relating to the mind: *a mental image; mental arithmetic.* **2.** Relating to mental disease: *a mental patient; a mental hospital.* —**men′tal·ly** *adv.*

men·tal·i·ty (měn tǎl′ĭ tē) *n., pl.* **men·tal·i·ties. 1.** [U] Mental ability or capacity; intelligence: *a group of students of high mentality.* **2.** [C] A characteristic way of thinking: *a cautious mentality.*

men·thol (měn′thôl′) *n.* [U] A compound made from peppermint oil and used in perfumes, as a flavoring, and as a mild anesthetic. —*adj.* Made with menthol: *menthol cigarettes.*

men·tion (měn′shən) *tr.v.* To speak or write about (sbdy./sthg.) briefly; refer to: *I mentioned your idea during my conversation with him.* —*n.* The act of referring to sthg. or sbdy. briefly or casually: *He made no mention of the problem in his report.* ♦ **Don't mention**

ă–cat; ā–pay; âr–care; ä–father; ĕ–get; ē–be; ĭ–sit; ī–nice; îr–here; ŏ–got; ō–go; ô–saw; oi–boy; ou–out; ōō–took; ōō–boot; ŭ–cut; ûr–word; th–thin; *th*–this; hw–when; zh–vision; ə–about; N–French bon

it. *Informal.* You're welcome: *"Thanks for your help." "Don't mention it."*

men·tor (mĕn′tôr′ *or* mĕn′tər) *n.* A wise and trusted advisor. —*tr.v.* To serve as a trusted advisor or teacher to (sbdy.), as at work: *The senior attorney enjoyed mentoring young attorneys new to the law firm.*

men·u (mĕn′yōō) *n.* **1.** A list of foods and drinks served at a restaurant: *Waiter, could I please see what desserts are on the menu?* **2.** A list of computer commands shown on a monitor to a user: *Choose the command Save from the menu by clicking on it with the mouse.*

me·ow (mē ou′) *n.* The sound made by a cat. —*intr.v.* To make such a sound: *The cat meowed for her food.*

mer·can·tile (mûr′kən tēl′ *or* mûr′kən tīl′) *adj.* Relating to merchants or trade: *mercantile law.*

mer·ce·nar·y (mûr′sə nĕr′ē) *adj.* **1.** Guided only by or working only out of a desire for money: *mercenary ambitions.* **2.** Hired for service as a soldier in a foreign army: *mercenary forces.* —*n., pl.* **mer·ce·nar·ies.** A soldier hired to serve for money in a foreign army.

mer·chan·dise (mûr′chən dīz′ *or* mûr′chən dīs′) *n.* [U] Things that may be bought or sold; commercial goods: *The merchandise was displayed in the store window.* —*tr.v.* (mûr′chən dīz′). **mer·chan·dised, mer·chan·dis·ing, mer·chan·dis·es. 1.** To buy and sell (goods). **2.** To promote the sale of (goods), as through advertising: *merchandising a new product.* —**mer′chan·dis′ing** *n.* [U]

mer·chant (mûr′chənt) *n.* A person who runs a retail business; a shopkeeper: *neighborhood merchants.* —*adj.* Relating to trade or commerce; commercial: *a merchant bank serving large businesses.*

mer·ci·ful (mûr′sĭ fəl) *adj.* Having or showing mercy; compassionate: *The boy's mother begged the judge to be merciful.* —**mer′ci·ful·ly** *adv.*

mer·ci·less (mûr′sĭ lĭs) *adj.* Having or showing no mercy; cruel: *a merciless dictator.* —**mer′ci·less·ly** *adv.* —**mer′ci·less·ness** *n.* [U]

mer·cu·ri·al (mər kyŏŏr′ē əl) *adj.* **1.** Clever or quick: *the mercurial wit of a comedian.* **2.** Changeable; unstable: *She was confused by her friend's mercurial nature.* **3.** Containing or caused by the action of the element mercury. —**mer′cu′ri·al·ly** *adv.*

mer·cu·ry (mûr′kyə rē) *n.* [U] **1.** *Symbol* **Hg** A silvery white poisonous metallic element that is a liquid at room temperature. Atomic number 80. See table at **element. 2.** The column of mercury in a thermometer: *The mercury only rose to 25°F today.*

mer·cy (mûr′sē) *n.* [U] Kindness or compassion toward another person: *The soldiers showed great mercy toward their prisoners.*

♦ **at the mercy of.** Without any protection against: *Drifting in the boat, they were at the mercy of the weather.*

mercy killing *n.* [U] The killing of a person or animal that is suffering greatly and likely to die; euthanasia.

mere (mîr) *adj.* Superlative **mer·est. 1.** Being nothing more than: *The king at that time was a mere child.* **2. the merest.** The smallest or least important: *She was so nervous that the merest sound made her jump.*

mere·ly (mîr′lē) *adv.* Only; simply: *He asked my opinion not because he respects it but merely to be polite.*

merge (mûrj) *v.* **merged, merg·ing, merg·es.** —*tr.* To bring (things) together so they become one; unite: *The new management merged the two departments.* See Synonyms at **mix.** —*intr.* To come together to form one; blend together: *two lanes of traffic that merge into one.*

merg·er (mûr′jər) *n.* The action of merging, especially the union of two or more corporations or organizations: *a bank merger.*

me·rid·i·an (mə rĭd′ē ən) *n.* **1.a.** An imaginary circle passing around the earth and through the North and South geographic poles. **b.** Either half of such a circle from pole to pole. **2.** The highest point: *High office is the meridian of a career in politics.*

me·ringue (mə răng′) *n.* [C; U] A mixture of stiffly beaten egg whites and sugar, often baked as a topping for cakes or pies.

mer·it (mĕr′ĭt) *n.* **1.** [U] Superior worth; excellence: *a painting of great merit.* **2.** [C] Something deserving of praise or reward: *the merits of a good education.* **3. merits.** The facts of a matter, whether good or bad: *The judge will base her decision on the merits of the case.* —*tr.v.* To be worthy of (sthg.); deserve: *Hard work merits praise.*

mer·i·to·ri·ous (mĕr′ĭ tôr′ē əs) *adj. Formal.* Having merit; deserving praise: *a soldier rewarded for meritorious conduct.* —**mer′i·to′ri·ous·ly** *adv.*

mer·maid (mûr′mād′) *n.* An imaginary sea creature with the head and upper body of a woman and the tail of a fish.

mer·ri·ment (mĕr′ĭ mənt) *n.* [U] Amusement and fun: *Sounds of merriment came from the party.*

mer·ry (mĕr′ē) *adj.* **mer·ri·er, mer·ri·est.** Full of fun and high spirits: *a merry and festive crowd; a merry celebration.* —**mer′ri·ly** *adv.*

mer·ry-go-round (mĕr′ē gō round′) *n.* **1.** A circular platform with seats, usually in the form of horses, on which people ride for fun as it turns round and music plays; a carousel. **2.** A rapid series of activities: *Graduation week was a merry-go-round of parties.*

mer·ry·mak·ing (mĕr′ē mā′kĭng) *n.* [U] Fun and enjoyment, especially with a festive party or celebration: *We invited our friends to join in the merrymaking.* —**mer′ry•mak′er** *n.*

me•sa (mā′sə) *n.* A high land area with a flat top and steep sides, common in the southwest United States.

mesh (mĕsh) *n.* **1.** [C; U] A net, screen, or fabric made from loosely woven cords, threads, or wires: *a screen made of wire mesh; a fine mesh of interlacing threads.* **2. meshes.** Something that catches and holds; a trap: *They were caught in the meshes of their own bad decisions.* **3.** [C; U] The engagement or interlocking of two sets of gear teeth. —*v.* —*tr.* To cause (gear teeth) to become engaged. —*intr.* **1.** To become engaged or interlocked: *The bicycle didn't work because the teeth of the gears failed to mesh.* **2.** To fit together effectively; be coordinated: *We can't arrange a meeting because our schedules don't mesh.*

mes•mer•ize (mĕz′mə rīz′) *tr.v.* **mes•mer•ized, mes•mer•iz•ing, mes•mer•iz•es.** To fascinate or completely hold the interest of (sbdy.): *The performance mesmerized the audience.*

mes•quite (mĕ skēt′) *n.* [U] Any of several thorny shrubs or trees of southwest North America.

mess (mĕs) *n.* **1.a.** A disorderly or dirty condition: *The kitchen is in a mess.* **b.** A person or thing that is in such a condition: *The house is a mess.* **2.** A confusing or troublesome situation: *We're in a mess because we have no more money.* **3.** *Informal.* A quantity of food: *We caught and cooked a mess of fish.* **4.** A meal served to a military group: *The soldiers lined up for morning mess.* —*v.* ◆ **mess around.** *intr.v. Informal.* To pass time with no goal or purpose, often playfully: *He was just messing around with his friends.* **mess up.** *intr.v.* To make a mistake, especially from nervousness or confusion: *The goalie messed up and dropped the ball.* —*tr.v.* [sep.] **1.** To make (sthg.) disorderly or dirty: *We took off our muddy boots so as not to mess up the house.* **2.** To manage (sthg.) badly; ruin or spoil: *Losing my notes messed up my chances of doing well on the examination.* **mess with.** *tr.v.* [insep.] To play with (sthg.) in an interfering way: *Who messed with my camera?*

mes•sage (mĕs′ĭj) *n.* **1.** A communication sent from one person or group to another: *I found the message you left at my desk.* **2.** A basic theme, lesson, or moral: *a movie with a message about life.*

mes•sen•ger (mĕs′ən jər) *n.* A person who carries messages or runs errands: *The messenger delivered the flowers.*

mes•si•ah (mĭ sī′ə) *n.* A leader who is expected to save or free a people: *waiting for a messiah to lead them.*

mess•y (mĕs′ē) *adj.* **mess•i•er, mess•i•est.** **1.** In a mess; disorderly: *a messy house.* **2.** Causing a mess: *the messy work of car repair.* **3.** Difficult or unpleasant; complicated: *a messy situation.* —**mess′i•ly** *adv.* —**mess′i•ness** *n.* [U]

met (mĕt) *v.* Past tense and past participle of **meet.**

met•a•bol•ic (mĕt′ə bŏl′ĭk) *adj.* Relating to metabolism: *metabolic rate.* —**met′a•bol′i•cal•ly** *adv.*

me•tab•o•lism (mĭ tăb′ə lĭz′əm) *n.* The processes in a living thing that make growth and action possible.

met•al (mĕt′l) *n.* [C; U] **1.** Any of the elements, such as iron, gold, copper, lead, or magnesium, that usually reflect light and conduct heat and electricity well. **2.** An alloy, such as steel or bronze, made of two or more metals.

HOMONYMS: metal, mettle (courage).

---

me•tal•lic (mə tăl′ĭk) *adj.* **1.** Relating to a metal: *a metallic shine.* **2.** Containing metal: *a metallic chemical compound.*

met•al•lur•gy (mĕt′l ûr′jē) *n.* [U] The science and technology of getting metals from ores, refining them for use, and creating alloys and useful objects from metals. —**met′al•lur′gi•cal** *adj.* —**met′al•lur′gist** *n.*

met•a•mor•phic (mĕt′ə môr′fĭk) *adj.* **1.** Changed by metamorphism: *metamorphic rock.* **2.** Relating to metamorphosis: *the metamorphic stages of an insect's life.*

met•a•mor•phism (mĕt′ə môr′fĭz′əm) *n.* [U] The process by which rocks are changed by great heat or pressure.

met•a•mor•phose (mĕt′ə môr′fōz′) *tr. & intr.v.* **met•a•mor•phosed, met•a•mor•phos•ing, met•a•mor•phos•es.** [into] To change by metamorphism or metamorphosis: *The tadpoles will metamorphose into frogs. Heat and pressure metamorphosed the limestone into marble.*

met•a•mor•pho•sis (mĕt′ə môr′fə sĭs) *n.*, *pl.* **met•a•mor•pho•ses** (mĕt′ə môr′fə sēz′). [C; U] **1.** A marked or complete change in appearance or form: *His college years effected a metamorphosis in him.* **2.** A change in the form and habits of an animal during natural development after birth: *Caterpillars become butterflies by metamorphosis.*

met•a•phor (mĕt′ə fôr′) *n.* A figure of speech in which a word or phrase that is usually used with one thing is applied to sthg. else, to make a comparison between the two. For example, *That boy is an early bird* is a metaphor.

ă–cat; ā–pay; âr–care; ä–father; ĕ–get; ē–be; ĭ–sit; ī–nice; îr–here; ŏ–got; ō–go; ô–saw; oi–boy; ou–out; o͝o–took; o͞o–boot; ŭ–cut; ûr–word; th–thin; th–this; hw–when; zh–vision; ə–about; N–French bon

met·a·phor·i·cal (mĕt′ə fôr′ĭ kəl *or* mĕt′-
ə fŏr′ĭ kəl) *adj.* Relating to metaphors: *She
used a metaphorical expression in calling her
vacation a dream.* —**met′a·phor′i·cal·ly**
adv.

met·a·phys·ics (mĕt′ə fĭz′ĭks) *n.* [U] *(used
with a singular verb).* The branch of philosophy that examines the nature of reality,
including the relationship between mind and
matter. —**met′a·phys′i·cal** *adj.* —**met′a·
phys′i·cal·ly** *adv.*

me·tas·ta·sis (mə tăs′tə sĭs′) *n., pl.* **me·
tas·ta·ses** (mə tăs′tə sēz′). [C; U] The
spread of sthg., usually cancer, from one
place in the body to other places.

me·tas·ta·size (mə tăs′tə sīz′) *intr.v.* **me·
tas·ta·sized, me·tas·ta·siz·ing, me·tas·
ta·siz·es.** To spread from one part of the body
to another: *The cancer has metastasized.*

mete (mēt) *v.* **met·ed, met·ing, metes.**
♦ **mete out.** *tr.v.* [sep.] To distribute (sthg.)
as by measuring amounts or shares: *The
judge meted out a punishment to fit the crime.*

HOMONYMS: mete, meat (animal flesh), **meet**
(come upon).

me·te·or (mē′tē ər *or* mē′tē ôr′) *n.* A bright
trail or streak in the night sky, formed when a
meteoroid enters the atmosphere and is so
heated by friction that it glows. Meteors are
sometimes called shooting stars.

me·te·or·ic (mē′tē ôr′ĭk *or* mē′tē ŏr′ĭk)
adj. **1.** Relating to meteors: *a meteoric flash.*
2. Like a meteor in speed, brilliance, or briefness: *the book's meteoric rise in popularity.*

me·te·or·ite (mē′tē ə rīt′) *n.* A meteoroid
that has reached the earth without burning up.

me·te·or·oid (mē′tē ə roid′) *n.* An object
that travels through interplanetary space and
becomes a meteor when it enters the earth's
atmosphere.

me·te·or·ol·o·gist (mē′tē ə rŏl′ə jĭst) *n.*
A person who specializes in meteorology:
*The meteorologist on Channel 5 gives enter-
taining weather reports.*

me·te·or·ol·o·gy (mē′tē ə rŏl′ə jē) *n.* [U]
The science that deals with atmospheric conditions, especially as they relate to weather.
—**me′te·or·o·log′i·cal** (mē′tē ər ə lŏj′-
ĭ kəl) *adj.*

me·ter[1] (mē′tər) *n.* The basic unit of length
in the metric system, equal to 39.37 inches.
See table at **measurement.**

me·ter[2] (mē′tər) *n.* A device used to measure
and record speed, temperature, or distance, or
to show the amount of sthg. used, as gas or
electricity: *a water meter.* —*tr.v.* To measure
(sthg.) with a meter: *The electric company
meters the electricity used by customers.*

me·ter[3] (mē′tər) *n.* [C; U] **1.** The arrangement of accented and unaccented syllables in
a line of poetry: *A line of poetry has meter*

when the words form a rhythmic pattern. **2.**
The pattern of beats in a measure of music;
musical rhythm: *the meter of a waltz.*

—**meter** *suff.* A suffix that means measuring
device: *speedometer; thermometer.*

meter maid *n. Informal.* A woman traffic
control officer who gives out tickets for parking violations.

meth·ane (mĕth′ān′) *n.* [U] A colorless,
odorless, flammable gas that has the formula
CH_4. It is found in natural gas and forms by
the decomposition of plants, as in marshes
and coal mines.

meth·od (mĕth′əd) *n.* **1.** [C] A regular or
orderly way of doing sthg.: *Boiling is one
method of cooking rice.* **2.** [U] Orderliness;
regularity: *Lack of method in solving problems wastes time.*

SYNONYMS: method, system, routine, manner.
These nouns refer to the plans or procedures followed to accomplish a task or reach a goal.
Method suggests a detailed, logically ordered
plan: *The student developed a method for finishing his homework in half the time.* **System**
means a coordinated group of methods: *Their
system of doing experiments was well planned.*
Routine means a habitual, often tiresome
method: *His routine for cleaning the house never
changes.* **Manner** means a personal or distinctive method of action: *I'm probably the only one
with my manner of folding shirts.*

me·thod·i·cal (mə thŏd′ĭ kəl) *also* **me·
thod·ic** (mə thŏd′ĭk) *adj.* **1.** Arranged or
done in regular order; systematic: *a methodical inspection.* **2.** Characterized by orderly
habits or behavior: *She's very methodical in
her approach to teaching.* —**me·thod′i·
cal·ly** *adv.* —**me·thod′i·cal·ness** *n.* [U]

Meth·od·ist (mĕth′ə dĭst) *n.* A member of
a Protestant church founded in England in the
18th century on the teachings of John and
Charles Wesley. —**Meth′od·is′m** *n.* [U]

me·tic·u·lous (mĭ tĭk′yə ləs) *adj.*
Extremely careful and precise; showing great
concern for details: *a meticulous housekeeper; meticulous attention to spelling.* —**me·
tic′u·lous·ly** *adv.* —**me·tic′u·lous·ness**
n. [U]

me·tre (mē′tər) *n. Chiefly British.* Variant
of **meter.**

met·ric (mĕt′rĭk) *adj.* Relating to the metric
system: *a metric ton.*

metric system *n.* [U] A decimal system of
weights and measures based on the meter as
its unit of length, the kilogram as its unit of
mass, and the liter as its unit of volume: *The
metric system is slowly gaining in use in the
United States.*

metric ton *n.* A unit of mass or weight equal
to 1,000 kilograms (2,205 pounds). See table
at **measurement.**

met•ro (mĕt′rō) *n., pl.* **met•ros.** A subway system: *Let's take the metro.* —*adj. Informal.* Metropolitan: *the metro area.*

met•ro•nome (mĕt′rə nōm′) *n.* An adjustable device that makes a series of regular clicks at different speeds: *A metronome provides a steady beat for practicing music.*

me•trop•o•lis (mĭ trŏp′ə lĭs) *n. (usually singular). Formal.* A large important city, especially the largest or most important city of a country, state, or region: *Chicago is the metropolis of the Midwest.*

met•ro•pol•i•tan (mĕt′rə pŏl′ĭ tən) *adj.* Relating to or characteristic of a major city: *metropolitan bus routes.*

—metry *suff.* A suffix that means process or science of measurement: *optometry.*

met•tle (mĕt′l) *n.* [U] **1.** Spirit; daring; courage: *soldiers who showed their mettle.* **2.** Basic character or temperament: *Your mettle will be tested in times of stress.*

Homonyms: mettle, metal (element).

mew (myōō) *intr.v.* To make the high-pitched cry of a cat or kitten: *The tiny kittens were mewing for their mother.* —*n.* The crying sound of a cat.

Mex. *abbr.* An abbreviation of: **1.** Mexican. **2.** Mexico.

mez•za•nine (mĕz′ə nēn′ *or* mĕz′ə nēn′) *n.* **1.** A partial story between two main stories of a building: *a stairway between the first floor and the mezzanine.* **2.** The lowest balcony in a theater or the first few rows of the balcony: *seats in the mezzanine.*

mg *abbr.* An abbreviation of milligram.

Mg The symbol for the element **magnesium.**

mgr. *abbr.* An abbreviation of manager.

MHz *abbr.* An abbreviation of megahertz.

MI *abbr.* An abbreviation of Michigan.

mi. *abbr.* An abbreviation of mile.

mice (mīs) *n.* Plural of **mouse.**

Mich. *abbr.* An abbreviation of Michigan.

micro— or **micr—** *pref.* A prefix that means: **1.** Small or smaller: *microcircuit.* **2.** Involving magnification or enlargement: *microscope.* **3.** One millionth: *microsecond.*

Word Building: micro— The basic meaning of the prefix **micro—** is "small." **Micro—** has been chiefly used to form science words. It is the opposite of the prefix **macro—** ("large") in pairs such as **microcosm/macrocosm** and **micronucleus/macronucleus. Micro—** is also sometimes the opposite of the prefix **mega—**, as in *microvolt* ("one millionth of a volt") and *megavolt* ("one million volts").

mi•crobe (mī′krōb′) *n.* A microorganism that causes disease, especially a bacterium: *Scientists study microbes.*

mi•cro•bi•ol•o•gy (mī′krō bī ŏl′ə jē) *n.* [U] The branch of biology that deals with microorganisms. —**mi′cro•bi′o•log′i•cal** (mī′krō bī′ə lŏj′ĭ kəl) *adj.* —**mi′cro•bi•ol′o•gist** *n.*

mi•cro•chip (mī′crə chĭp′) *n.* An extremely small square of semiconducting material on which an electronic component or integrated circuit is etched: *microchips for use in computers.*

mi•cro•cir•cuit (mī′krō sûr′kĭt) *n.* A miniaturized electronic circuit made up of small chips of semiconductor material containing elements of the circuit.

mi•cro•com•put•er (mī′krō kəm pyōō′tər) *n.* A small computer, such as a personal computer, containing a microprocessor and designed to be used by one person at a time.

mi•cro•cosm (mī′krə kŏz′əm) *n.* [C; U] Something regarded as a small representation of sthg. much larger: *The problems of the family are the nation's problems in microcosm.*

mi•cro•film (mī′krə fĭlm′) *n.* [C; U] A film on which written or printed material can be reproduced in much smaller size: *the library's collection of newspapers on microfilm.* —*tr.v.* To reproduce (sthg.) on microfilm: *The government microfilms documents to save storage space.*

mi•crom•e•ter (mī krŏm′ĭ tər) *n.* A device for measuring very small distances, angles, or objects: *Micrometers are used to measure the accuracy of machines.*

mi•cron (mī′krŏn′) *n.* A unit of length equal to one millionth (10⁻⁶) of a meter.

mi•cro•or•gan•ism (mī′krō ôr′gə nĭz′əm) *n.* A living thing, such as a bacterium or a protozoan, so small that it can be seen only with a microscope.

mi•cro•phone (mī′krə fōn′) *n.* A device that converts sound waves into electric current, as in recording or radio broadcasting: *Speak into the microphone.*

mi•cro•proc•es•sor (mī′krō prŏs′ĕs ər) *n.* An integrated circuit that contains the entire central processing unit of a computer on a single chip.

mi•cro•scope (mī′krə skōp′) *n.* An instrument consisting of a lens or combination of lenses for magnifying very small objects so they can be seen.

microscope

mi·cro·scop·ic (mī′krə skŏp′ĭk) *adj.* **1.** Extremely small: *microscopic cells.* **2.** Relating to a microscope: *microscopic study of a specimen.* **3.** Done with great attention to detail: *a microscopic analysis of the city's budget.* —**mi′cro·scop′i·cal·ly** *adv.*

mi·cro·sec·ond (mī′krō sĕk′ənd) *n.* A unit of time equal to one millionth (10^{-6}) of a second.

mi·cro·wave (mī′krō wāv′) *n.* **1.** A high frequency electromagnetic wave, usually one millimeter to one meter in wavelength. **2.** An oven in which microwaves are used to heat and cook food. —*tr.v.* **mi·cro·waved, mi·cro·wav·ing, mi·cro·waves.** To cook or heat (food) in a microwave oven: *I microwaved the frozen pizza.*

mid— *pref.* A prefix that means middle: *midsummer; temperatures in the mid-20s.*

WORD BUILDING: mid— The prefix **mid**—, which means "middle," combines primarily with nouns to form compounds, most of which represent a time (**midmorning, midsummer, midyear**) or place (**midstream, midtown**). When **mid**— is added to a word beginning with a capital letter, it is always necessary to use a hyphen: *mid-November, mid-Atlantic states.*

---

mid·air (mĭd′âr′) *n.* [U] A point or region in the air: *The basketball player seemed suspended in midair.*

mid·day (mĭd′dā′) *n.* [U] The middle of the day; noon: *We ate lunch at midday.*

mid·dle (mĭd′l) *adj.* **1.** Equally distant from the ends or extremes; central: *the middle seats of the row.* **2.** Being halfway in a series: *the middle child of three in the family.* —*n.* **1.** An area or point equally distant from the ends, edges, or extremes; a center: *the middle of the room.* **2.** Something between a beginning and an end: *A story has a beginning, a middle, and an end.* **3.** *Informal.* The middle part of the human body; the waist: *This belt won't fit round my middle.*

middle age *n.* [U] The time of human life between youth and old age, usually seen as the years between 40 and 60.

mid·dle-aged (mĭd′l ājd′) *adj.* Relating to middle age: *a middle-aged man with graying hair.*

Middle Ages *pl.n.* The period in European history between ancient times and the Renaissance, usually dated from about 500 to about 1450.

middle class *n.* The people of a society in a social and economic position between the lower working classes and the rich: *The middle class includes business people, skilled workers, and professionals.*

mid·dle·man (mĭd′l măn′) *n.* A trader who buys goods from producers and sells to retailers or consumers: *Buy direct from the manufacturer and avoid paying a middleman.*

midg·et (mĭj′ĭt) *n.* **1.** An offensive term for a very small person of normal proportions. **2.** A small or miniature version of sthg., such as a camera or car.

mid·night (mĭd′nīt′) *n.* [U] Twelve o'clock at night: *We left the party at midnight.*

mid·point (mĭd′point′) *n.* A point halfway between limits or endpoints: *the midpoint of a semester.*

mid·riff (mĭd′rĭf′) *n.* The middle part of the human body, from just below the chest to the waist: *a bare midriff.*

midst (mĭdst) *n.* [U] **1.** The middle position or part; the center: *a tree in the midst of the garden.* **2.** The condition of being surrounded by sthg.: *trouble in the midst of good fortune.*

mid·stream (mĭd′strēm′) *n.* [U] **1.** The middle of a stream. **2.** The middle of a course of action: *We changed plans in midstream.*

mid·sum·mer (mĭd′sŭm′ər) *n.* [U] **1.** The middle of the summer: *We're planning a vacation for midsummer.* **2.** The summer solstice, about June 21.

mid·term (mĭd′tûrm′) *n.* **1.** [U] The middle of a school term or a political term of office: *an assessment of progress at midterm.* **2.** [C] An examination given at the middle of a school term: *He's studying for midterms.*

mid·town (mĭd′toun′) *n.* [U] The central part of a town or city: *We can catch a bus at midtown.*

mid·way (mĭd′wā′) *n.* The area of a fair, carnival, or circus where side shows and other amusements are located: *We played games along the midway.* —*adv.* In the middle of a distance or period of time: *Midway through college, she changed her major.*

mid·week (mĭd′wēk′) *n.* [U] The middle of the week: *By midweek, people are looking forward to the weekend.*

mid·wife (mĭd′wīf′) *n.*, *pl.* **mid·wives** (mĭd′-wīvz′). A person, such as a nurse, trained to help women in childbirth: *Many women use midwives when they give birth at home.*

mid·win·ter (mĭd′wĭn′tər) *n.* [U] **1.** The middle of the winter: *heavy snows in midwinter.* **2.** The winter solstice, about December 22.

mid·wives (mĭd′wīvz′) *n.* Plural of **midwife.**

mid·year (mĭd′yîr′) *n.* **1.** [U] The middle of the year: *All students will be changing courses at midyear.* **2.** [C] An examination given in the middle of a school year: *The student got good grades on her midyears.*

mien (mēn) *n. Formal.* A person's manner of behavior or appearance: *the mien of a dignified professor.*

HOMONYMS: mien, mean (signify, unkind, middle point).

---

miff (mĭf) *tr.v.* To offend or annoy (sbdy.): *I was miffed by their failure to do the job properly.*

M

might¹ (mīt) *n.* [U] **1.** Great power or force: *the might of a great army.* **2.** Physical strength: *I pushed with all my might.* See Synonyms at **strength.**

HOMONYMS: might (power, past tense of may), **mite** (tiny animal).

might² (mīt) *aux.v.* **1.** Used to show possibility or probability: *We might go to the beach tomorrow.* **2.** Past tense of **may.** Used to express permission: *She asked if she might stay out late.*

might•y (mī′tē) *adj.* **might•i•er, might•i• est. 1.** Having great power, strength, or skill: *a mighty hunter.* **2.** Great in size or intensity: *a mighty stone fortress.* —*adv. Informal.* Very; extremely: *They've been gone a mighty long time.* —**might′i•ly** *adv.*

mi•graine (mī′grān′) *n.* A very severe headache that usually affects one side of the head and tends to happen repeatedly: *My aunt has suffered from migraines all her life.*

mi•grant (mī′grənt) *n.* A farm worker who travels from one area to another in search of work: *migrants picking grapes.* —*adj.* Migratory; migrating: *migrant labor.*

mi•grate (mī′grāt′) *intr.v.* **mi•grat•ed, mi•grat•ing, mi•grates. 1.** To move from one country or region and settle in another: *Many people migrated to the cities to look for work.* **2.** To move regularly to a different region, especially at a particular time of the year: *Many birds migrate to southern regions in the fall.* —**mi•gra′tion** *n.* [C; U]

mi•gra•to•ry (mī′grə tôr′ē) *adj.* **1.** Traveling from one place to another at regular times: *migratory birds.* **2.** Relating to migration: *long migratory flights.*

mike (mīk) *n. Informal.* A microphone: *The speaker adjusted the mike.*

mild (mīld) *adj.* **1.** Gentle or kind in manner or behavior: *a mild grandparent.* **2.** Moderate in type, degree, effect, or force: *a mild soap; a mild climate.* —**mild′ly** *adv.* —**mild′ness** *n.* [U]

mil•dew (mĭl′dōō′) *n.* [U] Any of various fungi that form a white or grayish coating on surfaces, especially under damp warm conditions: *The old leather shoes were covered with mildew.* —*intr.v.* To become covered or spotted with mildew: *The leather coat mildewed in the damp closet.*

mile (mīl) *n.* **1.** A unit of length equal to 5,280 feet or 1,760 yards (about 1,609 meters): *We drove 300 miles yesterday.* **2.** A nautical mile. See table at **measurement.**

mile•age (mī′lĭj) *n.* [U] **1.** Length or distance in miles: *The mileage between the two cities is great.* **2.** Total miles covered or traveled over a given time: *We haven't put much mileage on the car in the last month.* **3.** The distance a motor vehicle can travel on a given amount of fuel: *a car that gets good mileage.* **4.** An amount given for traveling expenses at a certain rate per mile: *The company pays a mileage of 30¢ per mile when I use my car for business travel.*

mile•stone (mīl′stōn′) *n.* **1.** A stone marker set up on a roadside to show the distance in miles from a given point. **2.** An important event: *The Bill of Rights was a milestone in the history of human rights.*

mil•i•tant (mĭl′ĭ tənt) *adj.* **1.** Fighting or making war: *militant bands of revolutionaries.* **2.** Aggressive or ready to fight, especially in the service of a cause: *Militant strikers blocked the entrances to the business.* —*n.* A militant person: *The government tried to control the militants.* —**mil′i•tan•cy** *n.* [U] —**mil′i•tant•ly** *adv.*

mil•i•ta•rism (mĭl′ĭ tə rĭz′əm) *n.* [U] **1.** The policy of keeping strong armed forces: *a political party promoting militarism.* **2.** The giving of high honor to military spirit or ideals: *a culture with a history of militarism.* —**mil′i•ta•rist** *n.* —**mil′i•ta•ris′tic** *adj.*

mil•i•ta•rize (mĭl′ĭ tə rīz′) *tr.v.* **mil•i• ta•rized, mil•i•ta•riz•ing, mil•i•ta• riz•es. 1.** To equip or train (sbdy.) for war. **2.** To fill (sbdy.) with the spirit of militarism. —**mil′i•ta•ri•za′tion** (mĭl′ĭ tər ĭ- zā′shən) *n.* [U]

mil•i•tar•y (mĭl′ĭ tĕr′ē) *adj.* **1.** Relating to the armed forces: *a military base.* **2.** Relating to war: *military history.* —*n., pl.* **military** also **mil•i•tar•ies.** The armed forces of a country: *a career in the military.* —**mil′i•tar′i•ly** (mĭl′ĭ târ′ə lē) *adv.*

mil•i•tate (mĭl′ĭ tāt′) *intr.v.* **mil•i•tat•ed, mil•i•tat•ing, mil•i•tates.** [*against*] To have force or influence: *Carelessness militates against doing a good job.*

mi•li•tia (mə lĭsh′ə) *n.* An army of citizens who are not professional soldiers and who may be called for military service in times of emergency: *Civilian militia fought in the Revolutionary War.*

mi•li•tia•man (mə lĭsh′ə mən) *n.* A member of a militia.

milk (mĭlk) *n.* [U] **1.a.** A white liquid produced by female mammals to feed their young. **b.** The milk of cows, used as food by human beings. **2.** A liquid resembling milk: *coconut milk.* —*tr.v.* **1.a.** To squeeze milk from the teats or udder of (a cow, goat, or other mammal). **b.** To draw out a liquid from (sthg.): *The researcher milked the snake of its venom.* **2.** *Informal.* To get money or benefits from (sbdy./sthg.), for personal gain or advantage: *She milked her parents of every penny they had.*

milk shake or **milk•shake** *n.* A drink made of milk, flavoring, and ice cream, stirred until foamy: *Do you want a chocolate milk shake?*

milk•y (mĭl′kē) *adj.* **milk•i•er, milk•i•est.** Resembling milk, especially in color: *milky water.* —**milk′i•ness** *n.* [U]

mill (mĭl) *n.* **1.** A building with machines for grinding grain into flour: *The old mill had been in use for 200 years.* **2.** A device or machine for grinding, crushing, or pressing: *a pepper mill.* **3.** A building or group of buildings equipped with machinery for processing a material of some kind: *a steel mill.* —*tr.v.* **1.** To grind or crush (sthg.) into powder or fine grains: *They milled the wheat into flour.* **2.** To process or produce (steel, paper, or another product) in a mill. ♦ **mill about** or **around.** *intr.v.* To move around in a confused or disorderly manner: *During the fire drill, the students milled about on the playground.*

mil•len•ni•um (mə lĕn′ē əm) *n., pl.* **mil•len•ni•ums** or **mil•len•ni•a** (mə lĕn′ē ə). **1.** A period of one thousand years: *the end of the millenium.* **2.** A period of joy, prosperity, and peace: *Many people wait for the approaching millenium.* —**mil′len′ni•al** *adj.*

mill•er (mĭl′ər) *n.* A person who owns or operates a mill for grinding grain.

mil•let (mĭl′ĭt) *n.* [U] The grain or seeds of a cereal grass widely used as a food grain in Asia and Europe.

milli— *pref.* A prefix that means one thousandth: *millimeter.*

mil•li•gram (mĭl′ĭ grăm′) *n.* A unit of mass or weight equal to one thousandth of a gram.

mil•li•li•ter (mĭl′ə lē′tər) *n.* A unit of fluid volume or capacity equal to one thousandth (10^{-3}) of a liter. See table at **measurement.**

mil•li•li•tre (mĭl′ə lē′tər) *n. Chiefly British.* Variant of **milliliter.**

mil•li•me•ter (mĭl′ə mē′tər) *n.* A unit of length equal to one thousandth (10^{-3}) of a meter. See table at **measurement.**

mil•li•me•tre (mĭl′ə mē′tər) *n. Chiefly British.* Variant of **millimeter.**

mil•li•ner•y (mĭl′ə nĕr′ē) *n., pl.* **mil•li•ner•ies.** [C; U] The business of making, designing, or selling women's hats. —**mil′li•ner** (mĭl′ə nər) *n.*

mil•lion (mĭl′yən) *n., pl.* **million** or **mil•lions. 1.** The number, written as 10^6 or 1 followed by six zeros, that is equal to 1,000 $\times$ 1,000: *ten million.* **2.** A very large number: *There are millions of things to do in a big city.* —**mil′lion** *adj.* —**mil′lionth** *n.* [U]

USAGE: After a number, use **million** (not **millions**), as in **50 million** or **18 million people.**

mil•lion•aire (mĭl′yə nâr′) *n.* A person who has at least a million dollars or a similar amount in another currency: *In the 1800s there were few millionaires.*

mime (mīm) *n.* **1.** [U] Acting with gestures and movements but without speech; pantomime: *the art of mime.* **2.** [C] An actor in pantomime: *The mime's face was painted white.* —*tr.v.* **mimed, mim•ing, mimes. 1.** To act out (sthg.) with gestures and body movements: *The game involved miming movie titles for other players to guess.* **2.** To make fun of (sbdy./sthg.) by imitation: *She mimed his way of walking.*

mim•e•o•graph (mĭm′ē ə grăf′) *n.* **1.** An old type of machine that makes copies of material written on a stencil. **2.** A copy made by such a machine. —*tr.v.* To copy (a document) with a mimeograph: *The teacher mimeographed the test for her students.*

mim•ic (mĭm′ĭk) *tr.v.* **mim•icked, mim•ick•ing, mim•ics. 1.** To copy or imitate (sbdy./sthg.) closely, as in speech, expression, or gesture, often so as to ridicule: *Children often mimic their parents.* See Synonyms at **imitate. 2.** To resemble (sthg.) closely: *an insect that mimics a small leaf.* —*n.* A person who imitates, especially a performer or comedian skilled in pantomime.

mim•ic•ry (mĭm′ĭ krē) *n.* [U] **1.** The art or practice of mimicking. **2.** The resemblance of one living thing to another or to an object in its environment so as to hide or protect itself: *Mimicry is common among insects.*

min. *abbr.* An abbreviation of: **1.** Minimum. **2.** Minute.

min•a•ret (mĭn′ə rĕt′) *n.* A tall slender tower on a mosque from which people are called to prayer: *The graceful minarets rise above the city.*

mince (mĭns) *v.* **minced, minc•ing, minc•es.** —*tr.* To cut or chop (sthg.) into very small pieces: *Mince the onions for the soup.* —*intr.* To walk in an affected way or with very short steps: *mincing along on high heels.* —*n.* [U] Mincemeat. ♦ **mince words.** *(usually in the negative).* To make words less harsh or disturbing, especially to be polite: *The doctor minced no words in describing the patient's condition.*

mince•meat (mĭns′mēt′) *n.* [U] A mixture of finely chopped fruit, spices, and sometimes meat, used especially as a pie filling: *Mincemeat pie is a Christmas tradition in many homes.*

mind (mīnd) *n.* **1.** [C; U] The human consciousness originating in the brain; the center of thought, emotion, memory, and imagination: *healthy in mind and body.* **2.** [C] A healthy mental condition: *I was afraid I was losing my mind.* **3.** [C] A person of great intelligence: *Newton was one of the great minds of science.* —*v.* —*tr.* **1.** To pay attention to (sbdy./sthg.): *Mind what I'm saying.* **2.** To obey (sbdy.): *The children were told to mind*

M

the baby sitter. **3.** To take care of (sbdy./sthg.): *He stayed home to mind the baby.* **4.** To object to or dislike (sbdy./sthg.): *I don't mind washing the dishes.* —*intr.* **1.** To be troubled or concerned: *I don't mind if you borrow the car.* **2.** To behave obediently: *That child refuses to mind.* ♦ **a mind of (one's) own.** An independent way of thinking: *We tried to persuade her, but she has a mind of her own.* **change (one's) mind.** To change an opinion, attitude, or point of view: *It's not too late to change your mind.* **keep in mind.** To continue to think about (sbdy./sthg.): *Keep our invitation in mind.* **keep (one's) mind on.** To hold one's attention on (sthg.): *Sometimes it's hard to keep your mind on your work.* **mind (one's) own business.** *Informal.* To keep from getting involved in another person's life or problems: *I told my brother to mind his own business.* **mind's eye.** The ability to imagine or remember: *Picture a beautiful beach in your mind's eye.* **of one mind.** In agreement: *We're of one mind about the proposed tunnel.*

mind•bog•gling (mīnd′bŏg′lĭng) *adj. Informal.* Overwhelming to the mind or emotions: *She was faced with a mind-boggling problem.*

mind•ed (mīn′dĭd) *adj.* **1.** *Formal.* Wanting to do sthg.: *Come over for a visit if you are so minded.* **2.** (*often used with a hyphen*). Having a specific kind of mind: *a strong-minded person.*

mind•ful (mīnd′fəl) *adj.* Attentive; aware: *My parents are always mindful of the importance of reading.* —**mind′ful•ly** *adv.*

mind•less (mīnd′lĭs) *adj.* **1.** Lacking intelligence; foolish: *a mindless question.* **2.** Having no purpose or meaning: *a mindless act.* **3.** [*of*] Giving or showing little attention or care: *She was mindless of the dangers.* —**mind′less•ly** *adv.*

mind reading *n.* [U] The ability to know another's thoughts through extrasensory communication; telepathy: *You should have told me you wanted to come; I'm not good at mind reading.* —**mind reader** *n.*

mind•set or **mind-set** (mīnd′sĕt′) *n.* A particular attitude or feeling towards a situation: *Thanks to his positive mindset, he was able to keep trying until he succeeded.*

mine¹ (mīn) *n.* **1.** A hole or passage dug in the earth to get metals, coal, salt, or other minerals: *a gold mine.* **2.** A rich supply or source: *The encyclopedia is a mine of information.* **3.** An explosive device that can be buried in the ground or hidden underwater: *a land mine.* —*v.* **mined, min•ing, mines.** —*tr.* **1.** To take (ores or minerals) from the earth: *The company mined coal from these mountains.* **2.** To

place explosive mines in or under (sthg.): *The ship mined the harbor.* —*intr.* To dig in the earth to extract ore or minerals: *The company is mining for diamonds.*

mine² (mīn) *pron.* (used with a singular or plural verb). The one or ones belonging to me: *Your car is different from mine. These books are mine.*

min•er (mī′nər) *n.* A person who works in a mine.

HOMONYMS: miner, minor (under legal age).

min•er•al (mĭn′ər əl) *n.* **1.** An inorganic solid substance found in nature, especially one such as gold, iron ore, or stone, that is taken from the earth by mining or quarrying. **2.** An inorganic element, such as calcium, iron, or potassium, that is needed by living things for good nutrition: *a daily dose of vitamins and minerals.* —*adj.* Of or containing a mineral or minerals: *mineral water.*

min•e•stro•ne (mĭn′ĭ strō′nē) *n.* [C; U] An Italian soup containing vegetables, pasta, and herbs in a meat or vegetable broth.

min•gle (mĭng′gəl) *v.* **min•gled, min•gling, min•gles.** —*tr.* To mix or combine (different things): *The poem mingled humor and sadness.* See Synonyms at **mix.** —*intr.* **1.** To become mixed or united: *Fresh water and salt water mingle at the mouth of the river.* **2.** To move among or join with others: *The guests mingled freely at the party.*

min•i (mĭn′ē) *n., pl.* **min•is.** Something smaller or shorter than others of its kind: *She changed her long skirt for a mini.* —**min′i** *adj.*

mini— *pref.* A prefix that means small: *minibike; miniskirt.*

min•i•a•ture (mĭn′ē ə chər *or* mĭn′ə chər) *n.* A copy or reproduction in a small size: *The architects placed a miniature of the proposed building on the table.* —*adj.* Made much smaller in size or scale. See Synonyms at **little.**

min•i•a•tur•ize (mĭn′ē ə chə rīz′ *or* mĭn′ə chə rīz′) *tr.v.* **min•i•a•tur•ized, min•i•a•tur•iz•ing, min•i•a•tur•iz•es.** To plan or make (sthg.) in a very small size: *The company miniaturized a camera for use in surgery.*

min•i•bike (mĭn′ē bīk′) *n.* A small motorcycle: *Minibikes are smaller and less powerful than motorcycles.*

min•i•com•put•er (mĭn′ē kəm pyoo′tər) *n.* A small computer with more memory and speed than a microcomputer.

min•i•mal (mĭn′ə məl) *adj.* Smallest in amount or degree; least possible: *an easy job requiring minimal effort.* —**min′i•mal•ly** *adv.*

min·i·mize (mĭn′ə mīz′) *tr.v.* **min·i·mized, min·i·miz·ing, min·i·miz·es. 1.** To reduce (sthg.) to the smallest possible amount or degree: *In winter, we try to minimize the amount of heat that escapes our house.* **2.** To represent (sthg.) as having little importance, value, or size: *He minimized the dangers of his job when he told his wife about it.*

min·i·mum (mĭn′ə məm) *n.* **1.** The smallest amount or degree possible: *We need a minimum of an hour to make dinner.* **2.** The lowest amount or degree reached or recorded: *The temperature's minimum yesterday was 45°.* *—adj.* Representing the least possible or the lowest amount or degree: *You must make a minimum payment of ten percent of what you owe.*

minimum wage *n.* The lowest wage that an employer can legally pay an employee: *Congress has raised the minimum wage.*

min·ing (mī′nĭng) *n.* [U] **1.** The work, process, or business of extracting coal, minerals, or ore from the earth: *He wrote a report on mining in the Rocky Mountains.* **2.** The process of placing explosive mines.

min·i·skirt (mĭn′ē skûrt′) *n.* A short skirt with a hemline above the knees.

min·is·ter (mĭn′ĭ stər) *n.* **1.** A person who performs religious functions in a Protestant church: *They were married by a Baptist minister.* **2.** A person in charge of a government department: *the minister of finance.* *—intr.v.* [*to*] To attend to another person's needs; give help or comfort: *The nurses ministered to the sick.* **—min′is·te′ri·al** (mĭn′ĭ stîr′ē əl) *adj.*

min·is·try (mĭn′ĭ strē) *n., pl.* **min·is·tries. 1.** The position and duties of a Christian minister: *the ministry of a small church.* **2.** The Christian clergy considered as a group: *the majority of the Protestant ministry.* **3.** A department of government under the charge of a minister: *officials in the labor ministry.*

mink (mĭngk) *n.* **1.** [C; U] A mammal of North America that has thick soft brown fur and lives around water. **2.** [U] The fur of this animal, often used to make or decorate clothing: *an expensive coat of dark mink.*

Minn. *abbr.* An abbreviation of Minnesota.

min·now (mĭn′ō) *n.* Any of various small freshwater fish often used as bait for fishing.

mi·nor (mī′nər) *adj.* **1.** Small in degree, size, or importance: *a minor change; a minor role in the play.* **2.** Less serious: *a minor injury.* **3.** Not yet at the legal age of an adult: *minor children.* **4.** Relating to a minor musical scale: *a minor key.* *—n.* **1.** A person who is not yet the legal age of an adult: *Minors cannot buy alcohol or tobacco.* **2.** A secondary area of a person's academic studies: *She graduated from college with a major in physics and a minor in philosophy.* *—intr.v.* To do academic work in a minor: *This year many students are minoring in history.*

mi·nor·i·ty (mə nôr′ĭ tē *or* mə nŏr′ĭ tē *or* mī nôr′ĭ tē *or* mī nŏr′ĭ tē) *n., pl.* **mi·nor·i·ties. 1.** The smaller of two groups that form a whole: *A minority of the voters opposed the tax cut.* **2.** A racial, religious, political, or other group different from the majority of people in a country: *laws protecting the rights of minorities.* **3.** *Formal.* The period of being under legal adult age.

min·strel (mĭn′strəl) *n.* **1.** In medieval times, a musician who traveled from place to place, singing and reciting poetry. **2.** A performer in a minstrel show.

minstrel show *n.* An old type of comic variety show in which performers presented songs, dances, and comic skits. Often white performers made themselves up as African Americans.

mint[1] (mĭnt) *n.* **1.** A place where the official coins of a country are made. **2.** *Informal.* A large amount, especially of money: *That painting is worth a mint.* *—tr.v.* **1.** To produce (money) by stamping metal; coin. **2.** To invent or make up (sthg.): *The scientist minted a name for the newly discovered chemical.* ◆ **in mint condition.** In original condition; undamaged: *an antique car in mint condition.*

mint[2] (mĭnt) *n.* **1.** [C; U] Any of various plants, such as the spearmint and peppermint, having leaves with a strong pleasant smell and taste: *Mint oil is used as a flavoring and the leaves are used in cooking and for tea.* **2.** [C] A candy flavored with mint: *breath mints.*

min·u·end (mĭn′yōō ĕnd′) *n.* A number from which another is to be subtracted. For example, in the expression 100 − 23 = 77, the minuend is 100.

min·u·et (mĭn′yōō ĕt′) *n.* A slow graceful dance from 17th-century France or the music for this dance.

mi·nus (mī′nəs) *prep.* **1.** Reduced by the subtraction of; decreased by: *Seven minus four equals three.* **2.** *Informal.* Without; lacking: *We arrived at the theater minus our tickets.* *—adj.* **1.** Less than zero; negative: *temperatures dropping into the minus numbers.* **2.** Slightly lower or less than: *a grade of A minus.* *—n.* **1.** The minus sign. **2.** A negative number or quantity: *My answer was a minus in that problem.* **3.** A disadvantage or drawback: *He needs to consider all the pluses and minuses of the job before deciding whether to accept it.*

min·us·cule (mĭn′ə skyōōl′ *or* mĭ nŭs′kyōōl′) *adj.* Very small; tiny: *a job with minuscule pay.*

minus sign *n.* The symbol −, as in 4 − 2 = 2, that is used to indicate subtraction or a negative quantity.

min·ute[1] (mĭn′ĭt) *n.* **1.** A unit of time equal to ¹⁄₆₀ of an hour or 60 seconds. **2.** A unit for measuring angles that is equal to ¹⁄₆₀ of a degree or 60 seconds. **3.** A short period of time; a moment: *Wait a minute.* **4. minutes.** An official record of the events or discussion at a meeting: *Members read and approved the minutes of the previous meeting.*

mi·nute² (mī nōot′) *adj.* **1.** Extremely small; tiny: *minute dust particles.* **2.** Not worth noticing; unimportant: *a minute problem.* **3.** Marked by careful study of small details: *a minute inspection.* —**mi·nute′ly** *adv.*

mi·nu·ti·a (mǐ nōo′shē ə) *n., pl.* **mi·nu·ti·ae** (mǐ nōo′shē ē′). A small or trivial detail: *My assistant is learning all the minutiae of running a business.*

mir·a·cle (mǐr′ə kəl) *n.* **1.** An event believed to be an act of a supernatural power because it is impossible to explain by the laws of nature: *Only a miracle could cure the patient.* **2.** A person, a thing, or an event that causes great admiration, awe, or wonder: *medical miracles.* See Synonyms at **wonder.**

mi·rac·u·lous (mǐ răk′yə ləs) *adj.* **1.** Having the nature of a miracle: *a miraculous event.* **2.** Having the power to work miracles: *a miraculous drug.* —**mi·rac′u·lous·ly** *adv.* —**mi·rac′u·lous·ness** *n.* [U]

mi·rage (mǐ räzh′) *n.* An illusion in which one seems to see bodies of water and upside-down reflections of distant objects: *mirages in the desert.*

mire (mīr) *n.* [C; U] **1.** An area of wet muddy ground. **2.** A difficult situation: *caught in the mire of debt.* —*tr.v.* **mired, mir·ing, mires.** **1.** To cause (sbdy./sthg.) to sink or become stuck in mire. **2.** To hold or trap (sbdy./sthg.) as if stuck in mire: *The family was mired in poverty.*

mir·ror (mǐr′ər) *n.* **1.** A surface that can reflect light to form an image of sthg. in front of it: *I looked at myself in the mirror while brushing my hair.* **2.** Something that reflects or gives a true picture of sthg. else: *The city's progress is a mirror of the nation's progress.* —*tr.v.* To reflect (sthg.) as if in a mirror: *The lake mirrored the clouds.*

mirror image *n.* An image that is the exact likeness of another one, but is reversed like an image in a mirror.

mirth (mûrth) *n.* [U] Happy laughter or merriment: *shouts of mirth.* —**mirth′ful** *adj.* —**mirth′ful·ly** *adv.*

mirth·less (mûrth′lǐs) *adj.* Showing no happiness: *He gave only a mirthless smile in response to my joke.* —**mirth′less·ly** *adv.*

mis— *pref.* A prefix that means: **1.** Error or wrongness: *misspell.* **2.** Badness or lack of proper standards: *misbehave.* **3.** Failure or lack of: *misfire; mistrust.*

WORD BUILDING: mis— The basic meaning of the prefix **mis—** is "bad; badly; wrong; wrongly." Thus **misfortune** means "bad fortune" and **misbehave** means "to behave badly." Likewise, a **misspelling** is "a wrong spelling" and **misdo** means "to do wrongly." **Mis—** usually forms compounds by attaching to verbs: *misunderstand, misremember.* **Mis—** also forms compounds by attaching to nouns that come from verbs: **miscalculation, mismanagement, mispronunciation.**

---

mis·ad·ven·ture (mǐs′əd věn′chər) *n.* A mishap; an unlucky accident: *A series of misadventures led to the loss of his business.*

mis·ap·ply (mǐs′ə plī′) *tr.v.* **mis·ap·plied, mis·ap·ply·ing, mis·ap·plies.** To use or apply (sthg.) wrongly: *You misapplied the equation in that math problem.* —**mis·ap′pli·ca′tion** (mǐs ăp′lǐ kā′shən) *n.* [C; U]

mis·ap·pre·hend (mǐs ăp′rǐ hěnd′) *tr.v.* *Formal.* To fail to understand (sthg.) correctly: *The soldier misapprehended the order.* —**mis·ap′pre·hen′sion** (mǐs ăp′rǐ hěn′shən) *n.* [C; U]

mis·ap·pro·pri·ate (mǐs′ə prō′prē āt′) *tr.v.* **mis·ap·pro·pri·at·ed, mis·ap·pro·pri·at·ing, mis·ap·pro·pri·ates.** To take (sthg.) dishonestly for one's own use: *A state employee misappropriated government funds.* —**mis·ap′pro′pri·a′tion** *n.* [C; U]

mis·be·got·ten (mǐs′bǐ gŏt′n) *adj.* **1.** A term used in the past in describing a child born to unmarried parents. **2.** Not lawfully obtained: *misbegotten wealth.*

mis·be·have (mǐs′bǐ hāv′) *intr.v.* **mis·be·haved, mis·be·hav·ing, mis·be·haves.** To behave badly: *Children who misbehave in class will miss play time.* —**mis′be·hav′ior** (mǐs′bǐ hāv′yər) *n.* [U]

misc. *abbr.* An abbreviation of miscellaneous.

mis·cal·cu·late (mǐs kăl′kyə lāt′) *tr. & intr.v.* **mis·cal·cu·lat·ed, mis·cal·cu·lat·ing, mis·cal·cu·lates.** To calculate or estimate incorrectly: *We miscalculated our travel time. They miscalculated and didn't have enough food.* —**mis·cal′cu·la′tion** *n.* [C; U]

mis·car·riage (mǐs′kăr′ǐj *or* mǐs kăr′ǐj) *n.* **1.** The birth of a fetus before it is developed enough to survive: *The woman suffered a miscarriage.* **2.** Failure to achieve the proper or desired result: *a miscarriage of justice.*

mis·car·ry (mǐs′kăr′ē *or* mǐs kăr′ē) *intr.v.* **mis·car·ried, mis·car·ry·ing, mis·car·ries.** **1.** To have a miscarriage: *She miscarried two months into her pregnancy.* **2.** To fail; go wrong: *The plan miscarried.*

mis·cast (mǐs kăst′) *tr.v.* **mis·cast, mis—**

---

cast·ing, mis·casts. To cast (a performer) in an unsuitable role: *The actor was miscast in the role.*

mis·cel·la·ne·ous (mĭs′ə lā′nē əs) *adj.* Composed of or concerned with a variety of different elements: *a miscellaneous assortment of books; miscellaneous travel expenses.*

mis·chief (mĭs′chĭf) *n.* [U] **1.** Annoying or improper behavior: *The father warned his boys to stay out of mischief.* **2.** A tendency to play tricks or cause trouble: *a lively child full of fun and mischief.*

mis·chie·vous (mĭs′chə vəs) *adj.* **1.** Causing mischief; naughty: *a mischievous child.* **2.** Showing a desire to play tricks or tease: *a mischievous look on her face.* —**mis′chie·vous·ly** *adv.* —**mis′chie·vous·ness** *n.* [U]

mis·con·cep·tion (mĭs′kən sĕp′shən) *n.* [C; U] A mistaken idea: *The President wants to clear up public misconceptions about his new tax proposal.*

mis·con·duct (mĭs kŏn′dŭkt) *n.* [U] Improper behavior: *a soldier guilty of misconduct.*

mis·con·strue (mĭs′kən strōō′) *tr.v.* **mis·con·strued, mis·con·stru·ing, mis·con·strues.** *Formal.* To mistake the meaning of (sthg.); misinterpret: *We misconstrued the teacher's words.*

mis·count (mĭs kount′) *v.* —*tr.* To count (sthg.) incorrectly: *She was accused of miscounting the money.* —*intr.* To make an incorrect count. —*n.* (mĭs′kount′). An inaccurate count: *A miscount of the votes was discovered and corrected.*

mis·deal (mĭs dēl′) *tr. & intr.v.* **mis·dealt** (mĭs dĕlt′), **mis·deal·ing, mis·deals.** To deal (playing cards) incorrectly: *The dealer misdealt the cards. I misdealt and had to start again.* —**mis′deal′** *n.*

mis·deed (mĭs dēd′) *n. Formal.* A wrong or illegal act: *They should be punished for their misdeeds.*

mis·de·mean·or (mĭs′dĭ mē′nər) *n.* In law, an offense less serious than a felony: *The amount he stole was small, so he was charged with only a misdemeanor.*

mis·di·rect (mĭs′dĭ rĕkt′) *tr.v.* **1.** To give incorrect or inaccurate instructions to (sbdy.): *misdirect a tourist.* **2.** To put a wrong address on (a piece of mail): *I must have misdirected the letter.* —**mis′di·rec′tion** *n.* [C; U]

mi·ser (mī′zər) *n.* A person who hates to spend or share money, especially one who lives poorly in order to save it: *The old miser lived in a house with no running water but had a million dollars in the bank.* —**mi′ser·li·ness** *n.* [U] —**mi′ser·ly** *adj.*

mis·er·a·ble (mĭz′ər ə bəl *or* mĭz′rə bəl) *adj.* **1.** Very unhappy or uncomfortable: *This cold is making me feel miserable.* **2.** Causing discomfort or unhappiness: *miserable weather.* **3.** Terribly poor or inadequate: *miserable food.* —**mis′er·a·bly** *adv.*

mis·er·y (mĭz′ə rē) *n.* [U] **1.** Long-time suffering or unhappiness: *The earthquake caused great misery.* **2.** Miserable conditions of life; extreme poverty: *living in misery in the inner city.*

mis·fire (mĭs fīr′) *intr.v.* **mis·fired, mis·fir·ing, mis·fires.** **1.** To fail to fire or go off: *The gun misfired.* **2.** To fail to achieve the desired result: *Their plan misfired.* —**mis′fire′** *n.*

mis·fit (mĭs′fĭt′) *n.* A person who cannot adjust to his or her situation in life or is seen as too different from other people: *Now he is called a genius, but when he was a child people just thought him a misfit.*

mis·for·tune (mĭs fôr′chən) *n.* **1.** [U] Bad luck or fortune: *Misfortune followed him wherever he went.* **2.** [C] An unfortunate event: *The hurricane was a great misfortune for the fishing industry.*

mis·giv·ing (mĭs gĭv′ĭng) *n.* [C; U] A feeling of doubt or concern: *We had misgivings about using our savings to buy a new car.*

mis·guid·ed (mĭs gī′dĭd) *adj.* Acting or done out of mistaken opinions or beliefs: *His misguided efforts to help only made things worse.* —**mis·guid′ed·ly** *adv.*

mis·han·dle (mĭs hăn′dl) *tr.v.* **mis·han·dled, mis·han·dling, mis·han·dles.** **1.** To handle (sthg.) roughly: *My package was mishandled in the mail.* **2.** To manage (sthg.) badly: *The singer's manager mishandled her money.*

mis·hap (mĭs′hăp′) *n.* [C; U] **1.** Bad luck. **2.** An unlucky accident: *They had a terrible mishap on their trip.*

mish·mash (mĭsh′măsh *or* mĭsh′mäsh′) *n. Informal.* A mixture of unrelated things: *The candidate presented nothing but a mishmash of other people's ideas.*

mis·in·form (mĭs′ĭn fôrm′) *tr.v.* To give wrong or inaccurate information to (sbdy.): *I'm afraid someone has misinformed you about the purpose of the meeting.* —**mis·in′for·ma′tion** (mĭs ĭn′fər mā′shən) *n.* [U]

mis·in·ter·pret (mĭs′ĭn tûr′prĭt) *tr.v.* To interpret, understand, or explain (sthg.) incorrectly: *He misinterpreted their remarks and thought they had insulted him.* —**mis′in·ter′pre·ta′tion** *n.* [C; U]

mis·judge (mĭs jŭj′) *v.* **mis·judged, mis·judg·ing, mis·judg·es.** —*tr.* To judge (sbdy./sthg.) incorrectly: *misjudge a person.* —*intr.* To be wrong in judging sthg.: *I thought it was only a mile away, but I misjudged.*

mis·lay (mĭs lā′) *tr.v.* **mis·laid** (mĭs lād′), **mis·lay·ing, mis·lays.** **1.** To lay or put (sthg.) down in a place one cannot remember: *I've mislaid my glasses.* **2.** To put (sthg.) down incorrectly: *The workers mislaid the carpet.*

mis·lead (mĭs lēd′) *tr.v.* **mis·led** (mĭs lĕd′), **mis·lead·ing, mis·leads.** **1.** To lead or guide (sbdy.) in the wrong direction: *The*

M

road sign completely *misled us.* **2.** To lead (sbdy.) into wrong ideas or actions, especially by giving false or incomplete information: *He misled investors into believing the company was financially healthy.* —**mis•lead′ing** *adj.*

mis•led (mĭs lĕd′) *v.* Past tense of **mislead.**

mis•man•age (mĭs măn′ĭj) *tr.v.* **mis•man•aged, mis•man•ag•ing, mis•man•ag•es.** To manage (sthg.) badly or carelessly: *He was accused of mismanaging his department.* —**mis•man′age•ment** *n.* [U]

mis•match (mĭs măch′) *tr.v.* To match (things) in an unsuitable way: *His socks are mismatched.* —*n.* (**mĭs′măch′**). An unsuitable match: *a mismatch between two tennis players of very different abilities.*

mis•no•mer (mĭs nō′mər) *n.* A wrong name or label for sbdy. or sthg.: *To call a whale a fish is to use a misnomer.*

mi•sog•y•nist (mĭ sŏj′ə nĭst) *n.* A person who hates women. —**mi•sog′y•nis′tic** *adj.* —**mi•sog′y•ny** *n.* [U]

mis•place (mĭs plās′) *tr.v.* **mis•placed, mis•plac•ing, mis•plac•es.** **1.** To put (sthg.) in a wrong place: *That painting is misplaced on that wall.* **2.** To lose (sthg.): *She always misplaces her keys.* **3.** To place (trust, for example) in a person or idea that is undeserving: *She misplaced her faith when she trusted him.*

mis•print (mĭs prĭnt′) *tr.v.* To print (sthg.) incorrectly: *misprint a name in the newspaper.* —*n.* (**mĭs′prĭnt′**). An error in printing.

mis•pro•nounce (mĭs′prə nouns′) *tr.v.* **mis•pro•nounced, mis•pro•nounc•ing, mis•pro•nounc•es.** To pronounce (sthg.) incorrectly: *Please excuse me if I mispronounced your name.*

mis•quote (mĭs kwōt′) *tr.v.* **mis•quot•ed, mis•quot•ing, mis•quotes.** To quote (sbdy./sthg.) incorrectly: *The singer angrily accused the reporter of misquoting her remarks.* —**mis′quo•ta′tion** *n.* [C; U]

mis•read (mĭs rēd′) *tr.v.* **mis•read** (mĭs-rĕd′), **mis•read•ing, mis•reads.** **1.** To read (sthg.) incorrectly: *misread a sign.* **2.** To draw the wrong conclusion from (sthg.); misinterpret: *I misread your nod to mean "yes."*

mis•rep•re•sent (mĭs rĕp′rĭ zĕnt′) *tr.v.* To describe or explain (sbdy./sthg.) in a false or misleading manner: *The newspaper misrepresented the mayor's statements.* —**mis•rep′re•sen•ta′tion** *n.* [C; U]

miss¹ (mĭs) *tr.v.* **1.** To fail to hit, catch, or make contact with (sbdy./sthg.): *The ball missed the basket.* **2.** To fail to see or notice (sthg.): *We missed the television special last night.* **3.** To fail to attend or be present for (sthg.): *My brother never missed a day of school.* **4.** To fail to understand (sthg.):

You're missing my point. **5.** To fail to accomplish (sthg.): *You just missed winning the race.* **6.** To be too late for (sthg.); not reach in time: *miss a bus.* **7.** To feel the absence or loss of (sbdy./sthg.): *I miss my hometown.* **8.** To notice the absence or loss of (sthg.): *When did you first miss your wallet?* **9.** To lack (sthg.): *The book is missing a few pages.* —*n.* A failure to hit, succeed, or find: *two hits and a miss.* ◆ **miss out.** *intr.v.* [*on*] To lose a chance for sthg.: *Don't miss out on this great opportunity. Hurry or you'll miss out!* **miss the boat.** *Informal.* To fail to take advantage of an opportunity: *He waited too long to apply for the job and so missed the boat.* **miss the mark.** To fail to be correct or exact: *His comments missed the mark.*

miss² (mĭs) *n.* **1. Miss.** A title of courtesy used before the last name or full name of an unmarried woman or girl: *Do you prefer to be called Miss or Ms. Baker?* **2.** Used as a form of polite address for a young woman or girl: *Excuse me, miss.* **3. misses.** A range of clothing sizes for girls and women: *She wears a misses size ten.* —SEE NOTE at **Ms.**

Miss. *abbr.* An abbreviation of Mississippi.

mis•shap•en (mĭs shā′pən) *adj.* Badly shaped; not normal in shape: *The first cake I baked was misshapen but still tasted good.*

mis•sile (mĭs′əl) *n.* An object or a weapon that is thrown, fired, dropped, or otherwise launched at a target: *ballistic missiles.*

miss•ing (mĭs′ĭng) *adj.* **1.** Lost: *missing persons.* **2.** Not present; absent: *Who is missing from class today?*

mis•sion (mĭsh′ən) *n.* **1.** An assignment that a person or group of persons is sent to complete: *a rescue mission.* **2.** A combat operation, especially a flight into a combat zone by military aircraft: *The pilot flew ten missions during the war.* **3.** Something that a person feels is the main task of his or her life: *My mission in life is to become a teacher.* **4.** A group sent to a foreign country for a specific purpose: *a trade mission; a diplomatic mission.* **5.** A group or an establishment of missionaries in some territory or foreign country: *Los Angeles started as a small Spanish mission.*

mis•sion•ar•y (mĭsh′ə nĕr′ē) *n., pl.* **mis•sion•ar•ies.** A person sent, especially by a Christian organization, to do religious work or help people in a foreign country: *The missionaries worked to convert the villagers.*

mis•sive (mĭs′ĭv) *n. Formal.* A letter or written message: *a missive from the President.*

mis•speak (mĭs spēk′) *tr. & intr.v.* **mis•spoke** (mĭs spōk′), **mis•spo•ken** (mĭs-spō′kən), **mis•speak•ing, mis•speaks.** To pronounce or speak incorrectly: *The actor misspoke his lines.*

mis•spell (mĭs spĕl′) *tr.v.* **mis•spelled** or **mis•spelt** (mĭs spĕlt′), **mis•spell•ing, mis•spells.** To spell (a word) incorrectly: *On the test, I misspelled five words.*

mis•spend (mĭs spĕnd′) *tr.v.* **mis•spent** (mĭs spĕnt′), **mis•spend•ing, mis•spends.** To spend (sthg.) improperly, foolishly, or wastefully: *He misspent his money on gambling.*

mis•spoke (mĭs spōk′) *v.* Past tense of **mis-speak.**

mis•spo•ken (mĭs spō′kən) *v.* Past participle of **misspeak.**

mis•state (mĭs stāt′) *tr.v.* **mis•stat•ed, mis•stat•ing, mis•states.** To state (sthg.) wrongly or falsely: *Don't misstate anything on your job application.* —**mis•state′ment** *n.*

mis•step (mĭs stĕp′) *n.* **1.** A misplaced or awkward step. **2.** A mistake in action or behavior: *A single misstep by the thief allowed the police to catch him.*

mist (mĭst) *n.* [C; U] **1.** A mass of tiny droplets of water in the air, close to or touching the earth. **2.** Water vapor that condenses on and clouds a surface: *mist on a window-pane.* **3.** A mass of tiny drops of a liquid, such as perfume, sprayed into the air. —*intr.v.* To rain in a fine shower: *It began to mist at four o'clock.* ✦ **mist over.** *intr.v.* **1.** To be covered with mist: *The car windows misted over, so the driver had trouble seeing.* **2.** To become blurred by tears: *Her eyes misted over at the thought of her new grandchild.* —**mist′i•ly** *adv.* —**mist′i•ness** *n.* [U] —**mist′y** *adj.*

mis•take (mĭ stāk′) *n.* An error resulting from a lack of judgment, knowledge, or care: *careless mistakes.* —*tr.v.* **mis•took** (mĭ-stook′), **mis•tak•en** (mĭ stā′kən), **mis•tak•ing, mis•takes. 1.** To understand (sthg.) incorrectly: *We mistook politeness as friendliness.* **2.** To recognize or identify (sbdy./sthg.) incorrectly: *She mistook satin for silk.*

mis•tak•en (mĭ stā′kən) *adj.* Wrong; in error: *If I am not mistaken, you were here yesterday, too.* —**mis•tak′en•ly** *adv.*

Mis•ter (mĭs′tər) *n.* **1.** Used as a courtesy title before the last name or full name of a man, usually as the abbreviation **Mr. 2.** *Informal.* Used as a form of address for a man.

mis•tle•toe (mĭs′əl tō′) *n.* [U] A plant with evergreen leaves and white berries. It is often used as a Christmas decoration: *Traditionally, people kiss under a sprig of mistletoe that is hung in a doorway.*

mis•took (mĭ stook′) *v.* Past tense of **mis-take.**

mis•treat (mĭs trēt′) *tr.v.* To treat (sbdy./sthg.) badly; abuse: *People shouldn't mistreat animals.* —**mis•treat′ment** *n.* [U]

mis•tress (mĭs′trĭs) *n.* **1.** *Formal.* A woman in a position of authority, control, or ownership, as the head of a household. **2.** A female lover of a man who is usually married and pays to support her.

mis•tri•al (mĭs trī′əl *or* mĭs trīl′) *n.* **1.** A trial that a judge stops and calls invalid because of an error in procedure: *The judge declared a mistrial.* **2.** A trial in which the jurors fail to agree on a verdict.

mis•trust (mĭs trŭst′) *n.* [U] Lack of trust; suspicion: *Her mistrust makes it hard for her to keep friends.* See Synonyms at **uncertainty.** —*tr.v.* To have no trust in (sbdy./sthg.); regard with suspicion: *They mistrust stangers.* —**mis-trust′ful** *adj.* —**mis•trust′ful•ly** *adv.*

mis•un•der•stand (mĭs′ŭn dər stănd′) *tr.v.* **mis•un•der•stood** (mĭs′ŭn dər-stood′), **mis•un•der•stand•ing, mis•un•der•stands.** To understand (sbdy./sthg.) incorrectly or imperfectly: *I misunderstood the teacher's instructions.*

mis•un•der•stand•ing (mĭs′ŭn dər stăn′-dĭng) *n.* **1.** A failure to understand: *a misunderstanding about the meeting time.* **2.** A quarrel or disagreement: *The two sisters had a misunderstanding and never spoke to each other again.*

mis•un•der•stood (mĭs′ŭn dər stood′) *v.* Past tense of **misunderstand.**

mis•use (mĭs yōos′) *n.* [U] Wrong or improper use: *the misuse of drugs.* —*tr.v.* (mĭs-yōoz′). **mis•used, mis•us•ing, mis•us-es. 1.** To use (sthg.) wrongly or incorrectly: *She misused the word in that sentence.* **2.** To make improper use of (sthg.); abuse: *Let's not misuse our natural resources.*

mite (mīt) *n.* **1.** Any of various very small animals related to spiders that often live on other animals or plants: *dust mites.* **2.** A very small, pitiful creature or child: *The poor little mite seemed so cold.*

HOMONYMS: mite, might (power, past tense of may).

---

mit•i•gate (mĭt′ĭ gāt′) *tr.v.* **mit•i•gat•ed, mit•i•gat•ing, mit•i•gates.** To make (sthg.) less severe: *The judge mitigated the sentence.* —**mit′i•gat′ing** *adj.*

mitt (mĭt) *n.* **1.** A padded glove worn to protect the hand: *a catcher's mitt; an oven mitt.* **2.** *Slang. (usually plural).* A hand: *Keep your mitts off my things!*

mit•ten (mĭt′n) *n.* A covering for the hand, with a separate section for the thumb and one wide section for all four fingers.

mix (mĭks) *v.* —*tr.* **1.** To blend (things) into a single mass by pouring, stirring, or shaking: *Mix flour, water, and eggs to form the dough.* **2.** To combine or join (sthg.): *mix joy with sorrow.* **3.** To bring (people) into social contact: *The new league mixes boys with girls on the teams.*

mitten

—*intr.* **1.** To become blended together: *Oil and water do not mix.* **2.** [*with*] To spend time socially: *Don't mix with troublemakers.* —*n.* [C; U] **1.** A blend of different elements: *a mix of comedy and romance.* **2.** A mixture, especially of ingredients packaged and sold commercially: *a cake mix.* ◆ **mix up.** *tr.v.* [*sep.*] **1.** To confuse (sbdy.): *Your directions mixed us up even more.* **2.** To confuse (two people or things): *I always mix up the twins.*

SYNONYMS: mix, blend, merge, fuse, mingle.
These verbs mean to put into or come together in one mass. **Mix** is the most general term: *The artist mixed the blue and yellow paints together.* **Blend** means to mix thoroughly so that the parts lose their separate characteristics: *They blend coffee and cocoa to make a special mocha drink.* **Merge** means to absorb one thing into another to make a new whole: *The two companies merged.* **Fuse** means to make a strong union by merging: *Extreme heat fused the two metals together.* **Mingle** means to mix without changing the component parts: *They mingled outside the theater.* **ANTONYM: separate.**

---

mixed (mĭkst) *adj.* **1.** Blended together into one mass: *a drink of mixed juices.* **2.** Composed of various elements: *a mixed reaction from the critics.* ◆ **mixed bag.** *Informal.* A collection of things that are unlike each other: *a four-screen movie theater showing a mixed bag of films.*

mixed number *n.* A number, such as 7⅜, consisting of a whole number and a fraction.

mix•er (mĭk′sər) *n.* **1.** A device that mixes or blends ingredients, especially by mechanical action: *a cement mixer; He used the mixer to beat the eggs.* **2.** A person who meets and talks with new people easily: *He's a good mixer at parties.* **3.** An informal party where people can meet. **4.** A beverage, such as soda water, used in alcoholic drinks.

mix•ture (mĭks′chər) *n.* [C; U] **1.** A combination of different ingredients, things, or kinds: *a mixture of roses and carnations in the vase.* **2.** Something made of substances that are not chemically combined: *a mixture of several gases.*

mix-up also **mix•up** (mĭks′ŭp′) *n.* A state of confusion; a misunderstanding: *There was a mix-up over the starting time of the game.*

ml or **mL** *abbr.* An abbreviation of milliliter.

mm *abbr.* An abbreviation of millimeter.

Mn The symbol for the element **manganese.**

mne•mon•ic (nĭ mŏn′ĭk) *adj.* Relating to the memory: *a mnemonic device for remembering the names of presidents.* —*n.* Something, such as a formula or rhyme, that helps one to remember sthg. For example, *i before e except after c* is a mnemonic.

MO or **Mo.** *abbr.* An abbreviation of Missouri.

mo. *abbr.* An abbreviation of month.

moan (mōn) *n.* A long, low sound, usually of sorrow or pain: *The nurse heard the patient's moan.* —*v.* —*intr.* **1.** To make the sound of a moan or moans: *The dog moaned in its sleep.* **2.** To complain or grieve: *They moaned about the lost opportunity.* —*tr.* To say (sthg.) with a moan: *"We can't seem to win a game,"* moaned the coach.

moat (mōt) *n.* A wide deep ditch, usually filled with water, especially one surrounding a medieval town or fortress.

mob (mŏb) *n.* **1.** A large disorderly crowd: *The mob rioted in the streets.* **2.** Often **Mob.** Organized crime: *The FBI kept a close watch on the Mob's activities.* —*tr.v.* **mobbed, mob•bing, mobs.** **1.** To crowd around and press against or annoy (sbdy.), especially in anger or enthusiasm: *Autograph seekers mobbed the stars.* **2.** To crowd into or fill (a place): *Visitors mobbed the museum.*

mo•bile (mō′bəl *or* mō′bīl′) *adj.* **1.** Capable of being moved from place to place: *a mobile hospital.* **2.** Capable of moving or changing easily: *a face with mobile features.* **3.** Fluid or flowing freely: *Mercury is a mobile metal.* **4.** Allowing movement from one social class to another: *a mobile society.* —*n.* (mō′bēl′). A type of sculpture consisting of parts that move, especially as the air moves. —**mo•bil′i•ty** (mō bĭl′ĭ tē) *n.* [U]

mobile home *n.* A house trailer that is used as a permanent house and usually has utilities such as water and electricity.

mo•bi•lize (mō′bə līz′) *v.* **mo•bi•lized, mo•bi•liz•ing, mo•bi•liz•es.** —*tr.* **1.** To bring together (sbdy./sthg.) to prepare for war or a similar emergency: *Troops were mobilized.* **2.** To assemble or coordinate (sbdy./sthg.) for a particular purpose: *She mobilized public opinion to support the cleanup of the river.* —*intr.* To organize or become ready: *Workers mobilized after the earthquake.* —**mo′bi•li•za′tion** (mō′bə lǐ zā′shən) *n.* [C; U]

mob•ster (mŏb′stər) *n. Informal.* A member of a criminal gang: *Mobsters control the drug trade.*

moc•ca•sin (mŏk′ə sĭn) *n.* A soft leather slipper first worn by Native Americans.

mo•cha (mō′kə) *n.* [U] A flavoring made of coffee mixed with chocolate.

mock (mŏk) *tr.v.* To make fun of (sbdy./ sthg.), often by imitating or describing in an insulting way; ridicule: *They mocked the way she laughed.* —*adj.* Not real; pretend: *a mock battle.* —**mock′er** *n.*

mock•er•y (mŏk′ə rē) *n.* **1.** [U] Ridicule: *The mockery of his classmates turned his face red.* **2.** [C] A false, offensive, or ridiculous

---

ă–**cat**; ā–**pay**; âr–**care**; ä–**father**; ĕ–**get**; ē–**be**; ĭ–**sit**; ī–**nice**; îr–**here**; ŏ–**got**; ō–**go**; ô–**saw**; oi–**boy**; ou–**out**;
ōō–**took**; ōō–**boot**; ŭ–**cut**; ûr–**word**; th–**thin**; *th*–**this**; hw–**when**; zh–**vision**; ə–**about**; N–French bon

imitation of sthg.: *The trial was a mockery of justice.*

mock·ing·bird (mŏk′ĭng bûrd′) *n.* Any of several birds of the southern and eastern United States that often imitate the songs of other birds.

mock·up also **mock-up** (mŏk′ŭp′) *n.* A model, as of an airplane or a building, used for demonstration, study, or testing: *a mockup of the new engine.*

mod·al or **modal auxiliary** (mōd′l) *n.* In grammar, one of a set of English verbs, including *can, may, must, ought, shall, should, will,* and *would,* that are used with other verbs to express mood or tense.

mode (mōd) *n.* **1.** A way, manner, or style of doing sthg.: *a mode of living; a mode of travel.* **2.** The current fashion or style in clothing: *a hat in the latest mode.*

mod·el (mŏd′l) *n.* **1.** A small-scale copy or representation of sthg.: *a model of a ship.* **2.** A style or design of sthg.: *This car is last year's model.* **3.** A person or thing serving as an ideal example of sthg.: *That farm is a model of efficient management.* **4.** A person hired to wear and show clothes: *a fashion model.* **5.** A person who poses for an artist or a photographer. **6.** In science, a description of a system that accounts for its known properties in a reasonable way. *—v.* *—tr.* **1.** [*after; on*] To plan or build (sthg.) according to a respected model: *The library was modeled after the Library of Congress in Washington.* **2.** To make sthg. by shaping (a plastic substance): *I like to model clay.* **3.** To show (clothing, for example) so others see how it looks: *She modeled her new dress.* *—intr.* To serve as a model: *She modeled for the photographer.* *—adj.* **1.** Serving or used as a model: *We visited the model home.* **2.** Serving as a standard of excellence: *She is a model child.*

mod·el·ing (mŏd′l ĭng) *n.* [U] **1.** The act of constructing a model out of a pliable material: *Children often enjoy modeling in clay.* **2.** The profession of being a model: *Modeling can be a brief career.*

mo·dem (mō′dĕm′) *n.* A device that changes data usable in data processing to another form usable in transmission by telephone: *The modem in my computer lets me connect to the Internet.*

mod·er·ate (mŏd′ər ĭt) *adj.* **1.** Within reasonable limits; not excessive: *That store has moderate prices.* **2.** Average in amount or quality: *a moderate income.* **3.** Not severe; mild: *a moderate climate.* **4.** Opposed to radical or extreme opinions or actions, especially in politics or religion: *a moderate approach to taxation.* *—n.* A person who holds moderate views or opinions, especially in politics or religion. *—v.* (mŏd′ə rāt′). **mod·er·at·ed, mod·er·at·ing, mod·er·ates.** *—tr.* **1.** To make (sthg.) less extreme: *You should moder-*

ate *your demands.* **2.** To direct (a meeting or panel discussion): *The reporter was chosen to moderate the Presidential debates.* *—intr.* **1.** To become less extreme: *Her views on taxes have moderated since her election.* **2.** To act as a moderator. *—***mod′er·ate·ly** *adv.* *—***mod′er·a′tion** *n.* [U]

mod·er·a·tor (mŏd′ə rā′tər) *n.* The person who directs a meeting or discussion: *The moderator asked the candidates the next question.*

mod·ern (mŏd′ərn) *adj.* **1.** Relating to the present or recent past: *modern history.* **2.** Relating to a recently developed style, technique, or technology: *modern methods of farming.* *—n.* A person with modern ideas, tastes, or beliefs: *He's a modern in everything but fashion.* *—***mo·der′ni·ty** (mŏ dûr′nĭ tē or mō dûr′nĭ tē) *n.* [U]

mod·ern·ize (mŏd′ər nīz′) *v.* **mo·dern·ized, mo·dern·iz·ing, mo·dern·iz·es.** *—tr.* To make (sthg.) modern in appearance, style, or character: *My parents modernized their kitchen.* *—intr.* To become modern; accept or adopt modern ways: *The business was forced to modernize.* *—***mod′ern·i·za′tion** (mŏd′ər nĭ zā′shən) *n.* [C; U]

mod·est (mŏd′ĭst) *adj.* **1.** Showing a moderate opinion of one's own talents, abilities, or accomplishments: *He remains modest in spite of his fame.* **2.** Reserved in dress and behavior: *too modest to wear a bikini.* **3.** Not fancy or showy; unpretentious: *a modest house.* **4.** Moderate in size or amount: *a modest salary.* *—***mod′est·ly** *adv.* *—***mod′es·ty** *n.* [U]

mod·i·cum (mŏd′ĭ kəm) *n.* (*usually singular*). Formal. A small amount: *Politics is a subject in which I have only a modicum of interest.*

mod·i·fi·ca·tion (mŏd′ə fĭ kā′shən) *n.* **1.** [U] The action of modifying sthg.: *The theory is still subject to some modification.* **2.** [C] A small change or limitation: *The design was approved with certain modifications.*

mod·i·fi·er (mŏd′ə fī′ər) *n.* In grammar, a word, phrase, or clause that qualifies or limits the sense of another word or phrase. In the phrase *a flower garden,* the noun *flower* is a modifier.

mod·i·fy (mŏd′ə fī′) *v.* **mod·i·fied, mod·i·fy·ing, mod·i·fies.** *—tr.* **1.** To change (sthg.); alter: *The lawyer modified the terms of the contract.* **2.** In grammar, to qualify or limit the meaning of (a word or phrase): *Adjectives often modify nouns.* *—intr.* To be or become modified; change: *My political views have gradually modified.*

mod·u·late (mŏj′ə lāt′) *tr.v.* **mod·u·lat·ed, mod·u·lat·ing, mod·u·lates.** **1.** To change or vary (one's voice or a musical instrument, for example): *The singer modulated her voice.* **2.** To vary the amplitude, frequency, or some other characteristic of (electromagnetic waves) in order to transmit a signal. *—***mod′u·la′tion** *n.* [C; U] *—***mod′u·la·tor** *n.*

M

mod•ule (mŏj′ōōl) *n.* **1.** A part of a larger unit in education: *We need to take two modules of English.* **2.** A standard element that is used over and over again in forming a building or structure: *The housing was built using prefabricated modules.* **3.** A self-contained unit of a spacecraft that is used for a particular job or set of jobs: *a lunar module.* —**mod′u•lar** (mŏj′ə lər) *adj.*

mo•gul (mō′gəl) *n.* A very rich or powerful person: *a real-estate mogul.*

mo•hair (mō′hâr′) *n.* [U] The soft silky hair of the Angora goat and cloth made from it.

moist (moist) *adj.* Slightly wet; damp: *a moist cake.* See Synonyms at **wet.** —**moist′ness** *n.* [U]

mois•ten (moi′sən) *tr.v.* To make (sthg.) a little wet: *We used a humidifier to moisten the dry air. She moistened her lips.*

mois•ture (mois′chər) *n.* [U] Wetness, especially water vapor in the air or water spread thinly over a surface: *Moisture causes steel to rust.*

mois•tur•ize (mois′chə rīz′) *tr.v.* **mois•tur•ized, mois•tur•iz•ing, mois•tur•iz•es.** To add or restore liquid to (sthg.): *skin cream that moisturizes the face.* —**mois′-tur•iz′er** *n.*

mo•lar (mō′lər) *n.* Any of the teeth located toward the back of the jaws, used for grinding food: *Humans normally have 12 molars.*

mo•las•ses (mə lăs′ĭz) *n.* [U] A thick syrup produced in refining sugar: *Can you taste the molasses in these cookies?*

mold¹ (mōld) *n.* **1.** A hollow container used for shaping a liquid or plastic substance: *Pour the plaster into a mold.* **2.** Something made or shaped from a mold: *the mold of a statue.* —*tr.v.* **1.** To shape (sthg.) in a mold: *mold a cake.* **2.** To shape (sbdy./sthg.) in a particular way: *mold clay; mold young people into soldiers.*

mold² (mōld) *n.* [C; U] Any of various fungi that often form a fuzzy coating on the surface of food and other plant or animal substances: *old bread spotted with mold.* —**mold′i•ness** *n.* [U] —**mold′y** *adj.*

mold•ing (mōl′dĭng) *n.* **1.** [U] The act of making a mold. **2.** [C; U] An ornamental strip used to decorate a surface: *We have wooden molding around the windows in our house.*

mole¹ (mōl) *n.* A small, usually dark growth on the skin: *The woman had the mole on her arm removed.*

mole² (mōl) *n.* **1.** Any of various small burrowing mammals with long claws, tiny eyes, and short silky fur. **2.** A spy who operates from inside an organization: *The mole had been passing secrets for years.*

mole³ (mōl) *n.* The amount of a substance that has a mass in grams numerically equal to the molecular weight of the substance.

mol•e•cule (mŏl′ĭ kyōol′) *n.* A stable arrangement of atoms. A molecule is the smallest and simplest unit that has the characteristic chemical and physical properties of a compound or an element. —**mo•lec′u•lar** (mə lĕk′yə lər) *adj.*

mole•hill (mōl′hĭl′) *n.* A small mound of earth dug up by a mole burrowing underground. ♦ **make a mountain out of a molehill.** To give too much importance to a minor problem: *Don't make a mountain out of a molehill!*

mo•lest (mə lĕst′) *tr.v.* **1.** To force unwanted or improper sexual activity on (sbdy.): *The man who molested the child was sent to prison.* **2.** *Formal.* To annoy, bother, or disturb (sbdy./sthg.). —**mo′les•ta′tion** (mō′lĕ stā′shən) *n.* [U] —**mo•lest′er** *n.*

mol•li•fy (mŏl′ə fī′) *tr.v.* **mol•li•fied, mol•li•fy•ing, mol•li•fies.** To lessen the anger of (sbdy.): *a new company policy designed to mollify angry workers.*

mol•lusk (mŏl′əsk) *n.* Any of numerous soft-bodied invertebrate animals, such as snails, clams, and oysters, that usually have a hard outer shell and live in water. Some mollusks, such as octopuses and squids, have no outer shell.

molt (mōlt) *v.* —*intr.* In animals, to lose an outer covering, such as skin or feathers, when it is replaced by a new growth: *Some snakes molt in spring.* —*tr.* To lose (an outer covering): *Birds molt their feathers, but dogs and cats shed their hair.*

mol•ten (mōl′tən) *adj.* Made liquid by heat; melted: *The molten metal was poured into the mold.*

mom (mŏm) *n. Informal.* Mother.

mom-and-pop (mŏm′ən pŏp′) *adj.* Relating to a small business that is run by the owners: *a mom-and-pop grocery store.*

mo•ment (mō′mənt) *n.* **1.** [C] A very short period of time; an instant: *I'll be ready in a moment.* **2.** [C] A certain important point in time: *the happiest moment of my life.* **3.** [U] The present time: *We are busy at the moment.* **4.** [U] *Formal.* Great importance: *an event of great moment.* ♦ **any moment.** Very soon: *The train should be here any moment.* **the moment (that).** Just as soon as: *He fell in love the moment he saw her.*

mo•men•tar•i•ly (mō′mən târ′ə lē) *adv.* **1.** For an instant or a moment: *I was momentarily at a loss for words.* **2.** At any moment; very soon: *The doctor will see you momentarily.*

mo•men•tar•y (mō′mən tĕr′ē) *adj.* Lasting only an instant or a moment: *a momentary look at a passing car.*

mo·men·tous (mō mĕn′təs) *adj.* Of the greatest importance: *The birth of the baby was a momentous occasion.*

mo·men·tum (mō mĕn′təm) *n.* [U] **1.** Force or speed of motion: *The car gained momentum as it raced down the hill. The economy is gaining momentum.* **2.** The product of the mass and velocity of a moving body.

mom·my (mŏm′ē) *n., pl.* **mom·mies.** *Informal.* Mother. Usually used by small children.

Mon. *abbr.* An abbreviation of Monday.

mon·arch (mŏn′ərk *or* mŏn′ärk′) *n.* A ruler, such as a king or queen, who reigns over a country: *The monarch greeted her people.* —**mo·nar′chic** (mə när′kĭk), **mo·nar′chi·cal** *adj.*

mon·ar·chy (mŏn′ər kē *or* mŏn′är′kē) *n., pl.* **mon·ar·chies. 1.** [U] Government by a monarch. **2.** [C] A country ruled by a monarch. —**mon′ar·chist** *n.*

mon·as·ter·y (mŏn′ə stĕr′ē) *n., pl.* **mon·as·ter·ies.** The building or buildings where monks live, work, and pray: *The monastery is three hundred years old.*

mo·nas·tic (mə năs′tĭk) *adj.* **1.** Relating to a monastery. **2.** Resembling life in a monastery: *a monastic lifestyle.*

Mon·day (mŭn′dē *or* mŭn′dā′) *n.* The second day of the week.

mon·e·tar·y (mŏn′ĭ tĕr′ē) *adj.* **1.** Relating to money: *the monetary value of a painting.* —**mon′e·tar′i·ly** *adv.*

mon·ey (mŭn′ē) *n.* [U] **1.** Something, such as gold or an official coin or paper note, that has a legal value and can be exchanged for all goods and services. **2.** Wealth; property and assets: *family money.* ♦ **for (one's) money.** According to one's opinion or choice: *For my money, it's not worth the trouble of making a complaint.* **get (one's) money's worth.** To get sthg. worth the price one paid: *It was an expensive trip, but we had such a great time that we think we got our money's worth.* **put (one's) money where (one's) mouth is.** *Slang.* To act according to one's own advice: *You say I should buy this stock, but why don't you put your money where your mouth is and buy it yourself?*

mon·eyed (mŭn′ēd) *adj.* Rich; wealthy: *a moneyed individual.*

mon·ey·grub·ber (mŭn′ē grŭb′ər) *n. Informal.* A person who is too interested in getting money: *He's such a moneygrubber that he refuses to go to the movies.* —**mon′ey·grub′bing** *adj. & n.* [U]

mon·ey·mak·ing (mŭn′ē mā′kĭng) *adj.* Successful in earning money: *a moneymaking business.* —**mon′ey·mak′er** *n.*

money market *n.* In economics, the trade in short-term, low-risk financial instruments: *She has $5,000 in a money market account.*

money order *n.* A check for a specific amount of money that can be bought for cash at a bank or post office.

mon·grel (mŭng′grəl *or* mŏng′grəl) *n.* An animal, especially a dog, of mixed breed: *The little mongrel had been rescued from the animal shelter as a puppy.*

mon·i·tor (mŏn′ĭ tər) *n.* **1.** A device like a television that shows computer information on a screen. **2.** A person who gives warnings or instruction: *The hall monitor watches students passing between classes.* **3.** An electronic device used to record or control a process or information: *a radiation monitor.* —*tr.v.* **1.** To keep watch over (sbdy.); supervise: *He will monitor the students on the bus.* **2.** To keep track of (sthg.) systematically: *This machine monitors a patient's heartbeat.*

monk (mŭngk) *n.* A member of a group of men living in a monastery and following the rules of a religious order.

mon·key (mŭng′kē) *n., pl.* **mon·keys. 1.** Any of various mammals related to apes and humans, with long tails and with hands and feet adapted for holding things. **2.** A playful or mischievous child. ♦ **make a monkey out of.** To make sbdy. appear stupid or foolish: *The lawyer made a monkey out of the witness.*

monkey around. *intr.v. Informal.* To behave in a silly or mischievous way: *Don't monkey around during the ceremony.* **monkey business.** *Slang.* Playful behavior or dishonest acts: *We suspected the treasurer of monkey business with club funds.* **monkey with.** *tr.v. Informal.* [insep.] To disturb or tamper with (sthg.): *Don't monkey with the VCR.*

monkey wrench *n.* A hand tool with adjustable jaws for turning nuts and bolts of various sizes. ♦ **throw a monkey wrench into.** To disrupt plans: *Bad weather threw a monkey wrench into our plans for the picnic.*

mono (mŏn′ō) *n.* [U] *Informal.* The disease infectious mononucleosis: *The doctor said I have mono.*

mono— *or* **mon—** *pref.* A prefix that means: **1.** One; only; single: *monogamy.* **2.** Containing a single atom, radical, or group: *monoxide.*

mon·o·chro·mat·ic (mŏn′ə krō măt′ĭk) *adj.* **1.** Consisting of a single color: *monochromatic light.* **2.** Consisting of a single wavelength of light or other radiation: *monochromatic x-rays.*

mon·o·cle (mŏn′ə kəl) *n.* A single eyeglass, usually with a cord attached, worn in front of one eye.

mo·nog·a·my (mə nŏg′ə mē) *n.* [U] The custom or condition of being married to only one person at a time. —**mo·nog′a·mous** *adj.*

mon·o·gram (mŏn′ə grăm′) *n.* A design made of one or more letters, usually the initials of a name: *I had my monogram sewn on my shirt.* —*tr.v.* **mon·o·grammed, mon·o·gram·ming, mon·o·grams.** To mark (sthg.) with a monogram: *She monogrammed the sheets and towels.*

M

mon•o•lin•gual (mŏn′ə lĭng′gwəl) *adj.*
Using or knowing only one language: *a
monolingual dictionary.*

mon•o•logue (mŏn′ə lôg′) *n.* **1.** A long
speech by an actor or by a character in a
story. **2.** A series of jokes and stories told by
a comedian on the stage alone.

mon•o•nu•cle•o•sis (mŏn′ō nōō′klē ō′sĭs)
n. [U] Infectious mononucleosis, a contagious
viral disease: *Mononucleosis is a common illness among college students.*

mo•nop•o•lize (mə nŏp′ə līz′) *tr.v.* **mo•
nop•o•lized, mo•nop•o•liz•ing, mo•
nop•o•liz•es. 1.** To gain and hold a monopoly over (sthg.): *monopolize the diamond
market.* **2.** To get or have control over (sthg.):
Don't monopolize the conversation. **—mo•
nop′o•li•za′tion** (mə nŏp′ə lĭ zā′shən) *n.*
[U] **—mo•nop′o•liz′er** *n.*

mo•nop•o•ly (mə nŏp′ə lē) *n., pl.* **mo•
nop•o•lies. 1.a.** Complete control by one
group over the producing or selling of a product
or service: *The early railroads had almost a
monopoly on freight and passenger transportation.* **b.** A company with such complete control:
Laws limit the power of monopolies. **2.** Sole
possession or control of sthg.: *The U.S. monopoly on the atomic bomb did not last long.*
—mo•nop′o•lis′tic (mə nŏp′ə lĭs′tĭk) *adj.*

mon•o•rail (mŏn′ə rāl′) *n.* A railway system using a track with a single rail: *The
monorail carries people around the amusement park.*

mon•o•syl•la•ble (mŏn′ə sĭl′ə bəl) *n.* A
word of one syllable: *He answered using
the monosyllables yes and no.* **—mon′o•
syl•lab′ic** (mŏn′ə sĭ lăb′ĭk) *adj.*

mon•o•the•ism (mŏn′ə thē′ĭz′əm) *n.* [U]
The belief that there is only one God: *Mono-
theism is a basic belief of Islam.* **—mon′o•
the′ist** *n.* **—mon′o•the•is′tic** *adj.*

mon•o•tone (mŏn′ə tōn′) *n.* **1.** A series of
sounds or words uttered in a single tone of
voice: *Try not to speak in a monotone.* **2.** A
boring repetition, as in sound, color, or style:
the gray monotone of a cloudy day.

mo•not•o•nous (mə nŏt′n əs) *adj.* **1.**
Spoken or sounded in one repeated tone: *The
monotonous lecture caused the students'
attention to wander.* **2.** Never different or
interesting; unchanging and dull: *a monotonous diet.* **—mo•not′o•nous•ly** *adv.*

mo•not•o•ny (mə nŏt′n ē) *n.* [U] Boring
sameness or repetition: *the monotony of a job
that never varies.*

mon•soon (mŏn sōōn′) *n.* **1.** A wind system
that produces the wet and dry seasons in
southern Asia. **2.** *(usually plural).* The season during which this wind blows from the
southwest, usually accompanied by heavy

rains: *The monsoons bring heavy rains and
flooding every year.* **3.** A heavy rain: *Several
inches of rain fell during the monsoon.*

mon•ster (mŏn′stər) *n.* **1.** An imaginary
creature that has body parts from various
human or animal forms, especially a frightening one: *Frankenstein's monster.* **2.** An animal or a plant that is very large or abnormal
in form or appearance.

mon•strous (mŏn′strəs) *adj.* **1.** Frightful;
shocking: *monstrous behavior.* **2.** Huge; enormous: *a monstrous iceberg.* **3.** Abnormal in
appearance or structure: *a monstrous building.* **—mon•stros′i•ty** (mŏn strŏs′ĭ tē) *n.*
—mon′strous•ly *adv.*

Mont. *abbr.* An abbreviation of Montana.

month (mŭnth) *n.* **1.** One of the twelve calendar divisions of the year, lasting about thirty
days. **2.** A period lasting from a date in one
calendar month to the same date in the following month: *The doctor will see you a month
from now.*

month•ly (mŭnth′lē) *adj.* **1.** Happening or
payable every month: *a monthly meeting;
monthly bills.* **2.** Continuing or lasting for
a month: *average monthly rainfall.* **—adv.**
Every month: *a magazine published monthly.*

mon•u•ment (mŏn′yə mənt) *n.* **1.** A structure, such as a tower or statue, built to honor
a person, a group, or an event. **2.** An excellent
work or achievement: *The book is a monument of scholarship.*

mon•u•men•tal (mŏn′yə mĕn′tl) *adj.* **1.**
Impressively large, strong, and long-lasting:
monumental dams and tunnels. **2.** Of very
special importance: *Einstein made monumental discoveries in physics.* **—mon′u•men′-
tal•ly** *adv.*

moo (mōō) *intr.v.* To make the deep sound of
a cow: *The cows mooed in the barn.* **—n., pl.**
moos. The deep sound made by a cow.

mooch (mōōch) *v. Slang.* **—tr.** To get or try to
get (sthg.) by begging: *He is always mooching food from me.* **—intr.** [off] To get or try to
get sthg. for free: *They lived by mooching off
friends.* **—mooch′er** *n.*

mood¹ (mōōd) *n.* A state of mind or feeling: *I
was in a good mood after the party.*

mood² (mōōd) *n.* In grammar, a set of verb
forms that tells how certain the speaker is of
the action expressed. In English, the indicative mood is used to make factual statements,
the imperative mood to give commands, and
the subjunctive mood to suggest doubt.

mood•y (mōō′dē) *adj.* **mood•i•er, mood•
i•est. 1.** Likely to change moods often, especially with periods of anger or gloom. **2.**
Feeling or showing low spirits; gloomy: *his
moody silence.* **—mood′i•ly** *adv.* **—mood′-
i•ness** *n.* [U]

moon (moon) *n.* **1.** The natural satellite of Earth, traveling around Earth at an average distance of about 237,000 miles (381,500 kilometers). **2.** A natural satellite of a planet: *the moons of Jupiter.* **3.** The moon as seen at a particular time in its cycle of phases: *a half moon.* —*v.* —*intr.* To daydream: *That child spends too much time mooning.* —*tr. Slang.* To bend over and show one's bare buttocks to (sbdy.) as a rude joke. ✦ **moon over.** *tr.v.* [insep.] *Informal.* To spend one's time thinking about one's love: *He mooned over his first girlfriend for months.*

moon•beam (moon'bem') *n.* A ray of moonlight.

moon•light (moon'līt') *n.* [U] The light that is reflected from the surface of the moon. —*intr.v. Informal.* To work at a second job, often at night, in addition to one's regular job: *The police officer moonlighted as a security guard.*

moon•lit (moon'lit') *adj.* Lighted by the moon: *a moonlit pond.*

moon•shine (moon'shīn') *n.* **1.** Moonlight. **2.** Whiskey that is made illegally.

moor[1] (moor) *v.* —*tr.* **1.** To secure (a boat or an aircraft, for example) with cables, lines, or anchors: *moored the boat to the dock.* —*intr.* **1.** To secure a boat or an aircraft with lines or anchors: *We moored out in the bay.* **2.** To be secured with lines or anchors: *The sailboat moored alongside the wharf.*

moor[2] (moor) *n.* (*usually plural*). A broad open land, often with wet areas and low shrubs: *England is known for its moors.*

moor•ing (moor'ĭng) *n.* **1.** A place where a boat or an aircraft may be secured. **2.** (*usually plural*). Equipment, such as anchors, chains, or lines, for securing a boat or aircraft: *In the storm the boat pulled free from its moorings.*

moose (moos) *n., pl.* **moose.** A large mammal of northern regions, related to the deer and with a large head and broad antlers in the male.

—————————————————————

Homonyms: moose, mousse (dessert).

—————————————————————

moot (moot) *adj.* **1.** Open to debate; arguable: *The price we should ask them to pay is a moot question.* **2.** No longer important; irrelevant: *Concerns for the President's safety became moot when he decided for political reasons not to make the trip.*

mop (mŏp) *n.* **1.** A tool for washing or dusting floors, consisting of a sponge or strips of cloth attached to a long handle: *The mop and bucket are in the kitchen.* **2.** A loosely tangled bunch or mass: *a mop of hair.* —*tr.v.* **mopped, mop•ping, mops.** To wash or wipe (sthg.) with or as if with a mop: *I mopped the hallway. She mopped her forehead with a towel.* ✦ **mop up.** *tr.v.* [sep.] To finish (a job), especially to clear (an area) of remaining enemy soldiers after a victory.

—*intr.v. Informal.* To finish a nearly completed task: *Let's mop up and go home.*

mope (mōp) *intr.v.* **moped, mop•ing, mopes.** To be in low spirits or quietly resentful; sulk: *He's moping because he didn't get the job.*

mo•ped (mō'pĕd') *n.* A lightweight motorized bicycle that can be pedaled.

mor•al (môr'əl *or* mŏr'əl) *adj.* **1.** Relating to the judgment of the goodness and badness of human action: *moral principles.* **2.** In accord with standards of what is good and just: *a moral way of living.* **3.** Coming from the inner sense of right and wrong: *She felt she had a moral duty to help.* **4.** Psychological rather than physical or concrete: *They gave me some moral support.* —*n.* **1.** The lesson or principle taught by a fable, a story, or an event: *What is the moral of the story?* **2. morals.** Standards of good or correct behavior: *He is a man of high morals.* —**mor'al•ly** *adv.*

mo•rale (mə răl') *n.* [U] The state of a person's or group's spirits, as shown in confidence, cheerfulness, and willingness to work toward a goal: *The party raised everyone's morale, and the staff finished the job on schedule.*

mor•al•ist (môr'ə lĭst *or* mŏr'ə lĭst) *n.* **1.** A person who is concerned with moral principles and questions. **2.** A person who is too much concerned with the morals of others. —**mor'al•is'tic** *adj.* —**mor'al•is'ti•cal•ly** *adv.*

mo•ral•i•ty (mə răl'ĭ tē) *n.* [U] **1.** A set of ideas about what is right and wrong in human behavior and relationships: *religious morality.* **2.** The quality of being moral; goodness or rightness: *People debate the morality of using animals in experiments.*

mor•al•ize (môr'ə līz' *or* mŏr'ə līz') *intr.v.* **mor•al•ized, mor•al•iz•ing, mor•al•iz•es.** To think about or express moral judgments: *It is useless to moralize to children unless you also act upon your beliefs.*

mo•rass (mə răs' *or* mô răs') *n.* **1.** An area of low soggy ground. **2.** A difficult or very confusing situation: *My paper started out fine, but then I got stuck in a morass of details.*

mor•a•to•ri•um (môr'ə tôr'ē əm) *n., pl.* **mor•a•to•ri•ums** *or* **mor•a•to•ri•a.** A stopping of some activity for a period of time; a temporary ban or pause: *The participating countries agreed to a moratorium on testing nuclear bombs.*

mor•bid (môr'bĭd) *adj.* **1.** Thinking too much about death, decay, or other unhealthy matters: *a morbid sense of humor.* **2.** Relating to disease: *morbid changes in body tissues.* —**mor•bid'i•ty** (môr bĭd'ĭ tē) *n.* [U] —**mor'bid•ly** *adv.* —**mor'bid•ness** *n.* [U]

more (môr) *adj.* Comparative of **many, much.** **1.a.** Greater in number: *More people came to the show tonight than ever before.* **b.** Greater in size, amount, or degree: *He does more work than anybody else.* **2.** Additional; extra: *I need more time to finish making dinner.* —*n.* A greater or additional number, degree, or amount: *More of our textbooks have arrived in the store.* —*pron.* **1.** *(used with a plural verb).* A greater number of persons or things: *I thought I had found all the empty bottles, but there were more in the basement.* **2.** *(used with a singular verb).* A greater amount of sthg.: *Do you want some tea? There's more in the pot.* —*adv.* Comparative of **much. 1.** To a greater degree or in a greater amount: *After seeing the movie again, we liked it even more.* **2.** Used to form the comparative of many adjectives and adverbs: *more difficult; more intelligently.* **3.** In addition; again: *I telephoned twice more, but got no answer.* ♦ **more and more.** To a steadily increasing degree: *Our neighbor got more and more annoyed at the noise.* **more or less.** About; approximately: *The trip takes six hours, more or less.*

more•o•ver (môr ō′vər *or* môr′ō′ vər) *adv. Formal.* Beyond what has been said; in addition: *We are, moreover, delighted to report that progress has been made.*

mo•res (môr′āz′) *pl.n. Formal.* **1.** The accepted customs and rules of behavior of a particular social group: *Mores vary in different cultures.* **2.** Attitudes about proper behavior: *the manners and mores of suburban life.*

morgue (môrg) *n.* An official place where bodies of persons found dead are kept until identified or claimed: *Police called her to the morgue to identify the body.*

mor•i•bund (môr′ə bŭnd′ *or* môr′ə bŭnd′) *adj. Formal.* At the point of death; about to die: *The patient was moribund.*

Mor•mon (môr′mən) *n.* A member of the Mormon Church. —*adj.* Relating to the Mormons or their church. —**Mor′mon•is′m** *n.* [U]

Mormon Church *n.* A Christian church founded by Joseph Smith in 1830, with doctrines based on the Bible and the Book of Mormo. Used to refer to the Church of Jesus Christ of Latter-Day Saints.

morn (môrn) *n.* A poetic word for morning.

HOMONYMS: morn, mourn (grieve).

---

morn•ing (môr′nĭng) *n.* [C; U] **1.** The early part of the day, from midnight to noon or from sunrise to noon. **2.** The first or early part of sthg.; the beginning: *the morning of a new nation.*

HOMONYMS: morning, mourning (grieving).

---

morning sickness *n.* [U] A sick feeling, often with vomiting, experienced by a preg-

nant woman: *Morning sickness kept her from eating much for the first three months of her pregnancy.*

mo•ron (môr′ŏn′) *n. Slang.* A person regarded as very stupid: *That moron was driving too fast.* —**mo•ron′ic** (mə rŏn′ĭk *or* mô rŏn′ĭk) *adj.*

mo•rose (mə rōs′ *or* mô rōs′) *adj.* Bad-tempered and depressed; gloomy: *She looked morose after speaking with her boss.* —**mo•rose′ly** *adv.* —**mo•rose′ness** *n.* [U]

mor•pheme (môr′fēm′) *n.* In grammar, a unit of language that has meaning and that cannot be divided into smaller meaningful parts. In the word *fires* both *fire* and -*s* are morphemes.

mor•phine (môr′fēn′) *n.* [U] An addictive narcotic drug extracted from opium and used in medicine as an anesthetic and sedative: *The doctor used morphine as a painkiller.*

mor•phol•o•gy (môr fŏl′ə jē) *n.* [U] **1.** The branch of biology that deals with the form and structure of living organisms. **2.** In linguistics, the study of the structure and form of words, including inflections and derivations: *We studied morphology and syntax in that course.* —**mor′pho•log′ic** (môr′fə lŏj′ĭk), **mor′pho•log′i•cal** *adj.*

Morse code (môrs) *n.* A code used for sending messages in which letters and numbers are represented by short and long sounds, known as dots and dashes.

mor•sel (môr′səl) *n.* **1.** A small piece of food: *We ate just a few morsels.* **2.** A small amount; a piece: *He had a morsel of gossip for us.*

mor•tal (môr′tl) *adj.* **1.** Not able to live forever: *All human beings are mortal.* **2.** Characteristic of human beings; human: *beyond the limits of mortal endurance.* **3.** Causing or accompanying death: *a mortal wound.* **4.** Being so wicked or evil as to bring eternal damnation: *a mortal sin.* **5.** Unrelenting; deadly: *mortal enemies.* **6.** Extreme; severe: *They lived in mortal fear.* —*n.* A human being: *We are all mortals.* —**mor′tal•ly** *adv.*

mor•tal•i•ty (môr tăl′ĭ tē) *n., pl.* **mor•tal•i•ties. 1.** [U] The condition of being subject to death: *A serious sickness made me aware of my own mortality.* **2.** [C; U] Death, especially of large numbers: *The war brought widespread civilian mortality.* **3.** [U] The proportion of people in a group that dies in a given period of time; the death rate: *That state has high infant mortality.*

mor•tar (môr′tər) *n.* **1.** [U] A building material, such as cement, used to hold together bricks, stones, or cement blocks. **2.** [C] A cannon used to fire shells: *The tanks were hit by mortar fire.* **3.** [C] A bowl used to hold substances while they are crushed or ground

---

ă–cat; ā–pay; âr–care; ä–father; ĕ–get; ē–be; ĭ–sit; ī–nice; îr–here; ŏ–got; ō–go; ô–saw; oi–boy; ou–out; o͞o–took; o͞o–boot; ŭ–cut; ûr–word; th–thin; *th*–this; hw–when; zh–vision; ə–about; N–French bon

with a pestle. —*tr.v.* To plaster or join (sthg.) with mortar.

mort·gage (môr′gĭj) *n.* A legal promise to give property to a creditor if payment is not made on a loan or debt: *That bank holds the mortgage on our house.* —*tr.v.* **mort·gaged, mort·gag·ing, mort·gag·es. 1.** To promise (property) as security for the payment of a debt: *We mortgaged our house for $50,000.* **2.** To put (sthg.) at risk for some immediate benefit: *He mortgaged his future by borrowing lots of money.*

mort·ga·gee (môr′gĭ jē′) *n.* The holder of a mortgage.

mort·ga·gor (môr′gĭ jôr′ *or* môr′gĭ jər) also **mort·gag·er** (môr′gĭ jər) *n.* A person who mortgages his or her property.

mor·ti·cian (môr tĭsh′ən) *n.* A person who prepares the bodies of dead people for burial and organizes the funeral; an undertaker: *The mortician discussed funeral plans with the family.*

mor·ti·fy (môr′tə fī′) *tr.v.* **mor·ti·fied, mor·ti·fy·ing, mor·ti·fies.** To cause (sbdy.) to feel shame or embarrassment; humiliate: *I was mortified by my cousin's rudeness at the ceremony.* —**mor′ti·fi·ca′·tion** (môr′tə fĭ kā′shən) *n.* [U]

mor·tu·ar·y (môr′chōō ĕr′ē) *n., pl.* **mor·tu·ar·ies.** A place where bodies of dead people are prepared or kept before burial or cremation: *Mortuaries provide burial services.*

mos. *abbr.* An abbreviation of months.

mo·sa·ic (mō zā′ĭk) *n.* **1.** A picture or design made on a surface by fitting together small colored pieces, as of glass or stone. **2.** Something that resembles a mosaic: *a mosaic of color in the flower garden.*

mo·sey (mō′zē) *intr.v. Informal.* **1.** To move slowly or at a relaxed pace: *We moseyed through the park.* **2.** To start moving; leave: *Let's mosey along so we don't miss the beginning of the play.*

Mos·lem (mŏz′ləm *or* mŏs′ləm) *n. & adj.* Variant of **Muslim.**

mosque (mŏsk) *n.* A Muslim house of worship.

mos·qui·to (mə skē′tō) *n., pl.* **mos·qui·toes** or **mos·qui·tos.** Any of various winged insects that carry diseases such as malaria and yellow fever. The female bites and sucks blood from people and other animals: *The mosquitoes were terrible last night, and we are covered with bites.*

moss (môs *or* mŏs) *n.* [C; U] A small green or brown plant that does not have flowers and that often forms a dense, soft growth on damp ground, rocks, or tree trunks. —**moss′y** *adj.*

most (mōst) *adj.* Superlative of **many, much.** **1.a.** Greatest in number: *Who won the most votes?* **b.** Largest in amount, size, or degree: *the most money.* **2.** In the greatest number of instances: *Most birds fly.* —*n.* The greatest amount or degree; the largest part: *Most of this*

land is good. —*pron. (used with a singular or plural verb).* The greatest part or number: *Most of the milk is gone. Some apples have been picked, but most are still on the trees.* —*adv.* Superlative of **more, much. 1.** In the greatest amount or to the highest degree. Used with many adjectives and adverbs to form the superlative: *most honest; most impatiently.* **2.** Very: *a most interesting piece of news.* **3.** *Informal.* Almost: *Most everybody's here already.* ♦ **at most** or **at the most.** At the maximum: *The professor spoke for ten minutes at most. We ran for two miles at the most.*

—**most** *suff.* A suffix that means most: *uppermost; innermost.*

most·ly (mōst′lē) *adv.* **1.** For the most part; mainly: *The strawberry plants are mostly growing well.* **2.** Generally; usually: *We mostly try to get to bed before midnight.*

mo·tel (mō tĕl′) *n.* A hotel for motorists, usually with rooms that open directly on a parking area: *We looked for an inexpensive motel near the highway.*

moth (môth *or* mŏth) *n., pl.* **moths** (môthz *or* mŏths). Any of numerous insects related to the butterfly but that fly at night and generally have a thicker body and feathery antennae: *The moth was attracted to the light.*

moth·ball (môth′bôl′) *n.* **1.** A marble-sized ball of naphthalene, stored with clothes to keep moths away. **2. mothballs.** A condition of long-term storage: *After decades of use, the ship was put into mothballs.* —*tr.v.* To put (sthg.) into protective storage: *The experimental airplane was mothballed after funds for more research ran out.*

moth-eat·en (môth′ēt′n) *adj.* **1.** Eaten away by moths: *a moth-eaten sweater.* **2.** Old and stale: *a moth-eaten saying.*

moth·er (mŭth′ər) *n.* **1.** A woman who gives birth to or raises a child. **2.** A female parent of an animal. **3.** A source or cause: *Poverty is the mother of many ills.* **4.** A woman who starts or creates sthg.: *Susan B. Anthony was one of the mothers of the women's suffrage movement.* —*adj.* **1.** Being a mother: *a mother hen.* **2.** Relating to a mother: *mother love.* **3.** Being the source or origin: *the mother church.* **4.** Native: *one's mother country.* —*tr.v.* **1.** To give birth to (sbdy./sthg.): *Our dog mothered a litter of six puppies.* **2.** To watch over or care for (sbdy./sthg.): *She's always mothering her little brother.* —**moth′er·ly** *adj.*

moth·er·hood (mŭth′ər hŏŏd′) *n.* [U] The condition of being a mother: *She was looking forward to motherhood.*

moth·er-in-law (mŭth′ər ĭn lô′) *n., pl.* **moth·ers-in-law** (mŭth′ərz ĭn lô′). The mother of one's wife or husband: *My mother-in-law calls often to chat.*

moth·er·land (mŭth′ər lănd′) *n.* The country of one's birth or of one's ancestors: *She returned to her motherland.*

moth·er·less (mŭ*th*′ər ləs′) *adj*. With no living mother: *motherless puppies*.

Mother Nature *n*. [U] A term for the forces and processes that control the world of living things: *Let's hope that Mother Nature will give us a mild winter*.

Moth·er's Day (mŭ*th*′ərz) *n*. In the United States and Canada the second Sunday in May, celebrated as a holiday in honor of mothers: *I sent my mother a dozen roses for Mother's Day*.

mother tongue *n*. One's native language: *Spanish is his mother tongue*.

mo·tif (mō tēf′) *n*. **1.** An idea or a symbol used repeatedly in a literary or artistic work: *The idea that people cannot control their fates is a recurrent motif in that writer's novels*. **2.** A repeated figure or design in architecture or decoration: *a necktie with a floral motif*.

mo·tion (mō′shən) *n*. **1.** [C; U] The process of moving; change of position: *I was feeling sick from the motion of the ship*. **2.** [U] The ability to move: *The motion in his arm returned after physical therapy*. **3.** [U] Operation; activity: *Put the engine in motion*. **4.** [C] A formal proposal put to a vote in a group: *I moved to adjourn the meeting, and the motion passed by voice vote*. —*v*. —*tr*. To direct (sbdy.) by a wave of the hand or another gesture; signal: *The driver stopped and motioned us to cross*. —*intr*. To make a gesture expressing one's wishes: *He motioned for the waiter to bring coffee*. ◆ **go through the motions.** To do sthg. in a way that shows lack of purpose or interest: *We thought he was sincere, but he was only going through the motions*.

mo·tion·less (mō′shən lĭs) *adj*. Not moving: *The cat was motionless while watching the bird*. —**mo′tion·less·ly** *adv*.

motion picture *n*. **1.** A movie. **2. motion pictures.** The movie industry: *She works in motion pictures*.

motion sickness *n*. [U] Nausea and dizziness caused by motion, as from traveling in a car or a ship: *I can't ride in the back seat because of motion sickness*.

mo·ti·vate (mō′tə vāt′) *tr.v*. **mo·ti·vat·ed, mo·ti·vat·ing, mo·ti·vates.** To provide (sbdy.) with a reason to act; move to action: *The gymnastics coach motivated us to practice, and we improved greatly*.

mo·ti·va·tion (mō′tə vā′shən) *n*. **1.** [U] The process of providing motives: *a teacher who is good at motivation*. **2.** [U] The condition of being motivated, especially to perform well: *These students have a high level of motivation*. **3.** [C] A motive or set of motives: *They questioned the motivation of people who run for public office*.

mo·tive (mō′tĭv) *n*. An emotion or need that causes a person to act in a certain way: *Our motive in writing the book was to make people aware of the issue*.

mot·ley (mŏt′lē) *adj*. Made up of a strange collection of different types: *a motley group of people from different neighborhoods*.

mo·tor (mō′tər) *n*. **1.** A device that changes electric energy into mechanical energy: *The washer needs a new motor*. **2.** A device that produces mechanical energy from a fuel; an engine: *We left the motor running in the car*. —*adj*. **1.** Caused to move by an engine or a motor: *a motor boat*. **2.** Relating to motors or engines: *motor oil*. **3.** Relating to movements of the muscles: *a motor reflex*. —*intr.v*. To travel in a motor vehicle: *The students motored through New England*.

mo·tor·bike (mō′tər bīk′) *n*. A lightweight motorcycle: *The motorbike was very economical to use*.

mo·tor·boat (mō′tər bōt′) *n*. A boat powered by an engine.

mo·tor·cade (mō′tər kād′) *n*. A procession of motor vehicles: *The President's motorcade passed through town*.

mo·tor·cy·cle (mō′tər sī′kəl) *n*. A vehicle with two wheels, similar to a bicycle but larger and heavier, powered by an engine: *The motorcycle roared down the highway*. —**mo′tor·cy′clist** *n*.

mo·tor·ist (mō′tər ĭst) *n*. A person who drives or rides in an automobile: *Many motorists die in auto accidents each year*.

mo·tor·ize (mō′tə rīz′) *tr.v*. **mo·tor·ized, mo·tor·iz·ing, mo·tor·iz·es.** To equip (sthg.) with a motor or motors: *motorize a bicycle*.

motor vehicle *n*. A motorized vehicle that travels on wheels but does not run on rails: *Cars, trucks, and buses are motor vehicles*.

mot·tled (mŏt′ld) *adj*. Spotted or streaked with different colors: *the mottled bird*.

mot·to (mŏt′ō) *n*., *pl*. **mot·toes** or **mot·tos.** **1.** A phrase or statement expressing a principle, a goal, or an ideal: *Kentucky's state motto is "United We Stand, Divided We Fall."* **2.** A brief expression of a guiding principle; a slogan: *His motto has always been "He who hesitates is lost."*

mound (mound) *n*. **1.** A pile of earth or rocks: *a mound of soil in the garden; a burial mound*. **2.** A pile or mass of sthg.: *Grandma served everyone mounds of mashed potatoes*.

mount[1] (mount) *v*. —*tr*. **1.** To climb (sthg.); go up: *The woman mounted the stairs*. **2.** To get up on (sthg.): *mount a bicycle; mount a horse*. **3.** To plan and start to do (sthg.): *The city mounted a campaign for literacy*. **4.** To set (sthg.) in a raised position: *The photographer mounted the camera on a tall tripod*.

—*intr.* **1.** To go upward; rise: *We watched the airplane mount into the sky.* **2.** To get up on sthg., such as a horse: *You can mount now.* **3.** To increase; grow higher: *Expenses are mounting quickly.* —*n.* **1.** A horse or another animal for riding: *Your mount is ready.* **2.** A frame or structure for holding or supporting sthg.: *the mounts of a telescope.*

mount² (mount) *n. (often used in names).* A mountain: *They climbed Mount McKinley.*

moun•tain (moun′tən) *n.* **1.** A raised portion of the earth's surface, generally very large and rising to a great height: *The mountains rose above the plains.* **2.** A large heap or quantity: *The director has a mountain of paperwork.* —**moun′tain•ous** *adj.*

moun•tain•eer (moun′tə nîr′) *n.* A person who climbs mountains for sport: *Our guide was an excellent mountaineer.* —*intr.v.* To climb mountains for sport.

mountain lion *n.* A large wild cat of mountainous regions of western North America and South America.

mountain range *n.* A row or group of connected mountains: *The Rockies are the highest mountain range in North America.*

Mount•ie (moun′tē) *n., pl.* **Mount•ies.** *Informal.* A member of the Royal Canadian Mounted Police.

mount•ing (moun′tĭng) *n.* A supporting structure or frame: *a mounting for a diamond.* —*adj.* Increasing: *Mounting excitement filled the crowd.*

mourn (môrn) *v.* —*intr.* To feel or express sorrow, especially for a person's death; grieve: *The dead man's family came together to mourn.* —*tr.* **1.** To grieve over (a person who has died): *We mourned our uncle.* **2.** To feel or express regret about (sthg.): *He sat mourning his bad luck.* —**mourn′er** *n.*

mourn•ful (môrn′fəl) *adj.* **1.** Feeling or showing deep sadness: *She had a mournful look on her face.* **2.** Suggesting deep sadness: *the mournful sound of a foghorn.* —**mourn′ful•ly** *adv.*

mourn•ing (môr′nĭng) *n.* [U] **1.** The expression of deep sadness and respect for a person who has died: *The flag was flown at half-mast as a sign of mourning.* **2.** The condition of a person feeling sadness over a death: *in mourning for a friend.* **3.** Traditional signs of grief for the dead, such as black clothes: *They wore mourning for a year.*

mouse (mous) *n., pl.* **mice** (mīs). **1.** A small rodent with a pointed nose, rounded ears, and a long thin tail. **2.** A person who is shy or easily frightened. **3.** *pl.* **mice** or **mous•es**

(mous′ĭz). A small device moved by hand along a surface to control the movement of a cursor on a computer screen.

mous•er (mou′zər) *n.* An animal, especially a cat, that catches mice: *Our cat is a good mouser.*

mouse•trap (mous′trăp′) *n.* A trap for catching mice: *Try putting some cheese in the mousetrap.*

mousse (mōos) *n.* [C; U] **1.** A cold dessert made from whipped cream or beaten egg whites, gelatin, and flavoring: *Do you like chocolate mousse?* **2.** A molded dish made from meat, fish, or shellfish and whipped cream: *salmon mousse.* **3.** A styling foam for hair: *She uses too much mousse in her hair.*

mous•tache (mŭs′tăsh′ *or* mə stăsh′) *n.* Variant of **mustache.**

mous•y also **mous•ey** (mou′sē *or* mou′zē) *adj.* **mous•i•er, mous•i•est. 1.** Like a mouse, especially in color: *mousy brown hair.* **2.** Timid and shy: *a mousy person.*

mouth (mouth) *n., pl.* **mouths** (mouthz). **1.** The opening of the body through which an animal takes in food: *Open your mouth and show me your tooth.* **2.** A natural opening, such as the opening of a cave or the part of a river that empties into a larger body of water: *The city is at the mouth of the river.* **3.** An opening into a container or an enclosure: *the mouth of a bottle.* —*tr.v.* (mouth). **1.** To move the mouth as if saying (sthg.) but without sounds: *She mouthed the words to the song.* **2.** To say (sthg.) mechanically or insincerely: *mouthing polite phrases.* **3.** To hold or move (sthg.) around in the mouth: *The baby was mouthing her spoon.* ◆ **mouth off.** *intr.v.* *Slang.* To speak rudely and boldly: *The boy was punished after he mouthed off to his father.*

mouth•ful (mouth′fŏol′) *n.* **1.** An amount taken into the mouth at one time: *We enjoyed every mouthful of the dessert.* **2.** An important or intelligent remark: *You just said a mouthful.* **3.** A word or phrase that is long and hard to pronounce: *That's quite a mouthful!*

mouth•piece (mouth′pēs′) *n.* **1.** The part of a device that is in or near the mouth when in use: *the mouthpiece of a telephone.* **2.** A protective piece of rubber worn over the teeth, as by an athlete: *The football player put in his mouthpiece.* **3.** *Informal.* A person who expresses the opinion of another person or of a group: *He's just a mouthpiece for the union.*

mouth-to-mouth resuscitation (mouth′-tə mouth′) *n.* [U] A method of giving air to a person who has stopped breathing, in which the rescuer presses his or her mouth to the mouth of the victim and blows air into the victim's lungs at regular intervals.

mouth•wash (mouth′wŏsh′ *or* mouth′-

wôsh′) *n.* [C; U] A liquid used to cleanse the mouth and freshen the breath: *Rinse your mouth with the mouthwash.*

mouth•wa•ter•ing or **mouth-wa•ter•ing** (**mouth′**wô′tə rĭng *or* **mouth′**wŏt′ə rĭng) *adj.* Appealing to the sense of taste: *the mouthwatering smell of a cake baking.*

move (mo͞ov) *v.* **moved, mov•ing, moves.** —*intr.* **1.** To change in position from one place or point to another: *The speaker moved to the middle of the stage.* **2.** To follow a specified course: *Earth moves around the sun.* **3.** To change one's place of living or doing business: *Our family moved here last year.* **4.** To advance; progress: *Work on the house was moving slowly.* **5.** To make a formal request or proposal: *I move to postpone the vote until our next meeting.* **6.** To take action: *If we don't move quickly, someone else will get the land.* —*tr.* **1.** To change the place or position of (sbdy./sthg.): *Let's move the desk against the wall.* **2.** To persuade or motivate (sbdy.): *What moved her to change schools?* **3.** To cause strong emotions in (sbdy.): *That song moved me the first time I heard it.* **4.** To propose or request (sthg.) in a formal way, as at a meeting: *I move that we form a committee to study the issue.* **5.** To empty (the bowels). —*n.* **1.** The act of moving: *He made a move to open the door.* **2.** An action planned to achieve an end: *a move aimed at stopping the arms race.* **3.a.** An act of changing the position of a piece in a board game: *That was a good move.* **b.** A player's turn to move a game piece: *It's your move.* ♦ **get a move on.** *Informal.* To get started: *We had better get a move on or we'll be late.* **move in.** *intr.v.* To begin to occupy a home or place of business: *The new tenant moved in on the first of the month.* **move out.** *intr.v.* To leave a home or place of business permanently: *When do you have to move out of your apartment?* **on the move. 1.** Moving from one place to another: *The taxi driver was on the move all day.* **2.** Making progress; advancing: *This area of research is really on the move.* —**mov′a•ble** also **move′a•ble** *adj.*

move•ment (mo͞ov′mənt) *n.* **1.** [C; U] The act or an instance of moving: *She picked up the ball in a quick movement.* **2.** [C] The activities of a group of people working toward a specific goal: *the civil rights movement.* **3.** [C] A tendency or trend: *a movement toward smaller cars.* **4.** [C] An emptying of the bowels. **5.** [C] A large section of a classical musical composition. **6.** [U] A mechanical device or system that produces or transmits motion: *the movement of a watch.*

mov•er (mo͞o′vər) *n.* **1.** A person or thing that moves: *The railroad became a prime mover of people and products during the 19th century.*

2. A person or company that is hired to move furniture and other belongings from one place to another. **3.** *Informal.* A person who makes important things happen: *He's known as a real mover in banking and finance.* ♦ **mover and shaker.** A person who has power and influence in an area of activity: *the movers and shakers in the Hollywood film industry.*

mov•ie (mo͞o′vē) *n.* **1.** A series of photographs rapidly projected on a screen so that what is in the pictures seems to move as in real life; a film. **2. the movies.** A showing of a movie: *We went to the movies last night.*

mov•ing (mo͞o′vĭng) *adj.* **1.** Changing or capable of changing position: *the moving parts of an engine.* **2.** Relating to the transfer of furniture from one location to another: *a moving van.* **3.** Involving a motor vehicle in motion: *He got a ticket for a moving violation.* **4.** Affecting the emotions: *That is a moving love story.* —**mov′ing•ly** *adv.*

mow (mō) *v.* **mowed, mowed** or **mown** (mōn), **mow•ing, mows.** —*tr.* To cut down (grass or grain) with a cutting tool or a machine such as a lawn mower: *Mow the grass before it gets too high.* —*intr.* To cut down grass or other growth. ♦ **mow down.** *tr.v.* [sep.] To cause (great numbers of people) to fall as if by cutting them down: *The protesters were mowed down by the troops.* —**mow′er** *n.*

moz•za•rel•la (mŏt′sə rĕl′ə) *n.* [U] A soft white Italian cheese: *Mozzarella is often used on pizza.*

MP or **M.P.** *abbr.* An abbreviation of military police.

mpg or **m.p.g.** *abbr.* An abbreviation of miles per gallon.

mph or **m.p.h.** *abbr.* An abbreviation of miles per hour.

Mr. (mĭs′tər) *n.* Used as a courtesy title before the last name or full name of a man.

Mrs. (mĭs′ĭz) *n.* **1.** Used as a courtesy title before the last name or full name of a married, widowed, or divorced woman. **2.** Used before a man's full name when addressing both husband and wife: *Mr. and Mrs. George Brown.* —SEE NOTE at **Ms.**

MS *abbr.* An abbreviation of: **1.** Mississippi. **2.** Multiple sclerosis.

Ms. also **Ms** (mĭz) *n.* Used as a courtesy title before the last name or full name of a woman or girl.

USAGE: Ms. The courtesy title **Ms.** has come to be widely used. It is especially good to use when you do not know if the woman you are addressing is married. It is similar to **Mr.,** the courtesy title for men, which does not change with marriage. A woman may prefer **Mrs.** or

Miss, so it is best to use the term preferred by the woman whom you are addressing.

M.S. *abbr.* An abbreviation of Master of Science: *She earned an M.S. in civil engineering.*

mt. or **Mt.** *abbr.* An abbreviation of: **1.** Mount. **2.** Mountain.

much (mŭch) *adj.* **more** (môr), **most** (mōst). *(used with uncountable nouns).* Great in amount, degree, or extent: *much talk and little action.* —*n.* [U] **1.** A large quantity or amount: *Do you have much to do?* **2.** Something special or important: *In spite of all our work, the experiment did not teach us much.* —*adv.* **more**, **most. 1.** *Formal.* To a large extent; greatly: *We are much impressed with the results of your research.* **2.** Just about; almost: *The patient is much the same today.* ◆ **much as.** Even though: *Much as I love skating, I'd rather go to the movies.* **much less.** And certainly not: *The caller didn't want to tell me his name, much less leave a message.* **so much for.** Used to express that sthg. done in the past was wasted or useless: *She refused to speak to me. So much for my efforts to help.*

USAGE: much The adjective **much** is used with uncountable nouns: *much money.* With countable nouns, use **many**: *many children.*

muck (mŭk) *n.* [U] **1.** A moist sticky mixture, as of mud: *Our boots were covered with muck.* **2.** Moist animal manure.

muck•rake (mŭk′rāk′) *intr.v.* **muck•raked, muck•rak•ing, muck•rakes.** To search for and expose corruption in public affairs: *a newspaper with a reputation for muckraking.* —**muck′rak′er** *n.*

mu•cous (myōō′kəs) *adj.* Relating to mucus: *mucous membranes.*

HOMONYMS: mucous, mucus (gland secretion).

mu•cus (myōō′kəs) *n.* [U] The sticky, slippery liquid material released by the body as a protective coating.

mud (mŭd) *n.* [U] **1.** Wet, sticky, soft earth: *Don't track mud through the house.* **2.** Things said to hurt a person's reputation: *sling mud at a political opponent.*

mud•dle (mŭd′l) *tr.v.* **mud•dled, mud•dling, mud•dles. 1.** To make a mess of (sthg.); bungle: *muddle a task.* **2.** To confuse (sbdy.): *I was muddled by the complicated math problem.* —*n.* A jumble; a mess: *The room was a muddle of clothes and toys.* ◆ **muddle through.** *tr.v.* [insep.] To manage to do (sthg.) without really knowing how or without necessary tools: *The band muddled through the rest of the song.*

mud•dy (mŭd′ē) *adj.* **mud•di•er, mud•di•est. 1.** Covered or soiled with mud: *muddy*

shoes. **2.** Cloudy with or as if with mud: *a muddy creek; muddy coffee.* **3.** Confused; vague: *muddy thinking.* —*tr.v.* **mud•died, mud•dy•ing, mud•dies. 1.** To soil (sthg.) with mud: *He muddied his boots crossing the yard.* **2.** To make (sthg.) cloudy as if with mud: *Soil erosion muddies the rivers.* **3.** To confuse (sthg.): *His remarks only muddied the issue.* ◆ **muddy the waters.** *Informal.* To make sthg. more difficult or confusing than it should be: *The new information just muddied the waters.* —**mud′di•ly** *adv.* —**mud′di•ness** *n.* [U]

mud•sling•ing (mŭd′slĭng′ĭng) *n.* [U] The practice of making false and harmful statements against an opponent, especially in a political campaign: *The mayor accused his opponent of mudslinging.* —**mud′sling′er** *n.*

muff[1] (mŭf) *tr.v.* To perform or handle (sthg.) clumsily: *She played the first song well, but muffed the second.*

muff[2] (mŭf) *n.* A tubelike cover of fur or cloth with open ends where the hands are warmed.

muf•fin (mŭf′ĭn) *n.* A small, sweet bread shaped like a cup: *He ordered a blueberry muffin and coffee.*

muf•fle (mŭf′əl) *tr.v.* **muf•fled, muf•fling, muf•fles. 1.** To make (sthg.) less loud or less clearly heard: *Snow muffled the sound of our footsteps.* **2.** To wrap up (sbdy./sthg.) in order to keep warm, hide, or protect: *I muffled the baby in a blanket.*

muf•fler (mŭf′lər) *n.* **1.** A device that quiets noise, especially one used on an automobile engine: *My car needs a new muffler.* **2.** A scarf worn around the neck for warmth.

mug[1] (mŭg) *n.* A large heavy cup, usually with a handle and used for hot drinks.

mug[2] (mŭg) *n. Informal.* A person's face: *The comic has an interesting mug.* —*v.* **mugged, mug•ging, mugs.** —*tr. Informal.* To attack (sbdy.) with the intent of robbing: *Somebody mugged the old man and took his wallet.* —*intr.* To make facial expressions, especially to be funny: *mugging for the amusement of the baby.* —**mug′ger** *n.*

mug•gy (mŭg′ē) *adj.* **mug•gi•er, mug•gi•est.** Warm and humid with little or no breeze: *a muggy day in August.* —**mug′gi•ness** *n.* [U]

mulch (mŭlch) *n.* [C; U] A protective covering, as of leaves or hay, placed around growing plants to keep the soil moist, prevent the roots from freezing, and prevent weeds from growing. —*tr.v.* To cover (sthg.) with mulch: *mulch the garden.*

mule (myōōl) *n.* **1.** An offspring of a male donkey and a female horse: *Mules are known for being stubborn.* **2.** *Informal.* A stubborn person.

mul•ish (myōō′lĭsh) *adj.* Stubborn and unreasonable: *He has a mulish disposition.* See Synonyms at **obstinate.** —**mul′ish•ly** *adv.* —**mul′ish•ness** *n.* [U]

mull¹ (mŭl) *tr.v.* To heat and add sugar and spices to (wine or cider).

mull² (mŭl) *v.* ◆ **mull over.** *tr.v.* [sep.] To think or consider (sthg.) for a time: *After I told him my idea, he mulled it over for days.*

multi— *pref.* A prefix that means: **1.** Many; much: *multicolored.* **2.** More than two: *multiracial.* **3.** Many times over: *multimillionaire.*

mul·ti·col·ored (mŭl'tĭ kŭl'ərd) *adj.* With many colors: *a multicolored jacket.*

mul·ti·fac·et·ed (mŭl'tē făs'ĭ tĭd) *adj.* With many sides or aspects: *a multifaceted study of changes in the environment.*

mul·ti·lat·er·al (mŭl'tĭ lăt'ər əl) *adj.* Involving more than two sides: *a multilateral trade agreement.*

mul·ti·me·di·a (mŭl'tē mē'dē ə) *adj.* Relating to several media, such as video, music, and computerized images and text, especially for education or entertainment.

mul·ti·mil·lion·aire (mŭl'tē mĭl'yə nâr' or mŭl'tē mĭl'yə nâr) *n.* A person whose financial worth equals several million dollars.

mul·ti·na·tion·al (mŭl'tē năsh'ə nəl) *adj.* **1.** With operations or smaller divisions in more than two countries: *a multinational corporation.* **2.** Involving more than two countries: *a multinational agreement.* —*n.* A company that operates in more than two countries.

mul·ti·ple (mŭl'tə pəl) *adj.* Relating to more than one element, part, or individual: *a plan with multiple advantages.* —*n.* A number that may be divided evenly by another number: *The numbers 4, 6, 8, and 12 are multiples of 2.*

multiple-choice *adj.* Offering several answers from which to choose the correct one: *There were 20 multiple-choice questions on the test.*

multiple sclerosis *n.* [U] A disease of the central nervous system, causing muscular weakness and loss of coordination.

mul·ti·pli·cand (mŭl'tə plĭ kănd') *n.* A number that is to be multiplied by another number.

mul·ti·pli·ca·tion (mŭl'tə plĭ kā'shən) *n.* [U] **1.** The process of multiplying: *the rapid multiplication of environmental problems.* **2.** A mathematical operation performed by multiplying a pair of numbers to arrive at a third number called a product: *Multiplication of 2 × 4 produces the same product as 4 × 2.*

multiplication sign *n.* The sign (×) placed between a pair of numbers to show multiplication of those numbers. This sign is usually read as "times." For example, 3 × 4 can be said "3 times 4."

mul·ti·plic·i·ty (mŭl'tə plĭs'ĭ tē) *n., pl.* **mul·ti·plic·i·ties.** A great number or variety: *a multiplicity of courses to choose from.*

mul·ti·pli·er (mŭl'tə plī'ər) *n.* **1.** The number by which another number is multiplied. **2.** An instrument or a device that causes an increase of a force or current.

mul·ti·ply (mŭl'tə plī') *v.* **mul·ti·plied, mul·ti·ply·ing, mul·ti·plies.** —*intr.* **1.** To increase in number or amount: *The problems seem to multiply.* See Synonyms at **increase. 2.** To perform multiplication. —*tr.* To perform multiplication on (a pair of numbers): *She multiplied 4 by 5 and got 20.*

mul·ti·ra·cial (mŭl'tē rā'shəl) *adj.* Involving various races: *Hawaii is an example of a multiracial society.*

mul·ti·tude (mŭl'tĭ tōōd') *n.* **1.** A large number: *We face a multitude of challenges.* **2.** The common people: *The multitude rejected both candidates in the election.*

mul·ti·tu·di·nous (mŭl'tĭ tōōd'n əs) *adj.* Formal. Existing in great numbers: *the multitudinous stars of our galaxy.*

mum¹ (mŭm) *adj.* Not talking; silent: *Keep mum about the plan.*

mum² (mŭm) *n.* A chrysanthemum.

mum·ble (mŭm'bəl) *tr. & intr.v.* **mum·bled, mum·bling, mum·bles.** To speak in an unclear manner, as by lowering the voice and partly closing the mouth: *He mumbled his name. I can't understand you when you mumble.* —*n.* Something said in a low unclear way: *The student answered the teacher in a mumble.* —**mum'bler** *n.*

mum·bo jum·bo (mŭm'bō jŭm'bō) *n.* [U] *Informal.* Speech or writing that is unclear or impossible to understand: *Give me a straight answer, not a lot of mumbo jumbo!*

mum·mi·fy (mŭm'ə fī') *v.* **mum·mi·fied, mum·mi·fy·ing, mum·mi·fies.** —*tr.* To make (a dead body) into a mummy. —*intr.* To become dry and smaller like a mummy: *The body had mummified.* —**mum'mi·fi·ca'tion** (mŭm'ə fĭ kā'shən) *n.* [U]

mum·my¹ (mŭm'ē) *n., pl.* **mum·mies.** The body of a human or an animal preserved after death, as practiced by the ancient Egyptians or by a natural process: *The mummies were at least 3,000 years old.*

mum·my² (mŭm'ē) *n., pl.* **mum·mies.** *Informal.* Mother. Usually used by small children.

mumps (mŭmps) *pl.n.* [U] *(used with a singular or plural verb).* A contagious viral disease that causes glands to swell, especially those at the back of the jaw: *Mumps was once a common childhood disease.*

munch (mŭnch) *v.* —*tr.* To chew (food) in a

noisy steady manner: *munch popcorn.* —*intr.* To chew food noisily and steadily: *They found the cow munching in a pasture.*

mun•chies (mŭn′chēz) *pl.n. Slang.* **1.** Food for snacking: *We bought popcorn and pretzels for munchies.* **2.** A hunger for snack foods: *An attack of the munchies sent me to the kitchen for cookies and milk.*

mun•dane (mŭn dān′ *or* mŭn′dān′) *adj.* **1.** Not interesting; ordinary: *mundane housekeeping chores.* **2.** *Formal.* Worldly; not spiritual: *mundane interests.*

mu•nic•i•pal (myōō nĭs′ə pəl) *adj.* Relating to a city or town: *municipal politics; the municipal airport.*

mu•nic•i•pal•i•ty (myōō nĭs′ ə păl′ĭ tē) *n., pl.* **mu•nic•i•pal•i•ties.** A city or town that is self-governing in local matters.

mu•ni•tions (myōō nĭsh′ənz) *pl.n.* Supplies for warfare, especially weapons and ammunitions.

mu•ral (myōōr′əl) *n.* A large painting or decoration created directly on a wall or ceiling: *The painter was famous for his murals of village life.*

mur•der (mûr′dər) *n.* [C; U] The unlawful and deliberate killing of one person by another: *The man was accused of murder.* —*tr.v.* **1.** To kill (sbdy.) with deliberate intent: *He murdered his wife.* **2.** To ruin or spoil (sthg.): *a writer who murders the language.* ♦ **get away with murder.** To escape punishment or discipline for misbehavior: *The boy's grandmother is too easy on him; she lets him get away with murder.* —**mur′der•er** *n.*

mur•der•ous (mûr′dər əs) *adj.* **1.** Capable of or planning on murder: *a murderous crowd.* **2.** Angry or savage, as if planning murder: *a murderous look.*

murk•y (mûr′kē) *adj.* **murk•i•er, murk•i•est.** **1.** Dark; gloomy: *a murky night.* See Synonyms at **dark.** **2.** Cloudy and dark with sediment: *the swamp's murky water.* —**murk′i•ly** *adv.* —**murk′i•ness** *n.* [U]

mur•mur (mûr′mər) *n.* **1.** A low continuous sound: *the murmur of the crowd.* **2.** An abnormal sound made by the heart: *The infant has a slight heart murmur.* —*v.* —*intr.* **1.** To make a low continuous sound: *The brook murmured through the forest.* **2.** To speak or complain in a low voice: *The students murmured among themselves about the new rules.* —*tr.* To say (sthg.) in a low and possibly unclear voice: *He murmured his approval.*

mus•cle (mŭs′əl) *n.* **1.** [C; U] A type of body tissue made of fibers that can contract and relax to cause movement or apply force: *She exercised to strengthen her muscles.* **2.** [U] Muscular strength: *The swimming team has plenty of muscle.* **3.** [U] *Informal.* Power or authority: *a law that had no muscle.* —*v.* ♦ **muscle in.** *intr.v. Informal.* [on] To force one's way into a place or situation where one

is not wanted: *He had the nerve to muscle in on someone else's job.*

HOMONYMS: muscle, mussel (mollusk).

mus•cle•bound also **mus•cle-bound** (mŭs′əl bound′) *adj.* With muscles that are too big and stiff, usually as a result of too much exercise: *a musclebound athlete.*

mus•cu•lar (mŭs′kyə lər) *adj.* With strong well-developed muscles: *a muscular gymnast.* —**mus′cu•lar′i•ty** (mŭs′kyə lăr′ĭ tē) *n.* [U] —**mus′cu•lar•ly** *adv.*

SYNONYMS: muscular, athletic, brawny, burly, sinewy. These adjectives all mean physically strong. *I lift weights because I want a more muscular body. The athletic young woman is good at soccer, basketball, and tennis. They need some brawny friends to help move that piano. A group of burly men unloaded the ship's cargo. Professional dancers are usually lean and sinewy.* **ANTONYM: scrawny.**

mus•cu•la•ture (mŭs′kyə lə chōōr′) *n.* [U] The system of muscles of a person or an animal.

muse (myōōz) *intr.v.* **mused, mus•ing, mus•es.** [*over; about*] To think or consider for a time: *He was musing over his chances of winning tomorrow's game.*

mu•se•um (myōō zē′əm) *n.* A building in which objects of artistic, historical, or scientific interest are shown: *The museum is planning an exhibit of Da Vinci's work.*

mush (mŭsh) *n.* [U] **1.** A thick hot cereal made of cornmeal and water or milk. **2.** A thick soft mass: *The tomato had turned to mush.* **3.** *Informal.* Too much sentimentality: *That love story was just a lot of mush.* —**mush′i•ly** *adv.* —**mush′i•ness** *n.* [U] —**mush′y** *adj.*

mush•room (mŭsh′rōōm *or* mŭsh′rōōm′) *n.* A fungus with a stalk topped by a fleshy umbrella-shaped cap: *Some mushrooms are used as food, but many kinds are poisonous.* —*intr.v.* To grow, multiply, or spread quickly: *The population in that suburb mushroomed during the last few years.* —*adj.* **1.** Relating to mushrooms: *mushroom soup.* **2.** Like a mushroom in shape: *a mushroom cloud.*

mu•sic (myōō′zĭk) *n.* [U] **1.** Vocal or instrumental sounds that have rhythm, melody, harmony, or some combination of these. **2.** A musical composition or a group of such compositions: *the music of Bach.* **3.** A pleasing sound or combination of sounds: *the music of the wind in the trees.* ♦ **music to (one's) ears.** Information one is happy to hear: *Praise for her children is always music to her ears.* **put on some music.** To turn on a radio or CD player: *Let's put on some music while we eat dinner.*

mu•si•cal (myōō′zĭ kəl) *adj.* **1.** Relating to

M

music: *a musical instrument; musical training.* **2.** Devoted to or skilled in music: *a musical family.* **3.** Pleasing to the ear: *a musical voice.* —*n.* A play or movie that includes singing along with the dialogue: *Do you like musicals?* —**mu′si•cal•ly** *adv.*

mu•si•cian (myōō zĭsh′ən) *n.* A person who is skilled in performing or composing music: *Musicians practice long hours.*

musk (mŭsk) *n.* [U] A strong-smelling substance produced by certain glands of some animals, sometimes used in making perfume.

mus•ket (mŭs′kĭt) *n.* A long-barreled gun used before the invention of the rifle: *Muskets were used during the American Revolution.*

Mus•lim (mŭz′ləm *or* mōōs′ləm) or **Mos•lem** (mŏz′ləm *or* mŏs′ləm) *n.* A believer in Islam. —*adj.* Relating to Islam or its believers.

muss (mŭs) *tr.v.* [*up*] To make (sthg.) untidy or messy: *The wind mussed up my hair.*

mus•sel (mŭs′əl) *n.* A saltwater or freshwater mollusk with a pair of narrow, often dark blue shells.

HOMONYMS: **mussel, muscle** (tissue fiber).

must (mŭst) *aux.v.* **1.** To be required or obliged to: *Human beings must have oxygen to live.* **2.** Used to express a command or a warning: *You must be careful when working on a ladder.* **3.** Used to show sthg. is certain or cannot be avoided: *All good things must come to an end.* **4.** To insist on sthg.: *If you must talk, do so quietly.* —*n.* Something that is required or necessary: *A good tent is a must when you go camping.*

mus•tache *also* **mous•tache** (mŭs′tăsh′ *or* mə stăsh′) *n.* The hair growing on a man's upper lip, especially when it is trimmed and shaped.

mus•tang (mŭs′tăng′) *n.* A small wild horse of the plains of western North America: *Mustangs are descendants of the horses that were brought to the Americas by Spanish explorers.*

mus•tard (mŭs′tərd) *n.* [U] **1.** A plant of Europe and Asia with yellow flowers and small sharp-tasting seeds. **2.** A spicy sauce made from the powdered seeds of this plant. **3.** A dark brownish yellow color. —*adj.* Dark brownish yellow. ◆ **cut the mustard.** To perform as well as expected or to meet a required standard: *You should quit if you can't cut the mustard.*

mus•ter (mŭs′tər) *tr.v.* **1.** To bring (people) together into a group: *The general mustered his troops for inspection.* **2.** To call forth or bring out (some quality): *She mustered enough courage to ask the boss for a raise.* —*n.* ◆ **pass muster.** To be good enough: *You've prepared*

well for this presentation, so I think you'll pass muster.*

must•n't (mŭs′ənt). Contraction of *must not.*

must•y (mŭs′tē) *adj.* **must•i•er, must•i•est.** Stale or moldy: *a musty smell.* —**must′-i•ness** *n.* [U]

mu•tant (myōōt′nt) *n.* **1.** A living thing that, as a result of mutation, is different from its parents. **2.** *Slang.* A creature or thing that is so strange it suggests a genetic mutant: *Movies set in the future often feature frightening mutants.* —*adj.* Changed as a result of mutation: *a mutant animal.*

mu•tate (myōō′tāt *or* myōō tāt′) *intr. & tr.v.* **mu•tat•ed, mu•tat•ing, mu•tates.** To change, especially by mutation: *Chemicals can cause genes to mutate.*

mu•ta•tion (myōō tā′shən) *n.* **1.** [C; U] A change in the genes or chromosomes of a living thing that can be passed on to its offspring: *The mutation of this strain of bacteria has made it more resistant to antibiotics.* **2.** [C] A mutant.

mute (myōōt) *adj.* **1.** Unable to speak: *The illness left him mute.* **2.** Choosing not to speak; silent: *The suspect remained mute under questioning.* **3.** Expressed without speech; unspoken: *the mute approval in his smile.* **4.** Not pronounced; silent: *the mute e in the word* house. —*tr.v.* **mut•ed, mut•ing, mutes.** To muffle or soften the sound of (sthg.): *The insulation in the walls muted the noise of the people living next door.* —**mute′ly** *adv.* —**mute′ness** *n.* [U]

mu•ti•late (myōōt′l āt′) *tr.v.* **mu•ti•lat•ed, mu•ti•lat•ing, mu•ti•lates.** **1.** To damage (sthg.) by cutting off or badly damaging a necessary part, such as an arm or leg. **2.** To damage (sthg.) badly; ruin: *The photo was mutilated in the mail.* —**mu′ti•la′tion** *n.* [C; U]

mu•ti•neer (myōōt′n îr′) *n.* A person, especially a soldier or sailor, who takes part in a mutiny.

mu•ti•nous (myōōt′n əs) *adj.* **1.** Relating to mutiny: *a mutinous act; a mutinous officer.* **2.** Behaving in an uncontrolled way; rebellious: *a mutinous child.* —**mu′ti•nous•ly** *adv.*

mu•ti•ny (myōōt′n ē) *n., pl.* **mu•ti•nies.** [C; U] Open rebellion against authority, especially rebellion of sailors against officers in charge on a ship: *The sailors were charged with mutiny.* —*intr.v.* **mu•ti•nied, mu•ti•ny•ing, mu•ti•nies.** To become involved in mutiny; rebel.

mutt (mŭt) *n. Informal.* A dog of mixed breed; a mongrel: *Many people prefer mutts to purebred dogs.*

mut•ter (mŭt′ər) *v.* **mut•tered, mut•ter•**

ing, mut·ters. —*intr.* **1.** To speak in low unclear tones: *She muttered to herself while she worked.* **2.** [*about*] To complain or grumble: *The shoppers muttered about the high price of food.* —*tr.* To say (sthg.) in low unclear tones: *He muttered something under his breath.*

mut·ton (mŭt′n) *n.* [U] The meat of a fully grown sheep: *Lamb is eaten more often than mutton in the United States.*

mu·tu·al (myōō′chōō əl) *adj.* **1.** With the same relationship to each other: *mutual enemies.* **2.** Possessed or shared in common: *We discovered that we had mutual friends.* —**mu′tu·al·ly** *adv.*

mutual fund *n.* In investments, a company that buys and sells its own shares and uses the pooled capital of its shareholders to invest in other companies: *Investing in mutual funds can be very profitable.*

muz·zle (mŭz′əl) *n.* **1.** The nose and jaws of certain animals, such as a dog or horse: *The dog touched me gently with his muzzle.* **2.** A leather or wire device fitted over an animal's jaws, usually to prevent biting: *The dog had to wear a muzzle.* **3.** The front end of the barrel of a gun: *Don't point the muzzle toward anyone.* —*tr.v.* **muz·zled, muz·zling, muz·zles. 1.** To put a muzzle on (an animal): *You'll have to muzzle your dog.* **2.** To prevent (abdy.) from expressing an opinion: *muzzle the opposition.*

MW *abbr.* An abbreviation of megawatt.

my (mī) *adj.* The possessive form of **I. 1.** Belonging or relating to me: *my pencil; my dentist.* **2.** Used before various forms of address to indicate politeness or affection: *My dear, you are so right.* **3.** Used in expressions of surprise or dismay: *My word! My goodness!* —*interj.* An expression used to show surprise or dismay: *My! What a mess!*

my·o·pi·a (mī ō′pē ə) *n.* [U] **1.** A common defect of the eye that makes distant objects appear blurred; nearsightedness: *Many people wear glasses because of myopia.* **2.** Lack of good judgment or thought about the distant future: *Myopia led the planners to ignore several important issues.* —**my·op′ic** (mī-ŏp′ĭk) *adj.*

myr·i·ad (mĭr′ē əd) *adj.* Amounting to a very large indefinite number: *the myriad fish in the ocean.* —*n.* A vast number: *a myriad of objections.*

my·self (mī sĕlf′) *pron.* **1.** The reflexive form of **me: a.** Used to show that the action of a verb refers back to the subject: *I injured myself. I gave myself some advice. I spent little money on myself.* **b.** Used to give emphasis: *I myself had to laugh.* **2.** My normal or

healthy self: *I was sick, but I'm feeling myself again.*

mys·te·ri·ous (mĭ stîr′ē əs) *adj.* Difficult or impossible to understand or explain: *the mysterious disappearance of the books.* —**mys·te′ri·ous·ly** *adv.* —**mys·te′ri·ous·ness** *n.* [U]

mys·ter·y (mĭs′tə rē) *n., pl.* **mys·ter·ies. 1.** [C] Something that is difficult to explain or understand: *How he got into the house is a mystery.* **2.** [C] Something that is a secret: *The teacher kept our grades a mystery.* **3.** [U] A quality that suggests sthg. unknown or unexplained: *The old house had an air of mystery.* **4.** [C] A novel, story, or film about a puzzling crime: *I love to read a good mystery.*

mys·tic (mĭs′tĭk) *adj.* **1.** Relating to mysticism; mystical. **2.** Causing a sense of mystery: *the mystic effects of a new moon.* —*n.* A person who practices or believes in mysticism.

mys·ti·cal (mĭs′tĭ kəl) *adj.* **1.** Relating to mysticism and its practices: *the mystical books of the alchemists.* **2.** Based on spiritual understanding rather than experience or reasoning: *a mystical belief in the power of numbers.* —**mys′ti·cal·ly** *adv.*

mys·ti·cism (mĭs′tĭ sĭz′əm) *n.* [U] **1.** The experience of spiritual union or direct communication with God. **2.** The belief that one can communicate directly with God through deep meditation. **3.** Confused and groundless thinking: *That theory is mysticism, not science.*

mys·ti·fy (mĭs′tə fī′) *tr.v.* **mys·ti·fied, mys·ti·fy·ing, mys·ti·fies.** To confuse or puzzle (sbdy.): *We were mystified by their response.* —**mys′ti·fi·ca′tion** (mĭs′tə fĭ-kā′shən) *n.* [U]

mys·tique (mĭ stēk′) *n.* A feeling of mystery or wonder that surrounds an activity, a person, or a group: *The mystique of the beautiful actress captured the public's imagination.*

myth (mĭth) *n.* **1.a.** [C] A traditional story dealing with the past or with supernatural beings, and usually trying to explain a belief, practice, or natural phenomenon: *the myth that gods built the mountains.* **b.** [U] Such stories considered as a group: *Greek myth.* **2.** [C] An imaginary story, person, or thing: *the myth of the giant fish in the lake.* **3.** [C] A false belief that is part of a set of ideas about society: *the myth that all tax increases are bad.* —**myth′ic, myth′i·cal** *adj.*

my·thol·o·gy (mĭ thŏl′ə jē) *n.* **1.** [C; U] A group of myths dealing with the origin, gods, and heroes of a specific people: *Roman mythology.* **2.** [C] The study of myths: *a professor of Greek history and mythology.* —**myth′o·log′i·cal** (mĭth′ə lŏj′ĭ kəl) *adj.*

M

Nn

n¹ or **N** (ĕn) *n.*, *pl.* **n's** or **N's.** The 14th letter of the English alphabet.

n² *n.* In mathematics, an indefinite number.

N¹ The symbol for the element **nitrogen.**

N² *abbr.* An abbreviation of: **1.** North. **2.** Northern.

n. *abbr.* An abbreviation of: **1.** Noun. **2.** Number.

Na The symbol for the element **sodium.**

N.A. *abbr.* An abbreviation of North America.

NAACP or **N.A.A.C.P.** *abbr.* An abbreviation of National Association for the Advancement of Colored People, usually pronounced as "N-double A-C-P."

nab (năb) *tr.v.* **nabbed, nab·bing, nabs.** *Informal.* **1.** To catch (sbdy.) doing sthg. illegal; arrest: *Police nabbed the bank robber.* **2.** To take (sthg.) quickly; grab: *People nabbed all the tickets before we could get any.*

na·cho (nä′chō′) *n.*, *pl.* **na·chos.** A snack food made from a small piece of tortilla, often topped with cheese or salsa and broiled.

na·dir (nā′dər *or* nā′dîr′) *n. (usually singular).* The lowest or worst point: *He was at the nadir of his life.*

nag¹ (năg) *v.* **nagged, nag·ging, nags.** —*tr.* **1.** To bother or annoy (sbdy.), as by complaining or scolding: *Don't nag me about cleaning my room.* **2.** To cause continuous pain or annoyance to (sbdy.): *My sore shoulder has been nagging me all day.* —*intr.* To scold or complain constantly: *The children have been nagging at me all day.* —*n.* A person who nags. —**nag′ger** *n.* —**nag′ging** *adj.*

nag² (năg) *n.* A horse, especially an old or worn-out horse: *The nag pulling the cart looked tired and lame.*

nail (nāl) *n.* **1.** A small, thin pointed piece of metal, often with a head, hammered into wood or other material to hold things. **2.** A fingernail or toenail. —*tr.v.* **1.** To join or attach (sthg.) with nails: *Nail the boards together.* **2.** *Slang.* To catch (sbdy.): *The police nailed the suspect in his car.* ◆ **nail down.** *tr.v.* [sep.] **1.** To make certain of (sthg.): *The reporters finally nailed down the facts of the story.* **2.** To force (sbdy.) to make a clear statement: *We need to nail him down on a price before we can decide to buy.*

nail polish *n.* [C; U] A clear or colored cosmetic paint for fingernails and toenails.

na·ive or **na·ïve** (nä ēv′) *adj.* **1.** Simple as a child; unexperienced: *He felt naive as he tried to bargain with the car salesman.* **2.** Showing a lack of experience or judgment: *naive remarks.* —**na·ive′ly** *adv.*

na·ive·té′ or **na·ïve′té** (nä′ēv tä′ *or* nä-ē′vĭ tä′) *n.* [U] The quality of being naive; natural simplicity: *The naiveté of the child's question made everyone smile.*

na·ked (nā′kĭd) *adj.* **1.** Not wearing clothing; nude. **2.** Having no vegetation or leaves: *trees with naked branches.* **3.** Not hidden: *the naked truth.* —**na′ked·ly** *adv.* —**na′ked·ness** *n.* [U]

naked eye *n.* [U] The eye alone, without the help of a device such as a telescope: *The planet Mars can be seen with the naked eye.*

name (nām) *n.* **1.** A word or words by which a person or thing is known: *My name is John.* **2.** A word or group of words used to describe sbdy., especially as an insult: *Stop calling me names!* **3.a.** General reputation: *That store has a bad name.* **b.** A respected reputation: *She has made a name for herself as a researcher.* **4.** A famous person: *He is a big name in the movies.* —*tr.v.* **named, nam·ing, names.** **1.** To give a name to (sbdy./sthg.): *Have you named the baby?* **2.** To mention or identify (sbdy./sthg.) by name: *Name the longest river in China.* **3.** To nominate or appoint (sbdy.), as to a specific duty, honor, or office: *He was named Secretary of Defense by the President.* ◆ **drop names.** To talk about famous or important people as if one knows them well: *I wish she would stop dropping names!* **in name only.** Officially but not in reality: *He is President in name only; the military controls the government.* **in the name of.** By the authority of: *Open this door in the name of the law!* **to (one's) name.** Belonging to one: *I don't have a dollar to my name.*

name brand *n.* A product with a trademark or name that identifies it and that belongs to the manufacturer: *That store sells name brands at discount prices.* —**name′-brand′** *adj.*

name-drop (nām′drŏp′) *intr.v.* **name-dropped, name-drop·ping, name-drops.** To mention the names of well-known people as if one knows them. —**name′-drop·per** *n.* —**name′-drop·ping** *n.* [U]

name·less (nām′lĭs) *adj.* **1.** Having no name: *nameless stars.* **2.** Not called by name; anony-

---

ă–**cat**; ā–**pay**; âr–**care**; ä–**father**; ĕ–**get**; ē–**be**; ĭ–**sit**; ī–**nice**; îr–**here**; ŏ–**got**; ō–**go**; ô–**saw**; oi–**boy**; ou–**out**; ōō–**took**; ōō–**boot**; ŭ–**cut**; ûr–**word**; th–**thin**; *th*–**this**; hw–**when**; zh–**vision**; ə–**about**; N–French **bon**

mous: *The person who gave the money wishes to remain nameless.* **3.** Impossible to describe: *nameless horror.* —**name′less•ly** *adv.*

name•ly (nām′lē) *adv.* That is to say; specifically: *First-class mail includes written matter, namely letters and post cards.*

name•sake (nām′sāk′) *n.* A person named after another: *John F. Kennedy, Jr., is his father's namesake.*

nan•ny (năn′ē) *n., pl.* **nan•nies.** A person employed to take care of a child, often living with a family: *We interviewed several young women before hiring her as a nanny.*

nanny goat *n.* A female goat.

nano— *pref.* A prefix that means one billionth (10^{-9}): *nanosecond.*

nan•o•sec•ond (năn′ə sĕk′ ənd) *n.* One billionth (10^{-9}) of a second.

nap (năp) *n.* A brief sleep, usually during the day: *The baby takes a nap every afternoon.* —*intr.v.* **napped, nap•ping, naps. 1.** To sleep for a short time. **2.** To be unaware of danger or trouble that is soon to happen: *We caught our competitors napping and won the contract.*

na•palm (nā′päm′) *n.* [U] A mixture of gasoline and chemicals that makes a flammable jelly for use in flame throwers and bombs: *The napalm exploded in flames.*

nape (nāp *or* năp) *n.* The back of the neck: *I felt the hair rise on the nape of my neck.*

naph•tha•lene (năf′thə lēn′ *or* năp′thə-lēn′) *n.* [U] A white crystalline compound used to repel moths.

nap•kin (năp′kĭn) *n.* **1.** A piece of cloth or soft paper used while eating to protect the clothes or to wipe the mouth and fingers. **2.** A sanitary napkin.

narc or **nark** (närk) *n. Slang.* A police officer who works to enforce drug laws; a narcotics agent.

nar•cis•sism (när′sĭ sĭz′ əm) *n.* [U] Excessive love or admiration of oneself: *His narcissism ruined his marriage.* —**nar′cis•sist** *n.* —**nar′cis•sist′ic** *adj.*

nar•cot•ic (när kŏt′ĭk) *n.* A drug, such as heroin or morphine, that reduces pain, causes sleep, and tends to cause addiction when used regularly: *Most narcotics are illegal drugs.* —*adj.* **1.** Relating to narcotics. **2.** Tending to cause sleep or stupor: *the narcotic effect of a boring movie.*

nar•rate (năr′āt′) *tr.v.* **nar•rat•ed, nar•rat•ing, nar•rates. 1.** To tell (a story, for example) in speech or writing: *He narrated his life story.* **2.** To provide a voiceover of (a film): *The actor narrated the documentary film.*

nar•ra•tion (nă rā′shən) *n.* [C; U] **1.** The act of narrating: *Her narration held our attention.* **2.** Something narrated; an account or a story: *a lengthy narration.*

nar•ra•tive (năr′ə tĭv) *n.* [C; U] A narrated account; a story. —*adj.* **1.** Telling a story:

narrative poems. **2.** Relating to narration: *the narrative skill of an author.*

nar•row (năr′ō) *adj.* **1.** Not wide, especially in comparison with length: *a narrow face.* **2.** Limited in variety: *a narrow selection of products.* **3.** Rigid in opinions and ideas; narrow-minded: *a narrow view of the world.* **4.** Almost unsuccessful; close: *a narrow escape; a narrow victory.* —*v.* —*tr.* **1.** To make (sthg.) narrow: *He narrowed his eyes.* **2.** To limit or restrict (sthg.): *Narrow down your topic to something you can handle.* —*intr.* To become narrower: *The road narrows just outside of town.* —**nar′row•ly** *adv.* —**nar′row•ness** *n.* [U]

nar•row-mind•ed (năr′ō mīn′dĭd) *adj.* Having no interest in the opinions or beliefs of other people: *Narrow-minded people have little respect for those who are not like themselves.* —**nar′row-mind′ed•ly** *adv.* —**nar′-row-mind′ed•ness** *n.* [U]

nar•y (nâr′ē) *adj. Formal.* Not one; no: *Nary a leaf was left on the tree.*

NASA (năs′ə) *abbr.* An abbreviation of National Aeronautics and Space Administration: *She is a NASA engineer working on the space shuttle.*

na•sal (nā′zəl) *adj.* **1.** Relating to the nose: *nasal irritation.* **2.a.** Spoken so that most of the air passes through the nose rather than the mouth: *a nasal sound, such as* m *or* n. **b.** Resembling a sound made in such a way: *the nasal twang of a guitar.*

nas•cent (năs′ənt *or* nā′sənt) *adj.* Coming into existence; starting: *a nascent movement toward democracy.*

nas•ty (năs′tē) *adj.* **nas•ti•er, nas•ti•est. 1.** Offensive; indecent: *a nasty word.* **2.** Mean and hurtful: *a nasty man.* **3.** Unpleasant; annoying: *nasty weather.* **4.** Painful and dangerous: *a nasty cut.* —**nas′ti•ly** *adv.* —**nas′-ti•ness** *n.* [U]

na•tal (nāt′l) *adj.* Relating to birth: *natal injuries.*

na•tion (nā′shən) *n.* **1.** A group of people organized under a single government; a country. **2.** The territory occupied by a country: *All across the nation new industries are developing.* **3.** A people who share customs and history and often speak the same language, especially a tribe of Native Americans.

na•tion•al (năsh′ə nəl) *adj.* **1.** Relating to a nation as a whole: *a national anthem; national elections.* **2.** Maintained by the government of a nation: *national parks.* —*n.* A citizen of a particular nation: *a Swedish national.* —**na′tion•al•ly** *adv.*

National Guard *n.* The military reserve units of each state of the United States.

na•tion•al•ism (năsh′ə nə lĭz′ əm) *n.* [U] **1.** Devotion to a particular nation: *During war, many countries experience a rise in nationalism.* **2.** A movement for political

N

independence by a group within a country. —**na′tion•al•ist** *n. & adj.* —**na′tion•al• is′tic** *adj.* —**na′tion•al•is′ti•cal•ly** *adv.*

na•tion•al•i•ty (năsh′ə năl′ĭ tē) *n., pl.* **na•tion•al•i•ties. 1.** [C; U] The status of belonging to a particular nation by origin, birth, or naturalization: *What is your nationality?* **2.** [C] A people having common origins or traditions: *Many nationalities have settled in the United States.*

na•tion•al•ize (năsh′ə nə līz′) *tr.v.* **na• tion•al•ized, na•tion•al•iz•ing, na•tion• al•iz•es.** To remove (sthg.) from private ownership and put it under the control of the government: *When did England nationalize its steel industry?* —**na′tion•al•i•za′tion** (năsh′ə nə lĭ zā′shən) *n.* [U]

national park *n.* Land declared public property by a national government in order to preserve and develop it for recreation and study.

na•tion•wide (nā′shən wīd′) *adv. & adj.* Across a whole nation: *The speech was broadcast nationwide. There is nationwide interest in recycling.*

na•tive (nā′tĭv) *adj.* **1.** Being born in a certain place: *He is a native Englishman.* **2.** Being one's own because of the place of one's birth: *Spanish is her native language.* **3.** Originally living or growing in a particular place: *a plant native to Asia.* **4.** Inborn; natural: *native ability.* **5.** Relating to the original inhabitants of a region: *a native custom.* —*n.* **1.** A person born in a particular place: *She is a native of New York now living in California.* **2.** One of the original inhabitants of a region.

Native American *n.* A member of any of the peoples who were living in the Western Hemisphere before the arrival of Europeans.

na•tive-born (nā′tĭv bôrn′) *adj.* Belonging to a place by birth: *a native-born Kenyan.*

na•tiv•i•ty (nə tĭv′ĭ tē or nā tĭv′ĭ tē) *n., pl.* **na•tiv•i•ties.** [C; U] **1.** *Formal.* Birth, especially the place, condition, or circumstances of being born. **2. Nativity. a.** The birth of Jesus. **b.** A representation, such as a painting, of Jesus's birth.

natl. *abbr.* An abbreviation of national.

NATO (nā′tō) *abbr.* An abbreviation of North Atlantic Treaty Organization.

nat•ty (năt′ē) *adj.* **nat•ti•er, nat•ti•est.** Neat and trim: *He's a natty dresser.* —**nat′ti•ly** *adv.*

nat•u•ral (năch′ər əl) *adj.* **1.** Present in nature; not artificial: *a natural pearl.* **2.** Relating to the physical world and the events that occur in it: *natural laws.* **3.** Following the usual course of nature: *a natural death.* **4.** With qualities or abilities that seem to be inborn: *She is a natural leader.* **5.** Not artificial or affected: *a natural way of speaking.* **6.** Expected; accepted: *Their friendship is a nat-*

ural result of their shared interest in art. —*n.* A person with the skills necessary for success: *You are a natural for this job.* —**nat′u• ral•ness** *n.* [U]

natural history *n.* [U] The study of living things and natural objects.

nat•u•ral•ist (năch′ər ə lĭst) *n.* A person who specializes in natural history, especially in the study of plants and animals in their natural surroundings.

nat•u•ral•ize (năch′ər ə līz′) *tr.v.* **nat• u•ral•ized, nat•u•ral•iz•ing, nat•u•ral• iz•es. 1.** To give full citizenship to (a person of foreign birth): *She was naturalized in a ceremony at the state capitol.* **2.** To accustom (a plant or an animal) to growing or living in new surroundings: *Dandelions are European plants that have been naturalized in North America.* —**nat′u•ral•i•za′tion** (năch′ər-ə lĭ zā′shən) *n.* [U] —**nat′u•ral•ized′** *adj.*

nat•u•ral•ly (năch′ər ə lē or năch′rə lē) *adv.* **1.** In a natural manner: *Try to behave naturally in front of the camera.* **2.** By nature: *Children are naturally curious.* **3.** Without a doubt; surely: *Naturally, the faster you grow, the more food you need.*

natural resource *n. (usually plural).* Something, such as a forest, a mineral deposit, or fresh water, that is found in nature and is necessary or useful to human beings.

natural selection *n.* [U] The principle that only those living things best suited to their environment tend to survive and pass on their genetic characteristics to their offspring, so these characteristics become more common with each generation of the species.

na•ture (nā′chər) *n.* **1.** [U] The physical world and the forces and processes that affect events in it: *the laws of nature.* **2.** [U] The world of living things and the outdoors: *Many people enjoy the beauties of nature.* **3.** [C] *(usually singular).* A kind or sort: *I like games of that nature.* **4.** [C; U] The basic characteristics and qualities of a person or thing: *It goes against her nature to complain. What is the nature of the problem?*

naught also **nought** (nôt) *Formal. n.* Zero; the digit 0. —*pron.* Nothing: *All their work was for naught.*

naugh•ty (nô′tē) *adj.* **naugh•ti•er, naugh• ti•est. 1.** Disobedient; mischievous: *You're a naughty boy for hiding Daddy's glasses!* **2.** Bad or improper: *a naughty word.* —**naugh′- ti•ly** *adv.* —**naugh′ti•ness** *n.* [U]

nau•se•a (nô′zē ə or nô′zhə) *n.* [U] A feeling of sickness in the stomach, characterized by the need to vomit.

nau•se•ate (nô′zē āt′ or nô′zhē āt′) *intr. & tr.v.* **nau•se•at•ed, nau•se•at•ing, nau• se•ates.** To feel or cause to feel nausea: *The*

ă–**cat**; ā–**pay**; âr–**care**; ä–**father**; ĕ–**get**; ē–**be**; ĭ–**sit**; ī–**nice**; îr–**here**; ŏ–**got**; ō–**go**; ô–**saw**; oi–**boy**; ou–**out**; o͞o–**took**; o͞o–**boot**; ŭ–**cut**; ûr–**word**; th–**thin**; *th*–**this**; hw–**when**; zh–**vision**; ə–**about**; N–French bon

smell of paint is nauseating. The thought of food nauseated her when she was pregnant.

nau·seous (nô′shəs *or* nô′zē əs) *adj.* **1.** Causing nausea; sickening: *The nauseous smell came from the garage.* **2.** Suffering from nausea: *She was feeling nauseous.*

USAGE: nauseous Traditionally **nauseous** is used only to mean "causing nausea," not "suffering from nausea." However, native speakers commonly use both **nauseated** and **nauseous** to mean "feeling or suffering from nausea."

nau·ti·cal (nô′tĭ kəl) *adj.* Relating to ships, sailors, or navigation. —**nau′ti·cal·ly** *adv.*

nautical mile *n.* A unit of length used in air and sea navigation, equal to about 6,076 feet (1,852 meters). See table at **measurement.**

na·val (nā′vəl) *adj.* **1.** Relating to a navy: *a naval officer.* **2.** Having a navy: *Spain was once a great naval power.*

HOMONYMS: naval, navel (bellybutton).

na·vel (nā′vəl) *n.* The scar left on the abdomen of mammals where the umbilical cord was attached before birth.

navel orange *n.* A sweet seedless orange with a mark like a navel.

nav·i·ga·ble (năv′ĭ gə bəl) *adj.* Deep enough or wide enough for travel by ships or boats: *The river is only navigable by small boats.* —**nav′i·ga·bil′i·ty** *n.* [U]

nav·i·gate (năv′ĭ gāt′) *v.* **nav·i·gat·ed, nav·i·gat·ing, nav·i·gates.** —*tr.* **1.** To plan and control the course of (a ship or an aircraft): *The captain navigated the ship through the islands.* **2.** To follow a planned course on, across, or through (sthg.): *navigate a stream.* —*intr.* To plan and control the course of a ship or an aircraft.

nav·i·ga·tion (năv′ĭ gā′shən) *n.* [U] **1.** The theory and practice of navigating, especially the science of planning a course for a ship or an aircraft: *He's studying navigation.* **2.** Travel or traffic by ships, especially commercial shipping: *an increase in navigation through the canal.* —**nav′i·ga′tion·al** *adj.*

nav·i·ga·tor (năv′ĭ gā′tər) *n.* **1.** A person who plots the course of a ship or an aircraft. **2.** A device that directs the course of an aircraft or a missile.

na·vy (nā′vē) *n.,* *pl.* **na·vies. 1.** All of a nation's warships. **2.** Often **Navy.** A nation's entire organization for sea warfare, including ships, people, and equipment at sea and on shore. **3.** Navy blue.

navy blue *n.* [U] A dark blackish blue color. —*adj.* Dark blackish blue.

nay (nā) *Formal. adv.* No: *All but four senators voted nay to the treaty.* —*n.* **1.** A vote of "no." **2.** A person who votes "no": *The nays carried it, and the bill was defeated.*

HOMONYMS: nay, neigh (whinny).

Na·zi (nät′sē *or* nät′sē) *n.,* *pl.* **Na·zis.** A member of the National Socialist German Workers' Party, founded in 1919 and brought to power by Adolf Hitler in 1933. —*adj.* Relating to Nazis. —**Na′zism** (nät′sĭz′ əm *or* nät′sĭz′ əm) *n.* [U]

NB also **N.B.** *abbr.* An abbreviation of New Brunswick.

n.b. or **N.B.** *abbr.* An abbreviation of nota bene (note well).

NC or **N.C.** *abbr.* An abbreviation of North Carolina.

Nd The symbol for the element **neodymium.**

ND *abbr.* An abbreviation of North Dakota.

N.Dak. *abbr.* An abbreviation of North Dakota.

Ne The symbol for the element **neon.**

NE *abbr.* An abbreviation of: **1.** Northeast. **2.** Nebraska.

near (nîr) *adv.* To, at, or within a short distance in space or time: *Don't come near!* —*adj.* **1.** Close in space, time, position, or degree: *near neighbors; near equals.* **2.** Close by family relationship: *near relatives.* **3.** Almost but not really happening: *a near victory.* **4.** Closer of two or more: *the near side of the house.* —*prep.* Close to, as in time, space, or degree: *a little inn near London.* —*v.* —*tr.* To come close or closer to (sbdy./sthg.): *The plane neared the runway.* —*intr.* To move near or nearer; approach: *The holiday season nears.* —**near′ness** *n.* [U]

near·by (nîr′bī′) *adj.* Located a short distance away: *a nearby supermarket.* —*adv.* Not far away; close by: *The bus stops nearby.*

near·ly (nîr′lē) *adv.* Almost but not quite: *That coat nearly fits.*

near·sight·ed (nîr′sī′tĭd) *adj.* Unable to see distant objects clearly; myopic: *She's nearsighted and wears glasses for driving.* —**near′sight′ed·ness** *n.* [U]

neat (nēt) *adj.* **1.** Orderly and clean; tidy: *a neat room.* **2.** Not careless or messy: *a neat person.* **3.** *Slang.* Wonderful; fine: *a neat idea.* —**neat′ly** *adv.* —**neat′ness** *n.* [U]

SYNONYMS: neat, tidy, trim, shipshape. These adjectives mean marked by good order and cleanliness. **Neat** means pleasingly clean and orderly: *You should keep your desk neat.* **Tidy** suggests precise arrangement and order: *Even their closets and drawers were kept tidy.* **Trim** stresses a pleasing appearance because of neatness, tidiness, and good proportions: *The trim little boat was all ready to set sail.* **Shipshape** means both neat and tidy: *We'll have the kitchen shipshape in no time.* **ANTONYMS: messy, sloppy.**

N

neb•u•la (nĕb′yə lə) *n., pl.* **neb•u•lae**
(nĕb′yə lē′) or **neb•u•las.** A thinly spread
mass of gas or dust in space.

neb•u•lous (nĕb′yə ləs) *adj.* Vague; unclear: *He has nebulous ideas about how
he'll earn a living as a musician.* —**neb′u•**
lous•ly *adv.* —**neb′u•lous•ness** *n.* [U]

nec•es•sar•i•ly (nĕs′ĭ sâr′ə lē) *adv.* As a
necessary result; inevitably: *Playing their
best does not necessarily mean that they'll
win the game.*

nec•es•sar•y (nĕs′ĭ sĕr′ē) *adj.* **1.** Important
and needed; essential: *Getting enough sleep
is necessary to stay healthy.* **2.** Needed for a
certain result or effect; required: *Fill out the
necessary forms.*

ne•ces•si•tate (nə sĕs′ĭ tāt′) *tr.v.* **ne•ces•**
si•tat•ed, ne•ces•si•tat•ing, ne•ces•si•
tates. *Formal.* To make (sthg.) necessary or
unavoidable: *The poor light necessitated the
use of a flash to take the picture.*

ne•ces•si•ty (nə sĕs′ĭ tē) *n., pl.* **ne•ces•**
si•ties. 1. [C] Something that is needed for
existence, success, or functioning: *Water is a
necessity of life.* **2.** [U] The quality of being
necessary: *the necessity of sleep.*

neck (nĕk) *n.* **1.** The part of the body that joins
the head to the shoulders: *A giraffe has a long
neck.* **2.** The part of a piece of clothing that
fits around the neck: *The neck is too tight on
that sweater.* **3.** A narrow part that extends or
connects: *the neck of a bottle; the neck of a
guitar.* —*intr.v. Informal.* An outdated expression meaning to kiss and caress. ◆ **neck and
neck.** Even in a close race: *The runners
were neck and neck at the finish line.* **pain in
the neck.** *Informal.* A bother: *That neighbor
is a pain in the neck; he's always borrowing
things.* **risk (one's) neck.** *Informal.* To put
oneself in physical or financial danger: *She
risked her neck in that business deal.* **up to
(one's) neck.** *Informal.* Very busy: *I'm up to
my neck with work right now.*

neck•er•chief (nĕk′ər chĭf *or* nĕk′ər chēf′)
n. A kerchief worn around the neck.

neck•lace (nĕk′lĭs) *n.* A string of beads
or jewels worn around the neck: *a pearl
necklace.*

neck•line (nĕk′līn′) *n.* The line formed by
the edge of a piece of clothing at or below the
neck: *I don't like the neckline on that dress.*

neck•tie (nĕk′tī′) *n.* A narrow band of cloth
worn around the neck beneath the shirt collar
and tied close to the throat.

nec•tar (nĕk′tər) *n.* **1.** [U] A sweet liquid in
certain flowers: *The hummingbird drank the
nectar from the flower.* **2.** [C; U] A fruit juice:
apricot nectar.

nec•tar•ine (nĕk′tə rēn′) *n.* A type of peach
with a smooth, shiny skin.

need (nēd) *n.* [C; U] **1.** A situation in which
sthg. is required: *The school has a need for a
new computer.* **2.** *(usually plural).* Something
required or wanted: *Our needs are simple.* **3.**
Necessity or obligation: *There wasn't any
need for you to pay me back.* —*v.* —*aux.* To
be required to do sthg.: *You need not come
today.* —*tr.* To require (sbdy./sthg.); have
need of: *I need two dollars for bus fare.* —*intr.*
To be in need: *You will never need if you
inherit a fortune.* ◆ **if need be.** If necessary:
If need be, I'll go by myself. **in need.**
Requiring help because of poverty or misfortune: *They lived in need because they lost
their jobs.*

HOMONYMS: need, knead (press and shape).

---

nee•dle (nēd′l) *n.*
1. A thin pointed
piece of metal used
in sewing or knit-
ting: *Do you have
a needle and some
thread? I need to
sew on a button.* **2.**

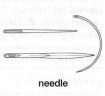

needle

The pointer on a dial, gauge, or compass:
Where is the needle pointing? **3.** A hypodermic needle used to give injections: *Doctors
must always use a new needle for each
patient.* **4.** A stiff pointed leaf of a pine tree.
—*tr.v.* **nee•dled, nee•dling, nee•dles.** *Informal.* To provoke or tease (sbdy.): *Older
children often needle younger ones.*

nee•dle•point (nēd′l point′) *n.* [U] Embroidery on canvas that resembles a woven
tapestry.

need•less (nēd′lĭs) *adj.* Not needed; unnecessary: *Pronouns help a writer avoid needless
repetition.* ◆ **needless to say.** Obviously:
Needless to say, we hope to do well on the test.
—**need′less•ly** *adv.*

nee•dle•work (nēd′l wûrk′) *n.* [U] Work,
such as sewing or embroidery, that is done
with a needle.

need•n't (nēd′nt). Contraction of *need not:*
*You needn't read that chapter for the next
class.*

need•y (nē′dē) *adj.* **need•i•er, need•i•est.**
Being in need; poor: *Our club donated food
to needy families.* —*n.* **the needy.** *(used with
a plural verb).* People in need: *They always
give to the needy.*

ne'er-do-well (nâr′dōō wĕl′) *n.* An irresponsible person who never does anything:
She is a ne'er-do-well who doesn't work.

ne•far•i•ous (nə fâr′ē əs) *adj. Formal.* Evil;
wicked: *the nefarious act of terrorism.*

ne•gate (nĭ gāt′) *tr.v.* **ne•gat•ed, ne•**
gat•ing, ne•gates. 1. To make (sthg.) inef-

---

fective or invalid; nullify: *This decision negates the previous agreement.* **2.** To rule (sthg.) out; deny: *There's no use trying to negate the seriousness of the problem.* —**ne·ga′tion** *n.* [U]

neg·a·tive (něg′ə tĭv) *adj.* **1.** Expressing denial or refusal: *a negative answer.* **2.** Not positive: *a negative attitude.* **3.** In medicine, indicating that a disease, condition, or microorganism is not present: *a negative result of a blood test.* **4.** Less than zero: *a negative number.* **5.** Relating to an electric charge like that of an electron. —*n.* **1.** A "no" answer. **2.** Something that lacks positive qualities: *There are many negatives in this proposal.* **3.** In grammar, a word or part of a word that expresses negation. For example, *no, not,* and *un-* are negatives. **4.** An image, especially in photography, in which the light areas appear dark and the dark areas appear light. **5.** A negative number. ◆ **in the negative.** In a sense or manner showing a refusal or denial: *She answered in the negative.* —**neg′a·tive·ly** *adv.*

ne·glect (nǐ glěkt′) *tr.v.* **1.** To ignore or pay no attention to (sbdy./sthg.): *He neglected his family.* **2.** To fail (to do sthg.), as through carelessness: *We neglected to tell the committee about the extra expenses.* —*n.* [U] **1.** The act of neglecting: *You got into trouble because of your neglect of your homework.* **2.** The condition of being neglected: *The garden has fallen into neglect.* —**ne·glect′ful** *adj.* —**ne·glect′ful·ly** *adv.*

neg·li·gee (něg′lǐ zhā′ *or* něg′lǐ zhā′) *n.* A woman's loose nightgown, often made of soft delicate material.

neg·li·gence (něg′lǐ jəns) *n.* [U] **1.** A failure to act with care or concern: *As a result of the man's negligence, the child was injured.* **2.** In law, failure to act with reasonable care: *The owner was charged with negligence after the accident.* —**neg′li·gent** *adj.* —**neg′li·gent·ly** *adv.*

neg·li·gi·ble (něg′lǐ jə bəl) *adj.* Not worth considering; very little: *a negligible difference.* —**neg′li·gi·bly** *adv.*

ne·go·tia·ble (nǐ gō′shə bəl) *adj.* **1.** Easy to negotiate: *a negotiable contract.* **2.** Able to be legally transferred from one person to another: *Traveler's checks are negotiable currency.* —**ne·go′tia·bil′i·ty** *n.* [U]

ne·go·ti·ate (nǐ gō′shē āt′) *v.* **ne·go·ti·at·ed, ne·go·ti·at·ing, ne·go·ti·ates.** —*tr.* **1.** To talk about (sthg.) with the hope of coming to an agreement: *The countries negotiated a peace treaty.* **2.** To succeed in doing (sthg.): *The car negotiated a sharp turn.* —*intr.* To talk with others to reach an agreement: *We must be prepared to compromise if we are going to negotiate.* —**ne·go′ti·a′tion** *n.* [C; U] —**ne·go′ti·a′tor** *n.*

Ne·gro (nē′grō) *n., pl.* **Ne·groes.** An out-

dated term for a person whose ancestors are from central and southern Africa; a black person; an African American.

neigh (nā) *n.* The long, high sound made by a horse. —*intr.v.* To make the sound of a horse; whinny: *The horse neighed at the barking dog.*

HOMONYMS: neigh, nay (no).

neigh·bor (nā′bər) *n.* **1.** A person who lives near or next to another: *Our new neighbors moved in last week.* **2.** A person or thing near another: *Earth's nearest neighbor is the moon.* —*tr.v.* To be near or next to (sthg.): *How many countries neighbor Thailand?*

neigh·bor·hood (nā′bər hŏŏd′) *n.* **1.** A district or an area in a town or city: *I live in a quiet neighborhood.* **2.** The people who live in a particular area: *The noise upset the entire neighborhood.* **3.** The area nearby; the vicinity: *I just happened to be in the neighborhood.* ◆ **in the neighborhood of.** Approximately: *That new car costs in the neighborhood of $20,000.*

neigh·bor·ly (nā′bər lē) *adj.* Having the quality of a friendly neighbor: *a neighborly act of kindness.* —**neigh′bor·li·ness** *n.* [U]

nei·ther (nē′thər *or* nī′thər) *adj.* Not either; not one nor the other: *Neither shoe fits comfortably.* —*pron.* Not either one; not the one nor the other: *Neither of the shoes fits.* —*conj.* **1.** Not either; not in either case. Used with *nor: They had neither seen the movie nor read the book.* **2.** Also not; nor: *If you won't go, neither will I.*

USAGE: neither When you use **neither** as a conjunction, you should follow it with **nor** rather than **or:** *Neither rain nor snow stopped her from going for a walk every day.*

nem·e·sis (něm′ĭ sĭs) *n., pl.* **nem·e·ses** (něm′ĭ sēz′). *(usually singular).* **1.** A source of great difficulty or harm: *Math was always his nemesis in college.* **2.** An unbeatable rival: *He met his nemesis in the tennis finals.*

neo- *pref.* A prefix that means new or recent: *neophyte, neonatal.*

WORD BUILDING: neo— The prefix **neo—** means "new or recent." Thus the word **neophyte** means "a beginner." Many words beginning with **neo—** refer to a new or modern form of a movement or political doctrine, such as **neoclassical** or **neofascism.** Many other formations are for recent science words, such as the word for the element **neodymium.**

ne·o·clas·si·cism (nē′ō klǎs′ ĭ sĭz′əm) *n.* [U] A movement that attempted to return to classical forms in such areas as literature, art, and architecture. —**ne′o·clas′sic, ne′o·clas′si·cal** *adj.*

N

ne•o•dym•i•um (nē′ō dĭm′ē əm) *n.* [U] *Symbol* **Nd** A metallic element used in lasers, glass, and medicine. Atomic number 60. See table at **element.**

ne•o•fas•cism (nē′ō făsh′ ĭz′ əm) *n.* [U] A movement based on the methods and beliefs of fascism. —**ne′o•fas′cist** *adj. & n.*

ne•on (nē′ŏn′) *n.* [U] *Symbol* **Ne** A colorless, chemically inert gaseous element. Tubes containing neon are used in electric signs or lamps. Atomic number 10. See table at **element.**

ne•o•na•tal (nē′ō nāt′l) *adj.* Relating to a newborn infant: *Seriously ill newborn babies are cared for in special neonatal care units in some hospitals.* —**ne′o•nate′** *n.*

ne•o-Na•zi (nē′ō-nät′sē) *n.* A member of a group following the beliefs of Adolf Hitler's Nazis. —**ne′o-Na′zism** *n.* [U]

ne•o•phyte (nē′ə fīt′) *n.* A beginner or novice: *He's a neophyte at politics.*

neph•ew (nĕf′yōō) *n.* The son of one's brother or sister, or the son of the brother or sister of one's spouse: *I have three nephews and two nieces.*

nep•o•tism (nĕp′ə tĭz′ əm) *n.* [U] Favoritism shown by people in government or the workplace to their relatives: *When the boss hired his daughter, he was accused of nepotism.*

nerd (nûrd) *n. Slang.* A person regarded as socially awkward, especially a person who is always occupied with science or computers: *a computer nerd.* —**nerd′y** *adj.*

nerve (nûrv) *n.* **1.** [C] A long fiber that carries messages from the central nervous system to the various parts of the body. **2.** [C] A sore point: *She touched a nerve when she criticized my English paper.* **3.** [U] Courage and control: *Don't lose your nerve; ask for the job.* **4. nerves.** Symptoms caused by the reaction of the nervous system to fear, anxiety, or stress: *She suffered an attack of nerves before an important speech.* ♦ **get on (one's) nerves.** To irritate sbdy.: *Their noisy children always get on my nerves.* **have a lot of nerve.** To take advantage of sbdy. or act rudely: *You have a lot of nerve taking my book!*

nerve-rack•ing (nûrv′răk′ĭng) *adj.* Intensely distressing or irritating: *The wait for the test results was nerve-racking.*

nerv•ous (nûr′vəs) *adj.* **1.** Having nerves that are easily affected; jittery: *a nervous person.* **2.** Uneasy; anxious: *nervous moments before the test.* **3.** Relating to the nervous system: *a nervous disorder.* —**nerv′ous•ly** *adv.* —**nerv′ous•ness** *n.* [U]

nervous system *n.* The system in the body that regulates internal functions and responses to stimuli. In vertebrates it includes the brain, spinal cord, and nerves.

nerv•y (nûr′vē) *adj.* **nerv•i•er, nerv•i•est.**

Extremely bold; rude: *Borrowing my books without asking is a nervy thing to do.*

—**ness** *suff.* A suffix that means state, condition, or quality: *brightness, cleanliness.*

> **WORD BUILDING: —ness** The suffix —**ness** commonly attaches to adjectives in order to form abstract nouns, such as **happiness, neighborliness,** and **destructiveness.** The suffix —**ness** also forms nouns from adjectives made of participles, such as **contentedness** and **willingness.** It can also form nouns from compound adjectives, such as **kindheartedness** and **straightforwardness.** The suffix —**ness** can even be used with phrases: **matter-of-factness.**

nest (nĕst) *n.* **1.** A shelter made by a bird or another animal to hold its young. **2.** A place of lodging or shelter: *The newlyweds' love nest is a small apartment.* —*v.* —*intr.* To build or stay in a nest: *Robins nested in the willow tree.* —*tr.* **1.** To place (sthg.) as if in a nest: *The diamond was nested in the velvet box.* **2.** To fit (things) inside one another: *You should nest the boxes for storage.*

nest

nest egg *n.* Money saved for future use; savings: *They plan to use their nest egg to buy a house.*

nes•tle (nĕs′əl) *v.* **nes•tled, nes•tling, nes•tles.** —*intr.* **1.** To settle down snugly and comfortably: *The child nestled close to his mother.* **2.** To lie half-sheltered: *Farms nestle in the valley.* —*tr.* **1.** To snuggle or press (sthg.) close: *The baby nestled her head on my shoulder.* **2.** To place or hold (sbdy./sthg.) as if in a nest: *I nestled the puppy in my arms.*

nest•ling (nĕst′lĭng) *n.* A bird too young to leave its nest: *We returned the nestling to its nest.*

net¹ (nĕt) *n.* **1.** [U] A loose fabric made of threads or ropes that are woven or knotted together. **2.** [C] A piece of net used for a special purpose, especially: **a.** A device used to catch fish, birds, or insects: *fishing nets.* **b.** A covering used as protection against insects: *a mosquito net over the bed.* **c.** A piece of mesh used to hold hair in place. **3.** [C] A barrier of mesh as in tennis or volleyball. —*tr.v.* **net•ted, net•ting, nets.** To catch (sthg.) in a net: *He netted a rare butterfly.*

net² (nĕt) *adj.* **1.** Remaining after all subtractions have been made: *What was your net income after expenses?* **2.** Final; ultimate: *What was the net result of your efforts?* —*n.*

[U] The net amount, as of profit, income, or weight: *What was your net last year?* —*tr.v.* **net·ted, net·ting, nets.** To bring (sthg.) in as profit: *The sale netted a huge profit.*

neth·er (nĕ*th*′ər) *adj. Formal.* Located below; lower or under: *In his fiction, Jules Verne wrote about travel in the nether regions of the earth.*

net·ting (nĕt′ĭng) *n.* [U] A fabric made with open spaces between crossing strands; net.

net·work (nĕt′wûrk′) *n.* **1.** A system made up of parts, lines, or routes that cross or interconnect: *a network of blood vessels; a transportation network.* **2.** A group of radio or television broadcasting stations, usually sharing many programs: *a television network.* **3.** A group of devices, such as computers, connected in order to share information. —*v.* —*intr.* To meet with people in order to advance one's career: *He networked at the party to meet new business contacts.* —*tr.* To connect (computers) for communication: *We networked our computers.*

neu·ral (nŏor′əl) *adj.* Relating to the nervous system.

neu·rol·o·gy (nŏo rŏl′ə jē) *n.* [U] The scientific and medical study of the nervous system and its diseases and disorders. —**neu′ro·log′i·cal** (nŏor′ə lŏj′ĭ kəl) *adj.* —**neu·rol′o·gist** *n.*

neu·ron (nŏor′ŏn) *n.* Any of the cells that make up the tissue of nerves: *The brain has many millions of neurons.*

neu·ro·sis (nŏo rō′sĭs) *n., pl.* **neu·ro·ses** (nŏo rō′sēz). [C; U] A disorder in which the function of the mind or emotions is disturbed, involving symptoms such as anxiety, depression, or obsession.

neu·rot·ic (nŏo rŏt′ĭk) *adj.* **1.** Relating to a neurosis: *neurotic symptoms.* **2.** Suffering from neurosis: *a neurotic patient.* **3.** Nervous or anxious in an unreasonable way: *She's one of the most neurotic people I know; she worries constantly.* —*n. Informal.* **1.** A person suffering from a neurosis. **2.** An unreasonably nervous or anxious person: *Don't be such a neurotic; the plane isn't going to crash.* —**neu·rot′i·cal·ly** *adv.*

neu·ter (nŏo′tər) *adj.* In grammar, neither masculine nor feminine in gender: *The word it is a neuter pronoun.* —*tr.v.* To castrate or spay (an animal): *We had the vet neuter our cat.*

neu·tral (nŏo′trəl) *adj.* **1.a.** Not supporting either side in a war, dispute, or contest: *a neutral nation.* **b.** Not belonging to either side in a conflict: *neutral territory.* **2.** Describing a color, such as gray, black, beige, or white, that lacks strong hue: *I bought a neutral-colored coat that goes with all of my clothes.* **3.** Without definite or distinctive characteristics: *a neutral flavor.* **4.** In chemistry, neither acid nor alkaline: *a neutral solution.* **5.** Having positive electric charges exactly bal-

anced by negative electric charges: *a neutral atom.* —*n.* [U] A position (especially in a vehicle) in which gears are not engaged, so no power can be transmitted: *Leave the car in neutral while I check the engine.*

neu·tral·i·ty (nŏo trăl′ĭ tē) *n.* [U] The condition, quality, or status of being neutral, especially a policy of not taking part in a war.

neu·tral·ize (nŏo′trə līz′) *tr.v.* **neu·tral·ized, neu·tral·iz·ing, neu·tral·iz·es. 1.** To cancel or counteract the effect of (sthg.): *neutralize a poison.* **2.** To counterbalance and reduce (sthg.) to zero: *neutralize an electric charge.* **3.** To cause (a chemical substance) to be neither acid nor alkaline: *neutralize a solution.* —**neu′tral·i·za′tion** (nŏo′trə lĭ zā′shən) *n.* [U] —**neu′tral·iz′er** *n.*

neu·tri·no (nŏo trē′nō) *n., pl.* **neu·tri·nos.** Any of three electrically neutral subatomic particles that travel at the speed of light and are thought to have a mass of zero if at rest.

neu·tron (nŏo′trŏn) *n.* An electrically neutral subatomic particle with the approximate mass of a proton.

Nev. *abbr.* An abbreviation of Nevada.

nev·er (nĕv′ər) *adv.* At no time; not ever: *I have never been here before.*

nev·er·more (nĕv′ər môr′) *adv. Formal.* Never again: *They will nevermore see each other.*

nev·er·the·less (nĕv′ər *th*ə lĕs′) *adv.* In spite of that; however: *His report was not long; nevertheless, it was full of interesting information.*

new (nŏo) *adj.* **1.** Recently made, built, or formed: *a new law; a new house.* **2.** Of the latest type; fashionable: *a new dance.* **3.** Never used or worn; not secondhand: *a new bicycle.* **4.** Fresh: *a new coat of paint.* **5.** Additional; further: *new sources of energy.* **6.** Recently arrived or established in a place, position, or relationship: *the new teacher; a new boyfriend.* —*adv. (usually used in combination).* Freshly; recently: *new-mown.* —**new′ness** *n.* [U]

N

HOMONYMS: **new, gnu** (antelope), **knew** (did know).

new·born (nŏo′bôrn′) *adj.* Just born: *newborn babies.* —*n.* A newborn child or animal.

new·com·er (nŏo′kŭm′ər) *n.* A person who has only recently arrived: *Our church held a dinner to welcome newcomers to the community.*

new·fan·gled (nŏo′făng′gəld) *adj. Informal. (often used in humorous situations).* New and often unnecessary or undesirable: *My grandfather always complains about our generation's newfangled ideas.*

new·ly (nŏo′lē) *adv.* **1.** Not long ago; recently: *A newly laundered shirt smells fresh and clean.* **2.** Freshly: *a newly painted room.*

new•ly•wed (nōō′lē wĕd′) *n.* A person recently married: *The newlyweds honeymooned in Florida.*

news (nōōz) *n.* [U] **1.a.** Information about recent events, especially when reported by newspapers, radio, or television. **b.** A presentation of such information, as on a television broadcast: *Did you watch the news last night?* **2.** New information: *The change in the bus schedule was news to me.*

news•cast (nōōz′kăst′) *n.* A radio or television program that broadcasts news reports: *We usually watch the 6:00 P.M. newscast.* —**news′cast′er** *n.*

news•let•ter (nōōz′lĕt′ər) *n.* A printed report giving news or information of interest to a special group: *Our company newsletter tells employees about benefits such as health insurance.*

news•pa•per (nōōz′pā′pər) *n.* A printed publication, usually issued daily or weekly, that contains current news, articles, and advertisements: *How often do you read the local newspaper?*

news•print (nōōz′prĭnt′) *n.* [U] Thin paper used to print newspapers.

news•stand (nōōz′stănd′) *n.* A small store, often with an open side, where newspapers, magazines, and snacks such as candy are sold.

news•wor•thy (nōōz′wûr′thē) *adj.* Interesting or important enough to report to the general public: *a newsworthy event.*

news•y (nōō′zē) *adj.* **news•i•er, news•i•est.** *Informal.* Full of news; informative: *My sister always writes newsy letters.*

new•ton (nōōt′n) *n.* A unit of force equal to the force needed to accelerate a mass of one kilogram one meter per second per second.

New Year *n.* The first day or days of a calendar year.

New Year's Day (yîrz) *n.* January 1, the first day of the year, celebrated as a holiday in many countries: *Many people enjoy watching parades and football games on New Year's Day.*

New Year's Eve *n.* The evening of December 31, celebrated as a holiday in many countries: *People celebrate New Year's Eve with parties that go on well past midnight.*

next (nĕkst) *adj.* **1.** Immediately following in time, order, or sequence: *next week; the next item on the list.* **2.** Nearest in space or position: *the next town; the next room.* —*adv.* **1.** In the time, order, or place immediately following: *our next oldest child.* **2.** On the first occasion after the present: *when you next wash the floor.* ◆ **next of kin.** A person's closest living relatives: *The police notified the accident victim's next of kin.* **next to. 1.** Adjacent to; beside: *Who is sitting next to you?* **2.** Coming immediately after in prefer-

ence: *Next to soccer, I like softball best.* **next to impossible.** Almost impossible: *It's next to impossible to find him at home.* **next to (the) last.** Coming one before the end: *She's next to last on the waiting list.*

next door *adv.* To or in the adjacent house, building, apartment, or room: *A large family just moved next door to us.* —*adj.* **next-door** (nĕkst′dôr′). Located or living in the adjacent house, building, apartment, or room: *our next-door neighbors.*

NH or **N.H.** *abbr.* An abbreviation of New Hampshire.

Ni The symbol for the element **nickel** (sense 1).

ni•a•cin (nī′ə sĭn) *n.* [U] A compound containing carbon, hydrogen, oxygen, and nitrogen: *Niacin is essential to living cells.*

nib•ble (nĭb′əl) *v.* **nib•bled, nib•bling, nib•bles.** —*tr.* **1.** To eat (sthg.) with small bites: *nibble cheese.* **2.** To bite at (sthg.) gently and repeatedly: *The fish nibbled the bait.* —*intr.* To take small bites: *We weren't very hungry, so we just nibbled at our food.* —*n.* A small bite of food: *Give me just a nibble of your sandwich, please.*

nice (nīs) *adj.* **nic•er, nic•est. 1.** Kind; friendly: *She's really nice.* **2.** Good; pleasant; agreeable: *a nice place to stay.* **3.** Having a pleasant appearance; attractive: *a nice dress.* **4.** Done with skill: *a nice bit of work.* **5.** Used as an intensive with *and: nice and warm; nice and easy.* —**nice′ly** *adv.* —**nice′ness** *n.* [U]

niche (nĭch *or* nēsh) *n.* **1.** A hollow, as in a wall: *I put my books in the niche by my bed.* **2.** A situation or an activity specially suited to a person's abilities or character: *She finally found her niche in life.*

nick (nĭk) *n.* A small cut or chip in a surface or edge: *a plate with a nick in it.* —*tr.v.* To make a small cut or notch in (sbdy./sthg.): *The barber nicked my ear.* ◆ **in the nick of time.** Just at the critical moment; just in time: *We arrived in the nick of time.*

nick•el (nĭk′əl) *n.* **1.** [U] *Symbol* **Ni** A silvery hard metallic element. Atomic number 28. See table at **element. 2.** [C] A U.S. or Canadian coin worth five cents, made of a nickel and copper alloy. ◆ **nickel-and-dime.** To force (sbdy.) to spend more money than wanted but in small amounts: *The owner of the local store has been nickel-and-diming customers to death.*

nick•nack (nĭk′năk′) *n.* Variant of **knick-knack.**

nick•name (nĭk′nām′) *n.* **1.** A descriptive name used instead of the real name of a person or animal: *My father's nickname is Shorty because he is not very tall.* **2.** A familiar or shortened form of a proper name: *Henry's nickname was Hank.* —*tr.v.* **nick•named,**

nick·nam·ing, nick·names. To give a nickname to (sbdy./sthg.): *New York is nicknamed the Big Apple.*

nic·o·tine (nĭk′ə tēn′) *n.* [U] A poisonous addictive alkaloid composed of carbon, hydrogen, and nitrogen. Nicotine is found in tobacco and is used as an insect poison.

niece (nēs) *n.* The daughter of one's brother or sister, or the daughter of the brother or sister of one's spouse: *She has two nieces and one nephew.*

nif·ty (nĭf′tē) *adj.* **nif·ti·er, nif·ti·est.** *Informal.* An outdated expression meaning nice; great: *a nifty new car.*

night (nīt) *n.* **1.** [C; U] The period between sunset and sunrise, especially the hours of darkness: *He tossed and turned all night.* **2.** [C] An evening or night devoted to some special purpose or event: *the opening night of a play.* **3.** [U] Darkness: *She ran out into the foggy night.* ◆ **night and day.** Two extremely different people or things: *The two brothers are as different as night and day.*

Homonyms: night, knight (soldier on horseback).

night·cap (nīt′kăp′) *n.* An alcoholic drink taken just before bedtime.

night·club (nīt′klŭb′) *n.* An establishment that stays open late at night and provides food, drink, and entertainment: *Some great bands play at that nightclub.*

night crawler *n.* An earthworm that comes out of the ground at night, often used as bait in fishing.

night·fall (nīt′fôl′) *n.* [U] The coming of night; dusk.

night·gown (nīt′goun′) *n.* A loose garment worn in bed by women and girls: *Do you prefer to wear a nightgown or pajamas?*

night·ie or **night·y** (nī′tē) *n.* A shortened form of nightgown: *My little sister likes her soft blue nightie with the kittens on it.*

night-light (nīt′līt′) *n.* A small light left on all night: *We leave a night-light on in the hallway.*

night·life (nīt′līf′) *n.* [U] Evening entertainment available in a community: *Some small towns don't have much nightlife.*

night·ly (nīt′lē) *adj.* **1.** Happening during the night: *The bears paid a nightly visit to the campground.* **2.** Happening or done every night: *the nightly news on TV.* —**night′ly** *adv.*

night·mare (nīt′mâr′) *n.* **1.** A dream that is very frightening: *The child awakens every night crying because of nightmares.* **2.** A very frightening or terrible experience: *Their vacation turned into a nightmare after their luggage was lost.* —**night′mar′ish** *adj.*

night owl *n.* *Informal.* A person who stays up late at night: *My brother is a night owl, but my sister-in-law always goes to bed early.*

night school *n.* A school that holds classes in the evening.

night shift *n.* **1.** A group of employees working during the night in a factory or business: *The night shift comes on at 11:00 P.M.* **2.** The period of time for such work: *She prefers working the night shift over the day shift.*

night·shirt (nīt′shûrt′) *n.* A loose shirt, often like a T-shirt, worn in bed.

night·stick (nīt′stĭk′) *n.* A club carried by a police officer.

night·time (nīt′tīm′) *n.* [U] The time between sunset and sunrise.

nil (nĭl) *n.* [U] Nothing; zero: *We received nil for our work on the project.*

nim·ble (nĭm′bəl) *adj.* **nim·bler, nim·blest.** **1.** Quick and light in movement; agile: *nimble fingers.* **2.** Quick and clever in thinking or understanding: *a nimble mind.* —**nim′bly** *adv.*

nin·com·poop (nĭn′kəm pōōp′ *or* nĭng′-kəm pōōp′) *n. Informal.* An outdated, mildly insulting expression for a foolish or silly person: *He was acting like a complete nincompoop.*

nine (nīn) *n.* **1.** The number, written 9, that is equal to 8 + 1. **2.** The ninth in a set or sequence. —**nine** *adj. & pron.*

nine·teen (nīn tēn′) *n.* **1.** The number, written 19, that is equal to 18 + 1. **2.** The 19th in a set or sequence. —**nine·teen′** *adj. & pron.*

nine·teenth (nīn tēnth′) *n.* **1.** The ordinal number matching the number 19 in a series. **2.** One of 19 equal parts: *One nineteenth of 190 is ten.* —**nine·teenth′** *adj. & adv.*

nine·ti·eth (nīn′tē ĭth′) *n.* **1.** The ordinal number matching the number 90 in a series. **2.** One of 90 equal parts: *One ninetieth of 90 is one.* —**nine′ti·eth** *adj. & adv.*

nine·ty (nīn′tē) *n., pl.* **nine·ties. 1.** The number, written 90, that is equal to 9 × 10. **2.** A decade or the numbers from 90 to 99. —**nine′ty** *adj. & pron.*

nin·ny (nĭn′ē) *n., pl.* **nin·nies.** *Informal.* A foolish or silly person: *Don't be such a ninny.*

ninth (nīnth) *n.* **1.** The ordinal number matching the number nine in a series. **2.** One of nine equal parts: *One ninth of 90 is ten.* —**ninth** *adj. & adv.*

nip[1] (nĭp) *tr.v.* **nipped, nip·ping, nips. 1.** To grab and bite (sbdy./sthg.): *One dog nipped the other.* **2.** To sting or chill (sbdy./sthg.) with the cold: *The wind nipped our ears.* —*n.* **1.** A small sharp bite: *The dog took a nip out of my finger.* **2.** Sharp biting cold or flavor: *a nip in the autumn air.* ◆ **nip and tuck.** Almost successful; close: *It was nip and tuck, but we got to the airport in time.*

nip in the bud. To stop the growth or development of sthg.: *The plan was nipped in the bud.* **nip off.** *tr.v.* [sep.] To remove (sthg.) by pinching or snipping: *Nip off the top leaf of the plant.* —**nip′py** *adj.*

N

nip² (nĭp) *n. Informal.* A small amount of liquor.

nip·ple (nĭp′əl) *n.* **1.** The tip of the breast, containing in females the outlets of the milk ducts. **2.** A soft rubber cap on a bottle from which a baby nurses: *Wash the nipple before you put it on the bottle.*

nipple

nir·va·na (nîr vä′nə *or* nər-vä′nə) *n.* [U] **1.** In Buddhism, the state of wisdom and compassion in which the self is freed from suffering and desire. **2.** An ideal condition of rest, harmony, or joy.

nit (nĭt) *n.* The egg or young of a louse or similar insect.

HOMONYMS: **nit, knit** (loop yarn).

nit·pick (nĭt′pĭk′) *intr.v.* To criticize others by finding fault with small, unimportant details: *Stop nitpicking!* —**nit′pick′er** *n.*

ni·trate (nī′trāt′ *or* nī′trĭt) *n.* [C; U] A chemical salt used in fertilizers.

ni·trite (nī′trīt′) *n.* [C; U] A chemical salt important in the nitrogen cycle.

ni·tro·gen (nī′trə jən) *n.* [U] *Symbol* **N** A colorless, odorless, gaseous element that makes up most of the atmosphere and is a necessary part of all animal and plant tissues. Nitrogen is used in explosives and fertilizers. Atomic number 7. See table at **element.**

ni·tro·glyc·er·in also **ni·tro·glyc·er·ine** (nī′trō glĭs′ər ĭn) *n.* [U] A thick explosive liquid, used in making dynamite and in medicine.

nit·ty-grit·ty (nĭt′ē grĭt′ē) *n.* [U] *Informal.* The specific or practical details; the heart of the matter: *We need to finish our project, so let's get down to the nitty-gritty.*

nit·wit (nĭt′wĭt′) *n. Informal.* A stupid or silly person.

nix (nĭks) *tr.v. Informal.* To forbid or veto (sthg.): *My parents nixed my idea of going to Europe.*

NJ or **N.J.** *abbr.* An abbreviation of New Jersey.

NM or **N.M.** *abbr.* An abbreviation of New Mexico.

N.Mex. *abbr.* An abbreviation of New Mexico.

no (nō) *adv.* **1.** Used to express a negative: *No, I'm not going.* **2.** Not at all. Often used with the comparative: *This car is no better than my old one.* —*adj.* **1.** Not any: *There are no cookies left.* **2.** Not at all; not close to being: *He's no child; he should know better.* **3.** Hardly any: *We got there in no time at all.* —*n., pl.*

noes. 1. A negative answer: *The suggestion met with a chorus of noes.* **2.** A negative vote or voter.

HOMONYMS: **no, know** (have knowledge).

no. *abbr.* An abbreviation of: **1.** North. **2.** Northern. **3.** Number.

no·bil·i·ty (nō bĭl′ĭ tē) *n.* [U] **1.** A class of people of high rank, often having wealth and power: *a member of the French nobility.* **2.** The quality of being noble in character: *There is nobility in devoting time to volunteer work.*

no·ble (nō′bəl) *adj.* **no·bler, no·blest. 1.** Having high rank in society. **2.** Having qualities of high moral character: *She has a noble spirit.* **3.** Excellent and admirable: *Working to help the poor is a noble cause.* —*n.* A member of the nobility: *the king and his nobles.* —**no′bly** *adv.*

no·ble·man (nō′bəl mən) *n.* A man of noble rank. —**no′ble·wom′an** (nō′bəl-wōōm′ən) *n.*

no·bod·y (nō′bŏd′ē *or* nō′bə dē) *pron.* No person; not anybody: *Nobody stayed after the lecture was over.* —*n., pl.* **no·bod·ies.** *Informal.* A person of no importance or influence: *He was just a nobody, so people paid no attention to his ideas.*

no-brain·er (nō′brā′nər) *n. Informal.* Something that is very easy to do or understand: *Predicting the winner of this election is a no-brainer.*

noc·tur·nal (nŏk tûr′nəl) *adj.* **1.** Relating to or happening at night: *a nocturnal breeze.* **2.** Relating to animals that are most active at night: *Owls are nocturnal birds.* —**noc·tur′nal·ly** *adv.*

nod (nŏd) *v.* **nod·ded, nod·ding, nods.** —*intr.* **1.** To lower and raise the head quickly in agreement: *When I asked him to the party, he nodded enthusiastically.* **2.** To let the head fall forward when getting sleepy: *He began to nod and soon was asleep.* **3.** To move up and down or sway: *flowers nodding in the breeze.* —*tr.* **1.** To lower and raise (the head) quickly, as when showing agreement, giving a greeting, or pointing to sthg.: *She nodded her head in agreement.* **2.** To express (approval) by lowering and raising the head: *He nodded his approval.* —*n.* A nodding movement of the head to show approval or point to sthg.: *She gave a nod of welcome.*

node (nōd) *n.* **1.** A swelling or lump: *Doctors found a node of cancer on the left lung.* **2.** The point on a plant stem where a leaf or stem is attached: *a leaf node.*

No·ël also **No·el** (nō ĕl′) *n.* **1.** Christmas. **2. no·ël.** A Christmas carol.

no-fault (nō′fôlt′) *adj.* **1.** Relating to auto-

ă–**cat**; ā–**pay**; âr–**care**; ä–**father**; ĕ–**get**; ē–**be**; ĭ–**sit**; ī–**nice**; îr–**here**; ŏ–**got**; ō–**go**; ô–**saw**; oi–**boy**; ou–**out**;
ōō–**took**; ōō–**boot**; ŭ–**cut**; ûr–**word**; th–**thin**; *th*–**this**; hw–**when**; zh–**vision**; ə–**about**; N–French **bon**

mobile insurance that pays accident victims regardless of who is responsible for the accident: *Many states have no-fault auto insurance.* **2.** Relating to a type of divorce in which no blame is placed on either husband or wife.

no-good (no′gŏŏd′) *adj. Informal.* Worthless; hateful: *a no-good criminal.*

noise (noiz) *n.* [C; U] **1.** A sound that is loud, unpleasant, or unexpected: *You're making too much noise. I was awakened by a noise in the street.* See Synonyms at **uproar. 2.** A sound of any kind: *The only noise was the wind in the trees.*

noise•less (noiz′lĭs) *adj.* Making little or no noise. —**noise′less•ly** *adv.* —**noise′less• ness** *n.* [U]

noise•mak•er (noiz′mā′kər) *n.* **1.** A person or thing that makes noise. **2.** A device, such as a horn or rattle, used to make noise at a celebration: *We all blew our noisemakers as the clock struck midnight.*

nois•y (noi′zē) *adj.* **nois•i•er, nois•i•est. 1.** Making a lot of noise: *a noisy engine.* **2.** Full of noise: *noisy streets.* —**nois′i•ly** *adv.* —**nois′i•ness** *n.* [U]

no•mad (nō′măd′) *n.* **1.** A member of a group of people who move from place to place seeking food, water, and grazing land for their animals: *The nomads moved to the valley during the rainy season.* **2.** A person who roams about instead of settling in one place: *He lived as a nomad after college, moving from city to city looking for work.* —**no•mad′ic** *adj.*

no man's land (mănz) *n.* [C; U] **1.** Land under dispute by two opposing countries or armies: *The soldiers shot at the man who had wandered into no man's land.* **2.** A remote area: *The hikers found themselves in no man's land, far from the nearest road.*

no•men•cla•ture (nō′mən klā′chər) *n.* [C; U] The system of names used in a particular science; terminology: *the nomenclature of anatomy.*

nom•i•nal (nŏm′ə nəl) *adj.* **1.** So small that it is meaningless: *They charged a nominal sum for admission.* **2.** In name only: *The queen is the nominal ruler, but the prime minister has the real power.* —**nom′i•nal•ly** *adv.*

nom•i•nate (nŏm′ə nāt′) *tr.v.* **nom•i• nat•ed, nom•i•nat•ing, nom•i•nates. 1.** To propose (sbdy.) as a candidate for an elected office: *I was nominated to be secretary.* **2.** To appoint (sbdy.) to an office or honor: *The President nominated a new chief of staff.* —**nom•i•na′tion** *n.* [C; U]

nom•i•na•tive (nŏm′ə nə′tĭv) *n.* [U] In grammar, the case of the subject of a verb. The pronouns *I* and *we* are in the nominative.

nom•i•nee (nŏm′ə nē′) *n.* **1.** A person nominated for an office or award: *the Democratic Party's presidential nominee.* **2.** A person

appointed to a position or an honor: *the President's nominee for FBI director.*

non— *pref.* A prefix that means not: *nonsense; nonstop.*

WORD BUILDING: non— The prefix **non—** can be added to almost any adjective. Some examples include **nonessential, nonmetallic,** and **nonproductive. Non—** also combines with many nouns, as in **nonentity, nonresident,** and **nonviolence. Non—** is used in combination with some verbs to form adjectives, as in **nonskid** and **nonstop.**

non•al•co•hol•ic (nŏn′ăl kə hô′lĭk *or* nŏn′ăl kə hŏl′ĭk) *adj.* Containing no alcohol: *We served only nonalcoholic beverages at the party.*

non•a•ligned (nŏn′ə līnd′) *adj.* Not in alliance with any other nation or group of allies; neutral: *a nonaligned nation.*

non•cha•lant (nŏn′shə länt′) *adj.* Seeming to be carefree and unconcerned: *a nonchalant attitude.* —**non′cha•lance′** *n.* [U] —**non′• cha•lant′ly** *adv.*

non•com•mit•tal (nŏn′kə mĭt′l) *adj.* Not showing how one feels or thinks: *She gave a noncommittal answer, "We'll see."* —**non′• com•mit′tal•ly** *adv.*

non•com•pli•ance (nŏn′kəm plī′əns) *n.* [U] Failure to obey a law: *Noncompliance with clean air laws by industry contributes to pollution.*

non•con•duc•tor (nŏn′kən dŭk′tər) *n.* A substance that conducts little or no electricity, heat, or sound: *Rubber is a nonconductor of electricity.*

non•con•form•ist (nŏn′kən fôr′mĭst) *n.* A person who does not follow generally accepted customs, beliefs, or ways of doing things: *She has always been a nonconformist; she hasn't owned a car in years and doesn't watch television.* —**non′con•form′i•ty** *n.* [U]

non•dairy (nŏn′dâr′ē) *adj.* Containing no milk or milk products: *She uses nondairy creamer in her coffee.*

non•de•duct•i•ble (nŏn′dĭ dŭk′tə bəl) *adj.* Referring to expenses that cannot be included as deductions for tax purposes: *The cost of getting to work is usually a nondeductible expense.*

non•de•nom•i•na•tion•al (nŏn′dĭ nŏm′ə nā′shə nəl) *adj.* Not associated with a particular religion: *We attended a nondenominational service.*

non•de•script (nŏn′dĭ skrĭpt′) *adj.* Difficult to describe because of a lack of distinctive qualities: *It was a nondescript house that looked like all the others.*

none (nŭn) *pron.* **1.** Not any: *None of the fruit was ripe.* **2.** Not one; nobody: *None dares to do it.* ♦ **none the worse.** Not harmed: *The*

N

cat was none the worse after falling out the window. **none too.** Not at all: *My teacher was none too pleased with my essay.*

HOMONYMS: none, nun (religious woman).

---

non•en•ti•ty (nŏn ĕn′tĭ tē) *n., pl.* **non•en•ti•ties.** A person or thing of no importance or significance: *She felt like a nonentity working for a large company.*

non•es•sen•tial (nŏn′ĭ sĕn′shəl) *adj.* Having little or no importance; not essential: *nonessential supplies.* —*n. (usually plural).* Something that is not essential: *Don't take any nonessentials on the trip.*

none•the•less (nŭn′thə lĕs′) *adv. Formal.* However; nevertheless: *Several people came for the meeting; nonetheless, the president decided to wait until next week to discuss the new plan.*

non•ex•ist•ent (nŏn′ĭg zĭs′tənt) *adj.* Not existing; entirely lacking: *planets with nonexistent atmospheres.* —**non′ex•ist′ence** *n.* [U]

non•fat (nŏn′făt′) *adj.* Without fat: *nonfat milk; nonfat foods.*

non•fic•tion (nŏn fĭk′shən) *n.* [U] Literature based on fact rather than fiction: *I've read his novels but not his nonfiction.*

non•flam•ma•ble (nŏn flăm′ə bəl) *adj.* Not flammable, especially not easily set fire to and burned: *Children's pajamas should always be made from nonflammable fabrics.* —**non•flam′ma•bil′i•ty** *n.* [U]

non•in•ter•ven•tion (nŏn′ĭn tər vĕn′shən) *n.* [U] Failure or refusal to intervene, especially in the affairs of another nation: *That country has a policy of nonintervention in its neighbors' affairs.*

non•judg•men•tal (nŏn′jŭj mĕn′tl) *adj.* Avoiding judging another person's actions based on one's personal standards: *He tried to remain nonjudgmental even though he would have behaved differently himself.*

non•me•tal•lic (nŏn′mə tăl′ĭk) *adj.* Not made of metal: *Nonmetallic materials generally conduct heat and electricity poorly.*

no-no (nō′nō′) *n., pl.* **no-noes.** *Informal.* Something that is not acceptable or allowed: *Chewing gum in class is a no-no.*

no-non•sense (nō nŏn′sĕns′) *adj.* Practical, serious, and businesslike: *a no-nonsense person.*

non•par•ti•san (nŏn pär′tĭ zən) *adj.* Not based on, influenced by, or supporting a political party or its interests: *nonpartisan opinions.*

non•plussed (nŏn plŭst′) *adj. Formal.* Shocked or surprised and not knowing what to think, say, or do; bewildered: *The announcement that the factory would close left the workers nonplussed.*

non•pre•scrip•tion (nŏn′prĭ skrĭp′shən) *adj.* Referring to medicines that do not require a written prescription from a doctor; over-the-counter: *nonprescription cold medicine.*

non•prof•it (nŏn prŏf′ĭt) *adj.* Not set up or managed for the purpose of making a profit: *The YMCA is a nonprofit organization.*

non•pro•lif•er•a•tion (nŏn′prə lĭf′ə rā′shən) *n.* [U] Limitation or control of the spread of sthg., usually of nuclear weapons: *The countries signed a treaty of nuclear nonproliferation.*

non•re•fund•a•ble (nŏn′rĭ fŭn′də bəl) *adj.* Referring to a purchase or a deposit that cannot be returned: *These airline tickets are nonrefundable.*

non•re•new•a•ble (nŏn′rĭ nōō′ə bəl) *adj.* Referring to natural resources that cannot be replaced, especially fuels: *Oil is a nonrenewable energy resource.*

non•res•i•dent (nŏn rĕz′ĭ dənt) *adj.* Not making one's permanent home in a particular place, especially relating to one's immigration status: *Many foreign students are nonresident aliens.* —*n.* A nonresident person.

non•re•stric•tive (nŏn′rĭ strĭk′tĭv) *adj.* In grammar, being a clause or phrase that describes a noun but does not restrict the meaning of the sentence and is set off by commas. In the sentence *The Smiths, who live in an apartment, have six cats,* the clause *who live in an apartment* is nonrestrictive.

non•sec•tar•i•an (nŏn′sĕk târ′ē ən) *adj.* Not limited to or associated with a particular religious denomination: *a nonsectarian college.*

non•sense (nŏn′sĕns′) *n.* [U] **1.** Words that have no meaning: *The message was nonsense because we weren't able to read his handwriting.* **2.** Foolish talk, writing, or behavior: *Stop the nonsense and pay attention.* **3.** Something that is not important or useful: *You shouldn't waste time on this nonsense.*

non•sen•si•cal (nŏn sĕn′sĭ kəl) *adj.* **1.** Making no sense: *a nonsensical message.* **2.** Foolish; absurd: *a nonsensical idea.*

non•sex•ist (nŏn sĕk′sĭst) *adj.* Not having negative references to gender, especially to the female gender: *Most writers are careful to use nonsexist language.*

non•stan•dard (nŏn stăn′dərd) *adj.* **1.** Varying from a standard: *The workers removed any apples that were nonstandard in size or color.* **2.** Relating to a kind of language that is not normally considered the accepted form: *Many slang words are considered nonstandard forms.*

---

words are not used by anyone. Rather, the term means that such words are not used in language that is considered standard, as in lectures by teachers or newscasts on television.

non•stop (nŏn′stŏp′) *adj.* Done without any stops: *a nonstop flight from New York to Paris.* —*adv.* Without making any stops: *We flew nonstop to Los Angeles.*

non•un•ion (nŏn yōōn′yən) *adj.* Not belonging to a labor union: *That company hires only nonunion workers.*

non•ver•bal (nŏn vûr′bəl) *adj.* Not using words: *Gestures, signs, and symbols are forms of nonverbal communication.*

non•vi•o•lence (nŏn vī′ə ləns) *n.* [U] The philosophy or practice of rejecting violence in favor of peaceful actions: *Mahatma Gandhi believed in nonviolence.* —**non•vi′-o•lent** *adj.* —**non•vi′o•lent•ly** *adv.*

noo•dle[1] (nōōd′l) *n.* A narrow strip of dried dough, usually made of eggs, flour, and water: *Mom always gave me chicken soup with noodles when I had a cold.*

noo•dle[2] (nōōd′l) *n. Slang.* The head: *Use your noodle to figure it out!*

nook (nŏŏk) *n.* **1.** A corner or recessed area, especially a part of a larger room: *a kitchen with a breakfast nook.* **2.** A hidden or private spot: *We found a quiet nook so that we could talk in private.* ◆ **nook and cranny.** Small, hidden places: *The little girl looked for her kitten in every nook and cranny in the house.*

noon (nōōn) *n.* [U] Twelve o'clock in the daytime; midday: *Lunch is served from noon until 2:00.*

no one *pron.* No person; nobody: *No one answered the phone, so I thought you were out.*

noose (nōōs) *n.* A loop formed in a rope used for hanging a person so that it becomes tighter as the rope is pulled: *The noose tightened around the man's neck.*

nope (nōp) *adv. Informal.* Used in speech as an answer meaning no: *Nope. I didn't find your gloves.*

nor (nôr; nər *when unstressed*) *conj.* **1.** *(used with neither).* Not either: *He has neither written nor telephoned me. These life forms are neither plants nor animals.* **2.** And not: *She can't go, nor can her brother.* —SEE NOTE at **neither.**

norm (nôrm) *n.* **1.** A standard or pattern that is considered to be typical of a group: *Learning to drive at age 16 is the norm in the United States.* **2.** An average or a statistical mode: *The norm on the first test was 79 percent.*

nor•mal (nôr′məl) *adj.* **1.** Standard or typical: *normal room temperature.* **2.** Functioning or happening in a natural healthy way: *normal digestion.* —*n.* [U] Something normal; the standard: *His body temperature was above normal.* —**nor′mal•ly** *adv.*

nor•mal•cy (nôr′məl sē) *n.* [U] *Formal.*

Normality: *After the holidays, life returned to normalcy.*

nor•mal•i•ty (nôr măl′ĭ tē) *n.* [U] The condition of being normal: *I used to think normality would be dull.*

nor•mal•ize (nôr′mə līz′) *tr.v.* **nor•mal•ized, nor•mal•iz•ing, nor•mal•iz•es.** To make (sthg.) normal: *The neighboring countries normalized relations with the new government.* —**nor′mal•i•za′tion** (nôr′mə-lĭ zā′shən) *n.* [U]

north (nôrth) *n.* [U] **1.** The compass direction to the left of sunrise, directly opposite south. **2.** A region in this direction: *Better farmlands lie in the north of the state.* **3. North.** The northern part of the United States, especially the Union states during the Civil War. —*adj.* **1.** To, toward, or in the north: *the north shore of the island.* **2.** From the north: *a north wind.* —*adv.* In, from, or toward the north: *The house faces north.*

north•bound (nôrth′bound′) *adj.* Going toward the north: *the northbound train.*

north•east (nôrth ēst′) *n.* [U] **1.** The direction halfway between north and east. **2.** An area or region lying in this direction. **3. Northeast.** The part of the United States including New England, New York, and sometimes Pennsylvania and New Jersey. —*adj.* **1.** To, toward, or in the northeast: *the northeast corner of the building.* **2.** Coming from the northeast: *northeast winds.* —*adv.* In, from, or toward the northeast. —**north•east′ern** *adj.*

north•east•er•ly (nôrth ē′stər lē) *adj.* **1.** Situated toward or facing the northeast: *a house with a northeasterly view.* **2.** Coming from the northeast: *northeasterly winds.* —**north•east′er•ly** *adv.*

north•er•ly (nôr′thər lē) *adj.* **1.** Situated toward or facing the north: *The compass needle points in a northerly direction.* **2.** Coming from the north: *northerly winds.* —**north′-er•ly** *adv.*

north•ern (nôr′thərn) *adj.* **1.** Situated in, toward, or facing the north: *the northern border.* **2.** Coming from the north: *northern winds.* **3.** also **Northern.** Relating to northern regions or the North: *a northern climate.*

north•ern•er also **North•ern•er** (nôr′thər-nər) *n.* A person who lives in or comes from the north, especially the northern United States: *We could tell she was a Northerner because of her accent.*

north•ern•most (nôr′thərn mōst′) *adj.* Farthest north: *the northernmost regions of the continent.*

north•ward (nôrth′wərd) *adv. & adj.* Toward, to, or in the north: *They turned the ship northward.* —**north′wards** *adv.*

north•west (nôrth wĕst′) *n.* [U] **1.** The direction halfway between north and west. **2.** An area or region lying in this direction. **3.**

N

Northwest. The part of the United States including Washington, Oregon, and Idaho. —*adj.* **1.** Of, in, or toward the northwest: *the northwest border.* **2.** Coming from the northwest: *northwest winds.* —*adv.* In, from, or toward the northwest. —**north•west′ern** *adj.*

north•west•er•ly (nôrth wĕs′tər lē) *adj.* **1.** Situated toward or facing the northwest: *a northwesterly course.* **2.** Coming from the northwest: *northwesterly breezes.* —**north•west′er•ly** *adv.*

nos. or **Nos.** *abbr.* An abbreviation of numbers.

nose (nōz) *n.* **1.** The part of the human or animal face that contains the nostrils and is used for smelling and breathing. **2.** The sense of smell: *a dog with a good nose.* **3.** The ability to detect things, as if by smell: *a nose for gossip.* **4.** The forward end of an airplane, a rocket, a submarine, or another pointed structure. —*v.* **nosed, nos•ing, nos•es.** —*tr.* **1.** To touch (sthg.) with the nose; nuzzle: *cats nosing the dead mouse.* **2.** To move or push (sthg.) with the nose: *The cow nosed the calf away from the fence.* **3.** To steer (a vehicle) ahead cautiously: *He nosed the car into the traffic.* —*intr.* To move forward cautiously: *He nosed along in the fog.* ♦ **by a nose.** By a narrow margin: *She won the race by a nose.* **look down (one's) nose.** To consider sbdy. with disapproval, contempt, or arrogance: *My rich aunt looks down her nose at her poor relations.* **nose around** or **about.** *intr.v.* To search persistently: *The police were nosing around for information.* **nose out.** *tr.v.* [sep.] **1.** To discover (sthg.): *He nosed out the source of the odor.* **2.** To defeat (sbdy./sthg.) by a narrow margin: *The black horse nosed out the brown one in the race.* **on the nose.** Exactly; precisely: *The cost of lunch was ten dollars on the nose.* **under (one's) nose.** In plain view: *I couldn't find my pencil even though it was right under my nose.*

nose•bleed (nōz′blēd′) *n.* An instance of bleeding from the nostrils: *I always get nosebleeds when the air is dry.*

nose•dive (nōz′dīv′) *n.* **1.** A very steep drop made by an airplane. **2.** In business, a sudden drop: *The price of that stock took a nosedive.*

nose-dive (nōz′dīv′) *intr.v.* **nose-dived** or **nose-dove** (nōz′dōv′), **nose-div•ing, nose-dives.** To drop sharply: *Prices will nose-dive if supply increases.*

nos•tal•gi•a (nŏ stăl′jə) *n.* [U] A desire for the past; homesickness: *an old song that filled us with nostalgia.* —**nos•tal′gic** *adj.* —**nos•tal′gi•cal•ly** *adv.*

nos•tril (nŏs′trəl) *n.* Either of the two external openings of the nose: *The horse's nostrils moved as he sniffed the air.*

nos•y or **nos•ey** (nō′zē) *adj.* **nos•i•er, nos•i•est.** *Informal.* Very curious about other people's affairs; prying: *a nosy neighbor.* See Synonyms at **curious.** —**nos′i•ly** *adv.* —**nos′i•ness** *n.* [U]

not (nŏt) *adv.* (*often shortened to* n't *as part of a contraction with auxiliary verbs*). In no way; to no degree. Used to express negation, denial, refusal, or prohibition: *I will not go. You may not borrow my book.* ♦ **not at all.** A response after an expression of thanks: *Not at all. It was my pleasure.* **not that.** Used to express the opposite of sthg. or negation: *Not that I want it, but are you finished with your sandwich?*

HOMONYMS: not, knot (tangle).

---

no•ta•ble (nō′tə bəl) *adj.* Worthy of notice; remarkable: *a notable success.* —*n.* A well-known person: *The party was attended by many notables.* —**no′ta•bly** *adv.*

no•ta•rize (nō′tə rīz′) *tr.v.* **no•ta•rized, no•ta•riz•ing, no•ta•riz•es.** To witness and certify (a signature on a document) to be authentic: *Contracts often must be notarized.*

no•ta•ry (nō′tə rē) *n., pl.* **no•ta•ries.** A notary public.

notary public *n., pl.* **notaries public.** A person with the legal authority to witness and certify the validity of signatures on documents: *You need to take this contract to a notary public before you go to the bank.*

no•ta•tion (nō tā′shən) *n.* **1.** [C] A written comment or explanation: *When you take notes, you can make notations in the margin of your book.* **2.** [U] A system of symbols or figures used in a particular field to represent quantities or other values: *musical notation.* —**no′tate** *v.*

notch (nŏch) *n.* **1.** A V-shaped cut: *Make a notch in the wood.* **2.** A level; a degree: *He loosened his belt a notch.* **3.** *Informal.* A social level; a step: *The defeat took him down a notch.* —*tr.v.* **1.** To cut a notch in (sthg.): *He notched each tree that he needed to trim.* **2.** To record (sthg.) by making notches: *We notched the score on a stick.*

note (nōt) *n.* **1.** (*usually plural*). A brief written record of what is heard, seen, or read, to help the memory: *She took notes during the lecture.* **2.** A short informal letter or message: *My husband left a note for me by the phone.* **3.** An explanation or comment at the bottom of a page or at the end of a chapter or book. **4.a.** A piece of paper money; a bill. **b.** A certificate representing an amount of money, issued by a government or bank. **5.a.** A symbol used to represent a musical tone. **b.** A musical tone. —*tr.v.* **not•ed, not•ing, notes. 1.** To observe

---

(sthg.); notice: *We noted the change in speed.* **2.** To write (sthg.) down: *In her diary, she noted the names of people she met.* ◆ **of note.** Of importance: *Nothing of note happened.* **take note of.** To notice (sbdy./sthg.); observe: *She looked out the window and took note of the weather.*

note·book (nōt′bŏŏk′) *n.* A book with blank pages for writing in: *I bought two new three-subject notebooks when the semester started.*

not·ed (nō′tĭd) *adj.* Well-known; famous: *a noted author.*

SYNONYMS: noted, celebrated, famous, illustrious, renowned. *These adjectives all mean widely known and esteemed.* Our library has invited a *noted* author to read from her new book. *The concert series features several* celebrated *musicians.* I'd like to be a *famous* scientist one day. *An* illustrious *judge presided over the case.* Several of the actors in that movie are *renowned.* ANTONYMS: unknown, obscure.

---

note·wor·thy (nōt′wûr′thē) *adj.* Deserving notice or attention; notable; significant: *The dinner welcoming the new ambassador was a noteworthy event.*

noth·ing (nŭth′ĭng) *pron.* **1.** Not anything: *I have nothing more to say.* **2.** No part; no portion: *Nothing is left of the old house.* —*n.* [U] **1.** Something that has no quantitative value; zero: *a score of two to nothing.* **2.** A person or thing of no importance: *That man is nothing to me.* —*adv.* Not at all: *My brother looks nothing like me.* ◆ **nothing but.** Only: *They ordered nothing but a cup of coffee.* **nothing doing.** *Informal.* Certainly not: *He wanted to borrow money, but I said, "Nothing doing!"* **nothing short of.** No less than: *The news was nothing short of spectacular.* —**noth′ing·ness** *n.* [U]

no·tice (nō′tĭs) *n.* **1.** [U] Perception; observation: *The mistake escaped her notice.* **2.** [C] A written announcement: *You should post a notice on the bulletin board.* —*tr.v.* **no·ticed, no·tic·ing, no·tic·es.** To perceive (sbdy./sthg.); become aware of: *We noticed a cloud of dust in the distance.* See Synonyms at **see**[1]. ◆ **give notice.** To inform a landlord or employer of one's intention to leave: *She gave a week's notice to her employer.*

no·tice·a·ble (nō′tĭ sə bəl) *adj.* Easily observed; evident: *a noticeable change in temperature.* —**no′tice·a·bly** *adv.*

no·ti·fi·ca·tion (nō′tə fĭ kā′shən) *n. Formal.* **1.** [U] The act of notifying. **2.** [C; U] Something, such as a letter, that gives official notice of sthg.: *Send me notification when you receive the check.*

no·ti·fy (nō′tə fī′) *tr.v.* **no·ti·fied, no·ti·fy·ing, no·ti·fies.** To give notice to (sbdy.); inform: *We notified the police about the burglary.*

no·tion (nō′shən) *n.* **1.** A belief or an opinion: *His notion of how math should be taught is interesting.* **2.** A mental image; an idea: *I have no notion of what you mean.* See Synonyms at **idea. 3.** An idea or impulse; a whim: *She had a notion to climb the hill.* **4. notions.** Small useful items, such as needles, buttons, and thread.

no·to·ri·e·ty (nō′tə rī′ĭ tē) *n.* [U] The condition of being widely and unfavorably known; bad reputation: *The murder investigation had given the actor a new kind of notoriety.*

no·to·ri·ous (nō tôr′ē əs) *adj.* Known widely and regarded unfavorably; infamous: *a notorious criminal.* —**no·to′ri·ous·ly** *adv.*

not·with·stand·ing (nŏt′wĭth stăn′dĭng) *prep.* In spite of: *Notwithstanding the rain, the teams played.*

nou·gat (nōō′gət) *n.* [U] A semi-hard, sticky candy made of sugar or honey and nuts.

noun (noun) *n.* In grammar, a word that is used to name a person, a place, a thing, a quality, or an action and that functions as the subject or object of a verb or as the object of a preposition. In the sentence *The man sent the box,* the words *man* and *box* are nouns.

USAGE: noun Every **noun** is either a **common noun** or a **proper noun.** A common noun is a noun such as *book* or *student.* Such nouns can stand for one particular item, as in *I want the fifth book on the pile.* Such a noun can also stand for all items referred to by the noun: *The book is the best means of communication ever invented.* A **proper noun** names sbdy. or sthg. that is unique: *Abraham Lincoln, British Columbia.*

---

nour·ish (nûr′ĭsh *or* nŭr′ĭsh) *tr.v.* **1.** To provide (a living thing) with food or other substances necessary for life and growth. **2.** To promote the growth or development of (sthg.); sustain: *She founded the business and nourished it with hard work.* **3.** To keep (sthg.) alive in the mind; harbor: *We nourished hope that the party would be a success.*

nour·ish·ment (nûr′ĭsh mənt *or* nŭr′ĭsh-mənt) *n.* [U] **1.** The act of nourishing. **2.** Something that nourishes; food: *Milk provides nourishment to children.*

Nov. *abbr.* An abbreviation of November.

no·va (nō′və) *n., pl.* **no·vae** (nō′vē) *or* **no·vas.** A star that suddenly becomes much brighter, then gradually returns to its original brightness over a period of weeks to years.

nov·el[1] (nŏv′əl) *n.* A long piece of writing that tells an invented story: *Her first novel sold over a million copies.*

nov·el[2] (nŏv′əl) *adj.* Strikingly new or different: *a novel idea.*

nov•el•ist (nŏv′ə lĭst) *n.* A writer of novels: *Who is your favorite novelist?*

nov•el•ty (nŏv′əl tē) *n., pl.* **nov•el•ties.** **1.** [U] The quality of being novel; newness: *We liked the new video camera until the novelty wore off.* **2.** [C] Something new and unusual: *Edison's light bulb was at first just an interesting novelty.* **3.** [C] A small mass-produced article, such as a toy or trinket.

No•vem•ber (nō vĕm′bər) *n.* The 11th month of the year, with 30 days.

nov•ice (nŏv′ĭs) *n.* A person new to a field or activity; a beginner: *He is taking a skating class for novices.*

now (nou) *adv.* **1.** At the present time: *Buildings now stand where there was once a park.* **2.** At once; immediately: *We'd better start now.* **3.** Very recently: *He left the room just now.* **4.** At this point in the series of events; then: *The ship now began to sink.* **5.** Nowadays: *You'll rarely see farming done with horses now.* **6.** Used to introduce a command, criticism, or request: *Now, why did you do that? Now remember to add the flour slowly.* **7.** Used to introduce an idea or a change of subject: *Now, dogs need more space than cats.* —*conj.* Since; seeing that: *Now that spring is here, we can expect warmer weather.* —*n.* [U] The present: *Up to now we couldn't afford a house.* ◆ **now and again** or **now and then.** Occasionally: *I like spicy food now and again.* **now, now.** Used to express sympathy: *Now, now, don't cry; we'll find your mother.*

now•a•days (nou′ə dāz′) *adv.* In the present times; in these days: *We try to eat less fat nowadays.*

no•way (nō′wā′) *adv. Informal.* In no way; not at all: *Noway are you going into the desert alone.*

no•where (nō′wâr′) *adv.* Not anywhere: *The book was nowhere to be found.* —*n.* [U] A remote or unknown place, especially a wilderness: *We stayed at a cabin in the middle of nowhere.* ◆ **get nowhere.** To make no progress; have no effect: *Fighting about it will get us nowhere.* **go nowhere.** To make no advancement in career: *She left the company because she was going nowhere.* **nowhere near. 1.** Not close to: *They live nowhere near me.* **2.** Not at all: *You have nowhere near enough money to buy that car.*

no-win (nō′wĭn′) *adj. Informal.* Certain to end in failure or disappointment: *We found ourselves in a no-win situation; no matter what we did, we were going to make someone angry.*

nox•ious (nŏk′shəs) *adj.* Harmful to the health of living things: *noxious chemicals.*

nozzle

noz•zle (nŏz′əl) *n.* A narrow part with an opening at the end of a hose, through which a liquid or gas is released under pressure: *Put the nozzle into the gas tank.*

nth (ĕnth) *adj.* In mathematics, relating to *n*, an indefinitely large whole number: *raise ten to the nth power.* ◆ **to the nth degree.** To the highest possible extent: *We checked and rechecked our results to the nth degree.*

nt. wt. *abbr.* An abbreviation of net weight.

nu•ance (nōō′äns′) *n.* A subtle variation in meaning: *writing with many nuances.*

nu•cle•ar (nōō′klē ər) *adj.* **1.** Relating to a nucleus. **2.** Relating to atomic energy: *a nuclear power plant.* **3.** Relating to atomic weapons: *Russia is one of the nuclear powers.*

nuclear energy *n.* [U] The energy that is released by changes to the nuclei of atoms.

nuclear family *n.* A family unit consisting of a mother and father and their children.

nuclear physics *n.* [U] *(used with a singular verb).* The scientific study of the structure and reactions of atomic nuclei.

nuclear reaction *n.* A reaction that changes the energy, structure, or composition of an atomic nucleus.

nuclear reactor *n.* A device in which a nuclear chain reaction is started and controlled, thus producing heat, which is usually used to generate electricity.

nu•cle•us (nōō′klē əs) *n., pl.* **nu•cle•i** (nōō′klē ī′) or **nu•cle•us•es. 1.** A structure within a living cell, containing the cell's genetic material. **2.** The positively charged central region of an atom. **3.** A basis for future growth; a starting point: *A few old paintings formed the nucleus of the art collection.* **4.** A central or essential part around which other parts are grouped; a core: *The oldest players formed the nucleus of the team.*

nude (nōōd) *adj.* Without clothing; naked: *That beach is open to nude bathers.* —*n.* **1.** [C] An unclothed human figure or a representation of it: *The artist was famous for his nudes.* **2.** [U] The condition of being unclothed: *He often sleeps in the nude.*

nudge (nŭj) *tr.v.* **nudged, nudg•ing, nudg•es.** To push or poke (sbdy./sthg.) gently: *He nudged her with his elbow.* —*n.* A gentle push.

nud•ist (nōō′dĭst) *n.* A person who wears no clothing in certain situations: *Nudists use that beach.* —**nud′is′m** *n.* [U]

N

nu·di·ty (n$\overline{oo}$′dĭ tē) *n.* [U] The condition of being unclothed: *Many people are embarrassed by nudity.*

nug·get (nŭg′ĭt) *n.* **1.** A hard lump of matter, especially of gold. **2.** A small unit or piece: *nuggets of information.*

nui·sance (n$\overline{oo}$′səns) *n.* A source of inconvenience or annoyance; a bother: *My little sister is a nuisance.*

nuke (n$\overline{oo}$k) *tr.v.* **nuked, nuk·ing, nukes.** *Slang.* **1.** To attack (sthg.) with nuclear weapons. **2.** To heat or cook (sthg.) in a microwave oven: *Nuke it for two minutes on high.*

null (nŭl) *adj.* **1.** Having no legal force; invalid: *The contract was made null by a later agreement.* **2.** Having the quantity or value of zero; amounting to nothing: *a null sum.*
♦ **null and void.** Having no legal force or effect; not binding: *That agreement is null and void after 30 days.*

nul·li·fy (nŭl′ə fī′) *tr.v.* **nul·li·fied, nul·li·fy·ing, nul·li·fies. 1.** To make (sthg.) legally invalid: *The Supreme Court has the right to nullify an act of Congress by finding it unconstitutional.* **2.** To cancel (sthg.): *The results of the game were nullified because of the illegal player.* —**nul′li·fi·ca′tion** (nŭl′ə fĭ kā′shən) *n.* [U]

numb (nŭm) *adj.* **1.** Lacking the power to feel or move normally. *My fingers and toes were numb with cold.* **2.** Showing little or no emotion: *His sudden death left her numb with grief.* —*tr. & intr.v.* To make or become numb: *The dentist numbed the tooth before she drilled it. My toes numbed with the cold.* —**numb′ly** *adv.* —**numb′ness** *n.* [U]

num·ber (nŭm′bər) *n.* **1.** [C] One of a set of symbols that have unique meaning and that can be derived in a fixed order by counting: *1, 2, and 3 are numbers.* **2. numbers.** Arithmetic: *She has always been good at numbers.* **3.** [C] One of a series in numerical order: *What number are you in this line?* **4.** [C] A series of numerals assigned to a person or thing for identification: *a telephone number.* **5.** [C] A quantity determined by adding up all units; a total; a sum: *The number of feet in a mile is 5,280.* **6.** [U] An indefinite quantity: *The crowd was small in number.* **7. numbers.** A large quantity: *There is strength in numbers.* **8.** [C] A song or piece of music in a program: *She sang two numbers from her new CD.* **9.** [U] In grammar, the indication by the form of a word of whether it is singular or plural: *The verb must agree in number with the subject.* —*v.* —*tr.* **1.** To assign a number to (sthg.): *Number each item in the list.* **2.** To amount to (sthg.); total: *The audience numbered nearly a thousand.* **3.** To include (sbdy./sthg.) in a certain category: *He was numbered among the best swimmers.* **4.** To mention (things) one by one: *I'll number the advantages of the plan.* —*intr.* To amount to a

group: *The crowd numbered in the thousands.*
♦ **by the numbers.** Exactly; fairly: *I always play by the numbers in my business.* **have (one's) number.** To know another person's true intentions: *We had his number all along; we always knew he was trying to trick us into selling the painting.* **look out for number one.** To protect one's own interests: *She's always looking out for number one.* **(one's) days are numbered.** To have little time left, often referring to approaching death or the end of a career: *His days at the company were numbered.* **without** or **beyond number.** Too many to be counted; countless: *Birds without number filled the sky.*

nu·mer·al (n$\overline{oo}$′mər əl) *n.* A symbol or mark used to represent a number. For example, 7 is a numeral.

nu·mer·ate (n$\overline{oo}$′mə rāt′) *tr.v.* **nu·mer·at·ed, nu·mer·at·ing, nu·mer·ates.** *Formal.* To enumerate (sthg.); count: *Numerate the reasons.* —**nu′mer·a′tion** *n.* [U]

nu·mer·a·tor (n$\overline{oo}$′mə rā′tər) *n.* The number written above the line in a common fraction to indicate the number of parts of the whole. In the fraction ⅔ the 2 is the numerator.

nu·mer·i·cal (n$\overline{oo}$ mĕr′ĭ kəl) *adj.* Relating to a number or series of numbers: *Put the totals in numerical order.* —**nu·mer′i·cal·ly** *adv.*

nu·mer·ous (n$\overline{oo}$′mər əs) *adj.* Amounting to a large number; many: *We found numerous items for sale.* —**nu′mer·ous·ly** *adv.*

nu·mis·mat·ics (n$\overline{oo}$′mĭz măt′ĭks) *n.* [U] (used with a singular verb). The collecting of coins or paper money: *Numismatics is a popular hobby.*

nun (nŭn) *n.* A woman who belongs to a religious order: *a Buddhist nun; a Catholic nun.*

HOMONYMS: nun, none (not any).

nup·tial (nŭp′shəl *or* nŭp′chəl) *Formal. adj.* Relating to marriage or the wedding ceremony: *a nuptial agreement.* —*n.* (usually plural). A wedding ceremony: *We attended the nuptials of two friends.*

nurse (nûrs) *n.* **1.** A person who is trained to care for sick, injured, or old people: *A nurse came to give my grandfather his shots.* **2.** A woman employed to take care of another's children; a nursemaid. —*v.* **nursed, nurs·ing, nurs·es.** —*tr.* **1.** To act as the nurse for (sbdy.); take care of: *She nursed her husband back to health.* **2.** To feed (an infant) from the breast. **3.** To try to cure (sthg.) by special care or treatment: *She's nursed that cough for a week.* **4.** To drink (sthg.) slowly, as if preserving: *He nursed his soda for an hour.* **5.** To keep (sthg.) alive in the mind; harbor: *Don't nurse a grudge.* —*intr.* To feed at the breast; suckle: *The baby nurses every two hours.* —**nur′sing** *n.* [U]

nurse•maid (nûrs′mād′) *n.* A woman employed to take care of children.

nurs•er•y (nûr′sə rē *or* nûrs′rē) *n., pl.* **nurs•er•ies. 1.** A room set apart for the use of small children: *The children played in the nursery.* **2.** A place where plants are raised for sale or experimentation: *We bought several trees and shrubs at the nursery.*

nursery rhyme *n.* A short rhymed poem for children: *My mother read me a Mother Goose nursery rhyme every night when I was a child.*

nursery school *n.* A school for children who are not old enough to attend kindergarten: *Most nursery schools are also daycare centers.*

nurs•ing home (nûr′sĭng) *n.* A place that provides living space and care for old people who cannot care for themselves and for people who are chronically ill: *We visited Grandfather at the nursing home every Sunday.*

nur•ture (nûr′chər) *tr.v.* **nur•tured, nur•tur•ing, nur•tures. 1.** To feed and protect (sbdy./sthg.); nourish: *He carefully nurtured the plants in a greenhouse.* **2.** To help (sbdy./sthg.) grow or develop; cultivate: *They nurtured their friendship.*

nut (nŭt) *n.* **1.a.** A fruit with a hard shell, such as an acorn. **b.** The often edible seed within such a fruit, as an almond. **2.** *Slang.* **a.** A crazy, funny, or eccentric person: *My uncle is such a nut.* **b.** An enthusiast: *a movie nut.* **3.** A small block of metal or wood designed to fit around and hold a bolt. ◆ **a tough** or **hard nut to crack.** A person or problem that is hard to handle: *He was a tough nut to crack, but the police finally got him to tell where he had hidden the money.*

nut
(hardware)

nut
(food)

nuts and bolts. Practical details and procedures: *We got down to nuts and bolts and started working on the new plan.*

nut•crack•er (nŭt′krăk′ər) *n.* A tool used for opening nuts, often consisting of two metal pieces between which the nut is squeezed.

nut•meg (nŭt′mĕg′) *n.* [U] A hard pleasant-smelling seed grated or ground and used as a spice: *I can taste the nutmeg in the cookies.*

nu•tri•ent (nōo′trē ənt) *n.* Something that nourishes, especially an ingredient in a food: *Vitamin A is an important nutrient.* —*adj.* Capable of nourishing; having nutritive value: *What is the nutrient value of chocolate?*

nu•tri•ment (nōo′trə mənt) *n.* Nourishment; food: *Milk is one of the best nutriments.*

nu•tri•tion (nōo trĭsh′ən) *n.* [U] **1.** The process of nourishing, especially the process by which a living thing uses food. **2.** Nourishment; diet: *We learned about good nutrition.* **3.** The study of food and nourishment: *She is taking a course in nutrition.* —**nu•tri′tion•al** *adj.* —**nu•tri′tion•al•ly** *adv.* —**nu•tri′tion•ist** *n.*

nu•tri•tious (nōo trĭsh′əs) *adj.* Providing nourishment; nourishing: *Cereal with milk and fruit is a nutritious breakfast.* —**nu•tri′tious•ly** *adv.* —**nu•tri′tious•ness** *n.* [U]

nu•tri•tive (nōo′trĭ tĭv) *adj.* Relating to nutrition: *Sugar has almost no nutritive value.*

nuts (nŭts) *Slang. adj.* **1.** Crazy; insane: *Don't listen to him; he's nuts.* **2.** [*about*] Very enthusiastic: *She's nuts about playing the drums.* —*interj.* Used to express disappointment: *Oh, nuts! I forgot my book.*

nut•shell (nŭt′shĕl′) *n.* The shell enclosing the meat of a nut. ◆ **in a nutshell.** In a few words; concisely: *In a nutshell, we need to finish this project and start the new one.*

nut•ty (nŭt′ē) *adj.* **nut•ti•er, nut•ti•est. 1.** Having the flavor of nuts: *nutty cookies.* **2.** *Slang.* Crazy; silly: *a nutty idea.* ◆ **(as) nutty as a fruitcake.** *Informal.* Crazy, often in a humorous way: *My neighbor is nutty as a fruitcake.* —**nut′ti•ness** *n.* [U]

nuz•zle (nŭz′əl) *tr.v.* **nuz•zled, nuz•zling, nuz•zles.** To rub or push (sbdy./sthg.) gently with the nose: *The dog nuzzled the boy.*

NV *abbr.* An abbreviation of Nevada.

NW *abbr.* An abbreviation of northwest.

NY or **N.Y.** *abbr.* An abbreviation of New York.

NYC or **N.Y.C.** *abbr.* An abbreviation of New York City.

ny•lon (nī′lŏn′) *n.* **1.** [C; U] A very strong elastic synthetic resin. **2.** [U] Cloth or yarn made from nylon. **3. nylons.** Women's stockings made of nylon: *She bought a new pair of nylons.*

nymph (nĭmf) *n.* **1.** In Greek and Roman mythology, a goddess of nature represented as a beautiful young woman. **2.** A young incompletely developed form of certain insects, such as the dragonfly.

nym•pho•ma•ni•ac (nĭm′fə mā′nē ăk′) *n.* A woman with an abnormally high sexual appetite. —**nym′pho•ma′ni•a** *n.* [U]

N

Oo

o or **O** (ō) *n., pl.* **o's** or **O's. 1.** The 15th letter of the English alphabet. **2.** A zero. **3.** One of the four types of blood in the ABO system: *type O blood.*

HOMONYMS: O, oh (exclamation), **owe** (have to pay).

O The symbol for the element **oxygen.**

oaf (ōf) *n.* A clumsy or stupid person: *That big oaf stepped on my foot!* —**oaf′ish** *adj.*

oak (ōk) *n.* **1.** [C] A tree that has acorns and leaves that are irregularly notched: *We have several oaks in our yard.* **2.** [U] The hard strong wood of such a tree: *oak furniture.*

oar (ôr) *n.* A long thin pole with a blade at one end, used to row a boat: *Use the oars to row the boat.*

HOMONYMS: oar, or (alternative), **ore** (mineral).

o·a·sis (ō ā′sĭs) *n., pl.* **o·a·ses** (ō ā′sēz). **1.** A small area in a desert with water and trees: *The nomads stopped at the oasis for water.* **2.** A pleasant place in an unpleasant area: *Her office was an oasis of calm.*

oat (ōt) *n. (usually used in the plural with a singular or plural verb).* A type of grain eaten by people and animals: *My horse's favorite food is oats.* ◆ **sow (one's) wild oats.** To act in a free, irresponsible way, especially having many sexual partners while a young man: *He's sowing his wild oats.*

oath (ōth) *n., pl.* **oaths** (ōthz *or* ōths). A promise to do sthg., calling on God or some sacred object as witness: *The President takes an oath to uphold the Constitution.* ◆ **be under oath.** To have promised to tell the truth: *The judge reminded the witness she was under oath.*

oat·meal (ōt′mēl′) *n.* [U] **1.** Crushed oats used for cooking: *oatmeal cookies.* **2.** Hot breakfast cereal made from oats: *Do you like milk or cream in your oatmeal?*

o·be·di·ence (ō bē′dē əns) *n.* [U] The act of obeying rules, laws, or requests: *Some parents demand absolute obedience.*

o·be·di·ent (ō bē′dē ənt) *adj.* Willing to obey: *an obedient dog.* —**o·be′di·ent·ly** *adv.*

ob·e·lisk (ŏb′ə lĭsk) *n.* A tall four-sided stone monument that comes to a point at the top.

o·bese (ō bēs′) *adj.* Extremely fat; very overweight: *He had been obese since childhood.* —**o·be′si·ty** *n.* [U]

o·bey (ō bā′) *v.* —*tr.* **1.** To comply with (a request, an order, or a law): *We always obeyed the traffic regulations.* **2.** To do what is commanded or requested by (sbdy.): *The girl obeyed her father and picked up her toys.* —*intr.* To be obedient: *My dog always obeys.*

o·bit·u·ar·y (ō bĭch′ōō ĕr′ē) *n., pl.* **o·bit·u·ar·ies.** A notice in the newspaper of a person's death, often with a short biography: *Do you usually read the obituaries?*

ob·ject (ŏb′jĕkt′) *n.* **1.** Something that can be seen or touched; a physical thing. **2.** A thing being studied or handled: *Place the object under the microscope.* **3.** Purpose; goal: *The object of the game is to hit the ball over the net.* **4.** In grammar, a noun, pronoun, or group of words that receives the action of a verb or that follows a preposition. In the sentence *I left my book in the classroom,* the phrase *my book* is the object of the verb; the phrase *the classroom* is the object of the preposition. —*intr.v.* (əb jĕkt′). To be against sthg.: *I object to killing animals for sport.* —**ob·jec′tor** *n.*

ob·jec·tion (əb jĕk′shən) *n.* **1.** A statement of an opposing idea: *She had no objection to the plan at first.* **2.** A reason not to do sthg.: *His only objection to buying the car was that it was too expensive.*

ob·jec·tion·a·ble (əb jĕk′shə nə bəl) *adj.* Causing objection; unpleasant: *objectionable language.* —**ob·jec′tion·a·bly** *adv.*

ob·jec·tive (əb jĕk′tĭv) *adj.* **1.** Existing in a physical form: *Science deals with objective facts.* **2.** Not influenced by emotion or personal feelings: *I can't be objective about my son's musical ability.* **3.** In grammar, relating to the case of a noun or pronoun that is the object of a verb or preposition. —*n.* **1.** A goal; a purpose: *Our objective is to plant more trees in town.* **2.** In grammar, the objective case. —**ob·jec′tive·ly** *adv.* —**ob·jec′tive·ness, ob′jec·tiv′i·ty** (ŏb′jĕk tĭv′i tē) *n.* [U]

ob·li·gate (ŏb′lĭ gāt′) *tr.v.* **ob·li·gat·ed, ob·li·gat·ing, ob·li·gates.** To force (sbdy.) to do sthg. by a social, legal, or moral law: *A doctor is obligated to help every patient.*

ob·li·ga·tion (ŏb′lĭ gā′shən) *n.* **1.** A legal, social, or moral duty: *an obligation to vote.* **2.** A debt owed as payment for a special service or favor: *a financial obligation; a social obligation.*

o·blig·a·to·ry (ə blĭg′ə tôr′ē *or* ŏb′lĭ gə-tôr′ē) *adj.* Legally or morally binding; required or compulsory: *obligatory attendance.* —**o·blig′a·to′ri·ly** *adv.*

o·blige (ə blīj′) *tr.v.* **o·bliged, o·blig·ing, o·blig·es.** *Formal.* To force (sbdy.) to do sth. through physical, legal, social, or moral pressure: *His mother obliged him to say "thank you."*

o·blig·ing (ə blī′jĭng) *adj.* Ready to do favors for others: *an obliging employee.* —**o·blig′ing·ly** *adv.*

o·blique (ō blēk′) *adj.* **1.** Describing two lines that meet at an angle; not parallel or perpendicular: *The roof forms an oblique angle with the wall.* **2.** Indirect; unclear: *She made an oblique comment about my new haircut.* —**o·blique′ly** *adv.* —**o·blique′ness** *n.* [U]

o·blit·er·ate (ə blĭt′ə rāt′) *tr.v.* **o·blit·er·at·ed, o·blit·er·at·ing, o·blit·er·ates. 1.** To remove or destroy (sth.): *The flood obliterated the cornfield.* **2.** To cover or hide from view: *The sun obliterated the moon.* —**o·blit′er·a′tion** *n.* [U]

o·bliv·i·on (ə blĭv′ē ən) *n.* [U] **1.** The state of being completely forgotten: *Many retired actors live in oblivion.* **2.** The state of being oblivious: *the oblivion of a deep sleep.*

o·bliv·i·ous (ə blĭv′ē əs) *adj.* Unaware of what is happening: *She is oblivious to her surroundings.* —**o·bliv′i·ous·ly** *adv.* —**o·bliv′i·ous·ness** *n.* [U]

ob·long (ŏb′lông′ *or* ŏb′lŏng′) *adj.* Shaped like a rectangle, with two long sides and two short sides: *an oblong table.* —*n.* An oblong object.

ob·nox·ious (ŏb nŏk′shəs) *adj.* Extremely unpleasant: *an obnoxious personality.* —**ob·nox′ious·ly** *adv.*

o·boe (ō′bō) *n.* A musical instrument made of black wood, played by blowing through a double reed.

o·bo·ist (ō′bō ĭst) *n.* A person who plays the oboe.

ob·scene (ŏb sēn′) *adj.* Extremely impolite; shocking: *obscene language.* —**ob·scene′ly** *adv.*

ob·scen·i·ty (ŏb sĕn′ ĭ tē) *n.*, *pl.* **ob·scen·i·ties.** [C; U] Extremely impolite behavior or language: *The driver shouted obscenities.*

ob·scure (əb skyoor′) *adj.* **1.** Not easy to see; unclear: *his small, obscure handwriting.* **2.** Difficult to understand; vague: *an obscure reference to ancient history.* See Synonyms at **vague. 3.** Not well known: *an obscure poet.* —*tr.v.* **ob·scured, ob·scur·ing, ob·scures. 1.** To block (sth.) from view; hide: *Clouds obscured the stars.* **2.** To make (sth.) difficult to understand: *His vague speech obscured his real plans.*

ob·scu·ri·ty (əb skyoor′ ĭ tē) *n.* [U] **1.** The condition of having little or no light; darkness: *the obscurity of the night.* **2.** The condition of being unknown or inconspicuous: *a great movie star, now in obscurity.* **3.** The condition of being hard to understand: *the obscurity of the poem.*

ob·se·qui·ous (əb sē′kwē əs) *adj. Formal.* Overly willing to serve, agree, or obey: *an obsequious person.* —**ob·se′qui·ous·ly** *adv.* —**ob·se′qui·ous·ness** *n.* [U]

ob·serv·a·ble (əb zûr′və bəl) *adj.* Possible to observe: *an observable change in the weather.* —**ob·serv′a·bly** *adv.*

ob·ser·vance (əb zûr′vəns) *n.* **1.** [U] The act of obeying a law or rule: *observance of the speed limit.* **2.** [C] The act of celebrating a holiday: *holiday observances.*

ob·ser·vant (əb zûr′ vənt) *adj.* **1.** Quick to notice things: *an observant student.* **2.** Following or observing a law or custom: *His parents are religious, but he is not observant.* —**ob·ser′vant·ly** *adv.*

ob·ser·va·tion (ŏb′ zər vā′shən) *n.* **1.** [U] The act of observing: *a tower used for the observation of aircraft.* **2.** [C] The act of noticing and recording a specific type of information with instruments: *my observation of the temperature on the thermometer.* **3.** [C] A comment or remark: *She made a funny observation about the movie they just saw.*

ob·ser·va·to·ry (əb zûr′və tôr′ē) *n.*, *pl.* **ob·ser·va·to·ries.** A building or room built for the purpose of looking at the sky through a telescope: *An astronomer studies the stars from an observatory.*

observatory
United States Naval Observatory in Washington, D.C.

ob·serve (əb zûrv′) *tr.v.* **ob·served, ob·serv·ing, ob·serves. 1.** To watch (sbdy./sth.) carefully; notice: *She observed a small child crossing the road.* See Synonyms at **see**[1]. **2.** To make a scientific observation of (sth.): *The researcher observed the migration of the birds.* **3.** To say (sth.); remark: *She observed that math was her best subject.* **4.** To obey (a law): *Please observe the speed limit.* **5.** To celebrate (a holiday): *We observed Independence Day together.* —**ob·serv′a·ble** *adj.* —**ob·serv′er** *n.*

ob·sess (əb sĕs′) *tr.v.* To occupy all of (sbdy.'s) attention all of the time: *Finding someone to blame for the accident obsessed them for years.* ◆ **obsessed with.** Passionately preoccupied with (sthg.): *He is obsessed with his new car.* —**ob•ses'sion** *n.* —**ob•ses'sive** *adj.* —**ob•ses'sive•ly** *adv.* —**ob•ses'sive•ness** *n.* [U]

ob•sid•i•an (ŏb sĭd'ē ən) *n.* [U] A shiny usually black glass of volcanic origin.

ob•so•les•cent (ŏb'sə lĕs'ənt) *adj. Formal.* Passing out of use or usefulness; becoming obsolete: *an obsolescent building.* —**ob'so•les'cence** *n.* [U]

ob•so•lete (ŏb'sə lēt' *or* ŏb'sə lēt') *adj.* No longer in use or in fashion: *obsolete technology.* —**ob'so•lete'ness** *n.* [U]

ob•sta•cle (ŏb'stə kəl) *n.* Something that stops progress or prevents success: *Lack of a high school diploma proved to be a huge obstacle.*

ob•ste•tri•cian (ŏb'stĭ trĭsh'ən) *n.* A doctor who specializes in obstetrics.

ob•stet•rics (ŏb stĕt'rĭks) *n.* [U] *(used with a singular verb).* The branch of medicine that deals with the care of women during pregnancy, childbirth, and the period following childbirth: *My friend works in obstetrics and gynecology.* —**ob•stet'ric, ob•stet'ri•cal** *adj.* —**ob•stet'ri•cal•ly** *adv.*

ob•sti•nate (ŏb'stə nĭt) *adj.* **1.** Stubbornly refusing to cooperate: *She was obstinate in her refusal to go.* **2.** Difficult to control or cure: *an obstinate headache.* —**ob'sti•na•cy** *n.* [U] —**ob'sti•nate•ly** *adv.*

SYNONYMS: obstinate, stubborn, mulish, headstrong. These adjectives mean unwilling to change or cooperate. **Obstinate** means extremely difficult to persuade: *My aunt is obstinate about doing things her own way.* **Stubborn** and **mulish** can mean that a person's personality makes him or her unwilling to cooperate: *He is too stubborn to admit he was wrong. It's mulish of you to refuse to look at the map until after we're lost.* **Headstrong** means impatient and stubborn: *That headstrong child will never follow advice.* **ANTONYMS: cooperative, flexible.**

---

ob•struct (əb strŭkt') *tr.v.* **1.** To close (sthg.); block: *The delivery truck obstructed the street.* **2.** To prevent (sthg.) from happening: *obstructing justice.* **3.** To prevent (sthg.) from being seen: *Buildings obstruct our view of the ocean.* —**ob•struc'tion** *n.*

ob•tain (əb tān') *tr.v.* To get or acquire (sthg.): *obtain a driver's license.* —**ob•tain'a•ble** *adj.*

ob•tru•sive (əb trōō'sĭv) *adj.* So noticeable as to be annoying: *obtrusive behavior.* —**ob•tru'sive•ly** *adv.* —**ob•tru'sive•ness** *n.* [U]

ob•tuse (əb tōōs') *adj.* **1.** Slow to understand; dull: *an obtuse person.* **2.** Between 90° and 180° in an angle. —**ob•tuse'ly** *adv.* —**ob•tuse'ness** *n.* [U]

obtuse angle *n.* An angle that contains more than 90° and less than 180°.

135°
obtuse angle

ob•vi•ate (ŏb'vē- āt') *tr.v.* **ob•vi•at•ed, ob•vi•at•ing, ob•vi•ates.** *Formal.* To make (sthg.) unnecessary: *I obviated the need for a plumber by fixing the leak myself.*

ob•vi•ous (ŏb'vē əs) *adj.* Easily seen or understood; evident: *an obvious advantage.* —**ob'vi•ous•ly** *adv.* —**ob'vi•ous•ness** *n.* [U]

oc•ca•sion (ə kā'zhən) *n.* **1.** An event or a happening: *enjoyable occasions.* **2.** An important event or happening: *Her party was quite an occasion.* **3.** A favorable or suitable time; an opportunity: *There were many occasions when we were able to go sailing.* **4.** A reason or cause: *What was the occasion for all that laughter?* —*tr.v. Formal.* To be the reason for (sthg.); cause: *The need to resolve the dispute occasioned the meeting.* ♦ **on occasion.** From time to time: *The friends call each other on occasion.*

oc•ca•sion•al (ə kā'zhə nəl) *adj.* **1.** Happening from time to time: *an occasional rainstorm.* **2.** Intended for use when needed: *occasional chairs.* —**oc•ca'sion•al•ly** *adv.*

oc•cult (ə kŭlt' *or* ŏk'ŭlt') *adj.* Relating to magic, astrology, or supernatural powers: *occult powers.* —*n.* [U] Occult practices or teachings: *a student of the occult.*

oc•cu•pan•cy (ŏk'yə pən sē) *n.* [U] **1.** The act of holding in possession; the act of occupying. **2.** The state of being occupied or rented: *a building with a high rate of occupancy.* ♦ **take occupancy of.** To begin to live in or use a space: *We can take occupancy of the new offices next week.*

oc•cu•pant (ŏk'yə pənt) *n.* A person who lives in or uses a space: *the occupants of a building.*

oc•cu•pa•tion (ŏk'yə pā'shən) *n.* **1.** [C] A way of earning money; a profession or job: *What is your occupation?* **2.** [C] An activity that keeps sbdy. busy: *His main occupation is fixing his house.* **3.** [U] The act of holding, possessing, or using a place: *the occupation of the cave by bears.* **4.** [U] The control of a nation or territory by a foreign military force: *military occupation.* —**oc'cu•pa'tion•al** *adj.*

oc•cu•pied (ŏk'yə pīd) *adj.* **1.** In use: *There was only one bathroom, and it was occupied.* **2.** Busy with sthg.: *Keep him occupied while I fix dinner.*

oc•cu•py (ŏk'yə pī') *tr.v.* **oc•cu•pied, oc•cu•py•ing, oc•cu•pies.** **1.** To fill (time or space): *Reading occupies his free time.* **2.** To live in (sthg.); inhabit: *They occupy a small apartment.* **3.** To hold (a position): *She* occupies the position of president. **4.** To control (sthg.) by force: *The army occupied the city.* **5.** To busy (oneself): *The children occupied themselves with the toys.*

oc•cur (ə kûr′) *intr.v.* **oc•curred, oc•cur•ring, oc•curs. 1.** To happen without planning: *The strangest thing occurred.* **2.** To come to one's mind: *That idea never occurred to me.* —**oc•cur′rence** *n.*

o•cean (ō′shən) *n.* **1.** [C; U] The mass of salt water that covers about 72 percent of the surface of the earth: *Little is known about life in the deep ocean.* **2.** [C] Any of the principal divisions of this body of water, including the Atlantic, Pacific, Indian, and Arctic oceans.

o•cean•og•ra•phy (ō′shə nŏg′rə fē) *n.* [U] The exploration and scientific study of the ocean. —**o•cean•og•ra•pher** *n.*

o•cher or **o•chre** (ō′kər) *n.* [U] **1.** A brownish orange mineral used in making paint and as a cosmetic. **2.** A yellowish or brownish orange color. —*adj.* Yellowish or brownish orange.

o'clock (ə klŏk′) *adv.* **1.** According to the clock: *3 o'clock.* **2.** According to an imaginary clock dial, with the observer at the center and 12 o'clock considered as straight ahead horizontally or straight up vertically: *enemy planes at 10 o'clock.*

Oct. *abbr.* An abbreviation of October.

oc•ta•gon (ŏk′tə gŏn′) *n.* A flat geometric shape with eight sides. —**oc•tag′o•nal** (ŏk tăg′ə nəl) *adj.*

oc•tane (ŏk′tān′) *n.* Any of several hydrocarbon compounds having the formula C_8H_{18} and occurring in petroleum.

oc•tave (ŏk′tĭv or ŏk′tāv′) *n.* **1.** Two notes in a musical scale that are eight tones apart. **2.** A series of eight consecutive notes in a musical scale: *A piano keyboard covers more than seven octaves.*

octo— or **octa—** or **oct—** *pref.* A prefix that means eight: *octane; octopus.*

Oc•to•ber (ŏk tō′bər) *n.* The tenth month of the year, with 31 days.

oc•to•ge•nar•i•an (ŏk′tə jə nâr′ē ən) *n.* A person between 80 and 90 years of age: *My grandmother is an octogenarian.*

oc•to•pus (ŏk′tə pəs) *n., pl.* **oc•to•pus•es** or **oc•to•pi** (ŏk′tə pī′). A sea creature with a soft rounded body and eight tentacles or "legs."

oc•u•lar (ŏk′yə lər) *adj.* Having to do with the eye or vision: *ocular measurements.* —*n.* The eyepiece of a microscope or telescope.

oc•u•list (ŏk′yə lĭst) *n.* **1.** An ophthalmologist. **2.** An optometrist.

odd (ŏd) *adj.* **1.** Unusual; peculiar; strange: *odd behavior; an odd name.* **2.** Being one of an incomplete set or pair: *an odd shoe.* **3.** Not

regular or expected: *The client telephoned at odd intervals.* **4.** Relating to whole numbers that are not divisible by two: *Three, five, and seven are odd numbers.* **5.** *(used with even numbers).* More than the number indicated: *There were 20-odd guests at the party.* ◆ **oddball.** *Informal.* A strange person: *He is something of an oddball.* **odd job.** A temporary job that doesn't require skill or training: *She worked at a series of odd jobs during college.* **odd man out.** A person not included in a group: *Without a date, I felt like the odd man out at the party.* —**odd′ly** *adv.* —**odd′ness** *n.* [U]

odd•i•ty (ŏd′ĭ tē) *n., pl.* **odd•i•ties. 1.** [C] A person or thing that is strange: *The three-legged cat was an oddity.* **2.** [U] The condition of being odd; strangeness: *The oddity of his behavior worried me.*

odds (ŏdz) *pl.n.* **1.** The likelihood or probability that sthg. will happen: *The odds are that it will rain tomorrow.* **2.** The chances for and against a certain event: *odds of 20 to 1.* ◆ **at odds.** In disagreement; in conflict: *They were at odds about what to do with the money.* **odds and ends.** Small items of various kinds: *a drawer filled with odds and ends.* **odds are.** It is likely: *The odds are that he'll fail the test.*

ode (ōd) *n.* A long, formal poem.

o•dom•e•ter (ō dŏm′ĭ tər) *n.* A device that measures the distance that a car or other vehicle has traveled: *What is the mileage on the odometer?*

o•dor (ō′dər) *n.* The smell of sthg.; scent: *Onions have a strong odor.* See Synonyms at **scent.** —**o′dor•ous** *adj.*

o•dor•if•er•ous (ō′də rĭf′ər əs) *adj. Formal.* Having an odor, especially a pleasant one.

o•dor•less (ō′dər lĭs) *adj.* Having no odor: *Carbon monoxide is a colorless, odorless gas.*

o•dour (ō′dər) *n. Chiefly British.* Variant of **odor.**

od•ys•sey (ŏd′ĭ sē) *n., pl.* **od•ys•seys.** An extended adventurous journey: *a European odyssey.*

of (ŭv or ŏv; əv *when unstressed*) *prep.* **1.** Coming from: *people of the north.* **2.** Caused by; resulting from: *He died of pneumonia.* **3.** At a distance from: *one mile east of here.* **4.** So as to be separated or relieved from: *a man robbed of his wallet; a patient cured of an infection.* **5.** From the total or group making up: *two of my friends.* **6.** Composed or made from: *shoes of the finest leather.* **7.** Belonging or connected to: *the hands of a watch; a person of her religion.* **8.** Possessing; having: *a man of honor.* **9.** Containing or carrying: *a bag of groceries.* **10.** Named or called: *the busy city of Chicago.* **11.** Centering on or directed toward: *a love of horses.* **12.** Produced by: *the fruits of our orchards.* **13.** Concerning; about: *We spoke of you last night.* **14.** Before; until: *five minutes of two.*

off (ôf *or* ŏf) *adv.* **1.** Away from a place: *They drove off.* **2.** At a distance in space or time: *a mile off; a week off.* **3.** So as to be no longer on or connected: *He shaved off his beard.* **4.** So as to be no longer continuing or functioning: *Turn the lights off.* **5.** So as to be smaller, fewer, or less: *Sales are dropping off.* **6.** So as to be away from work or duty: *taking the day off.* **7.** So as to be completely removed or finished: *dinosaurs dying off.* —*adj.* **1.** Not on, attached, or connected: *Her shoes were off.* **2.** Not continuing, operating, or functioning: *The oven is off.* **3.** No longer taking place; canceled: *The dance is off.* **4.** Less, fewer, or smaller: *Sales are off this year.* **5.** Below standard: *His performance was somehow off.* **6.** Started on the way; going: *I'm off to the movies.* **7.** In error: *off by several inches.* **8.** Away from work or duty: *I'm off tonight.* —*prep.* **1.** So as to be removed or distant from: *The girl stepped off the bus.* **2.** Away or relieved from: *off duty.* **3.** With the means or support provided by: *living off fruit; living off a pension.* **4.** Extending from: *a little alley off the main street.* **5.** Not equal to the usual standard of: *off her game.* **6.** Without: *staying off tobacco.* **7.** In the sea near: *a mile off the beach.* ◆ **off and on.** Occasionally; from time to time: *My knee still bothers me off and on.*

off·beat (ôf′bēt′ *or* ŏf′bēt′) *adj. Informal.* Not of an ordinary type; unconventional; different: *an offbeat way of dressing.*

off-col·or (ôf′kŭl′ ər *or* ŏf′kŭl′ər) *adj.* Improper; in poor taste: *an off-color joke.*

of·fence (ə fĕns′) *n. Chiefly British.* Variant of **offense.**

of·fend (ə fĕnd′) *v.* —*tr.* **1.** To cause (sbdy.) to become angry: *a remark that offended me.* **2.** To be displeasing to (sbdy.); be disagreeable to: *The smell from the chemicals offended everyone.* —*intr.* To be the cause of displeasure: *odors that offend.*

of·fend·er (ə fĕn′dər) *n.* A person or thing that offends, especially a person who is guilty of a crime: *The offenders were held in jail.*

of·fense (ə fĕns′) *n.* **1.** A violation of a moral, legal, or social code; a sin or crime: *an offense punishable by death.* **2.** Something that offends: *The building was an offense to the eye.* **3.** (ŏf′ĕns′). The act of attacking or assaulting: *The army went on the offense.* **4.** (ŏf′ĕns′). In sports, the team in possession of the ball or puck: *The offense moved the ball down the field.* ◆ **take offense.** To feel offended by sthg.: *She took offense at the remark.*

of·fen·sive (ə fĕn′sĭv) *adj.* **1.** Offending the senses; unpleasant: *an offensive smell.* **2.** Causing anger, displeasure, or resentment: *offensive language.* **3.** Relating to or

designed for attack: *offensive weapons.* **4.** (ŏf′ĕn sĭv). Relating to the offense of a sports team: *offensive players.* —*n.* An attack: *the third offensive of the war.* ◆ **on the offensive.** In an attitude of attack: *His thoughtless remark put her on the offensive.* —**of·fen′sive·ly** *adv.* —**of·fen′sive·ness** *n.* [U]

of·fer (ô′fər *or* ŏf′ər) *tr.v.* **1.** To present (sthg.) for acceptance or refusal: *They offered me dessert. May I offer my advice?* **2.** To present (sthg.) for sale: *a store offering suits at a discount.* **3.** To provide (sthg.): *The new apartment offers many advantages over our old one.* **4.** To present (sthg.) to the public: *The museum offered a program of music.* —*n.* **1.** [C] Something, such as a proposal, suggestion, or bid, that is offered: *an offer to teach; offers for the car.* **2.** [U] The act of offering: *the offer of his services.* ◆ **offer a prayer.** Say a prayer.

of·fer·ing (ô′fər ĭng *or* ŏf′ər ĭng) *n.* **1.** [U] The act of making an offer. **2.** [C] Something offered, such as a contribution, gift, or religious sacrifice: *an offering of food.*

off·hand (ôf′hănd′ *or* ŏf′hănd′) *adv. & adj.* Without preparation or previous thought: *Can you say offhand when they'll call? He gave an offhand reply.* —**off′hand′ed·ly** *adv.*

of·fice (ô′fĭs *or* ŏf′ĭs) *n.* **1.a.** [C] A place where business, clerical, or professional work is done: *the principal's office.* **b.** [U] The people working in such a place: *The office gave the boss a surprise party.* **2.** [C; U] A position of authority or trust, as in a government or a corporation: *the office of President.* **3.** [C; U] A branch of a department of a government: *the office of environmental affairs.* ◆ **in office.** Holding an elected or appointed position: *She has been in office for ten years.*

of·fice·hold·er (ô′fĭs hōl′dər *or* ŏf′ĭs-hōl′dər) *n.* A person who holds a public office: *City officeholders agreed to meet with the townspeople.*

of·fi·cer (ô′fĭ sər *or* ŏf′ĭ sər) *n.* **1.** A person who has a position of authority in a government, corporation, club, or other institution: *an officer of the court; club officers.* **2.** A person who holds a commission in the armed forces: *an officer in the Navy.* **3.** A police officer: *Officers searched for the lost child.*

of·fi·cial (ə fĭsh′əl) *adj.* **1.** Relating to an office or a position of authority: *official duties.* **2.** Properly authorized: *an official document.* **3.** Formal or ceremonious: *an official banquet.* —*n.* **1.** A person in a position of authority: *Officials ordered an investigation.* **2.** A referee or an umpire in a sports contest: *sports officials.* —**of·fi′cial·ly** *adv.*

of·fi·ci·ate (ə fĭsh′ ē āt′) *intr.v.* **of·fi·ci·at·ed, of·fi·ci·at·ing, of·fi·ci·ates.** [at] **1.** To perform the duties of a public official or a member of the clergy: *The mayor* *officiates at town meetings. The priest offici-ated at the wedding.* **2.** To serve as a referee or an umpire in a sports contest: *The new ref-eree officiated at the game.*

of•fi•cious (ə fĭsh′əs) *adj. Formal.* Self-impor-tant; bossy: *Stop being so officious.* **—of•fi′-cious•ly** *adv.* **—of•fi′cious•ness** *n.* [U]

off•ing (ô′fĭng *or* ŏf′ĭng) *n.* ◆ **in the offing.** In the near or immediate future; soon to come: *A raise is in the offing.*

off-key (ôf′kē′ *or* ŏf′kē′) *adj.* Higher or lower than the correct notes of a song: *The students were all off-key.* **—off′ key′** *adv.*

off-lim•its (ôf lĭm′ĭts *or* ŏf lĭm′ĭts) *adj.* Not to be entered by a certain group: *The teach-ers' lounge is off-limits to all students.*

off-line (ôf′līn′ *or* ŏf′līn′) *adj.* Not connect-ed to or controlled by a computer: *We went off-line at 8:00.*

off•set (ôf sĕt′ *or* ŏf sĕt′) *tr.v.* **off•set, off•set•ting, off•sets.** To counterbalance or counteract (sthg.); make up for: *The con-venience of having a car should offset the expense it involves.*

off•shoot (ôf′shōot′ *or* ŏf′shōot′) *n.* **1.** A part of a plant that branches out from the main stem: *The gardener trimmed the off-shoots.* **2.** Something that branches out or originates from a main source: *The new club was an offshoot of an older club.*

off•shore (ôf′shôr′ *or* ŏf′shôr′) *adj.* **1.** Moving away from the shore: *an offshore breeze.* **2.** Located at a distance from the shore: *offshore rocks.* **—adv. 1.** In a direction away from shore: *The breeze was blowing offshore.* **2.** At a distance from shore: *a boat sailing a half mile offshore.*

off•side (ôf′sīd′ *or* ŏf′sīd′) *also* **off•sides** (ôf′sīdz′ *or* ŏf′sīdz′) *adv. & adj.* In sports, such as soccer or football, ahead of the ball or line of scrimmage: *The referee called the guard offside. The offensive line was offside on the last play.*

off•spring (ôf′sprĭng′ *or* ŏf′sprĭng′) *n., pl.* **offspring.** The young or descendants of a person, an animal, or a plant: *The stallion produced 70 offspring during his life.*

off-stage *or* **off•stage** (ôf′stāj′ *or* ŏf′stāj′) *adj. & adv.* Taking place in an area of a stage that is not visible to the audience: *an off-stage change of costume; She walked off-stage.*

off-the-rec•ord (ôf′thə rĕk′ərd *or* ŏf′thə-rĕk′ərd) *adv. & adj.* Not to be published or acknowledged: *The senator spoke off-the-record to the press. She gave us an off-the-record interpretation.*

off-white (ôf′wīt′ *or* ŏf′wīt′) *n.* [U] A gray-ish or yellowish white color. **—adj.** Grayish or yellowish white.

of•ten (ô′fən *or* ŏf′ən) *adv.* Frequently;

many times: *She called often because she was homesick.*

o•gle (ō′gəl *or* ô′gəl) *tr.v.* **o•gled, o•gling, o•gles.** To stare at (sbdy.) in a flirtatious or overly attentive way: *The young men ogled the model.*

o•gre (ō′gər) *n.* **1.** In legends and fairy tales, a giant or monster that eats human beings. **2.** A person who is especially cruel or feared.

oh (ō) *interj.* **1.** An expression used to show emotion, such as surprise, anger, or pain: *Oh! I forgot my wallet!* **2.** An expression used to address a person directly: *Oh, waiter! Could we have the bill please?*

HOMONYMS: oh, O (letter), **owe** (have to pay).

OH *abbr.* An abbreviation of Ohio.

ohm (ōm) *n.* A measure of resistance to the flow of electricity through a wire.

ohm•me•ter (ōm′mē′tər) *n.* An instrument that measures electrical resistance in ohms.

—oid *suff.* A suffix that means like or resem-bling: *anthropoid.*

WORD BUILDING: —oid The basic meaning of the suffix **—oid** is "like" or "resembling." Words ending in **—oid** are generally adjectives but can also be nouns. Thus **humanoid** means "with human characteristics or form" (adjective sense) or "a being with human form" (noun sense). Nouns ending in **—oid** form adjectives by adding the suffix **—al: spheroid, spher-oidal; trapezoid, trapezoidal.**

---

oil (oil) *n.* [U] **1.** A slippery liquid made from animal or vegetable fats. It will not mix with water: *fish oil; olive oil.* **2.a.** Petroleum. **b.** A substance made from petroleum that is used to lubricate engines: *motor oil.* **3.** Often **oils.** Oil paint: *I like to paint with oils.* **—tr.v.** To lubricate, supply, cover, or polish (sthg.) with oil: *It will help if you oil the lock.* **—oil′y** *adj.*

oil well *n.* A hole dug or drilled in the earth to obtain petroleum.

oink (oingk) *n.* The sound made by pigs. **—intr.v.** To make the grunting sound of a pig.

oint•ment (oint′mənt) *n.* [U] A thick oily substance made to be rubbed on the skin as a medication or cosmetic; salve: *burn ointment.*

OK¹ *or* **o•kay** (ō kā′) *Informal. adj.* All right; acceptable; fine: *The plan is OK with me.* **—adv.** Fairly well; acceptably: *He feels OK.* **—n., pl.* **OK's** *or* **o•kays.** Approval; agree-ment: *Get your parents' OK before we start on the trip.* **—tr.v.* **OK'd, OK'ing, OK's** *or* **o•kayed, o•kay•ing, o•kays.** To approve (sthg.); agree to: *The governor OK'd the plans for the construction of a new highway.*

OK² *abbr.* An abbreviation of Oklahoma.

ă-**cat**; ā-**pay**; âr-**care**; ä-**father**; ĕ-**get**; ē-**be**; ĭ-**sit**; ī-**nice**; îr-**here**; ŏ-**got**; ō-**go**; ô-**saw**; oi-**boy**; ou-**out**; ōō-**took**; ōō-**boot**; ŭ-**cut**; ûr-**word**; th-**thin**; *th*-**this**; hw-**when**; zh-**vision**; ə-**about**; N-French **bon**

Okla. *abbr.* An abbreviation of Oklahoma.

o•kra (ō′krə) *n.* [U]
The long, green sticky
seed pods of a tall tropical plant, used in soups
or as a vegetable.

old (ōld) *adj.* **1.a.** Having lived for a long
time; of great age: *an
old pine tree.* **b.** Relatively advanced in age:
her older brothers and sisters. **2.** Of a certain
age: *She's ten years old today.* **3.** In existence
for a long time; made long ago: *an old part of
the city.* **4.** Showing the effects of time or
long use: *an old coat.* **5.** Belonging to or
associated with an earlier time: *visiting his
old neighborhood.* **6.** Known for a long time
and well liked: *an old friend.* *—n.* A person
or thing of a certain age: *That horse is a
three-year-old.*

okra

old-fash•ioned (ōld′făsh′ənd) *adj.* **1.** Belonging to or typical of an earlier time and
no longer in style: *old-fashioned clothes.*
2. Preferring or in keeping with ways or
ideas of an earlier time: *strict old-fashioned
grandparents.*

old maid *n.* **1.** An offensive term for a
woman, especially an older woman, who is
not married. **2.** A card game in which the
player who holds a certain card at the end
loses.

old man *n. Slang.* **1.** One's father. **2.** One's
husband. **3.** A man who is in charge; a boss.

o•le•o (ō′lē ō′) *n.* [U] Margarine.

ol•fac•to•ry (ŏl făk′tə rē *or* ōl făk′tə rē)
adj. Relating to the sense of smell: *olfactory
nerves.*

ol•i•garch (ŏl′ĭ gärk′ *or* ō′lĭ gärk′) *n.* A
member of an oligarchy.

ol•i•gar•chy (ŏl′ĭ gär′kē *or* ō′lĭ gär′kē) *n.*,
pl. **ol•i•gar•chies. 1.** A form of government
in which power is held by a small group of
people. **2.** The people forming such a group:
a member of the oligarchy.

ol•ive (ŏl′ĭv) *n.* **1.**
[C] The small, oval,
green or black fruit,
with a single hard
seed, of a tree that
grows in the Medi-
terranean: *Olives
are eaten whole or
pressed to produce
olive oil.* **2.** [U]
A dull yellowish
green color. *—adj.* Dull yellowish green.

olive

O•lym•pi•ad (ō lĭm′pē ad′) *n.* A celebration
of the modern Olympic games: *the 23rd
Olympiad.*

O•lym•pi•an (ō lĭm′pē ən) *n.* A contestant
in the Olympic games.

O•lym•pic games (ō lĭm′pĭk) *pl.n.* **1.** A
modern international athletic competition
now held every two years. **2.** An ancient
Greek festival of athletic competitions and
contests held every four years in honor of the
god Zeus.

O•lym′pics (ō lĭm′pĭks) *pl.n.* The Olympic
games.

om•buds•man (ŏm′bŭdz′mən) *n., pl.* **om•
buds•men.** A person who investigates and
resolves complaints, especially for an institution: *the university ombudsman.*

om•e•let (ŏm′lĭt) *n.* A dish of beaten eggs
cooked with a filling such as cheese.

o•men (ō′mən) *n.* An object or an event
regarded as a sign of future good or bad luck:
Do you believe in omens?

om•i•nous (ŏm′ə nəs) *adj.* Being a sign of
trouble or danger: *ominous clouds.* **—om′i•
nous•ly** *adv.*

o•mis•sion (ō mĭsh′ən) *n.* **1.** [U] The act of
omitting sthg.: *the omission of a letter from a
word.* **2.** [C] Something that has been omitted: *several omissions from the guest list.*

o•mit (ō mĭt′) *tr.v.* **o•mit•ted, o•mit•ting,
o•mits.** To leave out or fail to mention (sthg.):
Omit unnecessary words.

omni— *pref.* A prefix that means all: *omnidirectional; omnipotent.*

WORD BUILDING: omni— The prefix **omni—**
means "all." Because the meaning of **omni—** is
so clear and easily recognizable, the prefix has
long been used in English to make new words.
For example, the meanings of words such as
omnipurpose (all-purpose) and **omnipresent**
(always present) are easy to guess, even without a definition.

---

om•ni•di•rec•tion•al (ŏm′nē dĭ rĕk′shə-
nəl) *adj.* Capable of transmitting or receiving
signals in all directions: *an omnidirectional
antenna.*

om•nip•o•tent (ŏm nĭp′ə tənt) *adj.* Having unlimited power, authority, or force; all-
powerful. **—om•nip′o•tence** *n.* [U]

om•ni•pres•ent (ŏm′nĭ prĕz′ənt) *adj.*
Present everywhere at the same time.
—om′ni•pres′ence *n.* [U]

om•nis•cient (ŏm nĭsh′ənt) *adj.* Having total knowledge; knowing everything.
—om•nis′cience *n.* [U]

om•ni•vore (ŏm′nə vôr′) *n.* An organism
that eats both plant and animal food: *Bears
are omnivores.*

om•niv•o•rous (ŏm nĭv′ər əs) *adj.* Eating both plants and animals as food; eating
all kinds of food: *Rats are omnivorous.*
—om•niv′o•rous•ly *adv.*

on (ŏn *or* ôn) *prep.* **1.a.** In position upon: *a
plate on the table.* **b.** In contact with or
extending over: *a fly on the wall; a rash on
my arm.* **c.** Located at or along: *a house on
the beach.* **d.** Attached to or suspended from:

beads on a string. **2.** Used to show motion or direction toward or against: *throwing the books on the floor; a march on Washington.* **3.** Used to show when sthg. happens: *We met on Tuesday. On entering the room, she saw him.* **4.a.** Used to show the object affected by an action: *The spotlight fell on the actress.* **b.** Used to show the cause of an action: *He cut his foot on a piece of broken glass.* **5.a.** In the state of: *on vacation; on fire.* **b.** With or for the purpose of: *traveling on business.* **c.** Belonging to: *a doctor on the staff.* **6.** Concerning; about: *a book on carpentry.* **7.** *Informal.* In one's possession: *I don't have a cent on me.* **8.** *Informal.* At the expense of: *This meal is on me.* —*adv.* **1.** In or into a position of being attached to or covering sthg.: *He pulled his coat on.* **2.** Forward or ahead: *moving on to the next town.* **3.** In a continuous way: *We worked on quietly.* **4.** In or into operation: *Turn the television on.* **5.** In or at the present position or condition: *They decided to stay on a few more days.* —*adj.* **1.** Being in operation: *The television is on.* **2.a.** Planned; intended: *We have nothing on for the weekend.* **b.** Happening or soon to happen: *The party is on for tomorrow.* ♦ **and so on.** And more; et cetera: *We went to the store, got gas, picked up the children, and so on.* **on and off** or **off and on.** Stopping and starting; not continuously: *He has taken college courses on and off for years.* **on and on.** Without stopping; continuously: *The professor spoke on and on.*

once (wŭns) *adv.* **1.** One time only: *once a day.* **2.** In the past: *I was a child once too.* —*n.* [U] One single time or occurrence: *Let me go out just this once.* —*conj.* As soon as; if ever; when: *Once we get started, I'll show you what to do.* ♦ **at once. 1.** All at one time; simultaneously: *He picked up both children at once.* **2.** Immediately; instantly: *Come in here at once!* **once and for all.** Finally; conclusively: *She broke up with her boyfriend once and for all.* **once in a while.** Now and then: *I like to have ice cream once in a while.* **once upon a time.** *(used to start a fairy tale).* At some time in the past; long ago.

once-o·ver (wŭns'ō'vər) *n. Informal. (usually singular).* A quick but thorough examination of sbdy. or sthg.: *Dad gave my brothers the once-over before we left for church.*

on·com·ing (ŏn'kŭm'ĭng *or* ôn'kŭm'ĭng) *adj.* Coming toward a person or thing; approaching: *the oncoming train.*

one (wŭn) *adj.* **1.** Referring to a single person or thing: *one dog and three cats.* **2.** Referring to a single person or thing contrasted with another: *He was at one end of the hall and I was at the other.* **3.** Happening at some indef-

inite time: *One day you will be famous.* **4.** *Informal.* Used as an intensive: *That is one fine mess you've gotten us into!* **5.** Being the same in kind: *three animals of one species.* —*n.* **1.** The cardinal number, written 1, that designates the first unit in a series: *Turn to page 1.* **2.** A single person or unit: *This is the one I like best.* —*pron.* **1.** A single person or thing: *One of my teammates scored three goals.* **2.** An unspecified person; anyone: *One should be kind to one's neighbors.* **3.** The person or thing previously named: *He was looking for a TV and found one on sale.* ♦ **at one.** In accord or unity: *They lived at one with the environment.* **one and all.** Everyone: *Merry Christmas to one and all!* **one another.** Each other: *They talk to one another every day.* **one by one.** Individually: *She greeted her guests one by one.*

HOMONYMS: one, won (was victorious).

on·er·ous (ŏn'ər əs *or* ō'nər əs) *adj.* Troublesome or oppressive: *Cleaning the house was an onerous job.* —**on'er·ous·ly** *adv.*

one·self (wŭn sĕlf') *pron.* **1.** One's own self: *reading about oneself in the newspaper.* **2.** One's normal or healthy condition: *feeling like oneself again.*

one-sid·ed (wŭn'sī' dĭd) *adj.* **1.** Favoring one side or group; biased: *a one-sided version of the disagreement.* **2.** Having one side much stronger than another: *a one-sided game.*

one·time (wŭn' tīm') *adj.* At one time in the past; former: *a onetime TV star.*

one-time (wŭn' tīm') *adj.* Being true on a single occasion: *a one-time winner of the tournament.*

one-to-one (wŭn'tə wŭn') *adj.* Matching each member of a group with only one member of another group: *a one-to-one meeting to discuss the problem.*

one-track (wŭn'trăk') *adj.* Narrowly limited to a single idea or way of thinking: *a one-track mind.*

one-way (wŭn'wā') *adj.* Moving or permitting movement in one direction only: *a one-way street.*

on·go·ing (ŏn'gō'ĭng *or* ôn'gō'ĭng) *adj.* Continuing or progressing: *the ongoing development of the waterfront.*

on·ion (ŭn'yən) *n.* A plant with a small, round, white bulb that has a strong odor and taste.

on-line (ŏn'līn' *or* ôn'līn') *adj.* Connected to or controlled by a computer: *She went on-line to send her e-mail message.*

on·look·er (ŏn'lŏŏk' ər *or* ôn'lŏŏk' ər) *n.* A

person who watches or looks on: *Onlookers stood around at the crime scene.*

on•ly (ōn′lē) *adj.* **1.** Alone in kind; sole: *our only reason for going; their only child.* **2.** Most suitable of all: *the only real contenders for the championship.* —*adv.* **1.** Without anyone or anything else; alone: *We have only two sandwiches left.* **2.** Merely; just: *I only followed orders.* **3.** Exclusively; solely: *That train only runs on Sunday.* **4.** As recently as: *He called me only last month.* —*conj.* With the restriction that; but: *You may climb on the rocks, only be careful.* ◆ **be only too glad** or **happy to.** To be willing to do sthg.: *I would be only too glad to help.*

on•o•mat•o•poe•ia (ŏn′ə măt′ə pē′ə) *n.* [U] The forming or use of a word, such as *buzz,* that imitates the sound of the thing it refers to. —**on′o•mat′o•poe′ic** *adj.*

on•rush (ŏn′rŭsh′ *or* ôn′rŭsh′) *n.* A forward rush or flow: *the onrush of the crowd.* —**on′-rush′ing** *adj.*

on•set (ŏn′sĕt′ *or* ôn′sĕt′) *n.* A beginning; a start: *the onset of a disease.*

on•shore (ŏn′shôr′ *or* ôn′shôr′) *adj.* **1.** Moving toward the shore: *an onshore breeze.* **2.** Located on the shore: *an onshore patrol.* —*adv.* Toward the shore: *The wind shifted onshore.*

on•side (ŏn′sīd′ *or* ôn′sīd′) *adv. & adj.* In sports, in a position to receive the ball legally: *Try to stay onside. She's in an onside position.*

on-site (ŏn′sīt′ *or* ôn′sīt′) *adj.* At the physical location of a business or activity: *an on-site inspection.*

on•slaught (ŏn′slôt′ *or* ôn′slôt′) *n.* A violent attack or charge: *the enemy onslaught.*

Ont. *abbr.* An abbreviation of Ontario.

on•to (ŏn′tōō′ *or* ôn′tōō′) *prep.* **1.** On top of; to a position on or upon: *The dog jumped onto the chair.* **2.** *Informal.* Aware of; knowing about: *I'm onto his tricks.*

o•nus (ō′nəs) *n.* (*usually singular*). A difficult responsibility or necessity: *The onus is his to get the problem resolved.*

on•ward (ŏn′wərd *or* ôn′wərd) *adj.* Moving forward: *the onward rush of the train.* —*adv.* Also **on•wards** (ŏn′wərdz *or* ôn′wərdz). In a direction that is ahead in space or time; forward: *The ship sailed onward through the storm.*

—onym *suff.* A suffix that means name; word: *antonym; synonym.*

on•yx (ŏn′ĭks) *n.* [U] A type of quartz that occurs in bands of different colors, often black and white: *a black onyx ring.*

oo•dles (ōōd′lz) *pl.n. Informal.* A great amount or large number: *oodles of fun.*

ooze¹ (ōōz) *v.* **oozed, ooz•ing, ooz•es.** —*intr.* **1.** To flow or leak slowly: *Blood oozed from the cut on her finger.* **2.** To disappear slowly: *His courage oozed away.* —*tr.* To give off (sthg.) by flowing slowly: *The trees were oozing sticky sap.*

ooze² (ōōz) *n.* [U] Soft mud or slime, especially that covering the bottoms of oceans and lakes: *She could feel the ooze on the bottom of the pond.*

o•pac•i•ty (ō păs′ĭ tē) *n.* [U] The quality or condition of being opaque.

o•pal (ō′pəl) *n.* [C; U] A milky white mineral that has other colors in it. Opal is used as a gemstone.

o•pal•es•cent (ō′pə lĕs′ənt) *adj.* Having the milky iridescent colors of an opal. —**o′pal•es′cence** *n.* [U]

o•paque (ō pāk′) *adj.* **1.** Not letting light pass through: *Metal and wood are opaque.* **2.** Hard to understand; obscure: *an opaque explanation.* —**o•paque′ly** *adv.* —**o•paque′ness** *n.* [U]

OPEC (ō′pĕk′) *n.* An abbreviation of Organization of Petroleum Exporting Countries.

o•pen (ō′pən) *adj.* **1.** Not shut or closed: *an open door.* **2.** Allowing passage or view; not blocked: *open fields.* **3.** Uncovered; exposed: *an open wound.* **4.** Not sealed, fastened, or tied: *an open envelope.* **5.** Having spaces: *a fabric with a coarse open weave.* **6.a.** Free to be participated in; not restricted: *an open competition.* **b.** Available; not closed or decided: *The position is still open.* **7.a.** Vulnerable; susceptible: *The issue is open to question.* **b.** Willing or ready to consider: *I'm open to suggestions.* **8.** Honest and unreserved: *I'll be open with you about this.* **9.** Free from prejudice or fixed belief: *keeping an open mind.* **10.** Not hidden or secret: *showing open defiance.* **11.** Ready for business: *The store is open today.* —*v.* —*tr.* **1.** To make (sthg.) no longer shut or fastened: *I opened the window.* **2.** To remove the cover or wrapping from (sthg.): *Open the can.* **3.** To begin (sthg.): *The same topic opens this chapter.* **4.** To begin the operation of (sthg.): *They opened a new restaurant.* **5.** To make (sthg.) accessible or available for use: *open the new bridge; open new markets overseas.* —*intr.* **1.** To become open: *The door opened slowly.* **2.a.** To begin: *The meeting opened with her report.* **b.** To begin business or operation: *A new store opens tomorrow.* **3.** To have an opening: *Your room opens onto a terrace.* —*n.* [U] **1.** The outdoors: *camping in the open.* **2.** A condition free of secrecy: *Bring the facts into the open.* ◆ **open-and-shut.** Presenting no difficulties: *an open-and-shut case.* **open fire.** To begin firing guns: *The gunman opened fire on the crowd.* **open (one's) eyes.** To become aware of a risk or problem: *The accident opened our eyes to the danger of not wearing seatbelts.* **open up.** *intr.v. Informal.* To begin to speak freely and frankly: *At last the frightened witness opened up and told what he had seen.* —**o′pen•ly** *adv.* —**o′pen•ness** *n.* [U]

o·pen-air (ō'pən âr') *adj.* Outdoor: *an open-air concert.*

o·pen-end·ed (ō'pən ĕn'dĭd) *adj.* **1.** Not limited or restricted: *an open-ended contract.* **2.** Allowing for free response or discussion: *an open-ended question.*

o·pen·er (ō'pə nər) *n.* **1.** A person or thing that opens, especially a device used to cut open cans or remove bottle caps: *a can opener.* **2.** The first act or event in a show or a series of sporting events: *Our team won the opener.*

o·pen·hand·ed (ō'pən hăn'dĭd) *adj.* Giving freely; generous: *openhanded contributors to the campaign.*

o·pen·heart·ed (ō'pən här'tĭd) *adj.* Kind; generous: *She is an openhearted woman who always helps others.*

open house *n.* **1.** A party that may be attended by all who wish to do so: *He held an open house for his nephew's graduation.* **2.** An occasion in which a school or other institution is open for visiting and inspection: *We talked to our daughter's teacher at the open house.* **3.** A period during which a house for sale is open to the public: *The realtor held an open house on Sunday.*

o·pen·ing (ō'pə nĭng) *n.* **1.** The act of becoming open: *the opening of a new store.* **2.** A clear space or passage: *an opening in the woods; an opening in the wall.* **3.** An unfilled job or position; a vacancy: *an opening on the teaching staff.* **4.** A favorable opportunity: *He finally found an opening to tell his side of the story.* **5.** The first of sthg.: *at the opening of the movie.*

o·pen-mind·ed (ō'pən mīn'dĭd) *adj.* Willing to consider new ideas; unprejudiced: *He always tries to be open-minded about others' opinions.* —**o'pen-mind'ed·ly** *adv.* —**o'pen-mind'ed·ness** *n.* [U]

op·er·a (ŏp'ər ə *or* ŏp'rə) *n.* [C; U] A theatrical performance in which the words of a play are sung with an orchestra: *She enjoys listening to opera.* —**op'er·at'ic** (ŏp'ə-răt'ik) *adj.*

op·er·a·ble (ŏp'ər ə bəl *or* ŏp'rə bəl) *adj.* **1.** Being such that use or operation is possible: *a damaged but operable airplane.* **2.** Treatable by surgery: *an operable tumor.*

op·er·ate (ŏp'ə rāt') *v.* **op·er·at·ed, op·er·at·ing, op·er·ates.** —*intr.* **1.** To perform a function; work: *a machine that operates well.* **2.** To perform surgery: *Doctors operated on the patient.* **3.** To produce an effect: *This drug operates quickly.* —*tr.* **1.** To control the functioning of (sthg.); run: *operate a machine.* **2.** To direct the affairs of (sthg.); manage: *operate a business.*

op·er·at·ing system (ŏp'ə rā'tĭng) *n.* In computers, a set of programs designed to control the hardware of a computer system: *a new operating system.*

op·er·a·tion (ŏp'ə rā'shən) *n.* **1.** [U] The act or condition of operating or functioning: *a machine no longer in operation.* **2.** [C] A surgical treatment: *She had an operation to repair the torn ligament in her knee.* **3.** [C] A mathematical process or action performed according to specific rules: *Addition is a mathematical operation.* **4.** [C] A military action or series of actions. **5. operations.** *(used with a singular or plural verb).* The central administrative offices of a business or the military: *Operations is on the third floor.*

op·er·a·tion·al (ŏp'ə rā'shə nəl) *adj.* **1.** Relating to an operation or a series of operations. **2.** Able to be used; not broken: *an operational aircraft.*

op·er·a·tive (ŏp'ər ə tĭv *or* ŏp'rə tĭv) *adj.* **1.** In effect; in force: *a law of economics that is operative in the stock market.* **2.** Working correctly; efficient: *operative equipment.* —*n.* A secret agent; a spy: *operatives who gather information in other countries.*

op·er·a·tor (ŏp'ə rā'tər) *n.* **1.** A person who operates a machine or device: *a sewing machine operator.* **2.** A person who owns or manages a business or an industrial process: *a mine operator.* **3.** *Informal.* A person who uses shrewd or unfair methods: *He is known as quite an operator.*

oph·thal·mol·o·gy (ŏf'thəl mŏl'ə jē *or* ŏp'thəl mŏl'ə jē) *n.* [U] The branch of medicine that deals with the structure, functions, diseases, and treatment of the eye. —**oph'thal·mol'o·gist** *n.*

o·pin·ion (ə pĭn'yən) *n.* **1.** A belief based on what sbdy. thinks or feels, not supported by facts: *He has strong opinions about fashion.* **2.** A judgment based on special knowledge and given by an expert: *We asked the doctor for her opinion.* ♦ **have a high opinion.** To have the feeling that sbdy. or sthg. is valuable or important: *He has a high opinion of the candidate.*

o·pin·ion·at·ed (ə pĭn'yə nā'tĭd) *adj.* Holding stubbornly and often unreasonably to one's own opinions: *an opinionated critic.*

o·pi·um (ō'pē əm) *n.* [U] A drug that causes sleep, made from the seeds of the poppy plant: *Opium is the source of heroin and morphine.*

o·pos·sum (ə pŏs'əm *or* pŏs'əm) *n.* An animal of North and South America that lives mostly in trees, carries its young in a pouch, and has thick gray fur and a long bare tail.

opossum

op·po·nent (ə pō′nənt) *n.* A person or group that opposes another in a battle, contest, controversy, or debate: *Always watch your opponent carefully.*

op·por·tune (ŏp′ ər tōōn′) *adj.* **1.** Useful for a particular purpose: *an opportune suggestion.* **2.** Happening at a time that is advantageous: *Early morning is an opportune time to go running.*

op·por·tun·ist (ŏp′ ər tōō′nĭst) *n.* A person who advances his or her own position whether it is right or wrong to do so: *political opportunists.* —**op′por·tun′is′m** *n.* [U] —**op′por·tun·is′tic** *adj.*

op·por·tu·ni·ty (ŏp′ər tōō′ nĭ tē) *n., pl.* **op·por·tu·ni·ties. 1.** A time or an occasion that is suitable for a certain purpose: *This is your opportunity to speak.* **2.** A chance for progress or advancement: *The gift of $10,000 gave him the opportunity to go to college.*

op·pose (ə pōz′) *tr.v.* **op·posed, op·pos·ing, op·pos·es.** To offer resistance to (sbdy./sthg.): *oppose the enemy; oppose a plan of action.* ♦ **opposed to.** Against or disapproving of sthg.: *We are opposed to the use of pesticides.*

SYNONYMS: oppose, fight, combat, contest, resist. These verbs mean to try to defeat sbdy. or sthg. Oppose is the most general: *They opposed the plan to close the factory.* Fight and combat mean to oppose in an active way: *Citizens must work together to fight corruption in government. The development of vaccines was an important step toward combating disease.* Contest means to question sthg. and try to change it: *The losing candidate contested the election.* Resist means to try to prevent sthg. from happening: *The citizens united to resist the invasion.* ANTONYM: support.

---

op·po·site (ŏp′ ə zĭt) *adj.* **1.** Located directly across from sthg. else: *the opposite sides of a house.* **2.** Moving away from each other: *They went off in opposite directions.* **3.** Altogether different: *words with opposite meanings.* —*n.* A person or thing that is totally different from another: *What you're saying today is the exact opposite of what you were saying yesterday. In love, it seems that opposites attract.* —*adv.* In an opposite position: *He sat opposite from me.* —*prep.* Across from or facing: *Park your car opposite the school.*

op·po·si·tion (ŏp′ə zĭsh′ ən) *n.* [U] **1.** The act of opposing: *our active opposition to the law.* **2.** An opposing force or obstacle: *The old dog was the burglar's only opposition.* **3. Opposition.** A political party or organization opposed to the group, party, or government that has power at the present time.

op·press (ə prĕs′) *tr.v.* **1.** To control (sbdy./sthg.) by harsh and unjust treatment: *people oppressed by the current government.*

2. To cause (sbdy.) to feel distress or worry: *Grief oppressed her.* —**op·pres′sion** *n.* [U] —**op·pres′sor** *n.*

op·pres·sive (ə prĕs′ ĭv) *adj.* **1.** Difficult to bear; harsh and unjust: *The government became more oppressive during the war.* **2.** Causing physical or mental distress: *oppressive effects of bad weather; an oppressive silence.* —**op·pres′sive·ly** *adv.* —**op·pres′sive·ness** *n.* [U]

opt (ŏpt) *intr.v.* To make a choice or decision: *He opted to go to the party.*

op·tic (ŏp′ tĭk) *adj.* Relating to the eye or vision: *the optic nerve.*

op·ti·cal (ŏp′ tĭ kəl) *adj.* **1.** Relating to sight: *an optical defect.* **2.** Designed to assist sight: *optical instruments.* **3.** Relating to the science of optics. —**op′ti·cal·ly** *adv.*

optical scanner *n.* A device that converts images and text printed on paper into digital information that can be stored and processed by a computer.

op·ti·cian (ŏp tĭsh′ ən) *n.* A person who makes or sells eyeglasses.

op·tics (ŏp′ tĭks) *n.* [U] (*used with a singular verb*). The scientific study of light and vision.

op·ti·mal (ŏp′ tə məl) *adj.* Most favorable or desirable; optimum: *We picked the optimal time to leave for the airport.* —**op′ti·mal·ly** *adv.*

op·ti·mism (ŏp′ tə mĭz′əm) *n.* [U] A tendency to take a hopeful view of a situation or to expect the best possible outcome: *His optimism helped him get through the loss of his job.* —**op′ti·mist** *n.* —**op′ti·mis′tic** *adj.* —**op′ti·mis′ti·cal·ly** *adv.*

op·ti·mum (ŏp′ tə məm) *n., pl.* **op·ti·ma** (ŏp′ tə mə) or **op·ti·mums.** The most favorable point: *The engine is operating at its optimum.* —*adj.* Most favorable or advantageous; best: *The library provides optimum conditions for studying.* —**op′ti·mize′** (ŏp′ tə mĭz′) *v.*

op·tion (ŏp′ shən) *n.* **1.** [C] The act of choosing; choice: *We explored our options.* See Synonyms at **choice. 2.** [U] The power or right to choose; freedom to choose: *He had the option of attending college but decided not to.* **3.** [C] Something chosen or available as a choice: *A CD player is an option on some new cars.* **4.** [C] The exclusive right to buy or sell sthg. within a specified time at a set price: *We have a lease with an option to buy.* —**op′tion·al** *adj.* —**op′tion·al·ly** *adv.*

op·tom·e·trist (ŏp tŏm′ ĭ trĭst) *n.* A person who is trained and licensed to practice as a doctor of optometry.

op·tom·e·try (ŏp tŏm′ ĭ trē) *n.* [U] The profession of examining, measuring, and treating eye problems by means of corrective lenses or other methods.

op·u·lence (ŏp′ yə ləns) *n.* [U] Great wealth and luxury: *the opulence of the furnishings.* —**op′u·lent** *adj.* —**op′u·lent·ly** *adv.*

o·pus (ō′ pəs) *n., pl.* **o·pus·es.** A musical composition numbered to show the order of a composer's works.

or (ôr; ər *when unstressed*) *conj.* **1.a.** Used to show different possibilities: *hot or cold.* **b.** Used before the second of two possibilities when the first possibility is preceded by *whether: I don't know whether to laugh or cry.* **2.** Used with two equivalent expressions: *acrophobia, or the fear of great heights.* **3.** Used to indicate uncertainty: *He's called here three or four times already.* ◆ **or so.** Approximately; about: *It costs five dollars or so.*

HOMONYMS: or, oar (wooden pole), **ore** (mineral).

USAGE: or When you connect a series of singular nouns by **or**, the verb is singular: *Tom or Jack is coming.* When the elements are plural, the verb is plural: *Either the clowns or the monkeys make you laugh.* When the nouns do not agree in number, it is best to find other ways to express what you are trying to say: *Either Tom is coming or his sisters are.*

OR *abbr.* An abbreviation of Oregon.
—or[1] *suff.* A suffix that means a person or thing that performs an action: *competitor; accelerator.*
—or[2] *suff.* A suffix that means state, quality, or activity: *valor; honor.*
or·a·cle (ôr′ə kəl *or* ŏr′ə kəl) *n.* **1.** In ancient Greece, a person who transmitted messages from the gods to the people. **2.** The place where people find such a person. **3.** Any person considered to be a source of good advice.

HOMONYMS: oracle, auricle (heart atrium).

---

o·ral (ôr′əl) *adj.* **1.** Spoken rather than written: *an oral examination.* **2.** Relating to the mouth: *oral hygiene.* **3.** Used in or taken through the mouth: *an oral thermometer; oral medication.* **—o′ral·ly** *adv.*

HOMONYMS: oral, aural (of the ear).

---

or·ange (ôr′ĭnj *or* ŏr′ĭnj) *n.* **1.** [C] A round citrus fruit related to the grapefruit, lemon, and lime. **2.** [U] A color between yellow and red. *—adj.* Between yellow and red.
o·rang·u·tan (ô răng′ə tăn′ *or* ə răng′ə-tăn′) *n.* A large ape of the islands of Borneo and Sumatra, with long arms and reddish brown hair.
or·a·to·ry (ôr′ə tôr′ē *or* ŏr′ə tôr′ē) *n.* [U] The art of public speaking. **—or′a·tor** *n.*
orb (ôrb) *n. Formal.* A sphere or spherical object: *The moon is a great orb in the night sky.*

or·bit (ôr′bĭt) *n.* **1.** The path of a celestial body or artificial satellite as it travels around another celestial body: *the satellite's orbit.* **2.** The path of an electron around the nucleus of an atom. *—tr.v.* **1.** To put (sthg.) into orbit: *orbit a satellite.* **2.** To move in an orbit around (sthg.): *The moon orbits the earth.* **—or′bit·al** *adj.*
or·chard (ôr′chərd) *n.* **1.** A piece of land on which trees are grown for their fruit: *an old apple orchard.* **2.** The trees grown on such land: *The orchard was damaged in the storm.*
or·ches·tra (ôr′kĭ strə) *n.* **1.** A large group of musicians who play together on various instruments, such as violins, flutes, and horns: *a symphony orchestra.* **2.** The seats in the front part of the main floor of a theater. **—or·ches′tral** (ôr kĕs′trəl) *adj.*
or·ches·trate (ôr′ kĭ strāt′) *tr.v.* **or·ches·trat·ed, or·ches·trat·ing, or·ches·trates.** **1.** To compose or arrange (music) for performance by an orchestra. **2.** To organize (an event): *She orchestrated the wedding.* **—or′ches·tra′tion** *n.* [C; U]
or·chid (ôr′kĭd) *n.* **1.** [C] A tropical plant with colorful flowers. **2.** [U] A light reddish purple color. *—adj.* Light reddish purple.

orchid

or·dain (ôr dān′) *tr.v.* **1.** To appoint (sbdy.) as a minister, priest, or rabbi: *He was ordained by the bishop.* **2.** To control (an event or an outcome) by having superior power: *The government ordained an end to the strike.*
or·deal (ôr dēl′) *n.* A difficult or painful experience, especially one that severely tests a person's character or endurance: *the ordeal of losing a job.*
or·der (ôr′dər) *n.* **1.** [U] A sequence or arrangement of things one after the other: *alphabetical order.* **2.** [U] A condition in society marked by peaceful obedience to laws and authority: *The police restored order after the disturbance.* **3.** [C] A command and direction: *a court order.* **4.** [C] **a.** An instruction to buy, sell, or supply sthg.: *a government order for 10,000 blankets.* **b.** The thing supplied, bought, or sold: *The company ships orders postage paid.* **5.** [C] A portion of food in a restaurant: *an order of French fries.* **6.** [C] A group of persons living according to a religious rule: *an order of nuns.* **7.** [C] A social organization or club: *the Order of Elks.* *—v.* *—tr.* **1.** To issue a command or an instruction to (sbdy.): *The sergeant ordered the soldiers to attention.* **2.** To give a command or an instruction for (sthg.): *The president ordered a review of the budget.* **3.** To ask

---

ă-cat; ā-pay; âr-care; ä-father; ĕ-get; ē-be; ĭ-sit; ī-nice; îr-here; ŏ-got; ō-go; ô-saw; oi-boy; ou-out; ōo-took; ōō-boot; ŭ-cut; ûr-word; th-thin; th-this; hw-when; zh-vision; ə-about; N-French bon

to be supplied with (sthg.): *We ordered supplies for the camping trip.* **4.** To arrange (things) in a sequence: *We ordered the books according to subject.* —*intr.* To give a command or ask that sthg. be done or supplied: *Do as he orders.* ♦ **in order that.** *Formal.* So that: *The king divorced his queen, in order that he might marry again.* **in order to.** With the intention to; so as to: *We built the shed in order to store our tools.* **in short order.** With no delay; quickly: *He promised us an answer in short order.* **made to order.** According to the buyer's wishes: *a coat made to order.* **on order.** Requested but not yet delivered: *office supplies still on order.* **on the order of. 1.** Similar to; like: *a building on the order of a pyramid.* **2.** Approximately; about: *a building costing on the order of one million dollars.*
order around. *tr.v.* [sep.] To tell (sbdy.) what to do: *Stop ordering me around!* **out of order.** Not working; broken: *The soda machine is out of order.*
or•der•ly (ôr′dər lē) *adj.* **1.** Well arranged; neat: *an orderly kitchen.* **2.** Free from violence or disruption; peaceful: *The group protested in an orderly manner.* —*n., pl.* **or•der•lies.** An attendant who does nonmedical work in a hospital: *The orderly took the patient back to his room.* —**or′der•li•ness** *n.* [U]
or•di•nal (ôr′ dn əl) *adj.* Indicating a position in a series: *an ordinal rank of seventh.* —*n.* An ordinal number indicating position in a series. *First, second, third,* and so on are ordinals.
or•di•nance (ôr′dn əns) *n.* A rule or regulation, especially one enacted by a city government: *The city council passed an ordinance limiting parking on certain streets.*
or•di•nar•i•ly (ôr′dn âr′ə lē *or* ôr′dn ĕr′ə-lē) *adv.* As a general rule; usually: *We ordinarily go shopping for groceries on Tuesday.*
or•di•nar•y (ôr′dn ĕr′ē) *adj.* **1.** Usual; normal: *Yesterday was not an ordinary day.* **2.** Average in quality or size: *Their parents lived in an ordinary house.* ♦ **out of the ordinary.** Unusual: *Nothing out of the ordinary happened all week.*
or•di•na•tion (ôr′dn ā′shən) *n.* **1.** [C] The ceremony by which a person is admitted to the ministry of a Christian church. **2.** [U] The act of ordaining or the state of being ordained.
ord•nance (ôrd′nəns) *n.* Military supplies, including weapons, ammunition, and maintenance equipment.
ore (ôr) *n.* [C; U] A mineral or rock from which a valuable substance, especially a metal, can be taken: *iron ore.*

HOMONYMS: ore, oar (wooden pole), **or** (alternative).

Ore. *abbr.* An abbreviation of Oregon.

o•reg•a•no (ə rĕg′ə nō′) *n.* [U] An herb with strong-tasting small, green leaves used as flavoring for food.
or•gan (ôr′gən) *n.* **1.** A musical instrument consisting of a piano keyboard and a number of pipes that produce sound: *She played the organ in her church.* **2.** A distinct part of an organism, adapted for a particular function: *the stomach and other organs of digestion.*
or•gan•ic (ôr găn′ĭk) *adj.* **1.** Relating to living things: *decaying organic matter.* **2.** Relating to or produced using fertilizers of animal or vegetable matter and not artificial fertilizers or pesticides: *organic farming.* **3.** Made of related parts that work together as a unit: *an organic whole.* **4.** Relating to compounds containing carbon: *organic chemistry.* —**or•gan′i•cal•ly** *adv.*
or•gan•ism (ôr′gə nĭz′əm) *n.* A living thing, such as a plant or an animal.
or•gan•ist (ôr′gə nĭst) *n.* A person who plays the organ: *the church organist.*
or•gan•i•za•tion (ôr′gə nĭ zā′shən) *n.* **1.** [U] The act of organizing: *the organization of a vacation trip.* **2.** [U] The condition of being organized: *a high degree of organization.* **3.** [U] The way in which sthg. is organized: *The class has been studying the organization of corporations.* **4.** [C] A group of people united for some purpose or work: *a political organization.*
or•gan•ize (ôr′gə nīz′) *v.* **or•gan•ized, or•gan•iz•ing, or•gan•iz•es.** —*tr.* **1.** To arrange (sthg.) in an orderly systematic way: *organize one's thoughts before speaking.* **2.** To form or establish (a group) to work together for a particular purpose: *organize a singing group.* **3.** To cause (employees) to form or join a labor union: *The union is trying to organize the farm workers.* —*intr.* To form or join a group, especially a labor union: *The garment workers organized.* —**or′gan•iz′er** *n.*
or•gan•ized (ôr′ gə nīzd′) *adj.* **1.** Functioning within a formal structure: *organized crime.* **2.** Having membership in an organization, especially a union: *organized labor.* **3.** Efficient and methodical: *an organized student.*
or•gasm (ôr′găz′əm) *n.* [C; U] The highest point of sexual excitement.
or•gy (ôr′jē) *n., pl.* **or•gies.** A wild, drunken, and often indecent party or celebration.
o•ri•ent (ôr′ ē ənt *or* ôr′ē ĕnt′) *n.* [U] **Orient.** The countries of Asia, especially of eastern Asia. —*tr.v.* (ôr′ē ĕnt′). **1.** To set or place (sthg.) in a position relative to the points of the compass: *The designer oriented the swimming pool north and south.* **2.** To make (sbdy.) familiar with a new situation: *The book was designed to help orient new students to the campus.* ♦ **orient (oneself).** To locate oneself using a map, compass, or landmarks: *We used the sun to orient ourselves.* —**or′i•en•tate′** *v.*

o·ri·en·tal (ôr′ē ĕn′tl) *adj.* Often **Oriental.** Relating to the countries of the Orient or their peoples or cultures: *oriental art.*

o·ri·en·ta·tion (ôr′ē ĕn tā′shən) *n.* **1.** [U] Location or position with respect to the points of the compass: *the orientation of a rocket in space.* **2.** [U] A person's choices in religion, politics, or sexuality: *discrimination on the basis of sexual orientation.* **3.** [C] Introductory instruction concerning a new situation: *They attended an orientation for incoming students.*

or·i·fice (ôr′ə fĭs *or* ŏr′ə fĭs) *n.* An opening, especially into a cavity: *orifices such as the mouth and ears.*

or·i·gin (ôr′ə jĭn *or* ŏr′ə jĭn) *n.* **1.** [C; U] The source or beginning of sthg.: *the origin of a fire.* **2.** [U] Ancestry: *people of Swedish origin.* **3.** [C] The point at which the x-axis and the y-axis of a graph cross.

o·rig·i·nal (ə rĭj′ə nəl) *adj.* **1.** Existing before all others; first: *The original plan has been changed.* **2.** Fresh and newly created; not copied: *an original idea.* **3.** Frequently producing new ideas: *Einstein was an original thinker.* —*n.* The first form of sthg. from which other varieties are made: *Later models of the car retained many features of the original. Are these copies or the originals?* —**o·rig′i·nal′i·ty** (ə rĭj′ə năl′ ĭ tē) *n.* [U]

o·rig·i·nal·ly (ə rĭj′ ə nə lē) *adv.* **1.** At first; in the beginning: *I originally wanted to study French but decided against it.* **2.** By origin: *I am originally from Africa.*

o·rig·i·nate (ə rĭj′ ə nāt′) *v.* **o·rig·i·nat·ed, o·rig·i·nat·ing, o·rig·i·nates.** —*tr.* To bring (sthg.) into being: *Who originated the practice of giving birthday presents?* —*intr.* To come into existence; begin: *Supermarkets originated in the United States.* —**o·rig′i·na′tor** *n.*

or·na·ment (ôr′nə mənt) *n.* A decorative rather than useful object: *We hung ornaments on the tree.* —*tr.v.* (ôr′ nə mĕnt′). To decorate (sthg.) with ornaments: *You can ornament the tree for the holidays.* —**or′na·men′tal** (ôr′ nə mĕn′tl) *adj.* —**or′na·men·ta′tion** *n.* [U]

or·nate (ôr nāt′) *adj.* With a great many decorations: *an ornate palace.* —**or·nate′ly** *adv.* —**or·nate′ness** *n.* [U]

or·ner·y (ôr′nə rē) *adj.* **or·ner·i·er, or·ner·i·est.** *Informal.* Mean and stubborn: *an ornery old dog.*

or·ni·thol·o·gy (ôr′nə thŏl′ə jē) *n.* [U] The scientific study of birds. —**or′ni·thol′o·gist** *n.*

or·phan (ôr′fən) *n.* A child whose parents are dead. —*tr.v.* To make (a child) an orphan: *Many children were orphaned in the war.*

or·phan·age (ôr′fə nĭj) *n.* A public institu-

tion for the care and protection of children without parents: *The child was brought up in an orphanage.*

or·tho·don·tics (ôr′thə dŏn′tĭks) *n.* [U] (*used with a singular verb*). The dental practice of preventing and correcting abnormal positions of the teeth, often with braces. —**or′tho·don′tic** *adj.* —**or′tho·don′tist** *n.*

or·tho·dox (ôr′thə dŏks′) *adj.* **1.** Following traditional or officially approved beliefs: *orthodox theology.* **2. Orthodox. a.** Relating to the Eastern Orthodox Church. **b.** Relating to Orthodox Judaism. **3.** Following what is commonly accepted, customary, or traditional: *orthodox views on education.* —**or′tho·dox′y** *n.* [U]

or·thog·ra·phy (ôr thŏg′rə fē) *n.* [U] **1.** The correct spelling of words. **2.** The study of spelling. —**or′tho·graph′ic** (ôr′thə grăf′ĭk) *adj.* —**or′tho·graph′i·cal·ly** *adv.*

or·tho·pe·dics (ôr′thə pē′dĭks) *n.* [U] (*used with a singular verb*). The branch of medicine that deals with the treatment of disorders or injuries of the bones, joints, and associated muscles. —**or′tho·pe′dic** *adj.* —**or′tho·pe′dist** *n.*

—ory *suff.* A suffix that means: **1.** Relating to or characterized by: *advisory.* **2.** A place or thing used for a specific purpose: *reformatory.*

os·cil·late (ŏs′ə lāt′) *intr.v.* **os·cil·lat·ed, os·cil·lat·ing, os·cil·lates.** **1.** To swing back and forth with a steady rhythm: *The needle oscillated like the pendulum of a clock.* **2.** To move back and forth between two or more thoughts or courses of action; waver: *He was oscillating between two opinions.* —**os′cil·la′tion** *n.*

os·cil·la·tor (ŏs′ə lā′tər) *n.* A device that produces electromagnetic waves or an alternating current.

os·cil·lo·scope (ə sĭl′ə skōp′) *n.* An electronic instrument that produces a visual display on a screen showing the oscillation of an electrical current.

—ose¹ *suff.* A suffix that forms adjectives and means having; full of: *grandiose; comatose.*

—ose² *suff.* A suffix that means carbohydrate: *fructose.*

—osis *suff.* A suffix that means: **1.** Condition; process: *osmosis.* **2.** Diseased condition: *tuberculosis.*

os·mo·sis (ŏz mō′sĭs *or* ŏs mō′sĭs) *n.* [U] A process in which liquids pass through a membrane until all substances are in equal concentrations on both sides of the membrane. ♦ **by osmosis.** By observation rather than formal study: *He learned to cook by osmosis while watching his father prepare meals.*

os·ten·si·ble (ŏ stĕn′sə bəl) *adj.* Pretend; not actually true: *His ostensible rea-*

ă-cat; ā-pay; âr-care; ä-father; ĕ-get; ē-be; ĭ-sit; ī-nice; îr-here; ŏ-got; ō-go; ô-saw; oi-boy; ou-out; oo-took; oo-boot; ŭ-cut; ûr-word; th-thin; *th*-this; hw-when; zh-vision; ə-about; ɴ-French bon

son for calling was to ask how I was feeling, but his real reason was to ask for money. —**os·ten′si·bly** adv.

os·ten·ta·tious (ŏs′ těn tā′ shəs) adj. Characterized by a showy display of wealth; pretentious: an ostentatious house. —**os′ten·ta′tion** n. [U] —**os′ten·ta′tious·ly** adv.

os·te·o·path (ŏs′tē ə păth′) n. A doctor who practices osteopathy.

os·te·op·a·thy (ŏs′tē ŏp′ə thē) n. [U] A form of medical practice that stresses the manipulation of bones and muscles, along with conventional medical procedures, to treat disease: A doctor of osteopathy is an O.D. rather than an M.D. —**os′te·o·path′ic** adj.

os·te·o·po·ro·sis (ŏs′tē ō pə rō′sĭs) n. [U] A disease in which the bones become thin and easily broken: Many older women suffer from osteoporosis.

os·tra·cism (ŏs′trə sĭz′ əm) n. [U] Refusal to include sbdy. in a group, organization, or society in general: People often conform for fear of ostracism.

os·tra·cize (ŏs′trə sīz′) tr.v. **os·tra·cized, os·tra·ciz·ing, os·tra·ciz·es.** To refuse to include (sbdy.) in a group: Most societies ostracize criminals.

os·trich (ŏs′trĭch or ôs′trĭch) n. A very large African bird with a small head, a long neck, and long legs: Ostriches cannot fly, but they can run very fast.

oth·er (ŭth′ər) adj. **1.** Being the one that remains out of two or more items: Give me the other shoe. My other friends are away on vacation. **2.** Different: Any other answer would have been wrong. **3.** Additional; extra: I have no other shoes. **4.** Opposite or reverse: Get in on the other side of the boat. **5.** Recent: the other day. —n. **1.a.** The one that remains out of two or more: One took a taxi, and the other walked home. **b. others.** The remaining ones of several: How are the others doing now that I'm gone? **2.a.** A different person or thing: One boy after the other stood up. **b. others.** Additional people or things: If these are only a few of the guests, how many others are you expecting? —pron. A different or an additional person or thing: Someone or other will apply for the job. —adv. In another way; otherwise: He will never succeed other than by work. ♦ **every other.** Alternating: We play cards every other Friday night. **on the other hand.** From a different point of view: I like having expensive clothes. On the other hand, I like saving money.

oth·er·wise (ŭth′ər wīz′) adv. **1.** In another way; differently: She thought otherwise. **2.** Under other circumstances: The teacher explained some things I might not have understood otherwise.

ot·ter (ŏt′ər) n. A playful mammal that lives in or near water and has webbed feet and thick dark brown fur.

ouch (ouch) interj. An expression used in response to sudden pain: We heard her shout "Ouch!" when she broke the glass.

ought (ôt) aux.v. **1.** To be required by duty or obligation: We ought to clean up our room. **2.** To be required by good judgment: You ought to wear a raincoat. **3.** To be expected as probable or likely: Tonight ought to be a good night for looking at stars.

USAGE: ought Usually you follow **ought to** with a verb, as in We ought to go soon. Sometimes **ought to** is used without a following verb if the meaning is clear: Should we begin soon? Yes, we ought to.

ounce (ouns) n. **1.** [C] A unit of weight equal to 1/16 pound. See table at **measurement**. **2.** [C] A unit of volume used to measure liquids, equal to 1/16 pint. See table at **measurement**. **3.** [U] A tiny bit: He didn't get an ounce of respect.

our (our) adj. The possessive form of **we**. Of or belonging to us: our friends; our house.

HOMONYMS: our, hour (time unit).

ours (ourz) pron. (used with a singular or plural verb). The one or ones belonging to us: If your car doesn't work, take ours. Ours are on the desk.

our·selves (our sĕlvz′ or är sĕlvz′) pron. **1.a.** Used as a direct object, an indirect object, or an object of a preposition to show that the action of the verb refers back to the subject: We dressed ourselves. We made ourselves some breakfast. **b.** Used to give emphasis: We ourselves made the same discovery. **2.** Our normal or healthy condition: We were soon ourselves again after recovering from the flu.

—**ous** suff. A suffix that means having; full of: joyous; humorous.

WORD BUILDING: —ous The suffix **—ous**, which forms adjectives, has the basic meaning "having, full of, or characterized by." **Adventurous** for example, means "full of or characterized by adventure." Adjectives ending in **—ous** often have related nouns ending in **—ousness** or **—osity: joyousness, generosity.**

oust (oust) tr.v. To eject (sbdy.); remove: Voters ousted the official from office.

oust·er (ous′tər) n. An example of ousting or being ousted: The committee member blamed his ouster on a small group of opponents.

out (out) adv. **1.** Away from inside: The children ran out of the house. **2.** Away from the center: The searchers moved out into the woods around the cabin. **3.** From a container: Pour the soda out. **4.** Away from a usual place: She went out for a minute. **5.** Into or in the open air; outside: They went out to play. It's raining out. **6.** Into view: The moon came *out.* **7.** Without fear; boldly: *Speak out.* **8.** Into the possession of sbdy. else: *The performers gave out free tickets.* **9.** Into disuse or an unfashionable status: *Bell-bottom pants went out a long time ago.* **10.** Not in consideration: *Going to the movies is out because we don't have enough money.* **11.** In or into a nonworking condition: *The lights have gone out. My back went out.* —*adj.* No longer fashionable: *Long hair is out.* —*prep.* **1.** Through: *The bird flew out the window.* **2.** Beyond or outside of: *Out this door is the garage.* **3.** [*of*] See **out of.** —*n.* **1.** A means of escape: *Her lawyer discovered an out for her.* **2.** A play in which a batter or base runner is retired in baseball. —*tr.v.* Informal. To disclose information about (sbdy./ sthg.), especially about sexual preference: *The magazine outed a well-known politician last month.* ♦ **out-and-out.** Complete: *an out-and-out failure; an out-and-out liar.* **out-of-bounds.** Beyond the usual limits: *He kicked the ball out-of-bounds.* **out-of-date.** Old-fashioned; no longer useful: *an out-of-date computer.* **out of the closet.** Open about one's homosexuality: *In recent years, many gays and lesbians have decided to come out of the closet.* **out-of-the-way.** Away from an area usually visited: *an out-of-the-way place to have dinner.* **out—** *pref.* A prefix that means in a way that is better or greater: *outdistance; outsmart.*

WORD BUILDING: out— There are many words in English beginning with **out—**. In words such as **outbuilding, outcast, outpour,** and **outstanding, out—** has the same meaning as the adverb **out.** So an **outbuilding** is "a structure that is outside of a main building," and one who is **outstanding** "stands out or above the others." But in other cases **out—** takes on the sense of doing better or being greater, as in **outdo, outnumber,** and **outrun.** Although **out—** can attach to nouns, adjectives, or verbs to form other nouns, adjectives, or verbs, it most frequently attaches to verbs: **outdance, outcook, outride, outsing.**

---

out•age (ou′tĭj) *n.* An interruption in an operation, such as electric power: *The storm caused a power outage.*

out•bound (out′bound′) *adj.* Going away from a place: *the outbound train.*

out•break (out′brāk′) *n.* A sudden increase: *an outbreak of disease.*

out•burst (out′bûrst′) *n.* Sudden violent activity or emotion: *an outburst of laughter.*

out•cast (out′kăst′) *n.* A person who has been excluded from a society or group: *He was treated like an outcast even though he was found not guilty.*

out•class (out klăs′) *tr.v.* To surpass (sbdy.)

so as to be on a higher level: *She completely outclassed the other swimmers.*

out•come (out′kŭm′) *n.* A final result: *the outcome of an election.*

out•cry (out′krī′) *n., pl.* **out•cries. 1.** A loud cry. **2.** A strong protest: *The rise in prices produced a public outcry.*

out•dat•ed (out dā′tĭd) *adj.* Out-of-date; old-fashioned: *outdated methods.*

out•did (out dĭd′) *v.* Past tense of **outdo.**

out•dis•tance (out dĭs′təns) *tr.v.* **out•dis•tanced, out•dis•tanc•ing, out•dis•tanc•es. 1.** To run faster than (sbdy.), as in a long-distance race. **2.** To perform better than (sbdy.) by a wide margin: *The senator outdistanced her opponent.*

out•do (out dōō′) *tr.v.* **out•did** (out dĭd′), **out•done** (out dŭn′), **out•do•ing, out•does** (out dŭz′). To do better than (sbdy.): *Our team outdid theirs because we had practiced more.*

out•door (out′dôr′) *adj.* Located in, done in, or suitable for the outdoors: *an outdoor game; outdoor clothing.*

out•doors (out dôrz′) *adv.* In or into the open; outside: *We like to eat outdoors during the summer.* —*n.* [U] An area outside a house or building in the open air: *She loves to be in the outdoors.*

out•er (ou′tər) *adj.* **1.** Located on the outside; external: *outer walls.* **2.** Farther from the center: *the outer limits of the universe.*

out•er•most (ou′tər mōst′) *adj.* Most distant from the center: *the outermost reaches of the solar system.*

outer space *n.* [U] Any region of space beyond Earth: *Have you ever dreamed of traveling in outer space?*

out•field (out′fēld′) *n.* The playing area inside of the baselines in baseball beyond the infield. —**out′field′er** *n.*

out•fit (out′fĭt′) *n.* **1.** A set of clothing and accessories that go together: *She wore a dark blue outfit.* **2.** A military unit, business organization, or other association: *an army outfit.* —*tr.v.* **out•fit•ted, out•fit•ting, out•fits.** To provide (sbdy./sthg.) with the necessary equipment or clothing: *outfit a ship for a long trip.* —**out′fit′ter** *n.*

out•fox (out fŏks′) *tr.v.* To be smarter than (an opponent): *outfox the competition.*

out•go•ing (out′gō′ĭng) *adj.* **1.** Leaving; departing: *an outgoing ship.* **2.** Friendly; sociable: *an outgoing person.*

out•grow (out grō′) *tr.v.* **out•grew** (out grōō′), **out•grown** (out grōn′), **out•grow•ing, out•grows. 1.** To grow too large for (sthg.): *He outgrew his shoes.* **2.** To discard (sthg.) in the course of growing up or maturing: *She outgrew stuffed animals.*

ă-cat; ā-pay; âr-care; ä-father; ĕ-get; ē-be; ĭ-sit; ī-nice; îr-here; ŏ-got; ō-go; ô-saw; oi-boy; ou-out; ōō-took; ōō-boot; ŭ-cut; ûr-word; th-thin; *th*-this; hw-when; zh-vision; ə-about; N-French bon

out·house (out'hous') *n.* A small structure, separate from a main building, located over a hole and used as a toilet. Outhouses have no plumbing.

out·ing (ou'tĭng) *n.* A short trip for pleasure; an excursion: *an outing to the zoo.*

out·land·ish (out lăn'dĭsh) *adj.* Unconventional; strange: *outlandish clothes.*

out·last (out lăst') *tr.v.* To continue working longer than (sbdy./sthg.): *Do those batteries really outlast the other brands?*

out·law (out'lô') *n.* A person who repeatedly disobeys the law; a criminal. —*tr.v.* To declare (sthg.) illegal: *The state outlawed the sale of fireworks.*

out·lay (out'lā') *n.* The amount of money spent: *The total outlay was $50.*

out·let (out'lĕt') *n.* **1.** A passage or opening for letting sthg. out; a vent. **2.** A means of releasing energies: *Music was an outlet for her emotions.* **3.** A store that sells goods, especially bargains: *a clothing outlet.* **4.** An electric receptacle connected to a power line and equipped with a socket for a plug: *Plug the lamp into that outlet.*

out·line (out'līn') *n.* **1.** A line forming the outer edge of sthg. **2.** A drawing that consists of only the outer edge of an object: *Trace an outline of California from the map.* **3.** A short summary, usually arranged point by point: *an outline for a composition.* —*tr.v.* **out·lined, out·lin·ing, out·lines. 1.** To draw the outline of (sthg.): *The artist outlined the picture before drawing in the details.* **2.** To give the main points of (sthg.); summarize: *The team outlined a plan.*

out·live (out lĭv') *tr.v.* **out·lived, out·liv·ing, out·lives.** To live or last longer than (sbdy.): *Women tend to outlive men.*

out·look (out'lŏŏk') *n.* **1.** [C] A point of view; an attitude: *a happy outlook on life.* **2.** [U] The probable result; an expectation: *The outlook for new businesses is good.* **3.** [C] A place from which sthg. can be viewed: *a photograph taken from an outlook in the mountains.*

out·ly·ing (out'lī'ĭng) *adj.* Outside the limits or boundaries of a certain area: *Factories are being built in the outlying suburbs.*

out·ma·neu·ver (out'mə nōō' vər) *tr.v.* **1.** To overcome (sbdy./sthg.) by more careful planning or action: *The chess player outmaneuvered all opponents.* **2.** To excel in moving easily: *The car outmaneuvers all others of its size.*

out·mod·ed (out mō'dĭd) *adj.* **1.** No longer in fashion: *an outmoded style of dress.* **2.** No longer practical: *outmoded methods of transportation.*

out·num·ber (out nŭm'bər) *tr.v.* To be more numerous than (sbdy./sthg.); exceed in number: *Girls outnumber boys two to one in that class.*

out of *prep.* **1.a.** From within to the outside of:

The driver got out of the car. **b.** From a certain condition: *The baby came out of a deep sleep.* **c.** From a material or cause: *made out of wood.* **2.a.** Beyond the limits of: *The car drove out of view.* **b.** Away from what is expected or usual: *I'm out of practice.* **3.** From among: *five out of six votes.* **4.** In or into a state of being without: *We've run out of paint.*

out·pa·tient (out'pā'shənt) *n.* A person who receives treatment at a hospital or clinic without staying overnight: *You can have this surgery as an outpatient.*

out·play (out plā') *tr.v.* To surpass (one's opponent) in playing a game: *The basketball team outplayed the opponents.*

out·post (out'pōst') *n.* **1.** A station occupied by a group of military personnel far from the main station. **2.** A remote settlement: *an outpost in the desert.*

out·pour·ing (out'pôr'ĭng) *n. (usually singular).* **1.** The act of giving freely: *an outpouring of good wishes for the newly married couple.* **2.** Something that comes out: *an outpouring of lava from the volcano.*

out·put (out'pŏŏt') *n.* [U] **1.** An amount of sthg. produced, especially during a given period of time: *the output of a factory.* **2.a.** The energy, power, or work produced by a system or device: *the output of an engine; the output of a loudspeaker.* **b.** The information that a computer produces: *computer output.*

out·rage (out'rāj') *n.* **1.** [C] An extremely vicious or wicked act: *The attack was clearly an outrage.* **2.** [U] Great anger aroused by such an act: *public outrage over the murder.* —*tr.v.* **out·raged, out·rag·ing, out·rag·es. 1.** To offend (sbdy.) deeply: *Such an act outrages everyone's sense of justice.* **2.** To make (sbdy.) extremely angry or resentful: *We were outraged by his behavior.*

out·ra·geous (out rā'jəs) *adj.* Exceeding all bounds of what is right or proper: *an outrageous crime; outrageous prices.* —**out·ra'geous·ly** *adv.*

out·ran (out răn') *v.* Past tense of **outrun.**

out·rank (out răngk') *tr.v.* To rank above (sbdy.): *A president outranks a vice president.*

out·right (out'rīt' *or* out'rīt') *adv.* **1.** Completely; unconditionally: *The sellers rejected her offer outright.* **2.** Openly; straight to one's face: *I decided to tell him the news outright.* —*adj.* (out'rīt'). Complete; unconditional: *an outright gift; an outright lie.*

out·run (out rŭn') *tr.v.* **out·ran** (out răn'), **out·run, out·run·ning, out·runs. 1.** To run faster than (sbdy./sthg.): *The zebra outran the attacking lion.* **2.** To escape from (sbdy./sthg.); elude: *They outran three policemen.* **3.** To go beyond (sthg.); exceed: *Expenses are outrunning those of last year.*

out·sell (out sĕl') *tr.v.* **out·sold** (out sōld'), **out·sell·ing, out·sells. 1.** To sell faster or better than (sthg.): *The new model car has outsold all the others.* **2.** To sell more than (sbdy.): *That store consistently outsells the others.*

out·set (out'sĕt') *n.* [U] The beginning; the start: *Everyone knew something was wrong from the outset.*

out·shine (out shīn') *tr.v.* **out·shone** (out shōn'), **out·shin·ing, out·shines. 1.** To shine brighter than (sthg.): *The flashlight outshines the candle.* **2.** To be or appear better than (sbdy.): *She outshines the other players.*

out·side (out sīd' *or* out' sīd') *n.* **1.** The outer surface; exterior: *the outside of a house.* **2.** The external or surface appearance: *On the outside, it's very attractive.* —*adj.* **1.** External; outer: *an outside door.* **2.** Not belonging to or originating in a certain group: *problems caused by outside influences.* **3.** Beyond the limits of one's regular occupation: *His outside interests include music and photography.* **4.** Extreme: *The outside estimate on the car repair is $2,000.* **5.** Slight; remote: *an outside possibility.* —*adv.* On or to the external side: *Try to stay outside.* —*prep.* **1.** On or to the outer side of: *We stood outside the gate.* **2.** Beyond the limits of: *They were living outside the country.* **3.** Except: *We have no information outside the figures already given.* ◆ **at the outside.** At the most: *We'll be gone a week at the outside.*

outside of *prep.* Outside: *Outside of my window a bird is building a nest.*

out·sid·er (out sī'dər) *n.* A person who is not part of a certain group or activity: *Outsiders bought the business.*

out·skirts (out'skûrts') *pl.n.* The regions away from a central district; the surrounding areas: *We live on the outskirts of town.*

out·smart (out smärt') *tr.v.* To gain the advantage over (sbdy.) by cleverness; outwit: *Our company outsmarted the competition and won the contract.*

out·sold (out sōld') *v.* Past tense of **outsell.**

out·source (out'sôrs') *tr.v.* **out·sourced, out·sourc·ing, out·sources.** To purchase (essential services) from another company: *We are outsourcing most of our accounting.*

out·spo·ken (out spō'kən) *adj.* Frank and bold in speech: *an outspoken politician.* —**out·spo'ken·ly** *adv.* —**out·spo'ken·ness** *n.* [U]

out·stand·ing (out stăn'dĭng *or* out'-stăn'dĭng) *adj.* **1.** Unusually good; extraordinary: *one of the outstanding artists of our time; an outstanding example of modern architecture.* **2.** Not settled or resolved: *outstanding debts.* —**out·stand'ing·ly** *adv.*

out·strip (out strĭp') *tr.v.* **out·stripped, out·strip·ping, out·strips. 1.** To leave

(sbdy.) behind; outrun. **2.** To surpass (sthg.): *The sale of small cars soon outstripped that of large ones.*

out·ward (out'wərd) *adj.* **1.** Located on or moving toward the outside: *energy moving outward from the sun.* **2.** Visible on the surface: *an outward appearance of calm.* —*adv.* Also **outwards.** Away from the center: *Stand in a circle and face outward.* —**out'-ward·ness** *n.* [U]

out·ward·ly (out'wərd lē) *adv.* In appearance: *He seemed outwardly healthy.*

out·weigh (out wā') *tr.v.* **1.** To weigh more than (sbdy./sthg.): *That player outweighs everyone on the team.* **2.** To be of greater importance than (sthg.): *an objection that outweighs all others.*

out·wit (out wĭt') *tr.v.* **out·wit·ted, out·wit·ting, out·wits.** To prevail over (sbdy.) by using intelligence: *She outwitted her boss.*

out·work (out wûrk') *tr.v.* To work better or faster than (sbdy.): *The clerk outworks everyone else in the office.*

o·val (ō'vəl) *adj.* Resembling an egg in shape: *an oval face; an oval picture frame.* —*n.* An oval figure, form, or shape: *My sister's face is an oval.*

o·var·i·an (ō vâr'ē ən) *adj.* Relating to an ovary: *ovarian cancer.*

o·va·ry (ō'və rē) *n., pl.* **o·va·ries. 1.** Either of the two reproductive glands of female animals that produce egg cells. **2.** A plant part in which the seeds are formed.

o·va·tion (ō vā'shən) *n.* A loud and enthusiastic display of approval, usually in the form of applause: *The audience gave the singer a standing ovation.*

ov·en (ŭv'ən) *n.* An enclosed chamber used for baking, heating, or drying objects: *Most cakes are baked in a 350° oven.*

o·ver (ō'vər) *prep.* **1.** Above; higher than: *a sign over the door.* **2.** Above and across: *Hop over the fence.* **3.** To the other side of: *I walked over the bridge.* **4.** On the other side of: *a town over the border.* **5.** Upon the surface of: *a coat of varnish over the wood.* **6.** Through the extent of: *I read over the report.* **7.** Throughout or during: *over the years.* **8.** Through the medium of: *They talked over the telephone.* **9.** So as to cover: *She put a shawl over her shoulders.* **10.** In excess of; more than: *over ten miles.* **11.** In superiority to: *The team won a victory over the rivals.* **12.** On account of or with reference to: *an argument over methods.* —*adv.* **1.** Above the top: *The boys climbed the fence and looked over.* **2.a.** Across to another or opposite side: *They are flying over to Europe.* **b.** Across the edge or brim: *The coffee spilled over.* **3.** To another place: *Move the chair over here.* **4.** To one's home or office: *Let's invite them over.* **5.** To a different opinion: *After a long talk, I won her over.* **6.** To a different person, condition, or title: *The man signed the land over to his children.* **7.** So as to be completely covered: *The river froze over.* **8.** From beginning to end; through: *He is thinking it over.* **9.a.** From an upright position: *The girl knocked the vase over.* **b.** From an upward to an inverted or reversed position: *Turn the book over.* **10.** Again: *He had to do his homework over.* **11.** In addition or excess: *I have a dollar left over.* —*adj.* In excess: *My guess was $50 over.* ◆ **all over. 1.** Everywhere: *We looked all over for the cat.* **2.** Completely finished: *The party was all over by 11:00.* **over and over.** Many times without stopping: *They played the song over and over.* **over the counter.** Referring to medicines that are sold without a prescription: *Aspirin and cold remedies are over the counter drugs.* **over the hill.** *Informal.* Too old to do sthg.: *The swimmer was already over the hill at 22.*

o•ver•a•chiev•er (ō′vər ə chē′vər) *n.* A person who performs better than is expected: *an overachiever who speaks five languages and has three degrees.* —**o′ver•a•chieve′** *v.*

o•ver•ac•tive (ō′vər ăk′tĭv) *adj.* Active to an excessive or abnormal degree: *an overactive imagination.*

o•ver•all (o′vər ol′) *adj.* **1.** Including everything; total: *the overall cost of the project.* **2.** Viewed as a whole; general: *the overall effect created by the new furniture.*

o•ver•alls (ō′vər ôlz′) *pl.n.* Loose-fitting pants with straps and a top part that covers the chest: *Overalls are often worn over regular clothes to protect them from dirt.*

o•ver•ate (ō′vər āt′) *v.* Past tense of **overeat.**

o•ver•bear•ing (ō′vər-bâr′ĭng) *adj.* Arrogant and domineering in manner: *an overbearing person.*

overalls

o•ver•board (ō′vər-bôrd′) *adv.* Over the side of a boat: *The sailor fell overboard.* ◆ **go overboard.** To go to extremes: *Some grandparents go overboard on gifts for their grandchildren.*

o•ver•book (ō′vər book′) *tr.v.* To promise or sell more of (sthg.) than is available: *Airlines often overbook flights. The doctor is overbooked.*

o•ver•bur•den (ō′vər bûr′dn) *tr.v.* To give (sbdy.) too much work, care, or responsibility: *She has been overburdened by the responsibilities of work and family.*

o•ver•came (ō′vər kām′) *v.* Past tense of **overcome.**

o•ver•cast (ō′vər kăst′) *adj.* **1.** Covered over with clouds or mist; cloudy: *an overcast day.* **2.** Gloomy; dark: *an overcast look on her face.* —*n.* [U] A covering of mist or clouds: *We could hardly see through the overcast.*

o•ver•charge (ō′vər chärj′) *tr.v.* **o•ver•charged, o•ver•charg•ing, o•ver•charg•es.** To charge (sbdy.) too high a price for sthg.: *The clerk overcharged me on several items.* —*n.* (ō′vər chärj′). An excessive price or charge: *a three-dollar overcharge.*

o•ver•coat (ō′vər kōt′) *n.* A heavy coat worn over regular clothing in cold weather: *a winter overcoat.*

o•ver•come (ō′vər kŭm′) *v.* **o•ver•came** (ō′vər kām′), **o•ver•come, o•ver•com•ing, o•ver•comes.** —*tr.* **1.** To fight successfully against (sthg.): *She worked hard to overcome her problem.* **2.** To defeat (sbdy.) in a conflict or contest: *The home team overcame a powerful rival.* **3.** To affect (sbdy.) deeply; overpower: *Fear overcame him. Several firefighters were overcome by smoke.* —*intr.* To be victorious: *We shall overcome.*

o•ver•crowd (ō′vər kroud′) *tr.v.* To cause (sthg.) to be too full of people or things: *Eight people will overcrowd my car.*

o•ver•do (ō′vər dōō′) *tr.v.* **o•ver•did** (ō′vər dĭd′), **o•ver•done** (ō′vər dŭn′), **o•ver•do•ing, o•ver•does** (ō′vər dŭz′). **1.** To do or use (sthg.) to excess: *Don't overdo the studying or you will be too tired to take the exam. You overdid the salt.* **2.** To cook (sthg.) too much: *We overdid the meat.*

HOMONYMS: overdo, overdue (unpaid).

o•ver•dose (ō′vər dōs′) *n.* An excessively large dose, as of a drug: *a drug overdose.* —*intr.v.* (ō′vər dōs′). **o•ver•dosed, o•ver•dos•ing, o•ver•dos•es.** To take an overdose: *The man overdosed on drugs.*

o•ver•draft (ō′vər drăft′) *n.* **1.** The act of overdrawing an account: *an overdraft of $60 on a checking account.* **2.** The amount overdrawn: *a $30 overdraft.*

o•ver•draw (ō′vər drô′) *tr.v.* **o•ver•drew** (ō′vər drōō′), **o•ver•drawn** (ō′vər drôn′), **o•ver•draw•ing, o•ver•draws.** To take out more money than is available from (an account at a bank): *He overdrew his checking account twice last month.*

o•ver•dress (ō′vər drĕs′) *intr.v.* To dress in too formal or fancy a way for the occasion: *Don't overdress for the party.*

o•ver•drive (ō′vər drĭv′) *n.* [U] **1.** A gear in a motor vehicle that allows the driver to use less gas while driving at high speed. **2.** A state of increased activity: *He goes into overdrive when he has too much work.*

o•ver•due (ō′vər dōō′) *adj.* **1.** Unpaid after being due: *an overdue bill.* **2.** Later than scheduled or expected: *an overdue train.*

HOMONYMS: overdue, overdo (do to excess).

o·ver·eat (ō′vər ēt′) *intr.v.* **o·ver·ate** (ō′vər āt′), **o·ver·eat·en** (ō′vər ēt′n), **o·ver·eat·ing, o·ver·eats.** To eat too much: *A lot of people overeat during holidays.*

o·ver·es·ti·mate (ō′vər ĕs′tə māt′) *tr.v.* **o·ver·es·ti·mat·ed, o·ver·es·ti·mat·ing, o·ver·es·ti·mates. 1.** To rate or estimate (sthg.) too highly: *The mechanic overestimated the cost of repairing the car.* **2.** To value (sbdy./sthg.) too highly: *He overestimated his own abilities.*

o·ver·ex·pose (ō′vər ĭk spōz′) *tr.v.* **o·ver·ex·posed, o·ver·ex·pos·ing, o·ver·ex·pos·es. 1.** To display or expose (sbdy./sthg.) too much: *overexpose oneself to the sun.* **2.** To expose (a photographic film) too long. **—o′ver·ex·po′sure** *n.* [U]

o·ver·flow (ō′vər flō′) *v.* *—intr.* **1.** To run over the top or edge: *The sink overflowed.* **2.** To be filled beyond capacity: *The room was overflowing with people.* *—tr.* **1.** To flow over (the top or edge): *The river overflows its banks every year.* **2.** To fill (sthg.) beyond capacity: *The crowd overflowed the theater.* *—n.* (ō′vər flō′). **1.** [C] The act of overflowing. **2.** [U] An amount that overflows.

o·ver·grow (ō′vər grō′) *v.* **o·ver·grew** (ō′vər grōō′), **o·ver·grown** (ō′vər grōn′), **o·ver·grow·ing, o·ver·grows.** *—tr.* To cover (sthg.) over with vegetation: *The bushes overgrew the sidewalk.* *—intr.* To grow too much or larger than normal.

o·ver·growth (ō′vər grōth′) *n.* [U] Plants that grow over or upon sthg.: *an overgrowth of ivy on the house.*

o·ver·haul (ō′vər hôl′ *or* ō′vər hôl′) *tr.v.* To inspect (sthg.) and then repair or make changes: *The mechanic overhauled the engine.* *—n.* (ō′vər hôl′). The act or an example of overhauling: *a complete overhaul of an aircraft.*

o·ver·head (ō′vər hĕd′) *adj.* Located above the level of the head: *an overhead light.* *—n.* [U] The operating expenses of a business, such as rent, insurance, taxes, and electricity: *How much overhead does your business have?* *—adv.* (ō′vər hĕd′). Above one's head: *birds flying overhead.*

o·ver·hear (ō′vər hîr′) *tr.v.* **o·ver·heard** (ō′vər hûrd′), **o·ver·hear·ing, o·ver·hears.** To hear (sbdy./sthg.) accidentally: *She overheard her friends planning the surprise party.*

o·ver·heat (ō′vər hēt′) *tr. & intr.v.* To make or become too hot: *The furnace overheated the room. The engine overheated.*

o·ver·joyed (ō′vər joid′) *adj.* Extremely happy or delighted: *We were overjoyed to hear about the new baby.*

o·ver·kill (ō′vər kĭl′) *n.* [U] An amount in excess of what is necessary or appropriate: *Studying seven hours for the exam was overkill.*

o·ver·land (ō′vər lănd′ *or* ō′vər lənd) *adv. & adj.* Over or across land: *He traveled overland. We made an overland journey.*

o·ver·lap (ō′vər lăp′) *v.* **o·ver·lapped, o·ver·lap·ping, o·ver·laps.** *—tr.* **1.** To cover part of (sthg.): *The shingles overlap one another.* **2.** To have an area in common with (sthg.): *My vacation overlaps his.* *—intr.* **1.** To extend over part of another thing: *The scales of a fish overlap, forming a protective covering.* **2.** To have some part in common with sthg. else: *Mathematics and science overlap.* *—n.* (ō′vər lăp′). A part that overlaps or an example of overlapping: *The overlap in our schedules means we can eat lunch together.*

o·ver·load (ō′vər lōd′) *tr.v.* To put too large a load in or on (sthg.): *overload a bridge; overload an electric circuit.* *—n.* (ō′vər lōd′). An excessively large load.

o·ver·look (ō′vər lŏŏk′) *tr.v.* **1.** To provide a view of (sthg.): *The restaurant overlooks the bay.* **2.** To fail to notice or consider (sthg.): *You overlooked an important detail.* **3.** To ignore (sthg.) deliberately; disregard: *I overlooked her rude remark and kept on studying.* *—n.* (ō′vər lŏŏk′). A high place that provides a view of sthg.: *The bus stopped at the overlook so that the tourists could take pictures.*

o·ver·ly (ō′vər lē) *adv.* Excessively: *an overly long movie.*

o·ver·night (ō′vər nīt′) *adj.* **1.** Lasting for a night: *an overnight trip.* **2.** For use over a single night: *an overnight bag.* **3.** Happening as if in a single night; sudden: *an overnight success.* *—adv.* (ō′vər nīt′). **1.** During or for the length of a night: *Soak the dried beans overnight.* **2.** As if in one night; suddenly: *Our son grew six inches overnight.*

o·ver·pass (ō′vər păs′) *n.* A roadway or bridge that crosses above another roadway: *The car hit the overpass.*

o·ver·pay (ō′vər pā′) *v.* **o·ver·paid** (ō′vər-pād′), **o·ver·pay·ing, o·ver·pays.** *—tr.* To pay (sbdy.) too much: *I hope we didn't overpay them.* *—intr.* To pay too much: *You seem to have overpaid for your car.* **—o′ver·pay′ment** *n.*

o·ver·pop·u·late (ō′vər pŏp′yə lāt′) *tr.v.* **o·ver·pop·u·lat·ed, o·ver·pop·u·lat·ing, o·ver·pop·u·lates.** To fill (an area) with too many people or animals: *That park is overpopulated with deer.* **—o′ver·pop′-u·la′tion** *n.* [U]

o·ver·pow·er (ō′vər pou′ər) *tr.v.* **1.** To defeat or conquer (sbdy.) by superior force: *Police overpowered the thief.* **2.** To affect (sbdy.) strongly; overwhelm: *The heat over-*

powered the children, and they had to leave the beach.

o·ver·pow·er·ing (ō'vər pou'ər ĭng) *adj.* So strong as to be unbearable: *an overpowering smell.*

o·ver·pro·duce (ō'vər prə dōōs') *tr.v.* **o·ver·pro·duced, o·ver·pro·duc·ing, o·ver·pro·duc·es.** To produce too much or too many of (sthg.): *The factory overproduced that model of truck.* —**o'ver·pro·duc'tion** (ō'vər prə dŭk'shən) *n.* [U]

o·ver·rate (ō'vər rāt') *tr.v.* **o·ver·rat·ed, o·ver·rat·ing, o·ver·rates.** To rate (sthg.) too highly: *That movie is overrated; it wasn't very good.*

o·ver·ride (ō'vər rīd') *tr.v.* **o·ver·rode** (ō'vər rōd'), **o·ver·rid·den** (ō'vər rĭd'n), **o·ver·rid·ing, o·ver·rides. 1.** To be more important than (sthg.): *His concern for his son's safety overrode his fear of water.* **2.** To refuse to accept (sthg.): *Congress overrode the President's veto.* —*n.* A veto.

o·ver·rule (ō'vər rōōl') *tr.v.* **o·ver·ruled, o·ver·rul·ing, o·ver·rules.** To decide or rule against (sbdy./sthg.): *The judge overruled the objection of the lawyer. Her suggestion was to go out to eat, but she was overruled.*

o·ver·run (ō'vər rŭn') *tr.v.* **o·ver·ran** (ō'vər răn'), **o·ver·run, o·ver·run·ning, o·ver·runs. 1.** To invade and occupy (a place): *The enemy army overran the city.* **2.** To spread over and destroy (sthg.): *Weeds overran the garden.* **3.** To overflow (sthg.): *The river overran its banks.* **4.** To run or extend beyond (sthg.): *The plane overran the runway.*

o·ver·seas (ō'vər sēz' *or* ō'vər sēz') *adv.* Across the sea; abroad: *He was sent overseas.* —*adj.* From or situated across the sea: *We took an overseas flight to Asia.*

o·ver·see (ō'vər sē') *tr.v.* **o·ver·saw** (ō'vər sô'), **o·ver·seen** (ō'vər sēn'), **o·ver·see·ing, o·ver·sees.** To direct (sthg.); supervise: *The architect oversaw the contruction.* —**o'ver·se'er** *n.*

o·ver·shad·ow (ō'vər shăd'ō) *tr.v.* To make (sthg.) seem unimportant: *His intelligence overshadows that of his colleagues.*

o·ver·shoot (ō'vər shōōt') *tr.v.* **o·ver·shot** (ō'vər shŏt'), **o·ver·shoot·ing, o·ver·shoots. 1.** To shoot over or beyond (sthg.): *overshoot a target.* **2.** To fly beyond or past (sthg.): *The plane overshot the runway.*

o·ver·sight (ō'vər sīt') *n.* **1.** [C] An accidental omission or mistake: *Not inviting you to the party must have been an oversight.* **2.** [U] The act of overseeing: *Oversight of the project was his responsibility.*

o·ver·sleep (ō'vər slēp') *intr.v.* **o·ver·slept** (ō'vər slĕpt'), **o·ver·sleep·ing, o·ver·sleeps.** To sleep longer than planned: *I overslept and missed my exam.*

o·ver·state (ō'vər stāt') *tr.v.* **o·ver·**

stat·ed, o·ver·stat·ing, o·ver·states. To state (sthg.) too strongly; exaggerate: *Don't overstate the problem.* —**o'ver·state'ment** *n.*

o·ver·stay (ō'vər stā') *tr.v.* To stay past (a proper time): *When they started yawning, we realized we had overstayed our welcome.*

o·ver·step (ō'vər stĕp') *tr.v.* **o·ver·stepped, o·ver·step·ping, o·ver·steps.** To go beyond (a limit or bound): *She overstepped the rules.*

o·ver·stock (ō'vər stŏk') *tr.v.* To stock (a store) with more of sthg. than is necessary or desirable: *They overstocked the store with black socks and couldn't sell them all.* —*n.* (ō'vər stŏk'). [C; U] An excessive supply.

o·vert (ō vûrt' *or* ō'vûrt') *adj.* Not secret or hidden; open: *an overt act of war.* —**o·vert'ly** *adv.*

o·ver·take (ō'vər tāk') *tr.v.* **o·ver·took** (ō'vər tōōk'), **o·ver·tak·en** (ō'vər tā'kən), **o·ver·tak·ing, o·ver·takes. 1.** To come upon and pass (sbdy./sthg.): *We overtook the other hikers. The car overtook him on the road.* **2.** To come upon (sbdy./sthg.) unexpectedly: *A violent storm overtook him on the way to Chicago.*

o·ver·throw (ō'vər thrō') *tr.v.* **o·ver·threw** (ō'vər thrōō'), **o·ver·thrown** (ō'vər thrōn'), **o·ver·throw·ing, o·ver·throws.** To cause the defeat or destruction of (a government). *The generals overthrew the government.* —*n.* (ō'vər thrō'). The defeat or destruction of a government.

o·ver·time (ō'vər tīm') *n.* [U] **1.** Time worked in addition to regular working hours: *The employees have been working a lot of overtime.* **2.** Payment for this additional time worked: *She earns an hourly wage plus overtime.* **3.** A period in a sports contest added after the set time limit has passed: *The game went into overtime.* —*adv.* Beyond an established time limit, such as working hours: *We'll have to work overtime.*

o·ver·tone (ō'vər tōn') *n.* An idea that is suggested but not stated clearly: *overtones of anger in his voice.*

o·ver·ture (ō'vər chŏŏr') *n.* **1.** An instrumental composition: *The 1812 Overture is my favorite.* **2.** An offer or a proposal showing readiness to discuss sthg.: *making peace overtures.*

o·ver·turn (ō'vər tûrn') *v.* —*tr.* **1.** To turn (sthg.) over: *The wave overturned the boat.* **2.** To defeat (sbdy./sthg.): *The court overturned the law.* —*intr.* To turn over: *The car overturned.*

o·ver·use (ō'vər yōōz') *tr.v.* **o·ver·used, o·ver·us·ing, o·ver·us·es.** To use (sthg.) to excess: *Try not to overuse the passive voice in your writing.* —*n.* (ō'vər yōōs). [U] Too much or excessive use: *overuse of credit cards.*

o·ver·view (ō'vər vyōō') *n.* A general picture; a summary: *an overview of the plan.*

o·ver·weight (ō'vər wāt') *adj.* Weighing too much: *an overweight child; overweight packages.*

o·ver·whelm (ō'vər wĕlm') *tr.v.* **1.** To completely overpower (sbdy./sthg.): *The powerful army overwhelmed the enemy. The painting overwhelms the room.* **2.** To affect (sbdy.) deeply: *Sadness overwhelmed me.*

o·ver·whelm·ing (ō'vər wĕl' mĭng) *adj.* Overpowering in effect or strength: *an overwhelming problem.* —**o'ver·whelm'ing·ly** *adv.*

o·ver·work (ō'vər wûrk') *tr.v.* To cause (sbdy./sthg.) to work too hard: *The manager overworks her.* —*n.* (ō'vər wûrk'). [U] Too much work: *She is suffering from overwork.*

o·ver·wrought (ō'vər rôt') *adj.* Nervous or agitated: *The news left her overwrought.*

o·vu·late (ō'vyə lāt' *or* ŏv'yə lāt') *intr.v.* **o·vu·lat·ed, o·vu·lat·ing, o·vu·lates.** To produce or discharge an egg cell: *Women ovulate on average every 28 days.* —**o'vu·la'tion** *n.* [U]

o·vum (ō'vəm) *n., pl.* **o·va** (ō'və). A female reproductive cell; an egg: *a fertilized ovum.*

owe (ō) *tr.v.* **owed, ow·ing, owes. 1.** To have to pay (sbdy./sthg.): *He owes five dollars for the meal. We owe the plumber for fixing the pipe.* **2.** To have to give (sthg.): *We owe them an apology.* **3.** To describe the source of (sthg.): *She owes her good health to exercise.*

HOMONYMS: owe, O (letter), **oh** (exclamation).

ow·ing (ō'ĭng) *adj.* Still to be paid; owed: *the amount still owing.*

owing to *prep.* Because of; on account of: *Owing to the weather, we held the party indoors.*

owl (oul) *n.* A bird that usually flies at night and has a large head, large eyes, and a flat round face.

owl
Snowy owl

own (ōn) *adj.* Belonging to oneself: *Jim's own book; my own home.* —*n.* [U] Something that belongs to one: *He built the machine but the idea was my own.* —*tr.v.* To have or possess (sthg.): *I own a car.* ◆ **be on (one's) own.** To live away from one's family: *She's been on her own since she was 17.* **hold (one's) own.** To succeed in spite of difficulty: *She can hold her own in arguments.* **of (one's) own.** Belonging completely to oneself: *He wants a room of his own.* **on (one's) own.** Independently: *I found the answer on my own.* **own up.** *intr.v.* To admit: *You should own up to your mistake.* —**own'er** *n.*

own·er·ship (ō'nər shĭp') *n.* [U] The condition of being an owner; the legal right to possess sthg.: *home ownership.*

ox (ŏks) *n., pl.* **ox·en** (ŏk'sən). A large castrated male of domestic cattle used for heavy work.

ox·i·da·tion (ŏk'sĭ dā'shən) *n.* [U] **1.** The chemical combination of a substance with oxygen. **2.** A chemical reaction in which the atoms of an element lose electrons, thus undergoing an increase in valence.

ox·ide (ŏk'sīd') *n.* [C; U] A compound of oxygen and another element.

ox·i·dize (ŏk'sĭ dīz') *v.* **ox·i·dized, ox·i·diz·ing, ox·i·diz·es.** —*tr.* **1.** To combine (sthg.) with oxygen; make into an oxide. **2.** To coat (sthg.) with oxide: *Air oxidizes the surface of aluminum.* —*intr.* To become oxidized: *The metal oxidized.* —**ox'i·diz'er** *n.*

ox·y·gen (ŏk'sĭ jən) *n.* [U] *Symbol* **O** A colorless, odorless gas. This element occurs in many compounds, such as water: *Animals and plants cannot live without oxygen.* Atomic number 8. See table at **element.**

oys·ter (oi'stər) *n.* A flat shellfish that can be eaten. Some oysters produce pearls inside their shells.

o·zone (ō'zōn') *n.* [U] A poisonous, blue gas found in parts of the earth's atmosphere. Ozone is a form of oxygen that has three atoms per molecule rather than the usual two.

Pp

p or **P** (pē) *n.*, *pl.* **p's** or **P's**. The 16th letter of the English alphabet.

p or **P** *abbr.* An abbreviation of petite.

P The symbol for the element **phosphorus**.

p. *abbr.* An abbreviation of: **1.** Page. **2.** Participle. **3.** Pint.

pa (pä) *n. Informal.* Father.

PA *abbr.* An abbreviation of: **1.** Public-address system: *I heard an announcement over the PA that the train will be late.* **2.** Or **Pa.** Pennsylvania.

pace (pās) *n.* **1.** A step made in walking: *The man shortened his paces to match the child's.* **2.a.** The rate of speed at which a person or thing walks or runs: *The lead runner set a fast pace.* **b.** The speed at which an activity proceeds: *the slow pace of summer vacation.* —*v.* **paced, pac•ing, pac•es.** —*tr.* **1.** To walk back and forth across (a surface): *He paced the floor impatiently.* **2.** To set or regulate the speed of (sbdy./sthg.): *Our host paced the dinner very skillfully.* —*intr.* To walk with long deliberate steps: *The tiger paced in its cage.* ◆ **keep up the pace.** To do sthg. at a constant, usually fast, and tiring rate: *She's worked on her paper every night for a month; she can't keep up the pace much longer.* **pace off.** *tr.v.* [sep.] To measure (sthg.) by counting the steps needed to cover a distance: *I paced off the distance from the door to the stairs.* **pace (oneself).** To do sthg. in such a way that one's energy is not spent before the goal is reached: *She needs to learn to pace herself.* **put through (one's) paces.** To find out, by testing or another method, how well sbdy./sthg. performs: *I really put that car through its paces.*

pace•mak•er (pās′mā′kər) *n.* **1.** An electronic device used to regulate the heartbeat. **2.** A person or thing that sets the pace in a race.

pace•set•ter (pās′sĕt′ər) *n.* A leader in a field: *That company has become the pacesetter in software development.*

pa•cif•ic (pə sĭf′ĭk) *adj.* **1.** Loving peace; peaceful: *a pacific people.* **2.** Peaceful in nature: *a pacific scene.* —**pa•cif′i•cal•ly** *adv.*

pac•i•fi•er (păs′ə fī′ər) *n.* A rubber or plastic nipple for a baby to suck on: *The baby usually sleeps with a pacifier in her mouth.*

pac•i•fism (păs′ə fĭz′əm) *n.* [U] Opposition to war or violence as a means of solving problems or arguments. —**pac′i•fist** *n.* —**pac′i•fis′tic** *adj.* —**pac′i•fis′ti•cal•ly** *adv.*

pac•i•fy (păs′ə fī′) *tr.v.* **pac•i•fied, pac•i•fy•ing, pac•i•fies.** **1.** To quiet (sbdy.); calm: *Maybe the bottle will pacify the baby.* **2.** To establish peace in (a place): *pacify the frontier.* —**pac′i•fi•ca′tion** (păs′ə fi kā′shən) *n.* [U]

pack (păk) *n.* **1.** A collection of items tied up or wrapped together: *a pack of cigarettes.* **2.** A group of animals that run and hunt together: *a pack of wolves.* **3.** A large amount: *a pack of trouble.* **4.** A backpack or knapsack. **5.** Material, such as gauze, applied to a part of the body or a wound as treatment for an injury or a disorder: *Apply an ice pack to your sprained ankle.* —*v.* —*tr.* **1.** To put (sthg.) into a bag, box, or other container, as for storage, preserving, or selling: *pack groceries into shopping bags; pack clothes in a suitcase.* **2.** To fill (sthg.) with items: *pack a box.* **3.a.** To force or bring (people or things) together closely: *The college packed 200 students into the lecture hall.* **b.** To fill (sthg.) up completely: *The crowd packed the stadium.* **4.** To treat (a wound or body part) medically with a pack: *pack a wound.* —*intr.* **1.** To put one's clothes or things into a box or suitcase for traveling or storage: *I've already packed for my trip.* **2.** To become pressed together: *Brown sugar packs well for measuring.* ◆ **pack it in.** *Informal.* To stop work or activity: *Let's pack it in for today.* **pack off.** *tr.v.* [sep.] *Informal.* To send (sbdy.) away: *Their parents packed them off to bed.* **pack up.** *tr.v.* [sep.] To prepare (sthg.) for leaving: *The workers packed up their tools and left.*

pack•age (păk′ĭj) *n.* **1.** A wrapped or boxed object: *a package in the mail.* **2.** A container meant to hold sthg. for storage or transporting: *candy sold in colorful packages.* **3.** A plan or an offer made up of several items, each of which must be accepted: *That company has a good retirement package for its employees.* —*tr.v.* **pack•aged, pack•ag•ing, pack•ag•es.** To place in a package or make a package of (sthg.): *The company packages 100 tea bags to a box.*

package store *n.* A store that sells sealed bottles of alcoholic beverages; a liquor store.

pack•ag•ing (păk′ə jĭng) *n.* [U] **1.** Material used for making packages: *a new type of packaging.* **2.** The manner in which sthg., such as an idea or a product, or sbdy., such as a candidate or an author, is presented to the public: *The senator credited the advisors for* *the successful packaging of the President's tax proposal.*

pack•et (păk′ĭt) *n.* A small package or bundle, as of mail: *a packet of letters.*

pack•ing (păk′ĭng) *n.* [U] **1.** The act of one that packs, especially the processing and packaging of food products. **2.** Material put into a body opening or wound as part of a medical treatment. **3.** The processing and packaging of food, especially meat: *meat packing.* —**pack′er** *n.*

pack rat *n.* **1.** A North American rat that collects a variety of small objects in its nest. **2.** A person who keeps things that other people might throw away: *Never offer to help a pack rat move!*

pact (păkt) *n.* A formal agreement, as between nations; a treaty: *an economic pact.*

pad (păd) *n.* **1.** A cushion or mass of soft, firmly packed material used for stuffing, lining, or protection against injury: *chair pads; knee pads.* **2.** A small wad of material: *a steel-wool pad for cleaning pots and pans.* **3.** A number of sheets of paper of the same size stacked one on top of the other and glued together at one end: *The secretary wrote the message on a memo pad.* **4.** The fleshy underpart of the toes and feet of many animals. **5.** A muffled sound of soft footsteps: *the soft pad of the cat on the stairs.* **6.** A launch pad. —*v.* **pad•ded, pad•ding, pads.** —*tr.* **1.** To line, stuff, or cover (sthg.) with soft, firmly packed material: *pad the shoulders of a suit jacket.* **2.** To lengthen (sthg.) with unnecessary material: *pad a term paper.* **3.** To add false expenses or costs to (sthg.): *The mechanic padded the bill.* —*intr.* To go on foot, especially with very soft steps: *They like to pad about the house barefooted.*

pad•ding (păd′ĭng) *n.* [U] **1.** Material used to stuff, fill, protect, or line sthg. **2.** Unnecessary material added to a speech or written work to make it longer.

pad•dle (păd′l) *n.* **1.** A wooden tool with a flat blade at one end, used to move a small boat, such as a canoe. **2.** Any of various tools with a similar shape and various uses, such as for playing table tennis. —*v.* **pad•dled, pad•dling, pad•dles.** —*intr.* **1.** To move a boat with paddles: *The canoers paddled down the river.* **2.** To swim by repeated short strokes: *a dog paddling through the water.* —*tr.* **1.** To propel (a boat) with paddles: *I paddled the canoe downriver.* **2.** To beat or spank (sbdy.) with or as if with a paddle: *Teachers don't paddle students anymore.* —**pad′dler** *n.*

pad•dock (păd′ək) *n.* A fenced field or area, usually near a stable, in which horses are kept.

pad•dy (păd′ē) *n., pl.* **pad•dies.** A flooded or specially watered field in which rice is grown: *Farmers flooded the rice paddy.*

pad•lock (păd′lŏk′) *n.* A lock with a movable U-shaped bar at one end that is opened with a key or combination dial. —*tr.v.* To lock up (sthg.) with or as if with a padlock: *She padlocked her bicycle to a signpost.*

padlock

pa•gan (pā′gən) *n.* A person who is not a follower of one of the world's major religions and who worships other deities, such as nature deities. —*adj.* Relating to pagans or paganism: *pagan gods.* —**pa′gan•ism** *n.* [U]

page¹ (pāj) *n.* **1.** One side of a printed piece of paper, as of a book, letter, or newspaper. **2.** A memorable event: *a new page in the course of human history.* —*intr.v.* **paged, pag•ing, pag•es.** To turn pages: *I found him paging through a book.*

page² (pāj) *n.* **1.** A person employed to run errands, carry messages, or act as a guide, as in a hotel or club. **2.** A call for sbdy. over a loudspeaker: *The airport was so noisy I didn't hear the page for me.* —*tr.v.* **paged, pag•ing, pag•es.** To call (sbdy.), as over a loudspeaker or another device: *The doctor wears a beeper so her office staff can page her.*

pag•eant (păj′ənt) *n.* **1.** A play or dramatic presentation usually based on an event in history: *a church Christmas pageant about the birth of Jesus.* **2.** A procession or celebration.

pag•eant•ry (păj′ən trē) *n.* [U] **1.** Pageants and their presentation. **2.** Grand or showy display: *The crowd loved the pageantry of the royal wedding.*

pag•er (pā′jər) *n.* An electronic device that alerts a user about a phone message: *He wore a pager on his belt.*

pag•in•ate (păj′ə nāt′) *tr.v.* **pag•in•at•ed, pag•in•at•ing, pag•in•ates.** To number the pages of (sthg.): *paginate a document on a computer.*

pa•go•da (pə gō′də) *n.* A many-storied Buddhist tower, built as a memorial or shrine.

paid (pād) *v.* Past tense and past participle of **pay.**

pail (pāl) *n.* **1.** A rounded container, flat on the bottom, open at the top, and fitted with a handle; a bucket: *Fill this pail with water, please.* **2.** The amount that a pail holds: *Pour out a pail of sand.*

HOMONYMS: pail, pale (whitish).

---

pain (pān) *n.* **1.** [C; U] An unpleasant feeling resulting from injury or disease, usually limited to some part of the body: *chest pains; a pain in my side from running; a* *patient in pain.* **2.** [U] Mental or emotional suffering: *the pain of his divorce.* **3. pains.** Trouble, care, or effort: *She took great pains to do everything right.* **4.** [C] *Informal.* A source of annoyance: *He complains constantly; he's a real pain.* —*tr.v.* To cause (sbdy.) to suffer: *It pained her to see him so unhappy.* ♦ **on** or **under pain of.** Subject to the penalty of (a specified punishment): *The soldiers were ordered not to retreat, on pain of death.*

HOMONYMS: pain, pane (glass).

pained (pānd) *adj.* Showing hurt or worry: *a pained expression.*
pain•ful (pān′fəl) *adj.* **1.** Causing or full of pain: *a painful injury.* **2.** Causing suffering or anxiety: *a painful decision.* —**pain′ful•ly** *adv.* —**pain′ful•ness** *n.* [U]
pain•kill•er (pān′kĭl′ər) *n.* Something, such as a drug, that relieves pain: *addicted to painkillers.*
pain•less (pān′lĭs) *adj.* Not painful; causing no hurt: *a painless operation.* —**pain′less•ly** *adv.* —**pain′less•ness** *n.* [U]
pains•tak•ing (pānz′tā′kĭng) *adj.* Involving or showing great care or thoroughness: *painstaking research.* —**pains′tak′ing•ly** *adv.*
paint (pānt) *n.* **1.** [C; U] A liquid mixture, usually of a solid color, applied to surfaces to color or protect them: *Be careful not to touch the wet paint. I use oil paints.* **2.** [C] A spotted horse; a pinto: *The cowboy rode a paint.* —*v.* —*tr.* **1.** To coat or decorate (sthg.) with paint: *paint a house.* **2.** To make (a picture) with paints: *paint landscapes.* **3.** To describe (sbdy./sthg.) vividly in words: *The author painted her husband as a monster.* —*intr.* **1.** To paint pictures: *an artist who draws and paints beautifully.* **2.** To cover sthg. with paint: *The painter washed the walls before he painted.* —**paint′er** *n.*
paint•brush (pānt′brŭsh′) *n.* A brush for applying paint.
paint•ing (pān′tĭng) *n.* **1.** [U] The art or job of working with paints: *a painting class; house painting.* **2.** [C] A picture or design in paint: *Hang a painting on the wall.*
pair (pâr) *n., pl.* **pair** or **pairs. 1.** A set of two members that are matched or related in function or form: *a pair of boots.* **2.** An object consisting of two joined or similar parts: *a pair of pants; a pair of glasses.* **3.** Two persons, animals, or things that share sthg. and are considered together: *a pair of workhorses.* **4.** Two playing cards of the same value: *a pair of aces.* —*tr.* **1.** To arrange (sthg.) in sets of two: *Pair the questions with the correct answers.* **2.** To provide a partner for (sbdy.): *The teacher paired each child in the class with a tutor.* ♦ **pair off** or **up.** *intr.v.* To

form pairs or a pair: *The students paired off at the dance.*

HOMONYMS: pair, pare (peel), **pear** (fruit).

USAGE: pair The noun **pair** can be followed by a singular or plural verb. You use the singular when **pair** refers to the set taken as a whole: *This pair of shoes is on sale.* You use the plural when the two members are considered as individuals: *The pair are working together.* After a number other than one, **pair** can be either singular or plural, but the plural is now more common: *She bought six pairs* (or *pair*) *of shoes.*

pais•ley (pāz′lē) *adj.* With a colorful pattern of curved shapes and swirls: *a paisley dress.*
pa•ja•mas (pə jä′məz *or* pə jăm′əz) *pl.n.* A loose-fitting shirt and pants, usually worn to sleep in: *She prefers pajamas to nightgowns.*

paisley

pal (păl) *Informal. n.* A friend: *We were good pals.* —*v.* **palled, pal•ling, pals.** ♦ **pal around.** *intr.v.* To spend time together as friends: *We palled around during the summer.*
pal•ace (păl′ĭs) *n.* The official home of a royal person, such as a king: *We toured the palace.*
pal•at•a•ble (păl′ə tə bəl) *adj.* **1.** Acceptable to the taste; agreeable enough to eat: *palatable food.* **2.** Acceptable to the mind; agreeable: *I find her political views palatable.* —**pal′at•a•bil′i•ty** *n.* [U]
pal•ate (păl′ĭt) *n.* **1.** The roof of the mouth in vertebrates, forming a complete or partial separation between the mouth and the nose. **2.** The sense of taste: *a dessert pleasing to the palate.*

HOMONYMS: palate, palette (artist's mixing board), **pallet** (bed).

pa•la•tial (pə lā′shəl) *adj.* Like a palace; large and grand: *a palatial hotel.* —**pa•la′tial•ly** *adv.*
pale (pāl) *adj.* **pal•er, pal•est. 1.** Whitish or lighter than normal in complexion: *pale with fear.* **2.** Containing a large proportion of white; light: *a pale blue.* **3.** Not bright; faint: *a pale moon.* —*intr.v.* **paled, pal•ing, pales. 1.** To lose normal skin coloration: *She paled when she heard the knock at the door.* **2.** To become pale: *The sky grew red, then paled.* **3.** To become less important relative to sthg. else: *The success of his first book pales in comparison with sales of his new bestseller.*

P

HOMONYMS: pale, pail (bucket).

pa·le·on·tol·o·gy (pā′lē ŏn tŏl′ə jē) *n.* [U] The scientific study of fossils and ancient forms of life: *Paleontology includes the study of dinosaur fossils.* —**pa′le·on·tol′o·gist** *n.*

pal·ette (păl′ĭt) *n.* **1.** A thin board, often with a hole for the thumb, upon which an artist mixes colors. **2.** A range of colors: *The room was decorated in a palette of yellows and blues.*

HOMONYMS: palette, palate (roof of the mouth), pallet (bed).

pall (pôl) *n.* **1.** A cloth covering, often of black velvet, for a coffin. **2.** A coffin, especially one being carried to a grave. **3.** An atmosphere of low spirits and little hope: *The bad news cast a pall over the household.* —*intr.v.* To grow boring or annoying: *a clever idea that began to pall by the end of the meeting.*

pall·bear·er (pôl′bâr′ər) *n.* A person who helps carry the coffin at a funeral: *Several close friends acted as pallbearers at the funeral.*

pal·let (păl′ĭt) *n.* A narrow hard bed or straw-filled mattress.

HOMONYMS: pallet, palate (roof of the mouth), palette (artist's mixing board).

pal·lid (păl′ĭd) *adj.* **1.** Lacking healthy color; pale: *a pallid complexion.* **2.** Dull; not exciting: *a pallid response to my question.*

pal·lor (păl′ər) *n.* [U] Unhealthy paleness: *Her pallor frightened her parents into calling a doctor.*

palm¹ (päm) *n.* The inside surface of the hand between the wrist and the base of the fingers. —*tr.v.* **1.** To hide (an object) in the palm of the hand: *The magician palmed the coin.* **2.** To pick (sthg.) up secretly: *I palmed the money quickly.* ♦ **in the palm of (one's) hand.** Under one's control or influence: *She's so in love with him that he's got her in the palm of his hand.* **palm off.** *tr.v.* [sep.] To get sbdy. to buy or accept (sthg. fake or of little value): *palm off a copy of a painting; palm the tickets off on a friend.*

palm² (päm) *n.* A tree of tropical and subtropical regions, usually with a branchless trunk and a crown of large leaves shaped like feathers or fans.

palm²

pal·o·mi·no (păl′ə mē′nō) *n., pl.* **pal·o·mi·nos.** A horse with a golden or light tan coat and a whitish mane and tail.

pal·pa·ble (păl′pə bəl) *adj.* **1.** Capable of being touched or felt: *A palpable rush of fear ran down her back.* **2.** Easily noticed; obvious: *The excitement in the stadium was palpable.* —**pal′pa·bly** *adv.*

pal·pi·tate (păl′pĭ tāt′) *intr.v.* **pal·pi·tat·ed, pal·pi·tat·ing, pal·pi·tates.** *Formal.* **1.** To shake; tremble: *The leaves palpitated in the breeze.* **2.** To beat very rapidly: *That movie star makes my heart palpitate.* —**pal′pi·ta′tion** *n.* [C; U]

pal·try (pôl′trē) *adj.* **pal·tri·er, pal·tri·est.** *Formal.* Of little worth or importance: *The farmer sold the cow for a paltry sum of money.* —**pal′tri·ness** *n.* [U]

pam·per (păm′pər) *tr.v.* To treat (sbdy./ sthg.) with extreme favor and care, especially in an attempt to satisfy any desire: *She pampers her child with toys and treats.*

SYNONYMS: pamper, indulge, spoil, coddle, baby. These verbs mean to make too great efforts to please sbdy. **Pamper** means to satisfy someone's tastes or desires for luxurious things: *I pampered myself with a long hot bath.* **Indulge** means to yield to wishes or impulses, often ones that can do harm: *The twins indulged their craving for sweets by sharing a box of chocolates.* **Spoil** means to indulge sbdy. in a way that worsens his or her character: *You are spoiling that child, letting him have every toy he wants.* **Coddle** means to care for in a tender, overprotective way that can weaken character: *Don't coddle her and make her think she can't do the job all by herself.* **Baby** suggests giving sbdy. the kind of attention one might give a baby: *My brother likes to be babied when he is sick.* ANTONYMS: punish, abuse.

pam·phlet (păm′flĭt) *n.* A short book or other printed material with a paper cover and no binding; a booklet: *The pamphlet describes the new program.*

pan (păn) *n.* A wide shallow open container used for holding liquids and cooking: *Put the cake batter in a baking pan.* —*tr.v.* **panned, pan·ning, pans.** *Informal.* To review (sbdy./ sthg.) with strong criticism: *The critics panned the new film.* ♦ **pan out.** *intr.v.* To be successful: *My bid for a promotion didn't pan out.*

pan— *pref.* A prefix that means all: *panorama.*

pan·a·ce·a (păn′ə sē′ə) *n.* A cure for all diseases or problems: *There is no panacea for poverty.*

pa·nache (pə năsh′ *or* pə näsh′) *n.* [U] Great style: *She plays her violin with panache.*

ă–cat; ā–pay; âr–care; ä–father; ĕ–get; ē–be; ĭ–sit; ī–nice; îr–here; ŏ–got; ō–go; ô–saw; oi–boy; ou–out; o͝o–took; o͞o–boot; ŭ–cut; ûr–word; th–thin; *th*–this; hw–when; zh–vision; ə–about; N–French bon

pan•cake (păn′kāk′) *n.* A thin cake of batter, cooked on a hot flat surface: *We had pancakes with maple syrup for breakfast.*

pan•cre•as (păng′krē əs *or* păn′krē əs) *n.* A long irregularly shaped gland located behind the stomach: *The pancreas produces insulin and digestive juices.* —**pan′cre•at′ic** (păng′krē ăt′ĭk *or* păn′krē ăt′ĭk) *adj.*

pan•da (păn′də) *n.* A large mammal of the mountains of China and Tibet, resembling a bear and with black and white fur.

pan•dem•ic (păn děm′ĭk) *adj.* Spread quickly through a very wide area: *a pandemic outbreak of influenza.* —*n.* A pandemic disease.

pan•de•mo•ni•um (păn′də mō′nē əm) *n.* [U] Wild confusion and noise: *After the earthquake, there was pandemonium.*

pan•der (păn′dər) *intr.v.* To profit by making use of the needs and weaknesses of others: *His movies pander to popular tastes for violence.* —**pan′der•er** *n.*

pane (pān) *n.* A sheet of glass, especially one in a window or door: *The broken pane needs to be replaced.*

Homonyms: pane, pain (hurt).

pan•el (păn′əl) *n.* **1.** A flat piece, such as a wooden board, forming part of a surface or covering it: *a door with inlaid panels.* **2.** A board with instruments or controls: *the control panel of an airplane.* **3.** A group of persons gathered together to discuss or decide sthg.: *a panel of medical and legal experts.* —*tr.v.* To cover or decorate (sthg.) with panels: *panel the living room walls.*

pan•el•ing (păn′ə lĭng) *n.* [U] A set of wooden panels covering a wall or other surface: *We decided to use paneling instead of wallpaper.*

pan•el•ist (păn′ə lĭst) *n.* A person who is part of a panel: *Panelists took part in the discussion.*

pang (păng) *n.* **1.** A brief sharp feeling, as of pain: *hunger pangs.* **2.** A brief sharp feeling of strong emotion: *a pang of guilt.*

pan•han•dle (păn′hăn′dl) *intr.v.* **pan•han•dled, pan•han•dling, pan•han•dles.** *Informal.* To beg for money on the street or in a public area: *Several people were panhandling in the train station.* —**pan′han′dler** *n.*

pan•ic (păn′ĭk) *n.* [C; U] A sudden powerful terror: *She was in a panic before the test.* —*adj.* Relating to panic: *a panic reaction.* —*tr. & intr.v.* **pan•icked, pan•ick•ing, pan•ics.** To cause panic in or feel panic: *The dog panicked the cat. He always panics under pressure.* See Synonyms at **frighten.** —**pan′ick•y** *adj.*

pan•ic-strick•en (păn′ĭk strĭk′ən) *adj.* Filled with panic; terrified: *The tourist was panic-stricken when he lost his passport.*

pan•o•ram•a (păn′ə răm′ə) *n.* **1.** A view of everything visible over a wide area: *From the mountaintop we had a panorama of the whole valley.* **2.** A long series of events, stages, or things: *The book presents a panorama of world history.* —**pan′o•ram′ic** *adj.*

pan•sy (păn′zē) *n., pl.* **pan•sies.** A garden plant with flowers that have rounded velvety petals of various colors.

pant (pănt) *intr.v.* To breathe in short quick gasps: *The dog was panting from the heat.*

pan•the•on (păn′thē ŏn′) *n. (usually singular).* **1.** A temple dedicated to all of the gods. **2.** A public building honoring the great men and women of a nation. **3.** All the gods of a people.

pan•ther (păn′thər) *n.* The leopard in its black unspotted form.

pant•ies (păn′tēz) *pl.n. Informal.* Underpants for women or girls.

pan•to•mime (păn′tə mīm′) *n.* [C; U] **1.** Acting that consists of gestures and other body movement without speech: *perform a pantomime.* **2.** Movements of the face and body used in place of words to express a message or meaning: *Her pantomime meant it was time to leave.* —*tr.v.* **pan•to•mimed, pan•to•mim•ing, pan•to•mimes.** To perform or represent (sthg.) by gestures without speech: *He pantomimed the entire story of his escape.*

pan•try (păn′trē) *n., pl.* **pan•tries.** A small room or closet, usually next to a kitchen, where items are stored: *We keep dishes and canned foods in our pantry.*

pants (pănts) *pl.n.* Trousers: *a new pair of pants.*

pant•suit (pănt′sōōt′) *n.* A woman's suit with trousers and a jacket: *She often wears pantsuits to work.*

pant•y•hose (păn′tē hōz′) *pl.n.* Stockings and underpants woven together and worn by women as one piece of clothing: *a pair of pantyhose.*

pa•pa (pä′pə *or* pə pä′) *n. Informal.* Father.

pa•pa•cy (pā′pə sē) *n., pl.* **pa•pa•cies.** *(usually singular).* The office or authority of the pope. —**pa′pal** *adj.*

pa•pa•ya (pə pä′yə) *n.* The large orange-yellow fruit of a tropical American tree, with many small seeds and a sweet taste.

pa•per (pā′pər) *n.* **1.** [U] A material produced in thin sheets, mainly from wood, and used for writing, printing, drawing,

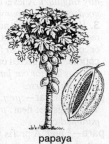

papaya

ing, wrapping, and covering walls: *Do you have a piece of writing paper? We used striped paper on the bedroom walls.* **2.** [C] A newspaper: *He* *read the morning paper.* **3.** [C] **a.** A report or essay assigned in school: *The student got an A on her history paper.* **b.** A scholarly essay: *The professor wrote a paper on the immune system.* **4. papers.** Documents that establish identity or give other information about a person: *Police demanded to see the man's papers.* **5. papers.** A collection of letters, diaries, and other personal writings: *President Lincoln's papers.* —*tr.v.* To cover or wrap (sthg.) in paper: *Photos of old movie stars papered the mirror.* —*adj.* Made of or producing paper: *paper plates; a paper mill.* —**pa′per•y** *adj.*

pa•per•back (pā′pər băk′) *n.* A book with a flexible paper cover: *Paperbacks cost much less than hardcover books do.*

pa•per•boy (pā′pər boi′) *n.* A boy who delivers newspapers: *Their son earns money as a paperboy.* —**pa′per•girl′** (pā′pər gûrl′) *n.*

paper clip *n.* A piece of wire that is bent and twisted and is used to hold papers together: *a box of paper clips.*

pa•per•weight (pā′pər wāt′) *n.* A small heavy object for holding down loose papers: *Some people collect glass paperweights.*

pa•per•work (pā′pər wûrk′) *n.* [U] Work involving the handling of reports, letters, and forms: *The police officer ended the day doing paperwork.*

pa•pier-mâ•ché (pā′pər mə shā′) *n.* [U] A material made from paper pulp mixed with glue or paste that can be shaped when wet. —*adj.* Made of this material: *a papier-mâché mask.*

pa•pri•ka (pă prē′kə *or* păp′rĭ kə) *n.* [U] A mild powdered spice made from sweet red peppers.

Pap smear *or* **Pap test** (păp) *n.* A test for cancer, especially of a woman's or girl's cervix, in which a group of cells is examined under a microscope.

pa•py•rus (pə pī′rəs) *n.* **1.** [C] A tall water plant similar to a reed, found in northern Africa and nearby regions. **2.** [U] A kind of paper made from this plant: *written on papyrus.*

par (pär) *n.* **1.** [U] An accepted or normal average: *below par in physical condition.* **2.** *(usually singular).* A level of equality: *The food is good, but not on a par with my grandmother's.* **3.** [U] In golf, the number of golf strokes regarded as necessary to complete a given hole or course: *This is a par four hole.* ♦ **par for the course.** As expected or as normally happens: *She was late for our lunch date, but that's just par for the course.*

para–[1] *or* **par–** *pref.* A prefix that means: **1.** Alongside; near: *parasite.* **2.** Assistant: *paramedic.*

para–[2] *pref.* A prefix that means parachute: *paratrooper.*

par•a•ble (păr′ə bəl) *n.* A simple story that gives a moral or religious lesson.

pa•rab•o•la (pə răb′ə lə) *n.* The curve formed by the set of points in a plane that are all equally distant from a given line and a given point not on the line. —**par′a•bol′ic** (păr′ə bŏl′ĭk) *adj.* —**par′a•bol′i•cal•ly** *adv.*

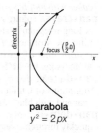

parabola
$y^2 = 2px$

par•a•chute (păr′ə sho͞ot′) *n.* **1.** A cloth device attached by cords to a harness and used to slow the fall of persons or objects from great heights. **2.** A similar device used to slow speeding vehicles: *Parachutes are used to slow the space shuttle when it lands.* —*v.* **par•a•chut•ed, par•a•chut•ing, par•a•chutes.** —*intr.* To descend by parachute: *He parachuted into enemy territory.* —*tr.* To drop (supplies, for example) by parachute: *The Red Cross parachuted medicine into the village.* —**par′a•chut′ist** *n.*

pa•rade (pə rād′) *n.* **1.** A public procession of people or vehicles, often with music, costumes, and colorful display: *a Fourth of July parade.* **2.** A line or group of moving people or things: *a parade of ants.* —*v.* **pa•rad•ed, pa•rad•ing, pa•rades.** —*intr.* **1.** To take part in a parade: *A company of firefighters paraded in uniform.* **2.** To show oneself proudly: *a peacock parading before his mate.* —*tr.* To exhibit (sbdy./sthg.) proudly or vainly: *He paraded his children before the guests.*

par•a•digm (păr′ə dīm′) *n.* **1.** An example of how sthg. should be done or treated; a model: *a paradigm for success.* **2.** A list of the inflectional forms of a word, considered as a model for determining the forms of other words like it: *a verb paradigm.*

par•a•dise (păr′ə dīs′) *n. (usually singular).* **1.** Heaven. **2.** A perfect or ideal place: *a paradise for birdwatchers.*

par•a•dox (păr′ə dŏks′) *n.* **1.** A statement that contradicts itself and therefore has an unclear meaning or no meaning. *We destroyed the town in order to save it* is an example of a paradox. **2.** A statement that appears to contradict itself or to be untrue but that may be true. *Light consists both of waves and of particles* is a paradox that can be demonstrated in experiments. **3.** A person or thing that seems contradictory or impossible to explain: *My mother remains a paradox to me.* —**par′a•dox′i•cal** (păr′ə dŏk′sĭ kəl) *adj.* —**par′a•dox′i•cal•ly** *adv.*

par•af•fin (păr′ə fĭn) *n.* [U] A waxy, white or

colorless, solid hydrocarbon mixture used in making candles, wax paper, and lubricating materials.

par•a•gon (păr′ə gŏn′) *n.* A model of excellence; a perfect example: *That businessman is a paragon of honesty.*

par•a•graph (păr′ə grăf′) *n.* A division of a piece of writing that begins on a new, usually indented line and that consists of one or more sentences on a single idea: *Don't forget to indent your paragraphs.*

par•a•keet (păr′ə kēt′) *n.* A small bird resembling a parrot and often kept as a pet.

par•a•le•gal (păr′ə lē′gəl) *n.* A person with specialized training who assists a lawyer: *working as a paralegal.* —*adj.* Relating to paralegals and their work.

par•al•lel (păr′ə lĕl′) *adj.* **1.** Lying in the same plane and not touching or crossing: *parallel lines.* **2.** With corresponding points always separated by the same distance: *a road parallel to the river.* **3.** Matching feature for feature; corresponding: *parallel economic developments in two countries.* —*adv.* In a parallel course or direction: *train tracks running parallel to the shore.* —*n.* **1.** Any of a set of parallel geometric figures, especially lines. **2.** Something closely resembling sthg. else; a corresponding case or instance: *Traditional stories of many different cultures contain parallels.* **3.** A comparison showing close resemblance: *The speaker drew a parallel between the operation of the factory and the activity of an ant colony.* **4.** Any of the lines considered to circle the earth parallel to the equator, used to represent degrees of latitude. —*tr.v.* **1.** To be or extend parallel to (sthg.): *The street paralleled a canal.* **2.** To be similar to (sthg.): *The growth of his personal fortune paralleled the economic development of the country.* **3.** [*to*] To compare (sthg.): *She paralleled the situation to a gathering storm.* —**par′al•lel′ism** *n.* [C; U]

par•al•lel•o•gram (păr′ə lĕl′ə grăm′) *n.* A flat four-sided geometric figure in which each pair of opposite sides is parallel.

pa•ral•y•sis (pə răl′ĭ sĭs) *n., pl.* **pa•ral•y•ses** (pə răl′ĭ sēz′). **1.** [U] Partial or complete loss of the ability to move or feel sensations in a part of the body, resulting from disease or injury that damages the nerves going to and from the part: *He suffered paralysis of his left side following a stroke.* **2.** [C] An inability to move or function normally: *a paralysis of the spirit.* —**par′a•lyt′ic** (păr′ə lĭt′ĭk) *adj. & n.*

par•a•lyze (păr′ə līz′) *tr.v.* **par•a•lyzed, par•a•lyz•ing, par•a•lyz•es.** **1.** To affect (sbdy.) with paralysis; make unable to move or feel: *The accident paralyzed her.* **2.a.** To make (sbdy.) helpless or motionless: *The victim was paralyzed by fear.* **b.** To block the normal functioning of (sthg.); bring to a standstill: *The heavy snows paralyzed the city.*

par•a•med•ic (păr′ə mĕd′ĭk) *n.* A person who is trained to give emergency treatment: *Paramedics treated the heart attack victim.*

pa•ram•e•ter (pə răm′ĭ tər) *n.* (*usually plural*). A fixed limit or boundary: *We must stay within the parameters of the budget.*

par•a•mil•i•tar•y (păr′ə mĭl′ĭ tĕr′ē) *adj.* Organized or functioning like a military unit but not a part of regular military forces: *a paramilitary group.*

par•a•mount (păr′ə mount′) *adj. Formal.* **1.** Supreme in rank or position; leading: *the paramount writer of our generation.* **2.** Of greatest importance or concern; primary: *our paramount need at this time.*

par•a•noi•a (păr′ə noi′ə) *n.* [U] **1.** A serious mental disorder marked by ideas that others want to cause one harm. **2.** Irrational fear for one's security.

par•a•noid (păr′ə noid′) *adj.* Relating to paranoia: *a paranoid reaction to a simple mistake.* —*n.* A person affected with paranoia: *That paranoid is always looking over his shoulder.*

par•a•pher•na•lia (păr′ə fər nāl′yə) *pl.n.* (*used with a singular or plural verb*). **1.** A person's personal belongings: *Gather up your paraphernalia so we can leave.* **2.** The equipment used in or associated with some activity: *the paraphernalia of camping.*

par•a•phrase (păr′ə frāz′) *n.* A restatement in other words: *A paraphrase of the question made it easier to understand.* —*tr.v.* **par•a•phrased, par•a•phras•ing, par•a•phras•es.** To restate (sthg.) in other words: *Try paraphrasing the passage to make its meaning clear.*

par•a•ple•gi•a (păr′ə plē′jē ə *or* păr′-ə plē′jə) *n.* [U] Paralysis of the entire lower part of the body, usually caused by injury to the spinal cord. —**par′a•ple′gic** *adj. & n.*

par•a•site (păr′ə sīt′) *n.* **1.** A plant or animal that lives in or on a different kind of living thing from which it feeds and to which it is sometimes harmful. Lice and tapeworms are parasites. **2.** A person who takes advantage of the generosity of others without giving anything in return: *Her husband should get a job; he's nothing but a parasite.* —**par′a•sit′ic** (păr′ə sĭt′ĭk) *adj.*

par•a•sol (păr′ə sôl′ *or* păr′ə sŏl′) *n.* A small light umbrella used as a protection against the sun: *In the past, many women used parasols on sunny days.*

par•a•troop•er (păr′ə trōō′pər) *n.* A soldier trained and equipped to parachute from airplanes.

par•boil (pär′boil′) *tr.v.* To boil (food) briefly: *Parboil tomatoes in order to peel them.*

par•cel (pär′səl) *n.* **1.** Something wrapped up in a bundle; a package: *A parcel was left for you.* **2.** A section or piece of land; a plot: *Our family owns a small parcel of land on the* *river.* —*v.* ◆ **parcel out.** *tr.v.* [sep.] To divide (sthg.) into parts and distribute: *He parcels out the work carefully.*

parch (pärch) *tr.v.* To make (sthg.) very dry, especially by intense heat: *A south wind parched the soil.*

parch•ment (pärch′mənt) *n.* [U] **1.** The skin of a sheep or goat, prepared as a material to write on. **2.** Heavy paper that looks like parchment: *The U.S. Constitution was written on parchment.*

par•don (pär′dn) *tr.v.* **1.** To release (sbdy.) from punishment or disfavor: *pardon a political prisoner.* See Synonyms at **forgive. 2.** To let (an offense) pass without punishment: *pardon a first offense.* **3.** To make allowance for (sbdy./sthg.); excuse: *Pardon me for asking.* —*n.* **1.** [U] Polite forgiveness, as for a discourtesy, interruption, or failure to hear: *We begged her pardon for being late.* **2.** [C; U] Freedom from punishment given by an official with authority over a legal case: *They asked the governor for a pardon.*

par•don•a•ble (pär′dn ə bəl) *adj.* Easily forgiven; excusable: *She displayed her gold medal with pardonable pride.*

pare (pâr) *tr.v.* **pared, par•ing, pares. 1.** To remove the skin or covering of (a fruit or vegetable) with a knife: *Pare the potatoes.* **2.** To make (sthg.) smaller as if by cutting: *They pared the budget to a bare minimum.* ◆ **pare away** or **off.** *tr.v.* [sep.] To remove (a surface part) with a knife: *I held the orange firmly and pared away the rind.* **pare down.** *tr.v.* [sep.] To reduce (sthg.) in amount: *We pared down expenses.*

HOMONYMS: pare, pair (two), **pear** (fruit).

par•ent (pâr′ənt *or* păr′ənt) *n.* A father or mother: *Her parents divorced last year.* —**par′ent•hood′** *n.* [U]

par•ent•age (pâr′ən tĭj *or* păr′ən tĭj) *n.* [U] Descent from parents or ancestors; origin: *refugee children of unknown parentage.*

pa•ren•tal (pə rĕn′tl) *adj.* Relating to or characteristic of a parent: *parental duty.*

pa•ren•the•sis (pə rĕn′thĭ sĭs) *n., pl.* **par•en•the•ses** (pə rĕn′thĭ sēz′). Either or both of the upright curved lines, (or), used to mark off additional or explanatory remarks in writing: *Extra information (such as related details) can be placed within parentheses.*

par•en•thet•i•cal (păr′ən thĕt′ĭ kəl) also **par•en•thet•ic** (păr′ən thĕt′ĭk) *adj.* **1.** Contained or grammatically capable of being contained within parentheses: *a parenthetical construction at the end of a sentence.* **2.** Forming a brief explanation or comment off the main topic: *a few parenthetical remarks*

during a speech. —**par′en•thet′i•cal•ly** *adv.*

par•fait (pär fā′) *n.* A dessert of layers, often of ice cream with various toppings, served in a tall glass.

pa•ri•ah (pə rī′ə) *n.* A person who has been excluded from society; an outcast: *Her unpopular beliefs will make a pariah of her.*

par•ish (păr′ĭsh) *n.* **1.** An area with its own Catholic or Anglican church: *our local parish.* **2.** An administrative district in Louisiana corresponding to a county in other states.

pa•rish•ion•er (pə rĭsh′ə nər) *n.* A member of a church parish: *Parishioners listened to the sermon.*

par•i•ty (păr′ĭ tē) *n.* [U] Equality, as in amount, status, value, or price: *Firefighters demanded parity of pay with police officers.*

park (pärk) *n.* **1.** A piece of land for recreational use inside a town or city, in its natural state or planted with gardens, grass, and trees: *New York's Central Park.* **2.** A large open area used for recreation or entertainment: *an amusement park.* **3.** A stadium or enclosed playing field: *a baseball park.* —*v.* —*tr.* **1.** To stop or leave (a vehicle) for a time in a place away from traffic: *I parked my car in the parking lot.* **2.** *Informal.* To place or leave (sthg.) temporarily: *He parked his lunch box on the porch while they played.* —*intr.* To park a motor vehicle: *We parked in front of the restaurant.*

par•ka (pär′kə) *n.* A warm fur or cloth jacket with a hood.

park•ing lot (pär′kĭng) *n.* An area for parking motor vehicles: *The city parking lot was full, so he parked on the street.*

parking meter *n.* A coin-operated device that allows a driver to park a motor vehicle for a specific period of time: *I got a ticket because the time had run out on the parking meter.*

park•way (pärk′wā′) *n.* A broad landscaped highway: *A parkway connects the two suburbs.*

par•lance (pär′ləns) *n.* [U] *Formal.* A special kind or style of language: *in the parlance of lawyers.*

par•lay (pär′lā′ *or* pär′lē) *tr.v.* **1.** To increase (money) to a much larger amount by repeated investments: *Her grandfather parlayed his small capital into a fortune.* **2.** To use (sthg.) to great advantage or profit: *She parlayed a talent for telling jokes into a career as an entertainer.*

par•lia•ment (pär′lə mənt) *n.* **1.** An assembly of persons that makes the laws of a nation. **2. Parliament.** The national legislature of the United Kingdom, made up of the House of Commons and the House of Lords. —**par′lia•men′ta•ry** (pär′lə mĕn′tə rē *or* pär′lə mĕn′trē) *adj.*

par·lia·men·tar·i·an (pär′lə mĕn târ′-
ē ən) *n.* An expert in parliamentary rules and
procedures.
par·lor (pär′lər) *n.* **1.** An old term for a room
in a home for entertaining visitors: *the front
parlor.* **2.** A room or a section of a building
designed for some special use: *She got her
hair done at the beauty parlor.*
par·lour (pär′lər) *n. Chiefly British.* Variant
of **parlor.**
Par·me·san (pär′mə zän′ *or* pär′mə zən)
n. [U] A hard dry Italian cheese, usually
served grated.
pa·ro·chi·al (pə rō′kē əl) *adj.* **1.** Relating to
a church parish: *a parochial priest; parochial
school.* **2.** Limited in range or understanding; narrow: *They accused him of having a
parochial mind.* **—pa·ro′chi·al·ism** *n.* [U]
—pa·ro′chi·al·ly *adv.*
par·o·dy (păr′ə dē) *n., pl.* **par·o·dies. 1.**
[C; U] A comic imitation, as of a person, literary work, or style, that exaggerates the characteristics of the original to make it seem
ridiculous: *The actors on that TV comedy
show often do amusing parodies of famous
films.* **2.** [C] Something so bad as to appear to
be a mockery: *The trial was a parody of justice.* *—tr.v.* **par·o·died, par·o·dy·ing,
par·o·dies.** To present, perform, or be a parody of (sbdy./sthg.): *The comic parodied the
rock star's style of singing and gesturing.*
pa·role (pə rōl′) *n.* [U] The early release of a
prisoner on condition of good behavior: *She
is on parole after serving only two years of
her sentence.* *—tr.v.* **pa·roled, pa·rol·ing,
pa·roles.** To release (sbdy.) on parole: *The
judge refused to parole the murderer.*
par·rot (păr′ət) *n.* **1.** A tropical bird with a
short hooked beak and brightly colored feathers: *Some parrots are kept as pets and can be
taught to imitate spoken words.* **2.** A person
who repeats or imitates sthg. without understanding it: *She's just her sister's parrot.*
—tr.v. To repeat or imitate (another's words
or another person), especially without understanding: *He parrots everything I say.*
par·ry (păr′ē) *tr.v.* **par·ried, par·ry·ing,
par·ries. 1.** To turn (a blow) aside so as not
to be hit: *Today we learned how to parry a
thrust in fencing.* **2.** To avoid (sthg.) skillfully: *The official parried questions from the
reporters.* *—n., pl.* **par·ries. 1.** The act of
turning aside a blow, especially in fencing. **2.**
An evasive action or answer: *The mayor met
the accusation with a clever parry that gave
away no information.*
pars·ley (pär′slē) *n.* [U] A plant with edible,
fragrant, feathery leaves used to flavor food and
as a garnish: *Top the dish with chopped parsley.*
pars·nip (pär′snĭp) *n.* The long whitish root of
a plant related to parsley, eaten as a vegetable.
par·son (pär′sən) *n.* A member of the Christian clergy, especially a Protestant minister.

par·son·age (pär′sə nĭj) *n.* The official
home of a parson, as provided by the church.
part (pärt) *n.* **1.** [C; U] A portion, division, or
segment of a whole: *We arrived late and
missed part of the movie. I gave her a part of
the orange.* **2.** [C] One of several equal portions that combine to make up a whole: *For
the salad dressing, we mixed two parts olive
oil with one part vinegar.* **3.** [C] A piece in a
machine or system that can be removed or
replaced: *The auto mechanic charged me for
parts and labor.* **4.** [C; U] A responsibility,
duty, or share in a common effort: *doing
one's part.* **5.** [C] A role: *a small part in the
play.* **6.** [U] A side in an argument or a controversy: *We took the part of the angry workers.* **7.** [C] *(usually plural).* A region, an area,
or a land: *exploring remote parts.* **8.** [C] The
line where the hair on the head is parted. *—v.*
—tr. **1.** To divide (sthg.) into two or more
parts; split: *She parted the log with an ax.* **2.**
To put or keep (persons) apart: *They were
good friends until a silly quarrel parted them.*
See Synonyms at **separate. 3.** To comb
(hair, for example) away from a dividing line,
as on the scalp: *My father parts his hair on
the left.* *—intr.* **1.** To become divided or separated: *The tree trunk parted into branches
higher up.* **2.** To leave one another; separate:
They finally parted when she moved west.
—adv. In part; partially: *Her dog is part collie, part German shepherd.* *—adj.* Not full;
partial: *part owner of a small business.* ♦ **for
(one's) part.** So far as one is concerned: *For
my part, I have no objections.* **for the most
part.** In most cases; chiefly: *She enjoys her
job for the most part.* **in part.** To some
extent; partly: *They're each responsible in
part.* **part and parcel.** A basic or essential
part: *Paying for moving was part and parcel
of the job offer.* **part company.** To break up a
relationship by separating: *He and his wife
have parted company.* **part with.** *tr.v.*
[insep.] To give up or let go of (sbdy./sthg.):
*She hated to part with her hard-earned
salary.* **take part.** To participate; be involved: *She took part in the discussion.*
part. *abbr.* An abbreviation of participle.
par·take (pär tāk′) *intr.v.* **par·took** (pär-
to͞ok′), **par·tak·en** (pär tā′kən), **par·tak·
ing, par·takes.** *Formal.* **1.** [*in*] To participate; be involved: *partake in the festivities.* **2.**
[*of*] To take a portion; eat or drink a helping:
We were invited to partake of their dinner.
par·tial (pär′shəl) *adj.* **1.** Not total; incomplete: *partial success.* **2.** Favoring one side;
biased: *partial to the other candidate; partial
comments.* **3.** [*to*] Especially attracted or
inclined: *She's partial to detective stories.*
—par′ti·al′i·ty (pär′shē ăl′ĭ tē) *n.* [C; U]
par·tial·ly (pär′shə lē) *adv.* To a certain degree or extent; incompletely: *an idea only
partially understood.*

par·tic·i·pant (pär tǐs′ə pənt) *n.* A person who participates: *participants in a card game.*

par·tic·i·pate (pär tǐs′ə pāt′) *intr.v.* **par·tic·i·pat·ed, par·tic·i·pat·ing, par·tic·i·pates.** To join with others in doing sthg.; be involved: *She participated in a discussion group.* —**par·tic′i·pa′tion** *n.* [U]

par·tic·i·pa·to·ry (pär tǐs′ə pə tôr′ē) *adj.* Involving the active participation of many people: *participatory democracy.*

par·ti·cip·i·al (pär′tǐ sǐp′ē əl) *adj.* In grammar, forming or formed from a participle: *a participial phrase; a participial adjective.*

par·ti·ci·ple (pär′tǐ sǐp′əl) *n.* In grammar, a verb form, in English usually ending in –*ing* or –*ed,* that is used with auxiliary verbs to form certain tenses and that can also function as an adjective. The past participle is also used to make the passive voice.

par·ti·cle (pär′tǐ kəl) *n.* **1.** A very small piece of solid matter: *particles of dust.* **2.** A subatomic particle. **3.** The smallest possible unit or amount: *She used every particle of strength she had left.* **4.** In grammar, any of a class of words, including many prepositions and conjunctions, that have little meaning by themselves but help to specify or connect the meanings of other words.

par·tic·u·lar (pər tǐk′yə lər) *adj.* **1.** Belonging to a specific person, group, or thing; not general: *the particular characteristics of the oak tree.* **2.** Distinct from others; certain: *on that particular day.* **3.** Greater than usual; special: *Pay particular attention to the speed limit.* **4.** Giving or demanding close attention to details; fussy: *She's very particular about her clothes.* —*n.* **particulars.** Items of information; detailed news: *Our friends reported the particulars of their voyage.* ◆ **in particular.** Particularly; especially: *I like that car in particular.*

par·tic·u·lar·ly (pər tǐk′yə lər lē) *adv.* **1.** As one specific case; specifically: *My daughter enjoys her science classes, particularly biology.* **2.** To a great degree; especially: *It's a particularly good play. They sing particularly well.*

part·ing (pär′tǐng) *n.* [C; U] A departure or time of going away: *a sad parting between friends.* —*adj.* Given or received at the moment of leaving: *a parting kiss.* ◆ **parting shot.** A rude or insulting comment offered just before leaving: *She didn't have the chance to respond to his parting shot.*

par·ti·san (pär′tǐ zən) *n.* **1.** A strong supporter of a party, a cause, a person, or an idea: *the President and his partisans in Congress.* **2.** A member of an organized group of fighters who attack an enemy within occupied territory; a guerrilla. —*adj.* **1.** Having a strong preference or bias: *too partisan to give a fair*

account of the battle. **2.** Relating to a partisan or partisans: *Partisan politics often blocks cooperation or progress.*

par·ti·tion (pär tǐsh′ən) *n.* **1.** [C] A thin structure, such as a panel, that divides a room. **2.** [U] The division of sthg. into parts: *the partition of the land into smaller lots.* —*tr.v.* To divide (sthg.) into separate spaces, parts, or sections: *The government partitioned the country after the war.* ◆ **partition off.** *tr.v.* [sep.] To form (sthg.) into a separate space by means of a partition: *They partitioned off the dining area from the kitchen.*

part·ly (pärt′lē) *adv.* To some extent; in part: *a journey partly by boat and partly on foot.*

part·ner (pärt′nər) *n.* **1.** One of two or more persons associated in some common activity, as: **a.** A member of a business partnership: *partners in a law firm.* **b.** A friend with whom one lives, travels, or works: *the cowboy and his partner.* **c.** Either of two persons dancing, singing, or skating together: *dance partners.* **d.** Either of two persons playing a game together: *tennis partners.* **2.** A husband or wife.

part·ner·ship (pärt′nər shǐp′) *n.* **1.** [U] The condition of being partners: *I bought the business in partnership with two friends.* **2.** [C] A business contract or relationship between two or more persons in which each agrees to work for a common enterprise and to share the profits or losses: *Their law firm is a partnership.* **3.** [C] A close relationship in which each member helps or cooperates with the other: *the partnership of science and industry.*

part of speech *n., pl.* **parts of speech.** One of the grammatical classes into which words are placed according to how they function. Traditionally, the parts of speech in English are *noun, pronoun, verb, adjective, adverb, preposition, conjunction,* and *interjection.* Sometimes *article* is considered a separate part of speech.

par·took (pär tŏŏk′) *v.* Past tense of **partake.**

part-time (pärt′tīm′) *adj.* During only part of the usual or standard working time: *a part-time job.* —**part′-time′** *adv.*

part·way (pärt′wā′) *adv. Informal.* To a part of the way; partly: *The child pushed the door partway open.*

par·ty (pär′tē) *n., pl.* **par·ties. 1.** A social gathering for pleasure or entertainment: *a birthday party.* **2.** A group of people participating together in some activity: *a search party looking for a lost child.* **3.** A group with shared political views, usually organized to nominate and support candidates for public office: *the Democratic Party.* **4.** A person or group involved in a legal proceeding: *the two parties in a lawsuit.*

ă-cat; ā-pay; âr-care; ä-father; ĕ-get; ē-be; ǐ-sit; ī-nice; îr-here; ŏ-got; ō-go; ô-saw; oi-boy; ou-out; ōō-took; ōō-boot; ŭ-cut; ûr-word; th-thin; *th*-this; hw-when; zh-vision; ə-about; N-French bon

pass (păs) *v.* —*intr.* **1.** To go or move; proceed: *passing from shop to shop.* **2.** To extend; run: *The river passes through our town.* **3.a.** To move by: *The crowd cheered as the band passed.* **b.** To move past another vehicle: *The sports car passed on the right.* **4.** To succeed in a course of study or an examination: *After studying hard, I passed.* **5.** To go by in time: *Time seems to pass quickly when you're on vacation.* **6.** To come to an end: *My anger passed.* **7.** To be allowed to happen without notice or action: *She let his rude remark pass.* **8.** To be transferred: *Ownership of the farm passed to his niece when he died.* **9.** To be approved: *The law passed by a large majority of senators.* **10.** In sports, to throw or propel a ball or puck to a teammate: *The player passed to her teammate just before stepping out of bounds.* —*tr.* **1.** To go by or ahead of (sbdy./sthg.): *She passed the lead runner and won the race.* **2.** To go beyond (sthg.): *The results of the experiment passed all our expectations.* **3.** To succeed in (an examination): *I hope to pass the test.* **4.** To cause (sthg.) to move or go in a certain way: *I passed the belt through the loops on my jeans.* **5.** To transfer or hand (sthg.) to sbdy.: *I passed the news to friends. Please pass the beans.* **6.** To allow (time) to go by: *He passed the winter in Vermont.* **7.a.** To approve or adopt (sthg.): *The Senate passed the bill.* **b.** To be approved or adopted by (sbdy./sthg.): *The bill passed the Senate.* **8.** In sports, to throw or propel (a ball or puck) to a teammate: *Pass the ball here!* —*n.* **1.** The act of passing: *The plane made two passes over the airport before landing.* **2.** A way by which one can go through or around an obstacle, especially a gap in a mountain range: *a mountain pass.* **3.** A permit or ticket giving sbdy. the right to come and go or giving free entrance or transportation: *a ten-day railroad pass.* **4.** A motion with the hand or with sthg. held in the hand: *The waiter made a pass with the sponge over the table.* **5.** An act of passing a ball or puck to a teammate: *What a great pass!* ◆ **bring to pass.** To cause (sthg.) to happen: *A small misunderstanding brought all this trouble to pass.* **come to pass.** *Formal.* To happen: *And so it came to pass.* **pass away** or **on.** *intr.v.* To die: *Her husband passed away last year.* **pass for.** *tr.v.* [insep.] To be accepted as or believed to be (sthg. one is not): *My mother can pass for my sister.* **pass off.** *tr.v.* [sep.] To describe, offer, or sell (sthg. fake) as genuine: *The man passed off the rhinestones as diamonds.* **pass out.** *intr.v.* To lose consciousness: *The patient passed out from loss of blood.* **pass over.** *tr.v.* [sep.] To leave (sbdy./sthg.) out; disregard: *He was disappointed at being passed over for an award. I passed over the dessert table.* **pass the buck.** *Slang.* To shift responsibility or blame from oneself to another: *Don't blame him; he'll just pass the buck.* **pass up.** *tr.v.* [sep.] *Informal.* To let (sthg. good) go by: *I won't pass up dessert.*

USAGE: pass The past tense and past participle of the verb **pass** is **passed**: *They passed our home. You have passed the exam.* **Past** is the corresponding adjective (*in the past week*), adverb (*drove past*), preposition (*past midnight; past the crisis*), and noun (*lived in the past*).

---

pass•a•ble (păs′ə bəl) *adj.* **1.** Capable of being passed or crossed: *a passable road.* **2.** Satisfactory but not excellent: *a passable job of acting.* —**pass′a•bly** *adv.*

pas•sage (păs′ĭj) *n.* **1.** [U] The act of passing: *They opened windows to allow the passage of air.* **2.** [C] A journey, especially by water: *a rough passage across the Atlantic.* **3.** [U] The right to travel on sthg., especially a ship: *We reserved passage to London.* **4.** [C] A narrow path or way between two points: *an underground passage.* **5.** [U] Creation by a legislature: *the passage of a law.* **6.** [C] A channel, duct, or path through or along which sthg. may pass: *the nasal passages.* **7.** [C] A section of a written work or speech: *a passage from the Bible.*

pas•sage•way (păs′ĭj wā′) *n.* A corridor or hallway.

pass•book (păs′book′) *n.* A bankbook.

pas•sé (pă sā′) *adj.* No longer in fashion: *His ideas about women in sports are passé.*

pas•sen•ger (păs′ən jər) *n.* A person riding in a train, an airplane, a ship, a bus, a car, or another vehicle: *The aircraft holds 260 passengers.*

pas•ser•by (păs′ər bī′) *n., pl.* **pas•sers•by** (păs′ərz bī′). A person who happens to be passing by, especially by chance: *Passersby were hit when gang members shot at police.*

pass•ing (păs′ĭng) *adj.* **1.** Going by: *a passing car.* **2.** Not lasting long; temporary: *a passing interest.* **3.** Allowing a person to pass a test or a course of study: *a passing grade.* —*n.* [U] **1.** The act of going by or the fact of having passed: *the passing of summer.* **2.** Death: *We mourned his passing.* ◆ **in passing.** As an aside; incidentally: *We noted, in passing, their late arrival.*

pas•sion (păsh′ən) *n.* **1.** [C; U] A powerful feeling such as love, joy, or hatred. See Synonyms at **feeling.** **2.** [C] **a.** Great enthusiasm for a certain activity or subject: *a passion for music.* **b.** Something greatly loved or enjoyed: *Golf is his passion.*

pas•sion•ate (păsh′ə nĭt) *adj.* **1.** Showing or expressing strong feeling: *a passionate speech; a passionate kiss.* **2.** Resulting from or marked by strong feeling: *passionate involvement in a cause.* —**pas′sion•ate•ly** *adv.*

P

pas·sive (păs'ĭv) *adj.* **1.** Affected by the actions of others but not acting in return: *He played a passive role and just agreed to anything the others wanted.* **2.** Offering no resistance; submissive: *She has a passive acceptance of her fate in life.* **3.** In grammar, relating to the passive voice. —*n.* **1.** [U] The passive voice in grammar. **2.** [C] A verb form in the passive voice. —**pas'sive·ly** *adv.* —**pas'sive·ness, pas·siv'i·ty** (păsĭv'ĭtē) *n.* [U]

passive voice *n.* [U] In grammar, a verb form or voice that shows that the subject receives the action expressed by the verb. In the sentence *The trees were planted in a row,* the verb form *were planted* is in the passive voice. —SEE NOTE at **verb.**

Pass·o·ver (păs'ō'vər) *n.* A Jewish holiday lasting eight days in the spring and recalling the escape of the Jews from Egypt.

pass·port (păs'pôrt') *n.* **1.** An official document, generally in booklet form, that identifies a person as a citizen of a country and permits travel outside the country. **2.** Something that assures the achievement of sthg. else: *Hard work is often a passport to success.*

pass·word (păs'wûrd') *n.* A secret word or phrase that one uses to get into a place or gain access to information: *I need to change the password on my computer.*

past (păst) *adj.* **1.** Gone by; completed: *That day is past.* **2.** Having existed or happened at an earlier time: *past victories.* **3.** Recently ended: *in the past few days.* **4.** Former; previous: *a past vice president, now retired.* **5.** In grammar, relating to the past tense. —*n. (usually singular).* **1.** [U] The time before the present: *memories of the past.* **2.** [C] A person's history, background, or former activities: *a woman with a distinguished past.* **3.** [U] The past tense. —*adv.* So as to pass by and go beyond: *He waved as he drove past.* —*prep.* **1.** Beyond in time: *It is past midnight.* **2.** Beyond in position: *My house is a mile past the river.* **3.** Beyond the number and amount of: *The child could not count past 20.*

pas·ta (päs'tə) *n.* [U] Dough made from flour and water, formed into shapes, dried, and boiled: *My favorite kind of pasta is spaghetti.*

paste (pāst) *n.* **1.** [U] A smooth sticky substance used to join light things together. **2.** [C] A food that has been made soft and creamy by pounding or grinding: *almond paste; tomato paste.* —*tr.v.* **past·ed, past·ing, pastes.** To fasten or attach (sthg.) with paste: *Paste the broken pieces together.*

pas·tel (păstĕl') *n.* **1.** A soft delicate color or hue: *She dressed her baby in pastels.* **2.** A crayon similar to chalk, used in drawing or marking: *She likes to work in pastels.* **3.** A picture drawn with this type of crayon: *He*

purchased a pastel. —*adj.* **1.** Pale and soft in color: *pastel blue.* **2.** Relating to or drawn with pastels: *a pastel portrait.*

pas·teur·i·za·tion (păs'chər ĭ zā'shən) *n.* [U] A process in which milk, beer, and other liquids are heated to a specific temperature for a certain amount of time to kill harmful germs or prevent further fermentation. —**pas'teur·ize'** (păs'chə rīz') *v.*

pas·time (păs'tīm') *n.* An activity that a person does for fun: *Hiking is his favorite pastime.*

pas·tor (păs'tər) *n.* A Christian minister or priest who is the leader of a congregation: *The new pastor led the prayer.*

pas·tor·al (păs'tər əl) *adj.* **1.** Relating to shepherds or country life: *a pastoral scene.* **2.** Relating to a pastor: *pastoral duties.*

past participle *n.* A participle that expresses past or completed action or time. It is used as an adjective, as in the phrase *finished product,* and also to form the passive voice and the perfect tenses of the active voice.

past perfect tense *n.* A verb tense that expresses action completed before a specified or implied past time. In English the past perfect tense is formed with the past participle of a verb and the auxiliary *had.* In the sentence *She had learned to drive before the month was over,* the verb form *had learned* is in the past perfect tense.

pas·tra·mi (pə strä'mē) *n.* [U] A seasoned smoked cut of beef: *a pastrami sandwich.*

pas·try (pā'strē) *n., pl.* **pas·tries. 1.** [U] Dough of flour, water, and shortening, used for the crusts of pies, tarts, and other baked foods. **2.** [C; U] Baked food, such as pies, made with such dough: *Danish pastries; some Viennese pastry.*

past tense *n.* A verb tense used to express an action or a condition that happened in or during the past. In the sentence *While you were sleeping, I wrote a letter,* the verbs *were sleeping* and *wrote* are in the past tense.

pas·ture (păs'chər) *n.* A piece of land covered with grass and other plants eaten by grazing animals such as cattle, horses, or sheep. —*tr.v.* **pas·tured, pas·tur·ing, pas·tures.** To put (animals) in a pasture to graze. ◆ **put out to pasture.** *Informal.* To make (sbdy.) retire: *The company's going to put me out to pasture when I turn 70.*

past·y (pā'stē) *adj.* **past·i·er, past·i·est.** Like flour paste in color or texture: *Her illness left her with a pasty complexion.* —**past'i·ness** *n.* [U]

pat¹ (păt) *tr.v.* **pat·ted, pat·ting, pats. 1.** To tap or stroke (sbdy./sthg.) gently with the open hand, often as a sign of affection: *The boy patted the friendly dog.* **2.** To flatten or shape (sthg.) by tapping gently with the hands: *She pats down the curls.* —*n.* **1.** A light touch or tap: *He gave his child a pat on the head.* **2.** A small piece: *a pat of butter.* ◆ **pat on the back.** A word or gesture of praise or approval: *He got a pat on the back for doing his job so well.*

pat² (păt) *adj.* Satisfactory but not thoughtful or sincere: *He gave a pat answer to the reporter's question.* ◆ **have down pat.** To know (sthg.) thoroughly or perfectly: *We have the new computer program down pat.*

pat. *abbr.* An abbreviation of patent.

patch (păch) *n.* **1.** A small piece of material used to cover a hole, rip, or worn place: *knee patches on the child's jeans.* **2.** A protective pad or bandage worn over a wound or an injured eye: *an eye patch.* **3.** A small piece of land, usually with plants growing on it: *a berry patch.* **4.** A small part or area that differs from what surrounds it: *a patch of blue sky.* —*tr.v.* **1.** To put a patch or patches on (sthg.): *I can patch a torn shirt.* **2.** To put together or mend (sthg.): *They patched together the table from broken pieces.* ◆ **patch up.** *tr.v.* [sep.] To settle or smooth (sthg.) over: *They patched up their quarrel.*

patch•work (păch'wûrk') *n.* **1.** [U] The sewing together of pieces of cloth of various colors, as in a quilt. **2.** [C] A mixture of many varied parts: *As seen from the plane, the farmers' fields formed a patchwork of colors.*

patch•y (păch'ē) *adj.* **patch•i•er, patch•i•est.** Uneven in quality or performance: *That carpenter does patchy work.* —**patch'i•ly** *adv.* —**patch'i•ness** *n.* [U]

pate (pāt) *n.* The human head, especially the top of the head: *a bald pate.*

pâ•té (pä tā') *n.* [U] A meat paste: *liver pâté.*

pat•ent (păt'nt) *n.* A grant made by a government that gives an inventor the exclusive right to make, use, and sell an invention for a stated period of time: *The inventor holds 17 patents.* —*adj.* (also pāt'nt). Obvious; plain: *No one believed his patent lies.* —*tr.v.* To get a patent on (sthg.): *The manufacturer of a new synthetic fabric patented the process.*

patent leather *n.* [U] Black leather with a smooth, hard, shiny surface, used for shoes, belts, handbags, and similar items.

pa•ter•nal (pə tûr'nəl) *adj.* **1.** Relating to or characteristic of a father; fatherly: *paternal care.* **2.** Related through one's father: *my paternal aunt.* —**pa•ter'nal•ly** *adv.*

pa•ter•nal•ism (pə tûr'nə lĭz'əm) *n.* [U] The policy or practice of treating or governing people in a fatherly manner by providing for their needs without giving them responsibility. —**pa•ter'nal•is'tic** *adj.*

pa•ter•ni•ty (pə tûr'nĭ tē) *n.* [U] The fact or condition of being a father: *He claimed paternity of his girlfriend's baby.*

paternity suit *n.* A lawsuit brought against

a man by a woman who states he is the father of her child and so must support the child financially.

path (păth) *n.*, *pl.* **paths** (păthz *or* păths). **1.** A track made by footsteps: *a path in the woods.* **2.** A road or way made for a particular purpose: *shovel a path through the snow.* **3.** The route along which sbdy. or sthg. moves: *step into her path to speak to her; the path of a hurricane.* **4.** A course or manner of conduct: *the path to success.*

pa•thet•ic (pə thĕt'ĭk) *adj.* **1.** Causing sympathy or sorrow: *a pathetic child living in poverty.* **2.** Causing scorn and low regard; worthless: *a pathetic effort at humor.* —**pa•thet'i•cal•ly** *adv.*

path•o•gen (păth'ə jən) *n.* Something that causes disease, especially a virus or microorganism: *preventing the spread of pathogens.* —**path'o•gen'ic** (păth'ə jĕn'ĭk) *adj.*

path•o•log•i•cal (păth'ə lŏj'ĭ kəl) also **path•o•log•ic** (păth'ə lŏj'ĭk) *adj.* **1.** Relating to a physical or mental disease: *a pathological liar.* **2.** Relating to pathology: *pathological processes.*

pa•thol•o•gy (pă thŏl'ə jē) *n.*, *pl.* **pa•thol•o•gies.** **1.** [U] The scientific and medical study of disease, its causes, its processes, and its effects. **2.** [C] The physical changes in the body and its functioning as a result of a disease or disorder. —**pa•thol'o•gist** *n.*

pa•thos (pā'thŏs' *or* pā'thôs') *n.* [U] A quality in a person or thing that causes others to feel pity, sympathy, or sorrow: *a song full of pathos.*

path•way (păth'wā') *n.* A path.

pa•tience (pā'shəns) *n.* [U] The capacity, quality, or fact of being patient: *Fishing demands patience.*

pa•tient (pā'shənt) *adj.* **1.** Enduring trouble, hardship, annoyance, or delay without complaint or anger: *being patient with a sick child.* **2.** Showing continued effort; persistent: *the patient collection of scientific evidence.* **3.** Showing or expressing patience: *a patient smile.* —*n.* A person who receives medical care or treatment: *patients in a hospital.* —**pa'tient•ly** *adv.*

pat•i•o (păt'ē ō') *n.*, *pl.* **pat•i•os.** An outdoor space for dining or recreation, next to a house or an apartment: *We often sit on the patio and chat during the summer.*

pat•ois (păt'wä' *or* pă twä') *n.*, *pl.* **pat•ois** (păt'wäz' *or* pă twä'). A regional dialect of a language: *Her patois was hard to understand.*

pa•tri•arch (pā'trē ärk') *n.* **1.** The father and leader of a family, clan, or tribe. **2.** A very old and respected man. —**pa'tri•ar'chal** *adj.*

pa•tri•ar•chy (pā'trē är'kē) *n.* [C; U] A society in which a man rules a family, clan, or tribe, and one's family line is traced through the father's side of the family.

pa·tri·cian (pə trĭsh′ən) n. **1.** A person of high social rank with refined manners and tastes: *The charity event was attended by local patricians.* **2.** A member of an aristocracy.

pat·ri·cide (păt′rĭ sīd′) n. [U] *Formal.* The act of murdering one's father. —**pat′ri·cid′al** *adj.*

pat·ri·mo·ny (păt′rə mō′nē) n. [U] Property or money inherited after the death of a father or other ancestor. —**pat′ri·mo′ni·al** *adj.*

pa·tri·ot (pā′trē ət) n. One who loves, supports, and defends his or her country: *We honor patriots who died defending our country.* —**pa′tri·ot′ic** (pā′trē ŏt′ĭk) *adj.* —**pa′tri·ot′i·cal·ly** *adv.*

pa·tri·ot·ism (pā′trē ə tĭz′əm) n. [U] Love of and devotion to one's country.

pa·trol (pə trōl′) v. **pa·trolled, pa·trol·ling, pa·trols.** —*tr.* To walk or travel through (an area) checking for possible trouble or inspecting: *Police patrol the streets.* —*intr.* To patrol an area: *We're patrolling from midnight until dawn.* —n. **1.** [U] The act of patrolling: *The soldiers are out on patrol.* **2.** [C] A group of persons, vehicles, ships, or aircraft that patrols an area: *a neighborhood patrol.*

patrol car n. A police car.

pa·trol·man (pə trōl′mən) n. A policeman who patrols an assigned area. —**pa·trol′wom′an** (pə trōl′wŏom′ən) n.

pa·tron (pā′trən) n. **1.** A regular customer of a store, restaurant, or other business: *Patrons are treated with respect.* **2.** A person who supports or promotes an activity or institution by giving money: *a patron of the arts.*

pa·tron·age (pā′trə nĭj or păt′rə nĭj) n. **1.** [U] The trade given to a store or restaurant by its customers: *We appreciate your patronage.* **2.** [C] *(usually singular).* Customers as a group: *The hotel has a very exclusive patronage.* **3.** [U] Support or encouragement from a patron: *an artist dependent upon the patronage of the rich.* **4.** [U] Support or encouragement given with an attitude of superiority: *She resented the patronage of her older sisters.*

pa·tron·ize (pā′trə nīz′ or păt′rə nīz′) tr.v. **pa·tron·ized, pa·tron·iz·ing, pa·tron·iz·es. 1.** To go to (a place) regularly as a customer: *I patronize that store.* **2.** To act as a patron to (sbdy./sthg.); support: *We try to patronize the arts.* **3.** To treat (sbdy.) as an inferior; talk down to: *Teachers shouldn't patronize students.*

pa·tron·iz·ing (pā′trə nīz ĭng or păt′rə nīz ĭng) *adj.* Showing that one considers others less able to think or act for themselves: *She had a patronizing attitude toward her coworkers.* —**pa′tron·iz·ing·ly** *adv.*

pat·sy (păt′sē) n., pl. **pat·sies.** *Slang.* A person who is cheated, taken unfair advantage of, or made the object of a joke: *I didn't enjoy being made their patsy.*

pat·ter (păt′ər) intr.v. **1.** To make a series of quick light taps: *Rain pattered on the roof.* **2.** To walk or move softly and quickly: *Children pattered through the halls.* —n. [U] **1.** A series of quick light tapping sounds: *the patter of tiny feet.* **2.** Smooth rapid speech, such as that used by a salesperson or comedian: *The comedian's patter had all of us laughing.*

pat·tern (păt′ərn) n. **1.** A person or thing that is used as a guide or considered worth imitating: *We should all follow his pattern for success.* **2.** An artistic or decorative design: *a tie with a floral pattern.* **3.** A diagram, plan, or model used to make things: *a dress pattern.* **4.** A combination of features, actions, or events that are repeated in the same arrangement: *patterns of behavior in monkeys.* ♦ **pattern after** or **on.** tr.v. [insep.] To form or design (sthg.) according to a certain model: *The country's constitution is patterned after our own. I pattern my speech on my mother's.*

pat·ty (păt′ē) n., pl. **pat·ties.** A small, rounded, flattened mass of ground or chopped food: *hamburger patties.*

pau·ci·ty (pô′sĭ tē) n. *Formal.* Short supply; scarcity: *That country is rich despite a paucity of natural resources.*

paunch (pônch or pänch) n. A somewhat fat stomach; potbelly: *As he got older, he developed a slight paunch.* —**paunch′y** *adj.* —**paunch′i·ness** n. [U]

pau·per (pô′pər) n. A term used in the past for a very poor person, often one who lived on charity.

pause (pôz) v. **paused, paus·ing, paus·es.** —*intr.* **1.** To stop briefly in the middle of an action or while speaking: *The speaker paused for a drink of water.* **2.** To stay for a time: *We paused under a tree before going on.* —*tr.* To stop (sthg.) briefly: *I paused the videotape while I answered the phone.* —n. A brief stop or break in action or speech: *She took a pause to answer questions.*

SYNONYMS: pause, intermission, recess, suspension. These nouns all mean a temporary stop in activity. *There was a brief pause in the conversation. They went to the restroom during the play's intermission. Enjoy yourselves during winter recess. The strike caused a suspension of repair work on the highway.*

pave (pāv) tr.v. **paved, pav·ing, paves.** To cover (sthg.) with pavement: *The city paved the dirt road.* ♦ **pave the way.** [for] To make progress or development easier: *His experi-*

ments paved the way for new discoveries.
—pav'ing *n.* [U]

pave•ment (pāv′mənt) *n.* [U] A hard smooth surface of concrete, asphalt, or a similar material, as for a road or parking lot.

pa•vil•ion (pə vĭl′yən) *n.* **1.** A fancy tent: *We held the party in a pavilion on the lawn.* **2.** An open structure with a roof, used at parks or fairs for amusement or shelter.

paw (pô) *n.* **1.** The clawed foot of an animal, especially of an animal that has four legs, such as a dog or bear: *A bear's paw is huge.* **2.** *Informal.* The human hand: *Keep your paws off me!* —*tr.v.* **1.** To touch, strike, or scrape (sbdy./sthg.) with a paw: *The dog pawed my leg to get my attention.* **2.** To handle (sbdy./sthg.) in a rough or sexually improper way: *She told her boyfriend to stop pawing her.*

pawn¹ (pôn) *tr.v.* To give or leave (sthg. of value) as security for the payment of money borrowed: *He pawned his watch.*

pawn² (pôn) *n.* **1.** A chess piece of lowest value: *The pawn can move forward one space.* **2.** A person or thing used or controlled by others: *The small nation was nothing but a pawn in the struggle between two superpowers.*

pawn•bro•ker (pôn′brō′kər) *n.* A person who lends money at interest in exchange for personal property left as security.

pawn•shop (pôn′shŏp′) *n.* The shop of a pawnbroker.

pay (pā) *v.* **paid** (pād), **pay•ing, pays.** —*tr.* **1.** To give money to (sbdy.) in return for goods or services: *I paid her for the newspaper.* **2.** [*for*] To give (money) in exchange for goods or services: *How much did you pay for the tickets?* **3.** To produce (sthg.) as return: *a bond paying eight percent interest.* **4.** To be profitable or worthwhile for (sbdy. to do sthg.): *It paid him to be careful.* **5.** To give or express (sthg.): *pay attention; pay someone a compliment.* —*intr.* **1.** To give money in exchange for goods or services: *The woman went to the cashier to pay.* **2.** To suffer a cost or penalty: *You'll pay for eating so much.* **3.** To be profitable or worthwhile: *It pays to be on time.* —*adj.* **1.** Relating to payments: *a pay raise.* **2.** Requiring payment to operate: *a pay telephone.* —*n.* [U] Money given in return for work done; wages; salary: *He gets good pay.*
♦ **pay back.** *tr.v.* [sep.] To reward or punish (sbdy.) for some action: *One day I'll pay him back for all the pain he's caused me.* **pay off.** *tr.v.* [sep.] **1.** To pay the full amount on (a debt): *We finally paid off the mortgage on our house.* **2.** *Informal.* To bribe (sbdy.): *The assassin paid off the witnesses so they wouldn't tell what they had seen.* —*intr.v.* To be profitable: *an investment that pays off.* **pay (one's) dues.** To earn respect through working and serving a group for years, especially during hard times: *She has already paid her*

dues. **pay (one's) own way.** To contribute (one's) own share; pay for oneself: *She always pays her own way when they go out.* **pay out.** *tr.v.* [sep.] To give (money) out; spend: *The business paid more money out than it took in.* **pay through the nose.** To pay a very high price: *I paid through the nose for my new car.* **pay up.** *intr.v. Informal.* To give all the money owed: *He was told to pay up or move out.*

pay•a•ble (pā′ə bəl) *adj.* **1.** Requiring payment on a certain date; due: *a bill payable on the first of each month.* **2.** Specifying payment to a particular person: *Make the check payable to me.*

pay•back (pā′băk′) *n.* [U] The money or other return gained from sthg.: *She took a chance on starting the company, although the payback was uncertain.*

pay•check (pā′chĕk′) *n.* **1.** A check issued to an employee in payment of salary or wages: *He cashed his paycheck.* **2.** Salary or wages: *The new job means a larger paycheck.*

pay•day (pā′dā′) *n.* [C; U] The day on which wages are paid: *Friday is payday for me.*

pay dirt *n.* [U] Earth that is profitable to mine.
♦ **hit pay dirt.** To discover sthg. useful or profitable: *The reporter spent days hunting for information before finally hitting pay dirt.*

pay•load (pā′lōd′) *n.* **1.** The part of a cargo carried for payment as distinguished from the weight of the vehicle: *a payload to be delivered.* **2.** The explosive charge in the warhead of a missile: *a nuclear payload.*

pay•ment (pā′mənt) *n.* **1.** [U] The act of paying: *Prompt payment of the bill will be appreciated.* **2.** [C] An amount of money paid: *I make monthly payments on my car.* **3.** [U] Reward or punishment: *To see the child healthy again is payment enough for my services.*

pay•off (pā′ôf′ *or* pā′ŏf′) *n.* **1.** The reward or payment on some activity: *a big payoff on the lottery.* **2.** *Informal.* The final result of one's efforts or of a series of events: *The payoff for all his hard work was a promotion.* **3.** *Informal.* A bribe: *The spy demanded a payoff in exchange for passing secret information.*

pay-per-view (pā′pər vyōō′) *n.* [U] A service offered by cable TV companies that allows subscribers to see special programs and movies for an extra charge.

pay•roll (pā′rōl′) *n.* **1.** A list of employees and the amounts they should be paid: *The accountant is working on the payroll right now.* **2.** The total amount of money paid to employees at a given time: *Robbers stole the company payroll.*

Pb The symbol for the element **lead²** (sense 1).

PC *abbr.* An abbreviation of: **1.** Personal computer: *I bought a new printer for my PC.* Or **p.c.** Politically correct: *He's careful to use PC terms when speaking in public.*

pct. *abbr.* An abbreviation of percent.

pd. *abbr.* An abbreviation of paid.

P.D. *abbr.* An abbreviation of police department.

P.E. *abbr.* An abbreviation of physical education: *Our P.E. teacher had us run a mile.*

pea (pē) *n.* The round green seed of a climbing vine, enclosed in long green pods and eaten as a vegetable. ◆ **like two peas in a pod.** The same; identical: *Those boys are like two peas in a pod.*

peace (pēs) *n.* [U] **1.** The absence of war or other hostilities. **2.** Calm; freedom from disturbance: *a little peace and quiet.* **3.** Public security; law and order: *He was arrested for disturbing the peace.* ◆ **at peace. 1.** In a state of calm; free from worry: *She is at peace with herself.* **2.** Free from conflict or fighting: *We all want to live in a world at peace.* **keep** or **hold (one's) peace.** To be silent: *No matter what she says, hold your peace.*

HOMONYMS: **peace, piece** (part).

---

peace•a•ble (pē′sə bəl) *adj.* **1.** Preferring peace; not liking to quarrel or rebel: *a man with a peaceable nature.* **2.** Not involving violence or war; peaceful: *a peaceable solution.* —**peace′a•bly** *adv.*

Peace Corps *n.* [U] A U.S. government program that sends volunteers abroad to work with people of developing countries.

peace•ful (pēs′fəl) *adj.* **1.** Preferring to be at peace: *a peaceful nation.* **2.** Calm; quiet: *a small, peaceful village.* See Synonyms at **calm.** —**peace′ful•ly** *adv.* —**peace′ful•ness** *n.* [U]

peace•keep•ing (pēs′kē′pĭng) *adj.* Relating to maintaining peace: *a peacekeeping force sent by the United Nations.*

peace•mak•er (pēs′mā′kər) *n.* A person who makes peace, especially by settling the disputes of others: *She's always been the peacemaker in the family.*

peace•time (pēs′tīm′) *n.* [U] A time free from war.

peach (pēch) *n.* **1.** [C] A sweet, round, juicy fruit with downy yellowish or reddish skin and a pit. **2.** [U] A light yellowish pink color. **3.** [C] *Informal.* An excellent or especially likeable person or thing: *My history teacher is a peach.* —*adj.* Light yellowish pink. ◆ **peaches and cream. 1.** *Informal.* Easy; without problems: *Life can't always be peaches and cream.* **2.** Perfect; without a flaw: *a peaches-and-cream complexion.*

pea•cock (pē′kŏk′) *n.* **1.** The male of a large bird with brilliant blue or green feathers and very long tail feathers that are marked with eyespots and can be spread out like a fan. **2.** A vain or showy person: *My boss struts around like a peacock.*

peak (pēk) *n.* **1.a.** The pointed top of a mountain: *We reached the peak at noon.* **b.** The mountain itself: *We could see the peaks on the horizon.* **2.** A tapering point that projects upward: *the peak of a roof.* **3.** The point of greatest development, value, or intensity: *a book written at the peak of her career.* —*intr.v.* **1.** To be formed into a peak or peaks: *Beat the egg whites until they peak.* **2.** To achieve the point of greatest development, value, or intensity: *Sales tend to peak just before the holidays.*

HOMONYMS: **peak, peek** (glance), **pique** (provoke).

---

peaked[1] (pēkt *or* pē′kĭd) *adj.* Ending in a peak; pointed: *a peaked cap.*

peak•ed[2] (pē′kĭd) *adj.* Looking a little sick: *You look peaked today.*

peal (pēl) *n.* **1.** *(usually singular).* A ringing of a set of bells. **2.** A loud burst of noise: *peals of laughter.* —*tr. & intr.v.* To sound loudly; ring: *The bells pealed joyfully. The church bells pealed the hour.*

HOMONYMS: **peal, peel** (rind).

---

pea•nut (pē′nŭt′) *n.* **1.** The oily edible seed of a vine that grows in warm regions. **2. peanuts.** *Informal.* A small amount of money: *The salary is peanuts, but my job has other benefits.*

peanut

peanut butter *n.* [U] A paste made from ground roasted peanuts: *a sandwich of peanut butter and jelly.*

pear (pâr) *n.* A sweet juicy fruit with a rounded base and a narrower stem end.

HOMONYMS: **pear, pair** (two), **pare** (peel).

---

pearl (pûrl) *n.* **1.** A smooth white or grayish rounded growth formed inside the shells of some kinds of oysters and valued as a gem: *a necklace of pearls.* **2.** A person or thing that is very highly thought of: *pearls of wisdom.* —**pearl′y** *adj.*

peas•ant (pĕz′ənt) *n.* A member of the class of poor farmers and farm laborers: *Few peasants own the land they work.*

peas•ant•ry (pĕz′ən trē) *n.* [U] *(used with a singular or plural verb).* The social class made up of peasants.

peat (pēt) *n.* [U] Rotted vegetable matter, found in low wetland and used as a fuel and as a fertilizer.

peb•ble (pĕb′əl) *n.* A small stone, especially one worn smooth by erosion. —**peb′bly** *adj.*

ă–cat; ā–pay; âr–care; ä–father; ĕ–get; ē–be; ĭ–sit; ī–nice; îr–here; ŏ–got; ō–go; ô–saw; oi–boy; ou–out; ōō–took; ōō–boot; ŭ–cut; ûr–word; th–thin; *th*–this; hw–when; zh–vision; ə–about; N–French bon

pe·can (pĭ kăn′ *or* pĭ kän′ *or* pē′kăn) *n.* A nut with a smooth oval shell or the tree that bears such nuts.

peck[1] (pĕk) *v.* —*tr.* **1.** To make (a hole, for example) by striking sthg. repeatedly with a beak or a pointed instrument: *Birds have pecked holes in the tree.* **2.** To pick up (sthg.) with a beak: *The hungry hens pecked corn off the ground.* —*intr.* To strike sthg. with the beak or a pointed instrument: *The bird pecked at the dead branch.* —*n.* **1.** A stroke or light blow with the beak or a pointed instrument. **2.** *Informal.* A light quick kiss: *She gave me a peck as she was leaving.* ◆ **pecking order.** *Informal.* A ranking in order of importance among a group of people, classes, or nations: *As a newcomer, he was low in the pecking order.*

peck[2] (pĕk) *n.* **1.** A unit of dry volume or capacity equal to 8 quarts: *a peck of apples.* See table at **measurement. 2.** *(usually singular). Informal.* A great deal: *a peck of trouble.*

pec·to·ral (pĕk′tər əl) *adj.* Related to the chest or breast: *a pectoral muscle.* —*n.* A muscle of the chest: *The weightlifter has large pectorals.*

pe·cu·liar (pĭ kyōōl′yər) *adj.* **1.** Unusual or strange: *A peculiar sound caught my attention.* **2.** [*to*] Belonging to only one person, group, or kind; unique: *a fish peculiar to this river.* —**pe·cu′liar·ly** *adv.*

pe·cu·li·ar·i·ty (pĭ kyōō′lē ăr′ĭ tē *or* pĭ kyōōl yăr′ĭ tē) *n., pl.* **pe·cu·li·ar·i·ties. 1.** [C; U] The quality or condition of being peculiar: *the peculiarity of such quiet in the city.* **2.** [C] A notable or special feature or characteristic: *the peculiarities of a New York accent.* **3.** [C] Something odd or strange in a person's behavior: *his peculiarities about money.*

ped·a·gogue (pĕd′ə gŏg *or* pĕd′ə gôg′) *n. Formal.* **1.** A schoolteacher; an educator. **2.** A person who teaches in a close-minded manner: *The elderly professor was a bit of a pedagogue.*

ped·a·go·gy (pĕd′ə gō′jē *or* pĕd′ə gŏj′ē) *n.* [U] *Formal.* The art or profession of teaching. —**ped′a·gog′ic** (pĕd′ə gŏj′ĭk) also **ped′a·gog′i·cal** (pĕd′ə gŏj′ĭ kəl) *adj.*

ped·al (pĕd′l) *n.* A lever operated by the foot, as on a machine such as an automobile or bicycle or on a musical instrument such as a piano or organ: *brake pedals.* —*v.* —*intr.* To ride a bicycle: *We pedaled down the hill.* —*tr.* To operate the pedals of (sthg.): *He pedaled the bike up the hill.*

pe·dan·tic (pə dăn′tĭk) *adj.* Characterized by too much emphasis on book learning and formal rules: *a pedantic mind.* —**pe·dan′ti·cal·ly** *adv.*

ped·dle (pĕd′l) *tr.v.* **ped·dled, ped·dling, ped·dles. 1.** To travel around selling (goods): *He tries to peddle souvenirs to tourists in the street.* **2.** *Informal.* To spread or deal out (sthg.): *Don't peddle lies.* —**ped′dler** *n.*

ped·es·tal (pĕd′ĭ stəl) *n.* A support or base, as for a column or statue: *a marble pedestal.* ◆ **put on a pedestal.** To have too high regard or admiration for sbdy.: *Putting people on pedestals can lead to disappointment.*

pe·des·tri·an (pə dĕs′trē ən) *n.* A person traveling on foot, especially on city streets: *Pedestrians have the right of way.* —*adj.* **1.** Relating to pedestrians: *She stopped the car at a pedestrian crossing.* **2.** Commonplace; ordinary: *The reviewer criticized the author for her pedestrian writing.*

pe·di·a·tri·cian (pē′dē ə trĭsh′ən) *n.* A doctor who specializes in pediatrics.

pe·di·at·rics (pē′dē ăt′rĭks) *n.* [U] *(used with a singular verb).* The branch of medicine that deals with the care of infants and children and the treatment of their diseases. —**pe′di·at′ric** *adj.*

ped·i·cure (pĕd′ĭ kyōōr′) *n.* A cosmetic treatment of the feet and toenails: *She treated herself to a pedicure.*

ped·i·gree (pĕd′ĭ grē′) *n.* [C; U] A list or record of ancestors, especially of a purebred animal: *a horse with a great pedigree; of uncertain pedigree.*

ped·i·greed (pĕd′ĭ grēd′) *adj.* With a line of purebred ancestors: *a show of pedigreed dogs.*

pee (pē) *Slang. intr.v.* **peed, pee·ing, pees.** To urinate: *I drank a lot and needed to pee.* —*n.* **1.** [U] Urine. **2.** [C] An act of urination: *He went to the bathroom to take a pee.*

peek (pēk) *intr.v.* **1.** To look or glance briefly, as from a hiding place: *She peeked out the window to see who was at the door.* **2.** To be partially visible; show: *The first spring flowers peeked through the snow.* —*n.* A quick sly glance or look: *Take a peek at him.*

peek·a·boo (pēk′ə bōō′) *n.* [U] A game for amusing a small child, in which one covers one's face or hides and then comes out saying "Peekaboo!" —*adj.* Made to be partially see-through: *a peekaboo blouse.*

peel (pēl) *n.* [C; U] The skin of certain fruits and vegetables: *orange peel; potato peels.* —*v.* —*tr.* **1.** To remove the skin or rind from (sthg.): *peel a banana.* **2.** To strip away or pull off (an outer covering): *peel the bark off a tree.* —*intr.* To come off in thin strips or layers, as skin or paint: *The paint is peeling off the house.*

P

HOMONYMS: **peel, peal** (ringing).

peel·ings (pē'lĭngz) *pl.n.* The parts of a fruit or vegetable that are cut off and not eaten.

peep[1] (pēp) *n.* A weak high-pitched chirping sound, like that made by a young bird. —*intr.v.* To make such a sound: *Baby birds peeped in their nest.*

peep[2] (pēp) *intr.v.* **1.** To look from a concealed place; peek: *The kittens peeped from their box.* **2.** To become visible gradually, as though coming out of a hiding place: *At dawn the sun peeped over the horizon.* —*n.* A quick look or glance; a peek: *I took a peep at the sleeping baby.*

peep·hole (pēp'hōl') *n.* A small hole through which one may peep: *Many people now have peepholes in the doors of their apartments.*

peer[1] (pîr) *intr.v.* To look intently or with difficulty: *The driver tried to peer through the fog.*

HOMONYMS: **peer** (look, equal), **pier** (dock).

peer[2] (pîr) *n.* A person who has equal standing with others, as in rank, class, or age: *His teacher reports that he is well liked by his peers.*

peer·less (pîr'lĭs) *adj.* With no equal; unmatched: *a peerless performance by the champion ice skater.* —**peer'less·ly** *adv.* —**peer'less·ness** *n.* [U]

peeve (pēv) *tr.v.* **peeved, peev·ing, peeves.** To annoy (sbdy.) or make irritable: *My neighbor's dog barks so much that it peeves me.* —*n.* Something that annoys: *Her biggest peeve is the noisy dog next door.*

pee·vish (pē'vĭsh) *adj.* Annoyed; irritable: *The old man gets peevish when he's sick.* —**pee'vish·ly** *adv.* —**pee'vish·ness** *n.* [U]

peg (pĕg) *n.* **1.** A short rod or rounded pin, often of wood, used to hang things, fasten things, or plug a hole: *a row of pegs on the wall for hanging up jackets.* **2.** A degree, as in regard or respect: *My opinion of him has gone up a few pegs.* —*tr.v.* **pegged, peg·ging, pegs. 1.** To fasten or plug (sthg.) with a peg. **2.** To set or fix (a price, for example): *The company agreed to peg pay raises to the rate of inflation.* **3.** *Informal.* To classify (sbdy.): *We pegged her as the math expert.* ◆ **take down a peg.** To make sbdy. feel less proud: *He is too sure of himself and needs to be taken down a peg.*

pe·jor·a·tive (pə jôr'ə tĭv *or* pə jŏr'ə tĭv) *adj.* Expressive of a low or negative opinion. For example, *egghead* is a pejorative word for an intellectual. —**pe·jor'a·tive·ly** *adv.*

pel·i·can (pĕl'ĭ kən) *n.* A large, web-footed water bird of warm regions, with a large pouch under the lower bill for holding fish.

pel·let (pĕl'ĭt) *n.* **1.** A small densely packed ball, as of food, wax, or medicine. **2.** A small bullet or shot.

pelican

pell-mell also **pell·mell** (pĕl'mĕl') *adv.* In a hurried and confused manner: *The ducks flew off pell-mell.* —**pell'-mell'** *adj.*

pelt[1] (pĕlt) *n.* An animal skin with the fur or hair still on it.

pelt[2] (pĕlt) *v.* —*tr.* **1.** To strike (sbdy./sthg.) repeatedly with blows or objects: *The children pelted the sign with snowballs.* **2.** To throw (objects): *We were pelting stones at tin cans.* —*intr.* To strike or beat heavily: *The rain pelted against the tent.*

pel·vis (pĕl'vĭs) *n.* A basin-shaped structure in the vertebrate skeleton that is formed of several different bones and rests on the legs, supporting the lower end of the spine. —**pel'vic** *adj.*

pen[1] (pĕn) *n.* Any of various instruments for writing with ink, including the ballpoint pen and the fountain pen. —*tr.v.* **penned, pen·ning, pens.** To write or compose (sthg.) with or as if with a pen: *She penned a poem.*

pen[2] (pĕn) *n.* A small fenced-in area, especially one in which animals are kept. —*tr.v.* **penned** or **pent** (pĕnt), **pen·ning, pens.** To keep (an animal, for example) in or as if in a pen: *We pen the dogs out back.*

pen[3] (pĕn) *n. Informal.* A penitentiary: *The criminal did six years in the pen.*

pe·nal (pē'nəl) *adj.* Relating to punishment, as for breaking the law: *criminals sent to work in a penal colony.*

pe·nal·ize (pē'nə līz' *or* pĕn'ə līz') *tr.v.* **pe·nal·ized, pe·nal·iz·ing, pe·nal·iz·es.** To make (sbdy.) suffer a penalty, as for breaking a law or rule: *Our team was penalized by the officials for rough play.*

pen·al·ty (pĕn'əl tē) *n., pl.* **pen·al·ties. 1.** A punishment set by law for a crime: *the penalty for murder.* **2.** Something, such as money, that must be given up for an offense: *He paid a late penalty of $15.* **3.** In sports, a punishment or disadvantage imposed on a team or competitor for breaking a rule: *a two-minute penalty.*

pen·ance (pĕn'əns) *n.* [U] An act of self-denial or devotion that one does to show sorrow for a sin or other wrongdoing: *You must do penance for your selfish actions.*

pence (pĕns) *n. Chiefly British.* A plural of **penny** (sense 2).

pen·chant (pĕn′chənt) *n.* A definite liking or a strong tendency: *a penchant for spicy cooking; a penchant for getting into trouble.*

pen·cil (pĕn′səl) *n.* **1.** A thin writing instrument consisting of a stick of graphite or some other material encased in wood or held in a mechanical holder: *colored pencils.* **2.** Something shaped or used like a pencil: *an eyebrow pencil.* —*tr.v.* To write or mark (sthg.) with a pencil: *Her father penciled a shopping list.*

pen·dant (pĕn′dənt) *n.* A hanging ornament, such as one worn on a necklace.

pend·ing (pĕn′dĭng) *adj.* **1.** Not yet decided or settled; awaiting action: *legislation pending before Congress.* **2.** Soon to happen: *his pending retirement.* —*prep.* While awaiting; until: *The bridge is closed pending an investigation of the accident.*

pen·du·lous (pĕn′jə ləs) *adj.* Hanging loosely; suspended so as to swing or sway: *the elephant's pendulous ears.*

pen·du·lum (pĕn′-jə ləm) *n.* A weight hung from a fixed support so that it swings freely, often used to regulate the action of clocks.

pen·e·trate (pĕn′ĭ-trāt′) *v.* **pen·e·trat·ed, pen·e·trat·ing, pen·e·trates.** —*tr.* **1.** To enter or force a way into (sbdy./sthg.):

pendulum

A shaft of light penetrated the dark room. **2.** To enter into and spread through (sthg.): *Cold penetrated my bones.* **3.** To gain understanding of (sthg.): *penetrating the workings of the immune system.* —*intr.* To pierce or enter sthg.; make a way in or through sthg.: *plans to penetrate into outer space.* —**pen′e·tra·bil′i·ty** (pĕn′ĭ-trə bĭl′ĭ tē) *n.* [U] —**pen′e·tra·ble** *adj.*

pen·e·trat·ing (pĕn′ĭ trā′tĭng) *adj.* **1.** Sharp and loud: *a penetrating shriek.* **2.** Able to enter and spread through sthg.: *a penetrating ointment.* **3.** Showing sharp understanding: *a penetrating glance; penetrating remarks.* —**pen′e·trat′ing·ly** *adv.*

pen·e·tra·tion (pĕn′ĭ trā′shən) *n.* [U] **1.** The act of penetrating: *successful penetration of the opposing team's defense.* **2.** The power or ability to penetrate: *a drill with great penetration.* **3.** The ability to understand: *a problem that will require great penetration.*

pen·guin (pĕng′gwĭn *or* pĕn′gwĭn) *n.* Any of various flightless sea birds that live mostly in or near Antarctica.

pen·i·cil·lin (pĕn′ĭ sĭl′ĭn) *n.* [U] A medicine used to treat various diseases and infections.

pen·in·su·la (pə nĭn′sə lə) *n.* A piece of land that projects into a body of water and is connected with a larger land mass: *the Cape Cod peninsula.* —**pen·in′su·lar** *adj.*

pe·nis (pē′nĭs) *n.* The male sex organ, also used for urination.

pen·i·tent (pĕn′ĭ tənt) *adj.* Feeling sorrow for one's sins or wrong actions: *I was penitent as soon as the words were out of my mouth.* —*n.* A person who is penitent: *The penitents prayed and fasted.* —**pen′i·tence** *n.* [U]

pen·i·ten·tia·ry (pĕn′ĭ tĕn′shə rē) *n., pl.* **pen·i·ten·tia·ries.** A prison: *The drug dealer was sentenced to 20 years in the state penitentiary.*

pen·man·ship (pĕn′mən shĭp′) *n.* [U] The art, skill, or manner of handwriting: *Why do doctors have such unreadable penmanship?*

Penn. *abbr.* An abbreviation of Pennsylvania.

pen name *n.* A fictitious name used by an author: *The famous physicist wrote science fiction under a pen name.*

pen·nant (pĕn′ənt) *n.* **1.** A long tapering flag, such as are used on ships for signaling or identification. **2.** The yearly championship in professional baseball: *Who won the pennant last year?*

pen·ni·less (pĕn′ē lĭs) *adj.* With little or no money; very poor: *The failure of his business left him almost penniless.* —**pen′ni·less·ness** *n.* [U]

pen·ny (pĕn′ē) *n., pl.* **pen·nies. 1.** In the United States and Canada, the coin worth one cent. **2.** *pl.* **pence** *or* **pen·nies.** A coin used in Great Britain since 1971, worth 1/100 of a pound. **3.** A small sum of money: *I don't even have a penny in the bank.*

pen pal *n.* A friend whom one knows only by exchanging letters: *a student in Florida writing to a pen pal in Brazil.*

pen·sion (pĕn′shən) *n.* A sum of money paid regularly as a benefit to people who are retired: *She receives a monthly pension of $1,500.* —*tr.v.* To give a pension to (sbdy.). ♦ **pension off.** *tr.v.* [sep.] To retire or dismiss (sbdy.) with a pension: *The company reduced its workforce by pensioning off some older workers.* —**pen′sion·er** *n.*

pen·sive (pĕn′sĭv) *adj.* **1.** In deep and serious thought: *You've been pensive all day.* **2.** Showing deep, often sad thoughtfulness: *pensive eyes.* —**pen′sive·ly** *adv.* —**pen′sive·ness** *n.* [U]

pent (pĕnt) *v.* A past tense and a past participle of **pen²**.

penta– *or* **pent–** *pref.* A prefix that means five: *pentagon.*

pen·ta·gon (pĕn′tə gŏn′) *n.* **1.** A geometric figure bounded by five line segments and containing five angles. **2. Pentagon.** A five-sided building near Washington, D.C., containing the U.S. Department of

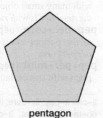

pentagon

Defense and the offices of the U.S. Armed Forces: *The commanding officer was sent to the Pentagon.* —**pen•tag′o•nal** (pĕn tăg′-ə nəl) *adj.*

pent•house (pĕnt′hous′) *n.* An expensive apartment located on the top floor of a tall building: *a penthouse view.*

pent-up (pĕnt′ŭp′) *adj.* Not expressed; held inside: *pent-up anger.*

pe•nul•ti•mate (pĭ nŭl′tə mĭt) *adj.* Next to last: *the penultimate chapter of the book.*

pe•on (pē′ŏn′ *or* pē′ən) *n.* **1.** A menial worker; a person who does low-level, routine work: *a peon in the company.* **2.** An unskilled laborer or farm worker in Latin America.

pe•o•ny (pē′ə nē) *n., pl.* **pe•o•nies.** A garden plant with large pink, red, or white flowers.

peo•ple (pē′pəl) *n., pl.* **people. 1.** Human beings considered as a group: *She prefers cats to people as companions.* **2.** A group of persons living under one government: *the people of Alaska.* **3.** *pl.* **peoples.** A group of persons sharing a common religion, culture, language, or condition of life: *the peoples of southwest Asia.* **4.** Family, relatives, or ancestors: *Her people are farmers.* —*tr.v.* **peo•pled, peo•pling, peo•ples.** To fill (a place) with or as if with people: *Many ethnic groups people the city.*

pep (pĕp) *Informal. n.* [U] Energy; high spirits: *Puppies have a lot of pep.* —*v.* **pepped, pep•ping, peps.** ◆ **pep up.** *tr.v.* [sep.] To make (sbdy./sthg.) more active, spirited, or interesting: *A cup of coffee will pep me up. A few jokes pepped up his speech.*

pep•per (pĕp′ər) *n.* **1.** [U] A black or white pungent spice made from the dried berries of a tropical vine: *added salt and pepper.* **2.** [C] The many-seeded red, yellow, or green fruit of any of several plants,

pepper

eaten as a vegetable or ground into seasonings: *bell peppers.* **3.** [U] Any of various seasonings, such as cayenne pepper or chili powder, made from hot red peppers. —*tr.v.* **1.** To season (sthg.) with pepper: *Let me pepper your food.* **2.** To supply (sbdy./sthg.) generously with small amounts of sthg.: *He likes to pepper a speech with jokes. She peppered me with ideas.* **3.** [U] To sprinkle or spray (sbdy./sthg.) with many small objects: *The guests peppered the newlyweds with rice.* —**pep′per•y** *adj.*

pep•per•corn (pĕp′ər kôrn′) *n.* A berry of the pepper vine: *The recipe uses green peppercorns.*

pep•per•mint (pĕp′ər mĭnt′) *n.* **1.** [U] A plant with leaves that produce an oil having a

strong pleasant taste and smell. **2.** [U] The oil or flavoring from this plant: *peppermint ice cream.* **3.** [C] A candy flavored with this oil: *chocolate-covered peppermints.*

pep•per•o•ni (pĕp′ə rō′nē) *n.* [C; U] A highly spiced pork and beef sausage.

pep talk *n. Informal.* A speech of encouragement: *The coach gave the team a pep talk.*

per (pûr) *prep.* **1.** To, for, or by each; for every: *Set the price at one dollar per dozen.* **2.** According to: *The publisher made changes to the book per instructions of the author.*

per annum (pûr ăn′əm) *adv. Formal.* By the year; annually: *This magazine subscription costs $25 per annum.*

per cap•i•ta (pər kăp′ĭ tə) *adv. & adj.* Per person: *the state's per capita income.*

per•ceive (pər sēv′) *tr.v.* **per•ceived, per•ceiv•ing, per•ceives. 1.** To become aware of (sbdy./sthg.) through the senses, especially to see or hear: *The baby sitter perceived that the child had been crying.* **2.** To achieve understanding of (sthg.): *We tried to perceive their intentions by analyzing their letter.*

per•cent also **per cent** (pər sĕnt′) *n.* One part in a hundred: *Sixty-two percent of the people we asked contributed some money.* —*adj.* Gaining interest at a given rate or percentage: *an eight percent savings account.*

per•cent•age (pər sĕn′tĭj) *n.* **1.** A fraction that has 100 understood as its denominator: *0.75 equals a percentage of 75.* **2.** A portion or share in relation to the whole: *A sizable percentage of the people at the meeting were teachers.*

per•cep•ti•ble (pər sĕp′tə bəl) *adj.* Capable of being perceived by the senses or by the mind: *a perceptible improvement in the patient's condition.* —**per•cep′ti•bly** *adv.*

per•cep•tion (pər sĕp′shən) *n.* **1.** [U] The ability, act, or process of perceiving: *quick in perception.* **2.** [C] Something perceived or understood: *You can't always trust your perception of a situation.* —**per•cep′tu•al** *adj.*

per•cep•tive (pər sĕp′tĭv) *adj.* **1.** Able to perceive; possessing good insight: *a perceptive student of physics.* **2.** Showing understanding and insight: *a perceptive thought.* —**per•cep′tive•ly** *adv.*

perch (pûrch) *n.* **1.** A branch or rod where a bird stands or rests: *The parrot stood on a perch.* **2.** A resting place or point for viewing sthg., especially one that is high up: *The girl slid down from a perch in the apple tree.* —*v.* —*intr.* **1.** To pause or rest as if on a perch: *She perched on the stool.* **2.** To occupy an elevated positon: *A village perched on the hillside.* —*tr.* To place (sthg.) as if on a perch: *She perched the straw hat on her head.*

per•co•late (pûr′kə lāt′) *v.* **per•co•lat•ed,**

per·co·lat·ing, per·co·lates. —*tr.* To cause (a liquid, for example) to pass through small holes or through a porous substance: *percolate oil through a filter.* —*intr.* **1.** To drain or pass slowly through a porous material or a filter: *Water percolated through the sand.* **2.** *Informal.* To become lively or active: *As she became aware of the new data, an idea began to percolate in her mind.* —**per′co·la′tion** *n.* [U]
per·co·la·tor (pûr′kə lā′tər) *n.* A coffeepot in which boiling water is forced up through a center tube and filters down through a basket of ground coffee.
per·cus·sion (pər kŭsh′ən) *n.* [U] **1.a.** The striking together of two objects, especially when noise is produced. **b.** A sound, vibration, or shock produced in this way. **2.** The group of musical instruments sounded by striking one object against another, such as the piano, drum, or triangle: *Percussion usually occupies the back row of an orchestra.*
per di·em (pər dē′əm) *adv. Formal.* Per day: *We are paid not by the hour but per diem.* —*adj.* On a daily basis; daily: *per diem expenses.* —*n.* An allowance for daily expenses: *The company gives traveling sales representatives a small per diem.*
per·emp·to·ry (pə rĕmp′tə rē) *adj.* **1.** Putting an end to all debate or action: *a peremptory order from the military governor.* **2.** Not to be denied, refused, or opposed: *a peremptory command.* **3.** Offensively self-assured; dictatorial: *his peremptory manner.* —**per·emp′to·ri·ly** *adv.*
per·en·ni·al (pə rĕn′ē əl) *adj.* **1.** Growing, flowering, and producing seeds for three or more years: *a perennial garden.* **2.** Lasting indefinitely: *perennial happiness.* **3.** Repeated regularly; appearing again and again: *perennial financial problems.* —*n.* A perennial plant: *Daisies are perennials.* —**per·en′ni·al·ly** *adv.*
per·fect (pûr′fĭkt) *adj.* **1.** With no faults, flaws, or defects: *a perfect diamond.* **2.a.** Lacking nothing; satisfying all requirements: *His understanding of the situation was perfect.* **b.** Completely accurate; exact: *a perfect copy.* **3.** Excellent in all respects: *perfect weather.* **4.** Complete: *a perfect fool.* **5.** Having a root that is a whole number; formed by raising an integer to an integral power. For example, 25 is a perfect square and 27 is a perfect cube. **6.** In grammar, relating to the perfect tense. —*n.* **1.** The perfect tense. **2.** A verb form in the perfect tense. —*tr.v.* (pər fĕkt′). To bring (sthg.) to perfection or completion: *He is trying to perfect his tennis serve.*

SYNONYMS: perfect, faultless, flawless, impeccable. These adjectives all mean without any defects or errors. *I think I have found the perfect solution. The lecturer argued her point with fault-*

less logic. That museum owns the largest flawless gem in the world. They spoke impeccable French after spending several years in Paris.

per·fect·i·ble (pər fĕk′tə bəl) *adj.* Capable of becoming or being made perfect: *perfectible writing.*
per·fec·tion (pər fĕk′shən) *n.* [U] **1.** The quality or condition of being perfect: *The factory owners demand perfection from the workers.* **2.** The act of perfecting: *Perfection of a recipe takes many attempts.* **3.** A person or thing considered to be a perfect example of excellence: *She is perfection on the dance floor.* ◆ **to perfection.** Flawlessly; without any mistakes: *a ballet performed to perfection.*
per·fec·tion·ism (pər fĕk′shə nĭz′əm) *n.* [U] A tendency to set extremely high standards and to be dissatisfied with anything less: *His perfectionism destroyed his marriage.* —**per·fec′tion·ist** *n.*
per·fect·ly (pûr′fĭkt lē) *adv.* **1.a.** In a perfect manner: *She played the piece perfectly.* **b.** To a perfect degree; precisely: *This circle is perfectly round.* **2.** Completely; wholly: *Those mushrooms are perfectly safe to eat.*
perfect tense *n.* In grammar, a verb tense that expresses an action completed prior to a fixed point in time. For example, *she has played* is in the present perfect tense, *she had played* is in the past perfect tense, and *she will have played* is in the future perfect tense.
per·fo·rate (pûr′fə rāt′) *tr.v.* **per·fo·rat·ed, per·fo·rat·ing, per·fo·rates.** **1.** To make holes in (sthg.); pierce: *Perforate the top of the pie to let the steam escape.* **2.** To pierce or stamp (sthg.) with rows of holes to allow easy separation: *A machine perforates sheets of postage stamps.*
per·fo·ra·tion (pûr′fə rā′shən) *n.* **1.** [C] A hole or series of holes, as those between postage stamps: *Tear the card off along the perforation.* **2.** [U] The act of perforating: *Perforation will cause the balloon to burst.*
per·form (pər fôrm′) *v.* —*tr.* **1.** To begin and carry (sthg.) through to completion: *perform an experiment.* **2.** To carry out or fulfill (a promise, duty, or task, for example): *perform one's job.* **3.** To present or enact (sthg.) before an audience: *perform a symphony.* —*intr.* **1.** To act or function in a specified manner: *The car performs well on curves.* **2.** To portray a role, present a musical work, or demonstrate a skill before an audience: *A famous pianist will perform on Tuesday.* —**per·form′er** *n.*
per·form·ance (pər fôr′məns) *n.* **1.** [U] The act or manner of performing: *Your performance on the job has been poor lately.* **2.** [U] The way in which a person or thing functions: *Look for good steady performance when buying a car.* **3.** [C] A public presentation of sthg., such as a musical or dramatic work: *a performance of Hamlet.*

per•fume (pûr′fyŏŏm′ *or* pər fyŏŏm′) *n.* **1.**
[C; U] A pleasant-smelling liquid made from
flowers or prepared synthetically: *a gift of
perfume.* **2.** [U] A pleasant scent or odor: *the
perfume of the garden at night. —tr.v.* (pər-
fyŏŏm′). **per•fumed, per•fum•ing, per•
fumes.** To fill (sthg.) with a fragrance or apply
a fragrance to (sthg.): *perfume the sheets.*

per•func•to•ry (pər fŭngk′tə rē) *adj.* Done
or acting routinely and with little interest or
care: *She gave a perfunctory wave and walked
away. —per•func′to•ri•ly adv.*

per•haps (pər hăps′) *adv.* Maybe; possibly:
Perhaps he'll come with us.

peri— *pref.* A prefix that means around,
about, or enclosing: *perimeter.*

per•il (pĕr′əl) *n. Formal.* **1.** [U] The condition
of being in danger or at risk of harm or loss:
The drought has put the crops in peril. **2.** [C]
Something that is dangerous or risky: *the per-
ils of a journey in a covered wagon. —per′-
il•ous adj. —per′il•ous•ly adv.*

pe•rim•e•ter (pə rĭm′ĭ tər) *n.* The outer limits of a figure or an area: *figure the perimeter
of a square; walk the perimeter of a cornfield.*

pe•ri•od (pîr′ē əd) *n.* **1.** An interval of time
with a specified length or characterized by
certain conditions: *a period of growth in the
economy.* **2.** A span of time known for a particular culture, set of beliefs, or technology; a
historical era: *the colonial period.* **3.** Any of
various intervals of time, as the divisions of
the school day or of playing time in a game: *I
have history in the fifth period.* **4.** An instance
or occurrence of menstruation: *She gets her
period about every 28 days.* **5.** A punctuation
mark (.) used at the end of declarative sentences and after many abbreviations.

pe•ri•od•ic (pîr′ē ŏd′ĭk) *adj.* **1.** Happening
or repeating at regular intervals; cyclic: *the
periodic motion of a pendulum.* **2.** Happening
repeatedly at irregular intervals: *periodic
inspections intended to take us by surprise.
—pe′ri•od′i•cal•ly adv.*

pe•ri•od•i•cal (pîr′ē ŏd′ĭ kəl) *adj.* **1.** Periodic: *periodical bouts with the flu.* **2.** Relating to a publication that is issued at regular
intervals of more than one day: *periodical
newspapers. —n.* A periodical publication,
especially a magazine that is issued at regular
intervals, such as once a week: *the periodi-
cals section of the library.*

periodic table *n.* A table in which the elements are presented in order of increasing
atomic number, with the elements that have
similar properties usually appearing in
columns.

per•i•o•don•tal (pĕr′ē ə dŏn′tl) *adj.* Relating to tissues and structures around the
teeth: *periodontal disease.*

per•i•o•don•tics (pĕr′ē ə dŏn′tĭks) *n.* [U]
(used with a singular verb). The branch
of dentistry that deals with the study and
treatment of periodontal disease. —**per′i•o•
don′tist** *n.*

pe•riph•er•al (pə rĭf′ər əl) *adj.* **1.** Located
on the periphery: *peripheral vision.* **2.** Of
minor importance: *Don't waste time on
peripheral issues. —n.* A device that can be
attached to a computer and controlled by
it: *Modems and printers are peripherals.
—pe•riph′er•al•ly adv.*

pe•riph•er•y (pə rĭf′ə rē) *n., pl.* **pe•riph•
er•ies. 1.** A line that forms a boundary; an
outer edge: *The strangers stayed at the
periphery of the crowd.* **2.** The outermost part
within a boundary: *He planted trees on the
periphery of his property.*

per•i•scope (pĕr′ĭ skōp′) *n.* An optical
instrument in which mirrors or prisms allow a
viewer to see objects that are not in a direct
line of sight: *a submarine periscope.*

per•ish (pĕr′ĭsh) *intr.v.* **1.** To die or be destroyed in a violent manner: *Many people
perished in the flood.* **2.** To pass from existence; disappear gradually: *The dinosaurs
perished from the earth.*

per•ish•a•ble (pĕr′ĭ shə bəl) *adj.* Likely to
decay or spoil easily: *perishable fruits and
vegetables. —n. (usually plural).* Something,
especially food, that may decay or spoil:
Keep perishables in the refrigerator.

per•jure (pûr′jər) *tr.v.* **per•jured, per•
jur•ing, per•jures.** To make (oneself) guilty
of perjury by telling lies under oath: *The witness perjured himself. —per′jur•er n.*

per•ju•ry (pûr′jə rē) *n.* [U] In law, the deliberate giving of false testimony while under
oath: *a witness found guilty of perjury.*

perk[1] (pûrk) *v. —tr.* **1.** To percolate (sthg.): *We
perked some fresh coffee.* **2.** To raise (sthg.) up:
The dog perked its ears at the noise. —intr. To
percolate: *The coffeepot was perking on the
stove.* ♦ **perk up.** *v.* [sep.] **1.** To cause (sbdy.)
to regain good spirits or liveliness: *A walk in the
fresh air perked me up.* **2.** To refresh the appearance of (sthg.): *New curtains perked up the
room. —intr.v.* To regain one's health or good
spirits: *She has perked up since the operation.*

perk[2] (pûrk) *n. Informal.* A perquisite: *Her
job has a lot of perks.*

perk•y (pûr′kē) *adj.* **perk•i•er, perk•i•est.**
Cheerful and lively: *a perky hat; a perky smile.
—perk′i•ly adv.*

perm (pûrm) *Informal. n.* A hair permanent:
She got a perm. —tr.v. To give a permanent to
(one's hair): *She permed her hair.*

per•ma•nence (pûr′mə nəns) *n.* [U] The
quality or condition of being permanent: *the
permanence of death.*

per·ma·nent (pûr′mə nənt) *adj.* Lasting or meant to last indefinitely; enduring: *a permanent settlement on the frontier.* —*n.* Long-lasting hair curls produced by setting the hair with chemicals. —**per′ma·nent·ly** *adv.*

per·ma·nent-press (pûr′mə nənt prĕs′) *adj.* Chemically treated for resistance to wrinkles and requiring no ironing: *permanent-press shirts.*

per·me·a·ble (pûr′mē ə bəl) *adj.* Capable of being passed through or permeated by liquids or gases: *rock that is permeable by water.* —**per′me·a·bil′i·ty** *n.* [U] —**per′me·a·bly** *adv.*

per·me·ate (pûr′mē āt′) *tr.v.* **per·me·at·ed, per·me·at·ing, per·me·ates. 1.** To spread or flow throughout (sthg.): *The smell of baking cookies permeated the house.* **2.** To pass through the tiny openings of (sthg.): *liquid permeating a membrane.*

per·mis·si·ble (pər mĭs′ə bəl) *adj.* Permitted; allowable: *a permissible error.* —**per·mis′si·bly** *adv.*

per·mis·sion (pər mĭsh′ən) *n.* [C; U] Consent, especially formal consent; authorization: *We have her permission to use her car.*

per·mis·sive (pər mĭs′ĭv) *adj.* Allowing freedom; lenient: *He has permissive parents.* —**per·mis′sive·ly** *adv.* —**per·mis′sive·ness** *n.* [U]

per·mit (pər mĭt′) *v.* **per·mit·ted, per·mit·ting, per·mits,** —*tr.* **1.** To allow the doing of (sthg.); consent to: *The town permits bicycle riding in the park.* **2.** To give consent or permission to (sbdy.): *The teacher does not permit students to chew gum in class.* **3.** To make (sthg.) possible: *The assembly line permitted mass production.* —*intr.* To give an opportunity; allow: *If weather permits, we will fly.* —*n.* (pûr′mĭt *or* pər mĭt′). A document or certificate giving permission to do sthg.: *a parking permit.*

per·mu·ta·tion (pûr′myoō tā′shən) *n.* **1.** *Formal.* A complete change; a transformation: *Spices undergo permutations when cooked.* **2.** Any of the ordered subsets that can be formed from the elements of a set. Some of the permutations of the set composed of *x, y,* and *z* are *xyz, xzy, yxz, yzx, zxy, zyx.*

per·ni·cious (pər nĭsh′əs) *adj. Formal.* **1.** Tending to cause death or serious injury; deadly: *a pernicious disease.* **2.** Causing great harm; destructive: *The nurse criticized smoking as a pernicious habit.* —**per·ni′cious·ly** *adv.*

per·ox·ide (pə rŏk′sīd′) *n.* [U] A colorless chemical liquid used primarily to bleach hair and destroy germs: *hydrogen peroxide.*

per·pen·dic·u·lar (pûr′pən dĭk′yə lər) *adj.* **1.** Intersecting at or forming a right angle: *graph paper covered with perpendicular lines.* **2.** At right angles to the horizontal; vertical: *the perpendicular walls of a deep canyon.* —**per′pen·dic′u·lar** *n.*

per·pe·trate (pûr′pĭ trāt′) *tr.v.* **per·pe·trat·ed, per·pe·trat·ing, per·pe·trates.** To be guilty of (sthg.); commit: *perpetrate a crime.* —**per′pe·tra′tion** *n.* [U] —**per′pe·tra′tor** *n.*

per·pet·u·al (pər pĕch′oō əl) *adj.* **1.** Lasting forever or for an indefinitely long time: *the perpetual ice of the polar regions.* **2.** Endlessly repeated or continuing without interruption: *She is tired of listening to her mother's perpetual nagging.* —**per·pet′u·al·ly** *adv.*

per·pet·u·ate (pər pĕch′oō āt′) *tr.v.* **per·pet·u·at·ed, per·pet·u·at·ing, per·pet·u·ates. 1.** To cause (sthg.) to continue indefinitely: *perpetuate bad feelings.* **2.** To cause (sthg.) to be remembered: *perpetuate a legend.* —**per·pet′u·a′tion** *n.* [U]

per·pe·tu·i·ty (pûr′pĭ toō′ĭ tē) *n.* [U] *Formal.* The quality or condition of being endless or eternal: *the perpetuity of greed.* ◆ **in perpetuity.** For an indefinite period of time; forever: *I have the use of the land in perpetuity.*

per·plex (pər plĕks′) *tr.v.* To confuse or puzzle (sbdy.): *Your behavior perplexes me.* —**per·plex′i·ty** (pər plĕk′sĭ tē) *n.* [U]

per·plexed (pər plĕkst′) *adj.* Confused or puzzled: *a perplexed look.*

per·qui·site (pûr′kwĭ zĭt) *n. Formal.* Something received in addition to a regular wage or salary; a special benefit: *Free use of a car was one of the supervisor's perquisites.*

per se (pər sā′) *adv. Formal.* In or by itself: *The law per se does not forbid smoking, but in combination with social pressures, it has greatly limited smoking.*

per·se·cute (pûr′sĭ kyoōt′) *tr.v.* **per·se·cut·ed, per·se·cut·ing, per·se·cutes.** To oppress or harass (sbdy.), especially because of politics, religion, or race, for example: *Nazis persecuted Jews during World War II.* —**per′se·cu′tion** (pûr′sĭ kyoō′shən) *n.* [U] —**per′se·cu′tor** *n.*

per·se·ver·ance (pûr′sə vîr′əns) *n.* [U] The act or quality of holding to a course of action, a belief, or a purpose: *It took great perseverance for the Wright Brothers to build a successful airplane.*

per·se·vere (pûr′sə vîr′) *intr.v.* **per·se·vered, per·se·ver·ing, per·se·veres.** [*at; in*] To hold to or persist in a course of action, a belief, or a purpose, in spite of opposition or discouragement: *Despite many difficulties, they persevered in their research.*

per·sist (pər sĭst′) *intr.v.* **1.** To insist or repeat in a stubborn manner: *She persisted in denying her guilt.* **2.** To hold firmly and steadfastly to a purpose, a state, or a project, despite difficulties or setbacks: *He persists in his efforts to find work.* **3.** To continue in existence; last: *The child's cough persisted for several weeks.*

P

per·sist·ent (pər sĭs'tənt) adj. **1.** Refusing to give up or let go; unwilling to stop: *a persistent salesman.* **2.** Insistently repetitive or continuous: *the persistent ringing of the telephone.* **3.** Existing in the same state for a long period of time; enduring: *The persistent problem of poverty won't just go away.* —**per·sist'ence** n. [U] —**per·sist'ent·ly** adv.

per·snick·e·ty (pər snĭk'ĭ tē) adj. Giving too much attention to unimportant details: *He quit his job because of a persnickety boss.*

per·son (pûr'sən) n. **1.** A living human being; an individual. **2.** A human being of a given characteristic: *a person of great talent.* **3.** *Formal.* The body or general appearance: *He had two wallets on his person.* **4.** In grammar, any of three groups of pronoun forms with corresponding verb forms that refer to the speaker (first person), the individual addressed (second person), or the individual or thing spoken of (third person). In the sentence *I spoke to you about her,* the pronoun *I* is in the first person, *you* is in the second person, and *her* is in the third person. ♦ **in person.** In one's physical presence; personally: *I'll deliver the book in person.*

per·so·na (pər sō'nə) n. *Formal.* **1.** *pl.* **per·so·nae** (pər sō'nē). A character in a literary work, especially one representing the speaker. **2.** *pl.* **personas.** The role that a person displays in public; one's public image or personality: *public persona.*

per·son·a·ble (pûr'sə nə bəl) adj. Pleasing in appearance or personality; attractive: *He's a personable fellow; you'll like him.*

per·son·al (pûr'sə nəl) adj. **1.** Relating to a particular person; private: *the personal letters of the college president.* **2.a.** Done, made, or performed in person: *a personal appearance.* **b.** For a particular person: *a personal favor.* **3.** Aimed at some aspect of a person, especially in a critical or unfriendly manner: *a highly personal remark.* **4.** Relating to the body or physical being: *personal cleanliness.* —n. *(usually plural).* A personal item or notice in a newspaper: *She reads the personals every day.*

personal computer or **PC** n. A microcomputer for use by an individual, as in an office or at home or school.

per·son·al·i·ty (pûr'sə năl'ĭ tē) n., pl. **per·son·al·i·ties. 1.** [C] The entire group of qualities and traits, of character or behavior, that are peculiar to each person: *He has a pleasing personality.* **2.** [U] The qualities that make sbdy./sthg. appealing: *Candidates can win more on personality than on capability. Colors give a room personality.* **3.** [C] A person of importance or fame: *television personalities.*

per·son·al·ize (pûr'sə nə līz) tr.v. **per·**

son·al·ized, per·son·al·iz·ing, per·son·al·iz·es. 1. To react to (sthg.) in a personal way: *You shouldn't personalize every little criticism.* **2.** To make (sthg.) personal, especially by marking as personal property: *Have them personalize the stationery.*

per·son·al·ly (pûr'sə nə lē) adv. **1.** In person or by oneself: *I thanked her personally rather than sending the standard letter.* **2.** As far as oneself is concerned: *Personally, I don't mind, but I can't speak for the others.* **3.** As a person: *I don't know him personally; we are just business acquaintances.* **4.** In a personal manner: *Try not to take criticism of your plan personally.*

personal pronoun n. In grammar, a pronoun that indicates the person speaking *(I, me, we, us),* the person spoken to *(you),* or the person or thing spoken about *(he, she, it, they, him, her, them).*

per·so·na non gra·ta (pər sō'nə nŏn grä'tə) adj. *Formal.* Fully unacceptable or unwelcome: *After he was fired, the man was persona non grata at the company.*

per·son·i·fy (pər sŏn'ə fī') tr.v. **per·son·i·fied, per·son·i·fy·ing, per·son·i·fies. 1.** To think of or represent (ideas or objects) as having human qualities or human form: *personifying justice as a blindfolded woman.* **2.** To be the perfect example of (a certain quality or idea): *The nurse personified compassion.* —**per·son'i·fi·ca'tion** (pər sŏn'ə fĭ kā'shən) n. [C; U]

per·son·nel (pûr'sə nĕl') n. **1.** *(used with a plural verb).* The group of persons employed by an organization, a business, or a service: *All of that company's personnel are pleasant to deal with.* **2.** *(used with a singular verb).* The division of an organization concerned with the selection, placement, and training of employees: *See someone in personnel about insurance. Personnel is down the hall.*

per·spec·tive (pər spĕk'tĭv) n. **1.** [C] A view: *the perspective of the city as seen from the rooftops.* **2.** [C] A mental outlook: *Try to get a new perspective on the issue.* **3.** [C; U] An idea of the relative importance of sthg.: *I don't want to lose perspective on our disagreement.* **4.** [U] The technique of representing three-dimensional objects and depth relationships on a flat surface: *a drawing of the building done in perspective.*

per·spi·ra·tion (pûr'spə rā'shən) n. [U] **1.** The salty moisture passed through the skin; sweat: *a shirt wet with perspiration.* **2.** The act or process of perspiring: *Perspiration cools the body.*

per·spire (pər spīr') intr.v. **per·spired, per·spir·ing, per·spires.** To give off perspiration: *Hard exercise makes me perspire.*

ă–cat; ā–pay; âr–care; ä–father; ĕ–get; ē–be; ĭ–sit; ī–nice; îr–here; ŏ–got; ō–go; ô–saw; oi–boy; ou–out; ōō–took; ōō–boot; ŭ–cut; ûr–word; th–thin; th–this; hw–when; zh–vision; ə–about; N–French bon

per•suade (pər swād') *tr.v.* **per•suad•ed, per•suad•ing, per•suades.** To cause (sbdy.) to do or believe sthg. by arguing, pleading, or reasoning; convince: *He tried to persuade them to come with us.* —**per•suad'er** *n.*

per•sua•sion (pər swā'zhən) *n.* **1.** [U] The act of persuading or the state of being persuaded: *It took a lot of persuasion to make him change his mind.* **2.** [C] A strong belief: *of a certain political persuasion.*

per•sua•sive (pər swā'sĭv) *adj.* Having the power to persuade: *You make a very persuasive argument.* —**per•sua'sive•ly** *adv.* —**per•sua'sive•ness** *n.* [U]

pert (pûrt) *adj.* **1.** Stylish: *a pert dress.* **2.** High-spirited; lively: *a pert little dog.* **3.** Bold and a little disrespectful: *a pert answer.* —**pert'ly** *adv.* —**pert'ness** *n.* [U]

per•tain (pər tān') *intr.v.* [*to*] **1.** To have reference; relate: *a discussion pertaining to art.* **2.** To belong to as a part or accessory of: *engineering skills that pertain to aeronautics.*

per•ti•nent (pûr'tn ənt) *adj.* Related to a specific matter at hand; relevant: *discussing pertinent topics.* —**per'ti•nence** *n.* [U]

per•turbed (pər tûrbd') *adj.* Uneasy or anxious; upset: *He was always perturbed over small matters.*

pe•ruse (pə rōōz') *tr.v.* **pe•rused, pe•rus•ing, pe•rus•es.** To read or examine (sthg.), especially with great care: *peruse a novel.* —**pe•rus'al** *n.* [C; U]

per•vade (pər vād') *tr.v.* **per•vad•ed, per•vad•ing, per•vades.** To spread or be present throughout (sthg.); permeate: *The sweet scent of gardenias pervaded the house.*

per•va•sive (pər vā'sĭv) *adj.* Tending to pervade or permeate: *a pervasive mood among voters.* —**per•va'sive•ly** *adv.* —**per•va'sive•ness** *n.* [U]

per•verse (pər vûrs') *adj.* **1.** Stubbornly opposing or resisting what is right, expected, or reasonable: *You're arguing just to be perverse.* **2.** Showing stubbornness or contrariness: *a perverse attitude.* —**per•verse'ly** *adv.* —**per•verse'ness** *n.* [U]

per•ver•sion (pər vûr'zhən *or* pər vûr'shən) *n.* **1.** [C; U] The act of perverting or the state of being perverted: *The cult leader accused the newspapers of printing perversions of his beliefs and teachings.* **2.** [C] A sexual act or practice that is considered abnormal or deviant.

per•ver•si•ty (pər vûr'sĭ tē) *n., pl.* **per•ver•si•ties.** [C; U] The quality of being perverse: *Her constant perversity frustrates everyone who tries to work with her.*

per•vert (pər vûrt') *tr.v.* **1.** To cause (sbdy./ sthg.) to turn from what is considered right, proper, or good; corrupt: *pervert the course of justice.* **2.** To put (sthg.) to a wrong or improper use: *The government perverted its responsibility by keeping files on ordinary*

citizens. **3.** To interpret (sthg.) wrongly: *He perverted the meaning of the poem.* —*n.* (pûr'vûrt'). A person who practices a sexual perversion.

per•vert•ed (pər vûr'tĭd) *adj.* **1.** Turned from what is considered right and correct; misguided: *a perverted notion of the truth.* **2.** Misinterpreted; distorted: *a perverted translation of the text.* **3.** Relating to a sexual perversion.

pes•ky (pĕs'kē) *adj.* **pes•ki•er, pes•ki•est.** *Informal.* Troublesome; annoying: *a pesky mosquito.* —**pes'ki•ly** *adv.* —**pes'ki•ness** *n.* [U]

pes•si•mism (pĕs'ə mĭz'əm) *n.* [U] A tendency to stress the negative or expect the worst: *Your pessimism makes you believe you'll fail.* —**pes'si•mist** *n.* —**pes'si•mis'tic** (pĕs'ə-mĭs'tĭk) *adj.* —**pes'si•mis'ti•cal•ly** *adv.*

pest (pĕst) *n.* **1.** *Informal.* An annoying person or thing; a nuisance: *Children sometimes make pests of themselves.* **2.** An animal or insect that is harmful to humans, domesticated animals, or crops: *The farmers learned new methods of dealing with pests.*

pes•ter (pĕs'tər) *tr.v.* To bother (sbdy.) with small annoyances: *Don't pester me while I'm busy.*

pes•ti•cide (pĕs'tĭ sīd') *n.* [C; U] A chemical used to kill harmful insects or rodents.

pes•ti•lence (pĕs'tə ləns) *n.* [C; U] **1.** An old term for a deadly disease that spreads quickly. **2.** An epidemic of such a disease. —**pes'ti•lent** *adj.*

pet (pĕt) *n.* **1.** An animal kept for companionship or amusement: *Dogs and cats are popular pets.* **2.** A person of whom one is especially fond; a favorite: *She's trying to be the teacher's pet.* —*adj.* **1.** Kept as a pet: *a pet cat.* **2.** Being a favorite: *a pet topic.* **3.** Expressing or showing affection: *a pet name.* —*v.* **pet•ted, pet•ting, pets.** —*tr.* To stroke or pat (an animal) gently: *petting and praising his dog.* —*intr. Informal.* To touch one another for sexual pleasure.

pet•al (pĕt'l) *n.* One of the brightly colored parts of a flower that are similar to leaves.

pe•ter (pē'tər) *v.* ◆ **peter out.** *intr.v.* **1.** To lessen slowly and come to an end; dwindle: *Our supplies petered out.* **2.** To become exhausted: *I petered out on the last lap of the race.*

pe•tite (pə tēt') *adj.* Small and slender; dainty: *a petite foot.*

pe•ti•tion (pə tĭsh'ən) *n.* **1.** A formal written document requesting a right or benefit from an authority: *collect signatures on a petition to change the law.* **2.** A pleading request, especially to a person or group in authority: *a petition for an audience with the king.* —*v.* —*tr.* To ask (sbdy.) for sthg. by petition: *Hawaii first petitioned Congress for statehood in 1902.* —*intr.* To make a formal request: *The lawyer petitioned for a retrial.* —**pe•ti'tion•er** *n.*

pe•tri dish (pē′trē) *n.* A shallow circular glass dish with a loose cover, used in the preparation of bacteria cultures.

pet•ri•fy (pĕt′rə fī′) *v.* **pet•ri•fied, pet•ri•fy•ing, pet•ri•fies.** —*tr.* **1.** To turn (wood or other organic material) into a stony mass: *petrified wood by replacing its internal structure with minerals.* **2.** To stun or paralyze (sbdy./sthg.) with terror: *We were petrified by the sound of the tornado.* —*intr.* To become stony: *The trees fell and then petrified.*

pet•ro•chem•i•cal (pĕt′rō kĕm′ĭ kəl) *n.* A chemical derived from petroleum or natural gas. —*adj.* Relating to petrochemicals: *petrochemical research.*

pet•rol (pĕt′rəl) *n.* [U] *Chiefly British.* Gasoline.

pe•tro•le•um (pə trō′lē əm) *n.* [U] A thick, dark, flammable liquid found between layers of rock below the surface of the earth: *Petroleum is refined into different types of fuels.*

petroleum jelly *n.* [U] A greasy, colorless substance obtained from petroleum and used in ointments and lubricants: *She uses petroleum jelly to protect the baby's skin.*

pet•ti•coat (pĕt′ē kōt′) *n.* An old term for a skirt or slip worn under another skirt or dress by girls and women.

pet•ty (pĕt′ē) *adj.* **pet•ti•er, pet•ti•est. 1.** Of small importance; trivial: *petty annoyances.* **2.** Narrow-minded; selfish: *petty quarrels.* **3.** Spiteful; mean: *He scolded her in a very petty way.* —**pet′ti•ly** *adv.* —**pet′ti•ness** *n.* [U]

petty cash *n.* A small fund of money for minor expenses in an office.

pet•u•lant (pĕch′ə lənt) *adj.* Ill-tempered: *a petulant response; a petulant child.* —**pet′u•lance** *n.* [U] —**pet′u•lant•ly** *adv.*

pe•tu•nia (pĭ tōōn′yə) *n.* A garden plant with white, reddish, or purple flowers shaped like funnels.

pew (pyōō) *n.* One of the long benches with backs arranged in rows for the seating of people in a church.

pew•ter (pyōō′tər) *n.* [U] **1.** A gray metal made of tin and lead: *a pewter vase; pewter eating utensils.* **2.** Articles made of pewter: *a collection of antique pewter.*

PG (pē′jē′) *n.* A movie rating that means persons of all ages may be admitted, but parental guidance should be used in the case of children.

pg. *abbr.* An abbreviation of page.

pH (pē′āch′) *n.* In chemistry, a numerical measure of the acidity or alkalinity of a solution, with 7 as the mark for neutral solutions, less than 7 for acid solutions, and more than 7 for alkaline solutions.

phal•lus (făl′əs) *n.* **1.** The penis. **2.** An image or representation of the penis as sexual power. —**phal′lic** *adj.*

phan•tom (făn′təm) *n.* **1.** A ghost. **2.** An image that appears only in the mind; an illusion: *chasing phantoms from the past.*

phar•ma•ceu•ti•cal (fär′mə sōō′tĭ kəl) *adj.* Relating to pharmacy or pharmacists: *pharmaceutical products.* —*n. (usually plural).* A pharmaceutical preparation or product; a medicinal drug.

phar•ma•col•o•gy (fär′mə kŏl′ə jē) *n.* [U] The scientific study of drugs and their composition, uses, and effects.

phar•ma•cy (fär′mə sē) *n., pl.* **phar•ma•cies. 1.** [U] The study and profession of preparing and dispensing drugs. **2.** [C] A place where drugs are sold; a drugstore: *She filled the prescription at the pharmacy on her way home.* —**phar′ma•cist** *n.*

phase (fāz) *n.* **1.** A distinct stage of development: *the next phase of our space program.* **2.** A temporary manner, attitude, or pattern of behavior: *He's just going through a phase.* **3.** An aspect; a part: *considering every phase of the problem.* **4.** Any of the forms, recurring in cycles, in which the moon or a planet appears. —*tr.v.* **phased, phas•ing, phas•es.** To plan or do (sthg.) so as to progress in stages: *The highway construction program was carefully phased.* ♦ **phase in.** *tr.v.* [sep.] To introduce (sthg.) one stage at a time: *phase in changes to the tax laws over the next two years.* **phase out.** *tr.v.* [sep.] To bring (sthg.) to an end, one stage at a time: *That model car is being phased out.*

HOMONYMS: phase, faze (upset).

Ph.D. *abbr.* An abbreviation of Doctor of Philosophy: *a professor with a Ph.D. in history.*

pheas•ant (fĕz′ənt) *n.* A large game bird, originally from Asia, that has a long tail and is often brightly colored in the male.

phe•nom•e•nal (fĭ nŏm′ə nəl) *adj.* Extraordinary; outstanding: *a phenomenal memory.* —**phe•nom′e•nal•ly** *adv.*

phe•nom•e•non (fĭ nŏm′ə nŏn′) *n.* **1.** *pl.* **phe•nom•e•na** (fĭ nŏm′ə nə). An occurrence or a fact that can be perceived by the senses or by instruments: *natural phenomena.* **2.** *pl.* **phenomena.** A fact or occurrence that is unusual or hard to explain: *supernatural phenomena.* **3.** *pl.* **phenomenons.** A remarkable or outstanding person: *He's a phenomenon on the basketball court.*

phi•lan•thro•pist (fĭ lăn′thrə pĭst) *n.* A person who gives money to promote good causes and human welfare: *Several philanthropists made it possible to save the museum.*

phi•lan•thro•py (fĭ lăn′thrə pē) *n., pl.* **phi•lan•thro•pies. 1.** [U] The desire or effort to help humankind, as by giving money to charities: *It's a good thing that philanthropy allows a tax deduction.* **2.** [C] Something, such as an institution or a cause, designed to promote human welfare: *Numerous philanthropies support cancer research.* —**phil′an•throp′ic** (fĭl′ən thrŏp′ĭk) *adj.* —**phil′an•throp′i•cal•ly** *adv.*

phi•lat•e•ly (fĭ lăt′l ē) *n.* [U] The collection and study of postage stamps. —**phil′a•tel′ic** (fĭl′ə tĕl′ĭk) *adj.* —**phi•lat′e•list** *n.*

phil•har•mon•ic (fĭl′här mŏn′ĭk) *n. Formal.* A symphony orchestra or the group of people that supports it.

phi•los•o•pher (fĭ lŏs′ə fər) *n.* **1.** A student of or specialist in philosophy. **2.** A person who lives and thinks according to a particular philosophy: *an existential philosopher.*

phil•o•soph•i•cal (fĭl′ə sŏf′ĭ kəl) also **phil•o•soph•ic** (fĭl′ə sŏf′ĭk) *adj.* **1.** Relating to a system of philosophy: *We have philosophical differences on questions of education.* **2.** Calm and rational under any circumstances: *She remained philosophical throughout the crisis.* —**phil′o•soph′i•cal•ly** *adv.*

phi•los•o•phize (fĭ lŏs′ə fīz′) *intr.v.* **phi•los•o•phized, phi•los•o•phiz•ing, phi•los•o•phiz•es.** To think or reflect in a philosophical manner: *She philosophized on the changes in her life.*

phi•los•o•phy (fĭ lŏs′ə fē) *n., pl.* **phi•los•o•phies. 1.** [U] The study by logical reasoning of such things as the universe, nature, life, and morals: *a philosophy major.* **2.** [C] A formal system of ideas based upon such study: *the philosophy of Plato.* **3.** [C] The system of values by which one lives: *"Might makes right" was the tyrant's philosophy.* **4.** [C] A basic theory; a viewpoint: *a successful philosophy of coaching.*

phlegm (flĕm) *n.* [U] Mucus produced by the mucous membranes of the respiratory tract: *The patient coughed up the phlegm from her throat.*

phleg•mat•ic (flĕg măt′ĭk) *adj. Formal.* Having or suggesting a calm temperament that is slow to respond emotionally: *His phlegmatic nature contrasted with his brother's excitability.* —**phleg•mat′i•cal•ly** *adv.*

pho•bi•a (fō′bē ə) *n.* An abnormal or unreasonable fear of sthg.: *a phobia about high places.*

phone (fōn) *n.* A telephone. —*v.* **phoned, phon•ing, phones.** —*intr.* To telephone: *He phoned to tell her about the movie.* —*tr.* **1.** To contact (sbdy.) by telephone: *Phone your sister.* **2.** To transmit (information) by telephone: *The reporter phoned the news to her editor.*

—**phone** *suff.* A suffix that means: **1.** Sound: *homophone.* **2.** A device that receives or emits sound: *earphone.*

pho•neme (fō′nēm′) *n.* In linguistics, the smallest unit of sound that can distinguish one word from another. For example, the *m* of *mat* and the *b* of *bat* are phonemes. —**pho•ne•mic** (fə nē′mĭk) *adj.*

pho•net•ic (fə nĕt′ĭk) *adj.* **1.** Relating to phonetics: *phonetic research.* **2.** Representing the sounds of speech with a set of symbols, each denoting a single sound. The word *lite* is a phonetic spelling of *light.* —**pho•net′i•cal•ly** *adv.*

pho•net•ics (fə nĕt′ĭks) *n.* [U] *(used with a singular verb).* The study of the sounds of speech and of their representation by symbols. —**pho′ne•ti′cian** (fō′nĭ tĭsh′ən) *n.*

phon•ic (fŏn′ĭk) *adj.* Of or involving sound, especially in speech. —**phon′i•cal•ly** *adv.*

phon•ics (fŏn′ĭks) *n.* [U] *(used with a singular verb).* A system used to teach reading that associates letters or groups of letters with the sounds they represent: *The children use phonics as they learn to read.*

phono— or **phon—** *pref.* A prefix that means sound, voice, or speech: *phonograph.*

pho•no•graph (fō′nə grăf′) *n.* A device that reproduces sound by means of a needle riding in the grooves of a record as it rotates. —**pho′no•graph′ic** *adj.*

pho•ny also **pho•ney** (fō′nē) *adj.* **pho•ni•er, pho•ni•est. 1.** Not genuine; fake: *a phony diamond.* **2.** Not sincere, true, or honest: *a phony smile.* —*n., pl.* **pho•nies** also **pho•neys. 1.** Something not genuine; a fake: *This emerald is a phony.* **2.** A person who is not sincere or honest; a fake or an impostor: *That television preacher is a phony who just wants to get rich.* —**pho′ni•ly** *adv.* —**pho′ni•ness** *n.* [U]

phoo•ey (fōō′ē) *interj.* An expression used to show disappointment or contempt: *Phooey! I didn't win the lottery again!*

phos•pho•res•cence (fŏs′fə rĕs′əns) *n.* [U] The process or phenomenon by which a body emits light: *The sea was lit up by the phosphorescence of tiny creatures.* —**phos′pho•res′cent** *adj.*

phos•pho•rus (fŏs′fər əs) *n.* [U] *Symbol* **P** A highly reactive, poisonous, nonmetallic element occurring in white (or sometimes yellow), red, and black forms. Atomic number 15. See table at **element.**

pho•to (fō′tō) *n., pl.* **pho•tos.** *Informal.* A photograph.

photo— or **phot—** *pref.* A prefix that means: **1.** Light: *photosynthesis.* **2.** Photographic: *photocopy.*

pho•to•cop•i•er (fō′tə kŏp′ē ər) *n.* A machine for photographically copying written, printed, or graphic material.

pho•to•cop•y (fō′tə kŏp′ē) *tr.v.* **pho•to•cop•ied, pho•to•cop•y•ing, pho•to•cop•ies.** To make a photographic reproduction of (printed, written, or graphic material): *photocopy a research article.* —*n., pl.* **pho•**

P

to·cop·ies. A photographic reproduction: *The lawyer made a photocopy of the letter for the file.*

pho·to·e·lec·tric (fō′tō ĭ lĕk′trĭk) *adj.* Relating to electrical effects caused by light. —**pho′to·e·lec′tri·cal·ly** *adv.*

pho·to·gen·ic (fō′tə jĕn′ĭk) *adj.* Attractive as a subject for photography: *She has a very photogenic smile.* —**pho′to·gen′i·cal·ly** *adv.*

pho·to·graph (fō′tə grăf′) *n.* An image formed on a light-sensitive surface by a camera and developed by chemical means to produce a positive print. —*v.* —*tr.* To take a photograph of (sbdy./sthg.): *We photographed everyone at the wedding.* —*intr.* To be a subject for photographs: *Some people photograph better than others.*

pho·to·graph·ic (fō′tə grăf′ĭk) *adj.* **1.** Relating to photography or a photograph: *a photographic lens.* **2.** Capable of forming accurate and lasting impressions: *a photographic memory.* —**pho′to·graph′i·cal·ly** *adv.*

pho·tog·ra·phy (fə tŏg′rə fē) *n.* [U] **1.** The art or process of creating images on light-sensitive surfaces. **2.** The practice or profession of making photographs. —**pho·tog′ra·pher** *n.*

pho·to·jour·nal·ism (fō′tō jûr′nə lĭz′əm) *n.* [U] Journalism in which news stories are presented primarily through photographs with added written information. —**pho·to·jour′nal·ist** *n.*

pho·ton (fō′tŏn′) *n.* A particle of light or other electromagnetic energy: *Photons have a mass of zero.*

pho·to·sen·si·tive (fō′tō sĕn′sĭ tĭv) *adj.* Capable of undergoing some change as a result of exposure to light: *photosensitive paper.* —**pho′to·sen′si·tiv′i·ty** *n.* [U]

pho·to·syn·the·sis (fō′tō sĭn′thĭ sĭs) *n.* [U] The chemical process by which plants that contain chlorophyll use light to change carbon dioxide and water into food.

phrasal verb *n.* In grammar, a verb form consisting of a verb and an adverb or a particle. As a unit, a phrasal verb has a meaning that differs from the meaning of its parts. Examples are *bring about* (to cause), *give up* (to surrender), or *pass away* (to die).

phrase (frāz) *n.* In grammar, a sequence of words that is meaningful but is less than a complete sentence. For example, *on the table* is a prepositional phrase. —*tr.v.* **phrased, phras·ing, phras·es.** To express (sthg.) in speaking or in writing: *He phrased his answer carefully.* —**phras′al** *adj.*

phy·lum (fī′ləm) *n., pl.* **phy·la** (fī′lə). One of the larger groups into which animals are

classified, ranking between a kingdom and a class.

phys. ed. *abbr. Informal.* Physical education: *All the children had phys. ed. twice a week.*

phys·i·cal (fĭz′ĭ kəl) *adj.* **1.** Relating to the body rather than the mind or emotions: *physical fitness; physical exercise.* **2.** Solid; material: *a physical object.* —*n.* A physical examination: *See your doctor for a yearly physical.* —**phys′-i·cal·ly** *adv.*

physical education *n.* [U] Education in the care and development of the human body, including athletics and hygiene.

physical science *n.* Any of the sciences, such as physics, chemistry, astronomy, and geology, that deal mainly with nonliving matter and energy.

physical therapy *n.* [U] The treatment of physical abnormality or injury by such means as exercise, massage, baths, or application of heat or cold.

phy·si·cian (fĭ zĭsh′ən) *n.* A person licensed to practice medicine; a medical doctor.

phys·ics (fĭz′ĭks) *n.* [U] *(used with a singular verb).* The science of matter and energy and the relations between them. —**phys′i·cist** (fĭz′ĭ sĭst) *n.*

phys·i·ol·o·gy (fĭz′ē ŏl′ə jē) *n.* [U] The scientific study of the processes, activities, and functions necessary to and characteristic of living organisms. —**phys′i·o·log′i·cal** (fĭz′ē ə lŏj′ĭ kəl) *adj.* —**phys′i·o·log′i·cal·ly** *adv.*

phy·sique (fĭ zēk′) *n.* The body considered in terms of its proportions, muscle development, and appearance: *the physique of a dancer.*

pi (pī) *n.* [U] *Symbol* π A number equal to the quotient of the circumference of a circle divided by its diameter, approximately 3.14159.

HOMONYMS: pi, pie (dessert).

pi·an·ist (pē ăn′ĭst *or* pē′ə nĭst) *n.* A person who plays the piano: *a concert pianist.*

pi·an·o (pē ăn′ō) *n., pl.* **pi·an·os.** A musical instrument with a keyboard. When a person's fingers hit the keys, hammers strike wire strings, producing sounds: *a grand piano.*

pic·co·lo (pĭk′ə lō′) *n., pl.* **pic·co·los.** A small flute with a higher range than an ordinary flute. —**pic′co·lo·ist** *n.*

pick¹ (pĭk) *v.* —*tr.* **1.** To choose or select (sbdy./sthg.): *pick the right person for the job.* **2.** To gather in (fruit or flowers, for example): *pick peas.* **3.** To poke and pull at (sthg.) with a toothpick or one's finger, for example: *pick one's teeth.* **4.** To open (a lock) without using a key, as with a piece of wire. **5.a.** To pluck (the strings) of a musical instrument.

b. To play (a tune or melody) in this way: *She picked a tune on the guitar.* —*intr.* **1.** To decide or choose with care: *Take your time to pick.* **2.** To find fault or make little criticisms: *He's always picking about something.* —*n.* [U] **1.** The act of selecting or choosing; choice: *They had first pick of the desserts.* **2.** Something selected as the best or choicest part: *the pick of the crop.* ◆ **pick and choose.** To select with great care: *There's no time to pick and choose.* **pick on.** *tr.v.* [insep.] To tease or bully (sbdy.): *Bigger children pick on him.* **pick (one's) brain.** To get information or ideas from a knowledgeable person through questioning: *We have to pick her brain about the project.* **pick (one's) pocket.** To steal sthg., especially a wallet, from sbdy.'s pocket. **pick out.** *tr.v.* [sep.] To choose or select (sbdy./sthg.): *We picked out the juiciest berries.* **pick up.** *tr.v.* [sep.] **1.a.** To take up (sthg.) by hand: *pick a book up off the floor.* **b.** To collect or gather (sthg.): *I picked up the pieces of broken glass.* **c.** To make (sthg.) orderly and neat: *He picked up the living room.* **2.** To take on (passengers or freight, for example): *I'll pick you up outside the train station.* **3.** To get (knowledge) by learning or experience: *The child picked up Spanish quickly.* **4.** To become sick with (a disease): *I picked up the flu last winter.* **pick up on.** *Informal.* To notice (sthg.): *He didn't pick up on the difference.*

pick² (pĭk) *n.* **1.** A tool for breaking hard surfaces, consisting of a slightly curved metal bar sharpened at both ends and fitted to a long handle. **2.** A pointed tool used for piercing, breaking, or picking: *an ice pick; a toothpick.* **3.** A small flat piece, as of plastic or bone, used to pluck the strings of an instrument: *a guitar pick.*

pick•et (pĭk′ĭt) *n.* **1.** A pointed stake or spike driven into the ground. **2.** A person or group of people stationed outside a building to demonstrate or protest: *Pickets marched outside the factory.* —*v.* —*tr.* To protest or demonstrate against (sbdy./sthg.), as during a strike: *Marchers picketed the United Nations today.* —*intr.* To act or serve as a picket: *Workers picketed all night.*

picket line *n.* A line or group of people stationed outside a building to demonstrate or protest.

pick•ing (pĭk′ĭng) *n.* **1.** [U] The act of one that picks: *strawberry picking.* **2. pickings. a.** Leftovers or scraps: *We got the last pickings.* **b.** A share of spoils: *Tourists provide easy pickings for thieves.*

pick•le (pĭk′əl) *n.* **1.** A food, such as a cucumber, that has been preserved and flavored in vinegar, salt, water, and spices: *homemade pickles.* **2.** *Informal.* A troublesome or difficult situation: *They're in a pickle now.* —*tr.v.* **pick•led, pick•ling, pick•les.** To preserve or flavor (food) in vinegar: *pickle vegetables.*

pick•led (pĭk′əld) *adj.* Preserved in a preparation of vinegar: *pickled beets.*

pick•pock•et (pĭk′pŏk′ĭt) *n.* A thief who steals from someone's pockets or purse.

pick•up (pĭk′ŭp′) *n.* **1.** [C] A pickup truck. **2.** [C] The act or process of picking up, as packages, work, or freight: *The truck made a pickup at 4:00.* **3.** [C] A person or thing that is picked up: *The taxi driver got a pickup at the airport.* **4.** [C] *Informal.* An improvement in condition or activity: *a pickup in attendance.* **5.** [U] The ability to gain speed rapidly: *a car with good pickup.*

pickup truck *n.* A light truck with an open body and low sides: *Pickup trucks are popular vehicles.*

pick•y (pĭk′ē) *adj.* **pick•i•er, pick•i•est.** *Informal.* Too careful; fussy: *He's very picky about food.*

pic•nic (pĭk′nĭk) *n.* A meal eaten outdoors, as on a pleasure trip to a park or in the country: *Let's go on a picnic.* —*intr.v.* **pic•nicked, pic•nick•ing, pic•nics.** To go on or participate in a picnic: *During the summer we picnic at outdoor concerts.* —*pic′nick•er n.*

pic•to•ri•al (pĭk tôr′ē əl) *adj.* **1.** Represented by pictures: *pictorial materials.* **2.** Composed of or illustrated by pictures: *pictorial representations of planets.* —*n.* An illustrated publication. —*pic•to′ri•al•ly adv.*

pic•ture (pĭk′chər) *n.* **1.** [C] A visual representation or image that is painted, drawn, photographed, or otherwise made on a flat surface: *drew a picture in pencil.* **2.** [C] An image created with words or in the mind: *a mental picture.* **3.** [U] A person or thing that looks much like another: *He is the picture of his father.* **4.** [U] A person or thing that is a good example of a certain emotion, mood, or state of mind: *The boy was the picture of happiness.* **5.** [U] A combination of circumstances; the situation: *How does an education figure in the picture?* **6.** [C] An image or a series of images on a television or movie screen: *That large-screen TV has a great picture.* **7.** [C] An old term for a movie: *Hollywood pictures.* —*tr.v.* **pic•tured, pic•tur•ing, pic•tures. 1.** To make a representation or picture of (sbdy./sthg.): *A graph is a good way to picture data.* **2.** To form a mental image of (sbdy./sthg.); imagine: *He pictured himself flying over the town.* ◆ **get the picture.** To grasp or understand sthg. after a period of effort: *She finally got the picture after a week of hints.* **in** or **out of the picture.** Able or unable to participate in an event, situation, or project: *If he's out of the picture now, there's no reason to keep him informed.* **the big picture.** *Informal.* The overall aspect of an event: *Don't lose sight of the big picture by worrying about details.*

pic•tur•esque (pĭk′chə rĕsk′) *adj.* **1.** Striking or interesting: *picturesque Alpine villages.*

2. Strikingly expressive; vivid: *picturesque language.* —**pic′tur•esque′ly** *adv.* —**pic′-tur•esque′ness** *n.* [U]

pid•dling (pĭd′lĭng) *adj.* Unimportant; trivial: *piddling objections.*

pidg•in (pĭj′ən) *n.* [C; U] A simple form of speech based on a mixture of two or more languages and used for communications between groups speaking different languages: *They spoke a Pidgin English together.*

HOMONYMS: **pidgin, pigeon** (bird).

pie (pī) *n.* A food consisting of a filling, such as fruit or meat, baked in a pastry shell and often covered with a crust or meringue: *as American as apple pie.*

HOMONYMS: **pie, pi** (number).

piece (pēs) *n.* **1.** Something considered as a part of a larger quantity or group: *The farmer gave a piece of his land to each of his children.* **2.** A portion or part that has been separated from a whole: *a piece of pizza.* **3.** An object that is one member of a set: *Each table setting has six pieces.* **4.** An artistic, musical, or literary work: *play a piece on the piano.* **5.** A coin: *a 50-cent piece.* **6.** An example or an instance: *a fine piece of detective work.* **7.** In certain board games, one of the small objects used in playing: *chess pieces.* **8.** *Slang.* A gun. —*tr.v.* **pieced, piec•ing, piec•es.** To join or unite the parts of (sthg.): *I pieced the puzzle together.* ♦ **a piece of cake.** Something very easy to do: *Passing the test was a piece of cake.* **a piece of (one's) mind.** Frank and severe criticism: *The principal gave me a piece of her mind for being late again.* **a piece of the action.** *Slang.* A share of an activity or of profits: *Now that business is good, everybody wants a piece of the action.* **a piece of work.** *Slang.* A person or thing that is overly complicated or difficult: *Fixing that car is a piece of work! That customer is always a piece of work.*

HOMONYMS: **piece, peace** (calm).

pièce de ré•sis•tance (pyĕs′də rā′zē stäns′) *n.* *(usually singular).* The most outstanding accomplishment: *Her performance was the pièce de résistance!*

piece•meal (pēs′mēl′) *adv.* **1.** By a small amount at a time; in stages: *built up his art collection piecemeal.* **2.** In pieces; apart: *The puzzle lay piecemeal on the floor.* —*adj.* Done or made in stages: *The city developed in a piecemeal fashion.*

piece•work (pēs′wûrk′) *n.* [U] Work paid for by the number of units produced: *In the past, many workers were paid by piecework.* —**piece′work′er** *n.*

pie chart *n.* A circular graph with lines extending out from the center to mark sections that vary in size according to the percentages represented.

pier (pîr) *n.* A platform extending from a shore over water and supported by rock or pillars, used to secure, protect, and provide access to ships or boats: *We walked to the end of the pier.*

pie chart

HOMONYMS: **pier, peer** (look, equal).

pierce (pîrs) *v.* **pierced, pierc•ing, pierc•es.** —*tr.* **1.** To pass into or through (sbdy./sthg.) with or as with a sharp instrument: *Arrows pierced the target.* **2.** To make a hole or opening in (sbdy./sthg.): *A nail pierced the tire. She had her ears pierced.* **3.** To sound sharply through (sthg.): *A cry pierced the air.* —*intr.* To penetrate into or through sthg.: *The rocket pierced through the clouds.*

pierc•ing (pîr′sĭng) *adj.* Sharp; penetrating: *piercing cold; piercing eyes.* —**pierc′ing•ly** *adv.*

pi•e•ty (pī′ĭ tē) *n.* [U] Religious devotion and reverence.

pig (pĭg) *n.* **1.** A hoofed mammal with short legs, bristly hair, and a blunt snout, used for food: *Ham, pork, and bacon come from pigs.* **2.** *Informal.* An insulting term for a person regarded as being like a pig, especially a greedy or gross person: *Don't be such a pig in front of guests.*

pi•geon (pĭj′ən) *n.* Any of various birds with short legs, a rounded chest, and a small head, especially one common in cities: *Don't feed the pigeons.*

HOMONYMS: **pigeon, pidgin** (speech form).

pi•geon•hole (pĭj′ən hōl′) *tr.v.* **pi•geon•holed, pi•geon•hol•ing, pi•geon•holes.** **1.** To put (sthg.) in a small compartment or recess: *pigeonhole unanswered letters.* **2.** To classify (sbdy./sthg.) into a group; categorize: *a tendency to pigeonhole people you meet.*

pig•gish (pĭg′ĭsh) *adj.* Greedy; sloppy: *piggish eating habits.* —**pig′gish•ly** *adv.* —**pig′-gish•ness** *n.* [U]

pig•gy•back (pĭg′ē băk′) *adv. & adj.* **1.** On the shoulders or back: *ride piggyback; a piggyback ride.* **2.** In or by means of truck trailers carried on railroad cars: *goods shipped piggyback.*

P

pig·gy bank (pĭg'ē) *n.* A child's bank for coins, often shaped like a pig.

pig·head·ed (pĭg'hĕd'ĭd) *adj.* Stupidly stubborn or uncooperative: *a pigheaded refusal to listen.* —**pig'head'ed·ly** *adv.* —**pig'head'ed·ness** *n.* [U]

pig·let (pĭg'lĭt) *n.* A young pig.

pig·ment (pĭg'mənt) *n.* **1.** [C; U] A substance or material used as coloring: *the pigments used in a paint.* **2.** [U] A substance that gives a characteristic color to plant or animal tissues: *pigment in the skin.* —**pig'men·ta'tion** (pĭg'mən tā'shən) *n.* [U]

pig·my (pĭg'mē) *n. & adj.* Variant of **pygmy.**

pig·pen (pĭg'pĕn') *n.* **1.** A pen for pigs. **2.** *Informal.* A dirty or very untidy place: *Your room is a pigpen again!*

pig·skin (pĭg'skĭn') *n.* **1.** [U] Leather made from the skin of a pig. **2.** [C] *Informal.* An American football: *Let's toss the old pigskin around.*

pig·sty (pĭg'stī') *n., pl.* **pig·sties. 1.** A shelter where pigs are kept. **2.** *Slang.* A dirty or very untidy place: *This house is a pigsty; we'll never get it clean.*

pig·tail (pĭg'tāl') *n.* A braid or braids of hair at the back or sides of the head: *She wore her hair in pigtails.*

pike (pīk) *n.* A turnpike: *Speed on the pike was reduced during the snowstorm.*

pi·laf (pĭ läf' *or* pē'läf') *n.* [U] A seasoned dish of steamed rice, often with vegetables: *Do you want rice pilaf or potatoes?*

pile¹ (pīl) *n.* **1.** A mass of objects stacked or thrown together in a heap: *a pile of firewood; piles of dirty clothes.* **2.** *Informal.* A large amount: *a pile of complaints.* **3.** *Slang.* A large sum of money; a fortune: *He made his pile and retired.* —*v.* **piled, pil·ing, piles.** —*tr.* **1.a.** To place or lay (sthg.) in or as if in a pile or heap: *They piled the dishes in the sink.* **b.** To load (sbdy./sthg.) with a heap or pile: *The children piled the table with books.* **2.** To place or heap (sthg.) in great amounts: *The committee piled honors on him.* ♦ **pile out.** *intr.v.* To leave, often in haste, in a disorderly group or mass: *The children piled out of the car.* **pile up.** *intr.v.* To form a heap or pile: *Our unpaid bills piled up.*

pile² (pīl) *n.* A heavy beam of timber, concrete, or steel, driven into the ground as a foundation or support for a structure.

pile³ (pīl) *n.* [C; U] *(usually singular).* Cut or uncut loops of yarn forming the surface of certain carpets or of fabrics such as velvet: *That rug has a thick pile.*

piles (pīlz) *pl.n.* Hemorrhoids.

pile·up or **pile-up** (pīl'ŭp') *n.* A serious collision usually involving several motor vehicles: *A pileup on the highway delayed traffic for hours.*

pil·fer (pĭl'fər) *tr.v. Formal.* To steal (a small amount or item): *He pilfered some apples from the orchard.* —**pil'fer·er** *n.*

pil·grim (pĭl'grəm) *n.* **1.** A person who travels to a shrine or sacred place for religious reasons. **2. Pilgrim.** One of the English colonists who settled Plymouth, Massachusetts, in 1620.

pil·grim·age (pĭl'grə mĭj) *n.* **1.** A journey to a sacred place or shrine: *a pilgrimage to Mecca.* **2.** A long journey with a meaningful purpose: *He made a pilgrimage to his childhood home.*

pill (pĭl) *n.* **1.** A small tablet of medicine taken by swallowing whole or chewing: *Have you taken your allergy pill?* **2.** Something distasteful or unpleasant that must be accepted: *Losing that promotion was a bitter pill for him to swallow.* **3.** *Slang.* An ill-natured or disagreeable person: *She can be such a pill when we don't do things her way.* ♦ **on the pill.** Taking birth control pills regularly: *You shouldn't smoke if you are on the pill.*

pil·lage (pĭl'ĭj) *v.* **pil·laged, pil·lag·ing, pil·lag·es.** —*tr.* To rob (sthg.) of goods by force: *The army pillaged the countryside.* —*intr.* To take booty. —*n.* [U] The act of pillaging: *the pillage of the city.* —**pil'lag·er** *n.*

pil·lar (pĭl'ər) *n.* **1.** A vertical structure used as a support for a building; a column. **2.** A person occupying a central position: *a pillar of the community.*

pil·low (pĭl'ō) *n.* A cloth case filled with soft material, such as feathers or foam rubber, used to cushion the head during sleep. —*tr.v.* To rest (sthg.) as if on a pillow: *She pillowed her head on her arms.*

pil·low·case (pĭl'ō kās') *n.* A removable cover for a pillow.

pi·lot (pī'lət) *n.* **1.** A person who operates an aircraft in flight. **2.** A licensed specialist who steers large ships in and out of port or through dangerous waters. **3.** A pilot light on a gas appliance: *Light the pilot.* **4.** A television program produced as a model of a series being considered for production by a network. —*tr.v.* **1.** To serve as the pilot of (a craft); steer: *Who'll pilot the plane?* **2.** To lead, guide, or conduct (sbdy.): *They piloted us through the difficult process the first time.* —*adj.* Serving as a small-scale model for future work: *a pilot project.*

pilot light *n.* A small jet of gas kept burning to ignite a gas burner, as in a stove or water heater: *The pilot light is out.*

pimp (pĭmp) *n.* A man who finds customers for a prostitute.

pim·ple (pĭm'pəl) *n.* A small swelling on the skin, often red and sore and sometimes containing pus. —**pim'ply** *adj.*

pin (pĭn) *n.* **1.** A short straight stiff piece of wire with a blunt head and a sharp point, used for fastening: *a dressmaker's pin.* **2.** Something that resembles a pin in shape or use: *a*

P

hairpin; a clothespin; a safety pin. **3.** A piece of jewelry fastened to clothing by means of a clasp: *gold earrings and a matching pin.* **4.** A rod of wood or metal that supports or fastens things, especially by passing through or into a series of prepared holes: *The doctor put a pin in her broken leg.* **5.** One of the wooden clubs in bowling. —*tr.v.* **pinned, pin•ning, pins. 1.** To fasten or secure (sthg.) with a pin: *Her date pinned the flower to her coat.* **2.** To hold (sbdy./sthg.) firmly in place: *The strong current pinned the canoe against the rock.* ♦ **on pins and needles.** Feeling nervous excitement: *We were on pins and needles waiting to hear the name of the winner.* **pin down.** *tr.v.* [sep.] **1.** To fix or establish (sthg.) clearly: *The researchers finally pinned down the cause of the disease.* **2.** To force (sbdy.) to give firm opinions or precise information: *The school committee pinned the superintendent down on the issue of budget cuts.* **pin on.** *tr.v.* [sep.] To put the blame (for sthg.) on sbdy.: *You can't pin this robbery on me!* **pin (one's) hopes on.** To trust in (sbdy./sthg.): *We pinned our hopes on winning the championship.*

pi•ña•ta (pēn yä′tə) *n.* A decorated container, often in the shape of an animal, filled with candy and toys and hung from the ceiling: *Blindfolded children try to break the piñata with a stick at birthday parties and Christmas celebrations in many Latin American countries.*

pin•cers (pĭn′sərz) *pl.n.* (used with a plural verb). **1.** A grasping tool with a pair of jaws and handles joined together to work in opposition: *The dentist used pincers to grab and pull the tooth.* **2.** A jointed grasping claw, as of a lobster or crab: *The crab held the fish firmly in its pincers.*

pinch (pĭnch) *v.* —*tr.* **1.** To squeeze (sbdy./sthg.) between the thumb and a finger or other edges: *The girl cried out when her little brother pinched her arm.* **2.** To squeeze or compress (sthg.) in a way that causes pain or discomfort: *The shoes pinched her feet.* **3.** To make (sthg.) appear wrinkled or unwell: *a face pinched by fear and fatigue.* **4.** *Slang.* To steal (sthg.): *He pinched some doughnuts from the tray.* **5.** *Slang.* To arrest (sbdy.): *The patrolman pinched the thief.* —*intr.* To press, squeeze, or bind painfully: *These shoes pinch!* —*n.* **1.** A squeeze or other pressure caused by pressing between the thumb and a finger or other edges: *I felt the crab give me a pinch on the toe.* **2.** The amount that can be held between the thumb and forefinger: *Add a pinch of salt.* ♦ **in a pinch. 1.** In an emergency situation: *He found himself in a pinch when he lost his job.* **2.** If necessary: *In a pinch she can do the work of two.* **pinch pennies.** *Informal.* To be thrifty or miserly: *He likes to pinch pennies.* —**pinch′er** *n.*

pinch-hit (pĭnch′hĭt′) *intr.v.* **pinch-hit, pinch-hit•ting, pinch-hits. 1.** In baseball, to bat as a substitute, especially when a hit is badly needed. **2.** *Informal.* To take the place of another: *I'm pinch-hitting for the regular mechanic today.* —**pinch hit** *n.* —**pinch hitter** *n.*

pin•cush•ion (pĭn′-kŏosh′ən) *n.* A small firm cushion into which pins and needles are stuck when not in use.

pine¹ (pīn) *n.* An evergreen tree that has cones and clusters of needle-shaped leaves.

pine² (pīn) *intr.v.* **pined, pin•ing, pines. 1.** [*for*] To feel a sad, often hopeless, desire: *pine for home.* **2.** To lose health or become weak from longing or grief: *The bird pined away and died.*

pine tree and cone

pine•ap•ple (pīn′-ăp′əl) *n.* [C; U] A large tropical fruit with yellow flesh, a rough spiny skin, and narrow prickly leaves at the top.

ping-pong (pĭng′pông′ or pĭng′pŏng′). *n.* [U] Table tennis.

pineapple

pin•ion¹ (pĭn′yən) *tr.v.* To hold or fasten (a person's arms) to prevent movement: *His arms were pinioned to his sides.*

pin•ion² (pĭn′yən) *n.* A small gearwheel that engages a larger gearwheel or a rack.

pink (pĭngk) *n.* **1.** [C; U] A light or pale red color. **2.** [U] The highest or best degree: *the pink of health.* —*adj.* Light or pale red: *pink cheeks.*

pink•ie also **pink•y** (pĭng′kē) *n.*, *pl.* **pink•ies.** *Informal.* The little finger: *a pinkie ring.*

pin•na•cle (pĭn′ə kəl) *n.* **1.** A tall pointed formation, as a mountain peak. **2.** The peak or summit of sthg.: *at the pinnacle of his fame.*

pin•point (pĭn′point′) *n.* **1.** A very small or sharp point. **2.** Something extremely small: *bright pinpoints of flame.* —*tr.v.* To locate and identify (sthg.) precisely: *We were able to pinpoint the reason for the change.* —*adj.* Showing care and precision: *pinpoint accuracy.*

pin•prick (pĭn′prĭk′) *n.* **1.** A slight hole made by or as if by a pin. **2.** A minor annoyance: *It's nothing but a pinprick to his pride.*

pin•stripe (pĭn′strīp′) *n.* A very thin stripe on a fabric.—*adj.* In a fabric with a pattern of very thin stripes: *a pinstripe suit.*

ă-**cat**; ā-**pay**; âr-**care**; ä-**father**; ĕ-**get**; ē-**be**; ĭ-**sit**; ī-**nice**; îr-**here**; ŏ-**got**; ō-**go**; ô-**saw**; oi-**boy**; ou-**out**; ŏŏ-**took**; ōō-**boot**; ŭ-**cut**; ûr-**word**; th-**thin**; *th*-**this**; hw-**when**; zh-**vision**; ə-**about**; N-French **bon**

pint (pīnt) *n.* **1.** A unit of measure for liquids, equal to 16 fluid ounces (about 0.473 liter). See table at **measurement**. **2.** The amount of a substance that can be held in a pint container: *a pint of milk.*

pin•to (pĭn′tō) *n., pl.* **pin•tos** or **pin•toes.** A horse with irregular spots or markings. —*adj.* Having irregular spots or markings: *pinto beans.*

pin•wheel (pĭn′wēl′) *n.* A toy made of blades of colored paper or plastic pinned to the end of a stick so that they turn round in the wind or when blown on.

pi•o•neer (pī′ə nîr′) *n.* **1.** A person who first enters or settles a region. **2.** A person who opens up new areas of research, thought, or development: *a pioneer in computer software.* —*adj.* **1.** Relating to early settlers: *pioneer life.* **2.** Leading the way: *pioneer research.* —*v.* —*tr.* **1.** To settle (a place): *The family pioneered North Dakota.* **2.** To be involved in the early development of (sthg.): *They say he pioneered television news reporting.* —*intr.* To act as a pioneer: *He pioneered in the use of antiseptics in surgery.*

pi•ous (pī′əs) *adj.* **1.** Having or showing religious reverence; devout: *pious followers of the faith.* **2.** Marked by a false devoutness: *a pious speech.* —**pi′ous•ly** *adv.*

pipe (pīp) *n.* **1.** A tube through which a liquid or gas can be made to flow: *The plumber fixed the pipe under the kitchen sink.* **2.** A device for smoking, made of a hollow clay or wood tube with a mouthpiece at one end and a small bowl at the other: *Grandpa filled his pipe with tobacco.* **3.a.** A simple tubular musical instrument similar to a flute. **b.** Any of the tubes used in an organ to produce musical tones. **4. pipes.** A bagpipe. —*tr.v.* **piped, pip•ing, pipes. 1.** To send (sthg.) by means of a pipe: *pipe oil from Alaska.* **2.** To play (music) on a pipe: *pipe a tune.* **3.** To speak or sing (sthg.) in a high voice: *The child piped a question.* ♦ **pipe down.** *intr.v.* Slang. To stop talking; be quiet: *I'm tired of hearing him complain; I wish he would pipe down.* **pipe up.** *intr.v.* To speak loud enough to be heard: *A child in the back row piped up with a question.* —**pip′er** *n.*

pipe dream *n.* A fantastic idea or unreasonable hope: *She talks about becoming a movie star, but it's just a pipe dream.*

pipe•line (pīp′līn′) *n.* **1.** A long series of pipes used to carry water, petroleum, or natural gas over great distances. **2.** A direct line of communication or route of supply: *After the snowstorm a plane was the town's only pipeline to the outside world.* ♦ **in the pipeline.** In preparation or under development but available soon: *The drug company announced it has a new vaccine in the pipeline.*

pipe organ *n.* A musical instrument with pipes that make tones when supplied with air and a keyboard that controls the flow of air.

pip•ing (pī′pĭng) *n.* [U] **1.** A system of pipes, such as those used in plumbing. **2.** The act of playing music on a pipe. **3.** A narrow tube of material, used as a trimming on fabric. ♦ **piping hot.** Very hot: *piping hot biscuits fresh from the oven.*

pip-squeak (pĭp′skwēk′) *n. Informal.* A person or thing that is small or unimportant: *My little brother is an annoying pipsqueak.*

pique (pēk) *tr.v.* **piqued, piqu•ing, piques. 1.** To cause (sbdy.) to feel resentful or indignant: *Her arrogant manner piqued her neighbors.* **2.** To arouse or provoke (sbdy./sthg.): *The unusual butterflies piqued his curiosity.*

Homonyms: pique, peak (pointed top), peek (glance).

pi•ra•cy (pī′rə sē) *n.* [U] **1.** Robbery committed at sea. **2.** The unauthorized use of another's invention or creation: *the piracy of her father's invention.*

pi•ra•nha (pĭ rän′yə *or* pĭ rä′nə) *n.* A small tropical American freshwater fish with very sharp teeth. Piranhas sometimes attack human beings and large animals.

pi•rate (pī′rĭt) *n.* A person who robs ships at sea. —*tr.v.* **pi•rat•ed, pi•rat•ing, pi•rates. 1.** To attack and rob (a ship at sea). **2.** To publish or reproduce (another's invention or creation) without permission: *It is illegal to pirate recordings of popular music and sell them.*

pir•ou•ette (pĭr′ōō ĕt′) *n.* In ballet, a full turn of the body on the toes or the ball of the foot. —*intr.v.* **pir•ou•et•ted, pir•ou•et•ting, pir•ou•ettes.** To perform a pirouette.

piss (pĭs) *Offensive Slang. intr.v.* To urinate. —*n.* [U] Urine. ♦ **piss off.** *tr.v.* [sep.] To make (sbdy.) angry: *Don't piss me off today; it's my birthday. I was pissed off when I left work.* —*intr.v.* Used as a rude response to sbdy.: *Her boss told her to piss off when she asked for another raise.*

pissed (pĭst) *adj. Offensive Slang.* Angry; very annoyed: *His mother was really pissed when he got home late.*

pis•ta•chi•o (pĭ stäsh′ē ō′) *n., pl.* **pis•ta•chi•os.** The small hard-shelled nut, with a sweet green kernel, of a tree of the Mediterranean region and western Asia.

pis•tol (pĭs′təl) *n.* A small gun designed to be held and fired with one hand.

pis•ton (pĭs′tən) *n.* A solid metal disk that fits snugly into a hollow cylinder and moves back and forth: *Many engines have pistons.*

pit¹ (pĭt) *n.* **1.** A large hole or cavity in the ground: *the pit of a mine.* **2.a.** A natural depression in the surface of a body or a part of one: *the pit of the stomach.* **b.** A small depression in the skin left by a disease or injury: *pits left by chicken pox.* **3.** The area directly in front of the stage of a theater in which the musicians sit: *the orchestra pit.* **4.** The area beside an automobile racecourse where cars are fueled and serviced during a race. **5.** An enclosed space in which animals are kept or are set to fight: *a snake pit.* —*v.* **pit·ted, pit·ting, pits.** —*tr.* **1.** To mark (sthg.) with cavities, depressions, or scars: *The moon appears to have been pitted by meteoroid impacts.* **2.** To set (sbdy./sthg.) in competition: *a tournament that pits one school against another.* ♦ **make a pit stop. 1.** To stop for refueling or repairs in a race. **2.** *Slang.* To stop briefly on a trip to use the bathroom: *Let's stop at the next rest area. I need to make a pit stop.* **the pits.** *Slang.* Something extremely bad: *Turn off the radio—that music is the pits!*

pit² (pĭt) *n.* The single hard-shelled seed of certain fruits, such as a peach or cherry; a stone. —*tr.v.* **pit·ted, pit·ting, pits.** To remove the pits from (sthg.): *We pitted the olives for the salad.*

pi·ta (pē′tə) *n.* [U] A round flat bread that can be opened into a pocket for filling: *a pita sandwich.*

pitch¹ (pĭch) *n.* [U] A sticky dark thick tar used for roofing, waterproofing, and paving.

pitch² (pĭch) *v.* —*tr.* **1.** To throw (sthg.), usually with careful aim: *pitching a baseball.* See Synonyms at **throw. 2.** To discard (sthg.) by throwing: *The child pitched the gum wrapper into the trash can.* **3.** To set up or establish (sthg.): *pitch a tent; pitch camp.* **4.** To set the musical pitch or key of (sthg.): *Pitch your voice so that it harmonizes with mine.* —*intr.* **1.** To toss or throw sthg., such as a baseball or horseshoe: *It's your turn to pitch.* **2.** To fall headfirst with sudden force: *He pitched over the ship's railing.* **3.** To move forcefully forward and backward alternately, as a ship at sea in a storm: *The choppy water made the boat pitch.* **4.** To move so that the front end lifts or falls in relation to the stern or tail: *The airplane pitched as it fought the headwind.* —*n.* **1.** [C] The act of pitching: *My pitch missed the wastebasket by a mile. The pitch of the boat made the passengers sick.* **2.** [C] In baseball, a throw of the ball by a pitcher to a batter: *On the next pitch, the batter hit the ball solidly.* **3.** [C] A degree or level of intensity: *The argument reached a feverish pitch.* **4.** [C; U] A steep slope: *the pitch of the roof.* **5.** [C; U] The quality of a sound, as determined mostly by its frequency, that makes it high or low: *She has perfect pitch.* **6.** [C] *Informal.* A line of talk designed to persuade: *a sales pitch.* ♦ **pitch in.** *intr.v. Informal.* To join forces with others; help or cooperate: *If everyone pitches in, the cleanup will soon be done.*

pitch-black (pĭch′blăk′) *adj.* Extremely

dark; black as pitch: *The house was pitch-black when we arrived.*

pitch-dark (pĭch′därk′) *adj.* Extremely dark: *It was a pitch-dark night.*

pitch·er¹ (pĭch′ər) *n.* The baseball player who pitches the ball to the batter.

pitch·er² (pĭch′ər) *n.* A container for liquids, usually with a handle and a spout for pouring: *a milk pitcher.*

pitch·fork (pĭch′fôrk′) *n.* A large fork with sharp, widely spaced prongs, used to lift and move hay.

pit·e·ous (pĭt′ē əs) *adj.* Demanding or arousing pity: *the piteous cries of a lost child.* —**pit′e·ous·ly** *adv.*

pit·fall (pĭt′fôl′) *n.* (usually plural). A hidden danger or unexpected difficulty: *Life is full of pitfalls.*

pith (pĭth) *n.* [U] **1.** The soft spongy substance in the center of the stems of many plants and under the skin of some fruits and vegetables: *Remove the pith from the orange.* **2.** The central or essential part; the heart or essence: *the pith of her argument.*

pith·y (pĭth′ē) *adj.* **pith·i·er, pith·i·est. 1.** Precisely meaningful; forceful and brief: *The judge made his meaning clear in a single pithy sentence.* **2.** Full of or resembling pith: *the pithy stem of a plant.* —**pith′i·ly** *adv.* —**pith′i·ness** *n.* [U]

pit·i·a·ble (pĭt′ē ə bəl) *adj.* Arousing or deserving of pity; sad: *His despair was pitiable.* —**pit′i·a·bly** *adv.*

pit·i·ful (pĭt′ĭ fəl) *adj.* **1.** Inspiring or deserving pity: *The cold and hungry puppy was a pitiful sight.* **2.** Arousing pity and scorn: *had only a pitiful excuse to offer.* —**pit′i·ful·ly** *adv.* —**pit′i·ful·ness** *n.* [U]

pit·i·less (pĭt′ĭ lĭs) *adj.* Having no pity; merciless: *Last winter the cold seemed truly pitiless.* —**pit′i·less·ly** *adv.* —**pit′i·less·ness** *n.* [U]

pit·tance (pĭt′ns) *n.* (usually singular). **1.** A very small wage: *The carpenter earns only a pittance at that job.* **2.** A very small amount: *a pittance of bread.*

pit·ted (pĭt′ĭd) *adj.* **1.** Marked by pits; with pits in the surface: *the pitted surface of the moon.* **2.** With the pit removed: *pitted olives.*

pit·ter-pat·ter (pĭt′ər păt′ər) *n.* [U] A rapid series of light tapping sounds: *the pitter-patter of mice in the walls.*

pit·y (pĭt′ē) *n.* **1.** [U] Sympathy and sadness in response to the bad luck or suffering of another: *We all felt pity for the hungry children.* **2.** [C] A matter of regret: *It's a pity you can't go.* —*tr.v.* **pit·ied, pit·y·ing, pit·ies. 1.** To feel pity for (sbdy./sthg.): *I pity her parents.* **2.** To consider (sbdy.) pitiful: *I pity you if you can't figure it out for yourself.*

◆ **have** or **take pity on.** To show understanding and give help to (sbdy./sthg.): *Have pity on your overworked employees.*

piv•ot (pĭv′ət) *n.* **1.** A short rod or shaft on which a related part rotates or swings: *The camera turns on a pivot in the tripod.* **2.** A person or thing on which sthg. depends: *She's the pivot in this project; we can't do it without her.* **3.** The act of turning as if on a pivot: *The pitcher made a nice pivot and threw to first base.* —*tr. & intr.v.* To turn or cause to turn as if on a pivot: *The movie pivots on the detective's refusal to believe a witness. The hair stylist pivoted my chair so I faced the mirror.* —**piv′ot•al** *adj.* —**piv′ot•al•ly** *adv.*

pix•el (pĭk′səl *or* pĭk′sĕl′) *n.* The smallest unit on a computer or television screen that with many others creates an electronic image.

pix•y or **pix•ie** (pĭk′sē) *n., pl.* **pix•ies.** A creature similar to a fairy or an elf, especially a mischievous playful one: *a pixy of a child.*

piz•za (pēt′sə) *n.* A baked Italian dish consisting of a shallow crust covered with tomato sauce, cheese, and often other toppings: *a pepperoni pizza.*

piz•zazz or **piz•zaz** (pĭ zăz′) *n.* [U] *Informal.* Dazzling style; exciting showiness: *Your new hat has pizzazz.*

piz•ze•ri•a (pēt′sə rē′ə) *n.* A place where pizzas are made and sold.

pj's or **PJ's** (pē′jāz′) *pl.n. Informal.* Pajamas.

pkg. *abbr.* An abbreviation of package.

pl. *abbr.* An abbreviation of plural.

plac•ard (plăk′ärd *or* plăk′ərd) *n.* A sign or notice for public display: *The striking workers carried placards.*

pla•cate (plā′kāt *or* plăk′āt′) *tr.v.* **pla•cat•ed, pla•cat•ing, pla•cates.** To calm the anger of (sbdy.), especially by agreeing to demands; pacify: *She placated the fussy child with a cookie.* —**pla′cat′er** *n.* —**pla•ca′tion** *n.* [U]

place (plās) *n.* **1.** A particular area or spot with definite or indefinite boundaries: *We chose a place on the wall to hang the painting.* **2.** A city or other locality: *What place were you born in?* **3.** A house, apartment, or other dwelling: *Come over to my place for supper.* **4.** Often **Place.** A public square or a short city street: *She lives on Butler Place.* **5.** A space for a person: *two empty places near the back of the theater; an extra place at the table for supper.* **6.** Position or rank: *The runner from Kenya won first place.* **7.** A particular situation or circumstance: *If you were in my place, would you act differently?* **8.** An appropriate duty, right, or social position: *It's not my place to tell you what to do.* **9.** A job or position: *She found a place with an accounting firm.* **10.** The position of a digit in relation to the other digits of a numeral: *In the number 1.8, the 8 is in the tenths place.* —*v.* **placed, plac•ing, plac•es.** —*tr.* **1.** To put

(sbdy./sthg.) in a particular position or order: *place cups and saucers on the table; place words in alphabetical order.* **2.** To find a place to live or work for (sbdy.): *The Career Office places graduates of the university with many area businesses.* **3.** To remember where or how (sbdy./sthg.) was first met or seen: *His face looks familiar, but I can't place him.* **4.** To put or let (sthg.) be: *place one's trust in the government.* **5.** To apply or arrange for (sthg.): *The bookstore placed an order for a dozen new textbooks.* —*intr.* To arrive among the first three finishers in a race, especially to finish second: *My horse failed to place.* ◆ **in place. 1.** In the appropriate or usual position or order: *Make sure everything is in place before we announce our plan.* **2.** In the same spot; without moving forwards or backwards: *We ran in place for ten minutes.* **in place of.** Instead of: *I gave her a watch in place of the one she had lost.* **out of place.** Out of the proper or usual position, order, time, or environment: *She felt out of place in her daughter's kitchen.*

pla•ce•bo (plə sē′bō) *n., pl.* **pla•ce•bos** or **pla•ce•boes.** A preparation containing no medicine, given to please a patient or used as the control in an experiment to test the effectiveness of a drug.

place mat *n.* A protective table mat for a single setting of dishes and flatware at meals.

place•ment (plās′mənt) *n.* **1.a.** [C; U] The act of placing or arranging: *her placement of the guests around the table.* **b.** [C] The state of being placed: *I'm looking for a new job placement.* **2.** [C] A particular arrangement: *a different placement of the pictures on the walls.*

pla•cen•ta (plə sĕn′tə) *n.* A spongy organ that develops in the uterus of a female mammal during pregnancy and nourishes the fetus. —**pla•cen′tal** *adj.*

plac•id (plăs′ĭd) *adj.* **1.** Calm; peaceful: *a placid lake.* See Synonyms at **calm. 2.** Satisfied; at ease: *a placid smile.* —**pla•cid′i•ty** (plə sĭd′ĭ tē) *n.* [U] —**plac′id•ly** *adv.*

pla•gia•rism (plā′jə rĭz′əm) *n.* **1.** [U] The act of plagiarizing: *The producers of the show were guilty of plagiarism.* **2.** [C] Something plagiarized: *His poems were plagiarisms from a magazine.* —**pla′gia•rist** *n.*

pla•gia•rize (plā′jə rīz′) *v.* **pla•gia•rized, pla•gia•riz•ing, pla•gia•riz•es.** —*tr.* To use as one's own (the ideas or writings of another): *The student plagiarized a newspaper article when writing her report.* —*intr.* To present as one's own work the ideas or words of another: *Do you think he intended to plagiarize?*

plague (plāg) *n.* **1.** A cause of widespread disaster and suffering: *a plague of locusts.* **2.** A very contagious, usually fatal epidemic disease. **3.** A sudden increase, as of sthg. destructive: *Poverty has become a plague in* *many countries.* **4.** A cause of annoyance; a nuisance: *The defective printer was a plague to our office.* —*tr.v.* **plagued, plagu•ing, plagues. 1.** To annoy or bother (sbdy.): *Stop plaguing me with your complaints.* **2.** To cause misery or trouble in or for (sbdy./sthg.): *Political problems have plagued that country for years.*

plaid (plăd) *n.* [C; U] Cloth with a pattern of perpendicular lines of different colors: *She often wears plaids.* —*adj.* With such a pattern: *a plaid shirt.*

plain (plān) *adj.* **1.** Open to view; clear: *The mountain stood out plain against the sky.* **2.** Obvious to the mind; perfectly clear: *His meaning was quite plain.* **3.** Not fancy; simple: *plain food.* **4.** Ordinary; average: *My dog is a plain old mutt.* **5.** Lacking beauty or special qualities: *a plain face.* **6.** Frank; candid: *plain talk.* **7.** Pure; natural: *plain water instead of soda water.* —*n. (usually plural).* A large, flat, mostly treeless area of land: *the plains of Nebraska.* —*adv. Informal.* Clearly; simply: *That's plain stupid.* —**plain'ly** *adv.* —**plain'ness** *n.* [U]

HOMONYMS: plain, plane (airplane, tool).

plain•clothes man or **plain•clothes•man** (plān'klōz'mən or plān'klōthz'mən) *n.* A member of a police force who wears civilian clothes on duty.

plain•tiff (plān'tĭf) *n.* The person, group, or institution that brings a lawsuit to a court.

plain•tive (plān'tĭv) *adj.* Expressing sorrow; sad: *a plaintive song.* —**plain'tive•ly** *adv.* —**plain'tive•ness** *n.* [U]

plait (plāt or plăt) *Chiefly British. n.* A braid, especially of hair. —*tr.v.* To braid (sthg.): *She plaited her hair.*

HOMONYMS: plait, plate (dish).

plan (plăn) *n.* **1.** A scheme, program, or method thought out ahead of time to achieve a goal: *a plan for reorganizing the town government.* **2.** A drawing or diagram showing how to build or assemble sthg.: *plans for a new house.* —*v.* **planned, plan•ning, plans.** —*tr.* **1.** To think out a scheme or program for accomplishing or gaining (sthg.): *plan one's trip.* **2.** To have (sthg.) in mind; intend: *She plans to go to Canada this summer.* **3.** To design (sthg.): *The architect will plan a new school.* —*intr.* To make a plan or plans: *He's always busy planning for the future.* —**plan'ner** *n.*

plane¹ (plān) *n.* **1.** An airplane. **2.** In geometry, a surface that contains all the straight lines required to connect any two points on it. **3.** A flat or level surface. **4.** A level of exis-

tence, development, or achievement: *a high moral plane.*

HOMONYMS: plane (airplane, tool), **plain** (clear).

plane² (plān) *n.* A carpenter's tool with an adjustable blade for smoothing and leveling wood. —*tr.v.* **planed, plan•ing, planes.** To smooth or finish (sthg.) with a plane: *She planed the wood for the table top.*

plan•et (plăn'ĭt) *n.* A celestial body that is larger than an asteroid or a comet and moves in an orbit around a star: *Mercury is the planet closest to the sun.* —**plan'e•tar'y** *adj.*

plan•e•tar•i•um (plăn'ĭ târ'ē əm) *n., pl.* **plan•e•tar•i•ums** or **plan•e•tar•i•a** (plăn'ĭ târ'ē ə). A building or room in which images of celestial bodies are projected onto the ceiling: *The audience sat in the planetarium gazing up at the images of the stars.*

plank (plăngk) *n.* **1.** A piece of lumber cut thicker than a board. **2.** One of the principles of a political platform: *Party members argued heatedly about each plank in the presidential platform.*

plank•ton (plăngk'tən) *n.* [U] The collection of plant and animal organisms, usually of very small size, that float or drift in great numbers in bodies of water: *whales feeding on plankton.*

plant (plănt) *n.* **1.** Any of various organisms that can manufacture their own food, cannot move under their own power, and have cells with walls made of cellulose: *plants and animals of the forest.* **2.** A factory where sthg. is produced or processed: *an automobile plant in Detroit.* **3.** A person or thing put into place to mislead or work secretly, especially a spy placed to deceive: *My new secretary turned out to be a plant from another company.* —*tr.v.* **1.** To place (seeds or young plants) in the ground or in soil for growing: *He planted tomatoes in the garden.* **2.** To fix or set (sthg.) firmly: *plant one's feet on the ground.* **3.** To start or establish (sthg.): *plant new colonies.* **4.** To fix (sthg.) firmly in the mind: *plant an idea.* **5.** To place (sbdy./sthg.) as a means of trapping or deceiving sbdy.: *plant spies in an organization.*

plan•tain (plăn'tən) *n.* A tropical fruit similar to the banana but not as sweet.

plan•ta•tion (plăn tā'shən) *n.* A large farm or estate on which certain crops are raised, often by resident workers: *a sugar plantation.*

plant•er (plăn'tər) *n.* **1.** A decorative container for a plant or small tree: *He placed several large planters filled with flowers on the patio.* **2.** A person or thing that plants, especially a tool or machine for planting seeds. **3.** The owner or manager of a plantation.

ă–cat; ā–pay; âr–care; ä–father; ĕ–get; ē–be; ĭ–sit; ī–nice; îr–here; ŏ–got; ō–go; ô–saw; oi–boy; ou–out; ōō–took; ōō–boot; ŭ–cut; ûr–word; th–thin; th–this; hw–when; zh–vision; ə–about; N–French bon

plaque (plăk) *n.* **1.** [C] A flat metal or stone plate used for decoration or engraved with an inscription to honor some special event or award: *a plaque honoring her 25 years of service.* **2.** [U] A film of mucus and bacteria that forms on the surface of the teeth: *Brushing helps prevent the buildup of plaque.*

plas•ma (plăz′mə) *n.* [U] The clear yellowish liquid part of blood in which cells are suspended: *blood plasma given to the patient.*

plas•ter (plăs′tər) *n.* [U] A mixture of sand, lime or gypsum, and water, sometimes with fiber added, that hardens to a smooth solid and is used for covering walls and ceilings: *The contractor put new plaster on the ceiling and walls.* —*tr.v.* **1.** To cover (sthg.) with plaster: *He plastered cracks in the ceiling.* **2.** To cover (sthg.) as if with plaster: *The students plastered the campus with posters.* **3.** To make (sthg.) stick to another surface: *I plastered posters on the wall.* —**plas′ter•er** *n.*

plas•ter•board (plăs′tər bôrd′) *n.* [U] A rigid board or sheet of layers of paper, used to cover walls.

plas•tic (plăs′tĭk) *n.* **1.** [C; U] A strong, lightweight chemical compound made from organic material such as petroleum. Plastics can be formed into almost any shape or into fibers to create fabrics: *Plastic has replaced metal in some auto body parts.* **2.** [U] *Informal.* A credit card or credit cards: *The restaurant accepts cash or plastic but no personal checks.* —*adj.* **1.** Made of plastic: *a plastic cup.* **2.** Capable of being shaped or formed: *Clay is a plastic material.* —**plas•tic′i•ty** (plăs tĭs′ĭ tē) *n.* [U]

plastic surgery *n.* [U] Surgery to repair, restore, or remodel body tissue or parts: *More men then ever before are having plastic surgery.*

plate (plāt) *n.* **1.** [C] A shallow usually circular dish from which food is eaten: *dinner plates.* **2.** [C] A thin flat sheet or piece of metal or other material, especially one on which sthg. is engraved: *a license plate; a name plate.* **3.** [C] A sheet of light-sensitive glass or metal upon which a photographic image can be recorded. **4.** [C] A piece of metal or plastic fitted to the gums to hold false teeth in place: *a partial plate.* **5.** [C] In baseball, home plate: *The batter stepped up to the plate.* **6.** [U] Dishes and other household articles coated with gold or silver: *silver plate.* **7.** [C] An electrode, as in a storage battery or capacitor. **8.** [C] In the geological theory of plate tectonics, one of the sections of the earth's crust. —*tr.v.* **plat•ed, plat•ing, plates.** To coat or cover (sthg.) with a thin layer of metal: *plate spoons with silver.*

HOMONYMS: plate, plait (braid).

pla•teau (plă tō′) *n.* **1.** An elevated, comparatively level expanse of land. **2.** A relatively stable level or stage of growth or development:

The economy has reached a new plateau. —*intr.v.* To reach a stage of little growth or development: *Prices have plateaued after months of rising.*

plate•let (plāt′lĭt) *n.* Any of the numerous microscopic bodies that are found in the blood of mammals and function in the clotting of blood.

plate tec•ton•ics (tĕk tŏn′ĭks) *n.* [U] *(used with a singular verb).* In geology, a theory that the earth's crust is divided into a series of vast platelike sections that move as distinct masses.

plat•form (plăt′fôrm′) *n.* **1.** A floor or horizontal surface higher than the area next to it: *a speakers' platform; a train arriving on platform number one.* **2.** A formal declaration of principles by a political party or candidate: *the new candidate's platform.*

plat•ing (plā′tĭng) *n.* [U] A thin layer or coating of metal, such as gold or silver, applied to a surface.

plat•i•num (plăt′n əm) *n.* [U] *Symbol* **Pt** A silver-white metallic element used as a catalyst, for chemical and industrial equipment, in dentistry, and in jewelry. Atomic number 78. See table at **element.**

plat•i•tude (plăt′ĭ tōod′) *n.* An often-repeated remark or statement, especially one expressed as if it were original or significant: *He's always mouthing platitudes; he has nothing meaningful to say.*

pla•ton•ic (plə tŏn′ĭk) *adj.* Relating to a friendly relationship that does not involve sex: *a platonic friendship.*

pla•toon (plə tōon′) *n.* A unit of soldiers smaller than a company but larger than a squad, normally commanded by a lieutenant.

plat•ter (plăt′ər) *n.* **1.** A large shallow dish or plate for serving food: *a meat platter.* **2.** A meal or course served on a platter: *a platter of fish.*

plau•si•ble (plô′zə bəl) *adj.* Seemingly true or reasonable: *a plausible excuse.* —**plau′si•bil′i•ty** *n.* [U] —**plau′si•bly** *adv.*

play (plā) *v.* —*intr.* **1.** To have fun; amuse oneself: *The children went outdoors to play.* **2.** To take part in a game: *The basketball star is injured and can't play.* **3.** To act in a certain way as a joke: *She looks angry, but she's just playing.* **4.** To be presented for an audience: *What movie is playing tonight?* **5.** To behave in a particular way: *You're not playing fair.* **6.** To perform or produce music: *The band played.* —*tr.* **1.** To perform or act (a role or part): *He's playing Hamlet. Advertising will play an important role in the campaign.* **2.** To pretend to be (sbdy.); mimic the activities of: *He was playing cowboy.* **3.a.** To engage in (a game or sport): *played tennis.* **b.** To have or work at (a position) in a game: *She plays goalie for her team.* **4.** To perform or put (sthg.) into effect, especially as a joke or trick: *play a joke on a friend.* **5.a.** To perform on (an instrument): *play the piano.* **b.** To perform (a piece of music) on an instrument or instruments: *Can you play a waltz?* **6.** To cause (a record, for example) to produce recorded sounds: *play a CD.* —*n.* **1.** [C] **a.** A literary work written for performance on the stage: *Shakespeare's plays.* **b.** The performance of such a work: *We went to a play last night.* **2.** [U] Activity done for fun: *Play is important for children and adults.* **3.** [U] A manner of dealing with people: *He believes in fair play.* **4.** [C] A move or an action in a game: *The catcher made a great play.* **5.** [U] Movement or freedom of movement: *the play of lights across a stage.* **6.** [U] Action; use: *The lobbyist brought her influence into full play.* **7.** [C] An attempt to get sthg.: *a play for sympathy.* ◆ **play along with.** To cooperate or pretend to cooperate: *The bank teller decided to play along with the robbers for a while.* **play down.** *tr.v.* [sep.] To make (sthg.) seem unimportant: *The economist played down the fall in stock prices.* **play hard to get.** To pretend not to be interested: *He wants to ask her out, but she's playing hard to get.* **play it safe.** To be cautious: *It usually takes an hour to get to the airport, but to play it safe, let's plan on two hours.* **play on** or **upon.** *tr.v.* [insep.] To take advantage of (another's attitudes or feelings) for one's own interests: *He played on my sympathy when asking for a loan.* **play (one's) cards right.** To arrange circumstances to one's advantage: *If you play your cards right, your trip might be paid for by the company.* **play the game.** To appear to agree with others in order to gain an advantage: *If you want to get ahead in business, you have to play the game.* **play up to.** To try to win the favor of (sbdy.): *We thought it would help to play up to the new teacher.* **play with fire.** To take part in sthg. dangerous or risky: *When he experiments with drugs, he's playing with fire.* —**play′a•ble** *adj.*

play•boy (plā′boi′) *n.* A man who devotes himself to pleasure, especially with women. —**play′girl′** *n.*

play-by-play (plā′bī plā′) *adj.* Relating to a detailed account of the action of an event, especially a sports event, as it is happening: *a play-by-play description of the ballgame.*

play•er (plā′ər) *n.* **1.** A person who takes part in a game or sport: *a professional tennis player.* **2.** A person who plays a musical instrument: *the band's bass player.* **3.** A device that reproduces recorded sound: *a CD player.*

play•ful (plā′fəl) *adj.* **1.** Full of fun and high spirits: *a playful cat.* **2.** Funny and lighthearted; not serious: *a playful discussion.* —**play′ful•ly** *adv.* —**play′ful•ness** *n.* [U]

play•ground (plā′ground′) *n.* An outdoor area for play, especially one with equipment such as slides and swings for children: *a new playground in the park.*

play•house (plā′hous′) *n.* **1.** A theater. **2.** A small house for children to play in.

play•ing card (plā′ĭng) *n.* A card marked with rank and suit and used to play a variety of games.

play•mate (plā′māt′) *n.* A child's companion in play or recreation: *Her daughter has lots of new playmates.*

play•off (plā′ôf′ *or* plā′ŏf′) *n.* In sports, a game or series of games played to determine a championship or break a tie: *The team made it to the playoffs.*

play•pen (plā′pĕn′) *n.* A portable enclosure in which a baby or a young child can be safely left to play: *The baby stood in his playpen and threw his toys out.*

play•room (plā′rōōm′) *n.* A room designed or set aside for play or recreation.

play•thing (plā′thĭng′) *n.* A thing to play with; a toy: *a child's collection of playthings.*

play•wright (plā′rīt′) *n.* A person who writes plays; a dramatist: *a great American playwright.*

pla•za (plä′zə *or* plăz′ə) *n.* **1.** A public square or similar open area in a town or city: *the plaza in Bogotá.* **2.** A shopping center.

plea (plē) *n.* **1.** An appeal or urgent request: *a plea for help.* **2.** In law, the answer of the accused to the charges: *The defendant entered a plea of guilty.*

plea-bar•gain (plē′bär′gən) *intr.v.* In law, to make an agreement in which a defendant pleads guilty to a lesser charge and the prosecutor does not bring more serious charges: *The lawyer for the accused man tried to plea-bargain for him.*

plead (plēd) *v.* **plead•ed** or **pled** (plĕd), **plead•ing, pleads.** —*intr.* **1.** To appeal earnestly; beg: *They were pleading with him to return.* **2.** To put forward a plea in a court of law: *How does the defendant plead?* —*tr.* **1.** To put forward (sthg.) as a defense or an excuse: *She pleaded illness as her reason for being absent.* **2.** To argue (a case) in a court of law: *pleaded the case before a judge.*

pleas•ant (plĕz′ənt) *adj.* **1.** Giving pleasure or enjoyment; agreeable: *a pleasant climate; a pleasant smell.* **2.** Pleasing in manner, behavior, or appearance: *a pleasant person to deal with.* —**pleas′ant•ly** *adv.* —**pleas′ant•ness** *n.* [U]

pleas•ant•ry (plĕz′ən trē) *n., pl.* **pleas•ant•ries.** A polite or humorous social remark: *We exchanged pleasantries before the concert.*

please (plēz) *v.* **pleased, pleas•ing,**

pleas•es. —*tr.* **1.** To give (sbdy./sthg.) pleasure or satisfaction: *The island pleased the tourists.* **2.** *Formal.* To be the will or desire of (sbdy.): *May it please the court.* —*intr.* **1.** To give satisfaction or pleasure; be agreeable: *I try to please when I can.* **2.** To have the will or desire; wish: *do exactly as they please.* —*adv.* If it is your desire or pleasure; if you will. Used to make a request or command more polite: *Would you please pass the salt? Please stand back.*

pleas•ing (plē′zĭng) *adj.* Giving pleasure or enjoyment; agreeable: *The young actor gave a pleasing performance.* —**pleas′ing•ly** *adv.*

pleas•ur•a•ble (plĕzh′ər ə bəl) *adj.* Agreeable; pleasant: *a pleasurable experience.* —**pleas′ur•a•bly** *adv.*

pleas•ure (plĕzh′ər) *n.* **1.** [U] The state or feeling of being pleased or glad: *She smiled with pleasure.* **2.** [C] A source of enjoyment or delight: *Reading is his chief pleasure.* **3.** [U] Amusement, entertainment, or enjoyment: *We grew vegetables for pleasure more than for food.*

pleat (plēt) *n.* A pressed or sewn fold in cloth made by doubling the material on itself. —*tr.v.* To make pleats in (sthg.): *pleat a ruffle.*

pleat•ed (plē′tĭd) *adj.* With pressed or sewn folds: *a pleated skirt; a pleated fan.*

ple•be•ian (plĭ bē′ən) *adj.* Coarse or vulgar: *plebeian tastes.* —*n.* A person considered to be coarse or vulgar.

pled (plĕd) *v.* A past tense and a past participle of **plead.**

pledge (plĕj) *n.* **1.** A formal vow; a solemn promise or agreement: *made a pledge to do their duty.* **2.** Something promised as security to guarantee payment of a debt: *a necklace left as a pledge for a loan.* **3.** Something given as a sign of love or friendship: *They exchanged rings as a pledge of love.* **4.** Someone who has been accepted for membership in a fraternity but has not yet been initiated. —*tr.v.* **pledged, pledg•ing, pledg•es. 1.** To guarantee (sthg.) by a solemn promise or vow: *They pledged their support.* See Synonyms at **vow. 2.** [*to*] To commit (oneself) in a solemn promise or vow: *They pledged themselves to secrecy.*

plen•ti•ful (plĕn′tĭ fəl) *adj.* **1.** In large amounts; ample: *plentiful food.* **2.** Producing large amounts: *a plentiful land.* —**plen′ti•ful•ly** *adv.*

plen•ty (plĕn′tē) *n.* [U] **1.** An adequate or large amount or supply: *plenty of time; plenty of food.* **2.** General prosperity: *a time of plenty.* —*adv.* *Informal.* Excessively; very: *They were plenty hungry.*

pli•a•ble (plī′ə bəl) *adj.* **1.** Easily bent or shaped; flexible: *pliable strips of wood.* **2.** Easily influenced or convinced: *a pliable mind.* —**pli′a•bil′i•ty** *n.* [U] —**pli′a•bly** *adv.*

pli•ant (plī′ənt) *adj.* Pliable.

pli•ers (plī′ərz) *pl.n.* A tool with two parts, similar to a pair of scissors, used for holding, bending, or cutting: *a pair of pliers.*

plight (plīt) *n.* A difficult or dangerous situation: *She told her parents of her financial plight, and they loaned her some money.*

pliers

plod (plŏd) *intr.v.* **plod•ded, plod•ding, plods. 1.** To walk heavily or slowly: *The horses plodded along.* **2.** To work or act slowly and wearily: *He plodded through his lessons.* —**plod′der** *n.*

plop (plŏp) *v.* **plopped, plop•ping, plops.** —*intr.* **1.** To fall with a sound like sthg. falling into water: *The carrots plopped into the soup.* **2.** To let one's body fall heavily or wearily: *She plopped into the chair.* —*tr.* To place or drop (sthg.) with a plopping sound: *He plopped the tomatoes onto the plate.* —*n.* A plopping sound: *The pebble fell with a plop into the pool.*

plot (plŏt) *n.* **1.** A small piece of ground; a lot: *a plot of good land.* **2.** The actions or events in a novel, movie, or play: *a mystery with a thrilling plot.* **3.** A secret plan to accomplish an often illegal purpose: *a plot to kill the queen.* —*tr.v.* **plot•ted, plot•ting, plots. 1.** To mark or note (sthg.) on a chart or map: *The captain plotted the ship's course.* **2.** To plan (sthg.) secretly: *plot revenge.* —**plot′ter** *n.*

plow also **plough** (plou) *n.* **1.** A farm implement with a heavy blade at the end of a beam, pulled either by animals or a vehicle, used for breaking up soil: *The farmer hooked the plow to the tractor.* **2.** A device or vehicle with a similar function: *a snowplow.* —*v.* —*tr.* **1.** To break (soil) with a plow: *The farmer plowed the field for planting.* **2.** To make (one's way) through sthg. steadily and with difficulty: *The girl plowed her way through the deep snow.* **3.** To remove snow from (sthg.) with a snowplow: *They plowed the streets after the storm.* —*intr.* To move steadily and with difficulty: *The boat plowed on.* ♦ **plow into.** *tr.v.* [insep.] *Informal.* To strike (sbdy./sthg.) with force: *The truck plowed into the fence.*

ploy (ploi) *n.* A trick designed to obtain advantage over an opponent: *His story was a ploy to get our trust.*

pluck (plŭk) *tr.v.* **1.** To pick (sthg.): *pluck a flower.* **2.** To pull out the feathers or hair of (sthg.): *pluck a chicken.* **3.** To pull (sthg.) suddenly; tug: *pluck a sleeve.* **4.** To sound (a string of an instrument) by stretching and releasing: *pluck a guitar.* —*n.* [U] Courage and spirit: *a reporter with a lot of pluck.*

pluck•y (plŭk′ē) *adj.* **pluck•i•er, pluck•i•est.** Showing spirit and courage in difficult circumstances: *a plucky child.*

plug (plŭg) *n.* **1.** A piece of wood, cork, or other material, used to fill a hole (in a pipe, for example). **2.** A device used to connect an electrical device to a power source. **3.** A spark plug. **4.** A hydrant: *a fire plug.* **5.** *Informal.* A favorable public mention of sthg., especially on television or radio: *In the interview, she made a plug for her new book.* —*tr.v.* **plugged, plug•ging, plugs. 1.** To fill (a hole) tightly as if with a plug or stopper: *Plug the leak!* **2.** *Informal.* To mention (sthg.) favorably; advertise: *plug a new movie.* ◆ **plug away at.** To work hard and without stopping: *We plugged away at the housecleaning.* **plug in.** *tr.v.* [sep.] To connect (an appliance) to an electrical outlet: *Plug the toaster in.* **plug into.** *tr.v.* [sep.] To connect (sthg.) to: *You can plug this CD player into the stereo. The computer plugs into a data bank.*

plum (plŭm) *n.* **1.** [C] The fruit of any of several small trees, with smooth often dark purple skin, juicy flesh, and a single pit. **2.** [U] A dark purple color. **3.** [C] Something very much wanted, such as a job that pays well: *His job in advertising is a real plum.* —*adj.* Dark purple.

HOMONYMS: plum, plumb (weight).

plum•age (plōō′mĭj) *n.* [U] The feathers on a bird: *brilliant blue-green plumage.*

plumb (plŭm) *n.* A weight hung from the end of a cord, used to measure water depth or test whether sthg. is vertical. —*adv.* Vertically; straight up and down: *the post stands plumb.* **2.** *Informal.* Completely; utterly: *plumb wrong.* —*adj.* **1.** Exactly vertical: *a plumb wall.* **2.** *Informal.* Complete; utter: *a plumb fool.* —*tr.v.* **1.** To test the depth or alignment of (sthg.) with a plumb: *plumb a well.* **2.** To examine (sthg.) closely; probe into: *plumb a criminal's mind.*

HOMONYMS: plumb, plum (fruit).

plumb•er (plŭm′ər) *n.* A person who installs and repairs pipes and plumbing.
plumb•ing (plŭm′ĭng) *n.* [U] **1.** The pipes and other equipment used to transport a liquid or gas. **2.** The work of a plumber.
plume (plōōm) *n.* **1.** A feather, especially a large or showy one used for decoration. **2.** Something that looks like a large feather: *A plume of smoke rose from the chimney.*
plum•met (plŭm′ĭt) *intr.v.* To fall straight down; plunge: *A rock plummeted down from the cliff. Stock prices plummeted.*
plump[1] (plŭmp) *adj.* Pleasantly rounded and full in form: *a plump figure; a plump peach.*

—*tr. & intr.v.* To make or become plump: *He plumped up the pillow. The child plumped out as she grew.* —**plump′ly** *adv.* —**plump′ness** *n.* [U]
plump[2] (plŭmp) *intr. & tr.v.* To drop or throw heavily or abruptly: *She plumped down on the grass. We plumped the books onto the table.* —*n.* A heavy abrupt fall: *She threw herself on the sofa with a plump.* —*adv.* With a heavy or abrupt drop: *He fell down plump on the ground.*
plun•der (plŭn′dər) *tr.v.* To take valuables from (sthg.); rob: *Pirates plundered the coastal city.* —*n.* [U] **1.** The act of taking property by force. **2.** Property stolen by force or by fraud: *digging a hole to hide their plunder.* —**plun′der•er** *n.*
plunge (plŭnj) *v.* **plunged, plung•ing, plung•es.** —*tr.* **1.** To thrust or place (sthg.) forcefully or suddenly into sthg.: *plunged the knife into the cake.* **2.** To cause (sbdy./sthg.) to enter suddenly or violently into a situation or activity: *events that plunged the world into war; a purchase that plunged him into debt.* —*intr.* **1.** To throw oneself suddenly or energetically into sthg., such as a body of water: *He plunged into the lake.* **2.** To fall steeply or sharply: *The cliff plunged into the sea.* **3.** To rush or move forward into or toward sthg. quickly and rapidly: *animals plunging through the undergrowth.* —*n.* **1.** The act of plunging: *a plunge into work.* **2.** A swim: *an early morning plunge.* ◆ **take the plunge.** *Informal.* To begin sthg. unfamiliar, especially after hesitating: *He decided to take the plunge and move to Houston.*
plung•er (plŭn′jər) *n.* **1.** A suction device used to clean out clogged drains and pipes. **2.** A machine part, such as a piston, that operates with a plunging movement.
plunk (plŭngk) *v.* —*tr.* **1.** *Informal.* To throw or place (sthg.) heavily or abruptly: *He plunked the nickel on the table.* **2.** To strum or pluck (the strings of a musical instrument): *plunking on a banjo.* —*intr.* **1.** To drop or sink heavily or wearily; plop: *They plunked down on the bench.* **2.** To make a short, hollow, metallic sound: *He plunked on his banjo.* —*n.* **1.** A short, hollow, twanging sound: *the plunk of a badly tuned guitar.* **2.** A heavy blow or hit.
plu•ral (plŏŏr′əl) *adj.* **1.** Relating to or composed of more than one. **2.** In grammar, relating to the form of a word that designates more than one. —*n.* The plural form of a word. *Children* is the plural of *child.* —**plu′ral•ly** *adv.*
plus (plŭs) *conj.* **1.** Added to: *Two plus three equals five.* **2.** Increased by; along with: *wages plus bonuses.* —*adj.* **1.** Greater than zero; positive: *a plus quantity.* **2.** Indicating a

positive electric charge. **3.** Slightly more than: *a grade of B plus.* —*n., pl.* **plus•es** or **plus•ses. 1.** The plus sign. **2.** A positive number. **3.** A favorable factor or condition: *We considered the pluses and minuses.*

plush (plŭsh) *n.* A fabric like velvet but with a deeper pile. —*adj.* **1.** Made of or covered with plush: *a plush sofa.* **2.** Luxurious; elegant: *a plush restaurant.* —**plush′y** *adj.*

plus sign *n.* The symbol (+), as in 2 + 2 = 4, that is used to show addition or a positive quantity.

plu•to•ni•um (ploo tō′nē əm) *n.* [U] *Symbol* **Pu** A naturally radioactive, silvery metallic element that is used as a source of energy in nuclear reactors and is highly poisonous. Atomic number 94. See table at **element.**

ply[1] (plī) *n., pl.* **plies** (plīz). **1.** A layer or thickness, as of cloth, paper or wood: *two-ply napkins.* **2.** One of the strands in yarn, rope, or thread: *three-ply yarn.*

ply[2] (plī) *tr.v.* **plied** (plīd), **ply•ing, plies** (plīz). **1.** *Formal.* To use (a tool): *ply a broom while cleaning the house.* **2.** To engage in (a trade or task); perform regularly: *ply the baker's trade.*

ply•wood (plī′wŏod′) *n.* [U] A building material made of layers of wood glued together.

P.M. also **p.m.** *abbr.* An abbreviation of post meridiem, used to indicate a time between noon and midnight: *3:30 P.M.*

pneu•mat•ic (noo măt′ĭk) *adj.* **1.** Relating to air or another gas: *pneumatic pressure.* **2.** Operated by compressed air: *a pneumatic drill.*

pneu•mo•nia (noo mōn′yə) *n.* [U] A disease in which the lungs become inflamed: *He died of pneumonia.*

PO or **P.O.** *abbr.* An abbreviation of post office.

poach[1] (pōch) *tr.v.* To cook (eggs or fish, for example) in a liquid that is gently boiling or simmering: *poached eggs on toast.*

poach[2] (pōch) *intr.v.* To hunt or fish illegally in a wildlife preserve or on private property: *They were poaching on the farmer's land when they were arrested.* —**poach′er** *n.*

pock (pŏk) *n.* A mark or scar of the skin left by smallpox or a similar disease; a pockmark.

pock•et (pŏk′ĭt) *n.* **1.** A small pouch, open at the top, sewn into or onto clothing and used to hold things: *Please put this in your pocket.* **2.** A small isolated area or group: *pockets of civilization in the desert; a pocket of unrest.* **3.** A small cavity in the earth where ore can be found: *a pocket of gold.* —*adj.* Suitable for being carried in a pocket: *a pocket watch.* —*tr.v.* **1.** To place (sthg.) as if in a pocket: *pocket a dime.* **2.** To take possession of (sthg.) dishonestly: *pocket the waiter's tip.* ◆ **in (one's) pocket.** In (one's) power, influence, or possession: *She has the*

election in her pocket. **line (one's) pockets.** To make a profit, especially by dishonest means: *He used his position with the city to line his pockets.*

pock•et•book (pŏk′ĭt book′) *n.* **1.** A container used to hold money, papers, cosmetics, and other small articles; a handbag or purse. **2.** A supply of money: *too expensive for our pocketbook.* **3.** A small book usually with a soft cover.

pock•et•ful (pŏk′ĭt fool′) *n., pl.* **pock•et•fuls** or **pock•ets•ful** (pŏk′ĭts fool′). The amount that a pocket will hold: *a pocketful of quarters.*

pock•et•knife (pŏk′ĭt nīf′) *n.* A small knife with a blade or blades that fold into the handle.

pock•mark (pŏk′märk′) *n.* A scar left on the skin as a result of acne or disease. —**pock′-marked′** *adj.*

pod (pŏd) *n.* A seed case of a pea, bean, or certain other plants.

po•di•a•try (pə dī′ə trē) *n.* [U] The branch of medicine that deals with the study and treatment of foot ailments. —**po•di′a•trist** *n.*

po•di•um (pō′dē əm) *n.* An elevated platform for an orchestra conductor or a lecturer.

po•em (pō′əm) *n.* A literary composition that conveys experiences, thoughts, or feelings in a vivid and imaginative way.

po•et (pō′ĭt) *n.* A person who writes poems.

po•et•ic (pō ĕt′ĭk) *adj* **1.** Relating to poetry: *poetic works.* **2.** Having a quality or style characteristic of poetry: *poetic language.* ◆ **poetic justice.** A particularly appropriate reward or punishment: *It was poetic justice that the car thief's own car was stolen the following week.*

po•et•ry (pō′ĭ trē) *n.* [U] **1.** The poems of a specific author, country, time period, or kind: *Renaissance poetry.* **2.** A quality that pleases or stirs the imagination; beauty: *poetry to my ears.*

poign•ant (poin′yənt) *adj.* **1.** Very distressing or painful: *poignant grief.* **2.** Deeply moving; touching: *poignant memories.* —**poign′an•cy** [U] —**poign′ant•ly** *adv.*

poin•set•ti•a (poin sĕt′ē ə *or* poin sĕt′ə) *n.* A tropical American plant with small yellowish flowers surrounded by showy, usually bright red leaves that resemble petals: *Many people display poinsettias during the Christmas holidays.*

point (point) *n.* **1.** [C] The sharp end of sthg.: *the point of a pencil.* **2.** [C] A piece of land that narrows as it extends into a body of water: *sailed around the point.* **3.** [C] A dot or period, as one used to separate the parts of a numeral. The number 2.5 is read *two point five.* **4.** [C] A geometric object with a location but no height, width, or length: *a line between two points.* **5.** [C] A position or place: *the highest point in the county.* **6.** [C; U] A specified degree or condition: *the boiling point of* *water.* **7.** [C] A specific moment in time: *At that point he noticed someone running away.* **8.** [U] The time immediately before an event: *on the point of quitting his job; at the point of death.* **9.** [C] The important or essential part or idea: *the point of a story.* **10.** [U] A purpose or goal: *What was the point of her visit?* **11.** [C] A distinctive quality or characteristic: *His sense of humor is one of his best points.* **12.** [C] A single unit in the score of a game, contest, or test: *scored two points for her team.* **13.** [C] A unit equal to one dollar and used to state the current prices of stocks: *The stock market fell ten points.* —*v.* —*tr.* **1.** To direct or aim (sthg.): *point the flashlight down the road.* **2.** To show (a direction or position) with or as if with a finger: *She pointed the way to the river.* —*intr.* **1.** To direct attention toward sthg. with the finger: *He pointed to the tree.* **2.** To be turned or directed in a given direction: *The compass needle pointed north.* **3.** To be a sign of sthg., especially of a likely event: *Employment figures point to an improvement in the economy.* ♦ **beside the point.** Unrelated or unimportant to the subject being discussed: *Whether you want to go or not is beside the point.* **make a point of.** To consider or treat (an action or activity) as of highest importance: *We made a point of being on time.* **point of no return.** A point beyond which one cannot turn back: *He reached a point of no return in his life when he participated in a robbery.*

point-blank (point′blăngk′) *adj.* **1.** Aimed straight at or very close to a mark or target: *a point-blank shot.* **2.** Without room for doubt; blunt: *a point-blank answer.* —*adv.* **1.** With a direct aim; straight: *He fired point-blank.* **2.** Without hesitating; bluntly: *She answered point-blank.*

point•ed (poin′tĭd) *adj.* **1.** With a sharp or tapered end or part: *pointed leaves.* **2.** Cutting; piercing: *a pointed manner.* **3.** Clearly directed or aimed, such as at a particular person: *a pointed remark.* —**point′ed•ly** *adv.* —**point′ed•ness** *n.* [U]

point•er (poin′tər) *n.* **1.** A marker that indicates a number on a scale, as in a clock or meter. **2.** A long stick used for indicating sthg., as on a map or blackboard. **3.** Any of a breed of dog often trained to point at an animal while hunting. **4.** A piece of advice: *pointers on buying a new car.*

point•less (point′lĭs) *adj.* With no purpose or meaning: *a pointless rule.* —**point′less•ly** *adv.* —**point′less•ness** *n.* [U]

point of view *n.*, *pl.* **points of view.** **1.** A manner of viewing things; an attitude: *a liberal point of view.* **2.** A position from which sthg. is observed or considered.

point•y (poin′tē) *adj.* **point•i•er, point•i•est.** With an end tapering to a point: *a pointy nose.*

poise (poiz) *v.* **poised, pois•ing, pois•es.** —*tr.* To balance or hold (sthg.) in equilibrium: *He poised the flashlight on the edge of the table.* —*intr.* **1.** To be balanced: *She poised on the end of the diving board.* **2.** To remain in one spot as if suspended: *A hummingbird poises over a flower.* —*n.* [U] A calm confident manner: *They answered our questions with unusual poise..* —**poised** *adj.*

poi•son (poi′zən) *n.* [C; U] A substance that causes injury, sickness, or death, especially by chemical means: *He put poison in her tea.* —*tr.v.* **1.** To kill or harm (sbdy./sthg.) with poison: *The dog had been poisoned.* **2.** To put poison on or into (sthg.): *poisoned the drink.* **3.** To have a harmful influence on (sbdy./sthg.): *Jealousy poisoned their minds.* —*adj.* Poisonous: *poison arrows.* —**poi′son•er** *n.*

poison ivy *n.* [U] A plant that has leaflets in groups of three and can cause a severe itching skin rash if touched.

poison oak *n.* [U] Either of two shrubs related to and resembling poison ivy and causing a similar skin rash.

poison ivy

poi•son•ous (poi′zə nəs) *adj.* **1.** Capable of harming or killing by poison: *poisonous fumes.* **2.** Full of ill will; malicious: *poisonous remarks.* —**poi′son•ous•ly** *adv.* —**poi′son•ous•ness** *n.* [U]

poke (pōk) *v.* **poked, pok•ing, pokes.** —*tr.* **1.** To push (sbdy.), as with a finger or elbow: *poke someone in the ribs.* **2.** To thrust (sthg.) forward; push: *The otter poked its head out of the water.* **3.** To make (sthg.) by thrusting or jabbing: *poke a hole in the canvas.* —*intr.* To make thrusts or jabs, as with a stick: *He poked at the fire.* ♦ **poke along.** *intr.v.* To move in a slow or lazy manner: *My old car is still poking along.* **poke around.** *intr.v.* To look or search in a relaxed manner: *I was just poking around in the closet when I found these old shoes.* **poke fun at.** To ridicule or gently tease (sbdy./sthg.): *They poke fun at me because I love the water but can't swim.*

pok•er[1] (pō′kər) *n.* A metal rod used to stir a fire.

pok•er[2] (pō′kər) *n.* [U] A card game played by two or more persons who bet on the outcome of the game.

pok•y also **poke•y** (pō′kē) *adj.* **pok•i•er, pok•i•est.** *Informal.* **1.** Slow: *a poky child.* **2.** Not lively; dull: *a poky little town.*

ă–cat; ā–pay; âr–care; ä–father; ĕ–get; ē–be; ĭ–sit; ī–nice; îr–here; ŏ–got; ō–go; ô–saw; oi–boy; ou–out; ōŏ–took; ōō–boot; ŭ–cut; ûr–word; th–thin; *th*–this; hw–when; zh–vision; ə–about; N–French bon

po•lar (pō′lər) *adj.* Relating to or near the North Pole or the South Pole: *a polar expedition.*

polar bear *n.* A large white bear of Arctic regions.

polar cap *n.* The mass of permanent ice that covers either of the earth's polar regions.

po•lar•i•ty (pō lăr′ĭ tē) *n., pl.* **po•lar•i•ties.** *(usually singular).* **1.** The condition of having or being directed toward poles, especially magnetic or electric poles. **2.** The condition of having opposite opinions: *political polarity.*

po•lar•ize (pō′lə rīz′) *v.* **po•lar•ized, po•lar•iz•ing, po•lar•iz•es.** —*tr.* **1.** To cause polarity in (sthg.); make polar. **2.** To set (sbdy./sthg.) at opposite extremes, leaving no middle ground: *polarize public opinion.* —*intr.* To become polarized. —**po′lar•i•za′tion** (pō′lər ĭ zā′shən) *n.* [U]

pole¹ (pōl) *n.* **1.** Either of the points of the earth's axis of rotation; the North Pole or South Pole. **2.** Either of a pair of oppositely charged electric terminals or ends of a magnet. **3.** Either end of the main axis of a nucleus, cell, or organism.

HOMONYMS: **pole** (point on an axis, rod), **poll** (voting place).

---

pole² (pōl) *n.* **1.** A long slender rod: *a fishing pole.* **2.** An upright post: *a telephone pole.*

po•lem•ic (pə lĕm′ĭk) *n., Formal.* A controversial argument, especially an attack on a specific belief: *a polemic on democracy.* —*adj.* Relating to a controversy, argument, or verbal attack.

pole vault *n.* An athletic contest in which each participant leaps over a high crossbar using a long pole. —**pole′-vault′** *v.* —**pole′-vault′er** *n.*

po•lice (pə lēs′) *n., pl.* **police.** *(used with a plural verb).* **1.** The department of government established to maintain order: *call the police.* **2.** Police officers considered as a group: *The police found the lost baby in the park.* —*tr.v.* **po•liced, po•lic•ing, po•lic•es.** To control or keep (sthg.) in order as if with a police force: *The principal policed the halls of the school.*

police force *n.* A body of persons trained and authorized by a government to enforce laws, detect crimes, and keep order among the public.

po•lice•man (pə lēs′mən) *n.* A man who is a member of a police force. —**po•lice′-wom′an** (pə lēs′wŏŏm′ən) *n.*

police officer *n.* A member of a police force.

pol•i•cy¹ (pŏl′ĭ sē) *n., pl.* **pol•i•cies.** A plan, principle, or course of action, as of a government or a business: *The bank has a strict lending policy. Honesty is the best policy.*

pol•i•cy² (pŏl′ĭ sē) *n., pl.* **pol•i•cies.** A written contract of insurance: *a life insurance policy.*

po•li•o (pō′lē ō′) *n.* [U] Poliomyelitis: *Polio was once a serious disease.*

po•li•o•my•e•li•tis (pō′lē ō mī′ə lī′tĭs) *n.* [U] A contagious viral disease causing inflammation of and damage to the central nervous system that often results in paralysis.

pol•ish (pŏl′ĭsh) *v.* —*tr.* **1.** To make (sthg.) smooth and shiny by rubbing, chemical action, or both: *polish silver.* **2.** To refine or perfect (sthg.): *polish one's writing.* —*intr.* To become smooth or shiny as if by being rubbed. —*n.* **1.** [U] Smoothness and shininess of a surface or finish: *the polish of the clean table.* **2.** [C; U] A substance containing chemicals or a scrubbing material for smoothing or shining a surface: *furniture polish.* **3.** [U] A high degree of refinement: *Her performance shows polish.* ♦ **polish off.** *tr.v.* [sep.] *Informal.* To finish (sthg.) quickly and easily: *He polished off his meal and left.* **polish up on.** To improve (a skill or an ability) by practicing: *I have to polish up on my French before visiting Paris.* —**pol′ish•er** *n.*

pol•ished (pŏl′ĭsht) *adj.* **1.** Made or naturally smooth and shiny: *a polished table; a polished stone.* **2.** Refined; polite: *polished manners.* **3.** Without errors: *a polished performance.*

po•lite (pə līt′) *adj.* **po•lit•er, po•lit•est.** **1.** With good manners; courteous: *a polite boy; a polite note.* **2.** Refined; elegant: *polite conversation.* —**po•lite′ly** *adv.* —**po•lite′ness** *n.* [U]

SYNONYMS: **polite, mannerly, civil, courteous.** These adjectives mean mindful of, conforming to, or marked by good manners. **Polite** and **mannerly** mean considerate of others or well-bred according to social standards: *You don't have to like all your relatives but you must be polite to them. Are rural people really more mannerly than city dwellers?* **Civil** means having a minimal amount of good manners; neither polite nor rude: *He is barely civil until he has his morning coffee.* **Courteous** means polite in a gracious way: *She wrote a courteous response accepting their invitation.*

---

pol•i•tic (pŏl′ĭ tĭk) *adj. Formal.* Showing good judgment; prudent: *a politic decision.*

po•lit•i•cal (pə lĭt′ĭ kəl) *adj.* **1.** Relating to the structure or affairs of government: *a political system.* **2.** Relating to or characteristic of politics or politicians: *a political party; a political campaign.* —**po•lit′i•cal•ly** *adv.*

politically correct *adj.* Relating to language or behavior that shows strict concern to treat all people fairly, regardless of race, age, gender, or physical ability. —**political correctness** *n.* [U]

politically incorrect *adj.* Relating to language or behavior that shows little concern to treat all people fairly. —**political incorrectness** *n.* [U]

political science *n.* [U] The study of the processes, principles, and structure of government and political institutions.

pol·i·ti·cian (pŏl'ĭ tĭsh'ən) *n.* A person active in politics, especially one holding a political office.

pol·i·tics (pŏl'ĭ tĭks) *n.* **1.** *(used with a singular verb).* The art or science of government or governing, as of a nation. **2.** *(used with a singular or plural verb).* The activities or affairs of a government, politician, or political party: *She never discusses politics at home.* **3.** *(used with a singular or plural verb).* Competition within a group: *office politics.* **4.** *(used with a singular or plural verb).* A person's political position or attitude: *His politics are conservative.*

pol·ka (pōl'kə *or* pō'kə) *n.* **1.** A lively round dance originating in eastern Europe and performed by couples. **2.** Music written for this dance. —*intr.v.* To dance the polka: *They polkaed around the dance floor.*

pol·ka dot (pō'kə) *n.* A pattern or fabric with many round dots that are evenly spaced. —*adj.* Marked with such a pattern: *a polka dot dress.*

poll (pōl) *n.* **1.** *(usually plural).* The place where votes are cast and counted: *Polls close at 8:00.* **2.** A survey of public opinion to acquire information: *The teacher took a poll of the class to find out who wanted to postpone the test.* —*tr.v.* To sample and record the opinions of (sbdy.): *poll the voters.*

HOMONYMS: poll, pole (point on an axis, rod).

---

pol·len (pŏl'ən) *n.* [U] Powdery yellow grains that contain the male reproductive cells of flowering plants: *Bees collect pollen.*

pol·li·nate (pŏl'ə nāt') *tr.v.* **pol·li·nat·ed, pol·li·nat·ing, pol·li·nates.** To fertilize (sthg.) with pollen. —**pol'li·na'tion** *n.* [U] —**pol'li·na'tor** *n.*

pol·li·wog *also* **pol·ly·wog** (pŏl'ē wŏg' *or* pŏl'ē wôg') *n.* A tadpole; a baby frog.

poll·ster (pōl'stər) *n.* A person who takes surveys of public opinion.

pol·lut·ant (pə lōot'nt) *n.* Something that pollutes: *industrial pollutants.*

pol·lute (pə lōot') *tr.v.* **pol·lut·ed, pol·lut·ing, pol·lutes.** **1.** To make (sthg.) unfit for or harmful to living organisms, especially by the addition of waste matter: *Sewage pollutes rivers.* **2.** To render (sbdy.) morally impure; corrupt: *pollute children's minds.* —**pol·lut'er** *n.* —**pol·lu'tion** *n.* [U]

po·lo (pō'lō) *n.* [U] A game in which two teams of players on horseback use long-handled mallets to drive a ball into the opposing team's goal.

poly— *pref.* A prefix that means more than one; many: *polygon.*

pol·y·es·ter (pŏl'ē ĕs'tər) *n.* [U] A resin used in the manufacture of plastic articles and cloth: *polyester pants.*

po·lyg·a·my (pə lĭg'ə mē) *n.* [U] The practice or condition of having more than one husband or wife at one time: *Polygamy is illegal in the United States.* —**po·lyg'a·mist** *n.* —**po·lyg'a·mous** *adj.* —**po·lyg'a·mous·ly** *adv.*

pol·y·glot (pŏl'ē glŏt') *adj.* Knowing or speaking many languages. —*n.* A person who speaks many languages.

pol·y·gon (pŏl'ē gŏn') *n.* A flat closed geometric shape with three or more straight sides. —**po·lyg'o·nal** (pə lĭg'ə nəl) *adj.*

pol·y·graph (pŏl'ē grăf') *n.* An instrument that records changes in blood pressure, pulse rate, and breathing rate and is used to determine if a person is lying.

pol·y·no·mi·al (pŏl'ē nō'mē əl) *n.* An algebraic expression that is represented as the sum of two or more terms.

pol·yp (pŏl'ĭp) *n.* An abnormal growth on a mucous membrane.

pol·y·syl·lab·ic (pŏl'ē sĭ lăb'ĭk) *adj.* Having more than three syllables. For example, the word *possibility* is polysyllabic.

pol·y·tech·nic (pŏl'ē tĕk'nĭk) *adj.* Dealing with or teaching many industrial arts and applied sciences: *She graduated from the local polytechnic college.* —*n.* A school specializing in the teaching of industrial arts and applied sciences.

pol·y·the·ism (pŏl'ē thē ĭz'əm) *n.* [U] The worship of or belief in more than one god.

pol·y·u·re·thane (pŏl'ē yŏor'ə thān') *n.* [U] A resin used in making tough resistant coatings, adhesives, and electrical insulation: *polyurethane varnish.*

pom·mel (pŭm'əl *or* pŏm'əl) *tr.v.* To beat (sbdy./sthg.) severely: *One boy pommeled the other.* —*n.* **1.** The raised part at the front of a saddle for a horse. **2.** A knob on the handle of a sword.

pomp (pŏmp) *n.* [U] Showy or solemn display: *the pomp of a royal wedding.*

pom·pon (pŏm'pŏn') *or* **pom·pom** (pŏm'pŏm') *n.* **1.** A small ball of material such as wool or ribbon, used as a decoration, especially on shoes or caps: *slippers with pompons on them.* **2.** pompom. A ball of colored paper or plastic that is waved by cheerleaders and sports fans: *The fans waved their pompoms.*

pom·pous (pŏm'pəs) *adj.* **1.** Showing excessive dignity and self-importance: *Stop being so pompous.* **2.** Full of high-sounding words and phrases: *a pompous speech.* —**pom·pos'i·ty** (pŏm pŏs'ĭ tē) *n.* [U] —**pom'pous·ly** *adv.* —**pom'pous·ness** *n.* [U]

ă–cat; ā–pay; âr–care; ä–father; ĕ–get; ē–be; ĭ–sit; ī–nice; îr–here; ŏ–got; ō–go; ô–saw; oi–boy; ou–out; ōo–took; ōō–boot; ŭ–cut; ûr–word; th–thin; th–this; hw–when; zh–vision; ə–about; N–French bon

pon•cho (pŏn′chō) *n.*, *pl.* **pon•chos.** A cloak, usually made of wool or a waterproof material, with a hole in the center for the head: *a rain poncho.*

pond (pŏnd) *n.* A quiet body of water smaller than a lake.

pon•der (pŏn′dər) *tr. & intr.v.* To think or consider carefully and thoroughly: *He pondered the meaning of his dream. She pondered over the decision.*

pon•der•ous (pŏn′dər əs) *adj.* **1.** Heavy and massive: *a ponderous dinosaur.* **2.** Dull, graceless, and difficult to read or understand: *a ponderous book.* —**pon′der•ous•ly** *adv.* —**pon′der•ous•ness** *n.* [U]

pon•tiff (pŏn′tĭf) *n.* The pope.

pon•tif•i•cate (pŏn tĭf′ĭ kāt′) *intr.v.* **pon•tif•i•cat•ed, pon•tif•i•cat•ing, pon•tif•i•cates.** *Formal.* To speak in a pompous, dogmatic way: *He was pontificating on lowering income taxes.*

pon•toon (pŏn tōōn′) *n.* **1.** A flat-bottomed boat or other floating structure, especially one used to support a bridge. **2.** One of the floats that supports a seaplane on water.

po•ny (pō′nē) *n.*, *pl.* **po•nies.** Any of several breeds of horses that are small in size when full-grown.

po•ny•tail (pō′nē tāl′) *n.* A hair style in which the hair is held back like a pony's tail.

pooch (pōōch) *n. Slang.* A dog.

poo•dle (pōōd′l) *n.* A breed of dog with thick curly hair that is usually cut into decorative shapes.

pooh-pooh (pōō′pōō′) *tr.v. Informal.* To express contempt for (sthg.): *He pooh-poohed the idea.*

pool[1] (pōōl) *n.* **1.** A small quiet body of water: *a deep pool in the stream.* **2.** A small collection of a liquid; a puddle: *a pool of blood.* **3.** A swimming pool: *We filled the pool.*

pool[2] (pōōl) *n.* **1.** [U] A game played with 15 balls on a table that has pockets on the sides and corners. **2.** [C] A game of chance in which players bet money on the outcome of an event, such as a football game: *She bet in the office pool.* **3.** [C] A way to share money or other resources for the advantage of all the participants: *forming a pool of talents.* —*tr. v.* To put (sthg.) into a common fund for use by all: *They agreed to pool their resources to finish the project quickly.*

poop[1] (pōōp) *n.* A raised structure at the back of a ship: *the poop deck.*

poop[2] (pōōp) *Slang. v.* ◆ **poop out.** *intr.v.* **1.** To quit because of exhaustion: *He pooped out of the race.* **2.** To decide not to participate, especially at the last minute: *Don't poop out on us! You said you would go!*

poop[3] (pōōp) *Slang. n.* [U] *Feces:* *She stepped in some dog poop.* —*intr.v.* To defecate: *The dog pooped on the sidewalk.*

poor (pōōr) *adj.* **1.** Having little or no money

and few or no possessions: *He was poor but proud.* **2.** Not adequate in quality; inferior: *a poor diet.* **3.** Causing sympathy or pity; unfortunate: *You poor thing; you must be exhausted!* —*n.* **the poor.** [U] *(used with a plural verb).* People with little or no money or possessions considered as a group: *He works with the urban poor.*

poor•ly (pōōr′lē) *adv.* In a poor way; badly: *I did poorly on the exam.*

pop[1] (pŏp) *v.* **popped, pop•ping, pops.** —*intr.* **1.** To make a short, sharp, explosive sound: *My knee popped when I sat down.* **2.** To burst open with a short, sharp, explosive sound: *The tire popped because you put too much air in it.* —*tr.* **1.** To cause (sthg.) to make a short explosive sound: *The boy popped his chewing gum.* **2.** To cause (sthg.) to burst open with a short explosive sound: *The baby popped a balloon.* **3.** To put (sthg.) somewhere quickly or suddenly: *He popped dinner into the microwave.* —*n.* **1.** A sudden sharp, explosive sound. **2.** A soft drink; a soda. ◆ **a pop.** Apiece; each: *They cost 25 cents a pop.* **pop in.** *intr.v.* To make a brief, unplanned visit: *Let's just pop in for a minute.* **pop open.** *intr.v.* To open wide suddenly: *His eyes popped open when he woke up.* —*tr.v.* [sep.] To open (a can): *Pop open the can.* **pop out.** *intr.v.* To come out suddenly: *The toys popped out of the box.* —*tr.v.* [sep.] **1.** To show (sthg.) quickly: *The bird popped her head out of the nest.* **2.** To remove (sthg.) by pushing on it: *Pop out the puzzle pieces.* **pop the question.** To propose marriage to sbdy.: *He popped the question last night.* **pop up.** *intr.v.* **1.** To jump upwards: *The child popped up from behind the couch.* **2.** To happen: *That problem keeps popping up.*

pop[2] (pŏp) *n. Informal.* Father.

pop[3] (pŏp) *adj. Informal.* Of or for the general public; popular: *pop culture.*

pop. *abbr.* An abbreviation of population.

pop•corn (pŏp′kôrn′) *n.* [U] A type of corn with hard kernels that burst when heated to form white irregularly shaped puffs: *I like eating hot buttered popcorn at the movies.*

pope or **Pope** (pōp) *n.* The bishop of Rome and head of the Roman Catholic Church.

pop•lar (pŏp′lər) *n.* A fast-growing tree with triangular leaves and soft light-colored wood.

pop•pa (pä′pə) *n.* Variant of **papa.**

pop•py (pŏp′ē) *n.*, *pl.* **pop•pies. 1.** [C] A plant with showy, often bright red flowers. The small dark seeds of some poppies are used in cooking and baking. **2.** [U] A vivid red to reddish orange color. —*adj.* Reddish orange.

pop•py•cock (pŏp′ē kŏk′) *n.* [U] *Informal.* Foolish talk; nonsense: *That's just poppycock!*

pop•u•lace (pŏp′yə lĭs) *n.* [U] *Formal.* The general public; the masses.

P

pop·u·lar (pŏp′yə lər) *adj.* **1.** Enjoyed by many people: *a popular pastime.* **2.** Liked by acquaintances; with many friends or admirers: *a popular teacher.* **3.** Representing or carried out by most of the people: *the popular vote.* **4.** Accepted or believed by many people; widespread: *a popular idea.*

pop·u·lar·i·ty (pŏp′yə lăr′ĭ tē) *n.* [U] The quality of being popular; the state of being liked by many people: *Her popularity helped her win the election.*

pop·u·lar·ize (pŏp′yə lə rīz′) *tr.v.* **pop·u·lar·ized, pop·u·lar·iz·ing, pop·u·lar·iz·es.** To make (sbdy./sthg.) popular; make known or understandable to the general public: *the popularization of African music.* —**pop′u·lar·i·za′tion** (pŏp′yə lər ĭ zā′shən) *n.* [U]

pop·u·lar·ly (pŏp′yə lər lē) *adv.* Commonly; generally: *The tomato is popularly thought to be a vegetable, but it is actually a fruit.*

pop·u·late (pŏp′yə lāt′) *tr.v.* **pop·u·lat·ed, pop·u·lat·ing, pop·u·lates.** **1.** To supply (sthg.) with inhabitants: *populate a remote region.* **2.** To live in (a place); inhabit.

pop·u·la·tion (pŏp′yə lā′shən) *n.* [C; U] **1.** All of the people that live in a specified area. **2.** All the plants or animals of the same kind in a region: *the rabbit population.*

pop·u·lous (pŏp′yə ləs) *adj.* Heavily populated; with many inhabitants: *California is the most populous state in the United States.*

por·ce·lain (pôr′sə lĭn *or* pôrs′lĭn) *n.* **1.** [U] A hard white material made by glazing a fine clay with colors and baking it at a high temperature: *a sink made of porcelain.* **2.** [C] An object made of this material: *fine porcelains.*

porch (pôrch) *n.* A platform with a roof at the entrance to a house: *They like to sit on the front porch.*

por·cu·pine (pôr′kyə-pīn′) *n.* A large rodent covered with long sharp spines that serve as protection.

porcupine

pore¹ (pôr) *intr.v.* **pored, por·ing, pores.** To read or study with great attention: *pore over old documents.*

HOMONYMS: pore (study, opening), **pour** (make flow).

---

pore² (pôr) *n.* A tiny opening, such as one in skin or on the surface of a leaf, through which liquids or gases may pass.

pork (pôrk) *n.* [U] The meat of a pig or hog used as food: *pork sausage; pork chops.*

por·nog·ra·phy (pôr nŏg′rə fē) *n.* [U] Writing, pictures, or other material meant to arouse sexual desire. —**por′no·graph′ic** (pôr′nə grăf′ĭk) *adj.*

po·rous (pôr′əs) *adj.* **1.** Full of pores: *porous soil.* **2.** With pores into or through which a liquid or gas can pass. —**po·ros′i·ty** (pô rŏs′ĭ tē) *n.* [U] —**po′rous·ly** *adv.* —**po′rous·ness** *n.* [U]

por·poise (pôr′pəs) *n.* A sea mammal related to the whale but smaller and usually with a short blunt snout.

por·ridge (pôr′ĭj *or* pŏr′ĭj) *n.* [U] Oatmeal or other meal boiled in water or milk until thick.

port¹ (pôrt) *n.* **1.** A city, town, or other place on a waterway with facilities for loading or unloading ships: *the port of Boston.* **2.** A place that gives shelter for ships; a harbor.

port² (pôrt) *n.* [U] The left side of a ship or an aircraft facing forward. —*adj.* Relating to or on the port: *a port cabin.*

port³ (pôrt) *n.* [U] A sweet strong wine.

port·a·ble (pôr′tə bəl) *adj.* Easily carried: *a portable radio.*

por·tend (pôr tĕnd′) *tr.v. Formal.* To serve as an advance indication of (sthg.): *The dark clouds portended rain.*

por·tent (pôr′tĕnt′) *n. Formal.* An indication that sthg. important or disastrous is about to occur; an omen: *The president's speech contained a portent of war.*

por·ter (pôr′tər) *n.* **1.** A person hired to carry baggage, as at a station or hotel: *We tipped the porter for each bag.* **2.** An attendant who waits on passengers in a railroad car: *A sleeping-car porter made our bed.*

por·ter·house (pôr′tər hous′) *n.* A cut of beef steak.

port·fo·li·o (pôrt fō′lē ō′) *n., pl.* **port·fo·li·os.** **1.** A flat portable case for holding loose papers or drawings. **2.** Samples of one's creative work: *an artist's portfolio.* **3.** A group of investments such as stocks and bonds: *a diversified portfolio.*

port·hole (pôrt′hōl′) *n.* A small circular window in the side of a ship or an airplane.

por·tion (pôr′shən) *n.* **1.** A part of a whole; a section of a larger thing: *A portion of your paycheck is withheld to pay taxes.* **2.** A single helping of food: *a portion of mashed potatoes.* —*v.* ♦ **portion out.** *tr.v.* [sep.] To distribute (sthg.) in portions: *The farmer portioned out the land among his children.*

port·ly (pôrt′lē) *adj.* **port·li·er, port·li·est.** Stout or heavy: *a portly old man.* —**port′li·ness** *n.* [U]

por·trait (pôr′trĭt) *n.* **1.** A painting, photograph, or drawing of a person, especially one showing the face. **2.** A picture or description in words, especially of a person.

por·tray (pôr trā′) *tr.v.* **1.** To show (sbdy./sthg.) by means of a picture. **2.** To describe or picture (sbdy./sthg.) through the use of

---

words: *The novel portrays life in Japan.* **3.** To play (sbdy.) on stage or on the screen: *portray a famous composer.* —**por•tray′al** *n.*

pose (pōz) *v.* **posed, pos•ing, pos•es.** —*intr.* **1.** To stand in a certain position for a portrait or photograph: *The children posed in front of the fireplace.* **2.** To pretend to be sbdy./sthg. that one is not: *caught posing as a detective.* —*tr.* **1.** To place (sbdy./sthg.) in a specific position, as for a photograph: *She posed us in the garden and took several pictures.* **2.** To present (a danger or a question): *pose a threat; pose a question.* —*n.* **1.** A position taken for a portrait or photograph: *an awkward pose.* **2.** A false appearance or attitude: *His seriousness is only a pose.*

posh (pŏsh) *adj.* Expensive and fashionable.

po•si•tion (pə zĭsh′ən) *n.* **1.** [C] The place where sbdy./sthg. is located: *the position of the sun in the sky.* **2.** [C] The way in which sbdy./sthg. is placed or arranged: *Try not to sit in one position too long.* **3.** [U] An advantageous place or location: *drivers maneuvering for position in the race.* **4.** [C] A point of view or an attitude on a certain question: *What is your position on the proposed tax?* **5.** [C] A job: *a position in the government.* **6.** [C] In sports, the area or role assigned to each member of a team: *defensive positions.* —*tr.v.* To put (sbdy./sthg.) in place or position: *position the chess pieces on the board.* ◆ **in a position to.** Able to do sthg.: *I'm not in a position to offer you a job today.* **in position** In the proper place: *The troops are in position.*

pos•i•tive (pŏz′ĭ tĭv) *adj.* **1.** Showing certainty, acceptance, or affirmation: *a positive answer; a positive statement.* **2.** Helpful; constructive: *positive steps to solve the problem.* **3.** Leaving no room for doubt or question: *positive proof.* **4.** Absolutely certain: *I'm positive about that.* **5.** Indicating that a suspected disease, condition, or microorganism is present: *a positive test result.* **6.** Greater than zero: *a positive number.* **7.** Relating to or having an electric charge that tends to attract electrons: *a positive charge.* —*n.* **1.** An affirmative degree, element, or characteristic: *His sincerity is a positive.* **2.** A photographic image in which light and dark appear as they do in nature. —**pos′i•tive•ly** *adv.*

poss. *abbr.* An abbreviation of possessive.

pos•se (pŏs′ē) *n.* In the past, a group of men, often riding horses, organized by a sheriff to help catch criminals.

pos•sess (pə zĕs′) *tr.v.* **1.** To have (sthg.); own: *They possess many thousands of acres of land.* **2.** To control the mind or thoughts of (sbdy.): *Ambition possessed her.* **3.** To have (sthg.) as a quality, characteristic, or other attribute: *possessed great talent.* —**pos•ses′sor** *n.*

pos•sessed (pə zĕst′) *adj.* **1.** Having or owning sthg.: *possessed of great wealth.* **2.** Controlled by or as if by a spirit or other force; obsessed: *possessed by a desire to become a*

musician. **3.** Calm; collected: *possessed even in time of trial.*

pos•ses•sion (pə zĕsh′ən) *n.* **1.** [U] The fact or condition of having or possessing sthg. **2.** [C] Something that is owned or possessed: *leaving most of their possessions behind.* **3.** [C] A territory subject to foreign control: *The Philippine Islands were once a possession of the United States.*

pos•ses•sive (pə zĕs′ĭv) *adj.* **1.** With a desire to dominate or control. **2.** Relating to ownership or possession. **3.** In grammar, relating to the case of a noun or pronoun that indicates possession. For example, the word *hers* is a possessive pronoun. —*n.* **1.** The possessive case. **2.** A word in the possessive case. —**pos•ses′sive•ly** *adv.* —**pos•ses′-sive•ness** *n.* [U]

possessive adjective *n.* In grammar, an adjective formed from a pronoun indicating possession. In the sentence *This is my duty,* the word *my* is a possessive adjective.

possessive pronoun *n.* In grammar, one of several pronouns indicating possession and capable of substituting for noun phrases. The possessive pronouns include *mine, hers, his, ours, yours,* and *theirs.*

pos•si•bil•i•ty (pŏs′ə bĭl′ĭ tē) *n., pl.* **pos•si•bil•i•ties. 1.** [U] The fact or condition of being possible: *the possibility of life on Mars.* **2.** [C] Something that is possible: *His promotion now seems a possibility.* **3. possibilities.** Potential for favorable results: *The idea has tremendous possibilities.*

pos•si•ble (pŏs′ə bəl) *adj.* **1.** Capable of happening, existing, being true, or being done: *It may be possible to get there by helicopter.* **2.** Capable of being used for a certain purpose: *a possible site for the new mall.*

pos•si•bly (pŏs′ə blē) *adv.* **1.** Perhaps: *He hesitated, possibly because he was afraid.* **2.** Under any circumstances: *I can't possibly do it.*

pos•sum (pŏs′əm) *n. Informal.* An opossum.

post¹ (pōst) *n.* **1.** A piece of wood or other material set upright in the ground to serve as a marker or support: *a fence post.* **2.** A terminal of a battery. **3.** The straight part of an earring that passes through a hole in a pierced earlobe. —*tr.v.* To put (sthg.) up in a prominent place for public viewing: *The winners' names will be posted on the bulletin board.*

post² (pōst) *n.* **1.** A military base: *an army post.* **2.** A local organization of military veterans. **3.** An assigned position of a guard: *a lookout post.* **4.** A position of employment, especially an appointed public office: *a high post in the government.* **5.** A place to which a person is assigned for duty: *an overseas post.* —*tr.v.* **1.** To assign (sbdy.) to a post or station: *post a guard.* **2.** To put (sthg.) forward; present: *post a reward.*

post³ (pōst) *Chiefly British. n.* Mail: *the morning post.* —*tr.v.* To mail (a letter): *I need*

to post my application before midnight.
♦ **keep posted.** To know or tell (sbdy.) the latest news: *I try to keep posted on current events. Keep me posted.*

post— *pref.* A prefix that means after in time; later: *postoperative.*

WORD BUILDING: post— The basic meaning of the prefix **post—** is "after." **Post—** is often used in opposition to the prefixes **ante—** and **pre—**: antedate/postdate and prewar/postwar. And **post—** occurs frequently in medical terminology. **Postnatal** is a common example, and there are many others.

---

post•age (pō'stĭj) *n.* [U] The charge for sending sthg. by mail: *airmail postage.*

postage stamp *n.* A small adhesive label issued by a government to show that postage has been paid.

post•al (pō'stəl) *adj.* Relating to the post office or mail service: *postal rates.*

postal service *n.* The post office.

post card also **post•card** (pōst'kärd') *n.* A card with space on one side for a postage stamp and an address, used for sending a short message through the mail.

post•date (pōst dāt') *tr.v.* **post•dat•ed, post•dat•ing, post•dates.** To put a date on (a check, for example) that is later than the actual date: *Most stores won't accept checks that are postdated.*

post•er (pō'stər) *n.* A large notice, announcement, or picture that is displayed on a wall: *a bedroom wall filled with posters of actors.*

pos•te•ri•or (pŏ stîr'ē ər) *n.* The buttocks.

pos•ter•i•ty (pŏ stěr'ĭ tē) *n.* [U] Future generations: *The author left several important books to posterity.*

post•grad•u•ate (pōst grăj'oō ĭt) *adj.* Relating to or pursuing advanced study after graduation from high school or college: *postgraduate courses.* —*n.* A person engaged in postgraduate study.

post•hu•mous (pŏs'chə məs) *adj.* Happening after one's death: *a posthumous award.* —**post'hu•mous•ly** *adv.*

post•man (pōst'mən) *n.* A mailman.

post•mark (pōst'märk') *n.* A mark printed over a postage stamp that cancels the stamp and records the date and place of mailing. —*tr.v.* To stamp (sthg.) with such a mark: *an envelope postmarked Chicago.*

post•mas•ter (pōst'măs'tər) *n.* A person who operates a local post office.

post•mor•tem (pōst môr'təm) *adj.* Happening or done after death: *a postmortem examination.* —*n.* **1.** An autopsy. **2.** An analysis of an event that has just taken place: *a postmortem on the failed plan.*

post•na•tal (pōst nāt'l) *adj.* Happening or done after birth: *postnatal care.*

post office *n.* **1.** The public department responsible for the transportation and delivery of the mail. **2.** A place where mail is received and stamps and other materials are sold.

post•op•er•a•tive (pōst ŏp'ər ə tĭv) *adj.* Happening after a surgical operation: *postoperative care.*

post•paid (pōst'pād') *adj.* With the postage paid in advance: *a postpaid reply card.*

post•par•tum (pōst pär'təm) *adj.* Happening in the period shortly after childbirth: *postpartum recovery.*

post•pone (pōst pōn') *tr.v.* **post•poned, post•pon•ing, post•pones.** To do (sthg.) at a later time: *You may want to postpone your visit.* —**post•pone'ment** *n.* [C; U]

post•script (pōst'skrĭpt') *n.* **1.** Information added at the end of a letter or document. **2.** A type of file in a computer.

pos•tu•late (pŏs'chə lāt') *tr.v.* **pos•tu•lat•ed, pos•tu•lat•ing, pos•tu•lates.** To assume the truth or existence of (sthg.): *Early scientists postulated that the sun moved around the earth.* —*n.* (pŏs'chə lĭt *or* pŏs'chə lāt'). Something assumed as being self-evident or generally accepted without proof.

pos•ture (pŏs'chər) *n.* **1.** [U] The way in which one holds one's body: *a person who has good posture.* **2.** [C] A position or an arrangement of the body or its parts: *a kneeling posture.* **3.** [U] A mental attitude with regard to sthg.: *a defensive posture.* —*intr.v.* **pos•tured, pos•tur•ing, pos•tures.** To assume an unnatural or exaggerated pose or mental attitude: *We all felt that the speaker was posturing.*

post•war (pōst'wôr') *adj.* Belonging to the period after a war: *postwar construction.*

po•sy (pō'zē) *n., pl.* **po•sies.** An old term for a flower or bunch of flowers.

pot (pŏt) *n.* **1.** [C] A deep rounded container made of metal, pottery, or glass, used especially for cooking or holding things: *a teapot; a flowerpot.* **2.** [C] The amount of sthg. that a pot can hold: *drank a pot of coffee.* **3.** [C; U] *(usually singular).* The total amount of bets made by all the players in one hand at cards: *Who won the pot?* **4.** [U] *Slang.* Marijuana: *Smoking pot is illegal.* —*tr.v.* **pot•ted, pot•ting, pots.** To plant or put (sthg.) in a pot: *He potted the tulip bulbs.* ♦ **go to pot.** To become ruined: *After his divorce, he really went to pot.*

po•ta•ble (pō'tə bəl) *adj.* Fit to drink: *potable water.*

po•tas•si•um (pə tăs'ē əm) *n.* [U] *Symbol* **K** A soft silver-white metallic element. Atomic number 19. See table at **element.**

---

po·ta·to (pə tā′tō) *n., pl.* **po·ta·toes.** A plant with brown or red-skinned starchy tubers that grow underground and are eaten cooked as vegetables.

potato chip *n.* A thin slice of potato fried until crisp and then salted.

po·ten·cy (pōt′n sē) *n.* [U] The quality or condition of being potent: *This medicine will lose its potency over time.*

po·tent (pōt′nt) *adj.* **1.** Strong; powerful: *a potent medicine.* **2.** With a powerful influence on the mind or feelings: *He made a potent argument for taking vitamins.*

po·ten·tial (pə tĕn′shəl) *adj.* Possible: *potential buyers; potential problems.* —*n.* [U] Capacity for growth, development, or coming into existence: *We see the potential for expanding our business in new markets.* —**po·ten′tial·ly** *adv.*

pot·hold·er (pŏt′hōl′dər) *n.* A small fabric pad used to handle hot cooking utensils.

pot·hole (pŏt′hōl′) *n.* A hole in a road surface.

po·tion (pō′shən) *n.* A liquid dose, especially of medicine or poison.

pot·luck (pŏt′lŭk′) *n.* **1.** [U] Whatever food happens to be available for a meal, especially when offered to a guest: *There's nothing special for lunch, just potluck.* **2.** [C] A meal at which each guest brings food to be shared by all: *a neighborhood potluck.*

pot·pie (pŏt′pī′) *n.* A meat or poultry pie with vegetables and a pastry crust.

pot·pour·ri (pō′pŏŏ rē′) *n., pl.* **pot·pour·ris.** **1.** [C] A miscellaneous collection: *The book was a potpourri of poems, legends, and sayings.* **2.** [U] A fragrant mixture of dried flowers and spices used to scent the air.

pot roast *n.* A cut of beef that is browned and then cooked until tender, often with vegetables, in a covered pot.

pot·shot (pŏt′shŏt′) *n. Informal.* A criticism made without careful thought: *Reporters took potshots at the mayor.*

pot·ted (pŏt′ĭd) *adj.* Placed in a pot: *a potted plant.*

pot·ter (pŏt′ər) *n.* A person who makes pottery.

pot·ter·y (pŏt′ə rē) *n., pl.* **pot·ter·ies.** **1.** [U] Objects, such as pots, vases, or dishes, made from moist clay and hardened by heat. **2.** [U] The work of a potter. **3.** [C] The place where a potter works.

pouch (pouch) *n.* **1.** A bag or sack: *a mail pouch.* **2.** A body part similar to a sac or pocket: *Kangaroos carry their young in a pouch.*

poul·tice (pōl′tĭs) *n.* A soft moist mass of a medicinal substance, usually heated, spread on cloth, and put on a sore or swollen part of the body: *a mustard poultice.*

poul·try (pōl′trē) *n.* (*used with a singular or plural verb*). Domestic birds, such as chickens, turkeys, ducks, or geese, raised for meat or eggs: *She doesn't eat poultry.*

pounce (pouns) *intr.v.* **pounced, pounc·ing, pounc·es.** **1.** To jump suddenly so as to seize sthg.: *The kitten pounced on the ball.* **2.** To seize sthg. swiftly and eagerly: *pounce at an opportunity.* —*n.* The act of pouncing: *With a pounce, the cat caught the mouse.*

pound¹ (pound) *n.* **1.** A unit of weight equal to 16 ounces (about 453.6 grams). See table at **measurement. 2.** The basic monetary unit of the United Kingdom, Cyprus, Lebanon, Sudan, Syria, and Egypt.

pound² (pound) *v.* —*tr.* **1.** To strike (sthg.) forcefully and repeatedly: *Pound the nail into the board.* **2.** To crush (sthg.) to a powder or pulp: *pounding corn into meal.* —*intr.* **1.** To strike or beat sthg. vigorously: *She pounded on the table.* **2.** To move along noisily and heavily: *They pounded up the stairs.* **3.** To pulsate rapidly and heavily; throb: *His heart pounded with excitement.* —**pound′ing** *adj.*

pound³ (pound) *n.* A place where stray or lost animals are kept: *We checked the pound to see if our dog was there.*

pound sterling *n.* The basic monetary unit of the United Kingdom.

pour (pôr) *v.* —*tr.* **1.** To cause (a fluid or loose particles) to flow as from a container: *pour the milk; pour salt.* **2.** To send forth (sthg.), as if in a stream: *poured money into the project.* —*intr.* **1.** To flow or run freely or strongly: *Salt pours easily. Blood poured from the wound.* **2.** To rain hard: *It isn't sprinkling; it's pouring.* **3.** To come or go in large numbers or amounts; swarm or flood: *Students poured into the school.* ♦ **pour out.** *tr.v.* [sep.] To tell (sthg.) freely: *He poured out his story.*

HOMONYMS: pour, pore (study, opening).

pout (pout) *intr.v.* To push out the lips, especially as a sign of annoyance or displeasure: *She's pouting in her room.* —*n.* A sullen expression made by pushing out the lips.

pov·er·ty (pŏv′ər tē) *n.* **1.** [U] The state of being poor: *She was raised in poverty.* **2.** [C] A lack of sthg.: *a poverty of imagination.*

poverty level or **poverty line** *n.* A minimum income level below which a person is officially considered to be living in poverty.

POW (pē′ō dŭb′əl yōō) *n., pl.* **POW's** also **POWs.** A prisoner of war.

pow·der (pou′dər) *n.* **1.** [C; U] A substance in the form of a great number of very fine particles: *face powder; soap powder.* **2.** [U] Gunpowder. **3.** [U] Light dry snow: *Skiers love powder.* —*tr.v.* To cover, dust, or sprinkle (sthg.) with powder: *I will powder the cookies with sugar. She powdered her nose.*

powder room *n.* A small bathroom without a bathtub or shower.

pow·der·y (pou′də rē) *adj.* **1.** Similar to powder: *powdery snow.* **2.** Covered or dusted with powder: *a lily that was powdery with* *pollen.* **3.** Easily made into powder; crumbly: *a soft powdery rock.*

pow·er (pou′ər) *n.* **1.** [C] *(usually plural).* A specific ability, capability, or skill: *He has great powers of concentration.* **2.** [U] Force or strength: *the pulling power of oxen.* See Synonyms at **strength. 3.** [U] Forcefulness; impact: *a book of unusual power.* **4.** [U] The official capacity to exercise control; authority: *The emperor ruled with absolute power.* **5.** [C] A source of authority or influence, especially a strong influential nation: *a world power.* **6.** [U] The rate at which work is done with respect to time, measured in units such as the watt or horsepower. **7.** [U] **a.** Energy that can be used for doing work: *atomic power.* **b.** Electricity: *The power failed during the storm.* **8.** [C] The number of times a number or an expression is multiplied by itself, as shown by an exponent: *The number 10^6 is read "ten to the sixth power."* **9.** [C] A number that represents the magnification of an optical instrument, such as a microscope or telescope. —*adj.* **1.** Relating to political, social, or economic control: *a power struggle.* **2.** Operating with mechanical or electrical energy in place of the user's energy: *power tools; power brakes.* **3.** Relating to electricity: *power lines.* —*tr.v.* To supply (sthg.) with power, especially mechanical power: *The truck is powered by a gasoline engine.*

pow·er·ful (pou′ər fəl) *adj.* **1.** With or capable of producing power: *powerful machines; a powerful nation.* **2.** Very effective; potent: *a powerful poison.* —**pow′er·ful·ly** *adv.*

pow·er·house (pou′ər hous′) *n.* **1.** A power plant. **2.** A person or thing that has great force or energy: *She's the powerhouse of the lecture committee.*

pow·er·less (pou′ər lĭs) *adj.* Without strength, power, or authority: *We are powerless to change the past.*

power of attorney *n., pl.* **powers of attorney.** A written document giving sbdy. legal authority to act on another person's behalf: *My daughter has my power of attorney.*

power plant *n.* A place that generates electric energy.

pow·wow (pou′wou′) *n.* **1.** A council or meeting of Native Americans. **2.** *Informal.* A conference or gathering: *We held a powwow to discuss sales.*

pox (pŏks) *n.* [U] A disease causing eruptions on the skin: *chickenpox; smallpox.*

PR *abbr.* An abbreviation of: **1.** Puerto Rico. **2.** Public relations.

prac·ti·ca·ble (prăk′tĭ kə bəl) *adj. Formal.* **1.** Capable of being done: *a practicable solution to the problem.* **2.** Usable for a certain purpose: *a practicable ski slope.*

prac·ti·cal (prăk′tĭ kəl) *adj.* **1.** Relating to experience, practice, or use rather than theory, study, or ideas: *practical knowledge instead of book learning.* **2.** Having or showing good judgment; sensible: *If we're practical, we can do the job quickly.* —**prac′ti·cal′i·ty** (prăk′-tĭ kăl′ĭ tē) *n.* [C; U]

practical joke *n.* A mischievous trick played on a person, especially one that causes embarrassment: *They put salt in the sugar bowl as a practical joke.*

prac·ti·cal·ly (prăk′tĭk lē) *adv.* **1.** In a practical way: *They dressed practically for the long hike.* **2.** Almost but not quite; nearly: *The school year is practically over.*

prac·tice (prăk′tĭs) *v.* **prac·ticed, prac·tic·ing, prac·tic·es.** —*tr.* **1.** To make a habit of (sthg.); do or perform regularly: *Learn to practice self-control.* **2.** To do or work on (sthg.) over and over in order to gain or improve a skill: *practice the piano.* **3.** To work at (sthg.), especially as a professional: *practice medicine.* **4.** To do (sthg.) because of a strong belief: *practice a religion; practice pacifism.* —*intr.* **1.** To do or perform sthg. regularly. **2.** To do sthg. repeatedly in order to gain or polish a skill: *If you want to improve, you'll have to practice.* **3.** To work at a profession. —*n.* **1.** [C] A habitual or regular action or way of doing sthg.: *makes a practice of being on time.* See Synonyms at **habit. 2.** [U] Experience or exercise in doing sthg. that develops, maintains, or improves one's skill: *Practice will improve your singing.* **3.** [U] Exercise of an occupation or a profession: *the practice of psychiatry.* **4.** [C] The business of a professional person: *She has her own law practice.* ◆ **out of practice.** Unable to do sthg. well because of lack of practice: *I love to ski, but I'm out of practice.* **practice what (one) preaches.** To do sthg. that one tells others to do: *He drives very carefully and practices what he preaches about road safety.*

prac·tic·ing (prăk′tĭ sĭng) *adj.* Active in a certain field: *a practicing attorney.*

prac·tise (prăk′tĭs) *v. & n. Chiefly British.* Variant of **practice.**

prac·ti·tion·er (prăk tĭsh′ə nər) *n.* A person who practices sthg., especially an occupation, a profession, or a technique: *a skilled practitioner of acupuncture.*

prag·mat·ic (prăg măt′ĭk) *adj.* Concerned with facts and actual occurrences; practical: *a pragmatic way of solving problems.* —**prag·mat′i·cal·ly** *adv.*

prag·ma·tism (prăg′mə tĭz′əm) *n.* [U] **1.** The philosophy that the meaning of an idea must be judged by its practical results. **2.** A practical way of thinking about situations or of solving problems: *This problem will be solved through pragmatism, not wild ideas.* —**prag′ma•tist** *n.*

prai•rie (prâr′ē) *n.* A wide area of flat grassland without trees, especially the large plain of central North America.

praise (prāz) *n.* [U] **1.** Expression of approval or admiration: *Praise from her family meant a lot to her.* **2.** Glory and honor given to a god. —*tr.v.* **praised, prais•ing, prais•es. 1.** To express approval of or admiration for (sbdy./sthg.): *Everyone praised her good sense.* **2.** To give (a god) glory and honor; worship.

praise•wor•thy (prāz′wûr′thē) *adj.* Deserving praise: *a praiseworthy act of courage.*

pram (prăm) *n. Chiefly British.* A baby carriage.

prance (prăns) *intr.v.* **pranced, pranc•ing, pranc•es. 1.** To move about by springing on the hind legs: *The horse pranced into the barn.* **2.** To walk or move in a proud or spirited way; strut: *The dancer pranced onstage.* —*n.* A prancing movement.

prank (prăngk) *n.* A mischievous trick or practical joke.

prank•ster (prăngk′stər) *n.* A person who plays tricks or pranks: *He's such a prankster that people are often angry with him.*

prat•tle (prăt′l) *intr.v.* **prat•tled, prat•tling, prat•tles.** To talk or chatter idly or foolishly: *prattling on about how much things cost.* —*n.* [U] Idle or meaningless chatter; babble: *an afternoon filled with prattle and gossip.*

prawn (prôn) *n.* A large type of edible shrimp.

pray (prā) *v.* —*intr.* **1.** To speak with God or a god, often silently, to show thanks or love, or to ask for sthg.: *She closed her eyes and prayed for an answer.* **2.** To make an earnest request: *They prayed for forgiveness.* —*tr.* **1.** To utter or say a prayer or prayers to (sbdy.); address by prayer. **2.** To make an earnest request for (sthg.): *I pray that you will return safely.*

HOMONYMS: pray, prey (hunted animal).

prayer (prâr) *n.* **1.** [U] The act of praying to God or a god: *Prayer can change people.* **2.** [C] A special set of words used in speaking with God: *a prayer of thanks.* **3.** [C] The slightest chance or hope, as for survival or success: *Without our best player we don't have a prayer.*

pray•ing mantis (prā′ĭng) *n.* A mantis.

pre— *pref.* A prefix that means: **1.** Earlier; before: *prehistoric.* **2.** In advance: *prepay.*

preach (prēch) *v.* —*tr.* **1.** To say or explain (sthg.) in a sermon: *preaches the gospel.* **2.** To teach or support (sthg.) and urge others to follow: *Our leaders preach tolerance of others.* **3.** To give (a sermon): *The minister*

preached the morning sermon. —*intr.* **1.** To deliver a sermon: *preaching on forgiveness.* **2.** To give religious or moral instruction, especially in a boring manner: *a writer with an unfortunate tendency to preach.*

preach•er (prē′chər) *n.* A person who preaches, especially one who tells about the gospel as an occupation: *a country preacher.*

pre•am•ble (prē′ăm′bəl) *n.* An introductory statement, especially the introduction to a formal document that explains its purpose: *the preamble to the Constitution.*

pre•ar•range (prē′ə rānj′) *tr.v.* **pre•ar•ranged, pre•ar•rang•ing, pre•ar•rang•es.** To arrange (sthg.) in advance: *We prearranged a meeting place.*

pre•car•i•ous (prĭ kâr′ē əs) *adj.* Unsafe; not steady: *He stood in a precarious position at the edge of the roof.* —**pre•car′i•ous•ly** *adv.*

pre•cau•tion (prĭ kô′shən) *n.* An action done in advance to guard against possible danger, error, or accident: *take safety precautions.*

pre•cau•tion•ar•y (prĭ kô′shə nĕr′ē) *adj.* Relating to or constituting a precaution: *precautionary measures; precautionary advice.*

pre•cede (prĭ sēd′) *tr.v.* **pre•ced•ed, pre•ced•ing, pre•cedes.** To come, exist, or occur before (sthg.) in time, order, position, or rank: *A short lecture will precede the movie.*

prec•e•dence (prĕs′ĭ dəns *or* prĭ sēd′ns) *n.* [U] The right to priority because of importance or rank: *The right to free speech takes precedence over your objections to their ideas.*

prec•e•dent (prĕs′ĭ dənt) *n.* [C; U] An act or instance that can be an example for similar circumstances in the future: *Our instructor set a precedent by giving an exam every six weeks.*

pre•ced•ing (prĭ sē′dĭng) *adj.* Coming before another or others in time, place, rank, or sequence: *the preceding winter; the preceding page.*

pre•cinct (prē′sĭngkt′) *n.* **1.** A subdivision or district of a city or town for election or police purposes: *Our town has three police precincts.* **2.** *(usually plural).* An area or enclosure with definite boundaries: *within the precincts of the university.*

pre•cious (prĕsh′əs) *adj.* **1.** Expensive; valuable: *precious metals.* **2.** Dear; beloved: *his precious children.* —*adv.* Used as an intensive; very: *We have precious little time.*

prec•i•pice (prĕs′ə pĭs) *n.* A very steep or overhanging mass of rock, such as a cliff.

pre•cip•i•tate (prĭ sĭp′ĭ tāt′) *v.* **pre•cip•i•tat•ed, pre•cip•i•tat•ing, pre•cip•i•tates.** —*tr.* **1.** To cause (sthg.) to happen suddenly: *The discovery of the stolen money precipitated the bank director's resignation.* **2.** To cause (water vapor) to condense and fall as rain or snow. **3.** To separate (sthg.) chemically from a solution as a solid: *We precipitated the minerals from the water by adding borax.* —*intr.* **1.** To condense and fall

P

from the air as rain or snow. **2.** To be separated from a solution as a solid. —*adj.* (prĭ sĭp′ĭ-tĭt). **1.** Acting or made hastily: *a precipitate decision.* **2.** Happening suddenly and unexpectedly: *a precipitate drop in prices.* —*n.* (prĭ sĭp′ĭ tāt′ *or* prĭ sĭp′ĭ tĭt). [C; U] A solid material separated from a solution by chemical means.

pre•cip•i•ta•tion (prĭ sĭp′ĭ tā′shən) *n.* [U] **1.** Rain or snow: *Last month's precipitation in our city was two inches.* **2.** The production of a precipitate, as in a chemical reaction.

pre•cip•i•tous (prĭ sĭp′ĭ təs) *adj.* Like a precipice; extremely steep: *a precipitous hill.* —**pre•cip′i•tous•ly** *adv.*

pre•cise (prĭ sīs′) *adj.* **1.** Clearly expressed; definite: *Please be precise in your instructions.* **2.** Distinct or correct: *Can you give me the precise pronunciation of that word?* **3.** Exact; accurate or correct: *a precise measurement.* —**pre•cise′ly** *adv.* —**pre•cise′ness** *n.* [U]

pre•ci•sion (prĭ sĭzh′ən) *n.* [U] The state or quality of being precise: *the precision of a chemist's scales.*

pre•clude (prĭ klo͞od′) *tr.v.* **pre•clud•ed, pre•clud•ing, pre•cludes.** To make (sthg.) impossible by action taken in advance; prevent: *The judge's decision precluded my testimony.*

pre•co•cious (prĭ kō′shəs) *adj.* Showing mental skills or abilities at an earlier age than is normal: *He was a precocious child who learned to read at three.* —**pre•co′cious•ly** *adv.* —**pre•co′cious•ness, pre•coc′i•ty** (prĭ kŏs′ĭ tē) *n.* [U]

pre•con•ceived (prē′kən sēvd′) *adj.* Relating to an opinion formed before enough information is available: *preconceived ideas about marriage.* —**pre′con•ceive′** *v.* —**pre′-con•cep′tion** (prē′kən sĕp′shən) *n.*

pre•con•di•tion (prē′kən dĭsh′ən) *n.* A condition that must be met before sthg. else can happen or be considered: *preconditions for a peace treaty.*

pre•cur•sor (prĭ kûr′sər *or* prē′kûr′sər) *n.* A person or thing that comes before another: *The phonograph record was a precursor of the CD.*

pre•date (prē dāt′) *tr.v.* **pre•dat•ed, pre•dat•ing, pre•dates.** **1.** To mark (sthg.) with a date earlier than the actual one: *predate a check.* **2.** To precede (sthg.) in time: *Dinosaurs predate elephants.*

pred•a•tor (prĕd′ə tər) *n.* An animal that lives by killing and eating other animals: *Lions and tigers are predators.*

pred•a•to•ry (prĕd′ə tôr′ē) *adj.* **1.** Living by killing and eating other animals: *a predatory animal.* **2.** Living by robbing or harming other people for personal gain.

pred•e•ces•sor (prĕd′ĭ sĕs′ər) *n.* **1.** A person who comes before another in time, especially in holding an office: *The new mayor's predecessor welcomed her.* **2.** Something that has been replaced by another: *The new building is bigger than its predecessor.*

pre•des•tine (prē dĕs′tĭn) *tr.v.* **pre•des•tined, pre•des•tin•ing, pre•des•tines.** To decide (sthg.) beforehand, especially by divine decree: *The Greeks believed that the gods predestined the early death of heroes.* —**pre•des′ti•na′tion** (prē dĕs′tə nā′shən) *n.* [U]

pre•de•ter•mine (prē′dĭ tûr′mĭn) *tr.v.* **pre•de•ter•mined, pre•de•ter•min•ing, pre•de•ter•mines.** To determine, decide, or establish (sthg.) in advance: *Climate predetermines the kinds of animals that can live in a region.* —**pre′de•ter′mi•na′tion** *n.* [U]

pre•dic•a•ment (prĭ dĭk′ə mənt) *n.* A situation, especially an unpleasant or troubling one, from which it is difficult to remove oneself: *Here's our predicament. Should we fix our car or sell it?*

pred•i•cate (prĕd′ĭ kāt′) *tr.v.* **pred•i•cat•ed, pred•i•cat•ing, pred•i•cates.** To base (a statement or an action) on sthg. else: *She predicated her argument on the assumption that inflation would not go up.* —*n.* (prĕd′ĭ kĭt). In grammar, the part of a sentence or clause that expresses the action or condition of the subject and includes the verb and the objects or phrases governed by the verb. The predicate in *Jane opened the door* is *opened the door.* —*adj.* (prĕd′ĭ kĭt). Belonging to the predicate of a sentence or clause. —SEE NOTE at **adjective.**

pre•dict (prĭ dĭkt′) *tr.v.* To tell about (sthg.) in advance; foretell: *The forecaster predicted snow for this evening.* —**pre•dict′a•ble** *adj.* —**pre•dic′tion** *n.*

WORD BUILDING: predict The word root —**dict**— in English words means "to say." Thus we have **predict**, "to say ahead of time, foretell" (using the prefix **pre—**, "before") and **contra-dict**, "to speak against" (**contra—**, "opposite, against").

pre•di•lec•tion (prĕd′l ĕk′shən *or* prēd′-l ĕk′shən) *n.* A tendency to like sthg.; a preference: *a predilection for fast cars.*

pre•dis•pose (prē′dĭ spōz′) *tr.v.* **pre•dis•posed, pre•dis•pos•ing, pre•dis•pos•es.** **1.** To incline or influence (sbdy.) beforehand: *Her warm smile may predispose people to like her.* **2.** To make (sbdy.) susceptible or liable: *working conditions that predispose miners to lung disease.* —**pre′dis•po•si′tion** (prē′dĭs pə zĭsh′ən) *n.*

ă-**cat**; ā-**pay**; âr-**care**; ä-**father**; ĕ-**get**; ē-**be**; ĭ-**sit**; ī-**nice**; îr-**here**; ŏ-**got**; ō-**go**; ô-**saw**; oi-**boy**; ou-**out**; o͞o-**took**; o͞o-**boot**; ŭ-**cut**; ûr-**word**; th-**thin**; th-**this**; hw-**when**; zh-**vision**; ə-**about**; N-French **bon**

pre·dom·i·nant (prĭ dŏm′ə nənt) *adj*. Most important, noticeable, or powerful: *the predominant nation.* —**pre·dom′i·nance** *n*. [U] —**pre·dom′i·nant·ly** *adv*.

pre·dom·i·nate (prĭ dŏm′ə nāt′) *intr.v*. **pre·dom·i·nat·ed, pre·dom·i·nat·ing, pre·dom·i·nates.** To be greater than others in number, force, or importance: *People of Italian descent predominate in this neighborhood.*

pre·em·i·nent (prē ĕm′ə nənt) *adj*. Superior to all others; outstanding: *the preeminent artist of the century.* —**pre·em′i·nence** *n*. [U] —**pre·em′i·nent·ly** *adv*.

pre·empt (prē ĕmpt′) *tr.v*. To take the place of (sthg.); displace: *The President's address will preempt the regular shows this evening.*

preen (prēn) *v*. —*tr*. **1.** To smooth or clean (fur or feathers) with the beak or tongue: *The cat preened itself.* **2.** To dress or groom (oneself) with elaborate care: *The bride preened her hair.* —*intr*. To primp: *He preened in front of the mirror.*

pre·fab (prē′făb′) *Informal. adj*. Prefabricated. —*n*. A prefabricated house or other structure.

pre·fab·ri·cate (prē făb′rĭ kāt′) *tr.v*. **pre·fab·ri·cat·ed, pre·fab·ri·cat·ing, pre·fab·ri·cates.** To build or manufacture (a building or section of a building) in advance, especially in sections than can be easily shipped and assembled. —**pre·fab′ri·ca′-tion** *n*. [U]

pref·ace (prĕf′ĭs) *n*. An introduction to a book or speech: *a preface to a lecture on travel.* —*tr.v*, [*with*] **pref·aced, pref·ac·ing, pref·ac·es.** To introduce (sthg.) with a preface: *The professor prefaced his lecture with a joke.* —**pref′a·to′ry** (prĕf′ə tôr′ē) *adj*.

pre·fer (prĭ fûr′) *tr.v*. **pre·ferred, pre·fer·ring, pre·fers.** To like (sbdy./sthg.) better: *I prefer tea to coffee.*

pref·er·a·ble (prĕf′ər ə bəl) *adj*. More desirable; preferred: *Milk is fine, but cream would be preferable.* —**pref′er·a·bly** *adv*.

pref·er·ence (prĕf′ər əns) *n*. **1.** [C; *for*]A liking for a person or thing over another or others: *Our guest had a preference for rice over potatoes.* **2.** [U] The act of preferring; the exercise of choice: *giving preference to family members.* See Synonyms at **choice.**

pref·er·en·tial (prĕf′ə rĕn′shəl) *adj*. Showing preference; favoring one over others: *The owner's friends always receive preferential treatment.* —**pref′er·en′tial·ly** *adv*.

pre·fix (prē′fĭks′) *n*. A word or syllable placed at the beginning of a word to change its meaning. *Un-* in *unable, pre-* in *preheat*, and *re-* in *replay* are prefixes.

preg·nan·cy (prĕg′nən sē) *n*., *pl*. **preg·nan·cies. 1.** [U] The condition of being pregnant: *Even the thought of pregnancy scared her.* **2.** [C] The time during which one is pregnant: *her third pregnancy.*

preg·nant (prĕg′nənt) *adj*. **1.** With developing young inside the body: *pregnant with twins.* **2.** Significant; full of meaning: *a pregnant pause in the campaign speech.*

pre·his·tor·ic (prē′hĭ stôr′ĭk *or* prē′hĭ-stŏr′ĭk) *adj*. Belonging to the time before history or events were recorded in writing: *a prehistoric animal.* —**pre′his·tor′i·cal·ly** *adv*.

prej·u·dice (prĕj′ə dĭs) *n*. **1.** [C; U] An unfair judgment or opinion formed before one knows the facts; a bias: *Many children have a prejudice against unfamiliar foods.* **2.** [U] Irrational suspicion or hatred of a particular race, religion, or group: *Ignorance and fear are the sources of prejudice.* —*tr.v*. **prej·u·diced, prej·u·dic·ing, prej·u·dic·es. 1.** To cause (sbdy.) to judge prematurely and irrationally: *an experience that prejudiced her against dogs.* **2.** To affect (sthg.) harmfully by a judgment or an act: *prejudiced her chances of admission.* —**prej′u·diced** *adj*.

prej·u·di·cial (prĕj′ə dĭsh′əl) *adj*. Harmful; detrimental: *made prejudicial comments about him.* —**prej′u·di′cial·ly** *adv*.

pre·lim·i·nar·y (prĭ lĭm′ə nĕr′ē) *adj*. Coming before or preparing for sthg. more important; introductory: *preliminary drawings for a building.* —*n*., *pl*. **pre·lim·i·nar·ies.** Something that leads to a main matter, action, or business: *She began her lecture without the usual preliminaries.*

prel·ude (prā′lōōd′ *or* prē′lōōd′) *n*. **1.** Something that precedes a more important action; a preliminary: *a prelude to our discussion.* **2.** A piece of music that acts as an introduction to a larger work.

pre·mar·i·tal (prē măr′ĭ tl) *adj*. Taking place before marriage: *premarital counseling.*

pre·ma·ture (prē′mə tŏŏr′ *or* prē′mə-chŏŏr′) *adj*. **1.** Happening before the usual time; unexpectedly early: *a premature death.* **2.** Born after too short a period of development: *a premature baby.* —**pre′ma·ture′ly** *adv*.

pre·med (prē′mĕd′) *Informal. adj*. Premedical. —*n*. [U] A premedical program of study: *She's in premed.*

pre·med·i·cal (prē mĕd′ĭ kəl) *adj*. Relating to studies that prepare one for the study of medicine.

pre·med·i·tate (prē mĕd′ĭ tāt′) *tr.v*. **pre·med·i·tat·ed, pre·med·i·tat·ing, pre·med·i·tates.** To plan or plot (a crime, for example) in advance: *premeditated the attack.* —**pre·med′i·ta′tion** *n*. [U]

pre·mier (prĭ mîr′ *or* prē′mîr) *adj*. First in status or importance; principal or chief: *the premier chef at the restaurant.* —*n*. (prĭ mîr′). A prime minister or a chief administrative officer, as of a country or province: *talks with the Israeli premier.*

pre·miere (prĭ mîr′ *or* prĭ myâr′) *n*. The first public performance of a play or movie.

prem·ise (prĕm'ĭs) *n.* **1.** A proposition or idea that forms the basis of an argument: *Your premise lacks logic.* **2. premises.** Property and the buildings on it: *The playground is part of the school premises.*

pre·mi·um (prē'mē əm) *n.* **1.** An extra or unexpected benefit or sum of money; a bonus: *The store gave out gifts as premiums to the first-day customers.* **2.** The amount paid or payable for an insurance policy: *monthly premiums.* **3.** An unusual or high value: *Many people place a premium on a good education.* —*adj.* Of very high quality or value: *premium gasoline.* ◆ **at a premium.** More valuable than usual, especially because it is difficult to obtain: *Gasoline was at a premium that summer.*

pre·mo·ni·tion (prē'mə nĭsh'ən *or* prĕm'ə nĭsh'ən) *n.* A feeling that sthg. (especially sthg. bad) will happen; a forewarning: *had a premonition of disaster.*

pre·na·tal (prē nāt'l) *adj.* Happening in the time before birth: *prenatal care.*

pre·oc·cu·pa·tion (prē ŏk'yə pā'shən) *n.* **1.** [U] The state of being preoccupied. **2.** [C] Something that preoccupies the mind: *Playing the piano was his only preoccupation.*

pre·oc·cu·pied (prē ŏk'yə pīd') *adj.* **1.** Thinking about sthg. else: *My mother-in-law was preoccupied and barely touched her lunch.* **2.** Overly concerned with sthg.: *He has always been preoccupied with his career.*

pre·oc·cu·py (prē ŏk'yə pī') *tr.v.* **pre·oc·cu·pied, pre·oc·cu·py·ing, pre·oc·cu·pies.** To hold the attention or interest of (sbdy.): *questions that have preoccupied scientists for years.*

prep. *abbr.* An abbreviation of preposition.

pre·paid (prēpād') *adj.* Paid for in advance: *a prepaid vacation tour.* —*v.* Past tense of **prepay.**

prep·a·ra·tion (prĕp'ə rā'shən) *n.* **1.** [U] The act of preparing: *the preparation of dinner for six persons.* **2.** [C] (*usually plural*). A preliminary step necessary in getting ready for sthg.: *final preparations for a rocket launch.* **3.** [C] A substance or mixture prepared for a certain use: *a preparation of herbs for seasoning vegetables.*

pre·par·a·to·ry (prĭ păr'ə tôr'ē *or* prĭ pâr'ə tôr'ē *or* prĕp'ər ə tôr'ē) *adj.* Serving to prepare; introductory: *preparatory exercises before a race.*

preparatory school *n.* A usually private secondary school that prepares students for college.

pre·pare (prĭ pâr') *v.* **pre·pared, pre·par·ing, pre·pares.** —*tr.* **1.** To make (sbdy./ sthg.) ready for some purpose, task, or event: *prepare the wood surface for painting by cleaning it.* **2.** To put together or make (sthg.) by combining various elements or ingredients: *prepare a book report; prepare the salad dressing.* —*intr.* To put things or oneself in readiness; get ready: *preparing to leave town.* —**pre·par'er** *n.*

pre·pared (prĭ pârd') *adj.* **1.** Ready: *We were prepared for any emergency.* **2.** Willing to do sthg.: *I'm not prepared to give in.* **3.** Written or organized ahead of time: *a prepared speech.*

pre·par·ed·ness (prĭ pâr'ĭd nĭs) *n.* [U] *Formal.* The state of being prepared, especially military readiness for combat: *military preparedness.*

pre·pay (prē pā') *tr.v.* **pre·paid, pre·pay·ing, pre·pays.** To pay for (sthg.) beforehand: *She agreed to prepay the rent.* —**pre·pay'ment** *n.* [C; U]

pre·pon·der·ance (prĭ pŏn'dər əns) *n.* *Formal.* Superiority in weight, force, or importance: *a preponderance of evidence proving him guilty.*

prep·o·si·tion (prĕp'ə zĭsh'ən) *n.* In grammar, a word placed before a noun or pronoun that shows the relationship, such as location, time, or direction, between that noun or pronoun and another word. *To, at,* and *in* are common prepositions. —**prep'o·si'tion·al** *adj.* —**prep'o·si'tion·al·ly** *adv.*

prep·o·si·tion·al phrase (prĕp'ə zĭsh'ə·nəl) *n.* In grammar, a phrase with a preposition and its object. In the sentence *The book is in the library,* the prepositional phrase is *in the library.*

pre·pos·ter·ous (prĭ pŏs'tər əs) *adj.* Contrary to reason or common sense; absurd: *He made such a preposterous suggestion that we all laughed.* —**pre·pos'ter·ous·ly** *adv.*

prep school (prĕp) *n. Informal.* A preparatory school.

pre·req·ui·site (prē rĕk'wĭ zĭt) *adj.* Required or necessary before sthg. can happen: *a course that is prerequisite to more advanced studies.* —*n.* A requirement: *I've completed all the prerequisites for my certificate.*

pre·rog·a·tive (prĭ rŏg'ə tĭv) *n.* A right or privilege, especially one that is associated with rank or status: *Using the private jet is the president's prerogative.*

pres. *abbr.* An abbreviation of: **1.** Present. **2.** Also **Pres.** President.

pres·age (prĭ sāj' *or* prĕs'ĭj) *tr.v.* **pre·saged, pre·sag·ing, pre·sag·es.** To indicate (sthg.) in advance; foretell: *A dark sky presaged the coming storm. The recession was presaged by many economists.*

pre·school (prē'skool') *adj.* Relating to the years of childhood that precede the beginning of elementary school. —*n.* (prē'skool'). A nursery school.

pre·scribe (prĭ skrīb′) *tr.v.* **pre·scribed, pre·scrib·ing, pre·scribes.** [*for*] **1.** To set (sthg.) down as a rule or guide; impose or direct: *The government prescribes standards for the purity of food.* **2.** To order or recommend the use of (a drug, for example): *The doctor prescribed bed rest for his injury.*

pre·scrip·tion (prĭ skrĭp′shən) *n.* **1.** [U] The act of prescribing. **2.** [C] A recommendation or rule: *prescriptions for correct usage in an English textbook.* **3.** [C] A written instruction from a doctor indicating what treatment or medication a patient is to receive: *Please take this prescription to the drugstore.* **4.** [C] A medicine ordered by prescription: *a prescription for headaches.*

pre·scrip·tive (prĭ skrĭp′tĭv) *adj.* Making or giving directions, laws, or rules: *a prescriptive grammar.* —**pre·scrip′tive·ly** *adv.*

pres·ence (prĕz′əns) *n.* **1.** [U] The condition of being present: *Your presence is required at the meeting.* **2.** [U] A person's way of moving or standing: *She has great presence on the stage.* **3.** [C] A supernatural influence felt to be nearby: *A mysterious presence frightened them away.* ◆ **presence of mind.** The ability to think and act calmly and efficiently, especially in an emergency: *Her presence of mind allowed her to escape the fire.*

pres·ent[1] (prĕz′ənt) *n.* [U] **1.** A period in time that is between past and future; now: *The present is important; the past isn't.* **2.** The present tense. —*adj.* **1.** Happening now; current: *the present situation.* **2.** Being in attendance: *Only three people were present at the meeting.* **3.** Existing in sthg.: *Oxygen is present in blood.* **4.** Relating to the present tense: *present participle.* ◆ **at present.** At the present time; right now: *I'm busy at present. Can I call you later?* **for the present.** For the time being; temporarily: *He's living with his parents for the present.*

pre·sent[2] (prĭ zĕnt′) *tr.v.* **1.** To introduce (sbdy.), especially with formal ceremony: *They presented me to their parents.* **2.** To bring (sthg.) before the public: *present a drama.* **3.** To make a gift or award of (sthg.): *She presented the prize to the winners.* **4.** To offer (sthg.) for observation, examination, or consideration: *Teachers present different ideas.* —*n.* **pres·ent** (prĕz′ənt). Something presented; a gift: *a birthday present.*

pre·sent·a·ble (prĭ zĕn′tə bəl) *adj.* Suitable for being given, shown, or offered: *Do I look presentable?*

pres·en·ta·tion (prĕz′ən tā′shən or prē′zən tā′shən) *n.* **1.** [C; U] The act of presenting, especially for acceptance or approval: *The presentation of our proposal went well.* **2.** [C] Something presented before an audience, as a play or lecture: *a presentation on ancient history.*

pres·ent-day (prĕz′ənt dā′) *adj.* Existing or happening now; current: *present-day attitudes about education.*

pres·ent·ly (prĕz′ənt lē) *adv.* **1.** In a short time; soon: *We'll be there presently.* **2.** At this time or period; now: *A team of scientists is presently exploring the area.*

present participle (prĕz′ənt) *n.* In grammar, a participle that expresses present action or condition. In the sentence *He is playing,* the word *playing* is the present participle.

pres·ent per·fect (prĕz′ənt pûr′fĭkt) *n.* In grammar, a verb tense used to refer to time up to and including the present. In the sentence *She has spoken to me,* the verb form *has spoken* is in the present perfect.

pres·ent tense (prĕz′ənt) *n.* In grammar, a verb tense used to refer to the present time. In the sentence *I am happy,* the verb *am* is in the present tense.

pre·ser·va·tive (prĭ zûr′və tĭv) *n.* Something used to preserve, especially a chemical added to a food: *juice made without preservatives.* —*adj.* Capable of preserving.

pre·serve (prĭ zûrv′) *tr.v.* **pre·served, pre·serv·ing, pre·serves.** **1.** To maintain (sbdy./sthg.) in safety; protect: *laws that help preserve wildlife.* See Synonyms at **defend.** **2.** To keep (sthg.) unchanged: *Both countries worked to preserve peaceful relations.* **3.** To protect (food) from spoilage, as by drying, pickling, or canning: *preserving fruits and vegetables.* —*n.* **1.** *(usually plural).* Fruit cooked with sugar to protect against decay or fermentation: *strawberry preserves.* **2.** An area maintained for the protection of wildlife or natural resources: *a nature preserve.* —**pres′er·va′tion** (prĕz′ər vā′shən) *n.* [U] —**pre·serv′er** *n.*

pre·side (prĭ zīd′) *intr.v.* **pre·sid·ed, pre·sid·ing, pre·sides.** To hold the position of authority; act as chairperson: *presided over a meeting.*

pres·i·den·cy (prĕz′ĭ dən sē) *n., pl.* **pres·i·den·cies.** **1.** The office or duties of a president: *Her presidency of the club improved our finances.* **2.** Often **Presidency.** The length of time a person serves as president: *a four-year Presidency.*

pres·i·dent (prĕz′ĭ dənt) *n.* **1.** The chief officer of an organization or institution, such as a club, corporation, or university: *He is our company president.* **2.** Often **President.** The chief executive of a republic, such as the United States.

pres·i·den·tial (prĕz′ĭ dĕn′shəl) *adj.* Relating to a president or presidency: *a presidential election.*

press (prĕs) *v.* —*tr.* **1.** To exert force or pressure against (sthg.): *Press the button.* **2.** To smooth (clothes or fabric, for example) by applying heat and pressure; iron: *He pressed the trousers.* **3.** To try hard to persuade or influence (sbdy.), especially by asking insis-

P

tently: *She pressed her aunt to stay for the holiday.* **4.** To urge or force (sbdy./sthg.) to action: *pressing the horses to go faster.* **5.** To lift (a weight): *He can press 200 pounds.* *—intr.* **1.** To advance eagerly; push forward: *The crowd pressed forward to catch a glimpse of the President.* **2.** To beg sbdy. or demand sthg.: *He pressed for the new assignment.* *—n.* **1.** [C] Any of various machines or devices used to squeeze or put pressure on sthg.: *an olive press.* **2.** [C] A printing press. **3.** [C] A place or a business where written materials are printed. **4. the press.** *(used with a singular or plural verb).* The people, such as editors and reporters, involved in collecting, publishing, or broadcasting news. **5.** [C; U] A crowd: *a press of people in the square.* **6.** [C; U] Pressure, haste, or urgency: *The press of business weighs heavily on her time.* ✦ **get good press.** To receive favorable comments or reports in the news media: *The company got good press for its efforts to reduce pollution.* **press charges.** To make an official accusation of an illegal act: *The police decided not to press charges against the driver after the accident.* **press on** or **ahead.** *intr.v.* To continue or advance forcefully despite difficulty: *We were determined to press on toward our goal.*

press agent *n.* A person in charge of advertising and publicity for a performer or business: *We spoke to the singer's press agent.*

press conference *n.* An interview held for news reporters by a political figure or a famous person.

pressed (prĕst) *adj.* [*for*] Under pressure, especially for lack of time or money: *We're pressed for time and can't stop to talk.*

press•ing (prĕs′ĭng) *adj.* Needing immediate attention; urgent: *the pressing problems of the world.*

press secretary *n.* A person who officially manages the public affairs and press conferences of a public figure: *the President's press secretary.*

pres•sure (prĕsh′ər) *n.* **1.** [U] The act of pressing: *Put pressure on the wound.* **2.** [C; U] The amount of force applied per unit of area of a surface: *air pressure.* **3.** [U] A strong, convincing influence, such as a moral force: *peer pressure.* **4.** [C; U] A condition of physical, mental, social, or economic distress: *the economic pressures on the farming community.* *—tr.v.* **pres•sured, pres•sur•ing, pres•sures.** To force (sbdy.) by influencing or persuading: *The movie studio pressured the star into making public appearances.*

WORD BUILDING: **pressure** The word root *—press—* in English words and the English

word **press** itself mean, "to squeeze." Thus we have the verbs **compress**, "to squeeze together" (using the prefix **com—**, "together, with"); **depress**, "to squeeze down" (**de—**, "down"); **express**, "to extract by pressure, expel, force" (**ex—**, "out, out of"); and **impress**, "to press on or against, drive in, imprint" (**in—** ², "into, in").

pressure cooker *n.* An airtight metal pot that uses steam under pressure to cook food quickly.

pres•sur•ize (prĕsh′ə rīz′) *tr.v.* **pres•sur•ized, pres•sur•iz•ing, pres•sur•iz•es.** **1.** To keep (a compartment) at normal atmospheric pressure: *pressurize the aircraft cabin.* **2.** To put (gas or liquid) under a greater pressure than normal. *—pres′sur•i•za′tion* (prĕsh′ər ĭ zā′shən) *n.* [U]

pres•tige (prĕ stēzh′ *or* prĕ stēj′) *n.* [U] Qualities that bring admiration or honor: *a lawyer with great prestige.*

pres•ti•gious (prĕ stē′jəs *or* prĕ stĭj′əs) *adj.* Respected; esteemed: *a prestigious occupation.* *—pres•tig′ious•ly adv.*

pre•sume (prĭ zōōm′) *v.* **pre•sumed, pre•sum•ing, pre•sumes.** *—tr.* **1.** To assume (sthg.) to be true in the absence of proof: *A person is presumed innocent until proved guilty.* **2.** To do (sthg.) without permission; dare: *He presumed to make arrangements for their vacation without her knowledge.* *—intr.* **1.** [*on*] To take unfair advantage of sthg.: *Their relatives presumed on their hospitality.* **2.** To assume that sthg. is true; suppose: *You're Ms. Brown, I presume?* *—pre•sum′-a•ble adj.* *—pre•sum′a•bly adv.*

pre•sump•tion (prĭ zŭmp′shən) *n.* The act of presuming or accepting sthg. as true without proof: *a presumption of innocence.*

pre•sump•tu•ous (prĭ zŭmp′chōō əs) *adj.* Going beyond what is right or proper; arrogant: *a presumptuous attitude.* *—pre•sump′tu•ous•ly adv.* *—pre•sump′tu•ous•ness n.* [U]

pre•sup•pose (prē′sə pōz′) *tr.v.* **pre•sup•posed, pre•sup•pos•ing, pre•sup•pos•es.** **1.** To believe or suppose (sthg.) in advance: *The teacher presupposed that we had studied algebra.* **2.** To require (sthg.) as a necessary prior condition: *The burned wood presupposed a fire.*

pre•teen (prē′tēn′) *adj.* **1.** Relating to children between ages 9 and 12: *preteen clothing.* **2.** Being a child between ages 9 and 12. *—n.* A preteen boy or girl: *a party for preteens.*

pre•tend (prĭ tĕnd′) *tr.v.* **1.** To give a false appearance of (sthg.): *pretend illness.* **2.** To make believe (sthg.): *Pretend that you are on another planet.* **3.** To claim (sthg.) falsely: *The woman pretended to be an expert.* *—pre•tend′er n.*

pre•tense (prē′tĕns′ *or* prĭ tĕns′) *n.* **1.** A

false appearance: *She made a pretense of being worried about us.* **2.** A false reason or excuse: *He spoke to us under false pretenses.*

pre·ten·tious (prǐ těn′shəs) *adj.* Extravagantly showy: *a pretentious house.* —**pre· ten′sion** *n.* —**pre·ten′tious·ly** *adv.* —**pre· ten′tious·ness** *n.* [U]

pret·er·ite or **pret·er·it** (prĕt′ər ǐt) *adj.* In grammar, relating to the verb tense that describes a past action or state. —*n.* A preterite tense.

pre·text (prē′těkst′) *n.* An excuse given to hide the real reason for sthg.: *She called on the pretext of asking about my health, but she really wanted to be sure I was at home.*

pret·ty (prǐt′ē) *adj.* **pret·ti·er, pret·ti· est.** Pleasing in a graceful or delicate way: *a pretty shell.* —*adv.* To a fair degree; moderately: *We are in pretty good shape.* —*v.* **pret·tied, pret·ty·ing, pret·ties.** ♦ **pretty much.** For the most part; mostly: *We were pretty much exhausted after the hike.* **pretty up.** *tr.v.* [sep.] To make (sthg.) pretty: *We can pretty up the spare room for you.* **sitting pretty.** In a good or favorable position: *He was sitting pretty after his promotion.* —**pret′ti·ly** *adv.* —**pret′ti·ness** *n.* [U]

pret·zel (prĕt′səl) *n.* A hard biscuit, salted on the outside and baked in the form of an open knot or stick.

pre·vail (prǐ vāl′) *intr.v.* **1.** To be stronger than sbdy./sthg.; triumph: *The army prevailed.* **2.** To be most common or frequent: *In this region, snow and ice prevail.* **3.** To be in use; be current: *an attitude that prevailed in the 1950s.* ♦ **prevail on** or **upon.** *tr.v.* [insep.] To convince (sbdy.) to do sthg.: *The salesperson prevailed upon me to buy a spare tire.*

pre·vail·ing (prǐ vā′lǐng) *adj.* **1.** Most frequent or common: *The prevailing winds come from the west.* **2.** Generally current; widespread: *the prevailing attitude.*

prev·a·lent (prĕv′ə lənt) *adj.* Widely existing or commonly occurring: *Certain diseases are more prevalent in hot humid areas.* —**prev′a· lence** *n.* [U] —**prev′a·lent·ly** *adv.*

pre·vent (prǐ věnt′) *tr.v.* **1.** To keep (sthg.) from happening: *Washing your hands can prevent illness.* **2.** To keep (sbdy.) from doing sthg.: *His snoring prevents me from sleeping.* —**pre·vent′a·ble** *adj.*

pre·ven·ta·tive (prǐ věn′tə tǐv) *adj. & n.* Variant of **preventive.**

pre·ven·tion (prǐ věn′shən) *n.* [U] The act of preventing: *the prevention of illness.*

pre·ven·tive (prǐ věn′tǐv) also **pre·ven· ta·tive** (prǐ věn′tə tǐv) *adj.* Designed to prevent or stop: *preventive steps against accidents.*

pre·view (prē′vyōō′) *n.* **1.** A private showing of a movie or an exhibition, before it is open to the public. **2.** An advance viewing of scenes of a movie that has not been released.

—*tr.v.* To view or exhibit (sthg.) in advance: *I previewed the new TV series and then allowed my daughter to watch it.*

pre·vi·ous (prē′vē əs) *adj.* Existing or happening before sthg. else in time or order: *in the previous chapter.* —**pre′vi·ous·ly** *adv.*

pre·war (prē′wôr′) *adj.* Existing or happening before a war: *prewar conditions.*

prey (prā) *n.* [U] **1.** An animal hunted for food: *The lion ate its prey under a tree.* **2.** A person or thing that is defenseless against attack; a victim. —*intr.v.* [on; upon] **1.** To hunt and kill other animals for food: *Owls prey on mice.* **2.** To take unfair advantage of other people: *The criminals preyed on widows.* **3.** To have a harmful or troublesome effect: *Worry preyed upon his mind.*

HOMONYMS: prey, pray (speak to a god).

---

price (prīs) *n.* **1.** [C] The amount of money or goods asked or given for sthg.: *The price of the book is $5.99.* **2.** [U] The cost, as in suffering, of getting sthg.: *The price of her success was hard work.* —*tr.v.* **priced, pric·ing, pric·es.** **1.** To establish a price for (sthg.): *priced beans at 89 cents a pound.* **2.** To find out the price of (sthg.): *Let's go in and price the shirts.*

price·less (prīs′lĭs) *adj.* **1.** With great worth: *priceless treasures.* **2.** Very funny or odd: *Little children often say priceless things.*

pric·ey also **pric·y** (prī′sē) *adj.* **pric·i·er, pric·i·est.** *Informal.* Expensive: *a pricey restaurant.* —**pric′ey·ness** *n.* [U]

prick (prĭk) *n.* **1.** The act of piercing or puncturing: *I gave my finger a prick while sewing.* **2.** The sensation of being pierced: *I felt a prick in my foot.* **3.** A hole or mark left by piercing: *tiny pricks made by a needle.* **4.** *Slang.* An offensive word for an unpleasant man. **5.** *Slang.* An offensive word for penis. —*tr.v.* **1.** To puncture (sthg.) lightly: *The thorn pricked my finger.* **2.** To sting (sbdy.) with emotional pain: *My conscience pricks me when I remember what I said.*

prick·le (prĭk′əl) *n.* **1.** A small sharp point or thorn. **2.** A tingling sensation. —*v.* **prick· led, prick·ling, prick·les.** —*tr.* **1.** To prick (sbdy./sthg.) as if with a thorn: *This sweater prickles me.* **2.** To cause (sthg.) to tingle: *This lotion will prickle your face.* —*intr.* To feel a tingling or pricking sensation: *Wool makes me prickle.*

prick·ly (prĭk′lē) *adj.* **prick·li·er, prick·li· est.** **1.** With prickles: *a prickly cactus.* **2.** Tingling: *a prickly feeling in my foot.* —**prick′li·ness** *n.* [U]

pride (prīd) *n.* **1.** [U] A sense of one's own worth; self-respect: *pride wounded by cruel remarks.* **2.** [U] A cause of satisfaction: *The painting was the pride of his collection.* **3.** [U] Too high an opinion of oneself; conceit.

4. [C] A group of lions. —*v.* **prid•ed, prid•ing, prides.** ♦ **pride (oneself) on.** To be pleased or satisfied with (sthg.): *He prided himself on his ability to fix cars.*

priest (prēst) *n.* A person with the authority to administer religious rites. —**priest′ly** *adj.*

priest•ess (prē′stĭs) *n.* A woman with the authority to perform and administer various rites, especially of a pagan religion.

priest•hood (prēst′hŏŏd′) *n.* [U] The office or role of a priest: *He entered the priesthood two years ago.*

prim (prĭm) *adj.* **prim•mer, prim•mest.** Stiffly proper in manner or appearance: *She looked prim and proper in her suit and shiny new shoes.* —**prim′ly** *adv.* —**prim′ness** *n.* [U]

pri•mal (prī′məl) *adj.* Of greatest importance; primary: *a primal necessity.*

pri•mar•i•ly (prī mâr′ə lē *or* prī měr′ə lē) *adv.* In the first place; chiefly: *a forest made up primarily of hardwoods.*

pri•mar•y (prī′měr′ē *or* prī′mə rē) *adj.* **1.** First in importance, rank, or quality: *The primary function of a window is to let in light.* **2.** First in time or sequence; original: *the primary stages of the project.* **3.** Fundamental; basic: *primary needs.* **4.** Relating to a primary school. **5.** Relating to a primary color. —*n., pl.* **pri•mar•ies.** A primary election.

primary color *n.* **1.** Any of the three colors of light, red, green, and blue, that can be mixed to make any other color. **2.** Any of the three colors of pigment, red, yellow, and blue, that can be mixed to make any other color.

primary election *n.* An election in which registered voters nominate candidates for office.

primary school *n.* A school that usually includes the first three or four grades of elementary school and sometimes kindergarten.

pri•mate (prī′māt′) *n.* An animal in the group of mammals that includes monkeys, apes, and humans.

prime (prīm) *adj.* **1.** Most important; chief: *my prime concern; the prime suspect.* **2.** First; original: *prime ideas.* **3.** Relating to a prime number. —*n.* **1.** [U] The stage of highest perfection: *She is in the prime of her life.* **2.** [U] The first or earliest part: *the prime of the day.* **3.** [C] A prime number. —*tr.v.* **primed, prim•ing, primes. 1.** To make (sbdy./sthg.) ready; prepare: *She primed him for the contest.* **2.** To prepare (sthg.) for operation: *prime a pump.* **3.** To prepare (a surface) for painting: *The painter primed the walls.*

prime minister *n.* The head of the Cabinet and often also the chief executive of a parliamentary democracy.

prime number *n.* A number that can only be divided by itself and 1, such as 7, 13, and 19.

prim•er¹ (prĭm′ər) *n.* **1.** A textbook for teaching children to read: *my first-grade primer.* **2.** A book that covers the basic elements of a subject: *a gardening primer.*

prim•er² (prī′mər) *n.* [C; U] A coat of paint used to prepare a surface.

prime time *n.* [U] The evening hours, between 8:00 and 10:00, when the largest television audience is watching: *televised during prime time.*

pri•me•val (prī mē′vəl) *adj.* Belonging to the earliest ages; ancient: *a primeval forest.*

prim•i•tive (prĭm′ĭ tĭv) *adj.* **1.** Relating to an early or original stage or state: *a primitive form of life.* **2.** Simple or crude: *a primitive form of rocket.* —**prim′i•tive•ly** *adv.*

pri•mor•di•al (prī môr′dē əl) *adj.* **1.** Being or happening first in sequence of time; original. **2.** Primary or fundamental: *play a primordial role.*

primp (prĭmp) *tr. & intr.v.* To dress or groom with considerable attention to detail: *She primped her hair. He primped for hours in front of the mirror.*

prince (prĭns) *n.* **1.** A son of a king or queen. **2.** The male ruler of some small countries.

prin•cess (prĭn′sĕs′ *or* prĭn sĕs′) *n.* **1.** A daughter of a king or queen. **2.** The female ruler of some small countries.

prin•ci•pal (prĭn′sə pəl) *adj.* First in rank, degree, or importance: *the principal character in the story.* —*n.* **1.** [C] The head of an elementary school or high school. **2.** [C] A main participant, as in a business deal: *The principals signed the contract.* **3.** [U] A sum of money owed as a debt, on which interest is calculated: *principal and interest on a mortgage.* —**prin′ci•pal•ly** *adv.*

HOMONYMS: principal, principle (belief).

USAGE: principal The words **principal** and **principle** are often confused but do not share any meanings. **Principle** is only a noun, and most of its senses refer to sthg. that is basic or to rules and standards: *She really sticks to her principles.* **Principal** is both a noun and an adjective. As a noun it generally refers to a person who has a high position or plays an important role, for example, *a principal of a school.* As an adjective **principal** means "chief" or "leading": *The principal ways to solve these problems are in the third chapter.*

prin•ci•ple (prĭn′sə pəl) *n.* **1.** A basic or fundamental belief: *the principles of democracy.* **2.** A rule or standard, especially of good behavior: *a man of high principles.* **3.** A law of nature: *the principle of conservation of energy.* ♦ **in principle.** With regard to the basics: *I agree in principle, but we'll see how the details work out.* **on principle.** According to or because of a principle: *I objected on principle.*

prin·ci·pled (prĭn′sə pəld) *adj.* Following a moral code: *a principled decision; a principled group of young people.*

print (prĭnt) *n.* **1.** [C] A mark made upon a surface by pressure: *prints in the sand.* **2.** [U] **a.** Lettering produced by printing: *Look at the print at the top of the page.* **b.** Printed material: *books in print.* **3.** [C] A picture made from an engraved plate: *They have several framed prints.* **4.** [C] Cloth marked with a pattern or design: *a paisley print.* **5.** [C] A photograph: *She ordered color prints.* —*v.* —*tr.* **1.** To produce (sthg.) with a printing press: *The government prints money.* **2.** To offer (sthg.) in printed form; publish: *The newspaper refused to print the letter.* **3.** To write (sthg.) in block letters: *Print your name on the line.* **4.** To produce (a photographic print): *Have you printed my pictures yet?* —*intr.* To write block letters similar to those used in print: *The children are learning to print.* ♦ **in print. 1.** In printed or published form: *My letter to the editor appeared in print.* **2.** Available from a publisher: *Her book has been in print for 20 years.* **out of print.** No longer available from a publisher: *That book's out of print.* **print out.** *tr.v.* [sep.] To print (sthg.) as a computer function; produce as printed output: *The printer is printing out the document now.*

print·er (prĭn′tər) *n.* **1.** A person whose job or business is printing. **2.** A device that prints: *a laser printer.*

print·ing (prĭn′tĭng) *n.* **1.** [U] The process or business of producing printed matter on a printing press or by similar means. **2.** [U] Block letters. **3.** [C] All the copies of a publication, such as a book, printed at one time: *the first printing of the dictionary.*

printing press *n.* A machine that prints newspapers, books, and similar materials.

print·out (prĭnt′out′) *n.* [C; U] Printed material produced by a printer connected to a computer.

pri·or (prī′ər) *adj.* Coming before in time, order, or importance: *his prior employment; a prior consideration.*

pri·or·i·ty (prī ôr′ĭ tē *or* prī ŏr′ĭ tē) *n., pl.* **pri·or·i·ties. 1.** [U] A ranking according to importance or urgency: *Safety is given high priority in factories.* **2.** [C] Something considered in terms of its importance relative to other matters: *Her first priority is finishing college.* —**pri·or′i·tize** *v.*

prism (prĭz′əm) *n.* **1.** A geometric solid with a flat base and three sides. **2.** A transparent block of glass that breaks up light into the colors of the spectrum: *Sunlight shining through a prism makes a rainbow.*

pris·on (prĭz′ən) *n.* **1.** A place where people convicted of crimes are kept. **2.** A place or feeling of confinement: *His job seemed a prison to him.*

pris·on·er (prĭz′ə nər *or* prĭz′nər) *n.* **1.** A person held in custody, especially in a prison or jail: *The guard brought the prisoner into his cell.* **2.** A person kept from freedom of action or expression: *He was a prisoner of his own fears.*

pris·tine (prĭs′tēn′ *or* prĭ stēn′) *adj.* Remaining in a clean or pure state; not spoiled: *the pristine beauty of the mountains; a car in pristine condition.*

pri·va·cy (prī′və sē) *n.* [U] **1.** The condition of being left alone: *Her privacy is important to her.* **2.** Freedom from interference: *the right of privacy.*

pri·vate (prī′vĭt) *adj.* **1.** Limited to one person: *a private room.* **2.** Not available for public use or participation: *a private party.* **3.** Owned by a person or group of persons rather than the public or government: *private property.* **4.** Not intended to be known publicly; secret: *private negotiations.* **5.** Not holding a public office: *a private citizen.* —*n.* An enlisted person of the lowest rank in the military. ♦ **in private.** Not in public; secretly or confidentially: *We met in private to discuss the business plans.*

private school *n.* A school that is not operated and supported by a government.

pri·va·tion (prī vā′shən) *n.* [C; U] Lack of the basic necessities of life: *Many people suffered privations after the war.*

priv·i·lege (prĭv′ə lĭj *or* prĭv′lĭj) *n.* [C; U] A special advantage, right, or permission given to an individual or a group: *He was given the privilege of using his brother's car.*

priv·i·leged (prĭv′ə lĭjd *or* prĭv′lĭjd) *adj.* Enjoying or having privileges: *the privileged classes.*

priv·y (prĭv′ē) *adj.* [to] Sharing knowledge of sthg. private or secret: *I'm not privy to the committee's discussions.* —*n., pl.* **priv·ies.** An outdoor toilet; an outhouse.

prize (prīz) *n.* An award, as in a competition or contest: *She won first prize in the singing contest.* —*adj.* **1.** Given as a prize: *prize money.* **2.** Given a prize or likely to win a prize: *a prize Siamese cat.* —*tr.v.* **prized, priz·ing, priz·es.** To value (sthg.) highly: *My family prizes learning.* See Synonyms at **appreciate.**

prize·fight (prīz′fīt′) *n.* A fight between professional boxers for money. —**prize′-fight′er** *n.* —**prize′fight′ing** *n.* [U]

prize·win·ning (prīz′wĭn′ĭng) *adj.* Having won a prize: *a prizewinning recipe.*

pro¹ (prō) *n., pl.* **pros.** An argument in favor

of sthg.: *We discussed the pros and cons.* —*adv.* In favor; in support: *argue pro and con.*

pro² (prō) *Informal. n., pl.* **pros.** A professional, especially in sports, or the group of professionals as a whole: *He wants to play in the pros.* —*adj.* Professional: *pro football.*

pro—¹ *pref.* A prefix that means: **1.** Favor or support: *pro-choice.* **2.** Acting as; substituting for: *pronoun.*

pro—² *pref.* A prefix that means before or earlier: *prologue.*

WORD BUILDING: pro— The prefix **pro—** usually means "favoring" or "supporting," as when it is prefixed to names of nationalities or social issues: pro-French. In this sense, the opposite of **pro—** would be **anti—**: proslavery/antislavery. Note that when **pro—¹** precedes a word beginning with a capital letter, a hyphen must be used. The prefix **pro—²** means "before" or "earlier." A **prologue** is a part of a play or other literary work that explains what comes later.

---

prob·a·bil·i·ty (prŏb′ə bĭl′ĭ tē) *n., pl.* **prob·a·bil·i·ties. 1.** [U] The condition of being probable; likelihood: *What is the probability of failure?* **2.** [C] *(usually plural).* A probable situation, condition, or event: *Don't decide until you've looked at the probabilities.*

prob·a·ble (prŏb′ə bəl) *adj.* Likely to happen or be true: *the probable cost of the trip.* —**prob′a·bly** *adv.*

pro·ba·tion (prō bā′shən) *n.* [U] **1.** A trial period for testing a person's abilities or personal qualities, as for a job or membership in a club: *New workers are on probation for two months.* **2.** The release of a convicted criminal on condition of good behavior: *on six months' probation for robbery.*

probation officer *n.* An official who supervises people who have been put on probation after being convicted of a crime.

probe (prōb) *n.* **1.** An examination or investigation of a remote or unknown region: *a space probe.* **2.** A long slender tool used to reach into or touch sthg., such as a wound, in order to examine it. —*v.* **probed, prob·ing, probes.** —*tr.* **1.** To explore or examine (sthg.) with a probe. **2.** To investigate or explore (sthg.): *The committee is probing the causes of the strike.* —*intr.* To conduct an investigation or search.

prob·lem (prŏb′ləm) *n.* **1.** A question to be considered, solved, or answered: *math problems; construction problems.* **2.** A situation or person that causes difficulty: *social problems.* —*adj.* Difficult to deal with or control: *a problem child.*

prob·lem·at·ic (prŏb′lə mǎt′ĭk) also **prob·lem·at·i·cal** (prŏb′lə mǎt′ĭ kəl) *adj.*

Posing a problem or question: *a problematic situation.*

pro·ce·dure (prə sē′jər) *n.* [C; U] A way of doing sthg. or getting sthg. done: *the procedure for getting a passport.* —**pro·ce′dur·al** *adj.*

pro·ceed (prə sēd′) *intr.v.* **1.** To move forward or onward, especially after an interruption; continue: *He finished work and then proceeded home.* **2.** To perform an action or process; continue: *After lunch, she proceeded to work on the report.* —*n.* **pro·ceeds** (prō′sēdz′). The amount of money derived from a fundraising event: *The proceeds from the bake sale will go to the children's hospital.*

pro·ceed·ing (prə sē′dĭng) *n.* **1.** An event or series of actions: *a reckless proceeding.* **2.** *(usually plural).* Legal action: *legal proceedings.*

proc·ess (prŏs′ĕs′) *n., pl.* **proc·ess·es** (prŏs′ĕs′ĭz *or* prŏs′ĭ sēz′). **1.** [C] A series of actions, changes, or functions leading to a desired result: *a manufacturing process; the process of digestion.* **2.** [U] Course of events or passage of time: *He started playing tennis, and in the process he lost ten pounds.* —*tr.v.* **1.** To put (sthg.) through a fixed series of steps: *process an application.* **2.** To prepare, treat, or convert (sthg.) by means of a special process: *process waste materials.*

pro·ces·sion (prə sĕsh′ən) *n.* **1.** [U] The act of moving along or forward; progression: *They entered the building in procession.* **2.** [C] A group of persons, vehicles, or objects moving along in an orderly line: *a royal procession.* —**pro·ces′sion·al** *adj.*

pro-choice (prō chois′) *adj.* Supporting the legal right of women and girls to choose whether or not to continue a pregnancy.

pro·claim (prə klām′) *tr.v.* To announce (sthg.) officially and publicly; declare: *proclaim that today is a holiday.*

proc·la·ma·tion (prŏk′lə mā′shən) *n.* **1.** [U] The act of proclaiming: *by royal proclamation.* **2.** [C] Something proclaimed, especially an official public announcement: *made several proclamations.*

pro·cras·ti·nate (prə krǎs′tə nāt′) *intr.v.* **pro·cras·ti·nat·ed, pro·cras·ti·nat·ing, pro·cras·ti·nates.** To put off doing sthg., especially out of habit: *She procrastinated until it was too late.* —**pro·cras′ti·na′tion** *n.* [U] —**pro·cras′ti·na′tor** *n.*

pro·cre·ate (prō′krē āt′) *intr.v.* **pro·cre·at·ed, pro·cre·at·ing, pro·cre·ates.** *Formal.* To produce children or baby animals. —**pro′cre·a′tion** *n.* [U]

proc·tor (prŏk′tər) *n.* In a school or university, an official appointed to supervise students during examinations: *a proctor for the psychology exam.* —*tr.v.* To supervise (an examination): *I proctored an exam today.*

---

pro·cure (prō kyŏŏr′) *tr.v.* **pro·cured, pro·cur·ing, pro·cures.** *Formal.* To get (sthg.) by special effort; obtain: *They procured tickets for the circus.* —**pro·cure′ment** *n.* [U]

prod (prŏd) *tr.v.* **prod·ded, prod·ding, prods. 1.** To jab or poke (sbdy./sthg.), as with a pointed object: *She prodded the cattle along.* **2.** To stir (sbdy.) to action; urge: *His parents continually prodded him to do his homework.* —*n.* **1.** A pointed object used to prod: *a cattle prod.* **2.** A stimulus to action: *Her remarks were a prod to do better.*

prod·i·gal (prŏd′ĭ gəl) *adj. Formal.* Recklessly or extravagantly wasteful: *our prodigal waste of natural resources.*

pro·di·gious (prə dĭj′əs) *adj.* **1.** Enormous: *She ate a prodigious amount of food.* **2.** Extraordinary: *a prodigious memory.* —**pro·di′gious·ly** *adv.*

prod·i·gy (prŏd′ə jē) *n., pl.* **prod·i·gies.** A person with exceptional talents or powers: *a child prodigy.*

pro·duce (prə dōōs′) *tr.v.* **pro·duced, pro·duc·ing, pro·duc·es. 1.** To bring forth (sthg.): *Seeds grow up to produce plants.* **2.** To create (sthg.) by mental or physical effort: *produce a painting.* **3.** To manufacture (sthg.): *produce parts for machines.* **4.** To cause (sthg.) to exist: *Industrial growth produced a new kind of business organization.* **5.** To supervise and finance the public presentation of (a movie, for example): *produce a play.* —*n.* (prŏd′ōōs). [U] Farm products, especially fruits or vegetables: *Excuse me, where can I find the produce?*

pro·duc·er (prə dōō′sər) *n.* **1.** A person or a business that produces, especially one that makes sthg. for sale: *a producer of cast iron.* **2.** A person who supervises and manages the making of a play, film, television show, or other entertainment: *a television producer.*

prod·uct (prŏd′əkt) *n.* **1.** Something produced by human effort or by nature: *farm products.* **2.** A direct result: *His discipline is the product of a strict education.* **3.** In mathematics, the result obtained when multiplication is performed.

pro·duc·tion (prə dŭk′shən) *n.* **1.** [U] The act of producing: *automobile production.* **2.** [C] An item that has been produced; a product: *literary productions.* **3.** [C] A movie, play, or television show: *This is the company's finest production to date.* **4.** [U] An amount produced: *Production is down this week.*

pro·duc·tive (prə dŭk′tĭv) *adj.* **1.** Producing abundantly; fertile: *productive farmlands.* **2.** Producing favorable results or conditions; constructive: *a productive life.* —**pro·duc′tive·ly** *adv.* —**pro·duc′tive·ness, pro′duc·tiv′i·ty** (prō′dŭk tĭv′ĭ tē or prŏd′ŭk tĭv′ĭ tē) *n.* [U]

prof. *abbr.* An abbreviation of: **1.** Professor. **2.** Professional.

pro·fane (prō fān′ *or* prə fān′) *adj.* **1.** Showing contempt for God or sacred things; irreverent: *profane language.* **2.** Not religious: *both sacred and profane music.* —**pro·fane′ly** *adv.*

pro·fan·i·ty (prō fān′ĭ tē) *n., pl.* **pro·fan·i·ties. 1.** [U] The quality of being profane; irreverence or vulgarity: *Profanity was not allowed in my parents' house.* **2.** [C] Abrasive, vulgar, or irreverent language: *The angry driver shouted profanities.*

pro·fess (prə fĕs′) *tr.v.* **1.** To declare (sthg.) openly; claim: *He professed an interest in learning to sail.* **2.** To declare faith in (a religion): *profess her beliefs.*

pro·fes·sion (prə fĕsh′ən) *n.* **1.** An occupation that requires training and specialized study: *the profession of engineering.* **2.** The act of professing; an open declaration: *a profession of faith.*

pro·fes·sion·al (prə fĕsh′ə nəl) *adj.* **1.** Relating to a profession: *lawyers, doctors, and other professional people.* **2.** Showing specialized skill: *She did a professional repair job on the car.* **3.** Consisting of persons receiving pay; not amateur: *professional golf.* —*n.* **1.** A person who earns a living in a given profession: *a golf professional.* **2.** A person who is skilled or experienced in a certain field; a qualified expert: *health care professionals.* —**pro·fes′sion·al·ly** *adv.*

pro·fes·sor (prə fĕs′ər) *n.* A teacher of the highest rank in a college or university. —**pro·fes′sor·ship′** *n.* [C; U]

pro·fes·so·ri·al (prō′fĭ sôr′ē əl *or* prŏf′ĭ sôr′ē əl) *adj.* Relating to or characteristic of a professor: *professorial duties, such as marking papers.* —**pro′fes·so′ri·al·ly** *adv.*

prof·fer (prŏf′ər) *Formal. tr.v.* To offer (sthg.): *proffered her legal services to our school.* —*n.* An offer: *the proffer of help.*

pro·fi·cient (prə fĭsh′ənt) *adj.* Skilled; competent: *proficient at playing the piano.* —**pro·fi′cien·cy** *n.* [U] —**pro·fi′cient·ly** *adv.*

SYNONYMS: proficient, adept, skilled, skillful, expert. These adjectives mean having or showing knowledge, ability, or skill, such as in a vocation, profession, or branch of learning. **Proficient** suggests advanced ability that was gained through training: *It takes many years of study and experience to become a proficient surgeon.* **Adept** suggests being naturally good at sthg. that can be improved through practice: *The dressmaker became adept at cutting fabric without a pattern.* **Skilled** suggests thorough ability and often mastery, such as in an art, a craft, or a trade: *Only the most skilled gymnasts are accepted for the Olympic team.* **Skillful** means with a natural talent: *She is especially skillful at measuring things by eye.* **Expert** applies to sbdy. with absolute skill and command: *A virtuoso is a person who is expert in playing a specific musical instrument.*

P

pro•file (prō′fīl′) *n.* **1.** [C; U] A side view of an object, especially of the human head: *the profile of Lincoln on the penny; a face seen in profile.* **2.** [C] The outline of sthg.: *the jagged profile of the city skyline.* **3.** [C] A short biography: *a profile of the president.* —*tr.v.* **pro•filed, pro•fil• ing, pro•files.** To give or write a short description of (sbdy./sthg.): *The millionaire was profiled in the story.* ♦ **a high** or **low profile.** A great or small amount of public visibility: *a politician with a high profile; an investigator keeping a low profile.*

prof•it (prŏf′ĭt) *n.* **1.** [C; U] The money made in a business venture: *The paperboy made a profit of five cents on every paper he sold.* **2.** [U] *Formal.* An advantage gained from doing sthg.; a benefit: *There was no profit in working hard.* —*v.* —*intr.* To gain an advantage; benefit: *profiting from the experience of others.* —*tr. Formal.* To be an advantage to (sbdy.): *It would profit you to listen.* —**prof′it•less** *adj.*

HOMONYMS: **profit, prophet** (person inspired by God).

prof•it•a•ble (prŏf′ĭ tə bəl) *adj.* **1.** Producing a profit; money-making: *a profitable business.* **2.** Producing benefits; rewarding: *She learned much that was profitable later.*

prof•it•eer (prŏf′ĭ tîr′) *n.* A person who makes excessive profits on goods in short supply. —*intr.v.* To act as a profiteer: *He profiteered during the war.*

prof•li•gate (prŏf′lĭ gĭt) *Formal. adj.* Wasteful: *profligate spending.* —*n.* A very wasteful person.

pro•found (prə found′) *adj.* **1.** Physically or emotionally deep; complete: *profound love of art.* **2.** Far-reaching: *a profound change in our society.* **3.** Wise and full of insight: *a profound remark.* —**pro•found′ly** *adv.* —**pro• fun′di•ty** (prə fŭn′dĭ tē) *n.* [U]

pro•fuse (prə fyo͞os′) *adj. Formal.* **1.** Abundant; plentiful: *a profuse variety of foods.* **2.** Extravagant; lavish: *profuse praise.* —**pro• fuse′ly** *adv.* —**pro•fuse′ness** *n.* [U]

pro•fu•sion (prə fyo͞o′zhən) *n.* [U] A large quantity or amount: *a profusion of flowers.*

pro•gen•i•tor (prō jĕn′ĭ tər) *n. Formal.* A direct ancestor.

prog•e•ny (prŏj′ə nē) *n., pl.* **progeny** or **prog•e•nies.** *(usually singular).* Descendants of a person or an animal considered as a group; offspring: *a list of the bull's progeny.*

pro•ges•ter•one (prō jĕs′tə rōn′) *n.* [U] A female hormone.

prog•no•sis (prŏg nō′sĭs) *n., pl.* **prog•no• ses** (prŏg nō′sēz). A prediction of the likely course or outcome of a disease: *His prognosis was for full recovery.*

pro•gram (prō′grăm′) *n.* **1.** A list of events and other information for a public presentation or entertainment: *a printed program of the concert.* **2.** A public performance, presentation, or entertainment: *We presented a program of folk music.* **3.** A radio or television show: *a program about African wildlife.* **4.** A list of activities, courses, or procedures; a schedule: *She arranged her program so that she could have Mondays off.* **5.** A course of academic study: *an excellent ESL program.* **6.** The coded information necessary for a computer to solve a problem or do a task: *a word-processing program.* —*tr.v.* **pro•grammed, pro•gram•ming, pro•grams** or **pro• gramed, pro•gram•ing, pro•grams. 1.** To provide (a computer) with a program: *She programmed the computer to answer the phone.* **2.** To train or regulate (sbdy.) to behave in a certain way: *We have been programmed to expect TV commercials.*

pro•gram•mer (prō′grăm ər) *n.* A person who writes programs for computers.

prog•ress (prŏg′rĕs′) *n.* [U] **1.** Forward movement; advance: *The taxi made slow progress through the traffic.* **2.** Steady improvement, as of civilization or an individual: *faith in human progress.* —*intr.v.* **pro•gress** (prə grĕs′). **1.** To move forward; advance: *Work on the new house has progressed rapidly.* **2.** To make steady improvements: *Medical technology is always progressing.* ♦ **in progress.** Going on; under way: *That research is in progress now.* **make progress.** To get better; improve: *We had problems at first, but now we're making progress.*

pro•gres•sion (prə grĕsh′ən) *n.* **1.** [U] Movement; progress: *the progression from beginner to expert.* **2.** [C] *(usually singular).* A series of things or events; a sequence: *a progression of speeches at the rally.*

pro•gres•sive (prə grĕs′ĭv) *adj.* **1.** Moving steadily forward; advancing: *the progressive motion of an ocean wave; progressive erosion of the riverbank.* **2.** Working for or favoring steady improvement: *progressive leadership.* **3.** In grammar, indicating a verb form used to express an action or a condition that is in progress. In the sentence *I am sitting,* the verb *sit* is in the progressive form. —*n.* A person who works for or wants steady improvements or reforms. —**pro•gres′sive•ly** *adv.* —**pro• gres′sive•ness** *n.* [U]

pro•hib•it (prō hĭb′ĭt) *tr.v.* **1.** To forbid (sthg.) by law or authority: *The new law prohibits use of fireworks.* **2.** To prevent (sbdy.) from doing sthg.: *Laws prohibit employers from discriminating against minorities.*

pro•hi•bi•tion (prō′ə bĭsh′ən) *n.* **1.** [U] The act of prohibiting. **2.** [C] A law that prohibits sthg.: *a prohibition on smoking.* **3.**

P

Prohibition. The period from 1920 to 1933, when the manufacture and sale of alcoholic beverages was illegal in the United States.

pro·hib·i·tive (prō hĭb′ĭ tĭv) *adj.* Preventing or discouraging the use or purchase of sthg.: *Prohibitive prices made it difficult to sell cars.* **—pro·hib′i·tive·ly** *adv.*

proj·ect (prŏj′ĕkt′) *n.* A plan or proposal (for a specific task): *a project to repair local roads.* **2.** A special assignment done by a student or group of students: *a science project.* **3.** *(usually plural). Informal.* A group of apartment buildings or houses built by the government for low-income families: *He grew up in the projects.* *—v.* **pro·ject** (prə jĕkt′). *—tr.* **1.** To push (sthg.) forward or outward: *He projected his jaw in defiance.* **2.** To shoot or throw (sthg.): *project an arrow.* **3.** To cause (an image) to appear on a surface: *projecting color slides onto a wall.* **4.** To calculate or predict (sthg. in the future) based on present information: *project next year's costs.* **5.** To direct (one's voice) so as to be heard clearly at a distance. *—intr.* To extend or jut out: *The second floor projects over the street.*

pro·jec·tile (prə jĕk′təl *or* prə jĕk′tīl′) *n.* An object, such as a bullet or an arrow, that is thrown or fired through space.

pro·jec·tion (prə jĕk′shən) *n.* **1.** [U] The act of projecting. **2.** [C] Something that extends outward beyond a surface: *an insect with spiny projections on its back.* **3.** [C] An estimate of what sthg. will be in the future, based on the present trends or information: *Projections indicate that sales will be up.*

pro·jec·tion·ist (prə jĕk′shə nĭst) *n.* A person who operates a movie or slide projector.

pro·jec·tor (prə jĕk′tər) *n.* A machine that uses lenses and a source of light to project images, as of movies or slides, onto a surface.

pro·le·tar·i·an (prō′lĭ târ′ē ən) *adj.* Connected with or characteristic of the working class: *a proletarian revolution.* *—n.* A member of the working class.

pro·le·tar·i·at (prō′lĭ târ′ē ĭt) *n.* *(used with a singular verb).* The working class.

pro-life (prō līf′) *adj.* Believing that human embryos or fetuses should have full legal protection and that deliberate abortions should be illegal.

pro·lif·er·ate (prə lĭf′ə rāt′) *intr.v.* **pro·lif·er·at·ed, pro·lif·er·at·ing, pro·lif·er·ates.** To grow, spread, or multiply at a fast rate: *Viruses proliferate in living tissue.* **—pro·lif′er·a′tion** *n.* [U]

pro·lif·ic (prə lĭf′ĭk) *adj.* Producing sthg., such as literary works or offspring, in great numbers: *a prolific author; Rabbits are prolific animals.* **—pro·lif′i·cal·ly** *adv.*

pro·logue (prō′lôg′ *or* prō′lŏg′) *n.* A beginning section of a play, an opera, or a literary work that introduces or explains what follows: *a prologue to Tom Sawyer.*

pro·long (prə lông′ *or* prə lŏng′) *tr.v.* **1.** To lengthen (sthg.) in duration: *a special diet for prolonging one's life.* **2.** To lengthen (sthg.) in time or space: *It is unwise to prolong a business letter.* **—pro′lon·ga′tion** (prō′lông gā′shən *or* prō′lŏng gā′shən) *n.* [C; U]

prom (prŏm) *n.* A formal dance held for a high-school class: *the junior prom.*

prom·e·nade (prŏm′ə nād′ *or* prŏm′ə näd′) *n.* A public place designed for a relaxed walk. *—intr.v.* **prom·e·nad·ed, prom·e·nad·ing, prom·e·nades.** To go on a relaxed walk: *promenading along the waterfront.*

prom·i·nence (prŏm′ə nəns) *n.* [U] The quality of being prominent; importance: *His father rose to a position of prominence in government.*

prom·i·nent (prŏm′ə nənt) *adj.* **1.** Projecting outward: *prominent brows.* **2.** Very noticeable; conspicuous: *You will find the checkout desk in a prominent place in your library.* **3.** Well-known; eminent: *a prominent politician.* **—prom′i·nent·ly** *adv.*

prom·is·cu·i·ty (prŏm′ĭ skyoō′ĭ tē) *n.* [U] The state or character of being promiscuous.

pro·mis·cu·ous (prə mĭs′kyoō əs) *adj.* Having sexual relations with many persons. **—pro·mis′cu·ous·ly** *adv.*

prom·ise (prŏm′ĭs) *n.* **1.** [C] A declaration that one will or will not do a certain thing; a vow: *She kept her promise to write home once a week.* See Synonyms at **vow.** **2.** [C; U] Indication of sthg. favorable to come or of future success: *a promise of spring in the warm breeze; a rookie baseball player who shows promise.* *—v.* **prom·ised, prom·is·ing, prom·is·es.** *—tr.* **1.** To declare (sthg.) with a promise; pledge: *I promised to come home early.* **2.** To give reasons for expecting (sthg.): *clouds that promised rain.* *—intr.* To make or give a promise.

prom·is·ing (prŏm′ĭ sĭng) *adj.* Likely to succeed: *a promising career.* **—prom′is·ing·ly** *adv.*

pro·mote (prə mōt′) *tr.v.* **pro·mot·ed, pro·mot·ing, pro·motes.** **1.** To raise (sbdy.) to a higher rank, position, or class: *promoted her to captain.* **2.** To aid the progress or growth of (sthg.); advance: *promoting reading ability.* **3.** To urge the adoption or use of (sthg.); advocate: *promote nonsmoking areas in restaurants.*

pro·mot·er (prə mō′tər) *n.* An active supporter; an advocate: *promoters of a longer school year for children.*

pro·mo·tion (prə mō′shən) *n.* **1.** [C] An advancement to a higher rank, position, or class: *a series of rapid promotions.* **2.** [C; U] Publicity, as for a product on sale; advertising: *promotion of new products.* **—pro·mo′tion·al** *adj.*

P

prompt (prŏmpt) *adj.* **1.** Being on time; punctual: *She was usually prompt in meeting deadlines.* **2.** Done without delay; immediate: *a prompt reply.* —*tr.v.* **1.** To urge (sbdy.) to some action: *an experience that prompted her to write her family.* **2.** To inspire or lead to (sthg.): *The poor test scores prompted a review of teaching methods.* **3.** To assist (sbdy.) by supplying a forgotten word, a cue, or another reminder: *prompt an actor.* —*n.* **1.** A reminder or cue. **2.** A symbol that appears on a computer screen to show that the computer is ready to receive data. —**prompt'er** *n.* —**prompt'ly** *adv.* —**prompt'ness** *n.* [U]

prom•ul•gate (prŏm'əl gāt') *tr.v.* **prom•ul•gat•ed, prom•ul•gat•ing, prom•ul•gates.** *Formal.* To announce (sthg.) publicly and officially; proclaim: *promulgate a new set of laws.* —**prom'ul•ga'tion** *n.* [U]

pron. *abbr.* An abbreviation of: **1.** Pronoun. **2.** Pronunciation.

prone (prōn) *adj.* **1.** Lying with the face downward. **2.** Tending; inclined: *prone to make hasty judgments; accident-prone.*

prong (prông *or* prŏng) *n.* One of the sharply pointed ends of a fork or other tool.

pronged (prôngd *or* prŏngd) *adj.* With prongs of a certain number or kind: *a three-pronged electrical plug.*

pro•noun (prō'noun') *n.* In grammar, any of a class of words used as substitutes for nouns or noun phrases. For example, *us* and *them* are pronouns.

pro•nounce (prə nouns') *tr.v.* **pro•nounced, pro•nounc•ing, pro•nounc•es.** To articulate or produce (a word or speech sound): *pronounce the letter A.* —**pro•nounce'a•ble** *adj.*

pro•nounced (prə nounst') *adj.* Distinct; easy to notice: *He was walking with a pronounced limp.*

pro•nounce•ment (prə nouns'mənt) *n.* *Formal.* An official expression of opinion or statement.

pron•to (prŏn'tō) *adv.* *Informal.* Right away; immediately: *We need to get there pronto.*

pro•nun•ci•a•tion (prə nŭn'sē ā'shən) *n.* **1.** [U] The act or way of pronouncing words: *She practiced her pronunciation.* **2.** [C] A written representation of the way a word is pronounced, using phonetic symbols: *Look up the word's pronunciation in the dictionary.*

proof (prōōf) *n.* **1.** [C; U] Evidence or demonstration of truth: *Accident figures give us undeniable proof of the value of using seat belts.* **2.** [C] A demonstration of the truth of a mathematical or logical statement. **3.** [U] The act of testing the truth of sthg. by experiment or trial. **4.** [C] A trial copy of sthg., such as a sheet of printed material. **5.** [U] The alcoholic content of a liquor: *eighty proof rum.* —*adj.* Fully resistant: *waterproof shoes.*

proof•read (prōōf'rēd') *tr.v.* **proof•read** (prōōf'rěd'), **proof•read•ing, proof•reads.** To read and mark corrections in (printed, typed, or written material): *She proofread the report once again before turning it in.* —**proof'read'er** *n.*

prop (prŏp) *n.* **1.** An object placed under or against a structure to keep it from falling: *Let's use the chair as a prop.* **2.** An object that is used to add realism in a play or movie. —*v.* **propped, prop•ping, props.** ♦ **prop up.** *tr.v.* [sep.] To keep (sthg.) from falling by placing an object beneath or against: *Prop up the shelf with a piece of wood.*

prop•a•gan•da (prŏp'ə găn'də) *n.* [U] Material that may not be completely true distributed for the purpose of winning people over to certain beliefs: *wartime propaganda.* —**prop'a•gan'dist** *n.* —**prop'a•gan'dize** *v.*

prop•a•gate (prŏp'ə gāt') *v.* **prop•a•gat•ed, prop•a•gat•ing, prop•a•gates.** —*tr.* **1.** To cause (sthg.) to produce offspring or new individuals; breed: *propagate plants.* **2.** To make (sthg.) known or accepted among many people; spread: *propagate a rumor.* —*intr.* To produce offspring. —**prop'a•ga'tion** *n.* [U]

pro•pane (prō'pān') *n.* [U] A colorless gas that has the formula C_3H_8 and is widely used as a fuel.

pro•pel (prə pěl') *tr.v.* **pro•pelled, pro•pel•ling, pro•pels.** To cause (sthg.) to move or continue in motion: *the rearward thrust that propels a jet airplane.*

pro•pel•lant *also* **pro•pel•lent** (prə pěl'ənt) *n.* [C; U] **1.** Something that produces forward movement, such as of a rocket. **2.** The compressed gas used in an aerosol spray container to force out the contents.

pro•pel•ler (prə pěl'ər) *n.* A rotary device, with two or more blades, driven by a motor and used to move an aircraft or a boat.

pro•pen•si•ty (prə pěn'sĭ tē) *n., pl.* **pro•pen•si•ties.** *Formal.* A natural tendency; an inclination: *her propensity to exaggerate.*

propeller

prop•er (prŏp'ər) *adj.* **1.** Correct, right, or suitable; appropriate: *the proper tools for repairing a leaky roof.* **2.** Strictly following the rules for social behavior: *a proper gentleman.* **3.** In the strict sense of the term: *We drove through the suburbs and entered the city proper.* —**prop'er•ly** *adv.*

proper noun *n.* In grammar, a noun that is

the name of a unique person, place, or thing. *London* is a proper noun. — SEE NOTE at **noun**.

prop•er•ty (prŏp′ər tē) *n., pl.* **prop•er•ties. 1.** [U] A possession or group of possessions: *He could put all his property into two suitcases.* **2.** [C; U] A piece of land owned by sbdy.: *A stream runs through our property.* **3.** [C] A characteristic quality, especially one that helps define or describe sthg.: *the chemical properties of a metal.* See Synonyms at **quality.**

proph•e•cy (prŏf′ĭ sē) *n., pl.* **proph•e•cies** (prŏf′ĭ sēz). [C; U] A declaration or warning of sthg. in the future; a prediction: *prophecies of financial disaster.*

proph•e•sy (prŏf′ĭ sī′) *v.* **proph•e•sied** (prŏf′ĭ sīd′), **proph•e•sy•ing** (prŏf′ĭ sī′ĭng), **proph•e•sies** (prŏf′ĭ sīz′). —*tr.* To use religious or magical knowledge to reveal (what will happen in the future): *The old man prophesied that the world would end in two years.* —*intr.* To predict the future.

proph•et (prŏf′ĭt) *n.* **1.** A person who speaks words inspired by God and gives God's message in this way. **2.** A person who can foretell the future.

HOMONYMS: **prophet, profit** (money).

pro•phet•ic (prə fĕt′ĭk) *adj.* **1.** Characteristic of a prophet. **2.** Predicting the future: *a warning that proved prophetic.* —**pro•phet′i•cal•ly** *adv.*

pro•po•nent (prə pō′nənt) *n.* A person who argues in support of sthg.; an advocate: *They are proponents of exercise and healthy eating.*

pro•por•tion (prə pôr′shən) *n.* **1.** [U] A relationship between amounts in which change in one results in change in the other. **2.** [C; U] The size, amount, or extent of one thing compared with that of another thing: *The proportion of flour to milk in the recipe is two to one.* **3.** [U] A pleasing relationship between the parts of a whole; balance: *The arm of the statue seems out of proportion.* **4.** [C] (*usually plural*). Size; dimensions: *a disease that reached epidemic proportions.* —*tr.v.* **1.** To adjust (sthg.) in order to reach a particular relation between parts: *Proportion the oil to the vinegar in the dressing.* **2.** To make the parts of (sthg.) harmonious or pleasing: *proportioned the statue nicely.* ♦ **in** or **out of proportion to.** In or not in accordance with the importance of (sthg.): *Her reaction was out of proportion to the problem.*

pro•por•tion•al (prə pôr′shə nəl) *adj. Formal.* Corresponding in size, amount, or degree; in proportion: *The effects of the drug were proportional to the dose.* —**pro•por′-tion•al•ly** *adv.*

pro•por•tion•ate (prə pôr′shə nĭt) *adj. Formal.* In proportion; corresponding: *taking a harder job with a proportionate increase in pay.* —**pro•por′tion•ate•ly** *adv.*

pro•pos•al (prə pō′zəl) *n.* **1.** The act of proposing; an offer: *a proposal to go fishing.* **2.** A plan or scheme offered for consideration: *The assistant made a proposal to work fewer hours.* **3.** An offer of marriage: *She accepted his proposal.*

pro•pose (prə pōz′) *v.* **pro•posed, pro•pos•ing, pro•pos•es.** —*tr.* **1.** To put (sthg.) forward for consideration; suggest: *propose a new law; propose a toast.* **2.** To declare an intention (to do sthg.); intend: *She proposed to buy me dinner this time.* —*intr.* [*to*] To make a proposal, especially an offer of marriage: *He proposed to his girlfriend on Valentine's Day.*

prop•o•si•tion (prŏp′ə zĭsh′ən) *n.* **1.** An offer; a proposal: *a business proposition.* **2.** A matter to be handled or dealt with: *Finding a cheap apartment is a difficult proposition.* —*tr.v.* **prop•o•si•tioned, prop•o•si•tion•ing, prop•o•si•tions.** *Informal.* To propose sexual relations to (sbdy.), usually in exchange for money.

pro•pri•e•tar•y (prə prī′ĭ tĕr′ē) *adj. Formal.* **1.** Relating to an owner or ownership: *She has a proprietary interest in the business.* **2.** Owned by an individual or a firm under a trademark or patent: *proprietary medicines.* —**pro•pri′e•tar′i•ly** *adv.*

pro•pri•e•tor (prə prī′ĭ tər) *n. Formal.* The owner and often manager of a business: *Speak to the proprietor about the job opening.*

pro•pri•e•ty (prə prī′ĭ tē) *n., pl.* **pro•pri•e•ties. 1.** [U] The quality of being proper; suitability; appropriateness: *She insisted on strict propriety at her dinner parties.* **2. pro•prieties.** The rules and conventions of polite social behavior.

pro•pul•sion (prə pŭl′shən) *n.* [U] **1.** The act of propelling sthg. forward. **2.** A force that pushes sthg. forward: *jet propulsion.*

pro•rate (prō rāt′ *or* prō′rāt′) *tr.v.* **pro•rat•ed, pro•rat•ing, pro•rates.** To divide (an expense) based on actual use: *The landlord prorated the first month's rent.*

prose (prōz) *n.* [U] Ordinary speech or writing as distinguished from poetry.

pros•e•cute (prŏs′ĭ kyо̄о̄t′) *tr.v.* **pros•e•cut•ed, pros•e•cut•ing, pros•e•cutes.** To bring or conduct a legal action against (sbdy.): *prosecuting people who break a law.*

pros•e•cu•tion (prŏs′ĭ kyо̄о̄′shən) *n.* **1.** [C; U] The act of prosecuting a person or case in a court of law: *They risked prosecution by breaking the law.* **2.** [U] A lawyer, or group of lawyers, who conducts legal cases on behalf of a government and its citizens: *The prosecution called the first witness.*

pros•e•cu•tor (prŏs′ĭ kyо̄о̄′tər) *n.* The person who starts a legal action, especially the public official who represents the government and the people in court.

pros•pect (prŏs′pĕkt′) *n.* **1.** [C; U] Something expected; a possibility: *The children hurried home with the prospect of a good dinner.* **2. prospects.** Chances for success or recovery: *Her prospects for a full recovery are excellent.* **3.** [C] A possible customer or client: *a sales prospect.* **4.** [C] A possible candidate, as for a team or job: *A football scout looked over the college prospects.* —*v.* —*tr.* To explore (a region) in search of mineral deposits or oil: *prospecting the mountains for silver.* —*intr.* To search for mineral deposits or oil. —**pros'pec•tor** *n.*

pro•spec•tive (prə spĕk'tĭv) *adj.* Expected to happen: *prospective tax increase.*

pro•spec•tus (prə spĕk'təs) *n.* A printed description of a business or other venture.

pros•per (prŏs'pər) *intr.v.* To be successful; thrive: *The town prospered for three centuries.*

pros•per•i•ty (prŏ spĕr'ĭ tē) *n.* [U] The condition of being prosperous; success: *We wished them long life and prosperity.*

pros•per•ous (prŏs'pər əs) *adj.* Successful; profitable: *a prosperous business.* —**pros'per•ous•ly** *adv.*

pros•tate (prŏs'tāt') *n.* An organ in males, surrounding the urethra at the base of the bladder, that controls the release of urine and secretes a fluid that is a major component of semen. —*adj.* Relating to the prostate: *prostate cancer.*

pros•ti•tute (prŏs'tĭ tōot') *n.* A person who performs sexual acts with others for pay. —*tr.v.* **pros•ti•tut•ed, pros•ti•tut•ing, pros•ti•tutes. 1.** To offer (oneself or sbdy. else) for sexual acts in return for pay. **2.** To sell (oneself or one's abilities) for an unworthy purpose: *prostituted their musical talents.*

pros•ti•tu•tion (prŏs'tĭ tōo'shən) *n.* [U] **1.** The practice of performing sexual acts for pay. **2.** The act of prostituting: *the prostitution of an artist's talents.*

pros•trate (prŏs'trāt') *tr.v.* **pros•trat•ed, pros•trat•ing, pros•trates. 1.** To throw (oneself) down flat. **2.** To exhaust (sbdy.) physically or emotionally: *a disease that prostrates its victims.* —*adj.* **1.** Kneeling or lying face down, as in submission: *He fell prostrate in front of the king.* **2.** Lying down at full length: *a sleeper prostrate on the floor.* **3.** [*with*] Exhausted physically or emotionally; helpless: *prostrate with fear.* —**pros•tra'tion** *n.* [C; U]

pro•tag•o•nist (prō tăg'ə nĭst) *n.* The main character in a drama or literary work.

pro•tect (prə tĕkt') *tr.v.* To keep (sbdy./sthg.) from harm; guard: *laws that protect certain species of birds.* See Synonyms at **defend.**

pro•tec•tion (prə tĕk'shən) *n.* **1.** [U] The act of protecting: *a hedge for protection*

against the wind. **2.** [C] A person or thing that protects: *The thin jacket was his only protection against the wind.*

pro•tec•tive (prə tĕk'tĭv) *adj.* Serving to protect: *a protective coat of paint.* —**pro•tec'tive•ly** *adv.* —**pro•tec'tive•ness** *n.* [U]

pro•tec•tor (prə tĕk'tər) *n.* **1.** A person who protects; a defender or guardian: *a protector of the working poor.* **2.** Something that protects: *wearing a chest protector.*

pro•té•gé (prō'tə zhā' *or* prō'tə zhā') *n.* A person whose welfare, training, or career is promoted by another more experienced person: *The retired singer prepared her protégé for his debut.*

pro•tein (prō'tēn) *n.* [C; U] A complex organic chemical compound that contains nitrogen and has a very high molecular weight. Proteins form the basis of living tissues.

pro•test (prə tĕst' *or* prō'tĕst') *v.* —*tr.* **1.** To express strong objections to (sthg.), as in a formal statement or public demonstration: *Demonstrators protested the new law.* **2.** To declare (sthg.) earnestly: *He protested his innocence.* —*intr.* To express strong objection: *You protest too much.* —*n.* (prō'tĕst'). [C; U] A formal statement of disapproval or objection: *Property owners sent a protest to the mayor's office.* ♦ **in protest.** Showing disapproval or objection: *He refused to buy imported cars in protest against the new tax. We'll march in protest of the law.* —**pro•test'er** *n.*

Prot•es•tant (prŏt'ĭ stənt) *n.* A member of one of the Christian churches descending from those that separated from the Roman Catholic Church in the 16th century. —*adj.* Relating to the Protestant religion: *the Protestant Bible.* —**Prot'es•tant•ism** *n.* [U]

prot•es•ta•tion (prŏt'ĭ stā'shən *or* prō'tĭ stā'shən) *n. Formal.* A serious declaration: *protestation of love.*

pro•to•col (prō'tə kôl' *or* prō'tə kŏl') *n.* [U] The rules of ceremony and social etiquette followed by diplomats and heads of state: *She broke protocol by leaving the party before the guest of honor.*

pro•ton (prō'tŏn') *n.* A particle with a positive charge, which forms part of an atomic nucleus.

pro•to•type (prō'tə tīp') *n.* An original example of sthg., which is used as a model for later prototypes: *The manufacturer builds many prototypes before deciding how the final product will look.*

pro•to•zo•an (prō'tə zō'ən) *n.*, *pl.* **pro•to•zo•ans** *or* **pro•to•zo•a** (prō'tə zō'ə). Any of a large group of very small one-celled organisms that are the simplest forms of animal life.

pro•tract (prō trăkt′) *tr.v.* To extend (sthg.) in time; lengthen: *We don't want to protract the negotiations.* —**pro•trac′tion** *n.* [U]

pro•trac•tor (prō trăk′tər) *n.* A semicircular instrument marked off in degrees, used for measuring and drawing angles.

pro•trude (prō trōōd′) *intr.v.* **pro•trud•ed, pro•trud•ing, pro•trudes.** To stick out from a surface: *Curly hair protruded from under the edges of his cap.* —**pro•trud′ing** *adj.*

pro•tru•sion (prō trōō′zhən) *n. Formal.* A part or an object that protrudes; a projection.

pro•tu•ber•ance (prō tōō′bər əns) *n. Formal.* A bulge, swelling, or knob: *a painful protuberance on his knee.*

pro•tu•ber•ant (prō tōō′bər ənt) *adj.* Bulging or swelling outward: *slightly protuberant eyes.*

proud (proud) *adj.* **1.** Feeling pleasure and satisfaction about sthg. one owns, makes, does, or is a part of: *proud to be a grandfather.* **2.** Unwilling to admit weakness or need: *too proud to ask for help.* **3.** Very respected; honored: *a proud name.* —**proud′ly** *adv.*

SYNONYMS: **proud, arrogant, haughty, disdainful.** These adjectives mean feeling or showing a high opinion of oneself and looking down on what one thinks is unworthy. **Proud** often means self-satisfied in a conceited way: *They were too proud to admit that they needed help.* **Arrogant** means too proud, demanding more power than is deserved: *The arrogant man refused to stand in line and wait his turn.* **Haughty** means proud in a condescending way because of one's high birth: *The duchess turned away with a haughty sniff, ignoring my question.* **Disdainful** means proud in a scornful, mocking way: *My teacher is disdainful of popular music.*

prove (prōōv) *v.* **proved, proved** or **prov•en** (prōō′vən), **prov•ing, proves.** —*tr.* **1.** To show (sthg.) to be true by giving evidence: *By measuring we proved that he was six feet tall.* **2.** To determine the quality of (sthg.) by testing; try out: *proving a new car on the open road.* —*intr.* To be shown to be such: *The original estimate proved too low.* —**prov′a•ble** *adj.*

prov•erb (prŏv′ûrb′) *n.* A short saying that is in frequent use and expresses a basic truth: *My favorite proverb is "Haste makes waste."*

pro•ver•bi•al (prə vûr′bē əl) *adj.* **1.** Like a proverb: *proverbial sayings.* **2.** Widely known; famous: *Her skill at cards is proverbial.* —**pro•ver′bi•al•ly** *adv.*

pro•vide (prə vīd′) *tr.v.* **pro•vid•ed, pro•vid•ing, pro•vides. 1.** To furnish (sthg.); supply: *generators that provide electricity.* **2.** To make (sthg.) available: *a gas station that provides restrooms.* **3.** To give (sthg.) as a condition: *The*

contract provides that we work on Saturday. ◆ **provide for.** *tr.v.* [insep.] **1.** To prepare for (sthg.): *provide for all weather conditions.* **2.** To supply the necessities of life, such as food and money, for (sbdy.): *He worked hard to provide for his large family.* **3.** To give (an instruction, rule, or condition): *He provided for a scholarship fund in his will.* —**pro•vid′er** *n.*

pro•vid•ed (prə vī′dĭd) *conj.* On the condition; if: *You may go, provided your homework is done.*

prov•i•dence (prŏv′ĭ dəns) *n.* [U] The control and protection of God; divine direction: *divine providence.*

prov•i•den•tial (prŏv′ĭ dĕn′shəl) *adj. Formal.* Happening at the right time; very fortunate: *The providential arrival of my paycheck enabled me to pay my monthly rent.*

pro•vid•ing (prə vī′dĭng) *conj.* On the condition; provided: *We are going to play volleyball, providing the court is free.*

prov•ince (prŏv′ĭns) *n.* **1.** A political division of a country or an empire: *Ontario and Quebec are provinces of Canada.* **2. provinces.** The rural areas of a country, away from the capital or population center.

pro•vin•cial (prə vĭn′shəl) *adj.* **1.** Relating to a province: *a provincial capital.* **2.** Characteristic of people from the provinces; not sophisticated or worldly: *provincial speech and dress.*

pro•vi•sion (prə vĭzh′ən) *n.* **1.** [U] The act of providing or supplying: *the provision of water to the drought victims.* **2. provisions.** Stocks of food and other necessary supplies: *We brought provisions for the week-long hike.* **3.** [C] *(usually plural).* A measure taken in preparation: *making provisions for her solo flight.* **4.** [C] A condition, especially in a legal document or an agreement: *a provision in my lease allowing me to keep a pet in the apartment.* —*tr.v.* To supply (sbdy.) with provisions: *The troops were provisioned with food for a week.*

pro•vi•sion•al (prə vĭzh′ə nəl) *adj.* Temporary: *a provisional government.* —**pro•vi′sion•al•ly** *adv.*

prov•o•ca•tion (prŏv′ə kā′shən) *n.* **1.** [U] The act of provoking; incitement. **2.** [C] Something that provokes: *Her comments were a provocation to me.*

pro•voc•a•tive (prə vŏk′ə tĭv) *adj.* **1.** Tending to provoke discussion or anger: *The scientist proposed a provocative new theory.* **2.** Sexually suggestive: *a provocative dress.* —**pro•voc′a•tive•ly** *adv.* —**pro•voc′a•tive•ness** *n.* [U]

pro•voke (prə vōk′) *tr.v.* **pro•voked, pro•vok•ing, pro•vokes. 1.** To make (sbdy.) angry: *His arguing provoked me.* **2.** To cause (sthg.): *Conscience provoked them to speak out.*

pro•vost (prō′vōst′) *n.* A high-ranking university administrator.

prow (prou) *n.* The forward part of a ship's hull; the bow.

prow·ess (prou′ĭs) *n.* [U] Superior skill or ability: *She showed prowess in mathematics.*

prowl (proul) *v.* —*tr.* To roam through (sthg.) quietly, as if in search of food: *Cats prowl the alleys at night.* —*intr.* To roam quietly as if hunting for sthg. —*n.* The act or an instance of prowling. ◆ **on the prowl.** Hunting for an animal or person to attack: *The tiger was on the prowl for prey.*

prowler (prou′lər) *n.* A person who moves around one's house, especially with the intention of harming sbdy. or stealing; a burglar: *We heard a prowler in the back yard.*

prox·im·i·ty (prŏk sĭm′ĭ tē) *n.* [U] The state, quality, or fact of being near; closeness: *people living in proximity to the airport.*

prox·y (prŏk′sē) *n., pl.* **prox·ies. 1.** [C] A person authorized to act for another; an agent. **2.** [C; U] The authority to act for another: *vote by proxy.*

prude (prōōd) *n.* A person who is too concerned with being proper or modest: *Don't be such a prude!* —**prud′ish** *adj.*

pru·dence (prōōd′ns) *n.* [U] Careful management; economy: *Through great prudence, they saved $10,000 in one year.*

pru·dent (prōōd′nt) *adj.* Wise in handling practical matters; sensible: *a prudent manager.* —**pru′dent·ly** *adv.*

prune¹ (prōōn) *n.* A dried plum.

prune² (prōōn) *tr.v.* **pruned, prun·ing, prunes. 1.** To cut or trim branches from (a tree or plant) to improve its growth or shape: *The gardener pruned the roses.* **2.** To shorten or improve (sthg.) by removing unnecessary parts: *prune a long composition.*

pry¹ (prī) *intr.v.* **pried** (prīd), **pry·ing, pries** (prīz). To look or investigate closely or curiously, often in a secret manner: *He can't help prying into his wife's past.*

pry² (prī) *tr.v.* **pried** (prīd), **pry·ing, pries** (prīz). **1.** To raise, move, or force (sthg.) open with a lever: *pry the lid off a box.* **2.** To get (sthg.) with difficulty: *pried answers from the child.*

P.S. *abbr.* An abbreviation of: **1.** Postscript. **2.** Public school.

psalm (säm) *n.* A sacred song; a hymn.

pseudo— or **pseud—** *pref.* A prefix that means false; deceptive: *pseudoscience.*

pseu·do·nym (sōōd′n ĭm′) *n.* A fictitious name used by an author; a pen name: *Mark Twain was the pseudonym of Samuel L. Clemens.*

pseu·do·sci·ence (sōō′dō sī′əns) *n.* A theory or method that is considered to be without scientific foundation.

pso·ri·a·sis (sə rī′ə sĭs) *n.* [U] A chronic noncontagious skin disease that causes inflammation.

psych (sīk) *v. Informal.* ◆ **psych out.** *tr.v.* [sep.] To damage the confidence of (sbdy.); intimidate: *The looks on our opponents' faces psyched us out.* **psych up.** *tr.v.* [sep.] To raise the level of excitement of (sbdy.): *The coach psyched the team up before the game.*

psy·che (sī′kē) *n.* **1.** The soul or spirit. **2.** The human mind.

psy·che·del·ic (sī′kĭ dĕl′ĭk) *adj.* **1.** Related to or causing hallucinations and altered mental states: *psychedelic drugs.* **2.** Brightly colored and patterned: *psychedelic art.*

psy·chi·a·try (sĭ kī′ə trē *or* sī kī′ə trē) *n.* [U] The branch of medicine that deals with the study and treatment of mental illness. —**psy′chi·at′ric** (sī′kē ăt′rĭk) *adj.* —**psy·chi′a·trist** *n.*

psy·chic (sī′kĭk) *n.* A person who is believed to be sensitive to forces that are not physical: *A psychic helped find the lost boys.* —*adj.* **1.** Relating to the human mind or psyche: *psychic distress.* **2.** Sensitive to forces that are not physical or capable of extraordinary mental processes, such as extrasensory perception: *strange psychic abilities.*

psycho— or **psych—** *pref.* A prefix that means the mind or mental processes: *psychoanalysis.*

psy·cho·a·nal·y·sis (sī′kō ə năl′ĭ sĭs) *n., pl.* **psy·cho·a·nal·y·ses** (sī′kō ə năl′ĭ sēz′). [U] A method of psychiatric therapy in which a patient speaks openly to a psychoanalyst about his or her childhood, family relations, behavior, and dreams: *They used psychoanalysis to treat his depression.* —**psy′cho·an′a·lyze** (sī′kō ăn′ə līz′) *v.*

psy·cho·an·a·lyst (sī′kō ăn′ə lĭst) *n.* A person who practices psychoanalysis.

psy·chol·o·gist (sī kŏl′ə jĭst) *n.* A person trained to perform psychological research, testing, and therapy.

psy·chol·o·gy (sī kŏl′ə jē) *n., pl.* **psy·chol·o·gies. 1.** [U] The scientific study of mental processes and behavior. **2.** [C; U] The emotional characteristics and behavior associated with an individual, a group, or an activity: *the psychology of war.* —**psy′cho·log′i·cal** (sī′kə lŏj′ĭ kəl) *adj.* —**psy′cho·log′i·cal·ly** *adv.*

psy·cho·path (sī′kə păth′) *n.* A person who has an antisocial personality disorder, especially one that is aggressive, perverted, or criminal: *The murders were committed by a psychopath.*

psy·cho·sis (sī kō′sĭs) *n., pl.* **psy·cho·ses** (sī kō′sēz). A serious mental disorder in which the mind cannot function normally and the ability to deal with reality is lost.

psy·cho·so·mat·ic (sī′kō sō măt′ĭk) *adj.*

P

Relating to disorders that start in the mind but affect the body: *psychosomatic illness.*

psy·cho·ther·a·py (sī′kō thĕr′ə pē) *n., pl.* **psy·cho·ther·a·pies.** [C; U] The treatment of mental and emotional problems using psychological techniques: *an unusual psychotherapy.*

psy·chot·ic (sī kŏt′ĭk) *adj.* Relating to psychosis. —*n.* A person who is affected by psychosis. —**psy·chot′i·cal·ly** *adv.*

Pt The symbol for the element **platinum.**

pt. *abbr.* An abbreviation of pint.

PTA or **P.T.A.** *abbr.* An abbreviation of Parent-Teachers Association.

Pu The symbol for the element **plutonium.**

pub (pŭb) *n.* A business where alcoholic beverages are sold and drunk: *the local pub.*

pu·ber·ty (pyoo′bər tē) *n.* [U] The stage during which a person first becomes able to produce children, usually between the ages of 12 and 16.

pu·bic (pyoo′bĭk) *adj.* Relating to the area around the sex organs in humans: *pubic hair.*

pub·lic (pŭb′lĭk) *adj.* **1.** Relating to the people or community: *public safety.* **2.** Kept for or used by the people or community; not private: *the public library.* **3.** Open to everybody: *The judge made the testimony public.* —*n.* [U] **1.** The community or people as a whole: *a building open to the public.* **2.** A group of people with a common interest: *the driving public.* ♦ **in public.** In such a way as to be visible to people: *They never speak to each other in public.* **in the public eye.** Often seen in public; famous: *He has been in the public eye since he was a child.* —SEE NOTE at **collective noun.**

pub·lic·ad·dress system (pŭb′lĭk ə drĕs′) *n.* A system that projects sound throughout a given area by using amplifiers.

pub·li·ca·tion (pŭb′lĭ kā′shən) *n.* **1.** [U] The act or process of publishing sthg. in printed or electronic form. **2.** [C] Something published, such as a magazine or newspaper.

public defender *n.* A publicly appointed lawyer who defends those who cannot get legal assistance otherwise.

pub·li·cist (pŭb′lĭ sĭst) *n.* A person who publicizes, especially a press or publicity agent.

pub·lic·i·ty (pŭ blĭs′ĭ tē) *n.* [U] **1.** Information given out, such as to the press, as a way of attracting public attention to a person, a group, or an event: *publicity for the show.* **2.** Public interest created by giving out such information: *The story created a lot of publicity for the actor.*

pub·li·cize (pŭb′lĭ sīz′) *tr.v.* **pub·li·cized, pub·li·ciz·ing, pub·li·ciz·es.** To give publicity to (sbdy./sthg.): *publicize the new movie.*

pub·lic·ly (pŭb′lĭk lē) *adv.* **1.** In a public way; openly: *They met publicly to discuss*

their problems. **2.** By or with the approval of the public: *a publicly owned water system.*

public relations *n.* **1.** [U] *(used with a singular verb).* The art or science of creating a good relationship with the public. **2.** [C] *(used with a plural verb).* The relationship between an organization and the public.

public school *n.* **1.** A local school supported by public money and providing free education for children. **2.** A private boarding school in Great Britain.

public servant *n.* A person who has a government job.

public television *n.* [U] Television that provides programs, especially of an educational nature, for the public, has no commercials, and receives public money to operate.

public utility *n.* A private company that provides an essential service, such as water or electricity, and is regulated by the government.

public works *pl.n.* Construction projects, such as highways or dams, paid for by public money and built by a government for the use of the general public.

pub·lish (pŭb′lĭsh) *tr.v.* **1.** To print and offer (sthg., such as a book) for public distribution or sale: *Her book was published last year.* **2.** To bring (sthg.) to public attention; announce: *Their parents published news of the engagement.*

pub·lish·er (pŭb′lĭ shər) *n.* A person or business that produces and distributes sthg., such as a book or magazine, in printed or electronic form.

puck (pŭk) *n.* A hard rubber disk used in ice hockey.

puck·er (pŭk′ər) *v.* —*tr.* To pull (sthg.) into small wrinkles or folds: *She puckered her lips.* —*intr.* To become gathered or wrinkled: *Her mouth puckered from the lemon.* —*n.* A small wrinkle, as in tightly stitched cloth: *a pucker in the seam of the shirt.*

pud·ding (pood′ĭng) *n.* [C; U] A sweet, soft dessert that has been boiled, steamed, or baked: *bread pudding; rice pudding.*

pud·dle (pŭd′l) *n.* A small pool of liquid: *Children love to step in puddles.*

pudg·y (pŭj′ē) *adj.* **pudg·i·er, pudg·i·est.** Short and stocky; chubby: *a pudgy baby.* —**pudg′i·ness** *n.* [U]

pueb·lo (pwĕb′lō) *n., pl.* **pueb·los.** A village or community of Native Americans in New Mexico and Arizona, typically made up of adobe or stone apartment buildings. —**pueb′lo** *adj.*

puff (pŭf) *n.* **1.** A short forceful discharge or gust, as of air, smoke, or vapor: *a puff of smoke.* **2.** Drawing in and blowing out the breath, as in smoking tobacco: *He took a long puff from the cigarette.* **3.** Something that looks light and fluffy: *little puffs of white clouds.* **4.** A light flaky pastry, often filled with custard or cream: *a cream puff.* —*v.*

—*intr.* **1.** To blow in puffs: *The old car puffed down the road.* **2.** To come forth in puffs: *Smoke puffed from the engine.* **3.** To breathe heavily and rapidly, as from fatigue: *He began to puff from the hard climb.* —*tr.* To send (sthg.) out in puffs: *The train puffed smoke.* ◆ **puff on.** *tr.v.* [insep.] To smoke (sthg.): *He puffed on his pipe.* **puff out.** *tr.v.* [sep.] To make (sthg.) larger by filling with air: *He puffed out his cheeks.* **puff up.** *tr.v.* [sep.] To fill (sbdy.) with pride: *Don't get all puffed up.* —*intr.v.* To swell: *My sprained ankle puffed up.*

puff•y (pŭf′ē) *adj.* **1.** Swollen: *the puffy eyes of a crying child.* **2.** Full and round, as if filled with air: *puffy sleeves.* —**puff′i•ness** *n.* [U]

pug•na•cious (pŭg nā′shəs) *adj. Formal.* Fond of fighting: *a pugnacious nature.* —**pug•na′cious•ly** *adv.* —**pug•na′cious• ness, pug•nac′i•ty** (pŭg năs′ĭ tē) *n.* [U]

puke (pyo͞ok) *Slang. intr. & tr.v.* **puked, puk•ing, pukes.** To vomit: *He felt like he was going to puke. The little girl puked her dinner.* —*n.* [U] Vomit.

pull (po͝ol) *v.* —*tr.* **1.a.** To apply force to (sthg.) to cause motion toward the source of the force: *horses pulling the plow.* **b.** To cause (sthg.) to move toward a point or center, as by using force: *The force of gravity pulls things toward the center of the earth.* **2.** To take (sbdy./sthg.) from a position or place; remove: *pull weeds from the garden; pull a player from the game.* **3.** To move (sthg.): *The driver pulled the car off the road.* **4.** To draw (sthg.) apart; tear or break: *The puppy pulled the towel into bits.* **5.** To injure (a muscle) by stretching or straining it too much. **6.** *Informal.* To attract the notice or attendance of (people): *The movie is pulling large crowds.* **7.** *Slang.* To draw out (a knife or gun): *pull a knife on the woman.* —*intr.* To use force in moving sthg. toward the source of that force: *We can move the desk if you push and I pull.* —*n.* **1.** [C; U] The act or process of pulling: *A hard pull opened the drawer.* **2.** [C] A continued effort: *a long pull to the summit of the mountain.* **3.** [C] Something, such as a knob on a drawer, that is used for pulling. **4.** [C] A deep drink of sthg. or a deep intake of breath, as on a cigarette. **5.** [U] *Slang.* Special influence: *He has a lot of pull in his hometown.* ◆ **pull away.** *intr.v.* **1.** To move away or backward; withdraw: *I pulled away from the edge of the cliff.* **2.** To move ahead: *Our candidate managed to pull away in the days before the election.* **pull for.** *tr.v.* [insep.] To express or feel sympathy or support for (sbdy.): *We're pulling for the mayor in the fall election.* **pull in.** *tr.v.*

[sep.] *Informal.* To earn (money): *He pulls in $200 a night working as a waiter.* —*intr.v.* To arrive: *The train pulled in at noon.* **pull off.** *tr.v.* [sep.] *Informal.* To perform (sthg.) in spite of difficulties or obstacles: *The team pulled off an upset victory.* **pull (oneself) together.** To get back one's calm and self-control: *pulled himself together after the shock.* **pull (one's) leg.** To tease or play a joke on sbdy.: *Relax, he's only pulling your leg.* **pull (one's) weight.** To do one's share, as of work: *They'll both be fired if they don't start pulling their weight.* **pull out.** *intr.v.* **1.** To leave: *We'll pull out early in the morning.* **2.** To withdraw, as from a situation or commitment: *Many investors pulled out.* **pull over.** *intr.v.* To stop one's vehicle at the side of the road: *I pulled over to look at the view.* —*tr.v.* [sep.] To bring (sbdy./sthg.) to a stop at the side of a road: *The police pulled her over for speeding.* **pull through.** *intr.v.* To come successfully through trouble or illness: *The doctor says my mother will pull through.* **pull together.** *intr.v.* To make a joint effort: *We'll meet the deadline if we all pull together.* —*tr.v.* [sep.] To collect (sthg.): *The teacher pulled the materials together for the class.*

SYNONYMS: pull, drag, draw, tow, tug. These verbs all mean to apply force to sthg., causing it to move toward that force. *The children pulled their sled up the hill. I had to drag my dog away from the cat in the tree. The weary traveler drew his chair closer to the fire. The car was towing a large trailer. I tugged my desk to the other side of the room.* **ANTONYM: push.**

---

pul•ley (po͝ol′ē) *n., pl.* **pul•leys.** A simple machine with a grooved wheel for a rope or chain, used for lifting heavy objects.

pull•o•ver (po͝ol′ō′vər) *n.* A sweater without buttons that is put on by being pulled over the head: *She prefers pullovers.*

pul•mo•nar•y (po͝ol′mə nĕr′ē *or* pŭl′mə-nĕr′ē) *adj.* Relating to

pulley
Simple fixed pulley

or affecting the lungs: *a pulmonary infection.*

pulp (pŭlp) *n.* **1.** [C; U] A soft mass of material: *paper pulp; beat to a pulp.* **2.** [U] The soft fleshy part of fruit or of certain vegetables: *orange pulp.* **3.** [U] A magazine containing sensational, often sexual, subject matter: *pulp fiction.* —**pulp′y** *adj.*

pul•pit (po͝ol′pĭt *or* pŭl′pĭt) *n.* A raised plat-

---

form or stand used in preaching or conducting a religious service.

pul•sar (pŭl′sär′) *n.* A celestial object that emits radio waves.

pul•sate (pŭl′sāt′) *intr.v.* **pul•sat•ed, pul•sat•ing, pul•sates.** To beat or vibrate rhythmically, as the heart does: *The music pulsated.* —**pul•sa′tion** *n.* [C; U]

pulse (pŭls) *n.* **1.** The rhythmic beat of the arteries: *The nurse checked the patient's pulse.* **2.** A regular or rhythmic beating: *the pulse of drums.* **3.** A short sudden change in a normally constant quantity: *a series of electrical pulses.* —*intr.v.* **pulsed, puls•ing, puls•es.** To pulsate; beat: *His heart pulsed wildly.*

pul•ver•ize (pŭl′və rīz′) *tr.v.* **pul•ver•ized, pul•ver•iz•ing, pul•ver•iz•es.** **1.** To grind (sthg.) into powder or dust: *pulverized the marble.* **2.** *Informal.* To defeat (sbdy.) completely in a game or sport: *The boxer pulverized his opponent.* —**pul′ver•i•za′tion** (pŭl′vər ĭ zā′shən) *n.* [U]

pu•ma (pyōō′mə *or* pōō′mə) *n.* A mountain lion; cougar.

pum•ice (pŭm′ĭs) *n.* [U] A porous lightweight volcanic rock used for cleaning and polishing.

pum•mel (pŭm′əl) *tr.v.* To beat or pound (sbdy./sthg.), as with the fists: *They pummeled each other.*

pump[1] (pŭmp) *n.* A machine for raising, compressing, or moving liquids or gases. —*tr.v.* **1.** To raise or cause (a liquid or gas) to flow by means of a pump: *She pumped the gas into her car.* **2.** To empty (sthg.) of liquid or gas by means of a pump: *They pumped the flooded cellar.* **3.** To cause (sthg.) to move up and down like a pump handle: *a bicyclist pumping the pedals.* **4.** To propel (sthg.) as if with a pump: *The police pumped bullets into a target.* ◆ **pump for information.** To question (sbdy.) closely: *We pumped him for information.* **pump up.** *tr.v.* [sep.] **1.** To inflate (sthg.) with gas using a pump: *I pumped my bicycle tires up.* **2.** To cause enthusiasm in (sbdy.): *The coach pumped up the team.*

pump[2] (pŭmp) *n.* A woman's shoe, usually with a heel and without laces, straps, or other fasteners.

pump[2]

pum•per•nick•el (pŭm′pər nĭk′əl) *n.* [U] A dark rye bread.

pump•kin (pŭmp′kĭn *or* pŭm′kĭn) *n.* [C; U] A large round fruit with a thick orange skin and pulp or the vine that produces it: *We always make pumpkin pie for Thanksgiving dessert.*

pumpkin

pun (pŭn) *n.* A humorous use of a word that has different meanings or of two words that sound the same. —*intr.v.* **punned, pun•ning, puns.** To make a pun.

punch[1] (pŭnch) *n.* A tool for making holes in sthg.: *a leather punch.* —*tr.v.* To use a punch on (sthg.): *punched a hole in the can.*

punch[2] (pŭnch) *tr.v.* To hit (sbdy./sthg.) with the fist: *punched me in the eye; punch down the bread dough.* —*n.* **1.** [C] A blow with the fist: *a punch in the nose.* **2.** [U] Energy; drive: *They were full of punch.* —**punch′er** *n.*

punch[3] (pŭnch) *n.* [C; U] A beverage of fruit juices and sometimes soda, sometimes mixed with wine or liquor.

punch line *n.* The ending of a joke or humorous story.

punch•y (pŭn′chē) *adj.* **punch•i•er, punch•i•est.** Dazed as if from a punch: *The boxer was punchy.*

punc•tu•al (pŭngk′chōō əl) *adj.* Acting or arriving exactly on time; prompt: *Her friend is always punctual.* —**punc′tu•al′i•ty** (pŭngk′chōō ăl′ĭ tē) *n.* [U] —**punc′tu•al•ly** *adv.*

punc•tu•ate (pŭngk′chōō āt′) *tr.v.* **punc•tu•at•ed, punc•tu•at•ing, punc•tu•ates.** **1.** To add punctuation to (written material): *punctuate the sentence.* **2.** To interrupt (sthg.) periodically: *The evening silence was punctuated by the sound of motorcycles.*

punc•tu•a•tion (pŭngk′chōō ā′shən) *n.* [U] The use of standard marks in writing to separate sentences and parts of sentences in order to make the meaning clear: *Check your punctuation before you hand in your paper.*

punctuation mark *n.* One of the marks or signs, such as the comma (,) or the period (.), used to punctuate written material.

punc•ture (pŭngk′chər) *v.* **punc•tured, punc•tur•ing, punc•tures.** —*tr.* **1.** To pierce (sthg.) with a pointed object: *I punctured the tomato with my fork.* **2.** To cause (sthg.) to collapse as if by piercing with sthg. sharp: *The setback punctured my ego.* —*intr.* To be pierced or punctured. —*n.* A hole made by sthg. sharp, especially a hole in an automobile tire: *This tire puncture can't be fixed.*

pun•dit (pŭn′dĭt) *n.* A very knowledgeable person, especially an expert or authority: *political pundits.*

pun•gent (pŭn′jənt) *adj.* **1.** Sharp to the taste or smell: *a pungent sauce; pungent smoke.* **2.** Hurtful, biting: *pungent remarks.* —**pun′gen•cy** *n.* [U] —**pun′gent•ly** *adv.*

pun•ish (pŭn′ĭsh) *tr.v.* **1.** To give (sbdy.) a penalty for doing sthg. wrong: *Society punishes criminals. She punished the naughty child.* **2.** To treat (sbdy./sthg.) roughly or harshly: *Heavy surf punished the small boat.* —**pun′ish•er** *n.*

pun•ish•a•ble (pŭn′ĭ shə bəl) *adj.* Liable to punishment: *a crime punishable by imprisonment.*

P

pun·ish·ment (pŭn′ĭsh mənt) *n.* **1.** [U] An act of punishing: *the punishment of wrongdoers.* **2.** [C] A penalty for a crime or wrongdoing: *What punishment was given for the crime?* **3.** [U] Rough or harsh treatment: *These shoes have taken a lot of punishment.*

pu·ni·tive (pyoo′nĭ tĭv) *adj.* Inflicting punishment: *a punitive decision.*

punk (pŭngk) *n. Slang.* An insulting term for a young person, especially a member of a rebellious group.

pun·ster (pŭn′stər) *n.* A person who makes puns.

punt (pŭnt) *n.* A kick in which a ball or other object is dropped and then kicked before it touches the ground. —*v.* —*tr.* To kick (a ball) by means of a punt: *The ball was punted 30 yards.* —*intr.* To execute a punt: *The team had to punt.* —**punt′er** *n.*

pu·ny (pyoo′nē) *adj.* **pu·ni·er, pu·ni·est.** *Informal.* Small or inferior in size or strength; weak: *a puny tomato.*

pup (pŭp) *n.* **1.** A young dog; a puppy. **2.** The young of certain other animals, such as the seal.

pu·pil[1] (pyoo′pəl) *n.* A student who learns sthg. from a teacher.

pu·pil[2] (pyoo′pəl) *n.* The dark opening in the center of the iris through which light enters the eye: *His pupils were dilated.*

pup·pet (pŭp′ĭt) *n.* **1.** A small doll or figure of a person or an animal, moved with the hand or strings: *The child received a hand puppet for her birthday.* **2.** A person whose behavior is controlled by the will of others: *The leader is a puppet ruled by the military.*

pup·pet·eer (pŭp′ĭ tîr′) *n.* A person who operates puppets.

pup·pet·ry (pŭp′ĭ trē) *n.* [U] The art of making and operating puppets.

pup·py (pŭp′ē) *n., pl.* **pup·pies.** A young dog: *Our dog had seven puppies.*

pur·chase (pûr′chĭs) *tr.v.* **pur·chased, pur·chas·ing, pur·chas·es.** To get (sthg.) in exchange for money; buy: *She purchased a new home.* —*n.* **1.** [C] Something that is bought: *The car was a wise purchase.* **2.** [C; U] The act of buying: *the purchase of land.* —**pur′chas·a·ble** *adj.* —**pur′chas·er** *n.*

pure (pyoor) *adj.* **pur·er, pur·est. 1.** With a uniform composition; not mixed: *pure oxygen.* **2.** Complete; total: *pure happiness.* **3.** Without evil; sinless: *a pure heart.* **4.** Of unmixed blood or ancestry: *a pure Siamese cat.* **5.** Not concerned with practical application; theoretical: *pure mathematics.*

pure·ly (pyoor′lē) *adv.* Completely and only: *They met purely by chance.*

pure·bred (pyoor′brĕd′) *adj.* With many generations of ancestors of the same breed or

kind: *a purebred dog.* —*n.* (pyoor′brĕd′). A purebred animal.

pu·rée (pyoo rā′ *or* pyoor′ā) *tr.v.* **pu·réed, pu·rée·ing, pu·rées.** To process (food) so that it becomes a soft pulp: *puréed some bananas for the baby.* —*n.* Food prepared in this way: *fruit purée.*

purge (pûrj) *v.* **purged, purg·ing, purg·es.** —*tr.* **1.** To cause (the bowels) to empty. **2.** To rid (sthg.) of sin or guilt: *purge one's soul.* **3.** To rid (a nation or a political party, for example) of persons considered undesirable. —*intr.* **1.** To become clean or pure. **2.** To cause or undergo an emptying of the bowels. —*n.* **1.** The act or process of purging: *a purge of workers involved in the scandal.* **2.** Something that purges.

pu·ri·fi·ca·tion (pyoor′ə fĭ kā′shən) *n.* [U] The act of cleansing or purifying: *ritual purification before burial.*

pu·ri·fy (pyoor′ə fī′) *tr.v.* **pu·ri·fied, pu·ri·fy·ing, pu·ri·fies. 1.** To rid (sthg.) of impurities; cleanse: *purify water.* **2.** To free (sbdy./sthg.) from sin or guilt: *purify the soul.* —**pu′ri·fi′er** *n.*

pur·ist (pyoor′ĭst) *n.* A person who practices or is in favor of strict or traditional correctness: *a purist about clothing who wears only cotton.*

Pu·ri·tan (pyoor′ĭ tn) *n.* **1.** A member of a Protestant group in England and New England in the 16th and 17th centuries that followed a strict moral code. **2. puritan.** A person considered excessively strict in morals: *She's a puritan who doesn't allow smoking or drinking at home.* —**pu·ri·tan′i·cal** (pyoor′ĭ tăn′ĭ kəl) *adj.*

pu·ri·ty (pyoor′ĭ tē) *n.* [U] **1.** The quality or condition of being pure: *the purity of mountain air.* **2.** Freedom from sin or guilt; chastity: *a life of great purity.*

pur·ple (pûr′pəl) *n.* [C; U] A color between blue and red. —*adj.* **1.** Of the color purple. **2.** Elaborate and ornate: *purple prose.*

pur·port (pər pôrt′) *tr.v. Formal.* To give the often false appearance of being (sthg.): *He purported to be related to the royal family.* —*n.* (pûr′pôrt′). [U] General meaning; significance: *the purport of a letter.* —**pur·port′ed·ly** (pər pôr′tĭd lē) *adv.*

pur·pose (pûr′pəs) *n.* **1.** [C] The intended or desired result; a goal: *The club's purpose is to promote sailing.* **2.** [U] Determination; resolve: *a woman of purpose.* ♦ **on purpose.** Intentionally; deliberately: *You did it on purpose.*

pur·pose·ful (pûr′pəs fəl) *adj.* With a purpose; intentional: *Her walk was strong and purposeful.* —**pur′pose·ful·ly** *adv.*

pur·pose·less (pûr′pəs lĭs) *adj.* Without

a purpose; meaningless: *purposeless talk.*
—**pur′pose·less·ly** *adv.*

pur·pose·ly (pûr′pəs lē) *adv.* With a specific purpose; deliberately: *He purposely hit my car!*

purr (pûr) *n.* A soft vibrant sound like that made by a cat: *the purr of the car's engine.* —*v.* —*intr.* To make a purr. —*tr.* To express (sthg.) by a purr: *The cat purred its contentment.*

purse (pûrs) *n.* **1.** A woman's bag for carrying personal items; a handbag: *a leather purse.* **2.** An amount of money given as a prize: *a race with a purse of $50,000.* —*tr.v.* **pursed, purs·ing, purs·es.** To pull (the lips or brow) into wrinkles or folds; pucker: *purse one's brow in thought.*

pur·sue (pər sōō′) *tr.v.* **pur·sued, pur·su·ing, pur·sues.** **1.** To follow (sbdy./sthg.) in order to catch up with or capture; chase: *The dogs pursued the fox.* **2.** To try to gain or accomplish (sthg.): *pursue a college degree.* **3.** To carry (sthg.) further: *Do you want to pursue this discussion?*

pur·suit (pər sōōt′) *n.* **1.** [U] The act of pursuing or chasing: *The pursuit lasted for two hours.* **2.** [C] (*usually plural*). An activity, such as a profession or hobby, engaged in regularly: *outdoor pursuits.*

pus (pŭs) *n.* [U] A thick yellowish white liquid that forms in infected places in the body.

push (pŏosh) *v.* —*tr.* **1.** To press against (sbdy./sthg.) to cause movement: *He pushed the rock, but it wouldn't move.* **2.** To pressure (sbdy./sthg.) for or to do sthg.: *They pushed him for an answer. They pushed her to try out for the basketball team.* **3.** To extend (sthg.): *Pioneers pushed their farms westward.* **4.** To press (sthg.) with one's finger: *push a button.* **5.** *Slang.* To promote or try to sell (sthg.): *push a new brand of toothpaste.* —*intr.* **1.** To use pressure or force against sthg.: *Let's all push to get the door open.* **2.** To advance despite difficulty or opposition: *We pushed ahead.* **3.** To use great effort: *She pushed to finish the report on time.* —*n.* **1.** [C] The act of pushing; a shove: *His car needed a push to get started.* **2.** [C] A vigorous effort: *a real push to finish the project.* **3.** [U] *Informal.* Energy; enterprise: *the push to be a great leader.* ◆ **push around.** *tr.v.* [sep.] *Informal.* To threaten to treat (sbdy.) roughly; intimidate: *The bully pushed a smaller child around.* **push off.** *intr.v.* **1.** To launch: *We pushed off from the dock.* **2.** *Informal.* To go away: *Push off! I don't want to talk to you now.* **push on.** *intr.v.* To continue despite difficulties: *Even though it was snowing, we pushed on toward home.* —*tr.v.* [sep.] To urge (sbdy.) forward: *We pushed them on.* **push (one's) luck.** To try sthg. risky, trusting to continued good luck: *She missed four days of work without penalty, but she'd better not push her luck again.*

push·er (pŏosh′ər) *n. Slang.* A person who sells drugs illegally.

push·o·ver (pŏosh′ō′vər) *n.* **1.** A person or group that is easy to defeat or take advantage of: *The team we played last week was a pushover.* **2.** Something that is easy to do: *an exam that was a pushover.*

push·up (pŏosh′ŭp′) *n.* An exercise performed by lying face down and pushing the body up and down with the arms: *She does 40 pushups every day.*

push·y (pŏosh′ē) *adj.* **push·i·er, push·i·est.** Too aggressive or forward: *a pushy salesman.*

puss[1] (pŏos) *n. Informal.* A cat.

puss[2] (pŏos) *n. Slang.* **1.** The mouth. **2.** The face: *a sour puss.*

puss·y (pŏos′ē) *n., pl.* **puss·ies.** *Informal.* A cat.

puss·y·foot (pŏos′ē fŏot′) *intr.v. Informal.* [*around*] To act cautiously or timidly: *Do what's necessary and stop pussyfooting around!* —**puss′y·foot′er** *n.*

put (pŏot) *tr.v.* **put, put·ting, puts. 1.** To place or set (sbdy./sthg.), as in a specified location: *Where did I put my umbrella? She put the baby to bed.* **2.** To cause (sbdy.) to be in a given condition: *Her friendly manner put me at ease.* **3.** To introduce (sthg.) for consideration: *I put a question to the teacher.* **4.** To express (sthg.); state: *I put my opinions honestly.* **5.** To apply (sthg.): *We'll do all right if we put our minds to it.* —*adj. Informal.* Without moving anywhere; stationary: *Just stay put for a minute.* ◆ **put across.** *tr.v.* [sep.] To state (sthg.) so as to be understood clearly or accepted readily: *I put across my ideas to the committee.* **put away.** *tr.v.* [sep.] **1.** To put (sthg.) back in the usual place: *I washed the dishes, dried them, and put them away.* **2.** *Informal.* To eat or drink (sthg.) quickly, often a large amount: *The boys put away the pizza in minutes.* **3.** *Informal.* To place (sbdy.) in prison or in an institution for the mentally ill: *put a criminal away for life.* **put by.** *tr.v.* [sep.] To save (sthg.) for later use: *We put by four quarts of stewed tomatoes.* **put down.** *tr.v.* [sep.] **1.** To write (sthg.) down: *Put your name down on the list.* **2.** To bring (sthg.) to an end: *put down a rebellion.* **3.** *Slang.* **a.** To speak about (sbdy./sthg.) as having no value or importance: *Don't put down your little sister.* **b.** To assign (sthg.) to a category: *We put his bad mood down to a lack of sleep.* **4.** To kill (an animal) in a painless way: *The injured horse had to be put down.* **put in.** *tr.v.* [sep.] To spend (time) at a location or job: *She put in four years with the armed services.* **put in for.** To submit (a request): *I put in for a transfer to Chicago.* **put off.** *tr.v.* [sep.] **1.** To delay (sthg.); postpone: *I put off taking the test until next week.* **2.** To cause disgust or distaste in (sbdy.), as from bad manners: *His harsh tone put me off.* **put on.** *tr.v.* [sep.] **1.** To dress oneself with (clothing): *We put on evening clothes for dinner.* **2.** *Slang.* To tease or mislead (sbdy.): *You're putting me on!* **3.** To add (sthg.): *put on weight.* **4.** To produce (sthg.); perform: *put on a play.* **put out.** *tr.v.* [sep.] **1.** To stop (sthg.) from burning or glowing: *The firefighters put the flames out. Please put out the lights when you leave.* **2.** To inconvenience or offend (sbdy.): *I hope we're not putting you out by arriving so late at night.* **put up to.** To cause (sbdy.) to commit a funny, mischievous, or harmful act: *I put her up to playing the practical joke.* **put over on.** To trick or fool (sbdy.): *Don't try to put anything over on her, because she'll surely catch you.* **put up.** *tr.v.* [sep.] **1.** To build (sthg.): *put up a skyscraper.* **2.** To provide (funds) in advance: *They put up money for the new show.* **3.** To provide lodgings for (a visitor): *The company put me up for the night in a good hotel.* **put up with.** To endure (sbdy./sthg.) without complaint: *How can you put up with all that noise?*

put·down or **put-down** (pŏŏt′doun′) *n. Slang.* A criticism or an insult: *She interpreted his remarks as a putdown.*

put-on (pŏŏt′ŏn′ *or* pŏŏt′ôn′) *adj.* Pretended; false: *a put-on air of friendliness.* —*n. Slang.* Something intended to deceive, often as a joke: *Her story was only a put-on.*

pu·tre·fy (pyŏŏ′trə fī′) *intr. & tr.v.* **pu·tre·fied, pu·tre·fy·ing, pu·tre·fies.** *Formal.* To become or cause to become decayed and have a foul odor: *The meat had putrefied. The fish was putrefied.* —**pu′-tre·fac′tion** (pyŏŏ′trə făk′shən) *n.* [U]

pu·trid (pyŏŏ′trĭd) *adj.* Decomposed and with a foul smell; rotten: *a putrid smell.*

putt (pŭt) *n.* A gentle golf stroke made to get the ball into the hole. —*v.* —*tr.* To hit (a golf ball) with such a stroke on the green. —*intr.* To putt a golf ball: *Is it my turn to putt?*

putt·er[1] (pŭt′ər) *n.* **1.** A short golf club used for putting. **2.** A golfer who is putting: *a good putter.*

put·ter[2] (pŭt′ər) *v.* ♦ **putter around.** *intr.v.* To do sthg. in an aimless or ineffective manner: *puttering around in the garden.* —**put′ter·er** *n.*

put·ty (pŭt′ē) *n.* [U] A soft cement used to fill holes in woodwork and secure panes of glass: *Put some putty in the hole.* —*tr.v.* **put·tied, put·ty·ing, put·ties.** To fill, cover, or fasten (sthg.) with putty: *puttied the new windowpane.*

puz·zle (pŭz′əl) *tr.v.* **puz·zled, puz·zling, puz·zles.** To confuse (sbdy.) by pre-

senting a difficult problem or matter: *Your explanation puzzles me.* —*n.* **1.** Something that confuses; a problem: *It's a puzzle to me how she can finish her homework so quickly.* **2.** A toy or game that presents a confusing problem or task: *a jigsaw puzzle.* ♦ **puzzle out.** *tr.v.* [sep.] To come to understand (sthg. confusing) by thought or study: *She puzzled out the algebra problem.* **puzzle over.** *tr.v.* [insep.] To think about (a problem): *Let me puzzle over that for a while.* —**puz′zler** *n.*

puz·zled (pŭz′əld) *adj.* Confused: *You look puzzled.*

puz·zling (pŭz′lĭng) *adj.* Confusing: *a puzzling explanation.*

puz·zle·ment (pŭz′əl mənt) *n.* [U] The state of being confused or baffled: *He expressed his puzzlement with a shrug of his shoulders.*

PVT or **Pvt** or **pvt.** *abbr.* An abbreviation of private.

pyg·my (pĭg′mē) *n., pl.* **pyg·mies. 1.** also **Pygmy.** An African or Asian people with an average height of less than five feet. **2.** An individual of unusually small size. —*adj.* Much smaller than the usual or typical kind: *a pygmy hippopotamus.*

py·ja·mas (pə jä′məz *or* pə jăm′əz) *pl.n. Chiefly British.* Variant of **pajamas.**

pyr·a·mid (pĭr′ə mĭd) *n.* **1.** A solid geometric shape with a polygon as its base and triangular faces that meet at a common vertex. **2.** A massive monument found especially in Egypt, built in this shape and serving as a tomb or temple.

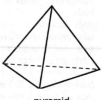
pyramid

py·ram·i·dal (pĭ răm′ĭ dl) *adj.* With the shape of a pyramid.

pyre (pīr) *n.* A pile of wood for burning a dead body as part of a funeral ceremony: *a funeral pyre.*

py·ro·ma·ni·a (pī′rō mā′nē ə) *n.* [U] An uncontrollable impulse to start fires. —**py′-ro·ma′ni·ac′** (pī′rō mā′nē ăk′) *adj. & n.*

py·ro·tech·nic (pī′rə tĕk′nĭk) *adj.* Relating to fireworks: *a pyrotechnic display for the Fourth of July.*

py·ro·tech·nics (pī′rə tĕk′nĭks) *n.* [U] *(used with a singular verb).* The art of manufacturing or setting off fireworks.

py·thon (pī′thŏn′) *n.* A very large nonpoisonous snake of Africa, Asia, and Australia that squeezes and suffocates its prey.

q or **Q** (kyōō) *n.*, *pl.* **q's** or **Q's.** The 17th letter of the English alphabet.

q. *abbr.* An abbreviation of quart.

qt or **qt.** *abbr.* An abbreviation of quart.

quack¹ (kwăk) *n.* The sound made by a duck. —*intr.v.* To make such a sound: *ducks quacking on the pond.*

quack² (kwăk) *n.* An untrained person who pretends to be a doctor and treats people. —*adj.* Characteristic of a quack: *a quack cure.*

quack·er·y (kwăk′ə rē) *n.* [U] The practice of a quack: *The man was accused of quackery.*

quad (kwŏd) *n.* **1.** A quadrangle. **2.** An apartment or suite for four people, as in a dormitory.

quad·ran·gle (kwŏd′răng′gəl) *n.* **1.** A flat geometric shape with four corners and four straight sides. **2.** A rectangular area bordered on all sides by buildings: *college dormitories forming a quadrangle.*

quad·rant (kwŏd′rənt) *n.* **1.a.** An arc of 90°. **b.** A quarter of a circle. **c.** Any of four regions into which a plane is divided by the axes of a coordinate system. **2.** An instrument with an arc of 90°, used to measure angles, as between the horizon and a star, for example.

quad·rat·ic equation (kwŏ drăt′ĭk) *n.* An equation of the general form $ax^2 + bx + c = 0$, where x is the independent variable and a, b, and c are constants.

quadri– or **quadru–** or **quadr–** *pref.* A prefix that means four: *quadrangle.*

quad·ri·ceps (kwŏd′rĭ sĕps′) *n.*, *pl.* **quad·ri·ceps.** The large four-part muscle at the front of the thigh.

quad·ri·lat·er·al (kwŏd′rə lăt′ər əl) *n.* A flat geometric shape with four sides. —*adj.* Having four sides: *Quadrilateral figures include squares and parallelograms.*

quad·ru·ped (kwŏd′rə pĕd′) *n.* A four-footed animal: *Dogs, cats, and horses are all quadrupeds.*

quad·ru·ple (kwŏ drōō′pəl or kwŏ drŭp′əl) *adj.* Multiplied by four: *quadruple population growth.* —*n.* *(usually singular).* A number or an amount four times as great as another: *He charges quadruple for transporting dangerous materials.* —*tr. & intr.v.* **quad·ru·pled, quad·ru·pling, quad·ru·ples.** To make or become four times as great: *We quadrupled enrollment by offering the course at night. The population of the town quadrupled.*

quad·ru·plet (kwŏ drŭp′lĭt or kwŏ drōō′plĭt) *n.* One of four children born in a single birth.

quag·mire (kwăg′mīr′ or kwŏg′mīr′) *n.* **1.** Land with a soft muddy surface. **2.** A difficult situation: *foreign involvement that became a quagmire for the government.*

quail (kwāl) *n.*, *pl.* **quail.** A small, plump, short-tailed bird with brownish feathers.

quaint (kwānt) *adj.* Pleasantly strange, especially in an old-fashioned way: *a quaint village.* —**quaint′ly** *adv.* —**quaint′ness** *n.* [U]

quake (kwāk) *intr.v.* **quaked, quak·ing, quakes.** **1.** To shake or vibrate: *The ground quaked as the elephants passed.* **2.** To shiver or tremble from fear or cold: *His legs quaked with fear.* —*n.* **1.** An instance of shaking or quivering: *a quake in one's voice.* **2.** An earthquake: *The quake lasted less than a minute.*

Quak·er (kwā′kər) *n.* A member of the Society of Friends, a Christian group that opposes war and rituals. —**Quak′er·ism** *n.* [U]

qual·i·fi·ca·tion (kwŏl′ə fĭ kā′shən) *n.* **1.** [U] The act of qualifying: *Her qualification as a surgeon took years of hard work.* **2.** [C] *(usually plural).* A skill or other quality that makes a person able for a particular job or task: *the qualifications for an airline pilot.* **3.** [C; U] A limit or change: *The group accepted the proposal without qualification.*

qual·i·fied (kwŏl′ə fīd′) *adj.* **1.** With the proper training and preparation, as for a job: *a fully qualified doctor.* **2.** Limited: *an attitude of qualified optimism.*

qual·i·fy (kwŏl′ə fī′) *v.* **qual·i·fied, qual·i·fy·ing, qual·i·fies.** —*tr.* **1.** To be evidence that (sbdy.) is eligible or qualified, as for a position or task: *Her grades qualify her for the Honor Society.* **2.** To make (sthg.) less harsh or extreme: *He qualified his remarks to avoid offending anyone.* **3.** To limit the meaning of (a word); modify: *Adjectives qualify nouns.* —*intr.* To be or become qualified: *She qualified for the final of the 400-meter run.* —**qual′i·fi′er** *n.*

qual·i·ta·tive (kwŏl′ĭ tā′tĭv) *adj.* Relating to quality, especially as distinguished from quantity or amount: *Each package holds the same number of items, so the only difference is qualitative.* —**qual′i·ta′tive·ly** *adv.*

qual·i·ty (kwŏl′ĭ tē) *n.*, *pl.* **qual·i·ties.** **1.** [C] A characteristic or property that sets sthg. apart from other things: *the sour quality of vinegar.* **2.** [C] A personal trait, especially a feature typical of one's character: *He has many good qualities.* **3.** [U] Excellence; superiority: *a store that sells only clothes of*

Q

quality. **4.** [U] Degree or grade of excellence: *meat of poor quality.*

SYNONYMS: quality, characteristic, property, attribute, trait. These nouns mean a feature that distinguishes or identifies a person or thing. **Quality** and **characteristic** are the most general: *The voice had a soft, musical quality. Name a common characteristic of mammals.* **Property** means a basic or essential quality possessed by all members of a group: *This experiment will illustrate some of the properties of crystals.* **Attribute** often means a quality that a person or thing is given credit for having: *What are the attributes of a good leader?* **Trait** means a single, clearly defined characteristic: *His jealous streak is a disturbing trait.*

---

quality control *n.* [C; U] A system used by a manufacturer to make sure that goods produced meet certain standards: *Our company does random testing of our products for quality control.*

qualm (kwäm *or* kwôm) *n.* **1.** A sudden disturbing feeling: *The child had qualms of homesickness.* **2.** A doubt or an uneasy feeling about the rightness of sthg.: *I have no qualms about trusting my friends.*

quan·da·ry (kwŏn′də rē *or* kwŏn′drē) *n.,* *pl.* **quan·da·ries.** A condition of uncertainty or doubt; a dilemma: *We were in a quandary over what to do next.*

quan·ti·fy (kwŏn′tə fī′) *tr.v.* **quan·ti·fied, quan·ti·fy·ing, quan·ti·fies.** To determine or describe the amount of (sthg.): *His value to his team is impossible to quantify.*

quan·ti·ta·tive (kwŏn′tĭ tā′tĭv) *adj.* Relating to quantity or number: *experiments that give quantitative proof of a theory.* **—quan′-ti·ta′tive·ly** *adv.*

quan·ti·ty (kwŏn′tĭ tē) *n.,* *pl.* **quan·ti·ties. 1.** [C] An amount or a number: *The elements are found in nature in various quantities.* **2.** [C; U] A large amount or number: *Pennsylvania was the first state to produce oil in quantity.*

quan·tum (kwŏn′təm) *n.,* *pl.* **quan·ta** (kwŏn′tə). A unit of energy, such as a photon, which cannot be divided into smaller parts.

quantum leap *n.* A sudden great change, especially in method or knowledge: *This discovery means a quantum leap in scientific understanding of the universe.*

quar·an·tine (kwôr′ən tēn′ *or* kwŏr′-ən tēn′) *n.* [C; U] An enforced confinement or isolation, especially one intended to keep a contagious disease from spreading: *a patient in quarantine.* *—tr.v.* **quar·an·tined, quar·an·tin·ing, quar·an·tines.** To keep

(sbdy./sthg.) confined or isolated, especially as a way to keep a disease from spreading: *The worker who was exposed to the virus has been quarantined.*

quark (kwôrk *or* kwärk) *n.* Any of a group of subatomic particles that have been proposed as fundamental units of matter.

quar·rel (kwôr′əl *or* kwŏr′əl) *n.* **1.** [C] An angry argument: *a noisy quarrel with his brother.* **2.** [U] A reason for argument or dispute: *I have no quarrel with what you say.* *—intr.v.* **1.** To engage in a quarrel; argue angrily: *The boys quarreled over the use of the tennis court.* **2.** To disagree or find fault: *quarrel with a court decision.*

quar·rel·some (kwôr′əl səm *or* kwŏr′əl-səm) *adj.* Tending to quarrel: *a quarrelsome family.*

quar·ry¹ (kwôr′ē *or* kwŏr′ē) *n.* [U] An animal hunted or chased: *The hunter's dogs led him to his quarry.*

quar·ry² (kwôr′ē *or* kwŏr′ē) *n., pl.* **quar·ries.** An open place in the ground from which stone is taken by digging, cutting, or blasting: *a limestone quarry.* *—tr.v.* **quar·ried, quar·ry·ing, quar·ries.** To take (stone) from a quarry.

quart (kwôrt) *n.* **1.** A liquid measure equal to two pints or 57.75 cubic inches. See table at **measurement. 2.** The amount of a substance that can be held in a quart-sized container: *a quart of juice.*

quar·ter (kwôr′tər) *n.* **1.** One of four equal parts: *I cut an orange into four quarters.* **2.** A U.S. or Canadian coin worth twenty-five cents. **3.** A period of fifteen minutes; one fourth of an hour: *It's a quarter to five.* **4.a.** A period of three months; one fourth of a year: *Sales picked up in the last quarter.* **b.** A school or college term lasting about three months: *a university on the quarter system.* **5.** One fourth of the period of the moon's revolution about Earth. **6.** In some sports, one of the four equal time periods in a game. **7.** A region or place: *People came from every quarter.* **8.** Often **Quarter.** A district or section, as of a city: *the French Quarter.* **9.** *(usually plural).* A living area: *She found quarters in a lovely part of town.* *—adj.* **1.** Being one of four equal parts: *Each daughter received a quarter share of the inheritance.* **2.** Being equal to one fourth of a particular unit of measure: *a quarter cup of flour.* *—tr.v.* **1.** To divide (sthg.) into four equal parts: *Peel and quarter the apples.* **2.** To supply (sbdy.) with housing: *The general quartered the troops in the town.*

quar·ter·back (kwôr′tər băk′) *n.* In football, the player who usually calls the signals to direct the plays.

ă–cat; ā–pay; âr–care; ä–father; ĕ–get; ē–be; ĭ–sit; ī–nice; îr–here; ŏ–got; ō–go; ô–saw; oi–boy; ou–out; ŏŏ–took; ōō–boot; ŭ–cut; ûr–word; th–thin; *th*–this; hw–when; zh–vision; ə–about; N–French bon

quar·ter·ly (kwôr′tər lē) *adj.* Happening or appearing every three months: *a quarterly magazine; a quarterly payment.* —*n., pl.* **quar·ter·lies.** A magazine published every three months. —*adv.* In or by quarter periods: *Shareholders receive dividends quarterly.*

quar·tet (kwôr tĕt′) *n.* **1.** A group of four musicians who sing or perform musical compositions together: *a string quartet.* **2.** A group of four people or things.

quartz (kwôrts) *n.* [U] A hard transparent mineral composed of silicon dioxide; the most common of all minerals. It occurs in rocks such as sandstone and granite, and in forms such as rock crystal, flint, and agate.

quartz

qua·sar (kwā′zär′ or kwā′sär′) *n.* An extremely large, radiant, and distant star-like body that gives off radio waves.

quash (kwŏsh) *tr.v.* To put down or suppress (sthg.) by force: *quash a rebellion.*

qua·si (kwā′zī′ or kwā′zē′) *adj.* Like but not being: *Astrology is a quasi science.*

qua·ver (kwā′vər) *intr.v.* To shake, as from weakness; tremble: *The old man's voice quavered.* —*n.* A quavering sound. —**qua′ver·y** *adj.*

quay (kē or kā) *n.* A wharf or reinforced bank where ships are loaded or unloaded.

Homonyms: quay, cay (island), **key** (lock opener, island).

Que. *abbr.* An abbreviation of Quebec.

quea·sy (kwē′zē) *adj.* **quea·si·er, quea·si·est. 1.** Sick to one's stomach; nauseated: *I get queasy on boats.* **2.** Easily troubled or squeamish: *too violent a movie for queasy viewers.* —**quea′si·ly** *adv.* —**quea′si·ness** *n.* [U]

queen (kwēn) *n.* **1.a.** A woman who rules a nation, usually inheriting her position for life. **b.** The wife or widow of a king. **2.** Something considered as the most outstanding in some way: *Paris is regarded as the queen of cities.* **3.a.** A playing card with a picture of a queen. **b.** In chess, a player's most powerful piece, able to move most freely. **4.** In a colony of bees, ants, or termites, a large specially developed female who is able to lay eggs. —**queen′ly** *adj.*

queen-size (kwēn′sīz′) also **queen-sized** (kwēn′sīzd′) *adj.* **1.** Extra large: *queen-size pantyhose.* **2.** Measuring about 60 inches by 80 inches (1.5 meters by 2.0 meters). Used of a bed: *queen-size sheets.*

queer (kwîr) *adj.* **1.** Unusual; odd or unconventional: *a queer expression on his face.* **2.** Feeling a little sick; queasy: *My stomach feels queer.* **3.** *Slang.* An offensive term meaning homosexual. —**queer′ly** *adv.* —**queer′ness** *n.* [U]

quell (kwĕl) *tr.v.* **1.** To put (sthg.) down by force; suppress: *quell a revolt.* **2.** To calm (sthg.): *quell one's fears.*

quench (kwĕnch) *tr.v.* [with] **1.** To put out or extinguish (a fire, for example): *The campers quenched the flames with water.* **2.** To satisfy (thirst): *He quenched his thirst with a can of soda.*

quer·u·lous (kwĕr′ə ləs or kwĕr′yə ləs) *adj.* **1.** Given to complaining or fretting: *a nervous and querulous old man.* **2.** Expressing complaints or a sense of being treated unfairly: *the querulous tone of his voice.* —**quer′u·lous·ly** *adv.* —**quer′u·lous·ness** *n.* [U]

que·ry (kwîr′ē) *n., pl.* **que·ries.** *Formal.* A question; an inquiry: *Please submit all queries in writing.* —*tr.v.* **que·ried, que·ry·ing, que·ries.** To express doubt about (sthg.); question: *Are you querying the wisdom of his decision?*

quest (kwĕst) *n.* A search, especially for sthg. considered valuable or very special: *Space exploration represents the latest quest for knowledge of the universe.*

ques·tion (kwĕs′chən) *n.* **1.** [C] An expression that asks for or requires information in reply: *Students ask questions of their teacher.* **2.** [C] A subject or point open to debate; an unsettled issue: *Your point raises broad constitutional questions.* **3.** [C] A matter; a problem: *It is only a question of money.* **4.** [U] Uncertainty; doubt: *There is no question about his ability to do the job.* —*tr.v.* **1.** To ask a question of (sbdy.): *My friends questioned me about my thoughts on the election.* See Synonyms at **ask.** **2.** To express doubt about (sthg.): *No one questions her decisions.* ✦ **out of the question.** Not to be considered; unthinkable or impossible: *Your going there alone is out of the question.* —**ques′tion·er** *n.*

ques·tion·a·ble (kwĕs′chə nə bəl) *adj.* Open to doubt; uncertain: *questionable motives.* —**ques′tion·a·bly** *adv.*

ques·tion·ing (kwĕs′chə nĭng) *adj.* Expressing curiosity or confusion: *a questioning glance.* —**ques′tion·ing·ly** *adv.*

question mark *n.* A punctuation mark (?) written at the end of a sentence or phrase to show that a question is being asked.

ques·tion·naire (kwĕs′chə nâr′) *n.* A printed form with a series of questions, often used to get information for statistics or to sample public opinion on a certain subject: *The doctor asks all new patients to complete a questionnaire.*

queue (kyoo) *n.* **1.** *Chiefly British.* A line of people waiting their turn, as at a ticket window. **2.** A sequence of stored data or programs waiting to be processed in a computer.

Q

—intr.v. **queued, queu·ing, queues.** *Chiefly British.* To get in line; wait in a queue: *We'll have to queue up for tickets.*

HOMONYMS: queue, cue (stick, signal).

---

quib·ble (kwĭb′əl) *intr.v.* **quib·bled, quib·bling, quib·bles.** To find fault or criticize for unimportant reasons: *Don't quibble over details.* *—n.* A minor criticism or an objection without much meaning or importance. **—quib′bler** *n.*

quiche (kēsh) *n.* A rich unsweetened custard baked in a pastry shell often with other ingredients such as cheese and vegetables.

quick (kwĭk) *adj.* **1.** Moving or acting with speed; fast: *quick on one's feet.* See Synonyms at **fast**[1]. **2.** Learning, thinking, or understanding with speed: *a quick mind.* **3.** Happening or done in a short time: *a quick recovery.* *—adv.* Quickly; promptly: *Come quick!* **—quick′ly** *adv.* **—quick′ness** *n.* [U]

quick·en (kwĭk′ən) *v.* *—tr.* **1.** To make (sthg.) more rapid; speed up: *quicken one's steps.* **2.** To make (sthg.) excited or lively: *Such stories quicken the imagination.* *—intr.* To become more rapid: *The runner's pace quickened.*

quick·sand (kwĭk′sănd′) *n.* [U] A dangerous bed of loose sand mixed with water, forming a soft shifting mass in which people or animals can be trapped and sink.

quick-tem·pered (kwĭk′tĕm′pərd) *adj.* Easily angered: *She becomes quick-tempered when tired.*

quick-wit·ted (kwĭk′wĭt′ĭd) *adj.* Quick to think and act; mentally alert and sharp: *a quick-witted driver.*

qui·et (kwī′ĭt) *adj.* **1.** Making little or no noise; silent or almost silent: *quiet neighbors; a quiet engine.* **2.** Not moving; still; calm: *a quiet lake.* **3.** Not active; slow: *January is a quiet time for businesses.* *—n.* [U] The quality or condition of being quiet: *the quiet of the forest in winter.* *—tr. & intr.v.* To make or become quiet: *The teacher quieted the class. The audience quieted down.* **—qui′et·ly** *adv.* **—qui′e·tude′** (kwī′ĭ to͞od′) *n.* [U]

quill (kwĭl) *n.* **1.** A long stiff bird feather. **2.** A writing pen made from a feather. **3.** One of the hollow spines of a porcupine.

quilt (kwĭlt) *n.* A bed covering made of two layers of cloth with a filling in between, held together by dec-

quilt

orative stitching: *My aunt gave me her antique quilt.* *—intr.v.* To work on or make a quilt: *They quilt together once a week.*

quilt·ing (kwĭl′tĭng) *n.* [U] **1.** The process of making quilts: *Quilting is a relaxing hobby.* **2.** Material that is sewn like a quilt: *The lining of the coat is made of quilting.*

qui·nine (kwī′nīn′) *n.* [U] A bitter colorless drug used to treat malaria.

quint·es·sen·tial (kwĭn′tə sĕn′shəl) *adj.* Being a perfect example of a certain type of person or thing: *the quintessential actor.* **—quin·tes′sence** (kwĭn tĕs′əns) *n.* [U]

quin·tet (kwĭn tĕt′) *n.* **1.** A group of five musicians who sing or perform musical compositions together: *He sings in a quintet.* **2.** A group of five people or things.

quin·tu·ple (kwĭn tŭp′əl *or* kwĭn to͞o′pəl) *adj.* Multiplied by five: *a quintuple increase.* *—tr. & intr.v.* **quin·tu·pled, quin·tu·pling, quin·tu·ples.** To make or become five times as great: *I quintupled the cookie recipe to make enough for the party. The population of that region has quintupled.*

quin·tu·plet (kwĭn tŭp′lĭt *or* kwĭn to͞o′plĭt) *n.* One of five children born in a single birth.

quip (kwĭp) *n.* A short, clever or witty remark: *a comedian known for his quips on politics.* *—intr.v.* **quipped, quip·ping, quips.** To make a quip or quips.

quirk (kwûrk) *n.* **1.** Something strange in a person's behavior: *Everyone has quirks.* **2.** An unpredictable event or act: *a quirk of fate.* **—quirk′y** *adj.*

quit (kwĭt) *v.* **quit** *or* **quit·ted** (kwĭt′ĭd), **quit·ting, quits.** *—tr.* **1.** To give up or resign from (a position): *quit one's job.* **2.** To discontinue or stop (doing sthg.): *Quit bothering me!* See Synonyms at **stop**. **3.** To leave or depart from (a place): *They decided to quit the city for the country.* *—intr.* **1.** To stop working or performing an action: *The motor quit when we were a few miles from home.* **2.** To give up, as in defeat: *We were sure to lose, but we refused to quit.*

quite (kwīt) *adv.* **1.** Completely: *I am not quite finished with that book.* **2.** Really; truly: *I'm quite sure you're wrong.* **3.** Somewhat; rather: *We plan to leave quite soon.*

quits (kwĭts) *adj.* [with] Even, as by payment or revenge: *One more payment and I'll be quits with the loan.* ♦ **call it quits.** *Informal.* **1.** To consider an argument settled or a debt paid: *Let's accept their offer and call it quits.* **2.** To stop working or trying: *We were all tired, so we called it quits.*

quit·ter (kwĭt′ər) *n.* A person who gives up easily: *The coach had no respect for quitters.*

quiv·er[1] (kwĭv′ər) *intr.v.* To shake with a slight vibrating motion; tremble: *His voice*

ă-**cat**; ā-**pay**; âr-**care**; ä-**father**; ĕ-**get**; ē-**be**; ĭ-**sit**; ī-**nice**; îr-**here**; ŏ-**got**; ō-**go**; ô-**saw**; oi-**boy**; ou-**out**; o͞o-**took**; o͞o-**boot**; ŭ-**cut**; ûr-**word**; th-**thin**; *th*-**this**; hw-**when**; zh-**vision**; ə-**about**; N-French **bon**

quivered as he spoke. —*n.* The act or motion of quivering: *a quiver in her voice.*

quiv•er² (kwĭv′ər) *n.* A case for holding and carrying arrows.

quiz (kwĭz) *tr.v.* **quizzed, quiz•zing, quiz•zes. 1.** To question (sbdy.) closely; interrogate: *The teenager's parents quizzed him about the party.* **2.** To test the knowledge of (sbdy.) by asking questions: *The teacher was quizzing students on geography.* See Synonyms at **ask.** —*n., pl.* **quiz•zes.** A short oral or written examination: *a spelling quiz.*

quiz show *n.* A television show in which contestants answer questions, usually for prizes.

quiz•zi•cal (kwĭz′ĭ kəl) *adj.* Showing a lack of understanding: *a quizzical look on his face.* —**quiz′zi•cal•ly** *adv.*

quo•rum (kwôr′əm) *n.* The minimum number of members of a group that must be present for decisions or actions to be valid: *We can't hold a vote without a quorum.*

quo•ta (kwō′tə) *n.* **1.** An amount of sthg. assigned to be done, made, or sold: *a machine shop's production quota.* **2.** The number or proportion of persons that may be admitted to a country or an institution: *immigration quotas.*

quot•a•ble (kwō′tə bəl) *adj.* Good for quoting: *a speech full of quotable phrases.* —**quot′a•bil′i•ty** *n.* [U]

quo•ta•tion (kwō tā′shən) *n.* **1.** [U] The act of quoting: *These remarks are not for direct*

quotation. **2.** [C] A phrase, sentence, or longer passage that is quoted: *The teacher read a quotation from Shakespeare.* **3.** [C] A statement of the price of a security or the price itself: *the latest stock market quotations.*

quotation mark *n.* Either of a pair of punctuation marks used at the beginning and end of a word or passage spoken or written by another person and repeated exactly. They take the form of double quotation marks (" ") and single quotation marks (' '). Single quotation marks usually indicate a quotation within another quotation.

quote (kwōt) *tr.v.* **quot•ed, quot•ing, quotes. 1.a.** To repeat (a sentence, for example): *quote a familiar proverb.* **b.** To repeat words written in (sthg.) or said by (sbdy.): *Can you quote the Constitution? The reporter quoted the mayor.* **2.** To mention or refer to (sbdy./sthg.) for illustration or proof: *quoted statistics to show he was right.* **3.** To state (a price) for securities, goods, or services: *She quoted a price for the repairs.* —*n.* **1.** *Informal.* A quotation: *a quote from* Romeo and Juliet. **2.** A quotation mark: *Enclose her words in quotes.* **3.** A statement of a price: *The mechanic gave me a quote on the repairs to my car.*

quo•tient (kwō′shənt) *n.* The number that results when one number is divided by another.

Qur•'an (kə răn′ *or* kə rän′) *n.* Variant of **Koran.**

Rr

r¹ or **R** (är) *n.*, *pl.* **r's** or **R's.** The 18th letter of the English alphabet.

r² or **R** *abbr.* An abbreviation of: **1.** Radius. **2.** Resistance.

R (är) *n.* A movie rating that means people under 17 may not be admitted unless accompanied by a parent or guardian: *My thirteen-year-old brother can't go to a movie that's rated R.*

R. *abbr.* An abbreviation of: **1.** River. **2.** Or **r.** Right.

Ra The symbol for the element **radium.**

rab·bi (răb'ī) *n.*, *pl.* **rab·bis.** A person trained in Jewish law, ritual, and tradition, who may lead a Jewish congregation.

rab·bit (răb'ĭt) *n.* **1.** [C] A small mammal with long ears, soft fur, and a short furry tail. **2.** [U] The fur of such an animal.

rabbit

rab·ble (răb'əl) *n.* [U] *Formal.* A noisy unruly crowd or mob: *The mayor refused to address the rabble in the streets.*

rab·ble-rous·er (răb'əl rou'zər) *n.* A leader or speaker who stirs up the emotions of the public: *He was known as a rabble-rouser who urged revolt.*

rab·id (răb'ĭd) *adj.* **1.** Affected by rabies: *a rabid dog.* **2.** Raging; uncontrollable: *rabid thirst.* **3.** Overzealous; fanatical: *a rabid baseball fan.* —**rab'id·ly** *adv.* —**rab'id·ness** *n.* [U]

ra·bies (rā'bēz) *n.* [U] An infectious viral disease that affects mammals, attacks the central nervous system, and causes death.

rac·coon (ră kōōn') *n.* A North American mammal with grayish brown fur, black face markings resembling a mask, and a bushy black-ringed tail.

raccoon

race¹ (rās) *n.* **1.** A group of people that share physical characteristics that are passed on genetically. **2.** A group of people who share a common history or place of birth. **3.** Human beings: *the human race.* —**ra'cial** *adj.* —**ra'cial·ly** *adv.*

race² (rās) *n.* **1.** A contest of speed, as in running or riding: *a horse race.* **2.** An extended competition for political control: *the presidential race.* —*v.* **raced, rac·ing, rac·es.** —*intr.* **1.** To take part in a race: *I race whenever I can.* **2.** To rush at top speed; dash: *We raced home.* —*tr.* **1.** To compete against (sbdy./sthg.) in a race: *I'll race you to the house.* **2.** To enter (sbdy./sthg.) into a race: *She races horses for a living.* **3.** To cause (sthg.) to run at high speed: *race an engine.* ◆ **race against the clock.** To try to do sthg. quickly: *We're racing against the clock trying to finish the job on time.* **race against time.** A situation in which sthg. must be finished or solved very quickly: *Finding a cure for AIDS is a race against time.* **rat race.** A fast, everyday way of living that gives sbdy. no time to rest or think clearly: *She needs to get out of that rat race.* —**rac'er** *n.*

race·course (rās'kôrs') *n.* A course laid out for racing; a racetrack.

race·horse (rās'hôrs') *n.* A horse bred and trained for racing.

race·track (rās'trăk') *n.* A usually oval course on which races are held.

rac·ism (rā'sĭz'əm) *n.* [U] **1.** The belief that a particular race is superior to others. **2.** Discrimination or prejudice based on that belief: *The all-white club was accused of racism.* —**rac'ist** *adj. & n.*

rack (răk) *n.* A frame, stand, or bar used to hang or display certain articles: *a coat rack; a magazine rack.* —*tr.v.* **1.** To place (sthg.) in or on a rack. **2.** [*with*] To torment or cause suffering in (sbdy./sthg.): *His grief was so great that his body was racked with sobs.* ◆ **rack (one's) brain.** To think long and hard: *I racked my brain but I couldn't recall your name.* **rack up.** *tr.v.* [*sep.*] *Informal.* To collect or score (points): *That skier has racked up enough points to win the championship.*

rack·et also **rac·quet** (răk'ĭt) *n.* In sports, a device used to strike a ball or shuttlecock, consisting of a frame with tight interwoven strings and a handle.

rack·et² (răk'ĭt) *n.* **1.** (*usually singular*). A loud unpleasant noise: *The children made a racket playing in the street.* See

racket

Synonyms at **uproar. 2.** A dishonest business, especially one that obtains money through fraud: *He's involved in some kind of racket.*

rack·et·eer (răk'ĭ tîr') *n.* A person who runs or works in a criminal racket. —**rack'·et·eer'ing** *n.* [U]

rac·quet·ball (răk'ĭt bôl') *n.* [U] A game played on an enclosed court by two or four players with short rackets and a hollow rubber ball.

rac·y (rā'sē) *adj.* **rac·i·er, rac·i·est.** Slightly improper or indecent: *a racy book.* —**rac'i·ly** *adv.* —**rac'i·ness** *n.* [U]

rad (răd) *n.* A unit of energy absorbed from ionizing radiation.

ra·dar (rā'där) *n.* **1.** [U] A way of detecting distant objects by using radio waves: *The plane is on radar.* **2.** [C] The equipment used in doing this: *The new radar can detect low-flying aircraft.*

radi— *pref.* Variant of **radio—**.

ra·di·al (rā'dē əl) *adj.* **1.** Arranged like or directed along a radius: *measurement of a radial segment.* **2.** Having parts that are arranged like radii: *the radial body of a starfish.* —*n.* A type of tire: *My car has steel-belted radials.* —**ra'di·al·ly** *adv.*

ra·di·ant (rā'dē ənt) *adj.* **1.** Sending forth light, heat, or other radiation: *a radiant star; radiant energy.* **2.** Filled with brightness; beaming: *a radiant smile.* —**ra'di·ance** *n.* [U] —**ra'di·ant·ly** *adv.*

ra·di·ate (rā'dē āt') *v.* **ra·di·at·ed, ra·di·at·ing, ra·di·ates.** —*intr.* **1.** To send out rays or waves: *The sun radiates brightly.* **2.** To be sent forth as radiation: *light that radiates from a star.* **3.** To extend in straight lines from a center: *The pain radiated down her arm.* —*tr.* **1.** To send forth (heat, light, or other energy): *The stove radiated warmth.* **2.** To give off (sthg.); project: *Our captain radiates confidence.*

ra·di·a·tion (rā'dē ā'shən) *n.* [U] **1.** Energy in the form of heat or light sent out in waves: *infrared radiation.* **2.** Nuclear energy that is harmful or deadly to living things, even in very small amounts: *She died after exposure to radiation.*

ra·di·a·tor (rā'dē ā'tər) *n.* **1.** A cooling device, as in a car, through which water or other fluids circulate. **2.** A heating device that circulates steam or hot water to give out heat, especially to warm a room.

rad·i·cal (răd'ĭ kəl) *adj.* **1.** Thorough and complete; basic: *She proposed a radical solution to the problem.* **2.** Advocating extreme or revolutionary changes, as in politics or government: *a radical wing of that political party.* —*n.* **1.** A person who advocates revolutionary changes: *Radicals are trying to overthrow the government.* **2.** A root, such as √2, especially as indicated by the radical sign √. —**rad'i·cal·ly** *adv.*

ra·di·i (rā'dē ī') *n.* A plural of **radius.**

ra·di·o (rā'dē ō) *n., pl.* **ra·di·os. 1.** [U] Electromagnetic waves that carry messages or information between points without the use of wires. **2.** [C] The equipment used to generate or receive such electromagnetic waves: *I listen to music on my radio.* **3.** [U] The sending of radio signals for entertainment or news programs, especially as a business; broadcasting: *His sister is in radio.* —*tr.v.* To send (messages) by radio: *The pilot radioed a question to the control tower.*

radio— or **radi—** *pref.* A prefix that means radiation: *radioactive; radiograph.*

ra·di·o·ac·tive (rā'dē ō ăk'tĭv) *adj.* Relating to or showing radioactivity: *Uranium is a radioactive element.*

ra·di·o·ac·tiv·i·ty (rā'dē ō ăk tĭv'ĭ tē) *n.* [U] **1.** The release of radiation by atomic nuclei. **2.** The radiation released: *The scientists were careful to guard against exposure to radioactivity.*

ra·di·ol·o·gy (rā'dē ŏl'ə jē) *n.* [U] The use of x-rays and other radiation in medical diagnosis and treatment. —**ra'di·ol'o·gist** *n.*

radio wave *n.* An electromagnetic wave used for radio and radar.

rad·ish (răd'ĭsh) *n.* An edible, strong-tasting, red-skinned or white root, usually eaten raw.

ra·di·um (rā'dē əm) *n.* [U] *Symbol* **Ra** A rare, white, highly radioactive metallic element. Atomic number 88. See table at **element.**

ra·di·us (rā'dē əs) *n., pl.* **ra·di·i** (rā'dē ī') or **ra·di·us·es. 1.a.** A line segment that joins the center of a circle with any point on its circumference. **b.** A line segment that joins the center of a sphere with any point on its surface. **2.** A circular area measured by a given radius: *all houses within a radius of 50 miles.*

radius

ra·don (rā'dŏn) *n.* [U] *Symbol* **Rn** A colorless, radioactive, inert gaseous element. Atomic number 86. See table at **element.**

raf·fle (răf'əl) *n.* A lottery in which people buy chances to win a prize: *When will they draw the winning ticket number for the raffle?* —**raf'fle** *v.*

raft (răft) *n.* A floating platform made of planks, logs, or barrels and used for transport or by swimmers.

raft·er¹ (răf'tər) *n.* A person who travels by raft.

raf·ter² (răf'tər) *n.* (*usually plural*). One of the beams supporting a roof.

raft·ing (răf'tĭng) *n.* [U] The sport of riding a rubber raft down a fast-moving river.

rag¹ (răg) *n.* **1.** A scrap of cloth: *a cleaning rag.* **2. rags.** Old clothing in terrible condition: *The poor child was dressed in rags.*

R

rag² (răg) *tr.v.* **ragged, rag·ging, rags.** *Slang.* To tease (sbdy.); taunt: *His friend ragged him for losing his keys again.*

rage (rāj) *n.* [C; U] **1.** Violent anger or a fit of such anger: *He flew into a rage.* See Synonyms at **anger. 2.** A fad or craze: *when miniskirts were the rage.* —*intr.v.* **raged, rag·ing, rag·es. 1.** To speak or act in violent anger: *The man raged about his car being stolen.* **2.** To move with great violence: *The storm raged outside.*

rag·ged (răg′ĭd) *adj.* **1.** Torn, frayed, or tattered: *ragged clothes.* **2.** Jagged or uneven: *the ragged edge of a torn paper.* **3.** Imperfect; sloppy: *The actor gave a ragged performance.* —**rag′ged·ly** *adv.* —**rag′ged·ness** *n.* [U]

rag·ged·y (răg′ĭ dē) *adj.* **rag·ged·i·er, rag·ged·i·est.** Worn-out or tattered; ragged: *a raggedy old dress.*

raid (rād) *n.* **1.** A sudden attack by an armed force: *an air raid.* **2.** A sudden and forcible entry into a place by police: *a raid on an illegal operation.* —*tr.v.* To carry out a raid on (a place): *He often raids the refrigerator at midnight.* —**raid′er** *n.*

rail¹ (rāl) *n.* **1.** [C] A horizontal bar such as that used in a fence. **2.** [C] A fence or barrier made of such bars. **3.** [C] A steel bar used, usually as one of a pair, as a track for railroad cars. **4.** [U] The railroad as a means of transportation: *travel by rail.*

rail² (rāl) *intr.v.* [*against*] To object or criticize in bitter, harsh, or abusive language: *Businessmen railed against the idea of more government control.*

rail·ing (rā′lĭng) *n.* [C; U] A handrail: *For safety, hold on to the railing.*

rail·road (rāl′rōd′) *n.* [C; U] A system of tracks, together with the stations, land, trains, and other related property under one management: *Railroads opened up the West.* —*tr.v. Informal.* **1.** To rush or push (sthg.) through without enough thought: *railroad a bill through the legislature.* **2.** To convict (sbdy.) without a fair trial or on false evidence: *The committee railroaded the leader to cover up their own crimes.*

rail·way (rāl′wā′) *n.* A railroad.

rain (rān) *n.* **1.** [U] Water that condenses from vapor in the atmosphere and falls to the earth as drops: *We are expecting rain this afternoon.* **2.** [C] (*usually plural*). A rainy season: *The rains came early this year.* —*v.* —*intr.* **1.** To fall in drops of water from the clouds: *It may rain tomorrow.* **2.** To release rain: *clouds that rain on the land.* —*tr.* **1.** To send (sthg.) down like rain: *They rained balloons on the guests at the party.* **2.** To give or offer (sthg.) in great amounts: *They rain gifts on their grandchil-*

dren. ◆ **rain cats and dogs.** *Informal.* To rain very heavily: *It was difficult to see because it was raining cats and dogs.* **rain down.** *intr.v.* To fall like rain: *Congratulations and good wishes rained down on the happy couple.* **rain out.** *tr.v.* [sep.] To force the cancellation or postponement of (an outdoor event) because of rain: *The baseball game was rained out again.* **When it rains, it pours.** An expression that means that bad things seem to happen all at once: *I failed my final exam, lost my dog, and had my bike stolen the same day. When it rains, it pours!*

HOMONYMS: rain, reign (rule), **rein** (strap).

rain·bow (rān′bō′) *n.* An arc-shaped band of colors seen in the sky opposite the sun, especially after rain.

rain check *n.* **1.** A ticket for admission to a future event if the scheduled event is canceled because of rain. **2.** A paper given to a customer as a promise that a sold-out sale item may be bought later at the sale price: *The store didn't have any more of the special lamps, so they gave me a rain check.*

rain·coat (rān′kōt′) *n.* A waterproof or water-resistant coat.

rain·drop (rān′drŏp′) *n.* A drop of rain.

rain·fall (rān′fôl′) *n.* [C; U] **1.** A fall of rain; a shower: *The weatherman is predicting heavy rainfall.* **2.** The amount of water, measured in inches, that falls during a specified time: *Rainfall is above average for the month.*

rain forest *n.* A dense tropical forest, usually with an annual rainfall of at least 100 inches (2.5 meters).

rain·storm (rān′stôrm′) *n.* A storm accompanied by rain.

rain·y (rā′nē) *adj.* **rain·i·er, rain·i·est.** Characterized by or bringing rain: *a rainy afternoon; cold and rainy weather.* —**rain′i·ness** *n.* [U]

raise (rāz) *tr.v.* **raised, rais·ing, rais·es. 1.** To move (sbdy./sthg.) to a higher position; lift: *Raise the window slightly, please.* **2.a.** To set (sthg.) in an upright position: *raise a flagpole.* **b.** To build (sthg.): *raise a barn.* **3.** To increase (sthg.) in size, quantity, or worth: *raise prices.* **4.** To increase (sthg.) in intensity or strength: *Don't raise your voice at me.* **5.** To grow or breed (sthg.): *raise corn; raise livestock.* **6.** To take care of (a growing child); bring up: *raise children.* **7.** To put (sthg.) forward for consideration: *raise a question.* **8.** To cause (a problem): *He raised a fuss because he didn't like his seat on the plane.* **9.** To gather (sthg.) together; collect: *The club needs to raise money.* —*n.* An increase in wages or salary: *It's time to ask for a raise.*

HOMONYMS: raise, raze (tear down).

---

rai·sin (rā′zĭn) *n.* A sweet dried grape: *raisin pie; oatmeal raisin cookies.*

rake (rāk) *n.* A long-handled tool with teeth or prongs at one end, used to gather leaves or to smooth earth: *a garden rake.* —*v.* **raked, rak·ing, rakes.** —*tr.* **1.** To gather or smooth (sthg.) with a rake: *rake leaves; rake the lawn.* **2.** To search or examine (sthg.) thoroughly: *The police raked the apartment for evidence.* —*intr.* To use a rake: *He's outside raking.* ◆ **rake in.** *tr.v.* [sep.] To gain (sthg.) in large amounts: *The business suddenly began raking in the money.* **rake over the coals.** To cause (sbdy.) extreme discomfort: *She was raked over the coals by her boss for losing the client.* **rake up.** *tr.v.* [sep.] To revive or bring (sthg.) to light; uncover: *raking up old anger.*

ral·ly (răl′ē) *v.* **ral·lied, ral·ly·ing, ral·lies.** —*tr.* **1.** To call (people) together for a common purpose: *The group was trying to rally supporters at the demonstration.* **2.** To rouse or revive (sbdy./sthg.) from inactivity or decline: *The coach rallied the team's confidence.* —*intr.* **1.** To come together for a common purpose: *We rallied for the cause.* **2.** To recover abruptly from a setback or disadvantage: *The stock market rallied in the final hour of trading.* **3.** To show a sudden improvement in health or spirits: *The patient rallied after four days of fever.* —*n., pl.* **ral·lies.** A gathering, especially one intended to inspire enthusiasm for a cause: *a political rally.* ◆ **rally around.** *tr.v.* [insep.] To show (sbdy./sthg.) support: *We rallied around our friend when she lost her job.*

ram (răm) *n.* A male sheep. —*tr.v.* **rammed, ram·ming, rams. 1.** To strike or drive against (sbdy./sthg.) with a heavy impact: *The ship rammed an iceberg.* **2.** To force (sthg.) into a narrow space; jam: *I rammed the clothes into a suitcase.*

RAM (răm) *abbr.* Random-access memory: *a personal computer with 16 megabytes of RAM.*

Ram·a·dan (răm′ə dän′ *or* răm′ə dän′) *n.* [U] The ninth month of the Muslim year, observed with fasting from sunrise to sunset.

ram·ble (răm′bəl) *intr.v.* **ram·bled, ram·bling, ram·bles. 1.** To wander aimlessly; stroll: *We rambled in the park.* See Synonyms at **wander. 2.** To follow an irregularly winding course of motion or growth: *The roses rambled over the fence.* —*n.* A leisurely stroll: *an early morning ramble.* ◆ **ramble on.** *intr.v.* To speak or write at length, often going off the subject: *He rambled on about his recent trip.* —**ram′bler** *n.*

ram·bling (răm′blĭng) *adj.* **1.** Often roaming: *a rambling herd of cattle.* **2.** Extending over an irregular area; sprawling: *a rambling ranch.* **3.** Long and tending to wander off the subject: *a rambling speech.*

ram·bunc·tious (răm bŭngk′shəs) *adj.* Noisy and out of control: *rambunctious children.*

ram·i·fi·ca·tion (răm′ə fĭ kā′shən) *n. Formal.* A result; a consequence: *We must consider all the ramifications of changes in the law.*

ramp (rămp) *n.* A sloping passage or roadway that leads from one level to another: *a wheelchair ramp; an exit ramp.*

ram·page (răm′pāj′) *n.* A course of wild, often violent action or behavior: *The escaped monkey went on a rampage.* —*intr.v.* (*also* răm pāj′). **ram·paged, ram·pag·ing, ram·pag·es.** To move about wildly or violently; rage: *a mob rampaging through the streets.*

ram·pant (răm′pənt) *adj.* Growing or extending in an out-of-control manner: *a rampant growth of weeds; rampant corruption.* —**ram′pant·ly** *adv.*

ram·shack·le (răm′shăk′əl) *adj.* Poorly made or taken care of; rickety: *A ramshackle building needs repair.*

ran (răn) *v.* Past tense of **run.**

ranch (rănch) *n.* A large farm, especially in the western United States, on which large herds of cattle, sheep, or horses are raised. —*intr.v.* To work on or manage a ranch: *My family ranches for a living.* —**ranch′er** *n.*

ran·cid (răn′sĭd) *adj.* Having the unpleasant smell or taste of rotten oils or fats: *rancid butter.*

ran·cor (răng′kər) *n.* [U] *Formal.* Strong resentment; deep-seated ill will: *She feels a great deal of rancor toward her former boss.* —**ran′cor·ous** *adj.*

ran·dom (răn′dəm) *adj.* With no specific pattern or purpose: *random movements.* ◆ **at random.** Without a clear method or purpose: *Choose a card at random from the deck.* —**ran′dom·ness** *n.* [U]

ran·dom-ac·cess memory (răn′dəm ăk′sĕs) *n.* [U] Computer memory that a user can add to or change. The information stored in it can be accessed in any order.

rang (răng) *v.* Past tense of **ring**[2].

range (rānj) *n.* **1.** [U] The extent of or area covered by sthg.: *within viewing range; the range of his interests.* **2.** [C] An extent or amount of difference: *a price range.* **3.** [C] An extended group or series, especially a row or chain of mountains: *a mountain range; a wide range of products.* **4.** [C] The area in which a kind of animal or plant normally lives or grows. **5.** [U] A large expanse of open land on which livestock wander and graze: *cowboys riding across the range.* **6.** [C] The greatest distance of operation, as of a sound, radio signal, or missile: *a radio* *receiver with a range of 200 miles.* **7.** [C] A place for practice in shooting at targets: *a firing range.* **8.** [C] A stove with spaces for cooking a number of things at the same time: *an electric range.* —*intr.v.* **ranged, rang•ing, rang•es. 1.** To vary or move between specified limits: *children whose ages ranged from four to ten.* **2.** To extend in a certain direction: *a river ranging westward.* **3.** To live or grow within a certain region: *Coyotes now range over the entire United States.*

rang•er (rān′jər) *n.* **1.** A person employed to maintain and protect a forest or other natural area: *a park ranger.* **2.** A member of a highly trained military group that goes on special missions.

rang•y (rān′jē) *adj.* **rang•i•er, rang•i•est.** With long slender arms and legs: *a tall rangy young man.*

rank¹ (răngk) *n.* **1.** [C; U] A position or degree of value in a group with different levels: *in the top rank of his class.* **2.** [C] *(usually plural).* A body of people classed together; numbers: *He has joined the ranks of factory workers.* —*v.* —*tr.* To give a particular order or position to (sbdy./sthg.); classify: *The teacher ranked the children according to age.* —*intr.* To hold a certain rank: *She ranked eighth in the class.* ◆ **pull rank.** To use one's superior rank to gain an advantage: *I wanted to watch a comedy, but my father pulled rank and we watched the news.*

rank² (răngk) *adj.* **1.** Strong and unpleasant in odor or taste: *a rank cigar.* **2.** Complete; absolute: *a rank amateur.*

rank and file *n.* [U] *(used with a plural verb).* The ordinary members of a group or organization, as distinguished from the leaders and officers.

rank•ing (răng′kĭng) *adj.* Of the highest rank; preeminent: *the ranking officer.*

ran•kle (răng′kəl) *v.* **ran•kled, ran•kling, ran•kles.** —*intr.* To cause persistent irritation or resentment: *That annoying noise really rankles.* —*tr.* To irritate (sbdy.): *His boasting rankles me.*

ran•sack (răn′săk′) *tr.v.* **1.** To search (sthg.) thoroughly: *ransack a drawer.* **2.** To rob (sthg.) of valuables and leave in disarray; pillage: *The thieves ransacked my apartment.*

ran•som (răn′səm) *n.* [U] **1.** The release of property or a person in return for payment of a demanded price: *The parents of the kidnapped child were anxious to arrange ransom.* **2.** The price or payment demanded: *a million-dollar ransom.* —*tr.v.* To obtain the release of (sbdy./sthg.) by paying a certain price: *The government has ransomed the hostages.*

rant (rănt) *intr.v.* To speak loudly or violently: *The property owner ranted against high taxes.*

rap¹ (răp) *tr.v.* **rapped, rap•ping, raps. 1.** To hit (sbdy./sthg.) sharply and swiftly; strike: *He rapped the table with his fist.* **2.** To criticize or blame (sbdy./sthg.): *The teacher rapped the student for losing her homework again.* —*n.* **1.** A quick light blow or knock: *a rap on the knuckles.* **2.** A knocking or tapping sound: *I heard a rap on the door.* **3.** *Slang.* A prison sentence: *a murder rap.* ◆ **take the rap.** *Slang.* To accept punishment or take the blame for a mistake: *I took the rap for my friend when he broke the dish.*

HOMONYMS: rap (knock, talk), **wrap** (envelop).

rap² (răp) *n.* [C; U] A form of popular music with a strong rhythm and spoken or chanted rhyming lyrics. —*intr.v.* **rap•ped, rap•ping, raps. 1.** *Informal.* To discuss (sthg.) freely and at length: *We rapped about our problems until 2 a.m.* **2.** To perform rap music: *The new group raps about crime.* —**rap′per** *n.*

rape (rāp) *n.* [C; U] The crime of forcing another person to submit to sexual acts. —*tr.v.* **raped, rap•ing, rapes.** To force (sbdy.) to submit to sexual acts, especially sexual intercourse. —**rap′ist** (rā′pĭst) *n.*

rap•id (răp′ĭd) *adj.* Fast; swift: *rapid progress; walking with rapid strides.* See Synonyms at **fast¹.** —*n. (usually plural).* An extremely fast-moving part of a river, caused by a steep descent in the riverbed: *We took our boat down the rapids.* —**ra•pid′i•ty** (rə pĭd′ĭ tē) *n.* [U] —**rap′id•ly** *adv.* —**rap′id•ness** *n.* [U]

rap•id-fire (răp′ĭd fīr′) *adj.* Happening very quickly one after another: *rapid-fire questions.*

rap•port (ră pôr′) *n.* [U] A relationship of shared trust and understanding: *There was an immediate rapport between the two students.*

rapt (răpt) *adj.* Deeply absorbed or delighted: *The children were listening with rapt attention.* —**rapt′ly** *adv.*

rap•ture (răp′chər) *n.* [U] The state of feeling overcome by great joy; ecstasy: *a look of rapture spread over his face.* —**rap′tur•ous** *adj.*

rare¹ (râr) *adj.* **rar•er, rar•est. 1.** Not occurring often; uncommon: *a rare disease.* **2.** Out of the ordinary; excellent: *a rare gift for art.* —**rare′ness** *n.* [U] —**rar′i•ty** *n.* [C; U]

rare² (râr) *adj.* **rar•er, rar•est.** Cooked a short time. Used of meat: *rare steak.* —**rare′ness** *n.* [U]

rare•ly (râr′lē) *adv.* Infrequently; seldom: *We rarely watch TV because we are so busy.* —SEE NOTE at **hardly.**

ras•cal (răs′kəl) *n.* **1.** A person who is playfully mischievous: *You rascal! You hid my shoes again!* **2.** A dishonest person; a scoundrel: *That rascal of a car salesman can't be trusted.*

rash¹ (răsh) *adj.* Too bold or hasty; reckless: *a rash decision to buy a new car.* —**rash′ly** *adv.* —**rash′ness** *n.* [U]

rash² (răsh) *n.* **1.** A red irritation of the skin: *Eating shrimp gives me a rash.* **2.** Several occurrences of the same kind of event in a brief period: *a rash of burglaries in the building.*

rasp•ber•ry (răz′běr′ē) *n. pl.* **rasp•ber•ries. 1.** A sweet, red or black berry that has many seeds and grows on prickly plants. **2.** *Slang.* A jeering sound made by vibrating the tongue between the lips while exhaling: *My little brother gave his friend the raspberry.*

raspberry

rasp•y (răs′pē) *adj.* **rasp•i•er, rasp•i•est.** Harsh or grating; rough: *a raspy voice.*

rat (răt) *n.* **1.** A long-tailed rodent related to and resembling the mouse but larger. **2.** *Informal.* A hateful sneaky person, especially one who gives out information about the wrongs of friends or associates. —*intr.v.* **rat•ted, rat•ting, rats.** *Slang.* [on] To betray sbdy. by giving information; squeal: *The boy ratted on his friends when they stole the magazines.*

rate (rāt) *n.* **1.** A quantity measured with respect to another measured quantity: *Our rate of speed was 85 miles per hour.* **2.** A measure of a part with respect to a whole; a proportion: *a national unemployment rate of 4.8 percent.* **3.** The cost or price charged for a service: *postal rates.* —*v.* **rat•ed, rat•ing, rates.** —*tr.* To place (sbdy./ sthg.) in a particular grade or rank: *The teachers rated her third in her class.* —*intr.* To hold a certain rank; be valued or placed in a certain class: *This movie rates as the best of the year.* ♦ **at any rate.** Whatever the case may be: *At any rate, I'd like to attend the play, in spite of high prices.*

rath•er (răth′ər) *adv.* **1.** Preferably: *I'd rather stay home tonight.* **2.** More exactly; more accurately: *She is a businesswoman, or rather a banker.* **3.** To a certain extent; somewhat: *I'm feeling rather sleepy.*

rat•i•fy (răt′ə fī′) *tr.v.* **rat•i•fied, rat•i•fy• ing, rat•i•fies.** To approve and thus make (sthg.) officially valid; confirm: *ratify a treaty.* —**rat′i•fi•ca′tion** (răt′ə fĭ kā′shən) *n.* [U]

rat•ing (rā′tĭng) *n.* **1.** A classification assigned according to quality or skill: *beef marked with a "choice" rating.* **2.** An evaluation of the financial status of sbdy./sthg.: *a company with a high credit rating.* **3.** *(usually plural).* The popularity of a television or radio program: *This comedy is doing well in the ratings.*

ra•tio (rā′shō *or* rā′shē ō′) *n., pl.* **ra•tios.** A relationship between the amounts or sizes of two things; a proportion: *The ratio of students to teachers in our school is 10 to 1.*

ra•tion (răsh′ən *or* rā′shən) *n.* **1.** A fixed amount, especially of food, given periodically: *a horse's daily ration of carrots.* **2.** **rations.** Food available to members of a group: *a soldier's rations.* —*tr.v.* To give or make (sthg.) available in fixed limited amounts: *A drought made it necessary to ration water.* See Synonyms at **distribute.**

ra•tion•al (răsh′ə nəl) *adj.* **1.** Having or using the ability to reason: *a rational person.* **2.** Based on reason; logical: *rational behavior.* —**ra′tion•al′i•ty** *n.* [U] —**ra′tion•al•ly** *adv.*

ra•tion•ale (răsh′ə năl′) *n.* A fundamental reason: *the rationale for raising prices.*

ra•tion•al•ize (răsh′ə nə līz′) *v.* **ra•tion• al•ized, ra•tion•al•iz•ing, ra•tion•al• iz•es.** —*tr.* To invent satisfactory but false explanations for (one's behavior): *She rationalized the fact that she didn't do her homework by saying the room was too cold.* —*intr.* To make excuses for one's behavior: *He often skips class but rationalizes about it.* —**ra′tion•al•i• za′tion** (răsh′ə nə lĭ zā′shən) *n.* [C; U]

rat•tan (ră tăn′) *n.* [U] The stems of a tropical palm tree, used for furniture. —*adj.* Made of rattan: *rattan chairs.*

rat•tle (răt′l) *v.* **rat•tled, rat•tling, rat• tles.** —*intr.* **1.a.** To make a series of short sharp sounds: *He was so frightened that his teeth rattled.* **b.** To move with such sounds: *The old train rattled along the track.* **2.** To talk rapidly and at length, usually without much thought: *My neighbor rattled on about his relatives.* —*tr.* **1.** To shake (sthg.) noisily: *I rattled the locked door.* **2.** *Informal.* To disturb the composure or confidence of (sbdy.): *His constant questions rattled me.* —*n.* **1.** A quick succession of short sharp sounds: *the rattle of the rain on the roof.* **2.** A device or object that rattles when shaken: *a baby's rattle.* ♦ **rattle off.** *tr.v.* [sep.] To say or perform (sthg.) rapidly or effortlessly: *rattle off a list of names.*

rat•tler (răt′lər) *n. Informal.* A rattlesnake.

rat•tle•snake (răt′l-snāk′) *n.* A poisonous American snake with several rings at the end of its tail that make a rattling sound.

rattlesnake

rat•ty (răt′ē) *adj. In-formal.* In bad shape; dirty and ugly: *They finally tore down that ratty building.*

rau•cous (rô′kəs) *adj.* **1.** Rough-sounding and harsh: *the bird's raucous cries.* **2.** Loud and out of control: *a raucous party.* —**rau′cous•ly** *adv.* —**rau′cous•ness** *n.* [U]

R

raun·chy (rôn′chē *or* rän′chē) *adj.* **raun·chi·er, raun·chi·est.** *Slang.* **1.** Obscene, lewd, or vulgar: *raunchy jokes.* **2.** Dirty; messy: *a raunchy old apartment.*

rav·age (răv′ĭj) *tr.v.* **rav·aged, rav·ag·ing, rav·ag·es.** To bring ruin to (sthg.); destroy: *A hurricane ravaged the houses along the coast.* —*n.* *(usually plural).* Severe damage: *the ravages of disease.*

rave (rāv) *intr.v.* **raved, rav·ing, raves. 1.** To speak wildly without making any sense: *He raved when he heard the bad news.* **2.** To speak with wild enthusiasm or praise: *She has been raving about her new skis.* —*adj.* *Informal.* Relating to an extravagantly enthusiastic review or opinion: *We went to see the movie after reading the rave reviews.*

rav·el (răv′əl) *tr. & intr.v.* To separate or become separated into single loose threads; fray: *She raveled the edge of the old sweater. The rug raveled where it was worn.*

ra·ven (rā′vən) *n.* A large black bird with a croaking cry like that of a crow. —*adj.* Black and shiny: *raven hair.*

rav·en·ous (răv′ə nəs) *adj.* **1.** Extremely hungry: *a ravenous appetite.* **2.** Greedy: *ravenous for power.* —**rav′en·ous·ly** *adv.*

ra·vine (rə vēn′) *n.* A deep narrow valley made by running water.

rav·ing (rā′vĭng) *adj.* **1.** Talking or behaving irrationally; wild: *The man was a raving drunk.* **2.** Worthy of admiration: *a raving beauty.*

rav·i·o·li (răv′ē ō′lē) *n., pl.* **ravioli** or **ra·vi·o·lis.** [C; U] A filled pasta usually served with sauce.

rav·ish (răv′ĭsh) *tr.v.* To seize and take (sbdy./sthg.) by force: *The troops ravished the countryside.*

rav·ish·ing (răv′ĭ shĭng) *adj.* Very beautiful: *a ravishing beauty.* —**rav′ish·ing·ly** *adv.*

raw (rô) *adj.* **1.** Uncooked: *raw meat.* **2.** In a natural condition: *furniture sanded down to raw wood.* **3.** Without training: *raw recruits.* **4.** Badly irritated; sore: *a raw open wound.* **5.** Unpleasantly damp and chilly: *raw weather.* ♦ **raw deal.** Something unfair: *What a raw deal! I never should have listened to your advice about buying a car.*

ray¹ (rā) *n.* **1.** A thin line or narrow beam of light or other radiation: *the sun's rays.* **2.** A small amount; a trace: *a ray of hope.*

ray² (rā) *n.* An ocean fish with a horizontally flat body, often with fins that resemble wings, and a long narrow tail.

ray·on (rā′ŏn) *n.* [U] A synthetic cloth made from wood fibers.

raze (rāz) *tr.v.* **razed, raz·ing, raz·es.** To destroy or tear down (a building) completely; level: *The city government decided to raze the old apartments.*

HOMONYMS: raze, raise (lift up).

ra·zor (rā′zər) *n.* A sharp cutting instrument, used for shaving the face or removing other body hair.

razz (răz) *tr.v. Slang.* To tease (sbdy.): *They razzed their friend about his girlfriend.*

rd. or **Rd.** *abbr.* An abbreviation of road.

re (rē) *prep. (usually written).* Concerning; about: *I'd like to speak to you re our meeting.*

re— *pref.* A prefix that means: **1.** Again; anew: *reread; redo.* **2.** Back; backward: *react; rewind.*

WORD BUILDING: re—. The primary meaning of the prefix re— is "again." Re— combines primarily with verbs, as in these examples: **rearrange, rebuild, recall, remake, rerun, rewrite.** The prefix is used with this meaning extensively. Sometimes it is necessary to use a hyphen with re— to distinguish between pairs such as **recreation** [rĕk′rē ā′shən] and **recreation** [rē′krē ā′shən]. A hyphen may also be used when the prefix re— precedes a word beginning with e, as in **re-enact** and **re-enter.**

reach (rēch) *v.* —*tr.* **1.** To touch or grasp (sbdy./sthg.) by stretching out: *The child couldn't reach the shelf.* **2.** To arrive at (sthg.); attain: *reach our destination; reach a conclusion.* **3.** To succeed in communicating with (sbdy.), especially by phone: *The neighbors reached the fire department in time to save the building.* **4.** To go or extend as far as (sthg.): *The property reaches the shore.* —*intr.* **1.** To try to grasp or touch sthg.: *She reached for a book.* **2.** To extend far in space or time: *a coat that reached to the knee; a career that reached over decades.* —*n.* **1.** [C] The act of stretching or thrusting out sthg.: *The frog caught the butterfly with a sudden reach of its tongue.* **2.** [U] The distance or extent to which sbdy. or sthg. can reach: *He has a long reach.* **3.** [U] The range of a person's understanding: *a subject beyond their reach.* ♦ **reach out to.** To try to contact (sbdy.) to give or get emotional support: *He reached out to his neighbors after the fire destroyed their home.*

SYNONYMS: reach, achieve, attain, gain. These verbs mean to succeed in arriving at a goal or an objective. **Reach** is the most general term: *They reached shelter just before the storm arrived.* **Achieve** suggests reaching by applying one's skill or initiative: *Through their research, the team of chemists achieved international fame.* **Attain** often means to reach an ambitious goal: *Soon she will attain her dream of becoming a lawyer.* **Gain** suggests making an effort to overcome

---

ă–**cat**; ā–**pay**; âr–**care**; ä–**father**; ĕ–**get**; ē–**be**; ĭ–**sit**; ī–**nice**; îr–**here**; ŏ–**got**; ō–**go**; ô–**saw**; oi–**boy**; ou–**out**; ŏŏ–**took**; ōō–**boot**; ŭ–**cut**; ûr–**word**; th–**thin**; *th*–**this**; hw–**when**; zh–**vision**; ə–**about**; N–French **bon**

obstacles: *Slowly the new management gained the workers' confidence.*

re•act (rē ăkt′) *intr.v.* **1.** To act in response to sthg.: *The eye reacts to bright light.* **2.** To act in opposition to sthg.: *The teenagers reacted against the curfew of 10:00 p.m.* **3.** To undergo a reaction: *The two chemicals reacted to form a dangerous gas.* —**re•ac′tive** *adj.*

re•ac•tion (rē ăk′shən) *n.* **1.** [C] A response to sthg.: *Her reaction surprised everyone.* **2.** [C] An unexpected problem with a drug: *She suffered an allergic reaction to penicillin.* **3.** [C; U] A chemical change.

re•ac•tion•ar•y (rē ăk′shə nĕr′ē) *adj.* Against progress or reform; very conservative: *a reactionary politician.* —*n.*, *pl.* **re•ac•tion•ar•ies.** An extreme conservative.

re•ac•ti•vate (rē ăk′tə vāt′) *tr.v.* **re•ac•ti•vat•ed, re•ac•ti•vat•ing, re•ac•ti•vates.** To make (sthg.) active again: *He reactivated his account at the bookstore.* —**re•ac′ti•va′tion** *n.* [U]

re•ac•tor (rē ăk′tər) *n.* The main part of a nuclear power plant.

read (rēd) *v.* **read** (rĕd), **read•ing, reads.** —*tr.* **1.** To look at and take in the meaning of (written characters, words, or sentences): *reading books.* **2.** To speak aloud the words of (sthg. written): *She read the poem while we listened.* **3.** To know (a language or system of notation) well enough to understand written and printed matter: *reads Chinese; reads music.* **4.** To take in the meaning of (sthg.): *reads American Sign Language; reading a map.* **5.** To detect (sthg.) by observing closely: *I read disappointment in her eyes.* **6.** To show or register (information): *The speedometer read 50 miles per hour.* —*intr.* **1.** To take in the meaning of written characters, as of words or music: *The child is learning to read.* **2.** To speak aloud the words one is reading: *He reads to his children every night.* **3.** [*about*] To learn by reading: *We read about the elections in the paper.* ♦ **read between the lines.** To find a hidden or unexpressed meaning in sthg. written or spoken: *We read between the lines and understood her "maybe" to mean "no."* **read out.** *tr.v.* [sep.] To read (sthg.) aloud: *The teacher read out the names.* **read up on.** To study or learn (sthg.) by reading: *We've been reading up on dinosaurs lately.*

read•a•ble (rē′də bəl) *adj.* **1.** Easily read; legible: *readable handwriting.* **2.** Pleasurable or interesting to read: *a readable story.* —**read′a•bil′i•ty** *n.* [U]

read•er (rē′dər) *n.* **1.** A person who reads: *She's an avid reader who always has a book in her hands.* **2.** A textbook with passages for practice in reading: *Bring your reader to*

class. **3.** A teaching assistant who reads and grades examination papers.

read•i•ly (rĕd′ə lē *or* rĕd′l ē) *adv.* **1.** In a cooperative way; willingly: *advice that was readily accepted.* **2.** Without difficulty; easily: *Tools are readily available at the hardware store.*

read•ing (rē′dĭng) *n.* **1.** [U] The act of a person who reads. **2.** [C] A public oral presentation of written material: *a poetry reading.* **3.** [C] A personal interpretation: *She described her reading of the political situation.* **4.** [U] Written or printed material. **5.** [C] The information shown by an instrument or a gauge: *He took a reading from the thermometer.*

re•ad•just (rē′ə jŭst′) *tr.v.* To arrange (sthg.) again: *You'll have to readjust the settings on the machine.* —**re′ad•just′ment** *n.* [C; U]

read•y (rĕd′ē) *adj.* **read•i•er, read•i•est.** **1.** Prepared for action or use: *getting ready for school; a garden ready for planting.* **2.** Willing: *ready to accept any reasonable offer.* **3.** Likely or about to do sthg.: *He seemed ready to answer.* **4.** Quick to react: *a ready response.* **5.** Available: *ready cash.* —*tr.v.* **read•ied, read•y•ing, read•ies.** To cause (sbdy./sthg.) to be ready: *They readied the boat to go fishing.* ♦ **at the ready.** Prepared to act: *We have a team of experts at the ready in case of a problem.* **make ready.** To make preparations: *They made ready to leave.* —**read′i•ness** *n.* [U]

read•y-made *or* **read•y•made** (rĕd′ē mād′) *adj.* Already prepared: *a ready-made dinner.*

re•al (rē′əl *or* rēl) *adj.* **1.** Not imaginary; actual: *This is a story about real people.* **2.** Authentic; not artificial: *a real diamond, not a fake one.* See Synonyms at **authentic.** **3.** Being no less than what is stated: *a real friend.* **4.** Serious; not to be taken lightly: *in real trouble.* —*adv.* *Informal.* Very: *I'm real sorry about that.* ♦ **for real.** *Slang.* Truly so in fact: *That description can't be for real.*

real estate *n.* [U] Land, including all the buildings and natural resources on it.

real estate agent *n.* A person who sells real estate professionally.

re•al•ism (rē′ə lĭz′əm) *n.* [U] **1.** A tendency to accept facts and be practical. **2.** The representation in art and literature of objects, actions, and social conditions as they actually are. —**re′al•ist** *n.*

re•al•is•tic (rē′ə lĭs′tĭk) *adj.* **1.** Accurately shown, as in artistic or literary realism: *realistic characters in a play.* **2.** Showing an awareness of facts and things as they actually are; practical: *a realistic estimate of the cost.* —**re′al•is′ti•cal•ly** *adv.*

re•al•i•ty (rē ăl′ĭ tē) *n.*, *pl.* **re•al•i•ties. 1.** [U] The quality of being actual or true: *Some scientists questioned the reality of life on other planets.* **2.** [C] A person or thing that is real: *seeing their dreams become realities.* **3.**

R

[U] The state of things as they actually exist: *The reality of the situation is that we've spent all the money in the budget.* ✦ **in reality.** In fact; actually: *He said he had finished the project, but in reality he still had several things to do.*

re·al·i·za·tion (rē′ə lǐ zā′shən) *n.* [U] **1.** The act of realizing: *They were shocked by the realization that they had run out of money.* **2.** The result of making sthg. real: *the realization of his hopes.*

re·al·ize (rē′ə līz′) *tr.v.* **re·al·ized, re·al·iz·ing, re·al·iz·es. 1.** To understand (sthg.) completely or correctly: *He realized that the situation was serious.* **2.** To make (sthg.) real; fulfill: *She realized her ambition to succeed as an artist.*

re·al·ly (rē′ə lē′ *or* rē′lē) *adv.* **1.** In actual fact: *The peanut isn't really a nut.* **2.** Truly; very: *a really beautiful morning.* **3.** Indeed: *Really, you shouldn't have done it.* —*interj.* An expression used to show surprise, especially with some doubt: *You just won a thousand dollars! Really?*

realm (rĕlm) *n.* **1.** A field or an area of interest: *the realm of science.* **2.** *Formal.* A kingdom.

re·al·tor (rē əl tər′ *or* rē əl tôr′) *n.* A person who sells real estate.

re·al·ty (rē′əl tē) *n.* [U] Real estate.

ream¹ (rēm) *n.* **1.** A standard quantity of paper of the same size and stock, now usually 500 sheets. **2.** *(usually plural).* A very large amount: *I have reams of homework.*

ream² (rēm) *tr.v.* To shape, enlarge, or adjust (a hole): *He reamed the hole in the wall after drilling it.* ✦ **ream out.** *tr.v.* [sep.] *Informal.* To criticize (sbdy.) harshly: *The boss reamed out the employee in front of everyone.*

reap (rēp) *tr.v.* **1.** To cut (grain or a similar crop) for harvest: *reap wheat.* **2.** To gain (sthg.) as a result of effort: *The scientist reaped fame from his many inventions.* —**reap′er** *n.*

re·ap·pear (rē′ə pîr′) *intr.v.* To appear again; return: *He disappeared into the kitchen and then reappeared with a platter of food.* —**re′ap·pear′ance** *n.* [C; U]

re·ap·ply (rē′ə plī′) *v.* **re·ap·plied, re·ap·ply·ing, re·ap·plies.** —*intr.* To apply for sthg. again: *She reapplied to the local college after she had been turned down.* —*tr.* To apply (sthg.) again: *We had to reapply the paint to the house after it rained.* —**re′ap·pli·ca′tion** *n.* [C; U]

re·ap·point (rē′ə point′) *tr.v.* To assign (sbdy.) to the same job again: *The new president reappointed her as the club's treasurer.* —**re′ap·point′ment** *n.* [C; U]

rear¹ (rîr) *n.* **1.** The part of sthg. that is farthest from the front: *the rear of the car.* **2.** *Informal.* The buttocks: *The baby fell on* his rear. —*adj.* Located in the rear: *a rear entrance.*

rear² (rîr) *v.* —*tr.* To care for (a child or animal) during the early stages of life; bring up: *My grandparents reared ten children.* —*intr.* To rise on the hind legs, as a horse: *The frightened horse reared and neighed.*

re·ar·range (rē′ə rānj′) *tr.v.* **re·ar·ranged, re·ar·rang·ing, re·ar·rang·es.** To change the arrangement of (objects): *rearrange the furniture.* —**re′ar·range′ment** *n.* [C; U]

rea·son (rē′zən) *n.* **1.** [C] The basis for an action, a decision, or a belief: *What are your reasons for quitting your job?* **2.** [C] A fact or cause that explains why sthg. exists or occurs: *reasons for being late.* **3.** [U] The ability to think, understand, and make decisions logically and sensibly; intelligence: *Humans have reason.* **4.** [U] A normal mental state; sanity: *That man has lost his reason!* **5.** [U] Sound judgment; good sense: *a woman of reason.* —*v.* —*intr.* **1.** To use the ability to think logically: *Animals cannot reason.* **2.** To argue logically and persuasively: *The police tried to reason with the angry crowd.* —*tr.* To determine or conclude (sthg.) by logical thinking: *He reasoned that the problem could be solved.* ✦ **listen to reason.** To accept good advice: *I tried to tell her not to buy that house, but she wouldn't listen to reason.* **within reason.** Within the bounds of good sense or what is possible: *I will pay any price within reason.* **without rhyme or reason.** Without a good plan or purpose: *His decisions are without rhyme or reason.*

rea·son·a·ble (rē′zə nə bəl) *adj.* **1.** In accordance with reason; logical: *a reasonable solution.* **2.** Not excessive or extreme; fair: *a reasonable price.* —**rea′son·a·ble·ness** *n.* [U] —**rea′son·a·bly** *adv.*

rea·son·ing (rē′zə nǐng) *n.* [U] The use of reason, especially to form conclusions and judgments: *I could not understand her reasoning, but her plan did work well.*

re·as·sem·ble (rē′ə sĕm′bəl) *v.* **re·as·sem·bled, re·as·sem·bling, re·as·sem·bles.** —*tr.* **1.** To fit or join the parts of (sthg.) together again: *reassemble an engine.* **2.** To bring or gather (people) together again: *reassemble old friends.* —*intr.* To gather together again, especially in a different place: *They were told to reassemble after the break.*

re·as·sure (rē′ə shŏŏr′) *tr.v.* **re·as·sured, re·as·sur·ing, re·as·sures. 1.** To assure (sbdy.) again: *He reassured me he would call.* **2.** To restore confidence to (sbdy.): *Their father's calm manner reassured the frightened children.* —**re′as·sur′ance** *n.* [C; U]

re·as·sur·ing (rē′ə shŏŏr′ĭng) *adj.* Comforting: *It's reassuring to know they arrived safely.* —**re′as·sur′ing·ly** *adv.*

re·bate (rē′bāt′) *n.* A return or deduction of part of a payment: *I got a rebate on the toothpaste I bought.*

re·bel (rĭ bĕl′) *intr.v.* **re·belled, re·bel·ling, re·bels.** [*against*] **1.** To violently oppose an established government or a ruling authority: *rebel against the king.* **2.** To resist or defy a rule or an accepted custom: *He rebelled against wearing a tie in summer.* —*n.* **reb·el** (rĕb′əl). A person who rebels or is in rebellion. —**re·bel′lion** (rĭ bĕl′yən) *n.* [C; U] —**re·bel′lious** *adj.*—**re·bel′lious·ly** *adv.*—**re·bel′lious·ness** *n.* [U]

re·birth (rē bûrth′ *or* rē′bûrth′) *n.* **1.** A new start: *That vacation gave me a rebirth of hope and energy.* **2.** A return to being popular: *the rebirth of jazz.*

re·boot (rē bōōt′) *tr. & intr.v.* To turn a computer off and then on again: *After you install the program, reboot your computer. If the system crashes, you'll have to reboot.*

re·born (rē bôrn′) *adj.* Emotionally or spiritually revived: *She felt reborn after her vacation.*

re·bound (rē′bound′ *or* rĭ bound′) *intr.v.* **1.** To bounce back after hitting sthg.: *The ball rebounded off the wall.* **2.** To recover, as from grief or illness: *She rebounded slowly after her dog died.* —*n.* (rē′bound′ *or* rĭ bound′). A bounce back: *He hit the tennis ball on the rebound.* ♦ **on the rebound.** Recovering after the end of a romantic relationship: *Two months after they broke up, he was on the rebound.*

re·buff (rĭ bŭf′) *n.* An unfriendly reply or response to an offer; a blunt refusal: *All she got for her kindness to him was a rebuff.* —*tr.v.* To reject (sbdy./sthg.) bluntly; snub: *They rebuffed our offer to help.*

re·build (rē bĭld′) *tr.v.* **re·built** (rē bĭlt′), **re·build·ing, re·builds.** To build (sthg.) again; reconstruct: *rebuild a school.*

re·buke (rĭ byōōk′) *tr.v.* **re·buked, re·buk·ing, re·bukes.** To criticize (sbdy.) sharply; scold: *The principal rebuked the late student.* —*n.* An expression of strong disapproval: *Just the way she looked at us was a rebuke.*

re·but (rĭ bŭt′) *tr.v.* **re·but·ted, re·but·ting, re·buts.** To prove (sthg.) false, especially by presenting opposing evidence or arguments: *They rebutted our remarks by showing new statistics.* —**re·but′tal** *n.* [C; U]

re·cal·ci·trant (rĭ kăl′sĭ trənt) *adj. Formal.* Not willing to do what sbdy. who has power tells one to do: *The recalcitrant child refused to go to sleep.* —**re·cal′ci·trance** *n.* [U]

re·call (rĭ kôl′) *tr.v.* **1.** To ask or order the return of (sbdy./sthg.): *The company recalled the cars for repair of defective brakes. The government recalled the ambassador.* **2.** To remember (sbdy./sthg.): *recalling his boyhood love of trains.* —*n.* (*also* rē′kôl′). **1.** [C] The act of calling back, especially an official order to return: *a product recall.* **2.** [U] The

ability to remember information or experiences: *He has total recall.*

re·cant (rĭ kănt′) *v. Formal.* —*tr.* To deny publicly (a statement or belief previously held): *The senator recanted his position on the new tax bill.* —*intr.* To make a formal denial of a previously held statement or belief: *When presented with the truth, she recanted.*

re·cap (rē′kăp′) *n.* A brief summary: *a recap of the top news stories.* —**re′cap′** *v.*

re·ca·pit·u·late (rē′kə pĭch′ə lāt′) *v.* **re·ca·pit·u·lat·ed, re·ca·pit·u·lat·ing, re·ca·pit·u·lates.** *Formal.* —*tr.* To repeat (sthg.) in shorter form; summarize: *She recapitulated the long story.* —*intr.* To make a summary: *After the lengthy lecture, the speaker recapitulated.* —**re′ca·pit′u·la′tion** *n.* [C; U]

re·cap·ture (rē kăp′chər) *n.* The act of taking again. —*tr.v.* **re·cap·tured, re·cap·tur·ing, re·cap·tures.** **1.** To capture (sbdy./sthg.) again: *recapture a city.* **2.** To recollect or recall (sthg.) vividly: *recapture a memory of better times.*

recd. *abbr.* An abbreviation of received.

re·cede (rĭ sēd′) *intr.v.* **re·ced·ed, re·ced·ing, re·cedes.** **1.** To move back from a limit or point: *His hairline has receded. The flood waters finally receded.* **2.** To become fainter or more distant: *The sound of the train receded.*

re·ceipt (rĭ sēt′) *n.* **1.** [U] The act of receiving: *receipt of a gift.* **2.** [C] (*usually plural*). The amount received: *tax receipts.* **3.** [C] A written statement that a specified article or amount of money has been received: *Don't forget to get a receipt from the salesclerk.*

re·ceiv·a·ble (rĭ sē′və bəl) *adj.* Awaiting or requiring payment; due: *accounts receivable.*

re·ceive (rĭ sēv′) *tr.v.* **re·ceived, re·ceiv·ing, re·ceives.** **1.** To get (sthg. given, offered, or sent): *receive payment.* **2.** To hear or see (information, for example): *We received good news.* **3.** *Formal.* To greet or welcome (sbdy.): *They received us as if we were royalty.* **4.** To regard (sbdy./sthg.) with approval or disapproval: *The movie was well received.*

re·ceiv·er (rĭ sē′vər) *n.* **1.** A person or thing that receives: *a telephone receiver.* **2.** The unit of a communications system, such as radio or television, that receives an incoming signal.

re·cent (rē′sənt) *adj.* Occurring at a time immediately before the present: *the recent past.* —**re′cent·ly** *adv.*

re·cep·ta·cle (rĭ sĕp′tə kəl) *n. Formal.* A container: *a trash receptacle.*

re·cep·tion (rĭ sĕp′shən) *n.* **1.** [U] The act of receiving. **2.** [C] A welcome or greeting: *a friendly reception.* **3.** [C] A social gathering, especially one honoring sbdy.: *a wedding reception.* **4.** [U] The act of receiving electrical

R

or electromagnetic signals or the quality of the signal: *a radio that gets good reception.*

re•cep•tion•ist (rĭ sĕp′shə nĭst) *n.* An office worker employed primarily to receive visitors and answer the telephone.

re•cep•tive (rĭ sĕp′tĭv) *adj.* Ready or willing to listen to sthg. favorably: *The company was receptive to change.* —**re•cep′tive•ly** *adv.* —**re•cep′tive•ness, re•cep•tiv′i•ty** *n.* [U]

re•cep•tor (rĭ sĕp′tər) *n.* A nerve ending specialized to sense or receive stimuli.

re•cess (rē′sĕs′ *or* rĭ sĕs′) *n.* **1.a.** [C] A temporary pause in usual activity: *a court recess ordered by the judge.* See Synonyms at **pause. b.** [U] The period of such a pause: *The children played games during recess.* **2.** [C] *(usually plural).* A distant or secret place: *the hidden recesses of her desk.* —*intr.v.* To take a recess: *The court recessed for lunch.*

re•ces•sion (rĭ sĕsh′ən) *n.* A time when economic activity has been weak: *Economists predicted a recession.*

rec•i•pe (rĕs′ə pē′) *n.* **1.** A set of written directions with a list of ingredients for preparing sthg., especially food: *a recipe for cookies.* **2.** A formula for accomplishing sthg.: *a recipe for success.*

re•cip•i•ent (rĭ sĭp′ē ənt) *n.* A person or thing that receives sthg.: *the recipient of an award.*

re•cip•ro•cal (rĭ sĭp′rə kəl) *adj. Formal.* Given or owed to each other: *The two countries made reciprocal trade agreements.* —**re•cip′ro•cal•ly** *adv.*

re•cip•ro•cate (rĭ sĭp′rə kāt′) *v.* **re•cip•ro•cat•ed, re•cip•ro•cat•ing, re•cip•ro•cates.** *Formal.* —*tr.* **1.** To give or take (sthg.) mutually: *reciprocate favors.* **2.** To show or feel (sthg.) in return: *He reciprocated her love.* —*intr.* To make a return for sthg. given or done: *You buy lunch today, and I'll reciprocate tomorrow.* —**re•cip′ro•ca′tion** *n.* [U]

re•cit•al (rĭ sīt′l) *n.* A performance of music or dance, especially one by a solo performer.

re•cite (rĭ sīt′) *v.* **re•cit•ed, re•cit•ing, re•cites.** —*tr.* To say aloud (sthg. prepared or memorized), especially before an audience: *The child recited the poem.* —*intr.* To repeat lessons prepared or memorized: *The teacher called on me to recite.* —**rec′i•ta′tion** (rĕs′ĭ-tā′shən) *n.* [C; U]

reck•less (rĕk′lĭs) *adj.* Lacking care or caution; careless: *reckless driving.* —**reck′less•ly** *adv.* —**reck′less•ness** *n.* [U]

reck•on (rĕk′ən) *v.* —*tr.* **1.** To count or calculate (sthg.); figure: *reckon time.* **2.** *Informal.* To think or assume (sthg.): *Do you reckon we'll be through in time?* —*intr.* To anticipate (expect): *We didn't reckon on so many guests.* ◆ **reckon with.** *tr.v.* [insep.] To resolve problems with

(sbdy.): *If you forget your homework, you'll have to reckon with the teacher.*

re•claim (rĭ klām′) *tr.v.* **1.** To make (land) usable for growing crops or living on: *The farmers reclaimed the valley and planted corn.* **2.** To extract (useful substances) from garbage or waste products: *The recycling team reclaimed paper from old magazines.* —**re•claim′a•ble** *adj.* —**rec′la•ma′tion** (rĕk′lə mā′shən) *n.* [U]

re•cline (rĭ klīn′) *intr.v.* **re•clined, re•clin•ing, re•clines.** To lie back or down: *The front seat of the car reclines.*

re•clin•er (rĭ klī′nər) *n.* An armchair that reclines when a sitter lowers the back and raises the front: *We put the new recliner in the living room for Dad to sit in when he watches TV.*

re•cluse (rĕk′loōs′ *or* rĭ kloōs′) *n.* A person who lives entirely alone and away from everyone else. —**re•clu′sive** (rĭ kloō′sĭv) *adj.*

rec•og•ni•tion (rĕk′əg nĭsh′ən) *n.* [U] **1.** The act of recognizing. **2.** Acknowledgment or approval: *an award in recognition of excellent service.*

rec•og•nize (rĕk′əg nīz′) *tr.v.* **rec•og•nized, rec•og•niz•ing, rec•og•niz•es. 1.** To know or identify (sbdy./sthg.) from past experience or knowledge: *I recognized friendliness in her smile.* **2.** To accept (sthg.) as valid or real: *recognize the concerns of taxpayers.* **3.** To acknowledge or approve of (sbdy./sthg.): *The court recognized his right to vote.* **4.** To accept officially the national status of (a new nation): *The UN recognized the new country.* **5.** *Formal.* To permit (sbdy.) to speak at a meeting: *The president of the club recognized the treasurer, who then gave her report.* —**rec′og•niz′a•ble** *adj.* —**rec′og•niz′a•bly** *adv.*

re•coil (rĭ koil′) *intr.v.* **1.** To move quickly backward like a gun when it is fired: *The rifle recoiled after being shot.* **2.** To shrink back in fear or dislike: *He recoiled when he saw the snake.* —*n.* (*also* rē′koil′). [U] **1.** The backward action of a gun when fired. **2.** The act of recoiling.

rec•ol•lect (rĕk′ə lĕkt′) *tr.v.* To remember (sthg.): *I don't recollect the details of the assignment.* —**rec′ol•lec′tion** *n.* [C; U]

rec•om•mend (rĕk′ə mĕnd′) *tr.v.* **1.** To praise or suggest (sbdy./sthg.) to another person: *I highly recommend him for the job.* **2.** To advise (a course of action): *He recommended that I see a doctor.*

rec•om•men•da•tion (rĕk′ə mĕn dā′shən) *n.* **1.** [U] The act of recommending. **2.** [C; U] A favorable statement about a person's qualifications or character: *I asked my teacher to write a letter of recommendation.*

rec•on•cile (rĕk′ən sīl′) *tr.v.* **rec•on•ciled,**

rec•on•cil•ing, rec•on•ciles. 1. To restore friendship between (people): *reconcile old enemies.* **2.** To resolve (a dispute): *reconcile the argument.* **3.** To bring (things) into harmony or agreement: *reconcile different points of view.* ◆ **reconcile (oneself) to.** To bring oneself to accept sthg. unwanted: *reconciling herself to the loss of her husband.* —**rec′on•cil′i•a′tion** (rĕk′ən sĭl′ē ā′shən) *n.* [U]

re•con•di•tion (rē′kən dĭsh′ən) *tr.v.* To restore (sthg.) by repairing or rebuilding: *He reconditioned an old car.*

re•con•nais•sance (rĭ kŏn′ə səns) *n.* [C; U] An inspection or exploration of an area, especially to gather information about military forces.

re•con•sid•er (rē′kən sĭd′ər) *tr.v.* To think about (sthg.) again, especially with the possibility of making a change: *He reconsidered taking the job, but the pay was too low.* —**re′con•sid′er•a′tion** *n.* [U]

re•con•struct (rē′kən strŭkt′) *tr.v.* **1.** To build (sthg.) again; restore: *We reconstructed the model house.* **2.** To determine or trace (sthg.) from information or clues: *reconstruct the events that preceded the accident.* —**re′con•struc′tion** *n.* [C; U]

re•cord (rĭ kôrd′) *tr.v.* **1.** To save (sthg.) in writing or another permanent form: *She recorded each change in the book.* **2.** To register or show (sthg.): *A thermometer records temperature.* **3.** To store (sound or images) in some permanent form as on a videotape or cassette tape: *record a movie.* —*n.* **rec•ord** (rĕk′ərd). **1.** An account, usually in writing, that saves knowledge: *a record of what happened on the trip.* **2.** The known history of performance or achievement: *your high-school record.* **3.** The highest or lowest measurement known, as in a sports event or the weather: *the record for most rainfall in a year; She holds the record in the 800-meter run.* **4.** A disk designed to be played on a phonograph: *Records have been replaced by tapes and CDs.* ◆ **off the record.** Not for publication: *The senator told the reporters that his remarks were off the record.* **on record.** Known to have been stated or to have taken a certain position: *She's on record as opposing the new law.*

re•cord•er (rĭ kôr′dər) *n.* **1.** A person or thing that records: *a tape recorder.* **2.** A type of flute.

re•cord•ing (rĭ kôr′dĭng) *n.* **1.** Something on which sound or visual images have been recorded, as a tape or a compact disk. **2.** A recorded sound or picture.

re•count (rĭ kount′) *tr.v.* To tell (sthg.) in detail: *The book recounts the battles of World War II.*

re•coup (rĭ kōōp′) *tr.v. Informal.* To receive sthg. equal to (sthg. lost); make up for: *He recouped his losses when the stock market improved.*

re•course (rē′kôrs *or* rĭ kôrs′) *n.* [U] **1.** A way to receive aid or protection: *You have recourse to the courts.* **2.** A person or thing to turn to for help or protection: *Her only recourse was legal action.*

re•cov•er (rĭ kŭv′ər) *v.* —*tr.* **1.** To get (sthg.) back; regain: *The police tried to recover the stolen bicycle.* **2.** To regain control over (oneself): *He recovered himself sufficiently to speak in public.* **3.** To make up for (sthg.); compensate for: *She recovered her losses.* —*intr.* To return to a normal or healthy condition: *recover after a long illness.* —**re•cov′er•a•ble** *adj.* —**re•cov′er•y** *n.* [C; U]

re•cre•ate (rē′krē āt′) *tr.v.* **re•cre•at•ed, re•cre•at•ing, re•cre•ates.** To make (sthg.) again: *re-create the scene.* —**re′-cre•a′tion** *n.* [C; U]

rec•re•a•tion (rĕk′rē ā′shən) *n.* [C; U] An activity, such as a sport or game, to refresh one's mind or body: *What do you like to do for recreation?* —**rec′re•a′tion•al** *adj.*

rec•re•a•tion•al vehicle (rĕk′rē ā′shə nəl) *n.* A large vehicle, such as a camper, with beds, kitchen, and often a bath, used to travel.

re•cruit (rĭ krōōt′) *tr.v.* **1.** To enlist (sbdy.) in military service: *The officer recruited young people for the army.* **2.** To supply (new members or employees) for sthg.: *They recruited new members for the club.* —*n.* **1.** A newly enlisted member of the armed forces. **2.** A new member of any organization. —**re•cruit′er** *n* —**re•cruit′ment** *n.* [U]

rec•tal (rĕk′təl) *adj.* Relating to the rectum.

rec•tan•gle (rĕk′tăng′gəl) *n.* A flat geometric shape with four sides and four right angles. —**rec•tan′gu•lar** (rĕk-tăng′gyə lər) *adj.*

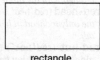
rectangle

rec•ti•fy (rĕk′tə fī′) *tr.v.* **rec•ti•fied, rec•ti•fy•ing, rec•ti•fies.** *Formal.* To set (sthg.) right; correct: *He plans to rectify his errors.*

rec•tum (rĕk′təm) *n.* The lower end of the digestive system, extending from the colon to the anus, where wastes are passed out of the body.

re•cu•per•ate (rĭ kōō′pə rāt′) *intr.v.* **re•cu•per•at•ed, re•cu•per•at•ing, re•cu•per•ates.** [*from*] To return to normal health or strength; recover: *recuperate from the flu.* —**re•cu′per•a′tion** *n.* [U] —**re•cu′per•a′tive** *adj.*

re•cur (rĭ kûr′) *intr.v.* **re•curred, re•cur•ring, re•curs.** To happen again or repeatedly; return: *an area where earthquakes recur.* —**re•cur′rence** *n.* [C; U]

re•cy•cle (rē sī′kəl) *tr. & intr.v.* **re•cy•cled, re•cy•cling, re•cy•cles.** To process and reuse useful substances found in garbage or waste: *She recycled the old newspapers and bottles. We always recycle.* —**re•cy′cla•ble** *adj. & n.* —**re•cy′cler** *n.*

red (rĕd) *n.* [C; U] The color of blood or of a

ripe strawberry. — *adj.* **red•der, red•dest.**
With a color resembling that of blood or a
ripe strawberry. ◆ **in the red.** Operating at a
loss; in debt: *Our company was in the red
after a year in business.* **see red.** To be very
angry: *When my brother took my CD player
without asking, I saw red.*

red-blood•ed (rĕd′blŭd′ĭd) *adj.* Strong and
full of vigor: *a red-blooded American who
loves television and baseball.*

red•den (rĕd′n) *tr. & intr.v.* To make or
become red: *His face reddened with embarrassment. The cold reddens my nose.*

red•dish (rĕd′ĭsh) *adj.* Somewhat red.

re•deem (rĭ dēm′) *tr.v.* **1.** To turn in (coupons,
for example) and receive sthg. in exchange:
redeem the winning ticket for a prize. **2.** To
exchange (stocks or bonds, for example) for
cash: *redeem his mutual fund account.* **3.** To
make up for (sthg.): *a deed that redeemed her
earlier mistake.* ◆ **have redeeming value** or
quality. To possess some positive characteristic: *That television program has no redeeming
value.* — **re•deem′a•ble** *adj.*

re•demp•tion (rĭ dĕmp′shən) *n.* [U] The
act of redeeming: *redemption of a winning
lottery ticket.*

red-eye (rĕd′ī′) *n.* An airplane flight that
leaves very late at night and arrives very early
in the morning: *I caught the red-eye from
New York to Los Angeles.*

red-hand•ed (rĕd′hăn′dĭd) *adv.* In the act of
doing sthg. wrong: *The thief was caught red-
handed with the money.*

red•head (rĕd′hĕd′) *n.* A person with red hair:
the only redhead in her family.—**red′head′ed**
adj.

red-hot (rĕd′hŏt′) *adj.* **1.** Hot enough to
glow red: *a red-hot bar of steel.* **2.** New; very
recent: *red-hot information.*

red-let•ter (rĕd′lĕt′ər) *adj.* Memorably
happy; important: *a red-letter day.*

red pepper *n.* **1.** [C] The ripened fruit of a
pepper plant. **2.** [U] Cayenne pepper.

red tape *n.* [U] Procedures or rules, especially
those connected with the official business of
government, that require great attention to
detail and often result in delay or inaction: *We
had to cut through a lot of red tape to open our
new business.*

re•duce (rĭ dōōs′) *v.* **re•duced, re•duc•
ing, re•duc•es.** —*tr.* **1.** To make (sthg.) less
in amount or degree; lessen: *reduce the volume of the music.* See Synonyms at **decrease.** **2.** To bring (sthg.) into a lower or
worse condition or state: *The explosion
reduced the building to rubble.* —*intr.* To lose
body weight, as by dieting: *After overeating
all month, I need to reduce.*

re•duc•tion (rĭ dŭk′shən) *n.* [C; U] The act

of reducing: *a reduction in unemployment.*

re•dun•dant (rĭ dŭn′dənt) *adj.* **1.** Involving
unnecessary repetition: *The editor took out a
redundant paragraph in the essay.* **2.** More
than what is needed; extra: *redundant machine parts.* — **re•dun′dan•cy** *n.* [C; U]
— **re•dun′dant•ly** *adv.*

red•wood (rĕd′wŏŏd′) *n.* A very tall cone-
bearing evergreen tree of northwest California, sometimes growing to a height of over
300 feet.

reed (rēd) *n.* **1.** A tall hollow-stemmed grass that
grows in wet places. **2.a.** A flexible strip of
cane or metal used in mouthpieces of certain
wind instruments. **b.** A woodwind instrument,
such as an oboe or a clarinet, with a reed.

HOMONYMS: reed, read (understand writing).

reed•y (rē′dē) *adj.* **reed•i•er, reed•i•est.**
1. Full of reeds: *a reedy swamp.* **2.** Resembling a reed: *a thin reedy girl.* **3.** With the
sound of a reed instrument: *the oboe's reedy
tone.* — **reed′i•ness** *n.* [U]

reef (rēf) *n.* A ridge of rock or coral that is
near the surface of a body of water.

reek (rēk) *intr.v.* To give off a strong or
unpleasant odor: *a salad reeking of garlic.*

HOMONYMS: reek, wreak (cause).

reel¹ (rēl) *n.* A device that turns on a central rod
or pin and is used for winding and storing rope,
film, tape, fishing line, and other flexible materials. —*tr.v.* **1.** To wind (sthg.) onto a reel: *reel
the yarn onto a spool.* **2.** [in] To pull in (a fish)
by winding on a reel: *reel in a shark.* ◆ **reel off.**
tr.v. [sep.] To recite (sthg.) fluently and usually
at length: *He reeled off a list of names.*

reel² (rēl) *intr.v.* **1.** To be thrown off balance:
The gymnast reeled when she hit the bar. **2.**
To stagger or sway: *After spinning around,
she reeled across the room.* **3.** To go round
and round in a whirling motion: *The events of
the day reeled in his mind.*

re•e•lect (rē′ĭ lĕkt′) *tr.v.* To elect (sbdy.)
again: *The president was reelected after a
close race.* — **re′e•lec′tion** *n.* [C; U]

re•en•try (rē ĕn′trē) *n., pl.* **re•en•tries.**
[C; U] The act of coming in or entering again:
the spacecraft's reentry into the atmosphere.

re•es•tab•lish (rē′ĭ stăb′lĭsh) *tr.v.* To
establish (sthg.) again; restore: *reestablish an
account that was closed.* — **re′es•tab′lish•
ment** *n.* [U]

re•ex•am•ine (rē′ĭg zăm′ĭn) *tr.v.* **re•ex•
am•ined, re•ex•am•in•ing, re•ex•am•
ines.** To consider or look over (sthg.) again;
review: *Let's reexamine the facts.*

re•fer (rĭ fûr′) *v.* **re•ferred, re•fer•ring,**

re·fers. —*tr.* To direct (sbdy.) to a person or an organization for help or information: *refer a patient to a heart specialist.* —*intr.* [*to*] **1.** To be about; concern: *questions that refer to today's lecture.* **2.** To mention or name as: *referring to her grandmother as "Nana."* **3.** To use as a source of information or authority: *refer to a dictionary.*

ref·e·ree (rĕf′ə rē′) *n.* **1.** In sports, an official supervising play. **2.** A person to whom sthg. is referred for a decision. —*tr. & intr.v.* To judge or act as a referee: *She refereed the soccer game. She referees every Saturday.*

ref·er·ence (rĕf′ər əns *or* rĕf′rəns) *n.* **1.** [U] An act of referring: *Let's file that article away for future reference.* **2.** [C] A mention of an occurrence, a situation, or a person: *He made frequent references to his trip to Europe.* **3.** [C] A note in a book or other publication that directs the reader to another part of the book or to another source of information. **4.** [C] A statement about a person's character or qualifications for sthg.: *I asked my boss for a reference.*

reference book *n.* A book, such as an encyclopedia, that provides information arranged for easy access.

ref·er·en·dum (rĕf′ə rĕn′dəm) *n., pl.* **ref·er·en·dums** *or* **ref·er·en·da.** A vote on an issue rather than a candidate: *The referendum on the school bond issue passed.*

re·fer·ral (rĭ fûr′əl) *n.* **1.** The act of referring: *the referral of the patient to a cancer specialist.* **2.** A person who has been referred to a specialist, such as a doctor or lawyer: *The doctor saw many of her own patients plus several referrals.*

re·fill (rē fĭl′) *tr.v.* To fill (sthg.) again: *He refilled the glass with water.* —*n.* (rē′fĭl′). **1.** A second or following filling: *She held out her glass for a refill.* **2.** A product for replacing the contents of a container when they have been used up: *I put a new refill in my pen.*

re·fine (rĭ fīn′) *tr.v.* **re·fined, re·fin·ing, re·fines.** **1.** To remove unwanted matter from (sthg.); make pure: *refine oil; refine sugar.* **2.** To improve or make (sthg.) elegant: *refine one's writing.*

re·fined (rĭ fīnd′) *adj.* **1.** Made pure, as through an industrial refining process: *refined sugar.* **2.** Free from rudeness; polite: *She is a refined person.*

re·fine·ment (rĭ fīn′mənt) *n.* **1.** [U] The act of improving: *Your writing has undergone much refinement.* **2.** [C] A small change or addition intended to improve sthg.: *We made some refinements to the computer program.* **3.** [U] Elegance; cultivation: *a person of refinement.*

re·fin·er·y (rĭ fī′nə rē) *n., pl.* **re·fin·er·ies.** An industrial plant for purifying a crude substance, such as petroleum or sugar.

re·flect (rĭ flĕkt′) *v.* —*tr.* **1.** To throw or bend back (light, for example) from a surface: *The*

water reflected the sunlight. **2.** To form an image of (sbdy./sthg.); mirror: *The shop window reflected his face.* **3.** To show (sthg.) as a result: *The price of a product reflects the cost of producing it.* —*intr.* **1.** To be thrown or bent back: *light reflecting from the water.* **2.** To think seriously; ponder: *I need time to reflect before answering your question.* ◆ **reflect on.** *tr.v.* [insep.] **1.** To form or express thoughts about (sthg.): *We reflected on the meaning of the poem.* **2.** To give evidence of the qualities of (sbdy.): *Keeping your room neat reflects positively on you.*

re·flec·tion (rĭ flĕk′shən) *n.* **1.** [U] The act of reflecting: *the reflection of light by a mirror.* **2.** [C] An image formed by reflected light: *the reflection of the trees in the river.* **3.** [U] Serious thought: *After long reflection, he decided to enroll in the course.* **4.** [C] A result: *Her achievements are a reflection of her hard work.* —**re·flec′tive** *adj.*

re·flec·tor (rĭ flĕk′tər) *n.* Something, such as a surface, that reflects: *We could see the reflector on the bicycle in the darkness.*

re·flex (rē′flĕks′) *n.* An involuntary or instinctive response to a stimulus: *Swatting at the bee was a reflex.*

re·flex·ive (rĭ flĕk′sĭv) *adj.* **1.** Relating to a reflex: *a reflexive movement.* **2.** In grammar, referring to: **a.** A verb that has an identical subject and direct object. In the sentence *She dressed herself,* the word *dressed* is a reflexive verb. **b.** A pronoun used as the direct object of a reflexive verb. In the sentence *He blames himself,* the word *himself* is a reflexive pronoun. —*n.* A reflexive verb or pronoun. —**re·flex′ive·ly** *adv.*

re·for·est (rē fôr′ĭst *or* rē fŏr′ĭst) *tr.v.* To replant (an area) with trees: *The ecologists reforested the burned area.* —**re′for·es·ta′tion** *n.* [U]

re·form (rĭ fôrm′) *v.* —*tr.* **1.** To improve (sthg.) by correcting errors or removing defects: *a plan to reform the health care system.* **2.** To cause (sbdy.) to give up harmful ways: *a program designed to reform criminals.* —*intr.* To become changed for the better: *He has reformed and no longer drinks.* —*n.* [C; U] A change or attempt to change for the better: *the reform of city government.* —**re·form′er** *n.*

ref·or·ma·tion (rĕf′ər mā′shən) *n.* [C; U] The act of reforming: *a total reformation of the school system.*

re·for·ma·to·ry (rĭ fôr′mə tôr′ē) *n., pl.* **re·for·ma·to·ries.** A place in which young lawbreakers are confined and disciplined.

re·frain¹ (rĭ frān′) *intr.v.* [*from*] To stop oneself from doing sthg.: *Please refrain from talking.*

re·frain² (rĭ frān′) *n.* A piece of music or group of words repeated several times in a song or poem.

R

re•fresh (rĭ frĕsh′) *tr.v.* **1.** To revive (sbdy.) with food, drink, or rest: *I refreshed myself with an afternoon nap.* **2.** To renew (sthg.) by stimulation: *refresh one's memory by rereading notes.* —**re•fresh′er** *n.* —**re•fresh′ing** *adj.* —**re•fresh′ing•ly** *adv.*

re•fresh•ment (rĭ frĕsh′mənt) *n.* **1.** [U] The act of refreshing. **2. refreshments.** A light meal or snack and drinks: *We offered our guests some refreshments.*

re•frig•er•ate (rĭ frĭj′ə rāt′) *tr.v.* **re•frig•er•at•ed, re•frig•er•at•ing, re•frig•er•ates.** **1.** To cool or chill (sthg.): *I refrigerated some water for drinking.* **2.** To preserve (food) by storing at a low temperature: *refrigerate leftover meat.* —**re•frig′er•a′tion** *n.* [U]

re•frig•er•a•tor (rĭ frĭj′ə rā′tər) *n.* An appliance for cooling food or other things.

ref•uge (rĕf′yōōj) *n.* **1.** [U] Protection; shelter: *They looked for refuge from the storm.* **2.** [C] A place that provides protection or shelter: *a wildlife refuge.*

ref•u•gee (rĕf′yōō jē′) *n.* A person who leaves a place in search of refuge in times of war or persecution.

re•fund (rĭ fŭnd′ or rē′ fŭnd′) *tr.v.* To pay back (money): *The store refunded the full price of the television set.* —*n.* (rē′ fŭnd′). [C; U] **1.** A repayment of money: *She demanded a refund.* **2.** An amount repaid: *How much was your tax refund?* —**re•fund′a•ble** *adj.*

re•fur•bish (rē fûr′bĭsh) *tr.v.* To freshen (sthg.) up: *refurbish a house.*

re•fus•al (rĭ fyōō′zəl) *n.* [C; U] The act of refusing: *His refusal of our offer surprised me.*

re•fuse[1] (rĭ fyōōz′) *v.* **re•fused, re•fus•ing, re•fus•es.** —*tr.* **1.** To be unwilling (to do sthg.): *I refuse to waste my money.* **2.** To be unwilling to accept (sthg.); turn down: *refuse an offer.* **3.** To be unwilling to give (sthg.); deny: *We were refused permission to leave early.* —*intr.* To decline to do, accept, give, or allow sthg.: *I'm sorry, but I must refuse.*

SYNONYMS: **refuse, decline, reject.** These verbs mean to be unwilling to accept, consider, or receive sbdy./sthg. **Refuse** can mean to oppose sthg. in an abrupt, rude way: *The captain refused to hear of any changes to the plan.* **Decline** means to refuse politely: *He declined the job promotion because he wanted to spend more time with his family.* **Reject** suggests turning away or discarding sbdy./sthg. as useless or defective: *The army would reject you because of your poor health.* ANTONYM: **accept.**

ref•use[2] (rĕf′yōōs) *n.* [U] *Formal.* Trash; waste: *City workers emptied the containers of refuse.*

re•fute (rĭ fyōōt′) *tr.v.* **re•fut•ed, re•**

fut•ing, re•futes. To prove (sthg.) to be false or wrong: *Their opponents in the debate refuted their statements.*

re•gain (rē gān′) *tr.v.* To recover possession of (sthg.); get back: *regain one's health.*

re•gal (rē′gəl) *adj.* **1.** Relating to a king; royal: *regal power.* **2.** Proper for a king: *a regal appearance.*

re•gale (rĭ gāl′) *tr.v.* **re•galed, re•gal•ing, re•gales.** [*with*] To entertain or amuse (sbdy.): *They regaled us with their stories and jokes.*

re•ga•lia (rĭ gāl′yə) *pl.n.* (*used with a singular or plural verb*). Fine or fancy clothes; finery: *the bride and groom in all their wedding regalia.*

re•gard (rĭ gärd′) *tr.v.* **1.** To look at (sbdy./sthg.) closely; observe: *The naturalist regarded the wolves carefully.* **2.** To hold (sbdy./sthg.) in affection or esteem: *He regards his teachers highly.* **3.** To relate to (sbdy./sthg.); concern: *This decision regards the future of our company.* —*n.* **1.** [U] Careful thought or attention: *She gives little regard to her appearance.* **2.** [U] Esteem or affection: *showing regard for his parents.* **3. regards.** Good wishes; greetings: *Send her my regards, will you?* ◆ **in** or **with regard to.** *Formal.* With respect to; about: *I'm calling in regard to the apartment you have for rent.*

re•gard•ing (rĭ gär′dĭng) *prep.* In reference to; about: *laws regarding sanitation.*

re•gard•less (rĭ gärd′lĭs) *adv.* In spite of everything; anyway: *She still loved him, regardless.*

re•gat•ta (rĭ gä′tə or rĭ găt′ə) *n.* A boat race or races, organized as a sporting event.

re•gen•er•ate (rĭ jĕn′ə rāt′) *tr.v.* **re•gen•er•at•ed, re•gen•er•at•ing, re•gen•er•ates.** **1.** To give new life to (sbdy./sthg.); revive: *The reforms were intended to regenerate the nation's economy.* **2.** To replace (a damaged or lost part or an organ) by growing new tissue: *A starfish can regenerate a lost arm.* —**re•gen′er•a′tion** *n.* [U] —**re•gen′er•a′tive** *adj.*

re•gent (rē′jənt) *n.* A member of the governing board of a state university or a state system of schools.

reg•gae (rĕg′ā) *n.* [U] Popular music of Jamaican origin.

re•gime (rā zhēm′ or rĭ zhēm′) *n.* **1.** A government or system of government: *a communist regime.* **2.** A system of care or treatment, such as a diet: *a beauty regime.*

reg•i•ment (rĕj′ə mənt) *n.* A unit of soldiers. —*tr.v.* (rĕj′ə mĕnt′). To control or put (sbdy./sthg.) into systematic order: *Our coach regiments our team strictly.* —**reg′i•men′tal** (rĕj′ə mĕn′tl) *adj.* —**reg′i•men•ta′tion** *n.* [U]

R

re·gion (rē′jən) *n.* **1.** ′A large portion of the earth's surface: *polar regions.* **2.** A large area of a surface or space: *the upper regions of the atmosphere.* **3.** A section or an area of the body: *the abdominal region.* —**re′gion·al** *adj.* —**re′gion·al·ly** *adv.*

reg·is·ter (rĕj′ĭ stər) *n.* **1.** An official record or list: *a register of all voters.* **2.** A device that automatically records or displays a number or amount: *a cash register.* —*v.* —*tr.* **1.** To record (sthg.) in a register: *register a birth.* **2.** To set (sthg.) down in writing; record: *register a complaint.* **3.** To indicate (sthg.) on a scale or device: *It registers 100°F on the thermometer.* **4.** To enroll (sbdy.) in order to vote or attend classes: *He registered himself in a chemistry course.* **5.** To show or express (sthg.): *His face registered no emotion.* —*intr.* **1.** To place one's name placed in a register: *You can register for the conference in the lobby.* **2.** To have one's name placed on a list of voters: *In order to participate in the election, you must first register.* **3.** To enroll as a student: *What day do you register for classes?* **4.** To be shown or expressed: *Recognition did not register on her face.* **5.** To make an impression: *Her name failed to register in my memory.*

reg·is·trar (rĕj′ĭ strär′ *or* rĕj′ĭ strär′) *n.* An official, especially at a university, who is responsible for keeping records.

reg·is·tra·tion (rĕj′ĭ strā′shən) *n.* **1.** [U] The act of registering, as of voters or students. **2.** [U] The number of people registered: *Voter registration in our town is 11,000.* **3.** [C] A document showing proof that (sthg.) has been registered: *The police officer asked to see my automobile registration.*

reg·is·try (rĕj′ĭ strē) *n., pl.* **reg·is·tries. 1.** [U] The act of registering; registration. **2.** [C] A place where official records are kept: *the Registry of Motor Vehicles.*

re·gress (rĭ grĕs′) *intr.v.* To go back to a previous condition; revert: *After not practicing her English, her knowledge of it regressed.* —**re·gres′sion** (rĭ grĕsh′ən) *n.* [U]

re·gret (rĭ grĕt′) *tr.v.* **re·gret·ted, re·gret·ting, re·grets. 1.** To feel sorry about (sthg.): *regret an error.* **2.** To remember (sthg.) with a sense of loss; mourn: *She regretted leaving her classmates.* —*n.* **1.** [C; U] A feeling of loss or disappointment: *She felt regret about what she had done.* **2. regrets.** A polite reply turning down an invitation: *send one's regrets.* —**re·gret′ta·ble** *adj.*

re·gret·ful (rĭ grĕt′fəl) *adj.* Full of regret; sorrowful or sorry: *I was regretful about my bad behavior.* —**re·gret′ful·ly** *adv.*

reg·u·lar (rĕg′yə lər) *adj.* **1.** Usual or normal: *the train's regular schedule.* **2.** Following an established procedure: *regular study habits.* **3.** Steady; habitual: *a regular customer.* **4.** Occurring at fixed intervals:

regular meals. **5.** Orderly, even, or symmetrical: *regular teeth.* **6.** *Informal.* Likable; nice: *He's a regular guy.* **7.** In grammar, conforming to the usual pattern of inflection, derivation, or word formation: *a regular verb.* —*n.* A habitual customer: *The waitress recognized him as one of the regulars.* —**reg′u·lar′i·ty** (rĕg′yə lăr′ĭ tē) *n.* [U] —**reg′u·lar·ly** *adv.*

reg·u·late (rĕg′yə lāt′) *tr.v.* **reg·u·lat·ed, reg·u·lat·ing, reg·u·lates. 1.** To control or direct (sthg.) according to a rule or law: *power to regulate trade.* **2.** To adjust (sthg.) for proper functioning: *regulate a heater.* **3.** To adjust or control (sthg.) according to a requirement: *This valve regulates the flow of water.* —**reg′u·la′tor** *n.*

reg·u·la·tion (rĕg′yə lā′shən) *n.* **1.** [C; U] The act of regulating: *government regulation.* **2.** [C] A rule, an order, or a law by which sthg. is regulated: *traffic regulations.*

reg·u·la·to·ry (rĕg′yə lə tôr′ē) *adj.* Having the ability to regulate or oversee: *a regulatory agency.*

re·gur·gi·tate (rē gûr′jĭ tāt′) *v.* **re·gur·gi·tat·ed, re·gur·gi·tat·ing, re·gur·gi·tates.** —*intr.* To vomit. —*tr.* **1.** To cause (partially digested food) to pour from the stomach through the mouth; vomit. **2.** To repeat (information) without understanding: *Students should not just regurgitate facts on the test.* —**re·gur′gi·ta′tion** *n.* [U]

re·ha·bil·i·tate (rē′hə bĭl′ĭ tāt′) *tr.v.* **re·ha·bil·i·tat·ed, re·ha·bil·i·tat·ing, re·ha·bil·i·tates. 1.** To restore (sbdy.) to useful life, as through training or therapy: *rehabilitate criminals for productive lives.* **2.** To restore (sthg.) to good condition or operation: *rehabilitate a house.* —**re′ha·bil′i·ta′tion** *n.* [U]

re·hash (rē hăsh′) *tr.v.* To present or go over (sthg.) again, without anything new resulting: *The sisters rehashed their disagreement.* —*n.* (rē′hăsh′). Something that is rehashed: *His book is a rehash of some earlier ideas.*

re·hears·al (rĭ hûr′səl) *n.* [C; U] The process of practicing in preparation for a performance or ceremony: *a wedding rehearsal; a play rehearsal.*

re·hearse (rĭ hûrs′) *v.* **re·hearsed, re·hears·ing, re·hears·es.** —*tr.* **1.** To practice (all or part of a program) in preparation for a performance: *The boys rehearsed their song.* **2.** To train (sbdy.) by rehearsal: *rehearse a choir.* —*intr.* To practice sthg., such as a speech, before presenting it publicly: *Before we sing publicly, we should rehearse.*

reign (rān) *n.* **1.** The exercise of political power by a monarch. **2.** The period during which a monarch rules: *the reign of Queen Elizabeth.* —*intr.v.* **1.** [over] To exercise the power of a monarch: *The queen reigns over her country.* **2.** To be widely felt or noticeable: *Quiet reigned after the storm.*

HOMONYMS: **reign**, **rain** (water drops), **rein** (strap).

re·im·burse (rē′ĭm bûrs′) *tr.v.* **re·im·bursed, re·im·burs·ing, re·im·burs·es.** To pay (sbdy.) back; compensate: *They reimbursed us for our travel expenses.* —**re′·im·burs′a·ble** *adj.* —**re′im·burse′ment** *n.* [C; U]

rein (rān) *n.* *(usually plural).* **1.** A long narrow strap attached to the bit in a horse's mouth and held by the rider or driver to control the horse. **2.** A means of restraint or guidance: *the reins of government.* —*tr.v.* To hold (sbdy./sthg.) back as if by reins: *The rider reined the horse.* ♦ **give free rein to.** To release (sbdy./sthg.) from restraints; allow to go unchecked: *She gave free rein to her feelings.* **keep a tight rein on.** To control (sbdy./sthg.) very closely: *Our teacher keeps a tight rein on the class.* **rein in.** *tr.v.* [sep.] To keep (sbdy./sthg.) under control: *That child's parents need to rein him in or he'll never learn manners.* **take the reins.** To take control of sthg.: *One of my classmates took the reins when our teacher had to leave for a minute.*

HOMONYMS: **rein**, **rain** (water drops), **reign** (rule).

re·in·car·na·tion (rē′ĭn kär nā′shən) *n.* [C; U] Rebirth in another body or form: *the reincarnation of that play as a movie.* —**re′in·car′nate** (rē′ĭn kär′nāt) *v.*

rein·deer (rān′dîr′) *n.* A deer of arctic regions of Europe, Asia, and North America, with large antlers in both the males and females.

reindeer

re·in·force (rē′ĭn fôrs′) *tr.v.* **re·in·forced, re·in·forc·ing, re·in·forc·es.** To make (sthg.) stronger by adding extra support to it; strengthen: *reinforce a bridge; reinforce safety.* —**re′in·force′a·ble** *adj.*

re·in·force·ment (rē′ĭn fôrs′mənt) *n.* **1.** [U] The act of reinforcing: *She needs a lot of positive reinforcement.* **2. reinforcements.** Additional troops or equipment sent to support a military action.

re·in·state (rē′ĭn stāt′) *tr.v.* **re·in·stat·ed, re·in·stat·ing, re·in·states.** To return (sbdy./sthg.) to a previous condition or position: *After a long leave of absence, she was reinstated in her job.* —**re′in·state′ment** *n.* [C; U]

re·it·er·ate (rē ĭt′ə rāt′) *tr.v.* **re·it·er·at·ed, re·it·er·at·ing, re·it·er·ates.** To say (sthg.) over again; repeat: *The coach reiterated his instructions.* —**re·it′er·a′tion** *n.* [C; U]

re·ject (rĭ jĕkt′) *tr.v.* **1.** To refuse to accept (sthg.): *We rejected the idea of working late.* See Synonyms at **refuse**[1]. **2.** To refuse to consider (sthg.): *My mother rejected my plans for a big party.* **3.** To fail to give affection or love to (sbdy.): *reject an old boyfriend.* **4.** To fail to accept (a transplanted organ or tissue) as part of one's own body: *reject the new liver after surgery.* —*n.* (rē′jĕkt). A person or thing that has been rejected: *rejects from military service.* —**re·jec′tion** *n.* [C; U]

re·joice (rĭ jois′) *intr.v.* **re·joiced, re·joic·ing, re·joic·es.** *Formal.* To feel joy; be delighted: *I rejoice in your good fortune.*

re·join (rē join′) *tr.v.* **1.** To join (things) together again: *The plumber rejoined the pipes that had separated.* **2.** To return to (sbdy./sthg.); reunite with: *The explorer rejoined his family.*

re·join·der (rĭ join′dər) *n.* *Formal.* An answer, especially in response to another's answer: *His criticism met with a rejoinder.*

re·ju·ve·nate (rĭ jōō′və nāt′) *tr.v.* **re·ju·ve·nat·ed, re·ju·ve·nat·ing, re·ju·ve·nates.** To make (sbdy./sthg.) young or vigorous again: *Her vacation completely rejuvenated her.* —**re·ju′ve·na′tion** *n.* [U]

re·lapse (rĭ lăps′) *intr.v.* **re·lapsed, re·laps·ing, re·laps·es. 1.** To fall back into an earlier condition: *We relapsed into our old sloppy habits.* **2.** To become sick again after a partial recovery: *He went back to work soon after having the flu, and then relapsed.* —*n.* (rē′lăps or rĭ lăps′). A falling back into an earlier condition, especially a return to illness: *Doctors feared the patient would suffer a relapse.*

re·late (rĭ lāt′) *v.* **re·lat·ed, re·lat·ing, re·lates.** —*tr.* **1.** To tell or narrate (sthg.): *relate a story.* **2.** To connect (sthg.): *I related his bad mood to a lack of sleep.* —*intr.* To interact with other persons in a meaningful way: *She relates well to her classmates.*

re·lat·ed (rĭ lā′tĭd) *adj.* **1.** Connected: *closely related topics.* **2.** Connected by kinship, marriage, or common origin: *We're related—he's my cousin.*

re·la·tion (rĭ lā′shən) *n.* **1.** [U] A connection between two or more things: *the relation of health and a good diet.* **2.** [C; U] A person connected to another by blood or marriage; a relative: *Is he any relation to you?* **3. relations.** The dealings or associations of persons, groups, or nations: *a country's foreign relations.*

R

re·la·tion·ship (rĭ lā′shən shĭp′) *n.* **1.** [U] The condition of being related; a connection. **2.** [C] A connection or tie between persons: *a business relationship.* **3.** [U] Family connection; kinship: *She claimed relationship to the millionaire.*

rel·a·tive (rĕl′ə tĭv) *adj.* **1.** Related; about: *your comments relative to my homework.* **2.** Considered in comparison with sthg. else: *the relative quiet of the suburbs.* **3.** Dependent on sthg. else for meaning; not absolute: *"Expensive" is a relative word.* **4.** In grammar, referring to an antecedent, as the pronoun *who* refers to *the woman* in the phrase *the woman who plays guitar.* —*n.* A person related by blood or marriage: *All the close relatives came to the wedding.*

relative clause *n.* In grammar, a dependent clause introduced by a relative pronoun. In the sentence *He who hesitates is lost,* the relative clause is *who hesitates.*

rel·a·tive·ly (rĕl′ə tĭv lē) *adv.* In comparison with sthg. else: *a relatively minor problem.*

relative pronoun *n.* In grammar, a pronoun that introduces a relative clause and refers to an antecedent. In the sentence *The house that I live in has a porch,* the relative pronoun is *that.*

rel·a·tiv·i·ty (rĕl′ə tĭv′ĭ tē) *n.* [U] **1.** The condition of being relative. **2.** The two-part theory of space and time developed by Albert Einstein.

re·lax (rĭ lăks′) *v.* —*tr.* **1.** To make (sthg.) less tight or tense: *relax one's muscles.* **2.** To make (sthg.) less severe or strict: *relax the rules.* **3.** To relieve (sbdy.) of tension or anxiety: *Listening to jazz relaxes me.* —*intr.* **1.** To rest: *I relaxed on the sofa.* **2.** To become less tight or tense: *My muscles relaxed in a hot bath.* **3.** To become less severe or strict: *My mother relaxed when she saw we did our work without being told.* **4.** To become less tense or anxious: *When I look at beautiful scenery, I always relax.*

re·lax·a·tion (rē′lăk sā′shən) *n.* **1.** [C; U] The act of relaxing: *a relaxation of the muscles.* **2.** [U] The condition of being relaxed: *She lay in bed in perfect relaxation.* **3.** [U] Refreshment of body or mind; fun; diversion: *What do you do for relaxation?*

re·laxed (rĭ lăkst′) *adj.* **1.** Not severe or strict: *a relaxed attitude.* **2.** Free from tension or anxiety: *a relaxed evening meal.*

re·lay (rē′lā) *n.* **1.** A race between two or more teams, in which each member of a team goes a part of the total distance. **2.** A switch that is operated by an electric current. —*tr.v.* (rē′lā *or* rĭ lā′). To pass or send (sthg.) along as if by relay: *relay the message to the boss.*

re·lease (rĭ lēs′) *tr.v.* **re·leased, re·leas·ing, re·leas·es. 1.** To set (sbdy.) free; liberate: *release prisoners.* **2.** To free (sthg.) from sbdy./sthg. that fastens or holds back; let go: *release balloons.* **3.** To make (sthg.)

available to the public: *release a film.* —*n.* **1.** [U] The act of releasing, as from prison or pain: *release of a prisoner.* **2.** [C] Something issued to the public: *a press release.*

rel·e·gate (rĕl′ĭ gāt′) *tr.v.* **rel·e·gat·ed, rel·e·gat·ing, rel·e·gates.** To send or remove (sbdy./sthg.) to a place or condition of less importance: *He has been relegated to a lower-paying job.* —**rel′e·ga′tion** *n.* [U]

re·lent (rĭ lĕnt′) *intr.v.* To agree to sthg. after first refusing: *After saying "no" repeatedly, my mother finally relented.*

re·lent·less (rĭ lĕnt′lĭs) *adj.* **1.** Very harsh; unyielding: *relentless criticism.* **2.** Not stopping: *a relentless wind.* —**re·lent′less·ly** *adv.*

rel·e·vant (rĕl′ə vənt) *adj.* Related to the matter being considered; pertinent: *relevant questions.* —**rel′e·vance, rel′e·van·cy** *n.* [U] —**rel′e·vant·ly** *adv.*

re·li·a·ble (rĭ lī′ə bəl) *adj.* Capable of being relied upon; dependable: *a reliable car that always works.* —**re·li′a·bil′i·ty** *n.* [U] —**re·li′a·bly** *adv.*

re·li·ance (rĭ lī′əns) *n.* [C; U] The act of relying; dependence: *a reliance on industry.*

re·li·ant (rĭ lī′ənt) *adj.* Showing reliance: *She is reliant on her job for food and shelter.*

rel·ic (rĕl′ĭk) *n.* An object or a custom surviving from an earlier culture or period: *relics of an ancient civilization.*

re·lief (rĭ lēf′) *n.* **1.** [U] The easing of distress, such as of pain or anxiety: *relief from a cold.* **2.** [C] Something that lessens pain or worry: *It was a relief to hear you'd arrived safely.* **3.** [U] Assistance and help, as in the form of food or money, given to the needy: *disaster relief.* **4.** [U] The variations in elevation of an area of the earth's surface: *a map that shows relief.* ◆ **on relief.** Receiving help from the government because of need: *After losing her job, she had to go on relief.*

re·lieve (rĭ lēv′) *tr.v.* **re·lieved, re·liev·ing, re·lieves. 1.** To lessen or reduce (pain or anxiety, for example); ease: *Aspirin relieves a headache.* **2.** To free (sbdy.) from pain or anxiety: *relieve them of worries.* **3.** To release (sbdy.), as from a duty or position, by acting as a substitute: *The second shift relieves us at 6 o'clock.* **4.** To give help to (sbdy.): *relieve the victims of the flood.* **5.** To make (sthg.) less unpleasant or boring: *We sang songs to relieve boredom on the job.* **6.** *Informal.* To rob (sbdy. of sthg.): *Two men relieved me of my wallet.* —**re·liev′er** *n.*

re·lig·ion (rĭ lĭj′ən) *n.* **1.** [U] Belief in and reverence for a supernatural being or beings, usually regarded as creator of the universe. **2.** [C] A particular organized system of such belief: *the Hindu religion.*

re·lig·ious (rĭ lĭj′əs) *adj.* **1.** Having belief in and reverence for a supernatural being: *a religious person.* **2.** Concerned with or teaching religion: *a religious book.* **3.** Very faithful;

R

conscientious: *a religious attention to detail.*
—**re·lig'ious·ly** *adv.* —**re·lig'ious·ness** *n.* [U]

re·lin·quish (rǐ lǐng'kwǐsh) *tr.v.* Formal. **1.** To give up, put aside, or surrender (sthg.): *relinquish claim to the land.* **2.** To let (sthg.) go; release: *She relinquished her grasp on the fishing pole.*

rel·ish (rěl'ǐsh) *n.* **1.** [U] Great enjoyment; pleasure; zest: *He began the task with relish.* See Synonyms at **love. 2.** [C; U] A spicy condiment, such as chopped pickles, served with food: *a hot dog with relish.* —*tr.v.* To take pleasure in (sthg.); enjoy: *He relished going to the beach at dawn.*

re·live (rē lǐv') *tr.v.* **re·lived, re·liv·ing, re·lives.** To undergo (an experience) again; live through another time: *We relived our childhood looking through the photo album.*

re·lo·cate (rē lō'kāt) *tr. & intr.v.* **re·lo·cat·ed, re·lo·cat·ing, re·lo·cates.** To establish or become established in a new place: *The company relocated the employee. We relocated to a new city.* —**re'lo·ca'tion** *n.* [U]

re·luc·tant (rǐ lŭk'tənt) *adj.* Unwilling: *reluctant to leave.* —**re·luc'tance** *n.* [U] —**re·luc'tant·ly** *adv.*

re·ly (rǐ lī') *intr.v.* **re·lied, re·ly·ing, re·lies.** [*on*] **1.** To be dependent for support or help: *She's relying on her parents to pay her rent.* **2.** To have trust or confidence: *I'm relying on you to be a good example for the others.*

re·main (rǐ mān') *intr.v.* **1.** To continue in the same condition: *This issue remains open to discussion.* **2.** To continue in the same place; stay: *The children remained at home after their mother left.* See Synonyms at **stay**[1]. **3.** To be left after the loss or destruction of others: *Only a few houses remain in the old neighborhood.* ♦ **remain to be seen.** To be undecided: *It remains to be seen whether they'll be able to come.*

re·main·der (rǐ mān'dər) *n.* **1.** The part left over; the rest: *the remainder of the year.* **2.** In math, the amount left over after division: *20 divided by 6 gives 3 with a remainder of 2.*

re·mains (rǐ mānz') *pl.n.* **1.** All that is left after the loss or destruction of other parts: *the remains of last night's supper.* **2.** A dead body; corpse.

re·mark (rǐ märk') *tr.v.* To express (sthg.) as a comment: *He remarked that the book was selling well.* —*n.* **1.** [C] A casual statement; a comment: *a remark about the weather.* **2.** [U] The act of noticing or observing; a mention: *a story worthy of remark.*

re·mark·a·ble (rǐ mär'kə bəl) *adj.* **1.** Worthy of notice: *The change in his personality was remarkable.* **2.** Extraordinary; uncommon: *a remarkable achievement.* —**re·mark'a·bly** *adv.*

re·match (rē mǎch' *or* rē'mǎch') *n.* A second contest between the same opponents.

re·me·di·al (rǐ mē'dē əl) *adj.* Supplying a treatment or solution: *a remedial operation; remedial reading.* —**re·me'di·al·ly** *adv.*

rem·e·dy (rěm'ǐ dē) *n., pl.* **rem·e·dies. 1.** Something, such as a medicine, that relieves pain, cures disease, or corrects a disorder. **2.** Something that corrects an error or a wrong: *a remedy for inflation.* —*tr.v.* **rem·e·died, rem·e·dy·ing, rem·e·dies. 1.** To relieve or cure (a disease or disorder): *The medicine remedied my allergies.* **2.** To set right or correct (an error, for example): *A change in government remedied the economic problems.*

re·mem·ber (rǐ měm'bər) *v.* —*tr.* **1.** To recall (sbdy./sthg.) to memory: *She remembered how to run the machine.* **2.** To keep (sthg.) carefully in memory: *Remember your doctor's appointment.* **3.** To give (sbdy.) a gift: *She remembered her nieces at Christmas.* **4.** To give greetings from (sbdy.): *Remember me to your parents.* —*intr.* To have or use the power of memory: *I just don't remember anymore.*

re·mem·brance (rǐ měm'brəns) *n.* **1.** [C] Something that serves to remind; a memento or souvenir: *a remembrance of our trip to Spain.* **2.** [U] The act of remembering: *the remembrance of our ancestors.*

re·mind (rǐ mīnd') *tr.v.* To cause (sbdy.) to remember or think of sthg.: *Remind her to water the plants.* —**re·mind'er** *n.*

rem·i·nisce (rěm'ə nǐs') *intr.v.* **rem·i·nisced, rem·i·nisc·ing, rem·i·nisc·es.** To remember and talk about past experiences or events: *My grandmother likes to reminisce about her childhood.*

rem·i·nis·cence (rěm'ə nǐs'əns) *n.* **1.** [U] The act of recalling the past: *lost in the reminiscence of childhood.* **2.** [C] Something remembered; a memory: *pleasant reminiscences of the summer.*

rem·i·nis·cent (rěm'ə nǐs'ənt) *adj.* Recalling to the mind; suggestive: *a melody reminiscent of a folk song.*

re·miss (rǐ mǐs') *adj.* Formal. Careless about duty; negligent: *She's remiss about returning phone calls.*

re·mis·sion (rǐ mǐsh'ən) *n.* [C; U] The lessening of a disease or disorder: *His cancer is in remission.*

re·mit (rǐ mǐt') *tr.v.* **re·mit·ted, re·mit·ting, re·mits.** Formal. To send (money) in payment: *remit a check for the phone bill.*

re·mit·tance (rǐ mǐt'ns) *n.* Formal. The money sent to sbdy.: *My remittance is in the mail.*

ă–cat; ā–pay; âr–care; ä–father; ĕ–get; ē–be; ĭ–sit; ī–nice; îr–here; ŏ–got; ō–go; ô–saw; oi–boy; ou–out; ōō–took; ōō–boot; ŭ–cut; ûr–word; th–thin; th–this; hw–when; zh–vision; ə–about; N–French bon

rem·nant (rĕm′nənt) *n.* **1.** A portion left over; a remainder: *remnants of an old document.* **2.** A surviving trace: *the last remnants of an ancient empire.* **3.** A leftover piece of cloth remaining after the rest has been sold.

re·mod·el (rē mŏd′l) *tr.v.* To make (sthg.) over in structure or style; rebuild: *remodel a kitchen.*

re·morse (rĭ môrs′) *n.* [U] Deep regret or guilt for having done sthg. wrong: *No matter what he does, he never shows remorse.*

re·morse·ful (rĭ môrs′fəl) *adj.* Filled with remorse: *a remorseful sob.* —**re·morse′·ful·ly** *adv.*

re·morse·less (rĭ môrs′lĭs) *adj.* Having no pity or compassion; merciless: *a remorseless criminal.* —**re·morse′less·ly** *adv.* —**re·morse′less·ness** *n.* [U]

re·mote (rĭ mōt′) *adj.* **1.** Located far away: *a remote Arctic island.* **2.** Distant in time: *the remote past.* **3.** Slight: *There is a remote possibility that it will snow today.* —*n. Informal.* A remote control: *I used the remote to change TV channels.* —**re·mote′ly** *adv.*

remote control *n.* A device used to control an appliance or a machine, such as a television or VCR, from a distance.

re·mov·al (rĭ mōo′vəl) *n.* **1.** [U] The act of removing: *The removal of the piano took four men.* **2.** [C] Dismissal, as from office or duties: *the removal of an adviser.*

re·move (rĭ mōov′) *tr.v.* **re·moved, re·mov·ing, re·moves.** **1.** To move (sthg.) from a position or place: *remove the pie from the oven.* **2.** To take (sthg.) off or away: *Our guest removed his coat.* **3.** To eliminate (sthg.): *remove a stain.* **4.** To dismiss (sbdy.) from office: *remove the governor after a scandal.* —*n. Formal.* Distance or degree of separation or remoteness: *We stood at a safe remove from the demolition site.* —**re·mov′a·ble** *adj.*

re·moved (rĭ mōovd′) *adj.* Emotionally distant; remote: *He felt removed from the events.*

re·mu·ner·ate (rĭ myōo′nə rāt′) *tr.v.* **re·mu·ner·at·ed, re·mu·ner·at·ing, re·mu·ner·ates.** *Formal.* To pay (sbdy.) for goods, services, or losses: *They remunerated us for the broken window.* —**re·mu′ner·a′tion** (rĭ myōo′nə rā′shən) *n.* [U]

ren·ais·sance (rĕn′ĭ säns′ *or* rĕn′ĭ säns′) *n.* **1.** A rebirth or revival: *a renaissance of downtown business.* **2. Renaissance.** The revival of classical art, literature, architecture, and learning in Europe from the 14th through the 16th century. —*adj.* **Renaissance.** Relating to the Renaissance or its artistic works or styles: *Renaissance music.*

re·nal (rē′nəl) *adj.* Relating to the kidneys: *renal failure.*

rend (rĕnd) *tr.v.* **rent** (rĕnt) or **rend·ed, rend·ing, rends.** *Formal.* To tear or pull (sthg.) apart violently: *The wind rent the flag.*

ren·der (rĕn′dər) *tr.v.* **1.** To cause (sthg.) to become; make: *The storm rendered the crop worthless.* **2.** To give (sthg.); provide: *render assistance.*

ren·dez·vous (rän′dā vōo′) *n., pl.* **ren·dez·vous** (rän′dā vōoz′). A prearranged meeting, often a secret one. —*intr.v.* **ren·dez·voused** (rän′dā vōod′), **ren·dez·vous·ing** (rän′dā vōo′ĭng), **ren·dez·vous** (rän′dā vōoz′). To meet together at a certain time and place: *We rendezvoused at the restaurant after the football game.*

ren·di·tion (rĕn dĭsh′ən) *n.* An interpretation or a performance of a musical composition or dramatic work.

ren·e·gade (rĕn′ĭ gād′) *n.* **1.** A person who rejects a cause or a group. **2.** An outlaw. —*adj.* Relating to or resembling a renegade; traitorous: *a renegade soldier.*

re·nege (rĭ nĭg′ *or* rĭ nĕg′) *intr.v.* **re·neged, re·neg·ing, re·neges.** [*on*] To fail to carry out a promise or duty: *renege on a commitment.*

re·new (rĭ nōo′) *tr.v.* **1.** To make (sthg.) as if new again; restore: *They plan to renew the old paint.* **2.** To take (sthg.) up again; resume: *She has renewed her study of music.* **3.** To arrange for an extension of (sthg.): *renew a prescription.*

re·new·a·ble (rĭ nōo′ə bəl) *adj.* **1.** Capable of being renewed: *a renewable membership in the club.* **2.** Capable of being replaced; replaceable: *Wood is a renewable source of energy.*

re·new·al (rĭ nōo′əl) *n.* [C; U] The act of renewing: *renewal of a magazine subscription.*

re·nounce (rĭ nouns′) *tr.v.* **re·nounced, re·nounc·ing, re·nounc·es.** **1.** To give up (a title, for example) by formal announcement: *renounce her title.* **2.** To reject (sbdy./sthg.): *In protest, she renounced her membership in the club.*

ren·o·vate (rĕn′ə vāt′) *tr.v.* **ren·o·vat·ed, ren·o·vat·ing, ren·o·vates.** To restore (sthg.) to an earlier condition by repairing or remodeling: *renovate a house.* —**ren′o·va′tion** *n.* [C; U] —**ren′o·va′tor** *n.*

re·nown (rĭ noun′) *n.* [U] The quality of having widespread honor and fame: *the renown of a great actress.*

re·nowned (rĭ nound′) *adj.* Having renown; famous: *a renowned scientist.* See Synonyms at **noted.**

rent[1] (rĕnt) *n.* [C; U] A payment made at regular intervals for the use of the property of another: *pay the monthly rent.* —*v.* —*tr.* **1.** To occupy or use (another's property) in return for regular payments: *rent an apartment; rent a bicycle.* **2.** To grant the use of (one's own property) in return for regular payments: *rent the car to a tourist.* —*intr.* To be for rent: *Rooms rent for $30 a day.* ♦ **for rent.** Available for use or service in return for payment: *sailboats for rent at $30 an hour.* —**rent′er** *n.*

R

rent[2] (rĕnt) v. A past tense and a past participle of **rend.** —n. **1.** An opening made by rending: *a rent in the curtain.* **2.** A break in relations between people or groups; a split: *a rent in the family.*

rent·al (rĕn'tl) n. **1.** [C] Property for rent: *The cottage where they are staying is a summer rental.* **2.** [U] The act of renting: *the rental of a car.*

re·nun·ci·a·tion (rĭ nŭn'sē ā'shən) n. [C; U] The act of renouncing: *the renunciation of a belief.*

re·o·pen (rē ō'pən) tr. & intr.v. **1.** To open or become open again: *They reopened a trail. The store will reopen after the holiday.* **2.** To take up again or be taken up again; resume: *They will reopen negotiations. The discussion will reopen.*

re·or·gan·ize (rē ôr'gə nīz') v. **re·or·gan·ized, re·or·gan·iz·ing, re·or·gan·iz·es.** —tr. To organize (sthg.) again or differently: *She reorganized her ideas and made a new outline for the paper.* —intr. To undergo or make changes in organization: *The group is reorganizing.* —**re·or'gan·i·za'·tion** (rē ôr'gə nĭ zā'shən) n. [U] —**re·or'·gan·iz'er** n.

Rep. abbr. An abbreviation of: **1.** Republic. **2.** Representative. **3.** Republican.

re·pair (rĭ pâr') tr.v. To restore (sthg.) to proper or useful condition after damage or injury; fix: *repair an automobile.* —n. **1.** [C; U] The work, act, or process of repairing: *cars in need of repair; the necessary repairs.* **2.** [U] General condition: *a truck in good repair.* —**re·pair'a·ble** adj.

re·pair·man (rĭ pâr'măn') n. A man whose job is making repairs. —**re·pair'wom'an** (rĭ pâr'wŏŏm'ən) n.

rep·a·ra·tion (rĕp'ə rā'shən) n. **1.** [U] Something done or paid to make amends; compensation. **2. reparations.** Compensation required from a defeated nation for damage or injury during a war.

re·pa·tri·ate (rē pā'trē āt') tr.v. **re·pat·ri·at·ed, re·pat·ri·at·ing, re·pat·ri·ates.** To restore or return (sbdy.) to the country of one's birth or citizenship: *The U.N. repatriated the refugees.*

re·pay (rĭ pā') tr.v. **re·paid** (rĭ pād'), **re·pay·ing, re·pays. 1.** To pay (sthg.) back: *We repaid our debt.* **2.** To make or do (sthg.) in return: *repay a-visit.* —**re·pay'a·ble** adj. —**re·pay'ment** n. [C; U]

re·peal (rĭ pēl') tr.v. To withdraw or cancel (sthg.) officially: *repeal a law.* —n. [U] The act of repealing: *the repeal of a law.*

re·peat (rĭ pēt') tr.v. **1.** To say (sthg.) again: *repeat a question.* **2.** To say (sthg.) in duplication of what another has said: *repeat the*

phrase after the teacher. **3.** To tell (sthg.) to sbdy. else: *repeat gossip.* **4.** To do, experience, or produce (sthg.) again: *We want to repeat our past successes.* **5.** To express (oneself) in the same words: *He's always repeating himself.* —n. **1.** The act of repeating: *the repeat of a performance.* **2.** Something repeated: *This television program is a repeat.* —adj. Relating to a person or thing that repeats: *a repeat offender.*

re·peat·ed (rĭ pē'tĭd) adj. Said, done, or happening again and again: *We heard repeated knocks at the door.* —**re·peat'ed·ly** adv.

re·pel (rĭ pĕl') tr.v. **re·pelled, re·pel·ling, re·pels. 1.** To drive off, force back, or keep (sbdy./sthg.) away: *repel an enemy attack.* **2.** To be resistant to (sthg.): *a fabric that repels water.* **3.** To refuse (sbdy./sthg.); reject: *He repelled her offer of help.* **4.** To cause aversion in (sbdy.): *Her rudeness repels us.*

re·pel·lent (rĭ pĕl'ənt) adj. **1.** Capable of repelling: *an odor that is repellent to dogs.* **2.** Causing disgust: *repellent behavior.* **3.** Resistant to a specific substance: *a water-repellent cloth.* —n. [C; U] **1.** A substance used to drive off pests: *an insect repellent.* **2.** A substance used to treat a fabric to make it resistant to water.

re·pent (rĭ pĕnt') v. —intr. **1.** To feel regret for sthg. one has done or failed to do: *We repented for not calling her.* **2.** To make a change for the better as a result of remorse or regret for one's sins. —tr. To feel regret or remorse for (sthg.): *I later repented my bad manners.* —**re·pen'tance** n. [U] —**re·pen'tant** adj.

re·per·cus·sion (rē'pər kŭsh'ən or rĕp'-ər kŭsh'ən) n. An indirect effect or result of an event or action: *His decision may have alarming repercussions.*

rep·er·toire (rĕp'ər twär') n. All of the songs, plays, or other works that a person or company is prepared to perform.

rep·e·ti·tion (rĕp'ĭ tĭsh'ən) n. [C; U] The act of repeating: *the repetition of a word.*

rep·e·ti·tious (rĕp'ĭ tĭsh'əs) adj. Filled with repetition, especially needless repetition: *repetitious arguments.* —**rep'e·ti'·tious·ly** adv. —**rep'e·ti'tious·ness** n. [U]

re·pet·i·tive (rĭ pĕt'ĭ tĭv) adj. Characterized by repetition: *a repetitive political speech.* —**re·pet'i·tive·ly** adv. —**re·pet'i·tive·ness** n. [U]

re·place (rĭ plās') tr.v. **re·placed, re·plac·ing, re·plac·es. 1.** To put (sthg.) back into position: *I replaced the dish in the cabinet.* **2.** To take or fill the place of (sbdy./sthg.): *Automobiles replaced horses.* **3.** To provide a substitute for (sbdy./sthg.): *replace a broken window.* —**re·place'a·ble** adj.

re•place•ment (rĭ plās′mənt) *n*. **1.** [U] The act of replacing: *the replacement of funds.* **2.** [C] A person or thing that replaces: *Stay at work until your replacement arrives.*

re•play (rē plā′) *tr.v.* To play (sthg.) again: *replay a tape.* —*n.* (rē′plā′). The act of replaying: *The referee decided there should be a replay.* ◆ **instant replay.** On television, the showing again of a play in a game, often in slow motion.

re•plen•ish (rĭ plĕn′ĭsh) *tr.v.* To restore a supply of (sthg.): *replenish the water in the tank.*

re•plete (rĭ plēt′) *adj.* [*with*] Formal. Full of: *a land replete with streams and forests.*

rep•li•ca (rĕp′lĭ kə) *n*. A copy or reproduction: *a replica of an early telephone.*

rep•li•cate (rĕp′lĭ kāt′) *v*. **rep•li•cat•ed, rep•li•cat•ing, rep•li•cates.** —*tr*. To duplicate, copy, reproduce, or repeat (sthg.): *replicate a scientific experiment.* —*intr*. To reproduce or become duplicated: *Cells replicate.* —**rep′li•ca′tion** (rĕp′lĭ kā′shən) *n*. [C; U]

re•ply (rĭ plī′) *v*. **re•plied, re•ply•ing, re•plies.** —*intr*. To say or give an answer: *He replied kindly.* —*tr*. To say or give (sthg.) as an answer: *She replied that she would go.* See Synonyms at **answer.** —*n., pl.* **re•plies.** [C; U] A response in speech or writing: *Send your written reply by next week.*

re•port (rĭ pôrt′) *n*. **1.** An oral or written account, often presented in detail: *a news report.* **2.** An explosive sound, as of a gun. —*v*. —*tr*. **1.** To make or present an account of (sthg.): *report the problem in a memo to the manager.* **2.** To write or provide (information) for publication or broadcast: *report the news.* **3.** To carry back and repeat (sthg.) to another: *The soldier reported a message.* **4.** To complain about or denounce (sbdy./sthg.): *report them to the police.* —*intr*. **1.** To make a report: *She reported on the evening news.* **2.** To present oneself: *report for duty.* **3.** To be accountable: *I report directly to the president.*

report card *n*. A written report of a student's achievement presented at regular intervals to a parent or guardian.

re•port•ed•ly (rĭ pôr′tĭd lē) *adv.* By report; supposedly: *Reportedly, the president will visit our town.*

re•port•er (rĭ pôr′tər) *n*. A person who investigates, writes, or presents news stories.

re•pose (rĭ pōz′) Formal. *n*. [U] **1.** The state of being at rest. **2.** Calmness; peace: *the repose of the lake.* —*intr.v*. **re•posed, re•pos•ing, re•pos•es.** **1.** To lie at rest; relax or sleep: *workers reposing at the end of day.* **2.** To lie supported by sthg.: *a dish reposing on the table.*

re•pos•i•to•ry (rĭ pŏz′ĭ tôr′ē) *n., pl.* **re•pos•i•to•ries.** A place where things are put for safekeeping: *a nuclear waste repository.*

re•pos•sess (rē′pə zĕs′) *tr.v.* To retake or regain possession of (sthg.): *The bank repossessed the car because he was late on his payments.* —**re′pos•ses′sion** (rē′pə zĕsh′ən) *n*. [C; U]

rep•re•hen•si•ble (rĕp′rĭ hĕn′sə bəl) *adj.* Worthy of blame: *a reprehensible act.* —**rep′re•hen′si•bly** *adv.*

rep•re•sent (rĕp′rĭ zĕnt′) *tr.v.* **1.** To stand for (sthg.); symbolize: *The rose represents beauty.* **2.** To communicate (sthg.) by sounds or symbols: *Letters represent sounds.* **3.** To portray (sbdy./sthg.), as in a picture: *The painting represents a girl with a shy smile.* **4.** To describe (sthg.) as having certain characteristics: *represented a product's quality falsely.* **5.** To serve as an example of (sthg.): *Her feelings represent those of the majority.* **6.** To be the equivalent of (sthg.): *The amount you eat and drink represents your total intake.* **7.** To act as the delegate or agent for (sbdy./sthg.): *represent a district; represent a client.*

rep•re•sen•ta•tion (rĕp′rĭ zĕn tā′shən) *n*. **1.** [U] The act of representing. **2.** [C] Something that represents, such as a picture or symbol. **3.** [C; U] The condition of serving as an official delegate or agent. **4.** [C; U] The right of being represented: *no taxation without representation.* **5.** [C] An account or a statement of facts, conditions, or arguments: *improper representations of a product.*

rep•re•sen•ta•tive (rĕp′rĭ zĕn′tə tĭv) *n*. **1.** A person or thing that serves as an example for others of the same class. **2.** A person who serves as a delegate or an agent for another. **3.** A member of the U.S. House of Representatives or of the lower house of a state legislature. —*adj*. **1.** Representing or able to do so: *representative of the facts.* **2.** Having power to act as an official delegate or agent. **3.** Relating to government by representation: *representative committees.* **4.** Serving as a typical example: *paintings representative of that era.*

re•press (rĭ prĕs′) *tr.v.* **1.** To hold (sthg.) back: *trying to repress his laughter.* **2.** To put (sbdy./sthg.) down by force; quell: *repress an uprising.* **3.** To force (painful memories, for example) out of the conscious mind: *He repressed memories of his difficult childhood.* —**re•pres′sion** *n*. [U] —**re•pres′sive** *adj.* —**re•pres′sive•ly** *adv.*

re•prieve (rĭ prēv′) *tr.v.* **re•prieved, re•priev•ing, re•prieves.** To postpone or cancel the punishment of (sbdy.): *The principal reprieved the tardy students.* —*n*. The putting off or cancellation of a punishment: *The prisoner was given a reprieve.*

rep•ri•mand (rĕp′rə mănd′) *tr.v.* To scold (sbdy.) severely or officially: *My mother reprimanded my brother for not doing his chores.* —*n*. A severe or official scolding: *The* *student received a reprimand for being late to class.*

re•print (rē′prĭnt′) *n.* A new printing of a book or article that is identical to an original. —*tr.v.* (rē prĭnt′). To print (sthg.) again: *They reprinted the popular article.*

re•pri•sal (rĭ prī′zəl) *n.* [C; U] Retaliation for injury or damage caused, often by one nation against another.

re•proach (rĭ prōch′) *tr.v.* To express disapproval of, criticism of, or disappointment in (sbdy.): *Our father reproached us for staying out too late.* —*n.* [C; U] Blame; rebuke: *The boy received a reproach for his careless behavior.* ♦ **above** or **beyond reproach.** Blameless: *Their behavior was beyond reproach.* —**re•proach′ful** *adj.* —**re•proach′ful•ly** *adv.*

re•pro•duce (rē′prə dōōs′) *v.* **re•pro•duced, re•pro•duc•ing, re•pro•duc•es.** —*tr.* **1.** To make an image or a copy of (sthg.): *A photocopier reproduces images.* **2.** To generate or produce (offspring). —*intr.* **1.** To generate or produce offspring: *These animals seldom reproduce in captivity.* **2.** To undergo copying: *Black-and-white photographs reproduce well.*

re•pro•duc•tion (rē′prə dŭk′shən) *n.* **1.** [U] The act of reproducing: *the reproduction of sound.* **2.** [C] Something that is reproduced; a copy: *a reproduction of a painting.* **3.** [U] The process by which organisms produce other organisms of the same kind. —**re′pro•duc′tive** (rē′prə dŭk′tĭv) *adj.*

rep•tile (rĕp′tĭl *or* rĕp′tīl′) *n.* Any of various cold-blooded animals, such as snakes, turtles, and crocodiles, that have a backbone, are covered with scales or horny plates, and breathe by means of lungs. —**rep•til′i•an** (rĕp tĭl′ē ən *or* rĕp tĭl′yən) *adj.*

reptile
River turtle

re•pub•lic (rĭ pŭb′lĭk) *n.* A nation whose head of state is not a monarch and in modern times is usually not a president.

re•pub•li•can (rĭ pŭb′lĭ kən) *adj.* **1.** Characteristic of a republic: *a republican form of government.* **2. Republican.** Relating to or belonging to the Republican Party. —*n.* **Republican.** A member of the Republican Party.

Republican Party *n.* One of the two major political parties of the United States.

re•pu•di•ate (rĭ pyōō′dē āt′) *tr.v.* **re•pu•di•at•ed, re•pu•di•at•ing, re•pu•di•ates.** *Formal.* To reject (sthg.) as untrue or unjust: *repudiate an accusation.* —**re•pu′di•a′tion** *n.* [U]

re•pug•nant (rĭ pŭg′nənt) *adj.* Causing disgust or dislike; repulsive: *the repugnant odor of rotting fish.* —**re•pug′nance** *n.* [U]

re•pulse (rĭ pŭls′) *tr.v.* **re•pulsed, re•puls•ing, re•puls•es.** **1.** To drive (sbdy./sthg.) back; repel: *repulse the enemy attackers.* **2.** To rebuff or reject (sbdy.) with rudeness or coldness: *She repulsed his offers to help.* —*n.* A firm rejection. —**re•pul′sion** *n.* [U] —**re•pul′sive** *adj.*

rep•u•ta•ble (rĕp′yə tə bəl) *adj.* Having a good reputation; honorable: *a reputable dealer.* —**rep′u•ta•bly** *adv.*

rep•u•ta•tion (rĕp′yə tā′shən) *n.* [C; U] **1.** The general opinion of sbdy. held by the public: *That lawyer has a good reputation.* **2.** A particular characteristic for which a person or thing is noted: *He has a reputation for honesty.*

re•pute (rĭ pyōōt′) *tr.v.* **re•put•ed, re•put•ing, re•putes.** To consider (sbdy./sthg.); suppose: *He is reputed to be honest.* —*n.* [U] *Formal.* Reputation: *a man of ill repute.*

re•put•ed (rĭ pyōō′tĭd) *adj.* Generally supposed to be sthg.: *the reputed leader of the movement.* —**re•put′ed•ly** *adv.*

re•quest (rĭ kwĕst′) *tr.v.* **1.** To express a desire for (sbdy./sthg.); ask for: *a letter requesting information.* **2.** To ask (sbdy.) to do sthg.: *I requested him to come along.* —*n.* **1.** [U] The act of asking: *Other sizes are available by request.* **2.** [C] Something asked for: *The band played several requests.*

re•quire (rĭ kwīr′) *tr.v.* **re•quired, re•quir•ing, re•quires.** **1.** To be in need of (sbdy./sthg.); need: *Do you require help?* **2.** To demand (sthg.): *Skiing requires practice.* **3.** To impose an obligation upon (sbdy.); order: *The school requires all students to study mathematics.*

re•quire•ment (rĭ kwīr′mənt) *n.* **1.** Something that is needed; a necessity: *a person's daily food requirement.* **2.** Something established as necessary for sthg. else: *What are the requirements for the job?*

req•ui•site (rĕk′wĭ zĭt) *adj. Formal.* Required; essential: *requisite courses for a degree.* —*n.* Something that is essential; a necessity: *the requisites for success.*

req•ui•si•tion (rĕk′wĭ zĭsh′ən) *n.* [C; U] A formal written request for sthg. needed: *Do you have a requisition for the supplies?* —*tr.v.* **1.** To demand (sthg.), as for military needs: *requisition food for the troops.* **2.** To make demands of (sbdy.): *requisitioned the department for additional supplies.*

re•run (rē′rŭn′) *n.* The repeating of a movie or a recorded television performance: *I'm tired of the same old reruns.* —*tr.v.* (rē rŭn′). **re•ran** (rē răn′), **re•run, re•run•ning,**

re•runs. To present a rerun of (a TV progam): *The station reran the old movie at midnight.*

re•scind (rĭ sĭnd′) *tr.v. Formal.* To make (sthg.) void; repeal: *He rescinded his offer.*

res•cue (rĕs′kyo͞o) *tr.v.* **res•cued, res•cu•ing, res•cues.** To set (sbdy./sthg.) free, as from danger or imprisonment; save: *Our neighbor rescued a cat from the tree.* —*n.* An act of rescuing or saving: *A lifeguard came to our rescue.* —**res′cu•er** *n.*

re•search (rĭ sûrch′ *or* rē′sûrch′) *n.* [U] Careful study of a certain subject, field, or problem to discover facts or principles: *I'm doing research on our town's history.* —*tr.v.* To do research on (sthg.); investigate: *He is researching the origins of football.* —**re•search′er** *n.*

re•sem•ble (rĭ zĕm′bəl) *tr.v.* **re•sem•bled, re•sem•bling, re•sem•bles.** To have a similarity to (sbdy./sthg.); be like: *My friend resembles his father in appearance.* —**re•sem′blance** (rĭ zĕm′bləns) *n.* [C; U]

re•sent (rĭ zĕnt′) *tr.v.* To feel angry at (sthg. considered mean, unjust, or offensive): *resent a rude remark.* —**re•sent′ful** *adj.* —**re•sent′ful•ly** *adv.* —**re•sent′ful•ness, re•sent′ment** *n.* [U]

res•er•va•tion (rĕz′ər vā′shən) *n.* **1.** [C] A way of having space, as in a hotel or on an airplane, saved or held in advance: *We made dinner reservations.* **2.** [C; U] (*usually plural*). A less than complete acceptance of sthg.: *He has certain reservations about the proposal.* **3.** [C] Land set apart by the federal government for a certain purpose, especially for the use of a Native American people.

re•serve (rĭ zûrv′) *tr.v.* **re•served, re•serv•ing, re•serves. 1.** To save (sthg.) for a particular purpose or later use: *reserve a tablecloth for special occasions.* See Synonyms at **keep. 2.** To order (sthg.) in advance for a specific time or date: *reserve a table in a restaurant.* **3.** To keep (sthg.) for oneself: *I reserve the evening for quiet relaxation.* —*n.* **1.** [C] Something saved for future use or a special purpose: *a fuel reserve.* **2.** [U] A tendency to talk little and keep one's feelings to oneself: *the quiet reserve of a shy friend.* **3.** [C] A reservation of public land: *a forest reserve.* **4.** [C] (*usually plural*). The part of a country's armed forces not on active duty but available in an emergency: *the Army reserves.*

re•served (rĭ zûrvd′) *adj.* **1.** Held in reserve; set aside: *a reserved seat.* **2.** Marked by self-restraint and quietness: *a shy, reserved person.* —**re•serv′ed•ly** (rĭ zûr′vĭd lē) *adv.*

res•er•voir (rĕz′ər vwär′ *or* rĕz′ər vwôr′) *n.* **1.** A pond or lake used for storing water. **2.** A container used for storing a fluid: *the reservoir of an ink bottle.* **3.** A large or extra supply; a reserve: *a reservoir of goodwill.*

re•side (rĭ zīd′) *intr.v.* **re•sid•ed, re•sid•**

ing, **re•sides.** *Formal.* To live in a place permanently: *She resides in Miami.*

res•i•dence (rĕz′ĭ dəns) *n.* **1.** [C] The place in which a person lives; a dwelling: *a private residence.* **2.** [U] The act of residing somewhere: *He learned Spanish during his residence in Mexico.*

res•i•den•cy (rĕz′ĭ dən sē) *n., pl.* **res•i•den•cies.** The period during which a doctor receives specialized clinical training: *The doctor did a two-year residency at a Boston hospital.*

res•i•dent (rĕz′ĭ dənt) *n.* **1.** A person who resides in a certain place permanently or for a long period: *a resident of Florida.* **2.** A doctor serving a period of residency: *a surgical resident.* —*adj.* Living in a certain place: *a resident alien.*

res•i•den•tial (rĕz′ĭ dĕn′shəl) *adj.* **1.** Relating to residence: *a residential college.* **2.** Suitable for or limited to homes rather than businesses: *a residential neighborhood.*

re•sid•u•al (rĭ zĭj′o͞o əl) *adj.* Remaining as sthg. left over: *the residual solids left when a liquid evaporates.* —**re•sid′u•al•ly** *adv.*

res•i•due (rĕz′ĭ do͞o′) *n.* Something that remains after another part is removed: *There's some kind of residue in the bottom of this glass.*

re•sign (rĭ zīn′) *v.* —*intr.* To give up one's job or office; quit, especially by formal notification: *When the company was sold, I resigned.* —*tr.* **1.** To give up (a position, for example), especially by formal notification: *She resigned her job as a bus driver.* **2.** To submit (oneself) passively: *I resigned myself to a long wait.*

res•ig•na•tion (rĕz′ĭg nā′shən) *n.* **1.** [C] The act of resigning: *The commissioner regretted his resignation.* **2.** [C] An oral or written statement that one is resigning a position or office: *She handed in her resignation.* **3.** [U] Acceptance of sthg. that seems impossible to avoid; a yielding: *There was a tone of resignation in her voice.*

re•signed (rĭ zīnd′) *adj.* Feeling or marked by unwilling acceptance: *a resigned look on his face.*

re•sil•ient (rĭ zĭl′yənt) *adj.* **1.** Having the ability to recover quickly, as from misfortune: *a resilient attitude.* **2.** Capable of returning to an original shape or position, as after having been compressed: *a resilient plastic.* —**re•sil′ience** *n.* [U]

res•in (rĕz′ĭn) *n.* [C; U] A natural or artificial clear or translucent liquid used in varnishes, lacquers, and plastics. —**res′in•ous** *adj.*

re•sist (rĭ zĭst′) *v.* —*tr.* **1.** To try to repel the actions or force of (sbdy./sthg.): *resist an attack.* See Synonyms at **oppose. 2.** To undergo little or no change as a result of the action of (sthg.); withstand: *a material that resists heat.* **3.** To keep oneself from giving in or yielding to (sthg.): *resist pressure; resist temptation.* —*intr.* To offer resistance: *When ordered to work late, we didn't resist.*

re·sis·tance (rĭ zĭs′təns) *n.* [U] **1.** The act of resisting: *The enemy offered little resistance.* **2.** A force that tends to oppose or slow down motion: *an automobile body shaped to lessen wind resistance.* **3.** The capacity of a living thing to defend itself against a disease: *resistance to a virus.* **4.** The opposition that an object offers to the passage of an electric current. —**re·sis′tant** *adj.*

re·sis·tor (rĭ zĭs′tər) *n.* A device used to control current in an electric circuit by providing resistance.

res·o·lute (rĕz′ə loōt′) *adj.* Firm or determined; unwavering: *a resolute voice.* —**res′o·lute·ly** *adv.* —**res′o·lute′ness** *n.* [U]

res·o·lu·tion (rĕz′ə loō′shən) *n.* **1.** [U] The quality of being resolute; firm determination: *face the future with resolution.* **2.** [C] A decision to do sthg.: *I made a resolution to get in shape.* **3.** [C] A formal statement of a decision or opinion by a legislature or another organization. **4.** [C; U] A solution or explanation; an answer: *the resolution of a problem.*

re·solve (rĭ zŏlv′) *tr.v.* **re·solved, re·solv·ing, re·solves.** **1.** To make a firm decision (to do sthg.): *He resolved to work harder.* **2.** To find a solution to (sthg.): *resolve a conflict.* —*n. Formal.* **1.** [U] Firmness of purpose; resolution: *work together with resolve.* **2.** [C] A decision or resolution: *a resolve to try harder.*

res·o·nant (rĕz′ə nənt) *adj.* **1.** Strong and deep in tone; resounding: *a resonant voice.* **2.** Continuing to sound in the ears or memory; echoing: *a resonant tone.* —**res′o·nance** *n.* [U]

re·sort (rĭ zôrt′) *intr.v.* [*to*] To go or turn for help or as a means of achieving sthg.: *The government resorted to censorship.* —*n.* A place where people go for relaxation or recreation: *a ski resort.* ◆ **last resort.** A person or thing turned to for aid or relief when everything else has failed: *I would ask him only as a last resort.*

re·sound (rĭ zound′) *intr.v.* **1.** To be filled with sound; echo: *The stadium resounded with cheers.* **2.** To make a loud, long, or echoing sound: *The music resounded through the hall.*

re·source (rē′sôrs′ *or* rĭ sôrs′) *n.* **1.** Something that can be used for support or help: *We used every resource we had to get the job done.* **2. resources.** An available supply of money that can be drawn on when needed: *We relied on our resources to buy the house.* **3.** Something that is a source of wealth to a country: *natural resources, such as coal and*

oil. **4.** The ability to deal with a situation effectively: *She didn't have the resources to deal with the pressure of that job.*

re·source·ful (rĭ sôrs′fəl) *adj.* Able to act effectively or imaginatively, especially in a difficult situation: *a resourceful leader.* —**re·source′ful·ly** *adv.* —**re·source′ful·ness** *n.* [U]

re·spect (rĭ spĕkt′) *tr.v.* **1.** To feel or show high regard for (sbdy./sthg.); esteem: *We respect her for her ability to listen carefully.* **2.** To avoid violation of (sthg.): *respect the speed limit.* —*n.* **1.** [U] A feeling of high regard; esteem: *respect for older people.* **2.** [U] The condition of being regarded with honor or esteem: *She is held in respect by her colleagues.* **3. respects.** Polite expressions of regard, especially those given after a death: *pay one's respects to the family of the deceased.* **4.** [C] A particular aspect or feature: *The two plans differ in one major respect.* ◆ **with respect to.** *Formal.* Regarding; concerning: *I have a comment with respect to your question.*

re·spect·a·ble (rĭ spĕk′tə bəl) *adj.* Worthy of respect or esteem: *respectable people.* —**re·spect′a·bil′i·ty** *n.* [U] —**re·spect′a·bly** *adv.*

re·spect·ful (rĭ spĕkt′fəl) *adj.* Showing or marked by proper respect: *a respectful tone of voice.* —**re·spect′ful·ly** *adv.*

re·spect·ing (rĭ spĕk′tĭng) *prep.* With respect to; concerning: *laws respecting personal property.*

re·spec·tive (rĭ spĕk′tĭv) *adj.* Relating to each of two or more persons or things; particular: *The delegates to the conference are experts in their respective fields.*

re·spec·tive·ly (rĭ spĕk′tĭv lē) *adv.* Each in the order named: *Albany, Augusta, and Atlanta are respectively the capitals of New York, Maine, and Georgia.*

res·pi·ra·tion (rĕs′pə rā′shən) *n.* [U] The process of inhaling and exhaling; breathing.

res·pi·ra·tor (rĕs′pə rā′tər) *n.* A device that helps sbdy. breathe. **2.** A filter worn over the mouth or nose, or both, to protect the respiratory system.

res·pi·ra·to·ry (rĕs′pər ə tôr′ē *or* rĭ spīr′ə tôr′ē) *adj.* Relating to or affecting breathing: *the human respiratory system.*

res·pite (rĕs′pĭt) *n.* [C; U] *Formal.* A short interval of rest or relief: *We stopped for a brief respite.*

re·splen·dent (rĭ splĕn′dənt) *adj. Formal.* Splendid or dazzling in appearance; brilliant: *She was resplendent in her jeweled gown.* —**re·splen′dence** *n.* [U]

re·spond (rĭ spŏnd′) *intr.v.* **1.** To make a reply; answer: *She responded quickly.* See

Synonyms at **answer. 2.** To act in return or in answer: *respond to a challenge.* **3.** To react positively or favorably: *The patient responded well to the treatment.*

re•sponse (rĭ spŏns′) *n.* [C; U] **1.** The act of responding: *the firefighter's response to the alarm.* **2.** An answer or a reply: *Your response to my letter was very kind.* **3.** A reaction, as that of a living thing or a mechanism: *a plant's response to light.*

re•spon•si•bil•i•ty (rĭ spŏn′sə bĭl′ĭ tē) *n., pl.* **re•spon•si•bil•i•ties. 1.** [U] The quality of being responsible: *Her children show amazing responsibility for their ages.* **2.** [C] Something that one is responsible for; a duty or an obligation: *Taking care of the cats is my responsibility.*

re•spon•si•ble (rĭ spŏn′sə bəl) *adj.* **1.** Dependable; reliable; trustworthy: *a mature and responsible person.* **2.** Accountable for anything that happens: *As the oldest, you'll be responsible while your parents are away.* **3.** Involving important duties: *a responsible job.* **4.** Being the cause of sthg.: *Viruses are responsible for many diseases.* —**re•spon′si•bly** *adv.*

re•spon•sive (rĭ spŏn′sĭv) *adj.* Answering or reacting readily: *a responsive student.* —**re•spon′sive•ly** *adv.* —**re•spon′sive•ness** *n.* [U]

rest[1] (rĕst) *n.* **1.** [C] A period of inactivity or sleep: *The hikers stopped for a brief rest.* **2.** [U] Peace or relaxation resulting from this: *Be sure to get plenty of rest.* **3.** [U] The calm of death: *go to one's eternal rest.* **4.** [C] A device used as a support: *a backrest.* —*v.* —*intr.* **1.** To stop motion, work, or activity: *The workers rested for a moment.* **2.** To lie down, especially to sleep: *rest after lunch.* **3.** To be at peace or ease: *Now that she's safely home I can rest easy.* **4.** To lie or lean on a support: *Her head rested on the pillow.* **5.** To be fixed or directed on sbdy./sthg.: *His gaze rested on the book.* **6.** To depend or rely: *The whole theory rests on one basic assumption.* **7.** To finish the presentation of evidence in a legal case: *The defense rests.* —*tr.* **1.** To give rest to (sthg.): *I rested my eyes.* **2.** To lay or lean (sthg.) for ease or support: *I rested the rake against the fence.* **3.** To base (sthg.): *We must rest our decision on the facts.* **4.** To fix or direct (the gaze, for example): *She rested her gaze on the man's face.* **5.** To finish the presentation of evidence in (a legal case): *The lawyer rested her case.*

HOMONYMS: rest (period of inactivity, remainder), **wrest** (pull away).

rest[2] (rĕst) *n.* [U] **1.** The part that is left after sthg. has been taken away; the remainder: *Pay ten percent now and the rest later.* **2.** That or those remaining: *Some guests are already here and the rest are coming.*

re•state (rē stāt′) *tr.v.* **re•stat•ed, re•stat•ing, re•states.** To state (sthg.) again or in a new form: *He restated the question when we misunderstood.* —**re•state′ment** *n.* [C; U]

res•tau•rant (rĕs′tər ənt *or* rĕs′tə ränt′) *n.* A place where meals are served to the public.

res•tau•ra•teur (rĕs′tər ə tûr′) *n.* The manager or owner of a restaurant.

rest•ful (rĕst′fəl) *adj.* Marked by or suggesting rest; calm: *a restful vacation.* —**rest′ful•ness** *n.* [U]

res•ti•tu•tion (rĕs′tĭ tōō′shən) *n.* [U] The act of repaying sbdy. for damage, loss, or injury: *She demanded restitution after the accident.*

res•tive (rĕs′tĭv) *adj.* **1.** Impatient or restless because of restriction or delay: *The crowd became restive waiting for the concert to begin.* **2.** Difficult to control: *a restive horse.* —**res′tive•ly** *adv.* —**res′tive•ness** *n.* [U]

rest•less (rĕst′lĭs) *adj.* **1.** Marked by a lack of quiet, rest, or sleep: *a restless night.* **2.** Unable to rest, relax, or be still: *a restless child.* —**rest′less•ly** *adv.* —**rest′less•ness** *n.* [U]

res•to•ra•tion (rĕs′tə rā′shən) *n.* **1.** [U] The action of restoring: *The restoration of the sculptures was difficult.* **2.** [C] Something restored: *This building is a restoration of a colonial farmhouse.*

re•stor•a•tive (rĭ stôr′ə tĭv) *adj.* Able to restore: *the restorative power of a long nap.*

re•store (rĭ stôr′) *tr.v.* **re•stored, re•stor•ing, re•stores. 1.** To bring (sthg.) back into existence or use; reestablish: *Such stories restore my faith in humanity.* **2.** To bring (sthg.) back to an original condition: *restore an old painting.* **3.** To bring (sbdy.) back to a prior position: *restore an emperor to the throne.*

re•strain (rĭ strān′) *tr.v.* **1.** To control (sbdy./sthg.): *She restrained her emotions.* **2.** To hold (sbdy.) back; prevent: *The police restrained them from going.*

re•straint (rĭ strānt′) *n.* **1.** [U] The condition of being restrained: *He had to be held in restraint.* **2.** [C] (*usually plural*). Something that holds back or restrains: *They put leg restraints on the prisoner.* **3.** [U] Control of feelings: *She showed great restraint even though she was angry.*

re•strict (rĭ strĭkt′) *tr.v.* To keep or confine (sbdy./sthg.) within limits: *Our dog is restricted to the back yard.*

re•strict•ed (rĭ strĭk′tĭd) *adj.* **1.** Kept within certain limits: *They accept a restricted number of students.* **2.** Excluding or unavailable except to certain people: *You can't enter because it's a restricted area.*

re•stric•tion (rĭ strĭk′shən) *n.* **1.** [C; U] The act of limiting or restricting: *restriction of immigration.* **2.** [C] Something that limits or restricts: *The students had to accept restrictions on their personal liberties.*

re·stric·tive (rĭ strĭk′tĭv) *adj.* **1.** Tending to restrict: *restrictive legislation.* **2.** In grammar, referring to a clause or phrase that describes a noun and restricts the meaning of the sentence. In the sentence *People who read a great deal have large vocabularies,* the clause *who read a great deal* is restrictive. —**re·stric′tive·ly** *adv.* —**re·stric′tive·ness** *n.* [U]

rest·room (rĕst′rōōm′ *or* rĕst′rŏŏm′) *n.* A room with toilets and sinks for public use.

re·sult (rĭ zŭlt′) *intr.v.* To happen as a consequence: *Nothing resulted from his efforts.* See Synonyms at **follow.** —*n.* [C; U] The consequence of a particular action; an outcome: *The book is the result of years of hard work.* ♦ **result in.** *tr.v.* [insep.] To have (sthg.) as an end: *The negotiations resulted in a new treaty.* —**re·sul′tant** *adj.*

re·sume (rĭ zōōm′) *v.* **re·sumed, re·sum·ing, re·sumes.** —*tr.* **1.** To begin (sthg.) again after a break: *We resumed our dinner after the interruption.* **2.** To occupy or take (sthg.) again: *The former prime minister resumed power.* —*intr.* To begin again or continue after a stop: *The meeting will resume after lunch.* —**re·sump′tion** (rĭ zŭmp′shən) *n.* [C; U]

ré·su·mé (rĕz′ōō mā′ *or* rĕz′ŏŏ mā′) *n.* **1.** An outline of one's professional history and experience, used to apply for a job: *Include your résumé with the job application.* **2.** A summary: *a brief résumé of the week's events.*

re·sur·gence (rĭ sûr′jəns) *n.* [U] A continuing after a stop; a renewal: *a resurgence in crime.* —**re·sur′gent** *adj.*

res·ur·rect (rĕz′ə rĕkt′) *tr.v.* **1.** To bring (sbdy.) back to life; raise from the dead. **2.** To bring (sthg.) back into practice or use: *resurrect an old custom.* —**res′ur·rec′tion** (rĕz′ə rĕk′shən) *n.* [U]

re·sus·ci·tate (rĭ sŭs′ĭ tāt′) *v.* **re·sus·ci·tat·ed, re·sus·ci·tat·ing, re·sus·ci·tates.** —*tr.* To return life or consciousness to (sbdy.); revive: *The lifeguard resuscitated the swimmer.* —*intr.* To come back to consciousness: *The swimmer resuscitated quickly.* —**re·sus′ci·ta′tion** *n.* [U]

re·tail (rē′tāl′) *n.* [U] The sale of goods to the general public: *The price at retail is higher than at wholesale.* —*adj.* Relating to the sale of goods at retail: *retail prices.* —*adv.* At a retail price: *The radio costs more retail than wholesale.* —*v.* —*tr.* To sell (things) directly to consumers: *The store retails lawn furniture.* —*intr.* To sell goods or be for sale at retail: *The camera retails at $300.* —**re′tail′er** *n.*

re·tain (rĭ tān′) *tr.v.* **1.** To keep possession of (sthg.); continue to have: *The new leader*

retained his job as head of finance. See Synonyms at **keep.** **2.** To keep or hold (sthg.): *Plants can retain moisture.* **3.** To keep (sthg.) in mind; remember: *Be sure to take notes since you can't possibly retain everything.* **4.** *Formal.* To hire (a lawyer, for example) by the payment of a fee: *She retained a lawyer.* —**re·ten′tion** (rĭ tĕn′shən) *n.* [U]

re·tain·er (rĭ tā′nər) *n.* **1.** A device used to hold teeth in position after orthodontic treatment: *She wears a retainer at night.* **2.** The fee paid to hire a professional adviser, such as a lawyer.

re·tal·i·ate (rĭ tăl′ē āt′) *intr.v.* **re·tal·i·at·ed, re·tal·i·at·ing, re·tal·i·ates.** To pay back an injury with one of the same kind; strike back: *retaliate against an enemy attack.* —**re·tal′i·a′tion** *n.* [U] —**re·tal′i·a·to′ry** (rĭ tăl′ē ə tôr′ē) *adj.*

re·tard (rĭ tärd′) *tr.v.* To slow the progress of (sthg.); delay: *A lack of sun retarded the growth of the plants.*

re·tar·da·tion (rē′tär dā′shən) *n.* [U] **1.** The act of retarding: *retardation of growth.* **2.** Slowness of growth or development: *mental retardation.*

re·tard·ed (rĭ tär′dĭd) *adj.* A somewhat offensive term meaning abnormally slow in mental development: *The child was born mentally retarded.*

retch (rĕch) *intr.v.* To strain or make an effort to vomit.

ret·i·cent (rĕt′ĭ sənt) *adj.* Tending not to speak out; quiet: *a reticent child.* —**ret′i·cence** *n.* [U]

ret·i·na (rĕt′n ə) *n.* A light-sensitive part at the back of the eye that is connected to the brain by the optic nerve. —**ret′i·nal** *adj.*

re·tire (rĭ tīr′) *v.* **re·tired, re·tir·ing, re·tires.** —*intr.* **1.** To give up one's work, usually because of age: *retire from teaching.* **2.** *Formal.* To withdraw to a quiet place: *The judge retired to her office.* **3.** *Formal.* To go to bed: *retire for the night.* —*tr.* **1.** To cause (sbdy.) to withdraw from an activity or work: *The coach retired the player.* **2.** To withdraw (sthg.) from use or active service: *retire an old battleship.* —**re·tire′ment** *n.* [U]

re·tir·ee (rĭ tīr′ ē′) *n.* A person who has retired from active working life.

re·tir·ing (rĭ tīr′ĭng) *adj.* Shy and quiet; modest: *He had a retiring manner.*

re·tort (rĭ tôrt′) *tr.v.* To say (an answer) in a quick, biting, or witty manner: *He retorted that he didn't care.* See Synonyms at **answer.** —*n.* A quick sharp reply: *His nasty retort surprised us.*

re·touch (rē tŭch′) *tr.v.* To make new details or touches to (sthg.) for correction or improvement; touch up: *retouch a photograph.*

re•trace (rē trās′) *tr.v.* **re•traced, re•trac•ing, re•trac•es.** To go back over (sthg.): *We retraced our steps looking for the lost keys.*

re•tract (rĭ trăkt′) *tr.v.* **1.** To take (sthg.) back: *He refused to retract his statement.* **2.** To pull (sthg.) back or in: *The airplane retracted its landing gear.* —**re•tract′a•ble** *adj.* —**re•trac′tion** *n.* [C; U]

re•treat (rĭ trēt′) *n.* **1.** [C; U] The act of withdrawing, especially from sthg. dangerous or unpleasant: *They made a hasty retreat.* **2.** [C] A place that is quiet or private: *We spent a week at the business retreat.* **3.** [C; U] The withdrawal of a military force. —*intr.v.* To fall or draw back; withdraw: *After a long battle, the troops retreated.*

re•tri•al (rē′trī′ əl *or* rē′trīl′) *n.* A second trial, as of a court case.

ret•ri•bu•tion (rĕt′rə byoō′shən) *n.* [U] Something given or demanded in repayment, especially punishment: *The robbery victim demanded retribution.*

re•trieve (rĭ trēv′) *v.* **re•trieved, re•triev•ing, re•trieves.** —*tr.* **1.** To get (sthg.) back; recover: *retrieve a lost glove.* **2.** To find and carry (sthg.) back; fetch: *The dog retrieved the toy.* **3.** To find and read (stored data) on a computer: *retrieve a file.* —*intr.* To find and bring back game that is hunted: *a dog trained to retrieve.* —**re•triev′al** (rĭ trē′vəl) *n.* [U]

re•triev•er (rĭ trē′vər) *n.* A type of dog trained to find and bring back birds or animals shot by hunters.

retro— *pref.* A prefix that means backward or back: *retrospective.*

ret•ro•ac•tive (rĕt′rō ăk′tĭv) *adj.* Applying to a previous time: *a retroactive pay increase.* —**ret′ro•ac′tive•ly** *adv.*

ret•ro•spect (rĕt′rə spĕkt′) *n.* ♦ **in retrospect.** Looking backward or reviewing the past: *In retrospect, it's easy to see what went wrong.*

ret•ro•spec•tive (rĕt′rə spĕk′tĭv) *Formal. adj.* Looking back on the past: *a retrospective examination of her career.* —*n.* An exhibition of the work of an artist over a period of years: *a retrospective of Monet's work.*

re•turn (rĭ tûrn′) *v.* —*intr.* **1.** To go or come back, as to a former condition or place: *return home.* **2.** To revert in speech, thought, or practice: *We finally returned to the discussion.* —*tr.* **1.** To send, put, or carry (sthg.) back: *We returned the book to the library.* **2.** To give (sthg.) back, as in exchange for sthg. else: *return merchandise for a refund.* **3.** To produce (interest or profit) as a payment for labor or investment: *Selling hot dogs returned him about ten percent.* —*n.* **1.** [U] The act of coming, going, bringing, or sending back: *a return to familiar places.* **2.** [C] Something brought or sent back: *Stores have many returns after Christmas.* **3.** [C] A happening again of an event: *the return of spring.*

4. [C] The profit or interest earned on an investment: *a five percent return.* **5.** [C] A formal tax statement on the required official form: *an income tax return.* **6.** [C] *(usually plural).* A report on the vote in an election: *early returns in the latest election.* **7.** [C] The key on a computer that positions the cursor at the beginning of a new line: *Hit the return to start a new line.* ♦ **in return.** In repayment: *If you do a favor for me, I'll do one for you in return.* —**re•turn′a•ble** *adj.*

re•un•ion (rē yoōn′yən) *n.* [C; U] A gathering of the members of a group who have been separated: *a yearly family reunion; a 20th class reunion.*

re•u•nite (rē′ yoō nīt′) *tr. & intr.v.* **re•u•nit•ed, re•u•nit•ing, re•u•nites.** To bring or come together again: *They reunited the family for a party. The friends reunited after a long separation.*

re•use (rē yoōz′) *tr.v.* **re•used, re•us•ing, re•us•es.** To use (sthg.) again: *Can you reuse this container?* —*n.* (rē yoōs′). [U] An act of using sthg. again: *The reuse of hypodermic needles is prohibited.* —**re•us′a•ble** *adj.*

rev (rĕv) *tr.v.* **revved, rev•ving, revs.** *Informal.* To increase the speed of (an engine or a motor): *Try not to rev the engine.*

re•vamp (rē vămp′) *tr.v.* To revise (sthg.) completely: *revamp a magazine's layout.*

re•veal (rĭ vēl′) *tr.v.* **1.** To make known (sthg. concealed or secret); disclose: *reveal a secret.* **2.** To bring (sthg.) to view; show: *The actor revealed his face.*

re•veal•ing (rĭ vē′lĭng) *adj.* **1.** Giving information about one's private feelings or attitudes: *a revealing letter.* **2.** Showing parts of the body that are usually covered: *a revealing negligee.*—**re•veal′ing•ly** *adv.*

rev•el (rĕv′əl) *intr.v.* **1.** [in] To take great pleasure or delight: *He revels in our lively discussions.* **2.** To engage in lively festivities: *They reveled until dawn in New Orleans.* —*n.* (*usually plural*). A noisy festivity or celebration; merrymaking: *all-night revels.* —**rev′el•er** *n.*

rev•e•la•tion (rĕv′ə lā′shən) *n.* **1.** [U] The act of revealing or disclosing. **2.** [C] Something revealed, especially sthg. surprising: *the revelation that they were already married.*

rev•el•ry (rĕv′əl rē) *n., pl.* **rev•el•ries.** [C; U] Noisy celebration: *Our revelry lasted till dawn.*

re•venge (rĭ vĕnj′) *tr.v.* **re•venged, re•veng•ing, re•veng•es.** To inflict punishment in return for (an injury or insult): *The character revenged his father's death.* —*n.* [U] The act or an example of revenging: *His revenge for the insult took an ugly form.* —**re•venge′ful** *adj.*

rev•e•nue (rĕv′ə noō) *n.* [C; U] **1.** The income that a government collects for payment of public expenses: *tax revenues*. **2.** Yield from property or investment; income: *Business revenue is down.*

re·ver·ber·ate (rĭ vûr′bə rāt′) *intr.v.* **re·ver·ber·at·ed, re·ver·ber·at·ing, re·ver·ber·ates.** To resound as in a series of echoes: *The concert hall reverberated with the sound of the piano.* —**re·ver′·ber·a′tion** *n.* [C; U]

re·vere (rĭ vîr′) *tr.v.* **re·vered, re·ver·ing, re·veres.** To regard (sbdy./sthg.) with awe and devotion: *The child revered his grandmother.*

SYNONYMS: revere, worship, adore, idolize. These verbs mean to regard with the deepest respect and honor. **Revere** means to honor and feel awed by sbdy./sthg.: *Their ancestor is revered as one of the town's founders.* **Worship** means to feel reverent or devoted love and often religious faith: *The ancient Greeks worshiped many different gods and goddesses.* **Adore** means to like sbdy./sthg. very much: *The little girl had such a sweet nature that everyone adored her.* **Idolize** means to worship sbdy. as if that person were perfect: *That girl still idolizes her older brother.*

---

rev·er·ence (rĕv′ər əns) *n.* [U] A feeling of deep awe and respect and often love: *He entered St. Patrick's Cathedral with reverence.* —**rev′er·ent, rev′er·en′tial** *adj.* —**rev′er·ent·ly** *adv.*

rev·er·end (rĕv′ər ənd) *n.* **1.** A minister in a Christian church: *The reverend will perform the ceremony.* **2. Reverend.** A title used for certain members of the Christian clergy: *the Reverend Martin Luther King, Jr.*

rev·er·ie (rĕv′ə rē) *n.* [C; U] A state of removed thought; daydreaming: *lost in reverie.*

re·ver·sal (rĭ vûr′səl) *n.* **1.** [C; U] The act of reversing: *a reversal of position.* **2.** [C] A change for the worse: *She suffered many reversals before finally succeeding in business.*

re·verse (rĭ vûrs′) *adj.* **1.** Turned backward in position, direction, or order: *The members of the choir filed back to their seats in reverse order.* **2.** Causing backward movement: *reverse gear.* —*n.* **1.** [U] The opposite or contrary of sthg.: *His opinion is the exact reverse of mine.* **2.** [U] The back or rear of sthg.: *the reverse of a page.* **3.** [U] A mechanism for moving backward, as a gear in an automobile: *Put the car in reverse.* **4.** [C] A change for the worse; a setback: *He has weathered the many reverses in his career.* —*v.* **re·versed, re·vers·ing, re·vers·es.** —*tr.* **1.** To turn (sthg.) around to the opposite direction: *She reversed the car.* **2.** To turn (sthg.) inside out or upside down: *You can*

reverse this jacket and wear it with the other side out. **3.** To exchange the positions of (things): *reverse the order of the numbers.* **4.** To make (a legal decision) invalid: *The higher court reversed the lower court's decision.*

re·vers·i·ble (rĭ vûr′sə bəl) *adj.* **1.** Capable of being reversed: *a reversible decision.* **2.** Wearable with either side turned outward: *a reversible vest.*

re·vert (rĭ vûrt′) *intr.v.* To return or go back to a former condition, belief, subject, or practice: *The writer reverted to her early style.* —**re·ver′sion** (rĭ vûr′zhən) *n.* [C; U]

re·view (rĭ vyōō′) *tr.v.* **1.** To look over, study, or examine (sthg.) again: *Let's review the last chapter.* **2.** To look back on (sthg.); think over: *review the day's events.* **3.** To examine (sthg.) in order to correct or criticize: *The scientist reviewed the data.* **4.** To write or give a critical report on (sthg.): *The newspaper's food critic reviewed the new restaurant favorably.* —*n.* **1.** [C; U] A reexamination or reconsideration. **2.** [C] A studying of sthg. covered earlier in school: *a review before the test.* **3.** [C] An inspection or examination. **4.** [C] A report that discusses sthg. new and judges its worth: *a book review.*

HOMONYMS: review, revue (show).

---

re·view·er (rĭ vyōō′ər) *n.* A person who reviews, especially one who writes critical reviews for a newspaper or magazine: *a movie reviewer.*

re·vile (rĭ vīl′) *tr.v.* **re·viled, re·vil·ing, re·viles.** *Formal.* To criticize (sbdy./sthg.) with abusive language: *He reviled his opponent in his speech.*

re·vise (rĭ vīz′) *tr.v.* **re·vised, re·vis·ing, re·vis·es.** **1.** To prepare a new version of (sthg. written): *revise an essay.* **2.** To reconsider and change or modify (sthg.): *revise an opinion.* —**re·vi′sion** (rĭ vĭzh′ən) *n.* [C; U]

re·vi·tal·ize (rē vīt′l īz′) *tr.v.* **re·vi·tal·ized, re·vi·tal·iz·ing, re·vi·tal·iz·es.** To make (sthg.) strong or active again, especially after a weak period: *plans to revitalize the city.* —**re·vi′tal·i·za′tion** *n.* [U]

re·vive (rĭ vīv′) *v.* **re·vived, re·viv·ing, re·vives.** —*tr.* **1.** To bring (sbdy.) back to life or consciousness: *revive someone who has fainted.* **2.** To give new strength or spirit to (sbdy./sthg.): *The music revived me.* **3.** To restore (sthg.) to use: *The studio revived the old TV program.* —*intr.* **1.** To return to life or consciousness: *She revived after a fainting spell.* **2.** To regain strength or good spirits: *He revived after a nap.* —**re·viv′al** *n.* [C; U]

re·voke (rĭ vōk′) *tr.v.* **re·voked, re·vok·ing, re·vokes.** To make (sthg.) void by

---

reversing, recalling, or withdrawing; cancel: *revoke a driver's license.*

re•volt (rĭ vōlt') *v.* —*intr.* **1.** To attempt to overthrow a government; rebel: *The peasants revolted after heavy taxation.* **2.** To oppose or refuse to accept sthg.: *We revolted against her idea of what the design should look like.* —*tr.* To fill (sbdy.) with disgust; repel: *The sight of the dirty kitchen revolted me.* —*n.* [C; U] An act of rebellion against authority; an uprising: *a prison revolt.*

re•volt•ing (rĭ vōl'tĭng) *adj.* Causing disgust; offensive: *revolting manners.* —**re• volt'ing•ly** *adv.*

rev•o•lu•tion (rĕv'ə lōō'shən) *n.* **1.** [C] Movement around a point, such as a rotation around an axis: *one revolution of the wheel.* **2.** [C; U] The overthrow of one government and its replacement with another: *the French Revolution.* **3.** [C] A sudden and important change: *the computer revolution.*

rev•o•lu•tion•ar•y (rĕv'ə lōō'shə nĕr'ē) *adj.* **1.** Relating to a revolution: *revolutionary war.* **2.** Tending to promote political or social revolution: *revolutionary writings.* **3.** Characterized by radical change: *a revolutionary new teaching idea.* —*n., pl.* **rev•o•lu•tion• ar•ies.** A person who is engaged in or favors revolution.

rev•o•lu•tion•ize (rĕv'ə lōō'shə nīz') *tr.v.* **rev•o•lu•tion•ized, rev•o•lu•tion•iz• ing, rev•o•lu•tion•iz•es.** To cause a radical change in (sthg.); change drastically: *The automobile revolutionized travel.*

re•volve (rĭ vŏlv') *intr.v.* **re•volved, re• volv•ing, re•volves.** **1.** To orbit a central point: *The earth revolves around the sun.* **2.** To turn on an axis; rotate: *The compass needle revolves on a point.*

re•volv•er (rĭ vŏl'vər) *n.* A pistol; a handgun.

re•volv•ing (rĭ vŏl'vĭng) *adj.* Tending to revolve or happen repeatedly: *a revolving door.*

re•vue (rĭ vyōō') *n.* A musical show consisting of songs, skits, and dances.

re•vul•sion (rĭ vŭl'shən) *n.* [U] A sudden strong feeling of violent disgust: *She felt revulsion at the sight of the accident.*

re•ward (rĭ wôrd') *n.* [C; U] **1.** Something given or received in return for a particular behavior: *the reward for her hard work.* **2.** Money offered or given for a special service, such as the return of a lost article or the capture of a criminal: *a $100 reward.* **3.** A satisfying result; a profit: *an investment with a handsome reward.* —*tr.v.* To give a reward to (sbdy.) or for (sthg.): *reward her for bravery; reward honesty.*

re•ward•ing (rĭ wôr'dĭng) *adj.* **1.** Offering satisfaction: *a rewarding experience.* **2.** Producing profit: *a rewarding investment.*

re•word (rē wûrd') *tr.v.* **1.** To change the

wording of (sthg.): *reword a contract.* **2.** To say (sthg.) again in different words: *The speaker reworded his answer to the question.*

re•work (rē wûrk') *tr.v.* To work (sthg.) over again; revise: *She reworked her paper.*

re•write (rē rīt') *tr.v.* **re•wrote** (rē rōt'), **re•writ•ten** (rē rĭt'n), **re•writ•ing, re• writes.** To write (sthg.) again, especially in a different or improved form: *He rewrote his letter to make it neater.* —*n.* (rē'rīt'). *Informal.* Something rewritten: *You need to do a rewrite.*

rhap•so•dy (răp'sə dē) *n., pl.* **rhap•so• dies.** A musical composition with an irregular form.

rhet•o•ric (rĕt'ər ĭk) *n.* [U] **1.** The art or study of using language effectively and persuasively. **2.** Elaborate, pretentious, or insincere writing or speech.

rhe•tor•i•cal (rĭ tôr'ĭ kəl *or* rĭ tŏr'ĭ kəl) *adj.* **1.** Relating to rhetoric. **2.** Used for persuasive effect: *rhetorical language.* —**rhe• tor'i•cal•ly** *adv.*

rhetorical question *n.* A question to which no answer is expected: *When the boss asked, "Are we going to let the competition take our customers?" it was just a rhetorical question.*

rheu•ma•tism (rōō'mə tĭz'əm) *n.* [U] A disease that affects the muscles and joints, causing pain and disability. —**rheu•mat'ic** (rōō măt'ĭk) *adj.*

rhine•stone (rīn'stōn') *n.* A colorless artificial gem of glass made to look like a diamond.

rhi•no (rī'nō) *n., pl.* **rhi•nos.** *Informal.* A rhinoceros.

rhi•noc•er•os (rī nŏs'ər əs) *n.* A large African or Asian mammal with short legs, thick tough skin, and one or two upright horns on the nose.

rho•do•den•dron (rō'də dĕn'drən) *n.* An evergreen shrub with clusters of white, pinkish, or purplish flowers.

rhyme (rīm) *n.* **1.** [U] Repetition of the final sounds of words or of lines of verse. **2.** [C] A poem with a regular repetition of sounds at the ends of lines: *nursery rhymes for small children.* **3.** [C] A word that has the same or similar final sound as another, as *baboon* and *cartoon.* —*v.* **rhymed, rhym•ing, rhymes.** —*intr.* **1.** To form a rhyme: *The word* hour *rhymes with* power. **2.** To make use of or have rhymes: *Not all poetry rhymes.* —*tr.* To put (sthg.) into a rhyme: *The boy rhymes words all the time.*

rhythm (rĭth'əm) *n.* **1.** [C; U] A musical pattern formed by a series of notes or beats that are of different lengths and stresses: *dancing to the rhythm.* **2.** [C; U] The pattern of stressed and unstressed syllables in poetry. **3.** [U] The regular sequence of repeated

R

actions or events: *the rhythm of the seasons.*
—**rhyth′mic, rhyth′mi•cal** *adj.* —**rhyth′-mi•cal•ly** *adv.*

rhythm and blues *pl.n. (used with a singular or plural verb).* A kind of popular music developed by black Americans that combines blues and jazz, characterized by a strong simple rhythm.

RI or **R.I.** *abbr.* An abbreviation of Rhode Island.

rib (rĭb) *n.* **1.** Any of a set of long curved bones that extend from the backbone to or toward the breastbone and enclose the chest cavity. **2.** A part similar to a rib and serving to shape or support: *a rib of an umbrella.* **3.** A cut of meat containing one or more ribs: *barbecued ribs.* —*tr.v.* **ribbed, rib•bing, ribs.** *Informal.* To make fun of or tease (sbdy.) in a friendly way: *She likes to rib her father.*

rib•bon (rĭb′ən) *n.* **1.** A narrow strip of fine cloth, such as satin or velvet, used for decorating: *The ribbons in her hair match the ribbons on the dress.* **2.** A strip or strips of cloth whose colors have special meanings, given as awards: *She won a blue ribbon for first place in the competition.*

rice (rīs) *n.* [U] The starchy seeds of a grass grown in warm wet regions as a source of food: *Rice is a popular food in Japan.*

rich (rĭch) *adj.* **1.** Having great wealth: *a rich industrial nation.* **2.** Having a large amount: *Milk is rich in protein.* **3.** Full of natural resources: *rich land.* **4.** Productive and therefore profitable: *rich soil.* **5.** Heavy and sweet: *a rich dessert.* **6.a.** Pleasantly full and mellow: *a rich tenor voice.* **b.** Warm and deep in color: *a rich brown velvet.* —*n. (used with a plural verb).* Wealthy people considered as a group: *tax laws that affect the rich.* —**rich′ly** *adv.* —**rich′ness** *n.* [U]

rich•es (rĭch′ĭz) *pl.n.* **1.** Great wealth. **2.** Valuable possessions.

Rich•ter scale (rĭk′tər) *n.* [U] A scale used to express the size or total energy of an earthquake: *a quake measuring 4.5 on the Richter scale.*

rick•et•y (rĭk′ĭ tē) *adj.* **rick•et•i•er, rick•et•i•est.** Likely to fall apart or break; shaky: *a rickety old bridge.*

ric•o•chet (rĭk′ə shā′ *or* rĭk′ə shā′) *intr.v.* **ric•o•cheted** (rĭk′ə shād′), **ric•o•chet•ing** (rĭk′ə shā′ĭng), **ric•o•chets** (rĭk′ə-shāz′). [*off*] To bounce at least once from a surface: *A bullet ricocheted off the rock.*

rid (rĭd) *tr.v.* **rid** or **rid•ded, rid•ding, rids.** [*of*] To free (sbdy./sthg.) of (sthg. unwanted): *How do we rid the dog of fleas? He rid himself of debt.* ✦ **get rid of. 1.** To throw away (sthg. unused or unwanted): *You need to get rid of some junk!* **2.** To make (sthg. unpleas-ant) stop: *I can't seem to get rid of this cough.* **3.** To make (sbdy.) leave: *You wait here while I get rid of whoever is at the door.*

rid•dance (rĭd′ns) *n.* ✦ **good riddance.** *Informal.* An expression used when one is glad that a person or thing is gone permanently: *She said "good riddance" when her boyfriend left.*

rid•den (rĭd′n) *v.* Past participle of **ride.** —*adj.* Full of or ruled by: *disease-ridden; worry-ridden.*

rid•dle¹ (rĭd′l) *n.* **1.** A puzzling question requiring thought to answer or understand: *In many ancient myths, the heroes are required to answer riddles.* **2.** Something that is difficult to understand: *It is a riddle to me why they are so excited.*

rid•dle² (rĭd′l) *tr.v.* **rid•dled, rid•dling, rid•dles. 1.** To pierce (sthg.) with many holes: *riddle a target with bullets.* **2.** To spread throughout (sthg.): *a government riddled with corruption.*

ride (rīd) *v.* **rode** (rōd), **rid•den** (rĭd′n), **rid•ing, rides.** —*intr.* **1.** To be carried or move, as in a vehicle or on horseback: *ride in a car.* **2.** To travel over a surface: *The car rides smoothly.* **3.** *Informal.* [*on*] To depend: *My grade rides on the results of the test.* **4.** To continue without interference: *Let the problem ride for now.* —*tr.* **1.** To sit on and move or drive (sthg.): *ride a bicycle; ride a horse.* **2.** To travel over, along, or through (sthg.): *a delivery van riding the back roads.* **3.** To be supported or carried on (sthg.): *surfers riding the waves.* **4.** *Informal.* To tease or ridicule (sbdy.): *The other children were always riding him.* —*n.* **1.** The act or an instance of riding, as in a vehicle or on an animal: *going for an elephant ride.* **2.** A device at an amusement park that one rides for pleasure or excitement: *The merry-go-round is my favorite ride.* **3.** A means of transportation: *waiting for her ride to come.* ✦ **ride out.** *tr.v.* [sep.] To survive or wait for the end of (sthg.): *We rode out the storm.* **ride shotgun.** *Slang.* To ride next to the driver of a vehicle: *Who wants to ride shotgun?* **take (one) for a ride.** To cheat or deceive (sbdy.): *That fast-talking salesperson really took me for a ride!*

rid•er (rī′dər) *n.* A person who rides, especially a person who rides horses.

ridge (rĭj) *n.* **1.** A long narrow upper section: *the ridge of a wave; the ridge of a roof.* **2.** A long narrow chain of hills or mountains.

rid•i•cule (rĭd′ĭ kyōol′) *n.* [U] Unkind words intended to cause laughter or scorn: *Her poor taste in clothing often left her open to ridicule.* —*tr.v.* **rid•i•culed, rid•i•cul•ing, rid•i•cules.** To laugh at or make fun of (sbdy./sthg.); mock in a very unkind way: *She often ridiculed her classmates.*

ri·dic·u·lous (rĭ dĭk′yə ləs) *adj.* Absurd or silly: *a ridiculous idea.* —**ri·dic′u·lous·ly** *adv.* —**ri·dic′u·lous·ness** *n.* [U]

rife (rīf) *adj.* **rif·er, rif·est. 1.** Being everywhere: *Malaria is rife in these regions.* **2.** Full of: *The article is rife with mistakes.*

riff·raff (rĭf′răf′) *n.* [U] *(used with a plural verb).* People regarded as worthless.

ri·fle[1] (rī′fəl) *n.* A gun with a long barrel, designed to be fired from the shoulder.

ri·fle[2] (rī′fəl) *tr.v.* **ri·fled, ri·fling, ri·fles.** [*through*] To look through (sthg.) very quickly, often to steal: *The spies rifled the diplomat's files. He rifled through the drawer looking for the money.*

rift (rĭft) *n.* **1.** A fault, as in a system of rock: *We climbed the small cliff by using rifts as hand holds.* **2.** A break in friendly relations: *A misunderstanding caused the rift between our countries.*

rig (rĭg) *tr.v.* **rigged, rig·ging, rigs. 1.** To provide (sthg.) with equipment: *rig a garage to store a boat.* **2.** To influence the result of (sthg.) dishonestly for personal gain: *rig a basketball game; rig an election.* —*n.* **1.** Special equipment or gear, especially equipment used for drilling oil wells: *a drilling rig.* **2.** *Informal.* A truck or tractor-trailer. *He drives a big rig.* ◆ **rig up.** *tr.v.* [sep.] To put (sthg.) together in a hurry because it is needed: *Do you think we could rig up a story to explain why we're so late?*

rig·ging (rĭg′ĭng) *n.* [U] **1.** The system of ropes, chains, and sails on a ship. **2.** The supporting material for construction work.

right (rīt) *adj.* **1.** Fitting with justice or morality: *We want to do the right thing.* **2.** Agreeing with fact or truth; correct: *the right answer.* **3.** Fitting or proper: *the right tool for the job.* **4.** In good mental or physical health: *not in her right mind; not feeling right.* **5.** Meant to be worn on the outside or on top: *Wear the jacket with the right side outward.* **6.** Advantageous or favorable: *I was lucky to be in the right place at the right time.* **7.** Relating to, directed toward, or located on the right side: *my right hand.* **8.** Often **Right.** Relating to the political Right. —*n.* **1.** [U] That which is just or morally good: *the difference between right and wrong.* **2.** [C] Something that a person has a moral or legal claim to: *the right of free speech.* **3.a.** [U] The right side: *the first door on the right.* **b.** [C] A turn in the direction of the right hand or side: *Make a right at the stop sign.* **4.** [U] Often **Right.** The people and groups who hold conservative ideas, especially in politics: *the religious right.* —*adv.* **1.** Toward or on the right: *turning right.* **2.** In a straight line; directly: *came right to the door.* **3.** In a correct manner; properly: *The shoes don't fit right.* **4.** Exactly: *The accident happened right next to*

where we were standing. **5.** Immediately: *He called right after breakfast.* **6.** Used as an intensive: *Keep right on going.* —*tr.v.* **1.** To put (sthg.) in or back in an upright or proper position: *They righted the canoe with difficulty.* **2.** To set (sthg.) right; correct: *right unfair hiring practices.* ◆ **by rights.** In a just manner; in fairness: *By rights, we should get equal pay for equal work.* **right away.** Without delay; immediately: *He answered right away.* **to rights.** In a satisfactory or orderly condition: *putting a messy room to rights.* —**right′ness** *n.* [U]

HOMONYMS: right, rite (ceremony), **write** (compose).

---

right angle *n.* An angle formed by the perpendicular intersection of two straight lines; an angle of 90°.

right·eous (rī′chəs) *adj.* Morally right; just: *a righteous cause.* —**right′eous·ly** *adv.* —**right′eous·ness** *n.* [U]

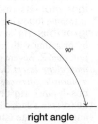
right angle

right·ful (rīt′fəl) *adj.* Relating to a just, proper, or legal claim: *the car's rightful owner.* —**right′ful·ly** *adv.*

right-hand (rīt′hănd′) *adj.* **1.** Relating to or located on the right: *the right-hand margin.* **2.** Designed for or done with the right hand: *a right-hand throw.* **3.** Helpful; reliable: *my right-hand assistant.*

right-hand·ed (rīt′hăn′dĭd) *adj.* **1.** Using the right hand more easily than the left: *a right-handed person.* **2.** Done with the right hand: *a right-handed throw.* Made to be worn on or used by the right hand: *right-handed scissors.* —*adv.* With the right hand: *She draws right-handed.* —**right′hand′ed·ly** *adv.* —**right′hand′ed·ness** *n.* [U]

right-hand·er (rīt′hănd′ər) *n.* A person who is right-handed.

right·ly (rīt′lē) *adv.* **1.** In a correct or proper manner: *act rightly.* **2.** *Informal.* Really: *I don't rightly know.*

right of way (rīt′əv wā′) *n., pl.* **rights of way** or **right of ways. 1.** The right to pass over property owned by sbdy. else: *A right of way allows the public to have access to the lake.* **2.** The strip of land over which structures such as highways, railroads, or power lines are built: *The bike path was built on an unused railroad right of way.* **3.** The legal right of a person or vehicle to pass in front of another: *Pedestrians in crosswalks have the right of way over vehicles.*

right-side up (rīt′sīd′) *adv. & adj.* **1.** With the top facing upward. **2.** In or into the correct position: *Turn the painting right-side up.*

right-to-life (rīt′tə līf′) *adj.* Pro-life. —**right-to-lifer** *n.*

right wing also **Right Wing.** *n.* The conservative faction of a group, especially of a political group. —**right′-wing′** *adj.* —**right′-wing′er** *n.*

right·y (rī′tē) *n., pl.* **right·ies.** *Informal.* A person who is right-handed.

rig·id (rĭj′ĭd) *adj.* **1.** Not changing shape or bending; stiff: *a rigid iron frame.* **2.** Strict: *rigid discipline.* —**ri·gid′i·ty** (rĭ jĭd′ĭ tē) *n.* [U] —**rig′id·ly** *adv.* —**rig′id·ness** *n.* [U]

rig·or (rĭg′ər) *n.* **1.** [U] Strictness or severe standards, as in action or judgment: *the rigor of mathematics.* **2.** [C] *(usually plural).* A harsh or difficult circumstance; a hardship: *the rigors of battle.*

rigor mor·tis (môr′tĭs) *n.* [U] Muscular stiffening following death.

rig·or·ous (rĭg′ər əs) *adj.* **1.** Characterized by or acting with rigor: *a rigorous training program.* **2.** Severe or harsh: *the rigorous climate of the desert.* **3.** Precisely accurate; strict: *a rigorous physical examination.* —**rig′or·ous·ly** *adv.* —**rig′or·ous·ness** *n.* [U]

rile (rīl) *tr.v.* **riled, ril·ing, riles.** *Informal.* To anger or irritate (sbdy.): *The endless delay riled the train's passengers.*

rim (rĭm) *n.* **1.** The border, edge, or margin of sthg.: *the rim of the cup.* See Synonyms at **margin. 2.** The outer part of a wheel around which a tire is fitted.

rime (rīm) *n.* [U] *Formal.* Frost or a coating of ice, as on grass or trees.

rind (rīnd) *n.* A tough outer covering, skin, or coating, as of fruit or cheese: *an orange rind.*

ring¹ (rĭng) *n.* **1.** A small circular band, often of precious metal, worn on a finger: *a gold wedding ring.* **2.** A circular object, form, or arrangement with an empty center: *a ring of flowers.* **3.** An enclosed area in which exhibitions, sports, or contests take place: *a circus ring; a boxing ring.* **4.** A group of persons acting privately or illegally for their own gain: *a ring of car thieves.* —*tr.v.* To surround (sbdy./sthg.) as if with a ring; encircle: *Let's ring the statue with flowers.*

ring² (rĭng) *v.* **rang** (răng), **rung** (rŭng), **ring·ing, rings.** —*intr.* **1.** To give forth a clear resonant sound, such as that of a bell: *The doorbell rang.* **2.** To sound a bell in order to call sbdy. to come: *ring for service at the hotel.* **3.** To hear a persistent hum-

ming: *ears ringing from the loud music.* **4.** To be filled with sound, talk, or rumors: *a room ringing with laughter; an office that rang with the good news.* —*tr.* **1.** To cause (a bell, for example) to ring: *ring a doorbell.* **2.** To announce or signal (sthg.) by or as if by ringing: *a clock that rings the hour.* **3.** To call (sbdy.) on the telephone: *Ring me this afternoon.* —*n.* **1.** The sound made by a bell or another vibrating object: *the ring of an alarm clock.* **2.** *Informal.* A telephone call: *Give me a ring from the hotel.* **3.** A sound or suggestion of a particular quality: *His offer has a suspicious ring.* ◆ **ring a bell.** *Informal.* To arouse a memory: *That name doesn't ring a bell with me.* **ring true.** To appear to be correct: *That story rings true.*

ring up. *tr.v.* [sep.] To record (a sale), especially by means of a cash register: *The clerk rang up my purchases.*

ringed (rĭngd) *adj.* Wearing, having, or surrounded by bands or rings: *A raccoon has a ringed tail.*

ring·er (rĭng′ər) *n.* **1.** *Slang.* A person who bears a striking resemblance to another: *Isn't she a ringer for her mother?* **2.** A person who sounds a bell or chime.

ring·lead·er (rĭng′lē′dər) *n.* A person who leads others, especially in unlawful or disorderly activities.

ring·let (rĭng′lĭt) *n.* A tight curl of hair: *a little girl with ringlets.*

ring·mas·ter (rĭng′măs′tər) *n.* A person who is in charge of and introduces the acts in a circus.

ring·side (rĭng′sīd′) *n.* A place providing a close view of an event, especially the seats next to the ring at a prizefight.

rink (rĭngk) *n.* An area with a smooth surface for skating: *an ice rink.*

rin·ky-dink (rĭng′kē dĭngk′) *adj.* *Slang.* **1.** Of cheap or poor quality: *a rinky-dink house.* **2.** Unimportant: *Who cares about your rinky-dink problems?*

rinse (rĭns) *tr.v.* **rinsed, rins·ing, rins·es. 1.** To wash (sthg.) lightly with water: *rinse the dishes.* **2.** To remove (soap, for example) by washing lightly with water: *She rinsed the shampoo from her hair.* —*n.* **1.** The act of washing lightly. **2.** The water or other solution used in rinsing: *a cold-water rinse.* **3.** A solution used in conditioning or coloring the hair: *a temporary hair rinse.* ◆ **rinse off** or **out.** *tr.v.* [sep.] **1.** To clean (sthg.) by washing with water: *rinse off the dishes.* **2.** To remove (sthg.) by washing with water: *I need to rinse the mud out of my jeans.*

ri•ot (rī′ət) *n.* **1.** A dangerous disturbance created by a large number of people: *a prison riot.* **2.** A colorful display: *The garden was a riot of colors.* **3.** *Slang.* An extremely funny person or thing: *That cartoon is a riot.* —*intr.v.* To take part in a riot: *Protesters rioted in the streets.* —**ri′ot•er** *n.*

ri•ot•ous (rī′ət əs) *adj.* **1.** Relating to or resembling a riot: *riotous mobs.* **2.** Loud and unrestrained: *riotous laughter.*

rip (rĭp) *v.* **ripped, rip•ping, rips.** —*tr.* To tear open or split apart (sthg.): *The cat's claws ripped the curtain.* —*intr.* To become torn or split apart: *My pants ripped.* —*n.* A torn or split place: *Sew up the rip.* ◆ **rip into.** *tr.v.* [insep.] To attack (sbdy.) verbally or physically: *She ripped into him for not telling the truth.* **rip off.** *tr.v.* [sep.] *Slang.* **1.** To steal (sthg.): *Someone ripped off my coat!* **2.** To exploit or cheat (sbdy.): *That salesman ripped me off!* **rip up.** *tr.v.* [sep.] To tear (paper or a document) into pieces: *She ripped the contract up.*

SYNONYMS: **rip, tear, shred, split.** These verbs mean to pull apart or separate by physical effort. **Rip** suggests separation by force, often along a dividing line such as a seam or joint: *The nurses ripped sheets into long strips to use as bandages.* **Tear** means to pull sthg. apart or into pieces: *He tore the napkin into bits.* **Shred** means to separate into long, irregular strips: *You should always shred confidential papers before throwing them away.* **Split** means to cut or break sthg. into parts or layers, especially along its entire length: *They split the logs with an ax to make firewood.*

ripe (rīp) *adj.* **rip•er, rip•est. 1.** Fully grown and developed: *ripe fruit.* **2.** Aged and ready to be used or eaten: *a ripe cheese.* **3.** Advanced in years: *the ripe age of 85.* **4.** Fully prepared; ready: *a team ripe for its first victory.* —**ripe′ly** *adv.* —**ripe′ness** *n.* [U]

rip•en (rī′pən) *intr.v.* To become ripe or riper; mature: *Allow the tomatoes to ripen on the vine.*

rip-off (rĭp′ôf′ *or* rĭp′ŏf′) *n. Slang.* **1.** A theft. **2.** Something that makes one feel cheated: *That movie was a rip-off.*

rip•ple (rĭp′əl) *v.* **rip•pled, rip•pling, rip•ples.** —*intr.* **1.** To form or show small waves on the surface: *The curtain rippled in the wind.* **2.** To flow with such small waves on the surface: *The stream rippled through the meadow.* —*tr.* To cause (sthg.) to form small waves: *A breeze rippled the prairie grass.* —*n.* **1.** A small wave, such as one formed on the surface of water when it is disturbed. **2.** A motion like that of a wave: *the ripple of muscles on the running horse.* **3.** A sound like that made by rippling water: *a ripple of laughter in the audience.*

rip-roar•ing (rĭp′rôr′ĭng) *adj. Informal.* Noisy, lively, and exciting: *We had a rip-roaring time at the party.*

rise (rīz) *intr.v.* **rose** (rōz), **ris•en, ris•ing, ris•es. 1.** To move from a lower to a higher position; ascend: *The plane rose quickly.* **2.** To stand up after sitting or lying: *The audience rose to their feet.* **3.** To get out of bed: *He rises early.* **4.** To increase in size, amount, level, or value: *The river rose after the heavy rain. Prices of imports rose.* **5.** To increase in intensity, force, or speed: *The wind has risen.* **6.** To increase in pitch or volume: *The sound of their voices rose and fell.* **7.** To advance in status or rank: *He wants to rise in the academic world.* **8.** To slope or extend upward: *Mt. McKinley rises to 20,320 feet.* **9.** To come to the mind or senses: *Old doubts rose to challenge me.* **10.** To come into existence: *Many streams rise in the snow-capped Andes.* **11.** To swell, as bread dough; become larger: *Let the dough rise for an hour.* —*n.* **1.** An act of rising; upward movement: *a balloon's rapid rise.* **2.** An increase in height, as of the level of water: *the rise of the tide.* **3.** An increase in price, worth, quantity, volume, or degree: *a rise in students' grades.* **4.** Elevation in status or rank: *her rise to stardom.* ◆ **get a rise out of.** *Slang.* To anger (sbdy./sthg.): *Stop trying to get a rise out of the dog.* **give rise to.** To bring (sthg.) into existence; cause: *Her shyness gave rise to the rumor that she was a snob.* **rise above.** *tr.v.* [insep.] **1.** To overcome (hardship, for example): *He's risen above his poor origins to become a successful lawyer.* **2.** To manage not to be affected by (sthg. unpleasant): *You will have to rise above their childish insults and do what is right.* **rise to the occasion.** To do sthg. well in spite of problems: *No matter what happens, she always rises to the occasion.* **rise up against.** To rebel against (sbdy./sthg.): *The people rose up against the tyrant and overthrew him.*

ris•er (rī′zər) *n.* **1.** A person who rises, especially from sleep: *Her husband is a late riser; she's an early riser.* **2.** A vertical part of a stair step.

risk (rĭsk) *n.* **1.** [C; U] The possibility of suffering harm or loss; danger: *Visiting someone with an infectious disease can be a foolish risk.* **2.** [C] A person or thing considered with respect to the possibility of loss: *People who pay their bills on time are good credit risks.* —*tr.v.* **1.** To put (sbdy./sthg.) in a situation where there is a chance of harm or loss: *He risked his savings in an investment scheme.* **2.** To subject oneself to the chance of (sthg.): *risking an accident.* ◆ **at (one's) own risk.** Accepting responsibility for the possibly dangerous or bad consequences of one's actions: *There's no lifeguard here, so you swim at*

R

your own risk. **at risk.** In danger: *She's at risk of failing in two subjects.* **risk (one's) neck.** *Informal.* To put (one's) life in danger: *She risked her neck climbing Mt. Everest.* —**risk′i•ness** *n.* [U] —**risk•y** (rĭs′kē) *adj.*

ris•qué (rĭs kā′) *adj.* Relating to sthg., such as clothing or a joke, that is close to being improper or indecent.

rite (rīt) *n. (usually plural).* A ceremonial act or series of acts: *the rites performed by various peoples before hunting.*

HOMONYMS: rite, right (direction), **write** (compose).

rit•u•al (rĭch′ōō əl) *n.* [C; U] **1.** A religious or other ceremony that involves special steps: *The priest performed the ritual.* **2.** A method or procedure faithfully followed: *Exercise was part of their daily ritual.* —**rit′u•al′ism** *n.* [U] —**rit′u•al•ly** *adv.*

ritz•y (rĭt′sē) *adj.* **ritz•i•er, ritz•i•est.** *Informal.* Elegant; fancy: *ritzy hotels.*

ri•val (rī′vəl) *n.* **1.** A person who tries to equal or outdo another; a competitor: *The two brothers have always been rivals.* **2.** A person or thing that equals or almost equals another: *a performance without rival.* —*tr.v.* To be the equal of (sbdy./sthg.); match in excellence: *The handling of this car rivals that of many more expensive cars.* —**ri′val•ry** *n.* [C; U]

riv•er (rĭv′ər) *n.* **1.** A large natural stream of water that flows into a larger body of water. **2.** A stream or flow resembling a river: *a river of tears.*

riv•et (rĭv′ĭt) *n.* A metal bolt or pin used to join objects. —*tr.v.* **1.** To fasten (sthg.) with a rivet: *rivet leather straps onto the suitcase.* **2.** To fasten or secure (sbdy./sthg.) firmly: *She stood riveted to the spot.* **3.** To attract or hold (one's attention, for example): *This book riveted my attention.*

Rn The symbol for the element **radon.**

RNA *n.* [U] A nucleic acid found in all living cells and functioning mainly in the synthesis of proteins; ribonucleic acid.

roach (rōch) *n.* A cockroach.

road (rōd) *n.* An open way for the passage of vehicles, persons, and animals. ♦ **hit the road.** To start on one's way; leave: *It's getting late, so we should hit the road.* **on the road. 1.** On tour, as a theatrical company. **2.** Traveling, especially as a salesperson.

HOMONYMS: road, rode (moved in a vehicle), **rowed** (used oars).

road•block (rōd′blŏk′) *n.* **1.** A barricade set up across a road to stop vehicles from moving. **2.** Something that prevents sbdy. from

achieving sthg.: *Some people create their own roadblocks in life.*

road•kill (rōd′kĭl′) *n.* [U] *Informal.* An animal that has been hit and killed accidentally on a highway.

road•run•ner (rōd′rŭn′ər) *n.* A long-tailed bird of southwest North America that runs very fast.

road•side (rōd′sīd′) *n.* The area along the side of a road.

roam (rōm) *v.* —*intr.* To move about without purpose or plan; wander: *Large herds of buffalo once roamed in the West.* See Synonyms at **wander.** —*tr.* To travel over or through (an area) without a purpose or plan; wander: *Bears roam the forest.*

roar (rôr) *v.* —*intr.* **1.** To produce a loud deep sound: *The crowd roared when the team finally scored a goal.* See Synonyms at **shout. 2.** To laugh loudly or excitedly: *She had us all roaring at her comic impressions of family members.* —*tr.* To express (sthg.) with a loud deep noise: *We roared our approval.* —*n.* **1.** The loud deep sound made by a wild animal: *the roar of the lion.* **2.** A loud deep sound or noise: *the roar of a rocket engine.*

roar•ing (rôr′ĭng) *adj. Informal.* Very lively or successful; doing well: *a roaring business.*

roast (rōst) *v.* —*tr.* **1.** To cook (sthg.) with dry heat, as in an oven: *roast a turkey.* **2.** To dry (sthg.) by heating: *They roasted coffee beans.* —*intr.* To cook in an oven: *The chicken should roast for an hour* —*n.* A cut of meat for roasting: *Put the roast into the oven at 2:00.* —*adj.* Roasted: *a roast duck.*

rob (rŏb) *tr.v.* **robbed, rob•bing, robs. 1.** To take valuables unlawfully from (sbdy./sthg.): *rob a bank.* **2.** To deprive (sbdy.) unjustly of sthg.: *Bad timing robbed her of the chance to get the job.* —**rob′ber** *n.*

rob•ber•y (rŏb′ə rē) *n., pl.* **rob•ber•ies.** [C; U] The act of unlawfully taking the property of another with the use of force.

robe (rōb) *n.* **1.** A bathrobe. **2.** *(usually plural).* An official garment worn over other clothes on formal occasions to show office or rank: *a judge's robes.*

rob•in (rŏb′ĭn) *n.* A North American songbird with a red breast and a dark gray back.

ro•bot (rō′bət *or* rō′bŏt′) *n.* **1.** A machine with the ability to perform human tasks or imitate human actions. **2.** A person who works or follows orders mechanically: *The people behind the counter were robots—never smiling, just doing their jobs.*

ro•bot•ics (rō bŏt′ĭks) *n.* [U] *(used with a singular verb).* The study and use of the technology of robots: *Many factories now use robotics.*

ro·bust (rō bŭst′ *or* rō′bŭst′) *adj.* **1.** Full of health and strength: *a robust rosebush with many blooms; an 80-year-old in robust health.* **2.** Very rich in flavor; full-bodied: *a robust blend of coffee beans.*

rock¹ (rŏk) *n.* **1.** A relatively hard material that is of mineral origin; a stone. **2.** A person or thing that resembles a rock in firmness or stability: *She's a rock in times of crisis.* ◆ **on the rocks. 1.** In a state of difficulty or ruin: *Their marriage is on the rocks.* **2.** Served over ice cubes, as an alcoholic drink.

rock² (rŏk) *v.* —*intr.* **1.** To be moved back and forth or from side to side: *The ship rocked gently.* **2.** To be shaken violently: *The buildings rocked during the earthquake.* —*tr.* **1.** To move (sbdy./sthg.) back and forth or from side to side to comfort or quiet: *I rocked the baby to sleep.* **2.** To shake (sbdy./sthg.) violently, as from a shock or blow: *The earthquake rocked the villages.* **3.** To stun or upset (sbdy.); shock: *A scandal rocked the town.* —*n.* [U] **1.** A rhythmic swaying motion: *the rock of the boat.* **2.** Rock 'n' roll. ◆ **rock the boat.** *Informal.* To upset the balance of a situation or group: *Don't rock the boat by bringing up old issues.*

rock-and-roll (rŏk′ən rōl′) *n.* [U] Variant of **rock 'n' roll.**

rock bottom *n.* [U] The lowest level or absolute bottom: *Prices have reached rock bottom.*

rock·er (rŏk′ər) *n.* **1.** A musician who plays rock 'n' roll. **2.** A rocking chair. **3.** One of the two curved pieces on which a cradle, rocking chair, or similar device rocks. ◆ **off (one's) rocker.** *Slang.* Out of one's mind; crazy: *Sometimes he goes off his rocker, but it doesn't mean anything.*

rock·et (rŏk′ĭt) *n.* **1.** A vehicle or device driven by one or more jet-propelled engines. **2.** A weapon carrying a warhead that is driven by rockets. **3.** A firework that is shot up into the sky. —*intr.v.* **1.** To travel in or by means of a rocket: *rocketing to the moon.* **2.** To move with great speed: *a train that went rocketing by.*

rocket engine *n.* An engine that is propelled by a jet of hot gases produced by burning fuel.

rock·ing chair (rŏk′ĭng) *n.* A chair mounted on rockers or springs.

rocking horse *n.* A toy horse large enough for a child to ride, mounted on rockers or springs.

rock 'n' roll or **rock-and-roll** (rŏk′ən rōl′) *n.* [U] A form of popular music that draws on rhythm and blues, country music, and gospel.

rocking chair

rock·y¹ (rŏk′ē) *adj.* **rock·i·er, rock·i·est.**

1. Containing rocks: *rocky soil.* **2.** Full of obstacles or difficulties: *a rocky career.*

rock·y² (rŏk′ē) *adj.* **rock·i·er, rock·i·est. 1.** Unsteady or shaky: *a rocky balance.* **2.** *Informal.* Weak, dizzy, or nauseated: *She's recovering from the flu, but still feels a little rocky.*

rod (rŏd) *n.* **1.** A thin, stiff, straight piece of metal, wood, or other material: *a curtain rod; a fishing rod.* **2.** Any of the long cells in the retina of the eye that are sensitive to dim light.

rode (rōd) *v.* Past tense of **ride.**

HOMONYMS: rode, road (passage), **rowed** (used oars).

ro·dent (rōd′nt) *n.* Any of various related mammals, such as a mouse, rat, squirrel, or beaver, with large front teeth used for gnawing.

ro·de·o (rō′dē ō′ *or* rō dā′ō) *n., pl.* **ro·de·os.** A cowboy show in which skills such as riding wild horses or bulls and roping calves are displayed.

roe (rō) *n.* [C; U] The eggs of a fish.

HOMONYMS: roe, row (continuous line, use oars).

rogue (rōg) *n.* A person who tricks or cheats others, a scoundrel: *a rogue preying on the elderly to get rich.*

rogu·ish (rō′gĭsh) *adj.* **1.** Dishonest; unprincipled: *That was a roguish thing to do to him!* **2.** Playfully teasing; mischievous: *a roguish sense of humor.* —**ro′guish·ly** *adv.*

role (rōl) *n.* **1.** A character or part played by a performer: *A famous actor played the role of the hero.* **2.** The characteristic or expected social behavior of a person: *confirming social roles of the past.*

HOMONYMS: role, roll (turn over).

role model *n.* A person who serves as a model for another person to imitate: *Children need good role models.*

roll (rōl) *v.* **rolled, roll·ing, rolls.** —*intr.* **1.** To move or travel along a surface by repeatedly turning: *The coin rolled across the sidewalk.* **2.** To move along on wheels or rollers: *The car rolled to a stop.* **3.** To begin to move or operate: *Come on, everybody, let's roll.* **4.** To make progress: *The campaign is really rolling now.* **5.** To take the shape of a ball or cylinder: *Yarn rolls easily.* **6.** To become flattened by applying pressure with a roller: *The dough rolls smoothly.* **7.** To move or extend in gentle rises and falls: *The sand dunes roll to the sea.* **8.** To move or rock from side to side: *The sailboat rolled and pitched in the storm.* **9.** To make a long deep sound: *Thunder rolled in the distance.* —*tr.* **1.** To cause (sthg.) to move or travel along a surface by repeatedly turning: *roll a ball.* **2.** To move or push (sthg.) along on wheels or rollers: *The secretary rolled the chair away from the desk.* **3.** To cause (sthg.) to begin moving or operating: *roll the movie cameras.* **4.** To say (a sound) with a trill: *You need to roll your* r*'s in Spanish.* **5.** To envelop or wrap (sthg.): *roll dirty laundry in a sheet.* —*n.* **1.** The act or an instance of rolling: *The golfer watched the roll of the ball toward the cup.* **2.** Something rolled up: *a roll of tape; a roll of film.* **3.** A swaying or rocking motion: *the roll of the ship on the waves.* **4.** A gentle rise and fall in a surface: *the roll of the plains.* **5.** A list of names of persons belonging to a group: *The teacher calls the roll before class begins.* **6.a.** A small rounded portion of bread: *a hamburger roll.* **b.** A portion of food shaped like a tube with a filling: *an egg roll.* **7.** A deep long sound: *a roll of thunder.* **8.** A rapid series of short sounds: *a drum roll.* ◆ **all rolled into one.** All together; combined: *My mother is a teacher, nurse, and best friend, all rolled into one.* **on a roll.** *Informal.* Experiencing continued, even increasing good fortune or success: *Let's get this work done now since we're on a roll.* **roll back.** *tr.v.* [sep.] **1.** To reduce (prices or wages, for example) to a previous lower level: *The candidate promised to roll back taxes.* **2.** To cause (sbdy./sthg.) to turn back or retreat: *roll back enemy forces.* **roll by** *or* **on.** *intr.v.* To go by; pass: *The years roll by more quickly as one gets older.* **roll in.** *intr.v.* **1.** To arrive: *He finally rolled in, three hours late.* **2.** To come often in large numbers: *Keep those cards and letters rolling in!* **roll off.** *tr.v.* [insep.] To appear from (a source): *New computers keep rolling off the assembly line.* **roll out.** *tr.v.* [sep.] To unroll: *We rolled out the red carpet for the visiting officials.* **roll over.** *tr.v.* [sep.] To reinvest (money): *Instead of cashing in his stock for a profit, he rolled it over.* **roll up.** *intr.v. Informal.* To arrive in a vehicle: *The star rolled up an hour late.* —*tr.v.* [sep.] To gain (sthg.) over time: *roll up a fortune.*

HOMONYMS: roll, role (part in a play).

---

roll call *n.* The reading aloud of a list of names of people to find out who is present.
roll•er (rō′lər) *n.* **1.** A small wheel, as on a roller skate: *Maybe you need to oil the rollers on the bed.* **2.** A small cylinder around which hair is wound to produce a soft curl: *She answered the door with her hair still in rollers.* **3.** A cylinder used to flatten, crush, or squeeze things. **4.** A cylinder for applying paint or a similar substance onto a surface: *I'll need a roller in order to paint this wall.*
Roll•er•blade (rō′lər blād) A trademark for a boot with a single row of rollers; an in-line

skate. —*intr.v.* To skate on in-line skates: *We went Rollerblading along the bike path.*
roller coaster *n.* An elevated railway with steep drops and sharp turns that is operated as a ride in an amusement park.
roller skate *n.* A shoe or boot with usually four wheels arranged in pairs or in a row, worn for skating on hard surfaces.
roll•er-skate (rō′lər skāt′) *intr.v.* **roll•er-skat•ed, roll•er-skat•ing, roll•er-skates.** To skate on roller skates. —**roller skater** *n.*
rol•lick•ing (rŏl′ĭ kĭng) *adj.* High-spirited and carefree; boisterous: *a rollicking song.*
roll•ing pin (rō′lĭng) *n.* A smooth cylinder, usually of wood, with a handle at each end, used for rolling out dough.
ro•ly-po•ly (rō′lē pō′lē) *Informal. adj.* Short and plump; roundish in shape: *a roly-poly baby.* —*n., pl.* **ro•ly-po•lies.** A short plump person or thing: *The puppy is a little roly-poly.*
ro•maine (rō mān′) *n.* [U] A type of lettuce with long crisp leaves forming a narrow head.
Ro•man Catholic (rō′mən) *adj.* Relating to the Christian church whose head is the pope in Rome. —*n.* A member of this church.
ro•mance (rō măns′ *or* rō′măns′) *n.* **1.** [C; U] A relationship involving love between two people: *She was looking for some romance in her life.* **2.** [C] A story about love, the adventures of heroes, and extraordinary events: *a medieval romance.* **3.** [U] A mysterious quality, as of sthg. adventurous: *an air of romance about the old castle.* —*tr.v.* (rō-măns′). **ro•manced, ro•manc•ing, ro•manc•es.** *Informal.* To court or carry on a love affair with (sbdy.): *He romanced her with candy and roses.*
Roman numeral *n.* Any of the numerals formed with the characters I, V, X, L, C, D, and M in the number system developed by the ancient Romans.
ro•man•tic (rō măn′tĭk) *adj.* **1.** Relating to or characteristic of romance: *a romantic story.* **2.** Given to thoughts or feelings of romance; sentimental: *a romantic young woman.* **3.** Relating to love or a love affair: *a romantic involvement.* —*n.* A romantic person: *an incurable romantic.* —**ro•man′ti•cal•ly** *adv.*
ro•man•ti•cize (rō măn′tĭ sīz′) *v.* **ro•man•ti•cized, ro•man•ti•ciz•ing, ro•man•ti•ciz•es.** —*tr.* To view or interpret (sbdy./sthg.) romantically: *romanticized ideas about marriage.* —*intr.* To think in a romantic way: *She romanticizes about him day and night.*
romp (rŏmp) *intr.v.* To play in an excited or lively manner: *dogs romping in a field.* —*n.* Lively high-spirited play: *a romp in the snow.*
roof (rŏŏf *or* rŏof) *n.* **1.** The exterior covering on the top of a building. **2.** The top part of

sthg.: *the roof of a car.* **3.** The upper surface of sthg.: *the roof of the mouth.* —*tr.v.* To cover (sthg.) with a roof: *a house roofed with shingles.*

roof•er (rōō′fər *or* roof′ər) *n.* A person who lays or repairs roofs.

roof•ing (rōō′fĭng *or* roof′ĭng) *n.* [U] Materials used to make a roof.

roof•top (rōōf′tŏp′ *or* roof′tŏp′) *n.* The outer surface of a roof: *We looked out over the rooftops of the city.*

rook (rook) *n.* A chess piece that may move in a straight line horizontally or vertically across any number of unoccupied squares.

rook•ie (rook′ē) *n.* **1.** A first-year player, especially in a major-league sport. **2.** *Slang.* A beginner; a novice: *We had to show the rookie how to do everything.*

room (rōōm *or* room) *n.* **1.** [C] **a.** An area of a building set off by walls or partitions: *How many rooms does your house have?* **b.** The people present in a room: *The whole room laughed.* **2.** [U] A space that is or may be occupied: *This big desk takes up too much room.* **3.** [U] Occasion; possibility: *There is room for doubt.* —*intr.v.* [with] To occupy a rented room as a lodger: *rooming with a private family.*

room and board *n.* [U] Lodging and meals earned, purchased, or provided: *The student's parents pay his college tuition and room and board.*

room•er (rōō′mər *or* room′ər) *n.* A person who rents a room; a lodger.

HOMONYMS: roomer, rumor (report).

room•mate (rōōm′māt′ *or* room′māt′) *n.* A person with whom one shares a room or an apartment.

room•y (rōō′mē *or* room′ē) *adj.* **room•i•er, room•i•est.** Having plenty of room; spacious: *a roomy closet.* —**room′i•ness** *n.* [U]

roost (rōōst) *n.* A branch, rod, or similar resting place on which birds perch or settle for the night. —*intr.v.* To rest or sleep on a roost.

roost•er (rōō′stər) *n.* A full-grown male chicken.

root[1] (rōōt *or* root) *n.* **1.** A part of a plant that usually grows down into the ground, absorbs water and minerals from the soil, and holds the plant securely in place. **2.** The part of an organ or body structure, such as a hair or tooth, that is fixed in other tissue and serves as a base. **3.** A source; an origin: *the ancient roots of democracy.* **4.** The essential part; core; heart: *the root of the problem.* **5. roots.** The condition of belonging to a particular culture, society, place, or environment: *We've lived here too short a time to have any roots here.* **6.** A word or base from which other words are formed, as by adding affixes. For

example, *cheer* is the root of *cheerful* and *cheerless.* **7.** A number that when multiplied by itself a given number of times produces a specified number. For example, since $2 \times 2 \times 2 = 16$, 2 is the fourth root of 16. —*v.* —*intr.* To send forth or start the growth of a root or roots: *Carrot tops will root in water.* —*tr.* **1.** To cause (sthg.) to put out roots and grow. **2.** To fix (sbdy./sthg.) in place by or as if by roots: *Our love of the mountains has rooted us here.* ◆ **root out.** *tr.v.* [sep.] To look for and destroy the cause of (a problem): *Police are trying to root out drugs.* **take root.** To become established: *The plant took root. An idea took root in my mind.*

HOMONYMS: root (plant part, dig, cheer), route (road).

root[2] (rōōt *or* root) *intr.v.* **1.** To dig with the snout or nose: *pigs rooting in the mud.* **2.** [through] To look for sthg. by moving things aside: *She rooted through the drawer looking for an eraser.*

root[3] (rōōt *or* root) *intr.v.* [for] To support by or as if by cheering: *They were rooting for their favorite team.*

root beer *n.* [C; U] A carbonated soft drink made from extracts of certain plant roots and herbs.

rope (rōp) *n.* [C; U] **1.** A heavy cord made of intertwined strands of fiber or some other material. **2. ropes.** *Informal.* The practices and techniques involved in a certain task or job: *learning the ropes; showing a new student the ropes.*—*tr.v.* **roped, rop•ing, ropes.** To tie or fasten (sbdy./sthg.) with or as if with a rope: *rope a calf.* ◆ **at the end of (one's) rope.** At the end of one's patience, endurance, or resources: *My mother is at the end of her rope with my sister's wild behavior.* **give plenty of rope to.** To let (sbdy./sthg.) do almost anything: *My boss gives her workers plenty of rope.* **rope into.** *tr.v.* [insep.] To talk (sbdy.) into (accepting a responsibility): *I got roped into going to the grocery store again.* **rope off.** *tr.v.* [sep.] To block off (a space): *The police roped off the crime scene.* —**rop′er** *n.*

Roque•fort (rōk′fərt) A trademark used for a strongly flavored French cheese that has veins of blue mold: *Roquefort dressing.*

rose[1] (rōz) *n.* **1.** [C] The red, pink, white, or yellow, often very fragrant flower of any of numerous usually prickly shrubs or vines. **2.** [U] A deep pink color. —*adj.* Deep pink.

rose

rose² (rōz) *v.* Past tense of **rise.**

rose-col•ored (rōz'kŭl'ərd) *adj.* **1.** Having the color rose. **2.** Cheerful or optimistic, especially too much so. ♦ **through rose-colored glasses.** With an unreasonably cheerful optimistic view of things: *Romantics often see the world through rose-colored glasses.*

rose•mar•y (rōz'mâr'ē) *n.* [U] The small grayish green leaves of an evergreen shrub, used as seasoning in cooking.

Rosh Ha•sha•nah also **Rosh Ha•sha•na** (rôsh' hə shô'nə *or* rôsh' hə shä'nə) *n.* The Jewish New Year, celebrated in September or October.

ros•ter (rŏs'tər *or* rô'stər) *n.* A list of names: *a class roster.*

ros•y (rō'zē) *adj.* **ros•i•er, ros•i•est. 1.** Having a reddish or deep pink color: *rosy cheeks.* **2.** Bright and cheerful: *The future looks rosy.* —**ros'i•ly** *adv.* —**ros'i•ness** *n.* [U]

rot (rŏt) *v.* **rot•ted, rot•ting, rots.** —*intr.* **1.** To spoil or decay: *The meat will rot if it is not refrigerated.* **2.** To become damaged or useless because of decay: *The roof of the old house had rotted away.* —*tr.* To cause (sthg.) to become rotten; decay: *Too much sugar will rot your teeth.* —*n.* [U] The process of rotting or the result of being rotted; decay.

ro•ta•ry (rō'tə rē) *n., pl.* **ro•ta•ries.** A traffic circle.— *adj.* Related to movement in a circle around a fixed point: *the rotary motion of a ceiling fan.*

ro•tate (rō'tāt) *v.* **ro•tat•ed, ro•tat•ing, ro•tates.** —*intr.* **1.** To turn around on an axis or a center: *The wheel rotates around the axle.* See Synonyms at **turn. 2.** To proceed in sequence; take turns: *The order of classes rotates each day.* —*tr.* **1.** To cause (sthg.) to turn on an axis or a center: *rotate a dial.* **2.** To plant or grow (crops) in a changing order: *Farmers rotate crops to protect the soil.* **3.** To cause (people or things) to alternate: *The coach rotates players in a game.*

ro•ta•tion (rō tā'shən) *n.* **1.a.** [U] The process of turning around a center or axis: *the rotation of the earth.* **b.** [C] A complete turn as a result of such motion: *turning at seven rotations per minute.* **2.** [C] Regular change or variation in a series or sequence: *the rotation of duties in a military unit.*

ROTC *abbr.* An abbreviation of Reserve Officers' Training Corps.

rote (rōt) *n.* [U] A process of memorizing by repetition, often without full understanding: *She learned the French song by rote.*

Homonyms: rote, wrote (formed letters).

ro•tis•se•rie (rō tĭs'ə rē) *n.* A broiler with a rotating metal rod for roasting meat.

ro•tor (rō'tər) *n.* A rotating part of a machine: *a rotor on a helicopter.*

rot•ten (rŏt'n) *adj.* **1.** Decayed or decomposed: *rotten meat.* **2.** Made weak or unsound by rot: *rotten wood.* **3.** Not honest, honorable, or decent; corrupt: *rotten politicians.* **4.** *Informal.* Very bad; terrible: *She has had some rotten luck.* —**rot'ten•ly** *adv.* —**rot'ten•ness** *n.* [U]

ro•tund (rō tŭnd') *adj.* Rounded in shape or figure; plump: *a rotund gentleman.*

ro•tun•da (rō tŭn'də) *n.* A round room or building, especially one with a dome.

rouge (rōōzh) *n.* [U] An outdated name for a pink or red cosmetic for coloring the cheeks or lips; blush. —*tr.v.* **rouged, roug•ing, roug•es.** To color (sthg.) with rouge: *rouged cheeks.*

rough (rŭf) *adj.* **1.** Having an irregular surface; not smooth or even: *a rough bumpy road.* **2.** Coarse to the touch: *rough wool; rough skin.* **3.** Marked by violent motion: *rough waters.* **4.** Difficult to endure: *a rough winter.* **5.** Not polite or refined: *rough manners.* **6.** Forceful: *a rough push.* **7.** Not finished; in a natural state: *a rough gem.* **8.** Not complete; tentative: *a rough draft.* —*tr.v.* To treat (sbdy.) with unnecessary physical violence, especially in certain sports: *He was penalized for roughing another player.* ♦ **rough it.** To live without the usual comforts and conveniences: *We roughed it in the mountains for a month.* **rough up.** *tr.v.* [sep.] To treat (sbdy.) with violence: *The boys roughed up the smaller child.* —**rough'ness** *n.* [U]

Homonyms: rough, ruff (fur or feathers).

rough•age (rŭf'ĭj) *n.* [U] Dietary fiber.

rough•en (rŭf'ən) *tr. & intr.v.* To make or become rough: *Washing dishes will roughen your hands. My hands have roughened since I started gardening.*

rough•house (rŭf'houz') *intr.v.* **rough•housed, rough•hous•ing, rough•hous•es.** *Informal.* To engage in noisy or rowdy play: *The children tired themselves out roughhousing.*

rough•shod (rŭf'shŏd') *adj.* ♦ **ride roughshod over.** To bully or treat (sbdy.) forcefully and unkindly: *He rode roughshod over everyone on his way to the top.*

rou•lette (rōō lĕt') *n.* [U] A gambling game in which players bet where a ball will come to rest on a rotating wheel with numbered slots.

round (round) *adj.* **1.a.** With a spherical or nearly spherical shape; ball-shaped: *An orange is round.* **b.** Moving in or forming a circle: *a round table.* **c.** Having a curved sur-

R

face: *a baby's round face.* **2.** Adjusted so as to be less exact; approximate: *round numbers.* —*n.* **1.** A round object: *a round of bread.* **2.** A complete course or series of events: *a round of negotiations.* **3.** *(usually plural).* A usual course of places visited or duties performed: *a doctor on her rounds.* **4.** A single shot from a gun or guns, or the ammunition for a single shot: *The police officer fired a round.* **5.** A specified period or unit of play in a game or contest: *play a round of golf.* **6.** A musical composition for two or more voices in which each voice enters at a different time with the same melody. —*v.* —*tr.* **1.** To make (sthg.) round: *You round your lips to pronounce "o."* **2.** To make a turn about or to the other side of (sthg.): *The car rounded a bend in the road.* **3.** To adjust (a number) to be less precise: *Let's round all the prices to the nearest dollar for an estimate of the total bill.* —*intr.* To become round: *Her shoulders have rounded with age.* —*adv.* Around: *a wheel spinning round and round.* —*prep.* Around: *Put the rope round the post.* ♦ **go round and round.** To talk without really doing anything: *We've gone round and round about his behavior but it's no better than it was.* **round off.** *tr.v.* [sep.] To adjust (a number) up or down to simplify: *The number 514 can be rounded off to 510 or to 500.* **round out.** *tr.v.* [sep.] To make (sthg.) more detailed or complete: *Round out your essay by adding more details.* **round up.** *tr.v.* [sep.] To find and bring together (people or things); gather: *Let's round up a group for a game of volleyball.* —**round′ness** *n.* [U]

round·a·bout (round′ə bout′) *adj.* Not going straight to the goal or conclusion; indirect: *We chose a roundabout course to avoid traffic.*

round·ed (roun′dĭd) *adj.* **1.** Having a curved shape: *a rounded edge.* **2.** Spoken with the lips shaped ovally: *a rounded vowel.*

round·ta·ble (round′tā′bəl) *n.* Often **round table.** A conference or discussion with several participants.

round-the-clock (round′thə klŏk′) *adj.* Lasting or continuing throughout the entire 24 hours of the day; continuous: *round-the-clock medical care.*

round·trip (round′trĭp′) *n.* A trip from one place to another and then back again: *a roundtrip ticket to Rome.*

round·up (round′ŭp′) *n.* A gathering up of persons or things: *a police roundup.*

rouse (rouz) *v.* **roused, rous·ing, rous·es.** —*tr.* **1.** To wake (sbdy.) up; arouse: *The train conductor roused the sleeping man.* **2.** To cause (sbdy./sthg.) to become active, attentive, or excited: *a sight that roused her curiosity.* —*intr.* To wake up; awaken: *She roused immediately on hearing the alarm.*

rous·ing (rou′zĭng) *adj.* **1.** Stirring; inspir-

ing: *a rousing call to action.* **2.** Energetic; vigorous: *a rousing dance tune.*

rout (rout) *n.* An overwhelming defeat: *a rout at the hands of the enemy.* —*tr.v.* To defeat (sbdy.) overwhelmingly; crush: *We routed the opposing team.*

route (rōōt *or* rout) *n.* **1.** A road or course for traveling from one place to another: *Route 66.* **2.** A fixed course, as of places or customers visited regularly by a salesperson or delivery person: *a newspaper route.* —*tr.v.* **rout·ed, rout·ing, routes.** To send or pass (sthg.) on in a certain way: *Please route the memo to the staff.*

HOMONYMS: route, root (plant part, dig, cheer).

rou·tine (rōō tēn′) *n.* **1.** [C; U] A series of activities performed or meant to be performed regularly; a standard or usual procedure: *her morning routine.* See Synonyms at **method. 2.** [C] A set piece of entertainment: *a comedy routine.* —*adj.* **1.** In accordance with standard procedure: *a routine check of passports.* **2.** Not special; ordinary: *another routine day.* —**rou·tine′ly** *adv.*

row¹ (rō) *n.* **1.** A series of persons or things placed next to each other, usually in a straight line: *a row of trees.* **2.** A line of connected seats, as in a theater: *Which row are we in?* **3.** A series without a break or gap in time: *She won the tennis title three years in a row.*

HOMONYMS: row (continuous line, use oars), **roe** (fish eggs).

row² (rō) *v.* —*intr.* To move a boat with oars: *We rowed down the river.* —*tr.* **1.** To propel (a boat) with oars. **2.** To carry (sbdy./sthg.) in a boat propelled by oars: *He rowed the dog across to the island.* —**row′er** *n.*

row·boat (rō′bōt′) *n.* A small boat moved by oars.

row·dy (rou′dē) *adj.* **row·di·er, row·di·est.** Rough and disorderly: *a rowdy and dangerous crowd.* —**row′di·ness** *n.* [U]

roy·al (roi′əl) *adj.* **1.** Relating to a king or queen. **2.** Fit for a king or queen: *a royal banquet.* **3.** *Informal.* Very big; huge: *You've made a royal mess of the kitchen.* —**roy′al·ly** *adv.*

roy·al·ty (roi′əl tē) *n., pl.* **roy·al·ties. 1.** [U] Members of a royal family. **2.** *(usually plural).* **a.** A share paid to an author or a composer out of the profits resulting from the sale or performance of his or her work. **b.** A share of profits paid to an inventor for the right to use his or her invention.

rpm or **r.p.m.** *abbr.* An abbreviation of revolutions per minute.

R.R. *abbr.* An abbreviation of railroad.

R.S.V.P. or **r.s.v.p.** *abbr.* An abbreviation of répondez s'il vous plaît (please reply).

rte. *abbr.* An abbreviation of route.

rub (rŭb) *v.* **rubbed, rub·bing, rubs.** —*tr.* **1.** To press sthg. against (a surface) and move it back and forth: *rub a window with a piece of cloth.* **2.** To cause (sthg.) to move along a surface with pressure: *rub a cloth against a windowpane.* —*intr.* To move along in contact with a surface; scrape: *machine parts with marks showing where they rub together.* —*n.* The act of rubbing: *a back rub.* ◆ **rub down.** *tr.v.* [sep.] To perform a brisk rubbing of (the body), as in massage: *He rubbed the boxer down.* **rub elbows** or **shoulders with.** To have contact with (other people): *rub elbows with the rich and famous.* **rub in.** *tr.v.* [sep.] To remind sbdy. repeatedly of (an unpleasant matter): *Please don't rub it in anymore! I know you beat me.* **rub off on. 1.** To make (other people) feel or act the same way; influence: *Don't let his bad attitude rub off on you.* **2.** To cling to (another surface) after touching: *The wet paint rubbed off on my coat.* **rub out.** *tr.v.* [sep.] *Slang.* To kill (sbdy.): *After he reported the gang's illegal activities, they rubbed him out.* **rub the wrong way.** To annoy (sbdy.); irritate: *It's the way you approach them that rubs people the wrong way.*

rub·ber (rŭb′ər) *n.* **1.** [U] An elastic material made from the milky sap of certain tropical plants or synthetically and used in a great variety of products. **2.** [C] A low overshoe made of rubber. **3.** [C] *Chiefly British.* An eraser. **4.** [C] *Slang.* A condom. —**rub′ber·y** *adj.*

rubber band *n.* An elastic loop of natural or synthetic rubber, used to hold objects together.

rub·ber·ize (rŭb′ə rīz′) *tr.v.* **rub·ber·ized, rub·ber·iz·ing, rub·ber·iz·es.** To coat or treat (sthg.) with rubber.

rub·ber·neck (rŭb′ər nĕk′) *intr.v. Slang.* [*at*] To turn one's head and stare while walking or driving: *Many drivers slowed down to rubberneck at the accident.*

rub·ber-stamp (rŭb′ər stămp′) *tr.v.* To support, vote for, or approve (sthg.) without question or thought: *The governor rubberstamped the legislation.*

rub·bish (rŭb′ĭsh) *n.* [U] **1.** Useless waste material; trash: *Throw your rubbish in the trash can.* **2.** Foolish talk or writing; nonsense: *Her ideas are pure rubbish.*

rub·ble (rŭb′əl) *n.* [U] Fragments of stone or other material left after the destruction or decay of a building: *The buildings were reduced to rubble in the earthquake.*

rub·down (rŭb′doun′) *n.* An energetic massage of the body.

ru·bel·la (rōō bĕl′ə) *n.* [U] An infectious disease that is caused by a virus; German measles.

ru·by (rōō′bē) *n., pl.* **ru·bies. 1.** [C] A deep red translucent mineral that is greatly valued as a precious stone. **2.** [U] A deep red color. —*adj.* Deep red.

ruck·us (rŭk′əs) *n. Informal.* A disturbance; confusion: *Our abrupt entrance caused a ruckus.*

rud·der (rŭd′ər) *n.* A flat movable structure at the back of a boat or the tail of an aircraft, used for steering.

rud·dy (rŭd′ē) *adj.* **rud·di·er, rud·di·est.** Having a healthy reddish color: *a ruddy complexion.*

rude (rōōd) *adj.* **rud·er, rud·est. 1.** Lacking courtesy; ill-mannered: *She apologized for being rude.* **2.** Relatively undeveloped; primitive: *a rude system of farming.* **3.** Sudden and jarring: *a rude shock.* —**rude′ly** *adv.* —**rude′ness** *n.* [U]

ru·di·ment (rōō′də mənt) *n. (usually plural).* **1.** A basic principle or skill: *learning the rudiments of grammar.* **2.** Something in a beginning or an undeveloped form: *The children have acquired the rudiments of social behavior.* —**ru′di·men′ta·ry** (rōō′də mĕn′tə rē or rōō′də mĕn′trē) *adj.*

rue (rōō) *tr.v.* **rued, ru·ing, rues.** To feel regret, remorse, or sorrow for (sthg.): *They rued the foolish decision.* —**rue′ful** *adj.* —**rue′ful·ly** *adv.*

ruff (rŭf) *n.* A growth of fur or feathers around the neck of an animal or a bird. —**ruffed** *adj.*

HOMONYMS: ruff, rough (not smooth).

---

ruf·fi·an (rŭf′ē ən) *n.* A tough or rowdy person; a thug.

ruf·fle (rŭf′əl) *n.* A strip of gathered or pleated cloth used for a trimming or decoration. —*tr.v.* **ruf·fled, ruf·fling, ruf·fles. 1.** To disturb the smoothness or evenness of (sthg.): *The wind ruffled the boy's hair.* **2.** To upset (sbdy.); fluster: *The unexpected events ruffled the speaker.* **3.** To cause (feathers) to stand up: *The bird ruffled his feathers.* **4.** To pleat or gather (fabric) into a ruffle: *ruffle a strip of satin.* ◆ **ruffle (one's) feathers.** To annoy (sbdy.); disturb: *Don't ruffle her feathers today; she's in a bad mood.*

rug (rŭg) *n.* **1.** A heavy fabric used to cover a floor. **2.** *Slang.* A hairpiece.

rug·by (rŭg′bē) *n.* [U] A form of football in which players may kick, dribble, or run with the ball, and play is continuous.

rug·ged (rŭg′ĭd) *adj.* **1.** Having a rough irregular surface: *rugged terrain.* **2.** Having wrinkles and rough features: *a rugged face.* **3.** Sturdy; hardy: *a rugged athlete.* **4.** Harsh

---

or difficult: *a rugged winter.* —**rug′ged•ly** *adv.* —**rug′ged•ness** *n.* [U]

ru•in (rōō′ĭn) *n.* **1.** [U] Total destruction or collapse. **2.** [U] The cause of such destruction: *A refusal to adopt new technology was the ruin of their business.* **3.** *(usually plural).* The remains of sthg. that has been destroyed or has fallen into pieces from age: *Aztec ruins.* —*tr.v.* **1.** To harm (sbdy./sthg.) greatly; make useless or worthless: *The recession ruined the new business.* **2.** To destroy (sthg.): *The crops were ruined by the flood.* —**ru′in•ous** *adj.* —**ru′in•ous•ly** *adv.*

rule (rōōl) *n.* **1. a.** [U] The power of governing; authority: *a democracy under the rule of law.* **b.** [C] A period of government: *during the rule of King George III.* **2.** [C] A statement that tells what may or may not be done: *the rules of tennis.* **3.** [C] A usual or customary course of action: *As a rule, I'm in bed by ten.* **4.** [C] A statement that tells what is true in most or all cases: *Most mammals are covered with fur, but human beings are an exception to this rule.* —*v.* **ruled, rul•ing, rules.** —*tr.* **1.** To have political control or authority over (sbdy./sthg.); govern: *She ruled her country wisely.* **2.** To have great influence over (sbdy./sthg.): *He allowed his passions to rule his judgment.* **3.** To declare or decide (sthg.). Used of a judge or court: *The Supreme Court ruled that the law was unconstitutional.* **4.** To mark (paper or another surface) with straight parallel lines: *ruled paper.* —*intr.* **1.** To be in control; exercise authority: *The queen has ruled wisely.* **2.** To make and express a judicial decision: *The judge ruled on the case.* ◆ **rule of thumb.** A general principle useful most of the time in making decisions or calculations: *As a rule of thumb, one pizza will serve four guests.* **rule out.** *tr.v.* [sep.] **1.** To prevent (sthg.) from happening: *The rain ruled out the picnic.* **2.** To remove (sbdy./sthg.) from consideration: *We have ruled him out as a candidate for the job.*

rul•er (rōō′lər) *n.* **1.** A person, such as a king or queen, who governs a country: *a wise ruler.* **2.** A flat, narrow piece of wood, metal, or plastic for drawing straight lines and measuring length: *a twelve-inch ruler.*

rul•ing (rōō′lĭng) *adj.* **1.** Having control, especially political control; governing: *a ruling body; the ruling classes.* **2.** Very powerful: *a ruling passion.* —*n.* An official decision: *a court ruling.*

rum (rŭm) *n.* [C; U] An alcoholic liquor distilled from sugar cane or molasses.

rum•ble (rŭm′bəl) *intr.v.* **rum•bled, rum•bling, rum•bles.** **1.** To make a deep, long, rolling sound: *thunder rumbling in the east.* **2.** To move with such a sound: *A heavy truck rumbled over the wooden bridge.* —*n.* **1.** A deep, long, rolling sound: *the rumble of the plane moving down the runway.* **2.** *Slang.* An outdated name for a gang fight.

ru•mi•nate (rōō′mə nāt′) *intr.v.* **ru•mi•nat•ed, ru•mi•nat•ing, ru•mi•nates.** **1.** To chew a cud, as a cow or sheep does. **2.** [on] To spend time thinking about a matter; meditate: *He ruminated on the proposal before making a decision.*

rum•mage (rŭm′ĭj) *intr.v.* **rum•maged, rum•mag•ing, rum•mag•es.** [through] To make an energetic search: *The boy rummaged through the drawers for a bathing suit.*

rummage sale *n.* A sale of old or unwanted objects, often donated to raise money for a charity.

rum•my (rŭm′ē) *n.* [U] A card game in which the players try to obtain sets of three or more cards of the same rank or suit.

ru•mor (rōō′mər) *n.* A story or report that is often repeated but may not be true: *Rumors spread quickly in an office.* —*tr.v.* To spread or tell (sthg.) by rumor: *It was rumored that he was leaving.*

rump (rŭmp) *n.* **1. a.** [C] The fleshy part above the hind legs of a four-footed animal: *the cow's rump.* **b.** [U] A cut of meat from this part: *a rump roast.* **2.** [C] *Informal.* The human buttocks.

rum•ple (rŭm′pəl) *v.* **rum•pled, rum•pling, rum•ples.** —*tr.* To wrinkle or crease (sthg.): *Don't rumple the suit.* —*intr.* To become wrinkled or creased: *Some fabrics rumple more easily than others.*

run (rŭn) *v.* **ran** (răn), **run, run•ning, runs.** —*intr.* **1.** To move on foot at a pace faster than walking: *running in an Olympic marathon.* **2.** To move away quickly: *At the first sign of danger, we ran.* **3.** To make a quick trip or visit: *Can I take the car to run to the store?* **4.** To compete in a race for elected office: *She's running for governor.* **5.** To move freely on or as if on wheels: *The wagon ran downhill.* **6.** To be in operation; work: *The engine is running.* **7.** To go along a regular course, especially on a schedule: *The*

R

trains are running late. **8.a.** To flow: *Turn on the faucet and let the water run.* **b.** To give off mucus or other fluid: *My nose is running.* **9.** To extend, spread, or reach: *This road runs all the way through town.* **10.** To take a particular form: *The report runs as follows.* **11.** To pass into a specified condition: *He ran into debt. We're running low on gas.* —*tr.* **1.** To travel over (a distance) on foot at a pace faster than a walk: *The boy ran two blocks.* **2.** To do or accomplish (sthg.) as if by running: *She ran some errands.* **3.** To cause (sthg.) to move quickly: *He ran his fingers over the piano keys.* **4.** To cause (sthg.) to function; operate: *run a machine.* **5.** To transport (sbdy./sthg.): *Can you run me into town?* **6.** To cause (sthg.) to flow: *run water into a tub.* **7.** To cause (sthg.) to extend or pass: *run a rope between trees.* **8.** To cause (a car, for example) to crash: *He ran his car into a tree.* **9.** To conduct, manage, or perform (sthg.): *run an experiment; run a business.* **10.** To import or export (sthg.) illegally: *run guns.* **11.** To process (a computer program or command). **12.** To expose oneself to (a risk). **13.** To have (a fever). —*n.* **1.** A pace faster than a walk: *He heard my call for help and came at a run.* **2.a.** An act of running: *go for a run.* **b.** A distance covered by or as if by running: *a short run.* **3.** A quick trip or visit: *a run into town.* **4.** A regular or scheduled route: *a delivery truck on its morning run.* **5.** A running race: *a five-mile run.* **6.** Unrestricted freedom or use: *They gave us the run of their place.* **7.** A continuous period of operation, especially of a machine or factory: *a trial run of a new engine.* **8.** An outdoor area enclosed for dogs or poultry, for example: *a chicken run.* **9.** A line of broken stitches in a knitted fabric: *a run in my stocking.* **10.** An unbroken series: *a run of victories.* **11.** A series of unexpected demands by depositors or customers: *a run on a bank.* **12.** An execution of a specific computer program or command. ◆ **a run for (one's) money.** Strong competition: *We might not be able to beat them, but we'll give them a good run for their money.* **have the run of.** To be able to move about freely or use a place that does not belong to one: *Their dog has the run of the apartment. I've always had the run of the house when she's out of town.* **in the long run.** Not immediately but eventually: *In the long run, your education will prove to be a good investment.* **in the short run.** In the immediate future: *If we don't make building repairs, we save money, but only in the short run.* **make a run for it.** To try to get away from danger: *When the dog came after me, I had to make a run for it.* **on the run. 1.** In

rapid retreat: *The soldiers had the enemy on the run.* **2.** In hiding: *fugitives on the run.* **3.** Hurrying busily from place to place: *I had lunch on the run.* **run across.** *tr.v.* [insep.] To find (sthg.) by chance: *Let me know if you run across my keys.* **run after.** *tr.v.* [insep.] **1.** To chase (sbdy./sthg.): *run after a bus.* **2.** To try to attract (sbdy.): *She's been running after him for years.* **run along.** *intr.v.* To go away; leave: *She told the children to run along and play.* **run around.** *intr.v.* To go to many places to get things done: *I spent all day running around trying to get ready for the party.* **run around with. 1.** To spend free time with (sbdy.): *My mother doesn't like the crowd I'm running around with.* **2.** To date (sbdy.), usually secretly: *I hear he's been running around with her best friend.* **run a temperature** or **fever.** To have a fever: *You must be running a temperature; you look sick.* **run away.** *intr.v.* To leave home: *The boy threatened to run away.* **run away with. 1.** To leave with (sbdy.) hurriedly: *Run away with me to Paris!* **2.** To steal (sthg.): *He ran away with all her money.* **3.** To start to control (sbdy.): overcome: *Children often allow their imaginations to run away with them.* **run by.** *intr.v.* To stop somewhere briefly: *I'll run by to see her after work.* —*tr.v.* **1.** [sep.] To ask one's opinion about (sthg.): *Do you mind if I run this idea by you?* **2.** [insep.] To stop briefly at (a place): *We can run by your place later.* **run down.** *intr.v.* To stop working because of lack of force or power: *The clock finally ran down.* —*tr.v.* [sep.] **1.** To chase and capture (sbdy./sthg.): *The police will run them down.* **2.** To say mean or unpleasant things about (sbdy./sthg.): *You're always running down my cooking.* **3.** To hit and knock down (sbdy.) with a vehicle: *He was run down by a speeding car.* **run for it.** To try to escape from danger: *When it began to hail, we ran for it.* **run for (one's) life.** To try to get away from danger: *When the bull charged, I ran for my life.* **run in.** *tr.v.* [sep.] To arrest (sbdy.): *The police ran him in for shoplifting.* **run in (one's) family.** To tend to be common in a family: *A talent for music runs in their family.* **run into.** *tr.v.* [insep.] **1.** To meet or find (sbdy.) by chance: *I ran into an old friend.* **2.** To meet with (difficulty): *He ran into trouble.* **3.** To reach (an amount); total: *These days, college costs can run into the tens of thousands.* **run low.** To be almost out of sthg.: *We ran low on heating fuel last winter.* **run off.** *tr.v.* [sep.] **1.** To print or copy (sthg.): *We ran off some more copies of the paper.* **2.** To force or drive off (trespassers, for example): *He found hunters on his land and ran them off.* —*intr.v.* To leave without returning: *One day* *he ran off, leaving his wife and children.* **run off at the mouth.** *Informal.* To talk too much: *I've stopped hearing what she says; she's always running off at the mouth.* **run off with.** **1.** To run away with (sbdy./sthg.): *She ran off with a boyfriend.* **2.** To steal (sthg.): *He ran off with my best coat.* **run on.** *intr.v.* **1.** To keep going; continue: *The meeting ran on for hours.* **2.** To talk without stopping, usually about unimportant matters: *He's always running on about something.* **run out.** *intr.v.* To become used up: *Supplies ran out.* —*tr.v.* [sep.] To force (sbdy.) to leave: *The sheriff ran them out of town.* **run out of.** To use all the supply of (sthg.): *We ran out of milk.* **run out on.** To leave (sbdy.) in a sudden irresponsible way: *Don't run out on your friends.* **run over.** *tr.v.* **1.** [sep.] To hit, knock down, and often pass over (sbdy./sthg.) with a vehicle: *She accidentally ran the dog over.* **2.** [insep.] To read or review (sthg.) quickly: *I just need to run over this article.* —*intr.v.* To go beyond a limit: *The meeting ran over. The soup ran over on the stove.* **run short.** To not have enough of sthg.: *Before we got paid, we ran short of money.* **run through.** *tr.v.* [insep.] **1.** To use (sthg.) up quickly: *She ran through all her money.* **2.** To rehearse or examine (sthg.) quickly: *Let's run through the scene again.* **run together.** To become smeared or blended: *The colors in the sign ran together when it got wet.* **run up.** *tr.v.* [sep.] To make (an expense, for example) greater or larger: *We ran up a huge bill at the restaurant.* **run up against.** To meet and have to deal with (a difficulty): *They ran up against unexpected delays.*

run·a·round (rŭn′ə round′) *n.* [U] Deception, usually in the form of vague excuses: *The salesman gave us the runaround when we asked what our old car was worth.*

run·a·way (rŭn′ə wā′) *n.* **1.** A person who has run away, as a teen from home: *shelter for runaways.* **2.** *Informal.* An easy victory: *Their team was so bad that the game was a runaway.* —*adj.* **1.** Escaping or having escaped: *runaway horses.* **2.** Out of control: *a runaway car rolling down the hill.* **3.** *Informal.* Easily won: *a runaway victory.*

run·down (rŭn′doun′) *n.* A point by point summary: *a rundown of the day's news.* —*adj.* also **run-down** (rŭn′doun′). **1.** Exhausted or weak: *feeling rundown.* **2.** Old and decayed: *rundown buildings.*

rung¹ (rŭng) *n.* **1.** A rod or bar forming a step of a ladder. **2.** A crosspiece between the legs of a chair.

HOMONYMS: **rung** (rod, sounded), **wrung** (twisted).

---

rung² (rŭng) *v.* Past participle of **ring²**.

run-in (rŭn′ĭn′) *n.* A quarrel or an argument: *I had a run-in with my mother this morning.*

run·ner (rŭn′ər) *n.* **1.** A person who runs, especially in a race. **2.** A messenger: *My lawyer sent a runner with the contract.* **3.** A part on which sthg. slides, as the blade of a skate: *a runner on a sled.* **4.** A long narrow strip of fabric used as a hall carpet or narrow tablecloth.

run·ner-up (rŭn′ər ŭp′) *n., pl.* **run·ners-up** (rŭn′ərz ŭp′). Somebody who finishes a competition in second place.

run·ning (rŭn′ĭng) *n.* [U] The act or an instance of running. —*adj.* Continuous; ongoing: *He gave us a running commentary on the game.* —*adv.* Consecutively: *for four years running.* ✦ **in the running.** With the possibility of winning or placing well in a competition: *She's in the running for the new job.* **out of the running.** With no possibility of winning or placing well in a competition: *Our team is out of the running for the championship.*

running mate *n.* The candidate for the lesser of two closely linked political offices: *The vice-presidential candidate is the running mate of the presidential candidate.*

run·ny (rŭn′ē) *adj.* **run·ni·er, run·ni·est.** Inclined to run or flow: *runny icing on the cake; a runny nose.*

run·off (rŭn′ôf′ *or* rŭn′ŏf′) *n.* **1.** [U] Water that is not taken in by the soil: *The river was filled with runoff from the melting snow.* **2.** [C] An extra contest held to break a tie: *candidates forced into a runoff.*

run-of-the-mill (rŭn′əv thə mĭl′) *adj.* Not special or outstanding; average: *a run-of-the mill restaurant.*

runt (rŭnt) *n.* A very small animal, especially the smallest in a litter: *My dog was the runt of the litter.*

run·way (rŭn′wā′) *n.* A strip of level, usually paved ground on which aircraft take off and land.

rup·ture (rŭp′chər) *n.* **1.** [C; U] The process of breaking open or bursting: *a rupture in the dam.* **2.** [C] A break in friendly relations: *a rupture in diplomatic relations.* **3.** [C] A hernia, especially in the groin or intestinal region. —*v.* **rup·tured, rup·tur·ing, rup·tures.** —*tr.* To break (sthg.) open; burst: *ruptured a water main.* —*intr.* To undergo or suffer a rupture: *The dam ruptured.*

ru·ral (rŏŏr′əl) *adj.* Relating to or characteristic of the country: *rural areas.*

ruse (rŏŏs *or* rŏŏz) *n.* A crafty trick or deception: *We used the ruse of shopping to get our mother to her surprise party.*

rush (rŭsh) *v.* —*intr.* **1.** To move or act swiftly; hurry: *Fire engines rushed past us.* **2.** To flow or surge rapidly and often with a continuous noise: *Water rushed over the falls.* —*tr.* **1.** To cause (sbdy.) to move or act with unusual haste: *Don't rush me.* **2.** To do or perform (sthg.) hastily: *She rushed the plans for the party.* **3.** To attack (sbdy./sthg.) sud-

R

denly; charge: *rushing the gates.* **4.** To carry or transport (sthg.) hastily: *The Red Cross rushed supplies to the camp.* —*n.* **1.** The act of rushing; a swift forward movement: *a rush to get inside.* **2.** An eager movement to or from a place in large numbers: *a rush for gold in the hills.* **3.** A flurry of hasty activity; a great hurry: *She left in such a rush that she forgot her purse.* **4.** A rapid, often noisy flow or passage: *a rush of air; a rush of words.*

rush hour *n.* A period of heavy traffic.

rust (rŭst) *n.* [U] **1.** Any of the various reddish brown oxides of iron that form when iron is exposed to oxygen in the presence of moisture at ordinary temperatures. **2.** A reddish brown color. —*adj.* Reddish brown. —*tr. & intr.v.* To make or become corroded or oxidized: *The bicycle rusted when it was left out in the rain.*

rus·tic (rŭs′tĭk) *adj.* Relating to or typical of country life or country people: *a rustic setting.*

rus·tle (rŭs′əl) *v.* **rus·tled, rus·tling, rus·tles.** —*intr.* **1.** To move with soft fluttering or crackling sounds: *leaves rustled in the*

wind. **2.** To steal cattle. —*tr.* **1.** To cause (sthg.) to rustle: *wind rustling the leaves.* **2.** To steal (cattle). ◆ **rustle up.** *tr.v.* [sep.] To get (food) quickly or briskly: *rustle up some dinner.* —**rus′tler** *n.*

rust·y (rŭs′tē) *adj.* **rust·i·er, rust·i·est. 1.** Covered with rust; corroded: *a rusty car.* **2.** Brownish red. **3.** Weak because of lack of use or practice: *My French is rusty. His knees are rusty.* —**rust′i·ness** *n.* [U]

rut (rŭt) *n.* A track, as in a dirt road, made by the passage of vehicles. ◆ **in a rut.** *Informal.* In a fixed, usually boring routine: *She was in a terrible rut at work.*

ruth·less (rōōth′lĭs) *adj.* Showing no pity; cruel: *a ruthless boss.* —**ruth′less·ly** *adv.* —**ruth′less·ness** *n.* [U]

RV *abbr.* An abbreviation of recreational vehicle.

rye (rī) *n.* [U] **1.** The seeds of a cereal grass, used for making flour and whiskey, or the plant. **2.** Whiskey made from this grain.

HOMONYMS: rye, wry (humorous).

Ss

s¹ or **S** (ĕs) *n., pl.* **s's** or **S's.** The 19th letter of the English alphabet.

s² *abbr.* An abbreviation of: **1.** second¹. **2.** Or **S.** Small.

S¹ The symbol for the element **sulfur.**

S² *abbr.* An abbreviation of: **1.** South. **2.** Southern.

—s¹ or **—es** *suff.* A suffix that is used to form plural nouns: *letters; dishes.*

—s² or **—es** *suff.* A suffix that is used to form the third person singular present tense of most verbs: *talks; washes.*

—s³ *suff.* A suffix that is used to form certain adverbs, such as *nights,* in *She works nights,* or *unawares,* in *We were caught unawares.*

—'s *suff.* A suffix that is used to form the possessive form of most nouns: *women's; boy's.*

's 1. Contraction of *is: She's happy.* **2.** Contraction of *has: He's been away.* **3.** Contraction of *us: Let's go to lunch.*

S.A. *abbr.* An abbreviation of: **1.** South Africa. **2.** South America.

Sab·bath (săb'əth) *n.* A day of rest and worship observed on Saturday by Jews and on Sunday by most Christians.

sab·bat·i·cal (sə băt'ĭ kəl) *n.* A leave of absence, often with pay, given to some college professors every seven years: *Professor Garcia is on sabbatical this year.* *—adj.* Relating to a sabbatical.

sa·ber (sā'bər) *n.* **1.** A heavy sword with a curved blade. **2.** A light sword used in fencing.

sab·o·tage (săb'ə täzh') *n.* [U] A deliberate attempt to damage or destroy property, a cause, or an activity. *—tr.v.* **sab·o·taged, sab·o·tag·ing, sab·o·tag·es.** To commit sabotage against (sthg.): *Our competitors sabotaged our plan.*

sab·o·teur (săb'ə tûr') *n.* A person who commits sabotage.

sa·bre (sā'bər) *n. & v. Chiefly British.* Variant of **saber.**

sac (săk) *n.* A part of an animal or a plant that resembles a bag, often containing a liquid.

HOMONYMS: **sac, sack** (bag, rob).

sac·cha·rin (săk'ər ĭn) *n.* [U] A white powder that tastes about 500 times sweeter than sugar and is used as a sweetener.

HOMONYMS: **saccharin, saccharine** (sweet).

sac·cha·rine (săk'ər ĭn *or* săk'ə rēn') *adj.* **1.** Relating to or characteristic of sugar; sweet. **2.** Insincerely sweet in tone or character: *a saccharine smile.*

sa·chet (să shā') *n.* A small bag filled with a perfumed substance and often kept in a drawer or closet to scent clothes.

HOMONYMS: **sachet, sashay** (walk casually).

sack¹ (săk) *n.* **1.a.** A large bag of strong coarse material used for holding objects in bulk: *a potato sack.* **b.** A similar bag of paper or plastic: *a brown paper sack.* **c.** The amount that such a container can hold: *a sack of groceries.* **2.** *Informal.* A bed, mattress, or sleeping bag: *He got in the sack and took a nap.* **3.** *Slang.* Dismissal from a job or position: *My friend got the sack because he was late too often for work.* *—tr.v.* **1.** To put (objects) into a sack: *The boy sacked the groceries.* **2.** *Slang.* To fire (sbdy.) from a job: *His boss sacked him for being late.* ♦ **hit the sack.** To go to sleep: *I hit the sack early last night.* **sack out.** *intr.v. Informal.* To go to sleep, usually in a place other than a bed: *My daughter sacked out on the couch.*

HOMONYMS: **sack** (bag, rob), **sac** (body part).

sack² (săk) *tr.v.* To rob (a captured city, for example) of its valuables; loot or plunder: *The enemy sacked the ancient city.* *—n.* The robbing or looting of a place captured by the enemy.

sac·ra·ment (săk'rə mənt) *n.* In Christian churches, one of the sacred rites or ceremonies that are considered to have been started by Jesus. *—sac'ra·men'tal* (săk'rə-mĕn'tl) *adj.*

sa·cred (sā'krĭd) *adj.* **1.** Worthy of religious worship; holy. **2.** Dedicated to or set apart for the worship of a god or religious figure: *a temple sacred to Buddha.* **3.** Relating to religious practices or objects: *sacred relics.* *—sa'cred·ly adv. —sa'cred·ness n.* [U]

sac·ri·fice (săk'rə fīs') *n.* **1.** The act of offering sthg., such as an animal's life, to a god or other religious figure in worship or to receive favor or forgiveness. **2.** The act of giving up sthg. highly valued for the sake of sthg. else considered to be of greater value: *Parents make many sacrifices for their children.* *—v.* **sac·ri·ficed, sac·ri·fic·ing,**

S

sac•ri•fic•es. —*tr.* **1.** To offer (sbdy./sthg.) as a sacrifice to a god or religious figure: *A lamb was sacrificed.* **2.** To give up (one thing) for another thing considered to be of greater value: *We sacrificed our time for a good cause.* —*intr.* To make or offer a sacrifice: *The ancient people sacrificed at the altar.* —**sac′ri•fi′cial** (săk′rə fĭsh′əl) *adj.*

sac•ri•lege (săk′rə lĭj) *n.* [C; U] An act of disrespect or violence toward sthg. sacred. —**sac′-ri•le′gious** (săk′rə lĭj′əs *or* săk′rə lē′jəs) *adj.*

sac•ro•sanct (săk′rō săngkt′) *adj.* Regarded as sacred and not to be violated: *the sacrosanct objects of the temple.*

sad (săd) *adj.* **sad•der, sad•dest. 1.** Showing, expressing, or feeling sorrow or unhappiness: *a sad face.* **2.** Causing sorrow, unhappiness, or regret: *sad memories.* **3.** Sorry; deplorable: *This old apartment is in sad shape.* —**sad′ly** *adv.* —**sad′ness** *n.* [U]

SYNONYMS: sad, unhappy, melancholy, sorrowful, desolate. These adjectives mean affected with or marked by a lack of joy. **Sad** and **unhappy** are the most general terms: *I was sad when that beautiful house was destroyed in the fire. He doesn't like movies that make him unhappy.* **Melancholy** means feeling a lingering or habitual sadness: *I kept telling jokes, trying to cheer up my melancholy friend.* **Sorrowful** means experiencing a painful sadness, especially one caused by loss: *One of the mourners let out a sorrowful cry.* **Desolate** means sorrowful beyond consolation: *He has been desolate ever since his girlfriend moved away.* **ANTONYM: glad.**

---

sad•den (săd′n) *tr. & intr.v.* To make or become sad: *The bad news saddened me. An unhappy memory often saddens.*

sad•dle (săd′l) *n.* **1.** A padded leather seat for a rider, strapped onto the back of a horse or other animal. **2.** The seat of a bicycle, motorcycle, or similar vehicle. —*v.* **sad•dled, sad•dling, sad•dles.** —*tr.* **1.** To put a saddle onto (a horse): *saddle a pony.* **2.** To load or burden (sbdy./sthg.); encumber: *She was saddled with all the responsibility.* —*intr.* To put a saddle on a horse: *Let's saddle up and go.*

sa•dism (sā′dĭz′ əm *or* săd′ĭz′ əm) *n.* [U] A psychological disorder in which a person gets pleasure from causing pain to others. —**sa′dist** *n.* —**sa•dis′tic** (sə dĭs′tĭk) *adj.* —**sa•dis′ti•cal•ly** *adv.*

sa•fa•ri (sə fär′ē) *n.* A trip to view or hunt animals, especially in Africa.

safe (sāf) *adj.* **saf•er, saf•est. 1.** Secure from danger, risk, or harm: *We were safe in the locked house.* **2.** Providing protection or security: *a safe hiding place.* **3.** Free from risk; sure: *a safe*

bet. —*n.* A strong locking metal box or room in which valuables, such as money and jewels, are kept for protection: ♦ **safe and sound.** Not hurt: *We arrived home from our vacation safe and sound.* —**safe′ly** *adv.*

safe-de•pos•it box (sāf′ dĭ pŏz′ĭt) *n.* A fireproof metal box, usually rented in a bank, for the safe storage of valuables.

safe•guard (sāf′gärd′) *n.* Something that provides protection or defense, as a safety precaution or a protective device: *safeguards to prevent accidents.* —*tr.v.* To protect (sbdy./sthg.) from danger; keep safe and secure: *laws to safeguard individual rights.*

safe•keep•ing (sāf′kē′pĭng) *n.* [U] The act of keeping or the condition of being kept safe; protection: *We left the money in her safekeeping.*

safe•ty (sāf′tē) *n., pl.* **safe•ties. 1.** [U] The condition of being safe; freedom from danger, risk, or injury: *Safety is an issue at school.* **2.** [C] A device designed to prevent accidents, especially a lock on a gun to keep it from firing accidentally.

safety belt *n.* A seat belt.

safety glass *n.* [U] Glass that resists shattering.

safety net *n.* **1.** A system that helps people in need, often one set up by the government: *Social Security is a safety net for the elderly.* **2.** A large net used to catch sbdy. who is high above the ground.

safety pin *n.* A pin made in the form of a clasp with a guard to cover and hold the pin.

safety valve *n.* **1.** A valve in a pressurized container, such as a steam boiler, that opens if the pressure reaches a dangerous level. **2.** Something that allows a person to release energy or emotion: *She needs a safety valve like exercise.*

saf•fron (săf′rən) *n.* [U] **1.** An orange-yellow spice or dye from flower parts. **2.** An orange-yellow color. —*adj.* Orange-yellow.

sag (săg) *intr.v.* **sagged, sag•ging, sags. 1.** To sink, droop, or settle from pressure or weight: *The large fish made the net sag.* **2.** To lose strength or firmness: *The old bed sagged in the middle.* **3.** To decline in amount or value: *Profits sagged.* —*n.* **1.** An instance of sagging or drooping: *the sag of the boards under our feet.* **2.** A sagging or sunken place: *a sag in the ceiling.*

sa•ga (sä′gə) *n.* A long adventure story that deals with historical or legendary heroes, families, deeds, and events.

sage[1] (sāj) *n.* A person who is highly respected for wisdom, experience, and judgment. —*adj.* **sag•er, sag•est.** Having or showing wisdom and sound judgment: *a sage judge.* —**sage′ly** *adv.*

sage[2] (sāj) *n.* [U] **1.** A plant with grayish

---

green spicy-smelling leaves used as flavoring in cooking. **2.** Sagebrush.

sage•brush (sāj′brŭsh′) *n.* [U] A shrub of dry regions of North America, with strong-smelling silver-green leaves and clusters of small white flowers.

Sag•it•tar•i•us (săj′ĭ târ′ē əs) *n.* **1.** The ninth sign of the zodiac in astrology. **2.** A person born under this sign, between November 22 and December 21.

sa•gua•ro (sə gwär′ō *or* sə wär′ō) *n., pl.* **sa•gua•ros.** A very large cactus of the southwest United States and Mexico, with upward-curving branches, white flowers, and edible red fruit.

said (sĕd) *v.* Past tense and past participle of **say.** *—adj.* In legal use, referring to sbdy./ sthg. previously named or mentioned: *The said tenant violated the lease.*

sail (sāl) *n.* **1.** A piece of fabric attached to a boat or ship and used to catch the wind and cause the boat or ship to move over water. **2.** A trip in a sail boat: *We went for a sail on the lake. —v. —intr.* **1.** To travel by ship or boat: *sail around the world.* **2.** To move across the surface of water, especially in a sailing vessel: *The boat sails smoothly.* **3.** To operate a sailing craft: *learn how to sail.* **4.** To start out on a voyage across a body of water: *The ship will sail at noon tomorrow. —tr.* **1.** To guide (a sailing vessel): *We sailed the boat across the lake.* **2.** To voyage upon or across (sthg.): *sail the Pacific Ocean.* ♦ **sail into.** *tr.v.* [insep.] To attack or criticize (sbdy.) forcefully: *Her boss sailed into her for being late.* **sail through.** *tr.v.* [insep.] To move swiftly, smoothly, or effortlessly through (sthg.): *She sailed through the math test.*

Homonyms: sail, sale (act of selling).

sail•boat (sāl′bōt′) *n.* A boat that has a sail or sails, so that it can be moved by the wind.

sail•ing (sā′lĭng) *n.* [U] **1.** The sport of operating or riding in a sailboat. **2.** The skill required to operate a vessel; navigation.

sail•or (sā′lər) *n.* A person who is a member of a ship's crew or who serves in a navy.

saint (sānt) *n.* **1.** A person who has been officially recognized as being worthy of special reverence. **2.** A person who is very virtuous: *My aunt is a saint. —saint′li•ness n.* [U] *—saint′ly adj.*

Saint Ber•nard (bər närd′) *n.* A breed of large strong dog developed in Switzerland, with a thick brown and white coat and originally used to rescue people lost in the Alps.

saint•hood (sānt′hood′) *n.* [U] The status, character, or condition of being a saint.

Saint Pat•rick's Day (păt′rĭks) *n.* March 17, a holiday observed in the United States and Ireland in honor of Saint Patrick, the patron saint of Ireland.

Saint Val•en•tine's Day (văl′ən tīnz′) *n.* February 14, a holiday celebrated by the exchange of valentine cards, candy, or other small gifts for one's special love.

sake[1] (sāk) *n.* **1.** Purpose; motive: *Our neighbors argue just for the sake of arguing.* **2.** Benefit or interest; welfare: *We bought a new heater for the baby's sake.* ♦ **for goodness'** or **for heaven's sake.** An expression used when one is strongly annoyed, impatient, or surprised: *For goodness' sake, don't smoke!*

sa•ke[2] (sä′kē) *n.* [U] A Japanese alcoholic beverage made from fermented rice.

sal•a•ble *also* **sale•a•ble** (sā′lə bəl) *adj.* Suitable to sell; capable of attracting buyers: *a salable car. —sal′a•bil′i•ty n.* [U]

sal•ad (săl′əd) *n.* [C; U] **1.** A dish made of raw vegetables, such as lettuce, often with cucumbers and tomatoes, served with a dressing. **2.** A cold dish of chopped fruit, potatoes, eggs, or other food, usually prepared with a dressing: *potato salad; fruit salad.*

salad bar *n.* A counter in a restaurant from which customers may serve themselves a variety of salad ingredients and dressings and other foods.

salad dressing *n.* [C; U] A sauce, as of mayonnaise or oil and vinegar, that is served on salad.

sal•a•man•der (săl′ə măn′dər) *n.* Any of various amphibians that resemble lizards but have smooth moist skin.

sa•la•mi (sə lä′mē) [C; U] *n.* A spiced and salted sausage of pork or beef or of both these meats.

sal•a•ried (săl′ə rēd) *adj.* Receiving or paying a salary: *a salaried position.*

sal•a•ry (săl′ə rē) *n., pl.* **sal•a•ries.** A fixed sum of money or other compensation paid to a person on a regular basis in return for work or service: *a good salary.*

sale (sāl) *n.* **1.** [C; U] The act or an instance of selling; an exchange of goods or services for money or other compensation. **2.** [C] An occasion when goods or services are offered at reduced prices: *a half-price sale on shirts at the store.* **3. sales. a.** The business of advertising and selling goods or services: *My father is in sales.* **b.** The amount of goods sold or of money brought in by selling goods: *Sales increased during the holidays.*

Homonyms: sale, sail (fabric used to catch wind).

sale•a•ble (sā′lə bəl) *adj.* Variant of **salable.**

sales•clerk (sālz′klûrk′) *n.* A person who is employed to sell goods in a store.

sales•man (sālz′mən) *n.* A man who is employed to sell goods or services. *—sales′-wom′an* (sālz′woom′ən) *n.*

sales•man•ship (sālz′mən shĭp′) *n.* [U] Skill, ability, or persuasiveness in selling.

S

sales•peo•ple (sālz′pē′pəl) *pl.n.* People who are employed to sell goods or services.

sales•per•son (sālz′pûr′sən) *n.* A salesman or saleswoman.

sales slip (sālz) *n.* A piece of paper given as proof that a person has paid for merchandise; a receipt: *You need your sales slip if you want to return what you bought.*

sales tax *n.* A fixed percentage of the purchase price on the sale of goods or services and usually collected by the seller for payment to the government.

sa•li•ent (sā′lē ənt *or* sāl′yənt) *adj.* Most obvious and important; striking or conspicuous: *the salient points of a plan.*

sa•line (sā′lēn′ *or* sā′līn′) *adj.* Relating to or containing salt; salty: *saline solution for contact lenses.* —*n.* A saline solution, especially one used in medicine and surgery. —**sa•lin′i•ty** (sə lĭn′ĭ tē) *n.* [U]

sa•li•va (sə lī′və) *n.* [U] The watery fluid that is secreted in the mouth and serves to moisten food as it is chewed and to promote digestion. —**sal′i•var′y** (săl′ə vĕr′ē) *adj.*

sal•i•vate (săl′ə vāt′) *intr.v.* **sal•i•vat•ed, sal•i•vat•ing, sal•i•vates.** To produce saliva: *The smell of fresh food made me salivate.* —**sal′i•va′tion** *n.* [U]

sal•low (săl′ō) *adj.* Of a sickly yellowish color or complexion: *a sallow face.*

salm•on (săm′ən) *n.* **1.** [C; U] A large food fish of northern waters with pinkish flesh. **2.** [U] A yellowish pink or pinkish orange color. —*adj.* Yellowish pink or pinkish orange.

sal•mo•nel•la (săl′mə nĕl′ə) *n.* [U] A type of bacteria that causes food poisoning.

sa•lon (sə lŏn′ *or* săl′ŏn′) *n.* **1.** A business offering a product or service related to fashion, expecially hairstyling: *a beauty salon.* **2.** A large room for entertaining guests.

sa•loon (sə lōōn′) *n.* A word used in the past for a place where alcoholic drinks were sold and drunk; a bar or tavern.

sal•sa (säl′sə) *n.* [U] **1.** A spicy sauce made of tomatoes, onions, and peppers, eaten with tortilla chips or other Mexican food. **2.** A popular form of Latin-American dance music.

salt (sôlt) *n.* [C; U] **1.** A natural white crystal, chiefly sodium chloride, widely used to season and preserve food. **2.** A chemical compound formed when one or more hydrogen ions of an acid are replaced by metallic ions. —*adj.* **1.** Containing or filled with salt: *a salt shaker.* **2.** Having the taste or smell of salt: *salt peanuts.* **3.** Preserved in salt or brine: *salt pork.* —*tr.v.* **1.** To season or sprinkle (sthg.) with salt: *Salt the stew.* **2.** To preserve (meat or fish) by treating with salt. **3.** To add interest or liveliness to (sthg.): *My professor salts his lectures with jokes.* ♦ **an old salt.** A

sailor. **salt away.** *tr.v.* [sep.] To put (money) aside; save: *He salted away half of his salary.* **take with a grain of salt.** To assume that sthg. may not be true: *My neighbor told me some news that I took with a grain of salt.* **worth (one's) salt.** Efficient and capable: *I have to prove that I'm worth my salt.*

sal•tine (sôl tēn′) *n.* A thin crisp cracker sprinkled with coarse salt.

salt•shak•er (sôlt′shā′kər) *n.* A container with holes in the top for holding and sprinkling salt.

salt•wa•ter *or* **salt-wa•ter** (sôlt′wô′tər *or* sôlt′wŏt′ər) *adj.* **1.** Consisting of water that contains a dissolved salt: *a saltwater solution.* **2.** Living in the sea or in salt water: *saltwater fish.*

salt•y (sôl′tē) *adj.* **salt•i•er, salt•i•est. 1.** Containing or seasoned with salt: *salty food.* **2.** Witty, often in a dry or biting way: *salty humor.* —**salt′i•ness** *n.* [U]

sal•u•ta•tion (săl′yə tā′shən) *n.* **1.** An expression or gesture of greeting or respect. **2.** The word or phrase of greeting used to begin a letter. *Dear Sir or Madam* is a salutation.

sa•lu•ta•to•ri•an (sə lōō′tə tôr′ē ən) *n.* In some schools and colleges, the student with the second highest academic rank, who gives the opening address at graduation.

sa•lu•ta•to•ry (sə lōō′tə tôr′ē) *n.*, *pl.* **sa•lu•ta•to•ries.** An opening address, especially one delivered at graduation exercises by a salutatorian. —*adj.* Relating to or expressing a greeting or welcome.

sa•lute (sə lōōt′) *v.* **sa•lut•ed, sa•lut•ing, sa•lutes.** —*tr.* **1.** To recognize (a superior officer) with a gesture according to military regulations, especially by raising the hand to the cap: *The soldier saluted the general.* **2.** To greet (sbdy.) with a polite, respectful, or friendly gesture: *They saluted us with a smile.* —*intr.* To make a gesture of greeting or respect: *The soldier saluted.* —*n.* **1.** An act, gesture, or display of respect, especially to a military superior. **2.** An act of greeting or recognizing, as a bow, wave, or nod.

sal•vage (săl′vĭj) *n.* [U] **1.** The act of saving endangered property from loss, especially a ship and its cargo from fire or shipwreck. **2.** Goods or property saved from destruction or disaster. —*tr.v.* **sal•vaged, sal•vag•ing, sal•vag•es. 1.** To save (sthg.) from loss or ruin: *We salvaged our photographs from the fire.* **2.** To save (discarded or damaged material) for further use: *The recycler salvaged glass for recycling.* —**sal′vage•a•ble** *adj.*

sal•va•tion (săl vā′shən) *n.* [U] **1.** Preservation or deliverance from destruction, difficulty, or evil. **2.** In Christianity, the saving of the soul from sin and punishment; redemp-

---

ă–cat; ā–pay; âr–care; ä–father; ĕ–get; ē–be; ĭ–sit; ī–nice; îr–here; ŏ–got; ō–go; ô–saw; oi–boy; ou–out; ōō–took; ōō–boot; ŭ–cut; ûr–word; th–thin; *th*–this; hw–when; zh–vision; ə–about; N–French bon

tion. 3. A person or thing that saves, rescues, or preserves: *The emergency supplies were our salvation during the hurricane.*

Salvation Army *n.* An international Christian organization established to spread religious teachings and do charitable work.

salve (săv *or* säv) *n.* [C; U] A soothing ointment applied to wounds, burns, or sores to heal them or relieve pain.

sal•vo (săl′vō) *n., pl.* **sal•vos** or **sal•voes. 1.** The first of a series of statements or actions, especially in an argument: *His opening salvo caught his opponent by surprise.* **2.** A simultaneous firing of several weapons.

Sa•mar•i•tan also **sa•mar•i•tan** (sə măr′ĭ tn) *n.* A person who helps others in trouble.

same (sām) *adj.* **1.** Similar in kind, quality, quantity, or degree: *These books are the same size.* **2.** Being the very one; identical: *This is the same seat I had yesterday.* **3.** Being the one previously mentioned: *The same novelist also wrote poetry.* —*adv.* In the same way: *The words* sail *and* sale *are pronounced the same.* —*pron.* A person or thing identical with another: *"Is she the one you mean?" "The same."*

same•ness (sām′nĭs) *n.* [U] **1.** The condition of being the same. **2.** A lack of variety or change; monotony: *the sameness of the flat landscape.*

sam•ple (săm′pəl) *n.* A part, piece, or selection that is considered representative of the whole: *Could I have a sample of that cake?* —*tr.v.* **sam•pled, sam•pling, sam•ples.** To take a sample of (sthg.), especially to test or examine: *We sampled the soil for nutrients.*

sam•pler (săm′plər) *n.* **1.** A piece of cloth embroidered with designs or sayings that displays fancy stitching or needlework. **2.** A representative selection of sthg.: *a sampler of chocolate candies.*

sam•u•rai (săm′ə rī′) *n., pl.* **sam•u•rai** or **sam•u•rais. 1.** The military aristocracy of feudal Japan. **2.** A professional warrior belonging to this class.

san•a•to•ri•um (săn′ə tôr′ē əm) *n.* An institution for the treatment of people with chronic diseases.

sanc•ti•fy (săngk′tə fī′) *tr.v.* **sanc•ti•fied, sanc•ti•fy•ing, sanc•ti•fies.** To make (sthg.) holy or sacred; purify: *sanctify the new church building.*

sanc•ti•mo•ni•ous (săngk′tə mō′nē əs) *adj.* Falsely pious or righteous: *a sanctimonious attitude.* —**sanc′ti•mo′ni•ous•ly** *adv.* —**sanc′ti•mo′ni•ous•ness** *n.* [U]

sanc•tion (săngk′shən) *n.* **1.** [U] Official permission or approval: *government sanction.* **2.** [C] An action taken by several nations acting together against a nation that has broken an international law: *The governments imposed sanctions because of human rights abuses.* —*tr.v.* To give official approval to (sthg.); authorize: *The committee sanctioned our proposal.*

sanc•ti•ty (săngk′tĭ tē) *n.* [U] Holiness of sthg.; sacredness: *sanctity of life.*

sanc•tu•ar•y (săngk′choo ĕr′ē) *n., pl.* **sanc•tu•ar•ies. 1.** [C] A sacred place, such as a church, temple, or mosque. **2.** [C; U] A place of refuge, asylum, or protection, especially from the law: *The refugees asked for sanctuary.* **3.** [C] A reserved area in which wildlife is protected by law: *a bird sanctuary.*

sand (sănd) *n.* **1.** [U] Loose grains or particles of disintegrated rock, finer than rice grains and coarser than salt grains. **2.** [C] *(usually plural).* Land, such as a beach or desert, covered with this material. —*tr.v.* **1.** To sprinkle or cover (sthg.) with or as if with sand: *sand an icy sidewalk.* **2.** To scrape or rub (sthg.) with sand or sandpaper: *She sanded the old table before painting it.*

san•dal (săn′dl) *n.* An open shoe made of a sole and straps used to fasten it to the foot.

sand•bag (sănd′băg′) *n.* A bag or sack filled with sand, often used to form protective walls: *Sandbags held back the water in the flood.*

sand•bar (sănd′bär′) *n.* A long mass or low ridge of sand built up in the water along a shore or beach by the action of waves or currents.

sand•blast (sănd′blăst′) *n.* A blast of air or steam carrying sand at high velocity to clean stone or metal surfaces, for example. —*tr.v.* To apply a sandblast to (a building, for example). —**sand′blast′er** *n.*

sand•box (sănd′bŏks′) *n.* A low box filled with sand for children to play in.

sand•er (săn′dər) *n.* **1.** A device, usually attached to a truck, that spreads sand on roads. **2.** A machine with a disk or belt of sandpaper, used for smoothing, polishing, or refinishing: *a floor sander.*

sand•man (sănd′măn′) *n. (singular only).* A character in fairy tales and folklore who makes children sleep by sprinkling sand in their eyes.

sand•pa•per (sănd′pā′pər) *n.* [U] Heavy paper coated on one side with sand or other abrasive material and used for smoothing surfaces. —*tr.v.* To rub (sthg.) with sandpaper: *Sandpaper the chair before painting it.*

sand•stone (sănd′stōn′) *n.* [U] A type of rock that is formed of sand-size grains of quartz and other minerals.

sand•storm (sănd′stôrm′) *n.* A strong wind carrying clouds of sand and dust through the air.

sand•wich (sănd′wĭch *or* săn′wĭch) *n.* Two or more slices of bread with a filling, such as meat or cheese, placed between them. —*tr.v.* **1.** [*between*] To insert (one thing) between two other things tightly: *sandwich a book between the bookends.* **2.** [*in*] To make room or time for (sthg.): *She sandwiched in a meeting despite her busy schedule.*

S

sand·y (săn′dē) *adj.* **sand·i·er, sand·i·est. 1.** Covered with, full of, or consisting of sand: *sandy beaches.* **2.** Of the color of sand; light yellowish brown. —**sand′i·ness** *n.* [U]

sane (sān) *adj.* **san·er, san·est. 1.** Of sound mind; mentally healthy: *a sane person.* **2.** Having or showing good judgment; reasonable: *a sane approach to the problem.* —**sane′ly** *adv.* —**sane′ness** *n.* [U]

sang (săng) *v.* A past tense of **sing.**

san·guine (săng′gwĭn) *adj. Formal.* **1.** Eagerly optimistic; cheerful: *She was sanguine about her new job.* **2.** Of the color of blood; red: *a sanguine complexion.* —**san′guine·ly** *adv.* —**san·guin′i·ty** *n.* [U]

san·i·tar·i·um (săn′ĭ târ′ē əm) *n.* A sanatorium.

san·i·tar·y (săn′ĭ tĕr′ē) *adj.* Free of germs; hygienic: *sanitary conditions of a hospital.* —**san′i·tar′i·ly** (săn′ĭ târ′ə lē) *adv.*

sanitary napkin *n.* A disposable pad of absorbent material worn by women to absorb menstrual flow.

san·i·ta·tion (săn′ĭ tā′shən) *n.* [U] **1.** The application of procedures and regulations that are meant to protect public health. **2.** The disposal of sewage and wastes.

san·i·tize (săn′ĭ tīz′) *tr.v.* **san·i·tized, san·i·tiz·ing, san·i·tiz·es. 1.** To make (sthg.) sanitary, as by cleaning: *sanitize the bathtub.* **2.** To make (sthg.) more acceptable by removing unpleasant or offensive features: *a movie sanitized for television.*

san·i·ty (săn′ĭ tē) *n.* [U] **1.** Soundness of mind; good mental health: *His sanity was in question.* **2.** The ability to make sound or reasonable judgments.

sank (săngk) *v.* A past tense of **sink.**

sans (sănz) *prep.* Without: *We went to the party sans our sister.*

San·ta Claus (săn′tə klôz′) *n.* A character who represents the spirit of Christmas, usually a jolly fat old man with a white beard and red suit, who brings gifts to children on Christmas Eve.

sap (săp) *n.* **1.** [U] The liquid that carries dissolved minerals and other food substances through various plant parts. **2.** [C] *Slang.* A foolish person; a dupe. —*tr.v.* **sapped, sap·ping, saps.** To weaken (sbdy./sthg.) gradually: *Heat sapped the runner's strength.*

sap·ling (săp′lĭng) *n.* A young tree.

sap·phire (săf′īr′) *n.* **1.** [C] A valuable blue gem. **2.** [U] The deep blue color of the gem sapphire. —*adj.* Deep blue.

sap·py (săp′ē) *adj.* **sap·pi·er, sap·pi·est.** *Slang.* Foolish; silly: *a sappy song.*

sar·casm (sär′kăz′əm) *n.* [U] **1.** A sharply mocking, often ironic remark intended to wound. **2.** The use of sarcasm.

sar·cas·tic (sär kăs′tĭk) *adj.* Characterized by or using sarcasm: *a sarcastic remark; a sarcastic person.* —**sar·cas′ti·cal·ly** *adv.*

sar·coph·a·gus (sär kŏf′ə gəs) *n.* A stone coffin, often decorated with sculpture.

sar·dine (sär dēn′) *n.* A small herring or similar small fish, often canned for use as food.

sa·ri (sä′rē) *n.* A type of dress worn chiefly by women of India and Pakistan, consisting of a length of cloth with one end wrapped around the waist to form a long skirt and the other end draped over the shoulder.

sa·rong (sə rông′ *or* sə rŏng′) *n.* A skirt of brightly colored cloth worn wrapped around the waist by men and women in Malaysia, Indonesia, and the Pacific islands.

sash¹ (săsh) *n.* A band or ribbon worn around the waist or over the shoulder as an ornament or symbol of rank.

sash² (săsh) *n.* A frame in which the panes of a window or door are set.

sa·shay (să shā′) *intr.v. Informal.* To move or walk in an easy or casual manner: *She sashayed into the room.*

HOMONYMS: sashay, sachet (perfumed bag).

---

sass (săs) *Informal. n.* [U] Disrespectful speech: *I've had enough of my son's sass.* —*tr.v.* To talk disrespectfully to (sbdy.): *She sassed her mother.* —**sas′si·ly** *adv.* —**sas′sy** *adj.*

sat (săt) *v.* Past tense and past participle of **sit.**

Sat. *abbr.* An abbreviation of Saturday.

Sa·tan (sāt′n) *n.* The evil opponent of God; the Devil.

sa·tan·ic (sə tăn′ĭk *or* sā tăn′ĭk) *adj.* **1.** Relating to the Devil or evil. **2.** Extremely cruel or evil.

satch·el (săch′əl) *n.* A small bag, often having a shoulder strap, used for carrying books, clothing, and other small items.

sate (sāt) *tr.v.* **sat·ed, sat·ing, sates.** To satisfy (an appetite) fully: *We sated our appetite with pizza.*

sat·el·lite (săt′l īt′) *n.* **1.** A mechanical device launched to orbit Earth or another celestial body: *a communications satellite.* **2.** A celestial body that travels in an orbit around a planet; a moon. **3.** A nation that is dominated politically and economically by another nation.

satellite dish *n.* A large circular device to receive satellite signals, especially for television.

sat·in (săt′n) *n.* [C; U] A smooth fabric with a glossy finish on one side. —*adj.* **1.** Made of or covered with satin: *a satin shirt.* **2.** Glossy and smooth: *satin skin.* —**sat′in·y** (săt′n ē) *adj.*

sat·ire (săt′īr′) *n.* A literary work in which

---

human behavior is attacked through humor or irony. —**sat′i·rist** (săt′ər ĭst) *n.*

sa·tir·i·cal (sə tĭr′ĭ kəl) or **sa·tir·ic** (sə-tĭr′ĭk) *adj.* Relating to or characterized by satire: *a satirical essay.* —**sa·tir′i·cal·ly** *adv.*

sat·i·rize (săt′ə rīz′) *tr.v.* **sat·i·rized, sat·i·riz·ing, sat·i·riz·es.** To ridicule or attack (sbdy./sthg.) by means of satire: *The writer satirized politicians.*

sat·is·fac·tion (săt′ĭs făk′shən) *n.* **1.** [U] Fulfillment or gratification of a desire or a need: *She had the satisfaction of seeing her daughter graduate from college.* **2.** [U] Pleasure derived from such fulfillment: *A look of satisfaction spread over his face.* **3.** [C] Something that gives fulfillment or gratification: *A good book is one of the satisfactions of life.*

sat·is·fac·to·ry (săt′ĭs făk′tə rē) *adj.* Sufficient to meet a demand or requirement; adequate: *a satisfactory grade.* —**sat′is·fac′to·ri·ly** *adv.*

sat·is·fy (săt′ĭs fī′) *tr.v.* **sat·is·fied, sat·is·fy·ing, sat·is·fies. 1.** To fulfill or gratify the need, desire, or expectation of (sbdy./sthg.): *The actor was satisfied with his performance.* **2.** To free (sbdy.) from doubt or question; convince: *The firefighters were satisfied that the fire was out.* **3.** To fulfill or meet (a standard, for example): *He satisfied the requirements to pass the course.*

sat·u·rate (săch′ə rāt′) *tr.v.* **sat·u·rat·ed, sat·u·rat·ing, sat·u·rates. 1.** To soak, fill, or load (sthg.) completely: *Water saturated the cloth.* **2.** To fill (sthg.) thoroughly: *The odor of fish saturated the kitchen.* —**sat′u·rat′ed** *adj.*

sat·u·ra·tion (săch′ə rā′shən) *n.* [U] **1.a.** The act or process of saturating. **b.** The condition of being saturated. **2.** Containing as much water vapor as is possible at a given temperature; having a relative humidity of 100 percent.

Sat·ur·day (săt′ər dē *or* săt′ər dā′) *n.* The seventh day of the week.

sauce (sôs) *n.* [C; U] **1.** A liquid dressing, seasoning, or topping for food: *spaghetti sauce.* **2.** Stewed fruit: *cranberry sauce.*

sauce·pan (sôs′păn′) *n.* A deep cooking pan with a long handle.

sau·cer (sô′sər) *n.* A small shallow dish for holding a cup.

sauc·y (sô′sē) *adj.* **sauc·i·er, sauc·i·est.** Disrespectful or impertinent, often in an entertaining way: *a saucy child.* —**sau′ci·ness** *n.* [U]

sau·er·kraut (sour′krout′) *n.* [U] Shredded cabbage, salted and fermented in its own juice.

sau·na (sô′nə *or* sou′nə) *n.* A steam bath in which the steam is produced by pouring water over heated rocks.

saun·ter (sôn′tər) *intr.v.* To walk at a leisurely pace; stroll: *He sauntered across the garden.* —*n.* A leisurely way of walking.

sau·sage (sô′sĭj) *n.* [C; U] Chopped and seasoned meat that is cooked fresh or cured.

sau·té (sō tā′ *or* sô tā′) *tr.v.* To fry (food) lightly in a shallow open pan: *He sautéed the onions.* —*n.* Sautéed food: *a vegetable sauté.*

sav·age (săv′ĭj) *adj.* **1.** Not cultivated; wild: *savage lands.* **2.** Violent; cruel: *a savage people.* **3.** Ferocious; vicious or fierce: *a savage attack.* —*n.* **1.** An insulting word for a person regarded as primitive or uncivilized. **2.** A person regarded as fierce or vicious. **3.** A rude person. —*tr.v.* **sa·vaged, sa·vag·ing, sa·va·ges.** To attack (sbdy./sthg.) brutally: *The critic savaged the actor in the review.* —**sav′age·ly** *adv.* —**sav′age·ness** *n.* [U]

sav·age·ry (săv′ĭj rē) *n.* [U] The quality or condition of being savage.

sa·van·na also **sa·van·nah** (sə văn′ə) *n.* A flat treeless grassland of warm regions.

save[1] (sāv) *v.* **saved, sav·ing, saves.** —*tr.* **1.** [*from*] To rescue (sbdy./sthg.) from harm, danger, or loss: *save the tree from disease.* **2.** To treat (sbdy./sthg.) with care to avoid damage; safeguard: *He tried to save his hearing by wearing ear plugs while on the job.* **3.** To prevent the loss or waste of (sthg.); conserve: *save money at a sale; save energy.* **4.** To make (sthg.) unnecessary; avoid: *He saved me a trip to the store.* **5.** To keep (sthg.) for future use; store: *save five dollars a week.* **6.** To set (sbdy.) free from sin; redeem: *saved the sinners.* **7.** To copy (a file) from a computer's main memory to a disk or other storage device for later use: *Save your document on the hard drive.* —*intr.* **1.** To avoid waste or expense; conserve: *save for future generations.* **2.** To accumulate money: *They are saving for a vacation.* —*n.* In sports, an act of preventing an opponent from scoring: *The goalie made a great save.* ♦ **save face.** To maintain respect: *The principal saved face when the teachers agreed not to go on strike.* —**sav′er** *n.*

save[2] (sāv) *prep.* Except; but: *All the trains arrived on time save one.* —*conj.* Were it not; except: *The day was perfect save for the rain.*

sav·ing (sā′vĭng) *n.* **1.** [U] Avoidance of waste or expense: *the saving of energy.* **2. savings.** Money saved: *a bank account for savings.* —*prep.* With the exception of: *All the books were ordered, saving this one.*

savings account (sā′vĭngz) *n.* An account that earns interest at a bank.

savings bond *n.* A registered bond issued by the U.S. Government.

sav·ior (sāv′yər) *n.* **1.** A person who saves or delivers another from danger, destruction, or loss. **2. Savior.** Jesus.

sa·vor (sā′vər) *n.* The taste or smell of sthg.: *the savor of cinnamon.* —*tr.v.* To taste or enjoy (sthg.) heartily; relish: *The team savored the moment of victory.*

sa·vor·y (sā′və rē) *adj.* **1.** Appetizing to the taste or smell: *a savory plate of spaghetti.* **2.** Salty or spicy; not sweet: *a savory cracker.*

sav·vy (săv′ē) *Informal. adj.* **sav·vi·er, sav·vi·est.** Well-informed; shrewd: *a savvy businesswoman.* —*n.* [U] Practical understanding; common sense: *She has a lot of business savvy.*

saw¹ (sô) *n.* Any of various hand-operated or power-driven tools with a thin metal blade or disk that has a sharp-toothed edge, used for cutting wood, metal, or other hard materials: *a hand saw; a circular saw.* —*v.*

saw¹

—*tr.* **1.** To cut or divide (sthg.) with a saw: *saw wood.* **2.** To produce or shape (sthg.) with a saw: *sawing curves in wood.* —*intr.* **1.** To use a saw: *The carpenter sawed all afternoon.* **2.** To be capable of being cut with a saw: *Pinewood saws easily.* ♦ **saw off.** *tr.v.* [sep.] To remove (sthg.) with a saw: *I need to saw off the dead branches on the tree.*

saw² (sô) *v.* Past tense of **see.**

saw·dust (sô′dŭst) *n.* [U] The small particles of wood or other material that fall from an object that is being sawed.

saw·horse (sô′hôrs′) *n.* A frame with legs, used to support a piece of wood that is being sawed.

saw·mill (sô′mĭl′) *n.* A place where lumber is sawed into boards.

sax (săks) *n.* A saxophone.

sax·o·phone (săk′sə fōn′) *n.* A wind instrument with a single-reed mouthpiece, a curved body made of metal, and keys operated by the player's fingers. —**sax′o·phon′ist** *n.*

say (sā) *v.* **said** (sĕd), **say·ing, says** (sĕz). —*tr.* **1.** To utter (sthg.) aloud; speak: *The children said, "Good morning."* **2.** To express (sthg.) in words;

saxophone

state: *The book says that the treaty was signed in 1945.* **3.** To give expression to (sthg.); show or indicate: *The clock says half past two.* **4.** To repeat or recite (sthg.): *saying the dialogue aloud.* **5.** To suppose (sthg.); assume: *Let's say that you're right.* —*intr.* To make a statement; express oneself: *The story is true, or so they said.* —*n.* **1.** A turn or chance to speak: *Let him*

have his say. **2.** The power to influence a decision: *We don't have any say in the matter.* —*adv.* **1.** Approximately: *Let's walk, say, five miles.* **2.** For example: *a tree, say a pine.* —*interj.* An expression used to attract attention or express wonder: *Say, that's some car!* ♦ **it goes without saying.** An expression used when sthg. is obviously true; of course: *It goes without saying that she will be angry.* **that is to say.** In other words. —**say′er** *n.*

say·ing (sā′ĭng) *n.* Something that is frequently said; a proverb.

say-so (sā′sō′) *n., pl.* **say-sos.** *Informal.* **1.** An unsupported statement: *I won't be convicted on your say-so alone.* **2.** An expression of permission or approval: *We can't act without our boss's say-so.*

SC or **S.C.** *abbr.* An abbreviation of South Carolina.

scab (skăb) *n.* **1.** The crust covering a healing wound. **2.** A worker who refuses to join a labor union or who takes a striker's job. —*intr.v.* **scabbed, scab·bing, scabs. 1.** To become covered with a scab: *The cut scabbed over.* **2.** To work as a scab.

scads (skădz) *pl.n. Informal.* A large number or amount: *Scads of people were at the party.*

scaf·fold (skăf′əld *or* skăf′ōld′) *n.* **1.** A temporary platform on which workers sit or stand when performing tasks high above the ground: *The painters put up a scaffold.* **2.** A platform used in the past for execution by hanging.

scaf·fold·ing (skăf′əl dĭng *or* skăf′ōl′dĭng) *n.* [U] A scaffold or system of scaffolds: *The scaffolding extended across the front of the building.*

scald (skôld) *tr.v.* **1.** To burn (sbdy./sthg.) with hot liquid or steam: *I scalded my hand making tea.* **2.** To cook (sthg.) slightly with boiling water: *scalded and peeled the peaches.* **3.** To heat (a liquid) almost to the boiling point: *scald milk.* —*n.* Injury or damage caused by scalding.

scale¹ (skāl) *n. (usually plural).* A small thin plate that is part of the outer covering of fish, reptiles, and certain other animals. —*tr.v.* **scaled, scal·ing, scales.** —*tr.* To clear or strip (sthg.) of scales: *scale and clean the fish.*

scale² (skāl) *n. (often used in the plural).* An instrument or a machine for weighing: *Put the fruit on the scale to weigh it.*

scale³ (skāl) *n.* **1.a.** [U] A system of ordered marks at fixed distances, used for measuring: *the metric scale.* **b.** [C] An instrument having such a system of marks: *a scale for converting inches to centimeters.* **2.** [C] **a.** The proportion used to determine the relationship between the actual dimensions of sthg. and the dimensions to which it is reduced or expanded when represented on a model, map, or drawing: *a scale of 1 inch to 50 miles.* **b.** A line with marks showing the actual dimensions of sthg. represented on a map, plan, or drawing. **3.** [C] *(usually singular).* A progressive classification, as of size, amount, importance, or rank: *a wage scale; on a scale of 1 to 10.* **4.** [C] The relative size or extent of sthg.: *on a large political scale.* **5.** [C] A series of musical tones. —*tr.v.* **scaled, scal‧ing, scales. 1.** To climb up or over (sthg.): *scale a mountain; scale a wall.* **2.** To draw or arrange (sthg.) in a particular proportion or scale. ♦ **scale back** or **down.** *tr.v.* [sep.] To adjust or regulate (sthg.) according to some standard: *scaling back oil production.*

sca‧lene (skā′lēn′ *or* skā lēn′) *adj.* Having three unequal sides: *scalene triangles.*

scal‧lion (skăl′yən) *n.* An onion with a small white bulb and long narrow green leaves.

scal‧lop (skŏl′əp *or* skăl′əp) *n.* **1.** A soft-bodied sea animal, used as food, with a fan-shaped shell. **2.** A thin boneless slice of meat: *a scallop of veal.*

scal‧loped (skŏl′əpt *or* skăl′əpt) *adj.* **1.** Baked in a casserole with milk or a sauce, often topped with bread crumbs: *scalloped potatoes.* **2.** Cut or formed with rounded, shell-like trim: *curtains with scalloped edges.*

scalp (skălp) *n.* The skin that covers the top of the human head. —*tr.v.* **1.** To cut or tear the scalp from (a head). **2.** *Slang.* To sell (tickets) at a price higher than their established value: *They scalped tickets to the sold-out game.*

scal‧pel (skăl′pəl) *n.* A small straight knife with a thin pointed blade, used in surgery.

scal‧y (skā′lē) *adj.* **scal‧i‧er, scal‧i‧est. 1.** Covered with scales: *scaly claws.* **2.** Dry or rough: *dry scaly skin.* —**scal′i‧ness** *n.* [U]

scam (skăm) *Slang. n.* A dishonest business scheme; a swindle: *a credit card scam.* —*tr.v.* **scammed, scam‧ming, scams.** To trick (sbdy.), especially in business: *The man had scammed customers.*

scamp (skămp) *n.* A playful mischievous person; a rascal.

scam‧per (skăm′pər) *intr.v.* To run quickly or lightly: *The puppy scampered across the lawn.*

scan (skăn) *tr.v.* **scanned, scan‧ning, scans. 1.** To examine (sthg.) quickly: *scan the report.* **2.** To look (sthg.) over quickly and systematically: *scan the ocean for signs of land.* **3.** To search (sthg.) electronically, as with a radar beam: *scan the skies for incoming aircraft.* **4.** *(used especially of an optical scanner).* **a.** To read (data) for use in a computer: *scan a product code.* **b.** To read and copy (an image or document) from paper to computer: *scan a photograph.* —*n.* **1.** [C; U] The act or an instance of scanning: *a brain scan.* **2.** [C] A computer image produced by scanning: *How much do they charge per scan?*

scan‧dal (skăn′dl) *n.* Something that shocks or offends the social community; a public disgrace: *the latest Hollywood scandal.*

scan‧dal‧ize (skăn′dl īz′) *tr.v.* **scan‧dal‧ized, scan‧dal‧iz‧ing, scan‧dal‧iz‧es.** To shock or offend (sbdy.): *The viewers were scandalized by the violent movie.*

scan‧dal‧ous (skăn′dl əs) *adj.* **1.** Causing scandal; shocking: *scandalous behavior.* **2.** Containing material damaging to a reputation: *scandalous gossip.* —**scan′dal‧ous‧ly** *adv.* —**scan′dal‧ous‧ness** *n.* [U]

scan‧ner (skăn′ər) *n.* **1.** A device that scans printed images; an optical scanner: *I bought a small scanner to use with my computer.* **2.** A radio receiver that continuously searches frequencies and plays aloud any signal it receives: *a police scanner.*

scant (skănt) *adj.* **1.** Barely sufficient; meager: *scant vegetation.* **2.** Short of an amount or measure: *a scant six miles away.* —**scant′ly** *adv.*

scant‧y (skăn′tē) *adj.* **scant‧i‧er, scant‧i‧est. 1.** Barely sufficient; meager: *a scanty water supply.* **2.** Not large enough: *a scanty bathing suit; scanty knowledge.* —**scant′i‧ly** *adv.* —**scant′i‧ness** *n.* [U]

—**scape** (skāp) *suff.* A suffix that means scene; view: *cityscape; landscape.*

scape‧goat (skāp′gōt′) *n.* A person, group, or thing that unjustly receives the blame of others. —**scape′goat′** *v.*

scar (skär) *n.* **1.** A mark left on the skin after a wound or an injury has healed: *a three-inch scar on his leg.* **2.** A mark or sign of damage, either physical or emotional: *scars from years of mental abuse.* —*v.* **scarred, scar‧ring, scars.** —*tr.* To mark (sbdy./sthg.) with a physical or emotional scar: *The burn scarred his hand.* —*intr.* To form a scar: *Her skin scarred from the burn.*

scarce (skârs) *adj.* **scarc‧er, scarc‧est. 1.** Not enough to meet a demand or requirement: *The pioneers' food and water were beginning to grow scarce.* **2.** Hard to find; rare: *Perfect diamonds are scarce.* ♦ **make (oneself) scarce.** *Informal.* To stay or go away; be absent: *Make yourself scarce before she gets here.* —**scarce′ness** *n.* [U]

scarce‧ly (skârs′lē) *adv.* **1.** Almost not; hardly: *I could scarcely see through the fog.* **2.** Certainly not: *They can scarcely complain after such a good meal.* —SEE NOTE at **hardly.**

scar‧ci‧ty (skâr′sĭ tē) *n., pl.* **scar‧ci‧ties.** An insufficient amount or supply; a shortage: *a scarcity of water.*

scare (skâr) *v.* **scared, scar‧ing, scares.** —*tr.* To frighten or alarm (sbdy./sthg.); terrify: *The dog scared the cat.* See Synonyms at **frighten.** —*intr.* To become frightened: *I don't scare easily.* —*n.* A condition, sensation, or state of fear or panic: *The accident gave us quite a scare.*

S

scare•crow (skâr′krō′) *n.* A crude figure of a person set up in a field to scare birds away from crops.

scarf¹ (skärf) *n.*, *pl.* **scarfs** (skärfs) or **scarves** (skärvz). A piece of cloth worn around the neck, head, or shoulders.

scarf² (skärf) *v.* *Slang.* ♦ **scarf down.** *tr.v.* [sep.] To eat (food) very quickly: *He scarfed down his lunch.* **scarf up.** *tr.v.* [sep.] To take (sthg.) very quickly: *Who scarfed all the concert tickets up?*

scar•let (skär′lĭt) *n.* [U] A bright red to reddish orange. —*adj.* Bright red to reddish orange.

scarves (skärvz) *n.* A plural of **scarf.**

scar•y (skâr′ē) *adj.* **scar•i•er, scar•i•est.** Causing fear or alarm: *a scary movie.* —**scar′i•ly** *adv.*

scat (skăt) *interj.* *Informal.* Used to tell a small animal, such as a cat or bird, to go away: *Scat! Get off the table!*

scath•ing (skā′thĭng) *adj.* Extremely severe; harshly critical: *a scathing verbal attack.* —**scath′ing•ly** *adv.*

scat•ter (skăt′ər) *v.* —*tr.* **1.** To cause (sthg.) to separate and go in various directions: *The wind scatters flower seeds.* **2.** To distribute (sthg.) loosely by sprinkling; strew: *scattering confetti during the parade.* **3.** To deflect a stream of (waves or particles) in different directions: *scatter light.* —*intr.* To separate and go in different directions; disperse: *After the parade, the crowd scattered.*

scat•ter•brain (skăt′ər brān′) *n.* *Informal.* A person regarded as thoughtless or disorganized. —**scat′ter•brained′** *adj.*

scat•ter•ing (skăt′ər ĭng) *n.* (*usually singular*). Something scattered, especially a small or irregular quantity or amount: *a scattering of applause from the audience.*

scav•enge (skăv′ənj) *v.* **scav•enged, scav•eng•ing, scav•eng•es.** —*tr.* To search through (sthg.) for material that can be used or food that can be eaten: *The cat scavenged the garbage cans for food.* —*intr.* To search for useful material: *We scavenged all morning and found little of value at the flea market.*

scav•en•ger (skăv′ən jər) *n.* **1.** An animal that feeds on dead or decaying plant or animal matter: *A vulture is a scavenger.* **2.** A person who searches through trash or discarded material for food or useful items.

sce•nar•i•o (sĭ nâr′ē ō′ or sĭ när′ē ō′) *n.*, *pl.* **sce•nar•i•os. 1.** Something that could happen: *In the worst scenario, our plan will still work.* **2.** A plot or an outline of a story or play.

scene (sēn) *n.* **1.** A place or an area seen by a viewer; a view from a particular point: *the scene from my window.* **2.** The place where an action or event occurs: *the scene of the crime.*

3. The place in which the action of a play, movie, or novel occurs; a setting. **4.** A part of a movie or play in which the setting is fixed and the action forms a connected unit: *The family reunion scene was the best part of the play.* **5.** A display of bad temper or behavior that attracts attention in public: *They caused a scene at the mall.* ♦ **behind the scenes.** In private: *Most of the work was done behind the scenes.*

HOMONYMS: scene, seen (viewed with the eye).

scen•er•y (sē′nə rē) *n.* [U] **1.** A view or views of natural features, especially in open country: *varied mountain scenery.* **2.** The painted backdrops and other structures used to create the setting for a theatrical production: *The crew painted scenery all night.*

sce•nic (sē′nĭk) *adj.* **1.** Having or offering natural scenery, especially attractive landscapes: *a scenic highway.* **2.** Relating to theatrical scenery: *scenic design.*

scent (sĕnt) *n.* **1.** A distinctive, often pleasing odor: *the scent of pine.* **2.** A perfume: *She is wearing a new scent.* **3.** The trail of a hunted animal or fugitive: *The dogs lost the deer's scent.* **4.** The sense of smell: *hunting by scent.* **5.** A hint of sthg.; a suggestion: *a scent of excitement with the approach of summer.* —*tr.v.* **1.** To perceive, identify, or detect (sthg.) by or as if by smelling: *scent danger.* **2.** To provide (sthg.) with an odor; perfume: *scent the room with flowers.*

HOMONYMS: scent, cent (penny), **sent** (transmitted).

SYNONYMS: scent, aroma, smell, odor. These nouns mean a quality that can be detected by sense organs in the nose. *The scent of pine needles filled the cabin. The aroma of frying onions always makes me hungry. We were alarmed by the smell of gas in the hall. The freshly painted room had a peculiar odor.*

scep•ter (sĕp′tər) *n.* A rod held by a ruler, such as a king or queen, as a sign of authority.

scep•tic (skĕp′tĭk) *n.* Variant of **skeptic.**

sched•ule (skĕj′ōōl or skĕj′ōō əl or skĕj′əl) *n.* **1.** A program of coming events or appointments: *Let me check my schedule.* **2.** A student's program of classes: *a heavy schedule of classes.* **3.** A timetable of departures and arrivals: *a bus schedule.* —*tr.v.* **sched•uled, sched•ul•ing, sched•ules. 1.** To place (sthg.) on a schedule: *schedule an exam.* **2.** To make up a schedule for (sthg.): *schedule all the appointments.* **3.** To plan or appoint (sbdy./sthg.) for a certain time or date: *schedule the trip for next week; schedule him to see the dentist.*

sche•mat•ic (skē măt′ĭk *or* skĭ măt′ĭk) *adj.* Relating to or in the form of a scheme or diagram: *a schematic drawing.* —**sche•mat′i•cal•ly** *adv.*

scheme (skēm) *n.* **1.** A secret plan; a plot: *a scheme to cheat investors.* **2.** An orderly combination or arrangement: *choosing a color scheme for the new kitchen.* —*v.* **schemed, schem•ing, schemes.** —*tr.* **1.** To make up a plan or scheme for (sthg.): *We schemed a surprise party.* **2.** To plot (sthg.): *prisoners scheming their escape.* —*intr.* To make plans, especially secret and devious ones: *They schemed all night.* —**schem′er** *n.*

schism (sĭz′əm *or* skĭz′əm) *n.* A separation or division into opposing groups: *a schism in a political party.*

schiz•o•phre•ni•a (skĭt′sə frē′nē ə *or* skĭt′sə frĕn′ē ə) *n.* [U] A severe mental disorder in which a person loses touch with reality and withdraws from other people. —**schiz′o•phren′ic** (skĭt′sə frĕn′ĭk) *adj.*

schlep (shlĕp) *v.* **schlepped, schlep•ping, schleps.** *Informal.* —*tr.* To carry (sthg.) or transport (sbdy.): *Would you schlep the groceries for me? Do I have to schlep you all over town?* —*intr.* To go somewhere tiredly or unwillingly: *It's too late to schlep all over town looking for a place to eat.* —*n.* **1.** A clumsy person; a bungler: *What a schlep! He dropped our pizza!* **2.** A long trip: *It's such a schlep to buy groceries.*

schlock (shlŏk) *n.* [U] Things that are useless or worthless: *My brother collects the most amazing schlock.*

schmaltz (shmälts) *n.* [U] Extreme sentimentality: *Why does she like all that schmaltz in the soap operas?* —**schmaltz′y** *adj.*

schmooze (shmo͞oz) *intr.v..* To talk casually: *She was outside, schmoozing with her friends.*

schmuck (shmŭk) *n.* An insulting word for a person seen as stupid, especially a man.

schol•ar (skŏl′ər) *n.* **1.** A learned person; an expert in a particular field: *a scholar of Russian history.* **2.** A student who has received a particular scholarship: *a Fullbright Scholar.* **3.** A pupil or student: *young scholars.*

schol•ar•ly (skŏl′ər lē) *adj.* Relating to or characteristic of scholars or scholarship: *scholarly research.*

schol•ar•ship (skŏl′ər shĭp′) *n.* **1.** [U] The methods, disciplines, and learning of a scholar. **2.** [U] Knowledge resulting from extensive research in a particular field. **3.** [C] A grant of financial aid awarded to a student, as for attending college.

scho•las•tic (skə lăs′tĭk) *adj.* Relating to schools or education; academic: *scholastic standards; scholastic achievement.* —**scho•las′ti•cal•ly** *adv.*

school¹ (sko͞ol) *n.* **1.** [C] An institution for teaching and learning. **2.** [C] A division of an educational institution, especially one for special study within a university: *a law school.* **3.** [C] The building or group of buildings housing an educational institution. **4.** [U] The instruction given at a school: *School ends early today.* **5.** [U] The process of being educated formally: *What are your plans when you finish school?* **6.** [C] A group of people, especially artists or writers, whose thought, work, or style shows common influences: *the realist school of art.* —*tr.v.* To instruct or train (sbdy.) in or as if in a school: *She is schooled in medicine.* See Synonyms at **teach.**

school² (sko͞ol) *n.* A large group of fish or other water animals that swim together: *a school of tuna.* —*intr.v.* To form or swim in such a group.

school•ing (sko͞o′lĭng) *n.* [U] **1.** Instruction or training given at school; formal education. **2.** Education obtained through experience or exposure: *Living on a farm has given her valuable schooling.*

school•room (sko͞ol′ro͞om′ *or* sko͞ol′ro͝om′) *n.* A classroom.

school•teach•er (sko͞ol′tē′chər) *n.* A person who teaches school below the college level.

school•work (sko͞ol′wûrk′) *n.* [U] Lessons done at school or to be done at home.

schoo•ner (sko͞o′nər) *n.* A sailing vessel with two or more masts.

schwa (shwä) *n.* A symbol (ə) used to represent certain vowel sounds that in English often occur in unstressed syllables; for example, the sounds of *a* in *alone* and the first *e* in *science* are represented by a schwa.

sci. *abbr.* An abbreviation of: **1.** Science. **2.** Scientific.

sci•ence (sī′əns) *n.* **1.a.** [U] The observation, study, and theoretical explanation of natural events. **b.** [C] A particular area of such activities: *the biological sciences.* **2.** [C] An activity that requires study and method: *the science of marketing.* **3.** [C; U] Systematic activity, discipline, or study: *I've got studying for tests down to a science.*

science fiction *n.* [U] Fiction in which real and imaginary scientific discoveries, such as life on other planets, form part of the plot or setting.

sci•en•tif•ic (sī′ən tĭf′ĭk) *adj.* Relating to or used in science: *scientific experiments.* —**sci′en•tif′i•cal•ly** *adv.*

sci•en•tist (sī′ən tĭst) *n.* A person who is an expert in one or more sciences, such as a physicist.

scin•til•late (sĭn′tl āt′) *intr.v.* **scin•til•lat•ed, scin•til•lat•ing, scin•til•lates.** **1.** To flash or sparkle. **2.** To be exciting or brilliant: *The conversation scintillated all evening.* —**scin′til•la′ting** *adj.* —**scin′til•la′tion** *n.*

S

scis•sors (sĭz′ərz) *pl.n.*
A cutting tool consist-
ing of two blades, each
with a ring-shaped han-
dle, joined in a way that
allows the cutting edges
to close against each
other.

scissors

scoff (skŏf *or* skôf) *intr.v.*
[*at*] To express opinions in a mocking disrespectful way; jeer: *They scoffed at the idea.*

scoff•law (skŏf′lô′ *or* skôf′lô′) *n.* A person
who habitually breaks the law.

scold (skōld) *tr.v.* To criticize (sbdy./sthg.)
harshly or angrily: *scold a puppy; The mother
scolded her child for running into the street.*

scone (skōn *or* skŏn) *n.* A small rich pastry
that resembles a biscuit.

scoop (skōōp) *n.* **1.** A small utensil shaped like
a shovel with a short handle and a deep curved
dish: *a flour scoop.* **2.** The amount that this
utensil can hold: *a scoop of sugar.* **3.a.** A utensil with a round bowl, used to serve balls of ice
cream or other semisoft food: *an ice cream
scoop.* **b.** A portion of food served with this
utensil: *two scoops of strawberry ice cream.* **4.**
A scooping movement or action: *She threw the
ball into the basket with a scoop.* **5.** *Informal.*
A news story reported by a broadcasting station or newspaper ahead of a competitor. **6.**
Informal. Current information or details:
What's the scoop on the new neighbors? — tr.v.
1. [*out; up*] To take (sthg.) up with a scoop:
scoop out the seeds; scoop up dirt. **2.** [*out*] To
hollow (sthg.) out or form by digging: *scoop
out a hole.* **3.** [*up*] To grab or gather (sthg.)
swiftly: *scoop up the dirty clothes.* **4.** *Informal.* To obtain and report a news story
before (a rival): *The small-town newspaper
scooped us on the fire story.*

scoop•ful (skōōp′fŏŏl′) *n.* The amount that
a scoop can hold: *a scoopful of coffee.*

scoot (skōōt) *intr.v.* [*off; away*] To go suddenly or quickly; hurry: *The rabbits scooted
off into the woods.*

scoot•er (skōō′tər) *n.* **1.** A child's vehicle
made of a long footboard between two small
wheels, controlled by a steering bar attached
to the front wheel. **2.** A motor scooter.

scope (skōp) *n.* **1.** [U] The area covered by an
activity, a situation, or a subject: *The book was
broad in scope.* **2.** [U] The range of one's
thoughts, actions, or abilities: *broaden one's
scope by reading.* **3.** [U] Room or opportunity
to function: *Give full scope to your imagination.* **4.** [C] A viewing instrument: *a rifle
scope.* ♦ **scope out.** *tr.v.* [sep.] *Slang.* To look
at or examine (sbdy./sthg.) carefully: *Let's
scope out this restaurant.*

—scope *suff.* A suffix that means an instru-

ment for viewing or observing: *microscope;
telescope.*

scorch (skôrch) *v. — tr.* **1.** To burn the surface
of (sthg.): *She scorched the shirt while ironing it.* **2.** To dry (sthg.) with intense heat: *The
sun scorched the desert. — intr.* To become
burned: *My dinner scorched when I left it on
the heat. — n.* **1.** A slight or superficial burn.
2. A discoloration caused by heat: *a scorch
left by the hot iron.*

scorch•er (skôr′chər) *n. Informal.* An extremely hot day: *Yesterday was a scorcher.*

score (skôr) *n.* **1.** The number of points made
by each competitor or team in a game or contest: *The score was 3 to 0.* **2.** A record of points
made in a game or contest: *The score was tied
late in the game.* **3.** A result of a test or an
examination: *a score of 90 on a math test.* **4.** A
reason: *You have nothing to worry about on
that score.* **5.** An old-fashioned word for a
group of 20 items, often years: *fourscore.* **6.**
scores. Large numbers: *scores of people.* **7.a.**
The written form of a musical composition. **b.**
A musical composition written for a film or
theater production. *— v.* **scored, scor•ing,
scores.** *— tr.* **1.** To gain (a point or points) in a
game or contest: *We scored ten goals in our
match.* **2.** To keep a written record of the score
or progress of (a game or contest): *It was my
job to score the baseball game.* **3.** To achieve,
gain, or win (sthg.): *score a goal; scored success in college.* **4.** To evaluate and assign a
grade to (sthg.): *The teacher scored the tests.*
5. To write music for (a film): *score the movie.*
6. *Slang.* To get (sthg.) such as illegal drugs.
— intr. **1.** To make a point in a game or contest:
Everyone cheered when we scored. **2.** *Slang.*
To get sthg. strongly desired, such as sex or
illegal drugs. ♦ **settle a score** or **have a score
to settle.** To get or to want revenge for some
wrong done to one: *I have an old score to settle
with him. — scor′er n.*

score•board (skôr′bôrd′) *n.* A large board that
indicates the score of a game for spectators.

score•card (skôr′kärd′) *n.* A printed card
used, as in golf, to record a score.

score•keep•er (skôr′kē′pər) *n.* An official
who records the score throughout a game
or competition.

scorn (skôrn) *n.* [U] A strong feeling that a person or thing is inferior or unworthy; contempt or
disdain. *— tr.v.* **1.** To consider or treat (sbdy./
sthg.) as inferior or unworthy: *The artist was
scorned by traditional painters.* **2.** To reject
or refuse (sbdy./sthg.) in an unkind way: *She
scorned their offer of help. — scorn′er n.*

scorn•ful (skôrn′fəl) *adj.* Full of or expressing scorn or contempt: *a scornful laugh.*
— scorn′ful•ly adv. — scorn′ful•ness n. [U]

Scor•pi•o (skôr′pē ō′) *n.* **1.** The eighth sign

S

of the zodiac in astrology. **2.** A person born under this sign, between October 24 and November 21.

scor·pi·on (skôr′pē ən) n. An animal related to the spider that has a narrow jointed body and a tail with a poisonous sting.

Scotch tape (skŏch) n. [U] A trademark for a clear adhesive tape.

Scotch or **Scotch whisky** n. [C; U] A smoky-flavored whiskey distilled in Scotland from malted barley.

scot-free (skŏt′frē′) adv. Informal. **1.** Without having to pay: We got into the games scot-free. **2.** Without incurring any punishment: He got off scot-free even though he was guilty.

scoun·drel (skoun′drəl) n. A wicked or dishonorable person; a villain.

scour¹ (skour) v. —tr. **1.** To clean or polish (sthg.) by scrubbing vigorously: scour a dirty pan. **2.** To remove (sthg.) by scrubbing: scour grease from a pan. —intr. To scrub sthg. vigorously: I scoured for hours in the kitchen.

scour² (skour) tr.v. To search (sthg.) thoroughly: The police scoured the scene of the crime for clues.

scourge (skûrj) n. A cause of widespread suffering, as a disease or war: the scourge of malaria.

scout (skout) v. —tr. **1.** To observe or explore (a place) carefully to obtain information: The soldier scouted the woods for enemy soldiers. **2.** To observe and evaluate (an athlete or entertainer, for example) for possible hiring: The coach scouted new players for the team. —intr. [around] To search: I scouted around for my baseball glove. —n. **1.** A person who goes out from a main body to gather information: The captain sent out a scout. **2.** Often **Scout. a.** A member of the Boy Scouts. **b.** A member of the Girl Scouts. **3.** A person employed to discover and recruit people with talent: a talent scout.

scout·ing also **Scout·ing** (skou′tĭng) n. [U] The activities of the Boy Scouts or Girl Scouts.

scout·mas·ter (skout′măs′tər) n. The adult leader of a troop of Boy Scouts.

scow (skou) n. A large flat-bottomed boat or barge that is used to transport sand, gravel, or garbage: a garbage scow.

scowl (skoul) intr.v. To frown in an expression of anger or disapproval: She scowled at the noisy spectators. —n. An angry frown: a scowl on my father's face. —**scowl′er** n.

scrag·gly (skrăg′lē) adj. **scrag·gli·er**, **scrag·gli·est**. Ragged and messy: scraggly hair; scraggly weeds; a scraggly dog.

scram (skrăm) intr.v. **scrammed**, **scram·ming**, **scrams**. Slang. To leave at once; go immediately: We told our friends to scram because our parents were coming home.

scram·ble (skrăm′bəl) v. **scram·bled**, **scram·bling**, **scram·bles**. —intr. **1.** To

move or climb hurriedly, especially on the hands and knees: The children scrambled over the stone wall. **2.** To struggle in order to get sthg.: We scrambled for the best seats. —tr. **1.** To mix (sthg.) together in a confused or disorderly way: scrambled the letters of a word. **2.** To cook (beaten eggs) until firm but moist and soft. **3.** To distort (an electronic signal) so that it cannot be used or understood without a special receiver: The police scrambled the radio signal. —n. **1.** A strenuous climb or hike: It was quite a scramble to reach the pass. **2.** A struggle for sthg.: a scramble for new territory.

scram·bler (skrăm′blər) n. An electronic device that scrambles a signal so that it can be received only with special equipment.

scrap¹ (skrăp) n. **1.** [C] A small piece or bit; a fragment: a scrap of paper. **2.** **scraps.** Leftover bits of food: The dog begged for scraps. **3.** [U] Discarded waste material, especially metal suitable for reprocessing: sold the old car as scrap. —tr.v. **scrapped**, **scrap·ping**, **scraps**. **1.** To break (sthg.) down into parts for disposal or salvage: scrap an old stove. **2.** Informal. To discard or abandon (sthg.) as useless; junk: scrap a plan.

scrap² (skrăp) intr.v. **scrapped**, **scrap·ping**, **scraps.** To fight, often with the fists: The boys scrapped over a disagreement. —n. Informal. A fight or quarrel: He was always getting into scraps.

scrap·book (skrăp′book′) n. A book with blank pages for placing pictures or other mementos.

scrape (skrāp) v. **scraped**, **scrap·ing**, **scrapes.** —tr. **1.** To remove (material) from a surface by forceful strokes with an edged instrument: I scraped ice from the windshield. **2.** To clean or smooth (sthg.) by rubbing: scrape a carrot. **3.** To cause (sthg.) to rub or move against sthg., often with a harsh sound: She scraped her fingernails on the blackboard. **4.** To damage or injure the surface of (sthg.) by rubbing against sthg. rough or sharp: I scraped my knee on the sidewalk. —intr. **1.** To rub or move with a harsh grating noise: The plow scraped over the road. **2.** To be frugal; scrimp: We really had to scrape to buy a new car. —n. **1.** The act or sound of scraping. **2.** A mark or an injury caused by scraping: a scrape on the knee. **3.a.** An embarrassing or difficult situation: She found herself in a scrape. **b.** A fight: The boy got into a scrape. ✦ **scrape by.** intr.v. To have barely enough money to live: They are just barely scraping by. We'll scrape by somehow.

scrape together. tr.v. [sep.] To gather or produce (sthg.) with difficulty: scrape together enough money for the rent.

scrap·er (skrā′pər) n. Something that scrapes, especially a tool for scraping off paint, ice, or other material.

S

scrap·py (skrăp′ē) *adj.* **scrap·pi·er, scrap·pi·est. 1.** Quarrelsome: *a scrappy child.* **2.** Full of fighting spirit: *a scrappy boxer.* **—scrap′pi·ness** *n.* [U]

scratch (skrăch) *v.* *—tr.* **1.** To make a thin shallow cut or mark on (a surface) with a sharp instrument: *I accidentally scratched my desk with the scissors.* **2.** To scrape or injure (sbdy./sthg.) with the nails or claws: *The cat scratched my arm.* **3.** To rub or scrape (the skin) to relieve itching: *My arm itched, so I scratched it.* **4.a.** To write or draw (sthg.) by scraping a surface: *scratched a name on a rock.* **b.** To write (sthg.) hastily; scrawl: *scratched notes on a pad.* **5.** [*out*] To strike out or cancel (a word, for example) by drawing lines across: *I scratched out each item from the list.* **6.** To withdraw (sbdy./sthg.) from competition: *scratch a runner from a race.* **7.** To make (a living) from hard work and saving money. *—intr.* **1.** To use the nails or claws to scrape or injure: *The dog scratched at the door.* **2.** To rub or scrape the skin to relieve itching: *If you get a rash, don't scratch; it will only get worse.* **3.** To make a thin scraping sound: *The pencil scratched on the paper.* *—n.* **1.** A mark or wound made by scratching. **2.** A sound made by scratching. *—adj.* **1.** Done hurriedly or haphazardly: *a scratch outline.* **2.** Assembled at random: *a scratch team.* ◆ **from scratch.** From the very beginning: *make a cake from scratch.* **scratch the surface.** To just begin: *She started her project yesterday but barely scratched the surface.* **up to scratch.** *Informal.* Meeting the requirements: *The sleepy student's work was not up to scratch.* **—scratch′er** *n.*

scratch·y (skrăch′ē) *adj.* **scratch·i·er, scratch·i·est. 1.** Rough, harsh, or irritating: *wearing a scratchy sweater.* **2.** Making a harsh scratching sound: *a scratchy voice.* **—scratch′i·ly** *adv.* **—scratch′i·ness** *n.* [U]

scrawl (skrôl) *v.* *—tr.* To write (sthg.) quickly or carelessly: *scrawl a note on a pad.* *—intr.* To write in an irregular manner: *Don't scrawl on the chalkboard.* *—n.* Unreadable handwriting. **—scrawl′er** *n.*

scraw·ny (skrô′nē) *adj.* **scraw·ni·er, scraw·ni·est.** Thin and bony; skinny: *a scrawny underfed dog.* See Synonyms at **lean²**. **—scraw′ni·ness** *n.* [U]

scream (skrēm) *v.* *—intr.* **1.** To produce a long, loud, piercing cry, as from fear or pain: *She screamed when the bee stung her.* **2.** To make a loud piercing sound: *The siren screamed.* *—tr.* To say (sthg.) in a screaming voice: *"Wait!" he screamed.* *—n.* **1.** A loud piercing cry or sound: *We heard a loud scream.* **2.** *Informal.* A person or thing that is very funny: *That joke is a scream.* **—scream′er** *n.*

screech (skrēch) *n.* A high-pitched harsh sound: *the screech of brakes.* *—v.* *—tr.* To say (sthg.) in a high-pitched harsh voice: *The children screeched an answer.* *—intr.* To make a shrill harsh sound like a screech: *The tires screeched on the wet pavement.*

screen (skrēn) *n.* **1.** A light movable device used to divide, hide, or protect sthg.: *She changed her clothes behind the screen.* **2.** Something that serves to conceal: *a screen of trees around the yard.* **3.** A frame with wire mesh, used in a window or door to keep out insects and allow air to pass in and out. **4.** A large flat white surface upon which slides or movies are projected. **5.** The surface on which an image appears, as on a television or computer monitor. *—tr.v.* **1.** To shelter, guard, or protect (sbdy./sthg.): *The stone wall screened us from the wind.* **2.** To hide (sbdy./sthg.) from view with a screen: *Trees screened the house from the street.* See Synonyms at **hide¹**. **3.** [*out*] To separate or sift (sthg.) out with a sieve: *to screen rocks out of the soil.* **4.** To examine (sbdy./sthg.) systematically to determine suitability: *screen job applicants.* **5.** To find out who is calling (on the phone) by using an answering machine instead of picking up the phone: *She always screens her calls.*

screen·ing (skrē′nĭng) *n.* A presentation of a movie.

screen·play (skrēn′plā′) *n.* The script for a movie.

screw (skrōō) *n.* A metal pin with spiral grooves, fitted with a slotted head so that it can be turned by a screwdriver and used to fasten things together. *—v.* *—tr.* **1.a.** To fasten, tighten, or attach (sthg.) by or as if by means of a screw: *We screwed the parts together.* **b.** To attach (a threaded cap or fitting) by twisting into place: *screw a valve onto the end of a pipe; screw the cap on the bottle.* **2.** *Offensive Slang.* To have sex with (sbdy.). **3.** *Offensive Slang.* To treat (sbdy.) badly: *My last boss really screwed me.* **4.** *Slang.* To cheat (sbdy.): *The salesperson screwed them on that car deal.* *—intr.* To become attached by means of a screw: *Those parts screw together easily.* ◆ **be (all) screwed up.** To be confused: *After my parents got divorced, my life was all screwed up.* **have a screw loose.** To be or act crazy: *They say that my neighbor has a screw loose because he talks to himself all the time.* **screw around.** *intr.v. Slang.* To waste time or behave in a childish way: *You should stop screwing around and study harder.* **screw up.** *tr.v.* [sep.] **1.** To gather

screw

or summon (sthg.) up: *I screwed up my courage to face the challenge.* **2.** *Slang.* To ruin (sthg.): *He screwed up his exam and got the answers wrong.* —*intr.v. Slang.* To make a mistake: *He's always screwing up.*

screw•ball (skrōō'bôl') *Slang. n.* A person regarded as strange or irrational. —*adj.* Strange or irrational: *That screwball idea will never work.*

screw•driv•er (skrōō'drī'vər) *n.* A tool used to turn screws.

screw•y (skrōō'ē) *adj.* **screw•i•er, screw• i•est.** *Slang.* **1.** Crazy or strange: *a screwy idea.* **2.** Odd or inappropriate: *There's something screwy with this computer.*

scrib•ble (skrĭb'əl) *v.* **scrib•bled, scrib• bling, scrib•bles.** —*tr.* **1.** To write or draw (sthg.) quickly or carelessly: *She scribbled a note to her boss.* **2.** To write or draw (doodles and meaningless marks): *The child scribbled marks on the wall.* —*intr.* To write or draw in a hurried careless way: *The student scribbled on the board.* —*n.* **1.** Careless hurried writing. **2.** Meaningless marks. —**scrib'bler** *n.*

scribe (skrīb) *n. Formal.* In the past, a person who copied manuscripts and documents.

scrim•mage (skrĭm'ĭj) *n.* A practice game, often between members of the same team: *The coach held a scrimmage.* —*intr.v.* **scrim• maged, scrim•mag•ing, scrim•mag•es.** To engage in a scrimmage: *The team scrimmaged for practice.*

scrimp (skrĭmp) *intr.v.* To be very frugal; economize severely: *We scrimped and saved for our trip.*

script (skrĭpt) *n.* **1.** [C; U] Letters or characters written by hand; handwriting: *written in neat script.* **2.** [C] The text of a play, movie, or broadcast: *The actor read the new script.*

Scrip•ture (skrĭp'chər) *n.* [C; U] **1.** A sacred writing or book. **2.** *(often used in the plural).* The sacred writings of the Bible. —**Scrip'- tur•al** *adj.*

scroll (skrōl) *n.* A roll of material used especially for writing a document. —*v.* —*tr.* To cause (text or graphics) to move vertically or horizontally across the screen of a computer monitor: *I scrolled the document off the screen.* —*intr.* To cause text or graphics to move vertically or hoizontally across the screen of a computer monitor: *Scroll down to the end of the document.*

Scrooge also **scrooge** (skrōōj) *n. Informal.* A person who hates to spend money.

scro•tum (skrō'təm) *n.* The external sac of skin that encloses the testes in most male mammals.

scrounge (skrounj) *v.* **scrounged, scroung• ing, scroung•es.** *Slang.* —*tr.* **1.** To obtain (sthg.) by rummaging or foraging: *scrounging old books out of the attic.* **2.** To obtain (sthg.) by begging or borrowing with no intention of returning or repaying: *scrounge*

a dollar from a friend. —*intr.* To search: *He scrounged in his pockets for money.*

scrub¹ (skrŭb) *v.* **scrubbed, scrub•bing, scrubs.** —*tr.* **1.** To rub (sthg.) hard in order to clean: *scrub the bathtub.* **2.** To remove (dirt or stains) by hard rubbing: *scrub the spots out of the carpet.* **3.** *Slang.* To cancel or abandon (sthg.): *scrub a space flight.* —*intr.* To clean or wash sthg. by hard rubbing: *I scrubbed and cleaned all day.* —**scrub'ber** *n.*

scrub² (skrŭb) *n.* [U] A growth of small scattered trees or shrubs, in a dry area.

scruff (skrŭf) *n.* The back of the neck or the loose skin covering it; the nape: *The mother cat picked up her kitten by the scruff of the neck.*

scruff•y (skrŭf'ē) *adj.* **scruff•i•er, scruff• i•est.** Shabby; untidy: *a scruffy little house.*

scrump•tious (skrŭmp'shəs) *adj.* Very pleasing to the taste; delicious: *a scrumptious chocolate cake.*

scru•ple (skrōō'pəl) *n. (usually plural).* A feeling of uneasiness that is produced by one's conscience and that stops one from doing sthg. bad: *His scruples prevented him from cheating.*

scru•pu•lous (skrōō'pyə ləs) *adj.* **1.** Showing extreme care about details; painstaking: *scrupulous attention to detail.* **2.** Having scruples; ethical: *a scrupulous attorney.* —**scru'- pu•lous•ly** *adv.* —**scru'pu•lous•ness** *n.* [U]

scru•ti•nize (skrōōt'n īz') *tr.v.* **scru•ti• nized, scru•ti•niz•ing, scru•ti•niz•es.** To observe or examine (sthg.) with great care: *We scrutinized the document for errors.*

scru•ti•ny (skrōōt'n ē) *n.* [U] **1.** A close careful examination or study: *close scrutiny of the documents.* **2.** Close observation; surveillance: *Doctors kept the patient under close scrutiny.*

scu•ba (skōō'bə) *n.* A portable device including one or more tanks of compressed air, used by divers to breathe underwater.

scuba

scuff (skŭf) *v.* —*intr. & tr.* To scrape or drag the feet while walking: *He scuffed across the floor. She scuffed the new linoleum.* —*n.* A worn or rough spot resulting from scraping: *scuffs on the newly painted wall.*

scuf•fle (skŭf'əl) *intr.v.* **scuf•fled, scuf• fling, scuf•fles.** To fight at close quarters: *The police scuffled with the thieves.* —*n.* A rough disorderly struggle at close quarters: *The coaches broke up the scuffle.*

sculpt (skŭlpt) *v.* —*tr.* To shape (sthg.), especially artistically: *sculpt a head; sculpt clay into a statue.* —*intr.* To be a sculptor; produce sculpture: *My mother sculpts in her free time.*

sculp•tor (skŭlp′tər) *n.* An artist who makes sculptures.

sculp•ture (skŭlp′chər) *n.* **1.** [U] The art of shaping or making figures or designs of wood, stone, clay, or metal. **2.a.** [C] A work of art created in this way: *a sculpture of a woman.* **b.** [U] Such works of art considered as a group: *African sculpture.* —*tr.v.* **sculp•tured, sculp•tur•ing, sculp•tures.** To form (sthg.) by sculpting: *sculpture a monument.*

scum (skŭm) *n.* [U] **1.** A filmy layer of matter that forms on the surface of a liquid or a body of water: *soap scum.* **2.** *Slang.* An extremely worthless person or group of people: *He treats everyone like scum.* ♦ **the scum of the earth.** *Informal.* The worst person or people in the world: *Many believe the leader of that country is the scum of the earth.*

scur•ri•lous (skûr′ə ləs *or* skŭr′ə ləs) *adj.* Expressed in coarse and abusive language: *a scurrilous attack.* —**scur′ril•ous•ly** *adv.* —**scur′ril•ous•ness** *n.* [U]

scur•ry (skûr′ē *or* skŭr′ē) *intr.v.* **scur•ried, scur•ry•ing, scur•ries. 1.** To move with light running steps; scamper: *The mouse scurried across the floor.* **2.** To rush or race about in a hurried or confused manner: *The shoppers scurried around before the store closed.*

scut•tle (skŭt′l) *v.* **scut•tled, scut•tling, scut•tles.** —*tr.* **1.** To sink (a ship) by cutting or opening holes in the hull. **2.** *Informal.* To discard or abandon (sthg.): *We scuttled our vacation plans.* —*intr.* To run or move with quick little steps; scurry: *The crab scuttled over the rocks.*

scut•tle•butt (skŭt′l bŭt′) *n.* [U] *Slang.* Gossip; rumor: *What's the scuttlebutt on the new boss?*

scythe (sīth) *n.* A tool with a long curved blade and a long bent handle, used for cutting grass or harvesting grain.

SD or **S.D.** *abbr.* An abbreviation of South Dakota.

S.Dak. *abbr.* An abbreviation of South Dakota.

SE *abbr.* An abbreviation of: **1.** Southeast. **2.** Southeastern.

sea (sē) *n.* **1.a.** The continuous body of salt water that covers most of the surface of the earth. **b.** A region of water within an ocean and partly enclosed by land: *the North Sea.* **c.** A large body of either fresh or salt water that is completely enclosed by land: *the Caspian Sea.* **2.** The condition of the ocean's surface, especially its motion or roughness: *a high sea.* **3.** A vast area: *a sea of ice.* ♦ **at sea. 1.** On the sea, especially on a sea voyage: *We were at sea for a month on a cruise.* **2.** In a state of confusion; lost: *I felt at sea when I tried to read the directions.*

sea•coast (sē′kōst′) *n.* Land along the sea.

sea•far•er (sē′fâr′ər) *n.* A sailor.

sea•far•ing (sē′fâr′ĭng) *n.* [U] The work of a sailor. —*adj.* Relating to ships or the people who sail them: *a seafaring life.*

sea•food (sē′food′) *n.* [U] Fish or shellfish from the sea eaten as food.

sea•go•ing (sē′gō′ĭng) *adj.* Made or used for ocean voyages: *a seagoing barge.*

sea gull also **sea•gull** (sē′gŭl′) *n.* A gull, especially one that lives along seacoasts.

sea horse *n.* A small ocean fish with a head like that of a horse, a body covered with bony plates, and a tail that can be curled around a supporting object.

seal¹ (sēl) *n.* **1.** A design used to identify a person or thing or to show that sthg. is authentic: *The notary's seal appears on every page of the contract.* **2.** Something that prevents a liquid or gas from entering or escaping: *a seal around a window.* **3.** A small paper sticker used to fasten or decorate an envelope. —*tr.v.* **1.** To close (sthg.) with or as if with a seal: *I sealed the envelope. The doctor sealed the wound with stitches.* **2.** To close (sthg.) so that a liquid or gas cannot enter or escape: *The plumber will seal the pipe joint.* **3.** To close (sthg.) tightly so that reopening is difficult or impossible: *Workers sealed the tunnel with concrete.* **4.** To apply a waterproof coating to (sthg.): *seal the driveway.* **5.** To establish or determine (sthg.) with no possibility of change: *Their fate was sealed.* ♦ **seal of approval.** Approval or acceptance, often verbal, of sthg.: *The architect gave his seal of approval to the plans.* **seal off.** *tr.v.* [sep.] To close tightly or surround (sthg.) with a barricade or rope: *They sealed off part of the road for repairs.* **seal (one's) lips.** To promise not to speak about sthg.: *Your secret is safe with me. My lips are sealed.* —**seal′er** *n.*

seal² (sēl) *n.* A sea mammal with a streamlined body, thick fur or hair, and flippers.

sea level *n.* [U] The level of the surface of the ocean, used as a standard in measuring land elevation or sea depths.

sea lion *n.* A large seal, mostly of Pacific waters, with a sleek body and brownish fur.

seam (sēm) *n.* A line formed by joining two pieces of material together at their edges, as by sewing or welding: *The dress tore along the seam.*

S

sea·man (sē′mən) *n.* A sailor.

HOMONYMS: seaman, semen (sperm).

---

sea·man·ship (sē′mən shĭp′) *n.* [U] Skill in sailing a boat or ship.

seam·stress (sēm′strĭs) *n.* A woman who sews, especially one who makes her living by sewing.

seam·y (sē′mē) *adj.* **seam·i·er, seam·i·est.** Unpleasant; nasty: *the seamy side of politics.*

sé·ance (sā′äns′) *n.* A meeting at which people attempt to communicate with the dead.

sea otter *n.* A large otter of Pacific waters, with soft dark brown fur.

sea·plane (sē′plān′) *n.* An airplane equipped with floats for taking off from or landing on water.

sea·port (sē′pôrt′) *n.* A harbor or town with facilities for seagoing ships: *San Francisco is a busy seaport.*

sear (sîr) *tr.v.* To burn the surface of (sthg.): *We seared the steaks on the grill.*

HOMONYMS: sear, seer (prophet).

---

search (sûrch) *v.* —*tr.* **1.** To make a careful examination of (sthg.) in order to find a missing person or thing: *She searched her room for the missing money.* **2.** To examine (sthg.) carefully: *searching his soul in order to make the proper decision.* —*intr.* To make a careful investigation; hunt: *searching for a lost dog.* —*n.* The act of searching: *the search for knowledge.* —**search′er** *n.*

search·ing (sûr′chĭng) *adj.* **1.** Examining closely or carefully: *a searching investigation of stock market dealings.* **2.** Keenly observant: *some searching insights.* —**search′ing·ly** *adv.*

search·light (sûrch′līt′) *n.* A light that produces a very bright beam and is used for searches.

search warrant *n.* A document giving a law officer permission to search a specified person, building, residence, or area for evidence to be used in a legal case.

sear·ing (sîr′ĭng) *adj.* Extremely sharp and painful; burning: *a searing pain in her stomach.*

sea·shell (sē′shĕl′) *n.* The hard shell that covers certain sea creatures.

sea·shore (sē′shôr′) *n.* Land next to the sea.

sea·sick·ness (sē′sĭk′nĭs) *n.* [U] Nausea or other discomfort as a result of the motions of a ship at sea. —**sea′sick′** *adj.*

sea·side (sē′sīd′) *n.* The seashore.

sea·son (sē′zən) *n.* **1.a.** One of four natural divisions of the year, spring, summer, autumn or fall, and winter: *the four seasons.* **b.** Either or the two parts, rainy and dry, into which the year is divided in tropical climates: *the rainy*

season. **2.** A period of the year marked by a certain activity or by the appearance of sthg.: *baseball season; the hurricane season.* —*tr.v.* **1.** To give (food) extra flavor by adding salt, pepper, spices, or other flavorings: *season the meat with garlic.* **2.** To train (sbdy.) through experience: *Hard training seasoned the players.* ◆ **in season.** **1.** Available for eating: *Strawberries are in season now.* **2.** In a specified period for legal hunting or fishing: *Deer are in season.* **out of season.** Not available, permitted, or ready to be eaten, caught, or hunted: *It is difficult to find wild mushrooms out of season.*

sea·son·a·ble (sē′zə nə bəl) *adj.* Suitable for the time or season: *seasonable weather; seasonable clothing.* —**sea′son·a·bly** *adv.*

sea·son·al (sē′zə nəl) *adj.* Dependent on a season or seasons: *seasonal variations in temperature.* —**sea′son·al·ly** *adv.*

sea·son·ing (sē′zə nĭng) *n.* [C; U] An ingredient that adds to the flavor of food: *Herbs are used as seasoning.*

season ticket *n.* A ticket for a specified period of time, as for a series of sporting events or performances: *We bought season tickets for baseball.*

seat (sēt) *n.* **1.** Something, such as a chair or bench, that may be sat on: *He offered his seat.* **2.** A place in which a person may sit: *a ticket for a seat on the plane.* **3.** The part of sthg. on which a person sits: *a bicycle seat.* **4.** The buttocks: *She fell on her seat.* **5.** The part of a garment covering the buttocks: *the seat of the pants.* **6.a.** The place where sthg. is located or based: *the seat of power.* **b.** A capital or center of authority: *the county seat.* —*tr.v.* **1.a.** To place (sbdy.) in or on a seat: *She seated the baby.* **b.** To assist (sbdy.) in sitting down: *The usher seated us in the front row.* **2.** To have seats for (a certain number of people): *an auditorium that seats 5,000.*

seat belt *n.* A safety strap or harness designed to hold a person securely in a seat, as in a car or airplane.

sea·weed (sē′wēd′) *n.* [U] Any of various plants or algae that live in ocean waters.

sea·wor·thy (sē′wûr′thē) *adj.* **sea·wor·thi·er, sea·wor·thi·est.** Suitable for crossing the sea: *a seaworthy ship.* —**sea′wor′thi·ness** *n.* [U]

sec *abbr.* An abbreviation of second (unit of time).

sec. *abbr.* An abbreviation of secant.

se·cant (sē′kănt′) *n.* A straight line or ray that intersects a curve, especially a circle, at two or more points.

se·cede (sĭ sēd′) *intr.v.* **se·ced·ed, se·ced·ing, se·cedes.** To withdraw formally from membership in an organization or union: *states that seceded before the Civil War.*

se·ces·sion (sĭ sĕsh′ən) *n.* [U] The act of seceding.

S

se·clude (sĭ klo͞od′) *tr.v.* **se·clud·ed, se·clud·ing, se·cludes.** To set or keep (sbdy./ sthg.) apart, as from social contact with others: *She secluded herself from the world.*

se·clud·ed (sĭ klo͞o′dĭd) *adj.* **1.** Removed or distant from others: *She lives a secluded life.* **2.** Screened or hidden from view: *a secluded pool.*

se·clu·sion (sĭ klo͞o′zhən) *n.* [U] The act or condition of being secluded: *She was in seclusion after the birth.*

sec·ond¹ (sĕk′ənd) *n.* **1.** A unit of time equal to ⅟₆₀ of a minute. **2.** A short period of time; a moment: *I'll see you in a second.*

sec·ond² (sĕk′ənd) *adj.* **1.** Coming next after the first in order, place, rank, time, or quality: *the second floor.* **2.** Alternate; every other: *every second year.* **3.** Inferior to another: *an accomplishment second only to yours.* **4.** Relating to the transmission gear used to produce speeds higher than those of first in a motor vehicle. *—n.* **1.** The ordinal number matching the number two in a series. **2.** *(usually plural).* A piece of merchandise of inferior quality: *The pants on sale are seconds.* **3. seconds.** *Informal.* A second serving of food: *Do you want seconds on the chicken?* **4.** The transmission gear used to produce speeds higher than those of first in a motor vehicle. *—tr.v.* **1.** To promote or encourage (sthg.): *I second the idea of a new school.* **2.** To endorse (a motion or nomination) as a means of bringing it to a vote: *The chairperson seconded the motion. —adv.* **1.** In the second order, place, or rank: *finished second in the race.* **2.** But for one other; except one: *the second-largest city.*

sec·ond·ar·y (sĕk′ən dĕr′ē) *adj.* **1.** Of the second rank; not primary: *a secondary cause.* **2.** Taken from sthg. primary or original: *secondary sources of information.* **3.** Relating to a secondary school: *secondary education.* *—sec′on·dar′i·ly* (sĕk′ən dâr′ə lē) *adv.*

secondary school *n.* A school for instruction between elementary school and college.

second class *n.* [U] **1.** Travel accommodations below first class, as on a train or an airplane. **2.** Second-class mail.

sec·ond-class (sĕk′ənd klăs′) *adj.* **1.** Considered to be of secondary status or importance: *a second-class citizen.* **2.** Relating to travel accommodations ranking next below first class: *a second-class passenger. —adv.* By means of second-class mail or travel accommodations: *We traveled second-class.*

sec·ond-de·gree burn (sĕk′ənd dĭ grē′) *n.* A burn that blisters the skin.

sec·ond-guess (sĕk′ənd gĕs′) *tr.v.* To criticize or correct (sbdy./sthg.) after a result is already known: *Don't second-guess my decision.*

sec·ond·hand (sĕk′ənd hănd′) *adj.* **1.** Previously used by another person; not new: *a secondhand coat.* **2.** Dealing in previously used goods: *a secondhand store.* **3.** Obtained from another source; not original: *secondhand information. —adv.* In an indirect way; indirectly: *news gathered secondhand.*

second hand *n.* The hand of a clock or watch that indicates the seconds.

sec·ond·ly (sĕk′ənd lē) *adv.* In the second place; second: *Secondly, we should work hard.*

second nature *n.* A behavior or characteristic that was originally learned, but that later seems natural because of long practice: *Swimming is second nature to him.*

second person *n.* **1.** A set of grammatical forms used in referring to the person addressed. **2.** One of these forms, such as *you* and *are* in *You are my friend.*

sec·ond-rate (sĕk′ənd rāt′) *adj.* Inferior in quality; mediocre: *second-rate work; a second-rate car that uses too much gas.*

se·cre·cy (sē′krĭ sē) *n.* [U] The condition of being secret or hidden: *work done in secrecy.*

se·cret (sē′krĭt) *adj.* **1.** Hidden from general knowledge or view: *secret plans.* **2.** Working in a hidden or confidential manner: *secret agents. —n.* **1.** Something known only to oneself or to a few: *Can you keep a secret?* **2.** Something beyond understanding or explanation: *the secret of the pyramids.* **3.** A method or formula for making or doing sthg: *the secret of making good bread.* ♦ **in secret. 1.** Not openly; in a manner unknown to the public: *The vote was counted in secret.* **2.** Privately: *We conducted the meeting in secret. —se′cret·ly adv.*

sec·re·tar·y (sĕk′rĭ tĕr′ē) *n., pl.* **sec·re·tar·ies. 1.** A person who does clerical work, such as typing, filing, and taking messages. **2.** An officer who takes minutes of meetings, answers correspondence, and keeps records for a club or organization. **3.** The head of a governmental department: *the Secretary of State. —sec′re·tar′i·al* (sĕk′rĭ târ′ē əl) *adj.*

se·crete¹ (sĭ krēt′) *tr.v.* **se·cret·ed, se·cret·ing, se·cretes.** To produce (a substance) from cells or bodily fluids: *That plant secretes liquid when touched.*

se·crete² (sĭ krēt′) *tr.v.* **se·cret·ed, se·cret·ing, se·cretes.** To conceal (sthg.) in a hiding place; hide: *She secreted her diary in a drawer.* See Synonyms at **hide¹.**

se·cre·tion (sĭ krē′shən) *n.* **1.** [U] The act or process of secreting a substance, especially one that is not a waste, from blood or cells. **2.** [C] A substance, such as tears or a hormone, that is secreted: *plant secretions.*

se·cre·tive (sē′krĭ tĭv) *adj.* Practicing or inclined to secrecy: *a secretive friend*

S

who doesn't gossip. —**se′cre•tive•ly** *adv.*
—**se′cre•tive•ness** *n.* [U]

Secret Service *n.* A branch of the U.S. Treasury Department whose work includes the protection of the President.

sect (sĕkt) *n.* A group of people forming a distinct unit within a larger group, usually a religious group.

sec•tar•i•an (sĕk târ′ē ən) *adj.* Relating to or characteristic of a sect. —**sec•tar′i•an•ism** *n.* [U]

sec•tion (sĕk′shən) *n.* **1.** One of several parts that make up sthg.; a piece: *a section of an orange.* **2.** A part of a written work: *the sports section of a newspaper.* **3.** A distinct area of a town, country, or city: *the business section of town.* **4.** A picture or diagram showing the internal structure of an object as it would appear if cut: *a cross section of the building showing all three floors.* **5.** A group of musical instruments or voices considered as a unit: *the string section of the orchestra.* —*tr.v.* To separate (sthg.) into parts: *Please section the orange.*

sec•tion•al (sĕk′shə nəl) *adj.* Composed of or divided into sections: *a sectional couch.*

sec•tor (sĕk′tər *or* sĕk′tôr′) *n.* A division of sthg.: *the manufacturing sector of the economy.*

sec•u•lar (sĕk′yə lər) *adj.* **1.** Worldly rather than spiritual: *secular interests.* **2.** Not related to religion or a religious organization: *a concert of secular music.*

se•cure (sĭ kyŏor′) *adj.* **se•cur•er, se•cur•est.** **1.** Free from danger, attack, or loss: *a secure building.* **2.** Free from fear, anxiety, or doubt; safe: *feeling secure at home.* **3.** Firmly fastened: *The handle is secure.* **4.** Assured; certain: *a secure peace.* —*tr.v.* **se•cured, se•cur•ing, se•cures. 1.** To guard (sbdy./sthg.) from danger or risk of loss: *Troops secured the city against attack.* **2.** To cause (sthg.) to remain firmly in position or place; fasten: *Secure the windows before it rains.* **3.** To make (sthg.) certain; ensure: *a constitution designed to secure our freedom.* **4.** To guarantee (sthg.) with a pledge: *They deposited collateral to secure the loan.* **5.** To get (sthg.); acquire: *secure a job.* **6.** To bring (sthg.) about; effect: *secured their release from prison.* —**se•cure′ly** *adv.*

se•cu•ri•ty (sĭ kyŏor′ĭ tē) *n., pl.* **se•cu•ri•ties. 1.** [U] Freedom from risk or danger; safety: *She worries about security in the apartment building.* **2.** [U] A pledge deposited or given to guarantee fulfillment of an obligation: *an extra month's rent given as security.* **3.** [C] *(usually plural).* A stock or bond: *the purchase of securities.*

secy. *abbr.* An abbreviation of secretary.

se•dan (sĭ dăn′) *n.* An automobile with two or four doors and a front and rear seat.

se•date¹ (sĭ dāt′) *adj.* Calm and dignified; composed: *a sedate meeting.* —**se•date′ly** *adv.* —**se•date′ness** *n.* [U]

se•date² (sĭ dāt′) *tr.v.* **se•dat•ed, se•dat•ing, se•dates.** To give a sedative to (a person or an animal): *The doctor sedated the patient.* —**se•da′tion** *n.* [U]

sed•a•tive (sĕd′ə tĭv) *adj.* Soothing, calming, or quieting: *a sedative effect.* —*n.* A sedative medicine or drug.

sed•en•tar•y (sĕd′n tĕr′ē) *adj.* **1.** Marked by or requiring much sitting: *Computer programming is sedentary work.* **2.** Accustomed to sitting or to taking little exercise: *She's a sedentary person who only watches TV.* —**sed′en•tar′i•ly** (sĕd′n târ′ə lē) *adv.*

sed•i•ment (sĕd′ə mənt) *n.* [C; U] Finely divided solid matter, such as dirt, that falls to the bottom of a liquid.

sed•i•men•ta•ry (sĕd′ə mĕn′tə rē *or* sĕd′ə mĕn′trē) *adj.* Relating to rocks formed from sediment deposited in water.

se•duce (sĭ dōōs′) *tr.v.* **se•duced, se•duc•ing, se•duc•es. 1.** To persuade (sbdy.) to have sexual intercourse. **2.** To persuade (sbdy.) to engage in wrongful or immoral behavior. —**se•duc′er** *n.* —**se•duc′tion** (sĭ dŭk′shən) *n.* [C; U]

se•duc•tive (sĭ dŭk′tĭv) *adj.* Tending to seduce; enticing: *the seductive power of advertising.* —**se•duc′tive•ly** *adv.* —**se•duc′tive•ness** *n.* [U]

see (sē) *v.* **saw** (sô), **seen** (sēn), **see•ing, sees.** —*tr.* **1.** To view (sbdy./sthg.) with the eye: *He saw a dog.* **2.** To have a mental picture of (sbdy./sthg.): *In her mind, she could see her hometown as it once was.* **3.** To understand (sthg.): *I see what you mean.* **4.** To consider (sbdy./sthg.) to be: *We see her as a world leader.* **5.** To imagine (sbdy./sthg.): *We can see him as an architect.* **6.** To be marked by or bring forth (sthg.): *The 1930s saw the development of antibiotics.* **7.** To find out (sthg.): *See whether that total is accurate.* **8.** To read or refer to (sthg.): *See the footnote on the next page.* **9.** To spend time with (sbdy.) often, as in dating: *They've been seeing each other for two years.* **10.** To meet (sbdy.) socially: *Will we see you tonight at the party?* **11.** To visit (sbdy.) for professional services: *He saw a lawyer.* **12.** To receive or admit (sbdy.): *The doctor will see you now.* **13.** To attend or view (sthg.): *We saw a good movie last night.* **14.** To go with (sbdy.) as an escort: *See her to the bus station.* **15.** To make sure or take care (that sthg. happens): *Always see that the door is locked.* —*intr.* **1.** To be able to view with the eye: *Can you see from there?* **2.** To understand: *If you explain, I'm sure he'll see.* **3.** To consider: *Let's see, what movie should we go to?* ♦ **see about.** *tr.v.* [insep.] To attend to (sthg.): *I'll see about getting tickets.* **see after.** *tr.v.* [insep.] To take care of (sbdy./sthg.): *Please see after your brother while I go to the store.* **see off.** *tr.v.* [sep.] To say good-bye to (sbdy. leaving): *We* *saw the guests off at the station.* **see out.** *tr.v.* [sep.] To go with (a guest) to the door: *Will you please see Ms. Smith out?* **see through.** *tr.v.* **1.** [insep.] To understand the true character or nature of (sbdy./sthg.): *She saw through his sales pitch.* **2.** [sep.] To support or continue with (sbdy./sthg.) in good times and bad: *I want to see the project through to the end.* **see to.** *tr.v.* [insep.] To attend to (sthg.): *See to the chores, please.*

HOMONYMS: see, sea (body of salt water).

SYNONYMS: see, notice, observe, view. These verbs mean to be visually aware of sthg. **See** is the most general term: *Did you see the full moon last night?* **Observe** can mean to look at sthg. carefully and closely: *We observed a change in the color of the water as it got deeper.* **Notice** can mean to observe sthg. closely and form a rather detailed impression: *He didn't notice that frost had formed on the window.* **View** can mean to examine sthg. with a particular purpose in mind or in a special way: *The tourists decided to view the art exhibit again.*

seed (sēd) *n., pl.* **seeds** or **seed. 1.** [C] A part of a flowering plant that will grow into a new plant: *tomato seeds; apple seeds.* **2.** [U] Seeds considered as a group: *We spread seed in the garden.* **3.** [C] *(usually plural).* A source or beginning: *This meeting holds the seeds of a lasting peace between the two countries.* —*v.* —*tr.* **1.** To plant seeds in (sthg.): *The farmer seeded the garden.* **2.** To remove the seeds from (fruit): *seeded an orange.* —*intr.* **1.** To plant seed: *We need to seed early if we want a full crop.* **2.** To go to seed: *The plants seeded before we could pick them.* ♦ **go to seed. 1.** To pass the seed-bearing stage: *The onion plants went to seed before we pulled them.* **2.** To become weak or run-down: *That neighborhood went to seed after the factory closed.* —**seed′less** *adj.*

HOMONYMS: seed, cede (give up).

seed·ling (sēd′lĭng) *n.* **1.** A young plant that is grown from a seed. **2.** A young tree less than three feet high.

seed·y (sē′dē) *adj.* **seed·i·er, seed·i·est. 1.** In poor condition and often in a bad location: *a seedy hotel.* **2.** Having many seeds: *Raspberries are seedy.* —**seed′i·ness** *n.* [U]

seek (sēk) *v.* **sought** (sôt), **seek·ing, seeks.** —*tr.* **1.** To try to locate (sthg.); search for: *The elephants moved, seeking a new source of water.* **2.** To try to obtain (sthg.): *seek money for her college education.* **3.** To make

an attempt (to do sthg.); try: *seek to learn a foreign language.* —*intr.* To make a search: *Seek and you will find it.* —**seek′er** *n.*

seem (sēm) *intr.v.* **1.** To appear to be: *She seems pleased to have a job.* **2.** To appear to oneself: *I seem to be lost.* **3.** To appear to be true: *There seems to be only one solution.*

HOMONYMS: seem, seam (line formed by joining).

seem·ing (sē′mĭng) *adj. Formal.* Having an appearance that may or may not be real; apparent: *I don't think we can trust his seeming honesty.*

seem·ing·ly (sē′mĭng lē) *adv.* In a way that seems to be true, but may not be: *a seemingly endless lecture.*

seem·ly (sēm′lē) *adj.* **seem·li·er, seem·li·est.** *Formal.* Following accepted standards of conduct and good taste; proper: *seemly behavior.*

seen (sēn) *v.* Past participle of **see.**

HOMONYMS: seen, scene (place).

seep (sēp) *intr.v.* To pass slowly through small openings: *Cold air seeped in through the crack under the door.*

seep·age (sē′pĭj) *n.* [U] **1.** The process of seeping; leakage: *Water seepage damaged the walls.* **2.** The amount of sthg. that has seeped in or out: *a lot of water seepage in the basement.*

seer (sîr) *n.* A person who can foresee or foretell events.

HOMONYMS: seer, sear (scorch).

see·saw (sē′sô′) *n.* A play apparatus with a long wooden board balanced on a central support. With a child riding on either end, one goes up as the other goes down. —*intr.v.* **1.** To ride on a seesaw: *The children seesawed in the park.* **2.** To move back and forth or up and down: *The table seesawed back and forth.*

seesaw

seethe (sēth) *intr.v.* **seethed, seeth·ing, seethes. 1.** To churn and foam as if boiling: *The ocean seethed in the storm.* **2.** To be violently agitated: *She seethed with anger.*

see-through (sē′thrōō′) *adj.* (usually used of fabrics). Transparent: *see-through curtains.*

seg·ment (sĕg′mənt) *n.* **1.** A part into which

sthg. is or can be divided; a section or division: *the various segments of American society; segments of an orange.* **2.** The portion of a line between any two of its points: *a line segment.* —*tr. & intr.v.* (sĕg **mĕnt′**). To divide or become divided into segments: *We segmented the cake into ten slices. The orange segmented easily.* —**seg′men•ta′tion** *n.* [U]

seg•re•gate (sĕg′rĭ gāt′) *tr.v.* **seg•re•gat•ed, seg•re•gat•ing, seg•re•gates. 1.** To separate or isolate (sbdy./sthg.) from others or from a group: *segregate the sick children from the others.* **2.** To separate (a race or class) from the rest of society: *In the past, schools segregated African Americans.*

seg•re•ga•tion (sĕg′rĭ gā′shən) *n.* [U] **1.** The act of segregating or the condition of being segregated. **2.** The policy and practice of segregating a race, as in schools, housing, and business, especially to discriminate against people. —**seg′re•ga′tion•ist** *adj. & n.*

seism— *pref.* Variant of **seismo—**.

seis•mic (sīz′mĭk) *adj.* Subject to or caused by an earthquake or earthquakes: *a seismic disturbance.*

seismo— or **seism—** *pref.* A prefix that means earthquake: *seismology.*

seis•mo•graph (sīz′mə grăf′) *n.* An instrument that detects and records movement in the earth's crust.

seis•mol•o•gy (sīz mŏl′ə jē) *n.* [U] The scientific study of earthquakes and other movements of the earth's crust.

seize (sēz) *tr.v.* **seized, seiz•ing, seiz•es. 1.** To grasp (sbdy./sthg.) suddenly and forcibly; take or grab: *The police officer seized his arm.* **2.** To take (sthg.) eagerly: *seize the opportunity to leave.* **3.** To take possession of (sthg.) by force: *The agents seized the drugs.*

sei•zure (sē′zhər) *n.* **1.** [C; U] The act of seizing: *the seizure of illegal drugs.* **2.** [C] A sudden fit or convulsion, as in epilepsy or a heart attack: *She suffered a seizure.*

sel•dom (sĕl′dəm) *adv.* Not often; rarely: *I seldom get ill.*

se•lect (sĭ lĕkt′) *tr.v.* To choose (sbdy./sthg.) from among several; pick out: *Select the nicest shoes.* —*adj.* **1.** Carefully chosen: *a select group of students.* **2.** Of special quality; choice: *a select cut of meat.*

se•lec•tion (sĭ lĕk′shən) *n.* **1.a.** [U] The act of selecting. See Synonyms at **choice**. **b.** [C] A person or thing selected: *He took his selection to the cash register.* **2.** [C] A carefully chosen or representative group of persons or things: *a selection of fine books.* **3.** [C] A literary or musical text chosen for reading or performance: *The next selection is by Mozart.* **4.** [U] A natural process by which certain animals or plants survive and produce offspring, while others die or do not breed: *natural selection.*

se•lec•tive (sĭ lĕk′tĭv) *adj.* **1.** Characterized by careful selection: *selective reading.* **2.**

Tending to select carefully; choosy: *He is very selective about his music.* —**se•lec′tive•ly** *adv.* —**se•lec′tiv′i•ty** (sĭ lĕk′ tĭv′ĭ tē) *n.* [U]

self (sĕlf) *n., pl.* **selves** (sĕlvz). The qualities that distinguish one person from another; individuality: *He's back to his cheerful self.*

self— *pref. (used with a hyphen).* A prefix that means: **1.** Oneself or itself: *self-evident.* **2.** Automatic or automatically: *self-cleaning.*

WORD BUILDING: self— The prefix **self—** usually forms compounds with adjectives, as in **self-conscious, self-employed,** and **self-governing,** and nouns, as in **self-confidence, self-improvement,** and **self-satisfaction,** and indicates sthg. about oneself.

self-ab•sorbed (sĕlf′ əb sôrbd′ *or* sĕlf′əb-zôrbd′) *adj.* So concerned with one's own life and problems that other people are ignored: *"You're very self-absorbed lately. Is something wrong?"*

self-ad•dressed (sĕlf′ ə drĕst′) *adj.* Addressed to oneself: *Include a self-addressed stamped envelope.*

self-ap•pointed (sĕlf′ ə poin′tĭd) *adj.* Believing that oneself is the best to lead or do sthg.: *Well, here comes our self-appointed leader.*

self-as•sured (sĕlf′ ə shoŏrd′) *adj.* Having or showing confidence: *a self-assured and mature person.* —**self′-as•sur′ance** (sĕlf′ə-shoŏr′ əns) *n.* [U]

self-cen•tered (sĕlf′sĕn′tərd) *adj.* Concerned only with one's own needs and interests; selfish: *a self-centered child.* —**self′-cen′tered•ness** *n.* [U]

self-clean•ing (sĕlf′klē′nĭng) *adj.* Describing an oven designed to clean itself: *a self-cleaning oven.*

self-con•fi•dence (sĕlf′kŏn′fĭ dəns) *n.* [U] Confidence in oneself or one's abilities: *He doesn't have much self-confidence.* —**self′-con′fi•dent** *adj.*

self-con•scious (sĕlf′kŏn′shəs) *adj.* **1.** Excessively conscious of one's appearance or manner; socially ill at ease: *a shy and self-conscious person.* **2.** Not natural: *a self-conscious laugh.* —**self′-con′scious•ly** *adv.* —**self′-con′scious•ness** *n.* [U]

self-con•tained (sĕlf′kən tānd′) *adj.* Not needing other things or people to operate or be complete: *She's lived a self-contained life since the divorce.*

self-con•trol (sĕlf′kən trōl′) *n.* [U] Control of one's emotions and behavior by one's own will. —**self′-con•trolled′** *adj.*

self-defeating (sĕlf′dĭ fē′tĭng) *adj.* Doing sthg. in a way that will end up being bad for oneself: *a self-defeating attitude.*

self-de•fense (sĕlf′dĭ fĕns′) *n.* [U] Defense of oneself against attack: *She shot the burglar in self-defense.*

S

self-denial (sĕlf′dĭ nī′əl) *n.* [U] The practice of denying oneself pleasures: *After years of self-denial, she now has time for herself.*

self-de·struc·tive (sĕlf′ dĭ strŭk′tĭv) *adj.* Bringing harm or pain to oneself: *She thinks driving too fast is self-destructive.* —**self′-de·struc′tion** *n.* [U]

self-dis·ci·pline (sĕlf′dĭs′ə plĭn) *n.* [U] Training and control of oneself and one's conduct, usually for personal improvement.

self-em·ployed (sĕlf′ĕm ploid′) *adj.* Earning one's living by working for oneself, rather than for an employer: *a self-employed consultant.*

self-es·teem (sĕlf′ĭ stēm′) *n.* [U] Pride in oneself; self-respect: *a child with low self-esteem.*

self-ev·i·dent (sĕlf′ĕv′ĭ dənt) *adj.* Requiring no proof or explanation: *The answer to that question is self-evident.*

self-ex·plan·a·to·ry (sĕlf′ĭk splăn′ə tôr′ē) *adj.* Requiring no explanation; obvious: *The directions are fairly self-explanatory.*

self-ful·fill·ing prophecy (sĕlf′fŏŏl fĭl′ĭng) *n.* A statement about sthg. in the future that becomes true because sbdy. expected it or acted so as to make it true: *The breakup of his marriage turned out to be a self-fulfilling prophecy.*

self-gov·ern·ment (sĕlf′gŭv′ərn mənt) *n.* [U] Political independence.

self-help (sĕlf′hĕlp′) *n.* [U] The act of helping or improving oneself.

self-i·mage (sĕlf′ĭm′ĭj) *n.* The way a person thinks of her- or himself: *You need to develop a better self-image.*

self-im·por·tance (sĕlf′ĭm pôr′tns) *n.* [U] Too high an opinion of one's own importance or position; conceit. —**self′-im·por′tant** *adj.*

self-im·prove·ment (sĕlf′ĭm prŏŏv′mənt) *n.* [U] Improvement of one's condition through one's own efforts.

self-in·dul·gent (sĕlf′ĭn dŭl′jənt) *adj.* Giving oneself pleasures that are not necessary: *A self-indulgent child can become a selfish adult.* —**self′in·dul′gence** *n.* [U]

self-in·ter·est (sĕlf′ĭn′trĭst *or* sĕlf′ĭn′tər-ĭst) *n.* [U] Selfish concern for one's personal advantage or interest.

self·ish (sĕl′fĭsh) *adj.* **1.** Concerned mainly with oneself with little or no regard for others: *a selfish person.* **2.** Showing lack of regard for others: *a selfish act.* —**self′ish·ly** *adv.* —**self′ish·ness** *n.* [U]

self·less (sĕlf′lĭs) *adj.* Having or showing no concern for oneself; unselfish: *a selfless act of kindness.* —**self′less·ly** *adv.* —**self′less·ness** *n.* [U]

self-made (sĕlf′mād′) *adj.* Having achieved success by one's own efforts: *a self-made woman.*

self-pit·y (sĕlf′pĭt′ē) *n.* [U] Pity for oneself.

self-por·trait (sĕlf′pôr′trĭt *or* sĕlf′pôr′trāt′) *n.* A painting of oneself made by oneself.

self-pos·sessed (sĕlf′pə zĕst′) *adj.* Confident and sure of oneself: *The self-possessed lawyer won over the jury.*

self-pres·er·va·tion (sĕlf′prĕz′ər vā′shən) *n.* [U] **1.** Protection of oneself from harm or destruction. **2.** The instinct for survival.

self-re·li·ance (sĕlf′rĭ lī′əns) *n.* [U] Dependence on one's own abilities or resources. —**self′-re·li′ant** *adj.*

self-re·spect (sĕlf′rĭ spĕkt′) *n.* [U] Proper respect for oneself, one's character, and one's actions. —**self′-re·spect′ing** *adj.*

self-re·straint (sĕlf′rĭ strānt′) *n.* [U] Control of one's emotions or desires; self-control.

self-right·eous (sĕlf′rī′chəs) *adj.* Too proud and sure of one's righteousness: *a self-righteous belief that he is always correct.* —**self′-right′eous·ly** *adv.* —**self′-right′eous·ness** *n.* [U]

self-sac·ri·fice (sĕlf′săk′rə fīs′) *n.* [U] Giving up of one's own interests or well-being for the sake of other people or for a cause. —**self′-sac′ri·fic′ing** *adj.*

self-sat·is·fac·tion (sĕlf′săt′ĭs făk′shən) *n.* [U] Contentment, especially smug contentment, with oneself. —**self′-sat′is·fied′** (sĕlf′săt′ĭs fīd′) *adj.*

self-serv·ice (sĕlf′sûr′vĭs) *adj.* Relating to a business or service in which customers help themselves: *a self-service laundry.*

self-serving (sĕlf′sûr′vĭng) *adj.* Showing concern only for one's own interests: *a speech full of self-serving remarks.*

self-start·er (sĕlf′ stär′tər) *n.* Someone who can work without the help of other people: *They'll do well. Everyone on the project is a self-starter.*

self-styled (sĕlf′stīld′) *adj.* Having assumed a title, role, or status without the right to it: *a self-styled literary critic.*

self-suf·fi·cient (sĕlf′sə fĭsh′ənt) *adj.* Providing for oneself without help; independent: *She is self-sufficient; she pays her own rent and tuition.* —**self′-suf·fi′cien·cy** *n.* [U]

self-sup·port·ing (sĕlf′sə pôr′tĭng *or* sĕlf′sə pôr′tĭng) *adj.* Able to earn enough money to not need any help: *a self-supporting hobby; When did your children become self-supporting?*

self-taught (sĕlf′tôt′) *adj.* Having taught oneself: *a self-taught painter.*

self-wind·ing (sĕlf′wīn′ding) *adj.* Describing a watch designed to wind itself.

sell (sĕl) *v.* **sold** (sōld), **sell·ing, sells.** —*tr.* **1.** To give (sthg.) in exchange for money: *sell a bike.* **2.** To offer (sthg.) for sale: *This store sells health foods.* **3.** To promote

(sthg.): *Advertising sells many products.*
—intr. 1. To engage in selling goods: *That store sells only on weekdays.* **2.** To be sold or to be on sale: *Fruit sells in this store.* **3.** To be popular on the market: *This tape is selling well.* ◆ **sell off.** *tr.v.* [sep.] To get rid of (sthg.) by selling, often at reduced prices: *They sold off their farm and moved to the city.* **sell out.** *tr.v.* [sep.] To put (all of one's goods or possessions) up for sale: *They sold out all of their inventory and closed the store.* **—intr.v.** To betray one's cause or colleagues: *They sold out when they gave up their beliefs for money.*

HOMONYMS: sell, cell (confining room).

sell•er (sĕl′ər) *n.* **1.** A person who sells; a vendor: *a bookseller.* **2.** An item that sells well or poorly: *This dress has been a very good seller.*

HOMONYMS: seller, cellar (basement).

sell•out (sĕl′out′) *n.* **1.** An event for which all tickets have been sold: *The concert was a sellout.* **2.** *Slang.* A person who has betrayed a principle or a cause.

selt•zer (sĕlt′sər) *n.* [C; U] **1.** A naturally bubbly mineral water. **2.** Soda water.

selves (sĕlvz) *n.* Plural of **self.**

se•man•tic (sĭ măn′tĭk) *adj.* Concerned with meaning, especially in language: *a semantic rule.*

se•man•tics (sĭ măn′tĭks) *n.* [U] *(used with a singular or plural verb).* In linguistics, the study of meaning in language forms.

sem•blance (sĕm′bləns) *n.* **1.** The appearance of a feeling, whether it is real or not; show: *keeping up a semblance of happiness.* **2.** A representation; a likeness: *He cupped his hands in the semblance of a bowl.*

se•men (sē′mən) *n.* [U] A whitish fluid that carries sperm cells, produced by the male reproductive organs.

HOMONYMS: semen, seaman (sailor).

se•mes•ter (sə mĕs′tər) *n.* One of two divisions of 15 to 18 weeks each of a school year.

semi— *pref.* A prefix that means: **1.** Half: *semicircle.* **2.** Partial or partially: *semiconscious.* **3.** Happening twice during a specific time: *semiannually.*

sem•i•an•nu•al (sĕm′ē ăn′yōō əl) *adj.* Happening or published twice a year: *semiannual payments; a semiannual magazine.* **—sem′i•an′nu•al•ly** *adv.*

sem•i•ar•id (sĕm′ē ăr′ĭd) *adj.* With little rainfall and able to produce only short grasses and shrubs: *a semiarid region.*

sem•i•au•to•mat•ic (sĕm′ē ô′tə măt′ĭk) *adj.* Relating to a firearm that ejects and loads

ammunition automatically after each shot: *a semiautomatic rifle.* **—n.** A semiautomatic firearm.

sem•i•cir•cle (sĕm′ĭ sûr′kəl) *n.* An arc of 180 degrees; a half circle. **—sem′i•cir′cu•lar** (sĕm′ĭ sûr′kyə lər) *adj.*

sem•i•co•lon (sĕm′ĭ kō′lən) *n.* A punctuation mark (;) used to connect independent clauses and indicating a closer relationship between them than a period does.

sem•i•con•duc•tor (sĕm′ē kən dŭk′tər) *n.* A solid crystalline substance, such as silicon, that conducts electricity less easily than a conductor.

sem•i•con•scious (sĕm′ē kŏn′shəs) *adj.* Partially conscious: *He was semiconscious after the accident.* **—sem′i•con′scious•ly** *adv.* **—sem′i•con′scious•ness** *n.* [U]

sem•i•fi•nal (sĕm′ē fī′nəl) *n.* A game, a competition, or an examination that precedes the final one: *The team lost in the semifinals.* **—sem′i•fi′nal** *adj.* **—sem′i•fi′nal•ist** *n.*

sem•i•month•ly (sĕm′ē mŭnth′lē) *adj.* Happening or published twice a month: *semimonthly visits.* **—n., pl.** **sem•i•month•lies.** A semimonthly publication. **—adv.** Twice a month: *We meet semimonthly.* **—SEE NOTE** at **biweekly.**

sem•i•nar (sĕm′ə när′) *n.* A short course or a special meeting about a particular subject: *We attended a two-day business seminar.*

sem•i•nar•i•an (sĕm′ə nâr′ē ən) *n.* A student at a seminary.

sem•i•nar•y (sĕm′ə nĕr′ē) *n., pl.* **sem•i•nar•ies.** A school for the training of priests, ministers, or rabbis.

sem•i•pre•cious stone (sĕm′ē prĕsh′əs) *n.* A gem, such as topaz, amethyst, or jade, that has commercial value but is less rare and expensive than a precious stone.

sem•i•pro•fes•sion•al (sĕm′ē prə fĕsh′ə nəl) *adj.* Taking part in a sport for pay, but not as a full-time occupation: *a semiprofessional baseball player.*

sem•i•skilled (sĕm′ē skĭld′) *adj.* **1.** Having some skills but not enough to do specialized work: *semiskilled workers.* **2.** Requiring limited skills: *a semiskilled job.*

sem•i•sol•id (sĕm′ē sŏl′ĭd) *adj.* Intermediate between a solid and a liquid. **—n.** (sĕm′ē sŏl′ĭd). A semisolid substance, such as a stiff dough or firm gelatin.

Se•mit•ic (sə mĭt′ĭk) *adj.* **1.** Relating to the Semites or their languages or cultures. **2.** Relating to a division of the Afro-Asiatic languages that includes Hebrew and Arabic. **—n.** [U] The Semitic languages.

sem•i•trail•er (sĕm′ē trā′lər) *n.* A large truck trailer.

sem•i•trop•i•cal (sĕm′ē trŏp′ĭ kəl) *adj.* Partly tropical; subtropical.

sem•i•week•ly (sĕm′ē wēk′lē) *adj.* Happening or published twice a week: *semiweekly* *treatments.* —*adv.* Twice a week. —SEE NOTE at **biweekly.**

sen. or **Sen.** *abbr.* An abbreviation of: **1.** Senate. **2.** Senator. **3.** Senior.

sen·ate (sĕn′ĭt) *n.* **1. Senate.** The upper house of the U.S. Congress, to which two members are elected by the people of each state for a six-year term. **2.** Often **Senate.** The upper house of the legislature in many states and some other countries.

sen·a·tor (sĕn′ə tər) *n.* A member of a senate.

sen·a·to·ri·al (sĕn′ə tôr′ē əl) *adj.* **1.** Relating or appropriate to a senator: *a senatorial decision.* **2.** Made up of senators: *a senatorial advisory group.*

send (sĕnd) *tr.v.* **sent** (sĕnt), **send·ing, sends.** —*tr.* **1.** To cause (sthg.) to be taken to a place: *We sent supplies to the disaster area.* **2.** To dispatch (sthg.), as by mail or telegraph; transmit: *Send me a letter. Send my regards.* **3.** To direct (sbdy./sthg.) to go to a place: *Mom sent me to the store to buy milk.* **4.** To enable (sbdy./sthg.) to go to a place, as by providing money: *She worked hard to send herself to college.* **5.** To hit (sthg.) so as to direct with force: *The batter sent the ball to left field.* **6.** To put (sthg.) into a given condition or kind of behavior: *The accident sent the train passengers into a panic.* ◆ **send away for.** To make a request or place an order for (sthg.), especially by mail: *send away for a catalog.* **send for.** *tr.v.* [insep.] To request (sbdy.) to come by means of a message or messenger; summon: *She sent for her driver.* **send in.** *tr.v.* [sep.] **1.** To send (sthg. for a specific purpose) by mail: *Did you send in your application for graduate school?* **2.** To send (sbdy.) into a place: *The coach sent in subs. The police were sent in.* **send out for.** To ask for sthg. to be delivered: *He sent out for pizza.* —**send′er** *n.*

send·off (sĕnd′ôf′ *or* sĕnd′ŏf′) *n.* A demonstration of affection and good wishes for the beginning of sthg. new: *They gave their son a big sendoff when he went to college.*

se·nile (sē′nīl′ *or* sĕn′īl′) *adj.* Showing or characteristic of senility: *Her dog was so old that he was becoming senile.*

se·nil·i·ty (sĭ nĭl′ĭ tē) *n.* [U] A weakening of mental abilities due to old age.

sen·ior (sēn′yər) *adj.* **1.** Referring to the older of two men, especially the older of two people with the same name, as father and son: *Bob Smith senior is Bob Smith junior's father.* **2.** Being in a higher position than other people in the same company: *a senior editor.* **3.** Relating to the fourth and last year of a high school or college: *the senior class.* —*n.* **1.** A person who is older than another: *My brother*

is my senior by four years. **2.** A senior citizen. **3.** A person in a higher position than another. **4.** A student in the fourth and last year of a high school or college.

senior citizen *n.* A person of or over the age of 65.

senior high school *n.* A high school in the United States and Canada, usually made up of the 10th, 11th, and 12th grades.

sen·ior·i·ty (sēn yôr′ĭ tē *or* sēn yŏr′ĭ tē) *n.* [U] **1.** The condition of being older or of higher rank. **2.** Priority over others, especially because of more years of service with a company: *Workers with the most seniority get longer vacations.*

sen·sa·tion (sĕn sā′shən) *n.* **1.a.** [C; U] A feeling that results from the stimulation of a sense organ or from some condition of the body: *the sensation of heat.* **b.** [U] The ability to feel: *a loss of sensation in the fingers due to cold.* **2.** [C] **a.** A condition of lively public interest and excitement: *News of the first artificial satellite caused a sensation.* **b.** A person, an event, or an object that causes interest, excitement, or admiration: *He is a singing sensation.* See Synonyms at **wonder.**

sen·sa·tion·al (sĕn sā′shə nəl) *adj.* **1.** Causing great interest or excitement, especially by shocking: *a sensational television report.* **2.** Extraordinary; outstanding: *a sensational dinner; a sensational tennis player.* —**sen·sa′tion·al·ly** *adv.*

sen·sa·tion·al·ism (sĕn sā′shə nə lĭz′əm) *n.* [U] The intentional use of sensational subject matter or highly dramatic style, especially in writing, journalism, or politics: *The newspaper was accused of sensationalism in reporting the story.*

sense (sĕns) *n.* **1.** [C] Any of the functions or abilities by which a living thing can perceive or feel its environment or its own internal conditions: *the sense of smell.* **2.** [C] A vague feeling about sthg.; an impression: *I have a sense that our team's going to win.* **3.** [U] Good judgment; practical intelligence: *I had the sense to go to bed early.* **4.** [U] **a.** Speech, thought, or reasoning that is sound and practical: *Talk sense!* **b.** Something reasonable: *We saw no sense in hurrying.* **5.** [C] One of the meanings of a word or phrase: *Words sometimes have many different senses.* **6.** [C] General opinion: *The sense of the group was that we should go ahead.* —*tr.v.* **sensed, sens·ing, sens·es. 1.** To become aware of (sthg.) through the senses: *He sensed an odor in the air.* **2.** To understand (sthg.); grasp: *The teacher sensed that we were confused.* **3.** To detect (sthg.) automatically: *A geiger counter senses radioactivity.* ◆ **come to (one's) senses.** To know what is logical or sensible:

You need to come to your senses! **make sense. 1.** To be understandable: *This memo doesn't make any sense.* **2.** To be logical: *It makes sense to go early if we want good seats.* **sense of humor.** An ability to understand or appreciate humor: *She has a wonderful sense of humor.*

sense•less (sĕns′lĭs) *adj.* **1.** Lacking meaning or sense: *senseless talk; a senseless death.* **2.** Lacking good judgment; foolish: *senseless drivers who cause accidents.* **3.** Unconscious: *The driver was knocked senseless in the accident.* —**sense′less•ly** *adv.*

sen•si•bil•i•ty (sĕn′sə bĭl′ĭ tē) *n., pl.* **sen•si•bil•i•ties.** [C; U] **1.** The ability to feel. **2.** The ability to receive and appreciate sensations and feelings in the mind: *her acute sensibility to the feelings of others.*

sen•si•ble (sĕn′sə bəl) *adj.* **1.** Showing good judgment; reasonable: *a sensible decision; He's not being very sensible about this.* **2.** Appropriate for a specific purpose: *a sensible winter coat.* —**sen′si•ble•ness** *n.* [U] —**sen′si•bly** *adv.*

sen•si•tive (sĕn′sĭ tĭv) *adj.* **1.** Able to perceive with a sense or senses: *Dogs are sensitive to sounds that we cannot hear.* **2.** Affected by an external condition or stimulus: *Photographic film is sensitive to light.* **3.** Responsive to the feelings of other people: *a sensitive and sympathetic listener.* **4.** Quick to take offense; touchy. *He was sensitive about his poor performance in the race.* **5.** Easily irritated: *sensitive skin.* **6.** Designed to indicate or measure small changes of condition: *a sensitive thermometer.* **7.** Requiring careful handling; delicate: *a matter too sensitive to be discussed.* —**sen′si•tive•ly** *adv.* —**sen′si•tive•ness, sen′si•tiv′i•ty** *n.* [U] —**sen′si•tize′** *v.*

sen•sor (sĕn′sər *or* sĕn′sôr′) *n.* A device that responds to a particular type of change in its condition or environment: *heat sensors.*

sen•so•ry (sĕn′sə rē) *adj.* Relating to the senses or sensation: *sensory stimulation; sensory nerves.*

sen•su•al (sĕn′shōō əl) *adj.* **1.** Relating to or giving pleasure to the body; physically gratifying: *the sensual experience of a warm bath.* **2.** Suggesting sexuality; voluptuous: *a sensual woman.* —**sen′su•al′i•ty** (sĕn′shōō ăl′ĭ tē) *n.* [U] —**sen′su•al•ly** *adv.*

sen•su•ous (sĕn′shōō əs) *adj.* **1.** Relating to or coming from the senses: *both a sensuous and an intellectual response to the music.* **2.** Appealing to the senses: *sensuous images.* —**sen′su•ous•ly** *adv.* —**sen′su•ous•ness** *n.* [U]

sent (sĕnt) *v.* Past tense and past participle of **send.**

HOMONYMS: sent, cent (penny), **scent** (smell).

sen•tence (sĕn′təns) *n.* **1.** An independent grammatical unit that has a subject that is either expressed or implied and a predicate with at least one finite verb. For example, *It's almost midnight* and *Stop!* are sentences. **2.a.** The judgment of a court of law; a verdict: *The judge handed down a sentence in the case.* **b.** The penalty given by a court to a convicted person: *a sentence of four years in prison.* —*tr.v.* **sen•tenced, sen•tenc•ing, sen•tenc•es.** To pass sentence upon (a defendant): *The judge sentenced the drug dealer to twenty years.*

sen•ti•ment (sĕn′tə mənt) *n.* **1.** [U] **a.** Emotion; feeling: *Music arouses different kinds of sentiment.* See Synonyms at **feeling. b.** Tender or romantic emotion. **2.** [U] A general attitude or inclination: *His sentiment is to support his home team.* **3.** [C] An opinion; a view: *I expressed my sentiments in favor of the idea.*

sen•ti•men•tal (sĕn′tə mĕn′tl) *adj.* **1.** Relating to the feelings; emotional: *We have a sentimental attachment to this town.* **2.** Marked by emotion that is excessive or foolish: *read a sentimental story.* **3.** Ruled or influenced by one's emotions rather than reason or practicality: *a sentimental man.* —**sen′ti•men•tal′i•ty** (sĕn′tə mĕn tăl′ĭ tē) *n.* [U] —**sen′ti•men′tal•ly** *adv.*

sen•ti•nel (sĕn′tə nəl) *n.* A guard; a sentry.

sen•try (sĕn′trē) *n., pl.* **sen•tries.** A guard, especially a soldier posted at a given spot to prevent the entry of unauthorized persons: *A sentry was posted at the border.*

sep•a•ra•ble (sĕp′ər ə bəl *or* sĕp′rə bəl) *adj.* Capable of being separated: *separable phrasal verbs.*

sep•a•rate (sĕp′ə rāt′) *v.* **sep•a•rat•ed, sep•a•rat•ing, sep•a•rates.** —*tr.* **1.** To put or keep (people/things) apart: *separated the puzzle pieces; I separated the children to stop them from fighting.* **2.** To keep (things) apart by occupying a position between: *the channel that separates Great Britain from France.* **3.** To place (things) in different categories; sort: *separating the list of words into nouns and verbs.* **4.** To make a distinction between (things); distinguish: *It was hard to separate facts from opinion in the editorial.* **5.** To divide (sthg.) into parts: *Draw a line that separates a square into two triangles.* **6.** To end a relationship with (sbdy.); part: *He was separated from his wife.* —*intr.* **1.** To come apart: *The satellite separated upon entry into the earth's atmosphere.* **2.** To withdraw; leave: *The state separated from the Union.* **3.** To part company: *We set out together, then separated at Miami.* **4.** To stop living together as a couple: *His parents separated after twenty years.* **5.** To become removed from a mixture: *The oil separated from the vinegar.* —*adj.* (sĕp′ər ĭt *or* sĕp′rĭt).

1. Set apart from the rest: *Libraries have a separate section for reference books.* **2.** Distinct from others; individual or independent: *a separate treaty between two of the members of the alliance.* —*n.* (**sĕp′ər ĭt** *or* **sĕp′rĭt**). *(usually plural).* A women's garment, such as a skirt, shirt, or pair of slacks, that may be bought separately and worn with other clothes in various combinations: *The store is having a sale on women's separates.* —**sep′a·rate·ly** *adv.*

SYNONYMS: separate, divide, part, sever. These verbs mean to cause to become disconnected or disunited. **Separate** means to put apart or to keep apart: *A mountain range separates France and Spain.* **Divide** means to separate by cutting, splitting, or branching into parts: *The orange was divided into segments.* **Part** often means to separate closely associated people or things: *A difference of opinion parted the old friends.* **Sever** often means to divide or end sthg. abruptly and violently: *The United States severed diplomatic relations with Cuba in 1961.*

sep·a·ra·tion (sĕp′ə rā′shən) *n.* **1.** [U] **a.** The act or process of separating: *the separation of cream from milk.* **b.** The condition of being separated: *her separation from the rest of the runners.* **2.** [C] An intervening space; a gap: *a separation between electrical circuits.* **3.** [C] A legal agreement by which a husband and wife live apart.

sep·a·ra·tist (sĕp′ər ə tĭst *or* sĕp′rə tĭst) *n.* **1.** A person who believes in the withdrawal of a group from a larger group, as from a political union or an established church. **2.** A person who believes in cultural, ethnic, or racial separation.

Sept. or **Sept** *abbr.* An abbreviation of September.

Sep·tem·ber (sĕp tĕm′bər) *n.* The ninth month of the year, with 30 days.

sep·tic (sĕp′tĭk) *adj.* Relating to or caused by the presence of disease-causing microorganisms or their toxins in the blood: *septic conditions of infection.*

septic tank *n.* An underground tank in which sewage is decomposed by bacteria.

sep·ul·cher (sĕp′əl kər) *n.* A burial tomb.

se·quel (sē′kwəl) *n.* **1.** A book or film complete in itself but continuing the story of an earlier work: *That movie is a sequel.* **2.** A thing or an event that follows; a continuation.

se·quence (sē′kwəns) *n.* **1.** [U] A following of one thing after another; succession: *the sequence of events.* **2.** [C] The order in which things or events occur or are arranged: *I followed the sequence of steps outlined in the*

book. **3.** [C] A related or continuous series: *a sequence of events that led to war.*

se·ques·ter (sĭ kwĕs′tər) *tr.v.* To cause (sbdy.) to go to a private place; seclude: *He sequestered himself in his room to think over what had happened.* —**se′ques·tra′tion** *n.* [U]

se·quin (sē′kwĭn) *n.* A small shiny disk or spangle, often sewn on cloth or clothes for decoration. —**se′quined** *adj.*

se·quoi·a (sĭ kwoi′ə) *n.* A very large cone-bearing evergreen tree of parts of Oregon and California; the redwood.

ser·e·nade (sĕr′ə nād′ *or* sĕr′ə nād′) *n.* A musical performance given to honor or express love for sbdy.: *He surprised his girlfriend with a serenade.* —*tr.v.* **ser·e·nad·ed, ser·e·nad·ing, ser·e·nades.** To perform a serenade for (sbdy.): *He serenaded her in the garden.*

ser·en·dip·i·tous (sĕr′ ən dĭp′ə təs) *adj.* Related to or happening through luck or good fortune: *a serendipitous discovery of gold.* —**ser′en·dip′i·tous·ly** *adv.*

ser·en·dip·i·ty (sĕr′ ən dĭp′ĭ tē) *n.* [U] The talent for making fortunate discoveries by accident.

se·rene (sə rēn′) *adj.* **1.** Peaceful; tranquil: *the serene face of a sleeping child.* See Synonyms at **calm. 2.** Unclouded; clear and bright: *serene skies.* —**se·rene′ly** *adv.*

se·ren·i·ty (sə rĕn′ĭ tē) *n.* [U] The quality of being serene; tranquillity.

serf (sûrf) *n.* A member of a class of laborers in Europe in the past who were considered property like the land where they lived and worked. —**serf′dom** *n.* [U]

HOMONYMS: serf, surf (waves).

ser·geant (sär′jənt) *n.* **1.** A noncommissioned officer in the U.S. Army, Air Force, or Marine Corps holding any of several ranks just below lieutenant. **2.** A police officer ranking below a captain, a lieutenant, or an inspector.

se·ri·al (sîr′ē əl) *adj.* **1.** Arranged in or forming a series: *serial publication.* **2.** Presented in installments: *a serial television drama.* —*n.* A story or play presented in installments: *Soap operas are serials.* —**se′ri·al·ly** *adv.*

HOMONYMS: serial, cereal (grain).

se·ri·al·ize (sîr′ē ə līz′) *tr.v.* **se·ri·al·ized, se·ri·al·iz·ing, se·ri·al·iz·es.** To write or publish (sthg.) in installments: *serialize a novel in a magazine.*

serial number *n.* A number that is one of a series of numbers and often letters and that is

ă-cat; ā-pay; âr-care; ä-father; ĕ-get; ē-be; ĭ-sit; ī-nice; îr-here; ŏ-got; ō-go; ô-saw; oi-boy; ou-out; ōō-took; ōō-boot; ŭ-cut; ûr-word; th-thin; *th*-this; hw-when; zh-vision; ə-about; N-French bon

used for identification, as of a machine: *The serial number of a car legally identifies it.*

se·ries (sîr'ēz) *n., pl.* **series.** A number of similar things or events that follow one another; a succession: *a series of storms.*

se·ri·ous (sîr'ē əs) *adj.* **1.** Thoughtful and sincere: *She gave me a serious look.* **2.** Deeply interested or involved: *a serious musician.* **3.** Intended to cause deep thought or emotion: *a serious play.* **4.** Not joking: *I'm serious. I'm leaving now.* **5.** Causing concern or anxiety: *a serious illness.* —**se'ri·ous·ly** *adv.* —**se'ri·ous·ness** *n.* [U]

ser·mon (sûr'mən) *n.* **1.** A talk on a religious subject given as part of a church service. **2.** A solemn, lengthy, and boring talk: *He had to listen to his father's sermon.* —**ser'mon·ize'** *v.*

ser·pent (sûr'pənt) *n.* **1.** A snake. **2.** A sly or treacherous person.

ser·pen·tine (sûr'pən tēn' *or* sûr'pən tīn') *adj.* **1.** Resembling or typical of a serpent: *serpentine movements.* **2.** Having many bends or curves: *a serpentine river.*

ser·rat·ed (sĕr'ā'tĭd) *adj.* Having an edge with notched projections resembling teeth: *a serrated knife.*

se·rum (sîr'əm) *n.* [C; U] **1.** A liquid extracted from the tissues of an immunized animal, used as a vaccine. **2.** The clear yellowish liquid obtained when all solid particles are removed from whole blood.

ser·vant (sûr'vənt) *n.* **1.** A person, such as a cook or housekeeper, who works for pay in the household of sbdy. else. **2.** A person publicly employed to perform services for the community: *police and other public servants.*

serve (sûrv) *v.* **served, serv·ing, serves.** —*tr.* **1.a.** To work for (sbdy./sthg.): *The mayor serves the city.* **b.** To be a servant to (sbdy.): *The soldiers served the king.* **2.a.** To prepare and offer (food): *serve dinner.* **b.** To provide food for (sbdy.): *serving the children first.* **3.** To provide goods and services for (customers), as in a store or restaurant. **4.** To assist or promote (sthg.): *serving the national interest.* **5.** To spend (a period of time) in fulfillment of an obligation: *He served 12 years in the Senate.* **6.** To give military service to (one's country, for example): *She served her country in the army.* **7.** To be used profitably by (sbdy./sthg.): *The airport serves a wide region.* **8.** To put (a ball, for example) in play by hitting it, as in tennis: *She served the ball.* —*intr.* **1.** To do a term of duty: *He served in the Air Force during the war.* **2.** To act in a given capacity: *serve as a clerk.* **3.** To be of use; function: *Let this serve as a reminder.* —*n.* The right to serve or the manner or act of serving a ball or shuttlecock: *a tennis player with a strong serve.* ◆ **serve (one) right.** To be deserved under the circumstances: *He has to pay a big fine for park-*

ing in a space reserved for the handicapped; *it serves him right.*

serv·er (sûr'vər) *n.* **1.** A person who serves food and drink; a waiter or waitress. **2.** Something, such as a tray or a bowl, used in serving food. **3.** A computer that provides information or services to other computers in a network: *a Web server.*

serv·ice (sûr'vĭs) *n.* **1.** [C; U] Work or employment for another or others: *Dad retired after years of loyal service.* **2.** [C] A branch of the government and its employees: *the diplomatic service.* **3.** [C] The armed forces or a branch of the armed forces: *Her brother joined the service.* **4.** [C; U] Work or duties done for another, as for a superior or a client: *provides full catering service; the services of a doctor.* **5.** [C; U] Installation, maintenance, or repairs provided by a dealer or manufacturer: *a warranty good for service for one year.* **6.** [U] A facility providing the public with use of sthg.: *Is there telephone service in this building?* **7.** [C] An act that helps another or others: *performing a valuable service for the family.* **8.a.** [U] The act or manner of serving food or fulfilling the needs of customers: *a hotel with poor service.* **b.** [C] A set of dishes and table utensils for serving and eating food: *a service for eight persons.* **9.** [C] A religious ceremony: *a church service.* —*tr.v.* **serv·iced, serv·ic·ing, serv·ic·es. 1.** To maintain or repair (sthg.): *The mechanic serviced my car.* **2.** To provide services to (sbdy./ sthg.): *Our business services the entire city.* —*adj.* **1.** Relating to the armed forces: *a service medal.* **2.** Reserved for the use of employees rather than the general public: *a service entrance to a hotel.* **3.** For the maintenance and repair of products sold: *a service guarantee.* **4.** Concerned with the serving of customers: *a service manager of a department store.*

serv·ice·a·ble (sûr'vĭ sə bəl) *adj.* **1.** Ready or fit for service; usable: *a serviceable old car.* **2.** Wearing well; sturdy: *serviceable work boots.* —**serv'ice·a·bil'i·ty** *n.* [U] —**serv'ice·a·bly** *adv.*

service charge *n.* An extra fee for a service: *The ticket agency adds a service charge of two dollars to the price of each ticket purchased.*

serv·ice·man (sûr'vĭs măn') *n.* **1.** A man who is a member of the armed forces. **2.** Also **service man.** A man whose job is to maintain and repair equipment. —**serv'ice·wom'an, service woman** (sûr'vĭs woॱŏm'ən) *n.*

service station *n.* A business that sells gasoline and often repairs motor vehicles.

ser·vile (sûr'vəl *or* sûr'vīl') *adj.* Acting like a servant: *a servile employee.*

serv·ing (sûr'vĭng) *n.* A single portion of food or drink; a helping: *three servings a day of fruits and vegetables.*

S

ser·vi·tude (sûr′vĭ tood′) *n.* [U] The condition of being a slave or serf.

ses·a·me (sĕs′ə mē) *n.* [U] The small flat seeds of a tropical Asian plant, used as food and as a source of oil.

ses·sion (sĕsh′ən) *n.* **1.** A period of time during the day or year when a school holds classes: *a summer session.* **2.** A meeting of a group to do or discuss sthg. of common interest: *a recording session; a gossip session.* **3.** A meeting or series of meetings of a government body: *a legislative session.*

set¹ (sĕt) *v.* **set, set·ting, sets.** —*tr.* **1.** To put (sbdy./sthg.) in a specified position; place: *set the book on the table; set the baby in her chair.* **2.** To put (sbdy./sthg.) in a specified condition: *setting him at liberty; set the wagon in motion.* **3.** To place (sthg.) in a firm or unmoving position: *set the post in concrete.* **4.** To put (a broken or dislocated bone) back in a proper or normal state. **5.** To adjust (an instrument, tool, or other device) to some desired condition of operation: *set the television to channel eight; set a mousetrap.* **6.** To arrange tableware on (a table) or at (a place) in preparation for a meal: *It's your turn to set the table.* **7.** To arrange (sthg.) in a certain manner: *set her hair with curlers; set a newspaper story for printing.* **8.** To compose music to fit (a text): *set a poem to music.* **9.** To represent (sthg.) as happening in a certain place or at a certain time: *The author set her story in Detroit.* **10.** To fix or establish (sthg.): *setting an example; set a record.* **11.** To decide on (sthg.): *They set June 9 as the date for the wedding.* **12.** To give (sbdy.) a certain task or position: *Our boss set us to work.* —*intr.* **1.** To disappear behind the horizon: *The sun sets in the west.* **2.** To become solid, hard, or fixed: *The builders poured the concrete and gave it time to set.* —*adj.* **1.** Fixed and established: *a set purpose.* **2.** Unwilling to change: *set in her ways.* **3.** Determined; intent: *He's set against going.* **4.** Ready: *We are set to leave in the morning.* —*n.* The manner in which sthg. is set: *the set of his cap.* ◆ **set about (doing).** To begin or start (sthg.): *She quickly set about solving the problem.* **set apart.** *tr.v.* [sep.] **1.** To reserve (sthg.) for a specific use: *money set apart to pay for college.* **2.** To make (sbdy./sthg.) different or noticeable: *characteristics that set them apart.* **set aside.** *tr.v.* [sep.] **1.** To separate and reserve (sthg.) for a special purpose: *He set aside a piece of cake for his wife.* **2.** To discard or reject (sbdy./sthg.): *He felt that management had set him aside in favor of a younger man.* **set back.** *tr.v.* [sep.] **1.** To slow down the progress of (sbdy./sthg.): *Bad weather set back the construction schedule.* **2.** *Informal.* To cost

(sbdy.): *That house must have set them back half a million dollars.* **set down.** *tr.v.* [sep.] **1.** To put (sthg.) in writing; record: *set down his thoughts in a letter.* **2.** To assign (sthg.) to a cause: *Let's set the mistake down to inexperience.* **set fire to.** To cause (sthg.) to start to burn: *Someone set fire to the building.* **set forth.** *tr.v.* [sep.] To present (sthg.) for consideration: *set forth a plan.* —*intr.v.* *Formal.* To start on a journey. **set in.** *intr.v.* To begin to happen or be apparent: *A storm was just setting in.* **set off.** *tr.v.* [sep.] **1. a.** To cause (sthg.) to happen: *set off a chemical reaction.* **b.** To cause (sthg.) to explode: *set off fireworks.* **2.** To direct attention to (sthg.) by contrast; accentuate: *set off a passage in the book by highlighting it in yellow.* —*intr.v.* To start on a journey: *set off for Mecca.* **set out.** *intr.v.* **1.** To begin an effort: *set out to solve the problem.* **2.** To start a journey: *We'll set out at sunrise.* —*tr.v.* [sep.] To display (sthg.) for exhibition or sale: *set out shoes in a store window.* **set sail.** To begin a voyage on water: *The boat set sail at dawn.* **set store by.** To think of (sthg.) as valuable: *I set great store by your opinion.* **set straight.** To correct (sbdy./sthg.) by giving full and accurate information: *He told his story publicly to set the record straight.* **set the pace.** To go at a speed or perform in a way that other competitors attempt to match or surpass. **set the stage for.** To provide the basis for (sthg.): *A series of conflicts set the stage for war.* **set up.** *tr.v.* [sep.] **1.** To assemble or erect (sthg.): *set up a stereo system.* **2.** To create or establish (sthg.): *set up a business.* **3.** To establish (sbdy.) in business by providing money, equipment, or other support: *Their parents set them up with a small store.* **4.** *Informal.* To put (sbdy.) into a difficult situation by trickery: *When the robber was surprised by the police, he realized that his partner had set him up.*

USAGE: set¹ The verb **set** is usually transitive and has an object: *He sets the table.* **Sit** is generally intransitive and has no object: *She sits at the table.* There are some exceptions: *The sun sets* (not *sits*). *A hen sets* (or *sits*) *on her eggs.*

set² (sĕt) *n.* **1.** A group of matching or related things that form a unit: *a set of dishes; a chess set.* **2. a.** The scenery built for a theatrical performance. **b.** The area in which a movie is filmed: *The director ordered quiet on the set.* **3.** The collection of parts that make up a television: *a new TV set.* **4.** In mathematics, a collection of distinct elements that have sthg. in common: *the set of all positive integers.* **5.** In tennis and other sports, a group of games

S

that forms one unit or part of a match: *She won the set.*

set•back (sĕt′băk′) *n.* A sudden reverse in progress; a change from better to worse: *The patient has suffered a setback and is not expected to live.*

set•ter (sĕt′ər) *n.* **1.** Any of several breeds of dog with smooth silky hair, often trained and used in hunting. **2.** A person or thing that sets: *a typesetter.*

set theory *n.* The mathematical study of the properties of sets.

set•ting (sĕt′ĭng) *n.* **1.** The way in which a control is set: *Change the setting on the heater, please.* **2.a.** A surrounding area; an environment: *animals in a natural setting.* **b.** The place where a story or movie takes place: *the setting for a novel.* **3.** A framework or border, as of precious metal, in which a jewel is firmly fixed: *a ruby in a gold setting.* **4.a.** The plates and eating utensils arranged on a table: *a lavish table setting.* **b.** A matched set of different sizes and types of dishes or eating utensils: *a five-piece place setting.* **5.** The act of setting: *the setting of the moon.*

set•tle (sĕt′l) *v.* **set•tled, set•tling, set•tles.** —*tr.* **1.** To put (sthg.) into order; fix: *settle the problem with the bank.* **2.** To put (sbdy.) securely into a desired position or place: *She settled herself by the fire.* **3.** To establish (sbdy.) as a resident or residents: *settled her family in Utah.* **4.** To establish residence in (a region): *pioneers who settled the West.* **5.** To restore calmness or comfort to (sbdy./sthg.): *The music settled her nerves.* **6.** To make compensation for (a claim): *The insurance company settled the claim for the accident.* **7.** To end or resolve (sthg.): *settle a dispute.* **8.** To decide (a lawsuit) by mutual agreement: *The two sides settled the lawsuit.* —*intr.* **1.** To stop moving and come to rest in one place: *Geese settled next to the river.* **2.** To descend or sink gradually: *Dust settled on the road.* **3.** To establish one's home: *settled in Mexico.* **4.** To reach a decision: *We finally settled on a solution to the problem.* ♦ **settle down.** *intr.v.* **1.** To begin living a stable and orderly life: *She decided to settle down and marry.* **2.** To become less nervous or restless: *The teacher asked the children to settle down.* **settle for.** *tr.v.* [insep.] To accept (sthg.) in spite of incomplete satisfaction: *That old car is not what I wanted, but I guess I'll settle for it.*

set•tle•ment (sĕt′l mənt) *n.* **1.** [U] The act of settling: *the settlement of differences; land open to settlement.* **2.** [C] A small community: *a settlement in the desert.* **3.** [C] An adjustment or understanding reached, as in business or finance: *They agreed on a settlement.*

set•tler (sĕt′lər) *n.* A person who settles in a new region.

set•up (sĕt′ŭp′) *n.* **1.** The way sthg. is organized or planned: *the setup of the new com-*

puter. **2.** A situation created to trick or trap sbdy.: *The robbery was a setup.*

sev•en (sĕv′ən) *n.* **1.** The number, written 7, that is equal to 6 + 1. **2.** The seventh in a set or sequence. —**sev′en** *adj. & pron.*

sev•en•teen (sĕv′ən tēn′) *n.* **1.** The number, written 17, that is equal to 16 + 1. **2.** The 17th in a set or sequence. —**sev′en•teen′** *adj. & pron.*

sev•en•teenth (sĕv′ən tēnth′) *n.* **1.** The ordinal number matching the number 17 in a series. **2.** One of 17 equal parts: *One seventeenth of 170 is ten.* —**sev′en•teenth′** *adj. & adv.*

sev•enth (sĕv′ənth) *n.* **1.** The ordinal number matching the number seven in a series. **2.** One of seven equal parts: *One seventh of 70 is ten.* —**sev′enth** *adj. & adv.*

Sev•enth-day Ad•ven•tist (sĕv′ənth dā′ ăd′vĕn′tĭst) *n.* A member of a Christian sect of Adventists who observe the Sabbath on Saturday.

sev•en•ty (sĕv′ən tē) *n., pl.* **sev•en•ties. 1.** The number, written 70, that is equal to 7 × 10. **2. seventies. a.** Often **Seventies.** The ten years from 70 to 79 in a century. **b.** A decade or the numbers from 70 to 79: *She's in her seventies.* —**sev′en•ty** *adj. & pron.*

sev•er (sĕv′ər) *tr.v.* **1.** To divide or separate (sthg.): *The Civil War severed the Union.* See Synonyms at **separate. 2.** To cut or break (sthg.) off from a whole: *sever a branch from a tree.*

sev•er•al (sĕv′ər əl *or* sĕv′rəl) *pron.* (used with a plural verb). An indefinite but small number; some or a few: *He saw several of his classmates.* —*adj.* Numbering more than two or three but not many: *several miles away.*

sev•er•ance (sĕv′ər əns *or* sĕv′rəns) *n.* [U] **1.** The act of severing: *the severance of political ties.* **2.** Severance pay: *She collected severance.*

severance pay *n.* [U] Extra pay given an employee when that person's job is ended: *two week's severance pay.*

se•vere (sə vîr′) *adj.* **se•ver•er, se•ver•est. 1.** Harsh or strict: *a severe law.* **2.** Grim or stern in manner or appearance: *a severe voice.* **3.** Causing great distress; sharp: *a severe pain.* **4.** Very serious or difficult; extreme: *severe damage.* —**se•vere′ly** *adv.* —**se•ver′i•ty** (sə vĕr′ĭ tē) *n.* [U]

sew (sō) *v.* **sewed, sewn** (sōn) *or* **sewed, sew•ing, sews.** —*tr.* To make or repair (sthg.) by stitching, as with a needle and thread or a sewing machine: *sew a new dress; sew up a seam.* —*intr.* To work with a needle and thread or a sewing machine: *She likes to sew.* ♦ **sew up.** *tr.v.* [sep.] *Informal.* To complete (sthg.) successfully: *Our volleyball team sewed up the championship.* —**sew′er** *n.*

HOMONYMS: sew, so (thus), **sow¹** (plant seeds).

sew•age (sōō′ĭj) *n*. [U] Liquid and solid waste carried away in sewers or drains.

sew•er[1] (sōō′ər) *n*. An underground pipe or channel built to carry away sewage or rainwater.

sew•er[2] (sō′ər) *n*. A person or thing that sews: *a sewer of fine clothing.*

sew•ing (sō′ĭng) *n*. [U] **1.** The act, occupation, or hobby of one who sews. **2.** The article on which a person is working with needle and thread.

sewing machine *n*. A machine for making or fixing clothing or similar items.

sewn (sōn) *v*. A past participle of **sew.**

sex (sĕks) *n*. **1.** [C] Either of two divisions, male and female, into which most organisms are grouped; a gender: *What sex is the kitten?* **2.** [U] The combination of characteristics that are typical of each of these two groups: *Sex is often marked by physical differences in size.* **3.** [C] The condition or character of being male or female: *the opposite sex.* **4.** [U] Sexual intercourse: *have sex.*

sex•ism (sĕk′sĭz′əm) *n*. [U] Discrimination based on sex, especially discrimination against women. —**sex′ist** *adj.* & *n.*

sex•tant (sĕk′stənt) *n*. A navigation instrument used to measure the altitude between the horizon and a celestial body.

sex•tet (sĕk stĕt′) *n*. **1.a.** A musical composition for six voices or instruments. **b.** A group of six musicians who perform such a composition. **2.** A group of six persons or things.

sex•ton (sĕk′stən) *n*. A person employed to take care of a church and its property.

sex•u•al (sĕk′shōō əl) *adj*. **1.** Affecting or typical of sex, sexuality, the sexes, or the sex organs and their functions: *sexual development.* **2.** Involving the union of male and female sex cells: *sexual reproduction.* —**sex′u•al•ly** *adv.*

sexual harassment *n*. [U] Unwanted and offensive sexual behavior or remarks, especially in the workplace: *She accused her employer of sexual harassment.*

sexual intercourse *n*. [U] Intimate physical contact between humans, usually involving insertion of the penis into the vagina.

sex•u•al•i•ty (sĕk′shōō ăl′ĭ tē) *n*. [U] **1.** A person's biological sex. **2.** The expression of a person's sexual feelings.

Sgt. *abbr.* An abbreviation of sergeant.

sh (sh) *interj*. An expression used to urge sbdy. to be silent: *Sh! No talking in the library.*

shab•by (shăb′ē) *adj*. **shab•bi•er, shab•bi•est. 1.** Dressed in old or worn-out clothes: *a shabby dresser.* **2.** Worn-out, frayed, and faded; threadbare: *shabby dress.* **3.** Old and

run-down; deteriorated: *shabby houses.* **4.** Despicable or unfair; mean: *shabby treatment.* —**shab′bi•ly** *adv.* —**shab′bi•ness** *n*. [U]

shack (shăk) *n*. A small crudely built cabin.

shack•le (shăk′əl) *n*. *(usually plural).* **1.** A metal ring fastened or locked around the wrist or ankle of a prisoner: *a prisoner in shackles.* **2.** Something that limits action or progress: *the shackles of ignorance.* —*tr.v.* **shack•led, shack•ling, shack•les. 1.** To put shackles on (sbdy.): *shackle a prisoner.* **2.** To confine, restrain, or limit (sbdy.): *shackle our imagination.*

shade (shād) *n*. **1.** [U] An area or a space of partial darkness: *shade under a tree.* **2.** [U] Cover or shelter from the sun or its rays: *Let's sit in the shade.* **3.** [C] A device used to reduce light or heat, as from the sun: *a window shade.* **4.** [C] The degree to which a color is mixed with black: *a deeper shade of red.* **5.** [C] A slight difference: *a shade of meaning.* **6.** [C] A small amount; a trace: *a shade under forty miles.* **7. shades.** *Informal.* Sunglasses. **8. shades.** Reminders; echoes: *shades of 1776.* —*tr.v.* **shad•ed, shad•ing, shades. 1.** To screen (sbdy./sthg.) from light or heat: *Trees shaded the street.* **2.** To represent or produce degrees of shade or shadow in (a drawing or painting): *The artist shaded the drawing.*

shad•ing (shā′dĭng) *n*. [U] **1.** A screening against light or heat. **2.** The lines or other marks used in a drawing or painting to represent changes in color or darkness.

shad•ow (shăd′ō) *n*. **1.** The image made by an object blocking rays of light: *shadows of leaves on the wall.* **2.** An imperfect imitation or copy: *a shadow of the original.* **3. shadows.** Darkness: *She waited in the shadows.* **4.** A person, such as a detective or spy, who follows another in secret. —*tr.v.* **1.** To cast a shadow on (sbdy./sthg.); shade: *The trees shadowed the walkway.* **2.** To follow after (sbdy./sthg.), especially in secret; trail: *The detective shadowed the suspect.* ♦ **afraid of (one's) own shadow.** Afraid of everything: *My brother is afraid of bugs, mice, and scary movies; he's even afraid of his own shadow!* **without** or **beyond a shadow of a doubt.** Without any doubt: *Without a shadow of a doubt, you should accept the job.*

shad•ow•y (shăd′ō ē) *adj*. **shad•ow•i•er, shad•ow•i•est. 1.** Resembling a shadow: *shadowy forms moving underwater.* **2.** Full of or dark with shadows: *shadowy woods.* See Synonyms at **dark. 3.** Vague; indistinct: *shadowy ideas.*

shad•y (shā′dē) *adj*. **shad•i•er, shad•i•est. 1.** Full of shade; shaded: *a shady street.* See Synonyms at **dark. 2.** Dishonest; ques-

S

tionable: *a shady deal.* —**shad′i•ly** *adv.*
—**shad′i•ness** *n.* [U]

shaft (shăft) *n.* **1.** A ray or beam of light: *a shaft of light.* **2.** The handle of any of various tools or implements: *the shaft of a hammer.* **3.** A long bar, especially one that turns and transmits power: *the drive shaft of an engine.* **4.** The long narrow body of a spear or an arrow. **5.** A long narrow passage or tunnel: *a mine shaft.* —*tr.v. Slang.* To cheat or mistreat (sbdy.): *His girlfriend shafted him.* ◆ **get the shaft.** *Slang.* To be cheated or ignored: *He didn't get promoted this year; he really got the shaft from his boss.*

shag•gy (shăg′ē) *adj.* **shag•gi•er, shag•gi•est. 1.** Having, covered with, or resembling long rough hair or wool: *a shaggy dog.* **2.** Rough and bushy: *shaggy hair.*

shah (shä) *n.* Used formerly as a title for the king of Iran.

shake (shāk) *v.* **shook** (sho͝ok), **shak•en** (shā′kən), **shak•ing, shakes.** —*tr.* **1.** To move or cause (sbdy.) to move back and forth with jerky movements: *The wet dog shook itself.* **2.** To cause (sbdy./sthg.) to tremble or vibrate: *The earthquake shook the ground.* **3.** To cause (sbdy./sthg.) to change an idea or belief: *Nothing could shake him from his belief.* **4.** To remove (sthg.) by jerky movements: *shake snow from the boots.* **5.** To make (sbdy.) uneasy; disturb: *The bad news shook her.* **6.** To wave (sthg.), especially in anger: *shake one's fist.* **7.** To clasp (hands) in greeting or leave-taking or as a sign of agreement: *They shook hands when they met.* —*intr.* **1.** To move back and forth in short, often jerky, movements: *The house shook in the storm.* **2.** To tremble, as from cold, fear, illness, or anger: *Her voice shook.* **3.** To shake hands: *Let's shake on it.* —*n.* **1.** The act of shaking: *a shake of the head.* **2.** A trembling or vibrating movement: *a shake in her hands.* **3.** A beverage mixed by shaking, especially a milk shake: *She ordered a chocolate shake.* **4. shakes.** *Informal.* Uncontrollable trembling: *I have the shakes from being so tired.* ◆ **shake a leg.** *Informal.* To hurry: *Let's shake a leg and leave for school now!*

shake off. *tr.v.* [sep.] To free oneself of (sthg.); get rid of: *We shook off our fears.*

shake up. *tr.v.* [sep.] **1.** To upset (sbdy.) by or as if by a physical jolt or shock: *The bad news shook us up.* **2.** To rearrange or reorganize (sthg.) completely: *The new director decided to shake up the entire organization.*

shak•er (shā′kər) *n.* A container used for shaking: *a salt shaker.*

shake•up (shāk′ŭp′) *n.* A major change or reorganization: *a shakeup of government personnel.*

shak•y (shā′kē) *adj.* **shak•i•er, shak•i•est. 1.** Trembling or quivering: *a shaky voice.* **2.** Unsteady or unsound: *a shaky old*

dock. **3.** Not to be depended on: *a shaky agreement.* —**shak′i•ly** *adv.*

shall (shăl) *aux.v.* past tense **should** (sho͝od). *Formal.* **1.** Used to express future action or condition: *I shall return tomorrow.* **2.** Used to express an order, a promise, a requirement, or an obligation: *You shall pay for your misdeeds.* **3.** Used to express determination: *I shall go if I want to.*

shal•low (shăl′ō) *adj.* **1.** Measuring little from the bottom to the top or surface; not deep: *a shallow lake; a shallow pan.* **2.** Lacking depth of thought, feeling, or knowledge; superficial: *shallow ideas.* —*n. (usually plural).* A shallow part of a body of water: *The children went swimming in the shallows.* —**shal′low•ly** *adv.* —**shal′low•ness** *n.* [U]

sham (shăm) *n.* Something false that is presented as genuine; a fraudulent imitation: *The contest turned out to be a sham.* —*adj.* Fake; not genuine: *sham jewels.*

sha•man (shä′mən *or* shā′mən) *n.* In certain societies a person who acts as an intermediary with the spirit world and who heals people and foretells future events.

sham•bles (shăm′bəlz) *n. (used with a singular verb).* A condition of great disorder or destruction: *The room was a shambles.*

shame (shām) *n.* **1.** [U] A painful emotion caused by a strong sense of guilt, embarrassment, or disgrace. **2.** [U] Capacity for such an emotion: *Have you no shame?* **3.** [C] A source of disgrace or embarrassment: *It's a shame that none of you offered to help the strangers.* **4.** [C] A great disappointment: *It would be a shame to miss the party.* —*tr.v.* **shamed, sham•ing, shames. 1.** To bring disgrace upon (sbdy./sthg.): *The incident shamed their good name.* **2.** [into] To force (sbdy.) by arousing a feeling of shame or guilt: *He was shamed into making an apology.* ◆ **put to shame.** To perform far better than (sbdy.); surpass: *Her high grades put the rest of us to shame.*

shame•ful (shām′fəl) *adj.* Causing shame; disgraceful: *shameful behavior.* —**shame′-ful•ly** *adv.*

shame•less (shām′lĭs) *adj.* **1.** Feeling no shame: *a shameless liar.* **2.** Marked by a lack of shame: *a shameless lie.* —**shame′less•ly** *adv.*

sham•poo (shăm po͞o′) *n., pl.* **sham•poos.** [C; U] **1.** A type of liquid soap used to wash the hair and scalp: *He tried a new shampoo.* **2.** A type of cleaner for rugs, upholstery, or cars: *rug shampoo.* **3.** The act of washing the hair or cleaning sthg. with shampoo: *I need a shampoo.* —*tr. & intr.v.* To wash or be washed with shampoo: *The man shampooed his daughter's hair. I'll shampoo in the shower.*

sham•rock (shăm′rŏk′) *n.* A clover or similar plant with three leaves on each stem, regarded as the national emblem of Ireland.

S

shan't (shănt). *Formal.* Contraction of *shall not.*

shan•ty (shăn′tē) *n., pl.* **shan•ties.** A roughly built cabin; a shack.

shape (shāp) *n.* **1.** The outward appearance of a thing; a form. **2.** Something distinguished from its surroundings by its outline: *dark shapes on the horizon.* **3.** The outline of a person's body, especially a woman's body; the figure: *a good shape.* **4.** A desirable form: *a fabric that holds its shape.* **5.** A form in which sthg. may appear: *relief in the shape of food and medical supplies.* —*tr.v.* **shaped, shap•ing, shapes. 1.** To give a certain shape or form to (sthg.): *shape clay into bowls.* **2.** To change (sthg.) to a particular shape or form; mold: *shape a sculpture out of ice.* **3.** To direct the course of (sthg.): *shaping a child's education.* ♦ **in** or **out of shape.** In or out of proper physical condition: *an athlete out of shape.*

shape up. *intr.v. Informal.* **1.** To turn out; develop: *I wondered how the game was shaping up.* **2.** To improve so as to meet a standard: *If you don't shape up, you'll fail this class.*

shape•less (shāp′lĭs) *adj.* **1.** Having no definite form or shape: *a shapeless cloud.* **2.** Lacking a pleasing shape; not shapely: *a shapeless dress.* —**shape′less•ly** *adv.* —**shape′less•ness** *n.* [U]

shape•ly (shāp′lē) *adj.* **shape•li•er, shape•li•est.** *(used especially of women).* Having a shape that is pleasing to look at; well-proportioned: *a shapely leg.* —**shape′li•ness** *n.* [U]

shard (shärd) *n.* A piece or fragment, as of glass or metal: *She stepped on a shard of glass.*

share (shâr) *n.* **1.** A part belonging to or contributed by a person or group; a portion: *He received a share of the profits. She paid her share of dinner.* **2.** A fair or full portion: *She did her share to make the play a success.* **3.** Any of the equal parts into which the capital stock of a business is divided: *buy 100 shares of stock.* —*v.* **shared, shar•ing, shares.** —*tr.* **1.** To divide and distribute (sthg.): *The little girl shared her cookie.* **2.** To use or experience (sthg.) in common with other people: *sharing the responsibility; share a room.* **3.** To tell or present (sthg.) to others: *He shared his adventure with the class.* —*intr.* To participate: *We shared in working on the project.* —**shar′er** *n.*

share•hold•er (shâr′hōl′dər) *n.* A person who owns shares in the stock of a company; a stockholder.

shark (shärk) *n.* **1.** Any of numerous often large and dangerous ocean fish with sharp teeth and tough skin. **2.** A person regarded as ruthless, greedy, or dishonest: *a loan shark.*

sharp (shärp) *adj.* **1.** With a thin edge or fine point for cutting or piercing: *a sharp razor; a sharp needle.* **2.** With an edge or a point: *sharp rocks.* **3.** Clear in form and detail: *a sharp image.* **4.** Sudden; not gradual: *a sharp drop to the sea.* **5.** Very accurate in understanding or use of the senses: *a sharp mind; the sharp eyes of a falcon.* **6.** Clever: *a sharp businessman.* **7.** Harshly critical: *a sharp tongue.* **8.a.** Sudden and forceful: *a sharp blow.* **b.** Felt suddenly and intensely: *a sharp pain.* **9.** With a strong odor and flavor: *a sharp cheese.* **10.** Higher in musical pitch than a natural tone or key: *a C sharp.* **11.** *Informal.* Stylish or attractive: *a sharp dresser.* —*adv.* **1.** In a sharp manner: *Look sharp when you cross the street.* **2.** Promptly; exactly: *at 3 o'clock sharp.* **3.** Above the correct pitch: *Nervousness caused him to sing sharp.* —*n.* **1.** A musical note or tone that is a half step higher than the natural note or tone. **2.** The symbol (♯) attached to a note to show that it is a sharp. —**sharp′ly** *adv.* —**sharp′ness** *n.* [U]

sharp•en (shär′pən) *tr. & intr.v.* To make or become sharp or sharper: *I sharpened the knife. The blade sharpens easily.* —**sharp′en•er** *n.*

sharp•shoot•er (shärp′shōō′tər) *n.* A person expert at shooting a gun.

shat•ter (shăt′ər) *v.* —*tr.* **1.** To cause (sthg.) to break suddenly into pieces; smash: *She shattered the glass by dropping it.* **2.** To destroy (sthg.) beyond hope of repair; ruin: *The loss of his job shattered his hopes.* —*intr.* To break into pieces; smash: *The glass shattered.* See Synonyms at **break.**

shave (shāv) *v.* **shaved, shaved** or **shav•en** (shā′vən), **shav•ing, shaves.** —*tr.* **1.a.** To remove hair from (sbdy./sthg.), especially with a razor: *shave a man's face.* **b.** To cut (the beard or hair) at the surface of the skin with a razor: *He shaved his beard off.* **2.** To cut thin slices from (sthg.): *shaving beef into thin slices.* —*intr.* To cut hair, especially the hair on a man's face, at the surface of the skin with a razor: *He shaves every morning.* —*n.* The act, process, or result of shaving: *a smooth shave.*

shav•er (shā′vər) *n.* A device for shaving, especially an electric razor.

shav•ing (shā′vĭng) *n.* **1.** [C] *(usually plural).* A thin slice or sliver, as of wood or metal: *wood shavings.* **2.** [U] The action of a person that shaves: *He hated shaving, so he grew a beard.*

shawl (shôl) *n.* A large piece of cloth worn as a covering for the shoulders or head.

she (shē) *pron.* **1.** The woman or girl previously mentioned: *Nancy left, but she will be back.* **2.** The female animal previously mentioned: *Our cat likes fish, but she won't eat*

ă-cat; ā-pay; âr-care; ä-father; ĕ-get; ē-be; ĭ-sit; ī-nice; îr-here; ŏ-got; ō-go; ô-saw; oi-boy; ou-out; ōō-took; ōō-boot; ŭ-cut; ûr-word; th-thin; *th*-this; hw-when; zh-vision; ə-about; N-French bon

chicken. —*n.* A female person or animal: *Is the baby a he or a she?*

sheaf (shēf) *n., pl.* **sheaves** (shēvz). A collection of things held or bound together: *a sheaf of papers.*

shear (shîr) *tr.v.* **sheared, sheared** or **shorn** (shôrn), **shear·ing, shears. 1.** To remove the hair from (sthg.): *shearing a sheep.* **2.** To cut (sthg.) with or as if with shears: *shearing a garden hedge.* —*n. (usually plural).* A pair of scissors or a similar cutting tool: *kitchen shears.* —**shear′er** *n.*

sheath (shēth) *n., pl.* **sheaths** (shēthz *or* shēths). **1.** A case into which the blade of a knife or sword fits. **2.** A similar covering. —*tr.v.* To sheathe (sthg.): *He sheathed his pen.*
sheathe (shēth) *tr.v.* **sheathed, sheath·ing, sheathes.** To insert (sthg.) into or provide (sthg.) with a sheath or protective covering: *sheathe a sword.*
sheaves (shēvz) *n.* Plural of **sheaf.**
shed¹ (shĕd) *v.* **shed, shed·ding, sheds.** —*tr.* **1.** To rid oneself of (sthg.): *He shed his clothes and jumped into the pool.* **2.** To send (sthg.) forth; give off: *The moon shed a pale light on the lake.* **3.** To repel (sthg.): *This coat sheds water.* **4.** To lose (sthg.) by a natural process: *Many trees shed their leaves in autumn. Snakes shed their skins.* **5.** To cause (sthg.) to pour forth: *shed tears; Cats shed hair.* —*intr.* To lose an outer covering of hair or skin by a natural process: *My dog sheds all the time.*
shed² (shĕd) *n.* A small structure for storage or shelter: *a tool shed.*
she'd (shĕd). Contraction of *she had* or *she would.*
sheen (shēn) *n.* Glistening brightness; luster: *the sheen of a new car.*
sheep (shēp) *n., pl.* **sheep.** Any of various hoofed mammals with a thick fleecy coat, widely raised for their wool, meat, and skin.
♦ **black sheep.** Someone who is not liked or appreciated by a group: *My cousin is the black sheep of the family.*

sheep

sheep·dog also **sheep dog** (shēp′dôg′ *or* shēp′dŏg′) *n.* A dog trained to guard and herd sheep.
sheep·herd·er (shēp′hûr′dər) *n.* A person who herds sheep; a shepherd.
sheep·ish (shē′pĭsh) *adj.* **1.** Embarrassed, as by being aware of a mistake: *a sheepish grin.* **2.** Meek or stupid: *a sheepish follower.* —**sheep′ish·ly** *adv.* —**sheep′ish·ness** *n.* [U]
sheer (shîr) *adj.* **1.** Thin, fine, and transparent: *sheer stockings.* **2.** Complete: *She dropped from sheer exhaustion.* **3.** Almost perpendicular; steep: *sheer cliffs.*

sheet (shēt) *n.* **1.** A large piece of cloth, used as a bed covering, especially in pairs, one under and one over the sleeper: *a new set of sheets for the bed.* **2.** A broad, thin, usually rectangular piece of material: *a sheet of paper; a sheet of metal.* **3.** A broad continuous expanse of material covering a surface: *a sheet of ice.*
sheet metal *n.* [U] Metal that has been rolled into a sheet.
sheet music *n.* [U] Music printed on individual sheets of paper.
sheik also **sheikh** (shēk *or* shāk) *n.* **1.** The leader of an Arab family or village. **2.** A Muslim religious official.

shelf (shĕlf) *n., pl.* **shelves** (shĕlvz). **1.** A flat rectangular piece of wood, metal, or glass, fastened at right angles to a wall or other vertical surface and used to hold or store objects: *a bookshelf; a kitchen shelf.* **2.** An object resembling a shelf, as a flat ledge of rock on a cliff.
shell (shĕl) *n.* **1.a.** The usually hard outer covering of certain animals, such as mollusks, insects, and turtles: *The turtle hid inside its shell. We collected shells on the beach.* **b.** A similar hard outer covering on an egg or nut: *Throw the eggshells in the trash.* **2.** An outer covering resembling a shell: *a pastry shell for a pie.* **3.** A projectile or piece of ammunition, especially the hollow tube containing explosives. —*v.* —*tr.* **1.** To remove the shells of (sthg.): *shell peanuts.* **2.** To fire shells at (sthg.): *shell a city.* ♦ **shell out.** *tr.v.* [sep.] *Informal.* To hand (payment) over; pay: *We had to shell out fifty dollars for the food.* —**shelled** *adj.*
she'll (shēl). Contraction of *she will* or *she shall.*
shell·fish (shĕl′fĭsh′) *n.* [U] A water animal, such as a clam or lobster, that has a shell: *Do you like to eat shellfish?*
shel·ter (shĕl′tər) *n.* **1.** [C; U] Something that provides cover or protection: *We used a*

tent as a shelter for the night. **2.** [C] An institution providing temporary housing: *a homeless shelter; an animal shelter.* —*tr.v.* To provide cover or protection for (sbdy./sthg.): *The trees sheltered us from the storm.*

shelve (shĕlv) *tr.v.* **shelved, shelv•ing, shelves. 1.** To place or arrange (sthg.) on a shelf: *We shelved the books according to author.* **2.** To put (sthg.) aside as though on a shelf; postpone: *The committee shelved the plans.*

shelves (shĕlvz) *n.* Plural of **shelf.**

shelv•ing (shĕl′vĭng) *n.* [U] Material for shelves.

she•nan•i•gan (shə năn′ĭ gən) *n. Informal. (usually plural).* A playful trick or prank: *Stop your shenanigans and sit down!*

shep•herd (shĕp′ərd) *n.* A person who herds, guards, and tends sheep. —*tr.v.* To herd, guard, tend, or guide (animals) in the manner of a shepherd. See Synonyms at **guide.**

sher•bet (shûr′bĭt) *n.* [C; U] A frozen fruit dessert: *lime sherbet.*

sher•iff (shĕr′ĭf) *n.* A law enforcement officer in a U.S. county.

sher•ry (shĕr′ē) *n., pl.* **sher•ries.** [C; U] An amber-colored dry or sweet Spanish wine.

she's (shēz). Contraction of *she is* or *she has.*

shield (shēld) *n.* **1.** A person or thing that provides protection: *She raised her arm as a shield against the bright light.* **2.** An emblem or a badge: *a police shield.* **3.** A piece of armor carried on the arm for protection against weapons. —*tr.v.* To protect (sbdy./ sthg.) with or as if with a shield: *She shielded the baby from the sun.* See Synonyms at **defend.**

shift (shĭft) *v.* —*tr.* **1.** To exchange (sthg.) for another of the same class: *The coach shifted game plans.* **2.** To move (sbdy./sthg.) from one place or position to another; transfer: *shift workers to another plant.* **3.** To change (gears), as in driving a car: *Shift gears as the car slows.* —*intr.* **1.** To change position, direction, place, or form: *The wind shifted suddenly.* **2.** To shift gears, as when driving a car: *She shifted into reverse.* —*n.* **1.** A change from one person or setup to another; a substitution: *a shift in plans for the party.* **2.** The period of time in which a group of workers are on duty at the same time, as at a factory: *the 9-to-5 shift.* **3.** A change in direction, attitude, judgment, or emphasis: *a shift in the wind; a shift toward greater tolerance.* **4.** A change in position: *a shift from one foot to the other.* ◆ **shift for (oneself).** To provide for one's needs; get along: *I can shift for myself.*

shift•less (shĭft′lĭs) *adj.* Lacking ambition or purpose; lazy: *a shiftless dog.* —**shift′-less•ly** *adv.*

shift•y (shĭf′tē) *adj.* **shift•i•er, shift•i•est.** Evasive or untrustworthy; deceitful: *a shifty character.* —**shift′i•ly** *adv.*

shil•ling (shĭl′ĭng) *n.* A coin used in the United Kingdom, worth one twentieth of a pound, 5 new pence, or 12 old pence prior to 1971.

shim•mer (shĭm′ər) *intr.v.* **1.** To shine with a flickering light; glimmer: *Candles shimmered in the windows.* **2.** To appear as a wavering or flickering image: *Heat waves shimmered on the road ahead.* —*n.* A flickering light; a glimmer: *the candles' shimmer.*

shim•my (shĭm′ē) *n., pl.* **shim•mies.** Abnormal vibration or movement back and forth, as of the wheels of an automobile: *My car has developed a bad shimmy.* —*intr.v.* **shim•mied, shim•my•ing, shim•mies.** To vibrate abnormally: *The whole car shimmies now.*

shin (shĭn) *n.* The front part of the leg below the knee and above the ankle. —*v.* **shinned, shin•ning, shins.** —*tr.* To climb (sthg.) by gripping and pulling with hands and legs: *shinning a tree.* —*intr.* To climb sthg. by shinning it: *She shinned up.*

shin•dig (shĭn′dĭg′) *n. Informal.* A large party, often with dancing.

shine (shīn) *v.* **shone** (shōn) or **shined, shin•ing, shines.** —*intr.* **1.** To emit or reflect light: *The sun shone on the mountains. We polished the table until it shone.* **2.** To distinguish oneself in an activity; excel: *Our band shines when we play the songs we know best.* **3.** To be apparent: *Happiness shone in his eyes.* —*tr.* **1.** To aim the beam of (a light): *Shine your flashlight over here.* **2.** *past tense and past participle* **shined.** To make (sthg.) glossy or bright by polishing: *Shine your shoes for school.* —*n.* **1.** [U] Brightness from a source of light; radiance: *the shine of headlights.* **2.** [C] Excellence in quality or appearance; splendor: *Her hair has a healthy shine.* **3.** [C] A shoeshine: *I need to get a shine.* ◆ **rain or shine.** Whatever the weather happens to be: *We'll have a picnic, rain or shine.* **take a shine to.** *Informal.* To like (sbdy.) at once: *The students took a shine to the new teacher.* —**shin′i•ness** *n.* [U] —**shin′y** *adj.*

shin•er (shī′nər) *n. Slang.* A black eye: *I got a shiner when I walked into the door.*

shin•gle (shĭng′gəl) *n.* **1.** *(usually plural).* A thin oblong piece of wood or other material laid in overlapping rows to cover the roof or sides of a building: *new roof shingles.* **2.** A small signboard, such as one hung outside the office of a professional: *The dentist hung out her shingle.* —*tr.v.* **shin•gled, shin•gling, shin•gles.** To cover (a roof or wall) with shingles: *The workers shingled the roof.*

ă–cat; ā–pay; âr–care; ä–father; ĕ–get; ē–be; ĭ–sit; ī–nice; îr–here; ŏ–got; ō–go; ô–saw; oi–boy; ou–out; o͞o–took; o͞o–boot; ŭ–cut; ûr–word; th–thin; *th*–this; hw–when; zh–vision; ə–about; N–French bon

shin·ny (shĭn′ē) *intr.v.* **shin·nied** (shĭn′ēd), **shin·ny·ing, shin·nies** (shĭn′ēz). [*up*] To climb by shinning: *shinny up a pole.*

Shin·to (shĭn′tō) *n.* [U] The traditional religion of the Japanese, marked by worship of ancestors and a lack of formal doctrine. —**Shin′to·ism** *n.* —**Shin′to·ist** *adj. & n.*

ship (shĭp) *n.* **1.** A large vessel for traveling over deep water. **2.** An aircraft or a spacecraft. **3.** A ship's crew: *Most of the ship was on deck.* —*tr.v.* **shipped, ship·ping, ships.** To send or transport (sbdy./sthg.): *shipping goods by truck.* ◆ **ship out.** *intr.v.* To leave, as for a distant place: *The sailors shipped out for Japan.* —*tr.v.* [sep.] To send (sbdy./sthg.), as to a distant place: *We shipped the package out last week.*

—**ship** *suff.* A suffix that means: **1.** Condition or quality: *friendship.* **2.** Rank or office: *professorship.* **3.** Art, skill, or craft: *penmanship.* **4.** A collective body: *readership.*

WORD BUILDING: —ship The suffix **—ship** has a long history in English. In the past, **—ship** was attached frequently to adjectives and nouns to indicate a particular state or condition: **hardship, friendship.** Today the suffix is added only to nouns and usually indicates a state or condition (**authorship, kinship, partnership, relationship**), the qualities belonging to a class of human beings (**craftsmanship, horsemanship, sportsmanship**), or rank or office (**ambassadorship**).

ship·ment (shĭp′mənt) *n.* **1.** [U] The act or an instance of shipping goods: *wheat for shipment abroad.* **2.** [C] A quantity of goods shipped together: *a new shipment of automobiles.*

ship·per (shĭp′ər) *n.* A person or company in the business of transporting or receiving goods.

ship·ping (shĭp′ĭng) *n.* [U] **1.** The act or business of transporting goods: *She's in shipping.* **2.** The body of ships belonging to one port, industry, or country: *French shipping.*

ship·shape (shĭp′shāp′) *adj.* Neatly arranged; in good order: *I want your room shipshape.* See Synonyms at **neat.**

ship·wreck (shĭp′rĕk′) *n.* **1.** The destruction of a ship, as by storm or collision. **2.** A wrecked ship. —*tr.v.* **1.** To cause (a ship) to be destroyed. **2.** To cause (sbdy.) to suffer shipwreck.

shirk (shûrk) *tr.v.* To avoid or neglect (a task or duty): *Don't shirk your household chores.* —**shirk′er** *n.*

shirt (shûrt) *n.* A garment for the upper part of the body, generally having a collar, sleeves, and a front opening.

shish ke·bab (shĭsh′ kə bŏb′) *n.* Pieces of seasoned meat and sometimes vegetables roasted on skewers.

shiv·er (shĭv′ər) *intr.v.* To shake with or as if with cold; tremble: *The kitten shivered under a bush.* —*n.* **1.** An instance of shivering: *She gave a shiver when the ghost appeared.* **2. the shivers.** Fear; disgust: *Snakes give me the shivers.*

shoal (shōl) *n.* A shallow place in a body of water, especially where sandbanks are located.

shock (shŏk) *n.* **1.** [C] A violent collision or impact; a heavy blow: *the shock of a volcano erupting.* **2.** [C] Something that upsets the mind or emotions as if with a violent unexpected blow: *the shock of his sister's death.* **3.** [U] A reaction to severe bodily injury, usually consisting of a loss of blood pressure and a slowing down of vital functions: *The accident victim went into shock.* **4.** [C] The sensation and muscular spasm caused by the passage of an electric current through the body or a body part: *I got a shock from the lamp's cord.* —*tr.v.* **1.** To surprise and disturb (sbdy.) greatly: *Princess Diana's death shocked the world.* **2.** To offend (sbdy.): *Her language shocked the group.* **3.** To give (sbdy./sthg.) an electric shock: *She was shocked by the iron.* —**shock′er** *n.*

shock·ing (shŏk′ĭng) *adj.* **1.** Highly disturbing emotionally: *I found that horror movie shocking.* **2.** Highly offensive; distasteful or indecent: *a shocking story.* —**shock′ing·ly** *adv.*

shock wave *n.* A wave formed through air, water, or the ground caused by explosions or objects moving at supersonic speeds.

shod (shŏd) *v.* Past tense and a past participle of **shoe.**

shod·dy (shŏd′ē) *adj.* **shod·di·er, shod·di·est. 1.** Of poor quality: *shoddy toys; a shoddy job.* **2.** Dishonest: *shoddy salesmen.*

shoe (shōō) *n.* **1.** An outer covering for the human foot, especially one of a pair having a rigid sole and heel and a flexible upper part. **2.** A horseshoe. **3.** The part of a brake that presses against a wheel or drum to slow its motion. —*tr.v.* **shod** (shŏd), **shod, shoe·ing, shoes.** To furnish or fit (sbdy./sthg.) with shoes: *shoe a horse.* ◆ **be in (one's) shoes.** *Informal.* To be in a person's place or position: *I'm glad I wasn't in his shoes when the boss caught him sleeping on the job.* **if the shoe fits, wear it.** If a description is accurate, don't deny it: *She was shocked when she was called a cheat, but I told her if the shoe fits, wear it.*

HOMONYMS: shoe, shoo (scare away).

shoe·horn (shōō′hôrn′) *n.* A curved implement, often of plastic or metal, used at the heel to help put on a shoe.

shoe·lace (shōō′lās′) *n.* A string or cord used for lacing and fastening shoes.

shoe·string (shōō′strĭng′) *n.* A shoelace. —*adj.* Consisting of a small amount of money: *a shoestring budget.* ◆ **on a shoe-**

S

string. With a small amount of money: *The company started out on a shoestring.*

shone (shōn) *v.* A past tense and a past participle of **shine.**

shoo (shōō) *interj.* An expression used to scare away animals or birds. —*tr.v.* To drive or scare (sbdy./sthg.) away by or as if by saying "shoo": *We shooed the children off to bed.*

shook (shŏŏk) *v.* Past tense of **shake.**

shoot (shōōt) *v.* **shot** (shŏt), **shoot·ing, shoots.** —*tr.* **1.a.** To hit, wound, or kill (sbdy./sthg.) with a weapon: *shoot a deer.* **b.** To fire (a gun, bow, or similar weapon): *shoot a gun at a target.* **c.** To fire (a bullet, arrow, or other missile) from or as if from a weapon: *shoot an arrow into the air; shoot a rocket toward the moon.* **2.** To force (sthg.) to move in a rapid stream or flow: *a volcano shooting lava.* **3.** To pass swiftly through (sthg.): *shooting the rapids on the Colorado River.* **4.a.** To record (sthg.) on film: *shot a scene for a movie.* **b.** To use (film) to take pictures. **5.** To throw or propel (a ball or puck, for example) in a specific direction or toward the goal: *She shot the ball at the goal.* —*intr.* **1.** To fire a missile from a weapon: *The captain ordered the soldiers not to shoot.* **2.** To appear or come out suddenly: *The sun shot through a break in the clouds.* **3.** To move quickly: *He shot across the street between the cars.* **4.** To take pictures or begin filming a scene in a movie: *The film studio will be shooting next week.* **5.** To propel a ball or other object toward the goal: *He shot at the goal and missed.* —*n.* A plant or plant part, such as a stem, leaf, or bud, that has just begun to grow or develop. —*interj.* A mild expression to show surprise, annoyance, or disappointment: *Shoot! I forgot my wallet.* ◆ **shoot down.** *tr.v.* [sep.] **1.** To bring down (an aircraft, for example) by hitting it with gunfire or a missile: *The plane was shot down over the ocean.* **2.** *Informal.* To ruin the hopes of (sbdy.): *He invited her to the dance, but she shot him down.* **3.** *Informal.* To put an end to (sthg.); defeat: *The boss shot down the proposal.* **shoot for** or **at.** *tr.v.* [insep.] *Informal.* To strive or aim for (sthg.); have as a goal: *The company is shooting for annual sales of one million.* **shoot up.** *intr.v.* **1.** *Informal.* To grow or get taller rapidly: *The corn shot up in July.* **2.** To increase dramatically in amount: *Prices have shot up.* **3.** *Slang.* To inject a drug into oneself with a needle. —**shoot′er** *n.*

shoot·ing star (shōō′tĭng) *n.* A meteor.

shop (shŏp) *n.* **1.** A small store: *a candy shop.* **2.** A workshop: *She has her shop in the basement.* —*intr.v.* **shopped, shop·ping, shops.** To visit stores to look at or buy things: *shopping for new shoes.* ◆ **set up shop.** To start a business: *My father set up shop and sold hardware in this town for years.* **shop around.** *intr.v.* **1.** To go from store to store in search of merchandise or bargains: *Let's shop around before we decide on a car.* **2.** To look for sthg., such as a better job: *He's shopping around for a better offer.* **talk shop.** To talk about one's work: *Let's not talk shop at lunch today.* —**shop′per** *n.*

shop·keep·er (shŏp′kē′pər) *n.* A person who owns or manages a shop.

shop·lift (shŏp′lĭft′) *v.* —*intr.* To steal merchandise from a store: *They were known to shoplift.* —*tr.* To steal (sthg.) from a store: *He shoplifted a pen and was arrested.*

shop·ping center (shŏp′ĭng) *n.* A group of stores, restaurants, and other businesses with a common parking lot and often in the same building.

shop·talk (shŏp′tôk′) *n.* [U] **1.** Talk or conversation about one's business: *Shoptalk is out of place at a party.* **2.** The jargon used in a specific business or field: *the shoptalk of dentists.*

shore¹ (shôr) *n.* [C; U] **1.** The land along the edge of a body of water. **2.** (*usually plural*). Land within national boundaries: *immigrants who came to these shores.*

shore² (shôr) *v.* **shored, shor·ing, shores.** ◆ **shore up** *tr.v.* [sep.] To support (sbdy./sthg.) by or as if by a prop: *shore up a sagging floor.*

shore·line (shôr′līn′) *n.* The edge of a body of water.

shorn (shôrn) *v.* A past participle of **shear.**

short (shôrt) *adj.* **1.a.** With little length; not long: *a short street.* **b.** With little height; not tall: *a short building.* **2.** Covering a small distance: *a short walk.* **3.** Lasting a brief time: *a short vacation.* **4.** Not sufficient in length or amount: *The ladder is 2 feet short. I'm short of money.* **5.** Relating to the vowel sounds in words such as *pat, pet, pit, pot, putt,* and *put.* **6.** Brief and impolite in speaking: *He was very short with the salesclerk.* **7.** Easily angered: *a short temper.* —*adv.* **1.** Abruptly; quickly: *I hit the car in front when the driver stopped short.* **2.** Before a given point or goal: *The arrow fell short of the target.* —*n.* A short circuit: *The electrician looked for the short.* —*v.* ◆ **for short.** As an abbreviation: *His name is Joseph, but he's called "Joe" for short.* **in short.** In summary; briefly: *In* short, you need to send in the forms as soon as possible. **short for.** An abbreviation of: *"Jo" is short for "Joanna."* **short of. 1.** Less than: *Nothing short of winning satisfies her.* **2.** Other than: *Nothing short of a police siren would have caught their attention.* **short out.** *tr.v.* [sep.] To cause a short circuit in (an electric circuit): *He accidentally shorted out the T.V.* —*intr.v.* To short-circuit: *The hair dryer shorted out.* —**short′ness** *n.* [U]

short•age (shôr′tĭj) *n.* [C; U] A lack in the amount needed; a deficiency: *a food shortage.*

short•bread (shôrt′brĕd′) *n.* [U] A cookie made of flour, sugar, and a lot of butter.

short•cake (shôrt′kāk′) *n.* [C; U] A dessert consisting of a biscuit or light cake served with fruit and often topped with whipped cream: *strawberry shortcake.*

short•change (shôrt′chānj′) *tr.v.* **short•changed, short•chang•ing, short•chang•es. 1.** To give (sbdy.) less change than is due: *The cashier in the supermarket short-changed me.* **2.** *Informal.* To swindle, cheat, or trick (sbdy.): *That car dealer shortchanges customers.* **3.** To underestimate (oneself): *Don't shortchange yourself.* —**short′chang′er** *n.*

short circuit *n.* A path that allows most of the current in an electric circuit to flow around or away from the principal elements or devices in the circuit.

short-cir•cuit (shôrt′sûr′kĭt) *v.* —*tr.* To cause (sthg.) to have a short circuit: *Rain short-circuited my car's ignition system.* —*intr.* To become affected with a short circuit: *The car is short-circuiting.*

short•com•ing (shôrt′kŭm′ĭng) *n.* An inadequacy; a flaw: *Try to ignore his shortcomings as a person.*

short•cut (shôrt′kŭt′) *n.* **1.** A route that is quicker or more direct than the one usually taken: *Let's take a shortcut to school.* **2.** A way of saving effort or time: *homework shortcuts.*

short•en (shôr′tn) *tr. & intr.v.* To make or become short or shorter: *shorten the work week; The days shorten in late summer.*

short•en•ing (shôr′tn ĭng *or* shôrt′nĭng) *n.* [U] A solid fat, usually made from vegetable oil, used to make cake or pastry.

short•fall (shôrt′fôl′) *n.* The amount by which a supply is less than expected or needed: *a shortfall of cash.*

short•hand (shôrt′hănd′) *n.* [U] A system of rapid handwriting using symbols to represent words, phrases, and letters.

short-hand•ed (shôrt′hăn′dĭd) *adj.* Lacking the usual or necessary number of employees, players, workers, or assistants: *I had to work overtime because the office was shorthanded last week.*

short-lived (shôrt′līvd′ *or* shôrt′lĭvd′) *adj.* Living or lasting only a short time: *a short-lived flower; short-lived happiness.*

short•ly (shôrt′lē) *adv.* **1.** In a short time; soon: *We will leave shortly.* **2.** In a few words; briefly: *To put it shortly, we've got to finish now or not at all.* **3.** In a rude or abrupt way: *"Why shouldn't I?" Charles demanded rather shortly.*

short-range (shôrt′rānj′) *adj.* **1.** Made for use over short distances: *short-range airlines.* **2.** Relating to the near future: *short-range goals.*

shorts (shôrts *or* shôrts) *pl.n.* Short pants with legs that end at or above the knee: *gym shorts.*

short•sight•ed (shôrt′sī′tĭd) *adj.* **1.** Near-sighted; not having clear vision of distant objects. **2.** Lacking foresight: *The city's plans were shortsighted and failed to account for population growth.* —**short′sight′ed•ly** *adv.* —**short′sight′ed•ness** *n.* [U]

short story *n.* A short piece of fiction.

short-tem•pered (shôrt′tĕm′pərd) *adj.* Easily losing one's temper; quickly angered: *Careful, he's short-tempered before lunch.*

shot¹ (shŏt) *n.* **1.** The shooting of a gun or similar weapon: *a rifle shot.* **2.** An attempt to score in a game: *The player had a shot at the goal.* **3.** *Informal.* A chance; a try: *He had a shot at a good job.* **4.** A bullet or other ammunition: *A shot ripped through the door.* **5.** A person who shoots, considered with regard to accuracy: *He is the best shot on the hockey team.* **6.a.** A photograph. **b.** A single, continuously photographed scene or view in a movie. **7.** An injection with a needle: *a shot of penicillin.* **8.** A drink of liquor that measures 1½ ounces. ◆ **a shot in the arm.** Something positive that increases confidence: *Winning a game was a shot in the arm for our team.* **a shot in the dark.** *Informal.* A wild guess: *I didn't know the answer, so I took a shot in the dark.* **big shot.** An important person: *a big shot from Hollywood.* **like a shot.** Very quickly: *I was out of that old house like a shot.*

shot² (shŏt) *v.* Past tense and past participle of **shoot.**

shot•gun (shŏt′gŭn′) *n.* A long gun, often used for hunting.

shot put *n.* [U] An athletic event in which participants throw a heavy metal ball as far as possible. —**shot′-put′ter** (shŏt′pŏŏt′ər) *n.*

should (shŏŏd) *aux.v.* Past tense of **shall. 1.** Used to express obligation or duty: *You should send her a note.* **2.** Used to express probability or expectation: *They should arrive at noon.* **3.** Used to express condition as opposed to present fact: *If they should call while I'm out, tell them I'll be right back.*

shoul•der (shōl′dər) *n.* **1.** The part of the body between the neck and upper arm. **2.** The part of a piece of clothing that covers the shoulder: *Your jacket is too big in the shoulders.* **3.** The edge or border running on either side of a roadway: *The car ran off the shoul-*

S

der of the road. —*tr.v.* **1.** To place (sbdy./ sthg.) on the shoulder or shoulders for carrying: *The woman shouldered the basket.* **2.** To take on (sthg.); bear: *shouldering the blame for the others.* —*intr.* To push with the shoulders. ◆ **a shoulder to cry on.** Someone who shows concern and listens to problems: *His best friend gave him a shoulder to cry on.*
shoulder to shoulder. 1. Side by side: *stand shoulder to shoulder.* **2.** In close cooperation: *They work shoulder to shoulder.*
should·n't (shŏŏd′nt). Contraction of *should not.*
shout (shout) *n.* A loud call: *We heard a shout from the street.* —*tr. & intr.v.* To say with or produce a shout: *The captain shouted orders. The coach shouted at the players.* ◆ **shout down.** *tr.v.* [sep.] To silence (sbdy.) by shouting loudly: *She tried to object, but everyone else shouted her down.*

SYNONYMS: shout, holler, howl, roar, yell. These verbs all mean to say with or make a loud, strong cry: *The children shouted and ran around the playground. She hollered a warning at the trespassers. The cook dropped the hot grease on his foot and howled with pain. The audience roared with laughter at the clowns. My neighbor yelled at the children who ran through her yard.*

---

shove (shŭv) *v.* **shoved, shov·ing, shoves.** —*tr.* **1.** To push (sbdy./sthg.) forward or along: *She shoved the table against the wall.* **2.** To push (sbdy.) roughly or rudely: *The shoppers started shoving each other.* —*intr.* To push a person or thing along: *Please stop shoving; you'll get your turn.* —*n.* The act of shoving; a push: *Give my car a shove so I can start it.*
shov·el (shŭv′əl) *n.* A tool with a handle and a wide scoop or blade for digging and moving material, such as dirt or snow. —*v.* —*tr.* **1.** To move or remove (sthg.) with a shovel: *shovel snow.* **2.** To clear or make (sthg.) with a shovel: *shovel the walk; shovel a path.* **3.** To place, throw, or move (sthg.) as if with a shovel: *shoveling food into his mouth.* —*intr.* To dig or work with a shovel: *After the blizzard, we shoveled for hours.*

shovel

show (shō) *v.* **showed, shown** (shōn) or **showed, show·ing, shows.** —*tr.* **1.a.** To cause or allow (sbdy./sthg.) to be seen: *She showed them her new computer programs.*

The dog showed its teeth. **b.** To present (sthg.) in public exhibition, for sale, or in competition: *show goods in a store.* **2.** To point out (sthg.) to sbdy.: *Show him the way.* **3.** To give a sign of (sthg.): *His expression showed interest.* **4.** To guide (sbdy.): *She showed us around the village.* **5.** To demonstrate (sthg.) by reasoning or example: *showed that her hypothesis was correct; showed us how to cook squash.* —*intr.* **1.** To be visible or become known: *Your intelligence shows in your selection of books.* **2.** *Slang.* To appear at an event or appointment: *We gave a party, but our friends didn't show.* —*n.* **1.** A display: *a show of affection.* **2.** An insincere display; a pretense: *put on quite a show of unity.* **3.a.** A dramatic appearance or display: *the fiery show of a volcanic eruption.* **b.** A display intended to impress others: *They rented the limousine just to make a show.* **4.a.** A public exhibition or entertainment: *a puppet show.* **b.** A radio or television program: *Did you watch the new show?* **5.** *Informal.* A planned event: *As chief organizer, she ran the whole show.* ◆ **get the show on the road.** *Slang.* To get started: *Let's get this show on the road.* **show off.** *intr.v.* To display or behave in a proud or showy manner: *That child is always showing off.* —*tr.v.* [sep.] To show (sbdy./sthg.) proudly to many people: *He's showing his new girlfriend off as though she were a car.* **show up.** *intr.v.* **1.** To be clearly visible: *The faces don't show up well in the photo.* **2.** To put in an appearance; arrive: *I waited half an hour, but they never showed up.* —*tr.v.* [sep.] *Informal.* To make (sbdy.) seem worse by comparison, as in ability or intelligence: *Their team really showed us up.*
show business *n.* [U] The entertainment industry.
show·case (shō′kās′) *n.* **1.** A display case, as in a store or museum: *Beautiful stones filled the showcase.* **2.** A setting in which sthg. may be displayed to advantage: *a showcase for her considerable talent.* —*tr.v.* **show·cased, show·cas·ing, show·cas·es.** To display (sbdy./sthg.) for pleasure or approval: *The company showcased its new products.*
show·down (shō′doun′) *n.* An event, especially a disagreement or confrontation, that forces an issue to a conclusion: *They'll probably have a showdown at the next meeting.*
show·er (shou′ər) *n.* **1.a.** A brief fall of rain or snow. **b.** A fall of a group of objects, especially from the sky: *a meteor shower.* **2.** An abundant flow: *a shower of praise.* **3.a.** A bath in which the water is sprayed on the bather from overhead: *I prefer to take a shower.*

b. The place in which such a bath is taken: *get into the shower.* **4.** A party held to honor and present gifts to sbdy. for a special event: *a bridal shower; a baby shower.* —*v.* —*tr.* **1.** To pour (sth.) down in a shower: *showered rose petals on the happy bride.* **2.** To give (sth.) abundantly: *The grandparents showered presents on the child.* —*intr.* **1.** To fall in or as if in a shower: *It showered all day.* **2.** To wash oneself in a shower: *I need to shower quickly.*

show•ing (shō′ĭng) *n.* **1.** The act of presenting or displaying: *a showing of the artist's paintings.* **2.** *(usually singular).* Performance, as in a competition or test of skill: *a good showing.* **3.** A presentation of evidence or figures: *Her showing of the statistics was revealing.*

show•man (shō′mən) *n.* **1.** A person who produces shows. **2.** A man with a flair for dramatic effectiveness. —**show′man•ship′** *n.* [U]

shown (shōn) *v.* A past participle of **show.**

HOMONYMS: shown, shone (put forth light).

---

show•off (shō′ôf′ *or* shō′ŏf′) *n.* A person who seeks attention by showing off: *Those children are terrible showoffs.*

show•piece (shō′pēs′) *n.* Something shown as an outstanding example of its kind: *The home is a showpiece.*

show room *n.* A room in which merchandise is displayed: *We looked at the washers in the show room.*

show•y (shō′ē) *adj.* **show•i•er, show•i•est.** Attracting attention: *a showy car.* —**show′i•ly** *adv.* —**show′i•ness** *n.* [U]

shrank (shrăngk) *v.* A past tense of **shrink.**

shrap•nel (shrăp′nəl) *n.* [U] Fragments of an artillery shell filled with metal balls and designed to explode in the air over enemy troops.

shred (shrĕd) *n.* **1.** *(usually plural).* A long irregular strip cut or torn from sth.: *shreds of cloth.* **2.** A small amount; a bit: *not a shred of evidence.* —*tr.v.* **shred•ded** or **shred, shred•ding, shreds.** To cut or tear (sth.) into small strips: *shred carrots.* See Synonyms at **rip[1].**

shrew (shrōō) *n.* **1.** Any of various small mammals that resemble a mouse and have pointed noses. **2.** An insulting term for an outspoken woman.

shrewd (shrōōd) *adj.* Clever, sharp, and practical: *a shrewd person.* —**shrewd′ly** *adv.* —**shrewd′ness** *n.* [U]

shrew•ish (shrōō′ĭsh) *adj.* Bad-tempered; nagging. —**shrew′ish•ly** *adv.* —**shrew′ish•ness** *n.* [U]

shriek (shrēk) *n.* A high, shrill, often frantic, cry: *shrieks of laughter; the shriek of a fire engine.* —*v.* —*intr.* To produce a shriek: *The children shrieked in play.* —*tr.* To say (sth.) with a shriek: *shriek a warning.*

shrill (shrĭl) *adj.* High-pitched and piercing: *a*

shrill whistle. —*tr. & intr.v.* To produce with or make a shrill sound or cry: *He shrilled his complaint. The wind shrilled outside.* —**shrill′ness** *n.* [U] —**shril′ly** *adv.*

shrimp (shrĭmp) *n., pl.* **shrimp** or **shrimps.** **1.** Any of various small, usually saltwater animals related to the lobsters and crayfish, often used as food. **2.** *Slang.* A small or unimportant person: *What a pesky shrimp his little brother is!*

shrine (shrīn) *n.* **1.** A place associated with a saint or other holy person: *People often light candles at religious shrines.* **2.** A place that is special because of its history or associations: *That university is considered a shrine of education.*

shrink (shrĭngk) *v.* **shrank** (shrăngk) or **shrunk** (shrŭngk), **shrunk** or **shrunk•en** (shrŭng′kən), **shrink•ing, shrinks.** —*intr.* **1.** To become reduced in size, amount, or value; become smaller: *His new sweater shrank in the wash.* **2.** To draw back, often in fear: *They shrank from the large black snake.* —*tr.* To cause (sth.) to shrink: *I shrank my new jeans when I washed them.* —*n. Slang.* A psychiatrist. —**shrink′a•ble** *adj.*

shrink•age (shrĭng′kĭj) *n.* [U] **1.** The process of shrinking; reduction in size: *shrinkage of the workforce.* **2.** The amount by which sth. shrinks: *You can expect some shrinkage with cotton.*

shriv•el (shrĭv′əl) *intr. & tr.v.* To become or make shrunken or wrinkled: *Leaves fall and shrivel in autumn. Heat shriveled the grapes into raisins.*

shroud (shroud) *n.* **1.** A cloth used to wrap a body for burial. **2.** Something that conceals, protects, or hides: *a shroud of silence.* —*tr.v.* **1.** To wrap (a corpse) in a shroud. **2.** To conceal (sth.); hide: *Huge trees shroud the path.*

shrub (shrŭb) *n.* A woody plant that is smaller than a tree and generally has several separate stems rather than a single trunk; a bush.

shrub•ber•y (shrŭb′ə rē) *n.* [U] A group of shrubs.

shrug (shrŭg) *v.* **shrugged, shrug•ging, shrugs.** —*tr.* To raise (the shoulders), especially to show doubt or lack of interest: *She shrugged her shoulders when asked the question.* —*intr.* To shrug the shoulders: *He shrugged and said he didn't know.* —*n.* The gesture of raising the shoulders to show doubt or lack of interest: *She gave a shrug and left without answering.* ♦ **shrug off.** *tr.v.* [sep.] **1.** To consider (sbdy./sth.) as being of little importance: *She shrugged off the insult and continued singing.* **2.** To get rid of (sbdy./sth.): *I can't seem to shrug off this cold.*

shrunk (shrŭngk) *v.* A past tense and a past participle of **shrink.**

shrunk•en (shrŭng′kən) *v.* A past participle of **shrink.**

shuck (shŭk) *n.* An outer covering, such as a

S

corn husk, a pea pod, or an oyster shell. —*tr.v.* **1.** To remove the husk or shell from (sthg.): *shuck corn; shuck oysters.* **2.** *Informal.* To remove or strip (clothing or a similar outer covering): *He shucked his jacket in the heat of the afternoon.* —*interj.* **shucks** (shŭks). An expression used to show disappointment or annoyance: *Shucks! I wish I could go.* —**shuck′er** *n.*

shud•der (shŭd′ər) *intr.v.* To tremble or shiver, as from fear or horror: *I shudder when I think about what might have happened.* —*n.* A shiver, as from fear or horror: *She gave a shudder.*

shuf•fle (shŭf′əl) *v.* **shuf•fled, shuf•fling, shuf•fles.** —*tr.* **1.** To slide (the feet) along the floor or ground: *Stop shuffling your feet.* **2.** To mix together (playing cards or game pieces) so as to make a random order of arrangement: *Shuffle the cards.* **3.** To move (sthg.) from one place to another: *shuffled the papers around.* —*intr.* To move with a dragging idle gait: *shuffled across the road.* —*n.* **1.** A short sliding step or movement. **2.** The mixing of cards or game pieces: *It's your shuffle.*

shun (shŭn) *tr.v.* **shunned, shun•ning, shuns.** To avoid (sbdy./sthg.) deliberately and consistently; keep away from: *Friends shunned her after the fight. He had been shunning his homework.*

shunt (shŭnt) *n.* The act of moving sbdy./ sthg. to an alternate course. —*tr.v.* To move (sbdy./sthg.) aside or onto an alternate course: *shunt traffic around a construction site.*

shush (shŭsh) *interj.* An expression used to demand silence: *Shush! Your sister is sleeping.* —*tr.v.* To demand silence from (sbdy.) by saying "shush": *She shushed the children.*

shut (shŭt) *v.* **shut, shut•ting, shuts.** —*tr.* **1.** To move (a door or lid, for example) to block an opening; close: *Don't forget to shut the door.* **2.** To block an entrance to or exit from (sthg.); close: *shut the garage.* **3.** To lock up or confine (sbdy./sthg.): *She shut herself up in her room to study.* **4.** To exclude (sbdy./sthg.) from a closed space: *Shut the cat out of the house.* **5.** To cause (sthg.) to stop operating: *School was shut for vacation.* —*intr.* To move or be moved to block passage; close: *a door that shuts by itself.* ◆ **shut down.** *tr.v.* [sep.] To close a business: *Strikers shut down the factory.* **shut off.** *tr.v.* [sep.] **1.** To stop the flow or passage of (sthg.); cut off: *Be sure to shut off the water when you finish washing.* **2.** To close (sbdy./sthg.) off; isolate: *During their camping trip, they were completely shut off from everybody.* —*intr.v.* To stop operating, especially automatically: *The light shuts off at dawn.* **shut up.** *tr.v.* [sep.] To cause (sbdy.) to stop speaking; silence: *Please shut that child up!* —*intr.v.* To stop speaking: *Will you shut up?*

shut•down (shŭt′doun′) *n.* A stoppage of operation, as of a factory: *a shutdown for repairs.*

shut-eye (shŭt′ī′) *n.* [U] *Informal.* Sleep: *Let's catch a little shut-eye now.*

shut-in (shŭt′ĭn′) *n.* A person who stays indoors because of illness or disability: *She has been a shut-in for years.*

shut•out (shŭt′out′) *n.* A game in which one side does not score: *The baseball game was a shutout.*

shut•ter (shŭt′ər) *n.* **1.** A device that opens and closes the lens opening of a camera to expose film. **2.** A hinged cover for a window, usually wooden with slanted slats.

shut•ter•bug (shŭt′ər bŭg′) *n.* *Informal.* Someone who likes to take a lot of photographs: *He's become a shutterbug since he got that new camera.*

shut•tle (shŭt′l) *n.* **1.** A vehicle that takes short frequent trips over an established route: *We took the shuttle to the airport.* **2.** A spacecraft that can be used more than once for trips into space: *A shuttle launch is scheduled for this week.* —*tr.* & *intr.v.* **shut•tled, shut•tling, shut•tles.** To move or cause to move back and forth by or as if by a shuttle: *shuttle between cities; shuttle children to school.*

shy (shī) *adj.* **shi•er** (shī′ər), **shi•est** (shī′ĭst) or **shy•er, shy•est.** **1.** Avoiding contact or uncomfortable with other people: *a shy person.* **2.** Easily startled; timid: *a shy deer.* **3.** Lacking: *He is three inches shy of six feet.* —*intr.v.* **shied** (shīd), **shy•ing, shies** (shīz). To move suddenly, as if startled: *The horse shied at the sound.* —**shy′ly** *adv.* —**shy′ness** *n.* [U]

shy•ster (shī′stər) *n.* *Slang.* An unethical or unscrupulous business person.

Si The symbol for the element **silicon.**

sib•ling (sĭb′lĭng) *n.* One of two or more people who have one or both parents in common; a brother or a sister: *How many siblings do you have?*

sic[1] (sĭk) *adv.* Used in written texts to show that a word or phrase that is misspelled or misused in a quotation appears this way in the original document.

HOMONYMS: sic (thus, attack), **sick** (ill).

---

sic[2] also **sick** (sĭk) *tr.v.* **sicced, sic•cing, sics** also **sicked, sick•ing, sicks.** To urge (sbdy./sthg.) to attack: *He sicced his dog on the burglar.*

sick[1] (sĭk) *adj.* **sick•er, sick•est. 1.a.** Suffering from or affected with a physical or mental illness; ill: *I'm feeling sick.* **b.** Of or for sick persons: *sick wards.* **2.** Morbid or not normal: *a sick sense of humor.* **3.a.** Deeply upset: *sick at heart.* **b.** Weary; tired: *sick of work.* ◆ **sick and tired.** Thoroughly weary, discouraged, or bored: *We're sick and tired of your complaining.*

HOMONYMS: sick, sic (thus, attack).

sick² (sĭk) *v.* Variant of **sic²**.

sick•en (sĭk′ən) *tr. & intr.v.* To make or become sick: *The smell of rotting fish sickened me. The dog sickened and died.*

sick•en•ing (sĭk′ə nĭng) *adj.* **1.** Extremely unpleasant or disgusting: *a sickening smell.* **2.** Causing strong anger or disapproval: *It's sickening to see what the river looks like after years of pollution.*

sick•le (sĭk′əl) *n.* A tool for cutting grain or tall grass, consisting of a semicircular blade attached to a short handle.

sick leave *n.* [C; U] A leave of absence given to a worker because of illness.

sick pay *n.* [U] Salary given to a worker during illness.

sick•ly (sĭk′lē) *adj.* **sick•li•er, sick•li•est. 1.** Tending to become sick easily; having delicate health: *a sickly child.* **2.** Of, caused by, or associated with sickness: *a sickly appearance.* —**sick′li•ness** *n.* [U]

sick•ness (sĭk′nĭs) *n.* **1.** [U] The condition of being sick; illness: *Sickness kept him out of school.* **2.** [C] A particular disease, disorder, or illness: *Malaria is a sickness.*

side (sīd) *n.* **1.** A line segment that forms a part of the boundary of a flat geometric figure: *A triangle has three sides.* **2.** A surface of an object, especially one joining a top and a bottom: *the four sides of the box.* **3.** Either of two surfaces of a flat object: *You can write on both sides of the paper.* **4.** Either the right or left half of a human or animal body: *I had been lying on my side.* **5.** The space immediately next to a person or thing: *walking at her side; drove onto the side of the road.* **6.** An area contrasted with another, especially when separated by sthg.: *this side of the river.* **7.** One of two or more opposing individuals, groups, teams, or sets of opinions: *Our side won the debate.* **8.** A distinct quality of sthg.: *the spiritual side of love.* **9.** Family line: *On my mother's side, there are five brothers.* —*adj.* **1.** Located on or to the side: *a side door.* **2.** From or to one side: *a side view.* **3.** Of secondary importance; minor: *a little side trip.* **4.** In addition to the main part: *a side order of French fries.* —*intr.v.* **sid•ed, sid•ing, sides.** [*with; against*] To be on a particular side in a dispute: *She's always siding with her brother and against her sister.* ◆ **on the side. 1.** In addition to the main portion: *We'll have some potatoes on the side.* **2.** In addition to the main occupation or activity: *He works as a doctor and plays violin on the side.* **side by side.** Next to each other; close together: *They stood side by side for the photo.*

side•burns (sīd′bûrnz′) *pl.n.* Growths of hair down the sides of a man's face in front of the ears.

sid•ed (sī′dĭd) *adj.* Having a specified number or kind of sides: *a three-sided figure.*

side dish *n.* Food served along with a main course, such as a vegetable.

side effect *n.* **1.** An undesirable reaction that results in addition to the intended effect of a drug: *the side effects of aspirin.* **2.** An activity or event that results in addition to another activity: *A side effect of the loss of jobs has been a drop in population.*

side•kick (sīd′kĭk′) *n.* Slang. A close friend or associate: *the criminal's sidekick.*

side•line (sīd′līn′) *n.* **1.** A boundary line along either of the two sides of a playing area, such as a soccer field. **2. sidelines.** The space immediately outside these lines: *The parents stood on the sidelines.* **3.** An activity pursued in addition to one's regular occupation: *As a sideline, he sells shoes.*

side•long (sīd′lông′ *or* sīd′lŏng′) *adj.* Directed to one side: *a sidelong glance.* —*adv.* Toward the side: *glancing sidelong.*

side•show (sīd′shō′) *n.* **1.** A small show offered as part of a larger one, as at a circus. **2.** A very confused event or situation: *Their wedding turned into a sideshow.*

side•step (sīd′stĕp′) *v.* **side•stepped, side•step•ping, side•steps.** —*intr.* **1.** To step aside: *The crowd sidestepped to make room for the runner.* **2.** To avoid an issue or a responsibility: *The politician sidestepped when asked about raising taxes.* —*tr.* **1.** To step out of the way of (sbdy./sthg.): *The quarterback sidestepped the tackler.* **2.** To evade (an issue or a responsibility): *The teacher sidestepped my question about the field trip.*

side•swipe (sīd′swīp′) *tr.v.* **side•swiped, side•swip•ing, side•swipes.** To strike (a vehicle, for example) along the side in passing: *The car sideswiped the truck as it started to turn.*

side•track (sīd′trăk′) *tr.v.* To divert (sbdy./sthg.) from a main issue or course: *Don't be sidetracked by unimportant details.*

side•walk (sīd′wôk′) *n.* A paved walkway along the side of a road.

side•ways (sīd′wāz′) also **side•way** (sīd′-wā′) *adv. & adj.* Toward one side: *turn sideways; a sideways glance.*

sid•ing (sī′dĭng) *n.* [U] Material, such as boards or shingles, used for covering the outside walls of a house.

si•dle (sīd′l) *intr.v.* **si•dled, si•dling, si•dles. 1.** To move sideways: *sidle along a steep cliff.* **2.** [*up*] To move forward in a quiet or sly manner: *sidle up to an old friend.*

siege (sēj) *n.* **1.** The surrounding and blockading of a place by an army attempting to capture it. **2.** A prolonged period, as of illness: *a siege of the flu.*

S

si·es·ta (sē ĕs′tə) *n.* A rest or nap after the midday meal.

sieve (sĭv) *n.* A kitchen utensil made of mesh or with very small holes, used to strain solids from liquids or to separate small pieces from large ones. —*tr.v.* **sieved, siev·ing, sieves.** To pass (sthg.) through a sieve: *The cook sieved the gravy to remove lumps.*

sift (sĭft) *v.* —*tr.* **1.** To put (sthg.) through a sieve or other straining device to remove large particles: *Sift a cup of flour.* **2.** To examine (sthg.) carefully: *sift the evidence.* —*intr.* To make a careful examination: *The reasearchers sifted through the data.* —**sift′er** *n.*

sigh (sī) *v.* —*intr.* **1.** To exhale a long deep breath while making a sound, as of tiredness, sadness, or relief: *The dog sighed and lay down.* **2.** To make a similar sound: *trees sighing in the wind.* —*tr.* To express (sthg.) with a sigh: *"Oh well," he sighed.* —*n.* The act or sound of sighing: *a loud sigh.*

sight (sīt) *n.* **1.** [U] The ability to see: *He lost his sight in an accident.* **2.** [U] The act of seeing: *The sight of land thrilled the sailors.* **3.** [U] The range that can be seen; the field of vision: *out of our sight.* **4.** [U] A brief view; a glimpse: *I tried to catch sight of her.* **5.** [C] Something worth seeing: *the sights of Rome.* **6.** [C] *(usually singular). Informal.* A messy place, person, or object: *We were a sight after crossing the swamp.* **7.** [C] A device used for aiming, as on a firearm or telescope. —*tr.v.* **1.** To see or observe (sbdy./sthg.): *sight land.* **2.** To observe (sbdy./sthg.) with the help of a sight: *sight a target.* ◆ **a sight for sore eyes.** Someone or sthg. that one enjoys seeing: *After her six months in Europe, home was a sight for sore eyes.* **out of sight, out of mind.** Forgotten when not visible or present: *I didn't think about my boss all weekend—out of sight, out of mind.*

HOMONYMS: sight, cite (quote), **site** (place).

S

sight·ed (sī′tĭd) *adj.* **1.** Having eyesight of a specified kind: *keen-sighted.* **2.** Having the ability to see: *Is the child sighted?*

sight·less (sīt′lĭs) *adj.* Unable to see; blind: *a sightless fish.*

sight·see·ing (sīt′sē′ĭng) *n.* [U] The act or pastime of touring places of interest: *We had plans for sightseeing in Chicago.* —**sight′-see′ing** *adj.* —**sight′se′er** *n.*

sign (sīn) *n.* **1.** Something that suggests a fact, quality, or condition not immediately evident: *A high temperature is a sign of an infection.* **2.** An act or a gesture that conveys an idea, information, or a command: *The officer gave the go-ahead sign.* **3.** A board or poster that has lettering or symbols and conveys information: *a street sign.* **4.** Remaining evidence; a trace: *Rescuers looked for signs of life.* **5.** An event thought to foretell sthg. in the future: *People once thought that eclipses were signs of coming disaster.* **6.** One of the 12 divisions of the zodiac, each named for a constellation and represented by a symbol: *What is your sign?* —*v.* —*tr.* **1.** To put one's signature as a way of showing agreement on (sthg.): *sign a document.* **2.** To write (one's signature): *Sign your name.* **3.** To communicate (sthg.) with sign language: *signed the lecture to a hearing-impaired audience.* —*intr.* **1.** To make a sign; signal: *She signed to me to be quiet.* **2.** To use sign language: *Can you sign?* **3.** To write one's signature: *Sign here, please.* ◆ **sign away.** *tr.v.* [sep.] To give up all right to (sthg.): *He signed away his inheritance.* **sign for.** *tr.v.* [insep.] To receive (sthg.) by signing one's name: *She signed for the package.* **sign in.** *intr. & tr.v.* To record one's arrival by signing a register: *She signed in at the front desk.* **sign off.** *intr.v.* To announce the end of a communication or broadcast: *The station signs off at midnight.* **sign off on.** To give approval for (sthg.): *We've already signed off on that project.* **sign out.** *intr. & tr.v.* To record one's departure by signing a register: *She signed out at noon.* **sign over.** *tr.v.* [sep.] To give up all rights to (sthg.): *She signed over her bank accounts to her son.* **sign up.** *intr.v.* To agree to participate by signing one's name; enlist: *I signed up for art classes.* —*tr.v.* [sep.] To register (sbdy.) as a participant: *She signed her daughter up for swimming lessons.* —**sign′er** *n.*

HOMONYMS: sign, sine (function of an acute angle).

sig·nal (sĭg′nəl) *n.* **1.** A sign, gesture, or device that conveys information: *a traffic signal; hand signals to the pitcher.* **2.** Something that is the cause of action: *He gave us the signal to begin.* **3.** The sound, image, or message transmitted or received, as in radio or television: *a radio signal.* —*v.* —*tr.* **1.** To make a signal to (sbdy./sthg.): *They signaled the engineer.* **2.** To make (sthg.) known by signals: *A period signals the end of a sentence.* —*intr.* To make a signal: *Our friends signaled when we arrived.* —**sig′nal·er** *n.*

sig·na·ture (sĭg′nə chər) *n.* **1.** One's name as written by oneself: *a messy signature.* **2.** The act of signing: *witness the signature of the will.*

sig·nif·i·cance (sĭg nĭf′ĭ kəns) *n.* [U] **1.** The state and quality of being significant; importance: *a political development of great significance.* **2.** The sense of sthg.; meaning: *He didn't understand the significance of her comment.*

sig·nif·i·cant (sĭg nĭf′ĭ kənt) *adj.* **1.** Having a meaning; meaningful: *a significant detail.* **2.** Having or likely to have a major effect;

important: *a significant historical event.*
—**sig·nif'i·cant·ly** *adv.*

sig·ni·fy (sĭg'nə fī') *tr.v.* **sig·ni·fied,
sig·ni·fy·ing, sig·ni·fies. 1.** To be a sign or an indication of (sthg.); represent or mean: *What does this monument signify?* **2.** To make (sthg.) known: *Her husband signified that he wanted to leave early.*

sign language *n.* [C; U] A language that uses hand movements to express words, grammar, and meaning.

sign·post (sīn'pōst') *n.* **1.** A post supporting a sign. **2.** An indication, a sign, or a guide: *a signpost on the road to success.*

Sikh (sēk) *n.* A member of a religion that was founded in India in the 16th century, believing in one God and combining elements of Hinduism and Islam.

si·lence (sī'ləns) *n.* [U] **1.** The quality or condition of being still and silent. **2.** The absence of sound; stillness: *the silence of the forest.* **3.** Refusal or failure to speak out: *a coward's silence.* —*tr.v.* **si·lenced, si·lenc·ing, si·lenc·es. 1.** To make (sbdy.) silent; quiet: *The teacher silenced the children.* **2.** To stop or prevent the expression of (sbdy./sthg.); suppress: *The government tried to silence all criticism.*

si·lent (sī'lənt) *adj.* **1.** Without sound or noise; quiet: *the silent night.* **2.** Not talking; saying nothing: *Everyone remained respectfully silent.* **3.** Not expressed; unspoken: *a silent admission of guilt.* **4.** Not pronounced or sounded, as a letter in a word: *The k in knight is silent.* —**si'lent·ly** *adv.*

sil·hou·ette (sĭl'oo ĕt') *n.* A drawing consisting of the outline of sthg., especially a human profile, filled in with a solid color. —*tr.v.* **sil·hou·et·ted, sil·hou·et·ting, sil·hou·ettes.** To cause (sbdy./sthg.) to be seen as a silhouette: *The mountains were silhouetted against the sky.*

sil·i·con (sĭl'ĭ kən *or* sĭl'ĭ kŏn') *n.* [U] *Symbol* **Si** A metalloid element that is used in glass, semiconductors, concrete, bricks, and ceramics. Atomic number 14. See table at **element.**

sil·i·cone (sĭl'ĭ kōn') *n.* [U] A chemical compound used in making adhesives, lubricants, protective coatings, and synthetic rubber.

silk (sĭlk) *n.* [C; U] **1.** A fine glossy fiber produced by a silkworm to form its cocoon. **2.** Thread or fabric made from this fiber. **3.** A fine silky material, such as the tuft at the end of an ear of corn. —*adj.* Made of or similar to silk. —**silk'i·ly** *adv.* —**silk'i·ness** *n.* [U] —**silk'y** *adj.*

silk·en (sĭl'kən) *adj.* **1.** Made of silk: *a silken scarf.* **2.** Having the look or feel of silk; smooth and glossy: *silken hair.*

silk·worm (sĭlk'wûrm') *n.* A caterpillar that produces silk cocoons, especially the caterpillar of a moth native to Asia.

sill (sĭl) *n.* A horizontal piece that holds up the vertical part of a window frame.

sil·ly (sĭl'ē) *adj.* **sil·li·er, sil·li·est. 1.** Showing lack of good sense or reason; stupid: *silly mistakes.* **2.** Lacking seriousness; playful: *a silly game.* —**sil'li·ness** *n.* [U]

silo (sī'lō) *n., pl.* **si·los. 1.** A tall cylindrical building in which grain is stored. **2.** An underground shelter for a missile.

silt (sĭlt) *n.* [U] A material consisting of small mineral particles, often found at the bottom of a body of water. ◆ **silt up.** *tr. & intr.v.* To fill or become filled with silt: *The flow of water had silted up the channel. A pond will silt up after a time.*

sil·ver (sĭl'vər) *n.* [U] **1.** *Symbol* **Ag** A soft, shiny, white metallic element that is superior to any other metal in its ability to conduct heat and electricity. Atomic number 47. See table at **element. 2.** Coins made of this metal. **3.** Tableware or other household articles made of or plated with this metal. **4.** A light, shiny, or metallic gray color. —*adj.* **1.** Made of or containing silver: *silver jewelry.* **2.** Having a light gray color like that of the metal silver: *silver hair.* —**sil'ver·y** *adj.*

silver lining *n.* A hopeful aspect of a bad situation: *He always looks for a silver lining in the worst situation.*

sil·ver·smith (sĭl'vər smĭth') *n.* A person who makes, repairs, or replates articles of silver.

sil·ver·ware (sĭl'vər wâr') *n.* [U] Metal eating and serving utensils.

sim·i·lar (sĭm'ə lər) *adj.* Related in appearance or nature; alike but not exactly the same: *a wild cat similar to but smaller than a lion.* —**sim'i·lar'i·ty** (sĭm'ə lăr'ĭ tē) *n.* —**sim'i·lar·ly** *adv.*

sim·i·le (sĭm'ə lē) *n.* A figure of speech in which unlike things are compared, often in a phrase introduced by *like* or *as.* For example, *She runs like a deer* and *That house is as big as a ship* are similes.

sim·mer (sĭm'ər) *v.* —*intr.* To be cooked gently or just at the boiling point: *Soup simmered on the stove.* —*tr.* To cook (sthg.) gently or just at the boiling point: *simmered the sauce.* —*n.* The condition or process of simmering: *Bring the sauce to a simmer.* ◆ **simmer down.** *intr.v.* To become calm after excitement or anger: *He finally simmered down after we explained the delay.*

sim·ple (sĭm'pəl) *adj.* **sim·pler, sim·plest. 1.** Not complicated; easy: *a simple explanation.* See Synonyms at **easy. 2.** Having no additions or qualifications; mere: *a simple "yes" or "no."* **3.** Not showy or elaborate; plain: *a simple wedding dress; simple everyday words.*

sim·ple-mind·ed *or* **sim·ple·mind·ed** (sĭm'pəl mīn'dĭd) *adj.* **1.** Not able to understand complicated things: *a simple-minded person.* **2.** Stupid or silly: *a simple-minded mistake.* —**sim'ple-mind'ed·ly** *adv.* —**sim'ple-mind'ed·ness** *n.* [U]

simple sentence *n.* A sentence consisting of

one independent clause with no dependent clauses, such as *The two boys played basketball.*

sim•plic•i•ty (sĭm plĭs′ĭ tē) *n.* [U] **1.** The property, condition, or quality of being simple; absence of complexity or difficulty: *the simplicity of the plan.* **2.** Absence of luxury or showiness; plainness: *a life of simplicity.* **3.** Absence of vanity or deceitfulness; sincerity: *childlike simplicity.*

sim•pli•fy (sĭm′plə fī′) *tr.v.* **sim•pli•fied, sim•pli•fy•ing, sim•pli•fies.** To make (sthg.) simple or simpler: *We decided to simplify our lifestyle.* —**sim′pli•fi•ca′tion** (sĭm′plə fĭ kā′shən) *n.* [U]

sim•ply (sĭm′plē) *adv.* **1.** In a simple way; plainly: *They live very simply.* **2.** Clearly: *She explained it quite simply.* **3.** Only; just: *We knew him simply as Joe.* **4.** Absolutely; altogether: *The meal was simply delicious.*

sim•u•late (sĭm′yə lāt′) *tr.v.* **sim•u•lat•ed, sim•u•lat•ing, sim•u•lates. 1.** To have the appearance, form, or sound of (sthg.); imitate: *a device that simulates space flight.* See Synonyms at **imitate. 2.** To pretend (sthg.): *The class simulated interest.* —**sim′u•la′tion** *n.* —**sim′u•la′tor** *n.*

si•mul•ta•ne•ous (sī′məl tā′nē əs) *adj.* Happening, existing, or done at the same time: *simultaneous cries of surprise.* —**si′mul•ta′ne•ous•ly** *adv.*

sin (sĭn) *n.* **1.** The act of breaking a religious or moral law. **2.** An act considered shameful or wrong: *It's a sin to waste food.* —*intr.v.* **sinned, sin•ning, sins. 1.** To violate a religious or moral law. **2.** To commit an offense; do wrong. —**sin′ner** *n.*

since (sĭns) *adv.* **1.** From then until now, or between then and now: *He left town and hasn't been here since.* **2.** Before now; ago: *long since forgotten.* —*prep.* From (a given time): *They've been friends since 1995.* —*conj.* **1.** During the period after the time when: *She hasn't been home since she graduated.* **2.** Continuously from the time when: *He hasn't spoken since he sat down.* **3.** Because: *Since you're not interested, I won't tell you about it.*

sin•cere (sĭn sîr′) *adj.* **sin•cer•er, sin•cer•est.** Not false or affected; genuine or true: *sincere friends; a sincere apology.* —**sin•cere′ly** *adv.*

sin•cer•i•ty (sĭn-sĕr′ĭ tē) *n.* [U] The quality or condition of being sincere; genuineness or honesty.

sine (sīn) *n.* In a right triangle, a function of an acute angle

equal to the length of the side opposite the angle divided by the length of the hypotenuse.

HOMONYMS: sine, sign (indication).

---

sin•ew (sĭn′yōō) *n.* **1.** [C] A tendon. **2.** [U] Vigorous strength; muscular power: *That horse has plenty of sinew.* —**sin′ew•y** *adj.*

sin•ful (sĭn′fəl) *adj.* Characterized by or full of sin; wicked. —**sin′ful•ly** *adv.* —**sin′ful•ness** *n.* [U]

sing (sĭng) *v.* **sang** (săng), **sung** (sŭng), **sing•ing, sings.** —*intr.* **1.** To perform songs or other vocal selections. **2.** To produce musical sounds: *birds that sing in the forest.* —*tr.* **1.** To produce the musical sound of (a song): *The performer sang a love song.* **2.** To bring (sbdy./sthg.) to a specified condition by singing: *She sang the baby to sleep.* **3.** To tell or proclaim (sthg.), especially in song or verse: *sang her praises.* ♦ **sing out.** *tr.v.* [sep.] To call out (sthg.) loudly: *She sang out her name.* —**sing′er** *n.*

sing. *abbr.* An abbreviation of singular.

singe (sĭnj) *tr.v.* **singed, singe•ing, sing•es. 1.** To burn (sthg.) slightly; scorch: *The picture had been singed in the fire.* **2.** To burn the ends of (sthg.): *He singed his hair.*

sin•gle (sĭng′gəl) *adj.* **1.** Not with another or others: *a single bird.* **2.** Consisting of one thing, part, or section: *a single layer.* **3.** Separate from others; individual: *Every single person will receive a free gift.* **4.** Intended or designed for use by one person: *a single bed.* **5.** Unmarried: *He's still single.* —*n.* **1.** An accommodation for one person, as a room in a hotel: *He asked for a single.* **2. singles.** Unmarried people considered as a group: *a club for singles.* —*v.* **sin•gled, sin•gling, sin•gles.** ♦ **single out.** *tr.v.* [sep.] To choose (sbdy./sthg.) from among a group: *He singled out two students for praise.*

single file *n.* [U] A line of people, animals, or things standing or moving one behind the other: *Please walk in single file.* —*adv.* In one line: *Please line up single file.*

sin•gle-hand•ed (sĭng′gəl hăn′dĭd) *adj. & adv.* Working or done without help; unassisted: *You should be able to do it single-handed.* —**sin′gle-hand′ed•ly** *adv.*

sin•gle-mind•ed (sĭng′gəl mīn′dĭd) *adj.* Having one purpose or opinion: *a single-minded approach to tax reform.* —**sin′gle-mind′ed•ly** *adv.* —**sin′gle-mind′ed•ness** *n.* [U]

sin•gly (sĭng′glē) *adv.* **1.** Without the company or help of others; alone: *She came to the board singly.* **2.** One by one; individually: *materials used singly or in combinations.*

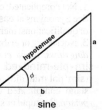

sine

S

sing·song (sĭng′sông′ or sĭng′sŏng′) n. *(usually singular).* A manner of speaking marked by a monotonous rising and falling of sound. —*adj.* Having a monotonous rhythm or manner of speaking: *a singsong way of talking.*

sin·gu·lar (sĭng′gyə lər) *adj.* **1.** In grammar: **a.** Relating to a noun, pronoun, or adjective that refers to a single person or thing or a group considered as a unit. For example, *I* and *he* are singular pronouns and *house* is a singular noun. **b.** Relating to a verb expressing the action or state of a single subject. For example, *comes* is a singular verb. **2.** Being the only one of a kind; unique: *a singular flower for its species.* **3.** Very strange; peculiar: *singular arrivals and departures at midnight.* —*n.* In grammar, the form taken by a word indicating one person or thing. For example, *he, book,* and *cat* are all singulars. —**sin′gu·lar·ly** *adv.*

sin·is·ter (sĭn′ĭ stər) *adj.* **1.** Suggesting or threatening evil: *a sinister smile.* **2.** Promising trouble; ominous: *sinister storm clouds.* —**sin′is·ter·ly** *adv.*

sink (sĭngk) *v.* **sank** (săngk) or **sunk** (sŭngk), **sunk, sink·ing, sinks.** —*intr.* **1.** To go to the bottom; submerge: *The anchor sank to the bottom.* **2.** To move to a lower level, especially slowly: *He sank into the chair.* **3.** To appear to move downward, as the sun or moon in setting: *The sun sank in the west.* **4.** To pass into a specified condition: *She sank into a deep sleep.* **5.** To worsen in condition or quality: *The business sank into bankruptcy.* **6.** To lessen or become weaker, as in strength or value: *His voice sank to a faint whisper. Farm prices sank steadily.* —*tr.* **1.** To cause (sthg.) to go below the surface: *Heavy storms can sink ships.* **2.** To cause (sthg.) to drop or lower: *He sank the spoon into the soup.* **3.** To bring (sthg.) to a worse condition or quality: *Poor management sank the project.* **4.** To invest (sthg.): *He sank a lot of money into real estate.* —*n.* An open, permanent water container with a drainpipe and usually a piped supply of water: *the kitchen sink.* ◆ **sink in.** *intr.v.* To become felt or understood: *Let the meaning sink in.* **sink or swim.** *Informal.* To succeed or fail without alternative: *If you ignore her advice, you can sink or swim.* —**sink′a·ble** *adj.*

sin·ner (sĭn′ər) *n.* A person who sins or does wrong.

sin·u·ous (sĭn′yōō əs) *adj.* With many curves or turns; winding: *a sinuous mountain road.* —**sin′u·ous·ly** *adv.*

si·nus (sī′nəs) *n.* Any of several air-filled cavities in the bones of the skull, especially one that connects with the nose.

si·nus·i·tis (sī′nə sī′tĭs) *n.* [U] Inflammation of the sinuses or a sinus, especially in the region near the nose.

sip (sĭp) *v.* **sipped, sip·ping, sips.** —*tr.* To drink (sthg.) in small quantities: *sip tea.* —*intr.* To drink sthg. in sips: *Sip at coffee when it's too hot.* —*n.* **1.** The act of sipping: *He smiled after his first sip.* **2.** A small quantity of liquid sipped: *I took a sip of coffee.*

si·phon (sī′fən) *n.* A tube filled with liquid and arranged so that the pressure of the atmosphere forces liquid from a container to flow through the tube and into a lower container. —*tr.v.* To draw off or transfer (a liquid) through or as if through a siphon: *siphon gas.*

sir (sûr) *n.* Used as a polite form of address for a man: *May I help you, sir?*

sire (sīr) *n.* **1.** The father of an animal, especially a domesticated animal such as a horse or cow. **2.** A father or forefather. —*tr.v.* **sired, sir·ing, sires.** To be the father or male ancestor of (sbdy./sthg.): *He sired ten children.*

si·ren (sī′rən) *n.* A device that makes a loud whistling or wailing sound as a signal or warning: *the ambulance siren.*

sir·loin (sûr′loin′) *n.* [C; U] A cut of meat, especially beef.

sis (sĭs) *n. Informal.* Sister.

sis·sy (sĭs′ē) *n., pl.* **sis·sies. 1.** An insulting term for a boy or man who is considered effeminate. **2.** A person considered timid or cowardly: *Don't be such a sissy. The snake isn't going to hurt you.*

sis·ter (sĭs′tər) *n.* **1.** A girl or woman with the same mother and father as sbdy. else. **2.** A girl or woman with one parent in common with sbdy. else; a half sister. **3.** A fellow woman or girl. **4.** A woman fellow member, as of a sorority. **5. Sister.** A nun.

sis·ter·hood (sĭs′tər hŏŏd′) *n.* [U] **1.** The relationship of being a sister or sisters. **2.** The quality of being sisterly. **3.** A group of women united by a common purpose or by vows.

sis·ter-in-law (sĭs′tər ĭn lô′) *n., pl.* **sis·ters-in-law** (sĭs′tərz ĭn lô′). **1.** The sister of one's husband or wife. **2.** The wife of one's brother. **3.** The wife of the brother of one's husband or wife.

sis·ter·ly (sĭs′tər lē) *adj.* **1.** Suitable for a sister or sisters: *took a sisterly interest in her education.* **2.** Showing affection: *a sisterly smile.* —**sis′ter·li·ness** *n.* [U]

sit (sĭt) *v.* **sat** (săt), **sit·ting, sits.** —*intr.* **1.** To rest with the body supported on the buttocks and the torso upright: *He sat on a chair.* **2.** To be located: *The farmhouse sits on a hill.* **3.** To remain inactive or unused: *The school building will sit empty until the next term begins.* **4.** To lie or rest: *dishes sitting on the shelf.* **5.** To pose for an artist or a photographer: *The college president sat for her portrait.* **6.** To occupy a place as one in a group of officials: *the first woman to sit on the Supreme Court.* **7.** To affect one as a burden: *Responsibility sat heavily on the President.* **8.** To be acceptable or agreeable: *The idea did not sit*

S

well with us. **9.** To keep watch or take care of a child; babysit: *The girl sits for a neighbor's child after school.* —*tr.* **1.** To cause (sbdy.) to sit; seat: *Let's sit them together.* **2.** To provide seating for (sbdy.): *This restaurant sits forty people.* —SEE NOTE at **set**[1].

♦ **sit down.** *intr.v.* To seat oneself (on a chair, for example): *Sit down and stay for a while.* **sit in.** *intr.v.* To attend or participate in sthg. as a visitor: *They invited me to sit in.* **sit out.** *tr.v.* [sep.] To not take part in (sthg.): *sit out a dance.* **sit pretty.** *Informal.* To be in a very favorable position: *With this big contract our company is sitting pretty.* **sit tight.** *Informal.* To be patient and wait: *Please sit tight while I find out what the problem is.* **sit up.** *intr.v.* **1.** To rise from lying down to a sitting position: *She sat up in bed when she heard the sound.* **2.** To stay up later than the usual bedtime: *They sat up waiting for their son to come home from a party.*

si•tar (sĭ tär′) *n.* A stringed instrument of India.

sit•com also **sit-com** (sĭt′kŏm′) *n. Informal.* A situation comedy on television.

site (sīt) *n.* The place where sthg. was, is, or will be located: *a good site for a park; the site of a historic battle.*

HOMONYMS: site, cite (quote), **sight** (vision).

---

sit-in (sĭt′ĭn′) *n.* A demonstration in which people protesting against certain conditions sit down in an appropriate place and refuse to move until their demands are considered or met.

sit•ter (sĭt′ər) *n.* A person who cares for children when the parents are not home; a baby sitter: *We need a sitter for the children.*

sit•ting duck (sĭt′ĭng) *n. Informal.* An easy target or victim: *The tourist was a sitting duck for thieves.*

sit•u•ate (sĭch′o͞o āt′) *tr.v.* **sit•u•at•ed, sit•u•at•ing, sit•u•ates.** To place (sbdy./ sthg.) in a certain spot or position; locate: *situate a factory on the edge of town.*

sit•u•a•tion (sĭch′o͞o ā′shən) *n.* **1.** A combination of circumstances at a given moment; a state of affairs: *He found himself in an awkward situation.* **2.** A person's position or status with respect to specified conditions: *a favorable financial situation.*

situation comedy *n.* A humorous television series with a regular cast of characters; a sitcom.

sit-up (sĭt′ŭp′) *n.* An exercise in which a person lying on his or her back rises to a sitting position using the abdominal muscles and then lies down again without moving the legs: *She does 50 sit-ups every morning.*

six (sĭks) *n.* **1.** The number, written 6, that is equal to 5 + 1. **2.** The sixth in a set or sequence. —**six** *adj. & pron.*

six•teen (sĭk stēn′) *n.* **1.** The number, written 16, that is equal to 15 + 1. **2.** The 16th in a set or sequence. —**six′teen′** *adj. & pron.*

six•teenth (sĭk stēnth′) *n.* **1.** The ordinal number matching the number 16 in a series. **2.** One of 16 equal parts. —**six•teenth′** *adj. & adv.*

sixth (sĭksth) *n.* **1.** The ordinal number matching the number six in a series. **2.** One of six equal parts: *a sixth of a pie.* —**sixth** *adj. & adv.*

sixth sense *n.* A special ability that is independent of the five senses; keen intuition.

six•ti•eth (sĭk′stē ĭth) *n.* **1.** The ordinal number matching the number 60 in a series. **2.** One of 60 equal parts. —**six′ti•eth** *adj. & adv.*

six•ty (sĭks′tē) *n., pl.* **six•ties. 1.** The number, written 60, that is equal to 6 × 10. **2. sixties. a.** Often **Sixties.** The ten years from 60 to 69 in a century: *She grew up in the Sixties.* **b.** A decade or the numbers from 60 to 69. —**six′ty** *adj. & pron.*

siz•a•ble also **size•a•ble** (sī′zə bəl) *adj.* Of considerable size; fairly large: *She has a sizable income.*

size (sīz) *n.* **1.** [U] The physical dimensions, proportions, or extent of an object: *an office of great size.* **2.** [C; U] Any of a series of standard measurements used to make objects such as clothing: *What size shirt do you wear?* —*tr.v.* **sized, siz•ing, siz•es.** To arrange, classify, or distribute (sthg.) according to size. ♦ **size up.** *tr.v.* [sep.] To make an estimate, an opinion, or a judgment of (sbdy./sthg.): *She sized up her opponent.*

sized (sīzd) *adj.* Having a particular or specified size: *a medium-sized car.*

siz•zle (sĭz′əl) *intr.v.* **siz•zled, siz•zling, siz•zles. 1.** To make the hissing sound characteristic of frying fat: *The potatoes sizzled in the pan.* **2.** To be very hot: *a summer day that sizzled.* —*n.* A hissing sound: *the sizzle of bacon frying.*

skate (skāt) *n.* **1.** An ice skate. **2.** A roller skate. —*intr.v.* **skat•ed, skat•ing, skates.** To glide or move along on or as if on skates: *He often skates to work.* ♦ **be skating on thin ice.** To be in an extremely dangerous situation: *If you don't do what she says, you'll be skating on thin ice.* —**skat′er** *n.*

skate•board (skāt′bôrd′) *n.* A short narrow board with a set of four wheels mounted under it that one rides on in a standing position. —*intr.v.* To ride on a skateboard. —**skate′board′er** *n.* —**skate′board′ing** *n.* [U]

skein (skān) *n.* A length of thread or yarn wound in a long loose coil: *a skein of yarn.*

skel•e•tal (skĕl′ĭ tl) *adj.* Relating to, forming, or like a skeleton: *skeletal remains.*

skel•e•ton (skĕl′ĭ tn) *n.* **1.** The internal structure composed of bone and cartilage that supports and protects the soft organs of a human or animal body. **2.** A supporting structure or framework, as of a building: *the skeleton of the church.* **3.** An outline of sthg. written: *the skeleton of a research paper.*

skep•tic (skĕp′tĭk) *n.* A person who habitually questions or doubts what others believe to be true. —**skep′ti•cal** *adj.* —**skep′ti•cal•ly** *adv.*

skep•ti•cism (skĕp′tĭ sĭz′əm) *n.* [U] A doubting or questioning attitude or state of mind.

sketch (skĕch) *n.* **1.** A rough preliminary drawing: *a sketch of the park.* **2.** A brief composition: *a biographical sketch.* —*v.* —*tr.* To make a sketch of (sbdy./sthg.): *I want to sketch his face.* —*intr.* To make a sketch: *She loves to sketch in the park.* —**sketch′er** *n.*

sketch•y (skĕch′ē) *adj.* **sketch•i•er, sketch•i•est.** Lacking in detail or completeness: *The police have only sketchy information about the robbery.* —**sketch′i•ly** *adv.* —**sketch′i•ness** *n.* [U]

skew (skyōō) *tr.v.* **1.** To turn or place (sthg.) at an angle, slant. *All that jumping skewed the pictures on the wall.* **2.** To distort (sthg.) in meaning or effect: *The article was skewed in favor of the proposal.* —*adj.* Turned or placed to one side: *a skewed row of trees.*

skew•er (skyōō′ər) *n.* A long, thin rod of wood or metal, used to hold meat during cooking. —*tr.v.* To hold together or pierce (sbdy./sthg.) with or as if with a skewer: *She skewered the meat.*

ski (skē) *n.*, *pl.* **skis.** One of a pair of long, narrow, flat runners of wood, metal, or plastic that are fastened to a boot or shoe for moving over snow. —*v.* —*intr.* To move on skis: *She skies well.* —*tr.* To travel over (sthg.) on skis: *She skied a new trail.* —**ski′er** *n.*

ski

skid (skĭd) *n.* The act of slipping or sliding over a surface: *The car went into a skid on the slippery pavement.* —*intr.v.* **skid•ded, skid•ding, skids.** To slip or slide out of control over a slippery surface: *The car skidded on the ice.* See Synonyms at **slide.**

ski lift *n.* An apparatus that transports skiers to the top of a ski trail or mountain.

skill (skĭl) *n.* **1.** [U] Ability that results from training or experience: *great skill as a teacher.* **2.** [C] An art, a trade, or a technique, especially one requiring use of the hands or body: *a carpenter's skills.* **3.** [C] (*usually plural*). A developed ability: *He has excellent writing skills.*

skilled (skĭld) *adj.* **1.** Having or showing skill; expert: *a skilled golfer.* See Synonyms at **proficient. 2.** Requiring specialized ability or training: *a skilled occupation.*

skil•let (skĭl′ĭt) *n.* A frying pan.

skill•ful (skĭl′fəl) *adj.* **1.** Having or using skill; expert: *a skillful cook.* See Synonyms at **proficient. 2.** Characterized by or requiring skill: *skillful violin playing.* —**skill′ful•ly** *adv.* —**skill′ful•ness** *n.* [U]

skim (skĭm) *v.* **skimmed, skim•ming, skims.** —*tr.* **1.** To remove (floating matter) from a liquid: *skim cream off the top of the milk.* **2.** To throw (sthg.) so as to bounce or slide: *skim stones over the pond.* **3.** To read or consider (sthg.) superficially: *skim a report.* —*intr.* **1.** [*across; over*] To move or glide lightly and quickly over a surface: *The sailboat skimmed across the lake.* **2.** [*through*] To give a quick and superficial reading or consideration: *skim through a novel.*

skim milk *n.* [U] Milk from which the cream has been removed.

skimp (skĭmp) *v.* —*tr.* To deal with (sthg.) carelessly: *I had to concentrate on my science project, skimping other things.* —*intr.* To be stingy or very thrifty: *She skimps on food.* —**skimp′i•ly** *adv.* —**skimp′i•ness** *n.* [U] —**skimp′y** *adj.*

skin (skĭn) *n.* **1.** [U] The tissue that forms the outer covering of the body of a person or an animal. **2.** [C; U] An outer layer, covering, or coating: *the skin of an apple.* —*tr.v.* **skinned, skin•ning, skins. 1.** To remove the skin from (sthg.): *skin a sheep.* **2.** To injure (sthg.) by scraping: *The little girl fell and skinned her knee.* **3.** To remove (an outer covering): *skinned off the thin bark of the tree.* **4.** Slang. To cheat (sbdy.); swindle: *They skinned us at that store.* ◆ **by the skin of (one's) teeth.** By the smallest margin; just barely: *We escaped getting hit by the skin of our teeth.* **get under (one's) skin.** To bother sbdy.: *The children were home all week and got under their mother's skin.* **have thin** or **thick skin.** To be or not be easily offended or upset: *Most entertainers have thick skin and don't let critics anger them.*

skin-deep (skĭn′dēp′) *adj.* Superficial; shallow: *Beauty is only skin-deep.*

skin diving *n.* [U] The sport of underwater swimming in which the swimmer is equipped with flippers and a face mask and usually a snorkel rather than a portable air supply. —**skin′dive′** *v.* —**skin diver** *n.*

skin•flint (skĭn′flĭnt′) *n.* A person who does not like to spend any money; a miser.

skin•head (skĭn′hĕd′) *n.* Slang. **1.** A person with a shaved head. **2.** A member of any of various groups who shave their heads and sometimes participate in racist activities.

S

skin·ny (skĭn′ē) *adj.* **skin·ni·er, skin·ni·est.** Very thin: *skinny legs.* See Synonyms at lean². —**skin′ni·ness** *n.* [U]

skin·tight (skĭn′tīt′) *adj.* Fitting or clinging closely to the skin: *skintight pants.*

skip (skĭp) *v.* **skipped, skip·ping, skips.** —*intr.* **1.** To move by hopping on one foot and then the other: *The girls skipped down the street.* **2.** To bounce over a surface: *The stone I threw skipped over the water six times.* **3.** To pass quickly from point to point: *skipping through the list hurriedly.* **4.** *Informal.* To leave hastily: *skip out on a debt.* —*tr.* **1.** To leap or jump lightly over (sthg.): *skip rope.* **2.** To pass over (sthg.) without mentioning; omit: *The reader skipped the unimportant details.* **3.** To cause (sthg.) to bounce over a surface; skim: *The boys were skipping rocks.* **4.** To leave (a place) hastily: *skip town.* —*n.* A gait in which hops and steps alternate.

skir·mish (skûr′mĭsh) *n.* A minor battle between small bodies of troops. —*intr.v.* To engage in a minor battle or dispute: *They skirmished over the last donut.*

skirt (skûrt) *n.* **1.** A garment that hangs from the waist and is usually worn by women and girls. **2.** A border, a margin, or an outer edge: *The sheep grazed at the skirt of the hill.* —*tr.v.* **1.** To form the border of (sthg.): *The road skirted the park.* **2.** To pass around rather than across or through (sthg.): *We skirted the marshes.* **3.** To evade (a topic or an issue, for example) in a roundabout way: *Don't try to skirt the issue.*

skit (skĭt) *n.* A short, usually humorous theatrical presentation.

skit·tish (skĭt′ĭsh) *adj.* Excitable or nervous: *a skittish colt.* —**skit′tish·ly** *adv.* —**skit′tish·ness** *n.* [U]

skulk (skŭlk) *intr.v.* To move about stealthily: *A cat skulked in the bushes.*

skull (skŭl) *n.* The part of the skeleton that forms the head.

skunk (skŭngk) *n.* **1.** A small mammal that has black and white fur and a bushy tail and can spray a bad-smelling liquid from glands near the base of the tail. **2.** *Slang.* An annoying or unlikeable person. —*tr.v.*

skunk

Slang. To defeat (sbdy./sthg.) overwhelmingly, especially by preventing from scoring: *Our team was skunked last week.*

sky (skī) *n., pl.* **skies** (skīz). **1.** The atmosphere, as seen from a given point on Earth's surface. **2.** *(usually plural).* The appearance of the upper atmosphere, especially with respect to weather: *We should have clear skies for the picnic tomorrow.*

sky·dive (skī′dīv′) *intr.v.* **sky·dived, sky·div·ing, sky·dives.** To jump and fall freely from an airplane, performing various maneuvers before opening a parachute. —**sky′div′er** *n.* —**sky′div′ing** *n.* [U]

sky-high (skī′hī′) *adv.* **1.** To a very high level: *Garbage was piled sky-high.* **2.** To pieces or in pieces; apart: *The explosives blew the old bridge sky-high.* —*adj.* Unreasonably high: *sky-high prices.*

sky·jack (skī′jăk′) *tr.v.* To hijack (an airplane) through the use or threat of force: *The plane was skyjacked and forced to fly to Cuba.* —**sky′jack′er** *n.*

sky·light (skī′līt′) *n.* A window in the roof of a building.

sky·line (skī′līn′) *n.* **1.** The line along which the earth and sky appear to meet; the horizon. **2.** The outline of a mountain range or group of buildings seen against the sky: *the Chicago skyline.*

sky·rock·et (skī′rŏk′ĭt) *intr.v.* To rise rapidly or suddenly: *Prices skyrocketed.*

sky·scrap·er (skī′skrā′pər) *n.* A very tall building.

sky·ward (skī′wərd) *adj. & adv.* Toward the sky: *a skyward glance; We looked skyward.* —**sky′wards** *adv.*

slab (slăb) *n.* A broad, flat, thick piece of sthg., as of food or stone: *a slab of bacon.*

slack (slăk) *adj.* **1.** Slow; sluggish: *a slack pace.* **2.** Not busy: *the slack moments of the day.* **3.** Not tense; loose: *a slack rope.* —*v.* —*tr.* To make (sthg.) slower or looser; slacken: *slack the rope.* —*intr.* **1.** To be or become slack: *The rope suddenly slacked.* **2.** To avoid work: *She always slacks on the job.* —*n.* [U] **1.** A loose part of sthg.: *take up some of the slack in the rope.* **2.** A period of little activity: *There is little slack in the schedule.* ◆ **give** or **cut (one) some slack.** *Informal.* **1.** To give (sbdy.) a chance to work less: *The teacher gave her students some slack and let them turn in their assignments late.* **2.** To give (sbdy.) the benefit of the doubt: *Why don't you cut him some slack?* **slack off.** *intr.v.* To decrease in activity or care: *We slacked off once we knew we'd meet the deadline.* —**slack′ness** *n.* [U]

slack·en (slăk′ən) *tr. & intr.v.* **1.** To make or become slower; slow down: *The dogs slackened their pace. The plane's air speed slackened.* **2.** To make or become less vigorous or intense: *High rates slackened the demand for loans. Business slackened.* **3.** To make or become less firm: *I slackened the leash to let the dog run. The tension in the room slackened.*

slack•er (slăk′ər) *n.* A person who tries to avoid work or responsibility.

slacks (slăks) *pl.n.* Casual pants that are not part of a suit.

slain (slān) *v.* Past participle of **slay.**

slake (slāk) *tr.v.* **slaked, slak•ing, slakes. 1.** To satisfy (a desire): *She slaked her thirst.* **2.** To lessen the force of (sthg.); moderate: *slaking his anger.*

sla•lom (slä′ləm) *n.* A skiing race down a zigzag course marked with flags.

slam (slăm) *v.* **slammed, slam•ming, slams.** —*tr.* **1.** To shut (sthg.) forcefully and with a loud noise: *slam a door.* **2.** To throw, move, or strike (sthg.) forcefully and loudly: *slammed down the telephone receiver.* —*intr.* **1.** To close or swing into place forcefully and with a loud noise: *The door slammed in the wind.* **2.** To hit sthg. with force; crash: *The car slammed into the tree.* —*n.* **1.** An act of slamming. **2.** The noise of a forceful impact; a bang.

slan•der (slăn′dər) *n.* [U] **1.** A false statement reported or said to damage a person's reputation. **2.** The act or crime of making or reporting such false statements. —*tr.v.* To make a false statement about (sbdy.): *slander the mayor.* —**slan′der•er** *n.*

slan•der•ous (slăn′dər əs) *adj.* Making or containing false and damaging charges about sbdy.: *a slanderous speech.* —**slan′der•ous•ly** *adv.*

slang (slăng) *n.* [U] **1.** A kind of language occurring most often in casual speech, consisting of made-up words and figures of speech that are deliberately used in place of standard terms to add interest, humor, irreverence, or other effect. For example, slang terms include *hot* meaning "excellent" and *split* meaning "to leave." **2.** Language peculiar to a certain group of people; jargon: *surfers' slang.* —**slang′y** *adj.*

slant (slănt) *v.* —*tr.* **1.** To give a direction other than horizontal or vertical to (sthg.); cause to slope. **2.** To present (news or information, for example) in a way that fits a particular opinion; bias: *She slanted her report to avoid certain conclusions.* —*intr.* To go in a direction other than horizontal or vertical; slope: *My handwriting slants to the right.* —*n.* **1.** A sloping line, direction, or course: *The house is on a slant.* **2.** A personal point of view or opinion: *What's your slant on health care?* **3.** A bias: *the reporter's slant on economics.*

slap (slăp) *n.* **1.** A sharp blow with the open hand or some other flat object: *She gave my shoulder a friendly slap.* **2.** An injury or sharp insult: *a slap to his pride.* —*v.* **slapped, slap•ping, slaps.** —*tr.* **1.** To strike (sbdy./sthg.) with a flat object, such as the palm of the hand: *Grandpa slapped his knee and chuckled.* **2.** To put or place (sthg.) with a loud sharp sound: *slapping a price tag on the*

package. —*intr.* To strike or beat with the force or sound of a slap: *waves slapping against the canoe.*

slap•dash (slăp′dăsh′) *adj.* Characterized by haste or carelessness: *slapdash work.* —*adv.* In a reckless, haphazard manner: *She ran slapdash through the store grabbing this and that.*

slap•stick (slăp′stĭk′) *n.* [U] A form of comedy marked by physical humor and crude practical jokes.

slash (slăsh) *v.* —*tr.* **1.** To cut or form (sthg.) with forceful sweeping strokes: *We slashed a path through the overgrown grass.* **2.** To make a gash in (sbdy./sthg.): *The burglar slashed the screen with a knife.* **3.** To reduce (sthg.) greatly: *The store will slash prices for the sale.* —*intr.* To make forceful sweeping strokes with or as if with a sharp instrument: *He was slashing at the ropes.* —*n.* **1.** A forceful sweeping stroke made with a sharp instrument: *took a slash at the thick vines.* **2.** A long cut or opening made by such a stroke: *The knife left a slash in my leg.* **3.** A sharp reduction: *Congress is making slashes in the national budget.*

slat (slăt) *n.* A flat narrow strip of metal or wood.

slate (slāt) *n.* **1.** [U] A fine-grained rock that splits into thin layers with smooth surfaces: *Slate was used for blackboards in the past.* **2.** [C] A record of past performance or activity: *starting with a clean slate.* **3.** [C] A list of the candidates of a political party running for office. —*tr.v.* **slat•ed, slat•ing, slates.** To schedule or designate (sbdy./sthg.): *slated the appointment for Tuesday.* ♦ **a clean slate.** A new beginning: *She started the year with a clean slate and quit smoking.*

slath•er (slăth′ər) *tr.v.* To spread (sthg.) thickly: *She slathered butter on her bread.*

slaugh•ter (slô′tər) *n.* [U] **1.** The killing of animals for food. **2.** The killing of a large number of people; a massacre. —*tr.v.* **1.** To kill (an animal) for food. **2.** To kill (people) brutally or in large numbers. —**slaugh′ter•er** *n.*

slave (slāv) *n.* **1.** A person who is owned by and forced to work for sbdy. else. **2.** A person completely controlled by a specified person or influence: *a slave to his appetites.* **3.** A person who works very hard: *a slave to his job.* —*intr.v.* **slaved, slav•ing, slaves.** To work very hard; toil: *She slaved at the stove for hours preparing dinner.*

slave driver *n. Informal.* An extremely demanding employer or supervisor: *Your boss must be a slave driver to make you work such long hours.*

slav•er•y (slā′və rē *or* slāv′rē) *n.* [U] **1.** The condition of being a slave: *Many Africans were sold into slavery.* **2.** The practice of owning slaves: *Slavery is against the law.* **3.** Hard work or poor conditions like that of a slave: *Working in a coal mine is slavery.*

slav·ish (slā′vĭsh) *adj.* **1.** Behaving in a fearful or submissive way: *slavish devotion.* **2.** Showing no originality; imitative: *a slavish copy of another artist's work.* —**slav′ish·ly** *adv.* —**slav′ish·ness** *n.* [U]

slay (slā) *tr.v.* **slew** (slōō), **slain** (slān), **slay·ing, slays. 1.** To kill (sbdy./sthg.) violently. **2.** *Slang.* To overwhelm (sbdy.), as with laughter: *Those old jokes still slay me.* —**slay′er** *n.*

HOMONYMS: slay, sleigh (sled).

slea·zy (slē′zē) *adj.* **slea·zi·er, slea·zi·est. 1.** Shabby and dirty: *a sleazy tavern.* **2.** Disreputable or dishonest; corrupt: *a sleazy character.* **3.** Made of low-quality materials; cheap: *sleazy clothes.* —**slea′zi·ly** *adv.* —**slea′zi·ness** *n.* [U]

sled (slĕd) *n.* **1.** A vehicle mounted on runners, used for carrying people or loads over snow and ice. **2.** A light frame mounted on runners, used by children for coasting over snow and ice. —*intr.v.* **sled·ded, sled·ding, sleds.** To ride on a sled: *The children sledded down the hill.*

sledge·ham·mer (slĕj′hăm′ər) *n.* A long heavy hammer, often held with both hands, used for heavy work.

sleek (slēk) *adj.* **1.** Smooth and glossy: *a sleek head of hair.* **2.** Neat, trim, and graceful in appearance: *a sleek racing car.* —**sleek′ly** *adv.* —**sleek′ness** *n.* [U]

sleep (slēp) *n.* [U] **1.** A natural condition of rest, occurring periodically in many animals, that is characterized by unconsciousness and a decrease in bodily movement. **2.** A period of this form of rest: *I had a good night's sleep.* —*v.* **slept** (slĕpt), **sleep·ing, sleeps.** —*intr.* **1.** To be in or pass into a state of sleep: *Be quiet! The baby is sleeping.* **2.** To be inactive or inattentive: *The sudden question caught me sleeping.* —*tr.* **1.** To pass or get rid of (sthg.) by sleeping: *slept away the afternoon.* **2.** To provide (a number of people) with beds: *This cabin sleeps four.* ◆ **put to sleep.** To give an animal a drug to kill it without pain: *The sick old dog had to be put to sleep.* **sleep around.** *intr.v. Informal.* To have sexual intercourse with many people: *People who sleep around are more likely to get AIDS than those who don't.* **sleep in.** *intr.v.* To sleep later than usual: *She likes to sleep in on Saturdays.* **sleep like a log.** To sleep deeply: *He sleeps like a log when he's in the country.* **sleep off.** *tr.v.* [sep.] To get rid of (sthg.) by sleeping: *She usually sleeps off a hangover.* **sleep on it.** *Informal.* To consider sthg. overnight before deciding: *I might*

accept your offer; let me sleep on it and I'll call you tomorrow. **sleep over.** *intr.v.* To spend the night as a guest in another's home: *Our daughter is sleeping over at her friend's.* **sleep through.** *tr.v.* [insep.] To continue to sleep and miss (sthg.) one had planned to see, do, or participate in: *I set the alarm but slept through my exam.* **sleep with.** *tr.v.* [insep.] *Informal.* To have sexual relations with (sbdy.): *She refuses to sleep with anyone until she's married.*

sleep·er (slē′pər) *n.* **1.** A person or an animal that sleeps: *a sound sleeper.* **2.** Something, such as a movie, play, or contestant, that gets little attention at first but then becomes unexpectedly popular or successful: *Some good movies have been sleepers.*

sleep·ing bag (slē′pĭng) *n.* A large warmly lined bag in which a person may sleep, especially outdoors: *We bought new sleeping bags for the camping trip.*

sleep·less (slēp′lĭs) *adj.* **1.** Marked by a lack of sleep; wakeful: *sleepless nights.* **2.** Never resting; always alert or active: *The worried parents kept a sleepless watch over the sick child.* —**sleep′less·ly** *adv.* —**sleep′less·ness** *n.* [U]

sleep·walk·ing (slēp′wô′kĭng) *n.* [U] The act of walking about while asleep. —**sleep′walk′er** *n.*

sleep·y (slē′pē) *adj.* **sleep·i·er, sleep·i·est. 1.** Ready for or needing sleep: *Are you sleepy yet?* **2.** Dulled from sleep: *sleepy eyes.* **3.** Quiet; inactive: *a sleepy town.* —**sleep′i·ly** *adv.* —**sleep′i·ness** *n.* [U]

sleep·y·head (slē′pē hĕd′) *n. Informal.* A sleepy person: *It's time to get up, sleepyhead.*

sleet (slēt) *n.* [U] Water that falls to the earth in the form of frozen or partially frozen raindrops: *Sleet covered the roads.* —*intr.v.* To fall as sleet.

sleeve (slēv) *n.* **1.** The part of a garment that covers all or part of the arm. **2.** A case or covering into which an object or a device fits: *a record sleeve.* ◆ **up (one's) sleeve.** Hidden but ready to be used: *I still have a few tricks up my sleeve.*

sleeved (slēvd) *adj.* Describing the sleeves of a piece of clothing: *a long-sleeved shirt; a short-sleeved dress.*

sleeveless (slēv′lĭs) *adj.* Without sleeves: *a sleeveless dress.*

sleigh (slā) *n.* A light vehicle on low runners for use on snow or ice, with one or more seats and usually drawn by a horse.

HOMONYMS: sleigh, slay (kill).

sleight of hand (slīt) *n., pl.* **sleights of hand.** [C; U] A trick or set of tricks per-

S

formed by a juggler or magician so quickly that one cannot see how it is done.

slen·der (slĕn′dər) *adj.* **1.** Long and thin: *a slender model.* See Synonyms at **lean²**. **2.** Small in amount or extent: *a slender chance of winning.* —**slen′der·ly** *adv.* —**slen′der·ness** *n.* [U]

slept (slĕpt) *v.* Past tense and past participle of **sleep.**

sleuth (slooth) *n.* An old-fashioned word for a detective.

slew¹ (sloo) *n. Informal.* A large amount or number: *We caught a whole slew of fish.*

slew² (sloo) *v.* Past tense of **slay.**

slice (slīs) *n.* **1.** A thin broad piece cut from a larger amount: *a slice of bread.* **2.** A share or portion: *a slice of the profits.* —*v.* **sliced, slic·ing, slic·es.** —*tr.* To cut (sthg.) into slices: *slice a loaf of bread.* —*intr.* To move like a knife: *The airplane sliced through the clouds.* —**slic′er** *n.*

slick (slĭk) *adj.* **1.** Smooth and slippery: *slick ice.* **2.** Acting or done with skill and ease: *a slick tennis shot.* **3.** Shrewd; crafty: *a slick business deal.* **4.** Attractive at first, but really shallow or insincere: *a slick writing style.* —*n.* A smooth or slippery surface or area: *an oil slick on the highway.* —*v.* ◆ **slick down** or **back.** *tr.v.* [sep.] To make (sthg.) smooth, glossy, or oily: *He slicked back his hair with water.*

slick·er (slĭk′ər) *n.* **1.** A raincoat made of a glossy or shiny material. **2.** *Informal.* A person with stylish clothing and fancy manners: *a city slicker.*

slide (slīd) *v.* **slid** (slĭd), **slid·ing, slides.** —*intr.* **1.** To move smoothly over a surface while maintaining continuous contact: *The car slid along the ice.* **2.** To move or pass quietly: *I slid past the door to his office so he wouldn't see me.* **3.** To lose a secure footing; slip: *I slid on the wet floor.* **4.** To move downward or into a less favorable position: *Prices began to slide.* **5.** To go without being acted on: *Let the matter slide.* —*tr.* To cause (sbdy./sthg.) to slip or slide: *Slide that box over here.* —*n.* **1.** A sliding action or movement: *a graceful slide across the ice.* **2.** A playground apparatus that includes a smooth chute for sliding down. **3.** A photographic image formed on a transparent piece of material for projection on a screen. **4.** A small glass plate on which things are placed for examination by microscope. **5.** A fall of a mass of rock, earth, or snow down a slope; an avalanche or a landslide: *The rock slide killed several tourists.*

slide

Synonyms: slide, glide, skid, coast. These verbs mean to move smoothly and continuously over or as if over a slippery surface. **Slide** suggests rapid, easy movement without loss of contact with the surface: *A tear slid down my cheek.* **Glide** means to move in a smooth, free-flowing, seemingly effortless way: *A submarine glided silently through the water.* **Skid** means to slide uncontrollably, often in a sideways direction: *The car skidded on a patch of ice.* **Coast** often means to slide downward, especially as a result of gravity: *We coasted down the hill on our sleds.*

---

slide projector *n.* A machine that projects an image from a slide onto a screen.

slight (slīt) *adj.* **1.** Small in size, amount, or degree: *a slight change in temperature.* **2.** Of little importance; trifling: *a slight misunderstanding.* **3.** Small and slender; delicate: *a slight girl.* —*tr.v.* To treat (sbdy./sthg.) rudely by making a person seem unimportant or by insulting: *He slighted my best friend.* —*n.* An act of slighting, especially an insult to one's pride or self-esteem: *She never forgets a slight.* —**slight′ness** *n.* [U]

slight·ly (slīt′lē) *adv.* **1.** To a small degree or extent; somewhat: *a slightly high price.* **2.** Slenderly; delicately: *slightly built.*

slim (slĭm) *adj.* **slim·mer, slim·mest. 1.** Small in thickness as compared to height; slender; thin: *a slim person.* **2.** Small in quantity or amount: *a slim chance of success.* —*v.* **slimmed, slim·ming, slims.** ◆ **slim down** *intr.v.* To become thinner: *She plans to slim down by exercising.* —*tr.v.* [sep.] To make (sthg.) smaller: *I hope to slim down my chances of losing the game.*

slime (slīm) *n.* [U] Thick, sticky, slippery mud or a similar substance. —**slim′i·ness** *n.* [U] —**slim′y** *adj.*

sling (slĭng) *n.* **1.** A band of cloth suspended from the neck to support an injured arm or hand. **2.** A looped rope, strap, or chain for lifting or supporting sthg. **3.** A slingshot. —*tr.v.* **slung** (slŭng), **sling·ing, slings. 1.** To carry (sbdy./sthg.): *Sling the pack over your shoulder.* **2.** To throw (sthg.) with or as if with a sling: *slinging rocks.* **3.** To place (sthg.) so as to hang loosely: *We slung the hammock between two trees.*

sling·shot (slĭng′shŏt′) *n.* A Y-shaped stick with an elastic strap attached to the prongs, used for shooting small stones.

slink (slĭngk) *intr.v.* **slunk** (slŭngk) also **slinked, slink·ing, slinks.** To move in a quiet sneaky way: *The cat slunk about in the bushes.*

slip (slĭp) *v.* **slipped, slip·ping, slips.** —*intr.* **1.** To move smoothly and quietly: *slipped past the guards.* **2.** To pass gradually or unnoticed: *weeks slipping away.* **3.** To lose one's balance or foothold: *He slipped and sprained his ankle.* **4.** To slide out of place; shift position: *The*

S

beams supporting the mine's roof were beginning to slip. **5.** To escape from a hold or grip: *The dog slipped out of its collar.* **6.** To fall into fault or error: *Since her mistakes were pointed out to her, she's only slipped once.* **7.** To decline from a former standard or level; fall: *The movie star's popularity has slipped.* —*tr.* **1.** To cause (sthg.) to move in a smooth, easy, or sliding motion: *slipped the rope over the branch.* **2.** To place or insert (sthg.) smoothly and quietly: *slip a note under the door.* **3.** To get loose or free from (sbdy./sthg.): *The cat slipped my grasp.* —*n.* **1.** The act or an instance of slipping or sliding: *a bad slip in the dark.* **2.** A small piece of paper: *Do you have a slip of paper that I can write the phone number on?* **3.** An error or oversight; a mistake: *With his record, he can't afford another slip.* **4.** A woman's undergarment that hangs from the shoulders or the waist and is worn under a dress or skirt. ◆ **give (one) the slip.** *Slang.* To escape from sbdy.: *The thief gave the police the slip.* **let slip.** To reveal sthg. without meaning to: *Before she could stop herself, she'd let the secret slip.* **slip of the tongue.** A statement that accidentally reveals sthg. the speaker wanted to keep secret: *One slip of the tongue could ruin our plans.* **slip on** or **off.** *tr.v.* [sep.] To put (sthg.) on or take (sthg.) off quickly and easily: *She slipped on her shoes.* **slip into** or **out of.** *tr.v.* [insep.] To put (sthg.) on or take (sthg.) off quickly and easily: *Let me slip out of this wet jacket.* **slip one over on.** To trick or deceive sbdy.: *We slipped one over on the boss today.* **slip (one's) mind.** To be forgotten: *Her birthday slipped my mind.* **slip through (one's) fingers.** To escape from (sbdy.), as an opportunity: *The promotion slipped through his fingers.*

slip up. *intr.v.* To make a mistake: *We can't afford to slip up again.*

slip•page (slĭp′ĭj) *n.* **1.** [U] The act or an instance of slipping: *slippage on a rocky mountain slope.* **2.** [C] The amount that sthg. has slipped: *a slippage of 20 points in the stock market.*

slip•per (slĭp′ər) *n.* A low shoe that can be slipped on and off easily and is usually worn indoors.

slip•per•y (slĭp′ə rē) *adj.* **slip•per•i•er, slip•per•i•est. 1.** Causing or tending to cause slipping, as a surface that is oily or wet: *slippery winter roads.* **2.** Not trustworthy; elusive or tricky: *a slippery character.* —**slip′per•i•ness** *n.* [U]

slip•shod (slĭp′shŏd′) *adj.* Done carelessly: *a slipshod job of writing.*

slip-up (slĭp′ŭp′) *n.* A careless mistake or an oversight: *Too many slip-ups cost him his job.*

slit (slĭt) *n.* A long, straight, narrow cut or opening: *a slit in the curtain.* —*tr.v.* **slit, slit•ting, slits.** To cut a slit in (sthg.): *slit an envelope.* —**slit′ter** *n.*

slith•er (slĭth′ər) *intr.v.* To move along by sliding or gliding like a snake: *The cat slithered noiselessly toward the bird.*

sliv•er (slĭv′ər) *n.* A thin piece cut, split, or broken off, as of wood or glass; a splinter: *cook beans with slivers of bacon.* —*tr.* & *intr.v.* To split or become split into thin pieces: *sliver wood for a fire; The fragile crystal slivered when it fell.*

slob (slŏb) *n. Informal.* A person regarded as dirty, lazy, or messy: *Her brother lives like a slob.*

slob•ber (slŏb′ər) *intr.v.* **1.** To let saliva or another liquid spill from the mouth; drool: *the baby was slobbering.* **2.** To express emotion in an overexcited or exaggerated way; gush: *Some children don't like to be slobbered over.* —*n.* Saliva or another liquid spilled from the mouth. —**slob′ber•y** *adj.*

slog (slŏg) *v.* **slogged, slog•ging, slogs.** —*intr.* **1.** To walk in a slow heavy way; plod: *slog down a muddy road.* **2.** To work very hard for long hours: *He's slogged all his life just to survive.* —*tr.* To make (one's way) slowly, heavily, and with great effort: *He slogged his way through the snow.*

slo•gan (slō′gən) *n.* A phrase expressing the goals or nature of a business, an organization, or a political candidate; a motto: *Their slogan is "Never wrong; never late."*

slop (slŏp) *n.* **1.** [U] Watery mud or a similar substance: *They trudged through the slop.* **2.** [U] Spilled or splashed liquid: *Clean up your slop.* **3.** [C] *(usually plural).* Waste food fed to animals. —*v.* **slopped, slop•ping, slops.** —*intr.* **1.** To be spilled or splashed: *Soup slopped over the edge of the bowl.* **2.** To walk heavily or messily, as through mud or puddles. —*tr.* **1.** To spill (liquid): *Don't slop your soup.* **2.** To feed slops to (animals): *slop the pigs.*

slope (slōp) *intr.v.* **sloped, slop•ing, slopes.** To incline upward or downward; be slanted: *The road slopes gently.* —*n.* **1.** An inclined line, surface, direction, or position. **2.** A part of Earth's surface forming an incline: *ski slopes.*

slop•py (slŏp′ē) *adj.* **slop•pi•er, slop•pi•est. 1.** Messy; untidy: *a sloppy room.* **2.** Carelessly done; full of mistakes: *a sloppy research paper.* **3.** *Informal.* Overly sentimental; gushy: *a sloppy greeting card.* **4.** Wet and messy: *a sloppy kiss.* —**slop′pi•ly** *adv.* —**slop′pi•ness** *n.* [U]

slosh (slŏsh) *v.* —*tr.* To spill or splash (a liquid): *He sloshed paint on the fence.* —*intr.* To splash in water or another liquid: *Elephants sloshed in the river.*

slot (slŏt) *n.* **1.** A narrow opening: *a mail slot.* **2.** An assigned place or position: *a new time slot for the TV program.* —*tr.v.* **slot•ted,**

slot·ting, slots. To cut or make a slot in (sthg.): *She slotted the pork chops to insert the seasoning.*

sloth (slôth *or* slōth *or* slŏth) *n.* **1.** [C] A slow-moving tropical American mammal that lives in trees and hangs upside-down from branches by its claws. **2.** [U] Dislike and avoidance of work; laziness: *Sloth will be her undoing.* —**sloth′ful** *adj.* —**sloth′ful·ness** *n.* [U]

slouch (slouch) *intr.v.* To sit, stand, or walk with a bent posture: *Don't slouch in your chair.* —*n.* **1.** An awkward, overly relaxed posture or gait: *walk with a slouch.* **2.** *Slang.* A lazy or incompetent person: *OK, so I'm a slouch.*

slough (slŭf) *n.* An outer layer or covering that is shed. —*v.* ♦ **slough off.** *tr.v.* [sep.] To cast (sthg.) off; shed: *The snake sloughed off its old skin.* —*intr.v.* To come off: *The scab on his knee sloughed off.*

slov·en·ly (slŭv′ən lē) *adj.* **1.** Messy or untidy in dress or appearance: *He dresses in slovenly clothing.* **2.** Careless: *She was fired because of slovenly work.* —**slov′en·li·ness** *n.* [U]

slow (slō) *adj.* **1.** Not moving or acting quickly: *a slow train.* **2.** Taking or requiring a long time: *a slow dinner.* **3.** Behind the correct time: *My watch is slow.* **4.** Not willing: *We were slow to volunteer for such a boring job.* **5.** Sluggish; not active. *Business is slow.* **6.** Not mentally quick: *a slow learner.* —*adv.* **1.** In a slow manner; not quickly or rapidly: *Go slow in heavy traffic.* **2.** So as to fall behind the correct time: *This watch runs slow.* —*tr. & intr.v.* To make or become slow or slower: *The brakes slowed the car. The pace of the runners slowed.* —**slow′ly** *adv.* —**slow′ness** *n.* [U]

slow·down (slō′doun′) *n.* The act of slowing down, especially an intentional slowing down of production by workers or management: *The recent slowdown hurt business.*

slow motion *n.* [U] A filmmaking technique in which the action as projected is slower than the original action.

slow·poke (slō′pōk′) *n. Informal.* A person who works, acts, or moves slowly: *Don't be such a slowpoke! We'll miss the bus.*

sludge (slŭj) *n.* [U] **1.** Semisolid material, as that formed from the treatment of sewage. **2.** Mud covering the ground or forming a deposit, as on a river bed.

slug¹ (slŭg) *n.* **1.** *Informal.* A bullet. **2.** A small metal disk for use in a vending or gambling machine, especially one used illegally.

slug² (slŭg) *n.* **1.** A snail-like creature, but without a shell. **2.** *Informal.* A lazy, idle person.

slug³ (slŭg) *tr.v.* **slugged, slug·ging, slugs.** To strike (sbdy./sthg.) hard, especially with the fist or a baseball bat. —*n.* A hard blow, as with the fist or a baseball bat. —**slug′ger** *n.*

slug·gish (slŭg′ĭsh) *adj.* **1.** Showing little activity or movement; slow: *a sluggish stream.*

2. Lacking alertness, vigor, or energy: *a sluggish response.* —**slug′gish·ly** *adv.* —**slug′gish·ness** *n.* [U]

slum (slŭm) *n.* An overcrowded urban area marked by dirt and poor housing conditions: *Poverty forces many people to live in slums.*

slum·ber (slŭm′bər) *intr.v.* **1.** To sleep: *The child slumbered in his crib.* **2.** To be calm or inactive: *The city slumbers.* —*n.* **1.** Sleep: *She fell into a deep slumber while watching TV.* **2.** A state of inactivity: *a bear in its winter slumber.* —**slum′ber·er** *n.*

slumber party *n.* A party in which a group of girls sleep overnight at one of the girls' houses.

slump (slŭmp) *intr.v.* **1.** To fall or sink heavily; collapse: *She slumped onto the sofa.* **2.** To decline or sink suddenly: *Business slumped badly during the spring.* —*n.* **1.** A sudden decline: *a stock market slump.* **2.** A drooping or slouching posture. **3.** An extended period of poor performance, especially in a sport: *a slump in his tennis game.*

slung (slŭng) *v.* Past tense and past participle of **sling.**

slunk (slŭngk) *v.* A past tense and a past participle of **slink.**

slur (slûr) *tr.v.* **slurred, slur·ring, slurs. 1.** To pronounce (sthg.) carelessly or indistinctly: *He was so tired that he began to slur his words.* **2.** To speak badly of (sbdy./sthg.): *slur a coworker's reputation.* —*n.* **1.** A discourteous or negative remark: *That slur hurt him deeply.* **2.** A slurred sound: *speak with a slight slur.*

slurp (slûrp) *tr. & intr.v.* To eat or drink noisily: *slurp through a straw; slurp soup.* —*n.* A sucking noise made when eating or drinking: *The sink drain made a series of slurps.*

slush (slŭsh) *n.* [U] Partially melted snow or ice. —**slush′i·ness** *n.* [U] —**slush′y** *adj.*

slut (slŭt) *n. Offensive.* A woman considered immoral because it is believed that she has sex with many people. —**slut′ty** *adj.*

sly (slī) *adj.* **sli·er** (slī′ər), **sli·est** (slī′ĕst) also **sly·er, sly·est. 1.** Clever or cunning: *a sly fox.* **2.** Secretive or dishonest: *a sly trick.* **3.** Playfully mischievous: *a sly wink.* ♦ **on the sly.** In a way intended to escape notice; secretly: *She took another job on the sly.* —**sly′ness** *n.* [U]

smack¹ (smăk) *tr.v.* **1.** To press together and open (the lips) quickly and noisily, as in eating: *The baby smacked his lips after he drank his bottle.* **2.** To kiss (sbdy.) noisily: *She smacked him on the cheek.* **3.** To slap or strike (sbdy./sthg.) with a loud sound: *He threatened to smack his dog if it didn't stop barking.* —*n.* **1.** The sound made by smacking the lips: *a loud smack.* **2.** A noisy kiss: *a smack on the cheek.* **3.** A sharp blow or loud slap: *We saw the man give his son a smack.* —*adv.* **1.** With a smack: *She fell smack on her back.* **2.** Directly: *We're smack in the middle of a big project.*

S

smack² (smăk) *intr.v.* To give an indication or suggestion: *This plan does not smack of success.*

smack³ (smăk) *n.* [U] *Slang.* Heroin.

small (smôl) *adj.* **1.** Being below the average in size, number, quantity, or extent; little: *a small car; a small business.* See Synonyms at **little. 2.** Limited in importance; trivial: *a small matter.* **3.** Carrying on an activity in a limited way: *a small farmer.* **4.** Not fully grown; very young: *a small child.* **5.** Narrow in outlook; petty: *a small mind.* **6.** Soft; low: *a small voice.* —*n.* **1.** Something that is smaller and especially narrower than the rest: *the small of the back.* **2.** A size of an article of clothing. —**small'ish** *adj.* —**small'ness** *n.* [U]

small change *n.* [U] **1.** Coins that are low in value. **2.** *Informal.* Something of little value or significance: *Treating all of us to dinner was just small change to her.*

small fry *n.* [U] *Informal.* **1.** Young or small children. **2.** People or things regarded as trivial or unimportant.

small intestine *n.* The part of the digestive system in which digestion is completed and nutrients are absorbed by the blood, extending from the outlet of the stomach to the beginning of the large intestine.

small-mind•ed (smôl'mīn'dĭd) *adj.* Having a narrow or selfish attitude: *She's a small-minded person.* —**small'-mind'ed•ly** *adv.* —**small'-mind'ed•ness** *n.* [U]

small potatoes *pl.n. Informal.* Unimportant or trivial matters: *Compared to yours, my problems seem like small potatoes.*

small•pox (smôl'pŏks') *n.* [U] A serious, often fatal, highly infectious viral disease with symptoms that include pimples that develop into pockmarks.

small talk *n.* [U] Ordinary conversation: *We engaged in small talk before the meeting.*

smart (smärt) *adj.* **1.** Intelligent, clever, or bright: *a smart student.* **2.** Expert in dealing with others: *a smart business person.* **3.** Rudely flippant; sassy: *That's enough of your smart talk!* **4.** Quick or energetic in movement: *a smart pace.* **5.** Fashionable; elegant: *a smart new coat.* —*intr.v.* To feel a sharp stinging pain: *My leg began to smart from the bee's sting.* —**smart'ly** *adv.* —**smart'ness** *n.* [U]

SYNONYMS: smart, intelligent, bright, brilliant, intellectual. These adjectives all mean talented in using one's mind. **Smart** means able to learn quickly and often also able to look out for oneself: *Her aunt was smart to tune up her bicycle before the long ride.* **Intelligent** means able to handle new situations and problems and good at figuring things out: *Only the most intelligent students can keep up with the teacher's rapid pace.* **Bright** means able to learn quickly and easily: *He is so bright, he learned to play chess in one hour.* **Brilliant** means unusually and impressively intelligent: *The most brilliant minds in the country have gathered for this meeting.* **Intellectual** means able to understand difficult or abstract concepts: *Her intellectual abilities help her to appreciate difficult poetry.*

smart al•eck (ăl'ĭk) *n. Informal.* A person who is rudely assertive or conceited: *My brother has always been a smart aleck.*

smart•en (smär'tn) *tr.v.* **1.** To improve (sthg.) in appearance: *smarten their kitchen.* **2.** To make (sthg.) quicker: *smarten the pace.* ◆ **smarten up.** *intr.v. Informal.* To make oneself smart or smarter: *He needs to smarten up and finish school.*

smash (smăsh) *v.* —*tr.* **1.** To break (sthg.) into pieces noisily and violently; shatter: *smash an egg.* **2.** To throw or strike (sthg.) violently and suddenly: *The wind smashed the tree into the house.* **3.** To destroy or crush (sbdy./sthg.) completely: *The troops smashed the rebellion.* —*intr.* **1.** To strike or collide noisily and violently: *The car smashed into the guard rail.* **2.** To break into pieces: *The vase smashed on the floor.* —*n.* **1.** The act or sound of smashing. **2.** *Informal.* A total success: *The new musical proved to be a smash.* —**smash'er** *n.*

smashed (smăsht) *adj. Informal.* Drunk: *He was smashed last night.*

smash•up (smăsh'ŭp') *n.* A serious collision of vehicles: *a three-car smashup.*

smat•ter•ing (smăt'ər ĭng) *n. (usually singular).* Superficial or incomplete knowledge: *He knows a smattering of Latin.*

smear (smîr) *v.* —*tr.* **1.** To spread, cover, or stain (sbdy./sthg.) with a sticky, greasy, or dirty substance: *The child smeared the wall with food.* **2.** To put (a substance) on a surface; apply: *I smeared suntan lotion on my arms.* **3.** To destroy the reputation of (sbdy.): *The ad campaign smeared the candidate.* —*intr.* To be or become stained or dirtied: *The paint on the wall had smeared.* —*n.* **1.** A stain or mark made by smearing. **2.** An attempt to destroy a person's reputation; slander.

smell (smĕl) *v.* **smelled** or **smelt** (smĕlt), **smell•ing, smells.** —*tr.* To detect or notice the odor of (sthg.) by means of the nose: *smell smoke.* —*intr.* **1.a.** To have or give off an odor: *Roses smell good.* **b.** To have or give off an unpleasant odor; stink: *That garbage smells.* **2.** To use the sense of smell; detect the scent of sthg. —*n.* **1.** [U] The sense by which odors are perceived; the ability to smell: *Dogs have a good sense of smell.* **2.** [C] The quality that permits sthg. to be perceived by the sense of smell; an odor: *the smell of food cooking.* See

S

Synonyms at **scent. 3.** [C] A distinctive quality; an aura or a feeling: *This plan has the smell of success.*

smell•y (smĕl′ē) *adj.* **smell•i•er, smell•i•est.** Having an unpleasant or offensive odor: *smelly feet.*

smelt¹ (smĕlt) *tr. & intr.* To melt or cause to melt in order to extract the metals from ore.

smelt² (smĕlt) *v.* A past tense and a past participle of **smell.**

smid•gen (smĭj′ən) *n.* A very small amount; a bit: *Add a smidgen of salt to the stew.*

smile (smīl) *n.* A facial expression formed by an upward curving of the corners of the mouth and indicating pleasure, affection, or amusement: *a happy smile.* —*v.* **smiled, smil•ing, smiles.** —*intr.* **1.** To have or form a smile: *She was smiling when she left the office.* **2.** To express approval: *The committee smiled on our proposal.* —*tr.* To express (sthg.) with a smile: *He smiled his agreement.* —**smil′er** *n.* —**smil′ing•ly** *adv.*

smirk (smûrk) *intr.v.* To smile in an annoying manner that expresses too much satisfaction with oneself: *smirk over an easy success.* —*n.* A smile made in such a way: *Wipe that smirk off your face!* —**smirk′er** *n.*

smith (smĭth) *n.* A person who forges and shapes metal: *a blacksmith.*

smith•er•eens (smĭth′ə rēnz′) *pl.n.* Informal. Splintered pieces, small bits: *The glass smashed to smithereens.*

smit•ten (smĭt′n) *adj.* Very attracted to or in love: *He's smitten with the new girl at school and thinks about nothing else.*

smock (smŏk) *n.* A long loose piece of clothing resembling a coat, worn over other clothes to protect them: *an artist's smock.*

smog (smŏg *or* smôg) *n.* [U] Fog that has become polluted with smoke and chemicals, usually present in large urban or industrial areas. —**smog′gy** *adj.*

smoke (smōk) *n.* **1.** [U] A gas, usually containing small pieces of soot or other solids and resulting from incomplete burning of materials. **2.** [C] The act of smoking tobacco: *Do you mind if I have a smoke?* —*v.* **smoked, smok•ing, smokes.** —*intr.* **1.** To draw in and exhale smoke from a cigarette, cigar, pipe, or another smoking material. **2.** To produce smoke: *The engine is smoking.* —*tr.* **1.** To draw in and exhale smoke from (a cigarette, cigar, or pipe). **2.** To preserve (meat or fish) by exposing it to wood smoke. ◆ **go up in smoke.** To be destroyed and leave nothing behind: *Our relationship went up in smoke when my girlfriend moved away.* **smoke out.** *tr.v.* [sep.] To force (sbdy./sthg.) out of a place of hiding by or as if by the use of smoke: *smoke out the guilty parties.*

smoke•less (smōk′lĭs) *adj.* Producing or giving off little or no smoke: *smokeless tobacco.*

smok•er (smō′kər) *n.* **1.** A person who

smokes tobacco. **2.** A device in which meat is smoked.

smoke screen *or* **smoke•screen** (smōk′-skrēn′) *n.* An action or a statement used to conceal actual plans or intentions: *They hid behind a smoke screen of vague promises.*

smoke•stack (smōk′stăk′) *n.* A large chimney or vertical pipe through which smoke and waste gases and vapors are discharged.

smok•y (smō′kē) *adj.* **smok•i•er, smok•i•est. 1.** Producing or giving off a large amount of smoke: *a smoky furnace.* **2.** Resembling smoke in smell, taste, or appearance: *a jacket of a smoky color.* —**smok′i•ness** *n.* [U]

smol•der (smōl′dər) *intr.v.* **1.** To burn with little smoke and no flame: *Logs smoldered in the fireplace.* **2.** To show signs of anger or hatred that is held inside or hidden: *He sat quietly, still smoldering from the insult.*

smooch (smōōch) *tr. & intr.v.* To kiss: *The dog smooched me on the face. The two of them are always smooching when they think no one's looking.*

smooth (smōōth) *adj.* **1.** Having a surface free from roughness; even: *smooth skin.* **2.** Having a fine consistency or texture: *the smooth side of the fabric.* **3.** Having an even or gentle motion or movement: *a smooth ride.* **4.** Calm; mild: *a smooth manner.* **5.** Flattering but not worthy of trust: *a smooth talker.* **6.** Having no difficulties: *a smooth operation.* See Synonyms at **easy.** —*tr.v.* **smoothed, smooth•ing, smoothes. 1.** To make (sthg.) smooth: *smooth out the wrinkles in a dress.* **2.** To make (sbdy./sthg.) calm; soothe: *He smoothed her quick anger.* **3.** To make (sthg.) less hard or crude; refine: *More people would like you if you smoothed the rough edges of your humor.* ◆ **smooth over.** *tr.v.* [sep.] To help solve (a problem or difficulty): *He tried to smooth the problem over by calling the client.* —**smooth′ly** *adv.* —**smooth′ness** *n.* [U]

smor•gas•bord (smôr′gəs bôrd′) *n.* [C; U] A buffet meal with a large variety of dishes.

smoth•er (smŭth′ər) *v.* —*tr.* **1.** To cause (sbdy.) to die from lack of oxygen; suffocate: *The mother dog accidentally smothered one of the pups.* **2.** To cause (a fire) to go out because of lack of oxygen: *We smothered the campfire.* **3.** To cover (food) with another food: *smother the hotdog with onions.* **4.** To lavish attention on (sbdy.): *smother a child with love.* —*intr.* To suffocate: *I feel like I'm smothering in this heat.*

smudge (smŭj) *v.* **smudged, smudg•ing, smudg•es.** —*tr.* To smear (sthg.): *The rain smudged the paint.* —*intr.* To become smudged: *The fresh paint smudged.* —*n.* A blotch or smear: *a smudge of lipstick.* —**smudg′y** *adj.*

smug (smŭg) *adj.* **smug•ger, smug•gest.** Satisfied or contented but not concerned for others: *She had a smug sense of well-being.* —**smug′ly** *adv.* —**smug′ness** *n.* [U]

S

smug·gle (smŭg′əl) *v.* **smug·gled, smug·gling, smug·gles.** —*tr.* To import or export (sthg.) illegally or without paying customs taxes: *smuggling diamonds.* —*intr.* To engage in smuggling. —**smug′gler** *n.*

smut (smŭt) *n.* [U] Obscene material, such as pictures or writing. —**smut′ty** *adj.*

Sn The symbol for the element **tin** (sense 1).

snack (snăk) *n.* **1.** A quick light meal: *Let's just have a snack.* **2.** Food eaten between meals: *an after-school snack of cookies and milk.* —*intr.v.* To eat a snack: *She snacked on potato chips.*

snag (snăg) *n.* **1.** A sharp, rough, or jagged projection: *a rocky snag.* **2.** A break, pull, or tear in fabric: *a snag in my dress.* **3.** An unforeseen or hidden obstacle: *Finishing the job was delayed when we hit a snag.* —*v.* **snagged, snag·ging, snags.** —*tr.* To catch, damage, or destroy (sthg.) by or as if by a snag: *I snagged my coat on a branch.* —*intr.* To be damaged by a snag: *The fishing line snagged on a log.*

snail (snāl) *n.* A slow-moving, soft-bodied land or water animal with a coiled spiral shell. ♦ **at a snail's pace.** Moving along very slowly: *Construction of the new highway is proceeding at a snail's pace.*

snake (snāk) *n.* **1.** A reptile with a long narrow body and no legs. Some snakes are poisonous. **2.** A sneaky or untrustworthy person. ♦ **snake in the grass.** A person who is sneaky or untrustworthy.

snap (snăp) *v.* **snapped, snap·ping, snaps.** —*intr.* **1.** To make a sharp cracking sound: *The burning log snapped in the fireplace.* **2.** To break suddenly with a sharp sound: *The twigs snapped underfoot.* **3.** To break under pressure or tension: *The rope snapped.* **4.** [*at*] To bite, seize, or grasp at suddenly and eagerly: *The dog snapped at my hand.* **5.** [*at*] To speak abruptly or sharply: *She snapped at him.* **6.** To open or close with a sharp sound: *The lid snapped shut.* —*tr.* **1.** To bite or snatch at (sbdy./sthg.) with the teeth: *The dog snapped the bone from my hand.* **2.** To break (sthg.) with a sharp sound: *snap twigs to start a fire.* **3.** To cause (sthg.) to make a cracking sound: *She snapped her fingers.* **4.** To close or shut (sthg.) with a sharp sound: *snap the lid on the jar.* **5.** To say (sthg.) sharply or abruptly: *snap orders.* **6.** To take (a photograph): *snap pictures.* —*n.* **1.** A sharp cracking sound: *The branch broke with a loud snap.* **2.** A sudden breaking of sthg. under strain. **3.** A fastener that closes and opens with a snapping sound. **4.** A brief spell of cold weather: *A cold snap is coming.* **5.** *Informal.* An easy task: *The math test was a snap.* —*adj.* Made or done without a lot of thought: *a snap decision.* ♦ **snap up.** *tr.v.* [*sep.*] To acquire (sthg.) quickly: *Fans snapped up the tickets.*

snap·py (snăp′ē) *adj.* **snap·pi·er, snap·pi·est. 1.** Lively; brisk: *a snappy rhythm.* **2.** *Informal.* Smart or chic in appearance: *a snappy dresser.* **3.** Irritable: *He was snappy because of lack of sleep.* —**snap′pi·ly** *adv.* —**snap′pi·ness** *n.* [U]

snap·shot (snăp′shŏt′) *n.* An informal photograph taken with a small hand-held camera.

snare (snâr) *n.* **1.** A trapping device used for capturing birds and small animals. **2.** Something that catches unsuspecting people: *The agents used stolen goods as part of a snare to catch thieves.* —*tr.v.* **snared, snar·ing, snares.** To trap (sbdy./sthg.) with or as if with a snare: *snare a rabbit; snare a thief.*

snarl¹ (snärl) *v.* —*intr.* **1.** To growl angrily or threateningly while showing the teeth: *The dog snarled.* **2.** To speak angrily or threateningly: *friends snarling at each other.* —*tr.* To say (sthg.) with anger or hostility: *snarled an answer.* —*n.* **1.** An angry or threatening growl, often made with teeth showing. **2.** A sound or tone of voice resembling this: *He made his demands in an angry snarl.*

snarl² (snärl) *n.* **1.** A tangled mass, as of hair or yarn: *Her hair was in snarls.* **2.** A confused, complicated, or tangled situation: *traffic snarl.* —*v.* —*intr.* To become tangled: *My fishing line snarled as I cast it into the water.* —*tr.* **1.** To tangle (sthg.): *The kitten snarled the wool.* **2.** To confuse (sthg.): *Snow snarled the morning commute.*

snatch (snăch) *v.* —*tr.* **1.** To grasp or grab (sbdy./sthg.) hastily or eagerly: *snatch an apple off the tree.* **2.** To steal (sthg.): *snatch a purse.* —*intr.* To try to hold or reach with the hands: *snatched at the rope.* —*n.* **1.** The act of snatching: *a snatch at the ball.* **2.** A small amount; a fragment: *a snatch of an old song.* —**snatch′er** *n.*

snaz·zy (snăz′ē) *adj.* *Slang.* Very fancy; stylish: *snazzy new clothes; a snazzy car.*

sneak (snēk) *v.* **sneaked** also **snuck** (snŭk), **sneak·ing, sneaks.** —*intr.* **1.** To go or move in a quiet secretive way: *She sneaked onto one of the boats.* **2.** To behave in a cowardly secretive way: *Don't sneak around.* —*tr.* To move, give, or take (sthg.) in a quiet secretive way: *He sneaked the photo into his pocket. Let's sneak a peek at the presents.* —*n.* A person regarded as cowardly and secretive: *My little brother is a sneak.* —**sneak′i·ly** *adv.* —**sneak′i·ness** *n.* [U] —**sneak′y** *adj.*

sneak·er (snē′kər) *n.* A sport shoe with a soft, flat rubber sole.

sneak·ing (snē′kĭng) *adj.* **1.** Acting in a secretive way. **2.** Not known or expressed: *a sneaking ambition to take over.* **3.** Gradually growing or persistent: *a sneaking suspicion.* —**sneak′ing·ly** *adv.*

sneer (snîr) *n.* A facial expression that shows lack of respect, made by raising one corner of the upper lip slightly: *The sneer on her face bothered me.* —*v.* —*tr.* To say (sthg.) with a sneer: *The man sneered an answer.* —*intr.* To show lack of respect with a sneer: *They sneered at my suggestion.* —**sneer'er** *n.*

sneeze (snēz) *intr.v.* **sneezed, sneez•ing, sneez•es.** To force air from the nose and mouth in an involuntary convulsive action: *Because of his allergies, he sneezes a lot.* —*n.* The act or the sound of sneezing: *I thought I heard a sneeze.*

snick•er (snĭk'ər) *intr.v.* To produce a partly covered laugh at sthg. that is not considered funny: *The children pointed at the mess and snickered.* —*n.* A sarcastic, partly covered laugh: *She tried to hide a snicker but failed.*

snide (snīd) *adj.* **snid•er, snid•est.** Sarcastic, slyly insulting, or cruel: *a snide remark.* —**snide'ly** *adv.*

sniff (snĭf) *v.* —*intr.* **1.** To inhale a short audible breath through the nose, as in smelling sthg.: *He sniffed at the food.* **2.** To regard sbdy./sthg. with contempt or scorn: *She sniffed at those who knew less than she.* —*tr.* **1.** To inhale (sthg.) through the nose: *sniffed the cold air.* **2.** To smell (sthg.), as in enjoyment or investigation: *sniffed the roses.* —*n.* **1.** The act or the sound of sniffing: *The dogs gave each other a sniff.* **2.** Something noticed or detected by or as if by sniffing: *a sniff of perfume.*

snif•fle (snĭf'əl) *intr.v.* **snif•fled, snif•fling, snif•fles.** To breathe noisily through a partially blocked nose, as when suffering from a head cold. —*n.* **1.** The act or sound of sniffling. **2. sniffles.** A condition, such as a head cold, that makes a person sniffle: *The baby has the sniffles.*

snip (snĭp) *tr.v.* **snipped, snip•ping, snips.** To cut or clip (sthg.) with short quick movements: *snip flowers.* —*n.* A small piece cut or clipped off: *a snip of parsley.*

snipe (snīp) *intr.v.* **sniped, snip•ing, snipes.** **1.** To shoot at others from a hiding place: *The gunman sniped at innocent people from a rooftop.* **2.** To criticize sbdy.: *He often snipes at his wife in public.* —**snip'er** *n.*

snip•pet (snĭp'ĭt) *n.* A small piece or amount: *snippets of gossip.*

snip•py (snĭp'ē) *adj.* **snip•pi•er, snip•pi•est.** *Informal.* Rude; insulting: *a snippy child; a snippy answer.*

snitch (snĭch) *Slang. v.* —*tr.* To steal (sthg. of little value): *snitch candy.* —*intr.* To tell on sbdy.; turn informer: *He snitched on his brother.* —*n.* **1.** A thief. **2.** An informer.

sniv•el (snĭv'əl) *intr.v.* **1.** To complain or whine tearfully: *Stop sniveling about your punishment.* **2.** To sniffle: *A bad cold made her snivel all the time.* —**sniv'el•er** *n.*

snob (snŏb) *n.* A person who thinks he or she is better than others: *We don't want snobs at our party.* —**snob'ber•y** (snŏb'ə rē) *n.* [U]

snob•bish (snŏb'ĭsh) *adj.* Characteristic of a snob; pretentious: *a snobbish attitude.* —**snob'bish•ly** *adv.* —**snob'bish•ness** *n.* [U]

snoop (snōōp) *intr.v.* To look or search in a sneaky secretive way: *Her brother is always snooping around.* —*n.* A person who snoops.

snoop•y (snōō'pē) *adj.* **snoop•i•er, snoop•i•est.** Likely to snoop; nosy: *the snoopiest person we know.* See Synonyms at **curious.**

snoot•y (snōō'tē) *adj.* **snoot•i•er, snoot•i•est.** *Informal.* Snobbish: *a snooty restaurant.* —**snoot'i•ly** *adv.* —**snoot'i•ness** *n.* [U]

snooze (snōōz) *intr.v.* **snoozed, snooz•ing, snooz•es.** To take a light nap; doze: *The cat snoozed in the window.* —*n.* A light nap: *I'm going to have a snooze.*

snore (snôr) *intr.v.* **snored, snor•ing, snores.** To breathe noisily through the nose and mouth while sleeping. —*n.* The act or the sound of snoring. —**snor'er** *n.*

snor•kel (snôr'kəl) *n.* A breathing device used by skin divers, consisting of a long tube curved at one end and fitted with a mouthpiece. —*intr.v.* To swim using a snorkel.

snorkel

snort (snôrt) *n.* **1.** A rough noisy sound made by breathing forcefully through the nostrils, as that made by an animal. **2.** A sound resembling this: *the snort of a steam engine.* —*v.* —*intr.* **1.** To breathe noisily and forcefully through the nostrils: *The frightened horses reared and snorted.* **2.** To make a noise expressing ridicule, disbelief, or contempt: *He snorted when she offered to pay for lunch.* —*tr.* To express (sthg.) with a snort: *She snorted her disapproval.*

snot (snŏt) *Slang.* **1.** Nasal mucus. **2.** An annoying or arrogant person. —**snot'ti•ly** *adv.* —**snot'ti•ness** *n.* [U] —**snot'ty** *adj.*

snout (snout) *n.* The nose, jaws, or front part of the head of an animal. —**snout'ed** *adj.*

snow (snō) *n.* **1.** [U] Crystals of ice that form from water vapor in the atmosphere and fall to earth. **2.** [C] A falling of snow; a snowstorm. —*v.* —*intr.* To fall to the earth as snow. —*tr.* **1.** To isolate, block, or cover (sbdy./sthg.) with or as if with snow: *We were snowed in.* **2.** To impress (sbdy.): *She really snowed her boss.*
♦ **be snowed under.** To be overwhelmed: *I was snowed under with work.*

snow•ball (snō'bôl') *n.* A mass of soft wet snow packed into a ball that can be thrown. —*intr.v.* To grow rapidly, as in importance or size: *The minor problems snowballed.*

snow•drift (snō'drĭft') *n.* A large mass of snow that has been piled up by the wind.

snow•fall (snō'fôl') *n.* **1.** [C] A falling of

S

snow. **2.** [U] The amount of snow in a given area over a given period of time.

snow•flake (snō′flāk′) *n.* A single crystal or flake of snow.

snow job *n. Slang.* An attempt to impress sbdy. by telling false stories: *He gave me a big snow job.*

snow•man (snō′măn′) *n.* A figure of a person made from packed and shaped snow, usually formed by piling large snowballs on top of each other.

snow•mo•bile (snō′mō bēl′) *n.* A vehicle with runners resembling skis that is used for recreation and travel on ice and snow.

snow•plow (snō′plou′) *n.* A vehicle or machine equipped with a flat or slightly curved surface used to remove snow from roads.

snow•storm (snō′stôrm′) *n.* A storm with heavy snowfall.

snow•y (snō′ē) *adj.* **snow•i•er, snow•i•est. 1.a.** Full of or covered with snow: *snowy fields.* **b.** Likely to have snowfall: *a snowy climate.* **2.** Resembling snow; white: *snowy petals.*

snub (snŭb) *tr.v.* **snubbed, snub•bing, snubs.** To treat (sbdy.) rudely by ignoring them: *She snubbed him at the party.* —*n.* A deliberate slight; scornful treatment: *The snub was obvious to all.*

snuck (snŭk) *v.* A past tense and a past participle of **sneak.**

snuff[1] (snŭf) *tr.v.* **1.** To put out (sthg.); extinguish: *snuff a candle.* **2.** To put an end to (sbdy./sthg.); destroy: *snuff a revolution.*

snuff[2] (snŭf) *n.* [U] A preparation of finely powdered tobacco that can be drawn up into the nostrils by inhaling. ◆ **up to snuff.** Up to standard; adequate: *Your work just isn't up to snuff.*

snuf•fle (snŭf′əl) *v.* **snuf•fled, snuf•fling, snuf•fles.** —*intr.* To breathe noisily through the nose; sniffle: *The children snuffled in the back seat.* —*tr.* To utter (sthg.) in a sniffling tone: *snuffle agreement.* —*n.* The act or sound of snuffling.

snug (snŭg) *adj.* **snug•ger, snug•gest. 1.** Pleasant and comfortable; cozy: *a snug apartment.* **2.** Close-fitting: *a snug sweater.* **3.** Secure; safe: *a snug hideout; a snug living.* —**snug′ly** *adv.*

snug•gle (snŭg′əl) *intr. & tr.v.* **snug•gled, snug•gling, snug•gles.** To lie or press close together; nestle or cuddle: *snuggle up under the covers; snuggle a kitten.*

so (sō) *adv.* **1.** To such an extent: *I'm so happy that I could cry.* **2.** To a great extent: *The idea is so brilliant.* **3.** Consequently; as a result: *He refused to study for the exam and so nearly failed.* **4.** In the same way; also; likewise: *She likes the book and so do I.*

5. Approximately that amount or number; thereabouts: *The student fare is only $10 or so.* **6.** Then; apparently: *So you think you've got troubles?* **7.** In truth; indeed: *"You aren't telling the truth." "I am so." * **8.** In a condition or manner expressed or indicated; thus: *I wish you wouldn't talk so; you are going to upset her.* —*adj.* True; factual: *I wouldn't have told you this if it weren't so.* —*conj.* **1.** With the result or consequence that: *He failed to show up, so we went without him.* **2.** In order that: *I stayed so I could see you.* —*interj.* An expression used to show surprise or comprehension: *So, you finished on time after all.* ◆ **and so on** or **and so forth.** And similarly; and continuing in a like manner. **so as to** or **so as not to.** In order to or in order not to: *You should go early so as to be sure to get a good seat.* **so far as.** To the extent that: *So far as I'm concerned, the project is finished.* **so much for.** Used when sthg. planned did not happen or work: *So much for going to the movies tonight. We'll go tomorrow instead.* **so that.** In order that: *I stopped so that you could catch up.* **so what?** An impolite expression used to indicate that one does not care: *"Your hair is messy." "So what?"*

---

so. or **So.** *abbr.* An abbreviation of: **1.** South. **2.** Southern.

soak (sōk) *v.* —*tr.* **1.** To make (sbdy./sthg.) thoroughly wet: *The sudden rain soaked everyone. Soak the beans in water until soft.* **2.** *Slang.* To overcharge (sbdy.): *That restaurant really soaked us for lunch.* —*intr.* **1.** To become completely wet: *Clothes soaked in the washer.* **2.** To penetrate: *She paused to let her words soak in.* —*n.* The act of soaking: *I'm going to have a good soak in the tub.* ◆ **soak up.** *tr.v.* [sep.] **1.** To absorb (liquid): *Sponges soak up moisture.* **2.** To enjoy (sthg.): *They were soaking up the warm sun.* **3.** *Informal.* To learn (sthg.) quickly and eagerly: *The students were soaking everything up.*

so-and-so (sō′ən sō′) *n., pl.* **so-and-sos.** *(often used in a negative way).* An unnamed or unspecified person or thing: *Those so-and-sos sold us a bad car.*

soap (sōp) *n.* **1.** [C; U] A product manufactured in the form of bars, granules, flakes, or liquid and used to clean. **2. soaps.** Soap operas. —*tr.v.* To treat or cover (sbdy./sthg.) with or as if with soap: *She soaped the baby thoroughly.*

soap•box (sōp′bŏks′) *n.* A temporary platform used in the past while making an unprepared public speech. ◆ **on (one's)**

---

soapbox. *Informal.* Giving people one's opinions: *Oh, he's on his soapbox about the medical profession again.*

soap opera *n.* A drama, typically performed as a serial on daytime television, showing daily life and melodrama.

soap•suds (sōp′sŭdz′) *pl.n.* Suds or foam from soapy water.

soap•y (sō′pē) *adj.* **soap•i•er, soap•i•est.** **1.** Covered or filled with soap: *soapy water.* **2.** Resembling soap: *a soapy film on the glass.* —**soap′i•ness** *n.* [U]

soar (sôr) *intr.v.* **1.** To rise, fly, or glide high: *The jet soared overhead.* **2.** To rise suddenly, especially above what is normal: *The cost of living soared.*

HOMONYMS: soar, sore (painful).

---

sob (sŏb) *v.* **sobbed, sob•bing, sobs.** —*intr.* To cry uncontrollably: *The child sobbed for her mother.* See Synonyms at **cry.** —*tr.* To say (sthg.) with sobs: *sob one's despair.* —*n.* The act or sound of sobbing.

so•ber (sō′bər) *adj.* **1.** Not intoxicated or affected by the use of alcoholic beverages or drugs. **2.** Serious or grave: *a sober temperament.* **3.** Plain or subdued: *sober clothing.* —*tr. & intr.v.* To make or become sober: *The news sobered us to the difficulties we could face. They sobered quickly when the police arrived.* ◆ **sober up.** *tr.v.* [sep.] To make (sbdy.) sober: *The cold air sobered her up.* —*intr.v.* To become sober: *Don't drive until you sober up.* —**so′ber•ly** *adv.* —**so′ber•ness** *n.* [U]

so•bri•e•ty (sə brī′ĭ tē) *n.* [U] **1.** Refusal to use alcoholic beverages or drugs. **2.** Seriousness in bearing, manner, or treatment; solemnity.

SOB or **S.O.B.** *abbr. Offensive Slang.* Son of a bitch.

sob story *n.* A sad story, true or untrue, told to gain sympathy: *We tired quickly of his sob stories.*

so-called (sō′kôld′) *adj.* Referring to a person or thing that is not as named: *a so-called musician.*

soc•cer (sŏk′ər) *n.* [U] A game in which two teams maneuver a ball, mainly by kicking it, the object being to get the ball into the opposing team's goal.

soccer

so•cia•ble (sō′shə bəl) *adj.* Liking company; friendly: *a sociable person.* —**so′cia•bil′i•ty, so′cia•ble•ness** *n.* [U] —**so′cia•bly** *adv.*

so•cial (sō′shəl) *adj.* **1.** Living together in communities or similar organized groups: *Bees and ants are social insects.* **2.** Relating to the upper classes: *wealth and social position.* **3.** Sociable or friendly: *a social person.* **4.** Relating to matters affecting human welfare: *the state's social policy.* —**so′cial•ly** *adv.*

social climber *n.* Someone who wants to rise into a high social class: *He's always surrounded by a bunch of social climbers.*

so•cial•ism (sō′shə lĭz′əm) *n.* [U] A social system in which the government or the whole community owns the means of production, such as land and factories, and controls the distribution of goods and services. —**so′cial•ist** *n.* —**so′cial•is′tic** (sō′shə lĭs′tĭk) *adj.* —**so′cial•is′ti•cal•ly** *adv.*

so•cial•ite (sō′shə līt′) *n.* A person who is prominent in fashionable society: *a socialite seen in all the right places.*

so•cial•ize (sō′shə līz′) *v.* **so•cial•ized, so•cial•iz•ing, so•cial•iz•es.** —*intr.* To take part in social activities: *She enjoys socializing.* —*tr.* **1.** To make (sbdy.) fit for companionship with others: *socialize children.* **2.** To place (sthg.) under government ownership or control: *a proposal to socialize the medical system* —**so′cial•i•za′tion** (sō′shə lĭ zā′shən) *n.* [U]

social science *n.* The study of human society and of individual relationships in and to society, including sociology, psychology, anthropology, economics, political science, and history. —**social scientist** *n.*

Social Security *n.* [U] A U.S. government program that provides financial assistance to the elderly, unemployed, or disabled, financed by a tax on employers and employees.

social studies *pl.n.* (*used with a singular or plural verb*). A course of study that includes geography, history, government, and sociology, taught in elementary and secondary schools.

social work *n.* [U] Organized work and social services intended to improve the social conditions of a community, especially of the poor, elderly, or disabled. —**social worker** *n.*

so•ci•e•ty (sə sī′ĭ tē) *n., pl.* **so•ci•e•ties. 1.** [C; U] A group of people distinct from other groups and sharing a common culture. **2.** [C] An organization or association of people sharing common interests or activities: *a historical society.* **3.** [U] The rich, privileged, and fashionable social class: *He travels only in society.* **4.** [U] Companionship or company: *enjoying the society of friends.* —**so•ci′e•tal** *adj.*

so•ci•ol•o•gy (sō′sē ŏl′ə jē *or* sō′shē ŏl′ə-jē) *n.* [U] The scientific study of human social behavior and its origins, development, organizations, and institutions. —**so′ci•o•log′-i•cal** (sō′sē ə lŏj′ĭ kəl *or* sō′shē ə lŏj′ĭ kəl) *adj.* —**so′ci•ol′o•gist** *n.*

sock¹ (sŏk) *n.*, *pl.* **socks** or **sox.** A short stocking reaching a point between the ankle and the knee.

sock² (sŏk) *tr.v.* To hit (sbdy./sthg.) forcefully: *The player socked the ball out of the park.* —*n.* A punch: *a sock in the eye.*

sock•et (sŏk′ĭt) *n.* **1.** An opening into which an inserted part is designed to fit: *a light bulb socket.* **2.** A hollow part or hole into which a body part fits: *an eye socket; a hip socket.*

sod (sŏd) *n.* [U] A piece of grass and soil held together; turf. —*tr.v.* **sod•ded, sod•ding, sods.** To cover (sthg.) with sod: *They've just sodded their yard.*

so•da (sō′də) *n.* **1.a.** [U] Carbonated water; soda water: *This drink doesn't have enough soda.* **b.** [C] A soft drink containing soda water: *Would you like a soda?* **2.** [C] A drink made from carbonated water and ice cream: *a chocolate soda.*

soda pop *n.* [C; U] A soft drink.

soda water *n.* [U] Water that has been charged with carbon dioxide under pressure, used in various drinks and refreshments.

sod•den (sŏd′n) *adj.* Thoroughly soaked with water: *sodden land.*

so•di•um (sō′dē əm) *n.* [U] *Symbol* **Na** A soft, light, silver-white metallic element that reacts explosively with water and is naturally abundant in combined forms, especially in common salt. Atomic number 11. See table at **element.**

sodium chloride *n.* [U] A colorless crystalline salt of sodium, NaCl, used in making chemicals and as a preservative and seasoning for foods; common salt.

sod•om•y (sŏd′ə me) *n.* [U] Sexual intercourse with an animal or anal intercourse.

so•fa (sō′fə) *n.* A long upholstered seat with a back and arms.

soft (sôft *or* sŏft) *adj.* **1.** Not hard or firm; easily molded or cut: *a soft melon; soft snow.* **2.** Smooth or fine to the touch: *the soft fur of a kitten.* **3.** Not loud or harsh; quiet: *a soft voice.* **4.** Not brilliant or glaring: *a soft pink.* **5.** Mild; balmy: *a soft breeze.* **6.** *Informal.* Easy: *a soft job.* **7.** *Informal.* Not stern; lenient: *The coach is never soft on his players.* **8.** Relating to the hissing sound of the letters *c* and *g* as they are pronounced in *receive* and *general.* ♦ **have a soft spot for.** To be fond of (sbdy./sthg.): *She has a real soft spot for her pets.* **soft in the head.** *Informal.* Foolish; stupid: *You must be soft in the head for lending her so much money.* **soft on.** *Informal.* Too easy or permissive in dealing with sthg. regarded as very bad: *People have begun to think that our mayor is soft on crime.* —**soft′ly** *adv.* —**soft′ness** *n.* [U]

soft•ball (sôft′bôl′ *or* sŏft′bôl′) *n.* [U] A game similar to baseball but played with a larger, softer ball that is pitched underhand.

soft-boiled (sôft′boild′ *or* sŏft′boild′) *adj.* Of an egg, boiled in the shell to a soft consistency.

soft drink *n.* A carbonated beverage with no alcohol, usually sold in cans or bottles.

soft•en (sô′fən *or* sŏf′ən) *tr.* & *intr.v.* To make or become soft or softer: *soften the blow; Her heart softened when she saw the puppy.* —**soft′en•er** *n.*

soft•heart•ed (sôft′här′tĭd *or* sŏft′här′tĭd) *adj.* Easily moved emotionally; kind: *He's softhearted with animals.* —**soft′heart′ed•ly** *adv.* —**soft′heart′ed•ness** *n.* [U]

soft-pedal *tr.v.* To make (sthg.) seem less serious or difficult than it is: *The boss soft-pedaled what was going to be required of us.*

soft sell *n.* [U] A way of selling (sthg.) without using a lot of pressure: *The soft sell often works best for many customers.*

soft-spo•ken (sôft′spō′kən *or* sŏft′spō′-kən) *adj.* Speaking with a soft or gentle voice: *a soft-spoken scholar.*

soft spot *n.* (*usually singular*). **1.** A tender or sentimental feeling: *a soft spot for the helpless.* **2.** A weak or vulnerable point: *The soft spot in that company is their marketing.*

soft touch *n.* Someone who is easy to approach with a request: *She's a soft touch when you need to borrow money.*

soft•ware (sôft′wâr′ *or* sŏft′wâr′) *n.* [U] The programs, routines, and symbolic languages that control the operation of a computer.

soft•y or **soft•ie** (sôf′tē *or* sŏf′tē) *n.*, *pl.* **soft•ies.** *Informal.* A kind person or one who is easily persuaded: *Ah, you're nothing but a softy when it comes to lending money.*

sog•gy (sŏg′ē *or* sô′gē) *adj.* **sog•gi•er, sog•gi•est. 1.** Soaked with moisture; wet: *soggy bread.* **2.** Hot and humid: *another soggy July day.* —**sog′gi•ly** *adv.* —**sog′gi•ness** *n.* [U]

soil¹ (soil) *n.* **1.** [U] The loose top layer of the earth's surface, a mixture of rock and mineral particles with organic matter, suitable for the growth of plant life: *soil washed away by erosion.* **2.** [C] A particular kind of earth or ground: *a sandy soil.* **3.** [U] Country; region: *native soil.*

soil² (soil) *v.* —*tr.* **1.** To make (sthg.) dirty: *The children soiled their clothes.* **2.** To harm (sthg.); tarnish: *soil his reputation.* —*intr.* To become dirty: *a fabric that soils easily.*

so•journ (sō′jûrn′ *or* sō jûrn′) *n.* *Formal.* A temporary stay: *a lengthy sojourn in France.* —**so′journ′er** *n.*

sol•ace (sŏl′ĭs) *n.* [U] **1.** Comfort from worry or sadness: *find solace in religion.* **2.** Something that gives such comfort: *Music has been her solace.*

so•lar (sō′lər) *adj.* **1.** Relating to the sun: *solar radiation.* **2.** Using or operating by energy from the sun: *a solar heating system.*

solar system *n.* The sun together with the planets and other bodies, such as asteroids and comets, that orbit the sun.

sold (sōld) *v.* Past tense and past participle of **sell.**

sol•der (sŏd′ər) *n.* [U] An alloy that melts at low temperatures and is used in the molten state to join metal parts. —*tr.v.* To join, mend, or unite (sthg.) with solder: *soldering the wires together.*

sol•dier (sōl′jər) *n.* A person who serves in an army. —*intr.v.* To be or serve as a soldier: *She soldiered for four years.*

sole¹ (sōl) *n.* **1.** The bottom surface of the foot. **2.** The bottom surface of a shoe or boot, often excluding the heel.

HOMONYMS: sole (bottom of foot, only, fish), **soul** (spirit).

sole² (sōl) *adj.* **1.** Being the only one; single; only: *Her sole purpose in coming is to see you.* **2.** Relating exclusively to one person or group: *She took sole command of the ship.*

sole³ (sōl) *n.* A fish related to the flounder and used as food.

sole•ly (sōl′lē *or* sō′lē) *adv.* **1.** Alone; singly: *solely responsible.* **2.** Entirely; exclusively: *based solely on this information.*

sol•emn (sŏl′əm) *adj.* **1.** Deeply serious: *a solemn scholar; a solemn occasion.* **2.** Having the force of a religious ceremony; sacred: *took a solemn oath.* **3.** Gloomy: *He looks solemn.* —**so•lem′ni•ty** (sə lĕm′nĭ tē) *n.* [U] —**sol′- emn•ly** *adv.* —**sol′emn•ness** *n.* [U]

sol•em•nize (sŏl′əm nīz′) *tr.v.* **sol•em• nized, sol•em•niz•ing, sol•em•niz•es. 1.** To celebrate or observe (sthg.) with dignity: *solemnize the occasion.* **2.** To perform (sthg.) with formal ceremony: *solemnize a marriage.*

so•lic•it (sə lĭs′ĭt) *v.* —*tr.* **1.** To seek to obtain (sthg.): *solicit votes.* **2.** To ask or petition (sbdy.) persistently: *He solicited all his coworkers for donations.* —*intr.* To ask or petition for sthg. desired: *He has been soliciting in the neighborhood.* —**so•lic′i•ta′tion** *n.* [C; U] —**so•lic′i•tor** *n.*

so•lic•i•tous (sə lĭs′ĭ təs) *adj.* Anxious and concerned; attentive: *a solicitous parent.* —**so•lic′i•tous•ly** *adv.* —**so•lic′i•tous• ness** *n.* [U]

so•lic•i•tude (sə lĭs′ĭ tōod′) *n.* [U] *Formal.* The state of being solicitous; care or concern: *Your solicitude is appreciated.*

sol•id (sŏl′ĭd) *adj.* **1.** Having a definite shape and volume; not liquid or gaseous: *a solid material.* **2.** Firm or compact in substance: *a solid wall.* **3.** Not hollow or empty inside: *a solid block of ice.* **4.** Being the same substance or color throughout: *solid gold; solid red.* **5.** Without breaks; continuous: *a solid line of people.* **6.** Of good quality or substance; well-

made: *a solid foundation.* **7.** Dependable: *a solid citizen.* —*n.* A substance that has a definite shape and volume: *Is it a solid, a liquid, or a gas?* —**so•lid′i•ty** (sə lĭd′ĭ tē) *n.* [U] —**sol′id•ly** *adv.* —**sol′id•ness** *n.* [U]

sol•i•dar•i•ty (sŏl′ĭ dăr′ĭ tē) *n.* [U] Unity of purpose or interest: *They joined the strike in solidarity with postal workers.*

solid geometry *n.* [U] The geometry of three-dimensional figures and surfaces.

so•lid•i•fy (sə lĭd′ə fī′) *tr. & intr.v.* **so• lid•i•fied, so•lid•i•fy•ing, so•lid•i•fies.** To make or become solid: *We solidified our agreement. The paste solidified overnight.*

sol•i•taire (sŏl′ĭ târ′) *n.* **1.** [U] A card game played by one person. **2.** [C] A diamond or other gemstone set alone, as in a ring.

sol•i•tar•y (sŏl′ĭ tĕr′ē) *adj.* **1.** Existing or living alone: *a solitary traveler.* See Synonyms at **alone. 2.** Happening, done, or made alone: *a solitary evening.* **3.** Remote; secluded: *solitary places.*

sol•i•tude (sŏl′ĭ tōod′) *n.* [U] The state or quality of being alone or remote from others; isolation: *living in solitude.*

so•lo (sō′lō) *n., pl.* **so•los. 1.** A musical composition or passage for a single voice or instrument. **2.** A performance by or intended for a single individual. —*adj.* **1.** Composed, arranged for, or performed by a single voice or instrument. **2.** Made or done by a single individual. —*adv.* Alone: *The pilot flew solo for the first time.* —*intr.v.* **1.** To perform a solo: *The violinist soloed.* **2.** To fly an airplane without an instructor or companion: *She soloed for the first time today.* —**so′lo•ist** *n.*

sol•u•ble (sŏl′yə bəl) *adj.* **1.** Capable of being dissolved: *a mineral that is soluble in water.* **2.** Capable of being solved or explained: *Some questions are not soluble.* —**sol′u•bil′i•ty** (sŏl′yə bĭl′ĭ tē) *n.* [U]

so•lu•tion (sə lōo′shən) *n.* **1.** [C; U] A mixture of two or more substances that is capable of forming by itself when the substances are in contact: *a solution of salt in water.* **2.** [C] An answer to a problem: *Not every problem has a simple solution.*

solv•a•ble (sŏl′və bəl *or* sôl′və bəl) *adj.* Capable of being solved: *a solvable riddle.*

solve (sŏlv *or* sôlv) *tr.v.* **solved, solv•ing, solves.** To find an answer or solution to (a problem or an equation, for example): *She solved all the math problems on the test.*

sol•vent (sŏl′vənt *or* sôl′vənt) *adj.* Capable of meeting financial obligations: *a solvent business.* —*n.* A liquid that is capable of dissolving another substance: *a solvent to remove rust.* —**sol′ven•cy** *n.* [U]

som•ber (sŏm′bər) *adj.* **1.** Dark; gloomy: *a somber color.* **2.** Melancholy; dismal: *a somber mood.* **3.** Serious; grave: *a somber ceremony.* —**som′ber•ly** *adv.* —**som′ber•ness** *n.* [U]

S

some (sŭm) *adj.* **1.** Being an unspecified number or amount; few or little: *some people; some sugar.* **2.** Unknown or unspecified by name: *Some student was just here and left you this note.* **3.** *Informal.* Considerable; remarkable: *She is some skier!* **4.** Used to accuse sbdy. of betrayal of a trust or confidence: *Some friend you are! I tell you a secret and you go and blab it all over town!* —*pron.* **1.** An indefinite or unspecified number or amount: *We took some of the books to the library.* **2.** An indefinite additional amount: *From here to the lake is 100 miles and then some.* —*adv.* **1.** Approximately; about: *Some 40 people were at the party.* **2.** *Informal.* Somewhat: *He's improved some but not much.* ◆ —**some.** Used vaguely, combined with a number like twenty, thirty, or sixty, to indicate a number believed to be within a ten-year span: *My favorite teacher must be seventy-some years old by now. I'd say that house burned down twenty-some years ago.*

HOMONYMS: some, sum (amount).

USAGE: some, somebody, or **someone.** When you think the answer to a question will be "yes," use **some, somebody,** or **someone:** *Can I borrow some money? Was somebody at the door? Did someone call me?* If you are not sure what the answer to a question will be, use **any, anybody,** or **anyone:** *Do you have any money I can borrow? Is anybody we know going to be at the party? Can anyone give me a ride home?*

—**some**¹ *suff.* A suffix that means characterized by a specified quality, condition, or action: *bothersome; troublesome.*

—**some**² *suff.* A suffix that means a group of a specified number of members: *twosome; threesome.*

some•bod•y (sŭm'bŏd'ē *or* sŭm'bŭd'ē *or* sŭm'bə dē) *pron.* An unspecified or unknown person; someone: *Somebody's been here, but who?* —*n., pl.* **some•bod•ies.** *Informal.* A person of importance: *They really think they're somebodies.* —SEE NOTE at **some.**

some•day (sŭm'dā') *adv.* At some time in the future: *Someday he'll be able to retire.*

some•how (sŭm'hou') *adv.* In a way that is not said or understood: *I couldn't remember the formula, but somehow I got the right answer.*

some•one (sŭm'wŭn') *pron.* Somebody: *Someone called, but she didn't leave her name.* —SEE NOTE at **some.**

some•place (sŭm'plās') *adv.* Somewhere: *I don't like it here, so let's go someplace else.*

som•er•sault (sŭm'ər sôlt') *n.* An acrobatic move in which the body rolls in a complete circle, heels over head. —*intr.v.* To perform a somersault: *Children were somersaulting on the grass.*

some•thing (sŭm'thĭng) *pron.* An unspecified or unknown thing: *Something's wrong, but I'm not sure what it is.* —*n.* [U] *Informal.* A remarkable or important thing or person: *That concert was really something.* —*adv.* **1.** Somewhat; more or less: *She looks something like her mother.* **2.** Used in combination with a number, such as *twenty, thirty,* or *seventy,* to indicate that the specific year might be within that ten-year span: *She says she's thirty-something, but I'll bet it's more like forty-something.* ◆ **something of.** To some extent: *He's something of a computer expert.*

some•time (sŭm'tīm') *adv.* At an indefinite or unstated time in the future: *I'll see you sometime around six.*

some•times (sŭm'tīmz') *adv.* Now and then: *I see them sometimes, but not often.*

some•way (sŭm'wā') *adv.* In some way or other; somehow: *Don't worry—I'll fix up something someway.*

some•what (sŭm'wŏt' *or* sŭm'wŭt' *or* sŭm'wət) *adv.* To some degree; a little: *He resembles his brother somewhat.*

some•where (sŭm'wâr') *adv.* **1.** At, in, or to a place not specified or known: *I lost my keys somewhere in your house.* **2.** To a place or state of further development or progress: *He hopes to go somewhere with his acting.* **3.** Approximately; roughly: *We're somewhere about halfway through the job.* —*n.* [U] An unknown or unspecified place: *I wish I had somewhere to park my bike.*

son (sŭn) *n.* **1.** A person's male child. **2.** A male descendant: *sons of Abraham.* **3.** A man or boy regarded as if in a relationship of child to parent: *sons of freedom.*

HOMONYMS: son, sun (star).

so•nar (sō'när') *n.* [U] A system that uses reflected sound waves to detect and locate objects.

so•na•ta (sə nä'tə) *n.* A classical musical composition for one to four instruments, one of which is usually a piano.

song (sông *or* sŏng) *n.* **1.** A brief musical composition that is meant to be sung. **2.** A distinctive or characteristic sound made by an animal, such as a bird: *the robin's song.* ◆ **for a song.** *Informal.* At a low price: *We bought the old books for a song.*

song and dance *n.* **1.** A stage performance that consists of singing and dancing. **2.** A long, complex, and usually untrue excuse for neglect or failure to do sthg.: *Don't give me that old song and dance about why you didn't do your homework.*

song•writ•er (sông′rĭ′tər *or* sŏng′rĭ′tər) *n.* A person who writes lyrics or composes tunes for songs.

son•ic (sŏn′ĭk) *adj.* Of sound, especially audible sound: *The jet produced a sonic boom.*

son-in-law (sŭn′ĭn lô′) *n.*, *pl.* **sons-in-law** (sŭnz′ĭn lô′). The husband of one's daughter.

son•net (sŏn′ĭt) *n.* A 14-line poem with one of several usual rhyme schemes.

son•ny (sŭn′ē) *n.*, *pl.* **son•nies.** Used as a familiar form of address for a boy or young man.

<hr>

Homonyms: sonny, sunny (cheerful).

<hr>

son of a bitch *n. Offensive Slang.* A term for sbdy. who has acted in a mean way, especially a man; a bastard.

so•no•rous (sə nôr′əs *or* sŏn′ər əs) *adj.* Having or producing sound, especially full, deep, or rich sound: *a sonorous voice.* —**so•no′rous•ly** *adv.* —**so•no′rous•ness** *n.* [U]

soon (sōn) *adv.* **1.** In the near future: *Soon you'll have to leave.* **2.** Before the usual or appointed time; early: *He got there not an instant too soon.* **3.** Immediately; promptly: *Phone your mother as soon as we get into the house.* **4.** Gladly; willingly: *I'd as soon leave right now.* ◆ **no sooner had. . .than.** Used when one event immediately follows another: *No sooner had we come in the house than it started raining.* **sooner or later.** At some time; eventually: *Sooner or later you'll have to pay that bill.* **the sooner. . .the better.** Used when it is important or necessary that sthg. happen soon: *The sooner she comes the better, because we need to use her car.*

soot (sŏot *or* sōot) *n.* [U] A fine black powdery substance consisting chiefly of carbon and produced when wood, coal, . or other fuels burn incompletely. —**soot′y** *adj.*

soothe (sōoth) *v.* **soothed, sooth•ing, soothes.** —*tr.* **1.** To calm or quiet (sbdy./sthg.): *The mother sang a lullabye to soothe the baby.* **2.** To ease or relieve (pain, discomfort, or distress): *The massage soothed the ache in his back.* —*intr.* To bring comfort, composure, or relief: *music that soothes.*

sooth•ing (sōo′thĭng) *adj.* Tending to soothe; bringing relief or comfort: *soothing words.* —**sooth′ing•ly** *adv.*

sop (sŏp) *tr.v.* **sopped, sop•ping, sops.** To dip, soak, or drench (sthg.) in a liquid: *sop the bread in the beaten eggs.* ◆ **sop up.** *tr.v.* [sep.] To take up (a liquid) by absorption; soak up: *Sop up the water with this towel.*

so•phis•ti•cat•ed (sə fĭs′tĭ kā′tĭd) *adj.* **1.** Having worldly knowledge and confidence: *sophisticated tastes.* **2.** Elaborate, complex,

or complicated: *sophisticated technology.* —**so•phis′ti•ca′tion** *n.* [U]

soph•o•more (sŏf′ə môr′ *or* sŏf′môr′) *n.* **1.** A second-year student in a U.S. college. **2.** A tenth-grade student in a U.S. high school.

soph•o•mor•ic (sŏf′ə môr′ĭk *or* sŏf′ə-môr′ĭk) *adj.* Immature and foolish: *a sophomoric attitude.*

sop•o•rif•ic (sŏp′ə rĭf′ĭk *or* sō′pə rĭf′ĭk) *adj.* **1.** Inducing or tending to cause sleep: *soporific music.* **2.** Drowsy: *Eating too much can make me feel soporific.* —*n.* A drug or other substance that causes sleep.

sop•ping (sŏp′ĭng) *adj.* Thoroughly soaked; drenched: *The dog was sopping after swimming in the river.* —*adv. (used with* wet). Extremely; very: *sopping wet.*

so•pran•o (sə prăn′ō *or* sə prä′nō) *n.*, *pl.* **so•pran•os.** **1.** [U] The highest singing voice of a woman or young boy. **2.** [C] A singer having such a voice.

sor•cer•y (sôr′sə rē) *n.* [U] The use of supernatural power over others through the aid of spirits; witchcraft. —**sor′cer•er, sor′cer•ess** *n.*

sor•did (sôr′dĭd) *adj.* **1.** Filthy and rundown: *a sordid neighborhood.* **2.** Immoral: *a sordid motive.* —**sor′did•ly** *adv.* —**sor′did•ness** *n.* [U]

sore (sôr) *adj.* **sor•er, sor•est.** **1.** Painful to the touch; tender: *His sore leg made him walk with a limp.* **2.** Causing embarrassment or irritation: *Our victory is still a sore subject with that team.* **3.** *Informal.* Angry; offended: *He's sore because we were late.* —*n.* An open skin wound or ulcer. —**sore′ness** *n.* [U]

<hr>

Homonyms: sore, soar (rise).

<hr>

sore•ly (sôr′lē) *adv.* Extremely; greatly: *She was sorely distressed. The company sorely needed expertise.*

so•ror•i•ty (sə rôr′ĭ tē *or* sə rŏr′ĭ tē) *n.*, *pl.* **so•ror•i•ties.** A social organization of women students at a college or university.

sor•row (sŏr′ō) *n.* **1.** [U] Mental pain or suffering caused by loss, injury, or despair: *Her mother's death filled her with sorrow.* **2.** [C] Something that causes sadness or grief; a misfortune: *a life plagued by sorrows.* **3.** [U] The expression of sadness or grief: *He looked at them with sorrow.* —*intr.v.* To feel or display sorrow; grieve: *She sorrowed for her beloved dog.* —**sor′row•er** *n.*

sor•row•ful (sŏr′ō fəl) *adj.* Causing, feeling, or expressing sorrow: *a sorrowful event; a sorrowful voice.* See Synonyms at **sad.** —**sor′row•ful•ly** *adv.* —**sor′row•ful•ness** *n.* [U]

sor•ry (sŏr′ē) *adj.* **sor•ri•er, sor•ri•est.** **1.** Feeling or expressing sympathy, pity, or regret: *I'm sorry I forgot your birthday.* **2.** Worthless or inferior; poor: *a sorry excuse.* **3.**

S

Causing sorrow or grief; sad: *a sorry development.* —**sor′ri•ly** *adv.*

sort (sôrt) *n.* **1.** A group or collection of similar people or things; a class; a kind: *What sort of machine is it?* **2.** The character or nature of sthg.; a type; a quality: *a person of an interesting sort.* —*tr.v.* To arrange (sthg.) according to class, kind, or size; classify: *sorted the mail.* ◆ **of sorts** or **of a sort. 1.** Of a mediocre or inferior kind: *a democracy of a sort.* **2.** Of one kind or another: *knew many stories of sorts.* **out of sorts. 1.** Slightly ill: *She was feeling out of sorts after eating lunch.* **2.** Irritable; cross: *Why are you so out of sorts today?* **sort of.** *Informal.* Somewhat; rather: *They were sort of interested in the question.* **sort out.** *tr.v.* [sep.] **1.** To separate (sthg.) from other, different things: *sort out the bad apples from the good ones.* **2.** To make sense of (sthg.); think through: *How are we going to sort this mess out?* —**sort′er** *n.*

S O S (ĕs′ō ĕs′) *n.* *(usually singular).* A signal for help.

so-so (sō′sō′) *adj.* Neither very good nor very bad: *a so-so party.* —*adv.* Indifferently; tolerably; passably: *I did so-so on the test.*

souf•flé (sŏŏ flā′) *n.* [C; U] A light, fluffy baked dish made of eggs combined with other ingredients: *cheese soufflé.*

sought (sôt) *v.* Past tense and past participle of **seek.**

soul (sōl) *n.* **1.** [C] The spiritual nature of a person, regarded as the source of thought and emotion, and often believed to separate from the body after death and live forever. **2.** [C] *(usually singular).* A human being: *Not a soul was in sight.* **3.** [U] The central or vital part of sthg.: *The soul of that business is its sales force.* **4.** [U] The sense of ethnic pride among African Americans. **5.** [U] A strong, deeply felt emotion expressed by a speaker or an artist: *She puts soul into her teaching.* **6.** [U] Soul music.

HOMONYMS: soul, sole (foot part, only, fish).

soul•ful (sōl′fəl) *adj.* Full of or expressing a deep feeling: *soulful cries.* —**soul′ful•ly** *adv.* —**soul′ful•ness** *n.* [U]

soul•less (sōl′lĭs) *adj.* Lacking sensitivity or the capacity for deep feeling: *a soulless analysis of the poem.* —**soul′less•ly** *adv.*

soul music *n.* [U] Popular music developed by African Americans and combining elements of gospel music and rhythm and blues.

sound¹ (sound) *n.* **1.** [U] Something that the ears can detect: *Sound is an element of speech.* **2.** [C] The sensation produced in the ears by sthg.: *I heard sounds coming from the attic.* **3.** [C] A distinctive noise: *the sound of laughter.* **4.** [U]

The distance over which sthg. can be heard; earshot: *within the sound of my voice.* **5.** [U] A mental impression; meaning: *He did not like the sound of that remark.* **6.** [U] Recorded material, as for a motion picture: *It was a good film, but the sound was bad.* —*v.* —*intr.* **1.** To make a sound: *The whistle sounded.* **2.** To produce a certain audible effect: *The words* break *and* brake *sound alike.* **3.** To seem to be: *The news sounds good.* —*tr.* To call, announce, or signal (sthg.) by a sound: *sound a warning.* ◆ **sound off.** *intr.v.* To express one's views vigorously: *He sounded off about the unexpected test.*

sound² (sound) *adj.* **1.** Free from defect, decay, or damage; in good condition: *The bridge is sound.* **2.** Free from disease or injury: *Her health is sound.* **3.** Solid and firm: *a sound foundation.* **4.** Financially secure: *a sound economy.* **5.** Complete or thorough: *a sound analysis of the problem.* **6.** Deep and unbroken: *a sound sleep.* —*adv.* Thoroughly; deeply: *sound asleep.* —**sound′ly** *adv.* —**sound′ness** *n.* [U]

sound³ (sound) *n.* A long body of water, wider than a strait or channel, connecting larger bodies of water.

sound⁴ (sound) *v.* —*tr.* To measure the depth of (water), especially by means of a weighted line. —*intr.* **1.** To measure depth: *sounding with a long pole.* **2.** To dive swiftly downward: *The whale sounded and did not reappear.* ◆ **sound out.** *tr.v.* [sep.] To find out what (sbdy.) thinks: *Let me sound him out before we do anything.*

sound bite *n.* A short phrase that is supposed to represent a philosophy: *Television often represents candidates' views in just sound bites.*

sound effects *pl.n.* Noises made artificially for a play, movie, or radio or television program, intended to make it sound more real.

sound•ing (soun′dĭng) *n.* [C; U] The act of making measurements of depth, especially of a body of water.

sounding board *n.* A person or group whose reactions to an idea or opinion can serve as a measure of its effectiveness or acceptability: *A good friend is often the best sounding board.*

sound•less (sound′lĭs) *adj.* Having or making no sound: *soundless footsteps.* —**sound′less•ly** *adv.*

sound•proof (sound′prŏŏf′) *adj.* Designed to allow no audible sound to pass through or enter: *a soundproof room.* —**sound′proof′** *v.*

sound•track (sound′trăk′) *n.* **1.** The music that accompanies a movie. **2.** A recording of such music available for purchase.

sound wave *n.* A series of vibrations carried through a material, such as air or water, by which sounds are transmitted.

soup (sŏŏp) *n.* [C; U] A liquid food prepared from meat, fish, or vegetables, often with other ingredients added: *Eat your soup. It's good for you.* ◆ **in the soup.** In trouble: *We knew we were in the soup when we broke a window.* **soup up.** *tr.v.* [sep.] To improve the performance of (sthg.): *soup an engine up.*

soup•y (sōō′pē) *adj.* **soup•i•er, soup•i• est. 1.** Having the consistency or appearance of soup: *The pudding was too soupy.* **2.** *Slang.* Foggy: *a soupy day in Seattle.* **3.** *Informal.* Sentimental: *listening to soupy music.*

sour (sour) *adj.* **1.** Having an acid taste; sharp, tart, or tangy: *sour lemonade.* **2.** Spoiled: *The milk became sour.* **3.** Bad-tempered; cross: *a sour temper.* **4.** Worse than expected or than usual; bad: *His career went sour.* —*tr. & intr.v.* To make or become sour: *Lemon juice will sour milk. After a few lessons, she soured on the guitar.* —**sour′ly** *adv.* —**sour′ness** *n.* [U]

source (sôrs) *n.* **1.** A place or thing from which sthg. comes; a point of origin: *People along the coast used the sea as a source of food.* **2.** The beginning of a stream or river: *the source of the Nile.* **3.** A person or thing that supplies information: *Who is your source for that story?*

sour cream *n.* [U] Cream that is soured naturally, used in cooking.

sour•dough (sour′dō′) *n.* [U] Sour fermented dough used for a type of bread.

sour grapes *pl.n.* Saying that sthg. is not worth having after one has failed to win it: *His criticisms are nothing but sour grapes because he didn't get the job.*

south (south) *n.* [U] **1.** The direction to the right of sunrise, directly opposite north. **2.** Often **South.** A region or part of a country in this direction. **3. South.** The southern part of the United States, especially the states that fought for the Confederacy in the Civil War. —*adj.* **1.** Of, in, or toward the south: *the south side of the mountain.* **2.** From the south: *a dry south wind.* —*adv.* In, from, or toward the south: *He pointed south. We hiked south.*

south•bound (south′bound′) *adj.* Going toward the south: *Take the southbound train.*

south•east (south ēst′) *n.* [U] **1.** The direction halfway between east and south. **2.** An area or a region that lies in this direction. **3. Southeast.** A part of the southeast United States generally including Alabama, Georgia, South Carolina, and Florida. —*adj.* **1.** To, toward, or in the southeast: *the southeast corner.* **2.** Coming from the southeast: *a southeast wind.* —*adv.* In, from, or toward the southeast: *walking southeast.* —**south•east′ern** *adj.*

south•er•ly (sŭth′ər lē) *adj.* **1.** Situated toward or facing the south: *a southerly direction.* **2.** Coming from the south: *a southerly wind.* —*n., pl.* **south•er•lies.** A storm or wind from the south. —**south′er•ly** *adv.*

south•ern (sŭth′ərn) *adj.* **1.** Situated in, toward, or facing the south: *the southern side of the mountain.* **2.** Coming from the south: *a*

southern breeze. **3.** Often **Southern.** Relating to or characteristic of southern regions or the South: *a southern climate.*

south•ern•er also **South•ern•er** (sŭth′ər-nər) *n.* A person who lives in or comes from the south, especially the southern United States.

south•ern•most (sŭth′ərn mōst′) *adj.* Farthest south.

south•paw (south′pô′) *n. Slang.* A left-handed person, especially a left-handed baseball pitcher.

south•ward (south′wərd) *adv. & adj.* Toward, to, or in the south: *He gazed southward. She went on a southward hike.* —*n.* A direction or region to the south: *traveled to the southward.* —**south′ward•ly** *adj. & adv.* —**south′wards** *adv.*

south•west (south wĕst′) *n.* [U] **1.** The direction halfway between south and west. **2.** An area or a region lying in this direction. **3. Southwest.** A region of the southwest United States generally considered to include New Mexico, Arizona, Texas, California, and Nevada, and sometimes Utah and Colorado. —*adj.* **1.** Of, in, or toward the southwest: *a southwest window.* **2.** Coming from the southwest: *a southwest wind.* —*adv.* In, from, or toward the southwest: *facing southwest.* —**south•west′ern** *adj.*

sou•ve•nir (sōō′və nîr′ or sōō′və nîr′) *n.* An object kept as a remembrance of a place or an occasion; a memento: *souvenirs of our last vacation.*

sov•er•eign (sŏv′ər ĭn or sŏv′rĭn) *n.* A person with supreme authority over a state, especially a king or queen. —*adj.* **1.** Independent; self-governing: *sovereign states.* **2.** Having supreme rank or power: *a sovereign leader.* —**sov′er•eign•ty** *n.* [U]

sow[1] (sō) *tr.v.* **sowed, sown** (sōn) or **sowed, sow•ing, sows. 1.** To plant (seeds) to produce a crop: *The farmer sowed wheat and corn.* **2.** To plant or scatter seed in or on (sthg.): *She sowed her fields in the spring.* **3.** To spread (sthg.): *sow rumors.*

Homonyms: sow[1], **sew** (stitch), **so** (thus).

sow[2] (sou) *n.* An adult female pig.

sown (sōn) *v.* A past participle of **sow**[1].

sox (sŏks) *n.* A plural of **sock**[1] (sense 1).

soy (soi) *n.* [U] **1.** The soybean. **2.** Soy sauce.

soy•bean (soi′bēn′) *n.* The edible, highly nutritious seed of a plant native to Asia, used to make vegetable oil, flour, and many other products, or the plant itself.

soy sauce *n.* [U] A brown salty liquid made by fermenting soybeans in brine and used to flavor food.

spa (spä) *n.* **1.** A resort area, often having mineral springs. **2.** A business offering facilities and equipment for physical exercise.

space (spās) *n.* **1.** [U] The familiar three-dimensional region or field of everyday experience. **2.** [U] The expanse in which the solar system, stars, and galaxies exist; the universe: *outer space.* **3.** [C] A blank or empty area: *Fill in the blank spaces.* **4.** [C] An area provided for a particular purpose: *a parking space.* **5.** [C] A period or interval of time: *Let's rest for a space.* **6.** [U] Sufficient freedom to develop or explore one's needs, interests, and individuality: *She needs some space to sort out her feelings.* —*tr.v.* **spaced, spac·ing, spac·es. 1.** To arrange or organize (sthg.) with spaces between: *Carefully space the words on the poster.* **2.** To separate or keep (sthg.) apart: *The chairs were carefully spaced in the living room.* ♦ **space out.** *Slang. intr.v.* **1.** To forget: *I'm sorry I spaced out about your birthday.* **2.** To stop paying attention; daydream: *She spaced out during the lecture.* —*tr.v.* [sep.] To make (sbdy.) groggy, as from drugs or tiredness: *That allergy medicine really spaces him out.*

space cadet *n. Slang.* A person who cannot be relied on; sbdy. who often forgets: *She's always late because she's a space cadet.*

space·craft (spās′krăft′) *n., pl.* **spacecraft.** A vehicle designed for space travel.

spaced out (spāst) *adj. Slang.* In a dreamy state of mind; distracted: *She was so spaced out she never heard a word I said.*

space·ship (spās′shĭp′) *n.* A spacecraft.

space shuttle *n.* A reusable space vehicle designed to transport astronauts between Earth and space.

space station *n.* A large satellite equipped to support a human crew and designed to remain in orbit around Earth for a long period.

space suit *n.* A protective pressurized suit designed to allow the wearer to move about freely in outer space.

space·y (spās′ē) *adj. Slang.* In a dreamy state of mind; distracted: *He's always spacey in the morning.*

spac·ing (spā′sĭng) *n.* [U] **1.** The act or result of arranging things so that they are separated by spaces: *He did a good job of allowing adequate spacing of the statues.* **2.** The spaces or a space between things: *Leave some spacing around each picture.*

spa·cious (spā′shəs) *adj.* **1.** Having much space; roomy: *a spacious room.* **2.** Vast in range or scope: *a spacious landscape.* —**spa′cious·ly** *adv.* —**spa′cious·ness** *n.* [U]

spade¹ (spād) *n.* A digging tool with a thick handle and a flat heavy blade that can be pressed into the ground with the foot; a shovel. —*tr.v.* **spad·ed, spad·ing, spades.** To dig (sthg.) with a spade: *The farmer spaded the garden.*

spade² (spād) *n.* **1.** A playing card with a black leaf-shaped figure on it. **2. spades.** *(used with*

a singular or plural verb). The suit of cards having this figure as its symbol.

spa·ghet·ti (spə gĕt′ē) *n.* [U] A pasta made into long solid strings and cooked by boiling.

span (spăn) *n.* **1.** The distance between two points or ends, as of a bridge: *a 65-foot span.* **2.** A period of time: *a span of four hours.* —*tr.v.* **spanned, span·ning, spans.** To extend across (space or time): *a career that spans 30 years.*

span·dex (spăn′dĕks) *n.* [U] A fabric made of a polymer containing polyurethane and used in elastic clothing: *spandex running shorts.*

span·gle (spăng′gəl) *n.* A small piece of sparkling metal or plastic sewn on clothes for decoration: *The ice skater's outfit had many bright spangles.* —*v.* **span·gled, span·gling, span·gles.** —*tr.* To decorate (sthg.) with spangles: *His mother spangled his costume for him.* —*intr.* To sparkle in the manner of spangles: *Waves spangled in the sunlight.*

span·iel (spăn′yəl) *n.* A small to medium-sized dog with drooping ears, short legs, and a silky wavy coat.

spank (spăngk) *tr.v.* To slap (sbdy./sthg.) on the buttocks with a flat object or the open hand. —*n.* A slap on the buttocks.

spank·ing (spăng′kĭng) *adv.* Used as an intensive: *a spanking new kitchen.* —*n.* [C; U] A series of slaps on the buttocks, given as punishment.

spar (spär) *intr.v.* **sparred, spar·ring, spars. 1.** To participate in a practice boxing match. **2.** To exchange words in a quarrel or an argument: *We sparred for an hour before he admitted I was right.*

spare (spâr) *tr.v.* **spared, spar·ing, spares. 1.** To treat (sbdy./sthg.) mercifully; deal with leniently: *The invaders spared only the children.* **2.** To refrain from destroying, harming, or using up (sthg.): *spared the trees.* **3.** To save (sbdy.) from experiencing or doing: *I spared you the trouble of returning the books.* **4.** To give (sthg.) out of one's resources: *Can you spare ten minutes? Can you spare a dollar?* —*adj.* **spar·er, spar·est. 1.a.** Kept in reserve: *a spare tire.* **b.** Being in excess of what is needed; extra: *spare cash.* **c.** Free for other use: *spare time.* **2.** Not abundant; meager: *a spare breakfast.* See Synonyms at **lean²**. —*n.* A replacement, such as a tire, reserved for future need. ♦ **spare no expense** or **effort.** To spend as much money or time as needed: *We spared no expense for the party.* **to spare.** In addition to what is needed: *We have ice cream to spare. We had $15 to spare.* —**spare′ly** *adv.* —**spare′ness** *n.* [U]

spare·ribs (spâr′rĭbz′) *pl.n.* Pork ribs, often cooked as barbecue.

spark (spärk) *n.* **1.** A glowing particle, such as one thrown out from a fire or one caused by friction: *Sparks flew when she threw the wood on the fire.* **2.** A flash of light, especially one produced by electric discharge. **3.** Something small that starts or remains; a seed or trace: *the spark of rebellion; no spark of interest in continuing the club.* —*tr.v.* To set (sthg.) in motion or push (sbdy.) to action: *His speech sparked a controversy.*

spar•kle (spär′kəl) *intr.v.* **spar•kled, spar•kling, spar•kles. 1.** To give off or reflect flashes of light; glitter: *Crystal glasses sparkled in the candlelight.* **2.** To be brilliant in performance: *She sparkled on the piano.* **3.** To be lively: *The conversation sparkled at the dinner table.* —*n.* **1.** [C] A small spark or glowing light: *the sparkle of diamonds.* **2.** [U] Liveliness; energy: *the sparkle of lively conversation.*

spar•kler (spär′klər) *n.* A type of firework that is held in the hand as it burns slowly and produces a shower of sparks.

spark plug *n.* A device that fits into an internal-combustion engine and produces an electric spark to ignite the fuel mixture.

spar•row (spăr′ō) *n.* A small brownish or grayish bird.

sparse (spärs) *adj.* **spars•er, spars•est.** Not dense or crowded: *sparse vegetation; a sparse population.* —**sparse′ly** *adv.* —**sparse′ness** *n.* [U] —**spar′si•ty** (spär′sĭ tē) *n.* [U]

spar•tan (spär′tn) *adj.* **1.** Simple, frugal, or self-disciplined: *spartan furnishings; a spartan lifestyle.* **2. Spartan.** Relating to Sparta or its people.

spasm (spăz′əm) *n.* **1.** A sudden involuntary contraction of a muscle or group of muscles. **2.** A sudden burst of energy, activity, or emotion: *a spasm of laughter.*

spas•mod•ic (spăz mŏd′ĭk) *adj.* **1.** Relating to, affected by, or resembling a spasm. **2.** Happening for short periods of time but not continuously: *She made several spasmodic attempts to change jobs.*

spas•tic (spăs′tĭk) *adj.* Relating to or marked by spasms: *a spastic colon.* —*n.* An old-fashioned and often insulting term for a person affected with spasms caused by a disease.

spat¹ (spăt) *v.* A past tense and a past participle of **spit¹.**

spat² (spăt) *n.* A brief quarrel.

spate (spāt) *n.* A lot of similar things happening in a short time: *a spate of trouble.*

spa•tial (spā′shəl) *adj.* Relating to or involving space: *a good sense of spatial relationships.* —**spa′tial•ly** *adv.*

spat•ter (spăt′ər) *v.* —*tr.* **1.** To scatter (sthg.) in drops or small splashes: *She spattered paint on her dress.* **2.** To spot or soil (sthg.) with a liquid: *He spattered his tie with gravy.* —*intr.* **1.** To come forth in drops or small splashes: *Mud from the passing car spattered on my shoes.* **2.** To fall in drops or splashes: *Rain spattered into the pool.* —*n.* **1.** [U] A spattering sound: *the spatter of rain-*

drops. **2.** [C] A drop, splash, or small amount: *spatters of grease on the stove.*

spat•u•la (spăch′ə lə) *n.* A tool with a broad, flat, flexible blade, used to mix, spread, or lift material, such as paint or food.

spawn (spôn) *n.* [U] **1.** The eggs of water animals such as fishes, amphibians, and mollusks. **2.** Offspring produced in large numbers: *Wars are the spawn of greed.* —*v.* —*intr.* To lay eggs; produce spawn: *Salmon swim upstream to spawn.* —*tr.* **1.** To produce (offspring) from such eggs: *Thousands of frogs were spawned in that pond.* **2.** To cause (sthg.); bring about: *an act that spawned a revolution.*

spay (spā) *tr.v.* To remove the ovaries of (a female animal): *His dog and cat have both been spayed.*

speak (spēk) *v.* **spoke** (spōk), **spo•ken** (spō′kən), **speak•ing, speaks.** —*intr.* **1.** To produce words; talk: *They spoke about the weather.* **2.** To express thoughts or feelings: *He spoke of his desire to travel.* **3.** To be on speaking terms: *They haven't spoken for years.* **4.** To deliver a speech or a lecture: *She's speaking tonight at the rally.* —*tr.* **1.** To pronounce (sthg.); say: *He spoke kind words.* **2.** To be able to converse in (a language): *She speaks Chinese.* **3.** To express (sthg.) in words; tell: *speak the truth.* ◆ **no. . .to speak of** or **not. . .to speak of.** Not enough of sthg. to consider: *She's very successful but has no education to speak of.* "*Do you have some money?*" "*Not much to speak of.*" **so to speak.** In a manner of speaking; as it were: *He was a friend of hers, so to speak.* **speak for.** *tr.v.* [insep.] To offer an opinion about sthg. for (another person): *I speak for everyone here when I say we could never have finished without you.* **speak for itself** or **themselves.** To be clear or obvious: *Don't trust him; his behavior speaks for itself.* **speak for (oneself).** To express an opinion held only by oneself: "*What a great movie!*" "*Ugh. Speak for yourself.*" **speaking of.** With regard to (sthg. just mentioned); about: *Speaking of travel, when are you leaving for Turkey?* **speak (one's) mind.** To say openly what one thinks about sthg.: *My grandmother always spoke her mind.* **speak out.** *intr.v.* To talk freely and fearlessly, as about a public issue: *We have to speak out on the issue of health care.* **speak up.** *intr.v.* **1.** To speak loud enough to be heard: *I can't hear you; please speak up.* **2.** To speak without fear or hesitation: *You have to speak up for your rights; no one else will.*

SYNONYMS: speak, talk, converse. These verbs mean to express one's thoughts by producing words. **Speak** and **talk** are both very general: *The movie star refuses to speak to reporters about her private life. I want to talk to you about your book report.* **Converse** means to exchange thoughts and ideas by talking: *They spent the evening laughing and conversing about old times.*

S

speak·er (spē′kər) *n.* **1.** A person who speaks: *speakers of English.* **2.** A person who gives a speech in public: *an excellent speaker.* **3.** Often **Speaker.** The presiding officer of a legislative body. **4.** The part of a radio, CD player, or similar device where the sound comes out; a loudspeaker.

speak·ing (spē′kĭng) *adj.* Involving speech: *a good speaking voice.* ◆ **on speaking terms.** Friendly enough to exchange superficial remarks: *We're on speaking terms with our neighbors.*

spear¹ (spîr) *n.* A weapon consisting of a long shaft with a sharply pointed head. —*tr.v.* To pierce (sbdy./sthg.) with or as if with a spear: *She speared the potato with the fork.*

spear² (spîr) *n.* A slender stalk, as of asparagus.

spear·head (spîr′hĕd′) *n.* **1.** The head of a spear. **2.** The force or leader behind an activity: *He was the spearhead in our effort to get better working conditions.* —*tr.v.* To lead (sthg.): *The company spearheaded the effort to develop solar energy.*

spear·mint (spîr′mĭnt′) *n.* [U] A common mint plant that produces an oil used as flavoring.

spe·cial (spĕsh′əl) *adj.* **1.** More than what is common or usual; exceptional: *a special occasion.* **2.** Distinct among others of a kind: *a special camera.* **3.** Peculiar to a specific person or thing: *special interests.* **4.** Having a specific function or application: *special training.* **5.** Particularly dear: *special friends.* **6.** Additional; extra: *a special flight.* —*n.* **1.** A featured attraction, such as a reduced price: *a special on peaches at the supermarket.* **2.** A single television production that features a specific work, topic, or performer: *a television special on wildlife.*

special interest *n.* A group or an organization attempting to influence legislators in favor of a particular interest or issue.

spe·cial·ist (spĕsh′ə lĭst) *n.* A person whose work is limited to a particular branch of study or research, such as a doctor who practices a particular type of medicine: *an eye specialist.*

spe·cial·ize (spĕsh′ə līz′) *intr.v.* **spe·cial·ized, spe·cial·iz·ing, spe·cial·iz·es. 1.** To focus on a special study, activity, or product: *a shop that specializes in sports clothes; She specialized in underwater photography.* **2.** To develop in a way that allows a living thing to become adapted to a particular environment, function, or way of life: *Some insects have specialized to life in the desert.* —**spe′cial·i·za′tion** (spĕsh′ə lĭ zā′shən) *n.* [C; U]

spe·cial·ized (spĕsh′ə līzd′) *adj.* **1.** Focused on a special area of study or a special product: *specialized medicine.* **2.** Adapted to a specific environment or way of life: *Some birds have beaks that are specialized for eating seeds.*

spe·cial·ly (spĕsh′ə lē) *adv.* **1.** Developed or adapted for a specific purpose: *clothing that is specially designed for cold weather; wings that are specially adapted for speed.* **2.** Especially: *We waited specially for you.*

spe·cial·ty (spĕsh′əl tē) *n., pl.* **spe·cial·ties. 1.** A special occupation, talent, or skill: *His specialty is portrait painting.* **2.** A special item or feature: *The restaurant's specialty is seafood.*

spe·cies (spē′shēz *or* spē′sēz) *n., pl.* **species.** A group of similar animals or plants that are considered to be the same kind and that are able to breed naturally and produce fertile offspring: *Cats and lions are different species.*

spe·cif·ic (spĭ sĭf′ĭk) *adj.* **1.** Stated clearly and in detail: *Be specific about what you want.* **2.** Special, distinctive, or unique: *a specific trait.* **3.** Intended for or acting on one particular thing: *a specific remedy for the infection.* **4.** Relating to a biological species: *The specific name of human beings is* Homo sapiens. —*pl.n.* **specifics.** Details; particulars: *Tell me what happened and give me the specifics.* —**spe·cif′i·cal·ly** *adv.*

spec·i·fi·ca·tion (spĕs′ə fĭ kā′shən) *n.* **1.** [U] The act of specifying. **2. specifications.** A statement giving an exact description, as of a product or a structure to be constructed: *a house built to specifications.*

spec·i·fy (spĕs′ə fī′) *tr.v.* **spec·i·fied, spec·i·fy·ing, spec·i·fies. 1.** To state (sthg.) clearly or in detail: *Specify how you want the package delivered.* **2.** To include (sthg.) in a specification: *Her wishes were specified in her will.*

spec·i·men (spĕs′ə mən) *n.* **1.** A representative of an entire set or group: *a plant specimen.* **2.** A sample, as of blood, tissue, or urine, used for analysis: *a specimen for lab work.*

spe·cious (spē′shəs) *adj. Formal.* Seemingly fair, sound, or true, but actually false: *specious reasoning.*

speck (spĕk) *n.* **1.** A small spot, mark, or discoloration: *brown specks on the paper.* **2.** A small amount; a bit: *a speck of dust.*

specked (spĕkt) *adj.* Marked with specks: *Her jeans were specked with mud.*

speck·le (spĕk′əl) *n.* A speck or small spot, especially a natural marking on skin, feathers, or leaves.

speck·led (spĕk′əld) *adj.* Covered with speckles or small spots: *speckled trout.*

spec·ta·cle (spĕk′tə kəl) *n.* **1.** A remarkable or impressive sight: *The rainbow was quite a* *spectacle.* **2.** A public performance or display, especially on a grand scale: *The royal wedding was an impressive spectacle.* **3.** A strange or embarassing display: *He got angry and made a spectacle of himself.* **4. spectacles.** An old word for a pair of eyeglasses.

spec•tac•u•lar (spĕk tăk′yə lər) *adj.* Of the nature of a spectacle; impressive or sensational: *a spectacular view.* —**spec•tac′u•lar•ly** *adv.*

spec•ta•tor (spĕk′tā′tər) *n.* Someone who watches an event: *The arena was filled with spectators.*

spec•ter (spĕk′tər) *n.* **1.** A ghost; a phantom. **2.** A haunting or disturbing image or possibility: *the specter of war.*

spec•trum (spĕk′trəm) *n.* **1.** A band of light waves, especially of the colors seen when white light is broken up according to wavelengths, as when passing through a prism or water drops: *the color spectrum.* **2.** A broad range of related qualities, ideas, or activities: *a wide spectrum of opinions.*

spec•u•late (spĕk′yə lāt′) *v.* **spec•u•lat•ed, spec•u•lat•ing, spec•u•lates.** —*intr.* **1.** To think deeply on a subject: *speculate about the reasons for the change in climate.* **2.** To buy or sell sthg. that involves a risk on the chance of making a profit: *speculating on the stock market.* —*tr.* To assume (sthg.) to be true without conclusive evidence: *Scientists speculated that there had been dinosaurs in that region of the country.* —**spec′u•la′tion** (spĕk′yə lā′shən) *n.* [C; U] —**spec′u•la′tor** *n.*

spec•u•la•tive (spĕk′yə lə tĭv *or* spĕk′yə-lā′tĭv) *adj.* **1.** Based on mental speculation: *in a speculative mood.* **2.** Given to making guesses: *a speculative sort of person.* **3.** Engaging in or involving financial speculation: *speculative investments.*

sped (spĕd) *v.* A past tense and a past participle of **speed.**

speech (spēch) *n.* **1.** [U] The act of speaking: *Clear speech is difficult when it's noisy.* **2.** [U] The ability to speak: *the speech of children.* **3.** [C] A talk or address: *He gave a speech to our garden club.* **4.** [U] The manner in which a person speaks: *His speech is somewhat slurred.* **5.** [U] The language or dialect of a nation or region: *Canadian speech.* **6.** [U] The study of oral communication.

speech•less (spēch′lĭs) *adj.* **1.** Unable to speak. **2.** Temporarily unable to speak, as through surprise: *Your rudeness left me speechless.* **3.** Not speaking; silent: *She remained speechless during his explanation.* **4.** Not expressed or not expressible in words: *speechless admiration.* —**speech′less•ly** *adv.* —**speech′less•ness** *n.* [U]

speed (spēd) *n.* **1.** [C] The rate at which an object moves from one point to another: *the speed of light.* **2.** [U] Swiftness of action: *react with speed in an emergency.* **3.** [U] The

condition or act of moving rapidly; swiftness: *He finished the race with a show of speed.* **4.** [C] A transmission gear or set of gears in a motor vehicle: *a five-speed transmission.* **5.** [U] *Slang.* An illegal drug that makes one very active; amphetamines. —*v.* **sped** (spĕd) *or* **speed•ed, speed•ing, speeds.** —*tr.* To cause (sthg.) to go or move rapidly: *I need to speed this letter on its way.* —*intr.* **1.** To drive at a speed that exceeds a legal limit: *She was speeding again.* **2.** To pass quickly: *The days sped by.* ◆ **speed off.** *intr.v.* To go or move quickly away: *She sped off in a cloud of dust. Don't just speed off when you still have work to do.* **speed up.** *tr.v.* [sep.] To increase the speed or rate of (sthg.): *He sped the car up.* —*intr.v.* To increase in speed or rate: *Let's speed up or we'll never finish on time.* **up to speed. 1.a.** Operating at maximum speed: *She brought the car up to speed.* **b.** Producing or performing at an acceptable rate or level: *His work is finally up to speed.* **2.** *Informal.* Fully informed: *Bring me up to speed on the issue.* —**speed′er** *n.*

speed•om•e•ter (spĭ dŏm′ĭ tər) *n.* An instrument that indicates the speed of a moving vehicle.

speedometer
Speedometer *(right)* and tachometer *(left)*

speed•up (spēd′ŭp′) *n.* **1.** An increase in speed; acceleration. **2.** Acceleration of production without increase in pay: *a speedup in production.*

speed•y (spē′dē) *adj.* **speed•i•er, speed•i•est. 1.** Swift; quick: *a speedy runner.* **2.** Done without delay; prompt: *a speedy reply.* —**speed′i•ly** *adv.* —**speed′i•ness** *n.* [U]

spell[1] (spĕl) *v.* **spelled** *or* **spelt** (spĕlt), **spell•ing, spells.** —*tr.* **1.** To name or write in order the letters forming (a word or part of a word): *Please spell your last name.* **2.** To be the letters of (a word or part of a word); form: *These letters spell animal.* **3.** To add up to (sthg.); signify: *Her efforts spelled success.* —*intr.* To form a word or words by letters: *The new students learned to spell in English.* ◆ **spell out.** *tr.v.* [sep.] To make (sthg.) perfectly clear and understandable: *Our teacher spelled out the instructions for us.*

spell[2] (spĕl) *n.* **1.** A word or group of words believed to have magic power: *cast a spell.* **2.** The condition of being bewitched or enchanted; a trance: *It was as if he was under a spell.* **3.** Fascination; charm: *the spell of the tropics.*

spell[3] (spĕl) *n.* **1.** A short indefinite period of time: *Let's sit for a spell.* **2.** *Informal.* A period of weather of a particular kind: *a cold spell.*

3. A period of work; a shift: *a spell at the plane's controls.* **4.** *Informal.* A brief period or symptom of illness: *He's been having coughing spells.* —*tr.v.* To relieve (sbdy.) from work temporarily by taking a turn: *Could you spell me at the computer?*

spell•bound (spĕl'bound') *adj.* Held as if under a spell; fascinated: *For an hour they were spellbound.*

spell•er (spĕl'ər) *n.* A person who spells words: *good spellers.*

spell•ing (spĕl'ĭng) *n.* **1.** [U] The forming of words with letters in an accepted order: *English spelling is hard to learn.* **2.** [C] The way a word is spelled: *the spelling of* engine.

spelling bee *n.* A spelling contest or competition.

spelt (spĕlt) *v.* A past tense and a past participle of **spell**¹.

spend (spĕnd) *v.* **spent** (spĕnt), **spend•ing, spends.** —*tr.* **1.** To use or put out (sthg.): *We spent a lot of energy practicing.* **2.** To pass (time) in a specified place or manner: *I spent my vacation hiking.* **3.** To pay out or waste (money): *I hated spending my last five dollars.* —*intr.* To pay out money: *How much have you spent so far?* —**spend'er** *n.*

spend•thrift (spĕnd'thrĭft') *n.* A person who spends money wastefully or foolishly. —*adj.* Wasteful; extravagant: *a spendthrift way of life.*

spent (spĕnt) *v.* Past tense and past participle of **spend**. —*adj.* **1.** Used up; consumed: *spent mineral resources.* **2.** Having no more energy, force, or strength: *The runner was spent at the end of the race.*

sperm (spûrm) *n., pl.* **sperm** or **sperms. 1.** [C] A male reproductive cell; a spermatozoon. **2.** [U] Semen.

sper•mat•o•zo•on (spər măt'ə zō'ŏn' or spûr'mə tə zō'ŏn') *n., pl.* **sper•mat•o•zo•a** (spər măt'ə zō'ə or spûr'mə tə zō'ə). A male reproductive cell, usually with a long tail and capable of uniting with an egg in the process of sexual reproduction.

spew (spyoō) *v.* —*tr.* **1.** To send or force (sthg.) out in or as if in a stream: *volcanoes spewing out lava.* **2.** To vomit or send out (sthg.) through the mouth: *He spewed his anger.* —*intr.* **1.** To flow or gush forth: *Water spewed out of the broken pipe.* **2.** To vomit.

sphere (sfîr) *n.* **1.** A three-dimensional geometric surface with all of its points the same distance from a given point. **2.** An object or a figure having this shape: *The earth is a sphere.* **3.** The extent of a person's knowledge, inter-

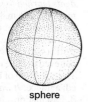

sphere

ests, or social position: *Calculus is outside his sphere.* **4.** An area of power, control, or influence: *Poland was once in the sphere of the Soviet Union.*

spher•i•cal (sfîr'ĭ kəl or sfĕr'ĭ kəl) *adj.* Having a round shape: *Planets are spherical.*

sphinx (sfĭngks) *n.* An Egyptian figure with the body of a lion and the head of a man.

spice (spīs) *n.* [C; U] **1.a.** A plant substance with a pleasant or strong smell and taste, used to flavor food. For example, cinnamon, nutmeg, pepper, and cloves are spices. **b.** Such substances considered as a group. **2.** Something that adds interest or flavor: *Variety is the spice of life.* —*tr.v.* **spiced, spic•ing, spic•es. 1.** To flavor (sthg.) with spices. **2.** To add interest or flavor to (sthg.): *She spiced her conversation with Spanish words.*

spick-and-span (spĭk'ən spăn') *adj.* Neat and clean; spotless: *His house is usually spick-and-span.*

spic•y (spī'sē) *adj.* **spic•i•er, spic•i•est. 1.** Having the flavor or smell of spice: *spicy pumpkin pie.* **2.** Slightly scandalous: *spicy stories.* —**spic'i•ly** *adv.* —**spic'i•ness** *n.* [U]

spi•der (spī'dər) *n.* Any of various small animals with eight legs and a body divided into two parts. Spiders usually spin webs to trap insects.

spider

spi•der•y (spī'də rē) *adj.* **1.** Resembling a spider in form, characteristics, or behavior: *the robot's spidery legs.* **2.** Resembling a spider's web in delicacy; very fine: *spidery handwriting.*

spiff•y (spĭf'ē) *adj.* **spiff•i•er, spiff•i•est.** *Informal.* Fashionable; stylish: *a spiffy dresser; a spiffy new car.*

spig•ot (spĭg'ət) *n.* A water faucet.

spike¹ (spīk) *n.* **1.** A long, thick, sharp-pointed piece of wood or metal. **2.** One of a number of sharp metal projections set in the soles of athletic shoes for grip. —*tr.v.* **spiked, spik•ing, spikes.** *Informal.* To add alcoholic liquor to (a drink): *The host spiked the punch.*

spike² (spīk) *n.* A long cluster of flowers: *a flower spike.*

spik•y (spī'kē) *adj.* **spik•i•er, spik•i•est.** Having sharp points: *The bird had a spiky tail.* —**spik'i•ness** *n.* [U]

spill (spĭl) *v.* **spilled** or **spilt** (spĭlt), **spill•ing, spills.** —*tr.* To cause or allow (sthg.) to flow or fall out of a container: *She spilled water from the bucket.* —*intr.* **1.** To run or fall out of a container: *Milk spilled over the top of the glass.* **2.** To spread beyond specific limits: *Fans spilled onto the playing field.* —*n.* **1.** An act of spilling: *pollution caused by oil spills.* **2.** A fall, as from a horse or bicycle: *She had a bad spill.* ◆ **spill the beans.** To tell a secret at the wrong time or to the wrong person: *Don't spill the beans about our party.*

spilt (spĭlt) *v.* A past tense and a past participle of **spill.**

spin (spĭn) *v.* **spun** (spŭn), **spin•ning, spins.** —*tr.* **1.** To twist (fibers, such as of cotton or wool) into thread: *spinning cotton.* **2.** To form (a web or cocoon, for example) as spiders and certain insects do: *The spider spun a web.* **3.** To tell (stories): *spin tales of the sea.* **4.** To cause (sthg.) to turn rapidly: *He spun the top.* —*intr.* **1.** To spin thread or yarn. **2.** To spin a web or cocoon. **3.** To turn rapidly: *wheels spinning in the mud.* See Synonyms at **turn. 4.** To seem to be whirling, as from dizziness; reel: *His head was spinning.* —*n.* **1.** The act of spinning: *The skater did a spin.* **2.** *Informal. (usually singular).* A short drive for pleasure: *Let's go for a spin in my new car.*

spin•ach (spĭn′ĭch) *n.* [U] A garden plant with dark green leaves eaten raw or cooked as a vegetable.

spi•nal (spī′nəl) *adj.* Relating to or near the spine: *a spinal injury.*

spin•dle (spĭn′dl) *n.* **1.** A rounded rod used for spinning and winding thread. **2.** A machine part that rotates or serves as an axis on which other parts rotate.

spin•dly (spĭnd′lē) *adj.* **spin•dli•er, spin•dli•est.** Long and thin; weak-looking: *spindly tree branches; spindly legs.*

spine (spīn) *n.* **1.** The series of connected bones along the back of a vertebrate; the backbone. **2.** A sharp-pointed plant or animal part, such as a thorn or quill: *a sea creature covered with spines.* **3.** The supporting part of a book, to which the covers are attached: *Be careful not to break the spine of the book.* —**spin′y** *adj.*

spine•less (spīn′lĭs) *adj.* **1.** Without courage or willpower. **2.** With no spiny plant or animal parts. **3.** Without a spinal column.

spinning wheel *n.* A machine for spinning fibers into thread or yarn.

spin•off or **spin-off** (spĭn′ôf′ *or* spĭn′ŏf′) *n.* Something developed from another thing that is larger or more complex: *The dolls are a spinoff from a children's TV show.*

spin•ster (spĭn′stər) *n.* An outdated, insulting term for a woman who has never married.

spi•ral (spī′rəl) *n.* **1.** A winding curve that moves upward or toward a fixed center: *She drew a spiral.* **2.** An object or a figure in the shape of a spiral: *A spiral of smoke came from the chimney.* —*intr.v.* **1.** To move in a spiral form: *Smoke spiraled from the chimney.* **2.** To rise or fall: *Costs are spiraling upward.*

spire (spīr) *n.* The pointed top of a tower: *a church spire.*

spir•it (spĭr′ĭt) *n.* **1.** [U] The human mind, will, and feelings: *Though they can't be here, they're with us in spirit.* **2.** [C] *(usually singular).* A central quality of a person, a thing, or a time: *the brave spirit of the early explorers.* **3.** [U] A particular mood showing energy, courage, or liveliness: *Their team showed a lot of spirit.* **4.** [C] *(usually singular).* A prevailing mood or attitude: *a spirit of rebellion in the land.* **5.** [C] A being without a body, such as a ghost, a fairy, an angel, or a devil. **6.** [C] *(usually singular).* The real meaning, sense, or intent of sthg.: *the spirit of the law.* **7. spirits.** Alcoholic drinks. —*tr.v.* [*away; off*] To carry (sbdy./sthg.) off mysteriously or secretly: *Someone spirited the papers away.*

spir•it•ed (spĭr′ĭ tĭd) *adj.* **1.** Showing life, energy, or courage: *a spirited defense of her rights.* **2.** With a particular mood or nature: *high-spirited.*

spir•it•less (spĭr′ĭt lĭs) *adj.* Without energy or enthusiasm: *a spiritless attempt to convince me.*

spir•i•tu•al (spĭr′ĭ chōō əl) *adj.* **1.** Relating to the spirit; not physical or material. **2.** Relating to God or religion; sacred: *spiritual gifts.* —*n.* A religious song originally sung by African American slaves. —**spir′i•tu•al•ly** *adv.*

spir•i•tu•al•i•ty (spĭr′ĭ chōō ăl′ĭ tē) *n.* [U] The state, quality, or fact of being spiritual: *a religious writer with great spirituality.*

spit[1] (spĭt) *n.* [U] The liquid in the mouth, especially when forced from the mouth; saliva. —*v.* **spat** (spăt) or **spit, spit•ting, spits.** —*tr.* [*out*] **1.** To force (sthg.) from the mouth: *Rinse your mouth with water and spit it out.* **2.** To say (sthg.) in a violent way: *He spat out an oath.* —*intr.* **1.** To force saliva from the mouth: *The boys were spitting at each other.* **2.** To make a hissing noise, as a cat does: *The wet wood spit as it burned.* ◆ **spit it out.** *Informal.* Used to encourage sbdy. to say sthg. he or she is reluctant to say: *Come on. Spit it out. Tell me what's bothering you.* **spit up.** *tr.v.* [sep.] To vomit (sthg.): *The baby spit up her breakfast.* **the spitting image of.** Exactly like (sbdy./sthg.): *She's the spitting image of her aunt.*

spit[2] (spĭt) *n.* **1.** A thin pointed rod used to hold and cook meat. **2.** A narrow point of sandy land reaching into a body of water.

spite (spīt) *n.* [U] Bad feeling that causes a person to want to hurt or humiliate another: *He spread the rumor out of spite.* —*tr.v.* **spit•ed, spit•ing, spites.** To show spite toward (sbdy.): *She did it to spite us.* ◆ **in spite of.** Not stopped by; regardless of: *They went on in spite of their fears.* —**spite′ful** *adj.* —**spite′ful•ly** *adv.* —**spite′ful•ness** *n.* [U]

spit•tle (spĭt′l) *n.* [U] Spit; saliva.

splash (splăsh) *v.* —*tr.* **1.** To throw (a liquid) around: *I accidentally splashed paint on the floor.* **2.** To throw liquid on (sthg.): *The waiter splashed my shirt with wine.* —*intr.* **1.** To fall into or move through liquid so that it moves: *Children were splashing in the ocean.* **2.** To spill or fall: *water splashing on rocks.* —*n.* **1.** The act or sound of splashing: *I heard a splash as the child fell into the pool.* **2.** A mark made by or as if by liquid: *splashes of color.* ♦ **make a splash.** To cause a strong but brief impression: *Her movie made a splash when it came out.* **splash down.** *intr.v.* To land in water: *The missile splashed down in the Atlantic.*

splash•down (splăsh′doun′) *n.* The landing of a missile or spacecraft in water: *a splashdown in the ocean.*

splash•y (splăsh′ē) *adj.* **splash•i•er, splash•i•est. 1.** Covered with splashes of color: *a splashy painting.* **2.** Showy: *a splashy wedding.*

splat•ter (splăt′ər) *v.* —*tr.* To splash (sthg.), especially so as to soil with liquid: *The grease splattered my shirt.* —*intr.* To move or fall so as to cause heavy splashes: *The paint splattered everywhere.* —*n.* A splash of liquid: *a splatter of red paint.*

spleen (splēn) *n.* An organ that stores and filters blood.

splen•did (splĕn′dĭd) *adj.* **1.** Grand; magnificent, especially in appearance: *splendid costumes.* **2.** Excellent; very fine: *a splendid vacation.* —**splen′did•ly** *adv.*

splen•dor (splĕn′dər) *n.* **1.** [U] Great beauty: *the splendor of a summer day.* **2.** [C] Something grand or of great beauty: *the splendors of Asia.*

splice (splīs) *tr.v.* **spliced, splic•ing, splic•es.** To join (film or rope, for example) at the ends: *spliced the videotapes.* —*n.* A connection made by splicing.

splint (splĭnt) *n.* A flat piece of rigid material used to keep a broken bone or a sprain from moving.

splin•ter (splĭn′tər) *n.* A sharp thin piece of wood, bone, or glass, split or broken off from a larger piece: *I have a splinter in my finger.* —*v.* —*intr.* To split or break into sharp slender pieces: *The glass splintered.* See Synonyms at **break.** —*tr.* To cause (sthg.) to splinter: *She splintered the glass when she hit the window.*

split (splĭt) *v.* **split, split•ting, splits.** —*tr.* **1.** To cut (sthg.) from end to end or along the length: *split the log.* See Synonyms at **rip**[1]. **2.** To separate (people or groups): *These issues split the party into two groups.* **3.** To divide and share (sthg.): *We split the reward.* —*intr.* **1.** To become separated into parts, especially lengthwise: *The tree trunk split with a crash.* **2.** To become open or ripped apart: *My pants split at the seam.* —*n.* **1.** The act or result of splitting. **2.** A division in a group: *a split in the party.* **3.** Something divided and given out; a share: *a split of the prize money.* —*adj.* **1.** Divided or separated: *split interests.* **2.** Broken lengthwise: *a split thumbnail.* ♦ **split hairs.** To see or make small distinctions: *Don't split hairs over the contract.* **split up.** *intr.v.* To end a relationship: *They split up after two years of marriage.* —*tr.v.* [sep.] To end (a relationship): *Financial problems split up the partnership.*

split-lev•el (splĭt′lĕv′əl) *adj.* Having the floor levels of rooms separated by about half a story: *a split-level ranch house.*

split second *n.* A brief instant; a flash: *I'll be there in a split second.*

split•ting (splĭt′ĭng) *adj.* Very severe and painful, as a headache: *a splitting headache.*

splotch (splŏch) *n.* An irregularly shaped stain, spot, or discolored area: *a splotch of blood.* —**splotch′y** *adj.*

splurge (splûrj) *intr.v.* **splurged, splurg•ing, splurg•es.** To spend money wastefully, as on luxuries: *He splurged and bought a new car.*

splut•ter (splŭt′ər) *v.* —*intr.* **1.** To make a spitting sound: *He spluttered and coughed as he come out of the water.* **2.** To speak in a hurried or confused way, as when angry: *He was so furious he could only splutter.* —*tr.* To utter or express (sthg.) in a hurried or confused way: *He spluttered out the wrong answer in his haste.* —*n.* A spluttering noise: *The car made a splutter and died.*

spoil (spoil) *v.* —*tr.* **1.** To damage the value or quality of (sthg.); ruin: *Rain spoiled our picnic.* See Synonyms at **hurt. 2.** To weaken (the character of a child or animal, for example) by being too kind or generous: *They spoiled their children.* See Synonyms at **pamper.** —*intr.* To decay or lose freshness: *Milk spoils quickly if it is not kept cold.* —*n.* **spoils.** Goods or property taken by the winner after a war: *To the victor go the spoils.* ♦ **spoiling for a fight.** In a mood to quarrel or fight: *He was clearly spoiling for a fight.*

spoke[1] (spōk) *n.* One of the bars or rods that connect the rim of a wheel to its center: *a bicycle spoke.*

spoke[2] (spōk) *v.* Past tense of **speak.**

spo•ken (spō′kən) *v.* Past participle of **speak.** —*adj.* **1.** Said; expressed orally: *spoken dialogue in an opera.* **2.** Speaking or using speech in a particular manner: *a soft-spoken man.* ♦ **be spoken for.** To be already claimed; be unavailable: *These seats are spoken for.*

spokes•man (spōks′mən) *n.* A person who speaks officially for another or others. —**spokes′per′son** (spōks′pûr′sən) *n.* —**spokes′wom′an** (spōks′wŏom′ən) *n.*

sponge (spŭnj) *n.* **1.** Any of numerous simple water animals that have a soft body with many small holes. **2.a.** The body of this animal, used for bathing, cleaning, and other purposes. **b.** A piece of sponge or man-made material that can hold water, used for washing or cleaning. **3.** A person who lives by relying on the generosity of others: *Her brother-in-law is a sponge.* —*v.* **sponged, spong·ing, spong·es.** —*tr.* **1.** To wash or wipe (sthg.) with or as if with a sponge: *She sponged her face with a wet hankerchief. Sponge the water off the table.* **2.** *Informal.* To get (sthg.) without paying for it: *She sponged a free meal from the cook at the cafeteria.* —*intr.* [*off*] To live by getting food, money, and other necessities from others: *She sponged off her friends until she found a job.*

spong·y (spŭn′jē) *adj.* **spong·i·er, spong·i·est.** Like sponge; soft and elastic: *a spongy bed of moss.* —**spong′i·ness** *n.* [U]

spon·sor (spŏn′sər) *n.* **1.** A person, group, or business that pays for a project, an event, or a program: *Most television shows have several corporate sponsors.* **2.** A person who takes responsibility, often financial, for another person or group: *the trip sponsors.* **3.** A member of a lawmaking body who proposes and works for passage of a new law: *The sponsors worked hard to get the bottle bill passed.* —*tr.v.* To act as a sponsor for (sbdy.): *They sponsored an immigrant family.* —**spon′sor·ship′** *n.* [U]

spon·ta·ne·i·ty (spŏn′tə nē′ĭ tē *or* spŏn′tə nā′ĭ tē) *n.* [U] The quality or condition of being spontaneous.

spon·ta·ne·ous (spŏn tā′nē əs) *adj.* Happening without an obvious cause; unplanned: *spontaneous cheers.* —**spon·ta′ne·ous·ly** *adv.*

spoof (spoof) *n.* An imitation of sthg. that makes fun of it; a light satire: *a spoof of grand opera.*

spook (spook) *Informal. n.* A ghost. —*v.* —*tr.* To frighten (sbdy./sthg.): *He spooked us by yelling, "Boo!"* —*intr.* To become frightened or nervous: *The horse spooked at the sound of thunder.*

spook·y (spoo′kē) *adj.* **spook·i·er, spook·i·est.** *Informal.* Frightening; eerie: *a spooky old house.* —**spook′i·ness** *n.* [U]

spool (spool) *n.* A cylinder for winding thread, wire, tape, or a similar material: *a spool of white thread.*

spoon (spoon) *n.* A utensil used in mixing, serving, or eating food. —*tr.v.* To lift or scoop (sthg.) up with a spoon: *She spooned the rice into the bowl.*

spoon-feed (spoon′fēd′) *tr.v.* **spoon-fed** (spoon′ fĕd′), **spoon-feed·ing, spoon-feeds.** **1.** To feed (sbdy.) with a spoon: *The nurse spoon-fed the patient.* **2.** To teach (sbdy.) with lessons that are too easy: *This school doesn't spoon-feed its students.*

spoon·ful (spoon′fool′) *n., pl.* **spoon·fuls.** The amount that a spoon holds: *a spoonful of sugar.*

spo·rad·ic (spə răd′ĭk) *adj.* Happening at irregular intervals; with no pattern or order: *sporadic applause; sporadic thunderstorms.* —**spo·rad′i·cal·ly** *adv.*

sport (spôrt) *n.* **1.** [C] An activity or game needing physical strength and skill that has rules: *What sports do you play?* **2.** [U] Light mockery; fun: *They made sport of my new hat.* —*tr.v.* To wear, display, or show (sthg.) off: *He sported a bright red necktie.* —*adj.* or **sports. 1.** Relating to or appropriate for sports: *sports medicine.* **2.** Suitable for outdoor or informal wear: *sport clothes; a sport shirt.* ◆ **be a good** or **bad sport.** To accept or fail to accept the results of sthg. gracefully, without becoming angry or upset: *She's always a good sport. Don't be a bad sport.*

sport·ing (spôr′tĭng) *adj.* **1.** Used in or appropriate for sports: *a sporting goods store.* **2.** Showing sportsmanship: *He needs a sporting chance.* —**sport′ing·ly** *adv.*

sports car (spôrts) *n.* A small automobile, often equipped for racing and designed to be driven at high speeds.

sports·man (spôrts′mən) *n.* **1.** A man who is active in sports. **2.** A man whose conduct and attitude show sportsmanship. —**sports′-man·like′** *adj.* —**sports′wom′an** (spôrts′woom′ən) *n.*

sports·man·ship (spôrts′mən shĭp′) *n.* [U] The attitude and conduct suitable to one who participates in sports, especially fair play, courtesy, and grace in losing.

sports·wear (spôrts′wâr′) *n.* [U] Clothes designed for comfort and casual wear.

sport·y (spôr′tē) *adj.* **sport·i·er, sport·i·est.** Appropriate to sports or participation in sports; casual: *a sporty outfit.*

spot (spŏt) *n.* **1.** A mark or stain, usually round, on a surface: *spots on the tablecloth.* **2.** A position; a location: *a good spot for watching the game.* **3.** *Informal.* A situation, especially a difficult one: *in a tight spot.* —*v.* **spot·ted, spot·ting, spots.** —*tr.* **1.** To cause (sthg.) to become marked with spots: *Soot spotted the curtains.* **2.** To recognize (sbdy./sthg.): *I spotted him on the subway.* **3.** *Informal.* To give (sbdy.) an advantage in points in a game: *I spotted him five points.* —*intr.* To become marked with spots. ◆ **on the spot. 1.** Without delay; at once: *I'll do it on the spot.* **2.** At the scene of action: *a report made on the spot.* **3.** In a difficult position: *Her comment put us on the spot.*

spot check *n.* A random or limited inspection: *Customs officers make spot checks of cars crossing the border.*

spot-check (spŏt′chĕk′) *tr.v.* To inspect (sbdy./sthg.) without warning: *That company spot-checks the workers for drug use.*

spot•less (spŏt′lĭs) *adj.* Perfectly clean: *spotless clothes; a spotless reputation.* See Synonyms at **clean.** —**spot′less•ly** *adv.* —**spot′less•ness** *n.* [U]

spot•light (spŏt′līt′) *n.* **1.** [C] A strong light that covers only a small area, often used to draw attention to an actor on a stage. **2.** [U] Public attention: *She was in the spotlight after winning the race.* —*tr.v.* **spot•light•ed** or **spot•lit** (spŏt′lĭt), **spot•light•ing, spot•lights. 1.** To shine a spotlight on (sbdy./sthg.): *spotlight her solo.* **2.** To focus attention on (sbdy./sthg.): *His advice spotlighted our problems.*

spot•ted (spŏt′ĭd) *adj.* Marked or stained with spots: *a spotted dog; spotted clothing.*

spot•ty (spŏt′ē) *adj.* **spot•ti•er, spot•ti•est. 1.** With or marked by spots; spotted. **2.** With uneven quality or frequency: *a spotty performance.* —**spot′ti•ly** *adv.* —**spot′ti•ness** *n.* [U]

spouse (spous) *n. Formal.* A husband or wife: *Have you met his spouse?.*

spout (spout) *v.* —*intr.* **1.** To come out in a rapid stream: *lava spouting from a volcano.* **2.** *Informal.* To speak in a wordy, dull, and pompous manner: *spouting about his awards.* —*tr.* **1.** To cause (sthg.) to flow out: *The radiator was spouting steam.* **2.** To say (sthg.) pompously: *spouting poetry.* —*n.* A tube or pipe used to pour liquid: *the spout of a coffeepot.* ◆ **spout off.** *intr.v.* To talk in a bragging or noisy way: *He's always spouting off about how much money he makes.*

sprain (sprān) *n.* An injury caused by twisting or tearing the ligaments of a joint: *an ankle sprain.* —*tr.v.* To cause a sprain to (a joint or muscle): *He sprained his wrist.*

sprang (sprăng) *v.* A past tense of **spring.**

sprawl (sprôl) *intr.v.* **1.** To sit or lie with the body, arms, and legs spread out awkwardly: *They sprawled on the floor to watch TV.* **2.** To spread out in a disordered fashion: *Shops and fast-food restaurants sprawled along the highway.* —*n.* [C; U] A sprawling postion or condition: *urban sprawl.*

spray (sprā) *n.* **1.** [U] Water or other liquid in a mist: *sea spray.* **2.** [C; U] A fine jet of liquid forced out of a container: *a spray of perfume.* **3.** [C; U] Any of a large number of products, such as paints or cosmetics, that are dispensed from containers in a spray: *air freshening spray.* —*v.* —*tr.* **1.** To shoot (a liquid) in the form of a spray: *spray paint on the board.* **2.** To put a spray on (a surface): *sprayed the table with polish.* —*intr.* To shoot sprays of liquid: *Soda sprayed out of the bottle.* —**spray′er** *n.*

spread (sprĕd) *v.* **spread, spread•ing, spreads.** —*tr.* **1.** To open (sthg.) to a full or fuller extent; unfold: *spread a tablecloth; a bird*

spreading its wings. **2.** To make the space between (things) bigger; move farther apart: *She spread her fingers.* **3.a.** To put (sthg.) on a surface in a layer: *spread varnish on the table.* **b.** To cover (sthg.) with a layer of sthg.: *spread bread with jelly.* **4.** To distribute (sthg.) over a large place or time: *storms that spread destruction; We spread the payments over six months.* **5.** To make (sthg.) widely known or visible: *spread the news.* —*intr.* **1.** To get bigger: *The fire spread to nearby houses.* **2.** To become distributed or well-known: *The news spread quickly.* **3.** To cover a surface with a layer: *The paint spreads nicely.* —*n.* **1.** [U] The act of spreading: *the spread of information.* **2.** [C] *(usually singular).* An open area of land: *a 300-acre spread.* **3.** [C] The size to which sthg. can be spread or unfolded: *wings with a six-foot spread.* **4.** [C] A cloth covering for a bed or other piece of furniture: *a new spread for the bed.* **5.** [C; U] A soft food that can be spread on bread or crackers: *cheese spread.* ◆ **spread out.** *tr.v.* [sep.] **1.** To open (sthg.) fully: *Spread the map out, please.* **2.** To move (people or things) farther apart: *Let's spread the plants out so that they have room to grow.* —*intr.v.* To move farther apart: *We need to spread out because it's too crowded.* —**spread′a•bil′i•ty** *n.* [U] —**spread′a•ble** *adj.*

spread-ea•gle (sprĕd′ē′gəl) *adj.* In a position with the arms and legs stretched out.

spree (sprē) *n.* A fun, wild activity, especially eating and drinking or spending money: *a shopping spree.*

sprig (sprĭg) *n.* A small branch of a plant with leaves: *a sprig of mint in the tea.*

spright•ly (sprīt′lē) *adj.* **spright•li•er, spright•li•est.** Active and happy; energetic: *a sprightly walk.* —**spright′li•ness** *n.* [U]

spring (sprĭng) *v.* **sprang** (sprăng) or **sprung** (sprŭng), **sprung, spring•ing, springs.** —*intr.* **1.** [*up*] To jump upward or forward; leap: *springing up from her chair.* **2.** To appear or happen suddenly: *A thought springs to mind.* —*tr.* **1.** To open or close (sthg.) suddenly: *spring a trap.* **2.** To present or produce (sbdy./sthg.) unexpectedly: *They sprang a surprise party on me.* —*n.* **1.** [C] A coil of wire that returns to its original shape after being compressed or stretched: *bed springs.* **2.** [C] The quality of being elastic: *a spring in her step.* **3.** [C] The act of springing, especially a leap or jump: *She made a spring at me.* **4.** [C] A small stream of water coming naturally from the earth. **5.** [C; U] The season of the year between winter and summer. —*adj.* Happening in or appropriate to the season of spring: *spring showers.* ◆ **spring a leak.** To begin to let liquid through a hole or crack: *The bucket sprang a leak.*

spring·board (sprĭng'bôrd') *n.* **1.** A flexible board, used for jumping or diving. **2.** Something that helps to start a career or an activity: *He won a speaking prize, which was his springboard to a life in politics.*

spring fever *n.* [U] A feeling of laziness or a need for change caused by the beginning of spring.

spring·time (sprĭng'tīm') *n.* [U] The season of spring.

spring·y (sprĭng'ē) *adj.* **spring·i·er, spring·i·est.** Elastic; bouncy: *a springy footstep.* —**spring'i·ly** *adv.* —**spring'i·ness** *n.* [U]

sprin·kle (sprĭng'kəl) *v.* **sprin·kled, sprin·kling, sprin·kles.** —*tr.* **1.** To scatter (sthg.) in drops or small pieces: *sprinkle sand on the icy steps.* **2.** To scatter drops or pieces on (sthg.): *sprinkle the garden with water.* —*intr.* To rain or fall in small or infrequent drops: *It sprinkled this morning, but now the sun is shining.* —*n.* **1.** A small amount: *a sprinkle of salt.* **2.** A light rainfall; a drizzle. **3.** The act of sprinkling: *I gave the flowers a sprinkle this morning.*

sprin·kler (sprĭng'klər) *n.* **1.** A device, attached to the end of a hose, for sprinkling water on a lawn: *Turn on the sprinkler.* **2.** One of the outlets in a sprinkler system in a building.

sprin·kling (sprĭng'klĭng) *n.* [*of*] A small amount of sthg.: *a sprinkling of sugar.*

sprint (sprĭnt) *n.* A short race or run at one's fastest speed: *a sprint to catch the bus.* —*intr.v.* To run or move at one's fastest speed for a short period: *The runner sprinted to the finish line.* —**sprint'er** *n.*

sprout (sprout) *v.* —*intr.* **1.** To begin to grow: *The corn sprouted from the ground after the rain.* **2.** To develop quickly: *New businesses sprouted up across the state.* —*tr.* To cause (sthg.) to begin to grow: *The wet soil sprouted mushrooms.* —*n.* **1.** A young plant growth, such as a bud or shoot. **2.** **sprouts.** Bean or alfalfa sprouts: *a sandwich with sprouts.*

spruce (sprōōs) *n.* **1.** [C] An evergreen tree with short needles. **2.** [U] The wood of such a tree. —*v.* **spruced, spruc·ing, spruc·es.** ♦ **spruce up.** *tr.v.* [sep.] To make (sbdy./sthg.) neat and clean: *We spruced up the house with a new coat of paint.* —*intr.v.* To become neat and clean: *He really spruced up for the date.*

sprung (sprŭng) *v.* A past tense and the past participle of **spring.**

spry (sprī) *adj.* **spri·er** (sprī'ər), **spri·est** (sprī'ĭst) or **spry·er, spry·est.** Active; lively: *a spry old man.* —**spry'ly** *adv.* —**spry'ness** *n.* [U]

spud (spŭd) *n. Slang.* A potato.

spun (spŭn) *v.* Past tense and past participle of **spin.**

spunk (spŭngk) *n.* [U] *Informal.* Spirit; courage: *His actions showed a lot of spunk.*

spunk·y (spŭng'kē) *adj.* **spunk·i·er, spunk·i·est.** *Informal.* Spirited; courageous: *a spunky young reporter.* —**spunk'i·ly** *adv.* —**spunk'i·ness** *n.* [U]

spur (spûr) *n.* **1.** A short spike or sharptoothed wheel that attaches to the heel of a rider's boot. **2.** Something that causes sbdy. to move or act: *Ambition was the spur for her great achievements.* —*tr.v.* **spurred, spur·ring, spurs.** **1.** To make (a horse) move with spurs: *The rider spurred the horse to a gallop.* **2.** To cause (sbdy.) to do sthg.: *The promise of a raise spurred us on.* ♦ **on the spur of the moment.** Without planning; suddenly: *We bought our tickets on the spur of the moment.*

spu·ri·ous (spyŏŏr'ē əs) *adj.* Not authentic; false; counterfeit: *spurious logic.* —**spu'ri·ous·ly** *adv.* —**spu'ri·ous·ness** *n.* [U]

spurn (spûrn) *tr.v.* To reject or refuse (sbdy./sthg.) in an unkind way: *He spurned my suggestions.*

spurt (spûrt) *n.* **1.** A sudden coming out of a liquid or gas: *a spurt of air.* **2.** A sudden short burst, as of energy or activity: *a spurt of activity.* —*v.* —*intr.* To come out suddenly: *Oil spurted from the broken pipe.* —*tr.* To force (sthg.) out in a sudden jet or squirt: *His wounds spurted blood.*

sput·ter (spŭt'ər) *intr.v.* **1.** To make weak spitting or coughing noises: *The engine sputtered and died.* **2.** To spit out words or sounds in an excited or confused way: *I was so nervous, I could only sputter.*

spy (spī) *n., pl.* **spies** (spīz). **1.** A person who works for a government or company to get secret information: *He was a spy during the war.* **2.** A person who secretly watches another or others: *Her little brother is such a spy.* —*v.* **spied** (spīd), **spy·ing, spies** (spīz). —*tr.* To see (sthg.) unexpected: *I spied a turtle on a log.* —*intr.* [*on*] To work as a spy: *She spied on the diplomats.*

sq. *abbr.* An abbreviation of square.

squab·ble (skwŏb'əl) *intr.v.* **squab·bled, squab·bling, squab·bles.** To have an argument, usually about sthg. that is not important: *The children were squabbling over the toy.* —*n.* A noisy quarrel: *a squabble with the neighbor.* —**squab'bler** *n.*

squad (skwŏd) *n.* A small group of people who are trained for a particular activity: *a football squad; an anticrime squad.*

squad car *n.* A police car.

squad·ron (skwŏd'rən) *n.* A military unit as of soldiers, planes, or ships.

squal·id (skwŏl'ĭd) *adj.* **1.** With a dirty, unhealthy, or poor appearance: *squalid buildings.* **2.** Morally low; sordid: *leading a squalid existence.* —**squal'id·ly** *adv.* —**squal'id·ness** *n.* [U]

squall (skwôl) *n.* A brief, sudden, and violent windstorm, often with rain or snow.

S

squal·or (skwŏl′ər) *n.* [U] The condition of being squalid: *They found themselves living in squalor.*

squan·der (skwŏn′dər) *tr.v.* To use or spend (sthg.) wastefully or extravagantly: *She squandered her money on expensive furniture and clothes.*

square (skwâr) *n.* **1.** An object with four equal sides. **2.** An L-shaped or T-shaped tool, used for drawing or testing right angles. **3.** The product that results when a number is multiplied by itself: *Twenty-five is the square of five.* **4.** An open area in a city at the place where two or more streets meet: *Their house is on Graves Square.* **5.** *Slang.* A person considered boring and out of touch with current fashion: *He dresses like a square.* —*adj.* **squar·er, squar·est. 1.** With four equal sides and four right angles. **2.** Forming a right angle: *a board with square corners.* **3.** Like a square in form: *a square field.* **4.** Using units that express the measure of area: *square miles.* **5.** Honest; direct: *a square answer.* **6.** *Slang.* Dull and conventional: *a square movie.* —*v.* **squared, squar·ing, squares.** —*tr.* **1.** To cut or form (sthg.) into a square or rectangular shape: *square a board.* **2.** To multiply (a number, a quantity, or an expression) by itself: *Three squared is nine.* **3.** To make (two things) agree: *We must square his story with ours.* **4.** To settle (sthg.): *square an account.* —*intr.* **1.** To be at right angles. **2.** [*with*] To agree: *That story doesn't square with the facts.* —*adv.* **1.** In a square shape or form. **2.** Directly; straight: *A truck ran square into the wall.* **3.** In a solid, honest, or firm way: *The salesmen dealt square with the customers.* ♦ **square away.** *tr.v.* [sep.] To put (sthg.) away or in order: *Square away your homework before dinner.* **square deal.** Fair treatment; honesty: *You'll always get a square deal at that store.* **square meal.** A good meal: *She eats three square meals a day.* **square off.** *intr.v.* To get ready to fight: *The boxers squared off.* **square one.** The beginning; starting point: *We changed our plans and went back to square one.* **square up.** *tr.v.* [sep.] To pay (a debt): *I need to square up my account with them.* —*intr.v.* To settle a debt: *Let's square up so we can leave.* —**square′ness** *n.* [U]

square dance *n.* A dance in which sets of four couples form squares: *There was a square dance at the county fair.*

square knot *n.* A double knot that is difficult to untie.

square

square·ly (skwâr′lē) *adv.* **1.** Exactly and directly: *He hit the nail squarely.* **2.** Directly and completely: *She was squarely to blame.*

square root *n.* A divisor of a number that when squared gives the number. The symbol for square root is $\sqrt{}$: *The square root of 9 is 3.*

squash¹ (skwŏsh *or* skwôsh) *n.* A vine with fleshy fruit related to the pumpkins and the gourds, eaten as a vegetable.

squash¹

squash² (skwŏsh *or* skwôsh) *v.* —*tr.* **1.** To flatten (sthg.); crush: *The little boy squashed the insect.* **2.** To force (sbdy./sthg.) into a small space: *We squashed the clothes into the suitcase.* —*intr.* **1.** To become crushed or flattened: *The tomato squashed when it hit the floor.* **2.** To become forced into a small space: *They squashed into the theater.* —*n.* [U] A game played in a walled court with a hard rubber ball and rackets.

squat (skwŏt) *intr.v.* **squat·ted, squat·ting, squats. 1.** To sit in a low position with bent knees: *The child squatted down to watch an ant.* **2.** To live in a place without permission: *They were squatting in an old school building.* —*adj.* **squat·ter, squat·test.** Short and thick; low and broad: *a squat shape.* —*n.* **1.** The act of squatting. **2.** A squatting position.

squat·ter (skwŏt′ər) *n.* A person who lives in a place without permission.

squaw (skwô) *n. Offensive.* A Native American woman.

squawk (skwôk) *intr.v.* **1.** To make a harsh scream: *The bird squawked and flew away.* **2.** *Informal.* To complain or protest loudly and angrily: *He squawked at his landlord.* —*n.* **1.** A loud screech: *the squawk of an automobile horn.* **2.** *Informal.* A loud angry complaint or protest. —**squawk′er** *n.*

squeak (skwēk) *v.* —*intr.* To make a short, high-pitched cry or sound: *The door squeaked as it opened.* —*tr.* To say (sthg.) in a thin, high-pitched voice: *squeaked an answer.* —*n.* **1.** A thin, high-pitched cry or sound: *the squeak of a mouse.* **2.** A difficult situation: *a tight squeak.* ♦ **squeak by** *or* **through.** To manage barely to pass, win, or survive sthg.: *He just squeaked by in his final exams.*

squeak·y (skwē′kē) *adj.* **squeak·i·er, squeak·i·est.** Making squeaking sounds: *a squeaky door; squeaky shoes.*

squeal (skwēl) *v.* —*intr.* **1.** To make a loud shrill cry or sound: *The bus squealed as it stopped.* **2.** *Slang.* To turn informer; betray another by giving away information: *She*

S

squealed on her brother for eating the cake. —*tr.* To say (sthg.) with a squeal. —*n.* A loud shrill cry or sound: *a squeal of delight from the baby.* —**squeal′er** *n.*

squea•mish (skwē′mĭsh) *adj.* Easily shocked or disgusted: *Nurses can't be squeamish about the sight of blood.* —**squea′mish•ly** *adv.* —**squea′mish•ness** *n.* [U]

squeeze (skwēz) *v.* **squeezed, squeez•ing, squeez•es.** —*tr.* **1.** To press hard on (sthg.): *The baby squeezed the rubber toy.* **2.** To put pressure on (sthg.), in order to get liquid, for example: *squeeze an orange.* **3.** [*from; out of*] To get (sthg.) by or as if by using pressure: *squeeze juice from a lemon; squeezed a confession out of a suspect.* **4.** To press (sthg.) gently, as with affection or sympathy: *squeezed her mother's hand.* —*intr.* **1.** To put pressure on: *She squeezed too hard.* **2.** To force one's way: *squeeze through a crowd.* —*n.* **1.** An act or instance of squeezing: *She gave his hand a squeeze.* **2.** *Informal.* Pressure exerted to obtain sthg.: *They put the squeeze on him and he confessed.* —**squeez′a•ble** *adj.* —**squeez′er** *n.*

squelch (skwĕlch) *v.* —*tr.* To silence (sthg.) to prevent its spread: *squelch a rumor.* —*intr.* To make a splashing squishing sound, such as when walking in mud. —*n.* A squishing sound. —**squelch′er** *n.*

squid (skwĭd) *n.* A soft-bodied sea animal with a long body and ten arms and related to the octopus.

squig•gle (skwĭg′əl) *n.* A small wiggly mark: *The child drew squiggles on the wall.*

squint (skwĭnt) *intr.v.* To look with the eyes partly closed: *The sun made the baby squint.* —*n.* The act of squinting.

squirm (skwûrm) *intr.v.* To twist with a wriggling motion, especially from nervousness or discomfort: *squirming on the hard bench.*

squir•rel (skwûr′əl *or* skwŭr′əl) *n.* A small rodent that lives in trees and has gray or reddish brown fur and a long bushy tail. —*v.* ◆ **squirrel away.** *tr.v.* [sep.] To hide or store (sthg.): *She squirreled away her money.*

squirrel

squirt (skwûrt) *v.* —*intr.* To come out in a thin strong stream: *Toothpaste squirted from the tube.* —*tr.* **1.** To force (liquid) in a thin stream through a narrow opening: *squirt juice from a lemon.* **2.** To wet (sthg.) with a spurt of liquid: *squirt the dishes with soap.* —*n.* **1.** The act of squirting: *She gave the soap a squirt.* **2.** *Informal.* An insignificant and annoying person, especially a young person: *Don't pay attention to that squirt.* —**squirt′er** *n.*

squish (skwĭsh) *v.* —*tr.* To squash or squeeze (sthg.) together: *Be careful not to squish the ripe tomato.* —*intr.* To make a noise like that

of soft mud being walked on: *She squished through the wet garden.* —*n.* A squishing sound.

Sr. *abbr.* An abbreviation of: **1.** Or **sr.** Senior. **2.** Sister (religious).

S.S. *abbr.* An abbreviation of Social Security.

St. *abbr.* An abbreviation of: **1.** Street. **2.** Saint.

stab (stăb) *v.* **stabbed, stab•bing, stabs.** —*tr.* **1.** To pierce or wound (sbdy./sthg.) with or as if with a pointed weapon: *stabbed the fish with a spear.* **2.** To push (a pointed weapon or instrument) into sthg.: *stabbed a fork into the meat.* —*intr.* **1.** To thrust with or as if with a pointed weapon: *He stabbed at the audience with his finger.* **2.** To make a wound with or as if with a pointed weapon. —*n.* **1.** A thrust made with a pointed weapon or instrument. **2.** A wound made with a pointed weapon. ◆ **take** or **make a stab at.** To try to do (sthg.): *He thought he would take a stab at painting for a living.* —**stab′ber** *n.*

sta•bil•i•ty (stə bĭl′ĭ tē) *n.* [U] The condition of being stable.

sta•bi•lize (stā′bə līz′) *v.* **sta•bi•lized, sta•bi•liz•ing, sta•bi•liz•es.** —*tr.* **1.** To make (sbdy./sthg.) stable: *The doctor stabilized the patient.* **2.** To maintain the stability of (a plane or ship, for example) by means of a stabilizer: *The pilot stabilized the aircraft.* **3.** To fix the level of (sthg.): *stabilize interest rates.* —*intr.* To become stable: *His condition stabilized.* —**sta′bi•li•za′tion** (stā′bə lĭ zā′shən) *n.* [U]

sta•bi•liz•er (stā′bə lī′zər) *n.* A device that stabilizes.

sta•ble[1] (stā′bəl) *adj.* **sta•bler, sta•blest. 1.** Not likely to change position or condition; firm: *a stable foundation of a house; a stable economy.* **2.** Not likely to be affected or overthrown: *a stable government.* **3.** Mentally or emotionally sound; sane or rational: *a very stable person.* —**sta′bly** *adv.*

sta•ble[2] (stā′bəl) *n.* A building for horses or other domestic animals.

stack (stăk) *n.* **1.** An orderly pile, especially one arranged in layers: *a stack of firewood.* **2.** *Informal.* A large quantity: *a stack of work to do.* —*v.* —*tr.* **1.** To arrange (sthg.) in a stack: *stacking hay; stack the books neatly.* **2.** To prearrange (sthg.) so as to increase one's chance of succeeding or failing: *stacked the deck against me.* —*intr.* To form a stack. ◆ **stack up.** *intr.v. Informal.* To measure up or be equal: *Our team stacks up well against the competition.*

sta•di•um (stā′dē əm) *n.* A large, usually open building for sports events with seating for spectators.

staff (stăf) *n., pl.* **staffs** or **staves** (stāvz). **1.** *pl.* **staffs.** A group of people who work for a person or organization: *We have a large staff at the office.* **2.** A long stick or cane used as a support, weapon, or symbol of authority.

S

—tr.v. To provide (sbdy./sthg.) with assistants or employees: *staffed the project.*

staff·er (stăf′ ər) *n. Informal.* A member of a staff: *White House staffers.*

staff·ing (stăf′ĭng) *n.* [U] The act of providing a staff: *What are your needs for staffing?*

stag (stăg) *n.* The adult male of various deer. *—adj. Slang.* Of or for men only: *a stag party.*

stage (stāj) *n.* **1.** [C] A raised and level platform, especially one in a theater on which actors and other entertainers perform. **2.** [U] Work in the theater: *The stage is her life.* **3.** [C] The scene or setting of an event or series of events: *The stage was set for a summit conference.* **4.** [C] Part of a process; a step in development: *a disease in its early stages.* *—tr.v.* **staged, stag·ing, stag·es. 1.** To produce or direct (a theatrical performance). **2.** To arrange and carry out (sthg.): *Students staged a protest march.*

stage·coach (stāj′kōch′) *n.* A closed horse-drawn vehicle with four wheels, used in the past to carry mail and passengers over a regular route.

stag·ger (stăg′ ər) *v. —intr.* To move or stand unsteadily, as if carrying a great weight: *He staggered under his heavy load. —tr.* **1.** To cause (sbdy.) to lose balance or sway: *The blow staggered him.* **2.** To overwhelm (sbdy.) with emotion or surprise: *Their news staggered us.* **3.** To arrange or schedule (sthg.) to come at different times: *The terms of U.S. senators are staggered, so that only one-third are elected every two years. —n.* An act of staggering; an unsteady motion or walk.

stag·ger·ing (stăg′ər ĭng) *adj.* Very surprising; unbelievable: *a staggering achievement.*

stag·nant (stăg′nənt) *adj.* **1.** Not moving or flowing and usually foul or polluted: *stagnant water.* **2.** Not changing or growing; inactive: *a stagnant industry.* —**stag′nan·cy** *n.* [U] —**stag′nant·ly** *adv.*

stag·nate (stăg′nāt′) *intr.v.* **stag·nat·ed, stag·nat·ing, stag·nates.** To be or become stagnant: *The fish pond stagnated. She has stagnated in her job.* —**stag·na′tion** *n.* [U]

staid (stād) *adj.* Serious and drab in style, manner, or behavior: *staid conversation.* —**staid′ly** *adv.* —**staid′ness** *n.* [U]

stain (stān) *v. —tr.* **1.** To discolor, soil, or spot (sthg.): *He accidentally stained his shirt with ink.* **2.** To ruin (a reputation, for example): *The incident stained his reputation.* **3.** To color (wood, for example) with a dye: *I plan to stain the table. —intr.* **1.** To cause a discoloration. **2.** To become discolored. —*n.* **1.** [C] A discolored or soiled spot: *a stain on my pants.* **2.** [C] A mark on one's character or reputation: *a stain on his good name.* **3.** [C; U] A liquid used to color wood.

stain·less (stān′lĭs) *adj.* **1.** Without stains or blemishes: *a stainless reputation.* **2.** Resisting stain or corrosion: *stainless alloys.*

stainless steel *n.* [U] A steel alloy that contains enough chromium to be resistant to rusting and corrosion.

stair (stâr) *n.* **1.** *(usually plural).* A series or flight of steps; a staircase: *The children ran up the stairs.* **2.** One of a flight of steps: *She tripped on the last stair.*

HOMONYMS: stair, stare (look fixedly).

stair·case (stâr′kās′) *n.* A flight of steps and its supporting structure.

stair·way (stâr′wā′) *n.* A staircase.

stake (stāk) *n.* **1.** A piece of wood or metal pointed on one end and driven into the ground as a marker, fence pole, or tent support. **2.** *(usually plural).* The amount of money or the property risked in a bet or gambling game: *playing poker for high stakes.* **3.** A share or an interest: *We all have a stake in completing this project on time. —tr.v.* **staked, stak·ing, stakes. 1.** [*off; out*] To mark the location or boundaries of (sthg.) with or as if with stakes: *stake out a piece of land.* **2.** To fasten, secure, or support (sthg.) with a stake: *stake a plant.* **3.** To gamble or risk (sthg.): *He staked two dollars on the game.* ◆ **at stake.** At risk; in jeopardy: *His business is at stake if he doesn't get the contract.* **stake out.** *tr.v.* [sep.] To keep close watch over (sbdy./sthg.): *The police staked out the jewelry store.*

HOMONYMS: stake, steak (meat).

stale (stāl) *adj.* **stal·er, stal·est. 1.** Not fresh: *stale bread.* **2.** Lacking originality; overused: *stale jokes.* **3.** Weakened by inactivity or boredom: *Some athletes work out on holidays, for fear of getting stale.*

stale·mate (stāl′māt′) *n.* [C; U] A situation in which further action is stopped: *The peace talks have reached a stalemate.*

stalk[1] (stôk) *n.* The main stem of a plant or a similar part supporting a leaf, flower, or fruit.

stalk[2] (stôk) *v. —intr.* **1.** To walk in a stiff or angry manner: *He stalked past me in stony silence.* **2.** To move in a threatening manner, as if following prey or a victim: *The hungry tiger stalked through the jungle. —tr.* To pursue or follow (sbdy./sthg.) in a threatening manner: *A wolf stalked the lamb.* —**stalk′er** *n.*

stall (stôl) *n.* **1.** A compartment for a domestic animal in a barn or stable. **2.** A small open-air shop used for selling or displaying goods: *a vegetable stall.* **3.** A small compartment: *a shower stall.* **4.** A sudden unintended loss of power or effectiveness in an engine: *The plane went into a stall.* —*v.* —*tr.* **1.** To slow down or stop the progress of (sthg.): *Opponents of the bill have stalled it in Congress.* **2.** To cause (an engine or a motor) to stop running: *I stalled the car in the rain.* —*intr.* **1.** To stop completely: *The project stalled because of a lack of money.* **2.** To stop running because of mechanical failure: *The car stalled at the top of the hill.*

stal•lion (stăl′yən) *n.* An adult male horse that has not been castrated.

stal•wart (stôl′wərt) *adj.* Brave and loyal: *stalwart defenders of their country.* —*n.* A loyal supporter; a dependable ally: *the President and his stalwarts.* —**stal′wart•ly** *adv.* —**stal′wart•ness** *n.* [U]

stam•i•na (stăm′ə nə) *n.* [U] Physical or mental strength that allows one to continue working hard for long periods; endurance: *Illness took away my stamina.*

stam•mer (stăm′ər) *v.* —*intr.* To speak with many pauses or repetitions, as from nervousness or confusion: *coughing and stammering from fear.* —*tr.* To say (sthg.) with many pauses or repetitions: *She stammered her complaint.* —*n.* A way of speaking marked by stammering: *He began his questions with a stammer.*

stamp (stămp) *v.* —*tr.* **1.** To bring down (the foot) forcefully: *We stamped our feet to shake off the snow.* **2.** To imprint or impress (sthg.) with a seal: *The border guard stamped our passports with a visa.* **3.** To put a postage stamp on (sthg.): *Don't forget to stamp the letter before mailing it.* —*intr.* To walk with heavy forceful steps: *stamped along the road.* —*n.* **1.** A postage stamp. **2.** A device used to impress, shape, or cut out sthg. **3.** A symbol of agreement or approval: *her stamp of approval.* ◆ **stamp out.** *tr.v.* [sep.] **1.** To put out (a fire) by stepping on it: *stamp out a fire.* **2.** To get rid of (sthg.) forcefully: *the effort to stamp out drugs.* **3.** To produce (a plan, for example) through intense effort: *stamped out a plan to improve education.*

stam•pede (stăm pēd′) *n.* A sudden violent rush of frightened people or large animals, as of a herd of cattle: *a stampede at the soccer game.* —*v.* **stam•ped•ed, stam•ped•ing, stam•pedes.** —*tr.* To cause (animals or people) to stampede: *Spectators stampeded the gates.* —*intr.* To run in a sudden rush: *The elephants stampeded.*

stance (stăns) *n.* **1.** The position or way of standing: *the erect stance of a diver.* **2.** An attitude or a point of view on some issue: *a judge with a tough stance on crime.*

stanch (stônch *or* stănch *or* stănch) *also* **staunch** (stônch *or* stănch) *tr.v.* To stop the flow of (blood or tears, for example): *She stanched her tears with a tissue.*

stand (stănd) *v.* **stood** (sto͞od), **stand•ing,**

stands. —*intr.* **1.** To rise to an upright position on the feet: *I stood up from my chair to answer the telephone.* **2.** To stay in an upright position on the feet or on a base: *The rocket stood on a launching pad.* **3.** To measure a certain height: *He stood six feet tall.* **4.** To be placed or situated: *The building stands at the corner.* **5.** To be at a specified level, position, or rank: *She was standing 12th in line.* **6.** To remain motionless or undisturbed: *Let the mixture stand overnight.* **7.** To remain in effect or existence: *Exceptions are made, but the rule still stands.* **8.** To hold a position or opinion: *How do you stand on the issue?* **9.** To be in a specified state or condition: *My client stands accused of a serious crime.* **10.** To be in a position of possible gain or loss: *She stands to make a fortune.* —*tr.* **1.** To cause (sthg.) to stand; place upright: *Stand the books in a row on the shelf.* **2.** To tolerate or endure (sthg.): *I can't stand all of this noise. This metal can stand high temperatures.* —*n.* **1.** An act of standing: *They endured a long stand in the line.* **2.** A place or station where sbdy. stands or sits: *a witness stand.* **3.** A place reserved for the stopping of certain vehicles: *a taxi stand.* **4.** A booth or counter for the display of goods for sale: *a flower stand.* **5.** A small rack or container for holding sthg.: *an umbrella stand.* **6. stands.** The seating area at a playing field or stadium: *We watched the game from the stands.* **7.** A desperate or final effort at defense or resistance, as in battle: *The troops made their stand at the river.* **8.** A position or an opinion that one is prepared to defend against the arguments of others: *She was never afraid to take a stand.* **9.** A group of tall plants or trees: *a stand of pine trees.* ◆ **could stand to.** An expression used to indicate what one should do or how sthg. should be changed: *She could stand to study harder. This room could stand to be cleaner.* **stand a chance.** To have a chance or hope for gaining or accomplishing sthg.: *I'm applying for the job, but I don't stand a chance.* **stand by.** *intr.v.* **1.** To be ready or available to act: *Medical staff are standing by in case of emergency.* **2.** To remain uninvolved; hold oneself back from acting: *People stood by and let the thief get away.* —*tr.v.* [insep.] **1.** To remain loyal to (sbdy.); aid or support: *She stood by her husband after his arrest.* **2.** To keep or maintain (sthg.): *I stand by my promise to you.* **stand for.** *tr.v.* [insep.] **1.** To represent or symbolize (sthg.): *The rose in the poem stands for beauty.* **2.** To advocate or support (sthg.): *We stand for freedom of the press.* **3.** To tolerate or accept (sthg.): *He won't stand for another delay.* **stand in for.** To act as a stand-in for (sbdy.): *The Vice President stood in for the President at the funeral.* **stand (one's) ground.** To remain firm against opposition or

S

attack: *She stood her ground until the company changed its policy.* **stand out.** *intr.v.* To be distinctive or prominent; attract attention: *Brightly colored clothing stands out in a crowd.* **stand up.** *intr.v.* To remain valid: *His claim will not stand up in court.* —*tr.v.* [sep.] *Informal.* To fail to keep a date with (sbdy.): *She was angry when he stood her up.* **stand up for.** To side with, defend, or be loyal to (sbdy./sthg.): *Stand up for what you believe in.* **stand up to.** To confront (sbdy./sthg.) fearlessly: *stood up to bigger children on the playground.* **where** or **how (one) stands.** What one's opinion is on some issue: *Where do you stand on gun control?*

stan·dard (stăn′dərd) *n.* **1.** A widely known and accepted measurement or weight used as a basis for a system of measurements: *the standard for a gallon.* **2.** A rule or model used to judge quality, behavior, weight, or value: *modern standards.* **3.** An acceptable level of quality: *an artist who sets high standards for herself.* —*adj.* **1.** Correct or acceptable in size, weight, or quality: *boards of standard length and thickness.* **2.** Normal; ordinary: *a standard excuse.*

stan·dard·ize (stăn′dər dīz′) *tr.v.* **stan·dard·ized, stan·dard·iz·ing, stan·dard·iz·es.** To make (sthg.) a standard: *standardized the test questions.* —**stan′dard·i·za′tion** (stăn′dər dĭ zā′shən) *n.* [U]

standard of living *n., pl.* **standards of living.** A level of comfort as measured by the goods, services, and luxuries available to a person, group, or nation.

stand·by (stănd′bī′) *n., pl.* **stand·bys.** A person or thing that is ready and available for service as a substitute, especially in an emergency: *If the power fails, we have a standby.* ◆ **on standby. 1.** Ready for use or available: *an extra crew on standby.* **2.** Ready to travel on an airplane flight if a seat becomes available: *We are going to try to fly on standby.*

stand-in (stănd′ĭn′) *n.* A person who takes over another person's job for a short time: *He worked as a stand-in for a famous actor.*

stand·ing (stăn′dĭng) *n.* [U] **1.** Rank, reputation, or position, as in society, a profession, or a sport: *a person of high standing in the community.* **2.** Continuation in time; duration: *a friend of long standing.* —*adj.* **1.** Remaining upright: *standing timber; a standing ovation.* **2.** Remaining in effect or existence; permanent: *a standing invitation; a standing army.* **3.** Not flowing or moving: *several feet of standing water.*

stand·off (stănd′ôf′ *or* stănd′ŏf′) *n.* A situation in which neither side can move or win: *a police standoff.*

stand·off·ish (stănd ô′fĭsh *or* stănd ŏf′ĭsh) *adj.* Unfriendly; aloof: *They haven't made many* friends because they are a bit standoffish.

stand·point (stănd′point′) *n.* A position from which things are seen or judged; a point of view: *From his standpoint, he should have gotten the job.*

stand·still (stănd′stĭl′) *n. (usually singular).* A complete stop: *Work came to a standstill.*

stank (stăngk) *v.* A past tense of **stink.**

stan·za (stăn′zə) *n.* A division of a poem, made up of a group of lines.

sta·ple¹ (stā′pəl) *n.* **1.** A major product grown or produced in a region: *Rice and rubber are the staples of this Asian country.* **2.** A basic food item, such as flour or rice: *a kitchen full of staples.* —*adj.* **1.** Produced or kept in large quantities to meet a steady demand: *Wheat is a staple crop.* **2.** Principal; main: *a staple textbook in this course.*

sta·ple² (stā′pəl) *n.* A U-shaped piece of wire, used for fastening papers together. —*tr.v.* **sta·pled, sta·pling, sta·ples.** To secure or fasten (sthg.) with a staple: *Staple the pages together.*

stapler (stā′plər) *n.* A tool used to fasten papers or other materials together with staples.

star (stär) *n.* **1.** A brightly burning celestial body. **2.** Any of the celestial bodies visible from Earth at night. **3. stars.** The celestial bodies, regarded as determining and influencing human events: *Thank your lucky stars. It was in the stars.* **4.** Something that looks like a star, especially a design with several points radiating from a center. **5.** An asterisk (*): *Please correct the items that have a star.* **6.** A famous or talented performer: *a movie star; a baseball star.* —*adj.* Relating to or being a talented and famous performer: *a star tennis player.* —*v.* **starred, star·ring, stars.** —*tr.* **1.** To decorate or mark (sthg.) with stars: *starred the good ideas in a text.* **2.** To present or feature (a performer) in a leading role: *The television series starred a famous actor.* —*intr.* **1.** To play the leading role in a theatrical or film production: *She's now starring in a Broadway show.* **2.** To perform excellently: *She starred at the piano.* ◆ **see stars.** To see flashing lights, especially because of a head injury: *I saw stars after the accident.*

star·board (stär′bərd) *n.* [U] The right-hand side of a ship or an aircraft as one faces forward. —*adj.* On the right-hand side as one faces forward: *the starboard bow.* —*adv.* To or toward the right-hand side as one faces forward: *looked starboard.*

starch (stärch) *n.* **1.** [U] A white tasteless powder that is found in plants, especially wheat, corn, rice, and potatoes: *foods high in starch.* **2.** [C] A food with a high content of starch, such as rice, beans, and potatoes: *Be careful not to eat too many starches.* **3.** [U] A substance, such as natural starch, used to stiffen fabrics: *Do you like starch in your shirts?* —*tr.v.* To stiffen (sthg.) with starch: *starch the tablecloth.* —**starched** *adj.*

starch•y (stär′chē) *adj.* **starch•i•er, starch• i•est. 1.a.** Containing starch: *starchy foods.* **b.** Stiffened with starch, as a fabric: *starchy collars.* **2.** Resembling starch: *a starchy face.* **3.** Stiff; formal: *starchy manners.*

star•dom (stär′dəm) *n.* [U] The status of a star performer: *She dreamed of stardom.*

stare (stâr) *v.* **stared, star•ing, stares.** —*intr.* [*at*] To look steadily and directly, often with a wide-eyed gaze: *Everyone stared at the newcomer.* —*tr.* To look at (sbdy./sthg.) steadily and directly: *She stared him in the eyes.* —*n.* An intent gaze.

HOMONYMS: stare, stair (step).

---

star•fish (stär′fĭsh′) *n.* A flat sea animal with a star-shaped body and usually five arms.

stark (stärk) *adj.* **1.** Bare and harsh: *the stark landscape of the moon.* **2.** Complete; total: *in stark contrast.* —*adv.* Utterly; completely: *stark raving mad.* —**stark′ly** *adv.* —**stark′- ness** *n.* [U]

star•light (stär′līt′) *n.* [U] The light that reaches Earth from the stars.

star•ling (stär′lĭng) *n.* A common bird with a short dark tail and dark glossy feathers.

star•ry (stär′ē) *adj.* **star•ri•er, star•ri•est. 1.** Shining like stars: *starry eyes.* **2.** Full of stars: *a starry night.* —**star′ri•ness** *n.* [U]

star•ry-eyed (stär′ē īd′) *adj. Informal.* Full of hope and confidence, often referring to young people: *starry-eyed young actors.*

Stars and Stripes *n. (used with a singular or plural verb).* The flag of the United States.

Star-Span•gled Banner (stär′spăng′gəld) *n.* **1.** The flag of the United States. **2.** The national anthem of the United States.

start (stärt) *v.* —*intr.* **1.** To begin an action or a movement: *We started at dawn and reached the peak of the mountain by nightfall.* See Synonyms at **begin. 2.** To come into operation or being; have a beginning: *School starts in September.* **3.** To move suddenly and involuntarily; startle: *The dog started at the loud noise.* —*tr.* **1.** To begin (sthg.): *start a new job; start reading a book.* **2.** To set (sthg.) into motion, operation, or activity: *start a car.* **3.** To found (sthg.); establish: *start a business.* **4.** To help or care for (sthg.) in an early stage of development: *start seedlings.* —*n.* **1.** A beginning: *a fresh start.* **2.** A place or time at which a person or thing begins: *At the start of our trip, we were cheerful.* **3.** A sudden or involuntary movement of the body; a startled reaction: *woke up with a start.* **4.** An opportunity to pursue a career or course of action: *She got her start by acting in commercials.* ◆ **for a start** or

to start with. Used at the beginning of a list: *For a start, it's cheap, and second, it's convenient.* **start back.** *intr.v.* To begin a return journey: *We started back for home at six.* **start off** or **out.** *intr.v.* **1.** To begin a journey away from home: *He starts off early tomorrow.* **2.** To begin a process or career: *She started out in anthropology, but changed her major to math.*

start•er (stär′tər) *n.* **1.** A person or thing that starts: *The starters began the race.* **2.** A device that makes an engine start: *The starter on the car is broken.*

star•tle (stär′tl) *v.* **star•tled, star•tling, star•tles.** —*tr.* **1.** To cause (sbdy.) to make a sudden movement: *A noise on the roof startled us.* **2.** To alarm, frighten, or surprise (sbdy.): *The ambassador's angry reaction startled our allies.* —*intr.* To become alarmed, frightened, or surprised. —*n.* A sudden mild shock: *We had a startle when you fell.*

star•tled (stär′tld) *adj.* Feeling shock, surprise, or alarm: *The startled man nearly fell out of his chair.*

star•tling (stär′tl ĭng) *adj.* Causing shock, surprise, or alarm: *We heard the startling news.*

starve (stärv) *v.* **starved, starv•ing, starves.** —*intr.* **1.** To suffer or die from lack of food: *Thousands starved as a result of the drought.* **2.** To suffer because of a lack of sthg., necessary: *a puppy starving for attention.* **3.** *Informal.* To be hungry: *He was starving after class.* —*tr.* To cause (sbdy./sthg.) to starve: *The invading troops starved the town into submission.* —**star•va′tion** *n.* [U]

stash (stăsh) *Slang. tr.v.* To hide or store (sthg.) in a secret place: *stashing her comic books under her mattress.* —*n.* **1.** A hiding place for money or valuables. **2.** Something hidden away: *a stash of old coins.*

state (stāt) *n.* **1.** [C] One of the smaller parts of a country such as the United States: *the state of Indiana.* **2.** [C; U] **a.** A group of people living under a single independent government; a nation: *the state of Israel.* **b.** The political organization or government of such a group: *medicine controlled by the state.* **3.** [C] A condition: *a state of confusion.* **4.** [C] *Informal.* A condition of excitement, confusion, or disorder: *They got into a state over the preparations for the party.* —*adj.* **1.** Owned and operated by a state: *state universities.* **2.** Relating to a nation or a political and geographic subdivision of a nation: *state security.* —*tr.v.* **stat•ed, stat•ing, states.** To say (sthg.) in words; declare: *stating a problem clearly.* ◆ **in state.** In an official and ceremonial way, especially when referring to the death of a high-ranking government official: *The king's body will lie in state for a week.*

state•less (stāt′lĭs) *adj.* Not being a citizen of any state or nation.

state•ly (stāt′lē) *adj.* **state•li•er, state•li• est. 1.** With a graceful dignity or formality: *a*

S

dance with a slow stately rhythm. **2.** Impressive in size or proportions; majestic: *stately columns; a stately oak.* —**state′li•ness** *n.* [U]

state•ment (stāt′mənt) *n.* **1.** Something stated or declared: *a statement of purpose.* **2.** A written summary of money paid, owed, or spent: *a monthly bank statement.*

state of the art *n.* [U] The highest level of development, as of a device, technique, or scientific field, at a particular time: *the state of the art in computers.* —**state′-of-the-art′** *adj.*

state•side (stāt′sīd′) *adj.* Of or in the continental United States: *Soldiers undergo stateside training before being sent abroad.* —*adv. Informal.* To or toward the continental United States: *returned stateside.*

states•man (stāts′mən) *n.* A person who is a leader in national or international affairs. —**states′man•ship′** *n.* [U] —**states′- wom′an** (stāts′woॕom′ən) *n.*

stat•ic (stăt′ĭk) *adj.* **1.** Without motion; stationary. **2.** Relating to or producing stationary electric charges: *clothes that cause static electricity.* —*n.* [U] Random noise, such as crackling in a radio or telephone receiver or specks on a television screen: *I can't hear you over the static.*

sta•tion (stā′shən) *n.* **1.** A place or building that is a center for a service or certain activities: *a gas station; a fire station.* **2.** A stopping place for taking on passengers: *a bus station; a train station.* **3.** A business that transmits radio or television signals: *a radio station.* **4.** A military base or location; a post: *a guard station.* —*tr.v.* To assign (sbdy.) to a position, especially a military or official position; post: *She was stationed in Germany.*

sta•tion•ar•y (stā′shə něr′ē) *adj.* Not moving or changing: *a stationary vehicle.*

HOMONYMS: stationary, stationery (paper).

sta•tion•er•y (stā′shə něr′ē) *n.* [U] Writing materials and office supplies, especially paper and envelopes.

station wagon *n.* An automobile with a door at the back, a large interior, and room for a lot of passengers or bags.

sta•tis•tic (stə tĭs′tĭk) *n.* An item of numerical data.

sta•tis•ti•cal (stə tĭs′tĭ kəl) *adj.* Relating to or using statistics: *statistical data.* —**sta• tis′ti•cal•ly** *adv.*

stat•is•ti•cian (stăt′ĭ stĭsh′ən) *n.* A person who studies or works with statistics.

sta•tis•tics (stə tĭs′tĭks) *n.* [U] **1.** (*used with a singular verb*). The branch of mathematics that deals with the collection, organization, analysis, and interpretation of numerical data.

2. (*used with a plural verb*). A collection or set of numerical data: *Statistics indicate a drop in unemployment.*

stat•ue (stăch′ॕoo) *n.* A form or likeness made of stone, clay, metal, or wood.

stat•u•esque (stăch′ॕoo ĕsk′) *adj.* Tall and elegant, usually used of women: *a statuesque woman.*

stat•u•ette (stăch′ॕoo ĕt′) *n.* A small statue.

stat•ure (stăch′ər) *n.* [U] *Formal.* **1.** The natural height of a person or an animal. **2.** A level of development or achievement: *chess players of equal stature.*

sta•tus (stā′təs *or* stăt′əs) *n.* [U] **1.** Social, legal, or professional position relative to that of others; rank or standing: *Her status is that of an observer.* **2.** High standing; prestige: *seeking status by buying an expensive car.*

status quo (kwō) *n.* (*usually singular*). The existing state of affairs: *We must be careful not to upset the status quo.*

stat•ute (stăch′ॕoot) *n.* A written law.

stat•u•to•ry (stăch′ə tôr′ē) *adj.* Defined by or regulated by statute.

staunch[1] (stônch *or* stänch) also **stanch** (stônch *or* stänch *or* stănch) *adj.* **1.** Firm and steadfast; loyal: *a staunch ally.* **2.** Strongly made or built: *staunch roots; staunch boards.* —**staunch′ly** *adv.* —**staunch′ness** *n.* [U]

staunch[2] (stônch *or* stänch) *v.* Variant of **stanch.**

stave (stāv) *n.* A strip of wood forming a part of the side of a barrel, tub, or similar structure. —*tr.v.* **staved** *or* **stove** (stōv), **stav• ing, staves.** [*in*] To break or smash a hole in (sthg.): *stove in the wall.* ◆ **stave off.** *tr.v.* [*sep.*] To keep or hold (sbdy./sthg.) off: *He tried to stave off hunger with chocolate bars.*

staves (stāvz) *n.* A plural of **staff.**

stay[1] (stā) *v.* —*intr.* **1.** To remain or continue in a place or condition: *stay home; stay awake.* **2.** To remain or reside in a place: *stay at a hotel.* **3.** To last; persist: *We voted to stay with the original plan.* **4.** To wait; pause: *Stay a little longer please.* —*tr.* **1.** To remain during (sthg.): *We stayed the week with my grandparents.* **2.** To postpone (sthg.): *stay a prisoner's execution.* —*n.* **1.** A brief period of residence or visiting: *a two-week stay at the beach.* **2.** A postponement, as of a legal action: *a stay of execution.* ◆ **stay on.** *intr.v.* To continue in a place beyond the normal time: *stayed on after closing.* **stay put.** *Informal.* To remain in one place without moving: *Stay put and I'll be right back.* **stay the course.** To last or continue: *She stayed the course in the marathon.*

SYNONYMS: stay, remain, wait, linger. These verbs mean to continue to be in a given place.

ă–cat; ā–pay; âr–care; ä–father; ĕ–get; ē–be; ĭ–sit; ī–nice; îr–here; ŏ–got; ō–go; ô–saw; oi–boy; ou–out; ॕoo–took; ॕoo–boot; ŭ–cut; ûr–word; th–thin; *th*–this; hw–when; zh–vision; ə–about; N–French bon

Stay is the most general: *We stayed at home all evening.* **Remain** often means to continue or to be left after others have gone: *One person should remain on watch at night.* **Wait** means to stay in readiness, anticipation, or expectation: *I was waiting for you in the car.* **Linger** means to be slow in leaving: *I lingered, enjoying the starry night after the fireworks had ended.*

stay² (stā) *tr.v.* To strengthen (sbdy.) mentally: *Her advice stayed us in a difficult time.* —*n.* **1.** A support or brace. **2.** A strip of plastic, or metal used to stiffen a garment or part, such as a shirt collar.

stead·fast (stĕd′făst′) *adj.* **1.** Not moving; steady: *standing steadfast.* **2.** Loyal or constant; faithful: *a steadfast friend.* —**stead′-fast′ly** *adv.* —**stead′fast′ness** *n.* [U]

stead·y (stĕd′ē) *adj.* **stead·i·er, stead·i·est. 1.** Firm in position, movement, or place: *a steady grip on the wheel.* **2.** Free or almost free from change or variation: *a steady wind; a steady income.* —*tr. & intr.v.* **stead·ied, stead·y·ing, stead·ies.** To make or become steady; stabilize: *She steadied her voice before giving an answer. The boat steadied in open water.* —*n., pl.* **stead·ies.** Someone's usual girlfriend or boyfriend. ♦ **go steady with.** To go out on dates only with a specific person: *Will you go steady with me?* —**stead′i·ly** *adv.* —**stead′i·ness** *n.* [U]

steak (stāk) *n.* [C; U] A slice of meat, typically beef or fish, usually broiled or fried.

Homonyms: steak, stake (post).

steal (stēl) *v.* **stole** (stōl), **sto·len** (stō′lən), **steal·ing, steals.** —*tr.* **1.** To take (property) without right or permission: *The thief stole the jewels.* **2.** To get or enjoy (sthg.) secretly: *steal an hour to play video games; steal a look in the teacher's grade book.* —*intr.* **1.** To commit theft: *She stole and was punished for it.* **2.** To move secretly: *The hours stole by.* —*n.* *Slang.* Something bought at a very low price; a bargain: *Her new coat was a steal at $75.* —**steal′er** *n.*

Homonyms: steal, steel (metal).

stealth (stĕlth) *n.* [U] **1.** The act of moving or proceeding in a quiet secretive way: *The leopard uses stealth to catch its prey.* **2.** The quality or characteristic of being secretive: *a man known for his stealth.*

stealth·y (stĕl′thē) *adj.* **stealth·i·er, stealth·i·est.** Quiet, secretive, and cautious: *stealthy steps.* —**stealth′i·ly** *adv.* —**stealth′i·ness** *n.* [U]

steam (stēm) *n.* [U] **1.** Water in the gaseous state; vapor: *steam from a hot shower.* **2.** Power generated by water vapor under pres-

sure: *a steam engine.* **3.** Power; energy: *soccer players running out of steam.* —*v.* —*intr.* **1.** To produce steam: *a kettle steaming on the stove.* **2.** To move by steam power: *The ship steamed into the harbor.* **3.** *Informal.* To become very angry: *I was steaming after the meeting.* —*tr.* To expose (sthg.) to steam, as in cooking: *Steam the rice for ten minutes.* ♦ **steam up.** *tr.v.* [sep.] To cause (sthg.) to fill with steam: *Try not to steam up the bathroom.* —*intr.v.* To become misted or covered with steam: *The bathroom mirror steams up when the shower is used.* **under (one's) own steam.** Alone; without help: *We finished the project under our own steam.*

steam·er (stē′mər) *n.* **1.** A steamship. **2.** A container in which sthg. is steamed: *a rice steamer.*

steam·roll (stēm′rōl) *v.* —*tr.* **1.** To smooth or level (a road) with a steamroller. **2.** To defeat or overwhelm (sbdy./sthg.) ruthlessly; crush: *She steamrolls anyone who opposes her.* —*intr.* To move or proceed with an overwhelming force: *The team steamrolled over every opponent.*

steam·rol·ler (stēm′rō′lər) *n.* **1.** A vehicle with a heavy roller for smoothing road surfaces. **2.** A crushing or overpowering force.

steam·ship (stēm′shĭp′) *n.* A large ship moved by one or more steam-driven engines.

steam·y (stē′mē) *adj.* **steam·i·er, steam·i·est. 1.** Filled with or producing steam: *a steamy kitchen.* **2.** Hot and humid: *another steamy August afternoon.* **3.** Very exciting sexually: *a steamy novel.* —**steam′i·ness** *n.* [U]

steed (stēd) *n.* *Formal.* A horse used for riding.

steel (stēl) *n.* [U] **1.** An alloy of iron and carbon, often with other metals added to give certain desired properties, widely used as a structural material. **2.** A quality suggestive of this alloy; hardness or strength: *nerves of steel.* —*adj.* **1.** Made with or relating to steel: *steel beams; the steel industry.* **2.** Very firm or strong. —*tr.v.* To strengthen (oneself) mentally: *He steeled himself for the bad news.*

Homonyms: steel, steal (take without right).

steel gray *n.* [U] A dark to purplish gray color. —*adj.* Dark to purplish gray: *a steel gray sky.*

steel·y (stē′lē) *adj.* **steel·i·er, steel·i·est.** Like steel, as in color or hardness: *They gave me a steely look.* —**steel′i·ness** *n.* [U]

steep¹ (stēp) *adj.* **1.** Rising or falling sharply: *a steep hill.* **2.** Very high; excessive: *a steep price to pay.* —**steep′ly** *adv.* —**steep′ness** *n.* [U]

steep² (stēp) *v.* —*tr.* **1.** To soak (sthg.) in a liquid: *steep tea in boiling water.* **2.** To involve (sbdy.) completely: *As a child, she steeped herself in adventure stories.* —*intr.* To soak in a liquid: *Let the tea steep for five minutes.*

S

stee·ple (stē′pəl)
n. A tall tower rising from the roof of a building, especially from a church or courthouse.
stee·ple·chase (stē′pəl chās′) *n.* A horse race across open country or over an obstacle course.
steer[1] (stîr) *v.* —*tr.* **1.** To direct the course of (an automobile, for example): *Steer the truck between the gates.* **2.** To set and follow (a course): *We steered a course around the rocks.* **3.** To guide or move (a person) into a place or course of action: *I steered the tourists toward downtown.* See Synonyms at **guide.** —*intr.* **1.** To guide a vehicle or vessel: *You are steering too close to the reef.* **2.** To follow a set course: *We steered through the narrow streets to the library.* **3.** To be guided: *This car steers easily.* ◆ **steer clear of.** *Informal.* To avoid (sbdy./sthg.): *You should steer clear of him if you want to avoid a fight.*
steer[2] (stîr) *n.* A young male of domestic cattle that is castrated and raised for beef.
steer·ing wheel (stîr′ĭng) *n.* A wheel that controls steering, as in an automobile.
stein (stīn) *n.* A large beer mug usually holding about a pint.
stel·lar (stĕl′ər) *adj.* **1.** Relating to stars. **2.** Relating to a star performer: *a stellar cast for the play.* **3.** Outstanding; prominent: *stellar achievements.*
stem[1] (stĕm) *n.* **1.** The main supporting part of a plant, usually long or slender and growing above the ground: *the stem of the rose.* **2.** A connecting or supporting part resembling a plant stem: *the stem of a pipe; the stem of a goblet.* **3.** The curving upright part at the front of a ship or boat. **4.** The main part of a word. —*v.* **stemmed, stem·ming, stems.** —*intr.* [*from*] To originate or come from sthg.: *His financial problems stem from his long illness.* —*tr.* To remove the stem of (sthg.): *stem strawberries.* ◆ **from stem to stern.** From one end to another: *The house was clean from stem to stern.*
stem[2] (stĕm) *tr.v.* **stemmed, stem·ming, stems.** To stop or hold (sthg.) back by or as if by damming: *He tried to stem the flood of paperwork.*
stemmed (stĕmd) *adj.* **1.** With a stem or a specific type of stem: *a stemmed goblet; a long-stemmed rose.* **2.** With the stems removed: *stemmed cherries.*
stench (stĕnch) *n.* A very strong unpleasant smell; a stink: *the stench of an open sewer.*

steeple

sten·cil (stĕn′səl) *n.* **1.** A sheet of plastic or cardboard in which letters or patterns have been cut. **2.** The lettering or pattern produced with such a sheet. —*tr.v.* To produce (sthg.) with a stencil: *stenciled her name on the bag.*
ste·nog·ra·phy (stə nŏg′rə fē) *n.* [U] The art or process of writing in shorthand. —**ste·nog′ra·pher** *n.*
step (stĕp) *n.* **1.** The single complete movement of raising one foot and putting it down in another spot, as in walking: *I took a step toward the door.* **2.** The sound of sbdy. walking: *I heard his step in the corridor.* **3.** A manner of walking: *moving with a light step.* **4.a.** The distance covered by moving one foot ahead of the other: *standing just a step away from the edge.* **b.** A short walking distance: *The bus stop is just a step from my front door.* **5.** A rest for the foot in going up or down, such as a stair or a rung of a ladder: *We climbed the steps.* **6.** One of a series of actions taken to achieve a goal or complete a process: *steps to program the computer.* —*v.* **stepped, step·ping, steps.** —*intr.* **1.** To put or press the foot: *Don't step on the grass.* **2.** To move with the feet in a certain manner: *step lively.* **3.** To move by taking a step: *Please step back.* —*tr.* To put or set (the foot) down: *step foot on land.* ◆ **out of step. 1.** Not moving in rhythm: *marching out of step.* **2.** Not conforming with others: *out of step with modern times.*
step by step. By degrees; little by little: *There's a lot to learn, so we'll do it step by step.*
step down. *intr.v.* To resign from a high post: *The Presidential advisor stepped down.* **step in.** *intr.v.* To enter into an activity or a situation, especially to intervene in a conflict: *Their friend stepped in to settle an argument.* **step on it.** *Informal.* To go faster; hurry: *We're late, so step on it!* **step up.** *tr.v.* [sep.] To increase (sthg.), especially in stages: *step up production.* —*intr.v.* To come forward: *Step up to the ticket counter, please.*

Homonyms: step, steppe (plain).

---

step— *pref.* A prefix that means related through the remarriage of a parent rather than by blood: *stepbrother; stepchild; stepparent.*
step·lad·der (stĕp′lăd′ər) *n.* A small portable ladder.
steppe (stĕp) *n.* A vast, dry, grass-covered plain as found in southeast Europe, Siberia, and central North America.

Homonyms: steppe, step (foot movement).

---

step·ping·stone (stĕp′ĭng stōn′) *n.* **1.** A stone that provides a place to step, as in crossing a stream. **2.** A step or means toward a goal: *a steppingstone to a better job.*

–ster *suff.* A suffix that means a person who does, performs, or takes part in sthg.: *gangster; youngster.*

ster•e•o (stĕr′ē ō′ *or* stîr′ē ō′) *n., pl.* **ster•e•os. 1.** [C] A stereophonic system or device: *I played jazz on my stereo.* **2.** [U] Stereophonic sound: *a performance reproduced in stereo.*

ster•e•o•phon•ic (stĕr′ē ə fŏn′ĭk) *adj.* Of or used in a system of sound reproduction that uses two or more separate channels to give a more natural distribution of sound.

ster•e•o•type (stĕr′ē ə tīp′ *or* stîr′ē ə tīp′) *n.* A conventional or oversimplified idea or image of sbdy., often based on race, gender, religion, or profession: *the stereotype of the meek librarian.* —*tr.v.* **ster•e•o•typed, ster•e•o•typ•ing, ster•e•o•types.** To make a stereotype of (sbdy./sthg.): *a movie that stereotypes farmers as unsophisticated fools.*

ster•e•o•typed (stĕr′ē ə tīpt′ *or* stîr′ē ə-tīpt′) *adj.* Based on stereotypes: *a stereotyped story of tragic love.*

ster•ile (stĕr′əl *or* stĕr′īl′) *adj.* **1.** Not able to produce offspring, seeds, or fruit: *a sterile bull.* **2.** Producing little or no plant life; barren: *a desolate sterile region.* **3.** Free from living microorganisms, especially those that cause disease: *a sterile bandage.* —**ster′-ile•ly** *adv.* —**ste•ril′i•ty** (stə rĭl′ĭ tē) *n.* [U]

ster•il•i•za•tion (stĕr′ə lĭ zā′shən) *n.* [U] **1.** The act or procedure of sterilizing. **2.** The condition of being sterile or sterilized.

ster•il•ize (stĕr′ə līz′) *tr.v.* **ster•il•ized, ster•il•iz•ing, ster•il•iz•es.** To make (sbdy./sthg.) sterile: *The dentist sterilized the equipment.* —**ster′il•iz′er** *n.*

ster•ling (stûr′lĭng) *n.* [U] **1.** Sterling silver. **2.** British money. —*adj.* **1.** Made of sterling silver: *sterling knives.* **2.** Consisting of or relating to British money: *sterling prices.* **3.** Of the highest quality; very fine: *She has sterling qualifications.*

sterling silver *n.* [U] **1.** An alloy containing 92.5 percent silver with copper or another metal. **2.** Objects made of this alloy.

stern[1] (stûrn) *adj.* Harsh or strict in manner or character: *a stern look from his mother.* —**stern′ly** *adv.* —**stern′ness** *n.* [U]

stern[2] (stûrn) *n.* The rear part of a ship or boat.

ster•oid (stîr′oid′ *or* stĕr′oid′) *n.* A drug that is used to treat diseases and injuries and sometimes illegally to increase muscle size. —**ster′oid′, ste•roi′dal** (stĭ roid′l *or* stĕ roid′l) *adj.*

steth•o•scope (stĕth′ə skōp′) *n.* A medical instrument used to listen to sounds, such as the heartbeat, made within the body.

stethoscope

stew (stōō *or* styōō) *v.* —*tr.* To cook (food) by simmering or boiling slowly: *stewing a chicken.* —*intr.* **1.** To undergo cooking by simmering or boiling slowly: *Let the food stew for an hour.* **2.** *Informal.* To suffer from intense heat; swelter: *stewing in an overheated room.* **3.** [about; over] *Informal.* To worry or be angry: *He stewed about his bad evaluation.* —*n.* [C; U] A dish cooked by stewing, especially a thick soup of meat or fish and vegetables. ◆ **in a stew.** Worried and upset: *My sister was in a stew over her lost keys.*

stew•ard (stōō′ərd) *n.* **1.** A man who is an attendant on a ship. **2.** An old-fashioned word for a man who is a flight attendant. **3.** A person who represents others, especially in a union: *a shop steward.* —**stew′ard•ship′** *n.* [U]

stew•ard•ess (stōō′ər dĭs) *n.* An old-fashioned word for a woman who is a flight attendant.

stewed (stōōd *or* styōōd) *adj.* Cooked by stewing: *stewed tomatoes.*

stick (stĭk) *n.* **1.** A long slender piece of wood, such as a branch from a tree. **2.** A piece of wood that is shaped for a specific purpose: *a walking stick; a hockey stick.* **3.** Something slender and often round in form: *a stick of dynamite.* **4.** A control lever for an airplane. **5. the sticks** *Informal.* A remote area or place regarded as dull or unsophisticated: *leaving the sticks for life in the big city.* —*v.* **stuck** (stŭk), **stick•ing, sticks.** —*tr.* **1.** To pierce or prick (sthg.) with a pointed instrument or object: *sticking her finger on a pin.* **2.** To push or force (sthg. pointed) into or through a surface: *stuck the knife in the board.* **3.** To fasten or attach (sthg.) with a pin or an adhesive material: *stick a note on the door; stick a stamp on an envelope.* **4.** To put or push (sthg.): *sticking her head out the window.* **5.** To hold back or delay (sbdy./sthg.): *We were stuck in traffic for an hour.* **6.** [with] *Informal.* To put blame, responsibility, or a burden on (sbdy.): *They stuck me with the bill.* —*intr.* **1.** To be or become fixed in place: *The arrow stuck in the tree. The wheels stuck in the mud.* **2.** To become attached or fastened: *Mud stuck to my shoes.* **3.** To be in close association: *Let's stick together or we'll get lost in this crowd.* **4.a.** [by; with] To remain faithful or loyal: *stick by a friend in trouble.* **b.** [with; at] To continue; persist: *I stuck with the lessons until the end.* ◆ **stick around.** *intr.v. Informal.* To remain: *We stuck around after the game to talk to the coach.* **stick out.** *intr.v.* To be obvious or easily noticed: *That hat sticks out in a crowd.* **stick up.** *intr.v.* To extend; project: *hair sticking up on his head.* **stick up for.** To defend or support (sbdy./sthg.): *Thanks for sticking up for me when everyone else criticized my decision.*

stick•er (stĭk′ər) *n.* A small piece of paper with a picture or writing on it that has adhesive and can be put on sthg.: *Children often enjoy collecting colorful stickers.*

stick•ler (stĭk′lər) *n.* A person who thinks sthg. is especially important: *Our instructor is a stickler for promptness.*

stick•up (stĭk′ŭp′) *n. Slang.* A robbery, especially one that involves a weapon.

stick•y (stĭk′ē) *adj.* **stick•i•er, stick•i•est.** **1.** With the quality of sticking to a surface; adhesive: *sticky paste; sticky candy.* **2.** Hot and humid: *sticky August weather.* **3.** *Informal.* Difficult or unpleasant: *a sticky situation.* —**stick′i•ly** *adv.* —**stick′i•ness** *n.* [U]

stiff (stĭf) *adj.* **1.** Not easily bent: *a stiff new pair of shoes.* **2.** Not moving or operating easily: *a stiff joint; a stiff doorknob.* **3.** Thick; almost solid: *a stiff mixture of flour and milk.* **4.** Rigidly formal; not friendly: *a stiff writing style.* **5.** Difficult to do: *a stiff entrance requirement.* **6.** Strong or undiluted: *a stiff dose of medicine; a stiff drink.* —*n. Slang.* **1.** A corpse: *The police found a stiff in the park.* **2.** A person thought of as dull and overly formal. —*tr.v. Slang.* To not pay (sbdy.) money that is owed: *The employees were stiffed a week's pay.* ♦ **bored stiff.** *Informal.* Very bored: *They were bored stiff during the lecture.* **frozen stiff.** *Informal.* Very cold: *She was frozen stiff after walking home.* **lucky stiff.** *Informal.* A lucky person: *You are such a lucky stiff! I never win anything.* **scared stiff.** *Informal.* Very scared: *The accident left them scared stiff.* —**stiff′ly** *adv.* —**stiff′ness** *n.* [U]

stiff•en (stĭf′ən) *tr. & intr.v.* To make or become stiff or stiffer: *Add more flour to stiffen the dough. His neck stiffened in anger.* —**stiff′en•er** *n.* [C; U]

stiff-necked (stĭf′nĕkt′) *adj.* Stubborn and arrogant: *They were very stiff-necked about the decision and refused to change their minds.*

sti•fle (stī′fəl) *v.* **sti•fled, sti•fling, sti•fles.** —*tr.* To keep (sbdy./sthg.) in or hold back; stop: *stifled a laugh.* —*intr.* To feel smothered or suffocated by or as if by a lack of air: *Open a window, I'm stifling in here!*

sti•fling (stī′flĭng) *adj.* Very hot or stuffy, almost suffocating: *a stifling room.*

stig•ma (stĭg′mə) *n.* A sign of shame or disgrace: *There should be no stigma attached to doing strenuous physical work.*

stig•ma•tize (stĭg′mə tīz′) *tr.v.* **stig•ma•tized, stig•ma•tiz•ing, stig•ma•tiz•es.** To mark (sbdy./sthg.) as shameful or disgraceful: *stigmatized by the scandal.* —**stig′ma•ti•za′tion** (stĭg′mə tĭ zā′shən) *n.* [U]

still¹ (stĭl) *adj.* **1.** Silent; quiet: *He was still for a moment and then started talking again.* **2.**

Not moving; motionless: *still water.* —*n.* [U] Silence; quiet; calm: *the still of the night.* —*adv.* **1.** Without movement: *Please stand still.* **2.** Up to or at a particular time: *We will still be here tomorrow.* **3.** In a larger amount or degree: *I've got still more good news for you.* **4.** Nevertheless; all the same: *a painful but still necessary decision.* —*tr.v.* **1.** To make (sthg.) quiet: *He stilled their objections.* **2.** To make (sthg.) calm: *stilled their fears.* —**still′ness** *n.* [U]

still² (stĭl) *n.* A device for distilling alcoholic drinks.

still•born (stĭl′bôrn′) *adj.* Dead at birth.

still life *n., pl.* **still lifes.** A painting, picture, or photograph of objects, such as flowers or fruit. —**still′-life′** *adj.*

stilt (stĭlt) *n.* One of a pair of long slender poles, each with a raised footrest, that allow the user to walk above the ground.

stilt•ed (stĭl′tĭd) *adj.* Stiffly or unnaturally formal: *stilted conversation.*

stim•u•lant (stĭm′yə lənt) *n.* **1.** Something, especially a drug, that temporarily increases activity. **2.** Something that gets a result; an incentive: *a stimulant to increase sales.*

stim•u•late (stĭm′yə lāt′) *v.* **stim•u•lat•ed, stim•u•lat•ing, stim•u•lates.** —*tr.* **1.** To cause activity or increased action in (sbdy./sthg.); encourage: *music that stimulates the imagination; changes to stimulate the economy.* **2.** To increase physical activity in (sbdy./sthg.) with a stimulant. —*intr.* To act or serve as a stimulant or stimulus. —**stim′u•la′tion** *n.* [U]

stim•u•lus (stĭm′yə ləs) *n., pl.* **stim•u•li** (stĭm′yə lī′). Something that causes a response: *Many hope the new airport will be a stimulus to the state's economy.*

sting (stĭng) *v.* **stung** (stŭng), **sting•ing, stings.** —*tr.* **1.** To pierce or wound (sbdy./sthg.) with a sharp-pointed part, as that of certain insects: *A bee may sting you.* **2.** To cause (sbdy.) to feel a sharp physical or emotional pain: *Smoke began to sting her eyes.* —*intr.* **1.** To have, use, or wound with a sharp-pointed part: *The bee stung twice.* **2.** To cause or feel a sharp physical or emotional pain: *Cruel comments sting.* —*n.* **1.** The act of stinging: *the sting of his words.* **2.** A wound or pain caused by or as if by stinging: *a bee sting.* —**sting′ing•ly** *adv.*

sting•er (stĭng′ər) *n.* Something that stings.

stin•gy (stĭn′jē) *adj.* **stin•gi•er, stin•gi•est.** **1.** Unwilling to give or spend money: *a stingy boss.* **2.** Scanty; meager: *a stingy meal.* —**stin′gi•ly** *adv.* —**stin′gi•ness** *n.* [U]

stink (stĭngk) *intr.v.* **stank** (stăngk) or **stunk** (stŭngk), **stunk, stink•ing, stinks.** **1.** To give off a strong foul odor: *The spoiled meat* stank. **2.** *Slang.* To be of very poor quality: *This movie stinks.* —*n.* A strong offensive odor: *the stink of old cheese.* ♦ **stink up.** *tr.v.* [sep.] To cause (sthg.) to stink: *The wet dog stunk up the room.* —**stink′y** *adj.*

stint (stĭnt) *v.* —*tr.* To limit (sbdy./sthg.) in amount or number: *He stinted his guests by serving only a little food.* —*intr.* [on] To be frugal: *Don't stint on food.* —*n.* A certain time of work: *She did a stint as a clerk in her family's business.*

sti·pend (stī′pĕnd′) *n.* A fixed or regular payment, such as a salary or an allowance.

stip·u·late (stĭp′yə lāt′) *tr.v.* **stip·u·lat·ed, stip·u·lat·ing, stip·u·lates.** To specify or demand (sthg.) as a condition of an agreement; require by contract: *The agreement stipulates monthly payments.* —**stip′u·la′tion** *n.*

stir (stûr) *v.* **stirred, stir·ring, stirs.** —*tr.* **1.** To move through (a liquid, for example) in circular motions: *Stir the soup. Stir flour into the sauce.* **2.** To cause (sbdy./sthg.) to move or change position: *The wind stirred the bird's feathers.* **3.** To excite strong feelings in (sbdy./sthg.): *The music stirred her heart.* —*intr.* **1.** To move or change position: *The dog stirred in his sleep.* **2.** To be affected by strong feelings or ideas: *A new plan began to stir in her brain.* —*n.* **1.** A stirring or mixing movement: *Give the soup a stir, please.* **2.** *(usually singular).* A public disturbance or an excited reaction: *a public stir over taxes.* ♦ **stir up.** *tr.v.* [sep.] **1.** To cause (sthg., such as trouble): *stirred up an argument.* **2.** To get (sbdy.) excited or angry: *He stirred them up with his speech.* —**stir′rer** *n.*

stir·ring (stûr′ĭng) *adj.* **1.** Causing strong feelings: *a stirring song of peace.* **2.** Lively: *a stirring march.* —**stir′ring·ly** *adv.*

stir·rup (stûr′əp *or* stĭr′əp) *n.* A metal loop with a flat base to support the rider's foot, hung by a strap from either side of a saddle on a horse.

stitch (stĭch) *n.* **1.** A complete movement of needle and thread, as in sewing fabric or closing a wound during surgery: *He needed 15 stitches to close the cut on his head.* **2.** *Informal.* An article of clothing: *a baby without a stitch on.* **3.** *(usually singular).* A sudden sharp pain, especially in the side: *She got a stitch while running.* —*tr.v.* To fasten or decorate (sthg.) with stitches: *stitch initials on a pocket; stitch a torn shirt.* ♦ **a stitch in time saves nine.** A little work done now saves a lot of work later. **in stitches.** Laughing hard: *His funny story had us all in stitches.* **stitch up.** *tr.v.* [sep.] To sew (a person or wound): *The doctor stitched the boy up.*

stock (stŏk) *n.* **1.** [C; U] A supply saved for future use: *Grain stocks are low.* **2.** [C; U] The total merchandise kept ready for sale or use by a merchant or business: *a large stock of furni-*

ture. **3.** [U] All the animals kept or raised on a farm. **4.** [U] A line or group of ancestors from which persons, animals, or plants are descended: *She comes from farming stock.* **5.** [C; U] Broth from boiled meat, fish, or vegetables, used in making soup, gravy, or sauces: *chicken stock.* **6.** [C; U] **a.** The money invested in a corporation by the buying of shares of ownership, each share giving the owner voting rights at meetings and often paying dividends. **b.** A number of shares owned by a stockholder: *I have stock in that company.* **7.** [U] Confidence or belief: *I put no stock in what he promises.* —*tr.v.* **1.** To provide (sthg.) with a supply: *stock a pond with fish; stock supermarket shelves.* **2.** To keep (sthg.) for future sale or use: *We stock canned goods.* —*adj.* **1.** Kept regularly available for sale or use: *Bread is a stock item.* **2.** Commonplace; not original: *a stock answer.* ♦ **in** or **out of stock.** Available or not available for sale or use: *Those shoes are not in stock.* **stock up.** *intr.v.* [on] To gather a supply of sthg.: *People stocked up on supplies before the hurricane.* **take stock. 1.** To count, list, or record all goods or materials in stock. **2.** To estimate or evaluate one's resources or oneself: *He took stock and decided to make some changes in his life.*

stock·ade (stŏ kād′) *n.* **1.** A fence made of upright wooden posts driven into the ground: *A stockade surrounded the fort.* **2.** A jail on a military base.

stock·bro·ker (stŏk′brō′kər) *n.* A person who buys or sells stocks.

stock exchange *n.* A place where stocks are bought and sold.

stock·hold·er (stŏk′hōl′dər) *n.* A person who owns shares of stock in a company.

stock·ing (stŏk′ĭng) *n.* A thin knitted covering for the foot and leg made from nylon, cotton, wool, and similar yarns.

stock market *n.* **1.** A stock exchange. **2.** *(usually singular).* The business carried out at a stock exchange: *He works in the stock market.* **3.** The average value of all stocks: *The stock market is up this week.*

stock·pile (stŏk′pīl′) *n.* A supply of material stored for future use: *a stockpile of weapons.* —*tr.v.* **stock·piled, stock·pil·ing, stock·piles.** To accumulate a stockpile of (sthg.): *stockpile supplies.*

stock·room *also* **stock room** (stŏk′rōōm′ *or* stŏk′rŏŏm′) *n.* A room in which goods or materials are kept.

stock-still (stŏk′stĭl′) *adj.* Completely still; motionless: *The deer stood stock-still in the road.*

stock·y (stŏk′ē) *adj.* **stock·i·er, stock·i·est.** Having a heavy solid body: *a stocky boy.* —**stock′i·ness** *n.* [U]

stock·yard (stŏk′yärd′) *n.* A large area in which animals, such as cattle or pigs, are kept until they are killed, sold, or shipped elsewhere.

stodg·y (stŏj′ē) *adj.* **stodg·i·er, stodg· i·est.** Dull and boring: *a stodgy person.* —**stodg′i·ly** *adv.* —**stodg′i·ness** *n.* [U]

sto·ic (stō′ĭk) *n.* A person who seems not to feel joy, sadness, pleasure, or pain. —*adj.* also **sto·i·cal** (stō′ĭ kəl). Seemingly unaffected by pleasure or pain: *He listened to the news with a stoic expression.* —**sto′i·cal·ly** *adv.* —**sto′i·cism** (stō′ĭ sĭz′ əm) *n.* [U]

stoke (stōk) *tr.v.* **stoked, stok·ing, stokes.** To add fuel to and take care of (a fire or furnace): *The man stoked the old coal boiler.*

stole¹ (stōl) *n.* A long scarf of cloth or fur worn by women around the shoulders: *a mink stole.*

stole² (stōl) *v.* Past tense of **steal.**

sto·len (stō′lən) *v.* Past participle of **steal.**

stol·id (stŏl′ĭd) *adj.* Having or showing little movement or emotion: *a stolid expression.* —**stol′id·ly** *adv.*

stom·ach (stŭm′ək) *n.* **1.** An organ shaped like a bag, where food is digested after eating: *My stomach hurts.* **2.** The part of the body that contains the stomach; the abdomen or belly: *She punched him in the stomach.* —*tr.v.* To tolerate or endure (sbdy./sthg.): *She had to stomach his rudeness.*

stom·ach·ache (stŭm′ək āk′) *n.* [C; U] Pain in the stomach or abdomen: *I had a stomachache from eating too much.*

stomp (stŏmp *or* stômp) *intr.v.* To walk heavily or violently: *He stomped out of the room in frustration.*

stone (stōn) *n.* **1.** [U] Hard or solid mineral or earthy matter; rock: *a wall made of stone.* **2.** [C] A small piece of rock: *I had some stones in my shoes.* **3.** [C] A gem or precious stone: *He gave her a big stone for their anniversary.* **4.** [C] A seed with a hard covering, such as of a cherry or plum; a pit. —*tr.v.* **stoned, ston·ing, stones. 1.** To throw stones at (sbdy./sthg.): *The crowd stoned the police.* **2.** To remove the stones or pits from (sthg.): *He was stoning peaches for a pie.* ♦ **a stone's throw.** A short distance: *They live a stone's throw from us.*

stoned (stōnd) *adj. Slang.* Drunk or drugged.

stone·ma·son (stōn′mā′sən) *n.* A person who prepares and uses stones in building.

stone·wall (stōn′wôl′) *intr. & tr.v. Informal.* To refuse to answer or cooperate: *The witness tried to stonewall as long as possible. The government official stonewalled the investigating committee.*

stone·ware (stōn′wâr′) *n.* [U] A hard heavy pottery.

stone·work (stōn′wûrk′) *n.* [U] **1.** The technique or process of building or making things from stone: *a mason skilled in stonework.* **2.** Something built or made of stone. —**stone′work′er** *n.*

ston·y (stō′nē) *adj.* **ston·i·er, ston·i·est.**

1. Covered with or full of stones: *stony soil.* **2.** Hardhearted and cruel: *a stony look.* —**ston′i·ly** *adv.* —**ston′i·ness** *n.* [U]

stood (stŏŏd) *v.* Past tense and past participle of **stand.**

stool (stŏŏl) *n.* **1.** A small single seat with no back or arms and supported on legs. **2.** Waste matter produced in a bowel movement.

stool pigeon *n. Slang.* A person who works as a decoy or an informer, especially for the police.

stoop¹ (stŏŏp) *v.* —*intr.* **1.** To bend forward and down from the waist or middle of the back: *stooping to pick up the newspaper.* **2.** To walk or stand with the head and upper back bent forward: *She stoops from years of hard work.* —*tr.* To bend (the head and body) forward and down: *stooped her head to enter the little house.* —*n.* **1.** The act of stooping. **2.** A forward bending of the head and body, especially when habitual: *walk with a stoop.* ♦ **stoop to (doing).** To engage in bad behavior: *I couldn't believe he'd stoop to telling lies.*

stoop² (stŏŏp) *n.* A small porch, staircase, or platform at the entrance of a house or building.

stop (stŏp) *v.* **stopped, stop·ping, stops.** —*tr.* **1.** To cause (sbdy./sthg.) to halt or cease moving, progressing, acting, or operating: *The officer stopped the car.* **2.** To bring (sthg.) to an end; cease: *stop running.* **3.** To close (an opening) by covering, plugging up, or filling in: *stop the drain.* **4.** To have a bank withhold payment of (sthg.): *stopped the check.* —*intr.* **1.** To cease moving, progressing, acting, or operating; come to a halt: *The clock stopped during the night.* **2.** To interrupt one's journey for a short visit or stay: *stop at the store on the way home.* —*n.* **1.** The act of stopping or the condition of being stopped: *The car came to a stop.* **2.** A stay or visit: *We made a stop at Austin.* **3.** A place at which a person or thing stops: *a bus stop.* **4.** Something that stops or blocks movement: *Put the stop in the sink.* ♦ **pull out all the stops.** To do everything necessary: *She pulled out all the stops to make her visit successful.* **stop by.** *intr.v.* To make a short visit to sbdy.: *Stop by if you're in town.* **stop off.** *intr.v.* To make a short visit while on the way to someplace else: *I need to stop off at the store before work.* **stop over.** *intr.v.* To make a short overnight visit on a longer journey: *We stopped over in New York before going on to Boston.* **stop short of (doing).** To stop before doing sthg. serious: *They punished the workers but stopped short of firing them.*

SYNONYMS: stop, cease, halt, quit. These verbs mean to bring or come to an end. **Cease** and **halt** are more formal than **stop** and **quit.** *Stop making so much noise; I'm trying to sleep!*

ă–cat; ā–pay; âr–care; ä–father; ĕ–get; ē–be; ĭ–sit; ī–nice; îr–here; ŏ–got; ō–go; ô–saw; oi–boy; ou–out; ŏŏ–took; ŏŏ–boot; ŭ–cut; ûr–word; th–thin; *th*–this; hw–when; zh–vision; ə–about; N–French bon

The siren ceased abruptly. We were halted at the checkpoint on the border. They quit riding at sundown.

stop•gap (stŏp′găp′) *n.* A temporary substitute: *a stopgap budget until the final one is approved.*

stop•light (stŏp′līt′) *n.* A traffic light.

stop•o•ver (stŏp′ō′vər) *n.* **1.** A short stay or visit in the course of a journey: *a flight to Seattle with a stopover in Chicago.* **2.** A place visited briefly: *We had stopovers in Paris and Rome.*

stop•page (stŏp′ĭj) *n.* [C; U] The act of stopping: *a work stoppage.*

stop•per (stŏp′ər) *n.* Something, such as a cork or plug, that is put into an opening to close it: *a tub stopper.*

stop•watch (stŏp′wŏch′) *n.* A watch that can be started and stopped by pushing a button, used for measuring exact lengths of time.

stor•age (stôr′ĭj) *n.* [U] **1.** The act of storing or the state of being stored: *goods in storage.* **2.** A space for storing: *We have a lot of storage in the attic.*

stopwatch

store (stôr) *n.* **1.** A place where goods are sold; a shop: *a department store.* **2.** A stock or supply of sthg. reserved for future use: *a store of grain.* **3. stores.** Supplies, especially of food, clothing, or arms. **4.** A large quantity or number: *a store of knowledge.* —*tr.v.* **stored, stor•ing, stores.** To put (sthg.) away for future use: *Squirrels store acorns for winter. We stored our winter clothes.* ♦ **in store.** In the near future: *A great opportunity was in store for her.* **set store by.** To feel that sbdy./sthg. is of a certain value: *We set little store by his words.*

store•house (stôr′hous′) *n.* **1.** A place or building where goods are stored; a warehouse. **2.** An abundant source or supply: *a storehouse of knowledge.*

store•keep•er (stôr′kē′pər) *n.* A person who runs a retail shop or store.

store•room (stôr′rōōm′ *or* stôr′rōōm′) *n.* A room where things are stored.

sto•ried (stôr′ēd) *adj.* Having a certain number of stories: *a five-storied house.*

stork (stôrk) *n.* A large wading bird with long legs and a long straight bill.

storm (stôrm) *n.* **1.** Rough weather, with strong winds and rain, snow, or other precipitation, often with thunder and lightning: *The storm kept us indoors all weekend.* **2.** A political or social disturbance: *a storm of protest over the judge's ruling.* —*v.* —*intr.* **1.** To be

stormy; blow forcefully and often rain, snow, hail, or sleet: *It stormed all night long.* **2.** To be very angry: *She was storming about the high phone bill.* **3.** To move or rush about angrily: *He stormed into the room.* —*tr.* To capture (sthg.) by a violent sudden attack: *storm the city.*

storm•y (stôr′mē) *adj.* **storm•i•er, storm•i•est.** **1.** With storms: *stormy weather.* **2.** Noisy or angry: *a stormy meeting.* —**storm′i•ly** *adv.* —**storm′i•ness** *n.* [U]

sto•ry[1] (stôr′ē) *n., pl.* **sto•ries.** **1.** An account of an event or a series of events, either true or fictitious: *a fairy story; a short story.* **2.** A newspaper or magazine article or radio or TV broadcast: *The reporter covered three stories today.* **3.** A lie: *Don't tell stories.*

sto•ry[2] (stôr′ē) *n., pl.* **sto•ries.** A floor or level of a building.

sto•ry•book (stôr′ē bŏok′) *n.* A book containing a collection of stories, usually for children. —*adj.* Happening in the style of a storybook: *a storybook romance.*

sto•ry•tell•er (stôr′ē tĕl′ər) *n.* A person who tells or writes stories.

stout (stout) *adj.* **1.** Determined, bold, or brave: *a stout heart.* **2.** Strong in body or structure; sturdy: *the stout back of a donkey.* **3.** Heavy in figure; fat: *a stout man.* —**stout′ly** *adv.* —**stout′ness** *n.* [U]

stout•heart•ed (stout′här′tĭd) *adj.* Brave; courageous: *a stouthearted old dog.* —**stout′heart′ed•ly** *adv.* —**stout′heart′ed•ness** *n.* [U]

stove[1] (stōv) *n.* A device that produces heat for warmth or cooking, using fuel or electricity as a source of power.

stove[2] (stōv) *v.* A past tense of **stave.**

stow (stō) *tr.v.* **1.** To place or arrange (sthg.), especially neatly: *She stowed her equipment in the locker.* **2.** To store (sthg.) for future use: *stow the wood in the cellar.* ♦ **stow away.** *intr.v.* To hide oneself aboard a train or ship, for example, in order to travel for free: *The men stowed away on the ship.*

stow•a•way (stō′ə wā′) *n.* A person who hides aboard a ship or other vehicle to get a free trip: *The stowaways were arrested.*

strad•dle (străd′l) *tr.v.* **strad•dled, strad•dling, strad•dles.** —*tr.* **1.** To sit or stand with a leg on each side of (sthg.): *She straddled the horse.* **2.** To appear to favor both sides of (sthg.): *straddle a political issue.* —**strad′dler** *n.*

strag•gle (străg′əl) *intr.v.* **strag•gled, strag•gling, strag•gles.** **1.** To move slower than others and fall behind: *One of the hikers straggled away from the path.* **2.** To move or spread out in a scattered or irregular group: *cows straggling into the barn.* —**strag′gler** *n.*

straight (strāt) *adj.* **1.** Without bends or curves: *a straight line; straight hair.* **2.** Level or upright: *a straight back.* **3.** Direct and hon-

833   stopgap / straight

S

est: *do some straight talking.* **4.** Neatly and orderly: *He can't keep his desk straight.* **5.** One after the other: *The team ended the season with six straight wins.* **6.** Not mixed with anything else; undiluted: *straight vodka.* **7.** *Slang.* Heterosexual. —*adv.* **1.** In a straight line; directly: *The arrow flew straight at the target.* **2.** Without stopping or delay: *went straight home.* ◆ **a straight face.** A serious expression; not smiling or laughing: *He told the joke with a perfectly straight face.* **set straight.** To tell (sbdy.) the truth, often in an unfriendly way: *He set us straight about the bills.* **straight off.** Immediately: *When she got my message, she called me straight off.* —**straight′ly** *adv.* —**straight′ness** *n.* [U]

HOMONYMS: straight, strait (channel).

straight angle *n.* An angle of 180 degrees.
straight•a•way (strāt′ə wā′) *adj.* Continuing in a straight line or course without a curve or turn. —*n.* A straight road, course, or track: *An accident on the straightaway ended the race.* —*adv.* (strāt′ə **wā′**). At once; immediately: *She came home straightaway from the party.*
straight•en (strāt′n) *tr. & intr.v.* To make or become straight or straighter: *straighten hair; She straightened as she stood up.* ◆ **straighten out.** *tr.v.* [sep.] To resolve or clarify (sthg.): *We straightened out the problems with the computer program.* **straighten up.** *intr.v.* To begin behaving well: *His father warned him to straighten up.* —*tr.v.* [sep.] To make (sthg.) neat and orderly: *We straightened up the house.*
straight•for•ward (strāt′ fôr′wərd) *adj.* **1.** Continuing in a straight course; direct: *a straightforward approach to a problem.* **2.** Honest and frank: *a straightforward reply.* —**straight′for′ward•ly** *adv.* —**straight′-for′ward•ness** *n.* [U]
strain¹ (strān) *v.* —*tr.* **1.** To pull, draw, or stretch (sthg.) tight: *The weight of the pulley strains the rope.* **2.** To force (sthg.) to make a strong effort: *She strained her lungs to play the horn.* **3.** To injure or impair (sthg.) by overuse: *strain a muscle.* **4.** To force or stretch (sthg.) beyond a proper limit: *It will strain my budget to buy a new coat.* **5.** To pass (sthg.) through a strainer; filter: *strain the tomatoes.* —*intr.* **1.** To make violent or steady efforts to do sthg.: *The runner strained to reach the finish line.* **2.** To pull violently: *The dog strained at its leash.* —*n.* **1.** [C] A pressure, stress, or force: *put a strain on our relationship.* **2.** [C; U] An injury resulting from excessive effort or twisting: *a muscle strain; back strain.* **3.** [U] Great pressure or demands on one's mind, body, or resources: *The students felt the strain of the extra homework.*

strain² (strān) *n.* **1.** A race, line, or breed: *a new strain of cattle; a strain of a virus.* **2.** *(usually plural).* A piece, passage, or sound of music: *the strains of the waltz.*
strained (strānd) *adj.* **1.** Passed through a strainer: *strained peaches.* **2.** Done with too much effort; stressed: *strained humor.* **3.** Tense; unfriendly: *a strained conversation.*
strain•er (strā′nər) *n.* A device used for separating liquids from solids.
strait (strāt) *n. (usually plural).* **1.** A narrow channel that connects two larger bodies of water: *the Straits of Gibraltar.* **2.** A position of difficulty, perplexity, distress, or need: *He was in desperate straits for money.*

HOMONYMS: strait, straight (erect).

strait•jack•et (strāt′jăk′ĭt) *n.* **1.** A long-sleeved garment used to bind the arms of a violent patient or prisoner. **2.** Something that restricts: *Their conditions were a straitjacket to our plan.*
strait-laced (strāt′lāst′) *adj.* Excessively strict: *old-fashioned, strait-laced ideas.*
strand¹ (strănd) *n.* The land along a body of water; a beach. —*tr.v.* **1.** To leave (sbdy./ sthg.) in a difficult or helpless position: *Travelers were stranded at the airport by bad weather.* **2.** To drive (sbdy./sthg.) ashore or aground: *The sailors had to strand the boat and save themselves.*
strand² (strănd) *n.* A single fiber or thread: *a strand of hair.*
strand•ed (străn′dĭd) *adj.* Left in a difficult position: *The stranded passengers tried to find another flight home.*
strange (strānj) *adj.* **strang•er, strang•est.** **1.** Unknown; unfamiliar: *a strange fish of tropical waters.* **2.** Out of the ordinary; unusual: *a strange feeling.* —**strange′ly** *adv.* —**strange′ness** *n.* [U]
strang•er (strān′jər) *n.* **1.** A person whom one does not know: *Don't get into cars with strangers.* **2.** A foreigner, a newcomer, or an outsider: *a stranger in town.*
stran•gle (străng′gəl) *tr.v.* **stran•gled, stran•gling, stran•gles.** To kill (sbdy./ sthg.) by pressing tightly around the neck. —**stran′gler** *n.* —**stran′gu•la′tion** *n.* [U]
strap (străp) *n.* **1.** A flexible narrow strip of material, used to hold things down, tie things together, or keep things in place: *the straps of an evening gown.* **2.** A narrow band formed into a loop for holding with the hand: *She pulled the suitcase along by its strap.* —*tr.v.* **strapped, strap•ping, straps.** To fasten or secure (sthg.) with a strap: *strapped an air tank to the diver's back.*

ă–cat; ā–pay; âr–care; ä–father; ĕ–get; ē–be; ĭ–sit; ī–nice; îr–here; ŏ–got; ō–go; ô–saw; oi–boy; ou–out; o͝o–took; o͞o–boot; ŭ–cut; ûr–word; th–thin; th–this; hw–when; zh–vision; ə–about; N–French bon

strap·ping (străp′ĭng) *adj.* With a sturdy muscular physique: *a strapping farm boy.*

stra·ta (strā′tə *or* străt′ə) *n.* A plural of **stratum.**

strat·a·gem (străt′ə jəm) *n.* A trick to deceive or surprise an enemy.

stra·te·gic (strə tē′jĭk) *adj.* **1.** Relating to strategy: *the strategic importance of the Panama Canal.* **2.** Necessary to a plan of action: *strategic locations.* —**stra·te′gi·cal·ly** *adv.*

strat·e·gist (străt′ə jĭst) *n.* A person who is skilled in strategy.

strat·e·gy (străt′ə jē) *n., pl.* **strat·e·gies. 1.** [C; U] A plan of action: *a winning strategy.* **2.** [U] The science of national planning during peace or war.

strat·i·fied (străt′ə fīd′) *adj.* Divided into layers or classes: *stratified societies.*

strat·i·fy (străt′ə fī′) *v.* **strat·i·fied, strat·i·fy·ing, strat·i·fies.** —*tr.* To form, arrange, or deposit (sthg.) in layers. —*intr.* To become layered; form layers. —**strat′i·fi·ca′tion** *n.* [U]

strat·o·sphere (străt′ə sfîr′) *n.* [U] The upper layer of the earth's atmosphere.

stra·tum (strā′təm *or* străt′əm) *n., pl.* **stra·ta** (strā′tə *or* străt′ə) *or* **stra·tums. 1.** A horizontal layer of material. **2.** A level of society made up of people with similar social, cultural, or economic status.

straw (strô) *n.* **1.a.** [U] Stalks of wheat, oats, or other grain used as bedding and food for animals, as stuffing or padding, and for making such items as hats and baskets. **b.** [C] A single stalk of such grain. **2.** [C] A slender paper or plastic tube used to drink liquids. —*adj.* Relating to or made of straw: *a straw hat.* ◆ **the last straw.** Something that finally makes a situation impossible: *I had a terrible day, and the last straw was losing my wallet.*

straw·ber·ry (strô′běr′ē) *n., pl.* **straw·ber·ries.** A plant with sweet, red, fleshy fruit with many small seeds on the surface.

stray (strā) *intr.v.* [*from*] To wander about or roam, especially beyond established limits: *Our cat seldom strays far from home. Don't stray from the topic.* —*n.* An animal that has strayed and is lost: *My friend has taken in several strays.* —*adj.* **1.** Strayed or lost: *a stray cat.* **2.** Scattered or separate: *stray shafts of sunlight.*

strawberry

streak (strēk) *n.* **1.** A line, mark, or smear: *a streak of chocolate on his face.* **2.** A part of a person's personality: *a mean streak.* **3.** *Informal.* A brief period, as of luck: *a winning streak.* —*v.* —*tr.* To mark (sthg.) with a streak:

Dog tracks streaked the floor. —*intr.* **1.** To form a streak or streaks: *The windows had streaked.* **2.** To move at high speed; rush: *Lightning streaked across the sky.* —**streak′y** *adj.*

stream (strēm) *n.* **1.** A flow of water that runs in a more or less regular course, as a brook or small river: *a quiet stream in the forest.* **2.** A steady flow of sthg.: *a stream of electrons; a stream of questions.* —*intr.v.* **1.** To flow in a stream: *Water streamed into the reservoir.* **2.** [*with*] To pour forth or give off a stream; flow: *His eyes streamed with tears.*

stream·er (strē′mər) *n.* A long narrow flag or strip of material used for decoration: *a hall decorated with colorful paper streamers.*

stream·line (strēm′līn′) *tr.v.* **stream·lined, stream·lin·ing, stream·lines. 1.** To construct or design (sthg.) so that it moves easily through wind or water: *streamline a boat.* **2.** To improve the appearance or efficiency of (sthg.); modernize: *streamline a computer design; streamline a factory.* —**stream′lined′** *adj.*

street (strēt) *n.* **1.** A public way or road in a city or town: *pave a street.* **2.** A public way along with its houses and buildings and the people living and working in them: *We live on a quiet street.* —*adj.* **1.** Happening in the street: *a street performance.* **2.** Living or working on the streets: *a street vendor.*

street·car (strēt′kär′) *n.* A public vehicle that runs on rails and provides transportation along a regular route.

strength (strĕngkth *or* strĕnth) *n.* **1.** [U] The quality of being strong: *a man of great physical strength.* **2.** [U] The power to resist force, stress, or attack: *the strength of steel.* **3.** [C] A source of power or force: *Religion is his strength.* ◆ **on the strength of.** On the basis of; because of: *Her professor gave her an "A" on the strength of her essay.*

---

strength·en (strĕngk′thən *or* strĕng′thən) *tr. & intr.v.* To make or become strong or stronger: *strengthened laws against drunk driving; Our resistance strengthened.*

stren·u·ous (strĕn′yōō əs) *adj.* **1.** Needing great effort or energy: *strenuous exercise.* **2.** Very strong; energetic: *strenuous objections.* —**stren′u·ous·ly** *adv.*

stress (strĕs) *n.* [C; U] **1.** Importance or emphasis placed on sthg.: *She puts too much stress on money.* **2.** The relative force given to a sound or syllable in a spoken word or phrase. **3.** A force that tends to strain physically or emotionally: *The stress of her job caused her to lose sleep.* —*tr.v.* **1.** To place stress on (sthg.); emphasize: *stress quality; stresses the first syllable.* **2.** To cause (sbdy./sthg.) to feel physical or mental pressure or strain: *This work is stressing me.* ◆ **stress out.** *tr.v.* [sep.] To cause (sbdy.) to worry: *Her job is stressing her out.* —*intr.v.* To worry about sthg.: *You shouldn't stress out about school.*

stretch (strĕch) *v.* —*tr.* **1.** To lengthen or widen (sthg.): *stretch a rubber band.* **2.** To cause (sthg.) to cover an area: *Stretch the canvas over the frame.* **3.** To extend (sthg.) beyond usual limits: *We've had to stretch our budget a little. Stretch your imagination.* —*intr.* **1.** To become lengthened or widened: *This shirt has stretched.* **2.** To cover a distance or an area: *The wheat field stretched to the north.* **3.** To extend one's muscles or limbs, as after sleep: *The cat stretched and jumped on the floor.* —*n.* **1.** [C] The act of stretching: *The cat made a big stretch.* **2.** [U] The extent to which sthg. can be stretched; elasticity: *a sock with a lot of stretch.* **3.** [C] An extension of sthg. beyond what is usual: *Believing your story is quite a stretch for us.* **4.** [C] [*of*] A continuous length or area: *a stretch of coastline.* **5.** [C] A continuous period of time: *She practices for two hours at a stretch.* —*adj.* Made of an elastic material: *stretch pants.* ◆ **stretch (one's) legs.** To go for a walk, especially after a long period of sitting: *I'm going to stretch my legs. Do you want to come?* **stretch out.** *tr.v.* [sep.] To extend (a part of the body): *She stretched out her hand.* —*intr.v.* To lie down: *He decided to stretch out on the couch for a while.* **stretch the truth.** To exaggerate: *She always stretches the truth.*

stretch•er (strĕch′ər) *n.* A movable object on which a sick or injured person can be carried.

strew (strōō) *tr.v.* **strewed, strewn** (strōōn) or **strewed, strew•ing, strews. 1.** To spread (sthg.) here and there: *strewed the papers on the floor.* **2.** To cover (an area or a surface) with scattered or sprinkled things: *The beach was strewn with trash.*

strick•en (strĭk′ən) *v.* A past participle of **strike.** —*adj.* Affected by sthg. difficult, such as disease, trouble, or painful emotion: *stricken by grief.*

strict (strĭkt) *adj.* **1.** Demanding strong discipline: *a strict teacher.* **2.** Precise; exact: *in strict accordance with the law.* **3.** Complete; absolute: *strict control.* —**strict′ly** *adv.* —**strict′ness** *n.* [U]

stride (strīd) *intr.v.* **strode** (strōd), **strid•den**
(strĭd′n), **strid•ing, strides. 1.** To walk vigorously with long steps: *striding along the sidewalk.* **2.** To take a single long step, as in passing over an obstruction: *strode across the puddle.* —*n.* **1.** The act of striding. **2.** A single long step. ◆ **make great strides.** To improve or progress: *The computer industry is making great strides in memory capacity.* **take in stride.** To cope with sthg. calmly: *He took the loss of his plane ticket in stride.*

stri•dent (strīd′nt) *adj.* Loud, harsh or shrill: *a strident voice.* —**stri′den•cy** *n.* [U]

strife (strīf) *n.* [U] A bitter conflict, disagreement, or struggle: *a period of strife.*

strike (strīk) *v.* **struck** (strŭk), **struck** or **strick•en** (strĭk′ən), **strik•ing, strikes.** —*tr.* **1.** To hit (sbdy./sthg.) with the hand, the fist, or a weapon: *She struck the child in anger.* **2.** To give (a blow): *strike a blow at injustice.* **3.** To make contact with or crash into (sbdy./sthg.) by accident: *The car struck a telephone pole.* **4.** To affect (sbdy.) suddenly, as with a disease: *struck by a heart attack.* **5.** To start (sthg.) burning, as by friction: *strike a match.* **6.** To impress (sbdy.) strongly: *It struck her as a good idea.* **7.** To reach or discover (sthg.): *strike gold.* **8.** To make or conclude (an agreement): *strike a bargain.* —*intr.* **1.** To give a blow with or as if with the fist, a hand, or a weapon; hit: *The cats struck at each other.* **2.** To make contact suddenly and violently: *Lightning struck.* **3.** To begin a military attack: *The army struck at dawn.* **4.** To mark the time with a sound: *The clock struck at noon.* **5.** To participate in a strike against an employer: *Workers struck for higher wages.* —*n.* **1.** The stopping of work by employees in an attempt to force an employer to meet certain demands: *a strike by miners demanding safer working conditions.* **2.** An attack, especially a military air attack: *air strikes.* **3.** An unfavorable condition; a disadvantage: *She has two strikes against her: little education and no work experience.* ◆ **on strike.** Refusing to work in an attempt to force an employer to meet a demand: *workers on strike for better wages.* **strike down.** *tr.v.* [sep.] **1.** To cause (sbdy.) to fall, suffer, or die, as if from a sudden blow: *He was struck down by cancer at an early age.* **2.** To make (sthg.) ineffective; cancel: *The court struck down the law.* **strike out.** *intr.v.* **1.** To start a journey energetically: *We struck out for the mountains on foot.* **2.** To fail three times to hit the ball in baseball: *The player struck out.* **3.** To fail in an effort to do sthg.: *I auditioned for a part in the play, but I struck out.* **strike up.** *tr.v.* [sep.] To initiate or begin (sthg.): *struck up a friendship with the new student.*

strik•er (strī′kər) *n.* An employee on strike against an employer.

strik•ing (strī′kĭng) *adj.* Catching the attention: *a striking outfit.* **—strik′ing•ly** *adv.*

string (strĭng) *n.* **1.** [C; U] A cord usually made of fiber, used for fastening or tying. **2.** [C] A set of things threaded together: *a string of beads.* **3.** [C] A cord stretched across a musical instrument to produce tones: *a violin string.* *—tr.v.* **strung** (strŭng), **string•ing, strings. 1.** To fit (sthg.) with a string or strings: *string a piano.* **2.** To thread (sthg.) on a string: *string beads.* **3.** To arrange (sthg.) in a string or series: *string words together.* **4.** To fasten, tie, or hang (sthg.) with a string or strings: *string a room with lights.*
♦ **pull strings.** To use influence: *She pulled strings to get tickets to the sold-out concert.* **string along.** *Informal. intr.v.* To go along with sbdy.: *Let me string along with your group.* *—tr.v.* [sep.] To fool, cheat, or deceive (sbdy.): *He strung us along without ever paying his share.* **string out.** *tr.v.* [sep.] To make (sthg.) take a long time: *She strung the story out until everyone lost interest.* **with no strings attached.** With no hidden conditions or limits: *He offered me the car with no strings attached.*

string bean *n.* A bean plant with long, narrow green or yellow bean pods eaten as a vegetable.

stringed instrument (strĭngd) *n.* A musical instrument such as a guitar or violin.

strin•gent (strĭn′jənt) *adj.* Rigorous; severe: *stringent requirements.* **—strin′gen•cy** *n.* [U] **—strin′gent•ly** *adv.*

string•y (strĭng′ē) *adj.* **string•i•er, string•i•est.** Like, made of, or with strings: *stringy hair; stringy meat.* **—string′i•ness** *n.* [U]

strip¹ (strĭp) *v.* **stripped, strip•ping, strips.** *—tr.* **1.** [*from; off*] To remove (sthg. closely held or attached); peel: *strip bark from a tree; strip paint off the wall.* **2.** [*of*] To deprive (sbdy./sthg.) of sthg.: *strip her of her title.* *—intr.* To take off all one's clothes: *We stripped before showering.*

strip² (strĭp) *n.* A long narrow piece of sthg.: *a strip of paper; a strip of land.*

stripe (strīp) *n.* A long narrow band that differs in color or texture from the area on either side: *a zebra's stripes; stripes on the flag.*

striped (strīpt) *adj.* With a pattern of stripes: *a striped shirt.*

strive (strīv) *intr.v.* **strove** (strōv), **striv•en** (strĭv′ən) or **strived, striv•ing, strives.** To use much effort or energy to do sthg.: *strive to improve working conditions.*

strobe light *n.* A lamp that produces very short, bright flashes of light.

strode (strōd) *v.* Past tense of **stride.**

stroke¹ (strōk) *n.* **1.** The act of striking, as with the hand or a weapon: *a stroke of the sword.* **2.** A sudden and unexpected action or event: *a stroke of luck; a stroke of genius.* **3.** Sudden damage to blood vessels in the brain that causes loss of muscular control: *Her grandfather suffered a stroke.* **4.** A single completed movement, as in swimming or rowing: *the long graceful strokes of a swimmer.*

stroke² (strōk) *tr.v.* **stroked, strok•ing, strokes.** To rub (sthg.) lightly; caress: *stroked the cat's head.* *—n.* A light caressing movement: *a stroke of her hand.*

stroll (strōl) *intr.v.* To walk at a slow pace: *People strolled about the park.* *—n.* A leisurely walk: *Would you like to go for a stroll?*

stroll•er (strō′lər) *n.* **1.** A four-wheeled chair for pushing small children. **2.** A person who strolls.

stroller

strong (strông) *adj.* **1.** Physically powerful; capable of great physical force: *The elephant is a strong animal.* **2.** With force of character, will, or intelligence: *a strong personality.* **3.** Not easily broken: *strong furniture.* **4.** Intense; concentrated: *a strong vinegar; a strong odor.* **5.** With a certain number of units or members: *Five hundred strong, they marched forward.* **—strong′ly** *adv.*

strong•box (strông′bŏks′) *n.* A metal box or safe for storing valuables.

strong•hold (strông′hōld′) *n.* An area dominated by people who share a special belief or interest: *a rebel stronghold.*

strove (strōv) *v.* Past tense of **strive.**

struck (strŭk) *v.* Past tense and a past participle of **strike.**

struc•tur•al (strŭk′chər əl) *adj.* Relating to the structure of sthg.: *structural defects.* **—struc′tur•al•ly** *adv.*

struc•ture (strŭk′chər) *n.* **1.** [C] Something made of a number of parts, such as a building: *a steel structure.* **2.** [U] The way in which parts are arranged or put together to form a whole: *good sentence structure.* *—tr.v.* **struc•tured, struc•tur•ing, struc•tures.** To give form or arrangement to (sthg.): *I structured my day around my dance lessons.*

strug•gle (strŭg′əl) *intr.v.* **strug•gled, strug•gling, strug•gles.** To use physical or emotional force to fight a person or thing: *We struggled against the fire.* *—n.* A hard fight or effort: *the struggle for survival.* **—strug′gler** *n.*

strum (strŭm) *tr.v.* **strummed, strum•ming, strums.** To play (a stringed instrument): *She strummed her guitar.* *—n.* The act or sound of strumming: *He gave the guitar a strum.*

strung (strŭng) *v.* Past tense and past participle of **string.**

strut (strŭt) *intr.v.* **strut•ted, strut•ting, struts.** To walk in a proud way: *The rooster strutted.* *—n.* A wood or metal bar used to brace a mechanical structure: *metal struts.*

stub (stŭb) *n.* **1.** The end remaining after sthg. bigger has been used up: *the stub of a pencil.*

S

2. The part of a check or ticket kept as a record: *Do you have your ticket stub?* —*tr.v.* **stubbed, stub·bing, stubs.** To strike (one's toe or foot) against sthg.: *She stubbed her toe on the chair leg.* ♦ **stub out.** *tr.v.* [sep.] To crush (a cigarette stub): *He stubbed out the cigarette in the ashtray.*

stub·ble (stŭb′əl) *n.* [U] The short stiff pieces of grain or hair left after it has been cut.

stub·born (stŭb′ərn) *adj.* **1.** Strong-willed, determined: *a stubborn child.* See Synonyms at **obstinate. 2.** Long-lasting; persistent: *a stubborn idea.* —**stub′born·ly** *adv.* —**stub′-born·ness** *n.* [U]

stub·by (stŭb′ē) *adj.* **stub·bi·er, stub·bi·est.** Short and stocky: *stubby legs.* —**stub′-bi·ness** *n.* [U]

stuck (stŭk) *v.* Past tense and past participle of **stick.**

stuck-up (stŭk′ŭp′) *adj. Informal.* Snobbish; conceited: *a stuck-up group of people.*

stud¹ (stŭd) *n.* **1.** A vertical post inside a wall. **2.** An earring, especially one for pierced ears: *diamond studs.* **3.** A removable button used to fasten and decorate, as on a dress shirt. —*tr.v.* **stud·ded, stud·ding, studs.** To cover (sthg.) with objects: *stud a bracelet with turquoise.*

stud² (stŭd) *n.* **1.** A male animal, especially a stallion, kept for breeding. **2.** *Slang.* A man who is very attractive. **3.** *Slang.* A man who is very active sexually.

stud·ded (stŭd′ĭd) *adj.* Covered with jewels: *a diamond-studded bracelet.*

stu·dent (stood′nt) *n.* **1.** A person who attends a school, college, or university. **2.** A person who studies sthg.: *a student of languages.*

stud·ied (stŭd′ēd) *adj.* Carefully considered; deliberate: *a studied pose.*

stu·di·o (stoo′dē ō) *n., pl.* **stu·di·os. 1.** An artist's workroom. **2.** A photographer's place of business. **3.** A room or building for movie, television, or radio productions. **4.** A one-room apartment.

stu·di·ous (stoo′dē əs) *adj.* **1.** Willing to study: *a studious life.* **2.** Careful: *a studious avoidance of work.* —**stu′di·ous·ly** *adv.* —**stu′di·ous·ness** *n.* [U]

stud·y (stŭd′ē) *n., pl.* **stud·ies. 1.** [C; U] The act of studying: *years of intense study.* **2.** [C; U] A branch of knowledge; a subject: *studies in geology.* **3.** [C] A scholarly work on a particular subject: *presented a study of dreams.* **4.** [C] A room for studying. —*v.* **stud·ied, stud·y·ing, stud·ies.** —*tr.* **1.** To use one's mind to gain knowledge and understand (a subject): *study French.* **2.** To read or examine (sthg.) carefully: *He studies law at night. She studied his face.* —*intr.* To follow a course of study: *studying at the local college.*

stuff (stŭf) *n.* [U] **1.** *Informal.* Unspecified material: *What is that stuff in your hair?* **2.** Unspecified articles: *I sold all my stuff before I moved.* **3.** The basic elements of sthg.; essence: *the stuff of which fear is made.* —*tr.v.* **1.** To fill (sthg.) tightly: *stuffed the hole in the window with cardboard.* **2.** To fill (sthg.) with an appropriate stuffing: *stuff a pillow with feathers.*

stuff·ing (stŭf′ĭng) *n.* [U] **1.** Padding put in things made of or covered with cloth: *a chair with cotton stuffing.* **2.** Food put into the cavity of a piece of meat or a hollowed-out vegetable: *We put bread stuffing in the turkey.*

stuff·y (stŭf′ē) *adj.* **stuff·i·er, stuff·i·est. 1.** Without fresh air: *an overheated stuffy room.* **2.** Having blocked breathing: *a stuffy nose.* **3.** Dull and boring: *a stuffy party.* —**stuff′i·ly** *adv.* —**stuff′i·ness** *n.* [U]

stum·ble (stŭm′bəl) *intr.v.* **stum·bled, stum·bling, stum·bles. 1.a.** To trip and almost fall: *The player stumbled.* **b.** To move in a clumsy way: *He stumbled out of bed.* **2.** [over] To speak in a clumsy way: *Do you stumble over words?* —*n.* **1.** The act of stumbling; a fall. **2.** A mistake. ♦ **stumble across** or **on.** *tr.v.* [insep.] To come upon (sthg.) by accident or by surprise: *They stumbled across the clue.* —**stum′bler** *n.*

stum·bling block (stŭm′blĭng) *n.* An obstacle: *His shyness was a stumbling block to his sales career.*

stump (stŭmp) *n.* A short or broken part left after the main part of sthg. has been cut away, broken off, or worn down: *a tree stump; a stump of a tail.* —*tr.v. Informal.* To puzzle or baffle (sbdy.) completely: *Their questions stumped us.* —**stump′y** *adj.*

stun (stŭn) *tr.v.* **stunned, stun·ning, stuns. 1.** To make (sbdy.) unconscious, by or as if by a blow. **2.** To shock (sbdy.) emotionally: *The scandal stunned the neighborhood.*

stung (stŭng) *v.* Past tense and past participle of **sting.**

stunk (stŭngk) *v.* A past tense and the past participle of **stink.**

stun·ning (stŭn′ĭng) *adj.* **1.** Causing or capable of causing emotional shock or loss of consciousness: *a stunning blow.* **2.** Of a strikingly attractive appearance: *a stunning suit.* **3.** Impressive or suprising: *a stunning performance.* —**stun′ning·ly** *adv.*

stunt¹ (stŭnt) *tr.v.* To stop the growth or development of (sthg.): *Air pollution may stunt many kinds of plants.*

stunt² (stŭnt) *n.* **1.** An act showing unusual strength, skill, or daring: *an action movie full of dangerous stunts.* **2.** An unusual action done to attract attention: *a publicity stunt.*

stu·pe·fy (stoo′pə fī′) *tr.v.* **stu·pe·fied, stu·pe·fy·ing, stu·pe·fies. 1.** To make

---

(sbdy.) unable to think: *The dull lecture stupefied them.* **2.** To amaze (sbdy.): *a record-breaking time that stupefied the sports world.* —**stu•pe•fac′tion** (stōō′pə făk′shən) *n.* [U]

stu•pen•dous (stōō pĕn′dəs) *adj.* Surprisingly great, dangerous, impressive, or powerful: *stupendous risks.* —**stu•pen′dous•ly** *adv.*

stu•pid (stōō′pĭd) *adj.* Foolish; silly: *a stupid answer.* —**stu•pid′i•ty** *n.* [C; U] —**stu′pid•ly** *adv.*

stu•por (stōō′pər) *n. (usually singular).* A state of being unable to think or use the senses; a daze: *She was in a stupor from the medicine.*

stur•dy (stûr′dē) *adj.* **stur•di•er, stur•di•est.** With rugged physical strength: *a chair made of sturdy canvas.* —**stur′di•ly** *adv.* —**stur′di•ness** *n.* [U]

stut•ter (stŭt′ər) *v.* —*intr.* To hesitate and repeat sounds in speaking. —*tr.* To say (sthg.) with constant hesitations or repetitions of sounds: *stuttered a response.* —*n.* The act or habit of stuttering. —**stut′ter•er** *n.*

sty¹ (stī) *n., pl.* **sties** (stīz). **1.** An enclosure for pigs. **2.** A very dirty or untidy place: *This kitchen is a sty!*

sty² (stī) *n., pl.* **sties** (stīz). Inflammation of an eyelid.

style (stīl) *n.* **1.** [C; U] The way of saying or doing sthg.: *a style of speech; a writing style.* **2.** [C] A sort or kind; a type: *a style of furniture.* **3.** [U] A comfortable and elegant way of life: *living in style.* **4.** [C] A particular fashion, especially of dressing: *the styles of the 1920s.* —*tr.v.* **styled, styl•ing, styles.** To arrange, design, or make (sthg.) in a special way: *styled the house after a country cottage.*

styl•ish (stī′lĭsh) *adj.* Very fashionable: *a stylish outfit.* —**styl′ish•ly** *adv.* —**styl′ish•ness** *n.* [U]

styl•ist (stī′lĭst) *n.* A designer of or an expert on styles in decorating, dress, or beauty: *a hair stylist.*

sty•lis•tic (stī lĭs′tĭk) *adj.* Relating to style, especially literary style.

styl•ize (stī′līz′) *tr.v.* **styl•ized, styl•iz•ing, styl•iz•es.** To restrict or make (sthg.) conform to a particular style: *stylize the stage sets.*

suave (swäv) *adj.* **suav•er, suav•est.** Smoothly polite: *a suave gentleman.* —**suave′ly** *adv.* —**suave′ness, suav′i•ty** *n.* [U]

sub¹ (sŭb) *n. Informal.* **1.** A submarine. **2.** A submarine sandwich.

sub² (sŭb) *Informal. n.* A substitute. —*intr.v.* **subbed, sub•bing, subs.** To act as a substitute: *She subbed for our teacher yesterday.*

sub— *pref.* A prefix that means: **1.** Under; beneath: *submarine.* **2.** A lower or secondary part: *subplot; subdivision.* **3.** Less than completely or normally; almost: *subtropical.*

WORD BUILDING: sub— The prefix **sub—** means "under." When **sub—** is used to form

words, it can mean "under" (**submarine, subsoil, subway**), "subordinate" (**subcommittee, subplot, subset**), or "less than completely" (**subhuman, substandard**). The prefix **sub—** can combine with verbs as well as with adjectives and nouns, as in **subdivide, sublease,** and **sublet.**

---

sub•com•mit•tee (sŭb′kə mĭt′ē) *n.* A smaller committee made up of members chosen from a main committee.

sub•con•scious (sŭb kŏn′shəs) *adj.* Relating to thoughts or feelings that one is not aware of having: *a subconscious desire for revenge.* —*n. (usually singular).* The subconscious mind. —**sub•con′scious•ly** *adv.*

sub•con•ti•nent (sŭb′kŏn′tə nənt *or* sŭb kŏn′tə nənt) *n.* A large landmass that is part of a continent but is considered as an independent entity: *the Indian subcontinent.*

sub•di•vide (sŭb′dĭ vīd′ *or* sŭb′dĭ vīd′) *v.* **sub•di•vid•ed, sub•di•vid•ing, sub•di•vides.** —*tr.* To divide (sthg.) into smaller parts, especially to divide (land) into lots: *subdivided the old farm for houses.* —*intr.* To form into subdivisions.

sub•di•vi•sion (sŭb′dĭ vĭzh′ən *or* sŭb′dĭ vĭzh′ən) *n.* **1.** [U] The act of subdividing. **2.** [C] A subdivided part.

sub•due (səb dōō′) *tr.v.* **sub•dued, sub•du•ing, sub•dues.** To quiet or bring (sbdy./sthg.) under control by physical force or persuasion: *She subdued the wild horse.*

sub•dued (səb dōōd′) *adj.* **1.** Gentle, quiet: *subdued colors; a subdued whisper.* **2.** Unusually quiet: *The accident left us subdued.*

sub•hu•man (sŭb hyōō′mən) *adj.* Not fully human: *subhuman intelligence.*

sub•ject (sŭb′jĭkt) *adj.* [*to*] **1.** Under the power or authority of another: *subject to the jurisdiction of a government.* **2.** Likely to have or get: *a statement subject to misinterpretation; subject to allergies.* —*n.* **1.** A person or thing about which sthg. is said or done: *a subject of discussion.* **2.** A theme of a musical composition, work of art, or book: *What is the subject of that book?* **3.** A course or an area of study: *Her favorite subject is math.* **4.** A person or animal used as the object of clinical study: *the subjects of an experiment.* **5.** The part of a sentence or clause that is related to the verb. In the sentence *I am hungry, I* is the subject. **6.** A person who owes allegiance to a government or ruler: *a subject of the throne.* —*tr.v.* (səb jĕkt′). **1.** To bring (sbdy./sthg.) under control or authority: *The ancient Romans subjected many peoples.* **2.** [*to*] To cause (sbdy./sthg.) to undergo or experience sthg.: *The doctors subjected me to many tests.* —**sub•jec′tion** *n.* [U]

S

SYNONYMS: subject, matter, topic, theme.
These nouns mean the principal idea or point of a speech, a piece of writing, or a work of art. **Subject** is the most general: *Many 18th-century paintings had historical subjects.* **Matter** often means the material that is the object of thought: *This will be an interesting matter for you to discuss.* **Topic** means a subject of discussion, argument, or conversation: *The hospital is giving a series of lectures on the topic of nutrition.* **Theme** often means a subject, idea, point of view, or perception that is developed in a work of art: *The theme of this poem is the healing power of love.*

sub·jec·tive (səb jĕk′tĭv) *adj.* Particular to a given person; personal: *a subjective opinion.*

sub·ju·gate (sŭb′jə gāt′) *tr.v.* **sub·ju·gat·ed, sub·ju·gat·ing, sub·ju·gates.** To bring (sbdy./sthg.) under control: *subjugated by the king.* —**sub′ju·ga′tion** *n.* [U]

sub·lease (sŭb′lēs′) *tr.v.* **sub·leased, sub·leas·ing, sub·leas·es.** To sublet (property): *We subleased the house for the summer.*

sub·let (sŭb′lĕt′) *tr.v.* **sub·let, sub·let·ting, sub·lets.** To rent (property one holds by lease) to another: *He sublet his apartment to me.* —*n.* (sŭb′lĕt′). Property, especially an apartment, rented by a tenant to another party: *an illegal sublet.*

sub·lime (sə blīm′) *adj.* Excellent; impressive: *a sublime performance.* —**sub·lime′ly** *adv.*

sub·ma·rine (sŭb′mə rēn′ *or* sŭb′mə ren′) *n.* **1.** A ship that can operate underwater. **2.** A large meat and cheese sandwich on a long roll. —*adj.* Used, grown, or existing beneath the surface of the sea; undersea: *a submarine volcano.*

submarine

sub·merge (səb mûrj′) *v.* **sub·merged, sub·merg·ing, sub·merg·es.** —*tr.* **1.** To put (sbdy./sthg.) under water: *submerged the dish.* **2.** To cover (sbdy./sthg.) with water: *The flood submerged the island.* —*intr.* To go under or as if under water.

sub·merse (səb mûrs′) *tr.v.* **sub·mersed, sub·mers·ing, sub·mers·es.** To submerge (sbdy./sthg.). —**sub·mer′sion** (səb mûr′zhən *or* səb mûr′shən) *n.* [U]

sub·mis·sion (səb mĭsh′ən) *n.* **1.** [U] The act of submitting to the power of another. **2.** [U] The condition of being submissive or compliant: *forced into submission.* **3.a.** [U] The act of submitting sthg. for consideration: *the submission of a manuscript to a publisher.* **b.** [C] Something submitted for consideration: *received many submissions in the mail.*

sub·mis·sive (səb mĭs′ĭv) *adj.* Inclined or willing to submit: *a submissive personality.*

sub·mit (səb mĭt′) *v.* **sub·mit·ted, sub·mit·ting, sub·mits.** —*tr.* **1.** [*to*] To surrender (oneself) to the will or authority of another: *They submitted themselves to his judgment.* **2.** To commit (sthg.) to the consideration of another: *We submitted our applications to her.* **3.** To offer (sthg.) as a proposition or contention: *I submit that the terms of the contract are unreasonable.* —*intr.* [*to*] To yield; surrender: *He submitted to their demands.* —**sub·mit′tal** *n.*

sub·or·di·nate (sə bôr′dn ĭt) *adj.* **1.** Belonging to a lower rank; secondary: *a subordinate position.* **2.** Subject to the authority or control of another: *a subordinate worker.* —*n.* A person or thing that is subordinate: *He is courteous to his subordinates.* —*tr.v.* (sə bôr′dn āt′). **sub·or·di·nat·ed, sub·or·di·nat·ing, sub·or·di·nates.** **1.** To put (sbdy./sthg.) in a lower rank or class. **2.** To treat (sthg.) as of lesser importance: *subordinating work to family.* —**sub·or′di·nate·ly** *adv.* —**sub·or′di·na′tion** *n.* [U]

sub·poe·na (sə pē′nə) *n.* A legal document requiring a person to appear in court and give testimony. —*tr.v.* To serve or summon (sbdy.) with such a document.

sub·scribe (səb skrīb′) *intr.v.* **sub·scribed, sub·scrib·ing, sub·scribes.** To pay regularly for sthg., such as issues of a magazine or tickets to a series of performances: *subscribe to the newspaper.* —**sub·scrib′er** *n.*

sub·scrip·tion (səb skrĭp′shən) *n.* An order to buy sthg., such as issues of a magazine or a series of tickets to performances: *a magazine subscription; a subscription to the ballet.*

sub·se·quent (sŭb′sĭ kwĕnt′) *adj.* Following sthg. else in time or order; succeeding: *heavy rains and subsequent floods.* —**sub′se·quent·ly** *adv.*

sub·ser·vi·ent (səb sûr′vē ənt) *adj.* **1.** Subordinate in capacity or function. **2.** Willing to submit to others; servile. —**sub·ser′vi·ence** *n.* [U]

sub·side (səb sīd′) *intr.v.* **sub·sid·ed, sub·sid·ing, sub·sides.** **1.** To go back to a lower or normal level: *The flood waters subsided.* **2.** To become less powerful or active: *The wind finally subsided.*

sub·sid·i·ar·y (səb sĭd′ē ĕr′ē) *adj.* Connected, but secondary in importance; subordinate: *a subsidiary aim of the project.* *—n., pl.* **sub·sid·i·ar·ies.** A company with more than half of its stock owned by another company: *a subsidiary of an international company.*

sub·si·dize (sŭb′sĭ dīz′) *tr.v.* **sub·si·dized, sub·si·diz·ing, sub·si·diz·es.** To assist or support (sbdy./sthg.) with a subsidy: *The committee asked for funds to subsidize farms.* *—sub′si·diz′er* *n.*

sub·si·dy (sŭb′sĭ dē) *n., pl.* **sub·si·dies.** Financial assistance, as that granted by a government to a private business: *Prices are controlled by farm subsidies.*

sub·sist (sab sĭst′) *intr.v.* To maintain life; live: *Horses can subsist on grass.* *—sub·sis′tence* *n.* [U]

sub·son·ic (sŭb sŏn′ĭk) *adj.* With a speed less than that of sound: *a subsonic airplane.*

sub·stance (sŭb′stans) *n.* **1.** [C] A material of a particular kind or composition: *a fatty substance.* **2.** [U] The essence of what is said or written; the gist: *the substance of the report.* **3.** [U] That which is solid or real: *a dream without substance.*

substance abuse *n.* Excessive use of addictive substances, especially alcohol and narcotic drugs.

sub·stan·dard (sŭb stăn′dərd) *adj.* Not good enough; below standard: *substandard goods.*

sub·stan·tial (sab stăn′shal) *adj.* **1.** Solidly built; strong: *substantial houses.* **2.** Considerable in importance, value, degree, amount, or extent: *making substantial progress.* *—sub·stan′tial·ly* *adv.*

sub·stan·ti·ate (sab stăn′shē āt′) *tr.v.* **sub·stan·ti·at·ed, sub·stan·ti·at·ing, sub·stan·ti·ates.** To support (sthg.) with proof or evidence: *substantiate a claim.* *—sub·stan′ti·a′tion* *n.* [U]

sub·sti·tute (sŭb′stĭ tōōt′) *n.* A person or thing that takes the place of another; a replacement: *a substitute for the regular organist.* *—v.* **sub·sti·tut·ed, sub·sti·tut·ing, sub·sti·tutes.** *—tr.* To put or use (sbdy./sthg.) in place of another: *substitute walnuts for pecans in the recipe.* *—intr.* To take the place of another: *I substituted for him in the game.* *—sub′sti·tu′tion* *n.* [C; U]

sub·ter·fuge (sŭb′tər fyōōj′) *n.* [C; U] A trick or deceptive device; deceit.

sub·ter·ra·ne·an (sŭb′tə rā′nē ən) *adj.* Located or operating beneath the earth's surface; underground: *subterranean houses.*

sub·ti·tle (sŭb′tīt′l) *n. (usually plural).* A printed translation of the dialogue of a foreign-language film shown at the bottom of the screen.

sub·tle (sŭt′l) *adj.* **sub·tler, sub·tlest.** **1.** Delicate; difficult to detect or analyze: *subtle changes.* **2.** Not immediately obvious: *a subtle problem.* **3.** Able to make fine distinc-

tions; clever: *a subtle mind.* *—sub′tle·ness* *n.* [U] *—sub′tly* *adv.*

sub·tle·ty (sŭt′l tē) *n., pl.* **sub·tle·ties. 1.** [U] The state or quality of being subtle: *the subtlety of his plan.* **2.** [C] Something subtle, especially an idea or a distinction: *a subtlety of meaning.*

sub·tract (sab trăkt′) *v.* *—tr.* [*from*] To take (sthg.) away; deduct: *subtract five from seven.* *—intr.* To perform the arithmetic operation of subtraction.

sub·trac·tion (sab trăk′shan) *n.* [C; U] **1.** The act of subtracting. **2.** The arithmetic operation of finding the difference between two amounts or numbers.

sub·urb (sŭb′ûrb′) *n.* A usually residential area or community outside or near a city: *the suburbs of Atlanta.* *—sub·ur′ban* *adj.*

sub·ur·bi·a (sa bûr′bē ə) *n.* [U] Suburbs considered as a group.

sub·vert (sab vûrt′) *tr.v.* To overthrow or destroy (sthg.): *subvert a government.* *—sub·ver′sion* *n.* [U] *—sub·ver′sive* *adj. & n.*

sub·way (sŭb′wā′) *n.* An underground urban railroad, usually operated by electricity: *You can take the subway to the theater.*

subway

suc·ceed (sak sēd′) *v.* *—intr.* **1.** To accomplish sthg. desired or attempted: *He succeeded in repairing the watch.* **2.** To follow or come next in time or order; replace another in an office or position: *She succeeded to the throne.* *—tr.* **1.** To come after (sbdy./sthg.) in time or order; follow: *This novel succeeded his first.* See Synonyms at **follow. 2.** To come after and take the place of (sbdy.): *Who succeeded Taft as President?*

suc·cess (sak sĕs′) *n.* **1.** [U] The achievement of sthg. desired, planned, or attempted: *the success of the experiment.* **2.** [C] A person or thing that is successful: *The project was a big success.*

suc·cess·ful (sak sĕs′fal) *adj.* With a favorable outcome: *a successful attempt.* *—suc·cess′ful·ly* *adv.*

suc·ces·sion (sak sĕsh′ən) *n.* **1.** [U] The act of following in order or sequence: *the succession of events.* **2.** [C] A group of persons or things arranged or following in order; a sequence: *We heard a succession of sharp sounds.* **3.** [U] The sequence or right of one

S

person after another to succeed to a position: *a war over the succession to the Spanish throne.*

suc•ces•sive (sək sĕs′ĭv) *adj.* Following one after the other: *three successive years.* —**suc•ces′sive•ly** *adv.*

suc•ces•sor (sək sĕs′ər) *n.* A person or thing that succeeds another: *the successor to the throne.*

suc•cinct (sək sĭngkt′) *adj.* Expressed in few words; concise: *gave a succinct explanation.* —**suc•cinct′ly** *adv.* —**suc•cinct′ness** *n.* [U]

suc•cor (sŭk′ər) *Formal. n.* [U] Assistance in time of distress; relief. —*tr.v.* To give assistance to (sbdy.) in difficulty.

HOMONYMS: **succor, sucker** (dupe).

---

suc•cu•lent (sŭk′yə lənt) *adj.* Full of juice or sap; juicy: *succulent berries.* —*n.* A succulent plant, such as a cactus. —**suc′cu•lence** *n.* [U] —**suc′cu•lent•ly** *adv.*

suc•cumb (sə kŭm′) *intr.v.* **1.** To submit to sthg. overpowering or overwhelming; give up or give in: *succumb to the pressures of one's friends.* **2.** [*to*] To die: *He succumbed to illness.*

such (sŭch) *adj.* **1.** Of this kind or a similar kind: *an eye specialist, one of many such doctors in the hospital.* **2.** Of a degree or quality indicated: *Their happiness was such that they were in tears.* **3.** Of so great a degree or quality: *We never dreamed of such wealth.* —*adv.* **1.** To so great a degree; so: *She is such a good friend.* **2.** Very; especially: *He has done such good work lately.* —*pron.* **1.** Such a person or persons or thing or things: *We expected problems, and such occurred.* **2.** A person or thing referred to: *Such are the fortunes of love.* **3.** Similar things or people; the like: *pins, needles, and such.* ◆ **such as.** For example: *vegetables such as peas and carrots.*

suck (sŭk) *v.* —*tr.* **1.** To pull (liquid) into the mouth by moving the tongue and lips. **2.** To pull in (sthg.) by lowering the pressure inside: *A vacuum cleaner can suck up dirt.* **3.** To hold or move (sthg.) inside the mouth: *suck a cough drop.* —*intr.* To suckle. —*n.* The act or sound of sucking.

suck•er (sŭk′ər) *n.* **1.** A part by which an animal or plant clings to sthg. by suction. **2.** *Informal.* A person who is easily fooled: *I can't believe I gave him the money—I'm such a sucker!*

HOMONYMS: **sucker, succor** (support).

---

suck•le (sŭk′əl) *v.* **suck•led, suck•ling, suck•les.** —*tr.* To allow (a baby) to take milk from the breast or udder: *Mammals suckle their young.* —*intr.* To suck at the breast or udder.

suck•ling (sŭk′lĭng) *n.* A baby or young animal that is still being nursed by its mother. —*adj.* Not yet weaned: *a suckling pig.*

suc•tion (sŭk′shən) *n.* [U] A force that causes a fluid or solid to be drawn into a space because of a difference in pressures. —*adj.* Creating, using, or done by suction: *a suction pump.*

sud•den (sŭd′n) *adj.* Happening without warning; unforeseen: *a sudden storm.* ◆ **all of a sudden.** Very quickly and unexpectedly; suddenly: *All of a sudden, he passed out.* —**sud′den•ly** *adv.* —**sud′den•ness** *n.* [U]

suds (sŭdz) *pl.n.* Bubbles or foam made by mixing soap and water: *soap suds.* —**sud′sy** *adj.*

sue (soo) *v.* **sued, su•ing, sues.** —*tr.* To bring legal action against (sbdy./sthg.) in order to satisfy a claim or grievance: *She sued them for breach of contract.* —*intr.* **1.** To begin legal proceedings: *He sued for his right to the property.* **2.** To make an appeal: *sue for peace.*

suede (swād) *n.* [U] Leather with a soft velvety nap: *a jacket made of suede.*

suf•fer (sŭf′ər) *v.* —*intr.* [*from*] To feel or endure pain or distress: *suffer from disease.* —*tr.* **1.** To undergo or be subject to (sthg. painful or unpleasant): *suffer a defeat.* **2.** To endure or bear (sbdy./sthg.); stand: *She does not suffer fools easily.* —**suf′fer•er** *n.*

suf•fer•ing (sŭf′ər ĭng *or* sŭf′rĭng) *n.* [C; U] Pain or distress: *The people endured great suffering after the flood.*

suf•fice (sə fīs′) *v.* **suf•ficed, suf•fic•ing, suf•fic•es.** —*intr.* **1.** To meet present needs; be sufficient: *The food will suffice until next week.* **2.** To be capable or competent: *No words can suffice to thank you.* —*tr.* To be sufficient or adequate for (sbdy./sthg.): *enough water to suffice them for three days.*

suf•fi•cient (sə fĭsh′ənt) *adj.* As much as is needed; enough: *Are these really sufficient reasons for going?* —**suf•fi′cient•ly** *adv.*

suf•fix (sŭf′ĭks) *n.* In grammar, an affix added to the end of a word. —*tr.v.* To add (sthg.) as a suffix.

suf•fo•cate (sŭf′ə kāt) *v.* **suf•fo•cat•ed, suf•fo•cat•ing, suf•fo•cates.** —*intr.* **1.** To die from a lack of oxygen: *The baby suffocated.* **2.** To feel discomfort from a lack of fresh air: *I am suffocating in this sweater.* —*tr.* **1.** To kill (sbdy./sthg.) by depriving of oxygen. **2.** To cause (sbdy./sthg.) to suffer discomfort by or as by cutting off a supply of air. —**suf′fo•ca′tion** *n.* [U]

suf•frage (sŭf′rĭj) *n.* [U] The right to vote.

suf•fuse (sə fyooz′) *tr.v.* **suf•fused, suf•fus•ing, suf•fus•es.** To spread through or over (sthg.), as with liquid, color, or light: *A greenish haze suffused the woods.*

S

sug•ar (shŏŏg′ər) *n.* **1.** [U] A sweet, white, edible substance, obtained from plants. **2.** [C] *Informal.* A sweetheart or loved one. **3.** [U] *Informal.* A kiss. —*tr.v.* To coat or sweeten (sthg.) with sugar or as if with sugar: *She sugared her words.*

sug•ar•less (shŏŏg′ər lĭs) *adj.* **1.** With no sugar: *sugarless apple juice.* **2.** Sweetened with a substance other than sugar: *sugarless gum.*

sug•ar•y (shŏŏg′ə rē) *adj.* **1.** Containing, resembling, or tasting like sugar. **2.** Too kind or sentimental: *sugary compliments.*

sug•gest (səg jĕst′ *or* sə jĕst′) *tr.v.* **1.** To offer (sthg.) for consideration or action: *I suggest that we take a walk.* **2.** To bring (sthg.) to mind by association; show signs of: *a cloud that suggests a dragon; a silence that suggests disapproval.*

sug•gest•i•ble (səg jĕs′tə bəl *or* sə jĕs′tə bəl) *adj.* Easily influenced by suggestions: *He's a suggestible person.*

sug•ges•tion (səg jĕs′chən *or* sə jĕs′chən) *n.* **1.** [U] The act of suggesting: *hypnotic suggestion.* **2.** [C] Something suggested: *Let's follow her suggestion.* **3.** [C] A trace; a touch: *a suggestion of sorrow in his eyes.*

sug•ges•tive (səg jĕs′tĭv *or* sə jĕs′tĭv) *adj.* **1.** Tending to bring sthg. to mind: *These ruins are suggestive of a highly developed civilization.* **2.** Hinting at sthg. improper or indecent, especially about sex: *suggestive song lyrics.* —**sug•ges′tive•ly** *adv.*

su•i•cid•al (sŏŏ′ĭ sīd′l) *adj.* **1.** Relating to or causing suicide: *suicidal tendencies.* **2.** Dangerous; destructive: *a suicidal plan to climb the mountain alone.*

su•i•cide (sŏŏ′ĭ sīd′) *n.* **1.** [C; U] The act of intentionally killing oneself: *He committed suicide by jumping off a bridge.* **2.** [U] The destruction or ruin of one's own interests: *Refusing to follow company policy would be professional suicide.*

suit (sŏŏt) *n.* **1.** A set of matching outer clothes, especially a jacket with trousers or a skirt. **2.** An outfit worn for a special activity or purpose: *a gym suit.* **3.** One of the four sets, spades, clubs, hearts, or diamonds, in a deck of playing cards. **4.** A court action to get a right or claim; a lawsuit. —*tr.v.* **1.** To meet the requirements of (sthg.): *The house suited them.* **2.** To be or make (sthg.) appropriate or acceptable for (sthg.): *The song suited the occasion.* **3.** To please (sbdy.); satisfy: *This choice suits me just fine.* ◆ **suit (oneself).** To do what one likes: *If he wants to walk in the rain, he can suit himself.*

suit•a•ble (sŏŏ′tə bəl) *adj.* Appropriate to a certain purpose or occasion: *suitable shelter; suitable clothes.* —**suit′a•bil′i•ty** *n.* [U] —**suit′a•bly** *adv.*

suit•case (sŏŏt′kās′) *n.* A usually rectangular piece of luggage for carrying clothing.

suite (swēt) *n.* **1.** A series of connected rooms used as a living unit: *a hotel suite.* **2.** (*or* sŏŏt) A set of matching furniture: *a bedroom suite.* **3.** An instrumental musical composition consisting of a set of pieces in the same or closely related keys.

HOMONYMS: suite, sweet (sugary).

---

suit•or (sŏŏ′tər) *n.* An old-fashioned term for a man who wants to marry a woman.

sul•fur *also* **sul•phur** (sŭl′fər) *n.* [U] *Symbol* **S** A pale yellow nonmetallic element. Atomic number 16. See table at **element.** —**sul•fu′ric** *adj.* —**sul′fur•ous** (sŭl′fər əs) *adj.*

sulk (sŭlk) *intr.v.* To be sullenly silent or withdrawn: *She sulked in her room.* —**sulk′y** *adj.*

sul•len (sŭl′ən) *adj.* Showing a brooding bad humor or resentment; sulky: *a sullen disposition.* —**sul′len•ly** *adv.* —**sul′len•ness** *n.* [U]

sul•ly (sŭl′ē) *tr.v.* **sul•lied, sul•ly•ing, sul•lies.** To stain (sthg.): *sullied his reputation.*

sul•phur (sŭl′fər) *n.* Variant of **sulfur.**

sul•tan (sŭl′tən) *n.* A ruler of a Muslim country.

sul•try (sŭl′trē) *adj.* **sul•tri•er, sul•tri•est.** Very hot and humid: *a sultry summer day.*

sum (sŭm) *n.* **1.** A number obtained as a result of adding numbers: *The sum of 8 and 6 is 14.* **2.** The whole amount, quantity, or number: *the sum of our knowledge.* **3.** An arithmetic problem: *He's good at sums.* —*v.* **summed, sum•ming, sums.** ◆ **sum up.** *tr.v.* [sep.] To present (material) in a condensed form; summarize: *I'd like to sum up my argument.*

HOMONYMS: sum, some (a few).

---

sum•ma cum lau•de (sŏŏm′ə kŏŏm lou′də) *adv. & adj.* With the greatest academic honor: *graduating summa cum laude from college; She's a summa cum laude graduate.*

sum•mar•i•ly (sə mĕr′ə lē) *adv.* In an abrupt way; speedily and without ceremony: *The dishonest banker was summarily fired.*

sum•ma•rize (sŭm′ə rīz′) *tr.v.* **sum•ma•rized, sum•ma•riz•ing, sum•ma•riz•es.** To make a summary of (sthg.): *She summarized his views.* —**sum′ma•ri•za′tion** (sŭm′ər ĭ zā′shən) *n.* [U]

sum•ma•ry (sŭm′ə rē) *n., pl.* **sum•ma•ries.** A brief statement mentioning the main points of sthg.: *a summary of our findings.*

HOMONYMS: summary, summery (like summer).

---

sum•mer (sŭm′ər) *n.* [C; U] The season of the year between spring and autumn when the weather is hot: *a lazy summer afternoon.* —*intr.v.* To spend the summer: *They summered at a beach resort.* —*adj.* Happening in or appropriate to the summer: *a summer wedding; summer clothing.*

S

sum·mer·y (sŭm′ə rē) *adj.* Intended for or like summer: *summery weather.*

HOMONYMS: summery, summary (brief statement).

---

sum·mit (sŭm′ĭt) *n.* The highest point or part; the top, especially of a mountain: *the summit of the moutain.*

sum·mon (sŭm′ən) *tr.v.* **1.** To call (a group) together: *summon a meeting of the delegates.* **2.** To send or ask for (sbdy.) to appear: *summoned her to the principal's office.* ♦ **summon up.** *tr.v.* [sep.] To call (sthg.) forth from within oneself: *I summoned up all my will power not to laugh.*

sum·mons (sŭm′ənz) *n., pl.* **sum·mons·es.** A legal document ordering sbdy. to appear in court as a defendant, witness, or juror.

sump·tu·ous (sŭmp′chōō əs) *adj.* Grand and expensive; lavish: *a sumptuous feast.* —**sump′tu·ous·ly** *adv.* —**sump′tu·ous·ness** *n.* [U]

sun (sŭn) *n.* **1.** [C] *(usually singular).* The star that supplies the energy that sustains life on Earth. **2.** [C] A star that is the center of a system of planets. **3.** [U] The light and heat given off by the sun: *She sat in the sun.* —*v.* **sunned, sun·ning, suns.** —*tr.* To expose (sbdy./sthg.) to the sun, as for warming, drying, or tanning: *The cat sunned herself.* —*intr.* To lie in the sun; sunbathe.

HOMONYMS: sun, son (male child).

Sun. *abbr.* An abbreviation of Sunday.

sun·bathe (sŭn′bāth′) *intr.v.* **sun·bathed, sun·bath·ing, sun·bathes.** To lie in the sun in order to get a tan: *We sunbathed all afternoon.*

sun·beam (sŭn′bēm′) *n.* A ray of sunlight.

sun·burn (sŭn′bûrn′) *n.* [U] Redness and soreness of the skin caused by too much strong sunlight. —*intr.v.* **sun·burned** or **sun·burnt** (sŭn′bûrnt′), **sun·burn·ing, sun·burns.** To be affected with sunburn: *She sunburns easily.*

sun·dae (sŭn′dē *or* sŭn′dā′) *n.* Ice cream with toppings such as syrup, fruit, and nuts.

Sun·day (sŭn′dē *or* sŭn′dā′) *n.* The first day of the week.

Sunday school *n.* [C; U] A school, usually associated with a church, that gives religious education on Sundays.

sun·di·al (sŭn′dī′əl) *n.* An instrument that shows the time of day by the shadow cast by a central pointer on a dial.

sun·down (sŭn′doun′) *n.* [U] The time of sunset.

sun·dry (sŭn′drē) *adj. Formal.* Various; miscellaneous: *a drawer full of pens, paper clips, and sundry items.*

sun·flow·er (sŭn′flou′ər) *n.* A tall plant with large flower heads with yellow rays and dark centers.

sunflower

sung (sŭng) *v.* A past tense and the past participle of **sing.**

sun·glass·es (sŭn′glăs′ĭz) *pl.n.* Eyeglasses with dark lenses to protect the eyes from the sun.

sunk (sŭngk) *v.* A past tense and the past participle of **sink.**

sunk·en (sŭng′kən) *adj.* **1.** Situated beneath the surface of the water or ground; submerged: *a sunken reef.* **2.** Below the surrounding level: *a sunken bathtub.*

sun·light (sŭn′līt′) *n.* [U] The light of the sun.

sun·lit (sŭn′lĭt′) *adj.* Illuminated by the sun: *a sunlit prairie.*

sun·ny (sŭn′ē) *adj.* **sun·ni·er, sun·ni·est.** **1.** Full of sunshine: *a sunny day.* **2.** Cheerful: *a sunny mood.*

sun·rise (sŭn′rīz′) *n.* [C; U] The time when the sun becomes visible above the eastern horizon: *We went fishing at sunrise.*

sun·screen (sŭn′skrēn′) *n.* [C; U] A cream or lotion used to protect the skin from the sun.

sun·set (sŭn′sĕt′) *n.* [C; U] The time when the sun disappears below the western horizon: *a brilliant winter sunset.*

sun·shine (sŭn′shīn′) *n.* [U] The light of the sun; sunlight.

sun·stroke (sŭn′strōk′) *n.* [U] A severe form of heat stroke caused by exposure to the sun.

sun·tan (sŭn′tăn′) *n.* A dark color of the skin resulting from exposure to the sun. —**sun′tanned′** *adj.*

sun·up (sŭn′ŭp′) *n.* [U] The time of sunrise: *They farm from sunup to sundown.*

su·per (sōō′pər) *Informal. adj.* **1.** Very large, great, or extreme: *a super skyscraper.* **2.** Excellent: *a super party.* —*n.* A superintendent in a building.

super— *pref.* A prefix that means: **1.** Above; over; upon: *superimpose.* **2.** Superior in size, quality, number, or degree: *superhuman.* **3.** Exceeding a standard or norm: *supersonic.* **4.** Excessive in degree or intensity: *supersensitive.*

su·perb (sōō pûrb′) *adj.* Excellent: *a superb meal.* —**su·perb′ly** *adv.*

su·per·fi·cial (sōō′pər fĭsh′əl) *adj.* **1.** Affecting, or being on or near the surface: *a superficial wound.* **2.** Interested only in what

---

is apparent or obvious; shallow: *a superficial person.* —**su′per•fi′ci•al′i•ty** (sōō′pər-fĭsh′ē ăl′ĭ tē) *n.* [U] —**su′per•fi′cial•ly** *adv.*

su•per•fine (sōō′pər fīn′) *adj.* **1.** Extremely delicate: *a superfine distinction.* **2.** With extremely fine texture: *superfine sandpaper.*

su•per•flu•ous (sōō pûr′flōō əs) *adj.* More than what is required or sufficient: *Many items on the new budget are superfluous.* —**su•per′flu•ous•ly** *adv.* —**su•per′flu•ous•ness** *n.* [U]

su•per•high•way (sōō′pər hī′wā′) *n.* **1.** A wide highway with six or more lanes for high-speed traffic. **2.** A worldwide system of computers: *the information superhighway.*

su•per•hu•man (sōō′pər hyōō′mən) *adj.* Seeming beyond ordinary or normal human ability or power: *superhuman strength.*

su•per•im•pose (sōō′pər ĭm pōz′) *tr.v.* **su•per•im•posed, su•per•im•pos•ing, su•per•im•pos•es.** To lay or place (sthg.) over or upon sthg. else: *She superimposed one photograph on another.*

su•per•in•ten•dent (sōō′pər ĭn tĕn′dənt) *n.* **1.** A person who is in charge of all the schools in a certain area in the United States. **2.** A janitor or custodian in a building.

su•pe•ri•or (sōō pîr′ē ər) *adj.* **1.** High or higher in order, degree, or rank: *a superior court; a superior officer.* **2.** Higher in quality: *a superior car.* **3.** Excellent: *a superior singer.* **4.** Greater in number: *a superior number of eagles nesting.* **5.** Conceited; snobbish: *What makes him act so superior?* —*n.* **1.** A person who is above another in rank: *I need to talk this over with my superiors.* **2.** The head of a religious community, such as a monastery or convent: *Mother Superior.* —**su•pe•ri•or•i•ty** (sōō pîr′ē ôr′ĭ tē or sōō pîr′ē ŏr′ĭ tē) *n.* [U]

su•per•la•tive (sōō pûr′lə tĭv) *adj.* **1.** In grammar, relating to the highest degree of comparison of an adjective or adverb, as in *best, brightest,* or *most comfortable.* **2.** Of the highest order, quality, or degree: *a superlative specimen.* —*n.* **1.** (*usually singular*). In grammar, the superlative degree of an adjective or adverb. **2.** An adjective or adverb in the superlative degree. *Brightest* is the superlative of the adjective *bright.*

su•per•man (sōō′pər măn′) *n.* A man with powers beyond what is normal or natural. —**su′per•wo′man** (sōō′pər wŏŏm′ ən) *n.*

su•per•mar•ket (sōō′pər mär′kĭt) *n.* A large store that sells food and household goods.

su•per•mom (sōō′pər mŏm′) *n. Informal.* A mother who takes care of children and the home while also holding a full-time job.

su•per•nat•u•ral (sōō′pər năch′ər əl) *adj.* Relating to existence outside the natural world: *belief in supernatural creatures.* —*n.* [U] Something supernatural: *Do you believe in the supernatural?*

su•per•pow•er (sōō′pər pou′ ər) *n.* A powerful and influential nation: *a meeting of the European superpowers.*

su•per•sede (sōō′pər sēd′) *tr.v.* **su•per•sed•ed, su•per•sed•ing, su•per•sedes.** To take the place of (sthg.): *Electric light bulbs superseded candles and kerosene lamps as the major source of indoor light.*

su•per•son•ic (sōō′pər sŏn′ĭk) *adj.* Relating to, traveling at, or caused by a speed greater than the speed of sound in a given medium, especially air: *supersonic transport.*

su•per•star (sōō′pər stär′) *n.* A very popular performer, as in films, music, or sports: *Sports superstars earn millions of dollars.*

su•per•sti•tion (sōō′pər stĭsh′ən) *n.* [C; U] An action or a practice that is based on faith in magic or chance: *the superstition that carrying a crystal will protect a person from bad luck.*

su•per•sti•tious (sōō′pər stĭsh′əs) *adj.* Influenced by superstition: *a superstitious person.* —**su′per•sti′tious•ly** *adv.* —**su′•per•sti′tious•ness** *n.* [U]

su•per•struc•ture (sōō′pər strŭk′chər) *n.* **1.** The part of a building that is above the foundation. **2.** The parts of a ship that are above the main deck.

su•per•tank•er (sōō′pər tăng′kər) *n.* An extremely large ship, usually used for transporting oil.

su•per•vise (sōō′pər vīz′) *tr.v.* **su•per•vised, su•per•vis•ing, su•per•vis•es.** To direct, oversee, and manage (sbdy./sthg.): *She supervises a staff of chemists. Who supervises your work?* —**su′per•vi′sor** (sōō′pər-vī′zər) *n.* —**su′per•vi′so•ry** *adj.*

su•per•vi•sion (sōō′pər vĭzh′ən) *n.* [U] The act of supervising; direction: *children under the supervision of their parents.*

sup•per (sŭp′ər) *n.* **1.** An evening meal, especially dinner when eaten in the evening: *We usually eat supper at 6:00.* **2.** A social gathering at which supper is served: *a church supper.*

sup•plant (sə plănt′) *tr.v. Formal.* To take the place of (sbdy./sthg.): *The word processor has supplanted the typewriter.*

sup•ple (sŭp′əl) *adj.* **sup•pler, sup•plest. 1.** Easily bent or folded: *supple leather.* **2.** Moving easily; agile: *a supple body.* **3.** Quick; adaptable: *a supple mind.* —**sup′ple•ly** *adv.* —**sup′ple•ness** *n.* [U]

sup•ple•ment (sŭp′lə mənt) *n.* **1.** Something added to complete a thing or to make up for a weakness or lack: *This book is a supplement to the regular required reading. She takes vitamin supplements.* **2.** A section added to a newspaper, book, or document to give further information: *a special advertising supplement in the Sunday paper.* —*tr.v.* (sŭp′lə mĕnt′). To provide a supplement to (sthg.): *The teacher supplemented our reading with films.* —**sup′ple•men′ta•ry** *adj.*

S

supplementary angle *n.* One of a pair of angles whose sum is 180 degrees.

sup•ply (sə plī′) *tr.v.* **sup•plied, sup•ply•ing, sup•plies. 1.a.** To make (sthg.) available for use; provide: *supply uniforms to the team.* **b.** To make sthg. available for the use of (sbdy.): *Most hotels supply their guests with towels.* **2.** To fill (sthg.) sufficiently; satisfy: *Orange juice supplies my need for vitamin C.* —*n., pl.* **sup•plies. 1.** The act of supplying: *War interrupted the supply of petroleum.* **2.** An amount available for use: *Our supply of milk is low.* **3.** *(usually plural).* Materials or provisions stored and given out when needed: *Where do you keep medical supplies?* —**sup•pli′er** *n.*

supply and demand *n.* [U] The amount of goods available for sale compared to people's need or desire to buy: *Prices on fish have gone up because the catch has been so small; it's the law of supply and demand.*

sup•port (sə pôrt′) *tr.v.* **1.** To hold or carry the weight of (a structure or an object): *Beams support the floor.* **2.** To hold (sthg.) up or in position: *He supported the baby's head with his hand.* **3.** To provide money or other necessities for the care of (sbdy.): *She supports two children.* **4.** To provide evidence for (sthg.); show to be true: *The experiment supports his theory.* **5.** To help the cause, policy, or interest of (sbdy./sthg.): *support a political candidate.* —*n.* **1.** [U] **a.** The act of supporting: *She spoke in support of the proposed law.* **b.** The condition of being supported: *The candidate has little support outside his own party.* **2.** [C] A person or thing that supports: *supports that hold up a roof.*

sup•port•a•ble (sə pôr′tə bəl) *adj. Formal.* Bearable; endurable: *The pain was bad but supportable.* —**sup•port′a•bly** *adv.*

sup•port•er (sə pôr′tər) *n.* **1.** A person who promotes or favors sbdy. or sthg.; an advocate: *the candidate's loyal supporters.* **2.** An athletic supporter.

sup•por•tive (sə pôr′tĭv) *adj.* Providing support, help, or sympathy: *She has been a very supportive friend since my accident.*

sup•pose (sə pōz′) *v.* **sup•posed, sup•pos•ing, sup•pos•es.** —*tr.* **1.** To assume (sthg.) to be true or real for the sake of an argument or illustration: *Suppose we were rich.* **2.** To believe (sthg.), especially without proof: *I suppose she could have missed the train.* **3.** To consider (sthg.) as a suggestion: *Suppose we stop and rest a minute.* —*intr.* To guess or imagine: *We'll just have to go inside, I suppose.* ✦ **be supposed to. 1.** To be intended or imagined to: *a medicine that is supposed to relieve pain.* **2.a.** To be required or expected to: *He's supposed to be at school.* **b.** *(used in the negative).* To be permitted to: *We are not supposed to be here at night.*

sup•posed (sə pō′zĭd) *adj.* Believed to be true or real: *the supposed sighting of a UFO.*

sup•po•sed•ly (sə pō′zĭd lē) *adv.* As it is claimed; according to what is believed: *He is supposedly the richest man in the world.*

sup•po•si•tion (sŭp′ə zĭsh′ən) *n.* **1.** [U] The act of supposing: *an argument based on supposition, not fact.* **2.** [C] Something supposed; an assumption: *They made plans based on the supposition of good weather.*

sup•pos•i•to•ry (sə pŏz′ĭ tôr′ē) *n., pl.* **sup•pos•i•to•ries.** A medication prepared in a solid form, designed to be put into an opening in the body other than the mouth, especially the rectum.

sup•press (sə prĕs′) *tr.v.* **1.** To put an end to (sthg.) forcibly; crush: *suppress a rebellion.* **2.** To restrict or forbid the activities of (sthg.): *The government was accused of suppressing the opposition party.* **3.** To keep (sthg. secret) from being made known: *suppress news of the leader's illness.* —**sup•pres′sion** (sə prĕsh′ən) *n.* [U]

su•prem•a•cist (soo prĕm′ə sĭst) *n.* A person who believes that a certain group or race is or should be supreme: *white supremacists.*

su•prem•a•cy (soo prĕm′ə sē) *n.* [U] The quality or condition of being supreme: *a struggle for supremacy among colonial powers.*

su•preme (soo prēm′) *adj.* **1.** Greatest in power, authority, or rank; dominant over others: *a supreme commander.* **2.** Greatest in importance, degree, or achievement: *supreme intelligence.* —**su•preme′ly** *adv.*

Supreme Court *n.* **1.** [U] The highest Federal court in the United States, with nine justices and legal authority over all other courts in the nation. **2.** [C] **supreme court.** The highest court in most states within the United States.

supt. or **Supt.** *abbr.* An abbreviation of superintendent.

sur•charge (sûr′chärj′) *n.* An additional amount added to the usual charges or cost: *a surcharge for transporting dangerous goods.* —*tr.v.* **sur•charged, sur•charg•ing, sur•charg•es.** To charge (sbdy.) an additional amount over the usual cost: *That company surcharges customers for special handling.*

sure (shoor) *adj.* **sur•er, sur•est. 1.** Confident, as of sthg. awaited or expected: *I'm sure the package will come today.* **2.** Careful (to do sthg.): *Be sure to brush your teeth.* **3.** Impossible to doubt; certain: *sure proof of her innocence.* **4.** Certain to happen: *a sure victory for the team.* **5.** Steady; firm: *a sure hold on the suitcase.* **6.** Dependable; reliable: *The surest way of seeing that something gets done right is to do it yourself.* —*adv. Informal.* Surely; certainly: *That sure was an exciting race.* ✦ **for**

sure. *Informal.* Certainly; unquestionably: *We'll win today for sure.* **make sure.** To make certain; establish sthg. without doubt: *I think the play starts at 5:00, but I'll call to make sure.* **Sure.** *Informal.* **1.** Yes: *"Can you come?" "Sure."* **2.** Used in reply when sbdy. says thank you: *"Thanks for your help." "Sure, no problem."* **3.** Used to show partial agreement with some statement but also to introduce conflicting information: *Sure, she came, but she was two hours late.* **sure enough.** *Informal.* Used to say that sthg. happened exactly as expected: *Sure enough, my brother asked me for $50.* **sure thing.** *Informal.* **1.** Used to express agreement: *"I'll see you later." "Sure thing."* **2.** Used as a response when sbdy. says thank you: *"Thanks!" "Sure thing."* **3.** Something that is certain to happen or succeed: *That horse is a sure thing in the next race.* —**sure′ness** *n.* [U]

sure-fire (shŏŏr′fīr′) *adj. Informal.* Certain to be successful: *a sure-fire solution to the problem.*

sure-foot•ed or **sure•foot•ed** (shŏŏr′-fŏŏt′ĭd) *adj.* Not likely to stumble or fall: *a sure-footed horse.* —**sure′foot′ed•ness** *n.* [U]

sure•ly (shŏŏr′lē) *adv.* **1.** Certainly; without doubt: *Surely you can't be serious.* **2.** Without fail: *Slowly but surely spring returns.*

surf (sûrf) *n.* [U] The waves of the sea as they break upon a shore or reef: *We sat on the beach watching the surf.* —*intr.v.* To ride on a surfboard: *She has gone to Hawaii to surf.* ◆ **channel surf.** To look for a television program by changing channels quickly: *He loves to channel surf with the remote control.* **surf the Web** or **Net.** To go from one site to another on the Internet. —**surf′er** *n.*

---

sur•face (sûr′fəs) *n.* **1.** The outermost layer or boundary of an object: *dust from the surface of the moon.* **2.** The outward appearance: *On the surface, the house looked new.* **3.** A portion of space that has length and width but no thickness; a geometric figure that has only two dimensions: *A line is a series of points on a surface.* —*v.* **sur•faced, sur•fac•ing, sur•fac•es.** —*tr.* To form or shape the surface of (sthg.): *Workers surfaced the driveway with asphalt.* —*intr.* **1.** To rise to the surface, as of a body of water: *The submarine surfaced.* **2.** To appear after being hidden: *She knew the lost book would surface when she cleaned her room.*

surf•board (sûrf′bôrd′) *n.* A long narrow board used for standing and riding on large waves.

surfboard

surf•ing (sûr′fĭng) *n.* [U] The sport of riding waves, especially while standing or lying on a surfboard.

surge (sûrj) *intr.v.* **surged, surg•ing, surg•es.** **1.** To move with a gathering force and fullness, in or as if in waves: *The crowd surged forward.* **2.** To increase suddenly: *Excitement surged through his body.* —*n.* **1.** A powerful swelling motion like that of a wave: *There was a surge in the crowd when the ticket window opened.* **2.** A sudden onrush or increase: *a surge of excitement.* **3.** A sudden increase or change in electric current or voltage: *This device will protect your computer from a power surge.*

sur•geon (sûr′jən) *n.* A doctor specializing in surgery.

Surgeon General *n., pl.* **Surgeons General.** The chief medical officer in the U.S. Public Health Service: *The Surgeon General advises the President.*

sur•ger•y (sûr′jə rē) *n.* [U] **1.** The branch of medicine that deals with health problems by operating on the body, often involving the cutting of body tissues and removal, repair, or replacement of organs. **2.** A surgical operation or procedure: *open-heart surgery; laser surgery.*

sur•gi•cal (sûr′jĭ kəl) *adj.* Relating to surgeons or surgery: *surgical instruments.* —**sur′gi•cal•ly** *adv.*

sur•ly (sûr′lē) *adj.* **sur•li•er, sur•li•est.** Bad-tempered; sullen: *He tends to be surly before he has his morning coffee.* —**sur′li•ness** *n.*

sur•mise (sər mīz′) *Formal. tr.v.* **sur•mised, sur•mis•ing, sur•mis•es.** To conclude or guess (sthg.) on little evidence; suppose: *Astronomers surmise that there is life elsewhere in the universe.* —*n.* An idea or opinion based on little evidence; a guess: *His surmise about her future plans proved incorrect.*

sur•mount (sər mount′) *tr.v. Formal.* To overcome (sthg.); triumph over: *She surmounted her medical problems to become a great swimmer.*

sur•name (sûr′nām′) *n.* One's family name or last name: *The British royal family's surname is Windsor.*

sur•pass (sər păs′) *tr.v.* **1.** To go beyond the limit, powers, or capacity of (sthg.): *a palace that surpasses description.* **2.** To be or go beyond (sthg.) in degree or quality: *The success of the program surpassed their expectations.*

sur•plus (sûr′pləs or sûr′plŭs′) *adj.* Being more than what is needed or required: *Surplus grain is usually sold abroad or stored.* —*n.* An amount or a quantity that is more than what is needed: *After paying expenses, the library will use any surplus of funds to buy new books.*

sur•prise (sər prīz′) *tr.v.* **sur•prised, sur•pris•ing, sur•pris•es.** **1.** To come upon (sbdy.) suddenly or unexpectedly: *A police officer surprised the thief climbing out a*

S

window. **2.** To cause (sbdy.) to feel wonder, astonishment, or amazement, as at sthg. unexpected: *The low price of the car surprised me.* —*n.* **1.** [U] The act of surprising or the condition of being surprised: *The news made him look at me in surprise.* **2.** [C] Something, such as an attack, a gift, or an event, that surprises: *We wanted the party to be a surprise.*

SYNONYMS: surprise, astonish, amaze, astound. These verbs mean to affect a person strongly because of sthg. unexpected or unusual. **Surprise** means to fill with sudden wonder or disbelief: *It surprises me that you would want a job like that.* **Astonish** means to overwhelm with surprise: *The sight of such an enormous crowd outside the house astonished them.* **Amaze** means to affect with great wonder: *The magician has amazed audiences around the world.* **Astound** means to shock with surprise: *They were astounded by the waiter's rudeness.*

sur•prised (sər prīzd′) *adj.* Having or experiencing a feeling of surprise: *He had a surprised look on his face. I was surprised that you called.*

sur•pris•ing (sər prī′zĭng) *adj.* Unusual; not expected: *a surprising answer to my question.* —**sur•pris′ing•ly** *adv.*

sur•re•al (sə rē′əl) *adj.* With strange qualities like those of a dream: *The accident was such a shock that it seemed surreal to me.* —**sur•re′al•ly** *adv.*

sur•re•al•ism (sə rē′ə lĭz′əm) *n.* [U] A 20th-century literary and artistic movement attempting to show dreams and other products of the unconscious mind. —**sur•re′al•ist′** *adj. & n.*

sur•re•al•is•tic (sə rē′ə lĭs′tĭk) *adj.* **1.** Relating to surrealism: *surrealistic paintings.* **2.** With a dreamlike or unreal quality: *a surrealistic experience.*

sur•ren•der (sə rĕn′dər) *v.* —*tr.* [*to*] **1.** To give up (sthg.) to another on demand or under pressure: *surrendered the coast to the invading army.* See Synonyms at **yield**. **2.** To give (oneself) completely to sthg., such as an emotion, influence, or effort: *She surrendered herself to tears.* —*intr.* To give oneself up, as to the enemy: *The general surrendered.* —*n.* [U] The act of surrendering: *He was forced to decide between death and surrender.*

sur•rep•ti•tious (sûr′ əp tĭsh′əs) *adj.* Taken or done in secret: *a surreptitious look at his watch.* —**sur′rep•ti′tious•ly** *adv.* —**sur′rep•ti′tious•ness** *n.* [U]

sur•ro•gate (sûr′ə gĭt *or* sûr′ə gāt′) *n.* A person or thing that takes the place of another; a substitute. —*adj.* Substitute: *a surrogate parent.*

surrogate mother *n.* A woman who has a baby for another woman who cannot have a baby for some medical reason.

sur•round (sə round′) *tr.v.* **1.** To extend on all sides of (sbdy./sthg.); encircle: *A field of gravitation surrounds the earth. Hills surround the town.* **2.** To shut in or enclose (sbdy./sthg.) on all sides to prevent escape: *Police surrounded the building.*

sur•round•ings (sə roun′dĭngz) *pl.n.* The things that affect and surround one; environment: *Getting used to new surroundings after a move is difficult.*

sur•tax (sûr′tăks′) *n.* An additional tax: *a surtax on cigarettes.*

sur•veil•lance (sər vā′ləns) *n.* [U] Close observation of a person or group, especially one under suspicion: *Keep the suspect under surveillance.*

sur•vey (sər vā′ *or* sûr′vā′) *tr.v.* **1.** To look over the parts or features of (sthg.) to see the entire area: *The mayor surveyed the damage from the fire.* **2.** To measure and map the area, boundaries, or elevation of (a region): *The site was surveyed before construction of the bridge.* —*n.* (sûr′vā′). *pl.* **sur•veys. 1.** A general or overall view of sthg.: *The course offers a survey of English literature.* **2.** A detailed study of a group's opinions or behavior: *a survey of public opinion.* **3.a.** The act of surveying: *a survey of the property.* **b.** A map or report of what has been surveyed.

sur•vey•ing (sər vā′ĭng) *n.* [U] The measurement and description of a region, part, or feature on the earth's surface, especially for use in locating property boundaries and making maps. —**sur•vey′or** *n.*

sur•viv•al (sər vī′vəl) *n.* **1.** [U] **a.** The act of surviving: *laws to ensure the survival of endangered animal species.* **b.** The fact of having survived: *Their survival is a miracle.* **2.** [C] A person or thing that has survived: *a custom that is a survival of an ancient tradition.*

sur•vive (sər vīv′) *v.* **sur•vived, sur•viv•ing, sur•vives.** —*intr.* To stay alive or in existence: *trying to survive in the woods; a story that has survived for centuries.* —*tr.* **1.** To live longer than (sbdy.): *We expect our children to survive us.* **2.** To live or persist through (sthg.): *The plants survived the frost.*

sur•vi•vor (sər vī′vər) *n.* **1.** A person who has survived an accident or disaster that caused the death of others: *a survivor of the crash.* **2.** A living relative of a person who has died: *The money will be divided among his survivors.*

sus•cep•ti•ble (sə sĕp′tə bəl) *adj.* [*to*] **1.** Easily influenced or affected: *She is very susceptible to persuasion.* **2.** With little resistance: *susceptible to colds.* —**sus•cep′ti•bil′i•ty** *n.* [C; U]

sus·pect (sə spĕkt′) *tr.v.* **1.** To believe (sthg.) to be true or probable without being sure: *The Greeks were the first to suspect that the earth is round. We suspected that she would come.* **2.** To have doubts about (sbdy./sthg.); distrust: *We suspected his intentions.* **3.** To consider (sbdy.) guilty without proof: *The police suspect her of fraud.* —*intr.* To imagine sthg. to be true or probable: *He'll be tired when he arrives, I suspect.* —*n.* (sŭs′pĕkt′). A person who is suspected, especially of having committed a crime: *Police questioned the suspects.* —*adj.* (sŭs′pĕkt′). Viewed with suspicion; suspicious: *suspect motives; a suspect policy.*

sus·pend (sə spĕnd′) *tr.v.* **1.** To block (sbdy.) temporarily from participation in sthg., usually as a punishment: *suspend a student from school.* **2.** To cause (sthg.) to stop for a period; interrupt: *She suspended her work to have lunch.* **3.** To make (sthg.) temporarily invalid or ineffective: *suspended his driver's license.* **4.** To hang (sthg.) so as to allow free movement: *He suspended a swing from the tree.* **5.** To support (sbdy./sthg.) without apparent attachment; cause to float: *For an instant the acrobat seemed to be suspended in midair.*

sus·pend·ers (sə spĕn′dərz) *pl.n.* A pair of straps worn over the shoulders to hold up one's pants.

sus·pense (sə spĕns′) *n.* [U] Excitement, worry, or fear resulting from an uncertain or mysterious situation: *voters in suspense awaiting election results; a movie filled with suspense.* —**sus·pense′ful** *adj.*

sus·pen·sion (sə spĕn′shən) *n.* **1.** The act of suspending or the condition of being suspended: *a suspension of the rules; his suspension from school.* See Synonyms at **pause. 2.** A liquid or gas with solid particles evenly mixed. **3.** The system of springs, shock absorbers, and other parts that connect the wheels of a vehicle to its frame: *a truck with good suspension.*

sus·pi·cion (sə spĭsh′ən) *n.* **1.** [C] The act of suspecting sthg. on little evidence or without proof: *She had a strong suspicion that she was being cheated.* **2.** [U] The condition of being suspected, especially of doing sthg. wrong: *held under suspicion of theft.* **3.** [U] A state of uncertainty; doubt: *Everyone looked at the stranger with suspicion.* See Synonyms at **uncertainty.**

sus·pi·cious (sə spĭsh′əs) *adj.* **1.** Causing suspicion: *suspicious behavior.* **2.** [*of*] Tending to suspect; distrustful: *She was suspicious of anything new or unusual.* **3.** Expressing suspicion: *The neighbors gave the newcomer a suspicious look.* —**sus·pi′cious·ly** *adv.* —**sus·pi′cious·ness** *n.* [U]

sus·tain (sə stān′) *tr.v.* **1.** To keep (sthg.) in existence; maintain: *sustain an effort.* **2.** To keep (sbdy./sthg.) alive by supplying needed nourishment: *the grasses that sustain antelope.* **3.** To support (sthg.) from below; keep from falling or sinking: *Strong beams sustain the weight of the roof.* **4.** To support the spirits of (sbdy.): *His words of encouragement sustained us.* **5.** To experience or suffer (sthg.): *They sustained minor injuries in the accident.* —**sus·tain′able** *adj.*

sus·te·nance (sŭs′tə nəns) *n.* [U] *Formal.* **1.** The act of sustaining: *She depended on her friends for sustenance during the crisis.* **2.** The support of life, as with food and other necessities: *Rain forests provide sustenance to countless species.*

su·ture (soo′chər) *n.* **1.** A stitch used in surgery: *Six sutures were needed to close the cut on my hand.* **2.** The line where bones connect in an immovable joint: *the sutures of the skull.* —*tr.v.* **su·tured, su·tur·ing, su·tures.** To join (body tissues) by means of sutures, as in surgery.

svelte (svĕlt) *adj.* **svelt·er, svelt·est.** Slender or graceful in figure; slim: *a svelte fashion model.*

SW *abbr.* An abbreviation of southwest.

swab (swŏb) *n.* A small piece of cotton, sponge, or other absorbent material attached to the end of a stick and used for cleaning or for applying medicine: *a cotton swab.* —*tr.v.* **swabbed, swab·bing, swabs. 1.** To use a swab on (sthg.): *The nurse swabbed the skin with antiseptic.* **2.** To clean (sthg.) with a swab: *swab the decks of the ship; swabbed the injury.*

swag·ger (swăg′ər) *intr.v.* To walk in an overly proud manner: *The champion boxer swaggered into the ring for the fight.* —*n.* A swaggering movement or manner of walking: *He walked in with a swagger.*

swal·low[1] (swŏl′ō) *v.* —*tr.* **1.** To cause (food or drink) to pass from the mouth through the throat and into the stomach: *She swallowed the medicine.* **2.** To tolerate (sthg. unpleasant): *swallow an insult without saying a word.* **3.** To keep from expressing (sthg.): *swallow one's feelings.* **4.** *Slang.* To believe (sthg. untrue) without question: *She swallowed their story about why they were late.* —*intr.* To perform the act of swallowing. —*n.* **1.** The act of swallowing: *finished the drink in two swallows.* **2.** An amount swallowed: *a swallow of water.* ◆ **swallow (one's) words.** To take back sthg. one has said: *He said they couldn't win, so when they did, he had to swallow his words.*

swal·low[2] (swŏl′ō) *n.* Any of various small swift-flying birds with narrow pointed wings, a forked tail, and a large mouth for catching flying insects.

swam (swăm) *v.* Past tense of **swim.**

swamp (swŏmp) *n.* A low-lying wet region: *alligators living in a swamp.* —*tr.v.* **1.** [*with*] To fill or cover (sthg.) with or as if with water:

The road is swamped with rain water. **2.** [with] To give (sbdy./sthg.) too much; overwhelm: The staff is swamped with work. **3.** To fill (a boat) with water to the point of sinking. **—swamp′y** adj.

swan (swŏn) n. Any of various large, usually white water birds with webbed feet and a long slender neck.

swan

swank•y (swăng′-kē) adj. **swank•i•er, swank•i•est.** Very fashionable or elegant: a swanky hotel. **—swank′i•ly** adv.

swap (swŏp) Informal. tr. & intr.v. **swapped, swap•ping, swaps.** To trade one thing for another; exchange: We swapped business cards. She didn't like her seat, so I offered to swap. —n. An exchange of one thing for another: We decided to trade our seats at the movie and quickly made the swap.

swarm (swôrm) n. **1.** A large number of actively moving insects or other small creatures: a swarm of bees; swarms of microbes. **2.** A group of people or animals, especially when excited or moving in mass: His friends came in a swarm to congratulate him. —intr.v. **1.** To move in or form a swarm, as bees or other insects: The bees swarmed around the flowers. **2.** To move or gather in large numbers: Fans swarmed onto the playing field after the game. **3.** To be filled with busily moving creatures: The old log swarmed with bugs.

swarth•y (swôr′thē) adj. **swarth•i•er, swarth•i•est.** Having a dark complexion: the actor's swarthy good looks. **—swarth′i•ly** adv. **—swarth′i•ness** n. [U]

swas•ti•ka (swŏs′tĭ kə) n. **1.** The symbol of Nazi Germany. **2.** An ancient religious symbol formed by a Greek cross with the ends of the arms bent at right angles.

swat (swŏt) tr.v. **swat•ted, swat•ting, swats.** To hit (sbdy./sthg.) with a sharp blow or slap: swat a mosquito. —n. A quick blow; a slap: She killed the fly with a quick swat. **—swat′ter** n.

swatch (swŏch) n. A small sample of cloth or other material: We looked at lots of swatches before deciding on the curtains.

swath (swŏth) n. A path of a uniform width cut through grass or grain by a blade. ◆ **cut a swath.** To create a dramatic impression: a bold figure cutting a swath across the political landscape.

swathe (swŏth or swāth) tr.v. **swathed, swath•ing, swathes. 1.** To wrap or bind (sthg.) with strips of cloth: His right ankle was swathed in bandages. **2.** To cover or wrap (sbdy./sthg.): The actress was swathed in a long black cape.

sway (swā) v. —intr. To move back and forth or from side to side: Trees swayed in the wind. She swayed and put out a hand to steady herself. —tr. **1.** To cause (sthg.) to move back and forth or from side to side: The wind swayed the trees. **2.** To influence or control (sbdy./sthg.): issues most likely to sway voters. —n. [U] **1.** The act of moving from side to side with a swinging motion: the sway of the train. **2.** Power; influence: when the liberals held sway.

swear (swâr) v. **swore** (swôr), **sworn** (swôrn), **swear•ing, swears.** —intr. **1.** To use offensive language; curse: He swore angrily at the other driver. **2.** To make a serious promise about the truth of a statement one makes: witnesses asked to swear in court. —tr. **1.** To declare the truth of (sthg.) by calling on a sacred being or thing: He swore to God that he was innocent. **2.** To promise (sthg.); vow: swore to do his duty; She swore that she would get even. See Synonyms at **vow. 3.** To hold (sbdy.) by means of an oath: swore them to secrecy. ◆ **swear by.** tr.v. [insep.] **1.** To express great confidence in (sbdy./sthg.): He swears by his personal physician. **2.** To take an oath by (sbdy./sthg.): They swear by all that's holy to fight to the end. **swear in.** tr.v. [sep.] To administer an oath of office to (sbdy.): swear in the new mayor. **swear off.** tr.v. [insep.] Informal. To promise to give up (sthg.): swore off sweets. **swear out a warrant.** To get a warrant for someone's arrest. **—swear′er** n.

sweat (swĕt) intr.v. **sweat•ed** or **sweat, sweat•ing, sweats. 1.** To give off a salty liquid through the skin; perspire: Hot weather makes me sweat. **2.** Informal. To work long and hard: The students sweated over their term papers. **3.** Informal. To worry: The boss let us sweat for a day before announcing his decision. —n. **1.** [U] The salty liquid given off by the sweat glands of the skin: a runner covered in sweat. **2.** [C; U] The act of sweating: work up a sweat exercising. **3.** [C] Informal. An anxious condition; a state of impatience: The painters were in a sweat to get started. **4. sweats.** A sweat suit. ◆ **no sweat.** Informal. Easily done or handled: "Can you do it?" "No sweat." **sweat blood.** Informal. To work extremely hard: The coach promised to make us sweat blood. **sweat out.** tr.v. [sep.] Slang. **1.** To endure (sthg.) anxiously: sweat out an examination. **2.** To wait (for sthg.) anxiously: sweat out one's final grades.

sweat•er (swĕt′ər) n. A knitted piece of clothing made especially of wool, cotton, or acrylic yarn and worn on the upper body.

sweat•pants (swĕt′pănts′) pl.n. Pants usually with a drawstring or elastic waistband, worn especially for exercising and often made of thick cotton fabric.

sweat·shirt (swĕt′shûrt′) *n.* A long-sleeved pullover usually made of thick cotton fabric.

sweat·shop (swĕt′shŏp′) *n.* A factory where employees work long hours for low wages under poor conditions: *clothing made cheaply in overseas sweatshops.*

sweat suit *n.* A set of pants and a sweatshirt, worn especially for exercising and often made of thick cotton fabric.

sweat·y (swĕt′ē) *adj.* **sweat·i·er, sweat·i·est. 1.** Covered with, wet with, or smelling of sweat: *sweaty socks.* **2.** Causing sweat: *a sweaty job.* —**sweat′i·ly** *adv.*

sweep (swēp) *v.* **swept** (swĕpt), **sweep·ing, sweeps.** —*tr.* **1.** To clean or clear (sthg.) with a broom or brush: *swept the floor.* **2.** To clear (sthg.) away with or as if with a broom or brush: *sweep snow from the steps.* **3.** To move, remove, or carry (sbdy./sthg.) by force: *Flood waters swept everything from their path.* **4.** To touch (sthg.) lightly: *branches sweeping the river's surface.* **5.** To search (a place) thoroughly: *Searchers swept the area looking for the lost child.* **6.** To win all the stages or parts of (a game or contest): *swept the playoffs.* **7.** To move through (sthg.) quickly, as a new fashion, goods, or information: *The game is sweeping the country* —*intr.* **1.** To clean or clear a surface with a broom or brush: *He was sweeping when you called.* **2.** To move swiftly with a strong steady force: *The wind swept over the plain.* **3.** To extend gracefully, especially in a curve: *wildflowers sweeping down the slopes.* **4.** To extend in a wide range: *Searchlights swept across the sky.* **5.** To move quickly, as with a new fashion, goods, or information: *The new style swept across the country. The rumors swept through the office.* —*n.* **1.** A cleaning with or as if with a broom or brush. **2.** A thorough search of an area: *Police made a sweep of the nearby woods.* **3.** A wide curving motion: *the sweep of the oars.* **4.** The area covered by sweeping: *the sweep of a flashlight beam.* **5.** Victory in all stages of a game or contest: *won in a clean sweep.* ◆ **sweep away.** *tr.v.* [sep.] To carry (sbdy./sthg.) away by force: *The car was swept away by the flood.* **sweep off.** *tr.v.* [sep.] To clean (sthg.) with or as if with a broom: *She used her hand to sweep off the car after it snowed.* —**sweep′er** *n.*

sweep·ing (swē′pĭng) *adj.* **1.** With wide-ranging influence or effect: *sweeping changes.* **2.** Moving in or as if in a long curve: *made sweeping gestures with his arms.* **3.** Overwhelming; complete: *a sweeping victory.* —**sweep′ing·ly** *adv.*

sweep·stakes (swēp′stāks′) *n.* (used with a singular or plural verb). **1.** A lottery in which the money bet creates a fund that is given as a prize to one or several winners: *He won a*

million dollars in a sweepstakes. **2.** An event or a contest, especially a horse race, that also determines the winner of such a lottery.

sweet (swēt) *adj.* **1.** With the taste of sugar: *She likes her tea sweet.* **2.** Pleasing to the senses, feelings, or mind; agreeable: *a sweet melody.* **3.** Nice and friendly; lovable: *a sweet child.* —*n.* **1. sweets.** *Informal.* Foods, such as candy or pastries, that are high in sugar content: *He has cut all sweets from his diet.* **2.** A dear or beloved person: *Give me a kiss, my sweet.* ◆ **have a sweet tooth.** To have a liking for sweets: *She has a sweet tooth and keeps candy on her desk.* —**sweet′ly** *adv.* —**sweet′ness** *n.* [U]

HOMONYMS: sweet, suite (series of rooms).

---

sweet·en (swēt′n) *v.* —*tr.* **1.** To make (sthg.) sweet or sweeter by adding sugar or another sweet substance: *sweetened his coffee.* **2.** To make (sthg.) more pleasant or agreeable: *sweeten a job offer with added benefits.* —*intr.* To become sweet: *Fruit sweetens as it ripens.*

sweet·en·er (swēt′n ər) *n.* **1.** [C; U] A substance, such as sugar or saccharin, that sweetens: *a low-calorie sweetener.* **2.** [C] *Informal.* Something added to attract or persuade: *They offered shares in the company as a sweetener, and we made a deal.*

sweet·heart (swēt′härt′) *n.* **1.** A person whom one loves: *They have been sweethearts since high school.* **2.** *Informal.* A person regarded as lovable: *What a sweetheart you are to help like this.*

sweet·ie (swē′tē) *n. Informal.* Sweetheart; dear: *Good night, sweetie.*

sweet potato *n.* The thick, sweet yellowish or reddish root of a tropical vine, cooked and eaten as a vegetable.

swell (swĕl) *v.* **swelled, swelled** or **swol·len** (swō′lən), **swell·ing, swells.** —*intr.* **1.** To grow in size or volume as a result of internal pressure; expand: *The balloon swelled as I filled it with helium.* **2.** To grow in size, number, or degree: *Membership in the club swelled.* **3.a.** To be or become filled, as with pride, arrogance, or anger: *His face swelled in fury.* **b.** To rise from within: *Pride swelled within me.* —*tr.* **1.** To cause (sthg.) to increase in volume, size, number, degree, or intensity: *The new students swelled our class.* **2.** To fill (sthg.) with emotion: *Joy swelled her heart.* —*n.* **1.** An increase in size, number, or degree: *a swell in the population.* **2.** A long wave that moves continuously through the water without breaking: *large ocean swells.* —*adj. Informal.* **1.** Okay: *That's swell.* **2.** Fine; excellent: *We had a swell time.*

swell·ing (swĕl′ĭng) *n.* **1.** [U] The condition of being swollen or expanded: *a sprained ankle with severe swelling.* **2.** [C] Something swollen, especially a part of the body that has become abnormally swollen, as through disease or injury: *There's a swelling where he was hit on the lip.*

swel·ter (swĕl′tər) *intr.v.* To suffer from too much heat: *We sweltered in the stuffy room.*

swel·ter·ing (swĕl′tər ĭng) *adj.* Extremely hot and humid: *Everyone suffered through a sweltering summer.*

swept (swĕpt) *v.* Past tense and past participle of **sweep.**

swerve (swûrv) *tr. & intr.v.* **swerved, swerv·ing, swerves.** To turn aside or be turned aside from a straight course: *I swerved my bike to avoid the tree. The bus swerved into the passing lane.* —*n.* The act of swerving: *The car made a sudden swerve to the right.*

swift (swĭft) *adj.* **1.** Moving or capable of moving with great speed; fast: *a swift deer.* See Synonyms at **fast¹. 2.** Happening or accomplished quickly: *a swift response.* —*adv.* Quickly: *swift-flowing streams.* —*n.* Any of various small, fast-flying, gray or blackish birds with long narrow wings: *a chimney swift.* —**swift′ly** *adv.* —**swift′ness** *n.* [U]

swig (swĭg) *Informal. n.* A large swallow of a liquid; a gulp: *I took a swig of water.* —*tr.v.* **swigged, swig·ging, swigs.** To drink (liquid) in large gulps: *She swigged her coffee.*

swill (swĭl) *tr.v.* **1.** To drink (sthg.) eagerly or greedily: *swilling beer.* **2.** To feed (animals) with swill. —*n.* [U] **1.** A mixture of liquid and solid food given to animals, especially pigs. **2.** Garbage; refuse.

swim (swĭm) *v.* **swam** (swăm), **swum** (swŭm), **swim·ming, swims.** —*intr.* **1.** To move through water by using arms and legs, fins, or tail: *Fish swim.* **2.** To be covered with a liquid: *The French fries swam in ketchup.* **3.** To experience a floating or unbalanced sensation: *a thought that made his head swim.* **4.** To appear blurred, as if moving or spinning: *The room swam before my eyes.* —*tr.* **1.** To move through or across (a body of water) by swimming: *swim the English Channel.* **2.** To perform (a swimming stroke): *swim the backstroke.* —*n.* **1.** The act of swimming: *go for a swim.* **2.** The period of time spent swimming: *a short swim.* —*adj.* Relating to or used for swimming: *a swim mask.* —**swim′mer** *n.* —**swim′ming** *adj. & n.*

swim·ming·ly (swĭm′ĭng lē) *adv. Formal.* With great ease and success: *School is going swimmingly.*

swimming pool *n.* A structure that is filled with water and used for swimming.

swim·suit (swĭm′so͞ot′) *n.* An article of clothing to be worn while swimming; a bathing suit.

swin·dle (swĭn′dl) *tr.v.* **swin·dled, swin·**

dling, swin·dles. 1. To cheat or trick (sbdy.) out of money or property: *The lawyer swindled clients who trusted him.* **2.** To get (money) by cheating or fraud: *swindled money from old people.* —*n.* The act of swindling; a fraud. —**swin′dler** *n.*

swine (swīn) *n., pl.* **swine. 1.** A pig. **2.** A person who is crude, rough, or dishonorable.

swing (swĭng) *v.* **swung** (swŭng), **swing·ing, swings.** —*intr.* **1.** To move back and forth, hanging from above: *a rope swinging from a tree branch.* **2.** To hit at sthg. with a sweeping motion of the arm: *swing at the ball.* **3.** To ride on a swing: *children swinging on the playground.* **4.** To turn on a hinge: *The door swung closed.* **5.** To move to the side: *The car swung to the curb.* —*tr.* **1.** To cause (sthg.) to move back and forth, as on a swing: *She swung her arms as she walked.* **2.** To lift (sthg.) with a sweeping motion: *She swung the leather bag over her shoulder.* **3.** To cause (sthg.) to move in a broad curve: *swing a bat.* **4.** *Informal.* To manage or arrange (sthg.) successfully: *swing a deal; I don't think we can swing that car payment.* —*n.* **1.** [C] The act of swinging, especially a back-and-forth movement: *The gate closed with a swing.* **2.** [C] A sweep or stroke of sthg. that swings: *a swing of his tennis racket.* **3.** [C] A shift from one attitude or condition to another: *a swing toward conservatism.* **4.** [U] Freedom of movement or action: *He was given full swing in operating the business.* **5.** [C] A seat hanging from above, on which one may ride back and forth for fun: *playground swings.* **6.** [U] A type of popular dance music that developed about 1935 from jazz and uses a large band. ◆ **in full swing.** At the highest level of activity or operation: *The party was already in full swing when we arrived.* **swing around.** *tr.v.* [sep.] To turn (sbdy./sthg.) quickly to face a person or thing: *She swung her chair around to face the teacher.* —*intr.v.* To turn quickly: *The boy swung around to look at me.* **swing by.** *tr.v.* [insep.] To make a quick visit to (a place), usually before going somewhere else: *I'll swing by your house after work.* —*intr.v.* To stop for a brief visit: *What time do you think you'll swing by?*

swing·ing (swĭng′ĭng) *adj. Slang.* **1.** Lively: *a swinging party.* **2.** Sexually promiscuous. —**swing′er** *n.*

swipe (swīp) *n.* **1.** A sweeping blow or stroke: *a swipe at a mosquito.* **2.** A negative remark: *made a swipe at the other candidate.* —*v.* **swiped, swip·ing, swipes.** —*tr.* **1.** To hit (sbdy./sthg.) with a sweeping blow: *The ball swiped my arm.* **2.** *Informal.* To steal (sthg.): *Somebody swiped my wallet.* —*intr.* To make a sweeping stroke: *The player swiped at the ball.*

swirl (swûrl) *v.* —*intr.* To move with a twisting whirling motion: *The dancers swirled around the room.* See Synonyms at **turn.** —*tr.* To cause (sbdy./sthg.) to move with a twisting or whirling motion: *swirl soap and water in a dirty pan.* —*n.* The motion of whirling or twisting: *She turned with a swirl.*

swish (swĭsh) *v.* —*intr.* **1.** To move with a whistling or hissing sound, as a whip: *The wind swished through the dry grass.* **2.** To rustle, as certain fabrics such as silk: *Her long skirt swished as she passed.* —*tr.* To cause (sthg.) to make a swishing sound or movement: *He swished the leaves away.* —*n.* A sharp hissing or rustling sound: *the swish of the blade through the tall grass.*

Swiss cheese (swĭs) *n.* [U] A firm whitish cheese with many large holes.

switch (swĭch) *n.* **1.** A device used to open or close an electric circuit or to make a connection to another circuit: *turned on the lights by flipping a switch.* **2.** A change, as of attention or opinion: *He has made the switch to a new political party.* **3.** A device used to transfer railroad cars from one track to another. **4.** A slender flexible stick, especially one used for whipping. —*v.* —*tr.* **1.** To shift, transfer, or change (sthg.): *switch the conversation to a more interesting topic.* **2.** To exchange (two things): *We switched seats.* —*intr.* To make or experience a change or an exchange: *People have switched from type writers to word processors.* ♦ **switch off** or **on.** *tr.v.* [sep.] To turn (a machine or light) off or on: *Switch off the vacuum. How do you switch on the lights?* —**switch′er** *n.*

switch•blade (swĭch′blād′) *n.* A pocketknife with a blade that is quickly opened by a spring when a button on the handle is pressed.

switch•board (swĭch′bôrd′) *n.* A piece of equipment for controlling electric circuits, especially telephone circuits: *An operator handles telephone calls at the company switchboard.*

swiv•el (swĭv′əl) *n.* A movable support designed so that attached parts can turn freely: *This TV table has a swivel that lets you turn the TV easily.* —*tr. & intr.v.* To turn or rotate on or as if on a swivel: *She swiveled her chair. He swiveled around to face me when I spoke to him.*

swol•len (swō′lən) *v.* A past participle of **swell.** —*adj.* Expanded by or as if by internal pressure: *a swollen eyelid; The swollen river threatened to flood.*

swoon (swo͞on) *intr.v.* An old-fashioned word meaning to faint. —*n.* A fainting spell; a faint.

swoop (swo͞op) *v.* —*intr.* To move with a sudden sweeping motion: *The owl swooped down and caught the mouse.* —*tr.* To pick up (sthg.) with a sudden sweeping motion: *She swooped the cat up in her arms.* —*n.* The act of swooping: *He gathered up the books with one swoop.*

swoosh (swo͞osh *or* swo͝osh) *intr.v.* To move with or make a rushing sound: *The jet swooshed over the airfield.*

sword (sôrd) *n.* A hand weapon consisting of a long pointed blade set in a handle. —**swords′-man** *n.* —**swords′man•ship′** *n.* [U]

sword•fish (sôrd′fĭsh′) *n.* A large ocean fish with a long pointed upper jaw that projects forward like a sword.

sword•play (sôrd′plā′) *n.* [U] The act or art of using a sword, as in fencing: *a romantic adventure film full of swordplay.*

swore (swôr) *v.* Past tense of **swear.**

sworn (swôrn) *v.* Past participle of **swear.**

swum (swŭm) *v.* Past participle of **swim.**

swung (swŭng) *v.* Past tense and past participle of **swing.**

syl•la•bi (sĭl′ə bī′) *n.* A plural of **syllabus.**

syl•lab•ic (sĭ lăb′ĭk) *adj.* Relating to a syllable: *syllabic stress.*

syl•lab•i•fy (sĭ lăb′ĭ fī′) *tr.v.* **syl•lab•i•fied, syl•lab•i•fy•ing, syl•lab•i•fies.** To form or divide (a word) into syllables: *rules for syllabifying words.* —**syl•lab′i•fi•ca′-tion** (sĭ lăb′ĭ fĭ kā′shən) *n.* [U]

syl•la•ble (sĭl′ə bəl) *n.* A single uninterrupted sound forming part of a word or in some cases an entire word. The word *house* has one syllable; *houses* has two.

syl•la•bus (sĭl′ə bəs) *n., pl.* **syl•la•bus•es** or **syl•la•bi** (sĭl′ə bī′). An outline or a summary of the main points of a text, lecture, or course of study: *The professor handed out copies of the course syllabus.*

sym•bol (sĭm′bəl) *n.* **1.** Something that represents sthg. else by association, resemblance, or custom: *The lamb is a symbol of innocence.* **2.** A printed or written sign used to represent an operation, element, quantity, quality, or relation, as in mathematics or music: *The plus sign (+) is a symbol for addition.*

HOMONYMS: symbol, cymbal (musical instrument).

---

sym•bol•ic (sĭm bŏl′ĭk) *adj.* **1.** Relating to a symbol or symbols: *symbolic language.* **2.** Serving as a symbol: *a flag symbolic of national pride.* **3.** Using symbolism: *symbolic art.* —**sym•bol′i•cal•ly** *adv.*

sym•bol•ism (sĭm′bə lĭz′əm) *n.* [U] **1.** The practice of representing objects, ideas, events, or relationships by means of symbols: *the use of symbolism in poetry.* **2.** A symbolic meaning or representation: *Do you understand the religious symbolism of the painting?*

sym•bol•ize (sĭm′bə līz′) *tr.v.* **sym•bol-ized, sym•bol•iz•ing, sym•bol•iz•es. 1.** To serve as a symbol of (sthg.): *The poet uses rain to symbolize grief.* **2.** To represent or identify (sthg.) by a symbol: *a white dove that symbolizes peace.*

sym·met·ri·cal (sĭ mĕt′rĭ kəl) also **sym·met·ric** (sĭ mĕt′rĭk) *adj.* Showing symmetry: *the symmetrical nature of the human body.*

sym·me·try (sĭm′ĭ trē) *n., pl.* **sym·me·tries.** [C; U] **1.** An exact matching of the two equal parts on opposite sides of a central boundary: *the symmetry of a butterfly.* **2.** A relationship in which there is a characteristic equivalence or identity between parts: *We admired the beautiful symmetry in the design of a Greek temple.*

sym·pa·thet·ic (sĭm′pə thĕt′ĭk) *adj.* **1.** Feeling, expressing, or resulting from sympathy: *a sympathetic person; a sympathetic look.* **2.** [*to*] In agreement; favorable: *They were sympathetic to the plan.* —**sym′pa·thet′i·cal·ly** *adv.*

sym·pa·thize (sĭm′pə thīz′) *intr.v.* **sym·pa·thized, sym·pa·thiz·ing, sym·pa·thiz·es.** **1.** To feel or express sympathy for another person: *She called me to sympathize when I lost my job.* **2.** [*with*] To share or understand the feelings or ideas of another person or group: *sympathized with the goals of the environmental organization.* —**sym′pa·thiz′er** *n.*

sym·pa·thy (sĭm′pə thē) *n., pl.* **sym·pa·thies.** **1.** [U] A feeling or expression of understanding, pity, or sadness for the condition of another person: *We gave money out of sympathy for victims of the earthquake.* **2.** [U] Favor; agreement: *in sympathy with their beliefs.* **3.** [C] *(often used in the plural).* Used to express one's support of another person at the death of a loved one: *I'm sorry to hear your uncle died. You have my sympathies.*

sym·pho·ny (sĭm′fə nē) *n., pl.* **sym·pho·nies.** **1.** A long and elaborate musical composition for orchestra, usually consisting of four movements. **2.** A large orchestra composed of string, wind, and percussion sections. —**sym·phon′ic** *adj.*

sym·po·si·um (sĭm pō′zē əm) *n., pl.* **sym·po·si·ums** or **sym·po·si·a** (sĭm pō′zē ə). A meeting or conference for discussion of a topic: *an annual symposium on public health.*

symp·tom (sĭm′təm *or* sĭmp′təm) *n.* **1.** A sign of disorder or disease, especially a change from normal bodily function, feeling, or appearance: *My symptoms included fever, headaches, and a sore throat.* **2.** A sign of the existence of sthg. else: *The scarcity of birds was a symptom of broader problems in the environment.*

syn. *abbr.* An abbreviation of: **1.** Synonym. **2.** Synonymous.

syn·a·gogue also **syn·a·gog** (sĭn′ə gŏg′ *or* sĭn′ə gôg′) *n.* A building or place of meeting for worship and religious instruction in the Jewish faith.

sync or **synch** (sĭngk) *n.* [U] ♦ **in** or **out of synch.** *Informal.* **1.** In or out of synchronization: *band members playing out of sync with each other.* **2.** In or out of harmony or accord: *in sync with today's fashions.*

syn·chro·ni·za·tion (sĭng′krə nĭ zā′shən *or* sĭn′krə nĭ zā′shən) *n.* [U] The state of happening or operating at the same time: *perfect synchronization of the dancers' movements.*

syn·chro·nize (sĭng′krə nīz′ *or* sĭn′krə-nīz′) *v.* **syn·chro·nized, syn·chro·niz·ing, syn·chro·niz·es.** —*intr.* To operate at the same rate and time: *We timed our trip to synchronize with the annual jazz festival.* —*tr.* To cause (sthg.) to occur or operate at the same rate and time: *Let's synchronize our watches.* —**syn′chro·nous** (sĭng′krə nəs *or* sĭn′krə nəs) *adj.*

syn·di·cate (sĭn′dĭ kĭt) *n.* **1.** An association of people or firms joined for a specific business purpose: *formed a syndicate to control the supply to the world market.* **2.** An agency that sells articles or photographs for publication in newspapers or magazines: *a news syndicate.* —*tr.v.* (sĭn′dĭ kāt′). **syn·di·cat·ed, syn·di·cat·ing, syn·di·cates.** **1.** To organize or manage (people or firms) as a syndicate. **2.** To sell (sthg.) for publication through a syndicate: *His political cartoons are syndicated to newspapers across the country.* —**syn′di·ca′tion** *n.* [C; U]

syn·di·cat·ed (sĭn′dĭ kā′tĭd) *adj.* Sold to several different newspapers, magazines, or television stations: *a syndicated column; a syndicated program on television.*

syn·drome (sĭn′drōm′) *n.* A set of symptoms and signs that together show the presence of a disease, mental disorder, or other abnormal condition.

syn·o·nym (sĭn′ə nĭm′) *n.* A word with the same or almost the same meaning as another word. For example, the words *wide* and *broad* are synonyms.

syn·on·y·mous (sĭ nŏn′ə məs) *adj.* Having the same or a similar meaning: *synonymous words.*

syn·op·sis (sĭ nŏp′sĭs) *n., pl.* **syn·op·ses** (sĭ nŏp′sēz). A brief summary or outline of a subject or written work: *a synopsis of a play.*

syn·tac·tic (sĭn tăk′tĭk) or **syn·tac·ti·cal** (sĭn tăk′tĭ kəl) *adj.* Relating to the rules or patterns of syntax: *syntactic complexity.* —**syn·tac′ti·cal·ly** *adv.*

syn·tax (sĭn′tăks′) *n.* [U] The way in which words are put together to form phrases and sentences: *Our class studied English syntax.*

syn·the·sis (sĭn′thĭ sĭs) *n., pl.* **syn·the·ses** (sĭn′thĭ sēz′). [C; U] **1.** The combination of separate elements or substances into a single unit or whole: *a musician known for her syn-*

thesis of different musical styles and traditions. **2.** The formation of a chemical compound by combining simpler compounds or elements.

syn•the•size (sĭn'thĭ sīz') *tr.v.* **syn•the•sized, syn•the•siz•ing, syn•the•siz•es.** To make or produce (sthg.) by a process of synthesis: *synthesize an antibiotic.*

syn•the•siz•er (sĭn'thĭ sī'zər) *n.* An electronic musical instrument that can be made to produce a wide range of musical sounds, including those of several instruments.

syn•thet•ic (sĭn thĕt'ĭk) *adj.* Produced by combining several materials; man-made: *synthetic rubber; synthetic fabrics.* —*n.* A synthetic chemical compound or material: *a shirt made of synthetics.* —**syn•thet'i•cal•ly** *adv.*

syph•i•lis (sĭf'ə lĭs) *n.* [U] A serious sexually transmitted disease, which can cause death. —**syph•i•lit•ic** (sĭf'ə lĭt'ĭk) *adj.*

sy•ringe (sə rĭnj' *or* sîr'ĭnj) *n.* A medical instrument with a needle used to inject fluids into the body or draw fluids from the body.

syr•up (sĭr'əp *or* sûr'əp) *n.* [C; U] **1.** A thick, sweet, sticky liquid, consisting of sugar, water, and flavoring or medicine. **2.** The juice of a fruit or plant boiled until thick and sticky: *maple syrup on pancakes; corn syrup in candy.* —**syr'up•y** *adj.*

sys•tem (sĭs'təm) *n.* **1.** Something formed of a group of elements or parts that work together, such as: **a.** A group of related organs or parts of the human body: *the skeletal system.* **b.** A set of mechanical or electrical parts that work together: *the transmission system of an automobile.* **c.** A network of pathways or channels, as for travel or communications: *a telephone system.* **2.** An organized set of related principles or rules: *The company set up a new system for handling orders.* See Synonyms at **method. 3.** A social, economic, or political form of organization: *a system of government.* —**sys'tem•a•tize'** *v.*

sys•tem•at•ic (sĭs'tə măt'ĭk) *adj.* **1.** Carried on or done in a step-by-step way: *a systematic review.* **2.** Organized or methodical: *a systematic worker.*

sys•tem•ic (sĭ stĕm'ĭk) *adj.* **1.** Relating to an entire system: *The recession is not limited to one area of the economy, but is systemic.* **2.** Relating to or affecting the entire body: *systemic poisoning.*

S

Tt

t or **T** (tē) *n., pl.* **t's** or **T's.** The 20th letter of the English alphabet. ♦ **to a T.** Perfectly; precisely: *The jacket fit me to a T.*

T *abbr.* An abbreviation of temperature.

tab (tăb) *n.* **1.** A flap or short strip attached to an object to aid in handling or identifying it: *a pull tab on a soda can.* **2.** *Informal.* A bill, as for a meal in a restaurant: *I'll pay the tab.* ♦ **keep tabs on.** To watch or observe (sbdy./sthg.) carefully: *The teacher kept tabs on the children during the trip to the museum.* **run a tab.** To have an ongoing list of charges: *He ran a tab at the bar.*

Ta·bas·co (tə băs′kō). A trademark used for a spicy sauce made from a strong-flavored red pepper.

tab·by (tăb′ē) *n., pl.* **tab·bies.** A cat with striped gray or tan fur.

tab·er·na·cle (tăb′ər năk′əl) *n.* **1.** Often **Tabernacle.** A case or box on a church altar containing the consecrated bread and wine of Communion. **2.** A place of worship.

ta·ble (tā′bəl) *n.* **1.** A piece of furniture supported by one or more vertical legs and with a flat horizontal surface: *a wooden table.* **2.** The food and drink served at a meal: *sets a fine table.* **3.** The people assembled at a table, especially for a meal: *The entire table burst into laughter.* **4.** An orderly presentation of data, especially one in which the data are arranged in columns and rows. — *tr.v.* **ta·bled, ta·bling, ta·bles.** To postpone consideration of (sthg.); shelve: *table a piece of legislation.* ♦ **bring to the table.** To offer sthg. in trade or as one's share: *What do you bring to the table that this company might want?* **lay (one's) cards on the table.** To tell everything; be honest: *Let me lay my cards on the table for you.* **turn the tables on.** To reverse a bad situation so that one has the advantage: *Our team was losing until we turned the tables on our opponents in the final seconds of the game.* **under the table.** In secret: *The business deal was under the table.*

ta·ble·cloth (tā′bəl klôth′ *or* tā′bəl klŏth′) *n.* A cloth to cover a table, especially during a meal.

ta·ble·spoon (tā′bəl spoon′) *n.* **1.** A large spoon used for serving food. **2.** A cooking measure equal to three teaspoons or ½ fluid ounce (about 15 milliliters). See table at **measurement.**

ta·ble·spoon·ful (tā′bəl spoon foŏl′) *n.* The amount that a tablespoon can hold.

tab·let (tăb′lĭt) *n.* **1.** A pad of writing paper glued together along one edge. **2.** A small flat pellet of medicine to be taken orally: *an aspirin tablet.* **3.** A slab or plaque, as of stone, with a surface that has writing on it.

table tennis *n.* [U] A game similar to tennis, played on a table with wooden paddles and a small hollow plastic ball.

ta·ble·ware (tā′bəl wâr′) *n.* [U] The dishes, glassware, and silverware used in setting a table for a meal.

tab·loid (tăb′loid′) *n.* A small newspaper that presents the news in brief form and often contains a lot of sensational material.

ta·boo (tə boō′ *or* tă boō′) *n., pl.* **ta·boos.** A ban or an inhibition resulting from social custom or tradition. — *adj.* Excluded or forbidden from use, approach, or mention: *a taboo subject.*

tab·u·late (tăb′yə lāt′) *tr.v.* **tab·u·lat·ed, tab·u·lat·ing, tab·u·lates.** To arrange (information) in the form of a table; condense and list: *tabulate the results of a poll.* — **tab′·u·la′tion** *n.* [C; U]

ta·chom·e·ter (tə kŏm′ĭ tər) *n.* An instrument used to measure the rotations per minute of a rotating shaft.

tachometer

tac·it (tăs′ĭt) *adj.* Implied from actions; not spoken or written: *a tacit agreement.*

tac·i·turn (tăs′ĭ tûrn′) *adj.* Not inclined to talk much; silent: *She has a taciturn nature.*

tack (tăk) *n.* **1.** A short light nail with a sharp point and a flat head; a thumbtack. **2.** A course of action or an approach, especially when differing from a previous one: *try a new tack.* — *tr.v.* To fasten or attach (sthg.) with or as if with a tack: *She tacked the notice to the bulletin board.* ♦ **tack on.** *tr.v.* [sep.] To add (sthg.) to sthg. else: *The senator tacked a new measure on to a bill that would be passed.*

tack·le (tăk′əl) *n.* **1.** [U] The equipment used in a sport or an occupation, especially in fishing; gear. **2.** [C] In football: **a.** Either of the two line players on a team positioned between the guard and the end. **b.** The act of stopping an opposing player carrying the ball by seizing and throwing the player down. —*tr.v.* **tack·led, tack·ling, tack·les. 1.** To take on and wrestle with (an opponent or a problem, for example): *She tackled her brother after he kicked her. Let's tackle these math problems together.* **2.** In football, to seize and throw down (an opposing player carrying the ball). —**tack′ler** *n.*

tack·y¹ (tăk′ē) *adj.* **tack·i·er, tack·i·est.** Slightly gummy to the touch; sticky: *a tacky surface.*

tack·y² (tăk′ē) *adj.* **tack·i·er, tack·i·est.** *Informal.* Lacking style or good taste: *tacky clothes.* —**tack′i·ness** *n.* [U]

ta·co (tä′kō) *n., pl.* **ta·cos.** A corn tortilla folded around a filling such as ground meat or cheese.

tact (tăkt) *n.* [U] The ability to speak or act without offending others: *He has no tact whatsoever.* —**tact′ful** *adj.* —**tact′ful·ly** *adv.* —**tact′ful·ness** *n.* [U]

tac·tic (tăk′tĭk) *n.* A plan or measure for achieving a goal; a maneuver: *That company needs new marketing tactics for its products.*

tac·ti·cal (tăk′tĭ kəl) *adj.* **1.** Relating to or using tactics: *a tactical maneuver.* **2.** Characterized by cleverness or skill: *a tactical decision.*

tac·tics (tăk′tĭks) *n.* **1.** *(used with a singular verb).* The military science of positioning and directing forces against an enemy. **2.** *(used with a plural verb).* A set of plans or methods used to achieve a goal: *The company's tactics allowed it to put the competition out of business.*

tac·tile (tăk′təl *or* tăk′tīl′) *adj.* **1.** Capable of being felt by the sense of touch; tangible. **2.** Used for feeling: *tactile organs such as antennae.*

tact·less (tăkt′lĭs) *adj.* Lacking or showing a lack of tact; rude: *That remark about her appearance was tactless.* —**tact′less·ly** *adv.* —**tact′less·ness** *n.* [U]

tad (tăd) *n. (usually singular). Informal.* A small amount or degree: *I'll have just a tad more of the mashed potatoes.*

tad·pole (tăd′pōl′) *n.* A frog or toad in its early, newly hatched stage, when it lives in the water and has a tail and gills that disappear as the legs develop and the adult stage is reached.

taf·fy (tăf′ē) *n.* [U] A sweet chewy candy of molasses or brown sugar boiled until very thick and then pulled until the candy is glossy and holds its shape.

tag (tăg) *n.* **1.** [C] A strip, as of paper, metal, or leather, attached to sthg. or worn by sbdy. for the purpose of identifying, classifying, or labeling: *a name tag; a price tag.* **2.** [U] A children's game in which one player chases the others until he or she is able to touch one of them. **3.** [C] *Slang.* A graffiti writer's initials, nickname, or other identifying mark. —*tr.v.* **tagged, tag·ging, tags. 1.** To label, recognize, or identify (sbdy./sthg.) with or as if with a tag: *She tagged the teacher as hard to please.* **2.** To touch (sbdy.) in a game of tag. ♦ **tag along.** *intr.v.* To follow after; go with: *My little sister always wants to tag along.*

tail (tāl) *n.* **1.** The rear part of an animal, especially when it extends beyond the main part of the body: *a wagging tail.* **2.** The rear or bottom part: *the tail of a kite.* **3.** The rear part of the fuselage of an aircraft. **4.** A braid of hair; a pigtail. **5. tails.** *(usually used with a plural verb).* The side of a coin not having the principal design and the date: *heads or tails.* **6.** *Informal.* A person assigned to follow and report on sbdy. else: *The police put a tail on the suspect.* **7. tails.** A formal evening costume typically worn by men: *white tie and tails.* —*tr.v. Informal.* To follow and watch (sbdy.): *The detective tailed the suspect.* —**tail′less** *adj.*

HOMONYMS: tail, tale (story).

tail end *n.* **1.** The rear or last part: *Stay away from the tail end of that cow!* **2.** The very end: *the tail end of the day.*

tail·gate (tāl′gāt′) *n.* A hinged board or panel at the rear of a vehicle, such as a station wagon, that can be raised or lowered for loading and unloading. —*v.* **tail·gat·ed, tail·gat·ing, tail·gates.** —*tr.* To drive too closely behind (another vehicle): *That driver tailgated me for several blocks.* —*intr.* **1.** To follow another vehicle too closely: *If you tailgate, you might cause an accident.* **2.** *Informal.* To have a party at the back of a parked car before a sporting event: *We tailgated at every football game.*

tail·light (tāl′līt′) *n.* A red light or one of a pair mounted on the rear of a vehicle.

tai·lor (tā′lər) *n.* A person who makes, repairs, and alters garments such as suits, coats, and dresses. —*tr.v.* To make (sthg.), especially to specific requirements or measurements: *tailor a suit; tailor an insurance plan.*

tai·lored (tā′lərd) *adj.* **1.** Made especially for sbdy. Usually used of clothes: *a closet full of expensive tailored suits.* **2.** Simply designed; not frilly: *The clothes she wears to work are usually tailored.*

tail·pipe (tāl′pīp′) *n.* The pipe through which exhaust gases from an engine are discharged.

tail·spin (tāl′spĭn′) *n.* The rapid fall of an aircraft in a steep spiral spin.

tail wind *n.* A wind blowing in the same direction as a vehicle is traveling: *We made good time on the flight because of the tail wind.*
taint (tānt) *tr.v.* **1.** To affect (sbdy./sthg.) slightly with sthg. bad or undesirable: *a reputation that was tainted by rumors of unlawful activity.* **2.** To affect (sthg.) with decay or rot; spoil: *The fish was tainted.* —*n. (usually singular).* An infecting influence or trace: *The taint of corruption bankrupted the company.*
take (tāk) *v.* **took** (tŏŏk), **tak·en** (tā′kən), **tak·ing, takes.** —*tr.* **1.** To carry, lead, or cause (sbdy./sthg.) to go along to another place: *Don't forget to take your umbrella.* **2.** To remove (sbdy./sthg.) from a place: *take the dishes from the sink.* **3.** To hold (sthg.) with the hands; grip: *Take your partner's hand.* **4.** To capture (sthg.) physically; seize: *take an enemy fortress.* **5.** To apply oneself to the study of (a subject, for example): *take art lessons; take Spanish.* **6.** To use (sthg.) as a means of transportation: *take a train to Philadelphia.* **7.** To choose and then follow (a particular route or direction): *Take a right at the next corner.* **8.** To find or catch (sbdy.) in a particular situation: *Your actions took me by surprise.* **9.a.** To put (food or drink, for example) into the body: *took an aspirin.* **b.** To draw (sthg.) in; inhale: *took a deep breath.* **10.** To claim (sthg.) for oneself: *take all the credit.* **11.** To promise one's obedience to (sthg.): *take an oath.* **12.** To require or have (sthg.) as a proper accompaniment: *Intransitive verbs take no direct object. She takes cream in her coffee.* **13.** To pick (sthg.) out; select: *Take any card.* **14.** To begin to occupy (a place or position): *take a seat; take office.* **15.** To need or require (sthg.): *It takes money to live in that town. This camera takes 35mm film.* **16.** To get (sthg.), as through measurement, for example: *took the patient's temperature.* **17.** To accept or endure (sthg.): *He does not take criticism well.* **18.** To accept or believe (sthg.) as true: *I'll take your word.* **19.** To follow (a suggestion, for example): *I took your advice and studied for the exam.* **20.** To experience or feel (an emotion): *She takes pride in her work.* **21.** To subtract (a number or amount): *take 15 from 30.* —*intr.* **1.** To start growing; root or germinate: *Have the seeds taken?* **2.** To have the intended effect; operate or work: *The transfusion apparently took.* —*n.* **1.** An amount collected at one time, especially the profit or receipts of a business: *The manager counted today's take.* **2.** *Informal.* Opinion, understanding, or interpretation: *What's your take on the political situation?* **3.a.** A scene filmed or televised without stopping the camera. **b.** A recording made in a single session. ♦ **have**

what it takes. To be able: *I think he has what it takes to run this department.* **on the take.** *Informal.* Taking or trying to get bribes or illegal payments: *policemen on the take.* **take a breather.** To rest briefly: *Let's take a breather. We've been working for five hours straight now.* **take advantage of. 1.** To put (sthg.) to good use: *take advantage of the sale.* **2.** To use (sbdy./sthg.) unfairly and selfishly: *They took advantage of our friendship just to get a ride to the movies.* **take after.** *tr.v.* [insep.] To be like (sbdy.) in appearance, temperament, or character: *He takes after his grandfather.* **take apart.** *tr.v.* [sep.] To divide (sthg.) into parts; disassemble: *We had to take the chair apart to refinish it.* **take back.** *tr.v.* [sep.] To retract (sthg. stated or written): *I took back my promise when I saw I had been cheated.* **take care.** To be careful: *Take care when you cross the street.* **take care of.** To have responsibility for the support or treatment of (sbdy./sthg.): *I'm taking care of the puppy now.* **take charge.** To assume control or command: *He asked his assistant to take charge while he was away.* **take effect.** To become operative, as under law or regulation: *The new rules will take effect today.* **take five.** To rest briefly: *You've been working hard, so why don't you take five?* **take for a ride.** To deceive (sbdy.): *I'm going to break up with him; I think he's taking me for a ride.* **take for granted. 1.** To consider (sthg.) as true, real, and sure to happen: *The student took it for granted that he would pass the test.* **2.** To fail to appreciate the value of (sbdy./sthg.): *Her husband is angry at being taken for granted.* **take hold. 1.** [*of*] To seize, as by grasping: *Take hold of my hand.* **2.** To become established: *The new shrubs took hold on the hill.* **take in.** *tr.v.* [sep.] **1.** To receive (sbdy.) as a guest: *took him in for the night.* **2.** To reduce (sthg.) in size; make smaller: *He had to take in the slacks before he could wear them.* **3.** To understand (sthg.): *She explained the process, but I didn't take it all in.* **4.** To trick or deceive (sbdy.): *He was taken in by false promises.* **take into account.** To take (sthg.) into consideration: *The judge took the defendant's illness into account.* **take it.** To understand or assume: *I take it you don't like the idea.* **take it easy. 1.** To relax: *She's not doing anything but taking it easy tonight.* **2.** [*on*] To treat (sbdy./sthg.) more kindly or gently: *Take it easy on him; he didn't break your glasses on purpose.* **3.** To use less than one wants: *Take it easy on the milk; that's all we have.* **take it hard.** To suffer greatly: *When he divorced her, she really took it hard.* **take it or leave it.** To accept or refuse sthg. without changes or conditions:

That's my final offer; take it or leave it. **take it out on.** *Informal.* To treat (sbdy.) badly because of anger at sthg. else: *I know you're upset about your job, but don't take it out on your family.* **take off.** *tr.v.* [sep.] To remove (sthg.), as clothing: *took off our coats in the hallway.* —*intr.v.* **1.** *Slang.* To go; leave: *She took off early from practice.* **2.** To rise in flight: *The plane took off late.* **take on.** *tr.v.* [sep.] **1.** To undertake or begin to handle (sthg.): *took on some extra duties while a coworker was out sick.* **2.** To hire (sbdy.): *take on a new secretary.* **3.** To oppose (sbdy.) in competition: *The boxer offered to take on any opponent.* **take (one) for. 1.** To regard (sbdy./sthg.) as: *Many take him for a genius.* **2.** To consider (sbdy./sthg.) mistakenly: *The teacher took me for my sister.* **3.** To cheat (sbdy. for an amount of money): *You took me for $10 on those tickets!* **take (one's) time.** To act slowly or at one's chosen pace: *There's no hurry; take your time.* **take (one) up on.** *Informal.* To accept what (sbdy.) has offered as an invitation, for example: *I'll take you up on your offer of a ride.* **take out.** *tr.v.* [sep.] **1.** To remove (sthg.): *I had to have two teeth taken out.* **2.** *Informal.* To escort (sbdy.), as a date: *My brother took her out to dinner.* **take over,** *tr.v.* [sep.] To accept or claim the control or management of (sthg.): *He took over the business when his father retired.* **take part.** [*in*] To join in; participate: *He won't take part in such tasteless pranks.* **take place.** To happen; occur: *When did the event take place?* **take potshots at.** To criticize (sbdy.) in a sneaky, cowardly way: *She's always taking potshots at me at parties.* **take shape.** To come into being; form: *Our business plan is beginning to take shape.* **take sides.** To associate with and support a particular group, cause, or person: *Their father refused to take sides in the dispute.* **take to.** *tr.v.* [insep.] **1.** To hurry to (a place), as for safety: *took to the hills.* **2.** To become fond of or attached to (sbdy.): *The new kitten really took to me.* **take up.** *tr.v.* [sep.] **1.** To accept (an option, a bet, or a challenge) as offered: *We took up the challenge.* **2.** To develop an interest in or devotion to (sthg.): *She decided to take up stamp collecting.* —*intr.v.* To begin again: *Let's take up where we left off.* **take up with. 1.** *Informal.* To begin to associate with (sbdy.): *take up with the wrong people.* **2.** To discuss (a problem or complaint) with sbdy.: *You should take up those concerns with your doctor.* —**tak′er** *n.*

tak•en (tā′kən) *v.* Past participle of **take.** —*adj.* [*with; by*] Charmed or attracted: *She is quite taken with the puppy.* ◆ **be** or **get taken. 1.** To be cheated: *You were taken on that new car; I could have gotten it for you cheaper.* **2.** Occupied: *We were so late for the concert that our seats were already taken.*

take•off (tāk′ôf′ *or* tāk′ŏf′) *n.* **1.** The act or process of rising in flight. Used of an airplane or a rocket. **2.** *Informal.* An amusing imitation or parody: *Their group did a takeoff on a popular TV show.*

take•out (tāk′out′) *n.* [U] Food prepared and sold to be eaten off the premises: *Let's do takeout tonight instead of cooking.* —*adj.* Relating to such food: *We ordered takeout pizza.*

take•o•ver (tāk′ō′vər) *n.* The act or an instance of assuming control or management of sthg., especially the seizure of power: *the recent military takeover of industry.*

talc (tălk) *n.* [U] A fine-grained white, greenish, or gray mineral that has a soft soapy texture.

tal•cum powder (tăl′kəm) *n.* [U] A fine, often perfumed powder made from purified talc for use on the skin.

tale (tāl) *n.* **1.** Something told or related; a story: *Our grandfather told us a tale of suspense.* **2.** A falsehood; a lie: *Don't tell tales.*

HOMONYMS: tale, tail (rear part).

---

tal•ent (tăl′ənt) *n.* **1.** A marked natural ability, as for artistic accomplishment: *a person of many talents.* **2.** A person or group of people with such ability: *a great literary talent.* —**tal′ent•ed** *adj.*

tal•is•man (tăl′ĭs mən) *n., pl.* **tal•is•mans.** An object believed to give supernatural powers or protection to its bearer.

talk (tôk) *v.* —*intr.* **1.** To communicate by means of spoken language: *We talked for hours.* **2.** To say or pronounce words: *The baby can talk.* **3.** To imitate the sounds of human speech: *The parrot talks.* **4.** To express one's thoughts or emotions by means of a spoken language: *The couple talked about the issue.* See Synonyms at **speak. 5.** To express one's thoughts in writing: *The author of this book talks about geology.* **6.** To spread rumors; gossip: *If you do that, people will talk.* **7.** To reveal information concerning oneself or others, especially under pressure: *Has the prisoner talked?* —*tr.* **1.** To speak of or discuss (sthg.): *talk music; talk treason.* **2.** To speak or know how to speak in (a language): *talked French with the flight crew.* —*n.* **1.** [C] An exchange of ideas or opinions; a conversation: *I had a good talk with her.* **2.** [C] A speech or lecture: *The professor gave a talk on Mozart.* **3.** [U] Rumor or speculation: *just talk, with no basis in fact.* **4.** [U] A subject of conversation: *a musical that is the talk of the town.* **5.** [U] Empty speech or unnecessary discussion: *all talk and no action.* **6.** [U] A particular manner of speech: *baby talk.* ◆ **big talk.** Exaggerated claims; bragging: *Don't believe half of what he tells you; it's all big talk.* **talk back.** *intr.v.* To make a rude reply: *You'll be sorry if you talk back.* **talk big.** To exaggerate about sthg.: *Oh,* *she talks big, but it amounts to nothing.* **talk down to.** To speak to (sbdy.) as if the listener were stupid or less important: *The speaker talked down to the young audience.* **talk (one) into.** To persuade (sbdy. to do sthg.): *He talked me into seeing that movie, and now I'm glad.* **talk (one) out of.** To persuade (sbdy. not to do sthg.): *They finally talked me out of buying that expensive sports car.* **talk (one's) ear off.** To talk at great length without letting the other person say anything: *Once she gets started on that subject she'll talk your ear off.* **talk (oneself) blue in the face.** To urge sbdy. to do sthg. without succeeding: *He's talked himself blue in the face about saving money, but his son won't listen.* **talk (one's) way out of.** To get out of a bad situation by talking: *She can talk her way out of anything.* **talk out.** *tr.v.* [sep.] To discuss (sthg.) until everyone is pleased: *If you're angry with me about something, let's talk it out.* **talk out of both sides of (one's) mouth.** To contradict oneself: *Corporate executives are talking out of both sides of their mouths when they try to justify downsizing: Look at how much money they're paid!* **talk over.** *tr.v.* [sep.] To consider (sthg.) thoroughly in conversation; discuss: *We talked over the problem and decided what to do.* **talk sense.** To give sensible opinions: *My parents are so upset that they aren't capable of talking sense.* **talk up.** *tr.v.* [sep.] To speak in favor of (sthg.); promote: *The salesman talked up the new product.*

talk·a·tive (tô′kə tĭv) *adj.* Tending to talk a great deal: *You aren't very talkative this morning.* —**talk′a·tive·ly** *adv.* —**talk′a·tive·ness** *n.* [U]

talk·er (tô′kər) *n.* A person who talks, especially a talkative person.

talk show *n.* A TV or radio program on which people answer questions about themselves or discuss a topic.

tall (tôl) *adj.* **1.** Having greater than ordinary height: *a tall tree.* **2.** Having a specified height: *a plant three feet tall.* **3.** *Informal.* Exaggerated or boastful: *a tall tale.* —*adv.* With proud bearing; straight: *stand tall.* —**tall′ness** *n.* [U]

tal·ly (tăl′ē) *n., pl.* **tal·lies.** A list or score: *Keep a tally of daily expenses.* —*v.* **tal·lied, tal·ly·ing, tal·lies.** —*tr.* **1.** To list or record (sthg.): *We tallied our bill.* **2.** To cause (sthg.) to correspond or agree: *Don't forget to tally the two columns.* —*intr.* To be alike; agree: *The two sets of figures don't tally.*

tal·on (tăl′ən) *n.* The claw of a bird or an animal that seizes other animals as prey.

tam·bou·rine (tăm′bə rēn′) *n.* A percussion instrument like a small drum with small metal disks fitted into the rim that jingle when the instrument is struck or shaken.

tame (tām) *adj.* **tam·er, tam·est. 1.** Brought from wildness into a domesticated state: *a tame wolf.* **2.** Naturally unafraid; not timid: *The dodo bird was very tame and soon became extinct.* **3.** Yielding; docile: *a tame gesture of defeat.* **4.** Unexciting; dull: *The ride home seemed very tame after watching the car race.* —*tr.v.* **tamed, tam·ing, tames. 1.** To make (sthg.) tame; domesticate: *tame a wild horse.* **2.** To subdue or curb (sthg.): *The child tamed her natural curiosity.* —**tame′ly** *adv.* —**tame′ness** *n.* [U] —**tam′er** *n.*

tam·per (tăm′pər) *intr.v.* [with] **1.** To interfere in a harmful manner: *caught tampering with the switches.* **2.** To engage in secret or improper dealings, as in an effort to influence: *a lawyer accused of trying to tamper with the jury.*

tam·pon (tăm′pŏn′) *n.* A plug of absorbent material that a woman inserts into her vagina to absorb menstrual blood.

tan[1] (tăn) *v.* **tanned, tan·ning, tans.** —*tr.* **1.** To convert (animal skins) into leather. **2.** To make (sthg.) brown by exposure to the sun: *tanned her arms.* —*intr.* To become brown from exposure to the sun: *She tans easily.* —*n.* **1.** [U] A light yellowish brown color. **2.** [C] The brown color that sun rays give to the skin: *got a tan at the beach.* —*adj.* **tan·ner, tan·nest. 1.** Light yellowish brown. **2.** Having a suntan: *a tan face.* —**tan′ning** *n.* [U]

tan[2] *abbr.* An abbreviation of tangent.

tan·dem (tăn′dəm) *n.* **1.** A two-wheeled carriage drawn by horses harnessed one before the other. **2.** An arrangement of two or more people or things placed one behind the other: *A tandem of cars waited in front of the hotel.* **3.** A bicycle built for two riders in such an arrangement. —*adv.* One behind the other: *riding tandem.* ♦ **in tandem.** Together: *The companies are working in tandem to develop new products.*

tang (tăng) *n.* [U] **1.** A sharp distinctive flavor, taste, or odor, as that of orange juice. **2.** A trace or hint of sthg.: *The tang of doubt remained in the air.* —**tang′y** *adj.*

tan·gent (tăn′jənt) *adj.* Making contact at a point or along a line; touching but not intersecting: *a dirt road tangent to the highway.* —*n.* **1.** A line, curve, or surface touching but not intersecting another. **2.** A sudden digression or change of course: *go off on a different tangent.* —**tan·gen′tial** (tăn jĕn′shəl) *adj.* —**tan·gen′tial·ly** *adv.*

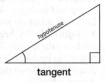

tangent

tan·ger·ine (tăn'jə rēn' *or* tăn'jə rēn') *n.* A fruit related to the orange but somewhat smaller, having deep orange skin that peels easily, or the tree it grows on.

tan·gi·ble (tăn'jə bəl) *adj.* **1.** Capable of being touched: *a tangible product like steel.* **2.** Capable of being treated as fact; real or concrete: *tangible evidence.* **3.** Capable of being understood or realized: *a tangible benefit.* —*n.* **1.** [U] Something concrete: *remain focused on the tangible.* **2. tangibles.** Material assets. —**tan'gi·bly** *adv.*

tan·gle (tăng'gəl) *v.* **tan·gled, tan·gling, tan·gles.** —*tr.* **1.** To mix or intertwine (sthg.) in a confused mass; snarl: *A bad cast tangled my fishing line.* **2.** To catch or hold (sthg.) in or as if in a net; entrap: *Don't tangle me in your office intrigues.* —*intr.* **1.** To be or become entangled: *The kite tangled in the tree's branches.* **2.** *Informal.* To enter into an argument, dispute, or conflict: *We tangled over the wording of our editorial.* —*n.* **1.** A confused snarled mass: *a tangle of vines.* **2.** A confused state or condition: *a tangle of lies.* **3.** *Informal.* An argument: *They got into a tangle over who should go first.*

tan·gled (tăng'gəld) *adj.* **1.** Snarled or twisted together: *tangled hair.* **2.** Confused and complicated: *tangled thoughts.*

tan·go (tăng'gō) *n., pl.* **tan·gos. 1.** A Latin American ballroom dance in 2/4 or 4/4 time. **2.** The music for this dance. —*intr.v.* To perform this dance.

tank (tăngk) *n.* **1.a.** A large, often metallic container for holding or storing fluids or gases: *a gasoline tank.* **b.** The amount that such a container can hold: *Buy a tank of gas.* **2.** An enclosed, heavily armored military vehicle with a cannon and guns and moving on treads. —*v.* ◆ **tank up.** *Informal. intr.v.* [*on*] To fill up: *Let's tank up on gas before we leave.* —*tr.v.* [*sep.*] To fill (sbdy./sthg.) up: *We tanked the baby up on milk before his nap.*

tank·er (tăng'kər) *n.* A ship, truck, or plane equipped to transport liquids, such as oil, in bulk: *an oil tanker.*

tank top *n.* A sleeveless, close-fitting, usually knit shirt with wide shoulder straps.

tan·ta·lize (tăn'tə līz') *tr.v.* **tan·ta·lized, tan·ta·liz·ing, tan·ta·liz·es.** To excite (sbdy.) by presenting sthg. desirable while keeping it out of reach: *His boss tantalized him with the promise of a raise.*

tan·ta·liz·ing (tăn'tə lī zǐng) *adj.* Very appealing and desirable; mouthwatering: *a tantalizing glimpse of the dessert.*

tan·ta·mount (tăn'tə mount') *adj.* Equivalent in effect or value: *a rule tantamount to a dictatorship.*

tan·trum (tăn'trəm) *n.* A fit of bad temper: *Your son had a tantrum in school today.*

tap¹ (tăp) *v.* **tapped, tap·ping, taps.** —*tr.* **1.** To strike (sbdy./sthg.) gently with a light blow or blows: *tap him on the shoulder.* **2.** To give a light rap with (sthg.): *tap a pencil on the desk.* —*intr.* To deliver a gentle light blow or blows: *tap on the window.* —*n.* **1.** A gentle blow: *give the jar a tap.* **2.** The sound made by such a blow: *I thought I heard a tap on the window.*

tap² (tăp) *n.* **1.** A valve and spout used to regulate the flow of a fluid at the end of a pipe. **2.** A small electronic device used to listen secretly to conversations: *The police put a tap on the phone.* —*tr.v.* **tapped, tap·ping, taps. 1.** To pierce (sthg.) in order to draw off liquid: *tap a maple tree.* **2.** To draw (liquid) from a vessel or container: *tap a barrel.* **3.** To put a tap on (a telephone). ◆ **on tap.** Ready to be drawn; in a tapped cask: *beer on tap.*

tap dance *n.* [U] A dance in which the rhythm is sounded out by the clicking taps on the heels and toes of a dancer's shoes. —**tap'-dance'** (tăp'dăns') *v.* —**tap dancer** *n.*

tape (tāp) *n.* **1.** [C; U] A continuous narrow, flexible strip of cloth, metal, paper, or plastic: *adhesive tape; magnetic tape; ticker tape.* **2.** [C] A blank or recorded audiotape or videotape: *I bought a new reggae tape.* —*tr.v.* **taped, tap·ing, tapes. 1.** To fasten, wrap, or bind (sthg.) with tape: *tape a bow on a package; tape a sprained wrist.* **2.** To record (sounds or pictures) on magnetic tape: *tape the show to watch it later.*

tape deck *n.* A tape recorder and player having no built-in amplifiers or speakers, used as a component in an audio system.

tape measure *n.* A tape of cloth, paper, or metal marked off in a scale, as of inches or centimeters, used for taking measurements.

tape player *n.* A machine for playing back recorded magnetic tapes, having a built-in amplifier and speakers.

ta·per (tā'pər) *n.* **1.** [C] A small or slender candle. **2.** [U] A gradual decrease in thickness or width of an elongated object: *the taper of a cone.* —*v.* —*intr.* To become gradually thinner toward one end: *a candle tapering to a point.* —*tr.* To make (sthg.) thinner or narrower at one end: *tapered the board to fit the slot.* ◆ **taper off.** *intr.v.* To lessen gradually: *The storm began to taper off.*

tape-re·cord (tāp'rǐ kôrd') *tr.v.* To record (sthg.) on magnetic tape: *tape-record a song.*

tape recorder *n.* A mechanical device for recording on magnetic tape and usually for playing back the recorded material.

tape recording *n.* **1.** [C] A magnetic tape on which sound or visual images have been recorded. **2.** [U] The act of recording on magnetic tape.

tap·es·try (tăp'ǐ strē) *n., pl.* **tap·es·tries.** A heavy cloth woven with rich, often many-colored designs and scenes, usually hung on walls for decoration and sometimes used to cover furniture.

T

taps (tăps) *pl.n. (used with a singular or plural verb).* A bugle call or drum signal sounded at night, as at a military camp as an order to put out lights, or at funerals and memorial services.

tar (tär) *n.* [U] A thick oily black mixture consisting mainly of hydrocarbons, used on roads and roofs. —*tr.v.* **tarred, tar·ring, tars.** To coat (sthg.) with or as if with tar: *The workers tarred the roof yesterday.*

ta·ran·tu·la (tə răn′chə lə) *n.* A large, hairy, mostly tropical spider that has a painful but not seriously poisonous bite.

tar·dy (tär′dē) *adj.* **tar·di·er, tar·di·est.** **1.** Late; delayed: *a tardy guest.* **2.** Moving slowly; sluggish: *tardy acceptance of new ideas.* —**tar′di·ly** *adv.* —**tar′di·ness** *n.* [U]

tar·get (tär′gĭt) *n.* **1.** An object that is shot at to test accuracy in rifle or archery practice: *She hit the target with the arrow.* **2.** Something aimed or fired at: *The target of the snowball was a trash can.* **3.** An object of criticism or attack: *the target of her anger.* **4.** A desired goal or aim: *the target of the research program.* ♦ **be on target.** To be correct or accurate: *Her predictions about the stock market were on target.*

target
Archery target

tar·iff (tăr′ĭf) *n.* **1.** A list or system of duties imposed by a government on imported or exported goods. **2.** A duty or duties imposed by a government on imported or exported goods: *a tariff on wool.*

tar·nish (tär′nĭsh) *v.* —*tr.* **1.** To dull the luster of (sthg.); discolor: *Being in the ground for so long had tarnished the old coins.* **2.** To detract from or stain (sthg.); disgrace: *The scandal tarnished his reputation.* —*intr.* **1.** To lose luster; become discolored: *The silver cup tarnished as it sat on the shelf.* **2.** To diminish or become tainted: *The luster of his fame has tarnished.* —*n.* [U] **1.** The condition of being tarnished. **2.** Discoloration of a metal surface, as from oxidation.

tarp (tärp) *n. Informal.* A tarpaulin.

tar·pau·lin (tär pô′lĭn *or* tär′pə lĭn) *n.* A sheet of material, such as waterproof canvas, used to cover and protect things from moisture: *Put a tarpaulin over the boat.*

tar·ra·gon (tăr′ə gŏn′) *n.* [U] The mildly spicy pleasant-smelling leaves of a plant native to Europe and Asia, used to flavor salads and cooked foods.

tar·ry (tăr′ē) *intr.v.* **tar·ried, tar·ry·ing, tar·ries.** *Formal.* **1.** To delay or be late in

coming, going, or doing: *The children tarry on the way to school.* **2.** To remain or stay temporarily, as in a place: *Tarry for just a moment.*

tart[1] (tärt) *adj.* **1.** Having a sharp pungent taste; sour: *tart apples.* **2.** Sharp or bitter in tone or meaning; biting: *a tart answer.* —**tart′ly** *adv.* —**tart′ness** *n.* [U]

tart[2] (tärt) *n.* A small pie with a sweet filling and no crust on top: *a strawberry tart.*

tar·tar (tär′tər) *n.* [U] A hard yellowish deposit that collects on the teeth, consisting of food particles and secretions.

tartar sauce *n.* [C; U] Mayonnaise mixed with chopped onion, olives, and pickles and served as a sauce with fish.

task (tăsk) *n.* **1.** A piece of work assigned or done as part of one's duties: *daily tasks.* **2.** A difficult or tedious undertaking: *the task of building a nation.* ♦ **take to task.** To scold sbdy.: *The teacher took all of us to task for not doing our homework.*

SYNONYMS: task, job, chore, assignment. These nouns mean a piece of work that one must do. **Task** means a well-defined responsibility that is sometimes burdensome and is usually required by sbdy. else: *The receptionist's main task is to answer the telephones.* **Job** often means a specific short-term piece of work: *We spent the day doing odd jobs around the house.* **Chore** often means a minor, routine, or odd job: *I have to finish my chores before I'm allowed to go out.* **Assignment** usually means a task given to one by a person in authority: *For tonight's assignment, read the first chapter.*

---

task force *n.* A temporary grouping of forces and resources for a specific goal: *a military task force.*

tas·sel (tăs′əl) *n.* **1.** A bunch of loose threads or cords bound at one end and hanging free at the other, used as an ornament on curtains and clothing. **2.** Something resembling such an ornament, especially the pollen-bearing flower cluster of a corn plant.

taste (tāst) *v.* **tast·ed, tast·ing, tastes.** —*tr.* **1.** To distinguish the flavor of (sthg.) by taking it into the mouth: *Taste this stew.* **2.** To eat or drink a small quantity of (sthg.): *I've already eaten, so I'll just taste the salmon.* **3.** To try (sthg.) for the first time; experience: *tasted freedom and loved it.* —*intr.* **1.** To distinguish flavors in the mouth: *I can't taste because I have a cold.* **2.** To have a distinct flavor: *The stew tastes salty.* **3.** To eat or drink a small amount: *She never eats; she just tastes.* —*n.* **1.** [C; U] The sense that distinguishes the sweet, sour, salty, and bitter qualities of substances in contact with the tongue. **2.** [C; U] A sensation produced by this sense; a flavor: *the taste of choco-late*. **3.** [C] *(usually singular)*. A distinctive perception as if by the sense of taste: *an experience that left a bad taste in my mouth*. **4.** [C] A small quantity eaten or tasted: *Have a taste of this*. **5.** [C] *(usually singular)*. A limited or first experience; a sample: *a taste of responsibility*. **6.** [C] *(usually singular)*. A personal preference or liking: *a taste for mysteries*. **7.** [U] The ability to appreciate what is beautiful or excellent: *good taste in clothes*. **8.** [U] The sense of what is least likely to offend in a given social situation: *a remark made in bad taste*.

taste•ful (tāst'fəl) *adj*. Having or showing good taste: *a tasteful reply*. —**taste'ful•ly** *adv*. —**taste'ful•ness** *n*. [U]

taste•less (tāst'lĭs) *adj*. **1.** Lacking in flavor: *a tasteless dish*. **2.** Having or showing poor taste: *a tasteless remark*. —**taste'-less•ly** *adv*. —**taste'less•ness** *n*. [U]

tast•y (tā'stē) *adj*. **tast•i•er, tast•i•est**. Having a pleasing flavor: *a tasty meal*. —**tast'i•ly** *adv*. —**tast'i•ness** *n*. [U]

tat•ter (tăt'ər) *n*. **1.** A torn and hanging piece of cloth; a shred. **2. tatters**. Torn and ragged clothing; rags. —*tr.v*. To make (sthg.) ragged: *That wind tattered the flag*.

tat•tered (tăt'ərd) *adj*. **1.** Torn into shreds; ragged: *tattered clothes*. **2.** Dressed in ragged clothes: *a tattered little boy*. **3.** Ruined: *tattered dreams*.

tat•tle (tăt'l) *intr.v*. **tat•tled, tat•tling, tat•tles. 1.** To reveal the plans or activities of another; gossip: *The boy tattled on his sister*. **2.** To talk idly; prattle: *He tattled endlessly over the book*. —**tat'tler** *n*.

tat•tle•tale (tăt'l tāl') *n*. A person who tattles on others: *My little sister is such a tattletale*.

tat•too (tă tōō') *n., pl*. **tat•toos**. A permanent mark or design made on the skin by a process of pricking and inserting dye or by raising scars. —*tr.v*. To mark (the skin) with a tattoo.

taught (tôt) *v*. Past tense and past participle of **teach**.

HOMONYMS: taught, taut (tight).

taunt (tônt) *tr.v*. To mock or reproach (sbdy.) in an insulting or scornful manner: *The bully taunted the small boy*. —*n*. A scornful remark; a jeer: *His taunts could be heard on the corner*.

Tau•rus (tôr'əs) *n*. **1.** [U] The second sign of the zodiac in astrology. **2.** [C] A person born under this sign, between April 20 and May 20.

taut (tôt) *adj*. **1.** Pulled or drawn tight: *sails taut with wind*. **2.** Strained; tense: *taut nerves*. **3.** Kept in trim shape; neat: *a taut, youthful body*. —**taut'ly** *adv*. —**taut'ness** *n*. [U]

HOMONYMS: taut, taught (instructed).

tav•ern (tăv'ərn) *n*. A place licensed to sell alcoholic beverages to be consumed on the premises.

taw•dry (tô'drē) *adj*. **taw•dri•er, taw•dri•est**. Cheap and gaudy in nature or appearance: *tawdry clothes; a tawdry remark*. —**taw'dri•ness** *n*. [U]

taw•ny (tô'nē) *adj*. Light brown to brownish orange in color.

tax (tăks) *n*. **1.** A contribution for the support of the government required of persons, groups, or businesses within the domain of that government: *a state gasoline tax*. **2.** A burdensome or excessive demand; a strain: *The extra orders are a tax on our system of production*. —*tr.v*. **1.** To place a tax on (sthg.): *tax cigarettes*. **2.** To require a tax from (sbdy.): *tax the people*. **3.** To make difficult or excessive demands upon (sbdy./sthg.): *Don't tax my patience*. —**tax'a•ble** *adj*.

tax•a•tion (tăk sā'shən) *n*. [U] The act or practice of imposing taxes: *no taxation without representation*.

tax•i (tăk'sē) *n., pl*. **tax•is** or **tax•ies**. A taxicab. —*intr.v*. **tax•ied, tax•i•ing** or **tax•y•ing, tax•ies** or **tax•is. 1.** To be transported by taxi: *We taxied up and down the island*. **2.** To move slowly over the surface of the ground or water before takeoff or after landing: *The airplane taxied to the runway*.

tax•i•cab (tăk'sē kăb') *n*. An automobile that carries passengers for a fare, usually calculated on a meter.

tax•ing (tăk'sĭng) *adj*. Difficult and physically or mentally exhausting: *Cleaning out the garage was taxing work*.

tax•on•o•my (tăk sŏn'ə mē) *n., pl*. **tax•on•o•mies**. [C; U] The science of classifying organisms into specially named groups based on shared characteristics and natural relationships: *plant taxonomies*. —**tax'o•nom'ic** (tăk'sə nŏm'ĭk) *adj*.

tax•pay•er (tăks'pā'ər) *n*. A person who pays or is required to pay taxes.

TB also **T.B.** *abbr*. An abbreviation of tuberculosis.

tbs. *abbr*. An abbreviation of: **1.** Tablespoon. **2.** Tablespoonful.

tbsp. *abbr*. An abbreviation of: **1.** Tablespoon. **2.** Tablespoonful.

tea (tē) *n*. **1.** [C; U] The young dried leaves of an eastern Asian evergreen shrub or small tree having fragrant white flowers and glossy leaves, or the plant that bears such leaves. **2.** [C; U] An aromatic beverage made by steeping tea leaves or other leaves and spices in hot water. **3.a.** *Chiefly British*. [U] A light afternoon meal consisting usually of sandwiches and cakes served with tea. **b.** [C] An afternoon reception or social gathering at which tea is served.

HOMONYMS: tea, tee (peg for a golf ball).

T

teach (tēch) *v.* **taught** (tôt), **teach·ing**, **teach·es.** —*tr.* **1.** To give knowledge or skill to (sbdy.): *He teaches children.* **2.** To provide knowledge of (sthg.); give instruction in: *She teaches math.* **3.** To advocate or preach (sthg.): *teach religious tolerance.* **4.** To carry on instruction on a regular basis in (sthg.): *taught third grade for years.* —*intr.* To give instruction or be employed as a teacher: *He's taught for six years.* —**teach'er** *n.*

SYNONYMS: teach, train, instruct, educate, school. These verbs mean to pass on knowledge or skill. **Teach** is the most general: *Your sister can teach you how to ride a bicycle.* **Train** means to teach particular skills intended to fit a person for a certain role, such as a job: *It is the manager's responsibility to train all new employees.* **Instruct** usually means to teach in an organized way: *The manual instructs you how to assemble the stereo.* **Educate** often means to instruct in a formal way: *They wanted their children to be educated in the very best schools.* **School** often means to teach with a hard, demanding process: *The violinist has been schooled to practice slowly.*

teach·a·ble (tē'chə bəl) *adj.* **1.** Capable of being taught: *Geometry is a teachable subject.* **2.** Able and willing to be taught: *teachable students.*

teach·ing (tē'chĭng) *n.* **1.** [U] The act, practice, occupation, or profession of a teacher: *Teaching is a challenging profession.* **2.** [C] Something taught, especially a precept or doctrine: *the teachings of Confucius.*

tea·cup (tē'kŭp) *n.* A small cup for drinking tea.

teak (tēk) *n.* [C; U] A tall Asian tree or its hard, strong, heavy wood, used for furniture and shipbuilding.

tea·ket·tle (tē'kĕt'l) *n.* A covered kettle with a spout and handle, used for boiling water, as for tea.

teal (tēl) *n.* [U] A dark blue-green color. —*adj.* Dark blue-green.

team (tēm) *n.* **1.** A group on the same side, as in a game: *a baseball team.* **2.** Two or more people organized to work together: *a team of scientists.* —*v.* —*tr.* To join (sbdy./sthg.) together so as to form a team: *We could team your sister with mine.* —*intr.* [up] To form a team or an association: *We teamed up to clean the beach.* —SEE NOTE at **collective noun.**

HOMONYMS: team, teem (abound).

team·mate (tēm'māt') *n.* A member of one's own team.

team·ster (tēm'stər) *n.* A truck driver.

team·work (tēm'wûrk') *n.* [U] Cooperative effort by members of a group or team to achieve a common goal: *Teamwork will enable us to finish on time.*

tea·pot (tē'pŏt') *n.* A covered pot with a handle and spout, used for making and pouring tea.

tear¹ (târ) *v.* **tore** (tôr), **torn** (tôrn), **tear·ing**, **tears.** —*tr.* **1.** To pull (sthg.) apart or into pieces by force: *Tear the paper in half.* See Synonyms at **rip. 2.** To make (an opening) by ripping: *I tore a hole in my pants.* **3.** To injure (sbdy./sthg.) by cutting or ripping: *I tore my elbow when I fell.* **4.** To separate (sthg.) forcefully: *We tore the wrapping off the present.* **5.** To divide or disrupt (sbdy.) emotionally: *He is torn between duty and loyalty to his friends.* —*intr.* **1.** To become torn: *Her pants tore.* **2.** To move with great speed; rush headlong: *He went tearing into town.* —*n.* **1.** The act of tearing: *I heard a tear as I got out of the car.* **2.** The result of tearing; a rip or rent: *a tear in his coat.* ◆ **tear around.** *intr.v.* To hurry; rush here and there: *She tears around but accomplishes nothing.* **tear at.** *tr.v.* [insep.] To claw at (sthg.): *Anxious to be in the lake, he tore at his clothes.* **tear down.** *tr.v.* [sep.] **1.** To demolish (sthg.): *They had to tear down what was left of the building after the fire.* **2.** To criticize (sbdy./sthg.) in a mean way: *He's always tearing her down in public.* **tear into.** *tr.v.* [sep.] **1.** To criticize (sbdy.) violently: *She tore into me for being late.* **2.** To eat (sthg.) quickly: *He tore into his food as if someone might take it from him.* **tear (oneself) away.** To leave (sbdy./sthg.) unwillingly: *Can you tear yourself away from the TV?* **tear up.** *tr.v.* [sep.] To tear (sthg.) to pieces: *Tear up the letter when you've read it.*

tear² (tîr) *n.* A drop of the clear salty liquid secreted by glands of the eyes. —*intr.v.* To fill with tears: *The vapor of an onion will make your eyes tear.*

HOMONYMS: tear², tier (row).

tear·drop (tîr'drŏp') *n.* **1.** A tear. **2.** An object shaped like a tear.

tear·ful (tîr'fəl) *adj.* **1.** Filled with or accompanied by tears: *a tearful farewell.* **2.** So piteous as to bring forth tears: *a tearful movie.* —**tear'ful·ly** *adv.* —**tear'ful·ness** *n.* [U]

tear gas (tîr) *n.* [U] Any of various chemicals that when dispersed as a gas or mist irritate the eyes and breathing passages severely, causing choking and heavy tears: *The police used tear gas on the crowd.*

tease (tēz) *v.* **teased, teas·ing, teas·es.** —*tr.* **1.** To annoy (sbdy./sthg.): *teasing the cat by* *pulling its tail.* **2.** To make fun of (sbdy.): *My sister used to tease me a lot.* **3.** To brush or comb (the hair) toward the scalp for a full, airy effect. —*intr.* To annoy or make fun of persistently: *Quit teasing!* —*n.* A person or a remark that teases: *Don't be such a tease.*

tea•spoon (tē′spo͞on′) *n.* **1.** The common small spoon used especially in serving and consuming coffee, tea, and desserts. **2.** A household cooking measure equal to ⅓ tablespoon (about 5 milliliters). See table at **measurement.**

tea•spoon•ful (tē′spo͞on fo͞ol′) *n.* The amount that a teaspoon can hold.

teat (tēt *or* tĭt) *n.* The part of an udder on a female animal through which milk is taken; a nipple.

tech. *abbr.* An abbreviation of: **1.** Technical. **2.** Technician.

tech•ni•cal (tĕk′nĭ kəl) *adj.* **1.** Relating to or derived from technique: *technical ability.* **2.** Used in or peculiar to a particular subject; specialized: *technical language.* **3.** Relating to or involving the practical, mechanical, or industrial arts or the applied sciences: *a technical school.* **4.** Industrial and mechanical; technological: *technical assistance overseas.* **5.** According to a principal or rule, especially in sports. *a technical foul.* —**tech′ni•cal′i•ty** (tĕk′nĭ kăl′ĭ tē) *n.* —**tech′ni•cal•ly** *adv.*

tech•ni•cian (tĕk nĭsh′ən) *n.* A person who is skilled in a certain technical field or process: *a dental technician.*

tech•nique (tĕk nēk′) *n.* **1.** [C] A method for performing a complicated task, as in a science or an art. **2.** [U] Skill in handling such methods: *As a pianist, she has nearly perfect technique.*

tech•nol•o•gy (tĕk nŏl′ə jē) *n., pl.* **tech•nol•o•gies.** **1.** [U] The use of scientific knowledge to solve practical problems, especially in industry and commerce. **2.** [C; U] The methods and materials used to solve practical problems: *aerospace technology.* —**tech′no•log′i•cal** (tĕk′nə lŏj′ĭ kəl) *adj.* —**tech′no•log′i•cal•ly** *adv.* —**tech•nol′o•gist** *n.*

ted•dy bear (tĕd′ē) *n.* A child's toy bear, usually stuffed with soft material.

te•di•ous (tē′dē əs) *adj.* Tiresome because of dullness or length; boring: *a tedious lecture.* See Synonyms at **boring.** —**te′di•ous•ly** *adv.* —**te′di•ous•ness** *n.* [U]

te•di•um (tē′dē əm) *n.* [U] The quality or condition of being tedious; boredom: *the tedium of waiting in lines all day.*

tee (tē) *n.* **1.** A small peg stuck in the ground to support a golf ball for a shot. **2.** A raised area from which a golfer hits the first shot toward a hole. —*v.* **teed, tee•ing, tees.** ✦ **tee off.** *intr.v.* To drive a golf ball from a tee or start a golf game: *They teed off at 10:00.* —*tr.v.* [sep.]

Slang. To make (sbdy.) angry or irritated: *Our boss was teed off again.*

HOMONYMS: tee, tea (drink).

teem (tēm) *intr.v.* To be full of things; swarm: *The pond teemed with insects.*

HOMONYMS: teem, team (group).

teen (tēn) *n.* **1. teens. a.** The numbers 13 through 19. **b.** The 13th through 19th items in a series or scale, as years of a century or degrees of temperature: *Temperatures fell into the teens last night.* **2.** A teenager.

teen•age or **teen-age** (tēn′āj′) also **teen•aged** or **teen-aged** (tēn′ājd′) *adj.* Relating to people aged 13 through 19: *a teenage boy.*

teen•ag•er (tēn′ā′jər) *n.* A person between the ages of 13 and 19.

tee•ny (tē′nē) also **teen•sy** (tēn′sē) *adj.* **tee•ni•er, tee•ni•est** also **teen•si•er, teen•si•est.** *Informal.* Tiny: *He has a teeny earring in his left ear.*

tee•pee (tē′pē) *n.* Variant of **tepee.**

tee shirt *n.* Variant of **T-shirt.**

tee•ter (tē′tər) *intr.v.* **1.** To walk or move unsteadily; totter: *The baby teetered at first when she started to walk.* **2.** To be in a dangerously unsteady position or condition: *The world teetered on the edge of war again.*

tee•ter-tot•ter (tē′tər tŏt′ər) *n.* A seesaw.

teeth (tēth) *n.* Plural of **tooth.**

teethe (tēth) *intr.v.* **teethed, teeth•ing, teethes.** To have teeth coming through the gums: *The baby is teething now.*

tee•to•tal•er or **tee•to•tal•ler** (tē′tōt′-l ər) *n.* A person who drinks no alcoholic beverages: *My uncle was a teetotaler.*

Tef•lon (tĕf′lŏn′) A trademark for a durable plastic used to coat certain cooking utensils and to prevent sticking of machine parts.

tel. *abbr.* An abbreviation of: **1.** Telegram. **2.** Telegraph. **3.** Telephone.

tele– *pref.* A prefix that means: **1.** Distance; distant: *telemetry.* **2.** Telegraph or telephone: *telegram.* **3.** Television: *telecast.*

tel•e•cast (tĕl′ĭ kăst′) *tr.v.* **tel•e•cast** or **tel•e•cast•ed, tel•e•cast•ing, tel•e•casts.** To broadcast (a program or programs) by television: *The presidential debate was telecast all over the world.* —*n.* A television broadcast.

tel•e•com•mu•ni•ca•tions (tĕl′ĭ kə-myo͞o′nĭ kā′shənz) *n.* [U] *(used with a singular verb).* The science and technology of sending messages over long distances, especially by electronic means: *Telecommunications is a rapidly changing field.*

tel•e•gram (tĕl′ĭ grăm′) *n.* A message transmitted by telegraph.

tel•e•graph (tĕl′ĭ grăf′) *n.* **1.** [U] A communications system in which a message in the form of electric impulses is sent, either by

T

wire or radio, to a receiving station. **2.** [C] A message sent by such a system; a telegram. —*tr.v.* **1.** To transmit (a message) by telegraph: *telegraph our congratulations.* **2.** To send or convey a message to (sbdy.) by telegraph. —**tel′e·graph′ic** *adj.* —**te·leg′ra·phy** (tə lĕg′rə fē) *n.* [U]

tel·e·mar·ket·ing (tĕl′ə mär′kĭ tĭng) *n.* [U] Use of the telephone in marketing goods or services. —**te′le·mar′ket·er** *n.*

te·lem·e·try (tə lĕm′ĭ trē) *n.* [U] The automatic measurement and transmission of data from a distant source to a receiving station.

te·lep·a·thy (tə lĕp′ə thē) *n.* [U] Communication from one mind to another through means other than the senses. —**tel′e·path′ic** (tĕl′ə păth′ĭk) *adj.*

tel·e·phone (tĕl′ə fōn′) *n.* A device for sending speech or other sounds over a distance. —*tr.v.* **tel·e·phoned, tel·e·phon·ing, tel·e·phones. 1.** To call or communicate with (sbdy.) by telephone: *She telephoned me last night.* **2.** To transmit (sthg.) by telephone: *We telephoned our thanks.*

tel·e·scope (tĕl′ĭ skōp′) *n.* A device that uses an arrangement of lenses, mirrors, or both to observe or photograph distant objects. —*tr.v.* **tel·e·scoped, tel·e·scop·ing, tel·e·scopes. 1.** To cause (sthg.) to slide inward or outward in overlapping sections, as the tube sections of a small hand telescope. **2.** To make (sthg.) briefer; condense: *telescoping several instructions for a recipe into one sentence.* —**tel′e·scop′ic** (tĕl′ĭ skŏp′ĭk) *adj.*

tel·e·thon (tĕl′ə thŏn′) *n.* A lengthy television program to raise funds for a charity.

tel·e·vise (tĕl′ə vīz′) *tr.v.* **tel·e·vised, tel·e·vis·ing, tel·e·vis·es.** To broadcast (sthg.) by television: *Four channels televised the presidential debate.*

tel·e·vi·sion (tĕl′ə vĭzh′ən) *n.* **1.** [U] The sending and receiving of visual images, usually with sound, as electrical waves through the air or through wires. **2.** [C] A device that receives such electrical waves and reproduces the images on a screen: *a brand-new television.* **3.** [U] The industry of producing and broadcasting television programs: *He works in television.*

tell (tĕl) *v.* **told** (tōld), **tell·ing, tells.** —*tr.* **1.** To give an account of (sthg.); describe or relate: *tell a story.* **2.** To express (sthg.) in words; say: *tell the truth.* **3.** To make (sthg.) known; indicate: *The temperature of something tells how hot or cold it is.* **4.** To discover (sthg.) by observation; identify: *It is hard to tell how far a teacher's influence extends.* **5.** To command (sbdy./sthg.); order: *told us to stand in line.* —*intr.* **1.** To give an account or a description of sthg.: *You said you'd tell about*

your vacation. **2.** [*on*] To reveal secrets; inform: *You shouldn't tell on your friends.* ♦ **tell apart.** *tr.v.* [sep.] To be able to identify (people or things); distinguish: *Can you tell the twins apart?* **tell it like it is.** To describe sthg. accurately; tell the truth: *Don't lie to me; tell it like it is.* **tell off.** *tr.v.* [sep.] To speak angrily to (sbdy. who has done wrong): *When he didn't call for two weeks, the woman told her friend off.* **tell the difference.** To be able to identify; distinguish: *He can't tell the difference between regular coffee and decaf.*

tell·er (tĕl′ər) *n.* **1.** A person who tells: *a teller of tall tales.* **2.** A bank employee who receives and pays out money: *The bank teller cashed the check for us.*

tell·ing (tĕl′ĭng) *adj.* Having force and producing a striking effect: *a telling remark.* —**tell′ing·ly** *adv.*

tell·tale (tĕl′tāl′) *adj.* Serving to indicate or reveal: *a telltale sign.*

temp (tĕmp) *n.* A person who performs office work on a temporary basis, as needed: *At Christmas, we hire temps to help with the extra work.*

temp. *abbr.* An abbreviation of: **1.** Temperature. **2.** Temporary.

tem·per (tĕm′pər) *tr.v.* **1.** To lessen the harshness or intensity of (sthg.); moderate: *tempering justice with mercy; temper your enthusiasm.* **2.** To harden or strengthen (metal or glass) by applying heat or by heating and cooling: *temper steel.* —*n.* **1.** [C; U] A state of mind or emotions: *an even temper.* **2.** [U] Calmness of mind or emotions; control: *Don't lose your temper.* **3.** [U] A tendency to become angry or irritable: *She has a quick temper.* **4.** [U] The degree of hardness and elasticity of steel.

tem·per·a·ment (tĕm′prə mənt *or* tĕm′-pər ə mənt) *n.* [C; U] The manner of thinking or behaving characteristic of a person: *a nervous temperament.*

tem·per·a·men·tal (tĕm′prə mĕn′tl *or* tĕm′pər ə mĕn′tl) *adj.* Very sensitive or irritable: *a temperamental person.*

tem·per·ate (tĕm′pər ĭt *or* tĕm′prĭt) *adj.* Characterized by moderate temperatures, weather, or climate; neither hot nor cold: *temperate weather; a temperate climate.*

tem·per·a·ture (tĕm′pər ə chŏŏr′ *or* tĕm′prə chŏŏr′) *n.* **1.a.** [C; U] The relative hotness or coldness of a body or an environment: *The temperature is below freezing.* **b.** [C] A numerical measure of hotness or coldness on a standard scale: *What's the temperature today?* **2.** [C] (*usually singular*). An abnormally high body temperature that is caused by a disease or disorder; a fever: *She has a temperature of 102°.*

ă-**cat**; ā-**pay**; âr-**care**; ä-**father**; ĕ-**get**; ē-**be**; ĭ-**sit**; ī-**nice**; îr-**here**; ŏ-**got**; ō-**go**; ô-**saw**; oi-**boy**; ou-**out**; ŏŏ-**took**; ōō-**boot**; ŭ-**cut**; ûr-**word**; th-**thin**; th-**this**; hw-**when**; zh-**vision**; ə-**about**; N-French **bon**

tem·pest (tĕm′pĭst) *n.* **1.** A violent storm. **2.** A violent fuss; an uproar. ◆ **tempest in a teapot.** Extreme upset about sthg. that is not important: *She was angry about the insult, but it was only a tempest in a teapot.*

tem·pes·tu·ous (tĕm pĕs′chōō əs) *adj.* **1.** Relating to or resembling a tempest: *tempestuous winds.* **2.** Violent; noisy: *a tempestuous meeting.* —**tem·pes′tu·ous·ly** *adv.* —**tem·pes′tu·ous·ness** *n.* [U]

tem·plate (tĕm′plĭt) *n.* A pattern or gauge, such as a thin metal plate cut to a definite pattern, used in making sthg. accurately, as in carpentry.

tem·ple¹ (tĕm′pəl) *n.* A building for religious ceremonies or worship: *the temple of Athena.*

tem·ple² (tĕm′pəl) *n.* Either of the flat regions at the sides of the head next to the forehead.

tem·po (tĕm′pō) *n., pl.* **tem·pos. 1.** The relative speed at which music is or ought to be played. **2.** A characteristic rate or rhythm of sthg.; a pace: *the tempo of life in a city.*

tem·po·ral (tĕm′pər əl *or* tĕm′prəl) *adj.* **1.** Relating to or limited by time: *temporal boundaries.* **2.** Relating to worldly affairs, especially as distinguished from religious concerns: *the temporal powers of the church.*

tem·po·rar·y (tĕm′pə rĕr′ē) *adj.* Used or enjoyed for a limited time only; not permanent: *a temporary job.* —*n., pl.* **tem·po·rar·ies.** *Informal.* An employee who works for a limited time only: *Her position is being filled for now by a temporary.*

tempt (tĕmpt) *tr.v.* **1.** To invite or attract (sbdy.): *Your offer tempts me.* **2.** To provoke or risk provoking (sbdy./sthg.): *Do not tempt fate.*

temp·ta·tion (tĕmp tā′shən) *n.* **1.** [U] The act of tempting or the condition of being tempted. **2.** [C] Something tempting or appealing: *Desserts were a real temptation for her.*

tempt·ing (tĕmp′tĭng) *adj.* Having strong appeal; attractive: *a tempting offer.*

ten (tĕn) *n.* **1.** The number, written 10, that is equal to 9 + 1. **2.** The tenth in a set or sequence. —**ten** *adj. & pron.*

te·na·cious (tə nā′shəs) *adj.* **1.** Holding or tending to hold firmly to sthg., such as a point of view: *a man tenacious in his convictions.* **2.** Tending to retain; retentive: *a tenacious memory.* —**te·nac′i·ty** (tə năs′ĭ tē) *n.* [U]

ten·an·cy (tĕn′ən sē) *n., pl.* **ten·an·cies. 1.** [U] Possession or occupancy of lands, buildings, or other property, as by lease or rent. **2.** [C] The period of a tenant's occupancy or possession.

ten·ant (tĕn′ənt) *n.* **1.** A person who pays rent to use or occupy property owned by another. **2.** A dweller in a place; an occupant.

tend¹ (tĕnd) *intr.v.* **1.** To incline toward: *Pressure at the office tends to make her grouchy.* **2.** To be inclined: *She tends toward conservatism in economic matters.*

tend² (tĕnd) *v.* —*tr.* To have the care of (sbdy./sthg.); look after: *tend a sick child; tend a sales counter.* —*intr.* [*to*] To apply one's attention; attend: *tend to one's own business.*

ten·den·cy (tĕn′dən sē) *n., pl.* **ten·den·cies. 1.** A characteristic likelihood: *Linen has a tendency to wrinkle.* **2.** A leaning or an inclination to think, act, or behave in a certain way: *He has a tendency to write long sentences.*

ten·der¹ (tĕn′dər) *adj.* **1.** Easily crushed or bruised; fragile: *tender flowers.* **2.** Easily chewed or cut: *a tender steak.* **3.** Young and vulnerable: *of tender age.* **4.a.** Easily hurt; sensitive: *tender skin.* **b.** Painful; sore: *a tender tooth.* **5.** Gentle and loving: *a tender heart; a tender glance.*

ten·der² (tĕn′dər) *n.* **1.** A formal offer or bid. **2.** Something, especially money, offered in payment: *legal tender.* —*tr.v.* To offer (sthg.) formally: *tender a letter of resignation.*

ten·der·heart·ed (tĕn′dər här′tĭd) *adj.* Easily moved by another's distress; compassionate.

ten·der·ize (tĕn′də rīz′) *tr.v.* **ten·der·ized, ten·der·iz·ing, ten·der·iz·es.** To make (meat) tender, as by marinating or pounding. —**ten′der·iz′er** *n.*

len·dor·loin (tĕn′dər loin′) *n.* The tenderest part, as of a loin of beef.

ten·don (tĕn′dən) *n.* A band of tough fibrous tissue that connects a muscle to a bone.

ten·dril (tĕn′drəl) *n.* **1.** One of the slender coiling parts resembling stems by means of which a climbing plant clings to sthg. for support. **2.** Something, such as a ringlet of hair, that is long, slender, and curling.

ten·e·ment (tĕn′ə mənt) *n.* An apartment house that is poorly maintained and often overcrowded.

ten·et (tĕn′ĭt) *n.* An opinion, a doctrine, or a principle held as being true by a person or an organization: *the tenets of democracy.*

ten·nis (tĕn′ĭs) *n.* [U] A game played with rackets and a light ball by two players or two pairs of players on a rectangular court, as of grass or clay, divided by a net.

tennis shoe *n.* A sneaker.

ten·or (tĕn′ər) *n.* **1.** [C] A continuous unchanging course: *The tenor of his career has been steadily upwards.* **2.** [U] The general meaning; drift: *He knew enough German to get the tenor of what was being said.* **3.** [C] **a.** The highest natural adult male voice. **b.** A man with such a voice.

tense¹ (tĕns) *adj.* **tens·er, tens·est. 1.** Taut; tightly stretched: *tense muscles.* **2.** Characterized by nervous tension or suspense: *a tense situation.* —*tr. & intr.v.* **tensed, tensing, tens·es.** To make or become tense: *When he's angry, he tenses his jaw. I could feel my neck muscles tense up.*

tense[2] (těns) *n.* In grammar: **1.** Any of the forms of a verb that show the time, such as past or present, and continuance or completion of the action or state. **2.** A set of verb forms indicating a particular time: *the future tense.*

ten·sion (těn'shən) *n.* **1.** [U] The condition of being stretched; tightness. **2.** [C; U] **a.** A force that tends to stretch out sthg. **b.** A measure of such a force: *a tension of 50 pounds.* **3.** [C; U] Mental, emotional, or nervous strain: *working under great tension.* **4.** [C; U] Unfriendliness or hostility between persons or groups: *tension among the teammates.*

tent (těnt) *n.* A portable shelter stretched over a supporting framework of poles with ropes and pegs.

ten·ta·cle (těn'tə kəl) *n.* One of the narrow, flexible parts extending from the body of certain animals, such as an octopus or a jellyfish, that are used for feeling, grasping, or moving.

ten·ta·tive (těn'tə tǐv) *adj.* **1.** Not fully worked out or agreed on: *a tentative production schedule.* **2.** Uncertain; hesitant: *After the accident, her movements were tentative.*

tenth (těnth) *n.* **1.** The ordinal number matching the number ten in a series. **2.** One of ten equal parts. —**tenth** *adv. & adj.*

ten·u·ous (těn'yōō əs) *adj.* **1.** Long and thin: *a tenuous nylon rope.* **2.** Having little substance; flimsy: *the tenuous character of his political ideas.* —**ten'u·ous·ly** *adv.* —**ten'u·ous·ness** *n.* [U]

ten·ure (těn'yər) *n.* **1.** [C; U] The holding of sthg. in one's possession, as an office; an occupation: *the tenure of a senator.* **2.a.** [C] The period of holding sthg.: *during our senator's tenure in office.* **b.** [U] The status of holding one's position on a permanent basis: *academic tenure.*

te·pee *also* **tee·pee** (tē'pē) *n.* A portable dwelling of certain Native American peoples, consisting of a conical framework of poles covered with skins or bark.

tep·id (těp'ĭd) *adj.* Moderately warm; lukewarm: *tepid water.*

te·qui·la (tə kē'lə) *n.* [U] An alcoholic liquor made from the juice of the Central American century plant.

term (tûrm) *n.* **1.a.** A limited period of time: *They worked in a mine for a term.* **b.** An assigned period for a person to serve: *She served a six-year term as senator.* **2.a.** A word or group of words having a particular meaning: *He used a few medical terms.* **b. terms.** Language of a certain kind; chosen words: *He praised her work in glowing terms.* **3.** (*usually plural*). An element of an agreement; a condition: *peace terms.* **4. terms.** The relation between two persons or groups: *We're on good* terms with the neighbors. —*tr.v.* To call (sbdy./ sthg.) by a particular term or name; designate: *They termed the freedom fighters "terrorists."*
♦ **bring to term.** To successfully complete a pregnancy: *The baby was brought to term in spite of some problems.* **come to terms. 1.** To reach an agreement: *Labor and management came to terms yesterday.* **2.** [*with*] To resolve or accept (sthg.): *She finally come to terms with her brother's death.* **in no uncertain terms.** Clearly and forcefully: *His father told him in no uncertain terms to be home by ten.* **in terms of.** Concerning; about: *We're uncertain in terms of his ability to do the job.*

ter·mi·nal (tûr'mə nəl) *adj.* Causing or ending in death; fatal: *a terminal disease.* —*n.* **1.** A point at which another conductor can be connected to an electric device or part. **2.** The station at the end of a railway, a bus line, or an airline. **3.** A device, often having a keyboard and a video display, through which data or information can enter or leave a computer system.

ter·mi·nate (tûr'mə nāt') *v.* **ter·mi·nat·ed, ter·mi·nat·ing, ter·mi·nates.** —*tr.* **1.** To bring (sthg.) to an end or a halt: *terminate an employee's contract.* **2.** To occur at or form the end of (sthg.); conclude: *A sonata terminated the concert.* —*intr.* **1.** To come to an end: *The lecture terminated in a question-and-answer period.* **2.** To have as an end or a result: *The negotiations terminated in a new treaty.* —**ter'mi·na'tion** *n.* [C; U]

ter·mi·nol·o·gy (tûr'mə nŏl'ə jē) *n., pl.* **ter·mi·nol·o·gies.** [C; U] The group of technical terms used in a particular trade, science, or art: *medical terminology.*

ter·mite (tûr'mīt') *n.* A white insect that lives in large colonies and feeds on and destroys wood.

tern (tûrn) *n.* A sea bird related to and resembling gulls, but generally smaller and with a forked tail.

HOMONYMS: tern, turn (rotate).

ter·race (těr'ĭs) *n.* **1.** A platform extending outdoors from a floor of a house or an apartment building. **2.** An open area adjacent to a house; a patio. —*tr.v.* **ter·raced, ter·rac·ing, ter·rac·es.** To form (sthg.) into a terrace or terraces: *terraced the hillside.*

ter·ra cot·ta (těr'ə kŏt'ə) *n.* [U] A hard, waterproof ceramic clay used in pottery and building construction.

terra fir·ma (fûr'mə) *n.* [U] Solid ground; dry land: *It was good to be back on terra firma after our long ocean voyage.*

ter·rain (tə rān′) *n*. [C; U] An area of land; a region: *The trail led us over some rough terrain.*

ter·res·tri·al (tə rĕs′trē əl) *adj*. **1.** Relating to the planet Earth or its inhabitants: *The craters of the moon look like some terrestrial craters.* **2.** Living or growing on land: *terrestrial snails.*

ter·ri·ble (tĕr′ə bəl) *adj*. **1.** Causing great alarm or fear; dreadful: *a terrible storm.* **2.** Extreme in extent or degree: *the terrible heat in the tropics.* **3.** Unpleasant; disagreeable: *We had a terrible time at the party.* **4.** Very bad in quality: *a terrible movie.* —**ter′ri·bly** *adv*.

ter·ri·er (tĕr′ē ər) *n*. A usually small active dog originally used for hunting.

ter·rif·ic (tə rĭf′ĭk) *adj*. **1.** Causing terror or great fear; terrifying: *a terrific storm.* **2.** Very bad or unpleasant: *a terrific headache.* **3.** Very good: *a terrific party.* **4.** Very great: *a train moving at a terrific speed.* —**ter·rif′i·cal·ly** *adv*.

ter·ri·fy (tĕr′ə fī′) *tr.v*. **ter·ri·fied, ter·ri·fy·ing, ter·ri·fies.** To fill (sbdy./sthg.) with terror; alarm: *Heights terrified her.* See Synonyms at **frighten**.

ter·ri·to·ri·al (tĕr′ĭ tôr′ē əl) *adj*. **1.** Relating to the geographic area under a given jurisdiction: *the territorial waters of Mexico.* **2.** Relating or limited to a particular territory; regional: *Dogs are territorial animals.*

ter·ri·to·ry (tĕr′ĭ tôr′ē) *n., pl*. **ter·ri·to·ries. 1.** [C; U] An area of land; a region. **2.** [C] The land and waters under the jurisdiction of a government. **3.** [C] Also **Territory.** A political subdivision of a country, especially one that is not a state but has its own legislature. **4.** [C] An area for which a person is responsible as a representative or an agent: *Oregon is his territory for sales.* **5.** [C] An area in which an animal lives and from which it keeps out intruders, especially others of the same species. ◆ **go** or **come with the territory.** To be included with or be part of a job: *No one likes to clean a house, but it comes with the territory.*

ter·ror (tĕr′ər) *n*. **1.** [C; U] Intense overpowering fear. **2.** [C] A cause of intense fear: *Outlaws were the terror of the ranchers.* **3.** [U] Violence committed by a group in order to frighten people or accomplish a goal, especially as part of a political policy: *Airplane hijacking is a tactic of terror.*

ter·ror·ism (tĕr′ə rĭz′əm) *n*. [U] The unlawful use of violence to frighten people or accomplish a goal, often for political reasons: *Nothing justifies terrorism.* —**ter′ror·ist** *adj. & n*.

ter·ror·ize (tĕr′ə rīz′) *tr.v*. **ter·ror·ized, ter·ror·iz·ing, ter·ror·iz·es. 1.** To fill or overpower (sbdy.) with terror: *You shouldn't terrorize small children.* **2.** To force (sbdy. to do sthg.) by fear and threats.

terse (tûrs) *adj*. **ters·er, ters·est.** Brief and to the point; concise: *Give that letter a terse reply.* —**terse′ly** *adv*. —**terse′ness** *n*. [U]

test (tĕst) *n*. **1.** A means of determining the presence, quality, or truth of sthg.; a trial: *a vision test.* **2.** A series of questions, problems, or physical responses designed to determine knowledge, intelligence, or ability: *Our class had a spelling test on Friday.* **3.** A basis for evaluation or judgment: *This slope will provide a good test of our skiing skills.* **4.** A process used to discover the presence of substances, such as disease germs of a particular type: *a blood test.* —*v*. —*tr*. To subject (sbdy./sthg.) to a test: *test one's strength; test a food for purity.* —*intr*. To undergo a test, especially with an indicated result: *The ore tested high in uranium content.* —**test′er** *n*.

tes·ta·ment (tĕs′tə mənt) *n*. **1.** Something that serves as tangible proof or evidence: *testament to his honesty.* **2.** A statement of belief; a credo. **3.** A document providing for the disposing of a person's property after death; a will: *prepare a last will and testament.*

test-drive (tĕst′drīv′) *tr.v*. **test-drove** (tĕst′drōv′), **test-driv·en** (tĕst′drĭv′ən), **test-driv·ing, test-drives.** To drive (a motor vehicle) to test its performance and condition: *Let's test-drive the car before we buy it.*

tes·tes (tĕs′tēz) *pl.n*. The pair of reproductive glands in the male in which sperm is produced.

tes·ti·cle (tĕs′tĭ kəl) *n*. One of the testes, especially one contained within a scrotum.

tes·ti·fy (tĕs′tə fī′) *v*. **test·i·fied, test·i·fy·ing, test·i·fies.** —*intr*. **1.** To make a declaration of truth or fact under oath: *Two witnesses testified against him in court.* **2.** To express or declare a strong belief. —*tr*. **1.** To declare (sthg.) publicly; make known: *I'll testify that he's a good cook.* **2.** To state or affirm (sthg.) under oath: *She testified in court that she saw the defendant.*

tes·ti·mo·ni·al (tĕs′tə mō′nē əl) *n*. **1.** A statement in support of a particular fact, truth, or claim: *The salesperson had testimonials for the quality of the rug.* **2.** A statement or letter affirming the quality of another's character or worth; a recommendation: *Testimonials poured in praising the mayor's performance.*

tes·ti·mo·ny (tĕs′tə mō′nē) *n., pl*. **tes·ti·mo·nies. 1.** [C; U] A declaration by a witness under oath: *give testimony in a case.* **2.** [U] Evidence in support of a fact or an assertion; proof: *testimony to your good character.*

tes·tos·ter·one (tĕs tŏs′tə rōn′) *n*. [U] A hormone produced primarily in the testes and responsible for male secondary sex characteristics.

tes·ty (tĕs′tē) *adj*. **tes·ti·er, tes·ti·est.** Easily angered; touchy or impatient: *I was testy after being stuck in traffic.* —**tes′ti·ly** *adv*. —**tes′ti·ness** *n*. [U]

T

tet·a·nus (tĕt′n əs) *n.* [U] A serious, often fatal disease caused by bacteria that generally enter the body through a deep wound.

tête-à-tête (tāt′ə tāt′ *or* tĕt′ə tĕt′) *n.* A private conversation between two people: *We had a tête-à-tête about her work.*

teth·er (tĕ*th*′ər) *n.* A rope or chain that keeps an animal within a small area. —*tr.v.* To fasten or restrict (sbdy./sthg.) with or as if with a tether: *Tether your horse to that post.* ◆ **at the end of (one's) tether** or **rope.** At the limits of one's resources or abilities: *He's an overworked intern at the end of his tether.*

tet·ra·he·dron (tĕt′-rə hē′drən) *n., pl.* **tet·ra·he·drons** or **tet·ra·he·dra** (tĕt′-rə hē′drə). A solid geometric shape with four triangular faces.

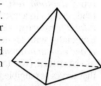
tetrahedron

Tex. *abbr.* An abbreviation of Texas.

text (tĕkst) *n.* **1.** [U] The main part of a written work. **2.** [C; U] A subject; a topic: *the text of a discussion.* **3.** [C] A textbook: *Open your texts to Chapter Three.* —**tex′tu·al** (tĕks′chōō əl) *adj.* —**tex′tu·al·ly** *adv.*

text·book (tĕkst′bŏŏk′) *n.* A book used in schools or colleges for the formal study of a subject.

tex·tile (tĕks′tīl′ *or* tĕks′təl) *n.* **1.** [C] A cloth or fabric, especially when woven or knitted. **2.** [U] Fiber or yarn for weaving or knitting into cloth.

tex·ture (tĕks′chər) *n.* [C; U] **1.** The structure of the interwoven threads or strands of a fabric: *Burlap has a coarse texture.* **2.** The feel of a surface: *The plaster gives the wall a rough texture.*

—**th** *suff.* A suffix used to form ordinal numbers: *seventh; hundredth.*

than (thăn *or* thən) *conj.* Used to introduce the second element or clause of an unequal comparison: *She's a better skier than I am.* —*prep.* In comparison with: *We admire no one more than him.*

thank (thăngk) *tr.v.* To express gratitude to (sbdy.): *We thanked her for the kind offer.*

thank·ful (thăngk′fəl) *adj.* Showing or feeling gratitude; grateful: *thankful to be alive.* —**thank′ful·ly** *adv.* —**thank′ful·ness** *n.* [U]

thank·less (thăngk′lĭs) *adj.* Not likely to be appreciated: *a thankless task.*

thanks (thăngks) *pl.n.* An acknowledgment of a favor or gift: *send thanks for a party.* —*interj.* An expression used to show gratitude: *Thanks!* ◆ **thanks to.** On account of; because of: *Thanks to you she has a job.*

Thanks·giv·ing (thăngks gĭv′ĭng) *n.* A holi-day for giving thanks, celebrated in the United States on the fourth Thursday of November and in Canada on the second Monday of October.

that (*thăt or thət*) *pron., pl.* **those** (*thōz*). **1.** Used to refer to the one mentioned or understood: *What kind of soup is that?* **2.** Used to indicate the farther or less immediate one: *That is for sale; this is not.* **3. those.** Used to indicate an unspecified number of people: *those who refused to join.* **4.** Used as a relative pronoun to introduce a clause, especially a restrictive clause: *the car that has the flat tire.* **5.** In, on, by, or with which: *each summer that the concerts are performed.* —*adj., pl.* **those.** **1.** Referring to the one identified or understood: *that place; those mountains.* **2.** Referring to the one less obvious: *That route is shorter than this one.* —*adv.* To such an extent or degree: *Is your problem that complicated?* —*conj.* **1.** Used to introduce a subordinate clause stating a result, wish, purpose, reason, or cause: *We hope that you will enjoy the book.* **2.a.** Used to introduce a subordinate clause modifying an adverb or adverbial expression: *The dogs will go anywhere that they are welcome.* **b.** Used to introduce a subordinate clause that is joined to an adjective or a noun as a complement: *I was sure that she was right. He has a feeling that interest rates will rise soon.* ◆ **all that.** Whatever remains; and so on: *At our fitness center, you can ride a bike, swim, lift weights, and all that.* **at that. 1.** The end of sthg.: *If he apologizes, maybe they'll leave it at that.* **2.** In addition; too: *He grabbed what he wanted and left, and didn't even pay us at that!*

that is. To explain more clearly; in other words: *The office is on the first floor, that is, the floor at street level.*

thatch (thăch) *n.* **1.** [U] Plant stalks or leaves, such as straw, reeds, or palm fronds, used for roofing. **2.** [C] Something resembling this, such as a thick growth of hair on the head: *a thatch of red hair.* —*tr.v.* To cover (sthg.) with or as if with thatch: *thatch a roof.*

thaw (thô) *v.* —*intr.* **1.** To change from a frozen solid to a liquid by gradual warming; melt: *The ice on the pond thawed in the warm sun.* **2.** To lose stiffness or numbness by being warmed: *My feet thawed by the fire.* **3.** To become warm enough for snow and ice to melt: *It often thaws in January.* **4.** To become less formal or reserved: *Relations between the countries began to thaw.* —*tr.* (sthg.) to thaw: *thaw the frozen chicken for dinner.* —*n.* A period of warm weather during which snow and ice melt: *the January thaw.*

the[1] (*thē* before a vowel; *thə* before a consonant) *def. art.* **1.** Used before nouns or noun phrases that refer to specified persons or things: *The pen that I was looking for was under the newspaper.* **2.** Used before a noun to stress its uniqueness or importance: *Last night's party was the event of the year.* **3.** Used before a singular noun to make it general: *The Siberian tiger is an endangered species.* **4.** Used before a proper name, as of a monument or ship: *the Alamo.* **5.** Used before an adjective to make it function as a noun and signify a class: *the rich and the powerful.* —SEE NOTE at **article.**

the² (thē before a vowel; thə before a consonant) *adv.* **1.** Because of that: *She thinks the better of you.* **2.** To that extent; by that much: *the sooner the better.* **3.** Used with a superlative: *Of all my cousins, I like you the best.*

the•a•ter or **the•a•tre** (thē′ə tər) *n.* **1.** [C] A building, a room, or an outdoor structure where plays or movies are presented. **2.** [U] Dramatic literature or its performance; drama: *He's majoring in theater.* **3.** [C] A place that is the setting for dramatic events: *the theater of politics.*

the•at•ri•cal (thē ăt′rĭ kəl) *adj.* **1.** Relating to or suitable for the theater. **2.** Marked by showy or exaggerated behavior; overly dramatic: *had a theatrical way of saying good-bye —n. (usually plural).* Stage performances, or a stage performance, especially by amateurs. —**the•at′ri•cal•ly** *adv.*

theft (thĕft) *n.* [C; U] The act or an instance of stealing; larceny: *the theft of our car.*

their (thâr) *adj.* The possessive form of **they.** Belonging to or relating to them: *Pittsburgh is their home town.*

HOMONYMS: their, there (at that place), **they're** (they are).

---

theirs (thârz) *pron. (used with a singular or plural verb).* The one or ones belonging to them: *If your car is not working, use theirs.*

them (thĕm *or* thəm) *pron.* The object pronoun form of **they: 1.** Used as the direct object of a verb: *I helped them fix their car.* **2.** Used as the indirect object of a verb: *I gave them an answer.* **3.** Used as the object of a preposition: *I saved the best seats for them.* —SEE NOTE at **me.**

the•mat•ic (thĭ măt′ĭk) *adj.* Relating to or being a theme or themes. —**the•mat′i•cal•ly** *adv.*

theme (thēm) *n.* **1.** A topic of speech or piece of writing. See Synonyms at **subject. 2.** A short written composition, especially a school composition.

theme park *n.* An amusement park with rides and activities relating to a single topic such as a historical event, science and technology, or wildlife.

them•selves (thĕm sĕlvz′ *or* thəm sĕlvz′) *pron.* The ones that are the same as them: **1.a.** Used as the direct or indirect object of a verb

or as the object of a preposition, to show that the action of the verb refers back to the subject: *They prepared themselves for the trip. The travelers gave themselves plenty of time. They saved the best for themselves.* **b.** Used to give emphasis: *The cooks themselves will eat in the kitchen.* **2.** Their normal or healthy selves: *After getting over their jet lag, they feel like themselves again.*

then (thĕn) *adv.* **1.** At that time: *We were younger then.* **2.** Next in time, space, or order: *We'll get ice cream, and then we'll go home.* **3.** Moreover; besides: *The meal was expensive, and then we also had to leave a tip.* **4.** In that case; therefore: *If x equals 11 and y equals 3, then xy equals 33. —n.* That time or moment: *From then on, we were close friends.* ♦ **and then some.** *Informal.* More in addition: *I made enough to serve all the guests and then some.* **then and there.** At that moment; immediately: *We decided then and there to buy this house.*

thence (thĕns *or* thĕns) *adv. Formal.* From there on: *We flew to Chicago and thence to St. Louis.*

thence•forth (thĕns fôrth′ *or* thĕns fôrth′) *adv. Formal.* From that time forward; thereafter: *Thenceforth she stopped attending class.*

the•o•lo•gi•an (thē′ə lō′jən) *n.* A person who has studied theology.

the•ol•o•gy (thē ŏl′ə jē) *n., pl.* **the•ol•o•gies.** [C; U] The study of the nature of God and religious ideas. —**the′o•log′i•cal** (thē′ə lŏj′ĭ kəl) *adj.*

the•o•rem (thē′ər əm *or* thîr′əm) *n.* A mathematical statement that can be proved true or false.

the•o•ret•i•cal (thē′ə rĕt′ĭ kəl) *adj.* **1.** Relating to theory: *a theoretical discussion.* **2.** Not proven; not practical: *theoretical physics.* —**the′o•ret′i•cal•ly** *adv.*

the•o•rize (thē′ə rīz′) *intr.v.* **the•o•rized, the•o•riz•ing, the•o•riz•es.** To make up a theory or theories; guess: *theorize about the purpose of life.*

the•o•ry (thē′ə rē *or* thîr′ē) *n., pl.* **the•o•ries. 1.** A statement or set of statements designed to explain an event or a group of events. **2.** A belief that guides action: *We went fishing on the theory that the rain would cause the fish to bite.* **3.** An assumption based on limited information or knowledge; a guess. —**the′o•re•ti′cian** (thē′ər ĭ tĭsh′ən), **the′o•rist** *n.*

ther•a•peu•tic (thĕr′ə pyōō′tĭk) *adj.* Used for healing or curing: *a therapeutic bath.* —**ther′a•peu′ti•cal•ly** *adv.*

ther•a•py (thĕr′ə pē) *n., pl.* **ther•a•pies. 1.** [C; U] A process designed to heal or cure an illness or a disability: *physical therapy.* **2.** [U] Psychotherapy: *a therapy group.* **3.** [U] Healing power or quality: *the therapy of fresh air and exercise.* —**ther′a•pist** *n.*

T

there (thâr) *adv.* **1.** At or in that place: *Set the package over there.* **2.** To or toward that place: *How long did it take to get there?* **3.** At that moment or point: *The violins come in there.* **4.** In that matter: *I can't agree with you there.* —*pron.* **1.** Used as the subject of *be* in a sentence or clause: *There are different kinds of pepper.* **2.** Used to indicate a person in direct address: *Hello there.* —*n.* That place or point: *I'll never know how we got out of there.* —*interj.* An expression used to show sympathy: *There, there, you'll be fine.*

Homonyms: there, their (belonging to them), **they're** (they are).

---

there·a·bouts (thâr′ ə bouts′) *adv. Informal.* **1.** Near that place: *somewhere in Iowa or thereabouts.* **2.** About that number, amount, or time: *at eight o'clock or thereabouts.*

there·af·ter (thâr ăf′tər) *adv. Formal.* From that time on: *Thereafter, people were glad to come to our concerts.*

there·by (thâr bī′) *adv.* Because of that: *We put in the storm windows to keep out the wind and thereby save heat.*

there·fore (thâr′fôr′) *adv.* For that reason; as a result: *It was raining; therefore we decided to stay home.*

there·in (thâr ĭn′) *adv. Formal.* In that place, time, or thing: *the house and everything therein.*

there·of (thâr ŭv′ *or* thâr ŏv′) *adv. Formal.* Relating to that: *his marriage and the joys thereof.*

there·up·on (thâr′ ə pŏn′ *or* thâr′ ə pôn′) *adv. Formal.* After that; directly following that: *He quit his job and thereupon left the country.*

ther·mal (thûr′məl) *adj.* **1.** Relating to or caused by heat: *thermal energy.* **2.** Intended or designed to help retain body heat: *thermal underwear.* —*n.* A current of air that rises because it is warmer than the air around it. —**ther′mal·ly** *adv.*

thermo— or **therm—** *pref.* A prefix that means heat: *thermometer.*

ther·mo·dy·nam·ic (thûr′mō dī năm′ĭk) *adj.* **1.** Relating to thermodynamics. **2.** Using mechanical power produced by heat.

ther·mo·dy·nam·ics (thûr′mō dī năm′ĭks) *n.* [U] *(used with a singular verb).* The part of physics that deals with the relationships between heat and other forms of energy.

ther·mom·e·ter (thər mŏm′ĭ tər) *n.* An instrument that measures temperature, especially one that uses colored liquid in a glass tube.

ther·mo·nu·cle·ar (thûr′mō nōō′klē ər) *adj.* **1.** Relating to the energy produced by a high-temperature atomic reaction. **2.** Relating to atomic weapons.

Ther·mos (thûr′məs). A trademark used for a brand of insulated beverage container.

ther·mo·stat (thûr′mə stăt′) *n.* A device that automatically controls a piece of heating or cooling equipment in such a way as to keep the temperature the same at all times.

the·sau·rus (thĭ sôr′əs) *n.* A book that groups together words and phrases that have similar meanings and, often, words with the opposite meaning.

these (thēz) *pron. & adj.* Plural of **this.**

the·sis (thē′sĭs) *n.*, *pl.* **the·ses** (thē′sēz). **1.** A statement put forth for discussion, often supported by an argument. **2.** A long essay resulting from original research written by a student seeking an academic degree.

they (thā) *pron.* **1.** The third person plural subject pronoun: *Paula and Dick worked here last summer, but now they are back in school.* **2.** People in general: *He's as smart as they come.* —SEE NOTE at **me.**

they'd (thād). Contraction of *they had* or *they would.*

they'll (thāl). Contraction of *they will.*

they're (thâr). Contraction of *they are.*

Homonyms: they're, their (belonging to them), **there** (at that place).

---

they've (thāv). Contraction of *they have.*

thick (thĭk) *adj.* **1.** Quite wide or deep; not thin: *a thick board.* **2.** Used to specify width or depth: *a board two inches thick.* **3.** Flowing slowly: *thick oil.* **4.** Dense or concentrated: *thick fog; a thick forest.* **5.** Very noticeable; obvious: *speaking with a thick accent.* **6.** *Informal.* Mentally slow; stupid: *He's very thick about matters of the heart.* ♦ **be thick with.** To have a very close relationship with (sbdy.): *She's very thick with that crowd these days, isn't she?* **in the thick of.** In the most active part of (sthg.): *in the thick of battle.* **lay it on thick.** To make sthg. sound greater or better than it is: *She'll lay it on thick if she thinks it will get her what she wants.* **thick as thieves.** Extremely close: *The new girl in class and my sister are thick as thieves.* **through thick and thin.** During good and bad times: *My family promised to be there to help through thick and thin.* —**thick′ly** *adv.*

thick·en (thĭk′ən) *tr. & intr.v.* To make or become thick or thicker: *We thickened the gravy. The pudding thickened as it cooled.* —**thick′en·er** *n.*

thick·en·ing (thĭk′ə nĭng) *n.* [U] The process of becoming thick.

thick-skinned (thĭk′skĭnd′) *adj.* **1.** With

ă-**cat**; ā-**pay**; âr-**care**; ä-**father**; ĕ-**get**; ē-**be**; ĭ-**sit**; ī-**nice**; îr-**here**; ŏ-**got**; ō-**go**; ô-**saw**; oi-**boy**; ou-**out**; ōō-**took**; ōō-**boot**; ŭ-**cut**; ûr-**word**; th-**thin**; *th*-**this**; hw-**when**; zh-**vision**; ə-**about**; N-French **bon**

a thick skin or rind. **2.** Not easily offended or insulted: *You have to be thick-skinned to work here.*

thief (thēf) *n., pl.* **thieves** (thēvz). A person who steals money or other valuables.

thigh (thī) *n.* The part of a human or animal leg between the hip and the knee.

thim·ble (thĭm′bəl) *n.* A small cup, usually of metal or plastic, worn to protect the finger that pushes the needle in sewing.

thin (thĭn) *adj.* **thin·ner, thin·nest. 1.** Quite narrow or shallow; not thick: *a thin board.* **2.** With a small diameter: *thin wire.* **3.** Lean or slender in form: *a thin man.* See Synonyms at **lean². 4.** Not dense or concentrated: *hair that was thin on top.* **5.** Flowing with relative ease: *thin oil.* —*adv.* So as to be thin: *Slice the bread thin.* —*tr. & intr.v.* **thinned, thin·ning, thins.** To make or become thin or thinner: *I thinned the gravy. Wait until the crowd thins.* —**thin′ly** *adv.* —**thin′ness** *n.* [U]

thing (thĭng) *n.* **1.** An object or idea that can be seen or thought about. **2.** A creature: *That kitten is the sweetest thing!* **3.** An article of clothing: *I can't wear that thing to the dance!* **4.** An action: *That was a nice thing to do for your sister.* **5.** The result of work or activity: *He's always drawing things.* **6.** A thought or an utterance: *What a rotten thing to say!* **7. things.** Personal possessions; belongings: *Have you packed your things for the weekend?* **8.** A matter of concern: *many things on my mind.* **9.** An event; a circumstance: *The flood was a terrible thing.* **10. things.** The general state of affairs; conditions: *Things are really looking up.* ◆ **do (one's) own thing.** To do what one likes to do: *Her boyfriend is always off doing his own thing.* **first thing.** *Informal.* Right away; before anything else: *We'll call him first thing in the morning.* **have a thing about.** To be annoyed by or concerned with: *My neighbor has a thing about children riding their bicycles in her driveway.* **have a thing for.** To like (sbdy./sthg.) a lot: *My best friend has a thing for chocolate.* **hear** or **see things.** To imagine sthg.: *I think my dog is seeing things because she barks so much.* **it's a good thing.** It's lucky: *It's a good thing I brought my medicine on the plane; the airline lost my luggage.* **make a big thing (out) of.** To make (sthg.) seem more important than it really is: *Don't make a big thing of doing the dishes.* **the (latest) thing.** A thing, event, or activity that is briefly popular: *Back then, wearing hoop skirts was the latest thing.* **the thing to do.** The right action to perform: *Helping your neighbor shovel snow was the thing to do.*

think (thĭngk) *v.* **thought** (thôt), **think·ing, thinks.** —*intr.* To have an idea in the mind; use the brain: *Think before you act; think carefully.* —*tr.* To hold (a specific idea or thought)

in the mind: *He always thinks he's right.* ◆ **think about.** *tr.v.* [insep.] **1.** To make a judgment about (sbdy./sthg.): *What do you think about the present government?* **2.** To consider (sthg.): *They're thinking about getting married.* **think better of.** To change one's mind about (doing sthg.): *I was going to ask him to my party and then thought better of it.* **think nothing of. 1.** To consider (sthg.) normal or unimportant: *She thinks nothing of calling you early in the morning.* **2.** Used to say that you thanks are not necessary: *I was going to the grocery store anyway when I got you the milk. Think nothing of it.* **think of.** *tr.v.* [insep.] **1.** To create (sthg. new): *No one had thought of bifocal glasses before.* **2.** To recall (sbdy./sthg.): *The movie made me think of my childhood.* **3.** To have consideration for (sbdy.): *Think of others before yourself.* **think out** or **through.** *tr.v.* [sep.] To plan (sthg.) well before acting: *Before you speak, think through what you want to say.* **think over.** *tr.v.* [sep.] To consider (sthg.) carefully before making a decision or acting: *Before you quit your job, think it over.* **think twice about. 1.** To consider (sthg.) carefully before acting: *Think twice before you speak.* **2.** To have (sbdy.) in one's mind: *During my vacation, I didn't think twice about my old girlfriend.* **think up.** *tr.v.* [sep.] To create (sthg.): *How did you think up such a crazy party game?*

think tank *n.* A group organized for intensive research and solving of problems in such areas as technology and politics.

thin·ner (thĭn′ər) *n.* [U] A liquid, such as turpentine, that is mixed with a paint to make it flow more easily as it is applied.

thin-skinned (thĭn′skĭnd′) *adj.* **1.** With a thin skin or rind. **2.** Easily offended or insulted: *She's so thin-skinned that it's hard to know what to say to her.*

third (thûrd) *n.* **1.** The ordinal number matching the number three in a series. **2.** One of three equal parts: *a third of a cup.* —**third** *adv. & adj.*

third degree *n.* ◆ **give the third degree.** To question (sbdy.) in great detail: *He gave me the third degree about why I was late to class.*

third-de·gree burn (thûrd′dĭ grē′) *n.* A severe burn in which the outer layer of skin is destroyed and sensitive nerve endings are exposed.

third party *n.* **1.** Someone not involved in a business deal between two people: *We don't need to be concerned with the interests of any third party.* **2.** A political party that is not one of the two major parties in the U.S. —**third-party** *adj.*

third person *n.* **1.** A set of grammatical forms used to refer to a person or thing other than the speaker or the one spoken to. **2.** A grammatical form belonging to such a set, as *he, she,* and *they.*

T

thirst (thûrst) *n*. **1.** [U] A sensation of dryness in the mouth and throat related to a need or desire to drink: *I'm dying of thirst.* **2.** [C] A strong desire: *a thirst for adventure.* —*intr.v.* **1.** To feel a need to drink. **2.** To have a strong craving; yearn: *thirsting for knowledge.*

thirst•y (thûr'stē) *adj.* **thirst•i•er, thirst•i•est. 1.** Desiring to drink: *Salty foods make me thirsty.* **2.** Very dry: *fields thirsty for rain.* **3.** Having a strong desire: *thirsty for travel.*

thir•teen (thûr tēn') *n*. **1.** The number, written 13, that is equal to 12 + 1. **2.** The 13th in a set or sequence. —**thir•teen'** *adj. & pron.*

thir•teenth (thûr tēnth') *n*. **1.** The ordinal number matching the number 13 in a series. **2.** One of 13 equal parts. —**thir'teenth'** *adv. & adj.*

thir•ti•eth (thûr'tē ĭth) *n*. **1.** The ordinal number matching the number 30 in a series. **2.** One of 30 equal parts. —**thir'ti•eth** *adv. & adj.*

thir•ty (thûr'tē) *n., pl.* **thir•ties. 1.** The number, written 30, that is equal to 3 × 10. **2. thirties. a.** Often **Thirties.** The ten years from 30 to 39 in a century. **b.** A decade or the numbers from 30 to 39: *The temperature was in the thirties last night.* —**thir'ty** *adj. & pron.*

this (thĭs) *pron., pl.* **these** (thēz). **1.** Used to refer to the person or thing present, nearby, or just mentioned: *This is my house. This is my friend's cousin.* **2.** Used to refer to what is about to be said: *This will really make you laugh.* **3.** Used to refer to the present occasion or time: *He's never been out later than this.* **4.** Used to indicate the nearer or the more immediate one: *That storm was weak compared to this.* —*adj., pl.* **these. 1.** Just mentioned or present in space, time, or thought: *We left early this morning.* **2.** Nearer or more immediate: *Walk on this side of the street, not that side.* **3.** About to be stated or described: *Just wait until you hear this story.* —*adv.* To this extent; so: *I never stayed up this late before.*

this•tle (thĭs'əl) *n*. A prickly plant with purplish flowers and seeds tufted with silky fluff.

thong (thông *or* thŏng) *n*. **1.** A narrow strip of leather or cloth used for tying two things together. **2.** A sandal held on the foot by a strip that passes between the toes. **3.** A very small bikini bathing suit.

thorn (thôrn) *n*. **1.** A sharp woody point growing from the stem of a plant. **2.** A person or thing that causes sharp pain, irritation, or discomfort: *He has been a thorn in my side for years.* —**thorn'less** *adj.*

thorn•y (thôr'nē) *adj.* **thorn•i•er, thorn•i•est. 1.** Covered with thorns: *thorny branches.* **2.** Difficult: *a thorny situation.*

thor•ough (thûr'ō *or* thŭr'ō) *adj.* **1.** Complete in all ways: *a thorough search.* **2.**

Extremely accurate or careful: *a thorough worker.* —**thor'ough•ly** *adv.* —**thor'ough•ness** *n*. [U]

thor•ough•bred (thûr'ō brĕd' *or* thŭr'ō-brĕd') *n*. An animal, especially a horse or dog, whose parents are both from the same pure breed. —*adj.* From a single pure breed.

thor•ough•fare (thûr'ō fâr' *or* thŭr'ō fâr') *n*. **1.** A main road or public highway. **2.** A heavily traveled waterway, such as a channel.

thor•ough•go•ing (thûr'ō gō'ĭng *or* thŭr'-ō gō'ĭng) *adj.* Very complete: *a thoroughgoing change in the tax laws.*

those (thōz) *pron. & adj.* Plural of **that.**

thou (thou) *pron.* An old usage that means the same as the second person singular *you,* often used in religious writing.

though (thō) *conj.* **1.** Despite the fact that; although: *Though it was raining, he walked to work.* **2.** Even if: *Though our chances of winning are slim, I think we should play.* —*adv.* However; nevertheless: *It's not going to snow; it may rain, though.*

thought (thôt) *v.* Past tense and past participle of **think.** —*n*. **1.** [U] The act or process of thinking: *spending hours in thought.* **2.** [C] A product of thinking; an idea: *Let me have your thoughts on this subject.* See Synonyms at **idea. 3.** [U] The ideas of a particular group of people: *ancient Greek thought.* **4.** [U] Consideration; attention: *giving serious thought to the matter.* ♦ **have second thoughts.** To rethink a decision; doubt: *When we heard the weather report, we had second thoughts about hiking in the mountains.*

thought•ful (thôt'fəl) *adj.* **1.** Busy thinking: *He was thoughtful for a minute.* **2.** Showing careful thought: *She wrote a thoughtful paper.* **3.** Showing concern for others; considerate: *Bringing flowers to the host was a thoughtful gesture.* —**thought'ful•ly** *adv.* —**thought'ful•ness** *n*. [U]

thought•less (thôt'lĭs) *adj.* Showing no care or concern: *It was thoughtless of her to forget your birthday.* —**thought'less•ly** *adv.* —**thought'less•ness** *n*. [U]

thou•sand (thou'zənd) *n*. The number, written 1,000 or 10³, that is equal to 10 × 100. —**thou'sand** *adj. & pron.*

thou•sandth (thou'zəndth *or* thou'zənth) *n*. **1.** The ordinal number matching the number 1,000 in a series. **2.** One of 1,000 equal parts. —**thou'sandth** *adv. & adj.*

thrash (thrăsh) *v.* —*tr.* **1.** To beat or flog (sbdy./sthg.), especially as a punishment: *His father used to thrash him for stealing.* **2.** To defeat (sbdy./sthg.) completely: *We thrashed their team yesterday.* —*intr.* To move wildly or violently: *a crocodile thrashing around in the water.*

ă–cat; ā–pay; âr–care; ä–father; ĕ–get; ē–be; ĭ–sit; ī–nice; îr–here; ŏ–got; ō–go; ô–saw; oi–boy; ou–out; o͞o–took; o͞o–boot; ŭ–cut; ûr–word; th–thin; *th*–this; hw–when; zh–vision; ə–about; N–French bon

thread (thrĕd) *n.* **1.** [C; U] Very fine cord made of cotton, silk, or nylon and used in sewing and weaving cloth. **2.** [C] Something that resembles a thread: *a thread of smoke coming out the chimney.* **3.** [C] Something that is continuous: *He lost the thread of his argument.* **4.** [C] A spiral ridge on a screw, nut, or bolt. —*tr.v.* **1. a.** To pass a thread through the eye of (a needle, for example): *thread the needle.* **b.** To pass (sthg.) through a narrow opening: *thread the film through the projector.* **2.** To connect (several things) by running a thread through them: *thread beads.* **3.** To make (one's way) cautiously through sthg.: *pedestrians threading their way through a crowd.* —**thread′like′** *adj.*

thread•bare (thrĕd′bâr′) *adj.* **1.** Shabby; old and worn: *a threadbare rug.* **2.** Overused; trite: *threadbare excuses.*

threat (thrĕt) *n.* **1.** An expression of an intention to inflict pain, injury, or punishment: *Don't listen to their threats.* **2.** A warning of probable danger or harm: *The night air held a threat of frost.* **3.** Something, such as a person, a thing, or an idea, regarded as a possible danger: *AIDS is a threat to everyone.*

threat•en (thrĕt′n) *v.* —*tr.* **1.** To make a threat against (sbdy.): *Don't threaten me.* **2.** To be a source of danger to (sbdy./sthg.): *Landslides threatened the mountain village.* **3.** To give signs or warning of (sthg.): *Dark skies threaten rain.* **4.** To announce the possibility of (sthg. unwanted): *They are always threatening to move to the suburbs.* —*intr.* To indicate danger or harm: *A thunderstorm threatened.*

threat•en•ing (thrĕt′n ĭng) *adj.* **1.** Expressing a threat: *a threatening letter.* **2.** Giving signs of danger: *threatening storm clouds.* —**threat′en•ing•ly** *adv.*

three (thrē) *n.* **1.** The number, written 3, that is equal to 2 + 1. **2.** The third in a set or sequence. —**three** *adj. & pron.*

3-D (thrē′dē′) *adj.* Three-dimensional: *3-D movies.*

three-di•men•sion•al (thrē′dĭ měn′shə-nəl) *adj.* **1.** Describing an image with three dimensions—height, width, and depth. **2.** Relating to visual images in which there is an illusion of depth and perspective: *a three-dimensional image projected with light from a laser.*

three•some (thrē′səm) *n.* **1.** A group of three persons or things. **2.** An activity, such as cards or a golf match, that involves three people.

thresh (thrĕsh) *v.* —*tr.* To separate out the seeds from (grain-bearing plants) by striking or beating: *The workers threshed the wheat with a machine.* —*intr.* To use a machine to separate grain or seeds from straw: *The farmer is threshing in the field.*

thresh•er (thrĕsh′ər) *n.* **1.** A person or thing that threshes. **2.** A threshing machine.

thresh•old (thrĕsh′ōld′ *or* thrĕsh′hōld′) *n.* **1.** The piece of wood or stone placed beneath a doorway; a doorsill. **2.** An entrance. **3.** The place where sthg. begins: *Science is on the threshold of finding a cure for cancer.* **4.** The lowest level at which sthg. can be seen, heard, or felt: *a sound at the threshold of hearing.*

threw (thrōō) *v.* Past tense of **throw.**

HOMONYMS: threw, through (in and out of).

thrice (thrīs) *adv. Formal.* Three times: *She was thrice named class president.*

thrift (thrĭft) *n.* [U] Careful management of money and other resources; frugality: *Thrift always pays off.* —**thrift′less** *adj.*

thrift•y (thrĭf′tē) *adj.* **thrift•i•er, thrift•i•est.** Practicing thrift; economical and frugal: *He's a thrifty shopper.* —**thrift′i•ly** *adv.* —**thrift′i•ness** *n.* [U]

thrill (thrĭl) *v.* —*tr.* To cause (sbdy.) to feel sudden joy, fear, or excitement: *The news of his promotion thrilled him.* —*intr.* To feel a sudden sense of excitement or emotion: *The children thrilled at the dolphin's tricks.* —*n.* **1.** Shivering caused by sudden excitement or emotion: *feeling thrills and chills.* **2.** A source or cause of excitement or emotion: *That rollercoaster ride was quite a thrill!*

thrill•er (thrĭl′ər) *n.* Something that thrills, especially an exciting book or movie.

thrill•ing (thrĭl′ĭng) *adj.* Exciting: *Meeting the President was a thrilling experience.*

thrive (thrīv) *intr.v.* **thrived, thriv•ing, thrives.** **1.** To grow in a healthy way; flourish: *Some plants thrive in sandy soil.* **2.** To make steady progress; prosper: *The town thrived and grew larger.*

throat (thrōt) *n.* **1. a.** The front portion of the neck: *The blouse ties at the throat.* **b.** The beginning of the passage that connects the mouth with the stomach and the lungs: *She had something stuck in her throat* **2.** A narrow part similar to the human throat: *the throat of a bottle.*

throat•y (thrō′tē) *adj.* **throat•i•er, throat•i•est.** With a sound made deep in the throat; hoarse or husky: *a throaty growl.* —**throat′i•ly** *adv.* —**throat′i•ness** *n.* [U]

throb (thrŏb) *intr.v.* **throbbed, throb•bing, throbs.** **1.** To beat rapidly or violently; pound: *His heart was throbbing with excitement.* **2.** To vibrate with a slow steady rhythm: *hearing the boat's engines throbbing all night.* —*n.* The act of throbbing; a beating or vibration: *the throb of a ship's engines.*

throe (thrō) *n. (usually plural).* A severe pain, as in childbirth. ♦ **in the throes of.** Experiencing great struggle or trouble with: *a country in the throes of an economic depression.*

throne (thrōn) *n.* **1.** [C] The chair occupied by a king or queen on ceremonial occasions: *The king sat on a golden throne.* **2.** [U] The power or authority of a king or queen: *The people feared the power of the throne.*

throng (thrông *or* thrŏng) *n.* A large group of people or things gathered or crowded closely together: *throngs of protesters.* —*v.* —*tr.* To crowd into (sthg.); fill: *People thronged the platforms of the subway station.* —*intr.* To gather or move in a throng: *People thronged to the new restaurant.*

throt·tle (thrŏt′l) *n.* **1.** A valve that regulates the flow of fuel in an engine. **2.** A pedal or lever that controls such a valve. —*tr.v.* **throt·tled, throt·tling, throt·tles. 1.** To control (an engine or its fuel supply) with a throttle. **2.** To strangle (sbdy.); choke: *He throttled the thief.* **3.** To suppress (sbdy./sthg.); control: *The dictator tried to throttle the press.*

through (thrōō) *prep.* **1.** In one side and out the opposite or another side of: *going through the door.* **2.** Among or between: *a walk through the flowers.* **3.** By way of: *He entered through a side door.* **4.** By means of: *getting an apartment through an agency.* **5.** Here and there in; around: *a tour through France.* **6.** From the beginning to the end of: *staying up through the night.* **7.** At or near the end of: *We are through our testing period.* **8.** Without stopping: *driving through a red light.* **9.** Because of; on account of: *We succeeded through hard work.* —*adv.* **1.** From one end or side to another or an opposite end or side: *I opened the window and climbed through.* **2.** From beginning to end; completely: *I glanced at the article but haven't read it through.* **3.** Thoroughly: *We got soaked through in the rain.* **4.** Over the total distance; all the way: *We drove straight through to Toledo.* **5.** To the end or conclusion: *I mean to see this matter through.* —*adj.* **1.** Allowing passage to the end: *a through street.* **2.** Going all the way to the end without stopping: *This is a through flight.* **3.** [*with*] Finished; done: *Are you through with your homework?* **4.** Finished; no longer effective or able: *If he injures that knee again, he's through as a basketball player.* **5.** Having no further dealings or connection: *She and her boyfriend are through.* ♦ **through and through.** Completely: *He loved her through and through.*

through·out (thrōō out′) *prep.* In, to, through, or during every part of: *throughout the country; throughout the night.* —*adv.* **1.** In or through all parts; everywhere: *The house is beautiful throughout.* **2.** During the entire time or extent: *She was questioned for two hours and remained calm throughout.*

through·way (thrōō′wā′) *n.* Variant of **thruway.**

throw (thrō) *tr.v.* **threw** (thrōō), **thrown** (thrōn), **throw·ing, throws. 1.** To send (sthg.) through the air with or as if with a forceful motion of the hand or arm: *throw a ball.* **2.** To move or send (sthg. or oneself) with great force and speed: *threw themselves at the food.* **3.** To send (sthg.) in a particular direction: *throw a glance at the window displays.* **4.** To put (clothing) on or off quickly or carelessly: *throwing a cape over her shoulders.* **5.** To send (sbdy./sthg.) forcefully to the ground or floor: *The horse threw its rider.* **6.** To arrange or give (a social event): *throw a party.* **7.** *Informal.* To lose (a fight, for example) purposely: *The boxer threw the fight.* **8.** To put (sbdy./sthg.) suddenly into a specified condition: *new regulations that threw the players into confusion.* **9.** To move (a switch or control lever) in order to operate a device: *The engineer threw the switch to start the motor.* **10.** *Informal.* To make (sbdy.) confused or uncertain: *Don't let his unfriendly manner throw you.* —*n.* **1.** The act or an instance of throwing: *a powerful throw.* **2.** The distance to which sthg. is or can be thrown: *a throw of 50 feet.* **3.** A scarf, shawl, or light blanket. ♦ **throw a fit.** To become suddenly and visibly angry: *She threw a fit when we showed up.* **throw around.** *tr.v.* [sep.] To scatter or distribute (sthg.) freely: *You shouldn't throw your money around.* **throw away.** *tr.v.* [sep.] **1.** To discard (sthg.) as useless: *He threw away the empty box.* **2.** To fail to take advantage of (sthg.): *My father threw away a chance to make a fortune.* **throw back.** *tr.v.* [sep.] To put (sthg.) back where it came from: *She threw the fish back because it was so small.* **throw in.** *tr.v.* [sep.] To add (an extra thing or amount) with no additional charge: *If you buy three apples, I'll throw in one more.* **throw off.** *tr.v.* [sep.] **1.** To remove (sthg.); rid oneself of: *It was so hot I threw off my blanket.* **2.** To trick (sbdy./sthg.); mislead: *The fox ran through a creek to throw the dogs off.* **throw out.** *tr.v.* [sep.] **1.** To reject or discard (sthg. unwanted): *I threw out yesterday's paper.* **2.** [*of*] To force (sbdy.) to leave a place or position, especially suddenly: *The officials threw the player out of the game.* **3.** To bring (sthg.) up for discussion: *She threw out the idea of going to a movie.* **throw the baby out with the bath water.** To get rid of sthg. that might be useful or valuable at the same time that one gets rid of what is not useful or valu-

T

able: *It's a good idea to look at one's beliefs carefully, but don't throw the baby out with the bath water.* **throw together.** *tr.v.* [sep.] **1.** To put together or make (sthg.) quickly: *She was able to throw dinner together in no time.* **2.** To meet (sbdy.) suddenly: *They were thrown together at a party, and now they're getting married.* **3.** To be made to bump into (sbdy.): *The passengers were thrown together by the rushing train.* **throw up.** *intr.v.* To vomit: *The sick child threw up several times.* —*tr.v.* [sep.] **1.** To vomit (sthg.): *I tried to eat a cracker, but just threw it up again.* **2.** To build (sthg.) quickly: *That house was thrown up in only a week.* —**throw′er** *n.*

SYNONYMS: throw, hurl, fling, pitch, toss. These verbs mean to shoot sthg. through the air with a motion of the hand or arm. **Throw** is the most general: *A sailor threw a life preserver to the struggling swimmer.* **Hurl** and **fling** mean to throw with great force: *In Greek mythology Zeus hurls lightning bolts from Olympus as if they were spears. The paper carrier had flung the newspaper onto the porch.* **Pitch** often means to throw with careful aim: *She pitched the wad of paper into the wastebasket.* **Toss** usually means to throw lightly or casually: *He tossed the day's mail onto the desk.*

throw•back (thrō′băk′) *n.* Something from an earlier period of time: *My mother collects dolls, a throwback to her childhood.*
thrown (thrōn) *v.* Past participle of **throw.**

HOMONYMS: thrown, throne (monarch's chair).

thru (thrōō) *Informal. prep., adv., & adj.* Through.
thrust (thrŭst) *tr.v.* **thrust, thrust•ing, thrusts. 1.** To push (sbdy./sthg.) forward quickly and forcibly: *She thrust the divorce papers at me.* **2.** To force (sbdy./sthg.) into a specified situation: *She thrust herself into our conversation.* —*n.* **1.** [C] A forceful shove or push. **2.** [U] A force that moves an object, especially an airplane or a rocket. **3.** [C] A piercing movement; a stab. **4.** [U] The main point: *the thrust of the governor's proposal.*
thru•way also **through•way** (thrōō′wā′) *n.* An expressway.
thud (thŭd) *n.* **1.** A dull sound. **2.** A blow or fall causing such a sound. —*intr.v.* **thud•ded, thud•ding, thuds.** To make a heavy dull sound.
thug (thŭg) *n. Informal.* A criminal.
thumb (thŭm) *n.* **1.** The short thick finger of the human hand, which can touch each of the other fingers: *I sprained my thumb.* **2.** A similar part of an animal's hand. **3.** The part of a glove or mitten that covers the thumb: *a hole in the thumb of the mitten.* —*v.* —*tr.* **1.** To scan (written matter) by turning pages with or as if

with the thumb. **2.** To soil or wear (sthg., as the pages of a book) by careless or frequent handling. **3.** *Informal.* To ask for (a ride) from a passing automobile by signaling with the thumb. —*intr. Informal.* To hitchhike. ♦ **all thumbs.** Clumsy; awkward: *She's all thumbs when she tries to sew.* **a rule of thumb.** A general rule for deciding sthg.: *As a rule of thumb, don't use the telephone while you're taking a bath.* **stick out like a sore thumb.** To be very obvious; be out of place: *He sticks out like a sore thumb when he wears that plaid coat.* **thumb a ride.** *Informal.* To get a ride in a passing vehicle by standing along a road and putting one's thumb in the air: *We thumbed a ride to Chicago.* **thumb (one's) nose at.** To refuse to obey; defy: *You cannot thumb your nose at laws against speeding.* **thumbs down.** An expression of rejection, refusal, or disapproval. **thumbs up.** An expression of approval, success, or hope. **thumb through.** *tr.v.* [insep.] To read (sthg.) quickly: *thumb through a file folder.* **under (one's) thumb.** Under the control or influence of (sbdy.): *He really has his wife under his thumb.*
thumb•nail (thŭm′nāl′) *n.* The nail of the thumb. —*adj.* **1.** Relating to or the size of a thumbnail. **2.** Brief; very short: *a thumbnail biography.*
thumb•tack (thŭm′tăk′) *n.* A tack with a fairly large, flat head that can be pressed into place with the thumb.
thump (thŭmp) *n.* **1.** A blow with a heavy object. **2.** The dull sound produced by such a blow; a thud: *We heard the thump on the stairs.* —*v.* —*tr.* To strike (sbdy./sthg.) with a heavy object, so as to produce a thud: *thumping the desk with her fist.* —*intr.* **1.** To beat, hit, or fall in such a way as to produce a thump: *The book thumped on the floor.* **2.** To make a repeated dull sound: *His heart thumped with fear.*
thun•der (thŭn′dər) *n.* [U] **1.** The loud noise that accompanies a stroke of lightning: *thunder and lightning.* **2.** A noise that resembles thunder: *the thunder of the engine.* —*v.* —*intr.* **1.** To produce thunder: *It stormed and thundered.* **2.** To produce sounds like thunder: *guns thundering in the distance.* —*tr.* To say (sthg.) loudly or threateningly: *The captain thundered orders to the sailors.*
thun•der•bolt (thŭn′dər bōlt′) *n.* A stroke of lightning accompanied by thunder.
thun•der•clap (thŭn′dər klăp′) *n.* A single sharp crash of thunder.
thun•der•cloud (thŭn′dər kloud′) *n.* A large dark cloud carrying an electric charge and producing lightning and thunder; a storm cloud.
thun•der•head (thŭn′dər hĕd′) *n.* The billowy upper part of a thundercloud.
thun•der•ous (thŭn′dər əs) *adj.* Producing thunder or a similar sound: *thunderous applause.* —**thun′der•ous•ly** *adv.*

T

thun·der·show·er (thŭn′dər shou′ər) *n.*
A short, often heavy rainstorm with thunder
and lightning.

thun·der·storm (thŭn′dər stôrm′) *n.* A
storm of heavy rain accompanied by lightning and thunder.

thun·der·struck (thŭn′dər strŭk′) *adj.*
Amazed; astonished: *He stood thunderstruck at
the sidelines watching his team lose the game.*

Thur. *abbr.* An abbreviation of Thursday.

Thurs·day (thûrz′dē *or* thûrz′dā′) *n.* The
fifth day of the week.

thus (thŭs) *adv. Formal.* **1.** In this manner:
Lay the pieces out thus. **2.** To a stated degree
or extent; so: *She has been the one who has
evaluated my work thus far.* **3.** Consequently;
therefore: *Thus, we decided to leave early.*

thwart (thwôrt) *tr.v.* To prevent (sthg.) from
happening; block: *They thwarted his plans.*

thy (thī) *adj.* The possessive form of **thou.**

thyme (tīm) *n.* [U] The spicy-smelling leaves
of a low-growing plant, used as a seasoning,
or the plant that bears such leaves.

HOMONYMS: thyme, time (moment).

thy·roid (thī′roid′) *n.* The gland in the neck
that controls growth and energy.

Ti The symbol for the element **titanium.**

ti·ar·a (tē ăr′ə *or* tē är′ə) *n.* A crown worn
on the head by women on formal occasions.

tic (tĭk) *n.* A recurring contraction or twitching of a set of muscles, usually in the face or
limbs: *a nervous tic.*

HOMONYMS: tic, tick (clicking sound, insect).

tick¹ (tĭk) *n.* **1.** A repeated clicking sound made
by a clock. **2.** A light mark used to call attention to an item. —*v.* —*intr.* To produce repeated clicking sounds. —*tr.* To count (sthg.): *a
clock ticking the hours.* ♦ **tick off.** *tr.v.* [sep.]
1. To make (sbdy.) angry: *Don't tick her off
now; she's had a rough day.* **2.** To check
(sthg.) off a list: *I ticked off the items we needed for the picnic as we packed the car.* **what
makes (one) tick.** What makes (sbdy.)
behave in a certain way: *After all these years I
still don't know what makes him tick.*

HOMONYMS: tick (clicking sound, bug), **tic**
(muscle contraction).

tick² (tĭk) *n.* A small animal related to the spider. Ticks attach themselves to and suck
blood from human beings and animals and
often carry disease.

tick·er (tĭk′ər) *n.* **1.** Any of various devices
that receive and record information, such
as stock-market quotations, by electronic

means. **2.** *Informal.* The heart: *a weak ticker.*

tick·et (tĭk′ĭt) *n.* **1.** A piece of paper that
allows sbdy. to enter a place or use a service:
a bus ticket; a theater ticket. **2.** A notice
given to a driver for a traffic violation: *I got a
ticket for speeding.* **3.** A tag attached to sthg.
sold in a store and giving information about
it; a label: *Is there a price on the ticket?* **4.** A
list of a political party's candidates in an election: *voting the Democratic ticket.* —*tr.v.* **1.**
To give (sbdy.) a ticket: *The police officer
ticketed the driver for speeding.* **2.** To attach
a tag to (sthg.); label: *The clerk ticketed the
sale items.* **3.** To mark or intend (sthg.) for a
specified use: *boxes ticketed for shipment.*
♦ **(just) the ticket.** Exactly what is needed:
On a hot day, lemonade is just the ticket.

tick·le (tĭk′əl) *tr.v.* **tick·led, tick·ling,
tick·les.** **1.** To touch (sbdy.) lightly, causing
laughter or twitching movements: *Stop tickling
your brother.* **2.** To delight or amuse (sbdy.):
His funny stories always tickle me. —*n.* The act
or sensation of tickling. ♦ **tickled pink.**
Informal. Pleased; delighted: *I was tickled pink
by the compliment.* **tickled to death.** Very
pleased; excited: *She was tickled to death by
the response to her first novel.* **tickle (one's)
fancy.** To amuse (sbdy.); please: *Where shall
we eat tonight? What tickles your fancy?*
—**tick′ler** *n.*

tick·lish (tĭk′lĭsh) *adj.* **1.** Sensitive to tickling: *a ticklish child.* **2.** Requiring skillful
handling: *a ticklish problem.* —**tick′lish·
ness** *n.* [U]

tick·tack·toe *also* **tick-tack-toe** (tĭk′tăk′-
tō′) *n.* [U] A game played by two persons,
each trying to make a line of three X's or
three O's on a grid with nine spaces.

tid·al (tīd′l) *adj.* Relating to tides: *tidal
marshes.*

tidal wave *n.* **1.** A great wave along a seacoast caused by wind and tide. **2.** A tsunami:
The earthquake caused a tidal wave.

tid·bit (tĭd′bĭt′) *n.* A choice piece of food or
gossip.

tide (tīd) *n.* [C; U] **1.a.** The periodic variation
in the surface level of the oceans caused by
the gravitational pull of the moon: *High tide
will be at 11:00 this morning.* **b.** The water
that moves when such a variation occurs: *The
tide came in.* **2.** Something that fluctuates
like the waters of the tide: *the rising tide of
immigration.* **3.** *Formal.* A time or season:
eveningtide; Christmastide. ♦ **tide (one)
over.** To support (sbdy.) through a difficult
period: *My brother lent me $100 to tide me
over until payday.*

tid·ings (tī′dĭngz) *pl.n. Formal.* News; information: *tidings of great joy.*

ti·dy (tī′dē) *adj.* **ti·di·er, ti·di·est.** **1.**

T

Orderly and neat: *a tidy room.* See Synonyms at **neat. 2.** *Informal.* Quite large: *a tidy sum of money.* —*tr.* & *intr.v.* **ti·died, ti·dy·ing, ti·dies.** To put in order; make neat: *Tidy your room. We tidied up after dinner.* —**ti′di·ly** *adv.* —**ti′di·ness** *n.* [U]

tie (tī) *v.* **tied, ty·ing** (tī′ĭng), **ties.** —*tr.* **1.** To fasten or secure (sthg.) with or as if with a cord, rope, or strap: *tie up a parcel; tie a dog to a fence.* **2.** To fasten by drawing together the parts of (sthg.) and knotting with strings or laces: *bending to tie her shoes.* **3.a.** To make (a knot) by fastening ends or parts. **b.** To put a knot or bow in (sthg.): *tie a necktie; tie a scarf.* **4.a.** To equal (an opponent or a score, for example) in a contest: *He tied the world record for the mile run.* **b.** To equal a score in (a contest): *They tied the game with minutes remaining.* **5.** To bring (people) together in a relationship; connect or unite: *people who are tied by marriage.* —*intr.* **1.** To be fastened or attached: *an apron that ties in back.* **2.** To achieve equal scores in a contest: *two teams that tied for first place.* —*n.* **1.** A cord, string, rope, or other means by which sthg. is tied. **2.** A necktie. **3.** Something that connects or unites: *the ties of friendship; family ties.* **4.** An equality of scores or votes in a contest: *The game ended in a tie.* **5.** One of the timbers laid across a railroad bed to support the rails. ◆ **tie down.** *tr.v.* [sep.] **1.** To limit the freedom of (sbdy.): *She can't stand to be tied down, so she never married.* **2.** To bind (sthg.) securely: *Is everything on the boat tied down?* **tie in.** *intr.v.* [with] To have a close relation; connect or coordinate: *Your story ties in with what she told me.* **tie up.** *tr.v.* [sep.] **1.** To secure (a boat) to a shore or pier; dock: *They tied up the boat at the dock.* **2.** To block or stop (sthg.): *an accident that tied up traffic.* **3.** To keep (sbdy.) busy: *I will be tied up in meetings all day.* **4.** To place or invest (money) so that it cannot be used freely: *She tied up her money in a new house.*

tier (tîr) *n.* One of a series of rows placed one above another: *a stadium with four tiers of seats.*

HOMONYMS: tier, tear² (eye drop).

tie-up (tī′ŭp′) *n.* A temporary stoppage, as of work or traffic: *The car accident caused a traffic tie-up.*

tiff (tĭf) *n.* A minor disagreement; a silly quarrel.

ti·ger (tī′gər) *n.* **1.** A very large wild cat of Asia, with dark yellow fur and black stripes. **2.** An enthusiastic, fierce, or aggressive person: *That new sales manager is a real tiger.*

tight (tīt) *adj.* **1.** Held in place firmly: *a tight knot; a tight lid.* **2.** Stretched as far as possible: *a tight rope.* **3.** So well built that water and air can't enter: *a tight roof.* **4.** With little empty space between; compact: *planes flying in tight*

formation. **5.** With little time to spare; full: *a tight schedule.* **6.** Fitting very close to some part of the body; snug: *His shoes were too tight.* **7.** Constricted: *a tight feeling in the chest.* **8.** Reluctant to give or spend money; stingy: *He's always been tight with his money.* **9.a.** Difficult to obtain: *Money was tight.* **b.** Affected by scarcity: *a tight money market.* **10.** Closely contested; close: *a tight race; a tight game.* —*adv.* Firmly; securely: *Screw the lid on tight.* ◆ **in a tight spot.** In a very difficult situation: *Not getting paid for his work left him in a tight spot.* **run a tight ship.** To maintain sthg. in an orderly manner: *Our teacher knows how to run a tight ship.* **sit tight.** To not move; wait: *Sit tight; help will be there soon.* **sleep tight.** To sleep well: *I hope you sleep tight.* —**tight′ly** *adv.* —**tight′ness** *n.* [U]

tight·en (tīt′n) *tr.* & *intr.v.* To make or become tight or tighter: *Tighten your grip. His fists tightened.*

tight·fist·ed (tīt′fĭs′tĭd) *adj.* Unwilling to spend money; stingy: *That guy is so tightfisted he hasn't bought new socks in years.*

tight·lipped also **tight-lipped** (tīt′lĭpt′) *adj.* **1.** With the lips pressed together: *She was tightlipped with pain.* **2.** Secretive; silent: *He was tightlipped about the meeting.*

tight·rope (tīt′rōp′) *n.* A tightly stretched wire on which acrobats perform high above the ground.

tights (tīts) *pl.n.* **1.** A snug stretchable garment covering the body from the waist down, designed for general wear by women and girls. **2.** A similar garment designed for athletics, worn especially by dancers and acrobats.

tight·wad (tīt′wŏd′) *n. Slang.* A stingy person: *The tightwad wouldn't donate to the charity.*

ti·gress (tī′grĭs) *n.* A female tiger.

tike (tīk) *n.* Variant of **tyke.**

tile (tīl) *n.* **1.** [C; U] A thin square of plastic, concrete, or other hard material used as a covering for floors, walls, and roofs. **2.** [C; U] A short length of clay or concrete pipe, used in sewers and drains. **3.** [C] A marked playing piece used in certain games. —*tr.v.* **tiled, til·ing, tiles.** To cover (sthg.) with tiles: *The contractor tiled the kitchen floor.*

til·ing (tī′lĭng) *n.* [U] **1.** The laying of tiles. **2.** Tiles considered as a group.

till¹ (tĭl) *tr.v.* To prepare (land) for the raising of crops by plowing; cultivate. —**till′a·ble** *adj.*

till² (tĭl) *prep.* Until: *I won't see you till tomorrow.* —*conj.* Until: *I can't help you till you tell me what's wrong.*

USAGE: till² You can usually use either **till** or **until.** Use **until** as the first word in a sentence, however: *Until you get that paper written, don't plan to go out.*

till³ (tĭl) *n*. A drawer where money is kept, especially in a store: *The clerk counted the money in the till.*

tilt (tĭlt) *v*. —*tr*. To cause (sthg.) to slant or lean; tip: *The children tilted the box to empty it.* —*intr*. **1.** To slope; incline: *That picture tilts to the left.* **2.** To favor one side over another in a dispute: *Her political views tilt to the right.* —*n*. **1.** A slant; a slope. **2.** A combat, especially a verbal duel. ♦ **at full tilt.** *Informal*. At full speed: *She always works at full tilt.*

tim•ber (tĭm′bər) *n*. [U] Trees that are used as a source of wood: *cut timber.*

tim•bered (tĭm′bərd) *adj*. Covered with trees: *a timbered slope.*

tim•ber•land (tĭm′bər lănd′) *n*. Wooded land, especially land used for the commercial production of timber.

tim•ber•line (tĭm′bər līn′) *n*. The level on the side of a mountain above which trees do not grow.

time (tīm) *n*. **1.** [U] A continuous quantity measurable in minutes, hours, and years, for example, and proceeding from the past through the present to the future. **2.a.** [C; U] A period limited by two points of this quantity, as by the beginning and end of an event: *the time it takes to go from one place to another.* **b.** [U] A number representing a given point, stated in hours and minutes: *The time was 5:15.* **c.** [U] A system by which such periods are measured or such numbers are calculated: *standard time; solar time.* **3.** [U] The characteristic beat of a musical rhythm: *a dance in 3/4 time.* **4.** [U] **a.** A moment or period for a given activity: *harvest time; time for bed.* **b.** A period that one is free: *Do you have time to talk?* **5.** [C] **a.** A period, especially of years marked by similar events and conditions: *Victorian times; a time of famine.* **b.** The present: *a sign of the times.* **6.** [U] **a.** A period of military service: *served his time in the army.* **b.** *Informal*. A prison sentence: *serve time for robbery.* **7.** [C] A person's experience during a specific period or occasion: *had a good time at the party.* **8.** [U] **a.** The customary period of work of an employee: *working full time.* **b.** The hourly pay rate: *She gets double time on weekends.* **9.** [C] **a.** One of several instances: *I let the phone ring three times.* **b. times.** Used to show the number by which sthg. is multiplied or divided: *This building is three times taller than that one.* —*adj*. Relating to or measuring time: *a time zone.* —*tr.v.* **timed, tim•ing, times. 1.** To set the time at which (sthg.) happens or is to happen: *timed his entrance for greatest effect.* **2.** To record or register the speed or duration of (sbdy./sthg.): *We timed the game at two hours even.* **3.** To regulate or adjust (sthg.) so

that an action occurs or force is applied at the correct time: *time a jump carefully; time an automobile engine.* **4.** To adjust (a clock or watch, for example) so that it keeps time accurately. ♦ **against time.** With a quickly approaching deadline: *working against time.* **ahead of (one's) time.** Seeing how sthg. will be before others do: *Great thinkers are always ahead of their time.* **ahead of time.** Before the expected time; early: *finished the work ahead of time.* **all in good time.** In enough time; at the proper time: *We'll deal with other issues all in good time.* **all the time.** Usually; often: *We eat pizza all the time.* **at one time. 1.** Simultaneously: *can't be in two places at one time.* **2.** At a period or moment in the past: *At one time they were classmates.* **at the same time.** However; nonetheless: *That coat is awfully expensive; at the same time, it is beautifully made.* **at times.** On occasion; sometimes. **behind the times.** Out-of-date; old-fashioned: *The writer called herself behind the times for continuing to work on a typewriter.* **do time.** To serve a prison sentence: *Her cousin has done time for shoplifting.* **for the time being.** Temporarily: *For the time being, he's living in a hotel.* **from time to time.** Once in a while: *I never see her but I call her from time to time.* **have the time. 1.** To know what time it is: *I didn't have a watch, so I asked someone else if he had the time.* **2.** To have enough time: *Do you have the time to see me now?* **have the time of (one's) life.** To enjoy oneself a lot: *I had the time of my life at your party.* **high time.** Past the appropriate time; long overdue: *It's high time that you went to bed.* **in no time.** Almost instantly; immediately: *We'll be finished in no time.* **in the nick of time.** Just before it is too late: *She arrived with the food in the nick of time.* **in time. 1.** Before a time limit ends: *They had to hurry to arrive in time for the movie.* **2.** In the end; eventually: *In time you will see that she is right.* **3.** In the proper musical tempo: *moving in time to the music.* **just in time. 1.** Before it is too late: *We should be able to finish just in time.* **2.** In business, a kind of inventory management that keeps up with demand while keeping inventory to a minimum. **kill time.** To do sthg. unimportant while waiting: *What should we do to kill time until the movie starts?* **lose time.** To be slowed down; be behind schedule: *We were late because we lost time in a highway traffic jam.* **make time. 1.** To go very quickly: *We made time because the highway had been cleared of snow.* **2.** *Slang*. [with] To have (sbdy.) as a romantic partner: *He's been trying to make time with her all week.* **make up time.** To get back time that has been lost: *We had to make up the time we lost on our trip by*

ă–**cat**; ā–**pay**; âr–**care**; ä–**father**; ĕ–**get**; ē–**be**; ĭ–**sit**; ī–**nice**; îr–**here**; ŏ–**got**; ō–**go**; ô–**saw**; oi–**boy**; ou–**out**; o͝o–**took**; o͞o–**boot**; ŭ–**cut**; ûr–**word**; th–**thin**; *th*–**this**; hw–**when**; zh–**vision**; ə–**about**; N–French **bon**

staying on the main highway. **one at a time.** In order, one by one: *The teacher will work with us one at a time.* **on (one's) own time.** After work; not on the employer's time: *She got promoted by working at home, on her own time.* **on time. 1.** According to schedule; at the expected time: *arrive on time for school each day.* **2.** By paying in installments: *buy a car on time.* **pass the time.** To sit around and do nothing special: *We played cards to pass the time.* **take time out. 1.** To stop doing sthg. and rest: *I took time out from my homework to have a snack.* **2.** In sports, to stop playing a game for a brief time to rest, plan strategy, or talk: *Our team took time out to talk over our next play.* **tell time.** To read a clock to know what time it is: *He's only five and can't tell time yet.* **time after time** or **time and again.** Again and again; repeatedly: *I've told you time after time not to do that.* **time off.** A break from work or school: *I had to take time off from work to go to the dentist.*

HOMONYMS: time, thyme (plant).

---

time bomb *n.* **1.** A bomb that can be set to explode at a certain time. **2.** A person who has an explosive temper who may become violent: *Since he lost his job he's been a walking time bomb.*

time clock *n.* A device that records the starting and quitting times of employees.

time frame *n.* A period during which sthg. takes place or is expected to take place: *Can you finish this job within the time frame?*

time-hon•ored (tīm′ŏn′ərd) *adj.* Done or observed over a long time; traditional: *time-honored customs.*

time•keep•er (tīm′kē′pər) *n.* A person who keeps track of time in a sports event.

time•less (tīm′lĭs) *adj.* Independent of time; eternal: *the timeless universe.* —**time′less•ness** *n.* [U]

time•ly (tīm′lē) *adj.* **time•li•er, time•li•est.** Occurring at a convenient time; well timed: *a timely remark.*

time-out also **time out** (tīm′out′) *n.* **1.** In sports, a brief rest period during which play is stopped: *The team called its last time-out.* **2.** A period of minutes that a young child must spend without playing or being with others as a means of discipline: *The four-year-old got a time-out for biting her brother.*

time•piece (tīm′pēs′) *n.* An instrument, such as a watch or clock, that measures time.

tim•er (tī′mər) *n.* **1.** A person or thing that measures time; a timekeeper. **2.** A timepiece used to measure intervals of time: *a cooking timer.* **3.** A device that turns a light or appliance on and off at a set time.

times (tīmz) *prep.* Multiplied by: *Eight times three equals twenty-four.*

time•ta•ble (tīm′tā′bəl) *n.* **1.** A schedule

listing the times at which certain events are expected to occur, as the arrival and departure of trains at a station. **2.** A schedule for completion of a project: *What is the timetable for completion of the building?*

time•worn (tīm′wôrn′) *adj.* **1.** Showing the effects of long use or wear. **2.** Used too often; trite: *a timeworn joke.*

time zone *n.* Any of 24 divisions along lines running north and south drawn on a map of standard time to establish a system worldwide: *The U.S. has six time zones.*

tim•id (tĭm′ĭd) *adj.* Easily frightened and fearful; shy: *a timid child.* —**ti•mid′i•ty** *n.* [U] —**tim′id•ly** *adv.*

tim•ing (tī′mĭng) *n.* [U] The process of regulating when sthg. happens to achieve the best effect, as in music, theater, sports, or mechanics: *His timing was off and he missed the catch.*

tin (tĭn) *n.* **1.** [U] *Symbol* **Sn** A soft, silvery metallic element used to protect the surface of other metals, or combined with other metals to produce alloys, such as pewter and bronze. Atomic number 50. See table at **element.** **2.** [C] A metal container or box: *a cookie tin.* —*tr.v.* **tinned, tin•ning, tins.** To plate or coat (sthg.) with tin. —*adj.* Relating to or made of tin.

tin can *n.* A container made of steel coated on the inside with tin or another corrosion-resistant material, used for preserving food.

tinc•ture (tĭngk′chər) *n.* [C; U] An alcohol solution of a medicine: *tincture of iodine.*

tin•der (tĭn′dər) *n.* [U] A material that catches fire easily, used to start fires: *We use dry twigs as tinder.*

tin•der•box (tĭn′dər bŏks′) *n.* **1.** A metal box for holding tinder. **2.** A potentially dangerous or explosive situation: *Those board members hate each other, so the meeting could be a real tinderbox.*

tine (tīn) *n.* A prong or similar narrow or pointed part, as of a fork.

tin•foil also **tin foil** (tĭn′foil′) *n.* [U] A thin, paperlike sheet of aluminum, used to wrap food: *baked potatoes in tinfoil.*

ting (tĭng) *n.* A light metallic sound, as of a small bell. —*intr.v.* To make a light metallic sound.

tinge (tĭnj) *tr.v.* **tinged, tinge•ing** or **ting•ing, ting•es. 1.** To color (sthg.) slightly; tint: *The sunset tinged the sky with red.* **2.** To affect (sthg.) slightly, as with a contrasting quality: *a smile tinged with pain.* —*n.* A small amount of color or some other quality: *a green tinge; a tinge of sadness in her remarks.*

tin•gle (tĭng′gəl) *intr.v.* **tin•gled, tin•gling, tin•gles.** To have a prickling stinging sensation, as from cold or excitement: *My hand tingled when I touched the electrical wire.* —*n.* A prickling or stinging sensation: *a tingle in the hand.*

T

tin·ker (tĭng′kər) *intr.v.* To make unskilled and experimental efforts at repair: *tinker with a car.*

tin·kle (tĭng′kəl) *intr.v.* **tin·kled, tin·kling, tin·kles. 1.** To make light metallic sounds, as of a small bell. **2.** *Informal.* To urinate. Often used with children: *She took her four-year-old to the bathroom because he needed to tinkle.* —*n.* A light clear metallic sound.

tin·ny (tĭn′ē) *adj.* **tin·ni·er, tin·ni·est. 1.** Containing tin. **2.** Tasting or smelling of tin: *tinny canned food.* **3.** Having a thin metallic sound: *a tinny voice.*

tin·sel (tĭn′səl) *n.* [U] **1.** Very thin strips of a silvery material used as a decoration: *tinsel on the Christmas tree.* **2.** Something that is showy but has no value: *Hollywood is called "Tinsel Town."*

tint (tĭnt) *n.* **1.** A shade of a color, especially a pale variation: *a blue tint.* **2.** A slight coloration; a tinge: *a tint of red in the sky.* —*tr.v.* To give a tint to (sthg.); color: *tint hair.*

ti·ny (tī′nē) *adj.* **ti·ni·er, ti·ni·est.** Extremely small: *tiny feet.* See Synonyms at **little.**

tip¹ (tĭp) *n.* **1.** The extreme end of sthg.: *a house on the tip of the island; asparagus tips.* **2.** A piece that fits on the end of sthg.: *the rubber tip of a cane.* —*tr.v.* **tipped, tip·ping, tips.** To provide (sthg.) with a tip.

tip² (tĭp) *v.* **tipped, tip·ping, tips.** —*tr.* **1.** To push or knock over (sthg.); overturn or topple: *The wind tipped over the vase on the table.* **2.** To slant (sthg.); tilt: *He tipped his cup as he drank.* —*intr.* To become tilted; slanted: *The boat's deck tipped as the wave passed.* ♦ **tip over.** *tr.v.* [sep.] To turn (sthg.) upside down: *He tipped his chair over.*

tip³ (tĭp) *tr.v.* **tipped, tip·ping, tips.** To tap or deflect (a ball or puck, for example), especially in scoring: *The player tipped the ball into the net.*

tip⁴ (tĭp) *n.* **1.** A small sum of money given to sbdy. for performing a service; a gratuity: *She left a 15% tip for the waiter.* **2.** Useful information; a helpful hint: *a book with tips on car repair.* —*tr.v.* **tipped, tip·ping, tips.** To give a tip to (sbdy.): *tipped the waiter generously.* —*intr.* To give tips or a tip: *tips generously.* ♦ **tip off.** *tr.v.* [sep.] To provide (sbdy.) with useful information: *He tipped off the police about the robbery.* —**tip′per** *n.* —**tip′ster** *n.*

tip-off (tĭp′ôf′ *or* tĭp′ŏf′) *n. Informal.* A piece of secret information: *Her smile was a tip-off that the test had gone well.*

tip·sy (tĭp′sē) *adj.* **tip·si·er, tip·si·est. 1.** Slightly drunk. **2.** Unsteady or crooked. —**tip′si·ly** *adv.* —**tip′si·ness** *n.* [U]

tip·toe (tĭp′tō′) *intr.v.* **tip·toed, tip·toe·ing, tip·toes.** To walk quietly on one's toes:

She tiptoed into the baby's room. —*n.* The tip of a toe or the toes: *She walked on tiptoe.*

tip·top (tĭp′tŏp′) *adj.* Excellent; first-rate: *feeling in tiptop shape.*

ti·rade (tī′rād′) *n.* A long angry speech, usually criticizing sbdy./sthg.: *The teacher delivered a tirade on lateness.*

tire¹ (tīr) *v.* **tired, tir·ing, tires.** —*intr.* **1.** To become weary or weak: *She does not tire easily.* **2.** To become bored; lose interest: *The audience tired after the first act of the play.* —*tr.* **1.** To make (sbdy.) tired: *The long walk tired me.* **2.** To exhaust the interest of (sbdy.); bore: *His long speech tired the listeners.*

tire² (tīr) *n.* A covering for a wheel, usually made of rubber and filled with compressed air.

tired (tīrd) *adj.* **1.a.** Exhausted; weary: *a tired athlete.* **b.** Impatient; bored: *a tired audience.* **2.** Overused: *a tired joke.*

tir·ing (tīr′ĭng) *adj.* Causing fatigue: *Driving eight hours was very tiring.*

tire·less (tīr′lĭs) *adj.* Not tiring easily: *a tireless worker.* —**tire′less·ly** *adv.*

tire·some (tīr′səm) *adj.* Causing fatigue or boredom: *a tiresome job; a long tiresome speech.* See Synonyms at **boring.**

'tis (tĭz). Contraction of *it is.*

tis·sue (tĭsh′ōo) *n.* **1.** [C; U] The substance that plants and animals are made of; a system of cells: *muscle tissue.* **2.** [U] Very thin paper: *a glass wrapped in tissue.* **3.** [C; U] A piece of soft absorbent paper used as a handkerchief: *wipe your nose with a tissue.*

tissue paper *n.* [U] Light thin paper used for wrapping gifts or protecting breakable objects.

tit (tĭt) *n.* An offensive word for a woman's breast.

ti·ta·ni·um (tī tā′nē əm *or* tĭ tā′nē əm) *n.* [U] *Symbol* **Ti** A shiny, white metallic element that is strong, light, and highly resistant to corrosion. Atomic number 22. See table at **element.**

tithe (tīth) *n.* A tenth of the money sbdy. earns given for the support of a religious institution. —*tr.v.* **tithed, tith·ing, tithes.** To give a religious institution one tenth of (the money one earns in a year).

tit·il·late (tĭt′l āt′) *tr.v.* **tit·il·lat·ed, tit·il·lat·ing, tit·il·lates.** To excite or stimulate (sbdy.) in a pleasurable, often sexual way: *an author expert in titillating the reader.* —**tit′il·la′tion** *n.* [U]

ti·tle (tīt′l) *n.* **1.** [C] **a.** A name given to a book, painting, or musical composition. **b.** A heading of a book chapter. **2.** [C] A word attached to a person's name to show rank or used as a sign of respect, as in: *Professor Lee; President Lincoln.* **3.a.** [U] The legal right to own sthg. **b.** [C] The document that shows such a legal right: *receiving the title to their car.* **4.** [C] A championship in sports: *Our team won the title last year.* —*tr.v.* **ti·tled, ti·tling, ti·tles.** To give a title to (sbdy./ sthg.): *What did you title your report?*

tit·ter (tĭt′ər) *intr.v.* To laugh in a quiet, nervous way; giggle: *The other children tittered when he blushed.* —*n.* A nervous giggle.

tiz·zy (tĭz′ē) *n., pl.* **tiz·zies.** *Slang.* A state of nervous excitement or confusion: *I was in a tizzy before the guests arrived.*

TNT (tē′ĕn tē′) *n.* [U] A chemical compound used mainly as an explosive.

to (tōō; tə *when unstressed*) *prep.* **1.** In the direction of; so as to reach: *a trip to Paris.* **2.** Toward: *He turned to me.* **3.** Reaching as far as: *The water was clear to the bottom.* **4.** Toward or reaching a certain state: *the governor's rise to power.* **5.** In contact with: *cheek to cheek.* **6.** In front of: *We stood face to face.* **7.** For the benefit of: *Tell it to me.* **8.** For the purpose of; for: *We went out to lunch.* **9.** Used to indicate belonging: *Do you have the belt to this dress?* **10.** Concerning or regarding: *Did you get an answer to your letter?* **11.** In a relationship with: *The river runs parallel to the road.* **12.** With the resulting condition of: *torn to shreds.* **13.** As an accompaniment of: *singing to an old tune.* **14.** Composing or constituting; in: *two pints to a quart.* **15.** In accord with: *That's not really to my liking.* **16.** As compared with: *This book is superior to her others.* **17.** Before: *The time is ten to five.* **18.** In honor of: *a toast to our visitors.* **19.a.** Used before a verb to indicate the infinitive: *I'd like to go.* **b.** Used alone when the infinitive is understood: *Go if you want to.* —*adv.* Into consciousness: *The patient came to.*

HOMONYMS: **to, too** (also), **two** (number).

toad (tōd) *n.* Any of numerous amphibians related to and resembling frogs, but with rougher, drier skin and living mostly on land.

HOMONYMS: **toad, toed** (having toes), **towed** (pulled).

to and fro *adv.* Back and forth: *She's always running to and fro.*

toast[1] (tōst) *tr.v.* **1.** To make and brown (bread or another food) by placing in a toaster, or close to a fire. **2.** To warm (sthg.) thoroughly, as before a fire: *toast one's feet by the fireplace.* —*n.* [U] Sliced bread that is heated and browned: *I'll just have toast and coffee for breakfast.*

toast[2] (tōst) *n.* **1.** The act of raising the glass and drinking in honor of sbdy./sthg. **2.** A person who receives much attention or acclaim: *The movie star became the toast of London.* —*tr.v.* To drink in honor of (sbdy./sthg.): *The guests toasted the bride.*

toast·er (tō′stər) *n.* An electrical appliance used to toast bread.

to·bac·co (tə băk′ō) *n., pl.* **to·bac·cos** or **to·bac·coes.** **1.** [C; U] The leaves of a tropical plant, processed for use in cigarettes, cigars, or snuff or for smoking in pipes. **2.** [U] Products, such as cigarettes or cigars, made from tobacco. **3.** [U] The habit of smoking tobacco: *He gave up tobacco years ago.*

to·day (tə dā′) *n.* [U] The present day or period of history: *the schedule for today; the composers of today.* —*adv.* **1.** During or on the present day: *He will arrive today.* **2.** During or at the present time: *Today more vitamins are sold than ever before.*

tod·dle (tŏd′l) *intr.v.* **tod·dled, tod·dling, tod·dles.** To walk with short unsteady steps, as a small child does.

tod·dler (tŏd′lər) *n.* A young child, usually between the ages of one and three.

to-do (tə dōō′) *n., pl.* **to-dos** (tə dōōz′). *Informal.* A commotion or fuss: *make a big to-do over the price.* —*adj.* Relating to things still to be done: *a to-do list.*

toe (tō) *n.* **1.** One of the extensions from the foot of a human or other animal: *He broke his big toe.* **2.** The part of a sock, stocking, shoe, or boot that fits over the toes: *I have a hole in the toe of my sock.* —*v.* **toed, toe·ing, toes.** —*tr.* To touch, kick, or reach (sthg.) with the toes. —*intr.* To walk, stand, or move with the toes pointed in a certain direction: *She toes out.* ◆ **on (one's) toes.** Ready to act; alert: *Be on your toes today. The boss is coming by.* **step on (one's) toes.** To hurt or offend the feelings of sbdy.: *You've stepped on my toes too many times.* **toe the line.** To behave properly: *She toes the line around her grandparents.*

HOMONYMS: **toe, tow** (pull).

toed (tōd) *adj.* Having toes, especially a certain kind or number of toes: *a long-toed bird; a two-toed sloth.*

HOMONYMS: **toed, toad** (animal), **towed** (pulled).

TOEFL (tō′fəl) *abbr.* An abbreviation of Test of English as a Foreign Language.

toe·nail (tō′nāl′) *n.* A nail on a toe.

tof·fee (tô′fē *or* tŏf′ē) *n.* [U] A hard chewy candy made of brown sugar or molasses and butter.

to·fu (tō′fōō) *n.* [U] A soft white food made from soybeans. Tofu is often used in salads and cooked foods, especially Asian dishes.

to·geth·er (tə gĕth′ər) *adv.* **1.** In a single group or place: *Many people were crowded together.* **2.** In contact: *rubbing one's hands together.* **3.** In relationship to another: *My cats get along together.* **4.** By cooperative

T

effort: *We painted the room together.* **5.** Simultaneously: *The bells rang out together.* **6.** *Informal.* Into an effective condition to do sthg.: *Get yourself together.* ◆ **have (one's) act together.** To have everything under control: *I admire her; she really has her act together.* —**to•geth'er•ness** *n.* [U]

toil (toil) *intr.v.* **1.** To labor continuously; work hard: *We toiled all day at cleaning up the yard.* **2.** To proceed with difficulty: *toiling up a steep hill.* —*n.* [U] Exhausting labor or effort. —**toil'er** *n.*

toi•let (toi'lĭt) *n.* **1.** A bathroom fixture that uses water to flush away waste products: *sitting on the toilet.* **2.** A room containing such a fixture: *Where is the toilet?*

toilet paper *n.* [U] Thin paper in rolls used to clean oneself when using the toilet.

toi•let•ry (toi'lĭ trē) *n., pl.* **toi•let•ries.** *(usually plural).* An article, such as soap or shampoo, used to clean or groom the body.

toilet water *n.* [U] A scented liquid used as a light perfume.

to•ken (tō'kən) *n.* **1.** Something that represents sthg. else; a sign: *A white flag is a token of surrender.* **2.** A keepsake; a souvenir: *She gave me this watch as a token of our friendship.* **3.** A piece of stamped metal used as a substitute for money: *subway tokens.* —*adj.* **1.** Done as a promise of an action in the future: *a token payment.* **2.** Minimal; merely symbolic: *token resistance to the new leader.* ◆ **by the same token.** In the same way; similarly: *By the same token, you can't spend more money than you have.* **in token of.** As an indication of: *a ring given in token of love.*

told (tōld) *v.* Past tense and past participle of **tell.**

tol•er•a•ble (tŏl'ər ə bəl) *adj.* **1.** Not too bad; not terrible: *tolerable food.* **2.** Fairly good: *in tolerable health.* —**tol'er•a•bly** *adv.*

tol•er•ance (tŏl'ər əns) *n.* **1.** [U] The ability to accept beliefs different from one's own. **2.** [C; U] The ability to endure hardship or pain. **3.** [C; U] The ability of a plant or animal to resist the effects of a poison or drug.

tol•er•ant (tŏl'ər ənt) *adj.* **1.** Able to accept the beliefs or practices of others: *a tolerant individual.* **2.** Able to endure a difficult situation or environmental condition: *plants tolerant of extreme heat; tolerant of his children's noisy games.*

tol•er•ate (tŏl'ə rāt') *tr.v.* **tol•er•at•ed, tol•er•at•ing, tol•er•ates.** **1.** To allow (sthg.) to happen; permit: *Why does she tolerate his interruptions?* **2.** To respect (the beliefs or practices of others). **3.** To put up with (sthg.); endure: *I won't tolerate your bad*

manners. **4.** To have a tolerance for (a drug or poison).

tol•er•a•tion (tŏl'ə rā'shən) *n.* [U] **1.** Accepting the actions or beliefs of others. **2.** Official recognition of the political and religious rights of all groups.

toll¹ (tōl) *n.* **1.** [C; U] A fee charged to cross a bridge or use a highway. **2.** [C; U] A charge for a service, as a long-distance telephone call. **3.** [U] An amount of loss or damage sthg. causes: *At the end of the war the toll was 5,000 dead and 9,000 injured.* ◆ **take a toll.** To cause loss or damage: *The hurricane took a heavy toll in lives and property.*

toll² (tōl) *v.* —*tr.* **1.** To ring (a bell) slowly: *tolling the church bells.* **2.** To announce (sthg.) by tolling: *The bell tolled the hour.* —*intr.* To ring in slowly repeated single tones.

toll•booth (tōl'bōōth') *n.* A booth where a toll is collected.

tom (tŏm) *n.* The male of various animals, especially a male cat or turkey.

tom•a•hawk (tŏm'ə hôk') *n.* A light ax used in the past as a weapon and tool by certain Native American peoples.

to•ma•to (tə mā'tō *or* tə mä'tō) *n., pl.* **to•ma•toes.** The soft red, fleshy fruit of a widely grown plant, eaten raw or cooked: *a chicken sandwich with lettuce and tomato.*

tomb (tōōm) *n.* **1.** A place where a dead person is buried; a grave. **2.** A room or structure for the burial of the dead.

tom•boy (tŏm'boi') *n.* An outdated term for an active, often athletic, girl.

tomb•stone (tōōm'stōn') *n.* A monument marking a tomb.

tom•cat (tŏm'kăt') *n.* A male cat.

tome (tōm) *n.* A large, heavy book, especially a scholarly one.

to•mor•row (tə môr'ō *or* tə mŏr'ō) *n.* [U] **1.** The day following today. **2.** The near future: *space flights of tomorrow.* —*adv.* On or for the day following today: *I will return your book tomorrow.*

ton (tŭn) *n.* **1.a.** A unit of weight equal to 2,000 pounds in the United States. **b.** A unit of weight equal to 2,240 pounds in Great Britain. **c.** A metric ton. See table at **measurement.** **2.** *Informal.* A very large quantity of sthg.: *I have to buy tons of books.*

tone (tōn) *n.* **1.** [C] A sound with a distinct pitch or quality; a note: *A musical scale has eight tones.* **2.** [C] The quality or character of sound: *The violin has a lovely tone.* **3.** [C] A color or shade of color: *a green tone.* **4.** [U] The tension of a muscle at rest: *good muscle tone.* **5.** [C] A manner of expression in speech or writing: *an angry tone of voice.* **6.** [C; U] A general quality or atmosphere: *the tone of the debate; a quiet tone of elegance in* *the room.* —v. **toned, ton•ing, tones. ♦ tone down.** *tr.v.* [sep.] To make (sthg.) less colorful or harsh; moderate: *We can tone down the room by painting it white.* **tone up.** *tr.v.* [sep.] To make (muscles) stronger and firmer: *He toned up his muscles.* —*intr.v.* To become more vigorous: *You need to tone up.*

tongs (tôngz *or* tŏngz) *pl.n.* A device with two movable arms used for lifting sthg., especially sthg. hot: *Use the tongs to turn the chicken.*

tongue (tŭng) *n.* **1.** [C] The fleshy muscular organ in the mouth that is used for tasting, eating, and speaking. **2.** [C; U] The tongue of an animal, such as a cow, used as food. **3.** [C] Something that looks like a tongue, such as the piece of material under the laces of a shoe. **4.** [C] A spoken language: *Her native tongue is Swedish.* **5.** [C; U] A manner of speech: *He has a sharp tongue.* ♦ **hold (one's) tongue.** To remain silent: *No matter what he does, hold your tongue.* **on the tip of (one's) tongue.** Almost, but not quite, remembered: *His name is on the tip of my tongue.* **tongue-in-cheek.** Said in a joking manner; not meant to be taken seriously: *a tongue-in-cheek comment.*

tongue-tied (tŭng′tīd′) *adj.* Unable to speak, speechless as from shyness or embarrassment: *She was completely tongue-tied when she stood up to speak.*

tongue twister *n.* **1.** A word or group of words that is difficult to say rapidly. **2.** Something that is difficult to pronounce: *His name is a real tongue twister.*

ton•ic (tŏn′ĭk) *n.* [C; U] **1.** A medicine that refreshes the body. **2.** A bitter-tasting carbonated drink. **3.** A word used in New England for a carbonated drink.

to•night (tə nīt′) *adv.* On or during the present or coming night: *I'll see you tonight at 10:00.* —*n.* [U] This night or the night of this day: *Tonight is a very special occasion.*

ton•nage (tŭn′ĭj) *n.* [U] **1.** Weight measured in tons. **2.** The number of tons of water a ship displaces when afloat.

ton•sil (tŏn′səl) *n.* Either of two small organs at the back of the throat, believed to help protect the body from respiratory infections.

ton•sil•lec•to•my (tŏn′sə lĕk′tə mē) *n., pl.* **ton•sil•lec•to•mies.** The removal of a tonsil or tonsils by means of surgery.

ton•sil•li•tis (tŏn′sə lī′tĭs) *n.* [U] An infection in the tonsils.

too (tōō) *adv.* **1.** In addition; also: *I can play the piano, too.* See Synonyms at **besides. 2.** More than enough; excessively: *You worry too much.* **3.** Very; extremely: *I'm only too happy to be of service.* **4.** *Informal.* Indeed; so: *You will too do it!*

took (tōok) *v.* Past tense of **take.**

tool (tōol) *n.* **1.** A device, such as a hammer or saw, held in the hand and used to make or repair sthg. **2.** A machine, such as an electric drill, used to make or repair sthg. **3.** Something used to accomplish a task: *Words are a writer's most important tools.*

toot (tōot) *v.* —*intr.* To sound a horn or whistle in short blasts. —*tr.* To blow or sound (a horn or whistle): *He tooted his car horn at his friend.* —*n.* A blast of a horn or whistle. ♦ **toot (one's) own horn.** To praise oneself; brag: *He's always tooting his own horn!*

tooth (tōoth) *n., pl.* **teeth** (tēth). **1.** The hard, white objects in the mouth used for biting and chewing. **2.** The toothlike parts of sthg., such as a comb or a saw. ♦ **fight tooth and nail.** To resist sbdy./sthg. fiercely: *She fought tooth and nail to keep her job.* **get (one's) teeth into.** To do a job with enthusiasm: *She really got her teeth into the project.* **set (one's) teeth on edge.** To cause sbdy. discomfort: *The sound of a dog barking sets my teeth on edge.*

tooth•ache (tōōth′āk′) *n.* [C; U] A pain in or near a tooth.

tooth•brush (tōōth′brŭsh′) *n.* A brush used for cleaning the teeth.

toothed (tōōtht *or* tōōthd) *adj.* Having teeth, especially a certain number or type: *sharp-toothed jaws; a fine-toothed comb.*

tooth•paste (tōōth′pāst′) *n.* [U] A paste used to clean the teeth.

tooth•pick (tōōth′pĭk′) *n.* A small piece of wood or other material for removing pieces of food from between the teeth.

top¹ (tŏp) *n.* **1.** The uppermost part, point, surface, or end: *the words at the top of the page; luggage on the top of the car.* **2.** Something that covers an uppermost part: *the top of a trash can.* **3.** The upper half of a two-piece article of clothing. **4.** The highest position: *He is at the top of the company.* —*adj.* **1.** Situated at the top: *the top drawer.* **2.** Of the highest amount or quality: *You pay top prices at a department store.* —*tr.v.* **topped, top•ping, tops. 1.** To serve as or supply a top to (sthg.): *top a cake with frosting.* **2.** To reach the top of (sthg.): *We topped the hill and started to climb down.* **3.** To exceed or surpass (sthg.): *He just topped the old record.* ♦ **blow (one's) top.** To lose one's temper: *He blew his top when he wasn't promoted.* **off the top of (one's) head.** *Informal.* Without preparation or previous thought: *I don't know how much it costs, but I can give you a guess off the top of my head.* **on top of.** *Informal.* **1.** In control of: *It's a big problem, but she's on top of it.* **2.** In addition to; besides: *two papers due next week and an exam on top of that.* **on top of the world.** Very happy: *She was on top of the world when she was selected for the Olympic team.* **over the top.** Beyond what was expected: *Our sales were over the top last quarter.*

top² (tŏp) *n.* A toy with one pointed end that spins around in a circle.

to·paz (tō′păz′) *n.* [C; U] A blue, yellow, brown, pink, or colorless gem used to make jewelry.

top·coat (tŏp′kōt′) *n.* A lightweight overcoat.

top·flight (tŏp′flīt′) *adj. Informal.* First-rate; excellent: *a topflight executive.*

top hat *n.* A man's tall, black hat used on formal occasions.

top-heav·y (tŏp′hĕv′ē) *adj.* Having too much weight at the top and therefore likely to fall over: *Careful! Those shelves are top-heavy.*

top·ic (tŏp′ĭk) *n.* **1.** The subject of a speech or a piece of writing: *What is the topic of your speech?* See Synonyms at **subject. 2.** A subject of discussion or conversation: *In geography class we discussed the topic of natural resources.*

top·i·cal (tŏp′ĭ kəl) *adj.* **1.** Relating to a particular location or place; local: *topical news items.* **2.** Currently of interest: *the economy and other topical issues.* **3.** On a particular part of the body: *topical application of a first-aid cream.* —**top′i·cal·ly** *adv.*

top·less (tŏp′lĭs) *adj.* Not wearing any clothes on the top of the body.

top·most (tŏp′mōst′) *adj.* Highest; uppermost: *the topmost shelf.*

top·notch (tŏp′nŏch′) *adj. Informal.* First-rate; excellent: *a topnotch tennis player.*

to·pog·ra·phy (tə pŏg′rə fē) *n.* [U] The physical features of a place, such as mountains and valleys. —**to·pog′ra·pher** *n.* —**top′o·graph′ic, top′o·graph′i·cal** *adj.*

top·ping (tŏp′ĭng) *n.* [C; U] A sauce, frosting, or decoration placed on food before serving.

top·ple (tŏp′əl) *v.* **top·pled, top·pling, top·ples.** —*tr.* To push or throw (sthg.) over; overturn or overthrow: *The army toppled the new government.* —*intr.* To totter and fall: *The pile of books toppled over.*

tops (tŏps) *adj. Slang.* First-rate; excellent: *He's tops in his field.*

top-se·cret (tŏp′sē′krĭt) *adj.* Containing information that only a few specific people are allowed to see.

top·soil (tŏp′soil′) *n.* [U] The layer of soil at the surface of the ground.

top·sy-tur·vy (tŏp′sē tûr′vē) *adv.* **1.** Upside-down. **2.** In a state of confusion: *I turned the room topsy-turvy looking for the keys.* —*adj.* Confused; disordered: *a topsy-turvy political situation.*

To·rah also **to·rah** (tôr′ə *or* tô rä′) *n.* **1.** A book containing the basic elements of Jewish religious law, literature, and teaching. **2.** A scroll containing this information, used during religious services.

torch (tôrch) *n.* **1.a.** A lighting device with a flame at the end of a handle. **b.** *Chiefly British.* A flashlight. **2.** A tool with a very hot flame at the end, used to cut metal or burn off paint; a blowtorch.

tore (tôr) *v.* Past tense of **tear¹.**

tor·ment (tôr′mĕnt′) *n.* [C; U] **1.** Great physical or mental pain: *the torment of a toothache; the torments of jealousy.* **2.** A bother or trouble: *That dog is the torment of its owners.* —*tr.v.* (tôr mĕnt′ *or* tôr′mĕnt′). **1.** To cause (sbdy.) great pain. **2.** To annoy, pester, or harass (sbdy.): *Stop tormenting me with silly questions.* —**tor·men′tor** *n.*

torn (tôrn) *v.* Past participle of **tear¹.**

tor·na·do (tôr nā′dō) *n., pl.* **tor·na·does** *or* **tor·na·dos.** A violent windstorm in the form of a column of air several hundred yards wide spinning at speeds of up to 500 miles (800 kilometers) per hour, accompanied by a funnel-shaped cloud.

tor·pe·do (tôr pē′dō) *n., pl.* **tor·pe·does.** A weapon shot from an airplane, boat, or submarine that travels underwater and explodes on a target. —*tr.v.* **tor·pe·doed, tor·pe·do·ing, tor·pe·does.** To attack (sthg.) with a torpedo.

torque (tôrk) *n.* [U] A force that causes twisting or rotation: *The car's engine produces enough torque to turn the wheels.*

tor·rent (tôr′ənt *or* tŏr′ənt) *n.* **1.** A swift-flowing stream. **2.** A heavy rainstorm: *rain falling in torrents.* **3.** A heavy uncontrolled outpouring: *a torrent of insults.* —**tor·ren′-tial** (tô rĕn′shəl *or* tə rĕn′shəl) *adj.*

tor·rid (tôr′ĭd *or* tŏr′ĭd) *adj.* **1.** Very dry and hot: *torrid weather.* **2.** Passionate: *a torrid romance.* —**tor′rid·ly** *adv.*

tor·so (tôr′sō) *n., pl.* **tor·sos.** The human body except for the head and limbs; the trunk.

torte (tôrt *or* tôr′tə) *n.* A rich cake.

tor·til·la (tôr tē′yə) *n.* A round, flat Mexican bread made from cornmeal or wheat flour.

tor·toise (tôr′tĭs) *n.* Any of various turtles that live on land.

tor·toise·shell (tôr′tĭs shĕl′) *n.* [U] The brownish outer covering of certain sea turtles or a similar synthetic material, used to make combs and jewelry.

tor·tu·ous (tôr′chōō əs) *adj.* **1.** Winding; twisting: *a tortuous road.* **2.** Confusing: *a tortuous argument.* —**tor′tu·ous·ly** *adv.* —**tor′tu·ous·ness** *n.* [U]

tor·ture (tôr′chər) *n.* **1.** [U] Causing extreme physical pain in order to punish sbdy. or force sbdy. to do sthg. or provide information: *The army resorted to torture to get the information.* **2.** [C; U] Extreme physical or mental pain: *the torture of a toothache.*

—*tr.v.* **tor·tured, tor·tur·ing, tor·tures.**
To cause (sbdy./sthg.) great pain: *the boy was torturing the cat, but we stopped him.*
—**tor′tur·er** *n.*

toss (tôs *or* tŏs) *v.* —*tr.* **1.a.** To throw (sthg.) lightly or casually: *toss a ball to a teammate.* See Synonyms at **throw. b.** To move (sthg.) around continuously: *Large waves tossed the ship around.* **2.** To move or lift (the head) with a sudden movement: *The horse tossed its head.* **3.** To flip (a coin) to decide sthg.: *Toss the coin to decide which team receives the ball.* **4.** To mix (a salad) lightly with a dressing: *You can toss the salad for me.* —*intr.* **1.** To be thrown here and there. **2.** To move about restlessly; twist and turn: *I tossed in my sleep all night.* —*n.* **1.** The act of tossing: *a toss of the coin.* **2.** A rapid upward movement, as of the head: *She gave her head a toss.* ♦ **toss off.** *tr.v.* [insep.] To do (sthg.) very quickly: *toss off a letter.*

toss·up (tôs′ŭp′ *or* tŏs′ŭp′) *n. Informal.* An even chance or choice: *It's a tossup as to who will win.*

tot (tŏt) *n.* A small child.

to·tal (tōt′l) *n.* **1.** An amount obtained by addition; a sum. **2.** A whole quantity. —*adj.* **1.** Relating to or constituting the whole: *the total population of the state.* **2.** Complete; absolute: *a total eclipse.* —*tr.v.* **1.** To find the sum of (several numbers); add up: *totaling expenses.* **2.** To equal (a total of); amount to: *Your bill totals $25.* —**to′tal·ly** *adv.*

to·tal·i·tar·i·an (tō tăl′ĭ târ′ē ən) *adj.* Relating to a form of government in which one political party exercises complete control and uses force to keep control. —*n.* A person who supports such a form of government. —**to·tal′i·tar′i·an·ism** *n.* [U]

to·tal·i·ty (tō tăl′ĭ tē) *n.* [U] **1.** The quality or state of being total. **2.** A total amount; a sum.

tote (tōt) *tr.v.* **tot·ed, tot·ing, totes.** *Informal.* To haul (sthg.); carry: *Tote the groceries home for me.*

tote bag *n.* A large handbag or shopping bag.

to·tem (tō′təm) *n.* **1.** An animal, a plant, or an object that serves as the symbol or emblem of a group of people: *The bear serves as the totem for some Native American tribes.* **2.** A statue representing such an object. —**to·tem′ic** *adj.*

totem pole *n.* A post carved and painted with a series of totemic symbols by certain Native American peoples of the northwest Pacific Coast.

tot·ter (tŏt′ər) *intr.v.* **1.** To sway as if about to fall: *A pile of books tottered at the edge of the table.* **2.** To walk unsteadily; stagger: *The baby tottered and fell down.*

touch (tŭch) *v.* —*tr.* **1.** To cause a part of the body, especially the hand or fingers, to feel (sbdy./sthg.): *I touched the statue.* **2.** To bring

sthg. into contact with (sthg.): *touched the sore spot with a probe; touching fire to a fuse.* **3.** To press or push (sthg.) lightly: *touch a control to improve the TV picture.* **4.** To disturb or move (sthg.) by handling: *Just don't touch anything in my room!* **5.** To meet (sthg.) without going beyond: *the line where his property touches mine.* **6.** To affect the emotions of (sbdy.); move to tears, sympathy, or gratitude: *an appeal that touched us deeply.* —*intr.* To be or come into contact: *Don't let the live wires touch.* —*n.* **1.** [C] The act or an instance of touching: *My teacher got my attention by a touch on my arm.* **2.** [U] The sense by which external objects or forces are perceived through contact with the body: *the sense of touch.* **3.** [C] A sensation experienced in touching sthg. with a characteristic texture: *the touch of silk.* **4.** [C] A light push; a tap: *a switch that requires just a touch.* **5.** [C] A small change or addition, or the effect achieved by it: *Candlelight provided just the right touch.* **6.** [C] A very small amount: *a touch of jealousy; a touch of pepper.* **7.** [C] A fine skill, especially with the hands: *She has a light touch.* **8.** [U] The state of being in contact or communication: *I've lost touch with most of my classmates.* ♦ **be a soft touch.** To respond easily to others, especially with money: *I can borrow the money from my brother; he's a soft touch.* **finishing touch.** The last detail of sthg.: *I put the finishing touches on my paper last night.* **have the touch.** To have a special skill with sthg.: *She has the touch for playing basketball.* **in touch.** [*with*] In contact (with sbdy./ sthg.): *in touch with his feelings; Let's stay in touch.* **touch base.** *Informal.* To communicate: *Let's touch base by phone before the weekend.*

touch down. *intr.v.* To make contact with the ground; land: *The plane touched down smoothly.* **touch off.** *tr.v.* [sep.] To cause (sthg.) to begin: *touch off a debate; touch off an explosion.* **touch on** or **upon.** *tr.v.* [insep.] To speak about or mention (a topic) briefly: *The news article only touched on the reasons for the strike.* **touch up.** *tr.v.* [sep.] To improve (sthg.) by making minor corrections, changes, or additions: *I touched up the painting before submitting it.*

touch-and-go (tŭch′ən gō′) *adj.* Dangerous and uncertain; precarious: *His heart was very weak; it was a touch-and-go situation.*

touch·down (tŭch′doun′) *n.* **1.** In football, the act of carrying the ball across the opponent's goal line for a score of six points. **2.** The contact of an aircraft or a spacecraft with the surface of the earth.

touched (tŭcht) *adj.* **1.** Emotionally affected; moved: *I was touched by your gesture.* **2.** *Informal.* Mentally unbalanced: *She's a little touched in the head.*

touch·ing (tŭch′ĭng) *adj.* Causing a sympathetic reaction: *a touching speech.* —**touch′-ing·ly** *adv.*

touch·y (tŭch′ē) *adj.* **touch·i·er, touch·i·est. 1.** Easily offended; oversensitive: *She's a little touchy today.* **2.** Delicate: *a touchy operation.*

tough (tŭf) *adj.* **1.** Not easy to tear or break; strong and resilient: *a tough substance.* **2.** Hard to cut or chew: *a tough steak.* **3.** Physically strong; rugged: *a tough athlete.* **4.** Requiring hard work; difficult: *a tough lesson.* **5.** Stubborn; resolute: *a tough man to convince.* **6.** Rough; violent: *tough criminals.* **7.** *Slang.* Too bad; unfortunate: *a tough break.* ◆ **as tough as nails.** Very strong and resolute: *I can't convince him—he's as tough as nails.* **a tough customer.** A person who is difficult to deal with: *Be sure your report is perfect before you hand it in to your teacher; she's a real tough customer.* **be** or **get tough with.** To be or become strict with (sbdy.): *After the fight, the school administration got tough with students.* **tough it out.** To stay throughout a hard or trying experience: *If the company cuts our wages again, some workers will be able to tough it out; others won't.* —**tough′ly** *adv.* —**tough′ness** *n.* [U]

tough·en (tŭf′ən) *tr. & intr.v.* To make or become tough: *Overcooking toughened the steak. With exercise, your body will toughen.*

tou·pee (tōō pā′) *n.* A small wig for men worn to cover a spot where hair no longer grows.

tour (tōōr) *n.* **1.** A trip with visits to many places of interest for business, pleasure, or instruction: *a tour of Europe.* **2.** A short trip to or through a place: *a tour of the printing plant.* **3.** A journey to fulfill a round of engagements in several places: *a concert tour.* **4.** A period of duty at a single place or job: *a short tour in Japan.* —*intr. & tr.v.* To go on a tour or make a tour of: *touring through Spain; touring Canada.*

tour de force (tōōr′ də fôrs′) *n., pl.* **tours de force** (tōōr′ də fôrs′). Something showing great skill or strength: *Her violin playing was a tour de force.*

tour·ism (tōōr′ĭz′əm) *n.* [U] **1.** The practice of traveling for pleasure: *an increase in international tourisim.* **2.** The business of providing tours and services for travelers: *studying tourism in Switzerland.*

tour·ist (tōōr′ĭst) *n.* A person who travels for pleasure.

tour·na·ment (tōōr′nə mənt or tûr′nə-mənt) *n.* A contest made up of a series of games or trials: *a tennis tournament.*

tour·ni·quet (tōōr′nĭ kĭt or tûr′nĭ kĭt) *n.* Something, such as a band of cloth, used to temporarily stop bleeding in a limb.

tou·sle (tou′zəl) *tr.v.* **tou·sled, tou·sling, tou·sles.** To disarrange or rumple (sthg., especially the hair): *She tousled the baby's hair.*

tout (tout) *tr.v.* To promote or praise (sthg.) energetically; publicize: *touting the proposal at the town meeting.*

tow (tō) *tr.v.* To pull (sthg.) along behind by a chain or line: *tow a car.* See Synonyms at **pull.** —*n.* The act of towing: *trying to get a tow from a police truck.* ◆ **in tow.** Along with; accompanying: *She always has a child or two in tow. The tugboat had a rowboat in tow.*

HOMONYMS: tow, toe (foot part).

to·ward (tôrd or tə wôrd′) also **to·wards** (tôrdz or tə wôrdz′) *prep.* **1.** In the direction of: *driving toward the river.* **2.** In a position facing: *She had her back toward me.* **3.** Not long before in time: *It started raining toward dawn.* **4.** In relation to; regarding: *a positive attitude toward the future.* **5.** For partial payment of: *a payment toward the house.*

USAGE: toward The words **toward** and **towards** mean the same thing. **Toward** is more commonly used by American English speakers. **Towards** is the main form used by British speakers of English.

tow·el (tou′əl) *n.* A piece of absorbent cloth or paper used for wiping or drying: *a dish towel; paper towels.* —*tr.v.* To wipe or rub (sbdy./sthg.) dry with a towel: *We toweled the dog off.*

tow·er (tou′ər) *n.* **1.** A tall building or part of a building: *the Eiffel Tower.* **2.** A tall structure used for observation, signaling, or pumping: *an airport control tower.* —*intr.v.* [*over; above*] To rise to a noticeable height: *skyscrapers towering over New York.* ◆ **a tower of strength.** A person who provides comfort, protection, or strength in difficult situations: *His father is a tower of strength.*

tower
Eiffel Tower

tow·er·ing (tou′ər-ĭng) *adj.* **1.** Of great height; very tall: *towering peaks.* **2.** Outstanding: *a towering scientific discovery.* **3.** Intense; extreme: *in a towering rage.*

town (toun) *n.* **1.** An area where people live that is larger than a village and smaller than a city: *my home town.* **2.** The residents of such a population center: *The whole town came out to welcome us.* **3.** The commercial center of

an area: *She goes into town every Tuesday.*
♦ **go out on the town.** To enjoy oneself in a town or city, especially at night: *We went out on the town to celebrate our engagement.* **go to town.** To behave in a free, unrestrained way, especially in spending money or eating: *After he won the lottery, he went to town and bought an expensive new sports car. She's going to town on that pizza.*

tox•ic (tŏk′sĭk) *adj.* Poisonous: *toxic industrial wastes.*

tox•i•col•o•gy (tŏk′sĭ kŏl′ə jē) *n.* [U] The scientific and medical study of poisons, their effects and detection, and the treatment of poisoning. —**tox′i•col′o•gist** *n.*

tox•in (tŏk′sĭn) *n.* A poison produced by a plant, an animal, or a microorganism.

toy (toi) *n.* **1.** An object for children to play with: *sand toys.* **2.** A dog of a very small breed: *a toy poodle.* —*intr.v.* [with] To amuse oneself idly: *talking on the phone and toying with a pencil.*

tr. *abbr.* An abbreviation of: **1.** Transitive. **2.** Treasurer.

trace (trās) *n.* **1.** [C; U] A visible mark made or left by a person, a thing, or an animal: *the dog's traces in the kitchen.* **2.** [C] An extremely small amount: *a trace of cinnamon in the cake.* —*tr.v.* **traced, trac•ing, trac•es.** **1.** To follow the course or trail of (sbdy./sthg.): *trace a lost letter.* **2.** To follow the history or development of (sthg.): *trace the beginnings of the Industrial Revolution.* **3.** To copy (sthg.) by following lines seen through a sheet of transparent paper: *trace a picture.* —**trace′a•ble** *adj.*

track (trăk) *n.* **1.** A mark or trail of marks left by sbdy./sthg. that has passed: *tire tracks.* **2.** A pathway or course over which sthg. moves: *a bicycle track in the park.* **3.** A rail or set of parallel rails on which a train or trolley runs: *railroad tracks.* **4.** A racetrack: *spend a day at the track.* **5.** Track and field: *She's going out for track.* **6.** A selection from a sound recording: *the title track of the album.* —*tr.v.* **1.** To follow the footprints or trail of (sbdy./sthg.): *They tracked the animal through the woods.* **2.** To carry (sthg.) on the feet and deposit as tracks: *Don't track mud on the floor.* **3.** To observe or follow the course or progress of (sbdy./sthg.): *Radar is used to track weather balloons.* ♦ **a one-track mind.** A tendency to pay attention to only one thing: *She has a one-track mind; she's only interested in sports.* **cover (one's) tracks.** To try to hide what one has done: *The thief was caught because he didn't cover his tracks well enough.* **in (one's) tracks.** Suddenly: *We stopped in our tracks when we saw the mess.* **keep** or **lose track of.** To be informed or uninformed about (sbdy./sthg.): *I like to keep track of my college friends.* **make tracks. 1.** [*for*] To go toward (sthg.) quickly: *Let's*

make tracks for the store. **2.** To leave quickly: *When we saw him coming, we made tracks.* **off the beaten track.** Away from a center of activity; not well known: *It's a nice hotel, but it's a little off the beaten track.* **off track.** *intr.v.* Not going in the right direction: *Her silly questions got the whole class off track.* **on the right** or **wrong track.** Doing or thinking sthg. correctly or incorrectly: *He's on the right track in his studies.* **stop in (one's) tracks.** To be surprised: *His appearance at the party stopped me in my tracks.*

track down. *tr.v.* [sep.] To follow and find (sbdy./sthg.): *We tracked her down in the library.* —**track′er** *n.*

track and field *n.* [U] Athletic events performed on a running track and the field associated with it. —**track′-and-field′** *adj.*

track•ing station (trăk′ĭng) *n.* A place with instruments for watching and maintaining contact with an artificial satellite or spacecraft.

track meet *n.* A track-and-field competition between two or more teams.

track record *n. Informal.* A record of actual performance or accomplishment: *The mayor's track record on crime is good.*

tract (trăkt) *n.* **1.** A large area of land or water. **2.** A system of body organs and tissues that together perform a specialized function: *the digestive tract.*

trac•ta•ble (trăk′tə bəl) *adj.* Easily controlled; tamed: *a tractable child.* —**trac′ta•bly** *adv.*

trac•tion (trăk′shən) *n.* [U] **1.** Pulling power, such as of a draft animal or an engine: *steam traction.* **2.** The friction that prevents a wheel or foot from slipping or skidding over the surface on which it runs or walks: *a car with good traction in the snow.*

trac•tor (trăk′tər) *n.* A motor vehicle used for pulling farm machinery and other heavy equipment.

tractor

trade (trād) *n.* **1.** [U] The business of buying and selling goods: *an expert in international trade.* See Synonyms at **business. 2.** [C] The people who work in a particular business or industry: *the building and construction trades.* **3.** [U] An exchange of one thing for another: *Everyone brings something to market for sale or trade.* **4.** [C; U] An occupation, especially one requiring special skill with the hands; a craft: *the tailor's trade.* —*v.* **trad•ed, trad•ing, trades.** —*intr.* **1.** [*for; in*] To buy, sell, or barter: *He traded for furs along the Oregon coast.* **2.** To exchange one thing for another: *Let's trade.* **3.** [*at*] To shop regularly: *He trades at the local grocery store.* —*tr.* **1.** To exchange or swap (sthg.): *trade books with a friend.* **2.** To buy and sell

T

(stocks, for example): *trade commodities futures.* ◆ **trade in.** *tr.v.* [sep.] To surrender or sell (sthg. old or used), as partial payment on a new purchase: *traded in the old car for a new one.*

trade-in (trād'ĭn') *n.* Something accepted as partial payment for a new purchase: *We used our old car as a trade-in for the new one.*

trade·mark (trād'märk') *n.* A name, symbol, or other legally restricted device identifying a product. —*tr.v.* To register (sthg.) as a trademark: *trademark a design.*

trade·off (trād'ôf' *or* trād'ŏf') *n.* An exchange of one thing for another, especially a giving up of sthg. desirable for sthg. else regarded as more desirable.

trad·er (trā'dər) *n.* A person who trades; a dealer.

trade school *n.* A school that offers training in skilled trades; a vocational school.

trade union *n.* A labor union.

trade wind *n. (usually plural).* A consistent system of winds blowing northeasterly in the Northern Hemisphere and southeasterly in the Southern Hemisphere.

trad·ing post (trā'dĭng) *n.* A station or store in a sparsely settled area established by traders.

tra·di·tion (trə dĭsh'ən) *n.* **1.** [U] The passing down of such things as beliefs and customs from generation to generation, especially orally: *a story from the Navajo tradition.* **2.** [C] A custom or usage handed down from generation to generation: *We follow our family traditions and have a reunion each fall.* —**tra·di'tion·al** *adj.* —**tra·di'tion·al·ly** *adv.*

traf·fic (trăf'ĭk) *n.* [U] **1.** Buying and selling of goods; trade: *illegal traffic in exotic birds.* See Synonyms at **business. 2.** The movement of vehicles, people, or messages along routes of transportation or communication: *Traffic is heavy during rush hour.* —*intr.v.* **traf·ficked, traf·fick·ing, traf·fics.** [in] To carry on trade or other dealings, especially illegally: *a country that traffics in illegal weapons.* —**traf'fick·er** *n.*

trag·e·dy (trăj'ĭ dē) *n., pl.* **trag·e·dies. 1.** [C] A serious play or literary work with a sad ending. **2.** [U] The branch of drama including such works. **3.** [C] A very sad event; a disaster: *His death was a tragedy for his family.* —**trag'ic** (trăj'ĭk) *adj.* —**trag'i·cal·ly** *adv.*

trail (trāl) *v.* —*tr.* **1.** To follow or allow (sthg.) to follow: *a child trailing a toy dog.* **2.** To follow the traces or scent of (sbdy./sthg.), as in hunting; track: *hounds trailing a bear.* —*intr.* **1.** To drag or be dragged along the ground: *Her long skirt was trailing on the floor.* **2.** To extend, grow, or droop loosely over a surface: *ivy trailing over the ground.* **3.** To walk with tired steps:

exhausted runners trailing along the road. —*n.* **1.** A path or beaten track: *a ski trail.* **2.** A mark or trace left by sbdy./sthg.: *The car left a trail of dust.* **3.** The scent of a person or an animal: *hounds following the trail of a bear.* **4.** Something that is drawn along or follows behind; a train: *The mayor came down the street followed by a trail of reporters.*

trail·blaz·er (trāl'blā'zər) *n.* **1.** A person who opens a trail. **2.** A leader in a field; a pioneer: *a trailblazer in medicine.*

trail·er (trā'lər) *n.* **1.** A large vehicle pulled by a tractor or truck: *a horse trailer.* **2.** A van that can be pulled by an automobile or a truck and used as a home or an office.

train (trān) *n.* **1.** A locomotive and a series of connected railroad cars. **2.** A long line of moving people, animals, or vehicles: *a wagon train.* **3.** A part of a gown that trails behind the wearer. **4.** An orderly sequence of related events or thoughts: *His question interrupted my train of thought.* **5.** A set of linked mechanical parts: *a gear train.* —*v.* —*tr.* **1.** To teach or show (sbdy./sthg.) a certain way of acting or behaving: *training a child to be polite.* **2.** To make (sbdy./sthg.) proficient with specialized instruction and practice: *She trains young musicians.* See Synonyms at **teach. 3.** To prepare (sbdy.) physically, as with regular exercise: *coaches training the players for the championship game.* **4.** To cause (a plant or one's hair) to take a desired course or shape: *trained a rose bush up the wall.* **5.** [on] To aim (sthg.): *trained a camera on the audience.* —*intr.* To give or carry out a course of training: *The runner trained daily for the marathon.*

train·ee (trā nē') *n.* A person who is being trained.

train·er (trā'nər) *n.* A person who trains, especially one who coaches athletes, racehorses, or show animals.

train·ing (trā'nĭng) *n.* [U] **1.** The process or routine of one who trains. **2.** The state of being trained. ◆ **in** or **out of training.** In or out of good physical condition: *I realized I was out of training when I tried to run up the hill.*

trait (trāt) *n.* **1.** A distinctive feature, as of a person's character: *She has many positive traits.* See Synonyms at **quality. 2.** A genetically determined characteristic or condition: *a recessive trait for blue eyes.*

trai·tor (trā'tər) *n.* A person who commits treason, or betrays a cause or trust. —**trai'tor·ous** *adj.*

tra·jec·to·ry (trə jĕk'tə rē) *n., pl.* **tra·jec·to·ries.** The path of a moving body or particle.

tramp (trămp) *v.* —*intr.* To walk with a heavy step: *tramp up the stairs.* —*tr.* To cross (sthg.) on foot: *tramp the fields in search of wild* *berries.* —*n.* **1.** The sound of heavy walking: *We heard a tramp in the hall.* **2.** A walking trip; a hike: *We took a long tramp through the woods.* **3.** *Informal.* A person who goes from place to place as a vagrant: *A tramp slept in our barn.* **4.** *Slang.* An old, very insulting word for a woman who has had many sexual partners.

tram·ple (trăm′pəl) *v.* **tram·pled, tram·pling, tram·ples.** —*tr.* To step on heavily so as to crush (sthg.): *The dog trampled the flowers.* —*intr.* To treat sbdy./sthg. harshly: *He is always trampling on her feelings.*

tram·po·line (trăm′pə lēn′ *or* trăm′pə lĭn) *n.* A sheet of strong canvas attached with springs to a metal frame and used for gymnastic jumping and acrobatics.

trance (trăns) *n.* **1.** A condition like sleep: *The hypnotist put me in a trance.* **2.** A condition in which one pays little or no attention to one's surroundings, as in daydreaming or deep thought: *He was in a trance and didn't hear my question.*

tran·quil (trăng′kwəl *or* trăn′kwəl) *adj.* Quiet, still, peaceful: *a tranquil lake.* See Synonyms at **calm.** —**tran′quil·ly** *adv.*

tran·quil·ize (trăng′kwə līz′ *or* trăn′kwə- līz′) *tr.v.* **tran·quil·ized, tran·quil·iz·ing, tran·quil·iz·es.** To sedate or calm (a person or animal) with a drug: *The vet tranquilized the frightened horse.*

tran·quil·iz·er (trăng′kwə līz′ ər *or* trăn′- kwə līz′ ər) *n.* A drug used to make a person or animal calm.

tran·quil·i·ty (trăng kwĭl′ĭ tē *or* trăn kwĭl′- ĭ tē) *n.* [U] The quality of being tranquil; calmness: *a painting with a feeling of tranquility.*

trans– *pref.* A prefix that means: **1.** Across; beyond: *transatlantic.* **2.** Through: *transcontinental.* **3.** Change; transfer: *translate.*

trans·act (trăn săkt′ *or* trăn zăkt′) *tr.v.* To do, carry out, or conduct (business or affairs): *transact the sale of a house.*

trans·ac·tion (trăn săk′shən *or* trăn zăk′- shən) *n.* [C; U] The act of transacting, especially a business agreement or exchange: *cash transactions only.*

trans·at·lan·tic (trăns′ət lăn′tĭk *or* trănz′- ət lăn′tĭk) *adj.* Crossing or involving people on both sides of the Atlantic Ocean: *a transatlantic flight.*

tran·scend (trăn sĕnd′) *tr.v.* To go or be beyond (sthg.): *an experience that transcends human understanding.* —**tran·scen′dence** *n.* [U] —**tran·scen′dent** *adj.*

trans·con·ti·nen·tal (trăns′kŏn tə nĕn′tl) *adj.* Crossing a continent: *a transcontinental flight.*

tran·scribe (trăn skrīb′) *tr.v.* **tran·scribed, tran·scrib·ing, tran·scribes.** To write or type a copy of (sthg.): *transcribe a dictated letter.*

tran·script (trăn′skrĭpt′) *n.* Something tran-

scribed, especially a copy of a record: *college transcript.*

tran·scrip·tion (trăn skrĭp′shən) *n.* [C; U] The act or process of transcribing.

trans·fer (trăns fûr′ *or* trăns′fər) *v.* **trans· ferred, trans·fer·ring, trans·fers.** —*tr.* **1.** To move or cause (sbdy./sthg.) to pass from one place, person, or thing to another: *Bees transfer pollen from one flower to another.* **2.** To shift the ownership of (property) to another. —*intr.* **1.** To move oneself from one location or job to another: *He plans to transfer to another school.* **2.** To change from one form of public transportation to another: *transferred to another bus.* —*n.* (trăns′fər). **1.** [C; U] Also **transferal.** The moving of sthg. from one place, person, or thing to another: *the transfer of land by purchase.* **2.** [C] A person who transfers or is transferred, as a student who changes schools: *college transfers.* **3.** [C] A ticket allowing a passenger to change from one form of public transportation to another: *a bus transfer.*

trans·fer·a·ble (trăns fûr′ə bəl) *adj.* Able to be transferred: *a check that is not transferable.*

trans·form (trăns fôrm′) *tr.v.* [*into*] **1.** To change the form or appearance of (sbdy./ sthg.): *A kiss transformed the frog into a prince.* **2.** To change the nature, function, or condition of (sthg.); convert: *A steam engine transforms heat into energy.*

trans·for·ma·tion (trăns′fər mā′shən) *n.* **1.** [C; U] The act or an instance of transforming. **2.** [U] The state of being transformed. **3.** [C] A noticeable change, as in appearance, usually for the better: *She is making many transformations in her home.* —**trans′for· ma′tion·al** *adj.*

trans·form·er (trăns fôr′mər) *n.* A device that increases or decreases the voltage of electrical energy.

trans·fuse (trăns fyōōz′) *tr.v.* **trans·fused, trans·fus·ing, trans·fus·es.** To give a transfusion of (sthg.) or to (sbdy.): *transfuse blood; transfuse a patient.* —**trans·fu′sion** (trăns fyōō′zhən) *n.* [C; U]

trans·gress (trăns grĕs′ *or* trănz grĕs′) *v.* *Formal.* —*tr.* **1.** To go beyond or over (a limit or boundary): *His conduct transgressed the boundaries of politeness.* **2.** To act in violation of (a law, for example). —*intr.* To commit an offense by violating a law or command. —**trans·gres′sion** (trăns grĕsh′ən *or* trănz- grĕsh′ən) *n.* [C; U] —**trans·gres′sor** *n.*

tran·sient (trăn′shənt *or* trăn′zhənt *or* trăn′zē ənt) *adj.* **1.** Lasting only a short time; transitory: *transient happiness.* **2.** Staying in a place only a brief time: *a transient guest at a hotel.* —*n.* A person or thing that is transient, especially a person making a brief stay at a hotel or boarding house: *transients spending time in the park.* —**tran′sience, tran′sien·cy** *n.* [U]

tran·sis·tor (trăn zĭs′tər *or* trăn sĭs′tər) *n.* **1.** An electrical device used for amplification and switching. **2.** A radio equipped with transistors.

tran·sit (trăn′sĭt *or* trăn′zĭt) *n.* [U] The moving of people or goods from one place to another, especially on a local public transportation system: *city funds to improve mass transit.*

tran·si·tion (trăn zĭsh′ən *or* trăn sĭsh′ən) *n.* [C; U] Passage from one form, condition, style, or place to another. —**tran·si′tion·al** *adj.*

tran·si·tive (trăn′sĭ tĭv *or* trăn′zĭ tĭv) *adj.* In grammar, relating to a verb that requires a direct object to complete its meaning. In the sentence *I bought a book on Monday,* the verb *bought* is transitive. —**tran′si·tive·ly** *adv.* —SEE NOTE at **verb.**

tran·si·to·ry (trăn′sĭ tôr′ē *or* trăn′zĭ tôr′ē) *adj.* Existing or lasting only for a short time: *transitory happiness.*

trans·late (trăns lāt′ *or* trănz lāt′) *v.* **trans·lat·ed, trans·lat·ing, trans·lates.** —*tr.* **1.** To express (sthg.) in another language: *translate a book from German to English.* **2.** To put (sthg.) into simpler words; explain or interpret: *translate his strange comments.* —*intr.* **1.** To make a translation. **2.** To be able to be expressed in another language or form: *Her poetry translates well. The book didn't translate well to film.* —**trans·la′tion** *n.* [C; U] —**trans·la′tor** *n.*

trans·lu·cent (trăns lōō′sənt *or* trănz-lōō′sənt) *adj.* Allowing light to pass through, but not transparent. —**trans·lu′cence, trans·lu′cen·cy** *n.* [U]

trans·mis·sion (trăns mĭsh′ən *or* trănz-mĭsh′ən) *n.* **1.** [U] The act or process of transmitting: *the transmission of news; the transmission of a disease.* **2.** [C] Something, such as a message, that is transmitted: *We've received your transmission.* **3.** [C] An automotive assembly of gears and associated parts by which power is carried from an engine to a driving axle.

trans·mit (trăns mĭt′ *or* trănz mĭt′) *tr.v.* **trans·mit·ted, trans·mit·ting, trans·mits.** **1.** To send or pass (sthg.) on from one person, place, or thing to another: *transmit a message; transmit an infection.* **2.** To send out (an electric or electronic signal), as by wire or radio. **3.** To cause or allow (sthg.) to travel or spread, as through a medium: *Glass transmits light.*

trans·mit·ter (trăns mĭt′ər *or* trănz mĭt′ər) *n.* **1.** A person or thing that transmits. **2.** A device used in a communications system to send forth information.

trans·o·ce·an·ic (trăns′ō shē ăn′ĭk *or*

trănz′ō shē ăn′ĭk) *adj.* **1.** Situated beyond or on the other side of the ocean. **2.** Crossing the ocean: *transoceanic flight.*

trans·par·en·cy (trăns pâr′ən sē *or* trăns-pâr′ən sē) *n., pl.* **trans·par·en·cies. 1.** [C] A transparent object, especially a photographic slide. **2.** [U] The condition or state of being transparent: *the transparency of a child's lie.*

trans·par·ent (trăns pâr′ənt *or* trăns-pâr′ənt) *adj.* **1.** Able to transmit light so that objects and images are clearly visible: *transparent glass.* **2.** So fine in texture that it can be seen through; sheer: *a transparent fabric.* **3.** Easily seen through or detected: *transparent lies.* —**trans·par′ent·ly** *adv.*

trans·spire (trăn spīr′) *intr.v.* **tran·spired, tran·spir·ing, tran·spires. 1.** To become known; come to light: *The plot transpired suddenly.* **2.** To happen; take place: *This story transpired in the Middle Ages.*

trans·plant (trăns plănt′) *tr.v.* **1.** To pull or dig up and replant (a growing plant): *transplant a rose bush.* **2.** To transfer (sbdy./sthg.) to and establish in a new place: *The early colonists transplanted their customs to the New World.* **3.** To transfer (tissue or an organ) from one body or body part to another: *transplanted a kidney.* —*n.* (trăns′plănt′). **1.** The act or process of transplanting: *a heart transplant.* **2.** A person or thing that is transplanted: *I didn't grow up here in Boston; I am a transplant.* —**trans·plant′a·ble** *adj.* —**trans′plan·ta′tion** *n.* [U]

trans·port (trăns pôrt′) *tr.v.* To carry (sbdy./sthg.) from one place to another; convey: *transport cargo; transport passengers.* —*n.* (trăns′pôrt′). **1.** [U] An act of transporting: *goods lost in transport.* **2.** [C] A vehicle, such as an aircraft, used to transport passengers, mail, or freight. **3.** [U] A system for transporting passengers: *public transport.*

trans·por·ta·tion (trăns′pər tā′shən) *n.* [U] **1.** The act or an instance of transporting: *the transportation of mail.* **2.** A means of transport: *Planes are fast transportation.* **3.** The business of moving passengers or goods: *a company engaged in transportation.*

trans·pose (trăns pōz′) *tr.v.* **trans·posed, trans·pos·ing, trans·pos·es.** To reverse or transfer the order or place of (sthg.); interchange: *transpose the letters of a word.* —**trans′po·si′tion** (trăns′pə zĭsh′ən) *n.* [C; U]

trans·verse (trăns vûrs′ *or* trănz vûrs′ *or* trăns′vûrs′ *or* trănz′vûrs′) *adj.* Situated or lying across; crosswise: *a transverse beam.* —**trans·verse′ly** *adv.*

trap (trăp) *n.* **1.** A device for catching and holding animals: *a mousetrap.* **2.** A plan for catching or tricking an unsuspecting person: *The police set a trap for the thief.* **3.** *Slang.* An insulting term for a mouth: *Keep your trap shut.* —*v.* **trapped, trap•ping, traps.** —*tr.* To catch (sbdy./sthg.) in or as if in a trap: *trapped a fox.* —*intr.* To trap animals, especially for their fur: *My uncle traps for a living.*

tra•peze (tră pēz′) *n.* A short horizontal bar hung from two parallel ropes, used for exercises or for acrobatic stunts.

trap•e•zoid (trăp′ĭ-zoid′) *n.* A flat geometric shape with four sides, two of which are parallel. —**trap′e•zoi′dal** *adj.*

trapezoid

trap•per (trăp′ər) *n.* A person who traps animals for their fur.

trap•pings (trăp′ĭngz) *pl.n.* Articles of dress or adornment, especially accessories: *They enjoyed their fancy car and all the trappings of success.*

trash (trăsh) *n.* [U] **1.** Worthless or discarded material or objects; refuse or rubbish. **2.** Empty expressions or ideas: *His poetry is utter trash.* **3.** *Slang.* An insulting term for a person or group of people regarded as worthless. —*tr.v.* *Informal.* **1.** To destroy (sthg.): *They trashed the hotel room.* **2.** To ruin (a person's reputation): *They trashed their friends.*

trash•y (trăsh′ē) *adj.* **trash•i•er, trash•i•est.** **1.** Resembling or containing trash: *a trashy back yard.* **2.** In very poor taste or of very poor quality: *a trashy motion picture.* —**trash′i•ness** *n.* [U]

trau•ma (trou′mə *or* trô′mə) *n.* **1.** [C] A serious wound or injury, as from violence or an accident. **2.** [C; U] An emotional shock that causes serious and lasting damage to one's personality: *childhood trauma.* —**trau′ma•tize′** *v.*

trau•mat•ic (trou măt′ĭk *or* trô măt′ĭk) *adj.* Relating to or caused by a trauma: *a traumatic experience.* —**trau•mat′i•cal•ly** *adv.*

trav•el (trăv′əl) *v.* —*intr.* **1.** To go from one place to another, as on a trip: *travel through Mexico.* **2.** To go from place to place as a salesperson or an agent: *He travels for a publishing house.* **3.** [through] To be transmitted, as light or sound; move or pass: *Sound waves travel through the air.* —*tr.* To pass or journey over or through (sthg.): *travel the countries of Africa.* —*n.* **1.** [U] The act or process of traveling: *Travel is slow in the mountains.* **2.** **travels.** A series of journeys: *on his travels through the Middle East.* —**trav′el•er** *n.*

trav•el•er's check (trăv′əl ərz *or* trăv′lərz) *n.* A check purchased in various amounts from a bank or travel agency and signed by a traveler upon purchase and again later in the presence of the person cashing it.

trav•el•ing salesman (trăv′ə lĭng *or*

trăv′lĭng) *n.* A man who travels from place to place soliciting business orders.

tra•verse (trə vûrs′ *or* trăv′ərs) *tr.v.* **tra•versed, tra•vers•ing, tra•vers•es.** To go across, over, or through (sthg.): *The soldiers traversed the desert safely.*

trav•es•ty (trăv′ĭ stē) *n., pl.* **trav•es•ties.** An imitation of sthg. that misrepresents it, such as a parody of a literary work: *a travesty of justice.*

trawl (trôl) *intr.v.* To fish with a net that is towed: *trawling for cod; trawling off Nova Scotia.* —**trawl′er** *n.*

tray (trā) *n.* A flat piece of wood or metal, for example, with a raised edge or rim, used for carrying, holding, or displaying articles: *a tea tray.*

treach•er•ous (trĕch′ər əs) *adj.* **1.** False; disloyal: *a treacherous friend.* **2.** Not to be relied on; not dependable: *He has a treacherous memory.* **3.** Dangerous: *a beach with a treacherous surf.*

treach•er•y (trĕch′ə rē) *n., pl.* **treach•er•ies.** [C; U] Willful betrayal of confidence or trust: *Taking the company records was an act of treachery.*

tread (trĕd) *v.* **trod** (trŏd), **trod•den** (trŏd′n) *or* **trod, tread•ing, treads.** —*tr.* **1.** To walk on, over, or along (sthg.): *people treading the sidewalks on their way to work.* **2.** To stamp or trample (sthg.): *They threshed the rice by treading it on a hard floor.* **3.** To make (a path or trail) by walking or trampling: *treading a path to the beach.* —*intr.* **1.** To go on foot; walk. **2.** To set down the foot; step. **3.** To press, crush, or injure sthg. by or as if by trampling: *Their careless remarks trod upon her feelings.* —*n.* **1.** [U] The act, manner, or sound of treading: *the swift tread of a horse.* **2.** [C] The part of a step in a staircase that is stepped on. **3.** [C; U] The part of a wheel or tire that makes contact with the road or rails. **4.** [C] The part of a shoe sole that touches the ground. ♦ **tread water. 1.** To keep the head above water while in an upright position by moving the legs up and down: *Try to tread water while I get help!* **2.** To use energy but make little or no progress toward achieving a goal: *Even though he studies every day, he's only treading water in his classes.*

tread•mill (trĕd′mĭl′) *n.* **1.** An exercise device consisting of an endless moving belt on which a person can walk or run while remaining in the same place. **2.** A boring task or routine: *I'm quitting this job; it's a treadmill!* ♦ **on a treadmill.** Working hard but not progressing: *Working all day and caring for her aging parents in her free time leaves her feeling like she's on a treadmill.*

treas. *abbr.* An abbreviation for: **1.** Treasurer. **2.** Treasury.

trea•son (trē′zən) *n.* [U] Betrayal of one's country; disloyalty: *convicted of treason*

for helping the enemy. —**trea′son•a•ble,
trea′son•ous** *adj.*

treas•ure (trĕzh′ər) *n.* **1.** [C; U] Stored money or jewels: *the king's treasure.* **2.** [C] A person or thing considered especially precious or valuable: *His daughter is his treasure.* —*tr.v.* **treas•ured, treas•ur•ing, treas•ures.** To value (sbdy./sthg.) highly; cherish: *He treasures the gold watch his colleagues gave him.* See Synonyms at **appreciate.**

treas•ur•er (trĕzh′ər ər) *n.* A person in charge of funds, especially the chief financial officer of a government, a corporation, or an association: *Pay membership dues to the club treasurer.*

treas•ur•y (trĕzh′ə rē) *n., pl.* **treas•ur•ies.** **1.** A place where private or public funds are controlled. **2.** A collection of literary or artistic treasures: *a treasury of good music.* **3. Treasury.** The department of a government in charge of collecting, managing, and paying out public funds.

treat (trēt) *v.* —*tr.* **1.** To act or behave in a specified manner toward (sbdy.): *We will treat you fairly.* **2.** To regard or handle (sthg.) in a certain way: *treated the matter seriously.* **3.** To deal with (sthg.) in speech, writing, or art; discuss: *The essay treats the subject with humor.* **4.** To provide (sbdy.) with food, entertainment, or gifts at one's own expense: *Did you say you'd treat us to lunch today?* **5.** [*by; with*] To subject (sthg.) to a physical or chemical process or action in order to change it in some way: *treating cloth with bleach.* **6.** [*for*] To give medical care to (a person) or for (a disease): *Doctors treated him for his injuries.* —*intr.* To pay for another's entertainment, food, or drink: *Let me treat.* —*n.* **1.** A meal, an entertainment, or sthg. similar that is paid for by sbdy. else: *Let this lunch be my treat.* **2.** A source of special delight or pleasure: *What a treat it was to visit the museum!*

treat•a•ble (trē′tə bəl) *adj.* Possible to treat; responsive to treatment: *a treatable disorder.*

trea•tise (trē′tĭs) *n.* A book that deals with a subject extensively and systematically: *a treatise on Mozart's symphonies.*

treat•ment (trēt′mənt) *n.* [C; U] The way of handling a person or thing: *equal treatment under the law; treatment for psychiatric problems.*

trea•ty (trē′tē) *n., pl.* **trea•ties.** A formal agreement, especially between two or more countries: *a peace treaty.*

treb•le (trĕb′əl) *adj.* Triple. —*tr. & intr.v.* **treb•led, treb•ling, treb•les.** To make or become triple: *They trebled their profits. Profits trebled last year.*

tree (trē) *n.* **1.** A tall woody plant with a trunk and branches: *a maple tree.* **2.** Something like

a tree, such as a pole with pegs or hooks for hanging clothes: *a coat tree.* **3.** A diagram with a branching form: *a family tree.* —*tr.v.* **treed, tree•ing, trees.** To force (an animal) up a tree: *The dogs treed a cat.* ◆ **up a tree.** *Informal.* In a situation of great difficulty or confusion; helpless: *She caught her son lying, and now he's up a tree.* —**tree′less** *adj.* —**tree′like′** *adj.*

trek (trĕk) *intr.v.* **trekked, trek•king, treks.** To make a slow or difficult journey, especially by foot: *trekked through the mountains.* —*n.* A journey, especially a long and difficult one: *an exhausting cross-country trek.*

trel•lis (trĕl′ĭs) *n.* A wooden support for climbing plants.

trem•ble (trĕm′bəl) *intr.v.* **trem•bled, trem•bling, trem•bles.** **1.** To shake involuntarily, especially from excitement, weakness, or anger: *trembling with cold.* **2.** To feel fear or anxiety: *I tremble to think what has happened.* **3.** To shake or quiver: *leaves trembling in the breeze.* —*n.* The act of trembling; a shudder: *the tremble of an earthquake.*

tre•men•dous (trĭ mĕn′dəs) *adj.* **1.** Very large in amount, extent, or degree; enormous: *traveling at a tremendous speed.* **2.** *Informal.* Marvelous; wonderful: *a tremendous party.* **3.** Terrible: *witnessed a tremendous accident.* —**tre•men′dous•ly** *adv.*

trem•or (trĕm′ər) *n.* **1.** A shaking or vibrating movement, as of the earth: *tremors before a big earthquake.* **2.** A rapid involuntary shaking or twitching of muscles: *tremors of fear.*

trem•u•lous (trĕm′yə ləs) *adj.* Trembling or shaking: *speaking with a tremulous voice.*

trench (trĕnch) *n.* **1.** A deep ditch, such as one used as protection for soldiers in warfare. **2.** A long deep valley on the ocean floor. ◆ **in the trenches.** The place in a game, war, or daily life where the most intense action takes place: *For years she's worked in the trenches to get help for battered women.*

trench coat *n.* A belted raincoat in a military style, with straps on the shoulders and deep pockets.

trend (trĕnd) *n.* A general direction or tendency; vogue: *the latest trend in fashion.* ◆ **set a trend.** To create a style that others follow: *Japan set a trend toward smaller cars.*

trend•y (trĕn′dē) *adj.* **trend•i•er, trend•i•est.** *Informal.* According to the latest fad or fashion: *trendy clothes.*

trep•i•da•tion (trĕp′ĭ dā′shən) *n.* [U] *Formal.* A state of alarm or dread; apprehension: *We approached the abandoned house with trepidation.*

tres•pass (trĕs′pəs *or* trĕs′păs′) *intr.v.* To go on the property of another without permis-

sion: *trespass on government land.* —*n.*
(**trĕs′păs′** *or* **trĕs′pəs**). [C; U] An act of trespassing. —**tres′pass•er** *n.*

tress•es (**trĕs′ĭz**) *pl.n.* Long, often curly hair.

tres•tle (**trĕs′əl**) *n.* A railroad bridge.

tri— *pref.* A prefix that means three: *triangular.*

tri•al (**trī′əl** *or* **trīl**) *n.* **1.** [C; U] The examination of evidence, charges, and claims in a law court: *Her trial lasted three days.* **2.** [C; U] The act or process of testing and trying sbdy./sthg.: *the trial of a new aircraft.* **3.** [C] An effort or attempt: *He succeeded on his second trial.* **4.** [C] Something, such as an annoying person or a state of difficulty, that is a test of one's patience: *The lack of water was a trial to the hikers.* ◆ **on trial.** In the process of being tried, as in a court of law: *He is on trial for murder.* **stand trial.** To be tried in a law court: *He is going to stand trial for murder.* **trial and error.** A way of solving problems by repeated testing until no errors remain: *We improved the design by trial and error.*

tri•an•gle (**trī′ăng′gəl**) *n.* **1.** A flat geometric shape with three sides. **2.** Something shaped like such a figure. **3.** A romantic situation involving three people. —**tri•an′gu•lar** (**trī ăng′gyə-lər**) *adj.*

triangle
(isosceles triangle)

tri•ath•lon (**trī ăth′lən** *or* **trī ăth′lŏn′**) *n.* An athletic competition with three events, usually swimming, bicycling, and running.

tribe (**trīb**) *n.* A group made up of a number of families, clans, or other groups with a common ancestry, culture, and leadership. —**trib′al** (**trī′bəl**) *adj.*

trib•u•la•tion (**trĭb′yə lā′shən**) *n.* **1.** [U] Great trouble or hardship; suffering: *a time of great tribulation.* **2.** [C] An experience that tests one's endurance, patience, or faith; a trial: *life's many tribulations.*

tri•bu•nal (**trī byōō′nəl** *or* **trĭ byōō′nəl**) *n.* *Formal.* **1.** A place or court of justice. **2.** A committee or board appointed to judge or settle special matters: *a military tribunal.*

trib•u•tar•y (**trĭb′yə tĕr′ē**) *n.*, *pl.* **trib•u•tar•ies.** A small stream that flows into a larger river or stream.

trib•ute (**trĭb′yōōt**) *n.* **1.** [C] A gift, praise, or payment made to show gratitude, respect, or admiration: *a tribute to her teaching.* **2.** [U] Money paid by one nation to another as acknowledgment of submission or as the price for protection by that nation.

tri•ceps (**trī′sĕps′**) *n.*, *pl.* **triceps.** A large muscle that runs along the back of the upper arm.

trick (**trĭk**) *n.* **1.** An act intended to deceive: *They used a trick to get us to agree.* **2.** A clever

action; a practical joke: *Did you play a trick on your brother?* **3.** A special skill; a knack: *There's no trick to making good coffee.* **4.** A feat of magic: *showed us a card trick.* **5.** *Slang.* **a.** An act of prostituting. **b.** A prostitute's client. —*v.* —*tr.* To cheat or deceive (sbdy.): *tricked us out of $50.* —*intr.* To practice trickery or deception. —*adj.* **1.** Relating to or involving tricks: *trick photography.* **2.** Able to do tricks: *a trick dog.* **3.** Used to play tricks: *a trick deck of cards.* ◆ **do the trick.** To get the desired result: *On a hot day a cold drink will do the trick.* **not miss a trick.** To be extremely alert: *a child who doesn't miss a trick.* **play tricks** or **a trick on.** To fool (sbdy.): *I thought I saw her; my eyes must be playing tricks on me.* **tricks of the trade.** Specialized methods used in a particular field: *That salesman knows all the tricks of the trade.*

trick•er•y (**trĭk′ə rē**) *n.* [U] The practice or use of tricks; deception: *He got the money by trickery.*

trick•le (**trĭk′əl**) *v.* **trick•led, trick•ling, trick•les.** —*intr.* **1.** To flow or fall in drops or in a thin stream: *Sand trickled through his fingers.* **2.** To move or proceed slowly or bit by bit: *The audience trickled in before curtain time.* —*tr.* To cause (sthg.) to trickle: *trickled the syrup on the waffle.* —*n.* A slow, small, or irregular flow: *a trickle of water from the roof; a trickle of orders in the mail.*

trick•ster (**trĭk′stər**) *n.* A person who cheats or plays tricks on others.

trick•y (**trĭk′ē**) *adj.* **trick•i•er, trick•i•est.** **1.** Deceitful; clever: *a tricky character.* **2.** Requiring caution or skill: *a tricky situation.*

tri•cy•cle (**trī′sĭk′ əl** *or* **trī′sĭ kəl**). A cycle used especially by small children, with three wheels and moved by pedals.

tried (**trīd**) *v.* Past tense and past participle of **try.** —*adj.* Thoroughly tested and proved to be good or trustworthy: *a tried recipe.*

tri•fle (**trī′fəl**) *n.* **1.** Something of little importance or value: *Don't worry about trifles.* **2.** A small amount; a little: *spent a trifle on her gift.* —*intr.v.* **tri•fled, tri•fling, tri•fles.** [*with*] **1.** To deal with sbdy./sthg. as if it were of little significance or importance: *Don't trifle with me!* **2.** To play with sthg.: *trifle with a pencil.* ◆ **a trifle.** Somewhat; slightly: *These shoes are a trifle large.*

tri•fling (**trī′flĭng**) *adj.* Of little worth or importance: *a trifling sum.*

trig•ger (**trĭg′ər**) *n.* The lever that releases a spring; especially to fire a gun. —*tr.v.* To start (sthg.); set off: *His thoughtless remark triggered an argument.*

trig•o•nom•e•try (**trĭg′ə nŏm′ĭ trē**) *n.* [U] The study of the relations between the sides and angles of triangles.

trill (**trĭl**) *n.* **1.** A vibrating or shaking sound, such as that made by certain birds; a warble: *a robin's trill.* **2.** A rapid vibration of one speech organ against another, such as of the tip of the tongue against the back of the upper front teeth. —*v.* —*tr.* **1.** To sound, sing, or play (sthg.) with a trill: *trilled the flute.* **2.** To make (a sound) with a trill: *In Spanish you trill the r.* —*intr.* To produce a trill.

tril•lion (trĭl′yən) *n.* The number, written as 10^{12} or 1 followed by 12 zeros, that is equal to one thousand times one billion. —**tril′lionth** *adv., adj. & n.*

tril•o•gy (trĭl′ə jē) *n., pl.* **tril•o•gies.** A single work in three books.

trim (trĭm) *tr.v.* **trimmed, trim•ming, trims.** **1.** To make (sthg.) neat, even, or tidy by clipping, smoothing, or pruning: *Trim the hedges.* **2.** To remove or reduce (sthg.) by cutting: *trim the crust off the bread; trim a budget.* **3.** To decorate (sthg.): *trim a Christmas tree with ornaments.* —*n.* **1.** [U] Proper shape, order, or condition: *in good trim for the game.* **2.** [U] Decoration on the surface of sthg.: *lace trim on her dress.* **3.** [C] A cutting or clipping to make sthg. neat: *Your beard needs a trim.* —*adj.* **trim•mer, trim•mest. 1.** In good or neat order: *He looked very trim in his new suit.* See Synonyms at **neat. 2.** Well-designed or proportioned, with simple or slim lines: *a trim schooner; a trim figure.* —**trim′ly** *adv.* —**trim′mer** *n.* —**trim′ness** *n.* [U]

tri•mes•ter (trī mĕs′tər *or* trī′mĕs′tər) *n.* A period or term of three months: *the first trimester of pregnancy.*

trim•ming (trĭm′ĭng) *n.* **1.** [U] The act of trimming. **2.** [U] An ornament: *fur trimming on a coat.* **3. trimmings.** Accessories; extras: *roast turkey with all the trimmings.*

trin•ket (trĭng′kĭt) *n.* A small ornament, such as a piece of jewelry: *The little girl kept her trinkets in a box.*

tri•o (trē′ō) *n., pl.* **tri•os. 1.** A group of three people or things. **2.a.** A musical composition for three performers. **b.** The group performing such a composition.

trip (trĭp) *n.* **1.** A journey from one place to another: *a trip from Cleveland to Pittsburgh.* **2.** A stumble or fall. **3.** *Slang.* A drug experience involving hallucinations: *an acid trip.* **4.** *Slang.* An intense or exciting experience: *The roller coaster at the amusement park was a real trip.* —*v.* **tripped, trip•ping, trips.** —*intr.* **1.** [*on; over*] To stumble: *He tripped over a root and fell.* **2.** To move with light rapid steps; skip: *The children tripped happily over the bridge.* **3.** *Slang.* To have hallucinations caused by drugs: *He was tripping on acid.* —*tr.* To cause (sbdy.) to stumble or fall: *I'm sorry. I didn't mean to trip you.* ◆ **trip up.** *tr.v.* [*sep.*] To catch or trap (sbdy.) in an error or an inconsistency: *The police tripped up the suspect during questioning.*

tripe (trīp) *n.* [U] **1.** The rubbery lining of the stomach of cattle or similar animals, used as food. **2.** *Informal.* Something with no value; rubbish: *His writing is tripe and not worth reading.*

tri•ple (trĭp′əl) *adj.* **1.** Made of three parts. **2.** Three times as much or as many. —*n.* **1.** A number or an amount three times as large as another. **2.** A group or set of three. —*tr. & intr.v.* **tri•pled, tri•pling, tri•ples.** To make or become three times as large in number or amount: *The store tripled its business in one year. Prices tripled in 20 years.*

trip•let (trĭp′lĭt) *n.* **1.** A group or set of three things of one kind. **2.** One of three children born at one birth: *He is a triplet.*

trip•li•cate (trĭp′lĭ kĭt) *n.* One of a set of three identical objects or copies: *file forms in triplicate.*

tri•pod (trī′pŏd′) *n.* An adjustable stand with three legs used to support a camera.

tripod

trite (trīt) *adj.* **trit•er, trit•est.** Without the power to create interest because of overuse or repetition: *a trite expression.* —**trite′ly** *adv.* —**trite′ness** *n.* [U]

tri•umph (trī′əmf) *intr.v.* [*over*] To be victorious or successful; win: *triumph over adversity.* —*n.* **1.** [U] Happiness over being successful: *Her political campaign ended in triumph.* **2.** [C] An important or notable success: *The bridge is a triumph of engineering.* —**tri•um′phant** (trī ŭm′fənt) *adj.*

triv•i•a (trĭv′ē ə) *pl.n. (used with a singular or plural verb).* Unimportant matters; trifles: *They spend too much time worrying about trivia.*

triv•i•al (trĭv′ē əl) *adj.* **1.** Of little importance or value: *trivial matters.* **2.** Ordinary; commonplace: *a trivial event.* —**triv′i•al′i•ty** (trĭv′ē ăl′ĭ tē) *n.* [C; U] —**triv′i•al•ly** *adv.*

trod (trŏd) *v.* Past tense and a past participle of **tread.**

trod•den (trŏd′n) *v.* A past participle of **tread.**

troll (trōl) *n.* A creature of Scandinavian folklore, described as either a friendly or mischievous dwarf or as a giant.

trol•ley (trŏl′ē) *n., pl.* **trol•leys.** A streetcar; an electric bus.

trom•bone (trŏm bōn′ *or* trəm bōn′) *n.* A brass musical instrument with a movable U-shaped slide.

troop (troop) *n.* **1.** A group or company of people, animals, or things: *a troop of students on a field trip.* **2. troops.** Military units; soldiers. **3.** A unit of Boy Scouts or Girl Scouts with an adult leader. —*intr.v.* To move or go as a group: *The children trooped home from school.*

HOMONYMS: troop, troupe (group of actors).

troop•er (trōo′pər) *n.* A state police officer.
tro•phy (trō′fē) *n.*, *pl.* **tro•phies. 1.** A prize or memento received as a symbol of victory, especially in sports: *a tennis trophy.* **2.** A specimen or part, such as the antlers of a deer, kept as a token of a successful hunt: *a hunting trophy.*

trophy
Hollis Stacy, winner of the U.S. Women's Open golf tournament

trop•ic (trŏp′ĭk) *n.* **1.** One of two lines of latitude on the earth at 23° 27' that are north and south of the equator. **2. Tropics** or **tropics.** The region of the earth bounded by these latitudes. —**trop′i•cal** *adj.* —**trop′i•cal•ly** *adv.*

trot (trŏt) *n.* **1.** A running gait of a person or an animal, faster than a walk; a jog: *moving at a trot.* **2.** A short, usually local, trip: *a trot around town.* —*v.* **trot•ted, trot•ting, trots.** —*intr.* **1.** To go or move at a trot: *The horses trotted down the road.* **2.** To move rapidly; hurry: *trotted up and down the stairs doing chores.* —*tr.* To cause (an animal) to trot: *She trotted her pony around the ring.* ◆ **trot out.** *tr.v.* [sep.] To bring (sbdy./sthg.) out and show for inspection or admiration: *The trainer trotted out the show dogs one by one.*

trou•ble (trŭb′əl) *n.* **1.** [U] A state of worry, danger, or need: *The ship was in trouble and signaled for help.* **2.** [C] A cause or source of worry or difficulty: *Running out of gas was only one of my troubles.* **3.** [U] An effort, especially one that causes inconvenience: *They went to a lot of trouble on our account.* **4.** [U] Pain or disease: *stomach trouble; engine trouble.* —*v.* **troub•led, troub•ling, troub•les.** —*tr.* **1.** To stir up (sbdy./sthg.): *A stiff wind troubled the lake.* **2.** To cause (sbdy.) pain or discomfort: *My stomach is troubling me.* **3.** To cause (sbdy.) distress or worry: *I am troubled by your lack of interest.* **4.** [*for; to*] To bother (sbdy.): *May I trouble you for the time?* —*intr.* To take pains: *Don't trouble to see me off.* ◆ **ask** or **look for trouble.** To act in a way that causes danger or difficulty: *She's asking for trouble by smoking so much.* **get into trouble. 1.** To be punished for sthg.: *The children got into trouble*

for painting the cat. **2.** To cause (sbdy.) to be punished for sthg.: *His lies got us into trouble.* **make trouble.** To cause sbdy. hardship or annoyance: *The gang made trouble for us by saying that we stole the car.*
trou•ble•mak•er (trŭb′əl mā′kər) *n.* A person or thing that causes trouble or strife: *Stay away from that boy—he's a real troublemaker!*
trou•ble•shoot•er (trŭb′əl shōo′tər) *n.* A person whose job is to locate and get rid of sources of trouble: *My daughter is a troubleshooter for that company.*
trou•ble•some (trŭb′əl səm) *adj.* Causing trouble or worry: *a troublesome car.*
trough (trôf *or* trŏf) *n.* **1.** A long, narrow, open box, especially one for feeding animals. **2.** A long narrow depression, as between waves or ridges. **3.** An extended region of low atmospheric pressure, often associated with a front.
trounce (trouns) *tr.v.* **trounced, trounc•ing, trounc•es.** To defeat (sbdy.) decisively: *We trounced the rival field hockey team.*
troupe (trōop) *n.* A company or group, especially of touring actors, singers, or dancers: *a ballet troupe.*

HOMONYMS: troupe, troop (group).

trou•sers (trou′zərz) *pl.n.* Pants.
trout (trout) *n.* [C; U] A fish, usually with a speckled body, that is valued as food.
trow•el (trou′əl) *n.* A hand tool with a flat blade for spreading mortar or cement or for gardening.
tru•an•cy (trōo′ən sē) *n.*, *pl.* **tru•an•cies.** [C; U] The act or condition of being absent without permission: *I was once suspended from school for truancy.*
tru•ant (trōo′ənt) *n.* A person who is absent without permission. —*adj.* Absent without permission, especially from school: *a truant pupil.*
truce (trōos) *n.* A temporary stopping of fighting by agreement between two enemies.
truck (trŭk) *n.* A heavy motor vehicle designed for carrying or pulling loads: *goods shipped by truck.* —*v.* —*tr.* To transport (goods) by truck: *truck apples from Washington.* —*intr.* To drive a truck: *I used to truck for a living.* ◆ **get trucking.** *Slang.* To start to do sthg.: *I should get trucking on my homework.* **keep on trucking.** *Slang.* To continue to do sthg.: *That rock group just keeps on trucking.* —**truck′er** *n.*
truck•load (trŭk′lōd′) *n.* The amount that a truck can hold: *a truckload of bananas.*
trudge (trŭj) *intr.v.* **trudged, trudg•ing, trudg•es.** To walk in a slow heavy-footed way: *trudging through heavy snow.*
true (trōo) *adj.* **tru•er, tru•est. 1.** Consistent with fact or reality: *Is this statement true or false?* **2.** Real, sincere, or genuine: *true gold.* See Synonyms at **authentic. 3.** Re-

T

liable; accurate: *a true prophecy.* **4.** Faithful; loyal: *Be true to your friends.* **5.** With the characteristics of a certain type: *The horse-shoe crab is not a true crab.* **6.** Exactly fitted: *The window wasn't true, and rain came in.* —*adv.* **1.** In accord with reality, fact, or truthfulness: *She speaks true.* **2.** Without leaving a course; exactly: *I'll sail the ship straight and true.*

true-blue (trōō′blōō′) *adj.* Loyal or faithful: *my true-blue friend.*

truf•fle (trŭf′əl) *n.* **1.** A blackish or light brown fungus that grows underground and is regarded as a food delicacy. **2.** A soft chocolate candy.

tru•ism (trōō′ĭz′əm) *n.* A statement of obvious truth. *The sky is above us* is a truism.

tru•ly (trōō′lē) *adv.* **1.** Sincerely; genuinely: *I am truly sorry.* **2.** Truthfully; accurately: *The newspaper reported the story truly.* **3.** Indeed: *The view from the hilltop is truly magnificent.*

trump (trŭmp) *n.* In card games, a suit declared to have a higher value than all other suits. —*v.* —*tr.* To take (a card or trick) with a trump. —*intr.* To play a trump. ◆ **play (one's) trump card.** To use sthg. to win: *Don't wait too long to play your trump card at the board meeting.* **trump up.** *tr.v.* [sep.] To devise (sthg.) fraudulently: *The dictator trumped up charges against his opponents.*

trum•pet (trŭm′pĭt) *n.* **1.** A high-pitched brass musical instrument with a mouthpiece at one end and a bell at the other. **2.** Something shaped like a trumpet: *the yellow trumpets of the daffodils.* **3.** A resounding call, as that of the elephant. —*v.* —*intr.* **1.** To play a trumpet. **2.** To make a loud resounding sound like that of a trumpet: *Elephants trumpeted in the distance.* —*tr.* To shout or announce (sthg.) loudly: *trumpeting the news of victory.* —**trum′pet•er** *n.*

trunk (trŭngk) *n.* **1.** The main stem of a tree. **2.** The main part of the body, not including the arms, legs, and head. **3.** A long flexible nose, especially of an elephant. **4.** A main part of sthg., not including parts that branch off: *the trunk of a nerve.* **5.** A covered compartment at the back of an automobile, used for luggage or storage. **6.** A large box or case with a lid, used as luggage or for storage. **7.** **trunks.** Men's shorts worn for swimming or athletics.

trust (trŭst) *n.* **1.** [U; *in*] Firm belief in the integrity, ability, or character of a person or thing: *trust in human nature.* **2.** [U] Custody; care: *The children are in my trust.* See Synonyms at **care.** **3.** [U] Responsibility: *violated a public trust.* **4.** [U] Reliance on sthg. in the future; hope: *trust in his invest-*

ments. **5.** [C; U] Legal control of property for the benefit of sbdy. else. **6.** [C] A group of businesses joined for the purposes of limiting competition and prices. —*v.* —*intr.* [*in*] To have or place confidence in; depend: *Trust in me.* —*tr.* **1.** To have or place confidence in (sbdy./sthg.); depend on: *Trust me.* **2.** To expect (sthg.); assume: *I trust that you will be on time.* **3.** To believe (sthg.): *I trust what you say.* ◆ **in trust.** In the possession or care of a trustee: *The land is held in trust for the people of the state.*

trus•tee (trŭ stē′) *n.* **1.** A person or firm that has legal control of property for another person's benefit. **2.** A member of a group or board that manages the affairs of an institution. —**trus•tee′ship** *n.* [C; U]

trust•ful (trŭst′fəl) *adj.* Inclined to believe or confide readily; full of trust: *a child's trustful eyes; a trustful person.* —**trust′ful•ly** *adv.* —**trust′ful•ness** *n.* [U]

trust fund *n.* Property placed under the legal control of a trustee for the benefit of sbdy. else, usually for a child.

trust•wor•thy (trŭst′wûr′thē) *adj.* Deserving trust; reliable: *a trustworthy assistant.*

trust•y (trŭs′tē) *adj.* **trust•i•er, trust•i•est.** Reliable; trustworthy: *my trusty companions.*

truth (trōōth) *n., pl.* **truths** (trōōthz *or* trōōths). **1.** [U] Agreement with fact or actuality: *a story with an appearance of truth.* **2.** [C] A statement proven to be or accepted as true: *scientific truths.* **3.** [U] Sincerity; integrity: *There was no truth in his speech.*

truth•ful (trōōth′fəl) *adj.* **1.** Consistently telling the truth; honest: *a truthful person.* **2.** True: *a truthful story of what happened.* —**truth′ful•ly** *adv.* —**truth′ful•ness** *n.* [U]

try (trī) *v.* **tried** (trīd), **try•ing, tries** (trīz). —*tr.* **1.** To make an effort (to do or accomplish sthg.); attempt: *Try to understand.* **2.** To taste, sample, or otherwise test (sthg.): *Let's try the pasta dish.* **3.** To examine or hear (a case) in a court of law. **4.** To put (sbdy./sthg.) under great strain or hardship: *a task that tried his strength.* —*intr.* To make an effort; strive: *I'll try as hard as I can.* —*n., pl.* **tries** (trīz). An attempt; an effort: *She made several tries before she got the window open.* ◆ **try on.** *tr.v.* [sep.] To put on (clothing) to test its fit: *He tried on the pants in the dressing room.* **try (one's) hand.** To attempt to do sthg. for the first time: *He thought he would try his hand at making an omelet.* **try (one's) patience.** To annoy; frustrate: *Any child can try your patience.* **try out.** *intr.v.* [*for*] To take a qualifying test, such as for a job or athletic team: *I wanted to try out for the basketball team.* —*tr.v.* [sep.] To test or use (sthg.) experimentally: *She tried out her new skis.*

T

try·ing (trī′ĭng) *adj.* Causing strain, hardship, or distress: *trying circumstances.*

try·out (trī′out′) *n.* A test to evaluate or find out qualifications of applicants, as for a theatrical role: *tryouts for chorus.*

tsar (zär *or* tsär) *n.* Variant of **czar** (sense 1).

T-shirt also **tee shirt** (tē′shûrt′) *n.* A short-sleeved collarless shirt or undershirt.

tsp. *abbr.* An abbreviation of teaspoon.

tsu·na·mi (tso͞o nä′mē) *n.* A very large ocean wave that is caused by an underwater earthquake or volcanic eruption and often causes extreme destruction when it strikes land.

Tu. *abbr.* An abbreviation of Tuesday.

tub (tŭb) *n.* **1.** An open, flat-bottomed container used for washing, packing, or storing. **2.** A bathtub: *She slipped and fell in the tub.*

tu·ba (to͞o′bə) *n.* A large brass musical instrument with a bass range and several valves to change its pitch.

tub·by (tŭb′ē) *adj.* **tub·bi·er, tub·bi·est.** Short and fat.

tube (to͞ob) *n.* **1.** [C; U] A hollow cylinder, especially one that holds a liquid or functions as a passage. **2.** [C] An organ of the body with the shape or function of a tube: *the bronchial tubes.* **3.** [C] A small flexible container with a narrow cap at one end: *a tube of toothpaste.* **4.** [U] *Slang.* Television: *What's on the tube?* ♦ **down the tubes.** *Slang.* Over; gone: *All that work is down the tubes.* —**tube′less** *adj.*

tu·ber (to͞o′bər) *n.* A swollen underground stem, such as a potato.

tu·ber·cu·lo·sis (to͞o bûr′kyə lō′sĭs) *n.* [U] An infectious disease of humans and animals that causes lesions in the lungs.

tub·ing (to͞o′bĭng) *n.* [U] **1.** A system of tubes. **2.** A piece or length of tube.

tu·bu·lar (to͞o′byə lər) *adj.* Made of, like, or being tubes or a tube.

tuck (tŭk) *tr.v.* To gather and fold (sthg.) under: *He tucked the shirt into his trousers.* —*n.* **1.** The act of tucking. **2.** A flattened pleat or fold, especially a narrow one stitched in place. ♦ **tuck away.** *tr.v.* [sep.] To put (sthg.) in a secret or little-known place: *I tucked some money away for emergencies. The cabin was tucked away among the pines.* ♦ **tuck in.** *tr.v.* [sep.] To cover or wrap (sbdy./sthg.) snugly in bed: *He tucked in the baby.*

tuck·er (tŭk′ər) *v. Informal.* ♦ **tucker out.** *tr.v.* [sep.] To make (sbdy.) weary; exhaust: *The long climb up the hill tuckered everyone out.*

Tue. *abbr.* An abbreviation of Tuesday.

Tues. *abbr.* An abbreviation of Tuesday.

Tues·day (to͞oz′dē *or* to͞oz′dā′) *n.* The third day of the week.

tuft (tŭft) *n.* A short bunch of strands, as of hair, grass, or yarn, attached at the base or growing close together.

tug (tŭg) *v.* **tugged, tug·ging, tugs.** —*tr.* **1.**

To pull at (sthg.) strongly; strain at: *The puppy was tugging the leash.* **2.** To move (sthg.) by pulling with great effort; drag: *I tugged a chair across the room.* See Synonyms at **pull.** —*intr.* To pull hard: *His mom kept tugging until the boot came off.* —*n.* **1.** A strong pull or pulling force: *Give it a tug.* **2.** A tugboat: *The tug guided the cargo ship into the harbor.*

tug·boat (tŭg′bōt′) *n.* A small powerful boat designed for pulling or pushing larger vessels.

tug of war *n., pl.* **tugs of war.** A contest of strength in which two teams pull on opposite ends of a rope.

tu·i·tion (to͞o ĭsh′ən) *n.* [U] A fee for instruction, especially at a college or private school.

tu·lip (to͞o′lĭp) *n.* A spring plant with a colorful cup-shaped flower that grows from a bulb.

tum·ble (tŭm′bəl) *v.* **tum·bled, tum·bling, tum·bles.** —*intr.* **1.** To perform acrobatic feats, such as somersaults, rolls, or twists. **2.** To fall or roll end over end: *The kittens tumbled over each other.* **3.** To spill or roll out in confusion or disorder: *School-children tumbled out of the bus.* **4.** To drop; decrease: *Prices tumbled.* **5.** To collapse: *The tower of blocks tumbled down.* —*tr.* To cause (sbdy./sthg.) to fall; bring down. —*n.* An act of tumbling; a fall: *take a bad tumble.*

tum·ble·down (tŭm′bəl doun′) *adj.* In bad condition; very rickety: *a tumbledown shack.*

tum·bler (tŭm′blər) *n.* **1.** An acrobat or a gymnast who tumbles. **2.** A drinking glass with no handle or stem. **3.** The part in a lock that releases the bolt when turned by a key.

tum·bling (tŭm′blĭng) *n.* [U] Gymnastics performed without specialized equipment.

tum·my (tŭm′ē) *n., pl.* **tum·mies.** *Informal.* The human stomach or belly: *a tummy ache.*

tu·mor (to͞o′mər) *n.* A mass of tissue in the body with an abnormal structure and rate of growth.

tu·mult (to͞o′mŭlt′) *n.* [C; U] **1.** The noise and commotion of a great crowd. **2.** Confusion of the mind or emotions.

tu·mul·tu·ous (to͞o mŭl′cho͞o əs) *adj.* Noisy and disorderly: *a tumultuous crowd.*

tu·na (to͞o′nə) *n.* [C; U] A large ocean fish that is used for food.

tun·dra (tŭn′drə) *n.* [U] A cold treeless area of Arctic regions, especially in Alaska, Canada, and Russia.

tune (to͞on) *n.* **1.** A melody, especially a simple and easily remembered one. **2.** Correct musical pitch: *She can't carry a tune.* **3.** Agreement or harmony: *ideas in tune with the times.* —*tr.v.* **tuned, tun·ing, tunes. 1.** To put (an instrument) in proper musical pitch: *tune a guitar.* **2.** To adjust (an engine, for example) for top performance: *tune the car every six months.* **3.** To adjust (a radio, for example) to a desired frequency: *tuned to 87.5 FM.* ♦ **change (one's) tune.** To change one's ideas about sthg.: *He changed his tune about paying me when my lawyer told him we'd sue him.* **in tune with.** In agreement with: *He tries to stay in tune with the times.* **stay tuned. 1.** To continue to listen to the same radio channel or watch the same television channel: *Stay tuned. Don't touch that dial!* **2.** To continue to pay attention to the same event or situation: *Stay tuned for the next bit of juicy gossip.* **to the tune of.** To the sum or extent of: *paid extra for the tickets to the tune of $20 each.* **tune in.** *intr.v.* To adjust an electronic receiver to receive signals at a particular frequency or to receive a desired program. **tune out.** *tr.v.* [sep.] **1.** To adjust (an electronic receiver) so as not to receive a particular signal. **2.** To stop listening to (sbdy./sthg.): *I was tired of her complaints, so I tuned her out.*

tun·er (tōō′nər) *n.* **1.** A person or thing that tunes: *a piano tuner.* **2.** A device for tuning, especially an electronic circuit or device used to select signals for a radio or television.

tune-up (tōōn′ŭp′) *n.* An adjustment, as of a motor or an engine, made to improve working order or efficiency: *My sewing machine needs a tune-up.*

tung·sten (tŭng′stən) *n.* [U] *Symbol* **W** A hard gray to white metallic element that is very resistant to corrosion and high temperatures. Atomic number 74. See table at **element.**

tu·nic (tōō′nĭk) *n.* **1.** A loose-fitting, knee-length garment. **2.** A long, plain military jacket, usually with a high stiff collar.

tun·nel (tŭn′əl) *n.* **1.** An underground or underwater passage. **2.** A passage through or under a barrier. *—v. —tr.* To make a tunnel under or through (sthg.): *tunneling the granite. —intr.* [through; under] To make a tunnel: *The crew tunneled under the harbor.*

tur·ban (tûr′bən) *n.* **1.** A traditionally Muslim headdress consisting of a long piece of cloth that is wound around a small cap or directly around the head. **2.** A similar headdress or hat.

tur·bine (tûr′bĭn *or* tûr′bīn′) *n.* A machine in which a wheel is turned by air or water.

tur·bu·lence (tûr′byə ləns) *n.* [U] **1.** The state or quality of being turbulent. **2.** An eddying motion of the atmosphere that interrupts the flow of wind.

tur·bu·lent (tûr′byə lənt) *adj.* Violent, uncontrolled, or disturbed: *turbulent waters; turbulent teenage years.*

tu·reen (tōō rēn′) *n.* A broad deep dish with a cover, used for serving soups at the table.

turf (tûrf) *n.* [U] **1.a.** A surface layer of earth with a dense growth of grass; sod. **b.** An arti-

ficial substitute surface, as on a playing field. **2.** *Slang.* The area claimed by a neighborhood gang as its territory: *gang turf.*

tur·key (tûr′kē) *n., pl.* **tur·keys. 1.** [C] A large, brownish North American bird with a bare head and fleshy neck. **2.** [U] The meat of a turkey: *We have turkey for Thanksgiving dinner.*

tur·mer·ic (tûr′mər ĭk) *n.* [U] A yellowish spicy powder used as a seasoning, especially in curries.

tur·moil (tûr′moil′) *n.* [U] A state of extreme confusion or commotion: *a country in turmoil because of war.*

turn (tûrn) *v. —tr.* **1.** To cause (sthg.) to move around an axis or a center: *The driver turned the steering wheel.* **2.** To cause (sthg.) to move around in order to achieve a result, such as opening or loosening: *turn the key; turn a screw.* **3.** To perform (sthg.) by rotating or revolving: *turn a somersault.* **4.** To change the position of (sthg.) so that the underside becomes the upper side: *turn a page.* **5.** To injure (a joint) by twisting: *turn an ankle.* **6.** To change the direction or course of (sthg. moving): *turn the car to the left.* **7.** To present or aim (sthg.) in a specified direction: *turn one's face to the wall; turn one's gaze to the sky.* **8.** To cause (sbdy./sthg.) to become opposed: *News of the scandal turned public opinion against the candidate.* **9.** To cause (sthg.) to change; transform: *Autumn turns the green leaves golden. —intr.* **1.** To move around an axis or a center; rotate or revolve: *How fast is the wheel turning?* **2.** To change position from side to side or back and forth: *I tossed and turned all through a sleepless night.* **3.** To progress through pages so as to arrive at a given place: *Please turn to page 361.* **4.** To direct one's way or course: *The truck turned into the service station.* **5.** To change or reverse one's course or direction: *Too tired to go farther, we turned and went home.* **6.** [against] To become hostile or opposed: *The peasants turned against the cruel king.* **7.** To direct one's attention, interest, or thought toward or away from sthg.: *Let's turn to another subject.* **8.a.** To change so as to be; become: *His hair turned gray. The night turned into day.* **b.** To reach and pass a certain age, for example: *My niece has turned three.* **9.** To change color: *The leaves turn in October. —n.* **1.** The act of turning or the condition of being turned; rotation or revolution: *a turn of the wheel.* **2.** A change of direction, motion, or position: *Make a left turn at the corner.* **3.** A curve, as in a road or path: *a sharp turn in the road.* **4.** One of a series of opportunities that happen in order: *waiting for her turn to roll the dice.* **5.** A movement or development in a particular direction: *The patient has suffered a turn for the worse.* **6.** An action having a good or bad effect on another: *She did me a good turn.* ◆ **at every turn.** In every place; at every moment: *He met with bad luck at every turn.* **in turn.** In the proper order or sequence: *You have to wait to play your cards in turn.* **out of turn.** Not in the proper order or sequence: *She went out of turn.* **turn a profit.** To make money: *Can we turn a profit on these old toys?* **turn away.** *tr.v.* [sep.] To send (sbdy.) away: *She turned away the salesman who came to the door.* **turn back.** *intr.v.* To reverse one's direction of motion: *stopped on the road and had to turn back.* —*tr.v.* [sep.] To fold (sthg.) down: *turned back the covers before getting into bed.* **turn blue.** To show signs of being cold: *My nose turned blue as soon as I stepped outside.* **turn down.** *tr.v.* [sep.] **1.** To lessen the speed, volume, intensity, or flow of (sthg.): *I turned down the radio.* **2.** To reject or refuse (a person, advice, or a suggestion): *He was turned down for the job.* **3.** To fold (sthg.) down: *turn down the bed covers.* **turn green. 1.** To show envy or jealousy: *When she saw my new car, she turned green.* **2.** To show signs of nausea: *After an hour on the boat, my friend started to turn green.* **turn in.** *tr.v.* [sep.] **1.** To give (sthg.) to an authority: *She turned in her keys at the end of the lease.* **2.** To inform an authority about (sbdy.): *One of his classmates found out he was cheating and turned him in.* —*intr.v. Informal.* To go to bed: *She was tired and so decided to turn in.* **turn loose.** To set (sbdy./sthg.) free; release: *Don't turn those kids loose in a toy store.* **turn off.** *tr.v.* [sep.] **1.** To stop the operation, activity, or flow of (sthg.): *Turn off the TV.* **2.** *Slang.* To cause dislike or disgust in (sbdy.): *Violent movies really turn me off.* **turn on.** *tr.v.* [sep.] **1.** To cause (sthg.) to begin operation or activity: *Turn on the porch light.* **2.** To begin to display or use (sthg.): *a politician who knows how to turn on the charm.* **3.** *Slang.* **a.** To cause (sbdy.) to become interested or excited: *My uncle turned me on to jazz.* **b.** To excite (sbdy.) sexually. —*intr.v.* To take drugs; get high. **turn (one's) stomach.** To cause a feeling of disgust or nausea in the mind or body: *That horror film turned my stomach.* **turn out.** *intr.v.* **1.** To arrive or assemble, as for a public event or entertainment: *A good crowd turned out for the picnic.* **2.** To end up; result: *The cake turned out beautifully.* —*tr.v.* [sep.] **1.** To force (sbdy.) to move out; evict: *They were turned out of the apartment when the lease was up.* **2.** To produce (sthg.): *a factory turning out cars.* **turn over.** *tr.v.* [sep.] **1.** To change the position of (sthg.) so that the bottom is on top: *turn over a mattress.* **2.** To think about (sthg.); consider: *turning over the lecture in my mind.* **3.** To transfer (sthg.) to another; surrender: *turned*

over *the keys to a more experienced driver.* —*intr.v.* To shift one's position by rolling from one side to the other: *turned over in bed.* **turn over a new leaf.** To change, especially to stop doing bad things: *He's stopped gambling and turned over a new leaf.* **turn to.** *tr.v.* [insep.] **1.** To consult or depend on (sbdy./sthg.) for help, support, or advice: *You can always turn to your parents.* **2.** To change into (sthg.); become different: *When a tree petrifies, it turns to stone.* **turn up.** *tr.v.* [sep.] **1.** To increase the speed, volume, intensity, or flow of (sthg.): *Turn up the radio so we can hear the news.* **2.** To find (sthg.): *Our investigation turned up several clues.* —*intr.v.* To make an appearance; arrive: *He turned up just in time for supper.* **turn up (one's) nose.** [at] To reject (sthg.): *He has always turned up his nose at green vegetables.*

HOMONYMS: turn, tern (sea bird).

SYNONYMS: turn, rotate, spin, whirl, swirl. These verbs all mean to move or cause to move in a circle. **Turn** is the most general: *The boy in front of me turned and stared at my desk.* **Rotate** means to move around an axis or a center: *The earth rotates once in 24 hours.* **Spin** means to rotate rapidly, often within a narrow space: *The sheets were spinning in the clothes dryer.* **Whirl** means to rotate or turn rapidly or forcefully: *They saw the whirling snowflakes and knew the blizzard had started.* **Swirl** often means to move rapidly in a circle: *Flood waters swirled wildly under the bridge.*

---

turn•a•round (tûrn′ə round′) *n.* **1.** A space, as in a driveway, permitting the turning around of a vehicle. **2.** A reversal: *a turnaround in stock prices.*

tur•nip (tûr′nĭp) *n.* A plant with a large yellowish or white root that is eaten as a vegetable.

turn•off (tûrn′ôf′ *or* tûrn′ŏf′) *n.* **1.** A branch of a road leading away from a main route, especially an exit on a highway. **2.** *Slang.* Something unpleasant, especially in a sexual way.

turn•out (tûrn′out′) *n.* **1.** [C] The number of people at a gathering; attendance: *a large turnout for the picnic.* **2.** [U] A number of things produced; output: *The factory increased its turnout of cars.*

turn•o•ver (tûrn′ō′vər) *n.* **1.** [C] An abrupt change; a reversal: *a turnover in public opinion.* **2.** [C] A small filled pastry: *an apple turnover.* **3.** [U] The amount of business done during a given period: *turnover doubled last year.* **4.** [U] The number of workers hired by an establishment to replace those who have left in a given period of time: *There isn't much turnover, so it's hard to get a job at that company.* **5.** [C] In sports, a loss of possession of the ball to the opposing team, as by a misplay or a violation of the rules: *a turnover that led to a touchdown.*

turn•pike (tûrn'pīk') *n.* A toll road, especially in the eastern United States.

turn•stile (tûrn'stīl') *n.* A gate that controls or counts the number of persons entering a public area by admitting them one at a time between horizontal bars revolving on a post.

turn•ta•ble (tûrn'tā'bəl) *n.* The rotating circular platform of a phonograph on which the record is placed.

tur•pen•tine (tûr'pən tīn') *n.* [U] A thin oil used as a paint thinner and solvent.

tur•quoise (tûr'kwoiz' *or* tûr'koiz') *n.* **1.** [C; U] A bluish green mineral often made into jewelry. **2.** [U] A light to brilliant bluish green color. —*adj.* Light to brilliant bluish green.

tur•tle (tûr'tl) *n.* Any of various reptiles that live either in water or on land and have a hard shell into which the head, legs, and tail can be pulled for protection.

turtle

tur•tle•neck (tûr'tl něk') *n.* A shirt or sweater with a high, tubular, turned-down collar that fits closely around the neck.

tusk (tŭsk) *n.* A long pointed tooth projecting outside of the mouth of certain animals, such as the elephant or walrus.

tus•sle (tŭs'əl) *intr.v.* **tus•sled, tus•sling, tus•sles.** To fight roughly; scuffle: *The boys tussled after the game.* —*n.* A rough or vigorous fight; a scuffle.

tu•tor (tōō'tər) *n.* A private instructor. —*tr.v.* To act as tutor to (sbdy.); instruct or teach privately: *We tutored the boy in math.*

tu•to•ri•al (tōō tôr'ē əl) *adj.* Relating to a tutor or private instructor. —*n.* A computer program that teaches one how to use or do sthg.: *a math tutorial.*

tux (tŭks) *n. Informal.* A tuxedo.

tux•e•do (tŭk sē'dō) *n., pl.* **tux•e•dos** or **tux•e•does.** A man's formal suit.

TV (tē'vē') *n., pl.* **TVs** or **TV's.** Television: *They bought a new big-screen TV.*

twang (twăng) *v.* —*intr.* To give off a sharp vibrating sound, as the string of a musical instrument does when plucked. —*tr.* **1.** To cause (sthg.) to make a sharp vibrating sound. **2.** To utter (sthg.) with a strongly nasal tone of voice. —*n.* **1.** A sharp vibrating sound, as that of a plucked string. **2.** A strongly nasal tone of voice: *a southern twang.*

tweak (twēk) *tr.v.* **1.** To pinch, pluck, or twist (sbdy./sthg.) sharply: *He tweaked her nose playfully.* **2.** To adjust (sthg.) slightly: *She tweaked the engine of her motorcycle.* —*n.* A sharp twisting pinch.

tweed (twēd) *n.* [C; U] A coarse woolen fabric used for suits and coats.

tweet (twēt) *n.* A chirping sound, as of a small bird. —*intr.v.* To produce a chirping sound: *The birds tweeted cheerfully.*

tweez•ers (twē'zərz) *pl.n.* A small metal tool used for pulling out single hairs or for handling small objects: *Use the tweezers to remove that splinter.*

twelfth (twĕlfth) *n.* **1.** The ordinal number matching the number 12 in a series. **2.** One of 12 equal parts: *One twelfth of 120 is ten.* —**twelfth** *adv. & adj.*

twelve (twĕlv) *n.* **1.** The number, written 12, that is equal to 11 + 1. **2.** The 12th in a set or sequence. —**twelve** *adj. & pron.*

twen•ti•eth (twĕn'tē ĭth) *n.* **1.** The ordinal number matching the number 20 in a series. **2.** One of 20 equal parts. —**twen'ti•eth** *adv. & adj.*

twen•ty (twĕn'tē) *n., pl.* **twen•ties. 1.** The number, written 20, that is equal to 2 × 10. **2. twenties. a.** Often **Twenties.** The ten years from 20 to 29 in a century. **b.** A decade or the numbers from 20 to 29: *She got married in her twenties.* —**twen'ty** *adj. & pron.*

twerp (twûrp) *n. Slang.* A person regarded as silly and unlikable.

twice (twīs) *adv.* **1.** In two cases or on two occasions; two times: *He saw the movie twice.* **2.** In doubled degree or amount: *She works twice as hard as her colleagues.*

twid•dle (twĭd'l) *v.* **twid•dled, twid•dling, twid•dles.** —*tr.* To turn (sthg.) over or around idly or lightly: *twiddling my hair.* —*intr.* To play with sthg. ♦ **twiddle (one's) thumbs.** To do little or nothing; be idle: *She was twiddling her thumbs in the doctor's office.*

twig (twĭg) *n.* A small branch or slender shoot of a tree or shrub.

twi•light (twī'līt') *n.* [U] **1.** The period between sunset and night. **2.** A period or condition of decline following growth or success: *a man in the twilight of his life.*

twin (twĭn) *n.* **1.** One of two offspring born at the same birth: *She had twins.* **2.** One of two identical or similar persons, animals, or things; a counterpart: *looking for a twin to a sock.* —*adj.* **1.** Being two or one of two offspring born at the same birth: *her twin sister; twin brothers.* **2.** Being two or one of two identical or similar persons, animals, or things: *a twin bed; twin cities.*

twine (twīn) *tr. & intr.v.* **twined, twin•ing, twines.** To twist or become twisted together; intertwine: *She twined the ribbons together. The snake twined around his arm.* —*n.* [U] A strong cord or string made of threads twisted together.

twinge (twĭnj) *n.* **1.** A sudden and sharp physical pain: *felt a twinge in my knees.* **2.** A mental or emotional pain: *felt a twinge of guilt.*

twin·kle (twĭng′kəl) *intr.v.* **twin·kled, twin·kling, twin·kles. 1.** To shine on and off; sparkle: *stars twinkling in the sky.* **2.** To be bright or sparkling, as with delight: *Her eyes twinkle.* —*n.* **1.** A glimmer: *a faint twinkle through the clouds.* **2.** A sparkle of merriment or delight in the eye: *a twinkle in his eye.* **3.** A brief interval; a twinkling: *I'll be back in a twinkle.*

twin·kling (twĭng′klĭng) *n.* **1.** [U] The act of blinking. **2.** [C] The time that it takes to blink; an instant: *We'll be done in a twinkling.*

twirl (twûrl) *tr. & intr.v.* To rotate or revolve briskly: *twirl a baton; pinwheels twirling in the wind.* —*n.* The act of spinning or the condition of being spun; a sharp quick spin or whirl: *give the wheel a twirl.* —**twirl′er** *n.*

twist (twĭst) *v.* —*tr.* **1.** To wind together (threads, for example) so as to produce a single strand: *twist a length of rope.* **2.** To turn (sthg.) so as to face another direction: *They twisted their heads around at the sound.* **3.** To injure (a joint) by a sudden turn: *twist one's ankle.* **4.** To change and distort the intended meaning of (sthg.): *The prosecutor twisted the words of the witness.* —*intr.* **1.** To be or become twisted: *fishing lines twisting underwater.* **2.** To move or progress in a winding course: *The river twisted toward the sea.* **3.** To turn to face in another direction: *The children twisted in their seats.* —*n.* **1.** A sliver of citrus peel twisted over a drink for flavoring. **2.** The act of twisting: *opened the bottle with a quick twist.* **3.** A change in direction; a turn: *a sharp twist in the path.* **4.** An unexpected change in a process or a departure from a pattern: *a story with a twist.* ◆ **twist off.** *tr.v.* [sep.] **1.** To turn (sthg.) so as to open: *twisted off the bottle cap.* **2.** To pull, break, or snap (sthg.) by turning: *twist off a dead branch.* **twist (one's) arm.** To use pressure to get sbdy. to do sthg.: *You won't have to twist my arm to get me to the party.* —**twist′a·ble** *adj.*

twist·ed (twĭs′tĭd) *adj.* Not normal; mean: *a twisted sense of humor.*

twist·er (twĭs′tər) *n. Informal.* A tornado.

twit (twĭt) *tr.v.* **twit·ted, twit·ting, twits.** To taunt or tease (sbdy.), especially for mistakes or faults: *They twitted her about her frequent coffee breaks.* —*n. Slang.* A person regarded as foolishly annoying.

twitch (twĭch) *v.* —*intr.* To move with a jerk or spasm: *muscles twitching.* —*tr.* To pull, jerk, or move (sthg.) sharply: *The bird twitched its tail.* —*n.* A sudden involuntary or spasmodic movement, as of a muscle.

twit·ter (twĭt′ər) *intr.v.* **1.** To utter a series of light chirping sounds made by certain birds. **2.** To speak rapidly and softly: *She twittered on and on about this and that.* —*n.*

1. The light chirping sound made by certain birds. **2.** A similar sound, especially light speech or laughter. **3.** A state of agitation or excitement: *Everyone's in a twitter about your visit.*

two (tōō) *n.* **1.** The number, written 2, that is equal to 1 + 1. **2.** The second in a set or sequence. —**two** *adj. & pron.*

HOMONYMS: two, to (toward), **too** (also).

---

two-bit (tōō′bĭt′) *adj.* **1.** *Informal.* Costing or worth 25 cents. **2.** *Slang.* Worth very little; petty or insignificant: *He's nothing but a two-bit crook.*

two-faced (tōō′fāst′) *adj.* Hypocritical or double-dealing; deceitful: *Who needs a two-faced friend?*

two·fer (tōō′fər) *n.* Two items on sale for the price of one: *I got a twofer on shirts yesterday and saved a lot of money.*

two-fisted (tōō′fĭs′tĭd) *adj.* Tough; serious: *a two-fisted approach to teaching.*

two-piece (tōō′pēs′) *adj.* Consisting of two parts: *a two-piece suit.*

two·some (tōō′səm) *n.* Two people or things together; a pair or couple: *They made quite a twosome.*

two-step (tōō′stĕp′) *n.* A ballroom dance in 2/4 time, characterized by long sliding steps.

two-time (tōō′tīm′) *tr.v.* **two-timed, two-tim·ing, two-times.** *Slang.* **1.** To be unfaithful to (a spouse or lover). **2.** To deceive (sbdy.); double-cross: *The thief two-timed his partner.* —**two′-tim′er** *n.*

two-way (tōō′wā′) *adj.* **1.** Moving or allowing motion in two directions: *a two-way street.* **2.** Permitting communication in two directions: *a two-way radio.*

—ty *suff.* A suffix that means condition or quality: *loyalty.*

ty·coon (tī kōōn′) *n.* A wealthy and powerful person in business or industry.

ty·ing (tī′ĭng) *v.* Present participle of **tie.**

tyke also **tike** (tīk) *n.* A small child.

type (tīp) *n.* **1.** [U] A number of people or things having in common traits or characteristics that set them apart as a class. **2.** [C] A person or thing with the characteristics of a group or class: *the type of hero popular in mystery novels.* **3.** [C] An example or a model with the ideal features of a group or class: *He was the perfect type of coach.* **4.** [U] Printed or typewritten characters; print. —*v.* **typed, typ·ing, types.** —*tr.* **1.** To write (sthg.) with a typewriter: *type an essay.* **2.** To classify (sthg.) according to a particular type or class: *type the rock samples by studying each; type an actor as a villain.* —*intr.* To write with a typewriter; typewrite: *He can't type very quickly.*

type·writ·er (tīp′rī′tər) *n.* A machine used for typing on paper.

ty·phoid fever (tī′foid′) *n.* [U] An infectious, often fatal, disease caused by bacteria transmitted in contaminated food or water.

ty•phoon (tī fo͞on′) *n.* A hurricane occurring in the western Pacific region.

ty•phus (tī′fəs) *n.* [U] An infectious disease caused by bacteria transmitted by fleas, lice, or mites.

typ•i•cal (tĭp′ĭ kəl) *adj.* Showing the traits or characteristics that identify a kind, group, or category: *a typical college campus.* —**typ′i•cal•ly** *adv.*

typ•i•fy (tĭp′ə fī′) *tr.v.* **typ•i•fied, typ•i•fy•ing, typ•i•fies.** To serve as a typical example of (sthg.): *That car typifies designs of the '60s.*

typ•ist (tī′pĭst) *n.* A person who operates a typewriter.

typo (tī′pō) *n., pl.* **typos.** An error in typing or word processing; a typographical error: *I found two typos in my essay.*

ty•pog•ra•phy (tī pŏg′rə fē) *n.* [U] The art

and technique of printing text. —**ty•pog′ra•pher** *n.* —**ty′po•graph′i•cal** (tī′pə gräf′ĭ kəl) *adj.*

ty•ran•ni•cal (tĭ răn′ĭ kəl *or* tī răn′ĭ kəl) *adj.* Relating to or characteristic of a tyrant or tyranny. —**ty•ran′ni•cal•ly** *adv.*

tyr•an•nize (tĭr′ə nīz′) *tr.v.* **tyr•an•nized, tyr•an•niz•ing, tyr•an•niz•es.** To treat or govern (sbdy./sthg.) as a tyrant: *That landlord tyrannizes his tenants.*

tyr•an•ny (tĭr′ə nē) *n., pl.* **tyr•an•nies. 1.** [C; U] A government in which a single ruler has absolute power. **2.** [U] Absolute power, especially when exercised unjustly or cruelly.

ty•rant (tī′rənt) *n.* **1.** An absolute ruler who governs without legal restrictions. **2.** A ruler who exercises power in a harsh cruel manner; an oppressor. **3.** A person who uses authority in a harsh or cruel manner: *I've heard that coach is a tyrant.*

tzar (zär *or* tsär) *n.* Variant of **czar** (sense 1).

Uu

u or **U** (yōō) *n.*, *pl.* **u's** or **U's.** The 21st letter of the English alphabet.

U The symbol for the element **uranium.**

U. or **U** *abbr.* An abbreviation of university.

u·biq·ui·tous (yōō bĭk′wĭ təs) *adj.* Being or seeming to be everywhere at the same time: *Television is a ubiquitous presence in modern society.* —**u·biq′ui·tous·ly** *adv.* —**u·biq′-ui·ty** *n.* [U]

ud·der (ŭd′ər) *n.* A bag-shaped part of a cow, goat, or certain other female mammals, in which milk is formed and stored.

UFO (yōō′ĕf ō′) *n.*, *pl.* **UFOs** or **UFO's.** An unidentified flying object: *The newspaper story covered UFOs.*

ugh (ŭg *or* ŭk) *interj.* An expression used to show disgust or horror: *"Ugh," she said, "rotten meat."*

ug·ly (ŭg′lē) *adj.* **ug·li·er, ug·li·est. 1.** Not pleasing to the eye: *an ugly building.* **2.** Nasty or offensive: *an ugly remark.* **3.** Disagreeable; unpleasant: *He has an ugly temper.* —**ug′li·ness** *n.* [U]

uh (ŭ) *interj.* An expression used to show hesitation or uncertainty: *"Uh, I'm not sure," he said.*

uhf or **UHF** *abbr.* An abbreviation of ultrahigh frequency.

uh-huh (ə hŭ′) *interj. Informal.* An expression used to show agreement: *"Uh-huh," she said, nodding. "I'll go."*

U.K. or **UK** *abbr.* An abbreviation of United Kingdom.

u·ku·le·le (yōō′kə lā′lē) *n.* A small four-stringed guitar, first popular in Hawaii.

ul·cer (ŭl′sər) *n.* An inflamed sore or lesion on the skin or inside the body: *a stomach ulcer.* —**ul′cer·ous** *adj.*

ul·te·ri·or (ŭl tîr′ē ər) *adj.* Beyond what can be seen or said, especially when purposely hidden: *ulterior motives.*

ul·ti·mate (ŭl′tə mĭt) *adj.* **1.** Final; last: *the ultimate stop on the subway.* **2.** Greatest possible in size or significance: *the ultimate act of courage.* **3.** Basic; fundamental: *ultimate truths.* —*n.* [U] The greatest extreme; the maximum: *the ultimate in automobiles.* —**ul′ti·mate·ly** *adv.*

ul·ti·ma·tum (ŭl′tə mā′təm) *n.* A final demand that carries the threat of penalties if specific terms are not accepted: *You need to give her an ultimatum or she'll never return your clothes.*

ul·tra (ŭl′trə) *adj.* Extreme, as in following a belief, fashion, or course of action: *an ultra conservative.*

ultra— *pref.* A prefix that means beyond the range, limit, or normal degree of: *ultrasonic; ultraviolet.*

ul·tra·high frequency (ŭl′trə hī′) *n.* [U] A band of radio frequencies from 300 to 3,000 megahertz.

ul·tra·ma·rine (ŭl′trə mə rēn′) *n.* [U] A bright or strong blue to purplish blue color. —*adj.* Bright blue to purplish blue.

ul·tra·son·ic (ŭl′trə sŏn′ĭk) *adj.* Relating to sound that is too high in frequency to be heard by human beings: *ultrasonic waves.*

ul·tra·sound (ŭl′trə sound′) *n.* **1.** [U] Ultrasonic sound. **2.** [C] The medical use of ultrasonic waves, especially to produce images of internal structures of the body or to observe a developing fetus: *She had an ultrasound at the hospital.*

ul·tra·vi·o·let (ŭl′trə vī′ə lĭt) *adj.* Relating to electromagnetic radiation with wavelengths shorter than those of visible light but longer than those of x-rays: *ultraviolet rays.* —*n.* [U] Ultraviolet light or the ultraviolet part of the spectrum.

um·ber (ŭm′bər) *n.* [U] **1.** A natural brown earth used as a pigment. **2.** A dark reddish brown color. —*adj.* Dark reddish brown.

um·bil·i·cal (ŭm bĭl′ĭ kəl) *adj.* Relating to a navel or an umbilical cord: *an umbilical hernia.*

umbilical cord *n.* The flexible cord-shaped structure connecting a fetus to its placenta.

um·brage (ŭm′brĭj) *n.* [U] *Formal.* Offense; resentment: *Don't take umbrage at my question.*

um·brel·la (ŭm-brĕl′ə) *n.* A device for protection from the rain or sun, made of a usually round piece of cloth or other material mounted on a rod along which it is raised or lowered.

umbrella

◆ **umbrella organization** or **group.** An organization that includes several smaller groups.

um·pire (ŭm′pīr′) *n.* A person who rules on plays, especially in baseball. —*v.* **um·pired, um·pir·ing, um·pires.** —*tr.* To act as an umpire for (sthg.): *umpire a game.* —*intr.* To be or act as an umpire: *He umpires for a living.*

ump·teen (ŭmp′tēn′) *adj. Informal.* Large but unspecified in number: *I have umpteen reasons for not going.* —**ump′teenth′** *adj.*

UN or **U.N.** *abbr.* An abbreviation of United Nations.

un–[1] *pref.* A prefix that means: **1.** Not: *unattached.* **2.** Contrary to: *unrest.*

> **WORD BUILDING: un–**[1] The prefix **un–**[1] has the basic meaning "not." Thus **unhappy** means "not happy." **Un–**[1] chiefly attaches to adjectives, as in **unable, unclean, unequal, uneven, unripe,** and **unsafe,** and adjectives made of participles, as in **unfeeling, unfinished, unflinching,** and **unsaid.** Less frequently **un–**[1] attaches to nouns: **uncertainty, unrest. un–**[2] is not related to **un–**[1]. Whereas **un–**[1] forms adjectives and nouns, **un–**[2] forms verbs and expresses removal or reversal: **undress, unnerve, unravel.**

un–[2] *pref.* A prefix that means: **1.** To reverse or undo an action: *unseal.* **2.** To deprive of or remove a thing: *unburden.* **3.** To release, free, or remove from: *untie.* **4.** Used as an intensive: *unloose.*

un•a•bashed (ŭn′ə băsht′) *adj.* Not embarrassed or ashamed: *unabashed greed.* —**un′a•bash′ed•ly** (ŭn′ə băsh′ĭd lē) *adv.*

un•a•ble (ŭn ā′bəl) *adj.* **1.** Lacking the necessary power, authority, or means to do sthg.: *unable to go to the party.* **2.** Lacking mental or physical ability to do sthg.: *With a sprained ankle, she was unable to walk to school.*

un•a•bridged (ŭn′ə brĭjd′) *adj.* Not shortened: *an unabridged book.*

un•ac•cent•ed (ŭn ăk′sĕn tĭd) *adj.* Having weak stress or no stress: *an unaccented syllable.*

un•ac•com•pa•nied (ŭn′ə kŭm′pə nēd) *adj.* Without a companion: *an unaccompanied guest.*

un•ac•count•a•ble (ŭn′ə koun′tə bəl) *adj.* **1.** Impossible to explain: *an unaccountable absence from class.* **2.** Not responsible to a higher authority; not responsible: *unaccountable for his actions.* —**un′ac•count′a•bly** *adv.*

un•ac•cus•tomed (ŭn′ə kŭs′təmd) *adj.* **1.** Not customary; unusual: *They treated me with unaccustomed politeness.* **2.** Not used to: *unaccustomed to the cold weather.*

un•ac•quaint•ed (ŭn′ə kwān′tĭd) *adj.* [*with*] Not familiar with or informed about: *unacquainted with the necessary procedures.*

un•a•dul•ter•at•ed (ŭn′ə dŭl′tə rā′tĭd) *adj.* **1.** Not mixed or diluted; pure: *unadulterated milk.* **2.** Thorough; complete: *unadulterated joy.*

un•af•fect•ed (ŭn′ə fĕk′tĭd) *adj.* **1.** Not changed or affected: *Our plans were unaffected by the rain.* **2.** Sincere: *an unaffected smile.*

un•aid•ed (ŭn ā′dĭd) *adv. & adj.* Without the help of tools or another person: *Three weeks after the operation, she walked unaided. The comet could be seen with the unaided eye.*

un•al•ter•a•ble (ŭn ôl′tər ə bəl) *adj.* Impossible to change: *an unalterable decision.* —**un•al′ter•a•bly** *adv.*

u•na•nim•i•ty (yōō′nə nĭm′ĭ tē) *n.* [U] The condition of being unanimous; complete agreement: *Unanimity is rare in a family of eight.*

u•nan•i•mous (yōō năn′ə məs) *adj.* **1.** Sharing the same opinion: *Critics were unanimous about the play.* **2.** Based on or characterized by complete agreement: *a unanimous vote.* —**u•nan′i•mous•ly** *adv.*

un•an•nounced (ŭn′ə nounst′) *adj. & adv.* Without prior notification: *There were several unannounced changes in the agenda. They walked in unannounced.*

un•ap•proach•a•ble (ŭn′ə prō′chə bəl) *adj.* Not friendly; aloof: *an unapproachable boss.*

un•armed (ŭn ärmd′) *adj.* Without weapons: *an unarmed security guard.*

un•as•sist•ed (ŭn′ə sĭs′tĭd) *adv. & adj.* Without help or support: *He could not get out of the swimming pool unassisted. He spoke of his unassisted rise from poverty.*

un•as•sum•ing (ŭn′ə sōō′mĭng) *adj.* Not pretentious; modest: *an unassuming friend.*

un•at•tached (ŭn′ə tăcht′) *adj.* **1.** Not attached or joined: *The pieces became unattached during shipping.* **2.** Not engaged, married, or involved in a serious romantic relationship: *There were several unattached people at the party.*

un•a•void•a•ble (ŭn′ə voi′də bəl) *adj.* Impossible to avoid; inescapable: *an unavoidable discussion.* —**un′a•void′a•bly** *adv.*

un•a•ware (ŭn′ə wâr′) *adj.* Not aware: *She was unaware of his presence.*

un•a•wares (ŭn′ə wârz′) *adv.* By surprise; unexpectedly: *I caught them unawares.*

un•bal•anced (ŭn băl′ənst) *adj.* **1.** Not in balance or in proper balance: *an unbalanced scale.* **2.** Not mentally sound; irrational: *an unbalanced mind.* **3.** Not balanced financially; having debits and credits that do not correspond to each other: *an unbalanced checkbook.*

un•bear•a•ble (ŭn bâr′ə bəl) *adj.* So unpleasant or painful as to be impossible to endure: *unbearable heat.* —**un•bear′a•bly** *adv.*

un•beat•a•ble (ŭn bē′tə bəl) *adj.* Impossible to surpass or defeat: *an unbeatable team.*

un•beat•en (ŭn bēt′n) *adj.* **1.** Never defeated: *an unbeaten swim team.* **2.** Not beaten or pounded, as in cooking: *unbeaten eggs.*

un•be•com•ing (ŭn′bĭ kŭm′ĭng) *adj.* **1.** Not attractive or flattering: *unbecoming clothes.* **2.** Not suitable or proper: *unbecoming behavior.*

un•be•liev•a•ble (ŭn'bĭ lē'və bəl) *adj.* Not to be believed; incredible: *an unbelievable story.* —**un'be•liev'a•bly** *adv.*

un•bi•ased (ŭn bī'əst) *adj.* Without bias or prejudice; impartial: *A judge must be unbiased.*

un•born (ŭn bôrn') *adj.* Not yet born: *an unborn child.*

un•bri•dled (ŭn brīd'ld) *adj.* Unrestrained; uncontrolled: *moments of unbridled joy.*

un•bro•ken (ŭn brō'kən) *adj.* **1.** Not broken; whole; intact: *the last unbroken cup of the set.* **2.** Not violated: *an unbroken promise.* **3.** Uninterrupted: *unbroken silence.* **4.** Not tamed or broken: *an unbroken pony.*

un•buck•le (ŭn bŭk'əl) *tr.v.* **un•buck•led, un•buck•ling, un•buck•les.** To loosen or undo the buckle of (sthg.): *You can unbuckle your seat belt now.*

un•bur•den (ŭn bûr'dn) *tr.v.* To free (sbdy./sthg.) from or relieve of a burden: *unburden one's mind.*

un•but•ton (ŭn bŭt'n) *tr.v.* To unfasten the buttons of (sthg.): *Unbutton your coat.*

un•but•toned (ŭn bŭt'nd) *adj.* Open and informal: *an unbuttoned discussion.*

un•called-for (ŭn kôld'fôr') *adj.* Unwanted, undeserved, or inappropriate: *an uncalled-for remark.*

un•can•ny (ŭn kăn'ē) *adj.* **un•can•ni•er, un•can•ni•est.** **1.** Arousing wonder and fear, as if supernatural; eerie: *an uncanny light coming out of the ruins.* **2.** So keen and perceptive as to seem supernatural: *uncanny wisdom.* —**un•can'ni•ly** *adv.*

un•ceas•ing (ŭn sē'sĭng) *adj.* Not stopping; continuous: *unceasing activity.* —**un•ceas'ing•ly** *adv.*

un•cer•tain (ŭn sûr'tn) *adj.* **1.** Not known or established; questionable: *The results of the experiment are uncertain.* **2.** Not definite; undecided: *uncertain plans.* **3.** Not having sure knowledge: *uncertain of the answers.* **4.** Subject to change: *uncertain weather.* —**un•cer'tain•ly** *adv.*

un•cer•tain•ty (ŭn sûr'tn tē) *n., pl.* **un•cer•tain•ties. 1.** [U] The condition of being uncertain: *The uncertainty of her husband's health distressed her.* **2.** [C] Something that is uncertain: *the uncertainties of life.*

SYNONYMS: **uncertainty, doubt, suspicion, mistrust.** These nouns mean a condition of being unsure about sbdy./sthg. **Uncertainty** is the least forceful: *I looked back on my decision with growing uncertainty.* **Doubt** refers to a questioning state of mind that leads to hesitation in accepting sthg. or making a decision: *If there is any doubt about his story, you can call his office to confirm it.* **Suspicion** often suggests an uneasy feeling that a person or thing is evil: *The leaders from the warring countries regarded each other with suspicion at the start*

of the conference. **Mistrust** means a lack of trust or confidence arising from suspicion: *After the strike, the company was filled with an atmosphere of general mistrust.*

un•char•i•ta•ble (ŭn chăr'ĭ tə bəl) *adj.* **1.** Not generous: *an uncharitable gift of 25 cents.* **2.** Unfair or unkind: *uncharitable remarks.*

un•chart•ed (ŭn chär'tĭd) *adj.* **1.** Not recorded on a map: *an uncharted island.* **2.** Unknown: *uncharted ideas.*

un•civ•i•lized (ŭn sĭv'ə līzd') *adj.* Not civilized; barbaric: *uncivilized behavior.*

un•cle (ŭng'kəl) *n.* **1.** The brother of one's mother or father. **2.** The husband of one's aunt.

un•clean (ŭn klēn') *adj.* **1.** Not clean; dirty: *an unclean room.* **2.** Morally impure: *unclean thoughts.* —**un•clean'li•ness** (ŭn klĕn'lē nĭs) *n.* [U] —**un•clean'ly** (ŭn klĕn'lē) *adj.* —**un•clean'ly** (ŭn klēn'lē) *adv.*

un•clear (ŭn klîr') *adj.* Not clear or explicit: *an unclear explanation.*

Uncle Sam (săm) *n.* A symbol of the United States government, represented as a tall thin man dressed in the national colors and wearing a white beard and a top hat.

un•clothe (ŭn klōth') *tr.v.* **un•clothed, un•cloth•ing, un•clothes.** To remove the clothing or cover from (sbdy.): *unclothe a baby for a bath.*

un•coil (ŭn koil') *tr. & intr.v.* To unwind or become unwound: *Uncoil the hose. The snake uncoiled.*

un•com•fort•a•ble (ŭn kŭm'fər tə bəl *or* ŭn kŭmf' tə bəl) *adj.* **1.** Experiencing physical discomfort: *She felt uncomfortable after her surgery.* **2.** Ill at ease; uneasy: *I'm uncomfortable with the committee's decision.* **3.** Causing discomfort: *an uncomfortable chair.* —**un•com'fort•a•bly** *adv.*

un•com•mon (ŭn kŏm'ən) *adj.* **1.** Not common; rare: *words used in uncommon ways.* **2.** Wonderful; remarkable: *uncommon happiness.* —**un•com'mon•ly** *adv.*

un•com•pro•mis•ing (ŭn kŏm'prə mī'zĭng) *adj.* Not willing to make compromises; rigid: *Their side took an uncompromising position during negotiations.* —**un•com'pro•mis'ing•ly** *adv.*

un•con•cerned (ŭn'kən sûrnd') *adj.* [*about*] **1.** Not interested; indifferent: *unconcerned about the problems of the poor.* **2.** Not worried or anxious: *She seemed unconcerned about the dog.* —**un'con•cern'ed•ly** (ŭn'kən sûr'nĭd lē) *adv.*

un•con•di•tion•al (ŭn'kən dĭsh'ə nəl) *adj.* Without conditions or limitations; absolute: *unconditional surrender; unconditional love.* —**un'con•di'tion•al•ly** *adv.*

un•con•quer•a•ble (ŭn kŏng'kər ə bəl) *adj.* Impossible to defeat: *With her unconquerable spirit, she will recover quickly.*

U

un•con•scion•a•ble (ŭn kŏn'shə nə bəl) *adj.* **1.** Without a conscience; without morality: *an unconscionable and evil act.* **2.** Beyond reason; extreme: *an unconscionable price.* —**un•con'scion•a•bly** *adv.*

un•con•scious (ŭn kŏn'shəs) *adj.* **1.** Temporarily lacking consciousness: *The patient was still unconscious from the anesthesia.* **2.** Without knowledge: *He was unconscious of their wishes.* **3.** Happening without one's awareness or conscious thought: *unconscious fears.* **4.** Not done on purpose; accidental: *an unconscious mistake.* —*n.* [U] The part of the mind that contains desires, fears, or memories that are not subject to conscious awareness or control. —**un•con'scious•ly** *adv.* —**un•con'scious•ness** *n.* [U]

un•con•sti•tu•tion•al (ŭn'kŏn stĭ tōō'shə nəl) *adj.* Not in agreement with the principles set forth in the constitution of a nation or state: *a unconstitutional law.*

un•con•trol•la•ble (ŭn'kən trō'lə bəl) *adj.* Impossible to control or govern: *an uncontrollable urge to laugh.* —**un'con•trol'la•bly** *adv.*

un•con•trolled (ŭn'kən trōld') *adj.* Not under control or restraint: *an uncontrolled drug; uncontrolled anger.*

un•con•ven•tion•al (ŭn'kən vĕn'shə nəl) *adj.* Not conforming to accepted social norms; out of the ordinary: *unconventional forms of art.* —**un'con•ven'tion•al•ly** *adv.*

un•cork (ŭn kôrk') *tr.v.* To remove the cork from (a bottle): *We uncorked the wine.*

un•count•a•ble (ŭn koun'tə bəl) *adj.* That cannot be counted: *uncountable tourists.*

uncountable noun *n.* A noun such as *milk* or *honesty* that has no plural form, cannot be counted, and is used with modifiers such as *some* or *much* rather than *a* or *one.*

un•count•ed (ŭn koun'tĭd) *adj.* **1.** Not counted: *The uncounted money is in the safe.* **2.** Too numerous to be counted: *uncounted millions calling for change.*

un•couth (ŭn kōōth') *adj.* Not refined; crude: *uncouth behavior.*

un•cov•er (ŭn kŭv'ər) *tr.v.* **1.** To remove a cover from (sbdy./sthg.): *uncover a jar.* **2.** To reveal or disclose (sthg.): *uncover a secret.*

un•cul•ti•vat•ed (ŭn kŭl'tə vā'tĭd) *adj.* **1.** Not prepared for growing crops: *uncultivated land.* **2.** Not refined or cultured: *an uncultivated person.*

un•cut (ŭn kŭt') *adj.* **1.** Not cut, trimmed, or sliced: *uncut hair; uncut bread.* **2.** Not ground or polished: *an uncut gem.* **3.** Not abridged or shortened: *an uncut movie.*

un•daunt•ed (ŭn dôn'tĭd *or* ŭn dän'tĭd) *adj.* Not discouraged; courageous: *The soldiers were undaunted in battle.*

un•de•cid•ed (ŭn'dĭ sī'dĭd) *adj.* **1.** Not yet settled; open: *plans still undecided.* **2.** Hav-

ing reached no decision: *She's undecided about whether to hire new workers.*

un•de•clared (ŭn'dĭ klârd') *adj.* Not formally declared: *an undeclared war; an undeclared candidate.*

un•de•ni•a•ble (ŭn'dĭ nī'ə bəl) *adj.* Difficult or impossible to deny: *undeniable facts.* —**un'de•ni'a•bly** *adv.*

un•der (ŭn'dər) *prep.* **1.** In a lower position or place than: *a cat under the table.* **2.** Beneath the surface of: *under the ground.* **3.** Beneath the pretense of: *under a false name.* **4.** Less than; smaller than: *under 20 years of age.* **5.** Less than the required amount or degree of: *under voting age.* **6.** Subject to the authority, rule, or control of: *under a dictatorship.* **7.** Receiving the effects of: *under the care of a doctor.* **8.** Subject to the obligation of: *under contract.* **9.** Within the group or classification of: *books listed under biology in the card catalog.* **10.** In the process of: *The proposal is under discussion.* **11.** In view of; because of: *Under these conditions, it would be wiser to wait.* —*adv.* In or into a place below or beneath: *The frog put its head under.* —*adj.* Located lower than or beneath sthg. else: *the under parts of a machine.* ♦ **keep under (one's) hat.** To keep (sthg.) a secret: *I shouldn't have told you that; keep it under your hat.* **under the gun.** Under the pressure of a deadline: *We're under the gun now to finish this project.*

under— *pref.* A prefix that means: **1.** Beneath or below in position: *underground.* **2.** Inferiority in rank or importance: *undersecretary.* **3.** Less in degree, rate, or quantity than normal or proper: *underestimate.*

WORD BUILDING: under— The prefix **under—** has essentially the same meaning as the preposition **under.** For example, in words such as **underarm, undercurrent, underlie,** and **undershirt, under—** denotes a position beneath or below. **Under—** also frequently conveys incompleteness or falling below a certain standard. Some examples are **undercharge, underdeveloped, underestimate,** and **underfeed.** Note that in this sense words beginning with **under—** often have counterparts beginning with **over—:** **overcharge, overestimate.**

---

un•der•a•chieve (ŭn'dər ə chēv') *intr.v.* **un•der•a•chieved, un•der•a•chiev•ing, un•der•a•chieves.** To perform worse or achieve less than expected: *It's clear she is underachieving in school this year.* —**un'der•a•chiev'er** *n.*

un•der•age (ŭn'dər āj') *adj.* Below the legal age for voting: *Underage people cannot buy alcoholic beverages.*

un•der•arm (ŭn'dər ärm') *adj.* Located, placed, or used under the arm: *underarm* *deodorant.* —*n.* The armpit. —**un′der·arm′** *adv.*

un·der·bid (ŭn′dər bĭd′) *tr.v.* **un·der·bid, un·der·bid·ding, un·der·bids.** To bid lower than (a competitor): *He underbid another builder for the construction project.*

un·der·brush (ŭn′dər brŭsh′) *n.* [U] Small trees, shrubs, or similar plants growing thickly beneath taller trees: *Look for the ball in the underbrush.*

un·der·charge (ŭn′dər chärj′) *tr.v.* **un·der·charged, un·der·charg·ing, un·der·charg·es.** To charge (a customer, for example) too little: *The cashier undercharged me for the meat.*

un·der·class (ŭn′dər klăs′) *n.* [C; U] The poorest group in a society.

un·der·clothes (ŭn′dər klōz′ *or* ŭn′dər-klōthz′) *pl.n.* Clothes worn next to the skin, beneath one's outer clothing; underwear.

un·der·cloth·ing (ŭn′dər klō′thĭng) *n.* [U] Underclothes.

un·der·coat (ŭn′dər kōt′) *n.* A coat of material applied to a surface to seal it or otherwise prepare it for a final coat, as of paint: *Give it an undercoat of primer first.*

un·der·cov·er (ŭn′dər kŭv′ər) *adj.* **1.** Performed or occurring in secret: *an undercover investigation.* **2.** Engaged in spying or secret investigations: *undercover police.*

un·der·cur·rent (ŭn′dər kûr′ənt *or* ŭn′dər-kûr′ənt) *n.* **1.** A current, as of air or water, flowing beneath a surface or another current. **2.** A partly hidden tendency, force, or influence that is often contrary to what is obvious: *His speech had an undercurrent of anger.*

un·der·cut (ŭn′dər kŭt′) *tr.v.* **un·der·cut, un·der·cut·ting, un·der·cuts.** **1.** To diminish or destroy the effectiveness of (sbdy./sthg.); undermine: *The scandal undercut the senator's influence.* **2.** To sell or work for less money than (a competitor): *The discount store undercut the department store.*

un·der·de·vel·oped (ŭn′dər dĭ vĕl′əpt) *adj.* **1.** Not developed in a full or normal way, as a living thing or one of its parts: *an underdeveloped plant.* **2.** Having a low level of economic development and technology in comparison to other societies: *an underdeveloped nation.*

un·der·dog (ŭn′dər dôg′ *or* ŭn′dər dŏg′) *n.* A person or thing that is expected to lose a contest or struggle, as in sports or politics: *Many fans cheer for the underdog.*

un·der·done (ŭn′dər dŭn′) *adj.* Not sufficiently cooked: *The chicken was underdone, so I put it back in the oven.*

un·der·em·ployed (ŭn′dər ĕm ploid′) *adj.* Employed in a job that requires less skill or training than one possesses or that offers fewer hours than one desires to work: *After finishing college, she was underemployed at her first job.*

un·der·es·ti·mate (ŭn′dər ĕs′tə māt′) *tr.v.* **un·der·es·ti·mat·ed, un·der·es·ti·mat·ing, un·der·es·ti·mates.** To make too low an estimate of the value, amount, or quality of (sthg.): *We underestimated how long it would take to build the shed.*

un·der·ex·pose (ŭn′dər ĭk spōz′) *tr.v.* **un·der·ex·posed, un·der·ex·pos·ing, un·der·ex·pos·es.** To expose (film) to light for too short a time to produce an image with good contrast: *The lab underexposed my photographs.* —**un′der·ex·po′sure** (ŭn′dər ĭk spō′zhər) *n.* [C; U]

un·der·feed (ŭn′dər fēd′) *tr.v.* **un·der·fed** (ŭn′dər fēd′), **un·der·feed·ing, un·der·feeds.** To feed (sbdy./sthg.) insufficiently: *She underfed the fish, and so they died.*

un·der·foot (ŭn′dər foot′) *adv.* **1.** Below or under the foot or feet: *The ice made it slippery underfoot.* **2.** In the way: *too many toys underfoot.*

un·der·gar·ment (ŭn′dər gär′mənt) *n.* An article of clothing worn under outer clothes, especially one worn next to the skin.

un·der·go (ŭn′dər gō′) *tr.v.* **un·der·went** (ŭn′dər wĕnt′), **un·der·gone** (ŭn′dər gôn′ *or* ŭn′dər gŏn′), **un·der·go·ing, un·der·goes.** **1.** To experience (sthg.): *Many insects undergo several changes in body form during their development.* **2.** To endure (sthg.); suffer through: *undergo hardship.*

un·der·grad·u·ate (ŭn′dər grăj′oo ĭt) *n.* A student who has entered a college or university but has not yet received a bachelor's or similar degree. —*adj.* **1.** For or characteristic of an undergraduate: *undergraduate courses.* **2.** Being an undergraduate: *undergraduate students.*

un·der·ground (ŭn′dər ground′) *adj.* **1.** Located or occurring below the surface of the earth: *an underground passage.* **2.** Acting or done in secret; hidden: *underground resistance to the tyrant.* **3.** Relating to an avant-garde or experimental movement or its films, publications, or art: *the underground press.* —*n.* [U] **1.** A secret organization working against a government in power. **2.** *Chiefly British.* A subway system. —*adv.* (ŭn′dər-ground′). **1.** Below the surface of the earth: *miners digging underground.* **2.** In secret: *spies working underground.*

un·der·growth (ŭn′dər grōth′) *n.* [U] Low-growing plants, shrubs, or young trees beneath taller trees in a forest.

un·der·hand (ŭn′dər hănd′) *also* **un·der·hand·ed** (ŭn′dər hăn′dĭd) *adj.* **1.** Deceptive, sly, or secretive: *an underhanded salesman.* **2.** In sports, performed with the hand brought forward and up from below the level of the shoulder: *an underhand throw.* —**un′der·hand′, un′der·hand′ed** *adv.*

un·der·lie (ŭn′dər lī′) *tr.v.* **un·der·lay** (ŭn′dər lā′), **un·der·lain** (ŭn′dər lān′),

U

un·der·ly·ing, **un·der·lies. 1.** To be located under or below (sthg.): *Roman roads underlie many modern European highways.* **2.** To be the basis for (sthg.); account for: *These ideas underlie her decision.*

un·der·line (ŭn′dər līn′ *or* ŭn′dər līn′) *tr.v.* **un·der·lined, un·der·lin·ing, un·der·lines. 1.** To draw a line under (sthg.); underscore: *underline the correct answer.* **2.** To stress or emphasize (sthg.): *He underlined their desire to cooperate.*

un·der·ly·ing (ŭn′dər lī′ĭng) *adj.* **1.** Located under or beneath sthg.: *the underlying layer of rock.* **2.** Basic; fundamental: *underlying values.* **3.** Present but not obvious; implied: *an underlying meaning.*

un·der·mine (ŭn′dər mīn′) *tr.v.* **un·der·mined, un·der·min·ing, un·der·mines.** To weaken or ruin (sthg.) by or as if by wearing away a base or foundation: *waters undermining the foundation of a house; bad habits undermining his health.*

un·der·neath (ŭn′dər nēth′) *adv.* In or to a place beneath; below: *The boys climbed the tree while we sat underneath.* *—prep.* Beneath; below; under: *put a plate underneath a cup.*

un·der·nour·ished (ŭn′dər nûr′ĭsht *or* ŭn′dər nŭr′ĭsht) *adj.* Without enough nourishment for proper health and growth: *an undernourished plant.*

un·der·pants (ŭn′dər pănts′) *pl.n.* Briefs or shorts worn as underwear, especially those of a child.

un·der·pass (ŭn′dər păs′) *n.* A passage underneath sthg., especially a part of a road that passes under another road or a railroad.

un·der·priv·i·leged (ŭn′dər prĭv′ə lĭjd) *adj.* Without the opportunities enjoyed by other members of one's society: *underprivileged children.*

un·der·rate (ŭn′dər rāt′) *tr.v.* **un·der·rat·ed, un·der·rat·ing, un·der·rates.** To judge or rate (sbdy./sthg.) too low; underestimate: *They underrated his ability.*

un·der·score (ŭn′dər skôr′) *tr.v.* **un·der·scored, un·der·scor·ing, un·der·scores. 1.** To underline (sthg.): *underscore the right word.* **2.** To emphasize (sthg.); stress: *underscore your main points in a speech.*

un·der·sea (ŭn′dər sē′) *adj.* Existing, done, used, or operating beneath the surface of the sea: *undersea life; undersea exploration.*

un·der·shirt (ŭn′dər shûrt′) *n.* An undergarment worn next to the skin under a shirt, especially one worn by a child or a man.

un·der·side (ŭn′dər sīd′) *n.* The side or surface that is underneath; the bottom side: *open a box from the underside.*

un·der·signed (ŭn′dər sīnd′) *adj.* Having signed at the end of a document: *the undersigned persons.* *—n., pl.* **undersigned.** A person whose name appears at the end of a document.

un·der·sized (ŭn′dər sīzd′) *also* **un·der·size** (ŭn′dər sīz′) *adj.* Smaller than the usual or required size: *an undersized coat.*

un·der·stand (ŭn′dər stănd′) *v.* **un·der·stood** (ŭn′dər stood′), **un·der·stand·ing, un·der·stands.** *—tr.* **1.** To grasp the nature and significance of (sthg.): *Do you understand how an engine works?* **2.** To know (sbdy./sthg.) well by long experience or close contact: *That teacher understands kids.* **3.** To grasp the meaning intended or expressed by (sbdy./sthg.): *She speaks Russian and can understand your new neighbors.* **4.** To be tolerant or sympathetic toward (sbdy./sthg.): *I don't agree, but I can still understand your point.* **5.** To learn (sthg.) indirectly, as by hearsay: *We understand she had a baby on Saturday.* **6.** To draw (sthg.) as a conclusion; infer: *Am I to understand that you are staying for the weekend?* **7.** To accept (sthg.) as an agreed fact: *Are the terms of our agreement understood?* **8.** To supply or add (words, for example) mentally: *The subject of an imperative verb is understood.* *—intr.* **1.a.** To have knowledge or understanding: *She understands quickly.* **b.** To have sympathy or tolerance: *When he heard the bad news, he understood and expressed his sorrow.* **2.** To learn sthg. indirectly; gather: *He's retiring, or so I understand.* **—un′der·stand′a·ble** *adj.—***un′der·stand′a·bly** *adv.*

un·der·stand·ing (ŭn′dər stăn′dĭng) *n.* **1.** [U] Comprehension. **2.** [U] The ability to understand; intelligence: *a person of great understanding.* **3.** [U] Individual judgment; opinion: *In my understanding, this plan makes sense.* **4.** [C] An agreement between two or more people or groups: *After long negotiations they finally reached an understanding.* **5.** [U] An attitude of appreciating the thoughts or feelings of others: *Show some understanding!* *—adj.* **1.** Characterized by or having comprehension or good sense: *an understanding student.* **2.** Compassionate; sympathetic: *a kind and understanding friend.*

un·der·state (ŭn′dər stāt′) *tr.v.* **un·der·stat·ed, un·der·stat·ing, un·der·states. 1.** To state (sthg.) incompletely or without full information: *They have understated the problem in order to avoid punishment.* **2.** To express (sthg.) with little emphasis, especially for an ironic effect.

un·der·stat·ed (ŭn′dər stā′tĭd) *adj.* Not showy; subtle: *an air of understated elegance.*

un·der·state·ment (ŭn′dər stăt′mənt *or* ŭn′dər stāt′mənt) *n.* **1.** [C] A statement that is less than complete. **2.** [U] Lack of emphasis in expression, especially for rhetorical effect: *He often uses understatement, as in saying "not bad" to mean "very good."*

un•der•stood (ŭn′dər sto͝od′) *v.* Past tense and past participle of **understand.** —*adj.* **1.** Agreed upon: *We recalled that the understood fee is 50 dollars.* **2.** Not expressed but implied: *You is the understood subject in the sentence* Please come in.

un•der•take (ŭn′dər tāk′) *tr.v.* **un•der•took** (ŭn′dər to͝ok′), **un•der•tak•en** (ŭn′dər tā′kən), **un•der•tak•ing, un•der•takes. 1.** To take (sthg.) upon oneself; decide or agree to do: *undertake a difficult job.* **2.** To agree or promise (sthg.): *She undertook to inspect the building.*

un•der•tak•er (ŭn′dər tā′kər) *n.* A funeral director.

un•der•tak•ing (ŭn′dər tā′kĭng) *n.* **1.** [C] A task or an assignment undertaken; a venture: *a risky undertaking.* **2.** [U] The occupation of a funeral director.

un•der•tone (ŭn′dər tōn′) *n.* An underlying or implied sense or meaning: *an undertone of hostility.*

un•der•took (ŭn′dər to͝ok′) *v.* Past tense of **undertake.**

un•der•tow (ŭn′dər tō′) *n.* [U] A current beneath the surface of a body of water flowing opposite to that of the current at the surface: *swimmers caught in the undertow.*

un•der•wa•ter (ŭn′dər wô′tər *or* ŭn′dər wŏt′ər) *adj.* Used, done, or existing under the surface of water: *underwater exploration.* —**un′der′wa′ter** *adv.*

un•der•way or **un•der•way** (ŭn′dər wā′) *adv. & adj.* **1.** In motion or operation: *The boat got under way.* **2.** In progress: *Plans for a new stadium are under way.*

un•der•wear (ŭn′dər wâr′) *n.* [U] Underclothes.

un•der•weight (ŭn′dər wāt′) *adj.* Weighing less than is normal or required: *an underweight child.*

un•der•went (ŭn′dər wĕnt′) *v.* Past tense of **undergo.**

un•der•world (ŭn′dər wûrld′) *n.* [U] The part of society engaged in crime and vice.

un•der•write (ŭn′dər rīt′) *tr.v.* **un•der•wrote** (ŭn′dər rōt′), **un•der•writ•ten** (ŭn′dər rĭt′n), **un•der•writ•ing, un•der•writes. 1.** To assume financial responsibility for (sthg.): *The corporation underwrote the movie.* **2.** To sign (an insurance policy) guaranteeing payment in case of losses or damage. —**un′der•writ′er** *n.*

un•de•sir•a•ble (ŭn′dĭ zīr′ə bəl) *adj.* Not wanted: *an undesirable effect.* —*n.* A person who is not wanted or whose behavior is objectionable: *We were treated as undesirables at the new school.* —**un′de•sir′a•bil′i•ty** *n.* [U] —**un′de•sir′a•bly** *adv.*

un•did (ŭn dĭd′) *v.* Past tense of **undo.**

un•dies (ŭn′dēz) *pl.n. Informal.* Underpants, especially those of a child.

un•dig•ni•fied (ŭn dĭg′nə fīd′) *adj.* Without dignity: *undignified behavior.*

un•do (ŭn do͞o′) *tr.v.* **un•did** (ŭn dĭd′), **un•done** (ŭn dŭn′), **un•do•ing, un•does** (ŭn dŭz′). **1.** To reverse the result or effect of (a previous action): *trying to undo mistakes.* **2.** To untie or loosen (sthg.): *undo a knot.* **3.** To open (sthg.); unwrap: *undo a package.* **4.** To cause the ruin or downfall of (sbdy./sthg.): *The old regime was undone by greed.*

HOMONYMS: undo, undue (extreme).

un•do•ing (ŭn do͞o′ĭng) *n.* [U] **1.** The act of unfastening or loosening: *The undoing of the package was harder than wrapping it.* **2.** A cause of ruin; a downfall: *Greed was his undoing.*

un•done (ŭn dŭn′) *v.* Past participle of **undo.**

un•doubt•ed (ŭn dou′tĭd) *adj.* Not doubted or questioned; accepted: *undoubted talent.* —**un•doubt′ed•ly** *adv.*

un•dress (ŭn drĕs′) *v.* —*tr.* To remove the clothing of (sbdy.): *She undressed her baby and put on his pajamas.* —*intr.* To take off one's clothing: *He undressed at the gym.* —*n.* [U] Nakedness: *in a state of undress.*

un•due (ŭn do͞o′) *adj.* **1.** Beyond what is normal or appropriate; extreme: *an undue amount of noise.* **2.** Not proper or legal: *undue powers.*

HOMONYMS: undue, undo (reverse).

un•du•late (ŭn′jə lāt′ *or* ŭn′dyə lāt′) *intr.v.* **un•du•lat•ed, un•du•lat•ing, un•du•lates.** To move in waves or with a smooth wavy motion: *wheat undulating in the breeze.* —**un′du•la′tion** *n.* [C; U]

un•du•ly (ŭn do͞o′lē) *adv.* To an extreme degree; immoderately: *unduly fearful.*

un•dy•ing (ŭn dī′ĭng) *adj.* Endless; everlasting: *undying gratitude.*

un•earned (ŭn ûrnd′) *adj.* **1.** Not gained by work: *unearned income from stock sales.* **2.** Not deserved: *unearned praise.* **3.** Not yet earned: *unearned interest on money.*

un•earth (ŭn ûrth′) *tr.v.* **1.** To bring (sthg.) up out of the earth; dig up: *Archeologists unearthed pottery.* **2.** To bring (sthg.) to public notice; uncover: *unearthing evidence about the crime.*

un•earth•ly (ŭn ûrth′lē) *adj.* **1.** Not of the earth or this world; supernatural: *unearthly creatures.* **2.** Unnaturally strange and frightening: *an unearthly scream.* **3.** Not customary or reasonable; absurd: *She gets up at an unearthly hour.* —**un•earth′li•ness** *n.* [U]

un•eas•y (ŭn ē′zē) *adj.* **1.** Lacking a sense of security: *The workers were uneasy about their jobs.* **2.** Awkward or unsure in manner:

U

The dog is uneasy with strangers. —**un•eas′-i•ly** *adv.* —**un•eas′i•ness** *n.* [U]

un•ed•u•cat•ed (ŭn ĕj′ə kā′tĭd) *adj.* Without an education, especially without formal schooling: *an uneducated worker.*

un•em•ploy•a•ble (ŭn′ĕm ploi′ə bəl) *adj.* Not able to find or hold a job: *He was unemployable because of his poor past performance.*

un•em•ployed (ŭn′ĕm ploid′) *adj.* **1.** Out of work; jobless: *She was unemployed for six months.* **2.** Not being used; idle: *an unemployed machine.* —*pl.n.* People who are out of work: *The number of unemployed has decreased.*

un•em•ploy•ment (ŭn′ĕm ploi′mənt) *n.* [U] **1.** The condition of being out of work: *a period of high unemployment.* **2.** *Informal.* Unemployment compensation: *The workers are collecting unemployment during the layoff.*

unemployment compensation *n.* [U] Money paid for a specified period by a state to a person who has lost a job for reasons other than poor performance.

un•e•qual (ŭn ē′kwəl) *adj.* **1.** Not the same in any measurable way; not equal: *unequal numbers.* **2.** Not the same in rank or social position: *unequal colleagues.* **3.** Not having the required ability; not adequate: *unequal to the task.* **4.** Not fair: *unequal shares.*

un•e•qualed (ŭn ē′kwəld) *adj.* Not matched by others of its kind; exceptional: *a musician unequaled in talent.*

un•e•quiv•o•cal (ŭn′ĭ kwĭv′ə kəl) *adj.* Without any doubt; clear: *an unequivocal success.* —**un′e•quiv′o•cal•ly** *adv.*

un•err•ing (ŭn ûr′ĭng *or* ŭn ĕr′ĭng) *adj.* Making no mistakes; consistently accurate: *an unerring sense of direction.* —**un•err′ing•ly** *adv.*

un•e•ven (ŭn ē′vən) *adj.* **1.** Not equal, as in size, length, or quality: *uneven hems on his pants.* **2.** Not the same; differing in quality or form: *an uneven performance; a lamp giving very uneven light.* **3.** Not level or smooth: *the uneven surface of the road.* **4.** Not straight or parallel: *a book with uneven margins.* —**un•e′ven•ly** *adv.* —**un•e′ven•ness** *n.* [U]

un•e•vent•ful (ŭn′ĭ vĕnt′fəl) *adj.* Having no significant events: *an uneventful evening of TV-watching.* —**un′e•vent′ful•ly** *adv.*

un•ex•cep•tion•al (ŭn′ĭk sĕp′shə nəl) *adj.* Not varying from what is usual or expected: *an unexceptional piano performance.* —**un′-ex•cep′tion•al•ly** *adv.*

un•ex•pect•ed (ŭn′ĭk spĕk′tĭd) *adj.* Not expected; coming without warning: *an unexpected gift.* —**un′ex•pect′ed•ly** *adv.*

un•fail•ing (ŭn fā′lĭng) *adj.* **1.** Not ending: *a source of unfailing amusement.* **2.** Constant; reliable: *an unfailing friend.* —**un•fail′-ing•ly** *adv.*

un•fair (ŭn fâr′) *adj.* Not fair, right, or just: *unfair laws.* —**un•fair′ly** *adv.* —**un•fair′-ness** *n.* [U]

un•faith•ful (ŭn fāth′fəl) *adj.* **1.** Disloyal: *an unfaithful friend.* **2.** Not true to one's spouse or lover: *an unfaithful husband.* **3.** Not reflecting the original contents; inaccurate: *an unfaithful copy.* —**un•faith′ful•-ness** *n.* [U]

un•fa•mil•iar (ŭn′fə mĭl′yər) *adj.* **1.** Not knowing about: *unfamiliar with that subject.* **2.** Not within one's knowledge; strange: *an unfamiliar face.* —**un′fa•mil′iar•ly** *adv.*

un•fas•ten (ŭn făs′ən) *v.* —*tr.* To separate the connected parts of (sthg.); open: *I unfastened the seat belt.* —*intr.* To become opened or untied: *The buckle unfastens easily.*

un•fa•vor•a•ble (ŭn fā′vər ə bəl *or* ŭn-fāv′rə bəl) *adj.* **1.** Likely to be a bad thing; not good: *unfavorable winds for sailing.* **2.** Opposed; against: *unfavorable criticism.* —**un•fa′vor•a•bly** *adv.*

un•feel•ing (ŭn fē′lĭng) *adj.* **1.** Without sensation; numb: *an unfeeling hand, numb from the cold.* **2.** Not sympathetic; hardened: *an unfeeling critic.*

un•fet•tered (ŭn fĕt′ərd) *adj.* Not restricted or tied down: *a week of unfettered freedom.*

un•fin•ished (ŭn fĭn′ĭsht) *adj.* **1.** Incomplete: *unfinished business.* **2.** Not processed in a specific way; natural: *unfinished furniture.*

un•fit (ŭn fĭt′) *adj.* **1.** Not suitable or adapted for a given purpose; inappropriate: *a paint that is unfit for use on metal.* **2.** Performing below a standard; incompetent or unqualified: *an unfit doctor.* **3.** Not in good health: *feeling unfit after a long illness.*

un•flap•pa•ble (ŭn flăp′ə bəl) *adj.* Not easily upset or excited; calm: *an unflappable attitude.* —**un•flap′pa•bil′i•ty** *n.* [U]

un•flinch•ing (ŭn flĭn′chĭng) *adj.* Not showing fear or indecision; steadfast: *an unflinching determination to find out all the facts.* —**un•flinch′ing•ly** *adv.*

un•fold (ŭn fōld′) *v.* —*tr.* **1.** To open or spread (sthg.) out: *He unfolded the map.* **2.** To reveal (sthg.) gradually; make known: *unfolding the details of her plans.* —*intr.* **1.** To become spread out or open: *The flower unfolded during the day.* **2.** To develop: *Their friendship unfolded over the summer.* **3.** To be revealed gradually: *The truth unfolded as the investigation proceeded.*

un•fore•seen (ŭn′fər sēn′ *or* ŭn′fôr sēn′) *adj.* Not expected: *unforeseen results of an experiment.*

un•for•get•ta•ble (ŭn′fər gĕt′ə bəl) *adj.* Permanently impressed on one's memory; memorable: *an unforgettable experience.* —**un′for•get′ta•bly** *adv.*

un·for·tu·nate (ŭn fôr′chə nĭt) *adj.* **1.** Having bad luck; unlucky: *an unfortunate player.* **2.** Causing bad luck; disastrous: *an unfortunate accident.* **3.** Regrettable or improper: *an unfortunate remark.* —*n.* A person who has undeserved bad luck: *the poor unfortunates of this world.* —**un·for′tu·nate·ly** *adv.*

un·found·ed (ŭn foun′dĭd) *adj.* Without any basis in fact; not supported: *They made several unfounded accusations.*

un·friend·ly (ŭn frĕnd′lē) *adj.* **1.** Not warm or friendly: *an unfriendly smile.* **2.** Unpleasant or unfavorable: *unfriendly clouds on the horizon.* —**un·friend′li·ness** *n.* [U]

un·furl (ŭn fûrl′) *tr. & intr.v.* To open and spread out or become open and spread out; unroll: *Let's unfurl the flag. The banner unfurled for everyone to see.*

un·gain·ly (ŭn gān′lē) *adj.* Without grace or ease of movement; clumsy: *an ungainly child.* —**un·gain′li·ness** *n.* [U]

un·god·ly (ŭn gŏd′lē) *adj.* **un·god·li·er, un·god·li·est.** **1.** Sinful; wicked. **2.** Outrageous: *waking him up at that ungodly hour.*

un·gram·mat·i·cal (ŭn′grə măt′ĭ kəl) *adj.* Not following the rules or standards of grammar: *an ungrammatical sentence.*

un·grate·ful (ŭn grāt′fəl) *adj.* Not feeling or expressing thanks. *His daughter was ungrateful for the advantages she received.* —**un·grate′ful·ly** *adv.* —**un·grate′ful·ness** *n.* [U]

un·guent (ŭng′gwənt) *n.* A salve for soothing or healing; an ointment: *Apply an unguent to the burn.*

un·hap·py (ŭn hăp′ē) *adj.* **un·hap·pi·er, un·hap·pi·est.** **1.** Not happy; sad: *He's feeling unhappy. See Synonyms at* **sad.** **2.** Not satisfied; displeased: *She's unhappy with her performance.* **3.** Not suitable; inappropriate: *an unhappy choice of words.* —**un·hap′pi·ly** *adv.* —**un·hap′pi·ness** *n.* [U]

un·health·y (ŭn hĕl′thē) *adj.* **un·health·i·er, un·health·i·est.** **1.** Being in a state of poor health; ill; sick: *He felt unhealthy because of the flu.* **2.** Being a sign or symptom of poor health: *a pale unhealthy appearance.* **3.** Causing or tending to cause poor health: *an unhealthy diet.* **4.** Harmful to character or moral health: *an unhealthy influence on her younger sister.* **5.** Risky; dangerous: *an unhealthy situation.*

un·heard-of (ŭn hûrd′ŭv′) *adj.* Not known or done before; without an earlier example: *living in unheard-of luxury.*

un·hook (ŭn hŏŏk′) *tr.v.* **1.** To release or remove (sthg.) from a hook: *I unhooked the porch screen.* **2.** To unfasten the hooks of (sthg.): *unhook a dress.*

uni— *pref.* A prefix that means one or single: *unicycle.*

WORD BUILDING: uni— The basic meaning of the prefix **uni—** is "one." The word **unicorn,** for example, refers to a one-horned animal. **Uniform** means "always the same" or literally "one shape." And **unison** means literally "one sound." Many new words with **uni—,** such as **unicellular, unicycle,** and **unilateral,** were created in the 19th century. **Uni—** can be compared to the prefix **mono—.**

u·ni·corn (yōō′nĭ kôrn′) *n.* An animal of myth resembling a horse with a single long horn growing out of its forehead.

u·ni·cy·cle (yōō′nĭ sī′kəl) *n.* A vehicle consisting of a frame and seat mounted over a single wheel and propelled by pedals.

un·i·den·ti·fied fly·ing object (ŭn′ī dĕn′tə fīd′) *n.* A flying object of an unknown nature, especially one suspected to have been sent by extraterrestrial beings.

u·ni·form (yōō′nə fôrm′) *adj.* **1.** Always the same; not changing or varying: *shirts of uniform color.* **2.** Being the same as or consistent with another or others: *rows of uniform brick houses.* —*n.* A suit of clothing intended to identify the persons who wear it as members of a specific group: *an army uniform.* —**u′ni·formed′** *adj.* —**u′ni·for′mi·ty** *n.* [U] —**u′ni·form′ly** *adv.*

unicycle

u·ni·fy (yōō′nə fī′) *tr. & intr.v.* **u·ni·fied, u·ni·fy·ing, u·ni·fies.** To make into or become a unit; unite: *The new government unified the nation. The classes unified to work on the project.* —**u′ni·fi·ca′tion** (yōō′nə fĭ kā′shən) *n.* [U]

u·ni·lat·er·al (yōō′nə lăt′ər əl) *adj.* Done or undertaken by only one side: *unilateral disarmament.* —**u′ni·lat′er·al·ly** *adv.*

un·im·peach·a·ble (ŭn′ĭm pē′chə bəl) *adj.* **1.** Correct; blameless: *unimpeachable behavior.* **2.** Beyond doubt or question; unquestionable: *unimpeachable honesty.*

un·im·por·tant (ŭn′ĭm pôr′tnt) *adj.* Not important; petty: *an unimportant question.* —**un′im·por′tance** *n.* [U]

un·in·hab·it·ed (ŭn′ĭn hăb′ĭ tĭd) *adj.* Not lived in; without residents: *a new building that is still uninhabited.*

un·in·hib·it·ed (ŭn′ĭn hĭb′ĭ tĭd) *adj.* **1.** Open and unrestrained: *uninhibited laughter.* **2.** Free from social or moral concerns: *uninhibited behavior at the party.*

un·in·tel·li·gent (ŭn′ĭn tĕl′ə jənt) *adj.*

Without intelligence; not smart: *an unintelligent decision.* —**un′in•tel′li•gent•ly** *adv.*

un•in•tel•li•gi•ble (ŭn′ĭn tĕl′ĭ jə bəl) *adj.* Hard to understand: *His speech was unintelligible because of the noise in the room.* —**un′in•tel′li•gi•bil′i•ty** *n.* [U] —**un′in•tel′li•gi•bly** *adv.*

un•in•ten•tion•al (ŭn′ĭn tĕn′shə nəl) *adj.* Not done or said on purpose: *She apologized for the unintentional insult.* —**un′in•ten′tion•al•ly** *adv.*

un•in•ter•est•ed (ŭn ĭn′trĭ stĭd *or* ŭn ĭn′tə rĕs′tĭd) *adj.* **1.** Without an interest; impartial: *Her finances are managed by an uninterested person.* **2.** Not interested; indifferent: *He was uninterested in the television show.*

un•in•vit•ed (ŭn′ĭn vī′tĭd) *adj.* Not invited or welcome: *She asked the uninvited guests to leave.*

un•ion (yoon′yən) *n.* **1.** [U] The act of uniting: *union of the two colleges into one.* **2.** [C] A mathematical set in which each element is also an element of two or more given sets. **3.** [C; U] A partnership in marriage: *a happy union.* **4.** [C] A labor union: *Workers decided to join the union.* **5. Union.** The United States of America, especially during the Civil War. —*adj.* **1. Union.** Relating to or loyal to the United States of America during the Civil War: *Union forces.* **2.** Relating to a labor union: *union negotiations.*

un•ion•ize (yoon′yə nīz′) *v.* **un•ion•ized, un•ion•iz•ing, un•ion•iz•es.** —*tr.* To organize (people or groups) into or cause to join a labor union: *unionize factory workers.* —*intr.* To organize or join a labor union. —**un′ion•i•za′tion** (yoon′yə nĭ zā′shən) *n.* [U]

Union Jack *n.* The flag of the United Kingdom.

u•nique (yoo nēk′) *adj.* **1.** Being the only one of its kind: *the unique manuscript of a medieval poem.* **2.** Without an equal: *a unique opportunity to buy a house.* —**u•nique′ly** *adv.* —**u•nique′ness** *n.* [U]

u•ni•sex (yoo′nĭ sĕks′) *adj.* Suitable to both males and females: *unisex clothes.*

u•ni•son (yoo′nĭ sən) *n.* [U] Agreement; harmony: *the unison of voices.* ♦ **in unison. 1.** In music, singing the same note at the same time: *The chorus sang in unison.* **2.** At the same time; at once: *They answered in unison.*

u•nit (yoo′nĭt) *n.* **1.** A thing, person, group, or structure regarded as a part of a whole: *We added an extra unit to a bookcase.* **2.** A single group regarded as a distinct part within a larger group: *an army unit.* **3.** A mechanical part or piece of equipment: *an air-conditioning unit.* **4.** A precisely defined quantity used as a standard for measuring quantities of the

same kind: *The meter is a unit of distance.* **5.** A section of a course of study focusing on one subject: *a unit on Native Americans.*

U•ni•tar•i•an (yoo′nĭ târ′ē ən) *n.* A person who believes in Unitarian Universalism. —**U′ni•tar′i•an** *adj.* —**U′ni•tar′i•an•ism** *n.* [U]

Unitarian U•ni•ver•sal•ism (yoo′nə vûr′sə lĭz′əm) *n.* [U] A religious association of Christian origin that has no official creed and that considers God to be a single being.

u•nite (yoo nīt′) *v.* **u•nit•ed, u•nit•ing, u•nites.** —*tr.* **1.** To bring together or join (things or people) to form a whole: *The chemist united the substances to form a new compound.* See Synonyms at **join. 2.** To join (things or people) together or to bring into close association for a common purpose: *a treaty to unite all nations in the fight against disease.* **3.** To join (a couple) in matrimony: *They were united in marriage today.* —*intr.* **1.** To become joined or combined into a unit: *The two firms united to form a large business.* **2.** To join and act together for a common purpose: *Let's unite and stop pollution.*

u•nit•ed (yoo nī′tĭd) *adj.* **1.** Combined into one: *a united group of workers.* **2.** Concerned with or resulting from joint action: *a united effort to preserve wildlife.* **3.** Being in harmony; agreed: *On that point we are united.*

u•ni•ty (yoo′nĭ tē) *n.* [U] **1.** Accord; harmony: *a period of great national unity and purpose.* **2.** The combination or arrangement of parts, as in a work of art or literature, into a complete whole.

univ. *abbr.* An abbreviation of: **1.** Universal. **2.** University.

u•ni•ver•sal (yoo′nə vûr′səl) *adj.* **1.** Relating to or affecting the whole world; worldwide: *universal peace.* **2.** Including or affecting all members of a class or group: *the universal agreement among scientists.* **3.** Relating to the universe: *universal laws.* —**u′ni•ver•sal′i•ty** (yoo′nə vər săl′ĭ tē) *n.* [C; U] —**u′ni•ver′sal•ly** *adv.*

Universal Product Code *n.* A series of vertical bars of varying widths printed on a package or tag and designed to be read by a computer scanner, so as to identify the item, tell its price, or keep track of inventory, for example; a bar code.

ISBN 0-395-81873-7

9 780395 818732

Universal Product Code

universal time *n.* [U] Greenwich, England time, used to figure time throughout the world.

u·ni·verse (yōo′nə vûrs′) *n.* All matter and energy considered as a whole; the cosmos.

u·ni·ver·si·ty (yōo′nə vûr′sĭ tē) *n.*, *pl.* **u·ni·ver·si·ties.** An institution of higher learning that includes one or more colleges and a graduate school and professional schools.

un·just (ŭn jŭst′) *adj.* Not just or fair; unfair: *unjust laws.* —**un·just′ly** *adv.*

un·kempt (ŭn kĕmpt′) *adj.* Not neat or tidy; messy: *an unkempt lawn; unkempt clothes.*

un·kind (ŭn kīnd′) *adj.* Not kind or sympathetic: *They exchanged unkind words.* —**un·kind′ly** *adv.* —**un·kind′ness** *n.* [C; U]

un·know·ing·ly (ŭn nō′ĭng lē) *adv.* Without awareness or deliberate intent: *She unknowingly led the police to her accomplice.*

un·known (ŭn nōn′) *adj.* **1.** Not known or familiar; strange: *a town unknown to us.* **2.** Not identified: *an unknown quantity.* **3.** Not widely known: *an unknown painter.* —*n.* [C; U] A person or thing that is unknown.

un·lace (ŭn lās′) *tr.v.* **un·laced, un·lac·ing, un·lac·es.** To loosen or undo the laces of (sthg.): *She unlaced her sneakers.*

un·latch (ŭn lăch′) *tr.v.* To unfasten or open (sthg.) by releasing a latch: *He unlatched the door and let the cat in.*

un·law·ful (ŭn lô′fəl) *adj.* Being in violation of the law; illegal: *He made an unlawful left turn.* —**un·law′ful·ly** *adv.*

un·lead·ed (ŭn lĕd′ĭd) *adj.* Not containing lead or lead compounds: *unleaded gasoline.*

un·leash (ŭn lēsh′) *tr.v.* To free (sthg.) from or as if from a leash: *unleashed the dog; unleashed his anger.*

un·leav·ened (ŭn lĕv′ənd) *adj.* Made without yeast or other leavening: *a flat, unleavened bread.*

un·less (ŭn lĕs′) *conj.* Except on the condition that: *You can't write the report unless you do the research first.*

un·like (ŭn līk′) *adj.* Not equal, as in amount: *unlike sums.* —*prep.* **1.** Different from; not like: *That band has a sound unlike any other.* **2.** Not typical of: *It is unlike him not to call if he cannot come.*

un·like·ly (ŭn līk′lē) *adj.* **un·like·li·er, un·like·li·est. 1.** Not likely; improbable: *Who would believe such an unlikely story?* **2.** Likely to fail: *an unlikely business venture.*

un·lim·it·ed (ŭn lĭm′ĭ tĭd) *adj.* Having no limits or bounds: *unlimited possibilities.*

un·list·ed (ŭn lĭs′tĭd) *adj.* Not appearing on a list: *She has an unlisted number, so it's not in the phone book.*

un·load (ŭn lōd′) *tr.v.* **1.a.** To remove the load or cargo from (sthg.): *unload a truck.* **b.** To remove (sthg. carried or transported): *unload furniture from the van.* **2.** *Informal.* To give expression to (one's troubles or feelings): *She unloaded her worries on her friend.* **3.** To remove the charge from (a gun): *Be sure to unload the gun before you clean it.*

4. To dispose of (sthg.), especially by selling in large quantities; dump: *unloading textiles at low prices.*

un·lock (ŭn lŏk′) *tr.v.* **1.** To undo (a lock), as by turning a key, for example. **2.** To undo the lock of (sthg.): *The banker unlocked the safe.* **3.** To set (sthg.) free; release: *The news unlocked a torrent of emotion.* **4.** To solve, disclose, or reveal (sthg.): *unlock a mystery.*

un·luck·y (ŭn lŭk′ē) *adj.* **un·luck·i·er, un·luck·i·est. 1.** Marked by or having bad luck: *an unlucky day; an unlucky person.* **2.** Seeming to cause bad luck: *an unlucky number.* —**un·luck′i·ly** *adv.*

un·made (ŭn mād′) *adj.* Not made: *an unmade bed.*

un·man·age·a·ble (ŭn măn′ĭ jə bəl) *adj.* Difficult or impossible to manage: *an unmanageable child; an unmanageable amount of work.*

un·man·ly (ŭn măn′lē) *adj.* Seen as not suitable for or expected of a man: *He was afraid people would consider his tears unmanly.*

un·manned (ŭn mănd′) *adj.* Lacking a crew or designed to operate without a crew: *an unmanned spacecraft.*

un·marked (ŭn märkt′) *adj.* Without an identifying mark: *an unmarked police car.*

un·mar·ried (ŭn măr′ēd) *adj.* Not married; single: *my unmarried sister.*

un·mask (ŭn măsk′) *v.* —*tr.* **1.** To remove a mask from (sbdy.). **2.** To show or tell the true nature of (sbdy./sthg.); reveal: *He finally unmasked his resentment.* —*intr.* To remove one's mask.

un·men·tion·a·ble (ŭn mĕn′shə nə bəl) *adj.* Not fit to be mentioned or discussed: *an unmentionable subject.* —*pl.n.* **unmentionables.** Underwear.

un·mer·ci·ful (ŭn mûr′sĭ fəl) *adj.* **1.** Having or showing no mercy; merciless: *unmerciful criticism.* **2.** Excessive; extreme: *unmerciful heat.* —**un·mer′ci·ful·ly** *adv.*

un·mind·ful (ŭn mīnd′fəl) *adj.* Not giving enough care or attention; careless: *unmindful of the time.* —**un·mind′ful·ly** *adv.*

un·mis·tak·a·ble (ŭn′mĭ stā′kə bəl) *adj.* Impossible to mistake: *the unmistakable cry of a hyena.* —**un′mis·tak′a·bly** *adv.*

un·mit·i·gat·ed (ŭn mĭt′ĭ gā′tĭd) *adj.* **1.** Not lessened in intensity; without relief: *unmitigated heat.* **2.** Absolute; total: *an unmitigated lie.*

un·moved (ŭn mōovd′) *adj.* Emotionally unaffected: *His sad story left the police unmoved.*

un·nat·u·ral (ŭn năch′ər əl) *adj.* **1.** Not in accord with what usually happens in nature; abnormal or unusual: *Such cold weather is unnatural for August.* **2.** Strained, stiff, or affected; artificial: *an unnatural manner.* —**un·nat′u·ral·ly** *adv.*

U

un•nec•es•sar•y (ŭn nĕs′ĭ sĕr′ē) *adj.* Not necessary; needless: *cutting unnecessary expenses.* —**un•nec′es•sar′i•ly** (ŭn nĕs′ĭ-sâr′ə lē) *adv.*

un•nerve (ŭn nûrv′) *tr.v.* **un•nerved, un•nerv•ing, un•nerves.** To cause (sbdy.) to lose strength or firmness of purpose: *The heated argument unnerved him.*

un•ob•served (ŭn′ əb zûrvd′) *adj.* **1.** Not seen or noticed: *We crept up the walkway unobserved.* **2.** Not kept or conformed to: *unobserved regulations; an unobserved holiday.*

un•ob•tru•sive (ŭn′ əb trōō′sĭv) *adj.* Not easily noticed; inconspicuous: *An unobtrusive visitor watched the rehearsal from the back of the hall.* —**un′ob•tru′sive•ly** *adv.* —**un′ob•tru′sive•ness** *n.* [U]

un•oc•cu•pied (ŭn ŏk′yə pīd′) *adj.* **1.** Not occupied or being used; vacant: *unoccupied seats.* **2.** Not busy; idle: *unoccupied workers.*

un•of•fi•cial (ŭn′ ə fĭsh′əl) *adj.* Not official; without formal approval or permission: *unofficial reports on the forest fire.* —**un′of•fi′cial•ly** *adv.*

un•op•posed (ŭn′ ə pōzd′) *adj.* Not challenged by another: *The candidate was unopposed.*

un•or•gan•ized (ŭn ôr′gə nīzd′) *adj.* **1.** Lacking order or unity; disorganized: *an unorganized pile of papers on his desk.* **2.** Not represented by a labor union: *unorganized workers.*

un•or•tho•dox (ŭn ôr′thə dŏks′) *adj.* Differing from tradition or custom: *Her unorthodox approach to the problem surprised us.*

un•pack (ŭn păk′) *v.* —*tr.* **1.** To remove the contents of (a suitcase, for example). **2.** To remove (sthg.) from a container or from packaging: *unpack groceries.* —*intr.* To remove objects from a container: *He went to his hotel room to unpack.*

un•paid (ŭn pād′) *adj.* **1.** Not yet paid: *an unpaid bill.* **2.** Receiving no pay: *an unpaid volunteer.*

un•par•al•leled (ŭn păr′ə lĕld′) *adj.* Without parallel or match; exceptional; unequaled: *unparalleled beauty.*

un•pleas•ant (ŭn plĕz′ənt) *adj.* Not pleasing; disagreeable: *an unpleasant smell.* —**un•pleas′ant•ly** *adv.*

un•plug (ŭn plŭg′) *tr.v.* **un•plugged, un•plug•ging, un•plugs.** To disconnect (an electric appliance) by removing a plug from an outlet: *Unplug the iron when you finish.*

un•pop•u•lar (ŭn pŏp′yə lər) *adj.* Lacking general approval; not generally well liked: *an unpopular student; an unpopular decision.*

un•prac•ticed (ŭn prăk′tĭst) *adj.* **1.** Not yet tested or tried: *unpracticed methods.* **2.** Lacking experience; unskilled: *unpracticed volunteers.*

un•prec•e•dent•ed (ŭn prĕs′ĭ dĕn′tĭd) *adj.* Never having happened before: *an unprecedented demand for housing.*

un•pre•dict•a•ble (ŭn′ prĭ dīk′tə bəl) *adj.* Difficult or impossible to be sure of in advance: *unpredictable weather; unpredictable behavior.* —**un′pre•dict′a•bil′i•ty** *n.* [U] —**un′pre•dict′a•bly** *adv.*

un•pre•pared (ŭn′ prĭ pârd′) *adj.* **1.** Having made no preparations: *unprepared for school.* **2.** Done without preparation: *an unprepared speech.*

un•pre•ten•tious (ŭn′ prĭ tĕn′shəs) *adj.* Without pretention; modest: *They were respected for their unpretentious lifestyle.*

un•prin•ci•pled (ŭn prĭn′sə pəld) *adj.* Lacking principles or honor; immoral: *an unprincipled attack on the opposing candidate.*

un•print•a•ble (ŭn prĭn′tə bəl) *adj.* Not proper for publication for legal or social reasons: *an unprintable story.*

un•pro•duc•tive (ŭn′ prə dŭk′tiv) *adj.* Not giving useful results; not effective: *an unproductive day on the job.*

un•pro•fes•sion•al (ŭn′ prə fĕsh′ə nəl) *adj.* Not meeting the standards of a profession: *unprofessional behavior.*

un•prof•it•a•ble (ŭn prŏf′ĭ tə bəl) *adj.* **1.** Bringing in no profit: *an unprofitable business.* **2.** Having no useful purpose: *We got into an unprofitable argument.* —**un•prof′it•a•bly** *adv.*

un•qual•i•fied (ŭn kwŏl′ə fĭd′) *adj.* **1.** [*for*] Without the necessary or required qualifications: *He's unqualified for the job.* **2.** Without reservation; complete: *an unqualified success.*

un•ques•tion•a•ble (ŭn kwĕs′chə nə bəl) *adj.* Without question or doubt; certain: *an unquestionable success.* —**un•ques′tion•a•bly** *adv.*

un•ques•tioned (ŭn kwĕs′chənd) *adj.* Not doubted or called into question: *his unquestioned honesty.*

un•ques•tion•ing (ŭn kwĕs′chə nĭng) *adj.* With no doubts or indecision: *She has an unquestioning faith in her religion.*

un•rav•el (ŭn răv′əl) *v.* —*tr.* **1.** To undo (a knitted fabric): *She unraveled her knitting and started again.* **2.** To separate the elements of (a mystery or problem): *Will the detective unravel this mystery?* —*intr.* To become unraveled: *a sweater unraveling at the neck.*

un•re•al (ŭn rē′əl *or* ŭn rēl′) *adj.* **1.** Not real; imaginary: *Most citizens were not fooled by unreal advances toward peace.* **2.** *Slang.* So remarkable as to be hard to believe: *food so good it was unreal.* —**un•re•al′i•ty** *n.* [U]

un·re·al·is·tic (ŭn′rē ə lĭs′tĭk) *adj.* Unreasonably idealistic: *unrealistic expectations for rapid improvement.* —**un′re·al·is′ti·cal·ly** *adv.*

un·rea·son·a·ble (ŭn rē′zə nə bəl) *adj.* **1.** Not governed by reason: *an unreasonable attitude.* **2.** Going beyond reasonable limits: *an unreasonable amount.* —**un·rea′son·a·bly** *adv.*

un·re·lent·ing (ŭn′rĭ lĕn′tĭng) *adj.* **1.** Not yielding, as in firmness or decision; inflexible: *an unrelenting opponent.* **2.** Not lessening in intensity: *She works at an unrelenting pace.*

un·re·li·a·ble (ŭn′rĭ lī′ə bəl) *adj.* Characterized by or showing a lack of dependability: *an unreliable worker who soon lost her job.* —**un′re·li·a·bil′i·ty** *n.* [U] —**un′re·li′a·bly** *adv.*

un·re·pent·ant (ŭn′rĭ pĕn′tənt) *adj.* Having or showing no regret for past wrongs: *an unrepentant sinner.*

un·re·quit·ed (ŭn′rĭ kwī′tĭd) *adj.* Not given back or returned equally: *unrequited love.*

un·re·served (ŭn′rĭ zûrvd′) *adj.* **1.** Not held for a particular person: *an unreserved seat.* **2.** Given without holding anything back: *unreserved praise.* **3.** Showing no reserve: *unreserved laughter.*

un·rest (ŭn rĕst′) *n.* [U] An uneasy or troubled condition: *social unrest.*

un·re·strained (ŭn′rĭ strānd′) *adj.* **1.** Not controlled: *the unrestrained spread of weeds.* **2.** Not held under emotional control: *unrestrained laughter.*

un·ripe (ŭn rīp′) *adj.* **1.** Not ripe; immature: *unripe fruit.* **2.** Not fully prepared or ready: *The time is yet unripe for such a plan.*

un·ri·valed (ŭn rī′vəld) *adj.* With no rival or equal: *the unrivaled champion.*

un·ruf·fled (ŭn rŭf′əld) *adj.* **1.** Not upset; calm: *He was unruffled after the coach yelled at him.* **2.** Regular and smooth, as the surface of water.

un·ru·ly (ŭn rōō′lē) *adj.* **un·ru·li·er, un·ru·li·est.** Difficult or impossible to discipline or control: *The little boy's parents think he is spirited, but his teacher finds him unruly.*

un·safe (ŭn sāf′) *adj.* Not safe; dangerous: *a bridge unsafe to cross.*

un·said (ŭn sĕd′) *adj.* Not said, especially not spoken out loud: *angry thoughts left unsaid.*

un·san·i·tar·y (ŭn săn′ĭ tĕr′ē) *adj.* Not sanitary; unclean: *Unsanitary conditions resulted in the closing of the restaurant.*

un·sat·is·fac·to·ry (ŭn săt′ĭs făk′tə rē) *adj.* Not satisfactory; not good enough: *unsatisfactory living conditions.*

un·sat·u·rat·ed (ŭn săch′ə rā′tĭd) *adj.* Relating to a chemical compound, especially of carbon, in which two atoms are joined by more than a single bond: *unsaturated fats.*

un·sa·vor·y (ŭn sā′və rē) *adj.* **1.** Distasteful or disagreeable: *an unsavory situation.* **2.** Morally offensive: *We warned her against that unsavory character.*

un·scathed (ŭn skā*th*d′) *adj.* Not harmed or injured: *The driver walked away from the accident unscathed.*

un·sci·en·tif·ic (ŭn′sī ən tĭf′ĭk) *adj.* **1.** Not according to the principles of science: *unscientific methods.* **2.** Not knowledgeable about science: *I can give you only an unscientific explanation.*

un·scram·ble (ŭn skrăm′bəl) *tr.v.* **un·scram·bled, un·scram·bling, un·scram·bles.** **1.** To straighten out or disentangle (a jumble or tangle): *He unscrambled the financial mess he had made.* **2.** To restore (a scrambled message) to understandable form: *She unscrambled the coded message.*

un·screw (ŭn skrōō′) *v.* —*tr.* **1.** To remove the screws from (sthg.): *I unscrewed the hinges.* **2.** To loosen, adjust, or remove (sthg.) by turning: *unscrew the lid off a jar.* —*intr.* To become or allow to become unscrewed: *This lid unscrews easily.*

un·scru·pu·lous (ŭn skrōō′pyə ləs) *adj.* Without scruples or principles; not honorable: *an unscrupulous salesman.* —**un·scru′pu·lous·ly** *adv.* —**un·scru′pu·lous·ness** *n.* [U]

un·seal (ŭn sēl′) *tr.v.* To break open or remove the seal of (sthg.); open: *He unsealed the package.*

un·sea·son·a·ble (ŭn sē′zə nə bəl) *adj.* Happening or done in the wrong season; not suitable for or characteristic of the season: *unseasonable weather.*

un·sea·soned (ŭn sē′zənd) *adj.* **1.** Inexperienced: *unseasoned campers.* **2.** Not ripe or mature: *unseasoned wood.* **3.** Having no added seasoning: *unseasoned meat.*

un·seat (ŭn sēt′) *tr.v.* **1.** To remove (sbdy.) from a seat, especially from a saddle: *The horse unseated the rider.* **2.** To remove or force (sbdy.) out of a position or office: *Voters unseated the senator in the election.*

un·seem·ly (ŭn sēm′lē) *adj. Formal.* Not in good taste; improper: *She was shocked by her granddaughter's unseemly behavior.*

un·seen (ŭn sēn′) *adj.* Not seen or noticed; invisible: *unseen benefits of education.*

un·self·ish (ŭn sĕl′fĭsh) *adj.* Not selfish; generous: *an unselfish act.* —**un·self′ish·ly** *adv.* —**un·self′ish·ness** *n.* [U]

un·set·tle (ŭn sĕt′l) *tr.v.* **un·set·tled, un·set·tling, un·set·tles.** **1.** To move (sthg.) from a settled condition: *strikes unsettling the economy.* **2.** To make (sbdy.) uneasy; disturb: *The news unsettled him.*

un·set·tled (ŭn sĕt′ld) *adj.* **1.** Not in a state of order or calmness; disturbed: *unsettled times.* **2.** Not determined or resolved: *an unsettled legal case.* **3.** Not paid: *unsettled*

U

accounts. **4.** Without people living there; not populated: *a vast unsettled region.*

un·sight·ly (ŭn sīt′lē) *adj.* **un·sight·li·er, un·sight·li·est.** Not pleasant to look at; unattractive: *the unsightly remains of a burned building.* —**un·sight′li·ness** *n.* [U]

un·skilled (ŭn skĭld′) *adj.* **1.** Without skill or technical training: *unskilled workers.* **2.** Requiring no special training or skills: *unskilled work.*

un·so·phis·ti·cat·ed (ŭn′sə fĭs′tĭ kā′tĭd) *adj.* **1.** Lacking worldly knowledge; simple and natural: *unsophisticated tastes and pleasures.* **2.** Not complex or complicated: *unsophisticated methods.*

un·sound (ŭn sound′) *adj.* **1.** Not dependably strong or solid: *a house with an unsound foundation.* **2.** Not physically or mentally healthy: *an unsound mind.* **3.** Not logical: *an unsound argument.*

un·spar·ing (ŭn spâr′ĭng) *adj.* **1.** Unmerciful; severe: *unsparing criticism.* **2.** Not holding back; generous: *unsparing in his efforts to help.* —**un·spar′ing·ly** *adv.*

un·speak·a·ble (ŭn spē′kə bəl) *adj.* **1.** Beyond description; impossible to describe: *unspeakable anxiety.* **2.** Bad beyond description: *unspeakable wickedness.* **3.** Not to be spoken: *an unspeakable word.* —**un·speak′-a·bly** *adv.*

un·spoiled (ŭn spoild′) *adj.* Not spoiled: *an unspoiled landscape.*

un·spo·ken (ŭn spō′kən) *adj.* Not expressed in words: *an unspoken wish.*

un·sports·man·like (ŭn spôrts′mən līk′) *adj.* Not showing the good behavior of sbdy. who follows the rules of a game, especially under stress: *He embarrassed his teammates with his unsportsmanlike conduct after their loss.*

un·sta·ble (ŭn stā′bəl) *adj.* **1.** Likely to change: *unstable prices.* **2.** Not firm; unsteady: *an unstable ladder.* **3.** Without control of one's emotions; characterized by unpredictable behavior: *an unstable character.* **4.** Tending to decompose easily, as a chemical compound.

un·stead·y (ŭn stĕd′ē) *adj.* **un·stead·i·er, un·stead·i·est. 1.** Not steady; unstable: *an unsteady chair.* **2.** Not firm; uneven: *an unsteady voice.* —**un·stead′i·ly** *adv.* —**un·stead′i·ness** *n.* [U]

un·stressed (ŭn strĕst′) *adj.* Not accented or stressed: *an unstressed syllable.*

un·strung (ŭn strŭng′) *adj.* Emotionally upset: *A series of disasters left her unstrung.*

un·stud·ied (ŭn stŭd′ēd) *adj.* Not produced for effect; natural: *unstudied grace.*

un·suc·cess·ful (ŭn′sək sĕs′fəl) *adj.* Not succeeding; without success: *an unsuccessful*

plan; *an unsuccessful person.* —**un′suc·cess′ful·ly** *adv.*

un·suit·a·ble (ŭn sōō′tə bəl) *adj.* Not appropriate: *an unsuitable dress for a wedding.* —**un·suit′a·bil′i·ty** *n.* [U] —**un·suit′a·bly** *adv.*

un·sung (ŭn sŭng′) *adj.* Not honored or praised; uncelebrated: *unsung heroes.*

un·sus·pect·ed (ŭn′sə spĕk′tĭd) *adj.* **1.** Not under suspicion: *He is unsuspected of any part in the deception.* **2.** Not known; unexpected: *Unsuspected wealth lay hidden there.*

un·sus·pect·ing (ŭn′sə spĕk′tĭng) *adj.* Not suspicious; trusting: *an unsuspecting child.* —**un′sus·pect′ing·ly** *adv.*

un·swerv·ing (ŭn swûr′vĭng) *adj.* Constant or unchanging, as in belief or attitude: *unswerving devotion to a cause; unswerving in her faith in him.*

un·tan·gle (ŭn tăng′gəl) *tr.v.* **un·tan·gled, un·tan·gling, un·tan·gles. 1.** To free (sthg.) from a tangle; disentangle: *untangle a fishing line.* **2.** To settle or resolve (sthg. puzzling or complicated): *untangle a problem.*

un·tapped (ŭn tăpt′) *adj.* Not used but offering possible profit or benefits: *untapped resources.*

un·taught (ŭn tôt′) *adj.* **1.** Not instructed; ignorant: *untaught children lacking in manners.* **2.** Not acquired by instruction; natural: *untaught musical skill.*

un·ten·a·ble (ŭn tĕn′ə bəl) *adj.* Not capable of being defended or maintained: *an untenable position.* —**un·ten′a·bly** *adv.*

un·think·a·ble (ŭn thĭng′kə bəl) *adj.* **1.** Impossible to imagine: *an unthinkable amount of money.* **2.** Not to be considered: *Raising taxes was politically unthinkable.* —**un·think′a·bly** *adv.*

un·think·ing (ŭn′ thĭng′kĭng) *adj.* **1.** Careless or thoughtless: *an unthinking remark that hurt my feelings.* **2.** Showing lack of thought: *an unthinking suggestion that made no sense.*

un·ti·dy (ŭn tī′dē) *adj.* Not tidy and neat; messy: *an untidy room.* —**un·ti′di·ly** *adv.* —**un·ti′di·ness** *n.* [U]

un·tie (ŭn tī′) *v.* **un·tied, un·ty·ing** (ŭn tī′ĭng), **un·ties.** —*tr.* **1.** To undo or loosen (a knot): *I untied my shoelaces.* **2.** To free (sthg.) from sthg. that binds or restrains: *We untied the dog and let her run.* —*intr.* To become untied.

un·til (ŭn tĭl′) *prep.* **1.** Up to the time of: *They danced until dawn.* **2.** Before (a specified time): *You can't have the bike until tomorrow.* —*conj.* **1.** Up to the time that: *We worked until it got dark.* **2.** Before: *Don't leave until we talk.* **3.** To the point or extent

that: *He talked until he could talk no more.*
— SEE NOTE at till[2].

un·time·ly (ŭn tīm′lē) *adj.* **un·time·li·er,
un·time·li·est.** **1.** Happening at an inappropriate or unsuitable time: *an untimely visit from my supervisor.* **2.** Happening too soon; premature: *an untimely death.*

un·tir·ing (ŭn tīr′ĭng) *adj.* **1.** Not tiring: *The swimmer seemed untiring during practice.* **2.** Not slowing or ending; persistent: *untiring efforts.* —**un·tir′ing·ly** *adv.*

un·to (ŭn′tŏŏ) *prep. Formal.* **1.** To: *what God said unto his angels.* **2.** Until: *a fast unto death.*

un·told (ŭn tōld′) *adj.* **1.** Not told or revealed: *untold secrets.* **2.** Without limit; beyond description: *untold millions.*

un·touch·a·ble (ŭn tŭch′ə bəl) *adj.* **1.** Not to be touched. **2.** Beyond the reach of criticism or attack: *His work has been untouchable.* —*n.* Also **Untouchable.** A member of the Hindu class considered ritually unclean by the other Hindu classes.

un·tried (ŭn trīd′) *adj.* Not tried, tested, or proved: *an untried vaccine against the virus.*

un·true (ŭn trŏŏ′) *adj.* **1.** Not true; false: *untrue statements.* **2.** [*to*] Not faithful; disloyal: *untrue to his religion.*

un·used (ŭn yŏŏzd′) *adj.* **1.** Not used or never having been used: *Please return any unused supplies.* **2.** (ŭn yŏŏst′). [*to*] Not accustomed: *He is unused to working so late.*

un·u·su·al (ŭn yŏŏ′zhŏŏ əl) *adj.* Not usual, common, or ordinary: *a rare and unusual species of fish.* —**un·u′su·al·ness** *n.* [U]

un·u·su·al·ly (ŭn yŏŏ′zhŏŏ ə lē) *adv.* More than is usual; very: *You're unusually quiet today.*

un·veil (ŭn vāl′) *tr.v.* **1.** To remove a veil or covering from (sbdy./sthg.): *unveil a statue at a ceremony.* **2.** To reveal (sthg.): *unveil secrets.*

un·war·rant·ed (ŭn wôr′ən tĭd *or* ŭn wŏr′ən tĭd) *adj.* Not needed or deserved; done without justification: *harsh and unwarranted criticism; a foolish and unwarranted expense.*

un·well (ŭn wĕl′) *adj.* In poor health; ill: *She had been unwell for years before she died.*

un·whole·some (ŭn hōl′səm) *adj.* Not healthful or healthy: *unwholesome foods.*

un·wield·y (ŭn wēl′dē) *adj.* Hard to hold because of shape or size: *an unwieldy package.* —**un·wield′i·ness** *n.* [U]

un·will·ing (ŭn wĭl′ĭng) *adj.* **1.** Not willing; hesitant or reluctant: *unwilling to face hard facts.* **2.** Done reluctantly: *unwilling help.* —**un·will′ing·ly** *adv.* —**un·will′ing·ness** *n.* [U]

un·wind (ŭn wīnd′) *v.* **un·wound** (ŭn-wound′), **un·wind·ing, un·winds.** —*tr.* To unroll (sthg.): *unwind a ball of string.* —*intr.* **1.** To become unrolled: *The spool of thread unwound as it fell.* **2.** To become free of worry or tension: *relax and unwind.*

un·wise (ŭn wīz′) *adj.* Not sensible or smart; foolish: *an unwise decision.* —**un·wise′ly** *adv.*

un·wit·ting (ŭn wĭt′ĭng) *adj.* **1.** Not knowing; unaware: *an unwitting victim of fraud.* **2.** Not intended; accidental: *an unwitting insult.* —**un·wit′ting·ly** *adv.*

un·world·ly (ŭn wûrld′lē) *adj.* **1.** Concerned with matters of the spirit or soul rather than of this world: *The priest spoke of unworldly concerns.* **2.** Not wise to the ways of the world; naive: *He came to the city as a young and unworldly man.*

un·wor·thy (ŭn wûr′thē) *adj.* [*of*] **1.** Not deserving: *a play unworthy of the award.* **2.** Not suiting, right, or appropriate: *a remark unworthy of her.* —**un·wor′thi·ness** *n.* [U]

un·wound (ŭn wound′) *v.* Past tense and past participle of **unwind.**

un·wrap (ŭn răp′) *tr.v.* **un·wrapped, un·wrap·ping, un·wraps.** To remove wrapping from (sthg.): *unwrap a gift.*

un·writ·ten (ŭn rĭt′n) *adj.* **1.** Not written or recorded: *an unwritten agreement.* **2.** Having authority based on custom or tradition rather than on a formal document: *an unwritten law.*

un·yield·ing (ŭn yēl′dĭng) *adj.* Not yielding or changing because of pressure or persuasion; firm: *unyielding in their insistence on equal rights.*

up (ŭp) *adv.* **1.** In or to a higher position: *We stood looking up at the sky.* **2.** In or to an upright or standing position: *She helped me up.* **3.a.** Above a surface: *The whale came up for air.* **b.** So as to detach or unearth: *pulling up weeds in the garden.* **4.** Into view or existence: *I'll have to write up a report.* **5.** Into consideration: *bring up a subject.* **6.** In or toward a position regarded as higher, as on a map: *going up to Canada.* **7.** To or at a higher price: *Fares are going up again.* **8.** So as to advance, increase, or improve: *His hopes keep going up.* **9.** With or to a greater intensity, pitch, or volume: *Turn the radio up.* **10.** Into a state of excitement or great activity: *A great wind came up.* **11.** Completely; entirely: *eat it all up; use up the rest.* **12.** Used as an intensive with certain verbs: *cleaning up the room; finishing up a project.* —*adj.* **1.** Being above an earlier position or level: *My grades are up.* **2.** Being out of bed: *Are you up yet?* **3.** Raised; lifted: *Leave the switch in the up position.* **4.** Moving or directed upward: *an up elevator.* **5.** Excited or cheerful: *Our spirits were up.* **6.** Actively functioning: *The computers are up.* **7.** Being considered: *a contract up for renewal.* **8.** Finished; over: *Time's up!* **9.** *Informal.* Well informed or prepared: *I'm not up on sports.* **10.** Being ahead of an opponent: *up by two points.* —*prep.* **1.** To or toward a higher point on: *up the mountain.* **2.** Toward or at a point farther along: *up the road.* **3.** In a direction toward the source of: *up the*

Amazon. *—n.* An upward movement or trend. *—v.* **upped, up•ping, ups.** *—tr.* To increase (sthg.): *upping prices.* *—intr. Informal.* To act suddenly or unexpectedly: *We voted his proposal down, so he upped and left the meeting.* ◆ **on the up-and-up** or **up and up.** *Informal.* Open and honest: *Is this deal on the up-and-up?* **up against.** Confronted with; facing: *up against a strong opponent.* **ups and downs.** Periods of good and bad luck or spirits: *We have our ups and downs, but in general, business is good.* **up to. 1.** Busy with, especially planning sthg. secret or dishonest: *up to more tricks.* **2.** Able to do or deal with (a challenge): *It was hard, but she proved up to it.* **3.** Dependent on (sbdy.): *Winning the game is up to us.* **what's up.** A question or an expression meaning "what's happening": *Tell me what's up—I just got back from vacation.*

up-and-com•ing (ŭp′ən kŭm′ĭng) *adj.* Showing signs of future success: *an up-and-coming actor.*

up•beat (ŭp′bēt′) *adj. Informal.* Optimistic or cheerful: *an upbeat mood.*

up•bring•ing (ŭp′brĭng′ĭng) *n.* [C; U] The care and training received during childhood: *a strict upbringing.*

UPC *abbr.* An abbreviation for Universal Product Code.

up•date (ŭp dāt′) *tr.v.* **up•dat•ed, up•dat•ing, up•dates.** To bring (sbdy./sthg.) up to date; inform of new information or recent changes: *update a map; update us on his medical condition.*

up•end (ŭp ĕnd′) *v.* *—tr.* To set or turn (sthg.) on one end: *upend a table.* *—intr.* To become upended: *The boat upended in the storm.*

up-front or **up•front** (ŭp′frŭnt′) *adj. Informal.* Honest, open, and direct; frank: *The boss promised to be up-front with his employees.*

up•grade (ŭp′grād′) *tr.v.* **up•grad•ed, up•grad•ing, up•grades.** To raise (sthg.) to a higher grade or standard: *upgrading all their products.* *—n.* **1.** [C; U] The act or an instance of upgrading: *planning an upgrade of office equipment; an upgrade to first class for the flight.* **2.** [U] Something that upgrades: *an upgrade for computer software.*

up•heav•al (ŭp hē′vəl) *n.* [C; U] **1.** A sudden and violent disturbance: *political upheaval.* **2.** A lifting or upward movement of the earth's crust.

up•hill (ŭp′hĭl′) *adj.* **1.** Going up a hill or slope: *an uphill street.* **2.** Difficult: *an uphill struggle to finish on time.* *—adv.* (ŭp′hĭl′). To higher ground: *going uphill.*

up•hold (ŭp hōld′) *tr.v.* **up•held** (ŭp hĕld′),

up•hold•ing, up•holds. 1. To prevent (sthg.) from falling; support: *The pillars uphold the roof.* **2.** To maintain (sthg.) against a challenge: *upholding her political opinions.*

up•hol•ster (ŭp hōl′stər *or* ə pōl′stər) *tr.v.* To supply (furniture) with stuffing, springs, cushions, and a fabric covering: *upholster a couch.* *—***up•hol′ster•er** *n.*

up•hol•ster•y (ŭp hōl′stə rē *or* ə pōl′stə rē) *n.* [U] **1.** The materials used in upholstering: *leather upholstery.* **2.** The craft, trade, or business of upholstering: *Upholstery is a dying art.*

up•keep (ŭp′kēp′) *n.* [U] **1.** Maintenance in good condition: *responsible for the upkeep of the building.* **2.** The cost of such maintenance: *I can no longer afford the upkeep on the boat.*

up•lift (ŭp lĭft′) *tr.v.* **1.** To raise (sthg.); elevate: *The good news uplifted our spirits.* **2.** To raise (sbdy.) to a higher social, moral, or intellectual level: *a talk aimed at uplifting the members of the church.*

up•on (ə pŏn′ *or* ə pôn′) *prep.* On: *We stopped and sat down upon a flat rock.*

up•per (ŭp′ər) *adj.* **1.** In a higher place, position, or rank: *the upper floors of a building; the upper classes of society.* **2.** Northern: *the upper east side of Manhattan.* *—n.* The part of a shoe or boot above the sole: *leather uppers.*

up•per•case (ŭp′ər kās′) *adj.* Written in capital letters: *an uppercase A.*

upper class *n.* [C; U] The highest social and economic class in a society. *—***up′per-class′** *adj.*

upper hand *n.* [U] A position of control or advantage: *Management had the upper hand in contract talks with the union.*

up•per•most (ŭp′ər mōst′) *adv. & adj.* In the highest place, position, or rank: *the team that finished uppermost in the standings; the uppermost rung of a ladder.*

up•pi•ty (ŭp′ĭ tē) *adj. Informal.* Acting as if one is better than other people; presumptuous: *The director has no patience with uppity young people.*

up•right (ŭp′rīt′) *adj.* **1.** In a vertical position: *an upright fence post.* **2.** Morally respectable; honorable: *an upright person.* *—adv.* Vertically: *I stood the book upright.* *—n.* **1.** A part of an object or structure that stands upright, as a beam. **2.** An upright piano. *—***up′right′ness** *n.* [U]

upright piano *n.* A piano in which the strings are mounted vertically, at right angles to the keyboard.

up•ris•ing (ŭp′rī′zĭng) *n.* A popular revolt against a government or its policies: *Government soldiers quickly put an end to the uprising.*

U

up·roar (ŭp′rôr′) *n.* [U] A condition of noisy excitement and confusion: *The announcement caused a public uproar.*

SYNONYMS: uproar, din, racket, noise. These nouns mean loud, confused, or disagreeable sound or sounds. **Uproar** means disorder with loud, confusing sound: *Even indoors we could hear the uproar of the crowd, cheering during the parade.* **Din** means a mix of loud sounds that usually clash: *The din in the factory ends abruptly when the noon whistle sounds.* **Racket** means loud, annoying noise: *The two little children were making a racket clanging pots and pans together.* **Noise** is the most general term: *Ear plugs cannot completely protect your hearing from damage caused by noise.*

---

up·roar·i·ous (ŭp rôr′ē əs) *adj.* **1.** Caused or accompanied by an uproar: *an uproarious New Year's celebration.* **2.** Loud and full: *uproarious laughter.* **3.** Causing loud laughter: *an uproarious comedy.* —**up·roar′i·ous·ly** *adv.*

up·root (ŭp rōōt′ *or* ŭp rŏŏt′) *tr.v.* **1.** To tear or remove (a plant and its roots) from the ground: *The storm uprooted the tree.* **2.** To destroy or get rid of (sthg.) completely: *It is not easy to uproot old customs.* **3.** To force (sbdy.) to leave a familiar or native place: *The government uprooted many people in order to build the highway.*

up·set (ŭp sĕt′) *tr.v.* **up·set, up·set·ting, up·sets.** **1.** To make (sbdy.) worried, unhappy, or distressed: *The bad news upset him.* **2.** To disturb the functioning, order, or course of (sthg.): *The move to the new building upset our schedule of deliveries.* **3.** To cause (sthg.) to overturn; tip over: *upset a vase of flowers.* **4.** (ŭp′sĕt′). To defeat unexpectedly (an opponent favored to win): *The new tennis player upset the world champion.* —*n.* (ŭp′sĕt′). [C; U] **1.** The act of upsetting or the condition of being upset: *Who is responsible for the upset of our plans?* **2.** A game or contest in which the favorite is defeated: *an upset over the best team in the league.* —*adj.* **1.** Worried and unhappy: *upset with him for failing to call.* **2.** Overturned: *an upset boat.* **3.** Showing signs of illness, especially indigestion: *an upset stomach.* **4.** Describing a surprise win: *an upset victory.*

up·shot (ŭp′shŏt′) *n.* (usually singular). The final result; outcome: *The upshot of all the discussion was a decision to postpone the vote.*

up·side down (ŭp′sīd′) *adv.* **1.** So that the upper or proper side is down: *Turn your cards upside down.* **2.** In great disorder: *The room had been turned upside down.*

up·stage (ŭp′stāj′) *adv.* On, at, to, or toward the rear of a stage. —*adj.* Relating to the rear of a stage. —*tr.v.* (ŭp stāj′). **up·staged, up·stag·ing, up·stag·es.** **1.** To take the

audience's attention from (another actor) by moving upstage. **2.** To steal attention or praise from (sbdy.): *He upstaged his rivals by announcing his discovery first.*

up·stairs (ŭp′stârz′) *adv.* **1.** Up the stairs: *I ran upstairs.* **2.** To or on a higher floor: *Everyone slept upstairs.* —*adj.* (ŭp′stârz′). Of or located on a higher floor: *an upstairs bedroom.* —*n.* (ŭp′stârz′). (used with a singular verb). The part of a building above the ground floor: *We're making the upstairs into a separate apartment.*

up·stand·ing (ŭp stăn′dĭng *or* ŭp′stăn′-dĭng) *adj.* Morally upright; honest: *a fine upstanding woman.*

up·start (ŭp′stärt′) *n.* A person of low beginnings who has suddenly risen to riches or high position, especially one who becomes arrogant because of success. —*adj.* **1.** Suddenly raised to an important position: *an upstart software company.* **2.** Self-important; too self-confident: *an upstart young man.*

up·state (ŭp′stāt′) *adv. & adj.* To, from, or in the northerly part of a state in the United States: *traveling upstate; upstate New York.*

up·stream (ŭp′strēm′) *adv. & adj.* In a direction opposite to the current of a stream: *fish swimming upstream; upstream waters.*

up·surge (ŭp′sûrj′) *n.* A rapid or sudden rise: *an upsurge in popular support for gun control.*

up·swing (ŭp′swĭng′) *n.* **1.** An upward swing or trend: *an upswing in the governor's popularity.* **2.** An increase, as in movement or business: *an upswing in the demand for new cars.*

up·take (ŭp′tāk′) *n.* Understanding; comprehension: *quick on the uptake.*

up·tight (ŭp′tīt′) *adj. Informal.* **1.** Tense or nervous: *feeling uptight before his performance.* **2.** Rigidly conventional, as in manner or opinions: *too uptight to try the new dance.*

up-to-date (ŭp′tə dāt′) *adj.* Based on the latest information, changes, improvements, or style: *an up-to-date encyclopedia.*

up·town (ŭp′toun′) *n.* [U] The upper part of a town or city. —*adv.* (ŭp′toun′). To, toward, or in the upper part of a town or city: *move uptown.* —*adj.* Relating to or located uptown: *an uptown store.*

up·turn (ŭp′tûrn′) *n.* An upward movement, curve, or trend, as in business: *An upturn in the economy pleases everyone.*

up·ward (ŭp′wərd) *adv.* In, to, or toward a higher place, level, or position: *The bird flew upward and out of sight.* —*adj.* Directed toward a higher place or position: *upward movement.* ♦ **upward of** or **upwards of.** More than; in excess of: *a concert attended by upward of 1000 people.*

u·ra·ni·um (yŏŏ rā′nē əm) *n.* [U] *Symbol* **U** A heavy, toxic, silvery white metallic element that is radioactive and easily oxidized. Uranium is the main source of nuclear energy. Atomic number 92. See table at **element.**

U

ur•ban (ûr′bən) *adj.* **1.** Relating to a city: *urban traffic; urban housing.* **2.** Characteristic of the city or city life: *urban pollution.*

ur•bane (ûr bān′) *adj.* Polite, refined, and often elegant: *an urbane gentleman.*

urban renewal *n.* [U] The rebuilding of poor urban neighborhoods by major repairs or reconstruction of housing and public works: *the president's plan for urban renewal.*

ur•chin (ûr′chĭn) *n.* **1.** A playful or mischievous child. **2.** A sea urchin.

—ure *suff.* A suffix that means: **1.** Act or process: *pressure.* **2.** Function or office: *legislature.*

u•re•thra (yōō rē′thrə) *n., pl.* **u•re•thras** or **u•re•thrae** (yōō rē′thrē). The duct or canal through which urine is passed out of the bladder in most mammals and through which semen is released in males.

urge (ûrj) *tr.v.* **urged, urg•ing, urg•es. 1.** To push, force, or drive (sbdy.) onward: *The captain urged her team on to victory.* **2.** To beg or ask (sbdy.) earnestly and repeatedly: *The coach urged us to stay in shape over summer vacation.* **3.** To speak earnestly in favor of doing, considering, or approving (sthg.): *urge the passage of new crime laws.* **—n.** An impulse that moves one to action or effort: *an urge to travel.*

ur•gen•cy (ûr′jən sē) *n.* [U] The quality or condition of being urgent: *the urgency of the political situation.*

ur•gent (ûr′jənt) *adj.* **1.** Needing immediate action or attention: *an urgent situation.* **2.** Carrying a sense of pressing importance or necessity: *an urgent tone of voice.* **—ur′gent•ly** *adv.*

u•ri•nal (yŏŏr′ə nəl) *n.* An upright wall fixture used by men and boys for urinating: *a row of urinals in the men's restroom.*

u•ri•nal•y•sis (yŏŏr′ə năl′ĭ sĭs) *n., pl.* **u•ri•nal•y•ses** (yŏŏr′ə năl′ĭ sēz′). [C; U] The chemical analysis of urine, used to diagnose disease or to check for the presence of a specific substance, such as a drug.

u•ri•nar•y (yŏŏr′ə nĕr′ē) *adj.* Relating to urine or its production, function, or excretion: *the urinary tract.*

u•ri•nate (yŏŏr′ə nāt′) *intr.v.* **u•ri•nat•ed, u•ri•nat•ing, u•ri•nates.** To discharge urine. **—u′ri•na′tion** *n.* [U]

u•rine (yŏŏr′ĭn) *n.* [U] A fluid containing body wastes taken from the blood by the kidneys, stored in the bladder, and passed from the body through the urethra.

urn (ûrn) *n.* **1.** A decorative vase or container, especially one used to hold the ashes of a dead person's body after cremation. **2.** A metal container with a spigot, used for serving tea or coffee.

us (ŭs) *pron.* The objective case of **we. 1.** Used as the direct object of a verb: *The movie impressed us greatly.* **2.** Used as the indirect object of a verb: *She gave us free tickets to the show.* **3.** Used as the object of a preposition: *He sent a letter to us.*

U.S. or **US** *abbr.* An abbreviation of United States.

USA *abbr.* An abbreviation of United States of America.

us•a•ble also **use•a•ble** (yōō′zə bəl) *adj.* **1.** Capable of being used: *separating usable material from waste.* **2.** Appropriate for use: *The little room seemed usable as an office.*

USAF also **U.S.A.F.** *abbr.* An abbreviation of United States Air Force.

us•age (yōō′sĭj) *n.* [U] **1.** The act, manner, or amount of using sthg.: *a gauge that measures water usage.* **2.** A usual or accepted practice: *a common usage in this region.* **3.** The way in which words or phrases are used, spoken, or written: *contemporary English usage.*

USCG also **U.S.C.G.** *abbr.* An abbreviation of United States Coast Guard.

U.S. Customary System *n.* The standard system of measurement in the United States, including linear measure, liquid measure, and dry measure, for example. A yard, an acre, a pint, and a bushel are all units of measure in the U.S. Customary System.

use (yōōz) *v.* **used, us•ing, us•es. —tr. 1.** To bring or put (sthg.) into service; employ for some purpose: *I used a fork to beat the eggs.* **2.** To practice or employ (sthg.): *Use caution when driving at night.* **3.** To achieve a goal by taking advantage of (sbdy./sthg.): *He used his connections to get a job in the mayor's office.* **—intr.** (yōōs). Used in the past tense followed by *to* to indicate a state, practice, or custom no longer followed or in existence: *I used to go there often.* **—n.** (yōōs). **1.** [C] The act of using sthg.: *the use of a pencil for writing.* **2.** [U] The condition or fact of being used: *The telephone is in use right now.* **3.** [C] The manner of using sthg.; usage: *the proper use of power tools.* **4.** [U] The power or ability of using sthg.: *He lost the use of one arm.* **5.** [C; U] The need or occasion to use sthg.: *Do you have any use for this book?* [U] The quality of being suitable for a purpose; usefulness: *old pieces of equipment of no practical use.* ♦ **it's** or **there's no use.** An expression used when there is no reason to do sthg. or to continue doing sthg.: *It's no use! I can't open this window. There's no use calling; she's not home.* **use up.** *tr.v* [sep.] To consume (sthg.) completely: *We used up the*

ă–cat; ā–pay; âr–care; ä–father; ĕ–get; ē–be; ĭ–sit; ī–nice; îr–here; ŏ–got; ō–go; ô–saw; oi–boy; ou–out; ōō–took; ōō–boot; ŭ–cut; ûr–word; th–thin; *th*–this; hw–when; zh–vision; ə–about; N–French bon

milk yesterday. We need to buy some more.
—SEE NOTE at **utilize.**

use•a•ble (yōō′zə bəl) *adj.* Variant of **usable.**

used (yōōzd) *adj.* **1.** Not new; secondhand: *I bought a used car.* **2.** (yōōst). [*to*] Accustomed: *It takes time to get used to the cold weather. She was used to taking a swim in the morning.*

use•ful (yōōs′fəl) *adj.* Capable of being used for some purpose; being of use or service: *a useful map.* —**use′ful•ly** *adv.* —**use′ful•ness** *n.* [U]

use•less (yōōs′lĭs) *adj.* **1.** Having no use: *a useless new invention.* **2.** Unable to function or assist: *As protection for the house, the dog is useless.* —**use′less•ly** *adv.* —**use′less•ness** *n.* [U]

us•er (yōō′zər) *n.* A person or thing that uses: *a personal computer user; a drug user.*

us•er-friend•ly (yōō′zər frĕnd′lē) *adj.* Easy to use or learn to use: *a user-friendly software program; a user-friendly form.*

ush•er (ŭsh′ər) *n.* **1.** A person who takes people to their seats, as in a theater. **2.** A man who forms part of a bridal party at a wedding. —*v.* —*tr.* **1.** To serve as an usher to (sbdy.); escort: *She ushered us to our seats.* See Synonyms at **guide. 2.** [*In*] To go before and introduce (sbdy./sthg.): *usher in a new era.* —*intr.* To work as an usher: *They ushered at the concert.*

USMC also **U.S.M.C.** *abbr.* An abbreviation of United States Marine Corps.

USN also **U.S.N.** *abbr.* An abbreviation of United States Navy.

u•su•al (yōō′zhōō əl) *adj.* **1.** Commonly experienced or observed; ordinary: *the usual traffic jams during rush hour.* **2.** Regularly or customarily used: *He ended his speech with the usual expressions of thanks.* **3.** In accord with regular practice or procedure: *Come at the usual time.* ◆ **as usual.** As commonly or regularly happens: *She jogged that morning as usual.* —**u′su•al•ly** *adv.*

u•surp (yōō sûrp′ *or* yōō zûrp′) *tr.v.* To take control of (the power or rights of another, for example) by force and without legal authority: *usurp a throne.* —**u•surp′er** *n.*

u•su•ry (yōō′zhə rē) *n.* [U] The practice of lending money at interest, especially at an excessively high or unlawfully high rate. —**u′su•rer** *n.*

u•ten•sil (yōō tĕn′səl) *n.* An instrument or an implement, such as one used in a kitchen: *Soup spoons are in the drawer with the other utensils.*

u•ter•us (yōō′tər əs) *n.* A hollow muscular organ of female mammals, in which the young can develop.

u•til•i•tar•i•an (yōō tĭl′ĭ târ′ē ən) *adj.* Showing or stressing usefulness over other values; practical: *a plain, utilitarian design for the building.*

u•til•i•ty (yōō tĭl′ĭ tē) *n., pl.* **u•til•i•ties. 1.** [U] The quality of being useful; usefulness: *a practice that is of little utility.* **2.** [C] (*usually plural*). A public service, such as electricity, water, or transportation: *Public utilities include sewer, gas, water, and electric service.*

u•til•ize (yōōt′l īz′) *tr.v.* **u•til•ized, u•til•iz•ing, u•til•iz•es.** *Formal.* To put (sthg.) to use, especially for a practical purpose: *utilizing the stream's water to run the mill.* —**u′ti•li•za′tion** (yōōt′l ĭ zā′shən) *n.* [U]

USAGE: utilize You can often simply say **use** instead of the longer word **utilize.** *Utilize,* however, can mean "to find a profitable or practical use for." Thus the sentence *They were unable to use the new computers* might mean only that people were unable to turn the computers on. The sentence *The teachers were unable to utilize the new computers* suggests that the teachers could not find ways to employ the computers in instruction.

ut•most (ŭt′mōst′) *adj.* Of the highest or greatest degree, amount, or intensity: *matters of the utmost importance.* —*n.* [U] The greatest possible degree, amount, or extent; the maximum: *We will try to our utmost to find a solution.*

u•to•pi•a (yōō tō′pē ə) *n.* Often **Utopia.** A place that is ideal, especially in morals and social and political life. —**u•to′pi•an** *adj. & n.*

ut•ter¹ (ŭt′ər) *tr.v.* **1.** To produce (a sound) with the voice: *utter a sigh.* **2.** To pronounce or speak (a word or words): *utter a prayer.*

ut•ter² (ŭt′ər) *adj.* Complete; absolute: *utter darkness.* —**ut′ter•ly** *adv.*

ut•ter•ance (ŭt′ər əns) *n. Formal.* **1.** [C] Something uttered or expressed; a statement. **2.** [U] The act of uttering: *She thought his continued utterance of old jokes was irritating.*

ut•ter•ly (ŭt′ər lē) *adv.* Completely; absolutely: *an utterly ridiculous idea.*

U-turn (yōō′tûrn′) *n.* A turn, as by a vehicle, completely reversing the direction of travel: *U-turns are not permitted on major highways.*

u•vu•la (yōō′vyə lə) *n.* The small cone-shaped mass of flesh that hangs from the end of the soft palate above the tongue.

Vv

v or **V** (vē) *n.*, *pl.* **v's** or **V's.** The 22nd letter of the English alphabet.

V[1] also **v** The Roman numeral for 5.

V[2] *abbr.* An abbreviation of: **1.** Velocity. **2.** Victory. **3.** Volt. **4.** Volume.

v. *abbr.* An abbreviation of: **1.** Verb. **2.** Verse. **3.** Versus. **4.** Volume (book). **5.** Vowel.

VA or **Va.** *abbr.* An abbreviation of Virginia.

va·can·cy (vā′kən sē) *n.*, *pl.* **va·can·cies.** A position, office, or space that is unfilled or unoccupied: *There are no vacancies at the hotel.*

va·cant (vā′kənt) *adj.* **1.** Containing nothing; empty: *vacant buildings.* See Synonyms at **empty. 2.** Not occupied or taken: *vacant seats.* **3.** Without expression; blank: *a vacant stare.* —**va′cant·ly** *adv.*

va·cate (vā′kāt′ *or* vā kāt′) *tr.* & *intr.v.* **va·cat·ed, va·cat·ing, va·cates.** To stop occupying or holding; give up: *vacate an apartment; hotel guests who must vacate by 10:00.*

va·ca·tion (vā kā′shən) *n.* [C; U] Time spent away from work or school: *summer vacation.* —*intr.v.* To take or spend a vacation: *He vacationed on the island.* —**va·ca′tion·er** *n.*

vac·ci·nate (văk′sə nāt′) *tr.v.* **vac·ci·nat·ed, vac·ci·nat·ing, vac·ci·nates.** [*against*] To give (a person or animal) an injection to protect against a disease: *We vaccinated the dog against rabies.*

vac·ci·na·tion (văk′sə nā′shən) *n.* **1.** [C; U] Inoculation with a vaccine in order to give immunity against an infectious disease. **2.** [C] A scar left on the skin where such an inoculation was made.

vac·cine (văk sēn′ *or* văk′sēn′) *n.* [C; U] An injection containing a weak form of a disease, used to protect a person or animal against the disease.

vac·il·late (văs′ə lāt′) *intr.v.* **vac·il·lat·ed, vac·il·lat·ing, vac·il·lates.** [*between*] To swing back and forth between two plans of action; hesitate: *She vacillated between going to the movies and staying home.* —**vac′il·la′tion** *n.* [C; U]

vac·u·ous (văk′yōō əs) *adj.* **1.** Empty: *a vacuous space.* **2.** Lacking intelligence; stupid: *a vacuous statement.* —**vac′u·ous·ly** *adv.*

vac·u·um (văk′yōōm *or* văk′yōō əm) *n.* **1.** A space from which everything, including air, has been removed. **2.** Total emptiness: *The death of her father left a vacuum in her life.* **3.** A vacuum cleaner: *May I use the vacuum?* —*tr.* & *intr.v.* To clean with or use a vacuum cleaner: *He vacuumed the carpet. We vacuum every week.*

vacuum cleaner *n.* An electrical appliance that cleans up dirt by suction.

vag·a·bond (văg′ə bŏnd′) *n.* A person who moves from place to place and has no permanent home. —*adj.* Characteristic of a wanderer: *leading a vagabond life.*

va·gi·na (və jī′nə) *n.* The passage leading from the uterus to the outside of the body in female mammals. —**vag′i·nal** (văj′ə nəl) *adj.* —**vag′i·nal·ly** *adv.*

va·grant (vā′grənt) *n.* A person who wanders from place to place and has no permanent home or job: *Police ordered the vagrants out of the subway station.* —*adj.* Wandering from place to place without a home or job. —**va′gran·cy** *n.* [U]

vague (vāg) *adj.* **vagu·er, vagu·est. 1.** Not clear; without details: *a vague statement; a vague promise.* **2.** Not clearly or strongly felt: *a vague sense of fear.* —**vague′ly** *adv.* —**vague′ness** *n.* [U]

SYNONYMS: vague, ambiguous, obscure, cryptic. These adjectives mean lacking a clear meaning. **Vague** means unclear because the details are missing: *I have only a vague idea of what the book is about.* **Ambiguous** means with two or more possible meanings: *I couldn't tell if he was happy or not because his smile was ambiguous.* **Obscure** suggests a hidden meaning: *The document makes several obscure references to a hidden treasure.* **Cryptic** suggests sthg. that is overly brief and is meant to be puzzling: *The club used cryptic abbreviations for everything in order to seem mysterious.*

---

vain (vān) *adj.* **1.** Not likely to succeed; useless: *a vain effort to get an A in math.* **2.** Overly proud of one's own looks or abilities: *She's vain about her cooking.* ♦ **in vain. 1.** Without success: *We tried in vain to open the window.* **2.** In an irreverent or disrespectful manner: *Their religion forbids taking God's name in vain.* —**vain′ly** *adv.*

HOMONYMS: vain, vane (weathervane), **vein** (blood vessel).

val. *abbr.* An abbreviation of value.
vale (vāl) *n.* A valley.

HOMONYMS: vale, veil (head covering).

val·e·dic·to·ri·an (văl′ĭ dĭk tôr′ē ən) *n.* The student with the highest rank in a high-school graduating class, who gives the valedictory speech at graduation.
val·e·dic·to·ry (văl′ĭ dĭk′tə rē) *n.*, *pl.* **val·e·dic·to·ries.** [C; U] A closing speech, especially one delivered at a graduation ceremony. —*adj.* Relating to a farewell speech.
va·lence (vā′ləns) *n.* A number that tells how many electrons an atom (or group of atoms) will add, lose, or share when it combines with another atom (or group of atoms).
val·en·tine (văl′ən tīn) *n.* **1.** A sentimental card sent to a boyfriend, girlfriend, or family member on Saint Valentine's Day. **2.** A person selected as one's sweetheart on Saint Valentine's Day: *Be my valentine.*
Val·en·tine's Day (văl′ən tīnz′) *n.* Saint Valentine's Day, a holiday celebrated in the United States and Canada on February 14 when people exchange valentine cards or gifts to show that they love each other.
val·et (văl′ĭt *or* văl′ā *or* vă lā′) *n.* **1.** An employee in a hotel who performs personal services for guests: *The valet picked up my laundry.* **2.** A person employed to park cars as at a restaurant or hotel: *The valet damaged the car.* **3.** A man's male servant, who takes care of his clothes and performs other personal services.
val·iant (văl′yənt) *adj.* Courageous; brave: *a valiant soldier; a valiant effort to save the child.* See Synonyms at **brave.** —**val′iant·ly** *adv.*
val·id (văl′ĭd) *adj.* **1.** Logical; convincing: *He had a valid reason for leaving work early.* **2.** Legal: *a valid passport.* —**va·lid′i·ty** (və lĭd′ĭ tē) *n.* [U]
val·i·date (văl′ĭ dāt′) *tr.v.* **val·i·dat·ed, val·i·dat·ing, val·i·dates. 1.** To give (sthg.) legal force; make valid: *validate a contract.* **2.** To establish the truth of (sthg.): *validate a theory.*
va·lise (və lēs′) *n.* An old word for a small piece of hand luggage.
val·ley (văl′ē) *n.*, *pl.* **val·leys.** A long narrow region of low land between ranges of mountains, often with a river or stream running along the bottom: *a peaceful valley.*
val·or (văl′ər) *n.* [U] Courage and boldness, bravery: *a medal for valor in wartime.*
val·or·ous (văl′ər əs) *adj.* Showing or having great personal bravery; valiant: *valorous deeds.*

val·our (văl′ər) *n. Chiefly British.* Variant of **valor.**
val·u·a·ble (văl′yoo ə bəl *or* văl′yə bəl) *adj.* **1.** Worth a lot of money: *a valuable piece of jewelry.* **2.** Very important: *acquire valuable information.* **3.** With admirable qualities: *a valuable friend.* —*n. (usually plural).* A valuable personal possession, as a piece of jewelry: *She insured her valuables against theft.*
val·ue (văl′yoo) *n.* **1.** [U] How much money sthg. is worth: *the value of a rare stamp.* **2.** [U] The usefulness of sthg. compared to how much it costs: *Those shoes were a good value.* **3.** [C] A belief or principle that sbdy. uses to make judgments: *traditional values such as honesty and fairness.* **4.** [C] A numerical quantity assigned to a letter: *In the equation x = 5, the value of x is five.* —*tr.v.* **val·ued, val·u·ing, val·ues.** To consider (sthg.) to be important: *He valued the team of horses highly.* See Synonyms at **appreciate.**
valve (vălv) *n.* **1.** Something attached to a pipe that opens and closes to control how much liquid or gas passes through. **2.** A similar part of a human or an animal's body: *the valves of the heart.*
vam·pire (văm′pīr′) *n.* **1.** An imaginary monster that lives on human blood. **2.** A person who victimizes others.
van (văn) *n.* **1.** An enclosed motor vehicle with rear or side doors and side panels, used especially for transporting people. **2.** A covered or enclosed truck or wagon used for transporting goods: *a moving van.*
van·dal (văn′dl) *n.* A person who destroys public or private property for no reason: *Vandals broke the school windows last night.*
van·dal·ism (văn′dl ĭz′əm) *n.* [U] Intentional damage to or destruction of public or private property.
van·dal·ize (văn′dl īz′) *tr.v.* **van·dal·ized, van·dal·iz·ing, van·dal·iz·es.** To destroy or damage (public or private property): *Somebody vandalized my garden.*
vane (văn) *n.* **1.** A blade attached to a shaft in a windmill or turbine in such a way that the air or water pushes against it, causing a circular motion. **2.** A weathervane.

HOMONYMS: vane, vain (proud), **vein** (blood vessel).

van·guard (văn′gärd) *n.* [U] **1.** The front or leading position in an army or a fleet. **2.** The leading position in a trend or movement.
va·nil·la (və nĭl′ə) *n.* [U] **1.** A tropical Central American plant with seedpods from which a flavoring extract is obtained. **2.** A flavoring extract made from the cured seedpods of this plant or produced artificially.
van·ish (văn′ĭsh) *intr.v.* **1.** To disappear quickly and completely: *The sun vanished*

behind a cloud. See Synonyms at **disappear.**
2. [*from*] To exist no longer: *The dinosaurs vanished from the earth.*

van·i·ty (văn′ĭ tē) *n., pl.* **van·i·ties. 1.** [U] Excessive pride; conceit. **2.** [C] A woman's dressing table: *Your comb is on the vanity.*

van·quish (văng′kwĭsh *or* văn′kwĭsh) *tr.v.* To defeat or conquer (sbdy.) in battle: *The army finally vanquished the enemy.* —**van′quish·er** *n.*

van·tage (văn′tĭj) *n.* A position that allows a wide view: *from his vantage above the river.*

va·por (vā′pər) *n.* [C; U] **1.** A faintly visible suspension of small particles of a gas or a solid in the air, as mist, fumes, or smoke. **2.** The gaseous form of a substance that is solid or liquid at room temperature: *water vapor.*

va·por·ize (vā′pə rīz′) *tr. & intr.v.* **va·por·ized, va·por·iz·ing, va·por·iz·es.** To convert or be converted into vapor: *He invented a device to vaporize medicine. Water vaporizes when it boils.* —**va′por·i·za′tion** (vā′pər ĭ zā′shən) *n.* [U]

va·por·iz·er (vā′pə rī′zər) *n.* A device that turns a liquid medicine into a vapor so that it can be inhaled.

va·pour (vā′pər) *n. Chiefly British.* Variant of **vapor.**

var. *abbr.* An abbreviation of: **1.** Variable. **2.** Variant. **3.** Variation. **4.** Variety. **5.** Various.

var·i·a·ble (vâr′ē ə bəl *or* văr′ē ə bəl) *adj.* **1.** Changeable: *a variable climate.* **2.** In mathematics, with more than one possible value: *a variable number.* —*n.* **1.** Something that varies or is prone to variation: *We need to consider all of the variables.* **2.** A variable mathematical quantity or a symbol that represents it. —**var′i·a·bil′i·ty** *n.* [U] —**var′i·a·bly** *adv.*

var·i·ance (vâr′ē əns *or* văr′ē əns) *n.* **1.** [C; U] A difference between what is expected and what actually happens. **2.** [C] An exception to a rule: *a variance to the building code.* ◆ **at variance.** *Formal.* In a state of discrepancy; differing: *Your view of the issue is at variance with mine.*

var·i·ant (vâr′ē ənt *or* văr′ē ənt) *adj.* Having or showing variation; differing: *words with variant spellings.* —*n.* Something that differs in form only slightly from sthg. else, as a different spelling or pronunciation of the same word. For example, *colour* is the British variant of *color.*

var·i·a·tion (vâr′ē ā′shən *or* văr′ē ā′shən) *n.* **1.** [C; U] The act of varying. **2.** [C] The extent to which sthg. varies: *temperature variations of more than 50 degrees Fahrenheit.* **3.** [C] Something that is slightly different from another of the same type: *a variation on a theme.*

var·i·cose veins (văr′ĭ kōs′) *pl.n.* A condition in which veins, especially of the legs, are abnormally swollen or knotted.

var·ied (vâr′ēd *or* văr′ēd) *adj.* With or consisting of various forms or types; diverse: *a varied assortment of candy.*

var·i·e·gat·ed (vâr′ē ĭ gā′tĭd *or* văr′ē ĭ-gā′tĭd) *adj.* With streaks or marks of a different color or colors: *plants with variegated leaves.*

va·ri·e·ty (və rī′ĭ tē) *n., pl.* **va·ri·e·ties. 1.** [U] Difference; diversity: *Variety is the spice of life.* **2.** [C] *(usually singular).* A collection of varied things, usually within the same general grouping; an assortment: *a variety of outdoor activities.* **3.** [C] A type of plant or animal that is related to another of the same species: *Broccoli is a variety of cabbage.*

var·i·ous (vâr′ē əs *or* văr′ē əs) *adj.* **1.** Of several different kinds: *We were unable to go for various reasons.* **2.** More than one; several: *He spoke to various members of the club.* **3.** Being an individual or separate member of a group or class: *The various members all agreed.* —**var′i·ous·ly** *adv.*

var·mint (vär′mĭnt) *n. Informal.* An outdated, often humorous word for a person or animal that is considered undesirable or annoying: *Get that varmint out of the house!*

var·nish (vär′nĭsh) *n.* [C; U] **1.** A paint used to coat a surface with a hard glossy transparent film: *Varnish is clear and shiny when it's dry.* **2.** The smooth coating or gloss that results from the use of this paint: *The table has two coats of varnish.* **3.** Something resembling a coat of varnish; outward appearance; gloss: *hiding his temper under a varnish of good manners.* —*tr.v.* To cover (sthg.) with varnish: *varnish a cabinet.* ◆ **varnish over.** *tr.v.* [sep.] To hide (sthg. unpleasant): *She tried to varnish over her lack of experience on her application.*

var·si·ty (vär′sĭ tē) *n., pl.* **var·si·ties.** The main team representing a university, college, or school in sports, games, or other competitions: *He plays on the varsity.*

var·y (vâr′ē *or* văr′ē) *v.* **var·ied, var·y·ing, var·ies.** —*tr.* **1.** To make changes in or cause (sthg.) to change; modify or alter: *I varied the speed of the drill to get it to work better.* **2.** To give variety to (sthg.): *vary one's diet.* —*intr.* **1.** To undergo or show change: *The temperature varied throughout the day.* **2.** To be different from others of its type: *vary from the norm.*

vas·cu·lar (văs′kyə lər) *adj.* With tubes or vessels that carry or circulate liquids such as blood or water within an animal or plant.

vase (vās *or* vāz *or* väz) *n.* An open container, usually of glass, used for holding flowers.

ă–cat; ā–pay; âr–care; ä–father; ĕ–get; ē–be; ĭ–sit; ī–nice; îr–here; ŏ–got; ō–go; ô–saw; oi–boy; ou–out; ŏŏ–took; ōō–boot; ŭ–cut; ûr–word; th–thin; *th*–this; hw–when; zh–vision; ə–about; N–French bon

va·sec·to·my (və sĕk'tə mē) *n., pl.*
va·sec·to·mies. [C; U] Surgical removal of
all or part of the tube that carries sperm in
males, usually for sterilization.
vast (văst) *adj.* **1.** Very great in size, number,
amount, or quantity: *She sold her art collection for a vast sum of money.* **2.** Very great in
area or extent; immense: *the vast expanse of
the Pacific Ocean.* **3.** Very great in degree or
intensity: *a vast difference between the two
policies.* —**vast'ly** *adv.* —**vast'ness** *n.* [U]
vat (văt) *n.* A large container, such as a tub
or barrel, used to hold or store liquids: *a vat
of wine.*
vaude·ville (vôd'vĭl') *n.* An old-fashioned
stage show with a variety of short acts such as
singing and dancing: *a vaudeville routine.*
vault¹ (vôlt) *n.* **1.** An arched structure that
supports a ceiling or roof. **2.** A room or compartment where valuables are kept: *a bank
vault.* **3.** An underground room. **4.** A burial
chamber, especially when underground.
vault² (vôlt) *tr. & intr.v.* To jump or leap over,
especially with a support such as the hands or
a pole: *The boy vaulted the stream. The gymnast vaulted.* —*n.* The act of vaulting; a leap.
vb. *abbr.* An abbreviation of verb.
VCR *n., pl.* **VCR's.** An electronic device for
recording and playing back video images and
sound through a television set; a videocassette recorder.
VD also **V.D.** *abbr.* An abbreviation of vene-
real disease.
VDT *n., pl.* **VDT's.** A screen on which computer data and graphic images are displayed;
video display terminal.
veal (vēl) *n.* [U] The meat of a calf.
vec·tor (vĕk'tər) *n.* **1.** In mathematics and
physics, a measurement that combines speed
and direction. **2.** The course followed by an
airplane.
veer (vîr) *v.* —*intr.* To turn aside from a
course, direction, or purpose; swerve: *The
plane veered east to avoid the oncoming
storm.* —*tr.* To alter the direction of (sthg.);
turn: *He veered the car sharply to the left.*
veg (vĕj) *Slang. v.* **vegged, veg·ging, veg·es.**
♦ **veg out.** *intr.v.* To relax and not do anything: *She spends Fridays vegging out in front
of the TV.*
veg·e·ta·ble (vĕj'tə bəl *or* vĕj'ĭ tə bəl) *n.* **1.**
A plant whose roots, leaves, stems, flowers,
seeds, or fruit are used as food: *Eat your vegetables.* **2.** A member of the plant kingdom; a
plant: *Is it animal, vegetable, or mineral?* **3.**
Informal. A person who is passive or not
responsive, especially one who has suffered
brain damage.
veg·e·tar·i·an (vĕj'ĭ târ'ē ən) *n.* A person
who eats only plants and plant products, or
one who also eats eggs and dairy products.
—*adj.* **1.** Relating to vegetarians or vegetari-
anism: *a vegetarian diet.* **2.** Consisting of

plants and plant products: *a vegetarian meal;
a vegetarian casserole.*
veg·e·tar·i·an·ism (vĕj'ĭ târ'ē ə nĭz' əm) *n.*
[U] The practice of following a vegetarian diet.
veg·e·tate (vĕj'ĭ tāt') *intr.v.* **veg·e·tat·ed,**
veg·e·tat·ing, veg·e·tates. 1. To grow or
sprout as a plant does. **2.** To be physically
inactive and mentally dull: *We vegetated on
weekends.* —**veg'e·ta'tive** *adj.*
veg·e·ta·tion (vĕj'ĭ tā'shən) *n.* [U] The
plants that grow in a certain area or region;
plant life: *the lush vegetation of the jungle.*
ve·he·ment (vē'ə mənt) *adj.* Intense; forceful:
a vehement critic of the city government.
—**ve'he·mence** *n.* [U] —**ve'he·ment·ly** *adv.*
ve·hi·cle (vē'ĭ kəl) *n.* **1.a.** A machine for
transporting people or things. **b.** A self-
propelled device with tires: *a motor vehicle.* **2.**
A means of expressing or accomplishing sthg.:
Oral tales are an important vehicle of culture.
ve·hic·u·lar (vē hĭk'yə lər) *adj.* Relating to or
intended for vehicles, especially motor vehicles: *vehicular traffic; vehicular regulations.*
veil (vāl) *n.* **1.** A piece of cloth worn by
women over the head, shoulders, and often
the face: *a bridal veil.* **2.** Something that covers or conceals like a veil: *a veil of secrecy.*
—*tr.v.* **1.** To cover (sthg.) with a veil: *veil
one's face.* **2.** To conceal or disguise (sthg.):
veiled their true reasons.

HOMONYMS: veil, vale (valley).

---

veiled (vāld) *adj.* **1.** Covered with a veil:
veiled women. **2.** Said indirectly: *a thinly
veiled threat.*
vein (vān) *n.* **1.** A blood vessel through which
blood returns to the heart. **2.** A narrow, usually branching tube in a leaf or an insect's
wing. **3.** A long, regularly shaped deposit
of an ore or a mineral in the earth: *a vein of
copper ore; a vein of coal.* **4.** A streak of a
different shade or color, as in marble or
wood. **5.** An attitude or mood: *He spoke in
a light playful vein.*

HOMONYMS: vein, vain (proud), **vane** (weathervane).

Vel·cro (vĕl'krō). A trademark used for
a fastening tape made of strips of cloth
that stick to each other, used on clothing and
luggage, for example.
ve·loc·i·ty (və lŏs'ĭ tē) *n., pl.* **ve·loc·
i·ties.** [C; U] **1.** The rate at which an object
moves in a specified direction: *The plane lost
velocity.* **2.** Speed: *the velocity of light.*
ve·lour (və loor') *n.* [C; U] A soft fabric
resembling velvet, used primarily for clothing and upholstery.
vel·vet (vĕl'vĭt) *n.* **1.** [C; U] A soft fabric of
silk, rayon, or nylon, with a smooth dense
pile on one side and a plain underside. **2.** [U]

Something resembling velvet: *leaves of velvet.* —**vel′vet•y** *adj.*

vel•vet•een (vĕl′vĭ tēn′) *n.* [C; U] A cotton fabric like velvet.

vend•er or **ven•dor** (vĕn′dər) *n.* **1.** A person who sells sthg.: *a street vender.* **2.** A vending machine.

ven•det•ta (vĕn dĕt′ə) *n.* A long, bitter fight or feud between two people or two groups of people, often with acts of revenge.

vend•ing machine (vĕn′dĭng) *n.* A machine that dispenses food, drinks, or other items after coins or bills are placed in it.

ve•neer (və nîr′) *n.* **1.** [C; U] A thin covering of wood or other material: *a cheap pine table with a mahagony veneer.* **2.** [C] A false outer appearance: *a veneer of friendliness.*

ven•er•a•ble (vĕn′ər ə bəl) *adj.* Worthy of respect due to age or position: *a venerable senator.* —**ven′er•a•bly** *adv.*

ven•er•ate (vĕn′ə rāt′) *tr.v.* **ven•er•at•ed, ven•er•at•ing, ven•er•ates.** To regard (sbdy./sthg.) with respect or reverence: *The senator was venerated in his hometown.* —**ven′er•a′tion** *n.* [U]

ve•ne•re•al disease (və nîr′ē əl) *n.* [C; U] Any of several diseases transmitted by sexual contact, such as syphilis and gonorrhea.

ve•ne•tian blind (və nē′shən) *n.* A window covering made of a number of thin horizontal slats that overlap when closed.

ven•geance (vĕn′jəns) *n.* [U] The act of hurting or punishing sbdy. who has done sthg. wrong: *She wanted vengeance for her son's death.* ◆ **with a vengeance.** With great violence or force: *The snowstorm hit with a vengeance.*

venge•ful (vĕnj′fəl) *adj.* Desiring vengeance: *a vengeful man.* —**venge′ful•ly** *adv.*

ven•i•son (vĕn′ĭ sən or vĕn′ĭ zən) *n.* [U] The meat of a deer used as food.

Venn diagram (vĕn) *n.* A diagram that uses circles to represent groups of ideas or objects in order to show which ones are separate from each other and which ones overlap.

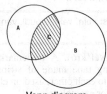

Venn diagram
A. People who like dogs
B. People who like cats
C. People who like dogs and cats

ven•om (vĕn′əm) *n.* **1.** [C; U] A poisonous substance that is produced by certain snakes, spiders, scorpions, and insects and can be injected into a victim by a bite or sting: *deadly snake venom.* **2.** [U] Anger; hatred: *We could hear the venom in his voice.*

ven•om•ous (vĕn′ə məs) *adj.* **1.** Containing venom: *a venomous snake.* **2.** Angry; hateful: *a venomous look.* —**ven′om•ous•ly** *adv.*

vent (vĕnt) *n.* An opening through which a liquid, gas, or vapor can escape: *a steam vent.* —*tr.v.* **1.** To give forceful expression to (sthg.): *venting their anger.* **2.** To release or discharge (steam, for example) through an opening. ◆ **give vent to.** To express (sthg.) freely and forcefully: *He finally gave vent to his feelings of frustration.*

ven•ti•late (vĕn′tl āt′) *tr.v.* **ven•ti•lat•ed, ven•ti•lat•ing, ven•ti•lates.** **1.** To let fresh air into (a room, for example): *ventilate the kitchen to remove cooking odors.* **2.** To expose (sthg.) to public discussion: *We ventilated our worries.*

ven•ti•la•tor (vĕn′tl ā′tər) *n.* **1.** A device that circulates fresh air and expels stale air. **2.** A respirator.

ven•tri•cle (vĕn′trĭ kəl) *n.* A chamber in an organ of the body, especially either of the chambers of the heart: *the left ventricle of the heart.* —**ven•tric′u•lar** (vĕn trĭk′yə lər) *adj.*

ven•tril•o•quism (vĕn trĭl′ə kwĭz′əm) *n.* [U] The art of projecting one's voice so that it seems to come from another source, as from a puppet. —**ven•tril′o•quist** *n.*

ven•ture (vĕn′chər) *n.* **1.** A project that is dangerous, daring, or uncertain. **2.** A business enterprise involving some financial risk. —*v.* **ven•tured, ven•tur•ing, ven•tures.** —*tr.* **1.** To expose (sthg.) to danger or risk: *The investor is venturing all his savings on this project.* **2.** To brave the dangers of (sthg.): *They ventured the high seas in a light boat.* **3.** To dare to say (sthg.); express at the risk of denial or criticism: *venture an opinion; venture a guess.* —*intr.* **1.** To take a risk; dare: *venture into a new business.* **2.** To proceed despite possible danger or risk: *The hikers ventured into the mountains.* —**ven′ture•some** *adj.*

ven•ue (vĕn′yōō) *n.* **1.** The locality in which a trial is held: *Lawyers asked for a change of venue.* **2.** The scene or setting in which sthg. takes place: *the venue of a play.*

ve•rac•i•ty (və răs′ĭ tē) *n.* [U] **1.** Truthfulness; honesty: *doubting the veracity of the witnesses.* **2.** Accuracy; precision: *checking the veracity of his report.*

ve•ran•da or **ve•ran•dah** (və răn′də) *n.* A porch or balcony, usually with a roof, extending along the outside of a building.

verb (vûrb) *n.* **1.** In grammar, a word, such as *be, run,* or *happen,* that shows existence, action, or occurrence. **2.** A phrase, such as *has been thinking,* that is used as a verb.

V

ver•bal (vûr′bəl) *adj.* **1.** Relating to or associated with words: *verbal aptitude tests.* **2.** Expressed in spoken rather than written words; oral: *a verbal agreement.* **3.** Relating to, having the nature or function of, or derived from a verb: *verbal constructions.* **4.** Used to form verbs: *a verbal suffix.* —*n.* A noun or adjective derived from a verb. —**ver′bal•ly** *adv.*

ver•bal•ize (vûr′bə līz′) *v.* **ver•bal•ized, ver•bal•iz•ing, ver•bal•iz•es.** —*tr.* To express (sthg.) in words: *He verbalized his fears.* —*intr.* To express oneself in words: *The baby is finally verbalizing.*

ver•ba•tim (vər bā′tĭm) *adj.* Using exactly the same words; corresponding word for word: *a verbatim quotation.* —*adv.* Word for word; in the same words: *He repeated the speech verbatim.*

ver•bi•age (vûr′bē ĭj *or* vûr′bĭj) *n.* [U] *Formal.* Too many words for the purpose; wordiness: *He cut the verbiage from his speech to make it more interesting.*

ver•bose (vər bōs′) *adj.* Using or containing more words than necessary; wordy. —**ver•bose′ly** *adv.* —**ver•bos′i•ty** (vər bŏs′ĭ tē) *n.* [U]

ver•dant (vûr′dnt) *adj.* **1.** Covered with green plants: *verdant meadows.* **2.** Green in color: *verdant leaves.*

ver•dict (vûr′dĭkt) *n.* **1.** The decision reached by a jury at the end of a trial: *The jury's verdict was "not guilty."* **2.** An opinion: *Our verdict is that we should sell.*

verge (vûrj) *n.* **1.** The extreme edge of sthg.; a border: *on the verge of the city's industrial section.* **2.** The point beyond which an action, a state, or a condition is likely to begin or occur: *on the verge of tears.* —*intr.v.* **verged, verg•ing, verg•es.** [*on*] To approach sthg. specified; come close: *strong interest verging on excitement.*

ver•i•fi•ca•tion (vĕr′ə fĭ kā′shən) *n.* [U] The act of finding or confirming the truth: *The bank needed verification of my address.*

ver•i•fy (vĕr′ə fī′) *tr.v.* **ver•i•fied, ver•i•fy•ing, ver•i•fies.** **1.** To prove the truth of (sthg.) by presenting evidence: *Astronomers have verified certain findings of the ancient Greeks.* **2.** To test the truth or accuracy of (sthg.): *verify his address.*

ver•i•ta•ble (vĕr′ĭ tə bəl) *adj. Formal.* Real or genuine: *a veritable success.*

ver•mil•ion also **ver•mil•lion** (vər mĭl′yən) *n.* [U] **1.** A bright red substance, used as a pigment. **2.** A vivid reddish orange color. —*adj.* Vivid reddish orange.

ver•min (vûr′mĭn) *n., pl.* **vermin. 1.** Small animals or insects, such as rats or cockroaches, that are destructive, annoying, or hazardous to one's health. **2.** A troublesome, nasty person. **3.** A group of such people. —**ver′min•ous** *adj.*

ver•mouth (vər mōōth′) *n.* [U] A sweet or dry wine flavored with herbs and used in mixed drinks and cooking.

ver•nac•u•lar (vər năk′yə lər) *n.* **1.** The ordinary spoken language of a country or area as distinct from the language taught in schools. **2.** The special language of a particular trade or profession: *the medical vernacular.* —*adj.* Commonly spoken by the members of a country or region.

ver•sa•tile (vûr′sə təl *or* vûr′sə tīl′) *adj.* **1.** Capable of doing many things well: *A versatile cook can make a wide variety of dishes.* **2.** With varied uses or functions: *a versatile piece of machinery.* —**ver′sa•til′i•ty** (vûr′sə tĭl′ĭ tē) *n.* [U]

verse (vûrs) *n.* **1.** [C] One line of poetry. **2.** [C] A stanza of a long poem or hymn: *Sing the next verse.* **3.** [U] The art or work of a poet; poetry: *She writes verse.*

versed (vûrst) *adj.* Skilled or knowledgeable in a certain area: *versed in foreign languages.*

ver•sion (vûr′zhən) *n.* **1.** A description of an event from a specific point of view: *His version of the accident disagreed with mine.* **2.** A translation of a written work: *an English version of a French story.* **3.** A form based on an earlier or original type: *a reworked version of the Ford Mustang.* **4.** An adaptation of a work of art into another medium: *the movie version of a play.*

ver•sus (vûr′səs *or* vûr′səz) *prep.* **1.** Against: *good versus evil.* **2.** As an alternative to or in contrast with: *studying to be a chemist versus working on a farm.*

vert. *abbr.* An abbreviation of vertical.

ver•te•bra (vûr′tə brə) *n., pl.* **ver•te•brae** (vûr′tə brā′) *or* **ver•te•bras.** The bones or segments of the spinal column.

ver•te•bral (vûr′tə brəl) *adj.* **1.** Relating to a vertebra. **2.** Made up of vertebrae: *the vertebral column.*

ver•te•brate (vûr′tə brĭt *or* vûr′tə brāt′) *adj.* **1.** With a backbone: *vertebrate animals.* **2.** Characteristic of a vertebrate or vertebrates: *the vertebrate brain.* —*n.* Any of a large group of animals with a backbone, including the fishes, amphibians, reptiles, birds, and mammals.

ver•tex (vûr′tĕks′) *n., pl.* **ver•tex•es** *or* **ver•ti•ces** (vûr′tĭ sēz′). **1.** *Formal.* The highest point of sthg.; the apex or summit. **2.a.** The point at which the sides of an angle intersect. **b.** The point of a triangle, a cone, or a pyramid that is opposite to and farthest away from its base.

ver•ti•cal (vûr′tĭ-kəl) *adj.* At right angles to the horizon; directly upright: *Hold the ruler in a vertical position.* —*n.* **1.** Something vertical, as a line or plane. **2.** A vertical position: *a post that leans slightly from the vertical.* —**ver′ti•cal•ly** *adv.*

vertical

ver•ti•go (vûr′tĭ gō′) *n.* [U] The sensation of dizziness caused by heights.

verve (vûrv) *n.* [U] Energy and enthusiasm: *His singing lacks verve.*

ver•y (vĕr′ē) *adv.* **1.** In a high degree; extremely: *feeling very happy.* **2.** Truly; absolutely: *the very best advice.* —*adj.* **1.** Absolute; utter: *the very end of the day.* **2.** Identical: *the very dress we saw yesterday.* **3.** Used to emphasize the importance of the thing described: *The very mountains crumbled.* **4.** Precise: *the very center of town.* **5.** Mere: *The very thought is frightening.* **6.** Actual: *He was caught in the very act of stealing.*

very high frequency *n.* [U] A radio-wave frequency of between 30 and 300 megahertz; VHF.

ves•sel (vĕs′əl) *n.* **1.** A hollow container, such as a bowl, pitcher, or tank, used to hold liquids. **2.** A large boat: *a sailing vessel.* **3.** A narrow tubular body part or plant part through which a fluid flows: *Veins and arteries are vessels.*

vest (vĕst) *n.* **1.** A sleeveless garment usually worn over a shirt. **2.** A sleeveless protective garment extending to the waist: *a bulletproof vest; a life vest.* —*tr.v.* To place (authority or power) in the control of a person or group: *The U.S. Constitution vests power in the President, Congress, and the Supreme Court.*

vest•ed (vĕs′tĭd) *adj.* Legally settled, absolute: *a vested right to the throne.*

vested interest *n.* A strong reason for wanting sthg. to happen: *She has a vested interest in his career.*

ves•ti•bule (vĕs′tə byoōl′) *n.* **1.** A small entrance hall or lobby. **2.** An enclosed area at the end of a railroad passenger car.

ves•tige (vĕs′tĭj) *n. Formal.* A visible trace or sign of sthg. that once existed: *barely a vestige of color left in the old curtains.* —**ves•tig′i•al** (vĕ stĭj′ē əl) *adj.*

vest•ment (vĕst′mənt) *n.* A garment, especially a robe, gown, or other article of dress, worn as an indication of office or by a cleric at a religious service.

vet (vĕt) *n. Informal.* **1.** A veterinarian. **2.** A veteran.

vet. *abbr.* An abbreviation of veteran.

vet•er•an (vĕt′ər ən *or* vĕt′rən) *n.* **1.** A person who has a lot of experience in a profession or other activity. **2.** A person who has served in the armed forces, especially in a war: *a veteran of the Vietnam War.*

Vet•er•ans Day (vĕt′ər ənz *or* vĕt′rənz) *n.* November 11, observed in honor of veterans of the armed services in the United States.

vet•er•i•nar•i•an (vĕt′ər ə nâr′ē ən *or* vĕt′rə nâr′ē ən) *n.* A doctor specially trained to give medical treatment to animals.

vet•er•i•nar•y (vĕt′ər ə nĕr′ē *or* vĕt′rə-nĕr′ē) *adj.* Relating to the medical treatment, diseases, or injuries of animals: *a veterinary college.*

ve•to (vē′tō) *n., pl.* **ve•toes.** [C; U] **1.a.** The power of a branch of government to reject a bill that has been passed: *The President has the right of veto.* **b.** Exercise of this right. **2.** The act of preventing sthg. from happening. —*tr.v.* **ve•toed, ve•to•ing, ve•toes.** **1.** To prevent (a bill) from becoming law by exercising the power of veto: *The governor vetoed the new bill.* **2.** To forbid or prohibit (sthg.): *The board vetoed all wage increases.*

vex (vĕks) *tr.v.* **1.** To irritate or annoy (sbdy.): *The father was vexed by the child's complaints.* **2.** To cause (sbdy.) to be confused; puzzle: *We were vexed by the problem.*

vex•a•tion (vĕk sā′shən) *n.* **1.** [U] The act of vexing or the condition of being vexed. **2.** [C] A source of irritation or annoyance.

vhf or **VHF** *abbr.* An abbreviation of very high frequency.

vi•a (vī′ə *or* vē′ə) *prep.* **1.** By way of: *going to Washington via New York.* **2.** By means of: *I sent the letter via airmail.*

vi•a•ble (vī′ə bəl) *adj.* **1.** Capable of continuing to live, grow, or develop: *viable seeds; a viable plan.* **2.** Capable of success: *a viable national economy.* —**vi′a•bil′i•ty** *n.* [U]

vi•a•duct (vī′ə dŭkt′) *n.* A bridge or series of bridges used to carry a road or railroad over a wide valley or other roads or railroads.

vi•al (vī′əl) *n.* A small glass container used for holding liquids: *a vial of perfume.*

vibe (vīb) *n. (usually plural). Informal.* A good or bad feeling given off by a person, place, or event: *They were getting good vibes about the party.*

vi•brant (vī′brənt) *adj.* **1.** Full of life; exciting: *a vibrant personality.* **2.** Very colorful: *a vibrant sunset.*

vi•brate (vī′brāt) *intr. & tr.v.* **vi•brat•ed, vi•brat•ing, vi•brates.** To move or cause to move back and forth rapidly: *The car is vibrating a lot. He vibrated a guitar string.*

vi·bra·tion (vī brā′shən) *n.* **1.** [U] **a.** The act of vibrating. **b.** The condition of being vibrated. **2.** [C] A rapid motion of a particle or an elastic solid back and forth in a straight line on both sides of a center position.

vi·bra·tor (vī′brā′tər) *n.* **1.** Something that vibrates. **2.** An electrical device used for massage.

vic·ar (vĭk′ər) *n.* A priest in charge of a local church.

vic·ar·age (vĭk′ər ĭj) *n.* **1.** [C] The home of a vicar. **2.** [U] The duties of a vicar.

vi·car·i·ous (vī kâr′ē əs *or* vī kăr′ē əs) *adj.* Felt or understood through another person's experience: *Reading about his adventures gave me vicarious pleasure.* — **vi·car′i· ous·ly** *adv.*

vice[1] (vīs) *n.* **1.** [U] Evil or immoral behavior: *a life of vice.* **2.** [C] A bad habit: *Smoking is my only vice.*

HOMONYMS: vice, vise (tool).

vice[2] (vīs) *n.* Variant of **vise.**

vice pres·i·dent *or* **vice-pres·i·dent** (vīs′-prĕz′ĭ dənt) *n.* An officer just below a president who has authority to take the president's place in case of absence, illness, or death. — **vice′-pres′i·den·cy** *n.* [U]

vi·ce ver·sa (vī′sə vûr′sə *or* vīs′ vûr′sə) *adv.* The same but in the opposite order: *She loves her daughter and vice versa.*

vi·cin·i·ty (vĭ sĭn′ĭ tē) *n.* [U] **1.** A nearby or surrounding region or place: *I live in the vicinity of the airport.* **2.** An approximate degree or amount: *houses priced in the vicinity of $100,000.*

vi·cious (vĭsh′əs) *adj.* **1.** Harmful; violent: *a vicious dog.* **2.** Intended to hurt a person's feelings: *a vicious comment.* **3.** Very strong or intense: *a vicious headache.* ◆ **vicious cir·cle.** A situation in which the solution of one problem creates a new problem and increases the difficulty of solving the original problem: *Quitting a nervous habit such as smoking can be a vicious circle.* — **vi′cious·ly** *adv.*

vic·tim (vĭk′tĭm) *n.* **1.** A person who is harmed or killed by another person or by an act, an agency, or a condition: *the victim of a burglar; the victims of an epidemic.* **2.** A person who is tricked, swindled, or taken advantage of: *a victim of fraud.*

vic·tim·ize (vĭk′tə mīz′) *tr.v.* **vic·tim·ized, vic·tim·iz·ing, vic·tim·iz·es.** To cause (sbdy.) to become a victim: *She felt victimized by her family.*

vic·tor (vĭk′tər) *n.* The winner in a fight, battle, contest, or struggle: *The victors celebrated the win by throwing water on the coach.*

Vic·to·ri·an (vĭk tôr′ē ən) *adj.* Relating to or belonging to the period of the reign of Queen Victoria of England from 1837 to 1905: *a Victorian novel; a Victorian house.*

vic·to·ri·ous (vĭk tôr′ē əs) *adj.* **1.** Being the winner in a contest or fight: *the victorious team.* **2.** Expressing a sense of victory: *a victorious cheer.* — **vic·to′ri·ous·ly** *adv.*

vic·to·ry (vĭk′tə rē) *n., pl.* **vic·to·ries.** [C; U] **1.** Defeat of an opponent or enemy: *victory over the opposing team.* **2.** Success in a struggle against difficulties: *victory in the battle against poverty.*

vid·e·o (vĭd′ē ō′) *n., pl.* **vid·e·os. 1.** [U] The visual part of a broadcast: *The sound was clear, but the video wasn't.* **2.** [C] A videocassette or videotape: *Let's watch a video.*

vid·e·o·cas·sette (vĭd′ē ō kə sĕt′) *n.* A cassette with blank or prerecorded videotape.

vid·e·o·disk *also* **vid·e·o·disc** (vĭd′ē ō-dĭsk′) *n.* A recording of a movie or TV show on an optical disk that is shown using a disk player attached to a TV set.

video game *n.* A computer game played by manipulating images on a video screen.

vid·e·o·tape (vĭd′ē ō tāp′) *n.* [C; U] A relatively wide magnetic tape used to record visual images and sound for later playback. — *tr.v.* **vid·e·o·taped, vid·e·o·tap·ing, vid·e·o·tapes.** To record (sthg.) on videotape: *videotape a wedding.*

videocassette recorder *n.* A VCR.

videotape recorder *n.* A device for making a videotape recording.

vie (vī) *intr.v.* **vied, vy·ing** (vī′ĭng), **vies.** [*for*] To try to win; compete: *Three teams vied for the national championship.*

view (vyōō) *n.* **1.** [C] An opinion; a personal perception: *her views on education.* **2.** [U] Range or field of sight: *The airplane disappeared from view.* **3.** [C] A scene; a vista: *the view from the top of the mountain.* **4.** [C] A way of showing sthg., from a particular position or angle: *a side view of the house.* — *tr.v.* **1.** To look at (sthg.); watch: *I viewed the stars through a telescope.* See Synonyms at **see**[1]. **2.** To examine or inspect (sthg.): *We viewed the house three times before buying it.* **3.** To regard (sbdy./sthg.); consider: *The president viewed the man as an enemy.* ◆ **in view of.** Taking into account; in consideration of: *In view of the difficulties he has had in his present job, he should not be hired.* **on view.** Placed so as to be seen; exhibited: *The photographs will be on view through next month.* **with a view to.** With the goal of: *They are saving money with a view to buying a house.*

view·er (vyōō′ər) *n.* **1.** A person who views sthg., especially a spectator: *television viewers.* **2.** A device that magnifies a picture so that it is easier to see.

view·find·er (vyōō′fīn′dər) *n.* The part of the camera one looks through while taking a picture.

view·point (vyōō′point′) *n.* An attitude or opinion: *He wants to hear your viewpoint, even though he may disagree with it.*

V

vig·il (vĭj′əl) *n.* [C; U] A period of silent watching or waiting: *a vigil at the bedside of her sick friend.*

vig·i·lance (vĭj′ə ləns) *n.* [U] Alert watchfulness: *Her vigilance had saved the baby from harm.*

vig·i·lant (vĭj′ə lənt) *adj.* Aware of what is happening; watchful: *vigilant parents.* **—vig′·i·lant·ly** *adv.*

vig·i·lan·te (vĭj′ə lăn′tē) *n.* A member of a group of people who decide to punish a suspected criminal without the legal right to do so.

vig·or (vĭg′ər) *n.* [U] **1.** Physical or mental energy or strength. **2.** The ability of a plant or animal to survive or grow. **3.** Strong feeling; enthusiasm: *He argued his point with great vigor.*

vig·or·ous (vĭg′ər əs) *adj.* **1.** Strong, energetic, and active: *a nest of vigorous young birds.* **2.** Done with force and energy: *vigorous exercise.* **—vig′or·ous·ly** *adv.*

vig·our (vĭg′ər) *n. Chiefly British.* Variant of **vigor.**

vile (vīl) *adj.* **vil·er, vil·est. 1.** Hateful; disgusting: *vile language.* **2.** Unpleasant or objectionable: *vile weather.* **—vile′ly** *adv.* **—vile′ness** *n.* [U]

vil·i·fy (vĭl′ə fī′) *tr.v.* **vil·i·fied, vil·i·fy·ing, vil·i·fies.** *Formal.* To make extremely negative statements about (sbdy./sthg.): *Even his family vilified his behavior.* **—vil′i·fi·ca′tion** (vĭl′ə fĭ kā′shən) *n.* [U]

vil·la (vĭl′ə) *n.* A large and luxurious country house.

vil·lage (vĭl′ĭj) *n.* **1.** A very small town: *a peaceful village.* **2.** The people who live in a village: *The entire village welcomed the newcomers.*

vil·lag·er (vĭl′ə jər) *n.* A person who lives in a village.

vil·lain (vĭl′ən) *n.* An evil person, especially the person opposite the hero in a drama: *He always plays the villain.*

vil·lain·ous (vĭl′ə nəs) *adj.* Appropriate to a villain, as in wickedness: *a villainous plot.*

vim (vĭm) *n.* [U] Liveliness and energy; enthusiasm: *full of vim and vigor.*

vin·ai·grette (vĭn′ĭ grĕt′) *n.* [U] A sauce or salad dressing of oil and vinegar.

vin·di·cate (vĭn′dĭ kāt′) *tr.v.* **vin·di·cat·ed, vin·di·cat·ing, vin·di·cates. 1.** To clear (sbdy.) of blame, suspicion, or doubt: *The jury vindicated him.* **2.** To justify or support (sthg.): *vindicate his claim to the money.*

vin·dic·tive (vĭn dĭk′tĭv) *adj.* Having or showing a desire for revenge; vengeful: *He was vindictive after his firing.* **—vin·dic′·tive·ly** *adv.* **—vin·dic′tive·ness** *n.* [U]

vine (vīn) *n.* A plant with a stem that climbs on sthg. for support: *a grape vine.*

vin·e·gar (vĭn′ĭ gər) *n.* [C; U] A liquid with an acid taste, often made from grapes or apples, used to flavor and preserve food: *I'll have oil and vinegar on my salad.*

vin·e·gar·y (vĭn′ĭ gə rē *or* vĭn′ĭ grē) also **vin·e·gar·ish** (vĭn′ĭ gər ĭsh *or* vĭn′ĭ grĭsh) *adj.* **1.** With the taste or smell of vinegar. **2.** Unpleasant.

vine·yard (vĭn′yərd) *n.* A place where grapes are grown.

vin·tage (vĭn′tĭj) *n.* **1.** [C; U] The wine produced by a particular vineyard or district in a single season. **2.** [C] The year in which a wine is bottled. **3.** [C; U] *Informal.* A year or period of origin: *He drives a car of 1950 vintage.* **—adj. 1.** Relating to a wine vintage. **2.** Old and of high quality; classic: *a vintage car.*

vi·nyl (vī′nəl) *n.* [U] A tough, flexible, shiny plastic, often used in upholstery and clothing.

vi·o·la (vē ō′lə) *n.* A stringed instrument of the violin family, slightly larger than a violin. **—vi·o′list** *n.*

vi·o·late (vī′ə lāt′) *tr.v.* **vi·o·lat·ed, vi·o·lat·ing, vi·o·lates. 1.** To break or disregard (sthg.): *violate a law; violate a promise.* **2.** To do harm to (sthg. sacred or highly respected); desecrate or defile: *violate a shrine.* **3.** To assault (sbdy.) sexually. **4.** To disturb rudely or interrupt (sthg.): *You violated his privacy.*

vi·o·la·tion (vī′ə lā′shən) *n.* [C; U] The act or an instance of violating or the condition of being violated: *the violation of a peace treaty; a traffic violation.*

vi·o·lence (vī′ə ləns) *n.* [U] **1.** Physical force used for the purpose of causing damage or injury: *crimes of violence.* **2.** Great force or intensity: *the violence of a hurricane.* **3.** An act of violent action or behavior: *protests that have led to violence.*

vi·o·lent (vī′ə lənt) *adj.* **1.** Acting with great physical force: *a violent attack.* **2.** With great emotional force: *a violent scream.* **3.** Very intense or strong: *a violent storm.* **4.** Caused by unexpected force or injury rather than by natural causes: *a violent death.* **—vi′o·lent·ly** *adv.*

vi·o·let (vī′ə lĭt) *n.* **1.** [C] A low-growing plant with flowers that are usually bluish purple but are sometimes yellow or white. **2.** [U] A bluish purple color. **—adj.** Bluish purple.

vi·o·lin (vī′ə lĭn′) *n.* A musical instrument with four strings that is held under the chin and played with a bow. **—vi′o·lin′ist** *n.*

violin

VIP (vē′ī pē′) *n.*, *pl.* **VIPs.** *Informal.* A very important person: *The VIPs arrived at the White House in limousines.*

vi·per (vī′pər) *n.* **1.** A small poisonous snake of northern Europe and Asia. **2.** A person regarded as wicked or hateful.

vi·ral (vī′rəl) *adj.* Relating to or caused by a virus: *viral diseases.*

vir·gin (vûr′jĭn) *n.* A person who has not had sexual intercourse. —*adj.* **1.** Relating to or being a virgin. **2.** Pure and natural; untouched: *virgin snow.* **3.** Unused, uncultivated, or unexplored: *virgin forests.*

vir·gin·al (vûr′jə nəl) *adj.* Relating to or appropriate to a virgin: *virginal modesty.*

vir·gin·i·ty (vər jĭn′ĭ tē) *n.* [U] The quality or condition of being a virgin.

Vir·go (vûr′gō) *n.* **1.** [U] The sixth sign of the zodiac in astrology, represented by a virgin. **2.** [C] A person born under this sign, between August 23 and September 22.

vir·ile (vîr′əl *or* vîr′īl′) *adj.* **1.** With the characteristics of an adult male. **2.** Showing masculine spirit, strength, vigor, or power. **3.** Able to perform sexually as a male. —**vi·ril′i·ty** (və rĭl′ĭ tē) *n.* [U]

vir·tu·al (vûr′choo əl) *adj.* Existing in effect but not in actual fact: *The book described the virtual extinction of the buffalo. After the rain, the lawn was a virtual lake.*

vir·tu·al·ly (vûr′choo ə lē) *adv.* **1.** In fact or for all practical purposes; almost completely: *The city was virtually paralyzed by the storm.* **2.** Almost but not quite; nearly: *Virtually every household has a TV these days.*

virtual reality *n.* [U] Computer technology that allows the user to experience a program as if the user were really in that environment.

vir·tue (vûr′choo) *n.* **1.a.** [U] Moral goodness: *a man of virtue.* **b.** [C] A particular example or kind of moral excellence: *the virtue of patience.* **2.** [C; U] A particularly beneficial quality; an advantage: *a plan with the virtue of being practical.* **3.** [C] Power; ability to produce a definite result: *believing in the virtue of vitamins to fight colds.* ◆ **by virtue of.** By reason of: *She has the reputation of being a great writer by virtue of her prize-winning books.*

vir·tu·os·i·ty (vûr′choo ŏs′ĭ tē) *n.* [U] A high level of technical skill or style.

vir·tu·o·so (vûr′choo ō′sō) *n.*, *pl.* **vir·tu·o·sos. 1.** A musical performer with great ability. **2.** A person of great skill or technique in the arts. —*adj.* Showing the ability, technique, or personal style of a virtuoso: *a virtuoso performance.*

vir·tu·ous (vûr′choo əs) *adj.* Showing great virtue, especially moral excellence: *virtuous behavior.* —**vir′tu·ous·ly** *adv.*

vir·u·lent (vîr′yə lənt *or* vîr′ə lənt) *adj.* **1.** Extremely infectious, malignant, or poison-

ous, as a disease: *a virulent form of cancer.* **2.** Very harsh or bitter: *virulent criticism.* —**vir′u·lence, vir′u·len·cy** *n.* [U]

vi·rus (vī′rəs) *n.* Any of various very small disease-producing particles that can infect plants and animals: *Viruses are smaller than bacteria.*

vi·sa (vē′zə) *n.* A document or stamp placed in a passport giving sbdy. permission to enter or leave a country: *a visa for Japan.*

vis·age (vĭz′ĭj) *n.* *Formal.* **1.** The face or facial expression of a person: *a stern visage.* **2.** Appearance: *the green visage of spring.*

vis·cos·i·ty (vĭ skŏs′ĭ tē) *n.* [U] **1.** The condition or property of being viscous. **2.** The degree to which a fluid resists flow when pressure is applied to it.

vis·cous (vĭs′kəs) *adj.* Tending to resist flow when pressure is applied, as a fluid; having a high viscosity: *Oil is highly viscous.*

vise also **vice** (vīs) *n.* A clamping device consisting of a pair of jaws that are opened and closed, used in carpentry or metalworking to hold an object so that it can be worked on.

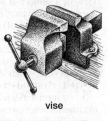

vise

HOMONYMS: vise, vice (evil behavior, tool).

vis·i·bil·i·ty (vĭz′ə bĭl′ĭ tē) *n.* [U] **1.** The fact or degree of being visible: *a celebrity with a lot of visibility.* **2.** The greatest distance one can see under given weather conditions: *Visibility during the storm was 100 feet.*

vis·i·ble (vĭz′ə bəl) *adj.* **1.** Possible to see: *a visible change of expression on her face.* **2.** Easily noticed; clear: *no visible solution to the problem.* —**vis′i·bly** *adv.*

vi·sion (vĭzh′ən) *n.* **1.** [U] The sense of sight; eyesight: *I have 20/20 vision.* **2.** [U] Unusual intelligence and foresight: *a leader of vision.* **3.** [C] A mental picture produced by the imagination: *having visions of warm summer days.* **4.** [C] The experience of seeing a supernatural being: *a vision of a ghost.* **5.** [C] A person or thing of great beauty: *The mountains were a vision of newly fallen snow.*

vi·sion·ar·y (vĭzh′ə nĕr′ē) *adj.* Characterized by vision or foresight: *visionary ideas for the future.* **2.** Marked by apparitions, prophecies, or revelations. —*n.*, *pl.* **vi·sion·ar·ies. 1.** A person who has ideas of what the future will be: *a great visionary.* **2.** A person who has visions; a seer.

vis·it (vĭz′ĭt) *v.* —*tr.* **1.** To go to see (sbdy.) for business or pleasure: *visit a dentist; visit one's family.* **2.** To spend time at (a place): *visiting Chicago over the weekend.* **3.** To stay with (sbdy.) as a guest: *visiting his former* *classmate in California.* —*intr.* **1.** To make a visit: *We were just visiting.* **2.** To have a talk: *I hope you'll be able to stay and visit.* —*n.* The act of visiting; a brief call or stay: *They paid us a visit.*

vis•i•ta•tion (vĭz′ĭ tā′shən) *n.* [U] *Formal.* The act of visiting, especially an official visit for the purpose of inspection or examination: *a visitation by state inspectors; visitation rights for parents separated from their children by divorce.*

vis•i•tor (vĭz′ĭ tər) *n.* A person who visits: *The United States has many foreign visitors.*

vi•sor also **vi•zor** (vī′zər) *n.* **1.** A piece on the front of a cap to shade and protect the eyes. **2.** A shield against direct sunlight attached above the windshield of an automobile.

vis•ta (vĭs′tə) *n.* **1.** A distant view, especially one seen through an opening between buildings or trees: *a waterfront vista.* **2.** A broad mental view of a subject: *a scientific discovery that opens up new vistas of human improvement.*

vi•su•al (vĭzh′ōō əl) *adj.* **1.** Relating to the sense of sight: *the visual arts such as painting and photography.* **2.** Able to be seen by the eye; visible: *visual information.*

vi•su•al•ize (vĭzh′ōō ə līz′) *v.* **vi•su•al•ized, vi•su•al•iz•ing, vi•su•al•iz•es.** —*tr.* To form a mental picture of (sthg.): *Try to visualize what our new house will look like.* —*intr.* To form a mental picture. —**vi•su•al•i•za′tion** (vĭzh′ōō ə lĭ zā′shən) *n.* [C; U]

vi•ta (vī′tə *or* vē′tə) *n., pl.* **vi•tae** (vī′tē *or* vē′tī). A short listing of one's education and work experience, used when looking for a job.

vi•tal (vīt′l) *adj.* **1.** Relating to life: *vital processes; vital signs.* **2.** Necessary to the continuation of life: *vital organs; vital functions.* **3.** Having great importance; essential: *Sleep is vital to good health.* **4.** Full of life; animated: *a vital senior citizen.* —**vi′tal•ly** *adv.*

vi•tal•i•ty (vī tăl′ĭ tē) *n.* [U] **1.** The capacity to live, grow, or develop. **2.** Physical or mental vigor; energy: *He has the vitality of a much younger man.* **3.** Power to survive: *the vitality of an old tradition.*

vital statistics *pl.n.* Facts about a person, such as one's sex, age, race, and marital status, especially for official records.

vi•ta•min (vī′tə mĭn) *n.* Any of various complex organic compounds that are needed in small amounts for normal growth and activity of the body and are found naturally in foods obtained from plants and animals: *Oranges contain vitamin C.*

vit•re•ous (vĭt′rē əs) *adj.* Relating to or resembling glass; glassy: *brick containing vitreous matter.*

vit•ri•ol•ic (vĭt′rē ŏl′ĭk) *adj.* *Formal.* Bitterly scathing; cruel: *a vitriolic remark.*

vi•va•cious (vĭ vā′shəs *or* vī vā′shəs) *adj.* Full of life; lively: *a charming and vivacious host.* —**vi•va′cious•ly** *adv.* —**vi•vac′i•ty** (vĭ văs′ĭ tē *or* vī văs′ĭ tē) *n.* [U]

viv•id (vĭv′ĭd) *adj.* **1.** Bright and distinct; brilliant: *a vivid star.* **2.** With bright color or colors: *a vivid sunset; a vivid blue.* **3.** Causing clear images within the mind: *a vivid description.* —**viv′id•ness** *n.* [U]

viv•i•sec•tion (vĭv′ĭ sĕk′shən *or* vĭv′ĭ sĕk′shən) *n.* [U] The act or practice of cutting into or dissecting a living animal, especially for scientific research.

vix•en (vĭk′sən) *n.* **1.** A female fox. **2.** An outdated term for a sharp-tempered or quarrelsome woman.

vi•zor (vī′zər) *n.* Variant of **visor.**

vo•cab•u•lar•y (vō kăb′yə lĕr′ē) *n., pl.* **vo•cab•u•lar•ies.** [C; U] **1.** All the words of a language. **2.** The total number of words used by or understood by a particular person or group: *a writer who uses a very rich vocabulary; the vocabulary of economics.*

vo•cal (vō′kəl) *adj.* **1.** Relating to or produced by the voice: *vocal quality; vocal organs.* **2.** Relating to singing: *vocal music; vocal group.* **3.** Tending to speak often and freely; outspoken: *He is very vocal in his opposition to new taxes.* —**vo′cal•ly** *adv.*

vocal cords *pl.n.* Muscles in the throat that produce sound as air passes through them.

vo•cal•ic (vō kăl′ĭk) *adj.* Relating to or having the nature of a vowel.

vo•cal•ist (vō′kə lĭst) *n.* A singer.

vo•cal•ize (vō′kə līz) *v.* **vo•cal•ized, vo•cal•iz•ing, vo•cal•iz•es.** —*tr.* **1.** To produce (sthg.) with the voice. **2.** To say (what one is thinking): *vocalize a popular opinion.* —*intr.* **1.** To use the voice: *The baby has begun to vocalize.* **2.** To sing: *singers vocalizing before a performance.* —**vo′cal•i•za′tion** (vō′kə lĭ zā′shən) *n.* [C; U]

vo•ca•tion (vō kā′shən) *n.* [C; U] **1.** A profession or an occupation, especially one for which a person is well qualified: *plans to make medicine her vocation.* **2.** A strong desire to do a particular type of work; a calling: *Her vocation led her to become a minister.* —**vo•ca′tion•al** *adj.*

vocational school *n.* A school that offers training in skilled trades such as mechanics, plumbing, carpentry, and construction; a trade school.

vo•cif•er•ous (vō sĭf′ər əs) *adj.* Noisy and demanding: *a vociferous crowd; vociferous protests.* —**vo•cif′er•ous•ly** *adv.*

vod•ka (vŏd′kə) *n.* [U] An alcoholic liquor originally made from wheat, but now also made from rye, corn, or potatoes.

vogue (vōg) *n.* **1.** The current fashion or style: *the colors currently in vogue.* **2.** Popular acceptance; popularity: *His novels enjoyed a great vogue in the 1930s.*

voice (vois) *n.* **1.** [C; U] **a.** The sound produced by the vocal organs of a human. **b.** The ability to produce such sounds: *He caught a bad cold and lost his voice.* **2.** [C; U] The condition or quality of a person's vocal sound: *a baritone in excellent voice; a hoarse voice from coughing.* **3.** [U] Expression of feelings or thoughts: *give voice to one's feelings.* **4.** [U] The right or opportunity to express a choice or opinion: *The children had no voice in deciding where to spend their vacation.* **5.** [U] In grammar, a property of a verb that indicates the relation between the subject and the action expressed by the verb. English has two voices, active and passive. —*tr.v.* **voiced, voic•ing, voic•es. 1.** To express (sthg.) in words: *She had a chance to voice her feelings.* **2.** To pronounce (sthg.) with vibration of the vocal cords: *Make sure to voice the first consonant.* ♦ **with one voice.** In complete agreement; unanimously: *Our group rejected the contract with one voice.*

voiced (voist) *adj.* **1.** Having a voice or a specific kind of voice: *a soft-voiced person.* **2.** Pronounced with vibration of the vocal cords, as the consonants *b* and *d.*

voice•less (vois′lĭs) *adj.* **1.** Without a voice; mute. **2.** Pronounced without vibration of the vocal cords, as the consonants *p* and *t.*

voice mail *n.* [U] A system in which telephone callers leave recorded messages that the people being called can listen to at a later time.

voice•o•ver (vois′ō′vər) *n.* In films and television, the words spoken by sbdy. who does not appear on screen.

void (void) *adj.* **1.** Containing nothing; empty: *a void area.* See Synonyms at **empty. 2.** Completely lacking: *void of all fear.* **3.** With no legal force or validity: *The judge declared the contract void.* —*n.* **1.** An empty space; a vacuum: *the void of outer space.* **2.** An empty feeling, as of sadness: *His death left a void.* —*tr.v.* **1.** *Formal.* To pass body wastes from (the bladder or bowels). **2.** To make (sthg.) invalid; invalidate: *void an old passport; void a sale.*

vol. *abbr.* An abbreviation of volume.

vol•a•tile (vŏl′ə tl *or* vŏl′ə tīl′) *adj.* **1.** Changing to vapor easily at normal temperatures: *Gasoline is a volatile substance.* **2.** Changeable; fickle: *the volatile preferences of the public.* **3.** Tending to become violent; explosive: *a volatile political situation.* —**vol′a•til′i•ty** (vŏl′ə tĭl′ĭ tē) *n.* [U]

vol•can•ic (vŏl kăn′ĭk *or* vôl kăn′ĭk) *adj.* **1.** Caused by or produced by a volcano: *volcanic eruptions; volcanic rock.* **2.** Powerfully explosive: *a volcanic temper.*

vol•ca•no (vŏl kā′nō) *n., pl.* **vol•ca•noes** or

vol•ca•nos. 1. An opening in the surface of the earth from which molten rock, dust, ash, and hot gases flow or are thrown out. **2.** A mountain formed by this action.

vo•li•tion (və lĭsh′ən) *n.* [U] Conscious choice or decision: *He left of his own volition.*

vol•ley (vŏl′ē) *n., pl.* **vol•leys. 1.** A series of bullets shot at the same time. **2.** A bursting forth of many things together: *a volley of questions.* **3.** In sports, especially tennis, a shot made by hitting the ball before it touches the ground. —*v.* —*tr.* **1.** To shoot (sthg.) out in a volley: *Reporters volleyed questions at the speaker.* **2.** To hit (a tennis ball, for example) before it touches the ground: *My partner volleyed the ball.* —*intr.* **1.** To be shot out in a volley. **2.** To make a volley, especially in tennis: *They volleyed back and forth.*

vol•ley•ball (vŏl′ē bôl′) *n.* **1.** [U] A game played by two teams on a rectangular court divided by a high net, in which a ball is hit back and forth over the net with the hands. **2.** [C] The ball used in this game.

volt (vōlt) *n.* A unit of electrical force, used to measure the flow of current: *a 12-volt battery.*

volt•age (vōl′tĭj) *n.* [C; U] Electrical force expressed in volts: *High-voltage lines carry electrical power over long distances.*

vol•ta•ic (vŏl tā′ĭk) *adj.* **1.** Relating to electricity that is produced by a chemical action. **2.** Producing electricity by chemical action: *a voltaic cell.*

vol•ume (vŏl′yoōm *or* vŏl′yəm) *n.* **1.** [U] The force or intensity of a sound; loudness: *Please lower the volume on the radio!* **2.** [U] Quantity; amount: *a large volume of mail.* **3.** [U] The amount of space occupied by a three-dimensional object: *the volume of a cube.* **4.** [C] A collection of printed sheets bound together into a book: *an encyclopedia published in 16 volumes.*

vo•lu•mi•nous (və loō′mə nəs) *adj.* **1.** With great volume, size, fullness, or number: *a voluminous trunk.* **2.** Filling or capable of filling several books: *a voluminous research project.*

vol•un•tar•y (vŏl′ən tĕr′ē) *adj.* **1.** Acting on one's own free will: *He made a voluntary contribution to his favorite charity.* **2.** Serving willingly and without expectation of reward: *voluntary community work.* **3.** Consciously controlled by an individual: *a voluntary muscle.* —**vol′un•tar′i•ly** (vŏl′ən târ′ə lē) *adv.*

vol•un•teer (vŏl′ən tîr′) *n.* A person who performs a service of his or her own free will, especially a service done without expecting a reward or pay: *hospital volunteers; The teacher asked for volunteers.* —*adj.* Done by volunteers: *volunteer firefighters.* —*v.* —*tr.* To give (sthg.) voluntarily: *She volunteered her services.* —*intr.* **1.** To perform or offer to perform a service of one's own free will: *She often volunteers in class.* **2.** To do charitable or helpful work without pay: *She volunteers at the hospital two days a week.*

vo·lup·tu·ous (və lŭp′chōō əs) *adj.* Suggesting physical or sensual pleasure and luxury: *a voluptuous piece of sculpture.*

vom·it (vŏm′ĭt) *v. —intr.* To eject the contents of the stomach through the mouth. *—tr.* To eject (the contents of the stomach) through the mouth. *—n.* [U] Matter discharged from the stomach by vomiting.

voo·doo (vōō′dōō) *n.* [U] A religion practiced chiefly in Caribbean countries, which includes belief in many deities and is derived from a mixture of African religions and Christianity.

vo·ra·cious (və rā′shəs) *adj.* **1.** Eating or eager to eat great amounts of food: *a voracious appetite.* **2.** Having a large appetite for an activity: *a voracious reader.*

vor·tex (vôr′tĕks′) *n., pl.* **vor·tex·es** or **vor·ti·ces** (vôr′tĭ sēz′). **1.** A powerful circular motion of water or wind that sucks everything near it toward its center. **2.** A place or situation that draws into its center all that surrounds it: *the vortex of war.*

vote (vōt) *n.* **1.** A formal expression of one's decision or choice, made in an election. **2.** *(usually singular).* The number of votes cast in an election: *a heavy vote in favor of the bill.* **3.** *(usually singular).* A group of voters alike in some way: *the labor vote.* **4.** The result of an election. *—v.* **vot·ed, vot·ing, votes.** *—intr.* To express one's preference; cast a vote: *voted early; voted for president.* *—tr.* To express one's preference for (sbdy./sthg.) by vote: *vote the Democratic ticket.*

vot·er (vō′tər) *n.* A person who votes or has the right to vote: *Few voters turned out for the election.*

vouch (vouch) *intr.v.* [*for*] To give a guarantee; supply assurance: *I can vouch for her honesty.*

vouch·er (vou′chər) *n.* A receipt, signed statement, or similar paper that serves as proof that sthg. has been paid for.

vow (vou) *n.* A solemn promise, especially to act in a specified way: *a vow to use his knowledge only for good; take the vows of a nun. —tr.v.* **1.** To promise or pledge (sthg.) solemnly: *She*

vowed that she would return home a success. **2.** To make a pledge or threat to accomplish (sthg.): *vowing revenge on the enemy.*

SYNONYMS: vow, promise, pledge, swear. These verbs all mean to declare solemnly that one will perform or avoid a particular course of action. *He vowed to quit smoking next week. I promise to write back soon. Several countries pledged to obey the ban on whale hunting. She swears she won't tell anyone my secret.*

vow·el (vou′əl) *n.* **1.** A speech sound created by the free passage of the breath through the larynx and mouth, usually forming the most prominent or central part of a syllable. **2.** A letter, such as *a, e, i, o, u,* and sometimes *y,* that represents such a sound.

voy·age (voi′ĭj) *n.* A long journey, especially by sea or through space: *a voyage to Mars. —intr.v.* **voy·aged, voy·ag·ing, voy·ag·es.** To make a voyage: *Explorers voyaged to unknown lands. —voy′ag·er n.*

VP or **V.P.** *abbr.* An abbreviation of vice president.

vs. *abbr.* An abbreviation of versus.

VT also **Vt.** *abbr.* An abbreviation of Vermont.

vul·gar (vŭl′gər) *adj.* Impolite; rude; offensive: *a vulgar joke. —vul′gar·ly adv.*

vul·gar·i·ty (vŭl găr′ĭ tē) *n., pl.* **vul·gar·i·ties.** **1.** [U] The quality of being vulgar. **2.** [C] Something that is impolite or offensive.

vul·ner·a·ble (vŭl′nər ə bəl) *adj.* **1.** Capable of being harmed or injured: *Baby birds are helpless and vulnerable.* **2.** Open to danger and attack; unprotected: *After the army left, the city was once again vulnerable.* **3.** Easily affected, as by persuasion or temptation: *She felt vulnerable to the urge to smoke. —vul′ner·a·bil′i·ty n.* [U] *—vul′ner·a·bly adv.*

vul·ture (vŭl′chər) *n.* **1.** Any of various large birds with dark feathers and a bare head and neck and that feed on dead animals. **2.** A greedy or ruthless person: *Vultures tried to take advantage of the accident victims by promising huge insurance settlements.*

vul·va (vŭl′və) *n.* The external female genital organs.

w or **W** (dŭb′əl yōō or dŭb′əl yōō) n., pl. **w's** or **W's.** The 23rd letter of the English alphabet.
W[1] The symbol for the element **tungsten.**
W[2] abbr. An abbreviation of: **1.** Watt. **2.** West.

wack•y (wăk′ē) adj. **wack•i•er, wack•i•est.** Slang. Crazy; silly: She wore a wacky outfit to the party. —**wack′i•ness** n. [U]

wad (wŏd) n. **1.** A small ball of soft material, often folded or rolled, used for padding, stuffing, or packing: a wad of wool. **2.** Informal. A large roll of paper money: a wad of bank notes. —v. **wad•ded, wad•ding, wads.** ◆ **wad up.** tr.v. [sep.] To squeeze, roll, or crush (sthg.) into a small mass: wad up a sheet of paper.

wad•dle (wŏd′l) intr.v. **wad•dled, wad•dling, wad•dles.** To walk with short steps that move the body from side to side: The ducklings waddled along behind the mother duck. —n. A swaying walk: Penguins walk with a waddle.

wade (wād) v. **wad•ed, wad•ing, wades.** —intr. To walk in or through water or another substance that makes normal movement difficult: We waded along the shore of the lake for hours. —tr. To cross (sthg.) by wading: The child waded the length of the pool. ◆ **wade through.** tr.v. [insep.] To make one's way through (sthg.) slowly and with difficulty: spend the day wading through paperwork.

wa•fer (wā′fər) n. **1.** A small, thin, crisp cookie, biscuit, or candy. **2.** A small thin disk of material on which an integrated circuit can be formed for use in computers.

waf•fle[1] (wŏf′əl) n. A light crisp breakfast cake with an indented surface, similar to a pancake, made by baking batter in a waffle iron.

waf•fle[2] (wŏf′əl) intr.v. **waf•fled, waf•fling, waf•fles.** Informal. To speak or write so as not to give a direct answer: Don't waffle; give me a simple yes or no.

waft (wäft or wăft) v. —tr. To cause (sthg.) to go or move gently through the air or over water: The breeze wafted the fog through the fields. —intr. To float easily and gently, as on the air; drift: The smell of the ocean wafted in when she opened the door. —n. Something, such as a scent, breeze, or sound, carried lightly through the air: a waft of perfume.

wag (wăg) v. **wagged, wag•ging, wags.** —intr. To move, swing, or wave back and forth or up and down: The puppy's tail wagged as we walked in. —tr. To move (a body part) from side to side or up and down, as in playfulness: The puppy wagged its tail eagerly. —n. The act or motion of wagging.

wage (wāj) n. Payment made to a worker for work done; salary or earnings: the minimum wage. —tr.v. **waged, wag•ing, wag•es.** To engage in (a war, for example): The World Health Organization has waged war on disease.

wa•ger (wā′jər) n. A bet: Place your wagers now. —tr. & intr.v. To bet or make a bet: I'll wager $5. Some people like to wager.

wag•gle (wăg′əl) intr. & tr.v. **wag•gled, wag•gling, wag•gles.** To move or cause to move with short quick motions; wag or wiggle: His finger waggled threateningly in front of my nose. The cow waggled her tail at the flies.

wag•on (wăg′ən) n. **1.** A four-wheeled, usually horse-drawn vehicle with a large rectangular body, used to transport loads. **2.** A station wagon. **3.** A child's low four-wheeled cart pulled by a long handle that controls the direction of the front wheels. ◆ **be** or **go on the wagon.** Informal. To stop drinking alcoholic beverages: Her father has been on the wagon for six months.

wagon

waif (wāf) n. A lost or homeless person or animal, especially an orphaned or abandoned child: Hungry waifs begged in the streets.

wail (wāl) intr.v. **1.** To make loud, long sounds of sadness: The crowd wailed for their dead leader. **2.** To make a prolonged sound suggesting a cry: The wind wailed through the trees. —n. A long high-pitched cry or sound: the lonesome wail of a train whistle.

HOMONYMS: wail, whale (sea mammal).

waist (wāst) n. **1.** The middle part of the human body between the bottom of the rib cage and the hips. **2.** The part of a piece of clothing that fits around the waist.

HOMONYMS: waist, waste (spend poorly).

waist•line (wāst′līn′) n. **1.** A line thought of as going around the body at the waist: I don't want to gain weight, so I'm watching my *waistline.* **2.** The point or line at which the skirt and the top of a dress join: *The dress is too tight at the waistline.*

wait (wāt) *v.* —*intr.* **1.** To remain in expectation: *waiting for the guests to arrive.* See Synonyms at **stay¹. 2.** To pause until another person catches up: *Wait for me!* **3.** To remain temporarily undone or postponed: *Dinner will have to wait.* **4.** To work serving tables, as in a restaurant. —*tr.* To remain or stay in expectation of (sthg.); await: *Wait your turn.* —*n.* The act of waiting or a period of time spent in waiting: *a short wait.* ◆ **can't wait (for).** To be eager or excited: *We can't wait for school to start.* **wait in vain.** To wait for sbdy. who doesn't come or sthg. that doesn't happen: *I waited in vain for you to come home.* **wait on** or **upon.** *tr.v.* [insep.] **1.** To serve the needs of (sbdy.): *The tall salesclerk waited on me.* **2.** To await (sbdy./sthg.): *They're waiting on my decision.* **wait on (one) hand and foot.** To serve (sbdy.) in every way: *While I was sick, she waited on me hand and foot.* **wait out.** *tr.v.* [sep.] To wait until (sbdy./ sthg.) has finished: *We thought she'd never stop talking, but we were able to wait her out.* **wait tables.** To work as a waiter or waitress, as at a restaurant: *wait tables to pay for school.* **wait up.** *intr.v.* **1.** To postpone going to bed: *Let's wait up to watch the late show.* **2.** *Informal.* To stop or pause so that another can catch up: *They got too far ahead, so I yelled to them to wait up.*

HOMONYMS: wait, weight (gravity force).

wait•er (wā'tər) *n.* A man who serves at a table, as in a restaurant.

wait•ing list (wā'tĭng) *n.* A list of people waiting, as for a table at a restaurant or for tickets to an event that is sold out.

waiting room *n.* A room, as in a doctor's office, for the use of people waiting.

wait•ress (wā'trĭs) *n.* A woman who serves at a table, as in a restaurant.

waive (wāv) *tr.v.* **waived, waiv•ing, waives. 1.** To give up (a right or claim) by one's own choice: *waive a jury trial.* See Synonyms at **yield. 2.** To set aside or postpone (sthg.): *Let's waive the formalities and start the discussion.*

HOMONYMS: waive, wave (move the hand).

waiv•er (wā'vər) *n.* An official statement giving up a right, claim, or privilege: *She signed a waiver saying she would not sue.*

HOMONYMS: waiver, waver (be uncertain).

wake¹ (wāk) *v.* **woke** (wōk) or **waked** (wākt), **waked** or **wok•en** (wō'kən), **wak•ing,**

wakes. —*intr.* **1.** To stop sleeping; become awake: *I woke before daybreak.* **2.** To remain awake: *Whether he sleeps or wakes, her little brother hugs his teddy bear.* —*tr.* To rouse (sbdy.) from sleep: *Wake me at nine o'clock.* —*n.* A watch or vigil kept over the body of a dead person before the burial: *We attended the wake at a funeral home.* ◆ **wake up.** *tr.v.* [sep.] To rouse (sbdy.) from sleep: *I woke him up early this morning.* —*intr.v.* To stop sleeping: *Wake up! You're late for work!*

USAGE: wake¹ The pairs **wake/waken** and **awake/awaken** have puzzled people for centuries. All four words have similar meanings, though there are some differences in use. **Wake** is more common than **waken** when used together with *up.* **Awake** and **awaken** are never used with *up: She woke up* (rarely *wakened up*; never *awakened up* or *awoke up*). In figurative senses *awake* and *awaken* are more common: *We awoke to the danger. You've awakened my memory.*

wake² (wāk) *n.* **1.** The visible track of waves, ripples, or foam left behind sthg. moving through water: *the wake of a ship.* **2.** The course, track, or condition left behind sthg. that has passed: *The hurricane left destruction in its wake.*

wake•ful (wāk'fəl) *adj.* Not sleeping or without sleep: *a wakeful night.* —**wake'ful• ness** *n.* [U]

wak•en (wā'kən) *v.* —*tr.* **1.** To rouse (sbdy.) from sleep; awake: *Waken me if he calls.* **2.** To stir (sbdy./sthg.), as from an inactive state: *Don't waken the competition to our plans.* —*intr.* To become awake; wake up: *I wakened before dawn.* —SEE NOTE at **wake¹.**

walk (wôk) *v.* —*intr.* **1.** To move over a surface by taking steps with the feet at a pace slower than a run: *The baby is just learning to walk.* **2.** To go or travel on foot: *I walked to school.* **3.** To move in a way that looks like walking: *an astronaut walking in space.* —*tr.* **1.** To pass over, on, or through (sthg.) by walking: *walking the historic section of the city.* **2.** To cause (sbdy./sthg.) to walk or go at a walk: *walk a horse uphill.* **3.** To accompany (sbdy.) on foot: *We walked our sister to the bus stop.* —*n.* **1.** The way of moving of a human or animal in which the feet are lifted alternately with at least one part of a foot always on the ground. **2.** A stroll or journey on foot: *take a walk.* **3.** A pathway or sidewalk on which to walk: *shovel snow off the walk.* **4.** An act, way, or speed of walking: *a slow walk; a brisk walk.* ◆ **all walks of life.** All the many kinds of people in society: *The candidate tried to appeal to people from all walks of life.* **walk all over.** To treat (sbdy.) badly and with a lack of respect: *Why does she let him walk all over her?* **walk away from.** To leave (sbdy./sthg.) completely and permanently: *Can you just walk away from a job you love?* **walk off.** *intr.v.* To leave in anger: *When they didn't get their way, they walked off without a word.* —*tr.v.* [sep.] **1.** To get rid of (sthg. unpleasant, as a feeling or pain) by walking: *I have a cramp, but I'll just walk it off.* **2.** To measure (sthg.) by steps: *I'll walk off the distance from the sidewalk to the front door.* **walk off with** or **walk away with. 1.** To steal (sthg.): *Who walked off with my hammer?* **2.** To win (a competition) easily: *Their school just walked away with the championship.* **walk on air.** To feel very good: *I was walking on air after I heard the good news.* **walk out.** *intr.v.* To leave a place suddenly, often as a signal of disapproval: *She said what she had to say and then walked out.* **walk out on.** To desert or abandon (sbdy./sthg.): *He left a good life when he walked out on her.*

walk•er (wô′kər) *n.* **1.** A person who walks, especially a contestant in a footrace. **2.** A frame used to support sbdy. while walking, as an infant learning to walk or an elderly person.

walk•out (wôk′out′) *n.* A labor strike or protest.

walk•way (wôk′wā′) *n.* A passage or path for walking.

wall (wôl) *n.* **1.** An upright structure of building material that encloses an area or separates two areas from each other. **2.** Something that is like a wall in appearance, function, or construction: *the wall of the stomach.* **3.** Something that is like a wall, as in hiding or dividing sthg.: *a wall of fog; a wall of secrecy.* —*v.* ◆ **climb the walls.** To be frustrated, irritated, or anxious: *She's trying to quit smoking, and it has her climbing the walls.* **drive (one) up the wall.** *Slang.* To irritate or frustrate (sbdy.): *Some kinds of music drive me up the wall.* **off the wall.** *Slang.* **1.** Extremely unconventional; strange: *His outfit is really off the wall.* **2.** Without any basis; ridiculous: *That explanation is really off the wall.* **wall off.** *tr.v.* [sep.] **1.** To divide or separate (sthg.) with or as if with a wall: *wall off compartments.* **2.** To enclose, surround, or fortify (sthg.) with a wall: *wall off a garden.*

wal•let (wŏl′ĭt) *n.* A small flat folding case, usually made of leather, for holding paper money, cards, or photographs; a billfold.

wal•lop (wŏl′əp) *Informal. tr.v.* **1.** To defeat (sbdy./sthg.) thoroughly: *They walloped their opponents.* **2.** To strike (sbdy./sthg.) with a hard blow: *The two boxers walloped each other.* —*n.* A hard blow or the ability to strike such a blow: *That storm really packed a wallop.*

wal•low (wŏl′ō) *intr.v.* **1.** To roll the body about, as in water or mud: *The pig wallowed in the mud.* **2.** To enjoy sthg. in an extreme way: *The millionaire wallowed in luxury.* **3.** To indulge in sthg. in an extreme manner:

Don't wallow in self-pity. —*n.* A pool of water or mud where animals go to wallow.

wall•pa•per (wôl′pā′pər) *n.* [U] Decorative paper used to cover walls. —*tr.v.* To cover (sthg.) with wallpaper: *wallpaper the bedroom.*

wall-to-wall (wôl′tə wôl′) *adj.* **1.** Completely covering a floor: *wall-to-wall carpeting.* **2.** Spreading through or filling an entire area: *wall-to-wall people at the party.*

wal•nut (wôl′nŭt′) *n.* **1.** [C] An edible nut with a hard rough shell. **2.** [U] The hard wood of the trees that bear such nuts.

wal•rus (wôl′rəs *or* wŏl′rəs) *n.* A large sea mammal of arctic regions, related to seals and sea lions and with tough wrinkled skin and large tusks.

waltz (wôlts *or* wôls) *n.* A slow ballroom dance with three beats, or the music for this dance. —*intr.v.* To dance the waltz. ◆ **waltz through.** *tr.v.* [insep.] To get through (sthg.) easily or without much effort: *He never studies; he just waltzes through all his classes.*

wan (wŏn) *adj.* **wan•ner, wan•nest. 1.** Unnaturally pale, as from physical or emotional distress: *a wan face.* **2.** Suggesting weariness, illness, or unhappiness: *a wan smile.* —**wan′ly** *adv.* —**wan′ness** *n.* [U]

wand (wŏnd) *n.* A slender rod or stick, especially one used by a magician.

wan•der (wŏn′dər) *v.* —*intr.* **1.** To move about without a destination or purpose: *wander in the woods on a fall day.* **2.** To go by an indirect route or stroll in a leisurely way: *wander home.* **3.** To follow an irregular winding or rambling course: *The brook wandered through the pasture.* **4.** To move away from a fixed course or topic: *The speaker's dull speech caused my attention to wander. Grandmother's mind wanders now.* —*tr.* To wander across or through (sthg.): *wander the backwoods.* ◆ **wander away** or **off.** *intr.v.* To move away from where one is supposed to be: *The child wandered away when her parents weren't looking.* —**wan′der•er** *n.*

SYNONYMS: wander, ramble, roam, meander. These verbs mean to move about without destination or purpose. **Wander** and **ramble** both mean to move about without a fixed course or goal: *He wandered from room to room looking for something interesting to do. After breakfast we can ramble through the hills.* **Roam** suggests wandering with freedom of movement, especially over a wide area: *Herds of bison once roamed across the Great Plains.* **Meander** suggests wandering slowly and sometimes aimlessly over an irregular or winding course: *Narrow roads meander through the countryside.*

wane (wān) *intr.v.* **waned, wan•ing, wanes. 1.** To decrease gradually in size, amount, intensity, or degree: *My interest waned as the*

W

speaker talked on and on. **2.** To come to an end: *The old year was waning.* —*n.* A time or phase of gradual decrease. ♦ **on the wane.** In a period of decline or decrease: *Hard times appear to be on the wane.*

wan•gle (wăng′gəl) *tr.v.* **wan•gled, wan•gling, wan•gles.** *Informal.* To make, achieve, or get (sthg.) by persuading or tricking: *I wangled an invitation to the exclusive party.*

wan•na (wŏn′ə *or* wô′nə) *aux.v. Informal.* A spoken form of: **1.** Want to: *Do you wanna go?* **2.** Want a: *Do you wanna hot dog?*

wan•na•be (wŏn′ə bē *or* wô′nə bē) *n. Informal.* Somebody who copies the behavior of a famous or popular person: *a roomful of rock-star wannabes.*

want (wŏnt *or* wônt) *v.* —*tr.* **1.** To desire (sthg.) greatly; wish for: *They wanted to play outdoors. He wants a guitar.* See Synonyms at **desire. 2.** To look for (sbdy.) with the intent to capture or arrest: *The fugitive is wanted by the police.* —*intr.* **1.** To have need: *They want for nothing.* **2.** To be disposed; wish: *Stop by after work if you want.* —*n.* **1.** [U] The condition or quality of lacking sthg. usual or necessary: *for want of a better word.* **2.** [U] Pressing need: *to live in want.* **3.** [C] Something desired: *That child has many wants.*

want ad *n. Informal.* A classified advertisement: *She looked for a job in the want ads.*

wan•ton (wŏn′tən) *adj.* **1.** Unnecessary or unjustified: *wanton killing.* **2.** Unrestrained; wild: *wanton luxury; wanton behavior.* —**wan′ton•ly** *adv.* —**wan′ton•ness** *n.* [U]

war (wôr) *n.* **1.** [C; U] A state of open armed conflict carried on between nations, states, or parties. **2.** [U] The techniques or procedures of war; military science. **3.** [C] A serious determined struggle or attack on sthg. considered harmful: *The President declared a war on poverty.* —*intr.v.* **warred, war•ring, wars. 1.** To carry on warfare. **2.** To struggle, contend, or fight: *warring with his conscience.*

war•ble (wôr′bəl) *tr. & intr.v.* **war•bled, war•bling, war•bles.** To sing high with melodic sounds like those of a bird: *The baby warbled happily. Birds warbled greetings from the trees.* —*n. (usually singular).* The act or an instance of singing with trills, runs, or quavers.

ward (wôrd) *n.* **1.a.** A large hospital room or section. **b.** A section of a hospital devoted to the care of a particular group of patients: *a maternity ward; the children's ward.* **2.** A person, especially a minor, placed under the care or protection of a guardian or court. **3.** An administrative division of a city or town, especially an election district: *She was elected councilor for the first ward.* —*v.* ♦ **ward off.** *tr.v.* [sep.] To turn (sbdy./sthg.) aside;

repel: *I warded off the bothersome insects by building a fire.*

—**ward** or —**wards** *suff.* A suffix that means: **1.** In a specified direction in time or space: *downward.* **2.** Toward a specified place or position: *homeward.*

WORD BUILDING: —**ward** The basic meaning of the suffix —**ward** is "having a particular direction or location." Thus **inward** means "directed or located inside." Other examples are **outward, forward, backward, upward, downward, earthward, homeward, eastward,** and **westward.** The suffix —**ward** forms adjectives and adverbs. Adverbs ending in —**ward** can also end in —**wards.** Thus *I stepped backward* and *I stepped backwards* are both correct. Only **backward** is an adjective: *a backward glance.*

---

war•den (wôr′dn) *n.* **1.** An official in charge of a prison. **2.** An official who enforces certain laws, such as hunting, fishing, or fire regulations: *a game warden; a fire warden.*

ward•robe (wôr′drōb′) *n.* **1.** Articles of clothing considered as a group, especially all the pieces of clothing belonging to one person or used for a specific purpose: *a business wardrobe.* **2.** A cabinet for holding clothes.

—**wards** *suff.* Variant of —**ward.**

ware (wâr) *n.* **1.** [U] Articles of the same general kind, made of a certain material or used in a specific way: *silverware; hardware.* **2. wares.** Articles for sale: *people displaying their wares in the market.*

HOMONYMS: ware, wear (have on).

---

ware•house (wâr′hous′) *n.* A place in which goods or articles of merchandise are stored, usually a large building.

war•fare (wôr′fâr′) *n.* [U] **1.** The waging of war against an enemy; armed conflict. **2.** A special type or method of military operation: *guerrilla warfare.* **3.** A state of disharmony or conflict; strife: *There's constant warfare among the company's executives.*

war•head (wôr′hĕd′) *n.* A section in the forward part of a bomb, missile, or torpedo that contains the explosive charge.

war•like (wôr′līk′) *adj.* **1.** Belligerent; hostile: *a warlike people.* **2.** Relating to war. **3.** Threatening or indicating war: *a warlike call to arms.*

war•lock (wôr′lŏk′) *n.* A male witch, sorcerer, wizard, or demon.

war•lord (wôr′lôrd′) *n.* A military leader who has control over a region.

warm (wôrm) *adj.* **1.** Moderately hot; neither cool nor very hot: *warm weather; warm air.* **2.** Giving off or keeping in heat: *the warm sun; a warm sweater.* **3.** Enthusiastic, friendly, or sincere: *a warm smile; warm greetings.* **4.** Showing liveliness, excitement, or disagreement; heated: *a warm debate.* **5.** Predominantly red or yellow in tone: *warm colors.* —*tr. & intr.v.* To make or become warm or warmer; heat up: *warm leftovers for supper; as the day gradually warmed.* ◆ **warm up.** *intr.v.* **1.** To prepare for an athletic event by exercising, stretching, or practicing for a short time beforehand: *The runner warmed up before the race.* **2.** To become ready for an event or operation: *She warmed up for her speech by practicing the opening lines.* —**warm′ly** *adv.* —**warm′ness** *n.* [U]

warm-blood·ed (wôrm′blŭd′ĭd) *adj.* **1.** With a relatively warm body temperature that stays about the same regardless of changes in the temperature of the surroundings: *Birds and mammals are warm-blooded.* **2.** Full of feeling; passionate: *a warm-blooded greeting.* —**warm′-blood′ed·ness** *n.* [U]

warm-heart·ed (wôrm′här′tĭd) *adj.* Characterized by kindness, sympathy, and generosity: *a warm-hearted person.* —**warm′-heart′ed·ness** *n.* [U]

war·mon·ger (wôr′mŭng′gər or wôr′-mŏng′gər) *n.* A person who encourages war.

warmth (wôrmth) *n.* [U] **1.** The state or quality of being warm; moderate heat: *This room needs some warmth.* **2.** The sensation of moderate heat: *find warmth near the fire.* **3.** Friendliness, kindness, or affection: *a person of great warmth.* **4.** Excitement or intensity, as of love or passion: *warmth of feeling.*

warm-up or **warm·up** (wôrm′ŭp′) *n.* **1.** The act or procedure of warming up: *a runner doing her warm-ups.* **2.** A period spent in warming up: *Are you finished with your warm-up?*

warn (wôrn) *v.* —*tr.* **1.** To tell (sbdy.) in advance of danger, harm, or evil: *The Coast Guard warned the sailors of bad weather.* **2.** To advise, caution, or counsel (sbdy.): *We warned them to be careful.* —*intr.* To give a warning: *The sky warned of a coming storm.*

warn·ing (wôr′nĭng) *n.* [C; U] **1.** A sign, indication, notice, or threat of coming danger: *The dog's low growl was a warning. Without warning, the shelf collapsed.* **2.** Advice to beware or to stop a given course of action: *How many warnings about smoking do you need?*

warp (wôrp) *v.* —*tr.* **1.** To turn or twist (wood, for example) out of shape: *an old table warped by sun and water.* **2.** To affect (sthg.) unfavorably, unfairly, or wrongly: *The fear of losing his fortune warped his personality.* —*intr.* To become bent or twisted out of shape: *In the damp basement, the boards warped.* —*n.* A bend or twist, especially in a piece of wood.

war·path (wôr′păth′) *n.* A course that leads to battle or warfare: *Watch out for the boss today; she's on the warpath.*

war·rant (wôr′ənt or wŏr′ənt) *n.* An official written order authorizing sthg., such as an arrest, a search, or a seizure: *a search war-*rant. —*tr.v.* **1.** To guarantee (sthg.): *warrant a product.* **2.** To call for or justify (sthg.): *There is enough evidence to warrant a trial.*

war·ran·ty (wôr′ən tē or wŏr′ən tē) *n., pl.* **war·ran·ties.** [C; U] A written guarantee given to a buyer by a company: *a five-year warranty on a car.*

war·ri·or (wôr′ē ər or wŏr′ē ər) *n.* A person who is or has been in battle; a soldier.

wart (wôrt) *n.* A hard rough lump growing on the skin, caused by a virus.

war·time (wôr′tīm′) *n.* [U] A period during which a war is in progress.

war·y (wâr′ē) *adj.* **war·i·er, war·i·est.** **1.** On guard; watchful: *We were wary of mistakes in our experiment.* **2.** Characterized by caution: *a wary look.* —**war′i·ness** *n.* [U]

was (wŭz or wŏz; wəz *when unstressed*) *v.* First and third person singular past tense of **be.**

wash (wŏsh or wôsh) *v.* —*tr.* **1.** To clean (sbdy./sthg.) by using water and often soap or detergent: *wash dishes.* **2.** To soak, rinse out, and remove (dirt or a stain) with water: *wash dirt out of the jeans.* **3.** To flow over and wet (sthg.) with water: *The waves washed the sandy shores.* **4.** To carry or remove (sthg.) by the action of moving water: *Rain falls and washes the soil downhill.* —*intr.* **1.** To clean sthg. or oneself in or with water: *He washes every day.* **2.** To undergo washing without fading or other damage: *Cotton washes well.* **3.** [against; over] To flow, sweep, or beat: *Waves washed over the rocks.* —*n.* [C; U] **1.** The act of washing or cleansing: *Give your face a quick wash.* **2.** A group of articles washed or intended for washing: *transfer the wash to the dryer.* **3.** A liquid preparation used in cleansing or coating sthg.: *mouthwash; whitewash.* ◆ **come out in the wash.** *Slang.* To be revealed eventually: *The truth will come out in the wash.* **wash down.** *tr.v.* [sep.] **1.** To swallow (food, for example) with a liquid: *He washed down the chips with some juice.* **2.** To clean (sthg.) by spraying with water: *wash the car down with a hose.* **wash (one's) hands of.** To refuse to accept responsibility for (sthg.): *I washed my hands of the problem.* **wash out.** *intr.v.* **1.** To be removed by washing: *That stain will wash out easily.* **2.** To fail at sthg., especially an educational program: *He washed out of law school.* **wash up.** *intr.v.* **1.** To wash one's hands: *Wash up before supper.* **2.** To be carried onto shore: *Look at the shells that have washed up!*

Wash. *abbr.* An abbreviation of Washington.

wash·a·ble (wŏsh′ə bəl or wôsh′ə bəl) *adj.* Capable of being washed without fading or other damage: *a washable skirt.*

wash-and-wear (wŏsh′ən wâr′ or wôsh′ən-wâr′) *adj.* Treated so as to be easily washed and to require little or no ironing: *a wash-and-wear shirt.*

wash·cloth (wŏsh′klôth′ or wŏsh′klŏth′ or wôsh′klôth′ or wôsh′klŏth′) *n.* A small cloth of absorbent material used for washing the face or body.

washed-out (wŏsht′out′ *or* wôsht′out′) *adj.* **1.** Without color or intensity; faded: *a washed-out photograph.* **2.** Exhausted or tired-looking: *You look washed-out today.*

washed-up (wŏsht′ŭp′ *or* wôsht′ŭp′) *adj.* No longer successful or needed; finished: *As an actor, he's washed-up.*

wash•er (wŏsh′ər *or* wô′shər) *n.* **1.** A person or thing that washes: *a window washer; a clothes washer.* **2.** A washing machine. **3.** An automatic dishwasher. **4.** A small disk, as of metal or rubber, used to tighten a nut.

wash•ing (wŏsh′ĭng *or* wô′shĭng) *n.* [U] **1.** The act or process of one that washes: *the washing of dishes.* **2.** A batch of clothes washed or to be washed at one time: *do the washing.*

washing machine *n.* An automatic machine for washing clothes.

wash•room (wŏsh′rōōm′ *or* wŏsh′rŏŏm′ *or* wôsh′rōōm′ *or* wôsh′rŏŏm′) *n.* A bathroom, especially one in a public place.

was•n't (wŭz′ənt *or* wŏz′ənt). Contraction of *was not.*

wasp (wŏsp) *n.* An insect with a body with a narrow midsection and two pairs of wings, often capable of giving a painful sting.

wasp

WASP or **Wasp** (wŏsp) *n.* An abbreviation of white Anglo-Saxon Protestant.

waste (wāst) *v.* **wast•ed, wast•ing, wastes.** —*tr.* **1.** To spend, consume, or use (sthg.) foolishly or needlessly; squander: *waste food by leaving it out to spoil; waste energy by leaving the lights on all night.* **2.** To cause (sbdy./sthg.) to lose strength or energy: *Disease wasted his body.* **3.** To fail to take advantage of or use (sthg.) for profit; lose: *I wasted my chance.* **4.** To destroy (sthg.) completely: *waste an opponent.* —*intr.* To pass without being used: *Time is wasting.* —*n.* **1.** [C; U] The act of wasting or the condition of being wasted: *a waste of resources.* **2.** [C] An area, a region, or a land that is uninhabited or uncultivated; a desert or wilderness: *dry desert wastes.* **3.** [C] Something used or worthless, as from a manufacturing process: *industrial wastes.* **4.** [U] Garbage; trash. **5.** [U] The material that remains after food has been digested and that is passed out of the body: *human waste.* ◆ **go to waste.** To pass by; not be used: *let good food go to waste; let an opportunity go to waste.* **lay waste to.** To destroy (sthg.) completely: *The storm laid waste to the beach.* **waste away.** *intr.v.* **1.** To die slowly: *We watched as he wasted away.* **2.** To become very thin and weak: *She's wasting away on that diet.*

waste (one's) breath. To get or accomplish nothing by speaking: *Don't waste your breath arguing; the decision's been made.*

HOMONYMS: waste, waist (body part).

waste•bas•ket (wāst′băs′kĭt) *n.* An open container for used paper and other trash.

waste•ful (wāst′fəl) *adj.* Characterized by or tending to waste; extravagant: *wasteful use of resources; a wasteful method.* —**waste′-ful•ly** *adv.* —**waste′ful•ness** *n.* [U]

waste•land (wāst′lănd′) *n. (usually singular).* Land that is lonely, empty, or ruined: *an industrial wasteland.*

waste•pa•per (wāst′pā′pər) *n.* [U] Discarded paper.

watch (wŏch) *v.* —*intr.* **1.** To look or observe closely or carefully: *We watched as the parade went by.* **2.** [*for*] To look and wait expectantly or in anticipation: *watch for an opportunity.* **3.** To stay awake and on guard: *She was watching and waiting.* —*tr.* **1.** To look at (sbdy./sthg.) steadily; observe: *I watched the pianist's hands as she played.* **2.** To take care of (animals or children, for example): *The baby sitter is watching the children.* —*n.* **1.** [C] A small portable timepiece, especially one worn on the wrist or carried in the pocket. **2.** [U] The act of keeping awake or mentally alert, especially for the purpose of guarding: *keep watch for signs of a tornado.* **3.** [C; U] The act of closely observing or the condition of being closely observed; surveillance: *There's a police watch on their house.* ◆ **watch it.** To be careful: *Watch it if you go out in that storm.* **watch (one's) step. 1.** To act or proceed with care and caution: *Watch your step in the desert; there may be scorpions.* **2.** To behave as it is demanded, required, or appropriate: *Watch your step around my parents.* **watch out.** *intr.v.* To be careful or on the alert; take care: *Watch out for drunken drivers.* **watch over.** *tr.v.* [insep.] To be in charge of (sbdy./ sthg.): *watch over a sick child.*

watch

watch•dog (wŏch′dôg′ *or* wŏch′dŏg′) *n.* **1.** A dog trained to protect people or property. **2.** A person or group who guards or protects against waste, loss, or illegal practices: *She's the family's watchdog when it comes to money.*

watch•ful (wŏch′fəl) *adj.* Carefully observant or alert: *a watchful teacher.* —**watch′-ful•ly** *adv.* —**watch′ful•ness** *n.* [U]

watch•mak•er (wŏch′mā′kər) *n.* A person who makes or repairs watches. —**watch′-mak′ing** *n.* [U]

ă–cat; ā–pay; âr–care; ä–father; ĕ–get; ē–be; ĭ–sit; ī–nice; îr–here; ŏ–got; ō–go; ô–saw; oi–boy; ou–out; ōō–took; ōō–boot; ŭ–cut; ûr–word; th–thin; *th*–this; hw–when; zh–vision; ə–about; ɴ–French bon

watch·man (wŏch′mən) *n.* A man employed to stand guard or keep watch; a security guard: *a night watchman.*

wa·ter (wô′tər *or* wŏt′ər) *n.* **1.** [U] A colorless liquid compound of hydrogen and oxygen (H_2O). Water freezes at 32°F (0°C) and boils at 212°F (100°C). **2.** [U] A body of water such as a sea, lake, river, or stream: *Stay away from the water if there's a storm.* **3. waters.** A particular stretch of sea or ocean, especially that of a state or country. **4.** [U] A supply of water: *Turn off the water when you're through.* **5.** [U] Any of various forms of water: *waste water; sparkling water.* —*v.* —*tr.* **1.** To pour water on or supply (sthg.) with water: *water the garden.* **2.** To give drinking water to (sthg.): *water the horses.* **3.** To mix or weaken (sthg.) with water: *water the wine.* —*intr.* To produce or discharge liquid, as from the eyes or mouth: *My mouth watered when I smelled the fresh bread. The smoke made his eyes water.* ♦ **hold water.** To be or seem true: *Her excuse for being late just doesn't hold water.* **in hot water.** In great trouble: *Because of your lie, we're all in hot water.* **water down.** *tr.v.* [sep.] **1.** To reduce the strength or effectiveness of (sthg.): *The cook had to water down the sweet syrup.* **2.** To provide water for (sthg.); spray with water: *water the sidewalks down to reduce the heat.* **water under the bridge.** A past event, especially sthg. unfortunate, that cannot be undone or made right and should be forgotten: *I hope our earlier disagreements are now water under the bridge.*

wa·ter·col·or (wô′tər kŭl′ər *or* wŏt′ər-kŭl′ər) *n.* **1.** [C] A paint in which water instead of oil is mixed with the coloring material before use. **2.** [C] A work of art done in this paint. **3.** [U] The art of using watercolors.

wa·ter·fall (wô′tər fôl′ *or* wŏt′ər fôl′) *n.* A natural stream of water falling from a high place.

water fountain *n.* A piece of equipment in a building or park that provides drinking water.

wa·ter·fowl (wô′tər foul′ *or* wŏt′ər foul′) *n., pl.* **waterfowl.** A water bird, especially a swimming bird: *Ducks and geese are waterfowl.*

wa·ter·front (wô′tər frŭnt′ *or* wŏt′ər-frŭnt′) *n.* (*usually singular*). **1.** Land that is at the edge of a body of water. **2.** The part of a town or city that is at the edge of the water, especially a wharf district where ships dock.

water hole *n.* A small natural depression in which water collects, especially a pool where animals come to drink during the dry season.

wa·ter·ing can (wô′tər ĭng *or* wŏt′ər ĭng) *n.* A container with a long spout, used to pour water on plants.

water lily *n.* A water plant with broad floating leaves and flowers in various colors.

wa·ter·logged (wô′tər lôgd′ *or* wô′tər-lŏgd′ *or* wŏt′ər lôgd′ *or* wŏt′ər lŏgd′) *adj.* Soaked or full of water: *a waterlogged field.*

wa·ter·mel·on (wô′tər mĕl′ən *or* wŏt′-ər mĕl′ən) *n.* [C; U] A very large melon with a hard green skin and sweet, watery, pink or reddish flesh, or the vine that produces it.

water polo *n.* [U] A water sport played by two teams of swimmers who try to throw a ball into the opponents' goal.

wa·ter·proof (wô′tər prōof′ *or* wŏt′ər-prōof′) *adj.* **1.** Able to prevent water from coming through: *An underwater camera must be waterproof.* **2.** Made of or treated with a substance to prevent penetration by water: *a waterproof jacket.* —*tr.v.* To make (sthg.) waterproof: *waterproof a tent.* —**wa′ter·proof′ing** *n.* [U]

wa·ter·re·pel·lent (wô′tər rĭ pĕl′ənt *or* wŏt′ər rĭ pĕl′ənt) *adj.* Resistant to water but not completely waterproof: *a water-repellent jacket; a water-repellent suntan lotion.*

wa·ter·shed (wô′tər shĕd′ *or* wŏt′ər shĕd′) *n.* **1.** A turning point in a course of events: *Losing her job turned out to be the watershed of her life.* **2.** A ridge forming the boundary between regions whose water drains into two different systems of rivers.

water ski *n.* A broad ski used for skiing on water.

wa·ter·ski (wô′tər skē′ *or* wŏt′ər skē′) *intr.v.* **wa·ter·skied, wa·ter·ski·ing, wa·ter·skis.** To ski on water while being pulled by a motorboat.

wa·ter·tight (wô′tər tīt′ *or* wŏt′ər tīt′) *adj.* **1.** So tightly made that no water can enter or escape: *a watertight boat.* **2.** With no weaknesses or flaws: *a watertight excuse.*

water vapor *n.* [U] Water in its gaseous state, especially in the atmosphere and at a temperature below the boiling point.

wa·ter·way (wô′tər wā′ *or* wŏt′ər wā′) *n.* A body of water, such as a river, canal, or channel, where boats can travel.

wa·ter·works (wô′tər wûrks′ *or* wŏt′ər-wûrks′) *pl.n.* (*used with a singular or plural verb*). The water system, including reservoirs, tanks, buildings, pumps, and pipes, of a city or town.

wa·ter·y (wô′tə rē *or* wŏt′ə rē) *adj.* **wa·ter·i·er, wa·ter·i·est. 1.** Filled with, made of, or soaked with water: *watery soil.* **2.** Containing too much water; thin: *watery soup.* **3.** Resembling water, as in paleness, thinness, or liquidity: *a watery blue sky.*

watt (wŏt) *n.* A unit of electrical power equal to one joule per second or about ¹/₇₄₆ horsepower. —**watt′age** *n.* [U]

wave (wāv) *v.* **waved, wav·ing, waves.** —*intr.* **1.** To make a signal with an up-and-down or back-and-forth movement of the hand: *She waved and said, "Good-bye!"* **2.** To move freely back and forth or up and down: *The flowers waved in the breeze.* **3.** To be or hang in curves or curls, as hair: *Her hair waves in the back.* —*tr.* **1.** To signal or express (sthg.)

by waving the hand: *We waved good-bye.* **2.** To move or swing (sthg.) as in giving a signal: *We all waved our hands wildly.* **3.** To cause (sthg.) to move back and forth or up and down: *She waved a fan in front of her face.* **4.** To arrange (hair) into curves or curls: *She waved her hair for the party.* —*n.* **1.** A ridge that moves along the surface of a body of water: *ocean waves.* **2.** A movement up and down or back and forth: *a wave of the hand.* **3.** An increase in a particular type of activity: *a wave of political problems; a crime wave.* **4.** A widespread persistent weather condition: *a heat wave.* **5.** A disturbance or vibration that passes through a medium or through space: *a sound wave.* ◆ **make waves.** *Informal.* To create problems: *I don't want to make waves, but I don't think you should talk to him.* **wave aside** or **away.** *tr.v.* [sep.] To dismiss (sbdy./ sthg.): *They waved aside our worries.* **wave on.** *tr.v.* [sep.] To signal (sbdy.) to continue: *I stopped at the accident, but a police officer waved me on.*

HOMONYMS: **wave, waive** (give up).

wave•length (wāv′lĕngkth′ *or* wāv′lĕngth′) *n.* The distance between the top or peak of one wave and the next, as in measuring sound or light: *Visible light and ultraviolet light have different wavelengths.* ◆ **on the same wavelength.** *Informal.* In complete agreement; in harmony: *We were on the same wavelength when we discussed the class trip.*

wa•ver (wā′vər) *intr.v.* To be or become unsteady or uncertain: *He wavered on the new contracts.*

HOMONYMS: **waver, waiver** (giving up).

wav•y (wā′vē) *adj.* **wav•i•er, wav•i•est. 1.** Full of or rising in waves: *wavy hair; a wavy sea.* **2.** With curves that resemble waves: *a wavy line.* —**wav′i•ness** *n.* [U]

wax¹ (wăks) *n.* [U] A solid or soft sticky substance that melts or softens easily when heated, used to make candles and to polish floors, furniture, and cars. —*tr.v.* To coat, treat, or polish (sthg.) with wax: *wax a floor; wax a car.*

wax² (wăks) *intr.v. Formal.* To increase gradually in size, number, or strength: *Civilizations have waxed and waned over the centuries.*

wax•en (wăk′sən) *adj.* **1.** Made of or covered with wax: *a waxen image.* **2.** Pale or smooth as wax: *a waxen face.*

wax•y (wăk′sē) *adj.* **wax•i•er, wax•i•est. 1.** Like wax in appearance or texture: *a flower with waxy petals.* **2.** Full of, made of, or covered with wax: *Polishing the car makes my hands waxy.*

way (wā) *n.* **1.** [C] **a.** A road, path, or highway to travel from one place to another: *Which way should I go to your house?* **b.** An opening that allows entry: *This door is the only way into the attic.* **2.** [C; U] Space or opportunity to proceed: *clear the way for the parade; open the way to peace.* **3.** [C] *(usually singular).* Progress or travel in a specific direction: *on his way north.* **4.** [C] A course of conduct or action: *the easy way out.* **5.** [C] *(usually singular).* A manner or method of doing: *no way to reach her; the American way of life.* **6.** [C] Distance: *It is a long way from here to Moscow.* **7.** [C] *(usually singular).* A specific direction: *He glanced my way.* **8.** [C] An aspect, a detail, or a feature: *Our jobs are in no way comparable.* **9.** [C] An ability or a skill: *That writer has a way with words.* **10.** [C] A state or condition: *He is in a bad way financially.* **11.** [U] A neighborhood or an area: *Drop in for a visit when you're out our way.* —*adv. Informal.* By a great distance or to a large degree; far: *way off base; way too much.* ◆ **by the way.** Used to signal a change in the subject of a conversation: *By the way, have you seen any good movies lately?* **by way of.** Through; via: *We walked to school by way of the park.* **get** or **have (one's) way.** To be able to get other people to agree to what one wants: *No matter what the issue is, he always gets his way.* **go (one's) own way.** To act as one chooses, independently of others: *I don't think we're going to agree; it's best if we go our own ways.* **go out of (one's) way.** To do sthg. that is inconvenient and beyond what is required: *My neighbors went out of their way to help me.* **have it both ways.** To be able to get two conflicting things one wants: *You can use the money for new skates or a winter coat, but you can't have it both ways.* **in a way.** In some manner; in part: *I like her approach to problems, in a way.* **in the way.** In a position that blocks or interferes: *There's nothing in the way of this project now.* **make way for.** To provide or clear a space for (sbdy./sthg.): *Many people lost their homes to make way for the new highway.* **no way.** Used to express firm refusal or disagreement: *We asked her to lend us the money for gas, but she said, "No way."* **on (one's) way.** In the process of coming, going, or traveling: *It's getting dark, so I'll be on my way.* **on the way.** On the route of a journey: *The travelers stopped at a diner on the way.* **out of the way.** In a position that does not block or interfere: *Tell them to keep out of the way while I fix the sink.*

HOMONYMS: **way, weigh** (measure weight).

way•lay (wā′lā′) *tr.v.* **way•laid** (wā′lād′), **way•lay•ing, way•lays.** To lie in wait for and attack (sbdy./sthg.) from ambush: *The thief waylaid my mother in the grocery store parking lot.*

way-out (wā′out′) *adj. Slang.* Very unconventional, unusual, or strange: *way-out clothes; way-out ideas.*

—ways *suff.* A suffix that means in a specified way, manner, direction, or position: *sideways.*

way•side (wā′sīd′) *n. (usually singular).* The side or edge of a road, path, or highway. ◆ **fall** or **go by the wayside.** To stop being a concern or stop being used: *Concern about fuel economy in cars has fallen by the wayside in recent years.*

way•ward (wā′wərd) *adj.* Stubborn or disobedient; willful or uncontrollable: *a wayward child.*

we (wē) *pron.* The person who is speaking or writing together with another or others: *We want to go swimming.*

HOMONYMS: we, wee (tiny).

weak (wēk) *adj.* **1.** Without physical strength or energy; feeble: *a weak handshake.* **2.** Tending to fail under pressure, stress, or strain; without resistance: *a weak link in a chain.* **3.** Without the proper or necessary strength or power: *weak coffee; weak eyesight.* **4.** Without ability or skill: *weak in math.* —**weak′ly** *adj.*

HOMONYMS: weak, week (seven days).

weak•en (wē′kən) *tr. & intr.v.* To make or become weak or weaker: *Too much water weakened the tea. After surgery, the patient gradually weakened.*

weak•ling (wēk′lĭng) *n.* A person or thing with a weak body or character.

weak•ness (wēk′nĭs) *n.* **1.** [U] The condition or quality of being weak: *physical weakness.* **2.** [C] A personal defect or failing: *Concentrate on overcoming your weaknesses.* **3.** [C] A special fondness or liking: *I have a weakness for good talkers. Ice cream is his weakness.*

wealth (wĕlth) *n.* **1.** [U] A large amount of money or valuable resources; riches: *Wealth doesn't always bring happiness.* **2.** [C] A large amount; an abundance: *a wealth of information.*

wealth•y (wĕl′thē) *adj.* **wealth•i•er, wealth•i•est. 1.** Having wealth; rich: *a wealthy family.* **2.** Well supplied; abundant: *a region wealthy in wildlife.* —**wealth′i•ly** *adv.* —**wealth′i•ness** *n.* [U]

wean (wēn) *tr.v.* **1.** To accustom (a baby or young animal) to food other than mother's milk: *The puppies were weaned at six weeks of age.* **2.** To stop (sbdy.) from doing sthg. that has become a habit: *She weaned herself from sweets.*

weap•on (wĕp′ən) *n.* **1.** An instrument of attack or defense in combat, such as a gun, missile, or sword. **2.** A way to defend against or defeat another: *Logic was her best weapon.* —**weap′on•ry** *n.* [U]

wear (wâr) *v.* **wore** (wôr), **worn** (wôrn), **wear•ing, wears.** —*tr.* **1.** To carry or have (sthg.) on the person as covering, decoration, or protection: *wear nice clothes.* **2.** To show (sthg.) in one's appearance: *He wore a smile.* **3.** To produce (sthg.), as by long or hard use, friction, or exposure: *I wore a hole in the old shoes.* **4.** To make (sbdy./sthg.) tired: *Your questions wear my patience.* —*intr.* **1.** To last under long or hard use: *That fabric wears well.* **2.** To break down as through use or friction: *The rear tires began to wear.* —*n.* [U] **1.** The act of wearing; use: *clothes for evening wear.* **2.** Clothing: *men's wear; sportswear.* **3.** Damage resulting from use or age: *The rug shows wear.* ◆ **wear away.** *tr.v.* [sep.] To make (sthg.) disappear through rubbing or use: *The paint on the stairs was worn away.* **wear down.** *tr.v.* [sep.] To reduce the strength or size of (sbdy./sthg.) by endless pressure or resistance: *The child's continual pleading finally wore her parents down.* **wear off.** *intr.v.* To be slowly reduced in effect: *My mouth hurt after the pain medication wore off.* **wear on.** *intr.v.* To pass slowly, as time: *The December day wore on toward night.* **wear out.** *tr.v.* [sep.] **1.** To make (sthg.) unusable through long or heavy use: *He wore out a pair of hockey skates.* **2.** To exhaust (sbdy.); tire: *Raking the leaves wore me out.* **wear thin.** To become less convincing, acceptable, or popular, as through repeated use: *Oversleeping is an excuse that has worn thin.* —**wear′er** *n.*

HOMONYMS: wear, ware (articles).

wea•ri•some (wîr′ē səm) *adj. Formal.* Tiresome or tedious: *Your constant excuses have become wearisome.*

wea•ry (wîr′ē) *adj.* **wea•ri•er, wea•ri•est. 1.** Physically or mentally tired: *She was weary after a day's work.* **2.** Showing or caused by tiredness: *The clerk gave a weary sigh.* **3.** With one's patience gone: *I am weary of your complaints.* —*tr. & intr.v.* **wea•ried, wea•ry•ing, wea•ries.** To make or become weary; tire: *The long hours of work had wearied Dad. Children sometimes weary quickly of new toys.* —**wea′ri•ly** *adv.* —**wea′ri•ness** *n.* [U]

wea•sel (wē′zəl) *n.* **1.** A mammal with a long narrow body, short legs, and a long tail, that feeds on small animals and birds. **2.** A person seen as clever, sneaky, or treacherous: *That weasel stole my wallet!* —*intr.v.* To be indirect or evasive in the use of words: *Stop weaseling about whether you like her.* ◆ **weasel out of.** *Informal.* To get out of a situation or commit-

W

ment in a sneaky or cowardly manner: *He weaseled out of helping us clean up after the dance.*

weath·er (wĕth′ər) *n.* [U] **1.** The condition of the atmosphere at a time or place: *warm and sunny weather.* **2.** Bad, rough, or stormy atmospheric conditions: *We didn't go on a picnic because of the weather.* —*v.* —*tr.* **1.** To change (sthg.) by the action of the weather: *The sun weathered the house paint.* **2.** To pass through (sthg.) safely; survive: *weather a storm.* —*intr.* **1.** To show the effects of exposure to the elements: *Some house paints weather quickly.* **2.** To withstand the effects of weather: *Our new roof will weather well.* ♦ **under the weather.** Somewhat ill: *He's been under the weather lately.*

weath·er-beat·en (wĕth′ər bēt′n) *adj.* Worn by exposure to the weather: *a weather-beaten house.*

weath·er·ing (wĕth′ər ĭng) *n.* [U] Any of the chemical or mechanical processes by which rocks exposed to the weather are broken down: *Those cliffs show the effects of weathering.*

weath·er·proof (wĕth′ər proof′) *adj.* Capable of withstanding exposure to weather without damage: *We need weatherproof siding for the house.* —*tr.v.* To make (sthg.) weatherproof: *I weatherproofed my house.*

weath·er·vane (wĕth′ər vān′) *n.* A device for showing wind direction.

weave (wēv) *v.* **wove** (wōv), **wo·ven** (wō′vən), **weav·ing, weaves.** —*tr.* **1.** To make (cloth) on a loom by interlacing threads. **2.** To make (sthg.) by interlacing long, thin pieces of material: *weave a basket.* **3.** To combine (things) into a whole made

weathervane

up of related parts: *She wove the separate incidents into a story.* **4.** To spin (a web, for example): *The spider wove her web.* **5.** Past tense **weaved.** To make (a path or way) by going in and out or from side to side: *The taxi weaved its way through the traffic.* —*intr.* **1.** To make cloth on a loom: *He was weaving in his studio when I arrived.* **2.** Past tense **weaved.** To move in a winding course or sway from side to side: *I saw a drunk driver weave down the road.* —*n.* The pattern or way of weaving a fabric: *a loose weave.* —**weav′er** *n.*

web (wĕb) *n.* **1.** A structure of fine silky strands made by spiders or other insects. **2.** Something that traps by entangling: *a web of lies.* **3.** A fold of skin or thin tissue connecting the toes of certain water birds or other animals: *Ducks have webs between their toes.* **4.** A woven structure: *A web of palm branches formed the roof of the hut.* **5. Web.** The World Wide Web. —**web′bing** *n.* [U]

webbed (wĕbd) *adj.* With the fingers or toes connected by a fold of skin or tissue: *the webbed foot of a duck.*

web-foot·ed (wĕb′foot′ĭd) *adj.* Having feet with webbed toes: *Frogs are web-footed.*

web·site or **Web·site** (wĕb′sīt′) *n.* A site on the World Wide Web.

wed (wĕd) *v.* **wed** or **wed·ded, wed** or **wed·ded, wed·ding, weds.** —*tr.* **1.** To take (sbdy.) as a husband or wife; marry: *She wed her husband 30 years ago.* **2.** To join (people) in marriage: *The minister will wed the young couple.* —*intr.* To take a husband or wife; marry: *They wed in a beautiful ceremony.* ♦ **be wedded to.** To be committed to (sthg.): *We're not wedded to that idea.*

Wed. *abbr.* An abbreviation of Wednesday.

we'd (wēd). Contraction of *we had, we should,* and *we would.*

wed·ding (wĕd′ĭng) *n.* **1.** [U] The act of marrying. **2.** [C] The ceremony or celebration of a marriage: *The wedding will be held at noon next Saturday.*

wedge (wĕj) *n.* **1.** A triangular piece of material, such as metal or wood, designed to be inserted into a crack or space to tighten or secure: *He put a wedge under the wheel of the car.* **2.** Something shaped like a wedge: *I ate a wedge of pie.* **3.** Something that causes division or disruption: *The issue drove a wedge between the party leaders.* —*v.* **wedged, wedg·ing, wedg·es.** —*tr.* **1.** To split or force (sthg.) apart with or as if with a wedge: *wedge open a log; wedge apart the opposition.* **2.** To fix in place or tighten (sthg.) with a wedge: *The carpenter wedged the windowpane so the glass fit tight against the frame.* —*intr.* To become lodged or jammed: *Our boat wedged between the rocks.*

wed·lock (wĕd′lŏk′) *n.* [U] *Formal.* The state of being married; matrimony: *holy wedlock.* ♦ **out of wedlock.** An old expression meaning outside of marriage: *She had a child out of wedlock.*

Wednes·day (wĕnz′dē *or* wĕnz′dā′) *n.* The fourth day of the week.

wee (wē) *adj.* **we·er, we·est. 1.** A term used in the past to mean very small; tiny: *a*

W

wee boy. See Synonyms at **little. 2.** Very early: *the wee hours.*

weed (wēd) *n.* A troublesome or useless plant, especially one growing where it is not wanted, as in a garden. —*tr. & intr.v.* To rid of or remove weeds: *We need to weed the garden. I hate to weed.* ◆ **weed out.** *tr.v.* [sep.] To remove (sbdy./sthg.) that is not wanted: *weed out old clothes; weed the lazy workers out.* —**weed′er** *n.* —**weed′y** *adj.*

week (wēk) *n.* **1.** A seven-day calendar period, especially one that begins on a Sunday and continues through Saturday: *the last week in June.* **2.** The part of a calendar week devoted to work, school, or business: *the business week.*

week•day (wēk′dā′) *n.* Any day of the week except Saturday and Sunday: *I prefer to shop on weekdays.*

week•end (wēk′ĕnd′) *n.* The end of the week, especially the period from Friday evening through Sunday evening: *go fishing over the weekend.*

week•ly (wēk′lē) *adv.* **1.** Once a week or every week: *She visits us weekly.* **2.** By the week: *I am paid weekly.* —*adj.* Done, happening, or coming once a week or every week: *a weekly trip; weekly earnings.* —*n., pl.* **week•lies.** A newspaper or magazine published once a week.

weep (wēp) *v.* **wept** (wĕpt), **weep•ing, weeps.** —*tr.* To shed (tears); cry: *She wept tears of joy at his safe return.* See Synonyms at **cry.** —*intr.* To show emotion by shedding tears. —**weep′y** *adj.*

weep•ing (wē′pĭng) *adj.* **1.** Shedding tears; tearful. **2.** Dropping rain: *weeping clouds.* **3.** With drooping branches: *a weeping cherry tree.*

weeping willow *n.* A widely cultivated tree with long, slender, drooping branches and narrow leaves.

wee•vil (wē′vəl) *n.* Any of numerous beetles that do great damage to plants.

weigh (wā) *v.* —*tr.* **1.** To measure the weight of (sbdy./sthg.) by using a scale or balance: *weigh a baby.* **2.** To consider (sthg.) carefully by balancing in the mind: *I weighed possible alternatives.* **3.** To choose (sthg.) carefully: *He weighed his words when answering the question.* —*intr.* **1.** To be of a specific weight: *weigh more than ten pounds.* **2.** To have consequence or influence: *That factor weighed*

heavily in the decision. ◆ **weigh down.** *tr.v.* [sep.] **1.** To cause (sbdy./sthg.) to bend down with added weight: *He was weighed down by a heavy suitcase.* **2.** To cause worry or concern to (sbdy.): *I'm weighed down with responsibility right now.* **weigh in.** *intr.v.* **1.** To be weighed in order to qualify for an athletic competition, such as wrestling: *Both boxers weighed in before the big fight.* **2.** To show support for sthg. in a dispute: *The governor finally weighed in on the workers' side.* **weigh on.** *tr.v.* [insep.] To concern (sbdy.) greatly; worry: *Her past rudeness to friends began to weigh on her.* **weigh out.** *tr.v.* [sep.] To measure (sthg.) by weight: *Weigh out a pound of hamburger for me.*

weight (wāt) *n.* **1.** [C] The measure of the heaviness of an object: *The car has a weight of 2,800 pounds.* **2.** [U] The force with which an object near the earth or another celestial body is attracted toward the center of the body by gravity. **3.** [C] A unit used as a measure of gravitational force: *a table of weights and measures.* **4.** [C] An object with a particular weight, used as a standard in weighing: *Place a two-pound weight on the scale.* **5.** [C] A heavy object, such as a paperweight or dumbbell: *You can lift weights to build muscles.* **6.** [C] A load or burden: *feeling a heavy weight of worry.* **7.** [U] Influence or importance: *Her opinion has a lot of weight in the medical community.* —*tr.v.* **1.** To make (sthg.) heavy or heavier with a weight or weights: *weight a fishing line.* **2.** To load down, burden, or oppress (sbdy.): *The heavy load weighted the delivery man.* **3.** To adjust (systems or measures) to help or hinder certain groups: *The school weights admissions decisions in favor of the children of alumni. The system is weighted against people who don't own property.* ◆ **carry weight.** To matter; be important: *Why should his opinion carry more weight than hers?* **pull (one's) weight.** To do (one's) share of work: *You'll have to pull your own weight if you want to work here.* **throw (one's) weight around.** To behave in a self-important, aggressive way: *Don't even try to throw your weight around with her!* **weight down.** *tr.v.* [sep.] To burden (sbdy./sthg.); overload: *The small boat was so weighted down that it sank.*

weight•less (wāt′lĭs) *adj.* **1.** With little or no weight: *The baby felt weightless in his arms.* **2.** Experiencing a gravitational force that is zero or very nearly zero: *The astronauts were weightless.* —**weight′less•ness** *n.* [U]

W

weight·lift·ing (wāt′lĭf′tĭng) *n.* [U] The lifting of heavy weights as an exercise or in athletic competition. —**weight′lift′er** *n.*

weight·y (wā′tē) *adj.* **weight·i·er, weight·i·est. 1.** With considerable weight; heavy: *a weighty package.* **2.** Very serious or important: *a weighty matter.*

weird (wîrd) *adj.* **1.** Of a very odd or unusual character; strange: *a weird character.* **2.** Relating to or suggesting the supernatural: *weird noises in the attic.* —**weird′ly** *adv.* —**weird′ness** *n.* [U]

weird·o (wîr′dō) *n., pl.* **weird·oes.** *Slang.* A person thought of as being very strange or eccentric.

wel·come (wĕl′kəm) *adj.* **1.** Received with pleasure and friendliness: *a welcome guest.* **2.** Giving pleasure or satisfaction: *a welcome break from hard work.* **3.** Warmly or willingly allowed or invited: *You are welcome to join us for dinner.* **4.** Used in response to an expression of thanks: *You're welcome. I was happy to help.* —*n.* **1.** A friendly greeting or reception. **2.** A response when sbdy. arrives: *They gave the stranger an unfriendly welcome.* —*tr.v.* **wel·comed, wel·com·ing, wel·comes. 1.** To greet, receive, or entertain (sbdy.) politely or warmly: *welcome guests.* **2.** To receive or accept (sthg.) gladly: *We would welcome a little privacy.* —*interj.* An expression used to greet a visitor: *Welcome! Please come in.*

weld (wĕld) *v.* —*tr.* **1.** To join (pieces of metal) by heating them. **2.** To join (people or organizations) closely: *A lifelong love of music welded the two friends.* —*intr.* To undergo welding or be capable of being welded: *metal that welds easily.* —*n.* The joint formed when metal parts are united by welding: *The weld didn't hold.* —**weld′er** *n.*

wel·fare (wĕl′fâr′) *n.* [U] **1.** Health, happiness, and good fortune; well-being: *the general welfare.* **2.** Financial or other aid provided, especially by the government, to people in need: *the budget for welfare.* ♦ **on welfare.** Receiving regular assistance from the government because of need.

well¹ (wĕl) *n.* **1.** A deep hole dug or drilled into the earth to obtain water, oil, or gas. **2.** A source to be drawn upon: *The dictionary is a well of information.* **3.** A vertical opening that passes through the floors of a building: *a stairwell.* —*intr.v.* To rise to the surface, ready to flow: *Tears welled in his eyes.* ♦ **well up.** *intr.v.* To rise; swell: *Anger welled up inside me.*

well² (wĕl) *adv.* **bet·ter** (bĕt′ər), **best** (bĕst). **1.** In a good or proper manner: *The children behaved very well on the trip.* **2.** Skillfully: *She plays the piano well.* **3.** Satisfactorily: *Did you sleep well?* **4.** Successfully or effectively: *The child gets along*

well with others. **5.** In a favorable or approving way: *They spoke well of you.* **6.** Thoroughly; completely: *Blend the ingredients well.* **7.** To a considerable degree or extent: *It was well after sunset.* **8.** With care or attention: *Listen well to what I say.* —*adj.* **better, best. 1.** In a satisfactory condition; right or proper: *All is well.* **2.** In good health; not sick: *She had the flu, but she's well now.* —*interj.* **1.** An expression used to show surprise or relief: *Well! You finally got here.* **2.** An expression used to introduce a remark or fill a pause during conversation: *Well, no one's perfect.* ♦ **as well.** In addition; also: *She took another class as well.* **leave well enough alone.** To not try to interfere with or change sbdy./sthg.: *He's happy with her; leave well enough alone.* **might** or **may as well.** With equal effect: *I might as well go.*

we'll (wēl). Contraction of *we will* and *we shall.*

HOMONYMS: we'll, wheel (circular frame).

---

well-bal·anced (wĕl′băl′ənst) *adj.* **1.** Evenly proportioned or balanced: *a well-balanced meal.* **2.** Mentally stable or sound: *a well-balanced man.*

well-be·ing (wĕl′bē′ĭng) *n.* [U] The state of being healthy, happy, or prosperous; welfare: *Be responsible for your own well-being.*

well-de·fined (wĕl′dĭ fīnd′) *adj.* With definite and distinct lines or features: *the well-defined shape of the mountains.*

well-done (wĕl′dŭn′) *adj.* Cooked all the way through: *a well-done steak.*

well-fed (wĕl′fĕd′) *adj.* Receiving plenty of healthy food: *a happy and well-fed baby.*

well-found·ed (wĕl′foun′dĭd) *adj.* Based on good judgment, reasoning, or evidence: *well-founded suspicions.*

well-groomed (wĕl′grōōmd′) *adj.* Neat and clean in dress or appearance: *well-groomed girls and boys.*

well-heeled (wĕl′hēld′) *adj.* Having plenty of money; prosperous: *His customers are all well-heeled.*

well-known (wĕl′nōn′) *adj.* Widely known; famous: *a well-known author.*

well-mean·ing (wĕl′mē′nĭng) *adj.* Having or showing good intentions: *well-meaning advice.*

well-nigh (wĕl′nī′) *adv.* Nearly; almost: *well-nigh impossible.*

well-off (wĕl′ôf′ or wĕl′ŏf′) *adj.* Rich or prosperous: *They seem to be quite well-off.*

well-read (wĕl′rĕd′) *adj.* Well informed because of extensive reading: *a well-read teacher.*

well-round·ed (wĕl′roun′dĭd) *adj.* **1.** Know-

W

ing or interested in a wide range or variety of subjects: *a well-rounded person.* **2.** Made up of a wide range of subjects: *a well-rounded education.*

well-thought-of (wĕl thôt′ŭv′ *or* wĕl thôt′ŏv′) *adj.* Respected: *Her work in physics is well-thought-of.*

well-timed (wĕl′tīmd′) *adj.* Happening or done at an appropriate time: *a well-timed remark.*

well-to-do (wĕl′tə dōō′) *adj.* Prosperous; rich: *His whole family is well-to-do.*

well-wish•er (wĕl′wĭsh′ər) *n.* A person who sends good wishes to another: *A crowd of well-wishers met the team at the airport.*

welsh (wĕlsh *or* wĕlch) also **welch** (wĕlch) *intr.v. Informal.* To cheat sbdy. by not paying a debt or bet or by not keeping a promise: *He welshed on the deal.*

welt (wĕlt) *n.* A ridge or bump raised on the skin by a blow or sometimes by an allergic reaction.

wench (wĕnch) *n.* An offensive term for a young woman or girl.

wend (wĕnd) *tr.v. Formal.* To proceed on or along (one's way); go: *People wended their way home after the fireworks.*

went (wĕnt) *v.* Past tense of **go.**

wept (wĕpt) *v.* Past tense and past participle of **weep.**

were (wûr) *v.* **1.** Second person singular and plural past tense of **be. 2.** First and third person plural past tense of **be. 3.** Past subjunctive of **be.**

HOMONYMS: were, whir (sound).

we're (wîr). Contraction of *we are.*

were•n't (wûrnt *or* wûr′ənt). Contraction of *were not.*

were•wolf (wâr′wŏŏlf′ *or* wîr′wŏŏlf′) *n.* A person in stories who is changed into a wolf or who can take the form of a wolf.

west (wĕst) *n.* [U] **1.** The compass direction in which the sun is seen to set, directly opposite east: *a wind blowing from the west.* **2.** Often **West. a.** A region or part of a country in this direction: *the west of Colombia.* **b.** The countries of western Europe and the Western Hemisphere. **c.** The region of the United States west of the Mississippi River: *She has always wanted to visit the West.* —*adj.* **1.** Of, in, or toward the west: *the west bank of the river.* **2.** From the west: *a west wind.* —*adv.* In, from, or toward the west: *a river flowing west.*

west•bound (wĕst′bound′) *adj.* Going toward the west: *a westbound train.*

west•er•ly (wĕs′tər lē) *adj.* **1.** Situated or moving toward the west: *a westerly direction.* **2.** Coming or being from the west: *westerly winds.*

west•ern (wĕs′tərn) *adj.* **1.** Situated in,

facing, or toward the west: *the western sky.* **2.** Coming from the west: *a western wind.* **3.** Native to, characteristic of, or growing in the west. **4.** Often **Western.** Relating to Europe and the countries of the Western Hemisphere, especially of North America. —*n.* Often **Western.** A book, film, or television program about frontier life in the western United States.

west•ern•er also **West•ern•er** (wĕs′tər-nər) *n.* A person who lives in the west, especially the western United States.

west•ern•ize (wĕs′tər nīz′) *tr.v.* **west•ern•ized, west•ern•iz•ing, west•ern•iz•es.** To cause (sbdy./sthg.) to adopt the customs of Western civilization: *a culture that is being westernized.*

west•ward (wĕst′wərd) *adv. & adj.* Toward, to, or in the west: *We sailed westward.*

wet (wĕt) *adj.* **wet•ter, wet•test. 1.** Covered or soaked with a liquid, such as water: *wet clothes.* **2.** Not yet dry or hardened: *wet paint; wet plaster.* **3.** Rainy, humid, or foggy: *a wet day; a wet climate.* —*n.* [U] Rainy or snowy weather: *The dog slept out in the wet.* —*tr.v.* **wet** *or* **wet•ted, wet•ting, wets.** To make (sthg.) wet: *She wet her hair.* —**wet′ly** *adv.* —**wet′ness** *n.* [U]

SYNONYMS: wet, moist, damp, humid. These adjectives mean covered with or filled with liquid. **Wet** is the most general: *She hung the wet towels on the clothesline.* **Moist** means slightly wet: *He wiped off the table with a moist sponge.* **Damp** means moist and often also unpleasantly sticky: *The damp cellar had a moldy smell.* **Humid** refers to a unpleasantly high degree of water vapor in the atmosphere: *The hot, humid weather made us want to jump in the pond.* **ANTONYM: dry.**

wet blanket *n. Informal.* A person or thing that ruins enjoyment or enthusiasm: *Don't spoil our fun by being a wet blanket.*

wet•land (wĕt′lănd′) *n. (usually plural).* A lowland area, such as a marsh or swamp, that is filled with moisture, especially when thought of as the home of wildlife: *laws to protect wetlands.*

wet suit *n.* A tight-fitting usually rubber suit worn in cold water, as by scuba divers, to keep in body heat.

we've (wēv). Contraction of *we have.*

HOMONYMS: we've, weave (make cloth).

whack (wăk *or* hwăk) *tr. & intr.v.* To strike with a sharp blow: *He was whacking at the wall with his hammer.* —*n.* **1.** A sharp swift blow: *Give this nail another whack.* **2.** The loud sound made by a sharp swift blow: *We heard several whacks from the kitchen.*

♦ **out of whack.** *Informal.* Out of order; not

working correctly: *I woke up late this morning because my alarm clock is out of whack.*
take a whack at. To try to do (sthg.): *I'll take a whack at bowling.*

whale (wāl *or* hwāl) *n.* Any of various very large sea mammals that resemble fish in form but breathe air. ◆ **a whale of a.** A very good (sthg.): *They had a whale of a party.*

HOMONYMS: whale, wail (cry).

---

whal·er (wā′lər *or* hwā′lər) *n.* **1.** A person who hunts whales. **2.** A ship or boat used in whaling.

whal·ing (wā′lĭng *or* hwā′lĭng) *n.* [U] The business or practice of hunting and killing whales.

wharf (wôrf *or* hwôrf) *n.*, *pl.* **wharves** (wôrvz *or* hwôrvz) *or* **wharfs.** A landing place or pier where ships may tie up and load or unload.

what (wŏt *or* hwŏt *or* wŭt *or* hwŭt; wət *or* hwət *when unstressed*) *pron.* **1.a.** Which thing or which particular one of many: *What are you having for dinner? What did she say?* **b.** Which kind, character, or name: *What are these objects?* **2.a.** That which; the thing that: *Listen to what I tell you.* **b.** Any thing that: *I intend to tell the truth, come what may.* **3.** *Informal.* Something: *I'll tell you one what: let's form a team.* —*adj.* **1.** Which one or ones of several or many: *What movie did you see?* **2.** Whatever: *They soon repaired what damage had been done.* **3.** How great; how surprising: *What a fool!* —*adv.* How much; in what way; how: *What does it matter?* —*interj.* An expression used to show surprise, disbelief, or other strong and sudden excitement: *What! I had no idea it was that late.* ◆ **and what have you.** And other things also: *We shopped for food, clothes, and what have you.* **and what not.** And other things also: *She brought cheese, crackers, and what not.* **what if.** What would occur if; suppose that: *What if you had a million dollars?* **what it takes.** The skill or qualities needed for success: *She's young, but she's got what it takes.* **what's in it for.** What good thing will (sbdy.) get as a result: *What's in it for me if I help you?* **what's what.** What is true or right: *I'll let him know what's what from the start.* **what's with.** *Informal.* What is the situation or issue with (sbdy./sthg.): *What's with you? You've been grouchy all week.* **what with.** Because of: *What with work and all, she hasn't had time to write.*

what·ev·er (wŏt ĕv′ər *or* hwŏt ĕv′ər *or* wŭt ĕv′ər *or* hwŭt ĕv′ər) *pron.* **1.** Everything or anything that: *Please do whatever you can to*

help. **2.** What amount that; the whole of what: *You may have whatever is left over.* **3.** No matter what: *Whatever you do, come early.* **4.** *Informal.* Which thing or things; what: *Whatever do you mean?* —*adj.* **1.** Of any number or kind; any: *Feel free to call on us for whatever help you need.* **2.** All of; the whole of: *He used whatever strength he had left to finish the job.* **3.** Of any kind at all: *He was left with nothing whatever.* —*interj.* An expression used to show that the speaker does not care: *"Do you want to go with me?" "Whatever."*

what·so·ev·er (wŏt′sō ĕv′ər *or* hwŏt′sō ĕv′ər *or* wŭt′sō ĕv′ər *or* hwŭt′sō ĕv′ər) *pron.* *Formal.* Whatever: *Do whatsoever you wish.* —*adj.* Whatever: *They have no power whatsoever.*

wheat (wēt *or* hwēt) *n.* [U] **1.** A grain-bearing grass grown in many parts of the world as an important source of food. **2.** The grain from this plant, often ground into flour.

whee·dle (wēd′l *or* hwēd′l) *tr.v.* **whee·dled, whee·dling, whee·dles.** To get (sthg.) by flattering or deceit: *He wheedled a promise out of me.*

wheel (wēl *or* hwēl) *n.* **1.** A solid disk or a rigid circular frame that turns around an axle in its center: *wagon wheels.* **2.** Something like a wheel or with a wheel for its main part: *a steering wheel; a potter's wheel.* **3. wheels.** Forces that provide energy, movement, or direction: *the wheels of commerce.* **4. wheels.** *Slang.* A car or small truck. —*v.* —*tr.* To move, roll, or transport (sbdy./sthg.) on wheels: *Put the books on the cart and wheel them to the library.* —*intr.* **1.** To turn or whirl around in place; pivot: *When the guard shouted, the thief wheeled and ran.* **2.** To move or fly in a curving or circular course: *A hawk wheeled over the meadow.* ◆ **at** *or* **behind the wheel. 1.** Steering a vehicle; driving: *Who was at the wheel when the accident happened?* **2.** In charge; responsible: *She's now behind the wheel of that company.* **big wheel.** *Slang.* A very powerful or influential person: *He's a big wheel in business.* **put the wheels in motion.** To start sthg.: *I'll go to the bank and put the wheels in motion for a loan.* **wheel and deal.** To make money or use influence, sometimes dishonestly: *He's always off wheeling and dealing somewhere.*

HOMONYMS: wheel, we'll (we will).

---

wheel·bar·row (wēl′băr′ō *or* hwēl′băr′ō) *n.* A small cart with one or two wheels, with handles at the rear, used to move small loads.

wheelbarrow

wheel·chair (wēl′châr′ or hwēl′châr′) n. A chair mounted on large wheels for use by a sick or disabled person.

wheel·er-deal·er (wē′lər dē′lər or hwē′lər dē′lər) n. Informal. A person who is smart, aggressive, and possibly dishonest, especially in business: Her brother was a wheeler-dealer, even in high school.

wheelchair

wheeze (wēz or hwēz) intr.v. **wheezed, wheez·ing, wheez·es. 1.** To breathe with difficulty, making a hoarse whistling sound: Asthma may cause a person to wheeze. **2.** To make a sound like heavy breathing: The steam engine chugged and wheezed. —n. A wheezing sound.

wheez·y (wē′zē or hwē′zē) adj. **wheez·i·er, wheez·i·est. 1.** Tending to wheeze. **2.** Making a wheezing sound: a wheezy old car.

when (wĕn or hwĕn) adv. At what time: When did you leave? —conj. **1.** At the time that: in April, when the snow melts. **2.** As soon as: I'll call you when I get there. **3.** At any time that; whenever: When the wind blows, the windows rattle. **4.** During the time at which; while: When I was out, she stopped by for a visit. **5.** Considering that; since: How are you going to pass when you won't study? —pron. What or which time: Since when has this been going on? —n. [U] The time or date: We knew the when but not the where of it.

when·ev·er (wĕn ĕv′ər or hwĕn ĕv′ər) adv. **1.** At any time: You can call me whenever. **2.** When: Whenever is she coming? —conj. **1.** At any time that: We can start whenever you're ready. **2.** Every time that: I smile whenever I think back on that day.

where (wâr or hwâr) adv. **1.** At or in what place or situation: Where is the phone? **2.** From what place or source: Where did you get that idea? **3.** To what place or end: Where does this road lead? —conj. **1.** At what or which place: I am going to my room, where I can study. **2.** In a place in which: She lives where the climate is mild. **3.** In any place that; wherever: Where there's smoke, there's fire. **4.** To a place in which: Let's go where it's quiet. —n. [U] **1.** The place or occasion: We know the when but not the where of it. **2.** What place, source, or cause: Where are you from?

where·a·bouts (wâr′ə bouts′ or hwâr′ə bouts′) adv. About where; in, at, or near what location: Whereabouts do you live? —n. [U] (used with a singular or plural verb): The approximate location of sbdy./sthg.: His whereabouts are unknown.

where·as (wâr ăz′ or hwâr ăz′) conj. Formal. **1.** Considering that: Whereas you have

worked hard to help us, so too will we work hard to help you. **2.** While on the contrary: We thought the meeting was tonight, whereas it was last night.

where·by (wâr bī′ or hwâr bī′) conj. By or through which: I had a plan whereby we could take two hours off our travel time.

where·in (wâr ĭn′ or hwâr ĭn′) adv. Formal. In what way; how: Wherein have I offended?

where·up·on (wâr′ə pŏn′ or hwâr′ə pŏn′ or wâr′ə pôn′ or hwâr′ə pôn′) conj. Formal. Closely following which: The metal cools until it hardens, whereupon it is removed from the sand.

wher·ev·er (wâr ĕv′ər or hwâr ĕv′ər) adv. **1.** In or to whatever place; situation: I used red pencil wherever needed. **2.** Where: Wherever have you been so long? —conj. In or to whatever place or situation: My thoughts are with you wherever you go.

where·with·al (wâr′wĭth ôl′ or hwâr′wĭth ôl′ or wâr′wĭth ôl′ or hwâr′wĭth ôl′) n. [U] The necessary means, especially financial means: We don't have the wherewithal to build a new pool.

wheth·er (wĕth′ər or hwĕth′ər) conj. **1.** Used in indirect questions to present one of two alternatives: We should find out whether the museum is open. **2.** Used to present alternative possibilities: Whether she wins or loses, this will be her last tournament.

HOMONYMS: whether, weather (state of the atmosphere).

whew (hwyōō or hwōō) interj. An expression used to show strong emotion, such as relief or amazement: Whew! We just made it in time!

which (wĭch or hwĭch) pron. **1.** What particular one or ones: Which is your house? **2.** The one or ones previously mentioned or implied: My house, which is near the ocean, stays cool in summer. **3.** Whatever one or ones; whichever: Choose which of these you want to take with you. **4.** A thing that: She left early, which was smart. —adj. **1.** What particular one or ones of a number of things or people: Which part of town do you mean? **2.** Any one or any number of; whichever: Use which door you please. **3.** Being previously mentioned or implied: It started to rain, at which point we ran.

which·ev·er (wĭch ĕv′ər or hwĭch ĕv′ər) pron. Whatever one or ones: Choose whichever you like, but choose. —adj. Being any one or any number of a group: Read whichever books you please.

whiff (wĭf or hwĭf) n. **1.** A brief passing odor carried in the air: a whiff of popcorn. **2.** A breath taken in, as of air or smoke: Take a whiff of this perfume.

while (wīl or hwīl) n. **1.** A period of time: stay for a while; singing all the while. **2.** The time, effort, or trouble taken in doing sthg.: *It will be worth your while to pay attention.* —*conj.* **1.** As long as; during the time that: *It was great while it lasted.* **2.** At the same time that; although: *My mother is tall while her sisters are short.* **3.** Whereas; and in contrast: *The soles of the shoes are leather, while the uppers are canvas.* —*v.* **whiled, whil•ing, whiles.** ◆ **while away.** *tr.v.* [sep.] To spend (time) idly or pleasantly: *while the summer away at the beach.*

HOMONYMS: while, wile (charm).

whim (wĭm *or* hwĭm) *n.* A sudden idea: *On a whim, we took the day off.*

whim•per (wĭm′pər *or* hwĭm′pər) *intr.v.* To cry or sob with soft broken sounds: *The child whimpered in pain.* See Synonyms at **cry.** —*n.* A low, broken, sobbing sound: *I thought I heard a whimper.*

whim•si•cal (wĭm′zĭ kəl *or* hwĭm′zĭ kəl) *adj.* **1.** Coming from whim: *a whimsical notion.* **2.** Irregular in behavior; unpredictable: *English spelling seems whimsical to many people.* —**whim′si•cal•ly** *adv.*

whim•sy (wĭm′zē *or* hwĭm′zē) *n., pl.* **whim•sies.** [C; U] An odd idea; a whim: *It was his whimsies that kept us busy.*

whine (wīn *or* hwīn) *intr.v.* **whined, whin•ing, whines.** **1.** To make a sad high-pitched sound, as in pain or complaint: *The dog whined at the door.* **2.** To complain or protest in a childish way: *Don't whine about every little thing!* —*n.* **1.** The act of whining: *A whine escaped her lips.* **2.** A whining sound or complaint: *the whine of a bullet.*

HOMONYMS: whine, wine (alcoholic drink).

whin•ny (wĭn′ē *or* hwĭn′ē) *intr.v.* **whin•nied, whin•ny•ing, whin•nies.** To neigh, especially in a gentle manner: *The horse whinnied when the girl approached.* —*n., pl.* **whin•nies.** The high, gentle sound made by a horse whinnying; a neigh.

whip (wĭp *or* hwĭp) *v.* **whipped whip•ping, whips.** —*tr.* **1.** To strike (sbdy./sthg.) repeatedly, as with a strap or rod: *whip a horse.* **2.** To affect (sbdy./sthg.) in a similar manner: *Icy winds whipped my face.* **3.** To beat (cream or eggs, for example) into a foam: *First, whip the egg whites.* **4.** To move, pull, or remove (sthg.) suddenly: *She whipped her notebook out of her bag.* **5.** *Informal.* To defeat (sbdy./sthg.): *You can't whip our team.* —*intr.* **1.** To move in a sudden quick way: *The car whipped around the corner.* **2.** To move like a whip: *Branches whipped against the windows.* —*n.* **1.** A flexible rod or piece of leather attached to a handle, used

for making animals move on or for striking sbdy. as punishment. **2.** Something that looks, bends, or moves about like a whip. ◆ **whip into shape.** To prepare or organize (sbdy./sthg.) in an efficient manner: *Don't worry; she'll whip the team into shape.* **whip up.** *tr.v.* [sep.] **1.** To cause (sthg.); excite: *The mayor tried to whip up support for the new library.* **2.** *Informal.* To prepare (sthg.) quickly: *We whipped up some sandwiches.*

whip•lash (wĭp′lăsh *or* hwĭp′lăsh′) *n.* [U] An injury to the neck or spine caused by a sudden backward or forward jerk of the head, as in a car accident.

whir (wûr *or* hwûr) *intr.v.* **whirred, whir•ring, whirs.** To move in a way that makes a buzzing or vibrating sound: *Bees whirred through the summer air.* —*n.* A sound of buzzing or vibration: *the whir of engines.*

HOMONYMS: whir, were (existed).

whirl (wûrl *or* hwûrl) *v.* —*intr.* **1.** To revolve rapidly around a center or an axis: *The airplane propeller whirled faster and faster.* See Synonyms at **turn.** **2.** To rotate or spin rapidly: *The dancer whirled on the stage.* **3.** To turn suddenly, changing direction: *The boy whirled around to face me.* **4.** To move or go quickly: *The bike racers whirled around the curve.* **5.** To have a spinning sensation; reel: *My head is whirling from the news.* —*tr.* **1.** To cause (sthg.) to rotate or turn rapidly: *whirl a pencil.* **2.** To move or drive (sthg.) in a circular or curving course: *The wind whirled the leaves.* —*n.* **1.** The act of rotating or revolving rapidly: *a whirl of dust.* **2.** A state of confusion: *Her mind was in a whirl.* **3.** A rapid series of events: *the social whirl.* **4.** *Informal.* A short trip or ride: *Let's go for a whirl in the car.* **5.** *Informal.* A brief or experimental try: *I've never skied before, but I'll give it a whirl.*

whirl•pool (wûrl′pōōl′ *or* hwûrl′pōōl′) *n.* **1.** A rapidly rotating current of water or other liquid; an eddy: *The whirlpool pulled the swimmer under.* **2.** A state of confusion; a tumult: *the whirlpool of local politics.* **3.** A bathtub or pool with jets of warm water that can be directed at body parts: *She soaked in the whirlpool.*

whirl•wind (wûrl′wĭnd′ *or* hwûrl′wĭnd′) *n.* **1.** A rapidly rotating column of air: *A whirlwind destroyed that house.* **2.** A confused rush: *shoppers caught in the holiday whirlwind.*

whisk (wĭsk *or* hwĭsk) *v.* —*tr.* **1.** To cause (sthg.) to move with quick, light, sweeping motions: *whisking the crumbs off the table.* **2.** To whip (eggs or cream). —*intr.* To move lightly, nimbly, and rapidly: *They whisked*

around the dance floor. —*n.* **1.** A quick, light, sweeping motion: *the whisk of a cow's tail.* **2.** A small short-handled broom. **3.** A kitchen tool used for whipping eggs or cream, for example: *a wire whisk.* ◆ **whisk away** or **off.** *intr.v.* To leave quickly: *They whisked off to dinner.* —*tr.v.* [sep.] To take (sbdy./sthg.) away quickly: *He whisked her away for a surprise dinner.*

whisk·er (wĭs′kər *or* hwĭs′kər) *n.* **1.a. whiskers.** The hair on a man's face. **b.** A single hair of a beard or mustache. **2.** One of the long hairs growing near the mouth of certain animals, such as cats, dogs, or rabbits.

whis·key also **whis·ky** (wĭs′kē *or* hwĭs′kē) *n.*, *pl.* **whis·keys** also **whis·kies.** [C; U] An alcoholic liquor distilled from grain, such as corn, rye, or barley.

whis·per (wĭs′pər *or* hwĭs′pər) *n.* **1.** Soft speech produced without full voice: *speak in a whisper.* **2.** A low rustling sound: *the whisper of wind in the trees.* —*v.* —*intr.* **1.** To speak softly: *whisper in the dark.* **2.** To make a soft rustling sound: *wind whispering in the leaves.* —*tr.* **1.** To say (sthg.) very softly: *Whisper the answer.* **2.** To say or tell (sthg.) privately or secretly: *The child whispered a secret.*

whis·tle (wĭs′əl *or* hwĭs′əl) *v.* **whis·tled, whis·tling, whis·tles.** —*intr.* **1.** To make a clear musical sound or call by forcing air through the teeth or through an opening in the lips: *whistling as she worked.* **2.** To make a clear, high musical sound by blowing on or through a device: *The referee whistled.* **3.** To move quickly so as to make a high-pitched sound: *The wind whistled through the trees.* —*tr.* **1.** To produce (sound) by whistling: *whistle a tune.* **2.** To call, direct, or signal (sbdy./sthg.) by whistling: *whistle a cab.* —*n.* **1.** A small wind instrument for making whistling sounds using one's breath: *The referee blew his whistle.* **2.** A device for making whistling sounds with forced air or steam: *a train whistle.* **3.** A whistling sound: *the whistle of bullets.* ◆ **blow the whistle on.** *Slang.* To expose wrongdoing in the hope of stopping it: *blow the whistle on corruption.* **wet (one's) whistle.** *Informal.* To have a drink: *Wet your whistle while you wait.*

white (wīt *or* hwīt) *n.* **1.** [C; U] The color of maximum lightness, as of milk, for example. **2.** [C] The white part of an egg: *Separate the white of the egg from the yolk.* **3.** [C] (usually plural). The white part of an eye, around the iris. **4. whites.** White trousers or a white outfit of a special type: *tennis whites.* **5.** [C] Also **White.** A member of a racial group of people with light skin, especially a person of European origin. —*adj.* **whit·er, whit·est. 1.** Of the color white, as new snow. **2.** Almost of the color white: *white wine; white hair.* **3.** Also **White.** Relating to a racial group with light skin, especially one of European origin.

4. Accompanied by or covered in snow: *a white Christmas.* **5.** Glowing with heat: *white flames.* —**white′ness** *n.* [U]

white blood cell *n.* Any of the white or colorless cells in the blood that have a nucleus and help protect the body against infections.

white-col·lar (wīt′kŏl′ər) *adj.* Relating to professionals or workers whose work usually does not involve manual labor.

white elephant *n.* **1.** A rare possession that is expensive to maintain: *Their old house is beautiful, but it's a white elephant.* **2.** Something of doubtful or limited value: *She bought a white elephant at a yard sale.*

white-hot (wīt′hŏt′ *or* hwīt′hŏt′) *adj.* So hot as to glow with a bright white light.

White House *n.* **1.** The executive branch of the U.S. government. **2.** The home and offices of the President of the United States.

white lie *n.* A small lie about a small matter, often told to keep a person's feelings from being hurt.

whit·en (wīt′n *or* hwīt′n) *tr.* & *intr.v.* To make or become white, especially by bleaching: *He whitened the clothes with bleach. The driftwood whitened in the sun.* —**whit′en·er** *n.*

white·wash (wīt′wŏsh′ *or* hwīt′wŏsh′ *or* wīt′wôsh′ *or* hwīt′wôsh′) *n.* **1.** [U] A mixture of lime and water, used in the past to whiten walls, fences, and other structures. **2.** [C] The hiding of flaws or failures: *a whitewash of his crimes.* —*tr.v.* **1.** To paint or coat (sthg.) with whitewash: *whitewash the fence.* **2.** To hide or make less of (a flaw, for example): *whitewash one's mistakes.*

white water *n.* [U] Turbulent, fast-moving water, as in rapids on a river.

whith·er (wĭth′ər *or* hwĭth′ər) *adv. Formal.* To what place, result, or condition: *Whither are we going?*

HOMONYMS: whither, wither (shrivel).

---

whit·ish (wī′tĭsh *or* hwī′tĭsh) *adj.* A little white: *whitish hair.*

whit·tle (wĭt′l) *v.* **whit·tled, whit·tling, whit·tles.** —*tr.* **1.** To cut small bits or peel shavings from (a piece of wood): *The boy whittled the block of pine.* **2.** To fashion or shape (sthg.) in this way: *whittle a toy boat.* **3.** [away; down] To reduce or eliminate (sthg.) gradually, as if by whittling: *He whittled down his debt by making regular payments.* —*intr.* To cut or shape wood with a knife: *He whittles as a hobby.* —**whit′tler** *n.*

whiz also **whizz** (wĭz *or* hwĭz) *v.* **whizzed, whiz·zing, whiz·zes.** —*intr.* **1.** To make a whirring sound, as of an object speeding through air: *The ball whizzed over my head.* **2.** To move rapidly; rush: *The train whizzed by.* —*tr.* To throw (sthg.) rapidly: *He whizzed the ball to me.* —*n.* **1.** A whirring sound: *the whiz of speeding bullets.* **2.** *Informal.* A

W

person who has remarkable skill: *He's a whiz at math.*

who (hōō) *pron.* **1.** What or which person or persons: *Who is calling?* **2.** Used as a relative pronoun to introduce a clause referring to a person: *The boy who came yesterday is now gone.*

whoa (wō *or* hwō) *interj.* **1.** An expression used as a command to stop, as to a horse. **2.** An expression used to stop sbdy. from moving or acting too quickly: *Whoa there! Is this wise?*

who'd (hōōd). Contraction of *who would* or *who had.*

who·dun·it (hōō dŭn′ĭt) *n. Informal.* A story about a crime and its solution; a mystery.

who·ev·er (hōō ĕv′ər) *pron.* **1.** Any person or persons: *Whoever comes should be welcomed into the house.* **2.** Who: *Whoever could have dreamed of such a thing?*

whole (hōl) *adj.* **1.** Containing all necessary parts; complete: *a whole outfit.* **2.** Not divided or separated; in one unit: *a whole acre of land.* **3.** Being the full amount, extent, or length: *The baby slept the whole night.* —*n.* **1.** All of a number, group, set, or thing: *We spent the whole of the class on review.* **2.** A complete system made up of interrelated parts: *the universe as a whole made up of the sun, planets, satellites, and other celestial bodies.* —*adv. Informal.* Entirely; completely: *a whole new idea.* ◆ **as a whole.** All parts or aspects considered; altogether: *As a whole, her work is quite good.* **on the whole.** Considering everything: *The damage doesn't look too bad, on the whole.*

whole·heart·ed (hōl′här′tĭd) *adj.* Showing full commitment; sincere: *wholehearted cooperation.* —**whole′heart′ed·ly** *adv.*

whole number *n.* Any of the set of numbers including 0 and all negative and positive multiples of 1.

whole·sale (hōl′sāl′) *n.* [U] The sale of goods in large quantities, especially to a retailer: *buy rugs at wholesale.* —*adj.* **1.** Relating to the sale of goods in large quantities for resale: *a wholesale dealer; wholesale prices.* **2.** Sold in large quantity, usually at a lower cost: *wholesale merchandise.* **3.** Done extensively and randomly: *wholesale destruction.* —*adv.* In large quantity: *sell wholesale.* —**whole′-sal′er** *n.*

whole·some (hōl′səm) *adj.* **1.** Leading to good health or well-being; healthy: *a wholesome diet.* **2.** Marked by a healthy physical, moral, or mental condition: *a wholesome rosy complexion; a wholesome attitude.* —**whole′-some·ly** *adv.* —**whole′some·ness** *n.* [U]

whole-wheat (hōl′wēt′) *adj.* **1.** Made from the entire grain of wheat, including the bran: *whole-wheat flour.* **2.** Made with whole-wheat flour: *whole-wheat bread.*

who'll (hōōl). Contraction of *who will* or *who shall.*

whol·ly (hō′lē) *adv.* Entirely; completely: *I'm not wholly sure I'll go.*

whom (hōōm) *pron.* The object form of **who:** *Whom were you calling?*

whom·ev·er (hōōm ĕv′ər) *pron.* The object form of **whoever:** *Call whomever you wish.*

whoop (hōōp *or* hwōōp *or* wōōp) *n.* **1.** A loud cry, as of celebration or excitement: *a victory whoop.* **2.** A hooting cry, as of a bird. —*v.* —*intr.* To make a loud shout or hooting cry: *Children whooped as they splashed in the lake.* —*tr.* To say (sthg.) with a whoop: *The fans whooped their delight.*

whoop·ing cough (hōō′pĭng *or* hōōp′ĭng *or* hwōō′pĭng *or* hwōōp′ĭng) *n.* [U] A bacterial infection of the lungs and respiratory passages that causes long periods of coughing.

whoops (wōōps *or* wŏŏps *or* hwōōps *or* hwŏŏps) *interj.* An expression used to show apology or mild surprise: *Whoops! I almost slipped on the ice.*

whop·per (wŏp′ər *or* hwŏp′ər) *n. Informal.* **1.** Something very big or remarkable: *That girl caught a whopper of a fish.* **2.** A big lie: *Fishermen are known for telling whoppers.*

whore (hôr) *n.* A prostitute.

whorl (wôrl *or* wûrl *or* hwôrl *or* hwûrl) *n.* **1.** A form that coils or spirals; a curl or swirl: *whorls of wood shavings.* **2.** One of the circular ridges of a fingerprint.

who's (hōōz). Contraction of *who is* or *who has.*

whose (hōōz) *adj.* **1.** The possessive form of **who:** *Whose watch is this?* **2.** The possessive form of **which:** *the dog whose foot is broken.*

who·so·ev·er (hōō′sō ĕv′ər) *pron. Formal.* Whoever.

why (wī *or* hwī) *adv.* For what purpose, reason, or cause: *Why is the door shut?* —*conj.* **1.** The reason, cause, or purpose for which: *I know why you're here.* **2.** Because of which;

for which: *The reason why I went swimming yesterday was that it was very hot.* —*n., pl.* **whys.** A cause or reason: *studying the whys of unemployment.* —*interj.* An expression used to show mild surprise, displeasure, or impatience: *Why, I'll be happy to help!*

wick (wĭk) *n.* A cord of loosely woven fibers, as in a candle or an oil lamp, that draws up fuel to the flame.

wick•ed (wĭk′ĭd) *adj.* **1.** Morally bad; evil: *Enjoying other people's pain is wicked.* **2.** Playfully malicious or mischievous: *Those boys played a wicked prank.* **3.** Severe and distressing: *He has a wicked cough.* **4.** *Slang.* Wonderful; terrific: *Her new car is wicked.* —*adv. Slang.* Extremely: *a wicked good movie.* —**wick′ed•ly** *adv.* —**wick′ed•ness** *n.* [U]

wick•er (wĭk′ər) *n.* [U] Items such as baskets or furniture made of interlaced plant branches or twigs: *She collects wicker.*

wide (wīd) *adj.* **wid•er, wid•est. 1.** Covering a large area from side to side: *a wide street.* **2.** With a specified distance from side to side: *a belt two inches wide.* **3.** Including much or many: *a wide selection of dresses.* **4.** Fully open or spread out: *with wide eyes.* **5.** At a distance from a desired point: *His first shot was wide of the goal by a foot.* —*adv.* **wider, widest. 1.** Over a great distance: *traveling far and wide.* **2.** To the fullest possible amount or degree; completely: *The door was wide open.* **3.** So as to miss the target: *Her shot went wide.* —**wide′ness** *n.* [U]

wide-a•wake (wīd′ə wāk′) *adj.* **1.** Completely awake: *I wasn't quite wide-awake when I answered the phone.* **2.** Alert; watchful: *a wide-awake police officer.*

wide-eyed (wīd′īd′) *adj.* **1.** With the eyes completely open: *He looked at me in wide-eyed surprise.* **2.** Innocent: *the wide-eyed belief of a child.*

wide•ly (wīd′lē) *adv.* **1.** In many places or by many people: *a TV star who is widely known; a reporter who has traveled widely.* **2.** To a large degree: *The two witnesses differed widely in their accounts of the accident.*

wid•en (wīd′n) *tr. & intr.v.* To make or become wide or wider: *construction to widen a road; eyes widened in surprise.*

wide•spread (wīd′sprĕd′) *adj.* **1.** Spread or scattered over a large area: *widespread damage from last month's storm.* **2.** Happening in many places or accepted by many people: *widespread agreement on the new proposal.*

wid•ow (wĭd′ō) *n.* A woman whose husband has died and who has not remarried. —*tr.v.* To make a widow or widower of (sbdy.): *She was widowed at a young age.*

wid•ow•er (wĭd′ō ər) *n.* A man whose wife has died and who has not remarried.

width (wĭdth *or* wĭtth) *n.* [U] The measurement of sth. from side to side: *a room ten feet in width and twenty in length.*

wield (wēld) *tr.v.* **1.** To handle (a weapon or tool) with skill and ease: *a woodsman wielding an ax.* **2.** To exercise (influence) effectively: *He wielded great power as Prime Minister.*

wie•ner (wē′nər) *n.* A hot dog.

wife (wīf) *n., pl.* **wives** (wīvz). A woman who is married to a man: *They became husband and wife.* —**wife′ly** *adj.*

wig (wĭg) *n.* An artificial covering of synthetic or human hair worn on the head, as a way to hide baldness or as part of a costume.

wig•gle (wĭg′əl) *intr. & tr.v.* **wig•gled, wig•gling, wig•gles.** To move or cause to move with short irregular motions from side to side: *She wiggled her toes. The dog's ears wiggled.* —*n.* A wiggling movement: *the wiggle of a rabbit's nose.*

wild (wīld) *adj.* **1.** Growing, living, or occurring in a natural state: *wild plants; wild animals.* **2.** Not lived in or developed by people: *wild unsettled country.* **3.** Uncivilized; savage: *wild outlaws robbing trains.* **4.** Lacking discipline or control: *a wild young boy.* **5.** Full of strong uncontrolled feeling: *wild with joy; wild laughter.* **6.** Very strange or unlikely: *a wild idea.* **7.** Far from the target: *a wild throw.* **8.** In card games, having a value determined by the cardholder's choice: *a wild card.* —*n. (usually plural).* A region not lived in or developed by human beings. *the wilds of northern Canada.* ◆ **be wild about.** *Informal.* To like (sbdy./sth.) very much: *I'm not wild about my brother's new girlfriend.* **in the wild.** In a natural state: *Have you ever seen moose in the wild?* —**wild′ly** *adv.* —**wild′ness** *n.* [U]

wild•cat (wīld′kăt′) *n.* **1.** Any of various wild small to medium-sized mammals, such as the lynx and the bobcat, related to the domestic cat. **2.** *Informal.* A quick-tempered or fierce person: *I thought she was calm, but she's a real wildcat.* —*adj.* **1.** Relating to an oil or a natural-gas well drilled in an area not known to be productive: *the risks of wildcat drilling.* **2.** Begun or done without official permission or approval: *a wildcat strike.*

wil•der•ness (wĭl′dər nĭs) *n.* [U] An unsettled, undeveloped region in its natural condition: *explorers in the wilderness.*

wild•fire (wīld′fīr′) *n.* **1.** [C] An intense and rapidly spreading fire: *The wildfire moved across the prairie.* **2.** [U] Something that acts very quickly and intensely: *the wildfire of revolution.*

wild•flow•er also **wild flow•er** (wīld′-flou′ər) *n.* A flowering plant that grows without being specially planted and cared for.

wild•fowl (wīld′foul′) *n., pl.* **wildfowl.** A wild bird that is hunted for food, such as a duck.

wild-goose chase (wīld′gōōs′) *n. Informal.* A useless or unsuccessful attempt to find sth.: *I wasted time on a wild-goose chase.*

wild•life (wīld′līf′) *n.* [U] Wild plants and

W

animals, especially animals living in the wild: *laws to protect wildlife.*

wild rice *n.* [U] A tall North American water grass and its narrow brownish seeds that are similar to rice and used as food.

Wild West *n.* [U] The western United States during the 19th and early 20th centuries: *stories of cowboys and outlaws in the Wild West.*

wile (wīl) *n. (usually plural).* **1.** A plan or trick intended to fool or catch sbdy.: *on guard against the salesman's wiles.* **2.** A manner or procedure used to attract, charm, or influence sbdy.: *She used all her wiles to persuade him.* —*tr.v.* **wiled, wil•ing, wiles.** To charm or fool (sbdy.): *They wiled him into betraying his friends.* ◆ **wile away.** *tr.v.* [sep.] To pass (time) agreeably: *wile away a Sunday afternoon.*

HOMONYMS: wile, while (during).

---

will[1] (wīl) *n.* **1.** [U] The power by which a person chooses a course of action: *the freedom of will.* **2.** [U] Strong attention to a purpose; determination: *the will to succeed.* **3.** [U] A desire or purpose, especially of one in authority: *They saw the flood as the will of God.* **4.** [U] Attitude toward others: *a man of goodwill.* **5.** [C] A legal document stating how a person wishes to give out his or her money and possessions after death: *Our lawyer helped us draw up a will.* —*v.* —*tr.* **1.** To influence (sbdy.) or cause (sthg.) by force of will: *The coach seemed to will us to find the strength to win.* **2.** To give (sthg.) in a legal will: *He willed his land to his grandchildren.* —*intr.* To make a choice; choose: *You're free to do as you will.* ◆ **at will.** Just as or when one wants: *free to come and go at will.*

will[2] (wīl) *aux.v.* Past tense **would** (wo͝od). **1.** Used to show future action or condition: *They will return later.* **2.** Used to show that sthg. is probable or seen as certain in the future: *You will regret this.* **3.** Used to show willingness: *Will you help me with this package?* **4.** Used to show command: *You will report to me afterward.* **5.** Used to show customary or habitual action: *People will talk about anyone who is different.* **6.** Used to show capacity or ability: *This metal will not crack.* —*tr. & intr.v. Formal.* To wish; desire: *Do what you will. Sit here if you will.*

will•ful also **wil•ful** (wīl′fəl) *adj.* **1.** Said or done on purpose; deliberate: *a willful waste of money.* **2.** Stubborn about doing what one wants: *a willful child.* —**will′ful•ly** *adv.* —**will′ful•ness** *n.* [U]

will•ing (wīl′ĭng) *adj.* **1.** In an agreeable state of mind; prepared: *I am willing to accept your apology.* **2.** Acting or ready to act gladly: *a willing worker.* —**will′ing•ly** *adv.* —**will′ing•ness** *n.* [U]

wil•low (wīl′ō) *n.* A tree with slender flexible twigs and narrow leaves.

wil•low•y (wīl′ō ē) *adj.* **wil•low•i•er, wil•low•i•est.** Like a willow, as in flexibility, slenderness, or gracefulness: *a tall and willowy fashion model.*

will•pow•er or **will pow•er** (wīl′pou′ər) *n.* [U] The strength of will to follow or complete one's decisions, wishes, or plans despite difficulties: *The runner needed all her willpower to finish the race.*

wil•ly-nil•ly (wīl′ē nĭl′ē) *adv. Informal.* **1.** Whether desired or not: *He must do what we've asked, willy-nilly.* **2.** Without order or plan: *a town that spread willy-nilly along the river.*

wilt (wīlt) *v.* —*intr.* **1.** To become limp or lose firmness; droop: *plants wilting in the heat.* **2.** To feel or show the effects of exhaustion: *We wilted after the long hike.* —*tr.* To cause (sthg.) to droop or lose freshness: *The sun wilted the flowers.*

wi•ly (wī′lē) *adj.* **wi•li•er, wi•li•est.** Full of clever tricks; cunning: *a wily fox.*

wimp (wĭmp) *n. Slang.* A person who is seen as weak or afraid. —**wimp′y** *adj.*

win (wĭn) *v.* **won** (wŭn), **win•ning, wins.** —*intr.* **1.** To finish first in a competition: *a horse that is sure to win.* **2.** To achieve success in an effort: *Okay, you win. We'll do it the way you want.* —*tr.* **1.** To finish first in (a race, for example): *He won the tennis game.* **2.** To receive (sthg.) as a prize or reward for performance: *Her horse won a blue ribbon.* **3.** To get or earn (sthg.) with effort: *Union leaders won benefits for the workers through talks with management.* **4.** To gain the affection and loyalty of (sbdy.): *The new student won many friends.* —*n.* A victory, especially in a competition: *The team has two wins, one loss, and one tie.* ◆ **win out.** *intr.v.* To succeed after difficulties: *The truth will win out.*

win over. *tr.v.* [sep.] To succeed in gaining the affection and support of (sbdy.): *Her speech won over the audience.*

wince (wĭns) *intr.v.* **winced, winc•ing, winc•es.** To move a little, involuntarily, as in pain, embarrassment, or distress: *She winced as the doctor pricked her finger to draw blood.* —*n.* A small, often sudden, movement or gesture back or away from sthg. unpleasant.

winch (wĭnch) *n.* A machine for pulling or lifting, made of a drum around which runs a rope or chain attached to the load being lifted.

wind[1] (wĭnd) *n.* **1.** [C; U] A current of air, especially a natural one that moves along or parallel to the ground: *a strong north wind; a fan that produces little wind.* **2.** [C] (*usually plural*). An influence, a tendency, or a destructive force: *the winds of change; the winds of war.* **3.** [U] Breath, especially nor-

---

W

mal breathing: *The soccer player had the wind knocked out of him.* **4.** [U] Gas produced in the stomach or intestines during digestion. **5. winds.** Wind instruments considered as a group. **6.** [U] Rumor or information: *There will be trouble if wind of this reaches the public.* —*tr.v.* To cause (sbdy.) to be short of breath: *The long hill winded the runners.* ◆ **in the wind.** Likely to happen soon: *new developments in the wind.*

wind² (wīnd) *v.* **wound** (wound), **wind·ing, winds.** —*tr.* **1.** [*around*] To wrap (sthg.) around itself or around sthg. else: *She wound the string into a ball. I wound the line around the pole.* **2.** To go or continue on (one's way) in a curving or twisting course: *The brook winds its way through the forest.* **3.** To turn (a crank, for example) in a series of circular motions: *Wind the crank to open the window.* **4.** To tighten the spring of (a mechanism) by turning a stem or cord, for example: *He wound his old watch.* —*intr.* **1.** To move in or have a curving or twisting course: *The river winds through the hills.* **2.** [*around*] To be coiled or spiraled: *The grapevine wound around the tree.* —*n.* A single turn, twist, or curve: *The mechanic gave the crank a wind.* ◆ **wind down.** *intr.v. Informal.* **1.** To gradually become less in energy, intensity, or activity: *Tourism really winds down at this time of year.* **2.** To relax; unwind: *winding down after a busy day.* **wind up.** *intr.v.* **1.** To come to an end: *The fishing season is winding up.* **2.** *Informal.* To arrive in a place or situation after or because of a course of action: *My watch was running slow, so I wound up being late.* —*tr.v.* [sep.] **1.** To bring (sthg.) to an end: *We wound the meeting up with lunch.* **2.** To turn (sthg.) around and around: *He is winding up the tape measure.* —**wind′er** *n.*

wind·break·er (wīnd′brā′kər) *n.* A jacket that protects against the wind.

wind·burn (wīnd′bûrn′) *n.* [U] Rough and reddened skin caused by wind.

wind-chill factor (wīnd′chĭl′) *n.* [U] The effect of the combination of wind speed and air temperature in cold weather.

wind·ed (wĭn′dĭd) *adj.* Breathing with difficulty, as after great physical effort: *a winded runner.*

wind·fall (wīnd′fôl′) *n.* A sudden unexpected piece of good fortune: *The money he won in the lottery was a windfall for his family.*

wind·ing (wīn′dĭng) *adj.* **1.** Turning or twisting: *a winding country road.* **2.** Spiral: *a winding staircase.*

wind instrument (wĭnd) *n.* A musical instrument, such as a clarinet or flute, in which sound is produced by a current of air, especially the breath.

wind·mill (wĭnd′mĭl′) *n.* A machine that

gets power from a wheel of adjustable blades turned by the wind.

win·dow (wĭn′dō) *n.* **1.** An opening in a wall or roof to let in light or air, usually framed and fitted with glass: *Open the window, please.* **2.** A pane of glass enclosed in such a framework; a windowpane: *The baseball broke the window.* **3.** An opening or transparent part that looks or functions like a window: *an envelope with a window.* **4.** A period of time during which an activity can or must take place: *a window of opportunity for saving endangered animals.* **5.** A small area on the screen of a computer monitor in which information is shown.

window box *n.* A long narrow box for growing plants, placed on a windowsill or ledge.

win·dow-dress·ing also **win·dow dress·ing** (wĭn′dō drĕs′ĭng) *n.* [U] **1.** Decorative show of goods for sale in store windows. **2.** A means of making sthg. look better than it really is: *The president of the company brought in new people just as window-dressing.*

win·dow·pane (wĭn′dō pān′) *n.* A piece of glass in a window.

win·dow-shop (wĭn′dō shŏp′) *intr.v.* **win·dow-shopped, win·dow-shop·ping, win·dow-shops.** To look at merchandise in store windows without intending to buy anything.

win·dow·sill (wĭn′dō sĭl′) *n.* The shelf-like part at the base of a window frame.

wind·shield (wĭnd′shēld′) *n.* A framed pane of glass or other transparent material in the front of a vehicle.

windshield wip·er *n.* (usually plural). A long thin metal arm with a rubber blade that moves across a windshield to clear it of rain.

wind·surf·ing (wĭnd′sûr′fĭng) *n.* [U] The sport of sailing while standing on a sailboard.

wind tunnel (wĭnd) *n.* A chamber through which wind can be forced at controlled speeds so its effect on an object, such as an aircraft or automobile, can be studied.

windsurfing

wind-up or **wind·up** (wīnd′ŭp′) *n.* A concluding part; a conclusion: *the wind-up of a long speech.* —*adj.* Operated by a spring that is wound up by hand: *a wind-up toy airplane.*

wind·y (wĭn′dē) *adj.* **wind·i·er, wind·i·est.** **1.** Characterized by or having wind: *a windy winter month.* **2.** Open to the wind; unprotected from winds: *the windy side of an apartment building.* **3.a.** Tending to talk for long periods: *a windy speaker.* **b.** Without substance; empty: *a windy speech.*

wine (wīn) *n.* **1.** [C; U] An alcoholic drink made of the fermented juice of grapes or other fruits or plants: *fine French wines; dandelion wine.* **2.** [U] The color of red wine: *a sweater available in gray, navy, or wine.* —*tr.v.* **wined, win·ing, wines.** To provide or entertain (sbdy.) with wines: *The mayor wined and dined the visiting businessmen.*

HOMONYMS: wine, whine (complain).

win·er·y (wī′nə rē) *n., pl.* **win·er·ies.** A place where wine is made.

wing (wĭng) *n.* **1.** One of a pair of specialized parts used for flying, as in birds, bats, or insects. **2.** A similar part of an animal that does not fly: *the wings of a penguin.* **3.** A part extending from the side of an aircraft that helps the craft to fly. **4. wings.** One of the areas on either side of a stage that are hidden from the audience. **5.** A structure attached to and connected with the side of a building: *building a new wing on the hospital.* **6.** A group that is part of or connected to an older or larger organization: *the conservative wing of the Party.* —*v.* —*intr.* To move on or as if on wings: *birds winging southward.* —*tr.* **1.** To throw (a ball, for example): *He winged a football at me.* **2.** To wound (a person or animal) slightly, as in the wing or arm: *The bullet only winged the victim.* ◆ **in the wings.** Close by in the background; available at short notice: *The future leaders of this political movement are waiting in the wings.* **on the wing.** In flight; flying: *birds on the wing.* **under (one's) wing.** Under one's protection; in one's care: *She took the new girl under her wing.* **wing it.** *Informal.* To say or do sthg. without preparation, planning, or enough experience: *He lost his notes for his speech, so he had to wing it.*

winged (wĭngd *or* wĭng′ĭd) *adj.* **1.** With wings or parts like wings: *winged insects; the winged seeds of the maple tree.* **2.** Moving on or as if on wings; flying: *on winged feet.*

wing·span (wĭng′spăn′) *n.* **1.** The distance between the tips of the wings on an aircraft. **2.** Wingspread.

wing·spread (wĭng′sprĕd′) *n.* The distance between the tips of the wings, as of a bird or an insect, when fully open: *a bird with a four-foot wingspread.*

wink (wĭngk) *v.* —*intr.* **1.** To close and open the eyelid of one eye on purpose, as to give sbdy. a message or signal: *He winked at me.* **2.** To shine on and off: *A lighthouse winked in the distance.* —*tr.* **1.** To close and open (an eye or the eyes) rapidly: *She winked her eyes to hold back tears.* **2.** To signal or express (sthg.) by winking: *I winked my approval of the idea.* —*n.* **1.a.** The act of winking. **b.** The very brief time required for a wink; an instant: *quick as a wink.* **2.** *Informal.* A brief period of sleep: *I got only a wink last night.* ◆ **wink at.** *tr.v.* [insep.] To pretend not to see (sthg.): *The mayor's staff all winked at police corruption.*

win·ner (wĭn′ər) *n.* A person or thing that wins, especially in sports, or a very successful person or thing: *The auto company's new model is sure to be a winner.*

win·ning (wĭn′ĭng) *adj.* **1.** Relating to the act of winning: *The judges chose the winning entry in the contest.* **2.** Successful; victorious: *the winning team.* **3.** Attractive; charming: *a winning personality.* —*n.* **1.** [U] The act of one that wins: *Her winning surprised us.* **2. winnings.** Something won, especially money: *The gambler took her winnings to the bank.* —**win′ning·ly** *adv.*

win·o (wī′nō) *n., pl.* **win·os.** *Slang.* A poor wine-drinking alcoholic: *winos on the sidewalk asking for money.*

win·some (wĭn′səm) *adj.* Charming, often in a childlike way: *a winsome smile.*

win·ter (wĭn′tər) *n.* [C; U] The season of the year between fall and spring. In the Northern Hemisphere, it is the coldest season, lasting from December until March. —*adj.* Occurring in or appropriate to the season of winter: *a winter storm; winter clothes.* —*intr.v.* To spend the winter: *Many retired people winter in Florida.*

win·ter·ize (wĭn′tə rīz′) *tr.v.* **win·ter·ized, win·ter·iz·ing, win·ter·iz·es.** To prepare (an automobile or a house, for example) for winter weather: *We winterized the car by changing the antifreeze.*

win·ter·time (wĭn′tər tīm′) *n.* [U] The season of winter.

win·try (wĭn′trē) *also* **win·ter·y** (wĭn′tə rē) *adj.* **win·tri·er, win·tri·est** *also* **win·ter·i·er, win·ter·i·est.** **1.** Characteristic of winter; cold: *wintry weather.* **2.** Suggestive of winter, as in coldness: *a wintry tone of voice.*

wipe (wīp) *tr.v.* **wiped, wip·ing, wipes.** **1.** To rub (sthg.), as with a cloth or paper, in order to clean or dry: *wipe the dishes with a towel.* **2.** [away; off] To remove (sthg.) by rubbing: *wiping the tears away.* **3.** To spread or apply (sthg.) by wiping: *She wiped furniture polish over the table.* —*n.* The act of wiping: *giving the table a wipe with a clean cloth.* ◆ **wipe out.** *tr.v.* [sep.] To destroy (sthg.) completely: *hoping to wipe out the disease.* —*intr.v.* *Informal.* To lose one's balance and fall: *The skier wiped out on her way down the mountain.*

wip·er (wī′pər) *n.* **1.** A person or thing that wipes. **2.** A device designed for wiping, especially a windshield wiper.

wire (wīr) *n.* **1.** [C; U] A usually flexible rod

or strand of metal, often covered with an electrical insulator, used to conduct electricity or to support parts of a structure: *telephone wires; a fence of barbed wire.* **2.** [C] A group of wire strands joined or twisted together; a cable. **3.** [C] **a.** A telegraph service. **b.** A telegram. **4.** [C] *Slang.* A hidden microphone, as on a person's body or in a building. —*v.* **wired, wir•ing, wires.** —*tr.* **1.** To join, connect, or attach (sthg.) with a wire or wires: *We've only wired the broken part onto the machine.* **2.** To equip (sthg.) with a system of electrical wires: *wire a house.* **3.** To send (a message, for example) by telegraph: *wire congratulations.* **4.** To send a telegram to (sbdy.): *The student wired home for money.* —*intr.* To send a telegram. ♦ **down to the wire.** *Informal.* To the very end, as in a race: *The horses ran neck and neck down to the wire.* **under the wire. 1.** At the finish line of a race. **2.** *Informal.* At the last moment: *He got his application in just under the wire.*

wire•less (wīr′lĭs) *adj.* Without a wire or wires: *wireless communication.* —*n.* A radio telegraph or radio telephone system.

wire•tap (wīr′tăp′) *n.* A hidden listening or recording device connected to a telephone or telegraph circuit. —*tr.v.* **wire•tapped, wire•tap•ping, wire•taps.** To listen in on (a telephone circuit) by means of a wiretap: *The FBI wanted to wiretap the suspect's phone.*

wir•ing (wīr′ĭng) *n.* [U] **1.** The act of attaching, connecting, or installing electric wires: *We hired an electrician to do the wiring.* **2.** A system of electric wires: *The fire started in the wiring.*

wir•y (wīr′ē) *adj.* **wir•i•er, wir•i•est. 1.** Like wire in form or quality, especially in stiffness: *wiry hair.* **2.** Strong and thin: *a basketball player with a wiry physique.* —**wir′i•ness** *n.* [U]

Wis. *abbr.* An abbreviation of Wisconsin.

wis•dom (wĭz′dəm) *n.* [U] **1.** Understanding of what is true, right, or of lasting importance: *gaining wisdom with age.* **2.** Common sense; good judgment: *We questioned the wisdom of their decision.*

wisdom tooth *n.* One of four molars, the last on each side of both jaws in humans, usually appearing much later than the other teeth.

wise (wīz) *adj.* **wis•er, wis•est. 1.** With wisdom: *a wise leader.* **2.** Showing common sense: *a wise decision.* **3.** Showing clever thinking: *a wise move.* **4.** [*to*] *Informal.* Provided with information; informed: *I'm wise to your tricks.* **5.** *Slang.* Rude and disrespectful: *Don't get wise with me, kid.* ♦ **wise up.** *intr.v. Slang.* To become aware or informed of worldly matters: *I used to pay full price until I wised up.* —**wise′ly** *adv.*

—**wise** *suff.* A suffix that means in a specified manner, position, or direction: *clockwise.*

wise•crack (wīz′krăk′) *Informal. n.* A joking or sarcastic remark. —*intr.v.* To make a

wisecrack: *His two friends stood watching him work and wisecracking to each other.*

wise guy *n. Slang.* An annoying person who talks as if he or she knew everything.

wish (wĭsh) *n.* **1.** A desire or longing for sthg.: *a secret wish for fame and fortune.* **2.** An expression of such a desire or longing: *Give them my best wishes for their health and happiness.* —*v.* —*tr.* **1.** To want (sthg.): *I wish you would hurry.* See Synonyms at **desire. 2.** To feel or express (for sbdy.) a hope of (sthg.): *wish him luck.* —*intr.* **1.** [*for*] To have or feel a desire: *He wished for a skateboard.* **2.** To make or express a wish: *wish upon a star.* —**wish′er** *n.*

wish•bone (wĭsh′bōn′) *n.* The forked bone in front of the breastbone in most birds. After eating, two people may pull the bone apart, and according to superstition, the person who gets the bigger part can make a wish.

wish•ful (wĭsh′fəl) *adj.* Having or expressing a wish or longing: *wishful eyes.* —**wish′ful•ly** *adv.*

wishful thinking *n.* [U] Mistaking one's wishes or desires for reality: *His claim that he can win this election is just wishful thinking.*

wish•y-wash•y (wĭsh′ē wŏsh′ē *or* wĭsh′ē-wô′shē) *adj.* **wish•y-wash•i•er, wish•y-wash•i•est.** *Informal.* Without much strength of character or purpose: *too wishy-washy to make a decision and stay with it.*

wisp (wĭsp) *n.* **1.** A small amount: *a wisp of smoke.* **2.** A person or thing that is thin, small, or weak: *a wisp of a girl.*

wist•ful (wĭst′fəl) *adj.* **1.** Full of wishful desire: *a wistful look at the toys in the store window.* **2.** Thoughtful and sad: *a wistful smile as she said good-bye.* —**wist′ful•ly** *adv.* —**wist′ful•ness** *n.* [U]

wit (wĭt) *n.* **1.** [U] The natural ability to understand; intelligence. **2.a.** [C] (*usually plural*). Creative ability to solve problems; resourcefulness: *We had to use our wits to find our way back to camp.* **b. wits.** Healthy mental processes; sanity: *I was scared out of my wits.* **3.** [C] **a.** The ability to say clever and humorous things: *He has a quick wit.* **b.** A person with this ability. ♦ **at (one's) wits' end.** Without any further ideas about how to solve a problem: *I've looked for my keys everywhere; I'm at my wits' end.*

witch (wĭch) *n.* **1.** A woman believed to have supernatural powers and practice magic. **2.** An extremely unpleasant woman; a hag.

witch•craft (wĭch′krăft′) *n.* [U] Magic; sorcery.

witch doctor *n.* A person believed to be able to cure sickness by magic or by driving away evil spirits, especially among African peoples.

witch-hunt (wĭch′hŭnt′) *n.* An investigation that is said to be done to uncover disloyalty or illegal activities, but is really done to make trouble for people with differing opinions or to gain publicity for the investigators.

with (wĭth *or* wĭth) *prep.* **1.** In the company of: *Did you go with her?* **2.** Next to; beside: *I sat with my friends.* **3.** Having as a possession or a characteristic: *They arrived with good news. He just sat there with his mouth open.* **4.a.** In a manner characterized by: *an operation performed with skill.* **b.** In the performance, use, or operation of: *I had trouble with the car.* **5.** In the care of: *We left the cat with the neighbors.* **6.** In the opinion of: *if it's all right with you.* **7.** Of the same opinion or belief as: *He is with us on that issue.* **8.** In the membership or employment of: *He's with a large law firm.* **9.** By the means or use of: *eat with a fork.* **10.** In spite of: *With all her experience, she could not get a job.* **11.** In the same direction as: *sail with the wind.* **12.** In regard or relation to: *We are pleased with her decision.* **13.** Having as a part; including: *The bill comes to $29.95 with postage and handling.* **14.** As a result or consequence of: *sick with the flu.* **15.** So as to be touching or joined to: *The dancers linked arms with their partners.*

with•draw (wĭth drô′ *or* wĭth drô′) *v.* **with•drew** (wĭth drōō′ *or* wĭth drōō′), **with•drawn** (wĭth drôn′ *or* wĭth drôn′), **with•draw•ing, with•draws.** *—tr.* **1.** [*from*] To take (sthg.) back or away; remove: *withdraw money from the bank.* **2.** To remove (sbdy./sthg.) from participation or consideration: *She withdrew her application.* *—intr.* **1.** To move or draw back: *The dinner guests withdrew to the den.* **2.** [*from*] To remove oneself from participation: *I decided to withdraw from one of my classes.*

with•draw•al (wĭth drô′əl) *n.* **1.** [C; U] The act of withdrawing: *the candidate's withdrawal from the race.* **2.** [C] A removal of sthg. that has been deposited: *a withdrawal from a bank account.* **3.** [U] The physical and mental reaction to stopping the use of an addictive substance: *a drug addict going through the pains of withdrawal.*

with•drawn (wĭth drôn′ *or* wĭth drôn′) *v.* Past participle of **withdraw.** *—adj.* **1.** Socially quiet; shy: *a withdrawn person.* **2.** Emotionally unresponsive: *He became withdrawn after the death of his wife.*

with•drew (wĭth drōō′ *or* wĭth drōō′) *v.* Past tense of **withdraw.**

with•er (wĭth′ər) *v.* *—intr.* **1.** To dry up from or as if from lack of water; shrivel: *The flowers withered in the vase.* **2.** To lose freshness, vitality, or force: *Her arm had withered during the many months in the cast.* *—tr.* **1.** To cause (sthg.) to shrivel or fade: *sun that withered the plants.* **2.** To make (sbdy.) speechless or incapable of action: *The principal withered the noisy student with a glance.* ◆ **wither away.**

intr.v. To dry up or lose vitality: *She seemed to wither away after her husband died.*

HOMONYMS: wither, whither (to where).

---

with•hold (wĭth hōld′ *or* wĭth hōld′) *tr.v.* **with•held** (wĭth hĕld′ *or* wĭth hĕld′), **with•hold•ing, with•holds. 1.** To keep (sthg.) in control; restrain: *withhold applause until the end of the act.* **2.** To keep from giving, granting, or permitting (sthg.): *Let's withhold judgment until we know the whole story.* See Synonyms at **keep. 3.** To deduct (withholding tax) from an employee's wages or salary: *My employer withholds state and federal taxes from my paychecks.*

with•hold•ing tax (wĭth hōl′dĭng *or* wĭth-hōl′ dĭng) *n.* [C; U] A share of an employee's pay kept back by an employer and paid to the government as the employee's income tax.

with•in (wĭth ĭn′ *or* wĭth ĭn′) *adv.* In or into the inner part; inside: *The girl kept all her dreams within.* *—prep.* **1.** In the inner part or parts of; inside: *within the body.* **2.** Inside the limits of sthg. in time or distance: *They arrived within an hour of us. We are within ten miles of home.* **3.** Not going beyond: *within the laws of the land.*

with•out (wĭth out′ *or* wĭth out′) *adv.* On the outside: *The building is in good condition within and without.* *—prep.* **1.** Not having; lacking: *without a car to get home.* **2.** Not accompanied by; in the absence of: *There's no smoke without fire.*

with•stand (wĭth stănd′ *or* wĭth stănd′) *tr.v.* **with•stood** (wĭth stōōd′ *or* wĭth stōōd′), **with•stand•ing, with•stands.** To resist or oppose (sthg.), especially with success: *The buildings withstood the hurricane.*

wit•less (wĭt′lĭs) *adj.* Lacking intelligence or wit; foolish: *a witless decision.*

wit•ness (wĭt′nĭs) *n.* **1.** A person who can give an account of sthg. seen, heard, or experienced personally: *a witness to the accident.* **2.** A person who is called to testify before a court of law: *a witness for the defense.* **3.** A person asked to be present at a transaction in order to serve as an observer: *a witness at a wedding.* **4.** A person who signs a document as a mark that it is real and true: *a witness to a will.* *—tr.v.* **1.** To be present at or have personal knowledge of (sthg.): *witness a volcanic eruption.* **2.** To sign (a document) as witness to its legality or authenticity: *witness a will.* ◆ **bear witness to.** To be proof of (sthg.): *His offer bears witness to his kindness.*

wit•ti•cism (wĭt′ĭ sĭz′əm) *n.* A witty remark.

wit•ty (wĭt′ē) *adj.* **wit•ti•er, wit•ti•est. 1.** Having or showing wit in speech or writing: *a* *witty person.* **2.** Characterized by wit; funny or clever: *a witty saying.* **—wit′ti•ly** *adv.* **—wit′ti•ness** *n.* [U]

wives (wīvz) *n.* Plural of **wife.**

wiz (wĭz) *n. Informal.* A person seen as especially talented or skilled: *She's a math wiz.*

wiz•ard (wĭz′ərd) *n.* **1.** A sorcerer or magician. **2.** A skilled or clever person: *a wizard with computers.*

wiz•ard•ry (wĭz′ər drē) *n.* [U] The art, skill, or practice of a wizard.

wiz•ened (wĭz′ənd) *adj.* Dried up or shriveled: *the wizened face of the old fisherman.*

wk. *abbr.* An abbreviation of week.

wkly. *abbr.* An abbreviation of weekly.

wob•ble (wŏb′əl) *v.* **wob•bled, wob•bling, wob•bles.** *—intr.* To move unsteadily from side to side: *The table wobbles because one leg is too short.* *—tr.* To cause (sthg.) to wobble: *Please don't wobble the desk while I'm writing.* *—n.* Unsteady motion: *The top spun with a wobble.*

wob•bly (wŏb′lē) *adj.* **wob•bli•er, wob•bli•est.** Tending to wobble; unsteady: *The patient is out of bed, but she is still wobbly.*

woe (wō) *n. Formal.* **1.** [U] Deep unhappiness, as from grief: *wishing for company in her woe.* **2.** [C] *(usually plural).* A misfortune or difficulty: *What is the cause of their financial woes?*

woe•be•gone (wō′bĭ gôn′ *or* wō′bĭ gŏn′) *adj.* Affected with or marked by sadness: *a woebegone expression on his face.*

woe•ful (wō′fəl) *adj.* **1.** Full of woe; mournful: *The poor man told a woeful tale.* **2.** Shamefully bad: *woeful treatment of the prisoners.* **—woe′ful•ly** *adv.*

wok (wŏk) *n.* A metal pan with a rounded bottom, used in Asian cooking for frying and steaming.

woke (wōk) *v.* A past tense of **wake**[1].

wok•en (wō′kən) *v.* A past participle of **wake**[1].

wolf (woŏlf) *n., pl.* **wolves** (woŏlvz). **1.** A meat-eating mammal related to the dog and living chiefly in northern regions. **2.** A person who is regarded as fierce, cruel, or dangerous. *—tr.v.* [*down*] To eat (sthg.) hungrily or greedily: *wolfed down the hamburger.* ◆ **wolf in sheep's clothing.** A person who pretends to be friendly while really planning to do harm.

wol•ver•ine (woŏl′və rēn′ *or* woŏl′və-rēn′) *n.* A small but fierce meat-eating mammal of northern regions, related to the weasel and with thick dark fur and a bushy tail.

wolves (woŏlvz) *n.* Plural of **wolf.**

wom•an (woŏm′ən) *n., pl.* **wom•en** (wĭm′ĭn). **1.** [C] An adult female human. **2.** [U] Women considered as a group; womankind: *The group discussed woman's role in the tribe's farming system.* ◆ **to a woman.** Without exception among a group of women:

They favored the proposal to a woman. —SEE NOTE at **man.**

wom•an•hood (woŏm′ən hoŏd′) *n.* [U] **1.** The condition of being an adult female person: *when a girl reaches womanhood.* **2.** Women considered as a group: *an insult to womanhood.*

wom•an•kind (woŏm′ən kīnd′) *n.* [U] Women considered as a group.

wom•an•ly (woŏm′ən lē) *adj.* With qualities generally considered characteristic and pleasing in a woman: *a womanly concern for people's feelings.* **—wom′an•li•ness** *n.* [U]

womb (woŏm) *n.* The uterus.

wom•en (wĭm′ĭn) *n.* Plural of **woman.**

wom•en•folk (wĭm′ĭn fōk′) *pl.n. Informal.* The women of a community or family: *soldiers concerned for their womenfolk back home.*

wom•en's room (wĭm′ĭnz) *n.* A public restroom for women.

won (wŭn) *v.* Past tense and past participle of **win.**

HOMONYMS: won, one (single).

won•der (wŭn′dər) *n.* **1.** [C] A person or thing that causes awe, surprise, or admiration: *a wonder of modern technology.* **2.** [U] Awe, astonishment, or admiration. *The sight of the whales filled us with wonder.* **3.** [C] An event that cannot be explained by the laws of nature; a miracle. **4.** [U] A feeling of puzzlement or doubt: *She heard his refusal with wonder.* *—v.* *—intr.* **1.** To have a feeling of awe or admiration: *They wondered at the sight of the canyon.* **2.** To be filled with curiosity or doubt: *He wondered about the future.* *—tr.* To feel curiosity or be in doubt about (sthg.): *I wonder what she is doing.* ◆ **little** or **small wonder.** It isn't surprising: *Small wonder you're cold—where's your coat?* **work wonders.** To produce surprising and effective results: *That medicine works wonders for my allergies.*

SYNONYMS: wonder, marvel, miracle, sensation. These nouns all mean sthg. that causes amazement or admiration in others. *If you want to see wonders of architecture, go see the Egyptian pyramids. That dinner was a marvel. The artificial heart is a miracle of medical science. Her latest book is a sensation; it has already won three literary prizes.*

won•der•ful (wŭn′dər fəl) *adj.* **1.** Capable of causing wonder; astonishing: *A soaring eagle is a wonderful sight.* **2.** Admirable; excellent: *a wonderful idea.* **—won′der•ful•ly** *adv.*

won•der•land (wŭn′dər lănd′) *n.* **1.** A marvelous imaginary place: *the wonderland described in the novel.* **2.** A marvelous real

W

place or scene: *We went camping in a won-derland of nature.*

won•der•ment (wŭn'dər mənt) *n.* [U] Astonishment, awe, or surprise: *The audience stared at the movie screen in wonderment.*

won•drous (wŭn'drəs) *adj.* Remarkable or extraordinary; wonderful: *wondrous results.* —**won'drous•ly** *adv.*

wont (wônt *or* wōnt *or* wŭnt) *Formal. adj.* Accustomed or used: *He was wont to go for long walks on the beach.* —*n. (usually singu-lar).* Customary practice: *She jogged that morning, as was her wont.*

won't (wōnt). Contraction of *will not.*

woo (wōō) *tr.v.* —*tr.* **1.** A term used in the past meaning to seek the romantic affection of (sbdy., usually a woman). **2.** To try to get or achieve (sthg.): *woo money from investors.* **3.** To try to get the favor of (sbdy.); try to per-suade: *Advertisers often woo teenagers.*

wood (wōōd) *n.* **1.** [U] **a.** The tough fibrous substance beneath the bark of trees and shrubs. **b.** This substance cut and prepared for use as building material and fuel: *a table made of wood.* **2.** [C] *(usually plural).* A dense growth of trees; a forest: *We went for a walk in the woods.* **3.** [C] Something made from wood, such as a golf club with a wooden head or a woodwind instrument.

HOMONYMS: wood, would (past tense of will).

---

wood•carv•ing (wōōd'kär'vĭng) *n.* **1.** [U] The art of creating or decorating wood objects by cutting and carving with a tool. **2.** [C] A carved wood object: *woodcarvings of animals.*

wood•chuck (wōōd'chŭk') *n.* A short-legged North American rodent with brownish fur that digs its home underground; a groundhog.

wood•ed (wōōd'ĭd) *adj.* Covered with trees or woods: *wooded hills.*

wood•en (wōōd'n) *adj.* **1.** Made of wood: *a wooden bridge.* **2.** Stiff and unnatural: *a wooden smile.* —**wood'en•ly** *adv.*

wood•land (wōōd'lənd) *n. (usually plural).* Land covered with trees and shrubs: *animals found in woodlands.*

wood•peck•er (wōōd'pĕk'ər) *n.* Any of various usually brightly colored birds with strong claws for holding onto and climbing trees and a strong pointed bill for drilling into bark and wood.

woods•man (wōōdz'mən) *n.* A man who works or lives in the woods or is skilled in things related to life in the woods, such as hunting or camping.

woods•y (wōōd'zē) *adj.* **woods•i•er,** **woods•i•est.** Relating to or typical of the woods: *an interest in woodsy activities.*

wood•wind (wōōd'wĭnd') *n.* **1.** A wind instrument, such as a bassoon, clarinet, or flute, made of a tube with holes and produc-ing sound when air is blown into or across a mouthpiece. **2. woodwinds.** The section of an orchestra or a band which includes such instruments.

wood•work (wōōd'wûrk') *n.* [U] Objects made of or work done in wood, especially wooden interior fittings in a house, as doors or windowsills. ◆ **out of the woodwork.** Out of places unknown, hidden, or unexpect-ed: *People come out of the woodwork to claim reward money.*

wood•work•ing (wōōd'wûr'kĭng) *n.* [U] The art, act, or trade of working with wood.

wood•y (wōōd'ē) *adj.* **wood•i•er, wood•i•est.** **1.** Forming or made up of wood: *woody tissue.* **2.** Characteristic or like of wood: *a woody smell.*

woof (wōōf) *n.* The characteristically deep bark of a dog: *The dog gave a low woof.* —*intr.v.* To make such a sound.

wool (wōōl) *n.* [U] **1.** The dense, soft, often curly hair of a sheep and certain other ani-mals, used to make yarn and fabric. **2.** Yarn, cloth, or clothing made of this hair. ◆ **pull the wool over (one's) eyes.** To fool or trick (sbdy.): *You really pulled the wool over my eyes about the surprise party.*

wool•en also **wool•len** (wōōl'ən) *adj.* **1.** Made of wool: *a woolen blanket.* **2.** Making or dealing in wool cloth or clothing: *a woolen mill.* —*n. (usually plural).* Fabric or clothing made from wool: *put woolens in storage for the summer.*

wool•ly (wōōl'ē) *adj.* **wool•li•er, wool•li•est.** **1.** Relating to or covered with wool: *a woolly coat; a woolly lamb.* **2.** Lacking detail or clarity: *woolly thinking.* ◆ **wild and wool-ly.** Rough and disorderly; lawless: *a wild and woolly frontier town.* —**wool'li•ness** *n.* [U]

wooz•y (wōō'zē *or* wōōz'ē) *adj.* **wooz•i•er, wooz•i•est.** **1.** Dazed or confused: *a patient feeling woozy after an operation.* **2.** Queasy or dizzy: *The amusement park ride left me a little woozy.* —**wooz'i•ness** *n.* [U]

word (wûrd) *n.* **1.** [C] A spoken sound or group of sounds that communicates a mean-ing: *The baby said her first word.* **2.** [C] A written letter or group of letters representing such a sound or group of sounds: *There are seven words in this sentence.* **3.** [C] A short conversation or a comment: *May I have a word with you?* **4.** [U] A promise: *keeping her word to be on time.* **5.** [C] A direction to do sthg.; an order: *Just say the word, and we'll come to help.* **6.** [U] News; information: *She sent word of her safe arrival.* **7. words.** Hostile or angry remarks made back and

W

---

forth; a quarrel: *He had words with his noisy neighbor.* —*tr.v.* To express (sthg.) in words: *I don't know how to word my invitation.* ♦ **good word. 1.** A favorable comment: *I'll put in a good word for you with the boss.* **2.** Favorable news: *What's the good word?* **in so many words.** In precisely those words; exactly: *They wanted us to leave, but wouldn't say it in so many words.* **of few words.** Not talkative: *a person of few words.* **take at (one's) word.** To believe (sbdy.) and act based on his or her statement: *We took him at his word that he would lock up when he left.* **word for word.** In exactly the same words: *She repeated the news she'd heard, word for word.*

word·ing (wûr′dĭng) *n.* [U] The act or style of expressing in words: *the formal wording of his letter.*

word·less (wûrd′lĭs) *adj.* **1.** Not expressed in words; unspoken: *a look that gave me her wordless thanks.* **2.** Speechless; silent: *wordless with gratitude.* —**word′less·ly** *adv.* —**word′less·ness** *n.* [U]

word of mouth *n.* [U] Spoken communication: *The news spread by word of mouth.*

word processing *n.* [U] The creation and production of documents and texts by means of computer systems.

word processor *n.* A computer system specially designed for or capable of word processing.

word·y (wûr′dē) *adj.* **word·i·er, word·i·est.** Using or expressed in too many words: *a wordy speaker; a wordy description.* —**word′i·ly** *adv.* —**word′i·ness** *n.* [U]

wore (wôr) *v.* Past tense of **wear.**

work (wûrk) *n.* **1.** [U] Physical or mental effort or activity directed toward producing or completing sthg.: *a project that will require a lot of work.* **2.** [U] Employment in a job or profession: *looking for work.* **3.** [U] Something that one is doing, making, or performing, especially as a job or a duty: *begin the day's work.* **4.** [U] **a.** The part of a day reserved for one's job: *I met her after work.* **b.** One's place of employment: *Should I call you at home or at work?* **5.** [C] **a.** A product of a particular kind of effort or activity: *This story is the work of an active imagination.* **b.** An act; a deed: *church members doing good works in the community.* **6.** [C] An artistic creation, such as a painting or musical composition. **7.** [U] In physics, the transfer of energy to a body, especially by applying force to move it. **8. works.** Engineering structures, such as bridges or dams. **9. works.** (*used with a singular or plural verb*). A factory, plant, or similar building for a specific type of business or industry: *a steelworks.* **10. works.** Internal mechanism: *the works of a watch.* **11. works.** *Informal.* The full range of possibilities; everything: *We ordered a pizza with the works.* —*v.* —*intr.* **1.**

To make a physical or mental effort to do, make, or accomplish sthg.: *work hard in the garden.* **2.** To be employed; have a job: *She quit school to work.* **3.** To function; operate: *How does this machine work? The telephone isn't working.* **4.** To have the desired effect or result; be successful: *This recipe seems to work.* **5.** To arrive at a specified condition through gradual or repeated movement: *The knot in my shoelaces worked loose.* **6.** To proceed or progress slowly and with difficulty: *We worked through the hardest math problems together.* —*tr.* **1.** To cause or effect (sthg.): *working miracles.* **2.** To cause (sthg.) to operate or function: *The pilot worked the controls.* **3.** To shape or forge (sthg.): *The artist worked the metal into a sculpture.* **4.** To knead or manipulate (a substance) in preparation: *Work the bread dough before shaping it.* **5.** To bring (sthg.) to a specified condition by gradual or repeated effort: *I finally worked the window open.* **6.** To make, achieve, or pay for (sthg.) by work or effort: *She worked her way through college.* **7.** To make (land, for example) productive: *work a farm.* **8.** To cause (sbdy./sthg.) to work: *The farmer works his horses hard.* **9.** To excite or provoke (sbdy.): *The speaker worked the crowd into a frenzy.* ♦ **in the works.** In preparation; under development: *There's a new movie in the works.* **out of work.** Without a job; unemployed. **work off.** *tr.v.* [sep.] To get rid of (sthg.) by work or effort: *He worked off some energy at the gym.* **work out.** *tr.v.* [sep.] To find a solution for (sthg.); solve: *Can you work out these math problems?* —*intr.v.* **1.** To prove successful or satisfactory: *Everything worked out in the end.* **2.** To have a specified result: *The arrangements worked out just fine.* **3.** To exercise for physical conditioning: *She works out at a health club.* **work up.** *tr.v.* [sep.] **1.** To excite the emotions of (sbdy.): *The loss of his job has worked him up pretty badly.* **2.** To develop or produce (sthg.): *work up a report; work up an appetite.*

work·a·ble (wûr′kə bəl) *adj.* **1.** Capable of being worked, dealt with, or handled: *Soften the material until it is workable.* **2.** Capable of being put into effective operation: *a workable plan.*

work·a·day (wûr′kə dā′) *adj.* Ordinary; commonplace: *the workaday concerns of housekeeping.*

work·a·hol·ic (wûr′kə hô′lĭk *or* wûr′kə-hŏl′ĭk) *n.* A person who has a compulsive need to work all the time: *a workaholic who refuses to take vacations.*

work·bench (wûrk′bĕnch′) *n.* A sturdy table or bench at which skilled manual work is done, as by a carpenter or machinist.

work·book (wûrk′bo͝ok′) *n.* A booklet containing problems and exercises that a student may do directly on its pages.

W

work•day (wûrk′dā′) *n.* **1.** A day on which work is done: *a shop open every workday.* **2.** The part of the day during which one works: *The client called just before the end of the workday.*

work•er (wûr′kər) *n.* **1.** A person who works: *a fast worker; an office worker.* **2.** A member of the working class: *the workers' political party.*

work•ers' compensation (wûr′kərz) *n.* [U] Payments made to an employee who is injured at work. Informally known as **workers' comp:** *She has been on workers' comp since she hurt her back.*

work force or **work•force** (wûrk′fôrs′) *n.* All the people working or available to work, as in a nation or a company: *The company plans to increase its work force by 20 employees.*

work•horse (wûrk′hôrs′) *n.* **1.** A person or thing that works tirelessly or under long-term use: *She's the real workhorse on the committee.* **2.** A horse that is used for labor.

work•ing (wûr′kĭng) *adj.* **1.** Capable of functioning: *a machine in working condition.* **2.** With a paying job; employed: *a working person.* **3.** Spent in work: *working hours.* **4.** Good enough for practical use: *a working knowledge of a language.* —*n.* (*usually plural*). The way in which sthg. operates or functions: *the workings of the brain.*

working class *n.* The part of society made up of those who work for wages, especially manual or industrial laborers.

work•ing•man (wûr′kĭng măn′) *n.* A man who works for wages. —**work′ing•wom′an** (wûr′kĭng woŏm′ən) *n.*

working papers *pl.n.* Legal documents stating the right to employment of a person who is underage or not a citizen.

work•load (wûrk′lōd′) *n.* **1.** The amount of work given to or expected from a worker in a specified period of time: *Her workload has increased in the past year.* **2.** The amount of work that can be produced in a specified period of time by a machine.

work•man (wûrk′mən) *n.* A man who performs manual or industrial labor for wages.

work•man•ship (wûrk′mən shĭp′) *n.* [U] The quality of sthg. made, as by a craftsperson or an artisan: *silver jewelry of fine workmanship.*

work•out (wûrk′out′) *n.* A period of exercise, as to improve physical condition: *the boxer's daily workout.*

work•shop (wûrk′shŏp′) *n.* **1.** A place where manual or light industrial work is done. **2.** An educational seminar held for a usually small number of participants: *a teachers' workshop.*

work•sta•tion (wûrk′stā′shən) *n.* An area, as in an office, equipped for one worker, often including a computer.

world (wûrld) *n.* **1.** The earth: *a flight around the world.* **2.** The people of the earth; the human race: *studying the history of the world.* **3.** Often **World.** A particular part of the earth: *the Western World.* **4.** A particular part of the earth and its people during a given period of history: *the Renaissance world.* **5.** A class or group of people, or their area of interest: *the scientific world.* **6.** A state of existence: *belief in the next world.* **7.** A large amount: *spent worlds of time; did a world of good.* ◆ **for all the world.** In all respects; exactly: *She looked for all the world like a movie star.* **for the world.** For any reason; by any possibility: *We wouldn't miss their party for the world.* **in the world.** Used as an intensive: *Where in the world did you find that hat?* **out of this world.** *Informal.* Extraordinary; superb: *a dinner that was out of this world.* **the world over.** Throughout the world: *a folk musician who is famous the world over.*

world-class (wûrld′klăs′) *adj.* Ranking among the best in the world: *a world-class athlete.*

world•ly (wûrld′lē) *adj.* **world•li•er, world•li•est.** **1.** Relating to the affairs of the world; not spiritual: *worldly concerns.* **2.** Well informed socially; sophisticated: *A year in the city saw the innocent girl become a worldly woman.* —**world′li•ness** *n.* [U]

world power *n.* A nation with the power to influence the course of world events: *The U.S. has been a world power for years.*

World Series *n.* In the United States, a series of professional baseball games played to decide the championship of the major leagues.

world•wide (wûrld′wīd′) *adj.* Involving the whole world: *a worldwide desire for peace.* —*adv.* Throughout the whole world: *distributed worldwide.*

World Wide Web *n.* [U] An information server on the Internet composed of sites and files connected to each other and accessible with a browser.

worm (wûrm) *n.* **1.** Any of various animals with a soft, long, rounded or flattened body and no backbone. **2. worms.** An infestation of the intestines or other parts of the body by parasitic worms. **3.** A person seen as deserving pity or contempt. —*v.* —*tr.* **1.** To make (one's way) with the crawling or twisting motion of a worm: *He wormed his way through the crowd to get a better view.* **2.** To cure (an animal) of intestinal worms: *The veterinarian wormed the dog.* ◆ **worm out of. 1.** To get (sthg.) from (sbdy.) by clever or dishonest means:

The spy wormed the information out of the messenger. **2.** To get out of (sthg.) by clever or tricky means: *He wormed out of the obligation.* —**worm′like′** *adj.*

worm•y (wûr′mē) *adj.* **worm•i•er, worm•i•est.** Full of or damaged by worms: *He threw away the wormy corn.*

worn (wôrn) *v.* Past participle of **wear.** —*adj.* **1.** Damaged by wear or use: *worn and faded blue jeans.* **2.** Showing the effects of worry, sickness, or strain: *a pale worn face.*

worn-out (wôrn′out′) *adj.* **1.** Used or worn until no longer usable: *She gave all her worn-out clothes to charity.* **2.** Extremely tired; exhausted: *We were worn-out from the long trip.*

wor•ri•some (wûr′ē səm *or* wŭr′ē səm) *adj.* Causing worry or anxiety: *The coming storm put them in a worrisome situation.*

wor•ry (wûr′ē *or* wŭr′ē) *v.* **wor•ried** (wûr′ēd *or* wŭr ′ēd), **wor•ry•ing, wor•ries** (wûr′ēz *or* wŭr′ēz). —*intr.* To feel uneasy or concerned about sthg.: *His mother worried about his health.* —*tr.* **1.** To cause (sbdy.) to feel anxious, distressed, or troubled: *Don't worry your parents!* **2.** To take hold of (sthg.) with the teeth and pull or tear repeatedly: *a cat worrying a ball of yarn.* —*n., pl.* **wor•ries. 1.** [U] Mental uneasiness or anxiety: *in a state of worry over her low grades.* **2.** [C] A source of anxiety or uneasiness: *He is a constant worry to his parents.* —**wor′ri•er** *n.*

wor•ry•wart (wûr′ē wôrt *or* wŭr′ē wôrt′) *n. Informal.* A person who worries too much: *Teenagers often feel their parents are worrywarts.*

worse (wûrs) *adj.* Comparative of **bad, ill. 1.** Of a more inferior quality, condition, or effect: *This restaurant is worse than the last one we ate at.* **2.** More severe or unfavorable: *The weather got worse during the night.* **3.** In poorer health; more ill: *The patient is worse today than yesterday.* —*n.* Something that is worse: *Of the two cars, the old one is the worse.* —*adv.* Comparative of **badly, ill.** In a worse manner; to a worse degree: *The team plays worse when we skip a practice.* ♦ **for better or worse.** Whether the situation or results be good or bad: *For better or worse, he trusts everyone.* **none the worse for.** Unharmed by: *The dog seems none the worse for spending the night out in the rain.*

wors•en (wûr′sən) *tr. & intr.v.* To make or become worse: *Arguing will only worsen our situation. The storm is worsening.*

wor•ship (wûr′shĭp) *n.* [U] **1.** The love and honor given to a god or an idol. **2.** A set of ceremonies, prayers, or other religious forms by which this love is expressed. **3.** Strong devotion; adoration: *the worship of sports heroes by young boys.* —*v.* —*tr.* **1.** To honor and love (a

god): *The ancient Greeks worshipped many gods.* **2.** To regard (sbdy.) with adoring respect: *He seems to worship his wife.* See Synonyms at **revere.** —*intr.* To participate in religious ceremonies: *She worships at the local Catholic church.* —**wor′ship•er** *n.*

worst (wûrst) *adj.* Superlative of **bad, ill. 1.** Of most inferior quality, condition, or effect: *one of the worst movies of the year.* **2.** Most severe or unfavorable: *the worst winter in years.* —*adv.* Superlative of **badly, ill.** In the worst manner or degree: *No one in the band played well, but the horn section clearly played worst.* —*n.* Something that is worst: *Cold pizza is the worst!* ♦ **get the worst of.** To suffer the most from (sthg.): *His wife got the worst of the divorce settlement.* **in the worst way.** *Informal.* Very much; a great deal: *The child wanted a kitten in the worst way.*

worth (wûrth) *n.* **1.** [U] The quality that gives value or usefulness to sthg.: *the worth of a good reputation.* **2.** [C] The value of sthg. expressed in money; market value: *property with a worth of a million dollars.* **3.** [U] The amount that a certain sum of money will buy: *$20 worth of nails.* **4.** [U] Wealth; riches: *the company's net worth.* —*adj.* **1.** Equal in value to sthg. specified: *a pen worth five dollars.* **2.** Deserving of: *a plan worth serious consideration.* **3.** With wealth amounting to: *a person worth $2,000,000.* ♦ **for what it's worth.** Even though it may not be important or valuable: *Let's listen to the proposal, for what it's worth.*

worth•less (wûrth′lĭs) *adj.* Without worth; of no use or value: *a worthless promise that won't be kept.* —**worth′less•ly** *adv.* —**worth′less•ness** *n.* [U]

worth•while (wûrth′wīl′) *adj.* Valuable or important enough for the time, effort, or interest involved: *a worthwhile effort to clean up the city.*

wor•thy (wûr′thē) *adj.* **wor•thi•er, wor•thi•est. 1.** Having worth, merit, or value; useful or valuable: *a worthy cause.* **2.** Honorable; admirable: *a worthy opponent.* **3.** Deserving: *worthy to be considered; worthy of praise.* —**wor′thi•ness** *n.* [U]

would (wŏŏd) *aux.v.* Past tense of **will².** **1.** Used in a dependent clause after a statement of desire, request, or advice: *I wish you would stay.* **2.** Used to make a polite request: *Would you please pass the salt?* **3.** Used to show uncertainty: *His statement would seem to mean he is guilty.* **4.** Used to show preference or willingness: *I would rather stay home tonight.* **5.** Used to show past intention: *He said that he would take us to the party.* **6.** Used to show customary or habitual behavior in the past: *Every day we would go to the beach.* **7.** Used to show probability: *We would be there by now if we had taken the train.*

HOMONYMS: would, wood (forest).

---

would-be (wŏŏd′bē′) *adj.* Desiring, attempting, or claiming to be: *would-be actors trying for a part in the film.*

would•n't (wŏŏd′nt). Contraction of *would not.*

wound¹ (wŏŏnd) *n.* **1.** An injury, especially one in which skin or tissue is cut, pierced, or broken: *the soldier's wounds.* **2.** An injury to one's feelings: *Time will heal the wounds of their divorce.* —*tr.v.* **1.** To inflict a wound or wounds on (sbdy./sthg.): *The hunter wounded a deer.* **2.** To hurt the feelings of (sbdy.): *His leaving wounded her deeply.*

wound² (wound) *v.* Past tense and past participle of **wind²**.

wove (wōv) *v.* Past tense of **weave**.

wo•ven (wō′vən) *v.* Past participle of **weave**. —*adj.* Made by weaving: *a woven rug.*

wow (wou) *Informal. interj.* An expression used to show wonder or great pleasure: *Wow! What a great surprise!* —*tr.v.* To have a strong and pleasant effect on (sbdy.): *The singer wowed the audience.*

wran•gle (răng′gəl) *v.* **wran•gled, wran•gling, wran•gles.** —*intr.* To argue noisily and angrily: *wrangling over the division of the money.* —*tr.* **1.** To win or get (sthg.) by argument: *The union wrangled better health insurance out of management.* **2.** To herd (horses or other livestock).

wran•gler (răng′glər) *n.* A cowboy or cowgirl, especially one who takes care of horses for riding.

wrap (răp) *v.* **wrapped, wrap•ping, wraps.** —*tr.* **1.** [*about; around*] To arrange or fold (a covering): *She wrapped a blanket about her.* **2.** To enclose (sthg.) within a covering: *wrap one's head in a scarf.* **3.** To clasp, fold, or coil (sthg.) around sthg.: *She wrapped the dog's leash around her hand.* **4.** To surround and hide (sthg.): *a plan wrapped in secrecy.* —*intr.* To coil or twist about or around sthg.: *The flag wrapped around the pole.* —*n.* An outer piece of clothing worn for warmth, as a cloak or coat. ◆ **under wraps.** *Informal.* Secret or hidden: *Plans for the project are still under wraps.*

wrapped up in. Completely involved in: *She was all wrapped up in a new mystery novel.*

wrap up. *tr.v.* [sep.] To bring (sthg.) to a conclusion; settle finally or successfully: *wrap up contract negotiations.* —*intr.v.* To put on warm clothing: *Wrap up well before you go out.*

HOMONYMS: wrap, rap (knock, talk).

---

wrap•per (răp′ər) *n.* **1.** A cover, as of paper, in which sthg. is wrapped: *a candy bar wrap-*

per. **2.** A person or device that wraps, as a store employee who wraps packages.

wrap•ping (răp′ĭng) *n.* [C; U] The material used for wrapping sthg.: *pretty wrapping for a birthday gift.*

wrap-up (răp′ŭp′) *n.* **1.** A short final summary, as of the news: *a wrap-up of the day's sports.* **2.** A concluding or final action: *the wrap-up of an election campaign.*

wrath (răth) *n.* [U] *Formal.* Violent anger: *The people feared the wrath of the gods.*

wrath•ful (răth′fəl) *adj. Formal.* Full of wrath: *wrathful fury.* —**wrath′ful•ly** *adv.*

wreak (rēk) *tr.v.* **1.** To force (vengeance or punishment) upon a person. **2.** To express or release (anger or resentment): *The emperor wreaked his anger upon his advisers.* **3.** To cause (sthg. violent): *wreak havoc.*

HOMONYMS: wreak, reek (smell bad).

---

wreath (rēth) *n., pl.* **wreaths** (rēthz *or* rēths). **1.** A ring of leaves, flowers, or branches worn on the head, placed on a memorial, or used as a decoration: *a wreath on the front door.* **2.** A ring or similar curving form: *a wreath of smoke.*

wreathe (rēth) *tr.v.* **wreathed, wreath•ing, wreathes.** **1.** To twist (leaves, for example) into a wreath or circular form: *wreathe flowers into a garland.* **2.** To coil (sthg.) so as to encircle sthg.: *The snake wreathed itself around the branch.* **3.** To encircle or decorate (sbdy./sthg.) with or as if with a wreath: *a poet wreathed with laurel.*

wreck (rĕk) *n.* **1.** The act of destroying: *the wreck of all my hopes.* **2.** Accidental destruction of a ship: *a shipwreck.* **3.** The remains of sthg. that has been ruined: *The car was a wreck and had to be towed away.* **4.** A person or thing in a disorderly or worn-out state: *The house was a wreck after the party.* —*tr.v.* **1.** To cause the destruction of (a vehicle) in a collision: *He wrecked the car.* See Synonyms at **ruin**. **2.** To tear down or destroy (sthg.): *The crew wrecked the building in five days.* **3.** To bring (sthg.) to a state of ruin: *A long period of overspending wrecked their finances.*

wreck•age (rĕk′ĭj) *n.* [U] The debris of sthg. wrecked: *looking for valuables among the wreckage.*

wreck•er (rĕk′ər) *n.* **1.** A person or thing that wrecks or destroys: *a wrecker of dreams.* **2.** A person who is in the business of taking down old buildings. **3.** A person who takes apart junk cars for useful parts. **4.** A truck with a hoist used to tow broken-down or wrecked cars.

wren (rĕn) *n.* A small brownish songbird with rounded wings, a slender bill, and a short tail.

wrench (rĕnch) *n.* **1.** A sudden sharp, forcible

ă-cat; ā-pay; âr-care; ä-father; ĕ-get; ē-be; ĭ-sit; ī-nice; îr-here; ŏ-got; ō-go; ô-saw; oi-boy; ou-out; ŏŏ-took; ōō-boot; ŭ-cut; ûr-word; th-thin; *th*-this; hw-when; zh-vision; ə-about; N-French bon

twist or turn: *He opened the jar with a wrench.* **2.** An injury produced by twisting or straining: *the wrench of an ankle.* **3.** A sudden pull on one's emotions; a surge of compassion, sorrow, or anguish: *The man felt a wrench when he had to leave his children.* **4.** A tool for gripping and turning objects such as nuts, bolts, or pipes. —*tr.v.* **1.** To pull or turn (sthg.) suddenly and forcibly: *The carpenter wrenched the nail out of the board.* **2.** To twist and sprain (a joint or other body part): *I wrenched my knee while running.*

wrest (rĕst) *tr.v.* **1.** To get (sthg.) by pulling and twisting forcefully: *trying to wrest the pen from her hand.* **2.** To gain or take (sthg.) away forcefully: *The rebels wrested power from the king.*

HOMONYMS: wrest, rest (period of inactivity, remainder).

wres•tle (rĕs′əl) *v.* **wres•tled, wres•tling, wres•tles.** —*intr.* **1.** To fight by holding and trying to bring one's opponent to the ground. **2.** To struggle or try for control: *wrestle with a problem.* —*tr.* **1.** To participate in a wrestling match with (an opponent): *wrestling the state champion.* **2.** To move or lift (sthg.) with great effort: *We wrestled the box up the stairs.*

wres•tler (rĕs′lər) *n.* A person who wrestles, especially as a sport: *a professional wrestler.*

wres•tling (rĕs′lĭng) *n.* [U] A sport in which two opponents try to throw or hold each other down.

wretch (rĕch) *n.* **1.** A miserable, unfortunate, or unhappy person: *The poor wretch has lost his wife.* **2.** A person seen as mean or terrible: *a hateful wretch.*

HOMONYMS: wretch, retch (vomit).

wretch•ed (rĕch′ĭd) *adj.* **1.** Very unhappy or unfortunate; miserable: *a wretched student.* **2.** Characterized by or causing suffering or unhappiness: *wretched working conditions.* **3.** Hateful or contemptible: *He's a wretched person to work for.* **4.** Of very bad quality: *a wretched performance.* —**wretch′ed•ly** *adv.* —**wretch′ed•ness** *n.* [U]

wrig•gle (rĭg′əl) *v.* **wrig•gled, wrig•gling, wrig•gles.** —*intr.* **1.** To turn or twist the body with winding writhing motions; squirm: *The child wriggled out of his mother's arms.* **2.** To move with writhing motions: *The snake wriggled under the rock.* **3.** To get into or out of a situation by clever means: *She wriggled out of having to baby-sit.* —*tr.* To move (sthg.) with a wriggling motion: *wriggle a toe.* —*n.* A wriggling movement.

wright (rīt) *n. (often used in a compound).* A person who constructs or repairs sthg.: *a playwright; a wheelwright.*

wring (rĭng) *tr.v.* **wrung** (rŭng), **wring•ing, wrings. 1.** [*out*] To twist, squeeze, or compress (sthg.), especially to get liquid out: *Wring the wet clothes out.* **2.** [*from; out*] To force or squeeze (liquid) out by or as if by twisting or pressing: *wring water from a towel.* **3.** To clasp and twist or squeeze (one's hands), as in distress: *He wrung his hands in despair.* **4.** To get (sthg.) out by force or pressure: *The lawyer wrung the truth out of the witness.* —*n.* A forceful squeeze or twist: *a quick wring of his hand.* ◆ **wringing wet.** Completely wet: *Those wringing wet clothes will give you a chill.*

HOMONYMS: wring, ring (circle, sound).

wring•er (rĭng′ər) *n.* A person or thing that wrings, especially a device in which laundry is pressed between rollers to get out water. ◆ **through the wringer.** Through the experience of a very difficult situation: *She felt like she had been put through the wringer during the job interview.*

HOMONYMS: wringer, ringer (one who resembles another).

wrin•kle (rĭng′kəl) *n.* **1.** A small ridge or crease on a normally smooth surface, such as cloth or skin: *The skirt was full of wrinkles.* **2.** A difficult aspect: *The project had a few wrinkles before we finished.* —*v.* **wrin•kled, wrin•kling, wrin•kles.** —*tr.* **1.** To make a wrinkle or wrinkles in (sthg.): *Don't wrinkle the suit.* **2.** To pull (sthg.) up into wrinkles: *She wrinkled her nose in distaste.* —*intr.* To form wrinkles: *Linen wrinkles easily.*

wrist (rĭst) *n.* The joint between the hand and the forearm: *He wears a watch on his left wrist.*

wrist•band (rĭst′bănd′) *n.* A band, as on a shirt sleeve or wristwatch, that goes around the wrist.

wrist•watch (rĭst′wŏch′) *n.* A watch worn on a band around the wrist.

writ (rĭt) *n.* A written court order telling a person to do or stop doing a certain act.

write (rīt) *v.* **wrote** (rōt) **writ•ten** (rĭt′n) **writ•ing, writes.** —*tr.* **1.** To form (letters, symbols, or words) on a surface with an instrument such as a pen: *The customer wrote his name on the check.* **2.** To compose and record (sthg.), as on paper: *write a poem; write music.* **3.** To create (a document) in legal form: *write a lease.* **4.** To express (sthg.) in writing: *writing down one's thoughts.* **5.** To communicate (sthg.) by writing: *She wrote that she planned to visit.* **6.** To show (sthg.) clearly; mark: *Happiness was written in her smile.* —*intr.* **1.** To form letters, words, or symbols on a

W

surface: *a child learning to write.* **2.** To produce written material, such as essays or books: *He writes for a Boston newspaper.* **3.** To compose a letter; communicate by mail: *Write to me.* ◆ **write in.** *tr.v.* [sep.] To vote by writing (a name not listed) on a ballot: *Voters wrote in the candidate's name.* **write off.** *tr.v.* [sep.] To consider (sthg.) as a loss or failure: *He wrote off his first paintings as mere practice.* **write out.** *tr.v.* [sep.] To write (sthg.) completely: *Write out your answers on the back of the test.* **write up.** *tr.v.* [sep.] To write a report or description of (sthg.), as for publication: *He told his supervisor about his idea, and she asked him to write it up.*

HOMONYMS: write, right (direction), **rite** (ceremony).

write-in (rīt′ĭn′) *n.* A vote made by writing in the name of a candidate not on the ballot.
writ•er (rī′tər) *n.* A person who writes, especially as an occupation.
write-off (rīt′ôf′ *or* rīt′ŏf′) *n.* **1.** Something that is completely ruined and worthless: *The burned building was a total write-off.* **2.** An income tax deduction: *Professional travel is a write-off.*
write-up (rīt′ŭp′) *n.* A published account, review, or notice, especially a favorable one: *The team got a nice write-up in the local paper.*
writhe (rīth) *intr.v.* **writhed, writh•ing, writhes.** To twist, as in pain, struggle, or embarrassment: *The injured player writhed in pain on the field.*
writ•ing (rī′tĭng) *n.* [U] **1.** The act of one who writes. **2.** Written form: *Make the request in writing.* **3.** Letters or characters that make up readable matter: *Can you read the writing in this note?* **4.** The occupation or style of a writer: *He earns little from his writing.*
writ•ten (rĭt′n) *v.* Past participle of **write.**
wrong (rông *or* rŏng) *adj.* **1.** Not correct; mistaken: *a wrong answer on a test.* **2.** Against conscience, morality, or law: *the wrong way to treat people.* **3.** Not required, intended, or wanted: *a wrong telephone number; the wrong direction.* **4.** Not fitting or suitable; inappropriate: *I said the wrong thing and hurt his feelings.* **5.** Not in agreement with a fixed custom, method, or procedure: *the wrong way to make pie.* **6.** Not functioning properly: *What is wrong with this machine?* —*adv.* **1.** Mistakenly; incorrectly: *You told the story wrong.* **2.** Immorally or

unjustly: *behave wrong.* —*n.* **1.** [C] An unjust or immoral act or circumstance: *They felt many wrongs had been committed against them.* **2.** [U] The condition of being mistaken or at fault: *The other driver was in the wrong.* —*tr.v. Formal.* To treat (sbdy.) unjustly or dishonorably: *You wrong him by saying he cheated.* ◆ **go wrong. 1.** To take a wrong turn or make a wrong move: *We went wrong at the fork in the road.* **2.** To proceed or end badly: *What went wrong with the project?* —**wrong′ly** *adv.* —**wrong′-ness** *n.* [U]
wrong•do•er (rông′dōō′ər *or* rŏng′dōō′ər) *n.* A person who does sthg. illegal or immoral: *The wrongdoers were punished.* —**wrong′-do′ing** *n.* [U]
wrong•ful (rông′fəl *or* rŏng′fəl) *adj.* **1.** Wrong; unjust: *wrongful criticism.* **2.** Unlawful: *wrongful death.*
wrong•head•ed (rông′hĕd′ĭd *or* rŏng′hĕd′ĭd) *adj.* Based on or refusing to change ideas or opinions that are wrong or unreasonable: *a wrongheaded insistence on doing everything himself.* —**wrong′head′ed•ly** *adv.* —**wrong′head′ed•ness** *n.* [U]
wrote (rōt) *v.* Past tense of **write.**

HOMONYMS: wrote, rote (routine).

wrought (rôt) *adj.* **1.** Made, formed, or fashioned: *a carefully wrought story.* **2.** Shaped by hammering with tools: *wrought metal.*
wrought iron *n.* [U] A highly purified form of iron that is easily shaped, forged, or welded. It is often used for decorative purposes.
wrung (rŭng) *v.* Past tense and past participle of **wring.**

HOMONYMS: wrung, rung (rod, sounded).

wry (rī) *adj.* **wri•er** (rī′ər), **wri•est** (rī′ĭst) *or* **wry•er, wry•est. 1.** Funny in an understated or ironic way: *wry humor.* **2.** Temporarily twisted in an expression of distaste or displeasure: *He made a wry face.* —**wry′ly** *adv.* —**wry′ness** *n.* [U]

HOMONYMS: wry, rye (grain).

wt. *abbr.* An abbreviation of weight.
WV *abbr.* An abbreviation of West Virginia.
W.Va. *abbr.* An abbreviation of West Virginia.
WWI *abbr.* An abbreviation of World War I.
WWII *abbr.* An abbreviation of World War II.
WY *abbr.* An abbreviation of Wyoming.
Wyo. *abbr.* An abbreviation of Wyoming.

W

ă–cat; ā–pay; âr–care; ä–father; ĕ–get; ē–be; ĭ–sit; ī–nice; îr–here; ŏ–got; ō–go; ô–saw; oi–boy; ou–out; ōō–took; ōō–boot; ŭ–cut; ûr–word; th–thin; *th*–this; hw–when; zh–vision; ə–about; N–French bon

Xx

x or **X** (ĕks) *n.*, *pl.* **x's** or **X's. 1.** The 24th letter of the English alphabet. **2.** A mark made in place of the signature of a person who cannot sign his or her name.

X¹ also **x** The Roman numeral for 10.

X² (ĕks) *n.* A movie rating that means children younger than 17 are not allowed.

x-ax·is (ĕks′ăk′sĭs) *n.*, *pl.* **x-ax·es** (ĕks′ăk′-sēz). The horizontal axis of a two-dimensional coordinate system.

Xe The symbol for the element **xenon.**

xe·non (zē′nŏn′) *n.* [U] *Symbol* **Xe** A colorless, odorless, gaseous element that is found in the atmosphere in small amounts. Atomic number 54. See table at **element.**

xen·o·pho·bi·a (zĕn′ə fō′bē ə *or* zē′nə-fō′bē ə) *n.* [U] Undue dislike or fear of foreign peoples or strangers: *When at war, many countries experience xenophobia.* — **xen′·o·phobe′** (zĕn′ə fōb′ *or* zō′nə fōb′) *n.* — **xen′o·pho′bic** *adj.*

xer·o·graph·ic (zîr′ə grăf′ĭk) *adj.* Used in or produced by xerography: *the xerographic method; xerographic prints.*

xe·rog·ra·phy (zĭ rŏg′rə fē) *n.* [U] A process for producing photographs or photocopies in which an image made up of particles of dry pigment is transferred to a sheet of paper and fixed to the paper by heat.

Xer·ox (zîr′ŏks). A trademark used for a photocopying process or machine. — *tr.v.* To photocopy (pages): *Please Xerox six copies of this letter.*

XL *abbr.* An abbreviation for extra large, usually used to refer to clothing.

X·mas (krĭs′məs *or* ĕks′məs) *n. Informal.* Christmas.

X-rat·ed (ĕks′rā′tĭd) *adj.* With the rating X: *an X-rated movie.*

x-ray (ĕks′rā′) *n.* **1.** *(usually plural).* High-energy electromagnetic radiation with a wavelength shorter than ultraviolet light. **2.** A photograph taken with x-rays: *a chest x-ray; an x-ray machine.* — *tr.v.* To photograph (a part of the body) with x-rays: *The doctor x-rayed his injured ankle.*

xy·lo·phone (zī′lə-fōn′) *n.* A percussion instrument made of a series of wooden bars of various sizes that produce various tones, played with two small mallets.

xylophone

Yy

y or **Y** (wī) *n.*, *pl.* **y's** or **Y's**. The 25th letter of the English alphabet.

Y *abbr.* A short form of YMCA or YWCA: *They took swimming lessons at the Y.*

—y¹ or **—ey** *suff.* A suffix that means: **1.** Characterized by; consisting of: *dusty; moldy.* **2.** Like: *summery; soupy.* **3.** To some degree; rather: *chilly.* **4.** Tending toward: *sleepy.*

—y² *suff.* A suffix that means: **1.** Condition; state: *jealousy.* **2.** Activity: *cookery.* **3.** Place for an activity: *cannery.* **4.** Result or product of an activity: *laundry.*

—y³ or **—ie** *suff.* A suffix that means: **1.** Small one: *doggy.* **2.** Dear one: *sweetie.*

yacht (yät *or* yŏt) *n.* A sailing or motor-driven vessel used for pleasure trips or racing. *—intr.v.* To sail, cruise, or race in a yacht: *The family yachts all summer.* **—yacht'ing** *n.* [U]

ya•hoo (yä'hōō *or* yā'hōō) *n.*, *pl.* **ya•hoos.** *Slang.* A person thought of as simple or not sophisticated. *—interj. Informal.* An expression of joy: *Yahoo! I got an A on my test.*

yak¹ (yăk) *n.* A long-haired ox of central Asia.

yak² (yăk) *intr.v.* **yakked, yak•king, yaks.** *Slang.* To talk for a long time about unimportant subjects; chatter: *They yakked on the phone all night.*

y'all (yôl) *pron.* Variant of **you-all.**

yam (yăm) *n.* **1.** A tropical vine with a starchy root, used as food. **2.** A reddish sweet potato.

yam•mer (yăm'ər) *intr. & tr.v.* To complain or say whimperingly; whine: *The children yammered all morning. My friend yammered his displeasure with the movie.*

yank (yăngk) *v. —tr.* **1.** To pull on (sth.) with a quick strong movement; jerk: *The baby yanked her hat off and threw it down.* **2.** *Informal.* To withdraw (a film or publication) from circulation because of poor sales or objectionable subject matter: *The studio yanked the film from the theaters because of its poor showing. —intr.* To pull with a quick strong movement: *I yanked on the bow until the knot came undone. —n.* A sudden sharp pull; a jerk: *Give the rope a yank.*

Yank (yăngk) *n. Informal.* A Yankee.

Yan•kee (yăng'kē) *n.* **1.** A person born or living in New England. **2.** A person born or living in a northern U.S. state, especially a Union soldier during the Civil War. **3.** *Slang.* An often insulting word for a person from the United States.

yap (yăp) *intr.v.* **yapped, yap•ping, yaps.** **1.** To bark sharply: *The puppy yapped all night.* **2.** *Slang.* To talk noisily or stupidly: *The children yapped happily about school. —n.* **1.** A sharp high-pitched bark. **2.** *Slang.* An insulting word for sbdy.'s mouth: *Shut your yap already!*

yard¹ (yärd) *n.* A unit of length equal to 3 feet or 36 inches (0.9144 meter). See table at **measurement.**

yard² (yärd) *n.* **1.** A piece of land near a building or group of buildings: *our back yard; the schoolyard.* **2.** An area, often enclosed, used for a particular kind of work, business, or other activity: *a lumberyard; a railroad yard.*

yard•age (yär'dĭj) *n.* [U] **1.** An amount or a length measured in yards: *yardage gained in a game.* **2.** Cloth sold by the yard.

yard sale *n.* A sale of used items, such as clothes, toys, and furniture, in one's yard.

yard•stick (yärd'stĭk') *n.* **1.** A marked measuring stick one yard in length. **2.** A standard used in comparing or judging: *Resale value is a good yardstick of a car's worth.*

yarn (yärn) *n.* **1.** [C; U] A continuous strand of spun material such as wool or nylon, used in weaving, knitting, or crocheting. **2.** [C] *Informal.* A story, often made-up or exaggerated: *He told quite a yarn about a fish that got away.* ◆ **spin** or **tell a yarn.** To tell a story, often untrue or exaggerated: *spinning yarns around the campfire.*

yawn (yôn) *v. —intr.* **1.** To open the mouth wide with a deep inward breath as when sleepy or bored: *He yawned repeatedly during the long lecture.* **2.** To open wide; gape: *The entrance to the tunnel yawned ahead of them. —tr.* To say (sth.) wearily, as if while yawning: *The guest of honor yawned a few bored remarks. —n.* The act of yawning: *She gave a yawn.*

y-axis (wī'ăk'sĭs) *n.*, *pl.* **y-axes** (wī'ak'sēz). The vertical axis of a two-dimensional coordinate system.

yd *abbr.* An abbreviation of yard¹ (measurement).

yeah (yĕ'ə *or* yă'ə) *adv. Informal.* Yes. *—interj.* (yā). An expression of joy: *Yeah! We won!*

ă–**cat**; ā–**pay**; âr–**care**; ä–**father**; ĕ–**get**; ē–**be**; ĭ–**sit**; ī–**nice**; îr–**here**; ŏ–**got**; ō–**go**; ô–**saw**; oi–**boy**; ou–**out**; ōō–**took**; ōō–**boot**; ŭ–**cut**; ûr–**word**; th–**thin**; *th*–**this**; hw–**when**; zh–**vision**; ə–**about**; N–French **bon**

year (yîr) *n.* **1.** The period of time during which the earth makes one complete revolution around the sun: *A year is about 365 days long.* **2.** A period of 12 months: *a year from June.* **3. years. a.** Age: *three years old.* **b.** Old age: *I'm feeling my years; it's hard to climb stairs.* **4. years.** A long time: *I haven't seen them in years. It'll be years before I try that again.* **5.** A period of time, often shorter than 12 months, used for a special activity or purpose: *The school year is from September to June.*

year•ling (yîr′lĭng) *n.* An animal that is one year old or between one and two years old.

year•ly (yîr′lē) *adj.* Happening once a year or every year; annual: *a yearly vacation to Paris in May.* —*adv.* Once a year; annually: *Maples and oaks shed their leaves yearly.*

yearn (yûrn) *intr.v.* [*for*] To have a strong, often rather sad desire: *She yearned for her school days.* —**yearn′ing** *n.* [C; U]

year-round (yîr′round′) *adj.* Existing, active, or lasting throughout the year: *year-round ice skating.*

yeast (yēst) *n.* [U] A one-celled fungus that causes the fermentation of carbohydrates, producing carbon dioxide and alcohol: *Yeast is used in baking.*

yell (yĕl) *v.* —*intr.* To cry out loudly, as in excitement or pain: *They yelled and jumped up and down.* See Synonyms at **shout.** —*tr.* To say (sthg.) with a loud cry; shout: *They yelled their hellos.* —*n.* A loud shout or cry: *a yell of triumph.*

yel•low (yĕl′ō) *n.* [C; U] The color of ripe lemons. —*adj.* **1.** Of the color yellow: *a yellow raincoat.* **2.** *Slang.* Cowardly: *The boxer accused his opponent of being yellow.* —*tr. & intr.v.* To make or become yellow: *Many washings had yellowed the linen tablecloth. The paper yellowed with age.*

yellow fever *n.* [U] An infectious tropical disease that causes the skin to turn yellow.

yel•low•ish (yĕl′ō ĭsh) *adj.* A little yellow: *a yellowish flower.*

yellow jacket *n.* A small wasp with yellow and black markings: *The yellow jackets spoiled the picnic.*

yelp (yĕlp) *v.* —*intr.* To give a short sharp bark or cry: *The dog yelped in pain.* —*tr.* To say (sthg.) with a short bark or cry: *The child yelped "ouch" when his cat scratched him.* —*n.* A short sharp bark or cry: *We heard the dog's yelp.*

yen¹ (yĕn) *n.* A strong desire or inclination: *a yen for chocolate; a yen to travel.*

yen² (yĕn) *n., pl.* **yen.** The basic monetary unit of Japan.

yes (yĕs) *adv.* Used to express affirmation, agreement, or consent: *Yes, I'll go to the movies.* —*n., pl.* **yes•es.** An affirmative or consenting reply: *His suggestion was met with a chorus of yeses.*

yes•ter•day (yĕs′tər dā′ *or* yĕs′tər dē) *n.* [U] **1.** The day before the present day: *Yesterday was cold and windy.* **2.** A time in the past, especially the recent past: *The science fiction of yesterday seems outdated today.* —*adv.* On the day before the present day: *I mailed the letter yesterday.*

yes•ter•year (yĕs′tər yîr′) *n.* [U] *Formal.* Time past: *The movies of yesteryear are my favorites.*

yet (yĕt) *adv.* **1.** At this time; for the present: *Dinner isn't ready yet.* **2.** Up to a specified time; thus far: *They have not started yet.* **3.** Even; still more: *a yet sadder story.* **4.** But; nevertheless: *young yet wise.* —*conj.* Nevertheless; and despite this: *She said she would be late, yet she arrived on time.* ◆ **as yet.** Up to the present time; up to now: *I haven't seen any qualified applicants as yet.*

yew (yōō) *n.* An evergreen tree or shrub with poisonous, flat, dark green needles and red berries.

HOMONYMS: yew, ewe (sheep), **you** (pronoun).

Yid•dish (yĭd′ĭsh) *n.* [U] A language spoken by Jews of Central and Eastern Europe and by their descendants in other parts of the world.

yield (yēld) *v.* —*tr.* **1.** To give (sthg.) by a natural process: *The garden yielded a variety of vegetables.* **2.** To provide (sthg.) as return for effort or investment: *an investment that yields high percentages.* **3.** To give over possession of (sthg.): *A driver should yield the road to a bicyclist.* —*intr.* **1.** To produce a return for effort or investment: *My stocks yielded significantly higher this year.* **2.** To give up, as in defeat: *Their team decided to yield because they were losing.* **3.** To give way to pressure or force: *The dough yields when pressed with a finger.* —*n.* An amount yielded or produced; a product: *a high yield of corn.*

SYNONYMS: yield, abandon, surrender, cede, waive. These verbs mean to let sthg. go or to give sthg. up. **Yield** means giving way, as to pressure or superior authority: *The diplomat had yielded a lot of ground by the time the conversation with the President was finished.* **Abandon** means to let sthg. go or give sthg. up with no expectation of returning to it or recovering it: *The shipwrecked family slowly abandoned all hope of being rescued.* **Surrender** means to abandon sthg. under force or demand: *The passengers surrendered their luggage to the customs agents.* **Cede** suggests giving up sthg. by formal transfer: *Germany ceded the region to France as part of the peace treaty.* **Waive** means voluntarily to do away with sthg., such as a claim: *The club members waived several of their privileges.*

Y

yip (yĭp) *n.* A short high-pitched bark. —*intr.v.*
yipped, yip·ping, yips. To make a sharp
high-pitched bark: *The dog yipped happily
when its master returned.*

yip·pee (yĭp′ē) *interj. Informal.* An expression used to show joy: *Yippee! We're going
camping!*

YMCA or **Y.M.C.A.** *abbr.* An abbreviation
of Young Men's Christian Association, an
organization that provides various services
and facilities, such as clubs, athletic activities, and sometimes inexpensive lodging: *We
went swimming at the YMCA.*

yo·del (yōd′l) *v.* —*intr.* To sing so that the
voice alternates rapidly between the normal
voice and a falsetto: *My uncle yodels beautifully.* —*tr.* To sing (a song) by yodeling: *She
yodeled a short tune.* —*n.* A song or cry that
is yodeled. —**yo′del·er** *n.*

yo·ga (yō′gə) *n.* [U] A system of exercises
emphasizing physical flexibility and strength
and spiritual calm.

yo·gi (yō′gē) *n., pl.* **yo·gis.** A person who
practices yoga.

yo·gurt also **yo·ghurt** (yō′gərt) *n.* [C; U] A
food made from milk curdled by bacteria and
often sweetened or flavored: *low-fat yogurt;
frozen strawberry yogurt.*

yoke (yōk) *n.* **1.** A crossbar with two U-
shaped pieces that fit around the necks of a
pair of animals working as a team. **2.** A
frame carried across a person's shoulders
with equal loads suspended from each end.
3. A part of a garment fitting closely around
the neck and shoulders: *The yoke of the
dress was embroidered.* **4.** The condition of
being dominated by or as if by a conqueror:
the yoke of tyranny. —*tr.v.* **yoked, yok·ing,
yokes.** **1.** To join or harness (sthg.) with a
yoke: *The farmer yoked the oxen to the cart.*
2. To join (sbdy./sthg.) closely as if with a
yoke; unite: *The two friends were yoked in a
long successful partnership.*

HOMONYMS: yoke, yolk (egg yellow).

yo·kel (yō′kəl) *n. Informal.* A mildly insulting term for a simple country person.

yolk (yōk) *n.* The yellow part of an egg of a
bird or reptile, surrounded by the white.

HOMONYMS: yolk, yoke (crossbar).

Yom Kip·pur (yôm′ kĭp′ər or yôm′ kē-
poor′) *n.* The Jewish Day of Atonement.

yon (yŏn) *adv. & adj.* An old word for there;
yonder: *Look yon at the sunset. Let's head for
yon house.*

yon·der (yŏn′dər) *adv.* In or at that indicated
place: *the village over yonder.* —*adj.* At a

distance, but usually within sight: *Let's go sit
under yonder oak tree.*

yore (yôr) *n.* [U] An old word for time long
past: *days of yore.*

you (yōō) *pron.* **1.** The one or ones being addressed: *You have very little time left. I'll lend
you the book.* **2.** An indefinitely specified
person; one: *You can't win them all.* ♦ **you
know.** Used in conversation to include the
other person or invite a comment: *She has
remarried, you know.* —SEE NOTE at **you-all.**

HOMONYMS: you, ewe (sheep), **yew** (shrub).

you-all (yōō′ôl′) also **y'all** (yôl) *pron.* You.
Used chiefly in the southern United States.

USAGE: you-all Residents of the southern
United States often use **you** and **you-all** (often
heard as **y'all**) to make a distinction between
one person and more than one person.

you'd (yōōd). Contraction of *you had* or *you
would.*

you'll (yōōl *or* yōōl; yəl *when unstressed*)
Contraction of *you will* or *you shall.*

HOMONYMS: you'll, Yule (Christmas).

young (yŭng) *adj.* **1.** In an early stage of life,
growth, or development: *A puppy is a young
dog.* **2.** At or near the beginning: *The evening
is young.* **3.** Belonging to or like youth or early
life: *He looks young for his age.* **4.** Without
experience or maturity: *a young teacher.* —*n.*
[U] **1.** Young people considered as a group;
youth: *Young and old voted for the candidate.*
2. Offspring: *a lioness with her young.*

young·ish (yŭng′ĭsh) *adj.* A little young: *a
youngish mother.*

young·ster (yŭng′stər) *n.* A child or young
person.

your (yŏŏr *or* yôr; yər *when unstressed*) *adj.* The
possessive form of **you.** **1.** Belonging to you:
your boots; your achievements. **2.** A person's;
one's: *The light switch is on your right.*

HOMONYMS: your, you're (you are).

you're (yŏŏr; yər *when unstressed*) Contraction of *you are.*

yours (yŏŏrz *or* yôrz) *pron. (used with a singular or plural verb).* **1.** The one or ones belonging to you: *Use my car if yours hasn't been
repaired. These letters are mine; yours are on
the table.* **2.** Used as a closing at the end of a letter: *sincerely yours.* ♦ **yours truly.** I, myself, or
me: *The work was done by yours truly.*

your·self (yŏŏr sĕlf′ *or* yôr sĕlf′ *or* yər sĕlf′)
pron. **1.** That one that is the same as you. **a.**

Y

Used as the direct or indirect object of a verb or as the object of a preposition to show that the action of a verb refers back to the subject: *You should not tire yourself. Give yourself enough time. Keep it for yourself.* **b.** Used for emphasis: *You yourself admitted it.* **2.** Your normal or healthy condition: *You were not feeling yourself when you did it.*

your•selves (yo͝or sĕlvz′ *or* yôr sĕlvz′ *or* yər sĕlvz′) *pron.* **1.** Those ones that are the same as you. **a.** Used as the direct or indirect object of a verb or as the object of a preposition to show that the action of a verb refers back to the subject: *Help yourselves. Have yourselves a good time. You should all watch out for yourselves.* **b.** Used for emphasis: *You'll have to take care of it yourselves.* **2.** Your normal or healthy condition: *Just relax and be yourselves.*

youth (yo͞oth) *n., pl.* **youths** (yo͞oths *or* yo͞othz). **1.** [U] The condition or time of being young or in one's early years: *During her youth, she lived in Ohio.* **2.** [C] A young person, especially one in late adolescence: *The police picked up several youths.* **3.** [U] *(used with a singular or plural verb).* Young people considered as a group: *the youth of our city.*

youth•ful (yo͞oth′fəl) *adj.* **1.** Characterized by youth: *the youthful hero.* **2.** Relating to or characteristic of youth: *youthful impatience.* —**youth′ful•ly** *adv.* —**youth′ful•ness** *n.* [U]

you've (yo͞ov). Contraction of *you have.*

yowl (youl) *intr.v.* To make a long, loud, sad cry; wail: *The cat yowled in the alley.* —*n.* A long, loud, mournful cry.

yo-yo (yō′yō′) *n., pl.* **yo-yos.** A toy made of a spool wound with string that is spun up and down using motions of the wrist.

yr. *abbr.* An abbreviation of: **1.** Year. **2.** Your.

yo-yo

Yule (yo͞ol) *n.* Christmas.

HOMONYMS: Yule, you'll (you will).

---

yum•my (yŭm′ē) *adj.* **yum•mi•er, yum•mi•est.** *Informal.* Delicious: *yummy chocolate cake.*

yup•pie (yŭp′ē) *n. Slang.* An insulting term for a materialistic person: *After he bought the sports car, his friends accused him of being a yuppie.*

YWCA or **Y.W.C.A.** *abbr.* An abbreviation of Young Women's Christian Association an organization that provides various services and facilities, such as clubs, athletic activities, and sometimes inexpensive lodging: *I take classes at the YWCA.*

Y

Zz

z or **Z** (zē) *n.*, *pl.* **z's** or **Z's.** The 26th letter of the English alphabet.

za·ny (zā'nē) *adj.* **za·ni·er, za·ni·est.** Very comical; clownish: *a zany movie.*

zap (zăp) *Slang. tr.v.* **zapped, zap·ping, zaps. 1.** To destroy or kill (sbdy./sthg.) with a burst of gunfire, flame, or electric current: *The new gadget zapped bugs effectively.* **2.** To expose (sthg.) to radiation: *Zap the leftovers in the microwave.* **3.** To use a remote control device to switch (channels on a television) or to turn off (a television). —*n.* A jolt or shock: *I got a zap when I touched the door knob.*

zeal (zēl) *n.* [U] Great interest in or dedication to a cause, an ideal, or a goal: *He approached the task with great zeal.*

zeal·ot (zĕl'ət) *n.* A person who is zealous, especially too much so: *religious zealots.*

zeal·ous (zĕl'əs) *adj.* Filled with or motivated by zeal; fervent: *zealous support of a cause.* —**zeal'ous·ly** *adv.* —**zeal'ous·ness** *n.* [U]

ze·bra (zē'brə) *n.* A black and white striped African mammal related to the horse.

zed (zĕd) *n. Chiefly British.* The letter *z.*

ze·nith (zē'nĭth) *n. (usually singular).* **1.** The point on the celestial sphere that is directly above the observer. **2.** The highest point; peak: *the zenith of success.*

zep·pe·lin (zĕp'ə lĭn) *n.* A rigid airship with a long cylindrical body that is filled with gas.

ze·ro (zîr'ō *or* zē'rō) *n.*, *pl.* **ze·ros** or **ze·roes. 1.** The numerical symbol 0. **2.** The temperature indicated by the numeral 0 on a thermometer. **3.** *Informal.* Nothing: *We have accomplished zero today.* —*tr.v.* **ze·roed, ze·ro·ing, ze·roes.** To adjust (an instrument or a device) to a setting of zero: *Zero the counter before starting the tape.* ◆ **zero in on.** To concentrate one's attention on; focus on: *The boy zeroed in on the toy display in the window.*

zest (zĕst) *n.* [U] **1.** Flavor or interest: *We can use spices to give zest to simple foods.* **2.** The outermost rind of an orange or a lemon, used as a flavoring: *lemon zest.* **3.** Spirited enjoyment; relish; gusto: *He ate his dinner with zest.* —**zest'ful** *adj.* —**zest'ful·ly** *adv.*

zig·zag (zĭg'zăg') *n.* A line or path that proceeds by sharp turns to the right and left. —*adj.* Moving

zig-zag

in or having a zigzag: *a zigzag path.* —*adv.* In a zigzag manner or pattern: *The blindfolded child went zigzag across the room.* —*intr.v.* **zig·zagged, zig·zag·ging, zig·zags.** To move in or form a zigzag: *The trail zigzagged up the mountain.*

zil·lion (zĭl'yən) *n. Informal.* An extremely large, indefinite number: *There were about a zillion people at the party.*

zinc (zĭngk) *n.* [U] *Symbol* **Zn** A shiny bluish white metallic element used as a coating for iron, in alloys such as brass, as a roofing material, and in electric batteries. Atomic number 30. See table at **element.**

zing (zĭng) *n.* **1.** [C] A high-pitched buzzing sound. **2.** [U] Spirit; liveliness: *She walks with zing in her step.* —*intr.v.* **1.** To make a zing: *The guitar zinged quietly.* **2.** To move swiftly with or as if with zing: *She zinged around the room.*

zing·er (zĭng'ər) *n. Informal.* A humorous insult: *The comedian had a lot of zingers in his act.*

zin·ni·a (zĭn'ē ə) *n.* A garden plant with brightly colored flowers.

zip (zĭp) *n.* **1.** [C] A brief, sharp, hissing sound. **2.** [U] Energy: *She has a lot of zip despite her age.* **3.** [U] *Informal.* Nothing: *That job pays zip.* **4.** [C] ZIP. ZIP Code: *Do you know your ZIP?* —*intr.v.* **zipped, zip·ping, zips. 1.** To move with a sharp hissing sound: *The cars zipped by us.* **2.** To move or act with a speed that suggests such a sound: *I'll zip over to the library and return these books.* ◆ **zip up.** *tr.v.* [sep.] **1.** To enclose (sbdy. in) sthg. with a zipper: *Zip me up, please.* **2.** To close the zipper on (sthg.): *Zip up your coat, please.*

ZIP Code (zĭp) *n.* A number used as part of an address that identifies the location of the recipient for mail delivery: *My ZIP Code is 94105.*

zip·per (zĭp'ər) *n.* A fastener made of two rows of interlocking teeth on adjacent edges of an opening closed or opened by a sliding tab.

zip·py (zĭp'ē) *adj.* **zip·pi·er, zip·pi·est.** Full of energy; lively: *a zippy song and dance.*

zipper

zir·con (zûr′kŏn′) *n.* [C; U] A mineral, essentially a silicate of zirconium, that can be heated, cut, and polished to form brilliant inexpensive gems that resemble diamonds.

zir·co·ni·um (zûr kō′nē əm) *n.* [U] *Symbol* **Zr** A shiny grayish white metallic element. Atomic number 40. See table at **element.**

zit (zĭt) *n. Slang.* Pimple.

Zn The symbol for the element **zinc.**

zo·di·ac (zō′dē ăk′) *n.* In astrology, the 12 divisions, or signs, of the celestial paths of the sun, moon, and planets, each with the name of a constellation: *My zodiac sign is Leo.*

zom·bie (zŏm′bē) *n., pl.* **zom·bies. 1.** According to voodoo belief, a dead person brought back to life by a supernatural power or spell. **2.** *Informal.* A person who looks or behaves like a zombie, as in mechanical movements or a sleep-like manner: *After sleeping only three hours, I was a zombie.*

zone (zōn) *n.* An area or region distinguished from a nearby one by a distinctive characteristic or reason: *a residential zone; a no-parking zone.* —*tr.v.* **zoned, zon·ing, zones.** To divide or mark (sthg.) off into zones: *The city council zoned the district for business use.* ♦ **zone out.** *intr.v. Informal.* To stop paying attention: *I zoned out during the meeting and didn't take notes.*

zoo (zōō) *n., pl.* **zoos. 1.** A place where living animals are kept and exhibited. **2.** *Slang.* A place or situation marked by confusion or disorder: *The office was a zoo today!*

zoo— *pref.* A prefix that means animal or animals: *zoology.*

WORD BUILDING: zoo— The prefix **zoo—**, which is pronounced with two syllables, means "animal, living being." We know this prefix best in the one-syllable word **zoo. Zoo** is a shortening of the longer, more formal **zoological garden,** which was originally a park where wild animals were kept on display. **Zoological** is the adjective form of the noun **zoology,** which means "the study of animals." **Zoology** is thus part of **biology,** which means "the study of life."

zo·o·log·i·cal (zō′ə lŏj′ĭ kəl) *also* **zo·o·log·ic** (zō′ə lŏj′ĭk) *adj.* Relating to animals or zoology: *a zoological collection.* —**zo′o·log′i·cal·ly** *adv.*

zo·ol·o·gy (zō ŏl′ə jē) *n.* [U] The branch of biology that deals with animals. —**zo·ol′o·gist** *n.*

zoom (zōōm) *intr.v.* **1.** To make a low-pitched buzzing or humming sound: *A hornet zoomed around my ear.* **2.** To move rapidly: *The cars zoomed past.* —*n.* [C; U] The sound or act of zooming: *the zoom of the jet.* ♦ **zoom in** or **out.** *intr.v.* To move a camera lens rapidly toward or away from a photographic subject: *The photographer zoomed in on the tiger.*

Zr The symbol for the element **zirconium.**

Zs or **Z's** *pl.n. Slang.* Sleep. ♦ **get** or **catch some Zs.** To sleep: *I need to catch some Zs, so I'm going to take a nap.*

zuc·chi·ni (zōō kē′nē) *n.* [C; U] A type of long narrow squash with a thin dark green skin.

zy·gote (zī′gōt′) *n.* The cell formed by the union of two gametes, especially a fertilized egg cell.

Numbers

	Cardinal	Ordinal
0	zero	
1	one	first
2	two	second
3	three	third
4	four	fourth
5	five	fifth
6	six	sixth
7	seven	seventh
8	eight	eighth
9	nine	ninth
10	ten	tenth
11	eleven	eleventh
12	twelve	twelfth
13	thirteen	thirteenth
14	fourteen	fourteenth
15	fifteen	fifteenth
16	sixteen	sixteenth
17	seventeen	seventeenth
18	eighteen	eighteenth
19	nineteen	nineteenth
20	twenty	twentieth
21	twenty-one	twenty-first
22	twenty-two	twenty-second
23	twenty-three	twenty-third
24	twenty-four	twenty-fourth
25	twenty-five	twenty-fifth
26	twenty-six	twenty-sixth
27	twenty-seven	twenty-seventh
28	twenty-eight	twenty-eighth
29	twenty-nine	twenty-ninth
30	thirty	thirtieth
40	forty	fortieth
50	fifty	fiftieth
60	sixty	sixtieth
70	seventy	seventieth
80	eighty	eightieth
90	ninety	ninetieth
100	one hundred	one hundredth
200	two hundred	two hundredth
1,000	one thousand	one thousandth
10,000	ten thousand	ten thousandth
100,000	one hundred thousand	one hundred thousandth
1,000,000	one million	one millionth
1,000,000,000	one billion	one billionth

Days of the Week

Day	Abbreviation
Sunday	S., Sun.
Monday	M., Mon.
Tuesday	T., Tu., Tue., Tues.
Wednesday	W., Wed.
Thursday	Th., Thur., Thurs.
Friday	F., Fr., Fri.
Saturday	S., Sat.

Months of the Year

Month	Abbreviation
January	Jan.
February	Feb.
March	Mar.
April	Apr.
May	
June	Jun.
July	Jul.
August	Aug.
September	Sept.
October	Oct.
November	Nov.
December	Dec.

Pronouns

Subject Pronouns

singular	*plural*
I	we
you	you
he, she, it	they

Object Pronouns

singular	*plural*
me	us
you	you
him, her, it	them

Possessive Pronouns

singular	*plural*
mine	ours
yours	yours
his, hers, its	theirs

Possessive Adjectives

singular	*plural*
my	our
your	your
his, her, its	their

Reflexive Pronouns

singular	*plural*
myself	ourselves
yourself	yourselves
himself, herself, itself	themselves

Irregular Verbs

Simple Form	Past	Past Participle
be	was, were	been
beat	beat	beaten
become	became	become
begin	began	begun
bend	bent	bent
bet	bet	bet
bite	bit	bitten
bleed	bled	bled
blow	blew	blown
break	broke	broken
breed	bred	bred
bring	brought	brought
build	built	built
burst	burst	burst
buy	bought	bought
catch	caught	caught
choose	chose	chosen
come	came	come
cost	cost	cost
cut	cut	cut
deal	dealt	dealt
do	did	done
draw	drew	drawn
drink	drank	drunk
drive	drove	driven
eat	ate	eaten
fall	fell	fallen
feed	fed	fed
feel	felt	felt
fight	fought	fought
find	found	found
fit	fit	fit
flee	fled	fled
fly	flew	flown
forget	forgot	forgotten
forgive	forgave	forgiven
freeze	froze	frozen
get	got	gotten
give	gave	given
go	went	gone
grind	ground	ground

Simple Form	Past	Past Participle
grow	grew	grown
hang	hung	hanged/hung
have	had	had
hear	heard	heard
hide	hid	hidden
hit	hit	hit
hold	held	held
hurt	hurt	hurt
keep	kept	kept
kneel	knelt	knelt
know	knew	known
lay	laid	laid
lead	led	led
leave	left	left
lend	lent	lent
let	let	let
light	lit	lit
lie (down)	lay	lain
lie (untruth)	lied	lied
lose	lost	lost
make	made	made
mean	meant	meant
meet	met	met
pay	paid	paid
prove	proved	proven/proved
put	put	put
quit	quit	quit
read	read	read
rid	rid	rid
ride	rode	ridden
ring	rang	rung
rise	rose	risen
run	ran	run
say	said	said
see	saw	seen
seek	sought	sought
sell	sold	sold
send	sent	sent
set	set	set
sew	sewed	sewn/sewed
shake	shook	shaken
shine	shone	shone
shoot	shot	shot
show	showed	shown/showed

Simple Form	Past	Past Participle
shrink	shrank	shrunk
shut	shut	shut
sing	sang	sung
sit	sat	sat
sleep	slept	slept
slide	slid	slid
speak	spoke	spoken
spend	spent	spent
spin	spun	spun
split	split	split
spread	spread	spread
stand	stood	stood
steal	stole	stolen
stick	stuck	stuck
sting	stung	stung
stink	stank	stunk
strike	struck	struck
string	strung	strung
swear	swore	sworn
sweep	swept	swept
swell	swelled	swollen/swelled
swim	swam	swum
swing	swung	swung
take	took	taken
teach	taught	taught
tear	tore	torn
tell	told	told
think	thought	thought
throw	threw	thrown
understand	understood	understood
wake	woke	woken
wear	wore	worn
wet	wet	wet
win	won	won
wind	wound	wound
wring	wrung	wrung
write	wrote	written

United States

Capital of the United States
District of Columbia, Washington, DC

State	Capital	Postal Abbreviation	Other Abbreviation
Alabama	Montgomery	AL	Ala.
Alaska	Juneau	AK	Alas.
Arizona	Phoenix	AZ	Ariz.
Arkansas	Little Rock	AR	Ark.
California	Sacramento	CA	Cal., Calif.
Colorado	Denver	CO	Col., Colo.
Connecticut	Hartford	CT	Ct., Conn.
Delaware	Dover	DE	Del.
Florida	Tallahassee	FL	Fla.
Georgia	Atlanta	GA	Ga.
Hawaii	Honolulu	HI	Hi.
Idaho	Boise	ID	Id.
Illinois	Springfield	IL	Ill.
Indiana	Indianapolis	IN	Ind.
Iowa	Des Moines	IA	Ia.
Kansas	Topeka	KS	Kans.
Kentucky	Frankfort	KY	Ky., Ken.
Louisiana	Baton Rouge	LA	La.
Maine	Augusta	ME	Me.
Maryland	Annapolis	MD	Md.
Massachusetts	Boston	MA	Mass.
Michigan	Lansing	MI	Mich.
Minnesota	St. Paul	MN	Minn.
Mississippi	Jackson	MS	Miss.
Missouri	Jefferson City	MO	Mo.
Montana	Helena	MT	Mont.
Nebraska	Lincoln	NE	Nebr.
Nevada	Carson City	NV	Nev.
New Hampshire	Concord	NH	N.H.
New Jersey	Trenton	NJ	N.J.
New Mexico	Santa Fe	NM	N.M., N.Mex.
New York	Albany	NY	N.Y.
North Carolina	Raleigh	NC	N.C.
North Dakota	Bismarck	ND	N.D., N.Dak.
Ohio	Columbus	OH	O.
Oklahoma	Oklahoma City	OK	Okla.
Oregon	Salem	OR	Ore.
Pennsylvania	Harrisburg	PA	Pa., Penn., Penna.
Rhode Island	Providence	RI	R.I.
South Carolina	Columbia	SC	S.C.

State	Capital	Postal Abbreviation	Other Abbreviation
South Dakota	Pierre	SD	S.D., S.Dak.
Tennessee	Nashville	TN	Tenn.
Texas	Austin	TX	Tex.
Utah	Salt Lake City	UT	Ut.
Vermont	Montpelier	VT	Vt.
Virginia	Richmond	VA	Va.
Washington	Olympia	WA	Wash.
West Virginia	Charleston	WV	W.Va.
Wisconsin	Madison	WI	Wis.
Wyoming	Cheyenne	WY	Wyo.

Territories

Guam	Agnes	GU	
Puerto Rico	San Juan	PR	P.R.
Virgin Islands	Charlotte Amalie	VI	V.I.

Canada

Capital of Canada
Ottawa

Province	Capital	Postal Abbreviation	Other
Alberta	Edmonton	AB	Alta.
British Columbia	Vancouver	BC	B.C.
Manitoba	Winnipeg	MB	Man.
New Brunswick	Fredericton	NB	N.B.
Newfoundland	St. John's	NF	Newf., Nfld.
Nova Scotia	Halifax	NS	N.S.
Ontario	Toronto	ON	Ont.
Prince Edward Island	Charlottetown	PE	P.E.I.
Quebec	Quebec	PQ	P.Q., Que.
Saskatchewan	Regina	SK	Sask.

Territories

Northwest Territories	Yellowknife	NT	NWT, N.W.T.
Yukon Territory	Whitehorse	YT	Y.T.

Countries of the World

Country	Nationality	Capital
Afghanistan	Afghan(s)	Kabul
Albania	Albanian(s)	Tiranë
Algeria	Algerian(s)	Algiers
Andorra	Andorran(s)	Andorra la Vella
Angola	Angolan(s)	Luanda
Antigua and Barbuda	Antiguan(s), Barbudan(s)	Saint John's
Argentina	Argentine(s), Argentinian(s)	Buenos Aires
Armenia	Armenian(s)	Yerevan
Australia	Australian(s)	Canberra
Austria	Austrian(s)	Vienna
Azerbaijan	Azerbaijani(s)	Baku
Bahamas	Bahamanian(s), Bahaman(s)	Nassau
Bahrain	Bahraini(s)	Manama
Bangladesh	Bangladeshi(s)	Dhaka
Barbados	Barbadian(s)	Bridgetown
Belarus	Belarusian(s)	Minsk
Belgium	Belgian(s)	Brussels
Belize	Belizean(s)	Belmopan
Benin	Beninese	Porto-Novo
Bhutan	Bhutanese	Thimphu
Bolivia	Bolivian(s)	Sucre, La Paz
Bosnia and Herzegovina	Bosnian(s), Herzegovinian(s)	Sarajevo
Botswana	Motswana (sing.), Batswana (pl.)	Gaborone
Brazil	Brazilian(s)	Brasília
Brunei	Bruneian(s)	Bandar Seri Begawan
Bulgaria	Bulgarian(s)	Sofia
Burkina Faso	Burkinabe	Ougadougou
Burundi	Burundian(s)	Bujumbura
Cambodia	Cambodian(s)	Phnom Penh
Cameroon	Cameroonian(s)	Yaoundé
Canada	Canadian(s)	Ottawa
Cape Verde	Cape Verdean(s)	Praia
Central African Republic	Central African(s)	Bangui
Chad	Chadian(s)	N'Djamena
Chile	Chilean(s)	Santiago
China	Chinese	Beijing
Colombia	Colombian(s)	Bogotá
Comoros	Comoran(s)	Moroni
Congo, Democratic Republic of (Zaire)	Congolese	Kinshasa

Country	Nationality	Capital
Congo, Republic of	Congolese	Brazzaville
Costa Rica	Costa Rican(s)	San José
Côte d'Ivoire (Ivory Coast)	Ivoirian(s), Ivorian(s)	Yamoussoukro, Abidjan
Croatia	Croatian(s)	Zagreb
Cuba	Cuban(s)	Havana
Cyprus	Cypriot(s)	Nicosia
Czech Republic	Czech(s)	Prague
Denmark	Dane(s)	Copenhagen
Djibouti	Djiboutian(s)	Djibouti
Dominica	Dominican(s)	Roseau
Dominican Republic	Dominican(s)	Santo Domingo
Ecuador	Ecuadorian(s)	Quito
Egypt	Egyptian(s)	Cairo
El Salvador	Salvadoran(s)	San Salvador
Equatorial Guinea	Equatorial Guinean(s)	Malabo
Eritrea	Eritrean(s)	Asmara
Estonia	Estonian(s)	Tallinn
Ethiopia	Ethiopian(s)	Addis Ababa
Fiji	Fijian(s)	Suva
Finland	Finn(s)	Helsinki
France	French, Frenchman, Frenchwoman	Paris
Gabon	Gabonese	Libreville
Gambia	Gambian(s)	Banjul
Georgia	Georgian(s)	Tbilisi
Germany	German(s)	Berlin, Bonn
Ghana	Ghanaian(s)	Accra
Greece	Greek(s)	Athens
Grenada	Grenadan(s)	Saint George's
Guatemala	Guatemalan(s)	Guatemala City
Guinea	Guinean(s)	Conakry
Guinea-Bissau	Guinea-Bissauan(s)	Bissau
Guyana	Guyanese	Georgetown
Haiti	Haitian(s)	Port-au-Prince
Honduras	Honduran(s)	Tegucigalpa
Hungary	Hungarian(s)	Budapest
Iceland	Icelander(s)	Reykjavik
India	Indian(s)	New Delhi
Indonesia	Indonesian(s)	Jakarta
Iran	Iranian(s)	Tehran
Iraq	Iraqi(s)	Baghdad
Ireland	Irish, Irishman, Irishwoman	Dublin
Israel	Israeli(s)	Jerusalem

Country	Nationality	Capital
Italy	Italian(s)	Rome
Jamaica	Jamaican(s)	Kingston
Japan	Japanese	Tokyo
Jordan	Jordanian(s)	Amman
Kazakstan	Kazakstani(s)	Almaty
Kenya	Kenyan(s)	Nairobi
Kiribati	I-Kiribati	Bairiki
Kuwait	Kuwaiti(s)	Kuwait
Kyrgyzstan	Kyrgyz(s)	Bishkek
Laos	Laotian(s)	Vientiane
Latvia	Latvian(s)	Riga
Lebanon	Lebanese	Beirut
Lesotho	Mesotho (sing.), Basotho (pl.)	Maseru
Liberia	Liberian(s)	Monrovia
Libya	Libyan(s)	Tripoli
Liechtenstein	Liechtensteiner(s)	Vaduz
Lithuania	Lithuanian(s)	Vilnius
Luxembourg	Luxembourger(s)	Luxembourg
Macedonia	Macedonian(s)	Skopje
Madagascar	Malagasy, Madagascan(s)	Antananarivo
Malawi	Malawian(s)	Lilongwe
Malaysia	Malaysian(s)	Kuala Lumpur
Maldives	Maldivian(s), Maldivan(s)	Male
Mali	Malian(s)	Bamako
Malta	Maltese	Valletta
Marshall Islands	Marshallese	Majuro
Mauritania	Mauritanian(s)	Nouakchott
Mauritius	Mauritian(s)	Port Louis
Mexico	Mexican(s)	Mexico City
Micronesia	Micronesian(s)	Palikir
Moldova	Moldovan(s)	Chisinau
Monaco	Monacan(s), Monegasque(s)	Monaco
Mongolia	Mongolian(s)	Ulan Bator
Morocco	Moroccan(s)	Rabat
Mozambique	Mozambican(s)	Maputo
Myanmar (Burma)	Burmese, Burman(s)	Yangon (Rangoon)
Namibia	Namibian(s)	Windhoek
Nauru	Nauruan(s)	Yaren
Nepal	Nepalese	Katmandu
Netherlands	Dutch, Dutchman, Dutchwoman	Amsterdam, The Hague

Country	Nationality	Capital
New Zealand	New Zealander(s)	Wellington
Nicaragua	Nicaraguan(s)	Managua
Niger	Nigerien(s)	Niamey
Nigeria	Nigerian(s)	Abuja, Lagos
Norway	Norwegian(s)	Oslo
North Korea	North Korean(s)	Pyongyang
Oman	Omani(s)	Muscat
Pakistan	Pakistani(s)	Islamabad
Palau	Palauan(s)	Koror
Panama	Panamanian(s)	Panama City
Papua New Guinea	Papua New Guinean(s)	Port Moresby
Paraguay	Paraguayan(s)	Asunción
Peru	Peruvian(s)	Lima
Philippines	Filipino(s)	Manila
Poland	Pole(s)	Warsaw
Portugal	Portuguese	Lisbon
Qatar	Qatari(s)	Doha
Romania	Romanian(s)	Bucharest
Russia	Russian(s)	Moscow
Rwanda	Rwandan(s)	Kigali
Saint Kitts and Nevis	Kittsian(s), Nevisian(s)	Basseterre
Saint Lucia	Saint Lucian(s)	Castries
Saint Vincent and the Grenadines	Saint Vincentian(s), Vincentian(s)	Kingstown
San Marino	Sammarinese	San Marino
São Tomé and Príncipe	São Toméan(s)	São Tomé
Saudi Arabia	Saudi Arabian(s)	Riyadh
Senegal	Senegalese	Dakar
Seychelles	Seychellois	Victoria
Sierra Leone	Sierra Leonean(s)	Freetown
Singapore	Singaporean(s)	Singapore
Slovakia	Slovakian(s)	Bratislava
Slovenia	Slovenian(s)	Ljubljana
Solomon Islands	Solomon Islander(s)	Honiara
Somalia	Somalian(s)	Mogadishu
South Africa	South African(s)	Pretoria, Cape Town, Bloemfontein
South Korea	South Korean(s)	Seoul
Spain	Spanish, Spaniard(s)	Madrid
Sri Lanka	Sri Lankan(s)	Colombo
Sudan	Sudanese	Khartoum
Suriname	Surinamese	Paramaribo
Swaziland	Swazi(s)	Mbabane

Country	Nationality	Capital
Sweden	Swede(s)	Stockholm
Switzerland	Swiss	Bern
Syria	Syrian(s)	Damascus
Taiwan	Taiwanese	Taipei
Tajikistan	Tajik(s)	Dushanbe
Tanzania	Tanzanian(s)	Dar es Salaam
Thailand	Thai	Bangkok
Togo	Togolese	Lomé
Tonga	Tongan(s)	Nuku'alofa
Trinidad and Tobago	Trinidadian(s), Tobagonian(s)	Port of Spain
Tunisia	Tunisian(s)	Tunis
Turkey	Turk(s)	Ankara
Turkmenistan	Turkmen(s)	Ashgabat
Tuvalu	Tuvaluan(s)	Funafuti
Uganda	Ugandan(s)	Kampala
Ukraine	Ukrainian(s)	Kiev
United Arab Emirates	Emirian(s)	Abu Dhabi
United Kingdom	British, Briton(s)	London
United States of America	American(s)	Washington, D.C.
Uruguay	Uruguayan(s)	Montevideo
Uzbekistan	Uzbek(s)	Tashkent
Vanuatu	Ni-Vanuatu	Vila
Vatican City		
Venezuela	Venezuelan(s)	Caracas
Vietnam	Vietnamese	Hanoi
Samoa	Samoan(s)	Apia
Yemen	Yemeni(s)	San'a
Yugoslavia	Yugoslavian(s)	Belgrade
Zambia	Zambian(s)	Lusaka
Zimbabwe	Zimbabwean(s)	Harare

Continents of the World

Country	Nationality
Africa	African(s)
Antarctica	
Asia	Asian(s)
Australia	Australian(s)
Europe	European(s)
North America	North American(s)
South America	South American(s)

Picture Credits

The editors wish to thank the individuals, organizations, and agencies that have contributed to the art program of this dictionary. The credits that follow are arranged alphabetically by entry word. For photographs, the name of the source appears first, followed by a slash and the photographer's name. Where two or more illustrations appear at one entry, the sources are separated by semicolons and follow the order of the illustrations.

abcissa Tech Graphics **accordion** Stock Boston/Jean-Claude Lejeune **alligator** Photo Researchers/Robert Wright **amphibian** Chris Costello **anchor** Laurel Cook Lhowe **antler** Gail Piazza **armadillo** Chris Costello **ATM** Zephyr Pictures/Denise DeLuise **ax** Chris Costello **bagpipes** AP Wide World **balance** Chris Costello **ballerina** Boston Ballet/John Burke **balloon** Picture Cube/Stanley Rowin **banjo** Stock Boston/Jean-Claude Lejeune **bar graph, barometer** Laurel Cook Lhowe **bear²**, **beaver** Leonard Rue Enterprises/ Leonard Lee Rue III **bicycle** Lightwave/S. E. Byrne **bison** Animals Animals/C. W. Perkins **blimp** The Goodyear Tire & Rubber Company **bolt** Laurel Cook Lhowe **bow** Laurel Cook Lhowe; Jeroboam/Kent Reno; Laurel Cook Lhowe **braid** Chris Costello **bridge** Stock Boston/Jeff Albertson **bureau** Laurel Cook Lhowe **butterfly** Animals Animals/ Stan Schroeder **cactus** Photo Researchers/ Jen & Des Bartlett **camcorder** Positive Images/Candace Cochrane **canoe** Stock Boston/Fredrik Bodin **carrot** Chris Costello **cell** Laurel Cook Lhowe **cello** Lightwave/ Steve Gravano **chain saw** Stock Boston/ Peter Menzel **circle** Laurel Cook Lhowe **comet** Lick Observatory **commencement** Picture Cube/Beringer-Dratch **compact disk, compass** Lightwave/Oscar Palmquist **computer** E. P. Jones & Co./Camerique **concave, concentric, convex** Laurel Cook Lhowe **coral** Grant Heilman Photography/ Runk & Schoenberger **courtyard** Positive Images/Jerry Howard **crane** Animals Animals/Miriam Agron; Photo Researchers/ Robert A. Isaacs **crescent** E. P. Jones & Co./ Camerique **cube, cylinder** Tech Graphics **daffodil** Laurel Cook Lhowe **deer** Animals Animals/Leonard Lee Rue III **derrick** Grant Heilman Photography/Alan Pitcairn **diagonal** Laurel Cook Lhowe **dish** Chris Costello; Grant Heilman Photography/Runk & Schoenberger **dog** © Houghton Mifflin Company—photograph by Evelyn Shafer **dolphin** Photo Researchers/Omikron **domino** Chris Costello **donkey** Positive Images/Jerry Howard **drawbridge** E. P. Jones & Co./ Harold M. Lambert **drill** Chris Costello **eagle** Animals Animals/Leonard Lee Rue III **ear** Laurel Cook Lhowe; Chris Costello **earphones** Photo Researchers/David M. Grossman **eclipse** Stock Boston/Ira Kirschenbaum **eggplant** Chris Costello **ellipse** Tech Graphics **equator, eye** Laurel Cook Lhowe **fair²** Grant Heilman Photography/Robert Barclay **farm** Picture Cube/Dede Hatch **faucet** Gail Piazza **fax** Lightwave/Oscar Palmquist **fir** Chris Costello **fire escape** Lightwave/Oscar Palmquist **flamingo** Chris Costello **floppy disk** Positive Images/Jerry Howard **flute** Stock Boston/Joseph Schuyler **forklift** E. P. Jones & Co. **fossil** Grant Heilman Photography/Runk & Schoenberger **frog** Chris Costello **fulcrum, gear** Laurel Cook Lhowe **goggles** Stock Boston/Jonathan Rawle **gourd** Chris Costello **graph** Laurel Cook Lhowe **guitar** PhotoEdit/Merritt A. Vincent **gyroscope** Grant Heilman Photography/Runk & Schoenberger **hammer, hammock** Chris Costello **handcuffs** Laurel Cook Lhowe **harmonica** Positive Images/Jerry Howard **hawk¹** Leonard Rue Enterprises/Mark Wilson **heart** Laurel Cook Lhowe **helicopter** Stock Boston/Peter Vandermark **helmet** Picture Cube/Paul Nurnberg **hexagon** Chris Costello **horizontal, hourglass** Laurel Cook Lhowe **hypotenuse, insect, instrument** Laurel Cook Lhowe **iron** Lightwave/Aldo Mastrocola **isosceles triangle, jack-o'-lantern** Laurel Cook Lhowe **joker** Chris Costello **kayak** Stock Boston/Peter Menzel **kerchief** Jeroboam/ Laimute Druskis **kiosk** Stock Boston/Owen Franken **kite** Laurel Cook Lhowe **knot** Tech Graphics **koala** H. Armstrong Roberts lamb Photo Researchers/Arthur W. Ambler lantern Laurel Cook Lhowe lighthouse Grant Heilman Photography/Hal H. Harrison line graph Laurel Cook Lhowe lobster Chris Costello magnet Laurel Cook Lhowe mask Chris Costello melon Laurel Cook Lhowe microscope Animals Animals/ George F. Godfrey mitten, needle Laurel Cook Lhowe nest Photo Researchers/Hal H. Harrison nipple Laurel Cook Lhowe nozzle Stock Boston/Bob Daemmrich nut Laurel Cook Lhowe observatory Grant Heilman Photography/Runk & Schoenberger obtuse angle, okra, olive Laurel Cook Lhowe opossum Grant Heilman Photography/Runk & Schoenberger orchid Chris Costello overalls Stock Boston/Jeffrey W. Myers owl Photo Researchers/Karl H. Maslowski padlock Gail Piazza paisley Allen Moore palm[2], papaya Chris Costello parabola, peanut Laurel Cook Lhowe pelican Picture Cube/Cynthia W. Sterling pendulum Gail Piazza pentagon, pepper, pie chart Laurel Cook Lhowe pine Chris Costello pineapple Laurel Cook Lhowe pliers Chris Costello poison ivy Laurel Cook Lhowe porcupine Chris Costello propeller National Center for Atmospheric Research/University Corporation for Atmospheric Research, National Science Foundation pulley Chris Costello pump[2], pumpkin Laurel Cook Lhowe pyramid Tech Graphics quartz Grant Heilman Photography/Barry L. Runk quilt © 1991 Judith Winters rabbit Chris Costello raccoon American Museum of Natural History, Courtesy Department Library Services, neg. no. 336665 racket[1], radius Laurel Cook Lhowe raspberry Chris Costello rattlesnake E. P. Jones & Co./Harold M. Lambert rectangle Laurel Cook Lhowe reindeer Wildlife Conservation Society, Bronx Zoo reptile Photo Researchers/Jack Dermid right angle Laurel Cook Lhowe rocking chair, rose[1] Chris Costello saw[1] Gail Piazza

saxophone Picture Cube/J. D. Sloan scissors Laurel Cook Lhowe screw Chris Costello scuba PhotoEdit/Tony Freeman seesaw E. P. Jones & Co. sheep Grant Heilman Photography/John Colwell shovel Chris Costello sine Tech Graphics ski E. P. Jones/Camerique skunk Chris Costello slide Positive Images/ Jerry Howard snorkel Stock Boston/Peter Vandermark soccer Globe Photos speedometer, sphere Laurel Cook Lhowe spider Cecile Duray-Bito square, squash[1] Laurel Cook Lhowe squirrel Chris Costello steeple Grant Heilman Photography/Alan Pitcairn stethoscope Chris Costello stopwatch Peter Vandermark strawberry Laurel Cook Lhowe stroller Positive Images/Jerry Howard submarine Archive Photos subway Globe Photos/ Camera Press sunflower Chris Costello surfboard E. P. Jones & Co./Camerique swan Chris Costello tachometer Laurel Cook Lhowe tangent Tech Graphics target E. P. Jones & Co./Harold M. Lambert tetrahedron Tech Graphics tower Stock Boston/ Peter Menzel tractor Stock Boston/Cary S. Wolinsky trapezoid, triangle Laurel Cook Lhowe tripod Stock Boston/Joseph Schuyler trophy Picture Cube/Jaye R. Phillips turtle Grant Heilman Photography/Hal II. Harrison umbrella Picture Cube/Carolyn Hine unicycle Stock Boston/Jean-Claude Lejeune Universal Product Code (UPC) Houghton Mifflin Company Venn diagram Chris Costello vertical Laurel Cook Lhowe violin Stock Boston/ Gale Zucker vise, wagon Chris Costello wasp Cecile Duray-Bito watch Laurel Cook Lhowe weathervane E. P. Jones & Co./Harold M. Lambert wheelbarrow Chris Costello wheelchair Picture Cube/Spencer Grant windsurfing Stock Boston/Peter Menzel xylophone Comstock, Inc./Russ Kinne yo-yo Lightwave/ Oscar Palmquist zigzag, zipper Laurel Cook Lhowe